KEY TO WORLD MAP PAGES

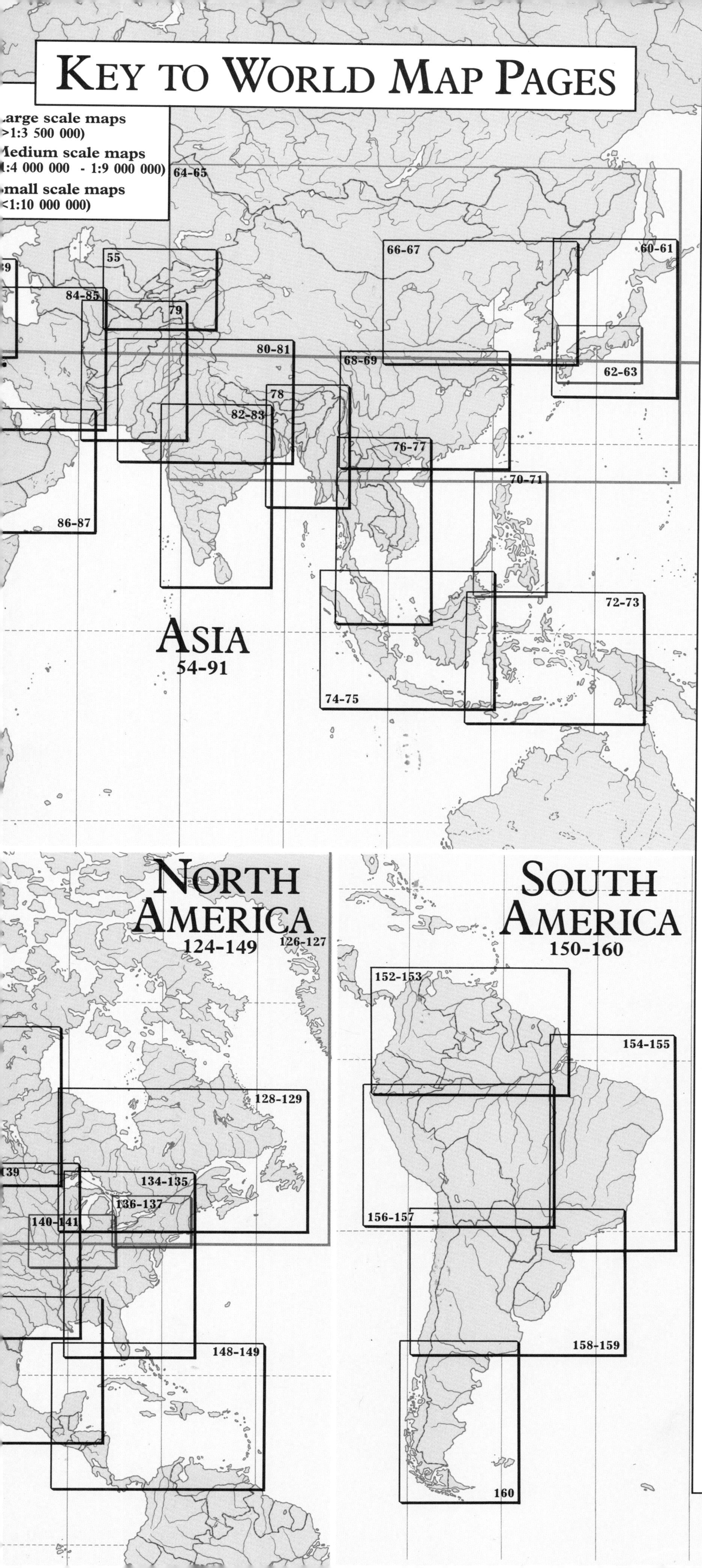

Large scale maps
(>1:3 500 000)

Medium scale maps
(1:4 000 000 - 1:9 000 000)

Small scale maps
(<1:10 000 000)

64-65

55

84-85

79

80-81

78

82-83

86-87

66-67

60-61

68-69

62-63

76-77

70-71

72-73

74-75

ASIA
54-91

NORTH AMERICA
124-149

126-127

128-129

134-135

136-137

140-141

148-149

SOUTH AMERICA
150-160

152-153

154-155

156-157

158-159

160

COUNTRY INDEX

PHILIP'S

ATLAS
OF THE
WORLD

Sixth Edition

PHILIP'S

ATLAS
OF THE
WORLD

Sixth Edition

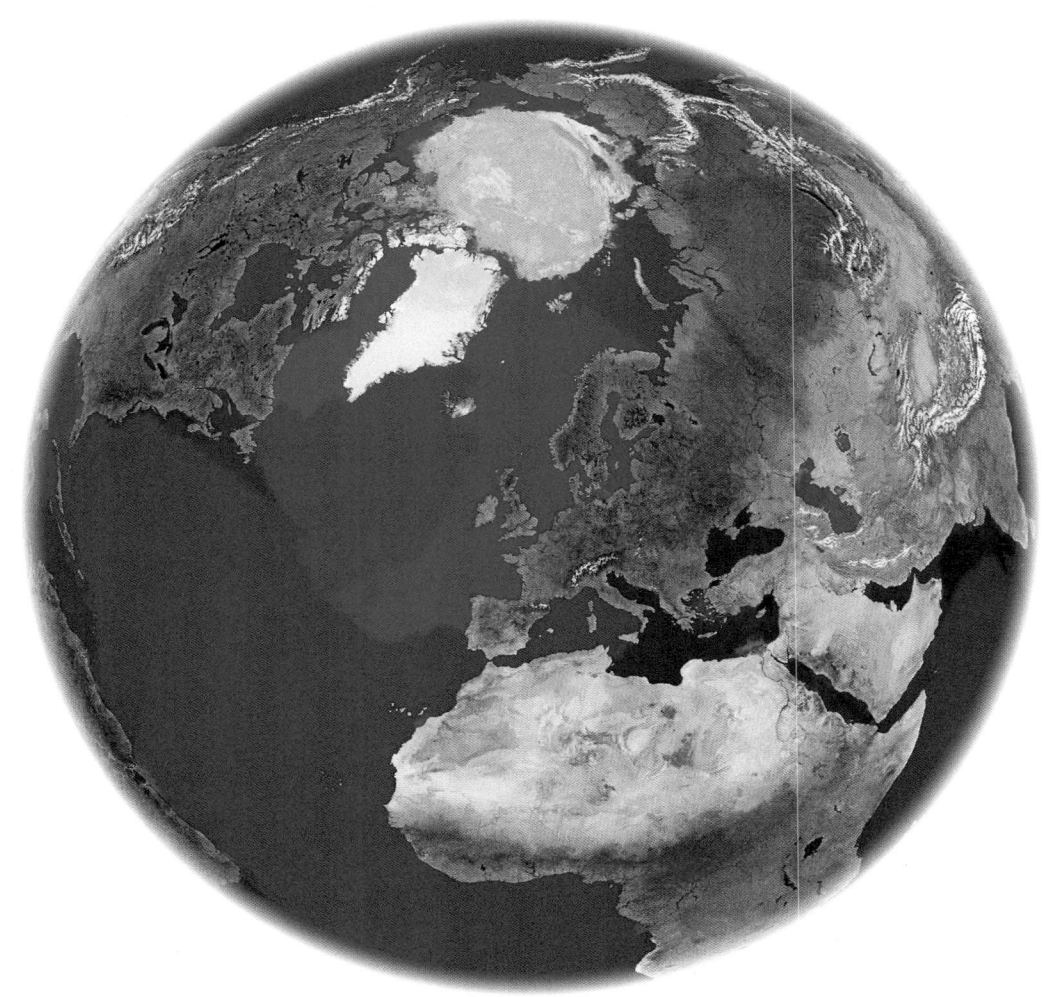

Picture Acknowledgements
Front cover / spine / main title page:
Zefa Picture Library/Tom V. Sant/Geosphere Project
DRA/Still Pictures/page 20

Introduction to World Geography
Cartography by Philip's

Geography Consultants
Professor M.J. Tooley, University of St Andrews, UK
Dr C. Clarke, Oxford University, UK
Professor M. Monmonier, Syracuse University, N.Y., USA

Illustrations
Stefan Chabluk

Published in Great Britain in 1996
by George Philip Limited,
an imprint of Reed Books,
Michelin House, 81 Fulham Road, London SW3 6RB,
and Auckland, Melbourne, Singapore and Toronto

Copyright © 1996 Reed International Books Limited

Cartography by Philip's

ISBN 0–540–06387–8

A CIP catalogue record for this book is available from the British Library

Printed in Italy

PHILIP'S WORLD MAPS

The reference maps which form the main body of this atlas have been prepared in accordance with the highest standards of international cartography to provide an accurate and detailed representation of the Earth. The scales and projections used have been carefully chosen to give balanced coverage of the world, while emphasizing the most densely populated and economically significant regions. A hallmark of Philip's mapping is the use of hill shading and relief colouring to create a graphic impression of landforms: this makes the maps exceptionally easy to read. However, knowledge of the key features employed in the construction and presentation of the maps will enable the reader to derive the fullest benefit from the atlas.

Map sequence

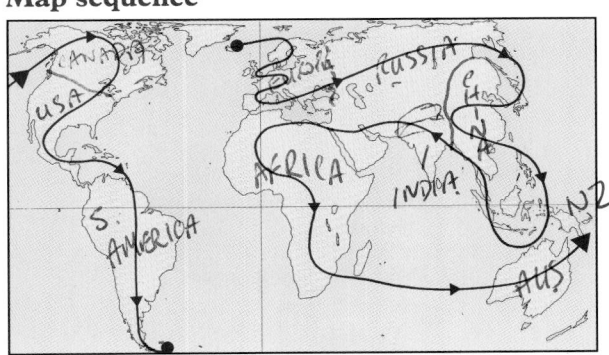

The atlas covers the Earth continent by continent: first Europe; then its land neighbour Asia (mapped north before south, in a clockwise sequence), then Africa, Australia and Oceania, North America and South America. This is the classic arrangement adopted by most cartographers since the 16th century. For each continent, there are maps at a variety of scales. First, physical relief and political maps of the whole continent; then a series of larger-scale maps of the regions within the continent, each followed, where required, by still larger-scale maps of the most important or densely populated areas. The governing principle is that by turning the pages of the atlas, the reader moves steadily from north to south through each continent, with each map overlapping its neighbours. A key map showing this sequence, and the area covered by each map, can be found on the endpapers of the atlas.

Map presentation

With very few exceptions (e.g. for the Arctic and Antarctic), the maps are drawn with north at the top, regardless of whether they are presented upright or sideways on the page. In the borders will be found the map title; a locator diagram showing the area covered and the page numbers for maps of adjacent areas; the scale; the projection used; the degrees of latitude and longitude; and the letters and figures used in the index for locating place names and geographical features. Physical relief maps also have a height reference panel identifying the colours used for each layer of contouring.

Map symbols

Each map contains a vast amount of detail which can only be conveyed clearly and accurately by the use of symbols. Points and circles of varying sizes locate and identify the relative importance of towns and cities; different styles of type are employed for administrative, geographical and regional place names. A variety of pictorial symbols denote landscape features such as glaciers, marshes and reefs, and man-made structures including roads, railways, airports, canals and dams. International borders are shown by red lines. Where neighbouring countries are in dispute, for example in the Middle East, the maps show the *de facto* boundary between nations, regardless of the legal or historical situation. The symbols are explained on the first page of the World Maps section of the atlas.

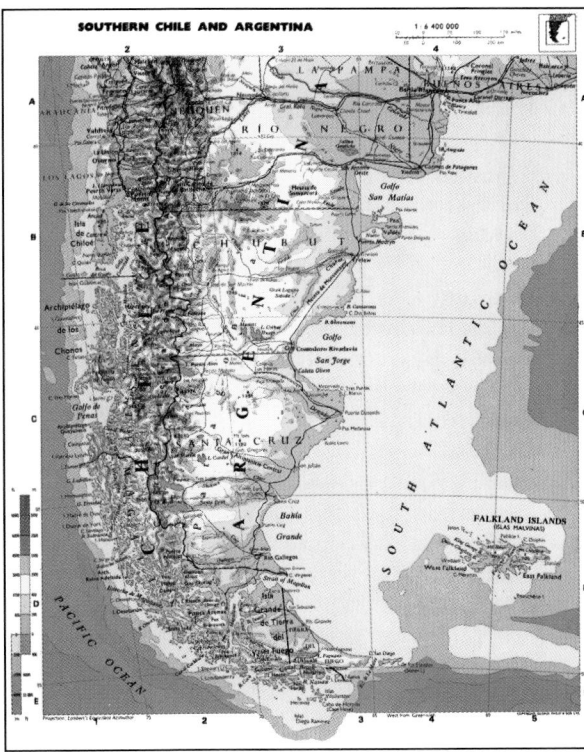

Map scales

1: 16 000 000
1 inch = 252 statute miles

The scale of each map is given in the numerical form known as the 'representative fraction'. The first figure is always one, signifying one unit of distance on the map; the second figure, usually in millions, is the number by which the map unit must be multiplied to give the equivalent distance on the Earth's surface. Calculations can easily be made in centimetres and kilometres, by dividing the Earth units figure by 100 000 (i.e. deleting the last five 0s). Thus 1:1 000 000 means 1 cm = 10 km. The calculation for inches and miles is more laborious, but 1 000 000 divided by 63 360 (the number of inches in a mile) shows that 1:1 000 000 means approximately 1 inch = 16 miles. The table below provides distance equivalents for scales down to 1:50 000 000.

LARGE SCALE		
1: 1 000 000	1 cm = 10 km	1 inch = 16 miles
1: 2 500 000	1 cm = 25 km	1 inch = 39.5 miles
1: 5 000 000	1 cm = 50 km	1 inch = 79 miles
1: 6 000 000	1 cm = 60 km	1 inch = 95 miles
1: 8 000 000	1 cm = 80 km	1 inch = 126 miles
1: 10 000 000	1 cm = 100 km	1 inch = 158 miles
1: 15 000 000	1 cm = 150 km	1 inch = 237 miles
1: 20 000 000	1 cm = 200 km	1 inch = 316 miles
1: 50 000 000	1 cm = 500 km	1 inch = 790 miles
SMALL SCALE		

Measuring distances

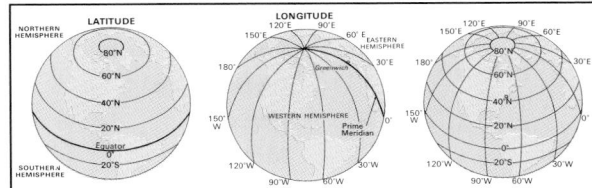

Although each map is accompanied by a scale bar, distances cannot always be measured with confidence because of the distortions involved in portraying the curved surface of the Earth on a flat page. As a general rule, the larger the map scale (i.e. the lower the number of Earth units in the representative fraction), the more accurate and reliable will be the distance measured. On small-scale maps such as those of the world and of entire continents, measurement may only be accurate along the 'standard parallels', or central axes, and should not be attempted without considering the map projection.

Map projections

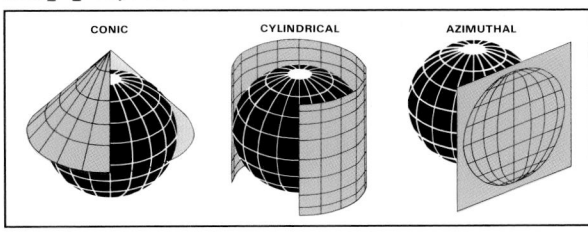

Unlike a globe, no flat map can give a true scale representation of the world in terms of area, shape and position of every region. Each of the numerous systems that have been devised for projecting the curved surface of the Earth on to a flat page involves the sacrifice of accuracy in one or more of these elements. The variations in shape and position of landmasses such as Alaska, Greenland and Australia, for example, can be quite dramatic when different projections are compared.

For this atlas, the guiding principle has been to select projections that involve the least distortion of size and distance. The projection used for each map is noted in the border. Most fall into one of three categories – conic, cylindrical or azimuthal – whose basic concepts are shown above. Each involves plotting the forms of the Earth's surface on a grid of latitude and longitude lines, which may be shown as parallels, curves or radiating spokes.

Latitude and longitude

Accurate positioning of individual points on the Earth's surface is made possible by reference to the geometrical system of latitude and longitude. Latitude *parallels* are drawn west–east around the Earth and numbered by degrees north and south of the Equator, which is designated 0° of latitude. Longitude *meridians* are drawn north–south and numbered by degrees east and west of the *prime meridian*, 0° of longitude, which passes through Greenwich in England. By referring to these co-ordinates and their subdivisions of minutes (1⁄60th of a degree) and seconds (1⁄60th of a minute), any place on Earth can be located to within a few hundred yards. Latitude and longitude are indicated by blue lines on the maps; they are straight or curved according to the projection employed. Reference to these lines is the easiest way of determining the relative positions of places on different maps, and for plotting compass directions.

Name forms

For ease of reference, both English and local name forms appear in the atlas. Oceans, seas and countries are shown in English throughout the atlas; country names may be abbreviated to their commonly accepted form (e.g. Germany, not The Federal Republic of Germany). Conventional English forms are also used for place names on the smaller-scale maps of the continents. However, local name forms are used on all large-scale and regional maps, with the English form given in brackets only for important cities – the large-scale map of Russia and Central Asia thus shows Moskva (Moscow). For countries which do not use a Roman script, place names have been transcribed according to the systems adopted by the British and US Geographic Names Authorities. For China, the Pin Yin system has been used, with some more widely known forms appearing in brackets, as with Beijing (Peking). Both English and local names appear in the index, the English form being cross-referenced to the local form.

CONTENTS

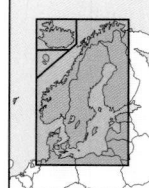
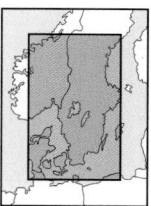
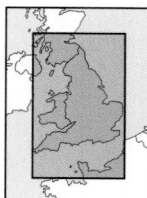
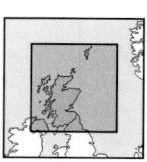
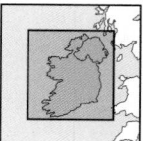
NOTE
The titles to the World Maps
list the main countries, states
and provinces covered by each
map. A name given in *italics*
indicates that only part of the
country is shown on the map.

Netherlands, Belgium and Luxembourg
1:1 000 000

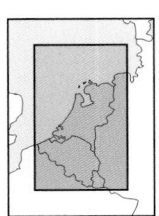

20–21

Northern France
1:2 000 000

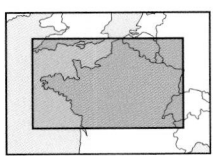

22–23

Southern France
1:2 000 000
Corsica, Monaco

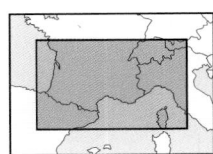

24–25

Germany
1:2 000 000

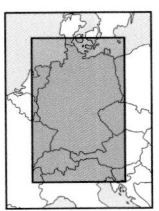

26–27

Switzerland
1:800 000
Liechtenstein

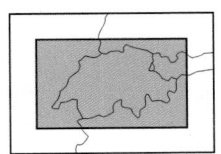

28–29

Austria, Czech Republic, Slovak Republic and Hungary
1:2 000 000
Poland

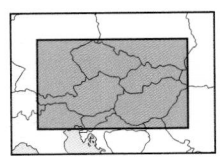

30–31

Malta, Crete, Corfu, Rhodes and Cyprus
1:800 000 / 1:1 040 000

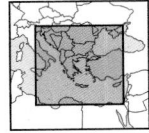

32

Balearics, Canaries and Madeira
1:800 000 / 1:1 600 00
Mallorca, Menorca, Ibiza

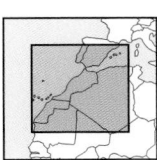

33

Eastern Spain
1:2 000 000
Andorra

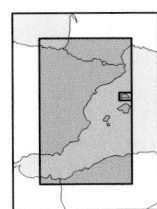

34–35

Western Spain and Portugal
1:2 000 000

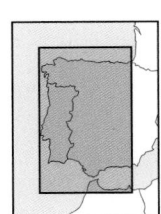

36–37

Northern Italy, Slovenia and Croatia
1:2 000 000
San Marino, Slovenia, *Croatia*

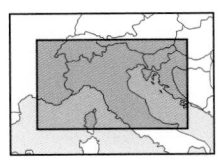

38–39

Southern Italy
1:2 000 000
Sardinia, Sicily

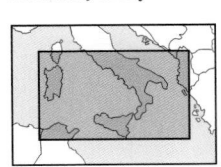

40–41

The Lower Danube
1:2 000 000
Bosnia-Herzegovina, Yugoslavia, Macedonia, Bulgaria

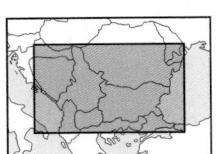

42–43

Greece and Albania
1:2 000 000

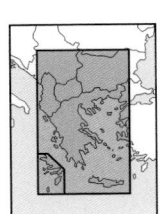

44–45

Romania
1:2 000 000

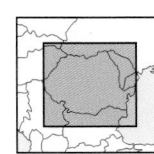

46

Poland
1:2 000 000

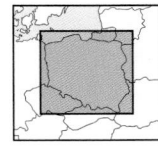

47

Eastern Europe and Turkey
1:8 000 000

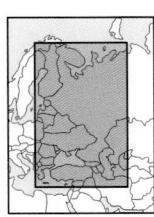

48–49

Baltic States, Belarus and Ukraine
1:4 000 000
Russia, Estonia, Latvia, Lithuania, Belarus, Moldova, *Ukraine*

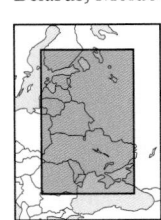

50–51

The Volga Basin and the Caucasus
1:4 000 000
Russia, Georgia, Armenia, Azerbaijan

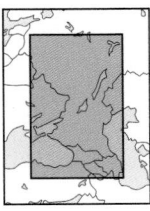

52–53

ASIA

Southern Urals
1:4 000 000
Russia

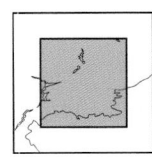

54

Central Asia
1:4 000 000
Kazakstan, Kyrgyzstan, Tajikistan, *Uzbekistan*

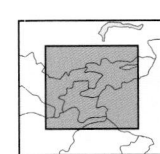

55

Russia and Central Asia
1:16 000 000
Russia, Kazakstan, Turkmenistan, Uzbekistan

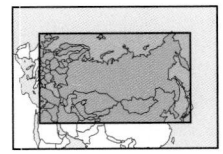

56–57

Asia: Physical
1:40 000 000

58

Asia: Political
1:40 000 000

59

Japan
1:4 000 000
Ryukyu Islands

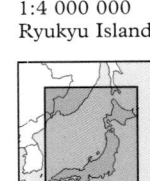
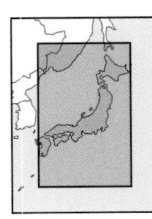

60–61

Southern Japan
1:2 000 000

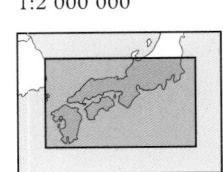

62–63

China and the Far East
1:12 000 000
Mongolia

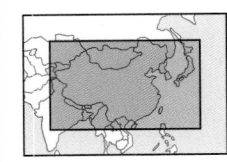

64–65

Northern China and Korea
1:4 800 000
North Korea, South Korea

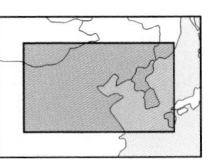

66–67

Southern China
1:4 800 000
Hong Kong, Taiwan, Macau

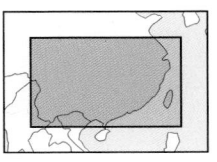

68–69

Philippines
1:3 200 000

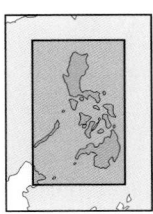

70–71

Eastern Indonesia
1:5 600 000

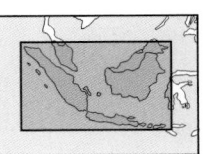

72–73

Western Indonesia
1:5 600 000
Malaysia, Singapore, Brunei

74–75

Mainland South-east Asia
1:4 800 000
Thailand, Vietnam, Cambodia, Laos

76–77

Bangladesh, North-eastern India and Burma
1:4 800 000
Bhutan

78

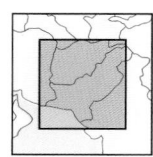
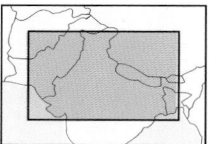
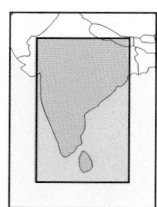
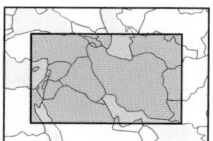
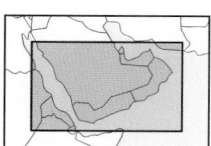
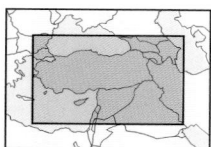
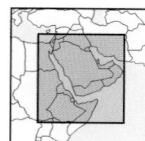
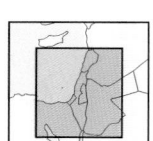
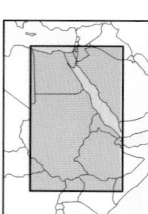
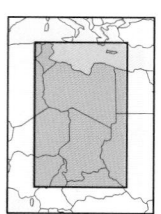
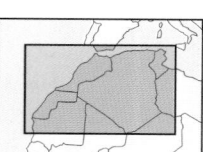
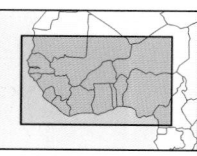
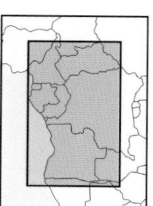
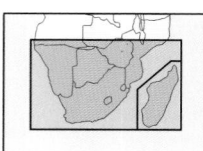
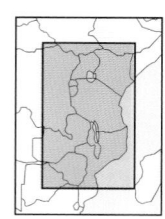
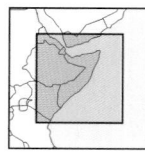
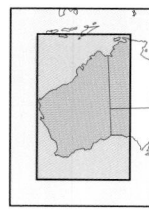

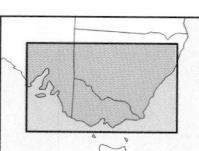

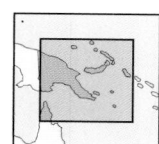

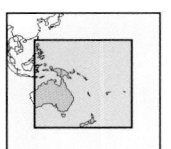
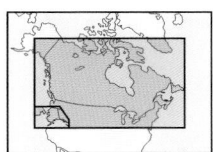
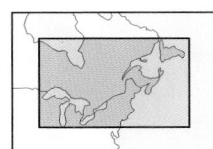
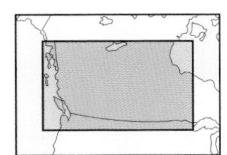
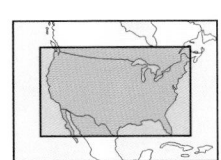
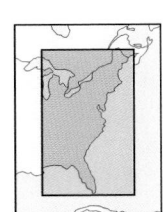
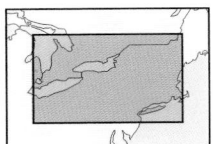
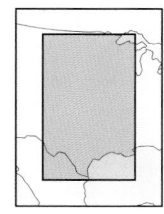
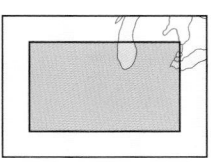
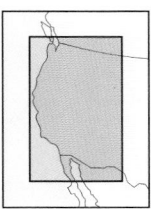
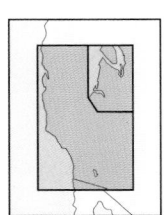
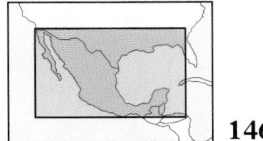
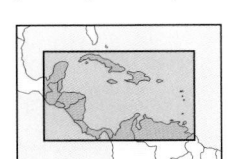
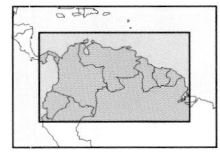
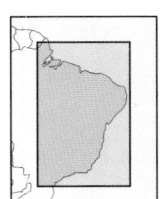
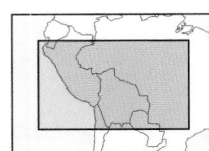
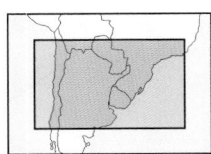
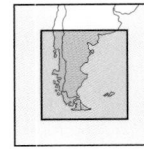

World Statistics: Countries

This alphabetical list includes all the countries and territories of the world. If a territory is not completely independent, then the country it is associated with is named. The area figures give the total area of land, inland water and ice. Units for areas and populations are thousands. The population figures are 1995 estimates. The annual income is the Gross National Product per capita in US dollars. The figures are the latest available, usually 1994.

Country/Territory	Area km² Thousands	Area miles² Thousands	Population Thousands	Capital	Annual Income US $
Adélie Land (Fr.)	432	167	0.03	–	–
Afghanistan	652	252	19,509	Kabul	220
Albania	28.8	11.1	3,458	Tirana	340
Algeria	2,382	920	25,012	Algiers	1,650
American Samoa (US)	0.20	0.08	58	Pago Pago	2,600
Amsterdam Is. (Fr.)	0.05	0.02	0.03	–	–
Andorra	0.45	0.17	65	Andorra La Vella	14,000
Angola	1,247	481	10,020	Luanda	600
Anguilla (UK)	0.1	0.04	8	The Valley	6,800
Antigua & Barbuda	0.44	0.17	67	St John's	6,390
Argentina	2,767	1,068	34,663	Buenos Aires	7,290
Armenia	29.8	11.5	3,603	Yerevan	660
Aruba (Neths)	0.19	0.07	71	Oranjestad	17,500
Ascension Is. (UK)	0.09	0.03	1.5	Georgetown	–
Australia	7,687	2,968	18,107	Canberra	17,510
Australian Antarctic Terr. (Aus.)	6,120	2,363	0	–	–
Austria	83.9	32.4	8,004	Vienna	23,120
Azerbaijan	86.6	33.4	7,559	Baku	730
Azores (Port.)	2.2	0.87	238	Ponta Delgada	–
Bahamas	13.9	5.4	277	Nassau	11,500
Bahrain	0.68	0.26	558	Manama	7,870
Bangladesh	144	56	118,342	Dhaka	220
Barbados	0.43	0.17	263	Bridgetown	6,240
Belarus	207.6	80.1	10,500	Minsk	2,930
Belgium	30.5	11.8	10,140	Brussels	21,210
Belize	23	8.9	216	Belmopan	2,440
Benin	113	43	5,381	Porto-Novo	420
Bermuda (UK)	0.05	0.02	64	Hamilton	27,000
Bhutan	47	18.1	1,639	Thimphu	170
Bolivia	1,099	424	7,900	La Paz/Sucre	770
Bosnia-Herzegovina	51	20	3,800	Sarajevo	2,500
Botswana	582	225	1,481	Gaborone	2,590
Bouvet Is. (Nor.)	0.05	0.02	0.02	–	–
Brazil	8,512	3,286	161,416	Brasília	3,020
British Antarctic Terr. (UK)	1,709	660	0.3	–	–
British Indian Ocean Terr. (UK)	0.08	0.03	0	–	–
Brunei	5.8	2.2	284	Bandar Seri Begawan	9,000
Bulgaria	111	43	8,771	Sofia	1,160
Burkina Faso	274	106	10,326	Ouagadougou	300
Burma (Myanmar)	677	261	46,580	Rangoon	950
Burundi	27.8	10.7	6,412	Bujumbura	180
Cambodia	181	70	10,452	Phnom Penh	600
Cameroon	475	184	13,232	Yaoundé	770
Canada	9,976	3,852	29,972	Ottawa	20,670
Canary Is. (Spain)	7.3	2.8	1,494	Las Palmas/Santa Cruz	–
Cape Verde Is.	4	1.6	386	Praia	870
Cayman Is. (UK)	0.26	0.10	31	George Town	20,000
Central African Republic	623	241	3,294	Bangui	390
Chad	1,284	496	6,314	Ndjaména	200
Chatham Is. (NZ)	0.96	0.37	0.05	Waitangi	–
Chile	757	292	14,271	Santiago	3,070
China	9,597	3,705	1,226,944	Beijing	490
Christmas Is. (Aus.)	0.14	0.05	2	The Settlement	–
Cocos (Keeling) Is. (Aus.)	0.01	0.005	0.6	West Island	–
Colombia	1,139	440	34,948	Bogotá	1,400
Comoros	2.2	0.86	654	Moroni	520
Congo	342	132	2,593	Brazzaville	920
Cook Is. (NZ)	0.24	0.09	19	Avarua	900
Costa Rica	51.1	19.7	3,436	San José	2,160
Croatia	56.5	21.8	4,900	Zagreb	4,500
Crozet Is. (Fr.)	0.51	0.19	35	–	–
Cuba	111	43	11,050	Havana	1,250
Cyprus	9.3	3.6	742	Nicosia	10,380
Czech Republic	78.9	30.4	10,500	Prague	2,730
Denmark	43.1	16.6	5,229	Copenhagen	26,510
Djibouti	23.2	9	603	Djibouti	780
Dominica	0.75	0.29	89	Roseau	2,680
Dominican Republic	48.7	18.8	7,818	Santo Domingo	1,080
Ecuador	284	109	11,384	Quito	1,170
Egypt	1,001	387	64,100	Cairo	660
El Salvador	21	8.1	5,743	San Salvador	1,320
Equatorial Guinea	28.1	10.8	400	Malabo	360
Eritrea	94	36	3,850	Asmara	500
Estonia	44.7	17.3	1,531	Tallinn	3,040
Ethiopia	1,128	436	51,600	Addis Ababa	100
Falkland Is. (UK)	12.2	4.7	2	Stanley	–
Faroe Is. (Den.)	1.4	0.54	47	Tórshavn	23,660
Fiji	18.3	7.1	773	Suva	2,140
Finland	338	131	5,125	Helsinki	18,970
France	552	213	58,286	Paris	22,360
French Guiana (Fr.)	90	34.7	154	Cayenne	5,000
French Polynesia (Fr.)	4	1.5	217	Papeete	7,000
Gabon	268	103	1,316	Libreville	4,050
Gambia, The	11.3	4.4	1,144	Banjul	360
Georgia	69.7	26.9	5,448	Tbilisi	560
Germany	357	138	82,000	Berlin/Bonn	23,560
Ghana	239	92	17,462	Accra	430
Gibraltar (UK)	0.007	0.003	28	Gibraltar Town	5,000
Greece	132	51	10,510	Athens	7,390
Greenland (Den.)	2,176	840	59	Godthåb (Nuuk)	9,000
Grenada	0.34	0.13	94	St George's	2,410
Guadeloupe (Fr.)	1.7	0.66	443	Basse-Terre	9,000
Guam (US)	0.55	0.21	155	Agana	6,000
Guatemala	109	42	10,624	Guatemala City	1,110
Guinea	246	95	6,702	Conakry	510
Guinea-Bissau	36.1	13.9	1,073	Bissau	220
Guyana	215	83	832	Georgetown	350
Haiti	27.8	10.7	7,180	Port-au-Prince	800
Honduras	112	43	5,940	Tegucigalpa	580
Hong Kong (UK)	1.1	0.40	6,000	–	17,860
Hungary	93	35.9	10,500	Budapest	3,330
Iceland	103	40	269	Reykjavik	23,620
India	3,288	1,269	942,989	New Delhi	290
Indonesia	1,905	735	198,644	Jakarta	730
Iran	1,648	636	68,885	Tehran	4,750
Iraq	438	169	20,184	Baghdad	2,000
Ireland	70.3	27.1	3,589	Dublin	12,580
Israel	27	10.3	5,696	Jerusalem	13,760
Italy	301	116	57,181	Rome	19,620
Ivory Coast	322	125	14,271	Yamoussoukro	630
Jamaica	11	4.2	2,700	Kingston	1,390
Jan Mayen Is. (Nor.)	0.38	0.15	0.06	–	–
Japan	378	146	125,156	Tokyo	31,450
Johnston Is. (US)	0.002	0.0009	1	–	–
Jordan	89.2	34.4	5,547	Amman	1,190
Kazakstan	2,717	1,049	17,099	Alma-Ata	1,540
Kenya	580	224	28,240	Nairobi	270
Kerguelen Is. (Fr.)	7.2	2.8	0.7	–	–
Kermadec Is. (NZ)	0.03	0.01	0.1	–	–
Kiribati	0.72	0.28	80	Tarawa	710
Korea, North	121	47	23,931	Pyŏngyang	1,100
Korea, South	99	38.2	45,088	Seoul	7,670
Kuwait	17.8	6.9	1,668	Kuwait City	23,350
Kyrgyzstan	198.5	76.6	4,738	Bishkek	830
Laos	237	91	4,906	Vientiane	290
Latvia	65	25	2,558	Riga	2,030
Lebanon	10.4	4	2,971	Beirut	1,750
Lesotho	30.4	11.7	2,064	Maseru	660

Country/Territory	Area km² Thousands	Area miles² Thousands	Population Thousands	Capital	Annual Income US $
Liberia	111	43	3,092	Monrovia	800
Libya	1,760	679	5,410	Tripoli	6,500
Liechtenstein	0.16	0.06	31	Vaduz	33,510
Lithuania	65.2	25.2	3,735	Vilnius	1,310
Luxembourg	2.6	1	408	Luxembourg	35,850
Macau (Port.)	0.02	0.006	490	Macau	7,500
Macedonia	25.7	9.9	2,173	Skopje	730
Madagascar	587	227	15,206	Antananarivo	240
Madeira (Port.)	0.81	0.31	253	Funchal	–
Malawi	118	46	9,800	Lilongwe	220
Malaysia	330	127	20,174	Kuala Lumpur	3,160
Maldives	0.30	0.12	254	Malé	820
Mali	1,240	479	10,700	Bamako	300
Malta	0.32	0.12	367	Valletta	6,800
Marshall Is.	0.18	0.07	55	Dalap-Uliga-Darrit	1,500
Martinique (Fr.)	1.1	0.42	384	Fort-de-France	3,500
Mauritania	1,025	396	2,268	Nouakchott	510
Mauritius	2.0	0.72	1,112	Port Louis	2,980
Mayotte (Fr.)	0.37	0.14	101	Mamoundzou	1,430
Mexico	1,958	756	93,342	Mexico City	3,750
Micronesia, Fed. States of	0.70	0.27	125	Palikir	1,560
Midway Is. (US)	0.005	0.002	2	–	–
Moldova	33.7	13	4,434	Chişinău	1,180
Monaco	0.002	0.0001	32	Monaco	16,000
Mongolia	1,567	605	2,408	Ulan Bator	400
Montserrat (UK)	0.10	0.04	11	Plymouth	4,500
Morocco	447	172	26,857	Rabat	1,030
Mozambique	802	309	17,800	Maputo	80
Namibia	825	318	1,610	Windhoek	1,660
Nauru	0.02	0.008	12	Yaren District	10,000
Nepal	141	54	21,953	Katmandu	160
Netherlands	41.5	16	15,495	Amsterdam/The Hague	20,710
Neths Antilles (Neths)	0.99	0.38	199	Willemstad	9,700
New Caledonia (Fr.)	19	7.3	181	Nouméa	6,000
New Zealand	269	104	3,567	Wellington	12,900
Nicaragua	130	50	4,544	Managua	360
Niger	1,267	489	9,149	Niamey	270
Nigeria	924	357	88,515	Abuja	310
Niue (NZ)	0.26	0.10	2	Alofi	–
Norfolk Is. (Aus.)	0.03	0.01	2	Kingston	–
Northern Mariana Is. (US)	0.48	0.18	47	Saipan	11,500
Norway	324	125	4,361	Oslo	26,340
Oman	212	82	2,252	Muscat	5,600
Pakistan	796	307	143,595	Islamabad	430
Palau	0.46	0.18	17	Koror	2,260
Panama	77.1	29.8	2,629	Panama City	2,580
Papua New Guinea	463	179	4,292	Port Moresby	1,120
Paraguay	407	157	4,979	Asunción	1,500
Peru	1,285	496	23,588	Lima	1,490
Peter 1st Is. (Nor.)	0.18	0.07	0	–	–
Philippines	300	116	67,167	Manila	830
Pitcairn Is. (UK)	0.03	0.01	0.06	Adamstown	–
Poland	313	121	38,587	Warsaw	2,270
Portugal	92.4	35.7	10,600	Lisbon	7,890
Puerto Rico (US)	9	3.5	3,689	San Juan	7,020
Qatar	11	4.2	594	Doha	15,140
Queen Maud Land (Nor.)	2,800	1,081	0	–	–
Réunion (Fr.)	2.5	0.97	655	Saint-Denis	3,900
Romania	238	92	22,863	Bucharest	1,120
Ross Dependency (NZ)	435	168	0	–	–
Russia	17,075	6,592	148,385	Moscow	2,350
Rwanda	26.3	10.2	7,899	Kigali	200
St Helena (UK)	0.12	0.05	6	Jamestown	–
St Kitts & Nevis	0.36	0.14	45	Basseterre	4,470
St Lucia	0.62	0.24	147	Castries	3,040
St Paul Is. (Fr.)	0.007	0.003	0	–	–
St Pierre & Miquelon (Fr.)	0.24	0.09	6	Saint Pierre	–
St Vincent & Grenadines	0.39	0.15	111	Kingstown	1,730
San Marino	0.06	0.02	26	San Marino	20,000
São Tomé & Príncipe	0.96	0.37	133	São Tomé	330
Saudi Arabia	2,150	830	18,395	Riyadh	8,000
Senegal	197	76	8,308	Dakar	730
Seychelles	0.46	0.18	75	Victoria	6,370
Sierra Leone	71.7	27.7	4,467	Freetown	140
Singapore	0.62	0.24	2,990	Singapore	19,310
Slovak Republic	49	18.9	5,400	Bratislava	1,900
Slovenia	20.3	7.8	2,000	Ljubljana	6,310
Solomon Is.	28.9	11.2	378	Honiara	750
Somalia	638	246	9,180	Mogadishu	500
South Africa	1,220	471	44,000	C. Town/Pretoria/Bloemfontein	2,900
South Georgia (UK)	3.8	1.4	0.05	–	–
South Sandwich Is. (UK)	0.38	0.15	0	–	–
Spain	505	195	39,664	Madrid	13,650
Sri Lanka	65.6	25.3	18,359	Colombo	600
Sudan	2,506	967	29,980	Khartoum	750
Surinam	163	63	421	Paramaribo	1,210
Svalbard (Nor.)	62.9	24.3	4	Longyearbyen	–
Swaziland	17.4	6.7	849	Mbabane	1,050
Sweden	450	174	8,893	Stockholm	24,830
Switzerland	41.3	15.9	7,268	Bern	36,410
Syria	185	71	14,614	Damascus	5,700
Taiwan	36	13.9	21,100	Taipei	11,000
Tajikistan	143.1	55.2	6,102	Dushanbe	470
Tanzania	945	365	29,710	Dodoma	100
Thailand	513	198	58,432	Bangkok	2,040
Togo	56.8	21.9	4,140	Lomé	330
Tokelau (NZ)	0.01	0.005	2	Nukunonu	–
Tonga	0.75	0.29	107	Nuku'alofa	1,610
Trinidad & Tobago	5.1	2	1,295	Port of Spain	3,730
Tristan da Cunha (UK)	0.11	0.04	0.33	Edinburgh	–
Tunisia	164	63	8,906	Tunis	1,780
Turkey	779	301	61,303	Ankara	2,120
Turkmenistan	488.1	188.5	4,100	Ashkhabad	1,400
Turks & Caicos Is. (UK)	0.43	0.17	15	Cockburn Town	5,000
Tuvalu	0.03	0.01	10	Fongafale	600
Uganda	236	91	21,466	Kampala	190
Ukraine	603.7	233.1	52,027	Kiev	1,910
United Arab Emirates	83.6	32.3	2,800	Abu Dhabi	22,470
United Kingdom	243.3	94	58,306	London	17,970
United States of America	9,373	3,619	263,563	Washington, DC	24,750
Uruguay	177	68	3,186	Montevideo	3,910
Uzbekistan	447.4	172.7	22,833	Tashkent	960
Vanuatu	12.2	4.7	167	Port-Vila	1,230
Vatican City	0.0004	0.0002	1	–	–
Venezuela	912	352	21,800	Caracas	2,840
Vietnam	332	127	74,580	Hanoi	170
Virgin Is. (UK)	0.15	0.06	20	Road Town	–
Virgin Is. (US)	0.34	0.13	105	Charlotte Amalie	12,000
Wake Is.	0.008	0.003	0.30	–	–
Wallis & Futuna Is. (Fr.)	0.20	0.08	13	Mata-Utu	–
Western Sahara	266	103	220	El Aaiún	300
Western Samoa	2.8	1.1	169	Apia	980
Yemen	528	204	14,609	Sana	800
Yugoslavia	102.3	39.5	10,881	Belgrade	1,000
Zaïre	2,345	905	44,504	Kinshasa	500
Zambia	753	291	9,500	Lusaka	370
Zimbabwe	391	151	11,453	Harare	540

WORLD STATISTICS: CITIES

This list shows the principal cities with more than 500,000 inhabitants (for China only cities with more than 700,000 inhabitants are included). The figures are taken from the most recent census or estimate available, and as far as possible are the population of the metropolitan area, e.g. greater New York, Mexico or London. All the figures are in thousands. Local name forms have been used for the smaller cities (e.g. Kraków).

Afghanistan
Kabul 1,424
Algeria
Algiers 1,722
Oran 664
Angola
Luanda 1,544
Argentina
Buenos Aires 11,256
Córdoba 1,198
Rosario 1,096
Mendoza 775
La Plata 640
San Miguel de Tucumán 622
Mar del Plata 520
Armenia
Yerevan 1,254
Australia
Sydney 3,657
Melbourne 3,081
Perth 1,193
Adelaide 1,050
Brisbane 777
Austria
Vienna 1,560
Azerbaijan
Baku 1,149
Bangladesh
Dhaka 6,105
Chittagong 2,041
Khulna 877
Rajshahi 517
Belarus
Minsk 1,613
Gomel 506
Belgium
Brussels 952
Bolivia
La Paz 1,126
Santa Cruz 695
Bosnia-Herzegovina
Sarajevo 526
Brazil
São Paulo 9,480
Rio de Janeiro 5,336
Salvador 2,056
Belo Horizonte 2,049
Fortaleza 1,758
Brasília 1,596
Curitiba 1,290
Recife 1,290
Nova Iguaçu 1,286
Pôrto Alegre 1,263
Belém 1,246
Manaus 1,011
Goiânia 921
Campinas 846
Guarulhos 781
São Gonçalo 748
São Luís 696
Duque de Caxias 665
Maceió 628
Santo André 614
Natal 607
Teresina 598
São Bernardo de Campo 565
Osasco 563
Campo Grande 526
Bulgaria
Sofia 1,221
Burkina Faso
Ouagadougou 634
Burma (Myanmar)
Rangoon 2,513
Mandalay 533
Cambodia
Phnom Penh 900
Cameroon
Douala 884
Yaoundé 750
Canada
Toronto 3,893
Montréal 3,127
Vancouver 1,603
Ottawa–Hull 921
Edmonton 840
Calgary 754
Winnipeg 652
Québec 646
Hamilton 599
Central African Rep.
Bangui 597
Chad
Ndjaména 530

Chile
Santiago 5,343
China
Shanghai 8,930
Beijing 6,690
Tianjin 5,000
Shenyang 4,050
Chongqing 3,870
Wuhan 3,870
Guangzhou 3,750
Harbin 3,120
Chengdu 2,760
Nanjing 2,490
Changchun 2,470
Xi'an 2,410
Dalian 2,400
Zibo 2,400
Qingdao 2,300
Jinan 2,150
Hangzhou 1,790
Taiyuan 1,720
Zhengzhou 1,690
Shijiazhuang 1,610
Changsha 1,510
Kunming 1,500
Nanchang 1,440
Fuzhou, Fujian 1,380
Lanzhou 1,340
Anshan 1,204
Fushun 1,202
Ürümqi 1,130
Hefei 1,110
Ningbo 1,100
Guiyang 1,080
Qiqihar 1,070
Tangshan 1,044
Jilin 1,037
Linhai 1,012
Macheng 1,010
Baotou 984
Nanning 960
Handan 838
Wuxi 827
Xuzhou, Jiangsu 806
Datong 798
Yichun, Heilongjiang 796
Benxi 767
Luoyang 760
Hohhot 730
Lichuan 718
Suzhou, Jiangsu 706
Huainan 704
Colombia
Bogotá 5,132
Cali 1,687
Medellin 1,608
Barranquilla 1,049
Cartagena 726
Congo
Brazzaville 938
Pointe-Noire 576
Croatia
Zagreb 931
Cuba
Havana 2,119
Czech Republic
Prague 1,216
Denmark
Copenhagen 1,337
Dominican Republic
Santo Domingo 2,200
Ecuador
Guayaquil 1,508
Quito 1,101
Egypt
Cairo 6,800
Alexandria 3,380
El Gîza 2,144
Shubra el Kheima 834
El Salvador
San Salvador 1,522
Ethiopia
Addis Ababa 2,213
Finland
Helsinki 516
France
Paris 9,319
Lyons 1,262
Marseilles 1,087
Lille 959
Bordeaux 696
Toulouse 650
Nice 516
Georgia
Tbilisi 1,279

Germany
Berlin 3,475
Hamburg 1,703
Munich 1,256
Cologne 693
Frankfurt 660
Essen 622
Dortmund 602
Stuttgart 594
Düsseldorf 575
Bremen 552
Duisburg 537
Hanover 525
Ghana
Accra 965
Greece
Athens 3,097
Guatemala
Guatemala 2,000
Guinea
Conakry 810
Haiti
Port-au-Prince 1,402
Honduras
Tegucigalpa 679
Hong Kong
Kowloon 2,031
Hong Kong 1,251
Tsuen Wan 690
Hungary
Budapest 2,009
India
Bombay (Mumbai) 12,572
Calcutta 10,916
Delhi 7,207
Madras 5,361
Hyderabad 4,280
Bangalore 4,087
Ahmadabad 3,298
Pune 2,485
Kanpur 2,111
Nagpur 1,661
Lucknow 1,642
Surat 1,517
Jaipur 1,514
Coimbatore 1,136
Vadodara 1,115
Indore 1,104
Patna 1,099
Madurai 1,094
Bhopal 1,064
Vishakhapatnam 1,052
Varanasi 1,026
Ludhiana 1,012
Agra 956
Jabalpur 887
Allahabad 858
Meerut 847
Vijayawada 845
Jamshedpur 834
Trivandrum 826
Dhanbad 818
Thane 797
Asansol 764
Nasik 722
Gwalior 720
Tiruchirappalli 711
Amritsar 709
Durg-Bhilai 689
Mysore 652
Rajkot 651
Jodhpur 649
Solapur 621
Faridabad 614
Ranchi 614
Bareilly 608
Srinagar 595
Aurangabad 592
Guwahati 584
Chandigarh 575
Salem 574
Cochin 564
Kota 536
Dharwad 527
Ghaziabad 520
Jullundur 520
Indonesia
Jakarta 8,259
Surabaya 2,421
Medan 1,686
Bandung 2,027
Palembang 1,084
Semarang 1,005
Ujung Pandang 913
Malang 650
Surakarta 504

Iran
Tehran 6,476
Mashhad 1,759
Esfahan 1,127
Tabriz 1,089
Shiraz 965
Ahvaz 725
Qom 681
Bakhtaran 624
Iraq
Baghdad 3,841
Diyala 961
As Sulaymaniyah 952
Arbil 770
Al Mawsil 644
Kadhimain 521
Ireland
Dublin 1,024
Israel
Jerusalem 544
Italy
Rome 2,723
Milan 1,359
Naples 1,072
Turin 953
Palermo 697
Genoa 668
Ivory Coast
Abidjan 1,929
Jamaica
Kingston 644
Japan
Tokyo 11,927
Yokohama 3,288
Osaka 2,589
Nagoya 2,159
Sapporo 1,732
Kobe 1,509
Kyoto 1,452
Fukuoka 1,269
Kawasaki 1,200
Hiroshima 1,102
Kitakyushu 1,020
Sendai 951
Chiba 851
Sakai 806
Kumamoto 640
Okayama 605
Hamamatsu 561
Sagamihara 560
Funabashi 540
Kagoshima 540
Higashiosaka 515
Jordan
Amman 1,272
Az-Zarqã 605
Kazakstan
Alma-Ata (Almaty) 1,147
Qaraghandy 613
Kenya
Nairobi 1,429
Korea, North
Pyŏngyang 2,639
Hamhung 775
Chŏngjin 754
Chinnampo 691
Sinŭiju 500
Korea, South
Seoul 10,628
Pusan 3,798
Taegu 2,229
Inchon 1,818
Kwangju 1,145
Taejŏn 1,062
Ulsan 683
Puch'on 668
Suwŏn 645
Sŏngnam 541
Chŏnju 517
Kyrgyzstan
Bishkek 628
Latvia
Riga 840
Lebanon
Beirut 1,500
Tripoli 500
Libya
Tripoli 990

Mali
Bamako 746
Mauritania
Nouakchott 600
Mexico
Mexico City 15,048
Guadalajara 2,847
Monterrey 2,522
Puebla 1,055
León 872
Ciudad Juárez 798
Tijuana 743
Culiacán Rosales 602
Mexicali 602
Acapulco de Juárez 592
Mérida 557
Chihuahua 530
San Luis Potosí 526
Aguascalientés 506
Moldova
Chişinău (Kishnev) 667
Mongolia
Ulan Bator 601
Morocco
Casablanca 3,079
Rabat-Salé 1,344
Fès 735
Marrakesh 665
Oujda 661
Mozambique
Maputo 1,070
Netherlands
Amsterdam 1,091
Rotterdam 1,069
The Hague 694
Utrecht 543
New Zealand
Auckland 896
Nicaragua
Managua 974
Nigeria
Lagos 1,347
Ibadan 1,295
Kano 700
Ogbomosho 661
Norway
Oslo 714
Pakistan
Karachi 5,181
Lahore 2,953
Faisalabad 1,104
Rawalpindi 795
Hyderabad 752
Multan 722
Gujranwala 659
Peshawar 556
Panama
Panama City 584
Paraguay
Asunción 945
Peru
Lima–Callao 6,601
Callao 638
Arequipa 620
Trujillo 509
Philippines
Manila 6,720
Quezon City 1,667
Davao 868
Cebu 641
Caloocan 629
Poland
Warsaw 1,655
Lódz 847
Kraków 751
Wroclaw 643
Poznań 590
Portugal
Lisbon 2,561
Oporto 1,174
Puerto Rico
San Juan 1,816
Romania
Bucharest 2,067
Russia
Moscow 8,957
St Petersburg 5,004
Novosibirsk 1,472
Nizhniy Novgorod 1,451
Yekaterinburg 1,413
Samara 1,271
Omsk 1,193
Chelyabinsk 1,170
Perm 1,108
Kazan 1,107

Ufa 1,100
Volgograd 1,031
Rostov 1,027
Voronezh 958
Krasnoyarsk 925
Saratov 916
Krasnodar 751
Togliatti 677
Vladivostok 675
Barnaul 665
Izhevsk 651
Irkutsk 644
Simbirsk 638
Yaroslavl 637
Khabarovsk 626
Novokuznetsk 614
Tula 591
Orenburg 574
Kemerovo 559
Penza 553
Tyumen 550
Ryazan 533
Naberezhnyye-Chelny 517
Astrakhan 512
Tomsk 506
Lipetsk 504
Saudi Arabia
Riyadh 2,000
Jedda 1,400
Mecca 618
Medina 500
Senegal
Dakar 1,730
Sierra Leone
Freetown 505
Singapore
Singapore 2,874
Somalia
Mogadishu 1,000
South Africa
Cape Town 1,912
Johannesburg 1,196
East Rand 1,379
Durban 1,137
Pretoria 1,080
Port Elizabeth 853
West Rand 870
Vanderbijlpark–Vereeniging 774
Soweto 597
Sasolburg 540
Spain
Madrid 3,041
Barcelona 1,631
Valencia 764
Sevilla 714
Zaragoza 607
Málaga 531
Sri Lanka
Colombo 1,863
Sudan
Khartoum 561
Omdurman 526
Sweden
Stockholm 1,539
Göteburg 783
Switzerland
Zürich 840
Syria
Damascus 1,451
Aleppo 1,445
Homs 518
Taiwan
Taipei 2,653
Kaohsiung 1,405
Taichung 817
Tainan 700
Panchiao 544
Tajikistan
Dushanbe 602
Tanzania
Dar-es-Salaam 1,361
Thailand
Bangkok 5,876
Togo
Lomé 590
Tunisia
Tunis 1,395
Turkey
Istanbul 6,620
Ankara 2,559
Izmir 1,757
Adana 916
Bursa 835
Gaziantep 603

Konya 513
Uganda
Kampala 773
Ukraine
Kiev 2,643
Kharkiv 1,622
Dnipropetrovsk 1,190
Donetsk 1,121
Odesa 1,096
Zaporizhzhya 898
Lviv 807
Kryvyy Rih 729
Mariupol 523
Mykolayiv 515
Luhansk 505
United Kingdom
London 6,967
Birmingham 1,220
Manchester 981
Glasgow 720
Liverpool 664
Leeds 529
Newcastle 525
United States
New York 19,670
Los Angeles 15,048
Chicago 8,410
San Francisco 6,410
Philadelphia 5,939
Boston 5,439
Detroit 5,246
Washington, DC 4,360
Dallas 4,215
Houston 3,962
Miami 3,309
Atlanta 3,153
Seattle 3,131
Cleveland 2,890
Minneapolis–St Paul 2,618
San Diego 2,601
St Louis 2,519
Baltimore 2,434
Pittsburgh 2,406
Phoenix 2,330
Tampa 2,107
Denver 2,089
Portland (Or.) 1,897
Cincinnati 1,865
Milwaukee 1,629
Kansas City (Mo.) 1,617
Sacramento 1,563
Norfolk 1,497
Indianapolis 1,424
Columbus (Oh.) 1,394
San Antonio 1,379
New Orleans 1,303
Charlotte 1,212
Buffalo 1,194
Hartford 1,156
Salt Lake City 1,128
Oklahoma 984
San Jose 801
Jacksonville 661
Omaha 656
Memphis 610
El Paso 544
Uruguay
Montevideo 1,384
Uzbekistan
Tashkent 2,094
Venezuela
Caracas 2,784
Maracaibo 1,364
Valencia 1,032
Maracay 800
Barquisimeto 745
Ciudad Guayana 524
Vietnam
Ho Chi Minh City 3,924
Hanoi 3,056
Haiphong 1,448
Yugoslavia
Belgrade 1,137
Zaïre
Kinshasa 3,804
Lubumbashi 739
Mbuji-Mayi 613
Kolwezi 544
Zambia
Lusaka 982
Zimbabwe
Harare 1,189
Bulawayo 622

WORLD STATISTICS: DISTANCES

The table shows air distances in miles and kilometres between thirty major cities. Known as 'Great Circle' distances, these measure the shortest routes between the cities, which aircraft use where possible. The maps show the world centred on six individual cities, and illustrate, for example, why direct flights from Japan to northern America and Europe are across the Arctic regions, and Singapore is on the direct line route from Europe to Australia. The maps have been constructed on an Azimuthal Equidistant projection, on which all distances measured through the centre point are true to scale. The circular lines are drawn at 5,000, 10,000 and 15,000 km from the central city.

Air distances between cities. In the printed table the upper-right of the diagonal is read in **Kms** and the lower-left of the diagonal is read in **Miles**.

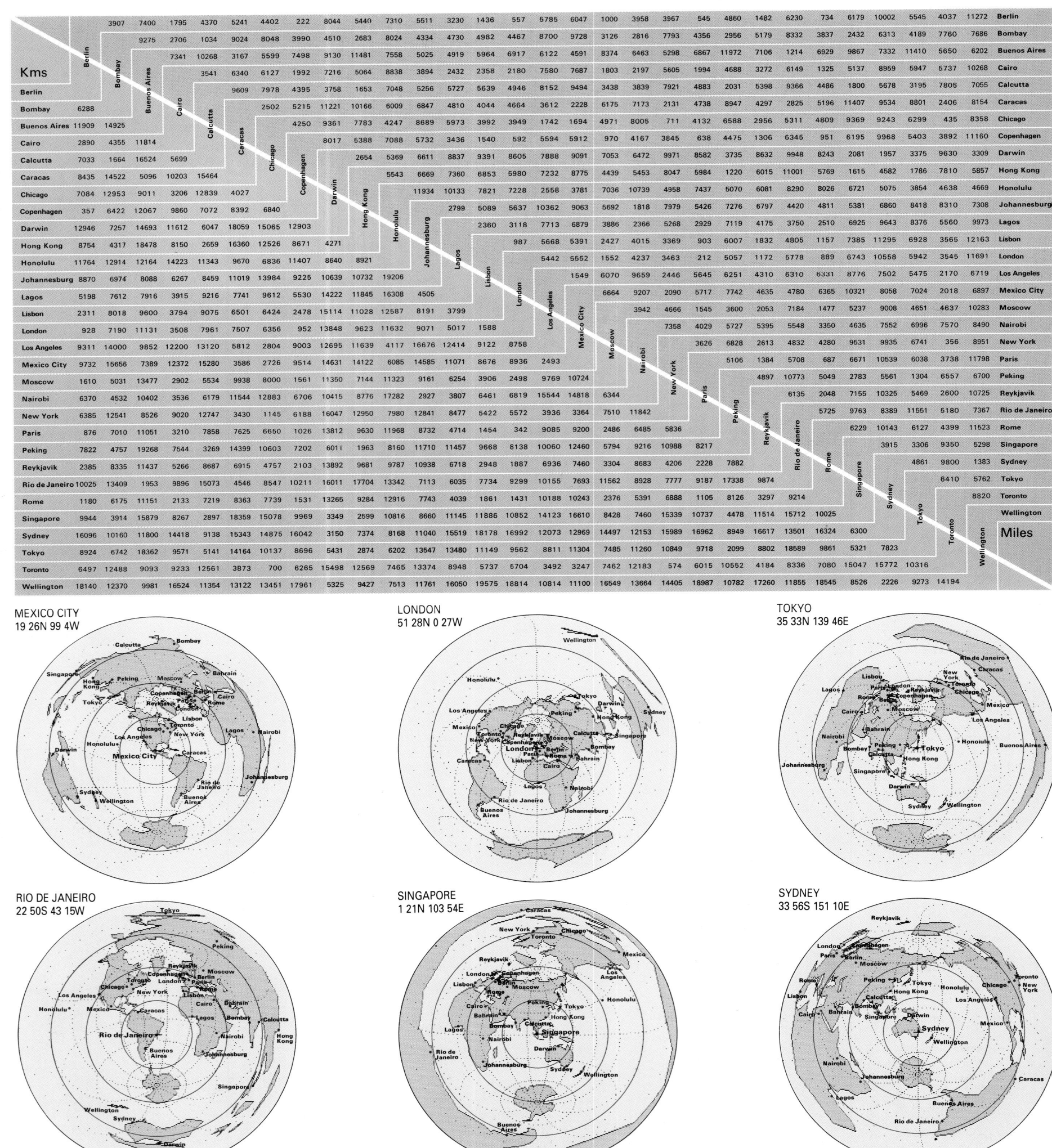

	Berlin	Bombay	Buenos Aires	Cairo	Calcutta	Caracas	Chicago	Copenhagen	Darwin	Hong Kong	Honolulu	Johannesburg	Lagos	Lisbon	London	Los Angeles	Mexico City	Moscow	Nairobi	New York	Paris	Peking	Reykjavik	Rio de Janeiro	Rome	Singapore	Sydney	Tokyo	Toronto	Wellington
Berlin		3907	7400	1795	4370	5241	4402	222	8044	5440	7310	5511	3230	1436	557	5785	6047	1000	3958	3967	545	4860	1482	6230	734	6179	10002	5545	4037	11272
Bombay	6288		9275	2706	1034	9024	8048	3990	4510	2683	8024	4334	4730	4982	4467	8700	9728	3126	2816	7793	4356	2956	5179	8332	3837	2432	6313	4189	7760	7686
Buenos Aires	11909	14925		7341	10268	3167	5599	7498	9130	11481	7558	5025	4919	5964	6917	6122	4591	8374	6463	5298	6867	11972	7106	1214	6929	9867	7332	11410	5650	6202
Cairo	2890	4355	11814		3541	6340	6127	1992	7216	5064	8838	3894	2432	2358	2180	7580	7687	1803	2197	5605	1994	4688	3272	6149	1325	5137	8959	5947		10268
Calcutta	7033	1664	16524	5699		9609	7978	4395	3758	1653	7048	5256	5727	5639	4946	8152	9494	3438	3839	7921	4883	2031	5398	8366	4486	1800	5678	3195	7805	7055
Caracas	8435	14522	5096	10203	15464		2502	5215	11221	10166	6009	6847	4810	4044	4664	3612	2228	6175	7173	2131	4738	8947	4297	2825	5196	11407	9534	8801	2406	8154
Chicago	7084	12953	9011	3206	12839	4027		4250	9361	7783	4247	8689	5973	3992	3949	1742	1694	4971	8005	711	4132	6588	2956	5311	4809	9369	9243	6299	435	8358
Copenhagen	357	6422	12067	9860	7072	8392	6840		8017	5388	7088	5732	3436	1540	592	5594	5912	970	4167	3845	638	4475	1306	6345	951	6195	9968	5403	3892	11160
Darwin	12946	7257	14693	11612	6047	18059	15065	12903		2654	5369	6611	8837	9391	8605	7888	9091	7053	6472	9971	8582	3735	8632	9948	8243	2081	1957	3375	9630	3309
Hong Kong	8754	4317	18478	8150	2659	16360	12526	8671	4271		5543	6669	7360	6853	5980	7232	8775	4439	5453	8047	5984	1220	6015	11001	5769	1615	4582	1786	7810	5857
Honolulu	11764	12914	12164	14223	11343	9670	6836	11407	8640	8921		11934	10133	7821	7228	2558	3781	7036	10739	4958	7437	5070	6081	8290	8026	6721	5075	3854	4638	4669
Johannesburg	8870	6974	8088	6267	8459	11019	13984	9225	10639	10732	19206		2799	5089	5637	10362	9063	5692	1818	7979	5426	7276	6797	4420	4811	5381	6860	8418	8310	7308
Lagos	5198	7612	7916	3915	9216	7741	9612	5530	14222	11845	16308	4505		2360	3118	7713	6879	3886	2366	5268	2929	7119	4175	3750	2510	6925	9643	8376	5560	9973
Lisbon	2311	8018	9600	3794	9075	6501	6424	2478	15114	11028	12587	8191	3799		987	5668	5391	2427	4015	3369	903	6007	1832	4805	1157	7385	11295	6928	3565	12163
London	928	7190	11131	3508	7961	7507	6356	952	13848	9623	11632	9071	5017	1588		5442	5552	1552	2237	3463	212	5057	1172	5778	889	6143	10558	5942	3545	11691
Los Angeles	9311	14000	9852	12200	13120	5812	2804	9003	12695	11639	4117	16676	12414	9122	8758		1549	6070	9659	2446	5645	6251	4310	6310	6331	8776	7502	5475	2170	6719
Mexico City	9732	15656	7389	12372	15280	3586	2726	9514	14631	14122	6085	14585	11071	8676	8936	2493		6664	9207	2090	5717	7742	4635	4780	6365	10321	8058	7024	2018	6897
Moscow	1610	5031	13477	2902	5534	9938	8000	1561	11350	7144	11323	9161	6254	3906	2498	9769	10724		3942	4666	1545	3600	2053	7184	1477	5237	9008	4651	4637	10283
Nairobi	6370	4532	10402	3536	6179	11544	12883	6706	10415	8776	17282	2927	3807	6461	6819	15544	14818	6344		7358	4029	5727	5395	5548	3350	4635	7552	6996	7570	8490
New York	6385	12541	8526	9020	12747	3430	1145	6188	16047	12950	7980	12841	8477	5422	5572	3936	3364	7510	11842		3626	6828	2613	4832	4280	9531	9935	6741	356	8951
Paris	876	7010	11051	3210	7858	7625	6650	1026	13812	9630	11968	8732	4714	1454	342	9085	9200	2486	6485	5836		5106	1384	5708	687	6671	10539	6038	3738	11798
Peking	7822	4757	19268	7544	3269	14399	10603	7202	6011	1963	8160	11710	11457	9668	8138	10060	12460	5794	9216	10988	8217		4897	10773	5049	2783	5561	1304	6557	6700
Reykjavik	2385	8335	11437	5266	8687	6915	4757	2103	13892	9681	9787	10938	6718	2948	1887	6936	7460	3304	8683	4206	2228	7882		6135	2048	7155	10325	5469	2600	10725
Rio de Janeiro	10025	13409	1953	9896	15073	4546	8547	10211	16011	17704	13342	7113	6035	7734	9299	10155	7693	11562	8928	7777	9187	17338	9874		5725	9763	8389	11551	5180	7367
Rome	1180	6175	11151	2133	7219	8363	7739	1531	13265	9284	12916	7743	4039	1861	1431	10188	10243	2376	5391	6888	1105	8126	3297	9214		6229	10143	6127	4399	11523
Singapore	9944	3914	15879	8267	2897	18359	15078	9969	3349	2599	10816	8660	11145	11886	10852	14123	16610	8428	7460	15339	10737	4478	11514	15712	10025		3915	3306	9350	5298
Sydney	16096	10160	11800	14418	9138	15343	14875	16042	3150	7374	8168	11040	15519	18178	16992	12073	12969	14497	12153	15989	16962	8949	16617	13501	16324	6300		4861	9800	1383
Tokyo	8924	6742	18362	9571	5141	14164	10137	8696	5431	2874	6202	13547	13480	11149	9562	8811	11304	7485	11260	10849	9718	2099	8802	18589	9861	5321	7823		6410	5762
Toronto	6497	12488	9093	9233	12561	3873	700	6265	15498	12569	7465	13374	8948	5737	5704	3492	3247	7462	12183	574	6015	10552	4184	8336	7080	15047	15772	10316		8820
Wellington	18140	12370	9981	16524	11354	13122	13451	17961	5325	9427	7513	11761	16050	19575	18814	10814	11100	16549	13664	14405	18987	10782	17260	11855	18545	8526	2226	9273	14194	

MEXICO CITY 19 26N 99 4W

LONDON 51 28N 0 27W

TOKYO 35 33N 139 46E

RIO DE JANEIRO 22 50S 43 15W

SINGAPORE 1 21N 103 54E

SYDNEY 33 56S 151 10E

WORLD STATISTICS: CLIMATE

Rainfall and temperature figures are provided for more than 70 cities around the world. As climate is affected by altitude, the height of each city is shown in metres beneath its name. For each month, the figures in red show average temperature in degrees Celsius, and in blue the total rainfall or snow in millimetres; the average annual temperature and total annual rainfall are at the end of the rows.

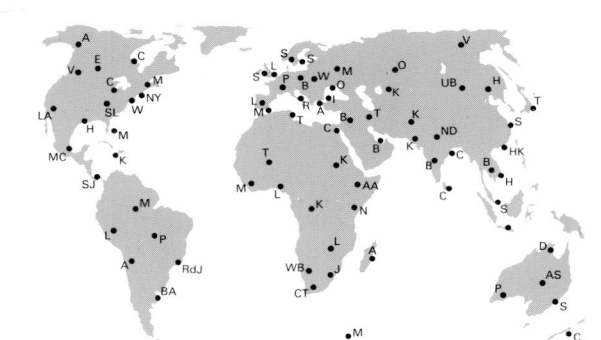

EUROPE

	Jan.	Feb.	Mar.	Apr.	May	June	July	Aug.	Sept.	Oct.	Nov.	Dec.	Year
Athens, Greece	62	37	37	23	23	14	6	7	15	51	56	71	402
107 m	10	10	12	16	20	25	28	28	24	20	15	11	18
Berlin, Germany	46	40	33	42	49	65	73	69	48	49	46	43	603
55 m	-1	0	4	9	14	17	19	18	15	9	5	1	9
Istanbul, Turkey	109	92	72	46	38	34	34	30	58	81	103	119	816
14 m	5	6	7	11	16	20	23	23	20	16	12	8	14
Lisbon, Portugal	111	76	109	54	44	16	3	4	33	62	93	103	708
77 m	11	12	14	16	17	20	22	23	21	18	14	12	17
London, UK	54	40	37	37	46	45	57	59	49	57	64	48	593
5 m	4	5	7	9	12	16	18	17	15	11	8	5	11
Málaga, Spain	61	51	62	46	26	5	1	3	29	64	64	62	474
33 m	12	13	16	17	19	29	25	26	23	20	16	13	18
Moscow, Russia	39	38	36	37	53	58	88	71	58	45	47	54	624
156 m	-13	-10	-4	6	13	16	18	17	12	6	-1	-7	4
Odesa, Ukraine	57	62	30	21	34	34	42	37	37	13	35	71	473
64 m	-3	-1	2	9	15	20	22	22	18	12	9	1	10
Paris, France	56	46	35	42	57	54	59	64	55	50	51	50	619
75 m	3	4	8	11	15	18	20	19	17	12	7	4	12
Rome, Italy	71	62	57	51	46	37	15	21	63	99	129	93	744
17 m	8	9	11	14	18	22	25	25	22	17	13	10	16
Shannon, Irish Republic	94	67	56	53	61	57	77	79	86	86	96	117	929
2 m	5	5	7	9	12	14	16	16	14	11	8	6	10
Stockholm, Sweden	43	30	25	31	34	45	61	76	60	48	53	48	554
44 m	-3	-3	-1	5	10	15	18	17	12	7	3	0	7

ASIA

	Jan.	Feb.	Mar.	Apr.	May	June	July	Aug.	Sept.	Oct.	Nov.	Dec.	Year
Bahrain	8	18	13	8	<3	0	0	0	0	0	18	18	81
5 m	17	18	21	25	29	32	33	34	31	28	24	19	26
Bangkok, Thailand	8	20	36	58	198	160	160	175	305	206	66	5	1,397
2 m	26	28	29	30	29	29	28	28	28	28	26	25	28
Beirut, Lebanon	191	158	94	53	18	3	<3	<3	5	51	132	185	892
34 m	14	14	16	18	22	24	27	28	26	24	19	16	21
Bombay, India	3	3	3	<3	18	485	617	340	264	64	13	3	1,809
11 m	24	24	26	28	30	29	27	27	27	28	27	26	27
Calcutta, India	10	31	36	43	140	297	325	328	252	114	20	5	1,600
6 m	20	22	27	30	30	30	29	29	29	28	23	19	26
Colombo, Sri Lanka	89	69	147	231	371	224	135	109	160	348	315	147	2,365
7 m	26	26	27	28	28	27	27	27	27	27	26	26	27
Harbin, China	6	5	10	23	43	94	112	104	46	33	8	5	488
160 m	-18	-15	-5	6	13	19	22	21	14	4	-6	-16	3
Ho Chi Minh, Vietnam	15	3	13	43	221	330	315	269	335	269	114	56	1,984
9 m	26	27	29	30	29	28	28	28	27	27	27	26	28
Hong Kong	33	46	74	137	292	394	381	361	257	114	43	31	2,162
33 m	16	15	18	22	26	28	28	28	27	25	21	18	23
Jakarta, Indonesia	300	300	211	147	114	97	64	43	66	112	142	203	1,798
8 m	26	26	27	27	27	27	27	27	27	27	27	26	27
Kabul, Afghanistan	31	36	94	102	20	5	3	3	<3	15	20	10	338
1,815 m	-3	-1	6	13	18	22	25	24	20	14	7	3	12
Karachi, Pakistan	13	10	8	3	3	18	81	41	13	<3	3	5	196
4 m	19	20	24	28	30	31	30	29	28	28	24	20	26
Kazalinsk, Kazakhstan	10	10	13	13	15	5	5	8	8	10	13	15	125
63 m	-12	-11	-3	6	18	23	25	23	16	8	-1	-7	7
New Delhi, India	23	18	13	8	13	74	180	172	117	10	3	10	640
218 m	14	17	23	28	33	34	31	30	29	26	20	15	25
Omsk, Russia	15	8	8	13	31	51	51	51	28	25	18	20	318
85 m	-22	-19	-12	-1	10	16	18	16	10	1	-11	-18	-1
Shanghai, China	48	58	84	94	94	180	147	142	130	71	51	36	1,135
7 m	4	5	9	14	20	24	28	28	23	19	12	7	16
Singapore	252	173	193	188	173	173	170	196	178	208	254	257	2,413
10 m	26	26	28	28	28	28	28	27	27	27	27	27	27
Tehran, Iran	46	38	46	36	13	3	3	3	3	8	20	31	246
1,220 m	2	5	9	16	21	26	30	29	25	18	12	6	17
Tokyo, Japan	48	74	107	135	147	165	142	152	234	208	97	56	1,565
6 m	3	4	7	13	17	21	25	26	23	17	11	6	14
Ulan Bator, Mongolia	<3	<3	3	5	10	28	76	51	23	5	5	3	208
1,325 m	-26	-21	-13	-1	6	14	16	14	8	-1	-13	-22	-3
Verkhoyansk, Russia	5	5	3	5	8	23	28	25	13	8	8	5	134
100 m	-50	-45	-32	-15	0	12	14	9	2	-15	-38	-48	-17

AFRICA

	Jan.	Feb.	Mar.	Apr.	May	June	July	Aug.	Sept.	Oct.	Nov.	Dec.	Year
Addis Ababa, Ethiopia	<3	3	25	135	213	201	206	239	102	28	<3	0	1,151
2,450 m	19	20	20	20	19	18	18	19	21	22	21	20	20
Antananarivo, Madagas.	300	279	178	53	18	8	8	10	18	61	135	287	1,356
1,372 m	21	21	21	19	18	15	14	15	17	19	21	21	19
Cairo, Egypt	5	5	5	3	3	<3	0	0	<3	<3	3	5	28
116 m	13	15	18	21	25	28	28	28	26	24	20	15	22
Cape Town, South Africa	15	8	18	48	79	84	89	66	43	31	18	10	508
17 m	21	21	20	18	16	13	12	13	14	16	18	19	17
Johannesburg, S. Africa	114	109	89	38	25	8	8	8	23	56	107	125	709
1,665 m	20	20	18	16	13	10	11	13	16	18	19	20	16

	Jan.	Feb.	Mar.	Apr.	May	June	July	Aug.	Sept.	Oct.	Nov.	Dec.	Year
Khartoum, Sudan	<3	<3	<3	<3	3	8	53	71	18	5	<3	0	158
390 m	24	25	28	31	33	34	32	31	32	32	28	25	29
Kinshasa, Zaïre	135	145	196	196	158	8	3	3	31	119	221	142	1,354
325 m	26	26	27	27	26	24	23	24	25	26	26	26	25
Lagos, Nigeria	28	46	102	150	269	460	279	64	140	206	69	25	1,836
3 m	27	28	29	28	28	26	26	25	26	26	28	28	27
Lusaka, Zambia	231	191	142	18	3	<3	<3	<3	0	10	91	150	836
1,277 m	21	22	21	21	19	16	16	18	22	24	23	22	21
Monrovia, Liberia	31	56	97	216	516	973	996	373	744	772	236	130	5,138
23 m	26	26	27	27	26	25	24	25	25	25	26	26	26
Nairobi, Kenya	38	64	125	211	158	46	15	23	31	53	109	86	958
1,820 m	19	19	19	19	18	16	16	16	18	19	18	18	18
Timbuktu, Mali	<3	<3	3	<3	5	23	79	81	38	3	<3	<3	231
301 m	22	24	28	32	34	35	32	30	32	31	28	23	29
Tunis, Tunisia	64	51	41	36	18	8	3		33	51	48	61	419
66 m	10	11	13	16	19	23	26	27	25	20	16	11	18
Walvis Bay, Namibia	<3	5	8	3	3	<3	<3	3	<3	<3	<3	<3	23
7 m	19	19	19	18	17	16	15	14	14	15	17	18	18

AUSTRALIA, NEW ZEALAND AND ANTARCTICA

	Jan.	Feb.	Mar.	Apr.	May	June	July	Aug.	Sept.	Oct.	Nov.	Dec.	Year
Alice Springs, Australia	43	33	28	10	15	13	8	8	8	18	31	38	252
579 m	29	28	25	20	15	12	12	14	18	23	26	28	21
Christchurch, N. Zealand	56	43	48	48	66	66	69	48	46	43	48	56	638
10 m	16	16	14	12	9	6	6	7	9	12	14	16	11
Darwin, Australia	386	312	254	97	15	3	<3	3	13	51	119	239	1,491
30 m	29	29	29	29	28	26	25	26	28	29	30	29	28
Mawson, Antarctica	11	30	20	10	44	180	4	40	3	20	0	0	362
14 m	0	-5	-10	-14	-15	-16	-18	-18	-19	-13	-5	-1	-11
Perth, Australia	8	10	20	43	130	180	170	149	86	56	20	13	881
60 m	23	23	22	19	16	14	13	13	15	16	19	22	18
Sydney, Australia	89	102	127	135	127	117	117	76	73	71	73	73	1,181
42 m	22	22	21	18	15	13	12	13	15	18	19	21	17

NORTH AMERICA

	Jan.	Feb.	Mar.	Apr.	May	June	July	Aug.	Sept.	Oct.	Nov.	Dec.	Year
Anchorage, Alaska, USA	20	18	15	10	13	18	41	66	66	56	25	23	371
40 m	-11	-8	-5	2	7	12	14	13	9	2	-5	-11	2
Chicago, Illinois, USA	51	51	66	71	86	89	84	81	79	66	61	51	836
251 m	-4	-3	2	9	14	20	23	22	19	12	5	-1	10
Churchill, Man., Canada	15	13	18	23	32	44	46	58	51	43	39	21	402
13 m	-28	-26	-20	-10	-2	6	12	11	5	-2	-12	-22	-7
Edmonton, Alta., Canada	25	19	19	22	43	77	89	78	39	17	16	25	466
676 m	-15	-10	-5	4	11	15	17	16	11	6	-4	-10	3
Honolulu, Hawaii, USA	104	66	79	48	25	18	23	28	36	48	64	104	643
12 m	23	18	19	20	22	24	25	26	26	24	22	19	22
Houston, Texas, USA	89	76	84	91	119	117	99	99	104	94	89	109	1,171
12 m	12	13	17	21	24	27	28	28	26	22	16	12	21
Kingston, Jamaica	23	15	23	31	102	89	38	91	99	180	74	36	800
34 m	25	25	25	26	26	28	28	28	27	27	26	26	26
Los Angeles, Calif., USA	79	76	71	25	10	3	<3	<3	5	15	31	66	381
95 m	13	14	14	16	17	19	21	22	21	18	16	14	17
Mexico City, Mexico	13	5	10	20	53	119	170	152	130	51	18	8	747
2,309 m	12	13	16	18	19	19	17	18	18	16	14	13	16
Miami, Florida, USA	71	53	64	81	173	178	155	160	203	234	71	51	1,516
8 m	20	20	22	23	25	27	28	28	27	25	22	21	24
Montréal, Que., Canada	72	65	74	74	66	82	90	92	88	76	81	87	946
57 m	-10	-9	-3	-6	13	18	21	20	15	9	2	-7	6
New York, N.Y., USA	94	97	91	81	81	84	107	109	86	89	76	91	1,092
96 m	-1	-1	3	10	16	20	23	23	21	15	7	2	11
St Louis, Mo., USA	58	64	89	97	114	114	89	86	81	74	71	64	1,001
173 m	0	1	7	13	19	24	26	26	22	15	8	2	14
San José, Costa Rica	15	5	20	46	229	241	211	241	305	300	145	41	1,798
1,146 m	19	19	21	21	22	21	21	21	21	20	20	19	20
Vancouver, B.C., Canada	154	115	101	60	52	45	32	41	67	114	150	182	1,113
14 m	3	5	6	9	12	15	17	17	14	10	6	4	10
Washington, D.C., USA	86	76	91	84	94	99	112	109	94	74	66	79	1,064
22 m	1	2	7	13	18	23	25	24	20	14	8	3	13

SOUTH AMERICA

	Jan.	Feb.	Mar.	Apr.	May	June	July	Aug.	Sept.	Oct.	Nov.	Dec.	Year
Antofagasta, Chile	0	0	0	<3	<3	3	5	3	<3	3	<3	0	13
94 m	21	21	20	18	16	15	14	14	15	16	18	19	17
Buenos Aires, Argentina	79	71	109	89	76	61	56	61	79	86	84	99	950
27 m	23	23	21	17	13	9	10	11	13	15	19	22	16
Lima, Peru	3	<3	<3	<3	<3	3	8	8	8	3	3	<3	41
120 m	23	24	24	22	19	17	16	16	17	18	19	21	20
Manaus, Brazil	249	231	262	221	170	84	58	38	46	107	142	203	1,811
44 m	28	28	28	28	28	28	28	29	29	29	29	28	28
Paraná, Brazil	287	236	239	102	13	<3	3	5	28	127	231	310	1,582
260 m	23	23	23	23	21	21	21	21	24	24	24	23	23
Rio de Janeiro, Brazil	125	122	130	107	79	53	41	43	66	79	104	137	1,082
61 m	26	26	25	24	22	21	21	21	21	22	23	25	23

WORLD STATISTICS: PHYSICAL DIMENSIONS

Each topic list is divided into continents and within a continent the items are listed in order of size. The order of the continents is as in the atlas, Europe through to South America. Certain lists down to this mark > are complete; below they are selective. The world top ten are shown in square brackets; in the case of mountains this has not been done because the world top 30 are all in Asia. The figures are rounded as appropriate.

WORLD, CONTINENTS, OCEANS

	km²	miles²	%
The World	509,450,000	196,672,000	–
Land	149,450,000	57,688,000	29.3
Water	360,000,000	138,984,000	70.7
Asia	44,500,000	17,177,000	29.8
Africa	30,302,000	11,697,000	20.3
North America	24,241,000	9,357,000	16.2
South America	17,793,000	6,868,000	11.9
Antarctica	14,100,000	5,443,000	9.4
Europe	9,957,000	3,843,000	6.7
Australia & Oceania	8,557,000	3,303,000	5.7
Pacific Ocean	179,679,000	69,356,000	49.9
Atlantic Ocean	92,373,000	35,657,000	25.7
Indian Ocean	73,917,000	28,532,000	20.5
Arctic Ocean	14,090,000	5,439,000	3.9

SEAS

Pacific	km²	miles²
South China Sea	2,974,600	1,148,500
Bering Sea	2,268,000	875,000
Sea of Okhotsk	1,528,000	590,000
East China & Yellow	1,249,000	482,000
Sea of Japan	1,008,000	389,000
Gulf of California	162,000	62,500
Bass Strait	75,000	29,000

Atlantic	km²	miles²
Caribbean Sea	2,766,000	1,068,000
Mediterranean Sea	2,516,000	971,000
Gulf of Mexico	1,543,000	596,000
Hudson Bay	1,232,000	476,000
North Sea	575,000	223,000
Black Sea	462,000	178,000
Baltic Sea	422,170	163,000
Gulf of St Lawrence	238,000	92,000

Indian	km²	miles²
Red Sea	438,000	169,000
The Gulf	239,000	92,000

MOUNTAINS

Europe		m	ft
Mont Blanc	France/Italy	4,807	15,771
Monte Rosa	Italy/Switzerland	4,634	15,203
Dom	Switzerland	4,545	14,911
Liskamm	Switzerland	4,527	14,852
Weisshorn	Switzerland	4,505	14,780
Taschorn	Switzerland	4,490	14,730
Matterhorn/Cervino	Italy/Switzerland	4,478	14,691
Mont Maudit	France/Italy	4,465	14,649
Dent Blanche	Switzerland	4,356	14,291
Nadelhorn	Switzerland	4,327	14,196
> Grandes Jorasses	France/Italy	4,208	13,806
Jungfrau	Switzerland	4,158	13,642
Barre des Ecrins	France	4,103	13,461
Gran Paradiso	Italy	4,061	13,323
Piz Bernina	Italy/Switzerland	4,049	13,284
Eiger	Switzerland	3,970	13,025
Monte Viso	Italy	3,841	12,602
Grossglockner	Austria	3,797	12,457
Wildspitze	Austria	3,772	12,382
Monte Disgrazia	Italy	3,678	12,066
Mulhacén	Spain	3,478	11,411
Pico de Aneto	Spain	3,404	11,168
Marmolada	Italy	3,342	10,964
Etna	Italy	3,340	10,958
Punta del'Argentera	Italy	3,297	10,817
Zugspitze	Germany	2,962	9,718
Musala	Bulgaria	2,925	9,596
Olympus	Greece	2,917	9,570
Triglav	Slovenia	2,863	9,393
Monte Cinto	France (Corsica)	2,710	8,891
Gerlachovka	Slovak Republic	2,655	8,711
Torre de Cerrado	Spain	2,648	8,688
Galdhöpiggen	Norway	2,468	8,100
Hvannadalshnúkur	Iceland	2,119	6,952
Kebnekaise	Sweden	2,117	6,946
Ben Nevis	UK	1,343	4,406

Asia		m	ft
Everest	China/Nepal	8,848	29,029
K2 (Godwin Austen)	China/Kashmir	8,611	28,251
Kanchenjunga	India/Nepal	8,598	28,208
Lhotse	China/Nepal	8,516	27,939
Makalu	China/Nepal	8,481	27,824
Cho Oyu	China/Nepal	8,201	26,906
Dhaulagiri	Nepal	8,172	26,811
Manaslu	Nepal	8,156	26,758
Nanga Parbat	Kashmir	8,126	26,660
Annapurna	Nepal	8,078	26,502
Gasherbrum	China/Kashmir	8,068	26,469
Broad Peak	China/Kashmir	8,051	26,414
Xixabangma	China	8,012	26,286
Kangbachen	India/Nepal	7,902	25,925
Jannu	India/Nepal	7,902	25,925
Gayachung Kang	Nepal	7,897	25,909
Himalchuli	Nepal	7,893	25,896
Disteghil Sar	Kashmir	7,885	25,869
Nuptse	Nepal	7,879	25,849
Khunyang Chhish	Kashmir	7,852	25,761
Masherbrum	Kashmir	7,821	25,659
Nanda Devi	India	7,817	25,646
Rakaposhi	Kashmir	7,788	25,551
Batura	Kashmir	7,785	25,541
Namche Barwa	China	7,756	25,446
Kamet	India	7,756	25,446
Soltoro Kangri	Kashmir	7,742	25,400
Gurla Mandhata	China	7,728	25,354
Trivor	Pakistan	7,720	25,328
> Kongur Shan	China	7,719	25,324
Tirich Mir	Pakistan	7,690	25,229
K'ula Shan	Bhutan/China	7,543	24,747
Pik Kommunizma	Tajikistan	7,495	24,590
Elbrus	Russia	5,642	18,510
Demavend	Iran	5,604	18,386
Ararat	Turkey	5,165	16,945
Gunong Kinabalu	Malaysia (Borneo)	4,101	13,455
Yu Shan	Taiwan	3,997	13,113
Fuji-San	Japan	3,776	12,388

Africa		m	ft
Kilimanjaro	Tanzania	5,895	19,340
Mt Kenya	Kenya	5,199	17,057
Ruwenzori (Margherita)	Uganda/Zaïre	5,109	16,762
Ras Dashan	Ethiopia	4,620	15,157
Meru	Tanzania	4,565	14,977
Karisimbi	Rwanda/Zaïre	4,507	14,787
Mt Elgon	Kenya/Uganda	4,321	14,176
Batu	Ethiopia	4,307	14,130
Guna	Ethiopia	4,231	13,882
Toubkal	Morocco	4,165	13,665
Irhil Mgoun	Morocco	4,071	13,356
Mt Cameroon	Cameroon	4,070	13,353
Amba Ferit	Ethiopia	3,875	13,042
Pico del Teide	Spain (Tenerife)	3,718	12,198
Thabana Ntlenyana	Lesotho	3,482	11,424
> Emi Koussi	Chad	3,415	11,204
Mt aux Sources	Lesotho/S. Africa	3,282	10,768
Mt Piton	Réunion	3,069	10,069

Oceania		m	ft
Puncak Jaya	Indonesia	5,029	16,499
Puncak Trikora	Indonesia	4,750	15,584
Puncak Mandala	Indonesia	4,702	15,427
> Mt Wilhelm	Papua New Guinea	4,508	14,790
Mauna Kea	USA (Hawaii)	4,205	13,796
Mauna Loa	USA (Hawaii)	4,170	13,681
Mt Cook	New Zealand	3,753	12,313
Mt Balbi	Solomon Is.	2,439	8,002
Orohena	Tahiti	2,241	7,352
Mt Kosciusko	Australia	2,237	7,339

North America		m	ft
Mt McKinley (Denali)	USA (Alaska)	6,194	20,321
Mt Logan	Canada	5,959	19,551
Citlaltepetl	Mexico	5,700	18,701
Mt St Elias	USA/Canada	5,489	18,008
Popocatepetl	Mexico	5,452	17,887
Mt Foraker	USA (Alaska)	5,304	17,401
Ixtaccihuatl	Mexico	5,286	17,342
Lucania	Canada	5,227	17,149
Mt Steele	Canada	5,073	16,644
Mt Bona	USA (Alaska)	5,005	16,420
Mt Blackburn	USA (Alaska)	4,996	16,391
Mt Sanford	USA (Alaska)	4,940	16,207
Mt Wood	Canada	4,848	15,905
Nevado de Toluca	Mexico	4,670	15,321
Mt Fairweather	USA (Alaska)	4,663	15,298
Mt Hunter	USA (Alaska)	4,442	15,573
Mt Whitney	USA	4,418	14,495
Mt Elbert	USA	4,399	14,432
Mt Harvard	USA	4,395	14,419
Mt Rainier	USA	4,392	14,409
Blanca Peak	USA	4,372	14,344
> Longs Peak	USA	4,345	14,255
Tajumulco	Guatemala	4,220	13,845
Grand Teton	USA	4,197	13,770
Mt Waddington	Canada	3,994	13,104
Mt Robson	Canada	3,954	12,972
Chirripó Grande	Costa Rica	3,837	12,589
Mt Assiniboine	Canada	3,619	11,873
Pico Duarte	Dominican Rep.	3,175	10,417

South America		m	ft
Aconcagua	Argentina	6,960	22,834
Bonete	Argentina	6,872	22,546
Ojos del Salado	Argentina/Chile	6,863	22,516
Pissis	Argentina	6,779	22,241
Mercedario	Argentina/Chile	6,770	22,211
Huascaran	Peru	6,768	22,204
Llullaillaco	Argentina/Chile	6,723	22,057
Nudo de Cachi	Argentina	6,720	22,047
Yerupaja	Peru	6,632	21,758
N. de Tres Cruces	Argentina/Chile	6,620	21,719
Incahuasi	Argentina/Chile	6,601	21,654
Cerro Galan	Argentina	6,600	21,654
Tupungato	Argentina/Chile	6,570	21,555
> Sajama	Bolivia	6,542	21,463
Illimani	Bolivia	6,485	21,276
Coropuna	Peru	6,425	21,079
Ausangate	Peru	6,384	20,945
Cerro del Toro	Argentina	6,380	20,932
Siula Grande	Peru	6,356	20,853
Chimborazo	Ecuador	6,267	20,561
Alpamayo	Peru	5,947	19,511
Cotapaxi	Ecuador	5,896	19,344
Pico Colon	Colombia	5,800	19,029
Pico Bolivar	Venezuela	5,007	16,427

Antarctica		m	ft
Vinson Massif		4,897	16,066
Mt Kirkpatrick		4,528	14,855
Mt Markham		4,349	14,268

OCEAN DEPTHS

Atlantic Ocean	m	ft	
Puerto Rico (Milwaukee) Deep	9,220	30,249	[7]
Cayman Trench	7,680	25,197	[10]
Gulf of Mexico	5,203	17,070	
Mediterranean Sea	5,121	16,801	
Black Sea	2,211	7,254	
North Sea	660	2,165	
Baltic Sea	463	1,519	
Hudson Bay	258	846	

Indian Ocean	m	ft
Java Trench	7,450	24,442
Red Sea	2,635	8,454
Persian Gulf	73	239

Pacific Ocean	m	ft	
Mariana Trench	11,022	36,161	[1]
Tonga Trench	10,882	35,702	[2]
Japan Trench	10,554	34,626	[3]
Kuril Trench	10,542	34,587	[4]
Mindanao Trench	10,497	34,439	[5]
Kermadec Trench	10,047	32,962	[6]
Peru–Chile Trench	8,050	26,410	[8]
Aleutian Trench	7,822	25,662	[9]
Middle American Trench	6,662	21,857	

Arctic Ocean	m	ft
Molloy Deep	5,608	18,399

LAND LOWS

		m	ft
Caspian Sea	Europe	−28	−92
Dead Sea	Asia	−403	−1,322
Lake Assale	Africa	−116	−381
Lake Eyre North	Oceania	−16	−52
Death Valley	N. America	−86	−282
Valdés Peninsula	S. America	−40	−131

Rivers

Europe

		km	miles	
Volga	*Caspian Sea*	3,700	2,300	
Danube	*Black Sea*	2,850	1,770	
Ural	*Caspian Sea*	2,535	1,575	
Dnepr (Dnipro)	*Volga*	2,285	1,420	
Kama	*Volga*	2,030	1,260	
Don	*Volga*	1,990	1,240	
Petchora	*Arctic Ocean*	1,790	1,110	
Oka	*Volga*	1,480	920	
Belaya	*Kama*	1,420	880	
Dnister (Dniester)	*Black Sea*	1,400	870	
Vyatka	*Kama*	1,370	850	
Rhine	*North Sea*	1,320	820	
N. Dvina	*Arctic Ocean*	1,290	800	
Desna	*Dnepr (Dnipro)*	1,190	740	
Elbe	*North Sea*	1,145	710	
Wisła	*Baltic Sea*	1,090	675	
Loire	*Atlantic Ocean*	1,020	635	
W. Dvina	*Baltic Sea*	1,019	633	

Asia

		km	miles	
Yangtze	*Pacific Ocean*	6,380	3,960	[3]
Yenisey–Angara	*Arctic Ocean*	5,550	3,445	[5]
Huang He	*Pacific Ocean*	5,464	3,395	[6]
Ob–Irtysh	*Arctic Ocean*	5,410	3,360	[7]
Mekong	*Pacific Ocean*	4,500	2,795	[9]
Amur	*Pacific Ocean*	4,400	2,730	[10]
Lena	*Arctic Ocean*	4,400	2,730	
Irtysh	*Ob*	4,250	2,640	
Yenisey	*Arctic Ocean*	4,090	2,540	
Ob	*Arctic Ocean*	3,680	2,285	
Indus	*Indian Ocean*	3,100	1,925	
Brahmaputra	*Indian Ocean*	2,900	1,800	
Syrdarya	*Aral Sea*	2,860	1,775	
Salween	*Indian Ocean*	2,800	1,740	
Euphrates	*Indian Ocean*	2,700	1,675	
Vilyuy	*Lena*	2,650	1,645	
Kolyma	*Arctic Ocean*	2,600	1,615	
Amudarya	*Aral Sea*	2,540	1,575	
Ural	*Caspian Sea*	2,535	1,575	
Ganges	*Indian Ocean*	2,510	1,560	
Si Kiang	*Pacific Ocean*	2,100	1,305	
Irrawaddy	*Indian Ocean*	2,010	1,250	
Tarim–Yarkand	*Lop Nor*	2,000	1,240	
Tigris	*Indian Ocean*	1,900	1,180	
Angara	*Yenisey*	1,830	1,135	
Godavari	*Indian Ocean*	1,470	915	
Sutlej	*Indian Ocean*	1,450	900	
Yamuna	*Indian Ocean*	1,400	870	

Africa

		km	miles	
Nile	*Mediterranean*	6,670	4,140	[1]
Zaïre/Congo	*Atlantic Ocean*	4,670	2,900	[8]
Niger	*Atlantic Ocean*	4,180	2,595	
Zambezi	*Indian Ocean*	3,540	2,200	
Oubangi/Uele	*Zaïre*	2,250	1,400	
Kasai	*Zaïre*	1,950	1,210	
Shaballe	*Indian Ocean*	1,930	1,200	
Orange	*Atlantic Ocean*	1,860	1,155	
Cubango	*Okavango Swamps*	1,800	1,120	
Limpopo	*Indian Ocean*	1,600	995	
Senegal	*Atlantic Ocean*	1,600	995	
Volta	*Atlantic Ocean*	1,500	930	
Benue	*Niger*	1,350	840	

Australia

		km	miles
Murray–Darling	*Indian Ocean*	3,750	2,330
Darling	*Murray*	3,070	1,905
Murray	*Indian Ocean*	2,575	1,600
Murrumbidgee	*Murray*	1,690	1,050

North America

		km	miles	
Mississippi–Missouri	*Gulf of Mexico*	6,020	3,740	[4]
Mackenzie	*Arctic Ocean*	4,240	2,630	
Mississippi	*Gulf of Mexico*	3,780	2,350	
Missouri	*Mississippi*	3,780	2,350	
Yukon	*Pacific Ocean*	3,185	1,980	
Rio Grande	*Gulf of Mexico*	3,030	1,880	
Arkansas	*Mississippi*	2,340	1,450	
Colorado	*Pacific Ocean*	2,330	1,445	
Red	*Mississippi*	2,040	1,270	
Columbia	*Pacific Ocean*	1,950	1,210	
Saskatchewan	*Lake Winnipeg*	1,940	1,205	
Snake	*Columbia*	1,670	1,040	
Churchill	*Hudson Bay*	1,600	990	
Ohio	*Mississippi*	1,580	980	
Brazos	*Gulf of Mexico*	1,400	870	
St Lawrence	*Atlantic Ocean*	1,170	730	

South America

		km	miles	
Amazon	*Atlantic Ocean*	6,450	4,010	[2]
Paraná–Plate	*Atlantic Ocean*	4,500	2,800	
Purus	*Amazon*	3,350	2,080	
Madeira	*Amazon*	3,200	1,990	
São Francisco	*Atlantic Ocean*	2,900	1,800	
Paraná	*Plate*	2,800	1,740	
Tocantins	*Atlantic Ocean*	2,750	1,710	
Paraguay	*Paraná*	2,550	1,580	
Orinoco	*Atlantic Ocean*	2,500	1,550	
Pilcomayo	*Paraná*	2,500	1,550	
Araguaia	*Tocantins*	2,250	1,400	
Juruá	*Amazon*	2,000	1,240	
Xingu	*Amazon*	1,980	1,230	
Ucayali	*Amazon*	1,900	1,180	
Marañón	*Amazon*	1,600	990	
Uruguay	*Plate*	1,600	990	
Magdalena	*Caribbean Sea*	1,540	960	

Lakes

Europe

		km²	miles²
Lake Ladoga	*Russia*	17,700	6,800
Lake Onega	*Russia*	9,700	3,700
Saimaa system	*Finland*	8,000	3,100
Vänern	*Sweden*	5,500	2,100
Rybinskoye Res.	*Russia*	4,700	1,800

Asia

		km²	miles²	
Caspian Sea	*Asia*	371,800	143,550	[1]
Aral Sea	*Kazak./Uzbek.*	33,640	13,000	[6]
Lake Baykal	*Russia*	30,500	11,780	[9]
Tonlé Sap	*Cambodia*	20,000	7,700	
Lake Balqash	*Kazakstan*	18,500	7,100	
Lake Dongting	*China*	12,000	4,600	
Lake Ysyk	*Kyrgyzstan*	6,200	2,400	
Lake Orumiyeh	*Iran*	5,900	2,300	
Lake Koko	*China*	5,700	2,200	
Lake Poyang	*China*	5,000	1,900	
Lake Khanka	*China/Russia*	4,400	1,700	
Lake Van	*Turkey*	3,500	1,400	
Lake Ubsa	*China*	3,400	1,300	

Africa

		km²	miles²	
Lake Victoria	*E. Africa*	68,000	26,000	[3]
Lake Tanganyika	*C. Africa*	33,000	13,000	[7]
Lake Malawi/Nyasa	*E. Africa*	29,600	11,430	[10]
Lake Chad	*C. Africa*	25,000	9,700	
Lake Turkana	*Ethiopia/Kenya*	8,500	3,300	
Lake Volta	*Ghana*	8,500	3,300	
Lake Bangweulu	*Zambia*	8,000	3,100	
Lake Rukwa	*Tanzania*	7,000	2,700	
Lake Mai-Ndombe	*Zaïre*	6,500	2,500	
Lake Kariba	*Zambia/Zimbabwe*	5,300	2,000	
Lake Albert	*Uganda/Zaïre*	5,300	2,000	
Lake Nasser	*Egypt/Sudan*	5,200	2,000	
Lake Mweru	*Zambia/Zaïre*	4,900	1,900	
Lake Cabora Bassa	*Mozambique*	4,500	1,700	
Lake Kyoga	*Uganda*	4,400	1,700	
Lake Tana	*Ethiopia*	3,630	1,400	
Lake Kivu	*Rwanda/Zaïre*	2,650	1,000	
Lake Edward	*Uganda/Zaïre*	2,200	850	

Australia

		km²	miles²
Lake Eyre	*Australia*	8,900	3,400
Lake Torrens	*Australia*	5,800	2,200
Lake Gairdner	*Australia*	4,800	1,900

North America

		km²	miles²	
Lake Superior	*Canada/USA*	82,350	31,800	[2]
Lake Huron	*Canada/USA*	59,600	23,010	[4]
Lake Michigan	*USA*	58,000	22,400	[5]
Great Bear Lake	*Canada*	31,800	12,280	[8]
Great Slave Lake	*Canada*	28,500	11,000	
Lake Erie	*Canada/USA*	25,700	9,900	
Lake Winnipeg	*Canada*	24,400	9,400	
Lake Ontario	*Canada/USA*	19,500	7,500	
Lake Nicaragua	*Nicaragua*	8,200	3,200	
Lake Athabasca	*Canada*	8,100	3,100	
Smallwood Res.	*Canada*	6,530	2,520	
Reindeer Lake	*Canada*	6,400	2,500	
Lake Winnipegosis	*Canada*	5,400	2,100	
Nettilling Lake	*Canada*	5,500	2,100	
Lake Nipigon	*Canada*	4,850	1,900	
Lake Manitoba	*Canada*	4,700	1,800	

South America

		km²	miles²
Lake Titicaca	*Bolivia/Peru*	8,300	3,200
Lake Poopo	*Peru*	2,800	1,100

Islands

Europe

		km²	miles²	
Great Britain	*UK*	229,880	88,700	[8]
Iceland	*Atlantic Ocean*	103,000	39,800	
Ireland	*Ireland/UK*	84,400	32,600	
Novaya Zemlya (N.)	*Russia*	48,200	18,600	
W. Spitzbergen	*Norway*	39,000	15,100	
Novaya Zemlya (S.)	*Russia*	33,200	12,800	
Sicily	*Italy*	25,500	9,800	
Sardinia	*Italy*	24,000	9,300	
N.E. Spitzbergen	*Norway*	15,000	5,600	
Corsica	*France*	8,700	3,400	
Crete	*Greece*	8,350	3,200	
Zealand	*Denmark*	6,850	2,600	

Asia

		km²	miles²	
Borneo	*S. E. Asia*	744,360	287,400	[3]
Sumatra	*Indonesia*	473,600	182,860	[6]
Honshu	*Japan*	230,500	88,980	[7]
Celebes	*Indonesia*	189,000	73,000	
Java	*Indonesia*	126,700	48,900	
Luzon	*Philippines*	104,700	40,400	
Mindanao	*Philippines*	101,500	39,200	
Hokkaido	*Japan*	78,400	30,300	
Sakhalin	*Russia*	74,060	28,600	
Sri Lanka	*Indian Ocean*	65,600	25,300	
Taiwan	*Pacific Ocean*	36,000	13,900	
Kyushu	*Japan*	35,700	13,800	
Hainan	*China*	34,000	13,100	
Timor	*Indonesia*	33,600	13,000	
Shikoku	*Japan*	18,800	7,300	
Halmahera	*Indonesia*	18,000	6,900	
Ceram	*Indonesia*	17,150	6,600	
Sumbawa	*Indonesia*	15,450	6,000	
Flores	*Indonesia*	15,200	5,900	
Samar	*Philippines*	13,100	5,100	
Negros	*Philippines*	12,700	4,900	
Bangka	*Indonesia*	12,000	4,600	
Palawan	*Philippines*	12,000	4,600	
Panay	*Philippines*	11,500	4,400	
Sumba	*Indonesia*	11,100	4,300	
Mindoro	*Philippines*	9,750	3,800	
Buru	*Indonesia*	9,500	3,700	
Bali	*Indonesia*	5,600	2,200	
Cyprus	*Mediterranean*	3,570	1,400	

Africa

		km²	miles²	
Madagascar	*Indian Ocean*	587,040	226,660	[4]
Socotra	*Indian Ocean*	3,600	1,400	
Réunion	*Indian Ocean*	2,500	965	
Tenerife	*Atlantic Ocean*	2,350	900	
Mauritius	*Indian Ocean*	1,865	720	

Oceania

		km²	miles²	
New Guinea	*Indon./Pap. NG*	821,030	317,000	[2]
New Zealand (S.)	*Pacific Ocean*	150,500	58,100	
New Zealand (N.)	*Pacific Ocean*	114,700	44,300	
Tasmania	*Australia*	67,800	26,200	
New Britain	*Papua NG*	37,800	14,600	
New Caledonia	*Pacific Ocean*	19,100	7,400	
Viti Levu	*Fiji*	10,500	4,100	
Hawaii	*Pacific Ocean*	10,450	4,000	
Bougainville	*Papua NG*	9,600	3,700	
Guadalcanal	*Solomon Is.*	6,500	2,500	
Vanua Levu	*Fiji*	5,550	2,100	
New Ireland	*Papua NG*	3,200	1,200	

North America

		km²	miles²	
Greenland	*Atlantic Ocean*	2,175,600	839,800	[1]
Baffin Is.	*Canada*	508,000	196,100	[5]
Victoria Is.	*Canada*	212,200	81,900	[9]
Ellesmere Is.	*Canada*	212,000	81,800	[10]
Cuba	*Caribbean Sea*	110,860	42,800	
Newfoundland	*Canada*	110,680	42,700	
Hispaniola	*Dom. Rep./Haiti*	76,200	29,400	
Banks Is.	*Canada*	67,000	25,900	
Devon Is.	*Canada*	54,500	21,000	
Melville Is.	*Canada*	42,400	16,400	
Vancouver Is.	*Canada*	32,150	12,400	
Somerset Is.	*Canada*	24,300	9,400	
Jamaica	*Caribbean Sea*	11,400	4,400	
Puerto Rico	*Atlantic Ocean*	8,900	3,400	
Cape Breton Is.	*Canada*	4,000	1,500	

South America

		km²	miles²
Tierra del Fuego	*Argentina/Chile*	47,000	18,100
Falkland Is. (E.)	*Atlantic Ocean*	6,800	2,600
South Georgia	*Atlantic Ocean*	4,200	1,600
Galapagos (Isabela)	*Pacific Ocean*	2,250	870

WORLD : REGIONS IN THE NEWS

Maps show the situation in May 1996

THE BREAK UP OF YUGOSLAVIA
The former country of Yugoslavia comprised six republics. In 1991 Slovenia and Croatia declared independence. Bosnia-Herzegovina followed in 1992 and Macedonia in 1993. Yugoslavia now comprises the remaining two republics, Serbia and Montenegro.

YUGOSLAVIA
Population : 10,763,000 (Serb 62.6%, Albanian 16.5%, Montenegrin 5%, Hungarian 3.3%, Muslim 3.2%)

Serbia
Population : 5,824,211 (Serb 87.7%) excluding the former autonomous provinces of Kosovo and Vojvodina
Kosovo
Population : 1,956,196
(Albanian 81.6%, Serb 9.9%)
Vojvodina
Population : 2,014,000
(Serb 56.8%, Hungarian 16.9%)

Montenegro Population : 615,035 (Montenegrin 61.9%, Muslim 14.6%, Albanian 6.6%)

CROATIA
Population : 4,504,000 (Croat 78.1%, Serb 12.2%)

SLOVENIA
Population : 1,942,000 (Slovene 88%, Croat 3%, Serb 2%)

MACEDONIA (F.Y.R.O.M.)
Population : 2,142,000 (Macedonian 64%, Albanian 21.7%, Turkish 5%, Romanian 3%, Serb 2%)

BOSNIA - HERZEGOVINA
Population : 3,527,000 (Muslim 49%, Serb 31.2%, Croat 17.2%)

The large scale map on the left shows the situation in Bosnia-Herzegovina in early 1996.

FORMER YUGOSLAVIA
0   50   100 150 200 km

- ·—· International boundaries
- ·—·· Republic boundaries
- —— Province boundaries
- ◎ Capital cities

BOSNIA-HERZEGOVINA
0   50   100 km

- ---- Dayton Peace Agreement Boundary
- Muslim-Croat Federation
- Bosnian Serb Republic

THE NEAR EAST
0   25   50 km

ISRAEL Population : 5,458,000 (inc. East Jerusalem and Jewish settlers in the areas under Israeli administration. (Jewish 82%, Arab Muslim 13.8%, Arab Christian 2.5%, Druze 1.7%)

West Bank Population : 973,500 (Palestinian Arabs 97% [of whom Arab Muslim 85%, Jewish 7%, Christian 8%])

Gaza Strip Population : 658,200 (Arab Muslim 98%)

JORDAN Population : 5,198,000 (Arab 99% [of whom about 50% are Palestinian Arab])

- ·—·· 1949 Armistice Line
- —— 1974 Cease-fire Lines
- *Efrata* ● Main Jewish settlements in the West Bank and Gaza Strip
- Halhul □ Main Palestinian Arab towns in the West Bank and Gaza Strip

THE CAUCASUS
0   100   200 km

- ·—· International boundaries
- ·—·· Republic boundaries

Georgia, Armenia and Azerbaijan achieved independence in 1991. Abkhazia, Ajaria and South Ossetia seek independence from Georgia.

Chechenia has been trying to break away from Russia since 1991, but Russia has resisted with military force. Hostility also continues between Armenia and Azerbaijan over the enclave of Nagorno-Karabakh.

RUSSIA

North Ossetia
Population : 695,000 (Ossetian 53%, Russian 29%, Chechen 5[%] Ingush 5% [expelled in 1992])

Chechenia
Population : 1,308,000 (Chech[en] and Ingush 70.7%, Russian 23[%])

Neighbouring **Ingushetia** (no[w] split from Chechenia)
Population : 250,000 (mainly Ingush)

GEORGIA
Population : 5,450,000 (Georg[ian] 70.1%, Armenian 8.1%, Russi[an] 6.3%, Azerbaijani 5.7%, Osset[ian] 3%, Greek 2%, Abkhazian 2%[)]

Abkhazia
Population : 537,500 (Georgia[n] 45.7%, Abkhazian 17.8%, Arm[enian] 14.6%, Russian 14.3%)

Ajaria
Population : 382,000 (Georgia[n] 82.8%, Russian 7.7%, Armeni[an])

South Ossetia
Population : 99,800 (Ossetian [ ], Georgian 29%)

ARMENIA
Population : 3,548,000 (Arme[nian] 93.3%, Azerbaijani 2.6%)

Nagorno-Karabakh
Population : 192,400 (Armeni[an] 76.9%, Azerbaijani 21.5%)

AZERBAIJAN
Population : 7,472,000 (Azerb[aijani] 82.7%, Russian 5.6%, Armeni[an] 5.6%, Lezgin 2.4%)

Naxçivan
Population : 300,400 (Azerbaijani 95.9%)

TAIWAN
0   50   100 150 200km

- Territory of People's Republic of China
- Territory of Republic of China (Taiwan)

S. CHINA SEA
0   250

- △ Philippin[es]
- ▽ Vietnam[ese]
- ◻ Chinese
- ● Taiwanes[e]
- —— Philippin[es]
- --- Vietnam[ese]
- —+— Chinese
- ····· Malaysia[n]

INTRODUCTION TO
WORLD
GEOGRAPHY

THE UNIVERSE

FOR MORE INFORMATION:

4: ORBITS OF THE PLANETS
PLANETARY DATA

About 15,000 million years ago, time and space began with the most colossal explosion in cosmic history: the so-called 'Big Bang' that is believed to have initiated the universe. According to current theory, in the first millionth of a second of its existence it expanded from a dimensionless point of infinite mass and density into a fireball about 30,000 million kilometres across; and it has been expanding ever since.

It took almost a million years for the primal fireball to cool enough for atoms to form. They were mostly hydrogen, still the most abundant material in the universe. But the new matter was not evenly distributed around the young universe, and a few 1,000 million years later atoms in relatively dense regions began to cling together under the influence of gravity, forming distinct masses of gas separated by vast expanses of empty space. To begin with, these first proto-galaxies were dark places: the universe had cooled. But gravitational attraction continued, condensing matter into coherent lumps inside the galactic gas clouds. About 3,000 million years later, some of these masses had contracted so much that internal pressure produced the high temperatures necessary to bring about nuclear fusion: the first stars were born.

There were several generations of stars, each feeding on the wreckage of its extinct predecessors as well as the original galactic gas swirls. With each new generation, progressively larger atoms were forged in stellar furnaces and the galaxy's range of elements, once restricted to hydrogen, grew larger. About 10,000 million years after the Big Bang, a star formed on the outskirts of our galaxy with enough matter left over to create a retinue of planets. Nearly 5,000 million years after that human beings evolved.

The Sun is one of more than 100,000 million stars in the home galaxy alone. Our galaxy, in turn, forms part of a local group of 25 or so similar structures, some much larger than our own; there are at least 100 million other galaxies in the universe as a whole. The most distant ever observed, a highly energetic galactic core known only as Quasar PKS 2000–330, lies about 15,000 million light-years away.

LIFE OF A STAR

For most of its existence, a star produces energy by the nuclear fusion of hydrogen into helium at its core. The duration of this hydrogen-burning period – known as the main sequence – depends on the star's mass; the greater the mass, the higher the core temperatures and the sooner the star's supply of hydrogen is exhausted. Dim, dwarf stars consume their hydrogen slowly, eking it out over 1,000 billion years or more. The Sun, like other stars of its mass, should spend about 10,000 million years on the main sequence; since it was formed less than 5,000 million years ago, it still has half its life left.

Once all a star's core hydrogen has been fused into helium, nuclear activity moves outwards into layers of unconsumed hydrogen. For a time, energy production sharply increases: the star grows hotter and expands enormously, turning into a so-called red giant. Its energy output will increase a thousandfold, and it will swell to a hundred times its present diameter.

After a few hundred million years, helium in the core will become sufficiently compressed to initiate a new cycle of nuclear fusion: from helium to carbon. The star will contract somewhat, before beginning its last expansion, in the Sun's case engulfing the Earth and perhaps Mars. In this bloated condition, the Sun's outer layers will break off into space, leaving a tiny inner core, mainly of carbon, that shrinks progressively under the force of its own gravity: dwarf stars can attain a density more than 10,000 times that of normal matter, with crushing surface gravities to match. Gradually, the nuclear fires will die down, and the Sun will reach its terminal stage: a black dwarf, emitting insignificant amounts of energy.

However, stars more massive than the Sun may undergo another transformation. The additional mass allows gravitational collapse to continue indefinitely: eventually, all the star's remaining matter shrinks to a point, and its density approaches infinity – a state that will not permit even subatomic structures to survive.

The star has become a black hole: an anomalous 'singularity' in the fabric of space and time. Although vast coruscations of radiation will be emitted by any matter falling into its grasp, the singularity itself has an escape velocity that exceeds the speed of light, and nothing can ever be released from it. Within the boundaries of the black hole, the laws of physics are suspended, but no physicist can ever observe the extraordinary events that may occur.

THE END OF THE UNIVERSE

The likely fate of the universe is disputed. One theory (top right) dictates that the expansion begun at the time of the Big Bang will continue 'indefinitely', with ageing galaxies moving further and further apart in an immense, dark graveyard. Alternatively, gravity may overcome the expansion (bottom right). Galaxies will fall back together until everything is again concentrated at a single point, followed by a new Big Bang and a new expansion, in an endlessly repeated cycle. The first theory is supported by the amount of visible matter in the universe; the second assumes there is enough dark material to bring about the gravitational collapse.

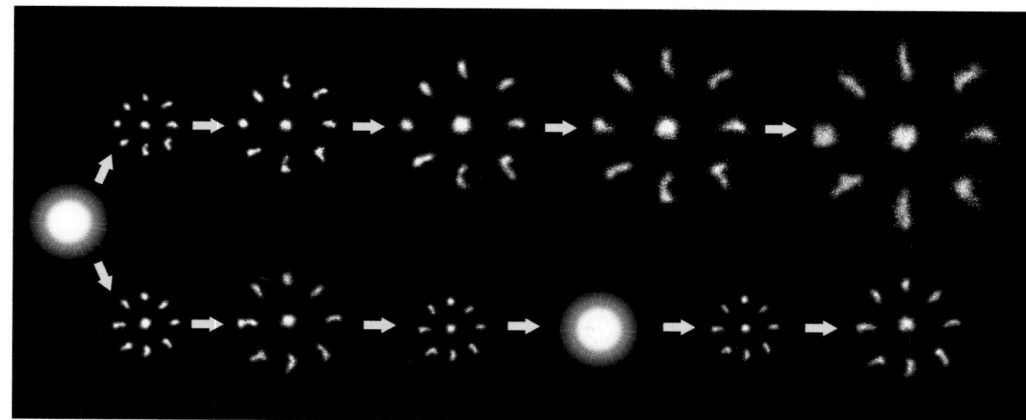

GALACTIC STRUCTURES

The universe's 100 million galaxies show clear structural patterns, originally classified by the American astronomer Edwin Hubble in 1925. Spiral galaxies like our own (top row) have a central, almost spherical bulge and a surrounding disk composed of spiral arms. Barred spirals (bottom row) have a central bar of stars across the nucleus, with spiral arms trailing from the ends of the bar. Elliptical galaxies (far left) have a uniform appearance, ranging from a flattened disk to a near sphere. So-called SO galaxies (left row, right) have a central bulge, but no spiral arms. A few have no discernible structure at all. Galaxies also vary enormously in size, from dwarfs only 2,000 light-years across to great assemblies of stars 80 or more times larger.

THE HOME GALAXY

The Sun and its planets are located in one of the spiral arms, a little less than 30,000 light-years from the galactic centre and orbiting around it in a period of more than 200 million years. The centre is invisible from the Earth, masked by vast, light-absorbing clouds of interstellar dust. The galaxy is probably around 12 billion years old and, like other spiral galaxies, has three distinct regions. The central bulge is about 30,000 light-years in diameter. The disk in which the Sun is located is not much more than 1,000 light-years thick but 100,000 light-years from end to end. Around the galaxy is the halo, a spherical zone 150,000 light-years across, studded with globular star-clusters and sprinkled with individual suns.

Globular clusters

Bulge

Disk

Solar System

Star charts are drawn as projections of a vast, hollow sphere with the observer in the middle. Each circle below represents one hemisphere, centred on the north and south celestial poles respectively – projections of the Earth's poles in the heavens. At the present era, the north pole is marked by the star Polaris; the south pole has no such convenient reference point. The rectangular

map shows the stars immediately above and below the celestial equator.

Astronomical co-ordinates are normally given in terms of 'Right Ascension' for longitude and 'Declination' for latitude or altitude. Since the stars appear to rotate around the Earth once every 24 hours, Right Ascension is measured eastwards – anti-clockwise – in hours and

minutes. One hour is equivalent to 15 angular degrees; zero on the scale is the point at which the Sun crosses the celestial equator at the spring equinox, known to astronomers as the First Point in Aries. Unlike the Sun, stars always rise and set at the same point on the horizon. Declination measures (in degrees) a star's angular distance above or below the celestial equator.

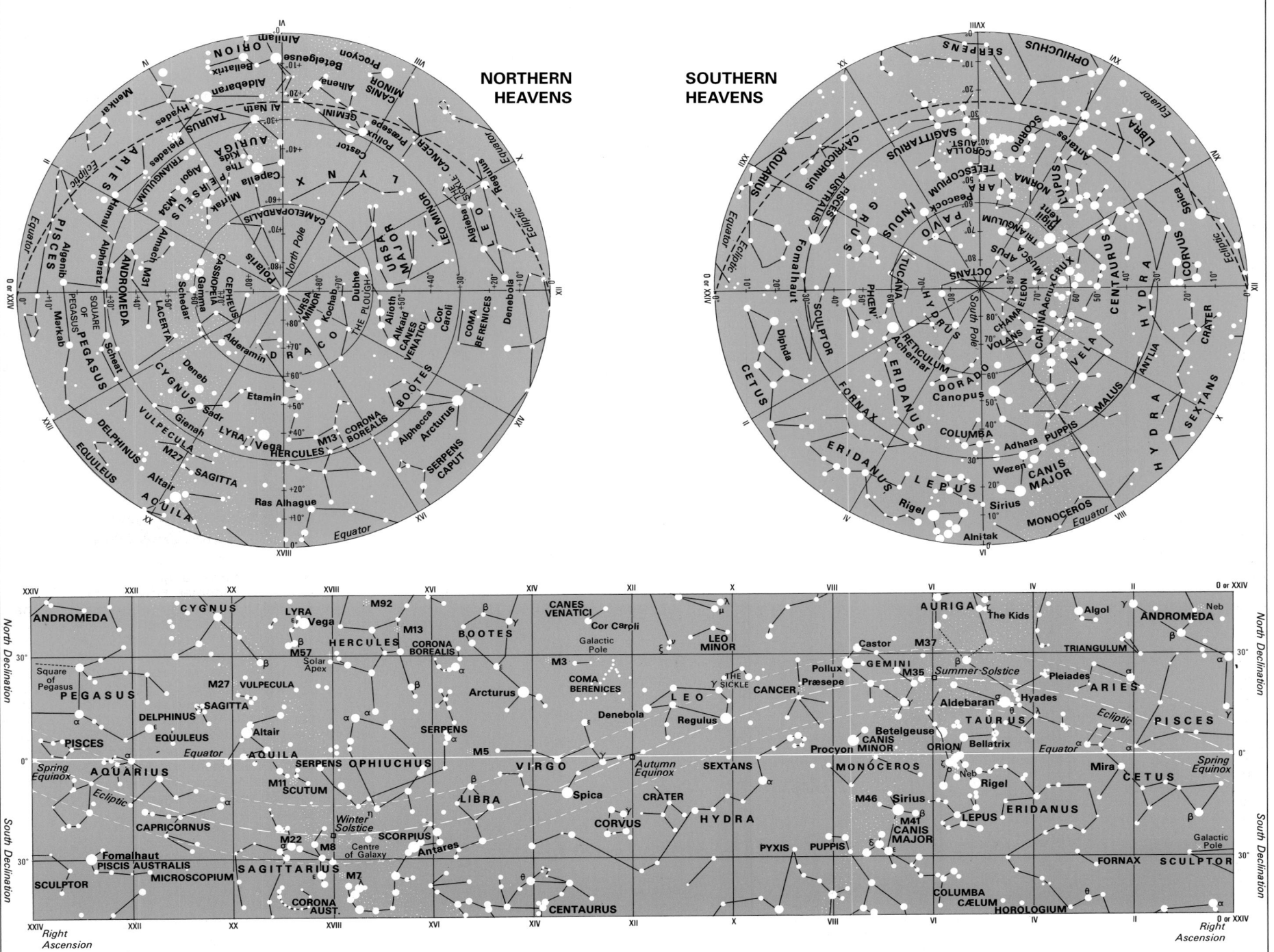

NORTHERN HEAVENS

SOUTHERN HEAVENS

THE CONSTELLATIONS

The constellations and their English names

Andromeda	Andromeda	Circinus	Compasses	Lacerta	Lizard
Antlia	Air Pump	Columba	Dove	Leo	Lion
Apus	Bird of Paradise	Coma Berenices	Berenice's Hair	Leo Minor	Little Lion
Aquarius	Water Carrier	Corona Australis	Southern Crown	Lepus	Hare
Aquila	Eagle	Corona Borealis	Northern Crown	Libra	Scales
Ara	Altar	Corvus	Crow	Lupus	Wolf
Aries	Ram	Crater	Cup	Lynx	Lynx
Auriga	Charioteer	Crux	Southern Cross	Lyra	Harp
Boötes	Herdsman	Cygnus	Swan	Mensa	Table
Caelum	Chisel	Delphinus	Dolphin	Microscopium	Microscope
Camelopardalis	Giraffe	Dorado	Swordfish	Monoceros	Unicorn
Cancer	Crab	Draco	Dragon	Musca	Fly
Canes Venatici	Hunting Dogs	Equuleus	Little Horse	Norma	Level
Canis Major	Great Dog	Eridanus	Eridanus	Octans	Octant
Canis Minor	Little Dog	Fornax	Furnace	Ophiuchus	Serpent Bearer
Capricornus	Goat	Gemini	Twins	Orion	Orion
Carina	Keel	Grus	Crane	Pavo	Peacock
Cassiopeia	Cassiopeia	Hercules	Hercules	Pegasus	Winged Horse
Centaurus	Centaur	Horologium	Clock	Perseus	Perseus
Cepheus	Cepheus	Hydra	Water Snake	Phoenix	Phoenix
Cetus	Whale	Hydrus	Sea Serpent	Pictor	Easel
Chamaeleon	Chamaeleon	Indus	Indian	Pisces	Fishes

Piscis Austrinus	Southern Fish
Puppis	Ship's Stern
Pyxis	Mariner's Compass
Reticulum	Net
Sagitta	Arrow
Sagittarius	Archer
Scorpius	Scorpion
Sculptor	Sculptor
Scutum	Shield
Serpens	Serpent
Sextans	Sextant
Taurus	Bull
Telescopium	Telescope
Triangulum	Triangle
Triangulum Australe	Southern Triangle
Tucana	Toucan
Ursa Major	Great Bear
Ursa Minor	Little Bear
Vela	Sails
Virgo	Virgin
Volans	Flying Fish
Vulpecula	Fox

THE NEAREST STARS

The 20 nearest stars, excluding the Sun, with their distance from Earth in light-years*

Proxima Centauri	4.25
Alpha Centauri A	4.3
Alpha Centauri B	4.3
Barnard's Star	6.0
Wolf 359	7.8
Lalande 21185	8.3
Sirius A	8.7
Sirius B	8.7
UV Ceti A	8.7
UV Ceti B	8.7
Ross 154	9.4
Ross 248	10.3
Epsilon Eridani	10.7
Ross 128	10.9
61 Cygni A	11.1
61 Cygni B	11.1
Epsilon Indi	11.2
Groombridge 34A	11.2
Groombridge 34B	11.2
L789-6	11.2
Procyon A	11.4
Procyon B	11.4

Many of the nearest stars, like Alpha Centauri A and B, are doubles, orbiting about the common centre of gravity and to all intents and purposes equidistant from Earth. Many of them are dim objects, with no name other than the designation given by the astronomers who investigated them. However, they include Sirius, the brightest star in the sky, and Procyon, the seventh brightest. Both are far larger than the Sun: of the nearest stars, only Epsilon Eridani is similar in size and luminosity.

* A light-year equals approx. 9,500,000,000,000 kilometres

THE SOLAR SYSTEM

Lying 27,000 light-years from the centre of one of billions of galaxies that comprise the observable universe, our Solar System contains nine planets and their moons, innumerable asteroids and comets, and a miscellany of dust and gas, all tethered by the immense gravitational field of the Sun, the middling-sized star whose thermonuclear furnaces provide them all with heat and light. The Solar System was formed about 4,600 million years ago, when a spinning cloud of gas, mostly hydrogen but seeded with other, heavier elements, condensed enough to ignite a nuclear reaction and create a star. The Sun still accounts for almost 99.9% of the system's total mass; one planet, Jupiter, contains most of the remainder.

By composition as well as distance, the planetary array divides quite neatly in two: an inner system of four small, solid planets, including the Earth, and an outer system, from Jupiter to Neptune, of four huge gas giants. Between the two groups lies a scattering of asteroids, perhaps as many as 40,000; possibly the remains of a planet destroyed by some unexplained catastrophe, they are more likely to be debris left over from the Solar System's formation, prevented by the gravity of massive Jupiter from coalescing into a larger body. The ninth planet, Pluto, seems to be a world of the inner system type: small, rocky and something of an anomaly.

By the 1990s, however, the Solar System also included some newer anomalies: several thousand spacecraft. Most were in orbit around the Earth, but some had probed far and wide around the system. The valuable information beamed back by these robotic investigators has transformed our knowledge of our celestial environment.

Much of the early history of science is the story of people trying to make sense of the errant points of light that were all they knew of the planets. Now, men have themselves stood on the Earth's Moon; probes have landed on Mars and Venus, and orbiting radars have mapped far distant landscapes with astonishing accuracy. In the 1980s, the US *Voyagers* skimmed all four major planets of the outer system, bringing new revelations with each close approach. Only Pluto, inscrutably distant in an orbit that takes it 50 times the Earth's distance from the Sun, remains unvisited by our messengers.

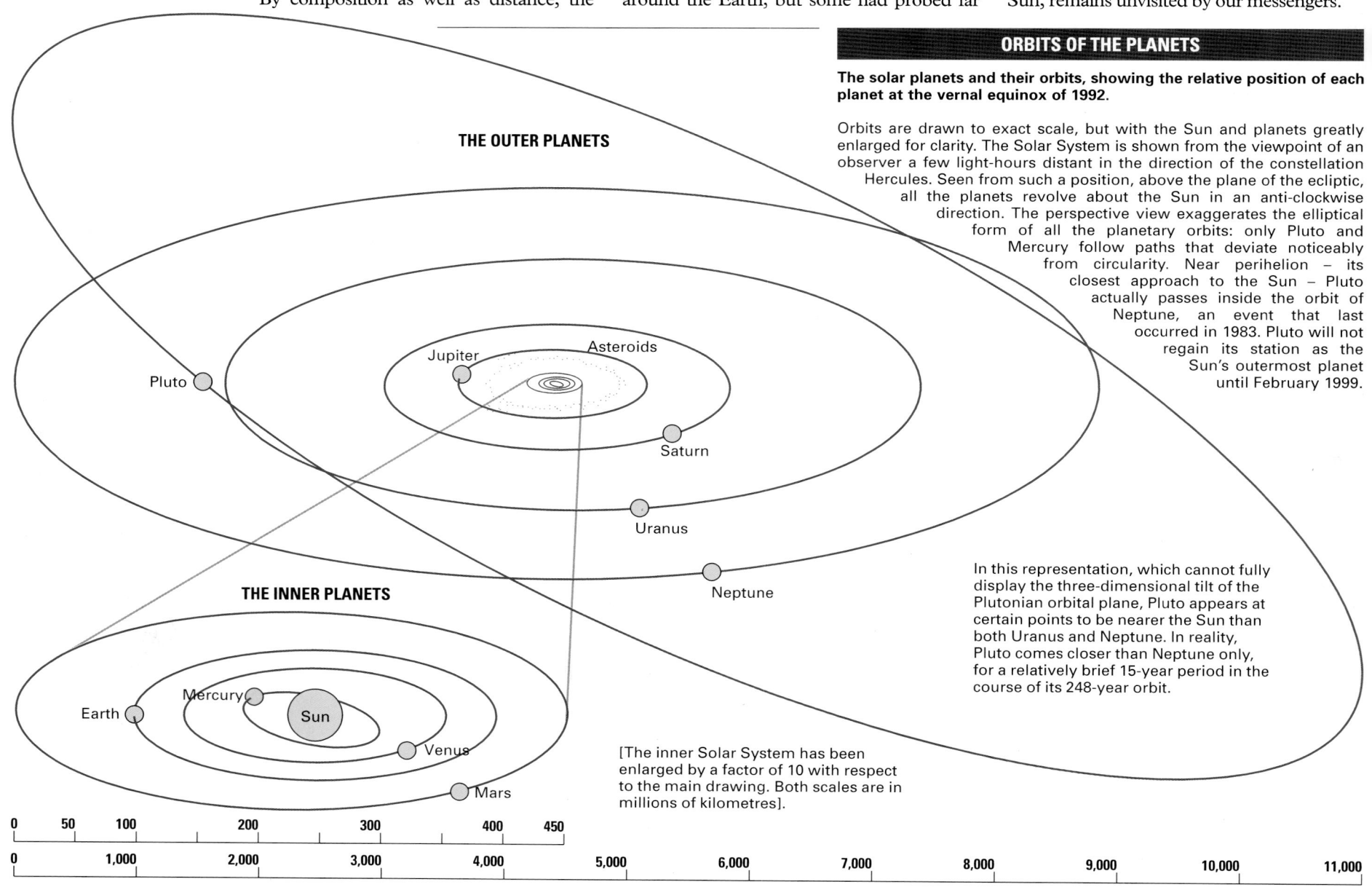

THE OUTER PLANETS

THE INNER PLANETS

[The inner Solar System has been enlarged by a factor of 10 with respect to the main drawing. Both scales are in millions of kilometres].

ORBITS OF THE PLANETS

The solar planets and their orbits, showing the relative position of each planet at the vernal equinox of 1992.

Orbits are drawn to exact scale, but with the Sun and planets greatly enlarged for clarity. The Solar System is shown from the viewpoint of an observer a few light-hours distant in the direction of the constellation Hercules. Seen from such a position, above the plane of the ecliptic, all the planets revolve about the Sun in an anti-clockwise direction. The perspective view exaggerates the elliptical form of all the planetary orbits: only Pluto and Mercury follow paths that deviate noticeably from circularity. Near perihelion – its closest approach to the Sun – Pluto actually passes inside the orbit of Neptune, an event that last occurred in 1983. Pluto will not regain its station as the Sun's outermost planet until February 1999.

In this representation, which cannot fully display the three-dimensional tilt of the Plutonian orbital plane, Pluto appears at certain points to be nearer the Sun than both Uranus and Neptune. In reality, Pluto comes closer than Neptune only, for a relatively brief 15-year period in the course of its 248-year orbit.

PLANETARY DATA

	Mean distance from Sun (million km)	Mass (Earth = 1)	Period of orbit (Earth years)	Period of rotation (Earth days)	Equatorial diameter (km)	Average density (water = 1)	Surface gravity (Earth = 1)	Escape velocity (km/sec)	Number of known satellites
Sun	–	332,946	–	25.38	1,392,000	1.41	27.9	617.5	–
Mercury	58.3	0.06	0.241	58.67	4,878	5.50	0.38	4.27	0
Venus	107.7	0.8	0.615	243.00	12,104	5.25	0.90	10.36	0
Earth	149.6	1.0	1.00	0.99	12,756	5.52	1.00	11.18	1
Mars	227.3	0.1	1.88	1.02	6,787	3.94	0.38	5.03	2
Jupiter	777.9	317.8	11.86	0.41	142,800	1.33	2.64	59.60	16
Saturn	1,427.1	95.2	29.46	0.42	120,000	0.706	1.16	35.50	20
Uranus	2,872.3	14.5	84.01	0.45	51,118	1.7	1.11	21.30	15
Neptune	4,502.7	17.1	164.79	0.67	49,528	1.77	1.21	23.30	8
Pluto	5,894.2	0.002	248.54	6.38	2,300	5.50	0.47	1.10	1

Planetary days are given in sidereal time – that is, with respect to the stars rather than the Sun. Most of the information in the table was confirmed by spacecraft and often obtained from photographs and other data transmitted back to the Earth. In the case of Pluto, however, only earthbound observations have been made, and no spacecraft will encounter it until well into the next century. Given the planet's small size and great distance, figures for its diameter and rotation period have only recently been confirmed.

Pluto is not massive enough to account for the perturbations in the orbits of Uranus and Neptune that led to its 1930 discovery, but it is now widely believed that these perturbations can be explained away as observational errors made by the earlier observers.

THE PLANETS

Mercury is the closest planet to the Sun and hence the fastest-moving. It has no significant atmosphere and a cratered, wrinkled surface very similar to that of Earth's Moon.

Venus has much the same physical dimensions as Earth. However, its carbon dioxide atmosphere is 90 times as dense, accounting for a runaway greenhouse effect that makes the Venusian surface, at 475°C, the hottest of all the planets in the Solar System. Radar mapping shows relatively level land with volcanic regions whose sulphurous discharges explain the sulphuric acid rains reported by soft-landing space probes before they succumbed to Venus' fierce climate.

Earth seen from space is easily the most beautiful of the inner planets; it is also, and more objectively, the largest, as well the only home of known life. Living things are the main reason why the Earth is able to retain a substantial proportion of corrosive and highly reactive oxygen in its atmosphere, a state of affairs that contradicts the laws of chemical equilibrium; the oxygen in turn supports the life that constantly regenerates it.

Mars was once considered the likeliest of the other planets to share Earth's cargo of life: the seasonal expansion of dark patches strongly suggested vegetation and the planet's apparent ice-caps indicated the vital presence of water. But close inspection by spacecraft brought disappointment: chemical reactions account for the seeming vegetation, the ice-caps are mainly frozen carbon dioxide, and whatever oxygen the planet once possessed is now locked up in the iron-bearing rock that covers its cratered surface and gives it its characteristic red hue.

Jupiter masses almost three times as much as all the other planets combined; had it scooped up a little more matter during its formation, it might have evolved into a small companion star for the Sun. The planet is mostly gas, under intense pressure in the lower atmosphere above a core of fiercely compressed hydrogen and helium. The upper layers form strikingly-coloured rotating belts, the outward sign of the intense storms created by Jupiter's rapid diurnal rotation. Close approaches by spacecraft have shown an orbiting ring system and discovered several previously unknown moons: Jupiter has at least 16 moons.

Saturn is structurally similar to Jupiter, rotating fast enough to produce an obvious bulge at its equator. Ever since the invention of the telescope, however, Saturn's rings have been the feature that has attracted most observers. *Voyager* probes in 1980 and 1981 sent back detailed pictures that showed them to be composed of thousands of separate ringlets, each in turn made up of tiny icy particles, interacting in a complex dance that may serve as a model for the study of galactic and even larger structures.

Uranus was unknown to the ancients. Although it is faintly visible to the naked eye, it was not discovered until 1781. Its composition is broadly similar to Jupiter and Saturn, though its distance from the Sun ensures an even colder surface temperature. Observations in 1977 suggested the presence of a faint ring system, amply confirmed when *Voyager 2* swung past the planet in 1986.

Neptune is always more than 4,000 million kilometres from Earth, and despite its diameter of almost 50,000 km, it can only be seen by telescope. Its 1846 discovery was the result of mathematical predictions by astronomers seeking to explain irregularities in the orbit of Uranus, but until *Voyager 2* closed with the planet in 1989, little was known of it. Like Uranus, it has a ring system; *Voyager*'s photographs revealed a total of eight moons.

Pluto is the most mysterious of the solar planets, if only because even the most powerful telescopes can scarcely resolve it from a point of light to a disk. It was discovered as recently as 1930, like Neptune as the result of perturbations in the orbits of the two then outermost planets. Its small size, as well as its eccentric and highly tilted orbit, has led to suggestions that it is a former satellite of Neptune, somehow liberated from its primary. In 1978 Pluto was found to have a moon of its own, Charon, apparently half the size of Pluto itself.

Mean distance from
Sun in million
kilometres

Mercury	58.3
Venus	107.7
Earth	149.6
Mars	227.9
Jupiter	777.9
Saturn	1,427.1
Uranus	2,872.3
Neptune	4,502.7
Pluto	5,894.2

THE EARTH: TIME AND MOTION

The basic unit of time measurement is the day, that is, one rotation of the Earth on its axis. The subdivision of the day into hours, minutes and seconds is arbitrary and simply for our convenience. Our present calendar is based on the solar year of 365.24 days, the time taken by the Earth to orbit the Sun. As the Earth rotates from west to east, the Sun appears to rise in the east and set in the west. When the Sun is setting in Shanghai, on the opposite side of the world New York is just emerging into sunlight. Noon, when the Sun is directly overhead, is coincident at all places on the same meridian, with shadows pointing directly towards the poles.

Calendars based on the movements of the Sun and Moon have been used since ancient times. The Julian Calendar, with its leap year, introduced by Julius Caesar, fixed the average length of the year at 365.25 days, which was about 11 minutes too long (the Earth completes its orbit in 365 days, 5 hours, 48 minutes and 46 seconds of mean solar time). The cumulative error was rectified by the Gregorian Calendar, introduced by Pope Gregory XIII in 1582, when he decreed that the day following 4 October was 15 October, and that century years did not count as leap years unless divisible by 400. England did not adopt the reformed calendar until 1752, when the country found itself 11 days behind the continent.

Britain imposed the Gregorian Calendar on all its possessions, including the American colonies. All dates preceding 2 September 1752 were marked 'OS', for 'Old Style'.

EARTH DATA

Maximum distance from Sun (Aphelion): 152,007,016 km
Minimum distance from Sun (Perihelion): 147,000,830 km
Obliquity of the ecliptic: 23° 27' 08"
Length of year – solar tropical (equinox to equinox): 365.24 days
Length of year – sidereal (fixed star to fixed star): 365.26 days
Length of day – mean solar day: 24h, 03m, 56s
Length of day – mean sidereal day: 23h, 56m, 04s

Superficial area: 510,000,000 sq km
Land surface: 149,000,000 sq km (29.2%)
Water surface: 361,000,000 sq km (70.8%)
Equatorial circumference: 40,077 km
Polar circumference: 40,009 km
Equatorial diameter: 12,756.8 km
Polar diameter: 12,713.8 km
Equatorial radius: 6,378.4 km
Polar radius: 6,356.9 km
Volume of the Earth: $1,083,230 \times 10^6$ cu km
Mass of the Earth: 5.9×10^{21} tonnes

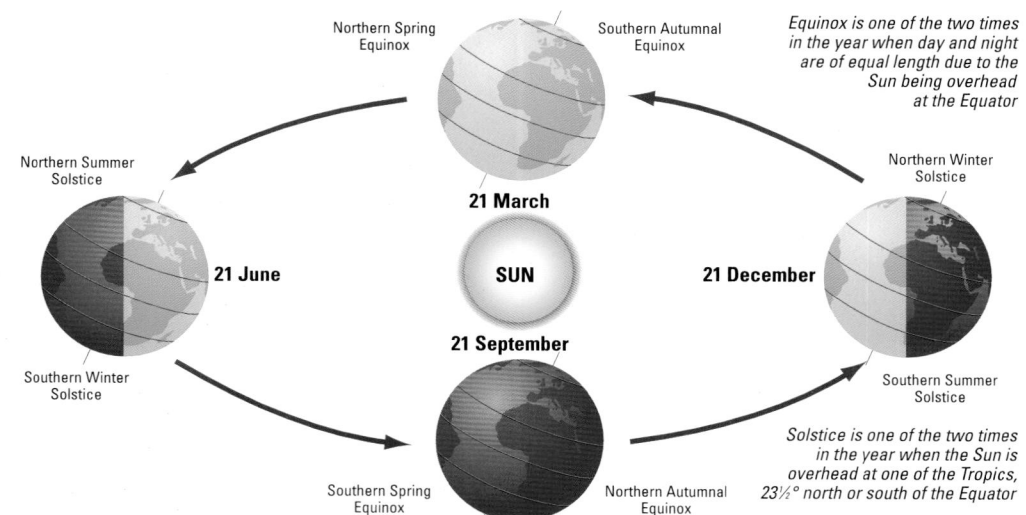

Equinox is one of the two times in the year when day and night are of equal length due to the Sun being overhead at the Equator

Solstice is one of the two times in the year when the Sun is overhead at one of the Tropics, 23½° north or south of the Equator

Northern Spring Equinox — Southern Autumnal Equinox
Northern Summer Solstice
Northern Winter Solstice
21 March
21 June — SUN — 21 December
21 September
Southern Winter Solstice
Southern Summer Solstice
Southern Spring Equinox — Northern Autumnal Equinox

THE SEASONS

The Earth revolves around the Sun once a year in an 'anti-clockwise' direction, tilted at a constant angle 23½° (the obliquity of the ecliptic). In June, the northern hemisphere is tilted towards the Sun: as a result, it receives more hours of sunshine in a day and therefore has its warmest season, summer. By December, the Earth has rotated halfway round the Sun so that the southern hemisphere is tilted towards the Sun and has its summer; the northern hemisphere has its winter. On 21 June the Sun is directly overhead at the Tropic of Cancer (23½°N), and this is midsummer in the northern hemisphere. Midsummer in the southern hemisphere occurs on 21 December, when the Sun is overhead the Tropic of Capricorn (23½°S).

The obliquity represents the greatest angular distance that the sun can lie north and south of the equator; it is decreasing by 0.47' per year.

DAY AND NIGHT

The Sun appears to rise in the east, reach its highest point at noon, and then set in the west, to be followed by night. In reality, it is not the Sun that is moving but the Earth rotating from west to east. The moment when the Sun's upper limb first appears above the horizon is termed sunrise; the moment when the Sun's upper limb disappears below the horizon is sunset.

At the summer solstice in the northern hemisphere (21 June), the Arctic has total daylight and the Antarctic total darkness. The opposite occurs at the winter solstice (21 December). At the Equator, the length of day and night are almost equal all year.

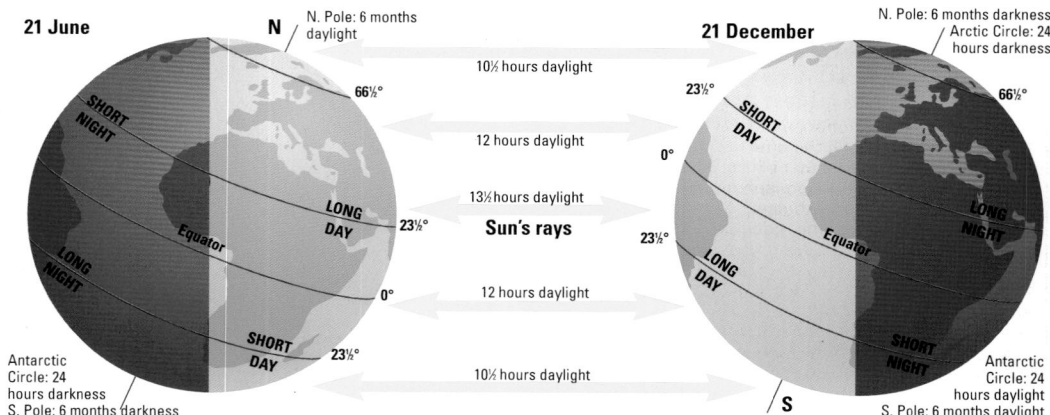

21 June
N. Pole: 6 months daylight
66½°
10½ hours daylight
12 hours daylight
13½ hours daylight
Equator 23½°
0°
12 hours daylight
Antarctic Circle: 24 hours darkness
S. Pole: 6 months darkness

Sun's rays

21 December
N. Pole: 6 months darkness / Arctic Circle: 24 hours darkness
23½° — 66½°
0°
Equator 23½°
12 hours daylight
Antarctic Circle: 24 hours daylight
S. Pole: 6 months daylight

THE SUN'S PATH

The diagrams on the left illustrate the apparent path of the Sun at (A) the Equator, (B) at mid-latitude (45°), (C) at the Arctic Circle (66½°), and (D) at the North Pole, where there are six months of continuous daylight and six months of continuous night.

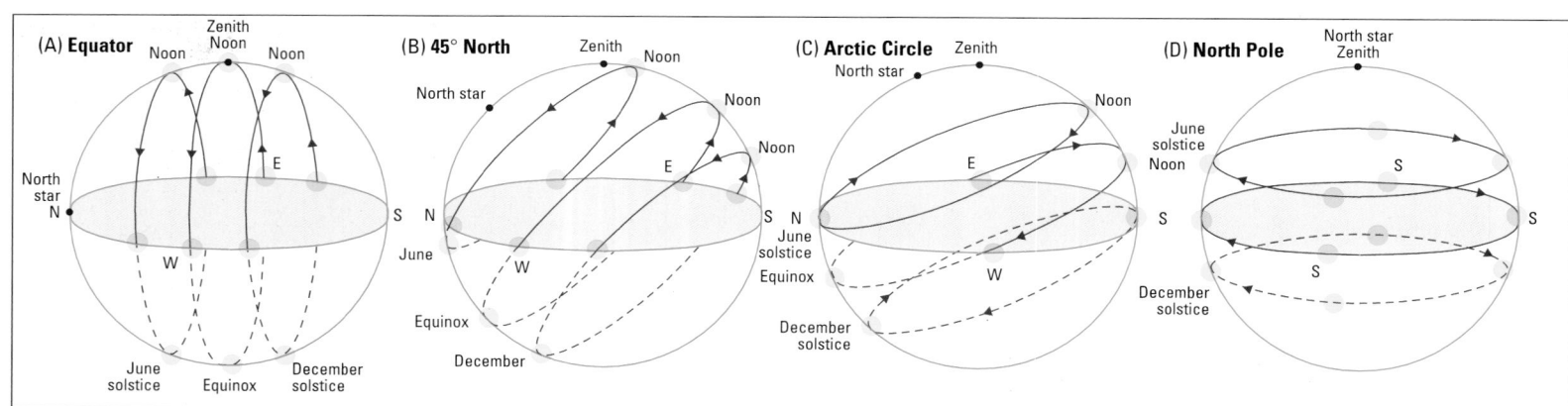

(A) Equator — (B) 45° North — (C) Arctic Circle — (D) North Pole

MEASUREMENTS OF TIME

Astronomers distinguish between solar time and sidereal time. Solar time derives from the period taken by the Earth to rotate on its axis: one rotation defines a solar day. But the speed of the Earth along its orbit around the Sun is not constant. The length of day – or 'apparent solar day', as defined by the apparent successive transits of the Sun – is irregular because the Earth must complete more than one rotation before the Sun returns to the same meridian. The constant sidereal day is defined as the interval between two successive apparent transits of a star, or the First Point of Aries, across the same meridian. If the Sun is at the equinox and overhead at a meridian one day, then the next day it will be to the east by approximately 1°. Thus, the Sun will not cross the meridian until four minutes after the sidereal noon.

From the diagrams on the right it is possible to discover the time of sunrise or sunset on a given date and for latitudes between 60°N and 60°S.

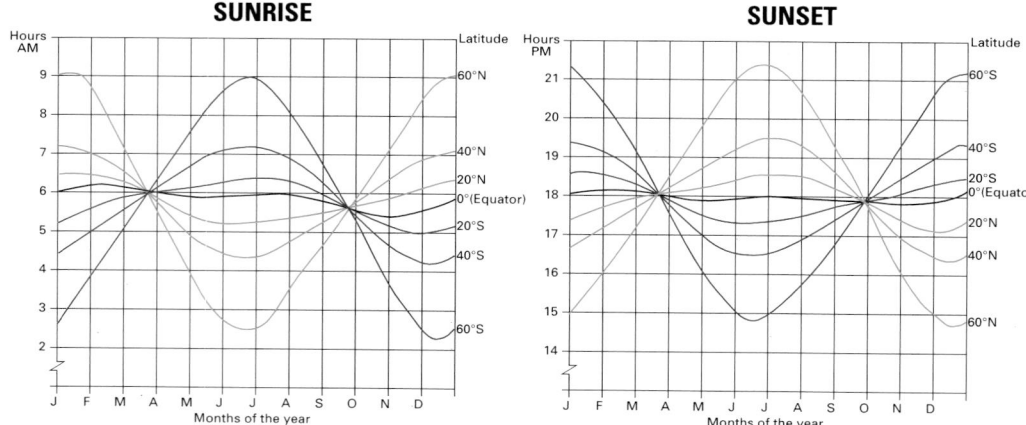

SUNRISE
Hours AM — Latitude
SUNSET
Hours PM — Latitude
Months of the year

THE MOON

Distance from Earth: 356,410 km – 406,685 km; Mean diameter: 3,475.1 km; Mass: approx. 1/81 that of Earth; Surface gravity: one-sixth of Earth's; Daily range of temperature at lunar equator: 200°C; Average orbital speed: 3,683 km/h

PHASES OF THE MOON

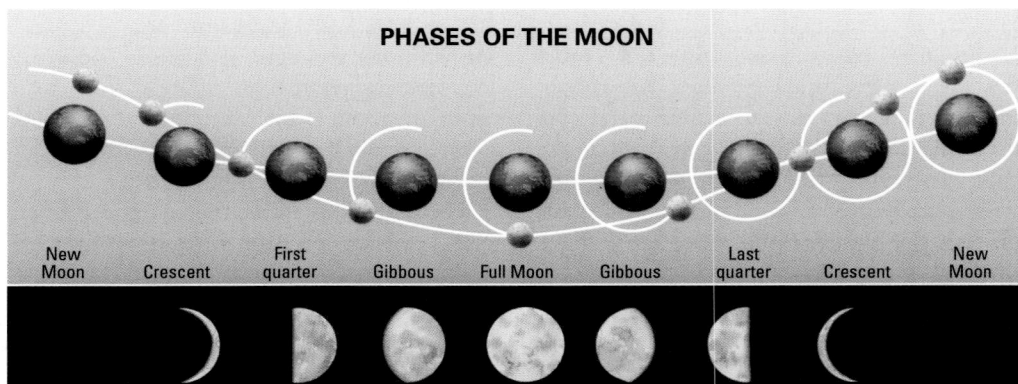

New Moon | Crescent | First quarter | Gibbous | Full Moon | Gibbous | Last quarter | Crescent | New Moon

The Moon rotates more slowly than the Earth, making one complete turn on its axis in just over 27 days. Since this corresponds to its period of revolution around the Earth, the Moon always presents the same hemisphere or face to us, and we never see 'the dark side'. The interval between one full Moon and the next (and between new Moons) is about 29½ days – a lunar month. The apparent changes in the shape of the Moon are caused by its changing position in relation to the Earth; like the planets, it produces no light of its own and shines only by reflecting the rays of the Sun.

Solar eclipse

Partial eclipse (1)

P   P   P

Total eclipse (2)

Lunar eclipse

ECLIPSES

When the Moon passes between the Sun and the Earth it causes a partial eclipse of the Sun (1) if the Earth passes through the Moon's outer shadow (P), or a total eclipse (2) if the inner cone shadow crosses the Earth's surface. In a lunar eclipse, the Earth's shadow crosses the Moon and, again, provides either a partial or total eclipse. Eclipses of the Sun and the Moon do not occur every month because of the 5° difference between the plane of the Moon's orbit and the plane in which the Earth moves. In the 1990s only 14 lunar eclipses are possible, for example, seven partial and seven total; each is visible only from certain, and variable, parts of the world. The same period witnesses 13 solar eclipses – six partial (or annular) and seven total.

TIDES

The daily rise and fall of the ocean's tides are the result of the gravitational pull of the Moon and that of the Sun, though the effect of the latter is only 46.6% as strong as that of the Moon. This effect is greatest on the hemisphere facing the Moon and causes a tidal 'bulge'. When the Sun, Earth and Moon are in line, tide-raising forces are at a maximum and Spring tides occur: high tide reaches the highest values, and low tide falls to low levels. When lunar and solar forces are least coincidental with the Sun and Moon at an angle (near the Moon's first and third quarters), Neap tides occur, which have a small tidal range.

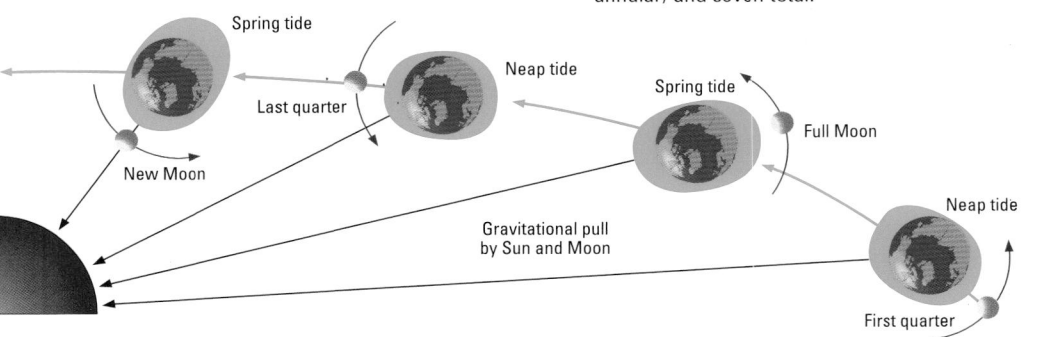

Spring tide · Neap tide · Last quarter · New Moon · Spring tide · Full Moon · Neap tide · First quarter · Gravitational pull by Sun and Moon

CARTOGRAPHY BY PHILIP'S, COPYRIGHT REED INTERNATIONAL BOOKS LTD

MOON DATA

Distance from Earth
The Moon orbits at a mean distance of 384,199.1 km, at an average speed of 3,683 km/h in relation to the Earth.

Size and mass
The average diameter of the Moon is 3,475.1 km. It is 400 times smaller than the Sun but is about 400 times closer to the Earth, so we see them as the same size. The Moon has a mass of 7,348 x 10¹⁹ tonnes, with a density 3.344 times that of water.

Visibility
Only 59% of the Moon's surface is directly visible from Earth. Reflected light takes 1.25 seconds to reach Earth – compared to 8 minutes 27.3 seconds for light to reach us from the Sun.

Temperature
With the Sun overhead, the temperature on the lunar equator can reach 117.2°C [243°F]. At night it can sink to –162.7°C [–261°F].

TIME ZONES

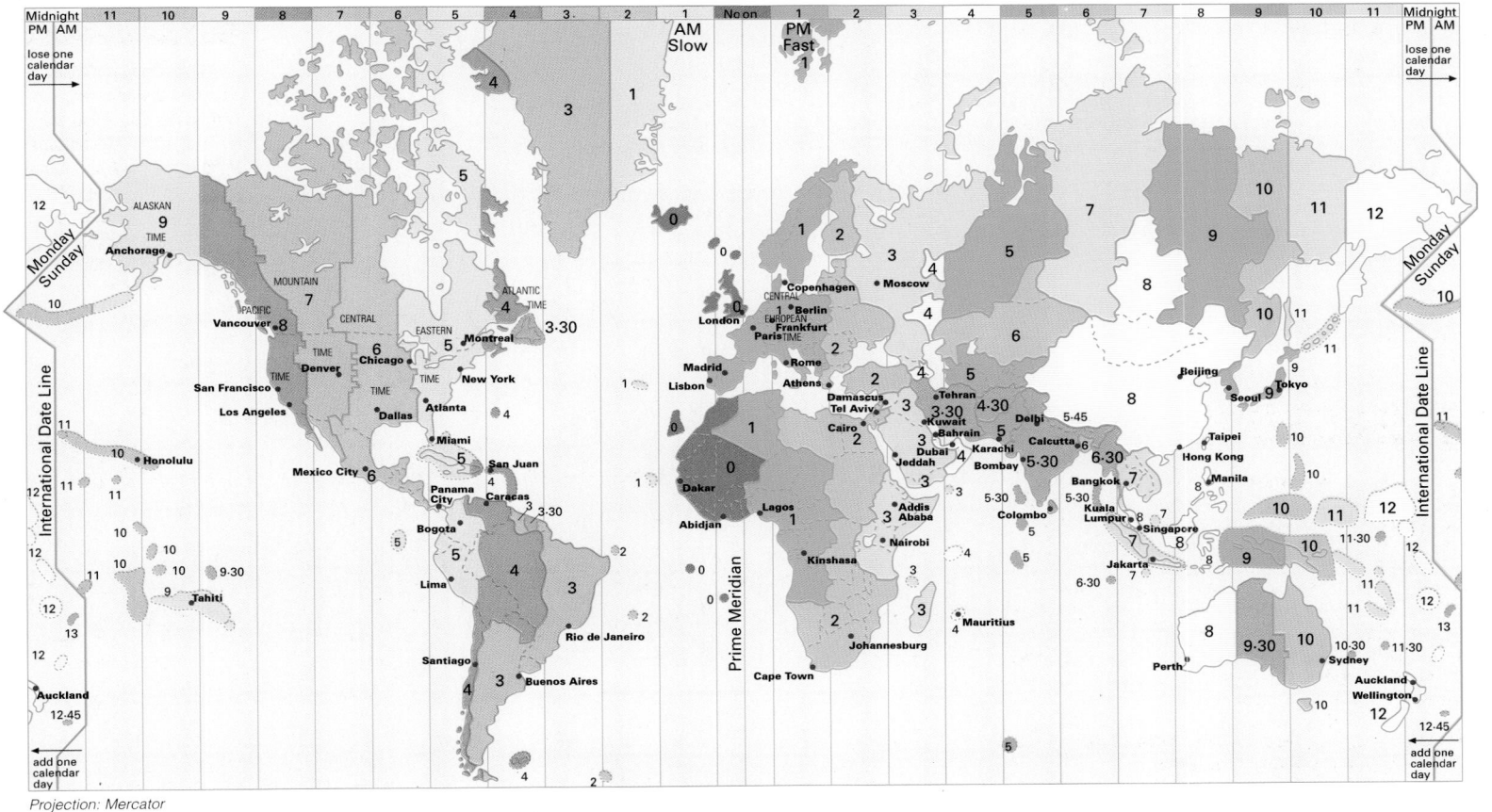

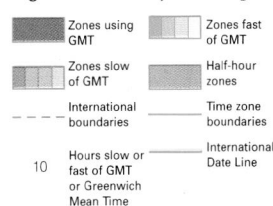

Projection: Mercator

The Earth rotates through 360° in 24 hours, and so moves 15° every hour. The world is divided into 24 standard time zones, each centred on lines of longitude at 15° intervals. At the centre of the first zone is the Prime meridian or Greenwich meridian. All places to the west of Greenwich are one hour behind for every 15° of longitude; places to the east are ahead by one hour for every 15°. When it is 12 noon at the Greenwich meridian, 180° east it is midnight of the same day – while 180° west the day is just beginning. To overcome this, the International Date Line was established, approximately following the 180° meridian. Thus, if you travelled eastwards from Japan (140° East) to Samoa (170° West), you would pass from Sunday night into Sunday morning.

Zones using GMT | Zones fast of GMT
Zones slow of GMT | Half-hour zones
--- International boundaries | Time zone boundaries
10 Hours slow or fast of GMT or Greenwich Mean Time | — International Date Line

THE EARTH: GEOLOGY

The complementary, almost jigsaw-puzzle fit of the Atlantic coasts led to Alfred Wegener's proposition of continental drift in Germany (1915). His theory suggested that an ancient super-continent, which he called Pangaea, incorporating all the Earth's landmasses, gradually split up to form the continents we know today.

By 180 million years ago, Pangaea had divided into two major groups and the southern part, Gondwanaland, had itself begun to break up with India and Antarctica-Australia becoming isolated.

By 135 million years ago, the widening of the splits in the North Atlantic and Indian Oceans persisted, a South Atlantic gap had appeared, and India continued to move 'north' towards Asia.

By 65 million years ago, South America had split completely from Africa.

To form today's pattern, India 'collided' with Asia (crumpling up sediments to form the Himalayas); South America rotated and moved west to connect with North America; Australia separated from Antarctica and moved north; and the familiar gap developed between Greenland and Europe.

The origin of the Earth is still open to conjecture, although the most widely accepted theory is that it was formed from a solar cloud consisting mainly of hydrogen about 4,600 million years ago. The cloud condensed, forming the planets. The lighter elements floated to the surface of the Earth, where they cooled to form a crust; the inner material remained hot and molten. The first rocks were formed over 3,500 million years ago, but the Earth's surface has since been constantly altered.

The crust consists of a brittle, low-density material, varying from 5 km to 50 km thick beneath the continents, which is predominantly made up of silica and aluminium: hence its name, 'sial'. Below the sial is a basaltic layer known as 'sima', comprising mainly silica and magnesium. The crust accounts for only 1.5% of the Earth's volume.

The mantle lies immediately below the crust, with a distinct change in density and chemical properties. The rock here is rich in iron and magnesium silicates, with temperatures reaching as high as 1,600°C. The rigid upper mantle extends down to a depth of about 1,000 km, below which is a more viscous lower mantle measuring about 1,700 km thick.

The outer core, measuring about 2,100 km thick, consists of molten iron and nickel at temperatures ranging from 2,100°C to 5,000°C, possibly separated from the less dense mantle by an oxidized shell. About 5,000 km below the planetary surface is a liquid transition zone, below which is the solid inner core, a sphere of about 1,350 km diameter, where rock is three times as dense as in the crust. The temperature at the centre of the Earth is probably about 5,000°C.

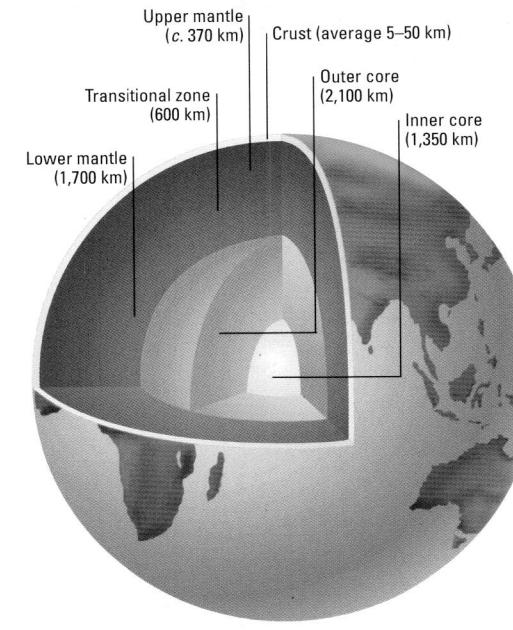

Upper mantle (c. 370 km) | Crust (average 5–50 km)
Transitional zone (600 km)
Outer core (2,100 km)
Inner core (1,350 km)
Lower mantle (1,700 km)

CONTINENTAL DRIFT

About 200 million years ago the original Pangaea landmass began to split into two continental groups, which further separated over time to produce the present-day configuration.

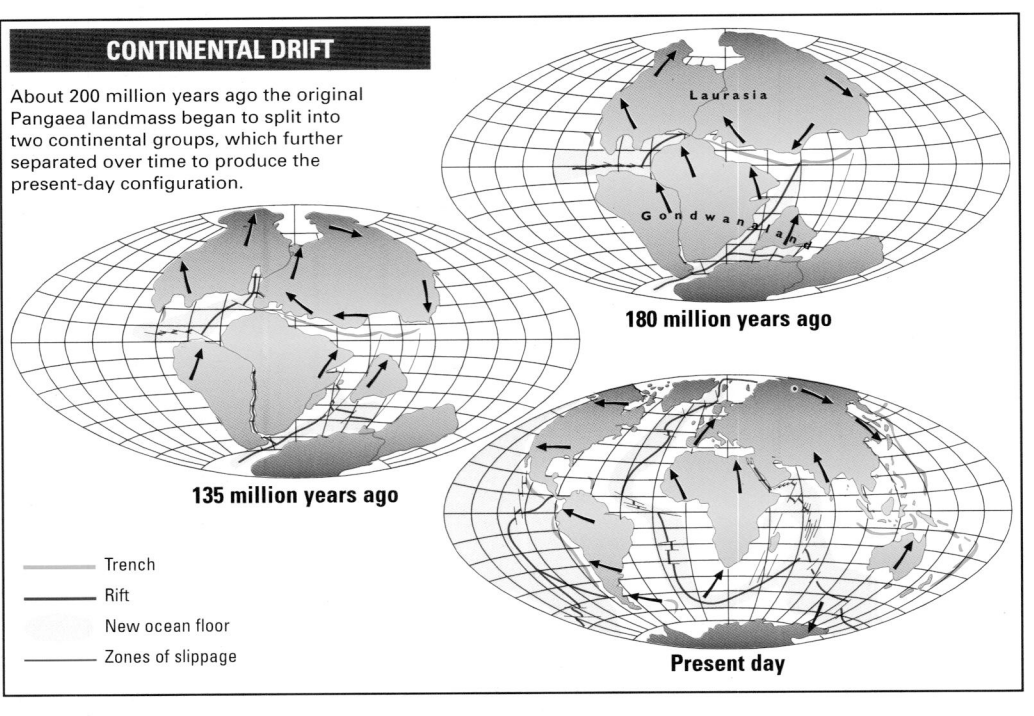

Laurasia
Gondwanaland

180 million years ago

135 million years ago

Present day

— Trench
— Rift
— New ocean floor
— Zones of slippage

PLATE TECTONICS

The original debate about the drift theory of Wegener and others formed a long prelude to a more radical idea: plate tectonics. The discovery that the continents are carried along on the top of slowly-moving crustal plates (which float on heavier liquid material – the lower mantle – much as icebergs do on water) provided the mechanism for the drift theories to work. The plates converge and diverge along margins marked by seismic and volcanic activity. Plates diverge from mid-ocean ridges where molten lava pushes up and forces the plates apart at a rate of up to 40 mm a year; converging plates form either a trench (where the oceanic plates sink below the lighter continental rock) or mountain ranges (where two continents collide).

The debate about plate tectonics is not over, however. In addition to abiding questions such as what force actually moves the plates (massive convection currents in the Earth's interior is the most popular explanation), and why so many volcanoes and earthquakes occur in mid-plate (such as Hawaii and central China), evidence began to emerge in the early 1990s that, with more sophisticated equipment and models, the whole theory might be in doubt.

VOLCANOES

Volcanoes occur when hot liquefied rock beneath the Earth's crust is pushed up by pressure to the surface as molten lava. There are some 550 known active volcanoes, around 20 of which are erupting at any one time. Some volcanoes erupt in an explosive way, throwing out rocks and ash (such as Anak Krakatoa in Indonesia); others are effusive, and lava flows out of the vent (Mauna Loa in Hawaii is a classic example); and there are volcanoes which are both (such as Mount Fuji, a composite volcano of the type shown opposite). Fast-flowing basaltic lava erupts at temperatures of between 1,000–1,200°C [1,800–2,200°F] close to the temperature of the upper mantle. An accumulation of lava and cinders around a vent creates cones of variable size and shape. As a result of many eruptions over centuries Mount Etna in Sicily has a circumference of over 120 km [75 miles].

Climatologists believe that volcanic ash, if ejected high enough into the atmosphere, can influence temperature and weather for several years afterwards. The eruption of Mount Pinatubo in the Philippines ejected more than 20 million tonnes of dust and ash 32 km [20 miles] into the atmosphere and is believed to have accelerated ozone depletion over a large part of the globe.

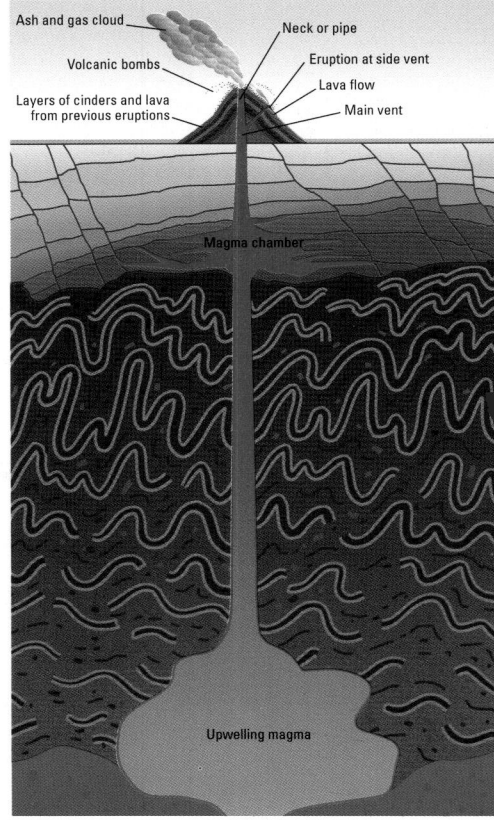

Ash and gas cloud
Volcanic bombs
Layers of cinders and lava from previous eruptions
Neck or pipe
Eruption at side vent
Lava flow
Main vent
Magma chamber
Upwelling magma

DISTRIBUTION

▲ Land volcanoes active since 1700

• Submarine volcanoes

◆ Geysers

5.5 ↗ Direction of movement (cm/year)

⌢ Boundaries of tectonic plates

Volcanoes can suddenly erupt after lying dormant for centuries: in 1991 Mount Pinatubo, in the Philippines, burst into life after sleeping for more than 600 years.

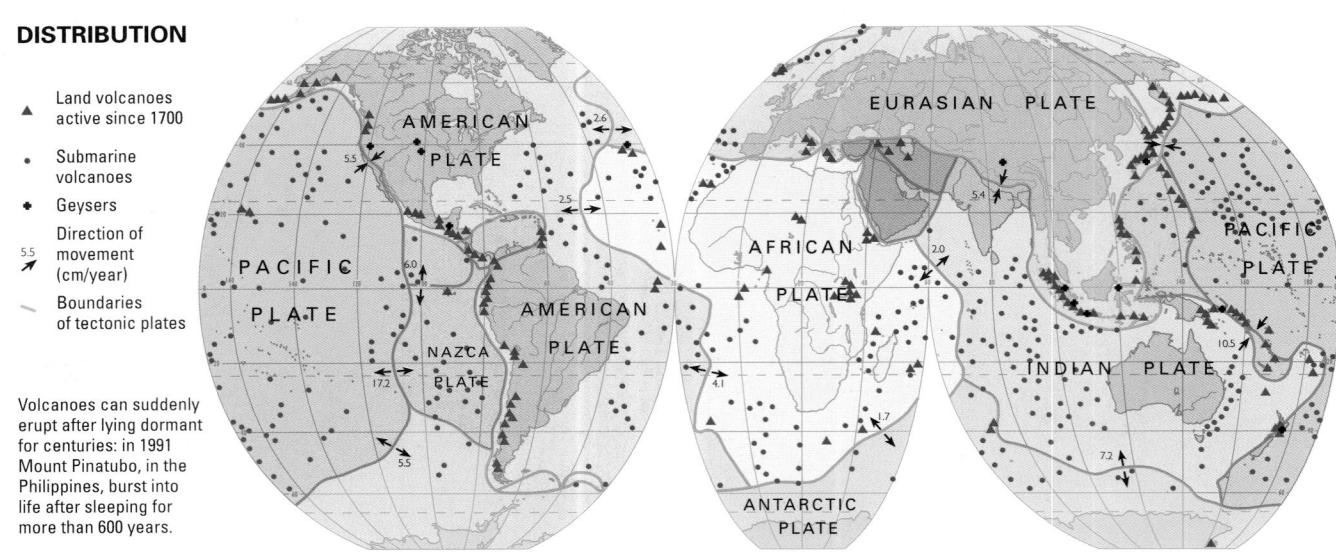

AMERICAN PLATE
PACIFIC PLATE
NAZCA PLATE
AMERICAN PLATE
EURASIAN PLATE
AFRICAN PLATE
PACIFIC PLATE
INDIAN PLATE
ANTARCTIC PLATE

GEOLOGICAL TIME

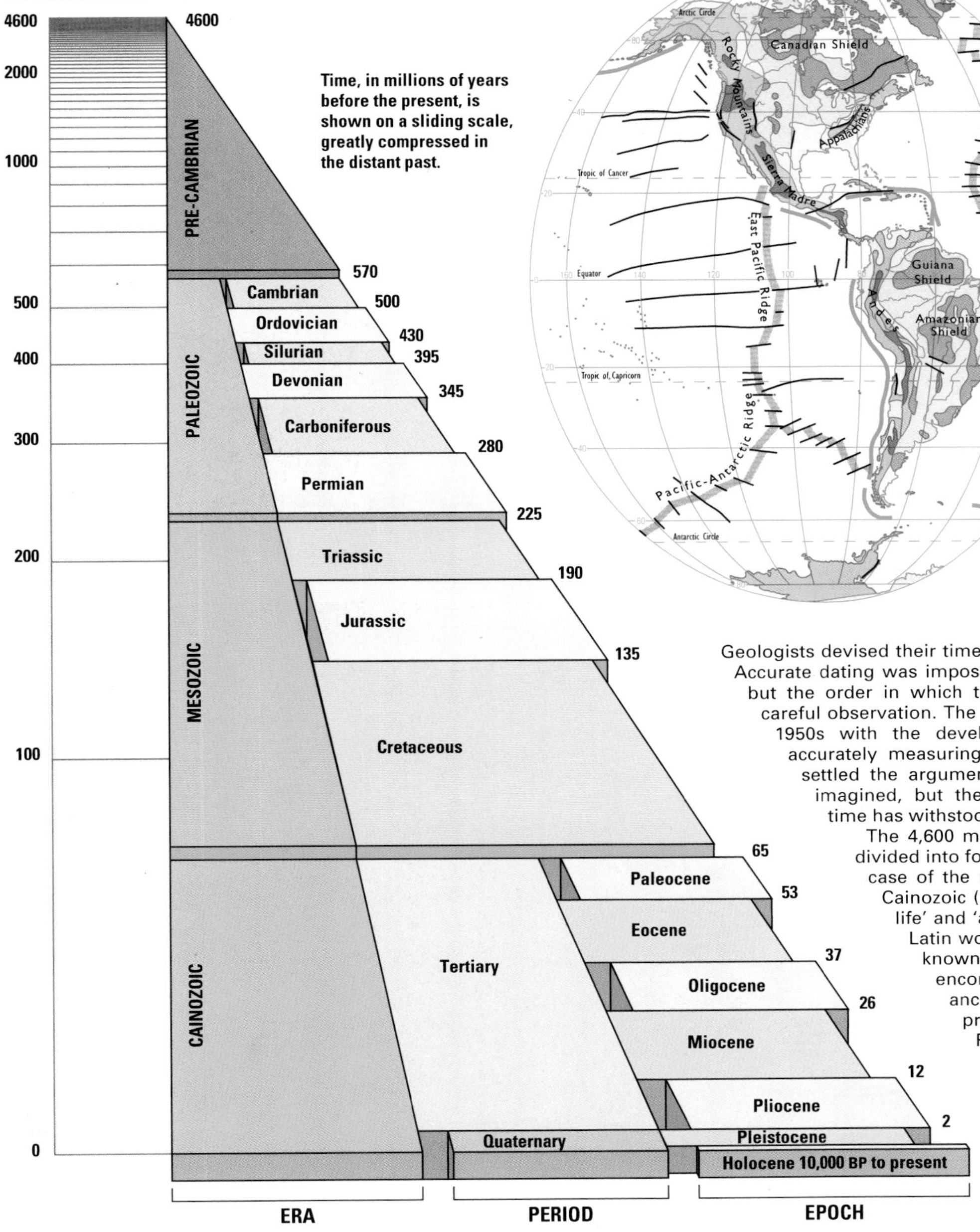

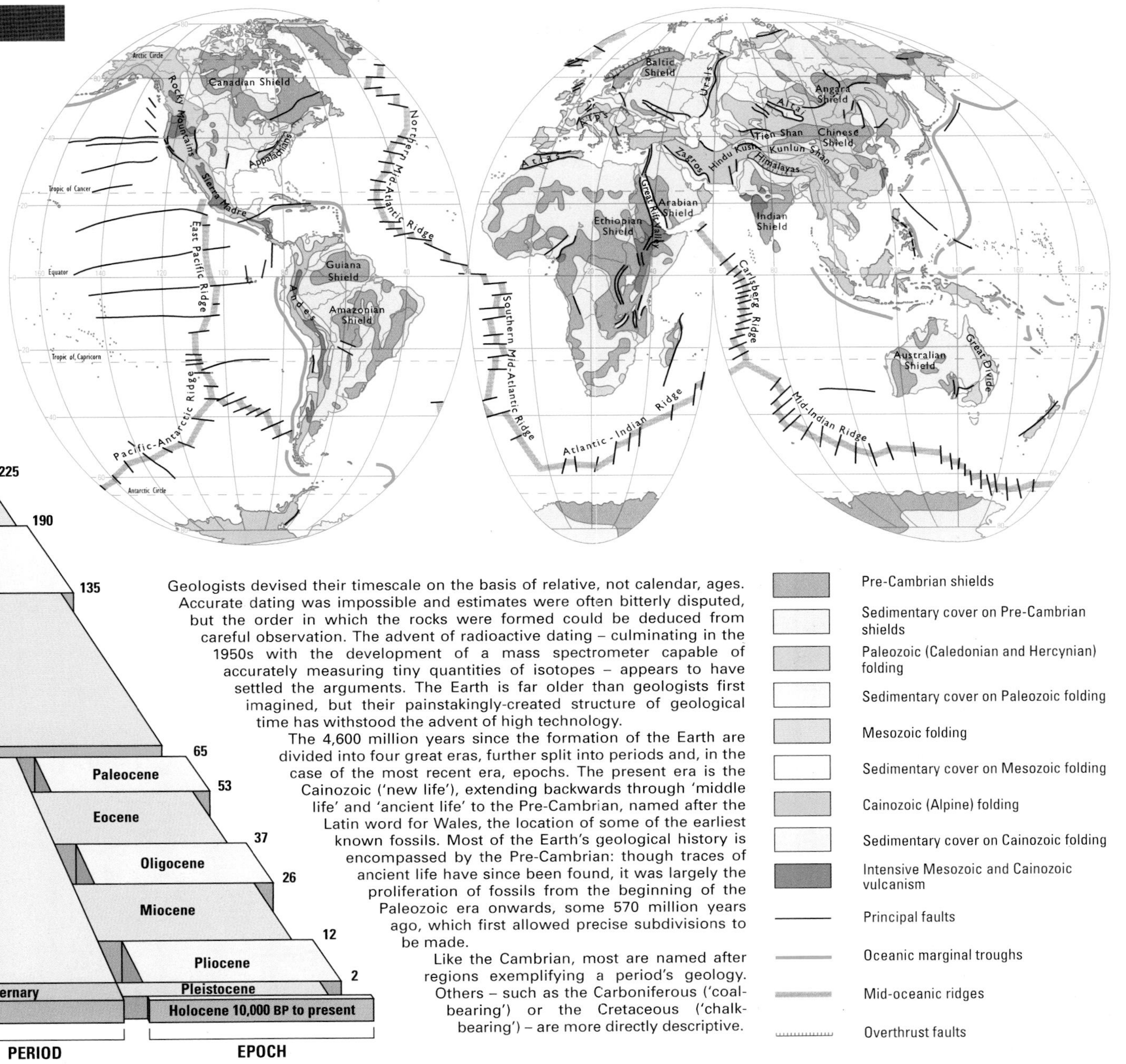

Time, in millions of years before the present, is shown on a sliding scale, greatly compressed in the distant past.

Time scale (millions of years):
- 4600 — PRE-CAMBRIAN (4600)
- 2000
- 1000
- 570 — Cambrian
- 500 — Ordovician (500)
- 430 — Silurian
- 400 — Devonian (395)
- 345 — Carboniferous
- 300 — Permian (280)
- 225 — Triassic
- 200 — Jurassic (190)
- 135 — Cretaceous
- 100
- 65 — Paleocene
- 53 — Eocene
- 37 — Oligocene
- 26 — Miocene
- 12 — Pliocene
- 2 — Pleistocene
- 0 — Holocene 10,000 BP to present

PALEOZOIC
MESOZOIC
CAINOZOIC
Tertiary
Quaternary

ERA — **PERIOD** — **EPOCH**

Geologists devised their timescale on the basis of relative, not calendar, ages. Accurate dating was impossible and estimates were often bitterly disputed, but the order in which the rocks were formed could be deduced from careful observation. The advent of radioactive dating – culminating in the 1950s with the development of a mass spectrometer capable of accurately measuring tiny quantities of isotopes – appears to have settled the arguments. The Earth is far older than geologists first imagined, but their painstakingly-created structure of geological time has withstood the advent of high technology.

The 4,600 million years since the formation of the Earth are divided into four great eras, further split into periods and, in the case of the most recent era, epochs. The present era is the Cainozoic ('new life'), extending backwards through 'middle life' and 'ancient life' to the Pre-Cambrian, named after the Latin word for Wales, the location of some of the earliest known fossils. Most of the Earth's geological history is encompassed by the Pre-Cambrian: though traces of ancient life have since been found, it was largely the proliferation of fossils from the beginning of the Paleozoic era onwards, some 570 million years ago, which first allowed precise subdivisions to be made.

Like the Cambrian, most are named after regions exemplifying a period's geology. Others – such as the Carboniferous ('coal-bearing') or the Cretaceous ('chalk-bearing') – are more directly descriptive.

Map legend:
- Pre-Cambrian shields
- Sedimentary cover on Pre-Cambrian shields
- Paleozoic (Caledonian and Hercynian) folding
- Sedimentary cover on Paleozoic folding
- Mesozoic folding
- Sedimentary cover on Mesozoic folding
- Cainozoic (Alpine) folding
- Sedimentary cover on Cainozoic folding
- Intensive Mesozoic and Cainozoic vulcanism
- Principal faults
- Oceanic marginal troughs
- Mid-oceanic ridges
- Overthrust faults

EARTHQUAKES

Earthquake magnitude is usually rated according to either the Richter or the Modified Mercalli scale, both devised by seismologists in the 1930s. The Richter scale measures absolute earthquake power with mathematical precision: each step upwards represents a ten-fold increase in the amplitude of the shockwave. Theoretically, there is no upper limit, but the largest earthquakes measured have been rated at between 8.8 and 8.9. The 12–point Mercalli scale, based on observed effects, is often more meaningful, ranging from I (earthquakes noticed only by seismographs) to XII (total destruction); intermediate points include V (people awakened at night; unstable objects overturned), VII (collapse of ordinary buildings; chimneys and monuments fall) and IX (conspicuous cracks in ground; serious damage to reservoirs).

NOTABLE EARTHQUAKES SINCE 1900

Year	Location	Mag.	Deaths
1906	San Francisco, USA	8.3	503
1906	Valparaiso, Chile	8.6	22,000
1908	Messina, Italy	7.5	83,000
1915	Avezzano, Italy	7.5	30,000
1920	Gansu (Kansu), China	8.6	180,000
1923	Yokohama, Japan	8.3	143,000
1927	Nan Shan, China	8.3	200,000
1932	Gansu (Kansu), China	7.6	70,000
1934	Bihar, India/Nepal	8.4	10,700
1935	Quetta, India*	7.5	60,000
1939	Chillan, Chile	8.3	28,000
1939	Erzincan, Turkey	7.9	30,000
1960	Agadir, Morocco	5.8	12,000
1962	Khorasan, Iran	7.1	12,230
1963	Skopje, Yugoslavia**	6.0	1,000
1968	N.E. Iran	7.4	12,000
1970	N. Peru	7.7	66,794
1972	Managua, Nicaragua	6.2	5,000
1974	N. Pakistan	6.3	5,200
1976	Guatemala	7.5	22,778
1976	Tangshan, China	8.2	650,000
1978	Tabas, Iran	7.7	25,000
1980	El Asnam, Algeria	7.3	20,000
1980	S. Italy	7.2	4,800
1985	Mexico City, Mexico	8.1	4,200
1988	N.W. Armenia	6.8	55,000
1990	N. Iran	7.7	36,000
1993	Maharashtra, India	6.4	30,000
1994	Los Angeles, USA	6.6	57
1995	Kobe, Japan	7.2	5,000
1995	Sakhalin Is., Russia	7.5	2,000
1996	Yunnan, China	7.0	240

The highest magnitude recorded on the Richter scale is 8.9, in Japan on 2 March 1933 (2,990 deaths). The most devastating quake ever was at Shaanxi (Shenshi) province, central China, on 3 January 1556, when an estimated 830,000 people were killed.

* now Pakistan
** now Macedonia

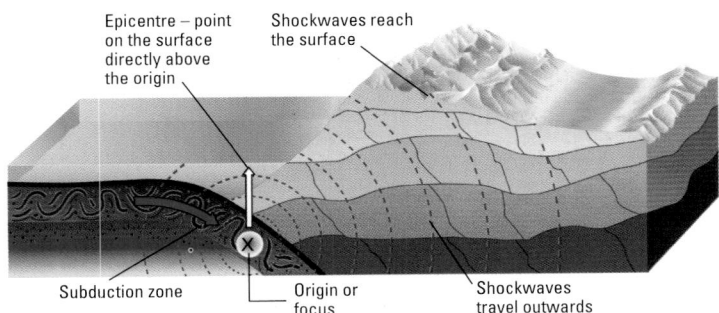
Epicentre – point on the surface directly above the origin
Shockwaves reach the surface
Subduction zone
Origin or focus
Shockwaves travel outwards

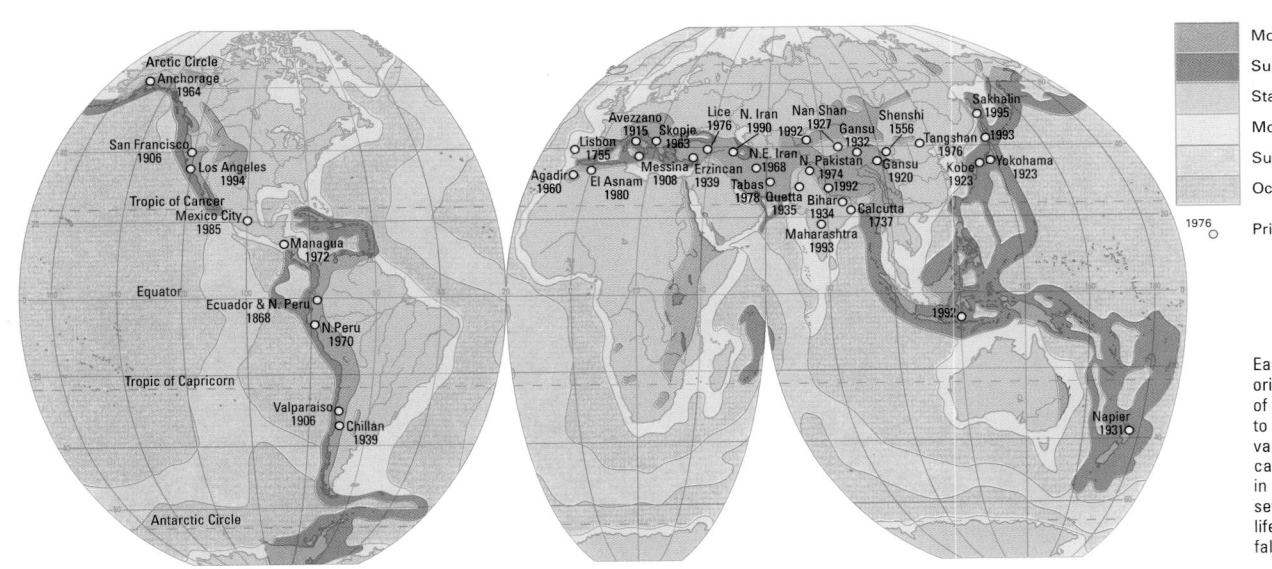

Earthquake map legend:
- Mobile land areas
- Submarine zones of mobile land areas
- Stable land platforms
- Mobile land areas
- Submarine extensions of land platforms
- Oceanic platforms
- Principal earthquakes & dates (1976)

Earthquakes are a series of rapid vibrations originating from the slipping or faulting of parts of the Earth's crust when stresses within build up to breaking point. They usually happen at depths varying from 8 km to 30 km. Severe earthquakes cause extensive damage when they take place in populated areas, destroying structures and severing communications. Most initial loss of life occurs due to secondary causes such as falling masonry, fires and flooding.

THE EARTH: OCEANS

SEAWATER

The chemical composition of the sea, by percentage, excluding the elements of water itself

Chloride (Cl)	55.04%
Sodium (Na)	30.61%
Sulphate (SO₄)	7.69%
Magnesium (Mg)	3.69%
Calcium (Ca)	1.16%
Potassium (K)	1.10%
Bicarbonate (HCO₃)	0.41%
Bromide (Br)	0.19%
Boric Acid (H₃BO₃)	0.07%
Strontium (Sr)	0.04%
Fluoride (Fl)	0.003%
Lithium (Li)	trace
Rubidium (Rb)	trace
Phosphorus (P)	trace
Iodine (I)	trace
Barium (Ba)	trace
Arsenic (As)	trace
Cesium (Cs)	trace

Eleven constituents account for over 99% of the salt content of seawater, but seawater also contains virtually every other element. In natural conditions, its composition is broadly consistent across the world's seas and oceans; but in coastal areas especially variations are sometimes substantial. The oceans are about 35 parts water to one part salt.

The Earth is a misnamed planet: more than 70% of its total surface area – 361,740,000 square kilometres – is covered by its oceans and seas. This great cloak of liquid water gives the planet its characteristic blue appearance from space, and is one of two obvious differences between the Earth and its near-neighbours in space, Mars and Venus. The other difference is the presence of life, and the two are closely linked.

Most geographers divide the world's water into four main oceans: the Pacific, Atlantic, Arctic and Indian Oceans; together accounting for 97.2% of all water. The oceans can be further divided into zones according to depth. The most active zone is the sunlit upper layer, home of most sea life and the vital interface between air and water. In this surface zone, huge energies are exchanged between the oceans and the atmosphere; it is also a kind of membrane through which the ocean breathes, absorbing great quantities of carbon dioxide and partially exchanging them for oxygen, largely through the phytoplankton, tiny plants that photosynthesize solar energy and provide the food base for all other marine life.

As depth increases, so light and colour gradually fade away, the longer wavelengths dying first. At 50 metres, the ocean is a world of green, blue and violet; at 100 metres, only blue remains; by 200 metres, there is only a dim twilight. The temperature falls away with the light, until just before 1,000 metres – the precise depth varies – there occurs a temperature change almost as abrupt as the transition between air and water far above. Below this thermocline, at a near-stable 3°C, the waters are forever unmoved by the winds of the upper world and are stirred only by the very slow action of deep ocean currents. The pressure is crushing, reaching 1,000 atmospheres in the deepest trenches: equivalent to a force of 1 tonne

LIFE IN THE OCEANS

An imaginary profile of the typical coastal and oceanic zones is shown, with a selection of the life forms that might occur in the water off the Pacific Coast of Central America. The animals illustrated are not drawn to scale as the range of sizes is too great. Most marine life is confined to the first 200 metres, the upper sunlit (photic) zone, where sunlight can still penetrate. Plant and animal plankton, the basis of life in the ocean, occur in great quantities in all zones.

In the pelagic environment (open sea), vertical gradients, including those of light, temperature and salinity, determine the distribution of organisms. From the tidal zone at the coastline, the continental shelf, geologically still part of the continental landmass, drops gently to about 200 metres – the sunlit zone. At the end of the shelf, the seabed falls away in the steeper angle of the continental slope. The subsequent descent to the deep ocean floor, known as the continental rise, is more gentle, with gradients between 1 in 100 and 1 in 700 until the abyssal plains, at between 2,500 and 6,000 metres below the surface.

For the most part, the sea bottom is flat, seldom descending below 6,000 metres. A few ocean trenches, however, slice almost twice as far into the Earth's crust, especially in the Pacific Ocean, where six trenches reach depths of more than 10,000 metres, including the 11,022-metre deep Mariana Trench.

Each of these zones contains a distinctive community of species adapted to the different conditions of salinity, temperature and light intensity. Indeed, a few organisms have been found even in the abyssal darkness of the great ocean trenches.

bearing down on every square centimetre.

Yet even here the oceans support life, and not only the handful of strange, deep-sea creatures that find a living in the near-empty abyss. The deep ocean serves as a gigantic storehouse, both for heat and for assorted atmospheric chemicals, regulating and balancing the proportions of various trace compounds and elements, and ensuring a large measure of stability for both the climate and the plants and animals that depend on it.

EL NIÑO

The importance of the ocean–atmosphere interaction is nowhere more dramatically demonstrated than in the Southern Pacific Ocean. Periodic weakening of the major wind patterns in this area leads to alterations in the surface currents in the southern gyre, suppression of the Peruvian upwelling, and changes to biological productivity, sea level and rainfall patterns.

These changes in the southern Pacific have considerable effects on the patterns of rainfall and weather in Australia and South-east Asia, where monsoon rainfall is reduced during El Niño years.

The El Niño phenomenon occurs every four to 12 years around Christmas. It is a warming of the surface waters by 2–6°C off the coast of South America and forms part of the ENSO (El Niño Southern Oscillation) pattern of climate in the southern hemisphere.

The occurrence of ENSO events is periodic and there is some worrying evidence that the frequency of the event may have increased during the last few decades. Due to the widespread changes that El Niño brings (a drastic reduction in fish life, for example), two programmes have been set up to monitor it: the Tropical Ocean Global Atmosphere programme (TOGA) and the World Circulation Experiment (WOCE).

ATOLL BUILDING

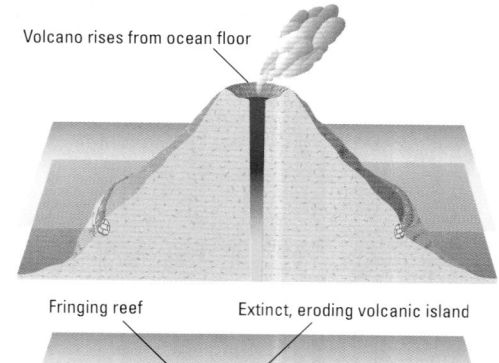

Volcano rises from ocean floor

Fringing reef   Extinct, eroding volcanic island

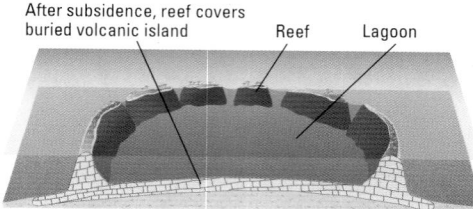

After subsidence, reef covers buried volcanic island   Reef   Lagoon

A coral atoll usually begins existence as a bare volcanic peak, thrusting above the surface of the ocean. A colony of coral – marine organisms called polyps, with skeletons of rigid calcium carbonate – forms itself in the shallow water around the peak. Its seafloor eruption over, the volcano is eroded and slowly sinks, leaving the coral forming a ring of hard limestone around its remnant. In time, all obvious trace of the volcano vanishes, and the barrier reef of an atoll is all that remains. Atolls can form either in the open ocean, such as those of the Pacific Ocean, or at continental margins, such as those of the Florida Keys.

Crab   Seaweed   SEA LEVEL
Jellyfish
Green turtle   Anchovy
Dolphin

SUNLIT ZONE
200 metres
[650 feet]

Marlin

Snake eel   Bonito
Blue Whale   TWILIGHT ZONE
1,000 metres
[3,000 feet]

Phytoplankton and zooplankton

Lantern fish

Ray

Sperm whale

Deep-sea squid   DARK ZONE
6,000 metres
[19,500 feet]

Anglerfish

Halosaur

Sea cucumber
Sponge

Isopod   TRENCH ZONE
10,000 metres
[33,000 feet]

JANUARY CURRENTS AND TEMPERATURES

(Northern Hemisphere: winter)

ACTUAL SURFACE
TEMPERATURE

°C
30
20
10
0
-10
-20
-30
-40

OCEAN CURRENTS

Cold	Warm	Speed (knots)
		Less than 0.5
		0.5 – 1.0
		Over 1.0

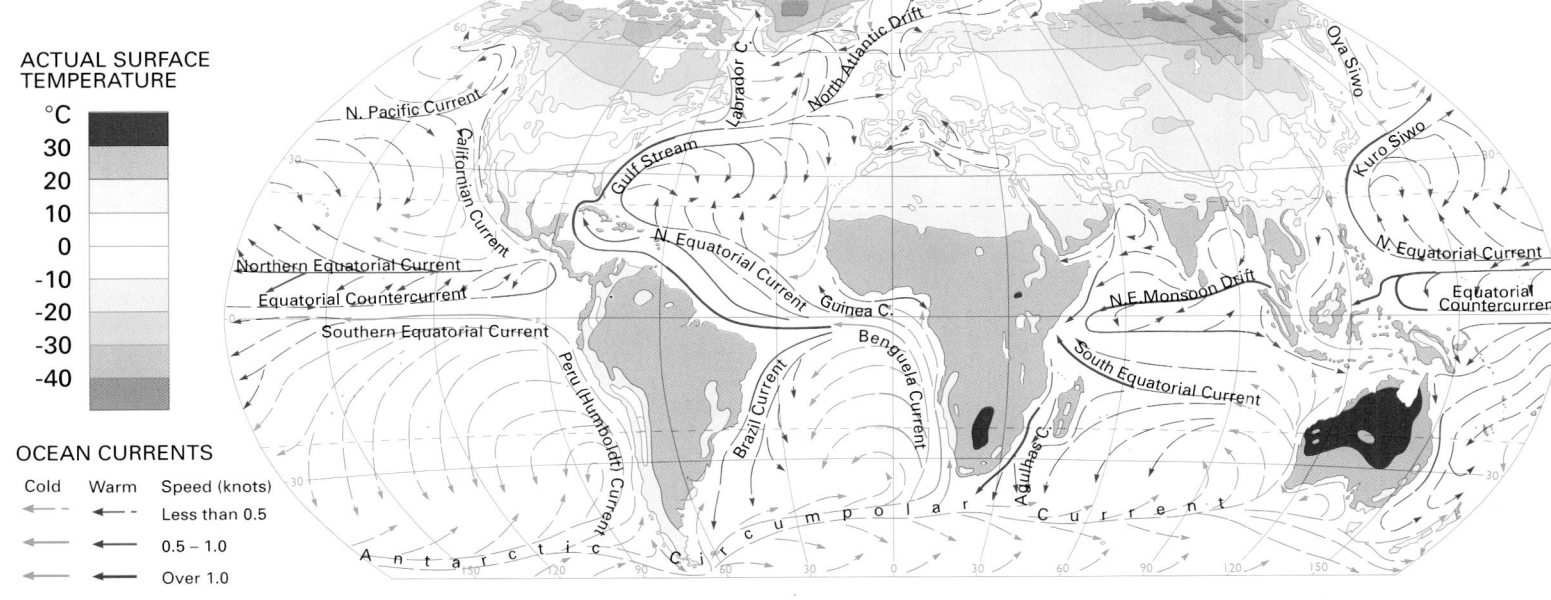

JULY CURRENTS AND TEMPERATURES

(Northern Hemisphere: summer)

ACTUAL SURFACE
TEMPERATURE

°C
30
20
10
0
-10

OCEAN CURRENTS

Cold	Warm	Speed (knots)
		Less than 0.5
		0.5 – 1.0
		Over 1.0

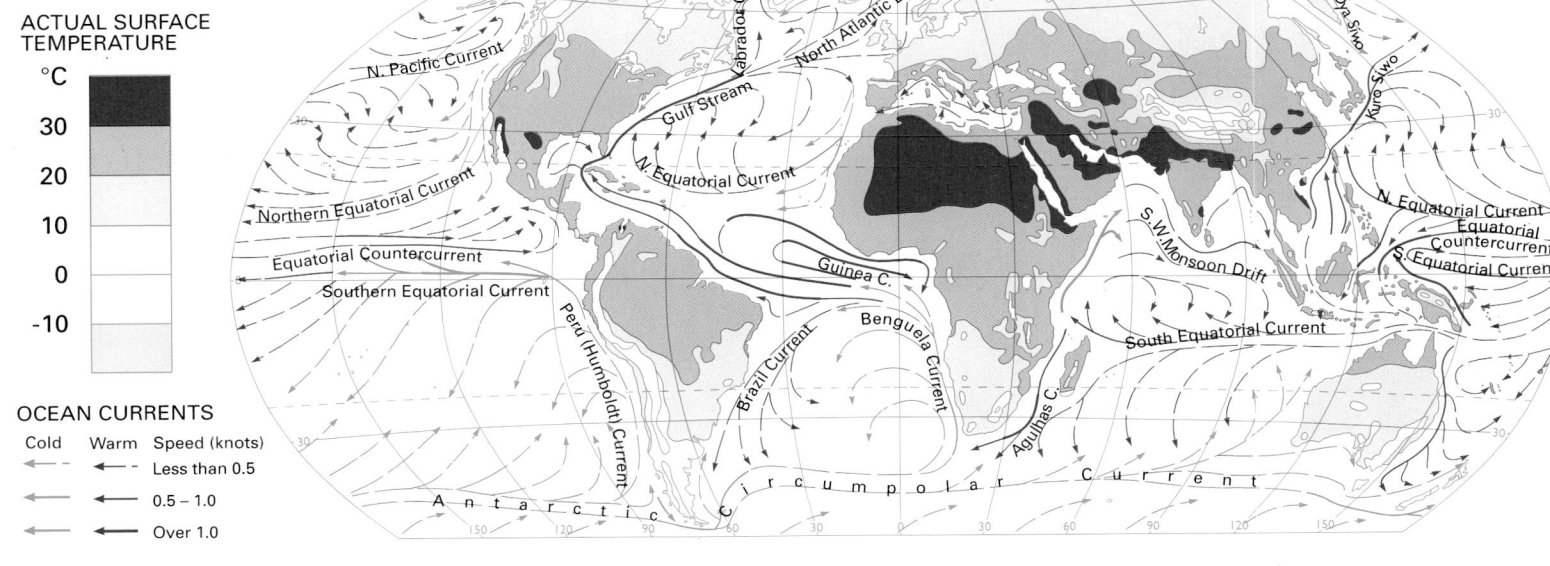

Moving immense quantities of energy as well as billions of tonnes of water every hour, the ocean currents are a vital part of the great heat engine that drives the Earth's climate. They themselves are produced by a twofold mechanism. At the surface, winds push huge masses of water before them; in the deep ocean, below an abrupt temperature gradient that separates the churning surface waters from the still depths, density variations cause slow vertical movements.

The pattern of circulation of the great surface currents is determined by the displacement known as the Coriolis effect. As the Earth turns beneath a moving object – whether it is a tennis ball or a vast mass of water – it appears to be deflected to one side. The deflection is most obvious near the Equator, where the Earth's surface is spinning eastwards at 1,700 km/h; currents moving polewards are curved clockwise in the northern hemisphere and anti-clockwise in the southern.

The result is a system of spinning circles known as gyres. The Coriolis effect piles up water on the left of each gyre, creating a narrow, fast-moving stream that is matched by a slower, broader returning current on the right. North and south of the Equator, the fastest currents are located in the west and in the east respectively. In each case, warm water moves from the Equator and cold water returns to it. Cold currents often bring an upwelling of nutrients with them, supporting the world's most economically important fisheries.

Depending on the prevailing winds, some currents on or near the Equator may reverse their direction in the course of the year – a seasonal variation on which Asian monsoon rains depend, and whose occasional failure can bring disaster to millions of people.

PROFILE OF THE ATLANTIC OCEAN

The deep ocean floor is no more uniform than the surface of the continents, although it was not until the development of effective sonar equipment that it was possible to examine submarine contours in detail. The Atlantic (below) and the Pacific show similar patterns. Offshore comes the continental shelf, sliding downwards to the continental slope and the steeper continental rise, after which the seabed rolls onwards into the abyssal plains. In the wide Pacific, these are interrupted by gently-rising abyssal hills; in both oceans, the plains extend all the way to the mid-oceanic ridges, where the upwelling of new crustal material is constantly forcing the oceans wider. Volcanic activity is responsible for the formation of seamounts and tablemounts, or guyots, their flat-topped equivalents.

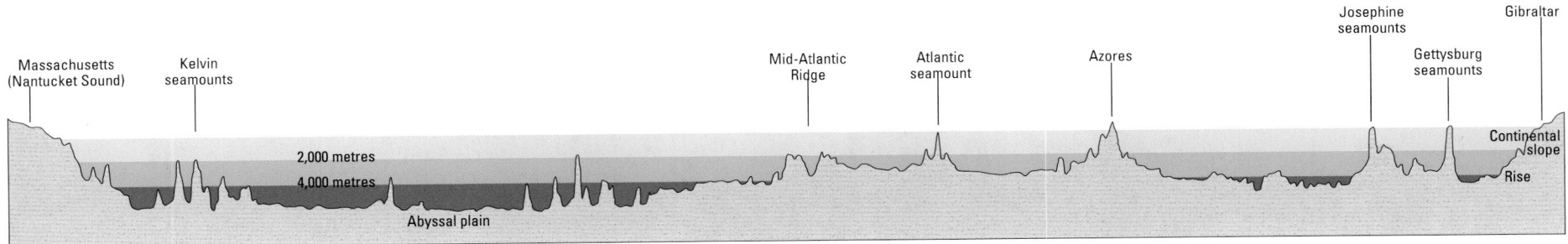

THE EARTH: ATMOSPHERE

Extending from the surface far into space, the atmosphere is a meteor shield, a radiation deflector, a thermal blanket and a source of chemical energy for the Earth's diverse inhabitants. Five-sixths of its mass is found in the first 15 kilometres, the troposphere, no thicker in relative terms than the skin of an onion. Clouds, cyclonic winds, precipitation and virtually all the phenomena we call weather occur in this narrow layer. Above, a thin layer of ozone blocks ultra-violet radiation. Beyond 100 kilometres, atmospheric density is lower than most laboratory vacuums, yet these tenuous outer reaches, composed largely of hydrogen and helium, trap cosmic debris and incoming high-energy particles alike.

CIRCULATION OF THE AIR

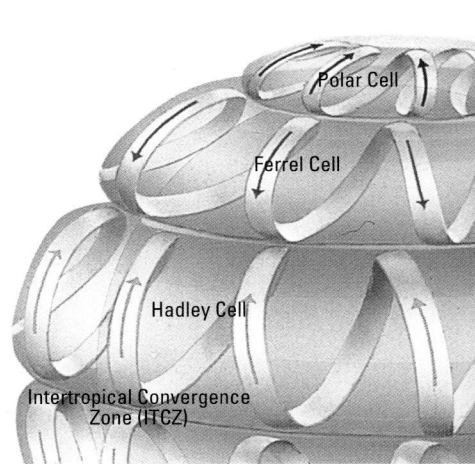

Polar Cell
Ferrel Cell
Hadley Cell
30°N
Equator
30°S
Intertropical Convergence Zone (ITCZ)

STRUCTURE OF ATMOSPHERE

F2
F1
E
D
Mesosphere
Ozone layer
Tropopause

TEMPERATURE

ca. 2,200°C
ca. 1,500°C
ca. 750°C

−58°C
−91°C
−93°C
−33°C
−8°C
−12°C
−38°C
−53°C
15°C

PRESSURE

$10^{-53}mb$
$10^{-47}mb$
$10^{-41}mb$
$10^{-35}mb$
$10^{-28}mb$
$10^{-22}mb$
$10^{-16}mb$
$10^{-10}mb$
$10^{-3}mb$
$10^{3}mb$

900 km
800 km
700 km
600 km
500 km
400 km
300 km
200 km
100 km
0

CHEMICAL STRUCTURE

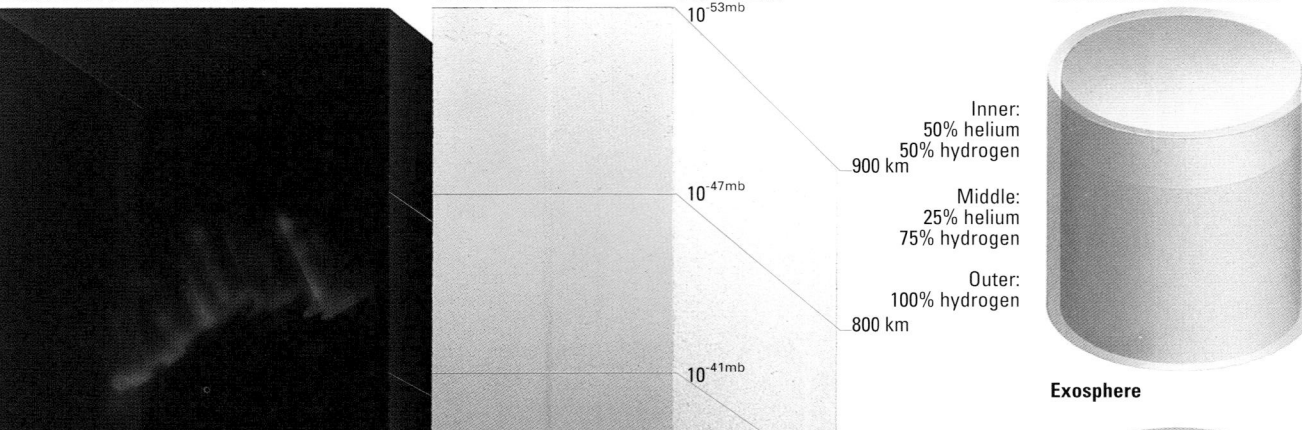

Inner:
50% helium
50% hydrogen

Middle:
25% helium
75% hydrogen

Outer:
100% hydrogen

Exosphere

15% helium
15% oxygen and atomic oxygen
70% nitrogen

Ionosphere

1% ozone
1% argon
18% oxygen
80% nitrogen

Stratosphere

1% argon
21% oxygen
78% nitrogen

Troposphere

Exosphere
The atmosphere's upper layer has no clear outer boundary, merging imperceptibly with interplanetary space. Its lower boundary, at an altitude of approximately 600 kilometres, is almost equally vague. The exosphere is mainly composed of hydrogen and helium in changing proportions, with a small quantity of atomic oxygen up to 600 kilometres. Helium vanishes with increasing altitude, and above 2,400 kilometres the exosphere is almost entirely composed of hydrogen.

Ionosphere
Gas molecules in the ionosphere, mainly helium, oxygen and nitrogen, are electrically charged – ionized – by the Sun's radiation. Within the ionosphere's range of 50 to 600 kilometres in altitude, they group themselves into four layers, known conventionally as D, E, F1 and F2, all of which can reflect radio waves of differing frequencies. The high energy of ionospheric gas gives it a notional temperature of more than 2,000°C, although its density is negligible. The auroras – aurora borealis and its southern counterpart, aurora australis – occur in the ionosphere when charged particles from the Sun interact with the Earth's magnetic fields, at their strongest near the poles.

Stratosphere
Separated at its upper and lower limits by the distinct thresholds of the stratopause and the tropopause, the stratosphere is a remarkably stable layer between 50 kilometres and about 15 kilometres. Its temperature rises from −55°C at its lower extent to approximately 0°C near the stratopause, where a thin layer of ozone absorbs ultra-violet radiation. 'Mother-of-pearl' or nacreous cloud occurs at about 25 kilometres' altitude. Stratospheric air contains enough ozone to make it poisonous, although it is in any case far too rarified to breathe.

Troposphere
The narrowest of all the atmospheric layers, the troposphere extends up to 15 kilometres at the Equator but only 8 kilometres at the poles. Since this thin region contains about 85% of the atmosphere's total mass and almost all of its water vapour, it is also the realm of the Earth's weather. Temperatures fall steadily with increasing height by about 1°C for every 100 metres above sea level.

AIR MASSES

Heated by the relatively high surface temperatures near the Earth's Equator, air expands and rises to create a belt of low pressure. Moving northwards towards the poles, it gradually cools, sinking once more and producing high-pressure belts at about latitudes 30°N and 30°S. Water vapour carried with the air falls as rain, releasing vast quantities of energy as well as liquid water when it condenses.

The high- and low-pressure belts are both areas of comparative calm, but between them, blowing from high-pressure to low-pressure areas, are the prevailing winds. The atmospheric circulatory system is enormously complicated by the Coriolis effect brought about by the spinning Earth: winds are deflected to the right in the northern hemisphere and to the left in the southern, giving rise to the typically cyclonic pattern of swirling clouds carried by the moving masses of air.

Although clouds appear in an almost infinite variety of shapes and sizes, there are recognizable features that form the basis of a classification first put forward by Luke Howard, a London chemist, in 1803 and later modified by the World Meteorological Organization. The system is derived from the altitude of clouds and whether they form hairlike filaments ('cirrus'), heaps or piles ('cumulus'), or layers ('stratus'). Each characteristic carries some kind of message – not always a clear one – to forecasters about the weather to come.

CLASSIFICATION OF CLOUDS

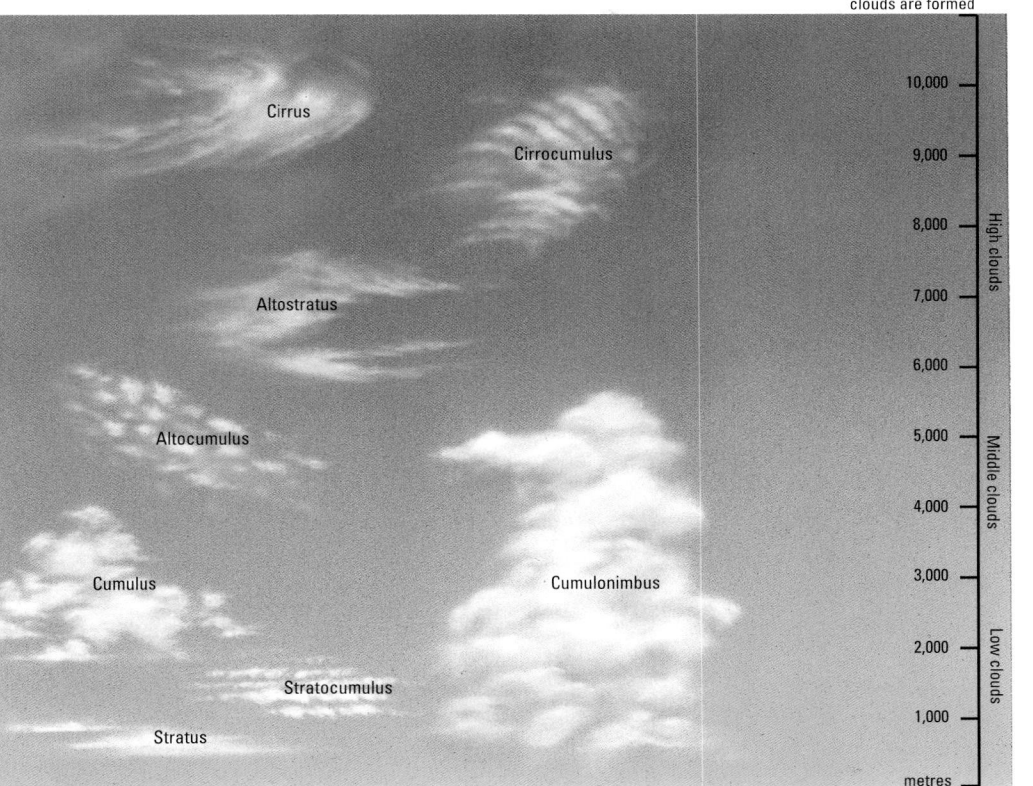

Clouds form when damp, usually rising, air is cooled. Thus they form when a wind rises to cross hills or mountains; when a mass of air rises over, or is pushed up by, another mass of denser air; or when local heating of the ground causes convection currents.

The types of clouds are classified according to altitude as high, middle or low. The high ones, composed of ice crystals, are cirrus, cirrostratus and cirrocumulus. The middle clouds are altostratus, a grey or bluish striated, fibrous or uniform sheet producing light drizzle, and altocumulus, a thicker and fluffier version of cirrocumulus.

The low clouds include nimbostratus, a dark grey layer that brings almost continuous rain or snow; cumulus, a detached 'heap' – brilliant white in sunlight but dark and flat at the base; and stratus, which forms dull, overcast skies at low altitudes.

Cumulonimbus, associated with storms and rains, heavy and dense with a flat base and a high, fluffy outline, can be tall enough to occupy middle as well as low altitudes.

PRESSURE AND SURFACE WINDS

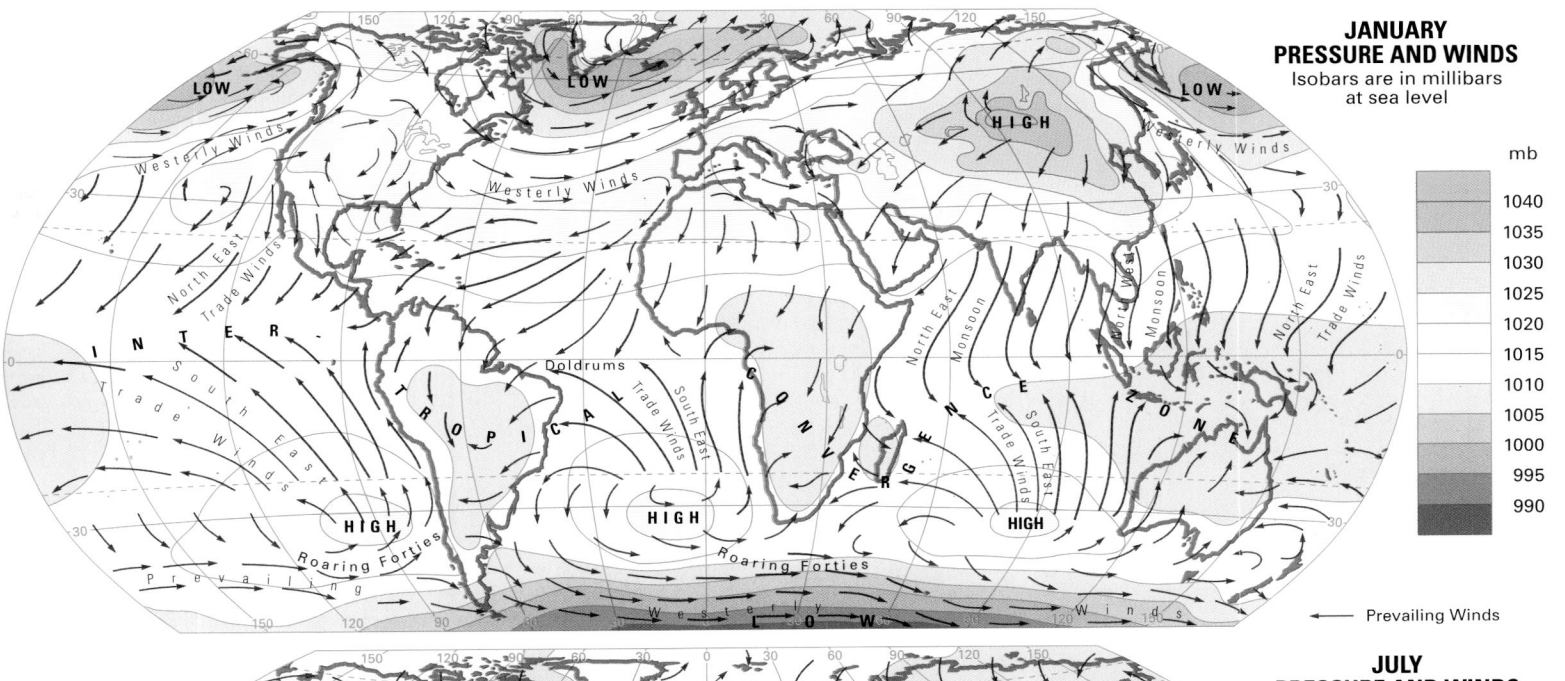

JANUARY PRESSURE AND WINDS
Isobars are in millibars at sea level

mb
1040
1035
1030
1025
1020
1015
1010
1005
1000
995
990

⟵ Prevailing Winds

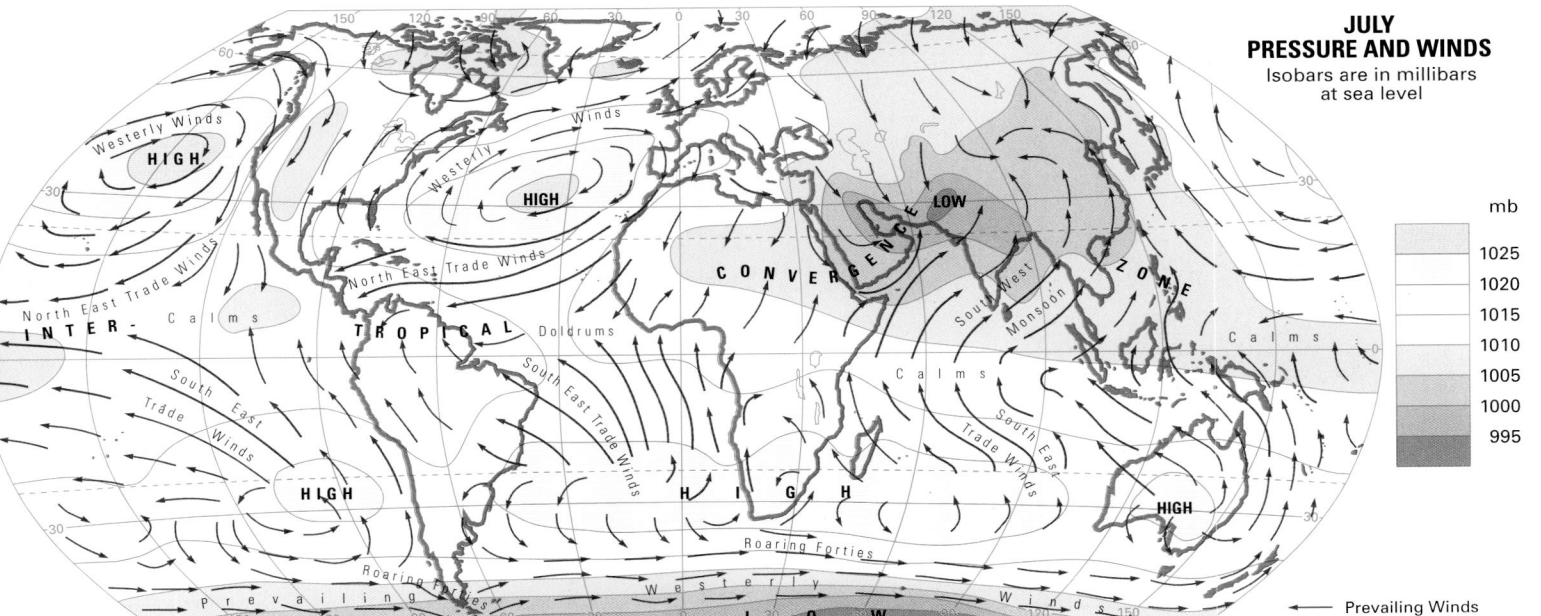

JULY PRESSURE AND WINDS
Isobars are in millibars at sea level

mb
1025
1020
1015
1010
1005
1000
995

⟵ Prevailing Winds

CLIMATE RECORDS

Pressure and winds

Highest barometric pressure: Agata, Siberia, 1,083.8 mb [32 in] at altitude 262 m [862 ft], 31 December 1968.

Lowest barometric pressure: Typhoon Tip, 480 km [300 mls] west of Guam, Pacific Ocean, 870 mb [25.69 in], 12 October 1979.

Highest recorded wind speed: Mt Washington, New Hampshire, USA, 371 km/h [231 mph], 12 April 1934. This is three times as strong as hurricane force on the Beaufort Scale.

Windiest place: Commonwealth Bay, George V Coast, Antarctica, where gales frequently reach over 320 km/h [200 mph].

Worst recorded storm: Bangladesh (then East Pakistan) cyclone*, 13 November 1970 – over 300,000 dead or missing. The 1991 cyclone, Bangladesh's and the world's second worst in terms of loss of life, killed an estimated 138,000 people.

Worst recorded tornado: Missouri/Illinois/Indiana, USA, 18 March 1925 – 792 deaths. The tornado was only 275 m [300 yds] wide.

* Tropical cyclones are known as hurricanes in Central and North America and as typhoons in the Far East.

THE EARTH: CLIMATE

Climate is weather in the long term: the seasonal pattern of hot and cold, wet and dry, averaged over time. At the simplest level, it is caused by the uneven heating of the Earth. Surplus heat at the Equator passes towards the poles, levelling out the energy differential. Its passage is marked by a ceaseless churning of the atmosphere and the oceans, further agitated by the Earth's diurnal spin and the motion it imparts to moving air and water. The heat's means of transport – by winds and ocean currents, by the continual evaporation and recondensation of water molecules – is the weather itself.

There are four basic types of climate, each of which is open to considerable subdivision: tropical, desert, temperate and polar. But although latitude is obviously a critical factor, it is not the only determinant. The differential heating of land and sea, the funnelling and interruption of winds and ocean currents by landmasses and mountain ranges, and the transpiration of vegetation: all these factors combine to add complexity. New York, Naples and the Gobi Desert share almost the same latitude, for example, but their climates are very different. And although the sheer intricacy of the weather system often defies day-to-day prediction in these or any other places their climatic patterns retain a year-on-year stability.

They are not indefinitely stable, however. The planet regularly passes through long, cool periods lasting about 100,000 years: these are the Ice Ages, probably caused by recurring long-term oscillations in the Earth's orbital path and fluctuations in the Sun's energy output. In the present era, the Earth is nearest to the Sun in the middle of the northern hemisphere's winter; 11,000 years ago, at the end of the last Ice Age, the northern winter fell with the Sun at its most distant.

Left to its own devices, the climate even now should be drifting towards another glacial period. But global warming caused by increasing carbon dioxide levels in the atmosphere, largely the result of 20th-century fuel-burning and deforestation, may well precipitate change far faster than the great, slow cycles of the Solar System.

Tropical rainy climates
All mean monthly temperatures above 18°C.

Af	Rainforest climate
Am	Monsoon climate
Aw	Savanna climate

Dry climates
Low rainfall combined with a wide range of temperatures

| BS | Steppe climate |
| BW | Desert climate |

Warm temperate rainy climates
The mean temperature is below 18°C but above –3°C and that of the warmest month is over 10°C.

Cw	Dry winter climate
Cs	Dry summer climate
Cf	Climate with no dry season

Cold temperate rainy climates
The mean temperature of the coldest month is below –3°C but that of the warmest month is still over 10°C.

| Dw | Dry winter climate |
| Df | Climate with no dry season |

Polar climates
The mean temperature of the warmest month is below 10°C, giving permanently frozen subsoil

| ET | Tundra climate |

The mean temperature of the warmest month is below 0°C, giving permanent ice and snow.

| EF | Polar climate |

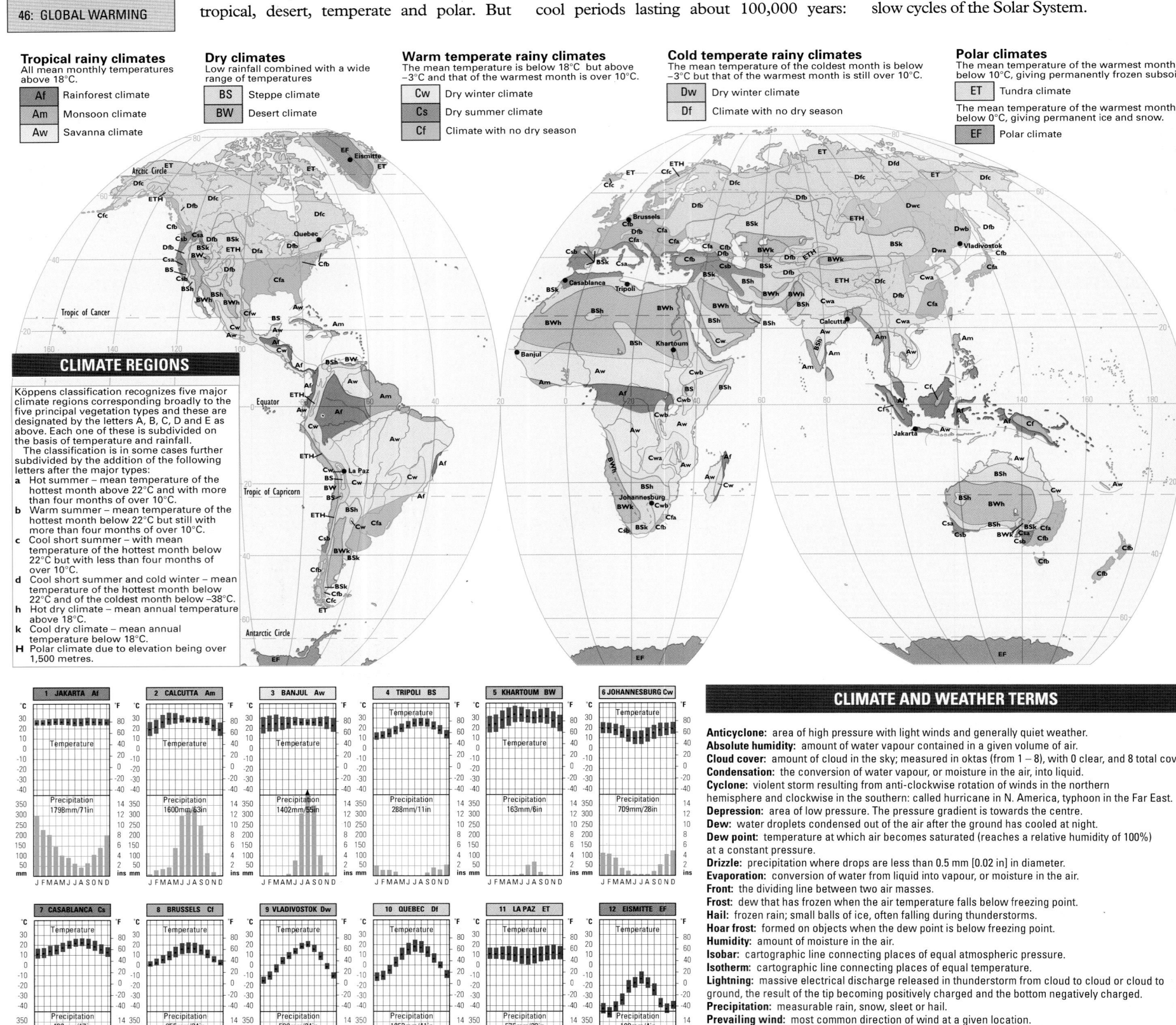

CLIMATE REGIONS

Köppens classification recognizes five major climate regions corresponding broadly to the five principal vegetation types and these are designated by the letters A, B, C, D and E as above. Each one of these is subdivided on the basis of temperature and rainfall.

The classification is in some cases further subdivided by the addition of the following letters after the major types:

a Hot summer – mean temperature of the hottest month above 22°C and with more than four months of over 10°C.

b Warm summer – mean temperature of the hottest month below 22°C but still with more than four months of over 10°C.

c Cool short summer – with mean temperature of the hottest month below 22°C but with less than four months of over 10°C.

d Cool short summer and cold winter – mean temperature of the hottest month below 22°C and of the coldest month below –38°C.

h Hot dry climate – mean annual temperature above 18°C.

k Cool dry climate – mean annual temperature below 18°C.

H Polar climate due to elevation being over 1,500 metres.

CLIMATE AND WEATHER TERMS

Anticyclone: area of high pressure with light winds and generally quiet weather.

Absolute humidity: amount of water vapour contained in a given volume of air.

Cloud cover: amount of cloud in the sky; measured in oktas (from 1 – 8), with 0 clear, and 8 total cover.

Condensation: the conversion of water vapour, or moisture in the air, into liquid.

Cyclone: violent storm resulting from anti-clockwise rotation of winds in the northern hemisphere and clockwise in the southern: called hurricane in N. America, typhoon in the Far East.

Depression: area of low pressure. The pressure gradient is towards the centre.

Dew: water droplets condensed out of the air after the ground has cooled at night.

Dew point: temperature at which air becomes saturated (reaches a relative humidity of 100%) at a constant pressure.

Drizzle: precipitation where drops are less than 0.5 mm [0.02 in] in diameter.

Evaporation: conversion of water from liquid into vapour, or moisture in the air.

Front: the dividing line between two air masses.

Frost: dew that has frozen when the air temperature falls below freezing point.

Hail: frozen rain; small balls of ice, often falling during thunderstorms.

Hoar frost: formed on objects when the dew point is below freezing point.

Humidity: amount of moisture in the air.

Isobar: cartographic line connecting places of equal atmospheric pressure.

Isotherm: cartographic line connecting places of equal temperature.

Lightning: massive electrical discharge released in thunderstorm from cloud to cloud or cloud to ground, the result of the tip becoming positively charged and the bottom negatively charged.

Precipitation: measurable rain, snow, sleet or hail.

Prevailing wind: most common direction of wind at a given location.

Rain: precipitation of liquid particles with diameter larger than 0.5 mm [0.02 in].

Relative humidity: amount of water vapour contained in a given volume of air at a given temperature.

Snow: formed when water vapour condenses below freezing point.

Thunder: sound produced by the rapid expansion of air heated by lightning.

Tornado: severe funnel-shaped storm that twists as hot air spins vertically (waterspout at sea).

Whirlwind: rapidly rotating column of air, only a few metres across, made visible by dust.

In sub-zero weather, even moderate winds significantly reduce effective temperatures. The chart below shows the windchill effect across a range of speeds. Figures in the pink zone are not dangerous to well-clad people; in the blue zone, the risk of serious frostbite is acute.

	Wind speed (km/h)				
	16	32	48	64	80
0°C	-8	-14	-17	-19	-20
-5°C	-14	-21	-25	-27	-28
-10°C	-20	-28	-33	-35	-36
-15°C	-26	-36	-40	-43	-44
-20°C	-32	-42	-48	-51	-52
-25°C	-38	-49	-56	-59	-60
-30°C	-44	-57	-63	-66	-68
-35°C	-51	-64	-72	-74	-76
-40°C	-57	-71	-78	-82	-84
-45°C	-63	-78	-86	-90	-92
-50°C	-69	-85	-94	-98	-100

BEAUFORT WIND SCALE

Named after the 19th-century British naval officer who devised it, Admiral Beaufort, the Beaufort Scale assesses wind speed according to its effects. It was originally designed as an aid for sailors, but has since been adapted for use on the land. It is used internationally.

Scale	Wind speed km/h	mph	Effect
0	0–1	0–1	**Calm** Smoke rises vertically
1	1–5	1–3	**Light air** Wind direction shown only by smoke drift
2	6–11	4–7	**Light breeze** Wind felt on face; leaves rustle; vanes moved by wind
3	12–19	8–12	**Gentle breeze** Leaves and small twigs in constant motion; wind extends small flag
4	20–28	13–18	**Moderate** Raises dust and loose paper; small branches move
5	29–38	19–24	**Fresh** Small trees in leaf sway; crested wavelets on inland waters
6	39–49	25–31	**Strong** Large branches move; difficult to use umbrellas; overhead wires whistle
7	50–61	32–38	**Near gale** Whole trees in motion; difficult to walk against wind
8	62–74	39–46	**Gale** Twigs break from trees; walking very difficult
9	75–88	47–54	**Strong gale** Slight structural damage
10	89–102	55–63	**Storm** Trees uprooted; serious structural damage
11	103–117	64–72	**Violent storm** Widespread damage
12	118+	73+	**Hurricane**

THE MONSOON

The term monsoon, is derived from the Arabic word for 'season', but is also the term given to the seasonal reversal of wind direction, most noticeably in South-east Asia.

The monsoon results from a number of factors: the extreme heating and cooling of large landmasses in relation to the less marked changes in temperature of the adjacent seas; the northwards movement of the Intertropical Convergence Zone (ITCZ – see Circulation of the Air diagram on page 12); and the effect of the Himalayas on the circulation of the air.

Summer Monsoon

In summer, which is the rainy season in South-east Asia, the ITCZ is drawn northwards. An area of low pressure develops over northern India and central Asia as a result of the intense heating of the land. Warm, moist winds blow north-eastwards from the Indian Ocean on to the land, bringing rain. Some monsoon regions are very wet. Cherrapunji in India, for example, receives over 11,000 mm [433 in] per annum.

Others regions, however, are very dry; in the Thar Desert between India and Pakistan annual rainfall is less than 250 mm [10 in].

The rainfall brought by monsoon conditions in Asia is cyclonic, but there is additional orographic rainfall in the mountains, which for this reason are often much wetter than the lowlands. Moreover, the great heat during the day often gives rise to thunderstorms, and convection rain occurs.

The major monsoon areas are in Asia where the seasonal reversal of wind is greatest. This is because the largest continent, Asia, is adjacent to the largest ocean, the Pacific. In the smaller continents of South America, Africa, Australia and North America, the

monsoonal effects are less marked. These areas do not have such wet summers or such dry winters, and are sometimes referred to as 'eastern marginal' rather than true monsoon.

Winter Monsoon

In winter, the ITCZ migrates southwards. The land-masses cool as the heat of the sun lessens and a high-pressure system develops over central Asia. The cool, dry winds blow from the interior to the sea, dumping any moisture on the Himalayas before descending to the coast. By the time they reach the lowlands the winds are dry and this region generally receives less than 100 mm [4 in] of rain in the eight-month winter period.

Average temperature in January

Average temperature

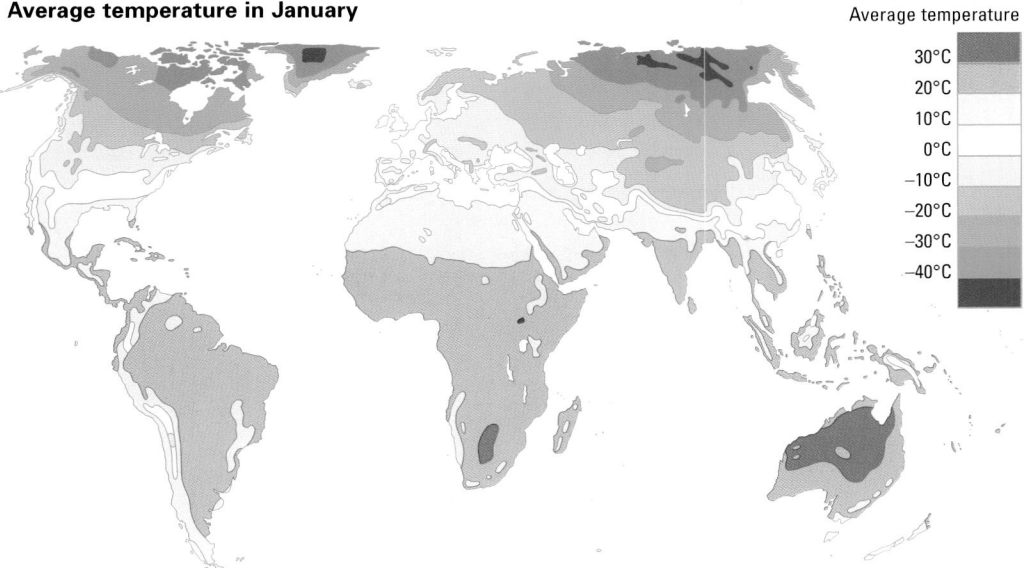

- 30°C
- 20°C
- 10°C
- 0°C
- −10°C
- −20°C
- −30°C
- −40°C

Average temperature in July

Average temperature

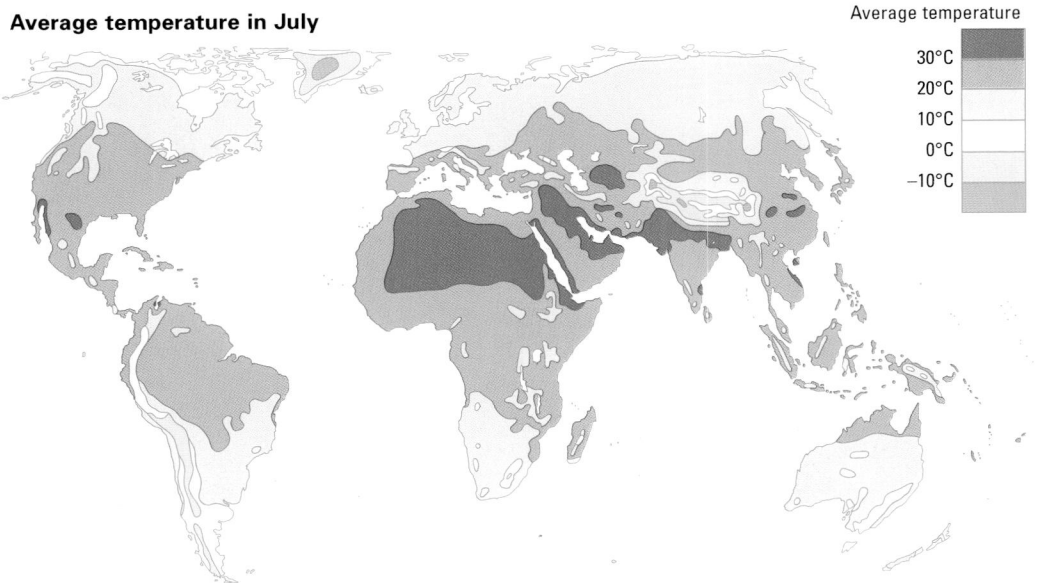

- 30°C
- 20°C
- 10°C
- 0°C
- −10°C

- 3,000 mm
- 2,000 mm
- 1,000 mm
- 500 mm
- 250 mm

Average annual precipitation

Temperature

Highest recorded temperature: Al Aziziyah, Libya, 58°C [136.4°F], 13 September 1922.

Highest mean annual temperature: Dallol, Ethiopia, 34.4°C [94°F], 1960–66.

Longest heatwave: Marble Bar, W. Australia, 162 days over 38°C [100°F], 23 October 1923 to 7 April 1924.

Lowest recorded temperature (outside poles): Verkhoyansk, Siberia, −68°C [−90°F], 6 February 1933. Verkhoyansk also registered the greatest annual range of temperature: −70°C to 37°C [−94°F to 98°F].

Lowest mean annual temperature: Polus Nedostupnosti, Pole of Cold, Antarctica, −57.8°C [−72°F].

Precipitation

Driest place: Arica, N. Chile, 0.8mm [0.03 in] per year (60-year average).

Longest drought: Calama, N. Chile: no recorded rainfall in 400 years to 1971.

Wettest place (average): Tututendo, Colombia: mean annual rainfall 11,770 mm [463.4 in].

Wettest place (12 months): Cherrapunji, Meghalaya, N.E. India, 26,470 mm [1,040 in], August 1860 to August 1861. Cherrapunji also holds the record for rainfall in one month: 930 mm [37 in], July 1861.

Wettest place (24 hours): Cilaos, Réunion, Indian Ocean, 1,870 mm [73.6 in], 15–16 March 1952.

Heaviest hailstones: Gopalganj, Bangladesh, up to 1.02 kg [2.25 lb], 14 April 1986 (killed 92 people).

Heaviest snowfall (continuous): Bessans, Savoie, France, 1,730 mm [68 in] in 19 hours, 5–6 April 1969.

Heaviest snowfall (season/year): Paradise Ranger Station, Mt Rainier, Washington, USA, 31,102 mm [1,224.5 in], 19 February 1971 to 18 February 1972.

THE EARTH: WATER AND LAND USE

Fresh water is essential to all terrestrial life, from the humblest bacterium to the most advanced technological society. Yet freshwater resources form a minute fraction of the Earth's 1.41 billion cubic kilometres of water: most human needs must be met from the 2,000 cubic kilometres circulating in rivers at any one time. Agriculture accounts for huge quantities: without large-scale irrigation, most of the world's people would starve. And since fresh water is just as essential for most industrial processes – smelting a tonne of nickel, for example, requires about 4,000 tonnes of water – the growth of population and advancing industry have together put water supplies under strain.

Fortunately, water is seldom used up: the planet's hydrological cycle circulates it with benign efficiency, at least on a global scale. More locally, though, human activity can cause severe shortages: water for industry and agriculture is being withdrawn from many river basins and underground aquifers faster than natural recirculation can replace it.

THE HYDROLOGICAL CYCLE

The world's water balance is regulated by the constant recycling of water between the oceans, atmosphere and land. The movement of water between these three reservoirs is known as the hydrological cycle. The oceans play a vital role in the hydrological cycle: 74% of the total precipitation falls over the oceans and 84% of the total evaporation comes from the oceans. Water vapour in the atmosphere circulates around the planet, transporting energy as well as the water itself. When the vapour cools it falls as rain or snow. The whole cycle is driven by the Sun.

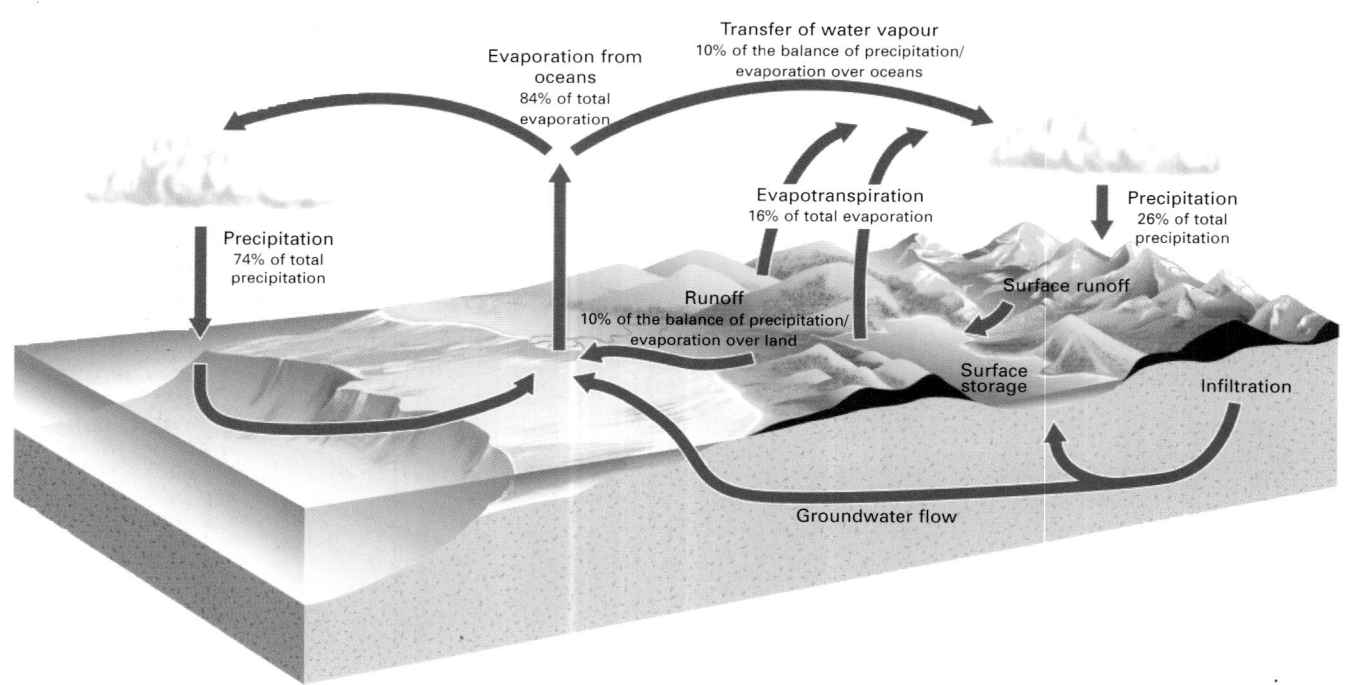

WATER DISTRIBUTION

The distribution of planetary water, by percentage. Oceans and ice-caps together account for more than 99% of the total; the breakdown of the remainder is estimated.

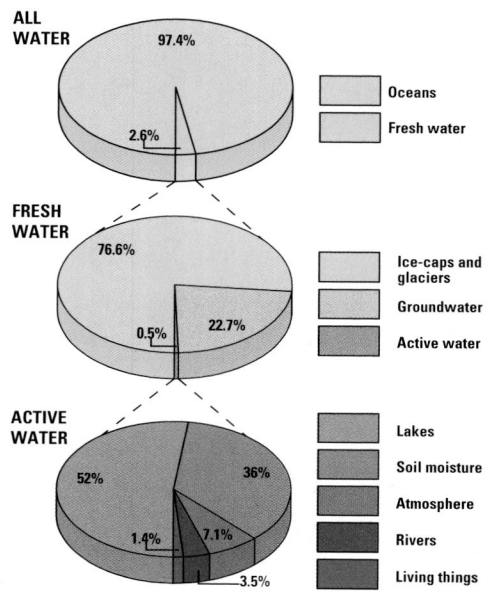

ALL WATER
- 97.4% Oceans
- 2.6% Fresh water

FRESH WATER
- 76.6% Ice-caps and glaciers
- 22.7% Groundwater
- 0.5% Active water

ACTIVE WATER
- 52% Lakes
- 36% Soil moisture
- 1.4% Atmosphere
- 7.1% Rivers
- 3.5% Living things

Almost all the world's water is 3,000 million years old, and all of it cycles endlessly through the hydrosphere, though at different rates. Water vapour circulates over days, even hours, deep ocean water circulates over millennia, and ice-cap water remains solid for millions of years.

WATER RUNOFF

Annual freshwater runoff by continent in cubic kilometres

- Asia
- North America
- South America
- Australasia
- Europe
- Africa

13,190 | 10,380 | 1,965 | 3,110 | 4,225 | 5,960

WATER UTILIZATION

The percentage breakdown of water usage by sector, selected countries (latest available year)

Domestic | Industrial | Agriculture

Mexico, UK, France, Saudi Arabia, Poland, Algeria, Egypt, CIS, USA, Ghana, India, Australia

WATER SUPPLY

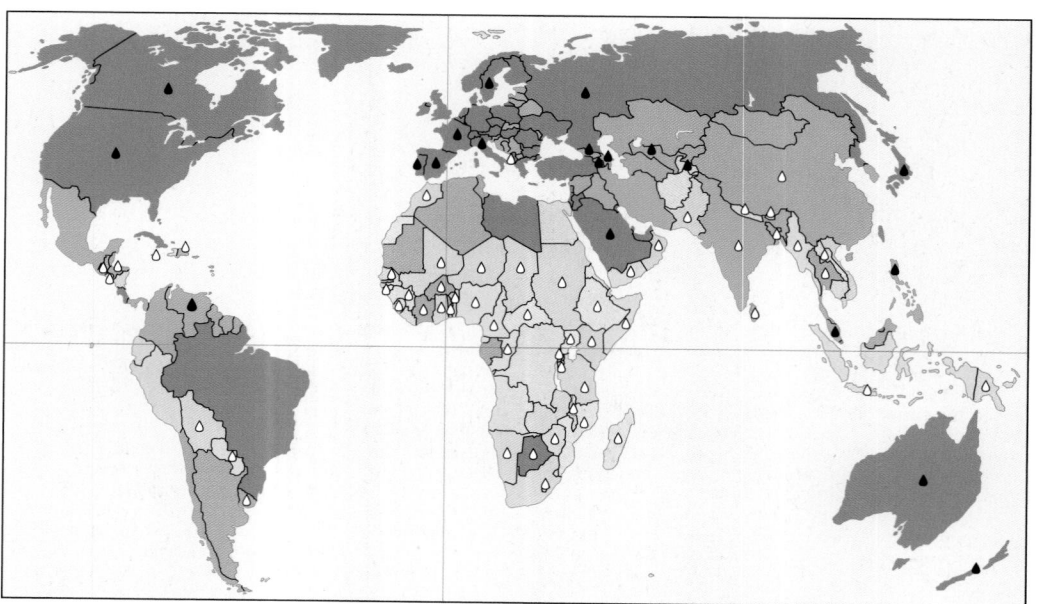

Percentage of total population with access to safe drinking water (1992)

- Over 90% with safe water
- 75 – 90% with safe water
- 60 – 75% with safe water
- 45 – 60% with safe water
- 30 – 45% with safe water
- Under 30% with safe water

◊ Under 80 litres average per capita daily water consumption

♦ Over 320 litres average per capita daily water consumption

Least well-provided countries

Central African Rep.	12%	Afghanistan	23%
Uganda	15%	Madagascar	23%
Ethiopia	18%	Guinea-Bissau	25%
Mozambique	22%	Laos	28%

The world's major rivers; the world's 20 longest are shown in square brackets, led by the Nile and the Amazon.

WHERE THE RIVERS RUN

- Pacific Ocean
- Indian Ocean
- Arctic Ocean
- Atlantic Ocean
- Caribbean Sea-Gulf of Mexico
- Mediterranean Sea
- Inland basins, ice-caps and deserts

The map shows the direction of freshwater flow on a continental scale; the chart opposite indicates the quantities involved. The rate of runoff varies seasonally and is affected by the surface vegetation. Most of the world's major rivers discharge into the Atlantic Ocean.

LAND USE BY CONTINENT

The proportion of productive land has reached its upper limit in Europe, and in Asia more than 80% of potential cropland is already under cultivation. Elsewhere, any increase is often matched by corresponding losses due to desertification and erosion; projections for 2025 show a decline in cropland per capita for all continents, most notably in Africa.

Legend:
- Forest
- Permanent pasture and rough grazing
- Permanent crops and plantations
- Arable
- Non-productive

NORTH AMERICA
37.6% / 12.6% / 0.3% / 17.3% / 32.2%

EUROPE
19.3% / 26.8% / 3% / 17.5% / 33.4%

ASIA
37.8% / 16% / 1.2% / 25% / 20.2%

SOUTH AMERICA
13.4% / 6.6% / 1.5% / 26.7% / 51.8%

AFRICA
44% / 5.6% / 0.6% / 26.6% / 23.2%

AUSTRALASIA
18.5% / 5.7% / 0.1% / 52.2% / 23.5%

NATURAL VEGETATION

Regional variation in vegetation (after Austin Miller)

- Tropical rainforest
- Subtropical and temperate rainforest
- Monsoon woodland and open jungle
- Subtropical and temperate woodland, scrub and bush
- Tropical savanna, with low trees and bush
- Tropical savanna and grasslands
- Dry semi-desert, with shrub and grass
- Desert shrub
- Desert
- Dry steppe and shrub
- Temperate grasslands, prairie and steppe
- Mediterranean hardwood forest and scrub
- Temperate deciduous forest and meadow
- Temperate deciduous and coniferous forest
- Northern coniferous forest (taiga)
- Mountainous forest, mainly coniferous
- High plateau steppe and tundra
- Arctic tundra
- Polar and mountainous ice desert

The map illustrates the natural 'climax vegetation' of a region, as dictated by its climate and topography. In most cases, human agricultural activity has drastically altered the vegetation pattern. Western Europe, for example, lost most of its broadleaf forest many centuries ago, while elsewhere irrigation has turned some natural semi-desert into productive land.

On the map, the blue line represents the northern limit of tree growth, and the red lines the northern and southern limits of palm growth.

17

THE EARTH: LANDSCAPE

Above and below sea level, the features of the Earth's crust are constantly changing. The phenomenal forces generated by convection currents in the molten core of the Earth carry the vast segments, or 'plates', of the crust across the globe in an endless cycle of creation and destruction. New crust emerges along the central depths of the oceans, where molten magma flows up from the mantle to the margins of neighbouring plates, forming the massive mid-ocean ridges. The sea floor spreads, and where oceanic plates meet continental plates, they dip back into the Earth's core to melt once again into magma.

Less dense, the continental plates 'float' among the oceans, drifting into and apart from each other at a rate which is almost imperceptibly slow: a continent may travel little more than 25 millimetres each year – in an average lifetime, Europe will move no more than a man's height – yet in the vast span of geological time, this process throws up giant mountain ranges and opens massive rifts in the land's surface.

The world's greatest mountain ranges have been formed in this way: the Himalayas by the collision of the Indo-Australian and Eurasian plates; the Andes by the meeting of the Nazca and South American plates. The Himalayas are a classic example of 'fold mountains', formed by the crumpling of the Earth's surface where two landmasses have been driven together. The coastal range of the Andes, by contrast, was formed by the upsurge of molten volcanic rock created by the friction of the continent 'overriding' the ocean plate.

However, the destruction of the landscape begins as soon as it is formed. Wind, water, ice and sea, the main agents of erosion, mount a constant assault that even the hardest rocks cannot withstand. Mountain peaks may dwindle by as little as a few millimetres each year, but if they are not uplifted by further movements of the crust they will eventually be reduced to rubble. Water is the most powerful destroyer – it has been estimated that 100 billion tonnes of rock is washed into the oceans every year.

When water freezes, its volume increases by about 9%, and no rock is strong enough to resist this pressure. Where water has penetrated tiny fissures or seeped into softer rock, a severe freeze followed by a thaw may result in rockfalls or earthslides, creating major destruction in a few minutes. Over much longer periods, acidity in rainwater breaks down the chemical composition of porous rocks, such as limestone, eating away the rock to form deep caves and tunnels. Chemical decomposition also occurs in riverbeds and glacier valleys, hastening the process of mechanical erosion.

Rivers and glaciers, like the sea itself, generate much of their effect through abrasion – pounding the landscape with the debris they carry with them. But, as well as destroying, they also create new landscapes, many of them spectacular: vast deltas, as seen at the mouth of the Mississippi or the Nile; cliffs, rock arches and stacks, as found along the south coast of Australia; and the fjords cut by long-melted glaciers in British Columbia, Norway and New Zealand.

THE SPREADING EARTH

The vast ridges that divide the Earth's crust beneath each of the world's oceans mark the boundaries between tectonic plates which are gradually moving in opposite directions. As the plates shift apart, molten magma rises from the mantle to seal the rift and the sea floor slowly spreads towards the continental landmasses. The rate of spreading has been calculated by magnetic analysis of the rock at around 40 mm [1.5 in] a year in the North Atlantic Ocean. Underwater volcanoes mark the line where the continental rise begins. As the plates meet, much of the denser ocean crust dips beneath the continental plate and melts back into the magma.

Sea-floor spreading in the Atlantic Ocean

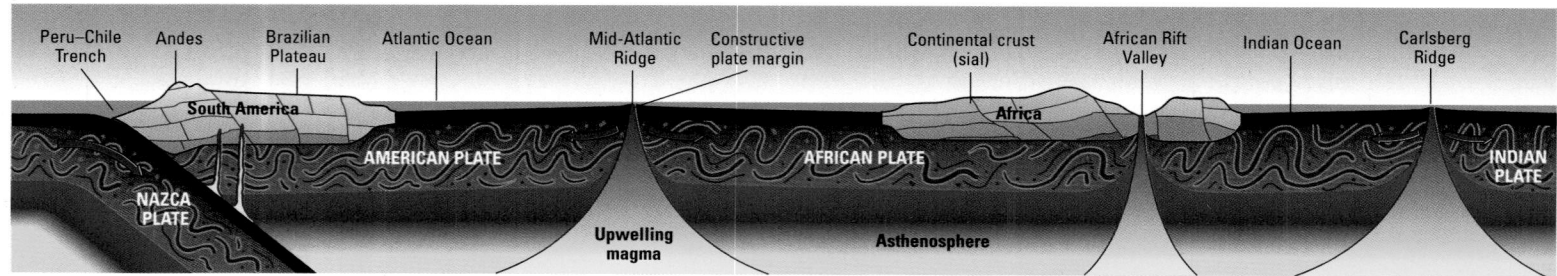

Sea-floor spreading in the Indian Ocean and continental plate collision

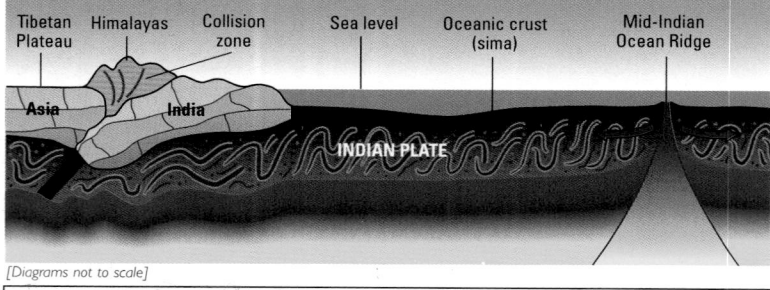

[Diagrams not to scale]

Oceanic and continental plate collision

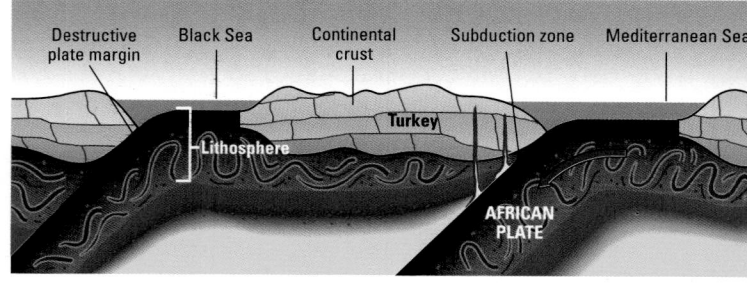

TYPES OF ROCK

Rocks are divided into three types, according to the way in which they are formed:

Igneous rocks, including granite and basalt, are formed by the cooling of magma from within the Earth's crust.

Metamorphic rocks, such as slate, marble and quartzite, are formed below the Earth's surface by the compression or baking of existing rocks.

Sedimentary rocks, like sandstone and limestone, are formed on the surface of the Earth from the remains of living organisms and eroded fragments of older rocks.

MOUNTAIN BUILDING

Mountains are formed when pressures on the Earth's crust caused by continental drift become so intense that the surface buckles or cracks. This happens where oceanic crust is subducted by continental crust or, more dramatically, where two tectonic plates collide: the Rockies, Andes, Alps, Urals and Himalayas resulted from such impacts. These are all known as fold mountains because they were formed by the compression of the rocks, forcing the surface to bend and fold like a crumpled rug. The Himalayas are formed from the folded former sediments of the Tethys Sea which was trapped in the collision zone between the Indian and Eurasian plates.

The other main mountain-building process occurs when the crust fractures to create faults, allowing rock to be forced upwards in large blocks; or when the pressure of magma within the crust forces the surface to bulge into a dome, or erupts to form a volcano. Large mountain ranges may reveal a combination of those features; the Alps, for example, have been compressed so violently that the folds are fragmented by numerous faults and intrusions of molten igneous rock.

Over millions of years, even the greatest mountain ranges can be reduced by the agents of erosion (especially rivers) to a low rugged landscape known as a peneplain.

Types of faults: Faults occur where the crust is being stretched or compressed so violently that the rock strata break in a horizontal or vertical movement. They are classified by the direction in which the blocks of rock have moved. A normal fault results when a vertical movement causes the surface to break apart; compression causes a reverse fault. Horizontal movement causes shearing, known as a strike-slip fault. When the rock breaks in two places, the central block may be pushed up in a horst fault, or sink (creating a rift valley) in a graben fault.

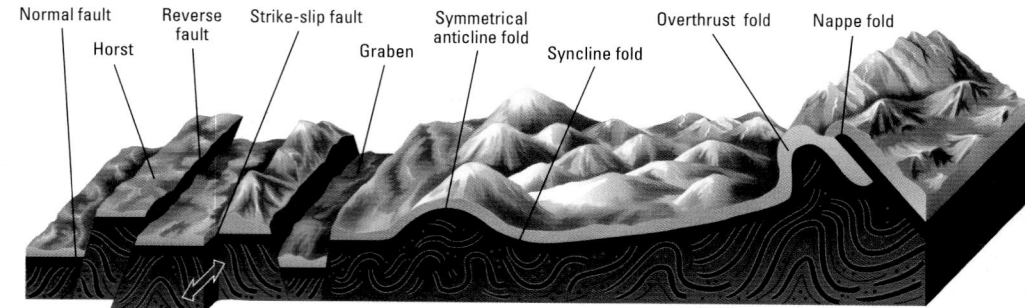

Types of fold: Folds occur when rock strata are squeezed and compressed. They are common, therefore, at destructive plate margins and where plates have collided, forcing the rocks to buckle into mountain ranges. Geographers give different names to the degrees of fold that result from continuing pressure on the rock. A simple fold may be symmetric, with even slopes on either side, but as the pressure builds up, one slope becomes steeper and the fold becomes asymmetric. Later, the ridge or 'anticline' at the top of the fold may slide over the lower ground or 'syncline' to form a recumbent fold. Eventually, the rock strata may break under the pressure to form an overthrust and finally a nappe fold.

The Earth's landscape comprises a huge variety of landforms, both large and small. The most dramatic landforms have been fashioned by plate tectonics and the agents of erosion; wind, water, ice and sea. Over million of years, mountains are gradually worn away, but in the process a variety of constantly changing landforms are created. The nature of the landforms is dependent on the erosive powers at work, the rock type, the local climatic conditions and the vegetation cover. Some of the major landforms are shown on the diagram below.

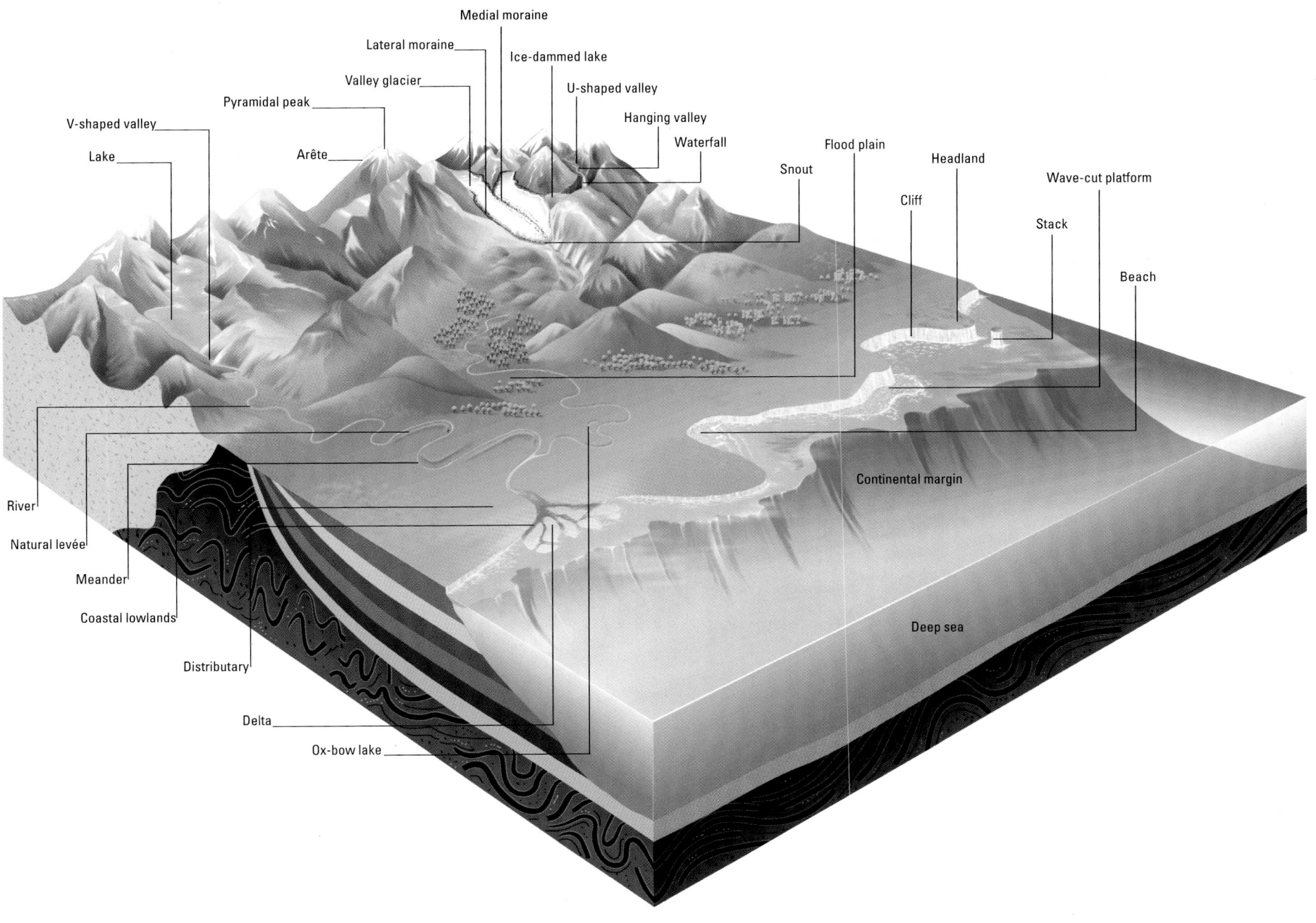

SHAPING FORCES: GLACIERS

Many of the world's most dramatic landscapes have been carved by ice sheets and glaciers. During the Ice Ages of the Pleistocene Epoch (over 10,000 years ago) up to a third of the land surface was glaciated; even today a tenth is covered in ice – the vast majority of this ice is locked up in vast ice sheets and ice-caps. The world's largest ice sheet covers most of Antarctica and is up to 4,800 m [15,750 ft] thick. It is extremely slow moving unlike valley glaciers which can move at rates of between a few centimetres and several metres a day.

Valley glaciers are found in mountainous regions throughout the world, except Australia. In the relatively short geological time scale of the recent ice ages, glaciers accomplished far more carving of the topography than did rivers and the wind. They are formed from compressed snow, called *névé*, accumulating in a valley head or cirque. Slowly the glacier moves downhill scraping away debris from the mountains and valleys through which it passes. The debris, or moraine, adds to the abrasive power of the ice. The amount of glacial debris is enormous – the sediments are transported by the ice to the edge of the glacier, where they are deposited or carried away by meltwater streams. The end of the glacier may not reach the bottom of the valley – the position of the snout depends on the rate at which the ice melts.

Glaciers create numerous distinctive landscape features from arête ridges and pyramidal peaks to ice-dammed lakes and truncated spurs, with the U-shape distinguishing a glacial valley from one cut by a river.

SHAPING FORCES: RIVERS

From their origins as small upland rills and streams channelling rainfall, or as springs releasing water that has seeped into the ground, all rivers are incessantly at work cutting and shaping the landscape on their way to the sea. The area of land drained by a river and all its tributaries is termed a drainage basin.

In highland regions stream flow may be rapid and turbulent, pounding rocks and boulders with enough violence to cut deep gorges and V-shaped valleys through softer rocks, or tumble as waterfalls over harder ones. Rocks and pebbles are moved along the stream bed either by saltation (bouncing) or traction (rolling), whilst lighter sediments are carried in suspension or dissolved in solution. This material transported by the river is termed its load.

As they reach more gentle slopes, rivers release some of the pebbles and heavier sediments they have carried downstream, flow more slowly and broaden out. Levées or ridges are raised along their banks by the deposition of mud and sand during floods. In lowland plains, where the gradient is minimal, the river drifts into meanders, depositing deep layers of sediment especially on the inside of each bend, where the flow is weakest. Here farmers may dig drainage ditches and artificial levées to keep the flood plain dry.

As the river finally reaches the sea, it deposits all its remaining sediments, and estuaries are formed where the tidal currents are strong enough to remove them; if not, the debris creates a delta, through which the river cuts outlet streams known as distributaries.

SHAPING FORCES: THE SEA

Under the constant assault from tides and currents, wind and waves, coastlines change faster than most landscape features, both by erosion and by the build-up of sand and pebbles carried by the sea. In severe storms, giant waves pound the shoreline with rocks and boulders; but even in much quieter conditions, the sea steadily erodes cliffs and headlands, creating new features in the form of sand dunes, spits and salt marshes. Beaches, where sand and shingle have been deposited, form a buffer zone between the erosive power of the waves and the coast. Because it is composed of loose material, a beach can rapidly adapt its shape to changes in wave energy.

Where the coastline is formed from soft rocks such as sandstones, debris may fall evenly and be carried away by currents from shelving beaches. In areas with harder rock, the waves may cut steep cliffs and wave-cut platforms; eroded debris is deposited as a terrace. Bays are formed when sections of soft rock are carved away between headlands of harder rock. These are then battered by waves from both sides, until the headlands are eventually reduced to rock arches and stacks.

A number of factors affect the rate of erosion in coastal environments. These vary from rock type and structure, beach width and supply of beach material, to the more complex fluid dynamics of the waves, namely the breaking point, steepness and length of fetch. Very steep destructive waves have more energy and erosive power than gentle constructive waves formed many kilometres away.

THE EARTH: ENVIRONMENT

Unique among the planets, the Earth has been the home of living creatures for most of its existence. Precisely how these improbable assemblies of self-replicating chemicals ever began remains a matter of conjecture, but the planet and its passengers have matured together for a very long time. Over 3,000 million years, life has not only adapted to its environment, but it has also slowly changed that environment to suit itself.

The planet and its biosphere – the entirety of its living things – function like a single organism. The British scientist James Lovelock, who first stated this 'Gaia hypothesis' in the 1970s, went further: he declared that the planet was actually a living organism, equipped on a colossal scale with the same sort of stability-seeking mechanisms used by lesser lifeforms like bacteria and humans to keep themselves running at optimum efficiency.

Lovelock's theory was inspired by a study of the Earth's atmosphere whose constituents he noted were very far from the state of chemical equilibrium observed elsewhere in the Solar System. The atmosphere has contained a substantial amount of free oxygen for the last 2,000 million years; yet without constant renewal, the oxygen molecules would soon be locked permanently in oxides. The nitrogen, too, would find chemical stability, probably in nitrates (accounting for some of the oxygen). Without living plants and algae to remove it, the carbon dioxide would steadily increase from its present-day 0.03%; in a few million years, it would form a thick blanket similar to the atmosphere of lifeless Venus, where surface temperatures reach 475°C.

It is not enough, however, for the biosphere simply to produce oxygen. While falling concentrations would first be uncomfortable and ultimately prove fatal for most contemporary life, at levels above the current 21% even moist vegetation is highly inflammable, and a massive conflagration becomes almost inevitable – a violent form of negative feedback to set the atmosphere on the path back to sterile equilibrium.

Fortunately, the biosphere has evolved over aeons into a subtle and complex control system, sensing changes and reacting to them quickly but gently, tending always to maintain the balance it has achieved.

Air–sea interface

The ocean surface is the location of most of the great systems of heat exchange that keep the Earth functioning properly. In addition, the ocean absorbs and circulates critical atmospheric gases.

The high atmosphere

On the edge of space, the ionized outer atmosphere shields the Earth from meteors and high-energy solar particles. Below, a layer of ozone traps ultraviolet radiation.

Tropical vegetation

The lush growth of rainforest and other vegetation in the Earth's tropical zones is one of the most important oxygen generators on the planet. Large-scale transpiration influences rainfall and climate patterns both locally and far afield.

Continental shelves

The warm, shallow fringes amount to 21% of the Earth's total ocean area but contain a far higher proportion of its plant and animal life. Vulnerable to coastal and marine pollution, plankton and other plants in these waters are key elements in the carbon and oxygen cycles upon which all life depends.

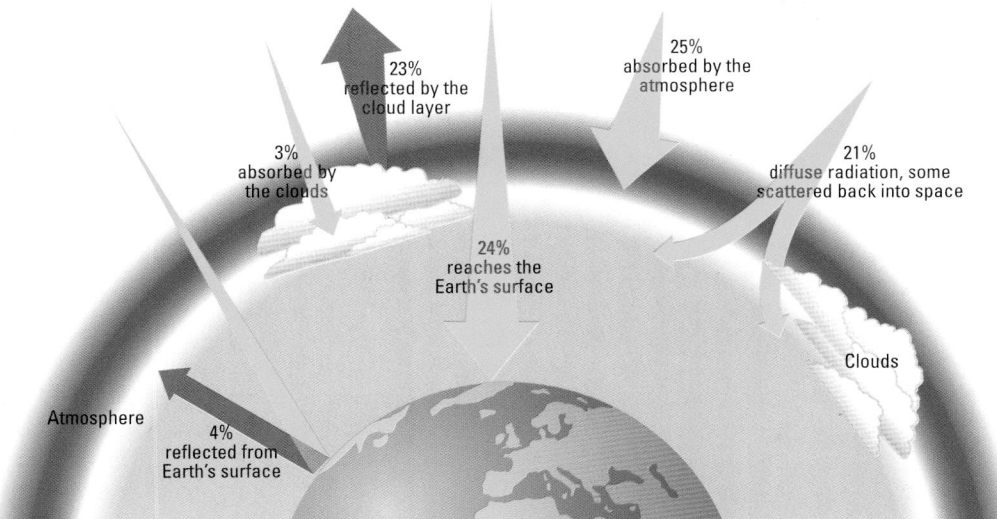

25%
absorbed by the
atmosphere

23%
reflected by the
cloud layer

3%
absorbed by
the clouds

21%
diffuse radiation, some
scattered back into space

24%
reaches the
Earth's surface

Clouds

Atmosphere

4%
reflected from
Earth's surface

THE EARTH'S ENERGY BALANCE

Apart from a modest quantity of internal heat from its molten core, the Earth receives all of its energy from the Sun. If the planet is to remain at a constant temperature, it must reradiate exactly as much energy as it receives. Even a minute surplus would lead to a warmer Earth, a deficit to a cooler one. The temperature at which thermal equilibrium is reached depends on a multitude of interconnected factors. Two of the most important are the relative brightness of the Earth – its index of reflectivity, called the 'albedo' – and the heat-trapping capacity of the atmosphere – the celebrated 'greenhouse effect' (see below).

Because the Sun is very hot, most of its energy arrives in the form of relatively short-wave radiation: the shorter the waves, the more energy they carry. Some of the incoming energy is reflected straight back into space, exactly as it arrived; some is absorbed by the atmosphere on its way towards the surface; some is absorbed by the Earth itself. Absorbed energy heats the Earth and its atmosphere alike. But since its temperature is very much lower that that of the Sun, the outgoing energy is emitted at much longer infra-red wavelengths. Some of the outgoing radiation escapes directly into outer space; some of it is reabsorbed by the atmosphere. Atmospheric energy eventually finds its way back into space, too, after a complex series of interactions. These include the air movements we call the weather and, almost incidentally, the maintenance of life on Earth.

This diagram does not attempt to illustrate the actual mechanisms of heat exchange, but gives a reasonable account (in percentages) of what happens to 100 energy 'units'. Short-wave radiation is shown in yellow, long-wave in orange.

THE CARBON CYCLE

Most of the constituents of the atmosphere are kept in constant balance by complex cycles in which life plays an essential and indeed a dominant part. The control of carbon dioxide, which if left to its own devices would be the dominant atmospheric gas, is possibly the most important, although since all the Earth's biological and geophysical cycles interact and interlock, it is hard to separate them even in theory and quite impossible in practice.

The Earth has a huge supply of carbon, only a small quantity of which is in the form of carbon dioxide. Of that, around 98% is dissolved in the sea; the fraction circulating in the air amounts to only 340 parts per million of the atmosphere, where its capacity as a greenhouse gas is the key regulator of the planetary temperature. In turn, life regulates the regulator, keeping carbon dioxide concentrations below danger level.

If all life were to vanish from the Earth tomorrow, the atmosphere would begin the process of change immediately, although it might take several million years to achieve a new, inorganic stability. First, the oxygen content would begin to fall away; with no more assistance than a little solar radiation, a few electrical storms and its own high chemical potential, oxygen would steadily combine with atmospheric nitrogen and volcanic outgassing. In doing so, it would yield sufficient acid to react with carbonaceous rocks such as limestone, releasing carbon dioxide. Once carbon dioxide levels exceeded about 1%, its greenhouse power would increase disproportionately. Rising temperatures – well above the boiling point of water – would speed chemical reactions; in time, the Earth's atmosphere would consist of little more than carbon dioxide and superheated water vapour.

Living things, however, circulate carbon. They do so first by simply existing: after all, the carbon

atom is the basic building block of living matter. During life, plants absorb carbon dioxide from the atmosphere and, along with various chemicals, as soluble salts from the soil, incorporating the carbon into their structure – leaves and trunks in the case of land plants, shells in the case of plankton and the tiny creatures that feed on it. The oxygen thereby freed is added to the atmosphere, at least for a time. The carbon is returned to circulation when the plants die or is passed up the food chain to the herbivores and then the carnivores that feed on them. As organisms at each of these trophic levels die, they decay, releasing the carbon which then combines once more with the oxygen released during life. However, a small proportion of carbon, about one part in 1,000, is removed almost permanently, buried beneath mud on land, or at sea sinking as dead matter to the ocean floor. In time, it is slowly compressed into sedimentary rocks such as limestone and chalk.

But in the evolution of the Earth, nothing is quite permanent. On an even longer timescale, the planet's crustal movements force new rock upwards in mid-ocean ridges. Limestone deposits are moved, and sea levels change; ancient carboniferous rocks are exposed to weathering, and a little of their carbon is released to be fixed in turn by the current generation of plants.

The carbon cycle has continued quietly for an immensely long time, and without gross disturbance there is no reason why it would not continue almost indefinitely in the future. However, human beings have found a way to release fixed carbon at a rate far faster than existing global systems can recirculate it. The fossil fuels, coal, oil, gas and peat deposits, represent the work of millions of years of carbon accumulation; but it has taken only a few human generations of high-energy scavenging to endanger the entire complex regulatory cycle.

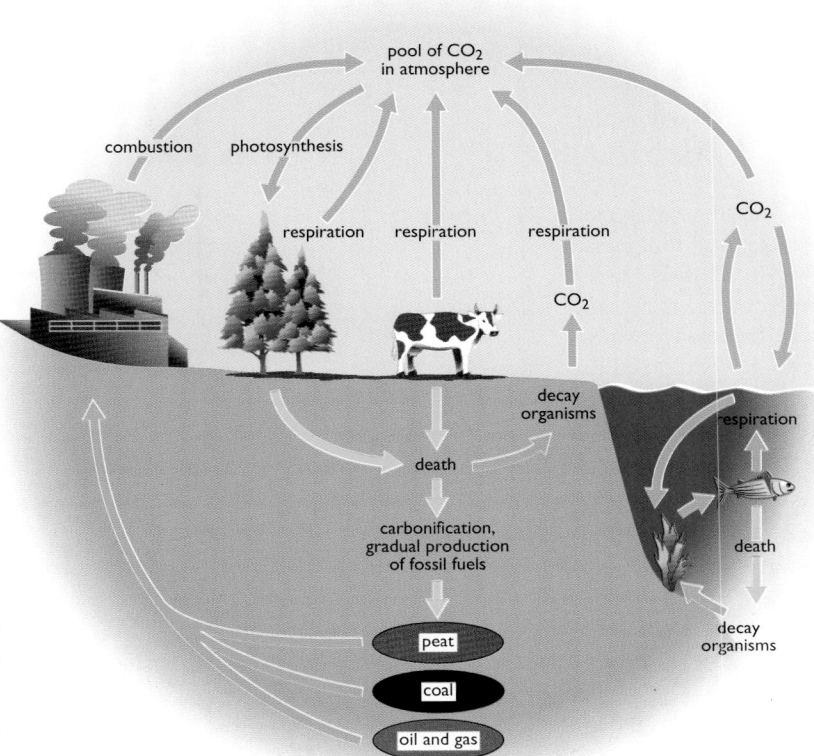

pool of CO_2
in atmosphere

combustion photosynthesis

respiration respiration respiration

CO_2

CO_2

decay
organisms

respiration

death

death

carbonification,
gradual production
of fossil fuels

decay
organisms

peat

coal

oil and gas

THE GREENHOUSE EFFECT

Constituting less than 1% of the atmosphere, the natural greenhouse gases (water vapour, carbon dioxide, methane, nitrous oxide and ozone) have a hugely disproportionate effect on the Earth's climate and even its habitability. Like the glass panes in a greenhouse, the gases are transparent to most incoming short-wave radiation, which passes freely to heat the planet beneath. But when the warmed Earth retransmits that energy, in the form of longer-wave infra-red radiation, the gases function as an opaque shield preventing some of it from escaping, so that the planetary surface (like the interior of a greenhouse) stays relatively hot.

Over the last 150 years, there has been a gradual increase in the levels of greenhouse gases (with the exception of water vapour which remains a constant in the system). These increases are causing alarm – global warming associated with a runaway greenhouse effect could bring disaster – and what is more, predictions suggest that there could be a further rise of 1.5°C–4.5°C by the year 2100. A serious reduction in the greenhouse gases would be just as damaging; a total absence of CO_2, for example, would leave the planet with a temperature roughly 33°C colder than at present.

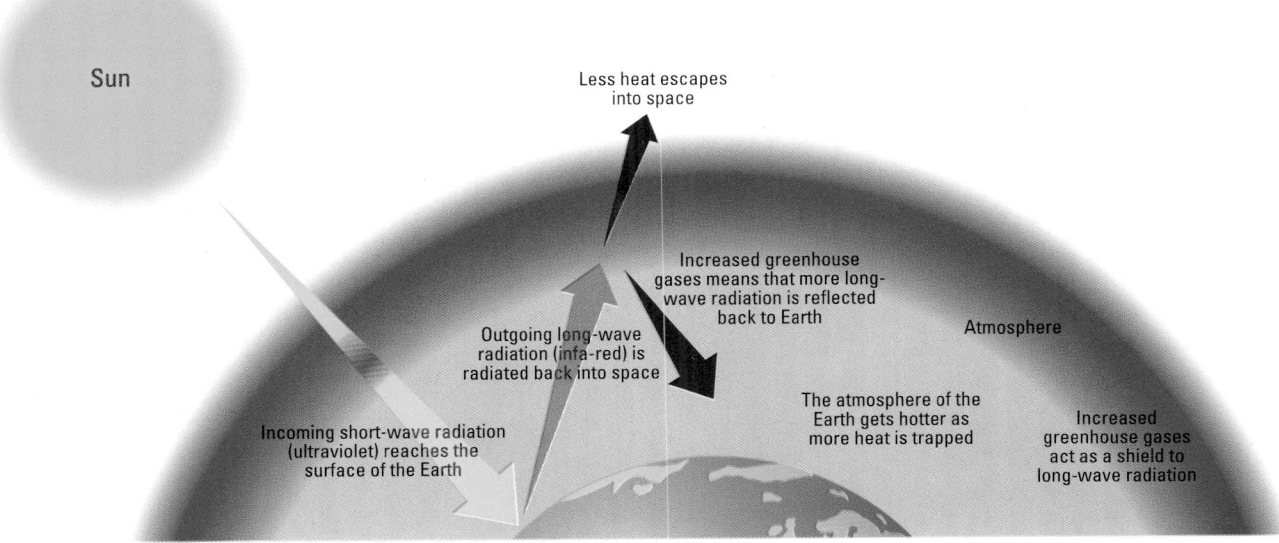

Sun

Less heat escapes
into space

Increased greenhouse
gases means that more long-
wave radiation is reflected
back to Earth

Outgoing long-wave
radiation (infra-red) is
radiated back into space

Atmosphere

The atmosphere of the
Earth gets hotter as
more heat is trapped

Increased
greenhouse gases
act as a shield to
long-wave radiation

Incoming short-wave radiation
(ultraviolet) reaches the
surface of the Earth

PEOPLE: DEMOGRAPHY

FOR MORE INFORMATION:

24: URBANIZATION OF
     THE EARTH
     URBAN POPULATION

25: LARGEST CITIES

31: FOOD AND
     POPULATION

40: WEALTH AND
     POPULATION

46: HUMAN EXPANSION

As the 20th century draws to its close, the Earth's population increases by nearly 10,000 every hour – enough to fill a new major city every week. The growth is almost entirely confined to the developing world, which accounted for 67% of total population in 1950 and is set to reach 84% by 2025. In developed countries, populations are almost static, and in some places, such as Germany, are actually falling. In fact, there is a clear correlation between wealth and low fertility: as incomes rise, reproduction rates drop.

The decline is already apparent. With the exception of Africa, the actual rates of increase are falling nearly everywhere. The population structure, however, ensures that human numbers will continue to rise even as fertility diminishes. Developed nations, like the UK, have an even spread across ages, and usually a growing proportion of elderly people: the over-75s often outnumber the under-5s, and women of child-bearing age form only a small part of the total. Developing nations fall into a pattern somewhere between that of Kenya and Brazil: the great majority of their people are in the younger age groups, about to enter their most fertile years. In time, even Kenya's population profile should resemble the developed model, but the transition will come about only after a few more generations' growth.

It remains to be seen whether the planet will tolerate the population growth that seems inevitable before stability is reached. More people consume more resources, increasing the strain on an already troubled environment. However, more people should mean a greater supply of human ingenuity – the only commodity likely to resolve the crisis.

LARGEST NATIONS

The world's most populous nations, in millions (1995)

1.	China	1,227
2.	India	943
3.	USA	264
4.	Indonesia	199
5.	Brazil	161
6.	Russia	148
7.	Pakistan	144
8.	Japan	125
9.	Bangladesh	118
10.	Mexico	93
11.	Nigeria	89
12.	Germany	82
13.	Vietnam	75
14.	Iran	69
15.	Philippines	67
16.	Egypt	64
17.	Turkey	61
18.	Thailand	58
19.	UK	58
20.	France	58
21.	Italy	57
22.	Ukraine	52
22.	Ethiopia	52
24.	Burma	47

CROWDED NATIONS

Population per square kilometre (1995), excl. nations of less than one million

1.	Hong Kong	5,602
2.	Singapore	4,838
3.	Bangladesh	822
4.	Mauritius	598
5.	Taiwan	586
6.	South Korea	455
7.	Puerto Rico	414
8.	Netherlands	373
9.	Belgium	332
10.	Japan	331
11.	Rwanda	300
12.	India	287
13.	Lebanon	286
14.	Sri Lanka	280
15.	El Salvador	273
16.	Trinidad & Tobago	252
17.	Jamaica	246
18.	UK	240
19.	Germany	230
20.	Israel	224

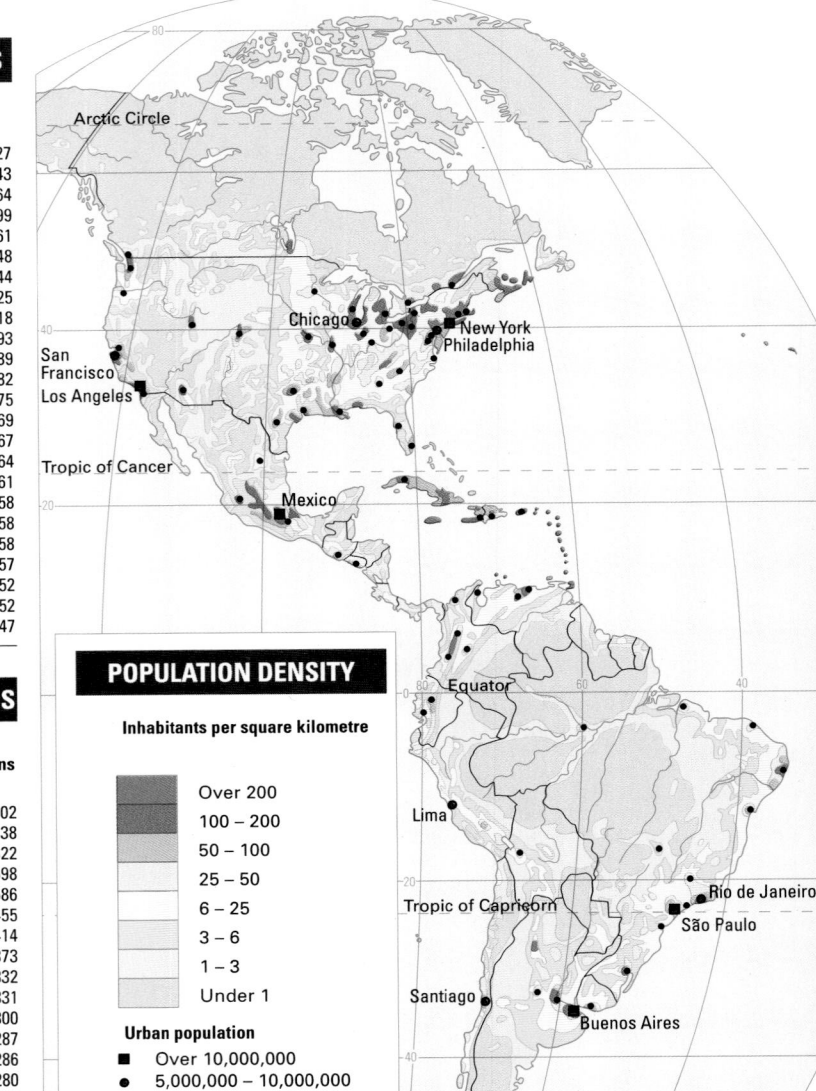

POPULATION DENSITY

Inhabitants per square kilometre

- Over 200
- 100 – 200
- 50 – 100
- 25 – 50
- 6 – 25
- 3 – 6
- 1 – 3
- Under 1

Urban population
- ■ Over 10,000,000
- ● 5,000,000 – 10,000,000
- • 1,000,000 – 5,000,000

Places marked are conurbations, not city limits; San Francisco itself, for example, has an official population of less than a million.

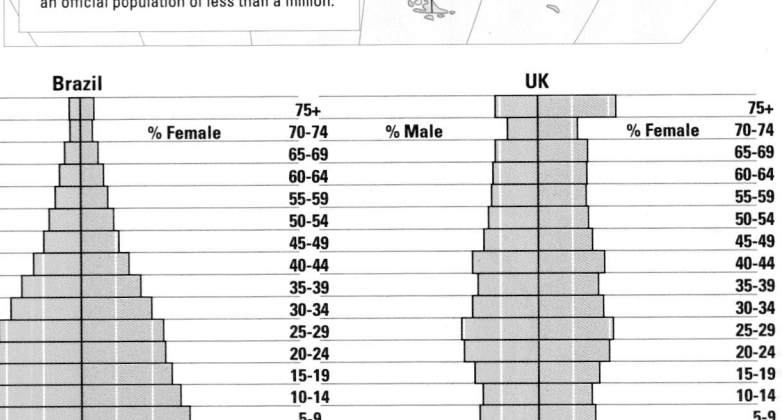

RATES OF GROWTH

Apparently small rates of population growth lead to dramatic increases over two or three generations. The table below translates annual percentage growth into the number of years required to double a population.

% change	Doubling time
0.5	139.0
1.0	69.7
1.5	46.6
2.0	35.0
2.5	28.1
3.0	23.4
3.5	20.1
4.0	17.7

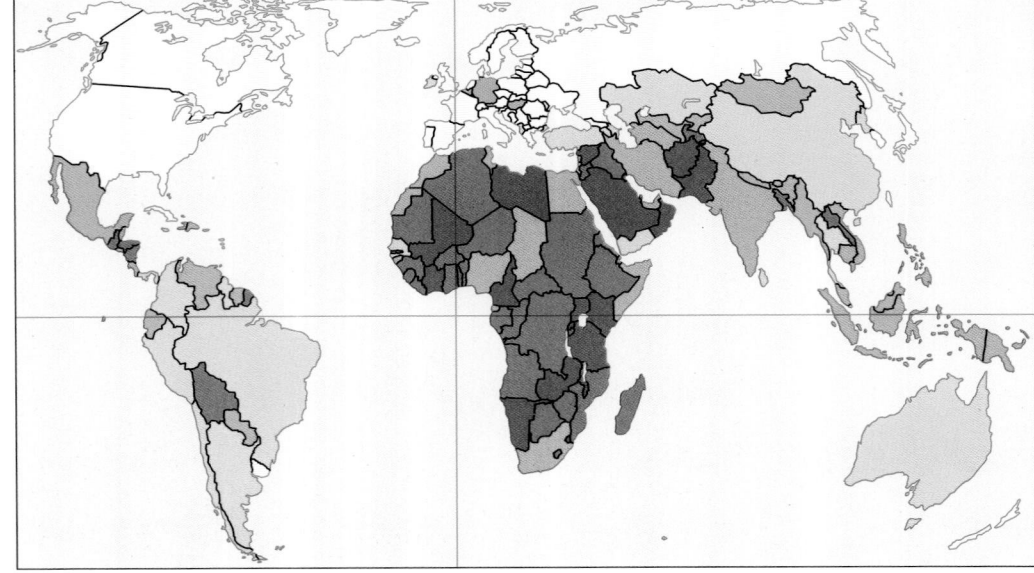

POPULATION CHANGE 1990–2000

The predicted population change for the years 1990–2000

- Over 40% population gain
- 30 – 40% population gain
- 20 – 30% population gain
- 10 – 20% population gain
- 0 – 10% population gain
- No change or population loss

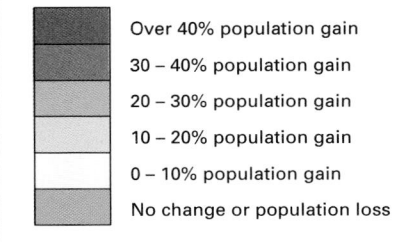

Top 5 countries		Bottom 5 countries	
Kuwait	+75.9%	Belgium	–0.1%
Namibia	+62.5%	Hungary	–0.2%
Afghanistan	+60.1%	Grenada	–2.4%
Mali	+55.5%	Germany	–3.2%
Tanzania	+54.6%	Tonga	–3.2%

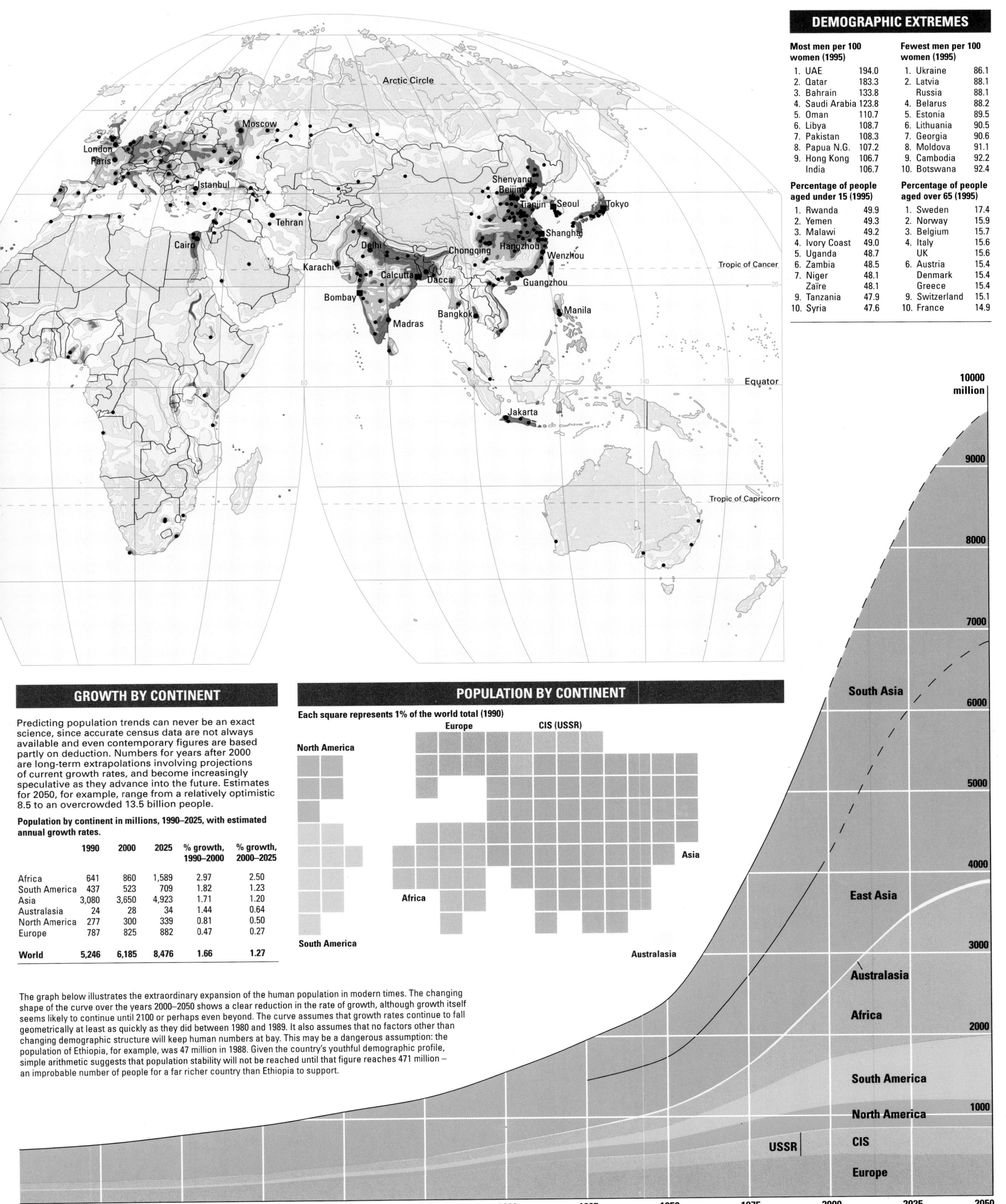

Arctic Circle

Moscow

London
Paris

Istanbul

Tehran

Cairo

Karachi

Delhi

Bombay

Calcutta
Dacca

Madras

Bangkok

Shenyang
Beijing
Tianjin Seoul
Shanghai
Chongqing Hangzhou
Wenzhou
Guangzhou

Tokyo

Manila

Jakarta

Tropic of Cancer

Equator

Tropic of Capricorn

DEMOGRAPHIC EXTREMES

Most men per 100 women (1995)		Fewest men per 100 women (1995)	
1. UAE	194.0	1. Ukraine	86.1
2. Qatar	183.3	2. Latvia	88.1
3. Bahrain	133.8	Russia	88.1
4. Saudi Arabia	123.8	4. Belarus	88.2
5. Oman	110.7	5. Estonia	89.5
6. Libya	108.7	6. Lithuania	90.5
7. Pakistan	108.3	7. Georgia	90.6
8. Papua N.G.	107.2	8. Moldova	91.1
9. Hong Kong	106.7	9. Cambodia	92.2
India	106.7	10. Botswana	92.4

Percentage of people aged under 15 (1995)		Percentage of people aged over 65 (1995)	
1. Rwanda	49.9	1. Sweden	17.4
2. Yemen	49.3	2. Norway	15.9
3. Malawi	49.2	3. Belgium	15.7
4. Ivory Coast	49.0	4. Italy	15.6
5. Uganda	48.7	UK	15.6
6. Zambia	48.5	6. Austria	15.4
7. Niger	48.1	Denmark	15.4
Zaïre	48.1	Greece	15.4
9. Tanzania	47.9	9. Switzerland	15.1
10. Syria	47.6	10. France	14.9

GROWTH BY CONTINENT

Predicting population trends can never be an exact science, since accurate census data are not always available and even contemporary figures are based partly on deduction. Numbers for years after 2000 are long-term extrapolations involving projections of current growth rates, and become increasingly speculative as they advance into the future. Estimates for 2050, for example, range from a relatively optimistic 8.5 to an overcrowded 13.5 billion people.

Population by continent in millions, 1990–2025, with estimated annual growth rates.

	1990	2000	2025	% growth, 1990–2000	% growth, 2000–2025
Africa	641	860	1,589	2.97	2.50
South America	437	523	709	1.82	1.23
Asia	3,080	3,650	4,923	1.71	1.20
Australasia	24	28	34	1.44	0.64
North America	277	300	339	0.81	0.50
Europe	787	825	882	0.47	0.27
World	5,246	6,185	8,476	1.66	1.27

The graph below illustrates the extraordinary expansion of the human population in modern times. The changing shape of the curve over the years 2000–2050 shows a clear reduction in the rate of growth, although growth itself seems likely to continue until 2100 or perhaps even beyond. The curve assumes that growth rates continue to fall geometrically at least as quickly as they did between 1980 and 1989. It also assumes that no factors other than changing demographic structure will keep human numbers at bay. This may be a dangerous assumption: the population of Ethiopia, for example, was 47 million in 1988. Given the country's youthful demographic profile, simple arithmetic suggests that population stability will not be reached until that figure reaches 471 million – an improbable number of people for a far richer country than Ethiopia to support.

POPULATION BY CONTINENT

Each square represents 1% of the world total (1990)

North America

Europe

CIS (USSR)

Asia

Africa

South America

Australasia

10000 million

9000

8000

7000

South Asia

6000

5000

East Asia

4000

Australasia

Africa

3000

South America

2000

North America

USSR CIS

1000

Europe

1750 1775 1800 1825 1850 1875 1900 1925 1950 1975 2000 2025 2050

23

PEOPLE: CITIES

In 1750, barely three humans in every hundred lived in a city; by 2000, more than half the world's population will find a home in some kind of urban area. In 1850, only London and Paris had more than a million inhabitants; by 2000, at least 24 cities will each contain over 10 million people. The increase is concentrated in the Third World, if only because levels of urbanization in most developed countries – more than 90% in the UK and Belgium, and almost 75% in the USA, despite that country's great open spaces – have already reached practical limits.

Such large-scale concentration is relatively new to the human race. Although city life has always attracted country dwellers in search of trade, employment or simply human contact, until modern times they paid a high price. Crowding and poor sanitation ensured high death rates, and until about 1850, most cities needed a steady flow of incomers simply to maintain their population levels: for example, there were 600,000 more deaths than births in 18th-century London, and some other large cities showed an even worse imbalance.

With improved public health, cities could grow from their own human resources, and large-scale urban living became commonplace in the developed world. Since about 1950, the pattern has been global. Like their counterparts in 19th-century Europe and the USA, the great new cities are driven into rapid growth by a kind of push-pull mechanism. The push is generated by agricultural overcrowding: only so many people can live from a single plot of land and population pressure drives many into towns. The pull comes from the possibilities of economic improvement – an irresistible lure to the world's rural hopefuls.

Such improvement is not always obvious: the typical Third World city, with millions of people living (often illegally) in shanty towns and many thousands existing homelessly on the ill-made streets, does not present a great image of prosperity. Yet modern shanty towns are healthier than industrializing Pittsburgh or Manchester in the last century, and these human ant-hills teem with industry as well as squalor: throughout the world, above-average rates of urbanization have gone hand-in-hand with above-average rates of economic growth. Surveys demonstrate that Third World city dwellers are generally better off than their rural counterparts, whose poverty is less concentrated but often more desperate. This only serves to increase the attraction of the city for the rural poor.

However, the sheer speed of the urbanization process threatens to overwhelm the limited abilities of city authorities to provide even rudimentary services. The 24 million people expected to live in Mexico City by 2000, for example, would swamp a more efficient local government than Mexico can provide. Improvements are often swallowed up by the relentless rise in urban population: although safe drinking water should reach 75% of Third World city dwellers by the end of the century – a considerable achievement – population growth will add 100 million to the list of those without it.

THE URBANIZATION OF THE EARTH

City-building, 1850–2000; each white spot represents a city of at least 1 million inhabitants.

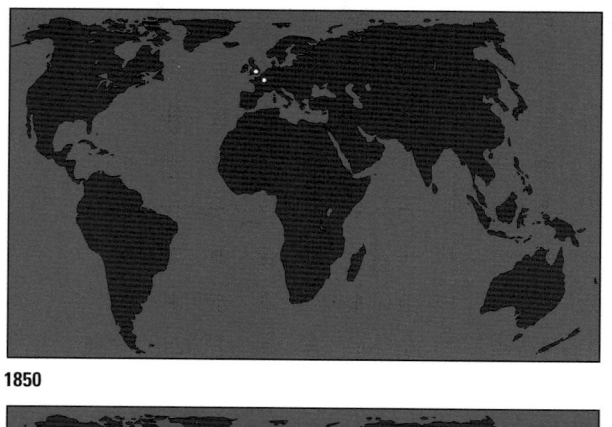

1850

1900

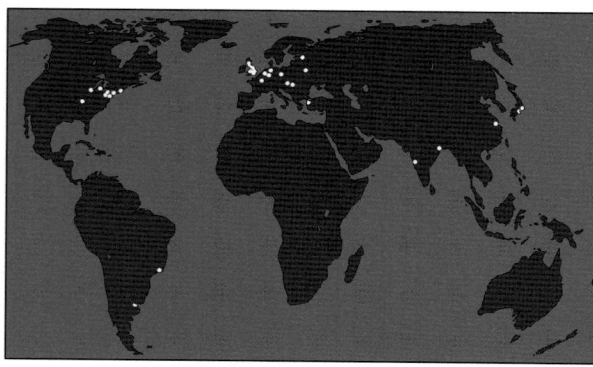

1925

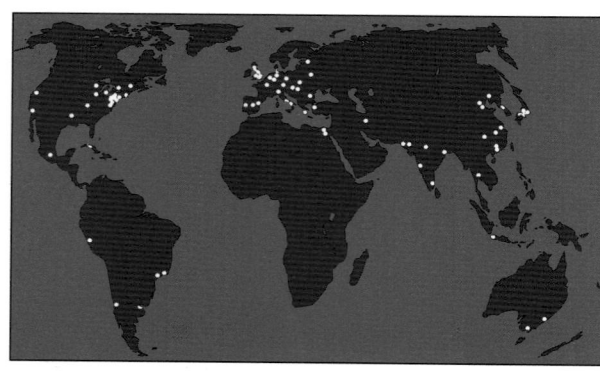

1950

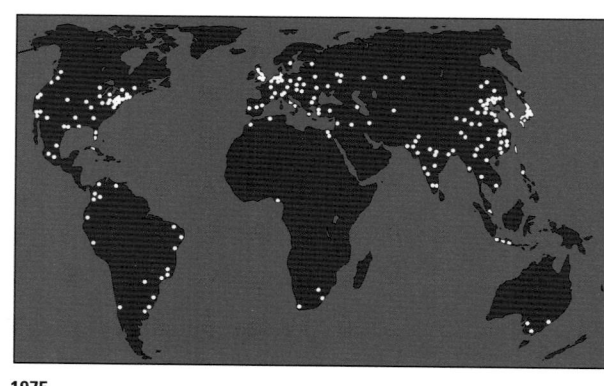

1975

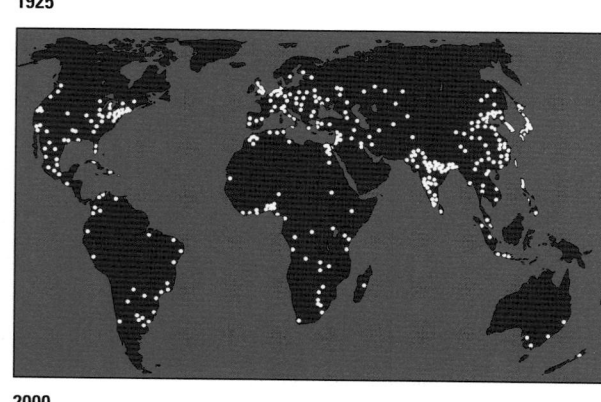

2000

URBAN POPULATION

Percentage of total population living in towns and cities (1992)

Over 75%	
50 – 75%	
25 – 50%	
10 – 25%	
Under 10%	

Most urbanized		Least urbanized	
Singapore	100%	Bhutan	6%
Belgium	97%	Rwanda	6%
Kuwait	95%	Burundi	7%
Hong Kong	94%	Malawi	12%
Venezuela	91%	Nepal	12%

[UK 89%   USA 76%]

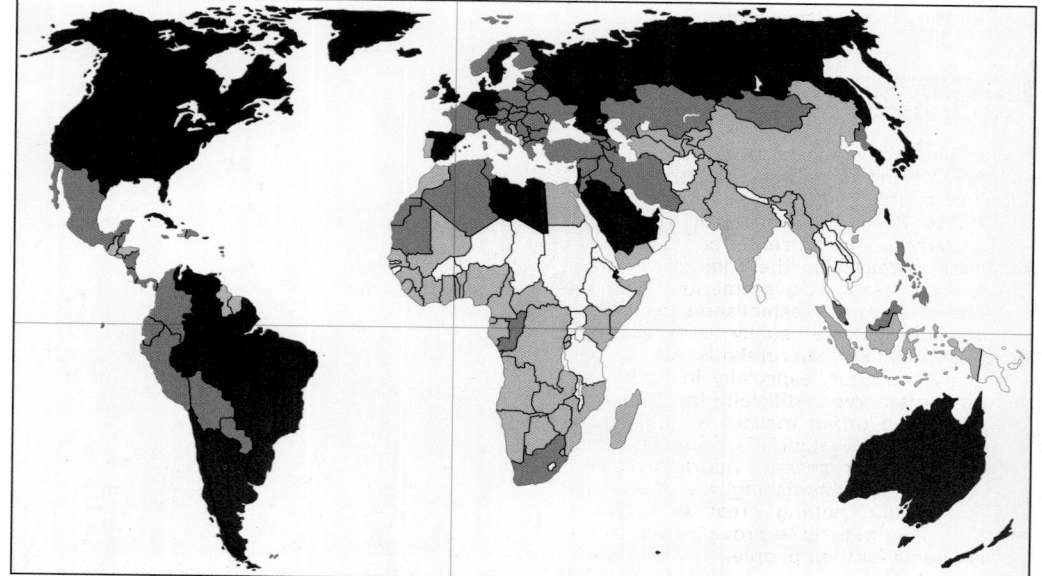

EXPANDING CITIES

The growth of the world's largest cities, 1950–2000. Intermediate rings indicate relative size in 1970 and 1985.

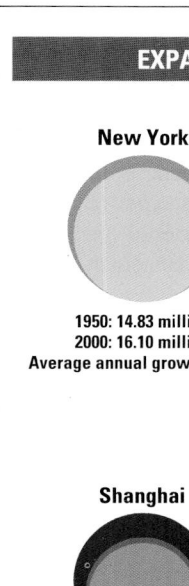

New York
1950: 14.83 million
2000: 16.10 million
Average annual growth: 0.16%

London
1950: 8.35 million
2000: 10.79 million
Average annual growth: 0.51%

Tokyo
1950: 6.25 million
2000: 21.32 million
Average annual growth: 2.5%

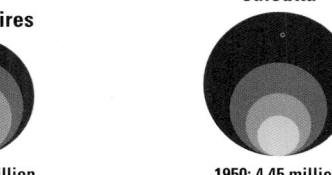

Buenos Aires
1950: 5.25 million
2000: 13.05 million
Average annual growth: 1.8%

Calcutta
1950: 4.45 million
2000: 15.94 million
Average annual growth: 2.6%

Shanghai
1950: 4.3 million
2000: 14.69 million
Average annual growth: 2.5%

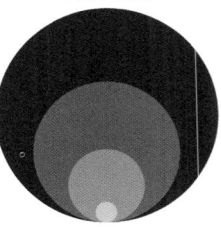

Mexico City
1950: 2.97 million
2000: 24.44 million
Average annual growth: 4.3%

Rio de Janeiro
1950: 2.94 million
2000: 13.0 million
Average annual growth: 3.0%

São Paulo
1950: 2.28 million
2000: 23.6 million
Average annual growth: 4.8%

Seoul
1950: 1.45 million
2000: 12.97 million
Average annual growth: 4.5%

Each set of circles illustrates a city's size in 1950, 1970, 1985 and 2000. In most cases, expansion has been steady and, often, explosive. New York and London, however, went through patches of negative growth during the period. In New York, the world's largest city in 1950, population reached a peak around 1970. London shrank slightly between 1970 and 1985 before resuming a very modest rate of increase. In both cases, the divergence from world trends can be explained in part by counting methods: each is at the centre of a great agglomeration, and definitions of where 'city limits' lie may vary over time. But their relative decline also matches a pattern often seen in mature cities in the developed world, where urbanization, already at a very high level, has reached a plateau.

CITIES IN DANGER

As the decade of the 1980s advanced, most industrial countries, alarmed by acid rain and urban smog, took significant steps to limit air pollution. Well into the 1990s, however, these controls have proved expensive to install and difficult to enforce, and clean air remains a luxury most developed as well as developing cities must live without.

Those taking part in the United Nations' Global Environment Monitoring System (see right) frequently show dangerous levels of pollutants ranging from soot to sulphur dioxide and photo-chemical smog; air in the majority of cities without such sampling equipment is likely to be at least as bad.

URBAN AIR POLLUTION

The world's most polluted cities: number of days each year when sulphur dioxide levels exceeded the WHO threshold of 150 micrograms per cubic metre (averaged over 4 to 15 years, 1970s – 1980s)

Sulphur dioxide is the main pollutant associated with industrial cities. According to the World Health Organization, more than seven days in a year above 150 µg per cubic metre bring a serious risk of respiratory disease: at least 600 million people live in urban areas where SO_2 concentrations regularly reach damaging levels.

Manila, Philippines
Calcutta, India
Milan, Italy
Zagreb, Croatia
Guangzhou, China
Madrid, Spain
Beijing, China
Xian, China
Seoul, South Korea
Tehran, Iran
Shenyang, China

120   90   60   30

SQUATTER SETTLEMENTS

Proportion of population living in squatter settlements, selected cities in the developing world (latest available years)

Urbanization in most Third World countries has been coming about far faster than local governments can provide services and accommodation for the new city dwellers. Many – in some cities, most – find their homes in improvised squatter settlements, often unconnected to power, water and sanitation networks. Yet despite their ramshackle housing and marginal legality, these communities are often the most dynamic part of a city economy. They are also growing in size; and given the squatters' reluctance to be counted by tax-demanding authorities, the percentages shown here are likely to be underestimates.

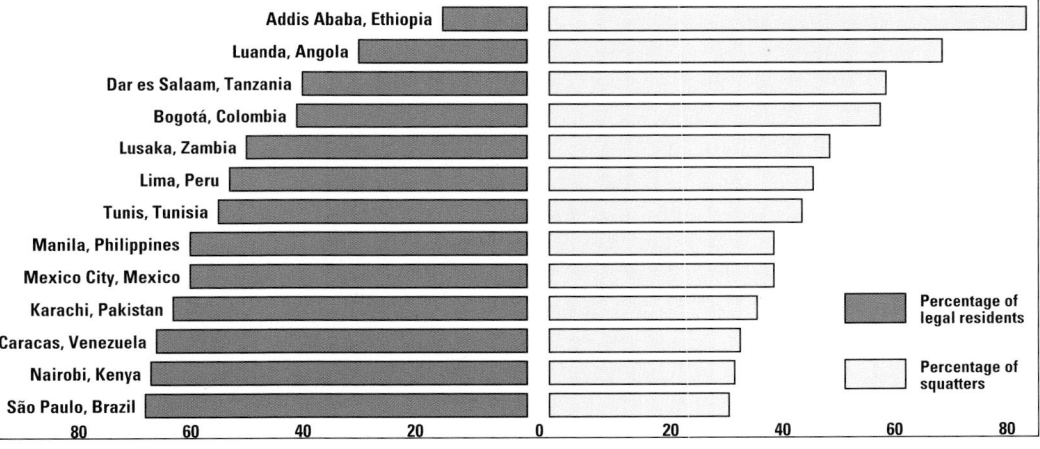

Addis Ababa, Ethiopia
Luanda, Angola
Dar es Salaam, Tanzania
Bogotá, Colombia
Lusaka, Zambia
Lima, Peru
Tunis, Tunisia
Manila, Philippines
Mexico City, Mexico
Karachi, Pakistan
Caracas, Venezuela
Nairobi, Kenya
São Paulo, Brazil

80 60 40 20 0 20 40 60 80

Percentage of legal residents

Percentage of squatters

LARGEST CITIES

By early next century for the first time in history, the majority of the world's population will live in cities. Below is a list of all the cities with more than 10 million inhabitants, based on estimates for the year 2015.*

1.	Tokyo–Yokohama	28.7
2.	Bombay	27.4
3.	Lagos	24.1
4.	Shanghai	23.2
5.	Jakarta	21.5
6.	São Paulo	21.0
7.	Karachi	20.6
8.	Beijing	19.6
9.	Dhaka	19.2
10.	Mexico City	19.1
11.	Calcutta	17.6
12.	Delhi	17.5
13.	New York	17.4
14.	Tianjin	17.1
15.	Manila	14.9
16.	Cairo	14.7
17.	Los Angeles	14.5
18.	Seoul	13.1
19.	Buenos Aires	12.5
20.	Istanbul	12.1
21.	Rio de Janeiro	11.3
22.	Lahore	10.9
23.	Hyderabad	10.6
24.	Bangkok	10.4
25.	Osaka	10.2
26.	Lima	10.1
27.	Tehran	10.0

City populations are based on urban agglomerations rather than legal city limits. In some cases where two adjacent cities have merged into one concentration, such as Tokyo–Yokohama, they have been regarded as a single unit.

* For a list of current city estimates, see page XI.

URBAN ADVANTAGES

Despite overcrowding and poor housing, living standards in the developing world's cities are almost invariably better than in the surrounding countryside. Resources – financial, material and administrative – are concentrated in the towns, which are usually also the centres of political activity and pressure. Governments – frequently unstable, and rarely established on a solid democratic base – are usually more responsive to urban discontent than rural misery.

In many countries, especially in Africa, food prices are often kept artificially low, appeasing underemployed urban masses at the expense of agricultural development. The imbalance encourages further cityward migration, helping to account for the astonishing rate of post-1950 urbanization and putting great strain on the ability of many nations to provide even modest improvements for their people.

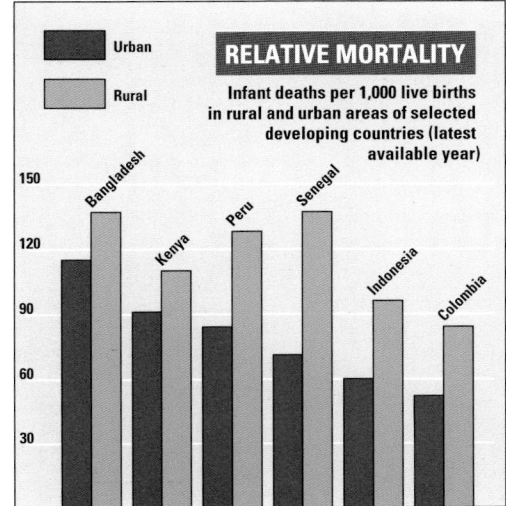

■ Urban
■ Rural

RELATIVE MORTALITY

Infant deaths per 1,000 live births in rural and urban areas of selected developing countries (latest available year)

150
120
90
60
30

Bangladesh Kenya Peru Senegal Indonesia Colombia

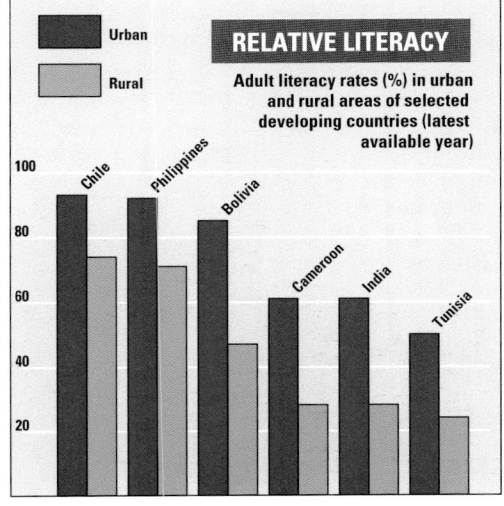

■ Urban
■ Rural

RELATIVE LITERACY

Adult literacy rates (%) in urban and rural areas of selected developing countries (latest available year)

100
80
60
40
20

Chile Philippines Bolivia Cameroon India Tunisia

PEOPLE: THE HUMAN FAMILY

Strictly speaking, all human beings belong to a single race – *Homo sapiens* has no subspecies. But although all humans are interfertile, anthropologists and geneticists distinguish three main racial types: Caucasoid, Negroid and Mongoloid. Racial differences reflect not so much evolutionary origin as long periods of separation.

Racial affinities are not always obvious. The Caucasoid group stems from Europe, North Africa and India, but still includes Australian aboriginals within its broad type; Mongoloid peoples comprise American Indians and Eskimos as well as most Chinese, central Asians and Malays; Negroids are mostly of African origin, but also include the Papuan peoples of New Guinea.

Migration in modern times has mingled racial groups to an unprecedented extent, and most nations now have some degree of racially mixed population.

Language is almost the definition of a particular human culture; the world has well over 5,000, most of them with only a few hundred thousand speakers. In one important sense, all languages are equal; although different vocabularies and linguistic structures greatly influence patterns of thought, all true human languages can carry virtually unlimited information. But even if, for example, there is no theoretical difference in the communicative power of English and one of the 500 or more tribal languages of Papua New Guinea, an English speaker has access to much more of the global culture than a Papuan who knows no other tongue.

Like language, religion encourages the internal cohesion of a single human group at the expense of creating gulfs of incomprehension between different groups. All religions satisfy a deep-seated human need, assigning men and women to a comprehensible place in what most of them still consider a divinely ordered world. But religion is also a means by which a culture can assert its individuality; the startling rise of Islam in the late 20th century is partly a response by large sections of the developing world to the secular, Western-inspired world order from which many non-Western peoples feel excluded. Like uncounted millions of human beings before them, they find in their religion not only a personal faith but also a powerful group identity.

WORLD MIGRATION

The greatest voluntary migration was the colonization of North America by 30–35 million European settlers during the 19th century. The greatest forced migration involved 9–11 million Africans taken as slaves to America 1550–1860. The migrations shown on the map are mostly international as population movements within borders are not usually recorded. Many of the statistics are necessarily estimates as so many refugees and migrant workers enter countries illegally and unrecorded. Emigrants may have a variety of motives for leaving, thus making it difficult to distinguish between voluntary and involuntary migrations.

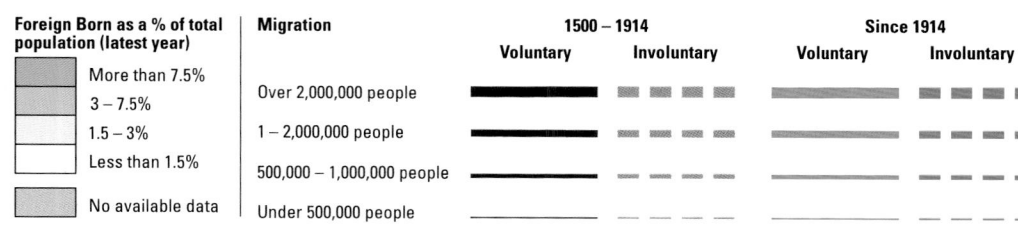

Foreign Born as a % of total population (latest year)	Migration	1500 – 1914		Since 1914	
		Voluntary	Involuntary	Voluntary	Involuntary
More than 7.5%	Over 2,000,000 people				
3 – 7.5%	1 – 2,000,000 people				
1.5 – 3%	500,000 – 1,000,000 people				
Less than 1.5%	Under 500,000 people				
No available data					

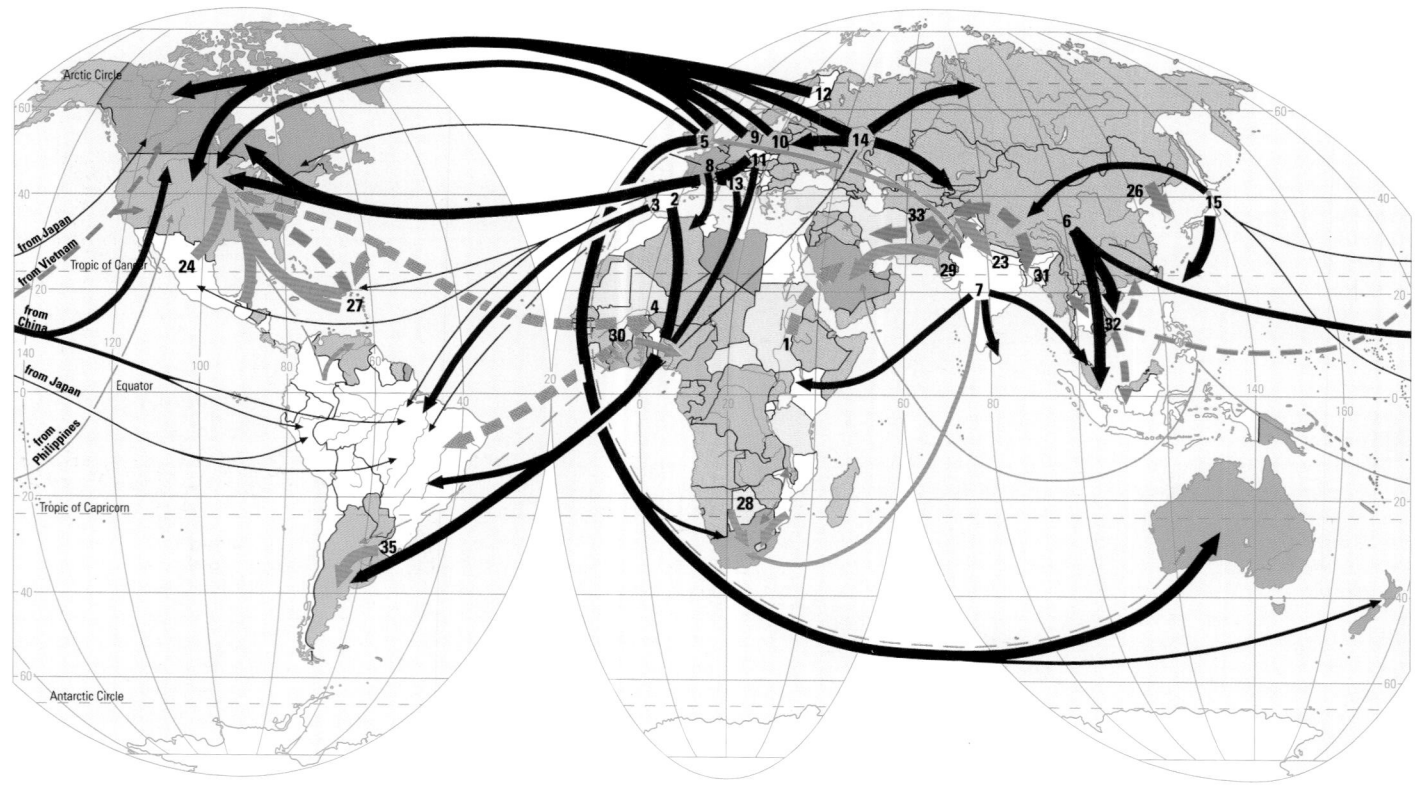

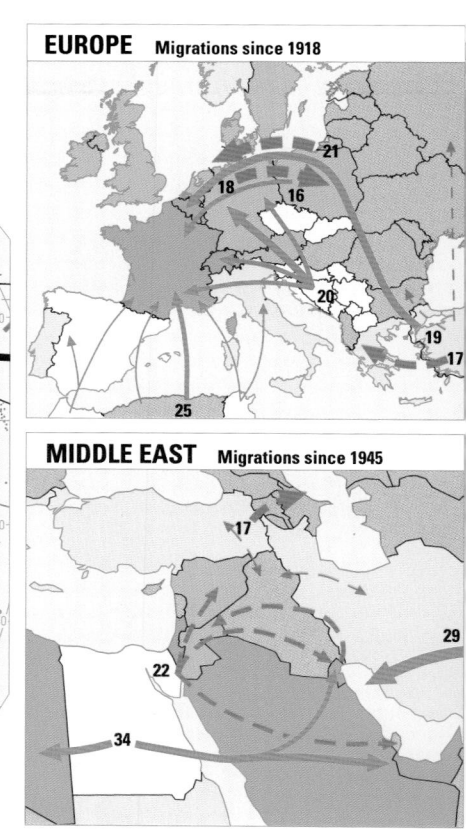

EUROPE   Migrations since 1918

MIDDLE EAST   Migrations since 1945

BUILDING THE USA

US Immigration 1820–1990

'Give me your tired, your poor/Your huddled masses yearning to breathe free....'

So starts Emma Lazarus's poem The New Colossus, inscribed on the Statue of Liberty. For decades the USA was the magnet that attracted millions of immigrants, notably from Central and Eastern Europe, the flow peaking in the early years of this century.

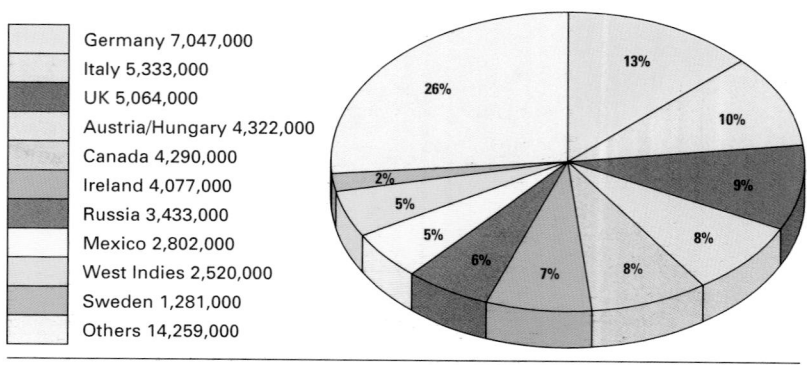

Germany 7,047,000
Italy 5,333,000
UK 5,064,000
Austria/Hungary 4,322,000
Canada 4,290,000
Ireland 4,077,000
Russia 3,433,000
Mexico 2,802,000
West Indies 2,520,000
Sweden 1,281,000
Others 14,259,000

Major world migrations since 1500 (over 1,000,000 people)

1. North African and East African slaves to Arabia (4.3m) 1500–1900
2. Spanish to South and Central America (2.3m) 1530–1914
3. Portuguese to Brazil (1.4m) 1530–1914
4. West African slaves to South America (4.6m) 1550–1860
   to Caribbean (4m) 1580–1860
   to North and Central America (1m) 1650–1820
5. British and Irish to North America (13.5m) 1620–1914
   to Australasia and South Africa (3m) 1790–1914
6. Chinese to South-east Asia (22m) 1820–1914
   to North America (1m) 1880–1914
7. Indian migrant workers (3m) 1850–1914
8. French to North Africa (1.5m) 1850–1914
9. Germans to North America (5m) 1850–1914
10. Poles to North America (3.6m) 1850–1914
11. Austro-Hungarians to North America (3.2m) 1850–1914
    to Western Europe (3.4m) 1850–1914
    to South America (1.8m) 1850–1914
12. Scandinavians to North America (2.7m) 1850–1914
13. Italians to North America (5m) 1860–1914
    to South America (3.7m) 1860–1914
14. Russians to North America (2.2m) 1880–1914
    to Western Europe (2.2m) 1880–1914
    to Siberia (6m) 1880–1914
    to Central Asia (4m) 1880–1914
15. Japanese to Eastern Asia, South-east Asia and America (8m) 1900–1914
16. Poles to Western Europe (1m) 1920–1940
17. Greeks and Armenians from Turkey (1.6m) 1922–1923
18. European Jews to extermination camps (5m) 1940–1944
19. Turks to Western Europe (1.9m) 1940–
20. Yugoslavs to Western Europe (2m) 1940–
21. Germans to Western Europe (9.8m) 1945–1947
22. Palestinian refugees (2m) 1947–
23. Indian and Pakistani refugees (15m) 1947
24. Mexicans to North America (9m) 1950–
25. North Africans to Western Europe (1.1m) 1950–
26. Korean refugees (5m) 1950–1954
27. Latin Americans and West Indians to North America (4.7m) 1960–
28. Migrant workers to South Africa (1.5m) 1960–
29. Indians and Pakistanis to The Gulf (2.4m) 1970–
30. Migrant workers to Nigeria and Ivory Coast (3m) 1970–
31. Bangladeshi and Pakistani refugees (2m) 1972
32. Vietnamese and Cambodian refugees (1.5m) 1975–
33. Afghan refugees (6.1m) 1979–
34. Egyptians to The Gulf and Libya (2.9m) 1980–
35. Migrant workers to Argentina (2m) 1980–

INDO-EUROPEAN FAMILY

1	Balto-Slavic group (incl. Russian, Ukrainian)
2	Germanic group (incl. English, German)
3	Celtic group
4	Greek
5	Albanian
6	Iranian group
7	Armenian
8	Romance group (incl. Spanish, Portuguese, French, Italian)
9	Indo-Aryan group (incl. Hindi, Bengali, Urdu, Punjabi, Marathi)

CAUCASIAN FAMILY

AFRO-ASIATIC FAMILY

11	Semitic group (incl. Arabic)
12	Kushitic group
13	Berber group

14	KHOISAN FAMILY
15	NIGER-CONGO FAMILY
16	NILO-SAHARAN FAMILY
17	URALIC FAMILY

ALTAIC FAMILY

18	Turkic group
19	Mongolian group
20	Tungus-Manchu group
21	Japanese and Korean

SINO-TIBETAN FAMILY

22	Sinitic (Chinese) languages
23	Tibetic-Burmic languages
24	TAI FAMILY

AUSTRO-ASIATIC FAMILY

25	Mon-Khmer group
26	Munda group
27	Vietnamese

28	DRAVIDIAN FAMILY (incl. Telugu, Tamil)
29	AUSTRONESIAN FAMILY (incl. Malay-Indonesian)
30	OTHER LANGUAGES

Languages form a kind of tree of development, splitting from a few ancient proto-tongues into branches that have grown apart and further divided with the passage of time. English and Hindi, for example, both belong to the great Indo-European family, although the relationship is only apparent after much analysis and comparison with non-Indo-European languages such as Chinese or Arabic; Hindi is part of the Indo-Aryan subgroup, whereas English is a member of Indo-European's Germanic branch; French, another Indo-European tongue, traces its descent through the Latin, or Romance, branch. A few languages – Basque is one example – have no apparent links with any other, living or dead. Most modern languages, of course, have acquired enormous quantities of vocabulary from each other.

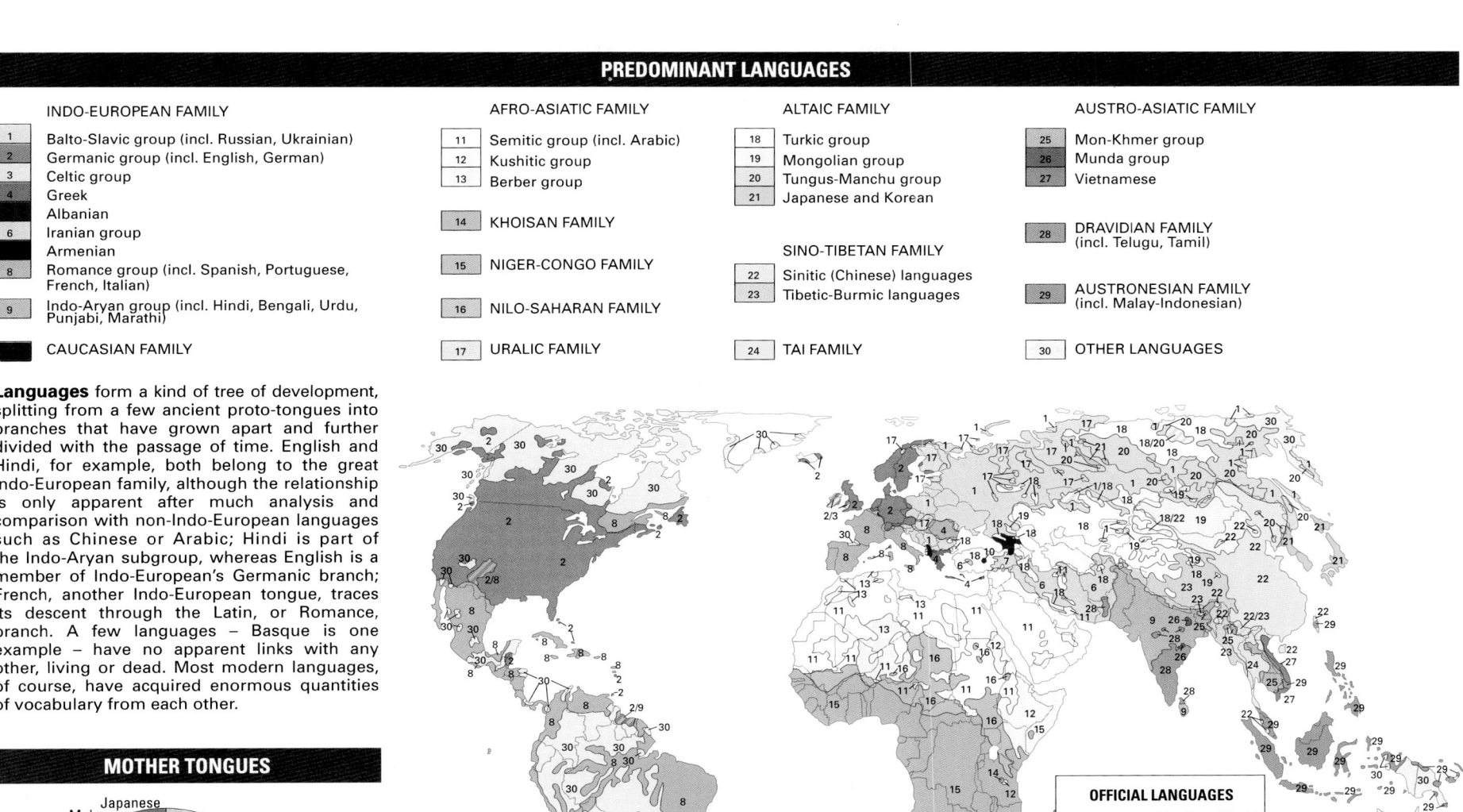

MOTHER TONGUES

Pie chart values:
Mandarin Chinese 834, English 443, Hindi 352, Spanish 341, Russian 293, Arabic 197, Bengali 184, Portuguese 173, Malay 142, Japanese 125

OFFICIAL LANGUAGES

Language	Total population	World %
English	1,400m	27.0%
Chinese	1,070m	19.1%
Hindi	700m	13.5%
Spanish	280m	5.4%
Russian	270m	5.2%
French	220m	4.2%
Arabic	170m	3.3%
Portuguese	160m	3.0%
Malay	160m	3.0%
Bengali	150m	2.9%
Japanese	120m	2.3%

- Roman Catholicism
- Orthodox and other Eastern Churches
- Protestantism
- Sunni Islam
- Shia Islam
- Buddhism
- Hinduism
- Confucianism
- Judaism
- Shintoism
- Tribal Religions

Religions are not as easily mapped as the physical contours of landscape. Divisions are often blurred and frequently overlapping: most nations include people of many different faiths – or no faith at all. Some religions, like Islam and Christianity, have proselytes worldwide; others, like Hinduism and Confucianism, are restricted to a particular area, though modern migrations have taken some Indians and Chinese very far from their cultural origins. It is also difficult to show the degree to which religion controls daily life: Christian Western Europe, for example, is now far less dominated by its religion than are the Islamic nations of the Middle East. Similarly, figures for the major faiths' adherents make no distinction between nominal believers enrolled at birth and those for whom religion is a vital part of existence.

RELIGIOUS ADHERENTS

Christian	1,667m
Roman Catholic	952m
Protestant	337m
Orthodox	162m
Anglican	70m
Other Christian	148m
Muslim	881m
Sunni	841m
Shia	40m
Hindu	663m
Buddhist	312m
Chinese Folk	172m
Tribal	92m
Jewish	18m
Sikhs	17m

CARTOGRAPHY BY PHILIP'S. COPYRIGHT REED INTERNATIONAL BOOKS LTD

FOR MORE INFORMATION:

26: MIGRATION

27: RELIGION

46: HUMAN EXPANSION

Humans are social animals, rarely functioning well except in groups. Evolution has made them so: hunter-gatherers in co-operative bands were far more effective than animals that prowled alone. Agriculture, the building of cities and industrialization are all developments that depended on human co-operative ability – and in turn increased the need for it.

Unfortunately, human groups do not always co-operate so well with other human groups, and friction between them sometimes leads to co-operatively organized violence. War is itself a very human activity, with no real equivalent in any other species. Always

murderous, it is sometimes purposeful and may even be effective. The colonization of the Americas and Australia, for example, was in effect the waging of aggressive war by well-armed Europeans against indigenous peoples incapable of offering a serious defence.

Most often, war achieves little but death and ruin. The great 20th-century wars accomplished nothing for the nations involved in them, although the world paid a price of between 50 and 100 million dead as well as immense material damage. The relative peace in the postwar developed world is at least partly due to the nuclear weapons with which rival powers have armed

themselves – weapons so powerful that their use would leave a scarcely habitable planet with no meaningful distinction between victor and vanquished.

Yet warfare remains endemic: the second half of the 20th century was one of the bloodiest periods in history, and death by organized violence remains common. The map below attempts to show the serious conflicts that have scarred the Earth since 1945. Most are civil wars in poor countries, rather than international conflicts between rich ones; some of them are still unresolved, while others may erupt again at intervals, adding to the world's population of refugees.

THE WORLD'S REFUGEES

Refugees and their national origin; the host nations and the relative size of their refugee populations (1991)

Refugee Destinations

Refugees in millions

Refugees as a proportion of host country's population

Origin of Refugees: Other, Cambodia, Somalia, Sudan, Angola, Ethiopia, Iraq, Mozambique, Palestine, Afghanistan

Destinations: India, Tanzania, Syria, Lebanon, Zaire, Somalia, Thailand, Turkey, Sudan, Ethiopia, Malawi, Jordan, Iran, Pakistan

3,500,000
3,000,000
2,500,000
2,000,000
1,500,000
1,000,000
500,000

The pie-chart shows the origins of the world's refugees, while the bar-chart below shows their destinations. According to the United Nations High Commissioner for Refugees, in 1990 there were almost 15 million refugees, a number that has continued to increase; indeed, by 1995 the number of refugees in the world had increased to 23 million. Some have fled from climatic change, some from economic disaster and others from political persecution; the great majority, however, are the victims of war.

All but a few who make it overseas seek asylum in neighbouring countries, which are often the least equipped to deal with them and where they are rarely welcome. Lacking any rights or power, they frequently become an embarrassment and a burden to their reluctant hosts.

Usually, the best any refugee can hope for is rudimentary food and shelter in temporary camps that all to often become semi-permanent, with little prospect of assimilation by host populations: many Palestinians, for example, have been forced to live in camps since 1948.

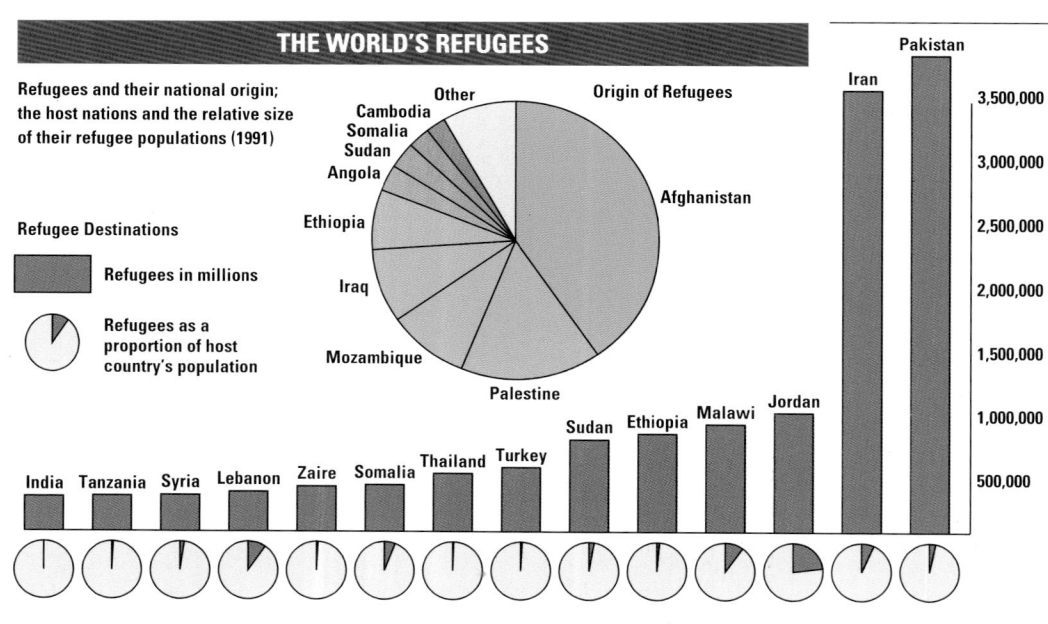

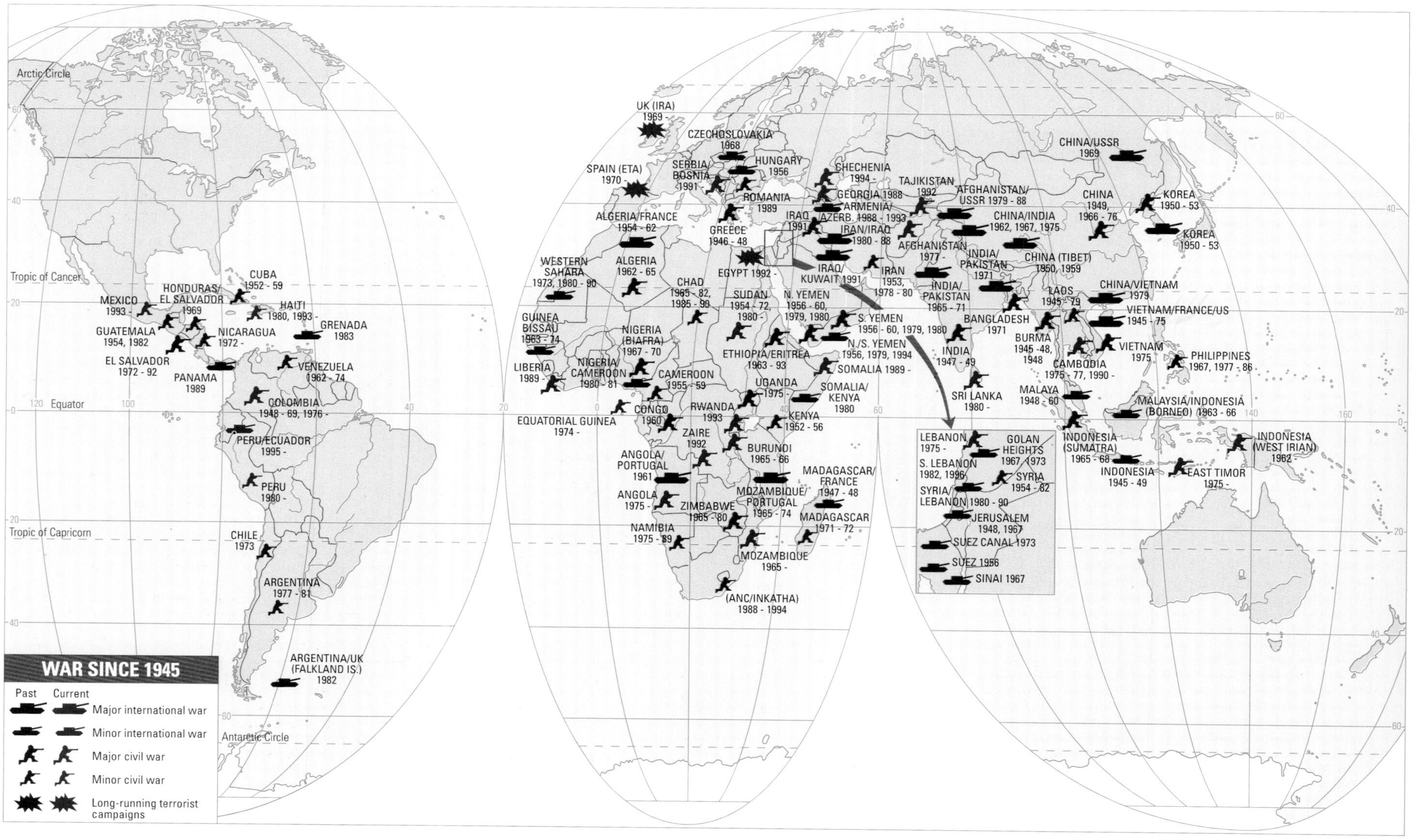

WAR SINCE 1945

Past	Current	
		Major international war
		Minor international war
		Major civil war
		Minor civil war
		Long-running terrorist campaigns

The United Nations Organization was born as World War II drew to its conclusion. Six years of strife had strengthened the world's desire for peace, but an effective international organization was needed to help achieve it. That body would replace the League of Nations which, since its inception in 1920, had signally failed to curb the aggression of at least some of its member nations. At the United Nations Conference on International Organization held in San Francisco, the United Nations Charter was drawn up. Ratified by the Security Council and signed by the 51 original members, it came into effect on 24 October 1945.

The Charter set out the aims of the organization: to maintain peace and security, and develop friendly relations between nations; to achieve international co-operation in solving economic, social, cultural and humanitarian problems; to promote respect for human rights and fundamental freedoms; and to harmonize the activities of nations in order to achieve these common goals.

By 1995, the UN had expanded to 185 member countries; it is the largest international political organization, employing over 25,000 people worldwide; its headquarters is in New York and accounts for 7,000 staff and it also has major offices in Rome, Geneva and Vienna.

The United Nations has six principal organs:

The General Assembly

The forum at which member nations discuss moral and political issues affecting world development, peace and security meets annually in September, under a newly-elected President whose tenure lasts one year. Any member can bring business to the agenda, and each member nation has one vote. Decisions are made by simple majority, save for matters of very great importance, when a two-thirds majority is required.

The Security Council

A legislative and executive body, the Security Council is the primary instrument for establishing and maintaining international peace by attempting to settle disputes between nations. It has the power to dispatch UN forces to stop aggression, and member nations undertake to make armed forces, assistance and facilities available as required. The Security Council has ten temporary members elected by the General Assembly for two-year terms, and five permanent members – China, France, Russia, UK and USA.

The Economic and Social Council

By far the largest United Nations executive, the Council operates as a conduit between the General Assembly and the many United Nations agencies it instructs to implement Assembly decisions, and whose work it co-ordinates. The Council also sets up commissions to examine economic conditions, collects data and issues studies and reports, and may make recommendations to the Assembly.

The Secretariat

This is the staff of the United Nations, and its task is to administer the policies and programmes of the UN and its organs, and to assist and advise the Head of the Secretariat, the Secretary-General – a full-time, non-political, appointment made by the General Assembly.

The Trusteeship Council

The Council administers trust territories with the aim of promoting their advancement. By the end of 1994, however, all the original 11 trust territories had become independent.

The International Court of Justice (the World Court)

The World Court is the judicial organ of the United Nations. It deals only with United Nations disputes and all members are subject to its jurisdiction. There are 15 judges, elected for nine-year terms by the General Assembly and the Security Council. The Court sits in The Hague.

United Nations agencies and programmes, and intergovernmental agencies co-ordinated by the UN, contribute to harmonious world development. Social and humanitarian operations include:

United Nations Development Programme (UNDP) Plans and funds projects to help developing countries make better use of their resources.
United Nations International Childrens' Fund (UNICEF) Created at the General Assembly's first session in 1945 to help children in the aftermath of World War II, it now provides basic health care and aid worldwide.
United Nations Fund for Population Activities (UNFPA) Promotes awareness of population issues and family planning, providing appropriate assistance.
Food and Agriculture Organization (FAO) Aims to raise living standards and nutrition levels in rural areas by improving food production and distribution.
United Nations Educational, Scientific and Cultural Organization (UNESCO) Promotes international co-operation through broader and better education.
World Health Organization (WHO) Promotes and provides for better health care, public and environmental health and medical research.

Membership There are seven independent states which are not members of the UN – Kiribati, Nauru, Switzerland, Taiwan, Tonga, Tuvalu and Vatican City. Official languages are Chinese, English, French, Russian, Spanish and Arabic.
Funding The UN budget for 1996–97 is US $2.61 billion. Contributions are assessed by the members' ability to pay, with the maximum 25% of the total, the minimum 0.01%. Contributions for 1994–95 were: USA 25.0%, Japan 12.45%, Germany 8.93%, Russia 6.71%, France 6.0%, UK 5.02%, Italy 4.29%, Canada 3.11% (others 28.49%).
Peacekeeping The UN has been involved in 43 peacekeeping operations worldwide since 1948 and there are currently 14 areas of UN patrol. In July 1993 there were 80,146 'blue berets' from 74 countries.

United Nations agencies are involved in many aspects of international trade, safety and security:

International Maritime Organization (IMO) Promotes unity amongst merchant shipping, especially in regard to safety, marine pollution and standardization.
International Labour Organization (ILO) Seeks to improve labour conditions and promote productive employment to raise living standards.
World Meteorological Organization (WMO) Promotes co-operation in weather observation, reporting and forecasting.
World Intellectual Property Organization (WIPO) Seeks to protect intellectual property such as artistic copyright, scientific patents and trademarks.
World Trade Organization (WTO) On 1 January 1995 the WTO replaced GATT. It advocates a common code of conduct and its aim is the liberalization of world trade.
Disarmament Commission Considers and makes recommendations to the General Assembly on disarmament issues.
International Atomic Energy Agency (IAEA) Fosters development of peaceful uses for nuclear energy, establishes safety standards and monitors the destruction of nuclear material designed for military use.

The World Bank comprises three United Nations agencies:

International Monetary Fund (IMF) Cultivates international monetary co-operation and expansion of trade.
International Bank for Reconstruction and Development (IBRD) Provides funds and technical assistance to developing countries.
International Finance Corporation (IFC) Encourages the growth of productive private enterprise in less developed countries.

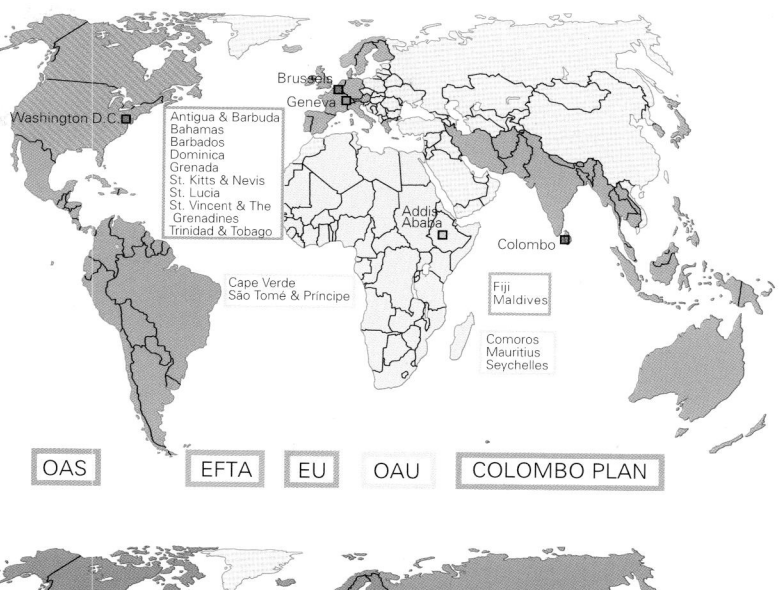

OAS | EFTA | EU | OAU | COLOMBO PLAN

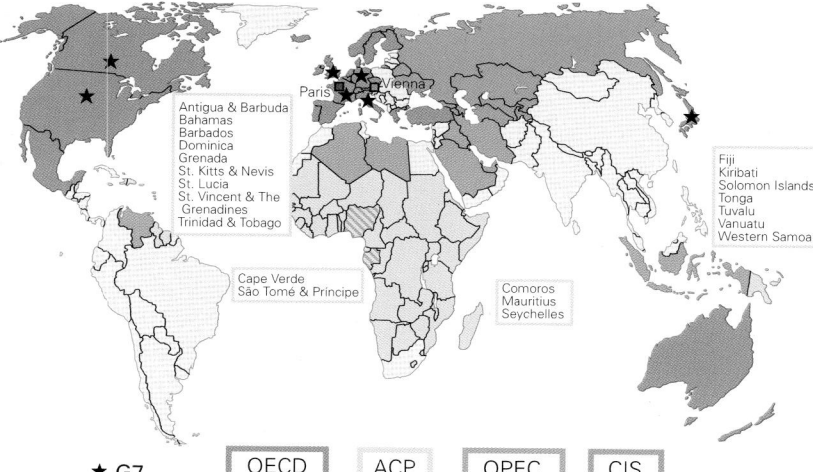

★ G7 | OECD | ACP | OPEC | CIS

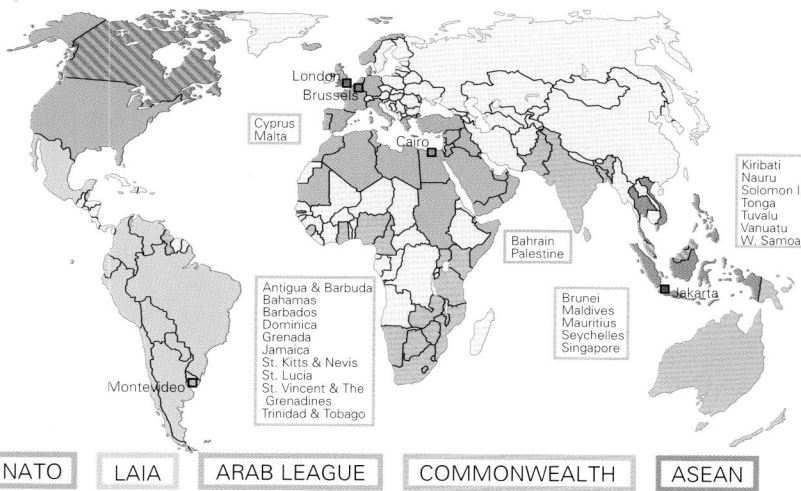

NATO | LAIA | ARAB LEAGUE | COMMONWEALTH | ASEAN

EU The European Union evolved from the European Community (EC) in 1993. The original body, the European Coal and Steel Community (ECSC), was created in 1951 following the signing of the Treaty of Paris. The 15 members of the EU – Austria, Belgium, Denmark, Finland, France, Germany, Greece, Ireland, Italy, Luxembourg, Netherlands, Portugal, Spain, Sweden and the UK – aim to integrate economies, co-ordinate social developments and bring about political union. These members of what is now the world's biggest market share agricultural and industrial policies and tariffs on trade.
EFTA European Free Trade Association (formed in 1960). Portugal left the original 'Seven' in 1989 to join what was then the EC, followed by Austria, Finland and Sweden in 1995. There are now only four members: Norway, Iceland, Liechtenstein and Switzerland.
ACP African-Caribbean-Pacific (formed in 1963). Member countries enjoy economic ties with the EU.
NATO North Atlantic Treaty Organization (formed in 1949). It continues after 1991 despite the winding up of the Warsaw Pact.
OAS Organization of American States (formed in 1948). It aims to promote social and economic co-operation between developed countries of North America and developing nations of Latin America.
ASEAN Association of South-east Asian Nations (formed in 1967). Vietnam joined in 1995.
OAU Organization of African Unity (1963). Its 53 members represent over 94% of Africa's population.
LAIA Latin American Integration Association (formed in 1980) superceded the Latin American Free Trade Association formed in 1961.
OECD Organization for Economic Co-operation and Development (formed in 1961). The 26 major Western free-market economies. The Czech Republic joined in December 1995. The 'G7' is its 'inner group' comprising Canada, France, Germany, Italy, Japan, USA and UK.
COMMONWEALTH The Commonwealth of Nations evolved from the British Empire; it comprises 16 nations recognizing the British monarch as head of state, 32 republics and 5 indigenous monarchies.
CIS The Commonwealth of Independent States (formed in 1991) comprises the countries of the former Soviet Union except for Estonia, Latvia and Lithuania.
OPEC Organization of Petroleum Exporting Countries (formed in 1960). It controls about three-quarters of the world's oil supply. Ecuador formally withdrew from OPEC on 1 January 1993.
ARAB LEAGUE (1945) The League's aim is to promote economic, social, political and military co-operation.
COLOMBO PLAN Its 26 members aim to promote economic and social development in Asia and the Pacific (formed in 1951).

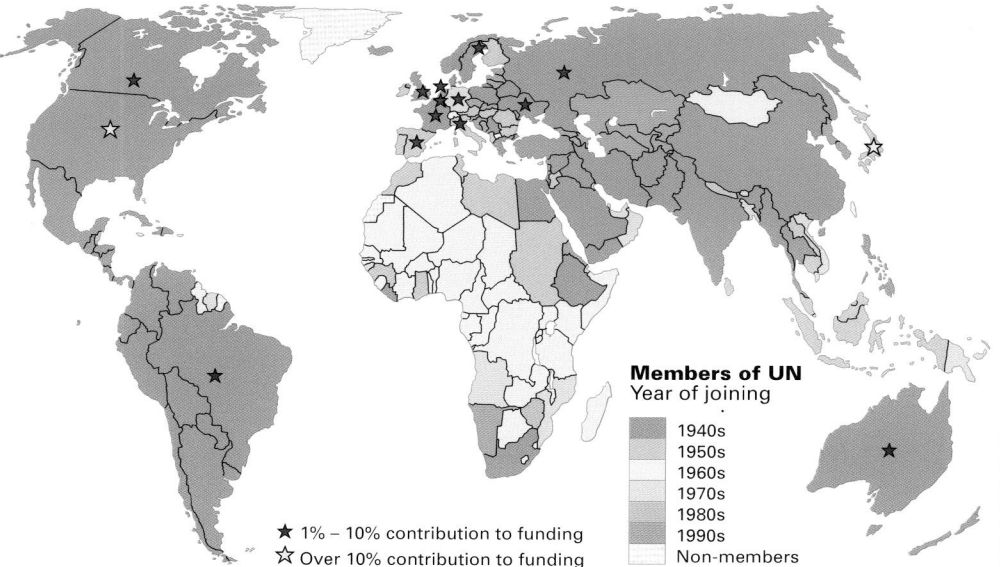

Members of UN
Year of joining

- 1940s
- 1950s
- 1960s
- 1970s
- 1980s
- 1990s
- Non-members

★ 1% – 10% contribution to funding
☆ Over 10% contribution to funding

PRODUCTION: AGRICULTURE

The invention of agriculture transformed human existence more than any other development, though it may not have seemed much of an improvement to its first practitioners. Primitive farming required brutally hard work, and it tied men and women to a patch of land, highly vulnerable to local weather patterns and to predators – drawbacks still apparent in much of the world today. It is difficult to imagine early humans being interested in such an existence while there were still animals around to hunt and wild seeds and berries to gather. Probably the spur was population pressure, with consequent overhunting and scarcity.

Despite its difficulties, the new life style had a few overwhelming advantages. It supported far larger populations, eventually including substantial cities, with all the varied cultural and economic activities they allowed. Later still, it furnished the surpluses that allowed industrialization – another enormous step in the course of human development.

Machines relieved many farmers of their burden of endless toil, and made it possible for relatively small numbers to provide food for more than 5,000 million people.

Now, as in the past, the whole business of farming involves the creation of a severely simplified ecology. Natural plant life is divided into crops, to be protected and nurtured, and weeds, the rest, to be destroyed. From the earliest days, crops were selectively bred to increase their yield, usually at the expense of their ability to survive, which became the farmer's responsibility; 20th-century plant geneticists have carried the technique to highly productive extremes. Due mainly to new varieties of rice and wheat, world grain production has increased by 70% since 1965, more than doubling in the developing countries, although such high yields demand equally high consumption of fertilizers and pesticides to maintain them. Mechanized farmers in North America and Europe continue to turn out huge surpluses,

although not without environmental costs.

Where production is inadequate, the reasons are as likely to be political as agricultural. Africa, the only continent where food production per capita is actually falling, suffers acutely from economic mismanagement, as well as from the perennial problems of war and banditry. Dismal harvests in the former USSR, despite its excellent farmland, helped bring about the collapse of the Soviet system.

There are other limits to progress too. Increasing population puts relentless pressure on farmers not only to maintain high yields but also to increase them. Most of the world's potential cropland is already under the plough. The overworking of marginal land is one of the prime causes of desertification; new farmlands burned out of former rain forests are seldom fertile for long. Human numbers may yet outrun the land's ability to feed them, as they did almost 10,000 years ago when sedentary agriculture began.

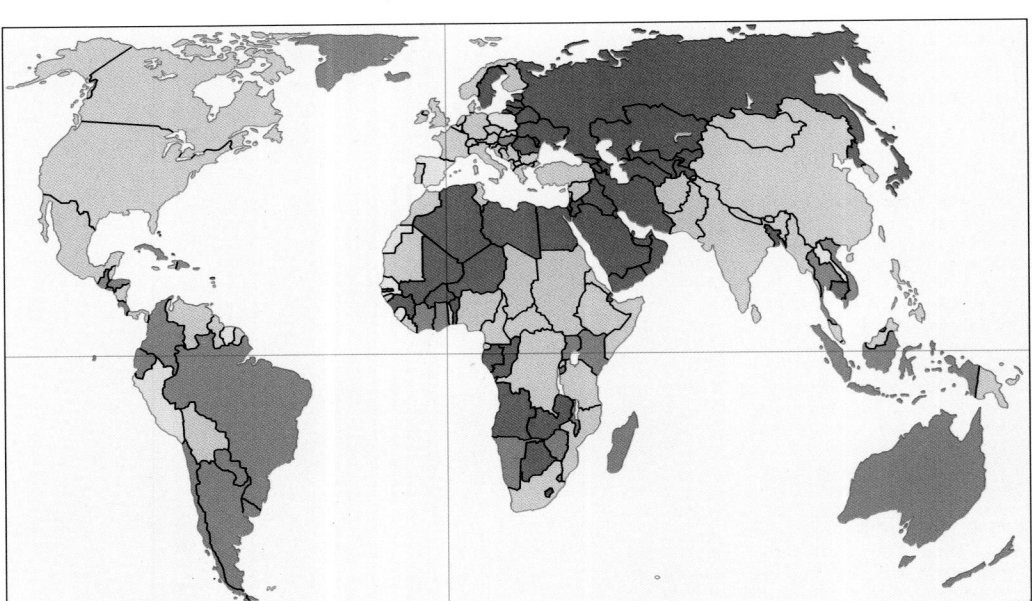

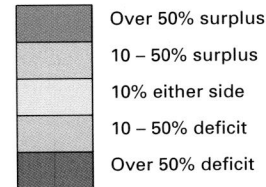

SELF-SUFFICIENCY IN FOOD

Balance of trade in food products as a percentage of total trade in food products – S.I.T.C. Classes 0, 1 and 4 (latest available year)

- Over 50% surplus
- 10 – 50% surplus
- 10% either side
- 10 – 50% deficit
- Over 50% deficit

Most self-sufficient		Least self-sufficient	
Argentina	95%	Algeria	−98%
Zimbabwe	87%	Djibouti	−97%
Honduras	81%	Yemen	−95%
Malawi	81%	Zambia	−95%
Costa Rica	79%	Japan	−91%
Iceland	78%	Gabon	−90%
Chile	75%	Kuwait	−75%
Uruguay	75%	Brunei	−89%
Ecuador	74%	Burkina Faso	−82%

LAND USE

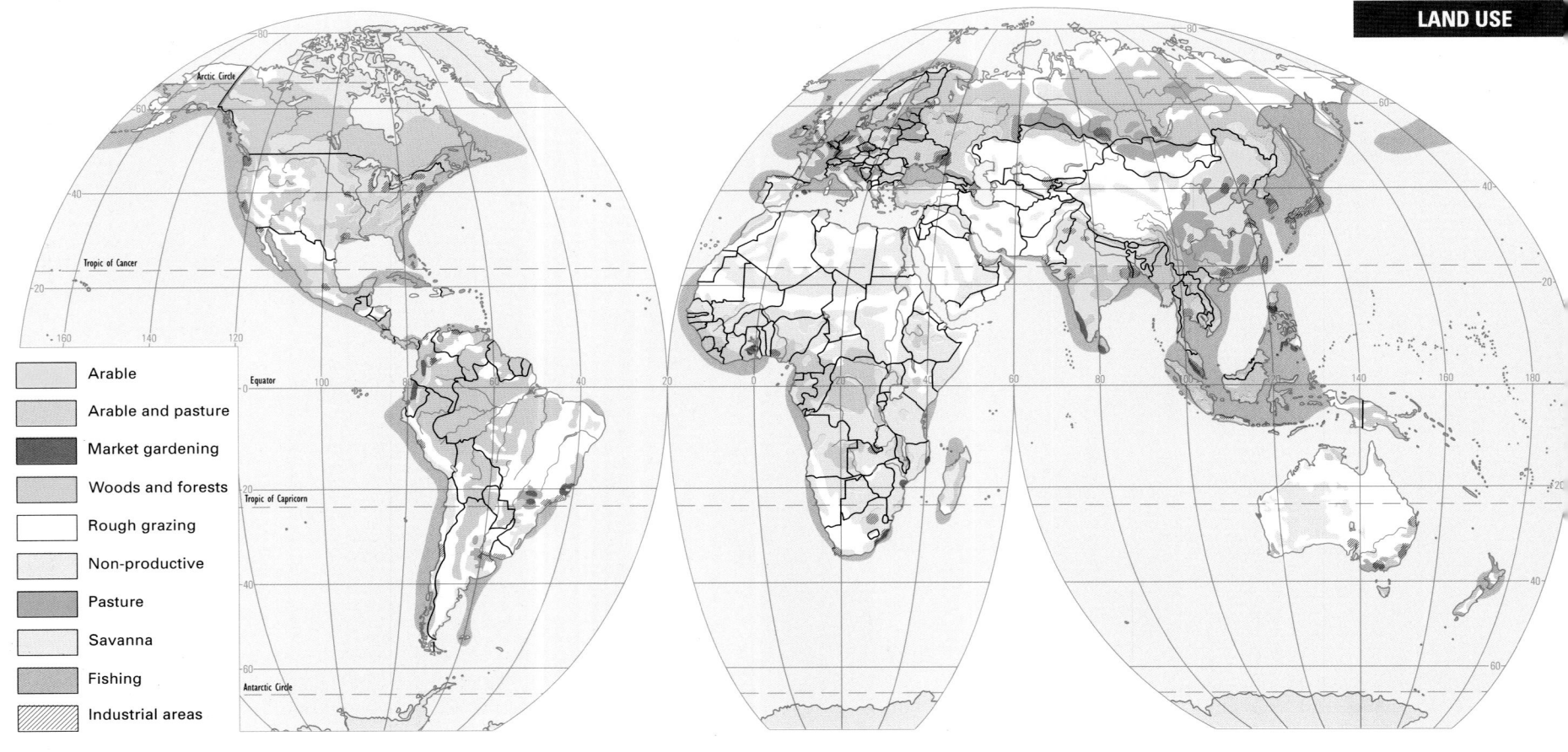

- Arable
- Arable and pasture
- Market gardening
- Woods and forests
- Rough grazing
- Non-productive
- Pasture
- Savanna
- Fishing
- Industrial areas

STAPLE CROPS

Wheat: Grown in a range of climates, with most varieties – including the highest-quality bread wheats – requiring temperate conditions. Mainly used in baking, it is also used for pasta and breakfast cereals.

China 18.6% · USA 11.6% · India 10.1% · Russia 7.5% · France 5.2% · Canada 4.3%

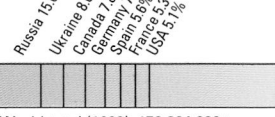

World total (1993): 564,457,000 tonnes

Maize: Originating in the New World and still an important human food in Africa and Latin America, in the developed world it is processed into breakfast cereals, oil, starches and adhesives. It is also used for animal feed.

USA 35.8% · China 22.9% · Brazil 6.7% · Mexico 4.1% · France 3.3%

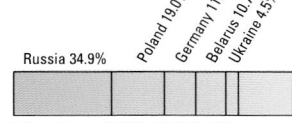

World total (1993): 450,570,000 tonnes

Oats: Most widely used to feed livestock, but eaten by humans as oatmeal or porridge. Oats have a beneficial effect on the cardiovascular system, and human consumption is likely to increase.

Russia 32.6% · Canada 10.2% · USA 8.4% · Germany 4.8% · Australia 4.7%

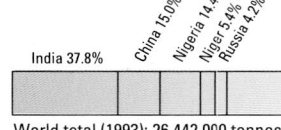

World total (1993): 35,443,000 tonnes

Millet: The name covers a number of small-grained cereals, members of the grass family with a short growing season. Used to produce flour, meal and animal feed, and fermented to make beer, especially in Africa.

India 37.8% · China 15.0% · Nigeria 14.4% · Niger 5.4% · Russia 4.2%

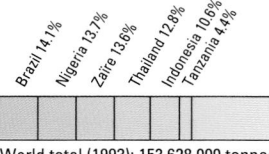

World total (1993): 26,442,000 tonnes

Cassava: A tropical shrub that needs high rainfall (over 1000 mm annually) and a 10–30 month growing season to produce its large, edible tubers. Used as flour by humans, as cattle feed and in industrial starches.

Brazil 14.1% · Nigeria 13.7% · Zaire 13.6% · Thailand 12.8% · Indonesia 10.0% · Tanzania 4.4%

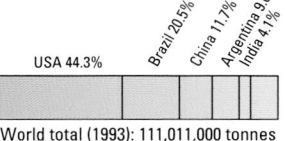

World total (1993): 153,628,000 tonnes

Cereals are grasses with starchy, edible seeds; every important civilization has depended on them as a source of food. The major cereal grains contain about 10% protein and 75% carbohydrate; grain is easy to store, handle and transport, and contributes more than any other group of foods to the energy and protein content of human diet. If all the cereals were consumed by man, there would be no shortage of food, but a large proportion of the total output is used as animal feed.

Starchy tuber crops or root crops, represented here by potatoes and cassava, are second in importance only to cereals as staple foods; easily cultivated, they provide high yields for little effort and store well – potatoes for up to six months, cassava for up to a year in the ground. Protein content is low (2% or less), starch content high, with some minerals and vitamins present, but populations that rely heavily on these crops may suffer from malnutrition.

Rice: Thrives on the high humidity and temperatures of the Far East, where it is the traditional staple food of half the human race. Usually grown standing in water, rice responds well to continuous cultivation, with three or four crops annually.

China 35.4% · India 21.0% · Indonesia 9.1% · Bangladesh 5.3% · Vietnam 4.2% · Thailand 3.6%

World total (1993): 527,413,000 tonnes

Barley: Primarily used as animal feed, but widely eaten by humans in Africa and Asia. Elsewhere, malted barley furnishes beer and spirits. Able to withstand the dry heat of subarid tropics, its growing season is only 80 days.

Russia 15.6% · Ukraine 8.0% · Canada 7.8% · Germany 7.0% · Spain 5.6% · France 5.3% · USA 5.1%

World total (1993): 170,364,000 tonnes

Rye: Hardy and tolerant of poor and sandy soils, it is an important foodstuff and animal feed in Central and Eastern Europe. Rye produces a dark, heavy bread as well as alcoholic drinks.

Russia 34.9% · Poland 19.0% · Germany 11.2% · Belarus 10.7% · Ukraine 4.5%

World total (1993): 26,200,000 tonnes

Potatoes: The most important of the edible tubers, potatoes grow in well-watered, temperate areas. Weight for weight less nutritious than grain, they are a human staple as well as an important animal feed.

Russia 13.2% · Poland 12.6% · China 12.2% · Ukraine 7.3% · USA 6.6% · India 5.5%

World total (1993): 288,183,000 tonnes

Soya: Beans from soya bushes are very high (30–40%) in protein. Most are processed into oil and proprietary protein foods. Consumption since 1950 has tripled, mainly due to the health-conscious developed world.

USA 44.3% · Brazil 20.5% · China 11.7% · Argentina 9.6% · India 4.1%

World total (1993): 111,011,000 tonnes

AGRICULTURAL POPULATION

Percentage of the total population dependent on agriculture (1994)

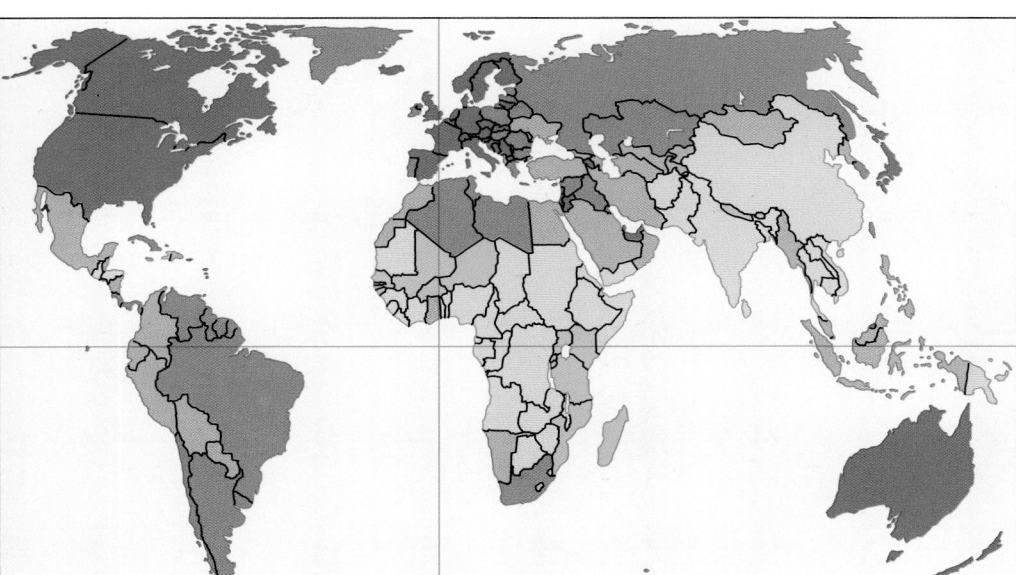

- Over 75% dependent
- 50 – 75% dependent
- 25 – 50% dependent
- 10 – 25% dependent
- Under 10% dependent

Top 5 countries		Bottom 5 countries	
Nepal	91%	Macau	0.4%
Rwanda	91%	Singapore	0.9%
Burundi	91%	Hong Kong	1.2%
Bhutan	90%	Kuwait	1.3%
Niger	86%	Guam	1.4%

FOOD & POPULATION

Comparison of food production and population by continent (latest available year). The left column indicates percentage shares of total world food production; the right shows population in proportion.

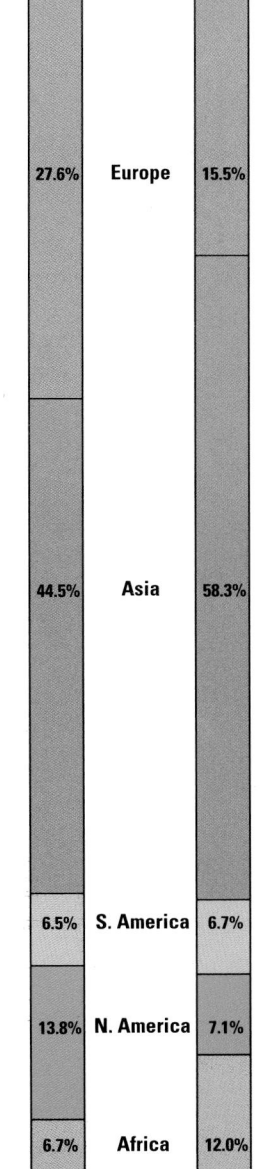

	FOOD	POPULATION
Australasia	1.2%	0.4%
Europe	27.6%	15.5%
Asia	44.5%	58.3%
S. America	6.5%	6.7%
N. America	13.8%	7.1%
Africa	6.7%	12.0%

ANIMAL PRODUCTS

Traditionally, food animals subsisted on land unsuitable for cultivation, supporting agricultural production with their fertilizing dung. But free-ranging animals grow slowly and yield less meat than those more intensively reared; the demands of urban markets in the developed world have encouraged the growth of factory-like production methods. A large proportion of staple crops, especially cereals, are fed to animals, an inefficient way to produce protein but one likely to continue as long as people value meat and dairy products in their diet.

Cheese: Least perishable of all dairy products, cheese is milk fermented with selected bacterial strains to produce a foodstuff with a potentially immense range of flavours and textures. The vast majority of cheeses are made from cow's milk, although sheep and goat cheeses are highly prized.

USA 24.2% · France 11.3% · Germany 9.5% · Italy 6.5% · Netherlands 4.7%

World total (1993): 13,533,000 tonnes

Lamb and Mutton: Sheep are the least demanding of domestic animals. Although unsuited to intensive rearing, they can thrive on marginal pastureland incapable of supporting beef cattle on a commercial scale. Sheep are raised as much for their valuable wool as for the meat that they provide, with Australia the world leader.

China 10.1% · Australia 9.2% · New Zealand 7.2% · UK 4.5% · Turkey 4.4% · Pakistan 4.2%

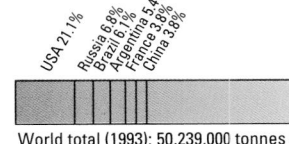

World total (1993): 6,914,000 tonnes

Beef and Veal: Most beef and veal is reared for home markets, and the top five producers are also the biggest consumers. The USA produces nearly a quarter of the world's beef and eats even more.

USA 21.1% · Russia 8.8% · Brazil 6.1% · Argentina 5.4% · France 3.8% · China 3.8%

World total (1993): 50,239,000 tonnes

Sugar cane: Confined to tropical regions, cane sugar accounts for the bulk of international trade in the commodity. Most is produced as a foodstuff, but some countries, notably Brazil and South Africa, distill sugar cane and use the resulting ethyl alcohol to make motor fuels.

Brazil 24.2% · India 22.2% · China 6.6% · Cuba 4.0% · Mexico 4.0% · Pakistan 3.7%

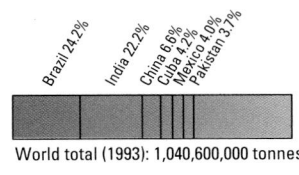

World total (1993): 1,040,600,000 tonnes

SUGARS

Milk: Many human groups, including most Asians, find raw milk indigestible after infancy, and it is often only the starting point for other dairy products such as butter, cheese and yoghurt. Most world production comes from cows, but sheep's milk and goats' milk are also important.

USA 15.1% · Russia 9.4% · India 8.6% · Germany 6.2% · France 5.5% · Ukraine 4.0%

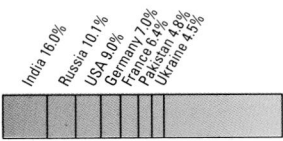

World total (1993): 453,733,000 tonnes

Butter: A traditional source of vitamin A as well as calories, butter has lost much popularity in the developed world for health reasons, although it remains a valuable food. Most butter from India, the world's largest producer, is clarified into ghee, which has religious as well as nutritional importance.

India 16.0% · Russia 10.1% · USA 9.0% · France 6.4% · Pakistan 4.8% · Ukraine 4.5%

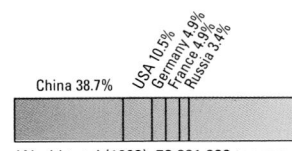

World total (1993): 6,956,000 tonnes

Pork: Although pork is forbidden to many millions, notably Muslims, on religious grounds, more is produced than any other meat in the world, mainly because it is the cheapest. It accounts for about 90% of China's meat output, although per capita meat consumption is relatively low.

China 38.7% · USA 10.5% · Germany 4.9% · France 4.9% · Russia 3.4%

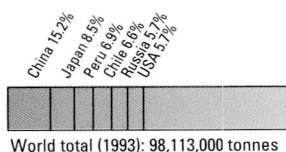

World total (1993): 73,891,000 tonnes

Fish: Commercial fishing requires large shoals of fish, often of only one species, within easy reach of markets. Although the great majority are caught wild in the sea, fish farming of both marine and freshwater species is assuming increasing importance, especially as natural stocks become depleted.

China 15.2% · Japan 8.5% · Peru 5.9% · Chile 6.6% · Russia 5.7% · USA 5.7%

World total (1993): 98,113,000 tonnes

Sugar beet: A temperate crop closely related to the humble beetroot, sugar beet's yield after processing is indistinguishable from cane sugar. Sugar beet is steadily replacing sugar cane imports in Europe, to the detriment of the developing countries that rely on it as a major cash crop.

Ukraine 12.0% · France 11.3% · Germany 10.2% · Russia 9.1% · USA 8.5% · Poland 5.5% · Turkey 5.5%

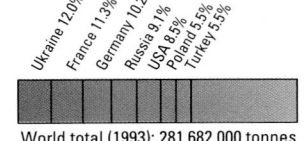

World total (1993): 281,682,000 tonnes

PRODUCTION: ENERGY

We live in a high-energy civilization. While vast discrepancies exist between rich and poor – a North American consumes 13 times as much energy as a Chinese, for example – even developing nations have more power at their disposal than was imaginable a century ago. Abundant energy supplies keep us warm or cool, fuel our industries and our transport systems, and even feed us: high-intensity agriculture, with its fertilizers, pesticides and machinery, is heavily energy-dependent.

Unfortunately, most of the world's energy comes from fossil fuels: coal, oil and gas deposits laid down over many millions of years. These are the Earth's capital, not its income, and we are consuming that capital at an alarming rate. New discoveries have persistently extended the known reserves: in 1989, the reserves-to-production ratio for oil assured over 45 years' supply, an improvement of almost a decade on the 1970 situation. But despite the effort and ingenuity of prospectors, stocks are clearly limited. They are also very unequally distributed, with the Middle East accounting for most oil reserves, and the CIS, especially Russia, possessing an even higher proportion of the world's natural gas. Coal reserves are more evenly shared, and also more plentiful: coal will outlast oil and gas by a very wide margin.

It is possible to reduce energy demand by improving efficiency: most industrial nations have dramatically increased output since the 1970s without a matching rise in energy consumption. But as fossil stocks continue to diminish, renewable energy sources – solar, wave and wind power, as well as hydro-electricity – must take on greater importance.

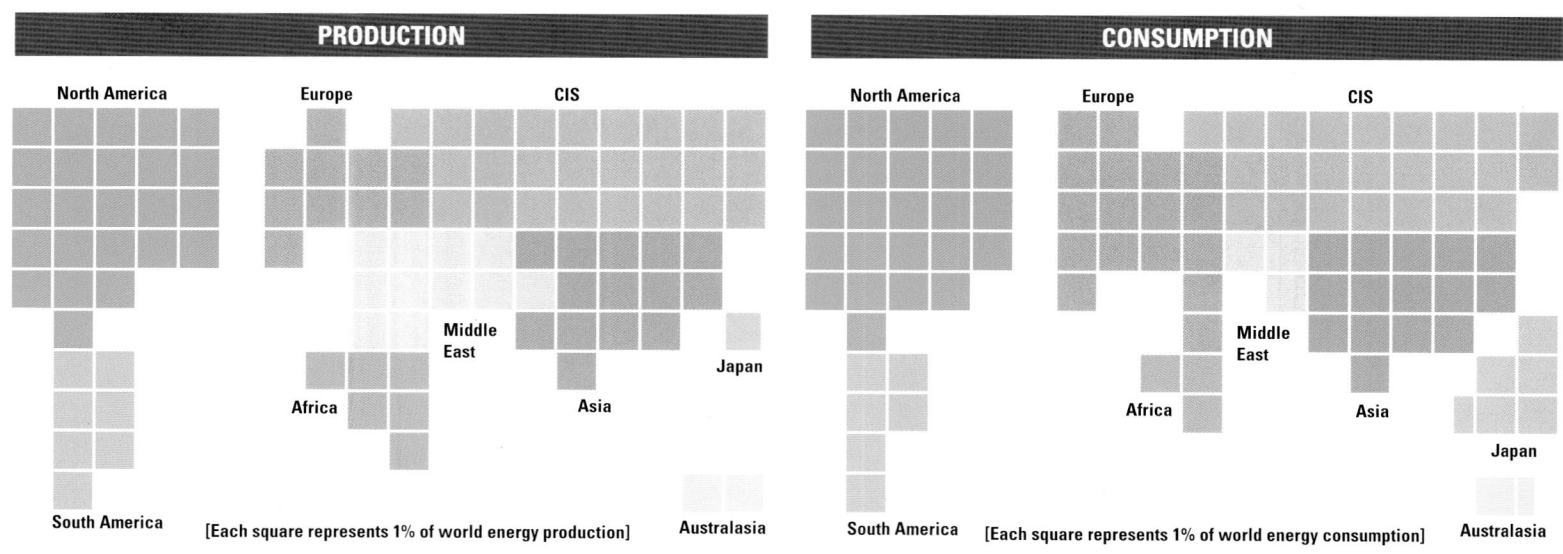

PRODUCTION

North America · Europe · CIS · Middle East · Japan · Africa · Asia · South America · Australasia

[Each square represents 1% of world energy production]

CONSUMPTION

North America · Europe · CIS · Middle East · Japan · Africa · Asia · South America · Australasia

[Each square represents 1% of world energy consumption]

CONVERSIONS

For historical reasons, oil is still traded in barrels. The weight and volume equivalents shown below are all based on average density 'Arabian light' crude oil, and should be considered approximate.

The energy equivalents given for a tonne of oil are also somewhat imprecise: oil and coal of different qualities will have varying energy contents, a fact usually reflected in their price on world markets.

1 barrel:

0.136 tonnes
159 litres
35 Imperial gallons
42 US gallons

1 tonne:

7.33 barrels
1185 litres
256 Imperial gallons
261 US gallons

1 tonne oil:

1.5 tonnes hard coal
3.0 tonnes lignite
12,000 kWh

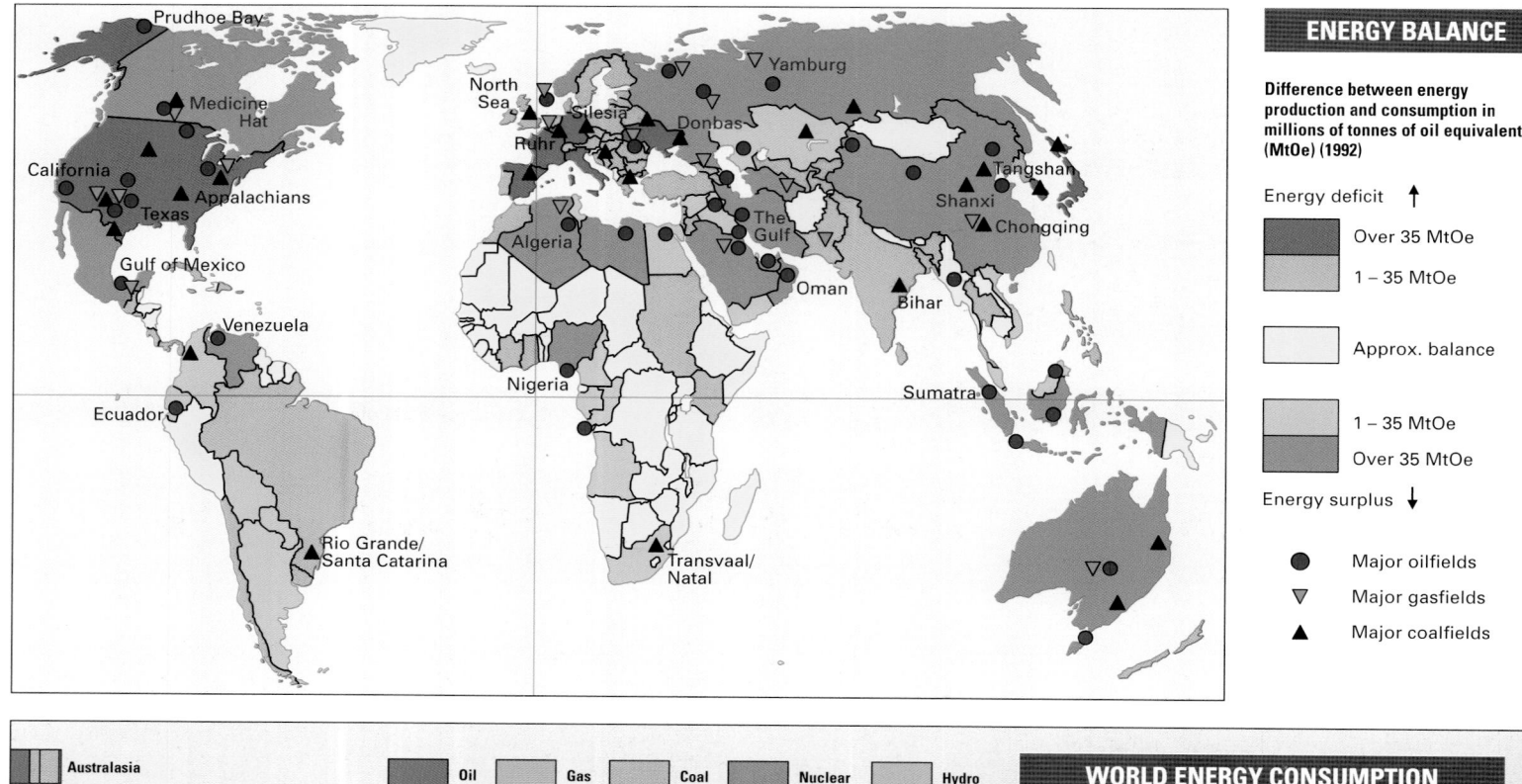

ENERGY BALANCE

Difference between energy production and consumption in millions of tonnes of oil equivalent (MtOe) (1992)

Energy deficit ↑

- Over 35 MtOe
- 1 – 35 MtOe
- Approx. balance
- 1 – 35 MtOe
- Over 35 MtOe

Energy surplus ↓

- ● Major oilfields
- ▽ Major gasfields
- ▲ Major coalfields

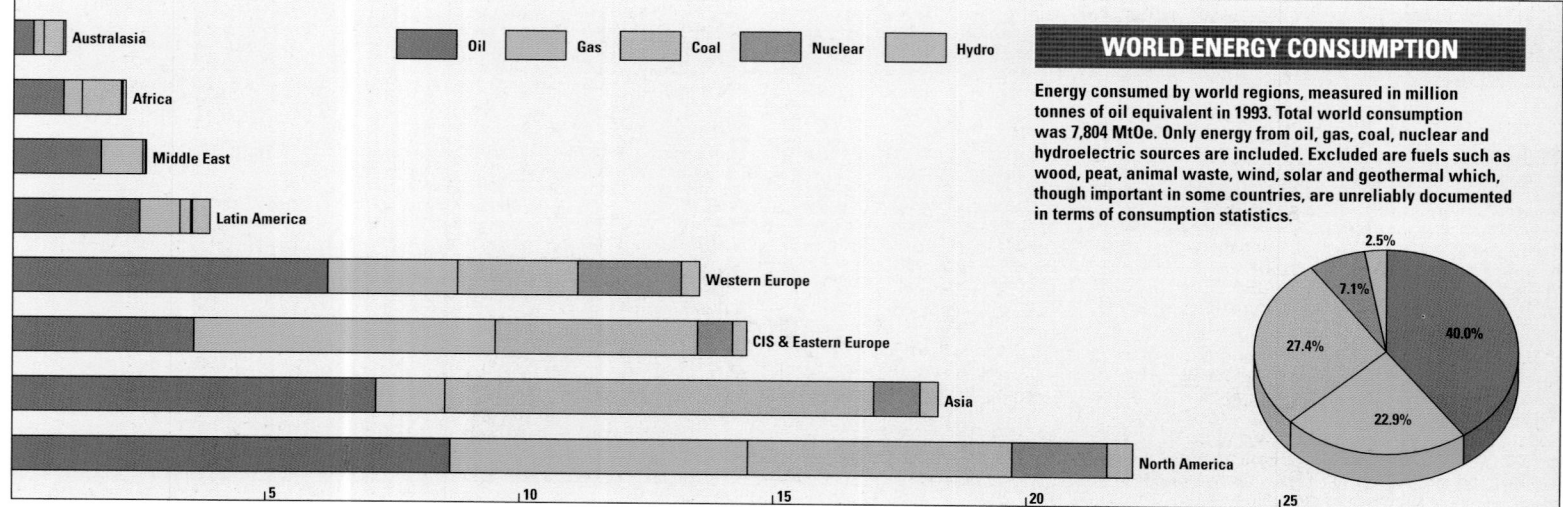

Oil · Gas · Coal · Nuclear · Hydro

Australasia · Africa · Middle East · Latin America · Western Europe · CIS & Eastern Europe · Asia · North America

WORLD ENERGY CONSUMPTION

Energy consumed by world regions, measured in million tonnes of oil equivalent in 1993. Total world consumption was 7,804 MtOe. Only energy from oil, gas, coal, nuclear and hydroelectric sources are included. Excluded are fuels such as wood, peat, animal waste, wind, solar and geothermal which, though important in some countries, are unreliably documented in terms of consumption statistics.

40.0% · 22.9% · 27.4% · 7.1% · 2.5%

FOSSIL FUEL RESERVES

Known world reserves in years as a multiple of annual production, 1970, 1980 and 1989

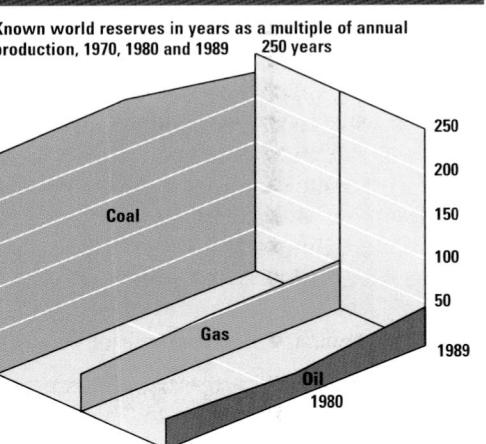

ENERGY AND OUTPUT

Tonnes of oil equivalent consumed to produce US $1,000 of GDP, four industrial nations (1973–89)

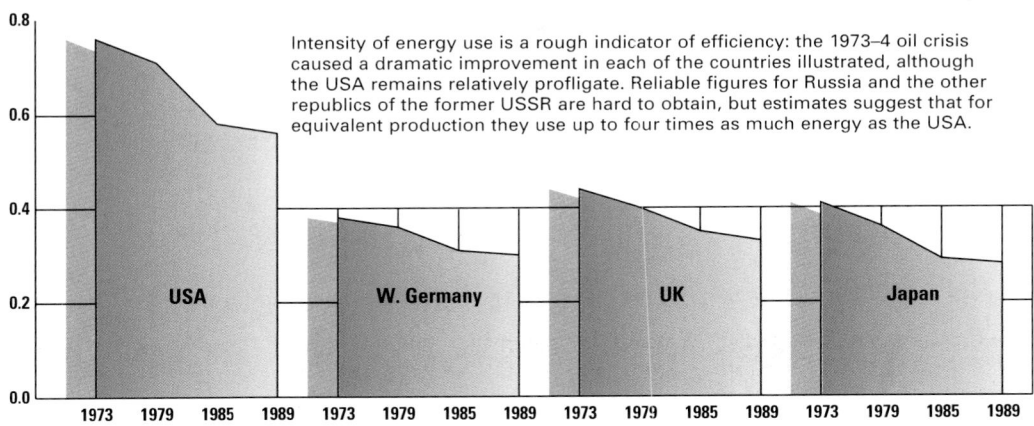

Intensity of energy use is a rough indicator of efficiency: the 1973–4 oil crisis caused a dramatic improvement in each of the countries illustrated, although the USA remains relatively profligate. Reliable figures for Russia and the other republics of the former USSR are hard to obtain, but estimates suggest that for equivalent production they use up to four times as much energy as the USA.

COAL RESERVES

World coal reserves by region and country, thousand million tonnes (latest available year)

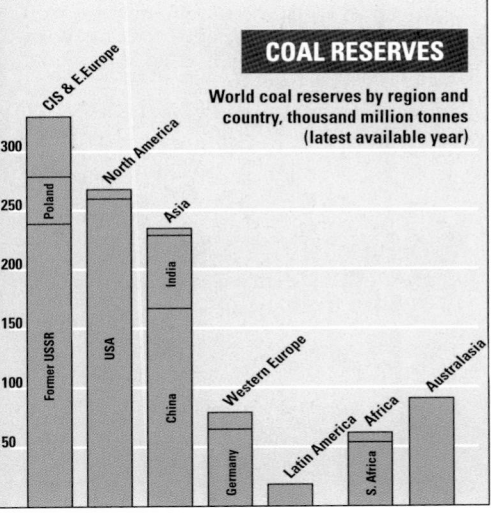

GAS RESERVES

World natural gas reserves by region and country, thousand million tonnes (latest available year)

Ca: Canada
In: Indonesia
Ma: Malaysia
AD: Abu Dhabi
SA: Saudi Arabia
Qa: Qatar
Iq: Iraq
No: Norway
Ne: Netherlands
Ve: Venezuela
Mx: Mexico
Al: Algeria
Ni: Nigeria

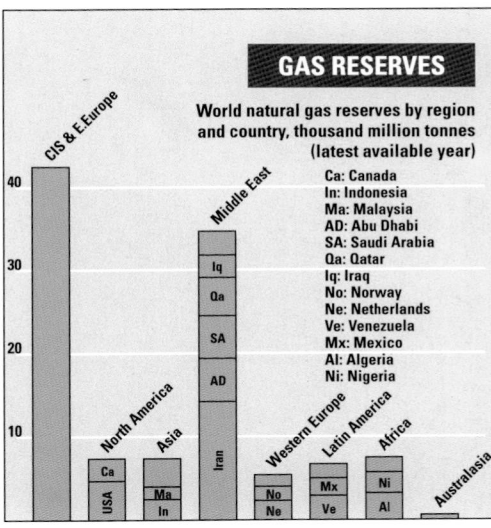

OIL RESERVES

World oil reserves by region and country, thousand million tonnes (latest available year)

A: Abu Dhabi
Ve: Venezuela
M: Mexico

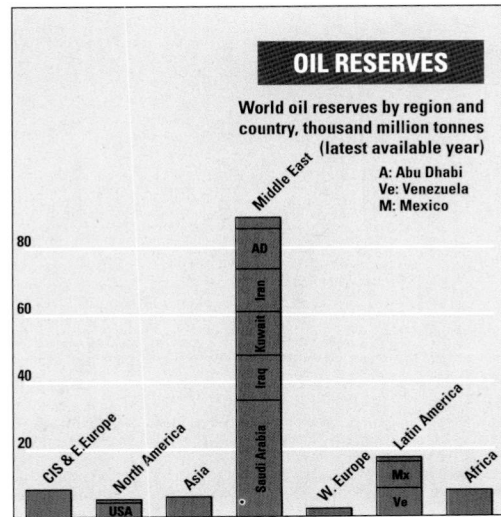

OIL MOVEMENTS

Major world movements of oil in millions of tonnes (1993)

Middle East to Western Europe	163
Middle East to Japan	126
Middle East to Asia (excl. Japan and China)	119
Mexico and Venezuela to Western Europe	100
Middle East to USA	82
Russia to Western Europe	49
Libya to Western Europe	47
Canada to USA	42
Nigeria to USA	36
Nigeria to Western Europe	27
Latin America to Western Europe	24
Western Europe (Norway and UK) to USA	21
Indonesia to Japan	18
Middle East to Latin America	16

Total world movements: 1,376 million tonnes

Only inter-regional movements in excess of 15 million tonnes are shown.

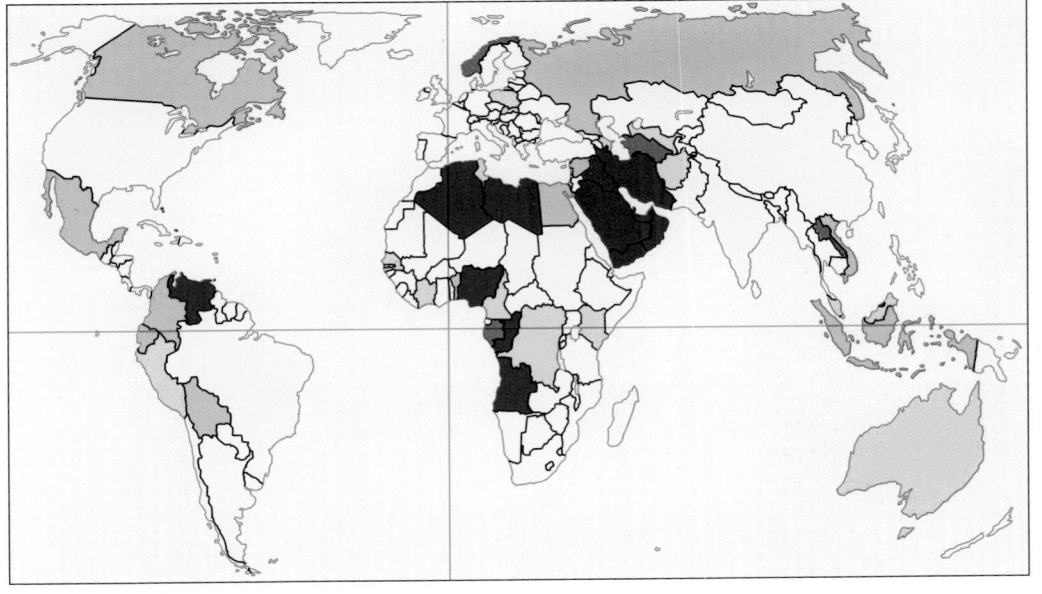

FUEL EXPORTS

Fuels as a percentage of total value of exports (latest available year)

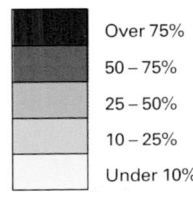

- Over 75%
- 50 – 75%
- 25 – 50%
- 10 – 25%
- Under 10%

NUCLEAR POWER

Percentage of electricity generated by nuclear power stations, leading nations (1994)

1. Lithuania	76%	11. Spain	35%
2. France	75%	12. Taiwan	32%
3. Belgium	56%	13. Finland	30%
4. Sweden	51%	14. Germany	29%
5. Slovak Rep.	49%	15. Ukraine	29%
6. Bulgaria	46%	16. Czech Rep.	28%
7. Hungary	44%	17. Japan	27%
8. Slovenia	38%	18. UK	26%
9. Switzerland	37%	19. USA	22%
10. South Korea	36%	20. Canada	19%

Although the 1980s were a bad time for the nuclear power industry (major projects ran over budget and fears of long-term environmental damage were heavily reinforced by the 1986 disaster at Chernobyl), the industry picked up in the early 1990s. Whilst the number of reactors is still increasing, however, orders for new plants have shrunk. This is partly due to the increasingly difficult task of disposing of nuclear waste.

HYDROELECTRICITY

Percentage of electricity generated by hydroelectric power stations, leading nations (1992)

1. Paraguay	99.9%	11. Zaïre	97.4%
2. Norway	99.6%	12. Cameroon	97.2%
3. Bhutan	99.6%	13. Albania	96.1%
4. Zambia	99.5%	14. Laos	95.3%
5. Ghana	99.3%	15. Iceland	94.8%
6. Congo	99.3%	16. Nepal	93.4%
7. Uganda	99.2%	17. Brazil	92.6%
8. Burundi	98.1%	18. Honduras	91.4%
9. Malawi	98.0%	19. Guatemala	89.7%
10. Rwanda	97.8%	20. Uruguay	89.0%

Countries heavily reliant on hydroelectricity are usually small and non-industrial: a high proportion of hydroelectric power more often reflects a modest energy budget than vast hydroelectric resources. The USA, for instance, produces only 9% of power requirements from hydroelectricity; yet that 9% amounts to more than three times the hydro-power generated by all of Africa.

ALTERNATIVE ENERGY SOURCES

Solar: Each year the Sun bestows upon the Earth almost a million times as much energy as is locked up in all the planet's oil reserves, but only an insignificant fraction is trapped and used commercially. In some experimental installations, mirrors focus the Sun's rays on to boilers, whose steam generates electricity by spinning turbines. Solar cells turn the sunlight into electricity directly, and although efficiencies are still low, advancing technology offers some prospect of using the Sun as the main world electricity source by 2100.

Wind: Caused by uneven heating of the Earth, winds are themselves a form of solar energy. Windmills have been used for centuries to turn wind power into mechanical work; recent models, often arranged in banks on gust-swept high ground, usually generate electricity.

Tidal: The energy from tides is potentially enormous, although only a few installations have been built to exploit it. In theory at least, waves and currents could also provide almost unimaginable power, and the thermal differences in the ocean depths are another huge well of potential energy. But work on extracting it is still in the experimental stage.

Geothermal: The Earth's temperature rises by 1°C for every 30 metres' descent, with much steeper temperature gradients in geologically active areas. El Salvador, for example, produces 39% of its electricity from geothermal power stations. More than 130 are operating worldwide.

Biomass: The oldest of human fuels ranges from animal dung, still burned in cooking fires in much of North Africa and elsewhere, to sugar cane plantations feeding high-technology distilleries to produce ethanol for motor vehicle engines. In Brazil and South Africa, plant ethanol provides up to 25% of motor fuel. Throughout the developing world, most biomass energy comes from firewood: although accurate figures are impossible to obtain, it may yield as much as 10% of the world's total energy consumption.

PRODUCTION: MINERALS

Even during the Stone Age, when humans often settled near the outcrops of flint on which their technology depended, mineral resources have attracted human exploiters. Their descendants have learned how to make use of almost every known element. These elements can be found, in one form or another, somewhere in the Earth's bountiful crust. Iron remains the most important, but modern industrial civilization has a voracious appetite for virtually all of them.

Mineral deposits once dictated the site of new industries; today, most industrial countries are heavily dependent on imports for many of their key materials. Most mining, and much refining of raw ores, is done in developing countries, where labour is cheap.

The main map below shows the richest sources of the most important minerals at present; some reserves – lead and mercury, for example – are running very low. The map takes no account of undersea deposits, most of which are considered inaccessible. Growing shortages, though, may encourage submarine mining: plans have already been made to recover the nodules of manganese found widely scattered on ocean floors.

MINERAL EXPORTS

Minerals and metals as a percentage of total exports (latest available year)

- Over 50%
- 10 – 50%
- 5 – 10%
- Under 5%

Direction of trade

- Copper
- Iron
- Bauxite (Aluminium)

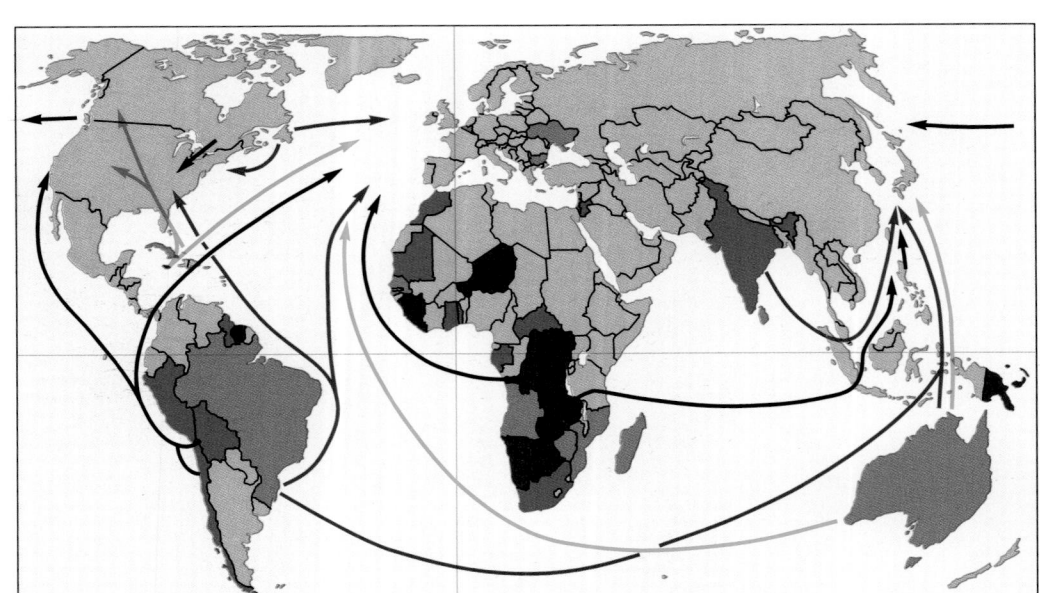

URANIUM

In its pure state, uranium is an immensely heavy, white metal; but although spent uranium is employed as projectiles in anti-missile cannons, where its mass ensures a lethal punch, its main use is as a fuel in nuclear reactors, and in nuclear weaponry. Uranium is very scarce: the main source is the rare ore pitchblende, which itself contains only 0.2% uranium oxide. Only a minute fraction of that is the radioactive U^{235} isotope, though so-called breeder reactors can transmute the more common U^{238} into highly radioactive plutonium.

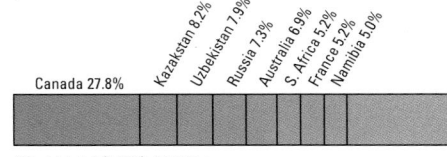

Canada 27.8% | Kazakstan 8.2% | Uzbekistan 7.9% | Russia 7.3% | Australia 6.9% | S. Africa 5.2% | France 5.2% | Namibia 5.0%

World total (1993): 33,000 tonnes

METALS

* Figures for aluminium are for refined metal; all other figures refer to ore production.

The world's leading producers of aluminium ore (bauxite) in 1993 were as follows:
1. Australia (36.2%)
2. Guinea (14.9%)
3. Jamaica (9.8%)
4. Brazil (8.3%),
5. Russia (6.7%)
6. China (5.7%)
7. India (4.6%)
8. Surinam (2.8%)
9. Venezuela (2.6%)
10. Greece (1.9%)

DIAMOND

Most of the world's diamond is found in kimberlite, or 'blue ground', a basic peridotite rock; erosion may wash the diamond from its kimberlite matrix and deposit it with sand or gravel on river beds. Only a small proportion of the world's diamond, the most flawless, is cut into gemstones – 'diamonds'; most is used in industry, where the material's remarkable hardness and abrasion resistance finds a use in cutting tools, drills and dies, as well as in styluses. Australia, not among the top 12 producers at the beginning of the 1980s, had by 1986 become world leader and by 1993 was the source of 40.6% of world production. The other main producers were Zaïre (16.3%), Botswana (14.6%), Russia (11.4%) and South Africa (9.7%). Between them, these five nations accounted for over 82% of the world total of 100,850,000 carats.

Aluminium: Produced mainly from its oxide, bauxite, which yields 25% of its weight in aluminium. The cost of refining and production is often too high for producer-countries to bear, so bauxite is largely exported. Lightweight and corrosion resistant, aluminium alloys are widely used in aircraft, vehicles, cans and packaging.

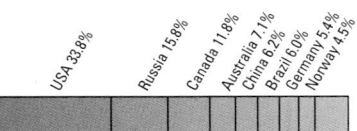

USA 33.8% | Russia 15.8% | Canada 11.8% | Australia 7.1% | China 6.2% | Brazil 6.0% | Germany 5.4% | Norway 4.5%

World total (1993): 19,609,000 tonnes *

Lead: A soft metal, obtained mainly from galena (lead sulphide), which occurs in veins associated with iron, zinc and silver sulphides. Its use in vehicle batteries accounts for the USA's prime consumer status; lead is also made into sheeting and piping. Its use as an additive to paints and petrol is decreasing.

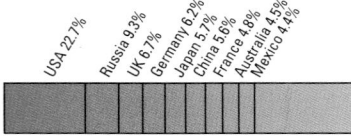

USA 22.7% | Russia 9.3% | UK 6.7% | Germany 6.2% | Japan 5.7% | China 5.6% | France 4.8% | Australia 4.5% | Mexico 4.4%

World total (1993): 5,400,000 tonnes *

Tin: Soft, pliable and non-toxic, used to coat 'tin' (tin-plated steel) cans, in the manufacture of foils and in alloys. The principal tin-bearing mineral is cassiterite (SnO_2), found in ore formed from molten rock. Producers and refiners were hit by a price collapse in 1991.

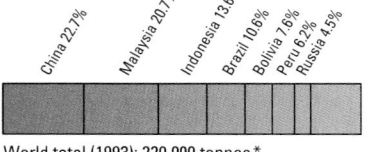

China 22.7% | Malaysia 20.7% | Indonesia 13.6% | Brazil 10.6% | Bolivia 7.6% | Peru 6.2% | Russia 4.3%

World total (1993): 220,000 tonnes *

Gold: Regarded for centuries as the most valuable metal in the world and used to make coins, gold is still recognized as the monetary standard. A soft metal, it is alloyed to make jewellery; the electronics industry values its corrosion resistance and conductivity.

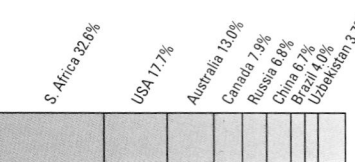

S. Africa 32.6% | USA 17.7% | Australia 13.0% | Canada 7.9% | Russia 6.8% | Brazil 4.0% | Uzbekistan 3.7%

World total (1993): 1,900 tonnes *

Copper: Derived from low-yielding sulphide ores, copper is an important export for several developing countries. An excellent conductor of heat and electricity, it forms part of most electrical items, and is used in the manufacture of brass and bronze. Major importers include Japan and Germany.

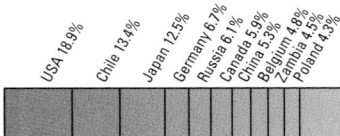

USA 18.9% | Chile 13.4% | Japan 12.5% | Germany 6.7% | Russia 6.1% | Canada 5.9% | China 5.3% | Belgium 4.8% | Zambia 4.5% | Poland 4.3%

World total (1993): 9,500,000 tonnes *

Mercury: The only metal that is liquid at normal temperatures, most is derived from its sulphide, cinnabar, found only in small quantities in volcanic areas. Apart from its value in thermometers and other instruments, most mercury production is used in anti-fungal and anti-fouling preparations, and to make detonators.

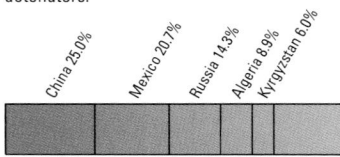

China 25.0% | Mexico 20.7% | Russia 14.3% | Algeria 8.9% | Kyrgyzstan 6.0%

World total (1993): 4,200 tonnes *

Zinc: Often found in association with lead ores, zinc is highly resistant to corrosion, and about 40% of the refined metal is used to plate sheet steel, particularly vehicle bodies – a process known as galvanizing. Zinc is also used in dry batteries, paints and dyes.

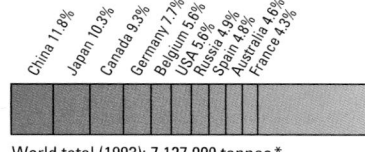

China 11.8% | Japan 10.3% | Canada 9.3% | Germany 7.7% | Belgium 5.6% | USA 5.6% | Spain 4.9% | Australia 4.6% | France 4.3%

World total (1993): 7,127,000 tonnes *

Silver: Most silver comes from ores mined and processed for other metals (including lead and copper). Pure or alloyed with harder metals, it is used for jewellery and ornaments. Industrial use includes dentistry, electronics, photography and as a chemical catalyst.

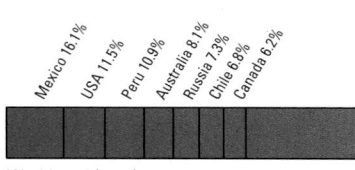

Mexico 16.1% | USA 11.5% | Peru 10.9% | Australia 8.1% | Russia 7.3% | Chile 6.8% | Canada 6.2%

World total (1993): 13,000 tonnes *

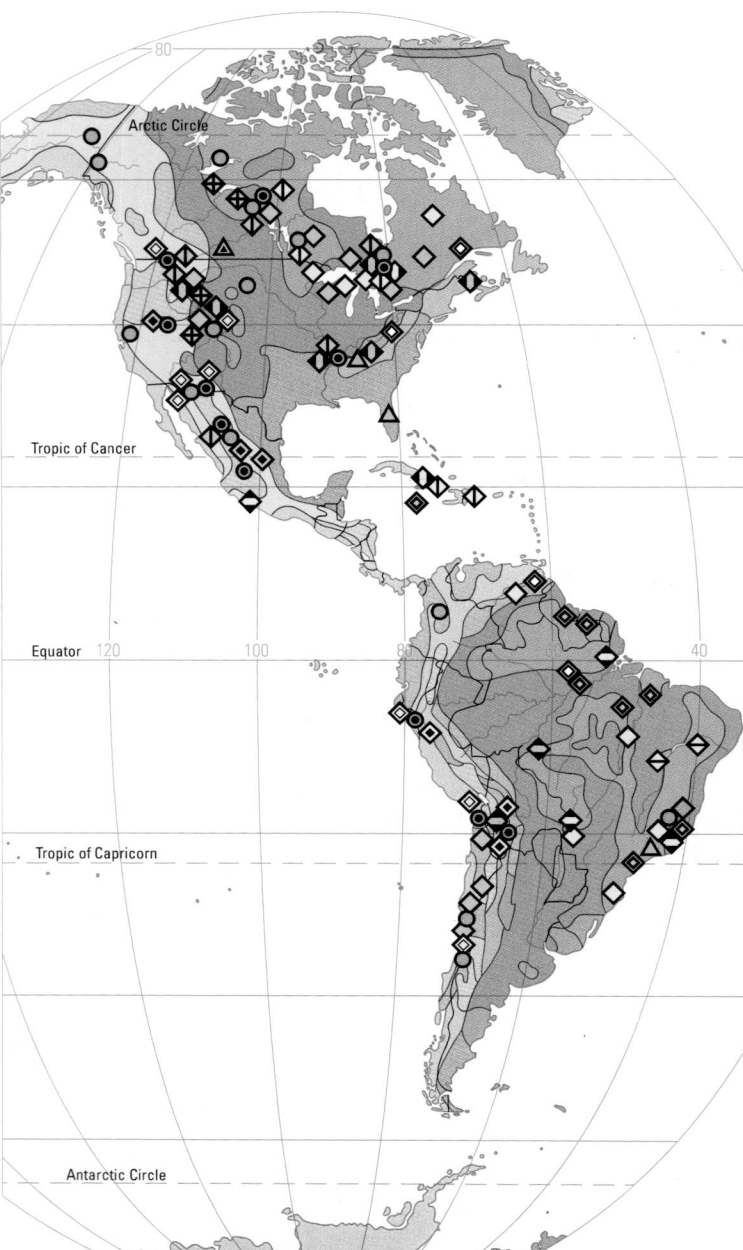

IRON AND FERRO-ALLOYS

Ever since the art of high-temperature smelting was discovered, some time in the second millennium BC, iron has been by far the most important metal known to man. The earliest iron ploughs transformed primitive agriculture and led to the first human population explosion, while iron weapons – or the lack of them – ensured the rise or fall of entire cultures.

Widely distributed around the world, iron ores usually contain 25–60% iron; blast furnaces process the raw product into pig-iron, which is then alloyed with carbon and other minerals to produce steels of various qualities. From the time of the Industrial Revolution, steel has been almost literally the backbone of modern civilization, the prime structural material on which all else is built.

Iron smelting usually developed close to the sources of ore and, later, to the coalfields that fuelled the furnaces. Today, most ore comes from a few richly-endowed locations where large-scale mining is possible. Iron and steel plants are generally built at coastal sites so that giant ore carriers, which account for a sizeable proportion of the world's merchant fleet, can easily discharge their cargoes.

World production of pig-iron and ferro-alloys (1993). All countries with an annual output of more than 1 million tonnes are shown

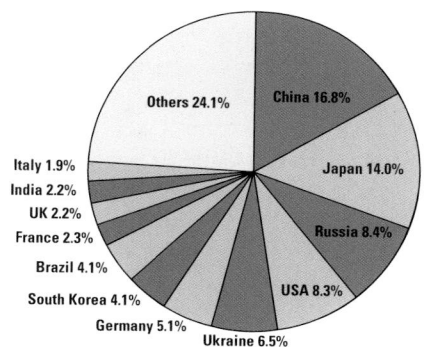

China 16.8%
Japan 14.0%
Russia 8.4%
USA 8.3%
Ukraine 6.5%
Germany 5.1%
South Korea 4.1%
Brazil 4.1%
France 2.3%
UK 2.2%
India 2.2%
Italy 1.9%
Others 24.1%

Total world production: 535 million tonnes

Development of world production of pig-iron and ferro-alloys (1945–93) in million tonnes. Data for a selection of years are shown.

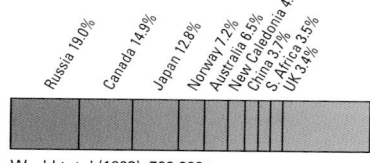

1945, 1950, 1955, 1960, 1965, 1970, 1975, 1976, 1977, 1978, 1979, 1980, 1982, 1984, 1986, 1988, 1990, 1991, 1992, 1993

Chromium: Most of the world's chromium production is alloyed with iron and other metals to produce steels with various different properties. Combined with iron, nickel, cobalt and tungsten, chromium produces an exceptionally hard steel, resistant to heat; chrome steels are used for many household items where utility must be matched with appearance – cutlery, for example. Chromium is also used in production of refractory bricks, and its salts for tanning and dyeing leather and cloth.

Manganese: In its pure state, manganese is a hard, brittle metal. Alloyed with chrome, iron and nickel, it produces abrasion-resistant steels; manganese-aluminium alloys are light but tough. Found in batteries and inks, manganese is also used in glass production. Manganese ores are frequently found in the same location as sedimentary iron ores. Pyrolusite (MnO_2) and psilomelane are the main economically-exploitable sources.

Nickel: Combined with chrome and iron, nickel produces stainless and high-strength steels; similar alloys go to make magnets and electrical heating elements. Nickel combined with copper is widely used to make coins; cupro-nickel alloy is very resistant to corrosion. Its ores yield only modest quantities of nickel – 0.5 to 3.0% – but also contain copper, iron and small amounts of precious metals. Japan, USA, UK, Germany and France are the principal importers.

China 25.0% | Brazil 16.4% | Australia 12.3% | Ukraine 7.4% | India 5.9% | USA 5.8% | Russia 4.3%

World total production of iron ore (1993): 940,000,000 tonnes

Kazakstan 35.2% | S. Africa 28.5% | India 9.1% | Turkey 7.0% | Zimbabwe 5.2% | Finland 4.5%

World total (1993): 9,930,000 tonnes

Ukraine 31.8% | China 19.1% | S. Africa 15.9% | Brazil 9.1% | Gabon 8.2% | Australia 6.6% | India 3.9%

World total (1993): 22,000,000 tonnes

Russia 19.0% | Canada 14.9% | Japan 12.8% | Norway 7.2% | Australia 8.5% | New Caledonia 4.7% | China 3.7% | S. Africa 3.5% | UK 3.4%

World total (1993): 790,000 tonnes

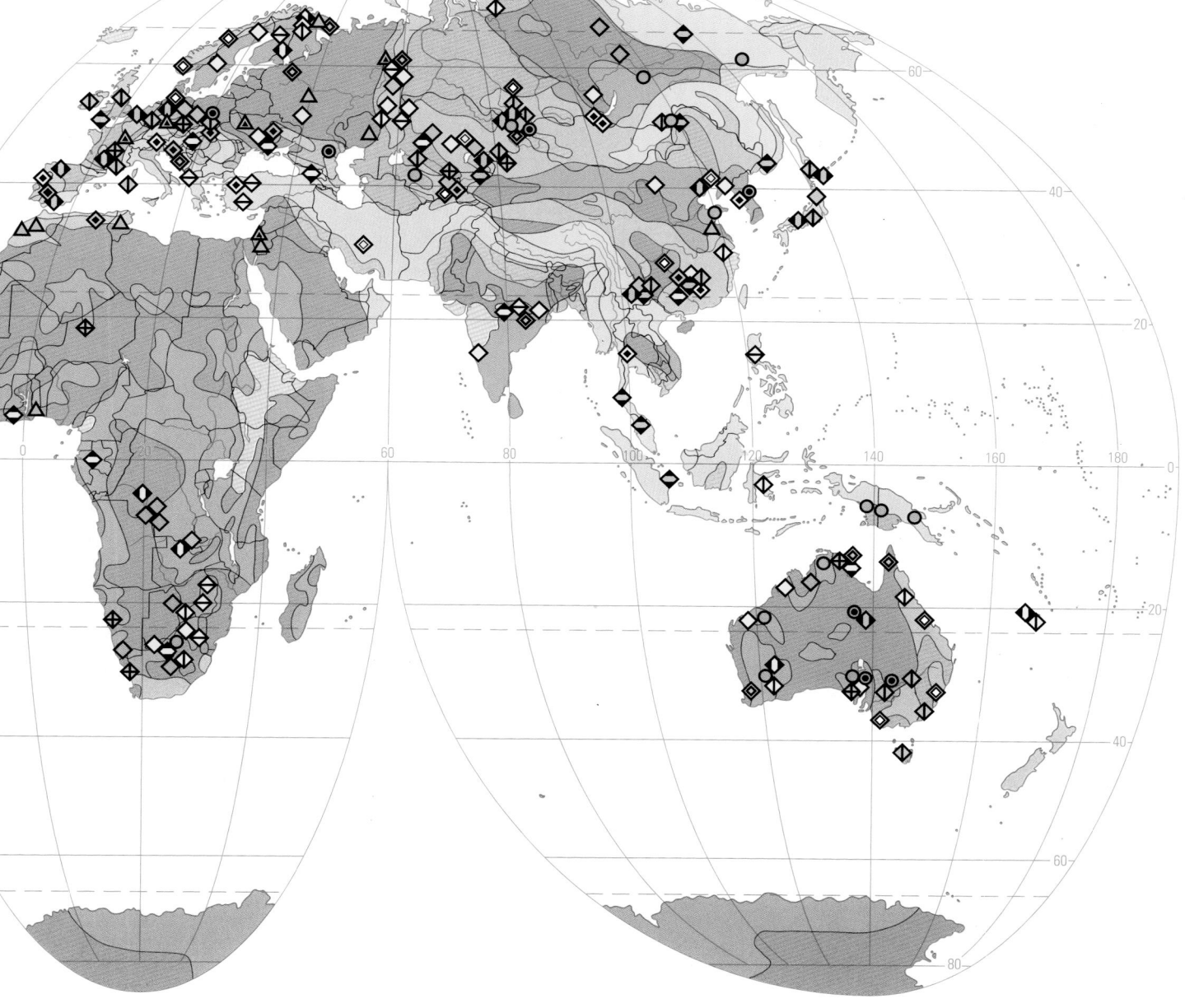

STRUCTURAL REGIONS

- Pre-Cambrian shields
- Sedimentary cover on Pre-Cambrian shields
- Paleozoic (Caledonian & Hercynian) folding
- Sedimentary cover on Paleozoic folding
- Mesozoic folding
- Sedimentary cover on Mesozoic folding
- Cainozoic (Alpine) folding
- Sedimentary cover on Cainozoic folding
- Intensive Mesozoic & Cainozoic vulcanism

DISTRIBUTION

Iron & ferro-alloys
- Chrome
- Cobalt
- Iron Ore
- Manganese
- Molybdenum
- Nickel Ore
- Tungsten

Non-ferrous metals
- Bauxite (Aluminium)
- Copper
- Lead
- Mercury
- Tin
- Zinc
- Uranium

Precious metals & stones
- Diamonds
- Gold
- Silver

Fertilizers
- Phosphates
- Potash

PRODUCTION: MANUFACTURING

In its broadest sense, manufacturing is the application of energy, labour and skill to raw materials in order to transform them into finished goods with a higher value than the various elements used in production.

Since the early days of the Industrial Revolution, manufacturing has implied the use of an organized workforce harnessed to some form of machine. The tendency has consistently been for increasingly expensive human labour to be replaced by increasingly complex machinery, which has evolved over time from water-powered looms to fully-integrated robotic plants.

Obviously, not all the world's industries – or manufacturing countries – have reached the same level. Textiles, for example, the foundation of the early Industrial Revolution in the West, can be mass-produced with fairly modest technology; today, they are usually produced in developing countries, mostly in Asia, where the low labour costs compensate for the large workforce that the relatively simple machinery requires. Nevertheless, the trend towards high-technology production, however uneven, seems inexorable. Gains in efficiency make up for the staggering cost of the equipment itself, and the outcome is that fewer and fewer people are employed to produce more and more goods.

One paradoxical result of the increase in industrial efficiency is a relative decline in the importance of the industrial sector of a nation's economy. The economy has already passed through one transition, generations past, when workers were drawn from the land into factories. The second transition releases labour into what is called the service sector of the economy: a diffuse but vital sector that includes not only such obvious services as transport and administration, but also finance, insurance and activities as diverse as fashion design or the writing of computer software.

The process is far advanced in the mature economies of the West, with Japan not far behind. Almost two-thirds of US wealth, for example, is now generated in the service sector, and less than half of Japan's Gross National Product comes from industry. The shrinkage, though, is only relative: between them, these two industrial giants produce almost twice the amount of manufactured goods as the rest of the world put together. And it is on the solid base of production that their general prosperity is founded.

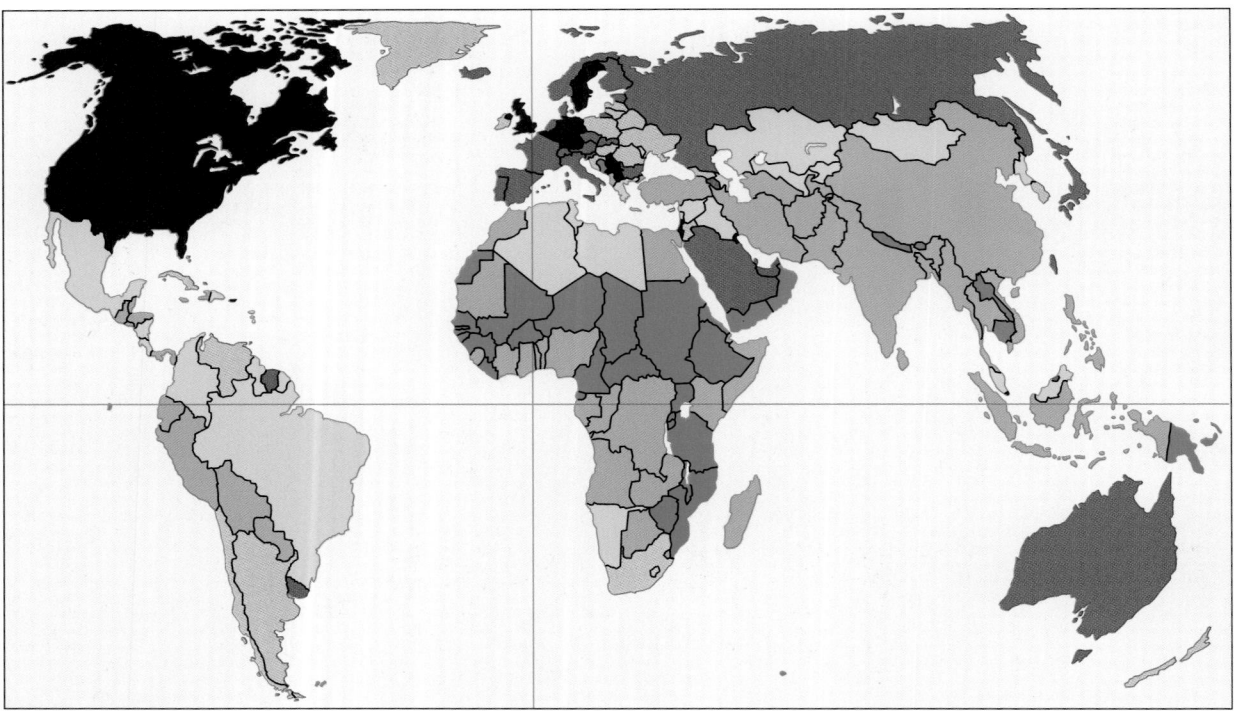

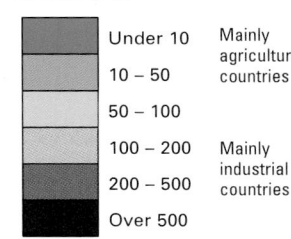

EMPLOYMENT

The number of workers employed in manufacturing for every 100 workers engaged in agriculture (latest available year)

- Under 10 — Mainly agricultural countries
- 10 – 50
- 50 – 100
- 100 – 200 — Mainly industrial countries
- 200 – 500
- Over 500

Selected countries (latest available year)

Singapore	8,860
Hong Kong	3,532
UK	1,270
Belgium	820
Former Yugoslavia	809
Germany	800
Kuwait	767
Bahrain	660
USA	657
Israel	633

DIVISION OF EMPLOYMENT

Distribution of workers between agriculture, industry and services, selected countries (latest available year)

The six countries selected illustrate the usual stages of economic development, from dependence on agriculture through industrial growth to the expansion of the services sector.

- Agriculture
- Industry
- Services

Nepal   Nigeria   Pakistan   Brazil   Hong Kong   USA

THE WORKFORCE

Percentages of men and women between 15 and 64 in employment, selected countries (latest available year)

The figures include employees and self-employed, who in developing countries are often subsistence farmers. People in full-time education are excluded. Because of the population age structure in developing countries, the employed population has to support a far larger number of non-workers than its industrial equivalent. For example, more than 52% of Kenya's people are under 15, an age group that makes up less than a tenth of the UK population.

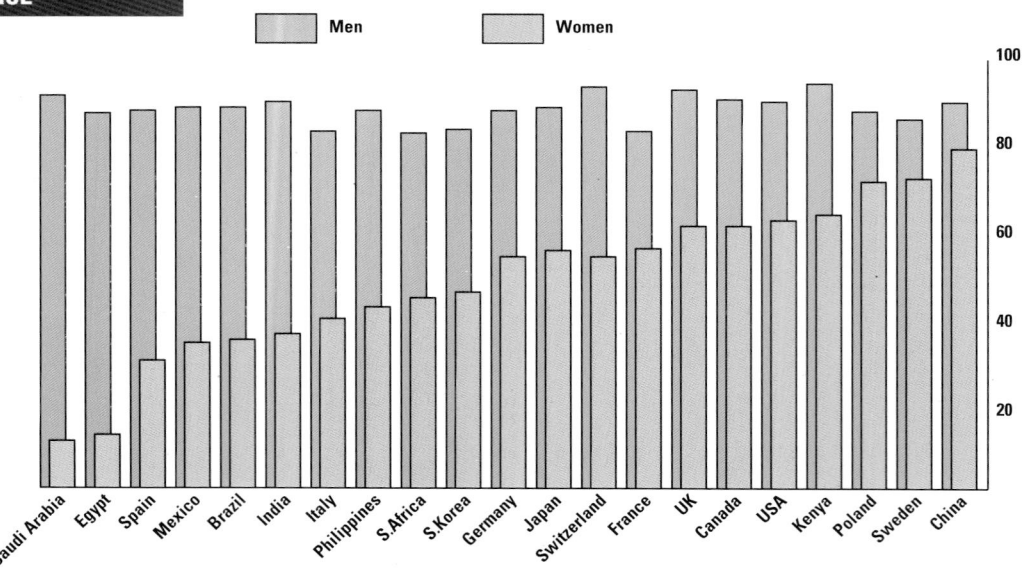

Men   Women

Saudi Arabia, Egypt, Spain, Mexico, Brazil, India, Italy, Philippines, S.Africa, S.Korea, Germany, Japan, Switzerland, France, UK, Canada, USA, Kenya, Poland, Sweden, China

WEALTH CREATION

The Gross National Product (GNP) of the world's largest economies, US $ billion (1993)

1.	USA	6,387,686	21. Sweden	216,294
2.	Japan	3,926,668	22. Belgium	213,435
3.	Germany	1,902,995	23. Austria	183,530
4.	France	1,289,235	24. Denmark	137,610
5.	Italy	1,134,980	25. Indonesia	136,991
6.	UK	1,042,700	26. Saudi Arabia	131,000
7.	China	581,109	27. Turkey	126,330
8.	Canada	574,884	28. Thailand	120,235
9.	Spain	533,986	29. South Africa	118,057
10.	Brazil	471,978	30. Norway	113,527
11.	Russia	348,413	31. Hong Kong	104,731
12.	South Korea	338,062	32. Ukraine	99,677
13.	Mexico	324,951	33. Finland	96,220
14.	Netherlands	316,404	34. Poland	87,315
15.	Australia	309,967	35. Syria	81,700
16.	Iran	300,000	36. Portugal	77,749
17.	India	262,810	37. Greece	76,698
18.	Switzerland	254,066	38. Israel	72,662
19.	Argentina	244,013	39. Malaysia	60,061
20.	Taiwan	225,000	40. Venezuela	58,916

PATTERNS OF PRODUCTION

Breakdown of industrial output by value, selected countries (latest available year)

	Food & agric. products	Textiles & clothing	Machinery & transport	Chemicals	Other
Algeria	26%	20%	11%	1%	41%
Argentina	24%	10%	16%	12%	37%
Australia	18%	7%	21%	8%	45%
Austria	17%	8%	25%	6%	43%
Belgium	19%	8%	23%	13%	36%
Brazil	15%	12%	24%	9%	40%
Burkina Faso	62%	18%	2%	1%	17%
Canada	15%	7%	25%	9%	44%
Denmark	22%	6%	23%	10%	39%
Egypt	20%	27%	13%	10%	31%
Finland	13%	6%	24%	7%	50%
France	18%	7%	33%	9%	33%
Germany	12%	5%	38%	10%	36%
Greece	20%	22%	14%	7%	38%
Hong Kong	6%	40%	20%	2%	33%
Hungary	6%	11%	37%	11%	35%
India	11%	16%	26%	15%	32%
Indonesia	23%	11%	10%	10%	47%
Iran	13%	22%	22%	7%	36%
Israel	13%	10%	28%	8%	42%
Ireland	28%	7%	20%	15%	28%
Italy	7%	13%	32%	10%	38%
Japan	10%	6%	38%	10%	37%
Kenya	35%	12%	14%	9%	29%
Malaysia	21%	5%	23%	14%	37%
Mexico	24%	12%	14%	12%	39%
Netherlands	19%	4%	28%	11%	38%
New Zealand	26%	10%	16%	6%	43%
Norway	21%	3%	26%	7%	44%
Pakistan	34%	21%	8%	12%	25%
Philippines	40%	7%	7%	10%	35%
Poland	15%	16%	30%	6%	33%
Portugal	17%	22%	16%	8%	38%
Singapore	6%	5%	46%	8%	36%
South Africa	14%	8%	17%	11%	49%
South Korea	15%	17%	24%	9%	35%
Spain	17%	9%	22%	9%	43%
Sweden	10%	2%	35%	8%	44%
Thailand	30%	17%	14%	6%	33%
Turkey	20%	14%	15%	8%	43%
UK	14%	6%	32%	11%	36%
USA	12%	5%	35%	10%	38%
Venezuela	23%	8%	9%	11%	49%

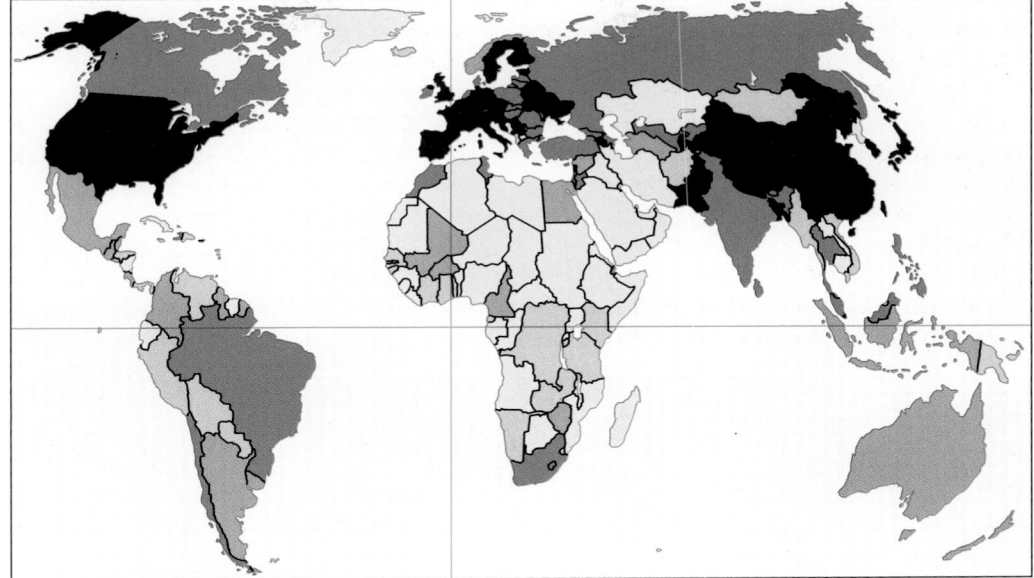
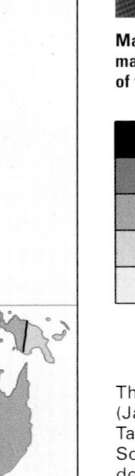

INDUSTRY AND TRADE

Manufactured goods (including machinery and transport) as a percentage of total exports (latest available year)

- Over 75%
- 50 – 75%
- 25 – 50%
- 10 – 25%
- Under 10%

The Far East and South-east Asia (Japan 98.3%, Macau 97.8%, Taiwan 92.7%, Hong Kong 93.0%, South Korea 93.4%) are most dominant, but many countries in Europe (e.g. Slovenia 92.4%) are also heavily dependent on manufactured goods.

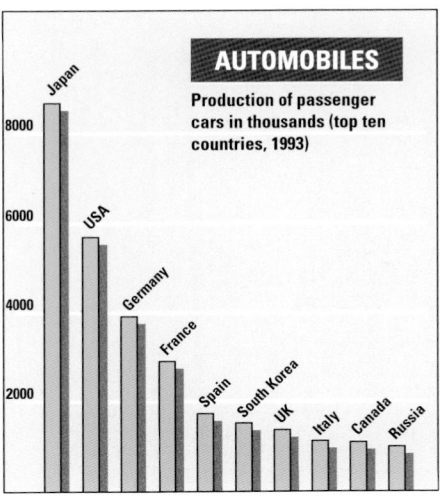

AUTOMOBILES
Production of passenger cars in thousands (top ten countries, 1993)

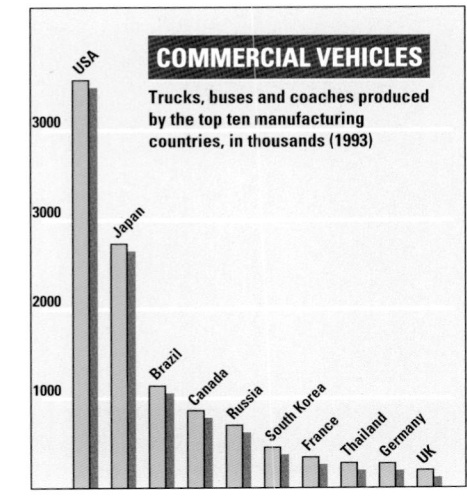

COMMERCIAL VEHICLES
Trucks, buses and coaches produced by the top ten manufacturing countries, in thousands (1993)

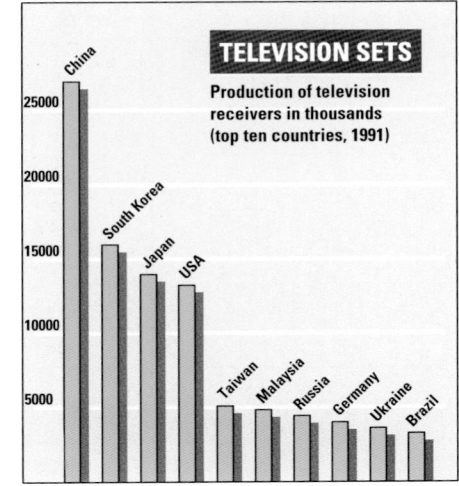

TELEVISION SETS
Production of television receivers in thousands (top ten countries, 1991)

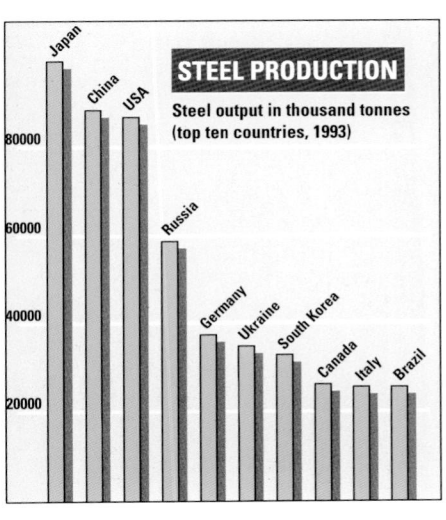

STEEL PRODUCTION
Steel output in thousand tonnes (top ten countries, 1993)

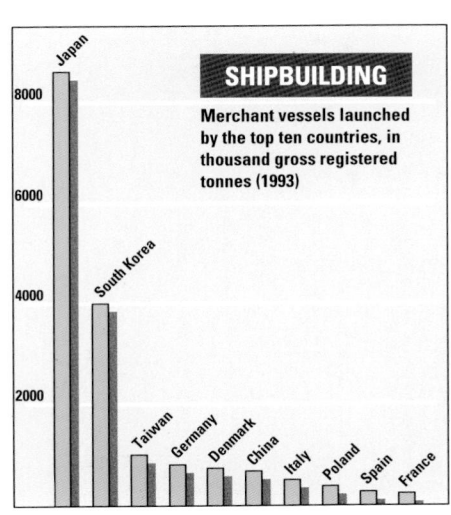

SHIPBUILDING
Merchant vessels launched by the top ten countries, in thousand gross registered tonnes (1993)

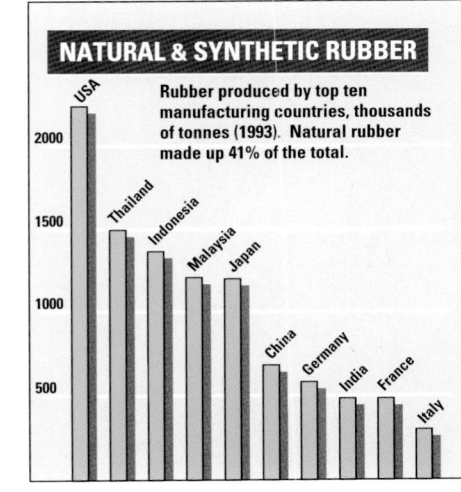

NATURAL & SYNTHETIC RUBBER
Rubber produced by top ten manufacturing countries, thousands of tonnes (1993). Natural rubber made up 41% of the total.

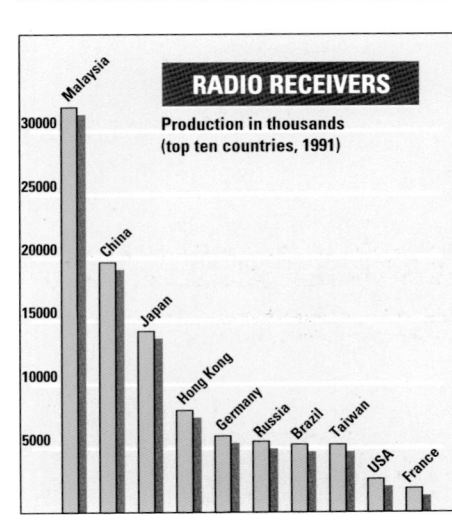

RADIO RECEIVERS
Production in thousands (top ten countries, 1991)

INDUSTRIAL POWER

Industrial output (mining, manufacturing, construction, energy and water production), top 40 nations, US $ billion (1991)

1. USA	1,627	21. Saudi Arabia 56
2. Japan	1,412	22. Indonesia 48
3. Germany	614	23. Spain 47
4. Italy	380	24. Argentina 46
5. France	348	25. Poland 39
6. UK	324	26. Norway 38
7. Former USSR	250	27. Finland 37
8. Brazil	161	28. Thailand 36
9. China	155	29. Turkey 33
10. South Korea	127	30. Denmark 31
11. Canada	117	31. Israel 23
12. Australia	93	32. Iran 20
Netherlands	93	33. Former
14. Taiwan	86	Czechoslovakia 19
15. Mexico	85	34. Hong Kong 17
16. Sweden	70	Portugal ('89) 17
17. Switzerland ('89)	61	36. Algeria 16
18. India	60	Greece 16
19. Austria	59	38. Iraq 15
Belgium	59	Philippines 15
		Singapore 15

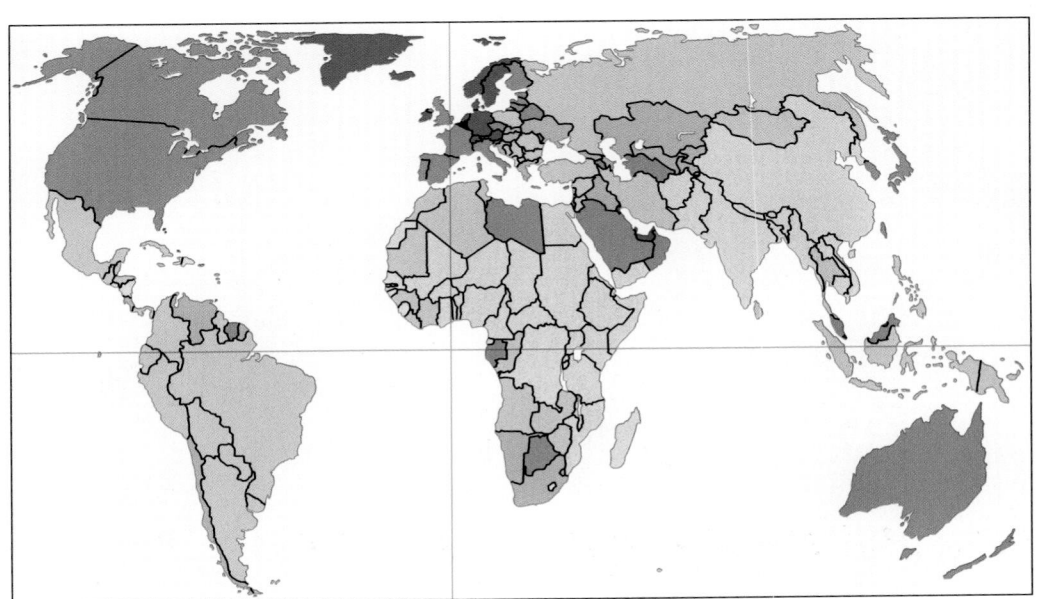

EXPORTS PER CAPITA

Value of exports in US $, divided by total population (latest available year)

- Over 10,000
- 5,000 – 10,000
- 1,000 – 5,000   [UK 3,135]
- 500 – 1,000   [USA 1,967]
- 100 – 500
- Under 100

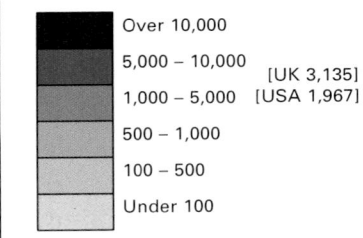

Highest per capita (1993)

Singapore	25,787
Hong Kong	22,339
Benelux	12,295
Brunei	8,778
Netherlands	8,578
Switzerland	8,457

PRODUCTION: TRADE

Trade plays an important role in most of the countries of the world and is a vital aspect of economic development. Despite local fluctuations, trade – the flow of commodities from producers to consumers – grew consistently faster than output throughout the 1980s. A worldwide recession in the first half of the 1990s, however, caused a slump in world trade.

International trade remains dominated by the wealthy, industrialized countries who are involved in 85% of all world trade. Nearly half of all trade flows between the advanced market economies of the EU, USA and Japan, although the Newly Industrialized Countries (NICs) of South-east Asia (predominantly Hong Kong, Singapore, South Korea and Taiwan) are proving increasingly competitive. By comparison, there is relatively little trade between the developing nations. In the poorer countries, trade in a single commodity (usually a mineral or foodstuff) may amount to 50% of GDP or more. Such raw materials are vulnerable to fluctuations in market prices and demand.

The 1990s have seen a widening of the gap between those countries producing raw materials (except oil) and those making a larger profit from the trade in manufactured products. According to the IMF and World Bank, Third World development rests on their ability to expand their trade links and to develop into export-led manufacturing.

WORLD TRADE

Percentage share of total world exports by value (1993)

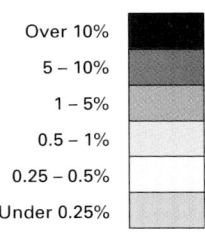

- Over 10%
- 5 – 10%
- 1 – 5%
- 0.5 – 1%
- 0.25 – 0.5%
- Under 0.25%

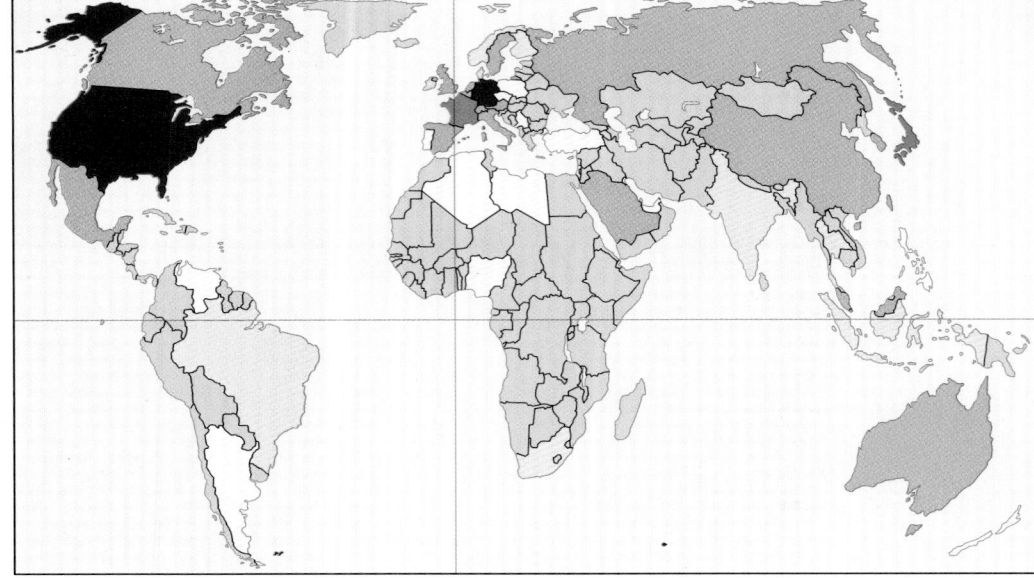

THE GREAT TRADING NATIONS

The imports and exports of the top ten trading nations as a percentage of world trade (latest available year). Each country's trade in manufactured goods is shown in orange.

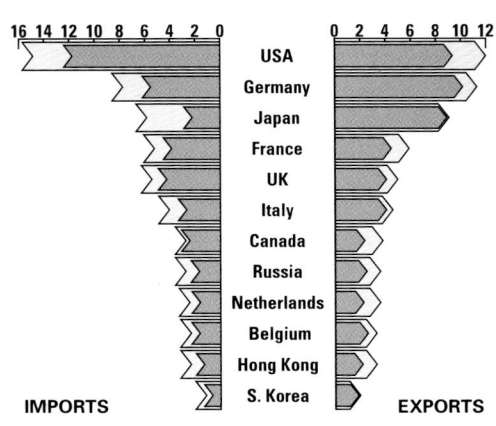

16 14 12 10 8 6 4 2 0   0 2 4 6 8 10 12

USA
Germany
Japan
France
UK
Italy
Canada
Russia
Netherlands
Belgium
Hong Kong
S. Korea

IMPORTS   EXPORTS

MAJOR EXPORTS

Leading manufactured items and their exporters, by percentage of world total in US $ (latest available year)

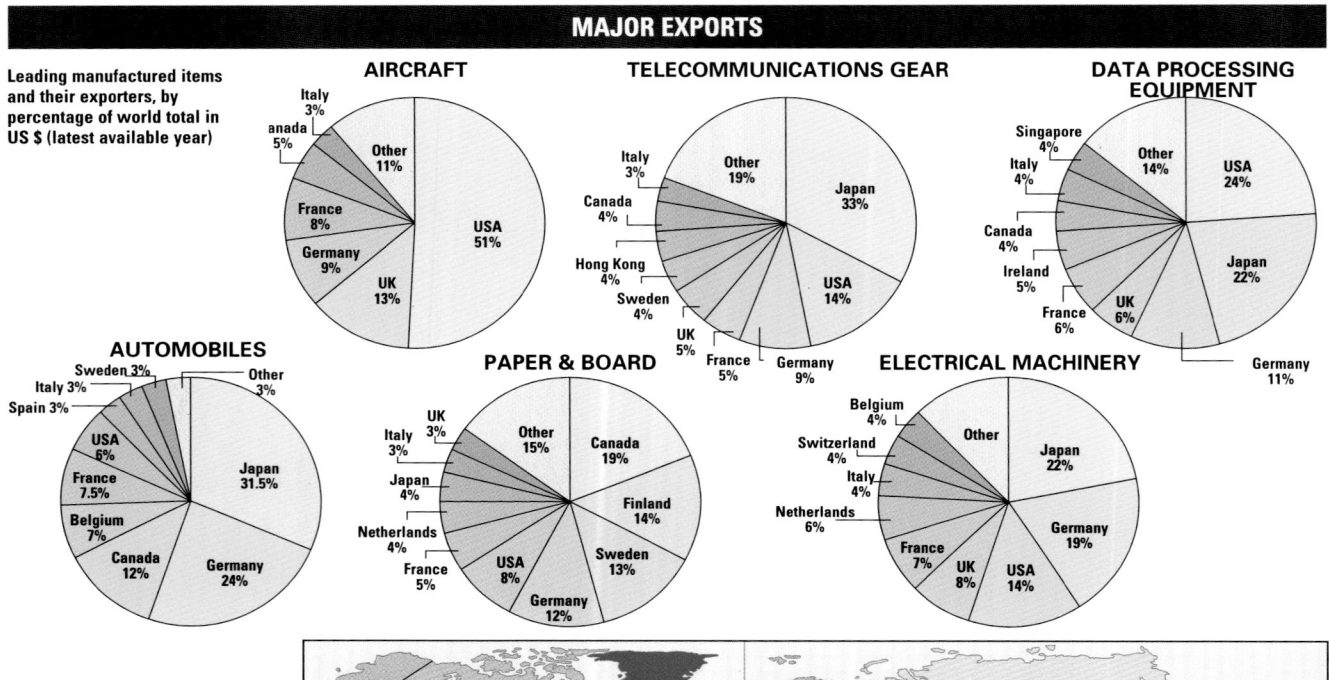

AIRCRAFT
USA 51%, UK 13%, Germany 9%, France 8%, Canada 5%, Italy 3%, Other 11%

TELECOMMUNICATIONS GEAR
Japan 33%, USA 14%, Germany 9%, France 5%, UK 5%, Sweden 4%, Hong Kong 4%, Canada 4%, Italy 3%, Other 19%

DATA PROCESSING EQUIPMENT
USA 24%, Japan 22%, Germany 11%, France 6%, UK 6%, Ireland 5%, Canada 4%, Italy 4%, Singapore 4%, Other 14%

AUTOMOBILES
Japan 31.5%, Germany 24%, Canada 12%, Belgium 7%, France 7.5%, USA 6%, Spain 3%, Italy 3%, Sweden 3%, Other 3%

PAPER & BOARD
Canada 19%, Finland 14%, Sweden 13%, Germany 12%, USA 8%, France 5%, Netherlands 4%, Japan 4%, Italy 3%, UK 3%, Other 15%

ELECTRICAL MACHINERY
Japan 22%, Germany 19%, USA 14%, UK 8%, France 7%, Netherlands 6%, Switzerland 4%, Italy 4%, Belgium 4%, Other

TRADED PRODUCTS

Top ten manufactures traded, by value in billions of US $ (latest available year)

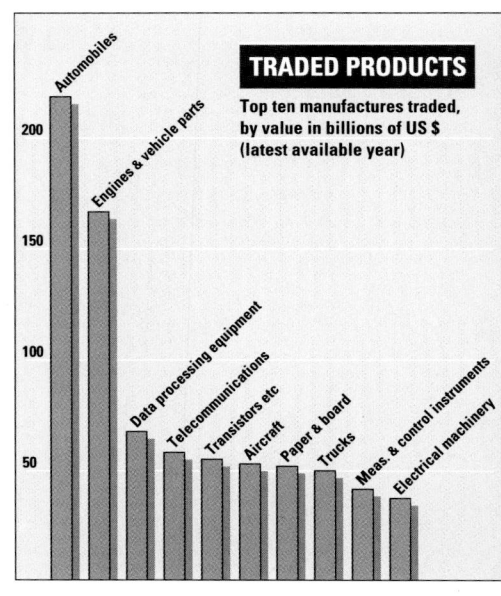

Automobiles
Engines & vehicle parts
Data processing equipment
Telecommunications
Transistors etc
Aircraft
Paper & board
Trucks
Meas. & control instruments
Electrical machinery

DEPENDENCE ON TRADE

Value of exports as a percentage of Gross National Product (1993)

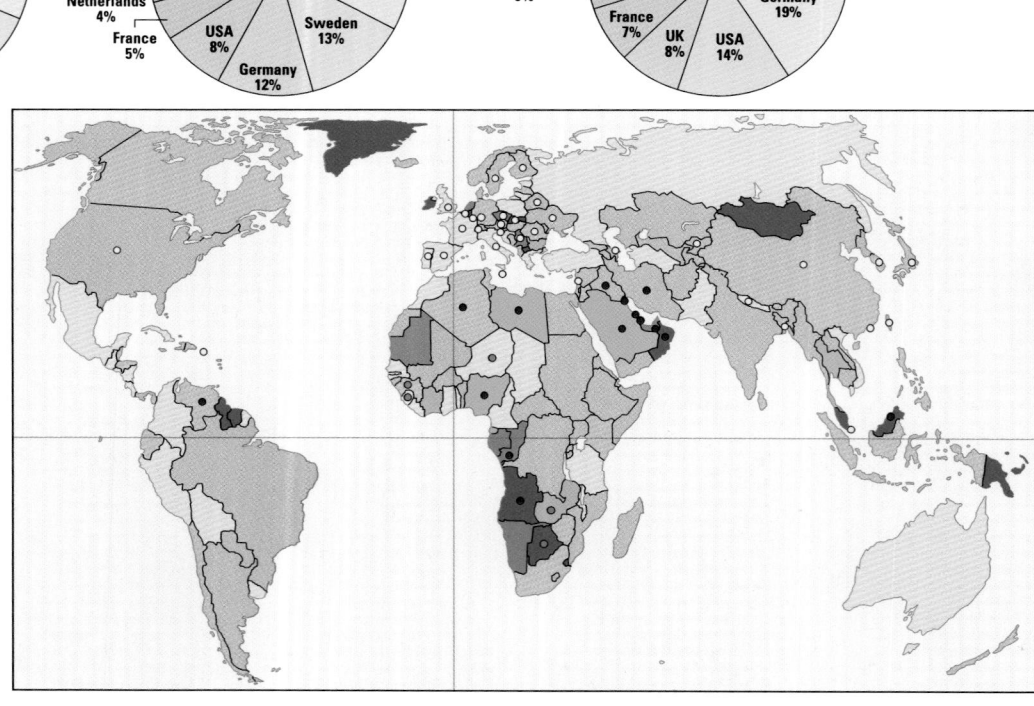

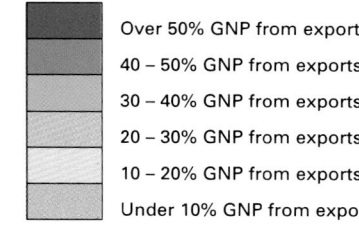

- Over 50% GNP from exports
- 40 – 50% GNP from exports
- 30 – 40% GNP from exports
- 20 – 30% GNP from exports
- 10 – 20% GNP from exports
- Under 10% GNP from exports

- ○ Most dependent on industrial exports (over 75% of total exports)
- ● Most dependent on fuel exports (over 75% of total exports)
- ● Most dependent on metal and mineral exports (over 75% of total exports)

WORLD SHIPPING

While ocean passenger traffic is nowadays relatively modest, sea transport still carries most of the world's trade. Oil and bulk carriers make up the majority of the world fleet, although the general cargo category was the fastest growing in 1989, a year in which total tonnage increased by 1.5%. Two innovations have revolutionized sea transport. The first is the development of the roll-on/roll-off (Ro-Ro) method where lorries or even trains loaded with freight are driven straight on to the ship, thus saving time. The second is containerization in which goods are packed into containers (the dimensions of which are fixed) at the factory, driven to the port and loaded on board by specialist machinery.

Almost 30% of world shipping sails under a 'flag of convenience', whereby owners take advantage of low taxes by registering their vessels in a foreign country the ships will never see, notably Panama and Liberia.

MERCHANT FLEETS

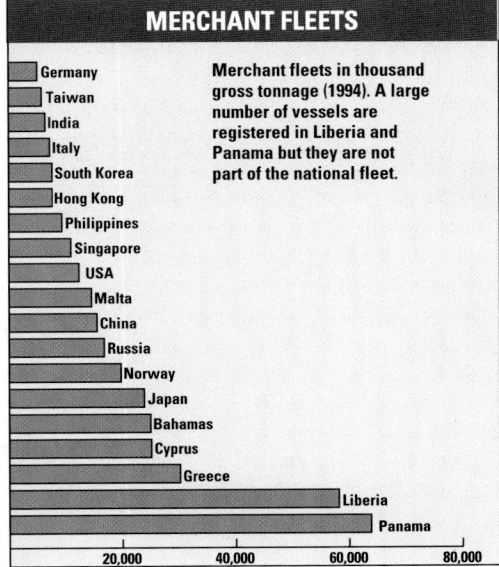

Merchant fleets in thousand gross tonnage (1994). A large number of vessels are registered in Liberia and Panama but they are not part of the national fleet.

Germany
Taiwan
India
Italy
South Korea
Hong Kong
Philippines
Singapore
USA
Malta
China
Russia
Norway
Japan
Bahamas
Cyprus
Greece
Liberia
Panama

20,000 40,000 60,000 80,000

FREIGHT

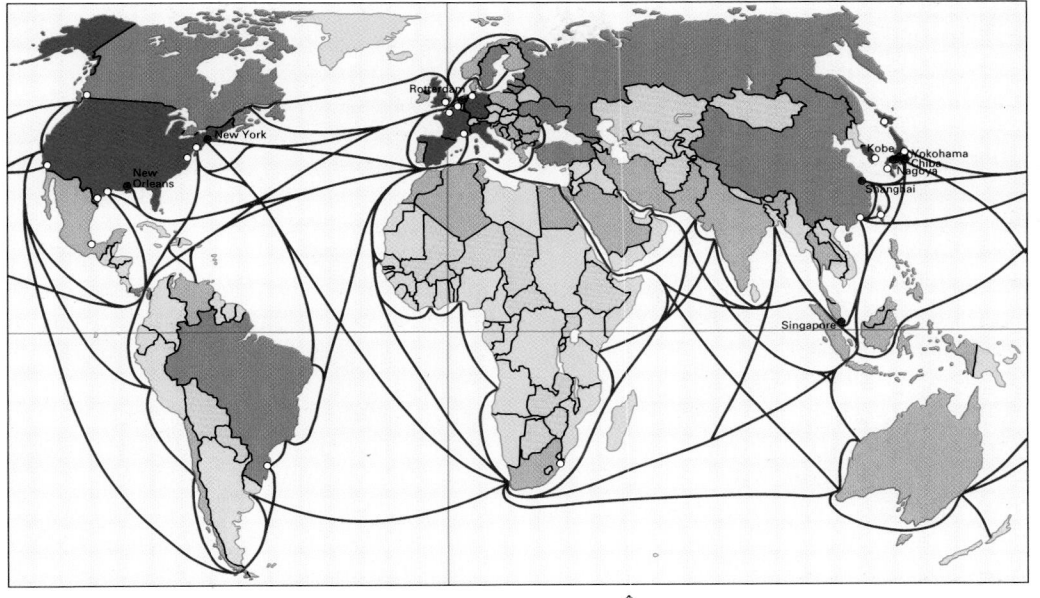

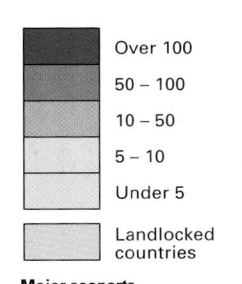

Freight unloaded in millions of tonnes (latest available year)

- Over 100
- 50 – 100
- 10 – 50
- 5 – 10
- Under 5
- Landlocked countries

Major seaports
- ● Over 100 million tonnes per year
- ○ 50 – 100 million tonnes per year

TYPES OF VESSELS

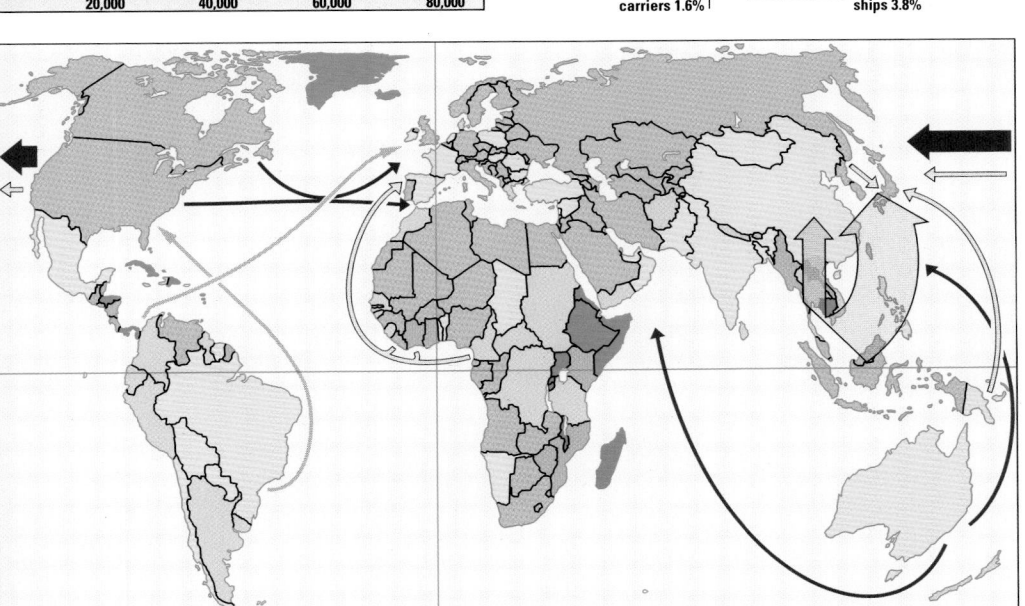

Oil tankers 38.4%
Ore & bulk carriers 29.9%
General cargo 16.1%
Others 9.7%
Ferries & passenger ships 0.5%
Liquid gas carriers 1.6%
Container ships 3.8%

THE GREAT PORTS

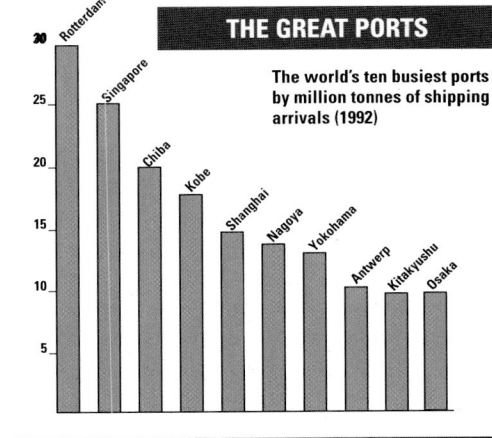

The world's ten busiest ports by million tonnes of shipping arrivals (1992)

Rotterdam, Singapore, Chiba, Kobe, Shanghai, Nagoya, Yokohama, Antwerp, Kitakyushu, Osaka

CARGOES

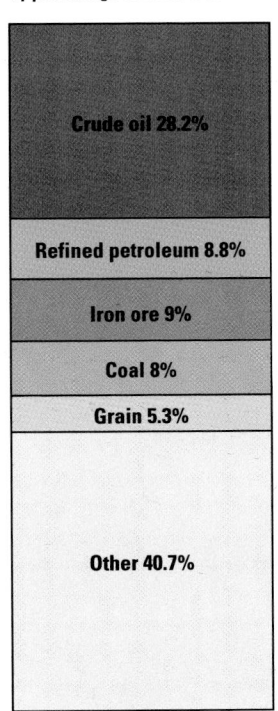

Types of seaborne freight, by percentage of world total

Crude oil 28.2%

Refined petroleum 8.8%

Iron ore 9%

Coal 8%

Grain 5.3%

Other 40.7%

TRADE IN PRIMARY PRODUCTS

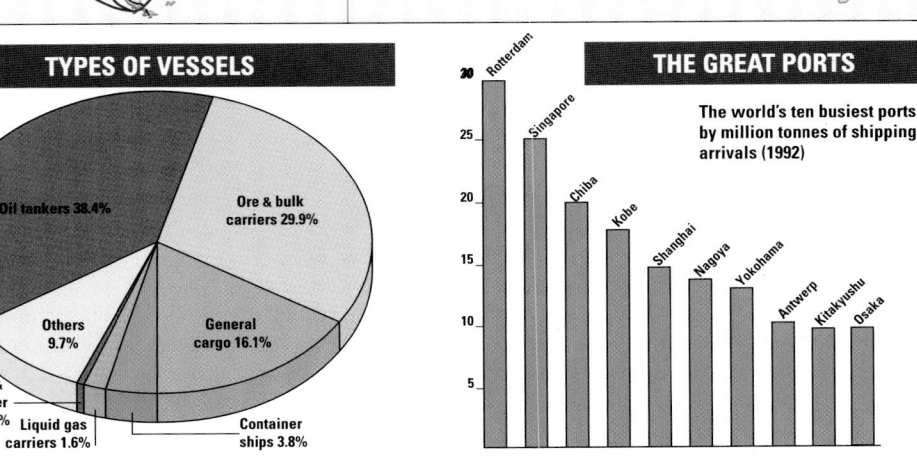

Primary products (excluding fuels, minerals and metals) as a percentage of total export value (latest available year)

- Over 75%
- 50 – 75%
- 25 – 50%
- 10 – 25%
- Under 10%

Direction of trade
- 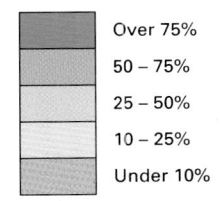 Major movements of cereals
- Major movements of coffee
- Major movements of hardwoods

Arrows show the major trade directions of selected primary products, and are proportional to export value.

BALANCE OF TRADE

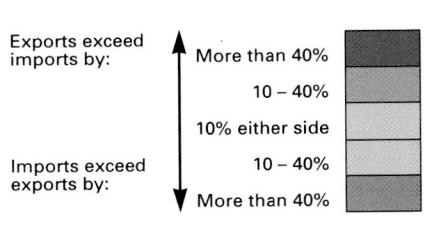

Value of exports in proportion to the value of imports (1993)

Exports exceed imports by:
- More than 40%
- 10 – 40%

10% either side

Imports exceed exports by:
- 10 – 40%
- More than 40%

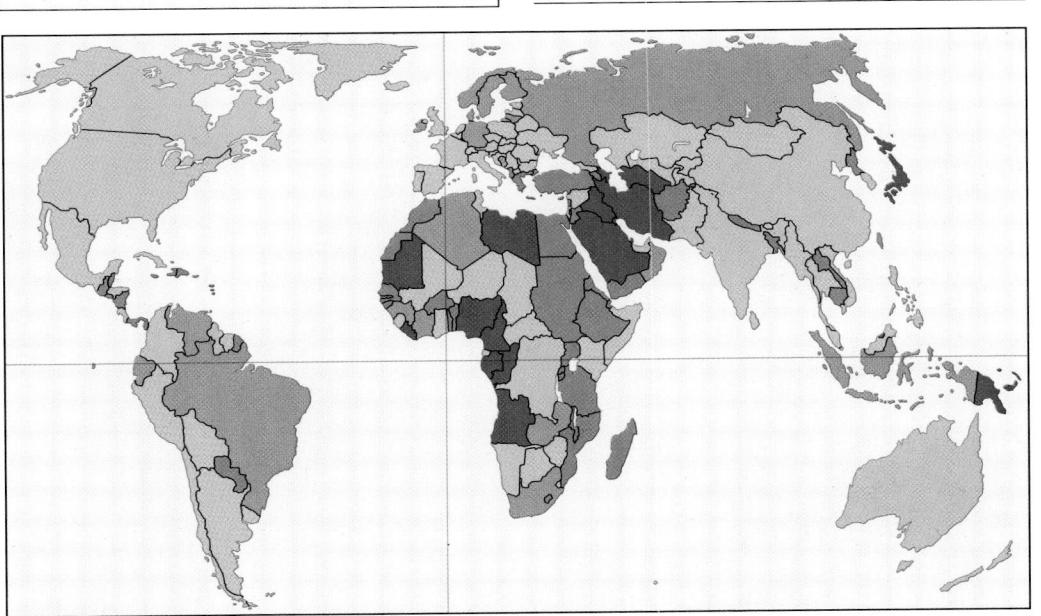

The total world trade balance should amount to zero, since exports must equal imports on a global scale. In practice, at least $100 billion in exports go unrecorded, leaving the world with an apparent deficit and many countries in a better position than public accounting reveals. However, a favourable trade balance is not necessarily a sign of prosperity: many poorer countries must maintain a high surplus in order to service debts, and do so by restricting imports below the levels needed to sustain successful economies.

QUALITY OF LIFE: WEALTH

CURRENCIES

Currency units of the world's most powerful economies

1. USA: US dollar ($, US $) = 100 cents
2. Japan: Yen (Y, ¥) = 100 sen
3. Germany: Deutsche Mark (DM) = 100 Pfennig
4. France: French franc (Fr) = 100 centimes
5. Italy: Italian lira (L, £, Lit)
6. UK: Pound sterling (£) = 100 pence
7. Canada: Canadian dollar (C$, Can$) = 100 cents
8. China: Renminbi yuan (RMBY, $, Y) = 10 jiao = 100 fen
9. Brazil: Cruzeiro real (BRC) = 100 centavos
10. Spain: Peseta (Pta, Pa) = 100 céntimos
11. India: Indian rupee (Re, Rs) = 100 paisa
12. Australia: Australian dollar ($A) = 100 cents
13. Netherlands: Guilder, florin (Gld, f) = 100 centimes
14. Switzerland: Swiss franc (SFr, SwF) = 100 centimes
15. South Korea: Won (W) = 100 chon
16. Sweden: Swedish krona (SKr) = 100 ore
17. Mexico: Mexican peso (Mex$) = 100 centavos
18. Belgium: Belgian franc (BFr) = 100 centimes
19. Austria: Schilling (S, Sch) = 100 Groschen
20. Finland: Markka (FMk) = 100 penniä
21. Denmark: Danish krone (DKr) = 100 øre
22. Norway: Norwegian krone (NKr) = 100 ore
23. Saudi Arabia: Riyal (SAR, SRI$) = 100 halalah
24. Indonesia: Rupiah (Rp) = 100 sen
25. South Africa: Rand (R) = 100 cents

Throughout the 1980s, most of the world became at least slightly richer. There were exceptions: in Africa, the poorest of the continents, many incomes actually fell, and the upheavals in Eastern Europe in 1989 left whole populations awash with political freedom but worse off financially in economies still teetering towards capitalism.

Most of the improvements, however, came to those who were already, in world terms, extremely affluent: the gap between rich and poor grew steadily wider. And in those developing countries that showed significant statistical progress, advances were often confined to a few favoured areas, while conditions in other, usually rural, districts went from bad to worse.

The pattern of world poverty varies from region to region. In most of Asia, the process of recognized development is generally under way, with production increases outpacing population growth. By 2000, less than 10% of the Chinese population should be officially rated 'poor': without the means to buy either adequate food or the basic necessities required to take a full part in everyday life. Even India's lower growth rate should be enough to reduce the burden of poverty for at least some of its people. In Latin America, average per capita production is high enough for most countries to be considered 'middle income' in world rankings. But although adequate resources exist, Latin American wealth is distributed with startling inequality. According to a 1990 World Bank report, a tax of only 2% on the richest fifth would raise enough money to pull every one of the continent's 437 million people above the poverty line.

In Africa, solutions will be much harder to find. The bane of high population growth has often been aggravated by incompetent administration, war and a succession of natural disasters. Population is the crux of the problem: numbers are growing anything up to twice as fast as the economies that try to support them. Aid from the developed world is only a partial solution; although Africa receives more aid than any other continent, much has been wasted on overambitious projects or lost in webs of inexperienced or corrupt bureaucracy. Yet without aid, Africa seems doomed to permanent crisis.

The rich countries can afford to increase their spending. The 26 members of the Organization for Economic Co-operation and Development comprise only 18% of the world's population, yet between them the nations produced over two-thirds of the world's goods and services, a share that is likely to increase as the year 2000 approaches.

CONTINENTAL SHARES

Shares of population and of wealth (GNP) by continent

Generalized continental figures show the startling difference between rich and poor, but mask the successes or failures of individual countries. Japan, for example, with less than 4% of Asia's population, produces almost 70% of the continent's output.

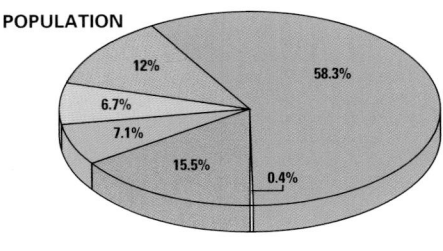

POPULATION

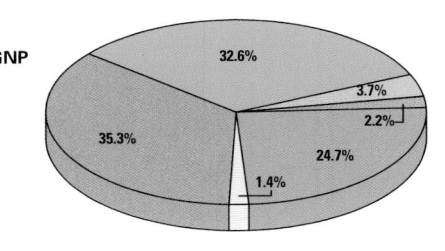

GNP

| Europe | Asia | South America |
| Australia | Africa | North America |

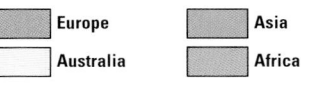
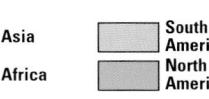

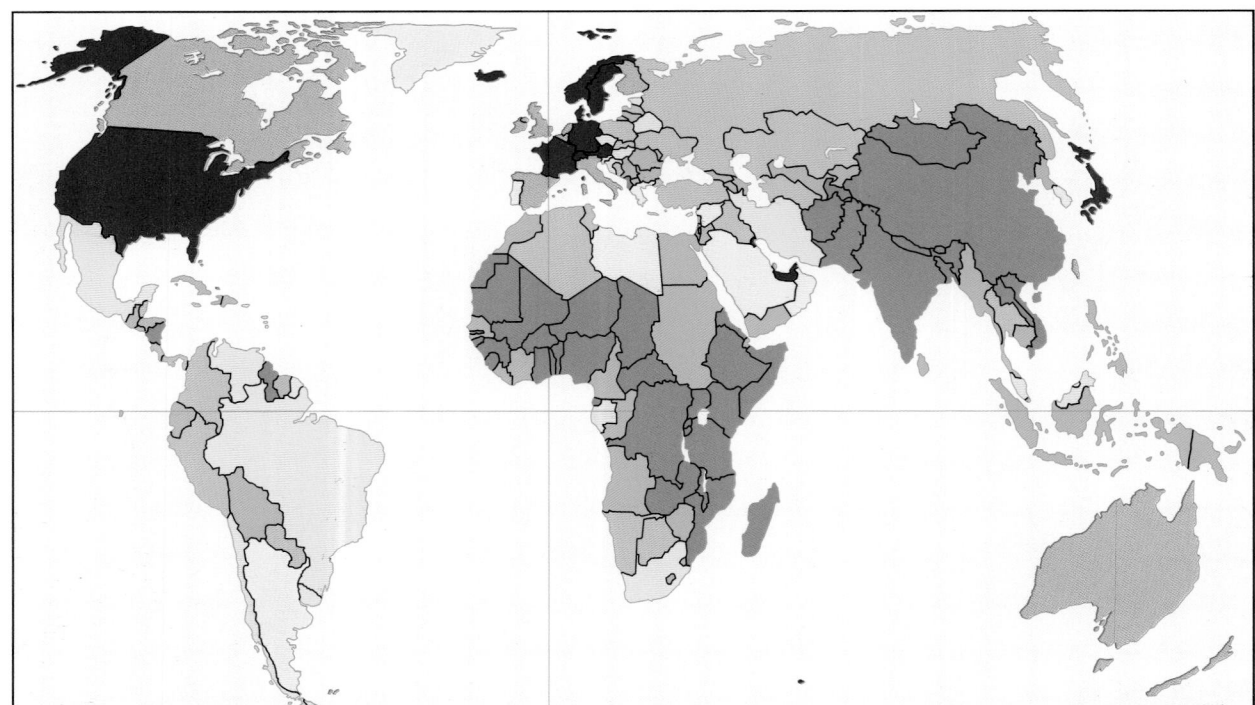

LEVELS OF INCOME

Gross National Product per capita: the value of total production divided by the population (1993)

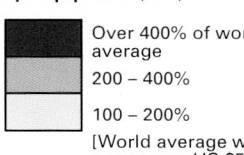

- Over 400% of world average
- 200 – 400%
- 100 – 200%
- [World average wealth per person US $5,359]
- 50 – 100%
- 25 – 50%
- 10 – 25%
- Under 10%

Richest countries

Switzerland .... $36,41(
Luxembourg .... $35,85(
Japan .... $31,45(
Bermuda .... $27,00(

Poorest countries

Mozambique .... $8(
Ethiopia .... $10(
Tanzania .... $10(
Sierra Leone .... $14(

INDICATORS

The gap between the world's rich and poor is now so great that it is difficult to illustrate on a single graph. Car ownership in the USA, for example, is almost 2,000 times as common as it is in Bangladesh. Within each income group, however, comparisons have some meaning: the Japanese on their overcrowded island have far fewer cars than the Americans; the Chinese, perhaps because of propaganda value, have many more TV sets than people in India, whose per capita income is similar, while people in Nigeria prefer to spend their money on vehicles.

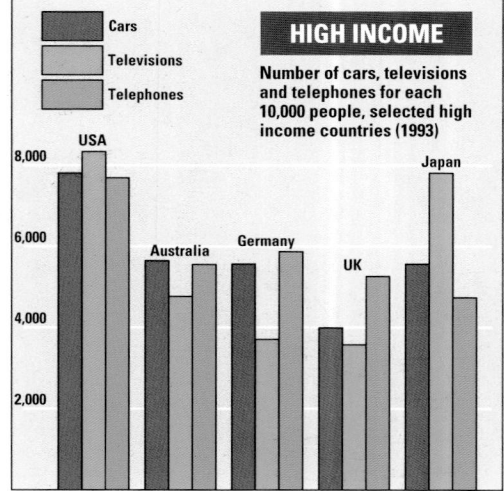

HIGH INCOME

Number of cars, televisions and telephones for each 10,000 people, selected high income countries (1993)

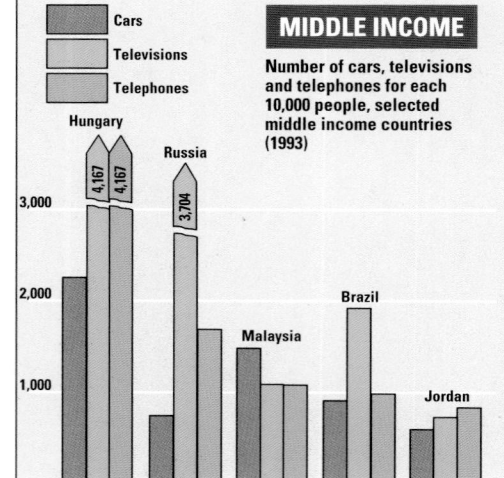

MIDDLE INCOME

Number of cars, televisions and telephones for each 10,000 people, selected middle income countries (1993)

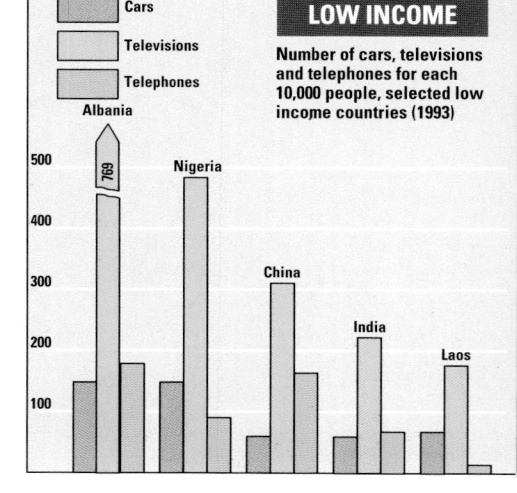

LOW INCOME

Number of cars, televisions and telephones for each 10,000 people, selected low income countries (1993)

DEBT AND AID

International debtors and the aid they receive (1993).

Although aid grants make a vital contribution to many of the world's poorer countries, they are usually dwarfed by the burden of debt that the devloping economies are expected to repay. In 1992, they had to pay US $160,000 million in debt service charges alone – more than two and a half times the amount of Official Development Assistance (ODA) the developing countries were receiving, and US $60,000 million more than total private flows of aid in the same year. In 1990, the debts of Mozambique, one of the world's poorest countries, were estimated to be 75 times its entire earnings from exports.

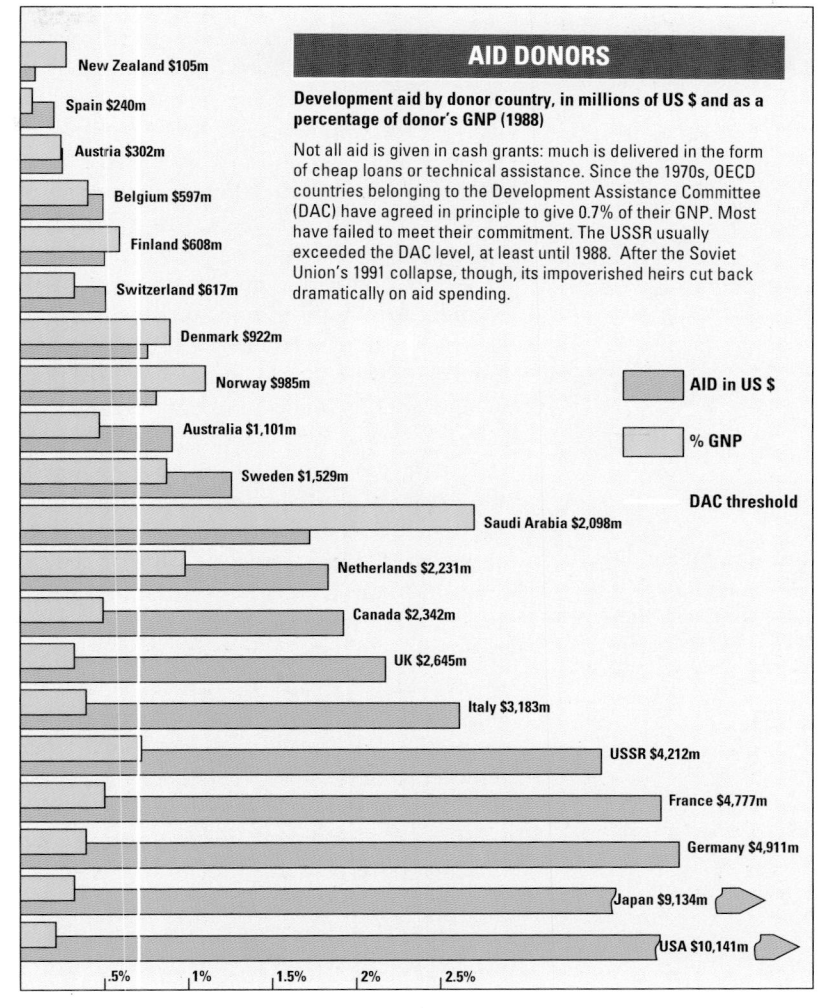

■ Debt, US $ per capita

■ Aid, US $ per capita

$4853

Countries (debt bars): India, Tanzania, Sierra Leone, Nigeria, Mozambique, Madagascar, Laos, Guinea-Bissau, Egypt, Honduras, Zambia, Papua New Guinea, Mauritania, Ecuador, Ivory Coast, Jordan, Jamaica, Nicaragua, Congo, Israel, Panama

$153 $279

AID DONORS

Development aid by donor country, in millions of US $ and as a percentage of donor's GNP (1988)

Not all aid is given in cash grants: much is delivered in the form of cheap loans or technical assistance. Since the 1970s, OECD countries belonging to the Development Assistance Committee (DAC) have agreed in principle to give 0.7% of their GNP. Most have failed to meet their commitment. The USSR usually exceeded the DAC level, at least until 1988. After the Soviet Union's 1991 collapse, though, its impoverished heirs cut back dramatically on aid spending.

■ AID in US $

■ % GNP

DAC threshold

New Zealand $105m
Spain $240m
Austria $302m
Belgium $597m
Finland $608m
Switzerland $617m
Denmark $922m
Norway $985m
Australia $1,101m
Sweden $1,529m
Saudi Arabia $2,098m
Netherlands $2,231m
Canada $2,342m
UK $2,645m
Italy $3,183m
USSR $4,212m
France $4,777m
Germany $4,911m
Japan $9,134m
USA $10,141m

.5% 1% 1.5% 2% 2.5%

Inflation (right) is an excellent index of a country's financial stability, and usually its prosperity or at least its prospects. Inflation rates above 20% are generally matched by slow or even negative growth; above 50%, an economy is left reeling. Most advanced countries during the 1980s had to wrestle with inflation that occasionally touched or even exceeded 10%; in Japan, the growth leader, price increases averaged only 1.8% between 1980 and 1988.

Government spending (below right) is more difficult to interpret. Obviously, very low levels indicate a weak state, and high levels a strong one; but in poor countries, the 10–20% absorbed by the government may well amount to most of the liquid cash available, whereas in rich countries most of the 35–50% that is typically in government hands is returned in services.

GNP per capita figures (below) should also be compared with caution. They do not reveal the vast differences in living costs between different countries: the equivalent of US $100 is worth considerably more in poorer nations than it is in the USA itself.

INFLATION

Average annual rate of inflation (1980–91)

- Over 50%
- 20 – 50%
- 7.5 – 20%
- 1 – 7.5%
- Negative inflation
- No data available

Highest average inflation
Nicaragua 584%
Argentina 417%
Brazil 328%

Lowest average inflation
Oman .... –3.1%
Kuwait .... –2.7%
Saudi Arabia .... –2.4%

THE WEALTH GAP

The world's richest and poorest countries, by Gross National Product per capita in US $ (1993)

1. Switzerland	36,410	1. Mozambique	80
2. Luxembourg	35,850	2. Ethiopia	100
3. Liechtenstein	33,510	3. Tanzania	100
4. Japan	31,450	4. Sierra Leone	140
5. Bermuda	27,000	5. Nepal	160
6. Denmark	26,510	6. Bhutan	170
7. Norway	26,340	7. Vietnam	170
8. Sweden	24,830	8. Burundi	180
9. USA	24,750	9. Uganda	190
10. Iceland	23,620	10. Chad	200
11. Germany	23,560	11. Rwanda	200
12. Kuwait	23,350	12. Afghanistan	220
13. Austria	23,120	13. Bangladesh	220
14. UAE	22,470	14. Guinea-Bissau	220
15. France	22,360	15. Malawi	220
16. Belgium	21,210	16. Madagascar	240
17. Netherlands	20,710	17. Kenya	270
18. Canada	20,670	18. Niger	270
19. Italy	19,620	19. India	290
20. Singapore	19,310	20. Laos	290

GNP per capita is calculated by dividing a country's Gross National Product by its population. The GNP per capita for the UK is $17,970.

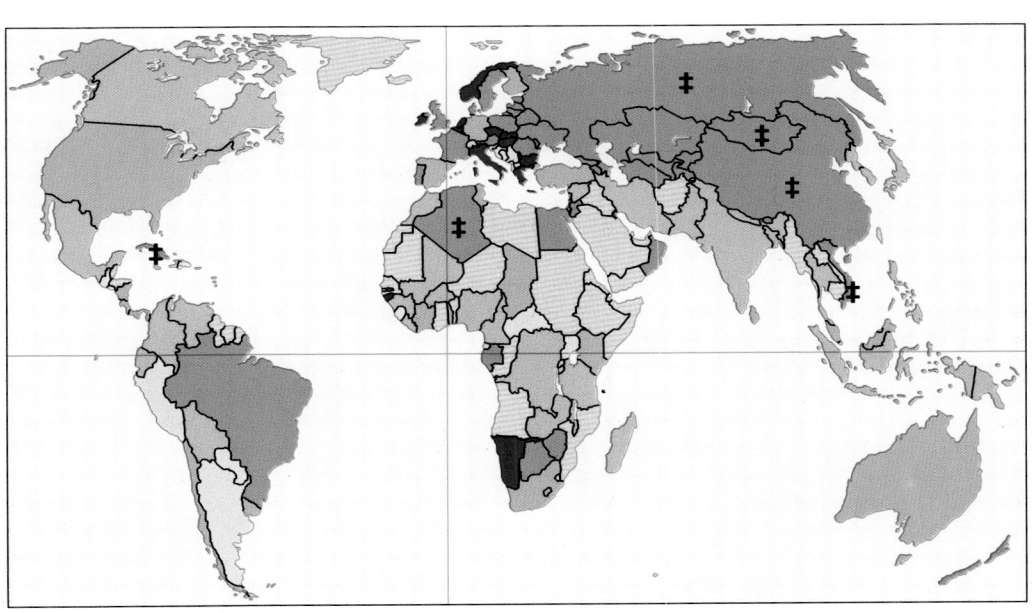
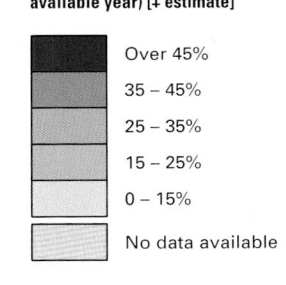

STATE SPENDING

Central government expenditure as a percentage of GNP (latest available year) [‡ estimate]

- Over 45%
- 35 – 45%
- 25 – 35%
- 15 – 25%
- 0 – 15%
- No data available

Top 5 countries
Bulgaria 77.3%
Guinea-Bissau 63.0%
Greece 60.0%
Ex-Czechoslovakia 55.6%
Hungary 54.7%

QUALITY OF LIFE: STANDARDS

At first sight, most international contrasts are swamped by differences in wealth. The rich not only have more money, they have more of everything, including years of life. Those with only a little money are obliged to spend most of it on food and clothing, the basic maintenance costs of existence; air travel and tourism are unlikely to feature on the lists of their expenditure. However, poverty and wealth are both relative: slum dwellers living on social security payments in an affluent industrial country have far more resources at their disposal than an average African peasant, but feel their own poverty none the less acutely. A middle-class Indian lawyer cannot command a fraction of the earnings of a counterpart in New York, London or Rome; nevertheless, he rightly sees himself as prosperous.

In 1990 the United Nations Development Programme published its first Human Development Index, an attempt to construct a comparative scale by which at least a simplified form of well-being might be measured. The index, expressed as a value between 0 and 0.999, combined figures for life expectancy and literacy with a wealth scale that matched incomes against the official poverty lines of a group of industrialized nations. National scores for 1992 ranged from 0.932 for Canada to a miserable 0.191 for Guinea, reflecting the all-too-familiar gap between rich and poor.

Comparisons between nations with similar incomes are more interesting, showing the effect of government policies. For example, Sri Lanka was awarded 0.665 against 0.382 for its only slightly poorer neighbour, India; Zimbabwe, with 0.474, had more than double the score of Benin, despite no apparent disparities in average income. Some development indicators may be interpreted in two ways. There is a very clear correlation, for example, between the wealth of a nation and the level of education that its people enjoy. Education helps create wealth, of course; but are rich countries wealthy because they are educated, or well-educated because they are rich? Women's fertility rates appear to fall almost in direct proportion to the amount of secondary education they receive; but high levels of female education are associated with rich countries, where fertility is already low.

Not everything, though, is married to wealth. The countries cited on these pages have been chosen to give a range covering different cultures as well as different economic power, revealing disparities among rich and among poor as well as between the two obvious groups. Income distribution, for example, shows that in Brazil (following the general pattern of Latin America) most national wealth is concentrated in a few hands; Bangladesh is much poorer, but what little wealth there is, is more evenly spread.

Among the developed countries the USA, with its poorest 20% sharing less than 5% of the national cake, has a noticeably less even distribution than Japan where, despite massive industrialization, traditional values act as a brake against poverty. Hungary, still enmeshed in Communism when these statistics were compiled, shows the most even distribution of all, which certainly matches with Socialist theory. However, the inequalities in Communist societies, a contributing factor in the demise of most of them in the late 1980s, are not easily measured in money terms. Communist élites are less often rewarded with cash than with power and privilege, commodities not easily expressed statistically.

There are other limits to statistical analysis. Even without taking account of such imponderables as personal satisfaction, it will always be more difficult to measure a reasonable standard of living than a nation's income or its productivity. Lack of money certainly brings misery, but its presence does not guarantee contentment.

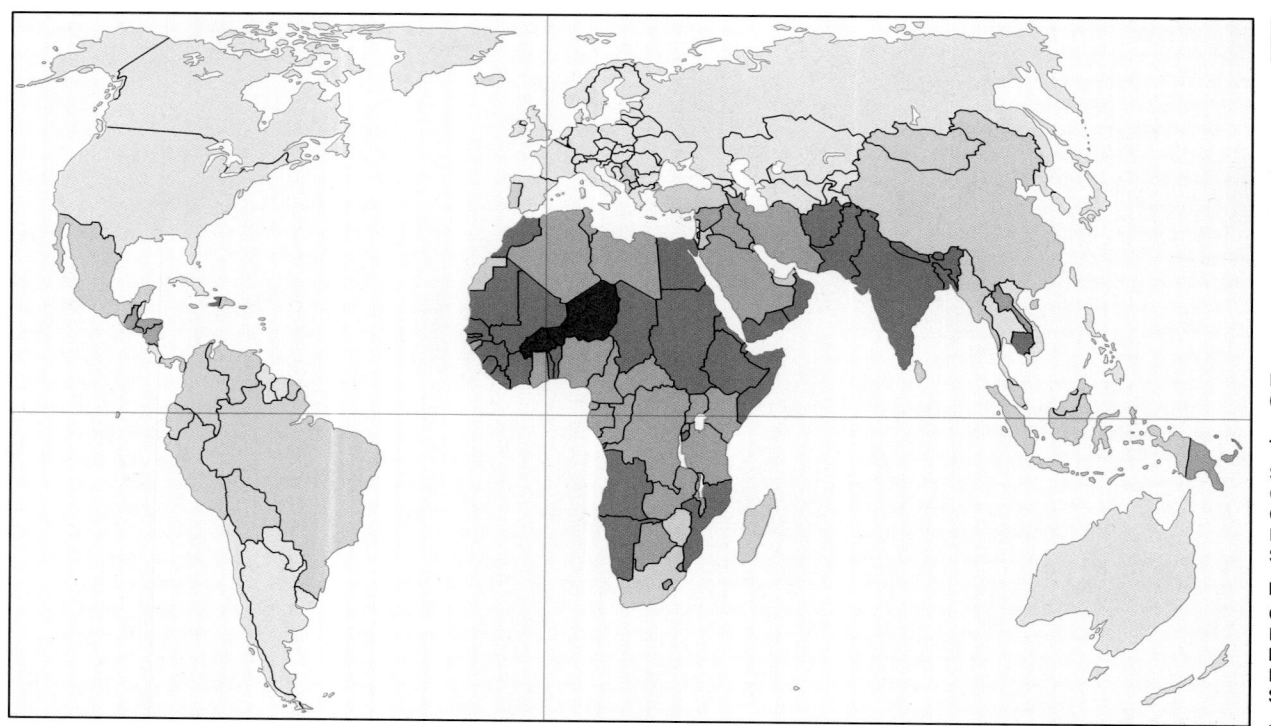

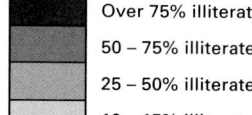

ILLITERACY

Percentage of the total population
unable to read or write (1992)

- Over 75% illiterate
- 50 – 75% illiterate
- 25 – 50% illiterate
- 10 – 15% illiterate
- Under 10% illiterate

Educational expenditure per person
(latest available year)

Top 5 countries

Sweden	$997
Qatar	$989
Canada	$983
Norway	$971
Switzerland	$796

Bottom 5 countries

Chad	$2
Bangladesh	$3
Ethiopia	$3
Nepal	$4
Somalia	$4

EDUCATION

The developing countries made great efforts in the 1970s and 1980s to bring at least a basic education to their people. Primary school enrolments rose above 60% in all but the poorest nations. Figures often include teenagers or young adults, however, and there are still an estimated 300 million children worldwide who receive no schooling at all. Secondary and higher education are expanding far more slowly, and the gap between rich and poor is probably even larger than it appears from the charts here, while the bare statistics provide no real reflection of educational quality.

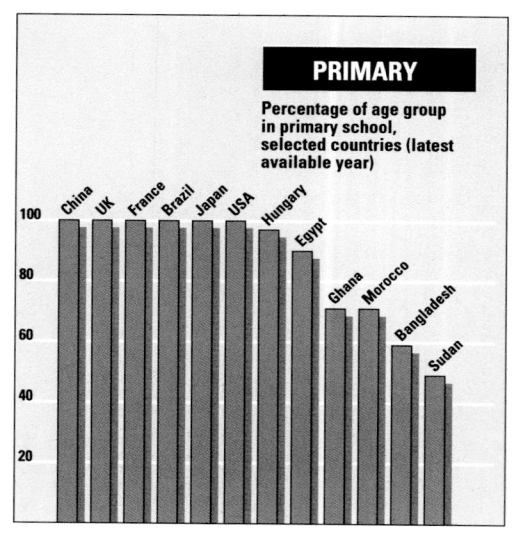

PRIMARY

Percentage of age group in primary school, selected countries (latest available year)

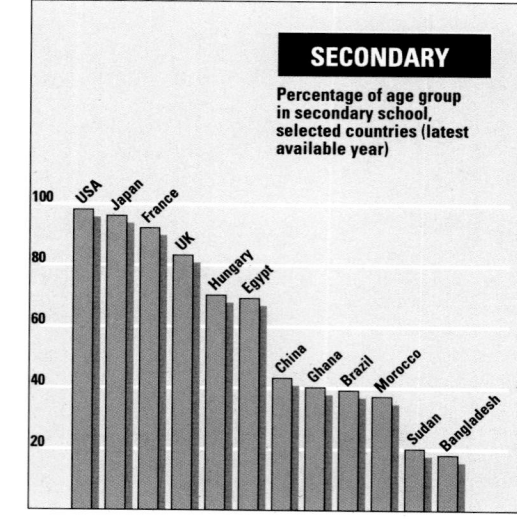

SECONDARY

Percentage of age group in secondary school, selected countries (latest available year)

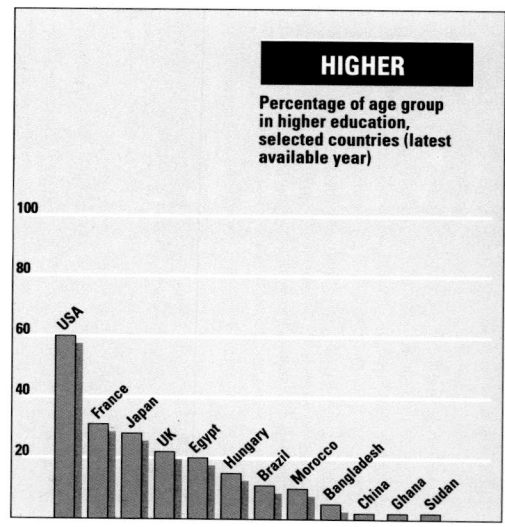

HIGHER

Percentage of age group in higher education, selected countries (latest available year)

DISTRIBUTION OF SPENDING

Percentage share of household spending

Food
Clothing
Energy & Housing
Medicine & Education
Transport
Other

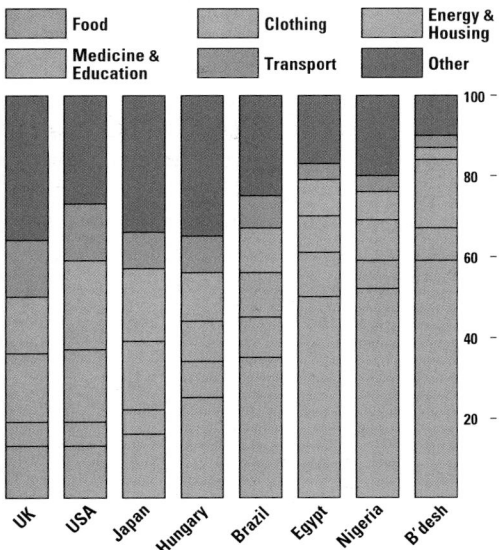

DISTRIBUTION OF INCOME

Percentage share of household income from poorest fifth to richest fifth, selected countries (latest available year)

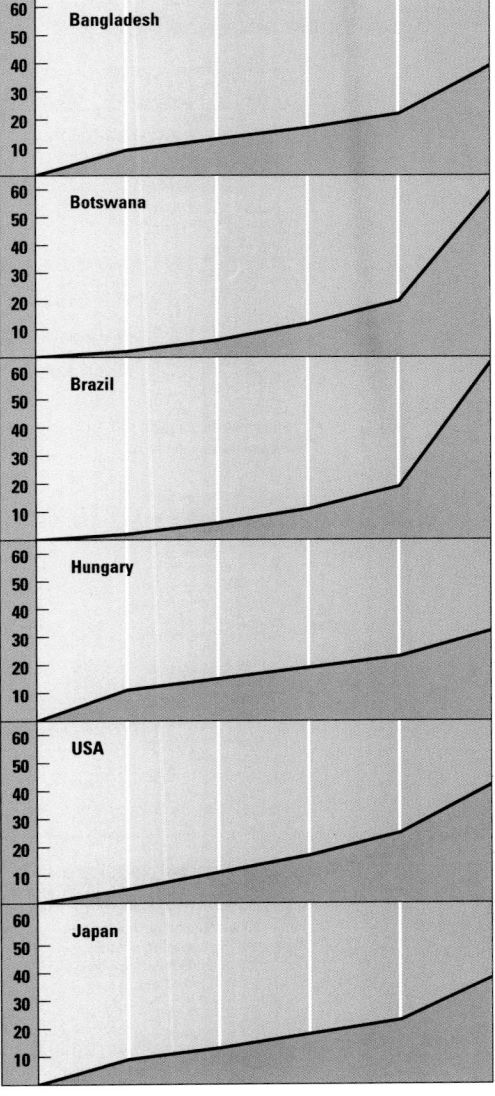

Bangladesh

Botswana

Brazil

Hungary

USA

Japan

FERTILITY AND EDUCATION

Fertility rate: average number of children borne per woman

Percentage of females aged 12–17 in secondary education

Fertility rates compared with female education, selected countries (1990–92)

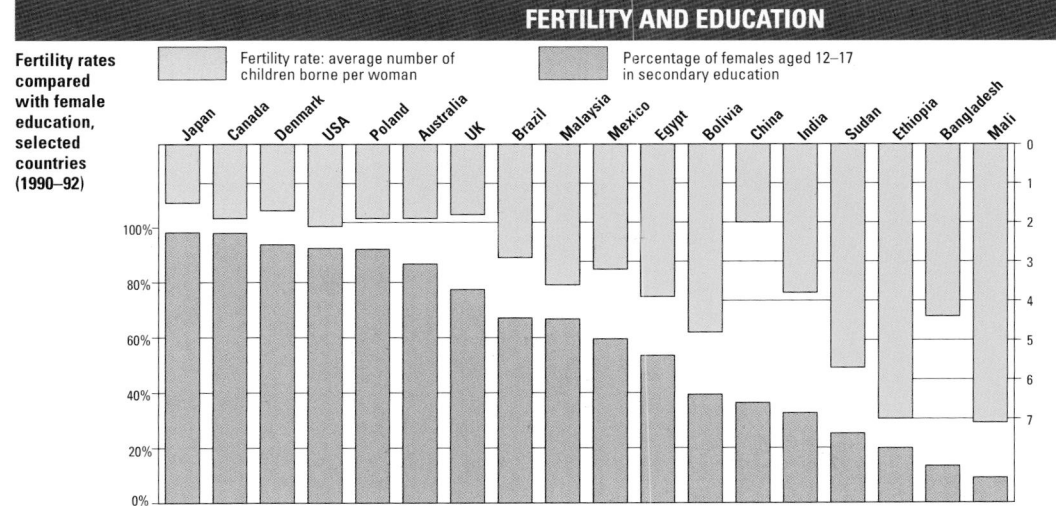

Since the age group for secondary schooling is usually defined as 12–17 years, percentages for countries with a significant number of 11- or 18-year-olds in secondary school may actually exceed 100.

A high proportion of employed women may indicate either an advanced, industrial economy where female opportunities are high, or a poor country where many women's lives are dominated by agricultural toil. The lowest rates are found in Islamic nations, whose religious precepts often exclude women even from fieldwork.

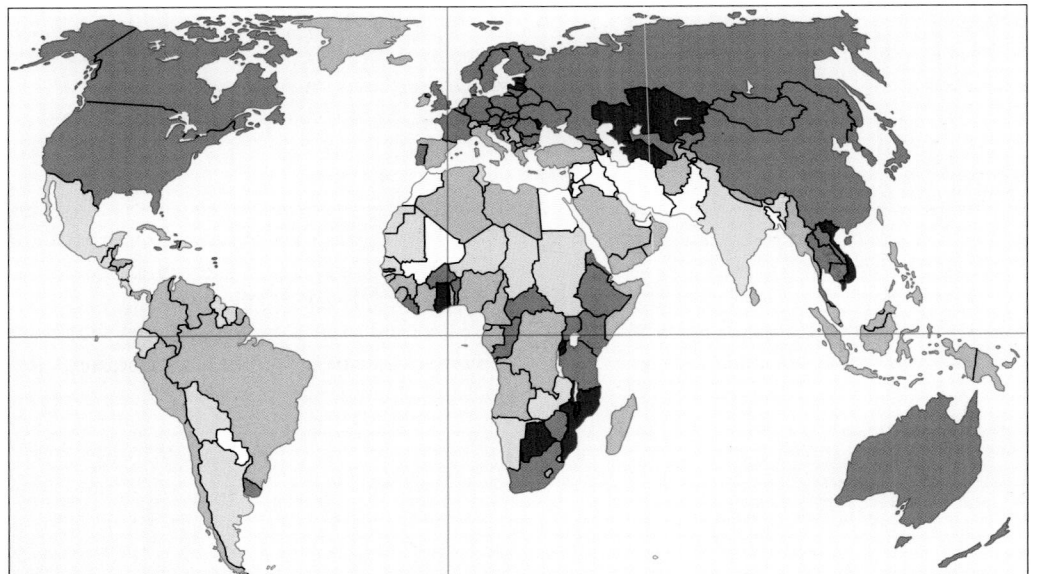

WOMEN AT WORK

Women in paid employment as a percentage of the total workforce (latest available year)

Over 50%
40 – 50%
30 – 40%
20 – 30%
10 – 20%
Under 10%

Most women in work

Kazakstan	54%
Rwanda	54%
Botswana	53%

Fewest women in work

Guinea-Bissau	3%
Oman	6%
Afghanistan	8%

TOURISM

Leisure and tourism is the world's second largest industry in terms of revenue generated. Small economies in attractive areas are often completely dominated by tourism: in some West Indian islands, tourist spending provides over 90% of the total income and is the biggest foreign exchange earner.

In cash terms the USA is the world leader: its 1992 earnings exceeded US $53.8 million, though that sum amounted to only 0.9% of its total GDP. Of the 39,538,000 visitors to the USA, 48% came from Canada.

TOURIST SPENDING

Countries spending the most on overseas tourism, US $ million (1993)

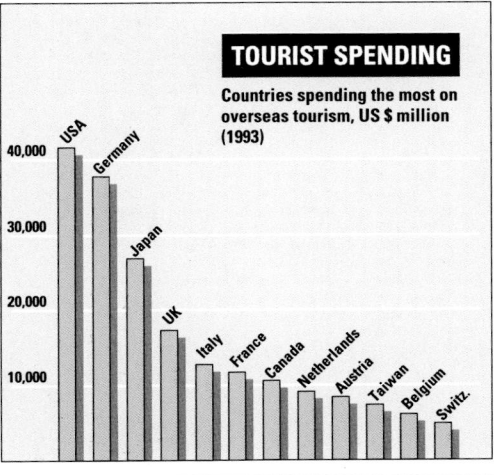

TOURIST EARNING

Countries receiving the most from overseas tourism, US $ million (1992)

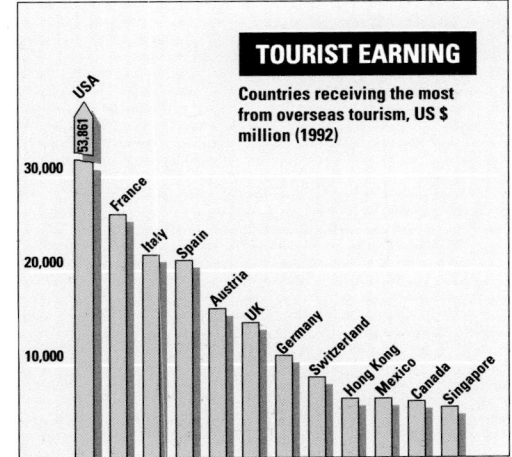

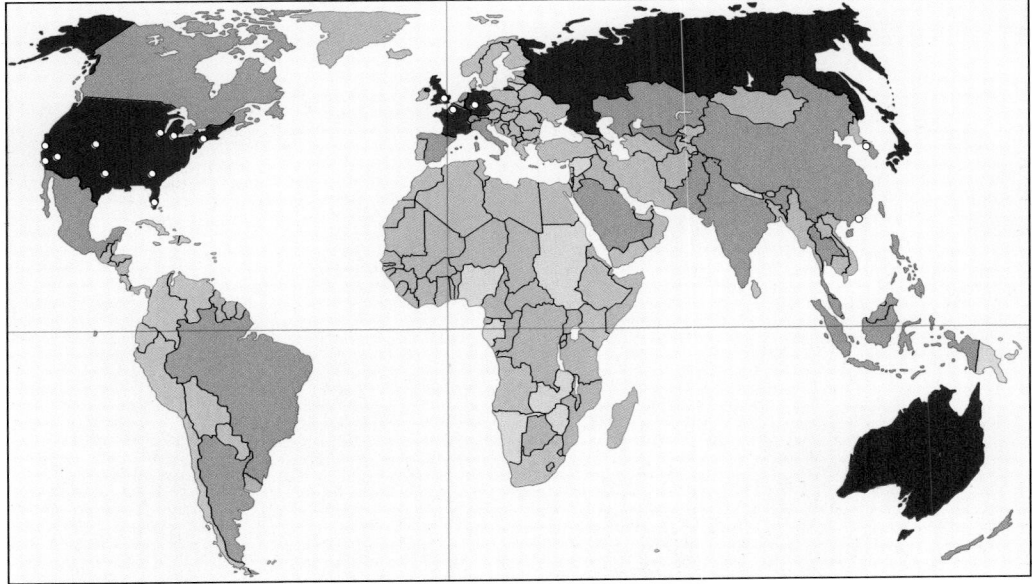

AIR TRAVEL

Millions of passenger km (the number of passengers carried, multiplied by distance flown from airport of origin) (1992)

Over 100,000
50,000 – 100,000
10,000 – 50,000
1,000 – 10,000
500 – 1,000
Under 500

○ Major airports (over 20 million passengers in 1991)

The world's busiest airport in terms of total passengers is Chicago's O'Hare; the busiest international airport is Heathrow, the largest of London's airports.

QUALITY OF LIFE: HEALTH

According to statistics gathered in the late 1980s and early 1990s, a third of the world's population has no access to safe drinking water: malaria is on the increase; cholera, thought vanquished, is reappearing in South America; an epidemic of the AIDS virus is gathering force in Africa; and few developing countries can stretch their health care budgets beyond US $2 per person per year.

Yet human beings, by every statistical index, have never been healthier. In the richest nations, where food is plentiful, the demands of daily work are rarely onerous and medical care is both readily available and highly advanced, the average life expectancy is often more than 75 years – approaching the perceived limits for human longevity. In middle-income nations, such as Brazil and the Philippines, life expectancy usually extends at least to the mid-60s; in China, it has already reached 70 years. Even in poverty-stricken Ethiopia and Chad, lifespans are close to 50 years. Despite economic crisis, drought, famine and even war, every country in the world reported an increase between 1965 and 1990.

It was not always so, even in countries then considered rich. By comparison, in 1880 the life expectancy of an average Berliner was under 30 years and infant mortality in the United Kingdom, then the wealthiest nation, stood at 144 per thousand births – a grim toll exceeded today only by three of the poorest African countries (Mali, Sierra Leone and Guinea). Even by 1910, European death rates were almost twice as high as the world average less than 80 years later; infant mortality in Norway, Europe's healthiest country, was then higher than in present-day Indonesia. In far less than a century, human prospects have improved beyond recognition.

In global terms, the transformation is less the result of high-technology medicine – still too expensive for all but a minority, even in rich countries – than of improvements in agriculture and hence nutrition, matched by the widespread diffusion of the basic concepts of disease and public health. One obvious consequence, as death rates everywhere continue to fall, is sustained population growth. Another is the rising expectation of continued improvement felt by both rich and poor nations alike.

In some ways, the task is easier for developing countries, striving with limited resources to attain health levels to which the industrialized world has only recently become accustomed. As the tables below illustrate, infectious disease is rare among the richer nations, while ailments such as cancer, which tend to kill in advanced years, do not seriously impinge on populations with shorter lifespans.

Yet infectious disease is relatively cheap to eliminate, or at least reduce, and it is likely to be easier to raise life expectancy from 60 to 70 years than from 75 to 85 years. The ills of the developed world and its ageing population are more expensive to treat – though most poor countries would be happy to suffer from the problems of the affluent. Western nations regularly spend more money on campaigns to educate their citizens out of overeating and other bad habits than many developing countries can devote to an entire health budget – an irony that marks the dimensions of the rich–poor divide.

Indeed, wealth itself may be the most reliable indicator of longevity. Harmful habits are usually the province of the rich; yet curiously, though the dangerous effects of tobacco have been proved beyond doubt, the affluent Japanese combine very high cigarette consumption with the longest life expectancy of all the major nations. Similarly, heavy alcohol consumption seems to have no effect on longevity: the French, world leaders in 1988 and in most previous surveys, outlive the more moderate British by a year, and the abstemious Indians by almost two decades.

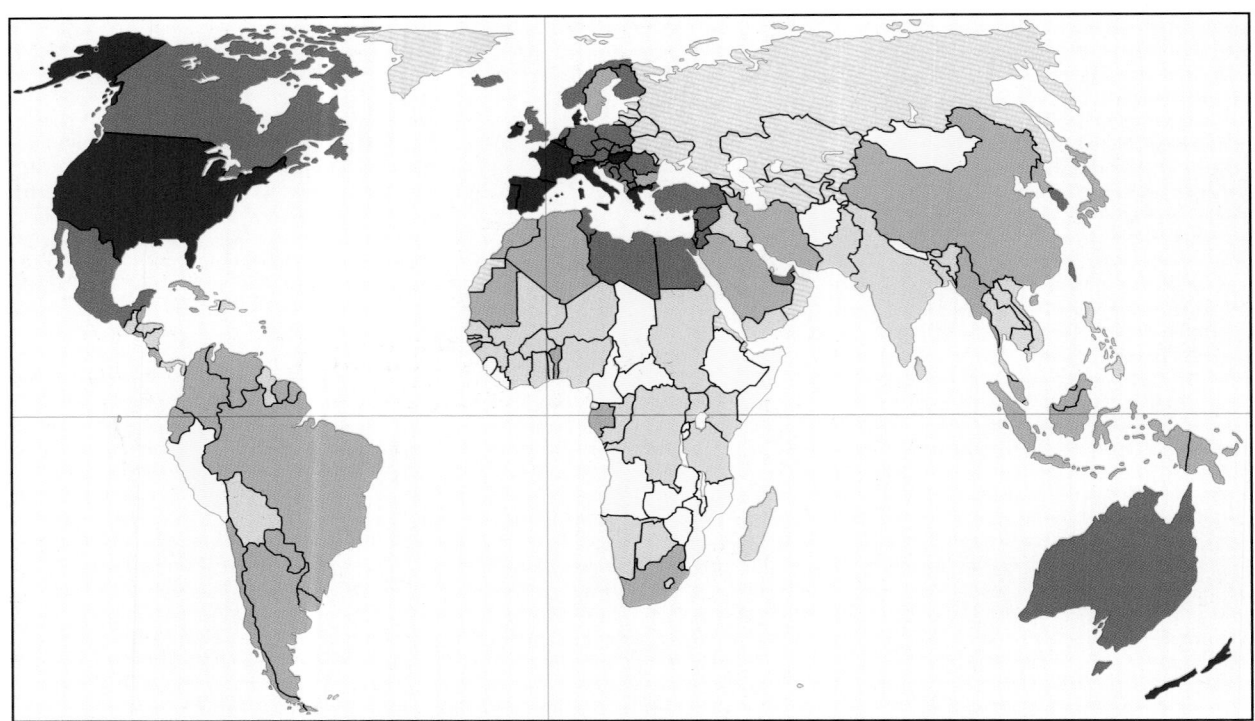

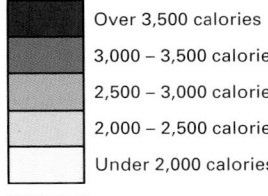

FOOD CONSUMPTION

Average daily food intake in calories per person (1992)

- Over 3,500 calories
- 3,000 – 3,500 calories
- 2,500 – 3,000 calories
- 2,000 – 2,500 calories
- Under 2,000 calories
- No available data

Top 5 countries

Ireland	3,847 cal
Greece	3,815 cal
Cyprus	3,779 cal
USA	3,732 cal
Spain	3,708 cal

Bottom 5 countries

Mozambique	1,680 cal
Liberia	1,640 cal
Ethiopia	1,610 cal
Afghanistan	1,523 cal
Somalia	1,499 cal

CAUSES OF DEATH

The rich not only live longer, on average, than the poor; they also die from different causes. Infectious and parasitic diseases, all but eliminated in the developed world, remain a scourge in poorer countries. On the other hand, more than two-thirds of the populations of OECD nations eventually succumb to cancer or circulatory disease; the proportion in Latin America is only about 45%. In addition to the three major diseases shown here, respiratory infection and injury also claim more lives in developing nations, which lack the drugs and medical skills required to treat them.

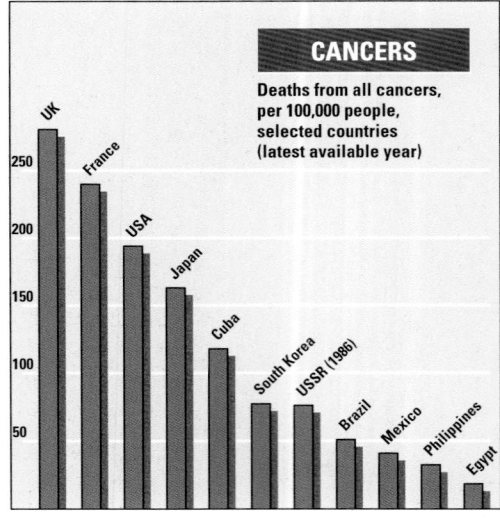

CANCERS

Deaths from all cancers, per 100,000 people, selected countries (latest available year)

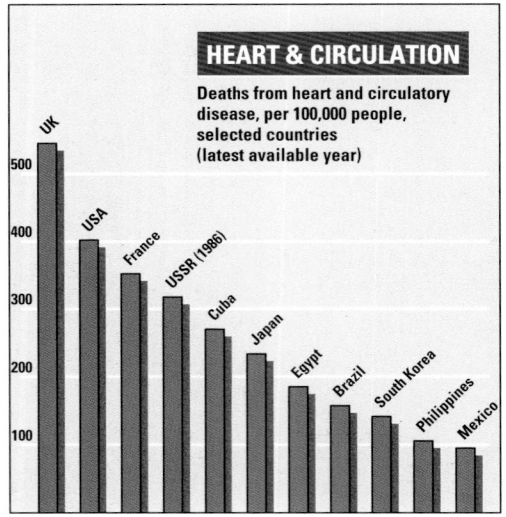

HEART & CIRCULATION

Deaths from heart and circulatory disease, per 100,000 people, selected countries (latest available year)

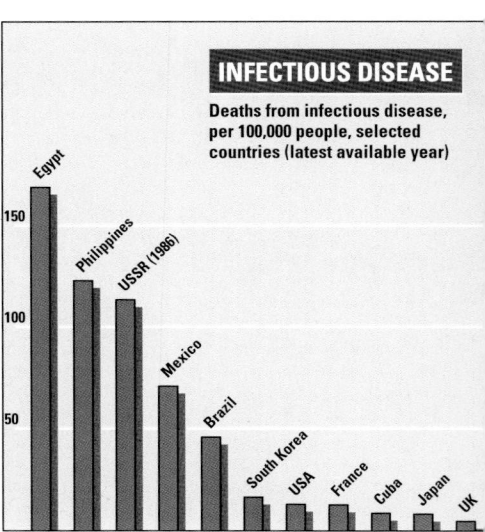

INFECTIOUS DISEASE

Deaths from infectious disease, per 100,000 people, selected countries (latest available year)

LIFE EXPECTANCY

Years of life expectancy at birth, selected countries (1990–95)

The chart shows combined data for both sexes. On average, women live longer than men worldwide, even in developing countries with high maternal mortality rates. Overall, life expectancy is steadily rising, though the difference between rich and poor nations remains dramatic.

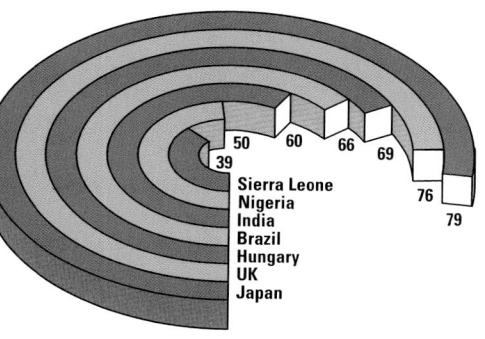

39 50 60 66 69 76 79

Sierra Leone
Nigeria
India
Brazil
Hungary
UK
Japan

CHILD MORTALITY

Number of babies who will die under the age of one, per 1,000 births (average 1990–95)

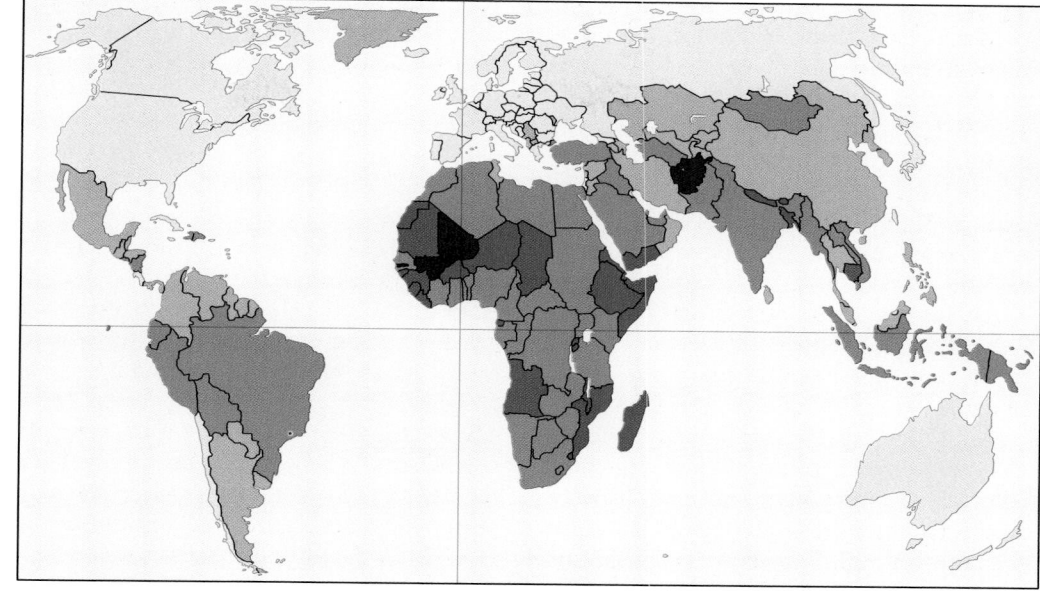

- Over 150 deaths
- 100 – 150 deaths
- 50 – 100 deaths
- 20 – 50 deaths
- 10 – 20 deaths
- Under 10 deaths

Highest child mortality
Afghanistan............ 162 deaths
Mali........................ 159 deaths

Lowest child mortality
Iceland...................... 5 deaths
Finland...................... 5 deaths

[UK 8 deaths USA 8 deaths]

EXPENDITURE ON HEALTH

Public expenditure on health as a percentage of GNP (1991)

Countries with the highest spending		Countries with the lowest spending	
Costa Rica	30.0	Syria	0.4
Panama	21.8	Sudan	0.5
Grenada	15.6	Indonesia	0.7
St Vincent & G.	15.1	Qatar	0.8
Bahamas	14.5	Zaïre	0.8
Bermuda	14.5	Morocco	0.9
USA	13.3	Somalia	0.9
Barbados	12.0	Cameroon	1.0
Lesotho	11.5	Laos	1.0
Puerto Rico	10.7	Philippines	1.0

[UK 6.6]

The allocation of limited funds for health care in the Third World is rarely evenly spread – the quality of treatment can vary enormously from place to place within the same country. Urban dwellers tend to have much better access to health provisions than those living in rural areas.

MEDICAL PROVISION

Doctors per 100,000 population, selected countries (latest available year, 1988–92)

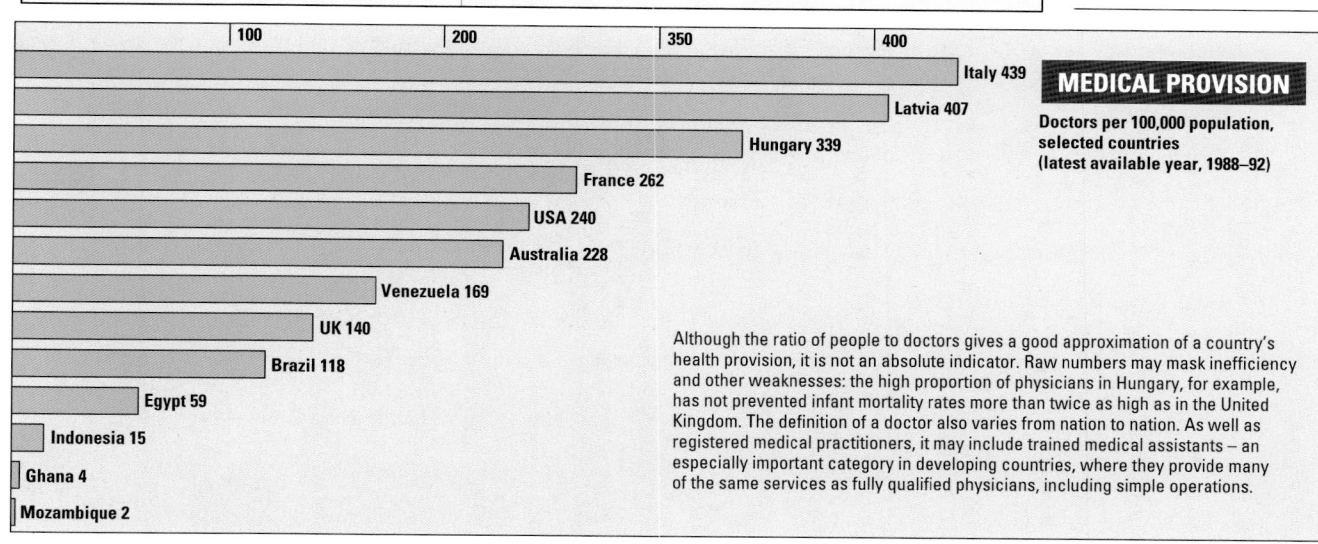

Italy 439
Latvia 407
Hungary 339
France 262
USA 240
Australia 228
Venezuela 169
UK 140
Brazil 118
Egypt 59
Indonesia 15
Ghana 4
Mozambique 2

Although the ratio of people to doctors gives a good approximation of a country's health provision, it is not an absolute indicator. Raw numbers may mask inefficiency and other weaknesses: the high proportion of physicians in Hungary, for example, has not prevented infant mortality rates more than twice as high as in the United Kingdom. The definition of a doctor also varies from nation to nation. As well as registered medical practitioners, it may include trained medical assistants – an especially important category in developing countries, where they provide many of the same services as fully qualified physicians, including simple operations.

THE AIDS CRISIS

The Acquired Immune Deficiency Syndrome was first identified in 1981, when American doctors found otherwise healthy young men succumbing to rare infections. By 1984, the cause had been traced to the Human Immunodeficiency Virus (HIV), which can remain dormant for many years and perhaps indefinitely: only half of those known to carry the virus in 1981 had developed AIDS ten years later.

By 1991 the World Health Organization knew of more than 250,000 AIDS cases worldwide and suspected the true number to be at least four times as high. In Western countries in the early 1990s, most AIDS deaths were among male homosexuals or needle-sharing drug-users. However, the disease is spreading fastest among heterosexual men and women, which is its usual vector in the Third World, where most of its victims live. Africa is the most severely hit: a 1992 UN report estimated that 2 million African children will die of AIDS before the year 2000 – and some 10 million will be orphaned.

TOBACCO

Annual consumption of cigarettes per capita (latest available year)

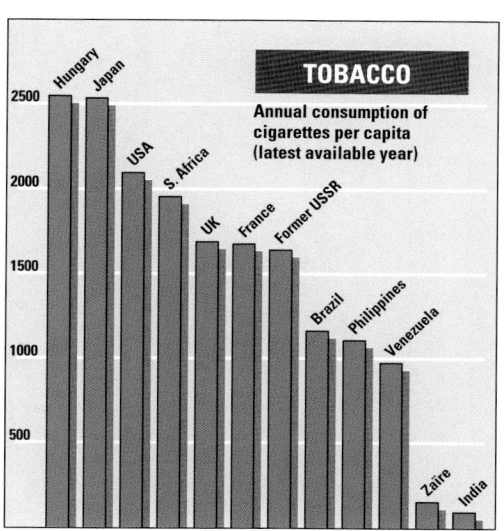

Hungary, Japan, USA, S. Africa, UK, France, Former USSR, Brazil, Philippines, Venezuela, Zaire, India

AIDS

Cases reported in 1993, per 100,000 population

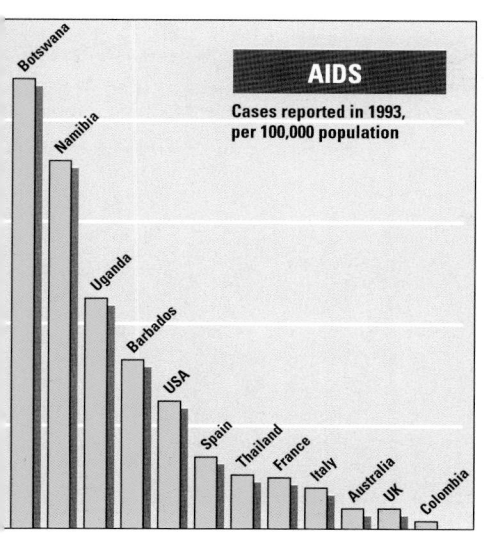

Botswana, Namibia, Uganda, Barbados, USA, Spain, Thailand, France, Italy, Australia, UK, Colombia

ALCOHOL

Annual consumption as litres of pure alcohol per capita (latest available year)

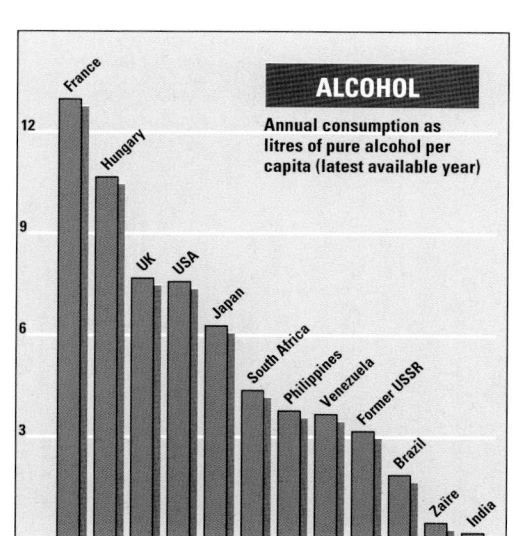

France, Hungary, UK, USA, Japan, South Africa, Philippines, Venezuela, Former USSR, Brazil, Zaire, India

CRIME AND PUNISHMENT

MURDER RATES

Murders per 100,000 population, selected countries (latest available year)

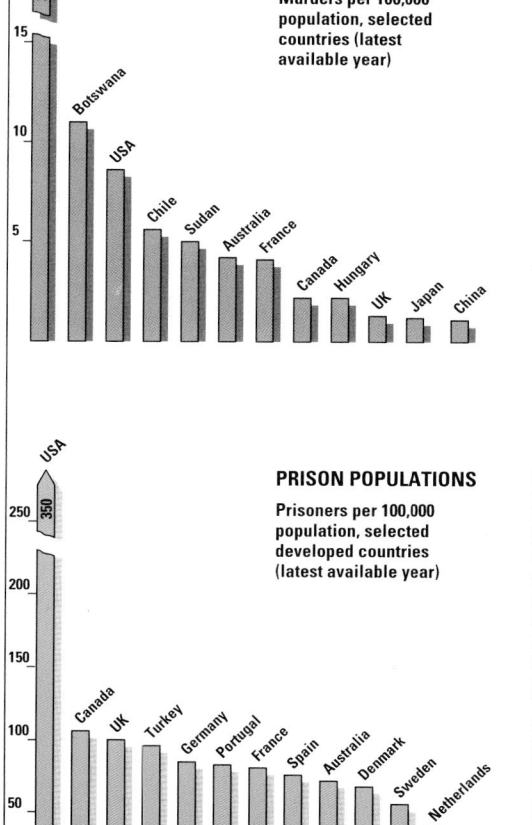

Philippines 38.7, Botswana, USA, Chile, Sudan, Australia, France, Canada, Hungary, UK, Japan, China

Crime rates are difficult to compare internationally. Standards of reporting and detection vary greatly, as do the definitions of many types of crime. Murder is probably the best detected as well as the most heinous, but different legal systems make different distinctions between murder and manslaughter or other forms of culpable homicide. By any reckoning, however, the USA's high murder rate stands out against otherwise similar Western countries, although it is dwarfed by the killings recorded in the very different culture of the Philippines.

PRISON POPULATIONS

Prisoners per 100,000 population, selected developed countries (latest available year)

USA 350, Canada, UK, Turkey, Germany, Portugal, France, Spain, Australia, Denmark, Sweden, Netherlands

Differences in prison population reflect penal policies as much as the relative honesty or otherwise of different nations, and by no means all governments publish accurate figures. In more than 50 countries, people are still regularly imprisoned without trial, in 60 torture is a normal part of interrogation, and some 130 retain the death penalty, often administered for political crimes and in secret. Over 2,000 executions were recorded in 1990 by the civil rights organization Amnesty International; the real figure, as Amnesty itself maintains, was almost certainly much higher.

QUALITY OF LIFE: ENVIRONMENT

Humans have always had a dramatic effect on their environment, at least since the invention of agriculture almost 10,000 years ago. Generally, the Earth has accepted human interference without any obvious ill effects: the complex systems that regulate the global environment have managed to absorb substantial damage while maintaining a stable and comfortable home for the planet's trillions of lifeforms. But advancing human technology and the rapidly expanding populations it supports are now threatening to overwhelm the Earth's ability to cope.

Industrial wastes, acid rainfall, expanding deserts and large-scale deforestation all combine to create environmental change at a rate far faster than the Earth can easily accommodate. Equipped with chain-saws

and flame-throwers, humans can now destroy more forest in a day than their ancestors could in a century, upsetting the balance between plant and animal, carbon dioxide and oxygen, on which all life ultimately depends. The fossil fuels that power industrial civilization have pumped enough carbon dioxide and other greenhouse gases into the atmosphere to make climatic change a near-certainty. Chlorofluorocarbons (CFCs) and other man-made chemicals are rapidly eroding the ozone layer, the planet's screen against ultraviolet radiation.

As a result, the Earth's average temperature has risen by about 0.5°C since the beginning of this century. Further rises seem inevitable, with 1990 marked as the hottest year worldwide since records began. A warmer Earth probably means a wetter Earth,

with melting ice-caps raising sea levels and causing severe flooding in some of the world's most densely populated regions. Other climatic models suggest an alternative doom: rising temperatures could increase cloud cover, reflecting more solar energy back into space and causing a new Ice Age.

Either way, the consequences for humans could be disastrous – perhaps the Earth's own way of restoring the ecological balance over the next few thousand years. Fortunately, there is a far faster mechanism available. Humans have provoked the present crisis, but human ingenuity can respond to it. CFC production is already almost at a standstill, and the first faltering steps towards stabilization and the reduction of carbon dioxide have been taken, with Denmark pioneering the way by taxing emissions in 1991.

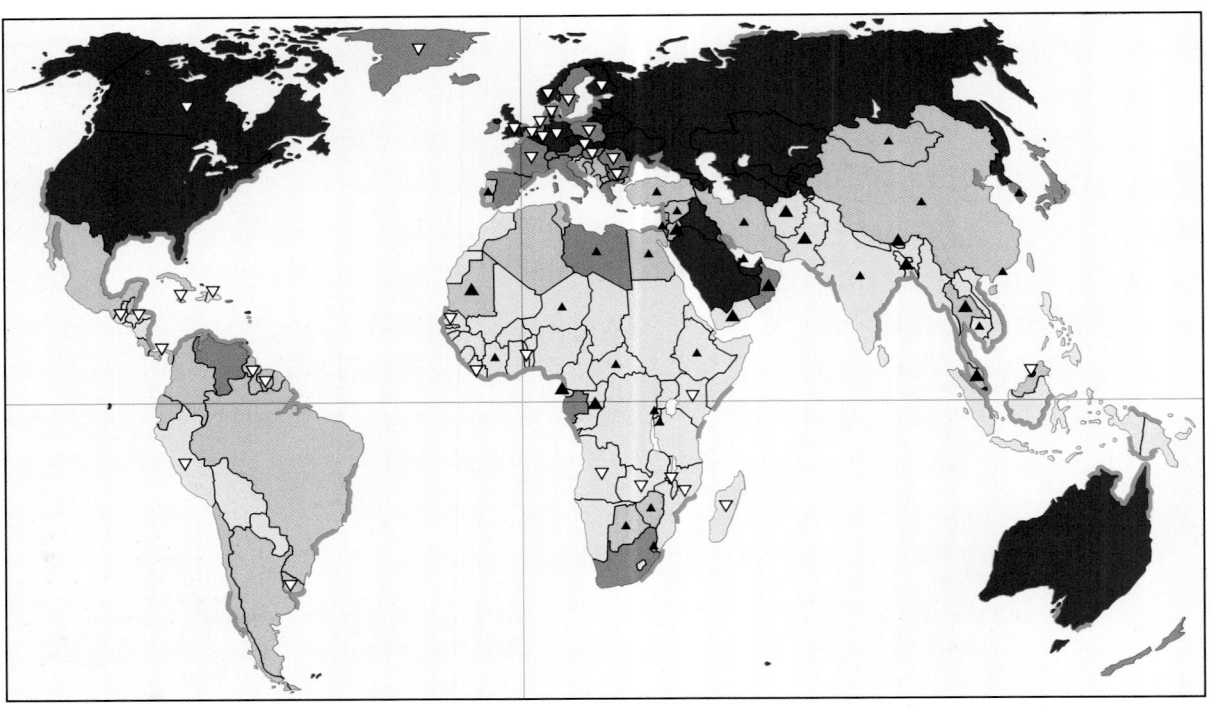

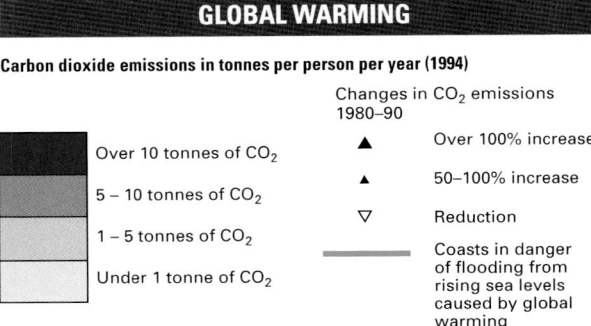

GLOBAL WARMING

Carbon dioxide emissions in tonnes per person per year (1994)

Over 10 tonnes of CO_2

5 – 10 tonnes of CO_2

1 – 5 tonnes of CO_2

Under 1 tonne of CO_2

Changes in CO_2 emissions 1980–90

▲ Over 100% increase

▲ 50–100% increase

▽ Reduction

— Coasts in danger of flooding from rising sea levels caused by global warming

THE RISE IN CARBON DIOXIDE

Emissions of carbon dioxide in millions of tonnes, 1950–91

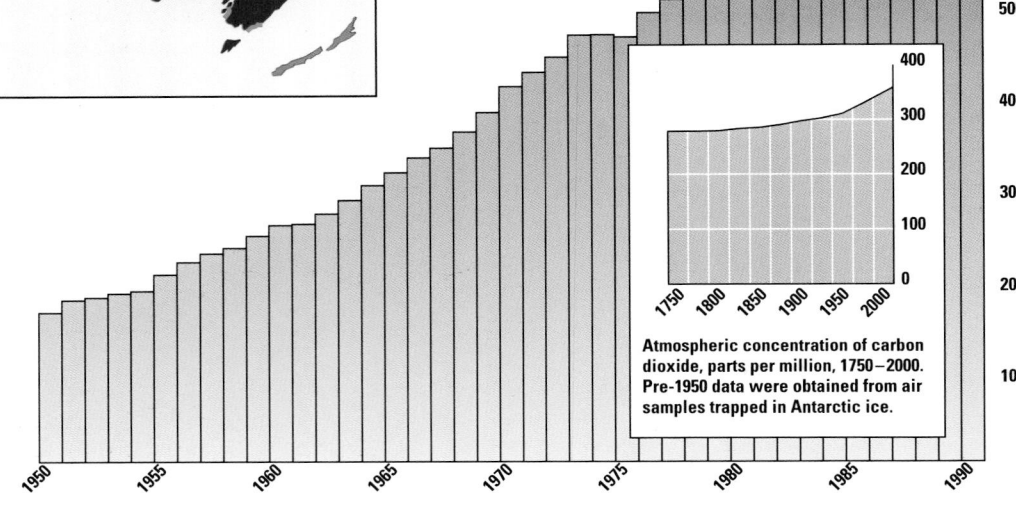

Atmospheric concentration of carbon dioxide, parts per million, 1750–2000. Pre-1950 data were obtained from air samples trapped in Antarctic ice.

Since the beginning of the Industrial Revolution, human activity has pumped steadily more and more carbon dioxide into the atmosphere. Most of it was quietly absorbed by the oceans, whose immense 'sink' capacity meant that 170 years were needed for levels to increase from the pre-industrial 280 parts per million to 300 parts per million (inset graph, right). But the vast increase in fuel-burning since 1950 (main graph) has overwhelmed even the oceanic sink. Atmospheric concentrations are now rising almost as steeply as carbon dioxide emissions themselves.

GREENHOUSE POWER

Relative contributions to the Greenhouse Effect by the major heat-absorbing gases in the atmosphere

The chart combines greenhouse potency and volume. Carbon dioxide has a greenhouse potential of only 1, but its concentration of 350 parts per million makes it predominate. CFC 12, with 25,000 times the absorption capacity of CO_2, is present only as 0.00044 ppm.

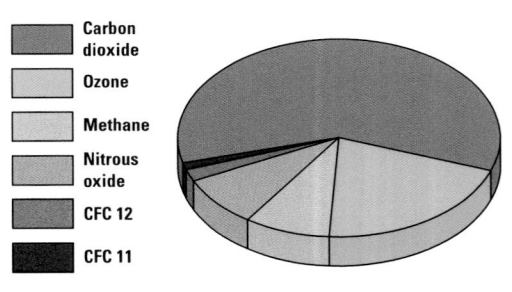

- Carbon dioxide
- Ozone
- Methane
- Nitrous oxide
- CFC 12
- CFC 11

CARBON DIOXIDE

Carbon dioxide released in millions of tonnes (1991)

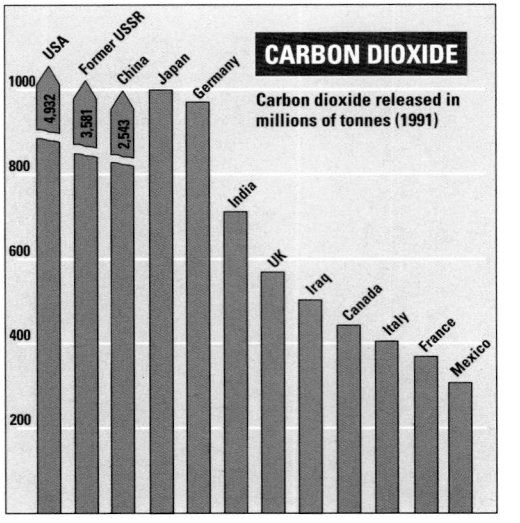

USA 4,932
Former USSR 3,581
China 2,543
Japan
Germany
India
UK
Iraq
Canada
Italy
France
Mexico

TEMPERATURE RISE

The rise in average temperatures caused by carbon dioxide and other greenhouse gases (1960–2020)

assumes present trends continue

assumes drastic emissions cuts in the 1990s

Recorded change

Projected changes

1960 1970 1980 1990 2000 2010 2020

Acid rain and sources of acidic emissions (latest available year)
Acid rain is caused by high levels of sulphur and nitrogen in the atmosphere. They combine with water vapour and oxygen to form acids (H_2SO_4 and HNO_3) which fall as precipitation.

 Regions where sulphur and nitrogen oxides are released in high concentrations, mainly from fossil fuel combustion

• Major cities with high levels of air pollution (including nitrogen and sulphur emissions)

Areas of heavy acid deposition
pH numbers indicate acidity, decreasing from a neutral 7. Normal rain, slightly acid from dissolved carbon dioxide, never exceeds a pH of 5.6.

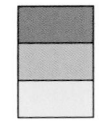

pH less than 4.0 (most acidic)

pH 4.0 to 4.5

pH 4.5 to 5.0

‒ ‒ ‒ Areas where acid rain is a potential problem

ANTARCTICA

The vast Antarctic ice-sheet, containing some 70% of the Earth's fresh water, plays a crucial role in the circulation of atmosphere and oceans and hence in determining the planetary climate. The frozen southern continent is also the last remaining wilderness – the largest area to remain free from human colonization.

Ever since Amundsen and Scott raced for the South Pole in 1911, various countries have pressed territorial claims over sections of Antarctica, spurred in recent years by its known and suspected mineral wealth: enough iron ore to supply the world at present levels for 200 years, large oil reserves and, probably, the biggest coal deposits on Earth.

However, the 1961 Antarctic Treaty set aside the area for peaceful uses only, guaranteeing freedom of scientific investigation, banning waste disposal and nuclear testing, and suspending the issue of territorial rights. By 1990, the original 12 signatories had grown to 25, with a further 15 nations granted observer status in subsequent deliberations. However, the Treaty itself was threatened by wrangles between different countries, government agencies and international pressure groups.

Finally, in July 1991, the belated agreement of the UK and the USA assured unanimity on a new accord to ban all mineral exploration for a further 50 years. The ban can only be rescinded if all the present signatories, plus a majority of any future adherents, agree. While the treaty has always lacked a formal mechanism for enforcement, it is firmly underwritten by public concern generated by the efforts of environmental pressure groups such as Greenpeace, which has been foremost in the campaign to have Antarctica declared a 'World Park'.

It now seems likely that the virtually uninhabited continent will remain untouched by tourism, staying nuclear-free and dedicated to peaceful scientific research.

DESERTIFICATION

Existing deserts

Areas with a high risk of desertification

Areas with a moderate risk of desertification

Former areas of rainforest

Existing rainforest

DEFORESTATION

5,200

1.5

Thousands of hectares of forest cleared annually, tropical countries surveyed 1981–85 and 1987–90. Loss as a percentage of remaining stocks is shown in figures on each column.

3,000

2,000

1,000

0

	Brazil	India	Indonesia	Burma	Thailand	Vietnam	Philippines	Costa Rica	Cameroon
1987–90		4.1	0.8	2.1	2.5	2.0	1.5	7.6	0.6
1981–85	0.4	0.3	0.5	0.3	2.4	0.7	1.0	4.0	0.4

■ 1987–90   ■ 1981–85

WATER POLLUTION

Severely polluted sea areas and lakes

Less polluted sea areas and lakes

Areas of frequent oil pollution by shipping

Major oil tanker spills ◤

Major oil rig blow-outs ▲

Offshore dumpsites for industrial and municipal waste ▼

Severely polluted rivers and estuaries ──

The most notorious tanker spillage of the 1980s occurred when the *Exxon Valdez* ran aground in Prince William Sound, Alaska, in 1989, spilling 267,000 barrels of crude oil close to shore in a sensitive ecological area. This rates as the world's 28th worst spill in terms of volume.

Poisoned rivers, domestic sewage and oil spillage have combined in recent years to reduce the world's oceans to a sorry state of contamination, notably near the crowded coasts of industrialized nations. Shipping routes, too, are constantly affected by tanker discharges. Oil spills of all kinds, however, declined significantly during the 1980s, from a peak of 750,000 tonnes in 1979 to under 50,000 tonnes in 1990. The most notorious tanker spill of that period – when the *Exxon Valdez* (94,999 grt) ran aground in Prince William Sound, Alaska, in March 1989 – released only 267,000 barrels, a relatively small amount compared to the results of blow-outs and war damage. Over 2,500,000 barrels were spilled during the Gulf War of 1991. The worst tanker accident in history occurred in July 1979, when the *Atlantic Empress* and the *Aegean Captain* collided off Trinidad, polluting the Caribbean with 1,890,000 barrels of crude oil.

CITY MAPS

Oslo, Copenhagen 2, Helsinki, Stockholm 3, London 4, Paris 5,The Ruhr 6, Berlin,
Hamburg, Munich 7, Madrid, Barcelona, Lisbon, Athens 8, Turin, Milan, Rome,
Naples 9, Prague, Warsaw, Vienna, Budapest 10, Moscow, St Petersburg 11,
Osaka, Hong Kong, Seoul 12, Tokyo 13, Peking, Shanghai, Tientsin, Canton 14,
Bangkok, Manila, Singapore, Jakarta 15, Delhi, Bombay, Calcutta 16,
Istanbul, Tehran, Baghdad, Karachi 17, Lagos, Cairo, Johannesburg 18, Sydney,
Melbourne 19, Montréal, Toronto 20, Boston 21, New York 22, Philadelphia 24,
Washington, Baltimore 25, Chicago 26, San Francisco 27, Los Angeles 28,
Mexico City 29, Havana, Caracas, Lima, Santiago 30, Rio de Janeiro,
São Paulo 31, Buenos Aires 32

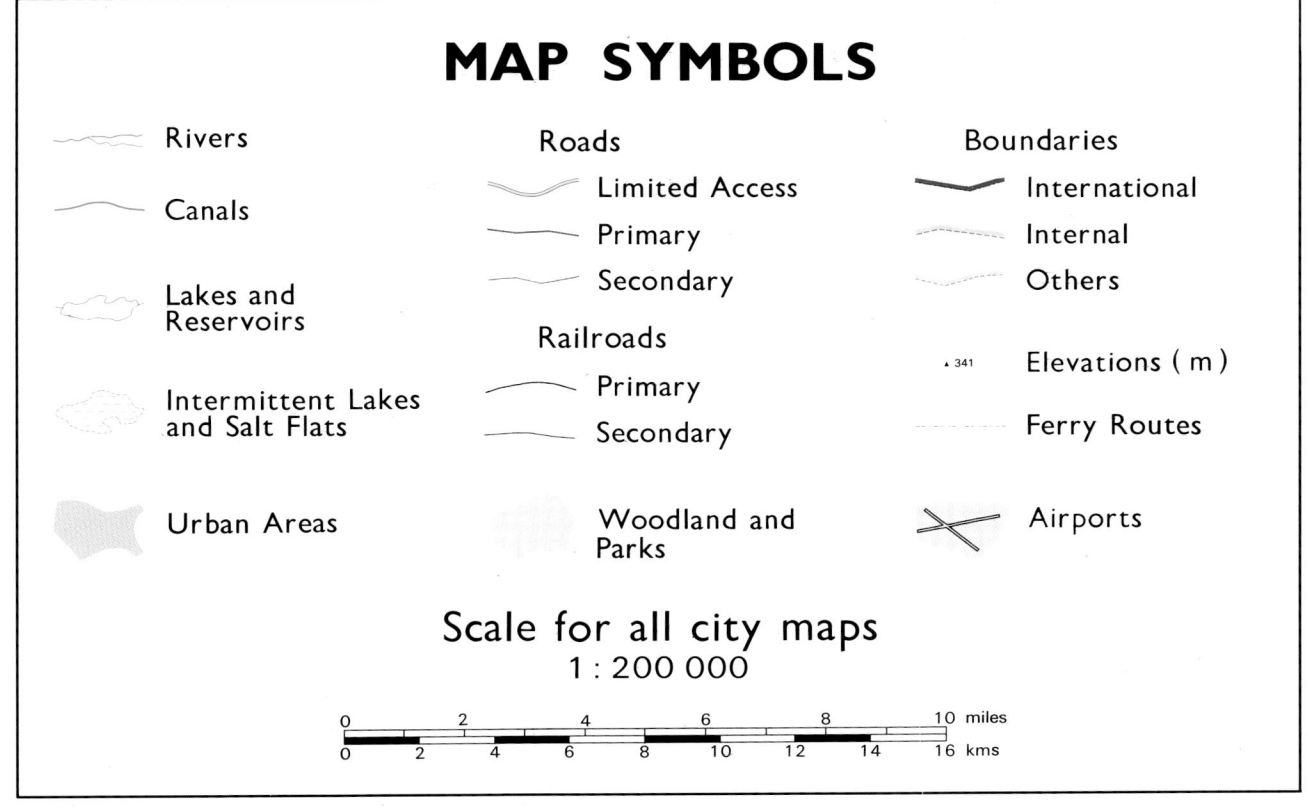

MAP SYMBOLS

Rivers	**Roads**		**Boundaries**	
Canals	Limited Access		International	
	Primary		Internal	
Lakes and Reservoirs	Secondary		Others	
	Railroads		• 341 Elevations (m)	
Intermittent Lakes and Salt Flats	Primary		Ferry Routes	
	Secondary			
Urban Areas	Woodland and Parks		Airports	

Scale for all city maps
1 : 200 000

0   2   4   6   8   10 miles
0   2   4   6   8   10   12   14   16 kms

1: 200 000

5 miles
8 km

Top map (Oslo)

Columns: 1 2 3 4 5 6

Rows: A B C

Utvika
Bruløkka
Glosli
Slakteren
Venner
Sørkedalen
Turter
Sandermosen
Slattum
Nittedal
Huseby
Heggelielva
N o r d m a r k a
Homledal
Tryvass-høgda 531
Maridalen
Skytta
407
Skedsmo
OSLO AKERSHUS FYLKE
Sollihøgda
Bogstadvatnet
418
Holmenkollen
Sognsvatn
Kjelsås
Alunsjøen
Vestli
Kjeller
Burudvatn
Ila
Ris
Røa
Ulleval
Grefsen
Grorud
Stovner
Strømmen
Lillestr
Bærums Verk
Rustad
Lijordet
OSLO
Sagene
Alnabru
Høybråten
Rud
Smestad
Bryn
379
Haslum
Skøyen
Universitet
Tøyen
Østre Aker
363
Lørenskog
Skui
Kolsås
Bærum
Lysaker
Domkirke
Sjøtrist
Gamlebyen
Lutvatn
Toverud
Stabekk
Bygdøy
Radhuset
Akershus festning
Ekeberg
Nordre Elvåga
Sylling
Hovik
Hovedøya
Bekkelaget
Oppsal
Bøler
Losby
Rælingen
Stovivatn
Tanum
Lindøya
Lambert Seter
Nordstrand
Nøklevatn
Ramstads
Sandvika
Snarøya
Ormøya
Østmark kapellet
Sandungen
Forneby
NESODDTANGEN
Malmøya
Sondre Elvåga
Slependen
Forneby
Ljan
Skullerud
Nordbysjøen
Semsvatn
Hvalstad
Nesøya
Ostøya
Flaskebekk
Oksval
Hauketo
Sørsdal
Brønnøya
Skoklefall
Klemetsrud
Tonekollen 368
Asker
Hvalstrand
Bonnefjorden
Sandbakken
Mosjøen
Lierskogen
Blakstad
OSLO AKERSHUS FYLKE
Ingierstrand
Siggerud
Vardå
Tranby
Vollen
215
Sørby
Kolbotn
Krokhøl
Skogen
Dikemark
Oslofjorden
Nesodden
Bru
Børtervatna
Lier
Gjellumvatn
Gjersjøen
Myrvoll
Binningsvatna
Frogner
Reistad
Fjellstrand
Hasle
Oppegård
134 Oppegård
Langen
Slemmestad
Svestad
Blylaget
Nærnes
Garder
East from Greenwich

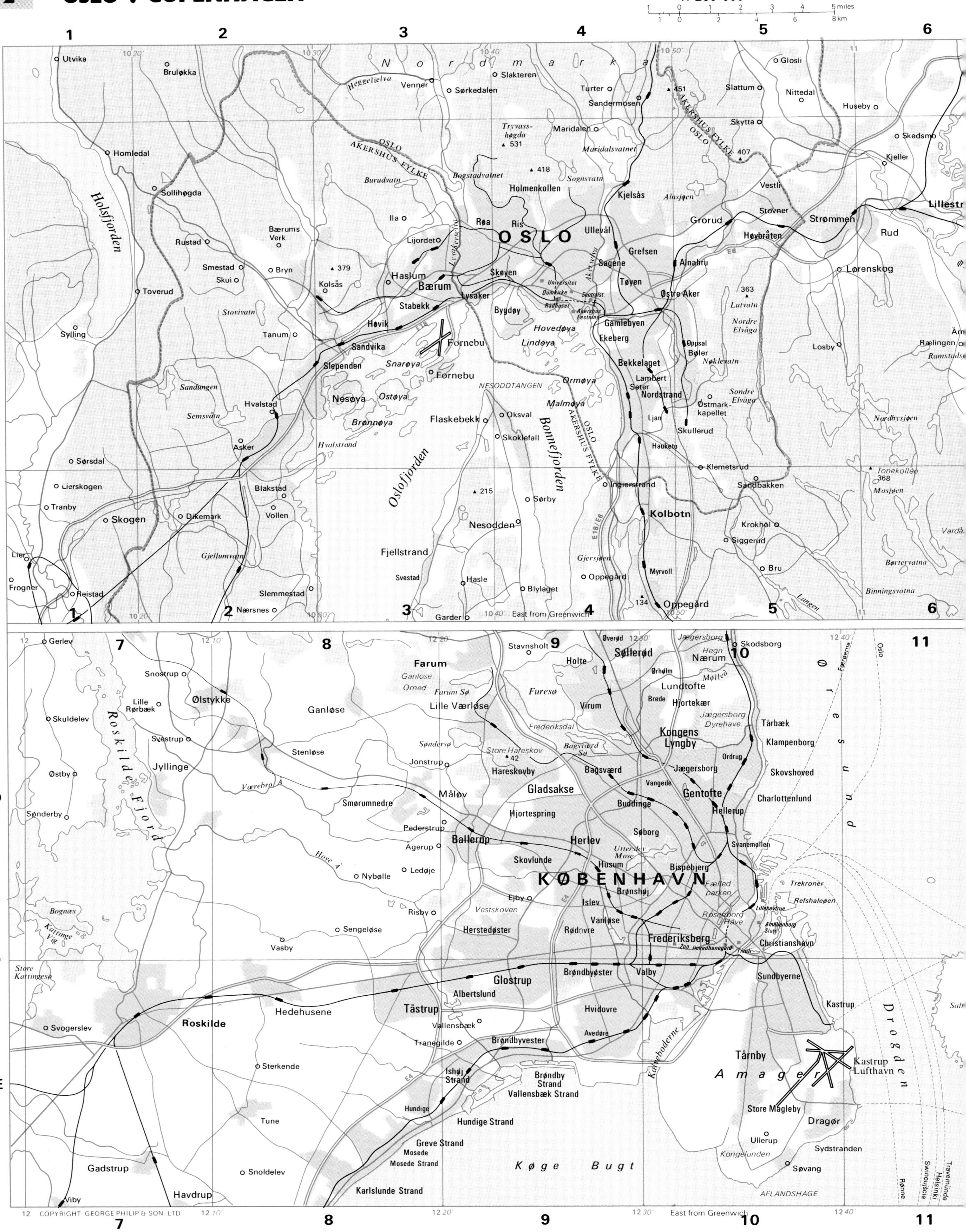

Bottom map (Copenhagen)

Columns: 7 8 9 10 11

Rows: D E

Gerlev
Øverød
Jægersborg
Skodsborg
Søllerød
Stavnsholt
Holte
Hegn
Nærum
Snostrup
Farum
Ganlose Orned
Furesø
Ørholm
Møllen
Lundtofte
Lille Rørbæk
Ølstykke
Ganløse
Farum Sø
Lille Værløse
Virum
Brede
Hjortekær
Tårbæk
Skuldelev
Frederiksdal
Jægersborg Dyrehave
Svestrup
Stenløse
Sønderø
Store Hareskov
Bagsværd Sø
Kongens Lyngby
Klampenborg
Østby
Jyllinge
Jonstrup
Hareskovby
42
Bagsværd
Ordrup
Skovshoved
Værebro Å
Målov
Gladsakse
Vangede
Jægersborg
Sønderby
Smørumnedre
Hjortespring
Buddinge
Gentofte
Charlottenlund
Hove Å
Pederstrup
Søborg
Hellerup
Ågerup
Ballerup
Herlev
Svanemøllen
Bognæs
Ledøje
Skovlunde
Husum
Uttersløv Mose
Bispebjerg
Nybølle
Ejby
KØBENHAVN
Risby
Islev
Brønshøj
Rosenborg Have
Trekroner
Refshaleøen
Sengeløse
Vestskoven
Vanløse
Fælledparken
Lillehavnœ
Kattinge Vig
Vasby
Herstedøster
Rødovre
Frederiksberg
Amalienborg Slot
Christianshavn
Store Kattingesø
Zoo Hovedbanegård
Tivoli
Svogerslev
Glostrup
Brøndbyøster
Valby
Sundbyerne
Roskilde
Albertslund
Hvidovre
Kastrup
Drogden
Hedehusene
Tåstrup
Brøndbyester
Avedøre
Vallensbæk
Tranegilde
Brøndbyvester
Køllevhaderne
Tårnby
Kastrup Lufthavn
Sterkende
Ishøj Strand
Brøndby Strand
Vallensbæk Strand
A m a g e r
Store Magleby
Dragør
Tune
Hundige
Hundige Strand
Ullerup
Sydstranden
Gadstrup
Greve Strand
Mosede
Mosede Strand
Kongelunden
Søvang
Viby
Havdrup
Snoldelev
Karlslunde Strand
K ø g e   B u g t
AFLANDSHAGE
Rønne
East from Greenwich

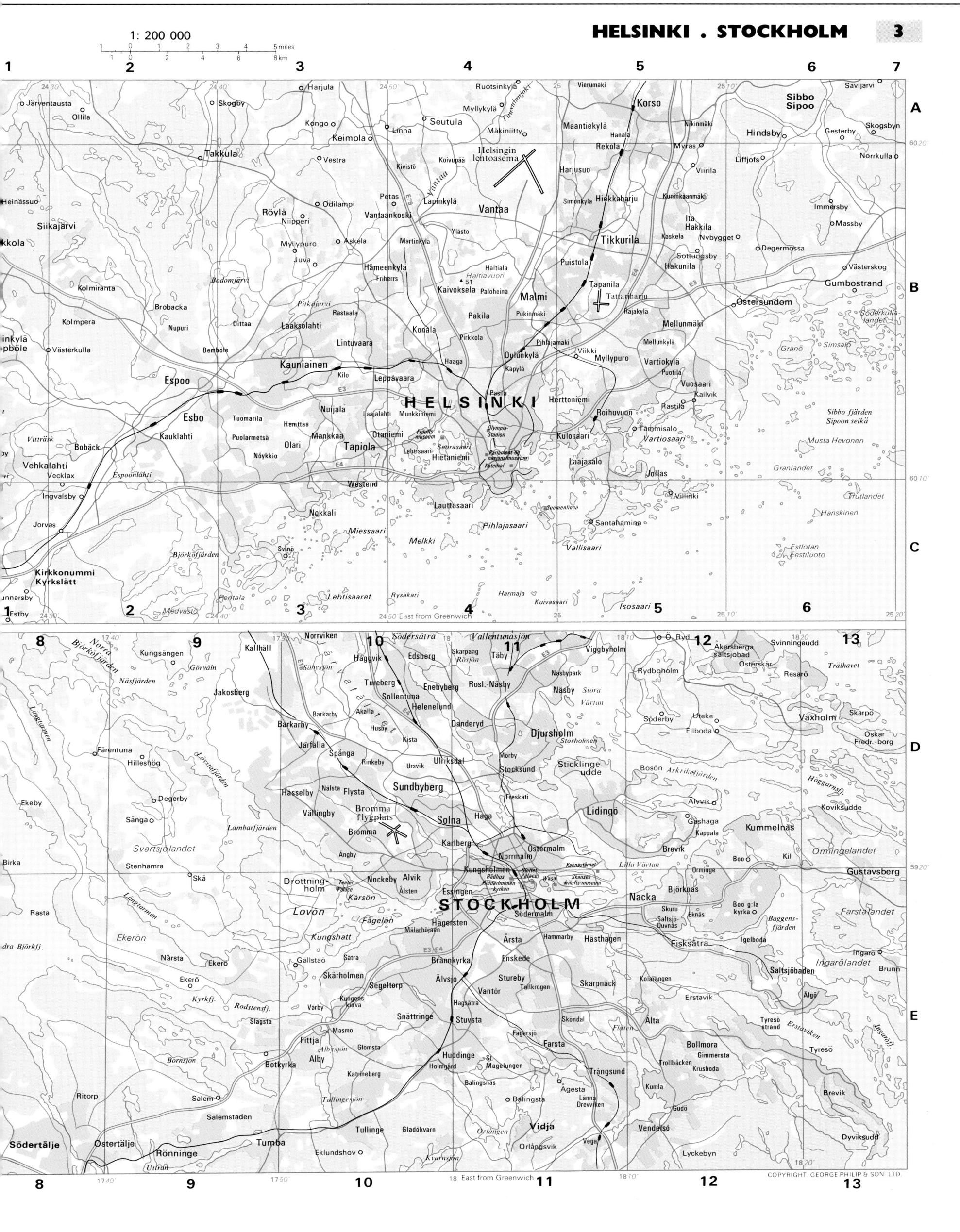

1: 200 000

0 1 2 3 4 5 miles
1 2 4 6 8 km

GREATER LONDON

River Thames

River Thames

Heathrow Airport

Brentwood · Shenfield · Ingrave · Herongate · Orsett · Chadwell St. Mary · Little Thurrock · Tilbury · Northfleet · Singlewell · Istead Rise · Meopham · New Ash Green · Wrotham · Culverstone Green · Stansted · Borough Green · Trottiscliffe

Blackmore · Doddinghurst · Mountnessing · Heybridge · Pilgrims Hatch · Brook Street · Harold Wood · Upminster · Hornchurch · Cranham · Corbets Tey · South Ockendon · North Stifford · Grays · Swanscombe · Greenhithe · Stone · Dartford · Wilmington · Hextable · Swanley · West Kingsdown · Hartley · Kemsing · Sevenoaks · Riverhead · Dunton Green · Otford

Chipping Ongar · Toot Hill · Kelvedon Hatch · Stapleford Abbotts · Abridge · Chigwell Row · Havering-atte-Bower · Romford · Harold Hill · Gidea Park · Gallows Corner · Squirrel's Heath · Emerson Park · Rush Green · Dagenham · Rainham · Aveley · Purfleet · West Thurrock · Erith · Belvedere · Slade Green · Bexley · Bexleyheath · Crayford · Barnehurst · Welling · Sidcup · St. Paul's Cray · St. Mary Cray · Orpington · Chelsfield · Pratts Bottom · Knockholt Pound · Badgers Mount · Shoreham · Eynsford · Farningham · Crockenhill

Epping · Theydon Bois · Loughton · Chigwell · Hainault · Barkingside · Newbury Park · Ilford · Barking · Beckton · Creekmouth · Abbey Wood · Plumstead · Woolwich · Charlton · Eltham · Mottingham · Chislehurst · Sidcup · Longlands · Blackfen · New Eltham · Petts Wood · Bromley Common · Keston · Downe · Cudham · Tatsfield · Biggin Hill · Leaves Green

Waltham Abbey · Cheshunt · Enfield Lock · Waltham Forest · Chingford · Woodford Green · Woodford Wells · Buckhurst Hill · Wanstead · Leytonstone · Stratford · West Ham · East Ham · Forest Gate · Upton · Canning Town · Silvertown · Greenwich · Blackheath · Lee · Lewisham · Catford · Bellingham · Grove Park · Southend · Shortlands · Bromley · Beckenham · Hayes · West Wickham · Shirley · Addington · New Addington · Selsdon · Sanderstead · Warlingham · Woldingham · Caterham · Chipstead

Potters Bar · Cuffley · Northaw · Enfield · Ponders End · Lower Edmonton · Upper Edmonton · Tottenham · Edmonton · Winchmore Hill · Southgate · Palmers Green · New Southgate · Wood Green · Haringey · Stoke Newington · Stamford Hill · Hackney · Bethnal Green · Bow · Poplar · Millwall · Bermondsey · Deptford · New Cross · Peckham · Nunhead · Brockley · Forest Hill · Sydenham · Penge · Upper Norwood · Thornton Heath · Croydon · Purley · Coulsdon · Kenley · Whyteleafe · Kingswood

Barnet · New Barnet · East Barnet · Cockfosters · Oakwood · Friern Barnet · Finchley · North Finchley · Whetstone · Totteridge · Muswell Hill · Highgate · Crouch End · Hornsey · Finsbury Park · Tufnell Park · Kentish Town · Camden Town · Islington · City · Holborn · Westminster · Shoreditch · Whitechapel · Stepney · Limehouse · Rotherhithe · Walworth · Camberwell · Dulwich · East Dulwich · West Dulwich · Penge · Anerley · Beckenham · Crystal Palace · Streatham · Norbury · Mitcham · Carshalton · Wallington · Beddington · Hackbridge · Waddon

Arkley · Hadley Wood · New Barnet · Church End · Mill Hill · Hendon · Colindale · Burnt Oak · Golders Green · Hampstead · Hampstead Garden Suburb · Cricklewood · Willesden · Brondesbury · Kilburn · Kensal Green · St. John's Wood · Regent's Park · Marylebone · Paddington · Bayswater · Notting Hill · Maida Vale · Kensington · Earls Court · Chelsea · Battersea · Clapham · Balham · Tooting · Upper Tooting · Wimbledon · Merton · Morden · St. Helier · North Cheam · Cheam · Sutton · Carshalton · Banstead · Burgh Heath · Tadworth · Walton on the Hill · Headley

Shenley · Borehamwood · Stone Grove · Edgware · Stanmore · Queensbury · Kingsbury · Wembley · Neasden · Dollis Hill · Stonebridge · Harlesden · Acton · East Acton · Park Royal · Ealing · Hanwell · Brentford · Chiswick · Turnham Green · Gunnersbury · Kew · Richmond · Mortlake · Barnes · East Sheen · Roehampton · Putney · Southfields · Wandsworth · Earlsfield · Raynes Park · New Malden · Worcester Park · Malden · Surbiton · Tolworth · Hook · Chessington · Epsom · Ashtead · Leatherhead · Fetcham · Great Bookham

Bushey · Watford · Belmont · Wealdstone · Harrow Weald · Harrow · Kenton · Pinner · North Harrow · West Harrow · South Harrow · Rayners Lane · Eastcote · Ruislip · Northolt · Greenford · Hanger Lane · Perivale · Northfields · Osterley · Heston · Isleworth · Twickenham · Teddington · Hampton · Hampton Hill · Hampton Court · Hampton Wick · Kingston upon Thames · Surbiton · Long Ditton · Thames Ditton · East Molesey · West Molesey · Esher · Claygate · Oxshott · Cobham · Stoke D'Abernon

Abbots Langley · Bricket Wood · Cassiobury Park · Croxley Green · Chorleywood · Rickmansworth · South Oxhey · Northwood · Pinner Green · West Ruislip · Ickenham · Uxbridge · Cowley · Yiewsley · West Drayton · Hayes · Hayes End · Hillingdon · Southall · Hounslow · Cranford · Harlington · Sipson · Harmondsworth · East Bedfont · Feltham · Hanworth · Ashford · Staines · Egham · Thorpe · Laleham · Shepperton · Chertsey · Sunbury · Walton-on-Thames · Weybridge · Byfleet · Ripley · Hersham · Whiteley Village · Wisley Gardens · East Horsley

Harefield · Denham · Denham Green · Iver · Chipperfield · Chorleywood · Chenies

River Lea · River Roding · River Brent · River Crane · River Colne · River Mole · River Wey · River Wandle · River Darent · River Cray · Grand Union Canal · Watling Street · Epping Forest · Hampstead Heath · Richmond Park · Wimbledon Common · Hatfield Forest

A

B

C

D

1 2 3 4 5 6 7

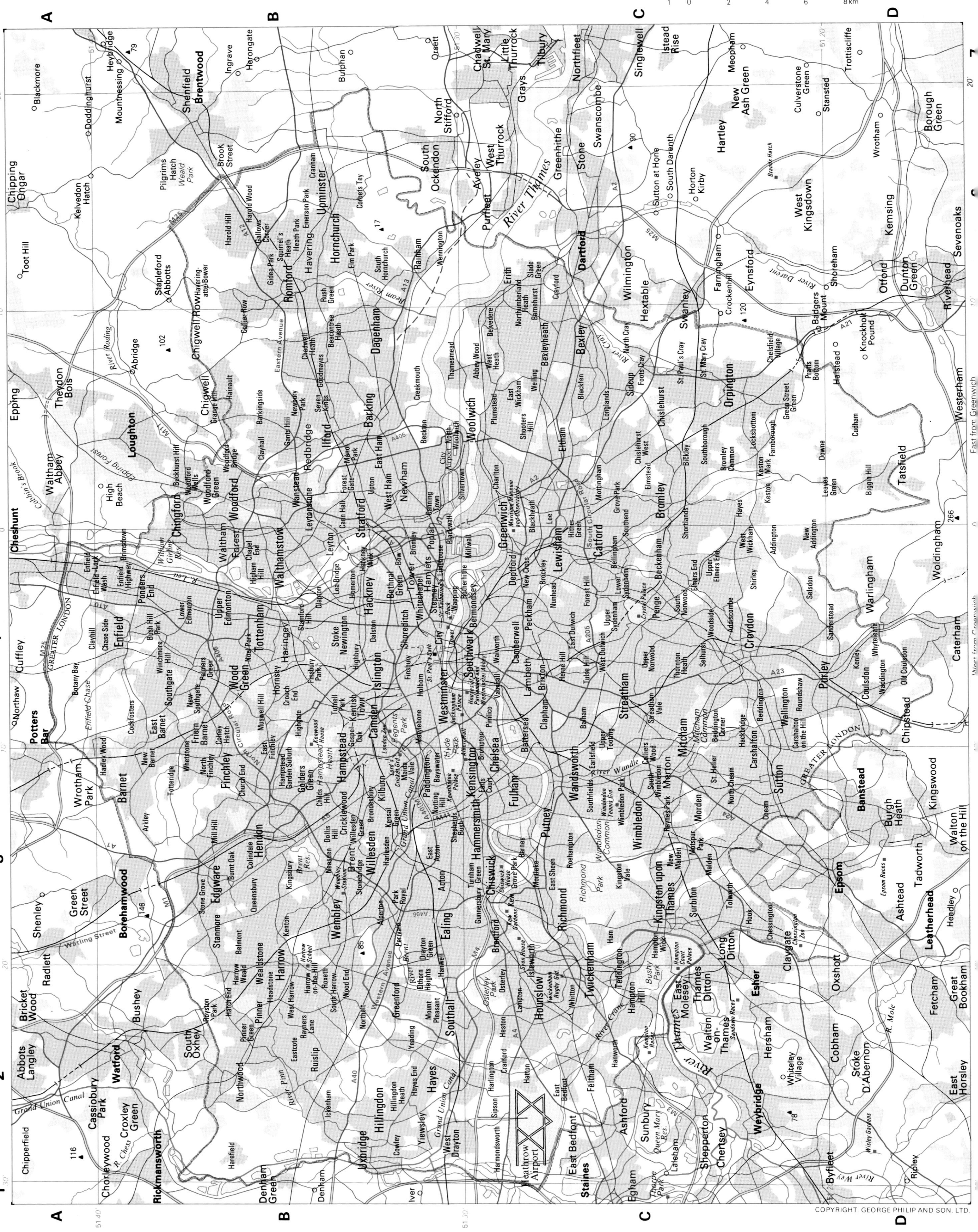

1: 200 000

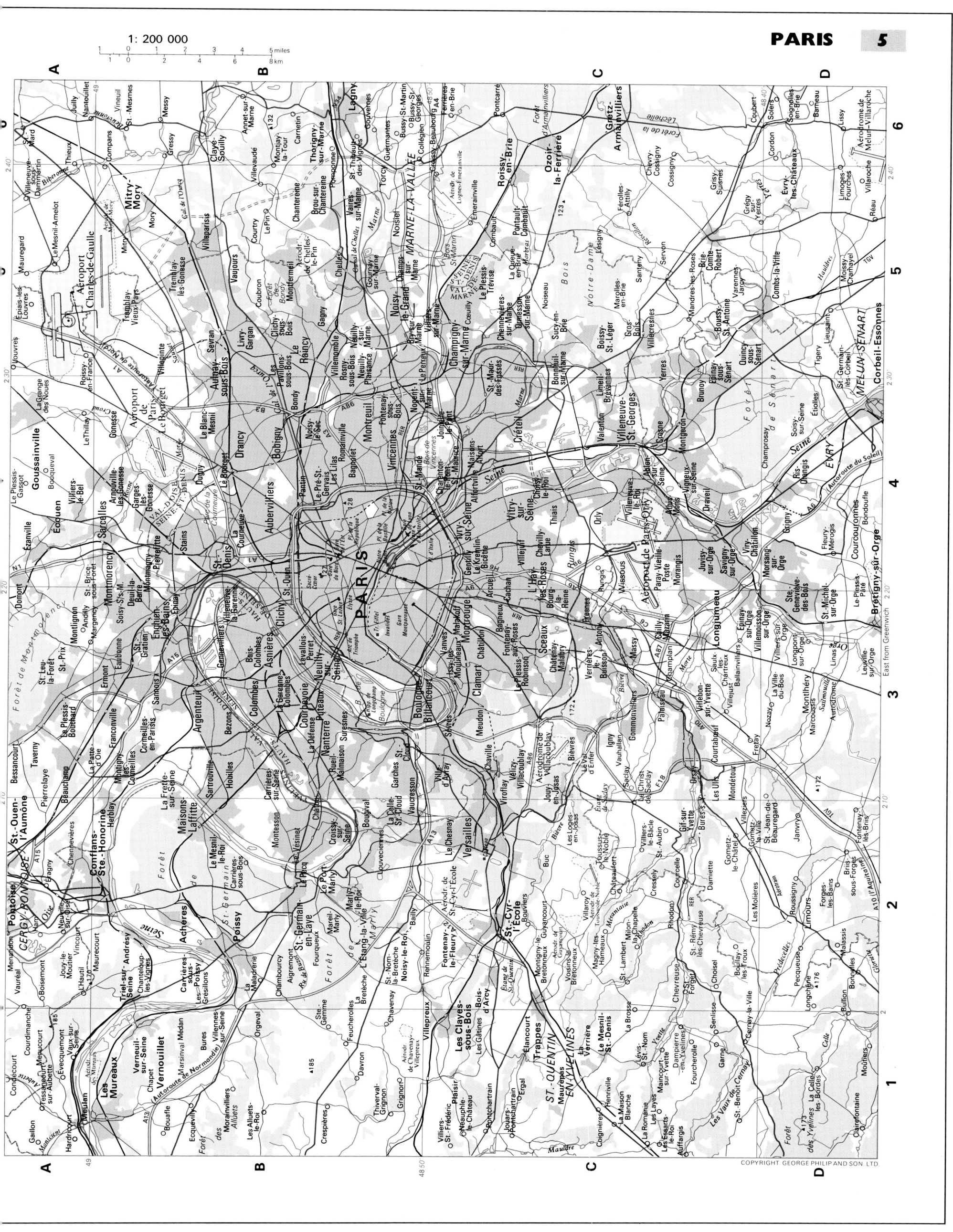

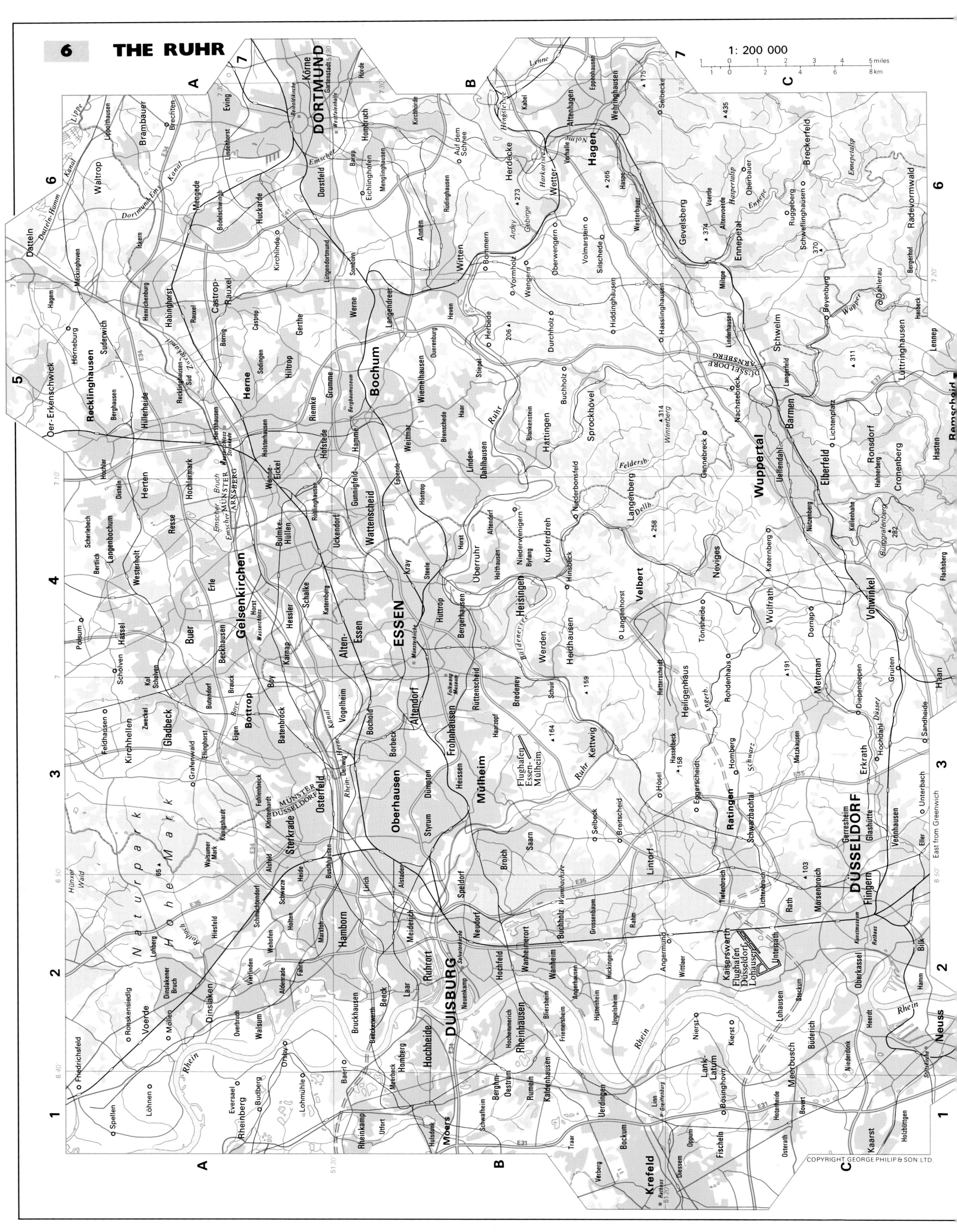

1 : 200 000

1 : 200 000

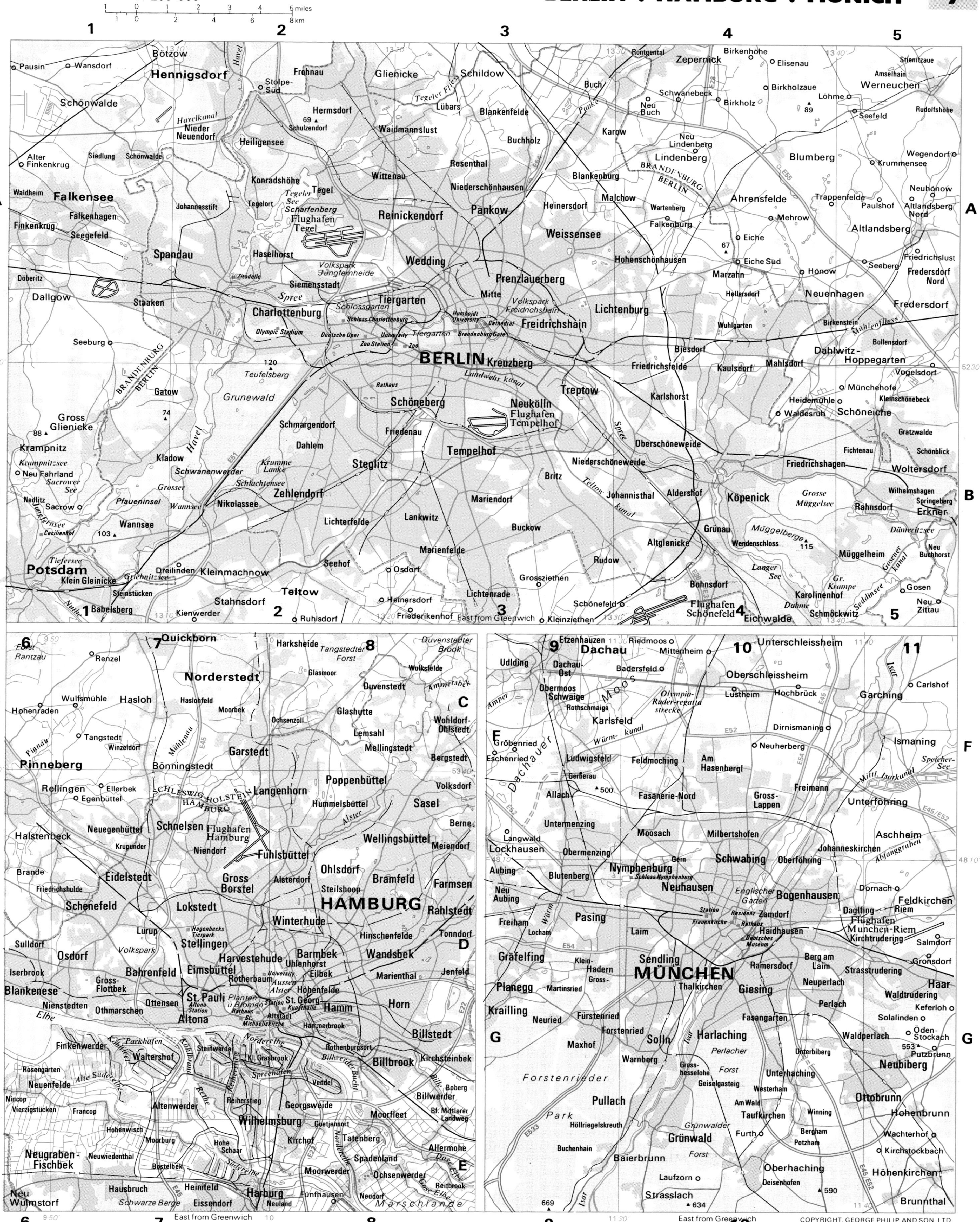

5 miles
8 km

Berlin map

Pausin · Wansdorf · Bötzow · Frohnau · Glienicke · Schildow · Röntgental · Zepernick · Birkenhöhe · Elisenau · Stienitzsee

Hennigsdorf · Stolpe-Süd · Buch · Schwanebeck · Birkholzaue · Werneuchen

Schönwalde · Hermsdorf · Lübars · Blankenfelde · Neu Buch · Birkholz · Löhme · Seefeld · Rudolfshöhe

Nieder Neuendorf · Schulzendorf · Waidmannslust · Karow · Neu Lindenberg · Wegendorf · Krummensee

Alter Finkenkrug · Siedlung Schönwalde · Heiligensee · Rosenthal · Buchholz · Lindenberg · Blumberg · Neuhonow

Waldheim · Falkensee · Konradshöhe · Tegel · Wittenau · Niederschönhausen · Blankenburg · BRANDENBURG BERLIN · Ahrensfelde · Trappenfelde · Paulshof · Altlandsberg Nord

Falkenhagen · Johannsthift · Tegelort · Scharfenberg · Pankow · Heinersdorf · Malchow · Wartenberg · Mehrow · Eiche · Hönow · Seeberg · Friedrichslust · Altlandsberg

Finkenkrug · Seegeld · Flughafen Tegel · Reinickendorf · Weissensee · Hohenschönhausen · Eiche Süd · Neuenhagen · Fredersdorf

Dallgow · Staaken · Haselhorst · Wedding · Mitte · Prenzlauerberg · Marzahn · Fredersdorf Nord

Döberitz · Spandau · Siemensstadt · Volkspark Jungfernheide · Tiergarten · Volkspark Friedrichshain · Lichtenburg · Hellersdorf · Birkenstein · Mühlenfliess

Gatow · Teufelsberg · Charlottenburg · Olympic Stadium · Deutsche Oper · University · Humboldt University · Brandenburg Gate · Cathedral · Freidrichshain · Bjesdorf · Dahlwitz-Hoppegarten · Bollensdorf

Seeburg · Grunewald · Schloss Charlottenburg · Zoo Station · Zoo · BERLIN Kreuzberg · Friedrichsfelde · Kaulsdorf · Mahlsdorf · Vogelsdorf

Gross Glienicke · Krampnitz · Rathaus · Schöneberg · Neukölln · Treptow · Karlshorst · Heidemühle · Münchehofe · Kleinschönebeck

Neu Fahrland · Sacrower See · Schwanenwerder · Friedenau · Flughafen Tempelhof · Oberschöneweide · Waldesruh · Schöneiche · Gratzwalde

Nedlitz · Sacrow · Pfaueninsel · Dahlem · Tempelhof · Niederschöneweide · Johannisthal · Aldershof · Grünau · Friedrichshagen · Fichtenau · Schönblick

Wannsee · Krumme Lanke · Steglitz · Mariendorf · Telton kanal · Köpenick · Grosse Müggelsee · Rahnsdorf · Wilhelmshagen · Springberg · Erkner

Cecilienhof · Grosser Wannsee · Schlachtensee · Zehlendorf · Lichterfelde · Lankwitz · Buckow · Grünau · Wendenschloss · Müggelberge · Müggelheim · Dämeritzsee

Tiefersee · Nikolassee · Marienfelde · Altglienicke · Langer See · Gr. Krampe · Neu Buchhorst

Potsdam · Klein Gleinicke · Kleinmachnow · Seehof · Osdorf · Grossziethen · Bohnsdorf · Karolinenhof · Gosen · Neu Zittau

Babelsberg · Kienwerder · Stahnsdorf · Teltow · Ruhlsdorf · Heinersdorf · Lichtenrade · Schönefeld · Flughafen Schönefeld · Eichwalde · Schmöckwitz

Friederikenhof · Kleinziethen · Dahme · Seddinsee

East from Greenwich

Hamburg map

Quickborn · Harksheide · Tangstedter Forst · Duvenstedter Brook

Forst Rantzau · Renzel · Norderstedt · Glasmoor · Wolksfelde · Duvenstedt · Ammersbek

Wulfsmühle · Hasloh · Haslohfeld · Ochsenzoll · Glashütte · Lemsahl · Mellingstedt · Wohldorf-Ohlstedt

Höhenraden · Tangstedt · Winzeldorf · Garstedt · Bergstedt

Pinneberg · Bönningstedt · Poppenbüttel · Volksdorf

Rellingen · Ellerbek · Egenbüttel · Schleswig-Holstein Hamburg · Langenhorn · Hummelsbüttel · Sasel · Berne

Halstenbeck · Neuegenbüttel · Krupunder · Schnelsen · Flughafen Hamburg · Niendorf · Fuhlsbüttel · Ohlsdorf · Wellingsbüttel · Meiendorf

Brande · Friedrichsruhe · Eidelstedt · Gross Borstel · Alsterdorf · Bramfeld · Farmsen

Schenefeld · Lokstedt · HAMBURG · Steilshoop · Rahlstedt

Sulldorf · Lurup · Hagenbecks Tierpark · Stellingen · Winterhude · Hinschenfelde · Tonndorf

Iserbrook · Osdorf · Volkspark · Harvestehude · Barmbek · Wandsbek · Jenfeld

Blankenese · Gross Flottbek · Bahrenfeld · Eimsbüttel · Uhlenhorst · Eilbek · Marienthal

Nienstedten · Ottensen · Rotherbaum · Hohenfelde · Horn

St. Pauli · Altona · Planten u Blomen · St. Georg · Hamm · Billstedt

Othmarschen · Elbe · Rathaus · Altstadt · St. Michaeliskirche · Hammerbrook · Billbrook

Finkenwerder · Parkhafen · Waltershof · Steinwerder · Kl. Grasbrook · Rothenburgsort · Billwerder · Kirchsteinbek

Rosengarten · Neuenfelde · Alte Süderelbe · Norderelbe · Spreehafen · Veddel · Boberg · Bf. Mittlerer Landweg

Nincop · Vierzigstücken · Francop · Reiherstieg · Georgswerder · Billwerder · Moorfleet

Neugraben-Fischbek · Altenwerder · Wilhelmsburg · Goetjensort · Tatenberg · Spadenland · Allermöhe

Neu Wulmstorf · Hohenwisch · Moorburg · Hohe Schaar · Kirchof · Moorwerder · Ochsenwerder

Hausbruch · Neuwiedenthal · Bostelbek · Schwarze Berge · Heimfeld · Eissendorf · Harburg · Fünfhausen · Neudorf · Reithbrook · Gr. Elbe · Marschlande

East from Greenwich

Munich map

Etzenhausen · Riedmoos · Mittenheim · Unterschleissheim

Dachau · Dachau-Ost · Badersfeld · Oberschleissheim · Carlshof

Udlding · Obermoos Schwaige · Rothschwaige · Olympia-Ruderregatta strecke · Lustheim · Hochbrück · Garching

Amper · Karlsfeld · Dirnismaning · MOOS · E52

Gröbenried · Eschenried · Ludwigsfeld · Feldmoching · Neuherberg · Ismaning · Speicher-See

Dachauer · Gerberau · Am Hasenbergl · Freimann · Unterföhring

Allach · Fasanerie-Nord · Gross-Lappen

Untermenzing · Moosach · Milbertshofen · Aschheim

Langwald · Obermenzing · Johanneskirchen

Lockhausen · Bern · Schwabing · Oberföhring · Ablanggraben

Aubing · Blutenberg · Nymphenburg · Schloss Nymphenburg · Englischer Garten · Bogenhausen · Dornach · Feldkirchen

Neu Aubing · Pasing · Station Frauenkirche · Residenz · Zamdorf · Dagifing · Riem

Würm · Freiham · Locham · Laim · Rathaus · Haidhausen · Flughafen München-Riem · Kirchtrudering · Salmdorf

Gräfelfing · Klein-Hadern · Gross-Hadern · Deutsches Museum · München · Ramersdorf · Berg am Laim · Strassrudering · Gronsdorf

Planegg · Martinsried · MÜNCHEN · Sendling · Thalkirchen · Giesing · Neuperlach · Haar

Krailling · Neuried · Fürstenried · Fasangarten · Perlach · Keferloh · Waldtrudering

Gräfelfing · Maxhof · Forstenried · Solln · Harlaching · Berg am Laim · Solalinden

Pullach · Warnberg · Grosshesselohe · Perlacher Forst · Unterbiberg · Waldperlach · Öden-Stockach · Neubiberg

Forstenrieder Park · Höllriegelskreuth · Geiselgasteig · Westerham · Am Wald · Unterhaching · Putzbrunn

Buchenhain · Grünwald · Furth · Bergham · Winning · Ottobrunn · Hohenbrunn

Baierbrunn · Taufkirchen · Grünwalder Forst · Potzham · Wächterhof · Kirchstockach · Höhenkirchen

Laufzorn · Deisenhofen · Brunnthal

Strasslach · Oberhaching

East from Greenwich

1: 200 000

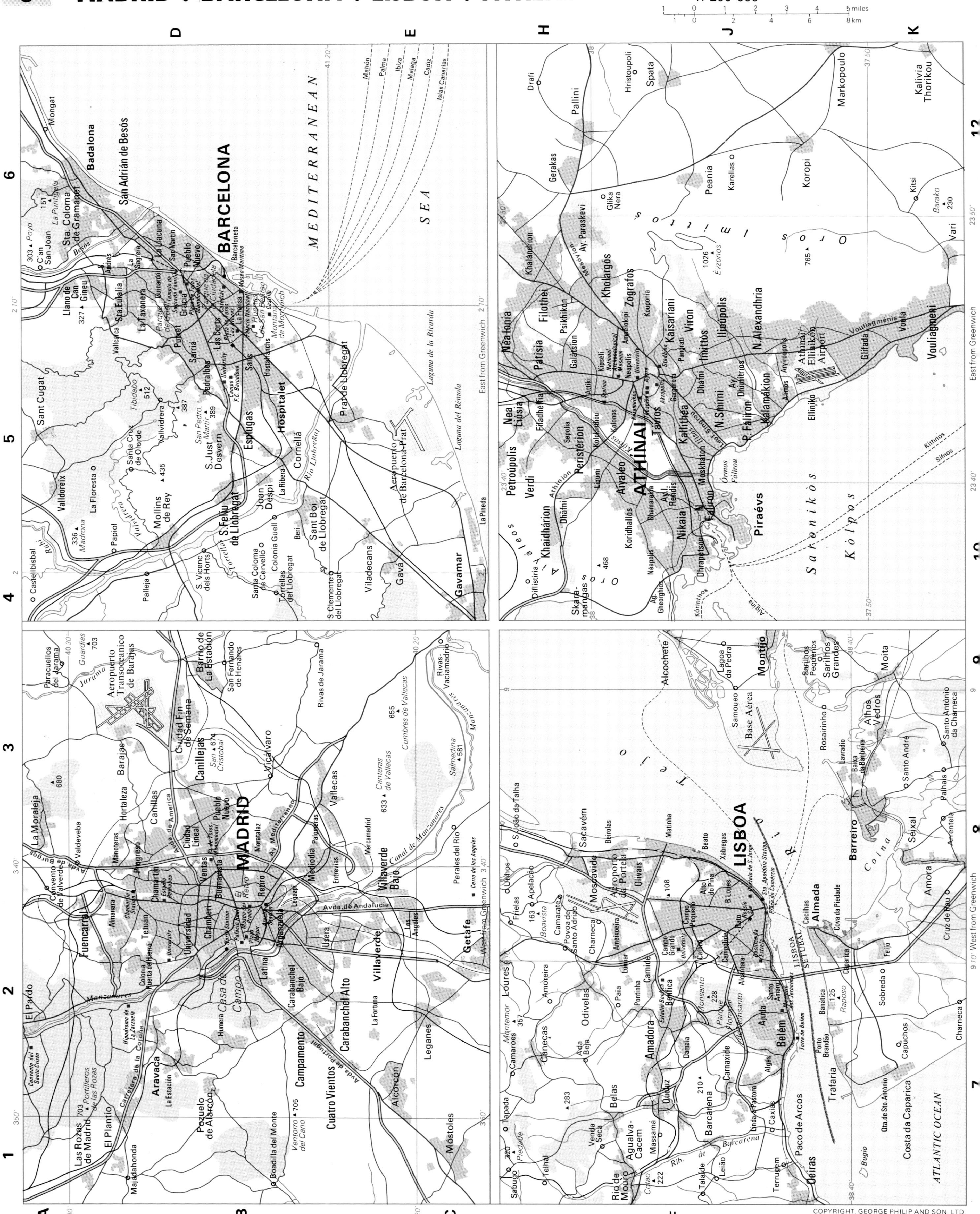

1 0 1 2 3 4 5 miles
1 0 2 4 6 8 km

MADRID . BARCELONA . LISBON . ATHENS

Barcelona

Mongat, Badalona, San Adrián de Besós, Sta. Coloma de Gramanet, La Puntiqua, San Joan, C'an, Poyo 303, 151, Sant Cugat, Llano de Can, Gineu, Llaretca, Sta. Eulalia, Andres, La Sagrera, Gracia, La Taxonera, Sarriá, Pedralbes, University, La Floresta, Valldoreix, Tibidabo 512, San Pedro, Santa Cruz de Olorde, S. Just Martín 389, 387, Las Corts, Sans, Hospitalet, Pueblo Nuevo, La Lacuna, Sant Martín, BARCELONA, Barceloneta, Montjuich, Puig, Valldrera 435, Esplugas, Cornellá, Mollins de Rey, S. Feliu de Llobregat, Joan Despí, Prat de Llobregat, Papiol, 336, Madrona, Sant Boi de Llobregat, Palleja, S. Vicenç dels Horts, Santa Coloma de Cervelló, Colonia Güell, La Ribera, Aeropuerto de Barcelona-Prat, Castellbisbal, Torrellas de Llobregat, Viladecans, Gavá, Gavamar, S. Clemente del Llobregat, La Pineda, Laguna de la Ricarda, Laguna del Remolá

MEDITERRANEAN SEA

East from Greenwich 2°10'

Mahón, Palma, Ibiza, Malaga, Cadiz, Islas Canarias

Madrid

Paracuellos del Jarama, Guardias 703, 703, Aeropuerto Transoceánico de Barajas, Barrio de La Estación, San Fernando de Henares, Jarama, La Moraleja, Barajas, Ciudad Fin de Semana, Canillejas, San Cristobal 674, Vicalvaro, Rivas de Jarama, Rivas-Vaciamadrid, Las Rozas de Madrid, Portilleros de las Rozas, Pozuelo de Alarcón, El Plantío, Majadahonda, Boadilla del Monte, El Pardo, Hipódromo de la Zarzuela, Convento del Santo Cristo, La Estación, Manzanares, Casa de Campo, Aravaca, Campamento, Cuatro Vientos, Ventoro 705, Alcorcón, Móstoles, Leganés, Carabanchel Alto, Carabanchel Bajo, La Fortuna, Villaverde, Villaverde Bajo, Mediodia, Entrevias, Vallecas, Cumbres de Vallecas, Canteras de Vallecas 633, 655, Salmedina 581, Cerro de los Angeles, Getafe, MADRID, Chamartín, Hortaleza, Canillas, Pueblo Nuevo, Ciudad Lineal, Moratalaz, Vallecas, Mercamadrid, Palaqueras, Perales del Río, Canal de Manzanares, Avda. de Andalucia

West from Greenwich 3°40'

Athens

Drafi, Pallini, Spata, Hristopoli, Markopoulo, Kalivia Thorikou, Gerakas, Peania, Karellas, Koropi, Kitsi, Barako 230, Neofonia, Khalápdrion, Glika Nera, Vari, Kholargós, Filothei, Psikhikón, Zografos, Kouponia, N. Alexandhria, Nea Ionia, Attiki, Galatsion, Kipseli, Pangrati, Kaisariani, Viron, Ilioupolis, Vouliagménis, Nea Liósia, Patisia, Neapolis, Ay. Paraskevi, Ay. Dhimitrios, N. Smirni, Kalamakion, Glifada, Petroúpolis, Verdi, Peristeri, Sepolia, Aivaléo, ATHINAI, P. Faliron, Ellinikó Airport, Vouliagméni, Athinón, Dháfni, Tavros, Kallithéa, Voula, Skarda-mangas, Khaidhárion, Dháfni, 468, Koridhallós, Nikaia, Moskhaton, N. Faliron, PIRAÉVS, Dhraptsona, Diflistiria, Ghergliios, Kórinthos, Aiyina, Kithnos, Sifnos, Saronikós Kólpos

Lisboa

Alcochete, Lagoa da Pedra, Montijo, Sarilhos Pequeños, Sarilhos Grandes, Moita, Base Aérea, Samoueo, Rosairinho, Santo António da Charneca, Alhos Vedros, Lavradio, Barreiro, Santo André, Palhais, Coina, Seixal, Amora, Corroios, Cruz de Pau, Arrentela, LISBOA, Ulhos, Apelação, S. João da Talha, Sacavém, Beirolas, Matinha, Xabregas, Beato, Povoa de Santo Adrião, Odivelas, Loures, Amoreira, Paio, Camarate, Charneca, Olivais, Aeroporto da Portela, Mosvavide, Amixoeira, Campo Grande, University, Benfica, Lumiar, Carnide, Estádio Benfica 357, Alto do Pina, Chelas, Campo Pequeno, Penha de França, Castelo de S. Jorge, Praça do Comercio, Cacilhas, Almada, Cova da Piedade, Feijó, Sobreda, Caparica, Pragal, Damaia, Amadora, Monsanto, Parque Florestal, Ajuda, Belém, Torre de Belém, Algés, Caxias, Oeiras, Paço de Arcos, Agualva-Cacem, Massamá, Queluz, Belas, Barcarena, Caparica, Trafaria, Costa da Caparica, ATLANTIC OCEAN, Rio de Mouro, Sabugo, Tapada, Piedade 220, Telhal, Venda Seca, Leião 222, Talaide, Porto Salvo, Linda a Pastora

West from Greenwich 9°10'

COPYRIGHT. GEORGE PHILIP AND SON LTD.

1 : 200 000

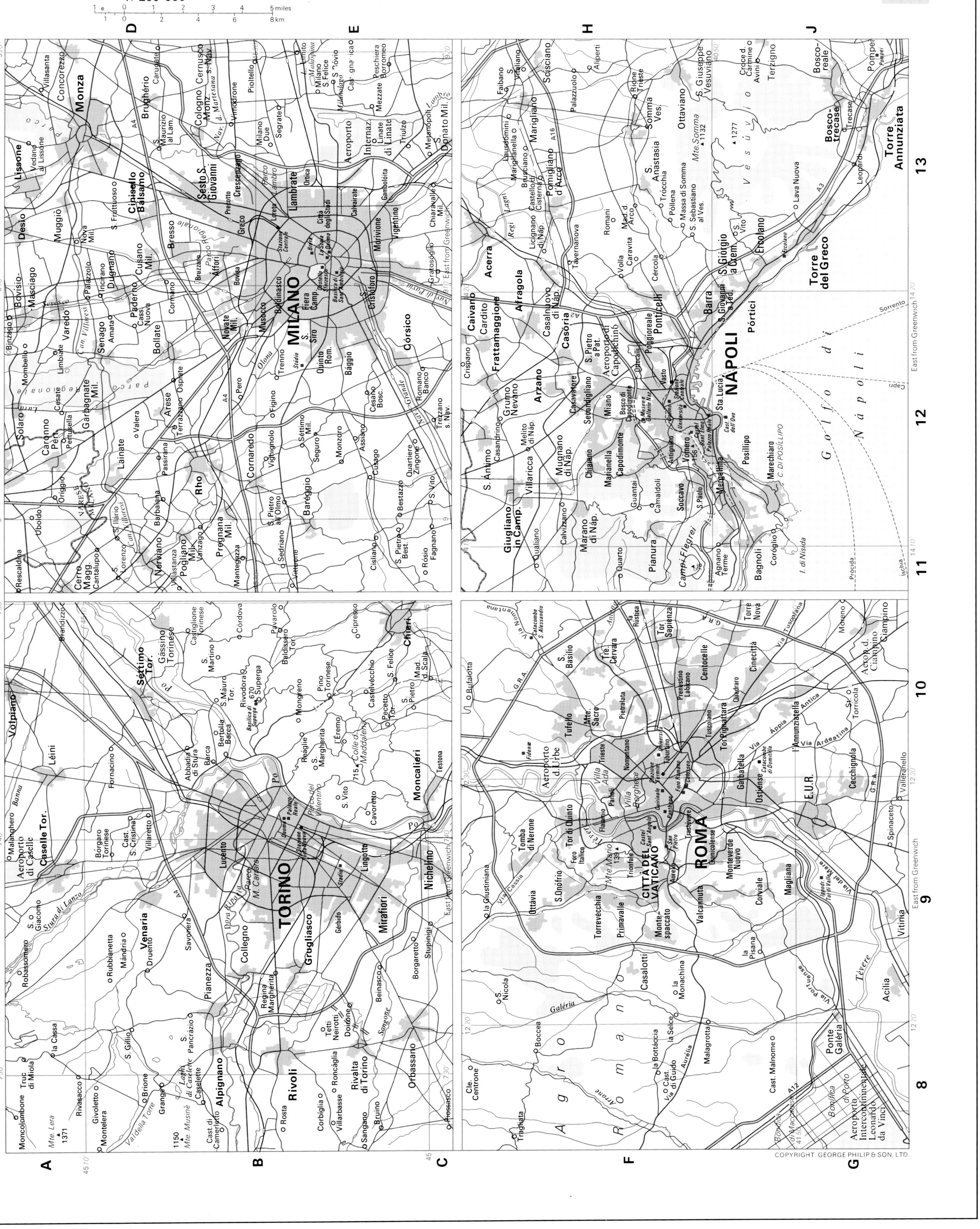

0 1 2 3 4 5 miles
0 1 2 3 4 5 6 7 8 km

MILANO

Monza
Lissone
Desio
Bovisio
Masciago
Muggiò
Cinisello Balsamo
Sesto S. Giovanni
Lambrate
Crescenzago
Brugherio
Cologno
Cernusco
Vimodrone
Segrate
Aeroporto
di Linate
Milano Due
Pioltello
Mezzate
Peschiera
Borromeo
Vedano al Lissone
Concorezzo
Carugate
Villasanta
Vimercate
Nova Mil.
S. Fruttuoso
Cusano
Bresso
Greco
Città degli Studi
Marivone
Vignentino
Gratosoglio
Corsico
Baggio
Quinto Rom.
Trenno
Figino
Assago
Rozzano
Opera
Novate Mil.
Bollate
Garbagnate Mil.
Rho
Arese
Pero
Cornaredo
Settimo Mil.
Barbaiana
Origgio
Uboldo
Caronno Pert.
Solaro
Ceriano
Limbiate
Varedo
Senago
Paderno Dug.
Cusano
Vigodarzere
Cornaredo
Passirana
Bareggio
Cisliano
Sedriano
Vittuone
Pregnana Mil.
Pogliano Mil.
Nerviano
Cerro Magg.
Rescaldina
S. Vittore Olona
Mantegazza

TORINO

Volpiano
Settimo Tor.
Gassino Torinese
Chieri
Leini
Caselle Tor.
Aeroporto di Caselle
Borgaro Torinese
Venaria
Rubbianetta
Mandria
Druento
Pianezza
Collegno
Grugliasco
Mirafiori
Lucento
Lingotto
Nichelino
Moncalieri
Testona
Superga
Pino Torinese
Baldissero Tor.
Castiglione Torinese
San Mauro Tor.
Abbadia di Stura
Cavoretto
Regina Margherita
Stupinigi
Orbassano
Rivalta di Torino
Alpignano
Rivoli
Beinasco
Borgaretto
Savonera
Pecetto Tor.
Castelvecchio
S. Felice

Monte Lera 1371
Monte Musinè 1150

ROMA

CITTÀ DEL VATICANO
EUR
Fidene
S. Basilio
Centocelle
Cinecittà
Ciampino
Aeroporto d. Urbe
Tor Sapienza
Mte. Sacro
Pietralata
Tiburtino
Prenestino
Labicano
Tuscolano
Gabatella
Ostiense
Magliana
Corviale
Monteverde Nuovo
Valcannuta
Monte Spaccato
Torrevecchia
Primavalle
Ottavia
la Giustiniana
Foro Italico
Trionfale
Castel Sant'Angelo
San Pietro
Trastevere
Testaccio
Via Appia Antica
Acilia
Vitinia
Casalotti
la Pisana
la Monachina
Malagrotta
Boccea
la Storta
la Bottaccia
la Selce
Ponte Galeria
Galéria
S. Nicola
Acquafredda
Tomba di Nerone
Via Aurelia
Via Cassia
Via Flaminia
Via Nomentana
Via Tiburtina
Via Casilina
Via Tuscolana
Via Appia
Via Ardeatina
Via Ostiense
Via Portuense
Via del Mare
Tévere
Via Salaria
G.R.A.
Mte. Mario 139
Monte Sacro
Spinaceto

Agro Romano

NÁPOLI

Vesuvio
Mte. Somma 1132
Vesuvio 1277
Faibano
Marigliano
Palazzuolo
Pomigliano d'Arco
Somma Ves.
Ottaviano
S. Giuseppe Vesuviano
Terzigno
Bosco-reale
Boscotrecase
Torre Annunziata
Pompei
Trecase
Torre del Greco
S. Giorgio a Crem.
Ercolano
Pòrtici
S. Giovanni a Ted.
Barra
Ponticelli
Poggioreale
Secondigliano
Miano
Capodimonte
Vomero
Posillipo
Marechiaro
C. di Posillipo
Bagnoli
Agnano Terme
Campi Flegrei
Pianura
Quarto
Marano di Náp.
Mugnano di Náp.
Chiaiano
Melito di Náp.
S. Antimo
Villaricca
Giugliano in Camp.
Qualiano
Calvizzano
Acerra
Afragola
Casoria
Casavatore
Arzano
Grumo Nevano
Frattamaggiore
Cardito
Crispano
Caivano
Casalnuovo di Náp.
S. Pietro a Pat.
Aeroporto di Capodichino
Casandrino
Camaldoli
Soccavo
Pianura

Golfo di Napoli
Sorrento
Capri
Ischia
Prócida
I. di Nisida

COPYRIGHT. GEORGE PHILIP & SON. LTD.

East from Greenwich

1 : 200 000

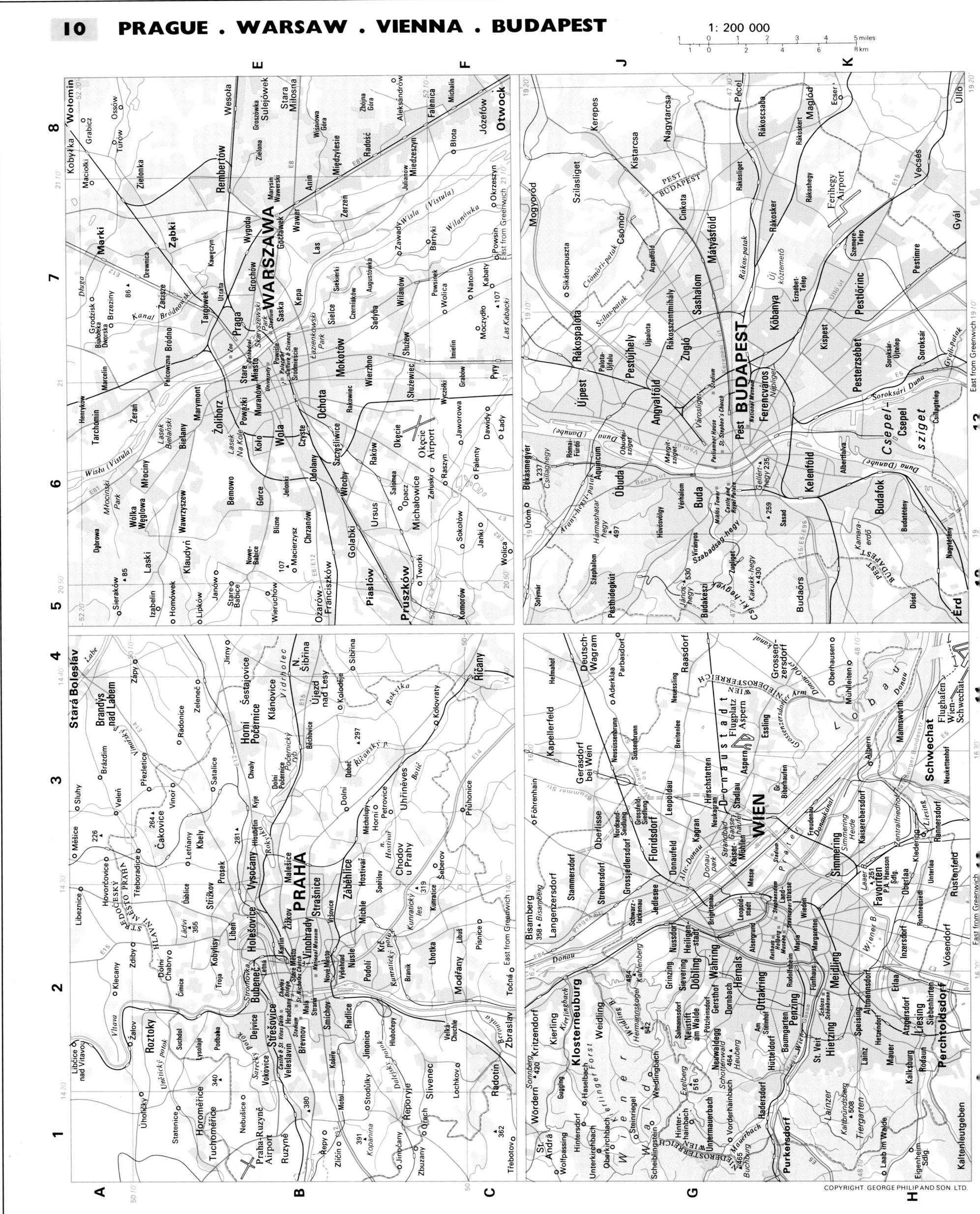

1: 200 000

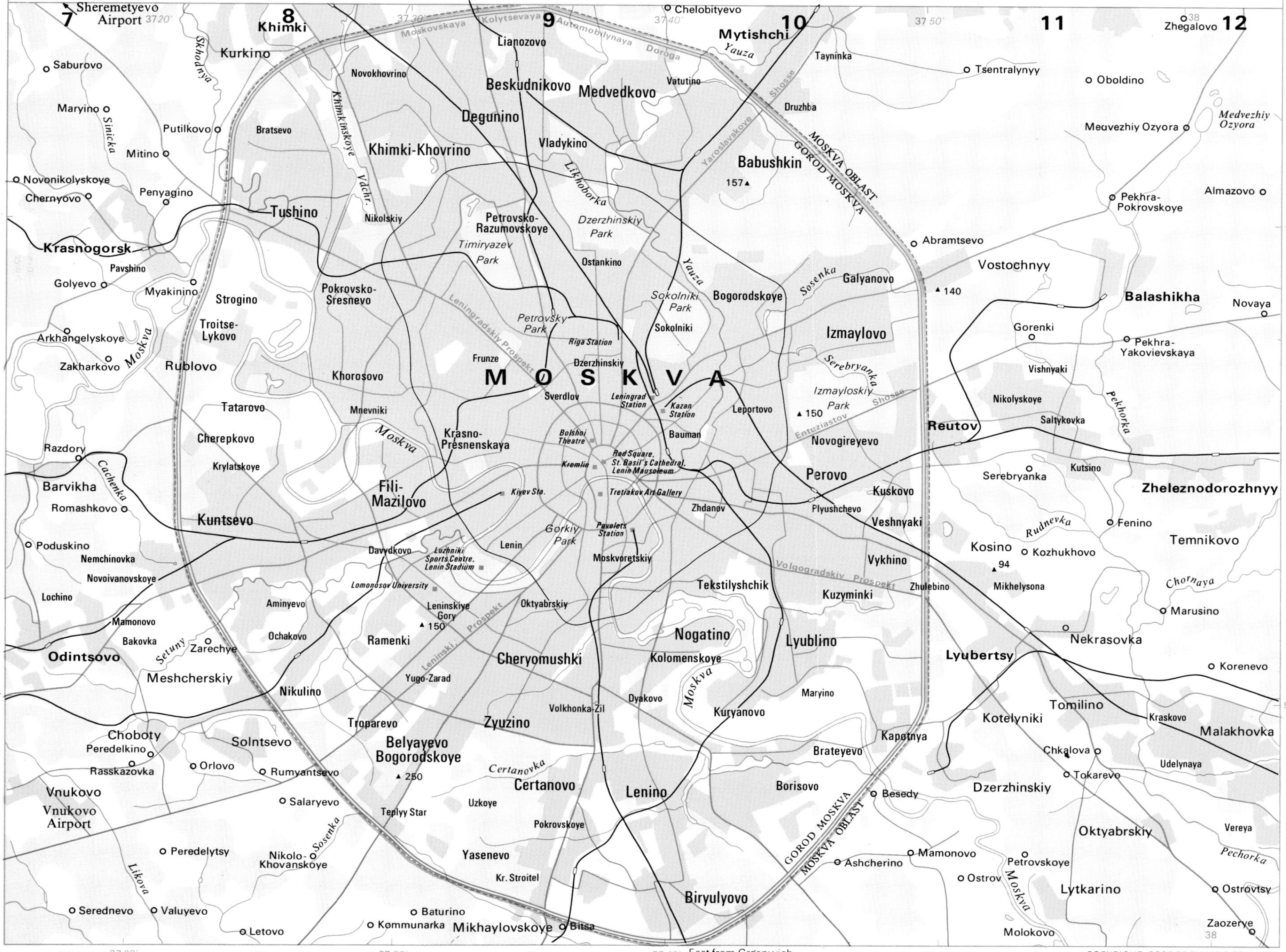

miles
km

(Top map — St. Petersburg)

1 2 3 4 5 6

Lisiy Nos
Olgino
Udelnaya
Ruchyi
Gorelly
Berngardovka
Vsevolozhsk
Lubya
O. Verperluda
Primorskoye Prospekt
Kolomyagi
Novaya Derevnya
Lesnoy
Grazhdanka
Rybatskaya
Rzhevka
Kalytino
Lakhtinskiy
Bobylyskaya
Staraya Derevnya
Bolshaya Nevka
O. Trudyashchikhsya
Noyoye Kovalyova
Krasnaya Gorka
Kirov Stadium
Ostrova Kirovskiye
Apterkarskiy Ostrov
Kara Marksa Prospekt
Polyustrovo
Selytsy
O. Volynyy
Petrogradskaya Storona
Vyborgskaya Storona
Finland Station
Bolshaya-Okhta
Khirvosti
Koltushi
Pavlovo
Matala Neva
O. Dekabristov
Fortress of St. Peter & St. Paul
Neva
Admiralteyskaya Storona
Okhta
Yanino
Staraya
Gulf of Finland
Ostrov Vasilyevskiy
Hermitage & Winter Palace
Old Admiralty
Zanevka
Oz. Korkinskoye
St. Isaac's Cathedral
Moskva Station
Alexander Nevsky Abbey
Malaya-Okhta
Okkervil
GOROD ST.-PETERBURG
Tavry
SANKT-PETERBURG
Vitebsk Station
Kudrovo
LENINGRAD OBLAST
Novosergiyevka
Razmitelevo
Fontanka
Obvodayy kanal
Warszawa Station
Volodarskoye
Ozerki
Ostrov Kanonerskiy
Ostrov Gutuyevskiy
Baltic Station
Volynkina-Derevnya
Vesolyy Posolok
Myaglovo
Obukhovo
Cornaya
Khaboye
Avtovo
Moskovskiy Prospekt
Farforovskaya
Neva
Volkovka
Lesnozavodskaya
Novosaratovka
Aleksandrovskoye
Strelyna
Kikenka
Posolok Lenina
Uritsk
Ulyanka
Ligovo
Dakhnoye
Airport
Srednaya Rogatka
Kupchino
Novoaleksandrovskoye
Rybatskoye
Ust-Slavyanka
Sosnovaya
Sinicka
1 2 3 Airport 4 5 6 East from Greenwich

(Bottom map — Moscow)

7 8 9 10 11 12

Sheremetyevo Airport
Khimki
Kolytsevaya
Moskovskaya
Automobilnaya Doroga
Chelobityevo
Mytishchi
Zhegalovo
Kurkino
Lianozovo
Yauza
Tayninka
Tsentralynyy
Oboldino
Saburovo
Novokhovrino
Beskudnikovo
Medvedkovo
Vatutino
Druzhba
Medvezhiy Ozyora
Medvezhiy Ozyora
Maryino
Putilkovo
Bratsevo
Degunino
Vladykino
Khimki-Khovrino
Khimkinskoye
Valchr
Likhoborka
MOSKVA OBLAST
GOROD MOSKVA
Almazovo
Novonikolyskoye
Chernyovo
Penyagino
Mitino
Nikolskiy
Petrovsko-Razumovskoye
Babushkin
Pekhra-Pokrovskoye
Tushino
Timiryazev Park
Dzerzhinskiy Park
157
Abramtsevo
Vostochnyy
Krasnogorsk
Ostankino
Yauza
Sosenka
Galyanovo
140
Golyevo
Pavshino
Myakinino
Strogino
Petrovsky Park
Sokolniki Park
Bogorodskoye
Gorenki
Balashikha
Novaya
Troitse-Lykovo
Riga Station
Sokolniki
Izmaylovo
Pekhra-Yakovievskaya
Arkhangelyskoye
Frunze
Dzerzhinskiy
Izmaylovskiy Park
150
Vishnyaki
Zakharkovo
Rublovo
Pokrovsko-Sresnevo
Khorosovo
Sverdlov
Serebryanka
Nikolyskoye
Saltykovka
Cachenka
Moskva
Mnevniki
Krasno-Presnenskaya
Leningrad Station
Kazan Station
Bauman
Reutov
Kutsino
Cherepkovo
Bolshoi Theatre
Red Square, St. Basil's Cathedral, Lenin Mausoleum
Kremlin
Novogireyevo
MOSKVA
Zheleznodorozhnyy
Barvikha
Krylatskoye
Perovo
Serebryanka
Romashkovo
Fili-Mazilovo
Kiyev Sta.
Tretiakov Art Gallery
Zhdanov
Kuskovo
Fenino
Kuntsevo
Paveletz Station
Plyushchevo
Veshnyaki
Poduskino
Nemchinovka
Gorkiy Park
Moskvoretskiy
Vykhino
Kosino
Kozhukhovo
Temnikovo
Novoivanovskoye
Davydkovo
Lenin
Zhulebino
Kuzminki
94
Mikhelysona
Lochino
Lomonosov University
Luzhniki Sports Centre, Lenin Stadium
Leninskiye Gory
150
Chornaya
Mamonovo
Aminyevo
Tekstilyshchik
Marusino
Bakovka
Ochakovo
Zarechye
Ramenki
Yugo-Zarad
Oktyabrskiy
Nogatino
Lyublino
Lyubertsy
Nekrasovka
Odintsovo
Setuny
Leninski Prospekt
Cheryomushki
Kolomenskoye
Maryino
Koreneva
Meshcherskiy
Nikulino
Dyakovo
Moskva
Kuryanovo
Zyuzino
Volkhonka-Zil
Tomilino
Kotelyniki
Kraskovo
Troparevo
Belyayevo Bogorodskoye
250
Certanova
Certanovo
Lenino
Kapotnya
Chkalova
Malakhovka
Choboty
Peredelkino
Solntsevo
Orlovo
Rumyantsevo
Brateyevo
Udelnaya
Dzerzhinskiy
Rasskazovka
Uzkoye
Pokrovskoye
Besedy
Borisovo
Vnukovo
Vnukovo Airport
Salaryevo
Teply Star
Yasenevo
Kr. Stroitel
GOROD MOSKVA
MOSKVA OBLAST
Oktyabrskiy
Vereya
Pechorka
Peredelytsy
Nikolo-Khovanskoye
Biryulyovo
Mamonovo
Ashcherino
Ostrov
Petrovskoye
Lytkarino
Ostrovtsy
Likora
Sosenka
Serednevo
Valuyevo
Letovo
Baturino
Kommunarka
Mikhaylovskoye
Bitsa
Molokovo
Zaozerye
Moskva
7 8 9 10 East from Greenwich 11 12

1 : 200 000

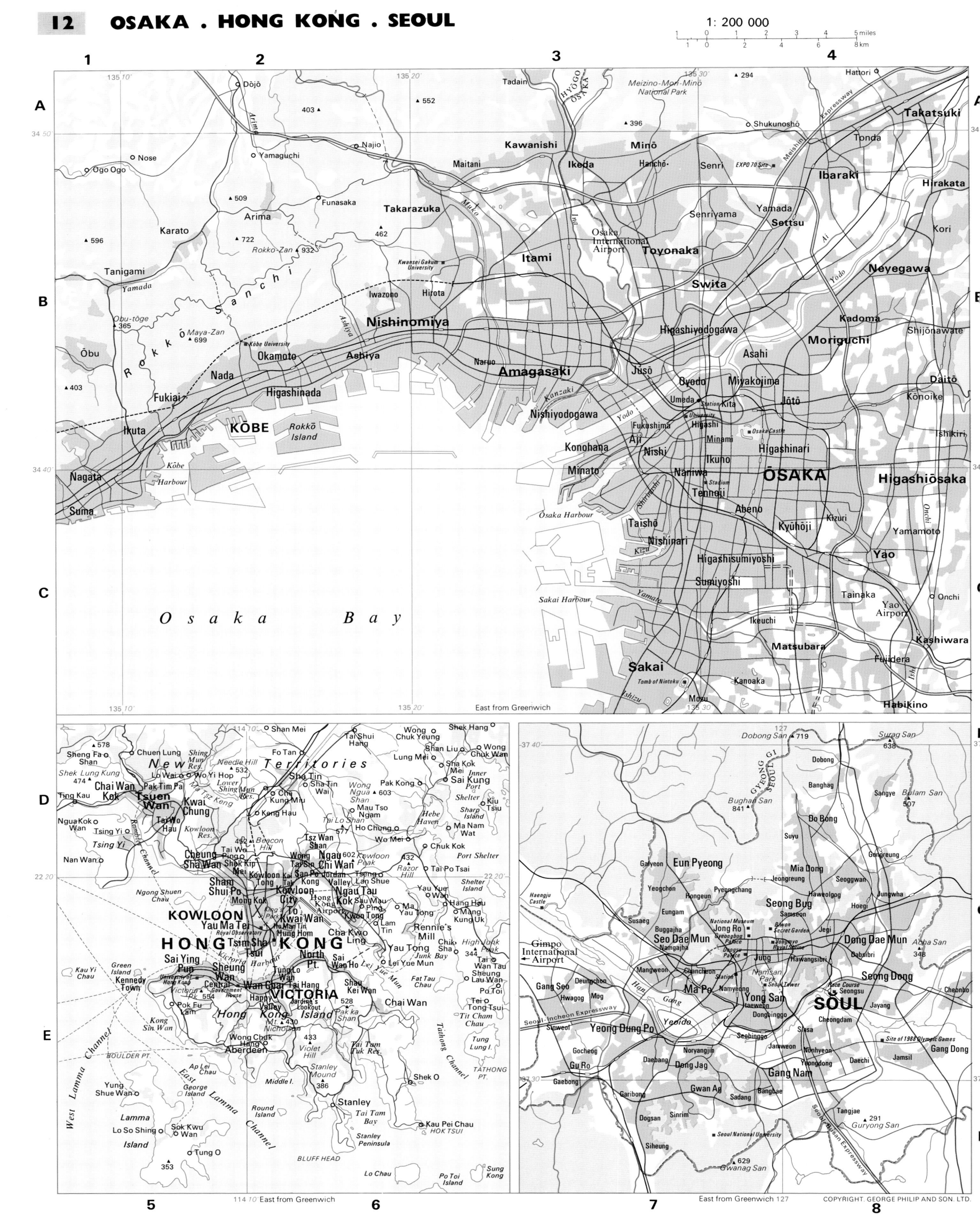

OSAKA

1   2   3   4

Dôjô
403 ▲
552 ○
Tadain
Meizino-Mori-Mino National Park
294 ▲
Hattori
Shukunoshō ○
A

Nose ○
Yamaguchi ○
Najio ○
Kawanishi
Minō
396 ▲
Tonda
Takatsuki
34 50

Ogo Ogo ○
Ikeda
Hanchō·
Senri
EXPO 70 Site
Ibaraki
Hirakata

509 ▲
Funasaka ○
Maitani
Senriyama
Yamada
Kori

Karato
Arima
462
Takarazuka
Yamada
Settsu

596 ▲
722 ▲
Rokko-Zan 932
Kwansei Gakuin University
Itami
Osaka International Airport
Toyonaka
Neyegawa

Tanigami
Yamada
Iwazono
Hirota
Higashiyodogawa
Kadoma
B

Obu-tôge 365
Maya-Zan 699 ▲
Nishinomiya
Naruo
Asahi
Moriguchi
Shijōnawate

Ôbu
Kōbe University
Okamoto
Ashiya
Amagasaki
Jūsō
Byōdo
Miyakojima
Jōtō
Dāitō

Nada
Higashinada
Kanzaki
Umeda
Kita
Kōnoike

Fukiai ○
Ikuta
KŌBE
Rokkō Island
Nishiyodogawa
Yodo
Fukushima
Higashi
Minami
Osaka Castle
Higashinari
Ishikiri

Konohana
Ajī
Nishi
Ikuno

Nagata ○
Kōbe Harbour
Minato
Naniwa
ŌSAKA
Higashiōsaka
34 40

Suma ○
Osaka Harbour
Taishō
Tennoji
Abeno
Kizuri
Yamamoto

Nishinari
Kyūhōji
Yāo

Higashisumiyoshi
Tainaka
Onchi

O s a k a   B a y
Sakai Harbour
Sumiyoshi
Yamato
Yao Airport
Ikeuchi
Matsubara
Kashiwara
C

Sakai
Tomb of Nintoku
Kanoaka
Fujidera

Mozu
Habikino
135 10'
135 20'
East from Greenwich
135 30'

HONG KONG

Shan Mei ○
Tai Shui Hang
Wong Chuk Yeung
Shek Hang
Dobong San 719 ▲
127
Surag San
638

Sheng Fa Shan 578 ▲
Chuen Lung ○
Shing Mun Res.
Needle Hill 532 ▲
Fo Tan
Territories
Shan Liu
Lung Mei
Wong Chuk Wan
37 40
Dobong

Shek Lung Kung
Lo Wai ○
Wo Yi Hop
Lower Shing Mun Res.
Sha Tin
Sha Kok Mei
Inner Sai Kung
Banghag
Sangye
Bulam San 507

Chai Wan Kok 474 ▲
Pak Tim Pa
Cha Kung Miu
Sha Tin Wai
Wong Ngau Shan 603 ▲
Pak Kong
Shelter
Kiu Tsiu
Bughan San 841 ▲
Do Bong

Ting Kau ○
Tsuen Wan
Kwai Chung
Kong Hau
Tai Lo Shan
Mau Tso Ngam
Ho Chung
Wo Mei
Ma Nam Wat
Suyu
Gangreung

Ngua Kok Wan
Tai Wo Hau
Kowloon Res.
452 ▲
Beacon Hill
Tsz Wan Shan 577
Chuk Kok
Port Shelter
Galyeon
Eun Pyeong
Mia Dong
Seoggwan

Tsing Yi
Cheung Sha Wan
Shek Kip Mei
Tai Wo
Wong Tai Sin
Ngau Chi Wan 602
Kowloon Peak
432 ▲
Razor Hill
Tai Po Tsai
Shelter Island
Yeogchon
Pyeongchang
Hongeun
Jeongreung
Hoegi

Nan Wan ○
Sham Shui Po
Kowloon Tong
San Po Kong
Jordan Valley
Lei Shue
Yau Yue Wan
Haengju Castle
Eungam
Susaeg
Buggahja
National Museum
Jong Ro
Jegi
Dong Dae Mun
348

Ngong Shuen Chau
Mong Kok
Kowloon City
Hung Hom
Kwun Tong
Ma Yau Tong
Ma Kung Uk
Hang Hau
Seongbug
Bawon Secret Garden
Seong Bug

KOWLOON
Yau Ma Tei
Royal Observatory
Kwai Wan
Cha Kwo Ling
Rennie's Mill
High Junk Peak
Namgajha
Seo Dae Mun
Gyeongbog Palace
Seongsu

Kau Yi Chau
Green Island
Kennedy Town
Tsim Sha Tsui
HONG KONG
North Pt.
Sai Wan Ho
Lei Yue Mun
Yau Tong
Fat Tau Chau
344 ▲
Gimpo International Airport
Mangweon
Jong
Gwanghwamun
Jung
Hawangsibri
Seong Dong
Chebnho

Sai Ying Pun
Sheung Wan
Victoria Harbour
Tung Lo Wan
Tai Hang
Shau Kei Wan
Tai Tam
Lau Sau
Po Toi
Yong San
Haeweon
Namyeong
Namsan Park
Seoul Tower
Race Course
Seongsu
Jayang

Pok Fu Lam
554 ▲
Central
Government House
Happy Valley
528
Pak ka Shan
Chai Wan
Tei O Tong Tsui
Tit Cham Chau
Yeong Dung Po
Yeoido
Dongbinggo
SOUL
Jamsil

Kong Sin Wan
Victoria
Mt. 430 ▲
Nicholson
Hong Kong Island
Tung Lung I.
Seoul-Incheon Expressway
Sinweol
Seobinggo
Sinsa
Site of 1988 Olympic Games

BOULDER PT.
Wong Chuk Hang
433 ▲
Violet Hill
Cheongdam
Gang Dong

Ap Lei Chau
Aberdeen
Middle I.
Stanley Mound 386
Shek O
TATHONG PT.
Gocheog
Daebang
Noryangjin
Banghae
Gang Nam

Yung Shue Wan ○
George Island
Lamma
Round Island
Stanley
Tai Tam Bay
Gu Ro
Dong Jag
Gwanak San 629 ▲
Tangjae
291 ▲
Guryong San

Lamma
Lo So Shing Island
Sok Kwu Wan ○
Tung O ○
353 ▲
Stanley Peninsula
Kau Pei Chau
HOK TSUI
Lo Chau
Po Toi Island
Sung Kong
BLUFF HEAD
Seoul National University
Gaebong
Dogsan
Sinrim
Siheung
Gwanag San

5   6   7   8
114 10' East from Greenwich
East from Greenwich 127

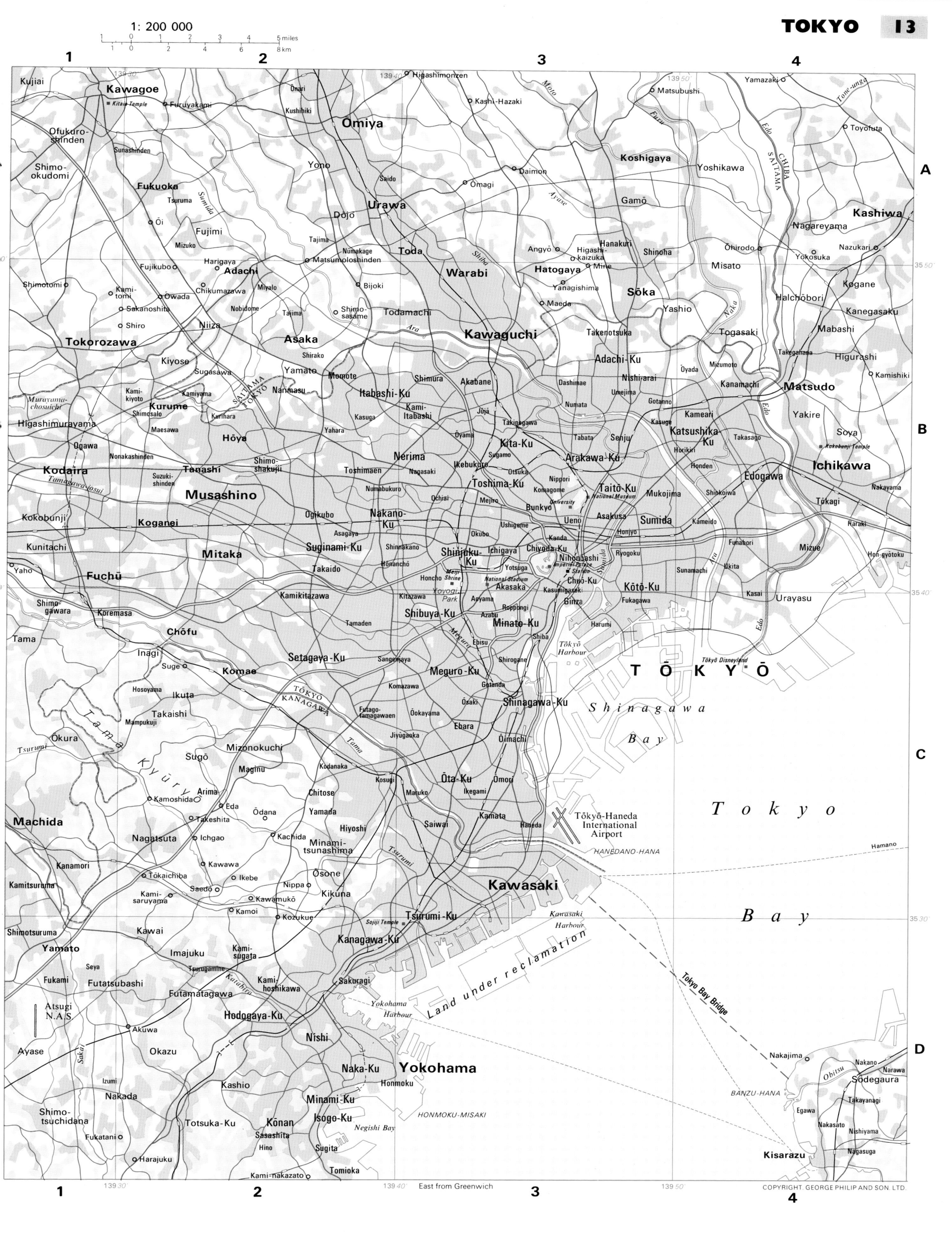

1: 200 000

0 1 2 3 4 5 miles
0 2 4 6 8 km

Kujiai
Kawagoe
• Kitain Temple
Furuyakami
Ōnari
Kushihiki
Higashimonzen
Matsubushi
Yamazaki
Toyofuta

Ōmiya
Kashi-Hazaki
Moto

Ofukuro-shinden
Yono
Kōshigaya
Yoshikawa

A

Shimo-okudomi
Saido
Ōmagi
Daimon
Gamō
Nagareyama
Kashiwa

Fukuoka
Tsuruma
Urawa
Dōjō
Ayase
Ōhirodo
Yokosuka
Nazukari

Ōi
Fujimi
Tajima
Numakage
Angyō
Higashi-kaizuka
Shinoha
Misato
Kōgane

Mizuko
Harigaya
Matsumoloshinden
Hanakuri
Mine
Halchōbori
Kanegasaku

Shimotomi
Fujikubo
Adachi
Chikumazawa
Miyalo
Bijoki
Shimo-sasame
Warabi
Hatogaya
Yanagishima
Sōka
Yashio
Togasaki
Mabashi
Higurashi

Kami-tomi
Ōwada
Nobidome
Tajima
Todamachi
Maeda
Takenotsuka
Takegamba
Kamishiki

Sakanoshita
Shiro
Niiza
Asaka
Shirako
Yamato
Momote
Shimura
Akabane
Kawaguchi
Adachi-Ku
Nishiarai
Ōyada
Mizumoto
Kanamachi
Matsudo

Tokorozawa
Kiyose
Sugasawa
Asaka
Itabashi-Ku
Kami-Itabashi
Jūjō
Dashimae
Numata
Umejima
Gotanno

Higashimurayama
Murayama-chosuichi
Kami-kiyoto
Kamiyama
Kurume
Shimdsalo
Maesawa
Kurihara
Yahara
Kasuga
Ōyama
Takinogawa
Senju
Kameari
Katsushika-Ku
Takasago
Kokubunji Temple

Ogawa
Nonakashinden
Hōya
Shimo-shakujii
Nerima
Toshimaen
Nagasaki
Kita-Ku
Sugamo
Tabata
Honden
Horikiri
Edogawa
Ichikawa

Kodaira
Tamagawa-josui
Tanashi
Numabukuro
Ikebukuro
Ōtsuka
Arakawa-Ku
Nippori
Komagome
Taitō-Ku
Mukojima
Shinkoiwa
Nakayama

Musashino
Ogikubo
Nakano-Ku
Ochiai
Mejiro
Bunkyo
University
National Museum
Asakusa
Sumida
Kameido
Haraki

Kokobunji
Koganei
Asagaya
Shinnakano
Okubo
Ushigome
Ueno
Honjyo
Funahori
Mizue
Hon-gyōtoku

Kunitachi
Mitaka
Suginami-Ku
Takaido
Hommachi
Shinjuku-Ku
Ichigaya
Chiyoda-Ku
Kanda
Nihonbashi
Station
Ryogoku
Ukita

Yaho
Fuchū
Honcho
Meiji Shrine
National Stadium
Yotsuya
Imperial Palace
Sunamachi

Shimo-gawara
Kamikitazawa
Kitazawa
Yoyogi Park
Akasaka
Kasumigaseki
Chūo-Ku
Kōtō-Ku
Kasai

Tama
Chōfu
Inagi
Suge
Komae
Shibuya-Ku
Aoyama
Roppongi
Ginza
Fukagawa
Urayasu

Sangenjaya
Azabu
Minato-Ku
Harumi

Ōkura
Hosoyama
Ikuta
Setagaya-Ku
Tamaden
Ebisu
Shiba
Tōkyō Harbour
Tōkyō Disneyland

Takaishi
Mampukuji
Futago-tamagawaen
Shirogane
T Ō K Y Ō

Sugō
Arima
Eda
Ōokayama
Meguro-Ku
Komazawa
Gotanda
Ōsaki
Shinagawa-Ku
Shinagawa Bay

Machida
Kamoshida
Ōdana
Chitose
Yamada
Ebara
Jiyūgaoka
Ōimachi

Nagatsuta
Ichgao
Takeshita
Minami-tsunashima
Hiyoshi
Kosugi
Matuko
Ōta-Ku
Ōmori
Ikegami
T o k y o

Kanamori
Kachida
Kawawa
Ōsone
Nippa
Kikuna
Saiwai
Kamata
Haneda
Tōkyō-Haneda International Airport
Hamano

Kamitsuruma
Tōkaichiba
Saedo
Kawamukō
Kozukue
Tsurumi
HANEDANO-HANA
B a y

Kami-saruyama
Kamoi
Kozukue
Tsurumi-Ku
Kawasaki
Kawasaki Harbour

Shimotsuruma
Kawai
Kami-sugata
Sojji Temple
Kanagawa-Ku
Tokyo Bay Bridge

Yamato
Seya
Imajuku
Tsurugamine
Kami-hoshikawa
Sakuragi
Nakajima
Nakano-Narawa

Fukami
Futatsubashi
Futamatagawa
Yokohama Harbour
Land under reclamation
Sōdegaura

Atsugi N.A.S
Hodogaya-Ku
Akuwa
Egawa
Takayanagi

Ayase
Okazu
Nishi
BANZU-HANA
Nakasato
Nishiyama

Izumi
Naka-Ku
Yokohama
Honmoku

Nakada
Minami-Ku
Kashio
Isogo-Ku
Kōnan
HONMOKU-MISAKI
Negishi Bay

Shimo-tsuchidana
Totsuka-Ku
Kōnan
Sasashita
Hino
Sugita

Fukatani
Harajuku
Tomioka
Kami-nakazato
Kisarazu
Nagasuga

C

D

East from Greenwich

1 : 200 000

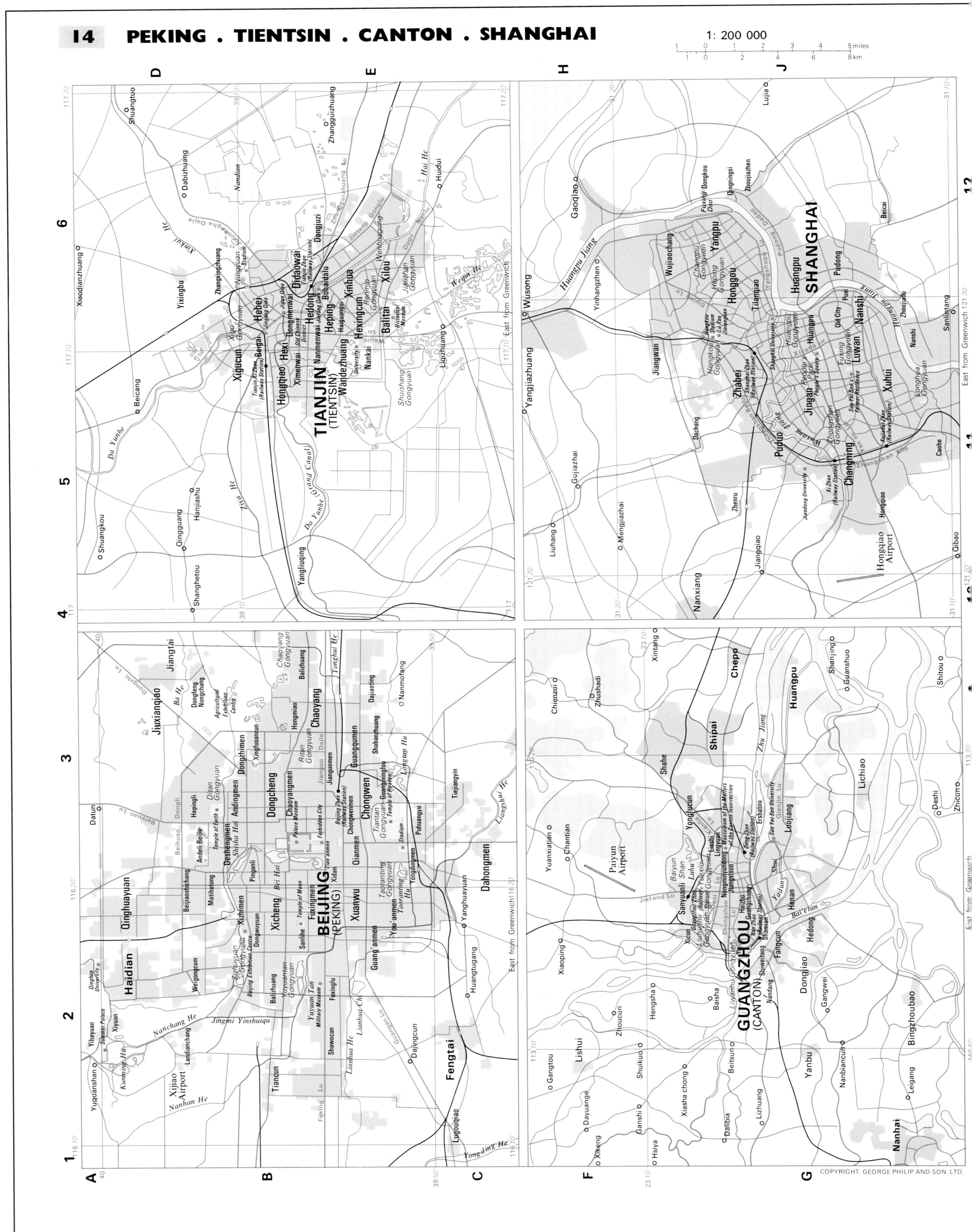

COPYRIGHT GEORGE PHILIP AND SON LTD.

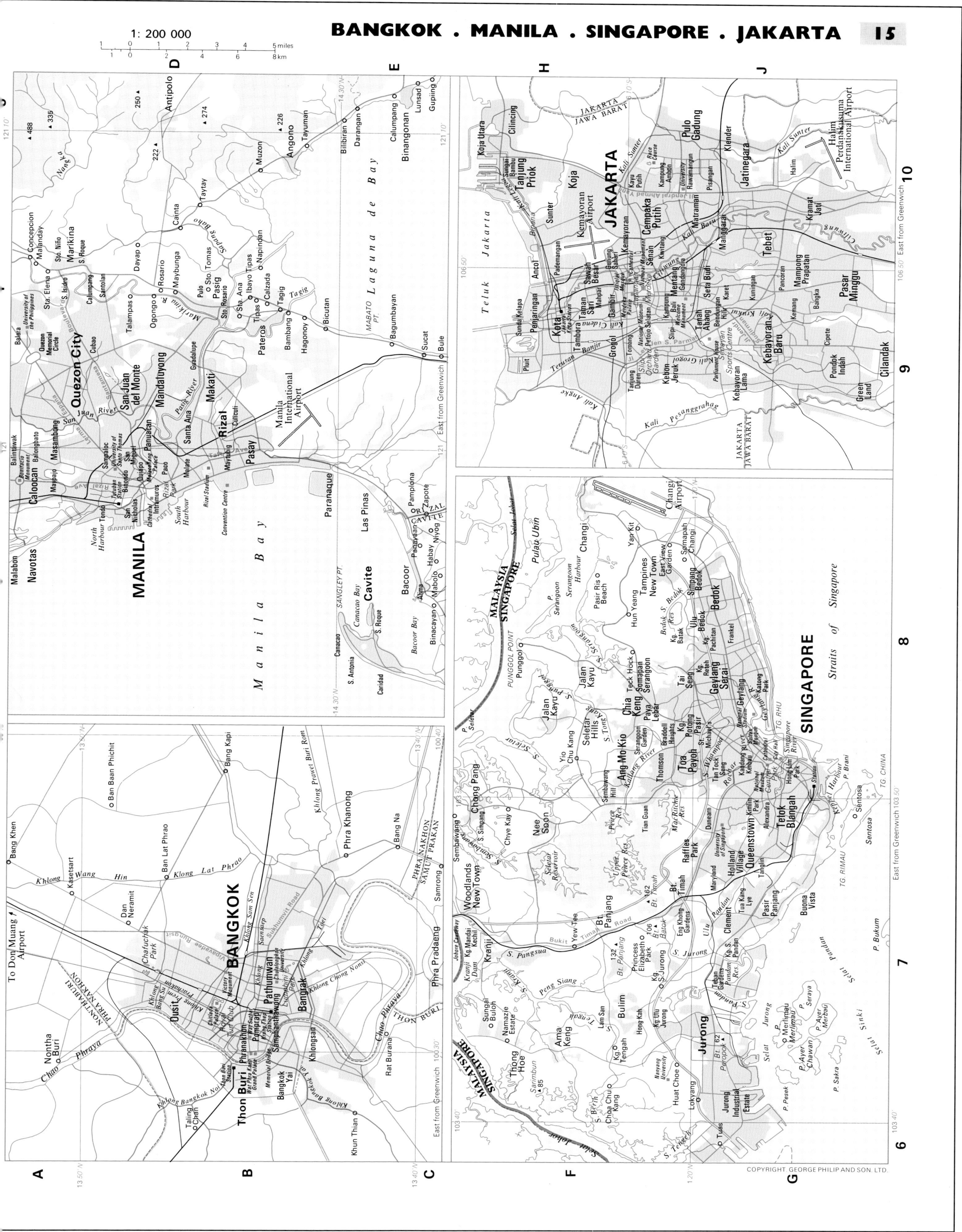

1: 200 000

1: 200 000

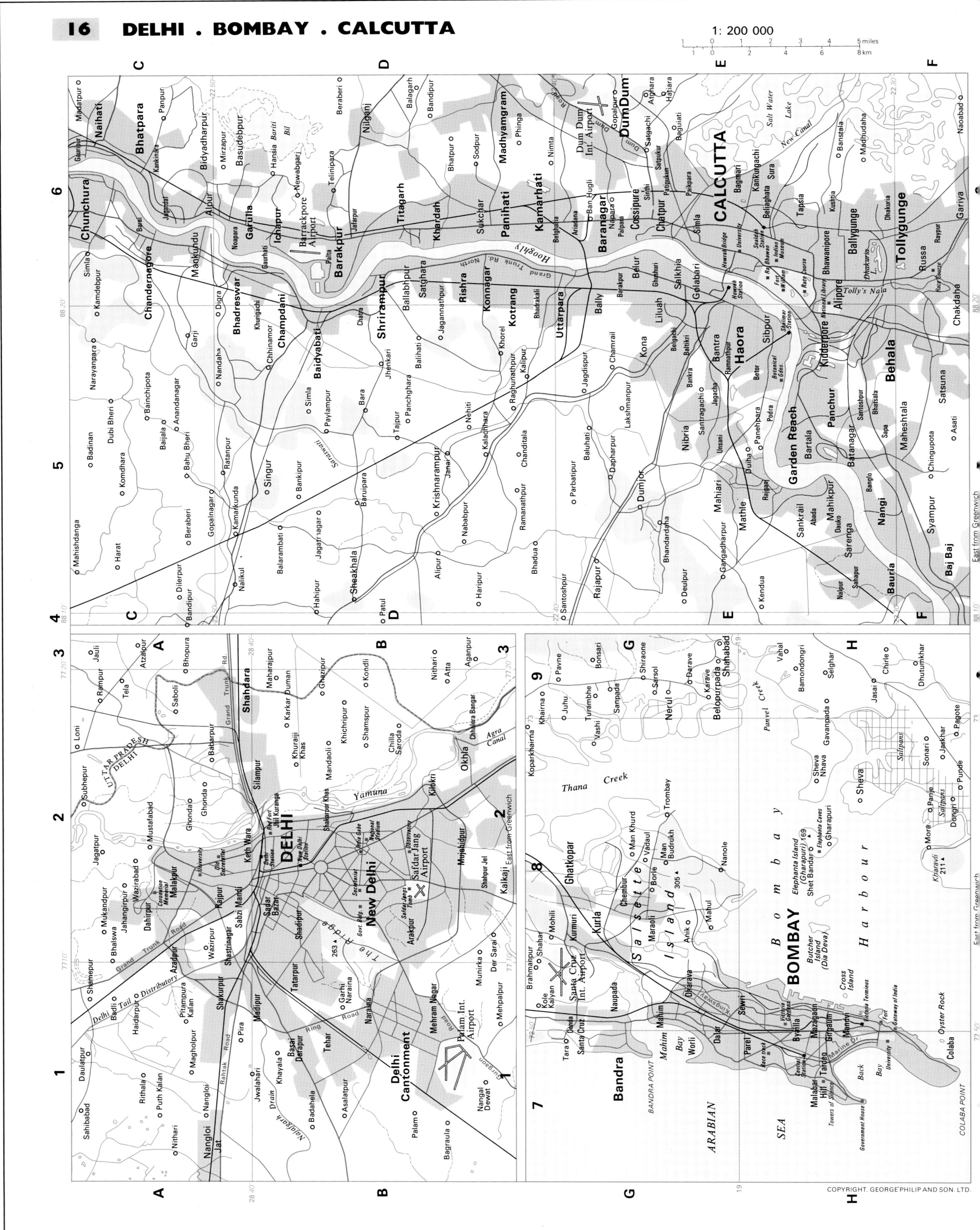

East from Greenwich

COPYRIGHT. GEORGE PHILIP AND SON. LTD.

1: 200 000

miles
8 km

TEHRAN

Tehrān Pars
Qasr-e-Firūzeh
Mesgarābād
Niāvarān
Qasemābād
Ekhtīyārīeh
Magidīyeh
Narmak
Shemīrānāt
Tolhak
Ehtratābād
Doshan Tappeh Airfield
Farahābād
Davūdīyeh
Evin
Pārk-e-Shāhanshāhī
Niru-ye Hava'i
Dulab
Kūy-e-Mekānir
Vanak
Yusofā'd
Kūy-e-Gīshā
Gulistan Palace
Bāzār
Dowlatābād
Kh.-e Khorāsān
Shahr-e-Rey
University
Amīrābād
Shah Reza
Imperial Palace
Jamshīdābād
Qual'eh Morghi Airfield
Bāgh-e-Feiz
Akbarābād
Jawādīyeh
Hasanābād
Wastanard
Nematābād
Kan
Mehrābād Airport
Yaftābād
Guldasteh
Firoz Bahram
Tepe Saif

KARACHI

Malir Cantonment
Drigh Road
Karachi Intl. Airport
Shares Fuisil
Phihāi
Bhambo Khān Qarmati
Korangi
Mahmiudabad
Ghizri Creek
Pitjāpur
Nazimabad
Goth Goli Mār
Sadr
Ghizri
Clifton
Ghandhi Zoo
Chhota Andai
Oyster Rocks
Barra Andai
Zoological Goth Garden
Sind
Sher Shah
Lat'āri
KARACHI CITY
Kīamari
Masroor
Chauki
Bunker
West Wharf
Napier Mole
Manora
Mauripur
Baba I.

ARABIAN SEA

East from Greenwich

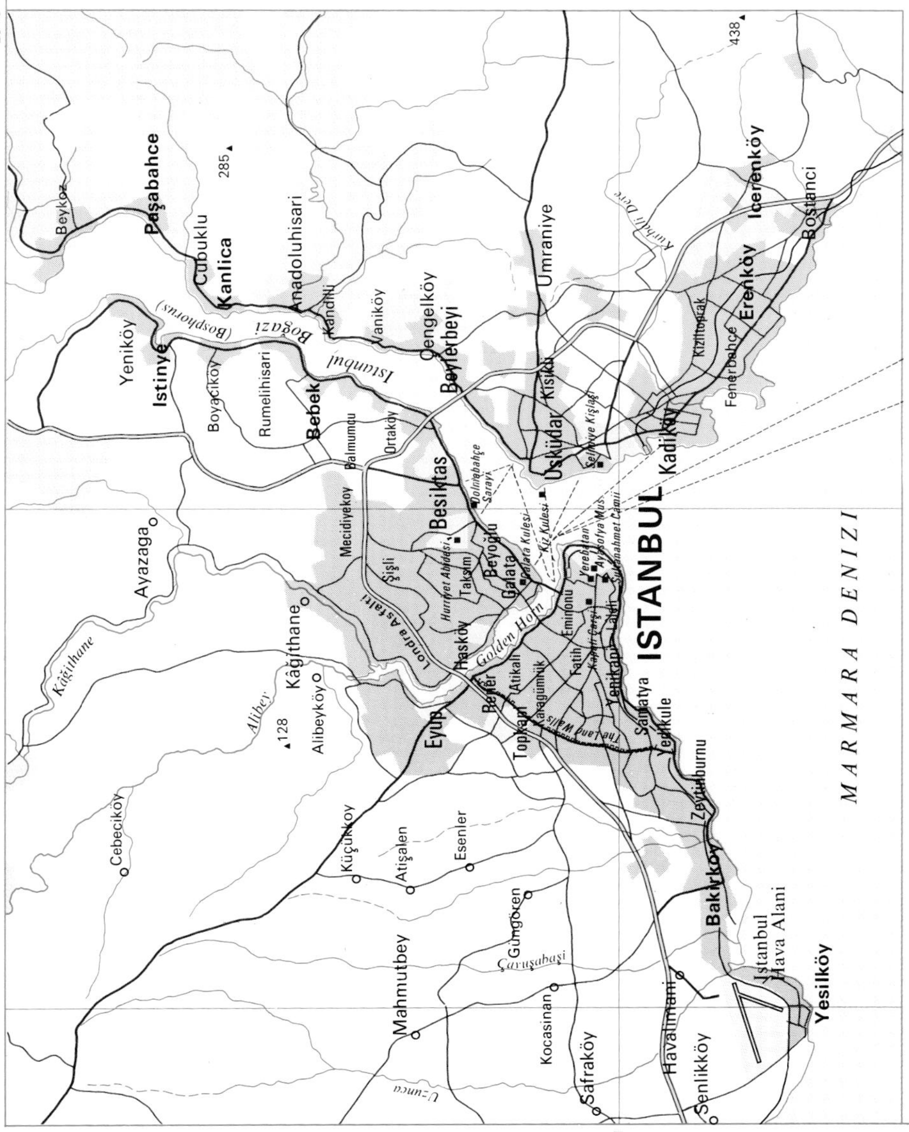

ISTANBUL

Beykoz
Paşabahçe
Çubuklu
Kanlıca
Anadoluhisari
Yeniköy
Istinye
Boyacıköy
Rumelihisari
Bebek
Yeniköy
Üsküdar
Çengelköy
Beylerbeyi
Avazaga
Kağıthane
Mecidiyeköy
Şişli
Beşiktaş
Galata
Beyoğlu
Taksim
Eyüp
Hasköy
ISTANBUL
Fatih
Kadıköy
Erenköy
İçerenköy
Bostancı
Üsküdar
Çebeciköy
Küçükköy
Alibeyköy
Topkapı
Zeytinburnu
Bakırköy
Istanbul Hava Alanı
Yeşilköy
Mahmutbey
Kocasinan
Şafraköy
Senlikköy
Havalimanı
Güngören
Bağcılar

MARMARA DENIZI

BAGHDAD

Dijail River
Saddam City
Khansā'
Amin
New Baghdad
Humaydi
Khalij
Muthanna
Rivad
Nuqel Hikmat Beg
Isbihiyā
Idris
Jizira
Dōra
Nил
Shaab
Nubai
Mahda
Dōra Expressway
Quds
Shaikh Omar
BAGHDAD
RUSAFA
Tunis
Magreb
Al 'Azamīyah
Tishriyaa
Jizā'er
Baghdad Univ.
KARKH
Karantin
Karratah
Ti imim
Salam
Atfiya
Aalam
Maarifa
Zahra
Medinah Al Mansir
Yarmuk
Site of Ancient Round City of Baghdad
Hurriya
Andalus
Khudra'
Jihad
Firdows
Adel Expressway
Shaala
Saddam Intl. Airport

AMANAT AL-ASIMA

East from Greenwich

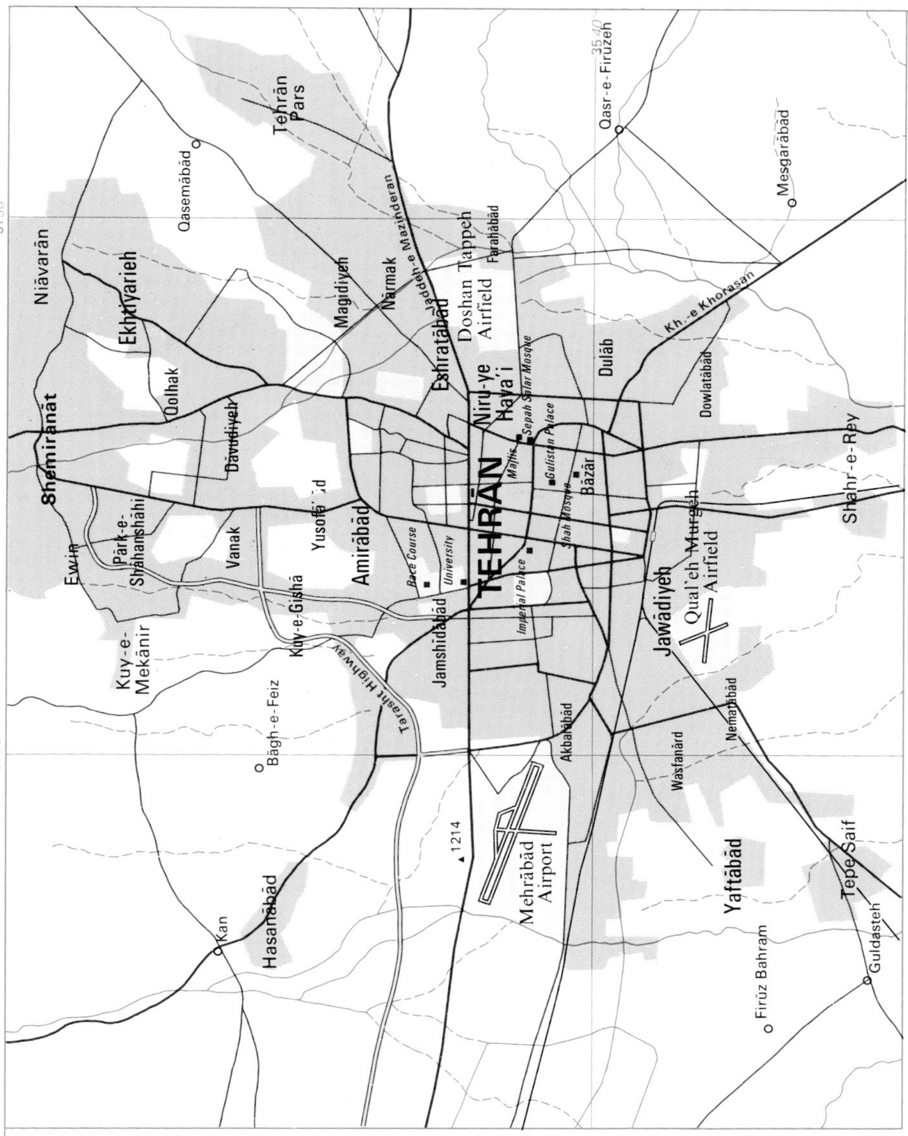

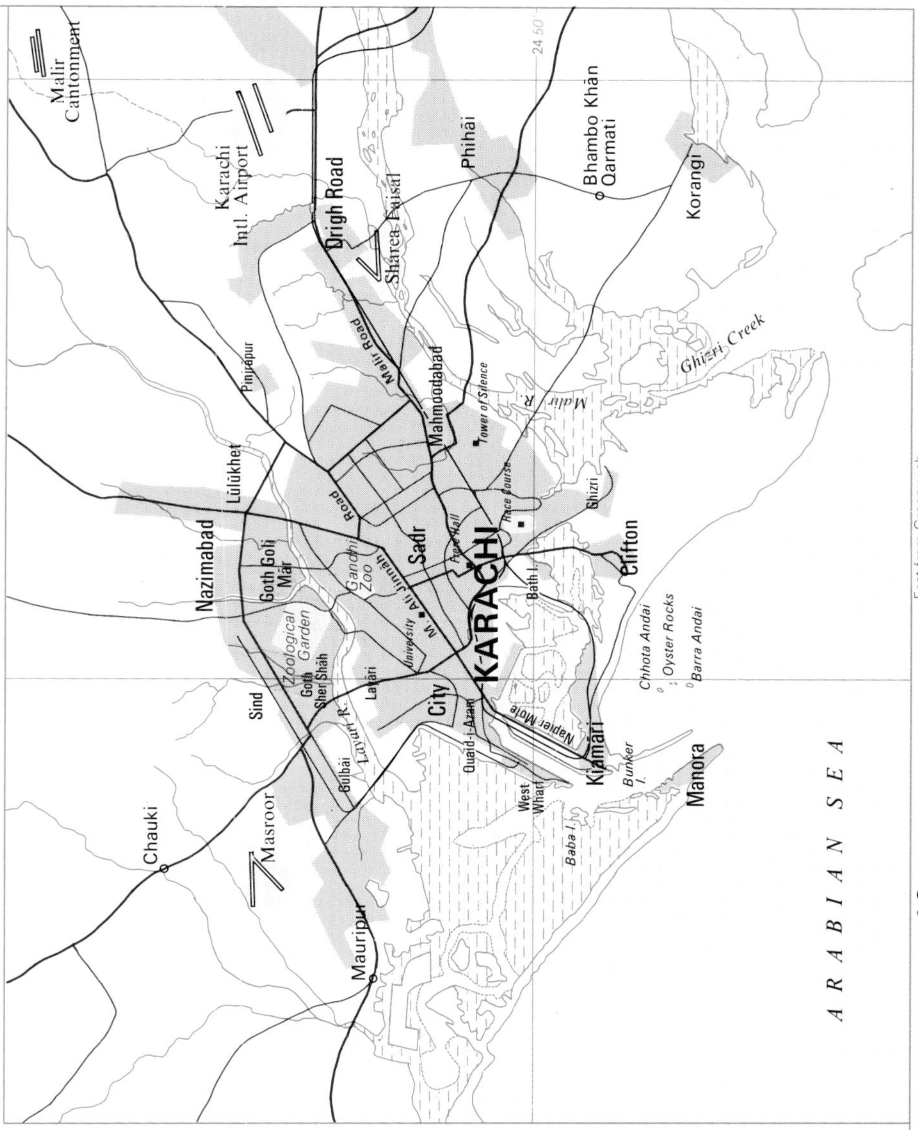

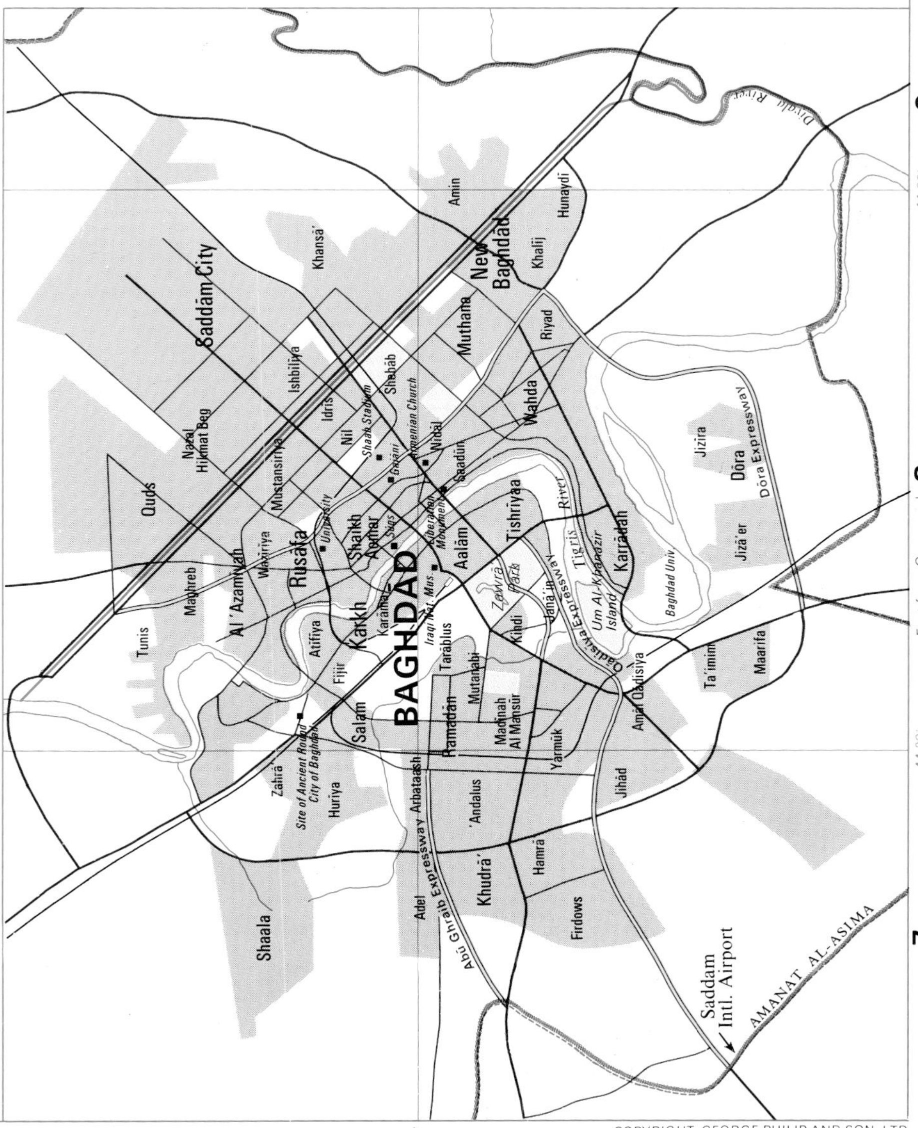

COPYRIGHT GEORGE PHILIP AND SON. LTD.

1: 200 000

5 miles
8 km

LAGOS

Lagos Lagoon

Bight of Benin

IKORODU
LAGOS MUNICIPALITY

LAGOS
Lagos Island
Victoria Island
Ebute-Metta
Apapa
Yaba
Shomolu
Mushin
Ikeja
Lagos-Ikeja Airport

Gbogbo, Igbpa, Malekete, Oreta, Iboju, Ogoyo, Alaguntan, Moba
Ason, Ofin, Osorun, Ebute-Ikorodu, Ibese
Oworonsoki, Oruba, Oguou, Onisigun, Ojota, Erunkan, Eregun, Ejigbo, Shogunle, Isolo, Oshodi, Ewu, Isagatedo, Jiesa-Tedo
Okunola, Cardoso, Olsheri-Olofin, Idimu, Arida, Iseri-Osun, Ikotun, Olute, Agboju, Amuwo, Kirikiri, Igbologun, Isunba, Imore, Badagri Creek
Okogbe, Ikuata, Okeogbe, Porto Novo Creek
Tarqua Bay, Ogogoro
Lagos Harbour, Lagos State Wharf
Oba's Palace, Station, National Stadium
Idi-Oro, Igbobi, Ijora, Okeita, Iganmu (Iponi), Coker, Ajeunle
University of Lagos, Agboyi Creek
Ivi-Owuro Creek, Falomo, Ikoyi, Obalende

El QÂHIRA (CAIRO)

Cairo International Airport
Almaza Airport

Masr el Gedida (Heliopolis)
EL QÂHIRA
MASR EL QÂHIRA
EL QÂHIRA
El Bahr el Ahmar
El Qâhira
Nahr en Nil
Masr el Qadima (Old Cairo)
El Gîza
El Tâlibîya
Shabrâmant

El Matarîya, El Zeitûn, Heliopolis, Mâdinet Nasr, Hilmîya, El Wayli el Kubrâ, El Qubba, El Abbâsîya, El Gamâlîya, El Misk, Mâdinet el Muqattam, Gebel el Muqattam, Gebel et Tura, El Ma'âdi, Tura, Tammûn, El Basâlîn, Saft el Laban, Birak el Kiyam, Et Talibîya, El Baragîl, Kafr es Sammân, Ausim, Zâwiyet Abû Musallam
Gebel el Ahmar, Wâdi el Nahdein, Wâdi Dîgla, Wâdi el Labîûbe
Shubrâ el Kheima, Bûlâq, El Zamâlik, El Awkât, El Duqqi, Imbâba, University Zoological Gardens, El Gîza Geziret ed Dahab
Bahtîm, Musturud, Gezîret el Hadar, Warrâq el Hadar, Gesîret Muhammad, Warrâq el Arab, El Kôm el Ahmar, Minshât el Bekkâri, Nahia, Kirdâsa, Hakim, Burtus
Pyramids Cheops, Chefren, Mykerinos, Sphinx
Citadel, Garden City, Gezirat el Rauda, President's Palace, Egyptian Museum
El Muhît Idkû el Gharbi, Bahr el Lubeini

256, 193, 204, 173, 83

JOHANNESBURG

Jan Smuts Airport
Rand Airport
Baragwanath Airfield
Diepkloof Airfield

JOHANNESBURG
Germiston
Benoni
Boksburg
Brakpan
Springs
Kwa-Thema
Kempton Park
Modderfontein
Edenvale
Alexandra
Sandton
Randburg
Krugersdorp
Roodepoort
Soweto
Alberton
Bedford View
Witfield
Eisburg

Daveyton, Petit, Geduld Dam, Brentwood Park, Rusville, Lakefield, New Kleinfontein, Benoni South, New Modder, Rynfield, Northmead, Morehill, Dalview, Brenthurst, Schagenrust, Finaalspan, Cinderella, Parkdene, Boksburg North, Boksburg South, Elandsfontein, Roodekop, Wadeville, Elspark, Dinwiddie, Florentia, New Redruth, Alberante, Randhart, Southcrest, South Hills, Klippoortje, Delville, Parkhill Gardens, Lambton, Fisher's Hill, Primrose, Dewetshof, North Germiston, Germiston South, Sunnyridge, Edenvale, Dunvegan, Edleen, Cresslawn, Rhodesfield, Allengrove, Linbropark, Lakeside, Thophill, Ahnwerp, Bonaero Park, Van Ryn Dam, Modderfontein Deep Levels, Van Dyks Park, Lecupan, Homestead Lake, Farrarmere
Sandown, Sandhurst, Hurlingham, Parkmore, Morningside, Kelvin, Lombardy East, Lyndhurst, Glenhazel, Sandringham, St. Andrews, Kew, Waverley, Highlands North, Oaklands, Orchards, Orange Grove, Observatory, Houghton, Norwood, Linksfield, Gardenvale, Malvern, Malvern East, Kensington, Troyeville, The Wilds, Parkwood, Saxonwold, Parktown North, Emmarentia, West Park, Greenside, Northcliff, Blackheath, Windsor Cresta, Robin Hills, Fontainebleau, Randpark, Bloemhof, Ferndale, Bordeaux, Blairgowrie, Craighall Park, Parkview, Parkhurst, Westcliff, Berea, Auckland Park, Melville, Westdene, Crosby, Newlands, Fairland, Weltevreden Park Ext., Raparkri, Discovery, Florida, Roodepoort-Wes, Hamberg, Kloofendal, Heldenkruin, Poortview, Amorosa, Witpoortjie, Manufacta, Kenmare, Luipaardsvlei, Silverfields, Culembeeck, Lewisham, Endeni, Honeydew
Turffontein, Forbsburg, Mayfair, Selby, Ophirton, Robertsham, New Canada, Noordgesig, Orlando East, Orlando West, Meadowlands, Mofolo, Jabulani, Molapo, Moroka, Mapetla, Chiawelo, Molatsane, Jabavu, Nancefield, Pimville, Meredale, Mondeor, Bloubosspruit, Glenwista, Mulbarton, Kibler Park, Klip River, Kliprivierberg, Rosettenville, Regents Park, Moffat Park, Rewlea, Crown Gardens, Riverlea, Marisburg, Bosmont, Triomf, New Canada Dam, Orlando Dam, Klipspruit
Rand Leases Gold Mines, Durban Roodepoort Deep Gold Mines, West Rand Cons Gold Mines
Jukskeirivier, Modderfontein, Van Ryn Dam, Geduld Dam, Cinderella Dam, Rand Airport, Simmer and Jack Mines, Victoria Lake, Elsburg Spruit, Klip River

East from Greenwich

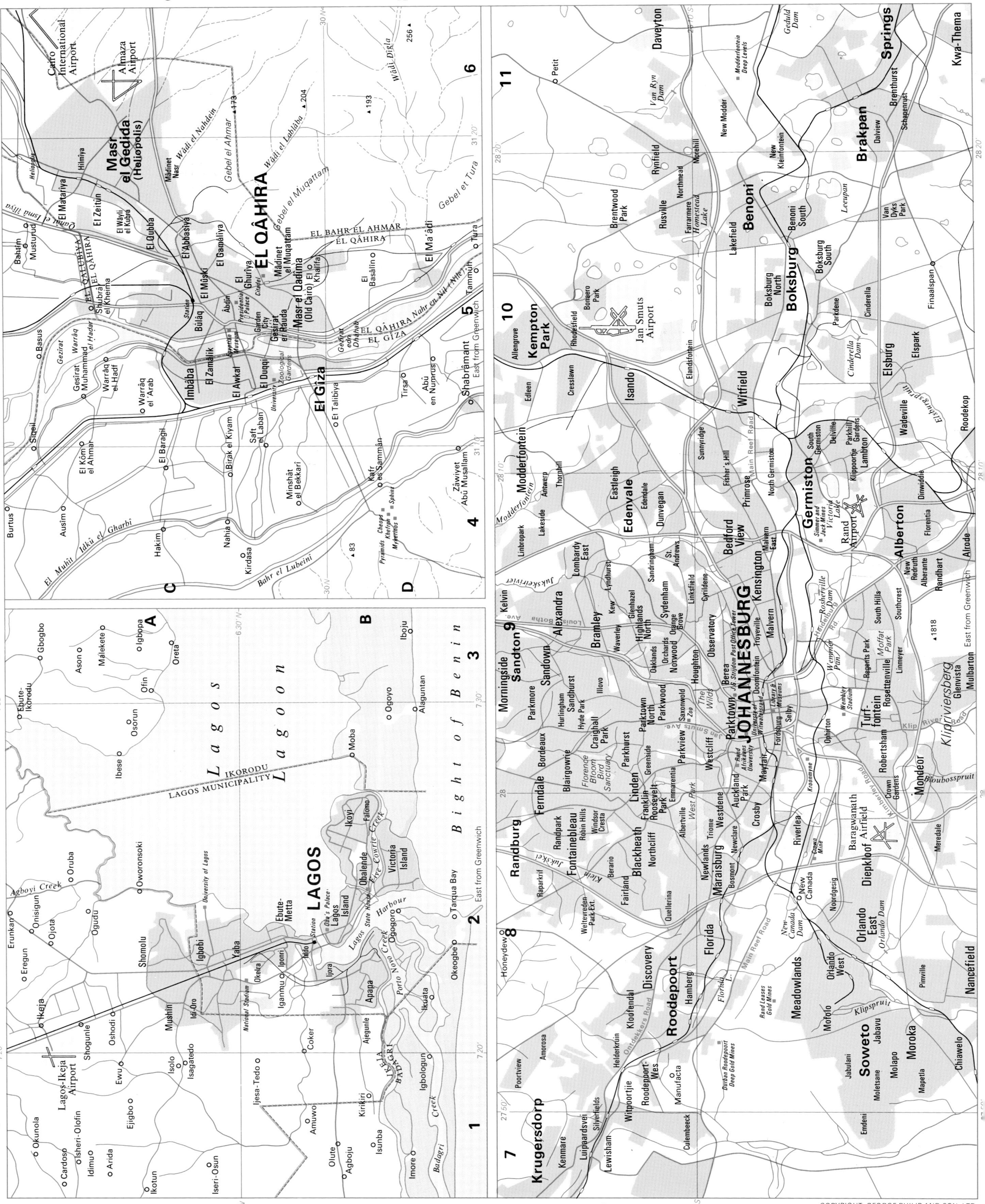

COPYRIGHT. GEORGE PHILIP AND SON. LTD.

26 10' S
27 50' S
28
28 20'
31 20'
31 10'
6 30' N
7 20'
7 30'
East from Greenwich
30 W

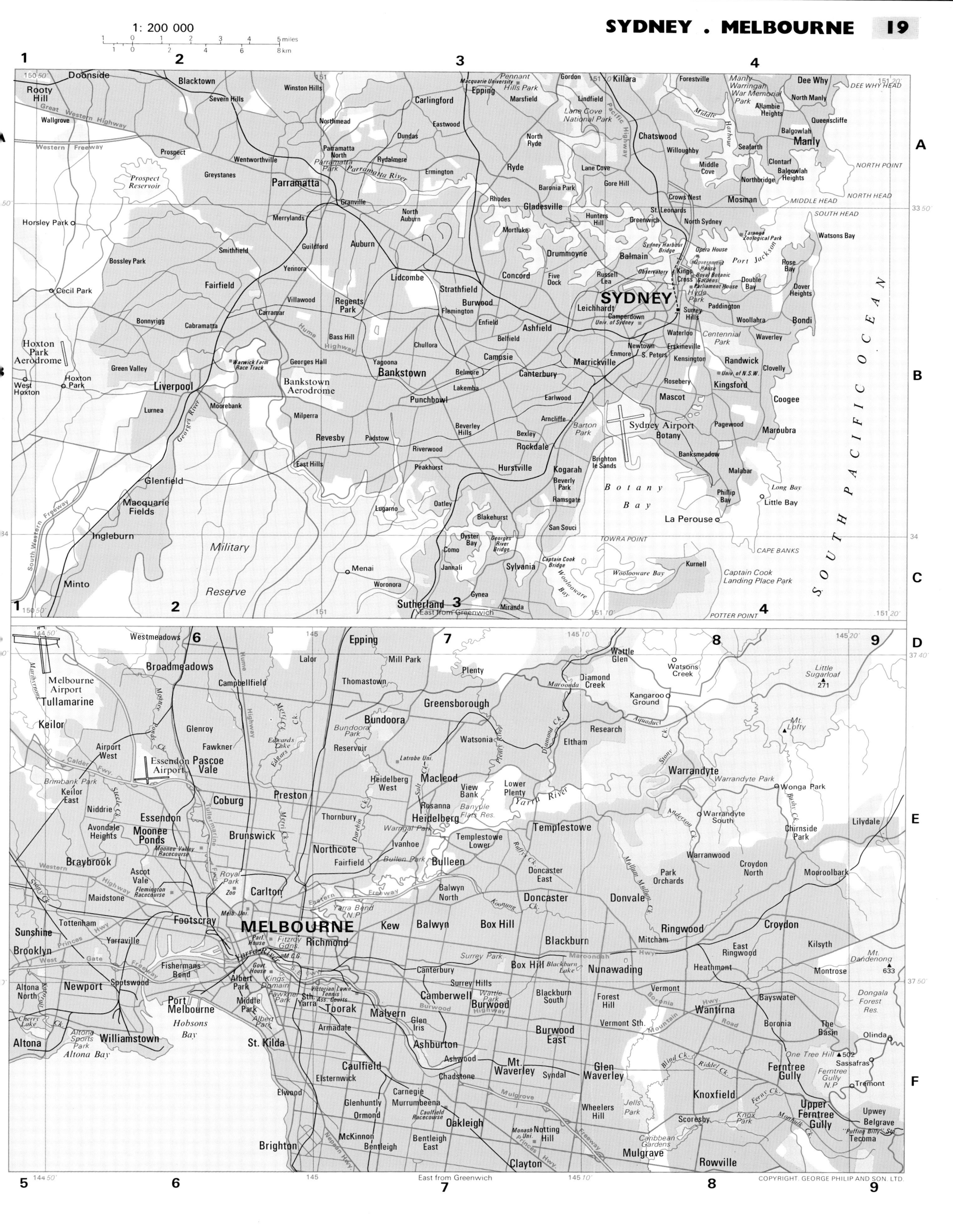

1 : 200 000

0   1   2   3   4   5 miles
0 1   2   4   6   8km

1   **2**   **3**   **4**   **5**

Lorraine

Ste-Thérèse

R. des Mille Îles

TERREBONNE

73.50'

73.40'

73.30'

St.-Augustin

Auteuil

Rivière-des-Prairies

Pointe-Aux-Trembles

R. des Prairies

A

Petit-Brûlé

Chicot

Chicot

Ste-Thérèse-Ouest

Ste-Rose

St-Vincent-de-Paul

Montréal-Est

Île de Boucherville

St. Lawrence

La Fresnière

St.-Eustache

Fabreville

Vimont

Duvernay

Montréal Nord

Anjou

Tetreauville

Longue Point

Boucherville

Ville de Laval

St-Léonard

St-Jean-de-dieu

Boulevard

Ave.

Sherbrook

St. Lawrence

Deux-Montagnes

Laval-Ouest

St-Martin

Bélanger

St-Michel

Boul Pie-IX

Pont-Viau

CHAMBLY

St.-Joseph-du-Lac

Ste-Marthe-sur-le-Lac

Laval-sur-le-Lac

Ste-Dorothée

Laval-des-Rapides

Chomedey

Abord à Plouffe

Ahuntsic

Bordeaux

Boulevard

St. Denis

Maisonneuve

Parc Olympique

Rue St. Denis

MONTRÉAL

Jacques Cartier

Mackayville

43.30'

DEUX MONTAGNES

Le Trappe

Pointe-Calumet

Île Bizard

Île-Bizard

R. des Prairies

Ste-Geneviève

Roxboro

Pierrefonds

Aéroport de Cartierville

St.-Laurent

Dollard-Des Ormeaux

Mont Royal

Parc Mont-Royal

Route

Outremont

Univ. McGill

Île Ste Hélène

Terre des Hommes

Longueuil

St.-Hubert

Dollard-des-Ormeaux

Univ. de Montréal

St-Lambert

43.30'

Pierrefonds

Kirkland

Pointe-Claire

Transcanadienne

Westmount

Hampstead

Côte-St-Luc

St-Pierre

Pont Victoria

Forum

Lemoyne

Préville

Greenfield Park

Notre-Dame

B

Lac des

Deux Montagnes

Île Cadieux

Beaconsfield

Dorval

Aéroport de Dorval

Lachine

Verdun

Lasalle

Île des Soeurs

Pont Champlain

Brossard

B

Vaudreuil-sur-le-Lac

Senneville

Baie-d'Urfé

Île aux Herons

St. Lawrence

St. Jacques

La Prairie

Pont Mercier

Canal de la Rive-Sud

La Prairie

Vaudreuil

Terrasse-Vaudreuil

Île-Perrot

Lac

Saint - Louis

Caughnawaga

Sainte Catherine

1

Dorion

Notre-Dame-de-L'Île Perrot

Île-Perrot

MONTREAL VAUDREUIL

West from Greenwich

73.40'

3

4

Candiac

5

1   **2**   73.50'   **3**   **4**   **5**

6   **7**   **8**   **9**   **10**

79.40'

Maple

79.30'

Richvale

Richmond Hill

Buttonville

79.20'

79.10'

Cherrywood

C

Kleinburg

Langstaff

East Don

Armadale

Markham

Milliken

DURHAM

Dunbarton

43.50'

Coleraine

Humber

East Barrie Highway

Concord

Thornhill

Markham

YORK

Brown

Little Rouge

Rouge

Fairport

Rouge Hill

West Rouge

Woodbridge

Pine Grove

Edgeley

Fisherville

Newton Brook

Willowdale

Agincourt

Malvern

Morningside Park

Highland Creek

Port Union

Rouge

New

G. Ross Lord Park

York University

Northmount

MacDonald

Cartier

Freeway

Woburn

West Hill

D

Beaumonde Heights

Humber Summit

Black Creek Pioneer Village

North York

Armour Heights

York Mills

Lansing

Wexford

Bendale

Scarborough

Highland Creek

Thistletown

Canada Forces Base

West Yonge

Don Mills

Cliffside

Scarborough

Kipling Heights

Downsview Dells Park

Lawrence Heights

Wilket Creek Park

Danforth

Rexdale

PEEL

Downsview

Ontario Science Centre

Thorncliffe

Kingston

Road

Malton

Humberlea

Avenue

Don

Leaside

Dentonia Park

Weston

Black Creek

Road

York

Birch Cliff

Humber

Cedarvale

Forest Hill

East York

Danforth Ave.

Don Valley Pkwy

43.40'

Toronto International Airport (Lester B. Pearson)

Humber Valley Village

Mount Dennis

York

Bloor

Parliament Buildings

Riverdale Park

Key Gardens

Hanlon

MacDonald Cartier Freeway

Mimico Creek

Humber

Lambton Mills

Humber Valley Park

Swansea

University of Toronto

Riverdale

Etobicoke

Kingsway

High Park

CN Tower

Gardiner Expressway

TORONTO

Islington

Etobicoke Creek

Parkdale

Exhibition Stadium

Toronto Harbour

E

Markland Wood

Burnhamthorpe

Summerville

The Queensway

Humber Bay

Humber Bay

Ontario Place

Toronto Island

Island Park

Browns Line

Mimico

Elizabeth Way

New Toronto

GIBRALTAR POINT

Cooksville

Mississauga

Lakeview

Long Branch

L a k e   O n t a r i o

79.40'

79.30'

West from Greenwich

79.20'

COPYRIGHT. GEORGE PHILIP AND SON LTD.

6   **7**   **8**   **9**   **10**

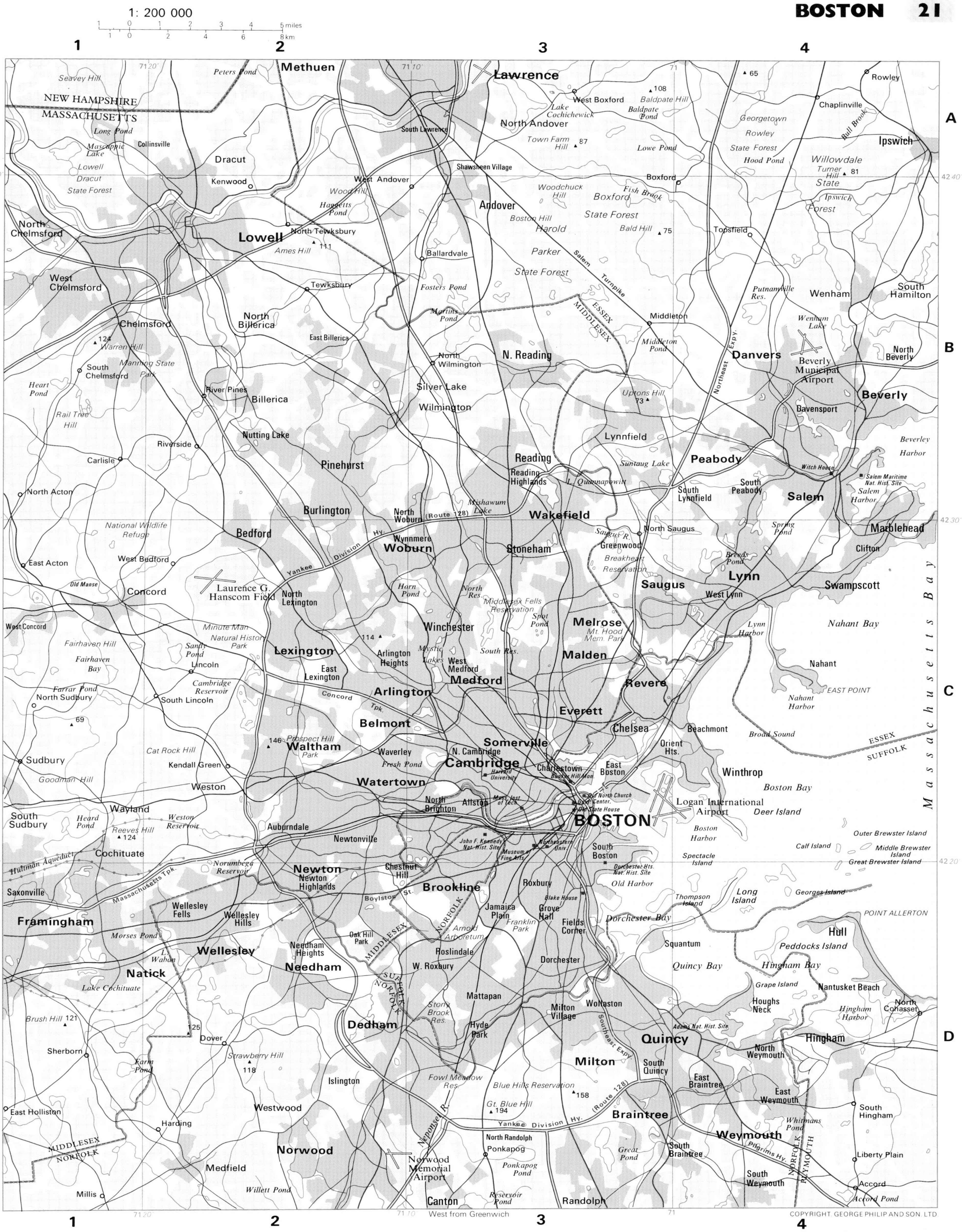

1: 200 000

0 1 2 3 4 5 miles
0 2 4 6 8 km

1 2 3 4

NEW HAMPSHIRE
MASSACHUSETTS

Seavey Hill
Peters Pond
Methuen
Lawrence
West Boxford
Baldpate Hill
65
Rowley
Chaplinville
Long Pond
Lake Cochichewick
Baldpate Pond
Georgetown
Ipswich
Muscapnie Lake
Collinsville
Dracut
North Andover
Town Farm Hill 87
Lowe Pond
Rowley State Forest
Willowdale
Lowell Dracut State Forest
Kenwood
South Lawrence
Boxford
Hood Pond
Turner Hill 81
State
North Chelmsford
Shawsheen Village
Andover
Woodchuck Hill
Boxford State Forest
Fish Brook
Ipswich Forest
Wood Hill
Haggetts Pond
Lowell
West Andover
Harold
Putnamville Res.
Wenham
South Hamilton
North Tewksbury
Ames Hill 111
Ballardvale
Parker State Forest
Salem Turnpike
Middleton
Wenham Lake
Danvers
North Beverly
Chelmsford
Warren Hill 124
Tewksbury
East Billerica
Fosters Pond
ESSEX MIDDLESEX
Middleton Pond
Beverly Municipal Airport
Beverly
South Chelmsford
Manning State Park
North Billerica
Martins Pond
N. Reading
Uptons Hill 73
Davensport
Heart Pond
River Pines
Billerica
North Wilmington
Silver Lake
Reading
Suntaug Lake
Lynnfield
Peabody
South Peabody
Salem Maritime Nat. Hist. Site
Beverley Harbor
Rail Tree Hill
Nutting Lake
Wilmington
Reading Highlands
L. Quannapowitt
South Lynnfield
Witch House
Salem
Salem Harbor
North Acton
Pinehurst
Mishawum Lake
Wakefield
North Saugus
Greenwood
Spring Pond
Marblehead
Carlisle
Riverside
Burlington
North Woburn (Route 128)
Stoneham
Saugus R.
Breakheart Reservation
Breed's Pond
Clifton
National Wildlife Refuge
Bedford
Woburn
Wynnmere Hy.
Lynn
West Lynn
Swampscott
East Acton
West Bedford
Yankee Division
Horn Pond
North Res.
Middlesex Fells Reservation
Saugus
Lynn Harbor
Nahant Bay
Old Manse
Laurence G. Hanscom Field
North Lexington
Winchester
Spot Pond
Melrose
Mt. Hood Mem. Park
Nahant
Concord
Minute Man Natural History Park
114
Arlington Heights
West Medford
South Res.
Malden
Revere
Nahant Harbor
West Concord
Fairhaven Hill
Sandy Pond
Lexington
East Lexington
Mystic Lakes
Medford
Everett
Chelsea
Beachmont
EAST POINT
Fairhaven Bay
Lincoln
Cambridge Reservoir
Arlington
Concord Tpk.
Belmont
Somerville
N. Cambridge
Charlestown
East Boston
Orient Hts.
Broad Sound
ESSEX SUFFOLK
Farrar Pond
North Sudbury
South Lincoln
146
Prospect Hill
Waltham
Waverley
Fresh Pond
Cambridge
Harvard University
Bunker Hill Mon.
Winthrop
Boston Bay
Sudbury
69
Cat Rock Hill
Kendall Green
Watertown
North Brighton
Allston
Mass. Inst. of Tech.
Old North Church
Logan International Airport
Deer Island
Goodman Hill
Weston
Wayland
Weston Reservoir
Auburndale
Newtonville
State House
South Boston
Boston Harbor
Calf Island
Outer Brewster Island
South Sudbury
Heard Pond
Reeves Hill 124
Norumbega Reservoir
John F. Kennedy Nat. Hist. Site
Museum of Fine Arts
Northeastern Univ.
Spectacle Island
Middle Brewster Island
Great Brewster Island
Cochituate
Hultman Aqueduct
Massachusetts Tpk.
Newton
Newton Highlands
Chestnut Hill
Brookline
Roxbury
Old Harbor
Thompson Island
Long Island
Georges Island
POINT ALLERTON
Saxonville
Wellesley Fells
Wellesley Hills
Boylston St.
Jamaica Plain
Grove Hall
Fields Corner
Dorchester Bay
Hull
Peddocks Island
Framingham
Morses Pond
Wellesley
Needham Heights
Oak Hill Park
Arnold Arboretum
Franklin Park
Blake House
Squantum
Quincy Bay
Hingham Bay
Natick
Lake Cochituate
Wellesley
Needham
MIDDLESEX NORFOLK
Roslindale
W. Roxbury
Dorchester
Grape Island
Nantasket Beach
North Cohasset
Brush Hill 121
Dover
Strawberry Hill 118
Needham
Mattapan
Stony Brook Res.
Milton Village
Wollaston
Houghs Neck
Hingham Harbor
East Weymouth
Sherborn
Farm Pond
Dedham
Hyde Park
Milton
Quincy
North Weymouth
Hingham
Islington
Fowl Meadow Res.
South Quincy
East Braintree
South Weymouth
Whitmans Pond
East Holliston
Westwood
Blue Hills Reservation
158
Gt. Blue Hill 194
Braintree
South Braintree
Weymouth
South Hingham
MIDDLESEX NORFOLK
Norwood
Medfield
Norwood Memorial Airport
North Randolph
Ponkapog
Ponkapog Pond
Great Pond
Route 128
Yankee Division Hy.
Southeast Expy.
Pilgrims Hy.
NORFOLK PLYMOUTH
Liberty Plain
South Weymouth
Accord
Millis
Harding
Willett Pond
Canton
Reservoir Pond
Randolph
Accord Pond
West from Greenwich

Massachusetts Bay

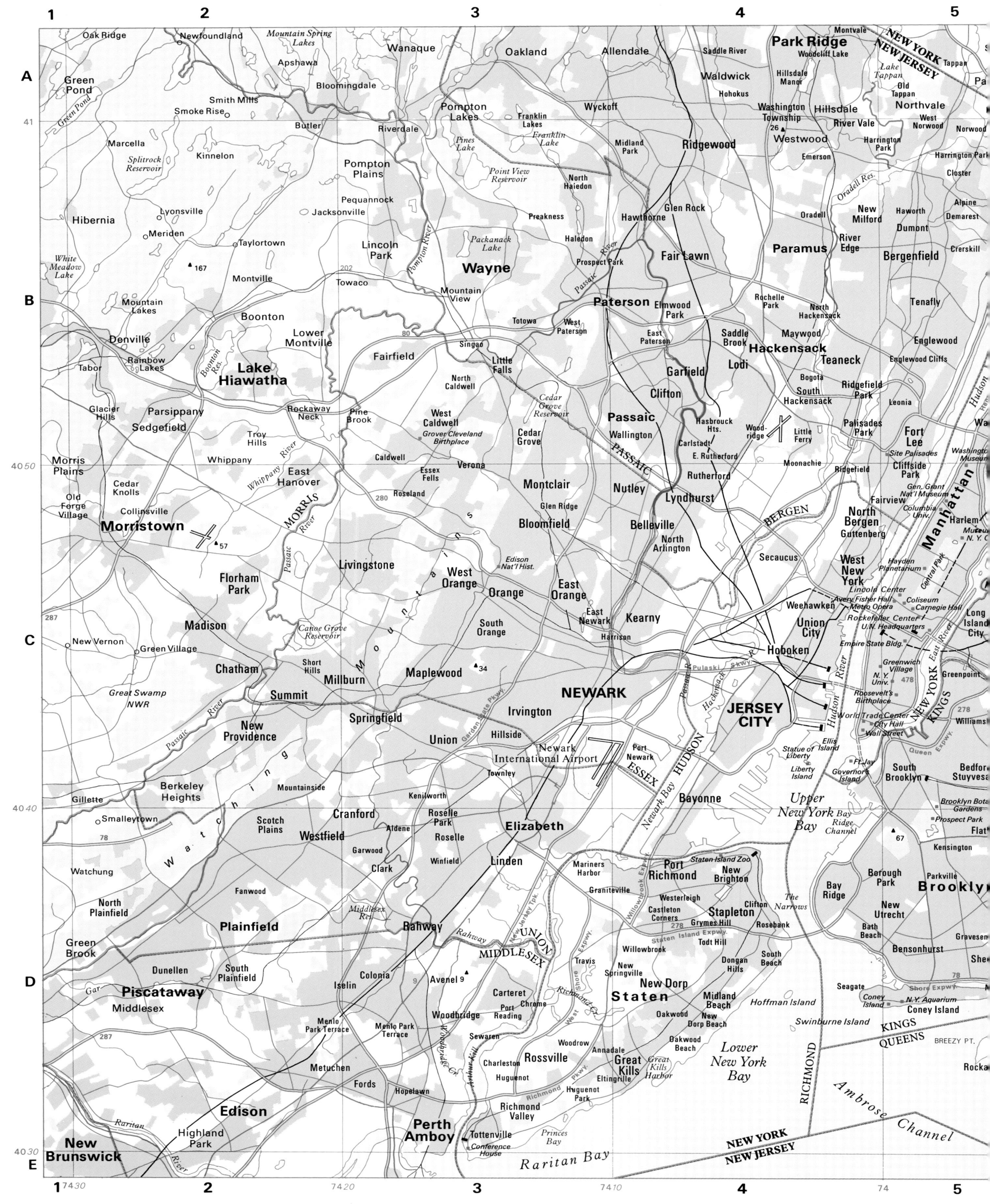

Oak Ridge
Newfoundland
Mountain Spring Lakes
Wanaque
Oakland
Allendale
Saddle River
Montvale
Park Ridge
NEW YORK NEW JERSEY
Tappan

Green Pond
Apshawa
Bloomingdale
Pompton Lakes
Woodcliff Lake
Waldwick
Hillsdale Manor
Washington Township
Lake Tappan
Old Tappan

A

Smith Mills
Smoke Rise
Butler
Riverdale
Franklin Lakes
Wyckoff
Hohokus
26
Westwood
Northvale
West Norwood
Norwood

41

Marcella
Kinnelon
Pines Lake
Franklin Lake
Midland Park
Ridgewood
Emerson
Oradell
New Milford
Haworth
River Vale
Harrington Park
Closter
Alpine
Demarest
Harrington Park

Splitrock Reservoir
Hibernia
Lyonsville
Pompton Plains
Point View Reservoir
North Haledon
Preakness
Hawthorne
Glen Rock
Paramus
River Edge
Bergenfield
Crerskill

White Meadow Lake
Meriden
Taylortown
167
Lincoln Park
202
Packanack Lake
Haledon
Wayne
Prospect Park
Fair Lawn
Passaic River
Rochelle Park
North Hackensack
Tenafly

B

Montville
Towaco
Mountain View
Totowa
West Paterson
Paterson
Elmwood Park
East Paterson
Saddle Brook
Maywood
Hackensack
Teaneck
Englewood

Mountain Lakes
Boonton
Lower Montville
Fairfield
Singac
Little Falls
Garfield
Lodi
Bogota
South Hackensack
Ridgefield Park
Englewood Cliffs

Denville
Rainbow Lakes
Boonton Rec.
80
North Caldwell
Clifton
Hasbrouck Hts.
Carlstadt
Wood-ridge
Little Ferry
Leonia

Tabor
Rockaway Neck
Pine Brook
West Caldwell
Cedar Grove Reservoir
Passaic
Wallington
E. Rutherford
Moonachie
Palisades Park

Glacier Hills
Parsippany
Sedgefield
Troy Hills
Grover Cleveland Birthplace
Cedar Grove
Rutherford
Ridgefield
Fort Lee

40 50
Morris Plains
Whippany
Caldwell
Verona
Montclair
Nutley
Lyndhurst
BERGEN
Fairview
Cliffside Park
Gen. Grant Nat'l Museum

Old Forge Village
Cedar Knolls
East Hanover
280
Roseland
Essex Fells
Glen Ridge
Belleville
North Bergen
Columbia Univ.

Collinsville
MORRIS River
Livingstone
West Orange
Bloomfield
North Arlington
Secaucus
Guttenberg
Harlem Museum N.Y.

Morristown
57
Florham Park
Canoe Grove Reservoir
Orange
East Orange
East Newark
Kearny
West New York
Hayden Planetarium
Lincoln Center
Avery Fisher Hall
Metro Opera

287
Madison
Mountains
South Orange
Harrison
Weehawken
Rockefeller Center
U.N. Headquarters
Coliseum
Carnegie Hall
Long Island City

C
New Vernon
Green Village
Chatham
Short Hills
34
Maplewood
Union City
Empire State Bldg.
Greenwich Village
Greenpoint

Great Swamp NWR
Summit
Millburn
NEWARK
Hoboken
Pulaski Skwy
N.Y. Univ.
478
Williamsb

New Providence
Springfield
Irvington
Hillside
JERSEY CITY
Roosevelt's Birthplace
World Trade Center
278

40 40
Berkeley Heights
Union
Newark International Airport
Townley
Port Newark
ESSEX
HUDSON
Statue of Liberty
Ellis Island
City Hall
Wall Street

Gillette
Mountainside
Kenilworth
Bayonne
Liberty Island
Ft. Jay
Governor's Island
South Brooklyn
Bedfor Stuyvesa

Smalleytown
78
Cranford
Roselle Park
Elizabeth
Newark Bay
Upper New York Bay
Bay Ridge Channel
Brooklyn Bota Gardens

Watchung
Scotch Plains
Aldene
Roselle
Mariners Harbor
Port Richmond
New Brighton
Staten Island Zoo
67
Prospect Park
Flat

North Plainfield
Westfield
Garwood
Winfield
Graniteville
Westerleigh
Castleton Corners
Clifton
The Narrows
Bay Ridge
Borough Park
Kensington
Brooklyn

Green Brook
Plainfield
Fanwood
Clark
Rahway
Stapleton
Rosebank
New Utrecht
Bath Beach

Dunellen
South Plainfield
Iselin
Colonia
Middlesex Rd.
278
Willowbrook
Todt Hill
New Springville
Grymes Hill
Bensonhurst
Gravesend

D
Piscataway
Middlesex
9
Avenel
Staten Island Expwy
Travis
Dongan Hills
South Beach
New Dorp
Seagate
Coney Island
N.Y. Aquarium
Coney Island

Carteret
Chrome
Richmond
UNION MIDDLESEX
Woodbridge
Port Reading
Woodrow
New Dorp Beach
Midland Beach
Hoffman Island
Swinburne Island
KINGS QUEENS
BREEZY PT.

287
Menlo Park Terrace
Sewaren
Charleston
Rossville
Huguenot
Oakwood Beach
Lower New York Bay
RICHMOND
Rocka

Metuchen
Fords
Hopelawn
Richmond Valley
Huguenot Park
Great Kills
Great Kills Harbor
Eltingville
Annadale
RICHMOND
Ambrose Channel

Edison
Highland Park
Perth Amboy
Tottenville
Conference House
Princes Bay
Raritan Bay
NEW YORK NEW JERSEY

40 30
New Brunswick
Raritan
River

E

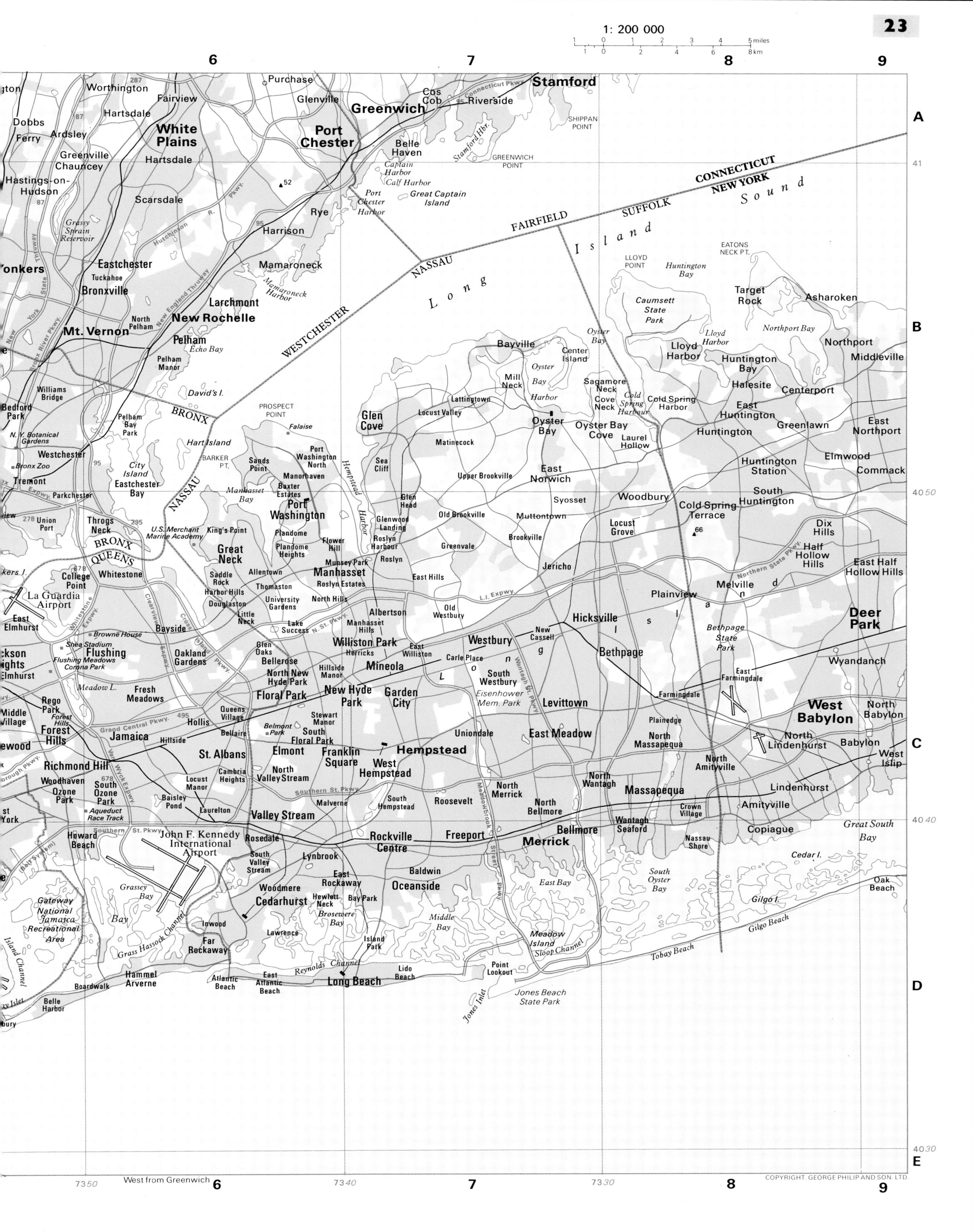

1:200 000

5 miles
8 km

A

B

C

D

E

41

40 50

40 40

40 30

6

7

8

9

Purchase
Worthington
Fairview
Glenville
Cos Cob
Riverside
Stamford
Greenwich
CONNECTICUT
NEW YORK

Dobbs Ferry
Ardsley
Hartsdale
White Plains
Port Chester
Belle Haven
SHIPPAN POINT

Greenville
Chauncey
Hartsdale
Captain Harbor
Calf Harbor
GREENWICH POINT

Hastings-on-Hudson
Scarsdale
52
Rye
Port Chester Harbor
Great Captain Island

FAIRFIELD
SUFFOLK
Long Island Sound

Harrison
NASSAU
EATONS NECK PT.

Yonkers
Eastchester
Tuckahoe
Bronxville
Mamaroneck
LLOYD POINT
Huntington Bay
Caumsett State Park
Lloyd Harbor
Northport Bay
Target Rock
Asharoken

Mamaroneck Harbor
WESTCHESTER
Bayville
Center Island
Lloyd Harbor
Huntington Bay
Northport

Mt. Vernon
North Pelham
New Rochelle
Larchmont
Mill Neck
Oyster Bay
Sagamore Neck
Cove Neck
Cold Spring Harbour
Cold Spring Harbor
Halesite
Centerport
East Huntington
Middleville

Pelham
Echo Bay
David's I.
Locust Valley
Matinecock
Oyster Bay
Oyster Bay Cove
Laurel Hollow
Huntington
Greenlawn
East Northport

Pelham Manor
PROSPECT POINT
Glen Cove
Sea Cliff
Upper Brookville
East Norwich
Huntington Station
Elmwood
Commack

Bedford Park
Williams Bridge
Pelham Bay Park
Falaise
Hart Island
Glen Head
Old Brookville
Woodbury
Cold Spring Terrace
Dix Hills

N.Y. Botanical Gardens
Westchester
City Island
BARKER PT.
Sands Point
Port Washington North
Glenwood Landing
Syosset
Half Hollow Hills

Bronx Zoo
Eastchester Bay
Manhasset Bay
Baxter Estates
Roslyn Harbour
Greenvale
Brookville
Muttontown
Locust Grove
66
East Half Hollow Hills

Tremont
Parkchester
Union Port
U.S. Merchant Marine Academy
Port Washington
Plandome
Flower Hill
Roslyn
Jericho
Melville

Throgs Neck
King's Point
Plandome Heights
Munsey Park
East Hills
Plainview
Northern State Pkwy

BRONX
QUEENS
Great Neck
Manhasset
Roslyn Estates
Old Westbury
Hicksville
Bethpage State Park
Deer Park

College Point
Whitestone
Saddle Rock
Harbor Hills
Thomaston
Roslyn Estates
North Hills
New Cassell
Bethpage

La Guardia Airport
Douglaston
University Gardens
Little Neck
Albertson
Manhasset Hills
Westbury
Levittown
East Farmingdale
Wyandanch

East Elmhurst
Browne House
Oakland Gardens
Lake Success
Williston Park
East Williston
Carle Place
South Westbury
Farmingdale

Jackson Heights
Shea Stadium
Flushing
Flushing Meadows Corona Park
Glen Oaks
Bellerose
Herricks
Eisenhower Mem. Park
Plainedge
West Babylon

Elmhurst
Meadow L.
Fresh Meadows
North New Hyde Park
Hillside Manor
Mineola
Levittown
North Massapequa
North Lindenhurst
North Babylon

Rego Park
Forest Hills
Floral Park
New Hyde Park
Garden City
East Meadow
North Amityville
West Islip

Middle Village
Hollis
Queens Village
Stewart Manor
Franklin Square
Uniondale
North Wantagh
Massapequa
Lindenhurst

Forest Hills
Jamaica
Hillside
Bellaire
Belmont Park
South Floral Park
West Hempstead
Hempstead
Crown Village
Amityville

Richmond Hill
St. Albans
Elmont
Cambria Heights
North Valley Stream
Malverne
South Hempstead
Roosevelt
North Merrick
North Bellmore
Seaford
Copiague

Woodhaven
Ozone Park
South Ozone Park
Locust Manor
Baisley Pond
Laurelton
Valley Stream
Rockville Centre
Freeport
Bellmore
Merrick
Wantagh
Nassau Shore
Great South Bay

Aqueduct Race Track
Rosedale
South Valley Stream
Lynbrook
Baldwin
Oceanside
East Bay
South Oyster Bay
Cedar I.
Oak Beach

Howard Beach
John F. Kennedy International Airport
East Rockaway
Gilgo I.

Grassey Bay
Woodmere
Cedarhurst
Hewlett Neck
Bay Park
Middle Bay
Meadow Island Sloop Channel
Gilgo Beach

Gateway National Jamaica Recreational Area
Inwood
Lawrence
Broadere Bay
Island Park
Point Lookout
Tobay Beach

Far Rockaway
Atlantic Beach
East Atlantic Beach
Long Beach
Lido Beach
Jones Beach State Park

Hammel
Arverne
Boardwalk
Reynolds Channel
Jones Inlet

Belle Harbor
Grass Hassock Channel

COPYRIGHT GEORGE PHILIP AND SON LTD.

West from Greenwich
73 50
73 40
73 30

6
7
8
9

1: 200 000

0 1 2 3 4 5 miles

1 0 2 4 6 8 km

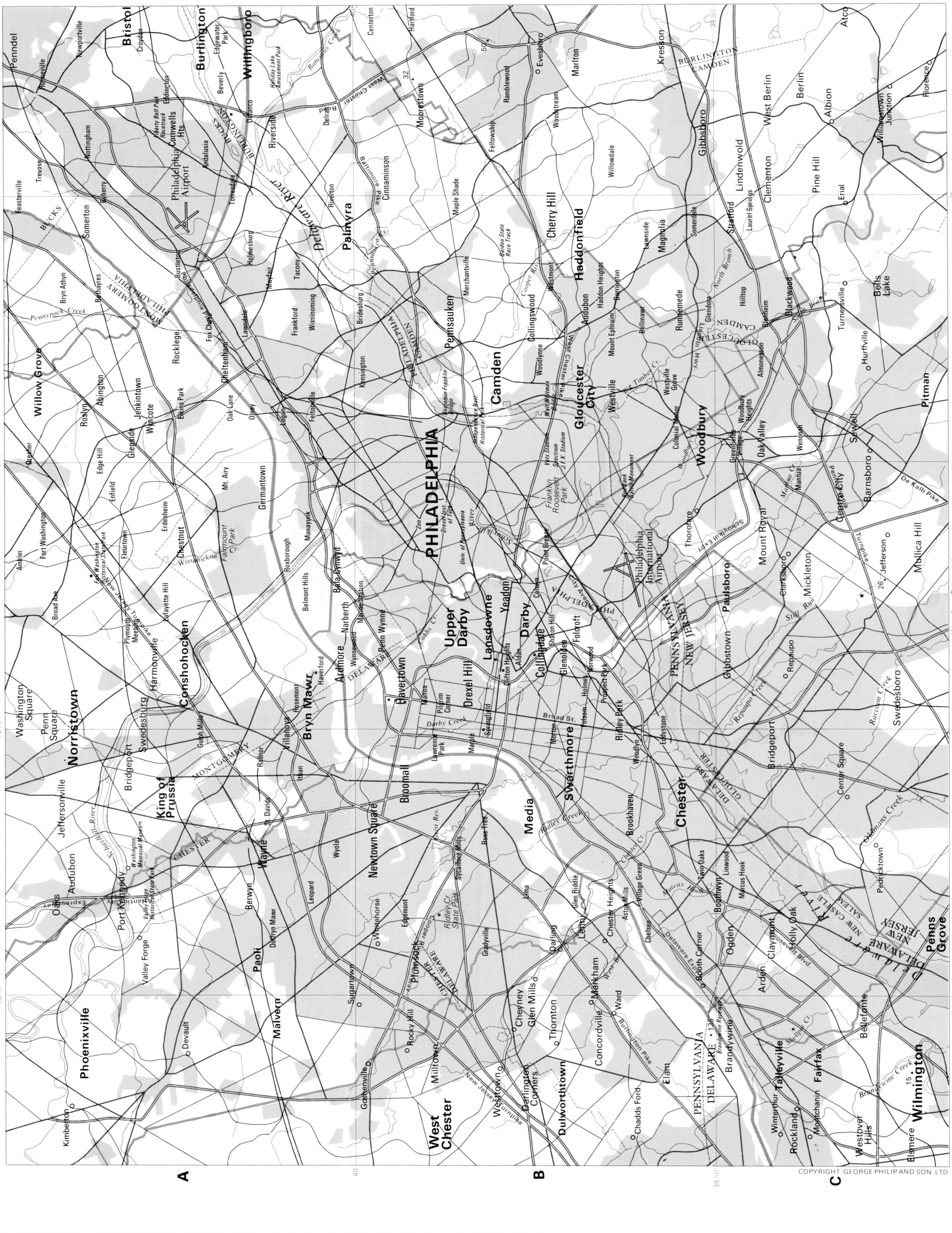
PHILADELPHIA
Camden
Gloucester City
Upper Darby
Lansdowne
Darby
Yeadon
Collingdale
Drexel Hill
Havertown
Ardmore
Bryn Mawr
Narberth
Bala-Cynwyd
Conshohocken
Norristown
King of Prussia
Wayne
Paoli
Malvern
Phoenixville
Valley Forge
West Chester
Media
Swarthmore
Chester
Wilmington
Penns Grove
Woodbury
Haddonfield
Cherry Hill
Pennsauken
Palmyra
Willingboro
Burlington
Bristol
Willow Grove
Germantown
Chestnut
Cheltenham
Philadelphia International Airport
Philadelphia Airport
Delaware River
Schuylkill River
Newtown Square
Broomall
Ridley Park
Paulsboro
Gibbstown
Mount Royal
Mickleton
Sewell
Pitman
Blackwood
Stratford
Gibbsboro
Berlin
West Berlin
Clementon
Lindenwold
Marlton
Evesboro
Moorestown
Cinnaminson
Riverside
Dulworthtown
Concordville
Brandywine
Talleyville
Fairfax
Claymont
Ogden
Brookhaven
Jefferson
Mullica Hill
Swedesboro
Bridgeport
PENNSYLVANIA
NEW JERSEY
DELAWARE
West from Greenwich
A
B
C
1
2
3
4
5

1: 200 000

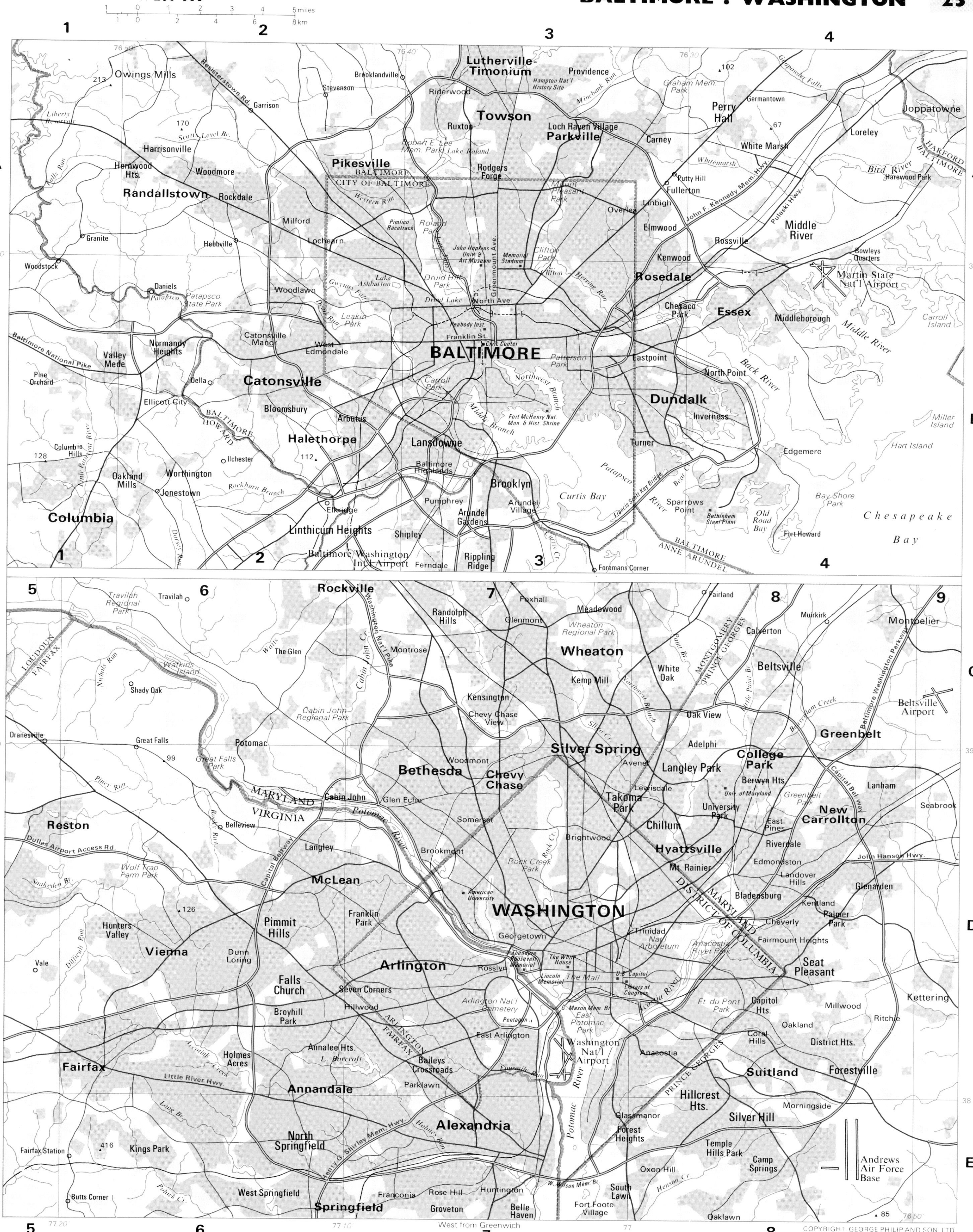

5 miles
8 km

1 **2** **3** **4**

Owings Mills
213
Resisterstown Rd.
Lutherville-Timonium
Brooklandville
Providence
Hampton Nat'l History Site
102
Graham Mem. Park
Germantown
Perry Hall
Loreley
Joppatowne

Stevenson
Riderwood
Garrison
170
Scott Level Br.
Minebank Run
67
White Marsh
Bird River
HARFORD
BALTIMORE

Harrisonville
Ruxton
Towson
Loch Raven Village
Carney
Putty Hill
Fullerton
Harewood Park

Hernwood Hts.
Woodmore
Pikesville
Parkville
Whitemarsh
John F. Kennedy Mem. Hwy
Pulaski Hwy
Bowleys Quarters

Randallstown
Rockdale
BALTIMORE CITY OF BALTIMORE
Rodgers Forge
Mt. Pleasant Park
Linbigh
Rossville
Middle River

A

Granite
Milford
Western Run
Pimlico Racetrack
Roland Park
Overlea
Elmwood
Kenwood

Hebbville
Lochearn
Druid Hill Park
North Ave.
Rosedale

Woodstock
39 20

Daniels
Patapsco State Park
Woodlawn
Gwynns Falls
Lake Ashburton
Druid Lake
John Hopkins Univ & Art Museum
Memorial Stadium
Clifton Park
Clifton
Chesaco Park
Martin State Nat'l Airport

Normandy Heights
Leakin Park
Catonsville Manor
West Edmondale
Franklin St.
Peabody Inst.
Civic Center
Herring Run
Eastpoint
Essex
Middleborough
Carroll Island

Valley Mede
Baltimore National Pike
Catonsville
BALTIMORE
North Point

Pine Orchard
Oella
Bloomsbury
Arbutus
Carroll Park
Fort McHenry Nat Mon & Hist Shrine
Patterson Park
Northwest Branch
Dundalk
Inverness

Ellicott City
BALTIMORE HOWARD
Halethorpe
Lansdowne
Middle Branch
Turner
Edgemere
Hart Island

Columbia Hills
128
Ilchester
112
Baltimore Highlands
Brooklyn
Patapsco River
Francis Scott Key Bridge
Miller Island

Oakland Mills
Worthington
Rockburn Branch
Pumphrey
Arundel Gardens
Arundel Village
Curtis Bay
Sparrows Point
Bethlehem Steel Plant
Bay Shore Park
Chesapeake Bay

Jonestown
Columbia
Elkridge
Linthicum Heights
Shipley
Rippling Ridge
Curtis Cr.
Old Road Bay
Fort Howard

Little Patuxent River
Baltimore Washington Int'l Airport
Ferndale
Foremans Corner
BALTIMORE ANNE ARUNDEL

1 **2** **3** **4**

5 **6** **7** **8** **9**

Travilah Regional Park
Travilah
Rockville
Foxhall
Meadewood
Fairland
Muirkirk
Montpelier

Randolph Hills
Glenmont
Wheaton Regional Park
Calverton
Beltsville

Shady Oak
Nichol's Run
Watkins Island
The Glen
Montrose
Wheaton
White Oak
Beltsville Airport

C

Dranesville
Great Falls
99
Cabin John Regional Park
Kensington
Kemp Mill
Oak View
Greenbelt

Great Falls Park
Chevy Chase View
Silver Spring
Adelphi
Greenbelt Park
39

Potomac
Silver Cr.
Montgomery Prince Georges
Baltimore Washington Parkway

Piney Run
Woodmont
Avenel
Langley Park
College Park
Lanham

Reston
MARYLAND VIRGINIA
Bethesda
Chevy Chase
Takoma Park
Berwyn Hts.
New Carrollton
Seabrook

Cabin John
Glen Echo
Somerset
Univ. of Maryland
University Park
East Pines

Belleview
Potomac River
Brightwood
Chillum
Hyattsville
Riverdale

Langley
Brookmont
Rock Creek Park
Mt. Rainier
Edmonston
John Hanson Hwy

McLean
American University
Glenarden

Wolf Trap Farm Park
Snakeden Br.
Bladensburg
Kentland
Palmer Park

Vienna
126
Pimmit Hills
Franklin Park
WASHINGTON
DISTRICT OF COLUMBIA
Cheverly
Fairmount Heights

Dunn Loring
Georgetown
Trinidad
Nat'l Arboretum
Anacostia River Park

D

Vale
Difficult Run
Falls Church
Rosslyn
The White House
The Mall
Capitol
Seat Pleasant
Kettering

Fairfax
LOUDOUN FAIRFAX
Arlington
Theodore Roosevelt Memorial
Lincoln Memorial
Library of Congress
Ft. du Pont Park
Capitol Hts.
Millwood
Ritchie

Seven Corners
Hillwood
Arlington Nat'l Cemetery
Mason Mem. Br.
East Potomac Park
Oakland
District Hts.

Holmes Acres
Broyhill Park
Pentagon
East Arlington
Coral Hills
Forestville

Accotink Creek
Little River Hwy
Annalee Hts.
L. Barcroft
Baileys Crossroads
Washington Nat'l Airport
Anacostia
Suitland

Annandale
Parklawn
Potomac River
Hillcrest Hts.
Morningside
Silver Hill
38 50

Long Br.
Alexandria
Glassmanor
Forest Heights
Temple Hills Park
Camp Springs

North Springfield
Andrews Air Force Base

Fairfax Station
416
Kings Park
Oxon Hill
Henson Cr.

Butts Corner
West Springfield
Franconia
Rose Hill
Huntington
South Lawn
85
76 50

Pohick Cr.
Springfield
Groveton
Belle Haven
W. Wilson Mem. Br.
Fort Foote Village
Oaklawn

E

West from Greenwich
77 10
77

COPYRIGHT GEORGE PHILIP AND SON LTD

5 **6** **7** **8** **9**

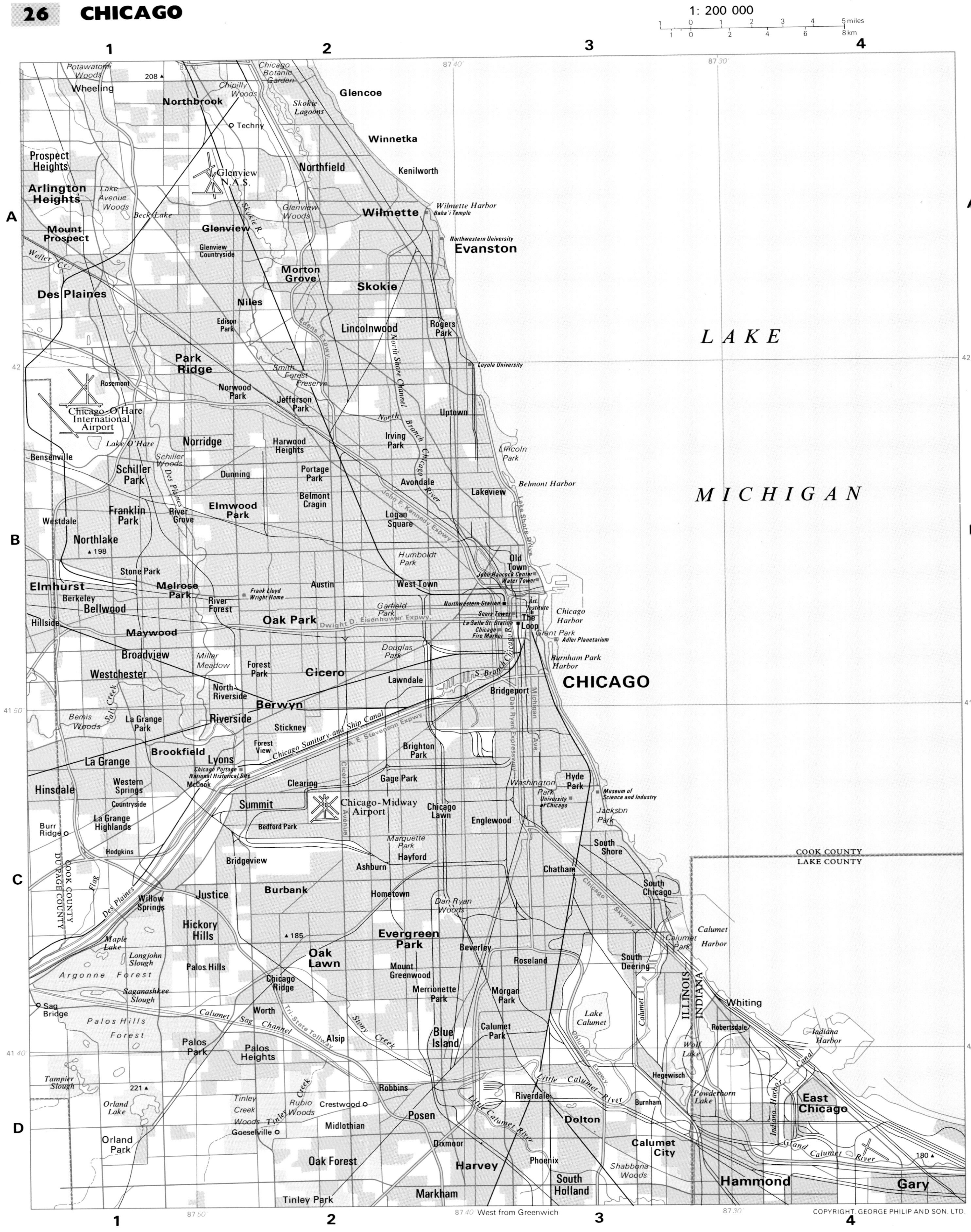

1 : 200 000

1 0 1 2 3 4 5 miles
1 0 2 4 6 8 km

1 **2** **3** **4**

Potawatomi Woods
208 ▲
Wheeling
Chipilly Woods
Chicago Botanic Garden
Glencoe
Northbrook
Techny
Skokie Lagoons
Winnetka
Prospect Heights
Northfield
Glenview N.A.S.
Kenilworth
Arlington Heights
Lake Avenue Woods
Beck Lake
Glenview Woods
Wilmette
Wilmette Harbor
Baha'i Temple

A

Mount Prospect
Glenview
Glenview Countryside
Northwestern University
Evanston

Des Plaines
Niles
Morton Grove
Skokie

Weller Cr.
Edison Park
Lincolnwood
Rogers Park

42
Park Ridge
Smith Forest Preserve
North Shore Channel
Loyola University

LAKE
42

Rosemont
Norwood Park
Jefferson Park
North Branch Chicago River
Uptown

Chicago-O'Hare International Airport
Lake O'Hare
Norridge
Harwood Heights
Portage Park
Irving Park
Lincoln Park

Bensenville
Schiller Woods
Des Plaines R.
Dunning
Belmont Cragin
Avondale
Lakeview
Belmont Harbor

MICHIGAN

Schiller Park
Elmwood Park
Logan Square
John F. Kennedy Expwy

Westdale
Franklin Park
River Grove
Lake Shore Drive

B
Northlake
198 ▲
Humboldt Park
Old Town
John Hancock Center
Water Tower

Stone Park
Austin
West Town

Elmhurst
Melrose Park
Frank Lloyd Wright Home
Northwestern Station
Art Institute
Chicago Harbor

Berkeley
River Forest
Garfield Park
Sears Tower
The Loop

Bellwood
Oak Park
Dwight D. Eisenhower Expwy
La Salle St. Station
Chicago Fire Market
Grant Park

Hillside
Maywood
Douglas Park
Adler Planetarium

Broadview
Miller Meadow
Forest Park
Cicero
Burnham Park Harbor

Westchester
Lawndale
CHICAGO

North Riverside
Berwyn
S. Branch
Bridgeport
Michigan Ave

41 50
Bemis Woods
Salt Creek
La Grange Park
Riverside
Stickney
Chicago Sanitary and Ship Canal
Dan Ryan Expressway
41

Brookfield
Lyons
Forest View
A. E. Stevenson Expwy
Brighton Park

La Grange
Chicago Portage National Historical Site
Cicero Avenue
Gage Park
Hyde Park

Hinsdale
Western Springs
McCook
Clearing
Washington Park
University of Chicago
Museum of Science and Industry

Countryside
Summit
Chicago-Midway Airport
Chicago Lawn
Jackson Park

Burr Ridge
La Grange Highlands
Bedford Park
Englewood

Hodgkins
Bridgeview
Marquette Park
South Shore

C
Flag
Justice
Burbank
Ashburn
Hayford
Chatham

COOK COUNTY DU PAGE COUNTY
Des Plaines
Willow Springs
Hometown
Dan Ryan Woods
South Chicago

COOK COUNTY LAKE COUNTY

Maple Lake
Hickory Hills
Evergreen Park
Beverley
Calumet
Calumet Park
Calumet Harbor

Longjohn Slough
Palos Hills
Oak Lawn
Mount Greenwood
Roseland
South Deering

Argonne Forest
185 ▲
Chicago Ridge
Merrionette Park
Morgan Park
Lake Calumet

Saganashkee Slough
Worth
Blue Island
Calumet Park
Calumet Skyway

ILLINOIS
INDIANA
Whiting

Sag Bridge
Palos Hills Forest
Calumet
Sag Channel
Alsip
Stony Creek
Wolf Lake
Robertsdale
Indiana Harbor

41 40
Palos Park
Palos Heights
Robbins
Riverdale
Hegewisch
Powderhorn Lake

221 ▲
Tinley Creek
Rubio Woods
Crestwood
Posen
Little Calumet River
Burnham
East Chicago

Tampier Slough
Orland Lake
Tinley Woods
Midlothian
Little Calumet River
Dolton
Shabbona Woods

D
Orland Park
Goeselville
Dixmoor
Calumet City
180 ▲

Oak Forest
Harvey
Phoenix
Hammond
Grand Calumet River
Gary

Tinley Park
Markham
South Holland

1 87 50 **2** 87 40 West from Greenwich **3** 87 30 **4**

1 : 200 000

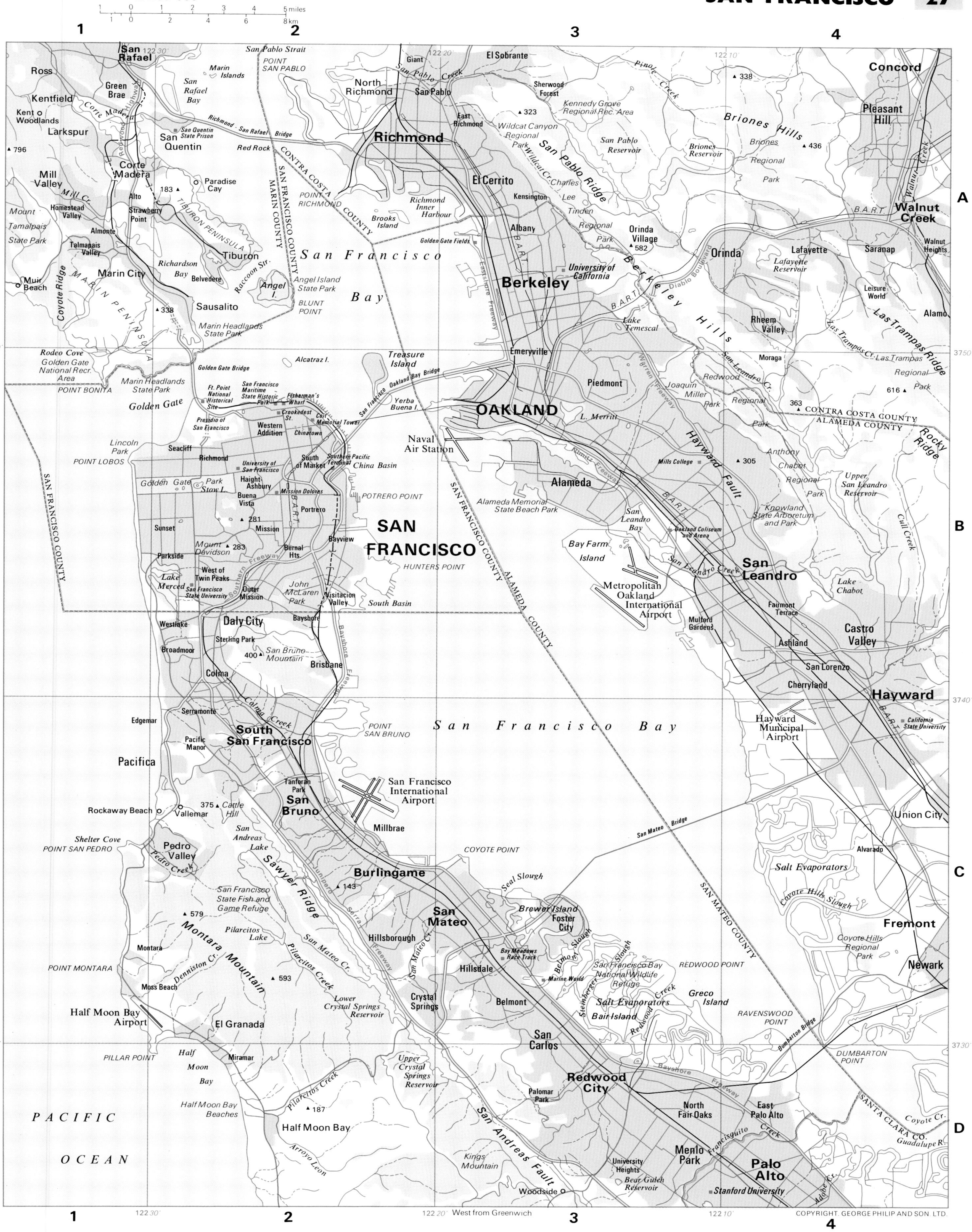

0 1 2 3 4 5 miles
0 2 4 6 8 km

1 **2** **3** **4**

San Rafael
Ross
Kentfield
Green Brae
Kent o Woodlands
Larkspur
▲796
Mill Valley
Corte Madera
San Quentin
San Quentin State Prison
Alto
Strawberry Point
183 o
Paradise Cay
Mount Tamalpais State Park
Homestead Valley
Almonte
Talmapais Valley
Tiburon
Marin City
Belvedere
Richardson Bay
Sausalito
▲338
Muir Beach
Coyote Ridge
MARIN PENINSULA
Angel I.
Angel Island State Park
BLUNT POINT
Rodeo Cove
Golden Gate National Recr. Area
POINT BONITA
Marin Headlands State Park
Golden Gate
Ft. Point National Historical Site
Presidio of San Francisco
Lincoln Park
POINT LOBOS
Seacliff
Richmond
Golden Gate Park
Stow L.
Sunset
Parkside
Mount Davidson ▲283
West of Twin Peaks
Lake Merced
San Francisco State University
Westlake
Broadmoor
Daly City
Sterling Park
Colma
400▲ San Bruno Mountain
Brisbane
Edgemar
Serramonte
South San Francisco
Pacifica
Pacific Manor
Rockaway Beach
Vallemar
375 o Cattle Hill
Shelter Cove
POINT SAN PEDRO
Pedro Valley
Montara
Moss Beach
POINT MONTARA
Half Moon Bay Airport
El Granada
Montara Mountain
▲579
▲593
Miramar
Half Moon Bay
Half Moon Bay Beaches
PILLAR POINT
187
PACIFIC OCEAN

San Pablo Strait
POINT SAN PABLO
Marin Islands
Giant
El Sobrante
North Richmond
San Pablo
East Richmond
▲323
Richmond
El Cerrito
Kensington
Albany
Berkeley
University of California
Red Rock
Brooks Island
Richmond Inner Harbour
Golden Gate Fields
Emeryville
Piedmont
OAKLAND
L. Merritt
Alameda
Naval Air Station
Treasure Island
Alcatraz I.
Golden Gate Bridge
Yerba Buena I.
San Francisco Maritime State Historic Park
Fisherman's Wharf
Coit Memorial Tower
Chinatown
Western Addition
Haight-Ashbury
Mission Dolores
Buena Vista
South of Market
Southern Pacific
China Basin
POTRERO POINT
Portrero
Mission
281▲
Bernal Hts.
Bayview
SAN FRANCISCO
HUNTERS POINT
John McLaren Park
Visitacion Valley
South Basin
Bayshore
SAN FRANCISCO COUNTY
POINT SAN BRUNO
San Francisco Bay
Tanforan Park
San Bruno
Millbrae
San Francisco International Airport
COYOTE POINT
Seal Slough
Brewer Island
Foster City
Burlingame
Hillsborough
San Mateo
Hillsdale
Crystal Springs
Belmont
San Carlos
North Fair Oaks
Redwood City
Menlo Park
Palo Alto
Stanford University
East Palo Alto
Woodside
Bear Gulch Reservoir
Kings Mountain
University Heights
San Mateo Bridge
Salt Evaporators
Union City
Alvarado
Fremont
Newark
Coyote Hills Regional Park
REDWOOD POINT
San Francisco Bay National Wildlife Refuge
Greco Island
Bair Island
RAVENSWOOD POINT
Dumbarton Bridge
DUMBARTON POINT
SANTA CLARA CO.

Concord
Pleasant Hill
Briones Hills
▲338
Sherwood Forest
Kennedy Grove Regional Rec. Area
San Pablo Reservoir
Briones Reservoir
Briones Regional Park
▲436
Walnut Creek
B.A.R.T.
Orinda Village 582
Orinda
Lafayette
Lafayette Reservoir
Saranap
Walnut Heights
Rheem Valley
Moraga
Leisure World
Alamo
Berkeley Hills
Lake Temescal
Hayward Fault
Joaquin Miller Park
Redwood Regional Park
363▲
CONTRA COSTA COUNTY
ALAMEDA COUNTY
616▲
Las Trampas Ridge
Las Trampas Regional Park
Rocky Ridge
▲305 Anthony Chabot Regional Park
Mills College
Knowland State Arboretum and Park
Upper San Leandro Reservoir
San Leandro Bay
Oakland Coliseum and Arena
San Leandro
Bay Farm Island
Metropolitan Oakland International Airport
Mulford Gardens
Lake Chabot
Fairmont Terrace
Castro Valley
Ashland
San Lorenzo
Cherryland
Hayward
California State University
Hayward Municipal Airport
Coyote Hills Slough
Coyote Cr.

West from Greenwich
COPYRIGHT. GEORGE PHILIP AND SON LTD.

A B C D

1: 200 000

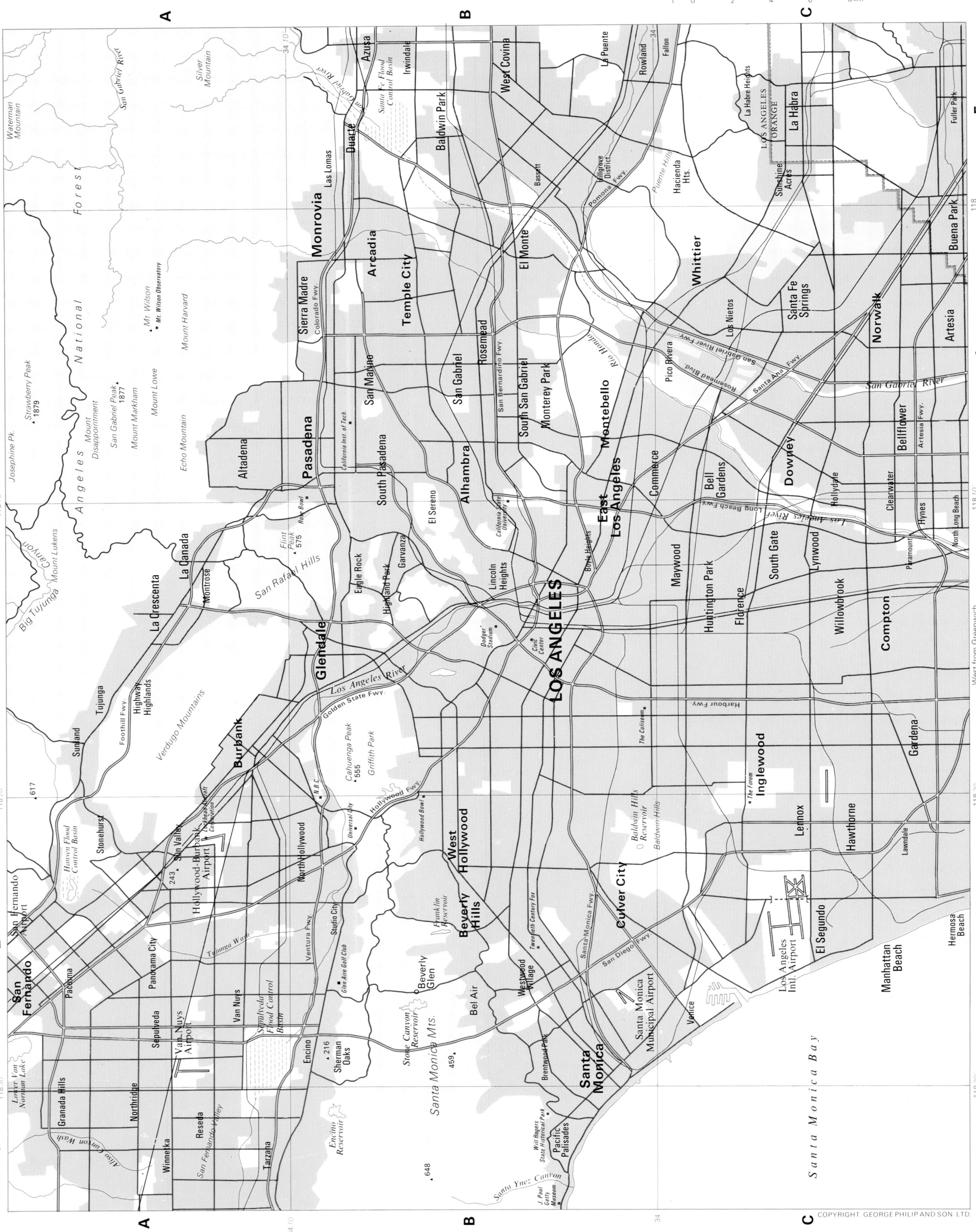

5 miles
8 km

A   B   C

5
4
3
2
1

Waterman Mountain
Silver Mountain
San Gabriel River
San Gabriel River
Azusa
Irwindale
Santa Fe Flood Control Basin
Duarte
West Covina
La Puente
Rowland
Fallon
La Habre Heights
LOS ANGELES / ORANGE
La Habra
Fuller Park

Angeles National Forest
Josephine Pk.
Strawberry Peak 1879
San Gabriel Peak 1877
Mount Markham
Mount Harvard
Mt. Wilson
Mt. Wilson Observatory
Mount Lowe
Echo Mountain
Mount Disappointment
Las Lomas
Monrovia
Sierra Madre
Arcadia
Temple City
Baldwin Park
Bassett
El Monte
Millgrove District
Pomona Fwy.
Puente Hills
Hacienda Hts.
Whittier
Sunshine Acres
Buena Park

Big Tujunga Canyon
Mount Lukens
La Cañada
Montrose
La Crescenta
Altadena
Pasadena
Rose Bowl
California Inst. of Tech.
San Rafael Hills
South Pasadena
San Marino
San Gabriel
Rosemead
San Bernardino Fwy.
South San Gabriel
Monterey Park
Montebello
Rio Hondo
Pico Rivera
Rosemead Blvd
Santa Ana Fwy.
San Gabriel River Fwy
Los Nietos
Santa Fe Springs
Norwalk
San Gabriel River
Artesia
Artesia Fwy.

Tujunga
Highway Highlands
Flint Peak 575
Eagle Rock
Garvanza
El Sereno
Alhambra
California State University
Boyle Heights
East Los Angeles
Commerce
Bell Gardens
Downey
Bellflower
Clearwater
Hynes
North Long Beach
West from Greenwich

Sunland
Foothill Fwy.
Verdugo Mountains
Glendale
Los Angeles River
Golden State Fwy.
Highland Park
Lincoln Heights
Dodger Stadium
Civic Center
LOS ANGELES
Los Angeles River
Long Beach Fwy.
Maywood
Huntington Park
Florence
South Gate
Lynwood
Willowbrook
Compton

617
Burbank
Hollywood Fwy.
Cahuenga Peak 555
Griffith Park
Harbour Fwy.
The Coliseum
Gardena

Hollywood Bowl
Universal City
N.B.C.
243
Hollywood-Burbank Airport
North Hollywood
West Hollywood
Beverly Hills
Hollywood
The Forum
Inglewood
Baldwin Hills
Baldwin Hills Reservoir
Hawthorne
Lennox
Lawndale

San Fernando Airport
San Fernando
Pacoima
Panorama City
Van Nuys
Studio City
Ventura Fwy.
Tujunga Wash
Sepulveda Flood Control Basin
Glen Aire Golf Club
Beverly Glen
Bel Air
Westwood Village
Twentieth Century Fox
Santa Monica Fwy.
Culver City
San Diego Fwy.
Los Angeles Intl. Airport
El Segundo
Manhattan Beach

Lower Van Norman Lake
Granada Hills
Northridge
Sepulveda
Van Nuys Airport
Reseda
216
Encino
Sherman Oaks
459
Stone Canyon Reservoir
Santa Monica Mts.
Brentwood Park
Santa Monica
Santa Monica Municipal Airport
Venice
Santa Monica Bay

Winneka
San Fernando Valley
Tarzana
Encino Reservoir
648
Santa Ynez Canyon
J. Paul Getty Museum
Will Rogers State Historical Park
Pacific Palisades
Franklin Reservoir

Alisa Canyon Wash

118

118

34 /10

34

COPYRIGHT GEORGE PHILIP AND SON LTD.

1: 200 000

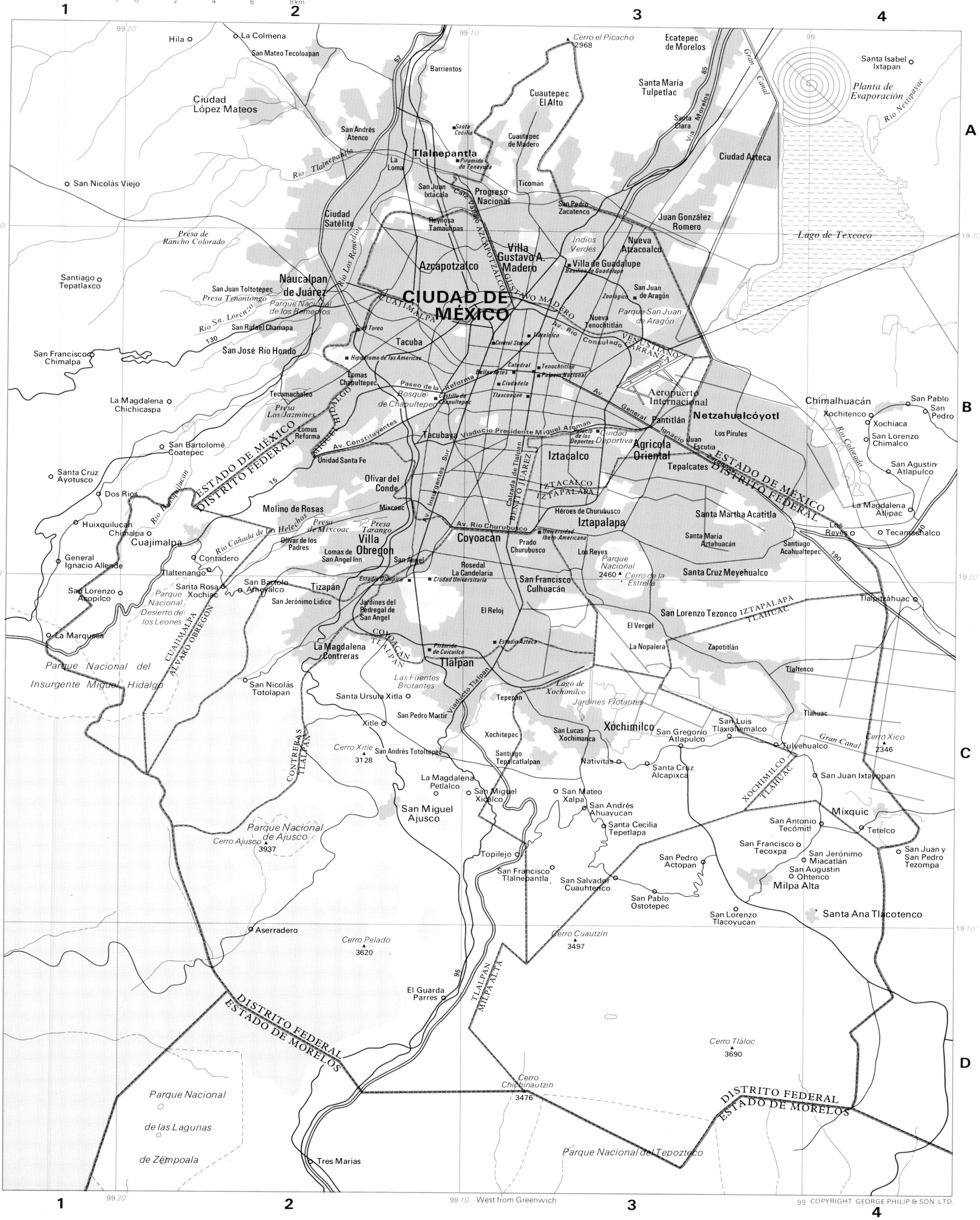

0 1 2 3 4 5 miles
0 2 4 6 8 km

1 **2** **3** **4**

Hila

La Colmena

San Mateo Tecoloapan

Barrientos

Cerro el Picacho 2968

Ecatepec de Morelos

Cuautepec El Alto

Santa María Tulpetlac

Santa Isabel Ixtapan

Planta de Evaporación

Río Nexipayac

Ciudad López Mateos

San Andrés Atenco

Santa Cecilia

Cuautepec de Madero

Santa Clara

A

San Nicolás Viejo

Tlalnepantla

Pirámide de Tenayuca

La Loma

Ticomán

Ciudad Azteca

San Juan Ixtacala

Progreso Nacional

San Pedro Zacatenco

Juan González Romero

Presa de Rancho Colorado

Ciudad Satélite

Reynosa Tamaulipas

Indios Verdes

Villa de Guadalupe

Basílica de Guadalupe

Nueva Atzacoalco

Lago de Texcoco

Santiago Tepatlaxco

Naucalpan de Juárez

Azcapotzalco

Villa Gustavo A. Madero

Zoológico

San Juan de Aragón

San Juan Toltotepec

Presa Tenantongo

Parque Nacional de los Remedios

CIUDAD DE MÉXICO

Parque San Juan de Aragón

San Rafael Chamapa

Río Sn. Loren-o

El Toreo

Nueva Tenochtitlán

San Francisco Chimalpa

San José Río Hondo

Tacuba

Central Station

Av. Río Consulado

Hipódromo de las Américas

Bellas Artes

Catedral

Tenochtitlan

Palacio Nacional

Lomas Chapultepec

Tecamachalco

Paseo de la Reforma

Bosque de Chapultepec

Castillo de Chapultepec

Ciudadela

Tlaxcoaque

Chimalhuacán

San Pablo San Pedro

La Magdalena Chichicaspa

Presa Los Jazmines

Lomas Reforma

Xochitenco

Xochiaca

San Lorenzo Chimalco

B

San Bartolomé Coatepec

Av. Constituyentes

Tacubaya

Viaducto Presidente Miguel Alemán

Palacio de los Deportes

Ciudad Deportiva

Agrícola Oriental

Ignacio Juan Escutia

San Agustín Atlapulco

Santa Cruz Ayotusco

Dos Ríos

Unidad Santa Fe

Iztacalco

Tepalcates

Los Pirules

La Magdalena Atlipac

Huixquilucan Chimalpa

Olivar del Conde

Mixcoac

IZTACALCO IZTAPALAPA

Santa Martha Acatitla

Los Reyes

Tecamachalco

Cuajimalpa

Contadero

Molino de Rosas

Presa de Mixcoac

Presa Tarango

Héroes de Churubusco

Iztapalapa

Santa María Aztahuacán

Santiago Acahualtepec

General Ignacio Allende

Tlaltenango

Olivar de los Padres

Lomas de San Angel Inn

Villa Obregón

Av. Río Churubusco

Coyoacán

Prado Churubusco

Universidad Ibero-Americana

Los Reyes

Parque Nacional 2460

Cerro de la Estrella

Santa Cruz Meyehualco

San Lorenzo Acopilco

San Rosa Xochiac

Tizapán

Estadio Olímpico

Ciudad Universitaria

San Angel

Rosedal La Candelaria

San Francisco Culhuacán

180

Parque Nacional Desierto de los Leones

San Bartolo Ameyalco

San Jerónimo Lidice

Jardines del Pedregal de San Angel

El Reloj

San Lorenzo Tezonco

IZTAPALAPA

Tlalpizáhuac

La Marquesa

La Magdalena Contreras

Pirámide de Cuicuilco

Estadio Azteca

El Vergel

La Nopalera

Zapotitlán

Tlaltenco

Parque Nacional del Insurgente Miguel Hidalgo

Tlalpan

Las Fuentes Brotantes

Lago de Xochimilco

Jardines Flotantes

Gran Canal

Cerro Xico 2346

C

San Nicolás Totolapan

Santa Ursula Xitla

Tepepan

Xochimilco

San Luis Tlaxialtemalco

Tulyehualco

Xitle

San Pedro Martir

Xochitepec

San Lucas Xochimanca

San Gregorio Atlapulco

San Juan Ixtayopan

Cerro Xitle 3128

San Andrés Totoltepec

Santiago Tepalcatlalpan

Nativitas

Santa Cruz Alcapixca

XOCHIMILCO TLAHUAC

La Magdalena Petlalco

San Mateo Xalpa

Mixquic

Tetelco

San Miguel Xicalco

San Andrés Ahuayucan

San Antonio Tecómitl

Parque Nacional de Ajusco

San Miguel Ajusco

Santa Cecilia Tepetlapa

San Francisco Tecoxpa

San Jerónimo Miacatlán

San Juan y San Pedro Tezompa

Cerro Ajusco 3937

Topilejo

San Pedro Actopan

San Augustín Ohtenco

Milpa Alta

San Francisco Tlalnepantla

San Salvador Cuauhtenco

San Pablo Ostotepec

San Lorenzo Tlacoyucan

Santa Ana Tlacotenco

Aserradero

Cerro Pelado 3620

Cerro Cuautzin 3497

D

El Guarda Parres

Cerro Tláloc 3690

DISTRITO FEDERAL ESTADO DE MORELOS

Parque Nacional

Cerro Chichinautzin 3476

DISTRITO FEDERAL ESTADO DE MORELOS

de las Lagunas

de Zempoala

Tres Marias

Parque Nacional del Tepozteco

1 **2** **3** **4**

1: 200 000

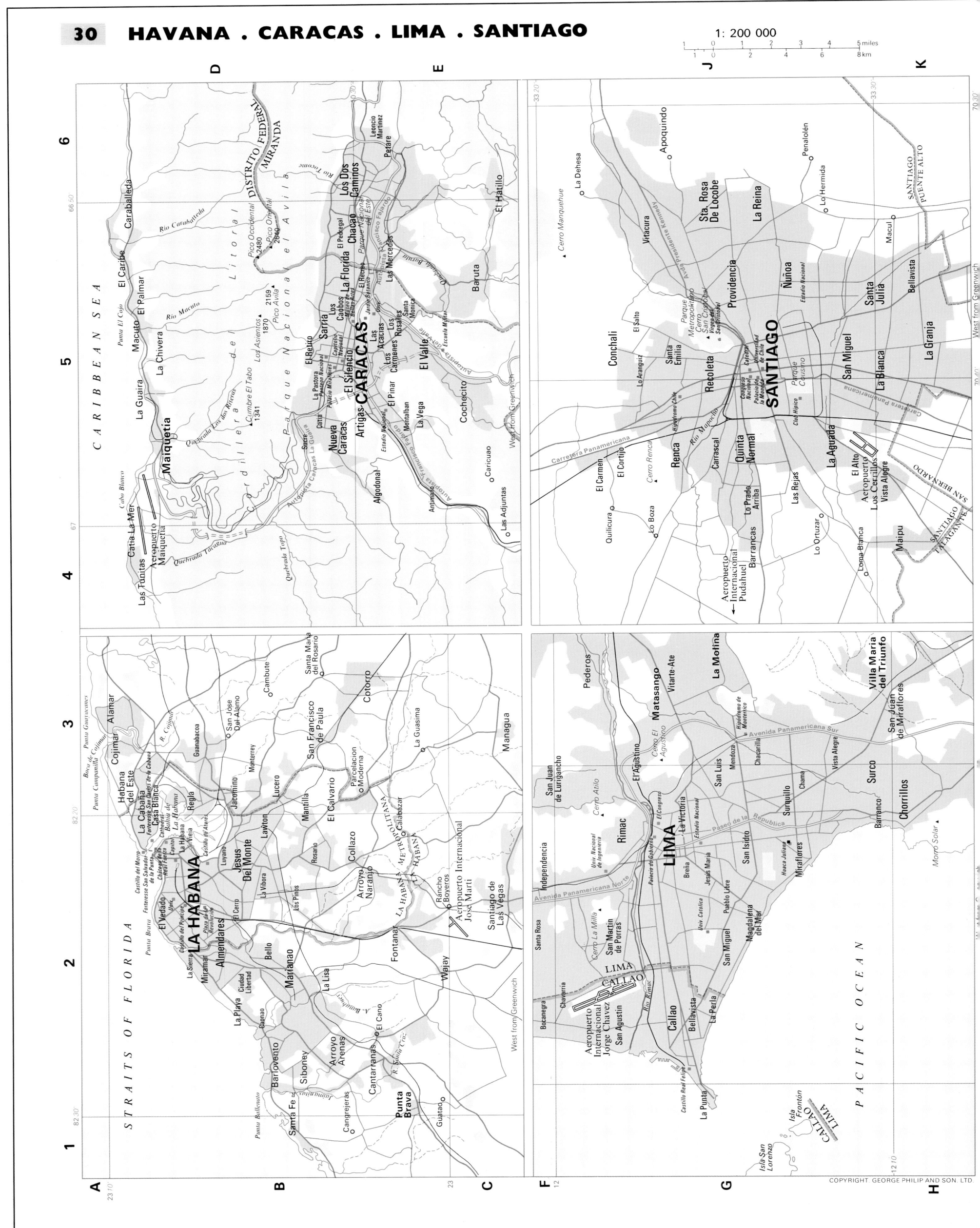

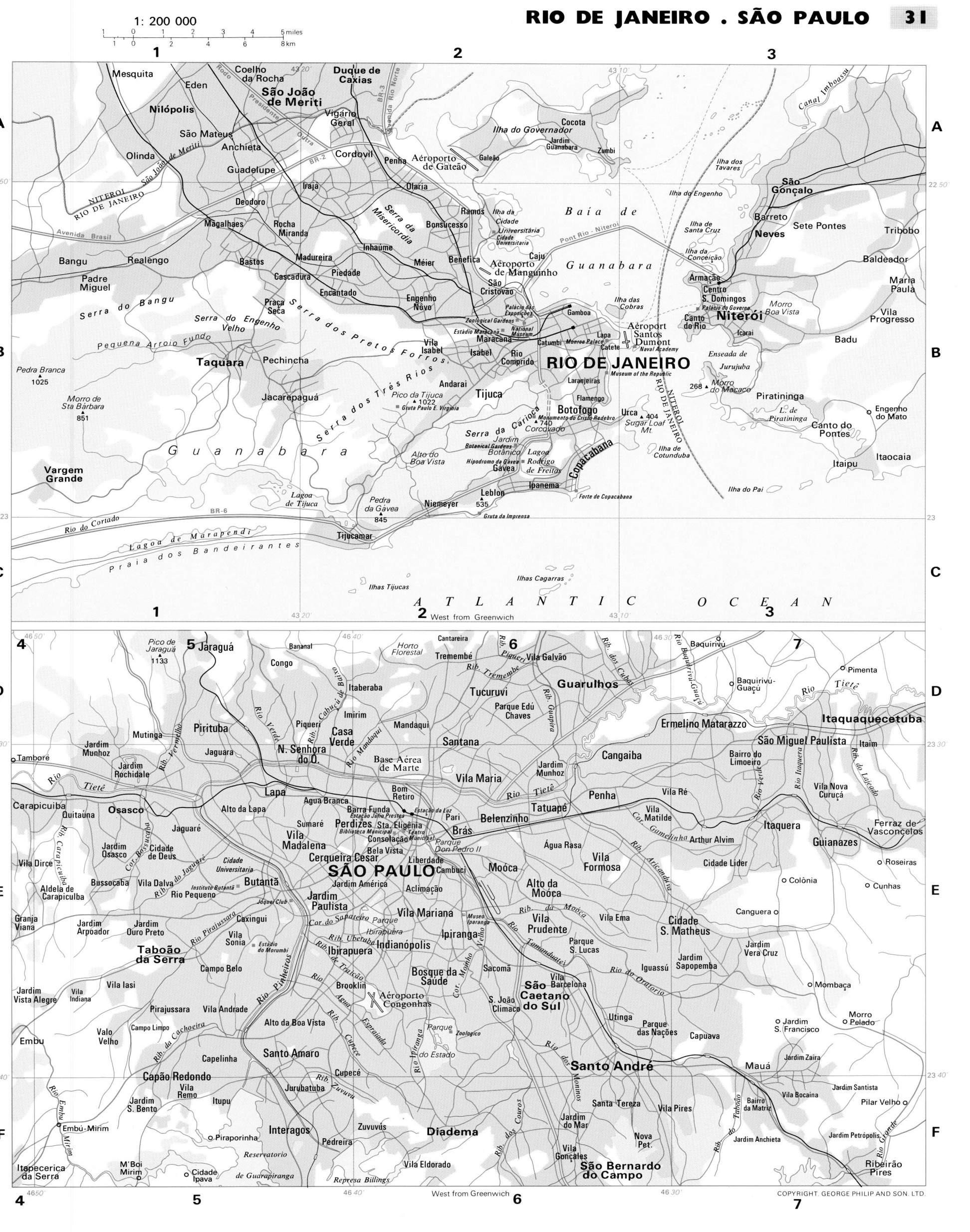

1: 200 000

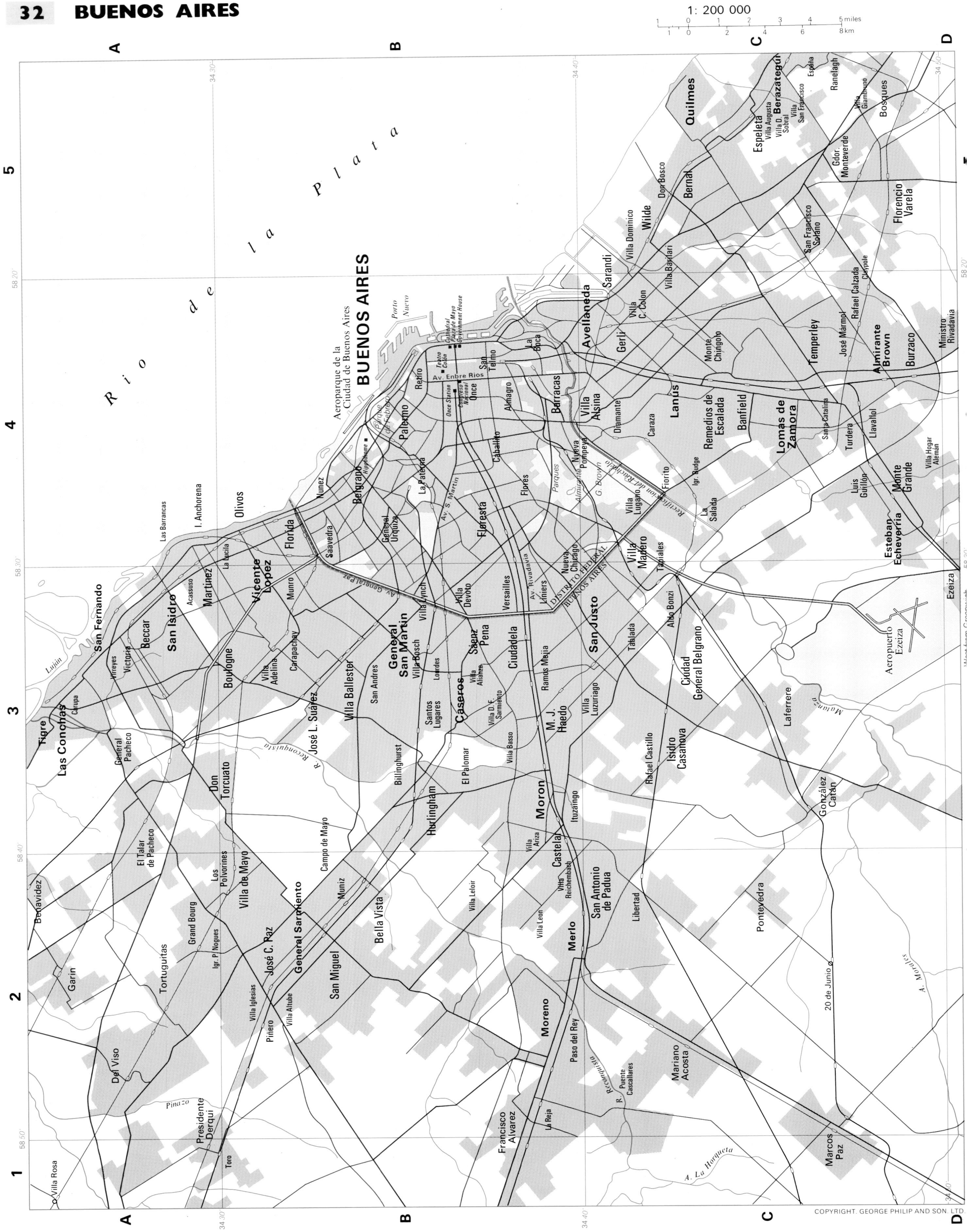

0 1 2 3 4 5 miles
0 1 2 4 6 8 km

BUENOS AIRES

Rio de la Plata

Aeroparque de la Ciudad de Buenos Aires

Quilmes
Espeleta
Berazátegui
Ranelagh
Espiña
Villa Augusta
Villa D. Sobral
San Francisco
Villa Giambruno
Bosques
Gdor. Monteverde
Florencio Varela
Dor Bosco
Bernal
Wilde
Villa Dominico
Sarandi
San Francisco Solano
Villa Baylari
Rafael Calzada
Claypole
Avellaneda
Gerli
Villa C. Colón
Temperley
José Mármol
Almirante Brown
Burzaco
La Boca
San Telmo
Barracas
Villa Alsina
Lanús
Monte Chingolo
Remedios de Escalada
Banfield
Lomas de Zamora
Luis Guillón
Monte Grande
Villa Hogar Alemán
Ministro Rivadavia
Retiro
Once
Almagro
Diamante
Caraza
Santa Catalina
Turdera
Llavallol
Palermo
Caballito
Nueva Pompeya
Villa Lugano
Fiorito
La Salada
Esteban Echeverría
La Paternal
Flores
Floresta
Parques
Villa Madero
Tapiales
Ezeiza
Belgrano
General Urquiza
Av. S. Martín
Nuñez
Olivos
Las Barrancas
I. Anchorena
Florida
Saavedra
Villa Lynch
Villa Devoto
Versalles
Liniers
Nueva Chicago
DISTRITO FEDERAL BUENOS AIRES
Aldo Bonzi
Ciudad General Belgrano
Aeropuerto Ezeiza
Vicente López
Martínez
Acassuso
La Lucila
Munro
Carapachay
Villa Adelina
San Andres
General San Martín
Villa Bosch
Lourdes
Sáenz Peña
Ciudadela
San Justo
Ramos Mejía
Tablada
Isidro Casanova
González Catán
San Fernando
Beccar
Victoria
San Isidro
Vireyes
Boulogne
Caseros
Villa Ballester
Santos Lugares
Villa Alsimre
Villa D.F. Sarmiento
Villa Basso
M. J. Haedo
Rafael Castillo
Laferrere
Tigre
Las Conchas
Catupa
General Pacheco
Don Torcuato
Campo de Mayo
Billinghurst
Hurlingham
El Palomar
Morón
Ituzaingó
Villa Ariza
Castelar
San Antonio de Padua
Pontevedra
Benávidez
El Talar de Pacheco
Los Polvorines
Villa de Mayo
Muniz
Bella Vista
Villa Leloir
Villa León
Villas Reichenbaht
Libertad
Del Viso
Grand Bourg
Igr. P. Nogues
José C. Paz
General Sarmiento
San Miguel
Moreno
Merlo
Paso del Rey
Mariano Acosta
Garín
Tortuguitas
Piñero
Villa Iglesias
Villa Altube
20 de Junio
Presidente Derqui
Pinazo
Francisco Alvarez
La Reja
Marcos Paz
Villa Rosa
Toro

INDEX TO CITY MAPS

Place names in this index are given a letter-figure reference to a map square made from the lines of latitude and longitude that appear on the city maps. The full geographic reference is provided in the border of each map.
The letter-figure reference will take the reader directly to the square, and by using the geographical coordinates the place sought can be pinpointed within that square.

The location given is the city or suburban center, and not necessarily the name. Lakes, airports and other features having a large area are given coordinates for their centers. Rivers that enter the sea, lake or main stream within the map area have the coordinates of that entrance.

If the river flows through the map, then the coordinates are given to the name. The same rule applies to canals. A river carries the symbol → after its name.

As an aid to identification, every place name is followed by the city map name or its abbreviation; for example, Oakland in California will be followed by S.F. Some of the place names so described will be completely independent of the main city.

An explanation of the alphabetical order rules is to be found at the beginning of the World Map Index.

ABBREVIATIONS USED IN THE INDEX

Ath. – Athinai (Athens)
B. – Baie, Bahía, Bay, Bucht
B.A. – Buenos Aires
Bagd. – Baghdad
Balt. – Baltimore
Bangk. – Bangkok
Barc. – Barcelona
Beij. – Beijing (Peking)
Berl. – Berlin
Bomb. – Bombay
Bost. – Boston
Bud. – Budapest
C. – Cabo, Cap, Cape
Calc. – Calcutta
Car. – Caracas
Chan. – Channel
Chic. – Chicago
Cr. – Creek
E. – East
El Qâ. – El Qâhira (Cairo)
G. – Golfe, Golfo, Gulf, Guba
Gzh. – Guangzhou (Canton)
H.K. – Hong Kong
Hbg. – Hamburg
Hd. – Head
Hels. – Helsinki
Hts. – Heights
I.(s) – Île, Ilha, Insel, Isla, Island, Isle
Ist. – Istanbul
J. – Jabal, Jebel
Jak. – Jakarta
Jobg. – Johannesburg
K. – Kap, Kapp
Kar. – Karachi
Kep. – Kepulauan
Købn. – København (Copenhagen)
L. – Lac, Lacul, Lago, Lagoa, Lake
L.A. – Los Angeles
La Hab. – La Habana (Havana)
Lisb. – Lisboa (Lisbon)
Lon. – London
Mdrd. – Madrid
Melb. – Melbourne
Méx. – México
Mil. – Milano
Mos. – Moskva (Moscow)
Mt. (e) – Mont, Monte, Monti, Montaña, Mountain
Mtrl. – Montréal
Mün. – München (Munich)
N. – Nord, Norte, North, Northern, Nouveau
Nápl. – Nápoli (Naples)
N.Y. – New York City
Os. – Ostrov
Oz. – Ozero
Pen. – Peninsula, Peninsule
Phil. – Philadelphia
Pk. – Park, Peak
Pra. – Praha (Prague)
Pt. – Point
Pta. – Ponta, Punta
Pte. – Pointe
R. – Rio, River
Ra. (s) – Range(s)
Res. – Reserve, Reservoir
Rio J. – Rio de Janeiro
S. – San, South
S.F. – San Francisco
S. Pau. – São Paulo
Sa. – Serra, Sierra
Sd. – Sound
Shang. – Shanghai
Sing. – Singapore
St. – Saint, Sankt, Sint
St-Pet. – St-Peterburg
Sta. – Santa, Station
Ste. – Sainte
Stgo. – Santiago
Sto. – Santo
Stock. – Stockholm
Str. – Strait, Stretto
Syd. – Sydney
Tehr. – Tehran
Tianj. – Tianjin (Tientsin)
Tori. – Torino (Turin)
Trto. – Toronto
W. – West
Wash. – Washington
Wsaw. – Warszawa (Warsaw)

A

Aalām, *Bagd.*	**17 F8**	33 19N	44 23 E
Abada, *Calc.*	**16 E5**	22 32N	88 13 E
Abbadia di Stura, *Tori.*	**9 B3**	45 7N	7 44 E
Abbey Wood, *Lon.*	**4 C5**	51 29N	0 7 E
Abbots Langley, *Lon.*	**4 A2**	51 42N	0 25W
Abeno, *Ōsaka*	**12 C4**	34 38N	135 31 E
Aberdeen, *H.K.*	**12 E6**	22 14N	114 8 E
Abfanggraben, *Mün.*	**7 F11**	48 10N	11 41 E
Abington, *Phil.*	**24 A4**	40 7N	75 7W
Ablon-sur-Seine, *Paris*	**5 C4**	48 43N	2 25 E
Abord à Plouffe, *Mtrl.*	**20 A3**	43 32N	73 43W
Abramtsevo, *Mos.*	**11 E10**	55 49N	37 49 E
Abridge, *Lon.*	**4 B5**	51 38N	0 7 E
Abû en Numrus, *El Qâ.*	**18 D5**	29 57N	31 12 E
Acassuso, *B.A.*	**32 A3**	34 29 S	58 30W
Accord, *Bost.*	**21 D4**	42 10N	70 52W
Accord Pond, *Bost.*	**21 D4**	42 10N	70 53W
Accotink Cr. →, *Wash.*	**25 D6**	38 51N	77 15W
Acerra, *Nápl.*	**9 H13**	40 56N	14 22 E
Acha San, *Sŏul*	**12 G8**	37 33N	127 5 E
Acheres, *Paris*	**5 B2**	48 57N	2 3 E
Acília, *Rome*	**9 G9**	41 47N	12 21 E
Aclimação, *S. Pau.*	**31 E6**	23 34 S	46 37W
Acostia →, *Wash.*	**25 D8**	38 51N	77 1W
Acton, *Lon.*	**4 B3**	51 30N	0 16W
Açúcar, Pão de, *Rio J.*	**31 B3**	22 56 S	43 9W
Ada Beja, *Lisb.*	**8 F7**	38 47N	9 13W
Adabe Cr. →, *S.F.*	**27 D4**	37 26N	122 6W
Adachi, *Tōkyō*	**13 B2**	35 49N	139 34 E
Adachi-Ku, *Tōkyō*	**13 B3**	35 47N	139 47 E
Adams Nat. Hist. Site, *Bost.*	**21 D4**	42 15N	71 0W
Addington, *Lon.*	**4 C4**	51 21N	0 1W
Addiscombe, *Lon.*	**4 C4**	51 22N	0 4W
Adel, *Bagd.*	**17 E7**	33 20N	44 17 E
Adelphi, *Wash.*	**25 C8**	39 0N	76 58W
Aderklaa, *Wien*	**10 G11**	48 17N	16 32 E
Admiralteyskaya Storona, *St-Pet.*	**11 B4**	59 56N	30 20 E
Áffori, *Mil.*	**9 D6**	45 31N	9 10 E
Aflandshage, *Købn.*	**2 E10**	55 33N	12 35 E
Afragola, *Nápl.*	**9 H12**	40 55N	14 18 E
Aganpur, *Delhi*	**16 B3**	28 33N	77 20 E
Agboju, *Lagos*	**18 B1**	6 27N	7 16 E
Agboyi Cr. →, *Lagos*	**18 A2**	6 33N	7 24 E
Ågerup, *Købn.*	**2 D8**	55 43N	12 19 E
Ågesta, *Stock.*	**3 E11**	59 12N	18 6 E
Agincourt, *Trto.*	**20 D9**	43 47N	79 16W
Agnano Terme, *Nápl.*	**9 J12**	40 49N	14 10 E
Agora, *Ath.*	**8 J11**	37 57N	23 43 E
Agra Canal, *Delhi*	**16 B2**	28 33N	77 17 E
Agricola Oriental, *Méx.*	**29 B3**	19 23N	99 4W
Agro Romano, *Rome*	**9 F8**	41 56N	12 17 E
Agua Branca, *S. Pau.*	**31 E5**	23 31 S	46 40W
Agua Espraiada →, *S. Pau.*	**31 E6**	23 36 S	46 41W
Água Rasa, *S. Pau.*	**31 E6**	23 32 S	46 33W
Agualva-Cacem, *Lisb.*	**8 F7**	38 46N	9 15W
Agustino, Cerro El, *Lima*	**30 G8**	12 3 S	76 59W
Ahrensfelde, *Berl.*	**7 A4**	52 34N	13 34 E
Ahuntsic, *Mtrl.*	**20 A3**	43 32N	73 41W
Ai →, *Ōsaka*	**12 B4**	34 46N	135 35 E
Aigremont, *Paris*	**5 B2**	48 54N	2 1 E
Airport West, *Melb.*	**19 E6**	37 42 S	144 52 E
Aiyaleo, *Ath.*	**8 J11**	37 59N	23 40 E
Ajegunle, *Lagos*	**18 B2**	6 26N	7 20 E
Aji, *Ōsaka*	**12 B3**	34 40N	135 27 E
Ajuda, *Lisb.*	**8 F7**	38 42N	9 12W
Ajusco, Parque Nacional de, *Méx.*	**29 C2**	19 12N	99 15W
Akabane, *Tōkyō*	**13 B3**	35 46N	139 42 E
Akalla, *Stock.*	**3 D10**	59 24N	17 55 E
Akasaka, *Tōkyō*	**13 B3**	35 40N	139 43 E
Akbarābād, *Tehr.*	**17 C5**	35 40N	51 20 E
Åkersberga Saltsjobad, *Stock.*	**3 D12**	59 26N	18 15 E
Akerselva →, *Oslo*	**2 B4**	59 54N	10 45 E
Akrópolis, *Ath.*	**8 J11**	37 57N	23 43 E
Akuwa, *Tōkyō*	**13 D2**	35 26N	139 30 E
Al 'Azamiyah, *Bagd.*	**17 E8**	33 22N	44 22 E
Alaguntan, *Lagos*	**18 B2**	6 25N	7 29 E
Alamar, *La Hab.*	**30 B3**	23 9N	82 16W
Alameda, *S.F.*	**27 B3**	37 46N	122 15W
Alameda Memorial State Beach Park, *S.F.*	**27 B3**	37 45N	122 16W
Alamo, *S.F.*	**27 A4**	37 51N	122 2W
Albany, *S.F.*	**27 A3**	37 53N	122 17W
Alberante, *Jobg.*	**18 F9**	26 16 S	28 7 E
Albern, *Wien*	**10 H10**	48 9N	16 29 E
Albert Hall, *Lon.*	**4 C3**	51 29N	0 10W
Albert Park, *Melb.*	**19 F6**	37 51 S	144 58 E
Albertfalva, *Bud.*	**10 K13**	47 26N	19 3 E
Alberton, *Jobg.*	**18 F9**	26 15 S	28 7 E
Albertslund, *Købn.*	**2 E9**	55 39N	12 21 E
Albertson, *N.Y.*	**23 C7**	40 46N	73 38W
Albertville, *Jobg.*	**18 E8**	26 9 S	27 58 E
Albion, *Phil.*	**24 C5**	39 46N	74 57W
Alby, *Stock.*	**3 E10**	59 14N	17 51 E
Albysjön, *Stock.*	**3 E10**	59 14N	17 52 E
Alcantara, *Lisb.*	**8 F7**	38 43N	9 10W
Alcatraz I., *S.F.*	**27 B2**	37 49N	122 25W
Alcochete, *Lisb.*	**8 F9**	38 45N	8 58W
Alcorcón, *Mdrd.*	**8 B2**	40 20N	3 48W
Aldan, *Phil.*	**24 B3**	39 55N	75 17W
Aldela de Carapiculba, *S. Pau.*	**31 E5**	23 34 S	46 49W
Aldene, *N.Y.*	**22 D3**	40 39N	74 17W
Aldenrade, *Ruhr*	**6 A2**	51 31N	6 44 E
Alder Planetarium, *Chic.*	**26 B3**	41 5N	87 36W
Aldershof, *Berl.*	**7 B4**	52 26N	13 33 E
Aldo Bonzi, *B.A.*	**32 C3**	34 42 S	58 31W
Aleksandrovskoye, *St-Pet.*	**11 B4**	59 51N	30 20 E
Aleksandrów, *Wsaw.*	**10 E8**	52 10N	21 14 E
Alexander Nevsky Abbey, *St-Pet.*	**11 B4**	59 54N	30 23 E
Alexandra, *Jobg.*	**18 E9**	26 6 S	28 5 E
Alexandra, *Sing.*	**15 G7**	1 17N	103 49 E
Alexandria, *Wash.*	**25 E7**	38 49N	77 5W
Alfortville, *Paris*	**5 C4**	48 48N	2 24 E
Algés, *Lisb.*	**8 F7**	38 42N	9 13W
Älgo, *Stock.*	**3 E13**	59 16N	18 20 E
Algodonal, *Car.*	**30 E5**	10 29N	66 58W
Alhambra, *L.A.*	**28 B4**	34 5N	118 7W
Alhos Vedros, *Lisb.*	**8 G8**	38 39N	9 1W
Alibey →, *Ist.*	**17 A2**	41 3N	28 56 E
Alibeyköy, *Ist.*	**17 A2**	41 4N	28 56 E
Alima, *Manila*	**15 E3**	14 27N	120 55 E
Alimos, *Ath.*	**8 J11**	37 52N	23 43 E
Aliperti, *Nápl.*	**9 H13**	40 53N	14 28 E
Alipore, *Calc.*	**16 E6**	22 31N	88 20 E
Alipur, *Calc.*	**16 D5**	22 43N	88 12 E
Aliso Canyon Wash →, *L.A.*	**28 A1**	34 15N	118 31W
Allach, *Mün.*	**7 F9**	48 11N	11 27 E
Allambie Heights, *Syd.*	**19 A4**	33 46 S	151 15 E
Allendale, *N.Y.*	**22 A4**	41 1N	74 9W
Allengrove, *Jobg.*	**18 E10**	26 5 S	28 14 E
Allentown, *N.Y.*	**23 C6**	40 47N	73 43W
Allermohe, *Hbg.*	**7 E8**	53 29N	10 7 E
Allerton, Pt., *Bost.*	**21 D4**	42 18N	70 52W
Allston, *Bost.*	**21 C3**	42 21N	71 7W
Alluets, Forêt des, *Paris*	**5 B1**	48 56N	1 55 E
Almada, *Lisb.*	**8 F8**	38 41N	9 8W
Almagro, *B.A.*	**32 B4**	34 38 S	58 24W
Almanara, *Mdrd.*	**8 B2**	40 28N	3 41W
Almaza Airport, *El Qâ.*	**18 C6**	30 5N	31 21 E
Almazovo, *Mos.*	**11 D12**	55 50N	38 3 E
Almendares, *La Hab.*	**30 B2**	23 6N	82 23W
Almendares →, *La Hab.*	**30 B2**	23 7N	82 24W
Almirante Brown, *B.A.*	**32 C4**	34 48 S	58 23W
Almirante G. Brown, Parques, *B.A.*	**32 C4**	34 40 S	58 28W
Almonesson, *Phil.*	**24 C4**	39 48N	75 5W
Almonte, *S.F.*	**27 A1**	37 53N	122 31W
Alnabru, *Oslo*	**2 B5**	59 55N	10 50 E
Alnsjøen, *Oslo*	**2 B5**	59 57N	10 51 E
Alperton, *Lon.*	**4 B3**	51 32N	0 17W
Alpignano, *Tori.*	**9 B1**	45 6N	7 31 E
Alpine, *N.Y.*	**22 B5**	40 57N	73 57W
Alpur, *Calc.*	**16 C6**	22 50N	88 23 E
Alrode, *Jobg.*	**18 F9**	26 17 S	28 7 E
Alsergrund, *Wien*	**10 G10**	48 13N	16 21 E
Alsfeld, *Ruhr*	**6 A3**	51 31N	6 50 E
Alsip, *Chic.*	**26 C2**	41 40N	87 44W
Alstaden, *Ruhr*	**6 B2**	51 28N	6 49 E
Ålsten, *Stock.*	**3 E10**	59 19N	17 57 E
Alster →, *Hbg.*	**7 D8**	53 38N	10 4 E
Alsterdorf, *Hbg.*	**7 D8**	53 36N	10 0 E
Älta, *Stock.*	**3 E12**	59 15N	18 11 E
Altadena, *L.A.*	**28 A4**	34 11N	118 8W
Alte-Donau →, *Wien*	**10 G10**	48 14N	16 25 E
Alte Süderelbe, *Hbg.*	**7 D7**	53 31N	9 52 E
Alten-Essen, *Ruhr*	**6 B4**	51 29N	7 1 E
Altendorf, *Ruhr*	**6 B3**	51 27N	6 58 E
Altenhagen, *Ruhr*	**6 B6**	51 22N	7 27 E
Altenvoerde, *Ruhr*	**6 C6**	51 18N	7 22 E
Altenwerder, *Hbg.*	**7 D7**	53 30N	9 55 E
Alter Finkenkrug, *Berl.*	**7 A1**	52 35N	13 3 E
Altglenicke, *Berl.*	**7 B4**	52 25N	13 32 E
Altlandsberg Nord, *Berl.*	**7 A5**	52 34N	13 43 E
Altmannsdorf, *Wien*	**10 H9**	48 9N	16 18 E
Alto, *S.F.*	**27 A1**	37 54N	122 30W
Alto da Boa Vista, *S. Pau.*	**31 E5**	23 38 S	46 42W
Alto da Lapa, *S. Pau.*	**31 E5**	23 31 S	46 43W
Alto da Moóca, *S. Pau.*	**31 E6**	23 34 S	46 33W
Alto do Pina, *Lisb.*	**8 F8**	38 44N	9 7W
Altona, *Hbg.*	**7 D7**	53 32N	9 56 E
Altona, *Melb.*	**19 F5**	37 51 S	144 49 E
Altona B., *Melb.*	**19 F6**	37 52 S	144 51 E
Altona North, *Melb.*	**19 F5**	37 50 S	144 49 E
Altona Sports Park, *Melb.*	**19 F6**	37 51 S	144 51 E
Altstadt, *Hbg.*	**7 D8**	53 32N	10 0 E
Alvarado, *S.F.*	**27 C4**	37 35N	122 4W
Alvik, *Stock.*	**3 E10**	59 19N	17 58 E
Älvsjo, *Stock.*	**3 E11**	59 16N	18 0 E
Älvvik, *Stock.*	**3 D12**	59 21N	18 15 E
Am Hasenbergl, *Mün.*	**7 F10**	48 12N	11 33 E
Am Steinhof, *Wien*	**10 G9**	48 12N	16 17 E
Am Wald, *Mün.*	**7 G10**	48 3N	11 36 E
Ama Keng, *Sing.*	**15 F7**	1 23N	103 41 E
Amadora, *Lisb.*	**8 F7**	38 45N	9 13W
Amagasaki, *Ōsaka*	**12 B3**	34 42N	135 23 E
Amager, *Købn.*	**2 E10**	55 36N	12 35 E
Amāl Qādisiya, *Bagd.*	**17 F8**	33 16N	44 20 E
Amalienborg Slott, *Købn.*	**2 D10**	55 41N	12 35 E
Amata, *Mil.*	**9 D5**	45 34N	9 8 E
Ambler, *Phil.*	**24 A3**	40 9N	75 13W
Ambrose Channel, *N.Y.*	**22 D5**	40 31N	73 50W
Ameixoeira, *Lisb.*	**8 F8**	38 46N	9 8W
Ames Hill, *Bost.*	**21 B2**	42 38N	71 13W
Amin, *Bagd.*	**17 F8**	33 19N	44 29 E
Aminyevo, *Mos.*	**11 E8**	55 41N	37 25 E
Amirābād, *Tehr.*	**17 C5**	35 43N	51 24 E
Amityville, *N.Y.*	**23 C8**	40 40N	73 23W
Ammersbek →, *Hbg.*	**7 C8**	53 42N	10 7 E
Amora, *Lisb.*	**8 G8**	38 37N	9 6W
Amoreira, *Lisb.*	**8 F7**	38 48N	9 11W
Amorosa, *Jobg.*	**18 E8**	26 5 S	27 52 E
Ampelokipi, *Ath.*	**8 J11**	37 58N	23 47 E
Amper →, *Mün.*	**7 F9**	48 14N	11 25 E
Amselhain, *Berl.*	**7 A5**	52 38N	13 43 E
Amuwo, *Lagos*	**18 B1**	6 28N	7 18 E
Anacostia, *Wash.*	**25 D8**	38 51N	76 59W
Anacostia River Park, *Wash.*	**25 D8**	38 54N	76 57W
Anadoluhisari, *Ist.*	**17 A3**	41 4N	29 3 E
Anandanagar, *Calc.*	**16 C5**	22 51N	88 16 E
Anchieta, *Rio J.*	**31 A1**	22 48 S	43 21W
Ancol, *Jak.*	**15 H9**	6 7 S	106 49 E
Andalus, *Bagd.*	**17 F7**	33 19N	44 18 E
Andalusia, *Phil.*	**24 A5**	40 4N	74 58W
Andarai, *Rio J.*	**31 B2**	22 56 S	43 14W
Andeli Beijie, *Beij.*	**14 B3**	39 57N	116 21 E
Anderson Cr. →, *Melb.*	**19 E8**	37 44 S	145 12 E
Andilly, *Paris*	**5 A3**	49 0N	2 17 E
Andingmen, *Beij.*	**14 B3**	39 55N	116 23 E
Andover, *Bost.*	**21 B3**	42 39N	71 7W
Andrésy, *Paris*	**5 B2**	48 58N	2 3 E
Andrews Air Force Base, *Wash.*	**25 E8**	38 48N	76 52W
Ang Mo Kio, *Sing.*	**15 F8**	1 22N	103 50 E
Ängby, *Stock.*	**3 D10**	59 20N	17 53 E
Angel I., *S.F.*	**27 A2**	37 52N	122 25W
Angel Island State Park, *S.F.*	**27 A2**	37 52N	122 25W
Angerbruch →, *Ruhr*	**6 C3**	51 18N	6 59 E
Angerhausen, *Ruhr*	**6 B2**	51 22N	6 43 E
Angermund, *Ruhr*	**6 C2**	51 19N	6 46 E
Angke, Kali →, *Jak.*	**15 H9**	6 6 S	106 46 E
Angono, *Manila*	**15 D4**	14 31N	121 8 E
Angyalföld, *Bud.*	**10 J13**	47 32N	19 5 E
Angyō, *Tōkyō*	**13 A3**	35 50N	139 45 E
Aniene →, *Rome*	**9 F10**	41 56N	12 35 E
Anik, *Bomb.*	**16 G8**	19 1N	72 53 E
Anin, *Wsaw.*	**10 E7**	52 13N	21 9 E
Anjou, *Mtrl.*	**20 A4**	43 36N	73 33W
Annadale, *N.Y.*	**22 D3**	40 32N	74 10W
Annalee Heights, *Wash.*	**25 D6**	38 51N	77 10W
Annandale, *Wash.*	**25 D6**	38 50N	77 11W
Annen, *Ruhr*	**6 B6**	51 27N	7 22 E
Annet-sur-Marne, *Paris*	**5 B6**	48 55N	2 43 E
Anthony Chabot Regional Park, *S.F.*	**27 B4**	37 46N	122 7W
Antignano, *Nápl.*	**9 H12**	40 51N	14 13 E
Antimano, *Car.*	**30 E5**	10 27N	66 59W
Antipolo, *Manila*	**15 D5**	14 35N	121 10 E
Antony, *Paris*	**5 C3**	48 44N	2 17 E
Antwerp, *Jobg.*	**18 E9**	26 5 S	28 9 E
Aoyama, *Tōkyō*	**13 C3**	35 39N	139 42 E
Ap Lei Chau, *H.K.*	**12 E5**	22 14N	114 9 E
Apapa, *Lagos*	**18 B2**	6 26N	7 21 E
Apelacão, *Lisb.*	**8 F8**	38 48N	9 7W
Apoquindo, *Stgo*	**30 J11**	33 23 S	70 30W
Apshawa, *N.Y.*	**22 A2**	41 1N	74 22W
Apterkarskiy Os., *St-Pet.*	**11 B4**	59 57N	30 20 E
Aquincum, *Bud.*	**10 J13**	47 33N	19 3 E
Ara →, *Tōkyō*	**13 B4**	35 41N	139 50 E
Arakawa-Ku, *Tōkyō*	**13 B3**	35 44N	139 48 E
Arakpur, *Delhi*	**16 B2**	28 35N	77 11 E
Arany-hegyi-patak →, *Bud.*	**10 J13**	47 34N	19 4 E
Aravaca, *Mdrd.*	**8 B2**	40 27N	3 47W
Arbataash, *Bagd.*	**17 E7**	33 20N	44 19 E
Arbutus, *Balt.*	**25 B2**	39 15N	76 41W
Arc de Triomphe, *Paris*	**5 B3**	48 52N	2 17 E
Arcadia, *L.A.*	**28 B4**	34 7N	118 1W
Arceuil, *Paris*	**5 C3**	48 48N	2 19 E
Arden, *Phil.*	**24 C2**	39 48N	75 29W
Ardey Gebirge, *Ruhr*	**6 B6**	51 24N	7 23 E
Ardmore, *Phil.*	**24 A3**	40 0N	75 17W
Ardsley, *N.Y.*	**23 A5**	41 0N	73 50W
Arese, *Mil.*	**9 D5**	45 32N	9 4 E
Arganzuela, *Mdrd.*	**8 B2**	40 23N	3 42W
Argenteuil, *Paris*	**5 B3**	48 56N	2 15 E
Argonne Forest, *Chic.*	**26 C1**	41 42N	87 53W
Ariadana, *Calc.*	**16 E6**	22 39N	88 22 E
Aricanduva →, *S. Pau.*	**31 E6**	23 31 S	46 33W
Arida, *Lagos*	**18 A1**	6 33N	7 16 E
Arima, *Ōsaka*	**12 B2**	34 47N	135 15 E
Arima, *Tōkyō*	**13 C2**	35 33N	139 33 E
Arima →, *Ōsaka*	**12 A2**	34 50N	135 14 E
Arkhangelyskoye, *Mos.*	**11 E7**	55 47N	37 17 E
Arkley, *Lon.*	**4 B3**	51 38N	0 13W
Arlington, *Bost.*	**21 C2**	42 24N	71 10W
Arlington, *Wash.*	**25 D7**	38 53N	77 7W
Arlington Heights, *Bost.*	**21 C2**	42 25N	71 10W
Arlington Heights, *Chic.*	**26 A1**	42 5N	87 55W
Arlington Nat. Cemetery, *Wash.*	**25 D7**	38 52N	77 4W
Armação, *Rio J.*	**31 B3**	22 52 S	43 6W
Armadale, *Melb.*	**19 F7**	37 51 S	145 0 E
Armadale, *Trto.*	**20 C9**	43 50N	79 14W
Armainvilliers, Forêt d', *Paris*	**5 C6**	48 46N	2 42 E
Armour Heights, *Trto.*	**20 D8**	43 45N	79 25W
Arncliffe, *Syd.*	**19 B3**	33 56 S	151 8 E
Arnold Arboretum, *Bost.*	**21 D3**	42 18N	71 8W
Arnouville-les-Gonesse, *Paris*	**5 B4**	48 59N	2 24 E
Arrentela, *Lisb.*	**8 G8**	38 37N	9 6W
Arrone →, *Rome*	**9 F8**	41 55N	12 16 E
Arroyo Arenas, *La Hab.*	**30 B2**	23 3N	82 27W
Arroyo Cr. →, *S.F.*	**26 D2**	37 27N	122 25W
Arroyo Naranjo, *La Hab.*	**30 B2**	23 2N	82 21W
Årsta, *Stock.*	**3 E11**	59 17N	18 3 E
Artesia, *L.A.*	**28 C4**	33 51N	118 4W
Arthur Alvim, *S. Pau.*	**31 E7**	23 32 S	46 28W
Arthur Kill →, *N.Y.*	**22 D3**	40 32N	74 15W
Artigas, *Car.*	**30 E5**	10 29N	66 56W
Arundel Gardens, *Balt.*	**25 B3**	39 12N	76 37W
Arundel Village, *Balt.*	**25 B3**	39 13N	76 35W
Aryiróupolis, *Ath.*	**8 J11**	37 52N	23 44 E
Arzano, *Nápl.*	**9 H12**	40 54N	14 16 E
Asagaya, *Tōkyō*	**13 B2**	35 41N	139 38 E
Asahi, *Ōsaka*	**12 B4**	34 43N	135 31 E
Asaka, *Tōkyō*	**13 B2**	35 47N	139 35 E
Asakusa, *Tōkyō*	**13 B3**	35 42N	139 47 E
Asalatpur, *Delhi*	**16 B1**	28 37N	77 4 E
Asati, *Calc.*	**16 F5**	22 28N	88 15 E
Aschheim, *Mün.*	**7 F11**	48 10N	11 42 E
Ascot Vale, *Melb.*	**19 E6**	37 46 S	144 53 E
Aserradero, *Méx.*	**29 D2**	19 10N	99 16W
Asharoken, *N.Y.*	**23 B8**	40 55N	73 21W
Ashburn, *Chic.*	**26 C2**	41 45N	87 43W
Ashburton, *Melb.*	**19 F7**	37 51 S	145 4 E

34 Ashburton, L.

Ashburton, L., Balt. 25 B2 39 19N 76 40W
Ashchherino, Mos. 11 F10 55 36N 37 46 E
Ashfield, Syd. 19 B3 33 53 S 151 7 E
Ashford, Lon. 4 C2 51 25N 0 26W
Ashiya, Ōsaka 12 B2 34 43N 135 18 E
Ashiya →, Ōsaka 12 B2 34 42N 135 18 E
Ashland, S.F. 27 B4 37 41N 122 7W
Ashstead, Lon. 4 D3 51 18N 0 17W
Ashwood, Melb. 19 F7 37 52 S 145 5 E
Asker, Oslo 2 B2 59 50N 10 25 E
Askisto, Hels. 3 B3 60 16N 24 47 E
Askrikefjärden, Stock. 3 D12 59 22N 18 13 E
Asnieres, Paris 5 B3 48 54N 2 16 E
Ason, Lagos 18 A3 6 34N 7 31 E
Aspern, Wien 10 G10 48 13N 16 29 E
Aspern, Flugplatz, Wien 10 G11 48 13N 16 30 E
Assiano, Mil. 9 E5 45 27N 9 3 E
Aston Mills, Phil. 24 B2 39 52N 75 26W
Astoria, N.Y. 22 C5 40 46N 73 55W
Atares, Castillo de, La Hab. 30 B2 23 7N 82 21W
Atco, Phil. 24 C5 39 46N 74 53W
Atghara, Calc. 16 E6 22 37N 88 26 E
Athens = Athínai, Ath. 8 J11 37 58N 23 43 E
Athínai, Ath. 8 J11 37 58N 23 43 E
Athinai-Ellinikón Airport, Ath. 8 J2 37 51N 23 44 E
Athis-Mons, Paris 5 C4 48 42N 2 23 E
Atīfīya, Bagd. 17 E8 33 21N 44 21 E
Atikali, Ist. 17 A2 41 1N 28 56 E
Atilo, Cerro, Lima 30 G8 12 2 S 77 2W
Atişalen, Ist. 17 A2 41 3N 28 52 E
Atlandsberg, Berl. 7 A5 52 33N 13 43 E
Atlantic Beach, N.Y. 23 D6 40 35N 73 44W
Atta, Delhi 16 B2 28 34N 77 19 E
Attiki, Ath. 8 H11 38 0N 23 43 E
Atzalpur, Delhi 16 A3 28 43N 77 20 E
Atzgersdorf, Wien 10 H9 48 8N 16 18 E
Aubervilliers, Paris 5 B4 48 54N 2 22 E
Aubing, Mün. 7 G9 48 9N 11 25 E
Auburn, Syd. 19 B3 33 51 S 151 1 E
Auburndale, Bost. 21 C2 42 20N 71 14W
Auckland Park, Jobg. 18 F9 26 11 S 28 0 E
Audubon, Phil. 24 A2 40 7N 75 25W
Auf-dem-Schnee, Ruhr 6 B6 51 26N 7 25 E
Auffargis, Paris 5 C1 48 42N 1 53 E
Augustówka, Wsaw. 10 E7 52 11N 21 5 E
Aulnay-sous-Bois, Paris 5 B4 48 56N 2 29 E
Aurelio, Rome 9 F9 51 54N 12 26 E
Ausîm, El Qâ. 18 C4 30 7N 31 8 E
Aussen Alster, Hbg. 7 D8 53 33N 10 0 E
Austerlitz, Gare d', Paris 5 B4 48 50N 2 22 E
Austin, Chic. 26 B2 41 53N 87 45W
Auteuil, Mtrl. 20 A3 43 37N 73 44W
Avedøre, Købn. 2 E9 55 37N 12 27 E
Aveley, Lon. 4 C6 51 29N 0 15 E
Avellaneda, B.A. 32 C4 34 40 S 58 22W
Avenel, N.Y. 22 D3 40 34N 74 16W
Avenel, Wash. 25 D8 38 59N 76 59W
Avila, Parque National el, Car. 30 D5 10 31N 66 52W
Avila, Pico, Car. 30 D5 10 32N 66 52W
Avini, Nápl. 9 J13 40 48N 14 28 E
Avondale, Chic. 26 B2 41 56N 87 41W
Avondale Heights, Melb. 19 E6 37 45 S 144 52 E
Avtovo, St-Pet. 11 B3 59 51N 30 16 E
Ayase, Tōkyō 13 D1 35 25N 139 26 E
Ayase →, Tōkyō 13 A3 35 52N 139 45 E
Ayazaga, Ist. 17 A2 41 6N 28 59 E
Ayer Chawan, P., Sing. 15 G7 1 16N 103 41 E
Ayer Merbau, P., Sing. 15 G7 1 16N 103 42 E
Ayía Paraskeví, Ath. 8 H11 38 1N 23 49 E
Áyios Dhimitrios, Ath. 8 J11 37 53N 23 44 E
Áyios Ioánnis Rendis, Ath. 8 J10 37 57N 23 39 E
Azabu, Tōkyō 13 C3 35 39N 139 43 E
Azadpur, Delhi 16 A2 28 42N 77 10 E
Azcapotzalco, Méx. 29 B2 19 28N 99 10W
Azteca, Estadia, Méx. 29 C3 19 8N 99 9W
Azusa, L.A. 28 B5 34 7N 117 54W

B

Ba He →, Beij. 14 B3 39 57N 116 27 E
Baba I., Kar. 17 H10 24 49N 66 57 E
Babarpur, Delhi 16 A2 28 41N 77 16 E
Babelsberg, Berl. 7 B1 52 22N 13 7 E
Babushkin, Mos. 11 D10 55 51N 37 42 E
Babylon, N.Y. 23 C9 40 42N 73 19W
Back →, Balt. 25 B4 39 17N 76 27W
Back B., Bomb. 16 H7 18 56N 72 48 E
Bacoor, Manila 15 E3 14 27N 120 56 E
Bacoor B., Manila 15 E3 14 27N 120 54 E
Badagri Cr. →, Lagos 18 B1 6 24N 7 17 E
Badahela, Delhi 16 B1 28 38N 77 4 E
Badalona, Barc. 8 D6 41 26N 2 14 E
Badersfeld, Mün. 7 F10 48 15N 11 31 E
Badgers Mt., Lon. 4 C5 51 20N 0 8 E
Badi, Delhi 16 A1 28 44N 77 8 E
Badinan, Calc. 16 C5 22 53N 88 14 E
Badu, Rio J. 31 B3 22 54 S 43 3W
Baerl, Ruhr 6 B2 51 29N 6 40 E
Bærum, Oslo 2 B3 59 54N 10 36 E
Bærums Verk, Oslo 2 B2 59 56N 10 28 E
Baggensfjärden, Stock. 3 E12 59 18N 18 19 E
Bággio, Mil. 9 E5 45 27N 9 6 E
Bāgh-e-Feiz, Tehr. 17 C4 35 44N 51 19 E
Baghdād, Bagd. 17 E8 33 20N 44 23 E
Bagmari, Calc. 16 E6 22 34N 88 23 E
Bagneux, Paris 5 C3 48 47N 2 18 E
Bagnolet, Paris 5 B4 48 52N 2 25 E
Bagnoli, Nápl. 9 J11 40 48N 14 9 E
Bagraula, Delhi 16 B1 28 34N 77 4 E
Bagsværd, Købn. 2 D9 55 45N 12 27 E
Bagsværd Sø, Købn. 2 D9 55 46N 12 28 E
Baguiati, Calc. 16 E6 22 36N 88 25 E
Bagumbayan, Manila 15 E4 14 28N 121 3 E
Baha'i Temple, Chic. 26 A2 42 4N 87 41W
Bahrenfeld, Hbg. 7 D7 53 34N 9 55 E
Bahtîm, El Qâ. 18 C5 30 8N 31 16 E
Bahu Bheri, Calc. 16 C5 22 50N 88 14 E
Baidyabati, Calc. 16 D5 22 46N 88 19 E
Baie-d'Urfé, Mtrl. 20 B2 43 25N 73 53W
Baierbrunn, Mün. 7 G10 48 1N 11 29 E
Baijala, Calc. 16 C5 22 51N 88 16 E
Baileys Crossroads, Wash. 25 D7 38 50N 77 6W
Bailly, Paris 5 B2 48 50N 2 4 E
Bainchipota, Calc. 16 C5 22 51N 88 16 E
Bair I., S.F. 27 C3 37 30N 122 13W
Bairro da Matriz, S. Pau. 31 F7 23 40 S 46 27W
Bairro do Limoeiro, S. Pau. 31 E7 23 30 S 46 27W
Baisha, Gzh. 14 G8 23 8N 113 11 E
Baisley Pond, N.Y. 23 C6 40 40N 73 47W
Baixa da Banheira, Lisb. 8 G8 38 39N 9 2W
Baiyun Shan, Gzh. 14 G8 23 8N 113 15 E
Baj Baj, Calc. 16 F5 22 28N 88 11 E
Bakirkoy, Ist. 17 B2 40 58N 28 52 E
Bakovka, Mos. 11 E8 55 40N 37 19 E
Bala-Cynwyd, Phil. 24 A3 40 0N 75 15W
Balagarh, Calc. 16 D6 22 44N 88 27 E
Balara, Manila 15 D4 14 39N 121 3 E
Balarambati, Calc. 16 D5 22 48N 88 12 E
Balashikha, Mos. 11 E11 55 48N 37 58 E
Bald Hill, Bost. 21 B3 42 38N 71 0W
Baldeador, Rio J. 31 B3 22 51 S 43 1W
Baldeneysee, Ruhr 6 B4 51 24N 7 1 E
Baldissero Torinese, Tori. 9 B3 45 4N 7 48 E
Baldpate Hill, Bost. 21 A3 42 42N 71 0W
Baldpate Pond, Bost. 21 A3 42 41N 71 0W
Baldwin, N.Y. 23 D7 40 38N 73 37W
Baldwin Hills, L.A. 28 B2 34 0N 118 21W
Baldwin Hills Res., L.A. 28 B2 34 0N 118 21W
Baldwin Park, L.A. 28 B5 34 5N 117 57W
Bal'etan →, Gzh. 14 G8 23 5N 113 14 E
Balgowlah, Syd. 19 A4 33 47 S 151 16 E
Balgowlah Heights, Syd. 19 A4 33 48 S 151 16 E
Balham, Lon. 4 C4 51 26N 0 8W
Balihati, Calc. 16 D5 22 44N 88 18 E
Balingsnäs, Stock. 3 E11 59 13N 18 0 E
Balingsta, Stock. 3 E11 59 12N 18 3 E
Balintawak, Manila 15 D3 14 39N 120 59 E
Balitai, Tianj. 14 E6 39 5N 117 11 E
Balizhuang, Beij. 14 B3 39 53N 116 28 E
Ballabhpur, Calc. 16 D6 22 44N 88 20 E
Ballainvilliers, Paris 5 C3 48 40N 2 17 E
Ballardvale, Bost. 21 B3 42 37N 71 9W
Ballenato, Pta., La Hab. 30 B2 23 55N 82 28W
Ballerup, Købn. 2 D9 55 43N 12 21 E
Bally, Calc. 16 E6 22 38N 88 20 E
Ballygunge, Calc. 16 E6 22 31N 88 21 E
Balmain, Syd. 19 B4 33 51 S 151 11 E
Balmumcu, Ist. 17 A3 41 3N 29 2 E
Balongbato, Manila 15 D3 14 39N 120 59 E
Baltikri, Calc. 16 E5 22 36N 88 18 E
Baltimore, Balt. 25 B3 39 17N 76 37W
Baltimore Highlands, Balt. 25 B3 39 14N 76 38W
Baltimore-Washington Int. Airport, Balt. 25 B3 39 11N 76 39W
Baluhati, Calc. 16 E5 22 39N 88 15 E
Balwyn, Melb. 19 E7 37 48 S 145 4 E
Balwyn North, Melb. 19 E7 37 47 S 145 4 E
Bambang, Manila 15 D4 14 31N 121 4 E
Bamondongri, Bomb. 16 H9 18 58N 73 1 E
Ban Baan Phichit, Bangk. 15 B2 13 49N 100 37 E
Ban Hugli, Calc. 16 E6 22 38N 88 22 E
Ban Lat Phrao, Bangk. 15 B2 13 47N 100 35 E
Banabuey →, La Hab. 30 B2 23 5N 82 27W
Bananal, S. Pau. 31 D5 23 27 S 46 41W
Banática, Lisb. 8 F7 38 40N 9 11W
Bandeirantes, Praia dos, Rio J. 31 C1 23 0 S 43 23W
Bandipur, Calc. 16 D6 22 43N 88 26 E
Bandipur, Calc. 16 C4 22 50N 88 9 E
Bandra, Bomb. 16 G7 19 3N 72 49 E
Bandra Pt., Bomb. 16 G7 19 2N 72 49 E
Banfield, B.A. 32 C4 34 44 S 58 24W
Bang Kapi, Bangk. 15 B2 13 45N 100 38 E
Bang Khen, Bangk. 15 A2 13 52N 100 35 E
Bang Na, Bangk. 15 B2 13 40N 100 36 E
Bang Su, Khlong →, Bangk. 15 B2 13 47N 100 31 E
Bangbae, Sŏul 12 H7 37 29N 126 59 E
Banghag, Sŏul 12 G8 37 38N 127 1 E
Bangka, Jak. 15 J9 6 15 S 106 48 E
Bangkok, Bangk. 15 B2 13 44N 100 30 E
Bangkok Noi, Khlong →, Bangk. 15 B1 13 45N 100 29 E
Bangkok Yai, Bangk. 15 B1 13 43N 100 29 E
Bangkok Yai, Khlong →, Bangk. 15 B1 13 44N 100 29 E
Banglo, Calc. 16 E5 22 31N 88 14 E
Bangrak, Bangk. 15 B2 13 43N 100 31 E
Bangu, Rio J. 31 B1 22 52 S 43 26W
Bangu, Sa. do, Rio J. 31 B1 22 53 S 43 24W
Bankipur, Calc. 16 D5 22 47N 88 13 E
Bankra, Calc. 16 E5 22 36N 88 17 E
Banks, C., Syd. 19 C4 34 0 S 151 16 E
Bankstown, Syd. 19 B3 33 55 S 151 2 E
Bankstown Aerodrome, Syd. 19 B2 33 55 S 150 59 E
Banna →, Tori. 9 A3 45 12N 7 42 E
Banstala, Calc. 16 E6 22 31N 88 24 E
Banstead, Lon. 4 D3 51 18N 0 12W
Bantra, Calc. 16 E5 22 35N 88 18 E
Banyule Flats Res., Melb. 19 E7 37 44 S 145 5 E
Baquirivú, S. Pau. 31 D7 23 26 S 46 28W
Baquirivú-Guaçu, S. Pau. 31 D7 23 28 S 46 28W
Bara, Calc. 16 D5 22 45N 88 16 E
Baragwanath Airfield, Jobg. 18 F8 26 14 S 27 58 E
Barai, Calc. 16 C6 22 52N 88 22 E
Barajas, Mdrd. 8 B3 40 28N 3 34W
Barajas, Aeropuerto Transoceanico de, Mdrd. 8 B3 40 28N 3 33W
Barakpur, Calc. 16 D6 22 47N 88 21 E
Baranagar, Calc. 16 E6 22 38N 88 22 E
Barbaiana, Mil. 9 D5 45 32N 9 1 E
Barca, Tori. 9 B3 45 6N 7 43 E
Barcarena, Lisb. 8 F7 38 43N 9 16W
Barcarena →, Lisb. 8 F7 38 41N 9 16W
Barcelona, Barc. 8 D6 41 22N 2 10 E
Barcelona-Prat, Aeropuerta de, Barc. 8 E5 41 17N 2 5 E
Barceloneta, Barc. 8 D6 41 22N 2 11 E
Barcroft, L., Wash. 25 D6 38 50N 77 9W
Baréggio, Mil. 9 E5 45 28N 9 0 E
Bariti Bil, Calc. 16 D6 22 48N 88 25 E
Barkarby, Stock. 3 D10 59 24N 17 52 E
Barker Pt., N.Y. 23 B6 40 50N 73 44W
Barking, Lon. 4 B5 51 32N 0 5 E
Barkingside, Lon. 4 B5 51 35N 0 4 E
Barlovento, La Hab. 30 B2 23 5N 82 28W
Barmbek, Hbg. 7 D8 53 34N 10 1 E
Barmen, Ruhr 6 C5 51 16N 7 12 E
Barneau, Paris 5 D6 48 38N 2 43 E
Barnes, Lon. 4 C3 51 28N 0 14W
Barnet, Lon. 4 B3 51 39N 0 11W
Barnsboro, Phil. 24 C4 39 45N 75 9W
Baronia Park, Syd. 19 A3 33 49 S 151 8 E
Barop, Ruhr 6 B6 51 29N 7 25 E
Barra, Nápl. 9 H12 40 50N 14 19 E
Barra Andai, Kar. 17 H11 24 47N 66 59 E
Barra Funda, S. Pau. 31 E6 23 31 S 46 39W
Barracas, B.A. 32 B4 34 39 S 58 24W
Barrackpore Airport, Calc. 16 D6 22 46N 88 21 E
Barrancas, Stgo 30 J10 33 26 S 70 44W
Barranco, Lima 30 G8 12 9 S 77 2W
Barreiro, Lisb. 8 G8 38 39N 9 5W
Barreto, Rio J. 31 B3 22 50 S 43 5W
Barrientos, Méx. 29 A2 19 34N 99 11W
Barrington, Phil. 24 B4 39 52N 75 3W
Barrio de La Estación, Mdrd. 8 B3 40 26N 3 32W
Bartala, Calc. 16 E5 22 32N 88 15 E
Barton Park, Syd. 19 B3 33 56 S 151 9 E
Bartyki, Wsaw. 10 F7 52 10N 21 6 E
Baru, Kali →, Jak. 15 J10 6 12 S 106 51 E
Baruipara, Calc. 16 D5 22 45N 88 13 E
Baruta, Car. 30 E5 10 26N 66 52W
Barvikha, Mos. 11 E7 55 44N 37 16 E
Basai Darapur, Delhi 16 B1 28 38N 77 6 E
Bass Hill, Syd. 19 B3 33 54 S 151 0 E
Bassett, L.A. 28 B5 34 3N 117 59W
Bastille, Place de la, Paris 5 B4 48 51N 2 22 E
Bastos, Rio J. 31 B1 22 52 S 43 21W
Basudebpur, Calc. 16 D6 22 49N 88 24 E
Basus, El Qâ. 18 C5 30 7N 31 12 E
Batanagar, Calc. 16 E5 22 31N 88 15 E
Batenbrock, Ruhr 6 A3 51 31N 6 57 E
Bath Beach, N.Y. 22 D4 40 36N 74 0W
Bath I., Kar. 17 H11 24 49N 67 1 E
Batok, Bukit, Sing. 15 F7 1 21N 103 46 E
Battersea, Lon. 4 C4 51 28N 0 9W
Baturino, Mos. 11 F9 55 35N 37 30 E
Bauman, Mos. 11 E10 55 45N 37 40 E
Baumgarten, Wien 10 G9 48 12N 16 17 E
Bauria, Calc. 16 E5 22 30N 88 10 E
Baxter Estates, N.Y. 23 B6 40 50N 73 42W
Bay Farm I., S.F. 27 B3 37 44N 122 14W
Bay Meadows Race Track, S.F. 27 C3 37 32N 122 17W
Bay Park, N.Y. 23 D7 40 37N 73 39W
Bay Ridge, N.Y. 22 D4 40 37N 74 1W
Bay Ridge Channel, N.Y. 22 D4 40 39N 74 1W
Bay Shore Park, Balt. 25 B4 39 13N 76 25W
Baykoz, Ist. 17 A3 41 7N 29 7 E
Bayonne, N.Y. 22 C4 40 40N 74 6W
Bayshore, S.F. 27 B3 37 42N 122 24W
Bayside, N.Y. 23 C6 40 45N 73 46W
Bayswater, Lon. 4 B3 51 30N 0 10W
Bayswater, Melb. 19 F8 37 50 S 145 17 E
Bayview, S.F. 27 B2 37 44N 122 23W
Bayville, N.Y. 23 B7 40 54N 73 33W
Bāzār, Tehr. 17 C5 35 40N 51 25 E
Beachmont, Bost. 21 C4 42 23N 70 59W
Beacon Hill, H.K. 12 D6 22 21N 114 10 E
Beaconsfield, Mtrl. 20 B2 43 25N 73 53W
Beacontree Heath, Lon. 4 B5 51 33N 0 9 E
Beam →, Lon. 4 B6 51 30N 0 10 E
Bear Cr. →, Balt. 25 B3 39 13N 76 30W
Bear Gulch Res., S.F. 27 D3 37 26N 122 13W
Beato, Lisb. 8 F8 38 44N 9 5W
Beauchamp, Paris 5 A3 49 0N 2 11 E
Beaumonte Heights, Trto. 20 D7 43 45N 79 34W
Beaverdam Cr. →, Wash. 25 C8 39 0N 76 5W
Bebek, Ist. 17 A3 41 4N 29 2 E
Beccar, B.A. 32 A3 34 27 S 58 32W
Běchovice, Pra. 10 B3 50 4N 14 36 E
Beck L., Chic. 26 A1 42 4N 87 52W
Beckenham, Lon. 4 C4 51 24N 0 1W
Beckhausen, Ruhr 6 A4 51 33N 7 1 E
Beckton, Lon. 4 B5 51 30N 0 4 E
Beddington, Lon. 4 C4 51 21N 0 8W
Beddington Corner, Lon. 4 C4 51 23N 0 9W
Bedford, Bost. 21 C2 42 27N 71 15W
Bedford Park, Chic. 26 C2 41 46N 87 46W
Bedford Park, N.Y. 23 B5 40 52N 73 52W
Bedford Stuyvesant, N.Y. 22 C5 40 41N 73 56W
Bedford View, Jobg. 18 F9 26 10 S 28 7 E
Bedok, Sing. 15 G8 1 19N 103 56 E
Beeck, Ruhr 6 B2 51 28N 6 44 E
Beeckerwerth, Ruhr 6 B2 51 28N 6 42 E
Behala, Calc. 16 E5 22 30N 88 18 E
Bei Hai, Beij. 14 B3 39 54N 116 21 E
Beicai, Shang. 14 J12 31 11N 121 32 E
Beicang, Tianj. 14 D5 39 13N 117 7 E
Beigai, Tianj. 14 E6 39 9N 117 10 E
Beijiaoshichang, Beij. 14 B2 39 57N 116 19 E
Beijing, Beij. 14 B2 39 53N 116 21 E
Beinasco, Tori. 9 B2 45 1N 7 34 E
Beirolas, Lisb. 8 F8 38 46N 9 5W
Beitsun, Gzh. 14 G8 23 7N 113 10 E
Békásmegyer, Bud. 10 J13 47 35N 19 3 E
Bekkelaget, Oslo 2 B4 59 53N 10 47 E
Bel Air, L.A. 28 B2 34 4N 118 27W
Bela Vista, S. Pau. 31 E6 23 33 S 46 38W
Bélanger, Mtrl. 20 A3 43 35N 73 42W
Belas, Lisb. 8 F7 38 46N 9 17W
Belém, Lisb. 8 F7 38 41N 9 12W
Belém, Torre de, Lisb. 8 F7 38 41N 9 12W
Belenzinho, S. Pau. 31 E6 23 32 S 46 34W
Belfield, Syd. 19 B3 33 53 S 151 6 E
Belgachi, Calc. 16 E5 22 36N 88 18 E
Belgharia, Calc. 16 E6 22 39N 88 22 E
Belgrano, B.A. 32 B4 34 33 S 58 27W
Belgrave, Melb. 19 F9 37 54 S 145 21 E
Bell Gardens, L.A. 28 C4 33 58N 118 9W
Bella Vista, B.A. 32 B2 34 34 S 58 41W
Bellaire, N.Y. 23 C6 40 42N 73 44W
Bellavista, Lima 30 G8 12 4 S 77 8W
Bellavista, Stgo 30 K11 33 31 S 70 35W
Belle Harbour, N.Y. 23 D5 40 34N 73 51W
Belle Haven, N.Y. 23 A7 41 0N 73 37W
Belle Haven, Wash. 25 E7 38 46N 77 3W
Bellefonte, Phil. 24 C1 39 45N 75 30W
Bellerose, N.Y. 23 C6 40 44N 73 42W
Belleview, Wash. 25 D6 38 57N 77 14W
Belleville, N.Y. 22 C4 40 48N 74 8W
Bellflower, L.A. 28 C4 33 53N 118 7W
Bellingham, Lon. 4 C4 51 25N 0 1W
Bellmawr, Phil. 24 B4 39 52N 75 5W
Bellmore, N.Y. 23 D7 40 39N 73 31W
Bello, La Hab. 30 B2 23 5N 82 24W
Bells Lake, Phil. 24 C4 39 45N 75 3W
Bellwood, Chic. 26 B1 41 52N 87 53W
Belmont, Bost. 21 C2 42 23N 71 10W
Belmont, Lon. 4 B3 51 36N 0 18W
Belmont, S.F. 27 C3 37 31N 122 17W
Belmont Cragin, Chic. 26 B2 41 56N 87 45W
Belmont Harbor, Chic. 26 B3 41 56N 87 38W
Belmont Hills, Phil. 24 A3 40 1N 75 15W
Belmont Slough, S.F. 27 C3 37 32N 122 15W
Belmore, Syd. 19 B3 33 55 S 151 5 E
Belopurpada, Bomb. 16 G9 19 0N 73 1 E
Beltsville, Wash. 25 C8 39 2N 76 54W
Beltsville Airport, Wash. 25 C9 39 1N 76 49W
Belur, Calc. 16 E6 22 37N 88 21 E
Belvedere, Lon. 4 C5 51 29N 0 9 E
Belvedere, S.F. 27 A2 37 52N 122 27W
Belyayevo Bogorodskoye, Mos. 11 F9 55 39N 37 31 E
Bemböle, Hels. 3 B2 60 13N 24 39 E
Bemis Woods, Chic. 26 C1 41 49N 87 54W
Bemowo, Wsaw. 10 E6 52 15N 20 53 E
Benavidez, B.A. 32 A2 34 24 S 58 41W
Bendale, Trto. 20 D9 43 45N 79 13W
Bendungan Hilir, Jak. 15 J9 6 12 S 106 48 E
Benefica, Rio J. 31 B2 22 52 S 43 14W
Benfica, Lisb. 8 F7 38 45N 9 11W
Benin B., Lagos 18 B2 6 24N 7 28 E
Benjamin Franklin Br., Phil. 24 B4 39 57N 75 8W
Benoni, Jobg. 18 F10 26 11 S 28 18 E
Benoni South, Jobg. 18 F10 26 12 S 28 17 E
Bensenville, Chic. 26 B1 41 57N 87 56W
Bensonhurst, N.Y. 22 D5 40 35N 73 59W
Bentleigh, Melb. 19 F7 37 54 S 145 2 E
Bentleigh East, Melb. 19 F7 37 54 S 145 4 E
Beraberi, Calc. 16 D6 22 46N 88 27 E
Berario, Jobg. 18 E8 26 7 S 27 57 E
Berazategui, B.A. 32 C5 34 45 S 58 15W
Berea, Jobg. 18 F9 26 10 S 28 3 E
Berg am Laim, Mün. 7 G10 48 7N 11 38 E
Bergbaumuseum, Ruhr 6 B5 51 29N 7 13 E
Bergenfield, N.Y. 22 B5 40 55N 73 59W
Berger, Oslo 2 B6 59 56N 11 7 E
Bergerhausen, Ruhr 6 B4 51 26N 7 2 E
Bergerhof, Ruhr 6 C6 51 12N 7 21 E
Bergham, Mün. 7 G10 48 2N 11 37 E
Berghausen, Ruhr 6 A5 51 36N 7 12 E
Berghm-Oestrum, Ruhr 6 B1 51 25N 6 39 E
Bergstedt, Hbg. 7 C8 53 40N 10 7 E
Beri, Barc. 8 D5 41 20N 2 1 E
Berih, Sungei →, Sing. 15 F7 1 22N 103 40 E
Berkeley, Chic. 26 B1 41 53N 87 54W
Berkeley, S.F. 27 A3 37 51N 122 16W
Berkeley Heights, N.Y. 22 C2 40 40N 74 26W
Berkeley Hills, S.F. 27 A3 37 51N 122 11W
Berlin, Berl. 7 A3 52 31N 13 23 E
Berlin, Phil. 24 C5 39 47N 74 55W
Bermondsey, Lon. 4 C4 51 29N 0 3W
Bernabeu, Estadio, Mdrd. 8 B2 40 27N 3 41W
Bernal, B.A. 32 C5 34 43 S 58 17W
Bernal Heights, S.F. 27 B2 37 44N 122 24W
Berne, Hbg. 7 D8 53 38N 10 8 E
Berngardovka, St-Pet. 11 A5 60 0N 30 34 E
Berthpage, N.Y. 23 C8 40 45N 73 29W
Bertlich, Ruhr 6 A4 51 36N 7 4 E
Bertolla Barca, Tori. 9 B3 45 6N 7 44 E
Berwyn, Chic. 26 B2 41 50N 87 47W
Berwyn, Phil. 24 A2 40 2N 75 26W
Berwyn Heights, Wash. 25 D8 38 59N 76 55W
Besedy, Mos. 11 F10 55 38N 37 47 E
Besiktas, Ist. 17 A3 41 2N 29 0 E
Beskudnikovo, Mos. 11 D9 55 52N 37 34 E
Besós →, Barc. 8 D6 41 24N 2 13 E
Bessancourt, Paris 5 A3 49 2N 2 12 E
Bestazzo, Mil. 9 E5 45 25N 9 0 E
Bethayres, Phil. 24 A4 40 7N 75 3W
Bethesda, Wash. 25 D7 38 59N 77 6W
Bethlehem Steel Plant, Balt. 25 B4 39 13N 76 29W
Bethnal Green, Lon. 4 B4 51 31N 0 2W
Bethpage State Park, N.Y. 23 C8 40 45N 73 25W
Betor, Calc. 16 E5 22 34N 88 17 E
Beuvronne →, Paris 5 B6 48 59N 2 40 E
Beverley, Chic. 26 C3 41 42N 87 39W
Beverley Hills, Syd. 19 B3 33 56 S 151 5 E
Beverley Park, Syd. 19 B3 33 58 S 151 8 E
Beverly, Bost. 21 B4 42 34N 70 53W
Beverly, Phil. 24 A5 40 3N 74 55W
Beverly Glen, L.A. 28 B2 34 6N 118 26W
Beverly Harbor, Bost. 21 B4 42 32N 70 51W
Beverly Hills, L.A. 28 B2 34 5N 118 24W
Beverly Municipal Airport, Bost. 21 B4 42 36N 70 55W
Bexley, Lon. 4 C5 51 26N 0 8 E
Bexley, Syd. 19 B3 33 56 S 151 7 E
Bexleyheath, Lon. 4 C5 51 27N 0 8 E
Beyenburg, Ruhr 6 C5 51 15N 7 19 E
Beylerbeyi, Ist. 17 A3 41 2N 29 2 E
Beyoğlu, Ist. 17 A2 41 1N 28 58 E
Bezons, Paris 5 B3 48 56N 2 13 E
Bhadrakali, Calc. 16 D6 22 40N 88 20 E
Bhadreswar, Calc. 16 D5 22 49N 88 22 E
Bhadua, Calc. 16 D5 22 40N 88 12 E
Bhalswa, Delhi 16 A2 28 44N 77 10 E
Bhambo Khān Qarmati, Kar. 17 H11 24 49N 67 7 E
Bhandardaha, Calc. 16 E5 22 37N 88 12 E
Bhatpara, Calc. 16 C6 22 52N 88 25 E
Bhatpur, Calc. 16 D6 22 43N 88 25 E
Bhatsala, Calc. 16 E5 22 30N 88 16 E
Bhawanipore, Calc. 16 E6 22 32N 88 21 E
Bhopura, Delhi 16 A2 28 41N 77 19 E
Białołeka Dworska, Wsaw. 10 E7 52 19N 21 1 E
Bickley, Lon. 4 C5 51 23N 0 3 E
Bicutan, Manila 15 D4 14 30N 121 3 E
Bidyadharpur, Calc. 16 C6 22 50N 88 24 E
Bielany, Wsaw. 10 E6 52 17N 20 57 E
Biesdorf, Berl. 7 A4 52 30N 13 33 E
Bièvre →, Paris 5 C2 48 44N 2 9 E
Bièvres, Paris 5 C3 48 45N 2 13 E
Big Timber Cr. →, Phil. 24 B4 39 52N 75 7W
Big Tujunga Canyon →, L.A. 28 A3 34 16N 118 12W
Biggin Hill, Lon. 4 D5 51 18N 0 1 E
Bijoki, Tōkyō 13 B2 35 49N 139 38 E
Bilibiran, Manila 15 E5 14 29N 121 10 E
Bilk, Ruhr 6 C2 51 12N 6 46 E
Billbrook, Hbg. 7 D8 53 31N 10 4 E
Bille →, Hbg. 7 D8 53 32N 10 4 E
Billerica, Bost. 21 B2 42 33N 71 16W
Billinghurst, B.A. 32 B3 34 34 S 58 37W
Billings, Represa, S. Pau. 31 F6 23 42 S 46 39W
Billstedt, Hbg. 7 D8 53 32N 10 6 E
Billwerder, Hbg. 7 D8 53 30N 10 7 E
Billwerder B., Hbg. 7 D8 53 31N 10 3 E
Binacayan, Manila 15 E3 14 27N 120 55 E
Binangonan, Manila 15 E5 14 28N 121 10 E
Binaria, Jak. 15 H10 6 7 S 106 51 E
Bingzhoubao, Gzh. 14 G8 23 2N 113 11 E
Binningsvatna, Oslo 2 C6 50 46N 11 3 E
Binondo, Manila 15 D3 14 36N 120 58 E
Binzago, Mil. 9 D5 45 37N 9 8 E
Birak el Kiyam, El Qâ. 18 C4 30 2N 31 9 E
Birch Cliff, Trto. 20 D9 43 41N 79 16W
Bird →, Balt. 25 A4 39 22N 76 22W
Birka, Stock. 3 D8 59 20N 17 33 E
Birkenhöhe, Berl. 7 A4 52 38N 13 36 E
Birkenstein, Berl. 7 A5 52 31N 13 40 E
Birkholz, Berl. 7 A4 52 37N 13 34 E
Birkholzaue, Berl. 7 A4 52 38N 13 36 E
Biryulyovo, Mos. 11 F10 55 35N 37 40 E
Bisamberg, Wien 10 G10 48 19N 16 21 E
Bispebjerg, Købn. 2 D10 55 42N 12 31 E
Bitsa, Mos. 11 F9 55 35N 37 36 E
Biwon Secret Garden, Sŏul 12 G7 37 34N 126 59 E
Bizard, Î., Mtrl. 20 B2 43 29N 73 53W
Björknas, Stock. 3 E12 59 19N 18 12 E
Björköfjärden, Hels. 3 C2 60 7N 24 38 E
Black Cr. →, Trto. 20 D8 43 40N 79 30W
Blackburn, Melb. 19 E7 37 48 S 145 9 E
Blackburn L., Melb. 19 E7 37 49 S 145 9 E
Blackburn South, Melb. 19 F7 37 50 S 145 9 E
Blackfen, Lon. 4 C5 51 26N 0 6 E
Blackheath, Jobg. 18 E8 26 8 S 27 57 E
Blackheath, Lon. 4 C5 51 28N 0 0 E
Blackmore, Lon. 4 A6 51 41N 0 19 E
Blacktown, Syd. 19 A2 33 46 S 150 56 E
Blackwall, Lon. 4 B4 51 30N 0 0 E
Blackwood, Phil. 24 C4 39 47N 75 4W
Bladensburg, Wash. 25 D8 38 55N 76 55W
Blairgowrie, Jobg. 18 E9 26 6 S 28 0 E
Blakehurst, Syd. 19 B3 33 59 S 151 6 E
Blakstad, Oslo 2 C2 50 49N 10 28 E
Blanco, C., Car. 30 D5 10 36N 66 59W
Blankenburg, Berl. 7 A3 52 35N 13 27 E
Blankenese, Hbg. 7 D6 53 33N 9 48 E
Blankenfelde, Berl. 7 A3 52 37N 13 23 E
Blankenstein, Ruhr 6 B5 51 24N 7 11 E
Blenheim, Phil. 24 C4 39 48N 75 4W
Bliersheim, Ruhr 6 B2 51 23N 6 42 E
Blind Cr. →, Melb. 19 F8 37 53 S 145 12 E
Blizne, Wsaw. 10 E6 52 14N 20 52 E
Bloomfield, N.Y. 22 C3 40 48N 74 12W
Bloomingdale, N.Y. 22 A3 41 0N 74 19W
Bloomsbury, Balt. 25 B2 39 15N 76 44W
Błota, Wsaw. 10 F8 52 9N 21 11 E
Bloubosspruit →, Jobg. 18 F9 26 16 S 28 0 E
Blue Hills Reservation, Bost. 21 D3 42 13N 71 5W
Blue Island, Chic. 26 C2 41 40N 87 40W
Bluff Hd., H.K. 12 E6 22 11N 114 12 E
Blumberg, Berl. 7 A4 52 36N 13 39 E
Blunt Pt., S.F. 27 A2 37 51N 122 25W
Blutenberg, Mün. 7 G9 48 9N 11 27 E
Blylaget, Oslo 2 C4 59 46N 10 41 E
Boa Vista, Alto do, Rio J. 31 B2 22 58 S 43 16W
Boa Vista, Morro, Rio J. 31 B3 22 53 S 43 5W
Boadilla del Monte, Mdrd. 8 B1 40 24N 3 52W
Boardwalk, N.Y. 23 D6 40 34N 73 49W
Boavista, Lisb. 8 F8 38 48N 9 8W
Bobäck, Hels. 3 B2 60 10N 24 31 E
Boberg, Hbg. 7 D8 53 30N 10 9 E
Bobigny, Paris 5 B4 48 54N 2 26 E
Bobylyskaya, St-Pet. 11 B3 59 59N 30 10 E
Bocanegra, Lima 30 F8 11 59 S 77 7W
Boccea, Rome 9 F8 41 57N 12 19 E
Bochold, Ruhr 6 B3 51 28N 6 57 E
Bochum, Ruhr 6 B5 51 28N 7 13 E
Bockum, Ruhr 6 B1 51 21N 6 37 E
Bodelschwingh, Ruhr 6 A6 51 33N 7 22 E
Bodomjärvi, Hels. 3 B3 60 15N 24 40 E
Bogenhausen, Mün. 7 G10 48 8N 11 36 E
Bognæs, Købn. 2 D7 55 41N 12 1 E
Bogorodskoye, Mos. 11 E10 55 48N 37 42 E
Bogota, N.Y. 22 B4 40 52N 74 2W
Bogstadvatnet, Oslo 2 B3 59 58N 10 37 E
Bohaidalu, Tianj. 14 E6 39 7N 117 12 E
Bohnsdorf, Berl. 7 B4 52 23N 13 34 E
Bois-Colombes, Paris 5 B3 48 55N 2 16 E
Bois-d'Arcy, Paris 5 C2 48 48N 2 1 E
Boisement, Paris 5 A2 49 1N 2 0 E
Boissy-St.-Léger, Paris 5 C5 48 44N 2 31 E
Boksburg, Jobg. 18 F10 26 12 S 28 15 E
Boksburg North, Jobg. 18 F10 26 12 S 28 15 E
Boksburg South, Jobg. 18 F10 26 13 S 28 16 E
Boldinasco, Mil. 9 E5 45 29N 9 8 E
Bøler, Oslo 2 B5 59 53N 10 50 E
Bollate, Mil. 9 D5 45 32N 9 7 E
Bollensdorf, Berl. 7 A5 52 30N 13 42 E
Bollmora, Stock. 3 E12 59 14N 18 14 E
Bolshaya Nevka, St-Pet. 11 B3 59 58N 30 18 E
Bolshaya-Okhta, St-Pet. 11 B4 59 56N 30 26 E
Bolshoi Theatre, Mos. 11 E9 55 45N 37 37 E
Bom Retiro, S. Pau. 31 E6 23 31 S 46 38W
Bombay, Bomb. 16 H8 18 56N 72 50 E
Bombay Harbour, Bomb. 16 H8 18 58N 72 55 E
Bombay Univ., Bomb. 16 H7 18 55N 72 49 E
Bommern, Ruhr 6 B6 51 25N 7 20 E
Bonaero Park, Jobg. 18 E10 26 7 S 28 15 E
Bondi, Syd. 19 B4 33 53 S 151 16 E
Bondoufle, Paris 5 D4 48 36N 2 22 E
Bondy, Paris 5 B4 48 54N 2 28 E
Bondy, Forêt de, Paris 5 B5 48 54N 2 33 E
Bonifacio Monument, Manila 15 D3 14 38N 120 58 E
Bonifica di Maccarese, Rome 9 F8 41 50N 12 15 E
Bonifica di Porto, Rome 9 G8 41 48N 12 16 E
Bonita, Pt., S.F. 27 B1 37 48N 122 31W
Bonnelles, Paris 5 D2 48 37N 2 1 E
Bonneuil-sur-Marne, Paris 5 C5 48 46N 2 30 E
Bönningstedt, Hbg. 7 C7 53 40N 9 54 E
Bonnyrigg, Syd. 19 B2 33 53 S 150 54 E
Bonsari, Bomb. 16 G9 19 4N 73 1 E
Bonsucesso, Rio J. 31 B2 22 51 S 43 15W
Boo, Stock. 3 D12 59 20N 18 16 E
Boonton, N.Y. 22 B2 40 54N 74 24W
Boonton Res., N.Y. 22 B2 40 53N 74 24W
Booth Corner, Phil. 24 B2 39 50N 75 29W
Boothwyn, Phil. 24 C2 39 49N 75 26W
Borbeck, Ruhr 6 B3 51 28N 6 56 E
Bordeaux, Jobg. 18 E9 26 5 S 28 1 E
Bordeaux, Mtrl. 20 A3 43 31N 73 43W
Borehamwood, Lon. 4 B3 51 39N 0 15W
Borgaretto, Tori. 9 B2 45 0N 7 35 E
Bórgaro Torinese, Tori. 9 B2 45 9N 7 39 E
Borghese, Villa, Rome 9 F9 41 54N 12 29 E
Borisovo, Mos. 11 F10 55 38N 37 44 E
Borle, Bomb. 16 G8 19 2N 72 54 E
Bornig, Ruhr 6 A5 51 33N 7 16 E
Bornsjön, Stock. 3 E9 59 14N 17 44 E
Boronia, Melb. 19 F8 37 51 S 145 17 E
Borough Green, Lon. 4 D6 51 17N 0 18 E
Borough Park, N.Y. 22 D5 40 38N 73 59W
Børtervatna, Oslo 2 C6 50 46N 11 3 E
Boscoreale, Nápl. 9 J13 40 46N 14 28 E
Boscotrecase, Nápl. 9 J13 40 46N 14 27 E
Bösinghovn, Ruhr 6 C1 51 18N 6 38 E
Bosmont, Jobg. 18 F8 26 10 S 27 57 E
Bosön, Stock. 3 D12 59 22N 18 11 E
Bosporus = Istanbul Boğazi, Ist. 17 A3 41 5N 29 3 E
Bosque da Saúde, S. Pau. 31 E6 23 36 S 46 37W
Bosques, B.A. 32 C5 34 48 S 58 15W
Bossley Park, Syd. 19 B2 33 51 S 150 53 E
Bossucaba →, S. Pau. 31 E5 23 31 S 46 46W
Bostanci, Ist. 17 B3 40 57N 29 5 E
Bostelbek, Hbg. 7 E7 53 28N 9 55 E
Boston, Bost. 21 C3 42 21N 71 3W
Boston B., Bost. 21 C4 42 22N 70 55W
Boston Harbor, Bost. 21 C4 42 20N 70 58W
Boston Hill, Bost. 21 B3 42 38N 71 5W
Botany, Syd. 19 B4 33 56 S 151 12 E
Botany B., Lon. 4 A4 51 40N 0 7W
Botany B., Syd. 19 B4 33 58 S 151 11 E
Botič →, Pra. 10 B3 50 4N 14 26 E
Botkyrka, Stock. 3 E9 59 15N 17 49 E
Botofogo, Rio J. 31 B2 22 56 S 43 10W
Bottrop, Ruhr 6 A3 51 32N 6 57 E
Bötzow, Berl. 7 A1 52 39N 13 8 E
Bouafle, Paris 5 B1 48 57N 1 54 E
Boucherville, Mtrl. 20 A5 43 36N 73 28W
Boucherville, Îs. de, Mtrl. 20 A5 43 36N 73 28W
Bougival, Paris 5 B2 48 51N 2 8 E
Boulder Pt., H.K. 12 E5 22 14N 114 6 E

Choisy-le-Roi 35

Boullay-les-Troux, *Paris* **5 C2** 48 40N 2 2 E
Boulogne, *B.A.* **32 B3** 34 30 S 58 33W
Boulogne, Bois de, *Paris* **5 B3** 48 51N 2 14 E
Boulogne-Billancourt, *Paris* **5 B3** 48 50N 2 14 E
Bouqueval, *Paris* **5 A4** 49 1N 2 25 E
Bourg-la-Reine, *Paris* **5 C3** 48 46N 2 19 E
Boussy-St.-Antoine, *Paris* **5 C5** 48 41N 2 33 E
Bouviers, *Paris* **5 C2** 48 46N 2 4 E
Bovert, *Ruhr* **6 C1** 51 16N 6 37 E
Bovisa, *Mil.* **9 D6** 45 30N 9 10 E
Bovísio-Masciago, *Mil.* **9 D5** 45 36N 9 8 E
Bow, *Lon.* **4 B4** 51 31N 0 1W
Bowleys Quarters, *Balt.* **25 A4** 39 20N 76 24W
Box Hill, *Melb.* **19 E7** 37 48 S 145 6 E
Boxford State Forest, *Bost.* **21 B3** 42 39N 71 2W
Boy, *Ruhr* **6 A3** 51 31N 7 0 E
Boyaciköy, *Ist.* **17 A3** 41 5N 29 2 E
Boye →, *Ruhr* **6 A3** 51 30N 6 59 E
Boyle Heights, *L.A.* **28 B3** 34 1N 118 12 E
Braddell Heights, *Sing.* **15 F8** 1 20N 103 51 E
Brahmanpur, *Bomb.* **16 G8** 19 5N 72 52 E
Braintree, *Bost.* **21 D3** 42 12N 71 0W
Brakpan, *Jobg.* **18 F11** 26 14 S 28 20 E
Brambauer, *Ruhr* **6 A6** 51 35N 7 26 E
Bramfeld, *Hbg.* **7 D8** 53 36N 10 5 E
Bramley, *Jobg.* **18 E9** 26 7 S 28 4 E
Brande, *Hbg.* **7 D6** 53 37N 9 49 E
Brandenburg Gate, *Berl.* **7 A3** 52 30N 13 21 E
Brandizzo, *Tori.* **9 A3** 45 10N 7 49 E
Brands Hatch, *Lon.* **4 C6** 51 21N 0 15 E
Brandýs nad Labem, *Pra.* **10 A3** 50 10N 14 39 E
Brandywine, *Phil.* **24 C1** 39 49N 75 32W
Brandywine Cr. →, *Phil.* **24 C1** 39 43N 75 31W
Brani, P., *Sing.* **15 G8** 1 15N 103 50 E
Branik, *Pra.* **10 B2** 50 1N 14 25 E
Brännkyrka, *Stock.* **3 E11** 59 17N 18 0 E
Brás, *S. Pau.* **31 E6** 23 32 S 46 36W
Brateyevo, *Mos.* **11 F10** 55 39N 37 45 E
Bratsevo, *Mos.* **11 D8** 55 51N 37 24 E
Brauck, *Ruhr* **6 A3** 51 32N 7 0 E
Brava, Pta., *La Hab.* **30 B2** 23 8N 82 23W
Braybrook, *Melb.* **19 E6** 37 46 S 144 51 E
Brázdim, *Pra.* **10 A3** 50 10N 14 35 E
Breakheart Reservation, *Bost.* **21 C3** 42 28N 71 1W
Brechten, *Ruhr* **6 A6** 51 34N 7 27 E
Breckerfeld, *Ruhr* **6 C6** 51 15N 7 28 E
Brede, *Købn.* **2 D10** 55 47N 12 30 E
Bredeney, *Ruhr* **6 B3** 51 24N 6 59 E
Breeds Pond, *Bost.* **21 C4** 42 28N 70 58W
Breezy Pt., *N.Y.* **22 D5** 40 33N 73 56W
Breitenlee, *Wien* **10 G11** 48 15N 16 30 E
Breitscheid, *Ruhr* **6 B3** 51 21N 6 51 E
Breña, *Lima* **30 G8** 12 3 S 77 3W
Brenschede, *Ruhr* **6 B5** 51 26N 7 12 E
Brent, *Lon.* **4 B3** 51 33N 0 15W
Brent →, *Lon.* **4 B2** 51 30N 0 20W
Brent Res., *Lon.* **4 B3** 51 34N 0 14W
Brentford, *Lon.* **4 C3** 51 28N 0 18W
Brenthurst, *Jobg.* **18 F11** 26 15 S 28 21 E
Brentwood, *Lon.* **4 B6** 51 36N 0 18 E
Brentwood Park, *Jobg.* **18 E10** 26 7 S 28 17 E
Brentwood Park, *L.A.* **28 B2** 34 3N 118 29W
Brera, *Mil.* **9 E6** 45 28N 9 11 E
Bresso, *Mil.* **9 D6** 45 32N 9 11 E
Brétigny-sur-Orge, *Paris* **5 D3** 48 36N 2 18 E
Brevik, *Stock.* **3 D12** 59 20N 18 12 E
Břevnov, *Pra.* **10 B2** 50 4N 14 22 E
Brewer I., *S.F.* **27 C3** 37 33N 122 16W
Bricket Wood, *Lon.* **4 A2** 51 42N 0 21W
Bridesburg, *Phil.* **24 B4** 39 59N 75 4W
Bridgeport, *Chic.* **26 B3** 41 50N 87 38W
Bridgeport, *Phil.* **24 A2** 40 6N 75 21W
Bridgeview, *Chic.* **26 C2** 41 45N 87 48W
Brie-Comte-Robert, *Paris* **5 C5** 48 41N 2 36 E
Brighton, *Melb.* **19 F6** 37 55 S 144 59 E
Brighton le Sands, *Syd.* **19 B3** 33 57 S 151 9 E
Brighton Park, *Chic.* **26 C2** 41 48N 87 41W
Brightwood, *Wash.* **25 D7** 38 57N 77 1W
Brigittenau, *Wien* **10 G10** 48 14N 16 22 E
Briis-sous-Forges, *Paris* **5 D2** 48 37N 2 7 E
Brimbank Park, *Melb.* **19 E6** 37 43 S 144 50 E
Brimsdown, *Lon.* **4 B4** 51 39N 0 0 E
Brione, *Tori.* **9 B1** 45 8N 7 28 E
Briones Hills, *S.F.* **27 A4** 37 56N 122 8W
Briones Regional Park, *S.F.* **27 A4** 37 55N 122 8W
Briones Res., *S.F.* **27 A3** 37 55N 122 11W
Brisbane, *S.F.* **27 B2** 37 40N 122 23W
Bristol, *Phil.* **24 A5** 40 6N 74 53W
Britz, *Berl.* **7 B3** 52 26N 13 27 E
Brixton, *Lon.* **4 C4** 51 27N 0 8W
Broad Axe, *Phil.* **24 A3** 40 8N 75 14W
Broad Sd., *Bost.* **21 C4** 42 23N 70 56W
Broadmeadows, *Melb.* **19 E6** 37 40 S 144 55 E
Broadmoor, *S.F.* **27 B2** 37 41N 122 29W
Broadview, *Chic.* **26 B1** 41 51N 87 52W
Brobacka, *Hels.* **3 B2** 60 15N 24 36 E
Brockley, *Lon.* **4 C4** 51 27N 0 2W
Bródno, *Wsaw.* **10 E7** 52 17N 21 1 E
Bródnowski, Kanal, *Wsaw.* **10 E7** 52 17N 21 3 E
Broich, *Ruhr* **6 B3** 51 25N 6 50 E
Bromley, *Lon.* **4 C5** 51 24N 0 0 E
Bromley-by-Bow, *Lon.* **4 B4** 51 31N 0 0 E
Bromley Common, *Lon.* **4 C5** 51 22N 0 2 E
Bromma, *Stock.* **3 D10** 59 21N 17 55 E
Bromma flygplats, *Stock.* **3 D10** 59 21N 17 56 E
Brompton, *Lon.* **4 C3** 51 29N 0 10W
Brøndby Strand, *Købn.* **2 E9** 55 36N 12 25 E
Brøndbyøster, *Købn.* **2 E9** 55 39N 12 26 E
Brøndbyvester, *Købn.* **2 E9** 55 37N 12 23 E
Brondesbury, *Lon.* **4 B3** 51 32N 0 12W
Brønnøya, *Oslo* **2 B3** 59 51N 10 32 E
Brønshøj, *Købn.* **2 D9** 55 41N 12 29 E
Bronx Zoo, *N.Y.* **23 B5** 40 50N 73 51W
Bronxville, *N.Y.* **23 B6** 40 56N 73 49W
Brook Street, *Lon.* **4 B6** 51 36N 0 17 E
Brookfield, *Chic.* **26 C1** 41 48N 87 50W
Brookhaven, *Phil.* **24 B2** 39 52N 75 23W
Brooklandville, *Balt.* **25 A2** 39 25N 76 40W
Brooklin, *S. Pau.* **31 E6** 23 37 S 46 39W
Brookline, *Bost.* **21 D3** 42 19N 71 8W
Brooklyn, *Balt.* **25 B3** 39 13N 76 36W
Brooklyn, *Melb.* **19 E5** 37 49 S 144 49 E
Brooklyn, *N.Y.* **22 D5** 40 37N 73 57W
Brookmont, *Wash.* **25 D7** 38 57N 77 7W
Brooks I., *S.F.* **27 A2** 37 53N 122 21W
Brookville, *N.Y.* **23 C7** 40 48N 73 33W
Broomall, *Phil.* **24 B2** 39 58N 75 22W
Brosewere B., *N.Y.* **23 D6** 40 37N 73 40W
Brossard, *Mtrl.* **20 B5** 43 27N 73 28W
Brou-sur-Chantereine, *Paris* **5 B5** 48 53N 2 37 E
Brown, *Trto.* **20 D9** 43 48N 79 14W
Browns Line, *Trto.* **20 E7** 43 36N 79 32W
Broyhill Park, *Wash.* **25 D6** 38 52N 77 12W
Bru, *Oslo* **2 C5** 59 47N 10 54 E
Bruckhausen, *Ruhr* **6 B2** 51 29N 6 43 E
Brughério, *Mil.* **9 D6** 45 33N 9 17 E
Bruino, *Tori.* **9 B1** 45 1N 7 27 E
Bruløkka, *Oslo* **2 A2** 60 1N 10 22 E
Brunn, *Stock.* **3 E13** 59 17N 18 25 E
Brunnthal, *Mün.* **7 G11** 48 0N 11 41 E
Brunoy, *Paris* **5 C4** 48 41N 2 29 E
Brunswick, *Melb.* **19 E6** 37 45 S 144 57 E
Brusciano, *Nápl.* **9 H13** 40 55N 14 25 E
Brush Hill, *Bost.* **21 D1** 42 15N 71 22W
Bruzzano, *Mil.* **9 D6** 45 31N 9 10 E
Bry-sur-Marne, *Paris* **5 B5** 48 50N 2 32 E
Bryn, *Oslo* **2 B2** 59 55N 10 27 E
Bryn Athyn, *Phil.* **24 A4** 40 8N 75 3W
Bryn Mawr, *Phil.* **24 A3** 40 1N 75 19W
Brzeziny, *Wsaw.* **10 E7** 52 19N 21 2 E
Bubeneč, *Pra.* **10 B2** 50 6N 14 24 E
Buc, *Paris* **5 C2** 48 46N 2 7 E
Buch, *Berl.* **7 A3** 52 38N 13 29 E
Buchburg, *Wien* **10 G9** 48 13N 16 11 E
Buchenhain, *Mün.* **7 G9** 48 1N 11 29 E
Buchholz, *Berl.* **7 A3** 52 36N 13 25 E
Buchholz, *Ruhr* **6 B2** 51 23N 6 46 E
Buckhurst Hill, *Lon.* **4 B5** 51 37N 0 2 E
Buckingham Palace, *Lon.* **4 B4** 51 30N 0 8W
Buckow, *Berl.* **7 B3** 52 25N 13 26 E
Buda, *Bud.* **10 J13** 47 30N 19 2 E
Budafok, *Bud.* **10 K13** 47 25N 19 2 E
Budakeszi, *Bud.* **10 J12** 47 30N 18 56 E
Budaörs, *Bud.* **10 K12** 47 27N 18 57 E
Budapest, *Bud.* **10 K13** 47 29N 19 3 E
Budatétény, *Bud.* **10 K13** 47 25N 19 1 E
Budberg, *Ruhr* **6 A1** 51 32N 6 38 E
Buddinge, *Købn.* **2 D10** 55 44N 12 30 E
Büderich, *Ruhr* **6 C2** 51 15N 6 41 E
Buena Park, *L.A.* **28 C4** 33 51N 118 1W
Buena Vista, *S.F.* **27 B2** 37 45N 122 26W
Buenavista, *Mdrd.* **8 B2** 40 25N 3 40W
Buenos Aires, *B.A.* **32 B4** 34 36 S 58 22W
Buenos Aires, Aeroparque de la Ciudad de, *B.A.* **32 B4** 34 34 S 58 25W
Buer, *Ruhr* **6 A4** 51 34N 7 2 E
Bufalotta, *Rome* **9 F10** 41 59N 12 33 E
Buggajha, *Sŏul* **12 G7** 37 34N 126 55 E
Bughan San, *Sŏul* **12 G7** 37 38N 126 58 E
Bugio, *Lisb.* **8 G7** 38 39N 9 18W
Bukit Panjang, *Sing.* **15 F7** 1 22N 103 45 E
Bukit Timah, *Sing.* **15 F7** 1 20N 103 47 E
Bulam San, *Sŏul* **12 G8** 37 38N 127 4 E
Bûlâq, *El Qâ.* **18 C5** 30 3N 31 14 E
Bule, *Manila* **15 E4** 14 26N 121 2 E
Bulim, *Sing.* **15 F7** 1 22N 103 43 E
Bull Brook →, *Bost.* **21 A4** 42 41N 70 52W
Bulleen, *Melb.* **19 E7** 37 46 S 145 4 E
Bullen Park, *Melb.* **19 E7** 37 46 S 145 4 E
Bullion, *Paris* **5 D1** 48 37N 1 59 E
Bulmke-Hüllen, *Ruhr* **6 A4** 51 31N 7 7 E
Bulphan, *Lon.* **4 B7** 51 32N 0 21 E
Bundoora, *Melb.* **19 E7** 37 41 S 145 2 E
Bundoora Park, *Melb.* **19 E7** 37 42 S 145 2 E
Bunker I., *Kar.* **17 H10** 24 48N 66 57 E
Bunkyo, *Tōkyō* **13 B3** 35 42N 139 45 E
Bunnefjorden, *Oslo* **2 B4** 59 50N 10 44 E
Buona Vista, *Sing.* **15 G7** 1 16N 103 47 E
Buquirivú-Guaçu →, *S. Pau.* **31 D7** 23 28 S 46 28W
Burbank, *Chic.* **26 C2** 41 44N 87 46W
Burbank, *L.A.* **28 A3** 34 12N 118 18W
Bures, *Paris* **5 B1** 48 56N 1 57 E
Bures-sur-Yvette, *Paris* **5 C2** 48 41N 2 9 E
Burggrafenberg, *Ruhr* **6 C4** 51 13N 7 7 E
Burgh Heath, *Lon.* **4 D3** 51 18N 0 13W
Burlingame, *S.F.* **27 C2** 37 34N 122 20W
Burlington, *Bost.* **21 B2** 42 30N 71 13W
Burlington, *Phil.* **24 A5** 40 4N 74 53W
Burnham, *Chic.* **26 D3** 41 38N 87 33W
Burnham Park Harbor, *Chic.* **26 B3** 41 51N 87 36W
Burnhamthorpe, *Trto.* **20 E7** 43 37N 79 35W
Burnt Oak, *Lon.* **4 B3** 51 36N 0 15W
Burr Ridge, *Chic.* **26 C1** 41 46N 87 54W
Burtus, *El Qâ.* **18 C4** 30 8N 31 8 E
Burudvatn, *Oslo* **2 B3** 59 58N 10 35 E
Burwood, *Melb.* **19 F7** 37 50 S 145 6 E
Burwood, *Syd.* **19 B3** 33 52 S 151 5 E
Burwood East, *Melb.* **19 F7** 37 51 S 145 8 E
Burzaco, *B.A.* **32 C4** 34 49 S 58 23W
Buschhausen, *Ruhr* **6 A3** 51 30N 6 50 E
Bush Hill Park, *Lon.* **4 B4** 51 38N 0 4W
Bushey, *Lon.* **4 B2** 51 38N 0 22W
Bushwick, *N.Y.* **23 C5** 40 41N 73 54W
Bushy Cr. →, *Melb.* **19 E8** 37 42 S 145 17 E
Bushy Park, *Lon.* **4 C2** 51 24N 0 20W
Bussocaba, *S. Pau.* **31 E5** 23 34 S 46 47W
Bussy-St.-Georges, *Paris* **5 B6** 48 50N 2 41 E
Bussy-St.-Martin, *Paris* **5 B6** 48 50N 2 41 E
Bustleton, *Phil.* **24 A4** 40 4N 75 2W
Butantã, *S. Pau.* **31 E5** 23 34 S 46 42W
Butcher I., *Bomb.* **16 H8** 18 57N 72 53 E
Butendorf, *Ruhr* **6 A3** 51 33N 6 59 E
Butler, *N.Y.* **22 B2** 40 59N 74 20W
Buttonville, *Trto.* **20 C8** 43 51N 79 20W
Butts Corner, *Wash.* **25 E6** 38 46N 77 19W
Byailla, *Bomb.* **16 H8** 18 58N 72 50 E
Byberry, *Phil.* **24 A5** 40 6N 74 59W
Byfang, *Ruhr* **6 B4** 51 24N 7 5 E
Byfleet, *Lon.* **4 D2** 51 19N 0 28W
Bygdøy, *Oslo* **2 B4** 59 54N 10 40 E

C

C.N. Tower, *Trto.* **20 E8** 43 38N 79 23W
Caballito, *B.A.* **32 B4** 34 37 S 58 25W
Cabin John, *Wash.* **25 D6** 38 58N 77 10W
Cabin John Cr. →, *Wash.* **25 C7** 39 2N 77 8W
Cabin John Regional Park, *Wash.* **25 C6** 39 0N 77 10W
Cabramatta, *Syd.* **19 B2** 33 53 S 150 56 E
Cabuçú de Baixo →, *S. Pau.* **31 D5** 23 30 S 46 40W
Cachan, *Paris* **5 C3** 48 47N 2 19 E
Cachenka →, *Mos.* **11 E7** 55 46N 37 17 E
Cachoeira →, *S. Pau.* **31 E5** 23 38 S 46 43W
Cacilhas, *Lisb.* **8 F8** 38 41N 9 8W
Cadieux, Î., *Mtrl.* **20 B1** 43 25N 74 1W
Cagarras, Is., *Rio J.* **31 C2** 23 1 S 43 12W
Cahuenga Pk., *L.A.* **28 B3** 34 8N 118 19 E
Cainta, *Manila* **15 D4** 14 34N 121 6 E
Cairo = El Qâhira, *El Qâ.* **18 C5** 30 2N 31 13 E
Cairo Int. Airport, *El Qâ.* **18 C6** 30 7N 31 23 E
Caivano, *Nápl.* **9 H12** 40 57N 14 18 E
Caju, *Rio J.* **31 B2** 22 52 S 43 12W
Čakovice, *Pra.* **10 B3** 50 9N 14 31 E
Calabazar, *La Hab.* **30 B2** 23 1N 82 20W
Calcutta, *Calc.* **16 E6** 22 34N 88 21 E
Caldwell, *N.Y.* **22 B3** 40 50N 74 19W
Calf Harbour, *N.Y.* **23 B7** 40 59N 73 37W
Calf I., *Bost.* **21 C4** 42 20N 70 53W
Calhua, *Lisb.* **8 F8** 38 44N 9 9W
California, Univ. of, *S.F.* **27 A3** 37 52N 122 16W
California Inst. of Tech., *L.A.* **28 B4** 34 8N 118 8W
California State Univ., *L.A.* **28 B3** 34 4N 118 10W
California State Univ., *S.F.* **27 C4** 37 39N 122 6W
Callao, *Lima* **30 G8** 12 3 S 77 8W
Caloocan, *Manila* **15 D3** 14 39N 120 58 E
Calumet →, *Chic.* **26 C3** 41 43N 87 31W
Calumet, L., *Chic.* **26 C3** 41 40N 87 35W
Calumet City, *Chic.* **26 D3** 41 36N 87 32W
Calumet Harbor, *Chic.* **26 C3** 41 43N 87 30W
Calumet Park, *Chic.* **26 C3** 41 40N 87 39W
Calumet Sag Channel →, *Chic.* **26 C2** 41 40N 87 47W
Calumpang, *Manila* **15 D4** 14 37N 121 5 E
Calvairate, *Mil.* **9 E6** 45 27N 9 13 E
Calverton, *Wash.* **25 C8** 39 3N 76 56W
Calvizzano, *Nápl.* **9 H12** 40 54N 14 11 E
Calzada, *Manila* **15 D4** 14 32N 121 4 E
Camarate, *Lisb.* **8 F8** 38 48N 9 7W
Camaroes, *Lisb.* **8 F7** 38 49N 9 14W
Camberwell, *Lon.* **4 C4** 51 28N 0 5W
Camberwell, *Melb.* **19 F7** 37 50 S 145 5 E
Cambria Heights, *N.Y.* **23 C6** 40 41N 73 44W
Cambridge, *Bost.* **21 C3** 42 23N 71 7W
Cambridge Res., *Bost.* **21 C2** 42 24N 71 16W
Cambuci, *S. Pau.* **31 E6** 23 33 S 46 47W
Cambute, *La Hab.* **30 B3** 23 5N 82 16W
Camden, *Lon.* **4 B4** 51 32N 0 8W
Camden, *Phil.* **24 B4** 39 56N 75 7W
Camp Springs, *Wash.* **25 E8** 38 48N 76 55W
Campamento, *Mdrd.* **8 B2** 40 23N 3 46W
Campanilla, Pta., *La Hab.* **30 A3** 23 10N 82 18W
Campbellfield, *Melb.* **19 E6** 37 40 S 144 57 E
Camperdown, *Syd.* **19 B4** 33 53 S 151 11 E
Campi Flegrei, *Nápl.* **9 H11** 40 50N 14 9 E
Campo, Casa de, *Mdrd.* **8 B2** 40 25N 3 45W
Campo Belo, *S. Pau.* **31 E5** 23 36 S 46 44W
Campo de Mayo, *B.A.* **32 B2** 34 32 S 58 40W
Campo Grando, *Lisb.* **8 F8** 38 45N 9 9W
Campo Limpo, *S. Pau.* **31 E5** 23 38 S 46 46W
Campo Pequeño, *Lisb.* **8 F8** 38 44N 9 8W
Campolide, *Lisb.* **8 F8** 38 43N 9 9W
Campsie, *Syd.* **19 B3** 33 54 S 151 6 E
C'an San Joan, *Barc.* **8 D6** 41 28N 2 11 E
Canacao, *Manila* **15 E3** 14 29N 120 54 E
Canacao B., *Manila* **15 E3** 14 29N 120 54 E
Cañada de los Helechos →, *Méx.* **29 B2** 19 21N 99 15W
Canarsie, *N.Y.* **23 D5** 40 38N 73 53W
Candiac, *Mtrl.* **20 B5** 43 23N 73 29W
Caneças, *Lisb.* **8 F7** 38 48N 9 13W
Cangaiba, *S. Pau.* **31 E6** 23 30 S 46 31W
Cangrejeras, *La Hab.* **30 B1** 23 3N 82 30W
Canguera, *S. Pau.* **31 E7** 23 34 S 46 26W
Canillas, *Mdrd.* **8 B3** 40 27N 3 38W
Canillejas, *Mdrd.* **8 B3** 40 26N 3 36W
Cann Hall, *Lon.* **4 B5** 51 33N 0 0 E
Canning Town, *Lon.* **4 B5** 51 30N 0 1 E
Canoe Grove Res., *N.Y.* **22 C2** 40 45N 74 21W
Cantalupo, *Mil.* **9 D4** 45 34N 8 58 E
Cantareira, *S. Pau.* **31 D6** 23 26 S 46 36W
Cantarranas, *La Hab.* **30 B2** 23 2N 82 28W
Canteras de Vallecas, *Mdrd.* **8 B3** 40 20N 3 37W
Canterbury, *Melb.* **19 E7** 37 49 S 145 4 E
Canterbury, *Syd.* **19 B3** 33 55 S 151 7 E
Canto do Rio, *Rio J.* **31 B3** 22 54 S 43 7W
Canton, *Bost.* **21 D3** 42 10N 71 8W
Caohe, *Shang.* **14 J11** 31 10N 121 24 E
Caonao, *La Hab.* **30 B2** 23 5N 82 24W
Capão Redondo, *S. Pau.* **31 E5** 23 39 S 46 45W
Caparica, *Lisb.* **8 F8** 38 40N 9 9W
Caparica, Costa da, *Lisb.* **8 G7** 38 38N 9 15W
Capelinha, *S. Pau.* **31 E5** 23 39 S 46 44W
Capitol Heights, *Wash.* **25 D8** 38 52N 76 55W
Capodichino, Aeroporto di, *Nápl.* **9 H12** 40 52N 14 17 E
Capodimonte, *Nápl.* **9 H12** 40 52N 14 14 E
Capodimonte, Bosco di, *Nápl.* **9 H12** 40 52N 14 15 E
Captain Cook Bridge, *Syd.* **19 C3** 34 0 S 151 7 E
Captain Cook Landing Place Park, *Syd.* **19 C4** 34 1 S 151 14 E
Captain Harbour, *N.Y.* **23 B7** 40 59N 73 37W
Capuava, *S. Pau.* **31 E7** 23 38 S 46 28W
Capuchos, *Lisb.* **8 G7** 38 38N 9 16W
Caraballeda, *Car.* **30 D5** 10 36N 66 50W
Carabanchel Alto, *Mdrd.* **8 B2** 40 22N 3 44W
Carabanchel Bajo, *Mdrd.* **8 B2** 40 23N 3 44W
Carabatteda →, *Car.* **30 D5** 10 37N 66 51W
Caracas, *Car.* **30 E5** 10 30N 66 54W
Carapachay, *B.A.* **32 B3** 34 31 S 58 32W
Carapicuiba, *S. Pau.* **31 E5** 23 31 S 46 49W
Carapicuiba →, *S. Pau.* **31 E5** 23 31 S 46 49W
Caravita, *Nápl.* **9 H13** 40 52N 14 21 E
Caraza, *B.A.* **32 C4** 34 41 S 58 25W
Cardito, *Nápl.* **9 H12** 40 56N 14 17 E
Cardoso, *Lagos* **18 A1** 6 34N 7 16 E
Caribbean Gardens, *Melb.* **19 F8** 37 54 S 145 12 E
Caricuao, *Car.* **30 E5** 10 25N 66 58W
Caridad, *Manila* **15 E3** 14 28N 120 53 E
Carioca, Sa. da, *Rio J.* **31 B2** 22 57 S 43 13W
Carle Place, *N.Y.* **23 C7** 40 44N 73 35W
Carlingford, *Syd.* **19 A3** 33 46 S 151 3 E
Carlisle, *Bost.* **21 B1** 42 31N 71 20W
Carlshof, *Mün.* **7 F11** 48 15N 11 41 E
Carlstadt, *N.Y.* **22 B4** 40 50N 74 6W
Carlton, *Melb.* **19 E6** 37 47 S 144 57 E
Carnaxide, *Lisb.* **8 F7** 38 43N 9 14W
Carnegie, *Melb.* **19 F7** 37 53 S 145 3 E
Carnegie Hall, *N.Y.* **22 C5** 40 45N 73 59W
Carnetin, *Paris* **5 B6** 48 54N 2 42 E
Carney, *Balt.* **25 A3** 39 23N 76 31W
Carnide, *Lisb.* **8 F7** 38 45N 9 10W
Caronno Pert, *Mil.* **9 D5** 45 35N 9 2 E
Carramar, *Syd.* **19 B2** 33 51 S 150 58 E
Carrascal, *Stgo* **30 J10** 33 25 S 70 42W
Carrières-sous-Bois, *Paris* **5 B2** 48 55N 2 6 E
Carrières-sous-Poissy, *Paris* **5 B2** 48 56N 2 2 E
Carrières-sur-Seine, *Paris* **5 B3** 48 55N 2 11 E
Carroll I., *Balt.* **25 B4** 39 19N 76 20W
Carroll Park, *Balt.* **25 B3** 39 16N 76 38W
Carshalton, *Lon.* **4 C3** 51 22N 0 10W
Carshalton on the Hill, *Lon.* **4 C4** 51 20N 0 9W
Carteret, *N.Y.* **22 D3** 40 34N 74 13W
Cartierville, Aéroport de, *Mtrl.* **20 A3** 43 31N 73 42 E
Carugate, *Mil.* **9 D6** 45 32N 9 20 E
Carupa, *B.A.* **32 A3** 34 25 S 58 33W
Casa Blanca, *La Hab.* **30 B3** 23 8N 82 19W
Casa Verde, *S. Pau.* **31 D5** 23 29 S 46 40W
Casalnuovo di Nápoli, *Nápl.* **9 H12** 40 54N 14 20 E
Casalotti, *Rome* **9 F9** 41 54N 12 22 E
Casandrino, *Nápl.* **9 H12** 40 56N 14 15 E
Casavatore, *Nápl.* **9 H12** 40 53N 14 15 E
Cascadura, *Rio J.* **31 B2** 22 52 S 43 19W
Caselette, *Tori.* **9 B1** 45 6N 7 28 E
Caselette, Laghi di, *Tori.* **9 B1** 45 7N 7 29 E
Caselle Torinese, *Tori.* **9 A3** 45 10N 7 38 E
Caseros, *B.A.* **32 B3** 34 36 S 58 34W
Casória, *Nápl.* **9 H12** 40 54N 14 17 E
Cassignanica, *Mil.* **9 E7** 45 27N 9 20 E
Cassiobury Park, *Lon.* **4 B2** 51 39N 0 25W
Castel di Camerletto, *Tori.* **9 B1** 45 6N 7 27 E
Castel di Guido, *Rome* **9 F8** 41 53N 12 17 E
Castel Malnome, *Rome* **9 F8** 41 50N 12 19 E
Castel San Cristina, *Tori.* **9 B3** 45 8N 7 40 E
Castel Sant'Angelo, *Rome* **9 F9** 41 54N 12 27 E
Castelar, *B.A.* **32 B3** 34 39 S 58 39W
Castellbisbal, *Barc.* **8 D4** 41 28N 1 58 E
Castello di Cisterna, *Nápl.* **9 H13** 40 54N 14 24 E
Castelvécchio, *Tori.* **9 B3** 45 1N 7 46 E
Castiglione Torinese, *Tori.* **9 B3** 45 6N 7 48 E
Castleton Corners, *N.Y.* **22 D4** 40 36N 74 8W
Castro Valley, *S.F.* **27 B4** 37 41N 122 5W
Castrop, *Ruhr* **6 A5** 51 32N 7 18 E
Castrop-Rauxel, *Ruhr* **6 A5** 51 33N 7 18 E
Cat Rock Hill, *Bost.* **21 C2** 42 23N 71 18W
Caterham, *Lon.* **4 D4** 51 16N 0 5W
Catete, *Rio J.* **31 B2** 22 54 S 43 10W
Catford, *Lon.* **4 C4** 51 26N 0 1W
Catia, *Car.* **30 D5** 10 31N 66 56W
Catia La Mer, *Car.* **30 D4** 10 36N 67 0W
Catonsville, *Balt.* **25 B2** 39 16N 76 43W
Catonsville Manor, *Balt.* **25 B2** 39 17N 76 44W
Cattle Hill, *S.F.* **27 C2** 37 36N 122 27W
Catumbi, *Rio J.* **31 B2** 22 54 S 43 12W
Caughnawaga, *Mtrl.* **20 B3** 43 24N 73 40W
Caulfield, *Melb.* **19 F7** 37 52 S 145 1 E
Caulfield Racecourse, *Melb.* **19 F7** 37 53 S 145 4 E
Caumsett State Park, *N.Y.* **23 B8** 40 55N 73 27W
Cavite, *Manila* **15 E3** 14 29N 120 54 E
Cavoretto, *Tori.* **9 B3** 45 1N 7 41 E
Caxias, *Lisb.* **8 F7** 38 42N 9 16W
Caxingui, *S. Pau.* **31 E5** 23 35 S 46 43W
Cebeciköy, *Ist.* **17 A2** 41 7N 28 53 E
Cecchignola, *Rome* **9 G10** 41 48N 12 29 E
Cecil Park, *Syd.* **19 B2** 33 52 S 150 51 E
Cecilienhof, *Berl.* **7 B1** 52 35N 13 5 E
Cedar Grove, *N.Y.* **22 B3** 40 50N 74 13W
Cedar Grove Res., *N.Y.* **22 B3** 40 51N 74 12W
Cedar I., *N.Y.* **23 D8** 40 38N 73 22W
Cedar Knolls, *N.Y.* **22 C2** 40 49N 74 27W
Cedarhurst, *N.Y.* **23 D6** 40 37N 73 43W
Cedarvale, *Trto.* **20 D8** 43 41N 79 26W
Celle →, *Paris* **5 D1** 48 36N 1 59 E
Cempaka Putih, *Jak.* **15 J10** 6 10 S 106 51 E
Çengelköy, *Ist.* **17 A3** 41 2N 29 3 E
Centennial Park, *Syd.* **19 B4** 33 53 S 151 14 E
Center Square, *Phil.* **24 C2** 39 46N 75 22W
Centerport, *N.Y.* **23 B8** 40 53N 73 22W
Centerton, *Phil.* **24 B5** 39 59N 74 53W
Centocelle, *Rome* **9 F10** 41 52N 12 34 E
Central Park, *N.Y.* **22 C5** 40 47N 73 58W
Central Park, *Sing.* **15 G8** 1 17N 103 50 E
Centre City, *Phil.* **24 C3** 39 46N 75 11W
Centre I., *N.Y.* **23 B7** 40 54N 73 31W
Cércola, *Nápl.* **9 H13** 40 51N 14 21 E
Cergy-Pontoise, *Paris* **5 A2** 49 1N 2 4 E
Cernay-la-Ville, *Paris* **5 C1** 48 40N 1 58 E
Cernusco sul Navíglio, *Mil.* **9 D6** 45 31N 9 19 E
Cerqueira Cesar, *S. Pau.* **31 E5** 23 33 S 46 40W
Cerro Ajusco, *Méx.* **29 C2** 19 12N 99 15W
Cerro de la Estrella, *Méx.* **29 B3** 19 20N 99 5W
Cerro de los Angeles, *Mdrd.* **8 C2** 40 18N 3 41W
Cerro el Picacho, *Méx.* **29 A3** 19 35N 99 6W
Cerro Maggiore, *Mil.* **9 D4** 45 35N 8 57 E
Certanovka →, *Mos.* **11 F9** 55 38N 37 48 E
Certanovo, *Mos.* **11 F9** 55 38N 37 36 E
Cesano Boscone, *Mil.* **9 E5** 45 26N 9 5 E
Cesate, *Mil.* **9 D5** 45 35N 9 4 E
Cha Kwo Ling, *H.K.* **12 E6** 22 18N 114 13 E
Chabot, L., *S.F.* **27 B4** 37 43N 122 6W
Chacao, *Car.* **30 D5** 10 30N 66 50W
Chacarilla, *Lima* **30 G9** 12 6 S 76 59W
Chadds Ford, *Phil.* **24 B1** 39 52N 75 35W
Chadstone, *Melb.* **19 F7** 37 52 S 145 5 E
Chadwell Heath, *Lon.* **4 B5** 51 34N 0 8 E
Chadwell St. Mary, *Lon.* **4 C7** 51 29N 0 20 E
Chai Wan, *H.K.* **12 E6** 22 16N 114 14 E
Chai Wan Kok, *H.K.* **12 D5** 22 22N 114 6 E
Chakdaha, *Calc.* **16 F5** 22 28N 88 19 E
Chama, *Lima* **30 G8** 12 7 S 77 0W
Chamartin, *Mdrd.* **8 B2** 40 27N 3 40W
Chamberi, *Mdrd.* **8 B2** 40 26N 3 42W
Chambourcy, *Paris* **5 B2** 48 54N 2 2 E
Champdani, *Calc.* **16 D5** 22 48N 88 19 E
Champigny-sur-Marne, *Paris* **5 C5** 48 49N 2 30 E
Champlain, Pont, *Mtrl.* **20 B4** 43 28N 73 31W
Champlan, *Paris* **5 C3** 48 42N 2 16 E
Champrosay, *Paris* **5 D4** 48 39N 2 25 E
Champs-sur-Marne, *Paris* **5 B5** 48 50N 2 34 E
Chamrail, *Calc.* **16 E5** 22 38N 88 17 E
Chancheon, *Sŏul* **12 G7** 37 33N 126 56 E
Chandernagore, *Calc.* **16 C6** 22 51N 88 21 E
Chanditala, *Calc.* **16 D5** 22 41N 88 15 E
Changi, *Sing.* **15 F8** 1 23N 103 59 E
Changi Airport, *Sing.* **15 F8** 1 21N 103 59 E
Changning, *Shang.* **14 J11** 31 13N 121 24 E
Changpu Gongyuan, *Shang.* **14 J12** 31 17N 121 31 E
Chanteloup-les-Vignes, *Paris* **5 B2** 48 58N 2 1 E
Chantereine, *Paris* **5 B5** 48 53N 2 37 E
Chantian, *Gzh.* **14 F8** 23 12N 113 16 E
Chao Phraya →, *Bangk.* **15 B2** 13 40N 100 31 E
Chaoyang, *Beij.* **14 B3** 39 53N 116 26 E
Chaoyang Gongyuan, *Beij.* **14 B3** 39 54N 116 28 E
Chaoyangmen, *Beij.* **14 B3** 39 54N 116 23 E
Chapel End, *Lon.* **4 B4** 51 35N 0 1W
Chapet, *Paris* **5 B1** 48 58N 1 55 E
Chaplinville, *Bost.* **21 A4** 42 42N 70 54W
Chapultepec, Bosque de, *Méx.* **29 B2** 19 25N 99 11W
Chapultepec, Castillo de, *Méx.* **29 B2** 19 25N 99 10W
Charenton-le-Pont, *Paris* **5 C4** 48 49N 2 25 E
Charles-de-Gaulle, Aéroport, *Paris* **5 A5** 49 0N 2 33 E
Charles Lee Tinden Regional Park, *S.F.* **27 A3** 37 53N 122 14W
Charleston, *N.Y.* **22 D3** 40 32N 74 14W
Charlestown, *Bost.* **21 C3** 42 22N 71 4W
Charlottenburg, *Berl.* **7 A2** 52 31N 13 14 E
Charlottenburg, Schloss, *Berl.* **7 A2** 52 31N 13 18 E
Charlottenlund, *Købn.* **2 D10** 55 44N 12 35 E
Charlton, *Lon.* **4 C5** 51 29N 0 1 E
Charneca, *Lisb.* **8 F8** 38 47N 9 8W
Charneca, *Lisb.* **8 G7** 38 37N 9 12W
Chase Side, *Lon.* **4 B4** 51 39N 0 4W
Châteaufort, *Paris* **5 C2** 48 44N 2 5 E
Châtenay-Malabry, *Paris* **5 C3** 48 46N 2 16 E
Chatham, *Chic.* **26 C3** 41 45N 87 36W
Chatham, *N.Y.* **22 C2** 40 44N 74 23W
Châtillon, *Paris* **5 C3** 48 48N 2 17 E
Chatou, *Paris* **5 B2** 48 53N 2 9 E
Chatpur, *Calc.* **16 E6** 22 36N 88 22 E
Chatra, *Calc.* **16 D5** 22 45N 88 19 E
Chatswood, *Syd.* **19 A4** 33 47 S 151 11 E
Chauki, *Kar.* **17 G10** 24 55N 66 56 E
Chavarria, *Lima* **30 G8** 12 0 S 77 7W
Chavenay, *Paris* **5 B1** 48 51N 1 59 E
Chavenay-Villepreux, Aérodrôme de, *Paris* **5 B1** 48 50N 1 58 E
Chaville, *Paris* **5 C3** 48 48N 2 11 E
Che Kung Miu, *H.K.* **12 D6** 22 22N 114 10 E
Cheam, *Lon.* **4 C3** 51 21N 0 12W
Chelles, *Paris* **5 B5** 48 53N 2 35 E
Chelles, Canal de, *Paris* **5 B5** 48 51N 2 35 E
Chells-le-Pin, Aérodrome, *Paris* **5 B5** 48 53N 2 36 E
Chelmsford, *Bost.* **21 B1** 42 35N 71 20W
Chelobityevo, *Mos.* **11 D10** 55 54N 37 40 E
Chelsea, *Bost.* **21 C3** 42 23N 71 1W
Chelsea, *Lon.* **4 C3** 51 29N 0 10W
Chelsea, *Phil.* **24 B2** 39 51N 75 27W
Chelsfield Village, *Lon.* **4 C5** 51 21N 0 8 E
Cheltenham, *Phil.* **24 A4** 40 3N 75 6W
Chembur, *Bomb.* **16 G8** 19 3N 72 53 E
Chennevières, *Paris* **5 A2** 49 0N 2 6 E
Chennevières-sur-Marne, *Paris* **5 C5** 48 47N 2 31 E
Cheongdam, *Sŏul* **12 G8** 37 31N 127 2 E
Cheonho, *Sŏul* **12 G8** 37 32N 127 6 E
Cheops, *El Qâ.* **18 D4** 29 58N 31 8 E
Chepo, *Gzh.* **14 G9** 23 7N 113 23 E
Cherepkovo, *Mos.* **11 E8** 55 45N 37 21 E
Chernyovo, *Mos.* **11 D7** 55 50N 37 17 E
Cherry Hill, *Phil.* **24 B4** 39 54N 75 1W
Cherry L., *Melb.* **19 F5** 37 51 S 144 49 E
Cherryland, *S.F.* **27 B4** 37 40N 122 7W
Cherrywood, *Trto.* **20 C10** 43 51N 79 8W
Chertsey, *Lon.* **4 C2** 51 23N 0 29W
Cheryomushki, *Mos.* **11 E9** 55 40N 37 35 E
Chesaco Park, *Balt.* **25 B3** 39 18N 76 30W
Chesapeake B., *Balt.* **25 B4** 39 12N 76 22W
Cheshunt, *Lon.* **4 A4** 51 42N 0 0 E
Chess →, *Lon.* **4 B2** 51 38N 0 27W
Chessington, *Lon.* **4 C3** 51 21N 0 18W
Chessington Zoo, *Lon.* **4 C3** 51 20N 0 19W
Chester, *Phil.* **24 B2** 39 50N 75 23W
Chester Cr. →, *Phil.* **24 B2** 39 50N 75 21W
Chester Heights, *Phil.* **24 B2** 39 53N 75 27W
Chestnut, *Phil.* **24 A3** 40 4N 75 13W
Chestnut Hill, *Bost.* **21 D2** 42 19N 71 10W
Cheung Sha Wan, *H.K.* **12 D5** 22 20N 114 8 E
Cheverly, *Wash.* **25 D8** 38 55N 76 54W
Chevilly-Larue, *Paris* **5 C4** 48 46N 2 21 E
Chevreuse, *Paris* **5 C2** 48 42N 2 2 E
Chevry-Cossigny, *Paris* **5 C5** 48 43N 2 39 E
Chevy Chase, *Wash.* **25 D7** 38 59N 77 4W
Chevy Chase View, *Wash.* **25 C7** 39 0N 77 4W
Cheyney, *Phil.* **24 B1** 39 55N 75 31W
Chhalera Bangar, *Delhi* **16 B2** 28 33N 77 17 E
Chhinamor, *Calc.* **16 D5** 22 48N 88 17 E
Chhota Andai, *Kar.* **17 H11** 24 48N 66 59 E
Chia Keng, *Sing.* **15 F8** 1 21N 103 52 E
Chiaíano, *Nápl.* **9 H12** 40 53N 14 13 E
Chiaravalle Milanese, *Mil.* **9 E6** 45 24N 9 16 E
Chiawelo, *Jobg.* **18 F8** 26 17 S 27 51 E
Chicago, *Chic.* **26 B3** 41 52N 87 38W
Chicago, Univ. of, *Chic.* **26 C3** 41 47N 87 35W
Chicago Harbor, *Chic.* **26 B3** 41 52N 87 36W
Chicago Lawn, *Chic.* **26 C2** 41 47N 87 40W
Chicago-Midway Airport, *Chic.* **26 C2** 41 47N 87 45W
Chicago-O'Hare Int. Airport, *Chic.* **26 B1** 41 58N 87 53W
Chicago Ridge, *Chic.* **26 C2** 41 41N 87 46W
Chicago Sanitary and Ship Canal, *Chic.* **26 C2** 41 49N 87 45W
Chichinautzin, Cerro, *Méx.* **29 D3** 19 6N 99 8W
Chicot, *Mtrl.* **20 A2** 43 35N 73 56W
Chicot →, *Mtrl.* **20 A2** 43 34N 73 51W
Chienzui, *Gzh.* **14 F9** 23 12N 113 22 E
Chieri, *Tori.* **9 B3** 45 0N 7 49 E
Chigwell, *Lon.* **4 B5** 51 36N 0 6 E
Chigwell Row, *Lon.* **4 B5** 51 37N 0 7 E
Chik Sha, *H.K.* **12 E6** 22 17N 114 16 E
Chikumazawa, *Tōkyō* **13 B2** 35 49N 139 32 E
Childs Hill, *Lon.* **4 B3** 51 33N 0 12W
Chilla Saroda, *Delhi* **16 B2** 28 35N 77 18 E
Chillum, *Wash.* **25 D8** 38 57N 76 58W
Chilly-Mazarin, *Paris* **5 C3** 48 42N 2 17 E
Chimalhuacán, *Méx.* **29 B4** 19 25N 89 57 E
Chimalpa, *Méx.* **29 B2** 19 21N 99 19W
China, Tg., *Sing.* **15 G8** 1 14N 103 50 E
China Basin, *S.F.* **27 B2** 37 46N 122 22W
Chingford, *Lon.* **4 B5** 51 37N 0 0 E
Chingupota, *Calc.* **16 F5** 22 29N 88 14 E
Chipilly Woods, *Chic.* **26 A2** 42 8N 87 48W
Chipperfield, *Lon.* **4 A2** 51 42N 0 29W
Chipping Ongar, *Lon.* **4 A6** 51 41N 0 15 E
Chipstead, *Lon.* **4 D4** 51 17N 0 8W
Chirle, *Bomb.* **16 H9** 18 55N 73 2 E
Chirnside Park, *Melb.* **19 E8** 37 45 S 145 18 E
Chislehurst, *Lon.* **4 C5** 51 24N 0 6 E
Chislehurst West, *Lon.* **4 C5** 51 25N 0 3 E
Chiswick, *Lon.* **4 C3** 51 29N 0 16W
Chiswick House, *Lon.* **4 C3** 51 28N 0 15W
Chitlade Palace, *Bangk.* **15 B2** 13 45N 100 31 E
Chitose, *Tōkyō* **13 C2** 35 33N 139 37 E
Chiyoda-Ku, *Tōkyō* **13 B3** 35 41N 139 44 E
Chkalova, *Mos.* **11 F11** 55 39N 37 56 E
Choa Chu Kang, *Sing.* **15 F7** 1 22N 103 40 E
Choboty, *Mos.* **11 F8** 55 39N 37 21 E
Chodov u Prahy, *Pra.* **10 B3** 50 1N 14 30 E
Chōfu, *Tōkyō* **13 C2** 35 38N 139 32 E
Choisel, *Paris* **5 C2** 48 41N 2 1 E
Choisy-le-Roi, *Paris* **5 C4** 48 46N 2 24 E

Chomedey, Mtrl. **20 A3** 43 32N 73 45W
Chong Nonsi,
Khlong →, Bangk. **15 B2** 13 42N 100 32 E
Chong Pang, Sing. .... **15 F7** 1 26N 103 49 E
Chongwen, Beij. ...... **14 B3** 39 52N 116 23 E
Chongwenmen, Beij. .. **14 B3** 39 52N 116 22 E
Chorleywood, Lon. **4 B2** 51 39N 0 29W
Chornaya →, Mos. .... **11 E12** 55 41N 38 0 E
Chorrillos, Lima ...... **30 H8** 12 10 S 77 1W
Christianshavn, Købn. .. **2 D10** 55 40N 12 35 E
Chrome, N.Y. **22 D3** 40 34N 74 13W
Chrzanów, Wsaw. .... **10 E6** 52 13N 20 53 E
Chuen Lung, H.K. .... **12 D5** 22 23N 114 6 E
Chuk Kok, H.K. ...... **12 D6** 22 20N 114 15 E
Chulalongkon Univ.,
Bangk. .... **15 B2** 13 44N 100 31 E
Chullora, Syd. .... **19 B3** 33 54 S 151 5 E
Chunchura, Calc. ..... **16 C6** 22 53N 88 23 E
Chuō-Ku, Tōkyō ..... **13 B3** 35 40N 139 46 E
Church End, Lon. **4 B3** 51 35N 0 11W
Chvaly, Pra. .... **10 B3** 50 6N 14 35 E
Chye Kay, Sing. ...... **15 F7** 1 25N 103 49 E
Ciampino, Rome ...... **9 G10** 41 47N 12 36 E
Ciampino, Aeroporto
di, Rome .... **9 G10** 41 47N 12 35 E
Cicero, Chic. **26 B2** 41 51N 87 44W
Cidade, I. da, Rio J. .. **31 B2** 22 51 S 43 13W
Cidade de Deus,
S. Pau. .... **31 E5** 23 33 S 46 45W
Cidade Ipava, S. Pau. **31 F5** 23 42 S 46 45W
Cidade Lider, S. Pau. .. **31 E7** 23 33 S 46 27W
Cidade São Matheus,
S. Pau. .... **31 E7** 23 35 S 46 29W
Cidena, Kali → Jak. .. **15 H9** 6 9 S 106 48 E
Cilandak, Jak. .... **15 J9** 6 17 S 106 47 E
Cilincing, Jak. .... **15 H10** 6 6 S 106 54 E
Ciliwung →, Jak. .... **15 J10** 6 6 S 106 47 E
Cîmice, Pra. .... **10 B2** 50 8N 14 25 E
Cinderella, Jobg. ..... **18 E10** 26 14 S 28 15 E
Cinderella Dam, Jobg. **18 F10** 26 14 S 28 14 E
Cinecittà, Rome ...... **9 F10** 41 51N 12 34 E
Ciniselló Bálsamo, Mil. **9 D6** 45 33N 9 13 E
Cinkota, Bud. .... **10 J14** 47 31N 19 14 E
Cinnaminson, Phil. ... **24 B5** 39 59N 74 59W
Cipete, Jak. .... **15 J9** 6 15 S 106 47 E
Cipresso, Tori. ...... **9 B3** 45 2N 7 48 E
Cisliano, Mil. .... **9 D5** 45 26N 8 59 E
Citénia, Mil. .... **9 E6** 45 28N 9 12 E
Città degli Studi, Mil.
Città del Vaticano,
Rome .... **9 F9** 41 54N 12 26 E
City I., N.Y. **23 B6** 40 50N 73 47W
Ciudad Azteca, Méx. .. **29 A3** 19 32N 99 1W
Ciudad Fin de Semana,
Mdrd. **8 B3** 40 26N 3 34W
Ciudad General
Belgrano, B.A. ..... **32 C3** 34 43 S 58 33W
Ciudad Libertad,
La Hab. **30 B2** 23 5N 82 25W
Ciudad Lineál, Mdrd. .. **8 B3** 40 26N 3 38W
Ciudad López Mateos,
Méx. **29 A2** 19 33N 99 16W
Ciudad Satélite, Méx. .. **29 A2** 19 30N 99 13W
Ciudad Universitaria,
Méx. **29 C2** 19 9N 99 10W
Ciudadela, B.A. ...... **32 B3** 34 38 S 58 32W
Ciudadela, Parque de
la, Barc. .... **8 D6** 41 23N 2 11 E
Clairefontaine, Paris .. **5 D1** 48 36N 1 54 E
Clamart, Paris .... **5 C4** 48 48N 2 15 E
Clapham, Lon. **4 B4** 51 27N 0 8W
Clapton, Lon. **4 B4** 51 33N 0 3W
Clark, N.Y. **22 D3** 40 38N 74 18W
Clarksboro, Phil. **24 C3** 39 48N 75 13W
Claye-Souilly, Paris ... **5 B6** 48 56N 2 41 E
Claygate, Lon. **4 C3** 51 21N 0 19W
Clayhall, Lon. .... **4 B5** 51 35N 0 3 E
Clayhill, Lon. **4 A4** 51 40N 0 5W
Claymont, Phil. **24 C2** 39 48N 75 27W
Claypole, B.A. .... **32 C4** 34 48 S 58 20W
Clayton, Melb. ...... **19 F7** 37 55 S 145 7 E
Clearing, Chic. **26 C2** 41 47N 87 45W
Clearwater, L.A. **28 C3** 33 52N 118 10W
Clement, Sing. ...... **15 G7** 1 18N 103 46 E
Clementon, Phil. **24 C5** 39 48N 74 59W
Clichy, Paris .... **5 B3** 48 54N 2 18 E
Clichy-sous-Bois, Paris **5 B4** 48 54N 2 32 E
Cliffside, Trto. **20 D9** 43 49N 79 14W
Cliffside Park, N.Y. .. **21 C4** 40 49N 73 59W
Clifton, Bost. **21 C4** 42 29N 70 52W
Clifton, Kar. .... **17 H11** 24 48N 67 1 E
Clifton, N.Y. **22 D4** 40 37N 74 4W
Clifton, N.Y. **22 B4** 40 51N 74 7W
Clifton, L., Balt. **25 B3** 39 19N 76 35W
Clifton Heights, Phil. .. **24 B3** 39 55N 75 17W
Clifton Park, Balt. **25 A3** 39 20N 76 35W
Clontarf, Syd. .... **19 A4** 33 48 S 151 16 E
Closter, N.Y. **22 B5** 40 58N 73 57W
Clovelly, Syd. .... **19 B4** 33 54 S 151 15 E
Cobbin's Brook →,
Lon. .... **4 A5** 51 40N 0 0 E
Cobbs Cr. →, Phil. ... **24 B3** 39 58N 75 18W
Cobham, Lon. **4 D2** 51 19N 0 23W
Cobras, I. das, Rio J. .. **31 B2** 22 53 S 43 9W
Coburg, Melb. .... **19 E6** 37 44 S 144 56 E
Cochecito, Car. **30 E5** 10 26N 66 55W
Cochickewick L., Bost. **21 A3** 42 42N 71 5W
Cochituate, Bost. **21 C1** 42 20N 71 21W
Cochituate L., Bost. .. **21 D1** 42 16N 71 21W
Cockfosters, Lon. **4 A4** 51 39N 0 8W
Cocota, Rio J. ...... **31 A2** 22 48 S 43 11W
Coelho da Rocha,
Rio J. .... **31 A1** 22 46 S 43 21W
Cœuilly, Paris .... **5 C5** 48 48N 2 32 E
Coignières, Paris ..... **5 C1** 48 44N 1 55 E
Coina, Lisb. **8 G8** 38 39N 9 5W
Cojimar, La Hab. **30 B3** 23 9N 82 17W
Cojimar →, La Hab. .. **30 B3** 23 9N 82 17W
Cojimar, Boca de,
La Hab. **30 A3** 23 10N 82 17W
Coker, Lagos .... **18 B2** 6 28N 7 20 E
Colaba, Bomb. ...... **16 H7** 18 53N 72 48 E
Colaba Pt., Bomb. .... **16 H7** 18 53N 72 48 E
Cold Spring Harbor,
N.Y. **23 B8** 40 52N 73 27W
Cold Spring Terrace,
N.Y. **23 B8** 40 49N 73 25W
Coleraine, Trto. **20 D6** 43 49N 79 40W
Colindale, Lon. **4 B3** 51 35N 0 15W
Collazo, La Hab. **30 B2** 23 2N 82 24W
College Park, Wash. .. **25 C5** 39 59N 76 55W
College Point, N.Y. ... **23 C5** 40 47N 73 50W
Collégien, Paris ..... **5 B6** 48 50N 2 41 E
Collegno, Tori. ...... **9 B2** 45 5N 7 34 E
Collier Row, Lon. .... **4 A5** 51 36N 0 10 E
Colliers Wood, Lon. .. **4 C3** 51 24N 0 10W
Collingdale, Phil. **24 B3** 39 54N 75 17W
Collingswood, Phil. ... **24 B4** 39 55N 75 5W
Collinsville, Mrtl. **20 B3** 45 40N 71 20W
Collinsville, N.Y. **23 C3** 40 48N 74 26W
Colma, S.F. **27 B2** 37 40N 122 27W
Colma, Cr. →, S.F. .. **27 C2** 37 38N 122 27W
Colney Hatch, Lon. ... **4 B4** 51 36N 0 9W
Cologno Monzese, Mil. **9 D6** 45 31N 9 17 E
Colombes, Paris ..... **5 B3** 48 55N 2 15 E
Colonia, N.Y. **22 D3** 40 35N 74 18W

Colônia, S. Pau. ..... **31 E7** 23 33 S 46 27W
Colonia Güell, Barc. .. **8 D5** 41 21N 2 2 E
Colonia Puerta de
Hierro, Mdrd. **8 B2** 40 27N 3 43W
Colonial Manor, Phil. .. **24 B4** 39 51N 75 9W
Colorado →, Méx. ... **29 B4** 19 23N 69 58 E
Colosseo, Rome ..... **9 F9** 41 53N 12 29 E
Columbia, Balt. **25 B1** 39 12N 76 50W
Columbia Hills, Balt. .. **25 B1** 39 14N 76 51W
Columbia Univ., N.Y. .. **23 B5** 40 48N 73 58W
Colwyn, Phil. **24 B3** 39 54N 75 14W
Combault, Paris ..... **5 C5** 48 48N 2 37 E
Combs-la-Ville, Paris .. **5 D5** 48 39N 2 33 E
Comércio, Praça do,
Lisb. **8 F8** 38 41N 9 9W
Commack, N.Y. **23 B9** 40 50N 73 19W
Commerce, L.A. **28 B4** 34 0N 118 9W
Como, Syd. .... **19 C3** 34 0 S 151 4 E
Compans, Paris ...... **5 B5** 48 59N 2 39 E
Compton, L.A. **28 C3** 33 53N 118 14W
Conceição, I. da, Rio J. **31 B3** 22 52 S 43 6W
Concepcion, Manila .. **15 D4** 14 39N 121 6 E
Conchali, Stgo ...... **30 J11** 33 22 S 70 39W
Concord, Bost. **21 C1** 42 27N 71 20W
Concord, S.F. **27 A4** 37 58N 122 3W
Concord, Trto. ...... **19 B3** 33 52 S 151 6 E
Concordville, Phil. **24 B1** 39 53N 75 31W
Concorezzo, Mil. .... **9 D6** 45 35N 9 19 E
Condécourt, Paris .... **5 A1** 49 2N 1 56 E
Coney Island, N.Y. ... **22 D4** 40 34N 74 0W
Conflans-Ste.-Honorine,
Paris .... **5 B2** 48 59N 2 6 E
Congo, S. Pau. ...... **31 D5** 23 27 S 46 42W
Congonhas, Aéroporto,
S. Pau. .... **31 E6** 23 38 S 46 39W
Conshohocken, Phil. .. **24 A3** 40 4N 75 18W
Contadero, Méx. **29 B2** 19 20N 99 17W
Convento de Valverde,
Mdrd. **8 A2** 40 30N 3 40W
Coogee, Syd. .... **19 B4** 33 55 S 151 16 E
Cooksville, Trto. **20 E7** 43 35N 79 38W
Cooper →, Phil. **24 B4** 39 57N 75 6W
Copacabana, Rio J. .. **31 B2** 22 58 S 43 11W
Copenhagen =
København, Købn. .. **2 D9** 55 40N 12 26 E
Copiague, N.Y. **23 D8** 40 39N 73 23W
Coral Hills, Wash. **25 D8** 38 51N 76 55W
Corbeil-Essonnes, Paris **5 D4** 48 36N 2 29 E
Corbets Tey, Lon. .... **4 B6** 51 32N 0 15 E
Corbiglia, Tori. ...... **9 B1** 45 3N 7 29 E
Corcovado, Rio J. ... **31 B2** 22 57 S 43 12W
Cordon, Paris .... **5 B5** 48 39N 2 41 E
Córdova, Tori. ...... **9 B3** 45 5N 7 48 E
Cordovil, Rio J. ..... **31 A2** 22 49 S 43 18W
Cormano, Mil. ...... **9 D6** 45 32N 9 10 E
Cormeilles-en-Parisis,
Paris .... **5 B3** 48 58N 2 11 E
Cornaredo, Mil. ..... **9 D5** 45 30N 9 1 E
Cornaya →, St-Pet. .. **11 B5** 59 53N 30 35 E
Cornellà, Barc. ...... **8 D5** 41 21N 2 4 E
Cornwells Heights, Phil. **24 A5** 40 4N 74 57W
Coróglio, Nápl. ...... **9 J12** 40 48N 14 10 E
Coronation Memorial,
Delhi .... **16 A2** 28 42N 77 12 E
Córsico, Mil. .... **9 E5** 45 25N 9 6 E
Corte Madera, S.F. ... **27 A1** 37 55N 122 30W
Corte Madera →, S.F. **27 A1** 37 55N 122 30W
Corviale, Rome ...... **9 F9** 41 51N 12 25 E
Cos Cob, N.Y. **23 A7** 41 1N 73 36W
Cossigny, Paris ...... **5 C6** 48 43N 2 40 E
Cossipure, Calc. ..... **16 E6** 22 37N 88 22 E
Cotao, Lisb. **8 F7** 38 45N 9 17W
Côte St.-Luc, Mtrl. ... **20 A4** 43 28N 73 39W
Cotorro, La Hab. **30 B3** 23 2N 82 15W
Cotunduba, I. de, Rio J. **31 B3** 22 57 S 43 8W
Coubert, Paris ...... **5 C6** 48 40N 2 41 E
Coubron, Paris ...... **5 B5** 48 54N 2 34 E
Coulsdon, Lon. **4 D4** 51 18N 0 7W
Countryside, Chic. ... **26 C1** 41 47N 87 52W
Courbevoie, Paris .... **5 B3** 48 53N 2 14 E
Courcouronnes, Paris **5 D4** 48 37N 2 24 E
Courdimanche, Paris .. **5 A2** 49 2N 2 1 E
Courelle, Paris ...... **5 C4** 48 43N 2 7 E
Couros →, S. Pau. ... **31 F6** 23 37 S 46 34W
Courtry, Paris .... **5 B5** 48 55N 2 35 E
Cousino, Parque, Stgo **30 J11** 33 27 S 70 40W
Cove Neck, N.Y. **23 B8** 40 52N 73 29W
Cowley, Lon. **4 B2** 51 31N 0 28W
Coyoacan, Méx. **29 B3** 19 21N 99 9W
Coyote Cr. →, S.F. .. **27 B4** 37 28N 122 4W
Coyote Hills Regional
Park, S.F. **27 C4** 37 32N 122 7W
Coyote Hills Slough,
S.F. **27 C4** 37 33N 122 7W
Coyote Pt., S.F. **27 B4** 37 35N 122 18W
Coyote Ridge, S.F. ... **27 A1** 37 51N 122 33W
Craighall Park, Jobg. .. **18 E9** 26 7 S 28 1 E
Crane →, Lon. **4 C2** 51 29N 0 29W
Cranford, Lon. **4 C2** 51 29N 0 24W
Cranford, N.Y. **22 D3** 40 39N 74 19W
Cranham, Lon. ...... **4 B6** 51 33N 0 16 E
Cray →, Lon. .... **4 C5** 51 28N 0 8 E
Crayford, Lon. ...... **4 C6** 51 27N 0 11 E
Creekmouth, Lon. .... **4 B5** 51 30N 0 6 E
Crerskill, N.Y. **22 B5** 40 56N 73 57W
Crescenzago, Mil. ... **9 D6** 45 30N 9 14 E
Crespières, Paris .... **5 B1** 48 52N 1 55 E
Cressely, Paris ...... **5 C2** 48 44N 2 4 E
Cresslawn, Jobg. .... **18 E10** 26 6 S 28 13 E
Crestwood, Chic. **26 D2** 41 38N 87 43W
Creteil, Paris .... **5 C4** 48 48N 2 27 E
Cricklewood, Lon. ... **4 B3** 51 33N 0 13W
Crispano, Nápl. ..... **9 H12** 40 57N 14 17 E
Cristo Redebro,
Monumento do,
Rio J. .... **31 B2** 22 56 S 43 12W
Crockenhill, Lon. .... **4 C5** 51 22N 0 9 E
Croissy-Beaubourg,
Paris .... **5 C5** 48 49N 2 39 E
Croissy-sur-Seine, Paris **5 B2** 48 50N 2 9 E
Cronenberg, Ruhr .... **6 C7** 51 11N 7 9 E
Crosby, Jobg. .... **18 F8** 26 11 S 27 59 E
Crosne, Paris .... **5 C4** 48 43N 2 27 E
Cross I., Bomb. ...... **16 H8** 18 56N 72 51 E
Crouch End, Lon. **4 B4** 51 34N 0 7W
Croud →, Paris ..... **5 B4** 48 57N 2 24 E
Crown Gardens, Jobg. **18 F9** 26 15 S 28 0 E
Crown Mines, Jobg. .. **18 F9** 26 12 S 27 57 E
Crown Village, N.Y. .. **23 C4** 40 40N 73 26W
Crows Nest, Syd. .... **19 A4** 33 49 S 151 12 E
Croxley Green, Lon. .. **4 B2** 51 39N 0 26W
Croydon, Lon. **4 C4** 51 22N 0 5W
Croydon, Melb. ..... **19 E8** 37 48 S 145 16 E
Croydon, N.Y. **24 A5** 40 5N 74 54W
Croydon North, Melb. **19 E8** 37 46 S 145 16 E
Cruz de Pau, Lisb. ... **8 G8** 38 37N 9 9W
Crystal Palace, Lon. .. **4 C4** 51 25N 0 4W
Crystal Springs, S.F. .. **27 C2** 37 31N 122 20W
Csepel, Bud. .... **10 K13** 47 25N 19 4 E
Csepelsziget, Bud. ... **10 K13** 47 25N 19 4 E
Csillaghegy, Bud. .... **10 J13** 47 35N 19 2 E
Csillagtelep, Bud. .... **10 K13** 47 25N 19 4 E
Cski-hegyek, Bud. ... **10 K12** 47 30N 18 57 E
Csömör, Bud. .... **10 J14** 47 33N 19 14 E

Cuajimalpa, Méx. **29 B2** 19 21N 99 17W
Cuatro Vientos, Mdrd. **8 B2** 40 22N 3 47W
Cuautepec de Madero,
Méx. **29 A3** 19 32N 99 8W
Cuautepec El Alto,
Méx. **29 A3** 19 33N 99 7W
Cuautzin, Cerro, Méx. **29 D3** 19 10N 99 4W
Cubao, Manila ...... **15 D4** 14 37N 121 3 E
Cubas →, S. Pau. .... **31 D6** 23 28 S 46 31W
Cubuklu, Ist. .... **17 A3** 41 5N 29 4 E
Cudham, Lon. .... **4 D5** 51 19N 0 4 E
Cuffley, Lon. **4 A4** 51 42N 0 6W
Cuicuilco, Pirámido de,
Méx. **29 C2** 19 17N 99 10W
Culembeeck, Jobg. ... **18 E7** 26 9 S 27 49 E
Culiculi, Manila ..... **15 D4** 14 33N 121 0 E
Cull Creek, S.F. **27 B4** 37 45N 122 2W
Culver City, L.A. **28 B2** 34 1N 118 24W
Culverstone Green,
Lon. .... **4 C7** 51 20N 0 20 E
Cumbre El Tabo, Car. **30 D5** 10 33N 66 56W
Cumbres de Vallecas,
Mdrd. **8 B3** 40 20N 3 33W
Cunhas, S. Pau. ..... **31 E7** 23 34 S 46 23W
Cupecé, S. Pau. ..... **31 E5** 23 39 S 46 40W
Cupece →, S. Pau. .. **31 E6** 23 37 S 46 42W
Curtis B., Balt. **25 B3** 39 12N 76 34W
Curtis Cr. →, Balt. .. **25 B3** 39 12N 76 34W
Cusago, Mil. .... **9 E5** 45 26N 9 1 E
Cusano Milanese, Mil. **9 D6** 45 33N 9 11 E
Çuvuşabaşi →, Ist. .. **17 A2** 40 58N 28 51 E
Çuvuşabaşi →, Ist. .. **18 F9** 26 10 S 28 6 E
Cyrildene, Jobg. ..... **18 F9** 26 10 S 28 6 E
Czernrakow, Wsaw. .. **10 E7** 52 11N 21 3 E
Czyste, Wsaw. ...... **10 E6** 52 13N 20 57 E

D

Da Yunhe →, Tianj. .. **14 D5** 39 19N 117 10 E
Dabizhuang, Tianj. ... **14 B2** 50 8N 14 29 E
Ďáblice, Pra. .... **12 G8** 37 33N 127 2 E
Dabsibri, Sŏul ...... **14 J11** 31 17N 121 24 E
Dachau, Shang. ..... **14 J11** 31 17N 121 24 E
Dachau, Mün. .... **7 F9** 48 15N 11 27 E
Dachau-Ost, Mün. ... **7 F9** 48 15N 11 27 E
Dachauer Moos, Mün. **7 F9** 48 14N 11 27 E
Daebang, Sŏul ...... **12 G7** 37 30N 126 55 E
Daechi, Sŏul .... **12 G8** 37 30N 127 2 E
Dagenham, Lon. ..... **4 B5** 51 32N 0 8 E
Dagfling, Mün. ...... **7 G10** 48 8N 11 39 E
Dahirpur, Delhi ..... **16 A2** 28 43N 77 11 E
Dahlem, Berl. .... **7 B2** 52 27N 13 16 E
Dahlerau, Ruhr ...... **6 C5** 51 13N 7 18 E
Dahlwitz-Hoppegarten,
Berl. .... **7 A5** 52 30N 13 41 E
Dahongmen, Beij. ... **14 C3** 39 48N 116 21 E
Daiman, Tōkyō ...... **13 A3** 35 53N 139 44 E
Daitō, Ōsaka .... **12 B4** 34 42N 135 38 E
Dajiaoting, Beij. ..... **14 B3** 39 50N 116 27 E
Dajingcun, Beij. ..... **14 B2** 39 50N 116 13 E
Dakhnoye, St-Pet. ... **11 C5** 59 49N 30 15 E
Dalar, Bomb. .... **16 G7** 19 0N 72 49 E
Dalejsky →, Pra. .... **10 B2** 50 2N 14 24 E
Dalhia, Gzh. .... **14 G7** 23 2N 113 6 E
Dallgow, Berl. ...... **7 A1** 52 32N 13 5 E
Dalston, Lon. **4 B4** 51 32N 0 4W
Dalview, Jobg. ...... **18 F11** 26 14 S 28 20 E
Daly City, S.F. **27 B2** 37 42N 122 27W
Damaia, Lisb. **8 F7** 38 44N 9 12W
Dämeritzsee, Berl. ... **7 B5** 52 34N 13 43 E
Damiette, Paris ...... **5 C2** 48 41N 2 7 E
Dampierre, Paris ..... **5 C1** 48 42N 1 59 E
Dan Neramit, Bangk. **15 B2** 13 48N 100 34 E
Dan Ryan Woods, Chic. **26 C2** 41 44N 87 40W
Dandenong, Mt., Melb. **19 E9** 37 49 S 145 21 E
Danforth, Trto. **20 D9** 43 43N 79 16W
Daniels, Balt. **25 B2** 39 19N 76 46W
Danvers, Bost. **21 B4** 42 34N 70 56W
Dapharpur, Calc. .... **16 E5** 22 38N 88 14 E
Darangan, Manila ... **15 E5** 14 29N 121 10 E
Darave, Bomb. ...... **16 G9** 19 1N 73 1 E
Darby, Phil. **24 B3** 39 55N 75 15W
Darby Cr. →, Phil. ... **24 B3** 39 50N 75 19W
Darent →, Lon. ..... **4 C6** 51 21N 0 12 E
Darling, Paris **24 B3** 39 54N 75 28W
Darlington Corners,
Phil. .... **4 C6** 51 30N 0 13 E
Dartford, Lon. ...... **16 E5** 22 31N 88 12 E
Dashi, Gzh. **24 B3** 39 55N 75 34W
Dashimae, Tōkyō .... **13 B3** 35 46N 139 44 E
Datteln, Ruhr .... **6 A6** 51 39N 7 20 E
Datteln-Hamm Kanal,
Ruhr .... **6 A6** 51 38N 7 24 E
Datun, Beij. .... **14 A3** 40 0N 116 23 E
Dauko, Calc. .... **16 E5** 22 31N 88 12 E
Daulatpur, Delhi .... **16 A1** 28 44N 77 6 E
Davenport, Bost. **21 B4** 42 33N 70 54W
Daveyton, Jobg. ..... **18 E11** 26 9 S 28 24 E
Davidkovo, Mos. .... **11 E8** 55 43N 37 29 E
David's I., N.Y. **23 B6** 40 53N 73 46W
Davron, Paris .... **5 B1** 48 52N 1 56 E
Davudiyeh, Tehr. .... **17 C5** 35 47N 51 26 E
Dawidy, Wsaw. ..... **10 F7** 52 6N 21 2 E
Dayap, Manila ...... **15 D4** 14 35N 121 4 E
Dayuange, Gzh. ..... **14 F7** 23 11N 113 7 E
Dead Run →, Balt. .. **25 B2** 39 18N 76 41W
Dee Why, Syd. ...... **19 A4** 33 46 S 151 17 E
Deer Park, N.Y. **23 C9** 40 46N 73 19W
Degermossa, Hels. ... **3 B6** 60 17N 25 12 E
Deguninno, Mos. .... **11 D9** 55 52N 37 33 E
Deisenhofen, Mün. ... **7 G10** 48 0N 11 35 E
Dejvice, Pra. .... **10 B2** 50 6N 14 24 E
Dekabristov →,
St-Pet. .... **11 B3** 59 56N 30 15 E
Del Viso, B.A. .... **32 A2** 34 27 S 58 47W
Delanco, Phil. **24 A5** 40 3N 74 57W
Delaware →, Phil. ... **24 A5** 40 1N 75 0W
Delbruch, Ruhr ...... **6 B4** 51 22N 7 0 E
Delhi, Delhi .... **16 B2** 28 39N 77 13 E
Delhi Cantonment,
Delhi .... **16 B1** 28 35N 77 7 E
Delhi Univ., Delhi ... **16 A2** 28 41N 77 12 E
Dellwig, Ruhr .... **6 A3** 51 29N 6 55 E
Delran, Phil. **24 A5** 40 1N 74 57W
Delville, Ruhr .... **6 B4** 51 20N 7 4 E
Demarest, N.Y. **22 B5** 40 57N 73 57W
Denham, Lon. **4 B2** 51 34N 0 30W
Denham Green, Lon. .. **4 B2** 51 34N 0 30W
Denia, N.Y. **23 C6** 40 45N 73 48W
Denontia Park, Trto. .. **20 D9** 43 41N 79 16W
Denville, N.Y. **22 B2** 40 53N 74 28W
Deodoro, Rio J. ..... **31 B1** 22 51 S 43 22W
Depgsu Palace, Sŏul .. **12 G7** 37 34N 126 58 E
Deptford, Lon. **4 C4** 51 28N 0 2W
Der Sarai, Delhi ..... **16 B2** 28 33N 77 10 E
Des Plaines, Chic. ... **26 B1** 42 2N 87 54W
Des Plaines →, Chic. **26 B1** 41 48N 87 49W
Deshengmen, Beij. ... **14 B3** 39 56N 116 21 E

Desierto de los Leones,
Parque Nacional,
Méx. **29 C2** 19 18N 99 18W
Desio, Mil. .... **9 D6** 45 36N 9 12 E
Deuil-la-Barre, Paris .. **5 B3** 48 58N 2 19 E
Deulpur, Calc. ...... **16 E5** 22 36N 88 11 E
Deungchon, Sŏul .... **12 G7** 37 33N 126 52 E
Deutsch-Wagram, Wien **10 G11** 48 17N 16 33 E
Deutsche Oper, Berl. .. **7 A2** 52 30N 13 19 E
Deutscher Museum,
Mün. .... **7 G10** 48 7N 11 35 E
Deux-Montagnes, Mtrl. **20 A2** 43 32N 73 53W
Deux Montagnes, L.
des, Mtrl. **20 B2** 43 27N 73 59W
Devault, Phil. **24 A1** 40 4N 75 32W
Dháfni, Ath. .... **8 J11** 37 55N 23 44 E
Dhakuria, Calc. ..... **16 E6** 22 30N 88 22 E
Dhakuria L., Calc. ... **16 E6** 22 30N 88 21 E
Dhamarakia, Ath. .... **8 J10** 37 58N 23 39 E
Dharava, Bomb. ..... **16 G8** 19 1N 72 51 E
Dhrapersón, Ath. .... **8 J10** 37 56N 23 37 E
Dhutumkhar, Bomb. .. **16 H9** 18 54N 73 1 E
Dia Deva, Bomb. .... **16 H8** 18 57N 72 53 E
Diadema, S. Pau. .... **31 F6** 23 41 S 46 37W
Diamante, B.A. ...... **32 C4** 34 41 S 58 25W
Diamond Cr. →,
Melb. .... **19 E7** 37 44 S 145 9 E
Diamond Creek, Melb. **19 E7** 37 40 S 145 10 E
Didaowai, Tianj. ..... **14 E6** 39 8N 117 12 E
Diepensiepen, Ruhr .. **6 C3** 51 14N 6 58 E
Diepkloof, Jobg. ..... **18 F8** 26 14 S 27 57 E
Diessem, Ruhr ...... **6 C1** 51 19N 6 34 E
Difficult Run →,
Wash. **25 D6** 38 55N 77 18W
Digla, W. →, El Qâ. .. **18 F9** 26 16 S 28 9 E
Digra, Calc. .... **16 D5** 22 49N 88 19 E
Dikemark, Oslo ..... **2 C2** 59 48N 10 22 E
Dilerpur, Calc. ...... **16 C5** 22 51N 88 10 E
Dinslaken, Ruhr ..... **6 A3** 51 34N 6 44 E
Dinslakener Bruch,
Ruhr .... **6 A2** 51 34N 6 44 E
Dinwiddie, Jobg. .... **18 F9** 26 16 S 28 9 E
Diósd, Bud. .... **10 K12** 47 24N 18 57 E
Dirstinmaning, Mün. . **7 F10** 48 13N 11 38 E
Disappointment, Mt.,
L.A. **28 A4** 34 15N 118 7W
Discovery, Jobg. .... **18 E8** 26 8 S 27 54 E
Distein, Ruhr .... **6 A4** 51 36N 7 0 E
District Heights, Wash. **25 D8** 38 51N 76 53W
Ditan Gongyuan, Beij. **14 B3** 39 56N 116 23 E
Dix Hills, N.Y. **23 C8** 40 48N 73 21W
Dixmoor, Chic. **26 D2** 41 37N 87 40W
Diyala →, Bagd. .... **17 F9** 33 13N 44 30 E
Djakarta =
Jak. .... **15 H10** 6 9 S 106 52 E
Djursholm, Stock. ... **3 D11** 59 24N 18 5 E
Do Bong, Sŏul ...... **12 G8** 37 39N 127 1 E
Dobbs, N.Y. **23 A5** 41 1N 73 52W
Döberitz, Berl. ...... **7 A1** 52 32N 13 3 E
Döbling, Wien ...... **10 G10** 48 14N 16 20 E
Dobong, Sŏul .... **12 G8** 37 39N 127 1 E
Dobong San, Sŏul ... **12 F8** 37 40N 127 0 E
Dobrowa, Wsaw. .... **10 E6** 52 19N 20 52 E
Doddinghurst, Lon. .. **4 A6** 51 40N 0 18 E
Dodger Stadium, L.A. **28 B3** 34 4N 118 14W
Dogan, Sŏul .... **12 H7** 37 28N 126 54 E
Doirone, Tori. ...... **9 B2** 45 3N 7 32 E
Dōjō, Ōsaka .... **12 A2** 34 51N 135 14 E
Dōjō, Tōkyō .... **13 A2** 35 51N 139 37 E
Dollard-des-Ormeaux,
Mtrl. **20 B3** 43 29N 73 49W
Dollis Hill, Lon. **4 B3** 51 33N 0 13W
Dolni, Pra. .... **10 B3** 50 3N 14 33 E
Dolni Chabry, Pra. ... **10 B2** 50 8N 14 26 E
Dolni Počernice, Pra. **10 B3** 50 5N 14 36 E
Dolton, Chic. **26 D3** 41 37N 87 35W
Domont, Paris ...... **5 A3** 49 1N 2 20 E
Don Bosco, B.A. ..... **32 C5** 34 42 S 58 17W
Don Mills, Trto. **20 D8** 43 44N 79 21W
Don Pedro II, Parque,
S. Pau. .... **31 E6** 23 33 S 46 36W
Don Torcuato, B.A. .. **32 A3** 34 29 S 58 38W
Donau →, Bud. ..... **10 J13** 47 33N 19 4 E
Donau-Oder Kanal,
Wien .... **10 G11** 48 12N 16 32 E
Donaufeld, Wien .... **10 G10** 48 15N 16 24 E
Donaukanal, Wien ... **10 G10** 48 13N 16 21 E
Donaupark, Wien .... **10 G10** 48 14N 16 24 E
Donaustadt, Wien ... **10 G10** 48 13N 16 29 E
Doncaster, Melb. .... **19 E7** 37 47 S 145 8 E
Doncaster East, Melb. **19 E7** 37 46 S 145 10 E
Dong Dae Mun, Sŏul **12 G8** 37 34N 127 2 E
Dong Jag, Sŏul ..... **12 G7** 37 30N 126 56 E
Dongala Forest
Reserve, Melb. .... **19 F9** 37 50 S 145 20 E
Dongan Hills, N.Y. ... **22 D4** 40 35N 74 5W
Dongbinggo, Sŏul ... **12 G7** 37 31N 126 58 E
Dongcheng, Beij. .... **14 B3** 39 57N 116 23 E
Dongfeng Nongchang,
Beij. .... **14 B3** 39 57N 116 28 E
Dongjiao, Gzh. ...... **14 F8** 23 5N 113 12 E
Dongguzi, Tianj. ..... **14 E6** 39 5N 117 14 E
Dongkou, Shang. .... **14 J12** 31 17N 121 33 E
Dongmenwai, Tianj. . **14 E6** 39 8N 117 11 E
Dongri, Bomb. ...... **16 H8** 18 53N 72 57 E
Dongwuyuan, Beij. .. **14 B3** 39 55N 116 18 E
Dongzhimen, Beij. ... **14 B3** 39 57N 116 26 E
Donvale, Melb. ...... **19 E8** 37 47 S 145 11 E
Doonside, Syd. ...... **19 A2** 33 46 S 150 51 E
Doornfontein, Jobg. .. **18 F9** 26 11 S 28 3 E
Dóra, Bagd. .... **17 F8** 33 16N 44 22 E
Dora Riparia →, Tori. **9 B2** 45 4N 7 38 E
Dorchester, Bost. **21 D3** 42 17N 71 3W
Dorchester B., Bost. .. **21 D3** 42 18N 71 1W
Dorchester Heights Nat.
Hist. Site, Bost. ... **21 D3** 42 19N 71 2W
Dorion, Mtrl. **20 B1** 43 23N 74 1W
Dornach, Mün. ...... **7 G11** 48 9N 11 41 E
Dornbach, Wien ..... **10 G9** 48 13N 16 18 E
Dorney Run →, Balt. **25 B1** 39 11N 76 47W
Dorstfeld, Ruhr ..... **6 A6** 51 30N 7 24 E
Dortmund, Ruhr ..... **6 A6** 51 30N 7 28 E
Dorval, Mtrl. **20 B3** 43 26N 73 45W
Dorval, Aéroport de,
Mtrl. **20 B3** 43 29N 73 49W
Dos Rios, Méx. **29 B1** 19 22N 99 20W
Doshan Tappeh
Airport, Tehr. ..... **17 C5** 35 41N 51 28 E
Dotmund-Ems Kanal,
Ruhr .... **6 A6** 51 35N 7 24 E
Double B., Syd. ..... **19 B4** 33 52 S 151 15 E
Douglas Park, Chic. .. **26 B2** 41 51N 87 42W
Douglaston, N.Y. **23 C6** 40 46N 73 44W
Dove Elbe →, Hbg. .. **7 E8** 53 28N 10 7 E
Dover Heights, Syd. .. **19 B4** 33 52 S 151 16 E
Dover Plains, Bost. ... **21 D4** 42 14N 71 16W
Dowlatābâd, Tehr. ... **17 D5** 35 38N 51 27 E
Downe, Lon. .... **4 D5** 51 19N 0 3 E
Downey, L.A. **28 C4** 33 56N 118 9W
Downsview, Trto. **20 D7** 43 43N 79 30W
Downsview Dells Park,
Trto. **20 D7** 43 44N 79 30W
Dracut, Bost. **21 A2** 42 40N 71 17W
Dragør, Købn. ...... **2 E10** 55 35N 12 38 E

Drancy, Paris .... **5 B4** 48 55N 2 26 E
Dranesville, Wash. ... **25 C5** 39 0N 77 20W
Draveil, Paris .... **5 C4** 48 41N 2 23 E
Drayton Green, Lon. . **4 B3** 51 30N 0 19W
Dreilinden, Berl. .... **7 B2** 52 24N 13 10 E
Dresher, Phil. **24 A4** 40 9N 75 9W
Drewnica, Wsaw. .... **10 E7** 52 18N 21 6 E
Drexel Hill, Phil. **24 B3** 39 56N 75 18W
Drexel Inst. of
Technology, Phil. .. **24 B3** 39 57N 75 11W
Drigh Road, Kar. .... **17 G11** 24 52N 67 7 E
Drogden, Købn. ..... **2 E11** 55 37N 12 42 E
Drottningholm, Stock. **3 E10** 59 19N 17 53 E
Druento, Tori. ...... **9 B2** 45 8N 7 34 E
Druid Hill Park, Balt. **25 B3** 39 20N 76 38W
Druid Lake, Balt. **25 B3** 39 19N 76 38W
Drummoyne, Syd. ... **19 B3** 33 51 S 151 8 E
Družhba, Mos. ...... **11 D10** 55 52N 37 44 E
Duarte, L.A. **28 B5** 34 8N 117 57W
Dubeč, Pra. .... **10 B3** 50 4N 14 35 E
Dubi Bheri, Calc. .... **16 C5** 22 52N 88 16 E
Duffryn Mawr, Phil. .. **24 A2** 40 2N 75 27W
Dugnano, Mil. ...... **9 D6** 45 33N 9 11 E
Dugny, Paris .... **5 B4** 48 57N 2 24 E
Duiha, Calc. .... **16 E5** 22 34N 88 15 E
Duisburg, Ruhr ..... **6 B2** 51 26N 6 45 E
Dulāb, Tehr. .... **17 D5** 35 39N 51 27 E
Dulwichtown, Phil. .. **24 B1** 39 54N 75 35W
Dum Dum, Calc. .... **16 E6** 22 38N 88 25 E
Dum Dum Int. Airport,
Calc. .... **16 E6** 22 38N 88 26 E
Dumbarton Pt., S.F. .. **27 D4** 37 29N 122 6W
Dumjor, Calc. .... **16 E5** 22 37N 88 13 E
Dumont, N.Y. **22 B5** 40 56N 73 59W
Dümpten, Ruhr ..... **6 B3** 51 27N 6 54 E
Duna →, Bud. ...... **10 J13** 47 33N 19 4 E
Dunbarton, Trto. **20 C10** 43 50N 79 6W
Dundalk, Balt. **25 B3** 39 17N 76 31W
Dundas, Syd. .... **19 A3** 33 47 S 151 3 E
Dunearn, Sing. ...... **15 G7** 1 19N 103 49 E
Dunellen, N.Y. **22 D2** 40 35N 74 26W
Dunn Loring, Wash. . **25 D6** 38 54N 77 13W
Dunning, Chic. **26 B2** 41 56N 87 48W
Dunton Green, Lon. .. **4 D6** 51 17N 0 11 E
Dunvegan, Jobg. .... **18 E9** 26 9 S 28 8 E
Duomo, Mil. .... **9 H12** 40 51N 14 15 E
Duomo, Nápl. .... **9 B3** 45 4N 7 45 E
Duomo, Tori. .... **9 B3** 45 4N 7 45 E
Duque de Caxias, Rio J. **31 A2** 22 46 S 43 18W
Durban Roodepoort
Deep Gold Mines,
Jobg. .... **18 F8** 26 11 S 27 52 E
Durchholz, Ruhr ..... **6 B5** 51 23N 7 18 E
Düssel →, Ruhr ..... **6 C3** 51 13N 6 58 E
Düsseldorf, Ruhr .... **6 C2** 51 13N 6 46 E
Düsseldorf-Lohausen,
Flughafen, Ruhr ... **6 C2** 51 17N 6 45 E
Duvensstedt, Hbg. ... **7 C8** 53 42N 10 6 E
Duvenstedter Brook,
Hbg. .... **7 C8** 53 43N 10 8 E
Duvernay, Mtrl. **20 A3** 43 35N 73 40W
Dyakovo, Mos. ...... **11 E9** 55 40N 37 39 E
Dyviksudd, Stock. ... **3 E13** 59 11N 18 23 E
Dzerzhinsky, Mos. ... **11 F11** 55 38N 37 51 E
Dzerzhinsky, Mos. ... **11 E9** 55 47N 37 37 E
Dzerzhinskiy Park, Mos. **11 E9** 55 50N 37 37 E

E

Eagle Rock, L.A. .... **28 B3** 34 8N 118 12 E
Ealing, Lon. **4 B3** 51 30N 0 18W
Earls Court, Lon. **4 C3** 51 29N 0 11W
Earlsfield, Lon. **4 C3** 51 26N 0 10W
Earlwood, Syd. ...... **19 B3** 33 55 S 151 8 E
East Acton, Bost. **21 C1** 42 28N 71 23W
East Acton, Lon. **4 B3** 51 30N 0 14W
East Arlington, Wash. **25 D7** 38 51N 77 4W
East Atlantic Beach,
N.Y. **23 D6** 40 35N 73 43W
East B., N.Y. **23 D7** 40 38N 73 32W
East Barnet, Lon. **4 C2** 51 26N 0 28W
East Bedfont, Lon. ... **4 C2** 51 26N 0 24W
East Billerica, Bost. .. **21 A3** 42 33N 71 15W
East Boston, Bost. ... **21 C3** 42 22N 71 1W
East Braintree, Bost. . **21 D4** 42 13N 70 58W
East Chicago, Chic. .. **26 D4** 41 38N 87 26W
East Dulwich, Lon. ... **4 C4** 51 27N 0 4W
East Elmhurst, N.Y. .. **23 C5** 40 45N 73 52W
East Farmingdale, N.Y. **23 C8** 40 44N 73 24W
East Finchley, Lon. .. **4 B3** 51 35N 0 10W
East Half Hollow Hills,
N.Y. **23 C9** 40 47N 73 19W
East Ham, Lon. ..... **4 B5** 51 32N 0 3 E
East Hanover, N.Y. .. **22 C2** 40 49N 74 21W
East Hills, N.Y. **23 C7** 40 47N 73 38W
East Hills, N.Y. ...... **19 B2** 33 57 S 150 59 E
East Holliston, Bost. . **21 D1** 42 12N 71 26W
East Horsley, Lon. ... **4 D2** 51 16N 0 26W
East Humber →, Trto. **20 D7** 43 47N 79 35W
East Huntington, N.Y. **23 B8** 40 52 S 73 24W
East Lamma Channel,
H.K. .... **12 E5** 22 13N 114 9 E
East Lexington, Bost. **21 C2** 42 27N 71 12W
East Los Angeles, L.A. **28 B3** 34 1N 118 10 E
East Meadow, N.Y. .. **23 C7** 40 43N 73 33W
East Molesey, Lon. ... **4 C2** 51 24N 0 21W
East New York, N.Y. . **23 C5** 40 40N 73 53W
East Newark, N.Y. ... **22 C4** 40 45N 74 9W
East Northport, N.Y. . **23 B8** 40 53N 73 18W
East Norwich, N.Y. .. **23 B7** 40 50N 73 31W
East Orange, N.Y. ... **22 C3** 40 45N 74 13W
East Palo Alto, S.F. .. **27 D4** 37 28N 122 8W
East Paterson, N.Y. .. **22 B4** 40 53N 74 8W
East Pines, Wash. ... **25 D8** 38 57N 76 54W
East Point, Bost. **21 C4** 42 25N 70 54W
East Potomac Park,
Wash. **25 D7** 38 52N 77 1W
East Richmond, S.F. .. **27 A3** 37 56N 122 19W
East Ringwood, Melb. **19 E8** 37 48 S 145 15 E
East River, N.Y. **23 C5** 40 44N 73 58W
East Rockaway, N.Y. **22 D6** 40 38N 73 40W
East Rutherford, N.Y. **22 B4** 40 50N 74 5W
East Sheen, Lon. **4 C3** 51 27N 0 16W
East View Garden,
Sing. .... **15 F8** 1 20N 103 57 E
East Weymouth, Bost. **21 D4** 42 13N 70 55W
East Wickham, Lon. .. **4 C5** 51 28N 0 8 E
East Williston, N.Y. .. **23 C7** 40 45N 73 38W
Eastchester, N.Y. **23 B6** 40 57N 73 49W
Eastchester B., N.Y. . **23 B6** 40 50N 73 47W
Eastcote, Lon. **4 B2** 51 34N 0 23W
Eastleigh, Jobg. ..... **18 E9** 26 7 S 28 8 E
Eastpoint, Bost. **21 C4** 42 22N 70 57W
Eastwood, Syd. ..... **19 A3** 33 47 S 151 4 E
Eatons Neck Pt., N.Y. **23 B8** 40 57N 73 24W
Eaubonne, Paris ..... **5 B3** 48 59N 2 16 E
Ebara, Tōkyō .... **13 C3** 35 35N 139 42 E
Ebisu, Tōkyō .... **13 C3** 35 38N 139 42 E
Ebute-Ikorodu, Lagos **18 A2** 6 35N 3 20 E

Gerthe 37

Ebute-Metta, *Lagos* **18 B2** 6 28N 7 23 E
Ecatepec de Morelos, *Méx.* **29 A3** 19 35N 99 2W
Echo B., *N.Y.* **23 B6** 40 54N 73 45W
Echo Mt., *L.A.* **28 A4** 34 12N 118 8W
Écouen, *Paris* **5 A4** 49 1N 2 22 E
Ecquevilly, *Paris* **5 B1** 48 57N 1 55 E
Ecser, *Bud.* **10 K14** 47 26N 19 19 E
Eda, *Tōkyō* **13 C2** 35 33N 139 33 E
Eddington, *Phil.* **24 A5** 40 5N 74 55W
Eddystone, *Phil.* **24 B2** 39 51N 75 20W
Eden, *Rio J.* **31 A1** 22 47 S 43 23W
Edendale, *Jobg.* **18 E9** 26 8 S 28 9 E
Edenvale, *Jobg.* **18 E9** 26 8 S 28 9 E
Edgars Cr. →, *Melb.* **19 E6** 37 43 S 144 58 E
Edge Hill, *Phil.* **24 A4** 40 7N 75 9W
Edgeley, *Trto.* **20 D7** 43 47N 79 31W
Edgemar, *S.F.* **27 C2** 37 39N 122 29W
Edgemere, *Balt.* **25 B4** 39 14N 76 26W
Edgemont, *Phil.* **24 B2** 39 58N 75 26W
Edgewater Park, *Phil.* **24 A5** 40 3N 74 54W
Edgware, *Lon.* **4 B3** 51 36N 0 15W
Edison, *N.Y.* **22 D2** 40 31N 74 23W
Edison Park, *Chic.* **26 A2** 42 1N 87 48W
Edleen, *Jobg.* **18 E10** 26 5 S 28 12 E
Edmondston, *Wash.* **25 D8** 38 56N 76 54W
Edo →, *Tōkyō* **13 C4** 35 38N 139 52 E
Edogawa, *Tōkyō* **13 B4** 35 43N 139 52 E
Edsberg, *Stock.* **3 D10** 59 26N 17 57 E
Edwards L., *Melb.* **19 E6** 37 42 S 144 59 E
Eestiluoto, *Hels.* **3 C6** 60 7N 25 13 E
Egawa, *Tōkyō* **13 D4** 35 22N 139 54 E
Egenbüttel, *Hbg.* **7 D7** 53 39N 9 51 E
Eggerscheidt, *Ruhr* **6 C3** 51 19N 6 53 E
Egham, *Lon.* **4 C1** 51 25N 0 30W
Eiche, *Berl.* **7 A4** 52 33N 13 35 E
Eiche Sud, *Berl.* **7 A4** 52 33N 13 35 E
Eichlinghofen, *Ruhr* **6 B6** 51 29N 7 24 E
Eichwalde, *Berl.* **7 B4** 52 22N 13 37 E
Eidelstedt, *Hbg.* **7 D7** 53 36N 9 54 E
Eiffel, Tour, *Paris* **5 B3** 48 51N 2 17 E
Eigen, *Ruhr* **6 A3** 51 32N 6 56 E
Eilbek, *Hbg.* **7 D8** 53 34N 10 2 E
Eimsbüttel, *Hbg.* **7 D7** 53 34N 9 57 E
Eissendorf, *Hbg.* **7 E7** 53 27N 9 57 E
Ejby, *Købn.* **2 D9** 55 41N 12 24 E
Ejigbo, *Lagos* **18 A1** 6 33N 7 18 E
Ekeberg, *Oslo* **2 B4** 59 53N 10 46 E
Ekeby, *Stock.* **3 D8** 59 21N 17 35 E
Ekerö, *Stock.* **3 E9** 59 17N 17 46 E
Ekerön, *Stock.* **3 E9** 59 18N 17 41 E
Ekhtiyarieh, *Tehr.* **17 C5** 35 46N 51 28 E
Eklundshov, *Stock.* **3 E10** 59 11N 17 54 E
Eknäs, *Stock.* **3 E12** 59 18N 18 13 E
El 'Abbasiya, *El Qâ.* **18 C5** 30 3N 31 16 E
El Agustino, *Lima* **30 G8** 12 2 S 77 0W
El Alto, *Stgo* **30 J10** 33 29 S 70 42W
El Awkal, *El Qâ.* **18 C5** 30 2N 31 12 E
El Baragil, *El Qâ.* **18 C4** 30 4N 31 9 E
El Basâlîn, *El Qâ.* **18 D5** 29 58N 31 16 E
El Calvario, *La Hab.* **30 B3** 23 3N 82 19W
El Cano, *La Hab.* **30 B2** 23 2N 82 27W
El Caribe, *Car.* **30 D5** 10 36N 66 52W
El Carmen, *Stgo* **30 J10** 33 22 S 70 43W
El Cerrito, *S.F.* **27 A3** 37 54N 122 18W
El Cerro, *La Hab.* **30 B2** 23 6N 82 23W
El Cojo, Pta., *Car.* **30 D5** 10 36N 66 53W
El Cortijo, *Stgo* **30 J10** 33 22 S 70 42W
El Duqqi, *El Qâ.* **18 C5** 30 1N 31 12 E
El Gamâlîya, *El Qâ.* **18 C5** 30 2N 31 15 E
El Ghurîya, *El Qâ.* **18 C5** 30 2N 31 15 E
El Gîza, *El Qâ.* **18 C5** 30 0N 31 12 E
El Granada, *S.F.* **27 C2** 37 30N 122 27W
El Guarda Parres, *Méx.* **29 D2** 19 9N 99 11W
El Hatillo, *Car.* **30 E6** 10 25N 66 49W
El Khalîfa, *El Qâ.* **18 C5** 30 0N 31 15 E
El Kôm el Ahmar, *El Qâ.* **18 C5** 30 6N 31 10 E
El Ma'âdi, *El Qâ.* **18 D5** 29 57N 31 15 E
El Matarîya, *El Qâ.* **18 C5** 30 7N 31 18 E
El Monte, *L.A.* **28 B4** 34 3N 118 1W
El Muhît Idkû el Gharbî →, *El Qâ.* **18 C4** 30 6N 31 6 E
El Mûskî, *El Qâ.* **18 C5** 30 3N 31 15 E
El Palmar, *Car.* **30 D5** 10 36N 66 53W
El Palomar, *B.A.* **32 B3** 34 36 S 58 37W
El Pardo, *Mdrd.* **8 A2** 40 30N 3 46W
El Pedregal, *Car.* **30 D5** 10 30N 66 51W
El Pinar, *Car.* **30 E5** 10 28N 66 56W
El Plantio, *Mdrd.* **8 B1** 40 28N 3 51W
El Qâhira, *El Qâ.* **18 C5** 30 2N 31 13 E
El Qubba, *El Qâ.* **18 C5** 30 4N 31 16 E
El Recreo, *Car.* **30 E5** 10 29N 66 52W
El Reloj, *Méx.* **29 C3** 19 19N 99 9W
El Retiro, *Car.* **30 D5** 10 31N 66 54W
El Salto, *Stgo* **30 J11** 33 22 S 70 38W
El Segundo, *L.A.* **28 C2** 33 55N 118 24W
El Sereno, *L.A.* **28 B3** 34 6N 118 10 E
El Silencio, *Car.* **30 D5** 10 30N 66 55W
El Sobrante, *S.F.* **27 A3** 37 58N 122 17W
El Talar de Pacheco, *B.A.* **32 A3** 34 27 S 58 38W
El Talibîya, *El Qâ.* **18 D5** 29 59N 31 10 E
El Valle, *Car.* **30 E5** 10 29N 66 54W
El Vedado, *La Hab.* **30 B2** 23 8N 82 23W
El Vergel, *Méx.* **29 C3** 19 18N 99 5W
El Wâyli el Kubra, *El Qâ.* **18 C5** 30 5N 31 17 E
El Zamalik, *El Qâ.* **18 C5** 30 3N 31 12 E
Elam, *Phil.* **24 B1** 39 51N 75 32W
Élancourt, *Paris* **5 C1** 48 47N 1 57 E
Elandsfortein, *Jobg.* **18 E10** 26 9 S 28 13 E
Elbe →, *Hbg.* **7 D6** 53 32N 9 49 E
Elberfeld, *Ruhr* **6 C4** 51 15N 7 9 E
Elephanta Caves, *Bomb.* **16 H8** 18 57N 72 57 E
Elephanta I., *Bomb.* **16 H8** 18 57N 72 56 E
Elisenau, *Berl.* **7 A4** 52 38N 13 37 E
Elizabeth, *N.Y.* **22 D3** 40 39N 74 13W
Elkins Park, *Phil.* **24 A4** 40 4N 75 8W
Elkridge, *Balt.* **25 B2** 39 13N 76 42W
Ellboda, *Stock.* **3 D12** 59 24N 18 15 E
Eller, *Ruhr* **6 C3** 51 12N 6 51 E
Ellerbek, *Hbg.* **7 D7** 53 39N 9 52 E
Ellicott City, *Balt.* **25 B2** 39 15N 76 49W
Ellinghorst, *Ruhr* **6 A3** 51 33N 6 57 E
Ellinikón, *Ath.* **8 J11** 37 50N 23 45 E
Ellis I., *N.Y.* **22 C4** 40 41N 74 2W
Elm Park, *Lon.* **4 B6** 51 32N 0 12 E
Elmers End, *Lon.* **4 C4** 51 23N 0 2W
Elmhurst, *Chic.* **26 B1** 41 53N 87 55W
Elmhurst, *N.Y.* **23 C5** 40 44N 73 53W
Elmont, *N.Y.* **23 C6** 40 42N 73 42W
Elmstead, *Lon.* **4 C5** 51 24N 0 2 E
Elmwood, *Balt.* **25 A3** 39 20N 76 31W
Elmwood, *N.Y.* **23 B8** 40 51N 73 20W
Elmwood Park, *Chic.* **26 B2** 41 55N 87 48W
Elmwood Park, *N.Y.* **22 B4** 40 54N 74 7W
Elsburg, *Jobg.* **18 F10** 26 15 S 28 13 E
Elsburgspruit →, *Jobg.* **18 F10** 26 16 S 28 12 E
Elsmere, *Phil.* **24 C1** 39 44N 75 35W
Elspark, *Jobg.* **18 F10** 26 15 S 28 13 E
Elsternwick, *Melb.* **19 F7** 37 52 S 145 0 E
Eltham, *Lon.* **4 C5** 51 27N 0 3 E
Eltham, *Melb.* **19 E7** 37 42 S 145 9 E
Elthorn Heights, *Lon.* **4 B2** 51 31N 0 20W
Eltingrille, *N.Y.* **22 D4** 40 32N 74 9W
Elwood, *Melb.* **19 F6** 37 53 S 144 59 E
Élysée, *Paris* **5 B3** 48 52N 2 19 E
Embu, *S. Pau.* **31 E4** 23 38 S 46 50W
Embu-Mirim, *S. Pau.* **31 F5** 23 41 S 46 49W
Embu Mirim →, *S. Pau.* **31 F5** 23 43 S 46 47W
Emdeni, *Jobg.* **18 F7** 26 14 S 27 49 E
Émerainville, *Paris* **5 C5** 48 48N 2 37 E
Emerson, *N.Y.* **22 B4** 40 57N 74 2W
Emerson Park, *Lon.* **4 B6** 51 34N 0 13 E
Emeryville, *S.F.* **27 B3** 37 49N 122 17W
Eminonu, *Ist.* **17 A2** 41 0N 28 57 E
Emmarentia, *Jobg.* **18 E9** 26 9 S 28 0 E
Emperor's Palace, *Tōkyō* **13 B3** 35 40N 139 45 E
Empire State Building, *N.Y.* **22 C5** 40 44N 73 59W
Emscher →, *Ruhr* **6 A6** 51 30N 7 26 E
Emscher Bruch, *Ruhr* **6 A4** 51 33N 7 8 E
Emscher Zweigkanal, *Ruhr* **6 A4** 51 33N 7 9 E
Encantado, *Rio J.* **31 B2** 22 53 S 43 19W
Encino, *L.A.* **28 B2** 34 9N 118 28W
Encino Res., *L.A.* **28 B1** 34 8N 118 30W
Enebyberg, *Stock.* **3 D10** 59 25N 17 59 E
Enfield, *Lon.* **4 B4** 51 39N 0 4W
Enfield, *Phil.* **24 A3** 40 6N 75 11W
Enfield, *Syd.* **19 B3** 33 53 S 151 6 E
Enfield Chase, *Lon.* **4 A4** 51 40N 0 8W
Enfield Highway, *Lon.* **4 B4** 51 39N 0 2W
Enfield Lock, *Lon.* **4 A4** 51 40N 0 1W
Enfield Wash, *Lon.* **4 B4** 51 39N 0 2W
Eng Khong Gardens, *Sing.* **15 F7** 1 20N 103 46 E
Engenho, I. do, *Rio J.* **31 B3** 22 50 S 43 6W
Engenho Nôvo, *Rio J.* **31 B2** 22 53 S 43 17W
Engenho Velho, Sa. do, *Rio J.* **31 B1** 22 54 S 43 21W
Engenno do Mato, *Rio J.* **31 B3** 22 56 S 43 2W
Enghein-les-Bains, *Paris* **5 B3** 48 58N 2 18 E
Englewood, *Chic.* **26 C3** 41 46N 87 38W
Englewood, *N.Y.* **22 B5** 40 53N 73 58W
Englewood Cliffs, *N.Y.* **22 B5** 40 53N 73 59W
Englischer Garten, *Mün.* **7 G10** 48 9N 11 35 E
Enmore, *Syd.* **19 B4** 33 54 S 151 10 E
Ennepe →, *Ruhr* **6 C6** 51 17N 7 23 E
Ennepetal, *Ruhr* **6 C6** 51 17N 7 21 E
Ennepetalsp →, *Ruhr* **6 C6** 51 14N 7 24 E
Enskede, *Stock.* **3 E11** 59 17N 18 4 E
Entrevias, *Mdrd.* **8 B2** 40 22N 3 40W
Épiais-les-Louvres, *Paris* **5 A5** 49 1N 2 33 E
Epinay, *Paris* **5 B3** 48 57N 2 19 E
Epinay-sous-Sénart, *Paris* **5 C5** 48 41N 2 30 E
Epinay-sur-Orge, *Paris* **5 C3** 48 40N 2 19 E
Eppende, *Ruhr* **6 B4** 51 28N 7 9 E
Eppenhausen, *Ruhr* **6 B6** 51 22N 7 29 E
Epping, *Lon.* **4 A5** 51 41N 0 6 E
Epping, *Melb.* **19 D7** 37 39 S 145 1 E
Epping, *Syd.* **19 A3** 33 46 S 151 5 E
Epping Forest, *Lon.* **4 B5** 51 39N 0 2 E
Epsom, *Lon.* **4 D3** 51 19N 0 15W
Epsom Racecourse, *Lon.* **4 D3** 51 18N 0 15W
Éragny, *Paris* **5 A2** 49 1N 2 5 E
Ercolano, *Nápl.* **9 J13** 40 48N 14 21 E
Érd, *Bud.* **10 K12** 47 23N 18 56 E
Erdenheim, *Phil.* **24 A3** 40 5N 75 12W
Eregun, *Lagos* **18 A2** 6 35N 7 22 E
Erenköy, *Ist.* **17 B3** 40 58N 29 3 E
Ergal, *Paris* **5 C1** 48 47N 1 55 E
Erial, *Phil.* **24 C4** 39 46N 75 0W
Erith, *Lon.* **4 C6** 51 28N 0 11 E
Erkner, *Berl.* **7 B5** 52 25N 13 44 E
Erkrath, *Ruhr* **6 C3** 51 13N 6 54 E
Erlaa, *Wien* **10 H9** 48 9N 16 19 E
Erle, *Ruhr* **6 A4** 51 33N 7 4 E
Ermelino Matarazzo, *S. Pau.* **31 D7** 23 29 S 46 28W
Ermington, *Syd.* **19 A3** 33 48 S 151 4 E
Ermont, *Paris* **5 B3** 48 59N 2 15 E
Ersébet-Telep, *Bud.* **10 K14** 47 27N 19 10 E
Ershatou, *Gzh.* **14 G8** 23 6N 113 18 E
Erskineville, *Syd.* **19 B4** 33 54 S 151 12 E
Erstavik, *Stock.* **3 E12** 59 16N 18 14 E
Erstaviken, *Stock.* **3 E12** 59 16N 18 20 E
Erunkan, *Lagos* **18 A2** 6 36N 7 23 E
Eschenried, *Mün.* **7 F9** 48 13N 11 24 E
Esenler, *Ist.* **17 A2** 41 1N 28 52 E
Esher, *Lon.* **4 C2** 51 22N 0 20W
Eshratābād, *Tehr.* **17 C5** 35 42N 51 27 E
España, *B.A.* **32 C5** 34 46 S 58 14W
Espeleta, *B.A.* **32 C5** 34 45 S 58 15W
Esplugas, *Barc.* **8 D5** 41 22N 2 5 E
Espoo, *Hels.* **3 B2** 60 13N 24 38 E
Espoonlahti, *Hels.* **3 B2** 60 9N 24 31 E
Esposizione Univ. di Roma (E.U.R.), *Rome* **9 G9** 41 49N 12 28 E
Essen, *Ruhr* **6 B4** 51 27N 7 0 E
Essen-Mülheim, Flughafen, *Ruhr* **6 B3** 51 24N 6 56 E
Essendon, *Melb.* **19 E6** 37 44 S 144 55 E
Essendon Airport, *Melb.* **19 E6** 37 43 S 144 54 E
Essex, *Balt.* **25 B4** 39 18N 76 28W
Essex Falls, *N.Y.* **22 C3** 40 49N 74 16W
Essingen, *Stock.* **3 E10** 59 19N 17 59 E
Essling, *Wien* **10 G11** 48 12N 16 30 E
Est, Gare de l', *Paris* **5 B4** 48 52N 2 21 E
Estado, Parque do, *S. Pau.* **31 E6** 23 38 S 46 38W
Estby, *Hels.* **3 C1** 60 5N 24 27W
Este, Parque Nacional del, *Car.* **30 E5** 10 29N 66 50W
Esteban Echeverria, *B.A.* **32 C4** 34 48 S 58 29W
Estlotan, *Hels.* **3 C6** 60 7N 25 13 E
Estrela, Basilica da, *Lisb.* **8 F8** 38 42N 9 9W
Étiolles, *Paris* **5 D4** 48 38N 2 28 E
Etobicoke, *Trto.* **20 E7** 43 39N 79 34W
Etobicoke Cr. →, *Trto.* **20 E7** 43 35N 79 32W
Etzenhauzen, *Mün.* **7 F9** 48 16N 11 27 E
Eun Pyeong, *Sŏul* **12 G7** 37 36N 126 56 E
Eungam, *Sŏul* **12 G7** 37 34N 126 55 E
Evanston, *Chic.* **26 A2** 42 3N 87 40W
Évecquemont, *Paris* **5 A1** 49 0N 1 56 E
Everett, *Bost.* **21 C3** 42 24N 71 3W
Evergreen Park, *Chic.* **26 C2** 41 43N 87 42W
Eversael, *Ruhr* **6 A1** 51 32N 6 39 E
Evesboro, *Phil.* **24 B5** 39 54N 74 55W
Eving, *Ruhr* **6 A6** 51 33N 7 28 E
Evry, *Paris* **5 D4** 48 38N 2 26 E
Évry-les-Châteaux, *Paris* **5 D5** 48 39N 2 38 E
Évzonos, *Ath.* **8 J11** 37 55N 23 49 E
Ewin, *Tehr.* **17 C5** 35 47N 51 23 E
Ewu, *Lagos* **18 A1** 6 33N 7 19 E
Exelberg, *Wien* **10 G9** 48 14N 16 15 E
Eynsford, *Lon.* **4 C6** 51 21N 0 12 E
Eyup, *Ist.* **17 A2** 41 2N 28 55 E
Ez Zeitûn, *El Qâ.* **18 C5** 30 6N 31 18 E
Ézanville, *Paris* **5 A4** 49 1N 2 21 E
Ezeiza, *B.A.* **32 D3** 34 50 S 58 31W
Ezeiza, Aeropuerto, *B.A.* **32 C3** 34 48 S 58 32W

F

Fabreville, *Mtrl.* **20 A2** 43 33N 73 51W
Fælledparken, *Købn.* **2 D10** 55 42N 12 34 E
Fågelön, *Stock.* **3 E10** 59 18N 17 55 E
Fagersjo, *Stock.* **3 E11** 59 14N 18 4 E
Fagnano, *Mil.* **9 E4** 45 24N 8 59 E
Fahrn, *Ruhr* **6 A2** 51 30N 6 45 E
Faibano, *Nápl.* **9 H13** 40 55N 14 27 E
Fair Lawn, *N.Y.* **22 B4** 40 55N 74 7W
Fairfax, *Phil.* **24 C1** 39 47N 75 33W
Fairfax, *Wash.* **25 D6** 38 50N 77 19W
Fairfax Station, *Wash.* **25 E6** 38 48N 77 19W
Fairfield, *Melb.* **19 E7** 37 46 S 145 2 E
Fairfield, *N.Y.* **22 B3** 40 53N 74 17W
Fairfield, *Syd.* **19 B2** 33 52 S 150 56 E
Fairhaven B., *Bost.* **21 C1** 42 25N 71 21W
Fairhaven Hill, *Bost.* **21 C1** 42 26N 71 21W
Fairland, *Jobg.* **18 E8** 26 8 S 27 57 E
Fairland, *Wash.* **25 C8** 39 4N 76 57W
Fairmont Terrace, *S.F.* **27 B4** 37 42N 122 7W
Fairmount Heights, *Wash.* **25 D8** 38 54N 76 54W
Fairmount Park, *Phil.* **24 A3** 40 3N 75 13W
Fairport, *Trto.* **20 D10** 43 49N 79 4W
Fairview, *N.Y.* **22 C5** 40 48N 73 59W
Fairview, *N.Y.* **23 A6** 41 1N 73 46W
Falenica, *Wsaw.* **10 F8** 52 9N 21 12 E
Falenty, *Wsaw.* **10 F6** 52 8N 20 55 E
Falkenburg, *Berl.* **7 A4** 52 34N 13 32 E
Falkenhagen, *Berl.* **7 A1** 52 34N 13 5 E
Falkensee, *Berl.* **7 A1** 52 34N 13 4 E
Fallon, *L.A.* **28 C5** 33 59N 117 54W
Falls Church, *Wash.* **25 D6** 38 53N 77 12W
Falls Run →, *Balt.* **25 A1** 39 21N 76 52W
Falomo, *Lagos* **18 B2** 6 26N 7 26 E
Fangcun, *Gzh.* **14 G8** 23 6N 113 13 E
Fanwood, *N.Y.* **22 D2** 40 37N 74 23W
Far Rockaway, *N.Y.* **23 D6** 40 36N 73 45W
Farahābād, *Tehr.* **17 C5** 35 41N 51 29 E
Färentuna, *Stock.* **3 D8** 59 23N 17 39 E
Farforovskaya, *St-Pet.* **11 B4** 59 52N 30 27 E
Farm Pond, *Bost.* **21 D2** 42 13N 71 20W
Farmingdale, *N.Y.* **23 C8** 40 43N 73 27W
Farmsen, *Hbg.* **7 D8** 53 36N 10 8 E
Farnborough, *Lon.* **4 C5** 51 21N 0 3 E
Farningham, *Lon.* **4 C6** 51 23N 0 12 E
Farrar Pond, *Bost.* **21 C1** 42 24N 71 21W
Farrarmere, *Jobg.* **18 E10** 26 9 S 28 18 E
Farsta, *Stock.* **3 E11** 59 14N 18 5 E
Farstalandet, *Stock.* **3 E13** 59 18N 18 23 E
Farum, *Købn.* **2 D8** 55 48N 12 21 E
Farum Sø, *Købn.* **2 D9** 55 48N 12 21 E
Fasanerie-Nord, *Mün.* **7 F10** 48 11N 11 32 E
Fasangarten, *Mün.* **7 G10** 48 5N 11 36 E
Fat Tau Chau, *H.K.* **12 E6** 22 16N 114 16 E
Fatih, *Ist.* **17 A2** 41 0N 28 56 E
Favoriten, *Wien* **10 H10** 48 9N 16 23 E
Fawkner, *Melb.* **19 E6** 37 42 S 144 56 E
Fawkner Park, *Melb.* **19 F6** 37 50 S 144 58 E
Feasterville, *Phil.* **24 A4** 40 9N 75 0W
Febrero, Parque de, *B.A.* **32 B4** 34 36 S 58 25W
Feijó, *Lisb.* **8 G8** 38 39N 9 9W
Feldersbruch →, *Ruhr* **6 B5** 51 23N 7 4 E
Feldhausen, *Ruhr* **6 A3** 51 36N 6 58 E
Feldkirchen, *Mün.* **7 G11** 48 8N 11 43 E
Feldmoching, *Mün.* **7 F10** 48 14N 11 32 E
Fellowship, *Phil.* **24 B5** 39 56N 74 57W
Feltham, *Lon.* **4 C2** 51 26N 0 24W
Feltonville, *Phil.* **24 A4** 40 1N 75 8W
Fenerbahce, *Ist.* **17 B3** 40 58N 29 2 E
Fengtai, *Beij.* **14 C2** 39 49N 116 14 E
Fenino, *Mos.* **11 E11** 55 43N 37 56 E
Ferencváros, *Bud.* **10 K13** 47 29N 19 5 E
Ferihegyi Airport, *Bud.* **10 K14** 47 26N 19 14 E
Ferndale, *Balt.* **25 B3** 39 11N 76 38W
Ferndale, *Jobg.* **18 E9** 26 5 S 28 0 E
Ferntree Gully, *Melb.* **19 F8** 37 52 S 145 17 E
Ferntree Gully Nat. Park, *Melb.* **19 F8** 37 52 S 145 19 E
Ferny Cr. →, *Melb.* **19 F8** 37 54 S 145 16 E
Férolles-Attilly, *Paris* **5 C5** 48 44N 2 37 E
Ferraz de Vasconcelos, *S. Pau.* **31 E7** 23 32 S 46 22W
Ferrières-en-Brie, *Paris* **5 C6** 48 49N 2 42 E
Ferry, *N.Y.* **23 A5** 41 0N 73 52W
Fetcham, *Lon.* **4 D2** 51 17N 0 21W
Feucherolles, *Paris* **5 B1** 48 52N 1 58 E
Fichtenau, *Berl.* **7 B5** 52 27N 13 42 E
Fields Corner, *Bost.* **21 D3** 42 18N 71 3W
Fiera Camp, *Mil.* **9 E5** 45 28N 9 9 E
Figino, *Mil.* **9 E5** 45 29N 9 4 E
Fijir, *Bagd.* **17 E8** 33 21N 44 21 E
Filadhélfia, *Ath.* **8 H11** 38 2N 23 43 E
Fili-Masilovo, *Mos.* **11 E8** 55 44N 37 29 E
Filothei, *Ath.* **8 H11** 38 2N 23 46 E
Finaalspan, *Jobg.* **18 F10** 26 16 S 28 16 E
Finchley, *Lon.* **4 B3** 51 36N 0 11W
Finkenkrug, *Berl.* **7 A1** 52 33N 13 3 E
Finkenwerder, *Hbg.* **7 D7** 53 32N 9 51 E
Finsbury, *Lon.* **4 B4** 51 31N 0 6W
Finsbury Park, *Lon.* **4 B4** 51 34N 0 6W
Fiorito, *B.A.* **32 C4** 34 42 S 58 26W
Firdows, *Bagd.* **17 F7** 33 17N 44 17 E
Firōz Bahram, *Tehr.* **17 D4** 35 37N 51 14 E
Fischeln, *Ruhr* **6 C1** 51 18N 6 35 E
Fish Brook →, *Bost.* **21 B3** 42 39N 71 1W
Fishermans Bend, *Melb.* **19 E6** 37 49 S 144 55 E
Fisher's Hill, *Jobg.* **18 F10** 26 10 S 28 10 E
Fisherville, *Trto.* **20 D8** 43 46N 79 28W
Fisksätra, *Stock.* **3 E12** 59 17N 18 13 E
Fittja, *Stock.* **3 E10** 59 14N 17 51 E
Fitzroy Gardens, *Melb.* **19 E6** 37 48 S 144 58 E
Five Cowrie Cr. →, *Lagos* **18 B2** 6 26N 7 25 E
Five Dock, *Syd.* **19 B3** 33 52 S 151 8 E
Fjellstrand, *Oslo* **2 C3** 59 47N 10 36 E
Flachsberg, *Ruhr* **6 C4** 51 11N 7 4 E
Flag →, *Chic.* **26 C1** 41 43N 87 55W
Flamengo, *Rio J.* **31 B2** 22 56 S 43 11W
Flaminio, *Rome* **9 F9** 41 55N 12 28 E
Flaskebekk, *Oslo* **2 B3** 59 51N 10 39 E
Flatbush, *N.Y.* **22 D5** 40 39N 73 56W
Flaten, *Stock.* **3 E11** 59 15N 18 9 E
Flemington, *Syd.* **19 B3** 33 53 S 151 4 E
Flemington Racecourse, *Melb.* **19 E6** 37 47 S 144 54 E
Fleury-Mérogis, *Paris* **5 D4** 48 37N 2 21 E
Flingern, *Ruhr* **6 C2** 51 13N 6 48 E
Flint Pk., *L.A.* **28 B3** 34 9N 118 11 E
Floral Park, *N.Y.* **23 C6** 40 43N 73 42W
Florence, *L.A.* **28 C3** 33 57N 118 13W
Florence, *Phil.* **24 C5** 39 44N 74 55W
Florence Bloom Bird Sanctuary, *Jobg.* **18 E9** 26 7 S 28 0 E
Florencio Varela, *B.A.* **32 C5** 34 49 S 58 18W
Florentia, *Jobg.* **18 F9** 26 16 S 28 8 E
Flores, *B.A.* **32 B4** 34 38 S 58 27W
Floresta, *B.A.* **32 B4** 34 37 S 58 27W
Florham Park, *N.Y.* **22 C2** 40 46N 74 23W
Florida, *B.A.* **32 B4** 34 31 S 58 28W
Florida, *Jobg.* **18 F8** 26 10 S 27 55 E
Florida L., *Jobg.* **18 F8** 26 10 S 27 54 E
Floridsdorf, *Wien* **10 G10** 48 15N 16 26 E
Flourtown, *Phil.* **24 A3** 40 6N 75 13W
Flower Hill, *N.Y.* **23 C6** 40 48N 73 40W
Flushing, *N.Y.* **23 C6** 40 45N 73 49W
Flushing Meadows Corona Park, *N.Y.* **23 C5** 40 44N 73 50W
Flysta, *Stock.* **3 D10** 59 22N 17 54 E
Fo Tan, *H.K.* **12 D6** 22 23N 114 11 E
Föhrenhain, *Wien* **10 G10** 48 19N 16 26 E
Folcroft, *Phil.* **24 B3** 39 53N 75 16W
Folsom, *Phil.* **24 B3** 39 53N 75 19W
Fontainebleau, *Jobg.* **18 E8** 26 6 S 27 57 E
Fontana, *La Hab.* **30 B2** 23 1N 82 24W
Fontanka, *St-Pet.* **11 B3** 59 54N 30 16 E
Fontenay-aux-Roses, *Paris* **5 C3** 48 47N 2 17 E
Fontenay-le-Fleury, *Paris* **5 C2** 48 48N 2 2 E
Fontenay-lès-Briis, *Paris* **5 D2** 48 37N 2 9 E
Fontenay-sous-Bois, *Paris* **5 B4** 48 51N 2 28 E
Foots Cray, *Lon.* **4 C5** 51 24N 0 7 E
Footscray, *Melb.* **19 E6** 37 48 S 144 56 E
Forbidden City, *Beij.* **14 B3** 39 53N 116 21 E
Fordham Univ., *N.Y.* **23 B5** 40 51N 73 51W
Fords, *N.Y.* **22 D3** 40 31N 74 19W
Fordsburg, *Jobg.* **18 F9** 26 12 S 28 2 E
Foremans Corner, *Balt.* **25 B3** 39 11N 76 33W
Forest Gate, *Lon.* **4 B5** 51 32N 0 1 E
Forest Heights, *Wash.* **25 E7** 38 48N 77 0W
Forest Hill, *Lon.* **4 C4** 51 26N 0 2W
Forest Hill, *Melb.* **19 F8** 37 50 S 145 10 E
Forest Hill, *Trto.* **20 D8** 43 41N 79 25W
Forest Hills, *N.Y.* **23 C5** 40 42N 73 51W
Forest Park, *Chic.* **26 B2** 41 51N 87 47W
Forest View, *Chic.* **26 C2** 41 48N 87 47W
Forestville, *Syd.* **19 A4** 33 46 S 151 12 E
Forestville, *Wash.* **25 D8** 38 50N 76 52W
Forges-les-Bains, *Paris* **5 D2** 48 37N 2 5 E
Fornacino, *Tori.* **9 B3** 45 9N 7 44 E
Fornebu, *Oslo* **2 B3** 59 53N 10 36 E
Fornebu Airport, *Oslo* **2 B3** 59 56N 10 37 E
Foro Italico, *Rome* **9 F9** 41 56N 12 26 E
Foro Romano, *Rome* **9 F9** 41 53N 12 29 E
Forst Rantzau, *Hbg.* **7 C6** 53 43N 9 49 E
Forstenried, *Mün.* **7 G9** 48 5N 11 29 E
Forstenrieder Park, *Mün.* **7 G9** 48 3N 11 27 E
Fort du Pont Park, *Wash.* **25 D8** 38 52N 76 56W
Fort Foote Village, *Wash.* **25 E7** 38 46N 77 1W
Fort Howard, *Balt.* **25 B4** 39 12N 76 26W
Fort Lee, *N.Y.* **22 B5** 40 50N 73 58W
Fort McHenry Nat. Mon., *Balt.* **25 B3** 35 15N 76 35W
Fort Washington, *Phil.* **24 A3** 40 8N 75 13W
Fort William, *Calc.* **16 E6** 22 33N 88 20 E
Foster City, *S.F.* **27 C3** 37 33N 122 15W
Fosters Pond, *Bost.* **21 B3** 42 36N 71 8W
Fourcherolle, *Paris* **5 C1** 48 42N 1 58 E
Fourmile Run →, *Wash.* **25 D7** 38 50N 77 2W
Fourqueux, *Paris* **5 B2** 48 53N 2 3 E
Fowl Meadow Res., *Bost.* **21 D3** 42 13N 71 8W
Fox Chase, *Phil.* **24 A4** 40 4N 75 5W
Foxhall, *Wash.* **25 C7** 39 4N 77 3W
Framingham, *Bost.* **21 D1** 42 18N 71 24W
Francisco Alvarez, *B.A.* **32 B1** 34 38 S 58 50W
Francisquito Cr. →, *S.F.* **27 D4** 37 27N 122 9W
Franconia, *Wash.* **25 E7** 38 47N 77 7W
Franconville, *Paris* **5 B3** 48 59N 2 13 E
Francop, *Hbg.* **7 D7** 53 30N 9 51 E
Frankel, *Sing.* **15 G8** 1 18N 103 55 E
Frankford, *Phil.* **24 A4** 40 1N 75 5W
Franklin L., *N.Y.* **22 B3** 40 59N 74 13W
Franklin Lakes, *N.Y.* **22 B3** 40 59N 74 13W
Franklin Park, *Bost.* **21 D3** 42 18N 71 5W
Franklin Park, *Chic.* **26 B1** 41 55N 87 52W
Franklin Park, *Wash.* **25 D7** 38 55N 77 9W
Franklin Res., *L.A.* **28 B2** 34 5N 118 24W
Franklin Roosevelt Park, *Jobg.* **18 E8** 26 8 S 27 59 E
Franklin Roosevelt Park, *Phil.* **24 B3** 39 54N 75 10W
Franklin Square, *N.Y.* **23 C6** 40 42N 73 40W
Frattamaggiore, *Nápl.* **9 H12** 40 56N 14 16 E
Frauenkirche, *Mün.* **7 G10** 48 8N 11 34 E
Frederiksberg, *Købn.* **2 D10** 55 40N 12 33 E
Frederiksdal, *Købn.* **2 D9** 55 46N 12 25 E
Fredersdorf, *Berl.* **7 A5** 52 31N 13 45 E
Fredersdorf Nord, *Berl.* **7 A5** 52 32N 13 45 E
Freeport, *N.Y.* **23 D7** 40 39N 73 35W
Freidrichshain, Volkspark, *Berl.* **7 A3** 52 31N 13 25 E
Freiham, *Mün.* **7 G9** 48 8N 11 25 E
Freimann, *Mün.* **7 F10** 48 11N 11 37 E
Fremont, *S.F.* **27 C4** 37 33N 122 2W
Fresh Meadows, *N.Y.* **23 C6** 40 43N 73 47W
Fresh Pond, *Bost.* **21 C3** 42 22N 71 8W
Freskati, *Stock.* **3 D11** 59 22N 18 3 E
Fresnes, *Paris* **5 C3** 48 45N 2 18 E
Fretay, *Paris* **5 C3** 48 40N 2 12 E
Freudenau, *Wien* **10 G10** 48 11N 16 25 E
Friedenau, *Berl.* **7 B3** 52 28N 31 20 E
Friederikenhof, *Berl.* **7 B3** 52 23N 13 21 E
Friedrichsfeld, *Ruhr* **6 A1** 51 37N 6 39 E
Friedrichsfelde, *Berl.* **7 B4** 52 29N 13 33 E
Friedrichshagen, *Berl.* **7 B4** 52 27N 13 37 E
Friedrichshain, *Berl.* **7 A3** 52 31N 13 25 E
Friedrichshulde, *Hbg.* **7 D7** 53 36N 9 51 E
Friedrichslust, *Berl.* **7 A5** 52 33N 13 43 E
Frielas, *Lisb.* **8 F8** 38 49N 9 6W
Friemersheim, *Ruhr* **6 B2** 51 23N 6 42 E
Friern Barnet, *Lon.* **4 B4** 51 37N 0 9W
Friherrs, *Hels.* **3 B3** 60 16N 24 49 E
Frogner, *Oslo* **2 A6** 60 1N 11 6 E
Frohnau, *Berl.* **7 A2** 52 38N 13 16 E
Frohnhausen, *Ruhr* **6 B3** 51 26N 6 56 E
Frontón, I., *Lima* **30 G7** 12 7 S 77 11W
Frunze, *Mos.* **11 E9** 55 47N 37 33 E
Fuchź, *Tōkyō* **13 B1** 35 40N 139 29 E
Fuencarral, *Mdrd.* **8 B2** 40 29N 3 42W
Fuhlenbrock, *Ruhr* **6 A3** 51 32N 6 54 E
Fuhlsbüttel, *Hbg.* **7 D8** 53 37N 10 1 E
Fujidera, *Ōsaka* **12 C4** 34 34N 135 36 E
Fujikubo, *Tōkyō* **13 B2** 35 49N 139 31 E
Fujimi, *Tōkyō* **13 A2** 35 50N 139 33 E
Fukagawa, *Tōkyō* **13 C3** 35 39N 139 48 E
Fukami, *Tōkyō* **13 D1** 35 28N 139 27 E
Fukiai, *Ōsaka* **12 B2** 34 42N 135 12 E
Fukuoka, *Tōkyō* **13 A2** 35 52N 139 31 E
Fukushima, *Ōsaka* **12 B3** 34 41N 135 28 E
Fulatani, *Tōkyō* **13 D1** 35 22N 139 30 E
Fulham, *Lon.* **4 C3** 51 28N 0 12W
Fuller Park, *L.A.* **28 C5** 33 51N 117 56W
Fullerton, *Balt.* **25 A3** 39 22N 76 30W
Funabori, *Tōkyō* **13 B4** 35 41N 139 52 E
Funasaka, *Ōsaka* **12 B2** 34 48N 135 16 E
Fünfhaus, *Wien* **10 G10** 48 11N 16 20 E
Fünfhausen, *Hbg.* **7 E8** 53 27N 10 2 E
Furesø, *Købn.* **2 D9** 55 47N 12 25 E
Fürstenried, *Mün.* **7 G9** 48 5N 11 28 E
Furth, *Mün.* **7 G10** 48 2N 11 35 E
Furu →, *Tōkyō* **13 A3** 35 54N 139 49 E
Furuyakami, *Tōkyō* **13 A2** 35 54N 139 31 E
Futago-tamagawaen, *Tōkyō* **13 C2** 35 36N 139 39 E
Futamatagawa, *Tōkyō* **13 D2** 35 27N 139 31 E
Futatsubashi, *Tōkyō* **13 D1** 35 28N 139 29 E
Fuxing Dao, *Shang.* **14 J12** 31 16N 121 33 E
Fuxing Gongyuan, *Shang.* **14 J11** 31 13N 121 27 E
Fuxinglu, *Beij.* **14 B2** 39 52N 116 16 E
Fuxingmen, *Beij.* **14 B2** 39 53N 116 19 E

G

Gadstrup, *Købn.* **2 E7** 55 34N 12 5 E
Gaebong, *Sŏul* **12 H7** 37 29N 126 52 E
Gage Park, *Chic.* **26 C2** 41 47N 87 42W
Gagny, *Paris* **5 B5** 48 53N 2 32 E
Gaillon, *Paris* **5 A1** 49 1N 1 53 E
Galata, *Ist.* **17 A2** 41 1N 28 58 E
Galátsion, *Ath.* **8 H11** 38 1N 23 45 E
Galeão, *Rio J.* **31 A2** 22 49 S 43 14W
Galéria →, *Rome* **9 F9** 41 57N 12 20 E
Gallows Corner, *Lon.* **4 B6** 51 35N 0 13 E
Gällstaö, *Stock.* **3 E10** 59 17N 17 51 E
Galyanovo, *Mos.* **11 E10** 55 48N 37 47 E
Galyeon, *Sŏul* **12 G7** 37 36N 126 55 E
Gambir, *Jak.* **15 H9** 6 9 S 106 48 E
Gamboa, *Rio J.* **31 B2** 22 53 S 43 11W
Gambolóita, *Mil.* **9 E6** 45 26N 9 13 E
Gamelinha →, *S. Pau.* **31 E6** 23 31 S 46 31W
Gamlebyen, *Oslo* **2 B4** 59 54N 10 46 E
Gamlebyen, *Shang.* **14 J11** 31 13N 121 29 E
Gamō, *Tōkyō* **13 A3** 35 52N 139 48 E
Gang Dong, *Sŏul* **12 G8** 37 30N 127 5 E
Gang Nam, *Sŏul* **12 G7** 37 30N 126 59 E
Gang Sea, *Sŏul* **12 G7** 37 32N 126 51 E
Gangadharpur, *Calc.* **16 E5** 22 35N 88 11 E
Gangtou, *Gzh.* **14 F7** 23 12N 113 8 E
Gangwei, *Gzh.* **14 G8** 23 4N 113 11 E
Ganløse, *Købn.* **2 D8** 55 47N 12 15 E
Ganløse Orned, *Købn.* **2 D8** 55 48N 12 18 E
Ganshi, *Gzh.* **14 F7** 23 10N 113 8 E
Gants Hill, *Lon.* **4 B5** 51 34N 0 4 E
Gaoqiao, *Shang.* **14 H12** 31 21N 121 34 E
Garbagnate Milanese, *Mil.* **9 D5** 45 34N 9 4 E
Garbatella, *Rome* **9 F10** 41 51N 12 30 E
Garches, *Paris* **5 B3** 48 50N 2 11 E
Garching, *Mün.* **7 F11** 48 14N 11 39 E
Garden City, *El Qâ.* **18 C5** 30 2N 31 14 E
Garden City, *N.Y.* **23 C7** 40 43N 73 37W
Garden Reach, *Calc.* **16 E5** 22 33N 88 15 E
Gardena, *L.A.* **28 C3** 33 53N 118 18W
Garder, *Oslo* **2 C3** 59 45N 10 38 E
Garfield, *N.Y.* **22 B4** 40 52N 74 7W
Garfield Park, *Chic.* **26 B2** 41 52N 87 42W
Gargareta, *Ath.* **8 J11** 37 57N 23 43 E
Garges-lès-Gonesse, *Paris* **5 B4** 48 58N 2 25 E
Garhi Naraina, *Delhi* **16 B1** 28 37N 77 8 E
Garibong, *Sŏul* **12 H7** 37 29N 126 54 E
Garin, *B.A.* **32 A2** 34 25 S 58 44W
Gariya, *Calc.* **16 F6** 22 28N 88 23 E
Garji, *Calc.* **16 C5** 22 50N 88 19 E
Garne, *Paris* **5 C1** 48 41N 1 58 E
Garrison, *Balt.* **25 A2** 39 24N 76 45W
Garstedt, *Hbg.* **7 C7** 53 40N 9 59 E
Gartenstadt, *Ruhr* **6 B6** 51 30N 7 30 E
Garulia, *Calc.* **16 D6** 22 48N 88 22 E
Garvanza, *L.A.* **28 B3** 34 6N 118 11 E
Garwood, *N.Y.* **22 D3** 40 38N 74 18W
Gary, *Chic.* **26 D4** 41 35N 87 23W
Gåshaga, *Stock.* **3 D12** 59 21N 18 13 E
Gássino Torinese, *Tori.* **9 B3** 45 7N 7 49 E
Gästerby, *Hels.* **3 C1** 60 8N 24 27 E
Gateão, Aéroporto de, *Rio J.* **31 A2** 22 49 S 43 15W
Gateway of India, *Bomb.* **16 H8** 18 55N 72 50 E
Gatow, *Berl.* **7 B1** 52 29N 13 11 E
Gaurhati, *Calc.* **16 D6** 22 48N 88 21 E
Gauripur, *Calc.* **16 C6** 22 53N 88 25 E
Gavá, *Barc.* **8 E5** 41 18N 2 0 E
Gavamar, *Barc.* **8 E4** 41 16N 1 58 E
Gavanpada, *Bomb.* **16 H9** 18 57N 73 0 E
Gávea, *Rio J.* **31 B2** 22 58 S 43 13W
Gávea, Pedra da, *Rio J.* **31 B2** 22 59 S 43 18W
Gbogbo, *Lagos* **18 A3** 6 35N 7 31 E
Gebel el Ahmar, *El Qâ.* **18 C5** 30 2N 31 19 E
Gebel el Muqattam, *El Qâ.* **18 C5** 30 1N 31 17 E
Gebel et Tura, *El Qâ.* **18 D5** 29 56N 31 15 E
Geduld Dam, *Jobg.* **18 F11** 26 12 S 28 24 E
Geiselgasteig, *Mün.* **7 G10** 48 3N 11 33 E
Geist Res., *Phil.* **24 B2** 39 57N 75 24W
Gellért hegy, *Bud.* **10 K13** 47 29N 19 3 E
Gelsenkirchen, *Ruhr* **6 A4** 51 32N 7 2 E
General Ignacio Allende, *Méx.* **29 B1** 19 20N 99 21W
General Pacheco, *B.A.* **32 A3** 34 27 S 58 36W
General San Martin, *B.A.* **32 B3** 34 35 S 58 32W
General Sarmiento, *B.A.* **32 B2** 34 32 S 58 43W
General Urquiza, *B.A.* **32 B4** 34 34 S 58 28W
Gennebreck, *Ruhr* **6 C5** 51 18N 7 12 E
Gennevilliers, *Paris* **5 B3** 48 56N 2 17 E
Gentilly, *Paris* **5 C4** 48 48N 2 21 E
Gentofte, *Købn.* **2 D10** 55 44N 12 32 E
Georges →, *Syd.* **19 B2** 33 56 S 150 55 E
Georges Hall, *Syd.* **19 B2** 33 54 S 150 59 E
Georges I., *Bost.* **21 D4** 42 19N 70 55W
Georges River Bridge, *Syd.* **19 C3** 34 0 S 151 6 E
Georgetown, *Wash.* **25 D7** 38 54N 77 3W
Georgetown Rowley State Forest, *Bost.* **21 A4** 42 41N 70 56W
Georgsweide, *Hbg.* **7 D8** 53 30N 10 1 E
Gerasdorf bei Wein, *Wien* **10 G10** 48 17N 16 28 E
Gerberau, *Mün.* **7 F9** 48 12N 11 27 E
Gérbido, *Tori.* **9 B2** 45 2N 7 36 E
Gerlev, *Købn.* **2 D7** 55 49N 12 0 E
Gerli, *B.A.* **32 C4** 34 41 S 58 22W
Germantown, *Balt.* **25 A4** 39 24N 76 28W
Germantown, *Phil.* **24 A3** 40 2N 75 11W
Germiston, *Jobg.* **18 F9** 26 13 S 28 10 E
Gerresheim, *Ruhr* **6 C3** 51 14N 6 51 E
Gersthof, *Wien* **10 G9** 48 14N 16 18 E
Gerthe, *Ruhr* **6 A5** 51 31N 7 16 E

38 Gesîrat el Rauda

Gesîrat el Rauda, *El Qâ.* 18 C5 30 1N 31 13 E
Gesîrat Muhammad, *El Qâ.* 18 C5 30 6N 31 11 E
Gesterby, *Hels.* 3 A6 60 20N 25 17 E
Getafe, *Mdrd.* 8 C2 40 18N 3 43W
Gevelsberg, *Ruhr* 6 C6 51 19N 7 21 E
Geylang, *Sing.* 15 G8 1 18N 103 53 E
Geylang →, *Sing.* 15 G8 1 18N 103 52 E
Geylang Serai, *Sing.* 15 G8 1 19N 103 53 E
Gezîrat edn Dhahab, *El Qâ.* 18 D5 29 59N 31 13 E
Gezîrat Warrâq el Hadar, *El Qâ.* 18 C5 30 6N 31 13 E
Gharapuri, *Bomb.* 16 H8 18 57N 72 57 E
Ghatkopar, *Bomb.* 16 G8 19 4N 72 54 E
Ghazipur, *Delhi* 16 B2 28 37N 77 19 E
Ghizri, *Kar.* 17 H11 24 49N 67 2 E
Ghizri Cr. →, *Kar.* 17 H11 24 47N 67 5 E
Ghonda, *Delhi* 16 A2 28 41N 77 16 E
Ghushuri, *Calc.* 16 E6 22 37N 88 21 E
Gianicolense, *Rome* 9 F9 51 53N 12 28 E
Giant, *S.F.* 27 A2 37 58N 122 20W
Gibbsboro, *Phil.* 24 B5 39 50N 74 57W
Gibbstown, *Phil.* 24 C3 39 49N 75 17W
Gibraltar Pt., *Trto.* 20 E8 43 36N 79 23W
Gidea Park, *Lon.* 4 B6 51 35N 0 11 E
Giesing, *Mün.* 7 G10 48 6N 11 35 E
Gif-sur-Yvette, *Paris* 5 C2 48 42N 2 8 E
Gilgo Beach, *N.Y.* 23 D8 40 36N 73 24W
Gilgo I., *N.Y.* 23 D8 40 37N 73 23W
Gillette, *N.Y.* 22 C2 40 40N 74 29W
Gimmersta, *Stock.* 3 E12 59 14N 18 14 E
Ginza, *Tōkyō* 13 C3 35 39N 139 46 E
Girgaum, *Bomb.* 16 H8 18 57N 72 50 E
Giugliano in Campània, *Nápl.* 9 H12 40 55N 14 12 E
Givoletto, *Tori.* 9 B1 45 9N 7 29 E
Gjellumvatn, *Oslo* 2 C2 59 47N 10 26 E
Gjersjøen, *Oslo* 2 C4 59 47N 10 47 E
Glacier Hills, *N.Y.* 22 B2 40 51N 74 28W
Gladbeck, *Ruhr* 6 A3 51 34N 6 58 E
Gladesville, *Syd.* 19 B3 33 50 S 151 8 E
Gladökvarn, *Stock.* 3 E10 59 11N 17 59 E
Gladsakse, *Købn.* 2 D9 55 45N 12 25 E
Glashutte, *Hbg.* 7 C8 53 41N 10 2 E
Glashütte, *Ruhr* 6 C3 51 13N 6 51 E
Glasmoor, *Hbg.* 7 C8 53 42N 10 1 E
Glassmanor, *Wash.* 25 E7 38 49N 77 0W
Glen Cove, *N.Y.* 23 B7 40 52N 73 38W
Glen Echo, *Wash.* 25 D7 38 58N 77 8W
Glen Hd., *N.Y.* 23 C7 40 49N 73 37W
Glen Iris, *Melb.* 19 F7 37 51 S 145 3 E
Glen Mills, *Phil.* 24 B2 39 55N 75 29W
Glen Oaks, *N.Y.* 23 C6 40 45N 73 43W
Glen Riddle, *Phil.* 24 B2 39 53N 75 26W
Glen Ridge, *N.Y.* 22 C3 40 48N 74 12W
Glen Rock, *N.Y.* 22 B4 40 57N 74 7W
Glen Waverley, *Melb.* 19 F8 37 52 S 145 10 E
Glenardon, *Wash.* 25 D8 38 56N 76 51W
Glencoe, *Chic.* 26 A2 42 7N 87 44W
Glendale, *L.A.* 28 B3 34 9N 118 15 E
Glendora, *Phil.* 24 B4 39 50N 75 4W
Glenfield, *Syd.* 19 B2 33 58 S 150 53 E
Glenhazel, *Jobg.* 18 E9 26 8 S 28 6 E
Glenhuntly, *Melb.* 19 F7 37 52 S 145 1 E
Glenmont, *Wash.* 25 C7 39 3N 77 4W
Glenolden, *Phil.* 24 B3 39 54N 75 17W
Glenroy, *Melb.* 19 E6 37 42 S 144 55 E
Glenside, *Phil.* 24 A4 40 6N 75 9W
Glenview, *Chic.* 26 A2 42 3N 87 48W
Glenview Countryside, *Chic.* 26 A2 42 3N 87 49W
Glenview Woods, *Chic.* 26 A2 42 4N 87 46W
Glenville, *N.Y.* 23 A6 41 1N 73 41W
Glenvista, *Jobg.* 18 F9 26 17 S 28 3 E
Glenwood Landing, *N.Y.* 23 C7 40 48N 73 38W
Glienicke, *Berl.* 7 A2 52 38N 13 18 E
Glömsta, *Stock.* 3 E10 59 14N 17 55 E
Glosli, *Oslo* 2 A5 60 1N 10 55 E
Glostrup, *Købn.* 2 E9 55 39N 12 23 E
Gloucester City, *Phil.* 24 B4 39 53N 75 7W
Gocheog, *Sŏul* 12 G7 37 30N 126 52 E
Goclawek, *Wsaw.* 10 E7 52 14N 21 7 E
Goeselville, *Chic.* 26 D2 41 37N 87 46W
Goetjensort, *Hbg.* 7 E8 53 29N 10 2 E
Golabari, *Calc.* 16 E6 22 35N 88 20 E
Golabki, *Wsaw.* 10 E6 52 12N 20 52 E
Golden Gate, *S.F.* 27 B2 37 48N 122 29W
Golden Gate Bridge, *S.F.* 27 B2 37 49N 122 28W
Golden Gate National Recreation Area, *S.F.* 27 B1 37 49N 122 31W
Golden Gate Park, *S.F.* 27 B2 37 46N 122 28W
Golden Horn, *Ist.* 17 A2 41 1N 28 57 E
Golders Green, *Lon.* 4 B3 51 34N 0 11W
Golyevo, *Mos.* 11 E7 55 48N 37 18 E
Gometz-la-Ville, *Paris* 5 C2 48 40N 2 7 E
Gometz-le-Châtel, *Paris* 5 C2 48 40N 2 8 E
Gondangdra, *Jak.* 15 J9 6 11 S 106 49 E
Gonesse, *Paris* 5 B4 48 59N 2 26 E
Gongreung, *Sŏul* 12 G8 37 36N 127 3 E
González Catán, *B.A.* 32 C3 34 46 S 58 38W
Goodman Hill, *Bost.* 21 C1 42 22N 71 23W
Goodmayes, *Lon.* 4 B5 51 33N 0 6 E
Gopalnagar, *Calc.* 16 C5 22 50N 88 13 E
Gopalpur, *Calc.* 16 E6 22 38N 88 26 E
Górce, *Wsaw.* 10 E6 52 15N 20 55 E
Gordon, *Syd.* 19 A3 33 46 S 151 8 E
Gore Hill, *Syd.* 19 A3 33 49 S 151 10 E
Gorelyy →, *St-Pet.* 11 A5 60 1N 30 30 E
Gorenki, *Mos.* 11 E11 55 47N 37 53 E
Gorkiy Park, *Mos.* 11 E9 55 43N 37 36 E
Görväln, *Stock.* 3 D9 59 26N 17 45 E
Gose Elbe →, *Hbg.* 7 E8 53 28N 10 6 E
Gosen, *Berl.* 7 B5 52 23N 13 43 E
Gosener kanal, *Berl.* 7 B5 52 24N 13 42 E
Goshenville, *Phil.* 24 B1 39 59N 75 32W
Gospel Oak, *Lon.* 4 B4 51 32N 0 9W
Gotanda, *Tōkyō* 13 C3 35 37N 139 43 E
Gotanno, *Tōkyō* 13 B3 35 45N 139 49 E
Goth Goli Mār, *Kar.* 17 G11 24 53N 67 1 E
Goth Sher Shāh, *Kar.* 17 G10 24 53N 66 59 E
Gournay-sur-Marne, *Paris* 5 B5 48 51N 2 34 E
Goussainville, *Paris* 5 A4 49 1N 2 27 E
Gouvernes, *Paris* 5 B6 48 51N 2 41 E
Governador, I. do, *Rio J.* 31 A2 22 48 S 43 13W
Governor's I., *N.Y.* 22 C4 40 41N 74 1W
Grabicz, *Wsaw.* 10 E8 52 19N 21 12 E
Grabów, *Wsaw.* 10 F6 52 8N 20 59 E
Gracia, *Barc.* 8 D6 41 24N 2 10 E
Gradyville, *Phil.* 24 B2 39 56N 75 27W
Gräfelfing, *Mün.* 7 G9 48 7N 11 25 E
Grafenwald, *Ruhr* 6 A3 51 34N 6 54 E
Graham Memorial Park, *Balt.* 25 A4 39 25N 76 29W
Gran Canal, *Méx.* 29 A3 19 34N 99 1W
Granada Hills, *L.A.* 28 A1 34 16N 118 30W
Grand Bourg, *B.A.* 32 A2 34 29 S 58 42W
Grand Calumet →, *Chic.* 26 D4 41 37N 87 28W
Grand Union Canal, *Lon.* 4 A2 51 42N 0 26W
Grande →, *S. Pau.* 31 F7 23 43 S 46 24W
Grange, *Tori.* 9 B1 45 7N 7 29 E
Grange Hill, *Lon.* 4 B5 51 36N 0 5 E
Granite, *Balt.* 25 A1 39 20N 76 51W
Graniteville, *N.Y.* 22 D3 40 37N 74 10W
Granja Viana, *S. Pau.* 31 E4 23 35 S 46 50W
Granlandet, *Hels.* 3 B6 60 10N 25 15 E
Granö, *Hels.* 3 B6 60 13N 25 14 E
Grant Park, *Chic.* 26 B3 41 52N 87 37W
Granville, *Syd.* 19 A3 33 49 S 151 1 E
Grape I., *Bost.* 21 D4 42 16N 70 55W
Grass Hassock Channel, *N.Y.* 23 D6 40 36N 73 47W
Grassey B., *N.Y.* 23 D6 40 37N 73 47W
Grassy Sprain Res., *N.Y.* 23 B5 40 58N 73 50W
Gratosóglio, *Mil.* 9 E6 45 24N 9 1 E
Gratzwalde, *Berl.* 7 B5 52 28N 13 42 E
Gravesend, *N.Y.* 22 D5 40 36N 73 56W
Grays, *Lon.* 4 C6 51 28N 0 19 E
Grazhdanka, *St-Pet.* 11 B4 59 59N 30 24 E
Great Blue Hill, *Bost.* 21 D3 42 12N 71 4W
Great Bookham, *Lon.* 4 D2 51 16N 0 21W
Great Brewster I., *Bost.* 21 C4 42 19N 70 53W
Great Captain I., *N.Y.* 23 B7 40 59N 73 37W
Great Falls, *Wash.* 25 D6 38 59N 77 17W
Great Falls Park, *Wash.* 25 D6 38 59N 77 14W
Great Kills, *N.Y.* 22 D4 40 32N 74 9W
Great Kills Harbour, *N.Y.* 22 D4 40 32N 74 8W
Great Neck, *N.Y.* 23 C6 40 48N 73 44W
Great Pond, *Bost.* 21 D3 42 11N 71 2W
Great South B., *N.Y.* 23 D9 40 39N 73 19W
Greco, *Mil.* 9 D6 45 30N 9 12 E
Greco I., *S.F.* 27 C3 37 30N 122 10W
Green Brae, *S.F.* 27 A1 37 57N 122 31W
Green Brook, *N.Y.* 22 D2 40 35N 74 26W
Green I., *H.K.* 12 E5 22 17N 114 6 E
Green Land, *Jak.* 15 J9 6 17 S 106 46 E
Green Pond, *N.Y.* 22 A2 41 1N 74 29W
Green Street, *Lon.* 4 A3 51 40N 0 16W
Green Street Green, *Lon.* 4 C5 51 21N 0 5 E
Green Valley, *Syd.* 19 B2 33 54 S 150 53 E
Green Village, *N.Y.* 22 C2 40 44N 74 27W
Greenbelt, *Wash.* 25 C8 39 0N 76 52W
Greenbelt Park, *Wash.* 25 D8 38 58N 76 53W
Greenfield Park, *Mtrl.* 20 B5 45 29N 73 28W
Greenfields Village, *Phil.* 24 C4 39 49N 75 9W
Greenford, *Lon.* 4 B2 51 31N 0 21W
Greenhithe, *Lon.* 4 C6 51 27N 0 17 E
Greenlawn, *N.Y.* 23 B8 40 52N 73 22W
Greenpoint, *N.Y.* 22 C5 40 43N 73 57W
Greensborough, *Melb.* 19 E7 37 41 S 145 5 E
Greenside, *Jobg.* 18 E9 26 8 S 28 1 E
Greenville, *N.Y.* 23 C7 40 48N 73 35W
Greenville Chauncey, *N.Y.* 23 B5 40 59N 73 50W
Greenwich, *Lon.* 4 C4 51 28N 0 0 E
Greenwich, *N.Y.* 23 A7 41 1N 73 37W
Greenwich, *Syd.* 19 B4 33 50 S 151 11 E
Greenwich Observatory, *Lon.* 4 C4 51 28N 0 0 E
Greenwich Pt., *N.Y.* 23 A7 41 0N 73 34W
Greenwich Village, *N.Y.* 22 C5 40 44N 73 59W
Greenwood, *Bost.* 21 C3 42 29N 71 2W
Grefsen, *Oslo* 2 B4 59 56N 10 47 E
Grégy-sur-Yerres, *Paris* 5 C5 48 40N 2 37 E
Greiffenburg, *Ruhr* 6 B1 51 20N 6 37 E
Gressy, *Paris* 5 B6 48 58N 2 40 E
Greve Strand, *Købn.* 2 E8 55 34N 12 18 E
Greystanes, *Syd.* 19 A2 33 49 S 150 58 E
Griebnitzsee, *Berl.* 7 B1 52 23N 13 8 E
Griffith Park, *L.A.* 28 B3 34 7N 118 18 E
Grignon, *Paris* 5 B1 48 50N 1 56 E
Grigny, *Paris* 5 D4 48 39N 2 23 E
Grinzing, *Wien* 10 G10 48 15N 16 20 E
Grisy-Suisnes, *Paris* 5 C6 48 41N 2 40 E
Gröbenried, *Mün.* 7 F9 48 13N 11 25 E
Grochów, *Wsaw.* 10 E7 52 15N 21 5 E
Grodzisk, *Wsaw.* 10 E7 52 19N 21 4 E
Grogol, *Jak.* 15 H9 6 9 S 106 47 E
Grogol, Kali →, *Jak.* 15 J9 6 11 S 106 47 E
Gronsdorf, *Mün.* 7 G11 48 7N 11 42 E
Grorud, *Oslo* 2 B5 59 57N 10 52 E
Gross Borstel, *Hbg.* 7 D7 53 36N 9 58 E
Gross Flottbek, *Hbg.* 7 D7 53 33N 9 53 E
Gross Glienicke, *Berl.* 7 B1 52 28N 13 6 E
Gross-Hadern, *Mün.* 7 G9 48 6N 11 29 E
Gross-Lappen, *Mün.* 7 F10 48 11N 11 35 E
Grosse Krampe, *Berl.* 7 B5 52 23N 13 40 E
Grosse Müggelsee, *Berl.* 7 B4 52 26N 13 38 E
Grossenbaum, *Ruhr* 6 B2 51 22N 6 46 E
Grossenzersdorf, *Wien* 10 G11 48 12N 16 33 E
Grossenzersdorfer Arm →, *Wien* 10 G11 48 12N 16 31 E
Grosser Biberhaufen, *Wien* 10 G10 48 12N 16 28 E
Grosser Wannsee, *Berl.* 7 B2 52 25N 13 10 E
Grossfeld-Siedlung, *Wien* 10 G10 48 16N 16 26 E
Grosshesselohe, *Mün.* 7 G10 48 3N 11 32 E
Grossjedlersdorf, *Wien* 10 G10 48 16N 16 23 E
Grossziethen, *Berl.* 7 B3 52 23N 13 26 E
Groszówka, *Wsaw.* 10 E8 52 14N 21 13 E
Grove Hall, *Bost.* 21 D3 42 18N 71 4W
Grove Park, *Lon.* 4 C5 51 25N 0 1 E
Grove Park, *Lon.* 4 C3 51 28N 0 15W
Groveton, *Wash.* 25 E7 38 46N 77 6W
Grugliasco, *Tori.* 9 B2 45 5N 7 34 E
Gruiten, *Ruhr* 6 C4 51 12N 7 0 E
Grumme, *Ruhr* 6 B5 51 30N 7 15 E
Grumo Nevano, *Nápl.* 9 H12 40 56N 14 15 E
Grünau, *Berl.* 7 B4 52 25N 13 34 E
Grunewald, *Berl.* 7 B2 52 29N 13 16 E
Grünwald, *Mün.* 7 G10 48 2N 11 31 E
Grünwalder Forst, *Mün.* 7 G10 48 2N 11 33 E
Grymes Hill, *N.Y.* 22 D4 40 36N 74 6W
Gu Ro, *Sŏul* 12 G7 37 30N 126 51 E
Guadalupe, *Manila* 15 D4 14 33N 121 2 E
Guadalupe →, *S.F.* 27 D4 37 28N 122 4W
Guadalupe, Basilica de, *Méx.* 29 B3 19 29N 99 7W
Guadelupe, *Rio J.* 31 A1 22 49 S 43 20W
Guanabacoa, *La Hab.* 30 B3 23 7N 82 17W
Guanabara, *Rio J.* 31 B1 22 57 S 43 27W
Guanabara, B. de, *Rio J.* 31 B2 22 52 S 43 10W
Guanabara, Jardim, *Rio J.* 31 A2 22 48 S 43 11W
Guang'anmen, *Beij.* 14 B2 39 51N 116 18 E
Guangminglou, *Beij.* 14 B3 39 51N 116 25 E
Guangqumen, *Beij.* 14 B3 39 52N 116 26 E
Guangzhou, *Gzh.* 14 G8 23 6N 113 13 E
Guanshuo, *Gzh.* 14 G9 23 4N 113 17 E
Guantai, *Nápl.* 9 H12 40 52N 14 11 E
Guapira →, *S. Pau.* 31 D6 23 30 S 46 33W
Guarapiranga, Res. de, *S. Pau.* 31 F5 23 42 S 46 43W
Guardias, *Mdrd.* 8 B3 40 29N 3 31W
Guarulhos, *S. Pau.* 31 D6 23 28 S 46 32W
Guatao, *La Hab.* 30 B2 23 0N 82 29W
Guayacanes, Pta., *La Hab.* 30 A3 23 10N 82 16W
Gubernador Monteverde, *B.A.* 32 C5 34 47 S 58 16W
Gudö, *Stock.* 3 E12 59 12N 18 12 E
Güell, Parque de, *Barc.* 8 D6 41 24N 2 10 E
Guermantes, *Paris* 5 B6 48 51N 2 42 E
Gugging, *Wien* 10 G9 48 18N 16 15 E
Guianazes, *S. Pau.* 31 E7 23 32 S 46 24W
Guildford, *Syd.* 19 B2 33 51 S 150 59 E
Guinardó, *Barc.* 8 D6 41 24N 2 10 E
Gujiazhai, *Shang.* 14 H11 31 21N 121 23 E
Gulbāi, *Kar.* 17 G10 24 52N 66 58 E
Guldasteh, *Tehr.* 17 D4 35 36N 51 15 E
Gulistan Palace, *Tehr.* 17 C5 35 40N 51 24 E
Gulph Mills, *Phil.* 24 A2 40 4N 75 20W
Gumbostrand, *Hels.* 3 B6 60 15N 25 17 E
Güngören, *Ist.* 17 A2 41 1N 28 52 E
Gunnarsby, *Hels.* 3 C1 60 6N 24 28W
Gunnersbury, *Lon.* 4 C3 51 29N 0 17W
Gunnigfeld, *Ruhr* 6 B4 51 29N 7 8 E
Gunpowder Falls →, *Balt.* 25 A4 39 23N 76 36W
Gunung Sahari, *Jak.* 15 H9 6 9 S 106 49 E
Gupiing, *Manila* 15 E5 14 27N 121 11 E
Guryong San, *Sŏul* 12 H8 37 28N 127 3 E
Gustavsberg, *Stock.* 3 E13 59 19N 18 23 E
Guttenberg, *N.Y.* 22 C4 40 48N 74 0W
Gutuyevskiy, Os., *St-Pet.* 11 B3 59 53N 30 15 E
Guyancourt, *Paris* 5 C2 48 46N 2 4 E
Guyancourt, Aérodrome de, *Paris* 5 C2 48 45N 2 3 E
Gvali-patak →, *Bud.* 10 K13 47 23N 19 7 E
Gwan Ag, *Sŏul* 12 H7 37 29N 126 57 E
Gwanag San, *Sŏul* 12 H7 37 27N 126 58 E
Gwynns Falls →, *Balt.* 25 B2 39 19N 76 42W
Gyál, *Bud.* 10 K14 47 23N 19 13 E
Gyeongbong Palace, *Sŏul* 12 G7 37 34N 126 58 E
Gynea, *Syd.* 19 C3 34 1 S 151 5 E

H

Haaga, *Hels.* 3 B4 60 13N 24 53 E
Haan, *Ruhr* 6 C3 51 11N 6 59 E
Haar, *Mün.* 7 G11 48 6N 11 43 E
Haar, *Ruhr* 6 B5 51 26N 7 13 E
Haarzopf, *Ruhr* 6 B3 51 25N 6 57 E
Habana del Este, *La Hab.* 30 B3 23 9N 82 19W
Habay, *Manila* 15 E3 14 27N 120 56 E
Habikino, *Ōsaka* 12 C4 34 33N 135 36 E
Habinghorst, *Ruhr* 6 A5 51 34N 7 18 E
Hacienda Heights, *L.A.* 28 C5 33 59N 117 59W
Hackbridge, *Lon.* 4 C4 51 23N 0 9W
Hackensack, *N.Y.* 22 B4 40 52N 74 4W
Hackney, *Lon.* 4 B4 51 32N 0 3W
Hackney Wick, *Lon.* 4 B4 51 32N 0 1W
Haddon Heights, *Phil.* 24 B4 39 53N 75 3W
Haddonfield, *Phil.* 24 B4 39 53N 75 2W
Hadersdorf, *Wien* 10 G9 48 12N 16 14 E
Hadley Wood, *Lon.* 4 B3 51 39N 0 10W
Haga, *Stock.* 3 D11 59 21N 18 1 E
Hagem, *Ruhr* 6 A5 51 38N 7 19 E
Hagen, *Ruhr* 6 B6 51 21N 7 27 E
Hägersten, *Stock.* 3 E10 59 18N 17 59 E
Haggetts Pond, *Bost.* 21 B2 42 39N 71 11W
Häggvik, *Stock.* 3 D10 59 26N 17 56 E
Hagonoy, *Manila* 15 D4 14 30N 121 4 E
Hagsätra, *Stock.* 3 E11 59 15N 18 0 E
Hahipur, *Calc.* 16 D5 22 47N 88 10 E
Hahnerberg, *Ruhr* 6 C4 51 12N 7 9 E
Hai He →, *Tianj.* 14 E6 39 4N 117 17 E
Haidarpur, *Delhi* 16 A1 28 43N 77 8 E
Haidhausen, *Mün.* 7 G10 48 7N 11 36 E
Haidian, *Beij.* 14 B2 39 59N 116 15 E
Haight-Ashbury, *S.F.* 27 B2 37 46N 122 26W
Haiguangsi, *Tianj.* 14 E6 39 7N 117 11 E
Hainault, *Lon.* 4 B5 51 36N 0 6 E
Haizhu Guangchang, *Gzh.* 14 G8 23 6N 113 14 E
Hakim, *El Qâ.* 18 C4 30 4N 31 7 E
Hakunila, *Hels.* 3 B5 60 16N 25 6 E
Halchōbori, *Tōkyō* 13 B4 35 48N 139 55 E
Haledon, *N.Y.* 22 B3 40 57N 74 11W
Halesite, *N.Y.* 23 B8 40 53N 73 24W
Halethorpe, *Balt.* 25 B2 39 14N 76 41W
Half Hollow Hills, *N.Y.* 23 C8 40 48N 73 21W
Half Moon B., *S.F.* 26 D2 37 27N 122 25W
Half Moon Bay Airport, *S.F.* 27 C1 37 31N 122 30W
Half Moon Bay Beaches, *S.F.* 26 D2 37 28N 122 28W
Halim, *Jak.* 15 J10 6 15 S 106 53 E
Halim Perdanakusuma Airport, *Jak.* 15 J10 6 16 S 106 53 E
Halstead, *Lon.* 4 D5 51 19N 0 8 E
Halstenbeck, *Hbg.* 7 D7 53 38N 9 50 E
Haltiala, *Hels.* 3 B4 60 16N 24 57 E
Haltiavuori, *Hels.* 3 B4 60 16N 24 58 E
Ham, *Lon.* 4 C3 51 25N 0 18W
Ham, *Paris* 5 A2 49 1N 2 3 E
Hamberg, *Jobg.* 18 E8 26 9 S 27 54 E
Hamborn, *Ruhr* 6 B2 51 29N 6 46 E
Hamburg, *Hbg.* 7 D8 53 33N 10 0 E
Hamburg Flughafen, *Hbg.* 7 D7 53 38N 9 59 E
Hämeenkylä, *Hels.* 3 B3 60 16N 24 48 E
Hamm, *Hbg.* 7 D8 53 33N 10 1 E
Hamm, *Ruhr* 6 C2 51 12N 6 44 E
Hammarby, *Stock.* 3 E11 59 17N 18 5 E
Hamme, *Ruhr* 6 B5 51 29N 7 12 E
Hammel Arverne, *N.Y.* 23 D6 40 35N 73 48W
Hammerbrook, *Hbg.* 7 D8 53 32N 10 1 E
Hammersmith, *Lon.* 4 C3 51 29N 0 14W
Hammond, *Chic.* 26 D4 41 36N 87 29W
Hampstead, *Lon.* 4 B3 51 33N 0 10W
Hampstead, *Mtrl.* 20 B4 45 28N 73 37W
Hampstead Garden Suburb, *Lon.* 4 B3 51 34N 0 11W
Hampstead Heath, *Lon.* 4 B3 51 33N 0 10W
Hampton Court Palace, *Lon.* 4 C2 51 24N 0 20W
Hampton Hill, *Lon.* 4 C2 51 25N 0 21W
Hampton Wick, *Lon.* 4 C3 51 24N 0 18W
Hamrā, *Bagd.* 17 F7 33 18N 44 21 E
Han Gang →, *Sŏul* 12 G7 37 32N 126 55 E
Hanakuri, *Tōkyō* 13 A3 35 50N 139 47 E
Hanala, *Hels.* 3 A5 60 20N 25 4 E
Hancho, *Ōsaka* 12 B3 34 48N 135 28 E
Haneda, *Tōkyō* 13 C3 35 32N 139 45 E
Hang Hau, *H.K.* 12 E6 22 19N 114 16 E
Hanjiashu, *Tianj.* 14 E5 39 11N 117 3 E
Hanlon, *Trto.* 20 E7 43 38N 79 39W
Hansen Flood Control Basin, *L.A.* 28 A2 34 15N 118 23W
Hansia, *Calc.* 16 D6 22 48N 88 24 E
Hanskinen, *Hels.* 3 C6 60 8N 25 18 E
Hanwell, *Lon.* 4 B2 51 30N 0 20W
Hanworth, *Lon.* 4 C2 51 26N 0 23W
Haora, *Calc.* 16 E5 22 34N 88 18 E
Happy Valley, *H.K.* 12 E6 22 16N 114 10 E
Harajuku, *Tōkyō* 13 D2 35 22N 139 30 E
Haraki, *Tōkyō* 13 B4 35 42N 139 56 E
Harat, *Calc.* 16 C5 22 52N 88 11 E
Harbor Hills, *N.Y.* 23 C6 40 46N 73 44W
Harburg, *Hbg.* 7 E7 53 27N 9 59 E
Harding, *Bost.* 21 D2 42 12N 71 19W
Hardricourt, *Paris* 5 A1 49 0N 1 53 E
Harefield, *Lon.* 4 B2 51 36N 0 28W
Hareskovby, *Købn.* 2 D9 55 45N 12 23 E
Harewood Park, *Balt.* 25 A4 39 22N 76 21W
Harigaya, *Tōkyō* 13 B2 35 49N 139 33 E
Haringey, *Lon.* 4 B4 51 34N 0 4W
Haripur, *Calc.* 16 D5 22 42N 88 10 E
Harjula, *Hels.* 3 A3 60 21N 24 45 E
Harjusuo, *Hels.* 3 B5 60 19N 25 0 E
Harkortsee, *Ruhr* 6 B6 51 23N 7 24 E
Harksheide, *Hbg.* 7 C8 53 43N 10 0 E
Harlaching, *Mün.* 7 G10 48 5N 11 33 E
Harlem, *N.Y.* 22 C5 40 48N 73 56W
Harlesden, *Lon.* 4 B3 51 32N 0 14W
Harlington, *Lon.* 4 C2 51 29N 0 25W
Harmaja, *Hels.* 3 C4 60 6N 24 58 E
Harmashatar hegy, *Bud.* 10 J13 47 33N 19 0 E
Harmondsworth, *Lon.* 4 C2 51 29N 0 29W
Harmonville, *Phil.* 24 A3 40 5N 75 18W
Harold Hill, *Lon.* 4 B6 51 36N 0 14 E
Harold Parker State Forest, *Bost.* 21 B3 42 37N 71 4W
Harold Wood, *Lon.* 4 B6 51 35N 0 14 E
Harrington Park, *N.Y.* 22 B5 40 59N 73 59W
Harrison, *N.Y.* 22 C4 40 44N 74 9W
Harrison, *N.Y.* 23 B6 40 57N 73 42W
Harrisonville, *Balt.* 25 A2 39 22N 76 49W
Harrow, *Lon.* 4 B2 51 34N 0 20W
Harrow on the Hill, *Lon.* 4 B2 51 34N 0 21W
Harrow School, *Lon.* 4 B2 51 34N 0 20W
Harrow Weald, *Lon.* 4 B2 51 36N 0 20W
Hart I., *Balt.* 25 B4 39 14N 76 23W
Hart I., *N.Y.* 23 B6 40 51N 73 46W
Hartford, *Phil.* 24 B5 39 58N 74 57W
Hartley, *Lon.* 4 C6 51 22N 0 18 E
Hartsdale, *N.Y.* 23 A6 41 1N 73 48W
Harumi, *Tōkyō* 13 C3 35 38N 139 47 E
Harvard, Mt., *L.A.* 28 A4 34 12N 118 4W
Harvard Univ., *Bost.* 21 C3 42 23N 71 7W
Harvestehude, *Hbg.* 7 D7 53 34N 9 58 E
Harvey, *Chic.* 26 D3 41 36N 87 39W
Harwood Heights, *Chic.* 26 B2 41 57N 87 46W
Hasanābād, *Tehr.* 17 C4 35 44N 51 16 E
Hasbrouck Heights, *N.Y.* 22 B4 40 51N 74 6W
Haselbach, *Wien* 10 G9 48 18N 16 14 E
Haselhorst, *Berl.* 7 A2 52 33N 13 14 E
Hasköy, *Ist.* 17 A2 41 2N 28 57 E
Hasle, *Oslo* 2 C3 59 46N 10 38 E
Hasloh, *Hbg.* 7 C7 53 41N 9 54 E
Haslohfeld, *Hbg.* 7 C7 53 41N 9 56 E
Haslum, *Oslo* 2 B3 59 55N 10 34 E
Haspe, *Ruhr* 6 B6 51 21N 7 25 E
Haspertalsp, *Ruhr* 6 C6 51 17N 7 24 E
Hasselbeck, *Ruhr* 6 C3 51 19N 6 56 E
Hässelby, *Stock.* 3 D10 59 22N 17 50 E
Hasslinghausen, *Ruhr* 6 C5 51 20N 7 16 E
Hasten, *Ruhr* 6 C5 51 11N 7 11 E
Hästhagen, *Stock.* 3 E11 59 18N 18 9 E
Hastings-on-Hudson, *N.Y.* 23 B5 40 59N 73 51W
Hatch End, *Lon.* 4 B2 51 36N 0 22W
Hatiara, *Calc.* 16 E6 22 36N 88 26 E
Hatogaya, *Tōkyō* 13 B3 35 49N 139 44 E
Hattingen, *Ruhr* 6 B5 51 23N 7 11 E
Hatton, *Lon.* 4 C2 51 28N 0 25W
Hattori, *Ōsaka* 12 A4 34 51N 135 36 E
Hauketo, *Oslo* 2 B4 59 50N 10 48 E
Hauldres →, *Paris* 5 D5 48 37N 2 37 E
Hausbruch, *Hbg.* 7 E7 53 28N 9 53 E
Havalimani, *Ist.* 17 B2 40 59N 28 50 E
Havana = La Habana, *La Hab.* 30 B2 23 7N 82 21W
Havdrup, *Købn.* 2 E7 55 33N 12 7 E
Havel →, *Berl.* 7 A2 52 37N 13 11 E
Havelkanal, *Berl.* 7 A2 52 36N 13 10 E
Haverford, *Phil.* 24 A3 40 0N 75 18W
Havering, *Lon.* 4 B6 51 33N 0 12 E
Havering-atte-Bower, *Lon.* 4 B6 51 37N 0 11 E
Havertown, *Phil.* 24 B3 39 58N 75 18W
Hawangsibri, *Sŏul* 12 G8 37 33N 127 1 E
Haweolgog, *Sŏul* 12 G8 37 35N 127 1 E
Haworth, *N.Y.* 22 B5 40 57N 73 59W
Hawthorne, *L.A.* 28 C2 33 54N 118 21W
Hawthorne, *N.Y.* 22 B4 40 57N 74 8W
Hayes, *Lon.* 4 C5 51 22N 0 0 E
Hayes, *Lon.* 4 B2 51 30N 0 25W
Hayes End, *Lon.* 4 B2 51 31N 0 25W
Hayford, *Chic.* 26 C2 41 45N 87 42W
Hayward, *S.F.* 27 B4 37 40N 122 4W
Hayward Fault, *S.F.* 27 B3 37 46N 122 10W
Haywood Municipal Airport, *S.F.* 27 C4 32 39N 122 9W
Headley, *Lon.* 4 D3 51 16N 0 16W
Headstone, *Lon.* 4 B2 51 35N 0 21W
Heard Pond, *Bost.* 21 C1 42 20N 71 23W
Heart Pond, *Bost.* 21 B1 42 33N 71 23W
Heath Park, *Lon.* 4 B6 51 34N 0 12 E
Heathmont, *Melb.* 19 E8 37 49 S 145 14 E
Heathrow Airport, *Lon.* 4 C2 51 28N 0 27W
Hebbville, *Balt.* 25 A2 39 20N 76 45W
Hebe Haven, *H.K.* 12 D6 22 21N 114 15 E
Hebei, *Tianj.* 14 E6 39 9N 117 11 E
Hedehusene, *Købn.* 2 E8 55 39N 12 11 E
Hedong, *Gzh.* 14 G8 23 5N 113 14 E
Hedong, *Tianj.* 14 E6 39 7N 117 11 E
Heerdt, *Ruhr* 6 C2 51 13N 6 42 E
Hegewisch, *Chic.* 26 D3 41 39N 87 33W
Heggelielva →, *Oslo* 2 B3 60 1N 10 36 E
Heide, *Ruhr* 6 A3 51 31N 6 50 E
Heidelberg, *Melb.* 19 E7 37 45 S 145 4 E
Heidelberg West, *Melb.* 19 E7 37 43 S 145 2 E
Heidemühle, *Berl.* 7 B5 52 29N 13 40 E
Heidhausen, *Ruhr* 6 B4 51 22N 7 1 E
Heiligenhaus, *Ruhr* 6 C3 51 19N 6 58 E
Heiligensee, *Berl.* 7 A2 52 36N 13 13 E
Heiligenstadt, *Wien* 10 G10 48 14N 16 21 E
Heimfeld, *Hbg.* 7 E7 53 28N 9 57 E
Heinässuo, *Hels.* 3 B1 60 18N 24 27 E
Heinersdorf, *Berl.* 7 A3 52 34N 13 26 E
Heisingen, *Ruhr* 6 B4 51 24N 7 4 E
Heissen, *Ruhr* 6 B3 51 26N 6 54 E
Helderkruin, *Jobg.* 18 E8 26 7 S 27 51 E
Helenelund, *Stock.* 3 D10 59 24N 17 58 E
Heliopolis, *El Qâ.* 18 C5 30 5N 31 19 E
Hellersdorf, *Berl.* 7 A4 52 32N 13 36 E
Hellerup, *Købn.* 2 D10 55 44N 12 33 E
Helmahof, *Wien* 10 G11 48 18N 16 34 E
Helsingfors = Helsinki, *Hels.* 3 B4 60 10N 24 55 E
Helsinki, *Hels.* 3 B4 60 10N 24 55 E
Helsinki Airport, *Hels.* 3 B4 60 18N 24 58 E
Hempstead, *N.Y.* 23 C7 40 42N 73 37W
Hempstead Harbor, *N.Y.* 23 B7 40 50N 73 39W
Henan, *Gzh.* 14 G8 23 5N 113 14 E
Hendon, *Lon.* 4 B3 51 35N 0 14W
Hengsha, *Gzh.* 14 G8 23 9N 113 12 E
Hengsteysee, *Ruhr* 6 B6 51 24N 7 27 E
Hennigsdorf, *Berl.* 7 A2 52 38N 13 12 E
Henrichenburg, *Ruhr* 6 A5 51 35N 7 19 E
Henriville, *Paris* 5 C1 48 44N 1 56 E
Henrykow, *Wsaw.* 10 E6 52 19N 20 58 E
Henson Cr. →, *Wash.* 25 E8 38 47N 76 58W
Henttaa, *Hels.* 3 B3 60 11N 24 45 E
Heping, *Tianj.* 14 E6 39 7N 117 11 E
Heping Gongyuan, *Shang.* 14 J12 31 16N 121 30 E
Hepingli, *Beij.* 14 B3 39 57N 116 23 E
Herbeck, *Ruhr* 6 C5 51 12N 7 18 E
Herbede, *Ruhr* 6 B5 51 25N 7 16 E
Herblay, *Paris* 5 B2 48 59N 2 9 E
Herdecke, *Ruhr* 6 B6 51 24N 7 25 E
Herlev, *Købn.* 2 D9 55 43N 12 27 E
Hermannskogel, *Wien* 10 G9 48 16N 16 17 E
Hermitage and Winter Palace, *St-Pet.* 11 B3 59 55N 30 19 E
Hermosa Beach, *L.A.* 28 C2 33 51N 118 23W
Hermsdorf, *Berl.* 7 A2 52 37N 13 18 E
Hernals, *Wien* 10 G10 48 13N 16 20 E
Herne, *Ruhr* 6 A5 51 32N 7 13 E
Herne Hill, *Lon.* 4 C4 51 27N 0 6W
Hernwood Heights, *Balt.* 25 A2 39 22N 76 49W
Héroes de Churubusco, *Méx.* 29 B3 19 21N 99 6W
Herongate, *Lon.* 4 B7 51 35N 0 21 E
Herons, Î. aux, *Mtrl.* 20 B4 43 25N 73 34W
Herricks, *N.Y.* 23 C7 40 45N 73 39W
Herring Run →, *Balt.* 25 B3 39 18N 76 30W
Hersham, *Lon.* 4 C2 51 21N 0 22W
Herstedøster, *Købn.* 2 D9 55 40N 12 22 E
Herten, *Ruhr* 6 A4 51 35N 7 8 E
Hertoniemi, *Hels.* 3 B5 60 12N 25 2 E
Hessler, *Ruhr* 6 A4 51 31N 7 8 E
Heston, *Lon.* 4 C2 51 28N 0 22W
Hetterscheidt, *Ruhr* 6 B3 51 20N 6 59 E
Hetzendorf, *Wien* 10 H9 48 9N 16 17 E
Heuberg, *Wien* 10 G9 48 13N 16 16 E
Heven, *Ruhr* 6 B5 51 26N 7 18 E
Hewlett Neck, *N.Y.* 23 D6 40 37N 73 41W
Hexi, *Tianj.* 14 E5 39 8N 117 9 E
Hexingcun, *Tianj.* 14 E6 39 6N 117 10 E
Hextable, *Lon.* 4 C6 51 24N 0 10 E
Heybridge, *Lon.* 4 B7 51 39N 0 22 E
Hibernia, *N.Y.* 22 B2 40 57N 74 29W
Hickory Hills, *Chic.* 26 C2 41 43N 87 49W
Hicksville, *N.Y.* 23 C7 40 46N 73 30W
Hiddinghausen, *Ruhr* 6 B5 51 21N 7 17 E
Hiekkaharju, *Hels.* 3 B5 60 18N 25 2 E
Hiesfeld, *Ruhr* 6 A2 51 33N 6 46 E
Hietaniemi, *Hels.* 3 B4 60 10N 24 54 E
Hietzing, *Wien* 10 G9 48 10N 16 17 E
Higashi, *Ōsaka* 12 B4 34 41N 135 31 E
Higashi-kaizuka, *Tōkyō* 13 A3 35 50N 139 46 E
Higashimonzen, *Tōkyō* 13 A3 35 55N 139 40 E
Higashimurayama, *Tōkyō* 13 B1 35 45N 139 26 E
Higashinada, *Ōsaka* 12 B3 34 42N 135 15 E
Higashinari, *Ōsaka* 12 B4 34 40N 135 32 E
Higashiōsaka, *Ōsaka* 12 C4 34 39N 135 37 E
Higashisumiyoshi, *Ōsaka* 12 C4 34 37N 135 31 E
Higashiyodogawa, *Ōsaka* 12 B3 34 44N 135 28 E
High Beach, *Lon.* 4 B5 51 39N 0 1 E
High Junk Pk., *H.K.* 12 E6 22 17N 114 17 E
High Park, *Trto.* 20 E8 43 38N 79 27W
Higham Hill, *Lon.* 4 B4 51 35N 0 2W
Highbury, *Lon.* 4 B4 51 33N 0 6W
Highgate, *Lon.* 4 B4 51 34N 0 8W
Highland Cr. →, *Trto.* 20 D9 43 45N 79 13W
Highland Creek, *Trto.* 20 D9 43 46N 79 8W
Highland Park, *L.A.* 28 B3 34 7N 118 13 E
Highland Park, *N.Y.* 22 D2 40 30N 74 25W
Highlands North, *Jobg.* 18 E9 26 8 S 28 5 E
Highway Highlands, *L.A.* 28 A3 34 14N 118 16W
Higurashi, *Tōkyō* 13 B4 35 47N 139 55 E
Hila, *Méx.* 29 A2 19 35N 99 17W
Hillcrest Heights, *Wash.* 25 E8 38 49N 76 57W
Hillerheide, *Ruhr* 6 A5 51 35N 7 12 E
Hilleshög, *Stock.* 3 D9 59 23N 17 42 E
Hillgrove District, *L.A.* 28 B5 34 1N 117 58W
Hillingdon, *Lon.* 4 B2 51 32N 0 27W
Hillingdon Heath, *Lon.* 4 B2 51 31N 0 26W
Hillsborough, *S.F.* 27 C2 37 32N 122 21W
Hillsdale, *N.Y.* 22 A4 41 0N 74 1W
Hillsdale, *S.F.* 27 C3 37 32N 122 18W
Hillsdale Manor, *N.Y.* 22 A4 41 1N 74 3W
Hillside, *Chic.* 26 B1 41 52N 87 55W
Hillside, *N.Y.* 23 C6 40 42N 73 48W
Hillside Manor, *N.Y.* 23 C6 40 44N 73 40W
Hilltop, *Phil.* 24 B4 39 49N 75 4W
Hillwood, *Wash.* 25 D7 38 52N 77 9W
Hilmīya, *El Qâ.* 18 C5 30 6N 31 19 E
Hiltrop, *Ruhr* 6 A5 51 31N 7 15 E
Hindsby, *Hels.* 3 A6 60 20N 25 13 E
Hingham, *Bost.* 21 D4 42 14N 70 54W
Hingham B., *Bost.* 21 D4 42 17N 70 56W
Hingham Harbor, *Bost.* 21 D4 42 15N 70 53W
Hino, *Tōkyō* 13 D2 35 23N 139 35 E
Hinsbeck, *Ruhr* 6 B4 51 22N 7 4 E
Hinschenfelde, *Hbg.* 7 D8 53 35N 10 0 E
Hinsdale, *Chic.* 26 C1 41 47N 87 55W
Hinterhainbach, *Wien* 10 G8 48 14N 16 12 E
Hintersdorf, *Wien* 10 G8 48 18N 16 13 E
Hirakata, *Ōsaka* 12 B4 34 48N 135 38 E
Hirota, *Ōsaka* 12 B2 34 44N 135 20 E
Hirschstetten, *Wien* 10 G10 48 14N 16 27 E
Hither Green, *Lon.* 4 C4 51 26N 0 0 E
Hiyoshi, *Tōkyō* 13 C2 35 33N 139 38 E
Hjortekær, *Købn.* 2 D10 55 47N 12 32 E
Hjortespring, *Købn.* 2 D9 55 44N 12 25 E
Hlubočepy, *Pra.* 10 B2 50 2N 14 23 E
Ho Chung, *H.K.* 12 D6 22 21N 114 14 E
Ho Man Tin, *H.K.* 12 E6 22 18N 114 11 E
Hoboken, *N.Y.* 22 C4 40 44N 74 1W
Hobsons B., *Melb.* 19 F6 37 51 S 144 55 E
Hochbrück, *Mün.* 7 F10 48 14N 11 37 E
Hochdahl, *Ruhr* 6 C3 51 13N 6 55 E
Hochemmerich, *Ruhr* 6 B2 51 24N 6 41 E
Hochfeld, *Ruhr* 6 B2 51 25N 6 45 E
Hochheide, *Ruhr* 6 B2 51 26N 6 41 E
Hochlar, *Ruhr* 6 A5 51 36N 7 11 E
Hochlarmark, *Ruhr* 6 A4 51 34N 7 9 E
Hodgkins, *Chic.* 26 C1 41 46N 87 53W
Hodogaya-Ku, *Tōkyō* 13 D2 35 26N 139 35 E
Hoegi, *Sŏul* 12 G8 37 35N 127 3 E
Hofberg, *Wien* 10 G10 48 12N 16 21 E
Hoffman I., *N.Y.* 22 D4 40 34N 74 3W
Hofstede, *Ruhr* 6 A5 51 30N 7 11 E
Höggarnsfjärden, *Stock.* 3 D13 59 22N 18 23 E
Hohe Mark, Naturpark, *Ruhr* 6 A2 51 35N 6 49 E
Hohe Schaar, *Hbg.* 7 E7 53 29N 9 58 E
Hohenbrunn, *Mün.* 7 G11 48 2N 11 42 E
Hohenfelde, *Hbg.* 7 D8 53 33N 10 1 E
Höhenkirchen, *Mün.* 7 G11 48 1N 11 43 E
Hohenraden, *Hbg.* 7 C6 53 41N 9 49 E
Hohenschönhausen, *Berl.* 7 A4 52 33N 13 30 E
Hohenwisch, *Hbg.* 7 E7 53 29N 9 53 E

Kennedy Grove Regional Rec. Area 39

Hohokus, N.Y. 22 A4 41 0N 74 5W
Hok Tsui, H.K. 12 E6 22 12N 114 15 E
Holborn, Lon. 4 B4 51 31N 0 7W
Holečovice, Pra. 10 B2 50 6N 14 28 E
Holland Village, Sing. 15 G7 1 18N 103 47 E
Hollis, N.Y. 23 C6 40 42N 73 45W
Höllriegelskreuth, Mün. 7 G9 48 2N 11 30 E
Holly Oak, Phil. 24 C2 39 47N 75 27W
Hollydale, L.A. 28 C4 33 55N 118 10W
Hollywood Bowl, L.A. 28 B2 34 6N 118 21W
Hollywood-Burbank Airport, L.A. 28 A2 34 11N 118 21W
Holmenkollen, Oslo 2 B4 59 57N 10 41 E
Holmes, Phil. 24 B3 39 53N 75 18W
Holmes Acres, Wash. 25 D6 38 51N 77 13W
Holmes Run →, Wash. 25 E7 38 48N 77 6W
Holmesburg, Phil. 24 A4 40 2N 75 2W
Holmgård, Stock. 3 E10 59 14N 18 0 E
Holsfjorden, Oslo 2 B1 59 58N 10 17 E
Holsterhausen, Ruhr 6 A5 51 32N 7 11 E
Holte, København. 2 D9 55 48N 12 27 E
Holten, Ruhr 6 A2 51 31N 6 47 E
Holthausen, Ruhr 6 B4 51 25N 7 5 E
Holzbüttgen, Ruhr 6 C1 51 13N 6 37 E
Homberg, Ruhr 6 B2 51 27N 6 41 E
Hombruch, Ruhr 6 B6 51 28N 7 27 E
Homerton, Lon. 4 B4 51 32N 0 2W
Homestead Lake, Jobg. 18 F10 26 10 S 28 17 E
Homestead Valley, S.F. 27 A1 37 53N 122 32W
Hometown, Chic. 26 C2 41 44N 87 42W
Homledal, Oslo 2 B1 59 59N 10 18 E
Homówek, Wsaw. 10 E5 52 17N 20 48 E
Hon-gyōtoku, Tōkyō 13 B4 35 41N 139 57 E
Hōnanchō, Tōkyō 13 B2 35 40N 139 39 E
Honcho, Tōkyō 13 B3 35 40N 139 41 E
Honden, Tōkyō 13 B4 35 43N 139 50 E
Honeydew, Jobg. 18 E8 26 4 S 27 55 E
Hong Kah, Sing. 15 F7 1 21N 103 43 E
Hong Kong, H.K. 12 E5 22 17N 114 11 E
Hong Kong, Univ. of, H.K. 12 E5 22 16N 114 8 E
Hong Kong Airport, H.K. 12 E6 22 19N 114 11 E
Hong Kong I., H.K. 12 E6 22 16N 114 11 E
Hong Lim Park, Sing. 15 G8 1 17N 103 50 E
Hongeun, Sŏul 12 G7 37 35N 126 56 E
Honggiao, Shang. 14 J11 31 12N 121 22 E
Honggou, Shang. 14 J11 31 16N 121 29 E
Hongkou Gongyuan, Shang. 14 J11 31 17N 121 28 E
Hongmiao, Beij. 14 B3 39 54N 116 26 E
Hongqiao, Tianj. 14 E5 39 8N 117 9 E
Hongqiao Airport, Shang. 14 J10 31 12N 121 19 E
Honjyo, Tōkyō 13 B3 35 41N 139 48 E
Honmoku, Tōkyō 13 D2 35 24N 139 39 E
Hönow, Berl. 7 A4 52 32N 13 38 E
Höntrop, Ruhr 6 B4 51 27N 7 9 E
Hood Pond, Bost. 21 A4 42 40N 70 57W
Hooghly →, Calc. 16 D6 22 41N 88 21 E
Hook, Lon. 4 C3 51 22N 0 17W
Hopelawn, N.Y. 22 D3 40 31N 74 17W
Hörde, Ruhr 6 B7 51 29N 7 30 E
Horikiri, Tōkyō 13 B4 35 44N 139 50 E
Horn, Hbg. 7 D8 53 33N 10 5 E
Horn Pond, Bost. 21 C2 42 28N 71 9W
Hornchurch, Lon. 4 B6 51 33N 0 14 E
Horneburg, Ruhr 6 A5 51 37N 7 17 E
Horni, Pra. 10 B3 50 2N 14 33 E
Horni Počernice, Pra. 10 B3 50 6N 14 36 E
Hornsey, Lon. 4 B4 51 35N 0 7W
Horoměřice, Pra. 10 B1 50 8N 14 20 E
Horsley Park, Syd. 19 B2 33 50 S 150 51 E
Horst, Ruhr 6 B4 51 26N 7 6 E
Horsthausen, Ruhr 6 A5 51 33N 7 12 E
Hortaleza, Mdrd. 8 B3 40 28N 3 38W
Horto Florestal, S. Pau. 31 D6 23 27 S 46 38W
Horton Kirby, Lon. 4 C6 51 23N 0 14 E
Hösel, Ruhr 6 B3 51 20N 6 53 E
Hosoyama, Tōkyō 13 C2 35 36N 139 31 E
Hospitalet, Barc. 8 D5 41 21N 2 6 E
Hostafranchs, Barc. 8 D5 41 21N 2 8 E
Hoterheide, Ruhr 6 C1 51 16N 6 37 E
Houbetin, Pra. 10 B3 50 6N 14 33 E
Houghs Neck, Bost. 21 D4 42 15N 70 57W
Houghton, Jobg. 18 F9 26 10 S 28 3 E
Houilles, Paris 5 B3 48 56N 2 11 E
Hounslow, Lon. 4 C2 51 28N 0 21W
Houses of Parliament, Lon. 4 C4 51 29N 0 7W
Hove Å →, Købn. 2 D8 55 43N 12 7 E
Hovedøya, Oslo 2 B4 59 53N 10 43 E
Høvik, Oslo 2 B3 59 54N 10 34 E
Hovorčovice, Pra. 10 A3 50 10N 14 31 E
Howard Beach, N.Y. 23 D5 40 39N 73 50W
Hoxton Park, Syd. 19 B2 33 55 S 150 51 E
Hoxton Park Aerodrome, Syd. 19 B2 33 54 S 150 50 E
Hōya, Tōkyō 13 B2 35 44N 139 34 E
Høybråten, Oslo 2 B5 59 56N 10 55 E
Hradčany, Pra. 10 B2 50 5N 14 24 E
Hsiya, Gzh. 14 G7 23 9N 113 6 E
Huangpu, Gzh. 14 G9 23 5N 113 23 E
Huangpu, Shang. 14 J12 31 14N 121 30 E
Huangpu Gongyuan, Shang. 14 J11 31 14N 121 29 E
Huangpu Jiang →, Shang. 14 J11 31 11N 121 29 E
Huangtugang, Beij. 14 C2 39 49N 116 15 E
Huat Choe, Sing. 15 F7 1 20N 103 41 E
Huckarde, Ruhr 6 A6 51 32N 7 24 E
Huckingen, Ruhr 6 B2 51 21N 6 44 E
Huddinge, Stock. 3 E11 59 14N 18 0 E
Hudson →, N.Y. 22 B5 40 43N 73 6W
Huertas de San Beltran, Barc. 8 D5 41 22N 2 9 E
Huguenot, N.Y. 22 D3 40 32N 74 13W
Huguenot Park, N.Y. 22 D3 40 31N 74 12W
Huidui, Tianj. 14 E6 39 4N 117 16 E
Huisquilucan →, Méx. 29 B2 19 24N 99 17W
Huixquilucan, Méx. 29 B1 19 21N 99 21W
Hull, Bost. 21 D4 42 18N 70 54W
Hulman Aqueduct, Bost. 21 C1 42 20N 71 23W
Hulmeville, Phil. 24 A5 40 8N 74 55W
Hulsdonk, Ruhr 6 B1 51 27N 6 36 E
Humaljärvi, Hels. 3 B1 60 10N 24 26 E
Humber →, Trto. 20 D7 43 47N 79 38W
Humber B., Trto. 20 E8 43 37N 79 27W
Humber Bay, Trto. 20 E8 43 38N 79 29W
Humber Summit, Trto. 20 D7 43 45N 79 32W
Humber Valley Park, Trto. 20 E8 43 39N 79 29W
Humber Valley Village, Trto. 20 D7 43 40N 79 31W
Humberlea, Trto. 20 D7 43 43N 79 31W
Humboldt Park, Chic. 26 B2 41 54N 87 42W
Humera, Mdrd. 8 B2 40 25N 3 46W
Hummelsbüttel, Hbg. 7 D8 53 39N 10 4 E
Hun Yeang, Sing. 15 F8 1 21N 103 55 E
Hunaydī, Bagd. 17 F8 33 18N 44 29 E
Hundige, Købn. 2 E8 55 35N 12 18 E
Hundige Strand, Købn. 2 E9 55 35N 12 20 E
Hung Hom, H.K. 12 E6 22 18N 114 11 E
Hunters Hill, Syd. 19 B3 33 50 S 151 9 E
Hunters Pt., S.F. 27 B2 37 43N 122 21W
Hunters Valley, Wash. 25 D6 38 54N 77 17W
Huntington, N.Y. 23 B8 40 51N 73 25W
Huntington, Wash. 25 E7 38 47N 77 4W
Huntington B., N.Y. 23 B8 40 54N 73 24W
Huntington Bay, N.Y. 23 B8 40 56N 73 26W
Huntington Park, L.A. 28 C3 33 58N 118 13W
Huntington Station, N.Y. 23 B8 40 50N 73 23W
Hünxer Wald, Ruhr 6 A2 51 37N 6 49 E
Hurffville, Phil. 24 C4 39 45N 75 6W
Hurīya, Bagd. 17 E7 33 21N 44 19 E
Hurlingham, B.A. 32 B3 34 35 S 58 37W
Hurlingham, Jobg. 18 E9 26 6 S 28 2 E
Hurstville, Syd. 19 B3 33 57 S 151 6 E
Husby, Stock. 3 D10 59 24N 17 56 E
Huseby, Oslo 2 A6 60 0N 11 1 E
Hustivař, Pra. 10 B3 50 3N 14 31 E
Husum, Købn. 2 D9 55 42N 12 27 E
Hütteldorf, Wien 10 G9 48 12N 16 15 E
Hüttenheim, Ruhr 6 B2 51 21N 6 43 E
Huttrop, Ruhr 6 B4 51 26N 7 3 E
Hüvösvölgy, Bud. 10 J13 47 32N 19 0 E
Hvalstad, Oslo 2 B2 59 51N 10 27 E
Hvalstrand, Oslo 2 B3 59 50N 10 30 E
Hvidovre, Købn. 2 E9 55 38N 12 27 E
Hwagog, Sŏul 12 G7 37 32N 126 51 E
Hyattsville, Wash. 25 D8 38 57N 76 57W
Hyde Park, Bost. 21 D3 42 15N 71 7W
Hyde Park, Chic. 26 C3 41 47N 87 35W
Hyde Park, Jobg. 18 E9 26 6 S 28 2 E
Hyde Park, Lon. 4 B3 51 30N 0 10W
Hyde Park, Syd. 19 B4 33 52 S 151 12 E
Hynes, L.A. 28 C3 33 52N 118 10W

I

Ibaraki, Ōsaka 12 B4 34 48N 135 34 E
Ibayo Tipas, Manila 15 D4 14 32N 121 4 E
Ibese, Lagos 18 A2 6 33N 7 28 E
Ibirapuera, S. Pau. 31 E5 23 36 S 46 40W
Ibirapuera, Parque, S. Pau. 31 E6 23 35 S 46 38W
Iboju, Lagos 18 B3 6 25N 7 31 E
Icarai, Rio J. 31 B3 22 54 S 43 6W
Icerenköy, Ist. 17 B3 40 58N 29 6 E
Ichapur, Calc. 16 D6 22 48N 88 22 E
Ichgao, Tōkyō 13 C2 35 32N 139 32 E
Ichigaya, Tōkyō 13 B3 35 41N 139 43 E
Ichikawa, Tōkyō 13 B4 35 43N 139 54 E
Ickenham, Lon. 4 B2 51 33N 0 26W
Ickern, Ruhr 6 A6 51 35N 7 21 E
Iddo, Lagos 18 B2 6 28N 7 22 E
Idi-Oro, Lagos 18 A2 6 31N 7 21 E
Idimu, Lagos 18 A1 6 34N 7 17 E
Idrīs, Bagd. 17 E8 33 22N 44 27 E
Iganmu, Lagos 18 B2 6 28N 7 22 E
Igbobi, Lagos 18 A2 6 31N 7 22 E
Igbologun, Lagos 18 B1 6 24N 7 19 E
Igbopa, Lagos 18 A3 6 32N 7 31 E
Igelboda, Stock. 3 E12 59 17N 18 17 E
Igny, Paris 5 C3 48 44N 2 13 E
Iguassú, S. Pau. 31 E6 23 36 S 46 30W
Ijesa-Tedo, Lagos 18 B1 6 29N 7 19 E
Ijora, Lagos 18 B2 6 27N 7 22 E
Ikebe, Tōkyō 13 C2 35 31N 139 34 E
Ikebukuro, Tōkyō 13 B3 35 43N 139 42 E
Ikeda, Ōsaka 12 B3 34 48N 135 25 E
Ikegami, Tōkyō 13 C3 35 33N 139 42 E
Ikeja, Lagos 18 A2 6 35N 7 20 E
Ikeuchi, Ōsaka 12 C4 34 35N 135 32 E
Ikotun, Lagos 18 A1 6 32N 7 16 E
Ikoyi, Lagos 18 B2 6 27N 7 26 E
Ikuata, Lagos 18 B2 6 24N 7 21 E
Ikuno, Ōsaka 12 B4 34 40N 135 30 E
Ikuta, Ōsaka 12 B2 34 41N 135 10 E
Ikuta, Tōkyō 13 C2 35 36N 139 32 E
Ila, Oslo 2 B3 59 57N 10 35 E
Ilchester, Balt. 25 B2 39 14N 76 46W
Ilford, Lon. 4 B5 51 33N 0 4 E
Ilioúpolis, Ath. 8 J11 37 54N 23 47 E
Illovo, Jobg. 18 E9 26 7 S 28 3 E
Ilsós →, Ath. 8 J11 37 55N 23 41 E
Imajuku, Tōkyō 13 D2 35 28N 139 32 E
Imbâba, El Qâ. 18 C5 30 3N 31 12 E
Imielin, Wsaw. 10 F7 52 9N 21 0 E
Imirim, S. Pau. 31 D6 23 29 S 46 39W
Imittós, Ath. 8 J11 37 55N 23 45 E
Immersby, Hels. 3 B6 60 18N 25 16 E
Imore, Lagos 18 B1 6 25N 7 17 E
Imperial Palace, Tōkyō 13 B3 35 41N 139 45 E
Ina →, Ōsaka 12 B3 34 48N 135 27 E
Inagi, Tōkyō 13 C2 35 38N 139 31 E
Incirano, Mil. 9 D5 45 34N 9 9 E
Independencia, Lima 30 F8 11 59 S 77 3W
Indian Gabe, Delhi 16 B2 28 36N 77 13 E
Indian Museum, Calc. 16 E6 22 33N 88 21 E
Indiana Harbor, Chic. 26 C4 41 40N 87 26W
Indiana Harbor Canal, Chic. 26 D4 41 39N 87 26W
Indianópolis, S. Pau. 31 E6 23 35 S 46 38W
Indios Verdes, Méx. 29 B3 19 29N 99 6W
Ingarö, Stock. 3 E13 59 17N 18 24 E
Ingaröfjärden, Stock. 3 E13 59 14N 18 25 E
Ingarölandet, Stock. 3 E13 59 17N 18 22 E
Ingenieur Budge, B.A. 32 C4 34 43 S 58 27W
Ingierstrand, Oslo 2 C4 59 49N 10 46 E
Ingleburn, Syd. 19 C2 34 0 S 150 52 E
Inglewood, L.A. 28 C3 33 57N 118 19W
Ingrave, Lon. 4 B7 51 35N 0 20 E
Ingvalsby, Hels. 3 C2 60 9N 24 32 E
Inhaúme, Rio J. 31 B2 22 51 S 43 17W
Inner Port Shelter, H.K. 12 D6 22 22N 114 17 E
Interagos, S. Pau. 31 F5 23 41 S 46 42W
Intramuros, Manila 15 D3 14 35N 120 57 E
Invalides, Paris 5 B3 48 51N 2 18 E
Inverness, Balt. 25 B4 39 15N 76 29W
Inwood, N.Y. 23 D6 40 36N 73 45W
Inzersdorf, Wien 10 H10 48 8N 16 21 E
Ipanema, Rio J. 31 B2 22 59 S 43 12W
Ipiranga, S. Pau. 31 E6 23 35 S 46 36W
Ipiranga →, S. Pau. 31 E6 23 37 S 46 37W
Iponri, Lagos 18 B2 6 28N 7 22 E
Ipswich, Bost. 21 A4 42 41N 70 50W
Ipswich →, Bost. 21 B4 42 39N 70 53W
Irajá, Rio J. 31 B2 22 50 S 43 19W
Irving Park, Chic. 26 B2 41 57N 87 42W
Irvington, N.Y. 23 A5 41 2N 73 52W
Irwindale, L.A. 28 B5 34 6N 117 54W
Isabel, Rio J. 31 B2 22 55 S 43 14W
Isagatedo, Lagos 18 A1 6 31N 7 19 E
Isando, Jobg. 18 E10 26 8 S 28 12 E
Isar →, Mün. 7 F11 48 15N 11 41 E
Iselin, N.Y. 22 D3 40 34N 74 19W
Iserbrook, Hbg. 7 D6 53 34N 9 49 E
Iseri-Osun, Lagos 18 A1 6 30N 7 16 E
Ishbīlīya, Bagd. 17 E8 33 21N 44 26 E
Isheri-Olofin, Lagos 18 A1 6 34N 7 16 E
Ishi →, Ōsaka 12 C4 34 34N 135 37 E
Ishikiri, Ōsaka 12 B4 34 40N 135 39 E
Ishizu →, Ōsaka 12 C3 34 33N 135 26 E
Ishøj Strand, Købn. 2 E9 55 36N 12 20 E
Isidro Casanova, B.A. 32 C3 34 42 S 58 36W
Island Channel, N.Y. 23 D5 40 35N 73 52W
Island Park, N.Y. 23 D7 40 36N 73 38W
Island Park, Trto. 20 E8 43 37N 79 22W
Islev, Købn. 2 D9 55 41N 12 27 E
Isleworth, Lon. 4 C3 51 28N 0 19W
Islington, Bost. 21 D2 42 13N 71 13W
Islington, Lon. 4 B4 51 32N 0 6W
Islington, Trto. 20 E7 43 38N 79 30W
Ismaning, Mün. 7 F11 48 13N 11 40 E
Ismayloskiypark, Mos. 11 E10 55 46N 37 46 E
Isogo-Ku, Tōkyō 13 D2 35 23N 139 37 E
Isolo, Lagos 18 A1 6 31N 7 19 E
Isosaari, Hels. 3 C5 60 6N 25 3 E
Issy-les-Moulineaux, Paris 5 C3 48 49N 2 15 E
Istanbul, Ist. 17 B2 41 0N 28 58 E
Istanbul Boğazi, Ist. 17 A3 41 5N 29 3 E
Istanbul Hava Alani, Ist. 17 B2 40 58N 28 50 E
Istead Rise, Lon. 4 C7 51 24N 0 21 E
Istinye, Ist. 17 A3 41 6N 29 3 E
Isunba, Lagos 18 B1 6 25N 7 17 E
Itä Hakkila, Hels. 3 B5 60 17N 25 7 E
Itabashi-Ku, Tōkyō 13 B2 35 46N 139 38 E
Itaberaba, S. Pau. 31 D6 23 28 S 46 39W
Itaeweon, Sŏul 12 G7 37 32N 126 58 E
Itaim, S. Pau. 31 D7 23 29 S 46 23W
Itaipu, Rio J. 31 B3 22 58 S 43 2W
Italie, Place d', Paris 5 C4 48 49N 2 22 E
Itami, Ōsaka 12 B3 34 46N 135 24 E
Itaocaia, Rio J. 31 B3 22 58 S 43 2W
Itapecerica da Serra, S. Pau. 31 F5 23 42 S 46 50W
Itaquaquecetuba, S. Pau. 31 D7 23 29 S 46 23W
Itaquera, S. Pau. 31 E7 23 32 S 46 27W
Itaquera →, S. Pau. 31 E7 23 28 S 46 26W
Ithan, Phil. 24 A2 40 1N 75 21W
Itupu, S. Pau. 31 F5 23 40 S 46 43W
Ituzaingo, B.A. 32 B3 34 39 S 58 38W
Ivanhoe, Melb. 19 E7 37 45 S 145 3 E
Iver, Lon. 4 B1 51 32N 0 30W
Ivry-sur-Seine, Paris 5 C4 48 49N 2 22 E
Iwazono, Ōsaka 12 B2 34 45N 135 18 E
Izabelin, Wsaw. 10 E5 52 17N 20 48 E
Izmaylovo, Mos. 11 E10 55 47N 37 47 E
Iztacalco, Méx. 29 B3 19 23N 99 6W
Iztapalapa, Méx. 29 B3 19 21N 99 6W
Izumi, Tōkyō 13 D1 35 25N 139 29 E

J

J. G. Strijdom Post Office Tower, Jobg. 18 F9 26 11 S 28 2 E
J. Paul Getty Museum, L.A. 28 B1 34 2N 118 33W
Jabavu, Jobg. 18 F8 26 14 S 27 52 E
Jabulani, Jobg. 18 F8 26 14 S 27 51 E
Jacarepaguá, Rio J. 31 B1 22 56 S 43 20W
Jackson Heights, N.Y. 23 C5 40 44N 73 53W
Jackson Park, Chic. 26 C3 41 46N 87 34W
Jacksonville, N.Y. 22 B3 40 57N 74 18W
Jacomino, La Hab. 30 B3 23 6N 82 19W
Jacques Cartier, Mtrl. 20 A5 43 31N 73 27W
Jægersborg, Købn. 2 D10 55 45N 12 31 E
Jægersborg Dyrehave, Købn. 2 D10 55 46N 12 33 E
Jægersborg Hegn, Købn. 2 D10 55 49N 12 33 E
Jafarpur, Calc. 16 D6 22 45N 88 22 E
Jagacha, Calc. 16 E5 22 35N 88 17 E
Jagannathpur, Calc. 16 D5 22 43N 88 18 E
Jagatdal, Calc. 16 C6 22 51N 88 23 E
Jagatmagar, Calc. 16 D5 22 46N 88 13 E
Jagatpur, Delhi 16 A2 28 44N 77 13 E
Jagdispur, Calc. 16 E5 22 39N 88 17 E
Jaguara, S. Pau. 31 E5 23 30 S 46 45W
Jaguaré, S. Pau. 31 E5 23 32 S 46 45W
Jaguaré →, S. Pau. 31 E5 23 32 S 46 45W
Jahangirpur, Delhi 16 A2 28 43N 77 12 E
Jaimanitas →, La Hab. 30 B2 23 5N 82 29W
Jakarta, Jak. 15 H10 6 9 S 106 52 E
Jakarta, Teluk, Jak. 15 H9 6 5 S 106 50 E
Jakosberg, Stock. 3 D9 59 25N 17 47 E
Jalan Kayu, Sing. 15 F8 1 24N 103 52 E
Jamaica, N.Y. 23 C6 40 42N 73 48W
Jamaica B., N.Y. 23 D6 40 36N 73 49W
Jamaica Plain, Bost. 21 D3 42 18N 71 6W
Jamshīdābād, Tehr. 17 C5 35 42N 51 22 E
Jamsil, Sŏul 12 G8 37 30N 127 4 E
Jamweon, Sŏul 12 G8 37 30N 127 0 E
Jan Smuts Airport, Jobg. 18 E10 26 7 S 28 14 E
Janai, Calc. 16 D5 22 43N 88 15 E
Janā'in, Bagd. 17 F8 33 18N 44 22 E
Janki, Wsaw. 10 F6 52 8N 20 52 E
Jannali, Syd. 19 C3 34 0 S 151 4 E
Jánoshegy, Bud. 10 J12 47 31N 18 57 E
Janów, Wsaw. 10 E6 52 16N 20 50 E
Janvry, Paris 5 D2 48 38N 2 9 E
Jaraguá, S. Pau. 31 D5 23 27 S 46 44W
Jaraguá, Pico de, S. Pau. 31 D5 23 27 S 46 46W
Jarama →, Mdrd. 8 B3 40 29N 3 32W
Jardim América, S. Pau. 31 E6 23 34 S 46 39W
Jardim Anchieta, S. Pau. 31 F7 23 41 S 46 27W
Jardim Arpoador, S. Pau. 31 E5 23 35 S 46 48W
Jardim do Mar, S. Pau. 31 F6 23 41 S 46 33W
Jardim Munhoz, S. Pau. 31 E6 23 30 S 46 33W
Jardim Osasco, S. Pau. 31 E5 23 33 S 46 47W
Jardim Ouro Preto, S. Pau. 31 E5 23 35 S 46 46W
Jardim Paulista, S. Pau. 31 E5 23 34 S 46 41W
Jardim Petrópolis, S. Pau. 31 F7 23 41 S 46 23W
Jardim Rochidale, S. Pau. 31 E5 23 30 S 46 46W
Jardim Santista, S. Pau. 31 F7 23 40 S 46 24W
Jardim São Bento, S. Pau. 31 F5 23 40 S 46 46W
Jardim São Francisco, S. Pau. 31 E7 23 38 S 46 26W
Jardim Sapopemba, S. Pau. 31 E7 23 36 S 46 29W
Jardim Vera Cruz, S. Pau. 31 E7 23 35 S 46 27W
Jardim Vista Alegre, S. Pau. 31 E5 23 37 S 46 49W
Jardim Zaira, S. Pau. 31 E7 23 39 S 46 25W
Jardines Flotantes, Méx. 29 C3 19 16N 99 6W
Jardine's Lookout, H.K. 12 E6 22 16N 114 11 E
Järfälla, Stock. 3 D10 59 23N 17 51 E
Järvafältet, Stock. 3 D10 59 25N 17 54 E
Järventausta, Hels. 3 A1 60 21N 24 28 E
Jasai, Bomb. 16 H9 18 56N 73 1 E
Jaskhar, Bomb. 16 H8 18 54N 72 58 E
Jatinegara, Jak. 15 J10 6 13 S 106 52 E
Jauli, Delhi 16 A3 28 44N 77 20 E
Jawādiyeh, Tehr. 17 D5 35 39N 51 22 E
Jaworowa, Wsaw. 10 F6 52 9N 20 56 E
Jayang, Sŏul 12 G8 37 32N 127 3 E
Jedlesee, Wien 10 G10 48 15N 16 23 E
Jefferson, Phil. 24 C3 39 45N 75 12W
Jefferson Park, Chic. 26 B2 41 58N 87 46W
Jeffersonville, Phil. 24 A2 40 8N 75 23W
Jegi, Sŏul 12 G8 37 34N 127 1 E
Jells Park, Melb. 19 F8 37 53 S 145 11 E
Jelonki, Wsaw. 10 E6 52 14N 20 54 E
Jenfeld, Hbg. 7 D8 53 34N 10 8 E
Jenkintown, Phil. 24 A4 40 6N 75 8W
Jeongreung, Sŏul 12 G8 37 35N 127 0 E
Jericho, N.Y. 23 C7 40 47N 73 32W
Jerónimes, Mosteiro dos, Lisb. 8 F7 38 41N 9 11W
Jersey City, N.Y. 22 C4 40 42N 74 4W
Jésus, Î., Mtrl. 20 A3 43 36N 73 44W
Jesus Del Monte, La Hab. 30 B2 23 6N 82 21W
Jesús Maria, Lima 30 G8 12 4 S 77 3W
Jhenkari, Calc. 16 D5 22 45N 88 18 E
Jhil Kuranga, Delhi 16 B2 28 39N 77 14 E
Jiangqiao, Shang. 14 J11 31 15N 121 20 E
Jiangtai, Beij. 14 B3 39 57N 116 28 E
Jianguomen, Beij. 14 B3 39 53N 116 24 E
Jiangwan, Shang. 14 J11 31 18N 121 28 E
Jianshan Gongyuan, Tianj. 14 E6 39 5N 117 12 E
Jihād, Bagd. 17 F7 33 17N 44 19 E
Jingan, Shang. 14 J11 31 14N 121 25 E
Jinočany, Pra. 10 B1 50 2N 14 16 E
Jinonice, Pra. 10 B2 50 3N 14 22 E
Jirny, Pra. 10 B4 50 7N 14 41 E
Jiuxianqiao, Beij. 14 B3 39 58N 116 28 E
Jiyźgaoka, Tōkyō 13 C3 35 35N 139 40 E
Jizā'er, Bagd. 17 F8 33 15N 44 23 E
Jizīra, Bagd. 17 F8 33 15N 44 25 E
Joan Despi, Barc. 8 D5 41 22N 2 2 E
Joaquin Miller Park, S.F. 27 B3 37 48N 122 11W
Johannesburg, Jobg. 18 F9 26 11 S 28 2 E
Johanneskirchen, Mün. 7 F10 48 10N 11 38 E
Johannesstift, Berl. 7 A2 52 34N 13 12 E
Johannisthal, Berl. 7 B4 52 26N 13 30 E
John F. Kennedy Int. Airport, N.Y. 23 D6 40 39N 73 45W
John F. Kennedy Nat. Hist. Site, Bost. 21 C3 42 20N 71 7W
John Hancock Center, Chic. 26 B3 41 53N 87 37W
John Hopkins Univ., Balt. 25 B3 39 19N 76 37W
John McLaren Park, S.F. 27 B2 37 43N 122 24W
Joinville-le-Pont, Paris 5 C4 48 49N 2 27 E
Jollas, Hels. 3 B5 60 10N 25 5 E
Jones Beach State Park, N.Y. 23 D7 40 35N 73 32W
Jones Falls →, Balt. 25 B3 39 20N 76 36W
Jones Inlet, N.Y. 23 D7 40 34N 73 34W
Jonestown, Balt. 25 B2 39 13N 76 48W
Jong Ro, Sŏul 12 G7 37 34N 126 58 E
Jongmyo Royal Shrine, Sŏul 12 G7 37 34N 126 59 E
Jonstrup, Købn. 2 D9 55 45N 12 20 E
Joppatowne, Balt. 25 A4 39 24N 76 20W
Jordan Valley, H.K. 12 D6 22 20N 114 12 E
Jorge Chavez, Aeropuerto Int., Lima 30 G8 12 2 S 77 8W
Jorvas, Hels. 3 C2 60 8N 24 30 E
José C. Paz, B.A. 32 B2 34 31 S 58 44W
José L. Suárez, B.A. 32 B3 34 32 S 58 34W
José Mármol, B.A. 32 C4 34 47 S 58 22W
Jose Marti, Aeropuerto Int., La Hab. 30 C2 22 59N 82 22W
Josephine Pk., L.A. 28 A4 34 17N 118 7W
Jōsō, Ōsaka 12 B3 34 42N 135 27 E
Jōtō, Ōsaka 12 B4 34 42N 135 33 E
Jouars-Pontchartrain, Paris 5 C1 48 47N 1 53 E
Jouy-en-Josas, Paris 5 C3 48 46N 2 10 E
Jouy-le-Moutier, Paris 5 A2 49 0N 2 2 E
Józefów, Wsaw. 10 F8 52 8N 21 13 E
Juan Escutia, Méx. 29 B3 19 23N 99 3W
Juan González Romero, Méx. 29 A3 19 30N 99 3W
Juhu, Bomb. 16 G9 19 5N 73 0 E
Juilly, Paris 5 A6 49 0N 2 42 E
Jūjā, Tōkyō 13 B3 35 45N 139 43 E
Jukskeirivier →, Jobg. 18 E9 26 5 S 28 6 E
Julianów, Wsaw. 10 E7 52 10N 21 9 E
Jung, Sŏul 12 G7 37 33N 126 59 E
Jungfernheide, Volkspark, Berl. 7 A2 52 32N 13 18 E
Jungfernsee, Berl. 7 B1 52 25N 13 6 E
Jungwha, Sŏul 12 G8 37 35N 127 3 E
Junk B., H.K. 12 E6 22 17N 114 15 E
Jurong, Sing. 15 G7 1 19N 103 40 E
Jurong, Selat, Sing. 15 G7 1 17N 103 42 E
Jurong, Sungei →, Sing. 15 G7 1 17N 103 45 E
Jurubatuba, S. Pau. 31 F5 23 40 S 46 41W
Jurujuba, Enseada de, Rio J. 31 B3 22 54 S 43 6W
Justice, Chic. 26 C2 41 44N 87 49W
Juusjärvi, Hels. 3 B1 60 12N 24 26 E
Juva, Hels. 3 B3 60 16N 24 45 E
Juvisy-sur-Orge, Paris 5 C4 48 41N 2 21 E
Jwalahari, Delhi 16 B1 28 40N 77 6 E
Jyllinge, Købn. 2 D7 55 45N 12 6 E

K

Kaarst, Ruhr 6 C1 51 13N 6 36 E
Kabaty, Wsaw. 10 F7 52 8N 21 4 E
Kabel, Ruhr 6 B6 51 24N 7 28 E
Kadiköy, Ist. 17 B3 40 59N 29 1 E
Kadoma, Ōsaka 12 B4 34 44N 135 35 E
Kafr es Sammân, El Qâ. 18 D4 29 58N 31 8 E
Kâğithane, Ist. 17 A2 41 4N 28 58 E
Kâğithane →, Ist. 17 A2 41 9N 28 56 E
Kagran, Wien 10 G10 48 14N 16 26 E
Kahlenberg, Wien 10 G9 48 16N 16 19 E
Kai Tak, H.K. 12 D6 22 20N 114 11 E
Kaisariani, Ath. 8 J11 37 57N 23 46 E
Kaiser-Mühlen, Wien 10 G10 48 13N 16 25 E
Kaiserebersdorf, Wien 10 H10 48 9N 16 26 E
Kaiserswerth, Ruhr 6 C2 51 18N 6 44 E
Kaivoksela, Hels. 3 B4 60 15N 24 53 E
Kakukk-hegy, Bud. 10 K12 47 29N 18 57 E
Kalachhara, Calc. 16 D5 22 42N 88 15 E
Kalamákion, Ath. 8 J11 37 52N 23 43 E
Kaldenhausen, Ruhr 6 B1 51 23N 6 39 E
Kalipur, Calc. 16 D5 22 40N 88 17 E
Kalkaji, Delhi 16 B2 28 32N 77 12 E
Kalksburg, Wien 10 H9 48 8N 16 15 E
Kallang →, Sing. 15 F8 1 21N 103 51 E
Kallhäll, Stock. 3 D9 59 26N 17 48 E
Kallithéa, Ath. 8 J11 37 56N 23 43 E
Kallvik, Hels. 3 B5 60 12N 25 8 E
Kaltbründsberg, Wien 10 G9 48 10N 16 13 E
Kaltenleutgeben, Wien 10 H9 48 7N 16 11 E
Kalveboderne, Købn. 2 E10 55 37N 12 31 E
Kalytino, St-Pet. 11 B5 59 59N 30 39 E
Kamaraerdö, Bud. 10 K12 47 26N 18 59 E
Kamarhati, Calc. 16 D6 22 40N 88 23 E
Kamarkunda, Calc. 16 D5 22 49N 88 12 E
Kamata, Tōkyō 13 C3 35 33N 139 43 E
Kamdebpur, Calc. 16 C5 22 53N 88 19 E
Kameari, Tōkyō 13 B4 35 45N 139 50 E
Kameido, Tōkyō 13 B4 35 42N 139 50 E
Kami-hoshikawa, Tōkyō 13 D2 35 27N 139 35 E
Kami-Itabashi, Tōkyō 13 B3 35 45N 139 40 E
Kami-nakazato, Tōkyō 13 D2 35 22N 139 36 E
Kami-saruyama, Tōkyō 13 C2 35 30N 139 31 E
Kami-sugata, Tōkyō 13 D2 35 28N 139 34 E
Kami-tomi, Tōkyō 13 B1 35 48N 139 29 E
Kamikitazawa, Tōkyō 13 C2 35 39N 139 36 E
Kamikiyoto, Tōkyō 13 B2 35 45N 139 30 E
Kamishiki, Tōkyō 13 B4 35 46N 139 57 E
Kamitsuruma, Tōkyō 13 C1 35 30N 139 26 E
Kamiyama, Tōkyō 13 B2 35 46N 139 32 E
Kamoi, Tōkyō 13 C2 35 30N 139 34 E
Kamoshida, Tōkyō 13 C2 35 33N 139 31 E
Kampong Batak, Sing. 15 F8 1 20N 103 54 E
Kampong Mandai Kechil, Sing. 15 F7 1 26N 103 46 E
Kampong Pachitan, Sing. 15 G8 1 19N 103 54 E
Kampong Potong Pasir, Sing. 15 F8 1 20N 103 52 E
Kampong Reteh, Sing. 15 G8 1 19N 103 53 E
Kampong Tengah, Sing. 15 F7 1 22N 103 42 E
Kampong Ulu Jurong, Sing. 15 F7 1 20N 103 42 E
Kampung Ambon, Jak. 15 J10 6 11 S 106 53 E
Kampung Bali, Jak. 15 J9 6 11 S 106 48 E
Kan, Tehr. 17 C4 35 45N 51 16 E
Kanagawa-Ku, Tōkyō 13 D2 35 29N 139 38 E
Kanamachi, Tōkyō 13 B4 35 46N 139 52 E
Kanamori, Tōkyō 13 C1 35 31N 139 27 E
Kanda, Tōkyō 13 B3 35 41N 139 45 E
Kandang Kerbau, Sing. 15 G8 1 18N 103 51 E
Kandilli, Ist. 17 A3 41 4N 29 3 E
Kanegasaku, Tōkyō 13 B4 35 48N 139 56 E
Kangaroo Ground, Melb. 19 E8 37 41 S 145 13 E
Kankinara, Calc. 16 C6 22 51N 88 24 E
Kankurgachi, Calc. 16 E6 22 34N 88 23 E
Kanlica, Ist. 17 A3 41 5N 29 3 E
Kanoaka, Ōsaka 12 C4 34 33N 135 31 E
Kanonerskiy, Os., St-Pet. 11 B3 59 53N 30 13 E
Kanzaki →, Ōsaka 12 B3 34 41N 135 24 E
Kapellerfeld, Wien 10 G10 48 18N 16 29 E
Kapotnya, Mos. 11 F10 55 39N 37 48 E
Käppala, Stock. 3 D12 59 21N 18 13 E
Käpylä, Hels. 3 B4 60 13N 24 57 E
Karachi, Kar. 17 G11 24 50N 67 0 E
Karachi Int. Airport, Kar. 17 G11 24 5N 67 9 E
Karachi Univ., Kar. 17 G11 24 51N 67 0 E
Karagümrük, Ist. 17 A2 41 1N 28 56 E
Karāma, Bagd. 17 E8 33 20N 44 22 E
Karato, Ōsaka 12 B2 34 46N 135 12 E
Karave, Bomb. 16 G9 19 0N 73 0 E
Karet, Jak. 15 J9 6 12 S 106 49 E
Karkar Duman, Delhi 16 B2 28 39N 77 18 E
Karkh, Bagd. 17 E8 33 20N 44 22 E
Karlberg, Stock. 3 D11 59 20N 18 1 E
Karlin, Pra. 10 B2 50 5N 14 26 E
Karlsfeld, Mün. 7 F9 48 13N 11 28 E
Karlshorst, Berl. 7 B4 52 29N 13 31 E
Karlslunde Strand, Købn. 2 E8 55 33N 12 15 E
Karnap, Ruhr 6 A4 51 31N 7 0 E
Karolinenhof, Berl. 7 B4 52 23N 13 38 E
Karow, Berl. 7 A3 52 36N 13 29 E
Karrādah, Bagd. 17 F8 33 17N 44 23 E
Kärsön, Stock. 3 E10 59 19N 17 54 E
Kasai, Tōkyō 13 C4 35 39N 139 52 E
Kasetsart, Bangk. 15 A2 13 50N 100 34 E
Kashi-Hazaki, Tōkyō 13 A3 35 54N 139 42 E
Kashio, Tōkyō 13 D2 35 24N 139 34 E
Kashiwa, Tōkyō 13 A4 35 51N 139 57 E
Kashiwara, Ōsaka 12 C4 34 34N 135 37 E
Kaskela, Hels. 3 B5 60 17N 25 6 E
Kastrup, Købn. 2 E10 55 38N 12 39 E
Kastrup Lufthavn, Købn. 2 E11 55 37N 12 14 E
Kasuga, Tōkyō 13 B2 35 45N 139 38 E
Kasuge, Tōkyō 13 B3 35 45N 139 49 E
Kasumigasek, Tōkyō 13 C3 35 40N 139 46 E
Katabira →, Tōkyō 13 D2 35 27N 139 38 E
Katernberg, Ruhr 6 A4 51 30N 7 4 E
Katong Park, Sing. 15 G8 1 18N 103 53 E
Katrineberg, Stock. 3 E10 59 13N 17 54 E
Katsushika-Ku, Tōkyō 13 B4 35 44N 139 51 E
Kattinge Vig, Købn. 2 D7 55 40N 12 1 E
Kau Pei Chau, H.K. 12 E6 22 12N 114 15 E
Kau Yi Chau, H.K. 12 E5 22 17N 114 4 E
Kauklahti, Hels. 3 B2 60 11N 24 36 E
Kaulsdorf, Berl. 7 B4 52 29N 13 34 E
Kauniainen, Hels. 3 B3 60 13N 24 44 E
Kawagoe, Tōkyō 13 A1 35 54N 139 29 E
Kawaguchi, Tōkyō 13 B3 35 47N 139 43 E
Kawai, Tōkyō 13 D2 35 29N 139 31 E
Kawamukō, Tōkyō 13 C2 35 30N 139 34 E
Kawanishi, Ōsaka 12 B3 34 49N 135 24 E
Kawasaki, Tōkyō 13 C3 35 31N 139 43 E
Kawasaki Harbour, Tōkyō 13 D3 35 30N 139 47 E
Kawawa, Tōkyō 13 C2 35 31N 139 33 E
Kawęczyn, Wsaw. 10 E7 52 16N 21 5 E
Kayu Putih, Jak. 15 J10 6 10 S 106 53 E
Kbely, Pra. 10 B3 50 8N 14 32 E
Kearny, N.Y. 22 C4 40 45N 74 8W
Kebayoran Baru, Jak. 15 J9 6 14 S 106 47 E
Kebayoran Lama, Jak. 15 J9 6 13 S 106 46 E
Kebon Jeruk, Jak. 15 J9 6 11 S 106 46 E
Keferloh, Mün. 7 G11 48 5N 11 43 E
Keilor, Melb. 19 E6 37 42 S 144 50 E
Keilor East, Melb. 19 E6 37 44 S 144 51 E
Keimola, Hels. 3 A3 60 20N 24 49 E
Kelenföld, Bud. 10 K13 47 27N 19 2 E
Kelvedon Hatch, Lon. 4 A6 51 40N 0 16 E
Kelvin, Jobg. 18 E9 26 4 S 28 5 E
Kemang, Jak. 15 J9 6 15 S 106 48 E
Kemayoran, Jak. 15 J10 6 10 S 106 51 E
Kemayoran Airport, Jak. 15 H10 6 8 S 106 50 E
Kemp Mill, Wash. 25 C7 39 0N 77 1W
Kempton Park, Jobg. 18 E10 26 5 S 28 14 E
Kempton Racecourse, Lon. 4 C2 51 24N 0 23W
Kemsing, Lon. 4 D6 51 18N 0 12 E
Kendall Green, Bost. 21 C2 42 22N 71 16W
Kendua, Calc. 16 E5 22 34N 88 10 E
Keng Hau, H.K. 12 D6 22 22N 114 10 E
Kenilworth, Chic. 26 A2 42 5N 87 42W
Kenilworth, N.Y. 22 C3 40 40N 74 16W
Kenley, Lon. 4 D4 51 19N 0 6W
Kenmare, Jobg. 18 E7 26 6 S 27 48 E
Kennedy Grove Regional Rec. Area, S.F. 27 A3 37 56N 122 14W

40 Kennedy Town

Kennedy Town, *H.K.* 12 E5 22 16N 114 6 E
Kensal Green, *Lon.* 4 B3 51 32N 0 13W
Kensington, *Jobg.* 18 F9 26 11 S 28 6 E
Kensington, *Lon.* 4 C3 51 29N 0 10W
Kensington, *N.Y.* 22 D5 40 38N 73 57W
Kensington, *Phil.* 24 B4 39 59N 75 6W
Kensington, *S.F.* 27 A3 37 54N 122 17W
Kensington, *Syd.* 19 B4 33 54 S 151 13 E
Kensington, *Wash.* 25 C7 39 1N 77 4W
Kensington Palace, *Lon.* 4 B3 51 30N 0 11W
Kent Woodlands, *S.F.* 27 A1 37 56N 122 34W
Kentfield, *S.F.* 27 A1 37 57N 122 33W
Kentish Town, *Lon.* 4 B4 51 32N 0 8W
Kentland, *Wash.* 25 D8 38 55N 76 53W
Kenton, *Lon.* 4 B2 51 34N 0 17W
Kenwood, *Balt.* 25 A4 39 20N 76 30W
Kenwood, *Bost.* 21 B2 42 40N 71 14W
Kenwood House, *Lon.* 4 B4 51 34N 0 9W
Kepa, *Wsaw.* 10 E7 52 13N 21 3 E
Keppel Harbour, *Sing.* 15 G7 1 15N 103 49 E
Kerameikos, *Ath.* 8 J11 37 58N 23 42 E
Kerepes, *Bud.* 10 J14 47 33N 19 17 E
Keston, *Lon.* 4 C5 51 21N 0 1 E
Keston Mark, *Lon.* 4 C5 51 21N 0 2 E
Keth Wara, *Delhi* 16 A2 28 40N 77 13 E
Kettering, *Wash.* 25 D9 38 53N 76 49W
Kettwig, *Ruhr* 6 B3 51 22N 6 56 E
Kew, *Jobg.* 18 E9 26 7 S 28 5 E
Kew, *Lon.* 4 C3 51 28N 0 17W
Kew, *Melb.* 19 E7 37 48 S 145 2 E
Kew Gardens, *Lon.* 4 C3 51 28N 0 17W
Key Gardens, *Trto.* 20 E9 43 39N 79 18W
Khaboye, *St-Pet.* 11 B6 59 53N 30 44 E
Khaidhárion, *Ath.* 8 H10 38 2N 23 38 E
Khairna, *Bomb.* 16 G9 19 5N 73 0 E
Khalándrion, *Ath.* 8 H11 38 3N 23 48 E
Khalij, *Bagd.* 17 F8 33 18N 44 28 E
Khansā, *Bagd.* 17 E8 33 21N 44 28 E
Kharavli, *Bomb.* 16 H8 18 54N 72 55 E
Khardah, *Calc.* 16 D6 22 43N 88 22 E
Khayala, *Delhi* 16 B1 28 39N 77 6 E
Khefren, *El Qâ.* 18 D4 29 58N 31 8 E
Khichripur, *Delhi* 16 B2 28 37N 77 18 E
Khimki, *Mos.* 11 D8 55 53N 37 24 E
Khimki-Khovrino, *Mos.* 11 D9 55 51N 37 31 E
Khimkinskoye Vdkr., *Mos.* 11 D8 55 51N 37 27 E
Khirvosti, *St-Pet.* 11 B5 59 56N 30 37 E
Khlongsan, *Bangk.* 15 B1 13 43N 100 29 E
Kholargós, *Ath.* 8 J11 37 59N 23 48 E
Khorel, *Calc.* 16 D5 22 41N 88 18 E
Khorosovo, *Mos.* 11 E8 55 46N 37 27 E
Khudrā, *Bagd.* 17 F7 33 19N 44 17 E
Khun Thian, *Bangk.* 15 B1 13 41N 100 27 E
Khuraiji Khas, *Delhi* 16 B2 28 38N 77 16 E
Khurigachi, *Calc.* 16 D5 22 48N 88 21 E
Kiamari, *Kar.* 17 H10 24 49N 66 58 E
Kidderpore, *Calc.* 16 E5 22 32N 88 19 E
Kienwerder, *Berl.* 7 B2 52 22N 13 11 E
Kierling, *Wien* 10 G9 48 18N 16 16 E
Kierlingbach →, *Wien* 10 G9 48 18N 16 19 E
Kierlinger Forst, *Wien* 10 G9 48 17N 16 14 E
Kierst, *Ruhr* 6 C2 51 18N 6 42 E
Kifisós →, *Ath.* 8 J11 37 58N 23 42 E
Kikenka →, *St-Pet.* 11 B2 59 50N 30 3 E
Kikuna, *Tōkyō* 13 C2 35 30N 139 37 E
Kil, *Stock.* 3 D12 59 20N 18 19 E
Kilburn, *Lon.* 4 B3 51 32N 0 11W
Killara, *Syd.* 19 A4 33 46 S 151 10 E
Kilo, *Hels.* 3 B3 60 13N 24 47 E
Kilokri, *Delhi* 16 B2 28 34N 77 15 E
Kilsyth, *Melb.* 19 E8 37 48 S 145 18 E
Kimberton, *Phil.* 24 A1 40 7N 75 34W
Kimlin Park, *Sing.* 15 G8 1 18N 103 49 E
Kindi, *Bagd.* 17 F8 33 18N 44 22 E
King of Prussia, *Phil.* 24 A2 40 5N 75 22W
Kings Cross, *Syd.* 19 B4 33 52 S 151 12 E
Kings Domain, *Melb.* 19 E6 37 49 S 144 58 E
Kings Mt., *S.F.* 27 D3 37 27N 122 19W
King's Park, *H.K.* 12 E6 22 18N 114 10 E
Kings Park, *Wash.* 25 E6 38 48N 77 17W
King's Point, *N.Y.* 23 C6 40 48N 73 45W
Kingsbury, *Lon.* 4 B3 51 34N 0 15W
Kingsford, *Syd.* 19 B4 33 55 S 151 14 E
Kingston upon Thames, *Lon.* 4 C3 51 24N 0 17W
Kingston Vale, *Lon.* 4 C3 51 25N 0 25W
Kingsway, *Trto.* 20 E7 43 38N 79 32W
Kingswood, *Lon.* 4 D4 51 17N 0 12W
Kinnelon, *N.Y.* 22 B2 40 59N 74 23W
Kipling Heights, *Trto.* 20 D7 43 43N 79 34W
Kipséli, *Ath.* 8 J11 37 59N 23 45 E
Kirchhellen, *Ruhr* 6 A3 51 36N 6 56 E
Kirchhörde, *Ruhr* 6 B6 51 27N 7 27 E
Kirchlinde, *Ruhr* 6 A6 51 31N 7 22 E
Kirchof, *Hbg.* 7 E8 53 29N 10 1 E
Kirchsteinbek, *Hbg.* 7 D8 53 31N 10 7 E
Kirchstockbach, *Mün.* 7 G11 48 1N 11 40 E
Kirchtrudering, *Mün.* 7 G11 48 7N 11 40 E
Kirdasa, *El Qâ.* 18 C4 30 2N 31 6 E
Kirikiri, *Lagos* 18 B1 6 26N 7 18 E
Kirkkonummi, *Hels.* 3 C1 60 6N 24 28W
Kirkland, *Mtrl.* 20 B2 43 26N 73 51W
Kirovskiye, Os., *St-Pet.* 11 B3 59 57N 30 14 E
Kisarazu, *Tōkyō* 13 D4 35 21N 139 54 E
Kisikli, *Ist.* 17 A3 41 1N 29 2 E
Kispest, *Bud.* 10 K13 47 27N 19 8 E
Kista, *Stock.* 3 D10 59 24N 17 57 E
Kistarcsa, *Bud.* 10 J14 47 32N 19 16 E
Kita, *Ōsaka* 12 B4 34 41N 135 30 E
Kita-Ku, *Tōkyō* 13 B3 35 44N 139 44 E
Kitain-Temple, *Tōkyō* 13 A1 35 54N 139 29 E
Kitazawa, *Tōkyō* 13 C3 35 39N 139 40 E
Kiu Tsiu, *H.K.* 12 D6 22 22N 114 17 E
Kivistö, *Hels.* 3 B4 60 18N 24 50 E
Kiyose, *Tōkyō* 13 B2 35 46N 139 31 E
Kiziltoprak, *Ist.* 17 B3 40 58N 29 3 E
Kizu →, *Ōsaka* 12 C3 34 37N 135 27 E
Kizuri, *Ōsaka* 12 C4 34 38N 135 34 E
Kjeller, *Oslo* 2 B6 59 58N 11 1 E
Kjelsås, *Oslo* 2 B4 59 57N 10 47 E
Kladow, *Berl.* 7 B1 52 27N 13 9 E
Klampenborg, *Købn.* 2 D10 55 46N 12 35 E
Klánovice, *Pra.* 10 B3 50 5N 14 40 E
Klaudyń, *Wsaw.* 10 E6 52 17N 20 50 E
Klecany, *Pra.* 10 A2 50 10N 14 24 E
Kledering, *Wien* 10 H10 48 8N 16 26 E
Klein Gleinicke, *Berl.* 7 B1 52 23N 13 5 E
Klein-Hadern, *Mün.* 7 G9 48 7N 11 28 E
Klein Jukskei →, *Jobg.* 18 E8 26 6 S 27 57 E
Kleinburg, *Trto.* 20 C7 43 51N 79 37W
Kleine Grasbrook, *Hbg.* 7 D7 53 31N 9 59 E
Kleinmachnow, *Berl.* 7 B2 52 24N 13 14 E
Kleinschönebeck, *Berl.* 7 B5 52 29N 13 42 E
Kleinziethen, *Berl.* 7 B3 52 22N 13 26 E
Klemetsrud, *Oslo* 2 B5 59 50N 10 51 E
Klender, *Jak.* 15 J10 6 12 S 106 53 E
Klippoortje, *Jobg.* 18 F9 26 14 S 28 10 E
Klipriviersberg, *Jobg.* 18 F8 26 16 S 28 2 E
Klipspruit →, *Jobg.* 18 F8 26 14 S 27 53 E
Kloofendal, *Jobg.* 18 E8 26 8 S 27 52 E
Klosterhardt, *Ruhr* 6 A3 51 32N 6 52 E
Klosterneuburg, *Wien* 10 G9 48 18N 16 19 E
Knockholt Pound, *Lon.* 4 D5 51 18N 0 7 E
Knowland State Arboretum and Park, *S.F.* 27 B4 37 45N 122 7W
Knox Park, *Melb.* 19 F8 37 54 S 145 15 E
Knoxville, *Melb.* 19 F8 37 53 S 145 14 E
Kōbanya, *Bud.* 10 K13 47 28N 19 9 E
Kobe, *Ōsaka* 12 B2 34 41N 135 13 E
Kōbe Harbour, *Ōsaka* 12 C2 34 39N 135 11 E
København, *Købn.* 2 D9 55 40N 12 26 E
Kobylisy, *Pra.* 10 B2 50 7N 14 26 E
Kobyłka, *Wsaw.* 10 D8 52 20N 21 10 E
Kocasinan, *Ist.* 17 A2 41 1N 28 50 E
Kočife, *Pra.* 10 B2 50 3N 14 21 E
Kodaira, *Tōkyō* 13 B1 35 43N 139 28 E
Kodanaka, *Tōkyō* 13 B2 35 34N 139 37 E
Koganei, *Tōkyō* 13 B4 35 49N 139 55 E
Koganei, *Tōkyō* 13 B2 35 42N 139 31 E
Kogarah, *Syd.* 19 B3 33 57 S 151 8 E
Køge Bugt, *Købn.* 2 E9 55 34N 12 24 E
Köhlbrand Rethe, *Hbg.* 7 D7 53 31N 9 56 E
Köhlfleet, *Hbg.* 7 D7 53 32N 9 53 E
Koivupää, *Hels.* 3 B4 60 18N 24 53 E
Koja, *Jak.* 15 H10 6 8 S 106 52 E
Koja Utara, *Jak.* 15 H10 6 5 S 106 53 E
Kokobunji, *Tōkyō* 13 B1 35 42N 139 27 E
Kokobunji-Temple, *Tōkyō* 13 B4 35 44N 139 55 E
Kol Scholven, *Ruhr* 6 A3 51 35N 6 59 E
Kolarängen, *Stock.* 3 E12 59 16N 18 10 E
Kolbotn, *Oslo* 2 C4 59 48N 10 48 E
Kole Kalyan, *Bomb.* 16 G8 19 5N 72 50 E
Kolmiranta, *Hels.* 3 B2 60 15N 24 31 E
Kolmperä, *Hels.* 3 B2 60 15N 24 32 E
Kolo, *Wsaw.* 10 E6 52 14N 20 56 E
Kolodeje, *Pra.* 10 B3 50 3N 14 38 E
Kolokinthou, *Ath.* 8 J11 38 0N 23 42 E
Kolomenskoye, *Mos.* 11 E10 55 40N 37 40 E
Kolomyagi, *St-Pet.* 11 A3 60 0N 30 19 E
Kolónos, *Ath.* 8 J11 37 59N 23 43 E
Kolovraty, *Pra.* 10 B3 50 0N 14 37 E
Kolsås, *Oslo* 2 B3 59 55N 10 30 E
Koltushi, *St-Pet.* 11 B5 59 55N 30 38 E
Komae, *Tōkyō* 13 C2 35 37N 139 34 E
Komagome, *Tōkyō* 13 B3 35 43N 139 45 E
Komazawa, *Tōkyō* 13 C3 35 37N 139 40 E
Komdhara, *Calc.* 16 C5 22 52N 88 14 E
Kommunarka, *Mos.* 11 F8 55 35N 37 29 E
Komorów, *Wsaw.* 10 F5 52 9N 20 48 E
Kona, *Calc.* 16 E5 22 37N 88 18 E
Konala, *Hels.* 3 B4 60 14N 24 52 E
Konan, *Tōkyō* 13 D2 35 23N 139 35 E
Kondli, *Delhi* 16 B2 28 36N 77 19 E
Kong Sin Wan, *H.K.* 12 E5 22 15N 114 7 E
Kongelunden, *Købn.* 2 E10 55 34N 12 34 E
Kongens Lyngby, *Købn.* 2 D10 55 46N 12 30 E
Kongo, *Hels.* 3 A3 60 20N 24 47 E
Königshardt, *Ruhr* 6 A3 51 33N 6 51 E
Konnagar, *Calc.* 16 D6 22 42N 88 21 E
Konohana, *Ōsaka* 12 B3 34 40N 135 26 E
Kōnoike, *Ōsaka* 12 B4 34 42N 135 37 E
Konradshöhe, *Berl.* 7 A2 52 35N 13 13 E
Koonung Cr. →, *Melb.* 19 E7 37 46 S 145 4 E
Kopanina, *Pra.* 10 B1 50 3N 14 17 E
Koparkhairna, *Bomb.* 16 G8 19 6N 72 59 E
Köpenick, *Berl.* 7 B4 52 26N 13 35 E
Korangi, *Kar.* 17 H11 24 47N 67 8 E
Koremasa, *Tōkyō* 13 C1 35 39N 139 29 E
Korenevo, *Mos.* 11 E12 55 40N 38 0 E
Kori, *Ōsaka* 12 B4 34 47N 135 38 E
Koridhallós, *Ath.* 8 J10 37 59N 23 39 E
Korkinskoye, Oz., *St-Pet.* 11 B6 59 55N 30 42 E
Körne, *Ruhr* 6 A7 51 30N 7 30 E
Korso, *Hels.* 3 A5 60 21N 25 5 E
Koshigaya, *Tōkyō* 13 A3 35 53N 139 47 E
Kosino, *Mos.* 11 E11 55 43N 37 50 E
Kosugi, *Tōkyō* 13 C2 35 34N 139 39 E
Kota, *Jak.* 15 H9 6 7 S 106 48 E
Kotelyniki, *Mos.* 11 F11 55 39N 37 52 E
Kōtō-Ku, *Tōkyō* 13 B3 35 40N 139 48 E
Kotrang, *Calc.* 16 D6 22 41N 88 20 E
Kouponia, *Ath.* 8 J11 37 57N 23 47 E
Koviksudde, *Stock.* 3 D13 59 21N 18 21 E
Kowloon, *H.K.* 12 E5 22 18N 114 10 E
Kowloon City, *H.K.* 12 E6 22 19N 114 11 E
Kowloon Pk., *H.K.* 12 E5 22 20N 114 13 E
Kowloon Res., *H.K.* 12 D5 22 21N 114 9 E
Kowloon Tong, *H.K.* 12 D5 22 20N 114 10 E
Kozhukhovo, *Mos.* 11 E11 55 43N 37 53 E
Kozukue, *Tōkyō* 13 C2 35 30N 139 35 E
Krailling, *Mün.* 7 G9 48 5N 11 24 E
Kramat Jati, *Jak.* 15 J10 6 15 S 106 51 E
Krampnitz, *Berl.* 7 B1 52 27N 13 3 E
Krampnitzsee, *Berl.* 7 B1 52 27N 13 3 E
Kranji, *Sing.* 15 F7 1 26N 103 45 E
Kranji, Sungei →, *Sing.* 15 F7 1 26N 103 44 E
Kranji Dam, *Sing.* 15 F7 1 26N 103 44 E
Kraskovo, *Mos.* 11 F11 55 39N 37 58 E
Krasnaya Gorka, *St-Pet.* 11 B5 59 58N 30 38 E
Krasno-Presnenskaya, *Mos.* 11 E9 55 45N 37 32 E
Krasnogorsk, *Mos.* 11 E7 55 49N 37 18 E
Krasnyj Stroitel, *Mos.* 11 F9 55 36N 37 36 E
Kray, *Ruhr* 6 B4 51 27N 7 4 E
Krč, *Pra.* 10 B2 50 2N 14 26 E
Krefeld, *Ruhr* 6 B1 51 20N 6 33 E
Kremlin, *Mos.* 11 E9 55 45N 37 38 E
Kresson, *Phil.* 24 B5 39 51N 74 54W
Kreuzberg, *Berl.* 7 A3 52 30N 13 24 E
Krishnarampur, *Calc.* 16 D5 22 43N 88 13 E
Kritzendorf, *Wien* 10 G9 48 19N 16 18 E
Krokhol, *Oslo* 2 C5 59 48N 10 57 E
Krugersdorp, *Jobg.* 18 E7 26 6 S 27 48 E
Krukut, Kali →, *Jak.* 15 J9 6 13 S 106 48 E
Krumme Lanke, *Berl.* 7 B2 52 27N 13 14 E
Krummensee, *Berl.* 7 A5 52 35N 13 42 E
Krupunder, *Hbg.* 7 D7 53 37N 9 53 E
Krusboda, *Stock.* 3 E12 59 13N 18 14 E
Krylatskoye, *Mos.* 11 E8 55 44N 37 23 E
Küçükkoy, *Ist.* 17 A2 41 3N 28 52 E
Kudrovo, *St-Pet.* 11 B5 59 55N 30 30 E
Kuivasaari, *Hels.* 3 C5 60 6N 25 0 E
Kujiai, *Tōkyō* 13 A1 35 57N 139 26 E
Küllenhahn, *Ruhr* 6 C4 51 14N 7 8 E
Kulosaari, *Hels.* 3 B5 60 11N 25 0 E
Kulturpalasset, *Wsaw.* 10 E7 52 14N 21 0 E
Kumla, *Stock.* 3 E12 59 14N 18 12 E
Kummelnäs, *Stock.* 3 D12 59 21N 18 16 E
Kungens kurva, *Stock.* 3 E10 59 15N 17 53 E
Kungsängen, *Stock.* 3 D9 59 26N 17 43 E
Kungshatt, *Stock.* 3 E10 59 17N 17 53 E
Kungsholmen, *Stock.* 3 D11 59 20N 18 2 E
Kuningan, *Jak.* 15 J9 6 13 S 106 49 E
Kuninkaanmäki, *Hels.* 3 B5 60 18N 25 7 E
Kunitachi, *Tōkyō* 13 B1 35 41N 139 27 E
Kunming Hu, *Beij.* 14 B2 39 59N 116 13 E
Kunratice, *Pra.* 10 B2 50 0N 14 29 E
Kunratický →, *Pra.* 10 B2 50 2N 14 24 E
Kunsthalle, *Hbg.* 7 D8 53 33N 10 0 E
Kuntsevo, *Mos.* 11 E8 55 43N 37 24 E
Kupchino, *St-Pet.* 11 B4 59 50N 30 23 E
Kupferdreh, *Ruhr* 6 B4 51 23N 7 5 E
Kurbali Dere →, *Ist.* 17 B3 40 58N 29 1 E
Kurihara, *Tōkyō* 13 B2 35 45N 139 34 E
Kurkino, *Mos.* 11 D8 55 53N 37 22 E
Kurla, *Bomb.* 16 G8 19 4N 72 52 E
Kurmuri, *Bomb.* 16 G8 19 4N 72 53 E
Kurnell, *Syd.* 19 C4 34 0 S 151 10 E
Kurume, *Tōkyō* 13 B2 35 45N 139 31 E
Kuryanovo, *Mos.* 11 F10 55 39N 37 42 E
Kushihiki, *Tōkyō* 13 A2 35 54N 139 36 E
Kushtia, *Calc.* 16 E6 22 31N 88 23 E
Kuskovo, *Mos.* 11 E10 55 44N 37 48 E
Kutsino, *Mos.* 11 E11 55 44N 37 55 E
Kuy-e-Gishā, *Tehr.* 17 C5 35 44N 51 23 E
Kuy-e-Mekānir, *Tehr.* 17 C5 35 46N 51 22 E
Kuzyminki, *Mos.* 11 E10 55 42N 37 46 E
Kvarnsjön, *Stock.* 3 E10 59 11N 17 58 E
Kwa-Thema, *Jobg.* 18 F11 26 17 S 28 23 E
Kwai Chung, *H.K.* 12 D5 22 22N 114 7 E
Kwitang, *Jak.* 15 J10 6 11 S 106 50 E
Kwun Tong, *H.K.* 12 E6 22 18N 114 13 E
Kyje, *Pra.* 10 B3 50 6N 14 33 E
Kyōhōji, *Ōsaka* 12 C4 34 38N 135 33 E
Kyrkfjärden, *Stock.* 3 E9 59 16N 17 45 E
Kyrkslätt, *Hels.* 3 C1 60 6N 24 28W

L

La Aguada, *Stgo* 30 J10 33 28 S 70 40W
La Ballena, *Stgo* 30 K11 33 30 S 70 40W
La Boca, *B.A.* 32 B4 34 38 S 58 22W
La Bottáccia, *Rome* 9 F8 41 54N 12 18 E
La Bretèche, *Paris* 5 B2 48 51N 2 1 E
La Brosse, *Paris* 5 C1 48 43N 1 20 E
La Cabana, *La Hab.* 30 B3 23 8N 82 20W
La Canada, *L.A.* 28 A3 34 12N 118 12W
La Cassa, *Tori.* 9 A2 45 11N 7 30 E
La Celle-les-Bordes, *Paris* 5 D1 48 38N 1 57 E
La Celle-St.-Cloud, *Paris* 5 B2 48 50N 2 9 E
La Chivera, *Car.* 30 D5 10 35N 66 54W
La Colmena, *Méx.* 29 A2 19 35N 99 16W
La Courneuve, *Paris* 5 B4 48 55N 2 22 E
La Crescenta, *L.A.* 28 A3 34 13N 118 14W
La Défense, *Paris* 5 B3 48 53N 2 12 E
La Dehesa, *Stgo* 30 J11 33 21 S 70 33W
La Estación, *Mdrd.* 8 B2 40 27N 3 48W
La Floresta, *Barc.* 8 D5 41 26N 2 3 E
La Florida, *Car.* 30 D5 10 30N 66 52W
La Fortuna, *Mdrd.* 8 B2 40 21N 3 46W
La Fransa, *Barc.* 8 D5 41 22N 2 9 E
La Fresnière, *Mtrl.* 20 A2 43 33N 73 58W
La Frette-sur-Seine, *Paris* 5 B3 48 58N 2 11 E
La Garenne-Colombes, *Paris* 5 B3 48 54N 2 15 E
La Giustiniana, *Rome* 9 F9 41 59N 12 24 E
La Grange, *Chic.* 26 C1 41 48N 87 53W
La Grange des Noues, *Paris* 5 A4 49 1N 2 28 E
La Grange Highlands, *Chic.* 26 C1 41 46N 87 53W
La Grange Park, *Chic.* 26 C1 41 49N 87 51W
La Granja, *Stgo* 30 K11 33 31 S 70 38W
La Guaira, *Car.* 30 D5 10 36N 66 55W
La Guardia Airport, *N.Y.* 23 C5 40 46N 73 52W
La Guasima, *La Hab.* 30 B3 23 0N 82 17W
La Habana, *La Hab.* 30 B3 23 7N 82 21W
La Habana, B. de, *La Hab.* 30 B3 23 7N 82 20W
La Habana Vieia, *La Hab.* 30 B2 23 7N 82 20W
La Habra, *L.A.* 28 C5 33 56N 117 57W
La Habre Heights, *L.A.* 28 C5 33 59N 117 56W
La Horqueta →, *B.A.* 32 C1 34 43 S 58 51W
La Lisa, *La Hab.* 30 B2 23 3N 82 25W
La Llacuna, *Barc.* 8 D6 41 24N 2 12 E
La Loma, *Méx.* 29 A2 19 31N 99 11W
La Lucila, *B.A.* 32 B4 34 30 S 58 29W
La Magdalena Atlipac, *Méx.* 29 B4 19 22N 89 56 E
La Magdalena Chichicaspa, *Méx.* 29 B2 19 24N 99 18W
La Magdalena Contreras, *Méx.* 29 C2 19 17N 99 13W
La Magdalena Petlalco, *Méx.* 29 C2 19 13N 99 10W
La Maison Blanche, *Paris* 5 C1 48 44N 1 54 E
La Maladrerie, *Paris* 5 B2 48 54N 2 1 E
La Marquesa, *Méx.* 29 C1 19 18N 99 22W
La Milla, Cerro, *Lima* 30 G8 12 2 S 77 5W
La Molina, *Lima* 30 G9 12 4 S 76 56W
La Monachina, *Rome* 9 F9 41 53N 12 21 E
La Moraleja, *Mdrd.* 8 A3 40 30N 30 38W
La Nopalera, *Méx.* 29 C3 19 18N 99 5W
La Pastora, *Car.* 30 D5 10 31N 66 55W
La Paterna, *B.A.* 32 B4 34 35 S 58 26W
La Patte-d'Oie, *Paris* 5 A3 49 0N 2 10 E
La Perla, *Lima* 30 G8 12 4 S 77 7W
La Perouse, *Syd.* 19 B4 33 59 S 151 14 E
La Pineda, *Barc.* 8 E5 41 15N 2 1 E
La Pisana, *Rome* 9 F8 41 51N 12 23 E
La Playa, *La Hab.* 30 B2 23 6N 82 26W
La Prairie, *Mtrl.* 20 B5 43 25N 73 29W
La Puente, *L.A.* 28 B5 34 1N 117 54W
La Punta, *Lima* 30 G7 12 4 S 77 10W
La Puntigala, *Barc.* 8 D6 41 27N 2 13 E
La Queue-en-Brie, *Paris* 5 C5 48 47N 2 34 E
La Reina, *Stgo* 30 J11 33 26 S 70 33W
La Reja, *B.A.* 32 B2 34 38 S 58 48W
La Ribera, *Barc.* 8 D5 41 21N 2 6 E
La Romanie, *Paris* 5 C1 48 43N 1 53 E
La Rústica, *Rome* 9 F10 41 54N 12 36 E
La Sagrera, *Barc.* 8 D6 41 25N 2 11 E
La Salada, *B.A.* 32 C4 34 43 S 58 28W
La Scala, *Mil.* 9 E6 45 28N 9 11 E
La Selce, *Rome* 9 F9 41 53N 12 20 E
La Sierra, *La Hab.* 30 B2 23 7N 82 24W
La Taxonera, *Barc.* 8 D6 41 25N 2 10 E
La Vega, *Car.* 30 E5 10 28N 66 56W
La Verrière, *Paris* 5 C1 48 45N 1 57 E
La Vibora, *La Hab.* 30 B2 23 5N 82 22W
La Victoria, *Lima* 30 G8 12 3 S 77 2W
La Ville-du-Bois, *Paris* 5 D3 48 39N 2 16 E
Laab im Walde, *Wien* 10 H9 48 9N 16 10 E
Laaer Berg, *Wien* 10 H10 48 9N 16 24 E
Laajalahti, *Hels.* 3 B3 60 11N 24 48 E
Laajasalo, *Hels.* 3 B5 60 10N 25 1 E
Laaksolahti, *Hels.* 3 B3 60 14N 24 45 E
Laar, *Ruhr* 6 B2 51 27N 6 44 E
Lablâba, W. el →, *El Qâ.* 18 C5 30 1N 31 19 E
Lachine, *Mtrl.* 20 B3 43 26N 73 42W
Ládví, *Pra.* 10 B2 50 8N 14 27 E
Ładý, *Wsaw.* 10 F6 52 8N 20 57 E
Lafayette, *S.F.* 27 A4 37 52N 122 6W
Lafayette Hill, *Phil.* 24 A3 40 5N 75 15W
Lafayette Res., *S.F.* 27 A4 37 53N 122 8W
Laferrere, *B.A.* 32 C3 34 45 S 58 35W
Lagny, *Paris* 5 B6 48 52N 2 42 E
Lagoa da Pedra, *Lisb.* 8 F9 38 43N 8 58W
Lagos, *Lagos* 18 B2 6 27N 7 23 E
Lagos Harbour, *Lagos* 18 B2 6 26N 7 23 E
Lagos-Ikeja Airport, *Lagos* 18 A1 6 34N 7 19 E
Lagos Island, *Lagos* 18 B2 6 26N 7 23 E
Lagos Lagoon, *Lagos* 18 B2 6 30N 7 28 E
Laguna de B., *Manila* 15 E4 14 29N 121 6 E
Laim, *Mün.* 7 G10 48 7N 11 30 E
Lainate, *Mil.* 9 D5 45 34N 9 1 E
Lainz, *Wien* 10 H9 48 10N 16 16 E
Lainzer Tiergarten, *Wien* 10 G9 48 10N 16 13 E
Lajeado →, *S. Pau.* 31 E7 23 28 S 46 24W
Lake Avenue Woods, *Chic.* 26 A1 42 4N 87 53W
Lake Hiawatha, *N.Y.* 22 B2 40 52N 74 23W
Lakefield, *Jobg.* 18 F10 26 11 S 28 17 E
Lakemba, *Syd.* 19 B3 33 55 S 151 5 E
Lakeside, *Jobg.* 18 E9 26 5 S 28 8 E
Lakeview, *Chic.* 26 B3 41 56N 87 38W
Lakeview, *Trto.* 20 E7 43 35N 79 32W
Lakhtinskiy, *St-Pet.* 11 B2 59 59N 30 9 E
Lakhtinskiy Razliv, Oz., *St-Pet.* 11 B3 59 59N 30 12 E
Lakshmanpur, *Calc.* 16 E5 22 38N 88 16 E
Laleham, *Lon.* 4 C2 51 24N 0 29W
Lâleli, *Ist.* 17 A2 41 0N 28 57 E
Lalor, *Melb.* 19 E6 37 40 S 144 59 E
Lam San, *Sing.* 15 F7 1 22N 103 43 E
Lam Tin, *H.K.* 12 E6 22 18N 114 14 E
Lambarfjärden, *Stock.* 3 D9 59 21N 17 48 E
Lambert, *Oslo* 2 B4 59 52N 10 48 E
Lambeth, *Lon.* 4 C4 51 28N 0 6W
Lambrate, *Mil.* 9 E6 45 28N 9 16 E
Lambro →, *Mil.* 9 E6 45 24N 9 17 E
Lambro, Parco, *Mil.* 9 E6 45 29N 9 14 E
Lambton, *Jobg.* 18 F10 26 14 S 28 10 E
Lambton Hills, *Trto.* 20 E7 43 39N 79 30W
Lamma I., *H.K.* 12 E5 22 12N 114 7 E
Lampton, *Lon.* 4 C2 51 28N 0 21W
Landianchang, *Beij.* 14 B2 39 57N 116 13 E
Landover Hills, *Wash.* 25 D8 38 56N 76 54W
Landstrasse, *Wien* 10 G10 48 12N 16 23 E
Landwehr kanal, *Berl.* 7 B3 52 29N 13 24 E
Lane Cove, *Syd.* 19 A3 33 48 S 151 9 E
Lane Cove National Park, *Syd.* 19 A3 33 47 S 151 8 E
Langen, *Oslo* 2 C5 59 44N 10 57 E
Langenberg, *Ruhr* 6 B4 51 20N 7 7 E
Langenbochum, *Ruhr* 6 A4 51 36N 7 6 E
Langendreer, *Ruhr* 6 B5 51 28N 7 18 E
Langenhorn, *Hbg.* 7 D7 53 39N 9 59 E
Langenhorst, *Ruhr* 6 B4 51 21N 7 1 E
Langenzersdorf, *Wien* 10 G10 48 18N 16 21 E
Langer See, *Berl.* 7 B4 52 24N 13 37 E
Langerfeld, *Ruhr* 6 C5 51 16N 7 14 E
Langley, *Wash.* 25 D6 38 57N 77 11W
Langley Park, *Wash.* 25 D8 38 59N 76 58W
Langstaff, *Trto.* 20 C8 43 50N 79 26W
Långtarmen, *Stock.* 3 D8 59 24N 17 36 E
Langwald, *Mün.* 7 F9 48 10N 11 23 E
Lanham, *Wash.* 25 D8 38 59N 76 51W
Lank-Latum, *Ruhr* 6 C2 51 18N 6 40 E
Lankwitz, *Berl.* 7 B3 52 25N 13 21 E
Länna Drevviken, *Stock.* 3 E11 59 12N 18 8 E
L'Annunziatella, *Rome* 9 G10 41 49N 12 33 E
Lansdowne, *Balt.* 25 B3 39 14N 76 38W
Lansdowne, *Phil.* 24 B3 39 56N 75 16W
Lansing, *Trto.* 20 D8 43 45N 79 24W
Lanús, *B.A.* 32 C4 34 42 S 58 23W
Lapa, *Rio J.* 31 B2 22 54 S 43 10W
Lapa, *S. Pau.* 31 E5 23 31 S 46 42W
Lapangan Merdeka, *Jak.* 15 J9 6 10 S 106 49 E
Lapinkylä, *Hels.* 3 B4 60 18N 24 51 E
Lapinkylä, *Hels.* 3 B1 60 13N 24 27 E
Lappböle, *Hels.* 3 B1 60 18N 24 27 E
Laranjeiras, *Rio J.* 31 B2 22 55 S 43 10W
Larchmont, *N.Y.* 23 B6 40 55N 73 44W
Larkspur, *S.F.* 27 A1 37 55N 122 31W
Las, *Wsaw.* 10 E7 52 13N 21 6 E
Las Acacias, *Car.* 30 E5 10 29N 66 54W
Las Adjuntas, *Car.* 30 E4 10 25N 67 0W
Las Barrancas, *B.A.* 32 A4 34 28 S 58 29W
Las Conchas, *B.A.* 32 A3 34 25 S 58 34W
Las Corts, *Barc.* 8 D5 41 23N 2 9 E
Las Fuentes Brotantes, *Méx.* 29 C2 19 16N 99 11W
Las Kabacki, *Wsaw.* 10 F7 52 7N 21 2 E
Las Lomas, *L.A.* 28 B5 34 8N 117 59W
Las Mercedes, *Car.* 30 E5 10 28N 66 51W
Las Pinas, *Manila* 15 E3 14 29N 120 58 E
Las Rejas, *Stgo* 30 J10 33 27 S 70 42W
Las Rozas de Madrid, *Mdrd.* 8 B1 40 29N 3 52W
Las Trampas Cr. →, *S.F.* 27 A4 37 53N 122 6W
Las Trampas Regional Park, *S.F.* 27 B4 37 49N 122 3W
Las Trampas Ridge, *S.F.* 27 A4 37 50N 122 3W
Las Tunitas, *Car.* 30 D4 10 36N 67 1W
Lasalle, *Mtrl.* 20 B4 43 26N 73 37W
Lasek Bielański, *Wsaw.* 10 E6 52 17N 20 57 E
Lasek Na Kole, *Wsaw.* 10 E6 52 15N 20 56 E
Laski, *Wsaw.* 10 E6 52 18N 20 51 E
Latina, *Mdrd.* 8 B2 40 24N 3 44W
Latrobe Univ., *Melb.* 19 E7 37 43 S 145 3 E
Lattingtown, *N.Y.* 23 B7 40 52N 73 34W
Laufzorn, *Mün.* 7 G10 48 0N 11 33 E
Laurel Hollow, *N.Y.* 23 B8 40 51N 73 28W
Laurel Springs, *Phil.* 24 C4 39 49N 75 0W
Laurelton, *N.Y.* 23 C6 40 40N 73 45W
Laurence Hanscom Field, *Bost.* 21 C2 42 28N 71 16W
Lausdomini, *Nápl.* 9 H13 40 55N 14 26 E
Lauttasaari, *Hels.* 3 C4 60 9N 24 53 E
Lava Nuova, *Nápl.* 9 J13 40 47N 14 23 E
Laval-des-Rapides, *Mtrl.* 20 A3 43 33N 73 41W
Laval-Ouest, *Mtrl.* 20 A2 43 32N 73 52W
Laval-sur-le-Lac, *Mtrl.* 20 A2 43 31N 73 52W
Lavradio, *Lisb.* 8 F8 38 40N 9 2W
Lawndale, *Chic.* 26 B2 41 50N 87 42W
Lawndale, *L.A.* 28 C2 33 52N 118 22W
Lawndale, *Phil.* 24 A4 40 3N 75 5W
Lawnside, *Phil.* 24 B4 39 51N 75 1W
Lawrence, *Bost.* 21 A3 42 43N 71 7W
Lawrence, *N.Y.* 23 D6 40 36N 73 43W
Lawrence Heights, *Trto.* 20 D8 43 43N 79 25W
Lawrence Park, *Phil.* 24 B2 39 57N 75 20W
Lawton, *La Hab.* 30 B2 23 5N 82 20W
Layāri, *Kar.* 17 G11 24 52N 67 0 E
Layāri →, *Kar.* 17 G10 24 52N 66 58 E
Lazienkowski Park, *Wsaw.* 10 E7 52 13N 21 1 E
Le Blanc-Mesnil, *Paris* 5 B4 48 56N 2 27 E
Le Bourget, *Paris* 5 B4 48 56N 2 25 E
Le Chesnay, *Paris* 5 B2 48 49N 2 7 E
Le Christ de Saclay, *Paris* 5 C3 48 43N 1 59 E
Le Kremlin-Bicêtre, *Paris* 5 C4 48 48N 2 21 E
Le Mesnil-Amelot, *Paris* 5 A5 49 1N 2 35 E
Le Mesnil-le-Roi, *Paris* 5 B2 48 56N 2 7 E
Le Mesnil-St.-Denis, *Paris* 5 C1 48 44N 1 57 E
Le Pecq, *Paris* 5 B2 48 53N 2 6 E
Le Perreux, *Paris* 5 B4 48 50N 2 29 E
Le Pin, *Paris* 5 B5 48 54N 2 37 E
Le Plessis-Bouchard, *Paris* 5 A3 49 0N 2 14 E
Le Plessis-Gassot, *Paris* 5 A4 49 2N 2 24 E
Le Plessis-Pâté, *Paris* 5 D3 48 36N 2 19 E
Le Plessis-Robinson, *Paris* 5 C3 48 47N 2 15 E
Le Plessis-Trévise, *Paris* 5 C5 48 48N 2 34 E
Le Port-Marly, *Paris* 5 B2 48 52N 2 6 E
Le Pré-St.-Gervais, *Paris* 5 B4 48 53N 2 23 E
Le Raincy, *Paris* 5 B5 48 53N 2 31 E
Le Thillay, *Paris* 5 A4 49 0N 2 28 E
Le Trappe, *Mtrl.* 20 B1 43 30N 74 1W
Le Val d'Enfer, *Paris* 5 C3 48 45N 2 11 E
Le Vésinet, *Paris* 5 B2 48 54N 2 8 E
Lea →, *Lon.* 4 B4 51 30N 0 2W
Lea Bridge, *Lon.* 4 B4 51 33N 0 2W
Leakin Park, *Balt.* 25 B2 39 18N 76 44W
Leaside, *Trto.* 20 D8 43 42N 79 22W
Leatherhead, *Lon.* 4 D3 51 17N 0 19W
Leaves Green, *Lon.* 4 D5 51 19N 0 1 E
Leblon, *Rio J.* 31 B2 22 59 S 43 14W
Léchelle, Forêt de la, *Paris* 5 C6 48 43N 2 41 E
Ledøje, *Købn.* 2 D8 55 42N 12 18 E
Lee, *Lon.* 4 C5 51 27N 0 0 E
Leeupan, *Jobg.* 18 F10 26 13 S 28 18 E
Leganes, *Mdrd.* 8 C2 40 19N 3 45W
Legazpi, *Mdrd.* 8 B2 40 23N 3 41W
Legoa, Kali →, *Jak.* 15 H10 6 6 S 106 52 E
Lehtisaari, *Hels.* 3 C3 60 6N 24 46 E
Lehtisaari, *Hels.* 3 B4 60 10N 24 51 E
Lei Yue Mun, *H.K.* 12 E6 22 17N 114 14 E
Leião, *Lisb.* 8 F7 38 43N 9 17W
Leichhardt, *Syd.* 19 B3 33 53 S 151 9 E
Leigang, *Gzh.* 14 G7 23 2N 113 6 E
Léini, *Tori.* 9 A3 45 11N 7 42 E
Leisure World, *S.F.* 27 A4 37 51N 122 4W
Lemoyne, *Mtrl.* 20 B5 43 29N 73 29W
Lemsahl, *Hbg.* 7 C8 53 41N 10 5 E
Lenin, *Mos.* 11 E9 55 43N 37 34 E
Leningrad = St. Petersburg, *St-Pet.* 11 B3 59 55N 30 15 E
Lenino, *Mos.* 11 F9 55 38N 37 39 E
Leninskiye Gory, *Mos.* 11 E9 55 41N 37 32 E
Lenne →, *Ruhr* 6 B7 51 25N 7 30 E
Lennep, *Ruhr* 6 C5 51 11N 7 15 E
Lenni, *Phil.* 24 B2 39 53N 75 27W
Lennox, *L.A.* 28 C2 33 56N 118 20W
Leonardo da Vinci, Aeroporto Int., *Rome* 9 G8 41 47N 12 15 E
Leoncio Martinez, *Car.* 30 E6 10 29N 66 48W
Leonia, *N.Y.* 22 B5 40 51N 73 59W
Leopard, *Phil.* 24 A2 40 1N 75 26W
Leopardi, *Nápl.* 9 J13 40 45N 14 24 E
Leopoldau, *Wien* 10 G10 48 15N 16 26 E
Leopoldstadt, *Wien* 10 G10 48 13N 16 22 E
Leportovo, *Mos.* 11 E10 55 46N 37 43 E
Leppävaara, *Hels.* 3 B3 60 13N 24 49 E
Lera, Mte., *Tori.* 9 A1 45 10N 7 27 E
L'Éremo, *Tori.* 9 B3 45 2N 7 44 E
Les Alluets-le-Roi, *Paris* 5 B1 48 54N 1 55 E
Les Clayes-sous-Bois, *Paris* 5 C1 48 49N 1 59 E
Les Essarts-le-Roi, *Paris* 5 C1 48 43N 1 53 E
Les Gâtines, *Paris* 5 C1 48 48N 1 58 E
Les Grésillons, *Paris* 5 B3 48 56N 2 1 E
Les Layes, *Paris* 5 C1 48 43N 1 55 E
Les Lilas, *Paris* 5 B4 48 52N 2 25 E
Les Loges-en-Josas, *Paris* 5 C2 48 45N 2 8 E
Les Molières, *Paris* 5 C2 48 40N 2 4 E
Les Mureaux, *Paris* 5 B1 48 59N 1 54 E
Les Pavillons-sous-Bois, *Paris* 5 B5 48 54N 2 30 E
Les Vaux de Cernay →, *Paris* 5 C1 48 41N 1 59 E
Lésigny, *Paris* 5 C5 48 44N 2 37 E
Lesnosavodskaya, *St-Pet.* 11 B4 59 51N 30 29 E
Lesnoy, *St-Pet.* 11 B4 59 59N 30 22 E
Lester B. Pearson Int. Airport, *Trto.* 20 D7 43 40N 79 38W
L'Étang-la-Ville, *Paris* 5 B2 48 52N 2 4 E
Letná, *Pra.* 10 B2 50 0S 14 26 E
Letňany, *Pra.* 10 B3 50 8N 14 30 E
Letovo, *Mos.* 11 F8 55 34N 37 24 E
Leuville-sur-Orge, *Paris* 5 D3 48 36N 2 15 E
Levallois-Perret, *Paris* 5 B3 48 53N 2 16 E
Lévis St.-Nom, *Paris* 5 C1 48 43N 1 57 E
Levittown, *N.Y.* 23 C7 40 43N 73 31W
Lewisdale, *Wash.* 25 D8 38 58N 76 59W
Lewisham, *Jobg.* 18 E7 26 7 S 27 49 E
Lewisham, *Lon.* 4 C4 51 27N 0 1W
Lexington, *Bost.* 21 C2 42 25N 71 12W
Leyton, *Lon.* 4 B4 51 33N 0 1W
Leytonstone, *Lon.* 4 B5 51 34N 0 0 E
L'Haütil, *Paris* 5 A2 49 0N 2 0 E
L'Hay-les-Roses, *Paris* 5 C4 48 46N 2 20 E
Lhotka, *Pra.* 10 B2 50 1N 14 26 E
Liangshui He →, *Beij.* 14 C3 39 48N 116 23 E
Lianhua Chi, *Beij.* 14 B2 39 52N 116 16 E
Lianhua He →, *Beij.* 14 B2 39 52N 116 13 E
Lianozovo, *Mos.* 11 D9 55 53N 37 34 E
Libčice nad Vltavou, *Pra.* 10 A2 50 11N 14 22 E
Liben, *Pra.* 10 B2 50 6N 14 27 E
Liberdade, *S. Pau.* 31 E6 23 33 S 46 37W
Libertad, *B.A.* 32 C2 34 41 S 58 40W
Liberty I., *N.Y.* 22 C4 40 41N 74 2W
Liberty Plain, *Bost.* 21 D4 42 14N 70 52W
Liberty Res., *Balt.* 25 A1 39 23N 76 52W
Libeznice, *Pra.* 10 A2 50 11N 14 29 E
Library of Congress, *Wash.* 25 D7 38 53N 77 0W
Libuč, *Pra.* 10 B2 50 0N 14 27 E
Lichiao, *Gzh.* 14 G8 23 3N 113 18 E
Lichtenbroich, *Ruhr* 6 C2 51 17N 6 49 E
Lichtenburg, *Berl.* 7 A4 52 31N 13 29 E
Lichtenplatz, *Ruhr* 6 C5 51 14N 7 11 E
Lichtenrade, *Berl.* 7 B3 52 23N 13 24 E
Lichterfelde, *Berl.* 7 B2 52 25N 13 19 E
Licignano di Nápoli, *Nápl.* 9 H13 40 54N 14 21 E
Lidcombe, *Syd.* 19 B3 33 52 S 151 3 E
Lidingö, *Stock.* 3 D11 59 21N 18 8 E
Lido Beach, *N.Y.* 23 D7 40 35N 73 37W
Lier, *Oslo* 2 C1 59 47N 10 15 E
Lierskogen, *Oslo* 2 C1 59 49N 10 14 E
Lieshi Lingyuan, *Gzh.* 14 G8 23 7N 113 16 E
Liesing, *Wien* 10 H9 48 8N 16 17 E
Liesing →, *Wien* 10 H10 48 8N 16 28 E
Lieusant, *Paris* 5 D5 48 38N 2 33 E
Liffjofs, *Hels.* 3 B6 60 13N 25 12 E
Ligovo, *St-Pet.* 11 C3 59 49N 30 10 E
Lijordet, *Oslo* 2 B3 59 56N 10 36 E
Likhoborka →, *Mos.* 11 D9 55 51N 37 30 E
Likova →, *Mos.* 11 F8 55 36N 37 20 E
Lilla Värtan, *Stock.* 3 D12 59 20N 18 11 E
Lille Rørbæk, *Købn.* 2 D7 55 47N 12 6 E

Midland Park 41

Lille Værløse, København 2 D9 55 47N 12 22 E
Lillehavfrue, København 2 D10 55 42N 12 35 E
Lillestrøm, Oslo 2 B6 59 57N 11 3 E
Liluah, Calc. 16 E5 22 37N 88 19 E
Lilydale, Melb. 19 E9 37 45 S 145 21 E
Lima, Lima 30 G8 12 3 S 77 2W
Lima, Phil. 24 B2 39 55N 75 26W
Limbiate, Mil. 9 D5 45 35N 9 7 E
Limehouse, Lon. 4 B4 51 30N 0 1W
Limeil-Brévannes, Paris 5 C4 48 44N 2 29 E
Limito, Mil. 9 E6 45 28N 9 19 E
Limoges-Fourches, Paris 5 D5 48 37N 2 39 E
Limours, Paris 5 D2 48 38N 2 4 E
Linas, Paris 5 D3 48 37N 2 16 E
Linate, Mil. 9 E6 45 26N 9 16 E
Linate, Aeroporto Internazionale di, Mil. 9 E6 45 26N 9 16 E
Linbigh, Balt. 25 A3 39 21N 76 31W
Linbropark, Jobg. 18 E9 26 5 S 28 7 E
Lincoln, Bost. 21 C2 42 25N 71 18W
Lincoln Center, N.Y. 22 C5 40 46N 43 59W
Lincoln Heights, L.A. 28 B3 34 4N 118 12 E
Lincoln Memorial, Wash. 25 D7 38 53N 77 2W
Lincoln Park, Chic. 26 B3 41 57N 87 38W
Lincoln Park, N.Y. 22 B3 40 56N 74 18W
Lincoln Park, S.F. 27 B1 37 47N 122 30W
Lincolnwood, Chic. 26 A2 42 1N 87 43W
Linda-a-Pastora, Lisb. 8 F7 38 42N 9 15W
Linden, Jobg. 18 E9 26 8 S 28 0 E
Linden, N.Y. 22 D3 40 38N 74 14W
Linden-Dahlhausen, Ruhr 6 B5 51 25N 7 10 E
Lindenberg, Berl. 7 A4 52 36N 13 31 E
Lindenhorst, Ruhr 6 A6 51 33N 7 27 E
Lindenhurst, N.Y. 23 C8 40 40N 73 22W
Lindenwold, Phil. 24 C5 39 49N 74 59W
Linderhausen, Ruhr 6 C5 51 17N 7 17 E
Lindfield, Syd. 19 A3 33 46 S 151 9 E
Lindøya, Oslo 2 B4 59 53N 10 42 E
Lingotto, Tori. 9 B2 45 1N 7 39 E
Liniers, B.A. 32 B3 34 39 S 58 30W
Linksfield, Jobg. 18 E9 26 9 S 28 6 E
Linmeyer, Jobg. 18 F9 26 15 S 28 4 E
Linn, Ruhr 6 B1 51 20N 6 38 E
Linna, Hels. 3 A4 60 20N 24 50 E
Linthicum Heights, Balt. 25 B2 39 12N 76 47W
Lintorf, Ruhr 6 B3 51 20N 6 50 E
Lintuvaara, Hels. 3 B3 60 14N 24 49 E
Linwood, Phil. 24 C2 39 49N 75 25W
Lioúmi, Ath. 8 J11 38 0N 23 40 E
Lipków, Wsaw. 10 E5 52 16N 20 48 E
Lippalthausen, Ruhr 6 A6 51 36N 7 26 E
Liqizhuang, Tianj. 14 E6 39 4N 117 10 E
Lirich, Ruhr 6 B2 51 29N 6 49 E
Lisboa, Lisb. 8 F8 38 42N 9 8W
Lisbon = Lisboa, Lisb. 8 F8 38 42N 9 8W
Lishui, Gzh. 14 F7 23 12N 113 9 E
Lisiy Nos, St-Pet. 11 A2 60 1N 30 0 E
Lissone, Mil. 9 D6 45 36N 9 14 E
Lissy, Paris 5 D6 48 38N 2 42 E
Litoral, Cord. del, Car. 30 D5 10 33N 66 54W
Little B., Syd. 19 B4 33 58 S 151 15 E
Little Calumet →, Chic. 26 D3 41 39N 87 34W
Little Falls, N.Y. 22 B3 40 52N 74 14W
Little Ferry, N.Y. 22 B4 40 50N 74 2W
Little Neck, N.Y. 23 C6 40 46N 73 43W
Little Paint Br. →, Wash. 25 C8 39 0N 76 55W
Little Patuxent →, Balt. 25 B1 39 13N 76 51W
Little Rouge →, Trto. 20 C9 43 45N 79 11W
Little Sugarloaf, Melb. 19 E8 37 40 S 145 18 E
Little Thurrock, Lon. 4 C7 51 29N 0 20 E
Liuhang, Shang. 14 H11 31 21N 121 21 E
Liuhuahu Gongyuan, Gzh. 14 G8 23 8N 113 14 E
Liverpool, Syd. 19 B2 33 55 S 150 55 E
Livingstone, N.Y. 22 C3 40 47N 74 19W
Livry-Gargan, Paris 5 B5 48 55N 2 31 E
Liwanhu Gongyuan, Gzh. 14 G8 23 7N 113 13 E
Lizhuang, Gzh. 14 G7 23 6N 113 7 E
Ljan, Oslo 2 B4 59 51N 10 48 E
Llano de Can Gineu, Barc. 8 D6 41 27N 2 10 E
Llavallol, B.A. 32 C4 34 48 S 58 25W
Llobregat →, Barc. 8 D5 41 19N 2 5 E
Lloyd Harbor, N.Y. 23 B8 40 54N 73 26W
Lloyd Pt., N.Y. 23 B8 40 56N 73 29W
Lo Aranguiz, Stgo 30 J11 33 23 S 70 40W
Lo Boza, Stgo 30 J10 33 23 S 70 43W
Lo Chau, H.K. 12 E6 22 11N 114 15 E
Lo Hermida, Stgo 30 J11 33 28 S 70 33W
Lo Ortuzar, Stgo 30 J10 33 28 S 70 43W
Lo Prado Arriba, Stgo 30 J10 33 26 S 70 42W
Lo So Shing, H.K. 12 E5 22 12N 114 7 E
Lo Wai, H.K. 12 D5 22 22N 114 8 E
Lobau, Wien 10 G11 48 10N 16 31 E
Lobos, Pt., S.F. 27 B1 37 46N 122 30W
Loch Raven Village, Balt. 25 A3 39 23N 76 34W
Locham, Mün. 7 G9 48 7N 11 26 E
Lochearn, Balt. 25 A2 39 20N 76 43W
Lochino, Mos. 11 E7 55 41N 37 17 E
Lochkov, Pra. 10 B2 50 0N 14 21 E
Lockhausen, Mün. 7 F9 48 10N 11 24 E
Locksbottom, Lon. 4 C5 51 21N 0 3 E
Locust Grove, N.Y. 23 C8 40 48N 73 29W
Locust Manor, N.Y. 23 C6 40 41N 73 45W
Locust Valley, N.Y. 23 B7 40 52N 73 36W
Lodi, N.Y. 22 B4 40 52N 74 5W
Lofty, Mt., Melb. 19 E8 37 42 S 145 17 E
Logan, Phil. 24 A4 40 2N 75 8W
Logan Int. Airport, Bost. 21 C4 42 22N 71 0W
Logan Square, Chic. 26 B2 41 55N 87 42W
Lognes-Emerainville, Aérodrome de, Paris 5 C5 48 49N 2 37 E
Lohausen, Ruhr 6 C2 51 16N 6 44 E
Lohberg, Ruhr 6 A2 51 34N 6 45 E
Löhme, Berl. 7 A5 52 37N 13 40 E
Lohmühle, Ruhr 6 A1 51 30N 6 39 E
Löhnen, Ruhr 6 A1 51 35N 6 39 E
Lokstedt, Hbg. 7 D7 53 36N 9 56 E
Lokyang, Sing. 15 G7 1 19N 103 40 E
Lölökhet, Kar. 17 G11 24 54N 67 2 E
Loma Blanca, Stgo 30 J10 33 29 S 70 43W
Lomas Chapultepec, Méx. 29 B2 19 25N 99 12W
Lomas de San Angel Inn, Méx. 29 B2 19 20N 99 13W
Lomas de Zamora, B.A. 32 C4 34 45 S 58 24W
Lombardy East, Jobg. 18 E9 26 6 S 28 7 E
Lomonosov Univ., Mos. 11 E9 55 42N 37 31 E
Lomus Reforma, Méx. 29 B2 19 24N 99 14W
London, Lon. 4 B4 51 30N 0 6W
London, City of, Lon. 4 B4 51 30N 0 6W
London, Tower of, Lon. 4 B4 51 30N 0 4W
London Zoo, Lon. 4 B4 51 31N 0 9W
Long B., Syd. 19 B4 33 59 S 151 15 E
Long Beach, N.Y. 23 D7 40 35N 73 39W
Long Branch, Trto. 20 E7 43 35N 79 31W
Long Brook →, Wash. 25 E6 38 49N 77 15W
Long Ditton, Lon. 4 C3 51 22N 0 19W
Long I., Bost. 21 D4 42 19N 70 59W
Long I., N.Y. 23 C7 40 45N 73 30W
Long Island City, N.Y. 22 C5 40 45N 73 56W
Long Island Sd., N.Y. 23 B7 40 57N 73 30W
Long Pond, Bost. 21 A1 42 41N 71 22W
Longchamp, Hippodrôme de, Paris 5 B3 48 51N 2 13 E
Longchêne, Paris 5 D2 48 38N 2 0 E
Longhua Gongyuan, Shang. 14 J11 31 10N 121 26 E
Longjohn Slough, Chic. 26 C1 41 42N 87 52W
Longjumeau, Paris 5 C3 48 41N 2 17 E
Longlands, Lon. 4 C5 51 25N 0 5 E
Longpont-sur-Orge, Paris 5 D3 48 38N 2 17 E
Longtan Hu →, Beij. 14 B3 39 51N 116 24 E
Longue Point, Mtrl. 20 A4 43 35N 73 31W
Longueuil, Mtrl. 20 A5 43 31N 73 29W
Loni, Delhi 16 A2 28 45N 77 17 E
Lord's Cricket Ground, Lon. 4 B3 51 31N 0 10W
Loreley, Balt. 25 A4 39 23N 76 24W
Lørenskog, Oslo 2 B5 59 55N 10 59 E
Loreto, Mil. 9 E6 45 29N 9 12 E
Lorraine, Mtrl. 20 A3 43 39N 73 46W
Los Angeles, L.A. 28 B3 34 3N 118 14 E
Los Angeles, Mdrd. 8 B2 40 20N 3 41W
Los Angeles →, L.A. 28 C3 33 55N 118 10W
Los Angeles Int. Airport, L.A. 28 C2 33 56N 118 23W
Los Asientos, Car. 30 D5 10 32N 66 53W
Los Caobos, Car. 30 D5 10 30N 66 53W
Los Carmenes, Car. 30 E5 10 28N 66 54W
Los Cerrillas, Aeroporto, Stgo 30 J10 33 29 S 70 42W
Los Dos Caminos, Car. 30 D6 10 30N 66 49W
Los dos Riteras →, Car. 30 D5 10 35N 66 57W
Los Jazmines, Presa, Méx. 29 B2 19 25N 99 15W
Los Nietos, L.A. 28 C4 33 57N 118 4W
Los Pinos, La Hab. 30 B2 23 4N 82 22W
Los Pirules, Méx. 29 B3 19 24N 99 2W
Los Polvorines, B.A. 32 B2 34 30 S 58 41W
Los Remedios →, Méx. 29 B2 19 28N 99 13W
Los Remedios, Parque Nacional de, Méx. 29 B2 19 27N 99 15W
Los Reyes, Méx. 29 B4 19 21N 99 6W
Los Rosales, Car. 30 E5 10 28N 66 53W
Losby, Oslo 2 B5 59 53N 10 59 E
Loughton, Lon. 4 B5 51 38N 0 4 E
Loures, Lisb. 8 F7 38 49N 9 10W
Louveciennes, Paris 5 B2 48 51N 2 8 E
Louvres, Paris 5 A5 49 2N 2 30 E
Lovön, Stock. 3 E10 59 18N 17 51 E
Lövstafjärden, Stock. 3 D9 59 23N 17 46 E
Lowe, Mt., L.A. 28 A4 34 13N 118 5W
Lowe Pond, Bost. 21 A3 42 41N 71 0W
Lowell, Bost. 21 B2 42 38N 71 16W
Lowell Dracut State Forest, Bost. 21 B1 42 39N 71 22W
Lower Crystal Springs Res., S.F. 27 C2 37 31N 122 21W
Lower Edmonton, Lon. 4 B4 51 37N 0 3W
Lower Montville, N.Y. 22 B2 40 53N 74 21W
Lower New York B., N.Y. 22 D4 40 32N 74 5W
Lower Plenty, Melb. 19 E7 37 44 S 145 7 E
Lower Shing Mun Res., H.K. 12 D5 22 22N 114 9 E
Lower Sydenham, Lon. 4 C4 51 25N 0 2W
Lower Van Norman L., L.A. 28 A2 34 17N 118 28W
Lübars, Berl. 7 A3 52 37N 13 21 E
Lubeinî, Bahr el →, El Qâ. 18 C4 30 1N 31 5 E
Lubya →, St-Pet. 11 A5 60 1N 30 39 E
Lucento, Tori. 9 B2 45 5N 7 39 E
Lucero, La Hab. 30 B3 23 5N 82 19W
Ludwigsfeld, Mün. 7 F9 48 12N 11 27 E
Lugarno, Syd. 19 B3 33 59 S 151 2 E
Lugouqiao, Beij. 14 C2 39 49N 116 10 E
Luhu, Gzh. 14 G8 23 9N 113 16 E
Luipaardsvei, Jobg. 18 E7 26 6 S 27 49 E
Luis Guillón, B.A. 32 C4 34 48 S 58 26W
Lujia, Shang. 14 J12 31 15N 121 37 E
Lukens, Mt., L.A. 28 A3 34 16N 118 12W
Lumiar, Lisb. 8 F8 38 46N 9 9W
Lundtofte, Købn. 2 D10 55 47N 12 30 E
Lung Mei, H.K. 12 D6 22 23N 114 15 E
Lunsad, Manila 15 E5 14 27N 121 11 E
Luojiang, Gzh. 14 G8 23 5N 113 17 E
Lura →, Mil. 9 D5 45 34N 9 5 E
Lurnea, Syd. 19 B2 33 56 S 150 54 E
Lurup, Hbg. 7 D7 53 35N 9 54 E
Lustheim, Mün. 7 F10 48 14N 11 34 E
Lütgendortmund, Ruhr 6 A6 51 30N 7 20 E
Lutherville-Timonium, Balt. 25 A3 39 25N 76 36W
Lüttringhausen, Ruhr 6 C5 51 12N 7 14 E
Lutvatn, Oslo 2 B5 59 54N 10 52 E
Luwan, Shang. 14 J11 31 12N 121 27 E
Luyano, La Hab. 30 B3 23 6N 82 21W
Luzhniki Sports Centre, Mos. 11 E9 55 43N 37 31 E
Lyckebyn, Stock. 3 E12 59 11N 18 13 E
Lynbrook, N.Y. 23 D6 40 39N 73 41W
Lyndhurst, Jobg. 18 E9 26 7 S 28 7 E
Lyndhurst, N.Y. 22 C4 40 49N 74 7W
Lynn, Bost. 21 C4 42 28N 70 57W
Lynn Harbor, Bost. 21 C4 42 27N 70 56W
Lynnfield, Bost. 21 B3 42 32N 71 2W
Lynwood, L.A. 28 C3 33 55N 118 11W
Lyon, Gare de, Paris 5 B4 48 50N 2 22 E
Lyons, Chic. 26 C2 41 48N 87 49W
Lyonsville, N.Y. 22 B2 40 57N 74 23W
Lysaker, Oslo 2 B3 59 54N 10 38 E
Lysakerselva →, Oslo 2 B3 59 54N 10 38 E
Lysolaje, Pra. 10 B2 50 7N 14 21 E
Lytkarino, Mos. 11 F11 55 35N 37 55 E
Lyubertsy, Mos. 11 E11 55 40N 37 51 E
Lyublino, Mos. 11 E10 55 41N 37 44 E

M

Ma Nam Wat, H.K. 12 D6 22 21N 114 16 E
Ma Po, Sŏul 12 G7 37 32N 126 56 E
Ma Tsz Keng, H.K. 12 D5 22 22N 114 7 E
Ma Yau Tong, H.K. 12 E6 22 19N 114 14 E
Maantiekylä, Hels. 3 A5 60 20N 25 0 E
Maarifa, Bagd. 17 F8 33 15N 44 21 E
Mabashi, Tōkyō 13 B4 35 48N 139 55 E
Mabato Pt., Manila 15 E4 14 29N 121 3 E
Mabolo, Manila 15 E3 14 26N 120 56 E
Macaco, Morro do, Rio J. 31 B3 22 56 S 43 6W
McCook, Chic. 26 C2 41 47N 87 49W
McGill Univ., Mtrl. 20 A4 43 30N 73 35W
Machida, Tōkyō 13 C1 35 32N 139 26 E
Macierzysz, Wsaw. 10 E6 52 13N 2[illegible] E
Maciolki, Wsaw. 10 E7 52 19N 21 [illegible] E
Mackayville, Mtrl. 20 A5 43 30N 7[illegible]6W
McKinnon, Melb. 19 F7 37 54 S 145 1 E
Mclean, Wash. 25 D6 38 56N 77 10W
Macleod, Melb. 19 E7 37 43 S 145 4 E
Macopocho →, Stgo 30 J10 33 24 S 70 40W
Macquarie Fields, Syd. 19 B2 33 59 S 150 53 E
Macquarie Univ., Syd. 19 A3 33 46 S 151 7 E
MacRitchie Res., Sing. 15 F7 1 20N 103 49 E
Macul, Stgo 30 K11 33 30 S 70 35W
Macuto, Car. 30 D5 10 36N 66 53W
Macuto →, Car. 30 D5 10 36N 66 53W
Madatpur, Calc. 16 C6 22 53N 88 27 E
Maddalena, Colle della, Tori. 9 B3 45 2N 7 43 E
Madhudaha, Calc. 16 E6 22 30N 88 24 E
Madhyamgram, Calc. 16 C6 22 41N 88 26 E
Madīnah Al Mansōr, Bagd. 17 F8 33 18N 44 20 E
Mâdinet el Muqattam, El Qâ. 18 C5 30 1N 31 15 E
Mâdinet Nasr, El Qâ. 18 C5 30 4N 31 18 E
Madipur, Delhi 16 B1 28 40N 77 8 E
Madison, N.Y. 22 C2 40 45N 74 24W
Madonna della Scala, Tori. 9 B3 44 59N 7 46 E
Madonna dell'Arco, Nápl. 9 H13 40 52N 14 23 E
Madrid, Mdrd. 8 B2 40 24N 3 42W
Madrona, Barc. 8 D5 41 27N 2 1 E
Madureira, Rio J. 31 B2 22 52 S 43 19W
Maeda, Tōkyō 13 B3 35 48N 139 45 E
Maesawa, Tōkyō 13 B3 35 44N 139 31 E
Magalhaes, Rio J. 31 B1 22 51 S 43 22W
Magdalena del Mar, Lima 30 G8 12 5 S 77 5W
Magholpur, Delhi 16 A1 28 41N 77 6 E
Maghreb, Bagd. 17 E8 33 23N 44 22 E
Magidiyeh, Tehr. 17 C5 35 43N 51 28 E
Maginu, Tōkyō 13 C2 35 34N 139 34 E
Magliana, Rome 9 F9 41 50N 12 26 E
Maglód, Bud. 10 K14 47 27N 19 18 E
Magnolia, Phil. 24 B4 39 51N 75 1W
Magny-les-Hameaux, Paris 5 C2 48 44N 2 3 E
Maharajpur, Delhi 16 B2 28 39N 77 19 E
Maheshtala, Calc. 16 F5 22 29N 88 15 E
Mahiari, Calc. 16 E5 22 35N 88 14 E
Mahikpur, Calc. 16 E5 22 32N 88 13 E
Mahim, Bomb. 16 G8 19 2N 72 50 E
Mahim B., Bomb. 16 G7 19 2N 72 49 E
Mahishdanga, Calc. 16 C6 22 53N 88 11 E
Mahlsdorf, Berl. 7 A4 52 30N 13 37 E
Mahmoodabad, Kar. 17 G11 24 51N 67 4 E
Mahmutbey, Ist. 17 A1 41 2N 28 49 E
Mahpar, Jak. 15 H9 6 9 S 106 49 E
Mahul, Bomb. 16 G8 19 0N 72 53 E
Maida Vale, Lon. 4 B3 51 31N 0 11W
Maidstone, Melb. 19 E6 37 47 S 144 52 E
Maincourt-sur-Yvette, Paris 5 C1 48 42N 1 58 E
Maipu, Stgo 30 K10 33 30 S 70 45W
Maiquetia, Car. 30 D5 10 35N 66 57W
Maiquetia Aeropuerto, Car. 30 D4 10 36N 67 0W
Maisons-Alfort, Paris 5 C4 48 48N 2 26 E
Maisons-Laffitte, Paris 5 B2 48 57N 2 8 E
Maissoneuve, Mtrl. 20 A4 43 32N 73 33W
Maitani, Ōsaka 12 B4 34 48N 135 22 E
Majadahonda, Mdrd. 8 B1 40 28N 3 52W
Majlis, Tehr. 17 C5 35 41N 51 25 E
Makati, Manila 15 D4 14 33N 121 7 E
Mäkiniitty, Hels. 3 A4 60 20N 24 58 E
Mala Straná, Pra. 10 B2 50 4N 14 24 E
Malabar, Syd. 19 B4 33 58 S 151 14 E
Malabar Hill, Bomb. 16 H7 18 57N 72 48 E
Malabon, Manila 15 D3 14 39N 120 56 E
Malacanang Palace, Manila 15 D3 14 35N 120 59 E
Malagrotta, Rome 9 F9 41 52N 12 20 E
Malakhovka, Mos. 11 F12 55 39N 38 0 E
Malakoff, Paris 5 C3 48 49N 2 18 E
Malakpur, Delhi 16 A2 28 42N 77 12 E
Malanday, Manila 15 D4 14 38N 121 5 E
Malanghero, Tori. 9 A2 45 12N 7 39 E
Mälarhöjaen, Stock. 3 E10 59 18N 17 58 E
Malaspina, L., Mil. 9 E6 45 28N 9 8 E
Malassis, Paris 5 C3 48 37N 2 3 E
Malate, Manila 15 D3 14 34N 120 59 E
Malaya Neva, St-Pet. 11 B3 59 56N 30 16 E
Malaya-Okhta, St-Pet. 11 B4 59 55N 30 25 E
Malchow, Berl. 7 A3 52 34N 13 29 E
Malden, Bost. 21 C3 42 26N 71 3W
Malden, Lon. 4 C3 51 23N 0 15W
Malečice, Pra. 10 B3 50 5N 14 30 E
Malekete, Lagos 18 A3 6 33N 7 32 E
Malir →, Kar. 17 H11 24 49N 67 4 E
Malir Cantonment, Kar. 17 G12 24 58N 67 10 E
Malmi, Hels. 3 B4 60 15N 24 59 E
Malmøya, Oslo 2 B4 59 52N 10 45 E
Måløv, Købn. 2 D9 55 44N 12 20 E
Malton, Trto. 20 D7 43 42N 79 38W
Malvern, Jobg. 18 F9 26 11 S 28 5 E
Malvern, Melb. 19 F7 37 50 S 145 2 E
Malvern, Phil. 24 A1 40 2N 75 31W
Malvern, Trto. 20 D9 43 47N 79 13W
Malvern East, Jobg. 18 F9 26 11 S 28 7 E
Malverne, N.Y. 23 C6 40 40N 73 40W
Mamaroneck, N.Y. 23 B6 40 56N 73 43W
Mamaroneck Harbour, N.Y. 23 B6 40 56N 73 42W
Mamonovo, Mos. 11 F10 55 36N 37 49 E
Mamonovo, Mos. 11 E8 55 43N 37 28 E
Mampong Prapatan, Jak. 15 J9 6 15 S 106 49 E
Mampukuji, Tōkyō 13 C2 35 36N 139 31 E
Man Budrukh, Bomb. 16 G8 19 2N 72 55 E
Man Khurd, Bomb. 16 G8 19 3N 72 55 E
Managua, La Hab. 30 C3 22 58N 82 17W
Manayunk, Phil. 24 A3 40 1N 75 12W
Mandaluyong, Manila 15 D4 14 35N 121 1 E
Mandaoli, Delhi 16 B2 28 37N 77 18 E
Mandaqui, S. Pau. 31 D6 23 29 S 46 37W
Mandaqui →, S. Pau. 31 D6 23 30 S 46 40W
Mandres-les-Roses, Paris 5 C5 48 42N 2 32 E
Mandvi, Bomb. 16 H8 18 56N 72 50 E
Mang Kung Uk, H.K. 12 E6 22 18N 114 16 E
Manggarai, Jak. 15 J10 6 12 S 106 50 E
Manguinho, Aeroporto de, Rio J. 31 B2 22 52 S 43 14W
Mangweon, Sŏul 12 G7 37 33N 126 55 E
Manhasset, N.Y. 23 C6 40 47N 73 40W
Manhasset B., N.Y. 23 C6 40 49N 73 43W
Manhasset Hills, N.Y. 23 C7 40 45N 73 39W
Manhattan, N.Y. 22 C5 40 48N 73 57W
Manhattan Beach, L.A. 28 C2 33 53N 118 24W
Manhatten, N.Y. 22 D5 40 34N 73 56W
Manila, Manila 15 D3 14 35N 120 58 E
Manila B., Manila 15 D3 14 32N 120 56 E
Manila Int. Airport, Manila 15 D4 14 31N 121 0 E
Mankkaa, Hels. 3 B3 60 11N 24 47 E
Mankunda, Calc. 16 C6 22 50N 88 22 E
Manly, Syd. 19 A4 33 47 S 151 17 E
Manly Warringah War Memorial Park, Syd. 19 A4 33 46 S 151 15 E
Manning State Park, Bost. 21 B1 42 34N 71 20W
Mannsworth, Wien 10 H11 48 8N 16 30 E
Manoa, Phil. 24 B3 39 58N 75 18W
Manor Park, Lon. 4 B5 51 32N 0 1 E
Manora, Kar. 17 H10 24 47N 66 58 E
Manorhaven, N.Y. 23 B6 40 50N 73 41W
Manoteras, Mdrd. 8 B3 40 28N 3 39W
Manquehue, Cerro, Stgo 30 J11 33 21 S 70 35W
Mantegazza, Mil. 9 D4 45 30N 8 58 E
Mantilla, La Hab. 30 B3 23 4N 82 20W
Mantua, Phil. 24 C3 39 47N 75 10W
Mantua Cr. →, Phil. 24 C3 39 47N 75 13W
Manufacta, Jobg. 18 E8 26 9 S 27 51 E
Manzanares, Canal de, Mdrd. 8 C3 40 19N 3 38W
Mapetla, Jobg. 18 F8 26 16 S 27 51 E
Maple, Trto. 20 C7 43 51N 79 30W
Maple L., Chic. 26 C1 41 43N 87 53W
Maple Shade, Phil. 24 B4 39 57N 75 0W
Maplewood, N.Y. 22 C3 40 43N 74 16W
Maracana, Rio J. 31 B2 22 54 S 43 13W
Maraisburg, Jobg. 18 F8 26 10 S 27 57 E
Marano di Nápoli, Nápl. 9 H12 40 53N 14 11 E
Maraoli, Bomb. 16 G8 19 2N 7[illegible] 53 E
Marapendi, L. de, Rio J. 31 C1 23 0 S 43 23W
Marblehead, Bost. 21 C4 42 29N 70 51W
Marcelin, Wsaw. 10 E6 52 19N 20 59 E
Marcella, N.Y. 22 B2 40 59N 74 29W
Marcos Paz, B.A. 32 C2 34 46 S 58 49W
Marcoussis, Paris 5 D3 48 38N 2 13 E
Marcus Hook, Phil. 24 C2 39 49N 75 25W
Marcus Hook Cr. →, Phil. 24 B2 39 49N 75 24W
Marechiaro, Nápl. 9 J12 40 48N 14 12 E
Mareil-Marly, Paris 5 B2 48 52N 2 4 E
Margareten, Wien 10 G10 48 11N 16 20 E
Margency, Paris 5 A3 49 0N 2 17 E
Margitsziget, Bud. 10 J13 47 31N 19 2 E
Maria, Wien 10 G10 48 11N 16 21 E
Maria Paula, Rio J. 31 B3 22 53 S 43 1W
Marianao, La Hab. 30 B2 23 4N 82 25W
Marianella, Nápl. 9 H12 40 53N 14 13 E
Mariano Acosta, B.A. 32 C2 34 42 S 58 47W
Mariano J. Haedo, B.A. 32 B3 34 39 S 58 35W
Maridalen, Oslo 2 B4 59 59N 10 45 E
Maridalsvatnet, Oslo 2 B4 59 59N 10 46 E
Mariendorf, Berl. 7 B3 52 26N 13 23 E
Marienfelde, Berl. 7 B3 52 24N 13 23 E
Marienthal, Hbg. 7 D8 53 34N 10 4 E
Mariglianella, Nápl. 9 H13 40 55N 14 26 E
Marigliano, Nápl. 9 H13 40 55N 14 27 E
Marikina, Manila 15 D4 14 38N 121 5 E
Marikina →, Manila 15 D4 14 33N 121 3 E
Marin City, S.F. 27 A1 37 52N 122 30W
Marin Headlands State Park, S.F. 27 A2 37 50N 122 28W
Marin Is., S.F. 27 A2 37 57N 122 27W
Marin Pen., S.F. 27 A1 37 50N 122 30W
Marine World, S.F. 27 C3 37 32N 122 16W
Mariners Harbour, N.Y. 22 D3 40 38N 74 10W
Mario, Mt., Rome 9 F9 41 55N 12 27 E
Markham, Chic. 26 D2 41 35N 87 40W
Markham, Phil. 24 B1 39 53N 75 30W
Markham, Trto. 20 C8 43 52N 79 15W
Markham, Mt., L.A. 28 A4 34 14N 118 6W
Marki, Wsaw. 10 E7 52 19N 21 6 E
Markland Wood, Trto. 20 E7 43 38N 79 34W
Marlton, Phil. 24 B5 39 53N 74 55W
Marly, Forêt de, Paris 5 B2 48 52N 2 4 E
Marly-le-Roi, Paris 5 B2 48 52N 2 5 E
Marne →, Paris 5 C4 48 47N 2 29 E
Marne-la-Vallée, Paris 5 B5 48 50N 2 37 E
Marolles-en-Brie, Paris 5 C5 48 44N 2 33 E
Maroonda Aquaduct, Melb. 19 E7 37 40 S 145 9 E
Maroubra, Syd. 19 B4 33 56 S 151 16 E
Marple, Phil. 24 B2 39 56N 75 20W
Marquette Park, Chic. 26 C2 41 46N 87 42W
Marrickville, Syd. 19 B3 33 54 S 151 9 E
Marschlande, Hbg. 7 E8 53 27N 10 6 E
Marsfield, Syd. 19 A3 33 46 S 151 7 E
Marte, Base Aérea de, S. Pau. 31 E6 23 30 S 46 38W
Martesana, Navíglio della, Mil. 9 D6 45 31N 9 17 E
Martin State Nat. Airport, Balt. 25 B4 39 19N 76 24W
Martinez, B.A. 32 A3 34 29 S 58 31W
Martinkylä, Hels. 3 B4 60 17N 24 51 E
Martins Pond, Bost. 21 B3 42 35N 71 7W
Martinsried, Mün. 7 G9 48 6N 11 27 E
Maruko, Tōkyō 13 C3 35 33N 139 40 E
Marusino, Mos. 11 E11 55 41N 37 58 E
Marxloh, Ruhr 6 A2 51 30N 6 47 E
Maryino, Mos. 11 E10 55 40N 37 45 E
Maryland, Sing. 15 G7 1 19N 103 47 E
Maryland, Univ. of, Wash. 25 D8 39 58N 76 56W
Marylebone, Lon. 4 B4 51 31N 0 9W
Marymont, Wsaw. 10 E6 52 16N 20 58 E
Marysin Wawerski, Wsaw. 10 E7 52 14N 21 9 E
Marzahn, Berl. 7 A4 52 32N 13 33 E
Masambong, Manila 15 D4 14 38N 121 0 E
Mascot, Syd. 19 B4 33 55 S 151 12 E
Mascuppic L., Bost. 21 A1 42 40N 71 23W
Masmo, Stock. 3 E10 59 15N 17 53 E
Maspeth, N.Y. 22 C5 40 43N 73 55W
Masr el Gedida, El Qâ. 18 C5 30 5N 31 19 E
Masr el Qadîma, El Qâ. 18 C5 30 0N 31 14 E
Masroor Airport, Kar. 17 G10 24 53N 66 56 E
Massa di Somma, Nápl. 9 H13 40 50N 14 22 E
Massachusetts B., Bost. 21 C4 42 24N 70 50W
Massachusett's Inst. of Tech., Bost. 21 C3 42 22N 71 6W
Massamá, Lisb. 8 F7 38 45N 9 16W
Massapequa, N.Y. 23 C8 40 40N 73 28W
Massby, Hels. 3 B6 60 17N 25 27 E
Massey →, Trto. 20 D9 43 42N 79 19W
Massy, Paris 5 C3 48 43N 2 16 E
Matarza →, B.A. 32 C3 34 47 S 58 35W
Matasango, Lima 30 G9 12 3 S 76 58W
Mathle, Calc. 16 E5 22 34N 88 13 E
Mathutong, Beij. 14 B2 39 56N 116 19 E
Matinecock, N.Y. 23 B7 40 51N 73 36W
Matinha, Lisb. 8 F8 38 45N 9 5W
Matramam, Jak. 15 J10 6 12 S 106 51 E
Matsubara, Ōsaka 12 C4 34 34N 135 33 E
Matsubushi, Tōkyō 13 A3 35 55N 139 49 E
Matsudo, Tōkyō 13 B4 35 46N 139 54 E
Matsumoloshinden, Tōkyō 13 B2 35 50N 139 36 E
Mattapan, Bost. 21 D3 42 16N 71 6W
Mátyásföld, Bud. 10 J14 47 30N 19 12 E
Mau Tso Ngam, H.K. 12 D6 22 20N 114 13 E
Mauá, S. Pau. 31 E7 23 39 S 46 27W
Mauer, Wien 10 H9 48 9N 16 16 E
Mauerbach →, Wien 10 G9 48 16N 16 13 E
Mauldre, Paris 5 C1 48 56N 1 58 E
Maurecourt, Paris 5 B2 48 59N 2 3 E
Mauregard, Paris 5 A5 49 2N 2 34 E
Maurepas, Paris 5 C1 48 46N 1 55 E
Mauripur, Kar. 17 G10 24 52N 66 55 E
Maxhof, Mün. 7 G9 48 4N 11 29 E
Maya-Zan, Ōsaka 12 B2 34 43N 135 12 E
Maybunga, Manila 15 D4 14 34N 121 4 E
Mayfair, Jobg. 18 F9 26 11 S 28 0 E
Mayfair, Phil. 24 A4 40 2N 75 3W
Maypajo, Manila 15 D3 14 38N 120 58 E
Maytubig, Manila 15 D3 14 33N 120 59 E
Maywood, Chic. 26 B1 41 52N 87 51W
Maywood, L.A. 28 C3 33 59N 118 12W
Maywood, N.Y. 22 B4 40 53N 74 3W
Mazagaon, Bomb. 16 H8 18 57N 72 50 E
M'Boi Mirim, S. Pau. 31 F5 23 42 S 46 46W
Meadow I., N.Y. 23 D7 40 36N 73 32W
Meadow L., N.Y. 23 C5 40 44N 73 50W
Meadowlands, Jobg. 18 F8 26 12 S 27 53 E
Meadowood, Wash. 25 C7 39 4N 77 0W
Měcholupy, Pra. 10 B3 50 3N 14 32 E
Měčice, Pra. 10 A3 50 11N 14 31 E
Mecidiyeköy, Ist. 17 A3 41 4N 29 0 E
Meckinghoven, Ruhr 6 A5 51 37N 7 19 E
Médan, Paris 5 B1 48 57N 1 59 E
Medfield, Bost. 21 D2 42 11N 71 18W
Medford, Bost. 21 C3 42 25N 71 7W
Media, Phil. 24 B2 39 55N 75 23W
Mediodia, Mdrd. 8 B3 40 22N 3 39W
Medvastö, Hels. 3 C2 60 5N 24 38 E
Medvedkovo, Mos. 11 D9 55 52N 37 37 E
Medvezhiy Ozyora, Mos. 11 D11 55 52N 37 59 E
Meerbeck, Ruhr 6 B1 51 28N 6 38 E
Meerbusch 6 C2 51 16N 6 40 E
Meguro [illegible], Tōkyō 13 C3 35 37N 139 45 E
Meguro-K[illegible], Tōkyō 13 C3 35 37N 139 42 E
Mehpalpur, Delhi 16 B1 28 3[illegible]N 77 E
Mehrābād Airport, Tehr. 17 C4 35 41N 51 18 E
Mehram Nagar, Delhi 16 B1 28 34N 77 8 E
Mehrow, Berl. 7 A4 52 34N 13 37 E
Meiderich, Ruhr 6 B2 51 27N 6 47 E
Meidling, Wien 10 G10 48 10N 16 20 E
Meiendorf, Hbg. 7 D8 53 37N 10 8 E
Méier, Rio J. 31 B2 22 52 S 43 15W
Meiji Shrine, Tōkyō 13 B3 35 41N 139 41 E
Meizino-Mori-Minō National Park, Ōsaka 12 A3 34 51N 135 28 E
Mejiro, Tōkyō 13 B3 35 43N 139 43 E
Melbourne, Melb. 19 E6 37 48 S 144 58 E
Melbourne Airport, Melb. 19 E6 37 40 S 144 50 E
Melbourne Univ., Melb. 19 E6 37 47 S 144 57 E
Melito di Nápoli, Nápl. 9 H12 40 55N 14 13 E
Melkki, Hels. 3 C4 60 8N 24 53 E
Mellingstedt, Hbg. 7 C8 53 40N 10 6 E
Mellunkylä, Hels. 3 B5 60 14N 25 5 E
Mellunmäki, Hels. 3 B5 60 14N 25 6 E
Melrose, Bost. 21 C3 42 27N 71 2W
Melrose, N.Y. 22 C5 40 49N 73 55W
Melrose Park, Chic. 26 B1 41 53N 87 50W
Melun-Sénart, Paris 5 D5 48 3N 2 31 E
Melun-Villaroche, Aérodrome de, Paris 5 D6 48 37N 2 41 E
Melville, N.Y. 23 C8 40 47N 73 24W
Menai, Syd. 19 C3 34 1 S 151 1 E
Menandon, Paris 5 A2 49 2N 2 3 E
Mendoza, Lima 30 G9 12 5 S 76 59W
Mengede, Ruhr 6 A6 51 34N 7 23 E
Mengjiazhai, Shang. 14 J11 31 19N 121 21 E
Menglinghausen, Ruhr 6 B6 51 28N 7 26 E
Menlo Park, S.F. 27 D3 37 27N 122 11W
Menlo Park Terrace, N.Y. 22 D3 40 34N 74 18W
Mentang, Jak. 15 J9 6 11 S 106 49 E
Menucourt, Paris 5 A1 49 1N 1 59 E
Meopham, Lon. 4 C7 51 22N 0 21 E
Mérantaise →, Paris 5 C2 48 42N 2 8 E
Mercamadrid, Mdrd. 8 B3 40 21N 3 39W
Merced, L., S.F. 27 B2 37 43N 122 29W
Merchantville, Phil. 24 B4 39 56N 75 3W
Mercier, Pont, Mtrl. 20 B3 43 24N 73 39W
Merdeka Palace, Jak. 15 J9 6 10 S 106 49 E
Meredale, Jobg. 18 F8 26 16 S 27 58 E
Mergellina, Nápl. 9 J12 40 49N 14 13 E
Meriden, N.Y. 22 B2 40 56N 74 27W
Merion Station, Phil. 24 B3 39 59N 75 15W
Merlimau, Sing. 15 G7 1 17N 103 42 E
Merlimau, P., Sing. 15 G7 1 17N 103 42 E
Merlo, B.A. 32 B2 34 39 S 58 43W
Merri Cr. →, Melb. 19 E6 37 47 S 144 59 E
Merrick, N.Y. 23 D7 40 39N 73 32W
Merrionette Park, Chic. 26 C2 41 41N 87 40W
Merritt, L., S.F. 27 B3 37 48N 122 15W
Merrylands, Syd. 19 B2 33 50 S 150 59 E
Merton, Lon. 4 C3 51 24N 0 11W
Mesgarābād, Tehr. 17 D6 35 27N 51 30 E
Meshcherskiy, Mos. 11 E8 55 40N 37 23 E
Mesquita, Rio J. 31 A1 22 46 S 43 25W
Messe, Wien 10 G10 48 13N 16 24 E
Messy, Paris 5 B6 48 58N 2 42 E
Metanópoli, Mil. 9 E6 45 24N 9 15 E
Methuen, Bost. 21 A2 42 42N 71 12W
Metropolitan Opera, N.Y. 22 C5 40 46N 74 59W
Mettman, Ruhr 6 C3 51 15N 6 58 E
Metuchen, N.Y. 22 D2 40 32N 74 21W
Metzkausen, Ruhr 6 C3 51 16N 6 57 E
Meudon, Paris 5 C3 48 48N 2 14 E
Meulan, Paris 5 A1 49 0N 1 54 E
México, Aeropuerto Int. de, Méx. 29 B3 19 25N 99 4W
México, Ciudad de, Méx. 29 B2 19 25N 99 7W
Mezzate, Mil. 9 E6 45 26N 9 17 E
Mia Dong, Sŏul 12 G8 37 36N 127 0 E
Miano, Nápl. 9 H12 40 53N 14 15 E
Miasto, Wsaw. 10 E7 52 15N 21 0 E
Michalin, Wsaw. 10 F8 52 9N 21 13 E
Michałowice, Wsaw. 10 E5 52 10N 20 52 E
Michle, Pra. 10 B2 50 3N 14 28 E
Mickleton, Phil. 24 C3 39 47N 75 14W
Middle →, Balt. 25 B4 39 18N 76 24W
Middle B., N.Y. 23 D7 40 36N 73 36W
Middle Branch →, Balt. 25 B3 39 15N 76 37W
Middle Brewster I., Bost. 21 C4 42 20N 70 51W
Middle Cove, Syd. 19 A4 33 48 S 151 13 E
Middle Harbour, Syd. 19 A4 33 47 S 151 14 E
Middle Hd., Syd. 19 A4 33 49 S 151 17 E
Middle I., H.K. 12 E6 22 16N 114 10 E
Middle Park, Melb. 19 F6 37 50 S 144 57 E
Middle River, Balt. 25 A4 39 20N 76 26W
Middle Village, N.Y. 23 C5 40 43N 73 52W
Middleborough, Balt. 25 B4 39 18N 76 26W
Middlesex, N.Y. 22 D2 40 34N 74 30W
Middlesex Fells Reservation, Bost. 21 C3 42 27N 71 6W
Middlesex Res., N.Y. 22 D3 40 37N 74 19W
Middleton, Bost. 21 B3 42 35N 71 0W
Middleton Pond, Bost. 21 B3 42 35N 71 1W
Middleville, N.Y. 23 B9 40 54N 73 19W
Midland Beach, N.Y. 22 D4 40 34N 74 5W
Midland Park, N.Y. 22 B4 40 59N 74 9W

42 Midlothian

Midlothian, *Chic.* 26 D2 41 37N 87 43W
Miedzeszyn, *Wsaw.* 10 E8 52 10N 21 11 E
Międzylesie, *Wsaw.* 10 E8 52 12N 21 10 E
Miessaari, *Hels.* 3 C3 60 8N 24 47 E
Mikhaylovskoye, *Mos.* 11 F9 55 35N 37 35 E
Mikhelysona, *Mos.* 11 E11 55 42N 37 52 E
Milano, *Mil.* 9 E5 45 28N 9 10 E
Milano Due, *Mil.* 9 E6 45 29N 9 16 E
Milano San Felice, *Mil.* 9 E6 45 28N 9 18 E
Milanolago, *Mil.* 9 E6 45 27N 9 17 E
Milbertshofen, *Mün.* 7 F10 48 10N 11 34 E
Milburn, *N.Y.* 22 C3 40 43N 74 19W
Milford, *Balt.* 25 A2 39 21N 76 43W
Mill Cr. →, *S.F.* 27 A1 37 53N 122 31W
Mill Hill, *Lon.* 4 B3 51 37N 0 14W
Mill Neck, *N.Y.* 23 B7 40 53N 73 33W
Mill Park, *Melb.* 19 E7 37 40 S 145 3 E
Mill Valley, *S.F.* 27 A1 37 54N 122 33W
Millbrae, *S.F.* 27 C2 37 35N 122 22W
Mille-Iles, R. des →, *Mtrl.* 20 A3 43 39N 73 46W
Miller I., *Balt.* 25 B4 39 15N 76 21W
Miller Meadow, *Chic.* 26 B2 41 51N 87 49W
Milliken, *Trto.* 20 D9 43 49N 79 17W
Millis, *Bost.* 21 D1 42 10N 71 21W
Mills College, *S.F.* 27 B3 37 46N 122 10W
Milltown, *Phil.* 24 B1 39 57N 75 32W
Millwall, *Lon.* 4 C4 51 29N 0 0 E
Millwood, *Wash.* 25 D8 38 52N 76 52W
Milon-la-Chapelle, *Paris* 5 C2 48 43N 2 3 E
Milpa Alta, *Méx.* 29 C3 19 11N 99 0W
Milperra, *Syd.* 19 B2 33 56 S 150 59 E
Milspe, *Ruhr* 6 C5 51 18N 7 19 E
Milton, *Bost.* 21 D3 42 14N 71 2W
Milton Village, *Bost.* 21 D3 42 15N 71 4W
Mimico, *Trto.* 20 E8 43 36N 79 29W
Mimico Cr. →, *Trto.* 20 E7 43 37N 79 33W
Minami, *Ōsaka* 12 B4 34 40N 135 30 E
Minami-Ku, *Tōkyō* 13 D2 35 24N 139 37 E
Minami-tsunashima, *Tōkyō* 13 C2 35 32N 139 37 E
Minato, *Ōsaka* 12 C3 34 39N 135 25 E
Minato-Ku, *Tōkyō* 13 C3 35 39N 139 44 E
Mine, *Tōkyō* 13 B3 35 49N 139 46 E
Minebank Run →, *Balt.* 25 A3 39 24N 76 33W
Mineola, *N.Y.* 23 C7 40 44N 73 38W
Ministro Rivadavia, *B.A.* 32 D4 34 50 S 58 22W
Minō, *Ōsaka* 12 B3 34 49N 135 28 E
Minshât el Bekkari, *El Qâ.* 18 C4 30 0N 31 8 E
Minto, *Syd.* 19 C2 34 1 S 150 51 E
Minute Man Nat. Hist. Park, *Bost.* 21 C2 42 25N 71 16W
Mirafiori, *Tori.* 9 B2 45 1N 7 36 E
Miraflores, *Lima* 30 G8 12 7 S 77 2W
Miramar, *La Hab.* 30 B2 23 7N 82 25W
Miramar, *S.F.* 27 D2 37 29N 122 27W
Miranda, *Syd.* 19 C3 34 2 S 151 6 E
Mirzapur, *Calc.* 16 D6 22 49N 88 24 E
Misato, *Tōkyō* 13 B4 35 49N 139 51 E
Misericordia, Sa. da, *Rio J.* 31 B2 22 51 S 43 17W
Mishawum L., *Bost.* 21 B3 42 30N 71 8W
Mission, *S.F.* 27 B2 37 44N 122 25W
Mississauga, *Trto.* 20 E7 43 35N 79 34W
Mitaka, *Tōkyō* 13 B2 35 41N 139 34 E
Mitcham, *Lon.* 4 C3 51 23N 0 10W
Mitcham, *Melb.* 19 E8 37 48 S 145 12 E
Mitcham Common, *Lon.* 4 C4 51 23N 0 8W
Mitino, *Mos.* 11 D8 55 51N 37 20 E
Mitry, *Paris* 5 B5 48 59N 2 36 E
Mitry-Mory, *Paris* 5 B5 48 59N 2 38 E
Mitry-Mory, Aérodrome de, *Paris* 5 B5 48 59N 2 37 E
Mitte, *Berl.* 7 A3 52 32N 13 24 E
Mittel Isarkanal, *Mün.* 7 F11 48 12N 11 40 E
Mittenheim, *Mün.* 7 F10 48 15N 11 33 E
Mixcoac, Presa de, *Méx.* 29 B2 19 21N 99 14W
Mixquic, *Méx.* 29 C4 19 13N 98 58W
Miyakojima, *Ōsaka* 12 B4 34 42N 135 31 E
Miyalo, *Tōkyō* 13 B2 35 49N 139 31 E
Mizonokuchi, *Tōkyō* 13 C2 35 35N 139 34 E
Mizue, *Tōkyō* 13 B4 35 41N 139 54 E
Mizuko, *Tōkyō* 13 A2 35 50N 139 32 E
Mizumoto, *Tōkyō* 13 B4 35 46N 139 52 E
Młocinski Park, *Wsaw.* 10 E6 52 19N 20 57 E
Młociny, *Wsaw.* 10 E6 52 18N 20 55 E
Mnevniki, *Mos.* 11 E8 55 45N 37 28 E
Moba, *Lagos* 18 B2 6 26N 7 28 E
Moczydło, *Wsaw.* 10 F7 52 8N 21 2 E
Modderfontein, *Jobg.* 18 E10 26 5 S 28 10 E
Modderfontein →, *Jobg.* 18 E9 26 5 S 28 10 E
Modřany, *Pra.* 10 B2 50 0N 14 24 E
Moers, *Ruhr* 6 B1 51 26N 6 37 E
Moffat Park, *Jobg.* 18 F9 26 15 S 28 4 E
Mofolo, *Jobg.* 18 F8 26 13 S 27 53 E
Mog, *Sŏul* 12 G7 37 32N 126 52 E
Mogyorod, *Bud.* 10 J14 47 35N 19 14 E
Mohili, *Bomb.* 16 G8 19 5N 72 52 E
Moinho Velho →, *S. Pau.* 31 E6 23 35 S 46 35W
Moissy-Cramayel, *Paris* 5 D5 48 37N 2 35 E
Moita, *Lisb.* 8 G9 38 39N 8 59W
Mokotów, *Wsaw.* 10 E7 52 12N 21 0 E
Molapo, *Jobg.* 18 F8 26 15 S 27 51 E
Mole →, *Lon.* 4 D2 51 14N 0 20W
Moletsane, *Jobg.* 18 F8 26 14 S 27 50 E
Molino de Rosas, *Méx.* 29 B2 19 21N 99 14W
Mølleå →, *Købn.* 2 D10 55 48N 12 35 E
Möllen, *Ruhr* 6 A2 51 35N 6 41 E
Mollins de Rey, *Barc.* 8 D5 41 24N 2 1 E
Molokovo, *Mos.* 11 F11 55 35N 37 53 E
Mombaça, *S. Pau.* 31 E7 23 37 S 46 25W
Mombello, *Mil.* 9 D5 45 36N 9 7 E
Momote, *Tōkyō* 13 B2 35 46N 139 37 E
Monash Univ., *Melb.* 19 F7 37 54 S 145 8 E
Monbulk Cr. →, *Melb.* 19 F8 37 55 S 145 12 E
Moncalieri, *Tori.* 9 B3 45 0N 7 41 E
Moncolombone, *Tori.* 9 A1 45 12N 7 28 E
Mondeor, *Jobg.* 18 F9 26 16 S 28 0 E
Moneda, Palacio de la, *Stgo* 30 J11 33 26 S 70 39W
Mong Kok, *H.K.* 12 E6 22 19N 114 10 E
Mongat, *Barc.* 8 D6 41 27N 2 16 E
Mongreno, *Tori.* 9 B3 45 3N 7 45 E
Moninos →, *S. Pau.* 31 F6 23 40 S 46 33W
Monrovia, *L.A.* 28 B4 34 9N 118 1W
Monsanto, *Lisb.* 8 F7 38 44N 9 12W
Monsanto, Parque Florestal de, *Lisb.* 8 F7 38 43N 9 11W
Mont Royal, *Mtrl.* 20 A4 43 30N 73 38W
Mont-Royal, Parc, *Mtrl.* 20 A4 43 30N 73 36W
Montalban, *Car.* 30 E5 10 28N 66 56W
Montana de Montjuich, *Barc.* 8 D5 41 21N 2 9 E
Montara, *S.F.* 27 C2 37 32N 122 30W
Montara, Pt., *S.F.* 27 C1 37 32N 122 31W
Montara Mt., *S.F.* 27 C2 37 32N 122 27W
Montchanin, *Phil.* 24 C1 39 47N 75 35W
Montclair, *N.Y.* 22 C3 40 49N 74 12W
Monte Chingolo, *B.A.* 32 C4 34 43 S 58 22W
Monte Grande, *B.A.* 32 C4 34 48 S 58 27W
Monte Sacro, *Rome* 9 F10 41 56N 12 32 E
Montebello, *L.A.* 28 B4 34 1N 118 8W
Montelera, *Tori.* 9 B1 45 9N 7 26 F
Montemor, *Lisb.* 8 F7 38 49N 9 12W
Monterey Park, *L.A.* 28 B4 34 3N 118 7W
Monterrey, *La Hab.* 30 B3 23 5N 82 18W
Montespaccato, *Rome* 9 F9 41 54N 12 23 E
Montesson, *Paris* 5 B2 48 54N 2 8 E
Monteverde Nuovo, *Rome* 9 F9 41 52N 12 26 E
Montfermeil, *Paris* 5 B5 48 54N 2 33 E
Montgeron, *Paris* 5 C4 48 42N 2 27 E
Montigny-le-Bretonneux, *Paris* 5 C2 48 46N 2 1 E
Montigny-les-Cormeilles, *Paris* 5 B3 48 59N 2 11 E
Montijo, *Lisb.* 8 F9 38 42N 8 58W
Montjay-la-Tour, *Paris* 5 B6 48 54N 2 40 E
Montlhéry, *Paris* 5 D3 48 38N 2 16 E
Montlignon, *Paris* 5 A3 49 0N 2 16 E
Montmagny, *Paris* 5 A4 48 58N 2 21 E
Montmorency, *Paris* 5 B4 48 59N 2 19 E
Montmorency, Forêt de, *Paris* 5 A3 49 2N 2 16 E
Montparnasse, Gare, *Paris* 5 B3 48 50N 2 19 E
Montpelier, *Wash.* 25 C8 39 3N 76 50W
Montréal, *Mtrl.* 20 A4 43 30N 73 33W
Montréal, Î. de, *Mtrl.* 20 A4 43 30N 73 40W
Montréal, Univ. de, *Mtrl.* 20 B4 43 29N 73 37W
Montréal-Est, *Mtrl.* 20 A4 43 37N 73 31W
Montréal Nord, *Mtrl.* 20 A4 43 36N 73 36W
Montreuil, *Paris* 5 B4 48 51N 2 27 E
Montrose, *L.A.* 28 A3 34 12N 118 12W
Montrose, *Melb.* 19 E8 37 49 S 145 19 E
Montrose, *Wash.* 25 C7 39 2N 77 7W
Montrouge, *Paris* 5 C3 48 48N 2 18 E
Montvale, *N.Y.* 22 A4 41 2N 74 1W
Montville, *N.Y.* 22 B2 40 55N 74 23W
Monza, *Mil.* 9 D6 45 35N 9 16 E
Monzoro, *Mil.* 9 E5 45 27N 9 2 E
Moóca, *S. Pau.* 31 E6 23 33 S 46 35W
Moóca →, *S. Pau.* 31 E6 23 35 S 46 35W
Moonachie, *N.Y.* 22 C4 40 50N 74 2W
Moonee Ponds, *Melb.* 19 E6 37 45 S 144 53 E
Moonee Valley Racecourse, *Melb.* 19 E6 37 45 S 144 55 E
Moorbek, *Hbg.* 7 C7 53 41N 9 58 E
Moorburg, *Hbg.* 7 E7 53 29N 9 55 E
Moorebank, *Syd.* 19 B2 33 56 S 150 56 E
Moorestown, *Phil.* 24 B5 39 58N 74 56W
Moorfleet, *Hbg.* 7 D8 53 30N 10 4 E
Mooroolbark, *Melb.* 19 E8 37 46 S 145 19 E
Moorwerder, *Hbg.* 7 E8 53 28N 10 3 E
Moosach, *Mün.* 7 F10 48 10N 11 30 E
Mora, *Bomb.* 16 H8 18 54N 72 55 E
Moraga, *S.F.* 27 B4 37 49N 122 7W
Morainvilliers, *Paris* 5 B1 48 55N 1 56 E
Morales →, *B.A.* 32 C2 34 47 S 58 35W
Morangis, *Paris* 5 C4 48 42N 2 20 E
Moratalaz, *Mdrd.* 8 B3 40 24N 3 39W
Morbras →, *Paris* 5 C5 48 46N 2 30 E
Mörby, *Stock.* 3 D11 59 23N 18 3 E
Morce →, *Paris* 5 B4 48 57N 2 22 E
Morden, *Lon.* 4 C3 51 24N 0 13W
Morehill, *Jobg.* 18 F11 26 10 S 28 20 E
Moreno, *B.A.* 32 B2 34 38 S 58 45W
Moreno, *Rome* 9 G10 41 48N 12 37 E
Morgan Park, *Chic.* 26 C3 41 41N 87 38W
Moriguchi, *Ōsaka* 12 B4 34 43N 135 34 E
Morivione, *Mil.* 9 E6 45 26N 9 12 E
Morningside, *Jobg.* 18 E9 26 4 S 28 3 E
Morningside, *Wash.* 25 E8 38 49N 76 53W
Morningside Park, *Trto.* 20 D9 43 46N 79 12W
Moroka, *Jobg.* 18 F8 26 15 S 27 52 E
Moron, *B.A.* 32 B3 34 39 S 58 37W
Morris Plains, *N.Y.* 22 C2 40 49N 74 29W
Morristown, *N.Y.* 22 C2 40 47N 74 28W
Morro, Castillo del, *La Hab.* 30 B2 23 8N 82 21W
Morro Pelado, *S. Pau.* 31 E7 23 38 S 46 24W
Morro Solar, *Lima* 30 H8 12 11 S 77 1W
Morsang-sur-Orge, *Paris* 5 D4 48 39N 2 21 E
Mörsenbroich, *Ruhr* 6 C2 51 15N 6 48 E
Morses Pond, *Bost.* 21 D2 42 17N 71 19W
Morte →, *Paris* 5 C3 48 40N 2 16 E
Mortlake, *Lon.* 4 C3 51 27N 0 15W
Mortlake, *Syd.* 19 B3 33 50 S 151 6 E
Morton, *Phil.* 24 B2 39 54N 75 19W
Morton Grove, *Chic.* 26 A2 42 2N 87 46W
Mory, *Paris* 5 B5 48 58N 2 37 E
Moscavide, *Lisb.* 8 F8 38 47N 9 6W
Moscow = Moskva, *Mos.* 11 E9 55 45N 37 37 E
Mosede, *Købn.* 2 E8 55 34N 12 17 E
Mosede Strand, *Købn.* 2 E8 55 34N 12 17 E
Mosjøen, *Oslo* 2 C6 59 49N 11 0 E
Moskhaton, *Ath.* 8 J11 37 55N 23 40 E
Moskva, *Mos.* 11 E9 55 45N 37 37 E
Moskvoretskiy, *Mos.* 11 E8 55 43N 37 30 E
Mosman, *Syd.* 19 A4 33 49 S 151 15 E
Moss Beach, *S.F.* 27 C2 37 31N 122 30W
Móstoles, *Mdrd.* 8 C1 40 18N 3 51W
Moto →, *Tōkyō* 13 A3 35 53N 139 45 E
Motol, *Pra.* 10 B1 50 3N 14 19 E
Motspur Park, *Lon.* 4 C3 51 23N 0 14W
Mottingham, *Lon.* 4 C5 51 26N 0 1 E
Mount Airy, *Phil.* 24 A3 40 3N 75 10W
Mount Dennis, *Trto.* 20 D8 43 40N 79 28W
Mount Ephraim, *Phil.* 24 B4 39 52N 75 5W
Mount Greenwood, *Chic.* 26 C2 41 42N 87 42W
Mount Hood Memorial Park, *Bost.* 21 C3 42 26N 71 1W
Mount Pleasant, *Lon.* 4 B2 51 30N 0 22W
Mount Pleasant Park, *Balt.* 25 A3 39 22N 76 34W
Mount Prospect, *Chic.* 26 A1 42 3N 87 54W
Mount Royal, *Phil.* 24 C3 39 48N 75 12W
Mount Tamalpais State Park, *S.F.* 27 A1 37 53N 122 34W
Mount Vernon, *N.Y.* 23 B5 40 54N 73 49W
Mount Waverley, *Melb.* 19 F7 37 52 S 145 7 E
Mount Wilson Observatory, *L.A.* 28 A4 34 13N 118 4W
Mountain Lakes, *N.Y.* 22 B2 40 54N 74 27W
Mountain Spring Ls., *N.Y.* 22 A2 41 2N 74 21W
Mountain View, *N.Y.* 22 B3 40 55N 74 15W
Mountainside, *N.Y.* 22 C2 40 40N 74 21W
Mountnessing, *Lon.* 4 B7 51 39N 0 21 E
Moûtiers, *Paris* 5 D1 48 39N 1 57 E
Mozu, *Ōsaka* 12 C3 34 33N 135 29 E
Müggelberge, *Berl.* 7 B4 52 25N 13 37 E
Müggelheim, *Berl.* 7 B5 52 24N 13 40 E
Muggiò, *Mil.* 9 D6 45 35N 9 13 E
Mugnano di Nápoli, *Nápl.* 9 H12 40 54N 14 12 E
Mühleiten, *Wien* 10 G11 48 10N 16 33 E
Mühlenau →, *Hbg.* 7 C7 53 41N 9 56 E
Mühlenfliess →, *Berl.* 7 A5 52 32N 13 42 E
Muir Beach, *S.F.* 27 B1 37 51N 122 34W
Muirkirk, *Wash.* 25 C8 39 3N 76 53W
Mujahidpur, *Delhi* 16 B2 28 33N 77 14 E
Mukandpur, *Delhi* 16 A2 28 44N 77 10 E
Muko →, *Ōsaka* 12 B3 34 48N 135 22 E
Mukojima, *Tōkyō* 13 B3 35 43N 139 49 E
Mulbarton, *Jobg.* 18 F9 26 17 S 28 3 E
Mulford Gardens, *S.F.* 27 B3 37 42N 122 10W
Mulgrave, *Melb.* 19 F8 37 55 S 145 12 E
Mülheim, *Ruhr* 6 B3 51 25N 6 53 E
Mullica Hill, *Phil.* 24 C3 39 44N 75 13W
Mullum Mullum Cr. →, *Melb.* 19 E8 37 44 S 145 10 E
Münchehofe, *Berl.* 7 B5 52 29N 13 40 E
München, *Mün.* 7 G10 48 8N 11 34 E
Munchen-Riem, Flughafen, *Mün.* 7 G11 48 7N 11 42 E
Munich = München, *Mün.* 7 G10 48 8N 11 34 E
Munirka, *Delhi* 16 B2 28 33N 77 10 E
Muniz, *B.A.* 32 B2 34 33 S 58 41W
Munkkiniemi, *Hels.* 3 B4 60 11N 24 52 E
Munro, *B.A.* 32 B3 34 31 S 58 31W
Munsey Park, *N.Y.* 23 C6 40 47N 73 40W
Münsterkirche, *Ruhr* 6 B4 51 27N 7 0 E
Muranów, *Wsaw.* 10 E6 52 14N 20 58 E
Murayama-chosuichi, *Tōkyō* 13 B1 35 45N 139 26 E
Murrumbeena, *Melb.* 19 F7 37 53 S 145 4 E
Musashino, *Tōkyō* 13 B2 35 42N 139 33 E
Mushin, *Lagos* 18 A2 6 31N 7 21 E
Musinè, Mte., *Tori.* 9 B1 45 7N 7 27 E
Musocco, *Mil.* 9 E5 45 29N 9 8 E
Musta Hevonen, *Hels.* 3 B6 60 11N 25 14 E
Mustafabad, *Delhi* 16 A2 28 43N 77 13 E
Mustansiriya, *Bagd.* 17 E8 33 22N 44 24 E
Musturud, *El Qâ.* 18 C5 30 8N 31 17 E
Muswell Hill, *Lon.* 4 B4 51 35N 0 8W
Mutanabi, *Bagd.* 17 F8 33 19N 44 21 E
Muthana, *Bagd.* 17 F8 33 19N 44 27 E
Mutinga, *S. Pau.* 31 D5 23 29 S 46 46W
Muttontown, *N.Y.* 23 C7 40 49N 73 32W
Muzon, *Manila* 15 D4 14 32N 121 8 E
Myaglovo, *St-Pet.* 11 B5 59 53N 30 39 E
Mykinino, *Mos.* 11 E8 55 48N 37 22 E
Mykerinos, *El Qâ.* 18 D4 29 28N 31 8 E
Myllykylä, *Hels.* 3 A4 60 21N 24 57 E
Myllypuro, *Hels.* 3 B5 60 13N 25 3 E
Myras, *Hels.* 3 B5 60 19N 25 6 E
Myrvoll, *Oslo* 2 C4 59 47N 10 48 E
Mystic Lakes, *Bost.* 21 C3 42 26N 71 8W
Mytishchi, *Mos.* 11 D10 55 53N 37 44 E

N

Nababpur, *Calc.* 16 D5 22 42N 88 12 E
Nações, Parque das, *S. Pau.* 31 E6 23 38 S 46 30W
Nachstebreck, *Ruhr* 6 C5 51 17N 7 14 E
Nacka, *Stock.* 3 E12 59 19N 18 10 E
Nada, *Ōsaka* 12 B2 34 42N 135 13 E
Nærsnes, *Oslo* 2 C2 59 45N 10 27 E
Nærum, *Købn.* 2 D10 55 48N 12 33 E
Nagareyama, *Tōkyō* 13 A4 35 51N 139 54 E
Nagasaki, *Tōkyō* 13 B3 35 43N 139 40 E
Nagasuga, *Tōkyō* 13 D4 35 21N 139 57 E
Nagata, *Ōsaka* 12 C1 34 39N 135 8 E
Nagatsuta, *Tōkyō* 13 C2 35 32N 139 31 E
Nagytarcsa, *Bud.* 10 J14 47 31N 19 17 E
Nagytétény, *Bud.* 10 K12 47 23N 18 59 E
Nahant, *Bost.* 21 C4 42 25N 70 54W
Nahant B., *Bost.* 21 C4 42 26N 70 55W
Nahant Harbor, *Bost.* 21 C4 42 25N 70 55W
Nahdein, W. el →, *El Qâ.* 18 C5 30 3N 31 19 E
Nahia, *El Qâ.* 18 C4 30 2N 31 7 E
Naihati, *Calc.* 16 C6 22 53N 88 25 E
Najafgarh Drain →, *Delhi* 16 B1 28 39N 77 4 E
Najio, *Ōsaka* 12 B2 34 49N 135 18 E
Naka →, *Tōkyō* 13 B4 35 49N 139 52 E
Naka-Ku, *Tōkyō* 13 D2 35 25N 139 38 E
Nakada, *Tōkyō* 13 D2 35 24N 139 30 E
Nakajima, *Tōkyō* 13 D4 35 25N 139 54 E
Nakano, *Tōkyō* 13 D4 35 25N 139 56 E
Nakano-Ku, *Tōkyō* 13 B3 35 42N 139 39 E
Nakasato, *Tōkyō* 13 D3 35 25N 139 42 E
Nakayama, *Tōkyō* 13 D3 35 43N 139 57 E
Nalikul, *Calc.* 16 D5 22 49N 88 10 E
Nalpur, *Calc.* 16 E5 22 31N 88 10 E
Namazie Estate, *Sing.* 15 F7 1 25N 103 42 E
Namgajha, *Sŏul* 12 G7 37 33N 126 55 E
Namsan Park, *Sŏul* 12 G7 37 32N 126 59 E
Namyeong, *Sŏul* 12 G7 37 32N 126 57 E
Nan Wan, *H.K.* 12 E5 22 20N 114 5 E
Nanbiancun, *Gzh.* 14 G7 23 4N 113 10 E
Nancefield, *Jobg.* 18 F8 26 17 S 27 54 E
Nanchang He →, *Beij.* 14 B2 39 58N 116 14 E
Nandaha, *Calc.* 16 D5 22 49N 88 16 E
Nandang, *Gzh.* 14 G8 23 6N 113 12 E
Nandian, *Tianj.* 14 D6 39 10N 117 16 E
Nangal Dewat, *Delhi* 16 B1 28 33N 77 5 E
Nangi, *Calc.* 16 E5 22 30N 88 13 E
Nangka →, *Manila* 15 D4 14 38N 121 8 E
Nangloi, *Delhi* 16 A1 28 41N 77 4 E
Nangloi Jat, *Delhi* 16 A1 28 41N 77 3 E
Nanhai, *Gzh.* 14 G7 23 2N 113 6 E
Nanhan He →, *Beij.* 14 B2 39 57N 116 11 E
Naniwa, *Ōsaka* 12 C3 34 39N 135 28 E
Nankai, *Tianj.* 14 E5 39 7N 117 10 E
Nanmenwai, *Tianj.* 14 E6 39 8N 117 12 E
Nanole, *Bomb.* 16 G8 19 10N 72 55 E
Nanshi, *Shang.* 14 J11 31 12N 121 29 E
Nanterre, *Paris* 5 B3 48 53N 2 12 E
Nantouillet, *Paris* 5 A6 49 0N 2 42 E
Nantucket Beach, *Bost.* 21 D4 42 16N 70 52W
Nanxiang, *Shang.* 14 J10 31 17N 121 18 E
Naoabad, *Calc.* 16 F6 22 28N 88 26 E
Napara, *Calc.* 16 E6 22 38N 88 23 E
Napier Mole, *Kar.* 17 H10 24 49N 66 58 E
Napindan, *Manila* 15 D4 14 32N 121 5 E
Naples = Nápoli, *Nápl.* 9 J12 40 50N 14 15 E
Nápoli, *Nápl.* 9 J12 40 50N 14 15 E
Nápoli, G. di, *Nápl.* 9 J12 40 46N 14 15 E
Naraina, *Delhi* 16 B1 28 36N 77 8 E
Narawa, *Tōkyō* 13 D3 35 25N 139 58 E
Narayanpara, *Calc.* 16 C5 22 53N 88 18 E
Narberth, *Phil.* 24 A3 40 0N 75 16W
Narimasu, *Tōkyō* 13 B2 35 46N 139 38 E
Nārmak, *Tehr.* 17 C5 35 42N 51 28 E
Nārsta, *Stock.* 3 E9 59 17N 17 43 E
Naruo, *Ōsaka* 12 B3 34 43N 135 22 E
Näsby, *Stock.* 3 D11 59 25N 18 5 E
Näsbypark, *Stock.* 3 D11 59 25N 18 5 E
Näsfjärden, *Stock.* 3 D9 59 25N 17 41 E
Nassau Shore, *N.Y.* 23 D8 40 39N 73 26W
Natick, *Bost.* 21 D2 42 17N 71 20W
Nation, Place de la, *Paris* 5 B4 48 51N 2 23 E
National Arboretum, *Wash.* 25 D8 39 54N 76 59W
Nativitas, *Méx.* 29 C3 19 15N 99 5W
Natolin, *Wsaw.* 10 F7 52 8N 21 4 E
Naucalpan de Juárez, *Méx.* 29 B2 19 28N 99 14W
Naupada, *Bomb.* 16 G8 19 3N 72 50 E
Navíglio di Pavia, *Mil.* 9 E5 45 24N 9 9 E
Navíglio Grande, *Mil.* 9 E5 45 25N 9 5 E
Navotas, *Manila* 15 D3 14 39N 120 56 E
Nazal Hikmat Beg, *Bagd.* 17 E8 33 23N 44 25 E
Nazimabad, *Kar.* 17 G11 24 54N 67 1 E
Nazukari, *Tōkyō* 13 A4 35 50N 139 57 E
Néa Alexandhria, *Ath.* 8 J11 37 52N 23 46 E
Néa Faliron, *Ath.* 8 J10 37 55N 23 39 E
Néa Ionía, *Ath.* 8 H11 38 3N 23 45 E
Néa Liósia, *Ath.* 8 H11 38 3N 23 43 E
Néa Smirni, *Ath.* 8 J11 37 54N 23 43 E
Neapolis, *Ath.* 8 J11 37 58N 23 45 E
Neasden, *Lon.* 4 B3 51 35N 0 16W
Neauphle-le-Château, *Paris* 5 C1 48 48N 1 53 E
Nebušice, *Pra.* 10 B1 50 6N 14 19 E
Nedlitz, *Berl.* 7 B1 52 25N 13 3 E
Nee Soon, *Sing.* 15 F7 1 24N 103 49 E
Needham, *Bost.* 21 D2 42 16N 71 13W
Needham Heights, *Bost.* 21 D2 42 17N 71 14W
Needle Hill, *H.K.* 12 D5 22 23N 114 9 E
Negishi B., *Tōkyō* 13 D2 35 23N 139 38 E
Nehiti, *Calc.* 16 D5 22 42N 88 16 E
Nekrasovka, *Mos.* 11 E11 55 41N 37 55 E
Nematābād, *Tehr.* 17 D5 35 38N 51 21 E
Nemchinovka, *Mos.* 11 E7 55 42N 37 19 E
Népliget, *Bud.* 10 K13 47 29N 19 7 E
Neponset →, *Bost.* 21 D3 42 12N 71 9W
Nerima, *Tōkyō* 13 B3 35 44N 139 40 E
Nerul, *Bomb.* 16 G9 19 2N 73 0 E
Nerviano, *Mil.* 9 D4 45 32N 8 58 E
Nesodden, *Oslo* 2 C4 59 48N 10 41 E
Nesoddtangen, *Oslo* 2 B4 59 52N 10 41 E
Nesøya, *Oslo* 2 B3 59 52N 10 31 E
Nestipayac →, *Méx.* 29 A4 19 33N 89 57W
Netzahualcóyotl, *Méx.* 29 B3 19 24N 99 2W
Neu Aubing, *Mün.* 7 G9 48 8N 11 25 E
Neu Buch, *Berl.* 7 A4 52 37N 13 31 E
Neu Buchhorst, *Berl.* 7 B5 52 24N 13 44 E
Neu Fahrland, *Berl.* 7 B1 52 26N 13 3 E
Neu Lindenberg, *Berl.* 7 A4 52 36N 13 33 E
Neu Wulmstorf, *Hbg.* 7 E6 53 27N 9 48 E
Neu Zittau, *Berl.* 7 B5 52 23N 13 44 E
Neubiberg, *Mün.* 7 G11 48 4N 11 40 E
Neudorf, *Hbg.* 7 E8 53 27N 10 4 E
Neudorf, *Ruhr* 6 B2 51 25N 6 47 E
Neuegenbüttel, *Hbg.* 7 D7 53 38N 9 54 E
Neuenfelde, *Hbg.* 7 D6 53 31N 9 48 E
Neuenhagen, *Berl.* 7 A4 52 32N 13 38 E
Neuenkamp, *Ruhr* 6 B2 51 26N 6 43 E
Neuessling, *Wien* 10 G11 48 15N 16 32 E
Neugraben-Fischbek, *Hbg.* 7 E6 53 28N 9 49 E
Neuhausen, *Mün.* 7 G10 48 9N 11 32 E
Neuherberg, *Mün.* 7 F10 48 13N 11 35 E
Neuhönow, *Berl.* 7 A5 52 34N 13 44 E
Neuilly-Plaisance, *Paris* 5 B5 48 51N 2 30 E
Neuilly-sur-Marne, *Paris* 5 B5 48 51N 2 31 E
Neuilly-sur-Seine, *Paris* 5 B3 48 53N 2 15 E
Neukagran, *Wien* 10 G10 48 14N 16 27 E
Neukettenhof, *Wien* 10 H10 48 7N 16 28 E
Neukölln, *Berl.* 7 B3 52 28N 13 25 E
Neuland, *Hbg.* 7 E8 53 27N 10 0 E
Neuperlach, *Mün.* 7 G10 48 6N 11 37 E
Neuried, *Mün.* 7 G9 48 5N 11 27 E
Neuss, *Ruhr* 6 C2 51 12N 6 42 E
Neustift am Walde, *Wien* 10 G9 48 14N 16 17 E
Neusüssenbrunn, *Wien* 10 G10 48 16N 16 29 E
Neuville-sur-Oise, *Paris* 5 A2 49 0N 2 4 E
Neuwaldegg, *Wien* 10 G9 48 14N 16 17 E
Neuwiedenthal, *Hbg.* 7 E7 53 28N 9 52 E
Neva →, *St-Pet.* 11 B4 59 56N 30 20 E
Neves, *Rio J.* 31 B3 22 51 S 43 5W
Neviges, *Ruhr* 6 C4 51 18N 7 5 E
New Addington, *Lon.* 4 C4 51 20N 0 0 E
New Ash Green, *Lon.* 4 C6 51 22N 0 18 E
New Baghdād, *Bagd.* 17 F8 33 18N 44 28 E
New Barnet, *Lon.* 4 B3 51 38N 0 10W
New Brighton, *N.Y.* 22 D4 40 38N 74 5W
New Brunswick, *N.Y.* 22 D2 40 30N 74 29W
New Canada, *Jobg.* 18 F8 26 12 S 27 56 E
New Canada Dam, *Jobg.* 18 F8 26 13 S 27 56 E
New Canal →, *Calc.* 16 E6 22 33N 88 25 E
New Carrollton, *Wash.* 25 D8 38 58N 76 52W
New Cassell, *N.Y.* 23 C7 40 45N 73 32W
New Cross, *Lon.* 4 C4 51 28N 0 1W
New Delhi, *Delhi* 16 B2 28 36N 77 11 E
New Dorp, *N.Y.* 22 D4 40 34N 74 7W
New Dorp Beach, *N.Y.* 22 D4 40 33N 74 6W
New Hyde Park, *N.Y.* 23 C7 40 43N 73 39W
New Kleinfontein, *Jobg.* 18 F11 26 10 S 28 20 E
New Malden, *Lon.* 4 C3 51 24N 0 15W
New Milford, *N.Y.* 22 B4 40 56N 74 0W
New Modder, *Jobg.* 18 F11 26 10 S 28 21 E
New Providence, *N.Y.* 22 C2 40 42N 74 23W
New Redruth, *Jobg.* 18 F9 26 15 S 28 7 E
New Rochelle, *N.Y.* 23 B6 40 55N 73 46W
New South Wales, Univ. of, *Syd.* 19 B4 33 55 S 151 14 E
New Southgate, *Lon.* 4 B4 51 37N 0 7W
New Springville, *N.Y.* 22 D3 40 35N 74 9W
New Territories, *H.K.* 12 D5 22 23N 114 10 E
New Toronto, *Trto.* 20 E7 43 35N 79 30W
New Utrecht, *N.Y.* 22 D5 40 36N 73 59W
New Vernon, *N.Y.* 22 C2 40 44N 74 30W
New York Aquarium, *N.Y.* 22 D5 40 33N 73 59W
New York Botanical Gdns., *N.Y.* 23 B5 40 51N 73 51W
New York Univ., *N.Y.* 22 C5 40 43N 74 59W
Newabgarj, *Calc.* 16 D6 22 47N 88 23 E
Newark, *N.Y.* 22 C3 40 43N 74 10W
Newark, *S.F.* 27 C4 37 32N 122 2W
Newark B., *N.Y.* 22 C4 40 40N 74 6W
Newark Int. Airport, *N.Y.* 22 C3 40 41N 74 10W
Newbury Park, *Lon.* 4 B5 51 34N 0 5 E
Newclare, *Jobg.* 18 F8 26 11 S 27 58 E
Newfoundland, *N.Y.* 22 A2 41 2N 74 25W
Newham, *Lon.* 4 B5 51 31N 0 1 E
Newlands, *Jobg.* 18 F8 26 10 S 27 57 E
Newport, *Melb.* 19 F6 37 50 S 144 51 E
Newportville, *Phil.* 24 A5 40 7N 74 53W
Newton, *Bost.* 21 D2 42 19N 71 13W
Newton Brook, *Trto.* 20 D8 43 47N 79 24W
Newton Highlands, *Bost.* 21 D2 42 19N 71 12W
Newtonville, *Bost.* 21 C2 42 20N 71 11W
Newtown, *Syd.* 19 B4 33 54 S 151 11 E
Newtown Square, *Phil.* 24 B2 39 59N 75 24W
Neyegawa, *Ōsaka* 12 B4 34 45N 135 36 E
Ngau Chi Wan, *H.K.* 12 D6 22 20N 114 12 E
Ngau Tau Kok, *H.K.* 12 E6 22 19N 114 12 E
Ngong Shuen Chau, *H.K.* 12 E5 22 19N 114 8 E
Ngua Kok Wan, *H.K.* 12 D5 22 21N 114 5 E
Niāvarān, *Tehr.* 17 C5 35 47N 51 29 E
Nibria, *Calc.* 16 E5 22 36N 88 16 E
Nichelino, *Tori.* 9 C2 44 59N 7 38 E
Nichols Run →, *Wash.* 25 C6 39 2N 77 17W
Nicholson, Mt., *H.K.* 12 E6 22 15N 114 11 E
Nidāl, *Bagd.* 17 F8 33 19N 44 25 E
Niddrie, *Melb.* 19 E6 37 44 S 144 51 E
Nieder Neuendorf, *Berl.* 7 A2 52 36N 13 12 E
Niederbonsfeld, *Ruhr* 6 B4 51 22N 7 8 E
Niederdonk, *Ruhr* 6 C2 51 14N 6 41 E
Niederschöneweide, *Berl.* 7 B3 52 27N 13 30 E
Niederschönhausen, *Berl.* 7 A3 52 35N 13 25 E
Niederwenigern, *Ruhr* 6 B4 51 24N 7 8 E
Niemeyer, *Rio J.* 31 B2 22 59 S 43 16W
Niendorf, *Hbg.* 7 D7 53 37N 9 57 E
Nienstedten, *Hbg.* 7 D7 53 33N 9 51 E
Nierst, *Ruhr* 6 C2 51 19N 6 43 E
Nihonbashi, *Tōkyō* 13 B3 35 41N 139 46 E
Niipperi, *Hels.* 3 B3 60 18N 24 45 E
Niiza, *Tōkyō* 13 B2 35 48N 139 33 E
Nikaia, *Ath.* 8 J10 37 57N 23 38 E
Nikinmäki, *Hels.* 3 A5 60 20N 25 8 E
Nikolassee, *Berl.* 7 B2 52 25N 13 12 E
Nikolo-Khovanskoye, *Mos.* 11 F8 55 36N 37 27 E
Nikolskiy, *Mos.* 11 E8 55 49N 37 29 E
Nikolyskoye, *Mos.* 11 E11 55 46N 37 53 E
Nikulino, *Mos.* 11 E8 55 40N 37 25 E
Nil, *Bagd.* 17 E8 33 21N 44 25 E
Nil, Nahr en →, *El Qâ.* 18 D5 29 57N 31 14 E
Nile = Nil, Nahr en →, *El Qâ.* 18 D5 29 57N 31 14 E
Niles, *Chic.* 26 A2 42 1N 87 48W
Nilganj, *Calc.* 16 D6 22 45N 88 25 E
Nilópolis, *Rio J.* 31 A1 22 47 S 43 23W
Nimta, *Calc.* 16 D6 22 40N 88 24 E
Nincop, *Hbg.* 7 D6 53 30N 9 48 E
Ningyuan, *Tianj.* 14 E6 39 9N 117 12 E
Nippa, *Tōkyō* 13 C2 35 31N 139 36 E
Nippori, *Tōkyō* 13 B3 35 43N 139 45 E
Niru-ye-Hava'i, *Tehr.* 17 C5 35 41N 51 26 E
Nishi, *Ōsaka* 12 B3 34 40N 135 28 E
Nishi, *Tōkyō* 13 D2 35 26N 139 37 E
Nishi-arai, *Tōkyō* 13 B3 35 46N 139 48 E
Nishinari, *Ōsaka* 12 C3 34 37N 135 28 E
Nishinomiya, *Ōsaka* 12 B2 34 44N 135 18 E
Nishiyama, *Tōkyō* 13 D4 35 22N 139 57 E
Nishiyodogawa, *Ōsaka* 12 B3 34 41N 135 24 E
Nisida, I. di, *Nápl.* 9 J11 40 47N 14 10 E
Niterói, *Rio J.* 31 B3 22 53 S 43 7W
Nithari, *Delhi* 16 B3 28 34N 77 20 E
Nittedal, *Oslo* 2 A5 60 0N 10 57 E
Niyog, *Manila* 15 E3 14 27N 120 57 E
Noapara, *Calc.* 16 D6 22 49N 88 22 E
Nobidome, *Tōkyō* 13 B2 35 48N 139 34 E
Nockeby, *Stock.* 3 E10 59 19N 17 56 E
Noel Park, *Lon.* 4 B4 51 35N 0 5W
Nogatino, *Mos.* 11 E10 55 41N 37 41 E
Nogent-sur-Marne, *Paris* 5 B4 48 50N 2 28 E
Noiseau, *Paris* 5 C5 48 46N 2 32 E
Noisiel, *Paris* 5 B5 48 51N 2 37 E
Noisy-le-Grand, *Paris* 5 B5 48 50N 2 33 E
Noisy-le-Roi, *Paris* 5 B2 48 50N 2 3 E
Noisy-le-Sec, *Paris* 5 B4 48 53N 2 27 E
Nokkala, *Hels.* 3 C3 60 8N 24 45 E
Nøklevatn, *Oslo* 2 B5 59 52N 10 52 E
Nolme →, *Ruhr* 6 B6 51 23N 7 26 E
Nomentano, *Rome* 9 F10 41 55N 12 30 E
Nonakashinden, *Tōkyō* 13 B2 35 44N 139 30 E
Nongminyundong Jiangxisuo, *Gzh.* 14 G8 23 7N 113 15 E
Nonhyeon, *Sŏul* 12 G8 37 30N 127 1 E
Nontha Buri, *Bangk.* 15 A1 13 50N 100 29 E
Noordgesig, *Jobg.* 18 F8 26 13 S 27 56 E
Nord, Gare du, *Paris* 5 B4 48 52N 2 21 E
Nordbysjøen, *Oslo* 2 B6 59 51N 11 1 E
Nordereble, *Hbg.* 7 D7 53 32N 9 59 E
Norderelbe →, *Hbg.* 7 E8 53 29N 10 3 E
Norderstedt, *Hbg.* 7 C7 53 42N 9 59 E
Nordmarka, *Oslo* 2 A4 60 1N 10 38 E
Nordrand-Seidlung, *Wien* 10 G10 48 16N 16 26 E
Nordre Elvåga, *Oslo* 2 B4 59 53N 10 54 E
Nordstrand, *Oslo* 2 B4 59 52N 10 48 E
Normandy Heights, *Balt.* 25 B2 39 17N 76 48W
Norra Björkföjärden, *Stock.* 3 D8 59 26N 17 39 E
Norridge, *Chic.* 26 B2 41 57N 87 49W
Norristown, *Phil.* 24 A2 40 7N 75 20W
Norrkula, *Hels.* 3 B6 60 19N 25 20 E
Norrmalm, *Stock.* 3 D11 59 20N 18 3 E
Norrviken, *Stock.* 3 D10 59 27N 17 52 E
North Acton, *Bost.* 21 B1 42 30N 71 23W
North Amityville, *N.Y.* 23 C8 40 41N 73 25W
North Andover, *Bost.* 21 A3 42 41N 71 7W
North Arlington, *N.Y.* 22 C4 40 47N 74 7W
North Auburn, *Syd.* 19 B3 33 50 S 151 3 E
North Babylon, *N.Y.* 23 C9 40 43N 73 19W
North Bellmore, *N.Y.* 23 C7 40 40N 73 32W
North Bergen, *N.Y.* 22 C4 40 48N 74 0W
North Beverly, *Bost.* 21 B4 42 34N 70 51W
North Billerica, *Bost.* 21 B2 42 35N 71 16W
North Branch →, *Phil.* 24 C4 39 50N 75 6W
North Branch Chicago River →, *Chic.* 26 B2 41 53N 87 42W
North Brighton, *Bost.* 21 C3 42 21N 71 8W
North Caldwell, *N.Y.* 22 B3 40 52N 74 15W
North Cambridge, *Bost.* 21 C3 42 24N 71 7W
North Cheam, *Lon.* 4 C3 51 22N 0 11W
North Chelmsford, *Bost.* 21 B1 42 38N 71 23W
North Cohasset, *Bost.* 21 D4 42 15N 70 50W
North Cray, *Lon.* 4 C5 51 25N 0 8 E
North Fair Oaks, *S.F.* 27 D3 37 28N 122 11W
North Finchley, *Lon.* 4 B3 51 36N 0 11W
North Germiston, *Jobg.* 18 F9 26 12 S 28 9 E
North Hackensack, *N.Y.* 22 B4 40 54N 74 2W
North Haledon, *N.Y.* 22 B3 40 58N 74 11W
North Harbour, *Manila* 15 D3 14 37N 120 57 E
North Hd., *Syd.* 19 A4 33 49 S 151 18 E
North Hills, *N.Y.* 23 C6 40 46N 73 40W
North Hollywood, *L.A.* 28 B2 34 9N 118 22W
North Lexington, *Bost.* 21 C2 42 27N 71 14W
North Lindenhurst, *N.Y.* 23 C8 40 42N 73 22W
North Long Beach, *L.A.* 28 C3 33 53N 118 10W
North Manly, *Syd.* 19 A4 33 46 S 151 17 E
North Massapequa, *N.Y.* 23 C8 40 42N 73 27W
North Merrick, *N.Y.* 23 C7 40 41N 73 33W
North New Hyde Park, *N.Y.* 23 C6 40 44N 73 42W
North Pelham, *N.Y.* 23 B6 40 54N 73 46W
North Plainfield, *N.Y.* 22 D2 40 37N 74 27W
North Point, *Balt.* 25 B4 39 16N 76 29W
North Pt., *H.K.* 12 E6 22 17N 114 12 E
North Pt., *Syd.* 19 A4 33 48 S 151 18 E
North Randolph, *Bost.* 21 D3 42 11N 71 4W
North Reading, *Bost.* 21 B3 42 34N 71 5W
North Res., *Bost.* 21 C3 42 27N 71 6W
North Richmond, *S.F.* 27 A2 37 57N 122 22W
North Riverside, *Chic.* 26 B2 41 50N 87 49W
North Ryde, *Syd.* 19 A3 33 47 S 151 7 E
North Saugus, *Bost.* 21 C3 42 29N 71 1W
North Shore Channel →, *Chic.* 26 B2 41 58N 87 42W

Pitampura Kalan 43

North Springfield, *Wash.* **25 E6** 38 48N 77 11W
North Stifford, *Lon.* **4 B6** 51 30N 0 18 E
North Sudbury, *Bost.* **21 C1** 42 24N 71 24W
North Sydney, *Syd.* **19 B4** 33 50 S 151 13 E
North Tewksbury, *Bost.* **21 B2** 42 38N 71 14W
North Valley Stream, *N.Y.* **23 C6** 40 41N 73 42W
North Wantagh, *N.Y.* **23 C7** 40 41N 73 30W
North Weymouth, *Bost.* **21 D4** 42 14N 70 56W
North Wilmington, *Bost.* **21 B3** 42 34N 71 9W
North Woburn, *Bost.* **21 B2** 42 30N 71 10W
North Woolwich, *Lon.* **4 B5** 51 30N 0 3 E
North York, *Trto.* **20 D8** 43 45N 79 27W
Northaw, *Lon.* **4 A4** 51 42N 0 8W
Northbridge, *Syd.* **19 A4** 33 49 S 151 15 E
Northbrook, *Chic.* **26 A1** 42 7N 87 50W
Northcliff, *Jobg.* **18 E8** 26 8 S 27 58 E
Northcote, *Melb.* **19 E7** 37 46 S 145 0 E
Northeastern Univ., *Bost.* **21 C3** 42 20N 71 4W
Northfield, *Chic.* **26 A2** 42 5N 87 45W
Northfleet, *Lon.* **4 C7** 51 26N 0 21 E
Northlake, *Chic.* **26 B1** 41 54N 87 53W
Northmead, *Jobg.* **18 E10** 26 9 S 28 19 E
Northmead, *Syd.* **19 A3** 33 47 S 151 0 E
Northmount, *Trto.* **20 D8** 43 46N 79 23W
Northolt, *Lon.* **4 B2** 51 32N 0 22W
Northport, *N.Y.* **23 B8** 40 54N 73 20W
Northport B., *N.Y.* **23 B8** 40 54N 73 22W
Northridge, *L.A.* **28 A1** 34 14N 118 30W
Northumberland Heath, *Lon.* **4 C6** 51 28N 0 10 E
Northvale, *N.Y.* **22 A5** 41 0N 73 59W
Northwest Branch →, *Balt.* **25 B3** 39 16N 76 35W
Northwest Branch →, *Wash.* **25 C8** 39 2N 76 56W
Northwestern Univ., *Chic.* **26 A2** 42 3N 87 40W
Northwood, *Lon.* **4 B2** 51 36N 0 25W
Norumbega Res., *Bost.* **21 D2** 42 19N 71 17W
Norwalk, *L.A.* **28 C4** 33 53N 118 4W
Norwood, *Bost.* **21 D2** 42 11N 71 13W
Norwood, *Jobg.* **18 E9** 26 9 S 28 4 E
Norwood, *N.Y.* **22 B5** 40 59N 73 57W
Norwood, *Phil.* **24 B3** 39 53N 75 17W
Norwood Memorial Airport, *Bost.* **21 D3** 42 11N 71 9W
Norwood Park, *Chic.* **26 B2** 41 59N 87 48W
Noryangjin, *Sŏul* **12 G7** 37 30N 126 56 E
Nose, *Ōsaka* **12 B2** 34 49N 135 10 E
Nossa Senhora do Ó, *S. Pau.* **31 E5** 23 30 S 46 41W
Notre-Dame, *Mtrl.* **20 B5** 43 28N 73 28W
Notre-Dame, *Paris* **5 B4** 48 51N 2 21 E
Notre-Dame, Bois, *Paris* **5 C5** 48 45N 2 34 E
Notre Dame de L'Île Perrot, *Mtrl.* **20 B2** 43 23N 73 53W
Notting Hill, *Lon.* **4 B3** 51 30N 0 12W
Notting Hill, *Melb.* **19 F7** 37 54 S 145 9 E
Nottingham, *Phil.* **24 A5** 40 7N 74 58W
Nova Milanese, *Mil.* **9 D6** 45 35N 9 12 E
Novate Milanese, *Mil.* **9 D5** 45 30N 9 8 E
Novaya Derevnya, *St-Pet.* **11 A3** 60 0N 30 19 E
Nové Mesto, *Pra.* **10 B2** 50 4N 14 25 E
Novoaleksandrovskoye, *St-Pet.* **11 B4** 59 50N 30 31 E
Novogireyevo, *Mos.* **11 E10** 55 45N 37 46 E
Novoivanovskoye, *Mos.* **11 E7** 55 42N 37 21 E
Novokhovrino, *Mos.* **11 D8** 55 53N 37 27 E
Novonikolyskoye, *Mos.* **11 D7** 55 50N 37 14 E
Novosaratovka, *St-Pet.* **11 B5** 59 50N 30 32 E
Novosergiyevka, *St-Pet.* **11 B5** 59 54N 30 34 E
Nowe-Babice, *Wsaw.* **10 E6** 52 15N 20 51 E
Nöykkiö, *Hels.* **3 B3** 60 10N 24 42 E
Noyoye Kovalyova, *St-Pet.* **11 B5** 59 58N 30 34 E
Nozay, *Paris* **5 D3** 48 39N 2 14 E
Nueva Atzacoalco, *Méx.* **29 B3** 19 29N 99 4W
Nueva Caracas, *Car.* **30 D5** 10 30N 66 57W
Nueva Chicago, *B.A.* **32 B4** 34 39 S 58 29W
Nueva Pompeya, *B.A.* **32 C4** 34 40 S 58 25W
Nueva Tenochtitlán, *Méx.* **29 B3** 19 27N 99 5W
Nuijala, *Hels.* **3 B3** 60 12N 24 46 E
Numabukuro, *Tōkyō* **13 B2** 35 43N 139 39 E
Numakage, *Tōkyō* **13 A2** 35 50N 139 37 E
Numata, *Tōkyō* **13 B3** 35 45N 139 46 E
Nunawading, *Melb.* **19 E8** 37 49 S 145 10 E
Nunez, *B.A.* **32 B4** 34 32 S 58 27W
Nunhead, *Lon.* **4 C4** 51 27N 0 3W
Ñuñoa, *Stgo* **30 J11** 33 27 S 70 35W
Nupuri, *Hels.* **3 B2** 60 14N 24 36 E
Nusle, *Pra.* **10 B2** 50 3N 14 26 E
Nussdorf, *Wien* **10 G10** 48 15N 16 21 E
Nuthe →, *Berl.* **7 B1** 52 22N 13 5 E
Nutley, *N.Y.* **22 C4** 40 49N 74 9W
Nutting L., *Bost.* **21 B2** 42 32N 71 16W
Nützenberg, *Ruhr* **6 C4** 51 15N 7 8 E
Nybølle, *Købn.* **2 D8** 55 42N 12 15 E
Nybygget, *Hels.* **3 B6** 60 17N 25 11 E
Nymphenburg, *Mün.* **7 G10** 48 9N 11 30 E
Nymphenburg, Schloss, *Mün.* **7 G10** 48 9N 11 30 E

O

Oak Beach, *N.Y.* **23 D9** 40 38N 73 19W
Oak Forest, *Chic.* **26 D2** 41 36N 87 44W
Oak Hill Park, *Bost.* **21 D2** 42 17N 71 11W
Oak Lane, *Phil.* **24 A4** 40 3N 75 8W
Oak Lawn, *Chic.* **26 C2** 41 42N 87 45W
Oak Park, *Chic.* **26 B2** 41 52N 87 47W
Oak Ridge, *N.Y.* **22 A2** 41 2N 74 28W
Oak Valley, *Phil.* **24 C4** 39 48N 75 9W
Oak View, *Wash.* **25 C8** 39 1N 76 58W
Oakland, *N.Y.* **22 A3** 41 1N 74 13W
Oakland, *S.F.* **27 B3** 37 48N 122 18W
Oakland, *Wash.* **25 D8** 38 52N 76 54W
Oakland Coliseum, *S.F.* **27 B3** 37 44N 122 11W
Oakland Gardens, *N.Y.* **23 C6** 40 45N 73 46W
Oakland Int. Airport, *S.F.* **27 B3** 37 43N 122 12W
Oakland Mills, *Balt.* **25 B2** 39 13N 76 49W
Oakland Naval Air Station, *S.F.* **27 B3** 37 47N 122 19W
Oaklands, *Jobg.* **18 E9** 26 8 S 28 4 E
Oaklawn, *Wash.* **25 E8** 38 46N 76 56W
Oakleigh, *Melb.* **19 F7** 37 54 S 145 5 E
Oaks, *Phil.* **24 A2** 40 8N 75 26W
Oakwood, *N.Y.* **22 D4** 40 34N 74 7W
Oakwood Beach, *N.Y.* **22 D4** 40 33N 74 7W
Oatley, *Syd.* **19 B3** 33 59 S 151 4 E
Obalende, *Lagos* **18 B2** 6 26N 7 25 E
Oba's Palace, *Lagos* **18 B2** 6 26N 7 22 E
Oberbauer, *Ruhr* **6 C6** 51 17N 7 25 E
Oberföhring, *Mün.* **7 G10** 48 10N 11 37 E
Oberhaching, *Mün.* **7 G10** 48 1N 11 35 E
Oberhausen, *Ruhr* **6 B3** 51 28N 6 54 E
Oberhausen, *Wien* **10 G11** 48 10N 16 34 E
Oberkassel, *Ruhr* **6 C2** 51 14N 6 45 E
Oberkirchbach, *Wien* **10 G9** 48 17N 16 12 E
Oberlaa, *Wien* **10 H10** 48 8N 16 24 E
Oberlisse, *Wien* **10 G10** 48 17N 16 26 E
Obermenzing, *Mün.* **7 F9** 48 10N 11 28 E
Obermoos Schwaige, *Mün.* **7 F9** 48 14N 11 27 E
Oberschleissheim, *Mün.* **7 F10** 48 15N 11 33 E
Oberschöneweide, *Berl.* **7 B4** 52 27N 13 31 E
Oberwengern, *Ruhr* **6 B6** 51 23N 7 22 E
Obitsu →, *Tōkyō* **13 D4** 35 25N 139 56 E
Oboldino, *Mos.* **11 D11** 55 53N 37 56 E
Observatory, *Jobg.* **18 F9** 26 10 S 28 4 E
Ōbu, *Ōsaka* **12 B1** 34 43N 135 8 E
Obu-tōge, *Ōsaka* **12 B1** 34 44N 135 9 E
Óbuda, *Bud.* **10 J13** 47 33N 19 2 E
Obudaisziget, *Bud.* **10 J13** 47 33N 19 3 E
Obukhovo, *St-Pet.* **11 B4** 59 53N 30 22 E
Occidental, Pico, *Car.* **30 D5** 10 32N 66 51W
Oceanside, *N.Y.* **23 D7** 40 38N 73 37W
Ochakovo, *Mos.* **11 E8** 55 41N 37 26 E
Ochiai, *Tōkyō* **13 B3** 35 43N 139 42 E
Ochota, *Wsaw.* **10 E6** 52 13N 20 58 E
Ochsenwerder, *Hbg.* **7 E8** 53 28N 10 4 E
Ochsenzoll, *Hbg.* **7 C8** 53 41N 10 0 E
Odana, *Tōkyō* **13 C2** 35 33N 139 35 E
Oden-Stockach, *Mün.* **7 G11** 48 5N 11 41 E
Odilampi, *Hels.* **3 B3** 60 18N 24 45 E
Odintsovo, *Mos.* **11 E7** 55 40N 37 16 E
Odivelas, *Lisb.* **8 F7** 38 47N 9 10W
Odolany, *Wsaw.* **10 E6** 52 13N 20 55 E
Oeiras, *Lisb.* **8 F7** 38 41N 9 18W
Oella, *Balt.* **25 B2** 39 16N 76 46W
Oer-Erkenschwick, *Ruhr* **6 A5** 51 38N 7 15 E
Oern, *Mün.* **7 G10** 48 10N 11 32 E
Ofin, *Lagos* **18 A3** 6 32N 7 30 E
Ofukuro-shinden, *Tōkyō* **13 A1** 35 53N 139 28 E
Ogawa, *Tōkyō* **13 B1** 35 44N 139 28 E
Ogden, *Phil.* **24 C2** 39 49N 75 27W
Ogikubo, *Tōkyō* **13 B2** 35 42N 139 37 E
Ogo Ogo, *Ōsaka* **12 B1** 34 49N 135 8 E
Ogogoro, *Lagos* **18 B2** 6 25N 7 24 E
Ogongo, *Manila* **15 D4** 14 35N 121 4 E
Ogoyo, *Lagos* **18 B2** 6 25N 7 29 E
Ogudu, *Lagos* **18 A2** 6 34N 7 24 E
O'Hare, L., *Chic.* **26 B1** 41 57N 87 53W
Ōhirodo, *Tōkyō* **13 A4** 35 50N 139 53 E
Ohlsdorf, *Hbg.* **7 D8** 53 37N 10 3 E
Ōi, *Tōkyō* **13 A2** 35 51N 139 31 E
Ōimachi, *Tōkyō* **13 C3** 35 35N 139 43 E
Oise →, *Paris* **5 A2** 49 2N 2 5 E
Oittaa, *Hels.* **3 B3** 60 15N 24 42 E
Ojota, *Lagos* **18 A2** 6 35N 7 23 E
Okamoto, *Ōsaka* **12 B2** 34 43N 135 15 E
Okazu, *Tōkyō* **13 D2** 35 25N 139 31 E
Okęcie, *Wsaw.* **10 E6** 52 11N 20 56 E
Okęcie Airport, *Wsaw.* **10 E6** 52 10N 20 57 E
Okelra, *Lagos* **18 B2** 6 29N 7 22 E
Okeogbe, *Lagos* **18 B2** 6 24N 7 23 E
Okhla, *Delhi* **16 B2** 28 33N 77 16 E
Okhta →, *St-Pet.* **11 B4** 59 56N 30 25 E
Okkervil →, *St-Pet.* **11 B4** 59 56N 30 30 E
Okrzeszyn, *Wsaw.* **10 F7** 52 8N 21 8 E
Oksval, *Oslo* **2 B4** 59 51N 10 40 E
Oktyabrskiy, *Mos.* **11 F11** 55 37N 37 58 E
Oktyabrskiy, *Mos.* **11 E9** 55 41N 37 35 E
Okubo, *Tōkyō* **13 B3** 35 41N 139 42 E
Okunola, *Lagos* **18 A1** 6 35N 7 17 E
Ōkura, *Tōkyō* **13 C1** 35 35N 139 27 E
Olari, *Hels.* **3 B3** 60 10N 24 44 E
Olaria, *Rio J.* **31 B2** 22 50 S 43 16W
Old Brookville, *N.Y.* **23 C7** 40 49N 73 35W
Old Cairo, *El Qâ.* **18 C5** 30 0N 31 14 E
Old Coulsdon, *Lon.* **4 D4** 51 17N 0 6W
Old Forge Village, *N.Y.* **22 C2** 40 48N 74 29W
Old Harbor, *Bost.* **21 D3** 42 19N 71 1W
Old Road B., *Balt.* **25 B4** 39 12N 76 27W
Old Tappan, *N.Y.* **22 A5** 41 0N 73 59W
Old Town, *Chic.* **26 B3** 41 54N 87 37W
Old Westbury, *N.Y.* **23 C7** 40 46N 73 35W
Oldmans Cr. →, *Phil.* **24 C2** 39 47N 75 26W
Olgino, *St-Pet.* **11 A3** 60 0N 30 10 E
Olimpico, Estadio, *Méx.* **29 C2** 19 19N 99 11W
Olinda, *Melb.* **19 F9** 37 51 S 145 21 E
Olinda, *Rio J.* **31 A1** 22 49 S 43 25W
Olivais, *Lisb.* **8 F8** 38 45N 9 7W
Olivar de los Padres, *Méx.* **29 B2** 19 21N 99 14W
Olivar del Conde, *Méx.* **29 B2** 19 22N 99 12W
Olivos, *B.A.* **32 B4** 34 30 S 58 28W
Ollila, *Hels.* **3 A2** 60 20N 24 32 E
Olney, *Phil.* **24 A4** 40 2N 75 8W
Olona →, *Mil.* **9 E5** 45 29N 9 6 E
Ølstykke, *Købn.* **2 D7** 55 47N 12 8 E
Olute, *Lagos* **18 B1** 6 27N 7 17 E
Olympia-Stadion, *Hels.* **3 B4** 60 11N 24 55 E
Olympique Parc, *Mtrl.* **20 A4** 43 33N 73 33W
Ōmagi, *Tōkyō* **13 A3** 35 52N 139 43 E
Ōmiya, *Tōkyō* **13 A2** 35 54N 139 37 E
Ōmori, *Tōkyō* **13 C3** 35 34N 139 43 E
Ōnari, *Tōkyō* **13 A2** 35 55N 139 36 E
Once, *B.A.* **32 B4** 34 37 S 58 24W
Onchi, *Ōsaka* **12 C4** 34 36N 135 38 E
Onchi →, *Ōsaka* **12 C4** 34 38N 135 37 E
One Tree Hill, *Melb.* **19 F8** 37 52 S 145 19 E
Onisigun, *Lagos* **18 A2** 6 35N 7 24 E
Ōokayama, *Tōkyō* **13 C3** 35 36N 139 40 E
Opacz, *Wsaw.* **10 E6** 52 10N 20 53 E
Ophirton, *Jobg.* **18 F9** 26 13 S 28 1 E
Oppegård, *Oslo* **2 C4** 59 45N 10 49 E
Oppsal, *Oslo* **2 B5** 59 53N 10 50 E
Oppum, *Ruhr* **6 C1** 51 19N 6 36 E
Oradell, *N.Y.* **22 B4** 40 57N 74 2W
Oradell Res., *N.Y.* **22 B4** 40 58N 74 0W
Orange, *N.Y.* **22 C3** 40 46N 74 15W
Orange Grove, *Jobg.* **18 E9** 26 9 S 28 5 E
Oratorio →, *S. Pau.* **31 E6** 23 36 S 46 32W
Orbassano, *Tori.* **9 B2** 45 0N 7 31 E
Orchards, *Jobg.* **18 E9** 26 9 S 28 4 E
Ordrup, *Købn.* **2 D10** 55 45N 12 34 E
Orech, *Pra.* **10 B1** 50 1N 14 17 E
Øresund, *Købn.* **2 D11** 55 45N 12 40 E
Oreta, *Lagos* **18 A3** 6 31N 7 31 E
Orge →, *Paris* **5 D3** 48 36N 2 17 E
Orgeval, *Paris* **5 B1** 48 55N 1 58 E
Orhølm, *Købn.* **2 D10** 55 48N 12 30 E
Orient Heights, *Bost.* **21 C4** 42 23N 70 59W
Oriental, Pico, *Car.* **30 D5** 10 32N 66 51W
Origgio, *Mil.* **9 D5** 45 35N 9 1 E
Orinda, *S.F.* **27 A3** 37 52N 122 10W
Orinda Village, *S.F.* **27 A3** 37 53N 122 12W
Orland L., *Chic.* **26 D1** 41 38N 87 52W
Orland Park, *Chic.* **26 D1** 41 37N 87 52W
Orlando Dam, *Jobg.* **18 F8** 26 15 S 27 55 E
Orlando East, *Jobg.* **18 F8** 26 14 S 27 55 E
Orlando West, *Jobg.* **18 F8** 26 13 S 27 54 E
Orlången, *Stock.* **3 E11** 59 11N 18 2 E
Orlångsvik, *Stock.* **3 E11** 59 11N 18 3 E
Orlovo, *Mos.* **11 F8** 55 38N 37 22 E
Orly, *Paris* **5 C4** 48 45N 2 23 E
Ormesson-sur-Marne, *Paris* **5 C5** 48 47N 2 32 E
Orminge, *Stock.* **3 E12** 59 19N 18 14 E
Ormingelandet, *Stock.* **3 D13** 59 20N 18 22 E
Ormond, *Melb.* **19 F7** 37 54 S 145 1 E
Órmos Fálirou, *Ath.* **8 J11** 37 54N 23 40 E
Ormøya, *Oslo* **2 B4** 59 52N 10 45 E
Oros Aiyáleos, *Ath.* **8 J10** 38 0N 23 36 E
Oros Imittoś, *Ath.* **8 J11** 37 53N 23 48 E
Örpadfold, *Bud.* **10 J14** 47 32N 19 12 E
Orpington, *Lon.* **4 C5** 51 22N 0 6 E
Orsay, *Paris* **5 C3** 48 41N 2 11 E
Orsby, *Ruhr* **6 A2** 51 31N 6 41 E
Orsett, *Lon.* **4 B7** 51 30N 0 22 E
Ortaköy, *Ist.* **17 A3** 41 3N 29 1 E
Ortica, *Mil.* **9 E6** 45 28N 9 16 E
Oruba, *Lagos* **18 A2** 6 34N 7 24 E
Ōsaka, *Ōsaka* **12 C4** 34 42N 135 30 E
Ōsaka B., *Ōsaka* **12 C2** 34 35N 135 18 E
Ōsaka Castle, *Ōsaka* **12 B4** 34 41N 135 30 E
Ōsaka Harbour, *Ōsaka* **12 C3** 34 38N 135 25 E
Ōsaka Univ., *Ōsaka* **12 B3** 34 41N 135 29 E
Ōsaki, *Tōkyō* **13 C3** 35 36N 139 42 E
Osasco, *S. Pau.* **31 E5** 23 31 S 46 46W
Osdorf, *Berl.* **7 B3** 52 24N 13 20 E
Osdorf, *Hbg.* **7 D7** 53 34N 9 50 E
Oshodi, *Lagos* **18 A2** 6 33N 7 21 E
Oskar Frederikborg, *Stock.* **3 D13** 59 24N 18 24 E
Oslo, *Oslo* **2 B4** 59 54N 10 43 E
Oslofjorden, *Oslo* **2 C3** 59 40N 10 35 E
Ōsone, *Tōkyō* **13 C2** 35 31N 139 37 E
Osorun, *Lagos* **18 A2** 6 33N 7 29 E
Ospiate, *Mil.* **9 D5** 45 32N 9 6 E
Ossów, *Wsaw.* **10 E8** 52 18N 21 12 E
Ostankino, *Mos.* **11 E9** 55 49N 37 37 E
Østby, *Købn.* **2 D7** 55 45N 12 2 E
Osterath, *Ruhr* **6 C1** 51 16N 6 36 E
Österby, *Hels.* **3 B1** 60 10N 24 25 E
Osterfeld, *Ruhr* **6 A3** 51 30N 6 53 E
Osterley, *Lon.* **4 C2** 51 28N 0 21W
Osterley Park, *Lon.* **4 C2** 51 29N 0 21W
Östermalm, *Stock.* **3 D11** 59 20N 18 4 E
Österskär, *Stock.* **3 D12** 59 26N 18 16 E
Östersundom, *Hels.* **3 B6** 60 15N 25 10 E
Ostertälje, *Stock.* **3 E8** 59 11N 17 39 E
Ostiense, *Rome* **9 F9** 41 51N 12 29 E
Østmarkkapellet, *Oslo* **2 B5** 59 52N 10 51 E
Ostøya, *Oslo* **2 B3** 59 52N 10 34 E
Östra Ryd, *Stock.* **3 D12** 59 27N 18 11 E
Østre Aker, *Oslo* **2 B4** 59 54N 10 49 E
Ostrov, *Mos.* **11 F11** 55 36N 37 50 E
Ostrovtsy, *Mos.* **11 F12** 55 36N 38 0 E
Ōta-Ku, *Tōkyō* **13 C3** 35 34N 139 41 E
Otaniemi, *Hels.* **3 B3** 60 11N 24 49 E
Otford, *Lon.* **4 D6** 51 18N 0 11 E
Othmarschen, *Hbg.* **7 D7** 53 33N 9 53 E
Otsuka, *Tōkyō* **13 B3** 35 43N 139 44 E
Ottakring, *Wien* **10 G9** 48 12N 16 18 E
Ottávia, *Rome* **9 F9** 41 57N 12 24 E
Ottaviano, *Nápl.* **9 H13** 40 50N 14 28 E
Ottensen, *Hbg.* **7 D7** 53 33N 9 55 E
Ottobrunn, *Mün.* **7 G11** 48 3N 11 40 E
Ottocalli, *Nápl.* **9 H12** 40 52N 14 17 E
Otwock, *Wsaw.* **10 F8** 52 8N 21 13 E
Ouerenburg, *Ruhr* **6 B5** 51 27N 7 16 E
Ouiapo, *Manila* **15 D3** 14 35N 120 59 E
Oulunkylä, *Hels.* **3 B4** 60 13N 24 58 E
Ourcq, Canal de l', *Paris* **5 B4** 48 54N 2 28 E
Ousit, *Bangk.* **15 B2** 13 47N 100 31 E
Outer Brewster I., *Bost.* **21 C4** 42 20N 70 52W
Outer Mission, *S.F.* **27 B2** 37 43N 122 26W
Outremont, *Mtrl.* **20 A4** 43 31N 73 36W
Overbruch, *Ruhr* **6 A2** 51 32N 6 43 E
Overlea, *Balt.* **25 A3** 39 21N 76 32W
Øverød, *Købn.* **2 D9** 55 48N 12 28 E
Ōwada, *Tōkyō* **13 B2** 35 48N 139 31 E
Owings Mills, *Balt.* **25 A2** 39 25N 76 47W
Oworonsoki, *Lagos* **18 A2** 6 32N 7 24 E
Oxon Hill, *Wash.* **25 E8** 38 48N 76 59W
Oxshott, *Lon.* **4 D2** 51 19N 0 21W
Oyada, *Tōkyō* **13 B4** 35 46N 139 50 E
Ōyama, *Tōkyō* **13 B3** 35 44N 139 42 E
Øyeren, *Oslo* **2 B6** 59 55N 11 6 E
Oyodo, *Ōsaka* **12 B3** 34 42N 135 29 E
Oyster B., *N.Y.* **23 B7** 40 52N 73 31W
Oyster B., *Syd.* **19 C3** 34 0 S 151 5 E
Oyster Bay Cove, *N.Y.* **23 B8** 40 51N 73 29W
Oyster Bay Harbour, *N.Y.* **23 B7** 40 53N 73 32W
Oyster Rock, *Bomb.* **16 H7** 18 54N 72 49 E
Oyster Rocks, *Kar.* **17 H11** 24 48N 66 59 E
Ozarów-Franciszków, *Wsaw.* **10 E5** 52 13N 20 48 E
Ozerki, *St-Pet.* **11 B6** 59 53N 30 42 E
Ozoir-la-Ferrière, *Paris* **5 C6** 48 46N 2 40 E
Ozone Park, *N.Y.* **23 C5** 40 40N 73 50W

P

Pacific Manor, *S.F.* **27 C2** 37 38N 122 27W
Pacific Palisades, *L.A.* **28 B1** 34 2N 118 32W
Pacifica, *S.F.* **27 C2** 37 37N 122 27W
Packanack L., *N.Y.* **22 B3** 40 56N 74 15W
Paco, *Manila* **15 D3** 14 35N 120 59 E
Paco de Arcos, *Lisb.* **8 F7** 38 41N 9 17W
Paddington, *Lon.* **4 B3** 51 30N 0 10W
Paddington, *Syd.* **19 B4** 33 53 S 151 14 E
Pademangan, *Jak.* **15 H9** 6 7 S 106 49 E
Paderno, *Mil.* **9 D5** 45 33N 9 9 E
Padre Miguel, *Rio J.* **31 B1** 22 52 S 43 25W
Padstow, *Syd.* **19 B3** 33 57 S 151 2 E
Pagewood, *Syd.* **19 B4** 33 56 S 151 14 E
Pagote, *Bomb.* **16 H8** 18 53N 72 59 E
Pai, I. do, *Rio J.* **31 B3** 22 59 S 43 5W
Paia, *Lisb.* **8 F7** 38 46N 9 11W
Paikpara, *Calc.* **16 E6** 22 36N 88 23 E
Paint Br. →, *Wash.* **25 C8** 38 57N 76 55W
Paiyun Airport, *Gzh.* **14 F8** 23 10N 113 15 E
Pak ka Shan, *H.K.* **12 E6** 22 16N 114 13 E
Pak Kong, *H.K.* **12 D6** 22 22N 114 15 E
Pak Tim Pa, *H.K.* **12 D5** 22 22N 114 7 E
Pakila, *Hels.* **3 B4** 60 15N 24 55 E
Palace Museum, *Beij.* **14 B3** 39 54N 116 21 E
Palaión Fáliron, *Ath.* **8 J11** 37 53N 23 42 E
Palaiseau, *Paris* **5 C3** 48 42N 2 14 E
Palam, *Delhi* **16 B1** 28 35N 77 4 E
Palam Int. Airport, *Delhi* **16 B1** 28 32N 77 8 E
Palazzo Reale, *Nápl.* **9 H12** 40 50N 14 15 E
Palazzo Reale, *Tori.* **9 B3** 45 4N 7 40 E
Palazzolo, *Mil.* **9 D5** 45 34N 9 9 E
Palazzuolo, *Nápl.* **9 H13** 40 54N 14 28 E
Palermo, *B.A.* **32 B4** 34 35 S 58 24W
Palhais, *Lisb.* **8 G8** 38 37N 9 2W
Palisades, *N.Y.* **22 A5** 41 1N 73 57W
Palisades Park, *N.Y.* **22 B4** 40 50N 74 1W
Palleja, *Barc.* **8 D5** 41 25N 2 0 E
Palmer Park, *Wash.* **25 D8** 38 55N 76 52W
Palmers Green, *Lon.* **4 B4** 51 36N 0 6W
Palmyra, *Phil.* **24 A4** 40 0N 75 1W
Palo Alto, *S.F.* **27 D4** 37 27N 122 8W
Paloheinä, *Hels.* **3 B4** 60 15N 24 56 E
Palomar Park, *S.F.* **27 D3** 37 29N 122 16W
Palomeras, *Mdrd.* **8 B3** 40 22N 3 39W
Palos Heights, *Chic.* **26 D2** 41 39N 87 47W
Palos Hills, *Chic.* **26 C2** 41 42N 87 49W
Palos Hills Forest, *Chic.* **26 C1** 41 40N 87 52W
Palos Park, *Chic.* **26 C1** 41 40N 87 50W
Palota-Üjfalu, *Bud.* **10 J13** 47 33N 19 7 E
Palpara, *Calc.* **16 E6** 22 38N 88 22 E
Palta, *Calc.* **16 D6** 22 46N 88 23 E
Pamplona, *Manila* **15 E3** 14 27N 120 58 E
Panayaan, *Manila* **15 E3** 14 27N 120 57 E
Panchghara, *Calc.* **16 D5** 22 44N 88 16 E
Panchur, *Calc.* **16 E5** 22 32N 88 16 E
Pancoran, *Jak.* **15 J9** 6 14 S 106 49 E
Pandan, Selat, *Sing.* **15 G7** 1 16N 103 45 E
Pandan, Sungei →, *Sing.* **15 G7** 1 18N 103 43 E
Pandan Res., *Sing.* **15 G7** 1 18N 103 44 E
Panehpara, *Calc.* **16 E5** 22 34N 88 15 E
Pangrati, *Ath.* **8 J11** 37 56N 23 45 E
Pangsua, Sungei →, *Sing.* **15 F7** 1 25N 103 45 E
Panihati, *Calc.* **16 D6** 22 41N 88 22 E
Panjang, Bukit, *Sing.* **15 F7** 1 22N 103 45 E
Panje, *Bomb.* **16 H8** 18 54N 72 57 E
Panke →, *Berl.* **7 A3** 52 31N 13 22 E
Pankow, *Berl.* **7 A3** 52 34N 13 23 E
Panorama City, *L.A.* **28 A2** 34 13N 118 26W
Panpur, *Calc.* **16 C6** 22 51N 88 26 E
Pantheon, *Rome* **9 F9** 41 53N 12 28 E
Pantin, *Paris* **5 B4** 48 53N 2 24 E
Pantitlán, *Méx.* **29 B3** 19 24N 99 4W
Panuacan, *Manila* **15 D4** 14 35N 121 0 E
Panvel Cr. →, *Bomb.* **16 H9** 18 59N 73 0 E
Paoli, *Phil.* **24 A2** 40 2N 75 28W
Papiol, *Barc.* **8 D5** 41 25N 2 0 E
Paracuellos del Jarama, *Mdrd.* **8 A3** 40 30N 3 31W
Paradise Cay, *S.F.* **27 A2** 37 54N 122 28W
Paramount, *L.A.* **28 C3** 33 53N 118 11W
Paramus, *N.Y.* **22 B4** 40 56N 74 2W
Paranaque, *Manila* **15 D3** 14 30N 120 59 E
Paray-Vieille-Poste, *Paris* **5 C4** 48 42N 2 20 E
Parbasdorf, *Wien* **10 G11** 48 16N 16 35 E
Parbatipur, *Calc.* **16 E5** 22 39N 88 13 E
Parcelacion Moderna, *La Hab.* **30 B3** 23 2N 82 19W
Parco Regionale, *Mil.* **9 D5** 45 35N 9 5 E
Parel, *Bomb.* **16 H7** 18 59N 72 49 E
Pari, *S. Pau.* **31 E6** 23 32 S 46 36W
Parioli, *Rome* **9 F9** 41 55N 12 29 E
Paris, *Paris* **5 B4** 48 53N 2 20 E
Paris-Le Bourget, Aéroport de, *Paris* **5 B4** 48 58N 2 26 E
Paris-Orly, Aéroport de, *Paris* **5 C4** 48 43N 2 22 E
Pārk-e-Shahānshāh, *Tehr.* **17 C5** 35 46N 51 24 E
Park Orchards, *Melb.* **19 E8** 37 46 S 145 13 E
Park Ridge, *Chic.* **26 A1** 42 0N 87 50W
Park Ridge, *N.Y.* **22 A4** 41 2N 74 2W
Park Royal, *Lon.* **4 B3** 51 31N 0 16W
Parkchester, *N.Y.* **23 C5** 40 49N 73 50W
Parkdale, *Trto.* **20 E8** 43 38N 79 25W
Parkdene, *Jobg.* **18 F10** 26 11 S 28 15 E
Parkhafen, *Hbg.* **7 D7** 53 32N 9 54 E
Parkhill Gardens, *Jobg.* **18 F10** 26 14 S 28 11 E
Parkhurst, *Jobg.* **18 E9** 26 8 S 28 1 E
Parklawn, *Wash.* **25 D7** 38 50N 77 7W
Parkmore, *Jobg.* **18 E9** 26 5 S 28 2 E
Parkside, *S.F.* **27 B2** 37 44N 122 29W
Parktown, *Jobg.* **18 F9** 26 10 S 28 2 E
Parktown North, *Jobg.* **18 E9** 26 8 S 28 2 E
Parkview, *Jobg.* **18 E9** 26 9 S 28 1 E
Parkville, *Balt.* **25 A3** 39 23N 76 34W
Parkville, *N.Y.* **22 D5** 40 38N 73 57W
Parkwood, *Jobg.* **18 E9** 26 9 S 28 2 E
Parque Edú Chaves, *S. Pau.* **31 D6** 23 29 S 46 34W
Parramatta, *Syd.* **19 A2** 33 49 S 150 59 E
Parramatta →, *Syd.* **19 A3** 33 49 S 151 3 E
Parramatta North, *Syd.* **19 A3** 33 48 S 151 0 E
Parramatta Park, *Syd.* **19 A3** 33 48 S 151 0 E
Parsippany, *N.Y.* **22 B2** 40 51N 74 26W
Paşabahce, *Ist.* **17 A3** 41 6N 29 5 E
Pasadena, *L.A.* **28 B4** 34 9N 118 8W
Pasar Minggu, *Jak.* **15 J9** 6 16 S 106 49 E
Pasay, *Manila* **15 D3** 14 32N 120 59 E
Pascoe Vale, *Melb.* **19 E6** 37 43 S 144 55 E
Pasig, *Manila* **15 D4** 14 33N 121 4 E
Pasig →, *Manila* **15 D4** 14 31N 121 6 E
Pasila, *Hels.* **3 B4** 60 12N 24 56 E
Pasing, *Mün.* **7 G9** 48 8N 11 28 E
Pasir Panjang, *Sing.* **15 G7** 1 17N 103 46 E
Pasir Ris Beach, *Sing.* **15 F8** 1 22N 103 56 E
Paso del Rey, *B.A.* **32 B2** 34 39 S 58 45W
Passaic, *N.Y.* **22 B4** 40 51N 74 9W
Passaic →, *N.Y.* **22 B3** 40 42N 74 10W
Passirana, *Mil.* **9 D5** 45 32N 9 2 E
Patapsco →, *Balt.* **25 B2** 39 19N 76 49W
Patapsco State Park, *Balt.* **25 B2** 39 18N 76 47W
Pateres, *Manila* **15 D4** 14 32N 121 3 E
Paterson, *N.Y.* **22 B4** 40 54N 74 9W
Pathumwan, *Bangk.* **15 B2** 13 44N 100 31 E
Patipukun, *Calc.* **16 E6** 22 36N 88 24 E
Patisia, *Ath.* **8 H11** 38 2N 23 45 E
Patterson Park, *Balt.* **25 B3** 39 17N 76 34W
Patul, *Calc.* **16 D4** 22 45N 88 9 E
Paulo E. Virginia, Gruta, *Rio J.* **31 B2** 22 56 S 43 16W
Paulsboro, *Phil.* **24 C3** 39 49N 75 14W
Paulshof, *Berl.* **7 A5** 52 34N 13 42 E
Pausin, *Berl.* **7 A1** 52 38N 13 2 E
Pavarolo, *Tori.* **9 B3** 45 4N 7 49 E
Pavlovo, *St-Pet.* **11 B5** 59 55N 30 38 E
Pavne, *Bomb.* **16 G9** 19 5N 73 1 E
Pavshino, *Mos.* **11 E7** 55 49N 37 20 E
Paya Lebar, *Sing.* **15 F8** 1 21N 103 52 E
Paylampur, *Calc.* **16 D5** 22 46N 88 15 E
Peabody, *Bost.* **21 B4** 42 32N 70 57W
Peabody Inst., *Balt.* **25 B3** 39 17N 76 37W
Peakhurst, *Syd.* **19 B3** 33 57 S 151 3 E
Pécel, *Bud.* **10 K14** 47 29N 19 20 E
Pecetto Torinese, *Tori.* **9 B3** 45 1N 7 44 E
Pechincha, *Rio J.* **31 B1** 22 55 S 43 20W
Pechorka →, *Mos.* **11 F12** 55 37N 38 2 E
Peckham, *Lon.* **4 C4** 51 28N 0 3W
Pecqueuse, *Paris* **5 D2** 48 38N 2 3 E
Peddocks I., *Bost.* **21 D4** 42 17N 70 56W
Pederstrup, *Købn.* **2 D9** 55 44N 12 20 E
Pedra Branca, *Rio J.* **31 B1** 22 55 S 43 26W
Pedralbes, *Barc.* **8 D5** 41 23N 2 7 E
Pedregal de San Angel, Jardines del, *Méx.* **29 C2** 19 19N 99 12W
Pedreira, *S. Pau.* **31 F5** 23 41 S 46 40W
Pedreros, *Lima* **30 G8** 12 2 S 76 57W
Pedricktown, *Phil.* **24 C2** 39 45N 75 24W
Pedro Cr. →, *S.F.* **27 C2** 37 35N 122 31W
Pedro Valley, *S.F.* **27 C2** 37 35N 122 29W
Peirce Res., *Sing.* **15 F7** 1 22N 103 49 E
Pekhra-Pokrovskoye, *Mos.* **11 D11** 55 50N 37 56 E
Pekhra-Yakovievskaya, *Mos.* **11 E11** 55 47N 37 57 E
Peking = Beijing, *Beij.* **14 B2** 39 53N 116 21 E
Pelado, Cerro, *Méx.* **29 D2** 19 10N 99 14W
Pelcowizna, *Wsaw.* **10 E7** 52 17N 21 0 E
Pelham, *N.Y.* **23 B6** 40 54N 73 46W
Pelham B. Park, *N.Y.* **23 B6** 40 52N 73 48W
Pelham Manor, *N.Y.* **23 B6** 40 53N 73 46W
Penalolén, *Stgo* **30 J11** 33 28 S 70 30W
Peng Siang →, *Sing.* **15 F7** 1 24N 103 43 E
Penge, *Lon.* **4 C4** 51 24N 0 3W
Penha, *Rio J.* **31 A2** 22 49 S 43 17W
Penha, *S. Pau.* **31 E6** 23 31 S 46 32W
Penjaringan, *Jak.* **15 H9** 6 7 S 106 48 E
Penn Square, *Phil.* **24 A3** 40 8N 75 19W
Penn Wynne, *Phil.* **24 B3** 39 59N 75 16W
Pennant Hills Park, *Syd.* **19 A3** 33 46 S 151 6 E
Penndel, *Phil.* **24 A5** 40 9N 74 54W
Penns Grove, *Phil.* **24 C2** 39 44N 75 27W
Pennsauken, *Phil.* **24 B4** 39 57N 75 5W
Pennsauken Cr. →, *Phil.* **24 B4** 39 59N 75 3W
Pennsylvania, Univ. of, *Phil.* **24 B3** 39 51N 75 11W
Pennypack Cr. →, *Phil.* **24 A4** 40 0N 75 3W
Pentala, *Hels.* **3 C3** 60 6N 24 40 E
Penyagino, *Mos.* **11 D8** 55 50N 37 20 E
Penzing, *Wien* **10 G9** 48 11N 16 18 E
Pequannock, *N.Y.* **22 B3** 40 57N 74 17W
Pequena Arroio Fundo →, *Rio J.* **31 B1** 22 58 S 43 21W
Perales del Rio, *Mdrd.* **8 C3** 40 18N 3 38W
Perchtoldsdorf, *Wien* **10 H9** 48 7N 16 17 E
Perdizes, *S. Pau.* **31 E6** 23 32 S 46 39W
Peredelkino, *Mos.* **11 F8** 55 38N 37 20 E
Peredelytsy, *Mos.* **11 F8** 55 36N 37 21 E
Peristérion, *Ath.* **8 H11** 38 1N 23 42 E
Perivale, *Lon.* **4 B3** 51 31N 0 18W
Perlach, *Mün.* **7 G10** 48 5N 11 37 E
Perlacher Forst, *Mün.* **7 G10** 48 4N 11 34 E
Pero, *Mil.* **9 D5** 45 30N 9 5 E
Peropok, Bukit, *Sing.* **15 G7** 1 19N 103 42 E
Perovo, *Mos.* **11 E10** 55 44N 37 45 E
Perrot, Î., *Mtrl.* **20 B2** 43 23N 73 56W
Perry Hall, *Balt.* **25 A4** 39 24N 76 28W
Perth Amboy, *N.Y.* **22 D3** 40 30N 74 16W
Pertusella, *Mil.* **9 D5** 45 35N 9 3 E
Pesanggrahag, Kali →, *Jak.* **15 J9** 6 10 S 106 44 E
Peschiera Borromeo, *Mil.* **9 E6** 45 26N 9 19 E
Pesek, P., *Sing.* **15 G7** 1 17N 103 41 E
Pest, *Bud.* **10 K13** 47 29N 19 4 E
Pesterzsébet, *Bud.* **10 K13** 47 26N 19 6 E
Pesthidegkút, *Bud.* **10 J12** 47 33N 18 57 E
Pestimre, *Bud.* **10 K14** 47 24N 19 11 E
Pestlörinc, *Bud.* **10 K14** 47 26N 19 11 E
Pestujhely, *Bud.* **10 J13** 47 32N 19 7 E
Petare, *Car.* **30 E6** 10 29N 66 48W
Petas, *Hels.* **3 B4** 60 15N 24 50 E
Peters Pond, *Bost.* **21 A2** 42 43N 71 15W
Petit, *Jobg.* **18 E11** 26 6 S 28 22 E
Petit-Brûlé, *Mtrl.* **20 A1** 43 35N 74 2W
Petojo Selatan, *Jak.* **15 J9** 6 10 S 106 48 E
Petrograd = St. Petersburg, *St-Pet.* **11 B3** 59 55N 30 15 E
Petrogradskaya Storona, *St-Pet.* **11 B4** 59 56N 30 20 E
Petroúpolis, *Ath.* **8 H11** 38 3N 23 40 E
Petrovice, *Pra.* **10 B3** 50 2N 14 33 E
Petrovsko-Rasumovskoye, *Mos.* **11 E9** 55 49N 37 34 E
Petrovskoye, *Mos.* **11 F11** 55 36N 37 53 E
Petrovsky Park, *Mos.* **11 E9** 55 47N 37 34 E
Pfaueninsel, *Berl.* **7 B1** 52 26N 13 7 E
Phihāi, *Kar.* **17 G11** 24 50N 67 8 E
Philadelphia, *Phil.* **24 B3** 39 57N 75 11W
Philadelphia Airport, *Phil.* **24 A5** 40 4N 75 0W
Philadelphia Int. Airport, *Phil.* **24 B3** 39 52N 75 16W
Phillip B., *Syd.* **19 B4** 33 58 S 151 14 E
Phinga, *Calc.* **16 D6** 22 41N 88 25 E
Phoenix, *Chic.* **26 D3** 41 36N 87 37W
Phoenixville, *Phil.* **24 A1** 40 7N 75 31W
Phra Khanong, *Bangk.* **15 B2** 13 40N 100 36 E
Phra Pradaeng, *Bangk.* **15 C2** 13 39N 100 33 E
Phranakhon, *Bangk.* **15 B1** 13 44N 100 29 E
Pianezza, *Tori.* **9 B2** 45 6N 7 32 E
Pianura, *Nápl.* **9 H11** 40 51N 14 10 E
Piaslów, *Wsaw.* **10 E5** 52 11N 20 49 E
Pico Rivera, *L.A.* **28 C4** 33 59N 118 5W
Piedade, *Lisb.* **8 F7** 38 49N 9 16W
Piedade, *Rio J.* **31 B2** 22 52 S 43 18W
Piedade, Cova da, *Lisb.* **8 F8** 38 40N 9 8W
Piedmont, *S.F.* **27 B3** 37 49N 122 14W
Pierrefitte, *Paris* **5 B4** 48 58N 2 21 E
Pierrefonds, *Mtrl.* **20 B2** 43 27N 73 52W
Pierrelaye, *Paris* **5 A2** 49 1N 2 8 E
Pietralata, *Rome* **9 F10** 41 55N 12 33 E
Pihlajamäki, *Hels.* **3 B4** 60 14N 24 58 E
Pihlajasaari, *Hels.* **3 C4** 60 8N 24 55 E
Pikesville, *Balt.* **25 A2** 39 22N 76 42W
Pilar Velho, *S. Pau.* **31 F7** 23 40 S 46 22W
Pilarcitos Cr. →, *S.F.* **27 C2** 37 33N 122 24W
Pilarcitos L., *S.F.* **27 C2** 37 33N 122 25W
Pilgrim Corner, *Phil.* **24 B3** 39 57N 75 19W
Pilgrims Hatch, *Lon.* **4 B6** 51 37N 0 17 E
Pillar Pt., *S.F.* **26 D2** 37 29N 122 30W
Pimenta, *S. Pau.* **31 D7** 23 27 S 46 24W
Pimlico, *Lon.* **4 C4** 51 29N 0 8W
Pimmit Hills, *Wash.* **25 D6** 38 54N 77 12W
Pimville, *Jobg.* **18 F8** 26 16 S 27 54 E
Pinazo →, *B.A.* **32 A2** 34 29 S 58 49W
Pine Brook, *N.Y.* **22 B3** 40 51N 74 18W
Pine Grove, *Trto.* **20 D7** 43 47N 79 34W
Pine Hill, *Phil.* **24 C5** 39 47N 74 59W
Pine Orchard, *Balt.* **25 B1** 39 16N 76 52W
Pinehurst, *Bost.* **21 B2** 42 31N 71 12W
Piñero, *B.A.* **32 B2** 34 31 S 58 46W
Pines Lake, *N.Y.* **22 B3** 40 59N 74 15W
Piney Run →, *Wash.* **25 D6** 38 58N 77 14W
Pinganli, *Beij.* **14 B3** 39 56N 116 20 E
Pinheiros →, *S. Pau.* **31 E5** 23 37 S 46 44W
Pinjrāpur, *Kar.* **17 G11** 24 53N 67 4 E
Pinn →, *Lon.* **4 B2** 51 30N 0 28W
Pinnau →, *Hbg.* **7 C6** 53 40N 9 49 E
Pinneberg, *Hbg.* **7 C6** 53 40N 9 48 E
Pinner, *Lon.* **4 B2** 51 35N 0 22W
Pinner Green, *Lon.* **4 B2** 51 35N 0 23W
Pino Torinese, *Tori.* **9 B3** 45 2N 7 46 E
Pinole Cr. →, *S.F.* **27 A3** 37 58N 122 12W
Pioltello, *Mil.* **9 D6** 45 30N 9 19 E
Piossasco, *Tori.* **9 C1** 44 59N 7 27 E
Piqueri, *S. Pau.* **31 D5** 23 29 S 46 41W
Piqueri →, *S. Pau.* **31 D6** 23 27 S 46 34W
Pira, *Delhi* **16 A1** 28 40N 77 7 E
Piraévs, *Ath.* **8 J10** 37 54N 23 39 E
Pirajussara, *S. Pau.* **31 E5** 23 37 S 46 46W
Pirajussara →, *S. Pau.* **31 E5** 23 33 S 46 42W
Piraporinha, *S. Pau.* **31 F5** 23 41 S 46 44W
Piratininga, *Rio J.* **31 B3** 22 56 S 43 4W
Piratininga, L. de, *Rio J.* **31 B3** 22 56 S 43 4W
Pirituba, *S. Pau.* **31 D5** 23 29 S 46 44W
Pirkkola, *Hels.* **3 B4** 60 14N 24 55 E
Pisangan, *Jak.* **15 J10** 6 12 S 106 52 E
Piscataway, *N.Y.* **22 D2** 40 34N 74 27W
Pisnice, *Pra.* **10 C2** 49 59N 14 28 E
Pitampura Kalan, *Delhi* **16 A1** 28 41N 77 7 E

44 **Pitkäjärvi**

Pitkäjärvi, *Hels.* **3 B3** 60 15N 24 45 E
Pitman, *Phil.* **24 C4** 39 44N 75 7W
Plainedge, *N.Y.* **23 C8** 40 43N 73 27W
Plainfield, *N.Y.* **22 D2** 40 36N 74 23W
Plainview, *N.Y.* **23 C8** 40 46N 73 27W
Plaisir, *Paris* **5 C1** 48 49N 1 56 E
Plandome, *N.Y.* **23 C6** 40 48N 73 42W
Plandome Heights, *N.Y.* **23 C6** 40 48N 73 42W
Planegg, *Mün.* **7 G9** 48 6N 11 25 E
Plazo Mayor, *Mdrd.* **8 B2** 40 25N 3 43W
Pleasant Hill, *S.F.* **27 A4** 37 56N 122 4W
Plenty, *Melb.* **19 E7** 37 40 S 145 5 E
Pluit, *Jak.* **15 H9** 6 7 S 106 47 E
Plumsock, *Phil.* **24 B2** 39 58N 75 28W
Plumstead, *Lon.* **4 C5** 51 29N 0 5 E
Plymouth Meeting, *Phil.* **24 A3** 40 6N 75 16W
Plyushchevo, *Mos.* **11 E10** 55 44N 37 45 E
Po →, *Tori.* **9 B3** 45 7N 7 46 E
Po Toi, *H.K.* **12 E6** 22 16N 114 17 E
Po Toi I., *H.K.* **12 E6** 22 10N 114 15 E
Podbaba, *Pra.* **10 B2** 50 7N 14 22 E
Podoli, *Pra.* **10 B2** 50 2N 14 25 E
Podra, *Calc.* **16 E5** 22 33N 88 16 E
Poduskino, *Mos.* **11 E7** 55 43N 37 15 E
Poggioreale, *Nápl.* **9 H12** 40 51N 14 17 E
Pogliano Milanese, *Mil.* **9 D4** 45 32N 8 59 E
Pohick Cr. →, *Wash.* **25 E6** 38 47N 77 16W
Point Breeze, *Phil.* **24 B3** 39 54N 75 13W
Point Lookout, *N.Y.* **23 D7** 40 35N 73 34W
Point View Res., *N.Y.* **22 B3** 40 58N 74 14W
Pointe-Aux-Trembles, *Mtrl.* **20 A4** 43 38N 73 30W
Pointe-Calumet, *Mtrl.* **20 B2** 43 29N 73 58W
Pointe-Claire, *Mtrl.* **20 B3** 43 27N 73 48W
Poissy, *Paris* **5 B2** 48 55N 2 2 E
Pok Fu Lam, *H.K.* **12 E5** 22 16N 114 7 E
Pokrovsko-Sresnevo, *Mos.* **11 E8** 55 48N 37 27 E
Pokrovskoye, *Mos.* **11 F9** 55 37N 37 36 E
Pόllena, *Nápl.* **9 H13** 40 51N 14 22 E
Polsum, *Ruhr* **6 A4** 51 37N 7 2 E
Polyustrovo, *St-Pet.* **11 B4** 59 57N 30 25 E
Pomigliano d'Arco, *Nápl.* **9 H13** 40 54N 14 23 E
Pompei, *Nápl.* **9 J13** 40 45N 14 29 E
Pomponne, *Paris* **5 B6** 48 52N 2 40 E
Pomprap, *Bangk.* **15 B2** 13 44N 100 30 E
Pompton →, *N.Y.* **22 B3** 40 53N 74 16W
Pompton Lakes, *N.Y.* **22 A3** 41 0N 74 15W
Pompton Plains, *N.Y.* **22 B3** 40 58N 74 18W
Ponders End, *Lon.* **4 B4** 51 38N 0 2W
Pondok Indah, *Jak.* **15 J9** 6 16 S 106 46 E
Ponkapog, *Bost.* **21 D3** 42 11N 71 4W
Ponkapog Pond, *Bost.* **21 D3** 42 11N 71 5W
Pont-Viau, *Mtrl.* **20 A3** 43 34N 73 41W
Pontault-Combault, *Paris* **5 C5** 48 47N 2 36 E
Pontcarré, *Paris* **5 C6** 48 47N 2 42 E
Pontchartrain, *Paris* **5 C1** 48 48N 1 54 E
Ponte Galéria, *Rome* **9 G8** 41 48N 12 19 E
Pontes, Canto do, *Rio J.* **31 B3** 22 56 S 43 3W
Pontevedra, *B.A.* **32 C2** 34 44 S 58 41W
Ponticelli, *Nápl.* **9 H12** 40 51N 14 19 E
Pontinha, *Lisb.* **8 F7** 38 45N 9 11W
Pontoise, *Paris* **5 A2** 49 2N 2 4 E
Poortview, *Jobg.* **18 E8** 26 5 S 27 51 E
Poplar, *Lon.* **4 B4** 51 30N 0 0 E
Poppenbüttel, *Hbg.* **7 D8** 53 39N 10 4 E
Port Chester, *N.Y.* **23 A6** 41 0N 73 40W
Port Chester Harbour, *N.Y.* **23 B7** 40 58N 73 38W
Port Jackson, *Syd.* **19 B4** 33 51 S 151 14 E
Port Kennedy, *Phil.* **24 A2** 40 6N 75 25W
Port Melbourne, *Melb.* **19 F6** 37 50 S 144 54 E
Port Newark, *N.Y.* **22 C4** 40 41N 74 9W
Port Reading, *N.Y.* **22 D3** 40 34N 74 13W
Port Richmond, *N.Y.* **22 D4** 40 38N 74 7W
Port Shelter, *H.K.* **12 D6** 22 20N 114 17 E
Port Union, *Trto.* **20 D10** 43 47N 79 7W
Port Washington, *N.Y.* **23 C6** 40 49N 73 42W
Port Washington North, *N.Y.* **23 B6** 40 50N 73 41W
Portage Park, *Chic.* **26 B2** 41 56N 87 45W
Portela, Aeroporto da, *Lisb.* **8 F8** 38 46N 9 7W
Pórtici, *Nápl.* **9 J12** 40 48N 14 19 E
Porto Brandão, *Lisb.* **8 F7** 38 40N 9 12W
Porto Novo Cr. →, *Lagos* **18 B2** 6 25N 7 22 E
Porto Nuevo, *B.A.* **32 B4** 34 35 S 58 22W
Portrero, *S.F.* **27 B3** 37 46N 122 25W
Posen, *Chic.* **26 D2** 41 38N 87 41W
Posíllipo, *Nápl.* **9 J12** 40 49N 14 13 E
Posíllipo, C. di, *Nápl.* **9 J12** 40 48N 14 12 E
Posolok Lenina, *St-Pet.* **11 C2** 59 50N 30 5 E
Potawatomi Woods, *Chic.* **26 A1** 42 8N 87 53W
Potomac, *Wash.* **25 D6** 38 59N 77 13W
Potomac →, *Wash.* **25 D7** 38 58N 77 9W
Potrero Pt., *S.F.* **27 B2** 37 45N 122 22W
Potsdam, *Berl.* **7 B1** 52 23N 13 3 E
Potter Pt., *Syd.* **19 C4** 34 2 S 151 13 E
Potters Bar, *Lon.* **4 A4** 51 41N 0 10W
Potzham, *Mün.* **7 G10** 48 1N 11 36 E
Pötzleinsdorf, *Wien* **10 G9** 48 14N 16 17 E
Povoa de Santo Adriao, *Lisb.* **8 F8** 38 47N 9 9W
Powderhorn L., *Chic.* **26 D3** 41 38N 87 31W
Powičle, *Wsaw.* **10 E7** 52 14N 21 1 E
Powōzki, *Wsaw.* **10 E6** 52 15N 20 58 E
Powsin, *Wsaw.* **10 F7** 52 8N 21 6 E
Powsinek, *Wsaw.* **10 F7** 52 9N 21 6 E
Poyo, *Barc.* **8 D6** 41 28N 2 12 E
Pozuelo de Alarcón, *Mdrd.* **8 B2** 40 25N 3 48W
Praça Seca, *Rio J.* **31 B1** 22 53 S 43 20W
Prado, Museo del, *Mdrd.* **8 B2** 40 25N 3 42W
Prado Churubusco, *Méx.* **29 B3** 19 20N 99 8W
Praga, *Wsaw.* **10 E7** 52 15N 21 2 E
Prague = Praha, *Pra.* **10 B2** 50 4N 14 25 E
Praha, *Pra.* **10 B2** 50 4N 14 25 E
Praha-Ruzyně Airport, *Pra.* **10 B1** 50 6N 14 16 E
Praires, R. des →, *Mtrl.* **20 A4** 43 38N 73 36W
Prat de Llobregat, *Barc.* **8 E5** 41 19N 2 5 E
Prater, *Wien* **10 G10** 48 12N 16 25 E
Pratts Bottom, *Lon.* **4 C5** 51 20N 0 7 E
Prawet Buri Rom, Khlong →, *Bangk.* **15 B2** 13 43N 100 38 E
Preakness, *N.Y.* **22 B3** 40 56N 74 12W
Precotto, *Mil.* **9 D6** 45 30N 9 13 E
Prédecelles →, *Paris* **5 D2** 48 36N 2 7 E
Pregnana Milanese, *Mil.* **9 D4** 45 30N 9 0 E
Prem Prachakan, Khlong →, *Bangk.* **15 B2** 13 46N 100 35 E
Prenestino Labicano, *Rome* **9 F10** 41 53N 12 33 E
Prenzlauerberg, *Berl.* **7 A3** 52 32N 13 24 E
Presidente Derqui, *B.A.* **32 A1** 34 29 S 58 50W
Presidente Outra, Rodo, *Rio J.* **31 A1** 22 47 S 43 21W
Preston, *Melb.* **19 E6** 37 44 S 144 59 E
Pretos Forros, Sa. dos, *Rio J.* **31 B2** 22 54 S 43 17W
Préville, *Mtrl.* **20 B5** 43 28N 73 29W
Přezletice, *Pra.* **10 B3** 50 9N 14 34 E
Primavalle, *Rome* **9 F9** 41 55N 12 25 E
Primrose, *Jobg.* **18 F9** 26 11 S 28 9 E
Princes B., *N.Y.* **22 D3** 40 30N 74 12W
Princess Elizabeth Park, *Sing.* **15 F7** 1 21N 103 45 E
Progreso, *Mdrd.* **8 B3** 40 27N 3 39W
Progreso Nacional, *Méx.* **29 A3** 19 30N 99 9W
Prosek, *Pra.* **10 B3** 50 7N 14 30 E
Prospect, *Syd.* **19 A2** 33 48 S 150 55 E
Prospect Heights, *Chic.* **26 A1** 42 5N 87 55W
Prospect Hill Park, *Bost.* **21 C2** 42 23N 71 13W
Prospect Park, *N.Y.* **22 B3** 40 55N 74 10W
Prospect Park, *Phil.* **24 B3** 39 53N 75 18W
Prospect Pt., *N.Y.* **23 B6** 40 52N 73 42W
Prospect Res., *Syd.* **19 A2** 33 49 S 150 53 E
Providence, *Balt.* **25 A3** 39 25N 76 34W
Providencia, *Stgo* **30 J11** 33 25 S 70 36W
Průhonice, *Pra.* **10 C3** 50 0N 14 33 E
Pruszków, *Wsaw.* **10 E5** 52 10N 20 48 E
Psikhikón, *Ath.* **8 H11** 38 1N 23 46 E
Pudong, *Shang.* **14 J12** 31 13N 121 30 E
Puduo, *Shang.* **14 J11** 31 15N 121 24 E
Pueblo Libre, *Lima* **30 G8** 12 5 S 77 4W
Pueblo Nuevo, *Barc.* **8 D6** 41 23N 2 11 E
Pueblo Nuevo, *Mdrd.* **8 B3** 40 25N 3 37W
Puente Cascallares, *B.A.* **32 C2** 34 41 S 58 48W
Puente Hills, *L.A.* **28 C5** 33 59N 117 59W
Puffing Billy Station, *Melb.* **19 F9** 37 54 S 145 20 E
Puhuangyu, *Beij.* **14 B3** 39 50N 116 22 E
Puistola, *Hels.* **3 B5** 60 16N 25 2 E
Pukinmäki, *Hels.* **3 B4** 60 15N 24 57 E
Pullach, *Mün.* **7 G9** 48 3N 11 31 E
Pulo, *Manila* **15 D4** 14 34N 121 4 E
Pulo Gadung, *Jak.* **15 J10** 6 11 S 106 54 E
Pumphrey, *Balt.* **25 B3** 39 13N 76 39W
Punchbowl, *Syd.* **19 B3** 33 55 S 151 3 E
Punde, *Bomb.* **16 H8** 18 53N 72 57 E
Punggol, *Sing.* **15 F8** 1 23N 103 54 E
Punggol, Sungei →, *Sing.* **15 F8** 1 24N 103 54 E
Punggol Pt., *Sing.* **15 F8** 1 24N 103 54 E
Punta Brava, *La Hab.* **30 B2** 23 1N 82 29W
Puolarmetsä, *Hels.* **3 B3** 60 11N 24 41 E
Puotila, *Hels.* **3 B5** 60 13N 25 6 E
Purchase, *N.Y.* **23 A6** 41 2N 73 43W
Purfleet, *Lon.* **4 C6** 51 29N 0 14 E
Purkersdorf, *Wien* **10 G9** 48 12N 16 11 E
Purley, *Lon.* **4 C4** 51 20N 0 6W
Puteaux, *Paris* **5 B3** 48 53N 2 14 E
Puth Kalan, *Delhi* **16 A1** 28 42N 77 4 E
Putilkovo, *Mos.* **11 D8** 55 51N 37 22 E
Putnamville Res., *Bost.* **21 B4** 42 36N 70 56W
Putney, *Lon.* **4 C3** 51 27N 0 13W
Putty Hill, *Balt.* **25 A3** 39 22N 76 30W
Putxet, *Barc.* **8 D5** 41 24N 2 8 E
Putzbrunn, *Mün.* **7 G11** 48 4N 11 42 E
Pyeongchang, *Sŏul* **12 G7** 37 35N 126 57 E
Pyramids, *El Qâ.* **18 D4** 29 58N 31 7 E
Pyry, *Wsaw.* **10 F6** 52 8N 21 0 E

Q

Qanât el Ismâîlîya, *El Qâ.* **18 C5** 30 7N 31 17 E
Qasemābād, *Tehr.* **17 C6** 35 4N 51 3 E
Qasr-e-Firōzeh, *Tehr.* **17 D6** 35 29N 51 31 E
Qianmen, *Beij.* **14 B3** 39 51N 116 21 E
Qibao, *Shang.* **14 K11** 31 9N 121 20 E
Qingguang, *Tianj.* **14 D5** 39 11N 117 2 E
Qinghua Univ., *Beij.* **14 A2** 40 0N 116 17 E
Qinghuayuan, *Beij.* **14 B2** 39 59N 116 19 E
Qingningsi, *Shang.* **14 J12** 31 16N 121 33 E
Qolhak, *Tehr.* **17 C5** 35 45N 51 26 E
Quadraro, *Rome* **9 F10** 41 51N 12 33 E
Quaid-i-Azam, *Kar.* **17 G10** 24 50N 66 59 E
Qual'eh Murgeh Airport, *Tehr.* **17 D5** 35 38N 51 22 E
Qualiano, *Nápl.* **9 H11** 40 55N 14 9 E
Quannapowitt, L., *Bost.* **21 B3** 42 30N 71 4W
Quartiere Zingone, *Mil.* **9 E5** 45 25N 9 3 E
Quarto, *Nápl.* **9 H11** 40 52N 14 8 E
Quds, *Bagd.* **17 E8** 33 23N 44 24 E
Quebrada Baruta →, *Car.* **30 E5** 10 29N 66 53W
Quebrada Tácagua →, *Car.* **30 D4** 10 36N 67 1W
Quebrada Topo →, *Car.* **30 D4** 10 32N 67 0W
Queen Mary Res., *Lon.* **4 C2** 51 24N 0 27W
Queens Village, *N.Y.* **23 C6** 40 43N 73 44W
Queensbury, *Lon.* **4 B3** 51 35N 0 16W
Queenscliffe, *Syd.* **19 A4** 33 47 S 151 17 E
Queenstown, *Sing.* **15 G7** 1 18N 103 48 E
Quellerina, *Jobg.* **18 E8** 26 9 S 27 56 E
Queluz, *Lisb.* **8 F7** 38 45N 9 14W
Quezon City, *Manila* **15 D4** 14 37N 121 2 E
Quickborn, *Hbg.* **7 C7** 53 43N 9 54 E
Quilicura, *Stgo* **30 J10** 33 22 S 70 43W
Quilmes, *B.A.* **32 C5** 34 43 S 58 15W
Quincy, *Bost.* **21 D3** 42 14N 71 0W
Quincy B., *Bost.* **21 D4** 42 16N 70 59W
Quincy-sous-Sénart, *Paris* **5 C5** 48 40N 2 32 E
Quinta Normal, *Stgo* **30 J10** 33 26 S 70 40W
Quinto Romano, *Mil.* **9 E5** 45 28N 9 7 E
Quirinale, *Rome* **9 F9** 41 53N 12 29 E
Quitaúna, *S. Pau.* **31 E5** 23 31 S 46 48W

R

Raasdorf, *Wien* **10 G11** 48 14N 16 33 E
Raccoon Cr. →, *Phil.* **24 C3** 39 48N 75 21W
Raccoon Str., *S.F.* **27 A2** 37 52N 122 26W
Radevormwald, *Ruhr* **6 C6** 51 12N 7 22 E
Radlett, *Lon.* **4 A3** 51 41N 0 19W
Radlice, *Pra.* **10 B2** 50 3N 14 23 E
Radnor, *Phil.* **24 A2** 40 2N 75 21W
Radonice, *Pra.* **10 B3** 50 8N 14 36 E
Radotin, *Pra.* **10 C2** 49 59N 14 21 E
Rælingen, *Oslo* **2 B6** 59 53N 11 5 E
Rafael Calzada, *B.A.* **32 C4** 34 47 S 58 21W
Rafael Castillo, *B.A.* **32 C3** 34 42 S 58 36W
Raffles Park, *Sing.* **15 G7** 1 19N 103 48 E
Raghunathpur, *Calc.* **16 D5** 22 41N 88 16 E
Rahlstedt, *Hbg.* **7 D8** 53 35N 10 7 E
Rahm, *Ruhr* **6 B2** 51 21N 6 47 E
Rahnsdorf, *Berl.* **7 B5** 52 25N 13 41 E
Rahway, *N.Y.* **22 D3** 40 36N 74 17W
Rail Tree Hill, *Bost.* **21 B1** 42 32N 71 22W
Rainbow Lakes, *N.Y.* **22 B2** 40 53N 74 27W
Rainham, *Lon.* **4 B6** 51 31N 0 11 E
Rainier, Mt., *Wash.* **25 D8** 38 56N 76 57W
Raj Bhawan, *Calc.* **16 E6** 22 33N 88 20 E
Rajakylä, *Hels.* **3 B5** 60 15N 25 5 E
Rajapur, *Calc.* **16 E5** 22 39N 88 11 E
Rajganj, *Calc.* **16 E5** 22 34N 88 14 E
Rajpur, *Delhi* **16 A2** 28 41N 77 12 E
Rákos-patak →, *Bud.* **10 K14** 47 29N 19 12 E
Rákoscsaba, *Bud.* **10 K14** 47 28N 19 17 E
Rákoshegy, *Bud.* **10 K14** 47 27N 19 14 E
Rákosker, *Bud.* **10 K14** 47 28N 19 14 E
Rákoskert, *Bud.* **10 K14** 47 27N 19 18 E
Rákosliget, *Bud.* **10 K14** 47 29N 19 16 E
Rákospalota, *Bud.* **10 J13** 47 34N 19 7 E
Rákosszentmihály, *Bud.* **10 J13** 47 31N 19 8 E
Raków, *Wsaw.* **10 E6** 52 11N 20 56 E
Rakowiec, *Wsaw.* **10 E6** 52 12N 20 58 E
Ramadān, *Bagd.* **17 F8** 33 19N 44 20 E
Ramanathpur, *Calc.* **16 D5** 22 41N 88 14 E
Rambler Channel, *H.K.* **12 D5** 22 21N 114 6 E
Ramblewood, *Phil.* **24 B5** 39 55N 74 56W
Ramenki, *Mos.* **11 E8** 55 41N 37 28 E
Ramersdorf, *Mün.* **7 G10** 48 6N 11 35 E
Ramnathpur, *Calc.* **16 E5** 22 35N 88 18 E
Ramos, *Rio J.* **31 B2** 22 50 S 43 14W
Ramos Mejia, *B.A.* **32 B3** 34 39 S 58 33W
Rampur, *Delhi* **16 A2** 28 44N 77 18 E
Ramsgate, *Syd.* **19 B3** 33 58 S 151 8 E
Ramstadjøen, *Oslo* **2 B6** 59 53N 11 3 E
Rancho Boyeros, *La Hab.* **30 C2** 22 59N 82 22W
Rancho Colorado, Presa de, *Méx.* **29 B2** 19 29N 99 16W
Rancocas Cr. →, *Phil.* **24 A5** 40 2N 74 58W
Rand Afrikaans Univ., *Jobg.* **18 F9** 26 11 S 28 0 E
Rand Airport, *Jobg.* **18 F9** 26 14 S 28 8 E
Randallstown, *Balt.* **25 A2** 39 21N 76 46W
Randburg, *Jobg.* **18 E8** 26 5 S 27 57 E
Randhart, *Jobg.* **18 F9** 26 16 S 28 7 E
Randolph, *Bost.* **21 D3** 42 10N 71 3W
Randolph Hills, *Wash.* **25 C7** 39 3N 77 6W
Randpark, *Jobg.* **18 E8** 26 6 S 27 58 E
Randwick, *Syd.* **19 B4** 33 54 S 151 14 E
Ranelagh, *B.A.* **32 C5** 34 47 S 58 14W
Rannersdorf, *Wien* **10 H10** 48 7N 16 27 E
Raparkrif, *Jobg.* **18 E8** 26 5 S 27 57 E
Raposo, *Lisb.* **8 F7** 38 40N 9 11W
Raritan →, *N.Y.* **22 D2** 40 30N 74 27W
Raritan B., *N.Y.* **22 E3** 40 29N 74 12W
Rasskazovka, *Mos.* **11 F8** 55 38N 37 20 E
Rasta, *Stock.* **3 E8** 59 18N 17 37 E
Rastaala, *Hels.* **3 B3** 60 15N 24 47 E
Rastila, *Hels.* **3 B5** 60 12N 25 7 E
Raszyn, *Wsaw.* **10 F6** 52 9N 20 54 E
Rat Burana, *Bangk.* **15 B2** 13 40N 100 30 E
Ratanpur, *Calc.* **16 D5** 22 49N 88 14 E
Rath, *Ruhr* **6 C2** 51 16N 6 49 E
Ratingen, *Ruhr* **6 C3** 51 18N 6 52 E
Rato, *Lisb.* **8 F8** 38 43N 9 8W
Rauxel, *Ruhr* **6 A5** 51 34N 7 18 E
Ravenswood Pt., *S.F.* **27 C4** 37 30N 122 8W
Rawamangun, *Jak.* **15 J10** 6 11 S 106 52 E
Rayners Lane, *Lon.* **4 B2** 51 34N 0 23W
Raynes Park, *Lon.* **4 C3** 51 24N 0 12W
Raypur, *Calc.* **16 F6** 22 28N 88 22 E
Razdory, *Mos.* **11 E7** 55 44N 37 17 E
Razmitelevo, *St-Pet.* **11 B5** 59 54N 30 39 E
Razor Hill, *H.K.* **12 D6** 22 20N 114 15 E
Reading, *Bost.* **21 B3** 42 31N 71 5W
Reading Highlands, *Bost.* **21 B3** 42 31N 71 5W
Reáglie, *Tori.* **9 B3** 45 3N 7 44 E
Real, Palacio, *Mdrd.* **8 B2** 40 25N 3 43W
Real Felipe, Castillo, *Lima* **30 G8** 12 4 S 77 9W
Real Fuerta, Château de la, *La Hab.* **30 B2** 23 8N 82 20W
Realengo, *Rio J.* **31 B1** 22 52 S 43 24W
Réau, *Paris* **5 D5** 48 36N 2 37 E
Recklinghausen, *Ruhr* **6 A5** 51 37N 7 12 E
Recklinghausen-Süd, *Ruhr* **6 A5** 51 34N 7 14 E
Recoleta, *Stgo* **30 J11** 33 25 S 70 40W
Reconquista →, *B.A.* **32 B3** 34 35 S 58 35W
Red Bank Battle Mon., *Phil.* **24 B3** 39 52N 75 11W
Red Fort, *Delhi* **16 B2** 28 39N 77 14 E
Red Rock, *S.F.* **27 A2** 37 55N 122 25W
Red Square, *Mos.* **11 E9** 55 45N 37 37 E
Redbridge, *Lon.* **4 B5** 51 34N 0 3 E
Redwood City, *S.F.* **27 D3** 37 29N 122 14W
Redwood Cr. →, *S.F.* **27 C3** 37 31N 122 11W
Redwood Pt., *S.F.* **27 C3** 37 32N 122 11W
Redwood Regional Park, *S.F.* **27 B4** 37 48N 122 8W
Reeves Hill, *Bost.* **21 C1** 42 20N 71 20W
Refshaleøen, *Købn.* **2 D10** 55 41N 12 36 E
Regents Park, *Jobg.* **18 F9** 26 14 S 28 3 E
Regents Park, *Lon.* **4 B4** 51 31N 0 9W
Regents Park, *Syd.* **19 B3** 33 52 S 151 1 E
Regi Lagni →, *Nápl.* **9 H13** 40 56N 14 23 E
Regina Margherita, *Tori.* **9 B2** 45 4N 7 34 E
Regla, *La Hab.* **30 B3** 23 7N 82 19W
Rego Park, *N.Y.* **23 C5** 40 43N 73 51W
Reiherstieg, *Hbg.* **7 D7** 53 30N 9 58 E
Reinickendorf, *Berl.* **7 A3** 52 34N 13 22 E
Reinoldikirche, *Ruhr* **6 A6** 51 30N 7 28 E
Reistad, *Oslo* **2 C1** 59 46N 10 16 E
Reitbrook, *Hbg.* **7 E8** 53 28N 10 8 E
Rekola, *Hels.* **3 B5** 60 19N 25 4 E
Rellingen, *Hbg.* **7 D7** 53 39N 9 50 E
Rembertów, *Wsaw.* **10 E7** 52 15N 21 9 E
Remedios de Escalada, *B.A.* **32 C4** 34 43 S 58 24W
Rémola, Laguna del, *Barc.* **8 E5** 41 16N 2 4 E
Remscheid, *Ruhr* **6 C5** 51 11N 7 11 E
Renca, *Stgo* **30 J10** 33 24 S 70 42W
Renca, Cerro, *Stgo* **30 J10** 33 23 S 70 40W
Rener, *Ist.* **17 A2** 41 1N 28 56 E
Renmin Gongyuan, *Tianj.* **14 E6** 39 6N 117 12 E
Rennemoulin, *Paris* **5 B2** 48 50N 2 2 E
Rennie's Mill, *H.K.* **12 E6** 22 18N 114 15 E
Renzel, *Hbg.* **7 C7** 53 43N 9 52 E
Repaupo, *Phil.* **24 C3** 39 48N 75 18W
Repaupo Cr. →, *Phil.* **24 C3** 39 49N 75 20W
Řeporyje, *Pra.* **10 B1** 50 1N 14 18 E
République, Place de la, *Paris* **5 B4** 48 52N 2 22 E
Repy, *Pra.* **10 B1** 50 4N 14 17 E
Resarö, *Stock.* **3 D13** 59 25N 18 20 E
Rescaldna, *Mil.* **9 D4** 45 36N 8 57 E
Research, *Melb.* **19 E8** 37 42 S 145 10 E
Reseda, *L.A.* **28 A1** 34 12N 118 31W
Reservoir, *Melb.* **19 E7** 37 42 S 145 1 E
Reservoir Pond, *Bost.* **21 D3** 42 10N 71 7W
Residenz, *Mün.* **7 G10** 48 8N 11 34 E
Resse, *Ruhr* **6 A4** 51 34N 7 6 E
Reston, *Wash.* **25 D6** 38 57N 77 20W
Retiro, *B.A.* **32 B4** 34 35 S 58 23W
Retiro, *Mdrd.* **8 B2** 40 24N 3 40W
Reutov, *Mos.* **11 E11** 55 45N 37 50 E
Réveillon →, *Paris* **5 C5** 48 42N 2 30 E
Revere, *Bost.* **21 C3** 42 25N 71 0W
Revesby, *Syd.* **19 B3** 33 57 S 151 0 E
Revolucion, Plaza de la, *La Hab.* **30 B2** 23 7N 82 23W
Rexdale, *Trto.* **20 D7** 43 43N 79 35W
Reynolds Channel, *N.Y.* **23 D6** 40 35N 73 41W
Reynosa Tamaulipas, *Méx.* **29 A2** 19 30N 99 10W
Rheem Valley, *S.F.* **27 A4** 37 50N 122 8W
Rhein-Herne Kanal, *Ruhr* **6 B3** 51 29N 6 59 E
Rheinberg, *Ruhr* **6 A1** 51 32N 6 37 E
Rheinhausen, *Ruhr* **6 B2** 51 24N 6 43 E
Rheinkamp, *Ruhr* **6 B1** 51 29N 6 36 E
Rho, *Mil.* **9 D5** 45 31N 9 2 E
Rhodes, *Syd.* **19 A3** 33 49 S 151 6 E
Rhodesfield, *Jobg.* **18 E10** 26 6 S 28 14 E
Rhodon, *Paris* **5 C2** 48 42N 2 3 E
Rhodon →, *Paris* **5 C2** 48 42N 2 4 E
Rhu, Tg., *Sing.* **15 G8** 1 17N 103 51 E
Ribeirão Pires, *S. Pau.* **31 F7** 23 42 S 46 23W
Říčanský →, *Pra.* **10 B3** 50 5N 14 36 E
Říčany, *Pra.* **10 C3** 49 59N 14 39 E
Ricarda, Laguna de la, *Barc.* **8 E5** 41 17N 2 6 E
Richardson B., *S.F.* **27 A2** 37 52N 122 29W
Richmond, *Lon.* **4 C3** 51 27N 0 17W
Richmond, *Melb.* **19 E7** 37 48 S 145 0 E
Richmond, *S.F.* **27 B2** 37 46N 122 27W
Richmond, *S.F.* **27 A2** 37 56N 122 21W
Richmond →, *N.Y.* **22 D3** 40 34N 74 11W
Richmond, Pt., *S.F.* **27 A2** 37 54N 122 23W
Richmond Hill, *N.Y.* **23 C5** 40 41N 73 51W
Richmond Hill, *Trto.* **20 C8** 43 51N 79 24W
Richmond Inner Harbour, *S.F.* **27 A2** 37 54N 122 20W
Richmond Park, *Lon.* **4 C3** 51 26N 0 16W
Richmond Valley, *N.Y.* **22 D3** 40 31N 74 13W
Richvale, *Trto.* **20 C8** 43 51N 79 26W
Rickers I., *N.Y.* **23 C5** 40 47N 73 53W
Rickmansworth, *Lon.* **4 B2** 51 38N 0 28W
Riddel Cr. →, *Melb.* **19 F8** 37 52 S 145 13 E
Riderwood, *Balt.* **25 A3** 39 24N 76 37W
Ridgefield, *N.Y.* **22 C4** 40 49N 74 0W
Ridgefield Park, *N.Y.* **22 B4** 40 52N 74 1W
Ridgewood, *N.Y.* **23 C5** 40 42N 73 53W
Ridley Cr. →, *Phil.* **24 B2** 39 51N 75 20W
Ridley Creek State Park, *Phil.* **24 B2** 39 57N 75 26W
Ridley Park, *Phil.* **24 B3** 39 52N 75 19W
Riedmoos, *Mün.* **7 F10** 48 16N 11 32 E
Riem, *Mün.* **7 G11** 48 8N 11 41 E
Riemke, *Ruhr* **6 A5** 51 30N 7 12 E
Rimac, *Lima* **30 G8** 12 2 S 77 2W
Rimau, Tg., *Sing.* **15 G7** 1 15N 103 48 E
Ringwood, *Melb.* **19 E8** 37 48 S 145 4 E
Rinkeby, *Stock.* **3 D10** 59 23N 17 55 E
Rio Comprido, *Rio J.* **31 B2** 22 55 S 43 12W
Rio de Janeiro, *Rio J.* **31 B2** 22 54 S 43 12W
Rio de Mouro, *Lisb.* **8 F7** 38 46N 9 15W
Rio Hondo →, *L.A.* **28 B4** 34 2N 118 15W
Rio Pequeno, *S. Pau.* **31 E5** 23 34 S 46 44W
Rione Trieste, *Nápl.* **9 H13** 40 52N 14 27 E
Ripley, *Lon.* **4 D2** 51 17N 0 29W
Rippling Ridge, *Balt.* **25 B3** 39 11N 76 37W
Ris, *Oslo* **2 B4** 59 56N 10 41 E
Ris-Orangis, *Paris* **5 D4** 48 38N 2 24 E
Risby, *Købn.* **2 D8** 55 41N 12 19 E
Rishra, *Calc.* **16 D6** 22 42N 88 20 E
Ritan Gongyuan, *Beij.* **14 B3** 39 53N 116 24 E
Ritchie, *Wash.* **25 D8** 38 52N 76 51W
Rithala, *Delhi* **16 A1** 28 43N 77 6 E
Ritorp, *Stock.* **3 E8** 59 12N 17 38 E
Rivalta di Torino, *Tori.* **9 B1** 45 2N 7 31 E
Rivas de Jarama, *Mdrd.* **8 B3** 40 22N 3 31W
Rivas-Vaciamadrio, *Mdrd.* **8 C3** 40 19N 3 30W
Rivasacco, *Tori.* **9 A1** 45 10N 7 29 E
Rive Sud, Canal de la, *Mtrl.* **20 B4** 43 24N 73 31W
River Edge, *N.Y.* **22 B4** 40 56N 74 1W
River Forest, *Chic.* **26 B2** 41 53N 87 49W
River Grove, *Chic.* **26 B1** 41 55N 87 50W
River Pines, *Bost.* **21 B2** 42 33N 71 [illegible]
River Vale, *N.Y.* **22 B4** 40 59N 74 [illegible]
Riverdale, *Chic.* **26 D3** 41 38N 87 3
Riverdale, *N.Y.* **22 B3** 40 59N 74 17W
Riverdale, *Trto.* **20 E8** 43 39N 79 21W
Riverdale, *Wash.* **25 D8** 38 57N 76 54W
Riverdale Park, *Trto.* **20 D8** 43 40N 79 21W
Riverhead, *Lon.* **4 D6** 51 16N 0 10 E
Riverlea, *Jobg.* **18 F8** 26 12 S 27 58 E
Riverside, *Bost.* **21 B2** 42 32N 71 18W
Riverside, *Chic.* **26 C2** 41 49N 87 49W
Riverside, *N.Y.* **23 B5** 40 54N 73 54W
Riverside, *N.Y.* **23 A7** 41 1N 73 34W
Riverside, *Phil.* **24 A5** 40 2N 74 57W
Riverton, *Phil.* **24 A4** 40 0N 75 0W
Riverwood, *Syd.* **19 B3** 33 57 S 151 3 E
Rivière-des-Praires, *Mtrl.* **20 A4** 43 38N 73 34W
Rivodora, *Tori.* **9 B3** 45 5N 7 47 E
Rivoli, *Tori.* **9 B1** 45 4N 7 30 E
Riyad, *Bagd.* **17 F8** 33 18N 44 27 E
Rizal, *Manila* **15 D4** 14 33N 121 0 E
Rizal Park, *Manila* **15 D3** 14 35N 120 58 E
Rizel Stadium, *Manila* **15 D3** 14 34N 120 59 E
Røa, *Oslo* **2 B3** 59 57N 10 39 E
Robassomero, *Tori.* **9 A2** 45 11N 7 34 E
Robbins, *Chic.* **26 D2** 41 38N 87 42W
Robert E. Lee Memorial Park, *Balt.* **25 A3** 39 23N 76 40 E
Robertsdale, *Chic.* **26 C3** 41 40N 87 30W
Robertsham, *Jobg.* **18 F9** 26 15 S 28 1 E
Robin Hills, *Jobg.* **18 E8** 26 6 S 27 58 E
Rocha Miranda, *Rio J.* **31 B1** 22 51 S 43 20W
Rochar →, *Sing.* **15 G8** 1 18N 103 52 E
Rochelle Park, *N.Y.* **22 B4** 40 54N 74 4W
Rock Cr. →, *Wash.* **25 D7** 38 54N 77 3W
Rock Creek Park, *Wash.* **25 D7** 38 56N 77 2W
Rockaway, *N.Y.* **22 D5** 40 32N 73 56W
Rockaway Beach, *S.F.* **27 C2** 37 36N 122 29W
Rockaway Islet, *N.Y.* **23 D5** 40 34N 73 53W
Rockaway Neck, *N.Y.* **22 B2** 40 51N 74 21W
Rockaway Point, *N.Y.* **23 D5** 40 33N 73 54W
Rockburn Branch →, *Balt.* **25 B2** 39 13N 76 43W
Rockdale, *Balt.* **25 A2** 39 21N 76 46W
Rockdale, *Syd.* **19 B3** 33 57 S 151 8 E
Rockland, *Phil.* **24 C1** 39 47N 75 34W
Rocklege, *Phil.* **24 A4** 40 4N 75 5W
Rockleigh, *N.Y.* **22 A5** 41 0N 73 55W
Rockville, *Wash.* **25 C6** 39 4N 77 10W
Rockville Centre, *N.Y.* **23 D7** 40 39N 73 38W
Rocky Hill, *Phil.* **24 B1** 39 58N 75 32W
Rocky Ridge, *S.F.* **27 B4** 37 47N 122 2W
Rocky Run →, *Wash.* **25 D6** 38 58N 77 14W
Rodaon, *Wien* **10 H9** 48 8N 16 16 E
Rodeo Cove, *S.F.* **27 B1** 37 49N 122 32W
Rodgers Forge, *Balt.* **25 A3** 39 22N 76 37W
Roding →, *Lon.* **4 B5** 51 30N 0 5 E
Rodość, *Wsaw.* **10 E8** 52 11N 21 11 E
Rødovre, *Købn.* **2 D9** 55 40N 12 26 E
Rodrigo de Freitas, L., *Rio J.* **31 B2** 22 58 S 43 12W
Rodstensfjärden, *Stock.* **3 E9** 59 16N 17 48 E
Roehampton, *Lon.* **4 C3** 51 27N 0 15W
Rogers Park, *Chic.* **26 A2** 42 0N 87 40W
Rohdenhaus, *Ruhr* **6 C4** 51 18N 7 0 E
Röhlinghausen, *Ruhr* **6 A4** 51 30N 7 9 E
Roihuvuori, *Hels.* **3 B5** 60 11N 25 2 E
Roissy, *Paris* **5 C5** 48 47N 2 39 E
Roissy-en-France, *Paris* **5 A5** 49 0N 2 30 E
Rokkō Sanchi, *Ōsaka* **12 B2** 34 44N 135 13 E
Rokko-Zan, *Ōsaka* **12 B2** 34 46N 135 16 E
Rokytka →, *Pra.* **10 B3** 50 6N 14 27 E
Roland Lake, *Balt.* **25 A3** 39 23N 76 38W
Roland Park, *Balt.* **25 A3** 39 20N 76 39W
Roma, *Rome* **9 F9** 41 54N 12 28 E
Római-Fürdö, *Bud.* **10 J13** 47 34N 19 4 E
Romainville, *Paris* **5 B4** 48 52N 2 26 E
Romani, *Nápl.* **9 H13** 40 52N 14 22 E
Romano Banco, *Mil.* **9 E5** 45 25N 9 6 E
Romashkovo, *Mos.* **11 E7** 55 43N 37 19 E
Rome = Roma, *Rome* **9 F9** 41 54N 12 28 E
Romford, *Lon.* **4 B6** 51 34N 0 11 E
Roncáglia, *Tori.* **9 B1** 45 2N 7 29 E
Rönninge, *Stock.* **3 E9** 59 12N 17 45 E
Ronsdorf, *Ruhr* **6 C5** 51 13N 7 11 E
Ronskensiedig, *Ruhr* **6 A2** 51 36N 6 41 E
Rontgental, *Berl.* **7 A4** 52 38N 13 31 E
Roodekop, *Jobg.* **18 F10** 26 17 S 28 11 E
Roodepoort, *Jobg.* **18 E8** 26 9 S 27 53 E
Roodepoort-Wes, *Jobg.* **18 E8** 26 8 S 27 51 E
Roosevelt, *N.Y.* **23 C7** 40 40N 73 35W
Rooty Hill, *Syd.* **19 A2** 33 46 S 150 50 E
Roppongi, *Tōkyō* **13 C3** 35 39N 139 44 E
Rosairinho, *Lisb.* **8 F8** 38 40N 9 0W
Rosanna, *Melb.* **19 E7** 37 44 S 145 4 E
Rosario, *La Hab.* **30 B2** 23 3N 82 21W
Rosario, *Manila* **15 D4** 14 35N 121 4 E
Rose B., *Syd.* **19 B4** 33 51 S 151 16 E
Rose Hill, *Wash.* **25 E7** 38 47N 77 6W
Rose Tree, *Phil.* **24 B2** 39 56N 75 23W
Rosebank, *N.Y.* **22 D4** 40 36N 74 4W
Rosebery, *Syd.* **19 B4** 33 55 S 151 12 E
Rosedal La Candelaria, *Méx.* **29 B3** 19 20N 99 10W
Rosedale, *Balt.* **25 B3** 39 19N 76 31W
Rosedale, *N.Y.* **23 D6** 40 39N 73 43W
Roseiras, *S. Pau.* **31 E7** 23 33 S 46 23W
Roseland, *Chic.* **26 C3** 41 42N 87 37W
Roseland, *N.Y.* **22 C3** 40 49N 74 17W
Roselle, *N.Y.* **22 D3** 40 39N 74 15W
Roselle Park, *N.Y.* **22 D3** 40 39N 74 16W
Rosemead, *L.A.* **28 B4** 34 4N 118 4W
Rosemere, *Mtrl.* **20 A2** 43 34N 73 50W
Rosemont, *Chic.* **26 B1** 41 59N 87 52W
Rosemont, *Phil.* **24 A3** 40 1N 75 19W
Rosenborg Have, *Købn.* **2 D10** 55 41N 12 33 E
Rosengarten, *Hbg.* **7 D6** 53 31N 9 49 E
Rosenthal, *Berl.* **7 A3** 52 35N 13 22 E
Rosettenville, *Jobg.* **18 F9** 26 15 S 28 3 E
Rosherville Dam, *Jobg.* **18 F9** 26 13 S 28 6 E
Rósio, *Mil.* **9 E4** 45 25N 8 57 E
Rösjön, *Stock.* **3 D11** 59 26N 18 0 E
Roskilde, *Købn.* **2 E7** 55 38N 12 5 E
Roskilde Fjord, *Købn.* **2 D7** 55 45N 12 4 E
Roslags-Näsby, *Stock.* **3 D11** 59 25N 18 2 E
Roslindale, *Bost.* **21 D3** 42 17N 71 7W
Roslyn, *N.Y.* **23 C7** 40 47N 73 38W
Roslyn, *Phil.* **24 A4** 40 7N 75 8W
Roslyn Estates, *N.Y.* **23 C6** 40 47N 73 40W
Roslyn Harbour, *N.Y.* **23 C7** 40 48N 73 38W
Rosne →, *Paris* **5 B4** 48 58N 2 25 E
Rosny-sous-Bois, *Paris* **5 B5** 48 52N 2 30 E
Ross, *S.F.* **27 A1** 37 57N 122 33W
Rosslyn, *Wash.* **25 D7** 38 53N 77 4W
Rossville, *Balt.* **25 A4** 39 20N 76 28W
Rossville, *N.Y.* **22 D3** 40 32N 74 12W
Rosta, *Tori.* **9 B1** 45 4N 7 27 E
Rotbach →, *Ruhr* **6 A2** 51 34N 6 41 E
Rothenburgsort, *Hbg.* **7 D8** 53 32N 10 2 E
Rotherbaum, *Hbg.* **7 D7** 53 33N 9 58 E
Rotherhithe, *Lon.* **4 C4** 51 29N 0 2W
Rothneusiedl, *Wien* **10 H10** 48 8N 16 23 E
Rothschmaige, *Mün.* **7 F9** 48 14N 11 27 E
Rouge →, *Trto.* **20 D9** 43 47N 79 12W
Rouge Hill, *Trto.* **20 D10** 43 48N 79 6W
Round I., *H.K.* **12 E6** 22 13N 114 11 E
Roundshaw, *Lon.* **4 C4** 51 20N 0 7W
Roussigny, *Paris* **5 D2** 48 38N 2 6 E
Rowland, *L.A.* **28 B5** 34 0N 117 55W
Rowley, *Bost.* **21 A4** 42 43N 70 52W
Rowville, *Melb.* **19 F8** 37 55 S 145 14 E
Roxboro, *Mtrl.* **20 A3** 43 30N 73 48W
Roxborough, *Phil.* **24 A3** 40 1N 75 13W
Roxbury, *Bost.* **21 D3** 42 19N 71 5W
Roxbury, *N.Y.* **23 D5** 40 33N 73 53W
Roxeth, *Lon.* **4 B2** 51 33N 0 20W
Royal Observatory, *H.K.* **12 E6** 22 18N 114 10 E
Royal Park, *Melb.* **19 E6** 37 46 S 144 57 E
Röylä, *Hels.* **3 B3** 60 18N 24 42 E
Royston Park, *Lon.* **4 B2** 51 36N 0 22W
Rozas, Portilleros de las, *Mdrd.* **8 B2** 40 29N 3 49W
Roztoky, *Pra.* **10 B2** 50 9N 14 23 E
Rubbianetta, *Tori.* **9 B2** 45 9N 7 34 E
Rubi →, *Barc.* **8 D5** 41 26N 2 0 E
Rubio Woods, *Chic.* **26 D2** 41 38N 87 45W
Rublovo, *Mos.* **11 E8** 55 47N 37 21 E
Ruchyi, *St-Pet.* **11 A4** 60 0N 30 25 E
Rud, *Oslo* **2 B6** 59 56N 11 0 E
Rüdinghausen, *Ruhr* **6 B6** 51 26N 7 22 E
Rudnevka →, *Mos.* **11 E11** 55 43N 37 56 E
Rudolfsheim, *Wien* **10 G10** 48 12N 16 20 E
Rudolfshöhe, *Berl.* **7 A5** 52 37N 13 44 E
Rudow, *Berl.* **7 B3** 52 24N 13 29 E
Rueil-Malmaison, *Paris* **5 B3** 48 52N 2 11 E
Ruffys Cr. →, *Melb.* **19 E7** 37 45 S 145 7 E
Ruggeberg, *Ruhr* **6 C6** 51 16N 7 23 E
Ruhlsdorf, *Berl.* **7 B2** 52 22N 13 15 E
Ruhr →, *Ruhr* **6 B3** 51 27N 6 56 E
Ruhrort, *Ruhr* **6 B2** 51 27N 6 44 E
Ruislip, *Lon.* **4 B2** 51 34N 0 24W
Rumelihisari, *Ist.* **17 A3** 41 4N 29 2 E
Rumeln, *Ruhr* **6 B1** 51 24N 6 39 E
Rumyantsevo, *Mos.* **11 F8** 55 38N 37 25 E
Rungis, *Paris* **5 C4** 48 44N 2 20 E
Runnemede, *Phil.* **24 B4** 39 50N 75 4W
Ruotsinkylä, *Hels.* **3 A4** 60 21N 24 57 E
Rusāfa, *Bagd.* **17 E8** 33 21N 44 23 E
Rush Green, *Lon.* **4 B6** 51 33N 0 10 E
Russa, *Calc.* **16 F6** 22 29N 88 21 E
Russell Lea, *Syd.* **19 B4** 33 52 S 151 10 E
Rustad, *Oslo* **2 B2** 59 56N 10 24 E
Rustenfeld, *Wien* **10 H10** 48 7N 16 23 E
Rusville, *Jobg.* **18 E10** 26 9 S 28 18 E
Rutherford, *N.Y.* **22 C4** 40 49N 74 6W
Rüttenscheid, *Ruhr* **6 B3** 51 25N 6 58 E
Ruxton, *Balt.* **25 A3** 39 23N 76 38W
Ruzyně, *Pra.* **10 B1** 50 5N 14 17 E
Rybatskaya, *St-Pet.* **11 B4** 59 59N 30 29 E
Rybatskoye, *St-Pet.* **11 B4** 59 50N 30 29 E
Rydalmere, *Syd.* **19 A3** 33 48 S 151 2 E
Rydboholm, *Stock.* **3 D12** 59 26N 18 12 E
Ryde, *Syd.* **19 A3** 33 48 S 151 6 E
Rye, *N.Y.* **23 B6** 40 58N 73 40W
Rynfield, *Jobg.* **18 E10** 26 9 S 28 19 E
Ryogoku, *Tōkyō* **13 B3** 35 40N 139 48 E
Rysäkari, *Hels.* **3 C4** 60 6N 24 50 E
Rzhevka, *St-Pet.* **11 B5** 59 59N 30 31 E

Serangoon Garden 45

S

Saadōn, Bagd. 17 F8 33 19N 44 25 E
Saarn, Ruhr 6 B3 51 24N 6 51 E
Saavedra, B.A. 32 B4 34 33 S 58 29W
Saboli, Delhi 16 A2 28 42N 77 18 E
Sabugo, Lisb. 8 F7 38 49N 9 17W
Saburovo, Mos. 11 D7 55 53N 37 15 E
Säbysjön, Stock. 3 D10 59 26N 17 52 E
Sabzi Mandi, Delhi 16 A2 28 40N 77 12 E
Sacavém, Lisb. 8 F8 38 47N 9 5W
Saclay, Paris 5 C3 48 43N 2 10 E
Saclay, Étang de, Paris 5 C2 48 44N 2 9 E
Sacoma, S. Pau. 31 E6 23 36 S 46 35W
Sacré-Coeur, Paris 5 B4 48 53N 2 20 E
Sacrow, Berl. 7 B1 52 25N 13 6 E
Sacrower See, Berl. 7 B1 52 26N 13 6 E
Sadang, Sŏul 12 H7 37 29N 126 58 E
Sadar Bazar, Delhi 16 B2 28 39N 77 11 E
Saddām City, Bagd. 17 E8 33 23N 44 27 E
Saddle Brook, N.Y. 22 B4 40 53N 74 5W
Saddle River, N.Y. 22 A4 41 1N 74 6W
Saddle Rock, N.Y. 23 C6 40 47N 73 45W
Sadr, Kar. 17 G11 24 51N 67 2 E
Sadyba, Wsaw. 10 E7 52 11N 21 3 E
Saedo, Tōkyō 13 C2 35 30N 139 33 E
Saensaep, Khlong →, Bangk. 15 B2 13 44N 100 32 E
Sáenz Pena, B.A. 32 B3 34 37 S 58 32W
Safdar Jang Airport, Delhi 16 B2 28 35N 77 12 E
Safdar Jangs Tomb, Delhi 16 B2 28 35N 77 12 E
Safraköy, Ist. 17 A1 41 0N 28 48 E
Saft el Laban, El Qâ. 18 C5 30 1N 31 10 E
Sag Bridge, Chic. 26 C1 41 41N 87 55W
Sagamore Neck, N.Y. 23 B8 40 53N 73 29W
Saganashkee Slough, Chic. 26 C1 41 41N 87 53W
Sagene, Oslo 2 B4 59 55N 10 46 E
Sagrada Família, Temple de, Barc. 8 D6 41 24N 2 10 E
Sahapur, Calc. 16 E5 22 31N 88 11 E
Sahibabad, Delhi 16 A1 28 45N 77 4 E
Sai Kung, H.K. 12 D6 22 22N 114 16 E
Sai Wan Ho, H.K. 12 E6 22 17N 114 12 E
Sai Ying Pun, H.K. 12 E5 22 17N 114 8 E
Saido, Tōkyō 13 A2 35 52N 139 39 E
Sailmouille →, Paris 5 D3 48 37N 2 17 E
St. Albans, N.Y. 23 C6 40 42N 73 44W
St. Andrä, Wien 10 G9 48 19N 16 12 E
St. Andrews, Jobg. 18 E9 26 9 S 28 7 E
St. Aubin, Paris 5 C2 48 44N 2 8 E
St. Augustin, Mtrl. 20 A2 43 37N 73 58W
St. Basil's Cathedral, Mos. 11 E9 55 45N 37 38 E
St.-Benoit, Paris 5 C1 48 40N 1 54 E
St.-Brice-sous-Forêt, Paris 5 A4 49 0N 2 21 E
St.-Cloud, Paris 5 B3 48 50N 2 12 E
St.-Cyr-l'École, Paris 5 C2 48 47N 2 4 E
St.-Cyr-l'École, Aérodrome de, Paris 5 C2 48 48N 2 4 E
St. Davids, Phil. 24 A2 40 2N 75 23W
St.-Denis, Paris 5 B4 48 56N 2 20 E
St. Eustache, Mtrl. 20 A2 43 33N 73 54W
St.-Forget, Paris 5 C2 48 42N 2 0 E
St. Georg, Hbg. 7 D8 53 33N 10 1 E
St.-Germain, Forêt de, Paris 5 B2 48 57N 2 5 E
St. Germain-en-Laye, Paris 5 B2 48 53N 2 4 E
St.-Germain-lès-Corbeil, Paris 5 D4 48 37N 2 29 E
St.-Gratien, Paris 5 B3 48 58N 2 17 E
St. Helier, Lon. 4 C3 51 23N 0 11W
St.-Hubert, Mtrl. 20 B5 43 29N 73 25W
St. Isaac's Cathedral, St-Pet. 11 B3 59 55N 30 19 E
St. Jacques →, Mtrl. 20 B5 43 26N 73 29W
St.-Jean-de-Beauregard, Paris 5 D3 48 39N 2 10 E
St.-Jean-de-dieu, Mtrl. 20 A4 43 34N 73 31W
St. Joseph-du-Lac, Mtrl. 20 A1 43 32N 74 0W
St. Katherine's Dock, Lon. 4 B4 51 30N 0 5W
St. Kilda, Melb. 19 F6 37 51 S 144 58 E
St. Lambert, Mtrl. 20 A5 43 30N 73 29W
St.-Lambert, Paris 5 C2 48 43N 2 1 E
St.-Laurent, Mtrl. 20 A3 43 30N 73 43W
St. Lawrence, Mtrl. 20 A5 43 26N 73 29W
St.-Lazare, Gare, Paris 5 B4 48 52N 2 19 E
St.-Léonard, Mtrl. 20 A4 43 35N 73 34W
St. Leonards, Syd. 19 A4 33 50 S 151 12 E
St.-Leu-la-Forêt, Paris 5 A3 49 1N 2 14 E
St.-Louis, L., Mtrl. 20 B3 43 24N 73 48W
St. Magelungen, Stock. 3 E11 59 13N 18 4 E
St.-Mandé, Paris 5 B4 48 50N 2 24 E
St.-Mard, Paris 5 A6 49 2N 2 41 E
St.-Martin, Mtrl. 20 A3 43 33N 73 45W
St.-Martin, Bois, Paris 5 C5 48 48N 2 35 E
St. Mary Cray, Lon. 4 C5 51 23N 0 7 E
St.-Maur-des-Fossés, Paris 5 C4 48 48N 2 29 E
St.-Maurice, Paris 5 C4 48 49N 2 24 E
St.-Mesmes, Paris 5 B6 48 59N 2 41 E
St. Michaeliskirche, Hbg. 7 D7 53 32N 9 59 E
St. Michael's, Sing. 15 G8 1 19N 103 51 E
St.-Michel, Mtrl. 20 A4 43 34N 73 37W
St.-Michel-sur-Orge, Paris 5 D3 48 38N 2 18 E
St. Nikolaus-Kirken, Pra. 10 B2 50 5N 14 23 E
St.-Nom-la-Bretèche, Paris 5 B2 48 51N 2 1 E
St.-Ouen, Paris 5 B4 48 56N 2 20 E
St.-Ouen-l'Aumône, Paris 5 A2 49 2N 2 6 E
St. Pauli, Hbg. 7 D7 53 33N 9 57 E
St. Pauls Cathedral, Lon. 4 B4 51 30N 0 5W
St. Paul's Cray, Lon. 4 C5 51 23N 0 6 E
St. Petersburg, St-Pet. 11 B3 59 55N 30 15 E
St.-Pierre, Mtrl. 20 B4 43 27N 73 38W
St. Prix, Paris 5 A3 49 0N 2 15 E
St.-Quentin, Étang de, Paris 5 C2 48 47N 2 0 E
St. Quentin-en-Yvelines, Paris 5 C1 48 46N 1 57 E
St.-Rémy-lès-Chevreuse, Paris 5 C2 48 42N 2 4 E
St.-Thibault-des-Vignes, Paris 5 B6 48 52N 2 41 E
St. Veit, Wien 10 G9 48 11N 16 16 E
St.-Vincent-de-Paul, Mtrl. 20 A4 43 36N 73 39W
Ste.-Anne-de-Bellevue, Mtrl. 20 B2 43 24N 73 55W
Ste.-Catherine, Mtrl. 20 B4 43 25N 73 34W
Ste.-Dorothée, Mtrl. 20 A3 43 31N 73 48W
Ste.-Gemme, Paris 5 B1 48 52N 1 59 E
Ste.-Geneviève, Mtrl. 20 B2 43 28N 73 51W
Ste.-Geneviève-des-Bois, Paris 5 D3 48 38N 2 19 E
Ste.-Hélène, Î., Mtrl. 20 A4 43 31N 73 32W
Ste. Marthe-sur-le-Lac, Mtrl. 20 A2 43 31N 73 56W
Ste.-Rose, Mtrl. 20 A3 43 37N 73 46W
Ste. Thérèse, Mtrl. 20 A3 43 38N 73 49W
Ste. Thérèse-Ouest, Mtrl. 20 A2 43 36N 73 50W
Saiwai, Tōkyō 13 C3 35 32N 139 41 E
Sakai, Ōsaka 12 C3 34 34N 135 27 E
Sakai →, Tōkyō 13 D1 35 27N 139 29 E
Sakai Harbour, Ōsaka 12 C3 34 36N 135 26 E
Sakanoshita, Tōkyō 13 B2 35 48N 139 30 E
Sakra, P., Sing. 15 G7 1 15N 103 41 E
Sakuragi, Tōkyō 13 D2 35 28N 139 38 E
Salam, Bagd. 17 E8 33 20N 44 20 E
Salaryevo, Mos. 11 F8 55 37N 37 25 E
Salem, Bost. 21 B4 42 30N 70 54W
Salem, Stock. 3 E9 59 13N 17 46 E
Salem Harbor, Bost. 21 B4 42 30N 70 52W
Salem Maritime Nat. Hist. Site, Bost. 21 B4 42 31N 70 52W
Salemstaden, Stock. 3 E9 59 13N 17 46 E
Salkhia, Calc. 16 E6 22 36N 88 21 E
Salmannsdorf, Wien 10 G9 48 14N 16 14 E
Salmdorf, Mün. 7 G11 48 7N 11 43 E
Salmedina, Mdrd. 8 C3 40 18N 3 35W
Salomea, Wsaw. 10 E6 52 11N 20 55 E
Salsette I., Bomb. 16 G8 19 2N 72 53 E
Salt Cr. →, Chic. 26 C1 41 51N 87 54W
Salt Cr. →, Melb. 19 E7 37 45 S 145 4 E
Salt Water L., Calc. 16 E6 22 33N 88 26 E
Saltholm, Købn. 2 E11 55 38N 12 46 E
Saltsjö-Duvnäs, Stock. 3 E12 59 18N 18 12 E
Saltsjöbaden, Stock. 3 E12 59 16N 18 18 E
Saltykovka, Mos. 11 E11 55 45N 37 54 E
Salvatorkirche, Ruhr 6 B2 51 26N 6 45 E
Sam Sen, Khlong →, Bangk. 15 B2 13 45N 100 33 E
Samatya, Ist. 17 B2 40 59N 28 55 E
Samoueo, Lisb. 8 F8 38 43N 8 59W
Sampaloc, Manila 15 D3 14 36N 120 59 E
Samphanthawong, Bangk. 15 B2 13 44N 100 31 E
Samrong, Bangk. 15 C2 13 39N 100 35 E
Samseon, Sŏul 12 G8 37 34N 127 0 E
San Agustin, Lima 30 G8 12 1 S 77 9W
San Agustin Atlapulco, Méx. 29 B4 19 23N 89 57 E
San Andreas Fault, S.F. 27 D3 37 27N 122 18W
San Andreas L., S.F. 27 C2 37 35N 122 25W
San Andrés, B.A. 32 B3 34 34 S 58 33W
San Andrés, Barc. 8 D6 41 26N 2 11 E
San Andrés Ahuayucan, Méx. 29 C3 19 13N 99 7W
San Andrés Atenco, Méx. 29 A2 19 32N 99 13W
San Andrés Totoltepec, Méx. 29 C2 19 15N 99 10W
San Andrián de Besós, Barc. 8 D6 41 25N 2 13 E
San Angel, Méx. 29 B2 19 20N 99 11W
San Antonia, Manila 15 E3 14 29N 120 53 E
San Antonio de Padua, B.A. 32 C2 34 40 S 58 42W
San Augustin Ohtenco, Méx. 29 C3 19 12N 99 0W
San Bartolo Ameyalco, Méx. 29 C2 19 19N 99 16W
San Bartolomé Coatepec, Méx. 29 B2 19 23N 99 18W
San Basilio, Rome 9 F10 41 56N 12 35 E
San Bóvio, Mil. 9 E6 45 27N 9 18 E
San Bruno, S.F. 27 C2 37 36N 122 24W
San Bruno, Pt., S.F. 27 B2 37 39N 122 22W
San Bruno Mt., S.F. 27 B2 37 41N 122 26W
San Carlos, S.F. 27 C3 37 30N 122 16W
San Carlos de la Cabana, Forteresse, La Hab. 30 B2 23 8N 82 20W
San Clemente del Llobregat, Barc. 8 E4 41 19N 1 59 E
San Cristobal, Mdrd. 8 B3 40 25N 3 35W
San Cristobal, Cerro, Stgo 30 J11 33 25 S 70 38W
San Cristoforo, Mil. 9 E5 45 26N 9 9 E
San Donato Milanese, Mil. 9 E6 45 24N 9 16 E
San Felice, Tori. 9 B3 45 1N 7 46 E
San Feliu de Llobregat, Barc. 8 D5 41 22N 2 2 E
San Fernando, B.A. 32 A3 34 26 S 58 32W
San Fernando, L.A. 28 A2 34 17N 118 26W
San Fernando Airport, L.A. 28 A2 34 17N 118 25W
San Fernando de Henares, Mdrd. 8 B3 40 25N 3 31W
San Fernando Valley, L.A. 28 A1 34 12N 118 31W
San Francisco, S.F. 27 B2 37 46N 122 23W
San Francisco, Univ. of, S.F. 27 B2 37 47N 122 27W
San Francisco B., S.F. 27 C3 37 39N 122 14W
San Francisco Chimalpa, Méx. 29 B1 19 26N 99 20W
San Francisco Culhuacán, Méx. 29 C3 19 19N 99 8W
San Francisco de Paula, La Hab. 30 B3 23 3N 82 17W
San Francisco Int. Airport, S.F. 27 C2 37 37N 122 22W
San Francisco Solano, B.A. 32 C5 34 46 S 58 19W
San Francisco State Univ., S.F. 27 B2 37 43N 122 28W
San Francisco Tecoxpa, Méx. 29 C3 19 12N 99 0W
San Francisco Tlalnepantla, Méx. 29 C3 19 12N 99 8W
San Fruttuoso, Mil. 9 D6 45 34N 9 14 E
San Gabriel, L.A. 28 B4 34 5N 118 5W
San Gabriel →, L.A. 28 C4 33 53N 118 6W
San Gabriel Pk., L.A. 28 A4 34 14N 118 5W
San Giacomo, Tori. 9 A2 45 11N 7 36 E
San Gillio, Tori. 9 B2 45 8N 7 32 E
San Giórgio a Crem, Nápl. 9 J13 40 50N 14 20 E
San Giovanni a Teduccio, Nápl. 9 J12 40 49N 14 18 E
San Giuseppe Vesuviano, Nápl. 9 H13 40 50N 14 29 E
San Gregorio Atlapulco, Méx. 29 C3 19 15N 99 4W
San Isidro, B.A. 32 A3 34 28 S 58 30W
San Isidro, Lima 30 G8 12 5 S 77 2W
San Isidro, Manila 15 D4 14 38N 121 5 E
San Jerónimo Lidice, Méx. 29 C2 19 19N 99 14W
San Jerónimo Miacatlán, Méx. 29 C4 19 12N 98 59W
San Jorge, Castelo de, Lisb. 8 F8 38 42N 9 8W
San Jose Del Alamo, La Hab. 30 B3 23 6N 82 17W
San José Rio Hondo, Méx. 29 B2 19 26N 99 14W
San Juan →, Manila 15 D4 14 35N 121 0 E
San Juan de Aragón, Méx. 29 B3 19 28N 99 4W
San Juan de Aragón, Parque, Méx. 29 B3 19 27N 99 4W
San Juan de Lurigancho, Lima 30 F8 11 59 S 77 0W
San Juan de Miraflores, Lima 30 H9 12 10 S 76 58W
San Juan del Monte, Manila 15 D4 14 36N 121 1 E
San Juan Ixtacala, Méx. 29 A2 19 31N 99 10W
San Juan Ixtayopan, Méx. 29 C4 19 14N 98 59W
San Juan Toltotepec, Méx. 29 B2 19 28N 99 15W
San Juan y San Pedro Tezompa, Méx. 29 C4 19 12N 98 57W
San Just Desvern, Barc. 8 D5 41 22N 2 4 E
San Justo, B.A. 32 C3 34 40 S 58 33W
San Leandro, S.F. 27 B4 37 43N 122 9W
San Leandro B., S.F. 27 B3 37 45N 122 13W
San Leandro Cr. →, S.F. 27 B3 37 44N 122 12W
San Lorenzo, Mil. 9 D4 45 34N 8 57 E
San Lorenzo, S.F. 27 B4 37 41N 122 6W
San Lorenzo →, Méx. 29 B2 19 28N 99 17W
San Lorenzo, I., Lima 30 G7 12 6 S 77 12W
San Lorenzo Acopilco, Méx. 29 C1 19 19N 99 20 E
San Lorenzo Chimalco, Méx. 29 B4 19 24N 89 58 E
San Lorenzo Tezonco, Méx. 29 C3 19 19N 99 3W
San Lorenzo Tlacoyucan, Méx. 29 C3 19 10N 99 2W
San Lucas Xochimanca, Méx. 29 C3 19 15N 99 6W
San Luis, Lima 30 G8 12 4 S 77 0W
San Luis Tlaxialtemalco, Méx. 29 C3 19 16N 99 2W
San Marino, L.A. 28 B4 34 7N 118 5W
San Martin, Barc. 8 D6 41 24N 2 11 E
San Martin de Porras, Lima 30 G8 12 1 S 77 5W
San Martino, Tori. 9 B3 45 6N 7 47 E
San Mateo, S.F. 27 C3 37 33N 122 19W
San Mateo Cr. →, S.F. 27 C2 37 31N 122 22W
San Mateo Tecoloapan, Méx. 29 A2 19 35N 99 14W
San Mateo Xalpa, Méx. 29 C3 19 13N 99 8W
San Máuro Torinese, Tori. 9 B3 45 6N 7 45 E
San Miguel, B.A. 32 B2 34 32 S 58 43W
San Miguel, Lima 30 G8 12 5 S 77 6W
San Miguel, Manila 15 D3 14 36N 120 59 E
San Miguel, Stgo 30 J11 33 29 S 70 39W
San Miguel Ajusco, Méx. 29 C2 19 13N 99 11W
San Miguel Xicalco, Méx. 29 C3 19 13N 99 9W
San Nicholas, Manila 15 D3 14 36N 120 57 E
San Nicola, Rome 9 F9 41 58N 12 21 E
San Nicolás Totolapan, Méx. 29 C2 19 16N 99 16W
San Nicolás Viejo, Méx. 29 A1 19 31N 99 21W
San Onófrio, Rome 9 F9 41 57N 12 25 E
San Pablo, Méx. 29 B4 19 25N 89 56 E
San Pablo, S.F. 27 A2 37 57N 122 20W
San Pablo, Pt., S.F. 27 A2 37 57N 122 25W
San Pablo Cr. →, S.F. 27 A2 37 58N 122 22W
San Pablo Ostotepec, Méx. 29 C3 19 11N 99 5W
San Pablo Res., S.F. 27 A3 37 55N 122 14W
San Pablo Ridge, S.F. 27 A3 37 55N 122 15W
San Pablo Str., S.F. 27 A2 37 58N 122 25W
San Pancrázio, Tori. 9 B2 45 6N 7 32 E
San Pedro, Méx. 29 B4 19 24N 89 55 E
San Pedro, Pt., S.F. 27 C1 37 35N 122 31W
San Pedro Actopan, Méx. 29 C3 19 12N 99 4W
San Pedro Martir, Barc. 8 D5 41 23N 2 6 E
San Pedro Martir, Méx. 29 C2 19 16N 99 10W
San Pedro Zacatenco, Méx. 29 A3 19 30N 99 6W
San Pietro, Rome 9 F9 41 53N 12 27 E
San Pietro, Tori. 9 B3 45 1N 7 45 E
San Pietro a Patierno, Nápl. 9 H12 40 53N 14 17 E
San Pietro all'Olmo, Mil. 9 E5 45 29N 9 0 E
San Po Kong, H.K. 12 D6 22 20N 114 11 E
San Quentin, S.F. 27 A2 37 56N 122 27W
San Rafael, S.F. 27 A1 37 58N 122 30W
San Rafael B., S.F. 27 A2 37 57N 122 28W
San Rafael Chamapa, Méx. 29 B2 19 27N 99 15W
San Rafael Hills, L.A. 28 A3 34 10N 118 12W
San Roque, Manila 15 D4 14 37N 121 5 E
San Salvador Cuauhtenco, Méx. 29 C3 19 11N 99 8W
San Salvador de la Punta, Forteresse, La Hab. 30 B2 23 8N 82 21W
San Sebastiano al Vesùvio, Nápl. 9 H13 40 50N 14 22 E
San Siro, Mil. 9 E5 45 28N 9 7 E
San Souci, Syd. 19 B3 33 59 S 151 8 E
San Telmo, B.A. 32 B4 34 37 S 58 23W
San Vicenc dels Horts, Barc. 8 D5 41 23N 2 0 E
San Vitaliano, Nápl. 9 H13 40 55N 14 28 E
San Vito, Mil. 9 E5 45 24N 9 0 E
San Vito, Nápl. 9 J13 40 49N 14 22 E
San Vito, Tori. 9 B3 45 2N 7 41 E
Sandbakken, Oslo 2 C5 59 49N 10 54 E
Sandermosen, Oslo 2 A4 60 0N 10 48 E
Sanderstead, Lon. 4 D4 51 19N 0 4W
Sandheide, Ruhr 6 C3 51 12N 6 56 E
Sandhurst, Jobg. 18 E9 26 6 S 28 3 E
Sandown, Jobg. 18 E9 26 5 S 28 4 E
Sandown Racecourse, Lon. 4 C2 51 22N 0 21W
Sandringham, Jobg. 18 E9 26 8 S 28 6 E
Sands Point, N.Y. 23 B6 40 50N 73 43W
Sandton, Jobg. 18 E9 26 5 S 28 4 E
Sandungen, Oslo 2 B2 59 52N 10 21 E
Sandvika, Oslo 2 B3 59 53N 10 32 E
Sandy Pond, Bost. 21 C2 42 26N 71 18W
Sånga, Stock. 3 D9 59 21N 17 42 E
Sangano, Tori. 9 B1 45 1N 7 26 E
Sangenjaya, Tōkyō 13 C2 35 37N 139 39 E
Sangley Pt., Manila 15 E3 14 29N 120 54 E
Sangone →, Tori. 9 B2 45 1N 7 32 E
Sangye, Sŏul 12 G8 37 38N 127 3 E
Sankrail, Calc. 16 E5 22 33N 88 13 E
Sanlihe, Beij. 14 B2 39 53N 116 18 E
Sanlintang, Shang. 14 K11 31 9N 121 29 E
Sannois, Paris 5 B3 48 58N 2 15 E
Sanpada, Bomb. 16 G9 19 3N 73 0 E
Sans, Barc. 8 D5 41 22N 2 7 E
Sant Ambrogio, Basilica di, Mil. 9 E6 45 27N 9 10 E
Sant Boi de Llobregat, Barc. 8 D5 41 20N 2 2 E
Sant Cugat, Barc. 8 D5 41 28N 2 5 E
Santa Ana, Manila 15 D4 14 34N 121 0 E
Santa Ana Tlacotenco, Méx. 29 C4 19 11N 98 58W
Santa Bárbara, Morro de, Rio J. 31 B1 22 56 S 43 26W
Santa Catalina, B.A. 32 C4 34 47 S 58 24W
Santa Cecilia Tepetlapa, Méx. 29 C3 19 13N 99 5W
Santa Clara, Méx. 29 A3 19 33N 99 3W
Santa Coloma de Cervelló, Barc. 8 D5 41 21N 2 0 E
Santa Coloma de Gramanet, Barc. 8 D6 41 27N 2 12 E
Santa Cruz, Bomb. 16 G7 19 4N 72 51 E
Santa Cruz →, La Hab. 30 B2 23 4N 82 29W
Santa Cruz, Ilhe de, Rio J. 31 B3 22 51 S 43 7W
Santa Cruz Alcapixca, Méx. 29 C3 19 14N 99 4W
Santa Cruz Ayotusco, Méx. 29 B1 19 22N 99 21W
Santa Cruz de Olorde, Barc. 8 D5 41 25N 2 3 E
Santa Cruz Int. Airport, Bomb. 16 G8 19 5N 72 51 E
Santa Cruz Meyehualco, Méx. 29 B3 19 20N 99 2W
Santa Elena, Manila 15 D4 14 38N 121 5 E
Santa Eligênia Consolação, S. Pau. 31 E6 23 32 S 46 38W
Santa Emilia, Stgo 30 J11 33 23 S 70 39W
Santa Eulalia, Barc. 8 D6 41 25N 2 10 E
Santa Fe, La Hab. 30 B2 23 4N 82 30W
Santa Fe Flood Control Basin, L.A. 28 B5 34 7N 117 57W
Santa Fe Springs, L.A. 28 C4 33 56N 118 3W
Santa Isabel Ixtapan, Méx. 29 A4 19 35N 89 57W
Santa Julia, Stgo 30 K11 33 30 S 70 35W
Santa Lucia, Nápl. 9 J12 40 49N 14 15 E
Santa Margherita, Tori. 9 B3 45 3N 7 43 E
Santa Maria Aztahuacán, Méx. 29 B3 19 21N 99 2W
Santa Maria del Rosario, La Hab. 30 B3 23 3N 82 15W
Santa Maria Tulpetlac, Méx. 29 A3 19 34N 99 3W
Santa Martha Acatitla, Méx. 29 B3 19 21N 99 2W
Santa Monica, Car. 30 E5 10 28N 66 53W
Santa Monica, L.A. 28 B2 34 1N 118 29W
Santa Monica B., L.A. 28 C1 33 58N 118 30W
Santa Monica Mt., L.A. 28 B2 34 6N 118 29W
Santa Rosa, Lima 30 F8 11 59 S 77 5W
Santa Rosa De Locobe, Stgo 30 J11 33 25 S 70 33W
Santa Rosa Xochiac, Méx. 29 C2 19 19N 99 17W
Santa Tereza, S. Pau. 31 F6 23 40 S 46 33W
Santa Ursula Xitla, Méx. 29 C2 19 16N 99 11W
Santa Ynez Canyon →, L.A. 28 B1 34 2N 118 33W
Santahamina, Hels. 3 C5 60 8N 25 2 E
Santana, S. Pau. 31 D6 23 29 S 46 36W
Sant'Anastasia, Nápl. 9 H13 40 51N 14 24 E
Sant'Ántimo, Nápl. 9 H12 40 56N 14 14 E
Santeny, Paris 5 C5 48 43N 2 34 E
Santiago, Stgo 30 J11 33 26 S 70 40W
Santiago Acahualtepec, Méx. 29 B3 19 20N 99 0W
Santiago de Las Vegas, La Hab. 30 C2 22 58N 82 22W
Santiago Tepalcatlalpan, Méx. 29 C3 19 14N 99 8W
Santiago Tepatlaxco, Méx. 29 B1 19 28N 99 20W
Sant'Ilário, Mil. 9 D4 45 34N 8 59 E
Santo Amaro, Lisb. 8 F7 38 42N 9 11W
Santo Amaro, S. Pau. 31 E5 23 39 S 46 42W
Santo Andre, Lisb. 8 G8 38 38N 9 3W
Santo André, S. Pau. 31 E6 23 39 S 46 41W
Santo António, Qta. de, Lisb. 8 G7 38 39N 9 15W
Santo António da Charneca, Lisb. 8 G8 38 37N 9 1W
Santo Niño, Manila 15 D4 14 38N 121 5 E
Santo Rosario, Manila 15 D4 14 33N 121 4 E
Santo Thomas, Univ. of, Manila 15 D3 14 36N 120 59 E
Santo Tomas, Manila 15 D4 14 33N 121 4 E
Santolan, Manila 15 D4 14 36N 121 4 E
Santos Dumont, Aéroport, Rio J. 31 B3 22 54 S 43 9W
Santos Lugares, B.A. 32 B3 34 35 S 58 35W
Santoshpur, Calc. 16 E5 22 31N 88 16 E
Santragachi, Calc. 16 E5 22 35N 88 17 E
Sanyuanli, Gzh. 14 G8 23 8N 113 14 E
São Bernardo do Campo, S. Pau. 31 F6 23 42 S 46 33W
São Caetano do Sul, S. Pau. 31 E6 23 37 S 46 34W
São Cristovão, Rio J. 31 B2 22 53 S 43 13W
São Domingos, Centro, Rio J. 31 B3 22 53 S 43 6W
São Gonçalo, Rio J. 31 A3 22 49 S 43 4W
São João Clímaco, S. Pau. 31 E6 23 37 S 46 35W
São João da Talha, Lisb. 8 F8 38 49N 9 5W
São João de Meriti, Rio J. 31 A1 22 47 S 43 18W
São Lucas, Parque, S. Pau. 31 E6 23 35 S 45 32W
São Mateus, Rio J. 31 A1 22 48 S 43 20W
São Miguel Paulista, S. Pau. 31 D7 23 29 S 46 26W
São Paulo, S. Pau. 31 E6 23 32 S 46 38W
Sapa, Calc. 16 E5 22 30N 88 15 E
Sapang Baho →, Manila 15 D4 14 33N 121 4 E
Sapateiro →, S. Pau. 31 E5 23 35 S 46 41W
Saranap, S.F. 27 A4 37 52N 122 4W
Sarandi, B.A. 32 C4 34 40 S 58 20W
Saraswati →, Calc. 16 D5 22 46N 88 15 E
Sarcelles, Paris 5 B4 48 59N 2 22 E
Sarecky →, Pra. 10 B2 50 7N 14 23 E
Sarenga, Calc. 16 E5 22 31N 88 12 E
Sarilhos Grandes, Lisb. 8 F9 38 40N 8 58W
Sarilhos Pequenos, Lisb. 8 F9 38 41N 8 59W
Sarimbun, Sing. 15 F7 1 24N 103 40 E
Saronikòs Kòlpos, Ath. 8 J10 37 52N 23 28 E
Sarriá, Barc. 8 D5 41 22N 2 8 E
Sarria, Car. 30 D5 10 30N 66 53W
Sarsol, Bomb. 16 G9 19 2N 73 0 E
Sartrouville, Paris 5 B3 48 56N 2 11 E
Sasad, Bud. 10 K13 47 28N 19 0 E
Sasashita, Tōkyō 13 D2 35 23N 139 35 E
Sasel, Hbg. 7 D8 53 39N 10 6 E
Sashalom, Bud. 10 J14 47 30N 19 10 E
Saska, Wsaw. 10 E7 52 14N 21 3 E
Sassafras, Melb. 19 F9 37 52 S 145 20 E
Satalice, Pra. 10 B3 50 7N 14 34 E
Satgachi, Calc. 16 E6 22 37N 88 25 E
Satghara, Calc. 16 D6 22 43N 88 21 E
Satpukur, Calc. 16 E6 22 37N 88 24 E
Sätra, Stock. 3 E10 59 17N 17 54 E
Satsuna, Calc. 16 F5 22 28N 88 17 E
Sau Mau Ping, H.K. 12 E6 22 19N 114 13 E
Saugus, Bost. 21 C3 42 28N 71 0W
Saugus →, Bost. 21 C3 42 27N 70 58W
Saulx-les-Chartreux, Paris 5 C3 48 41N 2 16 E
Sausalito, S.F. 27 A2 37 51N 122 28W
Sausset →, Paris 5 B5 48 56N 2 28 E
Savigny-sur-Orge, Paris 5 C4 48 40N 2 21 E
Savijärvi, Hels. 3 A6 60 21N 25 19 E
Savonera, Tori. 9 B2 45 7N 7 36 E
Sawah Besar, Jak. 15 H9 6 8 S 106 49 E
Sawyer Ridge, S.F. 27 C2 37 34N 122 24W
Saxonville, Bost. 21 D1 42 19N 71 24W
Saxonwold, Jobg. 18 E9 26 9 S 28 2 E
Scarborough, Trto. 20 D9 43 44N 79 14W
Scarsdale, N.Y. 23 B6 40 58N 73 47W
Sceaux, Paris 5 C3 48 46N 2 17 E
Schalke, Ruhr 6 A4 51 33N 7 4 E
Schapenrust, Jobg. 18 F11 26 15 S 28 21 E
Scharfenberg, Berl. 7 A2 52 35N 13 15 E
Scheiblingstein, Wien 10 G9 48 16N 16 13 E
Schenefeld, Hbg. 7 D7 53 36N 9 52 E
Scherlebech, Ruhr 6 A4 51 37N 7 8 E
Schildow, Berl. 7 A3 52 38N 13 22 E
Schiller Park, Chic. 26 B1 41 56N 87 52W
Schiller Woods, Chic. 26 B1 41 57N 87 51W
Schlachtensee, Berl. 7 B2 52 26N 13 13 E
Schlossgarten, Berl. 7 A2 52 31N 13 18 E
Schmachtendorf, Ruhr 6 A2 51 32N 6 48 E
Schmargendorf, Berl. 7 B2 52 28N 13 17 E
Schmöckwitz, Berl. 7 B5 52 22N 13 38 E
Schnelsen, Hbg. 7 D7 53 38N 9 54 E
Scholven, Ruhr 6 A4 51 36N 7 0 E
Schönblick, Berl. 7 B5 52 27N 13 43 E
Schönbrunn, Schloss, Wien 10 G9 48 10N 16 19 E
Schöneberg, Berl. 7 B3 52 28N 13 20 E
Schönefeld, Berl. 7 B4 52 23N 13 30 E
Schöneiche, Berl. 7 B5 52 28N 13 41 E
Schönwalde, Berl. 7 A1 52 37N 13 7 E
Schottenwald, Wien 10 G9 48 13N 16 16 E
Schuir, Ruhr 6 B3 51 23N 6 59 E
Schulzendorf, Berl. 7 A2 52 36N 13 16 E
Schuylkill →, Phil. 24 B3 39 53N 75 11W
Schwabing, Mün. 7 G10 48 10N 11 35 E
Schwafheim, Ruhr 6 B1 51 25N 6 36 E
Schwanebeck, Berl. 7 A4 52 37N 13 32 E
Schwanenwerder, Berl. 7 B2 52 26N 13 10 E
Schwarz →, Ruhr 6 C3 51 19N 6 44 E
Schwarzbachtal, Ruhr 6 C3 51 17N 6 51 E
Schwarze, Ruhr 6 A2 51 31N 6 48 E
Schwarze Berge, Hbg. 7 E7 53 27N 9 54 E
Schwarzlackenau, Wien 10 G10 48 17N 16 24 E
Schwechat, Wien 10 H10 48 8N 16 28 E
Schweflinghaüsen, Ruhr 6 C6 51 15N 7 24 E
Schwelm, Ruhr 6 C5 51 16N 7 16 E
Scisciano, Nápl. 9 H13 40 54N 14 28 E
Scoresby, Melb. 19 F8 37 54 S 145 14 E
Scotch Plains, N.Y. 22 D2 40 39N 74 22W
Scotts Level Br. →, Balt. 25 A2 39 23N 76 45W
Sea Cliff, N.Y. 23 B7 40 50N 73 38W
Seabrook, Wash. 25 D9 38 58N 76 49W
Seacliff, S.F. 27 B2 37 47N 122 28W
Seaforth, Syd. 19 A4 33 48 S 151 15 E
Seagate, N.Y. 22 D4 40 34N 74 0W
Seal Slough, S.F. 27 C3 37 34N 122 17W
Sears Tower, Chic. 26 B3 41 52N 87 38W
Seat Pleasant, Wash. 25 D8 38 53N 76 53W
Seavey Hill, Bost. 21 A1 42 42N 71 23W
Šeberov, Pra. 10 B3 50 0N 14 30 E
Secaucus, N.Y. 22 C4 40 47N 74 3W
Secondigliano, Nápl. 9 H12 40 53N 14 15 E
Seddinsee, Berl. 7 B5 52 23N 13 41 E
Sedgefield, N.Y. 22 B2 40 51N 74 26W
Sedriano, Mil. 9 E4 45 29N 8 58 E
Seeberg, Berl. 7 A5 52 33N 13 41 E
Seeburg, Berl. 7 A1 52 30N 13 7 E
Seefeld, Berl. 7 A5 52 37N 13 40 E
Seegefeld, Berl. 7 A1 52 33N 13 5 E
Seehof, Berl. 7 B2 52 24N 13 17 E
Segeltorp, Stock. 3 E10 59 16N 17 56 E
Segrate, Mil. 9 E6 45 29N 9 17 E
Seguro, Mil. 9 E5 45 28N 9 3 E
Seine →, Paris 5 C4 48 48N 2 25 E
Seixal, Lisb. 8 G8 38 38N 9 6W
Selbeck, Ruhr 6 B3 51 22N 6 51 E
Selbecke, Ruhr 6 C6 51 20N 7 28 E
Selby, Jobg. 18 F9 26 12 S 28 2 E
Seletar, P., Sing. 15 F8 1 26N 103 51 E
Seletar, Sungei →, Sing. 15 F8 1 25N 103 48 E
Seletar Hills, Sing. 15 F8 1 23N 103 52 E
Seletar Res., Sing. 15 F7 1 24N 103 48 E
Selghar, Bomb. 16 H9 18 57N 73 1 E
Selhurst, Lon. 4 C4 51 23N 0 5W
Selsdon, Lon. 4 C4 51 20N 0 3W
Selytsy, St-Pet. 11 B6 59 56N 30 42 E
Sembawang, Sing. 15 F7 1 26N 103 49 E
Sembawang, Sungei →, Sing. 15 F7 1 26N 103 48 E
Sembawang Hill, Sing. 15 F7 1 22N 103 49 E
Semsvatn, Oslo 2 B2 59 51N 10 25 E
Senago, Mil. 9 D5 45 34N 9 7 E
Senan, Jak. 15 J10 6 10 S 106 50 E
Sénart, Forêt de, Paris 5 D4 48 40N 2 28 E
Senayan Sports Centre, Jak. 15 J9 6 12 S 106 47 E
Sendling, Mün. 7 G10 48 7N 11 31 E
Sengeløse, Købn. 2 D8 55 40N 12 14 E
Senju, Tōkyō 13 B3 35 44N 139 48 E
Senlikköy, Ist. 17 B1 40 58N 28 47 E
Senlisse, Paris 5 C1 48 41N 1 59 E
Senneville, Mtrl. 20 B2 43 24N 73 57W
Senri, Ōsaka 12 B4 34 49N 135 30 E
Senriyama, Ōsaka 12 B4 34 47N 135 31 E
Sentosa, Sing. 15 G7 1 15N 103 49 E
Sentosa, P., Sing. 15 G7 1 15N 103 49 E
Seo Dae Mun, Sŏul 12 G7 37 34N 126 57 E
Seobinngo, Sŏul 12 G7 37 31N 126 58 E
Seoggwan, Sŏul 12 G8 37 35N 127 2 E
Seong Bug, Sŏul 12 G8 37 35N 127 0 E
Seong Dong, Sŏul 12 G8 37 33N 127 3 E
Seongsu, Sŏul 12 G8 37 32N 127 2 E
Seoul = Sŏul, Sŏul 12 G8 37 35N 127 3 E
Seoul National Univ., Sŏul 12 H7 37 28N 126 57 E
Seoul Tower, Sŏul 12 G7 37 32N 126 59 E
Sepah Salar Mosque, Tehr. 17 C5 35 40N 51 25 E
Sepolia, Ath. 8 H11 38 1N 23 42 E
Sepulveda, L.A. 28 A2 34 13N 118 27W
Sepulveda Flood Control Basin, L.A. 28 A2 34 10N 118 28W
Serangoon, P., Sing. 15 F8 1 23N 103 55 E
Serangoon, Sungei →, Sing. 15 F8 1 23N 103 55 E
Serangoon Garden, Sing. 15 F8 1 21N 103 51 E

46 Serangoon Harbour

Serangoon Harbour, *Sing.* **15 F8** 1 23N 103 57 E
Seraya, P., *Sing.* **15 G7** 1 16N 103 43 E
Serebryanka, *Mos.* **11 E11** 55 44N 37 53 E
Serebryanka →, *Mos.* **11 E10** 55 47N 37 44 E
Serednevo, *Mos.* **11 F7** 55 35N 37 18 E
Serramonte, *S.F.* **27 C2** 37 39N 122 28W
Servon, *Paris* **5 C5** 48 43N 2 35 E
Šestajovice, *Pra.* **10 B3** 50 6N 14 40 E
Sesto San Giovanni, *Mil.* **9 D6** 45 31N 9 13 E
Seta Budi, *Jak.* **15 J9** 6 12 S 106 49 E
Setagaya-Ku, *Tōkyō* **13 C2** 35 37N 139 36 E
Sete Pontes, *Rio J.* **31 B3** 22 50 S 43 4W
Seter, *Oslo* **2 B4** 59 52N 10 47 E
Séttimo Milanese, *Mil.* **9 E5** 45 28N 9 3 E
Séttimo Torinese, *Tori.* **9 B3** 45 8N 7 46 E
Settsu, *Ōsaka* **12 B4** 34 47N 135 33 E
Setuny →, *Mos.* **11 E8** 55 43N 37 21 E
Seurasaari, *Hels.* **3 B4** 60 11N 24 53 E
Seutula, *Hels.* **3 A4** 60 20N 24 52 E
Seven Corners, *Wash.* **25 D7** 38 53N 77 9W
Seven Kings, *Lon.* **4 B5** 51 33N 0 5 E
Sevenoaks, *Lon.* **4 D6** 51 16N 0 11 E
Severn Hills, *Syd.* **19 A2** 33 46 S 150 57 E
Sévesco →, *Mil.* **9 D5** 45 35N 9 9 E
Sevran, *Paris* **5 B5** 48 56N 2 31 E
Sèvres, *Paris* **5 C3** 48 49N 2 13 E
Sewaren, *N.Y.* **22 D3** 40 33N 74 15W
Sewell, *Phil.* **24 C4** 39 46N 75 8W
Sewri, *Bomb.* **16 H8** 18 59N 72 50 E
Seya, *Tōkyō* **13 D1** 35 28N 139 28 E
Sforzesso, Castello, *Mil.* **9 E6** 45 28N 9 10 E
Sha Kok Mei, *H.K.* **12 D6** 22 23N 114 16 E
Sha Tin, *H.K.* **12 D6** 22 23N 114 11 E
Sha Tin Wai, *H.K.* **12 D6** 22 22N 114 11 E
Shaala, *Bagd.* **17 E7** 33 22N 44 16 E
Shabanzhuang, *Beij.* **14 B3** 39 51N 116 25 E
Shabbona Woods, *Chic.* **26 D3** 41 36N 87 33W
Shabrâmant, *El Qâ.* **18 D5** 29 56N 31 11 E
Shadipur, *Delhi* **16 B2** 28 38N 77 11 E
Shady Oak, *Wash.* **25 C6** 39 1N 77 17W
Shahabad, *Bomb.* **16 G9** 19 0N 73 2 E
Shahar, *Bomb.* **16 G8** 19 5N 72 52 E
Shahdara, *Delhi* **16 A2** 28 40N 77 18 E
Shahe, *Gzh.* **14 G8** 23 9N 113 19 E
Shahpur Jel, *Delhi* **16 B2** 28 33N 77 12 E
Shahr-e-Rey, *Tehr.* **17 D5** 35 36N 51 25 E
Shaikh Aomar, *Bagd.* **17 E8** 33 20N 44 23 E
Shakarpor Khas, *Delhi* **16 B2** 28 37N 77 14 E
Shakurpur, *Delhi* **16 A1** 28 40N 77 8 E
Sham Shui Po, *H.K.* **12 E5** 22 19N 114 9 E
Shamepur, *Delhi* **16 A1** 28 44N 77 8 E
Shamian, *Gzh.* **14 G8** 23 6N 113 13 E
Shamspur, *Delhi* **16 B2** 28 36N 77 17 E
Shan Liu, *H.K.* **12 D6** 22 23N 114 16 E
Shan Mei, *H.K.* **12 D6** 22 24N 114 10 E
Shanghai, *Shang.* **14 J12** 31 14N 121 28 E
Shanghetou, *Tianj.* **14 D5** 39 11N 117 0 E
Shanjing, *Gzh.* **14 G9** 23 4N 113 23 E
Sharea Faisal, *Kar.* **17 G11** 24 52N 67 8 E
Sharon Hill, *Phil.* **24 B3** 39 54N 75 16W
Sharp I., *H.K.* **12 D6** 22 21N 114 17 E
Sharp Park, *S.F.* **27 C2** 37 38N 122 29W
Shau Kei Wan, *H.K.* **12 E6** 22 16N 114 13 E
Shawocun, *Beij.* **14 B2** 39 53N 116 13 E
Shawsheen Village, *Bost.* **21 A3** 42 40N 71 7W
Shea Stadium, *N.Y.* **23 C5** 40 45N 73 50W
Sheakhala, *Calc.* **16 D5** 22 45N 88 10 E
Shebāb, *Bagd.* **17 E8** 33 20N 44 26 E
Sheepshead B., *N.Y.* **22 D5** 40 35N 73 55W
Shek Hang, *H.K.* **12 D6** 22 24N 114 17 E
Shek Kip Mei, *H.K.* **12 D5** 22 20N 114 9 E
Shek Lung Kung, *H.K.* **12 D5** 22 23N 114 5 E
Shek O, *H.K.* **12 E6** 22 13N 114 15 E
Shellpot Cr. →, *Phil.* **24 C1** 39 44N 75 30W
Shelter Cove, *S.F.* **27 C1** 37 35N 122 30W
Shelter I., *H.K.* **12 E6** 22 19N 114 17 E
Shemirānāt, *Tehr.* **17 C5** 35 47N 51 25 E
Shenfield, *Lon.* **4 B6** 51 37N 0 19 E
Sheng Fa Shan, *H.K.* **12 D5** 22 23N 114 5 E
Shenley, *Lon.* **4 A3** 51 41N 0 16W
Shepherds Bush, *Lon.* **4 B3** 51 30N 0 13W
Shepperton, *Lon.* **4 C2** 51 23N 0 26W
Sherborn, *Bost.* **21 D1** 42 14N 71 22W
Sherman Oaks, *L.A.* **28 B2** 34 8N 118 29W
Sherwood Forest, *S.F.* **27 A3** 37 57N 122 16W
Shet Bandar, *Bomb.* **16 H8** 18 57N 72 55 E
Sheung Lau Wan, *H.K.* **12 E6** 22 16N 114 16 E
Sheung Wan, *H.K.* **12 E5** 22 16N 114 9 E
Sheva, *Bomb.* **16 H8** 18 56N 72 57 E
Sheva Nhava, *Bomb.* **16 H8** 18 57N 72 57 E
Shiba, *Tōkyō* **13 C3** 35 38N 139 45 E
Shiba →, *Tōkyō* **13 A3** 35 50N 139 44 E
Shibuya-Ku, *Tōkyō* **13 C3** 35 39N 139 41 E
Shijōnawate, *Ōsaka* **12 B4** 34 44N 135 37 E
Shimo-okudomi, *Tōkyō* **13 A1** 35 52N 139 27 E
Shimo-tsuchidana, *Tōkyō* **13 D1** 35 24N 139 27 E
Shimogawara, *Tōkyō* **13 C1** 35 39N 139 27 E
Shimosalo, *Tōkyō* **13 B2** 35 45N 139 31 E
Shimosasame, *Tōkyō* **13 B2** 35 48N 139 37 E
Shimoshakujii, *Tōkyō* **13 B2** 35 43N 139 35 E
Shimotomi, *Tōkyō* **13 B1** 35 49N 139 27 E
Shimotsuruma, *Tōkyō* **13 D1** 35 29N 139 26 E
Shimura, *Tōkyō* **13 B3** 35 46N 139 41 E
Shinagawa B., *Tōkyō* **13 C3** 35 35N 139 48 E
Shinagawa-Ku, *Tōkyō* **13 C3** 35 36N 139 44 E
Shing Mun Res., *H.K.* **12 D5** 22 23N 114 8 E
Shinjuku-Ku, *Tōkyō* **13 B3** 35 41N 139 42 E
Shinkoiwa, *Tōkyō* **13 B4** 35 43N 139 51 E
Shinnakano, *Tōkyō* **13 B3** 35 41N 139 40 E
Shinoha, *Tōkyō* **13 A3** 35 50N 139 49 E
Shipai, *Gzh.* **14 G9** 23 8N 113 20 E
Shipley, *Balt.* **25 B3** 39 12N 76 39W
Shippan Pt., *N.Y.* **23 A7** 41 1N 73 31W
Shirako, *Tōkyō* **13 B2** 35 47N 139 36 E
Shiraone, *Bomb.* **16 G9** 19 2N 73 1 E
Shirinashi →, *Ōsaka* **12 C3** 34 38N 135 27 E
Shirley, *Lon.* **4 C4** 51 22N 0 2W
Shiro, *Tōkyō* **13 B2** 35 48N 139 30 E
Shirogane, *Tōkyō* **13 C3** 35 37N 139 44 E
Shisha Hai, *Beij.* **14 B3** 39 55N 116 21 E
Shitou, *Gzh.* **14 G9** 23 1N 113 23 E
Shiweitang, *Gzh.* **14 G8** 23 6N 113 12 E
Shogunle, *Lagos* **18 A2** 6 34N 7 20 E
Shomolu, *Lagos* **18 A2** 6 32N 7 22 E
Shooters Hill, *Lon.* **4 C5** 51 28N 0 4 E
Shoreditch, *Lon.* **4 B4** 51 31N 0 4W
Shoreham, *Lon.* **4 D6** 51 19N 0 10 E
Short Hills, *N.Y.* **22 C2** 40 44N 74 21W
Shortlands, *Lon.* **4 C5** 51 23N 0 0 E
Shrirampur, *Calc.* **16 D5** 22 45N 88 21 E
Shuangkou, *Tianj.* **14 D5** 39 14N 117 2 E
Shuangtuo, *Tianj.* **14 D6** 39 13N 117 19 E
Shubrâ el Kheima, *El Qâ.* **18 C5** 30 6N 31 14 E
Shuikuo, *Gzh.* **14 F8** 23 10N 113 10 E
Shuishang Gongyuan, *Tianj.* **14 E5** 39 5N 117 9 E
Shukunoshō, *Ōsaka* **12 A4** 34 50N 135 31 E
Sibbo, *Hels.* **3 A6** 60 21N 25 14 E
Sibbo fjärden, *Hels.* **3 B6** 60 11N 25 17 E
Siboney, *La Hab.* **30 B2** 23 4N 82 28W
Sibpur, *Calc.* **16 E5** 22 34N 88 19 E
Sibřina, *Pra.* **10 B4** 50 3N 14 40 E
Sidcup, *Lon.* **4 C5** 51 25N 0 6 E
Siebenhirten, *Wien* **10 H9** 48 8N 16 17 E
Siedlung, *Berl.* **7 A1** 52 35N 13 7 E
Siekierki, *Wsaw.* **10 E7** 52 12N 21 4 E
Sielce, *Wsaw.* **10 E7** 52 12N 21 2 E
Siemensstadt, *Berl.* **7 A2** 52 32N 13 16 E
Sieraków, *Wsaw.* **10 E5** 52 19N 20 48 E
Sierra Madre, *L.A.* **28 B4** 34 9N 118 3W
Sievering, *Wien* **10 G10** 48 15N 16 20 E
Siggerud, *Oslo* **2 C5** 59 47N 10 52 E
Siheung, *Sŏul* **12 H7** 37 28N 126 54 E
Siikajärvi, *Hels.* **3 B2** 60 17N 24 31 E
Sikátorpuszta, *Bud.* **10 J14** 47 34N 19 10 E
Silampur, *Delhi* **16 B2** 28 39N 77 16 E
Silschede, *Ruhr* **6 B6** 51 21N 7 22 E
Silver Hill, *Wash.* **25 E8** 38 49N 76 55W
Silver L., *Bost.* **21 B3** 42 33N 71 9W
Silver Mt., *L.A.* **28 A5** 34 12N 117 55W
Silver Spring, *Wash.* **25 D7** 38 59N 77 2W
Silverfields, *Jobg.* **18 E7** 26 7 S 27 49 E
Silvertown, *Lon.* **4 C5** 51 29N 0 1 E
Simla, *Calc.* **16 E6** 22 35N 88 22 E
Simmer and Jack Mines, *Jobg.* **18 F9** 26 12 S 28 8 E
Simmering, *Wien* **10 G10** 48 10N 16 24 E
Simmering Heide, *Wien* **10 G10** 48 10N 16 26 E
Simonkylä, *Hels.* **3 B5** 60 18N 25 1 E
Simpang Bedok, *Sing.* **15 G8** 1 19N 103 56 E
Simsalö, *Hels.* **3 B6** 60 14N 25 17 E
Singao, *N.Y.* **22 B3** 40 53N 74 14W
Singapore, *Sing.* **15 G8** 1 17N 103 51 E
Singapore →, *Sing.* **15 G8** 1 17N 103 51 E
Singapore, Univ. of, *Sing.* **15 G7** 1 19N 103 49 E
Singapore Airport, *Sing.* **15 F8** 1 21N 103 54 E
Singlewell, *Lon.* **4 C7** 51 25N 0 21 E
Singur, *Calc.* **16 D5** 22 48N 88 13 E
Sinicka →, *Mos.* **11 D7** 55 52N 37 18 E
Sinki, Selat, *Sing.* **15 G7** 1 15N 103 42 E
Sinrim, *Sŏul* **12 H7** 37 28N 126 56 E
Sinsa, *Sŏul* **12 G8** 37 31N 127 0 E
Sinthi, *Calc.* **16 E6** 22 37N 88 23 E
Sinweol, *Sŏul* **12 G7** 37 31N 126 51 E
Sipoo, *Hels.* **3 A6** 60 21N 25 14 E
Sipoon selkä, *Hels.* **3 B6** 60 11N 25 17 E
Sipson, *Lon.* **4 C2** 51 29N 0 26W
Siqeil, *El Qâ.* **18 C4** 30 7N 31 10 E
Şişli, *Ist.* **17 A2** 41 3N 28 58 E
Skå, *Stock.* **3 E9** 59 19N 17 44 E
Skärholmen, *Stock.* **3 E10** 59 16N 17 53 E
Skarpäng, *Stock.* **3 D11** 59 26N 18 0 E
Skarpnäck, *Stock.* **3 E11** 59 16N 18 7 E
Skarpö, *Stock.* **3 D13** 59 24N 18 22 E
Skedsmo, *Oslo* **2 B6** 59 59N 11 2 E
Skhodnya →, *Mos.* **11 D8** 55 53N 37 23 E
Skodsborg, *Købn.* **2 D10** 55 49N 12 34 E
Skogby, *Hels.* **3 A2** 60 21N 24 40 E
Skogen, *Oslo* **2 C1** 59 48N 10 18 E
Skogsbyn, *Hels.* **3 A6** 60 20N 25 18 E
Skokie, *Chic.* **26 A2** 42 2N 87 43W
Skokie →, *Chic.* **26 A2** 42 3N 87 46W
Skokie Lagoons, *Chic.* **26 A2** 42 7N 87 46W
Skoklefall, *Oslo* **2 B4** 59 50N 10 40 E
Sköndal, *Stock.* **3 E11** 59 15N 18 6 E
Skovlunde, *Købn.* **2 D9** 55 42N 12 25 E
Skovshoved, *Købn.* **2 D10** 55 45N 12 35 E
Skøyen, *Oslo* **2 B4** 59 55N 10 40 E
Skui, *Oslo* **2 B2** 59 55N 10 25 E
Skuldelev, *Købn.* **2 D7** 55 46N 12 1 E
Skullerud, *Oslo* **2 B5** 59 51N 10 50 E
Skuru, *Stock.* **3 E12** 59 18N 18 12 E
Skytta, *Oslo* **2 B5** 59 59N 10 54 E
Slade Green, *Lon.* **4 C6** 51 27N 0 11 E
Slagsta, *Stock.* **3 E9** 59 15N 17 48 E
Slakteren, *Oslo* **2 A4** 60 1N 10 40 E
Slattum, *Oslo* **2 A5** 60 0N 10 55 E
Slemmestad, *Oslo* **2 C2** 59 46N 10 29 E
Slependen, *Oslo* **2 B3** 59 52N 10 30 E
Sligo Cr. →, *Wash.* **25 C7** 39 0N 77 1W
Slipi, *Jak.* **15 J9** 6 11 S 106 47 E
Slipi Orchard Garden, *Jak.* **15 J9** 6 10 S 106 46 E
Slivenec, *Pra.* **10 B2** 50 1N 14 21 E
Slone Canyon Res., *L.A.* **28 B2** 34 6N 118 27W
Sloop Channel, *N.Y.* **23 D7** 40 36N 73 31W
Sluhy, *Pra.* **10 A3** 50 11N 14 33 E
Służew, *Wsaw.* **10 E7** 52 10N 21 1 E
Służewiec, *Wsaw.* **10 E7** 52 10N 21 0 E
Smalleytown, *N.Y.* **22 D2** 40 39N 74 28W
Smestad, *Oslo* **2 B2** 59 55N 10 25 E
Smichov, *Pra.* **10 B2** 50 4N 14 23 E
Smith Forest Preserve, *Chic.* **26 B2** 41 59N 87 45W
Smith Mills, *N.Y.* **22 A2** 41 0N 74 23W
Smithfield, *Syd.* **19 B2** 33 51 S 150 56 E
Smoke Rise, *N.Y.* **22 A2** 41 0N 74 24W
Smørumnedre, *Købn.* **2 D8** 55 44N 12 7 E
Snakeden Br. →, *Wash.* **25 D6** 38 58N 77 17W
Snarøya, *Oslo* **2 B3** 59 52N 10 33 E
Snättringe, *Stock.* **3 E10** 59 15N 17 58 E
Snoldelev, *Købn.* **2 E8** 55 33N 12 10 E
Snostrup, *Købn.* **2 D7** 55 48N 12 7 E
Søborg, *Købn.* **2 D9** 55 43N 12 29 E
Sobreda, *Lisb.* **8 G7** 38 39N 9 11W
Soccavo, *Nápl.* **9 H12** 40 50N 14 11 E
Sodegaura, *Tōkyō* **13 D4** 35 24N 139 57 E
Söderby, *Stock.* **3 D12** 59 24N 18 12 E
Söderkullalandet, *Hels.* **3 B6** 60 14N 25 19 E
Södermalm, *Stock.* **3 E11** 59 18N 18 4 E
Södersätra, *Stock.* **3 D10** 59 27N 17 56 E
Södertälje, *Stock.* **3 E8** 59 11N 17 36 E
Sodingen, *Ruhr* **6 A5** 51 32N 7 15 E
Sodpur, *Calc.* **16 D6** 22 42N 88 24 E
Södra Björkfjärden, *Stock.* **3 E8** 59 17N 17 34 E
Soeurs, Î. des, *Mtrl.* **20 B4** 43 27N 73 32W
Sognsvatn, *Oslo* **2 B4** 59 58N 10 43 E
Soignolles-en-Brie, *Paris* **5 D6** 48 39N 2 43 E
Soisy-sous-Montmorency, *Paris* **5 B3** 48 59N 2 17 E
Soisy-sur-Seine, *Paris* **5 D4** 48 39N 2 27 E
Sojiji Temple, *Tōkyō* **13 D3** 35 29N 139 40 E
Sok Kwu Wan, *H.K.* **12 E5** 22 12N 114 7 E
Sōka, *Tōkyō* **13 B3** 35 49N 139 48 E
Sokolniki, *Mos.* **11 E10** 55 47N 37 40 E
Sokolniki Park, *Mos.* **11 E10** 55 48N 37 40 E
Sokołów, *Wsaw.* **10 F6** 52 9N 20 51 E
Solalinden, *Mün.* **7 G11** 48 5N 11 42 E
Solaro, *Mil.* **9 D5** 45 36N 9 6 E
Solers, *Paris* **5 D6** 48 39N 2 43 E
Solingen, *Ruhr* **6 C4** 51 10N 7 5 E
Sollentuna, *Stock.* **3 D10** 59 25N 17 56 E
Søllerød, *Købn.* **2 D9** 55 48N 12 29 E
Sollihøgda, *Oslo* **2 B2** 59 58N 10 21 E
Solln, *Mün.* **7 G10** 48 4N 11 31 E
Solna, *Stock.* **3 D10** 59 21N 17 59 E
Solntsevo, *Mos.* **11 F8** 55 39N 37 24 E
Solymár, *Bud.* **10 J12** 47 35N 18 56 E
Somapah Changi, *Sing.* **15 F8** 1 20N 103 57 E
Somapan Serangoon, *Sing.* **15 F8** 1 21N 103 53 E
Somborn, *Ruhr* **6 B6** 51 29N 7 20 E
Somerdale, *Phil.* **24 B4** 39 50N 75 1W
Somerset, *Wash.* **25 D7** 38 57N 77 5W
Somerton, *Phil.* **24 A4** 40 7N 75 1W
Somerville, *Bost.* **21 C3** 42 22N 71 5W
Somma, Mte., *Nápl.* **9 H13** 40 50N 14 25 E
Somma Vesuviana, *Nápl.* **9 H13** 40 52N 14 26 E
Sonari, *Bomb.* **16 H8** 18 54N 72 59 E
Sønderby, *Købn.* **2 D7** 55 44N 12 2 E
Søndersø, *Købn.* **2 D9** 55 46N 12 21 E
Sondre Elvåga, *Oslo* **2 B5** 59 51N 10 54 E
Sonnberg, *Wien* **10 G9** 48 19N 16 15 E
Sørby, *Oslo* **2 C4** 59 49N 10 41 E
Sørkedalen, *Oslo* **2 A3** 60 1N 10 37 E
Soroksár, *Bud.* **10 K13** 47 24N 19 7 E
Soroksár-Újtelep, *Bud.* **10 K13** 47 25N 19 7 E
Soroksari Duna →, *Bud.* **10 K13** 47 25N 19 5 E
Sørsdal, *Oslo* **2 B1** 59 50N 10 16 E
Sosenka →, *Mos.* **11 E10** 55 46N 37 42 E
Sosnovaya, *St-Pet.* **11 C2** 59 49N 30 8 E
Sottungsby, *Hels.* **3 B5** 60 16N 25 8 E
Sŏul, *Sŏul* **12 G8** 37 34N 127 51 E
Soundview, *N.Y.* **23 C5** 40 49N 73 53W
South Basin, *S.F.* **27 B2** 37 42N 122 22W
South Beach, *N.Y.* **22 D4** 40 35N 74 4W
South Boston, *Bost.* **21 C3** 42 20N 71 2W
South Braintree, *Bost.* **21 D4** 42 11N 70 59W
South Branch →, *Phil.* **24 C4** 39 50N 75 5W
South Brooklyn, *N.Y.* **22 C5** 40 41N 73 59W
South Chelmsford, *Bost.* **21 B1** 42 34N 71 22W
South Chicago, *Chic.* **26 C3** 41 44N 87 32W
South Darenth, *Lon.* **4 C6** 51 23N 0 15 E
South Deering, *Chic.* **26 C3** 41 42N 87 33W
South Floral Park, *N.Y.* **23 C6** 40 42N 73 41W
South Gate, *L.A.* **28 C3** 33 56N 118 12W
South Germiston, *Jobg.* **18 F10** 26 11 S 28 13 E
South Hackensack, *N.Y.* **22 B4** 40 51N 74 2W
South Hamilton, *Bost.* **21 B4** 42 36N 70 52W
South Harbour, *Manila* **15 D3** 14 34N 120 58 E
South Harrow, *Lon.* **4 B2** 51 33N 0 21W
South Hd., *Syd.* **19 B4** 33 50 S 151 16 E
South Hempstead, *N.Y.* **23 C7** 40 40N 73 37W
South Hills, *Jobg.* **18 F9** 26 14 S 28 5 E
South Hingham, *Bost.* **21 D4** 42 12N 70 53W
South Holland, *Chic.* **26 D3** 41 36N 87 35W
South Hornchurch, *Lon.* **4 B6** 51 32N 0 11 E
South Huntington, *N.Y.* **23 C8** 40 49N 73 23W
South Lawn, *Wash.* **25 E7** 38 47N 77 0W
South Lawrence, *Bost.* **21 A3** 42 41N 71 9W
South Lincoln, *Bost.* **21 C2** 42 24N 71 19W
South Lynnfield, *Bost.* **21 B4** 42 30N 70 59W
South Norwood, *Lon.* **4 C4** 51 23N 0 3W
South Ockendon, *Lon.* **4 B6** 51 30N 0 16 E
South of Market, *S.F.* **27 B2** 37 46N 122 24W
South Orange, *N.Y.* **22 C3** 40 45N 74 14W
South Oxley, *Lon.* **4 B2** 51 37N 0 23W
South Oyster B., *N.Y.* **23 D8** 40 38N 73 27W
South Ozone Park, *N.Y.* **23 C6** 40 41N 73 49W
South Pasadena, *L.A.* **28 B4** 34 7N 118 8W
South Peabody, *Bost.* **21 B4** 42 30N 70 57W
South Peters, *Syd.* **19 B4** 33 54 S 151 11 E
South Plainfield, *N.Y.* **22 D2** 40 35N 74 24W
South Quincy, *Bost.* **21 D3** 42 13N 71 0W
South Res., *Bost.* **21 C3** 42 26N 71 6W
South San Francisco, *S.F.* **27 C2** 37 38N 122 26W
South San Gabriel, *L.A.* **28 B4** 34 3N 118 6W
South Shore, *Chic.* **26 C3** 41 45N 87 34W
South Sudbury, *Bost.* **21 C1** 42 21N 71 24W
South Valley Stream, *N.Y.* **23 D6** 40 38N 73 43W
South Westbury, *N.Y.* **23 C7** 40 44N 73 34W
South Weymouth, *Bost.* **21 D4** 42 10N 70 56W
South Wimbledon, *Lon.* **4 C3** 51 24N 0 11W
South Yarra, *Melb.* **19 F6** 37 50 S 144 59 E
Southall, *Lon.* **4 B2** 51 30N 0 22W
Southborough, *Lon.* **4 C5** 51 23N 0 3 E
Southcrest, *Jobg.* **18 F9** 26 15 S 28 5 E
Southend, *Lon.* **4 C4** 51 25N 0 0 E
Southfields, *Lon.* **4 C3** 51 26N 0 11W
Southgate, *Lon.* **4 B4** 51 38N 0 7W
Southwark, *Lon.* **4 C4** 51 29N 0 5W
Søvang, *Købn.* **2 E10** 55 34N 12 37 E
Soweto, *Jobg.* **18 F8** 26 14 S 27 52 E
Soya, *Tōkyō* **13 B4** 35 44N 139 55 E
Spadenland, *Hbg.* **7 E8** 53 28N 10 3 E
Spandau, *Berl.* **7 A1** 52 33N 13 9 E
Spånga, *Stock.* **3 D10** 59 23N 17 53 E
Sparkhill, *N.Y.* **22 A5** 41 1N 73 55W
Sparrows Point, *Balt.* **25 B4** 39 13N 76 29W
Spectacle I., *Bost.* **21 C4** 42 19N 70 59W
Speicher-See, *Mün.* **7 F11** 48 12N 11 42 E
Speising, *Wien* **10 H9** 48 10N 16 17 E
Speldorf, *Ruhr* **6 B2** 51 26N 6 49 E
Spellen, *Ruhr* **6 A1** 51 36N 6 36 E
Sphinx, *El Qâ.* **18 D4** 29 58N 31 8 E
Spinaceto, *Rome* **9 G9** 41 47N 12 27 E
Splitrock Res., *N.Y.* **22 B2** 40 58N 74 26W
Spořilov, *Pra.* **10 B3** 50 2N 14 29 E
Spot Pond, *Bost.* **21 C3** 42 26N 71 4W
Spotswood, *Melb.* **19 F6** 37 50 S 144 52 E
Spree →, *Berl.* **7 A2** 52 32N 13 12 E
Spreehafen, *Hbg.* **7 D7** 53 31N 9 59 E
Spring Pond, *Bost.* **21 C4** 42 29N 70 56W
Springeberg, *Berl.* **7 B5** 52 26N 13 43 E
Springfield, *N.Y.* **22 C3** 40 42N 74 18W
Springfield, *Phil.* **24 B3** 39 56N 75 19W
Springfield, *Wash.* **25 E6** 38 46N 77 10W
Springs, *Jobg.* **18 F11** 26 15 S 28 23 E
Sprockhövel, *Ruhr* **6 B5** 51 22N 7 14 E
Squantum, *Bost.* **21 D3** 42 17N 71 0W
Squirrel's Heath, *Lon.* **4 B6** 51 34N 0 12 E
Srednaya Rogatka, *St-Pet.* **11 C4** 59 49N 30 22 E
Sródmieċcie, *Wsaw.* **10 E7** 52 13N 21 0 E
Staaken, *Berl.* **7 A1** 52 31N 13 8 E
Staatsoper, *Wien* **10 G10** 48 12N 16 21 E
Stabekk, *Oslo* **2 B3** 59 54N 10 36 E
Stadlau, *Wien* **10 G10** 48 13N 16 27 E
Stahnsdorf, *Berl.* **7 B2** 52 23N 13 12 E
Staines, *Lon.* **4 C2** 51 26N 0 29W
Stains, *Paris* **5 B4** 48 57N 2 22 E
Stamford, *N.Y.* **23 A7** 41 2N 73 32W
Stamford Harbor, *N.Y.* **23 A7** 41 0N 73 34W
Stamford Hill, *Lon.* **4 B4** 51 34N 0 4W
Stammersdorf, *Wien* **10 G10** 48 18N 16 24 E
Stanford Univ., *S.F.* **27 D4** 37 26N 122 10W
Stanley, *H.K.* **12 E6** 22 13N 114 12 E
Stanley Mound, *H.K.* **12 E6** 22 13N 114 12 E
Stanley Pen., *H.K.* **12 E6** 22 12N 114 12 E
Stanmore, *Lon.* **4 B3** 51 37N 0 18W
Stansted, *Lon.* **4 C6** 51 20N 0 18 E
Stapleford Abbotts, *Lon.* **4 B6** 51 37N 0 10 E
Stapleton, *N.Y.* **22 D4** 40 36N 74 5W
Stará Boleslav, *Pra.* **10 A3** 50 11N 14 39 E
Stara Milosna, *Wsaw.* **10 E8** 52 15N 21 12 E
Staraya, *St-Pet.* **11 B5** 59 55N 30 37 E
Staraya Derevnya, *St-Pet.* **11 B3** 59 58N 30 15 E
Stare, *Wsaw.* **10 E7** 52 15N 21 0 E
Stare Babice, *Wsaw.* **10 E5** 52 15N 20 49 E
Staré Mesto, *Pra.* **10 B2** 50 5N 14 25 E
State House, *Lagos* **18 B2** 6 26N 7 24 E
Staten, *N.Y.* **22 D4** 40 34N 74 7W
Staten Island Zoo, *N.Y.* **22 D4** 40 38N 74 6W
Statenice, *Pra.* **10 B1** 50 9N 14 19 E
Stavnsholt, *Købn.* **2 D9** 55 48N 12 24 E
Steele, *Ruhr* **6 B4** 51 27N 7 4 E
Steele Creek, *Melb.* **19 E6** 37 44 S 144 52 E
Steglitz, *Berl.* **7 B2** 52 27N 13 19 E
Stehstücken, *Berl.* **7 B1** 52 23N 13 7 E
Steilshoop, *Hbg.* **7 D8** 53 36N 10 2 E
Steinberger Slough, *S.F.* **27 C3** 37 32N 122 13W
Steinriegel, *Wien* **10 G9** 48 16N 16 12 E
Steinstücken, *Berl.* **7 B1** 52 21N 13 7 E
Steinwerder, *Hbg.* **7 D7** 53 32N 9 57 E
Stellingen, *Hbg.* **7 D7** 53 35N 9 56 E
Stenhamra, *Stock.* **3 D9** 59 20N 17 40 E
Stenløse, *Købn.* **2 D8** 55 46N 12 11 E
Stephansdom, *Wien* **10 G10** 48 12N 16 21 E
Stepney, *Lon.* **4 B4** 51 30N 0 3W
Sterkende, *Købn.* **2 E8** 55 36N 12 10 E
Sterkrade, *Ruhr* **6 A3** 51 31N 6 52 E
Sterling Park, *S.F.* **27 B2** 37 41N 122 27W
Stevenson, *Balt.* **25 A2** 39 24N 76 42W
Stewart Manor, *N.Y.* **23 C6** 40 43N 73 40W
Sticklinge udde, *Stock.* **3 D11** 59 23N 18 6 E
Stickney, *Chic.* **26 C2** 41 49N 87 46W
Stienitzaue, *Berl.* **7 A5** 52 38N 13 44 E
Stiepel, *Ruhr* **6 B5** 51 25N 7 14 E
Stiftskirche, *Ruhr* **6 C2** 51 12N 6 41 E
Still Run →, *Phil.* **24 C3** 39 47N 75 16W
Stockholm, *Stock.* **3 E11** 59 19N 18 4 E
Stocksund, *Stock.* **3 D11** 59 23N 18 3 E
Stockum, *Ruhr* **6 C2** 51 16N 6 44 E
Stodůlky, *Pra.* **10 B1** 50 3N 14 19 E
Stoke D'Abernon, *Lon.* **4 D2** 51 19N 0 23W
Stoke Newington, *Lon.* **4 B4** 51 33N 0 4W
Stolpe-Süd, *Berl.* **7 A2** 52 37N 13 14 E
Stone, *Lon.* **4 C6** 51 26N 0 16 E
Stone Grove, *Lon.* **4 B3** 51 37N 0 16W
Stone Park, *Chic.* **26 B1** 41 53N 87 52W
Stonebridge, *Lon.* **4 B3** 51 32N 0 16W
Stoneham, *Bost.* **21 C3** 42 29N 71 5W
Stonehurst, *L.A.* **28 A2** 34 15N 118 21W
Stony Brook Res., *Bost.* **21 D3** 42 15N 71 8W
Stony Cr. →, *Chic.* **26 C2** 41 40N 87 45W
Stony Cr. →, *Melb.* **19 E6** 37 49 S 144 53 E
Stora Värtan, *Stock.* **3 D11** 59 25N 18 7 E
Store Hareskov, *Købn.* **2 D9** 55 46N 12 23 E
Store Kattingesø, *Købn.* **2 E7** 55 39N 12 0 E
Store Magleby, *Købn.* **2 E10** 55 35N 12 35 E
Storholmen, *Stock.* **3 D11** 59 23N 18 8 E
Stovivatn, *Oslo* **2 B2** 59 54N 10 26 E
Stovner, *Oslo* **2 B5** 59 57N 10 55 E
Stow L., *S.F.* **27 B2** 37 46N 122 28W
Strašnice, *Pra.* **10 B2** 50 4N 14 28 E
Strandbad Gansehäufe, *Wien* **10 G10** 48 13N 16 26 E
Strasslach, *Mün.* **7 G10** 48 0N 11 30 E
Strasstrudering, *Mün.* **7 G11** 48 6N 11 41 E
Stratford, *Lon.* **4 B5** 51 33N 0 0 E
Stratford, *Phil.* **24 C4** 39 49N 75 0W
Strathfield, *Syd.* **19 B3** 33 52 S 151 5 E
Strawberry Hill, *Bost.* **21 D2** 42 14N 71 15W
Strawberry Pk., *L.A.* **28 A4** 34 16N 118 7W
Strawberry Pt., *S.F.* **27 A1** 37 53N 122 30W
Streatham, *Lon.* **4 C4** 51 25N 0 7W
Streatham Vale, *Lon.* **4 C4** 51 24N 0 8W
Strebersdorf, *Wien* **10 G10** 48 17N 16 23 E
Střešovice, *Pra.* **10 B2** 50 5N 14 23 E
Strelyna, *St-Pet.* **11 C1** 59 49N 30 0 E
Střížkov, *Pra.* **10 B2** 50 7N 14 28 E
Strogino, *Mos.* **11 E8** 55 48N 37 24 E
Strømmen, *Oslo* **2 B5** 59 56N 10 59 E
Stromovka, *Pra.* **10 B2** 50 6N 14 25 E
Strunkede Wasserschloss, *Ruhr* **6 A5** 51 33N 7 12 E
Studio City, *L.A.* **28 B2** 34 8N 118 24W
Stupinigi, *Tori.* **9 C2** 44 59N 7 36 E
Stura di Lanzo →, *Tori.* **9 A2** 45 11N 7 47 E
Stureby, *Stock.* **3 E11** 59 15N 18 4 E
Stuvsta, *Stock.* **3 E11** 59 15N 18 0 E
Styrum, *Ruhr* **6 B3** 51 27N 6 52 E
Subhepur, *Delhi* **16 A2** 28 44N 77 15 E
Sucat, *Manila* **15 E4** 14 27N 121 2 E
Success, L., *N.Y.* **23 C6** 40 45N 73 42W
Suchdol, *Pra.* **10 B2** 50 8N 14 22 E
Sucre, *Car.* **30 D5** 10 31N 66 57W
Sucy-en-Brie, *Paris* **5 C5** 48 46N 2 31 E
Sudberg, *Ruhr* **6 C4** 51 10N 7 6 E
Sudbury, *Bost.* **21 C1** 42 22N 71 24W
Suderelbe →, *Hbg.* **7 E7** 53 28N 9 58 E
Suderwich, *Ruhr* **6 A5** 51 36N 7 16 E
Sugamo, *Tōkyō* **13 B3** 35 44N 139 43 E
Sugar Loaf Mt. = Açúcar, Pão de, *Rio J.* **31 B3** 22 56 S 43 9W
Sugartown, *Phil.* **24 B1** 39 59N 75 30W
Sugasawa, *Tōkyō* **13 B2** 35 46N 139 32 E
Suge, *Tōkyō* **13 C2** 35 37N 139 32 E
Suginami-Ku, *Tōkyō* **13 B2** 35 41N 139 37 E
Sugita, *Tōkyō* **13 D2** 35 22N 139 37 E
Sugō, *Tōkyō* **13 C2** 35 34N 139 33 E
Suitland, *Wash.* **25 D8** 38 50N 76 55W
Sukchar, *Calc.* **16 D6** 22 42N 88 22 E
Sulejówek, *Wsaw.* **10 E8** 52 14N 21 14 E
Sulldorf, *Hbg.* **7 D6** 53 34N 9 49 E
Sultan Mosque, *Sing.* **15 G8** 1 18N 103 51 E
Suma, *Ōsaka* **12 C1** 34 38N 135 8 E
Sumaré, *S. Pau.* **31 E5** 23 32 S 46 41W
Sumida, *Tōkyō* **13 B3** 35 42N 139 49 E
Sumida →, *Tōkyō* **13 B3** 35 39N 139 45 E
Sumiyoshi, *Ōsaka* **12 C4** 34 36N 135 30 E
Summer Palace, *Beij.* **14 B2** 39 59N 116 13 E
Summerville, *Trto.* **20 E7** 43 37N 79 33W
Summit, *Chic.* **26 C2** 41 47N 87 47W
Summit, *N.Y.* **22 C2** 40 43N 74 22W
Sun Valley, *L.A.* **28 A2** 34 13N 118 21W
Sunamachi, *Tōkyō* **13 B4** 35 40N 139 50 E
Sunashinden, *Tōkyō* **13 A2** 35 53N 139 30 E
Sunbury, *Lon.* **4 C2** 51 25N 0 26W
Sunda Kelapa, *Jak.* **15 H9** 6 6 S 106 48 E
Sundbyberg, *Stock.* **3 D10** 59 22N 17 57 E
Sundbyerne, *Købn.* **2 E10** 55 39N 12 36 E
Sung Kong, *H.K.* **12 E6** 22 11N 114 17 E
Sungai Bambu, *Jak.* **15 H10** 6 6 S 106 53 E
Sungai Buloh, *Sing.* **15 F7** 1 25N 103 42 E
Sungei Simpang, *Sing.* **15 F7** 1 26N 103 49 E
Sunland, *L.A.* **28 A3** 34 15N 118 18W
Sunnyridge, *Jobg.* **18 F10** 26 10 S 28 10 E
Sunset, *S.F.* **27 B2** 37 44N 122 29W
Sunshine, *Melb.* **19 E5** 37 48 S 144 49 E
Sunshine Acres, *L.A.* **28 C5** 33 56N 117 59W
Suntaug L., *Bost.* **21 B3** 42 31N 71 0W
Sunter, *Jak.* **15 H10** 6 7 S 106 51 E
Sunter, Kali, *Jak.* **15 J10** 6 10 S 106 53 E
Suomenlinna, *Hels.* **3 C4** 60 9N 24 59 E
Superga, *Tori.* **9 B3** 45 4N 7 46 E
Superga, Basilica di, *Tori.* **9 B3** 45 5N 7 45 E
Sura, *Calc.* **16 E6** 22 33N 88 24 E
Surag San, *Sŏul* **12 F8** 37 40N 127 4 E
Surbiton, *Lon.* **4 C3** 51 23N 0 17W
Surco, *Lima* **30 G8** 12 9 S 77 0W
Suresnes, *Paris* **5 B3** 48 52N 2 13 E
Surquillo, *Lima* **30 G8** 12 6 S 77 1W
Surrey Hills, *Melb.* **19 F7** 37 50 S 145 5 E
Surrey Hills, *Syd.* **19 B4** 33 53 S 151 13 E
Surrey Park, *Melb.* **19 E7** 37 49 S 145 6 E
Susaeg, *Sŏul* **12 G7** 37 34N 126 54 E
Süssenbrunn, *Wien* **10 G10** 48 16N 16 29 E
Sutherland, *Syd.* **19 C3** 34 2 S 151 3 E
Sutton, *Lon.* **4 C3** 51 21N 0 11W
Sutton at Hone, *Lon.* **4 C6** 51 24N 0 14 E
Suyu, *Sŏul* **12 G8** 37 37N 127 0 E
Suzukishinden, *Tōkyō* **13 B2** 35 43N 139 31 E
Svanemøllen, *Købn.* **2 D10** 55 43N 12 34 E
Svartsjölandet, *Stock.* **3 D9** 59 20N 17 43 E
Sverdlov, *Mos.* **11 E9** 55 46N 37 36 E
Svestad, *Oslo* **2 C3** 59 46N 10 36 E
Svestrup, *Købn.* **2 D7** 55 46N 12 8 E
Svinningeudd, *Stock.* **3 D12** 59 26N 18 17 E
Švinö, *Hels.* **3 C3** 60 7N 24 44 E
Svogerslev, *Købn.* **2 E7** 55 38N 12 0 E
Swampscott, *Bost.* **21 C4** 42 28N 70 53W
Swanley, *Lon.* **4 C5** 51 23N 0 9 E
Swanscombe, *Lon.* **4 C6** 51 26N 0 18 E
Swansea, *Trto.* **20 E8** 43 39N 79 27W
Swarthmore, *Phil.* **24 B2** 39 54N 75 22W
Swedesboro, *Phil.* **24 C3** 39 45N 75 17W
Swedesburg, *Phil.* **24 A3** 40 5N 75 19W
Swinburne I., *N.Y.* **22 D4** 40 33N 74 3W
Swita, *Ōsaka* **12 B4** 34 45N 135 30 E
Syampur, *Calc.* **16 F5** 22 28N 88 12 E
Sycamore Mills, *Phil.* **24 B2** 39 57N 75 25W
Sydenham, *Jobg.* **18 E9** 26 9 S 28 5 E
Sydney, *Syd.* **19 B4** 33 52 S 151 12 E
Sydney, Univ. of, *Syd.* **19 B4** 33 54 S 151 11 E
Sydney Airport, *Syd.* **19 B4** 33 56 S 151 10 E
Sydney Harbour Bridge, *Syd.* **19 B4** 33 51 S 151 12 E
Sydstranden, *Købn.* **2 E10** 55 34N 12 38 E
Sylling, *Oslo* **2 B1** 59 54N 10 16 E
Sylvania, *Syd.* **19 C3** 34 0 S 151 7 E
Syndal, *Melb.* **19 F7** 37 52 S 145 9 E
Syon House, *Lon.* **4 C3** 51 28N 0 18W
Syosset, *N.Y.* **23 C7** 40 49N 73 30W
Szabadság-hegy, *Bud.* **10 J12** 47 30N 18 59 E
Szczęsliwice, *Wsaw.* **10 E6** 52 12N 20 57 E
Szemere-Telep, *Bud.* **10 K14** 47 26N 19 13 E
Śzephalom, *Bud.* **10 J12** 47 34N 18 57 E
Szilasliget, *Bud.* **10 J14** 47 34N 19 16 E

T

Tabata, *Tōkyō* **13 B3** 35 44N 139 46 E
Tablada, *B.A.* **32 C3** 34 41 S 58 32W
Taboão →, *S. Pau.* **31 F7** 23 40 S 46 27W
Taboão da Serra, *S. Pau.* **31 E5** 23 36 S 46 45W
Tabor, *N.Y.* **22 B2** 40 52N 74 28W
Täby, *Stock.* **3 D11** 59 26N 18 2 E
Tacony, *Phil.* **24 A4** 40 1N 75 2W
Tacuba, *Méx.* **29 B2** 19 26N 99 11W
Tacubaya, *Méx.* **29 B2** 19 24N 99 10W
Tadain, *Ōsaka* **12 A3** 34 51N 135 24 E
Tadworth, *Lon.* **4 D3** 51 17N 0 14W
Tagig, *Manila* **15 D4** 14 31N 121 4 E
Tagig →, *Manila* **15 D4** 14 31N 121 5 E
Tai Hang, *H.K.* **12 E6** 22 16N 114 11 E
Tai Lo Shan, *H.K.* **12 D6** 22 21N 114 13 E
Tai Po Tsai, *H.K.* **12 D6** 22 20N 114 15 E
Tai Seng, *Sing.* **15 F8** 1 20N 103 53 E
Tai Shui Hang, *H.K.* **12 D6** 22 24N 114 13 E
Tai Tam B., *H.K.* **12 E6** 22 12N 114 13 E
Tai Tam Tuk Res., *H.K.* **12 E6** 22 14N 114 13 E
Tai Wan Tau, *H.K.* **12 E6** 22 17N 114 17 E
Tai Wo Hau, *H.K.* **12 D5** 22 21N 114 7 E
Tai Wo Ping, *H.K.* **12 D5** 22 20N 114 9 E
Ta'imim, *Bagd.* **17 F8** 33 15N 44 21 E
Tainaka, *Ōsaka* **12 C4** 34 36N 135 35 E
Taishō, *Ōsaka* **12 C3** 34 38N 135 27 E
Taitō-Ku, *Tōkyō* **13 B3** 35 43N 139 47 E
Tajima, *Tōkyō* **13 B2** 35 48N 139 36 E
Tajpur, *Calc.* **16 D5** 22 44N 88 15 E
Takaido, *Tōkyō* **13 B2** 35 40N 139 37 E
Takaishi, *Tōkyō* **13 C2** 35 36N 139 31 E
Takarazuka, *Ōsaka* **12 B2** 34 47N 135 20 E
Takasago, *Tōkyō* **13 B4** 35 44N 139 52 E
Takatsuki, *Ōsaka* **12 A4** 34 50N 135 37 E
Takayanagi, *Tōkyō* **13 D4** 35 23N 139 57 E
Takegahana, *Tōkyō* **13 B4** 35 47N 139 54 E
Takenotsuka, *Tōkyō* **13 B3** 35 47N 139 47 E
Takeshita, *Tōkyō* **13 C2** 35 33N 139 32 E
Takinegawa, *Tōkyō* **13 B3** 35 45N 139 44 E
Takkula, *Hels.* **3 B2** 60 19N 24 38 E
Takoma Park, *Wash.* **25 D7** 38 58N 77 0W
Taksim, *Ist.* **17 A2** 41 2N 28 58 E
Talaide, *Lisb.* **8 F7** 38 44N 9 18W
Talampas, *Manila* **15 D4** 14 36N 121 4 E
Taling Chan, *Bangk.* **15 B1** 13 46N 100 27 E
Talleyville, *Phil.* **24 C1** 39 48N 75 32W
Tallkrogen, *Stock.* **3 E11** 59 16N 18 4 E
Talmapais Valley, *S.F.* **27 A1** 37 52N 122 32W
Tama, *Tōkyō* **13 C1** 35 38N 139 26 E
Tama →, *Tōkyō* **13 C2** 35 32N 139 39 E
Tama Kyźryō, *Tōkyō* **13 C2** 35 34N 139 30 E
Tamaden, *Tōkyō* **13 C2** 35 39N 139 38 E
Tamagawa-josui →, *Tōkyō* **13 B1** 35 41N 139 47 E
Taman Sari, *Jak.* **15 H9** 6 8 S 106 48 E
Tamanduatei →, *S. Pau.* **31 E6** 23 37 S 46 38W
Tambora, *Jak.* **15 H9** 6 8 S 106 47 E
Tamboré, *S. Pau.* **31 E4** 23 30 S 46 50W
Tammisalo, *Hels.* **3 B5** 60 11N 25 5 E
Tammûh, *El Qâ.* **18 D5** 29 55N 31 15 E
Tampier Slough, *Chic.* **26 D1** 41 39N 87 54W
Tan Tock Seng, *Sing.* **15 G8** 1 19N 103 50 E
Tanah Abang, *Jak.* **15 J9** 6 12 S 106 48 E
Tanashi, *Tōkyō* **13 B2** 35 43N 139 32 E
Tanforan Park, *S.F.* **27 C2** 37 37N 122 24W
Tangjae, *Sŏul* **12 H8** 37 29N 127 2 E
Tanglin, *Sing.* **15 G7** 1 18N 103 47 E
Tangstedt, *Hbg.* **7 C7** 53 40N 9 51 E
Tangstedter Forst, *Hbg.* **7 C8** 53 43N 10 3 E
Tanigami, *Ōsaka* **12 B2** 34 45N 135 10 E
Tanjung Duren, *Jak.* **15 J9** 6 10 S 106 46 E
Tanjung Priok, *Jak.* **15 H10** 6 6 S 106 52 E
Tanum, *Oslo* **2 B2** 59 53N 10 28 E
Taoranting Gongyuan, *Beij.* **14 B3** 39 51N 116 20 E
Taoranting Hu, *Beij.* **14 B3** 39 50N 116 20 E
Tapada, *Lisb.* **8 F7** 38 49N 9 16W
Tapanila, *Hels.* **3 B5** 60 15N 25 2 E
Tapiales, *B.A.* **32 C3** 34 42 S 58 30W
Tapiola, *Hels.* **3 B3** 60 10N 24 48 E
Tappan, *N.Y.* **22 A5** 41 1N 73 57W
Tappan, L., *N.Y.* **22 A5** 41 1N 73 59W
Tappeh, *Tehr.* **17 C5** 35 41N 51 29 E
Tapsia, *Calc.* **16 E6** 22 32N 88 23 E
Taquara, *Rio J.* **31 B1** 22 55 S 43 21W
Tara, *Bomb.* **16 G7** 19 5N 72 49 E
Tarāblus, *Bagd.* **17 F8** 33 19N 44 21 E
Tarango, Presa, *Méx.* **29 B2** 19 21N 99 12W
Tårbæk, *Købn.* **2 D10** 55 46N 12 35 E
Tarchomin, *Wsaw.* **10 E6** 52 19N 20 58 E
Tardeo, *Bomb.* **16 H7** 18 57N 72 48 E
Target Rock, *N.Y.* **23 B8** 40 55N 73 24W
Targówek, *Wsaw.* **10 E7** 52 16N 21 3 E
Tårnby, *Købn.* **2 E10** 55 37N 12 35 E

Villecresnes **47**

Taronga Zoo. Park, *Syd.* **19 B4** 33 50 S 151 14 E
Tarqua B., *Lagos* **18 B2** 6 24N 7 23 E
Tarzana, *L.A.* **28 A1** 34 10N 118 32W
Tåstrup, *Købn.* **2 E8** 55 39N 12 18 E
Tatarovo, *Mos.* **11 E8** 55 45N 37 24 E
Tatarpur, *Delhi* **16 B1** 28 38N 77 9 E
Tatenberg, *Hbg.* **7 E8** 53 29N 10 3 E
Tathong Channel, *H.K.* **12 E6** 22 15N 114 16 E
Tathong Pt., *H.K.* **12 E6** 22 14N 114 17 E
Tatsfield, *Lon.* **4 D5** 51 17N 0 1 E
Tattariharju, *Hels.* **3 B5** 60 15N 25 2 E
Tatuapé, *S. Pau.* **31 E6** 23 31 S 46 33W
Taufkirchen, *Mün.* **7 G10** 48 2N 11 36 E
Tavares, I. dos, *Rio J.* **31 A3** 22 49 S 43 6W
Tavernanova, *Nápl.* **9 H13** 40 54N 14 21 E
Taverny, *Paris* **5 A3** 49 1N 2 13 E
Távros, *Ath.* **8 J11** 37 57N 23 43 E
Tavry, *St-Pet.* **11 B6** 59 54N 30 40 E
Taylortown, *N.Y.* **22 B2** 40 56N 74 23W
Tayninka, *Mos.* **11 D10** 55 53N 37 45 E
Taytay, *Manila* **15 D4** 14 34N 121 7 E
Tayuman, *Manila* **15 D4** 14 31N 121 9 E
Teaneck, *N.Y.* **22 B4** 40 52N 74 1W
Teatro Colón, *B.A.* **32 B4** 34 36 S 58 23 E
Teban Gardens, *Sing.* **15 G7** 1 19N 103 44 E
Tebet, *Jak.* **15 J10** 6 14 S 106 50 E
Tecamachaleo, *Méx.* **29 B2** 19 25N 99 14W
Techny, *Chic.* **26 A2** 42 6N 87 48W
Teck Hock, *Sing.* **15 F8** 1 21N 103 54 E
Tecoma, *Melb.* **19 F9** 37 54 S 145 20 E
Teddington, *Lon.* **4 C2** 51 25N 0 20W
Tegel, *Berl.* **7 A2** 52 34N 13 16 E
Tegel, Flughafen, *Berl.* **7 A2** 52 35N 13 15 E
Tegeler Fliess →, *Berl.* **7 A3** 52 37N 13 21 E
Tegeler See, *Berl.* **7 A2** 52 34N 13 15 E
Tegelort, *Berl.* **7 A2** 52 34N 13 13 E
Tehar, *Delhi* **16 B1** 28 37N 77 7 E
Tehrān, *Tehr.* **17 C5** 35 41N 51 25 E
Tehrān Pars, *Tehr.* **17 C6** 35 44N 51 32 E
Tei Tong Tsui, *H.K.* **12 E6** 22 16N 114 17 E
Tejo →, *Lisb.* **8 F8** 38 45N 9 3W
Tekstilyshchik, *Mos.* **11 E10** 55 42N 37 41 E
Tela, *Delhi* **16 A2** 28 43N 77 19 E
Telhal, *Lisb.* **8 F7** 38 48N 9 18W
Telinipara, *Calc.* **16 D6** 22 46N 88 23 E
Telok Blangah, *Sing.* **15 G7** 1 17N 103 49 E
Teltow, *Berl.* **7 B2** 52 23N 13 17 E
Teltow kanal, *Berl.* **7 B3** 52 26N 13 29 E
Temescal, L., *S.F.* **27 A3** 37 50N 122 13W
Temnikovo, *Mos.* **11 E12** 55 43N 38 1 E
Tempelhof, *Berl.* **7 B3** 52 27N 13 23 E
Tempelhof, Flughafen, *Berl.* **7 B3** 52 28N 13 27 E
Temperley, *B.A.* **32 C4** 34 46 S 58 22W
Temple City, *L.A.* **28 B4** 34 6N 118 3W
Temple Hills Park, *Wash.* **25 E8** 38 48N 76 56W
Templestowe, *Melb.* **19 E7** 37 45 S 145 8 E
Templestowe Lower, *Melb.* **19 E7** 37 45 S 145 6 E
Tenafly, *N.Y.* **22 B5** 40 54N 73 58W
Tenantongo, Presa, *Méx.* **29 B2** 19 28N 99 15W
Tengah →, *Sing.* **15 F7** 1 23N 103 43 E
Tengeh, Sungei →, *Sing.* **15 F6** 1 20N 103 39 E
Tennoji, *Ōsaka* **12 C4** 34 39N 135 30 E
Tenochtitlán, *Méx.* **29 B3** 19 26N 99 7W
Tepalcates, *Méx.* **29 B3** 19 23N 99 3W
Tepe Saif, *Tehr.* **17 D4** 35 36N 51 17 E
Tepepan, *Méx.* **29 C3** 19 16N 99 9W
Teplyy Star, *Mos.* **11 F9** 55 37N 37 30 E
Tepozteco, Parque Nac. del, *Méx.* **29 D3** 19 3N 99 5W
Terrasse Vaudreuil, *Mtrl.* **20 B2** 43 23N 73 59W
Terrazzano, *Mil.* **9 D5** 45 32N 9 4 E
Terrugem, *Lisb.* **8 F7** 38 41N 9 17W
Terusan Banjir, *Jak.* **15 H9** 6 7 S 106 46 E
Terzigno, *Nápl.* **9 J13** 40 48N 14 29 E
Tessancourt-sur-Aubette, *Paris* **5 A1** 49 1N 1 55 E
Testona, *Tori.* **9 C3** 44 59N 7 42 E
Tetelco, *Méx.* **29 C4** 19 12N 98 57W
Tetreauville, *Mtrl.* **20 A4** 43 35N 73 32W
Tetti Neirotti, *Tori.* **9 B2** 45 3N 7 32 E
Tetuán, *Mdrd.* **8 B2** 40 27N 3 42W
Teufelsberg, *Berl.* **7 B2** 52 29N 13 14 E
Tévere →, *Rome* **9 F9** 41 56N 12 27 E
Tewksbury, *Bost.* **21 B2** 42 37N 71 12W
Texcoco, L. de, *Méx.* **29 B4** 19 30N 89 58 E
Thalkirchen, *Mün.* **7 G10** 48 6N 11 32 E
Thames Ditton, *Lon.* **4 C2** 51 23N 0 20W
Thamesmead, *Lon.* **4 B5** 51 30N 0 7 E
Thana Cr. →, *Bomb.* **16 G8** 19 4N 72 54 E
The Basin, *Melb.* **19 F8** 37 51 S 145 19 E
The Glen, *Wash.* **25 C6** 39 2N 77 12W
The Loop, *Chic.* **26 B3** 41 52N 87 37W
The Narrows, *N.Y.* **22 D4** 40 37N 74 3W
The Ridge, *Delhi* **16 B2** 28 37N 77 10 E
The White House, *Wash.* **25 D7** 38 53N 77 1W
The Wilds, *Jobg.* **18 F9** 26 10 S 28 2 E
Theseión, *Ath.* **8 J11** 37 57N 23 43 E
Theydon Bois, *Lon.* **4 A5** 51 40N 0 6 E
Thiais, *Paris* **5 C4** 48 46N 2 23 E
Thieux, *Paris* **5 A6** 49 0N 2 40 E
Thistletown, *Trto.* **20 D7** 43 44N 79 34W
Thiverval-Grignon, *Paris* **5 B1** 48 51N 1 55 E
Thomaston, *N.Y.* **23 C6** 40 47N 73 43W
Thomastown, *Melb.* **19 E7** 37 40 S 145 2 E
Thompson I., *Bost.* **21 D4** 42 19N 70 59W
Thomson, *Sing.* **15 F8** 1 20N 103 50 E
Thon Buri, *Bangk.* **15 B1** 13 45N 100 29 E
Thong Hoe, *Sing.* **15 F7** 1 25N 103 42 E
Thorigny-sur-Marne, *Paris* **5 B6** 48 53N 2 41 E
Thornbury, *Melb.* **19 E7** 37 44 S 145 1 E
Thorncliffe, *Trto.* **20 D8** 43 42N 79 20W
Thornhill, *Jobg.* **18 E9** 26 6 S 28 9 E
Thornhill, *Trto.* **20 D8** 43 48N 79 25W
Thornton, *Phil.* **24 B1** 39 54N 75 31W
Thornton Heath, *Lon.* **4 C4** 51 23N 0 6W
Thorofare, *Phil.* **24 B3** 39 50N 75 11W
Throgs Neck, *N.Y.* **23 C6** 40 48N 73 49W
Tian Guan, *Sing.* **15 F7** 1 21N 103 49 E
Tian'anmen, *Beij.* **14 B3** 39 53N 116 21 E
Tiancun, *Beij.* **14 B2** 39 54N 116 12 E
Tianjin, *Tianj.* **14 E5** 39 7N 117 12 E
Tiantan Gongyuan, *Beij.* **14 B3** 39 51N 116 22 E
Tiateloco, *Méx.* **29 B3** 19 27N 99 8W
Tibidabo, *Barc.* **8 D5** 41 25N 2 6 E
Tiburon, *S.F.* **27 A2** 37 52N 122 27W
Tiburon Pen., *S.F.* **27 A2** 37 53N 122 28W
Tiburtino, *Rome* **9 F10** 41 53N 12 30 E
Ticomán, *Méx.* **29 A3** 19 31N 99 8W
Tiefenbroich, *Ruhr* **6 C2** 51 18N 6 49 E
Tiefersee, *Berl.* **7 B1** 52 24N 13 5 E
Tiejiangyin, *Beij.* **14 C3** 39 49N 116 23 E
Tientsin = Tianjin, *Tianj.* **14 E5** 39 7N 117 12 E
Tiergarten, *Berl.* **7 A3** 52 31N 13 20 E
Tietê →, *S. Pau.* **31 D7** 23 28 S 46 24W
Tigery, *Paris* **5 D5** 48 38N 2 30 E
Tigre, *B.A.* **32 A3** 34 25 S 58 34W
Tigris →, *Bagd.* **17 F8** 33 17N 44 23 E
Tijuca, *Rio J.* **31 B2** 22 56 S 43 13W
Tijuca, L. de, *Rio J.* **31 B2** 22 59 S 43 20W
Tijuca, Pico da, *Rio J.* **31 B2** 22 56 S 43 15W
Tijucamar, *Rio J.* **31 C2** 23 0 S 43 18W
Tijucas, Is., *Rio J.* **31 C2** 23 1 S 43 17W
Tikkurila, *Hels.* **3 B5** 60 17N 25 2 E
Tilanqiao, *Shang.* **14 J11** 31 15N 121 29 E
Tilbury, *Lon.* **4 C7** 51 27N 0 21 E
Timah, Bukit, *Sing.* **15 F7** 1 21N 103 46 E
Timiryazev Park, *Mos.* **11 E9** 55 49N 37 33 E
Ting Kau, *H.K.* **12 D5** 22 22N 114 4 E
Tinley Cr. →, *Chic.* **26 D2** 41 39N 87 45W
Tinley Creek Woods, *Chic.* **26 D2** 41 38N 87 48W
Tinley Park, *Chic.* **26 D2** 41 35N 87 46W
Tipas, *Manila* **15 D4** 14 32N 121 4 E
Tirsa, *El Qâ.* **18 D5** 29 57N 31 12 E
Tishrīyaa, *Bagd.* **17 F8** 33 18N 44 24 E
Tit Cham Chau, *H.K.* **12 E6** 22 15N 114 17 E
Titagarh, *Calc.* **16 D6** 22 44N 88 22 E
Tivoli, *Købn.* **2 D10** 55 40N 12 35 E
Tizapán, *Méx.* **29 C2** 19 19N 99 13W
Tlalnepantla, *Méx.* **29 A2** 19 32N 99 11W
Tlalnepantla →, *Méx.* **29 A2** 19 30N 99 18W
Tláloc, Cerro, *Méx.* **29 D3** 19 7N 99 3W
Tlalpan, *Méx.* **29 C2** 19 17N 99 10W
Tlalpitzáhuac, *Méx.* **29 C4** 19 19N 98 56W
Tlaltenango, *Méx.* **29 B2** 19 20N 99 17W
Tlaltenco, *Méx.* **29 C3** 19 19N 99 0W
Tlaxcoaque, *Méx.* **29 B3** 19 25N 99 8W
To Kwai Wan, *H.K.* **12 E6** 22 18N 114 11 E
Toa Payoh, *Sing.* **15 F8** 1 20N 103 50 E
Tobay Beach, *N.Y.* **23 D8** 40 36N 73 26W
Točná, *Pra.* **10 C2** 49 58N 14 25 E
Tocome →, *Car.* **30 D6** 10 28N 66 49W
Toda, *Tōkyō* **13 A3** 35 50N 139 40 E
Todamachī, *Tōkyō* **13 B2** 35 48N 139 39 E
Todt Hill, *N.Y.* **22 D4** 40 36N 74 6W
Toei, Khlong →, *Bangk.* **15 B2** 13 43N 100 32 E
Togasaki, *Tōkyō* **13 B4** 35 47N 139 51 E
Tōkagi, *Tōkyō* **13 B4** 35 42N 139 55 E
Tōkaichiba, *Tōkyō* **13 C2** 35 31N 139 30 E
Tokarevo, *Mos.* **11 F11** 55 38N 37 54 E
Tokorozawa, *Tōkyō* **13 B1** 35 47N 139 28 E
Tōkyō, *Tōkyō* **13 C3** 35 43N 139 45 E
Tōkyō B., *Tōkyō* **13 C4** 35 33N 139 53 E
Tōkyō-Haneda Int. Airport, *Tōkyō* **13 C3** 35 33N 139 45 E
Tōkyō Harbour, *Tōkyō* **13 C3** 35 38N 139 46 E
Tokyo Univ., *Tōkyō* **13 B3** 35 42N 139 46 E
Tollygunge, *Calc.* **16 F6** 22 29N 88 21 E
Tolly's Nala, *Calc.* **16 E6** 22 33N 88 19 E
Tolworth, *Lon.* **4 C3** 51 22N 0 17W
Tomang, *Jak.* **15 J9** 6 10 S 106 47 E
Tomba di Nerone, *Rome* **9 F9** 41 58N 12 26 E
Tomilino, *Mos.* **11 F11** 55 39N 37 55 E
Tomioka, *Tōkyō* **13 D2** 35 22N 139 37 E
Tonda, *Ōsaka* **12 B4** 34 49N 135 35 E
Tondo, *Manila* **15 D3** 14 36N 120 57 E
Tone-unga →, *Tōkyō* **13 A4** 35 55N 139 56 E
Tonekollen, *Oslo* **2 C6** 50 49N 11 0 E
Tong Kang, Sungei →, *Sing.* **15 F8** 1 23N 103 53 E
Tonghui He →, *Beij.* **14 B3** 39 53N 116 28 E
Tönisheide, *Ruhr* **6 C4** 51 18N 7 3 E
Tonndorf, *Hbg.* **7 D8** 53 35N 10 8 E
Toorak, *Melb.* **19 F7** 37 50 S 145 1 E
Toot Hill, *Lon.* **4 A6** 51 41N 0 11 E
Topilejo, *Méx.* **29 C3** 19 12N 99 9W
Topkapi, *Ist.* **17 A2** 41 1N 28 55 E
Topsfield, *Bost.* **21 B4** 42 38N 70 57W
Tor di Quinto, *Rome* **9 F9** 41 56N 12 27 E
Tor Pignattara, *Rome* **9 F10** 41 52N 12 31 E
Tor Sapienza, *Rome* **9 F10** 41 53N 12 35 E
Torcy, *Paris* **5 B5** 48 51N 2 39 E
Torino, *Tori.* **9 B2** 45 5N 7 39 E
Toro, *B.A.* **32 B1** 34 30 S 58 50W
Toronto, *Trto.* **20 E9** 43 39N 79 13W
Toronto, Univ. of, *Trto.* **20 E8** 43 39N 79 23W
Toronto Harbour, *Trto.* **20 E8** 43 38N 79 21W
Toronto I., *Trto.* **20 E8** 43 37N 79 23W
Toronto Int. Airport, *Trto.* **20 D7** 43 40N 79 38 E
Torre Annunziata, *Nápl.* **9 J13** 40 45N 14 26 E
Torre Cervara, *Rome* **9 F10** 41 55N 12 35 E
Torre del Greco, *Nápl.* **9 J13** 40 47N 14 21 E
Torre Novo, *Rome* **9 F10** 41 51N 12 36 E
Torrellas →, *Barc.* **8 D5** 41 23N 2 1 E
Torrellas del Llobregat, *Barc.* **8 D4** 41 20N 1 59 E
Torresdale, *Phil.* **24 A5** 40 3N 74 59W
Torrevécchia, *Rome* **9 F9** 41 55N 12 25 E
Tortuguitas, *B.A.* **32 A2** 34 28 S 58 44W
Toshima-Ku, *Tōkyō* **13 B3** 35 43N 139 43 E
Toshimaen, *Tōkyō* **13 B2** 35 43N 139 38 E
Totowa, *N.Y.* **22 B3** 40 54N 74 13W
Totsuka-Ku, *Tōkyō* **13 D2** 35 23N 139 32 E
Tottenham, *Lon.* **4 B4** 51 35N 0 4W
Tottenham, *Melb.* **19 E6** 37 48 S 144 51 E
Tottenville, *N.Y.* **22 D3** 40 30N 74 14W
Totteridge, *Lon.* **4 B3** 51 37N 0 11W
Toussus-le-Noble, *Paris* **5 C2** 48 44N 2 6 E
Toussus-le-Noble, Aérodrome de, *Paris* **5 C2** 48 44N 2 6 E
Toverud, *Oslo* **2 B2** 59 55N 10 20 E
Towaco, *N.Y.* **22 B3** 40 55N 74 18W
Tower Hamlets, *Lon.* **4 B4** 51 31N 0 2W
Town Farm Hill, *Bost.* **21 A3** 42 40N 71 3W
Townley, *N.Y.* **22 C3** 40 41N 74 14W
Towra Pt., *Syd.* **19 C4** 34 0 S 151 10 E
Towson, *Balt.* **25 A3** 39 24N 76 36W
Tøyen, *Oslo* **2 B4** 59 55N 10 47 E
Toyofuta, *Tōkyō* **13 A4** 35 54N 139 55 E
Toyonaka, *Ōsaka* **12 B3** 34 46N 135 28 E
Traar, *Ruhr* **6 B1** 51 22N 6 36 E
Trafaria, *Lisb.* **8 F7** 38 40N 9 13W
Tragliata, *Rome* **9 F8** 41 58N 12 14 E
Traicão →, *S. Pau.* **31 E6** 23 35 S 46 41W
Trälhavet, *Stock.* **3 D13** 59 26N 18 22 E
Tranby, *Oslo* **2 C1** 59 49N 10 14 E
Tranegilde, *Købn.* **2 E9** 55 37N 12 20 E
Trångsund, *Stock.* **3 E11** 59 13N 18 8 E
Trappenfelde, *Berl.* **7 A4** 52 34N 13 39 E
Trappes, *Paris* **5 C1** 48 46N 1 59 E
Trastévere, *Rome* **9 F9** 51 53N 12 28 E
Travilah, *Wash.* **25 C6** 39 4N 77 15W
Travilah Regional Park, *Wash.* **25 C6** 39 4N 77 17W
Travis, *N.Y.* **22 D3** 40 35N 74 11W
Treasure I., *S.F.* **27 B2** 37 49N 122 22W
Třeboradice, *Pra.* **10 B3** 50 9N 14 31 E
Třebotov, *Pra.* **10 C1** 49 58N 14 17 E
Trecase, *Nápl.* **9 J13** 40 46N 14 26 E
Trekroner, *Købn.* **2 D10** 55 42N 12 36 E
Tremblay-lès-Gonesse, *Paris* **5 B5** 48 58N 2 30 E
Tremembé, *S. Pau.* **31 D6** 23 27 S 46 36W
Tremembe →, *S. Pau.* **31 D6** 23 27 S 46 34W
Tremont, *Melb.* **19 F9** 37 53 S 145 20 E
Tremont, *N.Y.* **23 B5** 40 50N 73 52W
Trenno, *Mil.* **9 E5** 45 29N 9 6 E
Treptow, *Berl.* **7 B3** 52 29N 13 27 E
Tres Marias, *Méx.* **29 D2** 19 3N 99 15W
Trés Rios, Sa. dos, *Rio J.* **31 B2** 22 56 S 43 17W
Tretiakov Art Gallery, *Mos.* **11 E9** 55 44N 37 38 E
Trevose, *Phil.* **24 A5** 40 8N 74 59W
Trezzano sul Navíglio, *Mil.* **9 E5** 45 24N 9 4 E
Tribobo, *Rio J.* **31 B3** 22 50 S 43 0W
Triel-sur-Seine, *Paris* **5 B2** 48 58N 2 0 E
Trieste, *Rome* **9 F10** 41 55N 12 30 E
Trinidad, *Wash.* **25 D8** 38 54N 76 59W
Triome, *Jobg.* **18 F8** 26 10 S 27 58 E
Trionfale, *Rome* **9 F9** 41 54N 12 26 E
Triulzo, *Mil.* **9 E6** 45 25N 9 16 E
Trócchia, *Nápl.* **9 H13** 40 51N 14 23 E
Troitse-Lykovo, *Mos.* **11 E8** 55 47N 37 23 E
Troja, *Pra.* **10 B2** 50 7N 14 25 E
Trollbäcken, *Stock.* **3 E12** 59 14N 18 12 E
Trombay, *Bomb.* **16 G8** 19 2N 72 56 E
Troparevo, *Mos.* **11 F8** 55 39N 37 29 E
Trottiscliffe, *Lon.* **4 D7** 51 18N 0 21 E
Troy Hills, *N.Y.* **22 B2** 40 50N 74 23W
Troyeville, *Jobg.* **18 F9** 26 11 S 28 4 E
Truc di Miola, *Tori.* **9 A2** 45 11N 7 30 E
Trudyashchikhsya, Os., *St-Pet.* **11 B3** 59 58N 30 18 E
Trutlandet, *Hels.* **3 C6** 60 9N 25 17 E
Tryvasshøgda, *Oslo* **2 B4** 59 59N 10 40 E
Tseng Lan Shue, *H.K.* **12 D6** 22 20N 114 14 E
Tsentralynyy, *Mos.* **11 D11** 55 53N 37 51 E
Tsim Sha Tsui, *H.K.* **12 E6** 22 17N 114 10 E
Tsing Yi, *H.K.* **12 D5** 22 21N 114 6 E
Tsuen Wan, *H.K.* **12 D5** 22 22N 114 7 E
Tsurugamine, *Tōkyō* **13 D2** 35 28N 139 33 E
Tsuruma, *Tōkyō* **13 A2** 35 52N 139 31 E
Tsurumi →, *Tōkyō* **13 C3** 35 32N 139 40 E
Tsurumi-Ku, *Tōkyō* **13 D3** 35 30N 139 41 E
Tsz Wan Shan, *H.K.* **12 D6** 22 20N 114 11 E
Tua Kang Lye, *Sing.* **15 G7** 1 18N 103 46 E
Tuas, *Sing.* **15 G6** 1 19N 103 39 E
Tuchoměřice, *Pra.* **10 B1** 50 7N 14 16 E
Tuckahoe, *N.Y.* **23 B6** 40 56N 73 49W
Tucuruvi, *S. Pau.* **31 D6** 23 28 S 46 35W
Tufello, *Rome* **9 F10** 41 56N 12 32 E
Tufnell Park, *Lon.* **4 B4** 51 33N 0 8W
Tujunga, *L.A.* **28 A3** 34 15N 118 16W
Tujunga Wash →, *L.A.* **28 A2** 34 12N 118 23W
Tullamarine, *Melb.* **19 E6** 37 41 S 144 50 E
Tullinge, *Stock.* **3 E10** 59 12N 17 54 E
Tullingesjön, *Stock.* **3 E10** 59 12N 17 52 E
Tulse Hill, *Lon.* **4 C4** 51 26N 0 6W
Tulyehualco, *Méx.* **29 C3** 19 15N 99 0W
Tumba, *Stock.* **3 E9** 59 12N 17 49 E
Tune, *Købn.* **2 E8** 55 35N 12 10 E
Tung Lo Wan, *H.K.* **12 E6** 22 17N 114 11 E
Tung Lung I., *H.K.* **12 E6** 22 15N 114 17 E
Tung O, *H.K.* **12 E5** 22 11N 114 8 E
Tunis, *Bagd.* **17 E8** 33 23N 44 21 E
Tuomarila, *Hels.* **3 B3** 60 11N 24 41 E
Tura, *El Qâ.* **18 D5** 29 55N 31 16 E
Turambhe, *Bomb.* **16 G9** 19 4N 73 0 E
Turdera, *B.A.* **32 C4** 34 48 S 58 26W
Tureberg, *Stock.* **3 D10** 59 25N 17 55 E
Turffontein, *Jobg.* **18 F9** 26 14 S 28 2 E
Turin = Torino, *Tori.* **9 B2** 45 5N 7 39 E
Turner, *Balt.* **25 B3** 39 14N 76 31W
Turner Hill, *Bost.* **21 A4** 42 40N 70 53W
Turnersville, *Phil.* **24 C4** 39 46N 75 3W
Turnham Green, *Lon.* **4 C3** 51 29N 0 16W
Turów, *Wsaw.* **10 E8** 52 19N 21 11 E
Turter, *Oslo* **2 A4** 60 0N 10 46 E
Tuscolano, *Rome* **9 F10** 41 52N 12 31 E
Tushino, *Mos.* **11 D8** 55 50N 37 24 E
Tuusulanjoki →, *Hels.* **3 A4** 60 20N 24 54 E
Twickenham, *Lon.* **4 C2** 51 26N 0 20W
Twickenham Rugby Ground, *Lon.* **4 C2** 51 27N 0 20W
Twin Oaks, *Phil.* **24 B2** 39 50N 75 25W
Twórki, *Wsaw.* **10 E5** 52 10N 20 49 E
Tyresö, *Stock.* **3 E13** 59 14N 18 20 E
Tyresö strand, *Stock.* **3 E12** 59 15N 18 17 E

U

Uberaba →, *S. Pau.* **31 E6** 23 35 S 46 41W
Uberruhr, *Ruhr* **6 B4** 51 25N 7 4 E
Ubin, P., *Sing.* **15 F8** 1 24N 103 57 E
Uboldo, *Mil.* **9 D5** 45 36N 9 0 E
Uckendorf, *Ruhr* **6 B4** 51 29N 7 7 E
Udelnaya, *St-Pet.* **11 A4** 60 0N 30 21 E
Udelynaya, *Mos.* **11 F11** 55 38N 37 59 E
Udlding, *Mün.* **7 F9** 48 15N 11 25 E
Uellendahl, *Ruhr* **6 C5** 51 16N 7 10 E
Ueno, *Tōkyō* **13 B3** 35 42N 139 46 E
Uerdingen, *Ruhr* **6 B1** 51 21N 6 38 E
Uhlenhorst, *Hbg.* **7 D8** 53 34N 10 1 E
Üholičky, *Pra.* **10 B1** 50 9N 14 19 E
Uhřiněves, *Pra.* **10 B3** 50 2N 14 35 E
Újezd nad Lesy, *Pra.* **10 B3** 50 4N 14 39 E
Újpalota, *Bud.* **10 J13** 47 32N 19 8 E
Újpest, *Bud.* **10 J13** 47 35N 19 4 E
Ukita, *Tōkyō* **13 B4** 35 40N 139 51 E
Ullerup, *Købn.* **2 E10** 55 34N 12 36 E
Ullevål, *Oslo* **2 B4** 59 56N 10 46 E
Üllo, *Bud.* **10 K14** 47 23N 19 20 E
Ulriksdal, *Stock.* **3 D10** 59 23N 17 59 E
Ulu Bedok, *Sing.* **15 G8** 1 19N 103 55 E
Ulu Pandan →, *Sing.* **15 G7** 1 19N 103 45 E
Ulyanka, *St-Pet.* **11 B3** 59 50N 30 14 E
Um Al-Khanazir, *Bagd.* **17 F8** 33 17N 44 22 E
Umeda, *Ōsaka* **12 B3** 34 41N 135 29 E
Umejima, *Tōkyō* **13 B3** 35 46N 139 48 E
Umraniye, *Ist.* **17 A3** 41 1N 29 4 E
Unětický →, *Pra.* **10 B2** 50 9N 14 24 E
Ungelsheim, *Ruhr* **6 B2** 51 21N 6 43 E
Unhos, *Lisb.* **8 F8** 38 49N 9 7W
Unidad Santa Fe, *Méx.* **29 B2** 19 23N 99 13W
Union, *N.Y.* **22 C3** 40 42N 74 16W
Union City, *N.Y.* **22 C4** 40 45N 74 2W
Union City, *S.F.* **27 C4** 37 36N 122 2W
Union Port, *N.Y.* **23 C5** 40 48N 73 51W
Uniondale, *N.Y.* **23 C7** 40 42N 73 35W
United Nations H.Q., *N.Y.* **22 C5** 40 45N 73 59W
Universal City, *L.A.* **28 B2** 34 8N 118 21W
Universidad de Chila, *Stgo* **30 J11** 33 26 S 70 39W
University Gardens, *N.Y.* **23 C6** 40 46N 73 42W
University Heights, *S.F.* **27 D3** 37 26N 122 13W
University Park, *Wash.* **25 D8** 38 58N 76 56W
Unsani, *Calc.* **16 E5** 22 35N 88 15 E
Unterbach, *Ruhr* **6 C3** 51 12N 6 53 E
Unterbiberg, *Mün.* **7 G10** 48 6N 11 38 E
Unterföhring, *Mün.* **7 F11** 48 11N 11 38 E
Unterhaching, *Mün.* **7 G10** 48 3N 11 37 E
Unterkirchbach, *Wien* **10 G9** 48 17N 16 12 E
Unterlaa, *Wien* **10 H10** 48 8N 16 24 E
Untermauerbach, *Wien* **10 G9** 48 14N 16 11 E
Untermenzing, *Mün.* **7 F9** 48 10N 11 28 E
Unterrath, *Ruhr* **6 C2** 51 16N 6 45 E
Unterschleissheim, *Mün.* **7 F10** 48 16N 11 35 E
Upminster, *Lon.* **4 B6** 51 33N 0 14 E
Upper Brookville, *N.Y.* **23 B7** 40 50N 73 35W
Upper Crystal Springs Res., *S.F.* **26 D2** 37 28N 122 20W
Upper Darby, *Phil.* **24 B3** 39 57N 75 16W
Upper Edmonton, *Lon.* **4 B4** 51 36N 0 3W
Upper Elmers End, *Lon.* **4 C4** 51 23N 0 1W
Upper Fern Tree Gully, *Melb.* **19 F8** 37 53 S 145 18 E
Upper New York B., *N.Y.* **22 D4** 40 39N 74 3W
Upper Norwood, *Lon.* **4 C4** 51 24N 0 6W
Upper Peirce Res., *Sing.* **15 F7** 1 22N 103 47 E
Upper San Leandro Res., *S.F.* **27 B4** 37 46N 122 6W
Upper Sydenham, *Lon.* **4 C4** 51 26N 0 4W
Upper Tooting, *Lon.* **4 C4** 51 25N 0 9W
Upton, *Lon.* **4 B5** 51 32N 0 1 E
Uptons Hill, *Bost.* **21 B3** 42 33N 71 0W
Uptown, *Chic.* **26 B2** 41 58N 87 40W
Upwey, *Melb.* **19 F9** 37 53 S 145 20 E
Urawa, *Tōkyō* **13 A2** 35 51N 139 39 E
Urayasu, *Tōkyō* **13 C4** 35 39N 139 53 E
Urbe, Aeroporto d', *Rome* **9 F10** 41 57N 12 30 E
Urca, *Rio J.* **31 B3** 22 56 S 43 9W
Uritsk, *St-Pet.* **11 C3** 59 49N 30 10 E
Üröm, *Bud.* **10 J13** 47 35N 19 1 E
Ursus, *Wsaw.* **10 E6** 52 11N 20 52 E
Ursvik, *Stock.* **3 D10** 59 23N 17 57 E
Usera, *Mdrd.* **8 B2** 40 22N 3 42W
Ushigome, *Tōkyō* **13 B3** 35 42N 139 44 E
Usküdar, *Ist.* **17 A3** 41 1N 29 0 E
Ust-Slavyanka, *St-Pet.* **11 C5** 59 51N 30 32 E
Uteke, *Stock.* **3 D12** 59 24N 18 15 E
Utfort, *Ruhr* **6 B1** 51 28N 6 37 E
Utinga, *S. Pau.* **31 E6** 23 38 S 46 31W
Utrata, *Wsaw.* **10 E7** 52 15N 21 4 E
Uttarpara, *Calc.* **16 E5** 22 39N 88 21 E
Utterslev Mose, *Købn.* **2 D9** 55 42N 12 29 E
Uttran, *Stock.* **3 E9** 59 12N 17 43 E
Utvika, *Oslo* **2 A1** 60 2N 10 15 E
Uxbridge, *Lon.* **4 B2** 51 32N 0 28W
Uzkoye, *Mos.* **11 F9** 55 37N 37 32 E
Uzunca →, *Ist.* **17 A1** 41 54N 28 50 E

V

Vadaul, *Bomb.* **16 G8** 19 2N 72 55 E
Værebro Å →, *Købn.* **2 D8** 55 47N 12 7 E
Vahal, *Bomb.* **16 H9** 18 58N 73 2 E
Vaires-sur-Marne, *Paris* **5 B5** 48 52N 2 38 E
Val della Torre, *Tori.* **9 B1** 45 8N 7 27 E
Valby, *Købn.* **2 E9** 55 39N 12 29 E
Valcannuta, *Rome* **9 F9** 41 52N 12 25 E
Valdeveba, *Mdrd.* **8 B3** 40 29N 3 39W
Vale, *Wash.* **25 D5** 38 55N 77 20W
Valentino, Parco del, *Tori.* **9 B3** 45 3N 7 41 E
Valenton, *Paris* **5 C4** 48 44N 2 27 E
Valera, *Mil.* **9 D5** 45 33N 9 3 E
Vallcarca, *Barc.* **8 D5** 41 25N 2 9 E
Valldoreix, *Barc.* **8 D5** 41 27N 2 3 E
Vallecas, *Mdrd.* **8 B3** 40 22N 3 37W
Vallemar, *S.F.* **27 C2** 37 36N 122 28W
Vallensbæk, *Købn.* **2 E9** 55 38N 12 21 E
Vallensbæk Strand, *Købn.* **2 E9** 55 36N 12 23 E
Vallentunasjön, *Stock.* **3 D11** 59 27N 18 1 E
Valleranello, *Rome* **9 G9** 41 46N 12 29 E
Valley Forge, *Phil.* **24 A2** 40 5N 75 27W
Valley Forge Hist. State Park, *Phil.* **24 A2** 40 5N 75 27W
Valley Mede, *Balt.* **25 B1** 39 16N 76 50W
Valley Stream, *N.Y.* **23 C6** 40 40N 73 43W
Vällingby, *Stock.* **3 D10** 59 21N 17 52 E
Vallisaari, *Hels.* **3 C5** 60 7N 25 0 E
Vallvidrera, *Barc.* **8 D5** 41 24N 2 6 E
Valo Velho, *S. Pau.* **31 E5** 23 38 S 46 47W
Valuyevo, *Mos.* **11 F8** 55 30N 37 21 E
Valvidrera →, *Barc.* **8 D5** 41 25N 2 0 E
Van Dyks Park, *Jobg.* **18 F10** 26 15 S 28 18 E
Van Nuys, *L.A.* **28 A2** 34 11N 118 27W
Van Nuys Airport, *L.A.* **28 A2** 34 12N 118 29W
Van Ryn Dam, *Jobg.* **18 E11** 26 8 S 28 21 E
Vanak, *Tehr.* **17 C5** 35 45N 51 23 E
Vangede, *Købn.* **2 D10** 55 45N 12 30 E
Vaniköy, *Ist.* **17 A3** 41 3N 29 3 E
Vanløse, *Købn.* **2 D9** 55 41N 12 28 E
Vantaa, *Hels.* **3 B4** 60 18N 24 56 E
Vantaa →, *Hels.* **3 B4** 60 13N 24 53 E
Vantaankoski, *Hels.* **3 B4** 60 18N 24 50 E
Vantör, *Stock.* **3 E11** 59 16N 18 2 E
Vanves, *Paris* **5 C3** 48 49N 2 17 E
Vanzago, *Mil.* **9 D4** 45 31N 8 59 E
Värby, *Stock.* **3 E10** 59 15N 17 52 E
Vardåsen, *Oslo* **2 C6** 50 48N 11 6 E
Varedo, *Mil.* **9 D5** 45 35N 9 8 E
Varennes-Jarcy, *Paris* **5 C5** 48 40N 2 33 E
Vargem Grande, *Rio J.* **31 B1** 22 58 S 43 27W
Városliget, *Bud.* **10 J13** 47 30N 19 5 E
Vartiokylä, *Hels.* **3 B5** 60 13N 25 6 E
Vartiosaari, *Hels.* **3 B5** 60 11N 25 5 E
Vasby, *Købn.* **2 D8** 55 40N 12 12 E
Vashi, *Bomb.* **16 G8** 19 4N 72 59 E
Vasilyevskiy, Os., *St-Pet.* **11 B3** 59 55N 30 16 E
Västerkulla, *Hels.* **3 B2** 60 16N 24 31 E
Västerskog, *Hels.* **3 B6** 60 16N 25 17 E
Vasto, *Nápl.* **9 H12** 40 51N 14 16 E
Vatutino, *Mos.* **11 D10** 55 52N 37 40 E
Vaucresson, *Paris* **5 B2** 48 50N 2 9 E
Vaudreuil, *Mtrl.* **20 B1** 43 24N 74 1W
Vaudreuil-sur-le Lac, *Mtrl.* **20 B1** 43 25N 74 1W
Vauhallan, *Paris* **5 C3** 48 44N 2 12 E
Vaujours, *Paris* **5 B5** 48 56N 2 34 E
Vauréal, *Paris* **5 A2** 49 2N 2 1 E
Vaux-sur-Seine, *Paris* **5 A1** 49 0N 1 57 E
Vauxhall, *Lon.* **4 C4** 51 29N 0 7W
Vaxholm, *Stock.* **3 D13** 59 24N 18 20 E
Vecklax, *Hels.* **3 B2** 60 10N 24 31 E
Vecsés, *Bud.* **10 K14** 47 24N 19 16 E
Vedano al Lissone, *Mil.* **9 D6** 45 36N 9 16 E
Veddel, *Hbg.* **7 D8** 53 31N 10 2 E
Vega, *Stock.* **3 E11** 59 11N 18 8 E
Vehkalahti, *Hels.* **3 B2** 60 11N 24 30 E
Veikkola, *Hels.* **3 B1** 60 17N 24 26 E
Velbert, *Ruhr* **6 B4** 51 21N 7 1 E
Veleň, *Pra.* **10 A3** 50 10N 14 33 E
Veleslavin, *Pra.* **10 B2** 50 5N 14 21 E
Vélizy-Villacoublay, *Paris* **5 C3** 48 47N 2 11 E
Velka-Chuchle, *Pra.* **10 B2** 50 0N 14 23 E
Venaria, *Tori.* **9 B2** 45 8N 7 37 E
Venda Seca, *Lisb.* **8 F7** 38 46N 9 15W
Vendelsö, *Stock.* **3 E12** 59 12N 18 11 E
Venice, *L.A.* **28 C2** 33 59N 118 27W
Venner, *Oslo* **2 A3** 60 1N 10 36 E
Vennhausen, *Ruhr* **6 C3** 51 13N 6 51 E
Ventas, *Mdrd.* **8 B2** 40 26N 3 40W
Ventorro del Cano, *Mdrd.* **8 B2** 40 23N 3 49W
Verberg, *Ruhr* **6 B1** 51 21N 6 34 E
Verde →, *S. Pau.* **31 E7** 23 29 S 46 27W
Verdi, *Ath.* **8 H11** 38 2N 23 40 E
Verdugo Mt., *L.A.* **28 A3** 34 12N 118 17W
Verdun, *Mtrl.* **20 B4** 43 27N 73 35W
Vereya, *Mos.* **11 F12** 55 37N 38 2 E
Vérhalom, *Bud.* **10 J13** 47 31N 19 1 E
Vermelho →, *S. Pau.* **31 E5** 23 30 S 46 46W
Vermont, *Melb.* **19 F8** 37 50 S 145 12 E
Vermont South, *Melb.* **19 F8** 37 51 S 145 11 E
Verneuil-sur-Seine, *Paris* **5 B1** 48 58N 1 59 E
Vernouillet, *Paris* **5 B1** 48 58N 1 56 E
Verona, *N.Y.* **22 C3** 40 49N 74 15W
Verperluda, Os., *St-Pet.* **11 B2** 59 59N 30 0 E
Verrières-le-Buisson, *Paris* **5 C3** 48 44N 2 16 E
Versailles, *B.A.* **32 B3** 34 38 S 58 31W
Versailles, *Paris* **5 C2** 48 48N 2 7 E
Veshnyaki, *Mos.* **11 E10** 55 43N 37 48 E
Vesolyy Posolok, *St-Pet.* **11 B4** 59 53N 30 28 E
Vestli, *Oslo* **2 B5** 59 58N 10 55 E
Vestra, *Hels.* **3 B3** 60 19N 24 46 E
Vestskoven, *Købn.* **2 D9** 55 41N 12 23 E
Vesuvio, *Nápl.* **9 J13** 40 49N 14 25 E
Vets Stadium, *Phil.* **24 B3** 39 54N 75 10W
Viby, *Købn.* **2 E7** 55 33N 12 1 E
Vicálvaro, *Mdrd.* **8 B3** 40 24N 3 36W
Vicente Lopez, *B.A.* **32 B4** 34 31 S 58 30W
Victoria, *B.A.* **32 A3** 34 27 S 58 32W
Victoria, *H.K.* **12 E6** 22 17N 114 11 E
Victoria, Pont, *Mtrl.* **20 B4** 43 29N 73 32W
Victoria Gardens, *Bomb.* **16 H8** 18 58N 72 50 E
Victoria Harbour, *H.K.* **12 E5** 22 17N 114 10 E
Victoria Island, *Lagos* **18 B2** 6 25N 7 25 E
Victoria L., *Jobg.* **18 F9** 26 13 S 28 9 E
Victoria Lawn Tennis Courts, *Melb.* **19 F7** 37 50 S 145 1 E
Victoria Park, *H.K.* **12 E5** 22 16N 114 8 E
Vidja, *Stock.* **3 E11** 59 12N 18 4 E
Vidrholec, *Pra.* **10 B3** 50 5N 14 39 E
Vienna = Wien, *Wien* **10 G10** 48 12N 16 22 E
Vienna, *Wash.* **25 D6** 38 54N 77 16W
Vieringhausen, *Ruhr* **6 C4** 51 10N 7 9 E
Vierlinden, *Ruhr* **6 A2** 51 32N 6 45 E
Vierumäki, *Hels.* **3 A5** 60 21N 25 2 E
Vierzigstücken, *Hbg.* **7 D6** 53 30N 9 49 E
View Bank, *Melb.* **19 E7** 37 43 S 145 6 E
Vigário Geral, *Rio J.* **31 A2** 22 48 S 43 18W
Vigentino, *Mil.* **9 E6** 45 26N 9 13 E
Viggbyholm, *Stock.* **3 D11** 59 26N 18 7 E
Vighignolo, *Mil.* **9 E5** 45 29N 9 2 E
Vigneux-sur-Seine, *Paris* **5 C4** 48 42N 2 24 E
Viikki, *Hels.* **3 B5** 60 13N 25 1 E
Viirilä, *Hels.* **3 B5** 60 19N 25 8 E
Vila Andrade, *S. Pau.* **31 E5** 23 37 S 46 44W
Vila Barcelona, *S. Pau.* **31 E6** 23 37 S 46 33W
Vila Bocaina, *S. Pau.* **31 F7** 23 40 S 46 26W
Vila Dalva, *S. Pau.* **31 E5** 23 34 S 46 46W
Vila Dirce, *S. Pau.* **31 E4** 23 33 S 46 50W
Vila Eldorado, *S. Pau.* **31 F6** 23 42 S 46 38W
Vila Ema, *S. Pau.* **31 E6** 23 35 S 46 31W
Vila Formosa, *S. Pau.* **31 E6** 23 36 S 46 44W
Vila Galvão, *S. Pau.* **31 D6** 23 27 S 46 34W
Vila Gonçales, *S. Pau.* **31 F6** 23 42 S 46 33W
Vila Iasi, *S. Pau.* **31 E5** 23 37 S 46 47W
Vila Indiana, *S. Pau.* **31 E5** 23 37 S 46 48W
Vila Isabel, *Rio J.* **31 B2** 22 54 S 43 15W
Vila Madalena, *S. Pau.* **31 E5** 23 32 S 46 41W
Vila Maria, *S. Pau.* **31 E6** 23 31 S 46 36W
Vila Mariana, *S. Pau.* **31 E6** 23 34 S 46 36W
Vila Matilde, *S. Pau.* **31 E6** 23 31 S 46 30W
Vila Nova Curuçá, *S. Pau.* **31 E7** 23 31 S 46 25W
Vila Pires, *S. Pau.* **31 F6** 23 41 S 46 30W
Vila Progresso, *Rio J.* **31 B3** 22 53 S 43 1W
Vila Prudente, *S. Pau.* **31 E6** 23 35 S 46 33W
Vila Ré, *S. Pau.* **31 E7** 23 31 S 46 29W
Vila Remo, *S. Pau.* **31 F5** 23 40 S 46 45W
Vila Sonia, *S. Pau.* **31 E5** 23 35 S 46 43W
Viladecans, *Barc.* **8 E5** 41 18N 2 1 E
Villa Ada, *Rome* **9 F10** 41 55N 12 30 E
Villa Adelina, *B.A.* **32 B3** 34 31 S 58 33W
Villa Alianza, *B.A.* **32 B3** 34 37 S 58 33W
Villa Alsina, *B.A.* **32 C4** 34 40 S 58 24W
Villa Altube, *B.A.* **32 B2** 34 31 S 58 45W
Villa Ariza, *B.A.* **32 B3** 34 38 S 58 39W
Villa Augusta, *B.A.* **32 C5** 34 45 S 58 15W
Villa Ballester, *B.A.* **32 B3** 34 33 S 58 33W
Villa Barilari, *B.A.* **32 C4** 34 42 S 58 20W
Villa Basso, *B.A.* **32 B3** 34 38 S 58 36W
Villa Bosch, *B.A.* **32 B3** 34 35 S 58 33W
Villa C. Colon, *B.A.* **32 C4** 34 41 S 58 21W
Villa D. F. Sarmiento, *B.A.* **32 B3** 34 38 S 58 35W
Villa D. Sobral, *B.A.* **32 C5** 34 45 S 58 15W
Villa de Guadalupe, *Méx.* **29 B3** 19 29N 99 6W
Villa de Mayo, *B.A.* **32 B2** 34 30 S 58 40W
Villa Devoto, *B.A.* **32 B3** 34 36 S 58 31W
Villa Dominico, *B.A.* **32 C5** 34 41 S 58 19W
Villa Giambruno, *B.A.* **32 C5** 34 48 S 58 15W
Villa Gustavo A. Madero, *Méx.* **29 B3** 19 29N 99 8W
Villa Hogar Alemán, *B.A.* **32 C4** 34 49 S 58 26W
Villa Iglesias, *B.A.* **32 B2** 34 30 S 58 45W
Villa Leloir, *B.A.* **32 B2** 34 36 S 58 41W
Villa Leon, *B.A.* **32 B2** 34 38 S 58 41W
Villa Lugano, *B.A.* **32 C4** 34 41 S 58 27W
Villa Luzuriago, *B.A.* **32 C3** 34 40 S 58 34W
Villa Lynch, *B.A.* **32 B3** 34 35 S 58 31W
Villa Madero, *B.A.* **32 C3** 34 41 S 58 30W
Villa Maria del Triunfo, *Lima* **30 G9** 12 9 S 76 57W
Villa Obregon, *Méx.* **29 B2** 19 20N 99 12W
Villa Reichembach, *B.A.* **32 B2** 34 39 S 58 40W
Villa Rosa, *B.A.* **32 A1** 34 25 S 58 5W
Villa San Francisco, *B.A.* **32 C5** 34 46 S 58 15W
Villacoublay, Aérodrome de, *Paris* **5 C3** 48 46N 2 12 E
Village Green, *Phil.* **24 B2** 39 52N 75 26W
Villanova, *Phil.* **24 A2** 40 1N 75 20W
Villarbasse, *Tori.* **9 B1** 45 2N 7 27 E
Villaretto, *Tori.* **9 B3** 45 8N 7 41 E
Villaricca, *Nápl.* **9 H12** 40 55N 14 11 E
Villaroche, *Paris* **5 D5** 48 37N 2 39 E
Villaroy, *Paris* **5 C2** 48 46N 2 5 E
Villasanta, *Mil.* **9 D6** 45 36N 9 18 E
Villastanza, *Mil.* **9 D4** 45 32N 8 57 E
Villaverde, *Mdrd.* **8 B2** 40 21N 3 42W
Villaverde Bajo, *Mdrd.* **8 B2** 40 20N 3 40W
Villawood, *Syd.* **19 B2** 33 52 S 150 58 E
Ville-d'Avray, *Paris* **5 C3** 48 49N 2 11 E
Ville de Laval, *Mtrl.* **20 A3** 43 34N 73 43W
Villebon-sur-Yvette, *Paris* **5 C3** 48 41N 2 14 E
Villecresnes, *Paris* **5 C5** 48 43N 2 31 E

48 Villejuif

Villejuif, Paris 5 C4 48 47N 2 21 E
Villejust, Paris 5 C3 48 41N 2 15 E
Villemoisson-sur-Orge, Paris 5 C3 48 40N 2 19 E
Villemomble, Paris 5 B5 48 52N 2 30 E
Villeneuve-la-Garenne, Paris 5 B3 48 56N 2 19 E
Villeneuve-le-Roi, Paris 5 C4 48 43N 2 24 E
Villeneuve-St.-Georges, Paris 5 C4 48 43N 2 27 E
Villeneuve-sous-Dammartin, Paris 5 A5 49 2N 2 38 E
Villennes-sur-Seine, Paris 5 B1 48 56N 2 0 E
Villeparisis, Paris 5 B5 48 56N 2 36 E
Villepinte, Paris 5 B5 48 57N 2 30 E
Villepreux, Paris 5 C1 48 49N 1 59 E
Villevaudé, Paris 5 B5 48 55N 2 39 E
Villeziers, Paris 5 C3 48 40N 2 10 E
Villiers-le-Bâcle, Paris 5 C2 48 44N 2 8 E
Villiers-le-Bel, Paris 5 A4 49 0N 2 23 E
Villiers-St. Frédéric, Paris 5 C1 48 49N 1 53 E
Villiers-sur-Marne, Paris 5 C5 48 49N 2 32 E
Villiers-sur-Orge, Paris 5 D3 48 39N 2 18 E
Villinki, Hels. 3 C5 60 9N 25 6 E
Villoresi, Canale, Mil. 9 D4 45 33N 8 59 E
Vimodrone, Mil. 9 D6 45 30N 9 16 E
Vimont, Mtrl. 20 A3 43 36N 73 43W
Vincennes, Paris 5 B4 48 51N 2 26 E
Vincennes, Bois de, Paris 5 C4 48 49N 2 26 E
Vinohrady, Pra. 10 B2 50 4N 14 26 E
Vinoř, Pra. 10 B3 50 8N 14 34 E
Vinořský →, Pra. 10 A3 50 11N 14 39 E
Violet Hill, H.K. 12 E6 22 15N 114 11 E
Virányos, Bud. 10 J12 47 31N 18 59 E
Virgeo del San Cristóbal, Stgo 30 J11 33 25 S 70 38W
Viroflay, Paris 5 C3 48 48N 2 10 E
Viron, Ath. 8 J11 37 55N 23 46 E
Virreyes, B.A. 32 A3 34 27 S 58 33W
Virum, Købn. 2 D9 55 47N 12 27 E
Viry-Châtillon, Paris 5 C4 48 40N 2 21 E
Vishnyaki, Mos. 11 E11 55 46N 37 53 E
Visitacion Valley, S.F. 27 B2 37 42N 122 23W
Vista Alegre, Lima 30 G9 12 8 S 76 59W
Vista Alegre, Stgo 30 K10 33 30 S 70 43W
Vitacura, Stgo 30 J11 33 23 S 70 35W
Vitarte-Ate, Lima 30 G9 12 3 S 76 57W
Vitinia, Rome 9 G9 41 47N 12 24 E
Vitry-sur-Seine, Paris 5 C4 48 47N 2 23 E
Vitträsk, Hels. 3 B1 60 11N 24 29 E
Vittuone, Mil. 9 E4 45 28N 8 57 E
Vladykino, Mos. 11 D9 55 51N 37 35 E
Vltava →, Pra. 10 A2 50 10N 14 2 E
Vnukovo, Mos. 11 F7 55 37N 37 17 E
Voerde, Ruhr 6 C6 51 18N 7 23 E
Voerde, Ruhr 6 A2 51 35N 6 42 E
Vogelheim, Ruhr 6 B3 51 29N 6 59 E
Vohwinkel, Ruhr 6 C4 51 13N 7 4 E
Voisins-le-Bretonneux, Paris 5 C2 48 45N 2 3 E
Vokovice, Pra. 10 B2 50 5N 14 21 E
Volgelsdorf, Berl. 7 B5 52 30N 13 44 E
Volkhonka-Zil, Mos. 11 F9 55 39N 37 37 E
Volkovka →, St-Pet. 11 B4 59 54N 30 25 E
Volksdorf, Hbg. 7 D8 53 39N 10 8 E
Volla, Nápl. 9 H13 40 52N 14 20 E
Vollen, Oslo 2 C2 59 48N 10 27 E
Volmarstein, Ruhr 6 B6 51 22N 7 22 E
Volodarskoye, St-Pet. 11 B4 59 54N 30 23 E
Volpiano, Tori. 9 A3 45 12N 7 46 E
Volynkina-Derevnya, St-Pet. 11 B3 59 53N 30 18 E
Volynyy, Os., St-Pet. 11 B3 59 57N 30 14 E
Vōmero, Nápl. 9 H12 40 50N 14 13 E
Vorderhainbach, Wien 10 G9 48 13N 16 12 E
Vorhalle, Ruhr 6 B6 51 23N 7 26 E
Vormholz, Ruhr 6 B5 51 24N 7 19 E
Vösendorf, Wien 10 H10 48 7N 16 20 E
Vostochnyy, Mos. 11 E11 55 49N 37 51 E
Vouliagmeni, Ath. 8 K11 37 50N 23 46 E
Vrčovice, Pra. 10 B2 50 4N 14 28 E
Vsevolozhsk, St-Pet. 11 A5 60 0N 30 39 E
Vuosaari, Hels. 3 B5 60 13N 25 8 E
Vyborgskaya Storona, St-Pet. 11 B4 59 57N 30 22 E
Vyčehrad, Pra. 10 B2 50 3N 14 25 E
Vykhino, Mos. 11 E10 55 42N 37 48 E
Vysočany, Pra. 10 B2 50 6N 14 29 E

W

Waban, L., Bost. 21 D2 42 17N 71 18W
Wachterhof, Mün. 7 G11 48 2N 11 42 E
Waddington, Lon. 4 D4 51 18N 0 7W
Wadeville, Jobg. 18 F10 26 15 S 28 11 E
Wahda, Bagd. 17 F8 33 18N 44 26 E
Währing, Wien 10 G10 48 14N 16 20 E
Waidmannslust, Berl. 7 A3 52 36N 13 20 E
Wajay, La Hab. 30 B2 23 0N 82 25W
Wakefield, Bost. 21 B3 42 30N 71 5W
Wald, Ruhr 6 C4 51 11N 7 3 E
Waldesruh, Berl. 7 B4 52 28N 13 37 E
Waldheim, Berl. 7 A1 52 34N 13 3 E
Waldperlach, Mün. 7 G11 48 4N 11 40 E
Waldtrudering, Mün. 7 G11 48 6N 11 42 E
Waldwick, N.Y. 22 A4 41 1N 74 5W
Wall Street, N.Y. 22 C4 40 42N 74 0W
Wallgrove, Syd. 19 A2 33 47 S 150 51 E
Wallington, Lon. 4 C4 51 21N 0 8W
Wallington, N.Y. 22 B4 40 50N 74 8W
Walnut Cr. →, S.F. 27 A4 37 55N 122 3W
Walnut Creek, S.F. 27 A4 37 53N 122 3W
Walnut Heights, S.F. 27 A4 37 52N 122 2W
Walsum, Ruhr 6 A2 51 32N 6 42 E
Walsumer Mark, Ruhr 6 A3 51 33N 6 50 E
Walt Whitman Br., Phil. 24 B4 39 4N 75 9W
Waltershof, Hbg. 7 D7 53 31N 9 54 E
Waltham, Bost. 21 C2 42 23N 71 14W
Waltham Abbey, Lon. 4 A5 51 41N 0 1 E
Waltham Forest, Lon. 4 B4 51 36N 0 0 E
Walthamstow, Lon. 4 B4 51 34N 0 1W
Walton on Thames, Lon. 4 C2 51 22N 0 23W
Walton on the Hill, Lon. 4 D3 51 16N 0 14W
Waltrop, Ruhr 6 A6 51 36N 7 25 E
Walworth, Lon. 4 C4 51 29N 0 5W
Wambachsee, Ruhr 6 B2 51 23N 6 47 E
Wan Chai, H.K. 12 E6 22 16N 114 10 E
Wanaque, N.Y. 22 A3 41 1N 74 17W
Wandezhuang, Tianj. 14 E5 39 6N 117 10 E
Wandle →, Lon. 4 C3 51 27N 0 11W
Wandsbek, Hbg. 7 D8 53 34N 10 4 E
Wandsworth, Lon. 4 C3 51 27N 0 11W
Wang Hin, Khlong →, Bangk. 15 A2 13 50N 100 35 E
Wanheim, Ruhr 6 B2 51 23N 6 45 E
Wanheimerort, Ruhr 6 B2 51 24N 6 45 E
Wanne-Eickel, Ruhr 6 A4 51 31N 7 9 E
Wannsee, Berl. 7 B1 52 25N 13 9 E
Wansdorf, Berl. 7 A1 52 38N 13 5 E
Wanstead, Lon. 4 B5 51 34N 0 1 E
Wantagh Seaford, N.Y. 23 D8 40 39N 73 28W
Wantirna, Melb. 19 F8 37 50 S 145 14 E
Wapping, Lon. 4 B4 51 30N 0 3W
Warabi, Tōkyō 13 B3 35 49N 139 42 E
Ward, Phil. 24 B1 39 52N 75 30W
Warlingham, Lon. 4 D4 51 18N 0 2W
Warnberg, Mün. 7 G10 48 4N 11 31 E
Warngal Park, Melb. 19 E7 37 45 S 145 4 E
Warrandyte, Melb. 19 E8 37 43 S 145 13 E
Warrandyte Park, Melb. 19 E8 37 44 S 145 14 E
Warrandyte South, Melb. 19 E8 37 44 S 145 14 E
Warranwood, Melb. 19 E8 37 46 S 145 14 E
Warrâq el 'Arab, El Qâ. 18 C5 30 4N 31 11 E
Warrâq el Hadf, El Qâ. 18 C5 30 5N 31 12 E
Warren Hill, Bost. 21 B1 42 35N 71 21W
Warsaw = Warszawa, Wsaw. 10 E7 52 14N 21 0 E
Warszawa, Wsaw. 10 E7 52 14N 21 0 E
Wartenberg, Berl. 7 A4 52 34N 13 31 E
Warwick Farm Racetrack, Syd. 19 B2 33 54 S 150 56 E
Wasa, Stock. 3 E11 59 19N 18 5 E
Wasfanārd, Tehr. 17 D5 35 38N 51 20 E
Washington, Wash. 25 D7 38 53N 77 2W
Washington Heights, N.Y. 22 B5 40 51N 73 56W
Washington Memorial Museum, Phil. 24 A2 40 5N 75 26W
Washington Nat. Airport, Wash. 25 D7 38 51N 77 2W
Washington Park, Chic. 26 C3 41 47N 87 36W
Washington Square, Phil. 24 A3 40 9N 75 19W
Washington Township, N.Y. 22 A4 41 0N 74 3W
Wasserschloss, Ruhr 6 A4 51 32N 7 1 E
Watching Mts., N.Y. 22 C2 40 43N 74 20W
Watchung, N.Y. 22 D2 40 38N 74 29W
Waterloo, Syd. 19 B4 33 53 S 151 12 E
Waterman Mt., L.A. 28 A5 34 14N 117 56W
Watertown, Bost. 21 C2 42 22N 71 10W
Watford, Lon. 4 A2 51 40N 0 27W
Watkins Island, Wash. 25 C6 39 2N 77 15W
Watsonia, Melb. 19 E7 37 43 S 145 6 E
Watsons B., Syd. 19 B4 33 50 S 151 18 E
Watsons Creek, Melb. 19 E8 37 40 S 145 13 E
Wattenscheid, Ruhr 6 B4 51 28N 7 8 E
Wattle Glen, Melb. 19 D8 37 39 S 145 11 E
Wattle Park, Melb. 19 F7 37 50 S 145 6 E
Watts →, Wash. 25 C6 39 2N 77 15W
Waverley, Bost. 21 C2 42 23N 71 10W
Waverley, Jobg. 18 E9 26 7 S 28 4 E
Waverley, Syd. 19 B4 33 53 S 151 15 E
Wawer, Wsaw. 10 E7 52 13N 21 8 E
Wawrzyszew, Wsaw. 10 E6 52 17N 20 53 E
Wayland, Bost. 21 C1 42 21N 71 20W
Wayne, N.Y. 22 B3 40 55N 74 15W
Wayne, Phil. 24 A2 40 2N 75 24W
Wazirabad, Delhi 16 A2 28 43N 77 13 E
Wazīrīya, Bagd. 17 E8 33 22N 44 23 E
Wazirpur, Delhi 16 A2 28 41N 77 10 E
Weald Park, Lon. 4 B6 51 37N 0 16 E
Wedding, Berl. 7 A3 52 32N 13 21 E
Weehawken, N.Y. 22 C4 40 45N 74 2W
Wegendorf, Berl. 7 A5 52 36N 13 45 E
Wehofen, Ruhr 6 A2 51 31N 6 46 E
Wehringhausen, Ruhr 6 B6 51 21N 7 28 E
Weidling, Wien 10 G9 48 17N 16 18 E
Weidling →, Wien 10 G9 48 17N 16 19 E
Weidlingbach, Wien 10 G9 48 16N 16 15 E
Weigongcum, Beij. 14 B2 39 57N 116 16 E
Weijin He →, Tianj. 14 E6 39 3N 117 12 E
Weissensee, Berl. 7 A3 52 33N 13 27 E
Weitmar, Ruhr 6 B5 51 27N 7 11 E
Welcome Monument, Jak. 15 J9 6 12N 106 49 E
Weller Creek, Chic. 26 A1 42 2N 87 52W
Wellesley, Bost. 21 D2 42 17N 71 17W
Wellesley Fells, Bost. 21 D2 42 18N 71 18W
Wellesley Hills, Bost. 21 D2 42 18N 71 16W
Welling, Lon. 4 C5 51 27N 0 6 E
Wellingsbüttel, Hbg. 7 D8 53 38N 10 6 E
Weltevreden Park Extension, Jobg. 18 E8 26 7 S 27 56 E
Wembley, Lon. 4 B3 51 33N 0 17W
Wembley Stadium, Jobg. 18 F9 26 13 S 28 1 E
Wembley Stadium, Lon. 4 B3 51 33N 0 16W
Wemmer Pan, Jobg. 18 F9 26 13 S 28 3 E
Wendenschloss, Berl. 7 B4 52 24N 13 35 E
Wengern, Ruhr 6 B6 51 24N 7 20 E
Wenham, Bost. 21 B4 42 36N 70 53W
Wenham L., Bost. 21 B4 42 35N 70 53W
Wenhuagong, Tianj. 14 E6 39 5N 117 14 E
Wennington, Lon. 4 B6 51 30N 0 12 E
Wenonah, Phil. 24 C4 39 47N 75 9W
Wentworthville, Syd. 19 A2 33 48 S 150 58 E
Werden, Ruhr 6 B4 51 23N 7 1 E
Werne, Ruhr 6 B5 51 29N 7 18 E
Werneuchen, Berl. 7 A5 52 38N 13 44 E
Wesoła, Wsaw. 10 E8 52 15N 21 13 E
West Andover, Bost. 21 B2 42 39N 71 10W
West Babylon, N.Y. 23 C8 40 43N 73 21W
West Bedford, Bost. 21 C2 42 28N 71 18W
West Berlin, Phil. 24 C5 39 48N 74 56W
West Boxford, Bost. 21 A3 42 42N 71 3W
West Caldwell, N.Y. 22 B3 40 51N 74 16W
West Chelmsford, Bost. 21 B1 42 36N 71 23W
West Chester, Phil. 24 B1 39 57N 75 35W
West Concord, Bost. 21 C1 42 27N 71 24W
West Covina, L.A. 28 B5 34 4N 117 55W
West Don →, Trto. 20 D8 43 44N 79 24W
West Drayton, Lon. 4 B2 51 30N 0 28W
West Dulwich, Lon. 4 C4 51 26N 0 5W
West Edmondale, Balt. 25 B2 39 17N 76 42W
West Ham, Lon. 4 B5 51 31N 0 1 E
West Harrow, Lon. 4 B2 51 34N 0 21W
West Heath, Lon. 4 C5 51 29N 0 7 E
West Hempstead, N.Y. 23 C7 40 41N 73 38W
West Hill, Trto. 20 D9 43 46N 79 10W
West Hollywood, L.A. 28 B2 34 5N 118 21W
West Hoxton, Syd. 19 B1 33 55 S 150 49 E
West Islip, N.Y. 23 C9 40 41N 73 18W
West Kingsdown, Lon. 4 C6 51 20N 0 15 E
West Lamma Channel, H.K. 12 E5 22 14N 114 4 E
West Lynn, Bost. 21 C4 42 27N 70 58W
West Medford, Bost. 21 C3 42 25N 71 7W
West New York, N.Y. 22 C4 40 46N 74 1W
West Norwood, N.Y. 22 B5 40 59N 73 58W
West of Twin Peaks, S.F. 27 B2 37 43N 122 27W
West Orange, N.Y. 22 C3 40 46N 74 15W
West Park, Jobg. 18 E8 26 9 S 27 59 E
West Paterson, N.Y. 22 B3 40 54N 74 11W
West Rouge, Trto. 20 D10 43 48N 79 7W
West Roxbury, Bost. 21 D3 42 16N 71 9W
West Springfield, Wash. 25 E6 38 47N 77 13W
West Thurrock, Lon. 4 C6 51 28N 0 16 E
West Town, Chic. 26 B2 41 53N 87 42W
West Wharf, Kar. 17 H10 24 49N 66 58 E
West Wickham, Lon. 4 C4 51 22N 0 0 E
Westbury, N.Y. 23 C7 40 45N 73 34W
Westchester, Chic. 26 B1 41 51N 87 53W
Westchester, N.Y. 23 B5 40 51N 73 51W
Westcliff, Jobg. 18 F9 26 10 S 28 1 E
Westdale, Chic. 26 B1 41 55N 87 54W
Westdene, Jobg. 18 F8 26 10 S 27 59 E
Westend, Hels. 3 C3 60 9N 24 48 E
Westerbauer, Ruhr 6 B6 51 20N 7 23 E
Westerham, Lon. 4 D5 51 16N 0 4 E
Westerham, Mün. 7 G10 48 3N 11 36 E
Westerholt, Ruhr 6 A4 51 36N 7 5 E
Westerleigh, N.Y. 22 D4 40 37N 74 7W
Western Addition, S.F. 27 B2 37 47N 122 25W
Western Run →, Balt. 25 A2 39 22N 76 39W
Western Springs, Chic. 26 C1 41 47N 87 52W
Westfalenhalle, Ruhr 6 B6 51 29N 7 27 E
Westfield, N.Y. 22 D2 40 39N 74 21W
Westlake, S.F. 27 B2 37 42N 122 29W
Westmeadows, Melb. 19 D6 37 39 S 144 55 E
Westminster, Lon. 4 B4 51 30N 0 7W
Westminster Abbey, Lon. 4 C4 51 29N 0 7W
Westmont, Phil. 24 B4 39 54N 75 3W
Westmount, Mtrl. 20 B4 43 29N 73 35W
Weston, Bost. 21 C2 42 22N 71 16W
Weston, Trto. 20 D7 43 42N 79 30W
Weston Res., Bost. 21 C2 42 20N 71 11W
Westover Hills, Phil. 24 C1 39 45N 75 35W
Westtown, Phil. 24 B1 39 56N 75 32W
Westville, Phil. 24 B4 39 52N 75 7W
Westville Grove, Phil. 24 B4 39 51N 75 7W
Westwood, Bost. 21 D2 42 12N 71 14W
Westwood, N.Y. 22 B4 40 59N 74 3W
Westwood Village, L.A. 28 B2 34 3N 118 26W
Wetter, Ruhr 6 B6 51 23N 7 23 E
Wexford, Trto. 20 D9 43 45N 79 18W
Wey →, Lon. 4 D2 51 18N 0 27W
Weybridge, Lon. 4 C2 51 22N 0 27W
Weyer, Ruhr 6 C4 51 10N 7 1 E
Weymouth, Bost. 21 D4 42 12N 70 57W
Whampoa, Sungei →, Sing. 15 G8 1 18N 103 52 E
Wheaton, Wash. 25 C7 39 2N 77 2W
Wheaton Regional Park, Wash. 25 C7 39 3N 77 1W
Wheelers Hill, Melb. 19 F8 37 53 S 145 10 E
Wheeling, Chic. 26 A1 42 8N 87 54W
Whetstone, Lon. 4 B3 51 37N 0 10W
Whippany, N.Y. 22 B2 40 49N 74 24W
Whippany →, N.Y. 22 B2 40 50N 74 20W
White Marsh, Balt. 25 A4 39 23N 76 28W
White Meadow L., N.Y. 22 B1 40 55N 74 30W
White Oak, Wash. 25 C8 39 2N 76 59W
White Plains, N.Y. 23 A6 41 0N 73 46W
Whitechapel, Lon. 4 B4 51 31N 0 3W
Whitehorse, Phil. 24 B2 39 59N 75 28W
Whiteley Village, Lon. 4 C2 51 21N 0 25W
Whitemarsh →, Balt. 25 A4 39 22N 76 29W
Whitestone, N.Y. 23 C6 40 47N 73 48W
Whiting, Chic. 26 C4 41 41N 87 30W
Whitmans Pond, Bost. 21 D4 42 12N 70 55W
Whittier, L.A. 28 C4 33 58N 118 2W
Whitton, Lon. 4 C2 51 27N 0 21W
Whyteleafe, Lon. 4 D4 51 18N 0 5W
Wieden, Wien 10 G10 48 11N 16 22 E
Wiemelhausen, Ruhr 6 B5 51 27N 7 13 E
Wien, Wien 10 G10 48 12N 16 22 E
Wien-Schwechat, Flughafen, Wien 10 H11 48 6N 16 34 E
Wiener Berg, Wien 10 H10 48 9N 16 21 E
Wiener Wald, Wien 10 G9 48 16N 16 14 E
Wieruchów, Wsaw. 10 E5 52 14N 20 49 E
Wierzbno, Wsaw. 10 E7 52 11N 21 1 E
Wilanów, Wsaw. 10 E7 52 10N 21 4 E
Wilanówka →, Wsaw. 10 F7 52 13N 21 6 E
Wildcat Canyon Regional Park, S.F. 27 A3 37 56N 122 17W
Wildcat Cr. →, S.F. 27 A3 37 57N 122 15W
Wilde, B.A. 32 C5 34 24 S 58 18W
Wilhelmsburg, Hbg. 7 E7 53 29N 9 59 E
Wilhelmshagen, Berl. 7 B5 52 26N 13 42 E
Wilket Creek Park, Trto. 20 D8 43 43N 79 21W
Willesden, Lon. 4 B3 51 32N 0 15W
Willesden Green, Lon. 4 B3 51 32N 0 13W
Willett Pond, Bost. 21 D2 42 10N 71 14W
William Girling Res., Lon. 4 B4 51 38N 0 1W
Williams Bridge, N.Y. 23 B5 40 52N 73 51W
Williamsburg, N.Y. 22 C5 40 42N 73 56W
Williamstown, Melb. 19 F6 37 51 S 144 52 E
Williamstown Junction, Phil. 24 C5 39 45N 74 56W
Willingboro, Phil. 24 A5 40 2N 74 53W
Williston Park, N.Y. 23 C7 40 45N 73 38W
Willoughby, Syd. 19 A4 33 48 S 151 12 E
Willow Grove, Phil. 24 A4 40 8N 75 7W
Willow Springs, Chic. 26 C1 41 44N 87 51W
Willowbrook, L.A. 28 C3 33 54N 118 13W
Willowbrook, N.Y. 22 D4 40 35N 74 8W
Willowdale, Phil. 24 B5 39 52N 74 58W
Willowdale, Trto. 20 D8 43 46N 79 25W
Willowdale State Forest, Bost. 21 B4 42 39N 70 54W
Wilmette, Chic. 26 A2 42 4N 87 42W
Wilmette Harbor, Chic. 26 A2 42 4N 87 41W
Wilmington, Bost. 21 B3 42 33N 71 9W
Wilmington, Lon. 4 C6 51 25N 0 12 E
Wilmington, Phil. 24 C1 39 44N 75 33W
Wilson, Mt., L.A. 28 A4 34 13N 118 4W
Wimbledon, Lon. 4 C3 51 25N 0 13W
Wimbledon Common, Lon. 4 C3 51 26N 0 14W
Wimbledon Park, Lon. 4 C3 51 25N 0 11W
Wimbledon Tennis Ground, Lon. 4 C3 51 25N 0 12W
Winchester, Bost. 21 C3 42 26N 71 8W
Winchmore Hill, Lon. 4 B4 51 38N 0 5W
Windsor Cresta, Jobg. 18 E8 26 7 S 27 59 E
Winfield, N.Y. 22 D3 40 38N 74 16W
Winnetka, Chic. 26 A2 42 6N 87 43W
Winnetka, L.A. 28 A1 34 10N 118 32W
Winning, Mün. 7 G10 48 2N 11 37 E
Winston Hills, Syd. 19 A2 33 46 S 150 57 E
Winterberg, Ruhr 6 C5 51 19N 7 12 E
Winterhude, Hbg. 7 D8 53 35N 10 0 E
Winterthur, Phil. 24 C1 39 48N 75 35W
Winthrop, Bost. 21 C4 42 22N 70 58W
Winzeldorf, Hbg. 7 C7 53 40N 9 54 E
Wisley Gardens, Lon. 4 D2 51 18N 0 28W
Wiśniowa Góra, Wsaw. 10 E8 52 13N 21 12 E
Wissahickon Cr. →, Phil. 24 A3 40 0N 75 12W
Wissinoming, Phil. 24 A4 40 1N 75 4W
Wissous, Paris 5 C3 48 44N 2 19 E
Witch House, Bost. 21 B4 42 31N 70 54W
Witfield, Jobg. 18 F10 26 11 S 28 12 E
Witpoortjie, Jobg. 18 E8 26 8 S 27 50 E
Witten, Ruhr 6 B6 51 26N 7 20 E
Wittenau, Berl. 7 A2 52 35N 13 19 E
Wittlaer, Ruhr 6 C2 51 19N 6 44 E
Witwatersrand, Univ. of, Jobg. 18 F9 26 11 S 28 1 E
Włochy, Wsaw. 10 E6 52 12N 20 54 E
Wo Mei, H.K. 12 D6 22 21N 114 15 E
Wo Yi Hop, H.K. 12 D5 22 23N 114 8 E
Woburn, Bost. 21 C3 42 29N 71 9W
Woburn, Trto. 20 D9 43 46N 79 12W
Wohldorf-Ohlstedt, Hbg. 7 C8 53 41N 10 7 E
Wola, Wsaw. 10 E6 52 14N 20 57 E
Woldingham, Lon. 4 D4 51 16N 0 1W
Wolf Lake, Chic. 26 D3 41 39N 87 31W
Wolf Trap Farm Park, Wash. 25 D6 38 56N 77 17W
Wolfpassing, Wien 10 G9 48 18N 16 10 E
Wolica, Wsaw. 10 F7 52 9N 21 3 E
Wolica, Wsaw. 10 F6 52 7N 20 51 E
Wólka Węglowa, Wsaw. 10 E6 52 18N 20 52 E
Wollaston, Bost. 21 D3 42 15N 71 2W
Wołomin, Wsaw. 10 D8 52 20N 21 12 E
Woltersdorf, Berl. 7 B5 52 27N 13 44 E
Wong Chuk Hang, H.K. 12 E6 22 15N 114 10 E
Wong Chuk Wan, H.K. 12 D6 22 23N 114 17 E
Wong Chuk Yeung, H.K. 12 D6 22 24N 114 15 E
Wong Ngua Shan, H.K. 12 D6 22 22N 114 14 E
Wong Tai Sin, H.K. 12 D6 22 20N 114 11 E
Wonga Park, Melb. 19 E8 37 44 S 145 17 E
Wood End, Lon. 4 B2 51 33N 0 21W
Wood Green, Lon. 4 B4 51 36N 0 6W
Wood Hill, Bost. 21 B2 42 39N 71 11W
Woodbridge, N.Y. 22 D3 40 33N 74 16W
Woodbridge, Trto. 20 D7 43 47N 79 35W
Woodbridge Cr. →, N.Y. 22 D3 40 32N 74 15W
Woodbury, N.Y. 23 C8 40 49N 73 28W
Woodbury, Phil. 24 B4 39 50N 75 9W
Woodbury Cr. →, Phil. 24 B4 39 51N 75 11W
Woodbury Heights, Phil. 24 C4 39 49N 75 7W
Woodchuck Hill, Bost. 21 B3 42 39N 71 4W
Woodcliff Lake, N.Y. 22 A4 41 1N 74 2W
Woodford, Lon. 4 B5 51 36N 0 1 E
Woodford Bridge, Lon. 4 B5 51 36N 0 3 E
Woodford Green, Lon. 4 B5 51 36N 0 1 E
Woodford Wells, Lon. 4 B5 51 37N 0 1 E
Woodhaven, N.Y. 23 C5 40 41N 73 51W
Woodlands, Sing. 15 F7 1 26N 103 46 E
Woodlawn, Balt. 25 B2 39 19N 76 44W
Woodlyn, Phil. 24 B2 39 52N 75 21W
Woodlynne, Phil. 24 B4 39 54N 75 6W
Woodmere, N.Y. 23 D6 40 38N 73 43W
Woodmont, Wash. 25 D7 38 59N 77 5W
Woodmore, Balt. 25 A2 39 22N 76 47W
Woodridge, N.Y. 22 B4 40 50N 74 4W
Woodrow, N.Y. 22 D3 40 32N 74 11W
Woodside, Lon. 4 C4 51 23N 0 4W
Woodside, N.Y. 23 C5 40 44N 73 54W
Woodside, S.F. 27 D3 37 26N 122 16W
Woodstock, Balt. 25 B1 39 19N 76 52W
Woodstream, Phil. 24 B5 39 54N 74 57W
Woollahra, Syd. 19 B4 33 53 S 151 15 E
Woolooware B., Syd. 19 C3 34 1 S 151 8 E
Woolwich, Lon. 4 C5 51 29N 0 4 E
Wördern, Wien 10 G9 48 19N 16 12 E
World Trade Center, N.Y. 22 C4 40 42N 74 0W
Worli, Bomb. 16 G7 19 1N 72 49 E
Woronora, Syd. 19 C3 34 1 S 151 2 E
Worth, Chic. 26 C2 41 41N 87 47W
Worthington, Balt. 25 B2 39 14N 76 47W
Worthington, N.Y. 23 A6 41 2N 73 49W
Wrotham, Lon. 4 D6 51 18N 0 18 E
Wrotham Park, Lon. 4 A3 51 40N 0 10W
Wuhlgarten, Berl. 7 A4 52 31N 13 34 E
Wujiaochang, Shang. 14 J12 31 18N 121 31 E
Wülfrath, Ruhr 6 C4 51 16N 7 2 E
Wulfsmühle, Hbg. 7 C7 53 41N 9 51 E
Wulksfelde, Hbg. 7 C8 53 42N 10 6 E
Wupper →, Ruhr 6 C5 51 14N 7 18 E
Wuppertal, Ruhr 6 C5 51 17N 7 10 E
Würm →, Mün. 7 G9 48 8N 11 27 E
Würm-kanal, Mün. 7 F9 48 13N 11 29 E
Wusong, Shang. 14 H11 31 22N 121 29 E
Wusong Jiang →, Shang. 14 J11 31 15N 121 29 E
Wyandanch, N.Y. 23 C8 40 44N 73 20W
Wyckoff, N.Y. 22 A3 41 0N 74 10W
Wyczółki, Wsaw. 10 F6 52 9N 20 59 E
Wygoda, Wsaw. 10 E7 52 15N 21 7 E
Wyncote, Phil. 24 A4 40 5N 75 8W
Wynnewood, Phil. 24 A3 40 0N 75 17W
Wynnmere, Bost. 21 C3 42 29N 71 9W
Wyola, Phil. 24 A2 40 0N 75 24W

X

Xabregas, Lisb. 8 F8 38 43N 9 6W
Xiaodianzhuang, Tianj. 14 D6 39 14N 117 14 E
Xiaoping, Gzh. 14 F8 23 12N 113 13 E
Xiasha chong, Gzh. 14 G7 23 8N 113 9 E
Xicheng, Beij. 14 B2 39 54N 116 19 E
Xico, Cerro, Méx. 29 C4 19 15N 98 56W
Xicun, Gzh. 14 G8 23 8N 113 13 E
Xidan, Beij. 14 B3 39 52N 116 20 E
Xigu Gongyuan, Tianj. 14 D6 39 10N 117 10 E
Xigucun, Tianj. 14 D5 39 10N 117 9 E
Xijiao Airport, Beij. 14 B2 39 57N 116 12 E
Xikeng, Gzh. 14 F7 23 11N 113 6 E
Xilou, Tianj. 14 E6 39 5N 117 12 E
Ximenwai, Tianj. 14 E5 39 8N 117 9 E
Xingfusancun, Beij. 14 B3 39 55N 116 25 E
Xinhua, Tianj. 14 E6 39 6N 117 12 E
Xinkai He →, Tianj. 14 D6 39 12N 117 15 E
Xintang, Gzh. 14 G9 23 9N 113 24 E
Xitle, Méx. 29 C2 19 15N 99 12W
Xitle, Cerro, Méx. 29 C2 19 14N 99 12W
Xiyuan, Beij. 14 B2 39 59N 116 14 E
Xizhimen, Beij. 14 B2 39 55N 116 19 E
Xochiaca, Méx. 29 B4 19 24N 89 58 E
Xochimilco, Méx. 29 C3 19 15N 99 5W
Xochimilco, L. de, Méx. 29 C3 19 16N 99 7W
Xochitenco, Méx. 29 B4 19 24N 89 58 E
Xochitepec, Méx. 29 C3 19 15N 99 9W
Xuanwu, Beij. 14 B2 39 52N 116 19 E
Xuhui, Shang. 14 J11 31 11N 121 26 E

Y

Yaba, Lagos 18 A2 6 30N 7 22 E
Yadun Shui, Gzh. 14 G8 23 5N 113 15 E
Yaftābād, Tehr. 17 D4 35 37N 51 17 E
Yagoona, Syd. 19 B3 33 54 S 151 2 E
Yahara, Tōkyō 13 B2 35 44N 139 37 E
Yaho, Tōkyō 13 B1 35 40N 139 26 E
Yakire, Tōkyō 13 B4 35 45N 139 54 E
Yamada, Ōsaka 12 B4 34 47N 135 32 E
Yamada, Tōkyō 13 C2 35 33N 139 37 E
Yamada →, Ōsaka 12 B2 34 45N 135 10 E
Yamaguchi, Ōsaka 12 B2 34 49N 135 14 E
Yamamoto, Ōsaka 12 C4 34 38N 135 37 E
Yamato, Tōkyō 13 B2 35 46N 139 36 E
Yamato, Tōkyō 13 D1 35 29N 139 27 E
Yamato →, Ōsaka 12 C3 34 36N 135 26 E
Yamazaki, Tōkyō 13 A4 35 55N 139 53 E
Yamuna →, Delhi 16 B2 28 37N 77 15 E
Yan Kit, Sing. 15 F8 1 21N 103 58 E
Yanagishima, Tōkyō 13 B3 35 49N 139 45 E
Yanbu, Gzh. 14 G7 23 5N 113 9 E
Yanghuayuan, Beij. 14 C2 39 49N 116 18 E
Yangjiazhuang, Shang. 14 H11 31 22N 121 25 E
Yangliuqing, Tianj. 14 E5 39 8N 117 0 E
Yangpu, Shang. 14 J12 31 16N 121 32 E
Yanino, St-Pet. 11 B5 59 55N 30 36 E
Yao, Ōsaka 12 C4 34 37N 135 36 E
Yao Airport, Ōsaka 12 C4 34 35N 135 36 E
Yarmōk, Bagd. 17 F7 33 18N 44 19 E
Yarra →, Melb. 19 E6 37 51 S 144 53 E
Yarra Bend Nat. Park, Melb. 19 E7 37 47 S 145 0 E
Yarraville, Melb. 19 E6 37 48 S 144 53 E
Yasenevo, Mos. 11 F9 55 36N 37 21 E
Yashio, Tōkyō 13 B3 35 48N 139 49 E
Yau Ma Tei, H.K. 12 E5 22 18N 114 10 E
Yau Tong, H.K. 12 E6 22 17N 114 14 E
Yau Yue Wan, H.K. 12 E6 22 19N 114 15 E
Yauza →, Mos. 11 D10 55 54N 37 43 E
Yeading, Lon. 4 B2 51 31N 0 23W
Yeadon, Phil. 24 B3 39 55N 75 15W
Yedikule, Ist. 17 B2 40 59N 28 55 E
Yenikapi, Ist. 17 A2 41 0N 28 56 E
Yeniköy, Ist. 17 A3 41 6N 29 3 E
Yennora, Syd. 19 B2 33 51 S 150 58 E
Yeogchon, Sŏul 12 G7 37 35N 126 55 E
Yeoido, Sŏul 12 G7 37 31N 126 55 E
Yeong Dung Po, Sŏul 12 G7 37 31N 126 54 E
Yeongdong, Sŏul 12 G8 37 30N 127 1 E
Yerba Buena I., S.F. 27 B2 37 48N 122 21W
Yerres, Paris 5 C5 48 43N 2 30 E
Yerres →, Paris 5 C5 48 43N 2 26 E
Yesilköy, Ist. 17 B2 40 57N 28 50 E
Yew Tee, Sing. 15 F7 1 23N 103 45 E
Yiewsley, Lon. 4 B2 51 31N 0 27W
Yiheyuan, Beij. 14 A2 40 0N 116 14 E
Yinhangzhen, Shang. 14 H12 31 20N 121 31 E
Yio Chu Kang, Sing. 15 F8 1 23N 103 51 E
Yixingbu, Tianj. 14 D6 39 11N 117 12 E
Ylästö, Hels. 3 B4 60 17N 24 35 E
Yodo →, Ōsaka 12 B4 34 45N 135 35 E
Yokohama, Tōkyō 13 D3 35 26N 139 41 E
Yokohama Harbour, Tōkyō 13 D2 35 27N 139 39 E
Yokosuka, Tōkyō 13 A4 35 50N 139 54 E
Yong San, Sŏul 12 G7 37 32N 126 58 E
Yongding He →, Beij. 14 C1 39 49N 116 10 E
Yongdingmen, Beij. 14 B3 39 50N 116 20 E
Yongfucun, Gzh. 14 G8 23 8N 113 17 E
Yonkers, N.Y. 23 B5 40 56N 73 52W
Yono, Tōkyō 13 A2 35 52N 139 37 E
York, Trto. 20 D8 43 40N 79 26W
York Mills, Trto. 20 D8 43 45N 79 22W
Yoshikawa, Tōkyō 13 A4 35 53N 139 50 E
Yotsuga, Tōkyō 13 B3 35 40N 139 44 E
You'anmen, Beij. 14 B2 39 51N 116 19 E
Yoyogi Park, Tōkyō 13 C3 35 40N 139 41 E
Yuanxiatian, Gzh. 14 F8 23 12N 113 17 E
Yuexiu Gongyuan, Gzh. 14 G8 23 8N 113 16 E
Yugo-Zarad, Mos. 11 E9 55 40N 37 30 E
Yung Shue Wan, H.K. 12 E5 22 13N 114 6 E
Yuquanshan, Beij. 14 A2 40 0N 116 13 E
Yusofābād, Tehr. 17 C5 35 43N 51 24 E
Yuyuan Tan, Beij. 14 B2 39 53N 116 16 E
Yuyuantan Gongyuan, Beij. 14 B2 39 54N 116 16 E
Yvelines, Forêt des, Paris 5 D1 48 38N 1 53 E
Yvette →, Paris 5 C1 48 43N 1 57 E

Z

Záběhlice, Pra. 10 B2 50 3N 14 29 E
Żacisze, Wsaw. 10 E7 52 17N 21 4 E
Zahrā, Bagd. 17 E7 33 22N 44 19 E
Zakharkovo, Mos. 11 E7 55 46N 37 18 E
Žalov, Pra. 10 A2 50 10N 14 22 E
Załuski, Wsaw. 10 F6 52 9N 20 55 E
Zamdorf, Mün. 7 G10 48 8N 11 35 E
Zanevka, St-Pet. 11 B5 59 55N 30 31 E
Zaozerye, Mos. 11 F12 55 35N 38 1 E
Zapote, Manila 15 E3 14 27N 120 56 E
Zapotitlán, Méx. 29 C3 19 18N 99 2W
Zápy, Pra. 10 B4 50 9N 14 40 E
Zarechye, Mos. 11 E8 55 41N 37 22 E
Zawady, Wsaw. 10 E7 52 10N 21 6 E
Zâwiyet Abû Musallam, El Qâ. 18 D4 29 56N 31 9 E
Zawrā Park, Bagd. 17 F8 33 18N 44 23 E
Zbójna Góra, Wsaw. 10 E8 52 11N 21 13 E
Zbraslav, Pra. 10 C2 49 58N 14 23 E
Zbuzany, Pra. 10 B1 50 1N 14 17 E
Zdiby, Pra. 10 B2 50 9N 14 27 E
Zehlendorf, Berl. 7 B2 52 26N 13 16 E
Zeleneč, Pra. 10 B3 50 8N 14 39 E
Zempoala, Parque Nac. de las Lagunas de, Méx. 29 D2 19 5N 99 18W
Zepernick, Berl. 7 A4 52 38N 13 33 E
Żerań, Wsaw. 10 E6 52 18N 20 58 E
Zerzeń, Wsaw. 10 E7 52 12N 21 7 E
Zeytinburnu, Ist. 17 B2 40 58N 28 53 E
Zhabei, Shang. 14 J11 31 16N 121 26 E
Zhangguizhuang, Tianj. 14 E6 39 7N 117 19 E
Zhangxingzhuang, Tianj. 14 D6 39 10N 117 12 E
Zhdanov, Mos. 11 E10 55 44N 37 41 E
Zhegalovo, Mos. 11 D11 55 54N 37 59 E
Zheleznodorozhnyy, Mos. 11 E12 55 45N 38 0 E
Zhenru, Shang. 14 J11 31 16N 121 22 E
Zhicun, Gzh. 14 G8 23 0N 113 18 E
Zhongshan Gongyuan, Shang. 14 J11 31 13N 121 24 E
Zhoucun, Gzh. 14 F8 23 11N 113 11 E
Zhoujiadu, Shang. 14 J11 31 11N 121 29 E
Zhoujiazhen, Shang. 14 J12 31 16N 121 33 E
Zhu Jiang →, Gzh. 14 G9 23 6N 113 20 E
Zhulebino, Mos. 11 E11 55 42N 37 50 E
Zhushadi, Gzh. 14 F9 23 11N 113 22 E
Zielona, Wsaw. 10 E8 52 14N 21 11 E
Zielonka, Wsaw. 10 E7 52 18N 21 9 E
Zitadella, Berl. 7 A2 52 31N 13 11 E
Zizhuyuan Gongyuan, Beij. 14 B2 39 55N 116 17 E
Žižkov, Pra. 10 B2 50 5N 14 28 E
Zličin, Pra. 10 B1 50 3N 14 17 E
Zōbki, Wsaw. 10 E7 52 17N 21 6 E
Zografos, Ath. 8 J11 37 58N 23 47 E
Żoliborz, Wsaw. 10 E6 52 16N 20 57 E
Zugliget, Bud. 10 K12 47 30N 18 59 E
Zugló, Bud. 10 J13 47 31N 19 8 E
Zumbi, Rio J. 31 A2 22 49 S 43 10W
Zuvuvu →, S. Pau. 31 F5 23 40 S 46 42W
Zuvuvus, S. Pau. 31 F6 23 41 S 46 39W
Zweckel, Ruhr 6 A3 51 35N 6 57 E
Zyuzino, Mos. 11 F9 55 39N 37 34 E

WORLD MAPS

MAP SYMBOLS

SETTLEMENTS

⬡ **PARIS**   ▣ **Berne**   ◉ **Livorno**   ◉ **Brugge**   ◎ **Algeciras**   ○ *Fréjus*   ○ *Oberammergau*   ○ *Thira*

Settlement symbols and type styles vary according to the scale of each map and indicate the importance
of towns on the map rather than specific population figures

∴ Ruins or Archæological Sites   ◡ Wells in Desert

ADMINISTRATION

Boundaries

────── International

▄ ▄ ▄ International
(Undefined or Disputed)

········· Internal

National Parks

International boundaries
show the *de facto* situation
where there are rival claims
to territory.

Country Names
NICARAGUA

Administrative
Areas

KENT

CALABRIA

COMMUNICATIONS

Roads

────── Primary

╲───╴ Secondary

····╴─╴ Trails and Seasonal

Railroads

╱╲──╴ Primary

───── Secondary

····─── Under Construction

✧ Airfields

⊳⊲ Passes

╶┤---├╴ Railroad Tunnels

········ Principal Canals

PHYSICAL FEATURES

╲╴──╴ Perennial Streams

········ Intermittent Streams

◯ Perennial Lakes

⬭ Intermittent Lakes

Swamps and Marshes

Permanent Ice
and Glaciers

▲ 2259 Elevations (m)

▼ 2604 Sea Depths (m)

408 Elevation of Lake
Surface Above
Sea Level (m)

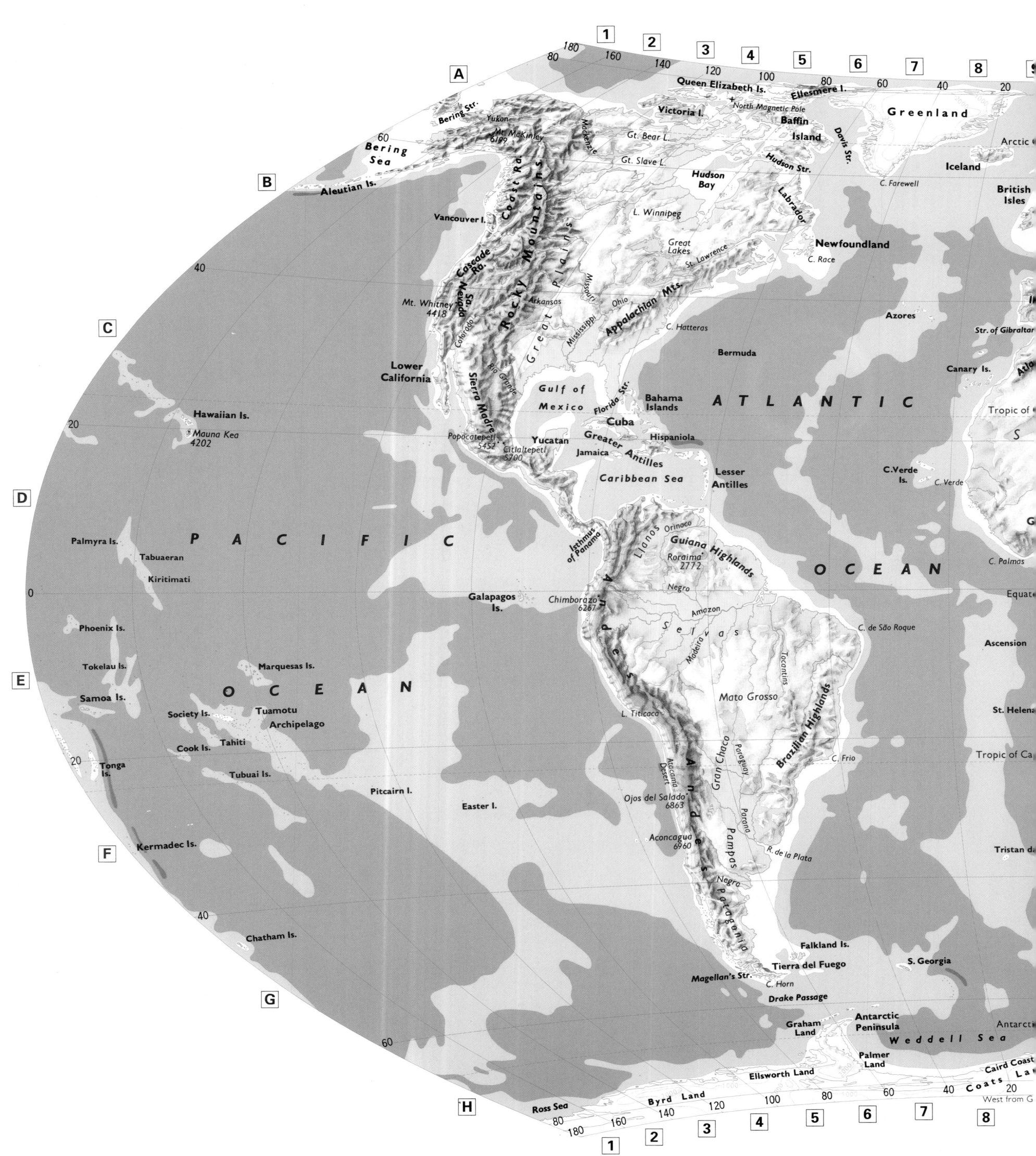

A

Bering Str.

Queen Elizabeth Is.

Ellesmere I.

+North Magnetic Pole

Victoria I.

Baffin

Island

Greenland

60

Yukon

Mt. McKinley
6199

Mackenzie

Gt. Bear L.

Davis Str.

Bering
Sea

Gt. Slave L.

Hudson Str.

Iceland

B

Aleutian Is.

Hudson
Bay

Labrador

C. Farewell

British
Isles

Vancouver I.

L. Winnipeg

Great
Lakes

St. Lawrence

Newfoundland

40

C. Race

Azores

Mt. Whitney
4418

Arkansas

Missouri

Ohio

Appalachian Mts.

C. Hatteras

Str. of Gibraltar

C

Colorado

Mississippi

Bermuda

Canary Is.

Atl

Lower
California

Gulf of
Mexico

Florida Str.

ATLANTIC

Tropic of

20

Hawaiian Is.

Rio Grande

Sierra Madre

Bahama
Islands

Cuba

S

Mauna Kea
4202

Popocatepetl
5452

Yucatan

Citlaltepetl
5700

Greater
Antilles

Jamaica

Hispaniola

C.Verde
Is.

C. Verde

Caribbean Sea

Lesser
Antilles

D

Palmyra Is.

Orinoco

Llanos

Guiana Highlands

OCEAN

C. Palmas

Tabuaeran

Isthmus
of Panama

Roraima
2772

Kiritimati

PACIFIC

Negro

Equate

0

Galapagos
Is.

Chimborazo
6267

Amazon

Ascension

Phoenix Is.

Andes

C. de São Roque

Madeira

Selvas

Tokelau Is.

Marquesas Is.

St. Hele

E

Samoa Is.

OCEAN

Mato Grosso

Tocantins

Society Is.

Tuamotu
Archipelago

L. Titicaca

Brazilian Highlands

Cook Is.

Tahiti

Tonga
Is.

20

Tubuai Is.

Paraguay

Tropic of Cap

Pitcairn I.

Easter I.

Ojos del Salado
6863

Paraná

C. Frio

Gran Chaco

Kermadec Is.

Atacama Desert

Pampas

F

Aconcagua
6960

R. de la Plata

Tristan da

40

Negro

Chatham Is.

Patagonia

G

Falkland Is.

S. Georgia

60

Tierra del Fuego

Magellan's Str.

C. Horn

Drake Passage

Graham
Land

Antarctic
Peninsula

Antarc

Palmer
Land

Weddell Sea

Ellsworth Land

Caird Coast

Coats La

H

Ross Sea

Byrd Land

West from G

Projection: Hammer Equal Area

3

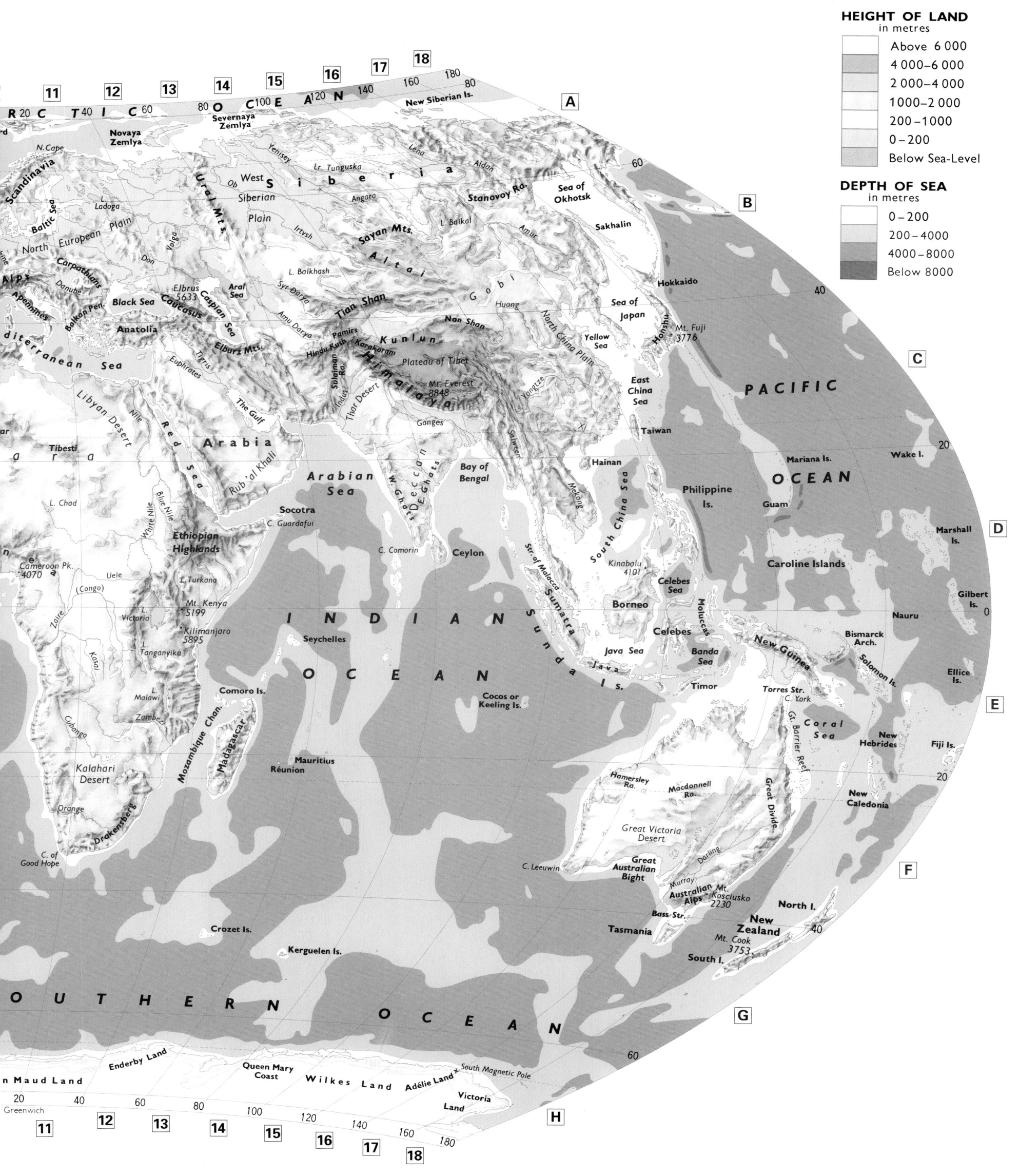

HEIGHT OF LAND
in metres

	Above 6 000
	4 000–6 000
	2 000–4 000
	1000–2 000
	200 –1000
	0 – 200
	Below Sea-Level

DEPTH OF SEA
in metres

	0 – 200
	200 – 4000
	4000 – 8000
	Below 8000

11 **12** **13** **14** **15** **16** **17** **18**

R 20 C 40 T I 60 C 80 O 100 C E 120 A N 140 160 180 80

N. Cape

Scandinavia

Baltic Sea

L. Ladoga

North European Plain

Novaya Zemlya

Severnaya Zemlya

New Siberian Is.

A

Yenisey

Ob West Siberian Plain

Lr. Tunguska

Lena

Aldan

S i b e r i a

Angara

Irtysh

Ural Mts.

Stanovoy Ra.

Sea of Okhotsk

B

Sayan Mts.

L. Baikal

Amur

Altai

Sakhalin

Volga

Don

Danube

Alps

Carpathians

Apennines

Balkan Pen.

Black Sea

Mediterranean Sea

Anatolia

Caucasus

Elbrus 5633

Caspian Sea

Aral Sea

Syr Darya

L. Balkhash

Amu Darya

Tian Shan

Gobi

Huang

Sea of Japan

Hokkaido

40

Elburz Mts.

Tigris

Euphrates

Hindu Kush

Pamirs

Karakoram

Kunlun

Nan Shan

North China Plain

Yellow Sea

Honshu

Mt. Fuji 3776

Sulaiman Ra.

Plateau of Tibet

C

Libyan Desert

Nile

Red Sea

Arabia

Thar Desert

Indus

Himalaya

Mt. Everest 8848

Ganges

Yangtze

East China Sea

Taiwan

PACIFIC

Tibesti

Deccan

W. Ghats

E. Ghats

Bay of Bengal

Salween

Mekong

Xi

Hainan

Mariana Is.

Wake I.

20

S a h a r a

Arabian Sea

Socotra

C. Guardafui

Ethiopian Highlands

Rub 'al Khali

Arabian Sea

C. Comorin

Ceylon

Str. of Malacca

South China Sea

Philippine Is.

Guam

OCEAN

Marshall Is.

L. Chad

Cameroon Pk. 4070

Uele

(Congo)

Zaire

L. Turkana

L. Victoria

Mt. Kenya 5199

Kilimanjaro 5895

L. Tanganyika

Seychelles

I N D I A N

Kinabalu 4101

Sumatra

Borneo

Celebes

Celebes Sea

Moluccas

New Guinea

Caroline Islands

Nauru

Gilbert Is.

0

D

Kasai

Comoro Is.

O C E A N

Java Sea

Banda Sea

Timor

Bismarck Arch.

Solomon Is.

Ellice Is.

E

L. Malawi

Madagascar

Mozambique Chan.

Zambezi

Cocos or Keeling Is.

Sunda Is.

Java

Torres Str.

C. York

Coral Sea

Gt. Barrier Reef

New Hebrides

Fiji Is.

20

Cubango

Kalahari Desert

Orange

Drakensberg

Mauritius

Réunion

Hamersley Ra.

Macdonnell Ra.

Great Divide

New Caledonia

C. of Good Hope

Great Victoria Desert

C. Leeuwin

Great Australian Bight

Murray

Darling

Australian Alps

Mt. Kosciusko 2230

North I.

F

Crozet Is.

Kerguelen Is.

Bass Str.

Tasmania

New Zealand

Mt. Cook 3753

South I.

40

S O U T H E R N   O C E A N

G

60

Maud Land

20 Greenwich 40

Enderby Land

60

Queen Mary Coast

80

Wilkes Land

100

Adélie Land

120

South Magnetic Pole

140

Victoria Land

160

180

H

11 **12** **13** **14** **15** **16** **17** **18**

A

1 2 3 4 5 6 7 8

Beaufort
Sea Parry Ch. Ellesmere I. GREENLAND
Banks I. Queen Elizabeth Is. (Denmark)
St. Lawrence Bering Strait Devon I.
ALASKA Fairbanks Victoria I. Devon I. *Baffin* Denmark Str.
(U.S.A.) Yukon *Bay* N
Anchorage Mackenzie Yellowknife Great Bear L. Baffin I. Godthåb ICELAND Arcti
G. of Great Slave L. Davis Str. Reykjavik Faroe Is.
Alaska Kodiak I. *Hudson* (Den.)

B

Aleutian Is. (U.S.A.) Queen Edmonton C A N A D A *Bay* UNITED
Charlotte Is. Calgary Churchill Nelson Schefferville KINGDOM
Vancouver Missouri Winnipeg L. Superior Québec Newfoundland Glasg
Vancouver I. Winnipeg L. Michigan Ottawa Montreal St. John's Dubli
Seattle UNITED STATES Minneapolis Milwaukee Detroit Toronto Boston Halifax IRELAND LON
Portland Missouri L. Huron CHICAGO Cleveland PORTUGAL
Salt Lake Denver Pittsburgh NEW YORK N O R T H Lisbon
City Kansas City St. Louis Cincinnati PHILADELPHIA Azores
SAN FRANCISCO Sacramento Colorado OF AMERICA Baltimore (Port.)

C

LOS ANGELES Phoenix El Paso Memphis Atlanta Washington D.C. A T L A N T I C Tangie
San Diego Dallas Jacksonville Bermuda Rabat
Ciudad Juárez Houston (U.K.) Madeira Casablanca
Tropic of Cancer New Miami (Port.) Marrakesh
Midway Is. Monterrey Orleans Gulf of BAHAMAS MOROCC
Hawaiian Is. Rio Grande Mexico Canary Is. El Aaiun
(U.S.A.) MEXICO León Havana CUBA (Sp.) O C E A N WESTERN
Honolulu Guadalajara Turks & Caicos SAHARA
Oahu MÉXICO Cayman Is.(U.K.) (U.K.) Nouakchott MAURITANIA
Hawaii Revilla Puebla HAITI DOMINICAN REP. Timb
Gigedo Is. BELIZE Port-au-Prince Santo Virgin Is.(U.S.A.)&(U.K.) CAPE VERDE SENEGAL
(Mexico) GUATEMALA JAMAICA Domingo PUERTO ANTIGUA & BARBUDA IS. Dakar
Guatemala Belmopan Kingston RICO ST. KITTS & NEVIS GAMBIA Barako

D

San Salvador HONDURAS Tegucigalpa Caribbean GUADELUPE (Fr.) DOMINICA Bissau GUINEA
EL SALVADOR NICARAGUA MARTINIQUE(Fr.) ST. LUCIA GUINEA-BISSAU
Clipperton I. Managua Sea ST. VINCENT & BARBADOS Conakry CO
(Fr.) San José Barranquilla THE GRENADINES GRENADA Freetown LIBERIA
P A C I F I C COSTA RICA Panamá NETH. TRINIDAD & Monrovia Ahd
PANAMA ANTILLES TOBAGO
Caracas Orinoco São Paulo G
Palmyra Is. Medellín VENEZUELA Georgetown (Brazil)
(U.S.A.) Cocos I. Cali Paramaribo
(C.Rica) GUYANA Cayenne
Howland I.(U.S.A.) Malpelo BOGOTÁ SURINAM FRENCH
Baker I.(U.S.A.) Jarvis I. (Colombia) COLOMBIA GUIANA
Equator (U.S.A.) Galápagos Quito Negro Belém
Kiritimati (Ecuador) ECUADOR Tapurá Manaus Amazon Fortaleza Fernando de Noronha
Abariringa Guayaquil Iquitos (Brazil)
KIRIBATI Malden I. Madeira B R A Z I L Natal Ascension I.

E

Phoenix Is. Starbuck I. Marajó Recife (U.K.)
Tokelau Is. Penrhyn I. PERU Tocantins St. Helen
(N.Z.) Manihiki Flint I. FRENCH São Francisco Salvador (U.K.)
WESTERN Callao LIMA
Wallis & SAMOA O C E A N Brasília S O U T H
Futuna AMERICAN Society Is. L. Titicaca
(Fr.) SAMOA Manihiki Tahiti La Paz Belo Horizonte Trindade
FIJI Marquesas Is. Arequipa BOLIVIA (Brazil)
TONGA Niue Cook Is. Tuamotu Sucre Belo Horizonte

F

Kermadec POLYNESIA Tubuai Is. Tropic of Capricorn SÃO PAULO RIO DE JANEIRO A T L A N T I
Is.(N.Z.) Pitcairn I. Antofagasta PARAGUAY Santos
(U.K.) Ducie I. Sala-y-Gómez Asunción Curitiba
Rapa (Chile) San Félix San Ambrosio Tucumán Pôrto Alegre
International Date Line Easter I. (Chile) Córdoba Paraná Rio Grande
(Chile) Juan Fernández Valparaíso URUGUAY O C E A N
Chatham Is. (Chile) SANTIAGO Rosario Montevideo Tristan d
(N.Z.) Talcahuano BUENOS AIRES
ARGENTINA Bahía Blanca

G

Chiloé I. Falkland Is. South Georgia
(U.K.) (U.K.)
Punta Arenas Tierra del Fuego South Sandwich
C. Horn Scotia Sea Is. (U.K.)
Drake Passage South Orkney Is.
H (U.K.)
South Shetland Is.
Antarctic Circle Bellingshausen Sea Weddell
(U.K.) Sea
Amundsen Sea A n t a

West from G

1 2 3 4 5 6 7 8

11 **12** **13** **14** **15** **16** **17** **18**

A R C T I C O C E A N

Barents Novaya *Kara* Severnaya *Laptev Sea* New Siberian Is. *East Siberian* Wrangel I.
Sea Zemlya *Sea* Zemlya *Sea*

d

Murmansk Norilsk Verkhoyansk Arctic Circle B

Oh *Yenisey* *Lena*

Arkhangelsk Salekhard Yakutsk Magadan Bering

SWEDEN FINLAND Perm Yekaterinburg R U S S I A Okhotsk Sea
Helsinki Tomsk Krasnoyarsk Sea of Petropavlovsk-
Stockholm EST. ST.PETERSBURG Kazan *Volga* Omsk Novosibirsk L. Baikal Okhotsk Kamchatskiy
openhagen LATVIA MOSCOW Samara Chelyabinsk Irkutsk Komsomolsk International
LITH. Minsk Saratov Barnaul Ulan Ude Khabarovsk Sakhalin Date Line
Berlin POLAND BELARUS Kiev Volgograd K A Z A K S T A N Ulan Bator *Amur* Vladivostok Sapporo
Prague REP. Warsaw UKRAINE Astrakhan *L. Balkhash* M O N G O L I A Harbin *Kuril Is.*
Budapest Odessa Aral Changchun
AUSTRIA Vienna REP. Bucharest *Black* GEORGIA Caspian Sea Bishkek Alma Ata Ürümqi SHENYANG Pyongyang SEOUL JAPAN 40
Milan Belgrade ROMANIA *Sea* Tbilisi KYRGYZSTAN BEIJING TIANJIN NORTH TŌKYŌ
Rome ITALY Sofia BULGARIA Yerevan UZBEKISTAN Tashkent Dalian KOREA
Naples GREECE ISTANBUL ARM. Baku Samarkand Dushanbe Lanzhou C H I N A Taiyuan SOUTH Kitakyūshū PACIFIC
editerranean Athens Izmir AZER. TURKMENISTAN TAJIKISTAN Xi'an KOREA Ōsaka
MALTA CYPRUS TURKEY Ankara Ashkhabad Mashhad Kābul Islamabad *Hwang-ho* Nanjing SHANGHAI OCEAN
TUNISIA Tripoli SYRIA Beirut Damascus TEHRĀN AFGHANISTAN Lahore Chengdu Wuhan *East China* Bonin Is.
Benghazi LEB. Baghdad Esfahān Kanpur T I B E T Lhasa CHONGQING *Sea* (Japan) Volcano Is.
Jerusalem ISR. Ammān IRAQ IRAN Shīrāz NEPAL Katmandu DELHI *Yangtze* Fuzhou (Japan) Marcus I. Tropic of Cancer
CAIRO JORDAN KUWAIT Abu Dhabi New Delhi BANGLA- Kunming GUANGZHOU Taipei (Japan)
L I B Y A EGYPT BAHRAIN QATAR KARACHI I N D I A DESH DACCA BURMA Hanoi TAIWAN Wake I. 20
Riyadh U.A.E. Ahmadabad CALCUTTA MYANMAR HONG KONG(U.K.) (U.S.A.)
NIGER Mecca SAUDI Muscat Nagpur *Bay of* *Hainan* NORTHERN
CHAD Omdurmān ARABIA OMAN BOMBAY *Bengal* Rangoon *South* MARIANAS
L.Chad Khartoum Aswān Asmara YEMEN *Arabian* Hyderabad Andaman Is. THAILAND VIET- *China* (U.S.A.) MARSHALL IS. D
Kano ERITREA Saná *Sea* MADRAS (India) BANGKOK NAM *Sea* GUAM
NIGERIA Ndjamena SUDAN DJIBOUTI Aden Bangalore Nicobar Is. Phnom CAMBODIA MANILA (U.S.A.) FEDERATED STATES PALAU
Abuja CENTRAL G. of Aden SOMALI Lakshadweep Is. (India) Penh Ho Chi Minh PHILIPPINES Truk
dan CAMEROON AFRICAN Addis Ababa (India) SRI LANKA City *Caroline Is.* Pohnpei
Douala REP. ETHIOPIA REP. Colombo Medan Kuala Lumpur SABAH OF MICRONESIA Gilbert Is.
Yaoundé Bangui MALDIVES PEN. MALAYSIA BRUNEI NAURU KIRIBATI
GABON UGANDA L. Turkana SINGAPORE Borneo
Libreville ZAÏRE Kampala KENYA *Zaïre* Kisangani L. Equator MALAYSIA Banjarmasin IRIAN TUVALU
Kigali RWANDA Victoria Nairobi *INDIAN* Palembang *Sumatra* I N D O N E S I A JAYA New
Brazzaville Bujumbura BURUNDI Mombasa SEYCHELLES Ireland
CABINDA Kinshasa Kananga Zanzibar Amirante OCEAN JAKARTA Ujung Pandang PAPUA New
(Angola) TANZANIA Dar es Salaam Is. Diego Garcia Bandung *Java* NEW Britain SOLOMON
Luanda Chagos Arch. GUINEA IS. Santa Cruz I.
ANGOLA Lubumbashi Aldabra Is. (U.K.) Surabaya *Arafura Sea* Port
Benguela COMOROS Agalega Is. Cocos Is. *Timor* Moresby C. York VANUATU
Mayotte (Austral.) Darwin
ZAMBIA Lilongwe (Fr.) Christmas I. Cairns FIJI
NAMIBIA Lusaka MALAWI MADAGASCAR Cargados Carajos (Austral.) Townsville Suva
Windhoek ZIMBABWE Harare Antananarivo Rodriguez NEW
BOTSWANA Bulawayo MOZAMBIQUE RÉUNION MAURITIUS Tropic of Capricorn Port Hedland CALEDONIA 20
Gaborone Pretoria (Fr.) Alice Springs
Johannesburg Maputo Geraldton A U S T R A L I A Rockhampton
SOUTH SWAZILAND Kalgoorlie- Brisbane
AFRICA LESOTHO Durban Perth Boulder *Darling* Lord Howe I. F
Cape Town Port Elizabeth Amsterdam I. *Great* Adelaide Newcastle (Austral.)
C. of Good Hope (Fr.) *Australian* Sydney Norfolk I.
St.Paul (Fr.) *Bight* Canberra Auckland (Austral.)
Melbourne *Tasman* North I.
Prince Edward Is. Crozet Is. Tasmania *Sea* NEW 40
(S.Africa) (Fr.) Wellington ZEALAND
Kerguelen Hobart Christchurch
(Fr.) South I.
McDonald Is. Heard I. Stewart I. Dunedin
(Austral.) (Austral.) Bounty Is.
(N.Z.)
UTHERN OCEAN Campbell I. Antipodes
(N.Z.) Is. (N.Z.)
Macquarie Is.
(Austral.) G
Antarctic Circle 60

c t i c a H
20 40 60 80 100 120 140 160 180
Greenwich *Ross Sea*

11 **12** **13** **14** **15** **16** **17** **18**

Hanoi ● Capital Cities

CARTOGRAPHY BY PHILIP'S. COPYRIGHT REED INTERNATIONAL BOOKS LTD.

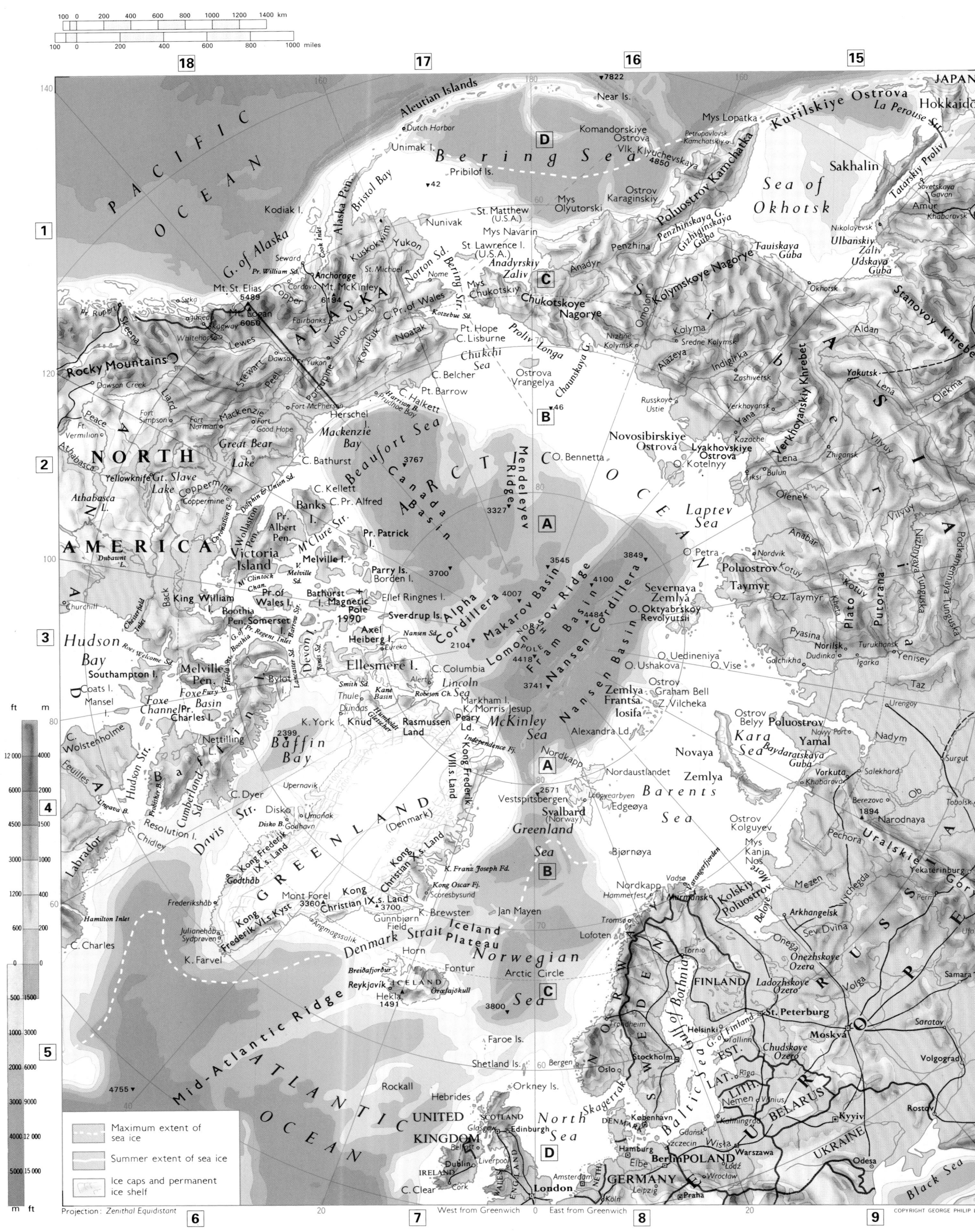

Projection: Zenithal Equidistant

West from Greenwich   East from Greenwich

Maximum extent of sea ice

Summer extent of sea ice

Ice caps and permanent ice shelf

COPYRIGHT GEORGE PHILIP LTD

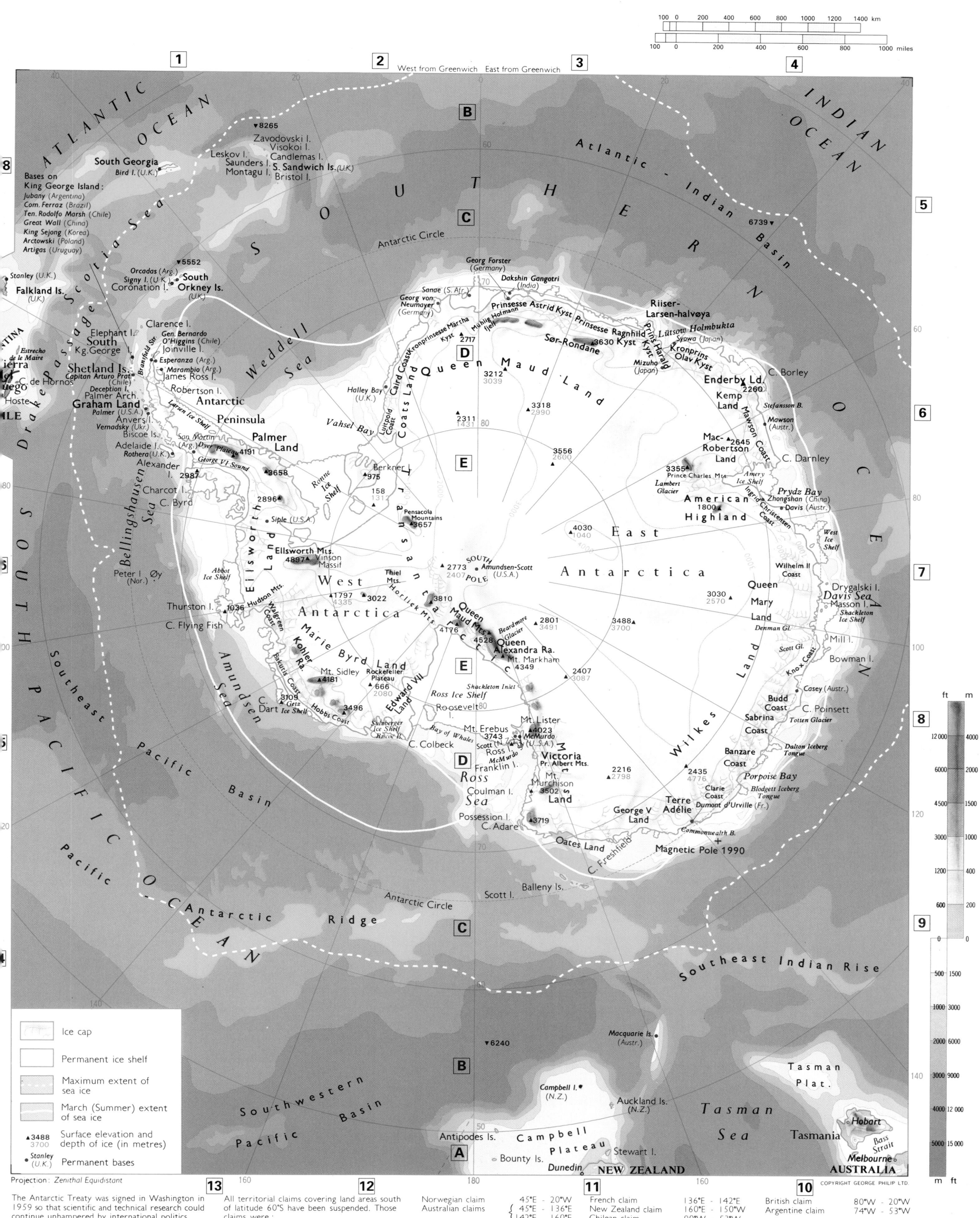

100 0 200 400 600 800 1000 1200 1400 km

100 0 200 400 600 800 1000 miles

Ice cap

Permanent ice shelf

Maximum extent of sea ice

March (Summer) extent of sea ice

▲3488 **Surface elevation and depth of ice (in metres)**
3700

● Stanley (U.K.) **Permanent bases**

Projection: Zenithal Equidistant

The Antarctic Treaty was signed in Washington in 1959 so that scientific and technical research could continue unhampered by international politics.

All territorial claims covering land areas south of latitude 60°S have been suspended. Those claims were:

Norwegian claim	45°E – 20°W	
Australian claims	{ 45°E – 136°E	
	142°E – 160°E	
French claim	136°E – 142°E	
New Zealand claim	160°E – 150°W	
Chilean claim	90°W – 53°W	
British claim	80°W – 20°W	
Argentine claim	74°W – 53°W	

COPYRIGHT GEORGE PHILIP LTD.

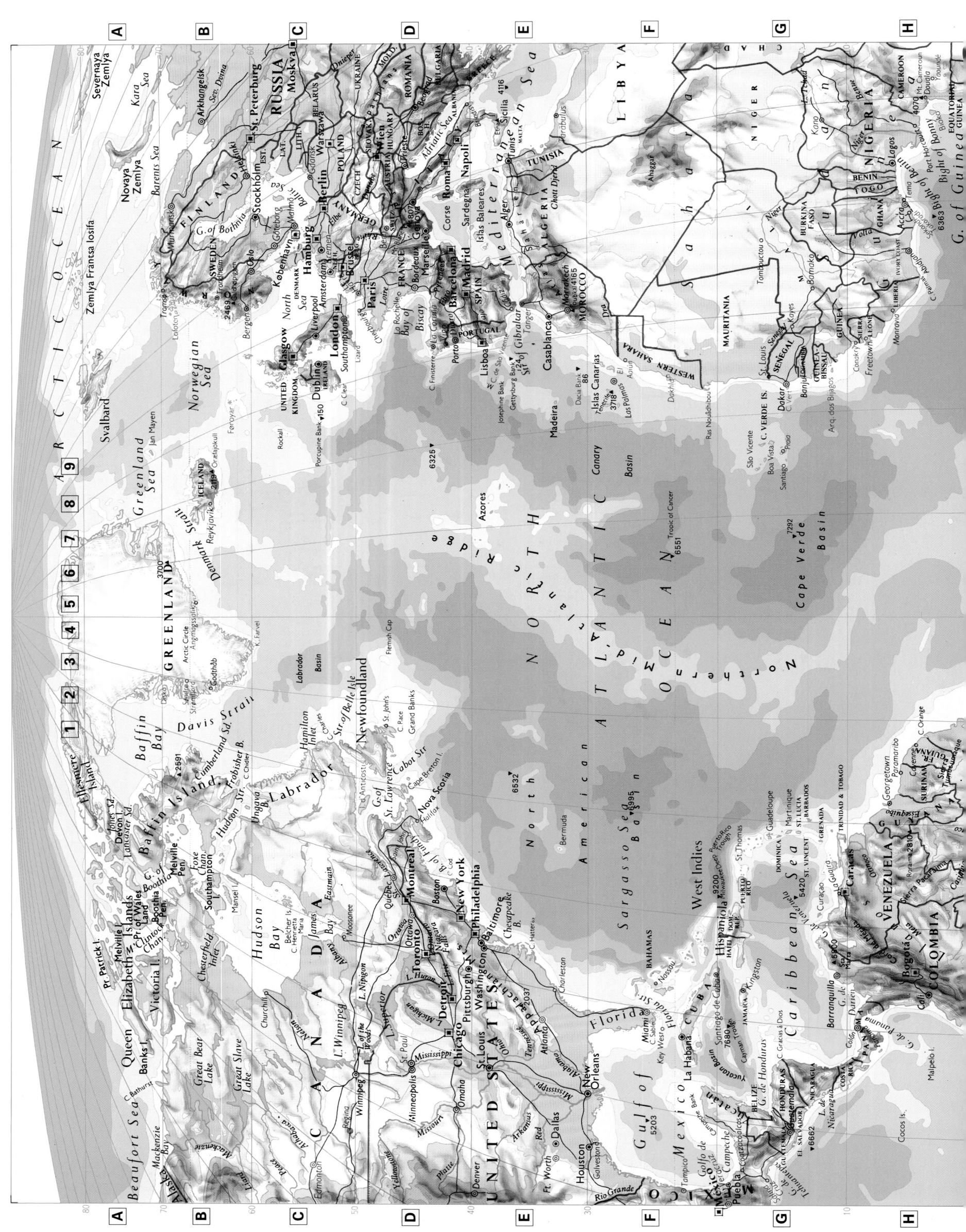

Projection: Mollweide

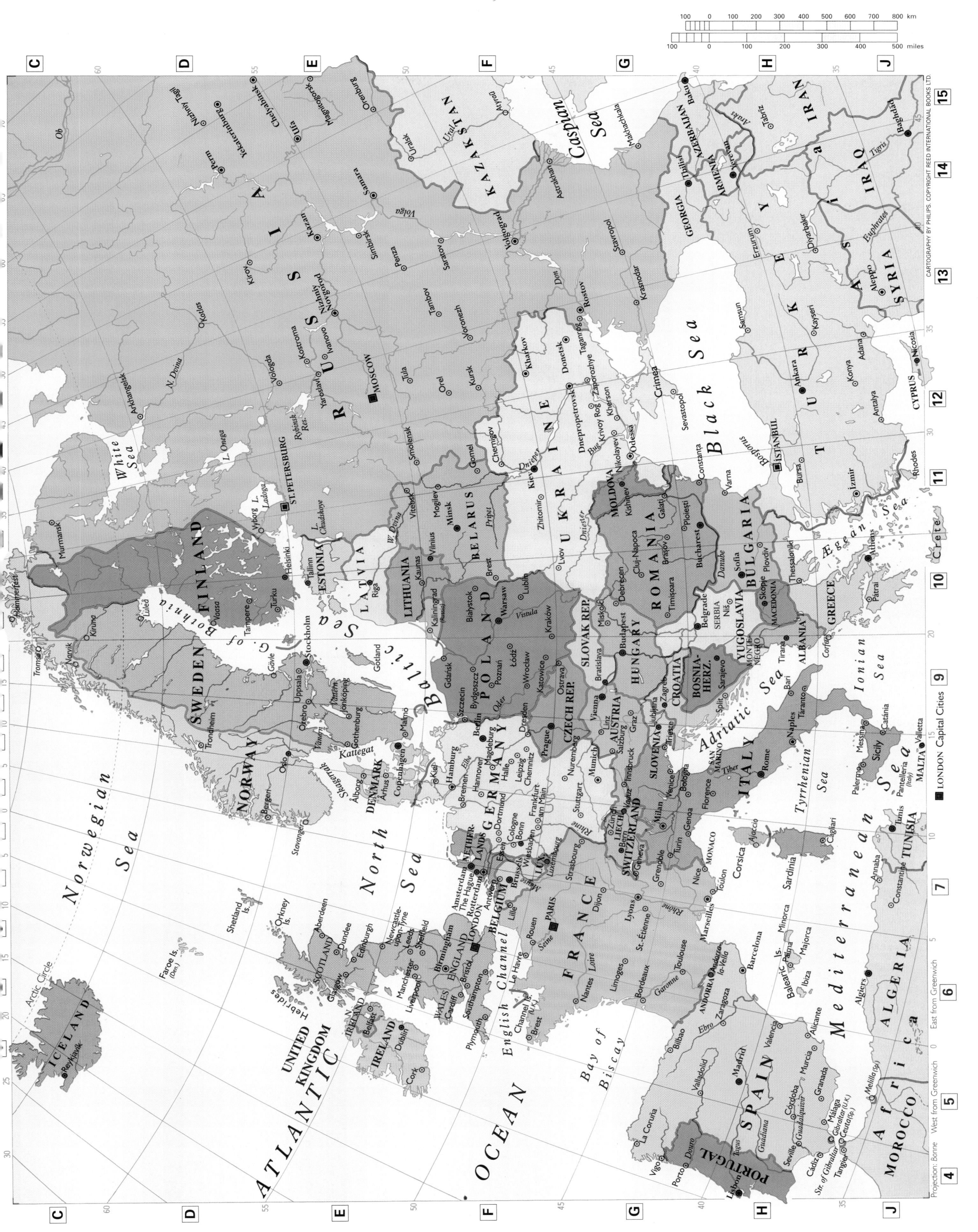

100 0 100 200 300 400 500 600 700 800 km

100 0 100 200 300 400 500 miles

Political : EUROPE

CARTOGRAPHY BY PHILIPS. COPYRIGHT REED INTERNATIONAL BOOKS LTD.

Projection: Bonne West from Greenwich East from Greenwich

SCANDINAVIA 1:4 000 000

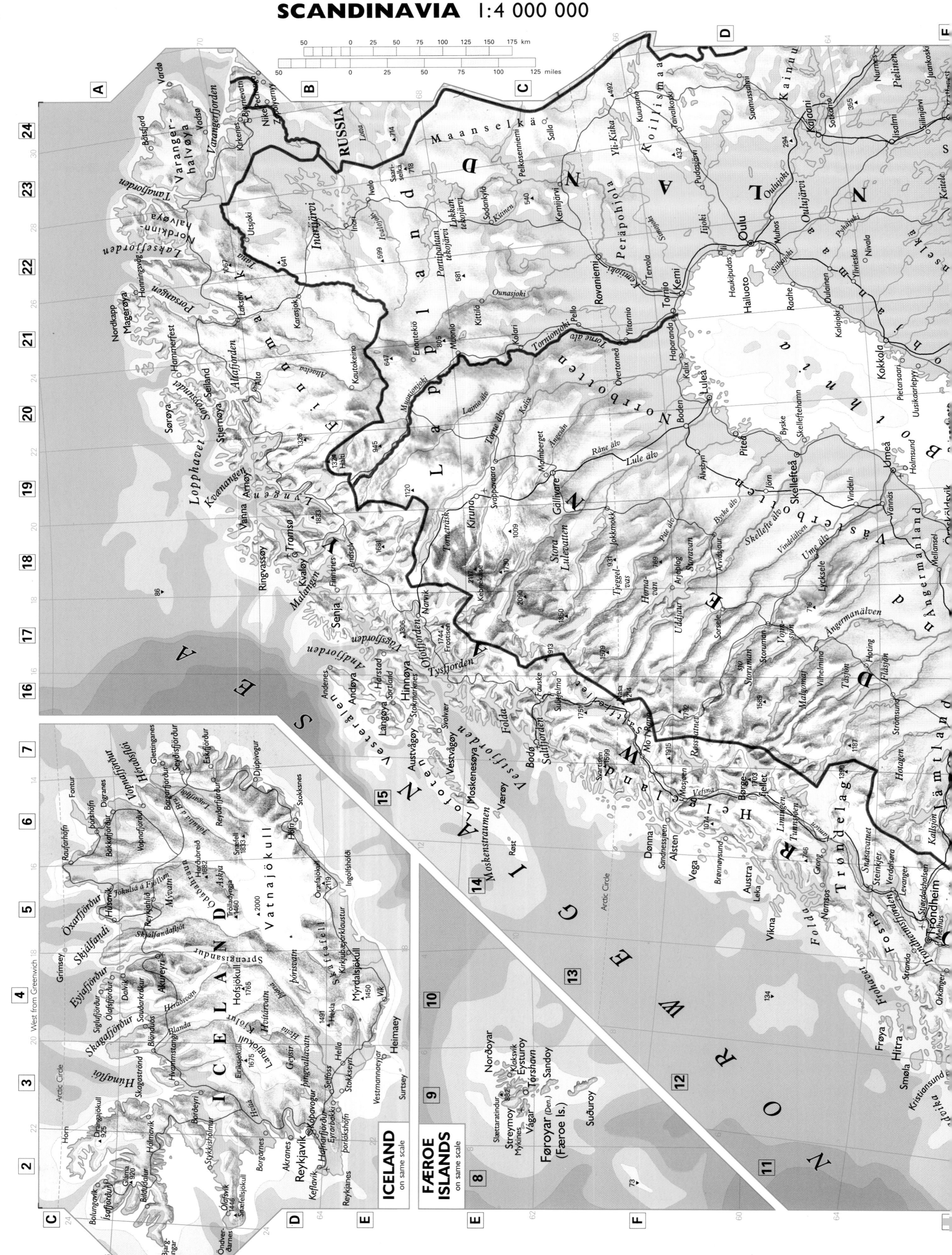

ICELAND
on same scale

FÆROE ISLANDS
on same scale

RUSSIA

NORWAY

SWEDEN

FINLAND

ICELAND

Reykjavik

Akureyri

Vatnajökull

Arctic Circle

West from Greenwich

Føroyar (Den.)
(Færoe Is.)

Tórshavn

NORWEGIAN SEA

ARCTIC OCEAN

Nordkapp

Hammerfest

Varangerfjorden

Kirkenes

Tromsø

Narvik

Bodø

Mo

Trondheim

Oulu

Kemi

Tornio

Rovaniemi

Luleå

Skellefteå

Umeå

Lappland

Norrbotten

Kiruna

F **G** **H** **J** **K**

21 **20** **19** **18** **17** **16** **15** **14** **13** **12**

Saimaa
Savonlinna
Mikkeli
Lappeenranta
Pekšämäki
Kouvola
Kotka
Heinola
Anjalankoski
Kymijoki
Hamina
Ostrov Bolshoy Tyuters

Jyväskylä
Keuruu
Mänttä
Jämsä
Lahti
Hämeenlinna
Hyvinkää
Kerava
Porvoo
Vantaa
Espoo
HELSINKI (Helsingfors)
Kirkkonummi

Tampere
Nokia
Valkeakoski
Riihimäki
Järvenpää
Lohja

Pori
Rauma
Uusikaupunki
Kankaanpää
Parkano
Turku (Åbo)
Salo
Naantali
Raisio
Paimio
Parainen

Kristiinankaupunki
Kaskinen
Kauhajoki
Jalasjärvi

Gulf of Finland
Narva
Gdov
Sillamäe
Jõhvi
Kohtla-Järve
Rakvere
Kunda
Tapa
Paide
Põltsamaa
Tartu
Põlva
Võru
Pskov
Ozero Chudskoye (Peipus)
Valga

TALLINN
Keila
Rapla
Viljandi
Paldiski
Naissaar
Haapsalu

ESTONIA
Vormsi
Hiiumaa (Dagö)
Orissaare
Saaremaa (Ösel)
Kuressaare
Muhu
Kärdla
Ruhnu saar
Kihnu
Pärnu
Kolkas Rags
Roja

LATVIA
Valmiera
Cēsis
Sigulda
Limbaži
RIGA
Jūrmala
Tukums
Ogre
Dobele
Saldus
Jelgava
Bauska
Talsi
Ventspils
Kuldīga
Aizpute
Priekule
Pāvilosta
Liepāja
Skuodas
Palanga

LITHUANIA
Šiauliai
Jonišķis
Biržai
Radviliškis
Panevėžys
Telšiai
Mažeikiai
Plungė
Kretinga
Klaipėda
Neringa
Šilutė
Tauragė
Jurbarkas
Kėdainiai
Ukmergė
VILNIUS
Kaunas
Jonava
Prienai
Marijampolė
Alytus
Varėna
Druskininkai

Daugava
Daugavpils
Zarasai
Rēzekne
Preiļi
Madona
Gulbene
Ludza

BELARUS
Braslaw
Vidzy
Pastavy
Lynttupy
Lida
Ashmyany

Gulf of Riga

BALTIC SEA

Gotland
Visby
Roma
Slite
Fårö
Gotska Sandön

Burgsvik
Hoburgen

Öland
Borgholm

Bornholm
Rønne
Nexø

Åland (Ahvenanmaa)
Mariehamn
Ålands hav

Härnösand
Sundsvall
Hudiksvall
Söderhamn
Gävle
Bollnäs
Ljusdal
Hofors
Sandviken

STOCKHOLM
Uppsala
Norrtälje
Märsta
Enköping
Västerås
Sala
Köping
Eskilstuna
Södertälje
Nyköping
Oxelösund
Katrineholm
Strängnäs
Mälaren

Falun
Borlänge
Mora
Siljan
Ludvika
Avesta
Hedemora
Fagersta
Hallefors
Filipstad
Karlskoga
Örebro
Kristinehamn
Karlstad
Arvika
Säffle
Åmål
Mariestad
Lidköping
Skövde
Skara
Falköping

Norrköping
Motala
Linköping
Finspång
Mjölby
Vadstena
Tranås
Nässjö
Eksjö
Västervik
Oskarshamn
Nybro
Kalmar
Vetlanda
Växjö
Huskvarna
Jönköping
Värnamo
Ljungby
Åsnen
Bolmen

Borås
Ulricehamn
Alingsås
Trollhättan
Vänersborg
Uddevalla
GÖTEBORG (Gothenburg)
Kungsbacka
Varberg
Falkenberg
Halmstad
Laholm
Kinna
Mölndal
Lysekil

Helsingborg
Landskrona
KØBENHAVN (Copenhagen)
Lund
MALMÖ
Trelleborg
Ystad
Simrishamn
Kristianstad
Hässleholm
Karlshamn
Karlskrona
Ronneby
Ängelholm
Blekinge
Skåne
Halland

Vänern
Vättern
Dalarna
Härjedalen
Värmland
Bohuslän
Dalsland
Västergötland
Östergötland
Småland
Uppland
Södermanland
Västmanland
Svealand

DENMARK
Ålborg
Hjørring
Frederikshavn
Thisted
Viborg
Randers
Århus
Silkeborg
Herning
Horsens
Vejle
Fredericia
Kolding
Esbjerg
Varde
Ribe
Haderslev
Åbenrå
Sønderborg
Odense
Svendborg
Nyborg
Korsør
Slagelse
Næstved
Roskilde
Holbæk
Kalundborg
Helsingør

Sjælland
Fyn
Lolland
Falster
Langeland
Møn
Bornholm
Als
Jylland

Kattegat
Skagerrak
Læsø
Anholt
Samsø

NORWAY
OSLO
Drammen
Hamar
Lillehammer
Gjøvik
Hønefoss
Kongsberg
Skien
Porsgrunn
Larvik
Sandefjord
Tønsberg
Horten
Moss
Fredrikstad
Sarpsborg
Halden
Kongsvinger
Elverum
Gol
Ski
Drøbak
Oslofjorden

Kristiansand
Arendal
Grimstad
Mandal
Lillesand
Flekkefjord
Farsund
Lista
Lindesnes

Stavanger
Sandnes
Haugesund
Bergen
Voss
Odda
Ål
Geilo
Flåm

Hardangervidda
Hardangerfjord
Sognefjord
Jotunheimen
Galdhøpiggen
Dovrefjell
Rondane
Gudbrandsdalen
Østerdalen
Valdres
Telemark
Glomma
Lågen
Femunden

GERMANY
Lübeck
Kiel
Neumünster
Flensburg
Schleswig
Husum
Rendsburg
Cuxhaven
Rostock
Wismar
Stralsund
Greifswald
Rügen
Usedom
Fehmarn
Mecklenburger Bucht
Kieler Bucht
Lübecker Bucht
Fehmarn Bælt
Little Bælt
Store Bælt
Schleswig-Holstein
Nordfriesische Inseln
Sylt
Föhr
Helgoland
Deutsche Bucht
Ost-Friesische Inseln
Elbe

POLAND
GDAŃSK
Gdynia
Sopot
Starogard Gdański
Tczew
Elbląg
Malbork
Słupsk
Koszalin
Kołobrzeg
Białogard
Darłowo
Ustka
Lębork
Wejherowo
Bytów

Kaliningrad (Russia)
Baltiysk
Zelenogradsk
Sovetsk
Chernyakhovsk
Gvardeysk
Bagrationovsk
Mys Taran
Kurshskiy Zaliv (Kuronský)
Wisła
Zalew Wiślany
Zatoka Gdańska

Augustów
Ełk
Giżycko
Kętrzyn
Suwałki

Projection: Conical with two standard parallels

East from Greenwich

CARTOGRAPHY BY PHILIP'S. COPYRIGHT REED INTERNATIONAL BOOKS LTD.

m / ft
6000 2000
3000 1000
1500 600
600 200
200
0
0 50
150 50
300 100
600 200
1500 500
3000 1000
6000 2000 m / ft

15

English Unitary Authorities
(from April 1996)

12. Hartlepool
13. Stockton-on-Tees
14. Middlesbrough
15. Redcar and Cleveland
16. Kingston upon Hull
17. York
18. South Gloucester
19. Bristol
20. North Somerset
21. Bath and N.E. Somerset

Welsh Unitary Authorities
(from April 1996)

1. Neath Port Talbot
2. Rhondda Cynon Taff
3. Bridgend
4. Merthyr Tydfil
5. Vale of Glamorgan
6. Caerphilly
7. Cardiff
8. Blaenau Gwent
9. Torfaen
10. Newport
11. Monmouthshire

9

E

Sizewell
Aldeburgh
Orford Ness
Southwold
Bungay
Diss
Waveney
Little Ouse
Thetford
Lark
SUFFOLK
Bury St. Edmunds
Saxmundham
Stowmarket
Mildenhall
Felixstowe
Walton-on-the-Naze
The Naze
Harwich
Ipswich
Orwell
Sudbury
Stour
Newmarket
Colchester
Cambridge
Saffron Walden
Braintree
Ouse
Mersea
St. Ives
CAMBRIDGE
Huntingdon
Royston
Letchworth
Bishop's Stortford
ESSEX
Maldon
Chelmsford
Clacton

F

Foulness
Shoeburyness
Southend
Basildon
Tilbury
Thames
Sheerness
Whitstable Bay
Herne Bay
Margate
North Foreland
Ramsgate
Deal
South Foreland
Dover
Folkestone
Hythe
New Romney
Dungeness
Romney Marsh
Rye
Ashford
Canterbury
KENT
Gillingham
Chatham
Rochester
Gravesend
Maidstone
Medway
Tonbridge
Tunbridge Wells
Rother
Hastings
Bexhill
Eastbourne
Beachy Hd.

Bedford
Northampton
Kettering
Wellingborough
Rushden
NORTHANTS
Market Harborough
Rugby
Leamington
WARWICK
Coventry
Nuneaton
Birmingham
WEST MIDLANDS
Redditch
Worcester
HEREFORD & WORCESTER
Dudley
Stourbridge
Kidderminster
Droitwich
Evesham
Stratford-on-Avon
Edge Hill
Banbury
Cherwell
OXFORD
Woodstock
Bicester
Aylesbury
BUCKS
Buckingham
Milton Keynes
Luton
Dunstable
Leighton Buzzard
Hitchin
Stevenage
HERTFORD
St. Albans
Hatfield
Welwyn
Hertford
Ware
Bishop's Stortford
Harlow
Epping
Enfield
Brentwood
Romford
Havering
LONDON
Barnet
Harrow
Brent
Ealing
Hillingdon
Uxbridge
Croydon
Bromley
Dartford
Gravesend
Sevenoaks
NORTH DOWNS
Reigate
Dorking
Leith Hill 294
Crawley
East Grinstead
WEST SUSSEX
Horsham
EAST SUSSEX
Lewes
Newhaven
Brighton
Hove
Worthing
Littlehampton
Bognor Regis
Selsey Bill
Chichester
SOUTH DOWNS
Arundel

G

CHANNEL

le Tréport
Dieppe
St. Valéry
St. Valéry
Fécamp
Étretat
C. d' Antifer
C. de la Hève
Le Havre
Seine
Honfleur
Trouville
Arromanches
Bayeux
Caen
Rouen
Elbeuf
Louviers
Pont l'Évêque
Lisieux
Bernay
Yvetot
Caudebec
FRANCE

East from Greenwich

8

H

SEINE

9

Rouen

8

Cherbourg
C. de la Hague
C. de la Hague
Barfleur
Quineville
Valognes
Carentan
Périers
Isigny
St. Lô
Vierville

7

West from Greenwich

Alderney
Guernsey
St. Peter Port
Sark
Channel Islands
Jersey
St. Helier
Barneville

6

5

0

7

6

5

4

3

2

1

Borth
Aberystwyth
CEREDIGION
Cardigan Bay
Aberaeron
Tregaron
Teifi
Newcastle Emlyn
Lampeter
Llandovery
Bay
Cardigan
St. David's Hd.
St. Davids
PEMBROKESHIRE
Fishguard
Haverfordwest
St. Bride's Bay
Milford Haven
Pembroke
Tenby
CARMARTHENSHIRE
Carmarthen
Carmarthen Bay
Llanelli
Burry Port
SWANSEA
Swansea
Gower
Port Talbot
Porthcawl
Bridgend
POWYS
Newtown
Llanidloes
Rhayader
Builth Wells
Llandrindod Wells
Radnor
Knighton
Presteigne
New Radnor
Brecon
Brecon Beacons 886
Merthyr Tydfil
Aberdare
Neath
Pontypridd
Rhondda
Cynon
Maesteg

BRECKNOCK
Black Mts.
Abergavenny
Ebbw Vale
Pontypool
Cwmbran
Newport
Cardiff
Barry

HEREFORD
Hereford
Ross
Ledbury
Malvern Hills
Great Malvern
Leominster
Ludlow
Clee Hills
Bridgnorth

Cheltenham
GLOUCESTER
Gloucester
Stroud
Cheltenham
Cleeve Hill 330
Cirencester
Severn
Forest of Dean
Chepstow
Avonmouth
Clevedon
Weston-super-Mare
Bristol
Bath
SOMERSET
Mendip Hills
Wells
Glastonbury
Bridgwater
Polden Hills
Quantock Hills
Taunton
Wellington
Minehead
Exmoor
Dunkery Beacon 520
Lynton
Ilfracombe
Barnstaple
Bideford
Braunton
Taw
Torridge
Hartland Point
Lundy

Bristol Channel

SCILLY ISLES
On same Scale

Isles of Scilly
St. Mary's

St. Ives
Penzance
Land's End

DEVON
Tiverton
Exe
Exeter
Crediton
Okehampton
Yes Tor 618
Dartmoor
Tavistock
Devonport
Plymouth
Plymouth Sound
Saltash
Launceston
Bodmin Moor
Brown Willy 419
Bodmin
Bude
Boscastle
Padstow
Newquay
St. Austell
CORNWALL
Truro
Redruth
Camborne
Helston
Penzance
St. Michael's Mount
Lizard
Fowey
Looe
Falmouth
St. Ives

Teignmouth
Dawlish
Exmouth
Sidmouth
Honiton
Chard
Axminster
Lyme Regis
Lyme Bay
Bridport
DORSET
Dorchester
Weymouth
Portland I.
Portland Bill
I. of Purbeck
Swanage
St. Alban's Hd.
Poole
Bournemouth
Christchurch
Avon
Lymington
New Forest
Southampton
HANTS
Winchester
Eastleigh
Portsmouth
Gosport
Fareham
Havant
ISLE OF WIGHT
Cowes
Newport
Ryde
Ventnor
St. Catherine's Point
Needles
Hayling I.

BERKS
Reading
Newbury
Kennet
Marlborough
Swindon
WILTS
Devizes
Trowbridge
Frome
Salisbury Plain
Stonehenge
Salisbury
Wilton
Shaftesbury
Blandford
Sherborne
Yeovil
Yeo
Parrett
Chard
Mere
Wylye
Avon
Stour

OXFORD
Oxford
Abingdon
Wantage
White Horse
Vale of White Horse
Faringdon
Witney
Thames
CHILTERN HILLS
High Wycombe
Windsor
Maidenhead
Henley
Aylesbury
Thame
SURREY
Guildford
Farnham
Aldershot
Farnborough
Basingstoke
Andover
Alton
Godalming
Haslemere
Woking
Esher
Kingston
Epsom
Sutton

F

m
ft
3000
1200
600
400
200
100
0

ft
1000
600
400
200
150
100
50
0
0
50
100
150
300
m

G

G

1

2

4

5

50

51

52

H

Projection: Conical with two standard parallels.

COPYRIGHT GEORGE PHILIP & SON, LTD.

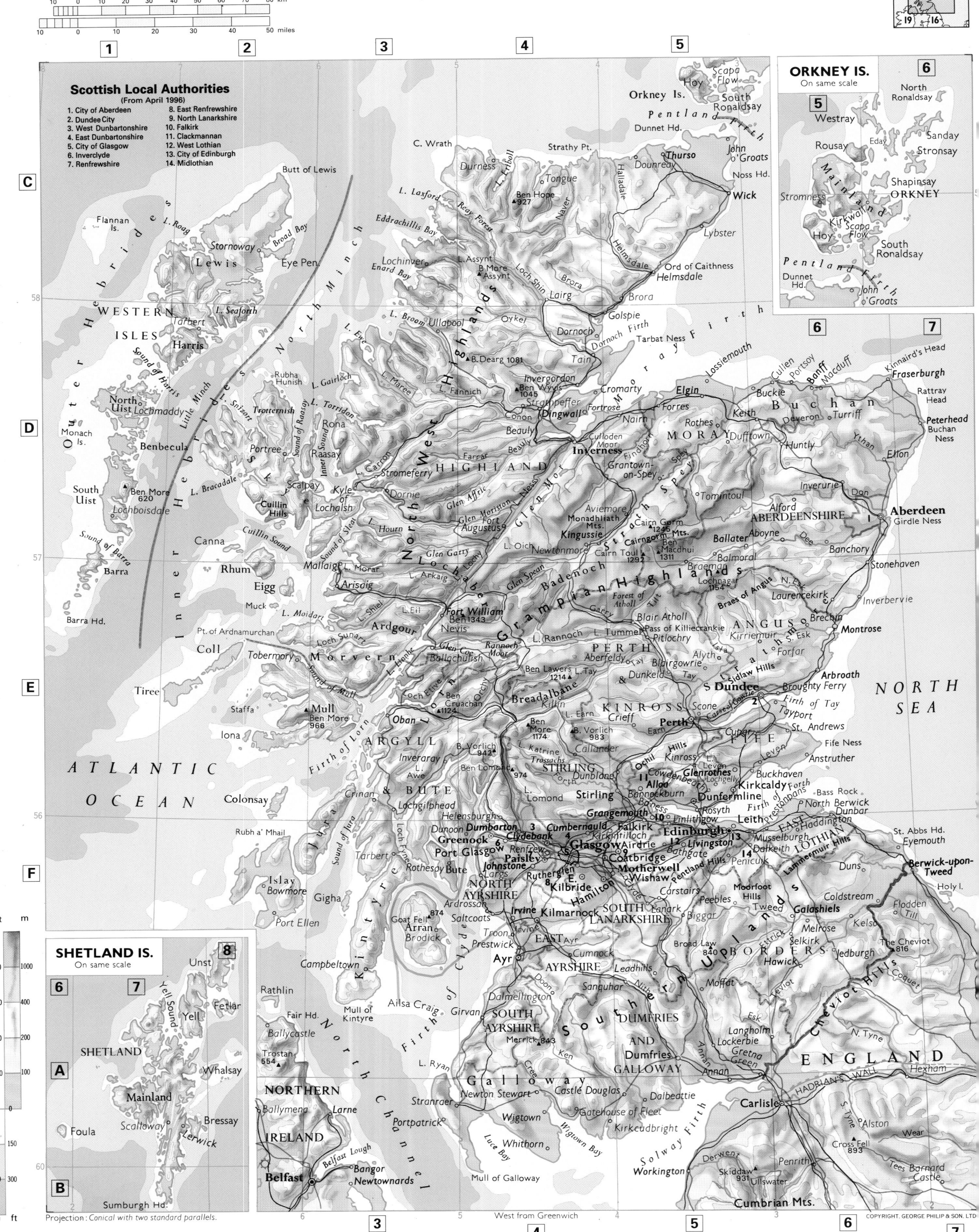

Scottish Local Authorities
(From April 1996)

1. City of Aberdeen   8. East Renfrewshire
2. Dundee City   9. North Lanarkshire
3. West Dunbartonshire   10. Falkirk
4. East Dunbartonshire   11. Clackmannan
5. City of Glasgow   12. West Lothian
6. Inverclyde   13. City of Edinburgh
7. Renfrewshire   14. Midlothian

ORKNEY IS.
On same scale

SHETLAND IS.
On same scale

Projection: Conical with two standard parallels.

West from Greenwich

COPYRIGHT. GEORGE PHILIP & SON. LTD.

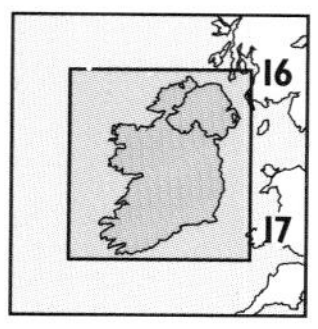

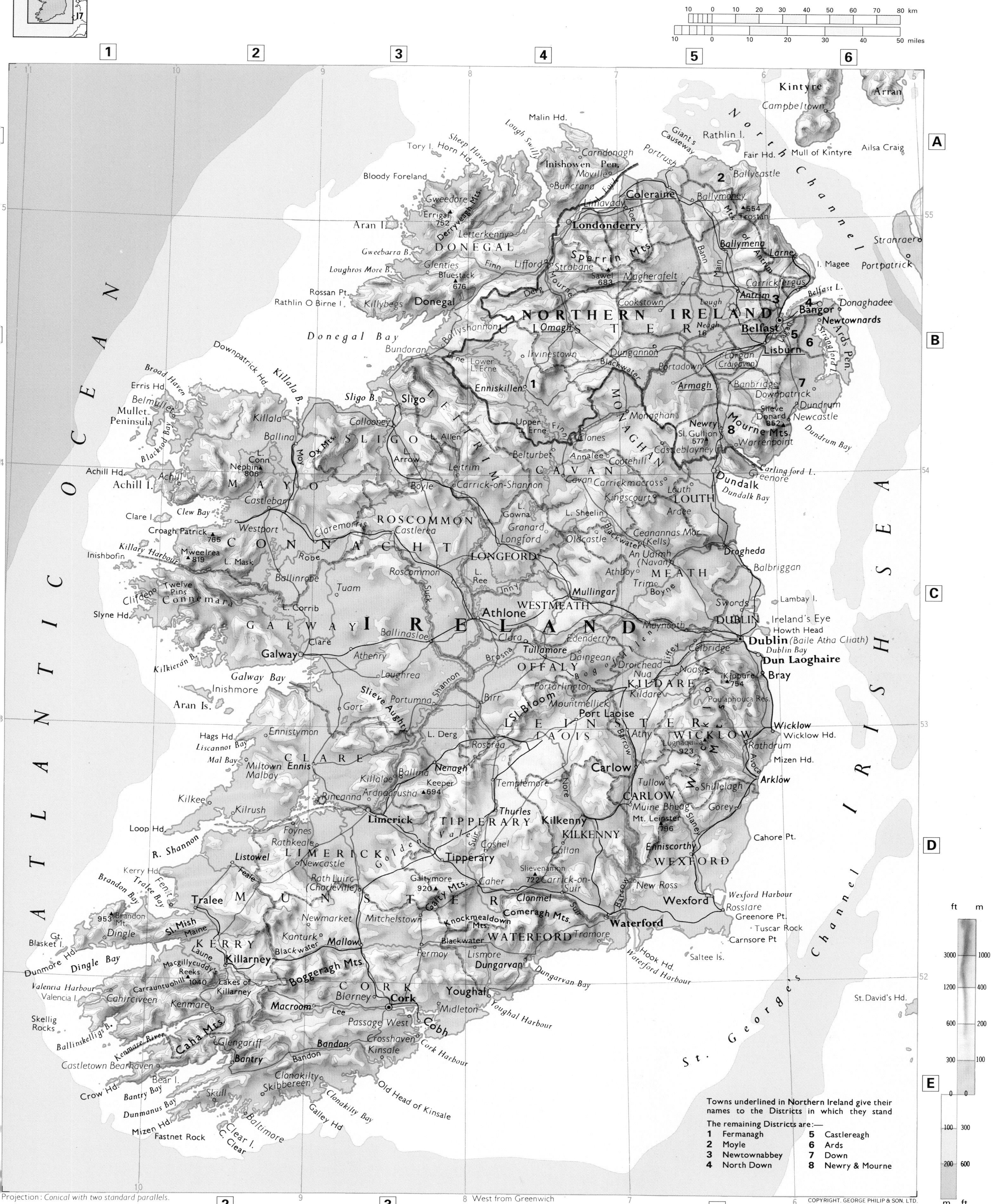

10 0 10 20 30 40 50 60 70 80 km
10 0 10 20 30 40 50 miles

NORTHERN IRELAND

ATLANTIC OCEAN

IRISH SEA

North Channel

St. George's Channel

Dublin (Baile Átha Cliath)

Belfast

Londonderry

Cork

Limerick

Waterford

Galway

DONEGAL
SLIGO
MAYO
LEITRIM
CAVAN
MONAGHAN
LOUTH
ROSCOMMON
LONGFORD
MEATH
WESTMEATH
CONNACHT
GALWAY
OFFALY
KILDARE
LEINSTER
WICKLOW
LAOIS
CLARE
TIPPERARY
KILKENNY
CARLOW
WEXFORD
LIMERICK
KERRY
MUNSTER
CORK
WATERFORD

Kintyre
Arran
Campbeltown
Mull of Kintyre
Ailsa Craig
Stranraer
Portpatrick

Malin Hd.
Inishowen Pen.
Carndonagh
Moville
Buncrana
Giant's Causeway
Portrush
Rathlin I.
Fair Hd.
Ballycastle
Ballymoney
Coleraine
Limavady
Ballymena
Larne
I. Magee
Carrickfergus
Antrim
Belfast L.
Bangor
Donaghadee
Newtownards
Ards Pen.
Strangford L.
Lisburn
Lurgan (Craigavon)
Portadown
Banbridge
Downpatrick
Dundrum
Newcastle
Newry
Sl. Gullion 577
Mourne Mts.
Slieve Donard 852
Warrenpoint
Carlingford L.
Greenore
Dundalk
Dundalk Bay

Sperrin Mts.
Sawel 683
Strabane
Lifford
Letterkenny
Derryveagh Mts.
Errigal 752
Gweedore
Aran I.
Bloody Foreland
Tory I.
Horn Hd.
Sheep Haven
Lough Swilly
Glenties
Bluestack 676
Killybegs
Donegal
Rossan Pt.
Rathlin O Birne I.
Loughros More B.
Gweebarra B.

Omagh
Cookstown
Magherafelt
Dungannon
Blackwater
Lough Neagh 16
Armagh
Monaghan
Castleblayney
Carrickmacross
Kingscourt
Ardee
Cootehill
Clones
Belturbet
Annalee
Cavan
Ceanannas Mór (Kells)
An Uaimh (Navan)
Trim
Boyne
Oldcastle
Granard
L. Sheelin
Gowna

Enniskillen
Upper L. Erne
Lower L. Erne
Irvinestown
Ballyshannon
Bundoran
Donegal Bay
Sligo B.
Sligo
Collooney
Ballina
Killala
Killala B.
Downpatrick Hd.
Killala
Broad Haven
Erris Hd.
Belmullet
Mullet Peninsula
Blacksod Bay
Achill Hd.
Achill I.
Achill
L. Conn
Nephin 806
Castlebar
Clew Bay
Clare I.
Croagh Patrick 765
Westport
Killary Harbour
Mweelrea 819
L. Mask
Inishbofin
Twelve Pins
Connemara
Slyne Hd.
Clifden
Ox Mts.
Moy
L. Allen
Arrow
Boyle
Leitrim
Carrick-on-Shannon
Roscommon
Castlerea
Claremorris
Ballinrobe
Robe
Tuam
L. Corrib
Athenry
Clare
Ballinasloe
Loughrea
Gort
Slieve Aughty
Portumna
L. Derg
Shannon
Suck
Athlone
Mullingar
Clara
Edenderry
Moynooth
Maynooth
Swords
Drogheda
Balbriggan
Lambay I.
Ireland's Eye
Howth Head
Dublin Bay
Dún Laoghaire
Bray
Celbridge
Naas
Droichead Nua
Kildare
Kippure 754
Poulaphouca Res.
Wicklow
Wicklow Hd.
Rathdrum
Mizen Hd.
Arklow
Lugnaquilla 923
Shillelagh
Gorey
Tullow
Muine Bheag
Mt. Leinster 796
Carlow
Athy
Barrow
Kilkenny
Callan
Enniscorthy
Wexford
Wexford Harbour
Rosslare
New Ross
Cahore Pt.
Tuscar Rock
Greenore Pt.
Carnsore Pt.
Saltee Is.
Hook Hd.
Waterford Harbour
Tramore
Dungarvan
Dungarvan Bay

Tullamore
Birr
Portarlington
Mountmellick
Port Laoise
Roscrea
Nenagh
Templemore
Thurles
Ballina
Killaloe
Keeper 694
Ardnacrusha
Limerick
Rathkeale
Newcastle
Listowel
Foynes
R. Shannon
Loop Hd.
Kilrush
Kilkee
Mal Bay
Miltown Malbay
Liscannor Bay
Hags Hd.
Ennistymon
Ennis
Rineanna
Golden Vale
Tipperary
Cashel
Caher
Galtymore 920
Galty Mts.
Clonmel
Carrick-on-Suir
Comeragh Mts.
Slievenamon 722
Knockmealdown Mts.
Lismore
Blackwater
Fermoy
Mitchelstown
Charleville (Rath Luirc)
Newmarket
Kanturk
Mallow
Macroom
Blarney
Cork
Cork Harbour
Cobh
Passage West
Midleton
Youghal
Youghal Harbour
Waterford
Dunmore Bay

Tralee
Tralee Bay
Brandon Bay
Brandon Mt. 953
Dingle
Dingle Bay
Gt. Blasket I.
Dunmore Hd.
Sl. Mish
Maine
Laune
Killarney
Lakes of Killarney
Macgillycuddy's Reeks
Carrauntoohill 1040
Kenmare
Cahirciveen
Valencia Harbour
Valencia I.
Skellig Rocks
Ballinskelligs B.
Kenmare River
Caha Mts.
Glengarriff
Bantry
Bantry Bay
Bear I.
Crow Hd.
Castletown Bearhaven
Dunmanus Bay
Mizen Hd.
Skull
Fastnet Rock
Clear I.
C. Clear
Baltimore
Galley Hd.
Clonakilty
Clonakilty Bay
Skibbereen
Old Head of Kinsale
Kinsale
Crosshaven
Bandon
Boggeragh Mts.
Lee

St. David's Hd.

Towns underlined in Northern Ireland give their
names to the Districts in which they stand

The remaining Districts are:—

1	Fermanagh	5	Castlereagh
2	Moyle	6	Ards
3	Newtownabbey	7	Down
4	North Down	8	Newry & Mourne

ft	m
3000	1000
1200	400
600	200
300	100
0	0
100	300
200	600
m	ft

Projection: Conical with two standard parallels.

West from Greenwich

COPYRIGHT. GEORGE PHILIP & SON. LTD.

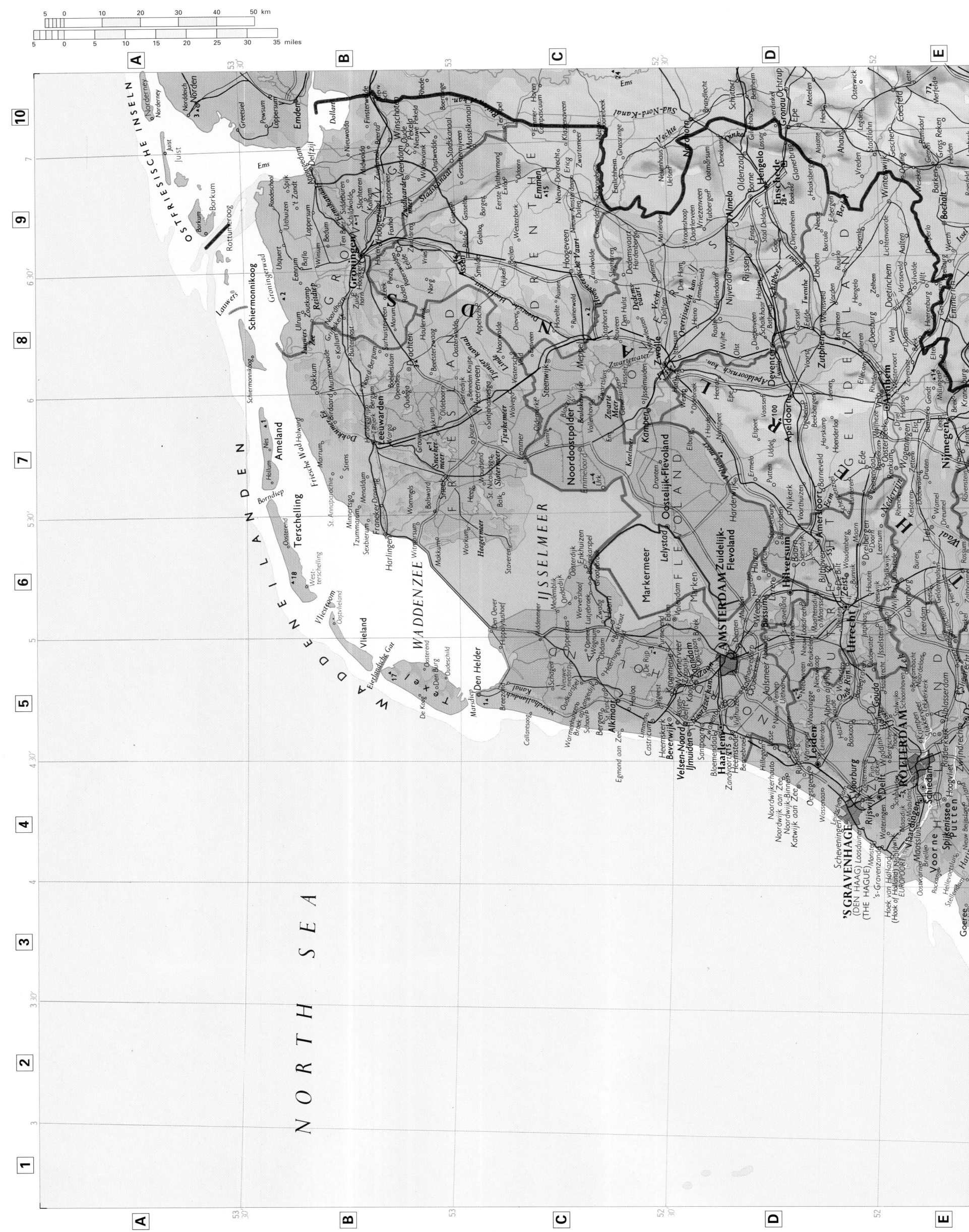

Projection: Conical with two standard parallels

East from Greenwich

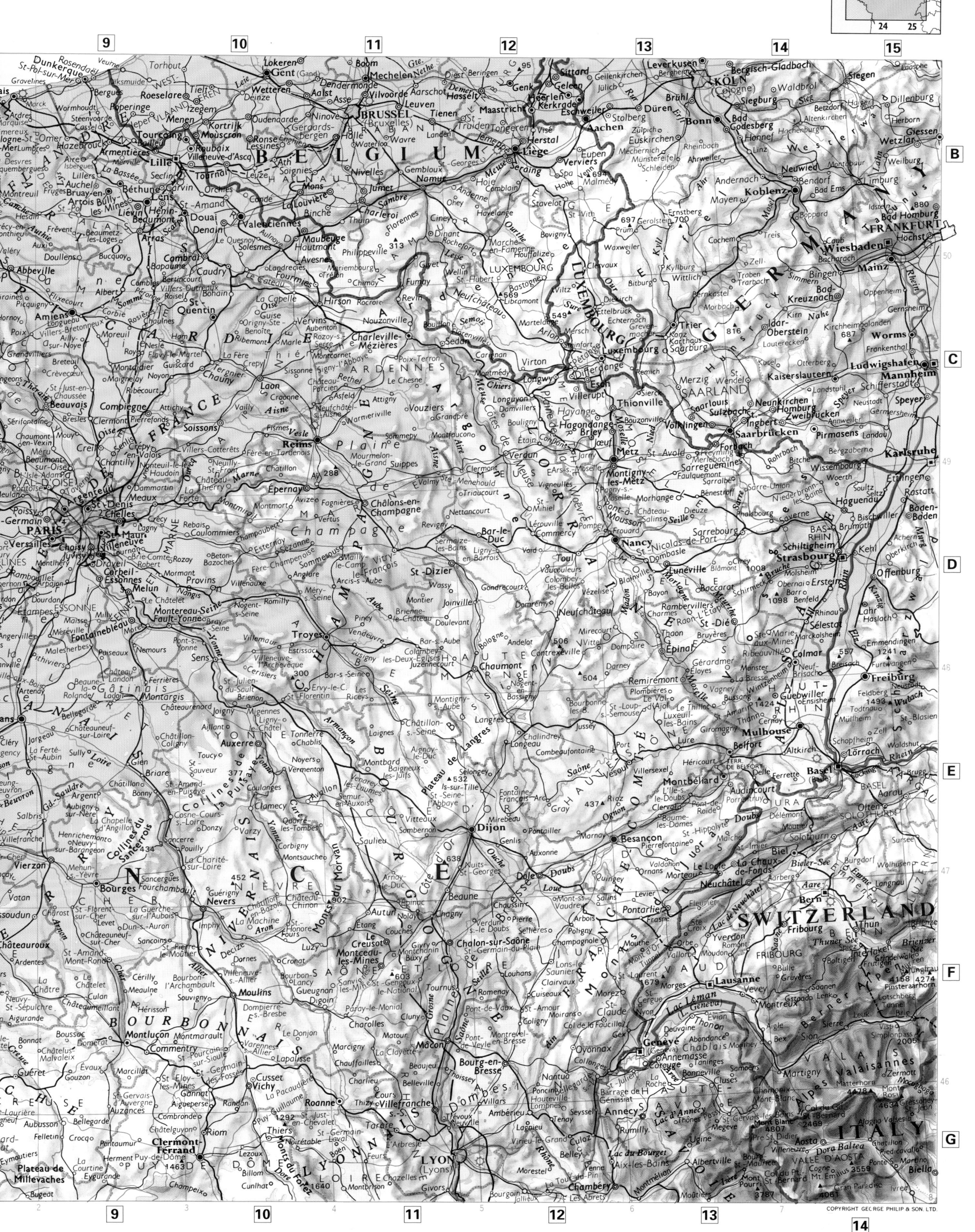

LIGURIAN SEA

Golfo di Génova

MEDITERRANEAN SEA

CORSE
(CORSICA)

HAUTE-CORSE

CORSE DU SUD

COPYRIGHT. GEORGE. PHILIP & SON. LTD.

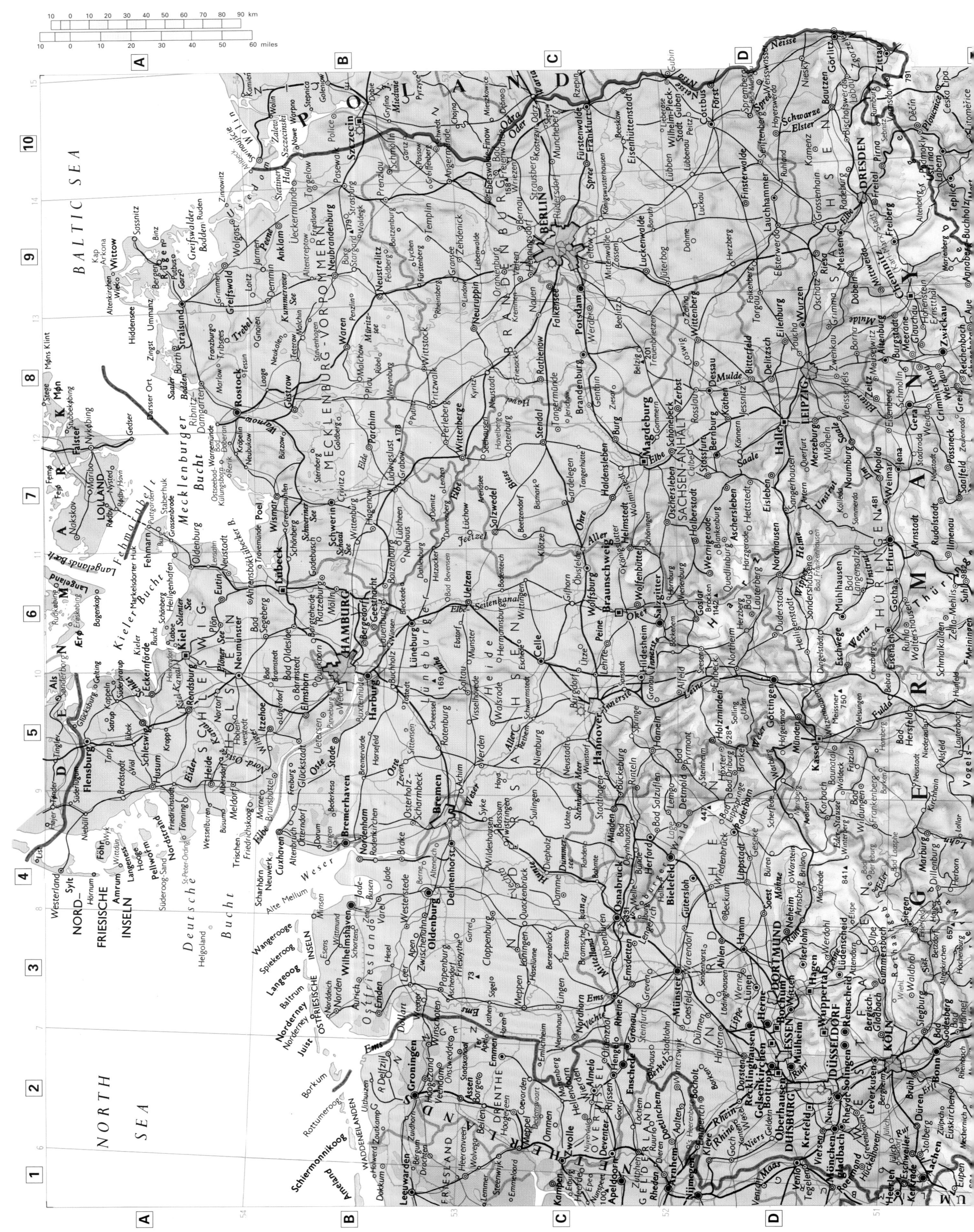

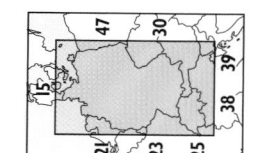

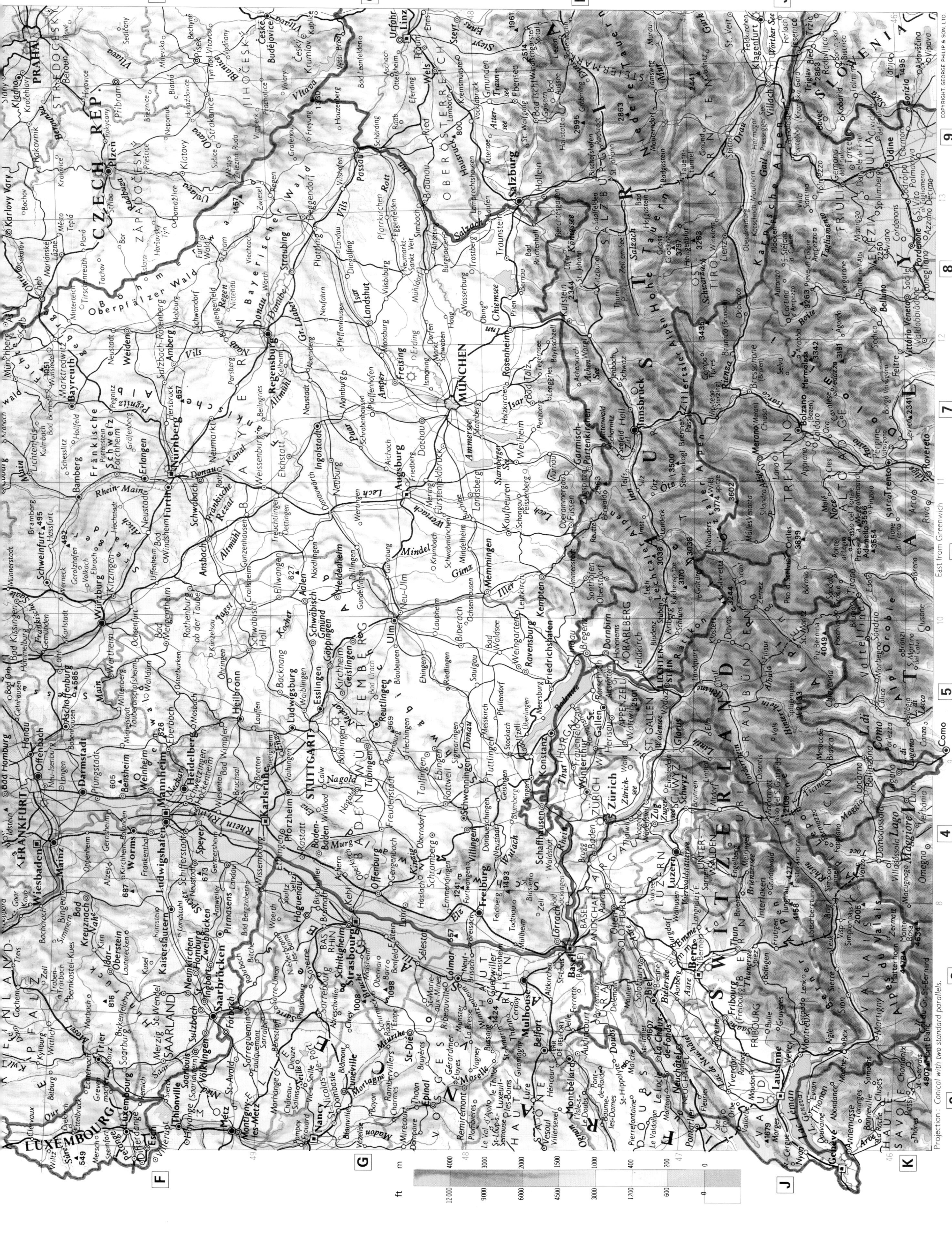

CZECH REP.
PRAHA
Plzeň
Karlovy Vary
České Budějovice
Linz
Salzburg
OBERÖSTERREICH
SALZBURG
TIROL
KÄRNTEN
Klagenfurt
Villach
SLOVENIA
Udine
FRIULI
VENEZIA GIULIA
Belluno
Bolzano
Trento
TRENTINO ALTO ADIGE
Innsbruck
AUSTRIA
München
Augsburg
Regensburg
Nürnberg
Würzburg
BAYERN
Ingolstadt
Landshut
Passau
Ulm
Stuttgart
BADEN-WÜRTTEMBERG
Karlsruhe
Mannheim
Heidelberg
Frankfurt
Wiesbaden
Mainz
Darmstadt
Saarbrücken
SAARLAND
RHEINLAND-PFALZ
LUXEMBOURG
Metz
Nancy
Strasbourg
Colmar
Mulhouse
Basel
Freiburg
Zürich
Bern
Luzern
Lausanne
Genève
SWITZERLAND
VALAIS
Lac Léman
Como
Lago Maggiore
VORARLBERG
LIECHTENSTEIN
Bodensee
Konstanz
Chiemsee
Vosges
Schwarzwald
Alpen
Projection: Conical with two standard parallels.
East from Greenwich
COPYRIGHT GEORGE PHILIP & SON, LTD
m
4000
3000
2000
1500
1000
400
200
0
ft
12 000
9000
6000
4500
3000
1200
600
0

Projection: Conical with two standard parallels

23 27
23   30
25
38
11

Projection: Conical with two standard parallels

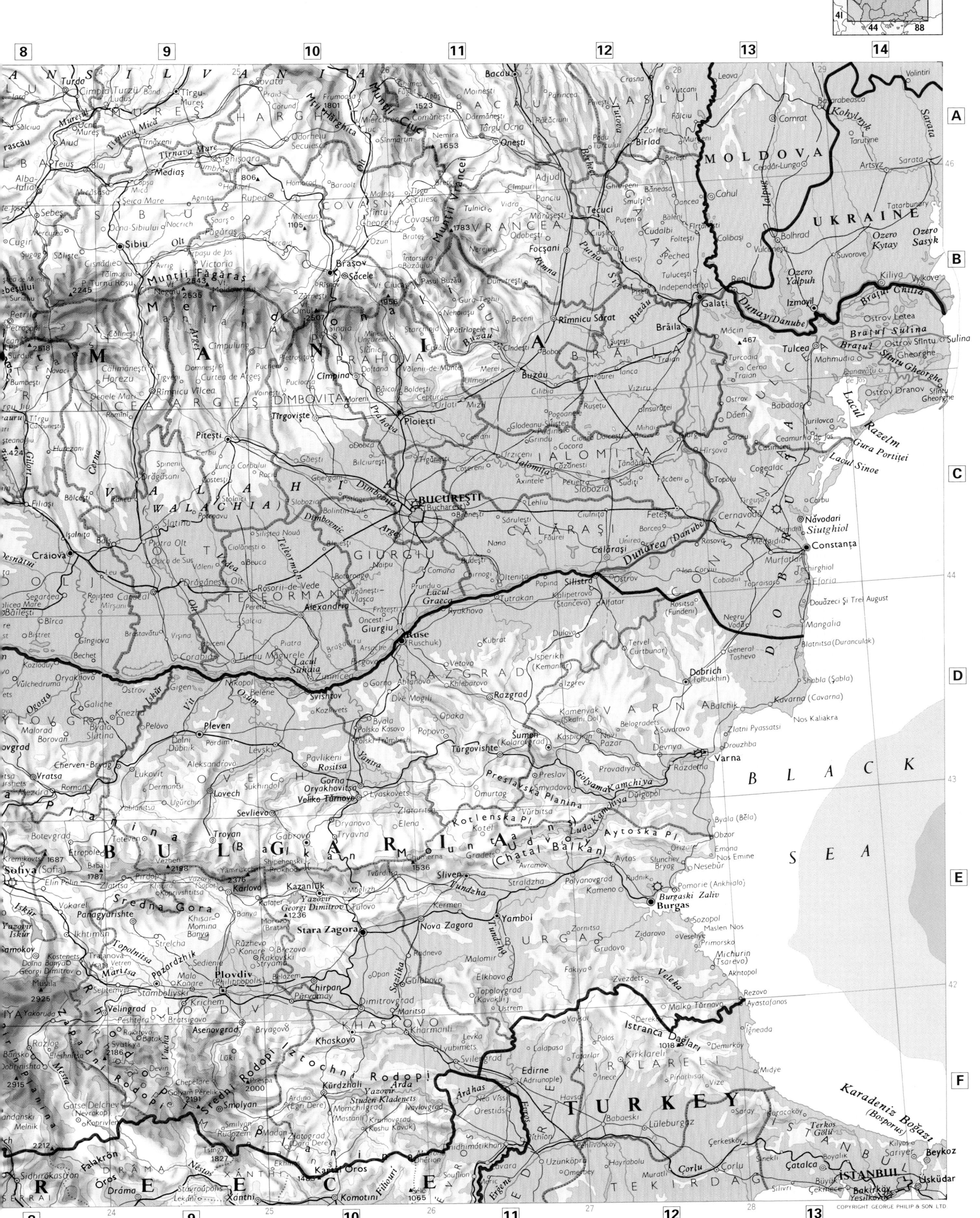

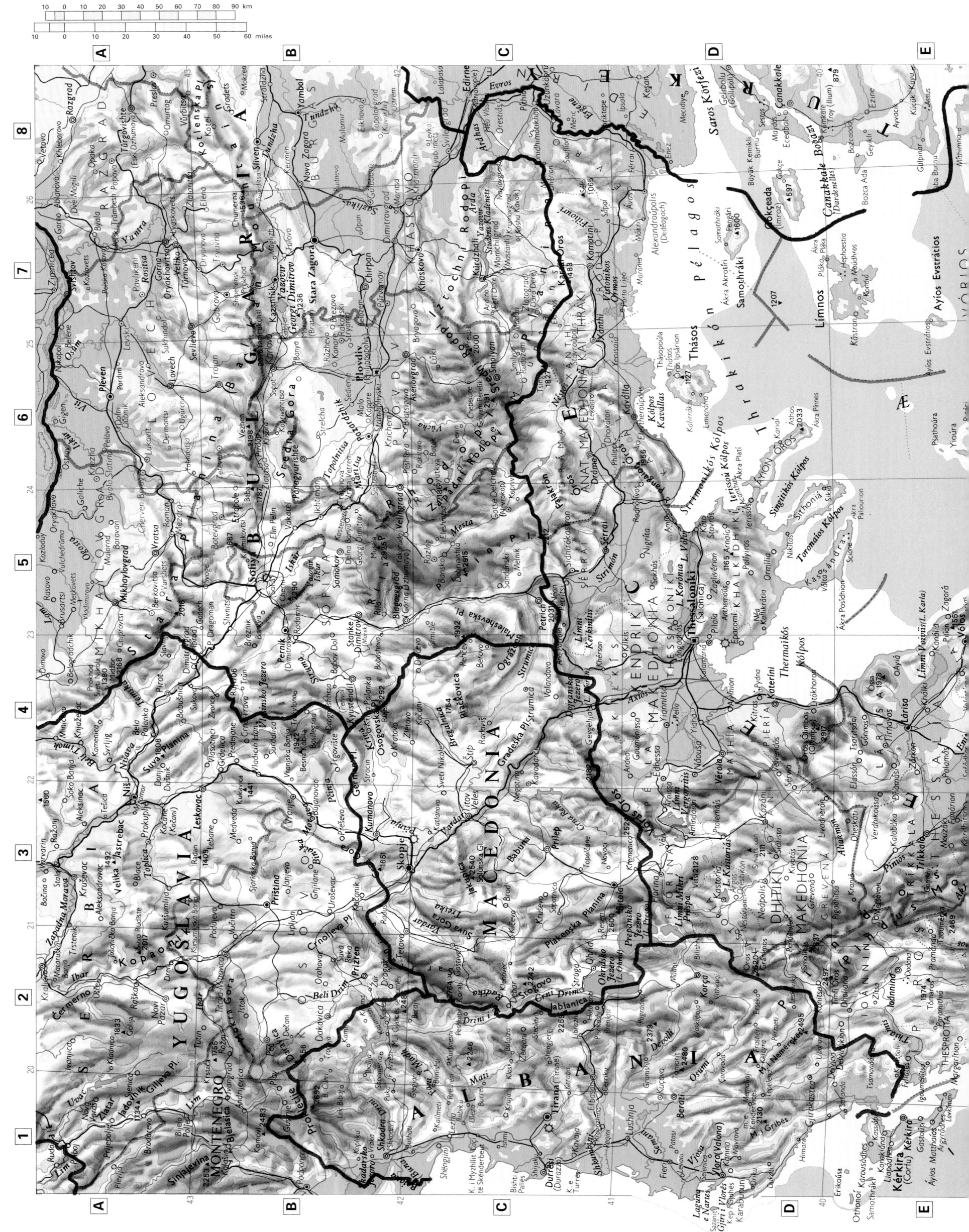

COPYRIGHT GEORGE PHILIP & SON LTD

East from Greenwich

Projection: Conical with two standard parallels

Continuation Eastwards
on same scale

KÓLPOS KÍN (Chios)

AIYAÍON

Psará

Khíos (Chios)

Ikaría

Mikonos

Ándros

Tinos

NÓTIOS

AIYAÍON

KIKLÁDHES
(CYCLADES)

Náxos

Páros

Síros

Kéa

Kíthnos

Sérifos

Sífnos

Mílos

Amorgós

Astipálaia

Levítha

Anáfi

Thíra

Íos

SEA OF CRETE
(Sea of Candia)

Iráklion
(Candia)

Khersónisos
Akrotíri
Kólpos Soúdhas

Kherónisos

Kólpos Mírabéllou

Kólpos Kisámou

Ándikíthira

Kíthira
(Cerigo)

SKÍ RO S

STEREÁ

ELLAS

Skópelos

Skíros

Okhi Óros

Vólos

ATTIKÍ

ATHÍNAI
ATHENS

Piraiévs
(Piraeus)

Saronikós
Kólpos

Khalkís
Chalcis

Levádhia

Thívai
(Thebes)

Kórinthos
Corinth

Corinth Canal

Návplion

PELOPÓNNISOS

Párnon Óros

LAKONÍA

Spárti
(Sparta)

Taíyetos Óros

Kalámai

MESSINÍA

Pátrai

AKHAÍA

ILÍA

Pírgos

Kiparissiakós
Kólpos

Messiniakós
Kólpos

Lakonikós
Kólpos

Argolikós
Kólpos

Ákra Maléa

Ákra Taínaron

Pýlos

Levkás
(Santa Maura)

Kefallinía
(Cephalonia)

Itháki
(Ithaca)

Zákinthos
(Zante)

IONIAN
ISLANDS

IÓNIOI NÍSOI

AITOLÍA

AKARNANÍA

Agrínion

Mesolóngion

Préveza

Neápolis

SÁMSUN
DAĞI

Sámos

Kuşadasi
Körfezi

Ephesus

Milétus

Kerme Körfezi

Mandalya Körfezi

Rhodes

Ródhos
(Rhodes)

Símí

Ástipálaia

Kos

Kálimnos

Léros

Pátmos

DODHEKÁNISOS
(DODECANESE)

Stenón Kárpathos

Kárpathos

Kásos

Stenón Kásos

m
ft

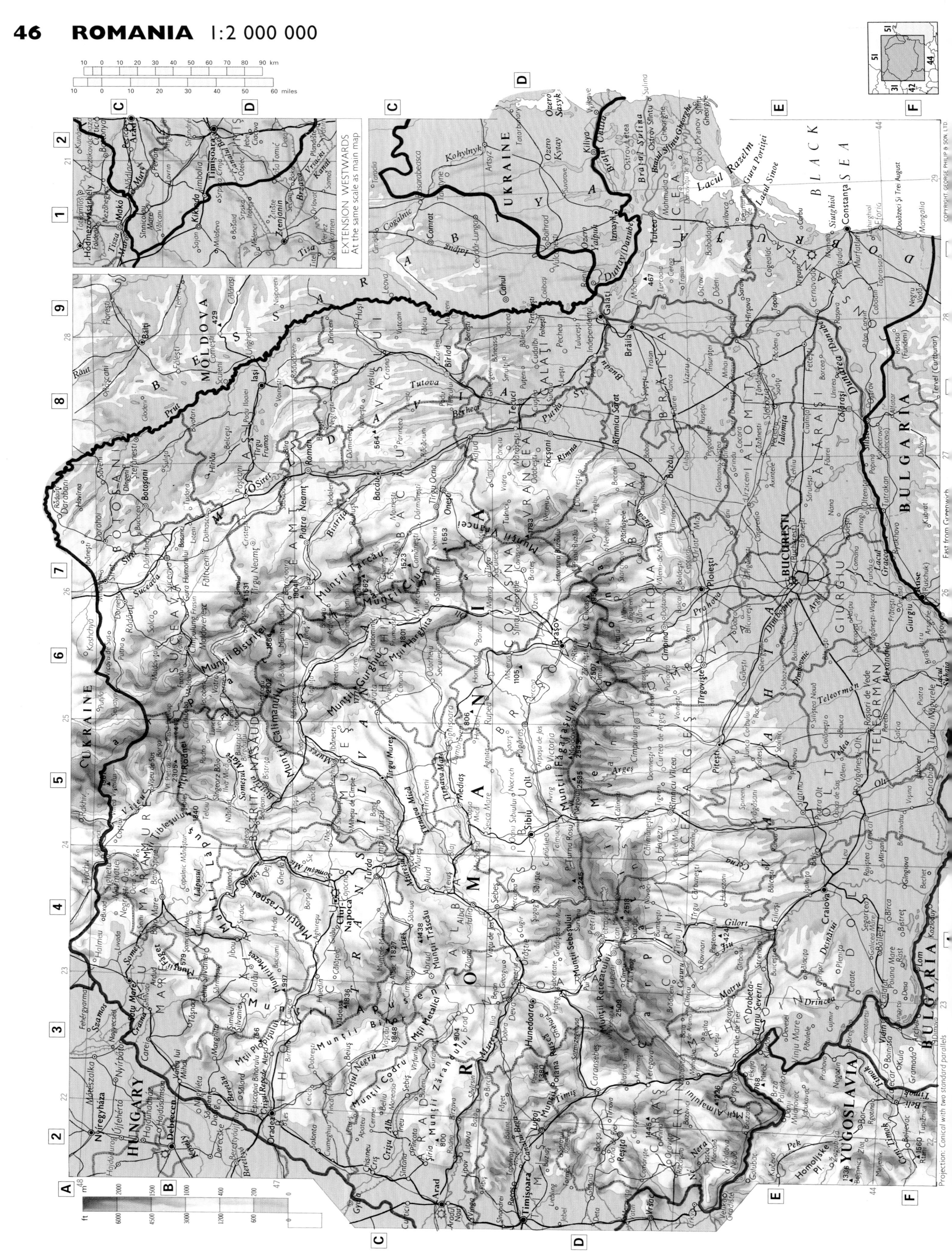

EXTENSION WESTWARDS
At the same scale as main map

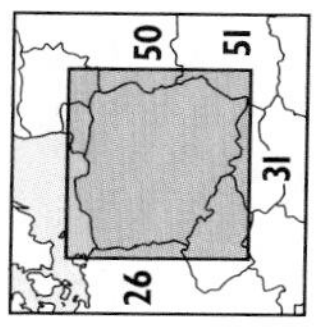

10 0 10 20 30 40 50 60 70 80 90 km

10 0 10 20 30 40 50 60 miles

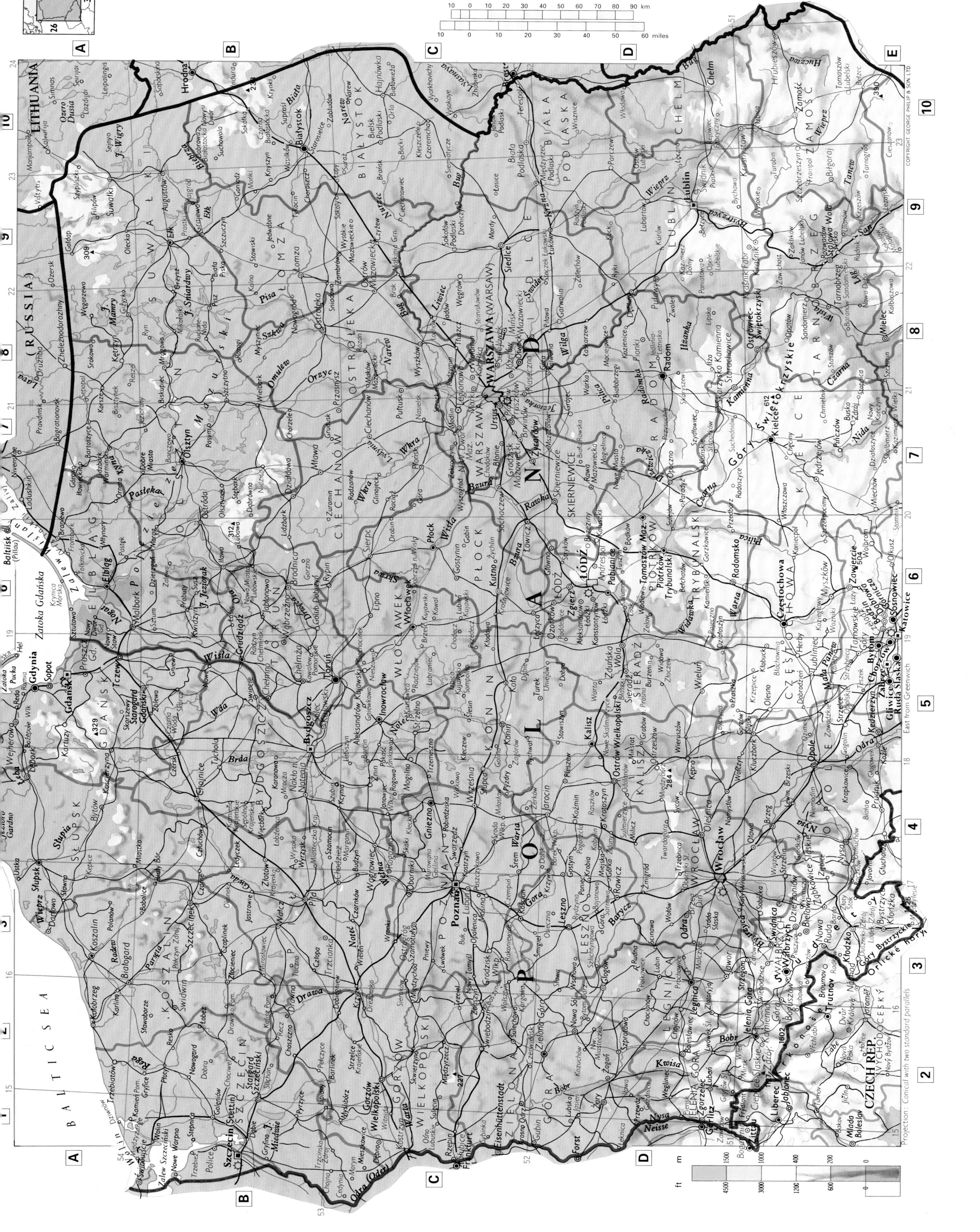

LITHUANIA

(RUSSIA)

BALTIC SEA

CZECH REP.

POLAND

Projection: Conical with two standard parallels

East from Greenwich

COPYRIGHT GEORGE PHILIP & SON LTD

m 4500 3000 1500 1200 600 400 200 0

ft

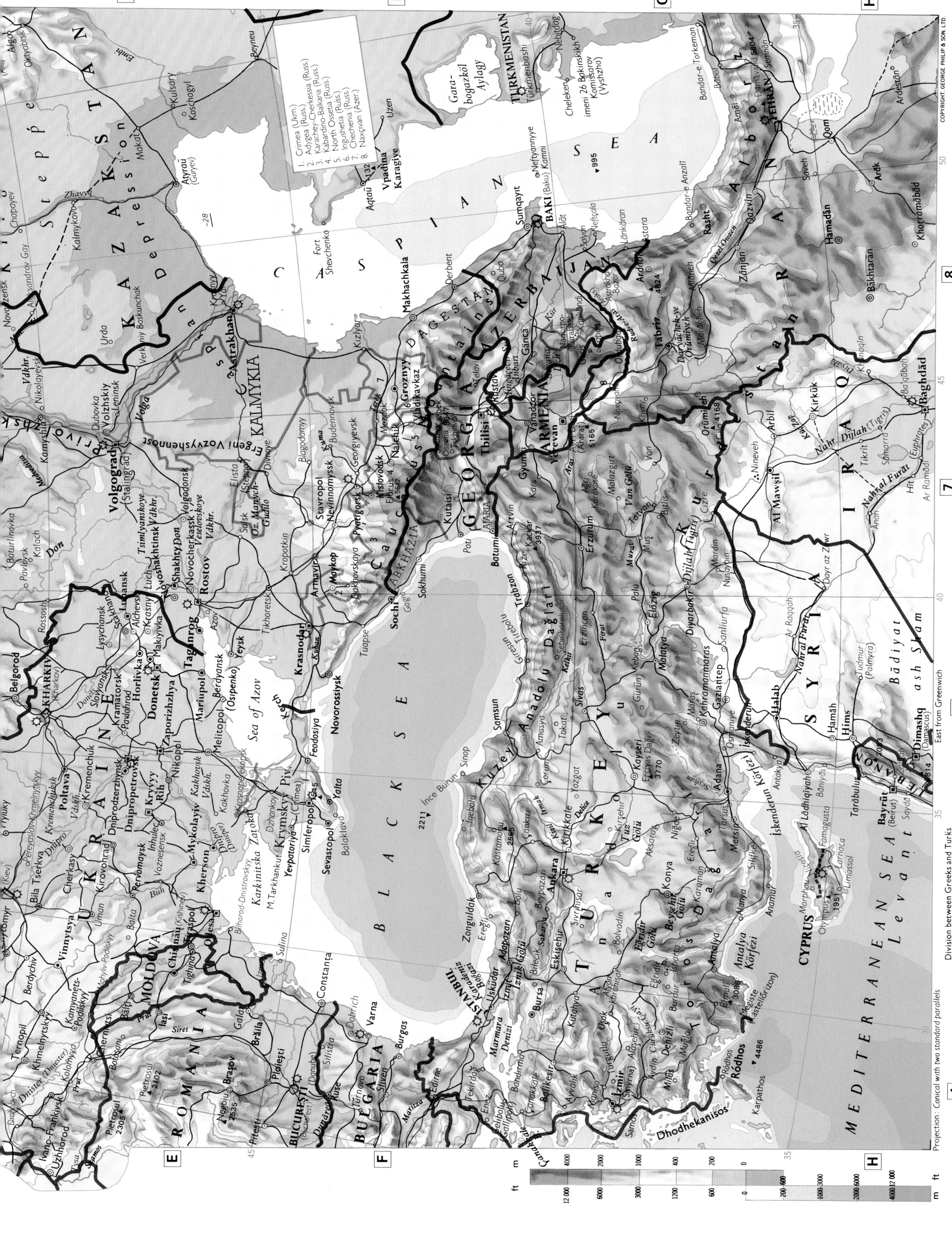
BLACK SEA
CASPIAN SEA
MEDITERRANEAN SEA
Levant
Sea of Azov
UKRAINE
KAZAKSTAN
TURKEY
IRAN
IRAQ
SYRIA
GEORGIA
ARMENIA
AZERBAIJAN
ROMANIA
BULGARIA
MOLDOVA
TURKMENISTAN
CYPRUS
LEBANON
KALMYKIA
ABKHAZIA
DAGESTAN
Caucasus
Anadolu
Kuzey Anadolu Dağları
Toros Dağları
Elburz
Caspian Depression
Ergeni Vozvyshennost
Bādiyat ash Shām
Gara-bogazköl Aylagy
ISTANBUL
ANKARA
BUCUREŞTI
TEHRĀN
BAKI (Baku)
TBILISI
YEREVAN
KHARKIV (Kharkov)
Volgograd (Stalingrad)
Astrakhan
Rostov
Donetsk
Odesa
Sevastopol
Simferopol
Trabzon
Tabrīz
Baghdād
Dimashq (Damascus)
Bayrūt (Beirut)
Halab
1. Crimea (Ukr.)
2. Adygea (Russ.)
3. Karachey-Cherkessia (Russ.)
4. Kabardino-Balkaria (Russ.)
5. North Ossetia (Russ.)
6. Ingushetia (Russ.)
7. Chechenia (Russ.)
8. Naxçivan (Azer.)
Division between Greeks and Turks in Cyprus; Turks to the North.
Projection: Conical with two standard parallels
East from Greenwich
COPYRIGHT GEORGE PHILIP & SON, LTD.
m
ft
4000
2000
1000
400
200
0
12 000
6000
3000
1200
600
200
600
1000
3000
2000
6000
4000
12 000
E
F
G
H
4
5
6
7
8
9

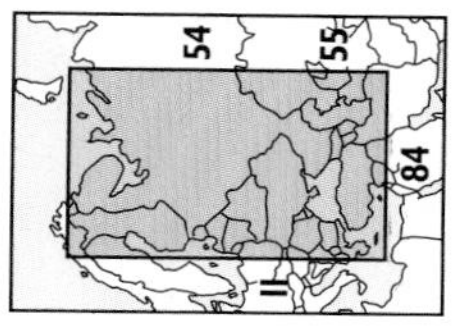
54
55
84

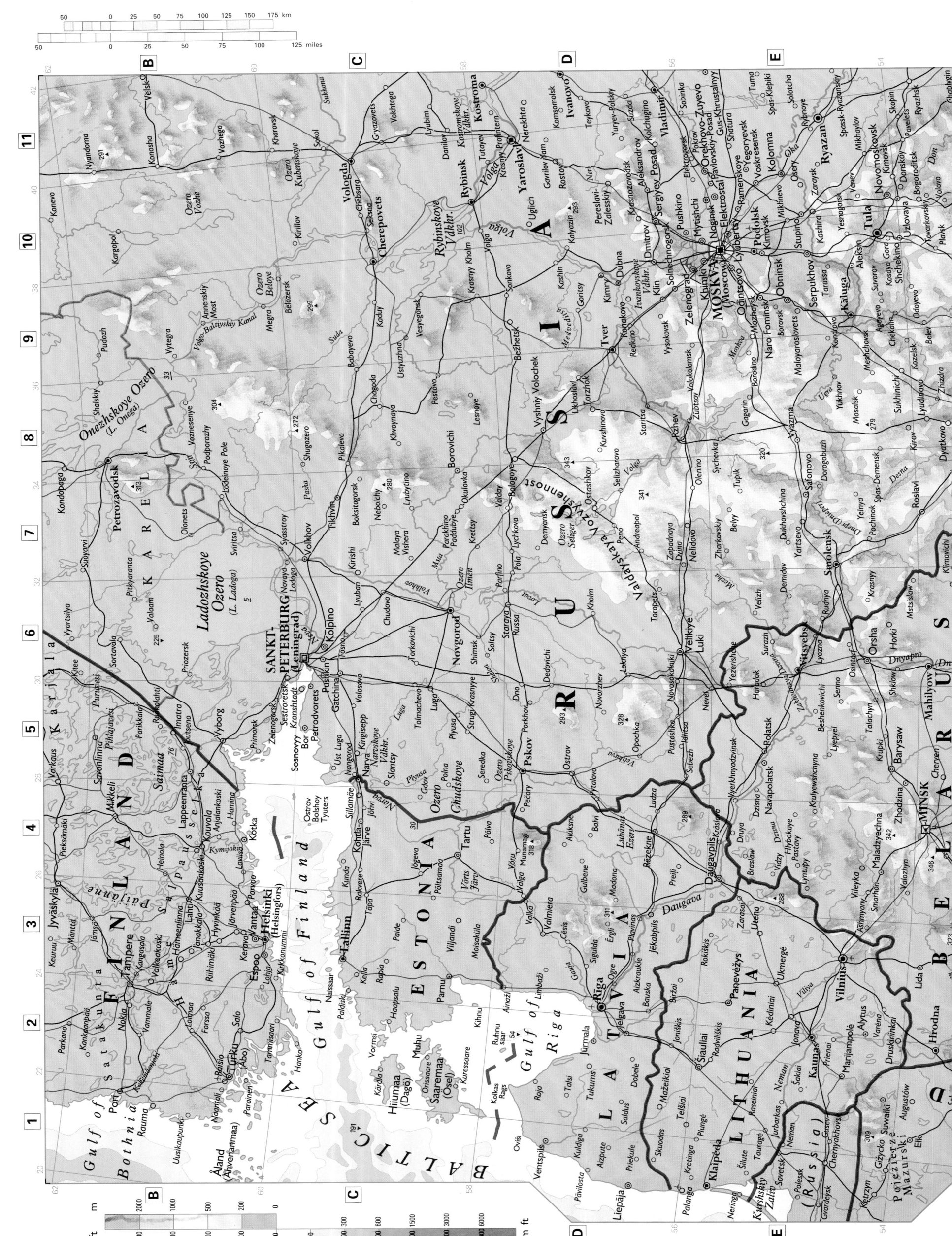

Projection: Conical with two standard parallels

East from Greenwich

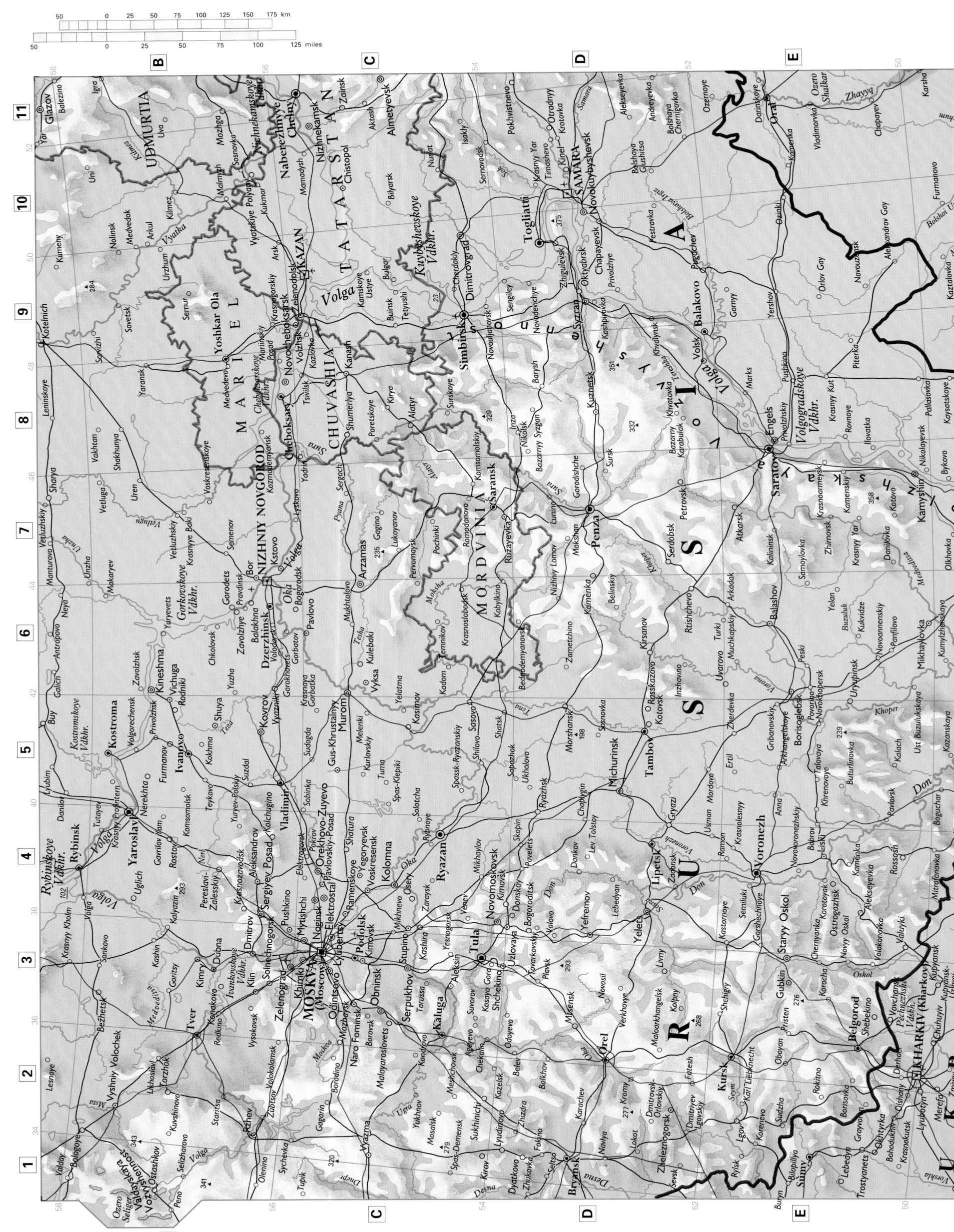

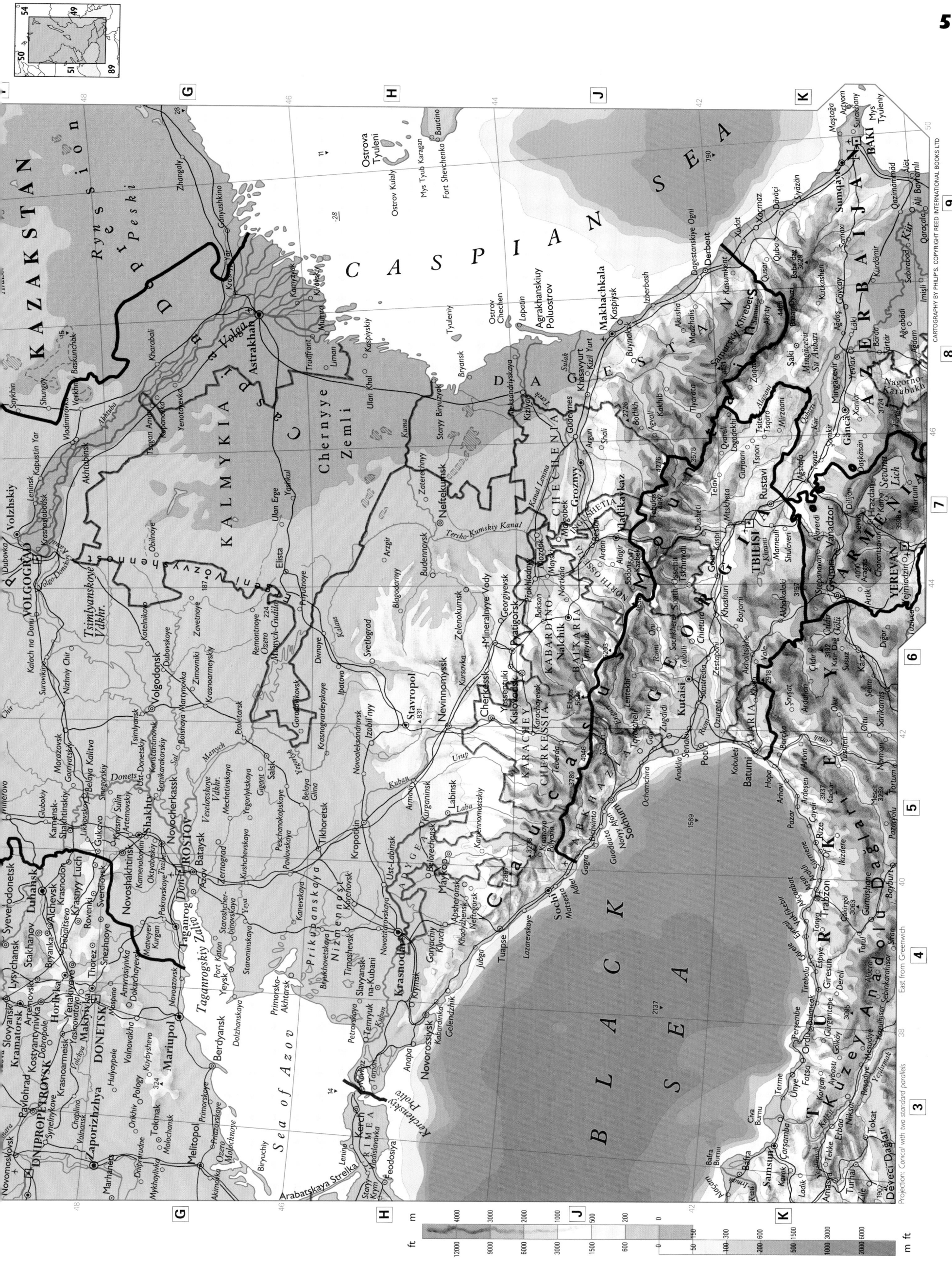

CASPIAN SEA

KAZAKSTAN

BLACK SEA

Sea of Azov

AZERBAIJAN

ARMENIA

GEORGIA

KALMYKIA

DAGESTAN

CHECHENIA

KABARDINO-BALKARIA

KARACHEY-CHERKESSIA

NORTH OSSETIA

INGUSHETIA

ABKHAZIA

ADYGEA

CRIMEA

VOLGOGRAD

ROSTOV

DONETSK

BAKI

TBILISI

YEREVAN

Makhachkala

Grozny

Astrakhan

Volgograd

Novorossiysk

Krasnodar

Stavropol

Nalchik

Kutaisi

Sochi

Batumi

Trabzon

CARTOGRAPHY BY PHILIP'S. COPYRIGHT REED INTERNATIONAL BOOKS LTD

Projection: Conical with two standard parallels

East from Greenwich

m   ft
4000 12000
3000 9000
2000 6000
1000 3000
500   1500
200   600
0

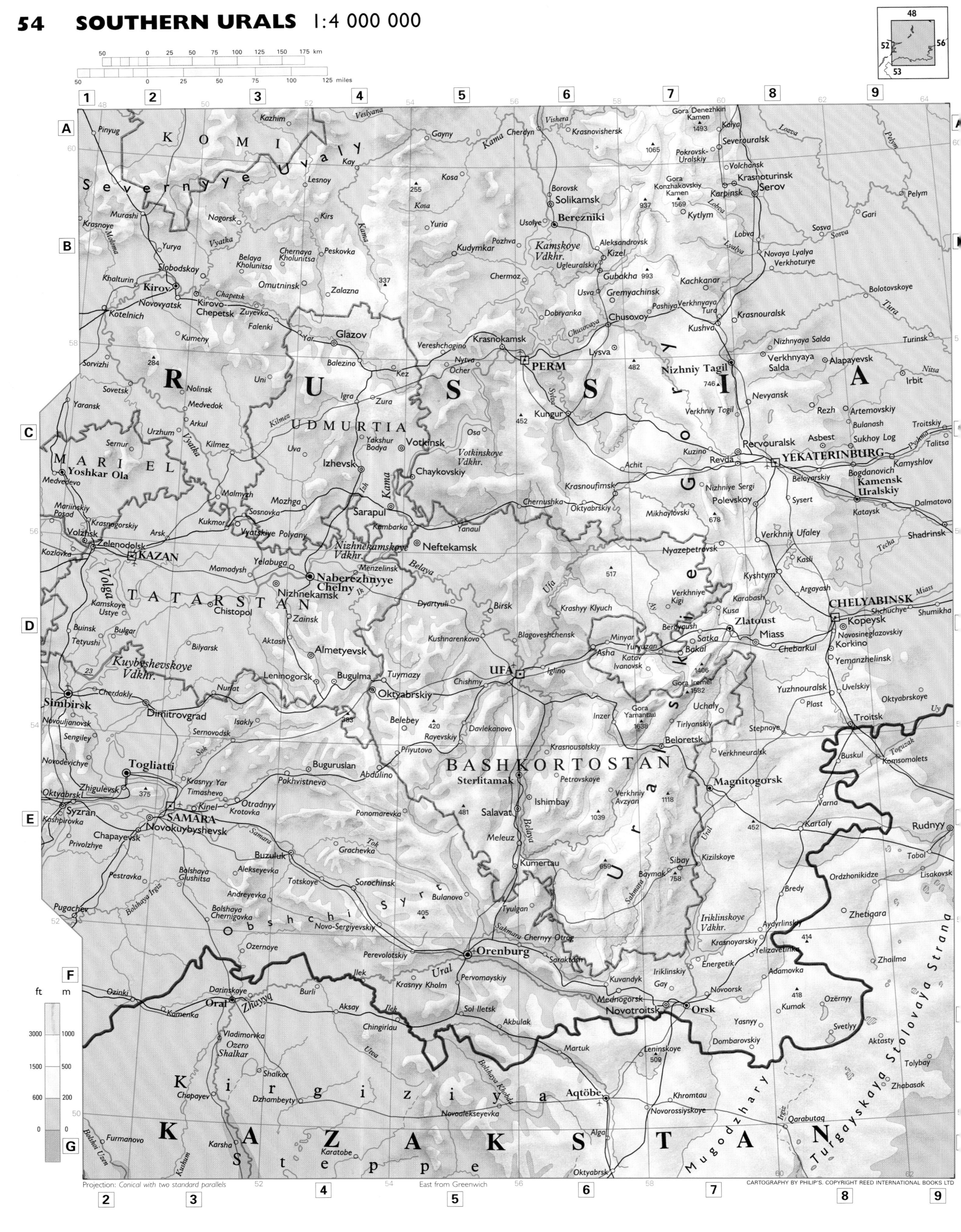

50   0   25 50 75 100 125 150 175 km
50   0   25   50   75   100 125 miles

1   **2**   **3**   **4**   **5**   **6**   **7**   **8**   **9**

K O M I   U r a l y

S e v e r n y y e

Pinyug
Murashi
Krasnoye
Molona
Yurya
Slobodskay
Khalturin
Novovyatsk
Kirov
Kirovo-
Chepetsk
Zuyevka
Kotelnich
Chapetsk
Kumeny
Falenki

Nagorsk
Kay
Lesnoy
Belaya
Kholunitsa
Chernaya
Kholunitsa
Peskovka
Zalazna
Yar
Glazov
Balezino
Kez
Igra
Zura

Kazhim
Veslyana
Gayny
Kosa
Kosa
255
Yuria
337
Vereshchagino
Ocher
Nytva
Krasnokamsk

Kama
Cherdyn
Vishera
Krasnovishersk
Borovsk
Solikamsk
Usolye
Berezniki
Pozhva
Kudymkar
Chermoz
Dobryanka
Usva

Gora Denezhkin
Kamen 1493
Kalya
Severouralsk
Pokrovsk-
Uralskiy
1065
Volchansk
Krasnoturinsk
Serov
Gora
Konzhakovskiy
Kamen
937 1569
Karpinsk
Kytlym
Aleksandrovsk
Kizel
Ugleuralskiy
Kamskoye
Vdkhr.
Gubakha 993
Gremyachinsk
Pashiya
Chusovoy
Verkhnyaya
Tura
Kushva
Lobva
Lyalya
Novaya Lyalya
Verkhoturye

Sosva
Gari
Sosva
Bolotovskoye
Tura
Turinsk

R   U   S   S   I   A

Sorvizhi
284
Nolinsk
Medvedok
Arkul
Uni
Balezino

Yaransk
Sovetsk
Urzhum
Sernur
Kilmez
Vyatka
Kilmez

U D M U R T I A

Yakshur
Bodya
Votkinsk
Izhevsk
Votkinskoye
Vdkhr.
Chaykovskiy

Osa
452
Kungur
Sylva
482
PERM
Lysva
Krasnokamsk

Nizhniy Tagil
746
Verkhniy Togil
Nevyansk
Rezh
Artemovskiy
Bulanash
Troitskiy
Verkhnyaya
Salda
Nizhnyaya Salda
Alapayevsk
Irbit
Nitsa

M A R I E L
Yoshkar Ola
Medvedevo
Mariinskiy
Posad
Krasnogorskiy
Volzhsk
Zelenodolsk
KAZAN
Kozlovka
Volga

Arsk
Kukmor
Malmyzh
Sosnovka
Mozhga
Sarapul
Kambarka
Vyatskiye Polyany
Yanaul
Neftekamsk

Kamskoye
Ustye
Buinsk
Bulgar
Tetyushi
Bilyarsk

T A T A R S T A N
Mamadysh
Yelabuga
Naberezhnyye
Chelny
Nizhnekamsk
Menzelinsk
Nizhnekamskoye
Vdkhr.
Belaya
Dyartyuli
Kushnarenkovo
Birsk

Chernushka
Oktyabrskiy
Mikhaylovsk
517
678
Achit
Krasnoufimsk
Nyazepetrovsk

Kuzino
Revda
Pervouralsk
YEKATERINBURG
Asbest
Sukhoy Log
Beloyarskiy
Bogdanovich
Kamensk
Uralskiy
Polevskoy
Sysert
Kamyshlov
Verkhnix Ufaley
Kataysk
Dalmatovo
Kasli
Techa
Shadrinsk

Chistopol
Zainsk
Aktash
Almetyevsk
Bugulma
Leninogorsk
Tuymazy
Oktyabrskiy

Verkhniye
Kigi
Krashyy Klyuch
Blagoveshchensk
Ufa
Minyar
Yuryuzan
Asha
Katav
Ivanovsk
Berdyaush
Zlatoust
Satka
Bakal
Gora Iremel
1582
1406

Verkhniye
Kigi
Karabash
Kyshtym
Argayash
Kusa
Miass
Chebarkul

CHELYABINSK
Kopeysk
Novosineglazovskiy
Korkino
Yemanzhelinsk
Miass
Shchuchye
Shumikha

Kuybyshevskoye
Vdkhr.
23
Buinsk
Simbirsk
Novoulyanovsk
Sengiley
Dimitrovgrad
Cherdakly
Novodevichye
Zhigulevsk
375
Togliatti
Oktyabrsk
Syzran
Kashpirovka

Nurlat
Isakly
383
Belebey
420
Rayevskiy
Davlekanovo
Priyutovo

BASHKORTOSTAN
Sterlitamak
Ishimbay
481
Salavat
Meleuz
Belaya
Petrovskoye
Verkhniy
Avzyan
1039
Gora
Yamantau
1638
Tirlyanskiy
Beloretsk
Verkhneuralsk
1118
Stepnoye
Yuzhnouralsk
Plast
Troitsk
Uchaly
Uy
452

Sernovodsk
Sok
Kinel
Krotovka
Otradnyy
Samara
Ponomarevka
Bugulma
Abdulino
Pokhvistnevo
Buguruslan
Grachevka
Sorochinsk
Buzuluk

Magnitogorsk
Varna
Kartaly
Rudnyy
452
Sibay
859
Baymak 758
Kizilskoye
Kumertau
Uy
Buskul
Komsomolets
Toguzak

SAMARA
Novokuybyshevsk
Chapayevsk
Privolzhye
Pestravka
Bolshaya
Glushitsa
Alekseyevka
Andreyevka
Totskoye

Ozernoye
Novo-Sergiyevskiy
405
Bulanovo
Tyulgan
Sakmara Chernyy Otrog
Chernyy Otrog
ORENBURG
Saraktash
Pervomayskiy
Krasnyy Kholm
Ilek
Ural

Iriklinskoye
Vdkhr.
Krasnoyarskiy
Energetik
Gay
Kuvandyk
Mednogorsk
Novotroitsk
Orsk
Yasnyy
414
Yelizavetinka
Zhaylma
Adamovka
Ordzhonikidze
Bredy
Lisakovsk
Zhetiqara

Pugachev
Bolshaya Irgiz
Bolshaya
Chernigovka
O b s h c h i y   S y r t
418
Dombarovskiy
Svetlyy
Kumak
Ozërnyy

Ozinki
Darinskoye
Oral
Zhaygyq
Kamenka
Chapayev
Burli
Aksay
Chingirlau
Ilek
Krasnyy Kholm
Sol Iletsk
Akbulak
Utva

Mednogorsk
Novotroitsk
Orsk
Leninskoye
509
Martuk
Novorossiyskoye
Khromtau
Aqtöbe

Vladimirovka
Ozero
Shalkar
Shalkar
Shalkar
Dzhambeyty
Aqtöbe
Novoalekseyevka
Oktyabrsk
Algai

K i r g i z i y a   **S t e p p e**

K   A   Z   A   K   S   T   A   N

Kushum
Furmanov
Karsha
Karatobe
Bolshaya Kobda
Irgiz
Qarabutaq
Tolybay
Zhabasak

Bolshoi Uzen
Uil

Projection: Conical with two standard parallels
East from Greenwich
CARTOGRAPHY BY PHILIP'S. COPYRIGHT REED INTERNATIONAL BOOKS LTD

ft   m
3000 1000
1500 500
600   200
       50
0   0

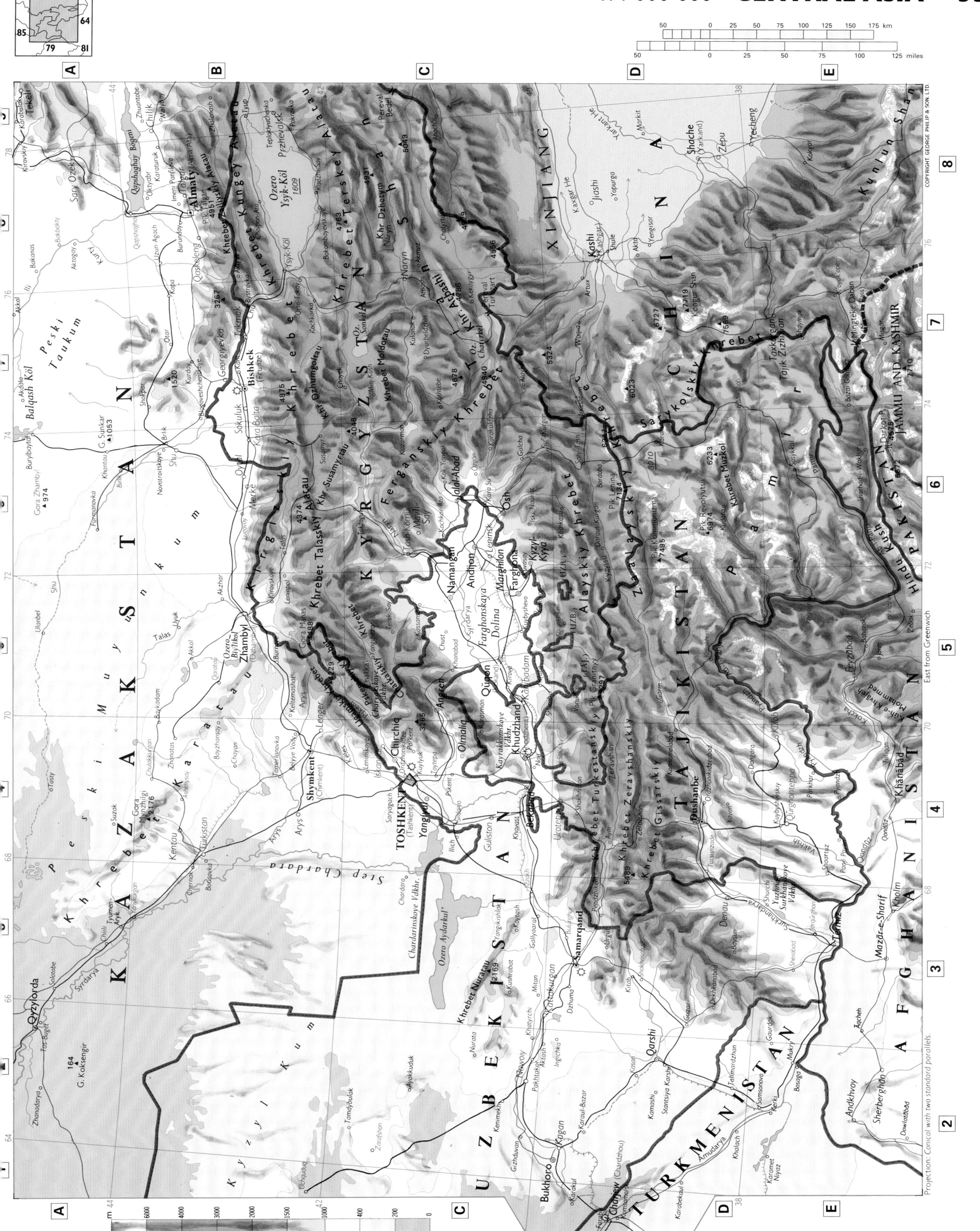

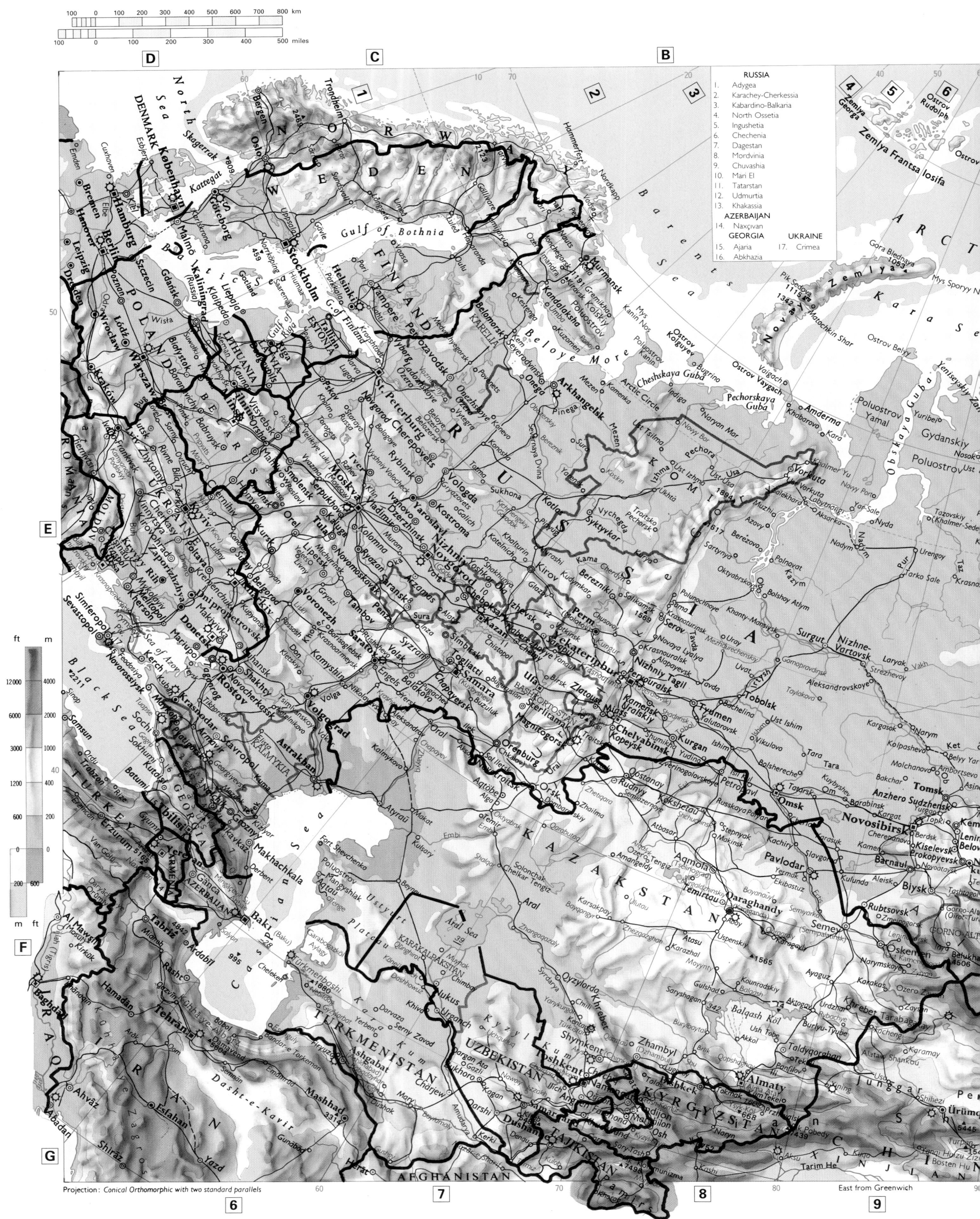

RUSSIA	
1.	Adygea
2.	Karachey-Cherkessia
3.	Kabardino-Balkania
4.	North Ossetia
5.	Ingushetia
6.	Chechenia
7.	Dagestan
8.	Mordvinia
9.	Chuvashia
10.	Mari El
11.	Tatarstan
12.	Udmurtia
13.	Khakassia
AZERBAIJAN	
14.	Naxçivan
GEORGIA	**UKRAINE**
15.	Ajana 17. Crimea
16.	Abkhazia

Projection: Conical Orthomorphic with two standard parallels

East from Greenwich

57

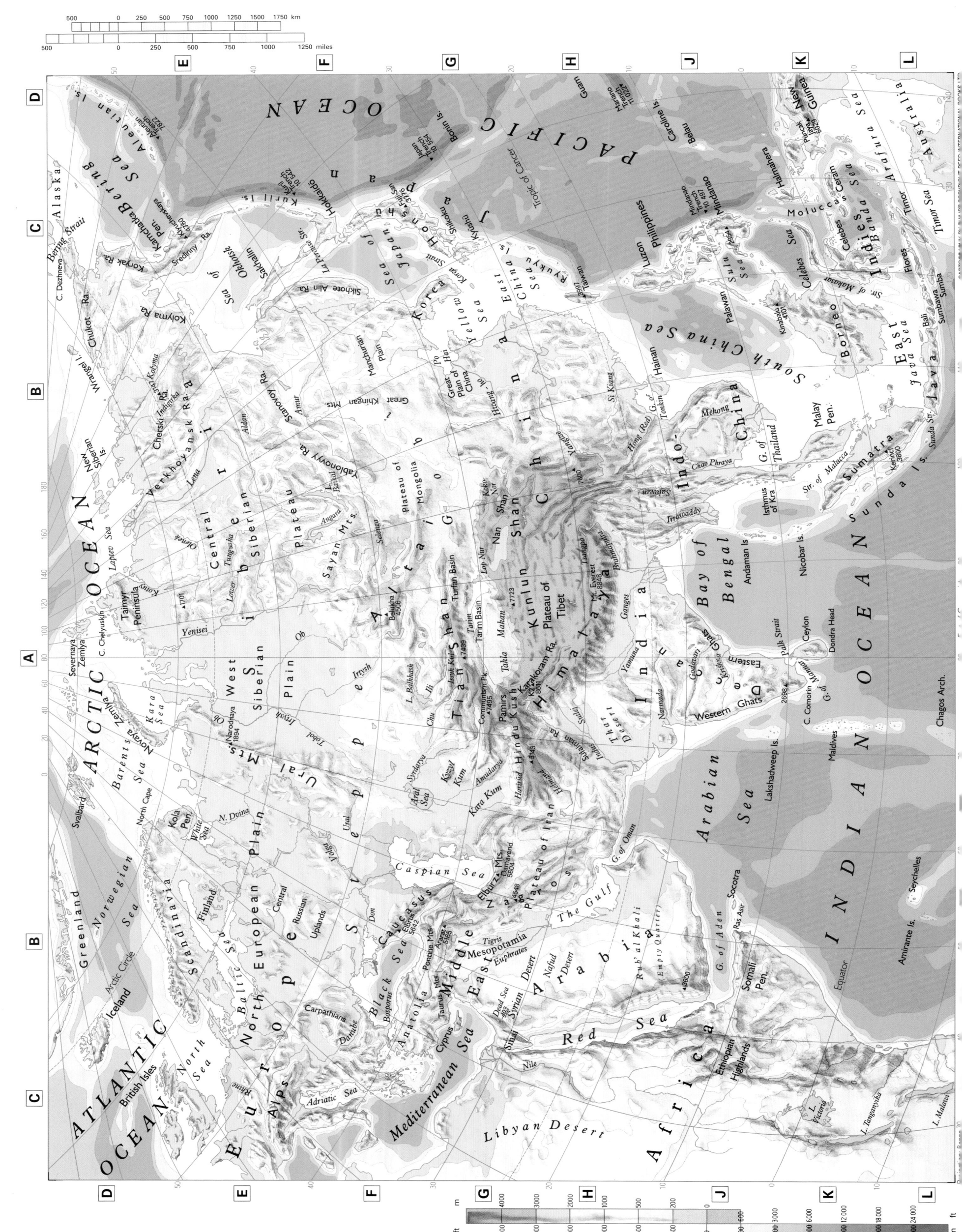

PACIFIC OCEAN

ARCTIC OCEAN

ATLANTIC OCEAN

INDIAN OCEAN

Bering Sea

Alaska

C. Dezhneva

Bering Strait

Wrangel I.

Chukot Pen.

Koryak Ra.

Kamchatka Pen.

Klyuchevskaya 4780

Sredinny Ra.

Sea of Okhotsk

Sakhalin

Kuril Is.

Aleutian Is.

Aleutian Trench 7822

Bonin Is.

Iwo Jima

Volcano Is.

Mariana Trench 11 022

Guam

Caroline Is.

Belau

New Guinea

Japan

Hokkaido

La Perouse Str.

Honshu

Sea of Japan

Korea Str.

Shikoku

Kyushu

Korea

Ryukyu Is.

Taiwan

East China Sea

Yellow Sea

Luzon

Philippines

Mindanao

Mindanao Trench 10 497

Halmahera

Molucca Sea

Celebes Sea

Celebes

Ceram

Banda Sea

Indonesia

Arafura Sea

Timor Sea

Australia

Irian

Manchurian Plain

Great Khingan Mts.

Amur

Hwang Ho

Great Plain of China

Po Hai

Si Kiang

Hainan

G. of Tonkin

Hong (Red)

Mekong

Indo-China

China

Malay Pen.

Chao Phraya

G. of Thailand

Str. of Malacca

Isthmus of Kra

Sumatra

Kinabalu 4101

Borneo

Str. of Macassar

Bali

Java Sea

Sumba

Sumbawa

Flores

Java

Sunda Is.

Sunda Str.

Kerinci 3800

Verkhoyansk Ra.

Cherski Ra.

Indigirka

Kolyma

New Siberian Is.

Laptev Sea

Kolyma Ra.

Lena

Aldan

Stanovoy Ra.

Yablonovyy Ra.

Central Siberian Plateau

Tunguska

Lower Tunguska

Angara

L. Baikal

Selenga

Sayan Mts.

Plateau of Mongolia

Altai

Kokonor

Nan Shan

Lop Nur

Tarim Basin

Makan

Takla

Tarim

Kunlun

Plateau of Tibet

Mt. Everest 8848

Himalaya

Ganges

Brahmaputra

India

Bay of Bengal

Andaman Is.

Nicobar Is.

Eastern Ghats

Godavari

Krishna

Western Ghats

C. Comorin 2698

Palk Strait

Ceylon

Dondra Head

Chagos Arch.

Maldives

Lakshadweep Is.

Amirante Is.

Seychelles

Socotra

Ras Asir

Somali Pen.

G. of Aden

Ethiopian Highlands

Taimyr Peninsula

C. Chelyuskin

Severnaya Zemlya

Kara Sea

Yenisei

Ob

Irtysh

West Siberian Plain

Tobol

Ural Mts.

Narodnaya 1894

Novaya Zemlya

Barents Sea

Svalbard

Greenland

Norwegian Sea

North Cape

Kola Pen.

White Sea

N. Dvina

Scandinavia

Finland

Baltic Sea

Volga

Don

Central Russian Uplands

North European Plain

Europe

Steppes

Rhine

Danube

Alps

Carpathians

Adriatic Sea

North Sea

British Isles

Iceland

Arctic Circle

Tian Shan

Communism Pk 7495

Pamirs

Hindu Kush 7690

Kara Kum

Kyzyl Kum

Syrdarya

Amudarya

Aral Sea

Chu

Ili

L. Balkhash

Issyk Kul

Irtysh

Belukha 4506

Karakoram Ra.

K2 8611

7723

7439

Helmand

Hamun

Suleiman Ra.

Thar Desert

Indus

Jhelum

Sutlej

Yamuna

Narmada

Caspian Sea

Elburz Mts. 5604

Damavend

Plateau of Iran

Zagros

The Gulf

G. of Oman

Arabian Sea

Caucasus 5642

Elbrus 5633

Black Sea

Bosporus

Pontine Mts.

Anatolia

Taurus Mts.

Ararat 5165

Tigris

Mesopotamia

Euphrates

Middle East

Dead Sea

Syrian Desert

An Nafud

Arabia

Rub' al Khali (Empty Quarter)

3600

4800

Cyprus

Sinai

Red Sea

Nile

Mediterranean Sea

Libyan Desert

Africa

L. Victoria

L. Tanganyika

Equator

Tropic of Cancer

L. Mobutu

Volcano

3776

1945

542

7397

South China Sea

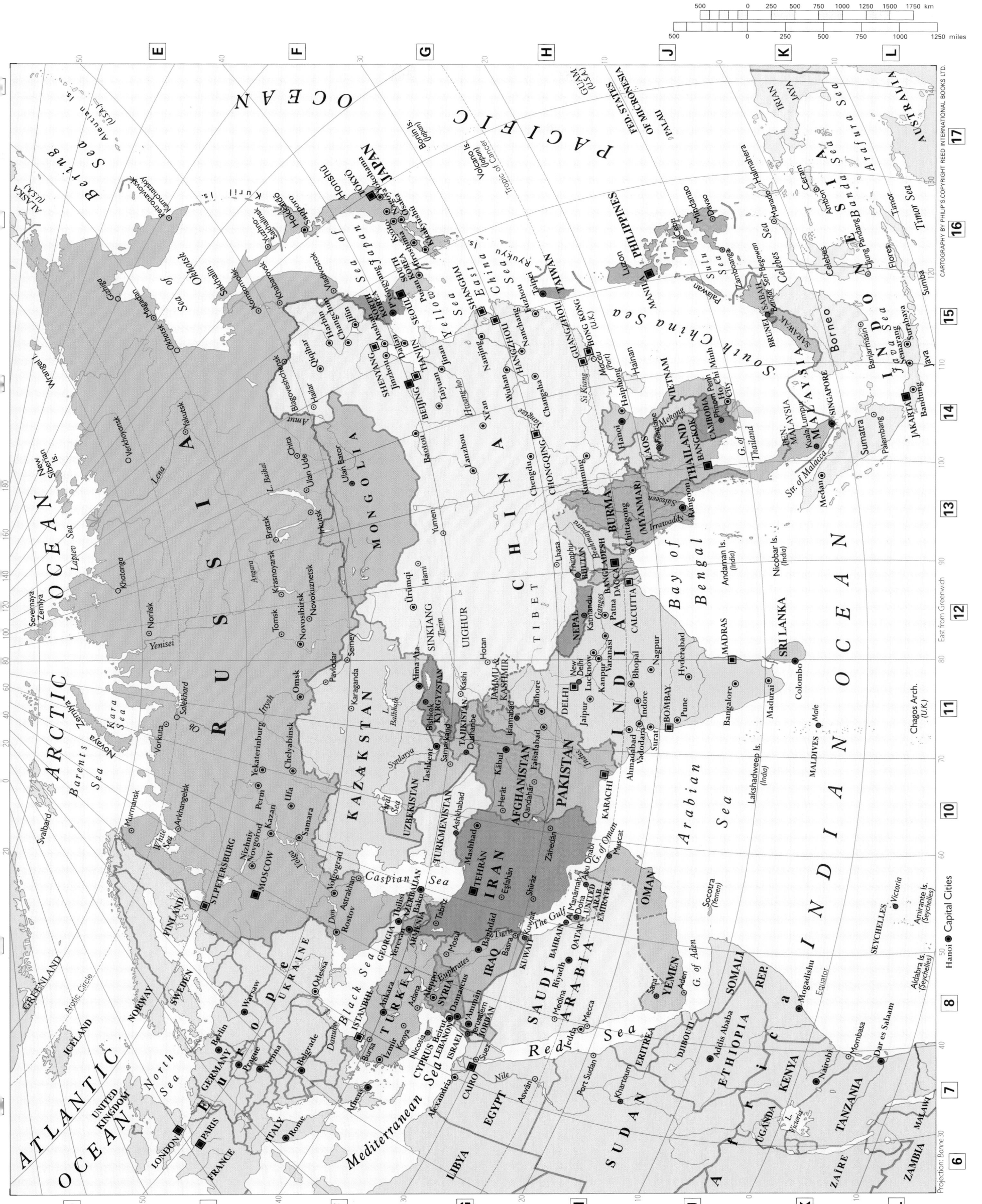

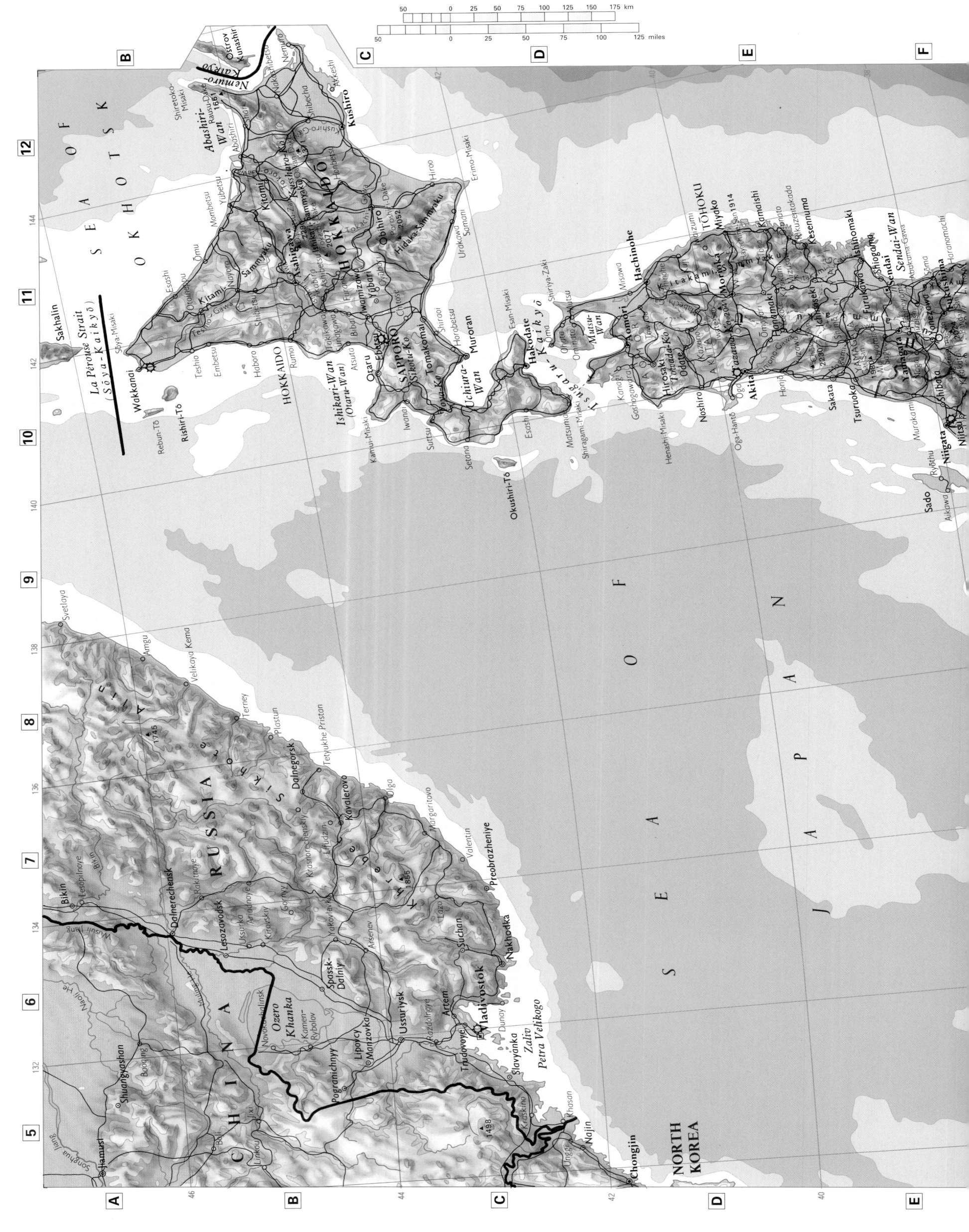

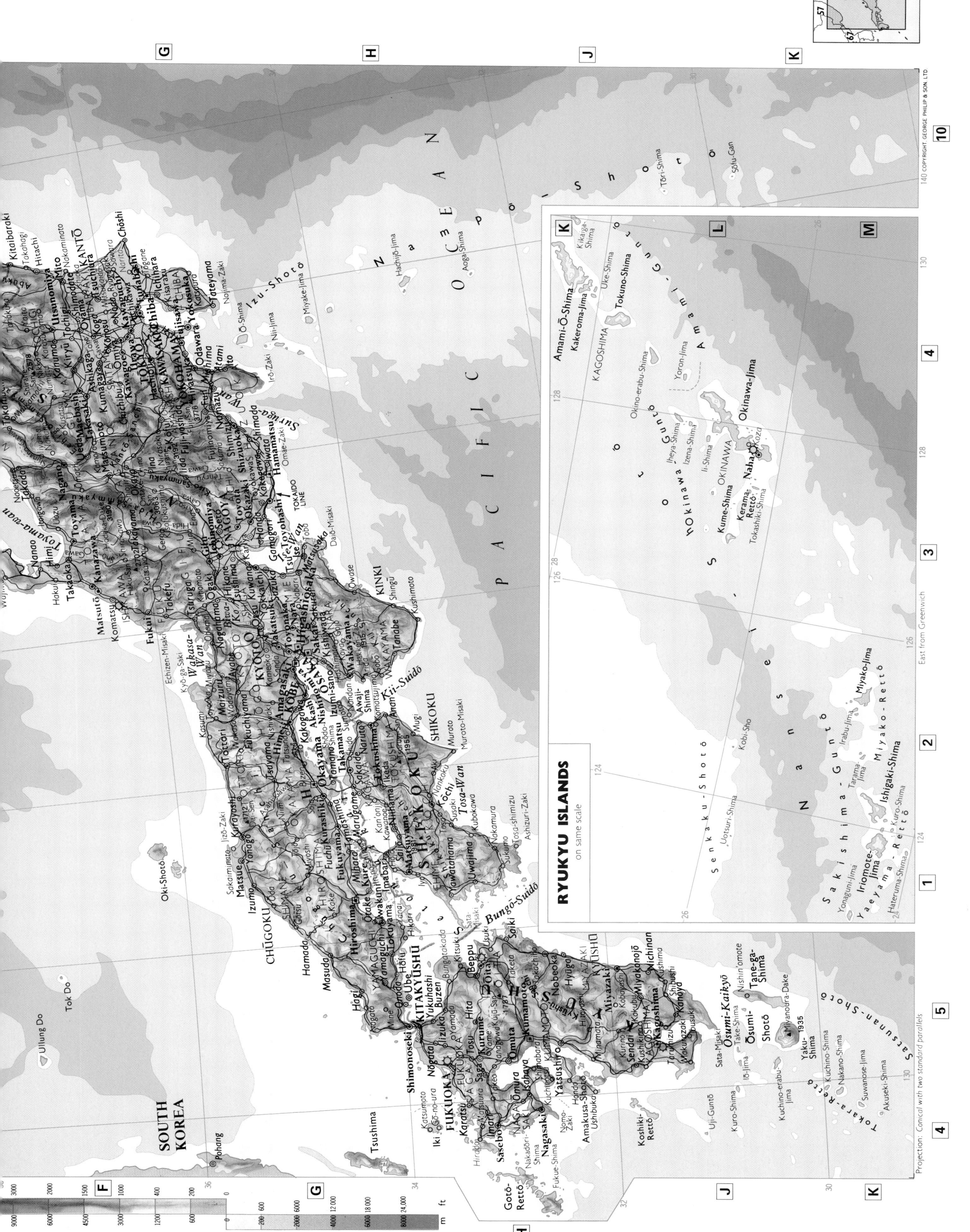

RYUKYU ISLANDS
on same scale

SOUTH
KOREA

PACIFIC   OCEAN

Projection: Conical with two standard parallels

140 COPYRIGHT GEORGE PHILIP & SON, LTD.

SEA OF JAPAN

SOUTH KOREA

Oki-Shotō
Dōgo ▲608 Daimanji-San
Saigō

CHŪGOKU-DISTRICT

H O N S

Shimane-Hantō
Jizō-Zaki
Iwami
Kasumi
Toyooka
Hi-no-Misaki
Hirata
Shinji
Matsue
Sakaiminato
Kurayoshi
Tottori
Hidaka
Taisha
Izumo
Ka
Yonago
Dai-Sen
Suga-no-Sen
Wadayama
Yasugi
Daito
Kisuki

Ōda
Sanbe-San ▲1126
Katsuyama
Tsuyama
Yamazaki
NISH

Gōtsu
Yōnotsu
Tōjō
Ochiai
Yanabara

Hamada
SHIMANE
Shōbara
Niimi
KA

Miyoshi
OKAYAMA
Tatsuno
Aioi
HYO

Masuda
HIROSHIMA
Fuchū
Takahashi
Okayama
Bizen
Himeji
Takasago

Ōmi-Shima
Aono-Yama
Kanmuri-Yama ▲1339
Saijō
Kasaoka
Saidaiji
Kakogawa

Hagi
Kake
Ōta-Gawa
Fukuyama
Tamashima
Tamano
Shōdo-Shima
Harima-Nada

Tsuno-Shima
Ōtake
Onomichi
In-no-Shima
Ieshima-Shotō
Awaji-Shim

Mi-Shima
YAMAGUCHI
Itsukuichi
HIROSHIMA
Mihara
Kurashiki
Marugame
Takamatsu

Nagato
Yamaguchi
Hōfu
Tokui
Takehara
In'no-Shima
Sakaide
KAGAWA
Hiketa

Hibiki-Nada
Mine
Nan'yō
Iwakuni
Hiroshima-Wan
Ondo
Zentsūji
Kotohira

Toyoura
Sanyō
Kure
Aki-Nada
Kurahashi-Jima
Takuma
Kamilla

Genkai-Nada
Ogōri
Kudamatsu
Tokuyama
Naga-Shima
Yashiro-Jima
Hiuchi-Nada
Kan'onji
Sanuki-Sammyaku
Naruto

Onoda
Ube
Hikari
Iwai-Jima
Hime-Jima
Imabari
Hōjō
Kawanoe
Anabuki
Tokush

Shimonoseki
KITAKYŪSHŪ
Suō-Nada
Heigun-To
Matsuyama
Niihama
Iyo-mishima
Komatsujima

Higasi-Suidō
Ō-Shima
Matsusaki
Saijō
TOKUSHIMA
Anan

Tsushima
Iki
Gō-no-ura
Fukuma
Nakama
Nōgata
Yukuhashi
Nakatsu
Futago-Yama
Kunisaki
Iyo-Nada
Hōjō
Iyo
Nyūgawa
Ishizuchi-San ▲1981
Tsuruki-San ▲1953
Mugi

Izuhara
Iki-Kaikyō
FUKUOKA
Iizuka
Takawa
Buzen
Usa
Bungotakada
EHIME
Shikoku-Sanchi
KOCHI

Kō-Saki
Katsumoto
Yobuko
FUKUOKA-Sanchi
Yamada
Hita
Yufu-Dake ▲1584
Beppu-Wan
Nagahama
Ozu
Uchiko
Sagawa
Tōyō

Ikitsuki-Shima
Maebaru
Setori-San
Amagi
Kusu
Beppu
Tsurusaki
Sada-Misaki-Hantō
Yawatahama
Susaki
Aki

Ō-Shima
Karatsu
Tsukushi
Aso
ŌITA
Ōita
Hōyo-Kaikyō
Uwa
Nankoku
Kubokawa
Muroto

Hirado
Matsuura
SAGA
Kurogi
Ōyama
Usuki
Saganoseki
Kōchi
Tosa
Tosa-Wan

Hirado-Shima
Imari
Tosu
Yame
Kuju-San ▲1787
Tsukumi
Uwajima
Hiromi
Muroto-Misaki

Takeo
Taku
Saga
Kurume
Oguni
Saiki
Ekawasaki
Saga

Sasebo
Kashima
Yanagawa
Chikugo
Taketa
Takachiho
Tsurumi-Saki
Jōhen
Nakamura
SHIKOKU

Omura-Wan
Tara
Okawa
Yamaga
Aso-San ▲1597
Kamae
Ōhama-Wan
Sukumo
SHIKOKU-DISTRICT

NAGASAKI
Tara-Dake
Ōmuta
Inomiya
Soba-Yama
Tsurumi-Saki-Suidō
Tosa-shimizu
Ashizuri-Zaki

Isahaya
Arao
Ōzu
Oki-no-Shima

Omura
Tamana
Kikuchi
Taketa

Nagasaki
Unzen-Dake ▲1360
Kumamoto
Mashiki

Nomo-Zaki
Shimabara
KUMAMOTO
Uto
Nobeoka

Amakusa-Shotō
Hondo
Kami-Jima
Misumi
Hinokage
Hyūga
Hososhima

Amakusa-Nada
Shimo-Jima
Yatsushiro
Kuma-Gawa
Shiba

Tachibana-Wan
Kuchinotsu
Oyana
Itsuki
Yatsushiro-Kai
Kyūshū-Sanchi
MIYAZAKI
Saito
Takanabe

Ushibuka
Naga-Shima
Minamata
Hitoyoshi
Yunomae

Izumi
KYŪSHŪ

Akune
Ōkuchi
Ebino
Kobayashi
KYŪSHŪ-DISTRICT
Miyazaki

Kami-koshiki Jima
Miyanojō
Kurino
Kirishima-Yama ▲1700

Koshiki-Rettō
Sendai
Kajiki
Kobun
Miyakonojō
Nichinan
Aburatsu

Shimo-koshiki-Jima
Kushikino
Ijuin
Hayato
KAGOSHIMA

Kagoshima
On-Take ▲1118

Taniyama
Satsuma-Hantō
Tarumizu
Shibushi
Kushima

Noma-Saki
Kaseda
Kanoya
Kōyama
Shibushi-Wan

Makurazaki
Chiran
Kagoshima-Wan
Ōsumi-Hantō

Bō-no-Misaki
Ibusuki
Yamagawa
Kaimon-Dake ▲924

Sata-Misaki

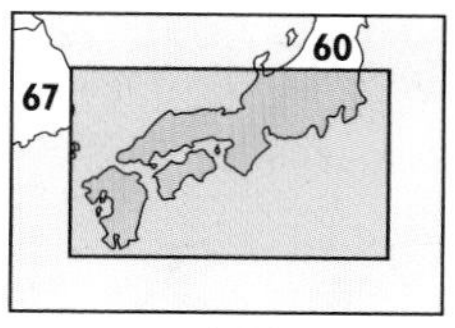

67 | 60

CHŪBU-DISTRICT

7 | 8 | 9 | 10 | 11 | 12

Himi
Takaoka
Shinminato
Uozu
Namerikawa
Nakano
Nikko
Chūzenji-Ko
Imaichi
Hitachi
Hitachi-ota
Kashima-
Tsubata
Ōyabe
Toyama
Nagano
Suzaka
Nakanojo
Numata
TOCHIGI
Karasuyama
Kanazawa
Tonami
Jōhana
Kōshoku
Shimonita
Kusatsu
Utsunomiya
Kanuma
Kasama
Mito
Nada
Matsutō
Neagari
Takayama
Ueda
Asama Yama
Shibukawa
GUMMA
Mo'oka
Motegi
Katsuta
Nakaminato
Komatsu
ISHIKAWA
Furukawa
Komoro
Maebashi
Annaka
Kiryū
Tochigi
Iwase
Tombe
Ōarai
Kaga
Kamioka
Matsumoto
Saku
Takasaki
Ashikaga
Ōta
Yūki
Shimodate
Ishioka
Kita-Ura
Mikuni
Katsuyama
Shiojiri
Okaya
Suwa
Tomioka
Fujioka
Isesaki
Honjo
Hanyu
Koga
Shimotsuma
Tsuchiura
IBARAK
Fukui
NAGANO
Suwa-Ko
Chino
Kumagaya
Gyoda
Konosu
Kasukabe
Mitsukaidō
Ryūgasaki
Itako
Kashima
Sabae
Ōno
Ina
Chichibu
Higashi-matsuyama
SAITAMA
Kawagoe
Noda
Shin-Tone-Gawa
Takefu
Hachiman
Nakatsugawa
Iida
Nirasaki
Ome
Tokorozawa
Omiya
Kashiwa
Narita
Asahi
Chōshi
Tsuruga
Hokuriku Tunnel
Seki
TOKYO
Kōdaira
Urawa
Kawaguchi
Matsudo
Ichikawa
CHIBA
Yokaichiba
Inubō-Zaki
Echizen-Misaki
GIFU
Mino-Kamo
Komagane
Kōfu
Enzan
Tachikawa
Musashino
Mitaka
Funabashi
Kyō-ga-Saki
Ōgaki
Mino
Mizunami
YAMANASHI
Hachioji
Machida
TŌKYŌ
Tōkyō-Wan
Gifu
Ichinomiya
Tajimi
Akaishi Sammyaku
Tsuru
Sagamihara
Yamato
Atsugi
KAWASAKI
Chichara
Mobara
Inazawa
Seto
Fuji yoshida
Tanzawa-Sanchi
YOKOHAMA
Nagahama
Hashima
Komaki
AICHI
KANAGAWA
Fujisawa
Kamakura
Kisarazu
Hikone
Kuwana
NAGOYA
Toyota
Fuji-San
Hatano
Hiratsuka
Yokosuka
Bōsō-Hantō
Biwa-Ko
Ōmi-hachiman
Tsushima
Okazaki
Fuji-no-miya
Gotemba
Odawara
Chigasaki
Ōtaki
KYŌTO
Ōtsu
Yokkaichi
Tōkai
Kariya
Shinshiro
Fuji
Mishima
Sagami-Wan
Miura
Uraga
Katsuura
Suzuka
Tokoname
Toyokawa
Shimizu
Atami
Kameyama
Handa
Shizuoka
Numazu
Tsu
Gamagori
Hamakita
Shimada
Kakegawa
Izu-Hantō
Ito
Su-no-Saki
Tateyama
Nabari
Matsusaka
Ise-Wan
Toyohashi
Fukuroi
Sagara
Suruga-Wan
Shimoda
Nojima-Zaki
Nara
MIE
Ise
Atsumi
Hamamatsu
Iwata
Yaizu
Shiio-Misaki
Irō-Zaki
OSAK
Shima-Hantō
Ago
Irako-Misaki
Omae-Zaki
Enshū-Nada
Mihara-Yama
Ō-Shima
To-Shima
Sakai
Kawachi-Nagano
Daiō-Misaki
Shikine-Jima
Nii-Jima
Kōzu-Shima
Hashimoto
Wakayama
Kumano-Nada
NARA
Kii Sanchi
Hakken-Zan
Kinki-District
Miyake-Jima
Kumano
Mikura-Jima
WAKAYAMA
Tanabe
Shingu
Nachikatsuura
Kushimoto
Shio-no-Misaki

Kii-Hantō

PACIFIC OCEAN

Hachijō-Jima

Aoga-Shima

Sumisu-Jima

COPYRIGHT GEORGE PHILIP & SON LTD

7 | 8 | 9 | 10 | 11 | 12

East from Greenwich

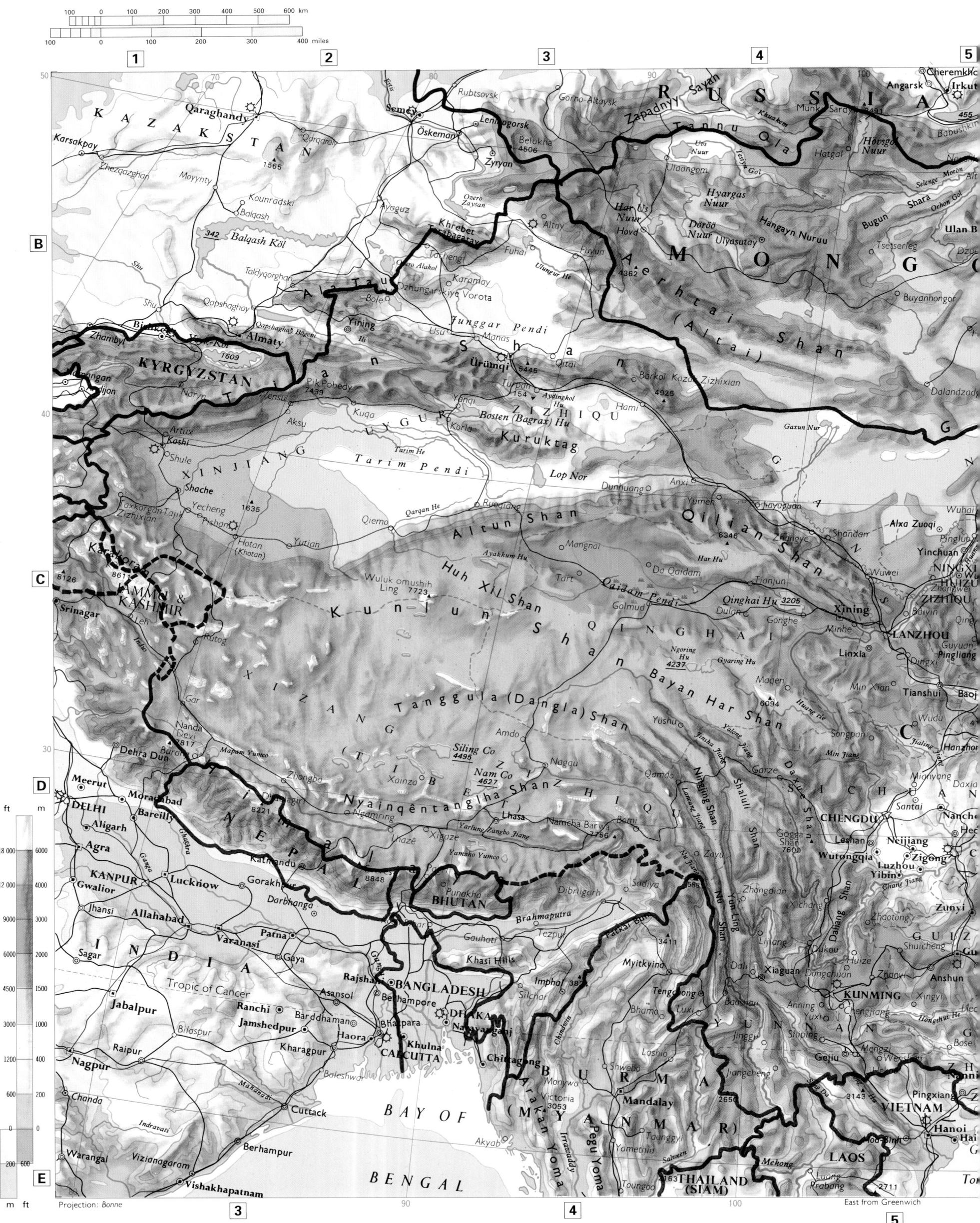

Projection: Bonne

East from Greenwich

55 57
79
76 70

7
6 8 9

120 140 50

Baykal
110
an Ude • **Chita** Sretensk
Bukachacha Gulian Shimanovsk
Nerchinsk Yilehuli Svobodny
lski Olovyannaya Borzya Shan Blagoveshchensk Chegdomyn
Chita Aihui Bureya Komsomolsk
Manzhouli Orogen Zizhiqi L. Bolon
Oroqen Zizhiqi Troitskoye Poronaysk
Dutulun Shan Hailar Nenjiang Obluchye C. Terpeniya B
Hulun Butha Qi Yichun Birobidzhan
Nur Solon Suihua Hegang Bikin **Sakhalin**
Choybalsan Arun Tamsaghulag Hulin Khabarovsk Dolinsk
Horqin Youyi Shuangcheng Hamusi Mishan Yuzhno-Sakhalinsk
Qianqi Qiqihar Shuangyashan
Tamsaghulag (Ulan Hot) Anda **HARBIN** Jixi Ozero Kholmsk
Baicheng Fuyu Mudanjiang Khanka La Perouse Str.
Saynshand Huolin Gol Tao'an Jilin Ussuriysk Wakkanai **Asahigawa**
Abagnar Qi CHANGCHUN Dunhua Artem **Hokkaido**
Dzamin Uud Erenhot Linxi Shuangliao Yanji Vladivostok Nakhodka **SAPPORO** Kushiro
Tongliao Siping Liaoyuan Songhua Hu Hunchun Partizansk Otaru Muroran C. Erimo
ONGGOL Duolun Chifeng Fuxin Songhua Chongjin Hakodate Tsugaru-kaikyo
Hohhot Jining FUSHUN SHENYANG Aomori Hachinohe
ou Zhangjiakou Chengde SHENYANG Benxi **NORTH** **SEA OF** Morioka
Datong Xuanhua Jinzhou ANSHAN Hungnam Akita Ishinomaki
Qinhuangdao Liaoyang Dandong Sakata
BEIJING Yingkou Yalu Wonsan **JAPAN** Sado Niigata **Sendai**
(Peking) Tangshan Liaodong P'YONGYANG Wajima
HEBEI Baoding BEIJING SHI Wan Korea Bay Kaesong Toyama
WALL **TIANJIN** DALIAN SOUL Kanazawa **TOKYO** C
Yuanping 2894 TIANJIN SHI Yantai Inch'on Okayama NAGOYA YOKOHAMA
TAIYUAN Shijiazhuang Cangzhou Bo Hai Weihai **SOUTH** HIROSHIMA **KOBE OSAKA** Yokosuka
Taihang Shan Handan Dezhou Ye Xian Taejon Taegu KOBE Sakai Shizuoka Hamamatsu
Fenyang Yangquan JINAN Weifang **YELLOW** PUSAN Kure Wakayama
Yuci Zibo Masan Shimonoseki Kochi
Changzhi Anyang Tai'an QINGDAO **SEA** Kwangju 1945 Hiroshima Shikoku Matsuyama
Linfen Jining **SHANDONG** KITAKYUSHU Fukuoka
XI'AN Luoyang Kaifeng Llanyungang FUKUOKA Kumamoto Kyushu
di **ZHENGZHOU** Shangqiu Xuzhou Qingjiang Yuncheng Cheju Do 1950 Sasebo **J** Kagoshima
Pingdingshan **HENAN** Hongze JIANGSU Nagasaki Kumamoto
Nanyang Shangshui Hu Nanjing Taizhou Tanega-shima
Han Shui Fuyang Bengbu Yangzhou Changzhou
Zhumadian Huainan **NANJING** Wuxi Suzhou **SHANGHAI SHI**
Xiangfan **ANHUI** Hefei Ma'anshan Wuhu Jiaxing **SHANGHAI**
Zhongxiang Tongling Wuxing **EAST CHINA**
han Yichang Dabie Shan **WUHAN** Anqing Hangzhou Amami-o-Shima
HU Shashi Huangshi Hangzhou Wan **SEA** Okinawa
Changde Hujiang Tunxi Shaoxing Ningbo
Yueyang **ZHEJIANG**
Yiyang Dongting Nanchang Jingdezhen Jinhua Qu Xian Wenzhou
HUNAN Hu Shangrao **Ryūkyū-rettō** **PACIFIC**
Changsha **JIANGXI** Naha
Xiangtan Pingxiang Shan Okinawa
Shaoyang Ji'an 2120
ma Hengyang Fuzhou Min Ch Nanping
Shaoyang Ganzhou **FUJIAN** Chilung **Tropic of Cancer**
Xing'an Longyan Hsinchu TAIPEI
Nan Ling Shaoguan Zhangzhou Fuzhou T'aichung
Ling Mei Xian Chao'an Quanzhou Changhua Kao Shan
XI Wuzhou **GUANGDONG** Xiamen Chiai TAIWAN
Zhaoqing **GUANGZHOU** Shantou 3997 (FORMOSA)
QU Jiangmen Huizhou T'ainan T'aitung
Maoming Foshan **HONG KONG** (Br.) Kaohsiung Pingtung
Zhanjiang Yangjiang **Macao** (Port.) **SOUTH CHINA**
gzhou Haixia Pratas Batan Is.
HAINAN **Haikou** **SEA**
Hainan Dao 1879 Babuyan Is.
zaoheng

110 120 130

COPYRIGHT GEORGE PHILIP & SON LTD

6 7 8

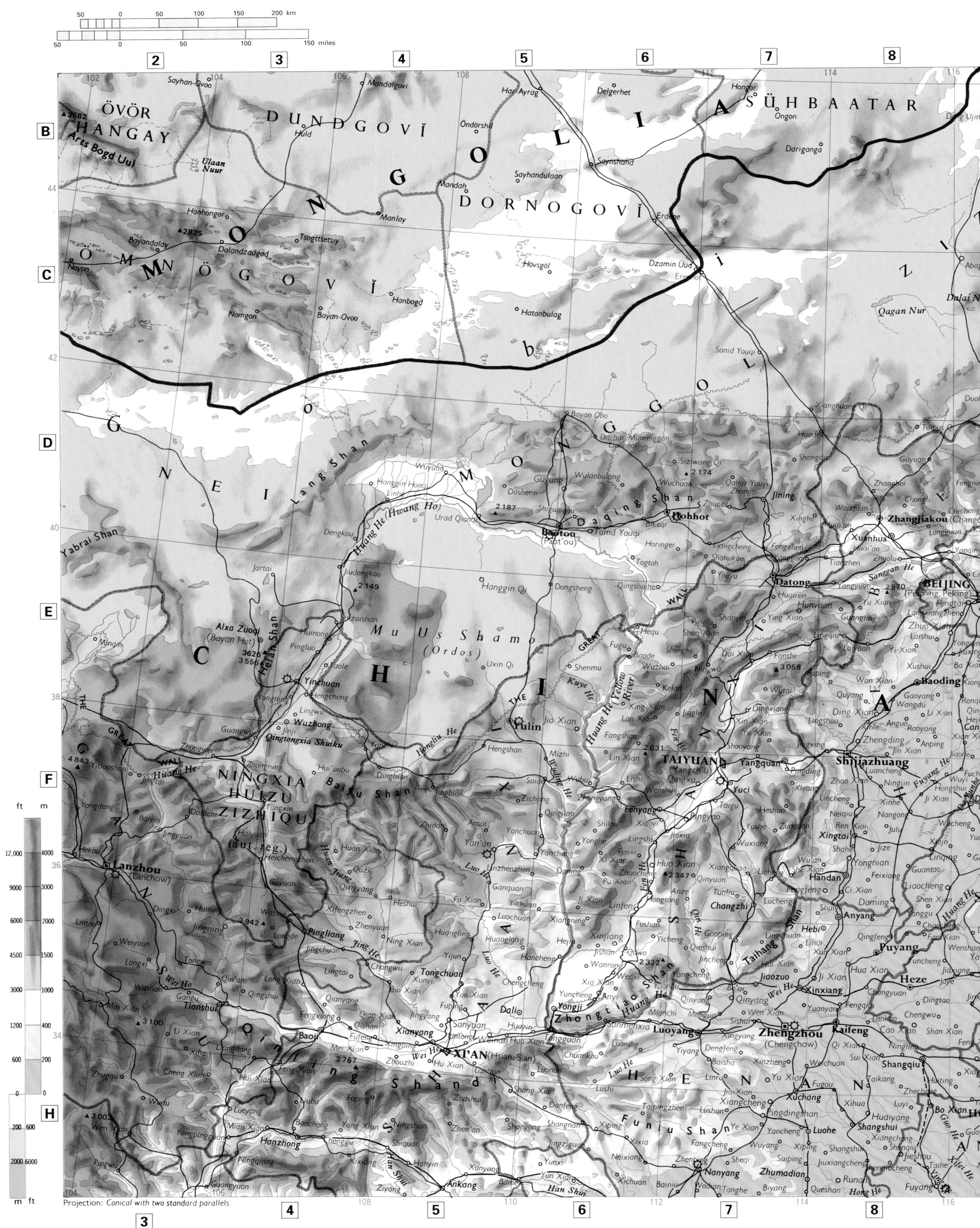

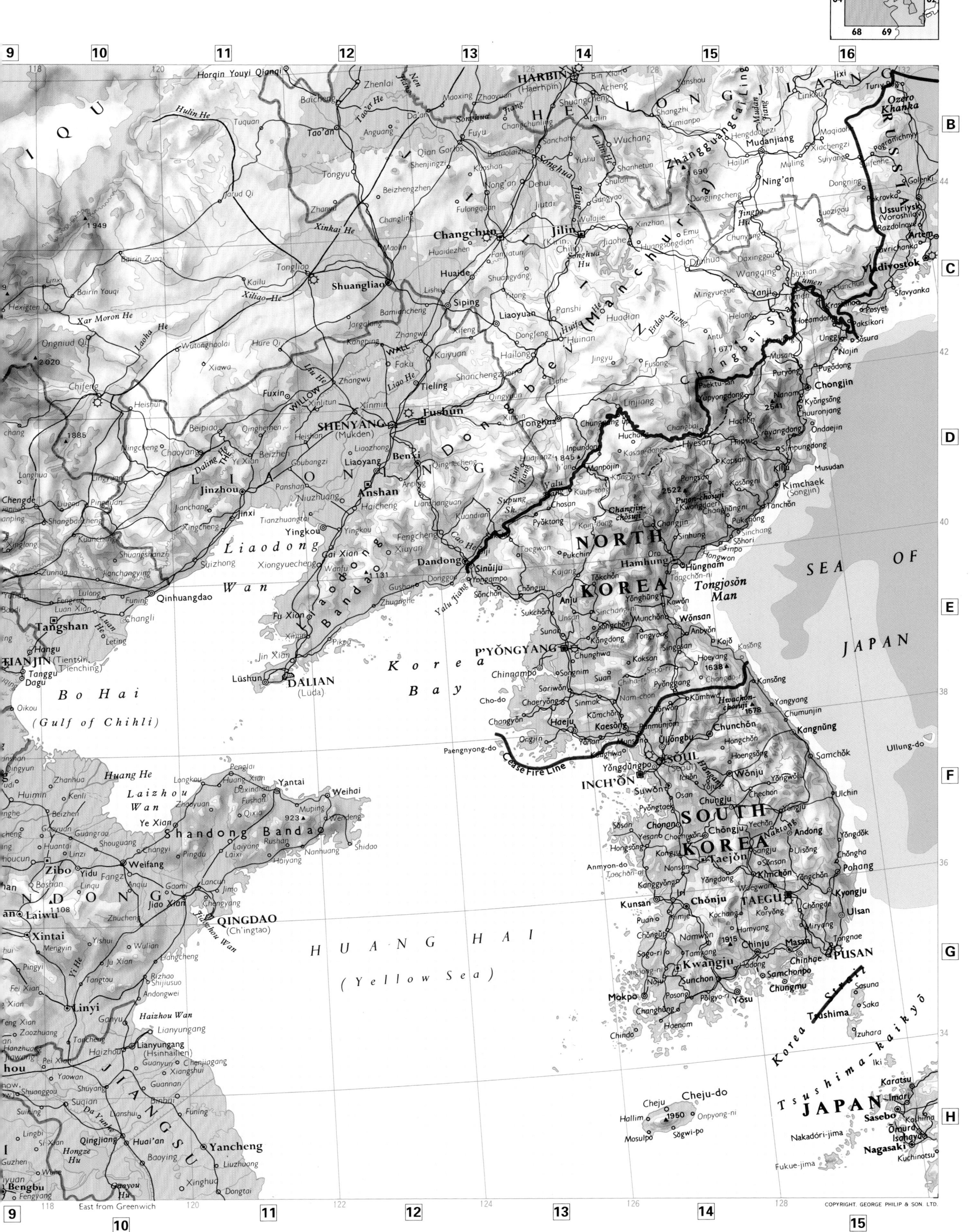

9   10   11   12   13   14   15   16

B

HORQIN YOUYI QIANQI

HEILONGJIANG

HARBIN
(Haerhpin)

RUSSIA

Ozero
Khanka

Ussuriysk
(Voroshilov)

Changchun

JILIN

Jilin
(Kirin)

Vladivostok

C

Shuangliao

Siping

Changbai Shan

Chongjin

42

Shenyang
(Mukden)

Fushun

D

LIAONING

NORTH
KOREA

Kimchaek
(Songjin)

40

Anshan

Benxi

Dandong

Sinŭiju

Hamhung

Hŭngnam

Liaodong
Wan

Lüshun

DALIAN
(Lüda)

Korea
Bay

P'YŎNGYANG

Tongjosŏn
Man

Wŏnsan

SEA   OF

E

Tangshan

TIANJIN (Tientsin,
Tienching)

Tanggu
Dagu

Bo Hai
(Gulf of Chihli)

JAPAN

38

Huang He

Laizhou
Wan

Yantai

Weihai

Cease Fire Line

SŎUL
(Seoul)

INCH'ŎN

F

Shandong Bandao

SOUTH
KOREA

Ullung-do

Zibo

Weifang

Taejŏn

36

QINGDAO
(Ch'ingtao)

Xintai

TAEGU

Kyongju

Ulsan

Linyi

HUANG   HAI

(Yellow Sea)

KWANGJU

PUSAN

G

JIANGSU

Lianyungang
(Hsinhailien)

Tsushima

JAPAN

34

Mokpo

Cheju-do

Yancheng

Karatsu

Nagasaki

H

Bengbu

East from Greenwich

9   10   11   12   13   14   15

COPYRIGHT. GEORGE PHILIP & SON. LTD.

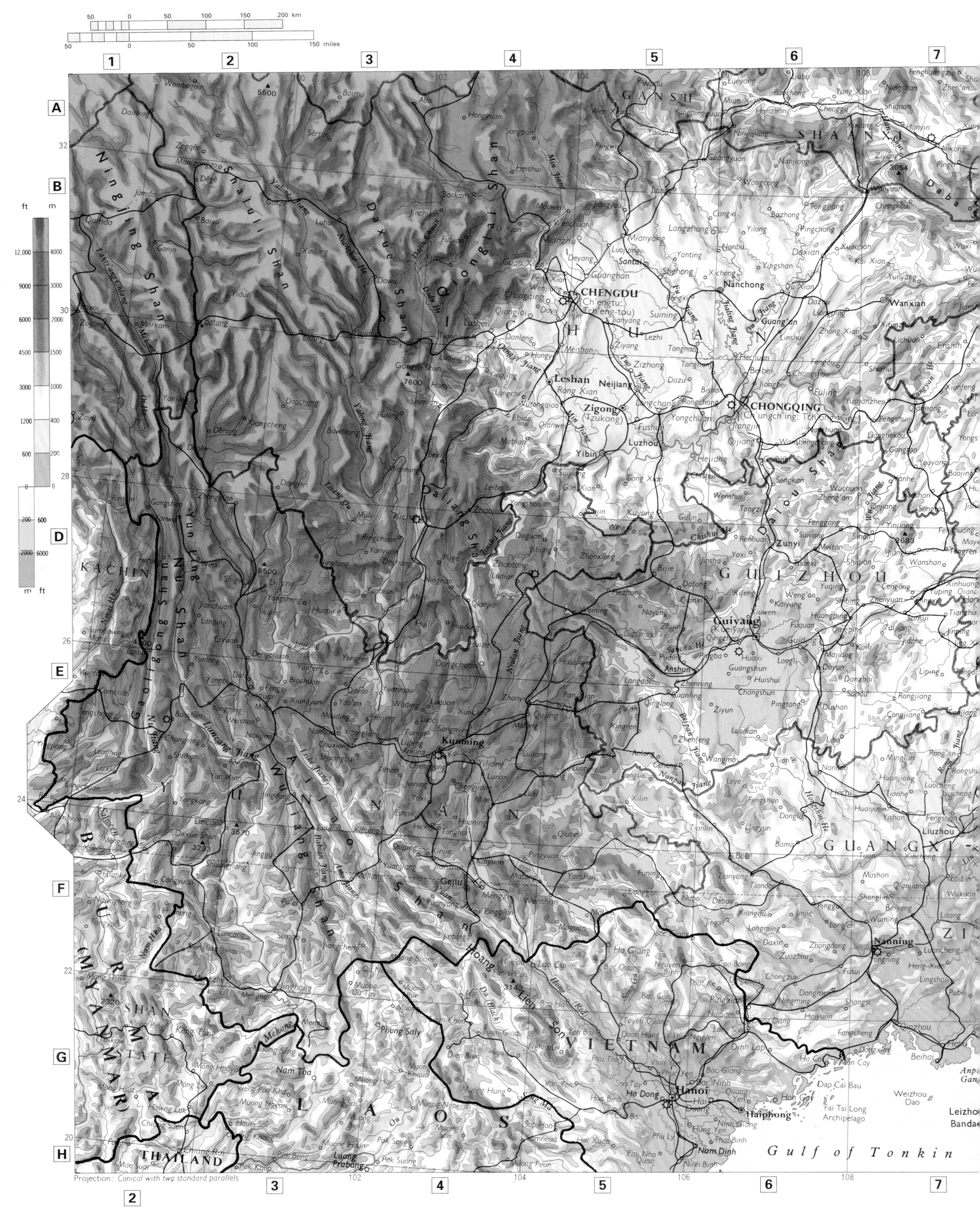

SOUTH CHINA SEA

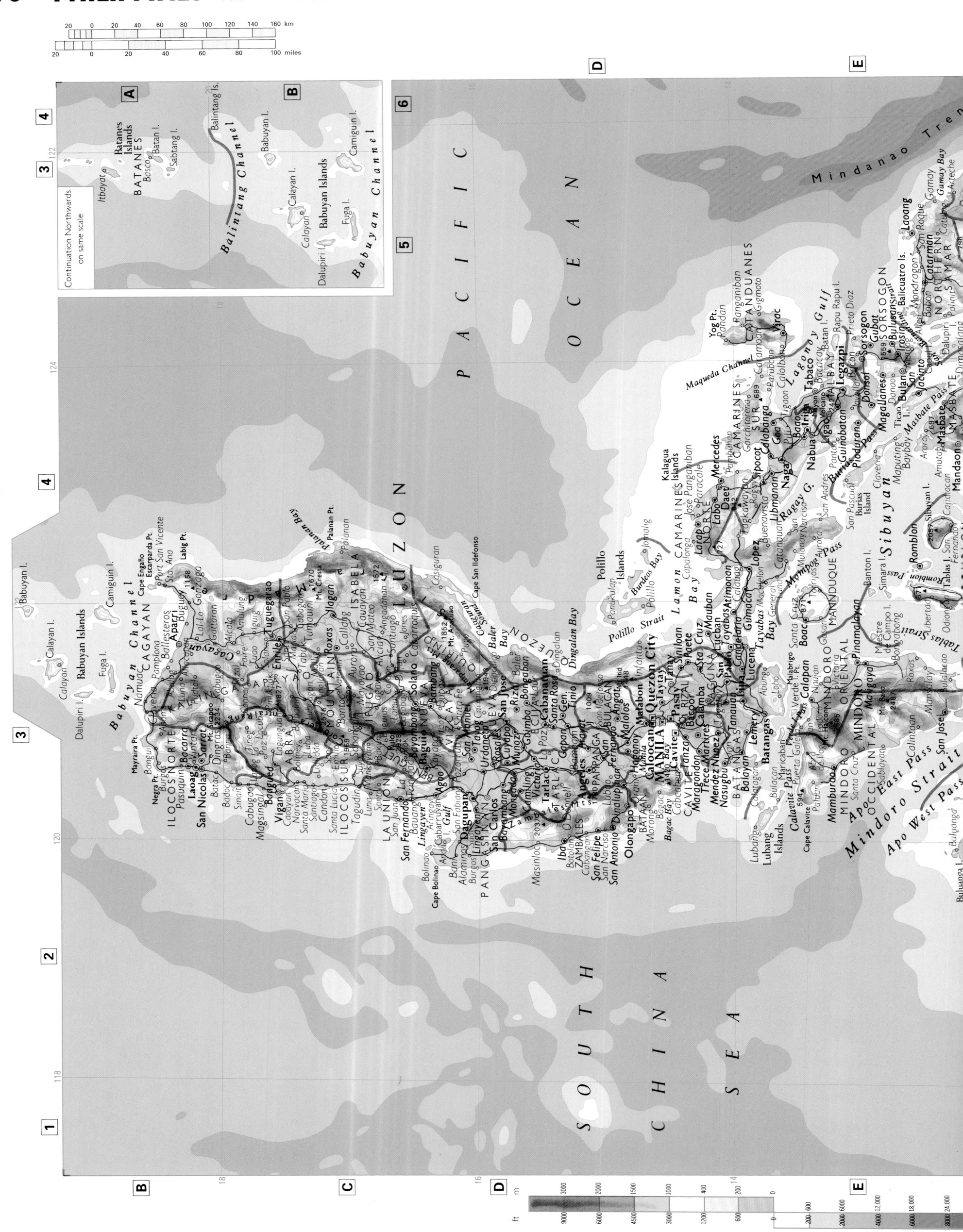

20 0 20 40 60 80 100 120 140 160 km
20 0 20 40 60 80 100 miles

A
B
C
D
E

1 2 3 4 5 6

Continuation Northwards
on same scale

Batanes
Islands
BATANES
Bosco
Batan I.
Sabtang I.
Itbayat
Balintang Is.

Balintang Channel

Babuyan I.
Babuyan I.
Calayan I.
Calayan
Babuyan Islands
Camiguin I.
Fuga I.
Dalupiri I.

Babuyan Channel

P A C I F I C   O C E A N

Mindanao Trench

S O U T H   C H I N A   S E A

L U Z O N

MANILA

Quezon City

m
3000
2000
1500
1000
400
200
0

ft
9000
6000
4500
3000
1200
600
0

-200
-2000
-4000
-6000
-8000

2000
4000
6000
8000

600
6000
12000
18000
24000

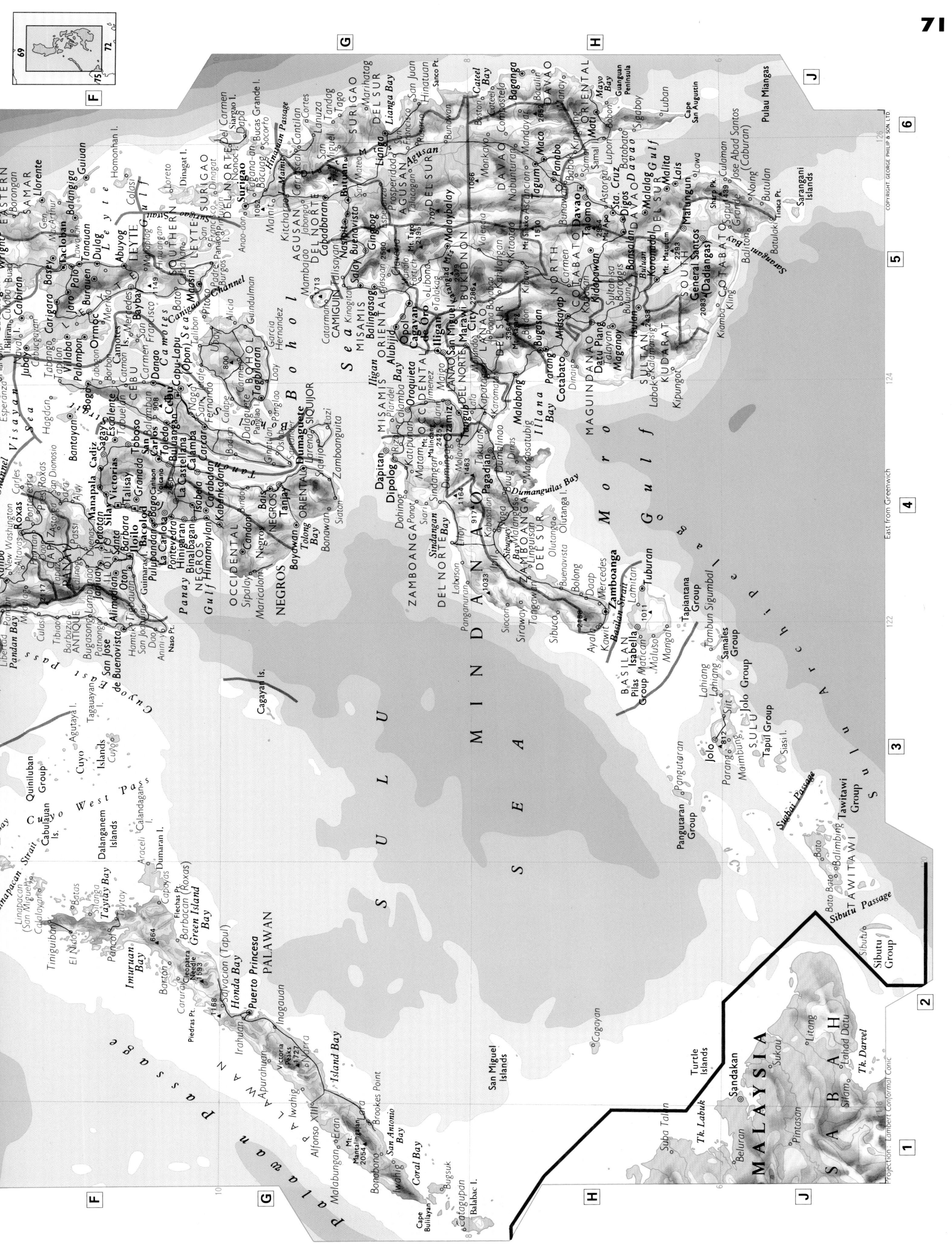

69 **72** **75**

F G H J

SAMAR
EASTERN
Llorente
Balangiga Guiuan
Homonhan I.
Borongan
Gen. MacArthur
Del Carmen
Socorro
Loreto
Dinagat I.
Dapa
Bucas Grande I.
Siargao I.
Gen. Cabunga-an
Hinatuan Passage
Cantilan
Cortes
Tandag
Sanco Pt.
San Juan
Hinatuan
Marihatag
Bunawan
Baganga
Cateel
Bay
Caraga
Baculin
Bay
DAVAO
ORIENTAL
Mayo
Manay
Guinan
Peninsula
Cape
San Agustin
Luban
Mati
Pulau Mangas

LEYTE
Tacloban
Palo
Burauen
Merida
Ormoc
Villaba
Palompon
Baybay
Maasin
SOUTHERN
LEYTE
Bato
Padre Burgos
Panaon I.
Liloan
Surigao
SURIGAO
DEL NORTE
Placer
Bacuag
Mainit
Gigaquit
Kitcharao
Tubay
Butuan
Cabadbaran
Buenavista
Nasipit
Prosperidad
AGUSAN
DEL SUR
Talacogon
Bunawan
Monkayo
Compostela
Mandaya
Nabunturan
Maco
Panabo
DAVAO
Samal I.
Davao
Sta. Cruz
Digos
Malita
Lais

J

SURIGAO
DEL SUR
Lianga Bay
Lanuza
Tago

VISAYAN SEA

Bantayan
CEBU
Bogo
Sogod
Tabuelan
Tuburan
Balamban
Toledo
Cebu
Lapu-Lapu
(Opon)
Mandaue
Carcar
Argao
Dalaguete
Bohol
Tagbilaran
Jagna
Anda

Camotes
Is.
Camotes
Sea

Bohol Sea

NEGROS
ORIENTAL
Dumaguete
SIQUIJOR
Larena
Zamboanguita

Tañon
Channel

CEBU

Mindanao Sea

Dipolog
Dapitan
Ozamiz
MISAMIS
OCCIDENTAL
Oroquieta
Jimenez
Tangub
Pagadian
ZAMBOANGA
DEL SUR

Iligan Bay
Cagayan
de Oro
MISAMIS
ORIENTAL
Alubijid
Balingasag
Balingoan
CAMIGUIN

Marawi
LANAO
DEL SUR
Lanao L.
Lala
LANAO
DEL NORTE
Kolambugan
Kapatagan
Malabang
Parang
Cotabato
Datu Piang
Maganoy
MAGUINDANAO
SULTAN
KUDARAT
Tacurong
Isulan
Kiamba
Maitum
Maasim
SOUTH
COTABATO
General Santos
Koronadal
NORTH
COTABATO
Kidapawan
Kabacan
BUKIDNON
Malaybalay
Valencia

MINDANAO

Iligan
Bay

Illana
Bay

Moro Gulf

ZAMBOANGA
DEL NORTE

ZAMBOANGA
DEL SUR
Tuburan
Zamboanga
Isabela
BASILAN
Pilas Group

Davao
Gulf

Sarangani
Bay
Sarangani
Islands

MALAYSIA
SABAH
Sandakan
Lahad Datu
Tk. Darvel
Turtle
Islands
Sibutu
Group
Sibutu Passage
TAWITAWI
Tawitawi
Group
(Dadiangas)
Sulu
Archipelago

SULU
SEA

SULU
Jolo Group
Tapul Group
Samales
Group
Jolo
Siasi

PALAWAN
Puerto Princesa
Honda Bay
Brooke's Point
Balabac I.
Cape
Buliluyan

Cagayan
Is.

Cuyo
Islands
Cuyo
Group
Quiniluban
Group
Agutaya I.

Palawan Passage

San Miguel
Islands

MOLUCCA SEA

Projection: Lambert Conformal Conic

East from Greenwich

116 118 120 122 124 126

F G H J

1 2 3 4 5 6

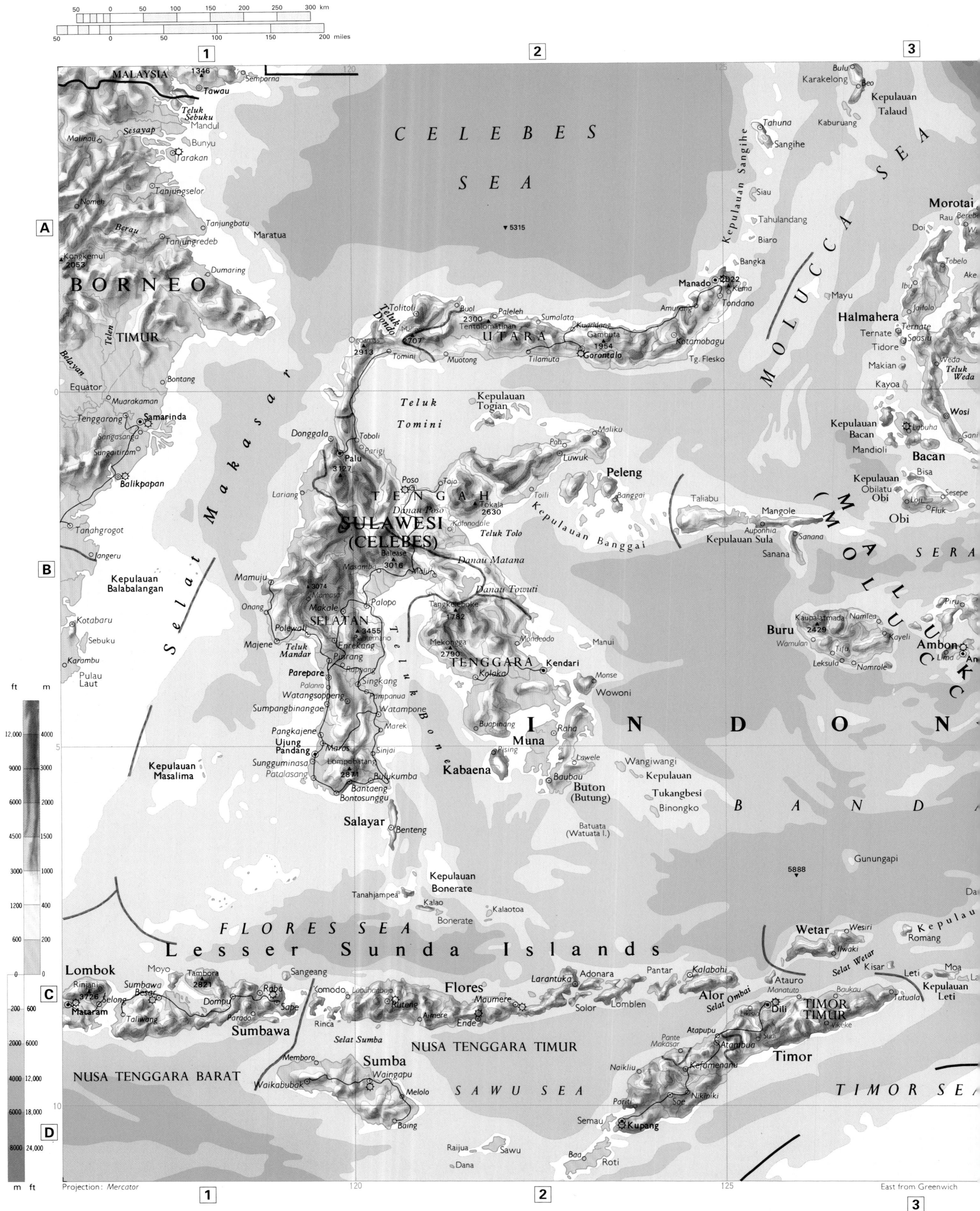

P A C I F I C

O C E A N

Tobi
(Belau)
Helen
Atoll

Kepulauan
Asia

Kepulauan
Mapia

Kepulauan
Ayu

Equator

4625

Gebe
Kabarai
Waibeem
Kwoka
3000
Kaironi
Warsa
Supiori
Kepulauan
Kumamba

Waigeo
Wakre
Jazirah Doberai
(Vogelkop)
Manokwari
Korim
Number
Sarmi
Ansudu

Selat Dampier
Saonek
Borong
Klamono
Biak
Bosnik
Jayapura

Batanta
Salawati
Wersar
3100
Ransiki
Wariap
Numfoor
Num
Selat Yapen
Tg. D'Urville
Mataboor
Genyem

Sailolof
Seget
Mogoi
Wasian
Yapen
Serui
Bonoi
Barapasi
Saberania
Krau
Sentani

Adua
Lermalu
Bira
Bintuni
Nuboai
Pegunungan Van Rees
Tariku
Taritatu

Misool
Saga
Babo
Wendesi
Wasior
Nabire
Wamena
Waru
Haya
3019
Susunu
Kwatisore
IRIAN JAYA
Puncak
Trikora
4750
Mandala
4702
Geser
Weri
Wenut
Ibonma
Kaimana
Enarotali
Waghete
Puncak
Jaya
5029
Pegunungan
Maoke

ram)
Kepulauan
Gorong
Karufa
Teluk
Kamrau
Pegunungan Sudirman
Pegunungan Jayawijaya
Wanapiri
Uta

Banda
Bandanaira
Kepulauan
Watubela
Manggawitu
Adi
Yapero
PAPUA NEW GUINEA

S I A
Kepulauan
Kai
Har
Teluk Flamingo
Agats
Pulau
Mindiptana

7440
Tual
Kai Besar
Gumzai
Kola
Dobo
Wokam
Pirimapun
Tanahmerah
Asike

Daya
Serua
Kai
Kecil
Bandar
Elat
Sewer
Kepulauan
Aru
Kobroor
Kepi

Nila
Wangal
Maikoor
Rebi
Koba
Kassue
Bade
Muting

Teun
Trangan
Tafermaar
Gomogomo
Okaba

Molu
Tg. Ngabordamlu
Pulau
Yos Sudarso
Kimaän
Merauke

Larat
Wuliaru
Selu
Alusi
Babar
Saumlaki
Yamdena
Selaru
Adaut
Eliase
Kepulauan Tanimbar
Tg. Vals
Pulau
Komoran

A R A F U R A   S E A

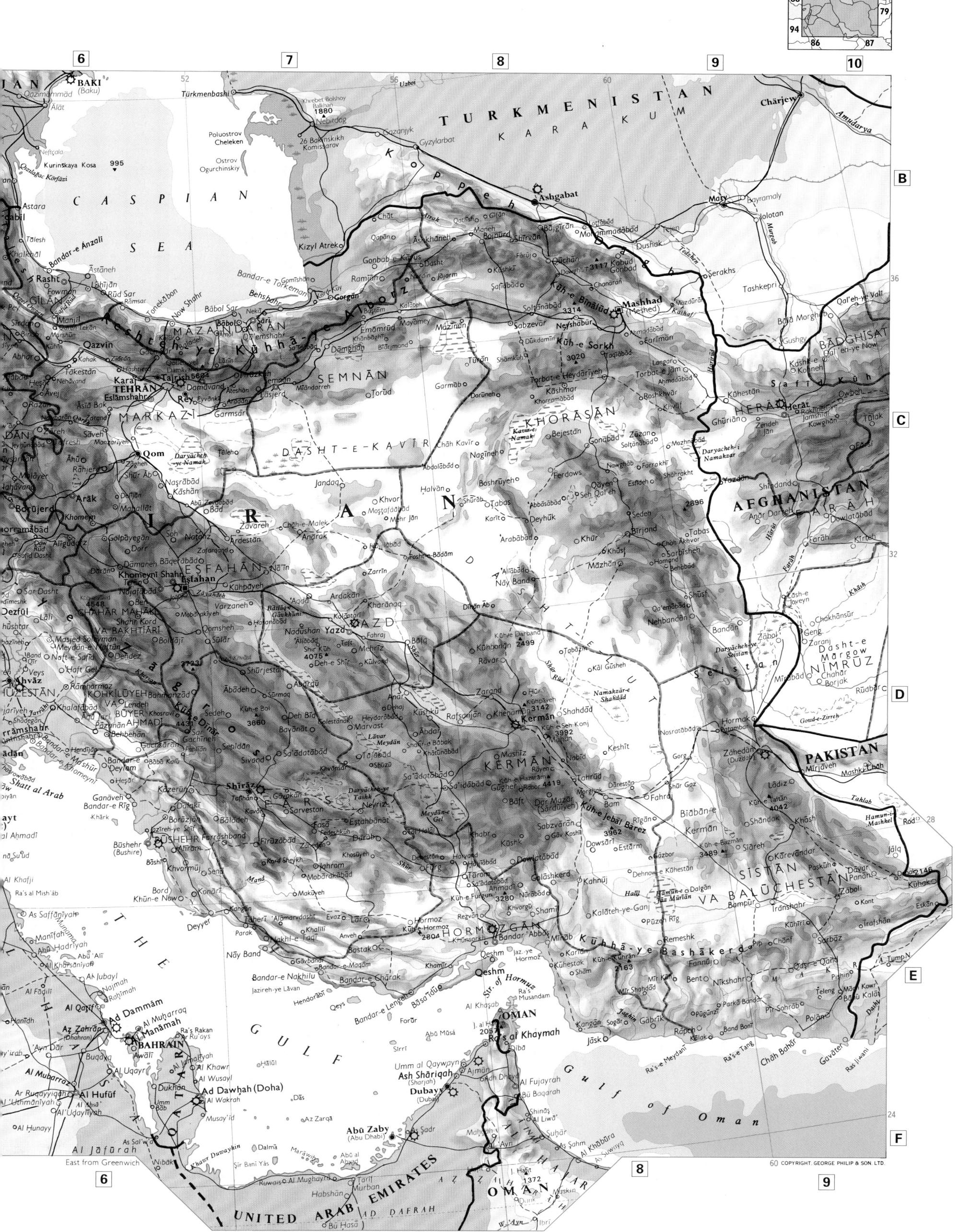

CASPIAN SEA

TURKMENISTAN

KARA KUM

IRAN

AFGHANISTAN

PAKISTAN

THE GULF

Gulf of Oman

UNITED ARAB EMIRATES

OMAN

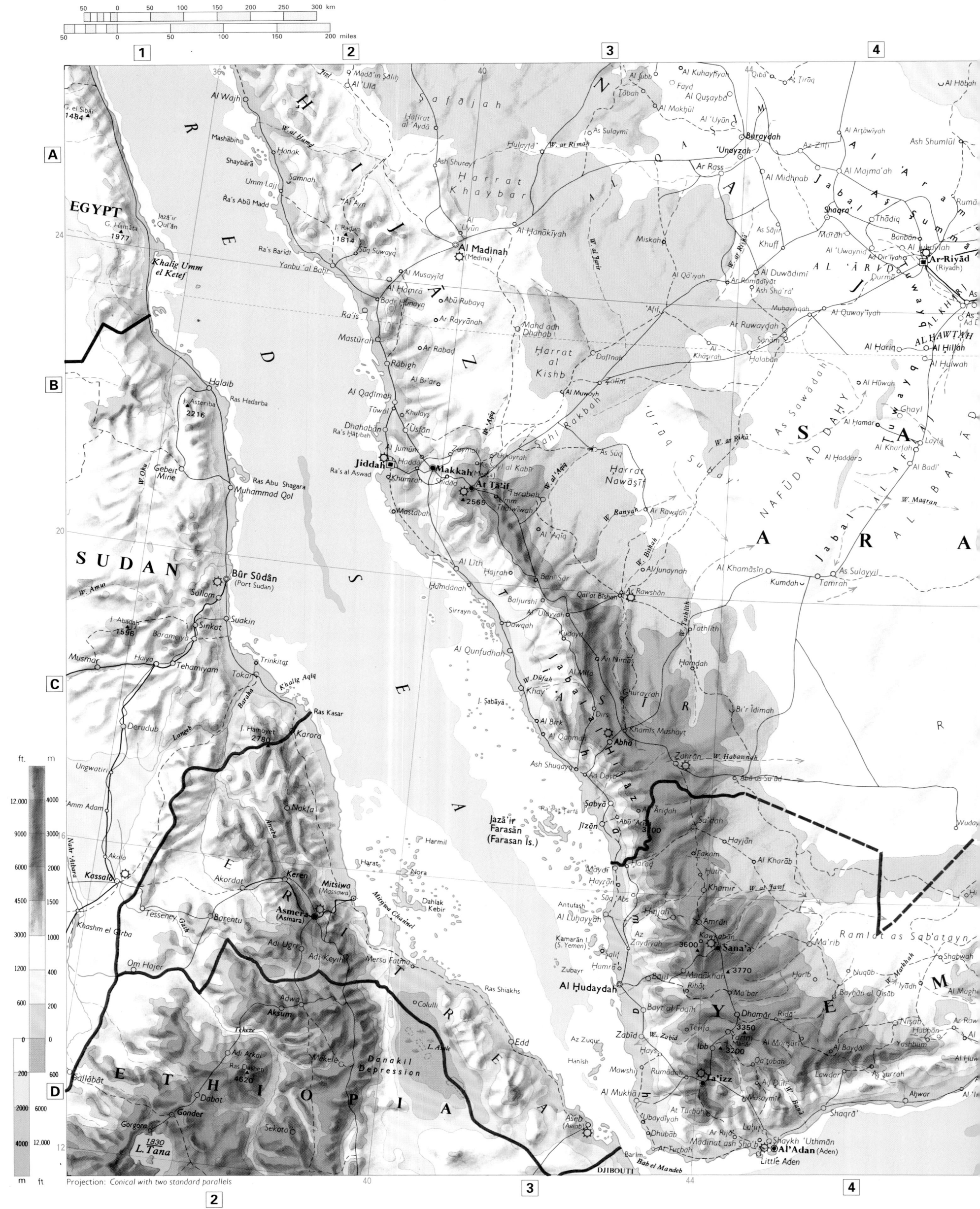

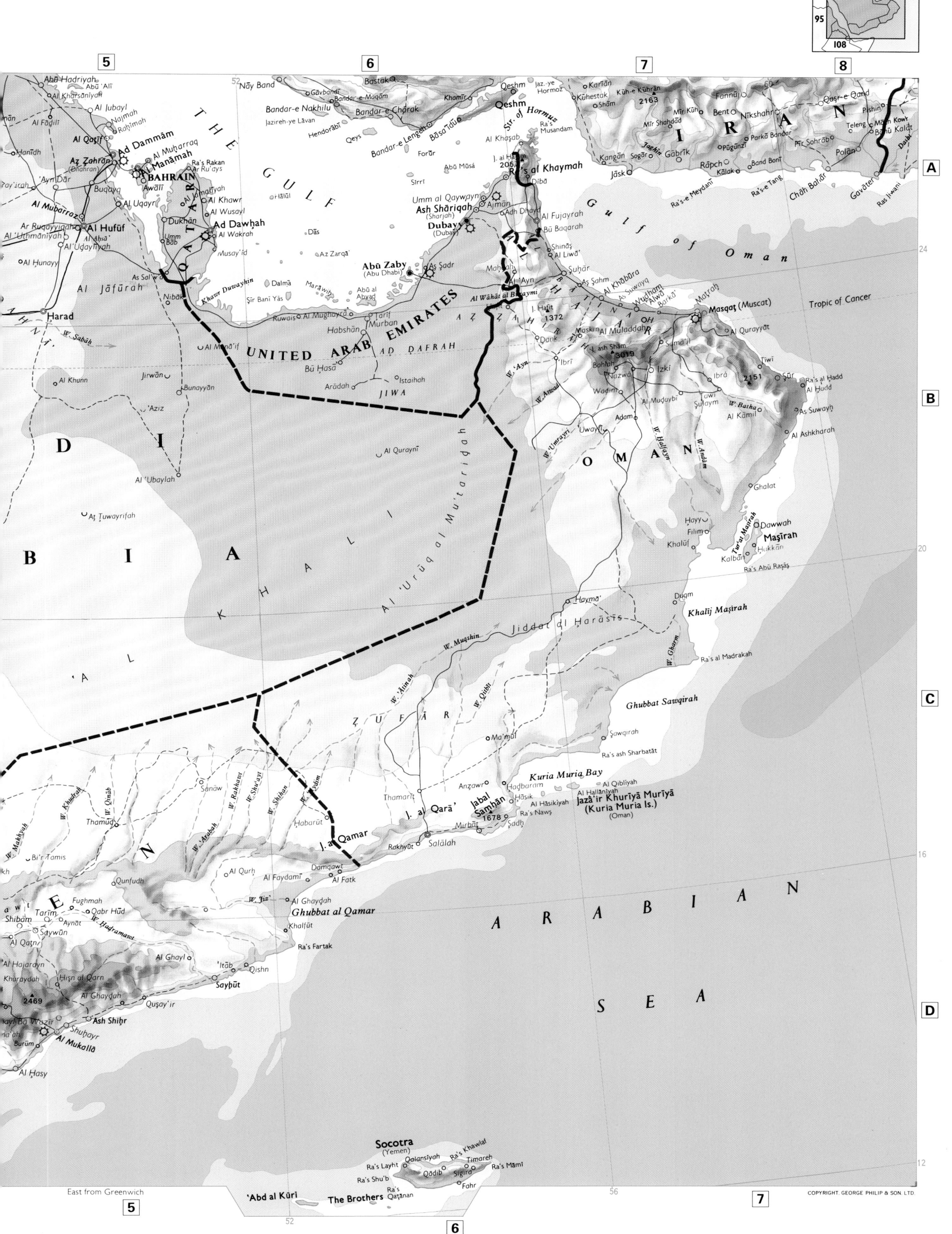

5   6   7   8

Abū Hadriyah
Abū 'Alī
Al Kharsāniyah
Al Jubayl
Najmah
Al Faqili
Raḥīmah
Al Qaṭīf
Ad Dammām
Az Zahrān (Dhahran)
Al Muḥarraq
Al Manāmah
BAHRAIN
Ra's Rakan
Ar Ru'ays
'Ayn Dār
Buqayq
'Ayrah
Al Mubarraz
Awālī
Al Ḥufūf
Al 'Uqayr
Ar Ruqayyiqah
Umm Bāb
Dukhān
Al 'Uthmāniyah
Al 'Ugayliyah
Al Ḥunayy

Nāy Band
Bastak
Gāvbandī
Bandar-e Maqām
Bandar-e Nakhilu
Jazireh-ye Lāvan
Hendorābī
Khamīr
Qeys
Bandar-e Lengeh
Bāsa'īdū
Qeshm
Jaz-ye Hormoz
Kārīān
Kūhestak
Shām
2163
Mīr Kūh
Fannūj
Bent
Nīkshahr
Forūr
Abū Mūsā
Al Khaṣab
Ra's Musandam
Siri
205?
Ra's al Khaymah
Dibā
J. al Ḥarīm
Jāsk
Kangān
Sogar
Gābrīk
Rāpch
Band Bont
Pūgūnzī
Juġīn
Mīr Shahdād
Qasr-e Qand
Pishīn
Teleng
Māsh Kowr
Pīr Sohrāb
Polān
Gavāter
Ras Jīwani
Bāh Kalāt
Dashṭ

THE GULF

IRAN

A

Umm al Qaywayn
Ash Shāriqah (Sharjah)
Ajmān
Adh Dhayd
Al Fujayrah
Dubayy (Dubai)
Bū Baqarah
Shināṣ
Al Liwā'
Ṣuḥār
Al Khābūra
Dās
Az Zarqā'
As Ṣadr
Mahḍah
Al 'Ayn
Aş Şaḥm
Al Khābūra
Aş Şuwayq
Wudham
Khaṣab

Abū Zaby (Abu Dhabi)

Musay'īd
Khawr Duwayhin
Dalmā
Marāwiḥ
Şīr Banī Yās
Abū al Abyad
As Sal'wā
Nibāk
Ruwais
Al Mughayrá
Tarif
Murbān
Habshān
UNITED ARAB EMIRATES
Al Minā'if
Bū Ḥasā
Arādah
Istaihah
JIWA
Al Wāhāt al Buraymi
J. Ḥafīt 1372
'Ibrī
Dank
Maskin
Al Muladdah
W. 'Ayn
J. ash Shām
3019
Baḥlah
Nazwá
Izkī
Ibrā
2151
Şūr
Ra's al Ḥadd
Al Ḥudd
As Suwayḥ
Al Ashkharah

Masqat (Muscat)
Tropic of Cancer
Al Quṟayyāt
Tīwī
W. Baṭha

Gulf of Oman

24

AD DAFRAH

'AZ ZĀH

AL BATINA

HAJAR

W. 'Ayn

W. Asʻard

Uwayl
Uwayfī
Adam
Al Muḍaybī
Ţuwī
Şulaym
W. Ḥalfayn
Al Kāmil
Ghalat

OMAN

W. Aridah

B

Al Khunn
Jirwān
Bunayyān
'Azīz
Al Qurayn
Al Quraynī

D

I

Aţ Ţuwayrifah

Al 'Ubaylah

Haylah
Filim
Khalūf
Ḥayy
Ţuwʻit Maṣīrah
Dawwah
Maṣīrah
Ḥukkān
Kalbān
Ra's Abū Raṣāṣ

20

B

I

A

KHALI

Al 'Urūq al Muʻtariḍah

Haymā'
Duqm

Khalij Maṣīrah

'A

L

Jiddat al Ḥarāsīs

Ra's al Madrakah

W. Muqshin

W. Aʻinah
W. Ghārm

Ghubbat Sawqirah

C

ZUFAR

W. Quitbī
Ma'mūl
Şawqirah
Ra's ash Sharbatāt

W. 'Amūt

Sānaw
W. Qhāb
W. Rakhaut
Thamūd
W. Shu'ayt
 Thamarīt
Anzawr
Ḥaqbaram
Al Qiblīyah
Al Ḥasikīyah
Al Qibliyah

Kuria Muria Bay

Al Ḥallānīyah

K. Khudrah
W. Arabah
Jabal Qarā'
Jabal Samḥān 1678
Murbāṭ
Şadḥ
Ra's Nawṣ

Jazā'ir Khurīyā Murīyā (Kuria Muria Is.) (Oman)

16

N

Bi'r Tamis
Ḥabarūt
Fūdmī
J. al Qamar
Rakhyūt
Salālah

Thamūd
Mukhby
Damqawt
Al Fatk
Al Qurh
Al Faydamī
W. Jiz

Ghubbat al Qamar

E

Fughmah
Tarīm
Aynāt
Sayḥūt
Al Ghaydah
Khalfūt
Ra's Fartak

W. Ḥadramawt
Al Ghayl
'Itāb
Qishn

2469
Al Hajaryn
Khuraydah
Ḥiṣn al Qarn
Al Ghaydah
Quşay'ir
Shibam
Şaywūn
Qaṭn
Ra's Shu'b

Ash Shiḥr
Shu'bayr
Al Mukallā
Burūm

Al Ḥasy

ARABIAN

SEA

D

Socotra (Yemen)
Qalansīyah
Ra's Khawlaf
Ra's Layht
Timareh
Qāḍib
Sigiro
Ra's Māmī
Fahr
Ra's Shu'b

East from Greenwich
'Abd al Kūri
The Brothers
Ra's Qaṭanān

52   56

5   6   7

Division between Greeks and Turks
in Cyprus; Turks to the North.

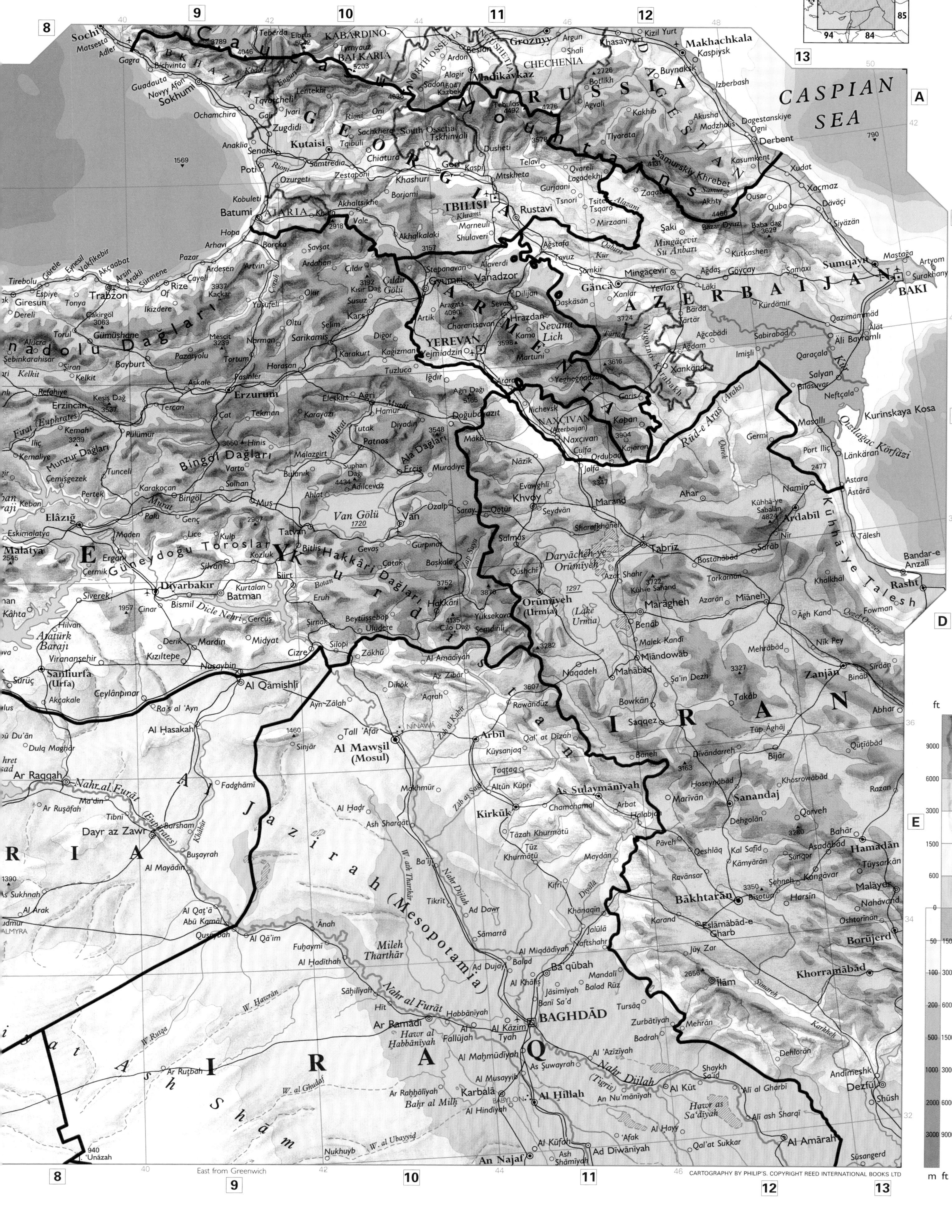

51 53
44
85
94 84
13

CASPIAN SEA

RUSSIA

Sochi
Matsesta
Adler
Gagra
Bichvinta
Guadauta
Novvy Afon
Sokhum
Ochamchira
Anaklia
Senaki
Poti
Kobuleti
Batumi
AJARIA
Khulo
Hopa
Arhavi
Borçka
Şavşat
Pazar
Ardeşen
Artvin
Ardahan
Çıldır

Teberda
Elbrus
5642
3789
Khaidi
4046
5203
Tyrnyauz
KABARDINO-BALKARIA
Lentekhi
Oni
Rioni
Jvari
Sachkhere
Zugdidi
Tqvarcheli
Gali
Tqibuli
South Ossetia
Tskhinvali
Kutaisi
Chiatura
Khashuri
Samtredia
Zestaponi
Ozurgeti
Rioni
Akhaltsikhe
Borjomi
Vale
2918
Akhalkalaki
Kars
3157
Shulaveri

NORTH OSSETIA
Alagir
Sadon
6047
Kazbek
4628
Vladikavkaz
Dusheti
Telavi
Mtskheta
Kaspi
Gori
TBILISI
Khrami
Marneuli
Rustavi
Mirzaani

Argun
GROZNYY
Shali
CHECHENIA
2726
Botlikh
4276
3578
Tyarata
Agvali
Kakhib
Akusha
Madzholis
Ogni

Khasavyurt
Kizil Yurt
Buynaksk
Izberbash
Kasumkent
Samurskiy Khrebet
4431
Samur
Akhty
4466
Zaqatala
Şaki

Makhachkala
Kaspiysk
Dagestanskiye Ogni
Derbent
790
Xudat
Xaçmaz
Qusar
Quba
Däväçi
Siyäzän

DAGESTAN

GEORGIA

Stepanavan
3192
Çıldır Gölü
Kısır Dağ
Susuz
Digor
Artik
Gyumri
Aragats
4090
Vanadzor
Dilijan
Sevan
Hrazdan
Charantsavan
Kamo
Sevana Lich
3598
YEREVAN
Yejmiadzin
Martuni
Yeghegnadzor

Agstafa
Tovuz
Şämkir
Ganca
Daşkäsän
Xanlar
3724
Yevlax
Mingäçevir
Su Anbarı
Ağdaş
Göyçay
Bärdä
Ağcäbädi
Ağdam
Xankändi
3616
Nagorno-Karabakh
Garis

Sumqayıt
Samaxı
BAKI
Surakhany
Artyom
Maştağa
Kürdämir
Qazımämmäd
Sabirabad
Äli Bayramlı
Salyan
Älät
Neftçala
Qaraçala
Imişli
Biläsuvar

AZERBAIJAN

ARMENIA

Trabzon
Akçaabat
Of
Sürmene
Rize
Çayeli
Çakırgöl
3063
İkizdere
Gümüşhane
Torul
3239
Bayburt
Mescit
Narman
Oltu
Şenkaya
Olur
Yusufeli
Tortum
Horasan
İspir
Şiran
Kelkit
Keşiş Dağ
3537
Erzincan
Tercan
Aşkale
Pasinler
Eleşkirt
Erzurum
Çat
Tekman
Karayazı
Ağrı
Tutak
Patnos
Doğubayazıt
Ağrı Dağı
5165
Diyadin
Ararat

Dağları
nadolu
Sebinkarahisar
Şebinkarahisar
Kelkit
Kemah
3650
Munzur Dağları
Kemaliye
Çemişgezek
Pülümür
Tunceli
Varto
Solhan
Bingöl Dağları
Karakoçan
Bingöl
Genç
Muş
2967
Malazgirt
Bulanık
Suphan Dağı
4434
Ahlat
Adilcevaz
Erciş
Muradiye
Van Gölü
1720
Van
Özalp
Saray
Qotür
Khoy
Evoghlu
3347
Nazik

Naxçıvan (Azerbaijan)
Nichevsk
Ordubad
Culfa
Jolfa
Marand
Ahar
Namin
2477
Kühhä-ye Sabalan
4821
Ardabil
Sarab
Kühhä-ye Talesh
Astara
Äştärä
Germi
Kuriņskaya Kosa
Qızılağac Körfäzi
Länkäran
Port İlic
Masallı

Rasht
Bandar-e Anzäli

IRAN

Elâzığ
Eskimalatya
Malatya
2545
Ergani
Cermik
Maden
Lice
Siverek
Diyarbakır
Kulp
Batman
Silvan
Kurtalan
Bismil
Dicle Nehri
Gerçüş
Mardin
Midyat
Derik
Kızıltepe
Nusaybin
Cizre
Silopi
Zakhu
Al-Amādiyah
Dihōk
Aqrah
Al Qāmishlī
Ayn Zālah

Güneydoğu Toroslar
Bitlis
Kozluk
Hakkâri Dağları
Çatak
Başkale
Gevaş
Gürpınar
Hakkâri
Yüksekova
Şemdinli
Cilo Dağı
4135
Rawāndūz
Qūshchī
3752
3810
Salmas
Şarafkhāneh
Tabrīz
Bostānābād
Azar Shahr
Küh-e Sahand
3722
Marāgheh
Azarān
Mīāneh
Zanjān
Bināb
Abhar

Daryācheh-ye Orūmīyeh
(Lake Urmia)
1297
Orūmīyeh
(Urmia)
3282
Naqadeh
Mahābād
Miāndowāb
3327
Bowkān
Sardaşt
Saqqez
Bijār
Takāb
Tüp Āghāj
Qūtīābād
Sırdān

Eruh
Beytüşşebap
Uludere
Şırnak
Az Zibār
An Najaf

Şanlıurfa (Urfa)
Akçakale
Ceylânpınar
Ra's al 'Ayn
Al Hasakah
1460
Tall 'Afar
Sinjār
Al Mawşil (Mosul)
NINAWÁ
Küysanjaq
Arbil
Qal'at Dizah
Taqtaq
Altūn Küpri
Kirkūk
Chamchamal
As Sulaymānīyah
Halabjah
3163
Hoseynābād
Dīvāndarreh
Mariwān
Sanandaj
Qorveh
Dehgolān
Sa'in Dezh
Bahār
3280
Asadābād
Hamadān
Tüysarkän
Malāyer
Nahāvand

Ar Raqqah
Nahr al Furāt
Ma'din
Ar Ruşāfah
Fadghāmī
Dulq Maghār
Ṣabkhat
Tibni
Dayr az Zawr
Buşayrah
Al Mayādīn
Şahneh
Kāmyārān
3350
Bisotūn
Bākhtarān
Harsin
Borūjerd
Khorramābād

As Sukhnah
Al Arak
Al Qaţ'a
Abū Kamāl
Qusaybah
Al Qā'im
Fuḥaymī
Mileh Tharthār
Tikrīt
Ad Dawr
Sāmarrā'
Kiffrī
Diyālá
Khānaqīn
Jalūlā'
Naftshahr
Qaşr-e Shīrīn
Karand
Islāmābād-e Gharb
Bisotūn
Jūy Zar
Sümäreh
Īlām
Dehlorān
Andīmeshk
Dezfūl
Shūsh

IRAQ

Al Jazīrah (Mesopotamia)

Ash Shām
W. al Tharthār
Al Hadīthah
Hīt
Habbānīyah
Hawr al Habbānīyah
Al Ramādī
Fallūjah
Al Kāzim
BAGHDĀD
Al Mahmūdīyah
As Suwayrah
Al Aẓīẓīyah
Jasīmīyah
Balad Rūz
Mandalī
Banī Sa'd
Tursāq
Mehrān
2656
Badrah
Zurbātīyah
Shaykh Sa'd
'Alī al Gharbī
'Alī ash Sharqī
Al Amārah
Süsangerd

Ar Ruţbah
W. Rutqa
W. Hawrān
Sāhilīyah
Nukhayb
W. al Ghudaf
W. al Ubayyid
Ar Rahhālīyah
Karbalā'
BABYLON
Al Hillah
An Nu'mānīyah
Al Kifl
Al Hindīyah
Ad Dīwānīyah
Ash Shāmīyah
Al Kūfah
An Najaf
Bahr al Milh
Hawr as Sa'dīyah
Qal'at Sukkar

'Ünäzah
940

East from Greenwich

SYRIA

ft m
9000 3000
6000 2000
3000 1000
1500 500
600 200
0 0
50 150
100 300
200 600
500 1500
1000 3000
2000 6000
3000 9000
m ft

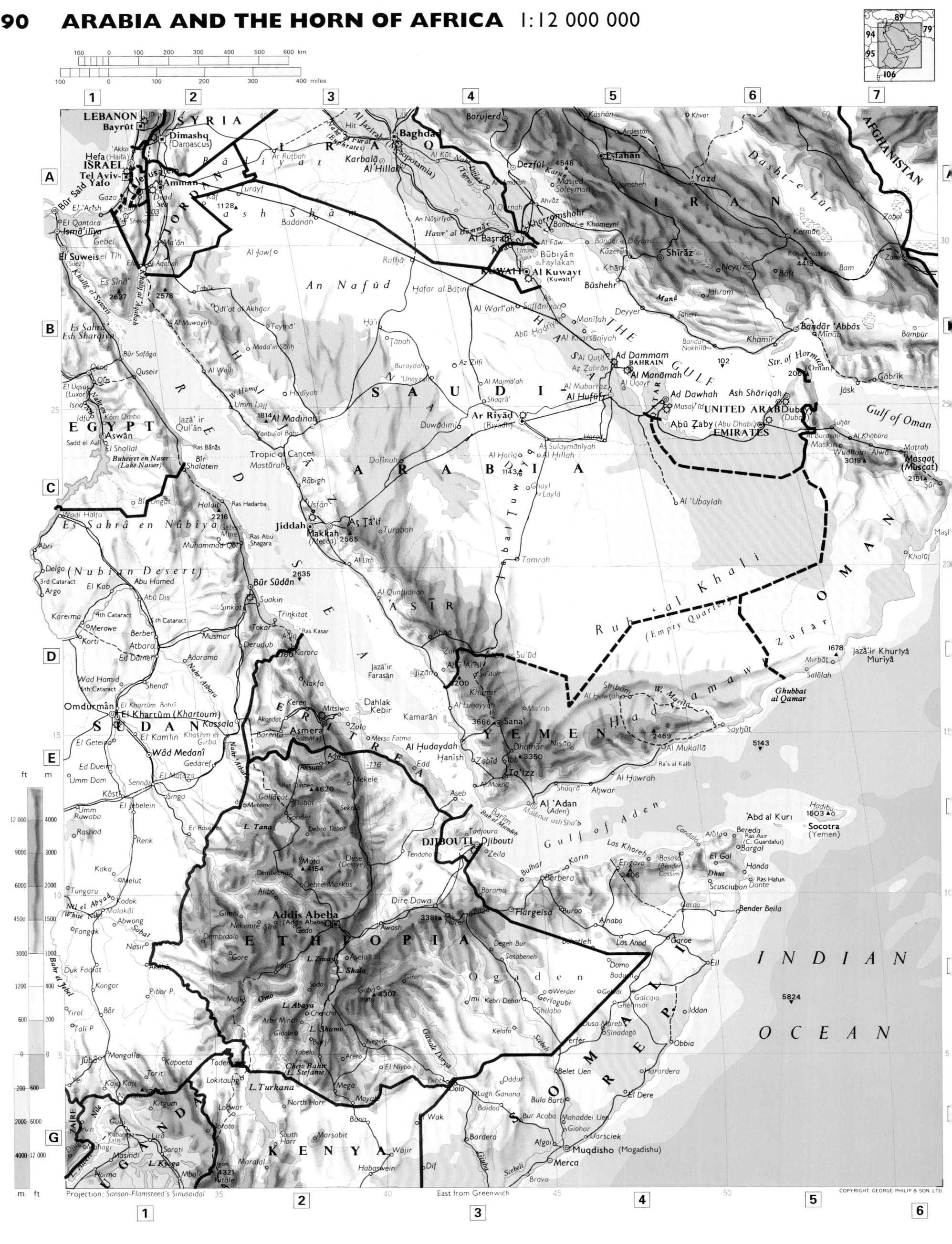

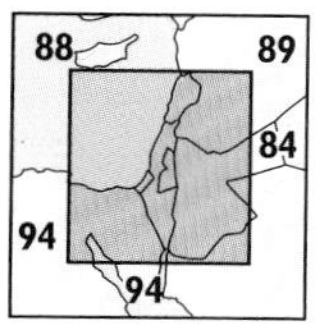

88 89
84
94
94

10 0 10 20 30 40 50 60 70 80 100 km
10 0 10 20 30 40 50 60 miles

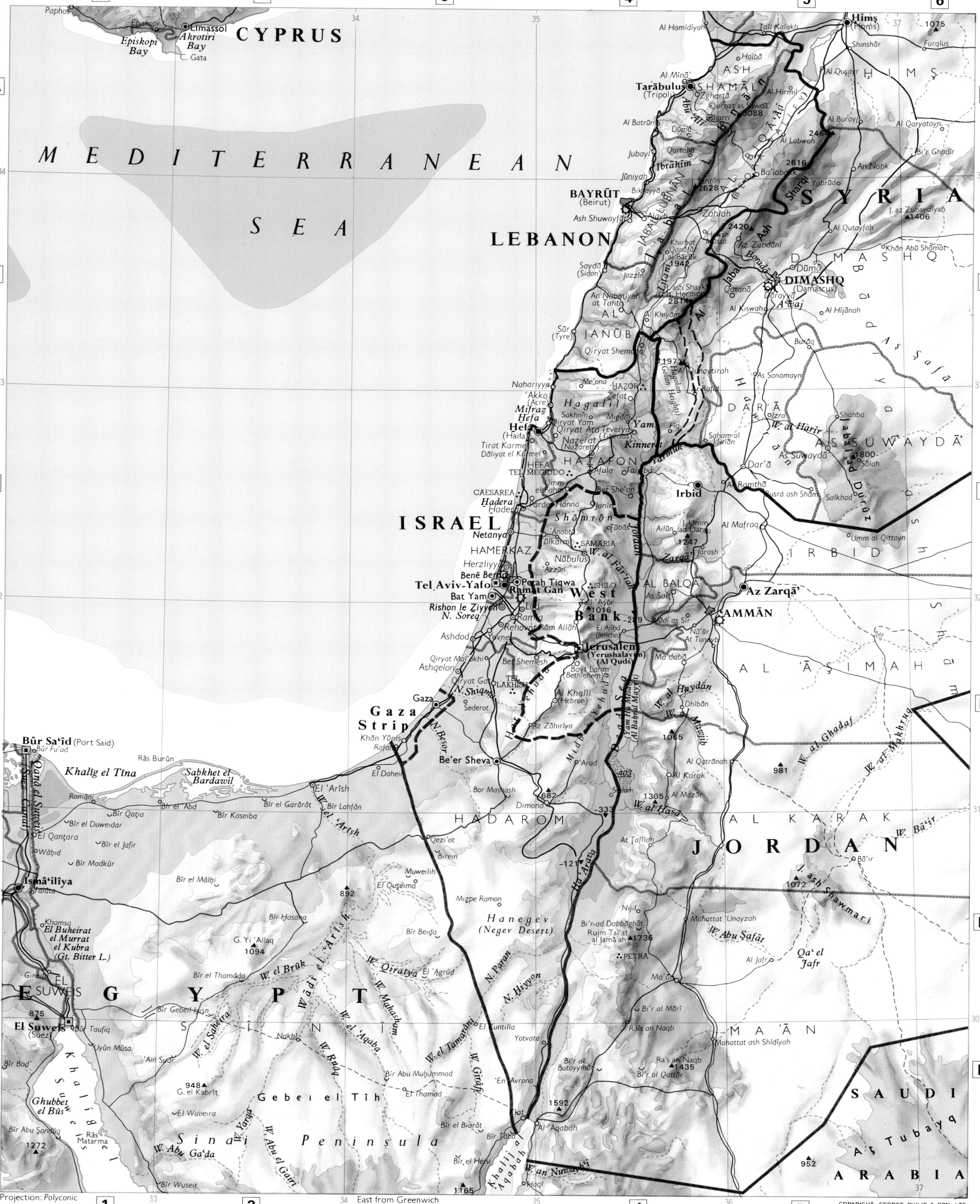

CYPRUS

Paphos
Episkopi
Episkopi Bay
Limassol
Akrotiri Bay
C. Gata

M E D I T E R R A N E A N

S E A

Al Hamidiyah
Tall Kalakh
Hims (Homs)
Shinshar
Furqlus
1075

ASH SHAMAL
Al Mina'
Tarabulus (Tripoli)
Zgharta
Al Qusayr
Al Qaryatayn
Halba
Al Hirmil
Al Batrun
Duma
Qurbat as Sawda'
3088
Al Burayj
Jubayl
Qartaba
2616
Ba'labakk
An Nabk
Ibrahim
2628
2465
Bi'r Ghadir

BAYRUT (Beirut)
Juniyah
Bikfayya
Zahlah
2420
Al Qutaylah
Ash Shuwayfat
Khirbat Qanafar
1947
Az Zabdani
DIMASHQ (Damascus)
Qatana
A'zaz
Al Kiswah
Al Hijanah
An Nabatiyah at Tahta
Mt Hermon 2814
Al Khiyam
J. az Zubaydiyah 1406

SYRIA

LEBANON

AL JANUB
Sur (Tyre)
Qiryat Shemona
1197
Al Qunaytirah
As Sanamayn
Buraq
DIMASHQ

Nahariyya
Me'ona
HAZOR
Golan Heights
Arida
W. al Harir
DAR'A
Jabal ash Shahba
'Akko (Acre)
Hagalil
Sefat
Midal
Fiq
Suham al Jawlan
AS SUWAYDA'
Mifraz Hefa
Sakhnin
Yam
Dar'a
As Suwayda'
1800
Hefa (Haifa)
Qiryat Yam
Qiryat Ata Teverya (Tiberias)
Kinneret
Yarmuk
Salah
Tirat Karmel
Nazerat (Nazareth)
HEFA
Daliyat el Karmel
HAZAFON
Afula
Tayba
Dar'a
Salkhad
TEL MEGIDDO
Bet She'an
Irbid
Umm al Qittayn
CAESAREA
el Fanna
Janin
Ajlun
'ad Dara
Al Mafraq
Hadera
Shomron
'Ubas
1247
Jarash
IRBID

ISRAEL

Netanya
Tulkarm
SAMARIA
W. al Fari'a
Zarqa
Az Zarqa'
HAMERKAZ
Anabta
Nablus
Herzliyya
'Azzun
AL BALQA
Bene Beraq
AMMAN
Tel Aviv-Yafo
Petah Tiqwa
SHILO
As Salt
Ramat Gan
West
Al Ashur
Bat Yam
1016
Wadi as Sir
Rishon le Ziyyon
Bank
Ram
219
Na'ur
N. Soreq
Rehovot
Ramallah
Jericho
Lod
AL 'ASIMAH
Ashdod
Yavne
Ma'daba
Qiryat Mal'akhi
Jerusalem (Yerushalayim) (Al Quds)
Bet Shemesh
Bayt Lahm (Bethlehem)
Ashqelon
TEL LAKHISH
Qiryat Gat
Al Khalil (Hebron)
Dhiban
W. al Mujib
Gaza
N. Shiqma
Sederot
Paz Zahiriya
Dimona
1065
W. al Ghadaf
Gaza Strip
Khan Yunis
Al Karak
981
Rafah
N. Besor
Be'er Sheva
Arad
1305
Al Mazar
W. al Hasa
Bur Sa'id (Port Said)
682
W. al Makhriq
Qana el Suways
333
AL KARAK
Khalig el Tina
Ras Burun
El Daheir
Bor Mashash
121
Sabkhet el Bardawil
El 'Arish
HADAROM
At Taffilah
Romani
Bir el Abd
Bir el Gararat
Bir Qatia
Bir el Duweidar
Bir Kaseiba
Bir el Lahfan
Qezi'ot
Ha 'Arava
Ba'ir
El Qantara
Wahid
Bir el Jafir
892
Birein
JORDAN
W. Ba'ir
Ismâ'iliya
Bir Madkur
Muweilih
El Quseima
Nijil
J. ash Shawmari
1072
El Suweis
Khamsa
El Buheirat el Murrat el Kubra (Gt. Bitter L.)
1094
Bir Hasana
Mizpe Ramon
Bi'r ad Dabbaghat
Mahattat 'Unayzah
Gineifa
Bir Beida
Hanegev (Negev Desert)
Ruim Tal'at al Jama'ah
1736
W. Abu Safar
Qa' el Jafr
G. Yi 'Allaq
W. Qiratya
El Agrud
875
W. el Bruk
El Thamada
N. Paran
N. Hiyyon
Bi'r al Mari
El Suweis (Suez)
Bur Taufiq
Uyun Musa
W. el Sahetra
Nakhl
W. el Tamayim
El Kuntilla
Ma'an
'En Avrona
Ras an Naqb
MA'AN
'Ain Sudr
948
G. el Kabrit
W. Raqa
Mahattat ash Shidiyah
Ghubbet el Bus
Bir Bad
Bir el Thamada
Bir Abu Muhammad
Ra's an Naqb
1435
Bir Abu Sanduq
Ras Matarma
W. Abu Ga'da
El Wabeira
Yotvata
Bi'r al Qattar
1272
SINAI Peninsula
W. Girafi
Elat
1592
Al 'Aqabah
SAUDI
Khalij el Suways
W. Yarqa
Bir el Biarat
Bir Taba
952
As Tubayq
1165
Khalij al 'Aqaba
W. an Nuwaybi
Haql
ARABIA

Projection: Polyconic

East from Greenwich

= = = 1974 Cease Fire Lines

ft m
9000 3000
6000 2000
4500 1500
3000 1000
1200 400
600 200
0 0
200 600
2000 6000
m ft

COPYRIGHT. GEORGE PHILIP & SON. LTD.

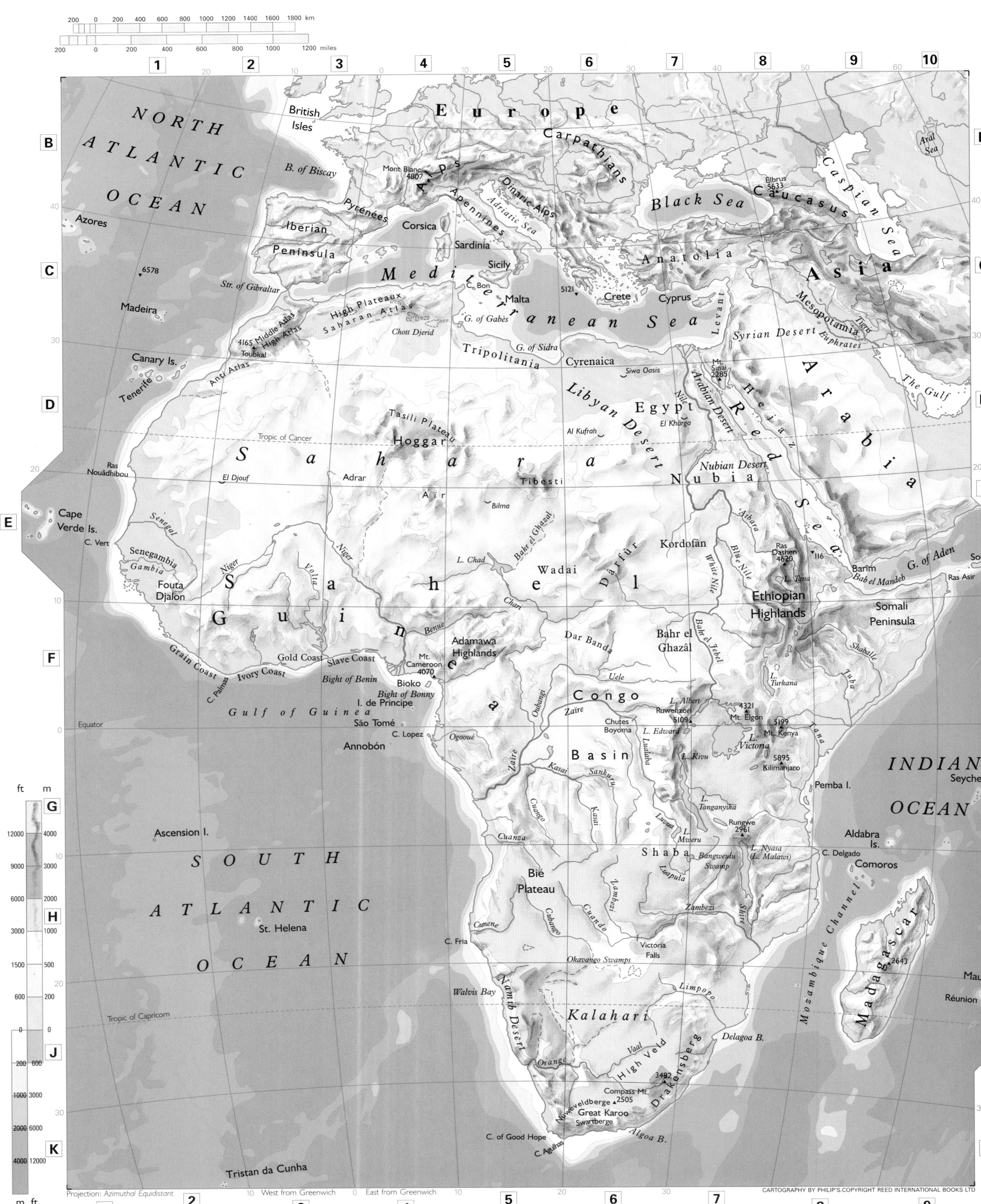

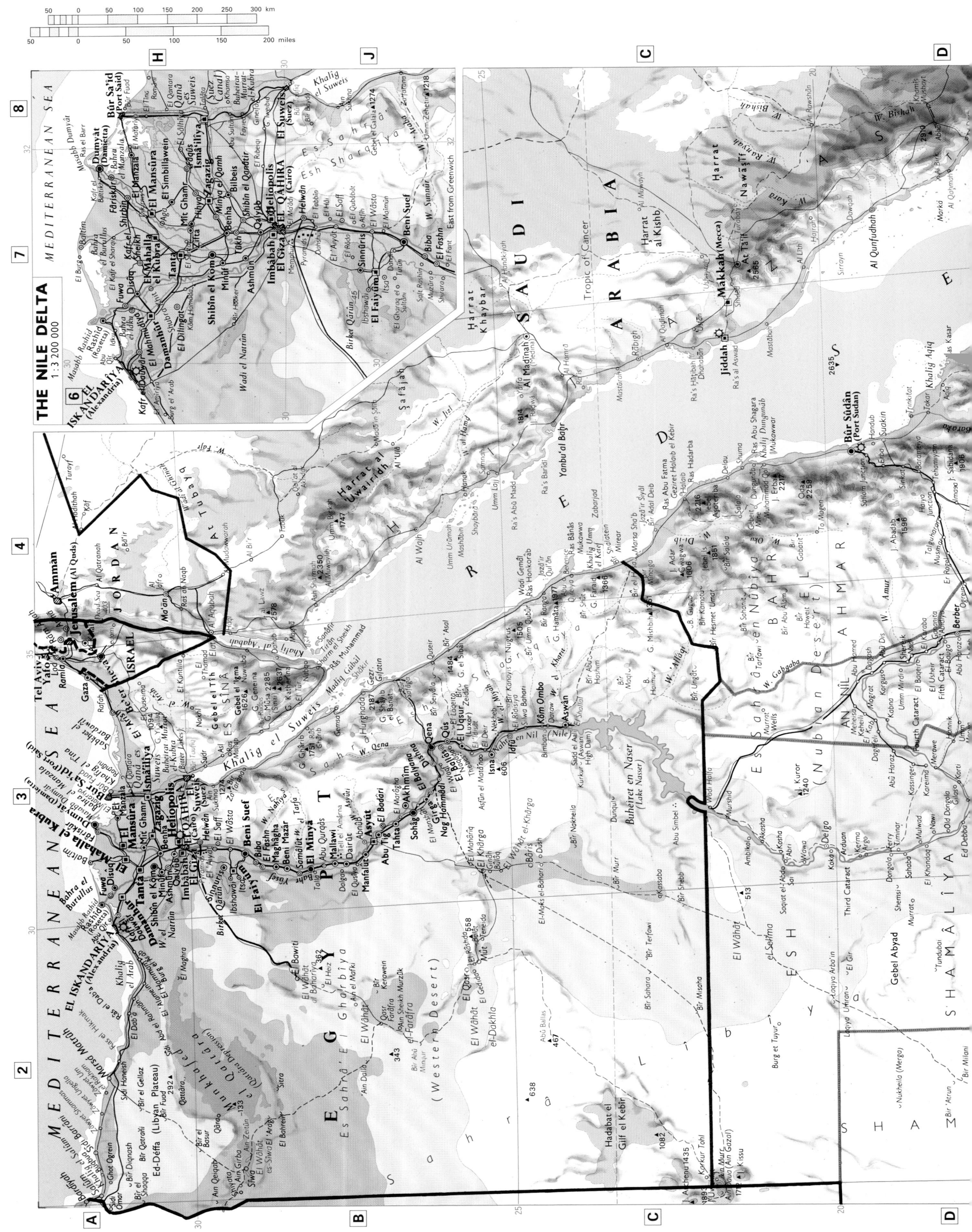

THE NILE DELTA
1:3 200 000

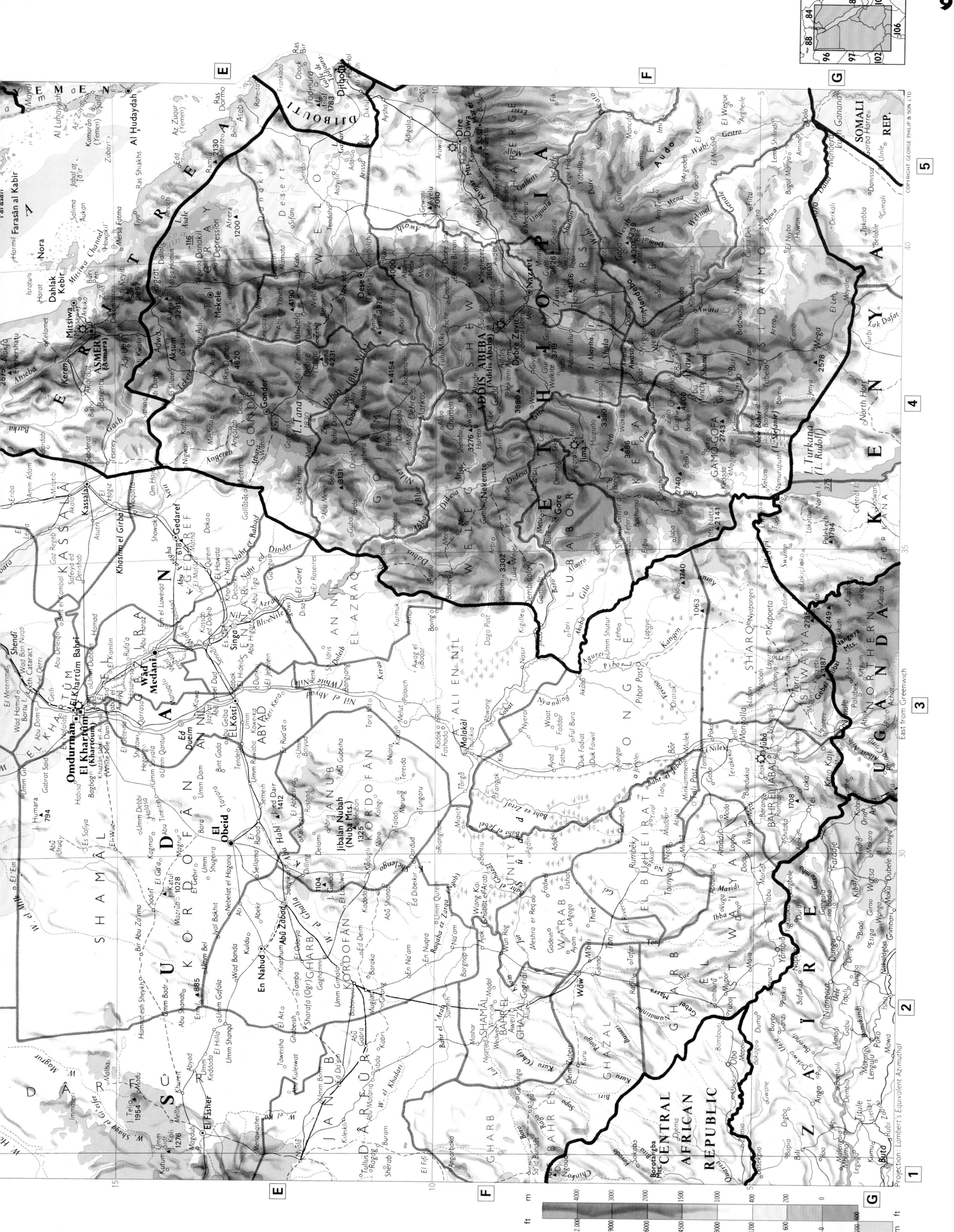

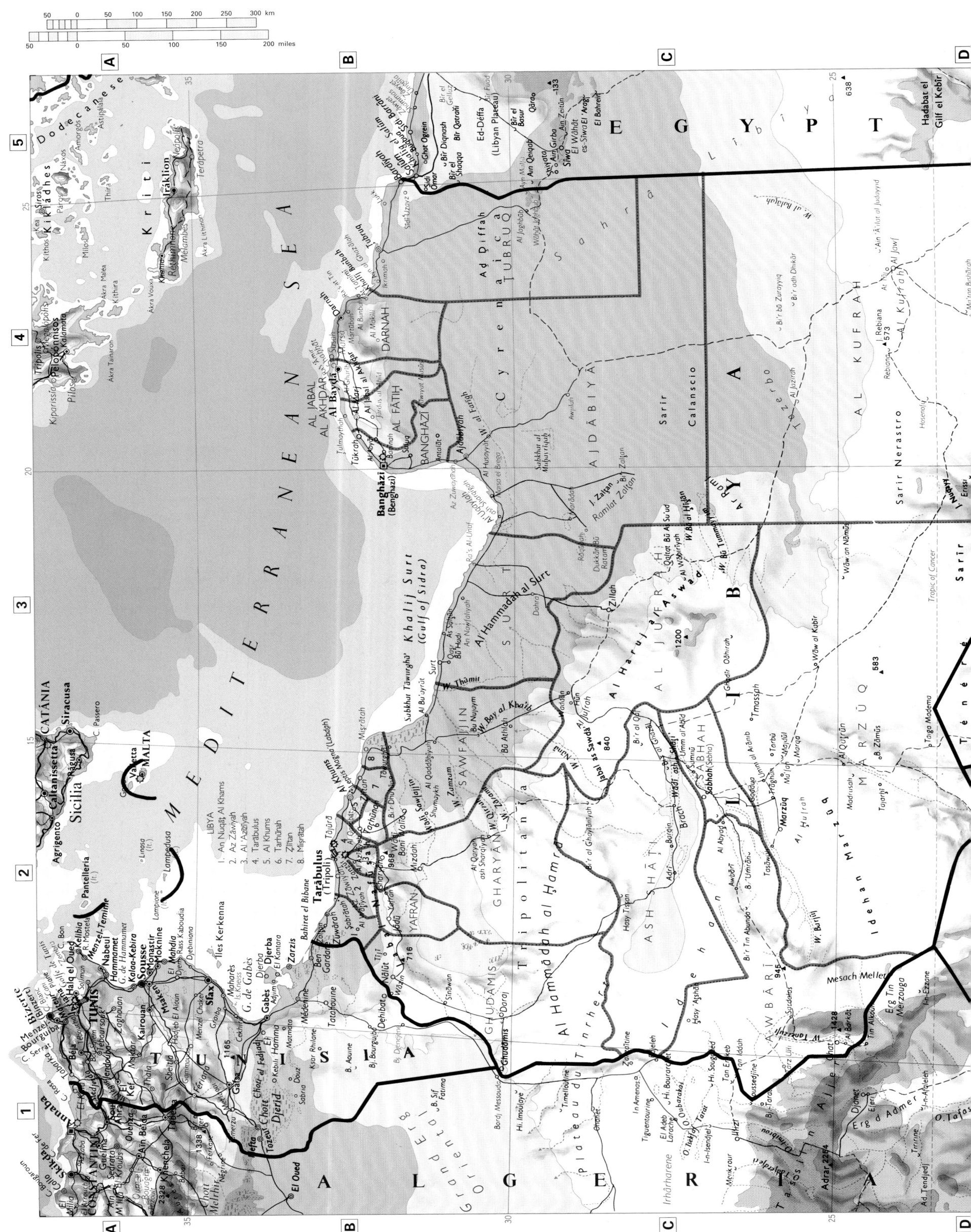

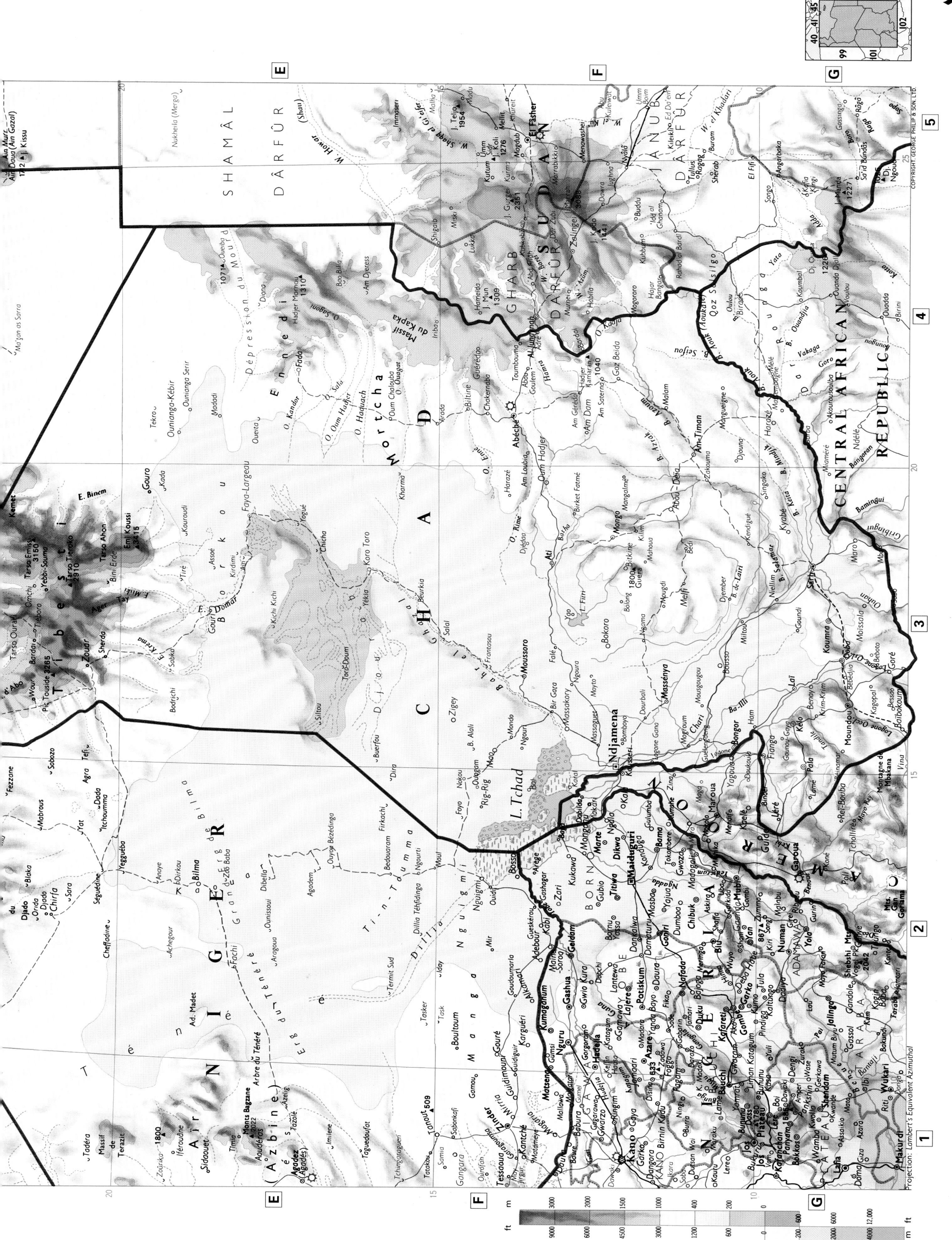

97

COPYRIGHT GEORGE PHILIP & SON, LTD.

Projection: Lambert's Equivalent Azimuthal

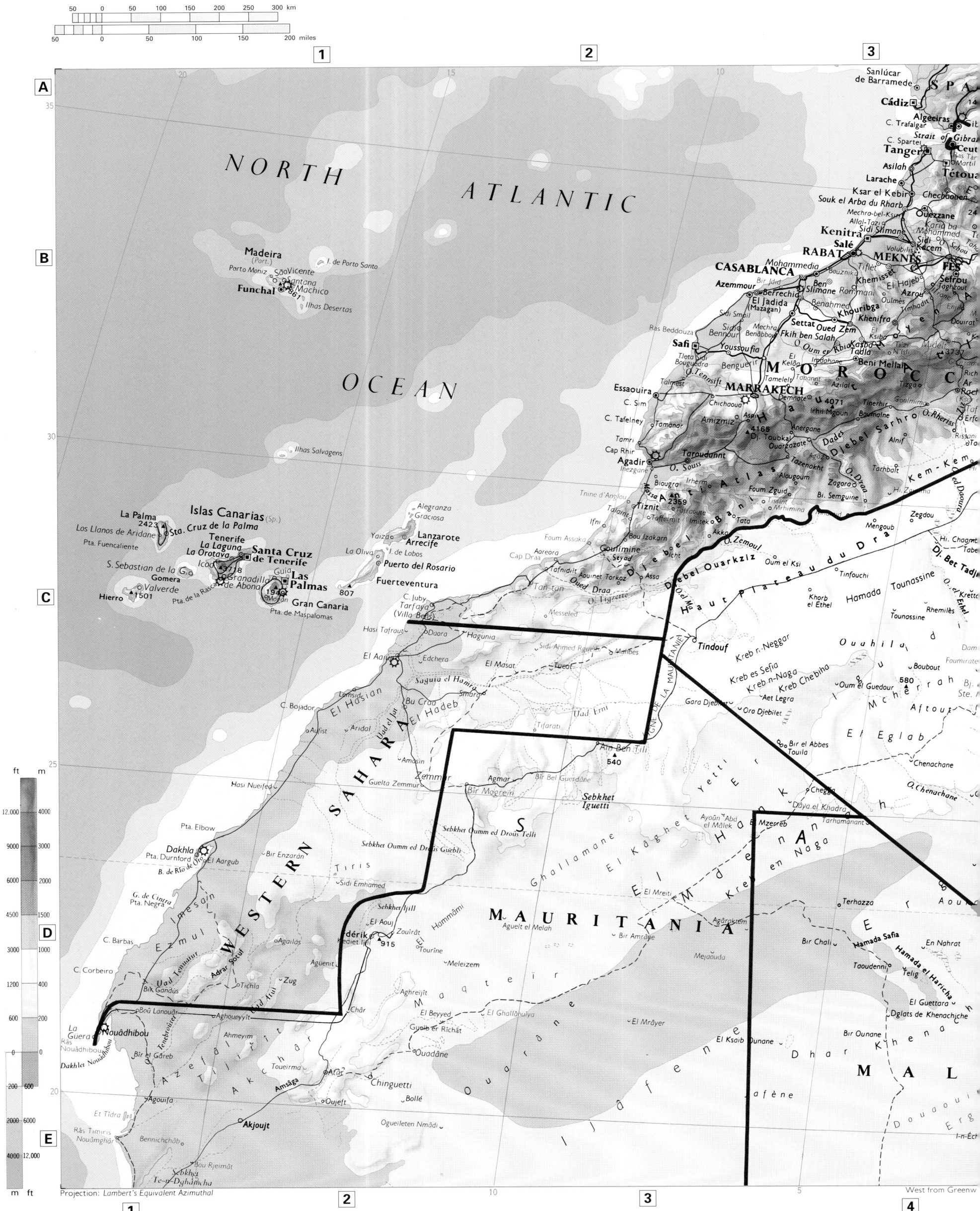

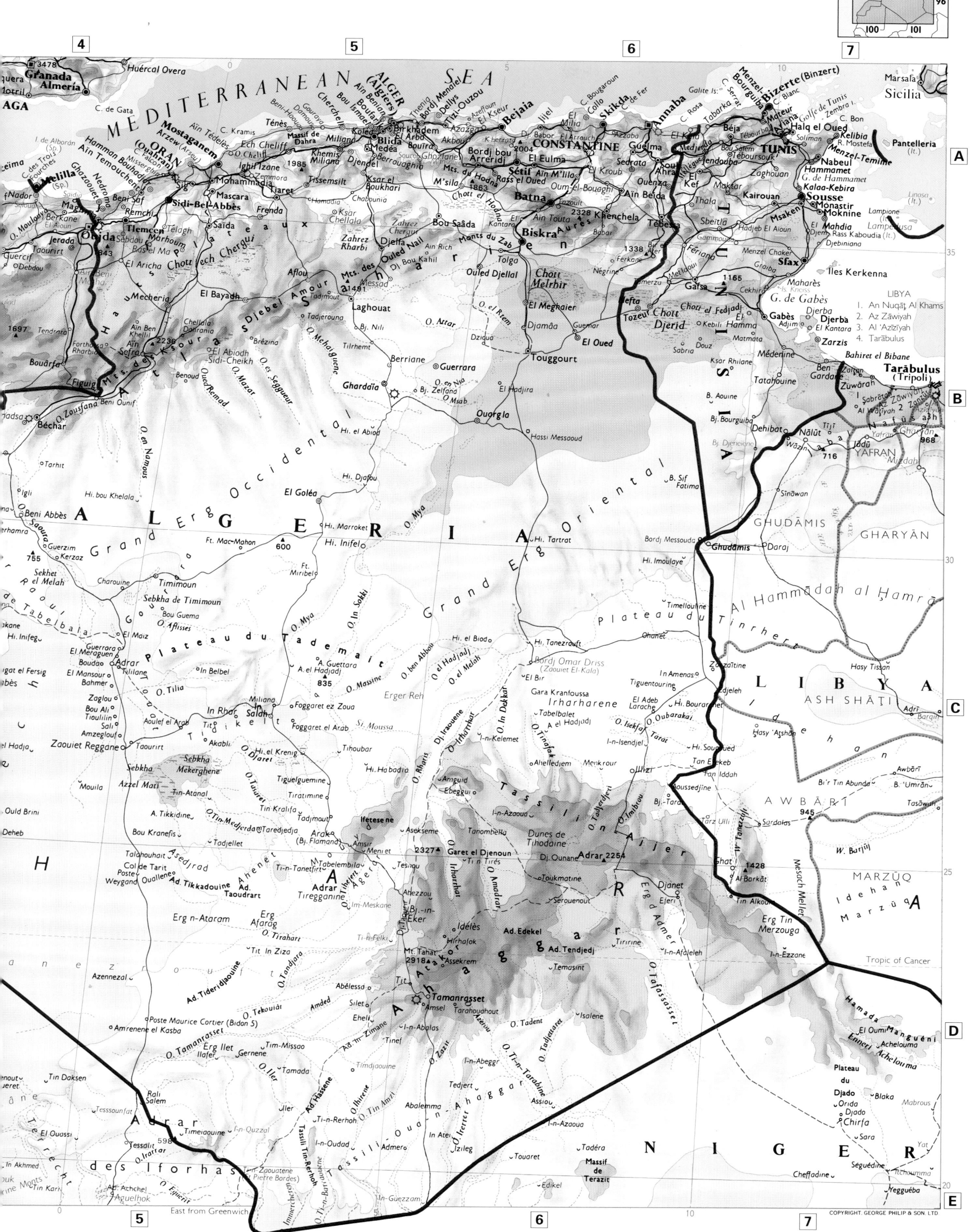

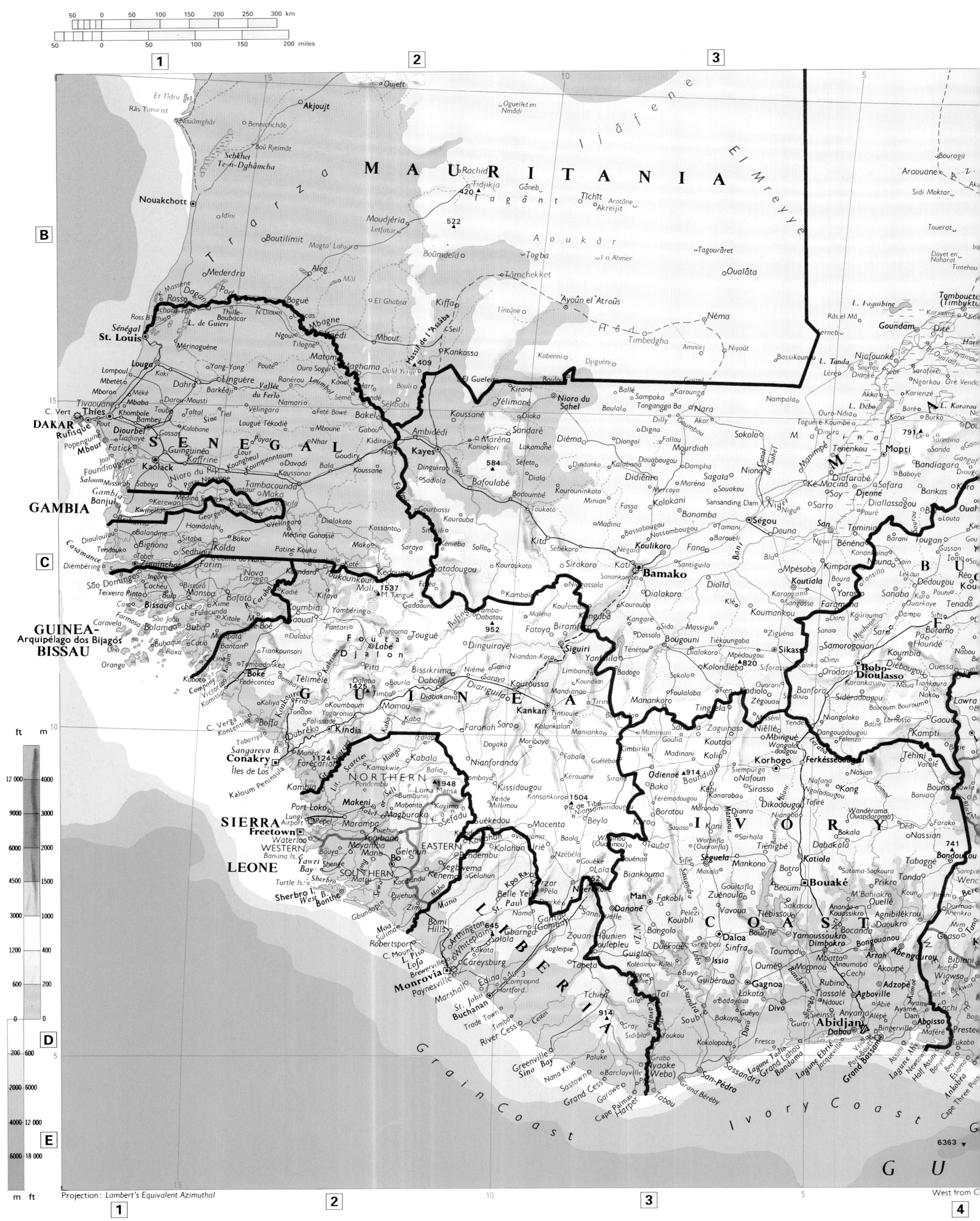

N. E. NIGERIA
on same scale as general map

East from Greenwich

COPYRIGHT. GEORGE PHILIP & SON. LTD.

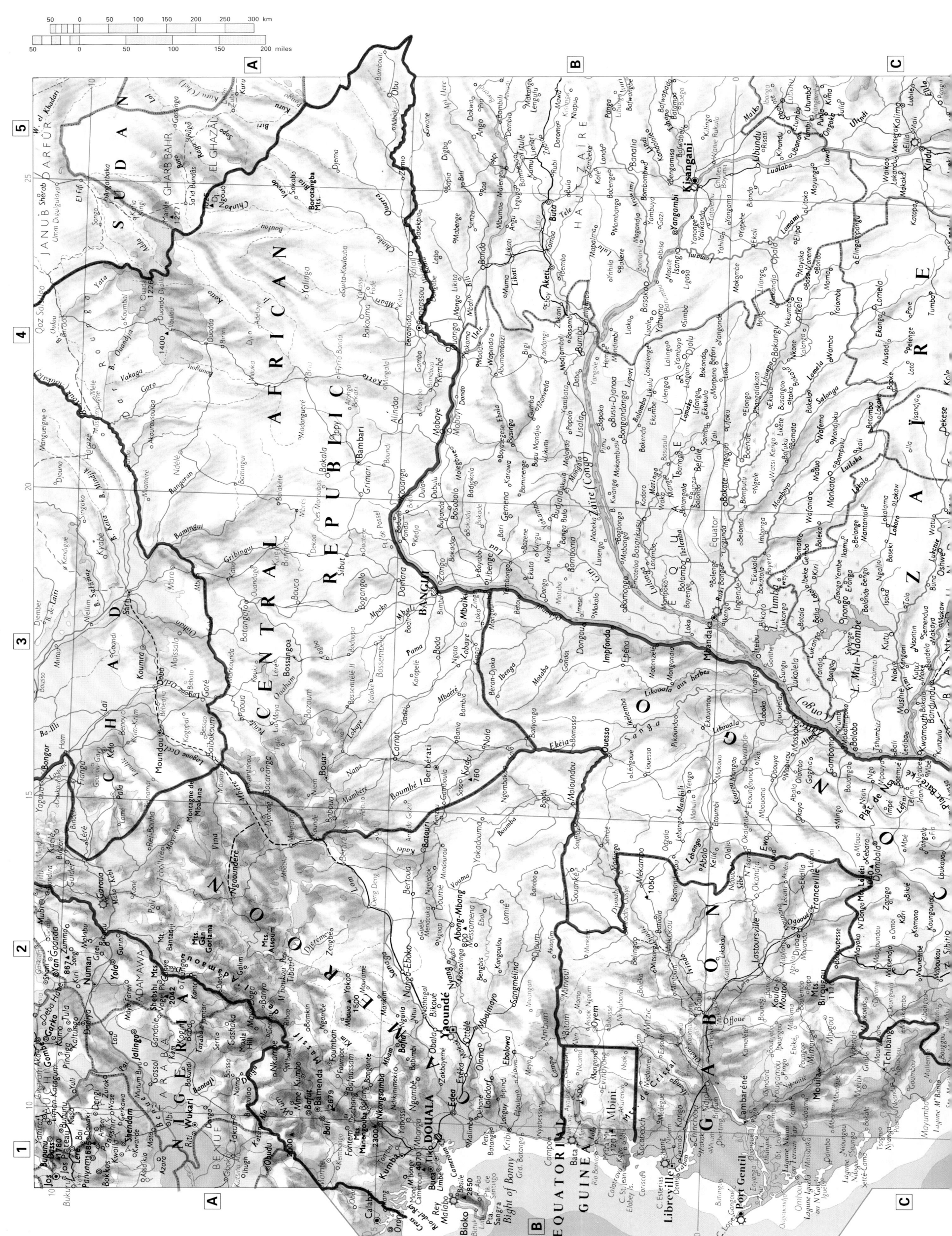

SÃO TOMÉ
AND PRÍNCIPE
At the same scale as main map

Projection: Lambert's Equivalent Azimuthal

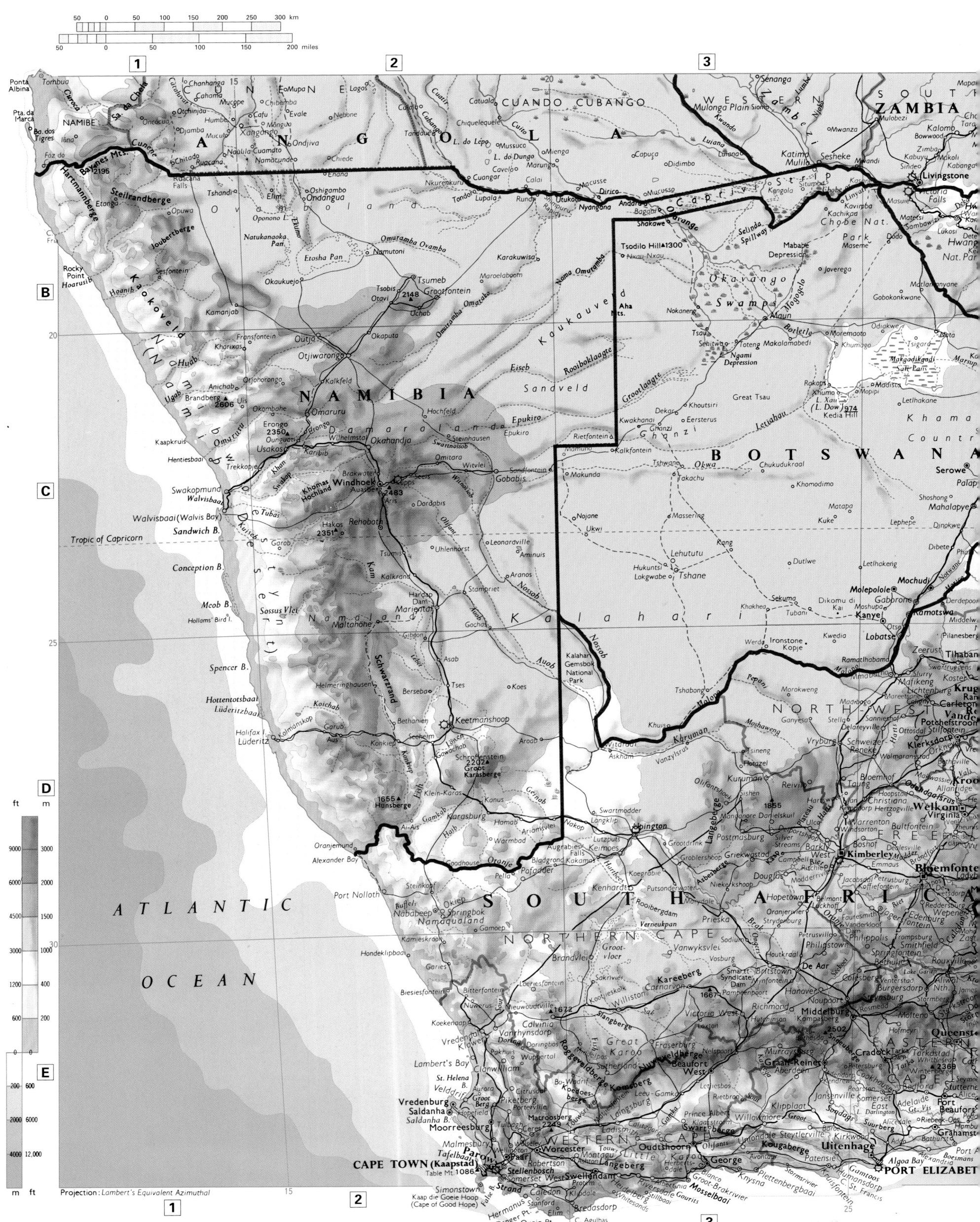

MADAGASCAR

On same scale as General Map

COPYRIGHT. GEORGE PHILIP & SON. LTD.

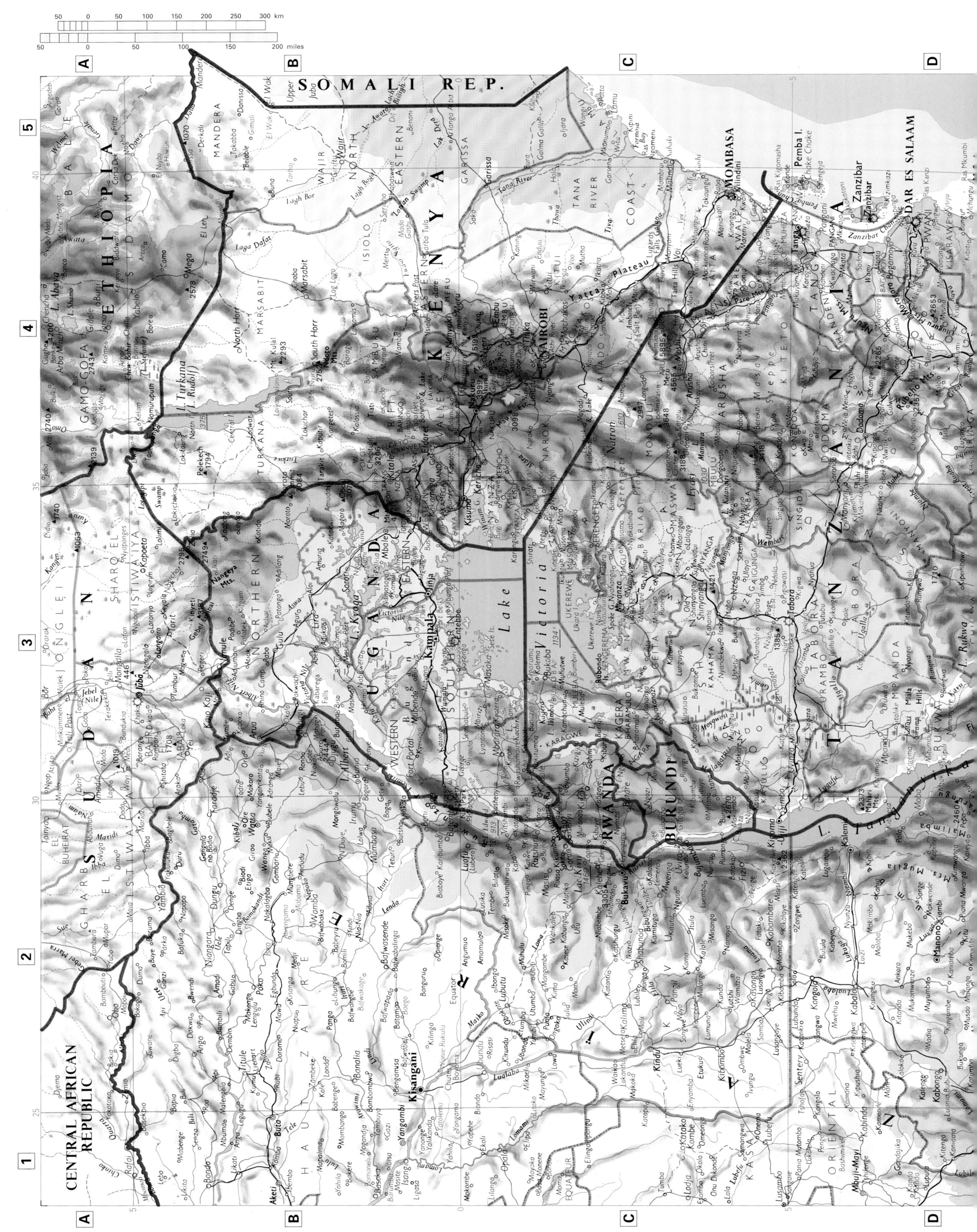

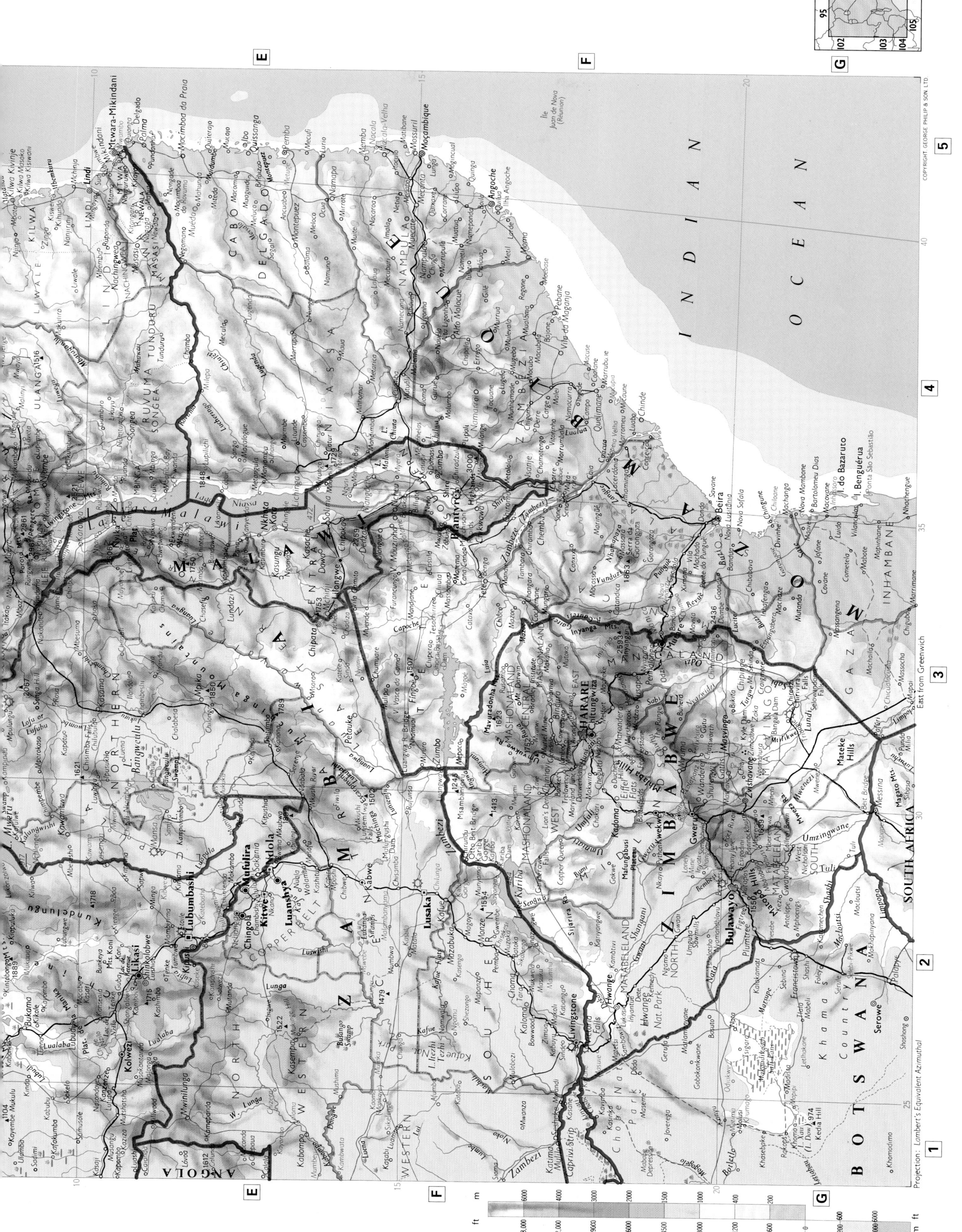

Projection: Lambert's Equivalent Azimuthal

East from Greenwich

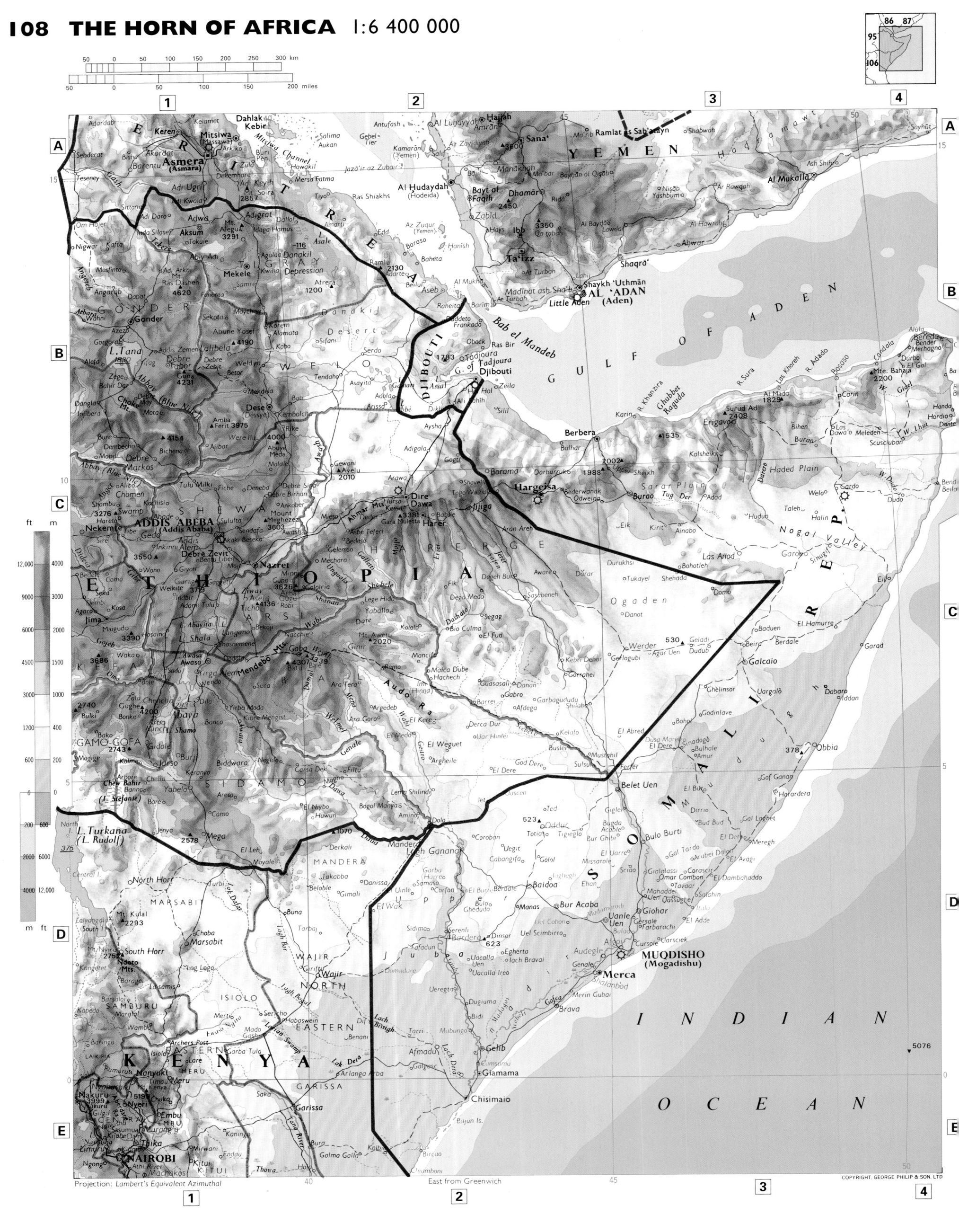

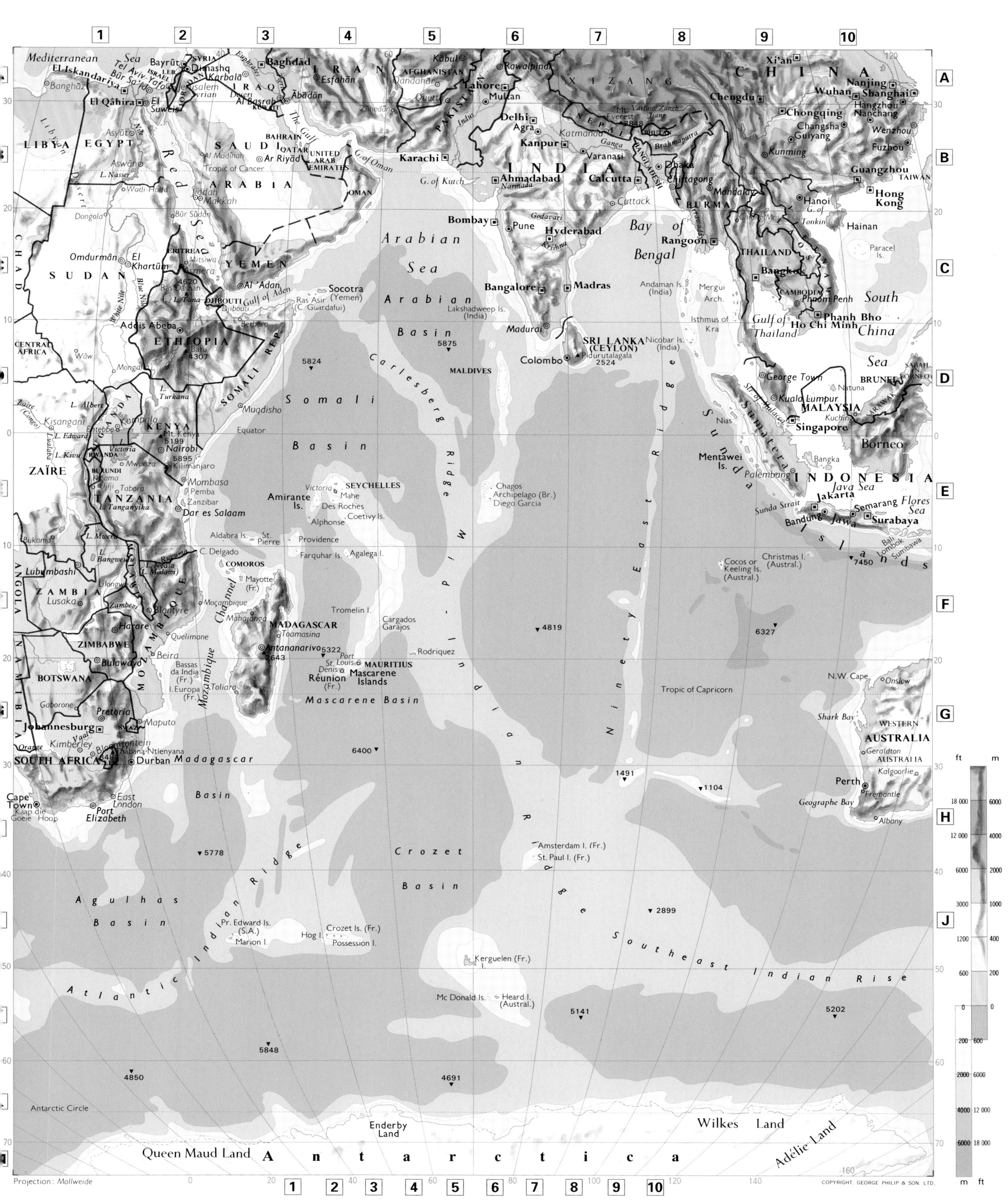

COPYRIGHT. GEORGE PHILIP & SON. LTD.

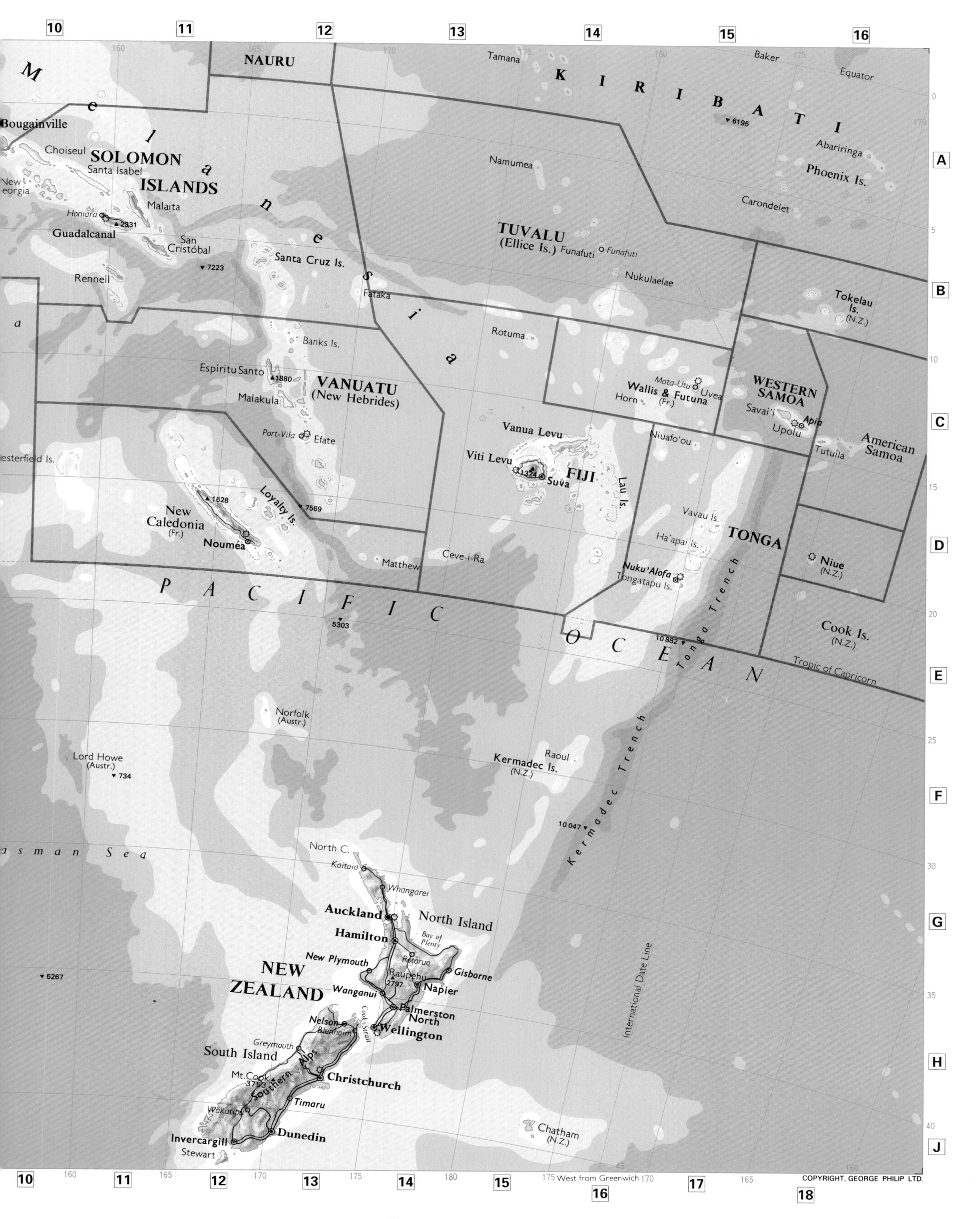

INDONESIA

TIMOR SEA

INDIAN OCEAN

NORTHERN TERRITORY

Tanami Desert

Great Sandy Desert

Joseph Bonaparte Gulf

Cambridge Gulf

Bonaparte Archipelago

King Leopold Ranges

Hamersley Range

Darwin

Melville I.

Bathurst I.

Port Hedland

Broome

Karratha

Tropic of Capricorn

Lombok
Sumbawa
Sumba
Sawu
Roti
Timor
Semau

Exmouth Gulf

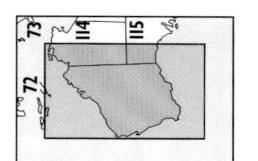

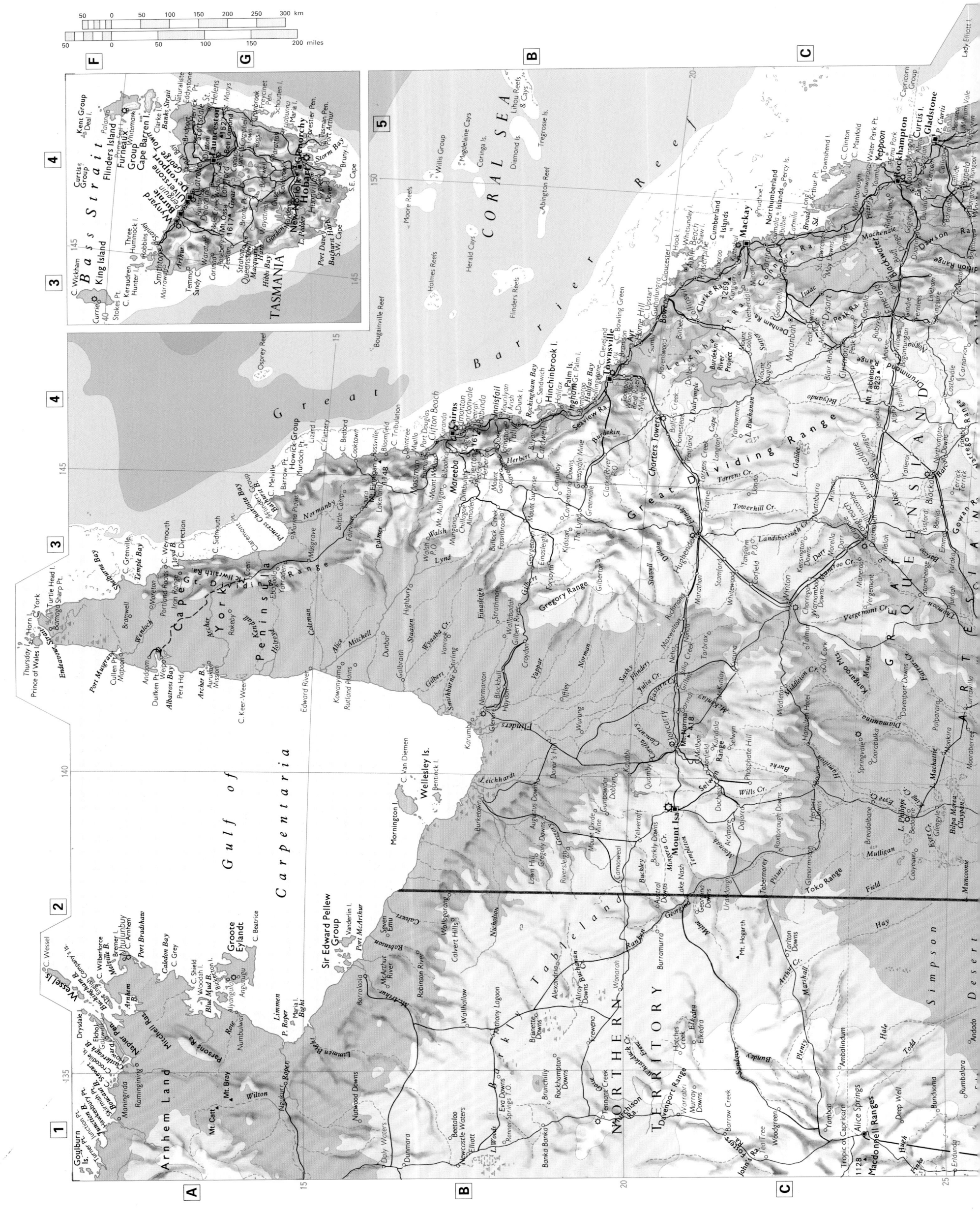

D E F

TASMAN SEA

SOUTH AUSTRALIA

NEW SOUTH WALES

VICTORIA

BRISBANE
Gold Coast
Coolangatta
Tweed Heads
Murwillumbah
Byron Bay
Ballina
Lismore
Coffs Harbour
Macksville
Kempsey
Port Macquarie
Taree
Newcastle
Gosford
Woy Woy
Manly
SYDNEY
Wollongong
Port Kembla
Shellharbour
Kiama
Ulladulla
Batemans Bay
Moruya
Narooma
Bega
Eden

Toowoomba
Ipswich
Warwick
Stanthorpe
Tenterfield
Inverell
Armidale
Tamworth
Muswellbrook
Mudgee
Dubbo
Orange
Bathurst
Parkes
Forbes
CANBERRA
Cooma
Goulburn

Charleville
Roma
Mitchell

Bourke
Broken Hill
Wilcannia
Cobar
Nyngan
Narromine
Griffith
Narrandera
Leeton
Hay
Deniliquin
Echuca
Shepparton
Bendigo
BALLARAT
MELBOURNE
Geelong
Colac
Warrnambool
Portland
Mount Gambier
Hamilton
Horsham
Mildura
Wentworth

Port Augusta
Whyalla
Port Pirie
Port Lincoln
ADELAIDE
Murray Bridge

Spencer Gulf
Gulf St. Vincent
Kangaroo I.
Lake Eyre North
Lake Torrens
Lake Gairdner
Lake Frome

Great Dividing Range
Flinders Ranges
Barrier Range
Grampians

King Island
Flinders Island
Furneaux Group
Cape Barren I.
Bass Strait
Wilsons Promontory

East from Greenwich

135 140 145 150

Projection: Bonne

m   ft
4500 15,000
3000 12,000
1500   6000
1000   4000
600   2000
400   1200
200   600
0   0
200   600
2000   4000
4000 12,000
ft   m

1 2 3 4 5

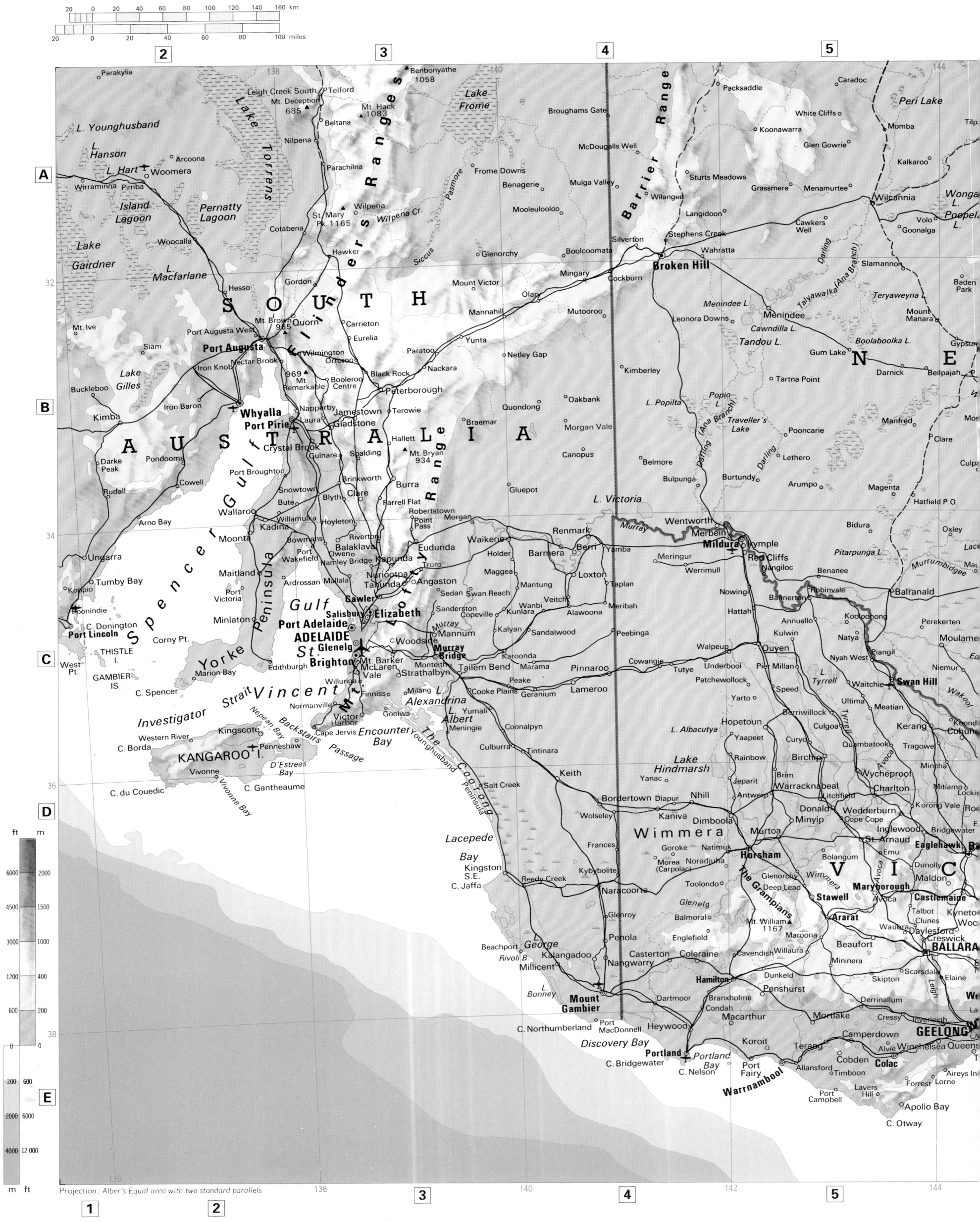

Projection: Alber's Equal area with two standard parallels

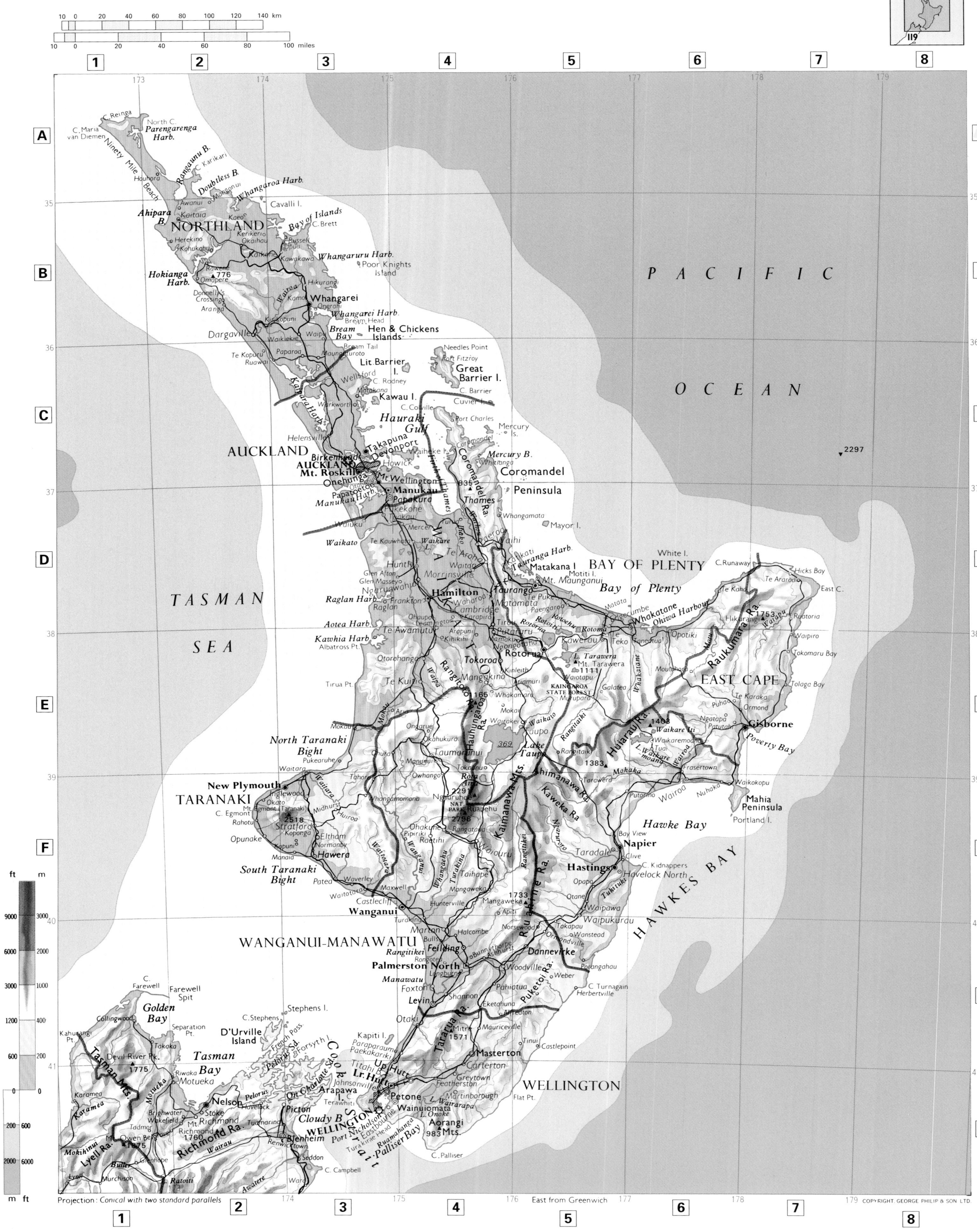

119

10 0 20 40 60 80 100 120 140 km
10 0 20 40 60 80 100 miles

A

C. Maria van Diemen
North C.
Reinga
Parengarenga Harb.
Ninety Mile Beach
Rangaunu B.
Karikari
Doubtless B.
C. Karikari
Awanui
Whangaroa Harb.

B

Ahipara B.
Kaitaia
Kaeo
Herekino
Kohukohu
Kerikeri
Okaihau
Bay of Islands
C. Brett
Russell
Kawakawa
Hokianga Harb.
Donnelly's Crossing
Omapere
Kaikohe
Hikurangi
*776
Cavalli I.
Poor Knights Island
Whangaruru Harb.
Aranga
Waima
Kamo
Whangarei
Onerahi
Dargaville
Waiotira
Waipu
Whangarei Harb.
Bream Head
Te Kopuru
Paparoa
Maungaturoto
Ruawai
Bream Bay
Hen & Chickens Islands
Bream Tail
Waikiekie

C

PACIFIC
OCEAN

NORTHLAND

Lit. Barrier I.
Port Fitzroy
Needles Point
Great Barrier I.
C. Barrier
Cuvier I.
Wellsford
C. Rodney
Kawau I.
C. Colville
Warkworth
Port Charles
Coromandel
Mercury Is.
Helensville
Hauraki Gulf
Takapuna
Cuvier I.
Mercury B.
AUCKLAND
Birkenhead
Devonport
Waiheke I.
Coromandel
Mt. Roskill
Howick
Whitianga
AUCKLAND
Onehunga
Mt. Wellington
Coromandel Peninsula
Papatoetoe
Manukau Harb.
Manukau
835
Tairua
Papakura
Thames
Pukekohe
Waiuku
Te Kauwhata
Mercer
Waihi
Mayor I.
Whangamata

D

TASMAN
Waikato
Te Aroha
Ngaruawahia
Huntly
Paeroa
Te Aroha
Katikati
Tauranga Harb.
BAY OF PLENTY
White I.
C. Runaway
Hicks Bay
Glen Afton
Mt. Maunganui
Matakana I.
Tauranga
Te Kaha
Te Araroa
Morrinsville
East C.
Glen Massey
Hamilton
Waharoa
Matamata
Motiti I.
Bay of Plenty
Matata
Edgecumbe
Whakatane
Ohiwa Harbour
Opotiki
Te Araroa
Raukumara Ra.
Frankton
Cambridge
Karapiro
Tirau
Putaruru
Rotorua
Rotoma
1753
SEA
Raglan
Raglan Harb.
Te Awamutu
Kihikihi
Arapuni
Rotorua
Kawerau
Teko
Ruatoria
Waipiro
Ohaupo
Tokomaru Bay

E

Aotea Harb.
Otorohanga
Kawhia Harb.
Albatross Pt.
Mangakino
Rotorua
L. Tarawera
Mt. Tarawera 1111
Galatea
KAINGAROA STATE FOREST
Murupara
Tolaga Bay
EAST CAPE
Te Karaka
Ormond
Ngatapa
Gisborne
Poverty Bay
Tirua Pt.
Te Kuiti
Waira
Tokoroa
Mangaokino
Atiamuri
1408
Rangitaiki
Waikaremoana
Tuai
Patutahi
Manganui
Taumarunui
Lake Taupo
369
Rangitaiki
1383
Mohaka
Wairoa
Waikokopu
Owhango
Turangi
Tarawera
Putorino
Mahia Peninsula
Portland I.

F

North Taranaki Bight
Pukearuhe
Waitara
Tahora
Okahukura
National Park
Raurimu
2796
Kaimanawa Mts.
Kaweka Ra.
Waikare Head
Hawke Bay
New Plymouth
Inglewood
Mt. Egmont 2518
TARANAKI
Okato
Mt. Taranaki
Midhurst
Whangamomona
229
Ruapehu
Mohaka
C. Egmont
Rahotu
Stratford
Koponga
Eltham
Ohakune
Pipiriki
Raetihi
Rangataua
Napier
Taradale
Clive
Opunake
Manaia
Normanby
Waiouru
Rangiwahia
Hastings
Havelock North
Kaponga
Hawera
South Taranaki Bight
Patea
Waverley
Waitotara
Wanganui
Taihape
Mangaweka
Apiti
C. Kidnappers
Otane
HAWKES BAY
Waipawa
Waipukurau
Maxwell
Hunterville
Castlecliff
1733
Turakina
Marton
Bulls
Wanganui
Halcombe
Norsewood
Weber
Takapau
WANGANUI-MANAWATU
Feilding
Rongotea
Bunnythorpe
Ashhurst
Dannevirke
Woodville
Potangahau
Rangitikei
Palmerston North
Pahiatua
Manawatu
Longburn
C. Turnagain
Foxton
Pahiatua
Herbertville
Shannon
Eketahuna
Levin
Mauriceville
Otaki
Tinui
Castlepoint
Kapiti I.
Paraparaumu
Mt. Bruce
1571
Masterton
Carterton
Paekakariki
Pukerua
Greytown
Featherston
Martinborough
WELLINGTON

Flat Pt.

ft m
9000 3000
6000 2000
3000 1000
1200 400
600 200
0 0
200 600
2000 6000
m ft

C. Farewell
Farewell Spit
Golden Bay
Collingwood
Stephens I.
C. Stephens
Kahurangi Pt.
Takaka
D'Urville Island
French Pass
Tasman Bay
Riwaka
Motueka
Pelorus Sd.
Forsyth I.
Cook Strait
Titahi
Petone
Wainuiomata
Upr. Hutt
Lr. Hutt
WELLINGTON
Tasman Mts.
1775
Devil River Pk.
Separation Pt.
Karamea
Brightwater
Wakefield
Nelson
Stoke
Mt. Richmond
Picton
Arapawa
Cloudy B.
Port Nicholson
Aorangi Mts.
983
Karamea
Murchison
Tadmor
Wai-iti
Havelock
Renwick
Tuamarina
Richmond Ra.
1760
Blenheim
Seddon
Mokihinui
Lyell Ra.
1675
Owen
Richmond Ra.
Wairau
C. Campbell
Lyell
Buller
Ratotti
Murchison
Inangahua
Wairau

WELLINGTON

Projection: Conical with two standard parallels
East from Greenwich
COPYRIGHT. GEORGE PHILIP & SON LTD.

173   174   175   176   East from Greenwich 177   178   179

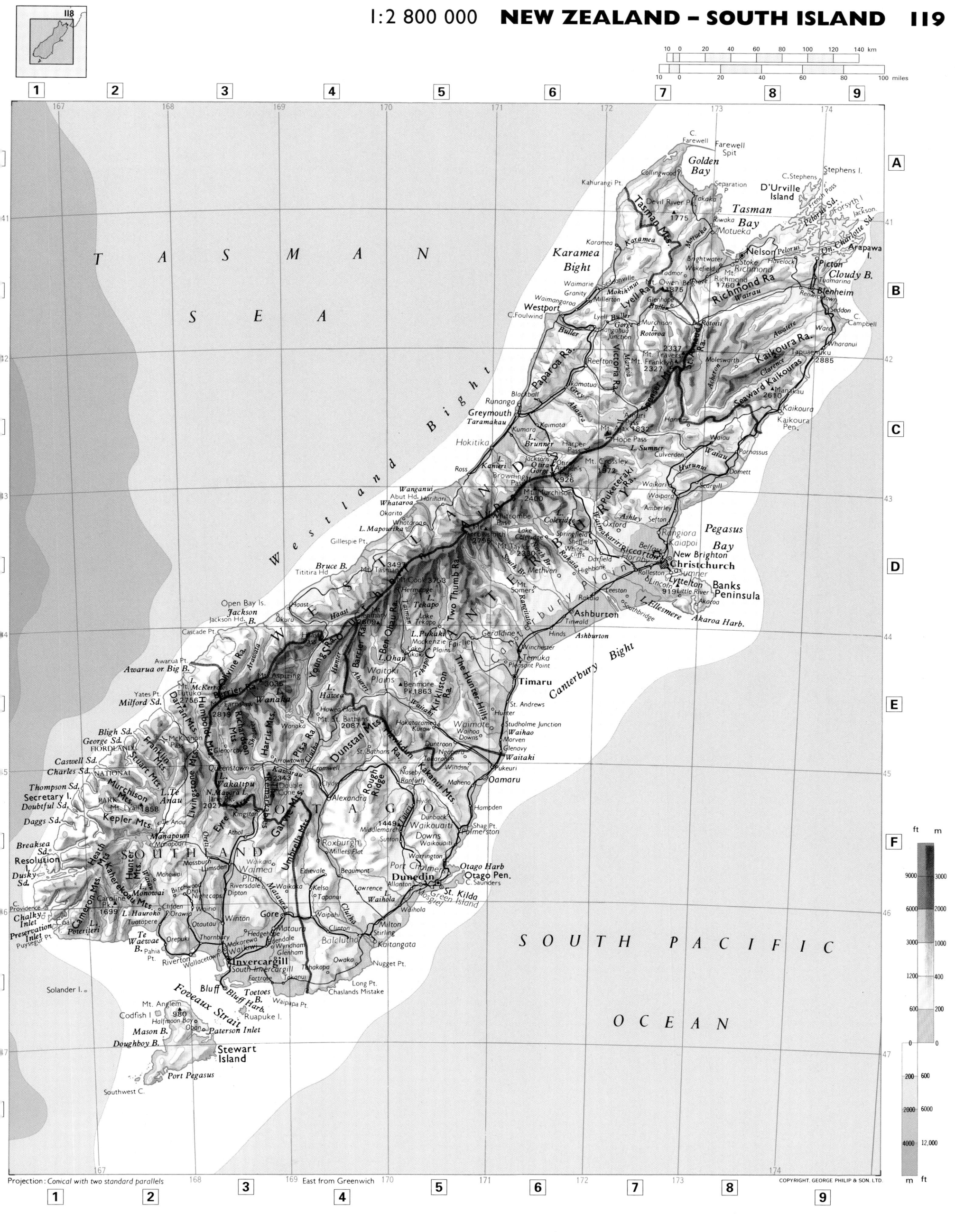

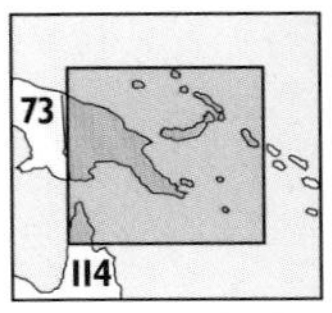

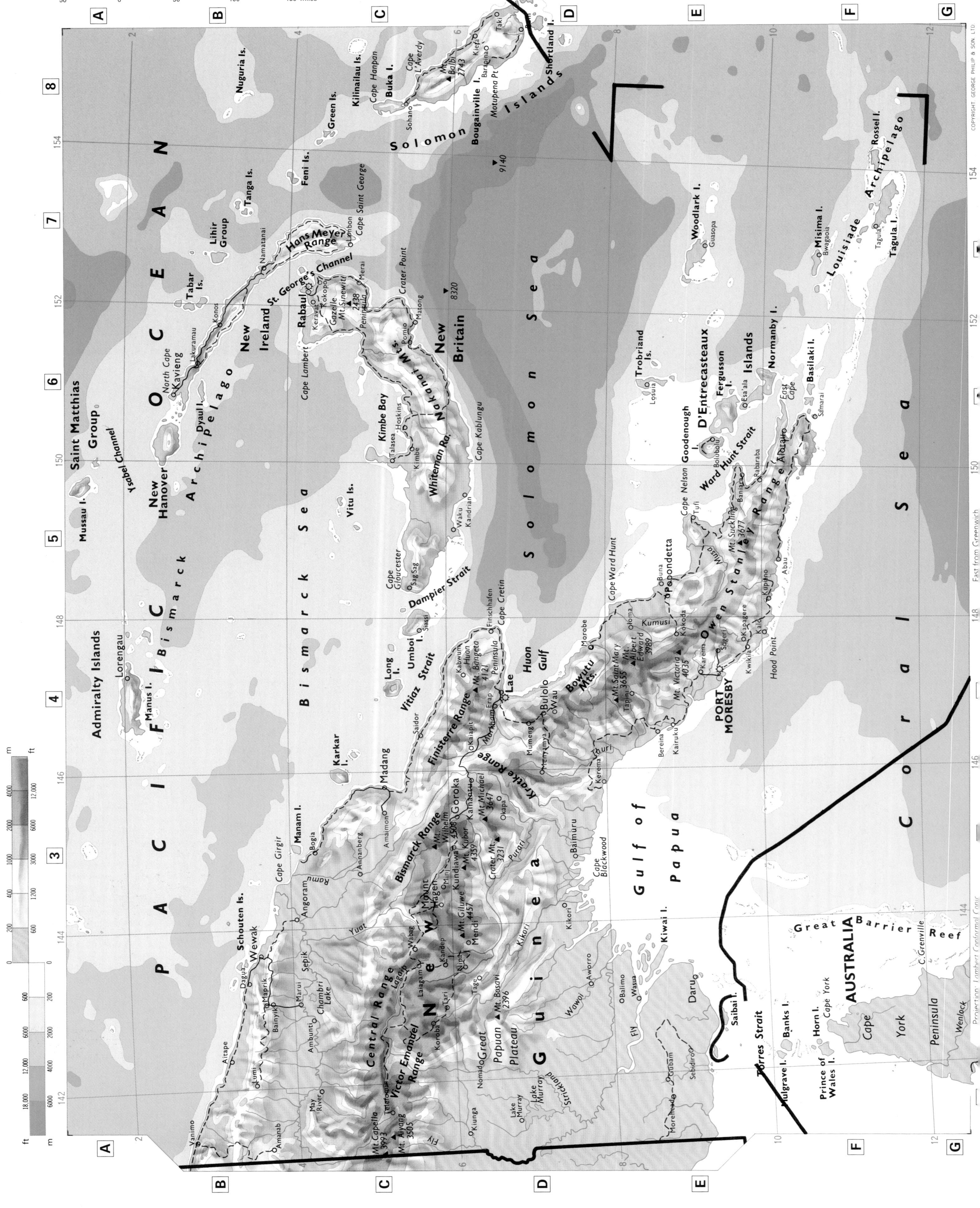

50 0 50 100 150 200 km

50 0 50 100 150 miles

73

114

COPYRIGHT GEORGE PHILIP & SON LTD.

East from Greenwich

Projection Lambert Conformal Conic

A B C D E F G

PACIFIC OCEAN

Nuguria Is.

Kilinailau Is.

Green Is.

Cape Hanpan

Buka I.

Cape L'Averdy

Mt. Balbi 2743

Taki

Kieta

Bariginao

Cape Shortland I.

Motupena Pt

Bougainville I.

Sohano

Solomon Islands

Solomon Sea

9140

8320

Crater Point

Pomio

Matong

Lombon

Cape Saint George

St. George's Channel

Hans Meyer Range

Namatanai

Konos

Lakuramau

Tabar Is.

Lihir Group

Tanga Is.

Feni Is.

North Cape

Kavieng

New Hanover

Ysabel Channel

Dyaul I.

New Ireland

Archipelago

Mussau I.

Saint Matthias Group

Bismarck

Bismarck Sea

Rabaul

Gazelle Peninsula

Keravat

Kokopo

Mt. Sinewit 2438

Cape Lambert

Hoskins

Kimbe Bay

Talasea

Kimbe

Waku

Kandrian

Cape Gloucester

Sag Sag

Dampier Strait

Whiteman Ra.

Nakanai Mts.

New Britain

Cape Kablungu

Vitu Is.

Long I.

Umboi I.

Siassi

Vitiaz Strait

Finschhafen

Cape Cretin

Huon Peninsula

Mt. Bangeta 4121

Kabwum

Huon Gulf

Lae

Erap

Markham

Bulolo

Wau

Morobe

Bowutu Mts.

Mumeng

Admiralty Islands

Lorengau

Manus I.

Karkar I.

Manam I.

Cape Girgir

Bogia

Madang

Saidor

Finisterre Range

Annanberg

Ramu

Yuat

Amaimon

Bismarck Range

Mt. Wilhelm 4508

Mt. Gilluwe 4368

Mt. Kubor 4359

Goroka

Kainantu

Mt. Michael 3647

Crater Mt. 3231

Kratke Range

Okapa

Purari

Baimuru

Kikori

Kikori

Cape Blackwood

Gulf of Papua

Kerema

Kairuku

Bereina

Kwikila

Hood Point

PORT MORESBY

Kupiano

Abau

Owen Stanley Range

Mt. Victoria 4035

Mt. Suckling 3677

East Cape

Samarai

Basilaki I.

Normanby I.

D'Entrecasteaux Islands

Fergusson

Goodenough

Esa'ala

Rabaraba

Baniara

Cape Nelson

Tufi

Buna

Popondetta

Kokoda

Kumusi

Oro Bay

Mt. Albert Edward 3989

Mt. Saint Mary 3655

Tapini

Cape Ward Hunt

Ward Hunt Strait

Trobriand Is.

Losuia

Kiriwina

Woodlark I.

Guasopa

Misima I.

Bwagaoia

Louisiade Archipelago

Tagula I.

Tagula

Rossell I.

Solomon Sea

Coral Sea

Great Barrier Reef

AUSTRALIA

C. Grenville

Cape York

York Peninsula

Wenlock

Torres Strait

Saibai I.

Daru

Kiwai I.

Mabudauan

Sebidiro

Morehead

Wassi

Balimo

Aworro

Wawoi

Lake Murray

Kiunga

Strickland

Fly

Nomad

Mt. Bosavi 2396

Tari

Koroba

Mendi

Laiagam

Wabag

Mt. Hagen

Mount Hagen

Central Range

Kandep

Victor Emanuel Range

Mt. Capella 3993

Mt. Aiyang 3505

Telefomin

Amanab

Vanimo

Aitape

May River

Green River

Lumi

Maprik

Dreikikir

Ambunti

Chambri Lake

Sepik

Wewak

Schouten Is.

Dagua

Angoram

New Guinea

Papuan Plateau

Great Papuan Plateau

m ft

4000 12 000

3000

2000 6000

1000

400 1200

200 600

0 0

ft m

18 000 6000

12 000 4000

6000 2000

0 0

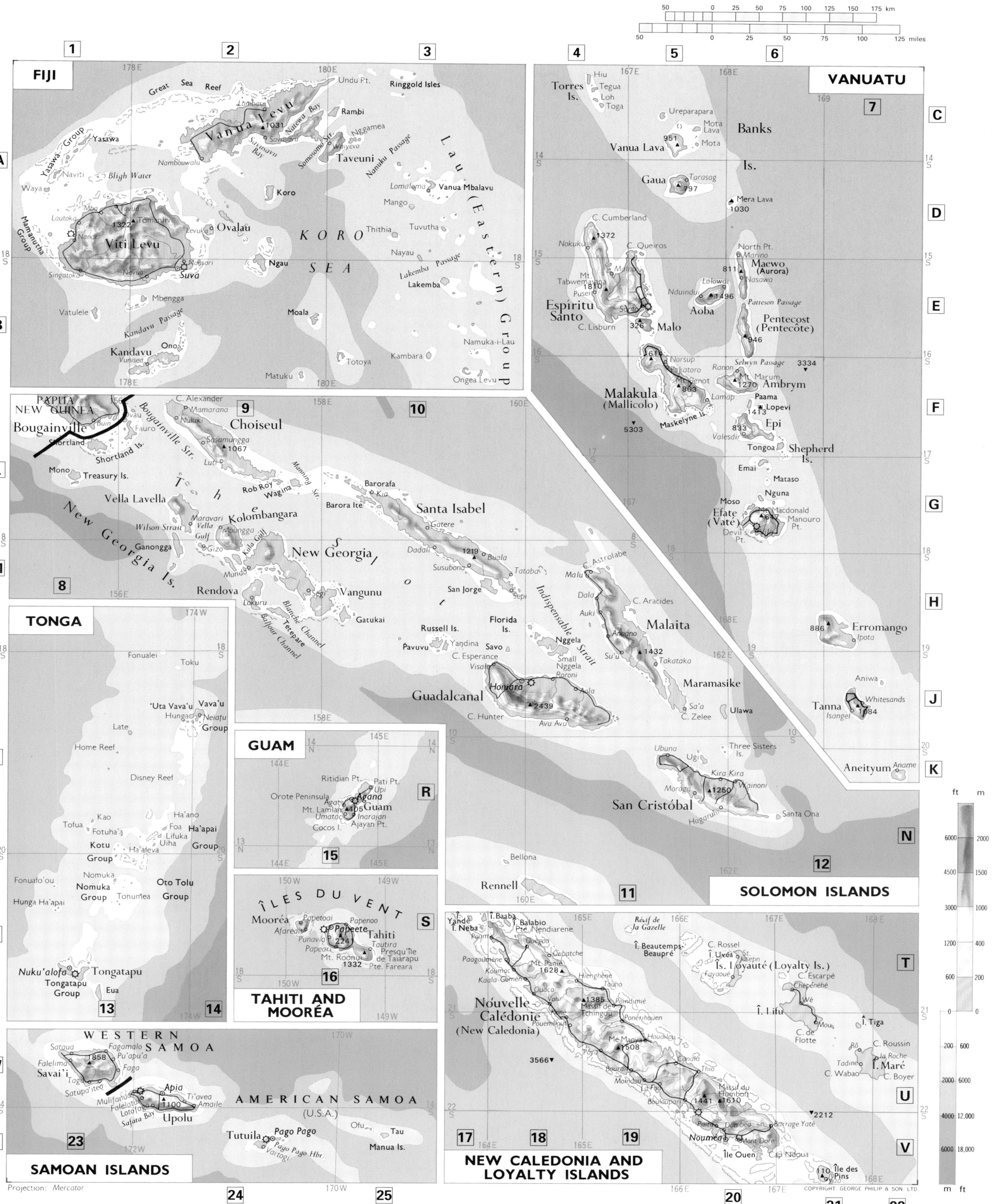

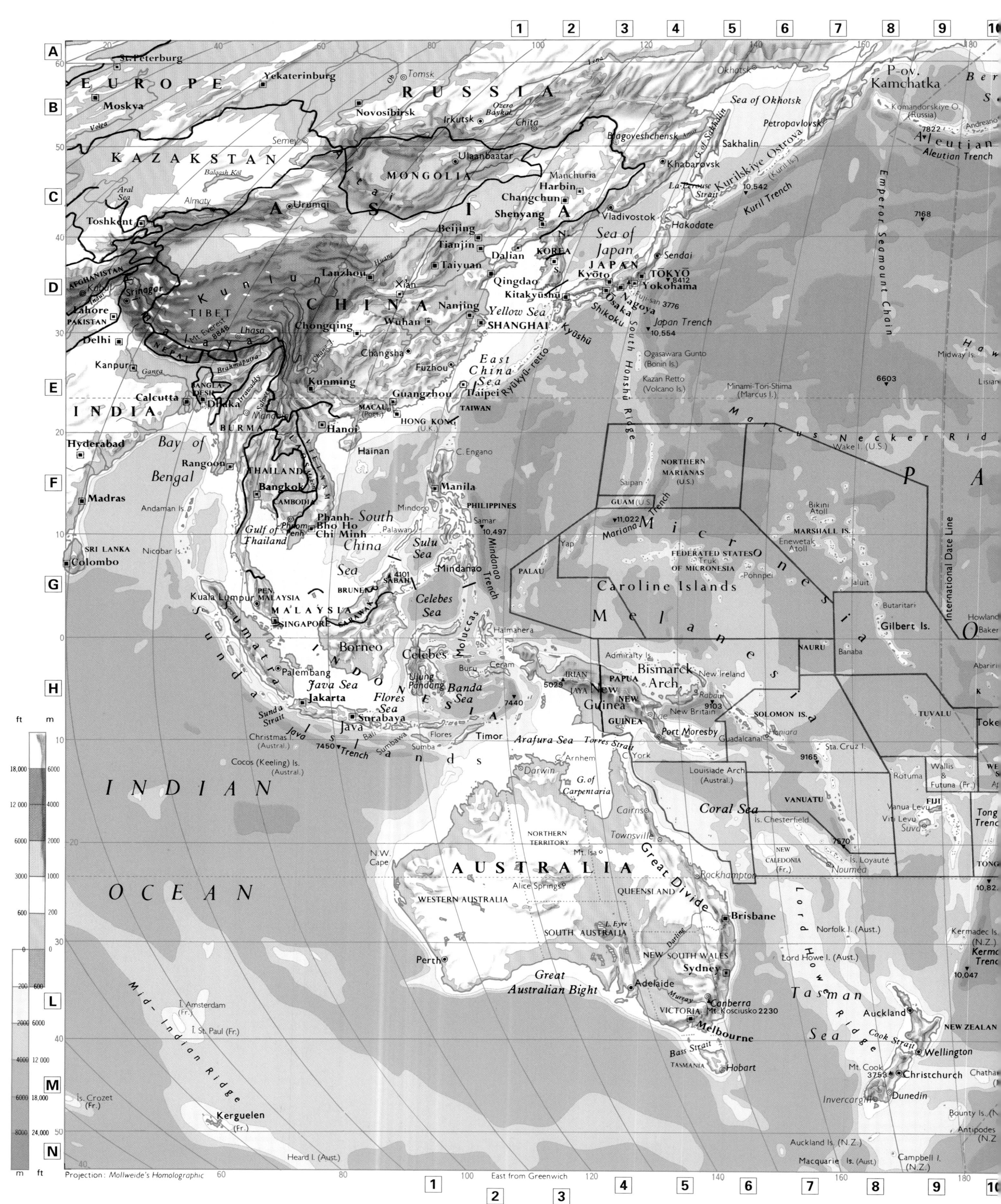

1 **12** **13** **14** **15** **16** **17** **18** **19** **20**

A

B

C

D

E

F

G

H

J

K

L

M

N

160   **12**   140   **13**   **14**   **15**   120   **16**   **17**   100   West from Greenwich   **18**   80   **19**   **20**   60   40   20

ALASKA (U.S.)

6959

Gulf of Alaska

Prince of Wales I.

Prince Rupert   Kitimat

Queen Charlotte Is.

Bristol Bay

GREENLAND   C. Farewell

R O C K Y   **C A N A D A**

N O R T H   A M E R I C A

Hudson Bay

Labrador

N O R T H

Edmonton

L. Winnipeg

Vancouver   Calgary   Regina   Winnipeg   L. Superior   St. Lawrence   Newfoundland

Vancouver I.   Victoria

Seattle   L. Michigan   Montréal   Québec   Pr. Edward I.

Portland   Boise   Missouri   Toronto   Ottawa   L. Ontario   Saint-John   C. Sable

Snake   Minneapolis   L. Erie   Buffalo   Boston

CHICAGO   Detroit   Pittsburgh   **NEW YORK**

Salt Lake City   Denver   Kansas City   St. Louis   Cincinnati   **Philadelphia**   Baltimore   Washington

C. Mendocino   **A T L A N T I C**

San Francisco   4418   **U N I T E D   S T A T E S**   Oklahoma   Memphis   Appalachian Mts.

6741   Los Angeles   Dallas   Atlanta   C. Hatteras

San Diego   Ciudad Juárez   Sierra Madre   Houston   New Orleans   Jacksonville   Bermuda (U.K.)

M E X I C O   San Antonio   **O C E A N**

Hawaiian Is. (U.S.)   Tropic of Cancer   I. Guadalupe (Mexico)   6225   Gulf of California   Monterrey   Gulf of Mexico   Miami   Florida Strait   BAHAMAS

Honolulu   Oahu   Guadalajara   C. México   CUBA   **West Indies**

4205   Hawaii   Is. Revilla Gigedo (Mexico)   Puebla   5700   Mérida   Yucatan Channel   La Habana   Hispaniola   DOM. REP.   9200

Acapulco   BELIZE   HAITI   JAMAICA   7680   Kingston   PUERTO RICO   Leeward Is.

I. Clipperton (Fr.)   GUATEMALA   HONDURAS   Caribbean Sea   BARBADOS

Guatemala   El Salvador   NICARAGUA   Windward Is.   TRINIDAD & TOBAGO

San Salvador   **CENTRAL AMERICA**   Managua   Barranquilla   Maracaibo   Caracas

Palmyra Is. (U.S.)   COSTA RICA   San José   Colón   Panama   Orinoco   VENEZUELA

Teraina   Tabuaeran   PANAMA Canal

Kiritimati   I. del Coco (Costa Rica)   Medellín   Bogotá

Jarvis I. (U.S.)   Equator   I. de Malpelo (Colombia)   Cali   COLOMBIA

Malden I.   Galápagos (Ecuador)   Quito   ECUADOR

Starbuck I.   Guayaquil   Iquitos   Manaus

Î. Marquises   C. Pariñas   Amazonas   **BRAZIL**

Tongareva   Penrhyn Is.   Caroline I.   Trujillo   **SOUTH**

Manihiki   Vostok I.   6369   PERU   **AMERICA**

Suwarrow Is.   Flint I.   Lima

Î. de la Société   Cuzco   Titicaca   Illampu & Ancohuma   6550

Cook Islands (N.Z.)   Î. Tuamotu   Arequipa   La Paz   BOLIVIA

Manuae   Tahiti   6866   Peru   East Pacific Ridge

FRENCH POLYNESIA   Iquique   Chile

Rarotonga   Tuamotu Ridge   PARAGUAY

Tropic of Capricorn   8050   Antofagasta   Trench   Asunción

Î. Tubuai (Îs. Australes)   Pitcairn I. (U.K.)   Ducie I. (U.K.)   San Félix (Chile)   Sala-y-Gomez (Chile)   Tucumán   Pto. Alegre

Rapa   I. de Pascua (Easter I.) (Chile)   San Ambrosio (Chile)   URUGUAY

Seamount Chain   6960   Córdoba   Rosario

Arch. de Juan Fernández (Chile)   Valparaíso   Santiago   Buenos Aires   Montevideo

Concepción   **ARGENTINA**   Río de la Plata

Chile Rise   Patagonia   **SOUTH**

Pacific-Antarctic Ridge   **ATLANTIC**

6212   **OCEAN**

Punta Arenas   Falkland Is. (U.K.)

Str. of Magellan   Tierra del Fuego   South Georgia (U.K.)

C. Horn

P A C I F I C   O C E A N

ALASKA
1:24 000 000

Projection: Bonne

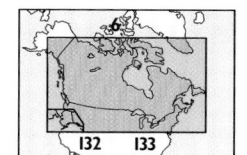

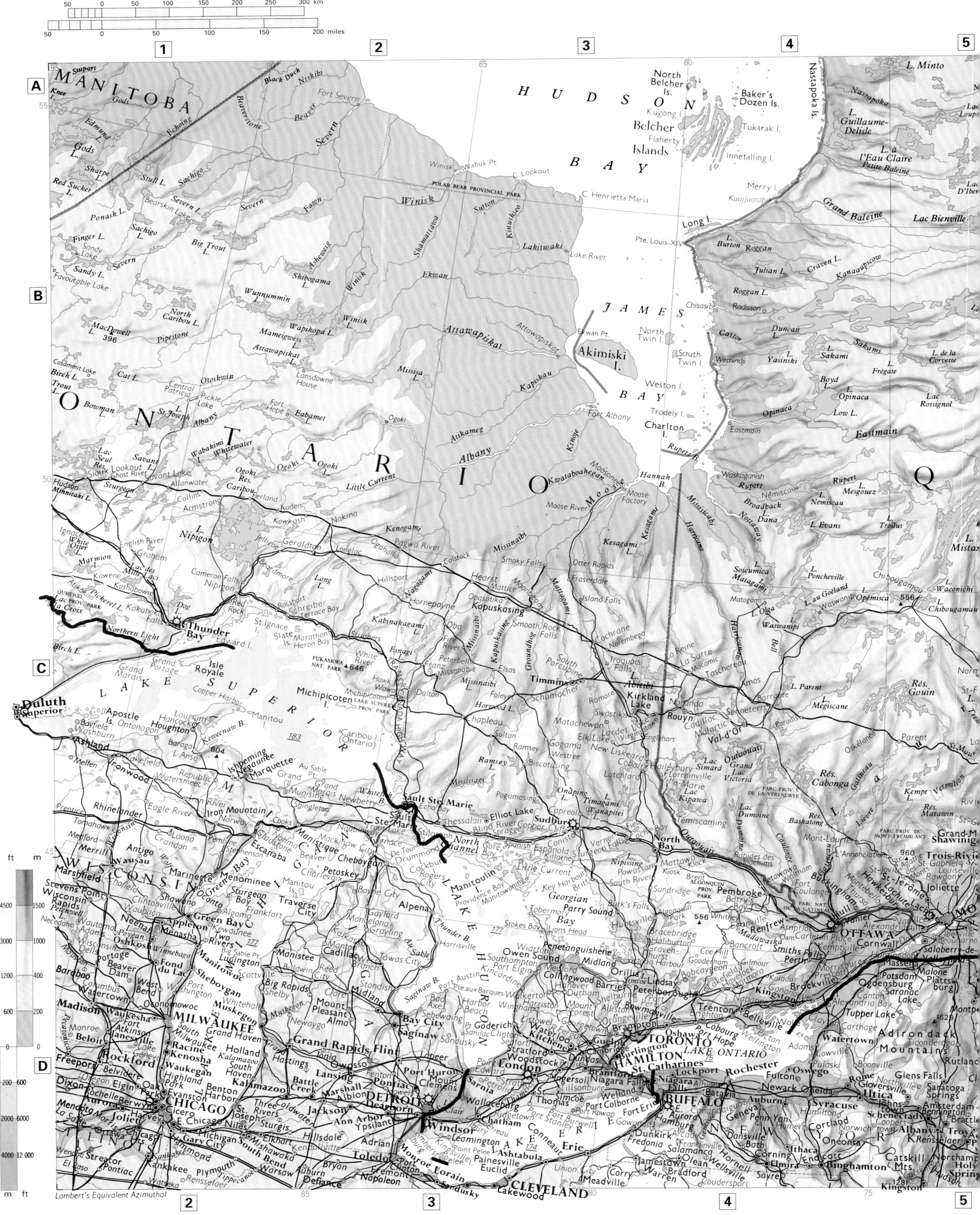

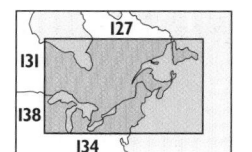

COPYRIGHT GEORGE PHILIP & SON LTD.

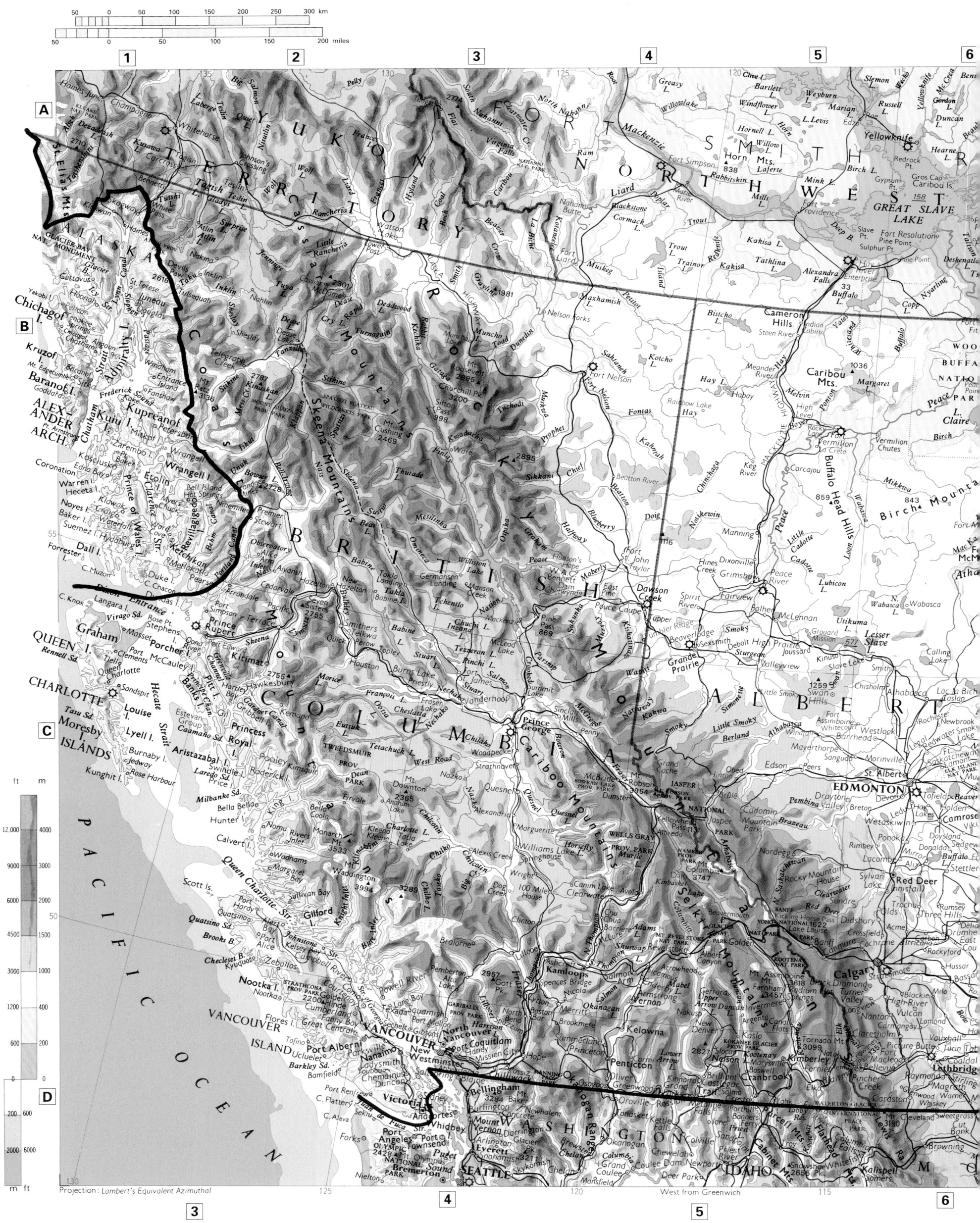

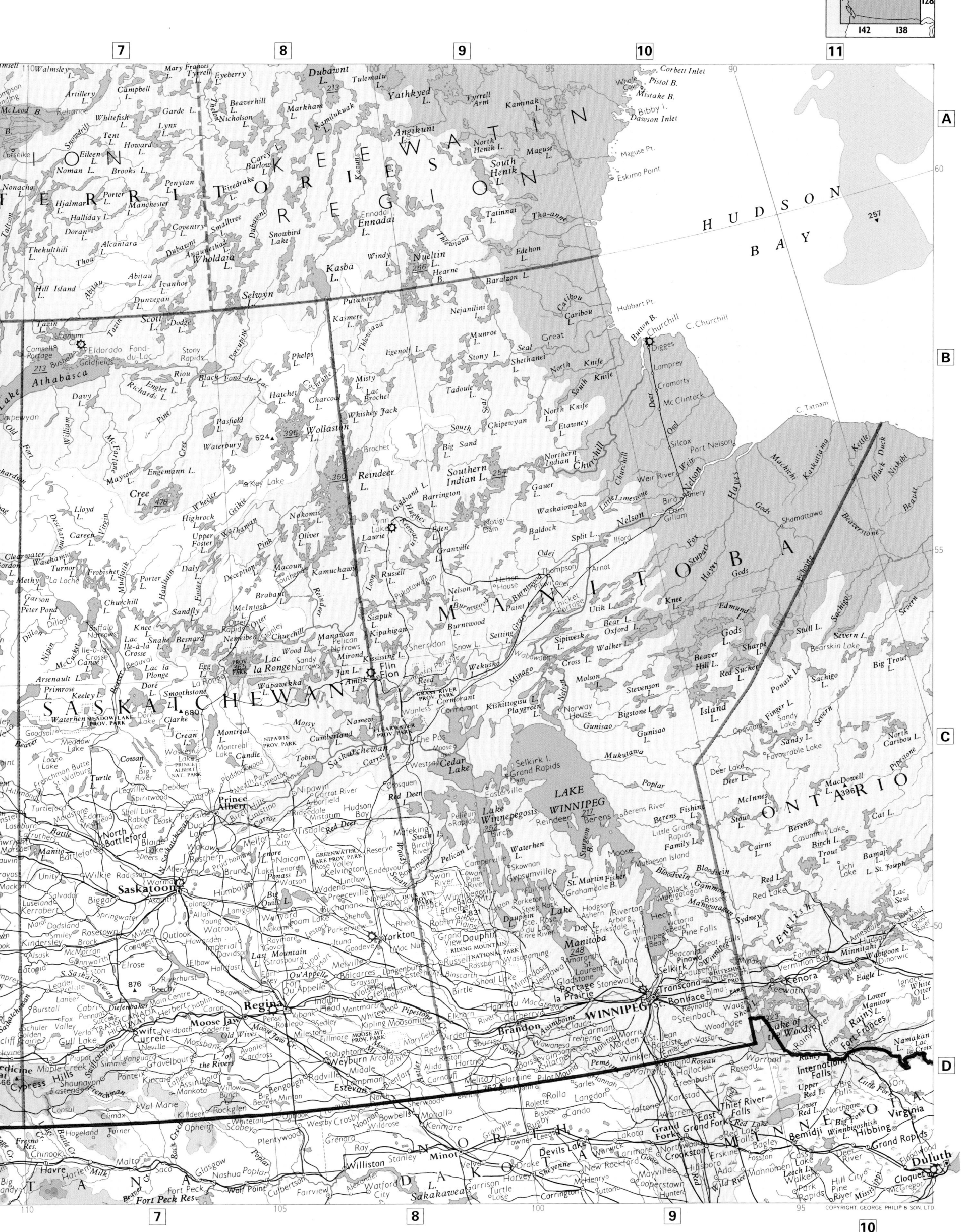

126
128
142 138

7 8 9 10 11

A

B

C

D

HUDSON
BAY

NORTH WEST TERRITORIES

KEEWATIN REGION

SASKATCHEWAN

MANITOBA

ONTARIO

LAKE WINNIPEG

Lake Athabasca

Reindeer L.

Wollaston L.

Churchill

Prince Albert

North Battleford

Saskatoon

Yorkton

Regina

Moose Jaw

Swift Current

Medicine
Cypress Hills

Brandon

WINNIPEG

St. Boniface

Transcona

Portage
la Prairie

Selkirk

Dauphin

The Pas

Flin Flon

Churchill

Kenora

Fort Frances

International
Falls

MONTANA

NORTH DAKOTA

MINNESOTA

Duluth

Grand Forks

Devils Lake

Minot

Williston

7 8 9 10

COPYRIGHT GEORGE PHILIP & SON LTD

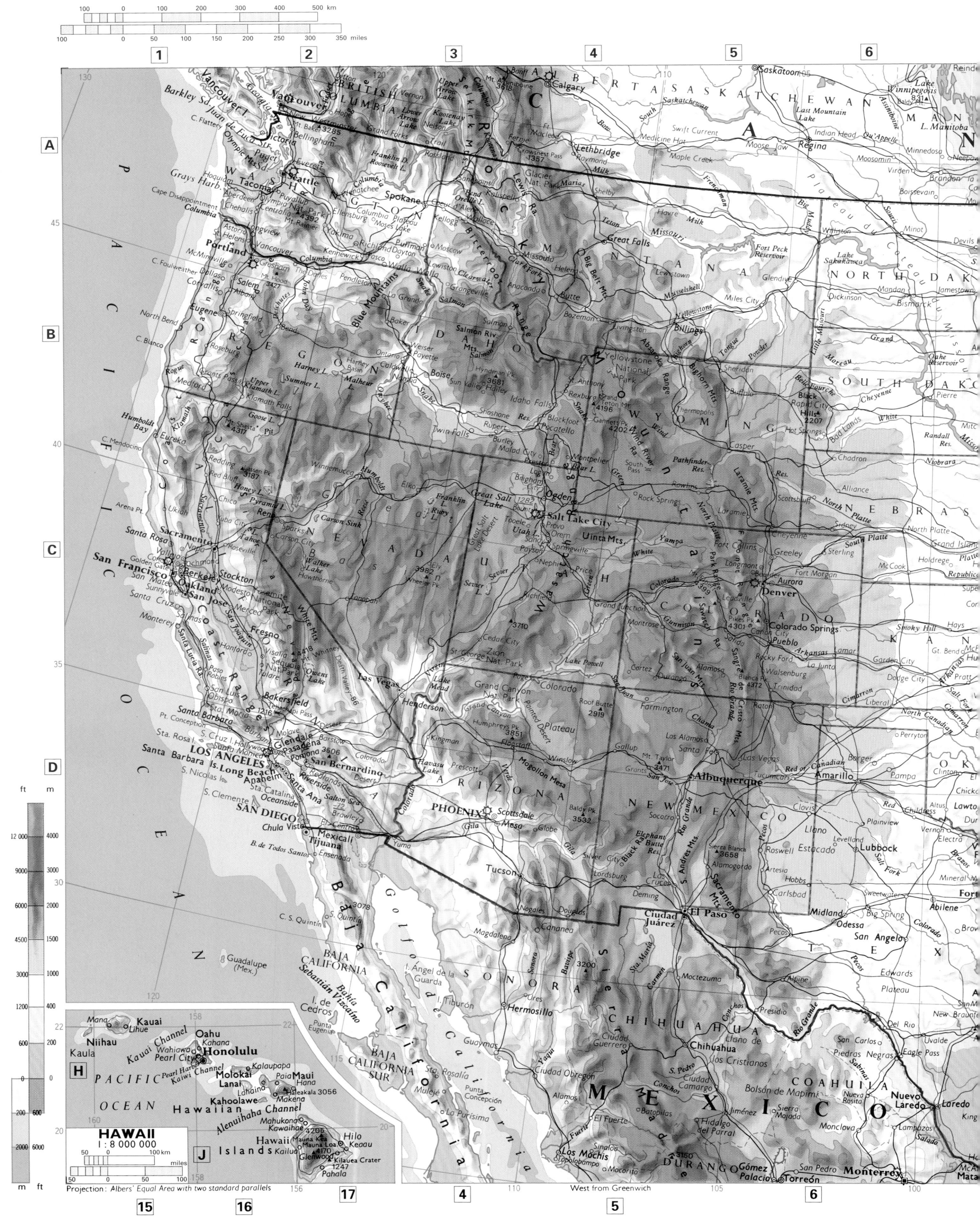

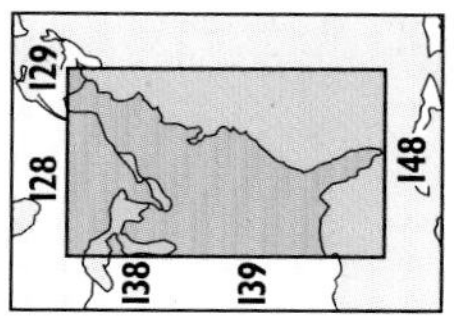

Projection: Alber's Equal Area with two standard parallels

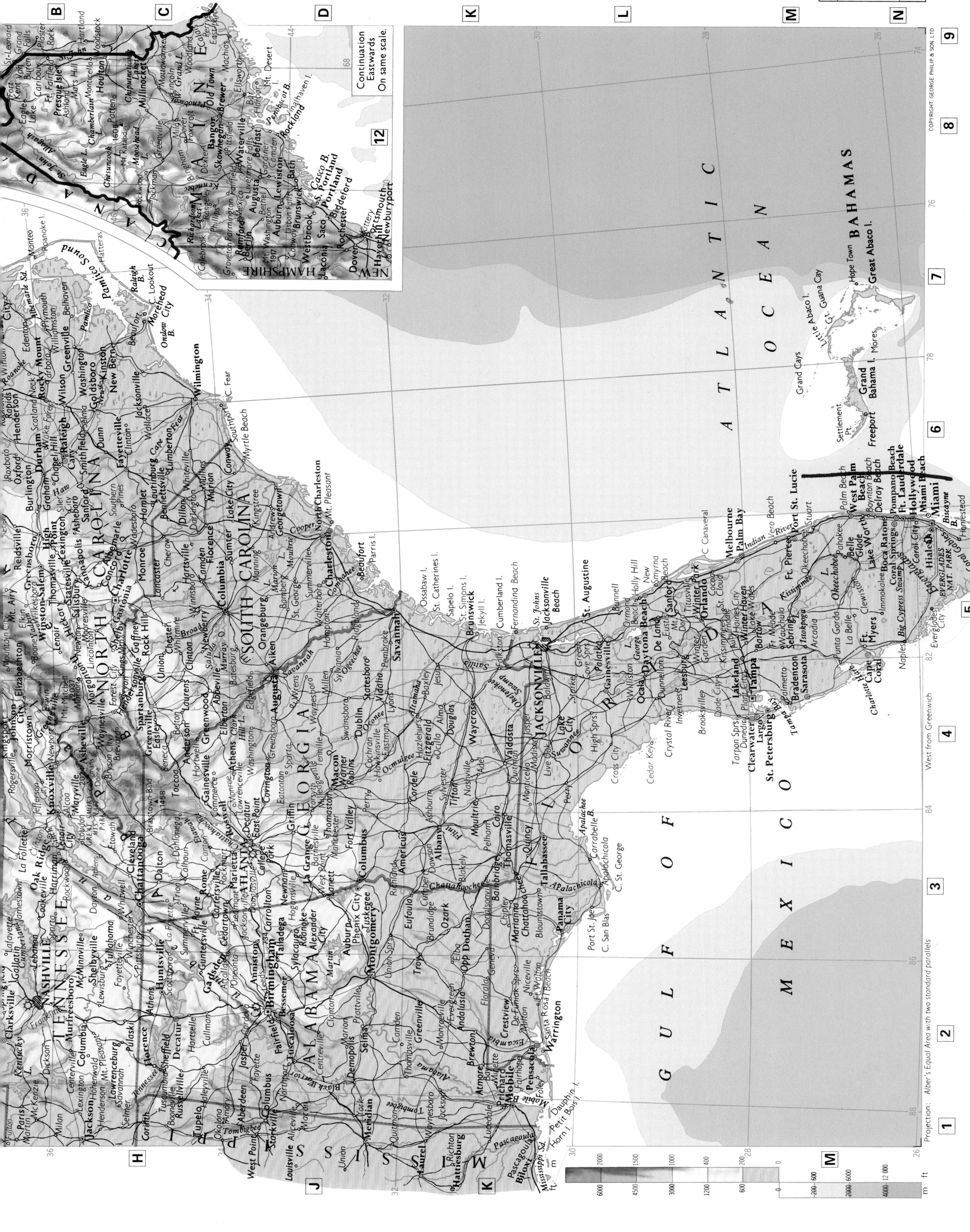

West from Greenwich

Continuation Eastwards
On same scale.

ATLANTIC OCEAN

GULF OF MEXICO

BAHAMAS

Great Abaco I.

Grand Bahama I.

NORTH CAROLINA

SOUTH CAROLINA

GEORGIA

ALABAMA

MISSISSIPPI

TENNESSEE

FLORIDA

MAINE

NEW HAMPSHIRE

ft. m
6000
4500
3000
1500
1200
600
400
200
0
m 0
200
600
2000
4000
12 000
ft

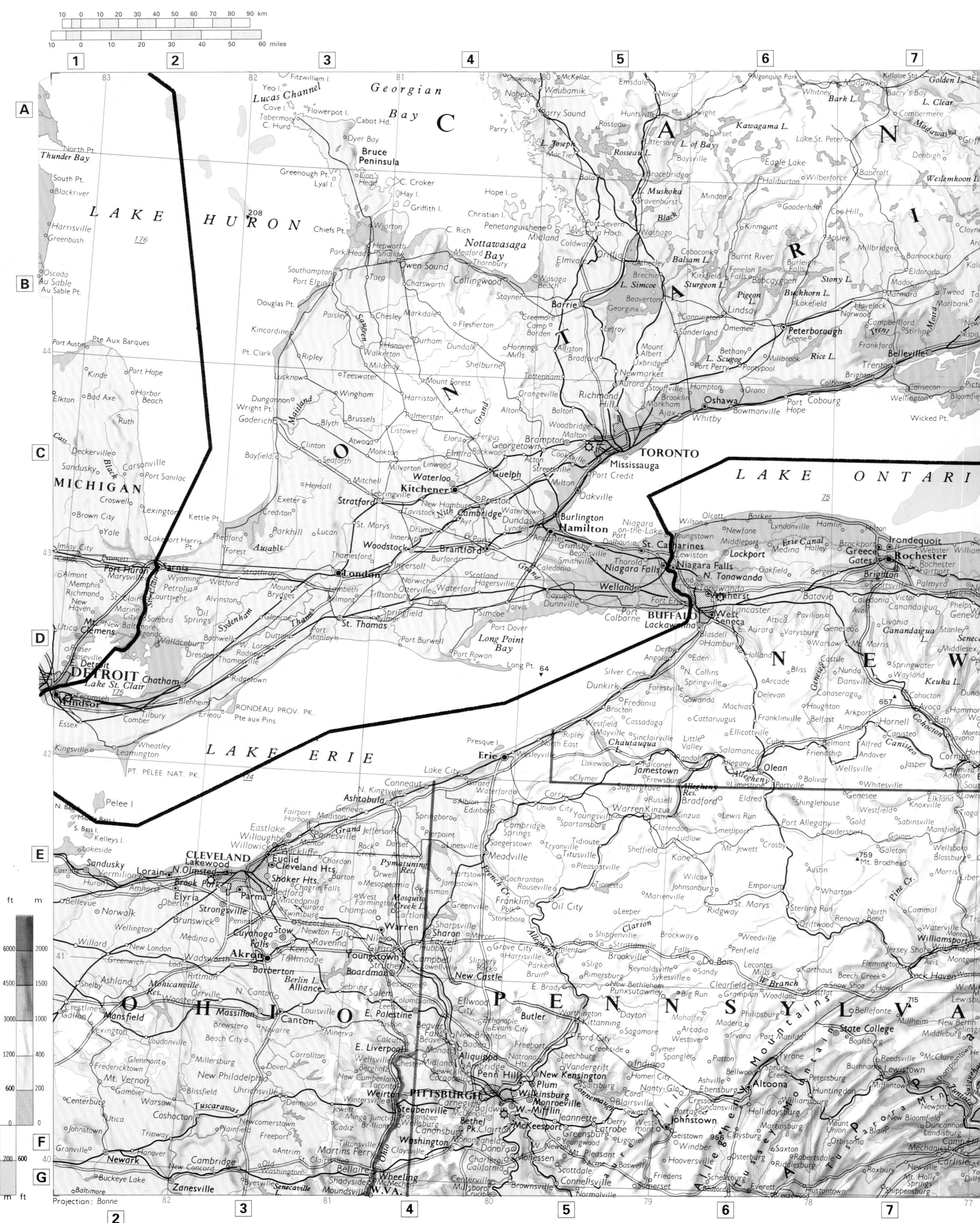

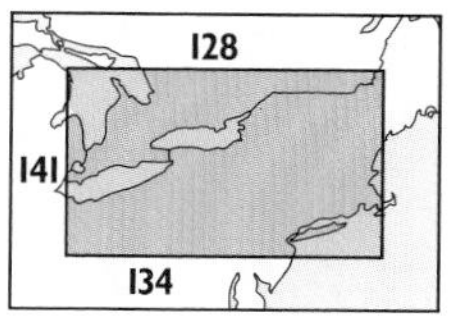
128
141
134

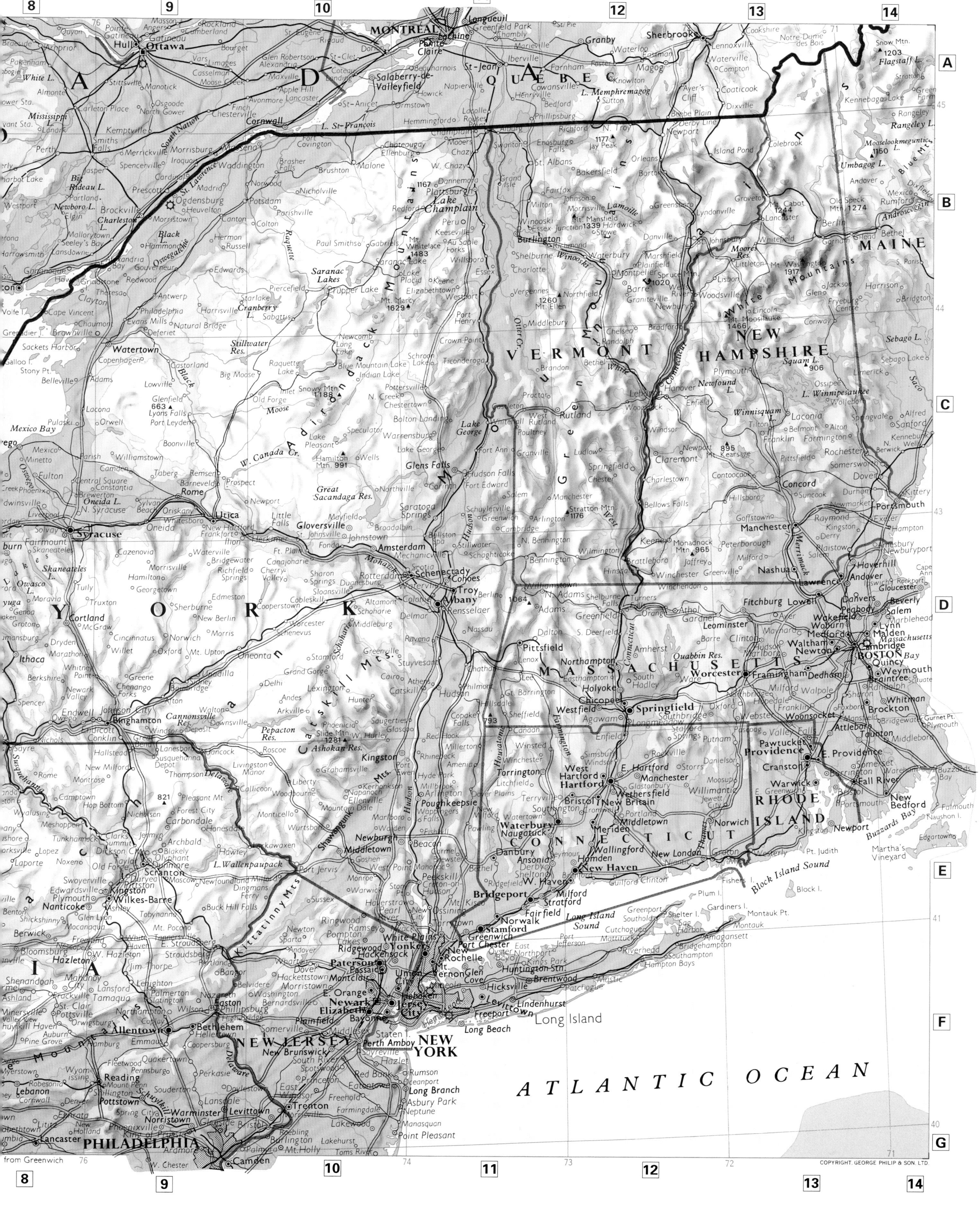
8
9
10
11
12
13
14
A
B
C
D
E
F
G
MONTREAL
Ottawa
Hull
Sherbrooke
Granby
Magog
Cornwall
Q U E B E C
L. Memphremagog
L. St-François
Plattsburg
Lake Champlain
Burlington
Montpelier
Barre
Watertown
Syracuse
Utica
Rome
Oneida L.
Amsterdam
Schenectady
Albany
Troy
Glens Falls
Saratoga Springs
Gloversville
Binghamton
Ithaca
Cortland
Kingston
Poughkeepsie
Newburgh
Middletown
Y O R K
V E R M O N T
NEW HAMPSHIRE
MAINE
MASSACHUSETTS
CONNECTICUT
RHODE ISLAND
NEW JERSEY
Concord
Manchester
Nashua
Portsmouth
Lawrence
Lowell
Haverhill
Fitchburg
Worcester
Springfield
Pittsfield
Northampton
Holyoke
BOSTON
Cambridge
Quincy
Brockton
Providence
Pawtucket
Newport
Fall River
New Bedford
Hartford
New Britain
Waterbury
New Haven
Bridgeport
Stamford
Norwalk
Middletown
New London
Mt. Washington 1917
White Mountains
Green Mountains
Adirondack Mountains
Catskill Mts.
Kittatinny Mts.
Scranton
Wilkes-Barre
Allentown
Bethlehem
Easton
Reading
Lancaster
PHILADELPHIA
Camden
Trenton
New Brunswick
Perth Amboy
Elizabeth
Newark
Jersey City
Paterson
Yonkers
NEW YORK
Long Island
Long Island Sound
Block Island Sound
Martha's Vineyard
Long Beach
Asbury Park
Long Branch
A T L A N T I C   O C E A N
from Greenwich
76
74
73
72
71
45
44
43
41
40

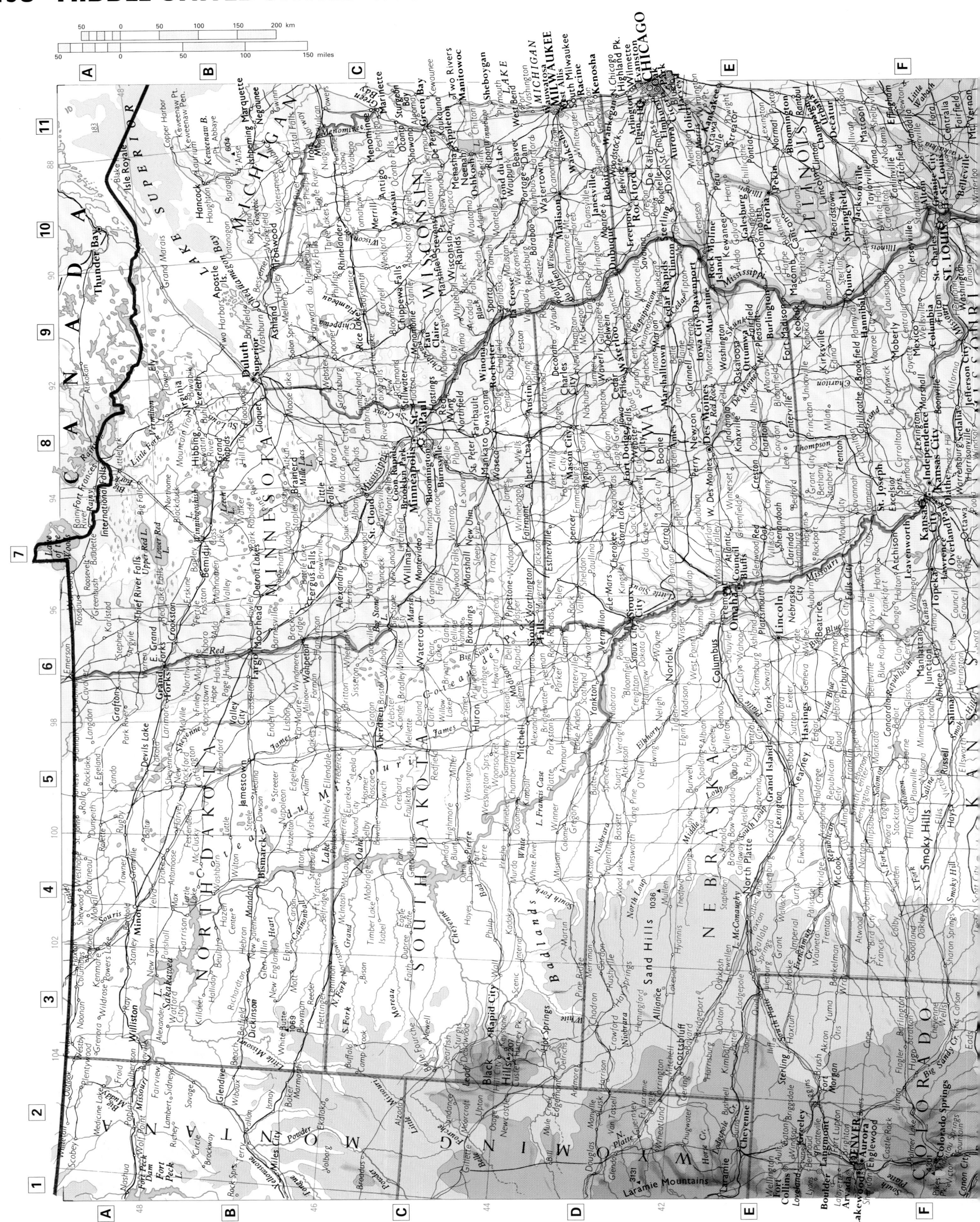

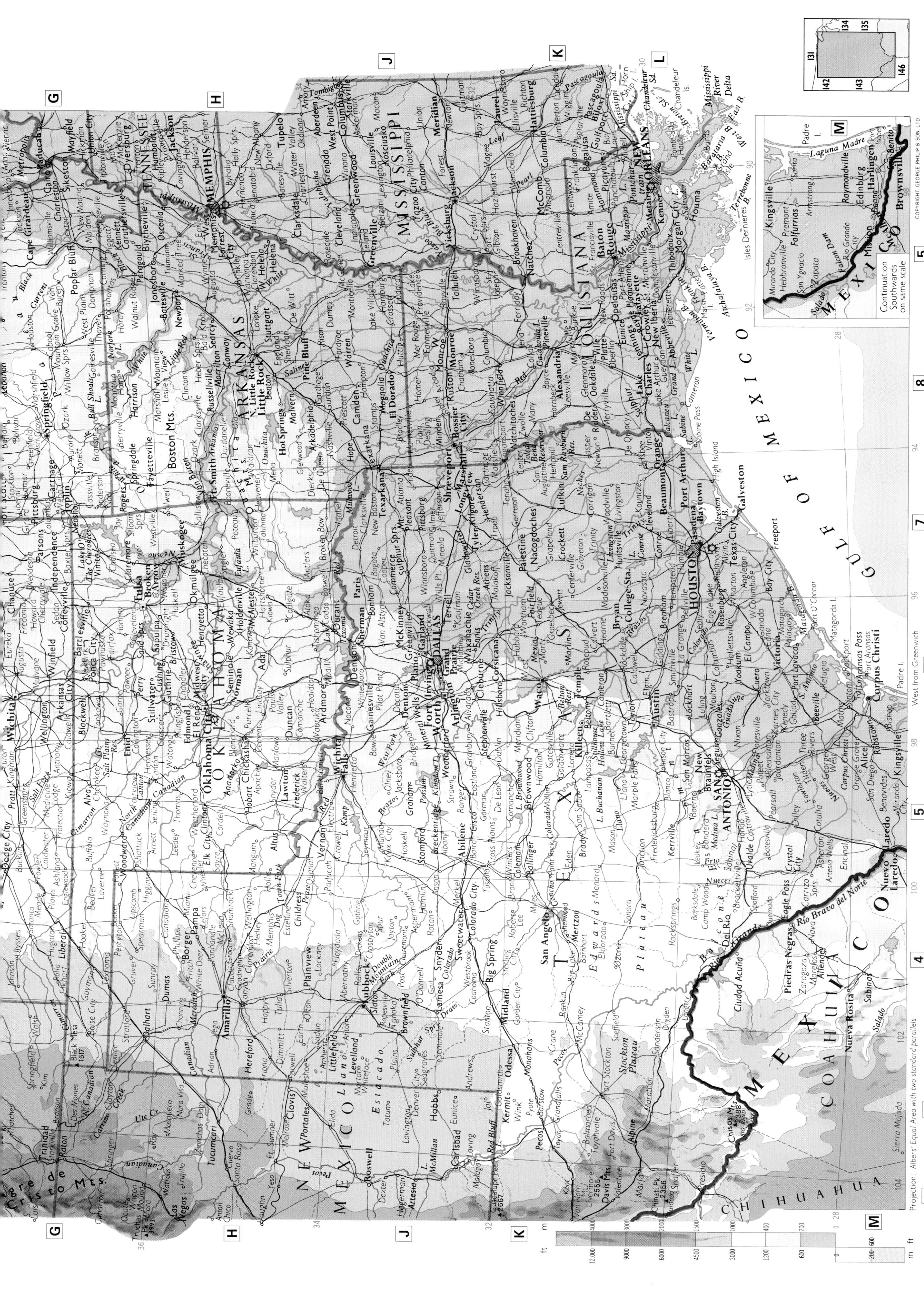

Map

TENNESSEE

MISSISSIPPI

LOUISIANA

ARKANSAS

OKLAHOMA

NEW MEXICO

TEXAS

MEXICO

COAHUILA

CHIHUAHUA

GULF OF MEXICO

MEMPHIS

NEW ORLEANS

DALLAS

Fort Worth

HOUSTON

SAN ANTONIO

Corpus Christi

Galveston

Little Rock

N. Little Rock

Oklahoma City

Tulsa

Wichita

Shreveport

Baton Rouge

Laredo

Nuevo Laredo

Brownsville

Matamoros

Laguna Madre

Padre I.

Mississippi River Delta

Chandeleur Is.

Balcones Escarpment

Edwards Plateau

Llano Estacado

Stockton Plateau

Sangre de Cristo Mts.

Boston Mts.

Ouachita Mts.

Rio Grande / Rio Bravo del Norte

Chisos Mts. 2356

Guadalupe Pk 2667

Projection: Albers' Equal Area with two standard parallels

West from Greenwich

COPYRIGHT GEORGE PHILIP & SON, LTD.

Continuation Southwards on same scale

Grid references: G H J K L M (columns); 2 3 4 5 6 7 8 (rows); 131 134 135 142 143 146

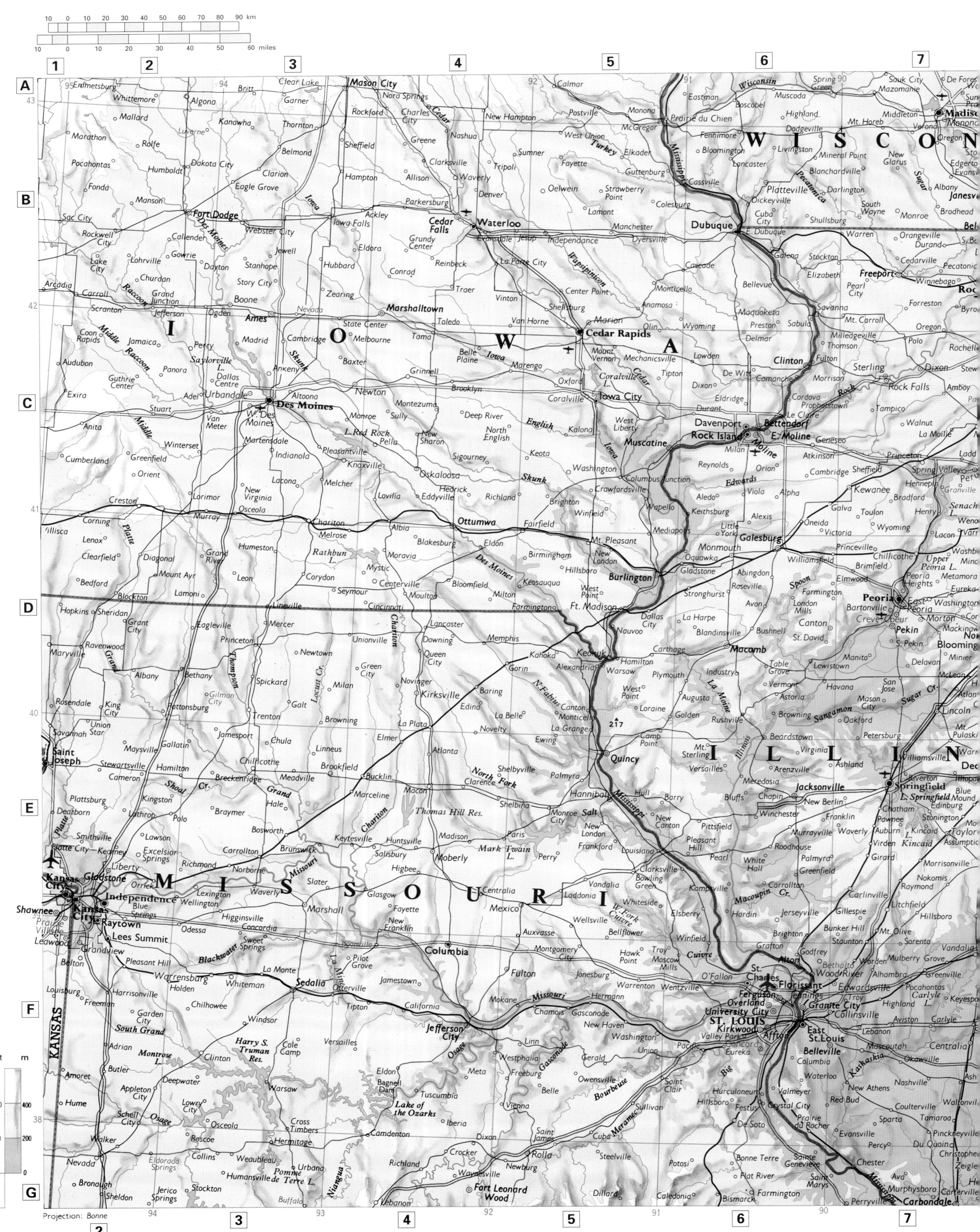

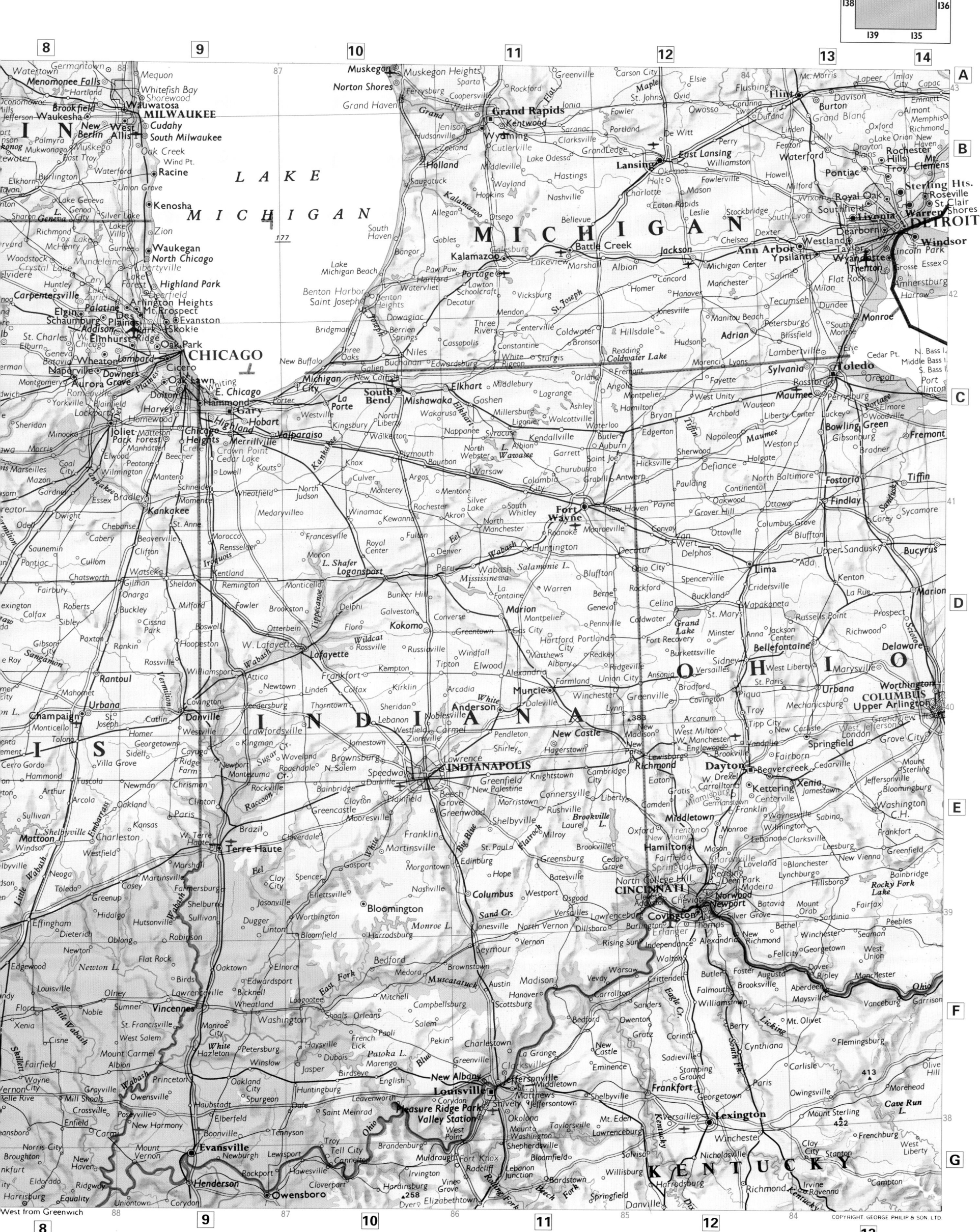

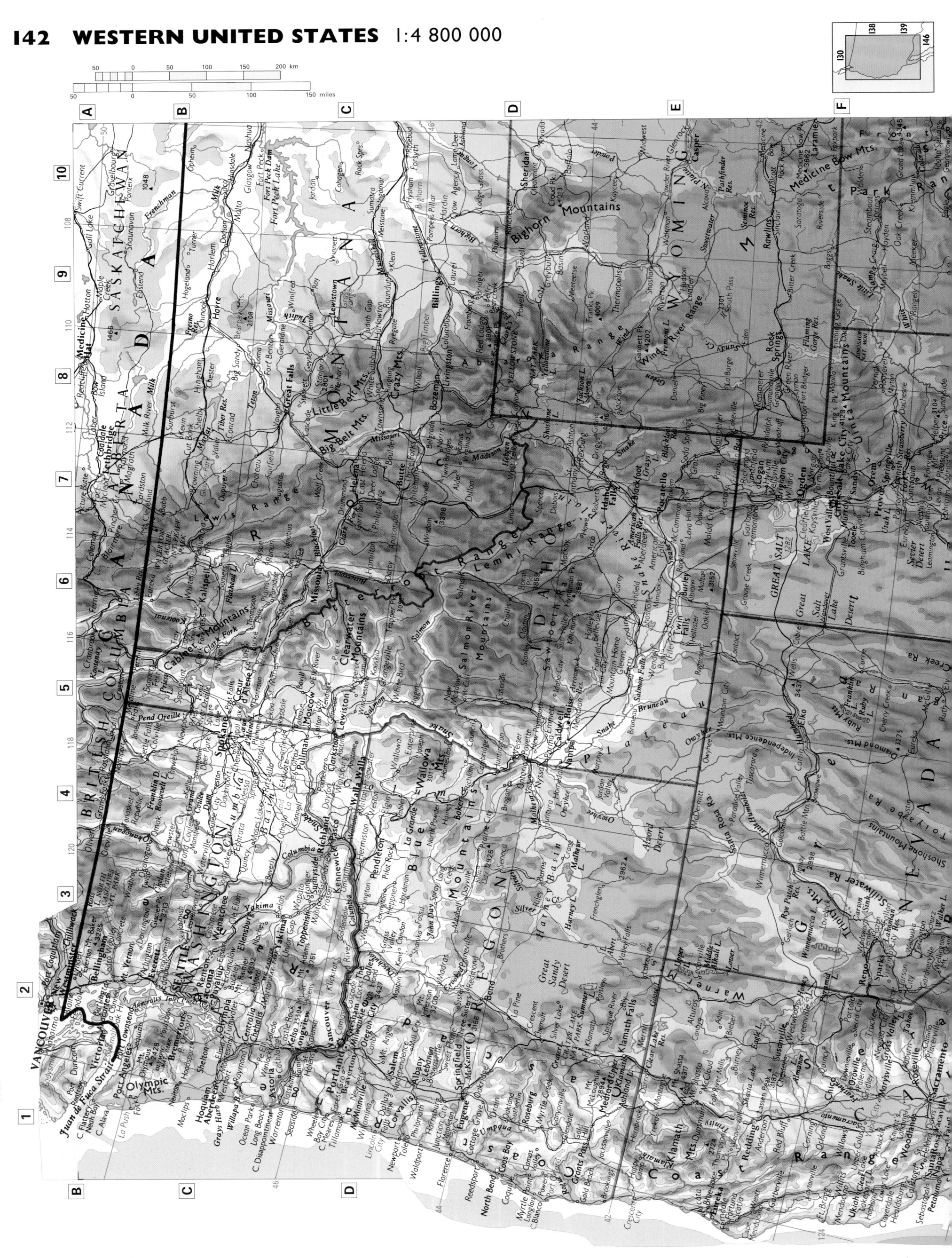

Projection: Albers' Equal Area with two standard parallels

West from Greenwich

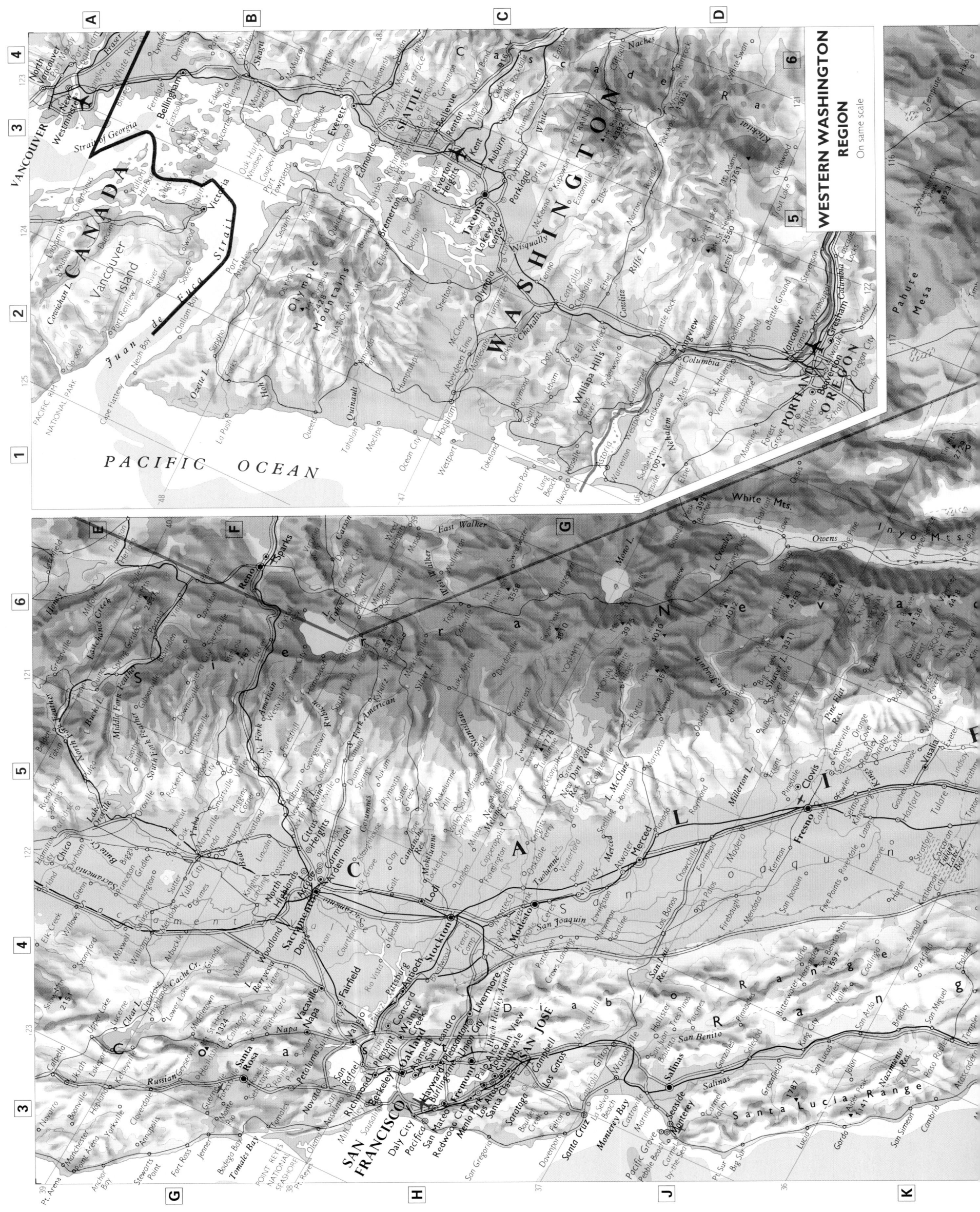

WESTERN WASHINGTON REGION
On same scale

J K L M H

10 0 10 20 30 40 50 60 70 80 90 km
0 10 20 30 40 50 60 miles

COPYRIGHT GEORGE PHILIP & SON LTD.

NEVADA

Meadow Valley Wash
Jumbo Peak 1175

Lake Mead
LAKE MEAD NATIONAL RECREATION AREA
Overton
Moapa
Hoover Dam
Henderson
Sunrise Manor
North Las Vegas
Las Vegas
Paradise
Arden
Sloan
Jean

Boulder City
L. Mohave
Davis Dam
Bullhead City
Needles
Topock
Kingman
Lake Havasu City
Parker Dam
Parker
Earp
Vidal
Bouse
Quartzsite
Vicksburg
Wickenburg

ARIZONA

Signal Peak 1457
Wenden
Hope
Salome
Aguila

Colorado R. Aqueduct
Sonora Mesa
Midland
Desert Center
Blythe
Ehrenberg
Ripley
Palo Verde
Cibola

Chocolate Mts.
Imperial Dam
Imperial Res.
Oglby
Yuma

Charleston Peak 3633
Mt. Charleston 2242
Pahrump
Tecopa
Shoshone

Death Valley
Amargosa Range
Amargosa
Telescope Peak 3366
Avawatz Mts. 1816

Silver Lake
Baker
Cima
Providence Mts.
Essex
Cadiz
Danby

Twentynine Palms
JOSHUA TREE NAT. MON.
Joshua Tree
Yucca Valley
Morongo Valley
Desert Hot Springs
Palm Springs 2633
Indio
Coachella
Salton Sea
Brawley
Westmorland
Imperial
El Centro
Holtville
Calexico
Mexicali

MOJAVE DESERT

Barstow
Yermo
Newberry Springs
Ludlow
Amboy
Bagdad

Ridgecrest
China Lake
Trona
Searles L.

Kramer Junction
Boron
Edwards
Mojave
California City
Rosamond
Lancaster
Palmdale
Victorville
Hesperia
Apple Valley
Adelanto
Hi Vista

San Bernardino Mts.
Big Bear City
Big Bear L. 2502
L. Arrowhead
Mt. San Gorgonio 3506

SAN BERNARDINO
Rialto
Fontana
Rancho Cucamonga
Upland
Redlands
Riverside
Moreno Valley
Perris
Hemet
San Jacinto 3293
Banning
Beaumont

ANZA-BORREGO DESERT ST. PARK
Borrego Springs
San Felipe
Ocotillo
Coyote Wells

Tehachapi Mts.
Tehachapi
Bakersfield
Oildale
Arvin
Lamont
Shafter
Wasco
Buena Vista L.

San Rafael Mts.
Santa Maria
Lompoc
Pt. Arguello
Pt. Conception

Santa Barbara
Goleta
Isla Vista
Ventura
Oxnard
Port Hueneme
Thousand Oaks
Simi Valley
Santa Clarita
San Fernando
Glendale
Pasadena
Burbank

LOS ANGELES
Beverly Hills
Santa Monica
Inglewood
Torrance
Redondo Beach
Palos Verdes Pt.
Palos Verdes
Downey
Norwalk
Compton
Long Beach
Anaheim
Fullerton
Garden Grove
Santa Ana
Orange
Corona
Costa Mesa
Huntington Beach
Newport Beach
Irvine
Mission Viejo
San Juan Capistrano

San Pedro Channel
Santa Catalina I.
Avalon
San Clemente I.
San Nicolas I.

Channel Islands
San Miguel I.
Santa Rosa I.
Santa Cruz I.
Santa Barbara I.

Laguna Beach
Dana Point
San Clemente
San Onofre
Pendleton
Oceanside
Carlsbad
Encinitas
Leucadia
Cardiff-by-the-Sea
Del Mar

Escondido
Vista
San Marcos
Poway
Ramona
Julian
Pine Valley

SAN DIEGO
National City
Coronado
Imperial Beach
Chula Vista
El Cajon
La Mesa
Spring Valley
Lemon Grove

Tijuana
Tecate
La Rumorosa

Gulf of Santa Catalina

M E X I C O

Is. los Coronados

P A C I F I C   O C E A N

West from Greenwich

Projection: Bonne

m ft
12,000
9000
6000
4500
3000
1200
600
0
200
2000
6000
ft m

13 12 11 10 9 8

114 115 116 117 118 119

34 33 32

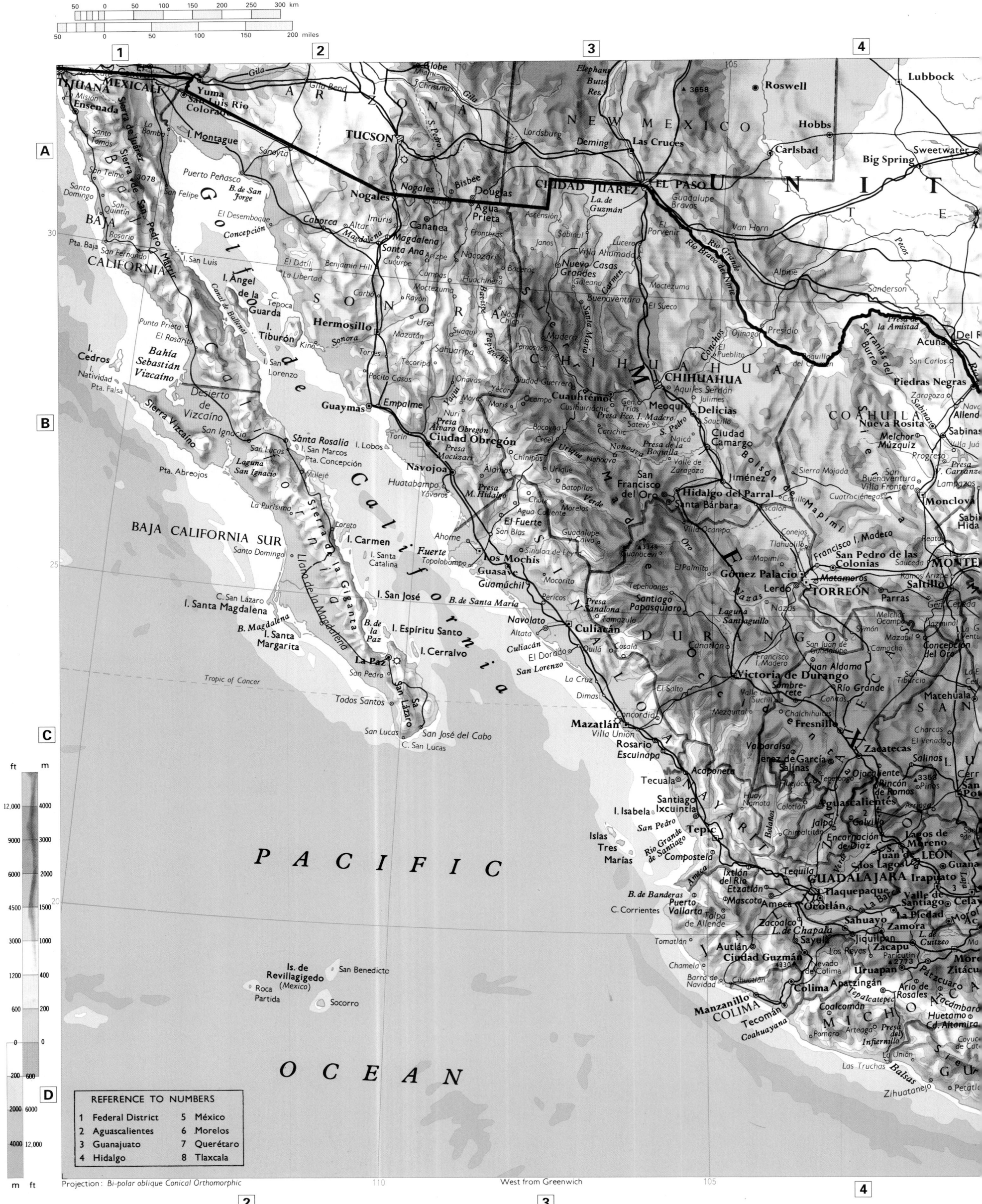

50 0 50 100 150 200 250 300 km
50 0 50 100 150 200 miles

1 **2** **3** **4**

Tijuana MEXICALI
La Misión
Ensenada Yuma
San Luis Rio
Colorado
Santo Tomás
Santo Domingo
San Telmo 3078
San Quintín
Rosario
San Fernando
Pta. Baja San Luis

ARIZONA
Globe
Christmas
Gila Bend
Gila
S. Pedro
TUCSON
Nogales
Nogales
Bisbee
Douglas
Agua Prieta

NEW MEXICO
Elephant Butte Res.
Lordsburg
Deming Las Cruces
CIUDAD JUAREZ EL PASO
La. de Guzmán
Guadalupe Bravos
Roswell
Hobbs
Carlsbad
Big Spring
Sweetwater
Lubbock

I. Montague
B. de San Jorge
Puerto Peñasco
B. de San Felipe
El Desemboque
Caborca
Altar
Imuris
Magdalena
Santa Ana
Cananea
Fronteras
Ascensión
Sabinal
Janos
Villa Ahumada
Lucero
El Porvenir
Van Horn
Alpine
Pecos
Sanderson

BAJA
CALIFORNIA
Concepción
El Dátil
Benjamin Hill
Compas
Cucurpe
Arizpe
Nacozari
Nuevo Casas Grandes
Galeana
Carmen
Buenaventura
El Sueco
Ojinaga
Presidio
Presa de la Amistad
Serranías del
Acuña
San Carlos
Del Rio

I. Angel de la Guarda
C. Tepoca
La Libertad
I. San Luis
HERMOSILLO
Ures
Mazatán
Moctezuma
Rayón
Carbó
Moctezuma
Baserac
Nácori Chico
Santa María
Madera
Temosachic
CHIHUAHUA
Aquiles Serdán
Julimes
Camargo
Jiménez
COAHUILA
Piedras Negras
Zaragoza
Allende
Sabinas

Punta Prieta
El Rosarito
I. Tiburón
Kino
Sonora
Torres
Sahuaripa
Suaqui
Yécora
Maicoba
Ciudad Guerrero
Cuauhtémoc
Cusihuiriáchic
Satevó
Bacoyna
Carichic
S. Pedro
Naica
Nueva Rosita
Melchor Múzquiz
Progreso
Villa Unión

I. Cedros
Natividad
Pta. Falsa
Bahía Sebastián Vizcaíno
Desierto de Vizcaíno
Pocito Casas
Guaymas
Empalme
Nuri
Presa Alvaro Obregón
Ciudad Obregón
Presa M. Hidalgo
Creel
Urique
Nonoava
Boquilla
Presa Fco. I. Madero
Delicias
Meoqui
CHIHUAHUA
Ciudad Camargo
Bolsón
Sierra Mojada
Jiménez
Valle de Zaragoza
San Buenaventura
Villa Frontera
Lampazos

Sierra Vizcaíno
San Ignacio
Santa Rosalía
I. San Marcos
I. Lobos
Torin
Navojoa
Alamos
Chinipas
Urique
Batopilas
San Francisco del Oro
Hidalgo del Parral
Santa Bárbara
Escalón
Villa Ocampo
Conejos
Mapimi
Cuatrociénegas
MONCLOVA

La Purísima
Laguna San Ignacio
Pta. Abreojos
Mulejé
Huatabampo
Yávaros
Agua Caliente
Morelos
Choix
San Blas
Sinaloa de Leyva
Guadalupe Calvo
3548
Guanaceví
El Palmito
Mapimi
Tlahualilo
Francisco I. Madero
San Pedro de las Colonias
Sauceda

BAJA CALIFORNIA SUR
Loreto
I. Carmen
I. Santa Catalina
Fuerte
Topolobampo
Ahome
Los Mochis
Guasave
Guamúchil
Mocorito
Tepehuanes
Santiago Papasquiaro
Gómez Palacio
Lerdo
Matamoros
TORREÓN
Parras
Saltillo

Santo Domingo
C. San Lázaro
I. Santa Magdalena
I. San José
B. de Santa María
Pericos
Presa Sanalona
Nazas
Laguna Santiaguillo
Cañatlán
Symón
Mazapil
Concepción del Oro
MONTE

B. Magdalena
I. Santa Margarita
B. de la Paz
I. Espíritu Santo
I. Cerralvo
Navolato
Culiacán
El Dorado
Quilá
Cosalá
DURANGO
Francisco I. Madero
Juan de Guadalupe
Camacho
San Juan de Guadalupe

La Paz
San Pedro
San Lázaro
Altata
Culiacán
El Dorado
La Cruz
Dimas
El Salto
Victoria de Durango
Sombrerete
Río Grande
Juan Aldama
Tiburcio
Matehuala
SAN

Tropic of Cancer
Todos Santos
San Lucas
San José del Cabo
C. San Lucas
Mazatlán
Villa Unión
Concordia
Mezquital
Chalchihuites
Fresnillo
Valparaíso
Jerez de García
Salinas
El Venado
Charcas

Rosario
Escuinapa
Acaponeta
Tecuala
Santiago Ixcuintla
Huajicori
Tepic
Huaynamota
Colotlán
Zacatecas
Aguascalientes
Rincón de Romos
Arroyo

PACIFIC
I. Isabela
San Pedro
Islas Tres Marías
Río Grande de Santiago
Compostela
Ameca
Ixtlán del Río
Etzatlán
Mascota
Ameca
Jalpa
Chimaltitán
Teocaltiche
Encarnación de Díaz
Juan
Lagos de Moreno
LEÓN
Guanajuato

Is. de Revillagigedo
San Benedicto
(Mexico)
Roca Partida
Socorro
B. de Banderas
Puerto Vallarta
Tolpa de Allende
Zacoalco
L. de Chapala
Sayula
Ameca
Ocotlán
Sahuayo
Zamora
La Piedad
Jiquilpan
Zacapu
Santiago
Valle de Santiago
Celaya
Irapuato

Tomatlán
Autlán
Ciudad Guzmán
Los Reyes
Zamora
Paricutín
Uruapan
Morelia
Zitácuaro
Pátzcuaro

OCEAN
Chamela
Barra de Navidad
Cihuatlán
Nevado de Colima
4330
COLIMA
Colima
Apatzingán
Arteaga
Coalcomán
Tepalcatepec
Ario de Rosales
Tacámbaro
Manzanillo
Tecomán
Coahuayana
MICHOACAN
Pómaro
Huetamo
Cd. Altamirano
La Unión
Zihuatanejo
Las Truchas
Balsas

REFERENCE TO NUMBERS
1 Federal District   5 México
2 Aguascalientes   6 Morelos
3 Guanajuato   7 Querétaro
4 Hidalgo   8 Tlaxcala

Projection: Bi-polar oblique Conical Orthomorphic
West from Greenwich

ft m
12,000 4000
9000 3000
6000 2000
4500 1500
3000 1000
1200 400
600 200
0 0
200 600
2000 6000
4000 12,000
m ft

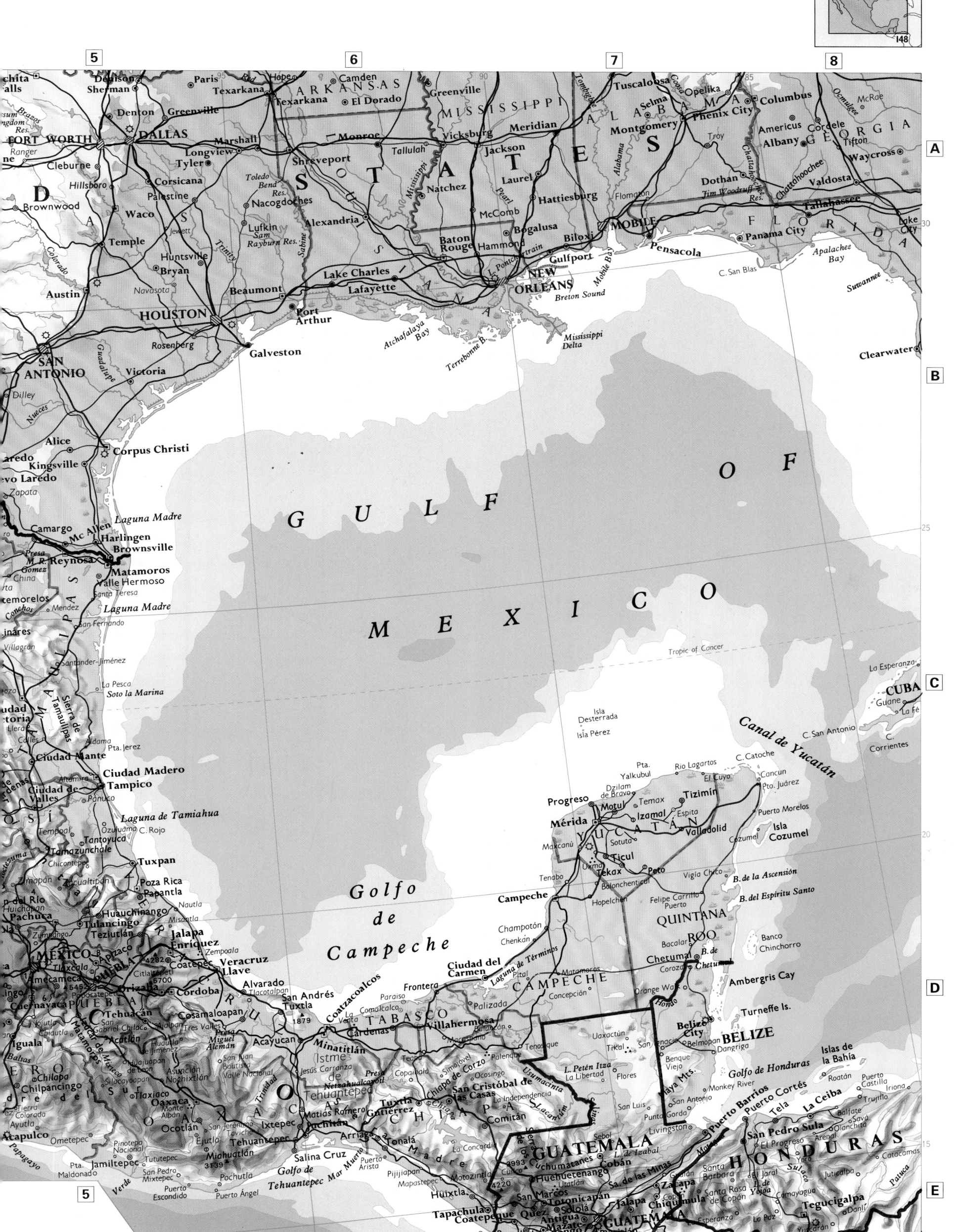

5 6 7 8

A

B

C

D

E

GULF OF MEXICO

Golfo de Campeche

CUBA

MEXICO

GUATEMALA **HONDURAS**

BELIZE

FORT WORTH · DALLAS

HOUSTON

SAN ANTONIO

NEW ORLEANS

MERIDA

YUCATÁN

QUINTANA ROO

TABASCO

CHIAPAS

OAXACA

GULF OF MEXICO

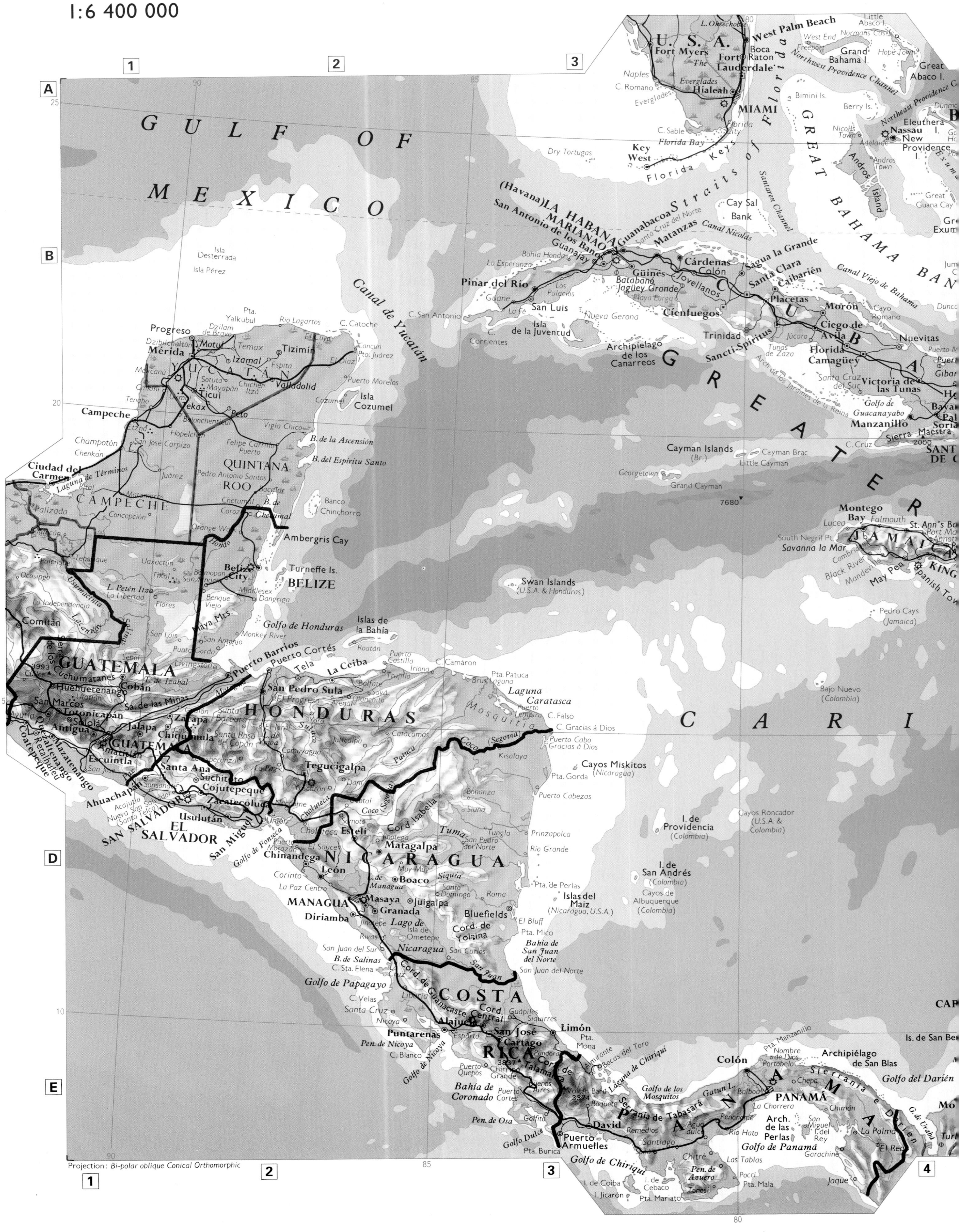

U.S.A.

Fort Myers · West Palm Beach · Boca Raton · Fort Lauderdale · Naples · MIAMI · Hialeah · Everglades · C. Romano · C. Sable · Florida Bay · Key West · Dry Tortugas · Florida Keys

Little Abaco I. · Grand Bahama I. · Hope Town · Great Abaco I. · Bimini Is. · Berry Is. · Nassau · New Providence I. · Andros Island · Eleuthera I. · Great Exuma I.

GREAT BAHAMA BANK

Straits of Florida

(Havana) LA HABANA · MARIANAO · Guanabacoa · San Antonio de los Baños · Guanajay · Pinar del Río · Guane · Los Palacios · La Fé · San Luis · Nueva Gerona · Isla de la Juventud · Corrientes · C. San Antonio

Matanzas · Cárdenas · Colón · Güines · Batabanó · Jagüey Grande · Jovellanos · Sagua la Grande · Santa Clara · Caibarién · Placetas · Morón · Cienfuegos · Trinidad · Sancti-Spíritus · Ciego de Ávila · Florida · Camagüey · Victoria de las Tunas · Manzanillo · Sierra Maestra

CUBA · GREATER

Archipiélago de los Canarreos · Golfo de Guacanayabo · Golfo de la Reina · Jardines de la Reina

Cayman Islands (Br.) · Georgetown · Grand Cayman · Cayman Brac · Little Cayman · 7680

Montego Bay · Falmouth · Lucea · Savanna la Mar · South Negril Pt. · Black River · JAMAICA · KINGSTON · Spanish Town · May Pen

Swan Islands (U.S.A. & Honduras)

Pedro Cays (Jamaica)

Bajo Nuevo (Colombia)

CARIBBEAN

Isla Desterrada · Isla Pérez

Progreso · Dzilam de Bravo · Pta. Yalkubul · Río Lagartos · C. Catoche · Mérida · Motul · Temax · Tizimín · Izamal · Espita · Cancún · Pto. Juárez · Valladolid · Chichén Itzá · Pto. Morelos · Isla Cozumel · Vigía Chico · B. de la Ascensión · B. del Espíritu Santo

YUCATAN · Ticul · Sotuta · Peto · Tekax · Mayapán

Campeche · Champotón · Hopelchén · Chenkán · CAMPECHE · Ciudad del Carmen · Palizada · Laguna de Términos · Escárcega · QUINTANA ROO · Pedro Antonio Santos · Felipe Carrillo Puerto · Banco Chinchorro · Chetumal · B. de Chetumal · Bacalar · Orange Walk · Corozal · Ambergris Cay · Turneffe Is.

Canal de Yucatán · C. San Antonio · Bahía Honda · La Esperanza

Palenque · Tenosique · Uaxactún · Tikal · Flores · L. Petén Itzá · La Libertad · BELIZE · Belize City · Middlesex · Dangriga · Benque Viejo · Maya Mts. · Monkey River · San Antonio

Comitán · La Independencia · Ocosingo · Usumacinta · Sebol

Golfo de Honduras · Islas de la Bahía · Roatán · Puerto Barrios · Livingston · Puerto Cortés · Tela · La Ceiba · Trujillo · C. Camarón · Pta. Patuca · Brus Laguna

GUATEMALA · Cuchumatanes · Cobán · L. de Izabal · Sa. de las Minas · Zacapa · Chiquimula · Santa Rosa de Copán · San Pedro Sula · El Progreso · Yoro · Sula · Santa Bárbara · Lago de Yojoa

Huehuetenango · Totonicapán · Sololá · Jalapa · GUATEMALA · Antigua · Escuintla · San Marcos · Quetzaltenango · Retalhuleu · Mazatenango · Coatepeque

HONDURAS · Tegucigalpa · Comayagua · Juticalpa · Catacamas · Danlí · Patuca · Coco

Santa Ana · Suchitoto · Cojutepeque · Zacatecoluca · Ahuachapán · Sonsonate · Nueva San Salvador · SAN SALVADOR · Usulután · San Miguel · EL SALVADOR · Golfo de Fonseca

Laguna Caratasca · Puerto · C. Falso · C. Gracias á Dios · Puerto Cabo Gracias á Dios · Segovia · Kisalaya · Cayos Miskitos (Nicaragua) · Pta. Gorda · Bonanza · Siuna · Puerto Cabezas

Estelí · Matagalpa · Chinandega · León · Boaco · NICARAGUA · Juigalpa · Tuma · Río Grande · Río San Pedro del Norte · Prinzapolka · Cord. Isabelia

MANAGUA · Masaya · Granada · Diriamba · Lago de Managua · Rivas · Lago de Nicaragua · Isla de Ometepe · Bluefields · El Bluff · Cord. de Yolaina · Siquia · Santo Domingo · Rama · Pta. de Perlas

B. de Salinas · C. Sta. Elena · Golfo de Papagayo · Cord. de Guanacaste · San Juan · San Carlos · San Juan del Norte · Bahía de San Juan del Norte · Islas del Maíz (Nicaragua, U.S.A.)

I. de Providencia (Colombia) · Cayos Roncador (U.S.A. & Colombia) · I. de San Andrés (Colombia) · Cayos de Albuquerque (Colombia)

COSTA RICA · Liberia · Santa Cruz · Nicoya · Pen. de Nicoya · Puntarenas · Alajuela · San José · Cartago · Cord. Central · Limón · C. Blanco · Golfo de Nicoya · Quepos · Bahía de Coronado · Pen. de Osa · Golfito · Golfo Dulce · Puerto Armuelles · Pta. Burica · Golfo de Chiriquí · Cord. de Talamanca · 3837

Colón · Portobelo · Nombre de Dios · Bocas del Toro · Laguna de Chiriquí · David · Santiago · Penonomé · La Chorrera · PANAMA · Chitré · Las Tablas · Golfo de Panamá · Pen. de Azuero · Pta. Mala · I. de Coiba · I. de Cebaco · Arch. de las Perlas · Isla del Rey · Golfo de San Miguel · La Palma · Serranía de San Blas · Golfo del Darién · El Real · Jaqué

Projection: Bi-polar oblique Conical Orthomorphic

50 0 50 100 150 200 250 300 km
50 0 50 100 150 200 miles

5 **6** **7** **8**

A

AS

A T L A N T I C

Tropic of Cancer

O C E A N

B

ft m
12,000 4000
9000 3000
6000 2000
4500 1500
3000 1000
1200 400
600 200
0 0

C

Town
e Bight
Cat I.
San Salvador
(Watling I., Guanahani)
Conception I.
Rum Cay
Long I.
Clarence Town
Crooked I. Passage
Richmond Crooked I.
Albert Town Snug Plana Cays
Verde Corner Mayaguana I.
Acklins I.
Mira por vos Cay
Hogsty Reef Little Inagua I.
Lake Rose Great
Matthew Inagua I.
Town

Caicos Passage
Caicos Islands (Br.)
Turks Islands (Br.)
Turks I. Passage

Baracoa
Moa
Pta. de Maisí
Cap. de Maisí
Paso de los Vientos
(Windward Passage)
Cap-à-Foux
tánamo
Gonâve
St.-Marc
Golfe de la Gonâve
Jérémie
Dame Marie
C.C.
Massif de la Hotte
Les Cayes
Pointe-à-Gravois
Î.-à-Vache

Î. de la Tortue
Port-de-Paix
Cap-Haïtien
Fort-Liberté
Santiago de Cabelleros
Gonaïves
Hinche
PORT- AU-PRINCE
San Juan
2280 Enriquillo
Aquin Jacmel

HAITI
HISPANIOLA

Monte Cristi
La Isabela
Puerto Plata
Vega
San Francisco de Macorís
Nagua
Sánchez
Sabana de La Mar
Cord. Central
3175
Hato Mayor
Higuay
C. Engaño
B. de Yuma
I. Saona
Isla Mona (U.S.A.)
Azua de Compostela
Baní San Cristóbal
San Pedro de Macorís
La Romana
Barahona
Pedernales
I. Beata C. Beata

DOMINICAN REP.
SANTO DOMINGO

Milwaukee Deep 9220
Puerto Rico Trench

Aguadilla
Arecibo
Mayagüez
Canal de la Mona

SAN JUAN
Bayamón Carolina
Caguas
Ponce 1338
Guayama

PUERTO RICO (U.S.A.)

Virgin Gorda
Virgin Is. (Br.)
Tortola
Road Town
St. Thomas
Charlotte Amalie
Virgin Is. (U.S.A.)
Christiansted St. Croix
Frederiksted

Anegada
Virgin Is.
Anegada Passage
Sombrero (Anguilla)
Anguilla (Br.)
St.-Martin (Guad.)
St. Maarten (Neth.)
St.-Barthélemy (Fr.)
Saba (Neth.)
St. Eustatius (Neth.)
Basseterre
Nevis
Redonda
Montserrat

Barbuda
ST. KITTS & NEVIS
ANTIGUA & BARBUDA
St. Johns
Antigua

LEEWARD ISLANDS
LESSER

Guadeloupe Passage
Ste-Rose Moule Désirade
(Fr.) **GUADELOUPE** Pointe-à-Pitre
Basse-Terre Grand-Bourg
Î. des Saintes (Guad.) Marie-Galante (Fr.)
Dominica Passage
Portsmouth **DOMINICA**
Roseau

I. de Aves (Bird I.) (Venezuela)

Martinique Passage
Mt. Pelée 1397 Ste-Marie
François
Rivière-Pil.
Fort-de-France
MARTINIQUE
St. Lucia Channel (Fr.)
Castries **ST. LUCIA**
Soufrière

St. Vincent Passage
Soufrière 1234 **ST. VINCENT**
Kingstown Speightstown
Bridgetown
BARBADOS

Hillsborough The Grenadines
St. George's **GRENADA**

ANTILLES

WINDWARD ISLANDS
LESSER ANTILLES

m ft
200 600
2000 6000
4000 12,000
6000 18,000
8000 24,000
m ft

D

BEAN SEA

LESSER ANTILLES

Aruba (Neth.)
Curaçao
Bonaire
Willemstad
NETH. ANTILLES

Pta. Gallinas
C. San Román
Pen. de la Guajira
Pta. Espada
Pen. de Paraguaná
Punto Fijo
Punta Cardón
Golfo de Venezuela

Is. de Aves (Ven.)
Is. Los Roques (Ven.)
I. Orchila (Ven.)
I. Blanquilla (Ven.)
I. Los Hermanos (Ven.)
I. Los Testigos (Ven.)
Tobago
Scarborough

Ríohacha
Uribia
GUAJIRA
C. San Juan de Guía
Santa Marta
Cienaga
Nevada de Santa Marta 5800
Soledad
Sabanalarga
Fundación
Valledupar
Agustín Codazzi
Zambrano
Calamar
Magangué
Mompós
El Banco

Coro
La Vela de Coro
FALCÓN
Altagracia
Mene de Mauroa
Tucacas
Puerto Cumarebo

Puerto Cabello
Maiquetía
La Guaira
CARACAS
Los Teques
DISTRITO FEDERAL
MIRANDA
Puerto La Cruz
Río Chico
Ocumare del Tuy
Villa de Cura
S. Juan de los Morros
El Sombrero

I. La Tortuga (Ven.)
I. Margarita
La Asunción
NUEVA ESPARTA
Porlamar
Pen. de Paria
Carúpano
Río Caribe
Güiria
SUCRE
Cumaná
Cariaco
Carúpano
Caripito

Dragon's Mouth
Port of Spain
Arima
Galera Pt.
Trinidad
TRINIDAD & TOBAGO
San Fernando
Serpent's Mouth

Ciudad Ojeda
Mene Grande
Machiques
La Concepción
Santa Rita
Cabimas
MARACAIBO
La Ceiba
Lago de Maracaibo
Betijoque
ZULIA
Villa del Rosario
San Carlos del Zulia
Catatumbo
El Tocuyo
Valera
Trujillo
TRUJILLO
MÉRIDA
Barinas
Ciudad Bolivia
Santa Bárbara
BARINAS
Bruzual

San Felipe
YARACUY
Chivacoa
Nirgua
Carora
Barquisimeto
LARA
Acarigua
Guanare
PORTUGUESA
El Baúl

Valencia
CARABOBO

San Carlos
COJEDES
Calabozo
GUÁRICO
Santa María de Ipire
Valle de la Pascua
Unare
El Pao
Aragua de Barcelona
Barcelona
Anaco
El Tigre
Cantaura
Pariaguán
ANZOÁTEGUI
Soledad
Maturín
MONAGAS
Tucupita
DELTA AMACU

Ciudad Guayana
Sierra Imataca
Upata
Guasipati
El Callao
Tumeremo
Ciudad Bolívar
Caroní
Emb. de Guri
El Pao

San Rafael
Cúcuta
NORTE DE SANTANDER
Ocaña
Cord. de Mérida
Cerro Bolívar
San Fernando de Apure
Apure
Arauca
San Juan de Nutrias
Achaguas
Mapire
Orinoco
Caicara
VENEZUELA

Ayapel
Caucasia
Simití
Corozal
BOLÍVAR
CÉSAR
Plato

E

West from Greenwich

5 **6** **7**

75 70 65 60
25 20 15 10

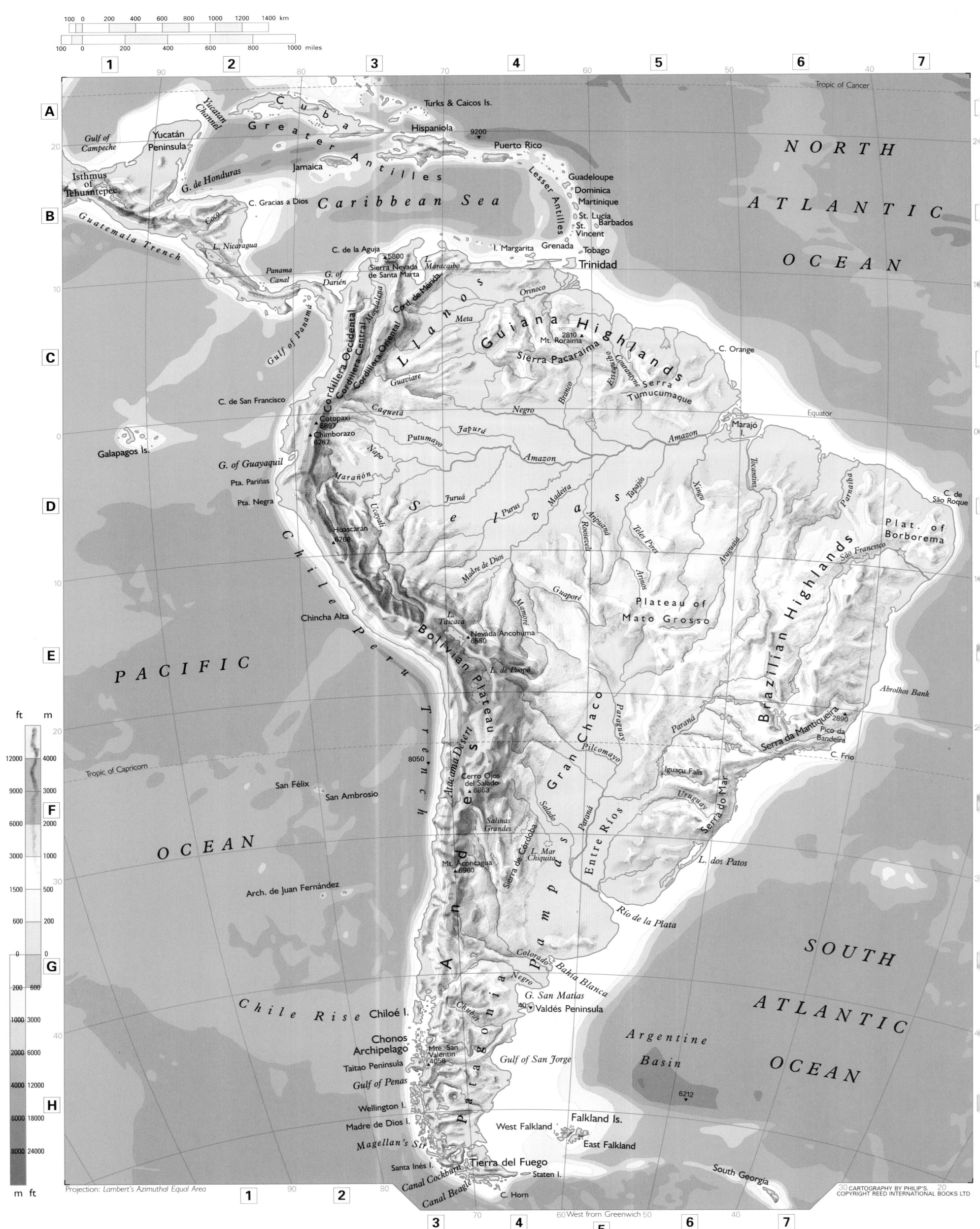

100 0 200 400 600 800 1000 1200 1400 km
100 0 200 400 600 800 1000 miles

1 2 3 4 5 6 7

90 80 70 60 50 40

Tropic of Cancer

A

Yucatán Channel *Cuba* Turks & Caicos Is.

Gulf of Campeche Yucatán Peninsula *Greater Antilles* Hispaniola 9200 Puerto Rico

20

Isthmus of Tehuantepec G. de Honduras Jamaica *Caribbean Sea* Guadeloupe Dominica Martinique St. Lucia St. Vincent Barbados Grenada Tobago Trinidad

NORTH ATLANTIC OCEAN

B

Guatemala Trench C. Gracias a Dios *Coco* L. Nicaragua C. de la Aguja 5800 Sierra Nevada de Santa Marta *Maracaibo* I. Margarita Lesser Antilles

Panama Canal G. of Darién *Orinoco* *Meta* 2810 Mt. Roraima C. Orange

10

Cord de Mérida *Llanos* *Guiana Highlands* *Serra*
Sierra Pacaraima *Cuaurinera Serra Tumucumaque*

C

C. de San Francisco *Cordillera Occidental* *Cordillera Central* *Cordillera Oriental* *Guaviare* *Caquetá* *Negro* *Branco*

Cotopaxi 5897 Chimborazo 6267 *Gulf of Panamá* *Putumayo* *Japurá* *Amazon* *Marajó I.*

Galapagos Is. G. of Guayaquil Pta. Pariñas Pta. Negra *Napo* *Marañón* *Amazon* *Tocantins* Equator

0

Juruá *Purus* *Madeira* *Xingu* *Tapajós* *Teles Pires* *Araguaia* *Tocantins* *Parnaiba* C. de São Roque

D

Huascarán 6768 *Ucayali* *S e l v a s* *Roosevelt* *Arinos* *São Francisco* Plat. of Borborema

10

Chile Peru Trench Chincha Alta *Madre de Dios* *Guaporé* Plateau of Mato Grosso *Brazilian Highlands*

L. Titicaca *Mamoré* Nevada Ancohuma 6550 *Bolivian Plateau* L. de Poopó

E

PACIFIC *Paraguay* *Paraná* Abrolhos Bank

20

Tropic of Capricorn San Félix San Ambrosio *Atacama Desert* 8050 *Gran Chaco* *Pilcomayo* *Uruguay* *Serra do Mar* Iguaçu Falls Serra da Mantiqueira 2890 Pico da Bandeira C. Frio

F

OCEAN Cerro Ojos del Salado 6863 Salinas Grandes *Salado* *Entre Ríos*

Arch. de Juan Fernández Mt. Aconcagua 6960 Sierra de Córdoba L. Mar Chiquita *Paraná* L. dos Patos

30

G

A n d e s *P a m p a s* *Río de la Plata*

Chile Rise Chiloé I. *Negro* *Colorado* Bahía Blanca *SOUTH ATLANTIC OCEAN*

Chonos Archipelago *Chubut* G. San Matías 40 Valdés Peninsula *Argentine Basin*

H

Taitao Peninsula Mte. San Valentín 4058 Gulf of San Jorge

40

Gulf of Penas *P a t a g o n i a* 6212

Wellington I.

Madre de Dios I. *Magellan's Str.* West Falkland Falkland Is. East Falkland

Santa Inés I. *Tierra del Fuego* Staten I. South Georgia

C. Horn

ft m

12000 4000
9000 3000
6000 2000
3000 1000
1500 500
600 200
0 0
200 600
1000 3000
2000 6000
4000 12000
6000 18000
8000 24000

m ft

1 2 3 4 5 6 7

90 80 70 60 West from Greenwich 50 40 30 20

CARTOGRAPHY BY PHILIP'S.
COPYRIGHT REED INTERNATIONAL BOOKS LTD

1 90   2   80   3   70   4   60   5   50   6   40   7

Tropic of Cancer

Havana   BAHAMAS   Turks & Caicos Is.   A
     CUBA   (U.K.)   20

                                                          Virgin Is.   NORTH
HAITI   DOMINICAN   (U.K.)
        REP.   San Juan   ANTIGUA &
JAMAICA Port-au-   PUERTO   BARBUDA   ATLANTIC
        Prince   Kingston RICO   ST. KITTS
                         (U.S.A.) & NEVIS
MEXICO   Basse-Terre GUADELOUPE (Fr.)
     BELIZE   DOMINICA (Fr.)   OCEAN   B
GUATEMALA   Fort-de-France MARTINIQUE
     HONDURAS   Caribbean Sea Castries ST. LUCIA
Guatemala Tegucigalpa   ST. VINCENT BARBADOS
San Salvador   Kingstown St. George's Bridgetown
EL SALVADOR NICARAGUA   GRENADA TRINIDAD &
        Managua   Port of TOBAGO
    COSTA   San José   C. de   Spain
    RICA   Panamá la Aguja Barranquilla Maracaibo Caracas
          PANAMA Cartagena   Barquisimeto Valencia   10
     G. of Darién   Orinoco Ciudad Guayana
Gulf of Panama   Cúcuta San Cristóbal   Georgetown
          Medellín Bucaramanga VENEZUELA GUYANA Paramaribo
                                          SURINAM Cayenne
          Bogotá   C. Orange
     Cali   GUYANA FRENCH C
          COLOMBIA   RORAIMA   GUIANA
                                        AMAPÁ
Galapagos Is.   Branco   Equator
(Ecuador)   Quito   Japurá
          ECUADOR   Putumayo   Marajó
     Guayaquil   Napo   Amazon Manaus Santarém I. Belém
G. of Guayaquil Marañón Iquitos   São Luís
                                 Amazon   Tocantins   Fortaleza
          Chiclayo   Ucayali AMAZONAS Madeira PARÁ   C. de
                    Juruá   MARANHÃO São Roque D
     Trujillo   ACRE   Purus   Tapajós Xingu Teresina RIO G.
     Chimbote   CEARÁ DO NORTE Natal
          PERU   Pôrto Velho Parnaíba   PARAÍBA
                    Madre de Dios RONDÔNIA PIAUÍ Campina Grande
     Callao LIMA   BRAZIL TOCANTINS PERNAMBUCO Recife
          Cuzco   ALAGOAS Maceió
     L.   Mamoré MATO GROSSO São Francisco SERGIPE Aracaju
     Titicaca   BAHÍA
          Arequipa BOLIVIA   Cuiabá GOIÁS   Salvador E
     Iquique   La Paz Cochabamba   DIS. FED Brasília
                 Santa Cruz   Goiânia MINAS GERAIS
          Sucre   MATO GROSSO
          PACIFIC   DO SUL   Belo
     Antofagasta   Paraguay   Ribeirão Horizonte ESPÍRITO
Tropic of Capricorn   Prêto   SANTO
San Félix   Salta PARAGUAY Paraná Juiz Vitória
(Chile)   San Ambrosio   de Fora
     (Chile)   San Miguel Pilcomayo   PARANÁ Campinas R. DE J. Campos F
          de Tucumán Resistencia Asunción SÃO PAULO SÃO Niterói
     OCEAN   Corrientes   PAULO RIO DE
Arch. de Juan Fernández Salado SANTA CATARINA Curitiba JANEIRO
     (Chile)   Córdoba Santa Fe RIO GRANDE
          San Juan Paraná DO SUL Pôrto Alegre
Viña del Mar Mendoza Rosario URUGUAY   G
Valparaíso   ARGENTINA Pelotas
SANTIAGO   Buenos Aires Montevideo   SOUTH
     Talca   CHILE   La Plata Río de la Plata
Concepción   Bahía   ATLANTIC
     Valdivia   Colorado Blanca Mar del Plata
                    Negro Viedma   OCEAN
Puerto Montt   Chubut
                                             H
          Gulf of San Jorge
     Comodoro Rivadavia
Gulf of Penas   West Falkland FALKLAND IS.
          Magellan's Str.   (U.K.)
     Punta Arenas Stanley East Falkland
          Tierra del Fuego
                    South Georgia
          C. Horn   (U.K.)

50 0   50 100 150 200 250 300 km
50 0   50   100   150   200 miles

A
B
C

ft   m
18,000 6000
12,000 4000
9000   3000
6000   2000
4500   1500
3000   1000
1200   400
600   200
0   0
200   600
2000   6000
4000   12,000
m   ft

CARIBBEAN   SEA

Aruba   NETH. ANTILLES
(Neth.) Curaçao Bonaire
Pta. Gallinas
Cabo de la Vela   C. San Román   Is. de Aves
Península   Pta. Espada   (Ven.)   Is. Los Roques
de la Guajira   Pen. de
Ríohacha   Paraguaná
                  Punto Fijo
LA   Punta Cardón   Puerto Cumarebo
GUAJIRA   Golfo de   Coro
Maicao   Venezuela   La Vela
Santa Marta   Mirimire
Ciénaga Sierra Nevada de   FALCÓN   Tucuyo de
BARRANQUILLA S. Juan   Dabajuro   la Costa   DISTRITO
Soledad   5800 del César   Mene de Mauroa Siquisique FEDERAL
ATLÁNTICO Santa Marta   Altagracia   Maiquetía
Sabanalarga Valledupar   San   Mene   San Felipe LA GUAIRA
Baranoa   Rafael Grande   Sta. Rita Yaritagua CARACAS
CARTAGENA Calamar   Villanueva MARACAIBO Cabimas Carora Los Teques
I. de Barú Ajona   La   BARQUISIMETO San Juan Victoria Alta
Turbaco   MAGDALENA Agustín   ZULIA Lago de Bachaquero El Tocuyo de los Morros de
Is. de San Bernardo Plato Codazzi   Maracaibo Mene   ARAGUA
Sincelejo Zambrano   La Ceiba   San Carlos
S. Onofre El Carmen Chimichagua CESAR   Trujillo   COJEDES Las Mercedes
SUCRE Magangué El Banco   San Carlos TRUJILLO Valera Guanare   Calabozo
Monteria Mompós   del Zulia MÉRIDA Boconó   PORTUGUESA GUARICO
CÓRDOBA BOLÍVAR Morales   Catatumbo Mérida 5007 Barinas Guanarito
Cereté Majagual   El Vigía   5007   BARINAS   Orituco
Planeta Rica Ayapel   NORTE Tovar La Grita BARINAS
Montelíbano Aguachica DE Cúcuta Sta. Bárbara Apure San Fernando
Tierralta Caucasia   OCAÑA Táriba Guasdualito de Apure
ANTIOQUIA SANTANDER   San Cristóbal Achaguas
MEDELLÍN BUCARAMANGA   Rubio VENEZUELA
CHOCÓ   Pamplona ARAUCA
Quibdó   ARAUCA
MANIZALES   Arauca
Bogotá   CASANARE
COLOMBIA   VICHADA
CALI   META
Popayán   GUAVIARE
CAUCA   GUAINÍA
Pasto   VAUPÉS
NARIÑO   AMAZONAS
ECUADOR
Quito
Guayaquil
PERU
LORETO

PACIFIC
OCEAN

Projection: Lambert's Equivalent Azimuthal

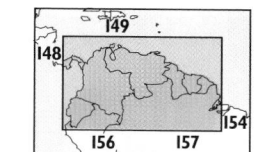

5   6   7

A T L A N T I C

O C E A N

A

B

C

D

La Blanquilla (Ven.)
Los Hermanos (Ven.)
St. George's **GRENADA**
Is. Los Testigos (Ven.)
Tobago
Scarborough

NUEVA ESPARTA
Margarita
La Asunción
Pta. Arenas
Porlamar
Coche
Carúpano
Río Caribe
Pen. de Paria
Güíria
Arima
Port of Spain
TRINIDAD
AND TOBAGO
Trinidad
Río Claro
Galeota Point

Pen. de Araya
Cumaná
SUCRE
Golfo de San Fernando
Cariaco
San Fernando
Barcelona 2596
Caicara
Caripito
Maturín
Amana
MONAGAS
Vincent's Mouth
Boca de la Sierpe
Guanta
Anaco
Cantaura
Guanipa
Tigre
Guarapiche
Morichal Largo
Caño Macareo
Boca Grande
I. Corocoro
Morawhanna

ANZOATEGUI
El Tigre
Pariaguán
Orinoco
Temblador
Barrancas
Tucupita
DELTA
Curiapo
Mabaruma
Barima
BARIMA-WAINI
Matthew's Ridge
Waini

Ciudad Guayana
Upata
AMACURO
La Horqueta
Kokerite
POMEROON-
SUPERNAAM
Charity
Anna Regina
ESSEQUIBO ISLANDS-
WEST DEMERARA

Ciudad Bolívar
Ciudad Piar
El Miamo
Guasipati
Tumeremo
Suddie
Parika
Georgetown
Buxton
DEMERARA-MAHAICA
Mahaicony
MAHAICA-BERBICE
Hyde Park
Port Mourant
New Amsterdam

Caura
Serranía Turagua
La Paragua
Embalse de Guri
El Callao
El Dorado
Cuyuni
Peter's Mine
Bartica
Rosignol
CUYUNI-
MAZARUNI
GUYANA
Mazaruni
Issano
Wismar
Linden (Mackenzie)
Mara
Skeldon
Nieuw Nickerie
Totness
Paramaribo
Nieuw Amsterdam

Angel Falls 2560
La Gran Sabana
Roraima 2772
Imbaimadai
Pakaraima
Kaieteur Falls
Mahdia
Tumatumari
UPPER-
ITUNI
Kwakwani
Ituni
Oreala
Epira
Tapoeripa
Wageningen
Groningen
CORONIE
Alliance
Iracoubo
Sinnamary
Is. du Diable
Iles du Salut
Kourou

Sierra del Zamura
Caroni
Paragua
Equeipa
Sta. Teresa
Orinduik
POTARO-
SIPARUNI
Wandaik
DEMERARA
Kwakwani
BERBICE
Kurupukari
Corantijn
Nickerie
PARA
Republiek
Brownsweg
Kwakpegron
COMMEWIJNE
Brokopondo
St. Laurent
Langatabbetje
CAYENNE
Gare Tigre
Cacao
Cayenne
Rémire

Serra Pacaraima
Toka
Apoteri
Yupukari
Lethem
Kato
UPPER TAKUTU-
UPPER ESSEQUIBO
Wichabai
Dadanawa
Shea
Kabalebo-stuwmeer
SURINAM
Wilhelmina Geb.
Julianatop 1280
SARAMACCA
Prof. Dr. Ir. W.J.
Van Blommestein Meer
Posoegroeno
Asidonhoppo
Amencankondre
MAROWIJNE
Tapanahoni
Benzdorp
Maripasoula
Saul
Paul Isnard
Grand Santi
St. Elie
Kaw
Régina
Cacao
Cabo Orange
Oyapoque

RORAIMA
Kamoa Mts.
Biloku
734
Essequibo
Isherton
Alalaparu
EAST-
BERBICE-
CORENTYNE
New River
Serra Acarai
690
FRENCH
GUIANA
Bienvenue
Alowike
Litani
Camopi
Oyapock
St. Georges
Oiapoque
Clevelândia do Norte
Vila Velha
Lourenço

Serra Tabatinga
San José do Anauá
Anauá
Boa Vista
Rupununi
Takutu
Tacutu
Boa Esperança
Maú
Caroebe
Caracaraí
Rewa
Maripa
Serra Tumucumaque
I. de Maracá
Araguari
AMAPÁ
Sucuriju

B R A Z I L
Branco
Caracaraí
Catrimani
Demini
Janaperí
Uatumã
Mapuera
Cuminá
Maroni
Maicuru
Jarí
Serra do Navio
Teresinha
Amapari
Porto Grande
Calçoene
Amapá
Aporema

Negro
Moreira
Barcelos
Caurés
Boiaçu
Alalaú
Represa de Balbina
Nhamundá
Jatapu
São Tiago
Cuminá
Maicuru
Cumina
Meriruma
Maloca
Arere
Macapá
Porto Santana
Mazagão
Cumã do Norte
I. Janaucu
I. Caviana
Ilha de Marajó

Cuiuni
Unini
Carvoeira
Moura
Jaú
Airão
Jauaperi
Santa Maria
Urubu
Uatumã
Faro
Óbidos
Alenquer
Prainha
Amazonas
Almeirim
Gurupá
Porto de Moz
Breves
Anajás
Araticu
I. Grande de Gurupá
Furo
Tajapuru
Portel

Agua Preta
Pauini
Mucura
Piorini
L. Amanã
L. Badajós
L. Piorini
Caapiranga
Anama
MANAUS
Manacapuru
Eva
Careiro
Itacoatiara
Barreirinha
Maués
Santarém
Belterra
Tapajós
Curuá
Uruará
Carvalho
Sousel
João
Anapu

Tefé
(Amazonas)
Coari
L. de Coari
Codajás
Beruri
Autazes
Ilha Tupinambaranas
Nova Olinda
Canumã
Aveiro
Brasília Legal
Altamira
Xingu

Purus
Itaboca
Abufari
Preto do Igapó-Açu
Madeira
Arumã
Novo Aripuanã
Borba
Abacaxis
Maués
Canuma
Munducurus
Itaituba
Iriri
Porto Alegre
Bacajá
Tapajós
Jacaré

P A R Á

A M A Z O N A S

West from Greenwich

COPYRIGHT GEORGE PHILIP & SON LTD

5   6   7

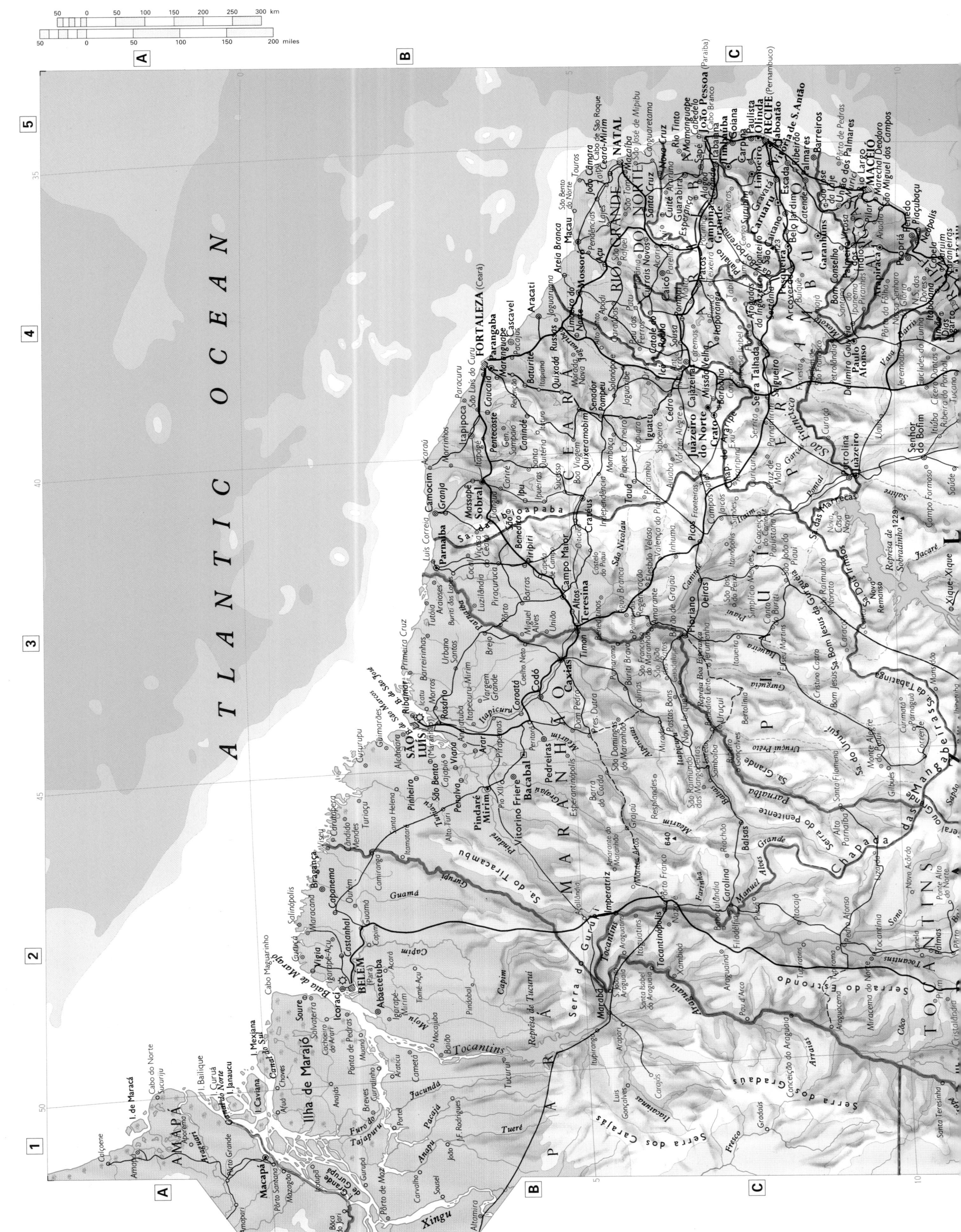

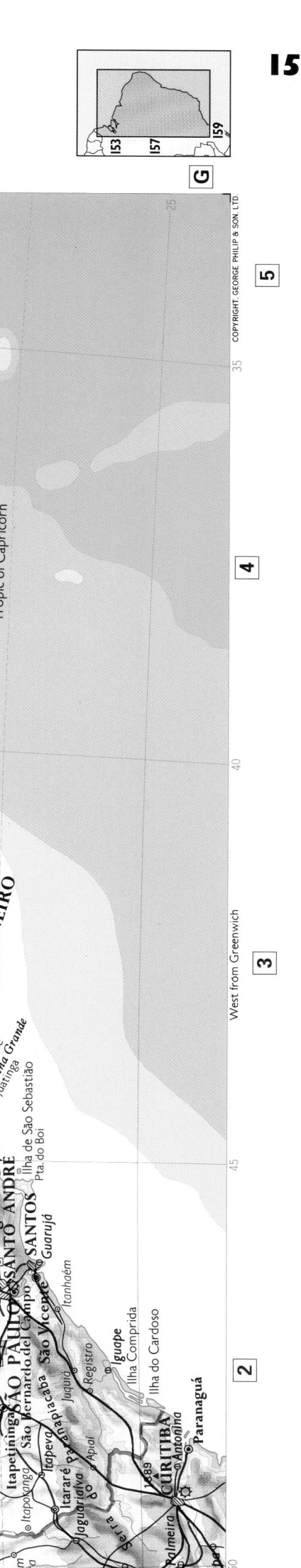

155

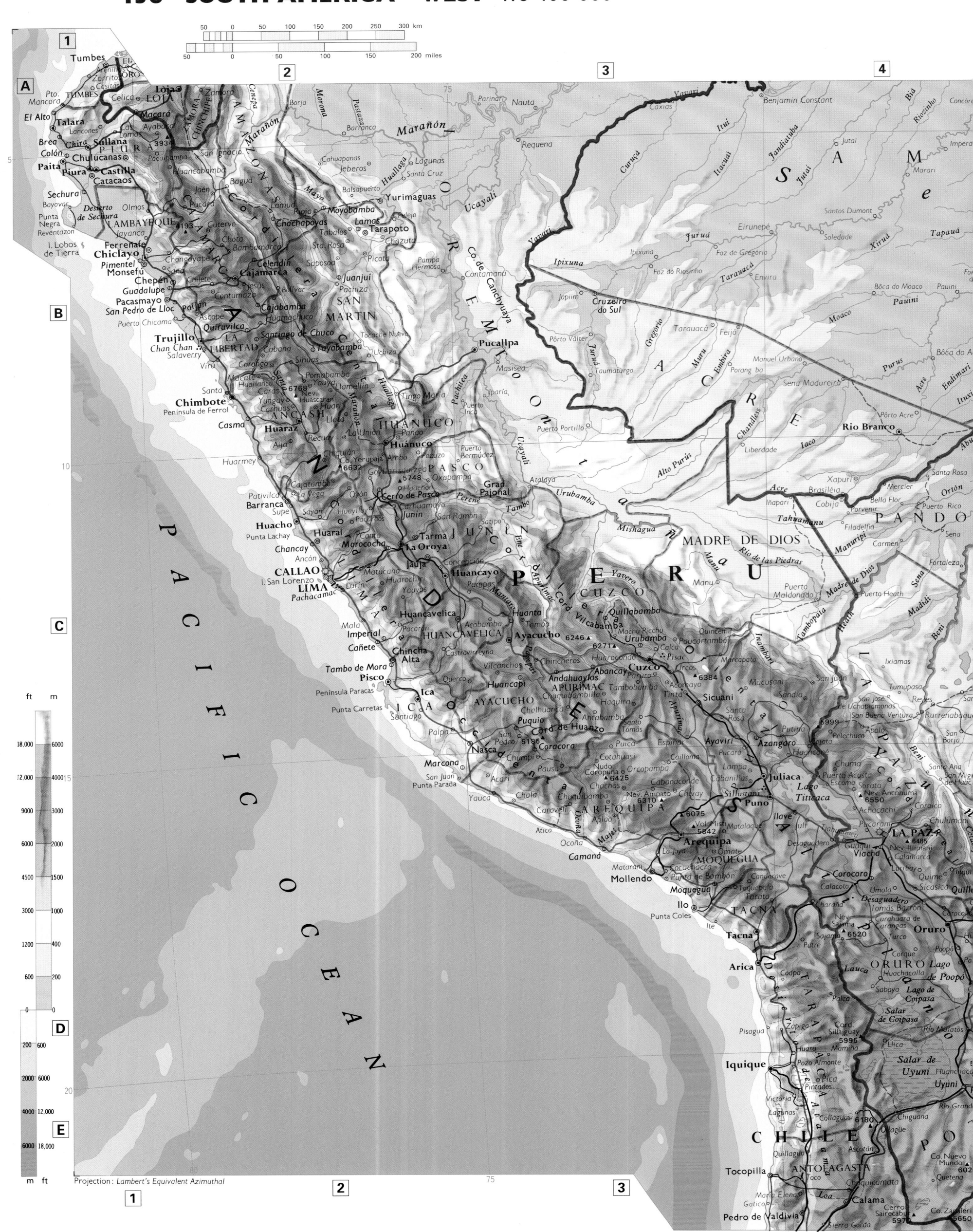

Projection: Lambert's Equivalent Azimuthal

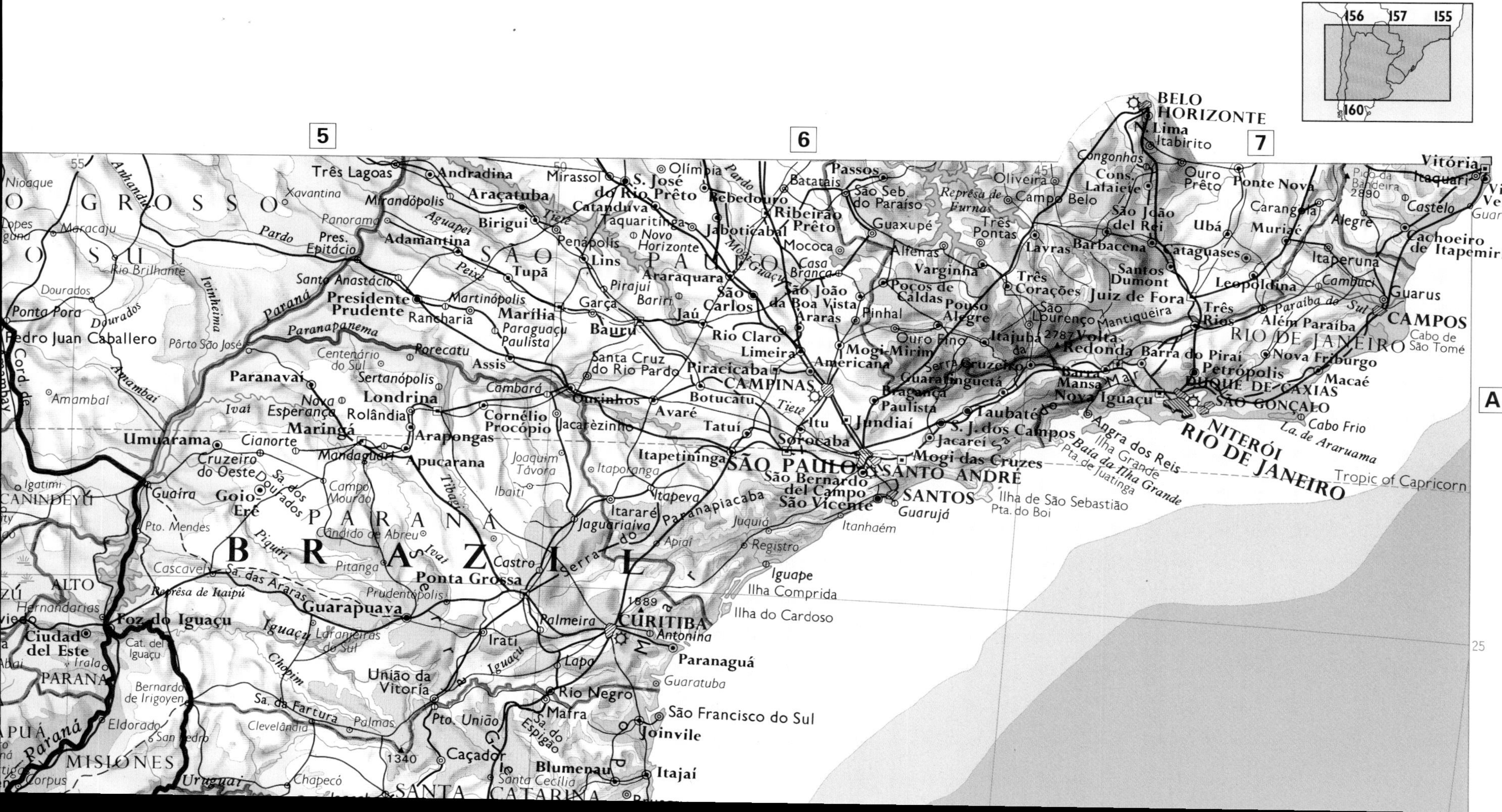

156 157 155
160

5 6 7

A

BELO HORIZONTE
Lima
Itabirito

Vitória
Itaquari
Vila Velha
Castelo

Três Lagoas
Andradina
Mirassol
Olímpia
S. José do Rio Prêto
Passos
Oliveira
Congonhas
Cons. Lafaiete
Ouro Prêto
Ponte Nova
Pico da Bandeira 2890
Guarapari

O GROSSO
Xavantina
Mirandópolis
Araçatuba
Catanduva
Batatais
São Seb. do Paraíso
Campo Belo
São João del Rei
Ubá
Carangola
Alegre
Cachoeiro de Itapemirim

Nioaque
Maracaju
Panorama
Biriguí
Taquaritinga
Ribeirão Prêto
Guaxupé
Três Pontas
Lavras
Barbacena
Cataguases
Muriaé
Itaperuna

DO SUL
Lopes
Pardo
Pres. Epitácio
Adamantina
Penápolis
Novo Horizonte
Jaboticabal
Prêto
Mococa
Alfenas
Varginha
Santos Dumont
Leopoldina
Cambuci

Dourados
Rio Brilhante
Santo Anastácio
Tupã
Lins
Araraquara
São João da Boa Vista
Poços de Caldas
Três Corações
Juiz de Fora
Três Rios
Além Paraíba
Guarus

Pedro Juan Caballero
Pôrto São José
Presidente Prudente
Martinópolis
Rancharia
Marília
Garça
Jaú
São Carlos
Araras
Pinhal
Pouso Alegre
São Lourenço
Mantiqueira
Paraíba do Sul
CAMPOS

Ponta Porã
Paraná
Paranapanema
Paraguaçu Paulista
Bauru
Rio Claro
Limeira
Mogi-Mirim
Ouro Fino
Itajubá 2787
Volta Redonda
Barra do Piraí
RIO DE JANEIRO
Cabo de São Tomé

Amambaí
Paranavaí
Centenário do Sul
Pirecicaba
Americana
Cruzeiro
Guaratinguetá
Barra Mansa
Nova Friburgo
Macaé

Ivaí
Nova Esperança
Sertanópolis
Assis
Cambará
CAMPINAS
Botucatu
Bragança Paulista
DUQUE DE CAXIAS
SÃO GONÇALO

Igatimi
Cianorte
Rolândia
Ourinhos
Avaré
Tietê
Taubaté
Nova Iguaçu
Cabo Frio
La. de Araruama

CANINDEYÚ
Guaíra
Maringá
Arapongas
Cornélio Procópio
Jacarèzinho
Tatuí
Itu
Jundiaí
S. J. dos Campos
NITERÓI
RIO DE JANEIRO

Mandaguari
Apucarana
Joaquim Távora
Itapetininga
Sorocaba
SÃO PAULO
Jacareí
Angra dos Reis
Tropic of Capricorn

Cruzeiro do Oeste
Campo Mourão
Ibaití
Itaporanga
Mogi das Cruzes
SANTO ANDRÉ
Ilha Grande
Pta. de Juatinga

UMUARAMA
Goio Erê
PARANÁ
Itararé
Itapeva
São Bernardo del Campo
São Vicente
SANTOS
Ilha de São Sebastião

Pto. Mendes
Dourados
Piquiri
Cândido de Abreu
Jaguariaíva
Paranapiacaba
Guarujá
Pta. do Boi

BRAZIL
Pitanga
Castro
Apiaí
Juquiá
Itanhaém

ALTO
Cascavel
Sa. das Araras
Prudentópolis
Ponta Grossa
Serra
Registro

Hernandarias
Represa de Itaipú
Guarapuava
1889
Iguape
Ilha Comprida

Ciudad del Este
Foz do Iguaçu
Iguaçu
Laranjeiras do Sul
Irati
Palmeira
CURITIBA
Antonina
Ilha do Cardoso

PARANÁ
Cat. del Iguaçu
Chopim
Lapa
Paranaguá

Bernardo de Irigoyen
União da Vitória
Rio Negro
Guaratuba

PUÁ
Eldorado
San Pedro
Sa. da Fartura
Palmas
Pto. União
Mafra
São Francisco do Sul

PARANÁ
Sa. do Espigão
MISIONES
1340
Clevelândia
Caçador
Blumenau
Itajaí

Corpus
Uruguai
Chapecó
Santa Cecília
SANTA CATARINA
Joinvile

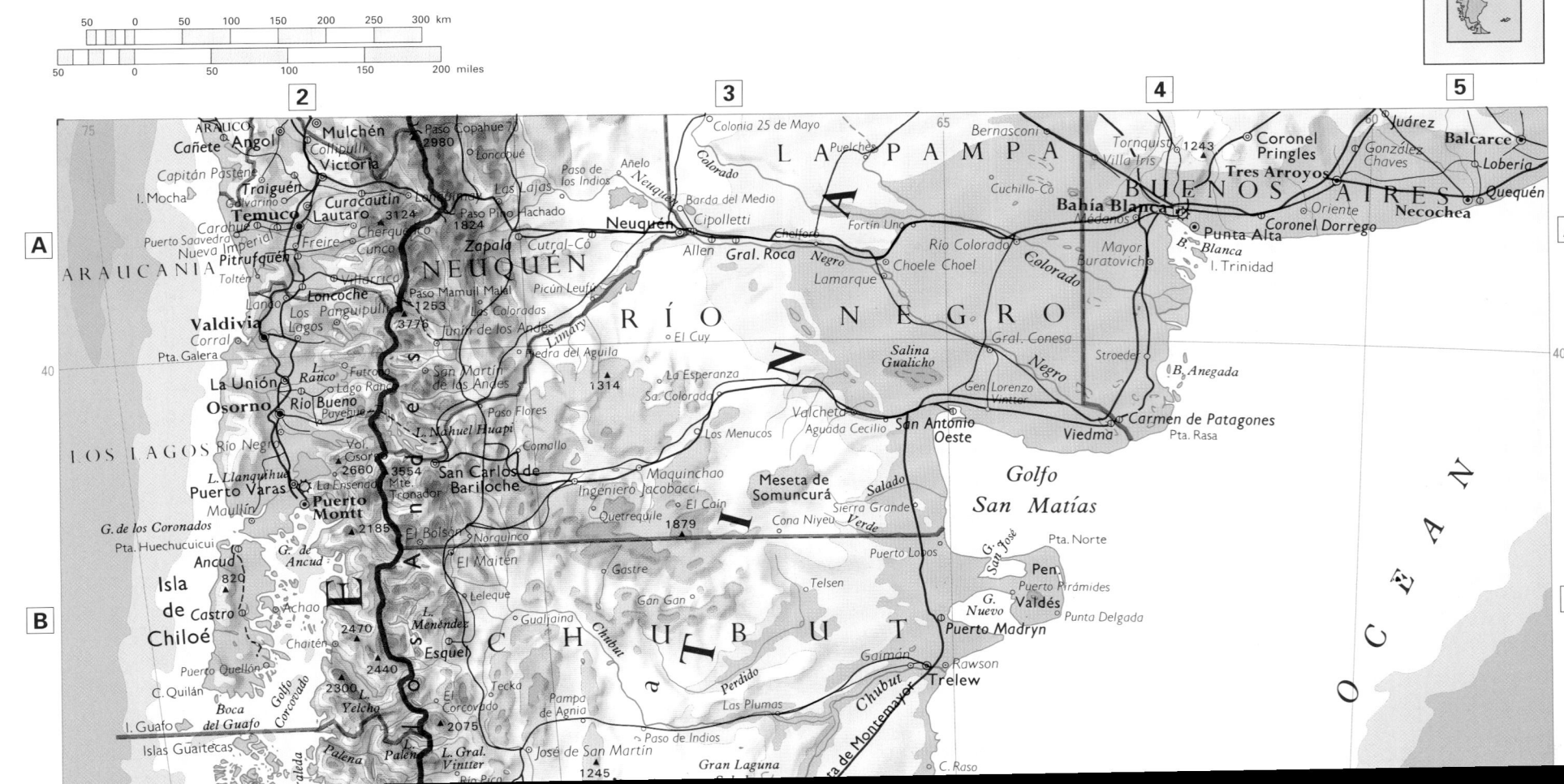

158 159

2   3   4   5

50 0 50 100 150 200 250 300 km

50 0 50 100 150 200 miles

A

B

75

ARAUCO
Cañete Angol
Capitán Pastene
Mulchén
Collipulli
Victoria
Paso Copahue
2980
Loncoué
Colonia 25 de Mayo
65
Bernasconi
Tornquist 1243
Coronel
Pringles
Gonzáles
Chaves
Balcarce
Loberia

Traiguén
I. Mocha
Galvarino
Temuco
Curacautín
Lautaro
3124
Paso Pino Hachado
1824
Las Lajas
Paso de
los Indios
Añelo
Barda del Medio
Colorado
Neuquén
Cipolletti
Fortín Uno
BUENOS
Bahía Blanca
Médanos
Punta Alta
Coronel Dorrego
AIRES
Quequén
Necochea

Capitán Pastene
Carahue
Puerto Saavedra
Nueva Imperial
Freire
Cunco
Cherquén
Zapala
Cutral-Có
Allen
Gral. Roca
Negro
Río Colorado
Colorado
Mayor
Buratovich
B. Blanca
I. Trinidad

ARAUCANIA
Pitrufquén
Toltén
Loncoche
Villarrica
Paso Mamuil Malal
1253
Picún Leufú
Lamarque
Choele Choel
Oriente

NEUQUÉN
RÍO
NEGRO

Valdivia
Corral
Pta. Galera
Lanco
Los
Lagos
L.
Panguipulli
3776
Junín de los Andes
Limay
El Cuy
Gral. Conesa
Stroeder
B. Anegada

40
40

La Unión
L.
Ranco
Futrono
Lago Ranco
San Martín
de los Andes
Piedra del Aguila
La Esperanza
1314
Sa. Colorada
Salina
Gualicho
Gen. Lorenzo
Vintter

Osorno
Río Bueno
Payehue
Paso Flores
Valcheta
Aguada Cecilio
San Antonio
Oeste
Carmen de Patagones
Pta. Rasa

LOS LAGOS
Río Negro
Vol.
Osorno
2660
L. Nahuel Huapi
Comallo
Los Menucos
Viedma

L. Llanquihue
La Ensenada
3554
Mte.
Tronador
San Carlos de
Bariloche
Maquinchao
Ingeniero Jacobacci
Meseta de
Somuncurá
Salado
Golfo
San Matías

Puerto Varas
Maullín
Puerto
Montt
2185
El Bolsón
Norquinco
El Cain
Quetrequile
1879
Cona Niyeu
Verde
Sierra Grande
G. San José
Pta. Norte

G. de los Coronados
Pta. Huechucuicui
Ancud
820
G. de
Ancud
El Maitén
Gastre
Puerto Lobos
G.
San José

Isla
de
Castro
Chiloé
Achao
L.
Menéndez
2470
Leleque
Gualjaina
Gan Gan
Telsen
Pen.
Valdés
Punta Delgada

Chiloé
Puerto Quellón
2440
Esquel
CHUBUT
Gaimán
Puerto Madryn
G.
Nuevo
Puerto Pirámides

C. Quilán
2300
L.
Yelcho
2075
El
Corcovado
Tecka
Pampa
de Agnia
Perdido
Las Plumas
Rawson
Trelew

Boca
del Guafo
Golfo
Corcovado
Palena
Palena
L. Gral.
Vintter
José de San Martín
Paso de Indios
Chubut
C. Raso

Islas Guaitecas
Río Pico
1245
Gran Laguna

OCEAN

INDEX

The index contains the names of all the principal places and features shown on the World Maps. Each name is followed by an additional entry in italics giving the country or region within which it is located. The alphabetical order of names composed of two or more words is governed primarily by the first word and then by the second. This is an example of the rule:

Mīr Kūh, *Iran*	**85 E8**	26 22 N	58 55 E
Mīr Shahdād, *Iran*	**85 E8**	26 15 N	58 29 E
Miraj, *India*	**82 F2**	16 50 N	74 45 E
Miram Shah, *Pakistan*	**79 B3**	33 0 N	70 2 E
Miramar, *Mozam.*	**105 C6**	23 50 S	35 35 E

Physical features composed of a proper name (Erie) and a description (Lake) are positioned alphabetically by the proper name. The description is positioned after the proper name and is usually abbreviated:

Erie, L., *N. Amer.*	**136 D3**	42 15 N	81 0 W

Where a description forms part of a settlement or administrative name however, it is always written in full and put in its true alphabetic position:

Mount Morris, *U.S.A.*	**136 D7**	42 44 N	77 52 W

Names beginning with M' and Mc are indexed as if they were spelt Mac. Names beginning St. are alphabetised under Saint, but Sankt, Sint, Sant', Santa and San are all spelt in full and are alphabetised accordingly. If the same place name occurs two or more times in the index and all are in the same country, each is followed by the name of the administrative subdivision in which it is located. The names are placed in the alphabetical order of the subdivisions. For example:

Jackson, *Ky., U.S.A.*	**134 G4**	37 33 N	83 23 W
Jackson, *Mich., U.S.A.*	**141 B12**	42 15 N	84 24 W
Jackson, *Minn., U.S.A.*	**138 D7**	43 37 N	95 1 W

The number in bold type which follows each name in the index refers to the number of the map page where that feature or place will be found. This is usually the largest scale at which the place or feature appears.

The letter and figure which are in bold type immediately after the page number give the grid square on the map page, within which the feature is situated. The letter represents the latitude and the figure the longitude.

In some cases the feature itself may fall within the specified square, while the name is outside. This is usually the case only with features which are larger than a grid square.

For a more precise location the geographical coordinates which follow the letter/figure references give the latitude and the longitude of each place. The first set of figures represent the latitude which is the distance north or south of the Equator measured as an angle at the centre of the earth. The Equator is latitude 0°, the North Pole is 90°N, and the South Pole 90°S.

The second set of figures represent the longitude, which is the distance East or West of the prime meridian, which runs through Greenwich, England. Longitude is also measured as an angle at the centre of the earth and is given East or West of the prime meridian, from 0° to 180° in either direction.

The unit of measurement for latitude and longitude is the degree, which is subdivided into 60 minutes. Each index entry states the position of a place in degrees and minutes, a space being left between the degrees and the minutes.

The latitude is followed by N(orth) or S(outh) and the longitude by E(ast) or W(est).

Rivers are indexed to their mouths or confluences, and carry the symbol → after their names. A solid square ■ follows the name of a country while, an open square □ refers to a first order administrative area.

ABBREVIATIONS USED IN THE INDEX

A.C.T. — Australian Capital Territory
Afghan. — Afghanistan
Ala. — Alabama
Alta. — Alberta
Amer. — America(n)
Arch. — Archipelago
Ariz. — Arizona
Ark. — Arkansas
Atl. Oc. — Atlantic Ocean
B. — Baie, Bahía, Bay, Bucht, Bugt
B.C. — British Columbia
Bangla. — Bangladesh
Barr. — Barrage
Bos.-H. — Bosnia-Herzegovina
C. — Cabo, Cap, Cape, Coast
C.A.R. — Central African Republic
C. Prov. — Cape Province
Calif. — California
Cent. — Central
Chan. — Channel
Colo. — Colorado
Conn. — Connecticut
Cord. — Cordillera
Cr. — Creek
Czech. — Czech Republic
D.C. — District of Columbia
Del. — Delaware
Dep. — Dependency
Des. — Desert
Dist. — District
Dj. — Djebel
Domin. — Dominica
Dom. Rep. — Dominican Republic
E. — East
El Salv. — El Salvador

Eq. Guin. — Equatorial Guinea
Fla. — Florida
Falk. Is. — Falkland Is.
G. — Golfe, Golfo, Gulf, Guba, Gebel
Ga. — Georgia
Gt. — Great, Greater
Guinea-Biss. — Guinea-Bissau
H.K. — Hong Kong
H.P. — Himachal Pradesh
Hants. — Hampshire
Harb. — Harbor, Harbour
Hd. — Head
Hts. — Heights
I.(s). — Île, Ilha, Insel, Isla, Island, Isle
Ill. — Illinois
Ind. — Indiana
Ind. Oc. — Indian Ocean
Ivory C. — Ivory Coast
J. — Jabal, Jebel, Jazira
Junc. — Junction
K. — Kap, Kapp
Kans. — Kansas
Kep. — Kepulauan
Ky. — Kentucky
L. — Lac, Lacul, Lago, Lagoa, Lake, Limni, Loch, Lough
La. — Louisiana
Liech. — Liechtenstein
Lux. — Luxembourg
Mad. P. — Madhya Pradesh
Madag. — Madagascar
Man. — Manitoba
Mass. — Massachusetts
Md. — Maryland

Me. — Maine
Medit. S. — Mediterranean Sea
Mich. — Michigan
Minn. — Minnesota
Miss. — Mississippi
Mo. — Missouri
Mont. — Montana
Mozam. — Mozambique
Mt.(e). — Mont, Monte, Monti, Montaña, Mountain
N. — Nord, Norte, North, Northern, Nouveau
N.B. — New Brunswick
N.C. — North Carolina
N. Cal. — New Caledonia
N. Dak. — North Dakota
N.H. — New Hampshire
N.I. — North Island
N.J. — New Jersey
N. Mex. — New Mexico
N.S. — Nova Scotia
N.S.W. — New South Wales
N.W.T. — North West Territory
N.Y. — New York
N.Z. — New Zealand
Nebr. — Nebraska
Neths. — Netherlands
Nev. — Nevada
Nfld. — Newfoundland
Nic. — Nicaragua
O. — Oued, Ouadi
Occ. — Occidentale
Okla. — Oklahoma
Ont. — Ontario
Or. — Orientale
Oreg. — Oregon

Os. — Ostrov
Oz. — Ozero
P. — Pass, Passo, Pasul, Pulau
P.E.I. — Prince Edward Island
Pa. — Pennsylvania
Pac. Oc. — Pacific Ocean
Papua N.G. — Papua New Guinea
Pass. — Passage
Pen. — Peninsula, Péninsule
Phil. — Philippines
Pk. — Park, Peak
Plat. — Plateau
P-ov. — Poluostrov
Prov. — Province, Provincial
Pt. — Point
Pta. — Ponta, Punta
Pte. — Pointe
Qué. — Québec
Queens. — Queensland
R. — Rio, River
R.I. — Rhode Island
Ra.(s). — Range(s)
Raj. — Rajasthan
Reg. — Region
Rep. — Republic
Res. — Reserve, Reservoir
S. — San, South, Sea
Si. Arabia — Saudi Arabia
S.C. — South Carolina
S. Dak. — South Dakota
S.I. — South Island
S. Leone — Sierra Leone
Sa. — Serra, Sierra
Sask. — Saskatchewan
Scot. — Scotland
Sd. — Sound

Sev. — Severnaya
Sib. — Siberia
Sprs. — Springs
St. — Saint, Sankt, Sint
Sta. — Santa, Station
Ste. — Sainte
Sto. — Santo
Str. — Strait, Stretto
Switz. — Switzerland
Tas. — Tasmania
Tenn. — Tennessee
Tex. — Texas
Tg. — Tanjung
Trin. & Tob. — Trinidad & Tobago
U.A.E. — United Arab Emirates
U.K. — United Kingdom
U.S.A. — United States of America
Ut. P. — Uttar Pradesh
Va. — Virginia
Vdkhr. — Vodokhranilishche
Vf. — Vîrful
Vic. — Victoria
Vol. — Volcano
Vt. — Vermont
W. — Wadi, West
W. Va. — West Virginia
Wash. — Washington
Wis. — Wisconsin
Wlkp. — Wielkopolski
Wyo. — Wyoming
Yorks. — Yorkshire
Yug. — Yugoslavia

162 A Coruña

A

A Coruña = La Coruña, Spain 36 B2 43 20N 8 25W
Aachen, Germany 26 E2 50 45N 6 6 E
Aadorf, Switz. 29 B7 47 30N 8 55 E
Aalborg = Ålborg, Denmark 15 G3 57 2N 9 54 E
Aalen, Germany 27 G6 48 51N 10 6 E
A'âli en Nîl □, Sudan 95 F3 9 30N 33 0 E
Aalsmeer, Neths. 20 D5 52 17N 4 43 E
Aalst, Belgium 21 G4 50 56N 4 2 E
Aalst, Neths. 21 F6 51 23N 5 29 E
Aalten, Neths. 20 E9 51 56N 6 35 E
Aalter, Belgium 21 F2 51 5N 3 28 E
Äänekoski, Finland 13 E21 62 36N 25 44 E
Aarau, Switz. 28 B6 47 23N 8 4 E
Aarberg, Switz. 28 B4 47 2N 7 16 E
Aardenburg, Belgium 21 F2 51 16N 3 28 E
Aare →, Switz. 28 A6 47 33N 8 14 E
Aargau □, Switz. 28 B6 47 26N 8 10 E
Aarhus = Århus, Denmark 15 H4 56 8N 10 11 E
Aarle, Neths. 21 E7 51 30N 5 38 E
Aarschot, Belgium 21 G5 50 59N 4 49 E
Aarsele, Belgium 21 G2 51 0N 3 26 E
Aartrijke, Belgium 21 F2 51 7N 3 6 E
Aarwangen, Switz. 28 B5 47 15N 7 46 E
Aba, China 68 A3 32 59N 101 42 E
Aba, Nigeria 101 D6 5 10N 7 19 E
Aba, Zaïre 106 B3 3 58N 30 17 E
Âbâ, Jazîrat, Sudan 95 E3 13 30N 32 31 E
Abacaxis →, Brazil 153 D6 3 54 S 58 47W
Ābādān, Iran 85 D6 30 22N 48 20 E
Abade, Ethiopia 95 F4 9 22N 38 3 E
Ābādeh, Iran 85 D7 31 8N 52 40 E
Abadin, Spain 36 B3 43 21N 7 29W
Abadla, Algeria 99 B4 31 2N 2 45W
Abaeté, Brazil 155 E2 19 9 S 45 27W
Abaeté →, Brazil 155 E2 18 2 S 45 12W
Abaetetuba, Brazil 154 B2 1 40 S 48 50W
Abagnar Qi, China 66 C9 43 52N 116 2 E
Abai, Paraguay 159 B4 25 58 S 55 54W
Abak, Nigeria 101 E6 4 58N 7 50 E
Abakaliki, Nigeria 101 D6 6 22N 8 2 E
Abakan, Russia 57 D10 53 40N 91 10 E
Abalemma, Niger 101 B6 16 12N 7 50 E
Abana, Turkey 88 B6 41 59N 34 1 E
Abancay, Peru 156 C3 13 35 S 72 55W
Abanilla, Spain 35 G3 38 12N 1 3W
Abano Terme, Italy 39 C8 45 22N 11 46 E
Abapó, Bolivia 157 D5 18 48 S 63 25W
Abarán, Spain 35 G3 38 12N 1 23W
Abariringa, Kiribati 122 H10 2 50 S 171 40W
Abarqū, Iran 85 D7 31 10N 53 20 E
Abashiri, Japan 60 B12 44 0N 144 15 E
Abashiri-Wan, Japan 60 B12 44 0N 144 30 E
Abau, Papua N. G. 120 F5 10 11 S 148 46 E
Abaújszántó, Hungary 31 C14 48 16N 21 12 E
Abay, Kazakstan 56 E8 49 38N 72 53 E
Abaya, L., Ethiopia 95 F4 6 30N 37 50 E
Abaza, Russia 56 D10 52 39N 90 6 E
Abbadia San Salvatore, Italy 39 F8 42 53N 11 41 E
'Abbāsābād, Iran 85 C8 33 34N 58 23 E
Abbay = Nîl el Azraq →, Sudan 95 D3 15 38N 32 31 E
Abbaye, Pt., U.S.A. 134 B1 46 58N 88 8W
Abbé, L., Ethiopia 95 E5 11 8N 41 47 E
Abbeville, France 23 B8 50 6N 1 49 E
Abbeville, La., U.S.A. 139 K8 29 58N 92 8W
Abbeville, S.C., U.S.A. 135 H4 34 11N 82 23W
Abbiategrasso, Italy 38 C5 45 24N 8 54 E
Abbieglassie, Australia 115 D4 27 15 S 147 28 E
Abbot Ice Shelf, Antarctica 7 D16 73 0 S 92 0W
Abbotsford, Canada 130 D4 49 5N 122 20W
Abbotsford, U.S.A. 138 C9 44 57N 90 19W
Abbottabad, Pakistan 80 B5 34 10N 73 15 E
Abcoude, Neths. 20 D5 52 17N 4 59 E
Abd al Kūrī, Ind. Oc. 87 D6 12 5N 52 20 E
Ābdar, Iran 85 D7 30 16N 55 19 E
'Abdolābād, Iran 85 C8 34 12N 56 30 E
Abdulino, Russia 54 E4 53 42N 53 40 E
Abéché, Chad 97 F4 13 50N 20 35 E
Abejar, Spain 34 D2 41 48N 2 47W
Abekr, Sudan 95 E2 12 45N 28 50 E
Abêlessa, Algeria 99 D5 22 58N 4 47 E
Abengourou, Ivory C. 100 D4 6 42N 3 27W
Åbenrå, Denmark 15 J3 55 3N 9 25 E
Abensberg, Germany 27 G7 48 48N 11 51 E
Abeokuta, Nigeria 101 D5 7 3N 3 19 E
Aber, Uganda 106 B3 2 12N 32 25 E
Aberaeron, U.K. 17 E3 52 15N 4 15W
Aberayron = Aberaeron, U.K. 17 E3 52 15N 4 15W
Aberconwy & Colwyn □, U.K. 16 D4 53 10N 3 44W
Abercorn = Mbala, Zambia 107 D3 8 46 S 31 24 E
Abercorn, Australia 115 D5 25 12 S 151 5 E
Aberdare, U.K. 17 F4 51 43N 3 27W
Aberdare Ra., Kenya 106 C4 0 15 S 36 50 E
Aberdeen, Australia 117 B9 32 9 S 150 56 E
Aberdeen, Canada 131 C7 52 20N 106 8W
Aberdeen, S. Africa 104 E3 32 28 S 24 2 E
Aberdeen, U.K. 18 D6 57 9N 2 5W
Aberdeen, Ala., U.S.A. 135 J1 33 49N 88 33W
Aberdeen, Idaho, U.S.A. 142 E7 42 57N 112 50W
Aberdeen, Ohio, U.S.A. 141 F13 38 39N 83 46W
Aberdeen, S. Dak., U.S.A. 138 C5 45 28N 98 29W
Aberdeen, Wash., U.S.A. 144 D3 46 59N 123 50W
Aberdeenshire □, U.K. 18 D6 57 17N 2 36W
Aberdovey = Aberdyfi, U.K. 17 E3 52 33N 4 3W
Aberdyfi, U.K. 17 E3 52 33N 4 3W
Aberfeldy, Australia 117 D7 37 42 S 146 22 E
Aberfeldy, U.K. 18 E5 56 37N 3 51W
Abergaria-a-Velha, Portugal 36 E2 40 41N 8 32W
Abergavenny, U.K. 17 F4 51 49N 3 1W
Abernathy, U.S.A. 139 J4 33 50N 101 51W
Abert, L., U.S.A. 142 E3 42 38N 120 14W
Aberystwyth, U.K. 17 E3 52 25N 4 5W
Abha, Si. Arabia 94 D5 18 0N 42 34 E
Abhar, Iran 89 D13 36 9N 49 13 E
Abhayapuri, India 78 B3 26 24N 90 38 E
Abia □, Nigeria 101 D6 5 30N 7 35 E
Abidiya, Sudan 94 D3 18 18N 34 3 E
Abidjan, Ivory C. 100 D4 5 26N 3 58W
Abilene, Kans., U.S.A. 138 F6 38 55N 97 13W
Abilene, Tex., U.S.A. 139 J5 32 28N 99 43W
Abingdon, U.K. 17 F6 51 40N 1 17W
Abingdon, Ill., U.S.A. 140 D6 40 48N 90 24W
Abingdon, Va., U.S.A. 135 G5 36 43N 81 59W
Abington Reef, Australia 114 B4 18 0 S 149 35 E
Abitau →, Canada 131 B7 59 53N 109 3W
Abitau L., Canada 131 A7 60 27N 107 15W
Abitibi L., Canada 128 C4 48 40N 79 40W
Abiy Adi, Ethiopia 95 E4 13 39N 39 3 E
Abkhaz Republic □ = Abkhazia □, Georgia 53 J5 43 12N 41 5 E
Abkhazia □, Georgia 53 J5 43 12N 41 5 E
Abkit, Russia 57 C16 64 10N 157 10 E
Abminga, Australia 115 D1 26 8 S 134 51 E
Abnûb, Egypt 94 B3 27 18N 31 4 E
Åbo = Turku, Finland 13 F20 60 30N 22 19 E
Abo, Massif d', Chad 97 D3 21 41N 16 8 E
Abocho, Nigeria 101 D6 7 35N 6 56 E
Abohar, India 80 D6 30 10N 74 10 E
Aboisso, Ivory C. 100 D4 5 30N 3 5W
Abolo, Congo 102 B2 0 8N 14 16 E
Abomey, Benin 101 D5 7 10N 2 5 E
Abondance, France 25 B10 46 18N 6 43 E
Abong-Mbang, Cameroon 102 B2 4 0N 13 8 E
Abongabong, Indonesia 74 B1 4 15N 96 48 E
Abonnema, Nigeria 101 E6 4 41N 6 49 E
Abony, Hungary 31 D13 47 12N 20 3 E
Aboso, Ghana 100 D4 5 23N 1 57W
Abou-Deïa, Chad 97 F3 11 20N 19 20 E
Abou Goulem, Chad 97 F4 13 37N 21 38 E
Aboyne, U.K. 18 D6 57 4N 2 47W
Abra □, Phil. 70 C3 17 35N 120 45 E
Abra de Ilog, Phil. 70 E3 13 27N 120 44 E
Abra Pampa, Argentina 158 A2 22 43 S 65 42W
Abrantes, Portugal 37 F2 39 24N 8 7W
Abraveses, Portugal 36 E3 40 41N 7 55W
Abreojos, Pta., Mexico 146 B2 26 50N 113 40W
Abreschviller, France 23 D14 48 39N 7 6 E
Abri, Esh Shamâliya, Sudan 94 C3 20 50N 30 27 E
Abri, Janub Kordofân, Sudan 95 E3 11 40N 30 21 E
Abrolhos, Banka, Brazil 155 E4 18 0 S 38 0W
Abrud, Romania 46 C4 46 19N 23 5 E
Abruzzi □, Italy 39 F10 42 15N 14 0 E
Absaroka Range, U.S.A. 142 D9 44 45N 109 50W
Abū al Khaṣīb, Iraq 85 D6 30 25N 48 0 E
Abū 'Alī, Si. Arabia 85 E6 27 20N 49 27 E
Abū 'Alī →, Lebanon 91 A4 34 25N 35 50 E
Abu 'Arīsh, Si. Arabia 86 C3 16 53N 42 48 E
Abû Ballas, Egypt 94 C2 24 26N 27 36 E
Abu Deleiq, Sudan 95 D3 15 57N 33 48 E
Abu Dhabi = Abū Ẓāby, U.A.E. 85 E7 24 28N 54 22 E
Abû Dis, Sudan 94 D3 19 12N 33 38 E
Abû Dom, Sudan 95 D3 16 18N 32 25 E
Abū Du'ān, Syria 89 D8 36 25N 38 15 E
Abu el Gairi, W. →, Egypt 91 F2 29 35N 33 30 E
Abû Gabra, Sudan 95 E2 11 2N 26 50 E
Abu Ga'da, W. →, Egypt 91 F1 29 15N 32 53 E
Abû Gubeiha, Sudan 95 E3 11 30N 31 15 E
Abu Habl, Khawr →, Sudan 95 E3 12 37N 31 0 E
Abū Ḥadrīyah, Si. Arabia 85 E6 27 20N 48 58 E
Abu Hamed, Sudan 94 D3 19 32N 33 13 E
Abu Haraz, An Nîl el Azraq, Sudan 95 E3 14 35N 33 30 E
Abû Haraz, Esh Shamâliya, Sudan 94 D3 19 8N 32 18 E
Abû Higar, Sudan 95 E3 12 50N 33 59 E
Abū Kamāl, Syria 89 E9 34 30N 41 0 E
Abū Madd, Ra's, Si. Arabia 84 E3 24 50N 37 7 E
Abu Matariq, Sudan 95 E2 10 59N 26 9 E
Abu Qir, Egypt 94 H7 31 18N 30 0 E
Abu Qireiya, Egypt 94 C4 24 5N 35 28 E
Abu Qurqâs, Egypt 94 J7 28 1N 30 44 E
Abū Raṣāş, Ra's, Oman 87 B7 20 10N 58 38 E
Abū Rubayq, Si. Arabia 86 B2 23 44N 39 42 E
Abu Ṣafāt, W. →, Jordan 91 E5 30 24N 36 7 E
Abū Simbel, Egypt 94 C3 22 18N 31 40 E
Abū Şukhayr, Iraq 89 G11 31 54N 44 30 E
Abu Tig, Egypt 94 B3 27 4N 31 15 E
Abu Tiga, Sudan 95 E3 12 47N 34 12 E
Abû Zabad, Sudan 95 E2 12 25N 29 10 E
Abū Ẓāby, U.A.E. 85 E7 24 28N 54 22 E
Abū Zeydābād, Iran 85 C6 33 54N 51 45 E
Abufari, Brazil 157 B5 5 25 S 62 59W
Abuja, Nigeria 101 D6 9 16N 7 2 E
Abukuma-Gawa →, Japan 60 E10 38 6N 140 52 E
Abukuma-Sammyaku, Japan 60 F10 37 30N 140 45 E
Abulug, Phil. 70 B3 18 27N 121 27 E
Abumombazi, Zaïre 102 B4 3 42N 22 10 E
Abunã, Brazil 157 B4 9 40 S 65 20W
Abunã →, Brazil 157 B4 9 41 S 65 20W
Abung, Phil. 70 E3 13 46N 121 26 E
Aburatsu, Japan 62 F3 31 34N 131 24 E
Aburo, Zaïre 106 B3 2 4N 30 53 E
Abut Hd., N.Z. 119 D5 43 7 S 170 15 E
Abwong, Sudan 95 F3 9 2N 32 14 E
Åby, Sweden 15 F10 58 40N 16 10 E
Aby, Lagune, Ivory C. 100 D4 5 15N 3 14W
Acacías, Colombia 152 C3 3 59N 73 46W
Acajutla, El Salv. 148 D2 13 36N 89 50W
Açallândia, Brazil 154 C2 5 0 S 47 30W
Acámbaro, Mexico 146 C4 20 0N 100 40W
Acanthus, Greece 44 D5 40 27N 23 47 E
Acaponeta, Mexico 146 C3 22 30N 105 20W
Acapulco, Mexico 147 D5 16 51N 99 56W
Acarai, Serra, Brazil 153 C6 1 50N 57 50W
Acaraú, Brazil 154 B3 2 53 S 40 7W
Acari, Brazil 154 C4 6 31 S 36 38W
Acarí, Peru 156 D3 15 25 S 74 36W
Acarigua, Venezuela 152 B4 9 33N 69 12W
Acatlán, Mexico 147 D5 18 10N 98 3W
Acayucan, Mexico 147 D6 17 59N 94 58W
Accéglio, Italy 38 D3 44 28N 7 0 E
Accomac, U.S.A. 134 G8 37 43N 75 40W
Accous, France 24 E3 43 0N 0 36W
Accra, Ghana 101 D4 5 35N 0 6W
Accrington, U.K. 16 D5 53 45N 2 22W
Acebal, Argentina 158 C3 33 20 S 60 50W
Aceh □, Indonesia 74 B1 4 15N 97 30 E
Acerenza, Italy 41 B8 40 48N 15 56 E
Acerra, Italy 41 B7 40 57N 14 22 E
Aceuchal, Spain 37 G4 38 39N 6 30W
Achacachi, Bolivia 156 D4 16 3 S 68 43W
Achaguas, Venezuela 152 B4 7 46N 68 14W
Achalpur, India 82 D3 21 22N 77 32 E
Achao, Chile 160 B2 42 28 S 73 30W
Achel, Belgium 21 F6 51 15N 5 29 E
Acheng, China 67 B14 45 30N 126 58 E
Achenkirch, Austria 30 D4 47 32N 11 45 E
Achensee, Austria 30 D4 47 26N 11 45 E
Acher, India 80 H5 23 10N 72 32 E
Achern, Germany 27 G4 48 37N 8 4 E
Acheron →, N.Z. 119 C8 42 16 S 173 4 E
Achill, Ireland 19 C2 53 56N 9 55W
Achill Hd., Ireland 19 C1 53 58N 10 15W
Achill I., Ireland 19 C1 53 58N 10 1W
Achill Sd., Ireland 19 C2 53 54N 9 56W
Achim, Germany 26 B5 53 1N 9 3 E
Achinsk, Russia 57 D10 56 20N 90 20 E
Achisay = Ashchysay, Kazakstan 55 B4 43 35N 68 53 E
Achit, Russia 54 C6 56 48N 57 54 E
Achol, Sudan 95 F3 6 35N 31 32 E
Acıgöl, Turkey 88 D3 37 50N 29 50 E
Acireale, Italy 41 E8 37 37N 15 10 E
Ackerman, U.S.A. 139 J10 33 19N 89 11W
Ackley, U.S.A. 140 B3 42 33N 93 3W
Acklins I., Bahamas 149 B5 22 30N 74 0W
Acme, Canada 130 C6 51 33N 113 30W
Acobamba, Peru 156 C3 12 52 S 74 35W
Acomayo, Peru 156 C3 13 55 S 71 38W
Aconcagua, Cerro, Argentina 158 C2 32 39 S 70 0W
Aconquija, Mt., Argentina 158 B2 27 0 S 66 0W
Acopiara, Brazil 154 C4 6 6 S 39 27W
Açores, Is. dos = Azores, Atl. Oc. 8 E6 38 44N 29 0W
Acorizal, Brazil 157 D6 15 12 S 56 22W
Acquapendente, Italy 39 F8 42 44N 11 52 E
Acquasanta Terme, Italy 39 F10 42 46N 13 24 E
Acquaviva delle Fonti, Italy 41 B9 40 54N 16 50 E
Acqui Terme, Italy 38 D5 44 41N 8 28 E
Acraman, L., Australia 115 E2 32 2 S 135 23 E
Acre = 'Akko, Israel 91 C4 32 55N 35 4 E
Acre □, Brazil 156 B3 9 1 S 71 0W
Acre →, Brazil 156 B4 8 45 S 67 22W
Acri, Italy 41 C9 39 29N 16 23 E
Acs, Hungary 31 D11 47 42N 18 2 E
Actium, Greece 45 F2 38 57N 20 45 E
Acton, Canada 136 C4 43 38N 80 3W
Açu, Brazil 154 C4 5 34 S 36 54W
Ad Dahnā, Si. Arabia 87 A5 24 30N 48 10 E
Ad Ḍāli', Yemen 86 D4 13 42N 44 44 E
Ad Dammām, Si. Arabia 85 E6 26 20N 50 5 E
Ad Darb, Si. Arabia 86 C3 18 2N 43 7 E
Ad Dawhah, Qatar 85 E6 25 15N 51 35 E
Ad Dawr, Iraq 89 E10 34 27N 43 47 E
Ad Ḍiffah, Libya 96 B4 30 30N 24 30 E
Ad Dilam, Si. Arabia 86 B4 23 55N 47 10 E
Ad Dir'īyah, Si. Arabia 84 E5 24 44N 46 35 E
Ad Dīwānīyah, Iraq 89 F11 32 0N 45 0 E
Ad Dujayl, Iraq 89 F11 33 51N 44 14 E
Ad Durūz, J., Jordan 91 C5 32 35N 36 40 E
Ada, Ghana 101 D5 5 44N 0 40 E
Ada, Serbia, Yug. 42 B5 45 49N 20 9 E
Ada, Minn., U.S.A. 138 B6 47 18N 96 31W
Ada, Ohio, U.S.A. 141 D13 40 46N 83 49W
Ada, Okla., U.S.A. 139 H6 34 46N 96 41W
Adad, Somali Rep. 108 C3 9 27N 46 49 E
Adaja →, Spain 36 D6 41 32N 4 52W
Ådalsliden, Sweden 14 A10 63 27N 16 55 E
Adam, Oman 87 B7 22 15N 57 28 E
Adam, Mt., Falk. Is. 160 D4 51 34 S 60 4W
Adamantina, Brazil 155 F1 21 42 S 51 4W
Adamaoua, Massif de l', Cameroon 101 D7 7 20N 12 20 E
Adamawa □, Nigeria 101 D7 9 20N 12 30 E
Adamawa Highlands = Adamaoua, Massif de l', Cameroon 101 D7 7 20N 12 20 E
Adamello, Mte., Italy 38 B7 46 9N 10 30 E
Adami Tulu, Ethiopia 95 F4 7 53N 38 41 E
Adaminaby, Australia 117 D8 36 0 S 148 45 E
Adamovka, Russia 54 F7 51 32N 59 56 E
Adams, Phil. 70 B3 18 28N 120 54 E
Adams, Mass., U.S.A. 137 D11 42 38N 73 7W
Adams, N.Y., U.S.A. 137 C8 43 49N 76 1W
Adams, Wis., U.S.A. 138 D10 43 57N 89 49W
Adam's Bridge, Sri Lanka 83 K4 9 15N 79 40 E
Adams L., Canada 130 C5 51 10N 119 40W
Adams Mt., U.S.A. 144 D5 46 12N 121 30W
Adam's Peak, Sri Lanka 83 L5 6 48N 80 30 E
Adamuz, Spain 37 G6 38 2N 4 32W
Adana, Turkey 88 D6 37 0N 35 16 E
Adanero, Spain 36 E6 40 56N 4 36W
Adapazarı, Turkey 88 B4 40 48N 30 25 E
Adarama, Sudan 95 D3 17 10N 34 52 E
Adare, C., Antarctica 7 D11 71 0 S 171 0 E
Adaut, Indonesia 73 C4 8 8 S 131 7 E
Adavale, Australia 115 D3 25 52 S 144 32 E
Adda →, Italy 38 C6 45 8N 9 53 E
Addis Ababa = Addis Abeba, Ethiopia 95 F4 9 2N 38 42 E
Addis Abeba, Ethiopia 95 F4 9 2N 38 42 E
Addis Alem, Ethiopia 95 F4 9 0N 38 17 E
Addison, Ill., U.S.A. 141 C8 41 55N 88 0W
Addison, N.Y., U.S.A. 136 D7 42 1N 77 14W
Addo, S. Africa 104 E4 33 32 S 25 45 E
Addyston, U.S.A. 141 E12 39 8N 84 43W
Adebour, Niger 97 F2 13 17N 11 50 E
Ādeh, Iran 84 B5 37 42N 45 11 E
Adel, Ga., U.S.A. 135 K4 31 8N 83 25W
Adel, Iowa, U.S.A. 140 C2 41 37N 94 1W
Adelaide, Australia 116 C3 34 52 S 138 30 E
Adelaide, Bahamas 148 A4 25 4N 77 31W
Adelaide, S. Africa 104 E4 32 42 S 26 20 E
Adelaide I., Antarctica 7 C17 67 15 S 68 30W
Adelaide Pen., Canada 126 B10 68 15N 97 30W
Adelaide River, Australia 112 B5 13 15 S 131 7 E
Adelanto, U.S.A. 145 L9 34 35N 117 22W
Adelboden, Switz. 28 D5 46 29N 7 33 E
Adele I., Australia 112 C3 15 32 S 123 9 E
Adélie, Terre, Antarctica 7 C10 68 0 S 140 0 E
Adélie Land = Adélie, Terre, Antarctica 7 C10 68 0 S 140 0 E
Ademuz, Spain 34 E3 40 5N 1 13W
Aden = Al 'Adan, Yemen 86 D4 12 45N 45 0 E
Aden, G. of, Asia 90 E4 12 30N 47 30 E
Adendorp, S. Africa 104 E3 32 15 S 24 30 E
Adh Dhayd, U.A.E. 85 E7 25 17N 55 53 E
Adhoi, India 80 H4 23 26N 70 32 E
Adi, Indonesia 73 B4 4 15 S 133 30 E
Adi Daro, Ethiopia 95 E4 14 20N 38 14 E
Adi Keyih, Eritrea 95 E4 14 51N 39 22 E
Adi Kwala, Eritrea 95 E4 14 38N 38 48 E
Adi Ugri, Eritrea 95 E4 14 58N 38 48 E
Adieu, C., Australia 113 F5 32 0 S 132 10 E
Adieu Pt., Australia 112 C3 15 14 S 124 35 E
Adigala, Ethiopia 95 E5 10 24N 42 15 E
Adige →, Italy 39 C9 45 9N 12 20 E
Adigrat, Ethiopia 95 E4 14 20N 39 26 E
Adilabad, India 82 E4 19 33N 78 20 E
Adilcevaz, Turkey 89 C10 38 47N 42 43 E
Adin, U.S.A. 142 F3 41 12N 120 57W
Adinkerke, Belgium 21 F1 51 5N 2 36 E
Adirondack Mts., U.S.A. 137 C10 44 0N 74 0W
Adıyaman, Turkey 89 D8 37 45N 38 16 E
Adjim, Tunisia 96 B2 33 47N 10 50 E
Adjohon, Benin 101 D5 6 41N 2 32 E
Adjud, Romania 46 C8 46 7N 27 10 E
Adjumani, Uganda 106 B3 3 20N 31 50 E
Adlavik Is., Canada 129 B8 55 2N 57 45W
Adler, Russia 53 J4 43 28N 39 52 E
Adliswil, Switz. 29 B7 47 19N 8 32 E
Admer, Algeria 99 D6 20 21N 5 27 E
Admer, Erg d', Algeria 99 D6 24 0N 9 5 E
Admiralty G., Australia 112 B4 14 20 S 125 55 E
Admiralty I., U.S.A. 126 C6 57 30N 134 30W
Admiralty Inlet, U.S.A. 142 C2 48 8N 122 58W
Admiralty Is., Papua N. G. 120 B4 2 0 S 147 0 E
Ado, Nigeria 101 D5 6 36N 2 56 E
Ado-Ekiti, Nigeria 101 D6 7 38N 5 12 E
Adok, Sudan 95 F3 8 10N 30 20 E
Adola, Ethiopia 95 E5 11 14N 41 44 E
Adonara, Indonesia 72 C2 8 15 S 123 5 E
Adoni, India 83 G3 15 33N 77 18 E
Adony, Hungary 31 D11 47 6N 18 52 E
Adour →, France 24 E2 43 32N 1 32W
Adra, India 81 H12 23 30N 86 42 E
Adra, Spain 35 J1 36 43N 3 3W
Adrano, Italy 41 E7 37 40N 14 50 E
Adrar, Algeria 99 C4 27 51N 0 11W
Adrasman, Tajikistan 55 C4 40 38N 69 58 E
Adré, Chad 97 F4 13 40N 22 20 E
Adrī, Libya 96 C2 27 32N 13 2 E
Ádria, Italy 39 C9 45 3N 12 3 E
Adrian, Mich., U.S.A. 141 C12 41 54N 84 2W
Adrian, Mo., U.S.A. 140 F2 38 24N 94 21W
Adrian, Tex., U.S.A. 139 H3 35 16N 102 40W
Adriatic Sea, Medit. S. 10 G9 43 0N 16 0 E
Adua, Indonesia 73 B3 1 45 S 129 50 E
Adula, Switz. 29 D8 46 30N 9 3 E
Adung Long, Burma 78 A6 28 7N 97 42 E
Adur, India 83 K3 9 8N 76 40 E
Adwa, Ethiopia 95 E4 14 15N 38 52 E
Adygea □, Russia 53 H5 45 0N 40 0 E
Adzhar Republic □ = Ajaria □, Georgia 53 K6 41 30N 42 0 E
Adzopé, Ivory C. 100 D4 6 7N 3 49W
Ægean Sea, Medit. S. 45 F7 38 30N 25 0 E
Aerhtai Shan, Mongolia 64 B4 46 40N 92 45 E
Ærø, Denmark 15 K4 54 52N 10 25 E
Ærøskøbing, Denmark 15 K4 54 53N 10 24 E
Aesch, Switz. 28 B5 47 28N 7 36 E
Aëtós, Greece 45 G3 37 15N 21 50 E
Afafi, Massif d', Niger 97 D3 22 11N 15 10 E
'Afak, Iraq 89 F11 32 4N 45 15 E
Afándou, Greece 32 C10 36 18N 28 12 E
Afarag, Erg, Algeria 99 D5 23 50N 2 47 E
Afdega, Ethiopia 108 C2 6 4N 43 30 E
Affreville = Khemis Miliana, Algeria 99 A5 36 11N 2 14 E
Affton, U.S.A. 140 F6 38 33N 90 20W
Afghanistan ■, Asia 79 B2 33 0N 65 0 E
Afgoi, Somali Rep. 108 D2 2 7N 44 59 E
'Afif, Si. Arabia 86 B3 23 53N 42 56 E
Afikpo, Nigeria 101 D6 5 53N 7 54 E
Aflou, Algeria 99 B5 34 7N 2 3 E
Afmadu, Somali Rep. 108 D2 0 31N 42 4 E
Afogados da Ingàzeira, Brazil 154 C4 7 45 S 37 39W
Afognak I., U.S.A. 126 C4 58 15N 152 30W
Afragola, Italy 41 B7 40 55N 14 18 E
Afrera, Ethiopia 95 E5 13 16N 41 5 E
'Afrīn, Syria 88 D7 36 32N 36 50 E
Afşin, Turkey 88 C7 38 14N 36 55 E
Afton, U.S.A. 137 D9 42 14N 75 32W
Aftout, Algeria 98 C4 26 50N 3 45W
Afuá, Brazil 153 D7 0 15 S 50 20W
Afula, Israel 91 C4 32 37N 35 17 E
Afyonkarahisar, Turkey 88 C4 38 45N 30 33 E
Aga, Egypt 94 H7 30 55N 31 10 E
Agadès = Agadez, Niger 97 E1 16 58N 7 59 E
Agadez, Niger 97 E1 16 58N 7 59 E
Agadir, Morocco 98 B3 30 28N 9 55W
Agaete, Canary Is. 33 F4 28 6N 15 43W
Agailás, Mauritania 98 D2 22 37N 14 22W
Agana, Guam 121 R15 13 28N 144 45 E
Agapa, Russia 57 B9 71 27N 89 15 E
Agar, India 80 H7 23 40N 76 2 E
Agaro, Ethiopia 95 F4 7 50N 36 38 E
Agartala, India 78 D3 23 50N 91 23 E
Agăş, Romania 46 C7 46 28N 26 15 E
Agassiz, Canada 130 D4 49 14N 121 46W
Agats, Indonesia 73 C5 5 33 S 138 0 E
Agbélouvé, Togo 101 D5 6 35N 1 14 E
Agboville, Ivory C. 100 D4 5 55N 4 15W
Ağcabädi, Azerbaijan 53 K8 40 5N 47 27 E
Agcogon, Phil. 70 E3 12 4N 121 57 E
Ağdam, Azerbaijan 53 L8 40 0N 46 58 E
Ağdaş, Azerbaijan 53 K8 40 44N 47 22 E
Agde, France 24 E7 43 19N 3 28 E
Agde, C. d', France 24 E7 43 16N 3 28 E
Agdz, Morocco 98 B3 30 47N 6 30W
Agdzhabedi = Ağcabädi, Azerbaijan 53 K8 40 5N 47 27 E

Al Khāliş 163

Agen, *France* 24 D4 44 12N 0 38 E
Ageo, *Japan* 63 B11 35 58N 139 36 E
Ager Tay, *Chad* 97 E3 20 0N 17 41 E
Agersø, *Denmark* 15 J5 55 13N 11 12 E
Ageyevo, *Russia* 52 C3 54 10N 36 27 E
Agger, *Denmark* 15 H2 56 47N 8 13 E
Ággius, *Italy* 40 B2 40 56N 9 4 E
Āgh Kand, *Iran* 89 D13 37 15N 48 4 E
Aghoueyyît, *Mauritania* 98 D1 21 10N 15 6W
Aginskoye, *Russia* 57 D12 51 6N 114 32 E
Agira, *Italy* 41 E7 37 39N 14 31 E
Ağlasun, *Turkey* 88 D4 37 39N 30 31 E
Agly →, *France* 24 F7 42 46N 3 3 E
Agnibilékrou, *Ivory C.* 100 D4 7 10N 3 11W
Agnita, *Romania* 46 D5 45 59N 24 40 E
Agnone, *Italy* 41 A7 41 48N 14 22 E
Ago, *Japan* 63 C8 34 20N 136 51 E
Agofie, *Ghana* 101 D5 8 27N 0 15 E
Agogna →, *Italy* 38 C5 45 4N 8 54 E
Agogo, *Sudan* 95 F2 7 50N 28 45 E
Agon, *France* 22 C5 49 2N 1 34W
Agön, *Sweden* 14 C11 61 34N 17 23 E
Agoo, *Phil.* 70 C3 16 20N 120 22 E
Ágordo, *Italy* 39 B9 46 18N 12 2 E
Agout →, *France* 24 E5 43 47N 1 41 E
Agra, *India* 80 F7 27 17N 77 58 E
Agrakhanskiy Poluostrov, *Russia* 53 J8 43 42N 47 36 E
Agramunt, *Spain* 34 D6 41 48N 1 6 E
Agreda, *Spain* 34 D3 41 51N 1 55W
Ağri, *Turkey* 89 C10 39 44N 43 4 E
Agri →, *Italy* 41 B9 40 13N 16 44 E
Ağri Daği, *Turkey* 89 C11 39 50N 44 15 E
Ağri Karakose, *Turkey* 49 G7 39 44N 43 3 E
Agrigento, *Italy* 40 E6 37 19N 13 34 E
Agrinion, *Greece* 45 F3 38 37N 21 27 E
Agrópoli, *Italy* 41 B7 40 21N 14 59 E
Ağstafa, *Azerbaijan* 53 K7 41 7N 45 27 E
Água Branca, *Brazil* 154 C3 5 50 S 42 40W
Agua Caliente, *Baja Calif., Mexico* 145 N10 32 29N 116 59W
Agua Caliente, *Sinaloa, Mexico* 146 B3 26 30N 108 20W
Agua Caliente Springs, *U.S.A.* 145 N10 32 56N 116 19W
Água Clara, *Brazil* 157 E7 20 25 S 52 45W
Agua Hechicero, *Mexico* 145 N10 32 26N 116 14W
Agua Preta →, *Brazil* 153 D5 1 41 S 63 48W
Agua Prieta, *Mexico* 146 A3 31 20N 109 32W
Aguachica, *Colombia* 152 B3 8 19N 73 38W
Aguada Cecilio, *Argentina* 160 B3 40 51 S 65 51W
Aguadas, *Colombia* 152 B2 5 40N 75 38W
Aguadilla, *Puerto Rico* 149 C6 18 26N 67 10W
Aguadulce, *Panama* 148 E3 8 15N 80 32W
Aguanga, *U.S.A.* 145 M10 33 27N 116 51W
Aguanish, *Canada* 129 B7 50 14N 62 2W
Aguanus →, *Canada* 129 B7 50 13N 62 5W
Aguapeí, *Brazil* 157 D6 16 12 S 59 43W
Aguapeí →, *Brazil* 155 F1 21 0 S 51 0W
Aguapey →, *Argentina* 158 B4 29 7 S 56 36W
Aguaray Guazú →, *Paraguay* 158 A4 24 47 S 57 19W
Aguarico →, *Ecuador* 152 D2 0 59 S 75 11W
Aguas →, *Spain* 34 D4 41 20N 0 30W
Aguas Blancas, *Chile* 158 A2 24 15 S 69 55W
Aguas Calientes, Sierra de, *Argentina* 158 B2 25 26 S 66 40W
Águas Formosas, *Brazil* 155 E3 17 5 S 40 57W
Aguascalientes, *Mexico* 146 C4 21 53N 102 12W
Aguascalientes □, *Mexico* 146 C4 22 0N 102 20W
Agudo, *Spain* 37 G6 38 59N 4 52W
Águeda, *Portugal* 36 E2 40 34N 8 27W
Agueda →, *Spain* 36 D4 41 2N 6 56W
Aguié, *Niger* 101 C6 13 31N 7 46 E
Aguilafuente, *Spain* 36 D6 41 13N 4 7W
Aguilar, *Spain* 37 H6 37 31N 4 40W
Aguilar de Campóo, *Spain* 36 C6 42 47N 4 15W
Aguilares, *Argentina* 158 B2 27 26 S 65 35W
Aguilas, *Spain* 35 H3 37 23N 1 35W
Agüimes, *Canary Is.* 33 G4 27 58N 15 27W
Aguja, C. de la, *Colombia* 152 A3 11 18N 74 12W
Agulaa, *Ethiopia* 95 E4 13 40N 39 40 E
Agulhas, C., *S. Africa* 104 E3 34 52 S 20 0 E
Agulo, *Canary Is.* 33 F2 28 11N 17 12W
Agung, *Indonesia* 75 D5 8 20 S 115 28 E
Agur, *Uganda* 106 B3 2 28N 32 55 E
Agusan →, *Phil.* 71 G5 9 0N 125 30 E
Agusan del Norte □, *Phil.* 71 G5 9 20N 125 10 E
Agusan del Sur □, *Phil.* 71 G5 8 30N 125 30 E
Agustín Codazzi, *Colombia* 152 A3 10 2N 73 14W
Agutaya I., *Phil.* 71 F3 11 9N 120 58 E
Agvali, *Russia* 53 J8 42 36N 46 8 E
Aha Mts., *Botswana* 104 B3 19 45 S 21 0 E
Ahaggar, *Algeria* 99 D6 23 0N 6 30 E
Ahamansu, *Ghana* 101 D5 7 38N 0 35 E
Ahar, *Iran* 89 C12 38 35N 47 0 E
Ahaura →, *N.Z.* 119 C6 42 21 S 171 34 E
Ahaus, *Germany* 26 C3 52 4N 7 0 E
Ahelledjem, *Algeria* 99 C6 26 37N 6 58 E
Ahimanawa Ra., *N.Z.* 118 F5 39 3 S 176 30 E
Ahipara B., *N.Z.* 118 B2 35 5 S 173 5 E
Ahiri, *India* 82 E5 19 30N 80 0 E
Ahlat, *Turkey* 89 C10 38 45N 42 29 E
Ahlen, *Germany* 26 D3 51 45N 7 53 E
Ahmad Wal, *Pakistan* 80 E1 29 18N 65 58 E
Ahmadabad, *India* 80 H5 23 0N 72 40 E
Aḩmadābād, *Khorāsān, Iran* 85 C9 35 3N 60 50 E
Aḩmadābād, *Khorāsān, Iran* 85 C8 35 49N 59 42 E
Aḩmadī, *Iran* 85 E8 27 56N 56 42 E
Ahmadnagar, *India* 82 E2 19 7N 74 46 E
Ahmadpur, *Pakistan* 80 E4 29 12N 71 10 E
Ahmar, *Ethiopia* 95 F5 9 20N 41 15 E
Ahmedabad = Ahmadabad, *India* 80 H5 23 0N 72 40 E
Ahmednagar = Ahmadnagar, *India* 82 E2 19 7N 74 46 E
Ahoada, *Nigeria* 101 D6 5 8N 6 36 E
Ahome, *Mexico* 146 B3 25 55N 109 11W
Ahr →, *Germany* 26 E3 50 32N 7 16 E
Ahram, *Iran* 85 D6 28 52N 51 16 E
Ahrax Pt., *Malta* 32 D1 35 59N 14 22 E
Ahrensbök, *Germany* 26 A6 54 8N 10 19 E
Ahrweiler, *Germany* 26 E3 50 31N 7 3 E
Āhū, *Iran* 85 C6 34 33N 50 2 E
Ahuachapán, *El Salv.* 148 D2 13 54N 89 52W
Ahuriri →, *N.Z.* 119 E5 44 31 S 170 12 E
Ahvāz, *Iran* 85 D6 31 20N 48 40 E
Ahvenanmaa = Åland, *Finland* 13 F16 60 15N 20 0 E
Aḩwar, *Yemen* 86 D4 13 30N 46 40 E
Ahzar, *Mali* 101 B5 15 30N 3 20 E
Aiari →, *Brazil* 152 C4 1 22N 68 36W
Aichach, *Germany* 27 G7 48 27N 11 8 E
Aichi □, *Japan* 63 B9 35 0N 137 15 E
Aidone, *Italy* 41 E7 37 25N 14 27 E
Aiello Cálabro, *Italy* 41 C9 39 1N 16 10 E
Aigle, *Switz.* 28 D3 46 18N 6 58 E
Aignay-le-Duc, *France* 23 E11 47 40N 4 43 E
Aigoual, Mt., *France* 24 D7 44 8N 3 35 E
Aigre, *France* 24 C4 45 54N 0 1 E
Aigua, *Uruguay* 159 C5 34 13 S 54 46W
Aigueperse, *France* 24 B7 46 3N 3 13 E
Aigues →, *France* 25 D8 44 7N 4 43 E
Aigues-Mortes, *France* 25 E8 43 35N 4 12 E
Aigues-Mortes, G. d', *France* 25 E8 43 31N 4 3 E
Aiguilles, *France* 25 D10 44 47N 6 51 E
Aiguillon, *France* 24 D4 44 18N 0 21 E
Aigurande, *France* 24 B5 46 27N 1 49 E
Aihui, *China* 65 A7 50 10N 127 30 E
Aija, *Peru* 156 B2 9 50 S 77 45W
Aikawa, *Japan* 60 E9 38 2N 138 15 E
Aiken, *U.S.A.* 135 J5 33 34N 81 43W
Ailao Shan, *China* 68 F3 24 0N 101 20 E
Aillant-sur-Tholon, *France* 23 E10 47 52N 3 20 E
Aillik, *Canada* 129 A8 55 11N 59 18W
Ailly-sur-Noye, *France* 23 C9 49 45N 2 20 E
Ailsa Craig, *U.K.* 18 F3 55 15N 5 6W
'Ailūn, *Jordan* 91 C4 32 18N 35 47 E
Aim, *Russia* 57 D14 59 0N 133 55 E
Aimere, *Indonesia* 72 C2 8 45 S 121 3 E
Aimogasta, *Argentina* 158 B2 28 33 S 66 50W
Aimorés, *Brazil* 155 E3 19 30 S 41 4W
Ain □, *France* 25 B9 46 5N 5 20 E
Ain →, *France* 25 C9 45 45N 5 11 E
Aïn Beïda, *Algeria* 99 A6 35 50N 7 29 E
Aïn Ben Khellil, *Algeria* 99 B4 33 15N 0 49W
Aïn Ben Tili, *Mauritania* 98 C3 25 59N 9 27W
Aïn Beni Mathar, *Morocco* 99 B4 34 1N 2 0W
Aïn Benian, *Algeria* 99 A5 36 48N 2 55 E
Ain Dalla, *Egypt* 94 B2 27 20N 27 23 E
Ain el Mafki, *Egypt* 94 B2 27 30N 28 15 E
Ain Girba, *Egypt* 94 B2 29 20N 25 14 E
Aïn M'lila, *Algeria* 99 A6 36 2N 6 35 E
Ain Qeiqab, *Egypt* 94 B1 29 42N 24 55 E
Aïn-Sefra, *Algeria* 99 B4 32 47N 0 37W
Ain Sheikh Murzûk, *Egypt* 94 B2 26 47N 27 45 E
'Ain Sudr, *Egypt* 91 F2 29 50N 33 6 E
Ain Sukhna, *Egypt* 94 J8 29 32N 32 20 E
Aïn Tédelès, *Algeria* 99 A5 36 0N 0 21 E
Aïn-Témouchent, *Algeria* 99 A4 35 16N 1 8W
Aïn Touta, *Algeria* 99 A6 35 26N 5 54 E
Ain Zeitûn, *Egypt* 94 B2 29 10N 25 48 E
Aïn Zorah, *Morocco* 99 B4 34 37N 3 32W
Ainabo, *Somali Rep.* 108 C3 9 0N 46 25 E
Ainaži, *Latvia* 13 H21 57 50N 24 24 E
Aínos Óros, *Greece* 45 F2 38 10N 20 35 E
Ainsworth, *U.S.A.* 138 D5 42 33N 99 52W
Aioi, *Japan* 62 C6 34 48N 134 28 E
Aipe, *Colombia* 152 C2 3 13N 75 15W
Aiquile, *Bolivia* 157 D4 18 10 S 65 10W
Aïr, *Niger* 97 E1 18 30N 8 0 E
Air Hitam, *Malaysia* 77 M4 1 55N 103 11 E
Airaines, *France* 23 C8 49 58N 1 55 E
Airão, *Brazil* 153 D5 1 56 S 61 22W
Airdrie, *U.K.* 18 F5 55 52N 3 57W
Aire →, *France* 23 C11 49 18N 4 49 E
Aire →, *U.K.* 16 D7 53 43N 0 55W
Aire, I. del, *Spain* 33 B11 39 48N 4 16 E
Aire-sur-la-Lys, *France* 23 B9 50 37N 2 22 E
Aire-sur-l'Adour, *France* 24 E3 43 42N 0 15W
Aireys Inlet, *Australia* 116 E6 38 29 S 144 5 E
Airlie Beach, *Australia* 114 C4 20 16 S 148 43 E
Airolo, *Switz.* 29 C7 46 32N 8 37 E
Airvault, *France* 22 F6 46 50N 0 8W
Aisch →, *Germany* 27 F7 49 49N 10 58 E
Aisen □, *Chile* 160 C2 46 30 S 73 0W
Aisne □, *France* 23 C10 49 42N 3 40 E
Aisne →, *France* 23 C9 49 26N 2 50 E
Aitana, Sierra de, *Spain* 35 G4 38 35N 0 24W
Aitape, *Papua N. G.* 120 B2 3 11 S 142 22 E
Aitkin, *U.S.A.* 138 B8 46 32N 93 42W
Aitolía Kai Akarnanía □, *Greece* 45 F3 38 45N 21 18 E
Aitolikón, *Greece* 45 F3 38 26N 21 21 E
Aiuaba, *Brazil* 154 C3 6 38 S 40 7W
Aiud, *Romania* 46 C4 46 19N 23 44 E
Aix-en-Provence, *France* 25 E9 43 32N 5 27 E
Aix-la-Chapelle = Aachen, *Germany* 26 E2 50 45N 6 6 E
Aix-les-Bains, *France* 25 C9 45 41N 5 53 E
Aixe-sur-Vienne, *France* 24 C5 45 47N 1 9 E
Aiyang, Mt., *Papua N. G.* 120 C1 5 10 S 141 20 E
Aiyansh, *Canada* 130 B3 55 17N 129 2W
Aíyina, *Greece* 45 G5 37 45N 23 26 E
Aiyínion, *Greece* 44 D4 40 28N 22 28 E
Aiyion, *Greece* 45 F4 38 15N 22 5 E
Aizawl, *India* 78 D4 23 40N 92 44 E
Aizenay, *France* 22 F5 46 44N 1 38W
Aizkraukle, *Latvia* 13 H21 56 36N 25 11 E
Aizpute, *Latvia* 13 H19 56 43N 21 40 E
Aizuwakamatsu, *Japan* 60 F9 37 30N 139 56 E
Ajaccio, *France* 25 G12 41 55N 8 40 E
Ajaccio, G. d', *France* 25 G12 41 52N 8 40 E
Ajaju →, *Colombia* 152 C3 0 59N 72 20W
Ajalpan, *Mexico* 147 D5 18 22N 97 15W
Ajanta Ra., *India* 82 D2 20 28N 75 50 E
Ajari Rep. = Ajaria □, *Georgia* 53 K6 41 30N 42 0 E
Ajaria □, *Georgia* 53 K6 41 30N 42 0 E
Ajax, *Canada* 136 C5 43 50N 79 1W
Ajax, Mt., *N.Z.* 119 C7 42 35 S 172 5 E
Ajayan Pt., *Guam* 121 R15 13 15N 144 43 E
Ajdâbiyah, *Libya* 96 B4 30 54N 20 4 E
Ajdovščina, *Slovenia* 39 C10 45 54N 13 54 E
Ajibar, *Ethiopia* 95 E4 10 35N 38 36 E
Ajka, *Hungary* 31 D10 47 4N 17 31 E
'Ajmān, *U.A.E.* 85 E7 25 25N 55 30 E
Ajmer, *India* 80 F6 26 28N 74 37 E
Ajo, *U.S.A.* 143 K7 32 22N 112 52W
Ajoie, *Switz.* 28 B4 47 22N 7 0 E
Ajok, *Sudan* 95 F2 9 15N 28 28 E
Ajuy, *Phil.* 71 F4 11 10N 123 1 E
Ak Dağ, *Turkey* 88 D3 36 30N 29 45 E
Ak Dağlar, *Turkey* 88 C7 39 32N 36 12 E
Akaba, *Togo* 101 D5 8 10N 1 2 E
Akabira, *Japan* 60 C11 43 33N 142 5 E
Akabli, *Algeria* 99 C5 26 49N 1 31 E
Akaishi-Dake, *Japan* 63 B10 35 27N 138 9 E
Akaishi-Sammyaku, *Japan* 63 B10 35 25N 138 10 E
Akaki Beseka, *Ethiopia* 95 F4 8 55N 38 45 E
Akala, *Sudan* 95 D4 15 39N 36 13 E
Akamas □, *Cyprus* 32 D11 35 3N 32 18 E
Akanthou, *Cyprus* 32 D12 35 22N 33 45 E
Akaroa, *N.Z.* 119 D7 43 49 S 172 59 E
Akaroa Harbour, *N.Z.* 119 D7 43 50 S 172 55 E
Akasha, *Sudan* 94 C3 21 10N 30 32 E
Akashi, *Japan* 62 C6 34 45N 134 58 E
Akbou, *Algeria* 99 A5 36 31N 4 31 E
Akbulak, *Russia* 54 F5 51 1N 55 37 E
Akçaabat, *Turkey* 89 B8 41 1N 39 34 E
Akçadağ, *Turkey* 88 C7 38 27N 37 43 E
Akçakale, *Turkey* 89 D8 36 41N 38 56 E
Akçakoca, *Turkey* 88 B4 41 5N 31 8 E
Akchâr, *Mauritania* 98 D2 20 20N 14 28W
Akdağmadeni, *Turkey* 88 C6 39 39N 35 53 E
Akdala, *Kazakstan* 55 A7 45 2N 74 35 E
Akechi, *Japan* 63 B9 35 18N 137 23 E
Akelamo, *Indonesia* 72 A3 1 35N 129 40 E
Akershus fylke □, *Norway* 14 E5 60 0N 11 10 E
Akeru →, *India* 82 F5 17 25N 80 5 E
Aketi, *Zaïre* 102 B4 2 38N 23 47 E
Akhaïa □, *Greece* 45 F3 38 5N 21 45 E
Akhalkalaki, *Georgia* 53 K6 41 27N 43 25 E
Akhaltsikhe, *Georgia* 53 K6 41 40N 43 0 E
Akharnaí, *Greece* 45 F5 38 5N 23 44 E
Akhelóös →, *Greece* 45 F3 38 19N 21 7 E
Akhendria, *Greece* 45 K7 34 58N 25 16 E
Akhéron →, *Greece* 44 E2 39 20N 20 29 E
Akhisar, *Turkey* 88 C2 38 56N 27 48 E
Akhladhókambos, *Greece* 45 G4 37 31N 22 35 E
Akhmîm, *Egypt* 94 B3 26 31N 31 47 E
Akhnur, *India* 81 C6 32 52N 74 45 E
Akhtopol, *Bulgaria* 43 E12 42 6N 27 56 E
Akhtuba →, *Russia* 53 G8 47 41N 46 55 E
Akhtubinsk, *Russia* 53 F8 48 13N 46 7 E
Akhty, *Russia* 53 K8 41 30N 47 45 E
Akhtyrka = Okhtyrka, *Ukraine* 51 G8 50 25N 35 0 E
Aki, *Japan* 62 D5 33 30N 133 54 E
Aki-Nada, *Japan* 62 C4 34 5N 132 40 E
Akiéni, *Gabon* 102 C2 1 11 S 13 53 E
Akimiski I., *Canada* 128 B3 52 50N 81 30W
Akimovka, *Ukraine* 51 J8 46 44N 35 0 E
Akita, *Japan* 60 E10 39 45N 140 7 E
Akita □, *Japan* 60 E10 39 40N 140 30 E
Akjoujt, *Mauritania* 100 B2 19 45N 14 15W
Akka, *Morocco* 98 C3 29 22N 8 9W
Akkeshi, *Japan* 60 C12 43 2N 144 51 E
'Akko, *Israel* 91 C4 32 55N 35 4 E
Akkol, *Kazakstan* 55 B5 43 36N 70 45 E
Akkol, *Kazakstan* 56 E8 45 0N 75 39 E
Akköy, *Turkey* 45 G9 37 30N 27 18 E
Akkrum, *Neths.* 20 B7 53 3N 5 50 E
Aklampa, *Benin* 101 D5 8 15N 2 10 E
Aklan □, *Phil.* 71 F4 11 50N 122 30 E
Aklavik, *Canada* 126 B6 68 12N 135 0W
Akmolinsk = Aqmola, *Kazakstan* 56 D8 51 10N 71 30 E
Akmonte, *Spain* 37 H4 37 13N 6 38W
Akmuz, *Kyrgyzstan* 55 C8 41 15N 76 10 E
Aknoul, *Morocco* 99 B4 34 40N 3 55W
Akō, *Japan* 62 C6 34 45N 134 24 E
Ako, *Nigeria* 101 C7 10 19N 10 48 E
Akobo →, *Ethiopia* 95 F3 7 48N 33 3 E
Akola, *India* 82 D3 20 42N 77 2 E
Akonolinga, *Cameroon* 101 E7 3 50N 12 18 E
Akordat, *Eritrea* 95 D4 15 30N 37 40 E
Akosombo Dam, *Ghana* 101 D5 6 20N 0 5 E
Akot, *India* 82 D3 21 10N 77 10 E
Akot, *Sudan* 95 F3 6 31N 30 9 E
Akpatok I., *Canada* 127 B13 60 25N 68 8W
Åkrahamn, *Norway* 13 G11 59 15N 5 10 E
Akranes, *Iceland* 12 D2 64 19N 22 5W
Akreïjit, *Mauritania* 100 B3 18 19N 9 11W
Akrítas Venétiko, Ákra, *Greece* 45 H3 36 43N 21 54 E
Akron, *Colo., U.S.A.* 138 E3 40 10N 103 13W
Akron, *Ind., U.S.A.* 141 C10 41 2N 86 1W
Akron, *Ohio, U.S.A.* 136 E3 41 5N 81 31W
Akrotiri, *Cyprus* 32 E11 34 36N 32 57 E
Akrotíri, Ákra, *Greece* 44 D7 40 26N 25 27 E
Akrotiri Bay, *Cyprus* 32 E12 34 35N 33 10 E
Aksai Chin, *India* 81 B8 35 15N 79 55 E
Aksaray, *Turkey* 88 C6 38 25N 34 2 E
Aksarka, *Russia* 56 C7 66 31N 67 50 E
Aksay, *Kazakstan* 54 F4 51 11N 53 0 E
Akşehir, *Turkey* 88 C4 38 18N 31 30 E
Akşehir Gölü, *Turkey* 88 C4 38 30N 31 25 E
Aksenovo Zilovskoye, *Russia* 57 D12 53 20N 117 40 E
Akstafa = Ağstafa, *Azerbaijan* 53 K7 41 7N 45 27 E
Aksu, *China* 64 B3 41 5N 80 10 E
Aksu →, *Turkey* 88 D4 36 52N 30 57 E
Aksum, *Ethiopia* 95 E4 14 5N 38 40 E
Aktash, *Russia* 52 C11 55 2N 52 0 E
Aktash, *Uzbekistan* 55 D2 39 55N 65 55 E
Aktasty, *Kazakstan* 54 F8 50 42N 61 42 E
Aktogay, *Kazakstan* 55 A8 44 25N 76 44 E
Aktogay, *Kazakstan* 56 E8 46 57N 79 40 E
Aktsyabrski, *Belarus* 51 F5 52 38N 28 53 E
Aktyubinsk = Aqtöbe, *Kazakstan* 54 F6 50 17N 57 10 E
Aktyuz, *Kyrgyzstan* 55 B8 42 54N 76 7 E
Aku, *Nigeria* 101 D6 6 40N 7 18 E
Akula, *Zaïre* 102 B4 2 22N 20 12 E
Akune, *Japan* 62 E2 32 1N 130 12 E
Akure, *Nigeria* 101 D6 7 15N 5 5 E
Akureyri, *Iceland* 12 D4 65 40N 18 6W
Akuseki-Shima, *Japan* 61 K4 29 27N 129 37 E
Akusha, *Russia* 53 J8 42 18N 47 30 E
Akwa-Ibom □, *Nigeria* 101 E6 4 30N 7 30 E
Akyab = Sittwe, *Burma* 78 E4 20 18N 92 45 E
Akyazı, *Turkey* 88 B4 40 40N 30 38 E
Akzhar, *Kazakstan* 55 B5 43 8N 71 37 E
Al Abyār, *Libya* 96 B4 32 9N 20 29 E
Al 'Adan, *Yemen* 86 D4 12 45N 45 0 E
Al Aḩsā, *Si. Arabia* 85 E6 25 50N 49 0 E
Al Ajfar, *Si. Arabia* 84 E4 27 26N 43 0 E
Al Amādīyah, *Iraq* 89 D10 37 5N 43 30 E
Al Amārah, *Iraq* 89 G12 31 55N 47 15 E
Al 'Aqabah, *Jordan* 91 F4 29 31N 35 0 E
Al' Aqīq, *Si. Arabia* 86 B3 20 39N 41 25 E
Al Arak, *Syria* 89 E8 34 38N 38 35 E
Al 'Aramah, *Si. Arabia* 84 E5 25 30N 46 0 E
Al 'Ariḑah, *Si. Arabia* 86 C3 17 3N 43 5 E
Al Arṭāwīyah, *Si. Arabia* 84 E5 26 31N 45 20 E
Al Ashkhara, *Oman* 87 B7 21 50N 59 30 E
Al 'Āşimah □, *Jordan* 91 D5 31 40N 36 30 E
Al' Assāfīyah, *Si. Arabia* 84 D3 28 17N 38 59 E
Al 'Ayn, *Oman* 85 E7 24 15N 55 45 E
Al 'Ayn, *Si. Arabia* 84 E3 25 4N 38 6 E
Al A'ẓamīyah, *Iraq* 84 C5 33 22N 44 22 E
Al 'Azīzīyah, *Iraq* 89 F11 32 54N 45 4 E
Al 'Azīzīyah, *Libya* 96 B2 32 30N 13 1 E
Al Bāb, *Syria* 88 D7 36 23N 37 29 E
Al Bad', *Si. Arabia* 84 D2 28 28N 35 1 E
Al Bādī, *Iraq* 84 C4 35 56N 41 32 E
Al Badī', *Si. Arabia* 86 B4 22 0N 46 35 E
Al Baḩrah, *Kuwait* 84 D5 29 40N 47 52 E
Al Balqā' □, *Jordan* 91 C4 32 5N 35 45 E
Al Barkāt, *Libya* 96 D2 24 56N 10 14 E
Al Bārūk, J., *Lebanon* 91 B4 33 39N 35 40 E
Al Başrah, *Iraq* 84 D5 30 30N 47 50 E
Al Baṭḩā, *Iraq* 84 D5 31 6N 45 53 E
Al Batrūn, *Lebanon* 91 A4 34 15N 35 40 E
Al Bayāḑ, *Si. Arabia* 86 B4 22 0N 47 0 E
Al Bayḑā, *Libya* 96 B4 32 50N 21 44 E
Al Bayḑā', *Yemen* 86 D4 14 5N 45 42 E
Al Bayḑā □, *Libya* 96 B4 32 0N 21 30 E
Al Bi'ār, *Si. Arabia* 86 B2 22 39N 39 40 E
Al Biqā □, *Lebanon* 91 A5 34 10N 36 10 E
Al Bi'r, *Si. Arabia* 84 D3 28 51N 36 16 E
Al Birk, *Si. Arabia* 86 C3 18 13N 41 33 E
Al Bu'ayrāt al Ḩasūn, *Libya* 96 B3 31 24N 15 44 E
Al Burayj, *Syria* 91 A5 34 15N 36 46 E
Al Fallūjah, *Iraq* 89 F10 33 20N 43 55 E
Al Fatk, *Yemen* 87 C6 16 31N 52 41 E
Al Fāw, *Iraq* 85 D6 30 0N 48 30 E
Al Faydamī, *Yemen* 87 C6 16 25N 52 26 E
Al Fujayrah, *U.A.E.* 85 E8 25 7N 56 18 E
Al Ghadaf, W. →, *Jordan* 91 D5 31 26N 36 43 E
Al Ghammās, *Iraq* 84 D5 31 45N 44 37 E
Al Gharīb, *Libya* 96 B4 32 35N 21 11 E
Al Ghayḑah, *Yemen* 87 C6 16 13N 52 11 E
Al Ghayḑah, *Yemen* 87 D5 14 55N 50 0 E
Al Ghayl, *Yemen* 87 D5 15 30N 50 54 E
Al Hābah, *Si. Arabia* 85 E5 27 10N 47 0 E
Al Ḩadd, *Oman* 87 B7 22 32N 59 48 E
Al Ḩaddār, *Si. Arabia* 86 B4 21 58N 45 57 E
Al Ḩadīthah, *Iraq* 89 E10 34 0N 41 13 E
Al Ḩadīthah, *Si. Arabia* 84 D3 31 28N 37 8 E
Al Ḩaḑr, *Iraq* 89 E10 35 35N 42 44 E
Al Hājānah, *Syria* 91 B5 33 20N 36 33 E
Al Hajarayn, *Yemen* 87 D5 15 29N 48 20 E
Al Hallānīyah, *Oman* 87 C7 17 30N 56 1 E
Al Hāmad, *Si. Arabia* 84 D3 31 30N 39 30 E
Al Ḩamar, *Si. Arabia* 86 B4 22 23N 46 12 E
Al Hamdāniyah, *Syria* 84 C3 35 25N 36 50 E
Al Hamidīyah, *Syria* 91 A4 34 42N 35 57 E
Al Hammādah al Ḩamrā', *Libya* 96 C2 29 30N 12 0 E
Al Ḩammār, *Iraq* 84 D5 30 57N 46 51 E
Al Ḩamrā', *Si. Arabia* 86 A2 24 2N 38 55 E
Al Ḩarīq, *Si. Arabia* 86 B4 23 29N 46 27 E
Al Ḩarīr, W. →, *Syria* 91 C4 32 44N 35 59 E
Al Harūj al Aswad, *Libya* 96 C3 27 0N 17 10 E
Al Ḩasā, W. →, *Jordan* 91 D4 31 4N 35 29 E
Al Ḩasakah, *Syria* 89 D9 36 35N 40 45 E
Al Hāsikīyah, *Oman* 87 C6 17 28N 55 36 E
Al Ḩasy, *Yemen* 87 D5 15 3N 48 40 E
Al Ḩawrah, *Yemen* 86 D4 13 50N 47 35 E
Al Ḩawṭah, *Yemen* 86 D4 14 23N 47 24 E
Al Ḩawṭah □, *Si. Arabia* 86 B4 23 30N 47 0 E
Al Haydān, W. →, *Jordan* 91 D4 31 29N 35 34 E
Al Ḩayy, *Iraq* 89 F12 32 5N 46 5 E
Al Ḩijāz, *Si. Arabia* 86 A2 26 0N 37 30 E
Al Ḩillah, *Iraq* 89 F11 32 30N 44 25 E
Al Ḩillah, *Si. Arabia* 86 B4 23 35N 46 50 E
Al Hindīyah, *Iraq* 89 F11 32 30N 44 10 E
Al Hirmil, *Lebanon* 91 A5 34 26N 36 24 E
Al Hoceïma, *Morocco* 98 A4 35 8N 3 58W
Al Ḩudaydah, *Yemen* 86 D3 14 50N 43 0 E
Al Ḩufrah, *Libya* 96 C2 25 32N 14 1 E
Al Hufūf, *Si. Arabia* 85 E6 25 25N 49 45 E
Al Ḩulwah, *Si. Arabia* 86 B4 23 24N 46 48 E
Al Ḩumaydah, *Si. Arabia* 84 D2 29 14N 34 56 E
Al Ḩunayy, *Si. Arabia* 85 E6 25 58N 48 45 E
Al Ḩurayḑah, *Yemen* 87 D5 15 36N 48 12 E
Al Husayyāt, *Libya* 96 B4 30 24N 20 37 E
Al Hūwah, *Si. Arabia* 86 B4 23 2N 45 48 E
Al Ḩuwaymī, *Yemen* 86 D4 13 23N 44 28 E
Al 'Irqah, *Yemen* 86 D4 13 39N 47 22 E
Al Īsāwīyah, *Si. Arabia* 84 D3 30 43N 37 59 E
Al Ittihad = Madīnat ash Sha'b, *Yemen* 86 D4 12 50N 45 0 E
Al Jafr, *Jordan* 91 E5 30 18N 36 14 E
Al Jaghbūb, *Libya* 96 C4 29 42N 24 38 E
Al Jahrah, *Kuwait* 84 D5 29 25N 47 40 E
Al Jalāmīd, *Si. Arabia* 84 D3 31 20N 39 45 E
Al Jamalīyah, *Qatar* 85 E6 25 37N 51 5 E
Al Janūb □, *Lebanon* 91 B4 33 20N 35 20 E
Al Jawf, *Libya* 96 D4 24 10N 23 24 E
Al Jawf, *Si. Arabia* 84 D3 29 55N 39 40 E
Al Jazirah, *Iraq* 89 E10 33 30N 44 0 E
Al Jazirah, *Libya* 96 C4 26 10N 21 20 E
Al Jithāmīyah, *Si. Arabia* 84 E4 27 41N 41 43 E
Al Jubayl, *Si. Arabia* 85 E6 27 0N 49 50 E
Al Jubaylah, *Si. Arabia* 84 E5 24 55N 46 25 E
Al Jubb, *Si. Arabia* 84 E4 27 11N 42 17 E
Al Jumūm, *Si. Arabia* 86 B2 21 37N 39 42 E
Al Junaynah, *Sudan* 97 F4 13 27N 22 45 E
Al Kabā'ish, *Iraq* 84 D5 30 58N 47 0 E
Al Kāmil, *Oman* 87 B7 22 13N 59 12 E
Al Karak, *Jordan* 91 D4 31 11N 35 42 E
Al Karak □, *Jordan* 91 E5 31 0N 36 0 E
Al Kāzim Tyah, *Iraq* 89 F11 33 22N 44 12 E
Al Khābūra, *Oman* 87 B7 23 57N 57 5 E
Al Khalīl, *West Bank* 91 D4 31 32N 35 6 E
Al Khāliş, *Iraq* 89 F11 33 49N 44 32 E

164 Al Khamāsīn

Al Khamāsīn, *Si. Arabia* . **86 B4** 20 29N 44 46 E
Al Kharāb, *Yemen* . . . . . . **86 C4** 16 29N 44 18 E
Al Kharfah, *Si. Arabia* . . **86 B4** 22 0N 46 35 E
Al Kharj, *Si. Arabia* . . . . **86 B4** 24 0N 47 0 E
Al Khāşirah, *Si. Arabia* . . **86 B3** 23 30N 43 47 E
Al Khawr, *Qatar* . . . . **85 E6** 25 41N 51 30 E
Al Khiḑr, *Iraq* . . . . **84 D5** 31 12N 45 33 E
Al Khiyām, *Lebanon* . . . . **91 B4** 33 20N 35 36 E
Al Khums, *Libya* . . . . **96 B2** 32 40N 14 17 E
Al Khums □, *Libya* . . . . . **96 B2** 31 20N 14 10 E
Al Kiswah, *Syria* . . . . **91 B5** 33 23N 36 14 E
Al Kūfah, *Iraq* . . . . **89 F11** 32 2N 44 24 E
Al Kufrah, *Libya* . . . . **96 D4** 24 17N 23 15 E
Al Kuhayfīyah, *Si. Arabia* **84 E4** 27 12N 43 3 E
Al Kūt, *Iraq* . . . . **89 F11** 32 30N 46 0 E
Al Kuwayt, *Kuwait* . . . . . **84 D5** 29 30N 48 0 E
Al Labwah, *Lebanon* . . . . **91 A5** 34 11N 36 20 E
Al Lādhiqīyah, *Syria* . . . . **88 E6** 35 30N 35 45 E
Al Līth, *Si. Arabia* . . . . . . **86 B3** 20 9N 40 15 E
Al Liwā', *Oman* . . . . **85 E8** 24 31N 56 36 E
Al Luḩayyah, *Yemen* . . . . **86 D3** 15 45N 42 40 E
Al Madīnah, *Iraq* . . . . **84 D5** 30 57N 47 16 E
Al Madīnah, *Si. Arabia* . . **84 E3** 24 35N 39 52 E
Al-Mafraq, *Jordan* . . . . . . **91 C5** 32 17N 36 14 E
Al Maghārīm, *Yemen* . . . . **86 D4** 15 1N 47 49 E
Al Maḩmūdīyah, *Iraq* . . . **89 F11** 33 3N 44 21 E
Al Majma'ah, *Si. Arabia* . **84 E5** 25 57N 45 22 E
Al Makhruq, W. →,
Jordan . . . . **91 D6** 31 28N 37 0 E
Al Makḩūl, *Si. Arabia* . . . **84 E4** 26 37N 42 39 E
Al Makīlī, *Libya* . . . . **96 B4** 32 10N 22 17 E
Al Manā'if, *Si. Arabia* . . . **87 B5** 23 49N 51 20 E
Al Manāmah, *Bahrain* . . . **85 E6** 26 10N 50 30 E
Al Manşūrī, *Yemen* . . . . . **86 D4** 14 17N 45 16 E
Al Maqwa', *Kuwait* . . . . . **84 D5** 29 10N 47 59 E
Al Marj, *Libya* . . . . **96 B4** 32 25N 20 30 E
Al Maţlā, *Kuwait* . . . . . . **84 D5** 29 24N 47 40 E
Al Mawjib, W. →,
Jordan . . . . **91 D4** 31 28N 35 36 E
Al Mawşil, *Iraq* . . . . **89 D10** 36 15N 43 5 E
Al Mayādin, *Syria* . . . . . . **89 E9** 35 1N 40 27 E
Al Mazār, *Jordan* . . . . **91 D4** 31 4N 35 41 E
Al Midhnab, *Si. Arabia* . . **84 E5** 25 50N 44 18 E
Al Mīfá, *Si. Arabia* . . . . . **86 C3** 18 54N 41 57 E
Al Minā', *Lebanon* . . . . . . **91 A4** 34 24N 35 49 E
Al Miqdādīyah, *Iraq* . . . . **89 E11** 34 0N 45 0 E
Al Mubarraz, *Si. Arabia* . . **85 E6** 25 30N 49 40 E
Al Muḑaybī, *Oman* . . . . . **87 B7** 22 34N 58 7 E
Al Mughayrā', *U.A.E.* . . . **85 E7** 24 5N 53 32 E
Al Muḩarraq, *Bahrain* . . . **85 E6** 26 15N 50 40 E
Al Mukallā, *Yemen* . . . . . . **87 D5** 14 33N 49 2 E
Al Mukhā, *Yemen* . . . . **86 D3** 13 18N 43 15 E
Al Muladdah, *Oman* . . . . . **87 B7** 23 45N 57 34 E
Al Musayjīd, *Si. Arabia* . . **84 E3** 24 5N 39 5 E
Al Musayyib, *Iraq* . . . . . . **89 F11** 32 49N 44 20 E
Al Muwaylih, *Si. Arabia* . **84 E2** 27 40N 35 30 E
Al Owuho = Otukpa,
Nigeria . . . . **101 D6** 7 9N 7 41 E
Al Qaddāhīyah, *Libya* . . . **96 B3** 31 15N 15 9 E
Al Qadīmah, *Si. Arabia* . . **86 B2** 22 20N 39 13 E
Al Qaḩmah, *Si. Arabia* . . **86 C3** 18 0N 41 41 E
Al Qā'im, *Iraq* . . . . **89 E9** 34 21N 41 7 E
Al Qalībah, *Si. Arabia* . . **84 D3** 28 24N 37 42 E
Al Qāmishlī, *Syria* . . . . . . **89 D9** 37 2N 41 14 E
Al Qaryah ash Sharqīyah,
Libya . . . . **96 B2** 30 28N 13 40 E
Al Qaryatayn, *Syria* . . . . . **91 A6** 34 12N 37 13 E
Al Qaşabát, *Libya* . . . . . . **96 B2** 32 39N 14 1 E
Al Qaṭ'ā, *Syria* . . . . **89 E9** 34 40N 40 48 E
Al Qaţīf, *Si. Arabia* . . . . . **85 E6** 26 35N 50 0 E
Al Qaţn, *Yemen* . . . . **87 D5** 15 51N 48 26 E
Al Qatrānah, *Jordan* . . . . **91 D5** 31 12N 36 6 E
Al Qaţrūn, *Libya* . . . . **96 D3** 24 56N 15 3 E
Al Qayşūmah, *Si. Arabia* **84 D5** 28 20N 46 7 E
Al Qiblīyah, *Oman* . . . . . **87 C7** 17 30N 56 20 E
Al Quds = Jerusalem,
Israel . . . . **91 D4** 31 47N 35 10 E
Al Qunaytirah, *Syria* . . . . **91 C4** 32 55N 35 45 E
Al Qunfudhah, *Si. Arabia* . **86 C3** 19 3N 41 4 E
Al Qurḩ, *Yemen* . . . . **87 C5** 16 44N 51 29 E
Al Qurnah, *Iraq* . . . . **84 D5** 31 1N 47 25 E
Al Quşayr, *Iraq* . . . . **84 D5** 30 39N 45 50 E
Al Quşayr, *Syria* . . . . **91 A5** 34 31N 36 34 E
Al Qutayfah, *Syria* . . . . . . **91 B5** 33 44N 36 36 E
Al Quway'īyah, *Si. Arabia* **86 A4** 24 3N 45 15 E
Al 'Ubaylah, *Si. Arabia* . **87 B5** 21 59N 50 57 E
Al' Uḑaylīyah, *Si. Arabia* **85 E6** 25 8N 49 18 E
Al 'Ulā, *Si. Arabia* . . . . . **84 E3** 26 35N 38 0 E
Al 'Ulayyah, *Si. Arabia* . **86 C3** 19 39N 41 54 E
Al Uqaylah ash Sharqīgah,
Libya . . . . **96 B3** 30 12N 19 10 E
Al Uqayr, *Si. Arabia* . . . . **85 E6** 25 40N 50 15 E
Al 'Uwaynid, *Si. Arabia* . **84 E5** 24 50N 46 0 E
Al 'Uwayqīlah, *Si. Arabia* **84 D4** 30 30N 42 10 E
Al 'Uyūn, *Si. Arabia* . . . . **84 E4** 26 30N 43 50 E
Al 'Uyūn, *Si. Arabia* . . . . **84 E3** 24 33N 39 35 E
Al Wajh, *Si. Arabia* . . . . . **84 E3** 26 10N 36 30 E
Al Wakrah, *Qatar* . . . . **85 E6** 25 10N 51 40 E
Al Wannān, *Si. Arabia* . . **85 E6** 26 55N 48 24 E
Al Waqbah, *Si. Arabia* . . **84 D5** 28 48N 45 33 E
Al Wari'āh, *Si. Arabia* . . **84 E5** 27 51N 47 25 E
Al Wātīyah, *Libya* . . . . . . **96 B2** 32 28N 11 57 E
Al Wusayl, *Qatar* . . . . **85 E6** 25 29N 51 29 E
Ala, *Italy* . . . . **38 C8** 45 45N 11 0 E
Ala Dağları, *Turkey* . . . . . **89 C10** 39 15N 43 33 E
Ala Tau Shankou =
Dzhungarskiye Vorota,
Kazakstan . . . . **64 B3** 45 0N 82 0 E
Alabama □, *U.S.A.* **135 J2** 33 0N 87 0W
Alabama →, *U.S.A.* **135 K2** 31 8N 87 57W
Alaca, *Turkey* . . . . **88 B6** 40 10N 34 51 E
Alaçam, *Turkey* . . . . **88 B6** 41 36N 35 36 E
Alaçam Dağları, *Turkey* . **88 C3** 39 18N 28 49 E
Alaçati, *Turkey* . . . . **45 F8** 38 16N 26 23 E
Alaejos, *Spain* **36 D5** 41 18N 5 13W
Alaérma, *Greece* . . . . **32 C9** 36 9N 27 57 E
Alagir, *Russia* . . . . **53 J7** 43 3N 44 14 E
Alagna Valsésia, *Italy* . . . **38 C4** 45 51N 7 56 E
Alagoa Grande, *Brazil* . . **154 C4** 7 3 S 35 35W
Alagoas □, *Brazil* . . . . . . **154 C4** 9 0 S 36 0W
Alagoinhas, *Brazil* . . . . . . **155 D4** 12 7 S 38 20W
Alagón, *Spain* **34 D3** 41 46N 1 12W
Alagón →, *Spain* **37 F4** 39 44N 6 53W
Alajero, *Canary Is.* **33 F2** 28 3N 17 13W
Alajuela, *Costa Rica* **148 D3** 10 2N 84 8W
Alakamisy, *Madag.* . . . . . **105 C8** 21 19 S 47 14 E
Alakurtti, *Russia* . . . . **48 A5** 67 0N 30 30 E
Alalapura, *Surinam* **153 C6** 2 20N 56 25W
Alalaú →, *Brazil* . . . . **153 D5** 0 30 S 61 9W
Alameda, *Spain* **37 H6** 37 12N 4 39W
Alameda, *Calif., U.S.A.* . . **144 H4** 37 46N 122 15W
Alameda, *N. Mex.,*
U.S.A. **143 J10** 35 11N 106 37W
Alaminos, *Phil.* . . . . **70 C2** 16 10N 119 59 E
Alamo, *U.S.A.* **145 J11** 36 21N 115 10W
Alamo Crossing, *U.S.A.* . **145 L13** 34 16N 113 33W
Alamogordo, *U.S.A.* **143 K11** 32 54N 105 57W
Alamos, *Mexico* **146 B3** 27 0N 109 0W
Alamosa, *U.S.A.* **143 H11** 37 28N 105 52W
Åland, *Finland* . . . . **13 F19** 60 15N 20 0 E
Aland, *India* . . . . **82 F3** 17 36N 76 35 E
Alandroal, *Portugal* **37 G3** 38 41N 7 24W
Ålands hav, *Sweden* . . . . . **13 F18** 60 0N 19 30 E
Alandur, *India* . . . . **83 H5** 13 0N 80 15 E
Alange, Presa de, *Spain* . **37 G4** 38 45N 6 18W
Alania = North
Ossetia □, *Russia* . . . . . **53 J7** 43 30N 44 30 E
Alanis, *Spain* **37 G5** 38 3N 5 43W
Alanya, *Turkey* . . . . **88 D5** 36 38N 32 0 E
Alaotra, Farihin', *Madag.* **105 B8** 17 30 S 48 30 E
Alapayevsk, *Russia* . . . . . **54 C8** 57 52N 61 42 E
Alar del Rey, *Spain* **36 C6** 42 38N 4 20W
Alaraz, *Spain* **36 E5** 40 45N 5 17W
Alaşehir, *Turkey* . . . . **88 C3** 38 23N 28 30 E
Alaska □, *U.S.A.* **126 B5** 64 0N 154 0W
Alaska, G. of, *Pac. Oc.* . **126 C5** 58 0N 145 0W
Alaska Highway, *Canada* **130 B3** 60 0N 130 0W
Alaska Peninsula, *U.S.A.* **126 C4** 56 0N 159 0W
Alaska Range, *U.S.A.* . . . **126 B4** 62 50N 151 0W
Alássio, *Italy* . . . . **38 D5** 44 0N 8 10 E
Älät, *Azerbaijan* . . . . **53 L9** 39 58N 49 25 E
Alatri, *Italy* . . . . **40 A6** 41 43N 13 21 E
Alatyr, *Russia* . . . . **52 C8** 54 55N 46 35 E
Alatyr →, *Russia* . . . . . . **52 C8** 54 52N 46 36 E
Alausi, *Ecuador* . . . . **152 D2** 2 0 S 78 50W
Álava □, *Spain* **34 C2** 42 48N 2 28W
Alava, C., *U.S.A.* **142 B1** 48 10N 124 44W
Alaverdi, *Armenia* . . . . . . **53 K7** 41 15N 44 37 E
Alavus, *Finland* . . . . **13 E20** 62 35N 23 36 E
Alawoona, *Australia* . . . . **116 C4** 34 45 S 140 30 E
'Alayh, *Lebanon* . . . . **91 B4** 33 46N 35 33 E
Alaykel, *Kyrgyzstan* . . . . **55 C7** 40 15N 74 25 E
Alayor, *Spain* . . . . **33 B11** 39 57N 4 8 E
Alayskiy Khrebet,
Kyrgyzstan . . . . **55 D6** 39 45N 72 0 E
Alazani →, *Azerbaijan* . . **53 K8** 41 5N 46 40 E
Alba, *Italy* . . . . **38 D5** 44 42N 8 2 E
Alba □, *Romania* . . . . **46 C4** 46 10N 23 30 E
Alba de Tormes, *Spain* . . **36 E5** 40 50N 5 30W
Alba-Iulia, *Romania* . . . . **46 C4** 46 8N 23 39 E
Albac, *Romania* . . . . **46 C4** 46 28N 23 1 E
Albacete, *Spain* **35 G3** 39 0N 1 50W
Albacete □, *Spain* **35 G3** 38 50N 2 0W
Albacutya, L., *Australia* . **116 C4** 35 45 S 141 58 E
Ålbæk, *Denmark* . . . . **15 G4** 57 36N 10 25 E
Ålbæk Bugt, *Denmark* . . . **15 G4** 57 35N 10 40 E
Albaida, *Spain* **35 G4** 38 51N 0 31W
Albalate de las Nogueras,
Spain **34 E2** 40 22N 2 18W
Albalate del Arzobispo,
Spain **34 D4** 41 6N 0 31W
Albania ■, *Europe* . . . . . . **44 C2** 41 0N 20 0 E
Albano Laziale, *Italy* . . . . **40 A5** 41 44N 12 39 E
Albany, *Australia* . . . . **113 G2** 35 1 S 117 58 E
Albany, *Ga., U.S.A.* **135 K3** 31 35N 84 10W
Albany, *Ind., U.S.A.* **141 D11** 40 18N 85 14W
Albany, *Minn., U.S.A.* . . . **138 C7** 45 38N 94 34W
Albany, *Mo., U.S.A.* **140 D2** 40 15N 94 20W
Albany, *N.Y., U.S.A.* **137 D11** 42 39N 73 45W
Albany, *Oreg., U.S.A.* . . . **142 D2** 44 38N 123 6W
Albany, *Tex., U.S.A.* **139 J5** 32 44N 99 18W
Albany, *Wis., U.S.A.* **140 B7** 42 43N 89 26W
Albany →, *Canada* **128 B3** 52 17N 81 31W
Albardón, *Argentina* . . . . **158 C2** 31 20 S 68 30W
Albarracín, *Spain* **34 E3** 40 25N 1 26W
Albarracín, Sierra de,
Spain **34 E3** 40 30N 1 30W
Albatross B., *Australia* . . **114 A3** 12 45 S 141 30 E
Albatross Pt., *N.Z.* . . . . . **118 E3** 38 7 S 174 44 E
Albay □, *Phil.* . . . . **70 E4** 13 13N 123 33 E
Albegna →, *Italy* . . . . **39 F8** 42 30N 11 11 E
Albemarle, *U.S.A.* **135 H5** 35 21N 80 11W
Albemarle Sd., *U.S.A.* . . . **135 H7** 36 5N 76 0W
Albenga, *Italy* . . . . **38 D5** 44 3N 8 13 E
Alberche →, *Spain* **36 F6** 39 58N 4 46W
Alberdi, *Paraguay* . . . . . . **158 B4** 26 14 S 58 20W
Alberes, Mts., *Spain* . . . . **34 C7** 42 28N 2 56 E
Alberique, *Spain* **35 F4** 39 7N 0 31W
Albersdorf, *Germany* . . . . **26 A5** 54 8N 9 17 E
Albert, *Australia* . . . . **117 B7** 32 22 S 147 30 E
Albert, *France* . . . . **23 B9** 50 0N 2 38 E
Albert, L., *Australia* . . . . **116 C3** 35 30 S 139 10 E
Albert Canyon, *Canada* . . **130 C5** 51 8N 117 41W
Albert Edward, Mt.,
Papua N. G. . . . . **120 E4** 8 20 S 147 24 E
Albert Edward Ra.,
Australia . . . . **112 C4** 18 17 S 127 57 E
Albert L., *Africa* . . . . **106 B3** 1 30N 31 0 E
Albert Lea, *U.S.A.* **138 D8** 43 39N 93 22W
Albert Nile →, *Uganda* . **106 B3** 3 36N 32 2 E
Albert Town, *Bahamas* . . **149 B5** 22 37N 74 33W
Alberta □, *Canada* **130 C6** 54 40N 115 0W
Alberti, *Argentina* . . . . . . **158 D3** 35 1 S 60 16W
Albertinia, *S. Africa* . . . . **104 E3** 34 11 S 21 34 E
Albertirsa, *Hungary* . . . . . **31 D12** 47 14N 19 37 E
Albertkanaal →, *Belgium* **21 F4** 51 14N 4 26 E
Alberton, *Canada* **129 C7** 46 50N 64 0W
Albertville = Kalemie,
Zaïre . . . . **106 D2** 5 55 S 29 9 E
Albertville, *France* . . . . . . **25 C10** 45 40N 6 22 E
Albi, *France* . . . . **24 E6** 43 56N 2 9 E
Albia, *U.S.A.* **140 C4** 41 2N 92 48W
Albina, *Surinam* **153 B7** 5 37N 54 15W
Albina, Ponta, *Angola* . . . **103 F2** 15 52 S 11 44 E
Albino, *Italy* . . . . **38 C6** 45 46N 9 47 E
Albion, *Idaho, U.S.A.* . . . **142 E7** 42 25N 113 35W
Albion, *Ill., U.S.A.* **141 F8** 38 23N 88 4W
Albion, *Ind., U.S.A.* **141 C11** 41 24N 85 25W
Albion, *Mich., U.S.A.* . . . **141 B12** 42 15N 84 45W
Albion, *Nebr., U.S.A.* . . . **138 E5** 41 42N 98 0W
Albion, *Pa., U.S.A.* **136 E4** 41 53N 80 22W
Alblasserdam, *Neths.* . . . **20 E5** 51 52N 4 40 E
Albocácer, *Spain* . . . . **34 E5** 40 21N 0 1 E
Alborán, *Medit. S.* **37 K7** 35 57N 3 0W
Alborea, *Spain* **35 F3** 39 17N 1 24W
Ålborg, *Denmark* . . . . **15 G3** 57 2N 9 54 E
Ålborg Bugt, *Denmark* . . **15 H4** 56 50N 10 35 E
Alborz, Reshteh-ye
Kūhhā-ye, *Iran* . . . . . . **85 C7** 36 0N 52 0 E
Albox, *Spain* **35 H2** 37 23N 2 8W
Albreda, *Canada* **130 C5** 52 35N 119 10W
Albufeira, *Portugal* **37 H2** 37 5N 8 15W
Albula →, *Switz.* . . . . **29 C8** 46 38N 9 28 E
Albuñol, *Spain* **35 J1** 36 48N 3 11W
Albuquerque, *Brazil* . . . . **157 D6** 19 23 S 57 26W
Albuquerque, *U.S.A.* **143 J10** 35 5N 106 39W
Albuquerque, Cayos de,
Caribbean **148 D3** 12 10N 81 50W
Alburg, *U.S.A.* **137 B11** 44 59N 73 18W
Alburno, Mte., *Italy* . . . . **41 B8** 40 33N 15 17 E
Alburquerque, *Spain* **37 F4** 39 15N 6 59W
Albury, *Australia* . . . . **117 D7** 36 3 S 146 56 E
Alby, *Sweden* . . . . **14 B9** 62 30N 15 28 E
Alcácer do Sal, *Portugal* . **37 G2** 38 22N 8 33W
Alcaçovas, *Portugal* **37 G2** 38 23N 8 9W
Alcala, *Phil.* . . . . **70 C3** 17 54N 121 39 E
Alcalá de Chisvert, *Spain* **34 E5** 40 19N 0 13 E
Alcalá de Guadaira, *Spain* **37 H5** 37 20N 5 50W
Alcalá de Henares, *Spain* **34 E1** 40 28N 3 22W
Alcalá de los Gazules,
Spain **37 J5** 36 29N 5 43W
Alcalá la Real, *Spain* **37 H7** 37 27N 3 57W
Alcamo, *Italy* . . . . **40 E5** 37 59N 12 55 E
Alcanadre, *Spain* **34 C2** 42 24N 2 7W
Alcanadre →, *Spain* **34 D4** 41 43N 0 12W
Alcanar, *Spain* . . . . **34 E5** 40 33N 0 28 E
Alcanede, *Portugal* **37 F2** 39 25N 8 49W
Alcanena, *Portugal* **37 F2** 39 27N 8 40W
Alcañices, *Spain* **36 D4** 41 41N 6 21W
Alcaníz, *Spain* **34 D4** 41 2N 0 8W
Alcântara, *Brazil* . . . . **154 B3** 2 20 S 44 30W
Alcántara, *Spain* **37 F4** 39 41N 6 57W
Alcantara L., *Canada* . . . **131 A7** 60 57N 108 9W
Alcantarilla, *Spain* **35 H3** 37 59N 1 12W
Alcaracejos, *Spain* **37 G6** 38 24N 4 58W
Alcaraz, *Spain* **35 G2** 38 40N 2 29W
Alcaraz, Sierra de, *Spain* **35 G2** 38 40N 2 20W
Alcaudete, *Spain* **37 H6** 37 35N 4 5W
Alcázar de San Juan,
Spain **35 F1** 39 24N 3 12W
Alchevsk, *Ukraine* . . . . . **51 H10** 48 30N 38 45 E
Alcira, *Spain* **35 F4** 39 9N 0 30W
Alcoa, *U.S.A.* **135 H4** 35 48N 83 59W
Alcobaça, *Portugal* **37 F2** 39 32N 8 58W
Alcobendas, *Spain* **34 E1** 40 32N 3 38W
Alcolea del Pinar, *Spain* . **34 D2** 41 2N 2 28W
Alcora, *Spain* **34 E4** 40 5N 0 14W
Alcorcón, *Spain* **36 E7** 40 20N 3 50W
Alcoutim, *Portugal* **37 H3** 37 25N 7 28W
Alcova, *U.S.A.* **142 E10** 42 34N 106 43W
Alcoy, *Spain* **35 G4** 38 43N 0 30W
Alcubierre, Sierra de,
Spain **34 D4** 41 45N 0 22W
Alcublas, *Spain* **34 F4** 39 48N 0 43W
Alcudia, *Spain* . . . . **33 B10** 39 51N 3 7 E
Alcudia, B. de, *Spain* . . . **33 B10** 39 47N 3 15 E
Alcudia, Sierra de la,
Spain **37 G6** 38 34N 4 30W
Aldabra Is., *Seychelles* . . **92 G8** 9 22 S 46 28 E
Aldama, *Mexico* **147 C5** 23 0N 98 4W
Aldan, *Russia* . . . . **57 D13** 58 40N 125 30 E
Aldan →, *Russia* . . . . **57 C13** 63 28N 129 35 E
Aldea, Pta. de la,
Canary Is. **33 G4** 28 0N 15 50W
Aldeburgh, *U.K.* . . . . **17 E9** 52 10N 1 37 E
Aldeia Nova, *Portugal* . . . **37 H3** 37 55N 7 24W
Alder, *U.S.A.* **142 D7** 45 19N 112 6W
Alder Pk., *U.S.A.* **144 K5** 35 53N 121 22W
Alderney, *U.K.* **17 H5** 49 42N 2 11W
Aldershot, *U.K.* **17 F7** 51 15N 0 44W
Aledo, *U.S.A.* **140 C6** 41 12N 90 45W
Alefa, *Ethiopia* . . . . **95 E4** 11 55N 36 55 E
Aleg, *Mauritania* **100 B2** 17 3N 13 55W
Alegranza, *Canary Is.* . . . **33 E6** 29 23N 13 32W
Alegranza, I., *Canary Is.* . **33 E6** 29 23N 13 32W
Alegre, *Brazil* . . . . **155 F3** 20 50 S 41 30W
Alegrete, *Brazil* . . . . **159 B4** 29 40 S 56 0W
Alegria, *Phil.* . . . . **71 F5** 11 47N 124 3 E
Aleisk, *Russia* . . . . **56 D9** 52 40N 83 0 E
Aleksandriya =
Oleksandriya, *Ukraine* . **51 H7** 48 42N 33 3 E
Aleksandriya =
Oleksandriya, *Ukraine* . **51 G4** 50 37N 26 19 E
Aleksandriyskaya, *Russia* **53 J8** 43 58N 47 14 E
Aleksandrov, *Russia* . . . . **52 B4** 56 23N 38 44 E
Aleksandrov Gay, *Russia* **52 E9** 50 9N 48 34 E
Aleksandrovac,
Serbia, Yug. . . . . **42 D6** 43 28N 21 3 E
Aleksandrovac,
Serbia, Yug. . . . . **42 C6** 44 28N 21 13 E
Aleksandrovka =
Oleksandrovka, *Ukraine* **51 H7** 48 55N 32 20 E
Aleksandrovo, *Bulgaria* . . **43 D9** 43 14N 24 51 E
Aleksandrovsk, *Russia* . . **54 B6** 59 9N 57 33 E
Aleksandrovsk-
Sakhalinskiy, *Russia* . . . **57 D15** 50 50N 142 20 E
Aleksandrovskiy Zavod,
Russia . . . . **57 D12** 50 40N 117 50 E
Aleksandrovskoye, *Russia* **56 C8** 60 35N 77 50 E
Aleksandrów Kujawski,
Poland . . . . **47 C5** 52 53N 18 43 E
Aleksandrów Łódźki,
Poland . . . . **47 D6** 51 49N 19 17 E
Alekseyevka, *Russia* . . . . **52 D10** 52 35N 51 17 E
Alekseyevka, *Russia* . . . . **52 E4** 50 43N 38 40 E
Aleksin, *Russia* . . . . **52 C3** 54 31N 37 9 E
Aleksinac, *Serbia, Yug.* . . **42 D6** 43 31N 21 42 E
Além Paraíba, *Brazil* . . . . **155 F3** 21 52 S 42 41W
Alemania, *Argentina* . . . . **158 B2** 25 40 S 65 30W
Alemania, *Chile* . . . . **158 B2** 25 10 S 69 55W
Ålen, *Norway* . . . . **14 B5** 62 51N 11 17 E
Alençon, *France* . . . . **22 D7** 48 27N 0 4 E
Alenuihaha Channel,
U.S.A. **132 H17** 20 30N 156 0W
Aleppo = Ḩalab, *Syria* . . **88 D7** 36 10N 37 15 E
Aléria, *France* . . . . **25 F13** 42 5N 9 26 E
Alert Bay, *Canada* **130 C3** 50 30N 126 55W
Alès, *France* . . . . **25 D8** 44 9N 4 5 E
Aleşd, *Romania* . . . . **46 B3** 47 3N 22 22 E
Alessándria, *Italy* . . . . . . **38 D5** 44 54N 8 37 E
Ålestrup, *Denmark* . . . . . **15 H3** 56 42N 9 29 E
Ålesund, *Norway* . . . . **13 E12** 62 28N 6 12 E
Alet-les-Bains, *France* . . . **24 F6** 42 59N 2 14 E
Aletschhorn, *Switz.* . . . . . **28 D6** 46 28N 8 0 E
Aleutian Is., *Pac. Oc.* **126 C2** 52 0N 175 0W
Aleutian Trench, *Pac. Oc.* **122 B10** 48 0N 180 0 E
Alexander, *U.S.A.* **138 B3** 47 51N 103 39W
Alexander, Mt., *Australia* **113 E3** 28 58 S 120 16 E
Alexander Arch., *U.S.A.* . **130 B2** 56 0N 136 0W
Alexander Bay, *S. Africa* **104 D2** 28 40 S 16 30 E
Alexander City, *U.S.A.* . . **135 J3** 32 56N 85 58W
Alexander I., *Antarctica* . **7 C17** 69 0 S 70 0W
Alexandra, *Australia* . . . . **117 D6** 37 8 S 145 40 E
Alexandra, *N.Z.* . . . . **119 F4** 45 14 S 169 25 E
Alexandra Falls, *Canada* . **130 A5** 60 29N 116 18W
Alexandria = El
Iskandarîya, *Egypt* . . . . **94 H6** 31 13N 29 58 E
Alexandria, *Australia* . . . **114 B2** 19 5 S 136 40 E
Alexandria, *B.C., Canada* **130 C4** 52 35N 122 27W
Alexandria, *Ont., Canada* **128 C5** 45 19N 74 38W
Alexandria, *Romania* . . . . **46 F6** 43 57N 25 24 E
Alexandria, *S. Africa* . . . . **104 E4** 33 38 S 26 28 E
Alexandria, *Ind., U.S.A.* . **141 D11** 40 16N 85 41W
Alexandria, *Ky., U.S.A.* . **141 F12** 38 58N 84 23W
Alexandria, *La., U.S.A.* . . **139 K8** 31 18N 92 27W
Alexandria, *Minn., U.S.A.* **138 C7** 45 53N 95 22W
Alexandria, *Mo., U.S.A.* . **140 D5** 40 27N 91 28W
Alexandria, *S. Dak.,*
U.S.A. **138 D6** 43 39N 97 47W
Alexandria, *Va., U.S.A.* . . **134 F7** 38 48N 77 3W
Alexandria Bay, *U.S.A.* . . **137 B9** 44 20N 75 55W
Alexandrina, L., *Australia* **116 C3** 35 25 S 139 10 E
Alexandroúpolis, *Greece* . **44 D7** 40 50N 25 54 E
Alexis, *U.S.A.* **140 C6** 41 4N 90 33W
Alexis →, *Canada* **129 B8** 52 33N 56 8W
Alexis Creek, *Canada* . . . **130 C4** 52 10N 123 20W
Alfabia, *Spain* . . . . **33 B9** 39 44N 2 44 E
Alfambra, *Spain* **34 E3** 40 33N 1 5W
Alfândega da Fé, *Portugal* **36 D4** 41 20N 6 59W
Alfaro, *Spain* **34 C3** 42 10N 1 50W
Alfatar, *Bulgaria* . . . . **43 D12** 43 59N 27 13 E
Alfeld, *Germany* . . . . **26 D5** 51 59N 9 50 E
Alfenas, *Brazil* . . . . **159 A6** 21 20 S 46 10W
Alfiós →, *Greece* . . . . **45 G3** 37 40N 21 33 E
Alfonsine, *Italy* . . . . **39 D9** 44 30N 12 3 E
Alfonso XIII, *Phil.* . . . . . . **71 G1** 9 15N 117 59 E
Alford, *U.K.* **16 D8** 57 14N 2 41W
Alfred, *Maine, U.S.A.* . . . **137 C14** 43 29N 70 43W
Alfred, *N.Y., U.S.A.* **136 D7** 42 16N 77 48W
Alfred Town, *Australia* . . **117 C7** 35 8 S 147 30 E
Alfredton, *N.Z.* . . . . **118 G4** 40 41 S 175 54 E
Alfreton, *U.K.* **16 D6** 53 6N 1 24W
Alga, *Kazakstan* . . . . **54 G6** 49 53N 57 20 E
Algaida, *Spain* . . . . **33 B9** 39 33N 2 53 E
Algar, *Spain* **37 J5** 36 40N 5 39W
Algård, *Norway* . . . . **13 G11** 58 46N 5 53 E
Algarinejo, *Spain* **37 H6** 37 19N 4 9W
Algarve, *Portugal* **37 J2** 36 58N 8 20W
Algeciras, *Spain* **37 J5** 36 9N 5 28W
Algemesí, *Spain* **35 F4** 39 11N 0 27W
Alger, *Algeria* . . . . **99 A5** 36 42N 3 8 E
Algeria ■, *Africa* . . . . **99 C5** 28 30N 2 0 E
Alghero, *Italy* . . . . **40 B1** 40 33N 8 19 E
Algiers = Alger, *Algeria* . **99 A5** 36 42N 3 8 E
Algoa B., *S. Africa* . . . . . **104 E4** 33 50 S 25 45 E
Algodonales, *Spain* **37 J5** 36 54N 5 24W
Algodor →, *Spain* **36 F7** 39 55N 3 53W
Algoma, *U.S.A.* **134 C2** 44 36N 87 26W
Algona, *U.S.A.* **140 A2** 43 4N 94 14W
Algonac, *U.S.A.* **136 D2** 42 37N 82 32W
Alhama de Almería, *Spain* **35 J2** 36 57N 2 34W
Alhama de Aragón, *Spain* **34 D3** 41 18N 1 54W
Alhama de Granada,
Spain **37 J7** 37 0N 3 59W
Alhama de Murcia, *Spain* **35 H3** 37 51N 1 25W
Alhambra, *Spain* **35 G1** 38 54N 3 4W
Alhambra, *Calif., U.S.A.* . **145 L8** 34 8N 118 6W
Alhambra, *Ill., U.S.A.* . . . **140 F7** 38 52N 89 45W
Alhaurín el Grande, *Spain* **37 J6** 36 39N 4 41W
Alhucemas = Al
Hoceïma, *Morocco* **98 A4** 35 8N 3 58W
'Alī al Gharbī, *Iraq* . . . . . **89 F12** 32 30N 46 45 E
Alī ash Sharqī, *Iraq* . . . . . **89 F12** 32 7N 46 44 E
Äli Bayramlı, *Azerbaijan* **53 L9** 39 59N 48 52 E
'Alī Khēl, *Afghan.* . . . . . . **79 B3** 33 57N 69 43 E
Ali Sahîh, *Djibouti* . . . . . **95 E5** 11 10N 42 44 E
Alī Shāh, *Iran* . . . . **84 B5** 38 9N 45 50 E
Ália, *Italy* . . . . **40 E6** 37 47N 13 43 E
'Alīābād, *Khorāsān, Iran* **85 C8** 32 30N 57 30 E
'Alīābād, *Kordestān, Iran* **84 C5** 35 4N 46 58 E
'Alīābād, *Yazd, Iran* . . . . **85 D7** 31 41N 53 49 E
Aliaga, *Spain* **34 E4** 40 40N 0 42W
Aliağa, *Turkey* . . . . **88 C2** 38 47N 26 59 E
Aliákmon →, *Greece* . . . . **44 D4** 40 30N 22 36 E
Alibag, *India* . . . . **82 E1** 18 38N 72 56 E
Alibo, *Ethiopia* . . . . **95 F4** 9 52N 37 5 E
Alibunar, *Serbia, Yug.* . . . **42 B5** 45 5N 20 57 E
Alicante, *Spain* **35 G4** 38 23N 0 30W
Alicante □, *Spain* **35 G4** 38 30N 0 37W
Alice, *S. Africa* . . . . **104 E4** 32 48 S 26 55 E
Alice, *U.S.A.* **139 M5** 27 45N 98 5W
Alice →, *Queens.,*
Australia . . . . **114 C3** 24 2 S 144 50 E
Alice →, *Queens.,*
Australia . . . . **114 B3** 15 35 S 142 20 E
Alice, Punta dell', *Italy* . . **41 C10** 39 24N 17 9 E
Alice Arm, *Canada* **130 B3** 55 29N 129 31W
Alice Downs, *Australia* . . **112 C4** 17 45 S 127 56 E
Alice Springs, *Australia* . . **114 C1** 23 40 S 133 50 E
Alicedale, *S. Africa* . . . . . **104 E4** 33 15 S 26 4 E
Aliceville, *U.S.A.* **135 J1** 33 8N 88 9W
Alicia, *Phil.* . . . . **71 G5** 9 54N 124 26 E
Alick Cr. →, *Australia* . . **114 C3** 20 55 S 142 20 E
Alicudi, I., *Italy* . . . . **41 D7** 38 33N 14 20 E
Alida, *Canada* **131 D8** 49 25N 101 55W
Aligarh, *Raj., India* . . . . . **80 G7** 25 55N 76 15 E
Aligarh, *Ut. P., India* . . . **80 F8** 27 55N 78 10 E
Alīgūdarz, *Iran* . . . . **85 C6** 33 25N 49 45 E
Alijó, *Portugal* **36 D3** 41 16N 7 27W
Alimena, *Italy* . . . . **41 E7** 37 42N 14 7 E
Alimnía, *Greece* . . . . **32 C9** 36 16N 27 43 E
Alimodian, *Phil.* . . . . **71 F4** 10 49N 122 26 E
Alindao, *C.A.R.* . . . . **102 A4** 5 2N 21 13 E
Alingsås, *Sweden* . . . . **15 G6** 57 56N 12 31 E
Alipur, *Pakistan* . . . . **80 E4** 29 25N 70 55 E
Alipur Duar, *India* . . . . . . **78 B2** 26 30N 89 35 E
Aliquippa, *U.S.A.* **136 F4** 40 37N 80 15W
Aliste →, *Spain* **36 D5** 41 34N 5 58W

Ampato, Nevado 165

Alitus = Alytus, Lithuania 13 J21 54 24N 24 3 E
Alivérion, Greece 45 F6 38 24N 24 2 E
Aliwal North, S. Africa 104 E4 30 45 S 26 45 E
Alix, Canada 130 C6 52 24N 113 11W
Aljezur, Portugal 37 H2 37 18N 8 49W
Aljustrel, Portugal 37 H2 37 55N 8 10W
Alkamari, Niger 97 F2 13 27N 11 10 E
Alken, Belgium 21 G6 50 53N 5 18 E
Alkmaar, Neths. 20 C5 52 37N 4 45 E
All American Canal, U.S.A. 143 K6 32 45N 115 15W
Allacapan, Phil. 70 B3 18 15N 121 35 E
Allada, Benin 101 D5 6 41N 2 9 E
Allah Dad, Pakistan 80 G2 25 38N 67 34 E
Allahabad, India 81 G9 25 25N 81 58 E
Allakh-Yun, Russia 57 C14 60 50N 137 5 E
Allal Tazi, Morocco 98 B3 34 30N 6 20W
Allan, Canada 131 C7 51 53N 106 4W
Allanche, France 24 C6 45 14N 2 57 E
Allanmyo, Burma 78 F5 19 30N 95 17 E
Allanridge, S. Africa 104 D4 27 45 S 26 40 E
Allansford, Australia 116 E5 38 26 S 142 39 E
Allanton, N.Z. 119 F5 45 55 S 170 15 E
Allanwater, Canada 128 B1 50 14N 90 10W
Allaqi, Wadi →, Egypt 94 C3 23 7N 32 47 E
Allariz, Spain 36 C3 42 11N 7 50W
Allassac, France 24 C5 45 15N 1 29 E
Alle, Belgium 21 J5 49 51N 4 58 E
Allegan, U.S.A. 141 B11 42 32N 85 51W
Allegany, U.S.A. 136 D6 42 6N 78 30W
Allegheny →, U.S.A. 136 F5 40 27N 80 1W
Allegheny Mts., U.S.A. 124 F11 38 15N 80 10W
Allegheny Plateau, U.S.A. 134 G6 38 0N 80 0W
Allegheny Reservoir, U.S.A. 136 E6 41 50N 79 0W
Allègre, France 24 C7 45 12N 3 41 E
Allen, Argentina 160 A3 38 58 S 67 50W
Allen, Phil. 70 E5 12 30N 124 17 E
Allen, Bog of, Ireland 19 C4 53 15N 7 0W
Allen, L., Ireland 19 B3 54 8N 8 4W
Allende, Mexico 146 B4 28 20N 100 50W
Allentown, U.S.A. 137 F9 40 37N 75 29W
Allentsteig, Austria 30 C8 48 41N 15 20 E
Alleppey, India 83 K3 9 30N 76 28 E
Aller →, Germany 26 C5 52 56N 9 12 E
Alleur, Belgium 21 G7 50 39N 5 31 E
Allevard, France 25 C10 45 24N 6 5 E
Alliance, Surinam 153 B7 5 50N 54 50W
Alliance, Nebr., U.S.A. 138 D3 42 6N 102 52W
Alliance, Ohio, U.S.A. 136 F3 40 55N 81 6W
Allier □, France 24 B6 46 25N 2 40 E
Allier →, France 23 F10 46 57N 3 4 E
Allingåbro, Denmark 15 H4 56 28N 10 20 E
Allison, U.S.A. 140 B4 42 45N 92 48W
Alliston, Canada 128 D4 44 9N 79 52W
Alloa, U.K. 18 E5 56 7N 3 47W
Allora, Australia 115 D5 28 2 S 152 0 E
Allos, France 25 D10 44 15N 6 38 E
Alluitsup Paa = Sydprøven, Greenland 6 C5 60 30N 45 35W
Alma, Canada 129 C5 48 35N 71 40W
Alma, Ga., U.S.A. 135 K4 31 33N 82 28W
Alma, Kans., U.S.A. 138 F6 39 1N 96 17W
Alma, Mich., U.S.A. 134 D3 43 23N 84 39W
Alma, Nebr., U.S.A. 138 E5 40 6N 99 22W
Alma, Wis., U.S.A. 138 C9 44 20N 91 55W
Alma Ata = Almaty, Kazakstan 55 B8 43 15N 76 57 E
Almada, Portugal 37 G1 38 40N 9 9W
Almaden, Australia 114 B3 17 22 S 144 40 E
Almadén, Spain 37 G6 38 49N 4 52W
Almagro, Spain 37 G7 38 50N 3 45W
Almagro I., Phil. 71 F5 11 56N 124 18 E
Almalyk = Olmaliq, Uzbekistan 55 C4 40 50N 69 35 E
Almanor, L., U.S.A. 142 F3 40 14N 121 9W
Almansa, Spain 35 G3 38 51N 1 5W
Almanza, Spain 36 C5 42 39N 5 3W
Almanzor, Pico del Moro, Spain 36 E5 40 15N 5 18W
Almanzora →, Spain 35 H3 37 14N 1 46W
Almas, Brazil 155 D2 11 33 S 47 9W
Almaş, Mţii., Romania 46 E3 44 49N 22 12 E
Almaty, Kazakstan 55 B8 43 15N 76 57 E
Almazán, Spain 34 D2 41 30N 2 30W
Almazora, Spain 34 F4 39 57N 0 3W
Almeirim, Brazil 153 D7 1 30 S 52 34W
Almeirim, Portugal 37 F2 39 12N 8 37W
Almelo, Neths. 20 D9 52 22N 6 42 E
Almenar, Spain 34 D2 41 43N 2 12W
Almenara, Brazil 155 E3 16 11 S 40 42W
Almenara, Spain 34 F4 39 46N 0 14W
Almenara, Sierra de, Spain 35 H3 37 34N 1 32W
Almendralejo, Spain 37 G4 38 41N 6 26W
Almería, Spain 35 J2 36 52N 2 27W
Almería □, Spain 35 H2 37 20N 2 20W
Almería, G. de, Spain 35 J2 36 41N 2 28W
Almetyevsk, Russia 52 C11 54 53N 52 20 E
Almirante, Panama 148 E3 9 10N 82 30W
Almirante Montt, G., Chile 160 D2 51 52 S 72 50W
Almiropótamos, Greece 45 F6 38 16N 24 11 E
Almirós, Greece 45 E4 39 11N 22 45 E
Almiroú, Kólpos, Greece 32 D6 35 23N 24 20 E
Almodôvar, Portugal 37 H2 37 31N 8 2W
Almodóvar del Campo, Spain 37 G6 38 43N 4 10W
Almogia, Spain 37 J6 36 50N 4 32W
Almonaster la Real, Spain 37 H4 37 52N 6 48W
Almont, U.S.A. 136 D1 42 55N 83 3W
Almonte, Canada 137 A8 45 14N 76 12W
Almonte →, Spain 37 F4 39 41N 6 28W
Almora, India 81 E8 29 38N 79 40 E
Almoradi, Spain 35 G4 38 7N 0 46W
Almorox, Spain 36 E6 40 14N 4 24W
Almoustarat, Mali 101 B5 17 35N 0 8 E
Almuñécar, Spain 37 J7 36 43N 3 41W
Alnif, Morocco 98 B3 31 10N 5 8W
Alnwick, U.K. 16 B6 55 24N 1 42W
Aloi, Uganda 106 B3 2 16N 33 10 E
Alon, Burma 78 D5 22 12N 95 5 E
Alor, Indonesia 72 C2 8 15 S 124 30 E
Alor Setar, Malaysia 77 J3 6 7N 100 22 E
Alora, Spain 37 J6 36 49N 4 46W
Alosno, Spain 37 H3 37 33N 7 7W
Alotau, Papua N. G. 120 F6 10 16 S 150 30 E
Alougoum, Morocco 98 B3 30 17N 6 56W
Aloysius, Mt., Australia 113 E4 26 0 S 128 38 E
Alpaugh, U.S.A. 144 K7 35 53N 119 29W
Alpedrinha, Portugal 36 E3 40 6N 7 27W
Alpena, U.S.A. 134 C4 45 4N 83 27W
Alpercatas →, Brazil 154 C3 6 2 S 44 19W
Alpes-de-Haute-Provence □, France 25 D10 44 8N 6 10 E
Alpes-Maritimes □, France 25 E11 43 55N 7 10 E
Alpha, Australia 114 C4 23 39 S 146 37 E
Alpha, U.S.A. 140 C6 41 12N 90 23W
Alphen, Neths. 21 F5 51 29N 4 58 E
Alphen aan den Rijn, Neths. 20 D5 52 7N 4 40 E
Alphonse, Seychelles 109 E4 7 0 S 52 45 E
Alpiarça, Portugal 37 F2 39 15N 8 35W
Alpine, Ariz., U.S.A. 143 K9 33 51N 109 9W
Alpine, Calif., U.S.A. 145 N10 32 50N 116 46W
Alpine, Tex., U.S.A. 139 K3 30 22N 103 40W
Alpnach, Switz. 29 C6 46 57N 8 17 E
Alps, Europe 10 F7 46 30N 9 30 E
Alpu, Turkey 88 C4 39 46N 30 58 E
Alrø, Denmark 15 J4 55 52N 10 5 E
Alroy Downs, Australia 114 B2 19 20 S 136 5 E
Alsace, France 23 D14 48 15N 7 25 E
Alsask, Canada 131 C7 51 21N 109 59W
Alsásua, Spain 34 C2 42 54N 2 10W
Alsdorf, Germany 26 E2 50 52N 6 10 E
Alsen, Sweden 14 A7 63 23N 13 56 E
Alsfeld, Germany 26 E5 50 44N 9 16 E
Alsónémedi, Hungary 31 D12 47 20N 19 15 E
Alsten, Norway 12 D15 65 58N 12 40 E
Alta, Norway 12 B20 69 57N 23 10 E
Alta, Sierra, Spain 34 E3 40 31N 1 30W
Alta Gracia, Argentina 158 C3 31 40 S 64 30W
Alta Lake, Canada 130 C4 50 10N 123 0W
Alta Sierra, U.S.A. 145 K8 35 42N 118 33W
Altaelva →, Norway 12 B20 69 54N 23 17 E
Altafjorden, Norway 12 A20 70 5N 23 5 E
Altagracia, Venezuela 152 A3 10 45N 71 30W
Altagracia de Orituco, Venezuela 152 B4 9 52N 66 23W
Altai = Aerhtai Shan, Mongolia 64 B4 46 40N 92 45 E
Altamachi →, Bolivia 156 D4 16 8 S 66 50W
Altamaha →, U.S.A. 135 K5 31 20N 81 20W
Altamira, Brazil 153 D7 3 12 S 52 10W
Altamira, Chile 158 B2 25 47 S 69 51W
Altamira, Colombia 152 C2 2 3N 75 47W
Altamira, Mexico 147 C5 22 24N 97 55W
Altamira, Cuevas de, Spain 36 B6 43 20N 4 5W
Altamont, Ill., U.S.A. 141 E8 39 4N 88 45W
Altamont, N.Y., U.S.A. 137 D10 42 43N 74 3W
Altamura, Italy 41 B9 40 49N 16 33 E
Altanbulag, Mongolia 64 A5 50 16N 106 30 E
Altar, Mexico 146 A2 30 40N 111 50W
Altata, Mexico 146 C3 24 30N 108 0W
Altavas, Phil. 71 F4 11 32N 122 29 E
Altavista, U.S.A. 134 G6 37 6N 79 17W
Altay, China 64 B3 47 48N 88 10 E
Altdorf, Switz. 29 C7 46 52N 8 36 E
Alte Mellum, Germany 26 B4 53 43N 8 10 E
Altea, Spain 35 G4 38 38N 0 2W
Altenberg, Germany 26 E9 50 45N 13 45 E
Altenbruch, Germany 26 B4 53 49N 8 46 E
Altenburg, Germany 26 E8 50 59N 12 25 E
Altenkirchen, Mecklenburg-Vorpommern, Germany 26 A9 54 38N 13 22 E
Altenkirchen, Rhld-Pfz., Germany 26 E3 50 41N 7 39 E
Altenmarkt, Austria 30 D7 47 43N 14 39 E
Altentreptow, Germany 26 B9 53 41N 13 14 E
Alter do Chão, Portugal 37 F3 39 12N 7 40W
Altıntas, Turkey 88 C4 39 4N 30 10 E
Altiplano, Bolivia 156 D4 17 0 S 68 0W
Altkirch, France 23 E14 47 37N 7 15 E
Altmühl →, Germany 27 G7 48 54N 11 52 E
Alto Adige = Trentino-Alto Adige □, Italy 38 B8 46 30N 11 20 E
Alto Araguaia, Brazil 157 D7 17 15 S 53 20W
Alto Cuchumatanes = Cuchumatanes, Sierra de los, Guatemala 148 C1 15 35N 91 25W
Alto Cuito, Angola 103 E3 13 27 S 18 49 E
Alto del Inca, Chile 158 A2 24 10 S 68 10W
Alto Garças, Brazil 157 D7 16 56 S 53 32W
Alto Iriri →, Brazil 157 B7 8 50 S 53 25W
Alto Ligonha, Mozam. 107 F4 15 30 S 38 11 E
Alto Molocue, Mozam. 107 F4 15 50 S 37 35 E
Alto Paraguai, Brazil 157 C6 14 30 S 56 31W
Alto Paraguay □, Paraguay 158 A4 21 0 S 58 30W
Alto Paraná □, Paraguay 159 B5 25 30 S 54 50W
Alto Parnaíba, Brazil 154 C2 9 6 S 45 57W
Alto Purús →, Peru 156 B3 9 12 S 70 28W
Alto Río Senguerr, Argentina 160 C2 45 2 S 70 50W
Alto Santo, Brazil 154 C4 5 31 S 38 15W
Alto Sucuriú, Brazil 157 D7 19 19 S 52 47W
Alto Turi, Brazil 154 B2 2 54 S 45 38W
Alton, Canada 136 C4 43 54N 80 5W
Alton, U.S.A. 140 F6 38 53N 90 11W
Alton Downs, Australia 115 D2 26 7 S 138 57 E
Altoona, Iowa, U.S.A. 140 C3 41 39N 93 28W
Altoona, Pa., U.S.A. 136 F6 40 31N 78 24W
Altopáscio, Italy 38 E7 43 49N 10 40 E
Altos, Brazil 154 C3 5 3 S 42 28W
Altötting, Germany 27 G8 48 12N 12 39 E
Altstätten, Switz. 29 B9 47 22N 9 33 E
Altūn Kūprī, Iraq 89 E11 35 45N 44 9 E
Altun Shan, China 64 C3 38 30N 88 0 E
Alturas, U.S.A. 142 F3 41 29N 120 32W
Altus, U.S.A. 139 H5 34 38N 99 20W
Alubijid, Phil. 71 G5 8 35N 124 29 E
Alucra, Turkey 89 B8 40 22N 38 47 E
Alūksne, Latvia 13 H22 57 24N 27 3 E
Alùla, Somali Rep. 108 B4 11 50N 50 45 E
Alunite, U.S.A. 145 K12 35 59N 114 55W
Alupka, Ukraine 51 K8 44 23N 34 2 E
Alur Gajah, Malaysia 74 B2 2 23N 102 13 E
Alushta, Ukraine 51 K8 44 40N 34 25 E
Alusi, Indonesia 73 C4 7 35 S 131 40 E
Alustante, Spain 34 E3 40 36N 1 40W
Al'Uzayr, Iraq 84 D5 31 19N 47 25 E
Alva, U.S.A. 139 G5 36 48N 98 40W
Alvaiázere, Portugal 36 F2 39 49N 8 23W
Älvängen, Sweden 15 G6 57 58N 12 8 E
Alvarado, Mexico 147 D5 18 40N 95 50W
Alvarado, U.S.A. 139 J6 32 24N 97 13W
Alvarães, Brazil 153 D5 3 12 S 64 50W
Alvaro Obregón, Presa, Mexico 146 B3 27 55N 109 52W
Alvdal, Norway 14 B4 62 6N 10 37 E
Alvear, Argentina 158 B4 29 5 S 56 30W
Alverca, Portugal 37 G1 38 56N 9 1W
Alveringen, Belgium 21 F1 51 1N 2 43 E
Alvesta, Sweden 13 H16 56 54N 14 35 E
Alvie, Australia 116 E5 38 14 S 143 30 E
Alvin, U.S.A. 139 L7 29 26N 95 15W
Alvinston, Canada 136 D3 42 49N 81 52W
Alvito, Portugal 37 G3 38 15N 8 0W
Älvkarleby, Sweden 13 F17 60 34N 17 26 E
Älvros, Sweden 14 B8 62 3N 14 38 E
Älvsborgs län □, Sweden 15 F6 58 30N 12 30 E
Älvsbyn, Sweden 12 D19 65 40N 21 0 E
Älvsered, Sweden 15 G6 57 14N 12 51 E
Alwar, India 80 F7 27 38N 76 34 E
Alwaye, India 83 J3 10 8N 76 24 E
Alxa Zuoqi, China 66 E3 38 50N 105 40 E
Alyaskitovyy, Russia 57 C15 64 45N 141 30 E
Alyata = Älät, Azerbaijan 53 L9 39 58N 49 25 E
Alyth, U.K. 18 E5 56 38N 3 13W
Alytus, Lithuania 13 J21 54 24N 24 3 E
Alzada, U.S.A. 138 C2 45 2N 104 25W
Alzano Lombardo, Italy 38 C6 45 44N 9 43 E
Alzette →, Lux. 21 J8 49 45N 6 6 E
Alzey, Germany 27 F4 49 45N 8 7 E
Am Dam, Chad 97 F4 12 40N 20 35 E
Am Géréda, Chad 97 F4 12 53N 21 14 E
Am-Timan, Chad 97 F4 11 0N 20 10 E
Amacuro □, Venezuela 153 B5 8 50N 61 5W
Amadeus, L., Australia 113 D5 24 54 S 131 0 E
Amâdi, Sudan 95 F3 5 29N 30 25 E
Amadi, Zaïre 106 B2 3 40N 26 40 E
Amadjuak, Canada 127 B12 64 0N 72 39W
Amadjuak L., Canada 127 B12 65 0N 71 8W
Amadora, Portugal 37 G1 38 45N 9 13W
Amagasaki, Japan 63 C7 34 42N 135 20 E
Amager, Denmark 15 J6 55 37N 12 35 E
Amagi, Japan 62 D2 33 25N 130 39 E
Amahai, Indonesia 73 B3 3 20 S 128 55 E
Amaimon, Papua N. G. 120 C3 5 12 S 145 30 E
Amakusa-Nada, Japan 62 E2 32 35N 130 5 E
Amakusa-Shotō, Japan 62 E2 32 15N 130 10 E
Åmål, Sweden 13 G15 59 3N 12 42 E
Amalapuram, India 83 F5 16 35N 81 55 E
Amalfi, Colombia 152 B2 6 55N 75 4W
Amalfi, Italy 41 B7 40 38N 14 36 E
Amaliás, Greece 45 G3 37 47N 21 22 E
Amalner, India 82 D2 21 5N 75 5 E
Amambaí, Brazil 159 A4 23 5 S 55 13W
Amambaí →, Brazil 159 A5 23 22 S 53 56W
Amambay □, Paraguay 159 A4 23 0 S 56 0W
Amambay, Cordillera de, S. Amer. 159 A4 23 0 S 55 45W
Amami-Guntō, Japan 61 L4 27 16N 129 21 E
Amami-Ō-Shima, Japan 61 L4 28 0N 129 0 E
Amana →, Venezuela 153 B5 9 45N 62 39W
Amaná, L., Brazil 153 D5 2 35 S 64 40W
Amanab, Papua N. G. 120 B1 3 40 S 141 14 E
Amanda Park, U.S.A. 144 C3 47 28N 123 55W
Amándola, Italy 39 F10 42 59N 13 21 E
Amangeldy, Kazakstan 56 D7 50 10N 65 10 E
Amantea, Italy 41 C9 39 8N 16 4 E
Amapá, Brazil 153 C7 2 5N 50 50W
Amapá □, Brazil 153 C7 1 40N 52 0W
Amapari, Brazil 153 C7 0 37N 51 39W
Amara, Sudan 95 E3 10 25N 34 10 E
Amarante, Brazil 154 C3 6 14 S 42 50W
Amarante, Portugal 36 D2 41 16N 8 5W
Amarante do Maranhão, Brazil 154 C2 5 36 S 46 45W
Amaranth, Canada 131 C9 50 36N 98 43W
Amarapura, Burma 78 E6 21 54N 96 3 E
Amaravati →, India 83 J4 11 0N 78 15 E
Amareleja, Portugal 37 G3 38 12N 7 13W
Amargosa, Brazil 155 D4 13 2 S 39 36W
Amargosa →, U.S.A. 145 J10 36 14N 116 51W
Amargosa Range, U.S.A. 145 J10 36 20N 116 45W
Amári, Greece 32 D6 35 13N 24 40 E
Amarillo, U.S.A. 139 H4 35 13N 101 50W
Amarnath, India 82 E1 19 12N 73 22 E
Amaro, Mte., Italy 39 F11 42 5N 14 5 E
Amaro Leite, Brazil 155 D2 13 58 S 49 9W
Amarpur, India 81 G12 25 5N 87 0 E
Amasra, Turkey 88 B5 41 45N 32 23 E
Amassama, Nigeria 101 D6 5 1N 6 2 E
Amasya, Turkey 88 B6 40 40N 35 50 E
Amataurá, Brazil 152 D4 3 29 S 68 6W
Amatikulu, S. Africa 105 D5 29 3 S 31 33 E
Amatitlán, Guatemala 148 D1 14 29N 90 38W
Amatrice, Italy 39 F10 42 38N 13 17 E
Amay, Belgium 21 G6 50 33N 5 19 E
Amazon = Amazonas →, S. Amer. 153 D7 0 5 S 50 0W
Amazonas □, Brazil 157 B5 5 0 S 65 0W
Amazonas □, Peru 156 B2 5 0 S 78 0W
Amazonas □, Venezuela 152 C4 3 30N 66 0W
Amazonas →, S. Amer. 153 D7 0 5 S 50 0W
Ambad, India 82 E2 19 38N 75 50 E
Ambahakily, Madag. 105 C7 21 36 S 43 41 E
Ambala, India 80 D7 30 23N 76 56 E
Ambalangoda, Sri Lanka 83 L5 6 15N 80 5 E
Ambalapulai, India 83 K3 9 25N 76 25 E
Ambalavao, Madag. 105 C8 21 50 S 46 56 E
Ambalindum, Australia 114 C2 23 23 S 135 0 E
Ambam, Cameroon 102 B2 2 20N 11 15 E
Ambanja, Madag. 105 A8 13 40 S 48 27 E
Ambarchik, Russia 57 C17 69 40N 162 20 E
Ambarijeby, Madag. 105 A8 14 56 S 47 41 E
Ambaro, Helodranon', Madag. 105 A8 13 23 S 48 38 E
Ambartsevo, Russia 56 D9 57 30N 83 52 E
Ambasamudram, India 83 K3 8 43N 77 25 E
Ambato, Ecuador 152 D2 1 5 S 78 42W
Ambato, Sierra de, Argentina 158 B2 28 25 S 66 10W
Ambato Boeny, Madag. 105 B8 16 28 S 46 43 E
Ambatofinandrahana, Madag. 105 C8 20 33 S 46 48 E
Ambatolampy, Madag. 105 B8 19 20 S 47 35 E
Ambatondrazaka, Madag. 105 B8 17 55 S 48 28 E
Ambatosoratra, Madag. 105 B8 17 37 S 48 31 E
Ambenja, Madag. 105 B8 15 17 S 46 58 E
Amberg, Germany 27 F7 49 26N 11 52 E
Ambergris Cay, Belize 147 D7 18 0N 88 0W
Ambérieu-en-Bugey, France 25 C9 45 57N 5 20 E
Amberley, N.Z. 119 D7 43 9 S 172 44 E
Ambert, France 24 C7 45 33N 3 44 E
Ambidédi, Mali 100 C2 14 35N 11 47W
Ambikapur, India 81 H10 23 15N 83 15 E
Ambikol, Sudan 94 C3 21 20N 30 50 E
Ambilobé, Madag. 105 A8 13 10 S 49 3 E
Ambinanindrano, Madag. 105 C8 20 5 S 48 23 E
Ambjörnarp, Sweden 15 G7 57 25N 13 17 E
Ambleside, U.K. 16 C5 54 26N 2 58W
Amblève, Belgium 21 H8 50 21N 6 10 E
Amblève →, Belgium 21 H7 50 25N 5 45 E
Ambo, Ethiopia 95 E4 12 20N 37 30 E
Ambo, Peru 156 C2 10 5 S 76 10W
Ambodifototra, Madag. 105 B8 16 59 S 49 52 E
Ambodilazana, Madag. 105 B8 18 6 S 49 10 E
Ambohimahasoa, Madag. 105 C8 21 7 S 47 13 E
Ambohimanga, Madag. 105 C8 20 52 S 47 36 E
Ambohitra, Madag. 105 A8 12 30 S 49 10 E
Amboise, France 22 E8 47 24N 1 2 E
Ambon, Indonesia 72 B3 3 43 S 128 12 E
Ambon, Indonesia 72 B3 3 35 S 128 20 E
Amboseli L., Kenya 106 C4 2 40 S 37 10 E
Ambositra, Madag. 105 C8 20 31 S 47 25 E
Ambovombé, Madag. 105 D8 25 11 S 46 5 E
Amboy, Calif., U.S.A. 145 L11 34 33N 115 45W
Amboy, Ill., U.S.A. 140 C7 41 44N 89 20W
Ambridge, U.S.A. 136 F4 40 36N 80 14W
Ambriz, Angola 103 D2 7 48 S 13 8 E
Ambrym, Vanuatu 121 F6 16 15 S 168 10 E
Ambunti, Papua N. G. 120 C2 4 13 S 142 52 E
Ambur, India 83 H4 12 48N 78 43 E
Amby, Australia 115 D4 26 30 S 148 11 E
Amchitka I., U.S.A. 126 C1 51 32N 179 0 E
Amderma, Russia 56 C7 69 45N 61 30 E
Ameca, Mexico 146 C4 20 30N 104 0W
Ameca →, Mexico 146 C3 20 40N 105 15W
Amecameca, Mexico 147 D5 19 7N 98 46W
Ameland, Neths. 20 B7 53 27N 5 45 E
Amélia, Italy 39 F9 42 33N 12 25 E
Amélie-les-Bains-Palalda, France 24 F6 42 29N 2 41 E
Amen, Russia 57 C18 68 45N 180 0 E
Amendolara, Italy 41 C9 39 57N 16 35 E
America, Neths. 21 F7 51 27N 5 59 E
American Falls, U.S.A. 142 E7 42 47N 112 51W
American Falls Reservoir, U.S.A. 142 E7 42 47N 112 52W
American Highland, Antarctica 7 D6 73 0 S 75 0 E
American Samoa ■, Pac. Oc. 121 X24 14 20 S 170 40W
Americana, Brazil 159 A6 22 45 S 47 20W
Americus, U.S.A. 135 J3 32 4N 84 14W
Amersfoort, Neths. 20 D6 52 9N 5 23 E
Amersfoort, S. Africa 105 D4 26 59 S 29 53 E
Amery, Australia 113 F2 31 9 S 117 5 E
Amery, Canada 131 B10 56 34N 94 3W
Amery Ice Shelf, Antarctica 7 C6 69 30 S 72 0 E
Ames, U.S.A. 140 B3 42 2N 93 37W
Amesbury, U.S.A. 137 D14 42 51N 70 56W
Amfíklia, Greece 45 F4 38 38N 22 35 E
Amfilokhía, Greece 45 F3 38 52N 21 9 E
Amfípolis, Greece 44 D5 40 48N 23 52 E
Ámfissa, Greece 45 F4 38 32N 22 22 E
Amga, Russia 57 C14 60 50N 132 0 E
Amga →, Russia 57 C14 62 38N 134 32 E
Amgu, Russia 57 E14 45 45N 137 15 E
Amgun →, Russia 57 D14 52 56N 139 38 E
Amherst, Canada 129 C7 45 48N 64 8W
Amherst, Mass., U.S.A. 137 D12 42 23N 72 31W
Amherst, N.Y., U.S.A. 136 D6 42 59N 78 48W
Amherst, Ohio, U.S.A. 136 E2 41 24N 82 14W
Amherst, Tex., U.S.A. 139 H3 34 1N 102 25W
Amherst I., Canada 137 B8 44 8N 76 43W
Amherstburg, Canada 128 D3 42 6N 83 6W
Amiata, Mte., Italy 39 F8 42 53N 11 37 E
Amiens, France 23 C9 49 54N 2 16 E
Amigdhalokefáli, Greece 45 J5 35 23N 23 30 E
Amili, India 78 A5 28 25N 95 52 E
Amindaion, Greece 44 D3 40 42N 21 42 E
Amīrābād, Iran 84 C5 33 20N 46 16 E
Amirante Is., Seychelles 58 K9 6 0 S 53 0 E
Amisk L., Canada 131 C8 54 35N 102 15W
Amistad, Presa de la, Mexico 146 B4 29 24N 101 0W
Amite, U.S.A. 139 K9 30 44N 90 30W
Amizmiz, Morocco 98 B3 31 12N 8 15W
Åmli, Norway 15 F2 58 45N 8 32 E
Amlwch, U.K. 16 D3 53 24N 4 20W
Amm Adam, Sudan 95 D4 16 20N 36 1 E
'Ammān, Jordan 91 D4 31 57N 35 52 E
Ammanford, U.K. 17 F3 51 48N 3 59W
Ammassalik = Angmagssalik, Greenland 6 C6 65 40N 37 20W
Ammerån, Sweden 14 A10 63 9N 16 13 E
Ammerån →, Sweden 14 A10 63 9N 16 13 E
Ammersee, Germany 27 G7 48 0N 11 7 E
Ammerzoden, Neths. 20 E6 51 45N 5 13 E
Amnat Charoen, Thailand 76 E5 15 51N 104 38 E
Amo Jiang →, China 68 F3 23 0N 101 50 E
Āmol, Iran 85 B7 36 23N 52 20 E
Amorebieta, Spain 34 B2 43 13N 2 44W
Amoret, U.S.A. 140 F2 38 15N 94 35W
Amorgós, Greece 45 H7 36 50N 25 57 E
Amory, U.S.A. 135 J1 33 59N 88 29W
Amos, Canada 128 C4 48 35N 78 5W
Åmot, Buskerud, Norway 14 E3 59 57N 9 54 E
Åmot, Telemark, Norway 14 E2 59 34N 8 0 E
Åmotsdal, Norway 14 E2 59 37N 8 26 E
Amour, Djebel, Algeria 99 B5 33 42N 1 37 E
Amoy = Xiamen, China 69 E12 24 25N 118 4 E
Ampang, Malaysia 77 L3 3 8N 101 45 E
Ampanihy, Madag. 105 C7 24 40 S 44 45 E
Ampasindava, Helodranon', Madag. 105 A8 13 40 S 48 15 E
Ampasindava, Saikanosy, Madag. 105 A8 13 42 S 47 55 E
Ampato, Nevado, Peru 156 D3 15 40 S 71 56W

Arima 167

Antufash, *Yemen* 86 D3 15 42N 42 25 E
Antwerp = Antwerpen, *Belgium* 21 F4 51 13N 4 25 E
Antwerp, *Australia* 116 D5 36 17 S 142 4 E
Antwerp, *N.Y., U.S.A.* 137 B9 44 12N 75 37W
Antwerp, *Ohio, U.S.A.* 141 C12 41 11N 84 45W
Antwerpen, *Belgium* 21 F4 51 13N 4 25 E
Antwerpen □, *Belgium* 21 F5 51 15N 4 40 E
Anupgarh, *India* 80 E5 29 10N 73 10 E
Anuradhapura, *Sri Lanka* 83 K5 8 22N 80 28 E
Anveh, *Iran* 85 E7 27 23N 54 11 E
Anvers = Antwerpen, *Belgium* 21 F4 51 13N 4 25 E
Anvers I., *Antarctica* 7 C17 64 30 S 63 40W
Anxi, *Fujian, China* 69 E12 25 2N 118 12 E
Anxi, *Gansu, China* 64 B4 40 30N 95 43 E
Anxiang, *China* 69 C9 29 27N 112 11 E
Anxious B., *Australia* 115 E1 33 24 S 134 45 E
Anyama, *Ivory C.* 100 D4 5 30N 4 3W
Anyang, *China* 66 F8 36 5N 114 21 E
Anyer, *Indonesia* 74 D3 6 4 S 105 53 E
Anyi, *Jiangxi, China* 69 C10 28 49N 115 25 E
Anyi, *Shanxi, China* 66 G6 35 2N 111 2 E
Anyuan, *China* 69 E10 25 9N 115 21 E
Anza, *U.S.A.* 145 M10 33 35N 116 39W
Anz̧awr, *Oman* 87 C6 17 28N 52 50 E
Anze, *China* 66 F7 36 10N 112 12 E
Anzhero-Sudzhensk, *Russia* 56 D9 56 10N 86 0 E
Ánzio, *Italy* 40 A5 41 27N 12 37 E
Anzoátegui □, *Venezuela* 153 B5 9 0N 64 30W
Aoba, *Vanuatu* 121 E5 15 25 S 167 50 E
Aoga-Shima, *Japan* 63 E11 32 28N 139 46 E
Aoiz, *Spain* 34 C3 42 46N 1 22W
Aomori, *Japan* 60 D10 40 45N 140 45 E
Aomori □, *Japan* 60 D10 40 45N 140 40 E
Aonla, *India* 81 E8 28 16N 79 11 E
Aono-Yama, *Japan* 62 C3 34 28N 131 48 E
Aorangi Mts., *N.Z.* 118 H4 41 28 S 175 22 E
Aosta, *Italy* 38 C4 45 45N 7 20 E
Aotea Harbour, *N.Z.* 118 D3 38 0 S 174 50 E
Aouderas, *Niger* 97 E1 17 45N 8 20 E
Aouinet Torkoz, *Morocco* 98 C3 28 31N 9 46W
Aoukar, *Mali* 98 D4 23 50N 2 45W
Aouker, *Mauritania* 100 B3 17 40N 10 0W
Aoulef el Arab, *Algeria* 99 C5 26 55N 1 2 E
Apa →, *S. Amer.* 158 A4 22 6 S 58 2W
Apache, *U.S.A.* 139 H5 34 54N 98 22W
Apalachee B., *U.S.A.* 135 L3 30 0N 84 0W
Apalachicola, *U.S.A.* 135 L3 29 43N 84 59W
Apalachicola →, *U.S.A.* 135 L3 29 43N 84 58W
Apapa, *Nigeria* 101 D5 6 25N 3 25 E
Apaporis →, *Colombia* 152 D4 1 23 S 69 25W
Aparecida do Taboado, *Brazil* 155 F1 20 5 S 51 5W
Aparri, *Phil.* 70 B3 18 22N 121 38 E
Aparurén, *Venezuela* 153 B5 5 6N 62 8W
Apateu, *Romania* 46 C2 46 36N 21 47 E
Apatin, *Serbia, Yug.* 42 B4 45 40N 19 0 E
Apàtity, *Russia* 48 A5 67 34N 33 22 E
Apatzingán, *Mexico* 146 D4 19 0N 102 20W
Apayao □, *Phil.* 70 B3 18 10N 121 10 E
Apeldoorn, *Neths.* 20 D7 52 13N 5 57 E
Apeldoornsch Kanal →, *Neths.* 20 D8 52 29N 6 5 E
Apen, *Germany* 26 B3 53 13N 7 48 E
Apennines = Appennini, *Italy* 38 D7 44 0N 10 0 E
Apere →, *Bolivia* 157 C4 13 44 S 65 18W
Apia, *W. Samoa* 121 W24 13 50 S 171 50W
Apiacás, Serra dos, *Brazil* 157 B6 9 50 S 57 0W
Apiaú →, *Brazil* 153 C5 2 39N 61 12W
Apiaú, Serra do, *Brazil* 153 C5 2 30N 62 0W
Apidiá →, *Brazil* 157 C5 11 39 S 61 11W
Apinajé, *Brazil* 155 D2 11 31 S 48 18W
Apiti, *N.Z.* 118 F4 39 58 S 175 54 E
Apizaco, *Mexico* 147 D5 19 26N 98 9W
Aplao, *Peru* 156 D3 16 0 S 72 40W
Apo, Mt., *Phil.* 71 H5 6 53N 125 14 E
Apo East Pass, *Phil.* 70 E3 12 40N 120 40 E
Apo West Pass, *Phil.* 70 E3 12 31N 120 22 E
Apodi, *Brazil* 154 C4 5 39 S 37 48W
Apolakkiá, *Greece* 32 C9 36 5N 27 48 E
Apolakkiá, Órmos, *Greece* 32 C9 36 5N 27 45 E
Apolda, *Germany* 26 D7 51 2N 11 32 E
Apollo Bay, *Australia* 116 E5 38 45 S 143 40 E
Apollonia = Marsá Susah, *Libya* 96 B4 32 52N 21 59 E
Apollonia, *Greece* 45 H6 36 58N 24 43 E
Apolo, *Bolivia* 156 C4 14 30 S 68 30W
Apónguao →, *Venezuela* 153 C5 4 48N 61 36W
Aporé, *Brazil* 157 D7 18 58 S 52 1W
Aporé →, *Brazil* 155 E1 19 27 S 50 57W
Aporema, *Brazil* 154 A1 1 14N 50 49W
Apostle Is., *U.S.A.* 138 B9 47 0N 90 40W
Apóstoles, *Argentina* 159 B4 28 0 S 56 0W
Apostolos Andreas, C., *Cyprus* 32 D13 35 42N 34 35 E
Apostolovo, *Ukraine* 51 J7 47 39N 33 39 E
Apoteri, *Guyana* 153 C6 4 2N 58 32W
Appalachian Mts., *U.S.A.* 134 G6 38 0N 80 0W
Appelscha, *Neths.* 20 C8 52 57N 6 21 E
Appennini, *Italy* 38 D7 44 0N 10 0 E
Appennino Ligure, *Italy* 38 D5 44 30N 9 0 E
Appenzell, *Switz.* 29 B8 47 20N 9 25 E
Appenzell-Ausser Rhoden □, *Switz.* 29 B8 47 23N 9 23 E
Appenzell-Inner Rhoden □, *Switz.* 29 B8 47 20N 9 25 E
Appiano, *Italy* 39 B8 46 28N 11 15 E
Appingedam, *Neths.* 20 B9 53 19N 6 51 E
Apple Hill, *Canada* 137 A10 45 13N 74 46W
Apple Valley, *U.S.A.* 145 L9 34 32N 117 14W
Appleby-in-Westmorland, *U.K.* 16 C5 54 35N 2 29W
Appleton, *U.S.A.* 134 C1 44 16N 88 25W
Appleton City, *U.S.A.* 140 F2 38 11N 94 2W
Approuague, *Fr. Guiana* 153 C7 4 20N 52 0W
Approuague →, *Fr. Guiana* 153 C7 4 30N 51 57W
Apricena, *Italy* 41 A8 41 47N 15 27 E
Aprigliano, *Italy* 41 C9 39 14N 16 21 E
Aprília, *Italy* 40 A5 41 36N 12 39 E
Apsheronsk, *Russia* 53 H4 44 28N 39 42 E
Apt, *France* 25 E9 43 53N 5 24 E
Apuane, Alpi, *Italy* 38 D7 44 7N 10 14 E
Apuaú, *Brazil* 153 D5 2 25 S 60 53W
Apucarana, *Brazil* 159 A5 23 55 S 51 33W
Apulia = Púglia □, *Italy* 41 B9 41 15N 16 15 E
Apurahuan, *Phil.* 71 G2 9 35N 118 20 E
Apure □, *Venezuela* 152 B4 7 10N 68 50W
Apure →, *Venezuela* 152 B4 7 37N 66 25W
Apurímac □, *Peru* 156 C3 14 0 S 73 0W
Apurimac →, *Peru* 156 C3 12 17 S 73 56W
Apuseni, Munţii, *Romania* 46 C3 46 30N 22 45 E
Aqabah = Al 'Aqabah, *Jordan* 91 F4 29 31N 35 0 E
'Aqabah, Khalīj al, *Red Sea* 84 D2 28 15N 33 20 E
Āqcheh, *Afghan.* 79 A2 36 56N 66 11 E
'Aqdā, *Iran* 85 C7 32 26N 53 37 E
Aqîq, *Sudan* 94 D4 18 14N 38 12 E
Aqîq, Khalîg, *Sudan* 94 D4 18 20N 38 10 E
'Aqīq, W. al →, *Si. Arabia* 86 B3 20 16N 41 40 E
Aqmola, *Kazakstan* 56 D8 51 10N 71 30 E
Aqrah, *Iraq* 89 D10 36 46N 43 45 E
Aqtöbe, *Kazakstan* 54 F6 50 17N 57 10 E
Aquidauana, *Brazil* 157 E6 20 30 S 55 50W
Aquidauana →, *Brazil* 157 D6 19 44 S 56 50W
Aquiles Serdán, *Mexico* 146 B3 28 37N 105 54W
Aquin, *Haiti* 149 C5 18 16N 73 24W
Ar Rabaḍ, *Si. Arabia* 86 B2 23 11N 39 52 E
Ar Rachidiya, *Morocco* 98 B4 31 58N 4 20W
Ar Rafīd, *Syria* 91 C4 32 57N 35 52 E
Ar Raḥḥālīyah, *Iraq* 89 F10 32 44N 43 23 E
Ar Ramādī, *Iraq* 89 F10 33 25N 43 20 E
Ar Ramādīyāt, *Si. Arabia* 86 A3 24 18N 43 52 E
Ar Raml, *Libya* 96 C3 26 45N 19 40 E
Ar Ramthā, *Jordan* 91 C5 32 34N 36 0 E
Ar Raqqah, *Syria* 89 E8 35 59N 39 8 E
Ar Rass, *Si. Arabia* 84 E4 25 50N 43 40 E
Ar Rawḍah, *Si. Arabia* 86 B3 21 16N 42 50 E
Ar Rawḍah, *Yemen* 86 D4 14 28N 47 17 E
Ar Rawshān, *Si. Arabia* 86 B3 20 2N 42 36 E
Ar Rayyānah, *Si. Arabia* 86 B2 23 32N 39 45 E
Ar Rifā'ī, *Iraq* 84 D5 31 50N 46 10 E
Ar Rijā', *Yemen* 86 D4 13 1N 44 35 E
Ar Riyāḍ, *Si. Arabia* 84 E5 24 41N 46 42 E
Ar Ru'ays, *Qatar* 85 E6 26 8N 51 12 E
Ar Rukhaymīyah, *Iraq* 84 D5 29 22N 45 38 E
Ar Ruqayyidah, *Si. Arabia* 85 E6 25 21N 49 34 E
Ar Ruṣāfah, *Syria* 89 E8 35 45N 38 49 E
Ar Ruṭbah, *Iraq* 89 F9 33 0N 40 15 E
Ar Ruwaydah, *Si. Arabia* 86 B4 23 40N 44 40 E
Ara, *India* 81 G11 25 35N 84 32 E
'Arab, Bahr el →, *Sudan* 95 F2 9 0N 29 30 E
Arab, Khalîg el, *Egypt* 94 H6 30 55N 29 0 E
'Arabābād, *Iran* 85 C8 33 2N 57 41 E
'Arabah, W. →, *Yemen* 87 C5 18 5N 51 26 E
Araban, *Turkey* 88 D7 37 28N 37 44 E
Arabatskaya Strelka, *Ukraine* 51 K8 45 40N 35 0 E
Arabba, *Italy* 39 B8 46 30N 11 52 E
Arabelo, *Venezuela* 153 C5 4 55N 64 13W
Arabia, *Asia* 90 C4 25 0N 45 0 E
Arabian Desert = Es Sahrâ' Esh Sharqîya, *Egypt* 94 B3 27 30N 32 30 E
Arabian Gulf = Gulf, The, *Asia* 85 E6 27 0N 50 0 E
Arabian Sea, *Ind. Oc.* 59 H10 16 0N 65 0 E
Araç, *Turkey* 88 B5 41 15N 33 21 E
Aracaju, *Brazil* 154 D4 10 55 S 37 4W
Aracataca, *Colombia* 152 A3 10 38N 74 9W
Aracati, *Brazil* 154 B4 4 30 S 37 44W
Araçatuba, *Brazil* 159 A5 21 10 S 50 30W
Araceli, *Phil.* 71 F2 10 33N 119 59 E
Aracena, *Spain* 37 H4 37 53N 6 38W
Aracena, Sierra de, *Spain* 37 H4 37 50N 6 50W
Aracides, C., *Solomon Is.* 121 M11 8 21 S 161 0 E
Araçuaí, *Brazil* 155 E3 16 52 S 42 4W
Araçuaí →, *Brazil* 155 E3 16 46 S 42 2W
'Arad, *Israel* 91 D4 31 15N 35 12 E
Arad, *Romania* 46 C2 46 10N 21 20 E
Arad □, *Romania* 46 C3 46 20N 22 0 E
Arada, *Chad* 97 F4 15 0N 20 20 E
Aradhippou, *Cyprus* 32 E12 34 57N 33 36 E
Aradu Nou, *Romania* 46 C2 46 8N 21 20 E
Arafura Sea, *E. Indies* 73 C5 9 0 S 135 0 E
Aragarças, *Brazil* 157 D7 15 55 S 52 15W
Aragats, *Armenia* 53 K7 40 30N 44 15 E
Aragón □, *Spain* 34 D4 41 25N 0 40W
Aragón →, *Spain* 34 C3 42 13N 1 44W
Aragona, *Italy* 40 E6 37 24N 13 27 E
Aragua □, *Venezuela* 152 B4 10 0N 67 10W
Aragua de Barcelona, *Venezuela* 153 B5 9 28N 64 49W
Araguacema, *Brazil* 154 C2 8 50 S 49 20W
Araguaçu, *Brazil* 155 D2 12 49 S 49 51W
Araguaia →, *Brazil* 154 C2 5 21 S 48 41W
Araguaiana, *Brazil* 157 D7 15 43 S 51 51W
Araguaína, *Brazil* 154 C2 7 12 S 48 12W
Araguari, *Brazil* 155 E2 18 38 S 48 11W
Araguari →, *Brazil* 153 C8 1 15N 49 55W
Araguatins, *Brazil* 154 C2 5 38 S 48 7W
Araioses, *Brazil* 154 B3 2 53 S 41 55W
Arak, *Algeria* 99 C5 25 20N 3 45 E
Arāk, *Iran* 85 C6 34 0N 49 40 E
Arakan □, *Burma* 78 F5 19 0N 94 15 E
Arakan Yoma, *Burma* 78 F5 20 0N 94 40 E
Arákhova, *Greece* 45 F4 38 28N 22 35 E
Arakkonam, *India* 83 H4 13 7N 79 43 E
Arakli, *Turkey* 89 B8 41 6N 40 2 E
Araks = Aras, Rūd-e →, *Azerbaijan* 53 K9 40 5N 48 29 E
Aral, *Kazakstan* 56 E7 46 41N 61 45 E
Aral Sea, *Asia* 56 E7 44 30N 60 0 E
Aral Tengizi = Aral Sea, *Asia* 56 E7 44 30N 60 0 E
Aralsk = Aral, *Kazakstan* 56 E7 46 41N 61 45 E
Aralskoye More = Aral Sea, *Asia* 56 E7 44 30N 60 0 E
Aralsor, Ozero, *Kazakstan* 53 F9 49 5N 48 12 E
Aramac, *Australia* 114 C4 22 58 S 145 14 E
Arambag, *India* 81 H12 22 53N 87 48 E
Aran Areh, *Ethiopia* 108 C2 9 2N 43 54 E
Aran I., *Ireland* 19 B3 55 0N 8 30W
Aran Is., *Ireland* 19 C2 53 6N 9 38W
Aranda de Duero, *Spain* 34 D1 41 39N 3 42W
Arandān, *Iran* 84 C5 35 23N 46 55 E
Aranđelovac, *Serbia, Yug.* 42 C5 44 18N 20 27 E
Aranga, *N.Z.* 118 B2 35 44 S 173 40 E
Arani, *India* 83 H4 12 43N 79 19 E
Aranjuez, *Spain* 36 E7 40 1N 3 40W
Aranos, *Namibia* 104 C2 24 9 S 19 7 E
Aransas Pass, *U.S.A.* 139 M6 27 55N 97 9W
Aranzazu, *Colombia* 152 B2 5 16N 75 30W
Arao, *Japan* 62 E2 32 59N 130 25 E
Araouane, *Mali* 100 B4 18 55N 3 30W
Arapahoe, *U.S.A.* 138 E5 40 18N 99 54W
Arapari, *Brazil* 154 C2 5 34 S 49 15W
Arapawa I., *N.Z.* 119 B9 41 11 S 174 17 E
Arapey Grande →, *Uruguay* 158 C4 30 55 S 57 49W
Arapgir, *Turkey* 89 C8 39 5N 38 30 E
Arapiraca, *Brazil* 154 C4 9 45 S 36 39W
Arapongas, *Brazil* 159 A5 23 29 S 51 28W
Arapuni, *N.Z.* 118 E4 38 4 S 175 39 E
Ar'ar, *Si. Arabia* 84 D4 30 59N 41 2 E
Araracuara, *Colombia* 152 D3 0 24 S 72 17W
Araranguá, *Brazil* 159 B6 29 0 S 49 30W
Araraquara, *Brazil* 155 F2 21 50 S 48 0W
Ararás, Serra das, *Brazil* 159 B5 25 0 S 53 10W
Ararat, *Armenia* 89 C11 39 48N 44 50 E
Ararat, *Australia* 116 D5 37 16 S 143 0 E
Ararat, Mt. = Ağrı Dağı, *Turkey* 89 C11 39 50N 44 15 E
Arari, *Brazil* 154 B3 3 28 S 44 47W
Araria, *India* 81 F12 26 9N 87 33 E
Araripe, Chapada do, *Brazil* 154 C3 7 20 S 40 0W
Araripina, *Brazil* 154 C3 7 33 S 40 34W
Araruama, L. de, *Brazil* 155 F3 22 53 S 42 12W
Araruna, *Brazil* 154 C4 6 52 S 35 44W
Aras, Rūd-e →, *Azerbaijan* 53 K9 40 5N 48 29 E
Araticu, *Brazil* 154 B2 1 58 S 49 51W
Arauca, *Colombia* 152 B3 7 0N 70 40W
Arauca □, *Colombia* 152 B3 6 40N 71 0W
Arauca →, *Venezuela* 152 B4 7 24N 66 35W
Arauco, *Chile* 158 D1 37 16 S 73 25W
Arauco □, *Chile* 158 D1 37 40 S 73 25W
Araújos, *Brazil* 155 E2 19 56 S 45 14W
Arauquita, *Colombia* 152 B3 7 2N 71 25W
Araure, *Venezuela* 152 B4 9 34N 69 13W
Arawa, *Ethiopia* 95 F5 9 57N 41 58 E
Arawata →, *N.Z.* 119 E3 44 0 S 168 40 E
Araxá, *Brazil* 155 E2 19 35 S 46 55W
Araya, Pen. de, *Venezuela* 153 A5 10 40N 64 0W
Arayat, *Phil.* 70 D3 15 10N 120 46 E
Arba Minch, *Ethiopia* 95 F4 6 0N 37 30 E
Arbat, *Iraq* 89 E11 35 25N 45 35 E
Arbatax, *Italy* 40 C2 39 56N 9 42 E
Arbedo, *Switz.* 29 D8 46 12N 9 3 E
Arbīl, *Iraq* 89 D11 36 15N 44 5 E
Arbois, *France* 23 F12 46 55N 5 46 E
Arboletes, *Colombia* 152 B2 8 51N 76 26W
Arbon, *Switz.* 29 A8 47 31N 9 26 E
Arbore, *Ethiopia* 95 F4 5 3N 36 50 E
Arboréa, *Italy* 40 C1 39 46N 8 35 E
Arborfield, *Canada* 131 C8 53 6N 103 39W
Arborg, *Canada* 131 C9 50 54N 97 13W
Arbrå, *Sweden* 14 C10 61 28N 16 22 E
Arbroath, *U.K.* 18 E6 56 34N 2 35W
Arbuckle, *U.S.A.* 144 F4 39 1N 122 3W
Arbus, *Italy* 40 C1 39 30N 8 33 E
Arc, *France* 23 E12 47 28N 5 34 E
Arc →, *France* 25 C10 45 34N 6 12 E
Arcachon, *France* 24 D2 44 40N 1 10W
Arcachon, Bassin d', *France* 24 D2 44 42N 1 10W
Arcade, *U.S.A.* 136 D6 42 32N 78 25W
Arcadia, *Fla., U.S.A.* 135 M5 27 13N 81 52W
Arcadia, *Ind., U.S.A.* 141 D10 40 11N 86 1W
Arcadia, *Iowa, U.S.A.* 140 B1 42 5N 95 3W
Arcadia, *La., U.S.A.* 139 J8 32 33N 92 55W
Arcadia, *Nebr., U.S.A.* 138 E5 41 25N 99 8W
Arcadia, *Pa., U.S.A.* 136 F6 40 47N 78 51W
Arcadia, *Wis., U.S.A.* 138 C9 44 15N 91 30W
Arcanum, *U.S.A.* 141 E12 39 59N 84 33W
Arcata, *U.S.A.* 142 F1 40 52N 124 5W
Arcévia, *Italy* 39 E9 43 30N 12 56 E
Archangel = Arkhangelsk, *Russia* 48 B7 64 38N 40 36 E
Archar, *Bulgaria* 42 D7 43 50N 22 54 E
Archbald, *U.S.A.* 137 E9 41 30N 75 32W
Archbold, *U.S.A.* 141 C12 41 31N 84 18W
Archena, *Spain* 35 G3 38 9N 1 16W
Archer →, *Australia* 114 A3 13 28 S 141 41 E
Archer B., *Australia* 114 A3 13 20 S 141 30 E
Archers Post, *Kenya* 106 B4 0 35N 37 35 E
Archidona, *Spain* 37 H6 37 6N 4 22W
Arci, Mte., *Italy* 40 C1 39 47N 8 45 E
Arcidosso, *Italy* 39 F8 42 52N 11 33 E
Arcila = Asilah, *Morocco* 98 A3 35 29N 6 0W
Arcis-sur-Aube, *France* 23 D11 48 32N 4 10 E
Arckaringa, *Australia* 115 D1 27 56 S 134 45 E
Arckaringa Cr. →, *Australia* 115 D2 28 10 S 135 22 E
Arco, *Italy* 38 C7 45 55N 10 53 E
Arco, *U.S.A.* 142 E7 43 38N 113 18W
Arcola, *Canada* 131 D8 49 40N 102 30W
Arcola, *U.S.A.* 141 E8 39 41N 88 19W
Arcoona, *Australia* 116 A2 31 2 S 137 1 E
Arcos, *Spain* 34 D2 41 12N 2 16W
Arcos de la Frontera, *Spain* 37 J5 36 45N 5 49W
Arcos de Valdevez, *Portugal* 36 D2 41 55N 8 22W
Arcot, *India* 83 H4 12 53N 79 20 E
Arcoverde, *Brazil* 154 C4 8 25 S 37 4W
Arctic Bay, *Canada* 127 A11 73 1N 85 7W
Arctic Ocean, *Arctic* 6 B18 78 0N 160 0W
Arctic Red River, *Canada* 126 B6 67 15N 134 0W
Arda →, *Bulgaria* 43 F11 41 40N 26 29 E
Arda →, *Italy* 38 D6 45 2N 10 2 E
Ardabīl, *Iran* 89 C13 38 15N 48 18 E
Ardahan, *Turkey* 89 B10 41 7N 42 41 E
Ardakān = Sepīdān, *Iran* 85 D7 30 20N 52 5 E
Ardales, *Spain* 37 J6 36 53N 4 51W
Årdalstangen, *Norway* 14 C1 61 14N 7 43 E
Ardea, *Greece* 44 D4 40 58N 22 3 E
Ardèche □, *France* 25 D8 44 42N 4 16 E
Ardèche →, *France* 25 D8 44 16N 4 39 E
Ardee, *Ireland* 19 C5 53 52N 6 33W
Arden, *Canada* 136 B8 44 43N 76 56W
Arden, *Denmark* 15 H3 56 46N 9 52 E
Arden, *Calif., U.S.A.* 144 G5 38 36N 121 33W
Arden, *Nev., U.S.A.* 145 J11 36 1N 115 14W
Ardenne, *Belgium* 23 C12 49 50N 5 5 E
Ardennes = Ardenne, *Belgium* 23 C12 49 50N 5 5 E
Ardennes □, *France* 23 C11 49 35N 4 40 E
Ardentes, *France* 23 F8 46 45N 1 50 E
Ardeşen, *Turkey* 89 B9 41 12N 41 2 E
Ardestān, *Iran* 85 C7 33 20N 52 25 E
Ardgour, *U.K.* 18 E3 56 45N 5 25W
Árdhas →, *Greece* 44 C8 41 36N 26 25 E
Ardila →, *Portugal* 37 G3 38 12N 7 28W
Ardino, *Bulgaria* 43 F10 41 34N 25 9 E
Ardlethan, *Australia* 117 C7 34 22 S 146 53 E
Ardmore, *Australia* 114 C2 21 39 S 139 11 E
Ardmore, *Okla., U.S.A.* 139 H6 34 10N 97 8W
Ardmore, *Pa., U.S.A.* 137 G9 39 58N 75 18W
Ardmore, *S. Dak., U.S.A.* 138 D3 43 1N 103 40W
Ardnacrusha, *Ireland* 19 D3 52 43N 8 38W
Ardnamurchan, Pt. of, *U.K.* 18 E2 56 43N 6 14W
Ardon, *Russia* 53 J7 43 10N 44 18 E
Ardooie, *Belgium* 21 G2 50 59N 3 13 E
Ardore, *Italy* 41 D9 38 11N 16 10 E
Ardres, *France* 23 B8 50 50N 1 59 E
Ardrossan, *Australia* 116 C2 34 26 S 137 53 E
Ardrossan, *U.K.* 18 F4 55 39N 4 49W
Ards □, *U.K.* 19 B6 54 35N 5 30W
Ards Pen., *U.K.* 19 B6 54 33N 5 34W
Ardud, *Romania* 46 B3 47 37N 22 52 E
Åre, *Sweden* 14 A7 63 22N 13 15 E
Arecibo, *Puerto Rico* 149 C6 18 29N 66 43W
Areia Branca, *Brazil* 154 B4 5 0 S 37 0W
Arena, Pt., *U.S.A.* 144 G3 38 57N 123 44W
Arenales, Cerro, *Chile* 160 C2 47 5 S 73 40W
Arenápolis, *Brazil* 157 C6 14 26 S 56 49W
Arenas, *Spain* 36 B6 43 17N 4 50W
Arenas de San Pedro, *Spain* 36 E5 40 12N 5 5W
Arendal, *Norway* 15 F2 58 28N 8 46 E
Arendonk, *Belgium* 21 F6 51 19N 5 5 E
Arendsee, *Germany* 26 C7 52 52N 11 27 E
Arenillas, *Ecuador* 152 D1 3 33 S 80 10W
Arenys de Mar, *Spain* 34 D7 41 35N 2 33 E
Arenzano, *Italy* 38 D5 44 24N 8 41 E
Arenzville, *U.S.A.* 140 E6 39 53N 90 22W
Areópolis, *Greece* 45 H4 36 40N 22 22 E
Arequipa, *Peru* 156 D3 16 20 S 71 30W
Arequipa □, *Peru* 156 D3 16 0 S 72 50W
Arere, *Brazil* 153 D7 0 16 S 53 52W
Arero, *Ethiopia* 95 G4 4 41N 38 50 E
Arès, *France* 24 D2 44 47N 1 8W
Arévalo, *Spain* 36 D6 41 3N 4 43W
Arezzo, *Italy* 39 E8 43 25N 11 53 E
Arga →, *Spain* 34 C3 42 18N 1 47W
Argalastí, *Greece* 44 E5 39 13N 23 13 E
Argamakmur, *Indonesia* 74 C2 3 35 S 102 0 E
Argamasilla de Alba, *Spain* 35 F1 39 8N 3 5W
Arganda, *Spain* 34 E1 40 19N 3 26W
Arganil, *Portugal* 36 E2 40 13N 8 3W
Argayash, *Russia* 54 D8 55 29N 60 52 E
Argelès-Gazost, *France* 24 F3 43 0N 0 6W
Argelès-sur-Mer, *France* 24 F7 42 34N 3 1 E
Argens →, *France* 25 E10 43 24N 6 44 E
Argent-sur-Sauldre, *France* 23 E9 47 33N 2 25 E
Argenta, *Italy* 39 D8 44 37N 11 50 E
Argenta, *U.S.A.* 141 E8 39 59N 88 49W
Argentan, *France* 22 D6 48 45N 0 1W
Argentário, Mte., *Italy* 39 F8 42 24N 11 9 E
Argentat, *France* 24 C5 45 6N 1 56 E
Argentera, *Italy* 38 D3 44 24N 6 57 E
Argentera, Monte del, *Italy* 38 D4 44 12N 7 5 E
Argenteuil, *France* 23 D9 48 57N 2 14 E
Argentia, *Canada* 129 C9 47 18N 53 58W
Argentiera, C. dell', *Italy* 40 B1 40 44N 8 8 E
Argentière, Aiguilles d', *Switz.* 28 E4 45 58N 7 2 E
Argentina ■, *S. Amer.* 160 B3 35 0 S 66 0W
Argentina Is., *Antarctica* 7 C17 66 0 S 64 0W
Argentino, L., *Argentina* 160 D2 50 10 S 73 0W
Argenton-Château, *France* 22 F6 46 59N 0 27W
Argenton-sur-Creuse, *France* 24 B5 46 36N 1 30 E
Argeş □, *Romania* 46 D5 45 0N 24 45 E
Argeş →, *Romania* 46 E7 44 11N 26 25 E
Arghandab →, *Afghan.* 79 C2 31 30N 64 15 E
Argo, *Sudan* 94 D3 19 28N 30 30 E
Argolikós Kólpos, *Greece* 45 G4 37 20N 22 52 E
Argolís □, *Greece* 45 G4 37 38N 22 50 E
Argonne, *France* 23 C12 49 10N 5 0 E
Árgos, *Greece* 45 G4 37 40N 22 43 E
Argos, *U.S.A.* 141 C10 41 14N 86 15W
Árgos Orestikón, *Greece* 44 D3 40 27N 21 26 E
Argostólion, *Greece* 45 F2 38 12N 20 33 E
Arguedas, *Spain* 34 C3 42 11N 1 36W
Arguello, Pt., *U.S.A.* 145 L6 34 35N 120 39W
Arguineguín, *Canary Is.* 33 G4 27 46N 15 41W
Argun, *Russia* 53 J7 43 18N 45 52 E
Argun →, *Russia* 57 D13 53 20N 121 28 E
Argungu, *Nigeria* 101 C5 12 40N 4 31 E
Argus Pk., *U.S.A.* 145 K9 35 52N 117 26W
Argyle, *U.S.A.* 138 A6 48 20N 96 49W
Argyle, L., *Australia* 112 C4 16 20 S 128 40 E
Argyll & Bute □, *U.K.* 18 E3 56 13N 5 28W
Arhavi, *Turkey* 89 B9 41 21N 41 18 E
Århus, *Denmark* 15 H4 56 8N 10 11 E
Århus Amtskommune □, *Denmark* 15 H4 56 15N 10 15 E
Aria, *N.Z.* 118 E4 38 33 S 175 0 E
Ariadnoye, *Russia* 60 B7 45 8N 134 25 E
Ariamsvlei, *Namibia* 104 D2 28 9 S 19 51 E
Ariana, *Tunisia* 96 A2 36 52N 10 12 E
Ariano Irpino, *Italy* 41 A8 41 9N 15 5 E
Ariano nel Polèsine, *Italy* 39 D9 44 56N 12 5 E
Ariari →, *Colombia* 152 C3 2 35N 72 47W
Aribinda, *Burkina Faso* 101 C4 14 17N 0 52W
Arica, *Chile* 156 D3 18 32 S 70 20W
Arica, *Colombia* 152 D3 2 0 S 71 50W
Arico, *Canary Is.* 33 F3 28 9N 16 29W
Arid, C., *Australia* 113 F3 34 1 S 123 10 E
Arida, *Japan* 63 C7 34 5N 135 8 E
Ariège □, *France* 24 F5 42 56N 1 30 E
Ariège →, *France* 24 E5 43 30N 1 25 E
Arieş →, *Romania* 46 C4 46 24N 23 20 E
Arīḥā, *Syria* 84 C3 35 49N 36 35 E
Arilje, *Serbia, Yug.* 42 D5 43 44N 20 7 E
Arílla, Ákra, *Greece* 32 A3 39 43N 19 39 E
Arima, *Trin. & Tob.* 149 D7 10 38N 61 17W

Azezo 169

At Turbah, *Yemen* **86 D4** 13 13N 44 7 E
At Turbah, *Yemen* **86 D3** 12 40N 43 30 E
Aţ Ţuwayrifah, *Si. Arabia* **87 B5** 21 30N 49 35 E
Atacama □, *Chile* **158 B2** 27 30 S 70 0W
Atacama, Desierto de, *Chile* **158 A2** 24 0 S 69 20W
Atacama, Salar de, *Chile* **158 A2** 23 30 S 68 20W
Ataco, *Colombia* **152 C2** 3 35N 75 23W
Atakor, *Algeria* **99 D6** 23 27N 5 31 E
Atakpamé, *Togo* **101 D5** 7 31N 1 13 E
Atalándi, *Greece* **45 F4** 38 39N 22 58 E
Atalaya, *Peru* **156 C3** 10 45 S 73 50W
Atalaya de Femes, *Canary Is.* **33 F6** 28 56N 13 47W
Ataléia, *Brazil* **155 E3** 18 3 S 41 6W
Atambua, *Indonesia* **72 C2** 9 7 S 124 54 E
Atami, *Japan* **63 B11** 35 5N 139 4 E
Atankawng, *Burma* **78 C6** 25 50N 97 47 E
Atapupu, *Indonesia* **72 C2** 9 0 S 124 51 E
Atâr, *Mauritania* **98 D2** 20 30N 13 5W
Ataram, Erg n-, *Algeria* **99 D5** 23 57N 2 0 E
Atarfe, *Spain* **37 H7** 37 13N 3 40W
Atascadero, *U.S.A.* **144 K6** 35 29N 120 40W
Atasu, *Kazakstan* **56 E8** 48 30N 71 0 E
Atatürk Barajı, *Turkey* **89 D8** 37 28N 38 30 E
Atauro, *Indonesia* **72 C3** 8 10 S 125 30 E
Atbara, *Sudan* **94 D3** 17 42N 33 59 E
'Atbara →, *Sudan* **94 D3** 17 40N 33 56 E
Atbasar, *Kazakstan* **56 D7** 51 48N 68 20 E
Atbashi, *Kyrgyzstan* **55 C7** 41 10N 75 48 E
Atbashi, Khrebet, *Kyrgyzstan* **55 C7** 40 50N 75 30 E
Atchafalaya B., *U.S.A.* **139 L9** 29 25N 91 25W
Atchison, *U.S.A.* **138 F7** 39 34N 95 7W
Atebubu, *Ghana* **101 D4** 7 47N 1 0W
Ateca, *Spain* **34 D3** 41 20N 1 49W
Aterno →, *Italy* **39 F10** 42 11N 13 51 E
Atesine, Alpi, *Italy* **38 B8** 46 55N 11 30 E
Atessa, *Italy* **39 F11** 42 4N 14 27 E
Ath, *Belgium* **21 G3** 50 38N 3 47 E
Athabasca, *Canada* **130 C6** 54 45N 113 20W
Athabasca →, *Canada* **131 B6** 58 40N 110 50W
Athabasca, L., *Canada* **131 B7** 59 15N 109 15W
Athboy, *Ireland* **19 C5** 53 37N 6 56W
Athenry, *Ireland* **19 C3** 53 18N 8 44W
Athens = Athínai, *Greece* **45 G5** 37 58N 23 46 E
Athens, *Ala., U.S.A.* **135 H2** 34 48N 86 58W
Athens, *Ga., U.S.A.* **135 J4** 33 57N 83 23W
Athens, *N.Y., U.S.A.* **137 D11** 42 16N 73 49W
Athens, *Ohio, U.S.A.* **134 F4** 39 20N 82 6W
Athens, *Pa., U.S.A.* **137 E8** 41 57N 76 31W
Athens, *Tenn., U.S.A.* **135 H3** 35 27N 84 36W
Athens, *Tex., U.S.A.* **139 J7** 32 12N 95 51W
Atherley, *Canada* **136 B5** 44 37N 79 20W
Atherton, *Australia* **114 B4** 17 17 S 145 30 E
Athiéme, *Benin* **101 D5** 6 37N 1 40 E
Athienou, *Cyprus* **32 D12** 35 3N 33 32 E
Athínai, *Greece* **45 G5** 37 58N 23 46 E
Athlone, *Ireland* **19 C4** 53 25N 7 56W
Athna, *Cyprus* **32 D12** 35 3N 33 47 E
Athni, *India* **82 F2** 16 44N 75 6 E
Athol, *N.Z.* **119 F3** 45 30 S 168 35 E
Atholl, Forest of, *U.K.* **18 E5** 56 51N 3 50W
Atholville, *Canada* **129 C6** 47 59N 66 43W
Áthos, *Greece* **44 D6** 40 9N 24 22 E
Athus, *Belgium* **21 J7** 49 34N 5 50 E
Athy, *Ireland* **19 D5** 53 0N 7 0W
Ati, *Chad* **97 F3** 13 13N 18 20 E
Ati, *Sudan* **95 E2** 13 5N 29 2 E
Atiak, *Uganda* **106 B3** 3 12N 32 2 E
Atiamuri, *N.Z.* **118 E5** 38 24 S 176 5 E
Atico, *Peru* **156 D3** 16 14 S 73 40W
Atienza, *Spain* **34 D2** 41 12N 2 52W
Atikokan, *Canada* **128 C1** 48 45N 91 37W
Atikonak L., *Canada* **129 B7** 52 40N 64 32W
Atimonan, *Phil.* **70 D3** 14 0N 121 55 E
'Ātinah, W. →, *Oman* **87 C6** 18 23N 53 28 E
Atirampattinam, *India* **83 J4** 10 28N 79 20 E
Atka, *Russia* **57 C16** 60 50N 151 48 E
Atkarsk, *Russia* **52 E7** 51 55N 45 2 E
Atkinson, *Ill., U.S.A.* **140 C6** 41 25N 90 1W
Atkinson, *Nebr., U.S.A.* **138 D5** 42 32N 98 59W
Atlanta, *Ga., U.S.A.* **135 J3** 33 45N 84 23W
Atlanta, *Ill., U.S.A.* **140 D7** 40 16N 89 14W
Atlanta, *Mo., U.S.A.* **140 E4** 39 54N 92 29W
Atlanta, *Tex., U.S.A.* **139 J7** 33 7N 94 10W
Atlantic, *U.S.A.* **138 E7** 41 24N 95 1W
Atlantic City, *U.S.A.* **134 F8** 39 21N 74 27W
Atlantic Ocean **8 H7** 0 0 20 0W
Atlántico □, *Colombia* **152 A2** 10 45N 75 0W
Atlas Mts. = Haut Atlas, *Morocco* **98 B3** 32 30N 5 0W
Atlin, *Canada* **130 B2** 59 31N 133 41W
Atlin, L., *Canada* **130 B2** 59 26N 133 45W
Atmakur, *India* **83 G4** 14 37N 79 40 E
Atmore, *U.S.A.* **135 K2** 31 2N 87 29W
Atō, *Japan* **62 C3** 34 25N 131 40 E
Atok, *Phil.* **70 C3** 16 35N 120 41 E
Atoka, *U.S.A.* **139 H6** 34 23N 96 8W
Átokos, *Greece* **45 F2** 38 28N 20 49 E
Atolia, *U.S.A.* **145 K9** 35 19N 117 37W
Atouguia, *Portugal* **37 F1** 39 20N 9 20W
Atoyac →, *Mexico* **147 D5** 16 30N 97 31W
Atrak = Atrek →, *Turkmenistan* **85 B8** 37 35N 53 58 E
Ätran, *Sweden* **15 G6** 57 7N 12 57 E
Atrato →, *Colombia* **152 B2** 8 17N 76 58W
Atrauli, *India* **80 E8** 28 2N 78 20 E
Atrek →, *Turkmenistan* **85 B8** 37 35N 53 58 E
Atri, *Italy* **39 F10** 42 35N 13 58 E
Atsbi, *Ethiopia* **95 E4** 13 52N 39 50 E
Atsoum, Mts., *Cameroon* **101 D7** 6 41N 12 57 E
Atsugi, *Japan* **63 B11** 35 25N 139 21 E
Atsumi, *Japan* **63 C9** 34 35N 137 4 E
Atsumi-Wan, *Japan* **63 C9** 34 44N 137 13 E
Atsuta, *Japan* **60 C10** 43 24N 141 26 E
Attalla, *U.S.A.* **135 H2** 34 1N 86 6W
Attáviros, *Greece* **32 C9** 36 12N 27 50 E
Attawapiskat, *Canada* **128 B3** 52 56N 82 24W
Attawapiskat →, *Canada* **128 B3** 52 57N 82 18W
Attawapiskat, L., *Canada* **128 B2** 52 18N 87 54W
Attendorn, *Germany* **26 D3** 51 8N 7 56 E
Attersee, *Austria* **30 D6** 47 55N 13 32 E
Attert, *Belgium* **21 J7** 49 45N 5 47 E
Attica, *U.S.A.* **141 D9** 40 18N 87 15W
Attichy, *France* **23 C10** 49 25N 3 3 E
Attigny, *France* **23 C11** 49 28N 4 35 E
Attikamagen L., *Canada* **129 A6** 55 0N 66 30W
Attikí □, *Greece* **45 F5** 38 10N 23 40 E
Attleboro, *U.S.A.* **137 E13** 41 57N 71 17W
Attock, *Pakistan* **80 C5** 33 52N 72 20 E
Attopeu, *Laos* **76 E6** 14 48N 106 50 E
Attunga, *Australia* **117 A9** 30 55 S 150 50 E
Attur, *India* **83 J4** 11 35N 78 30 E
'Atūd, *Yemen* **87 D5** 14 53N 48 10 E
Atuel →, *Argentina* **158 D2** 36 17 S 66 50W
Åtvidaberg, *Sweden* **15 F10** 58 12N 16 0 E
Atwater, *U.S.A.* **144 H6** 37 21N 120 37W
Atwood, *Canada* **136 C3** 43 40N 81 1W
Atwood, *U.S.A.* **138 F4** 39 48N 101 3W
Atyraū, *Kazakstan* **49 E9** 47 5N 52 0 E
Au Sable →, *U.S.A.* **134 C4** 44 25N 83 20W
Au Sable Pt., *U.S.A.* **128 C2** 46 40N 86 10W
Aubagne, *France* **25 E9** 43 17N 5 37 E
Aubange, *Belgium* **21 J7** 49 34N 5 48 E
Aubarca, C., *Spain* **33 B7** 39 4N 1 22 E
Aube □, *France* **23 D11** 48 15N 4 10 E
Aube →, *France* **23 D10** 48 34N 3 43 E
Aubel, *Belgium* **21 G7** 50 42N 5 51 E
Aubenas, *France* **25 D8** 44 37N 4 24 E
Aubenton, *France* **23 C11** 49 50N 4 12 E
Auberry, *U.S.A.* **144 H7** 37 7N 119 29W
Aubigny-sur-Nère, *France* **23 E9** 47 30N 2 24 E
Aubin, *France* **24 D6** 44 33N 2 15 E
Aubrac, Mts. d', *France* **24 D7** 44 40N 3 2 E
Auburn, *Ala., U.S.A.* **135 J3** 32 36N 85 29W
Auburn, *Calif., U.S.A.* **144 G5** 38 54N 121 4W
Auburn, *Ill., U.S.A.* **140 E7** 39 36N 89 45W
Auburn, *Ind., U.S.A.* **141 C11** 41 22N 85 4W
Auburn, *N.Y., U.S.A.* **137 D8** 42 56N 76 34W
Auburn, *Nebr., U.S.A.* **138 E7** 40 23N 95 51W
Auburn, *Wash., U.S.A.* **144 C4** 47 18N 122 14W
Auburn Ra., *Australia* **115 D5** 25 15 S 150 30 E
Auburndale, *U.S.A.* **135 L5** 28 4N 81 48W
Aubusson, *France* **24 C6** 45 57N 2 11 E
Auch, *France* **24 E4** 43 39N 0 36 E
Auchel, *France* **23 B9** 50 30N 2 29 E
Auchi, *Nigeria* **101 D6** 7 6N 6 13 E
Auckland, *N.Z.* **118 C3** 36 52 S 174 46 E
Auckland □, *N.Z.* **118 E6** 36 50 S 175 0 E
Auckland Is., *Pac. Oc.* **122 N8** 50 40 S 166 5 E
Aude □, *France* **24 E6** 43 8N 2 28 E
Aude →, *France* **24 E7** 43 13N 3 14 E
Audegle, *Somali Rep.* **108 D2** 1 59N 44 50 E
Auden, *Canada* **128 B2** 50 14N 87 53W
Auderghem, *Belgium* **21 G4** 50 49N 4 26 E
Auderville, *France* **22 C5** 49 43N 1 57W
Audierne, *France* **22 D2** 48 1N 4 34W
Audincourt, *France* **23 E13** 47 30N 6 50 E
Audo, *Ethiopia* **95 F5** 6 20N 41 50 E
Audubon, *U.S.A.* **140 C2** 41 43N 94 56W
Aue, *Germany* **26 E8** 50 35N 12 41 E
Auer = Ora, *Italy* **39 B8** 46 21N 11 18 E
Auerbach, *Germany* **26 E8** 50 30N 12 24 E
Aueti Paraná →, *Brazil* **152 D4** 1 51 S 65 37W
Aufist, *W. Sahara* **98 C2** 25 44N 14 39W
Augathella, *Australia* **115 D4** 25 48 S 146 35 E
Augrabies Falls, *S. Africa* **104 D3** 28 35 S 20 20 E
Augsburg, *Germany* **27 G6** 48 25N 10 52 E
Augusta, *Italy* **41 E8** 37 13N 15 13 E
Augusta, *Ark., U.S.A.* **139 H9** 35 17N 91 22W
Augusta, *Ga., U.S.A.* **135 J5** 33 28N 81 58W
Augusta, *Ill., U.S.A.* **140 D6** 40 14N 90 57W
Augusta, *Kans., U.S.A.* **139 G6** 37 41N 96 59W
Augusta, *Ky., U.S.A.* **141 F12** 38 47N 84 0W
Augusta, *Maine, U.S.A.* **129 D6** 44 19N 69 47W
Augusta, *Mont., U.S.A.* **142 C7** 47 30N 112 24W
Augusta, *Wis., U.S.A.* **138 C9** 44 41N 91 7W
Augustenborg, *Denmark* **15 K3** 54 57N 9 53 E
Augustów, *Poland* **47 B9** 53 51N 23 0 E
Augustus, Mt., *Australia* **112 D2** 24 20 S 116 50 E
Augustus Downs, *Australia* **114 B2** 18 35 S 139 55 E
Augustus I., *Australia* **112 C3** 15 20 S 124 30 E
Aukan, *Eritrea* **95 D5** 15 29N 40 50 E
Auki, *Solomon Is.* **121 M11** 8 45 S 160 42 E
Aukum, *U.S.A.* **144 G6** 38 34N 120 43W
Auld, L., *Australia* **112 D3** 22 25 S 123 50 E
Aulla, *Italy* **38 D6** 44 12N 9 58 E
Aulnay, *France* **24 B3** 46 2N 0 22W
Aulne →, *France* **22 D2** 48 17N 4 16W
Aulnoye-Aymeries, *France* **23 B10** 50 12N 3 50 E
Ault, *France* **22 B8** 50 8N 1 26 E
Ault, *U.S.A.* **138 E2** 40 35N 104 44W
Aulus-les-Bains, *France* **24 F5** 42 49N 1 19 E
Aumale, *France* **23 C8** 49 46N 1 46 E
Aumont-Aubrac, *France* **24 D7** 44 43N 3 17 E
Auna, *Nigeria* **101 C5** 10 9N 4 42 E
Aundh, *India* **82 F2** 17 33N 74 23 E
Aunis, *France* **24 B3** 46 5N 0 50W
Auponhia, *Indonesia* **72 B3** 1 58 S 125 27 E
Aups, *France* **25 E10** 43 37N 6 15 E
Aur, P., *Malaysia* **77 L5** 2 35N 104 10 E
Aura, *Burma* **78 B6** 26 59N 97 57 E
Auraiya, *India* **81 F8** 26 28N 79 33 E
Aurangabad, *Bihar, India* **81 G11** 24 45N 84 18 E
Aurangabad, *Maharashtra, India* **82 E2** 19 50N 75 23 E
Auray, *France* **22 E4** 47 40N 2 59W
Aurès, *Algeria* **99 A6** 35 8N 6 30 E
Aurich, *Germany* **26 B3** 53 28N 7 28 E
Aurilândia, *Brazil* **155 E1** 16 44 S 50 28W
Aurillac, *France* **24 D6** 44 55N 2 26 E
Auronzo di Cadore, *Italy* **39 B9** 46 33N 12 26 E
Aurora = Maewo, *Vanuatu* **121 E6** 15 10 S 168 10 E
Aurora, *Canada* **136 C5** 44 0N 79 28W
Aurora, *Isabela, Phil.* **70 C3** 16 59N 121 38 E
Aurora, *Quezon, Phil.* **70 E4** 13 21N 122 31 E
Aurora, *S. Africa* **104 E2** 32 40 S 18 29 E
Aurora, *Colo., U.S.A.* **138 F2** 39 44N 104 52W
Aurora, *Ill., U.S.A.* **141 C8** 41 45N 88 19W
Aurora, *Mo., U.S.A.* **139 G8** 36 58N 93 43W
Aurora, *Nebr., U.S.A.* **138 E6** 40 52N 98 0W
Aurora, *Ohio, U.S.A.* **136 E3** 41 21N 81 20W
Aursmoen, *Norway* **14 E5** 59 55N 11 26 E
Aurukun Mission, *Australia* **114 A3** 13 20 S 141 45 E
Aus, *Namibia* **104 D2** 26 35 S 16 12 E
Auschwitz = Oświęcim, *Poland* **31 A12** 50 2N 19 11 E
Austerlitz = Slavkov, *Czech.* **31 B9** 49 10N 16 52 E
Austin, *Ind., U.S.A.* **141 F11** 38 45N 85 49W
Austin, *Minn., U.S.A.* **138 D8** 43 40N 92 58W
Austin, *Nev., U.S.A.* **142 G5** 39 30N 117 4W
Austin, *Pa., U.S.A.* **136 E6** 41 38N 78 6W
Austin, *Tex., U.S.A.* **139 K6** 30 17N 97 45W
Austin, L., *Australia* **113 E2** 27 40 S 118 0 E
Austra, *Norway* **12 D14** 65 8N 11 55 E
Austral Downs, *Australia* **114 C2** 20 30 S 137 45 E
Austral Is. = Tubuai Is., *Pac. Oc.* **123 K12** 25 0 S 150 0W
Austral Seamount Chain, *Pac. Oc.* **123 K13** 24 0 S 150 0W
Australia ■, *Oceania* **122 K5** 23 0 S 135 0 E
Australian Alps, *Australia* **117 D8** 36 30 S 148 30 E
Australian Capital Territory □, *Australia* **115 F4** 35 30 S 149 0 E
Austria ■, *Europe* **30 E7** 47 0N 14 0 E
Austvågøy, *Norway* **12 B16** 68 20N 14 40 E
Autazes, *Brazil* **153 D6** 3 35 S 59 8W
Autelbas, *Belgium* **21 J7** 49 39N 5 52 E
Auterive, *France* **24 E5** 43 21N 1 29 E
Authie →, *France* **23 B8** 50 22N 1 38 E
Authon-du-Perche, *France* **22 D7** 48 12N 0 54 E
Autlán, *Mexico* **146 D4** 19 40N 104 30W
Autun, *France* **23 F11** 46 58N 4 17 E
Auvelais, *Belgium* **21 H5** 50 27N 4 38 E
Auvergne, *Australia* **112 C5** 15 39 S 130 1 E
Auvergne, *France* **24 C7** 45 20N 3 15 E
Auvergne, Mts. d', *France* **24 C6** 45 20N 2 55 E
Auvézére →, *France* **24 C4** 45 12N 0 50 E
Auxerre, *France* **23 E10** 47 48N 3 32 E
Auxi-le-Château, *France* **23 B9** 50 15N 2 8 E
Auxonne, *France* **23 E12** 47 10N 5 20 E
Auxvasse, *U.S.A.* **140 E5** 39 1N 91 54W
Auzances, *France* **24 B6** 46 2N 2 30 E
Auzat-sur-Allier, *France* **24 C7** 45 27N 3 19 E
Ava, *U.S.A.* **140 G7** 37 53N 89 30W
Avallon, *France* **23 E10** 47 30N 3 53 E
Avalon, *U.S.A.* **145 M8** 33 21N 118 20W
Avalon Pen., *Canada* **129 C9** 47 30N 53 20W
Avanigadda, *India* **83 G5** 16 0N 80 56 E
Avaré, *Brazil* **159 A6** 23 4 S 48 58W
Ávas, *Greece* **44 D7** 40 57N 25 56 E
Avawatz Mts., *U.S.A.* **145 K10** 35 40N 116 30W
Aveiro, *Brazil* **153 D6** 3 10 S 55 5W
Aveiro, *Portugal* **36 E2** 40 37N 8 38W
Aveiro □, *Portugal* **36 E2** 40 40N 8 35W
Āvej, *Iran* **85 C6** 35 40N 49 15 E
Avelgem, *Belgium* **21 G2** 50 47N 3 27 E
Avellaneda, *Argentina* **158 C4** 34 50 S 58 10W
Avellino, *Italy* **41 B7** 40 54N 14 47 E
Avenal, *U.S.A.* **144 K6** 36 0N 120 8W
Avenches, *Switz.* **28 C4** 46 53N 7 2 E
Averøya, *Norway* **14 A1** 63 0N 7 35 E
Aversa, *Italy* **41 B7** 40 58N 14 12 E
Avery, *U.S.A.* **142 C6** 47 15N 115 49W
Aves, I. de, *W. Indies* **149 C7** 15 45N 63 55W
Aves, Is. de, *Venezuela* **149 D6** 12 0N 67 30W
Avesnes-sur-Helpe, *France* **23 B10** 50 8N 3 55 E
Avesta, *Sweden* **13 F17** 60 9N 16 10 E
Aveyron □, *France* **24 D6** 44 22N 2 45 E
Aveyron →, *France* **24 D5** 44 5N 1 16 E
Avezzano, *Italy* **39 F10** 42 2N 13 25 E
Avgó, *Greece* **45 J7** 35 33N 25 37 E
Aviá Terai, *Argentina* **158 B3** 26 45 S 60 50W
Aviano, *Italy* **39 B9** 46 4N 12 36 E
Avigliana, *Italy* **38 C4** 45 5N 7 23 E
Avigliano, *Italy* **41 B8** 40 44N 15 43 E
Avignon, *France* **25 E8** 43 57N 4 50 E
Ávila, *Spain* **36 E6** 40 39N 4 43W
Ávila □, *Spain* **36 E6** 40 30N 5 0W
Ávila, Sierra de, *Spain* **36 E5** 40 40N 5 15W
Avila Beach, *U.S.A.* **145 K6** 35 11N 120 44W
Avilés, *Spain* **36 B5** 43 35N 5 57W
Avionárion, *Greece* **45 F6** 38 31N 24 8 E
Avísio →, *Italy* **39 B8** 46 7N 11 5 E
Aviston, *U.S.A.* **140 F7** 38 36N 89 36W
Aviz, *Portugal* **37 F3** 39 4N 7 53W
Avize, *France* **23 D11** 48 59N 4 1 E
Avoca, *Ireland* **19 D5** 52 51N 6 13W
Avoca, *U.S.A.* **136 D7** 42 25N 77 25W
Avoca →, *Australia* **116 C5** 35 40 S 143 43 E
Avola, *Canada* **130 C5** 51 45N 119 19W
Avola, *Italy* **41 F8** 36 56N 15 7 E
Avon, *Ill., U.S.A.* **140 D6** 40 40N 90 26W
Avon, *N.Y., U.S.A.* **136 D7** 42 55N 77 45W
Avon, *S. Dak., U.S.A.* **138 D5** 43 0N 98 4W
Avon →, *Australia* **113 F2** 31 40 S 116 7 E
Avon →, *Bristol, U.K.* **17 F5** 51 29N 2 41W
Avon →, *Dorset, U.K.* **17 G6** 50 44N 1 46W
Avon →, *Warks., U.K.* **17 F5** 52 10N 1 51W
Avondale, *Zimbabwe* **107 F3** 17 43 S 30 58 E
Avonlea, *Canada* **131 D7** 50 0N 105 0W
Avonmore, *Canada* **137 A10** 45 10N 74 58W
Avonmouth, *U.K.* **17 F5** 51 30N 2 42W
Avramov, *Bulgaria* **43 E11** 42 45N 26 38 E
Avranches, *France* **22 D5** 48 40N 1 20W
Avre →, *France* **22 D8** 48 47N 1 22 E
Avrig, *Romania* **46 D5** 45 43N 24 21 E
Avtovac, *Bos.-H.* **42 D3** 43 9N 18 35 E
Avu Avu, *Solomon Is.* **121 M11** 9 50 S 160 22 E
Awag el Baqar, *Sudan* **95 E3** 10 10N 33 10 E
A'waj →, *Syria* **91 B5** 33 23N 36 20 E
Awaji, *Japan* **63 C7** 34 32N 135 1 E
Awaji-Shima, *Japan* **62 C6** 34 30N 134 50 E
'Awālī, *Bahrain* **85 E6** 26 0N 50 30 E
Awantipur, *India* **81 C6** 33 55N 75 3 E
Awanui, *N.Z.* **118 B2** 35 4 S 173 17 E
Awarja →, *India* **82 F3** 17 5N 76 15 E
Awarua B., *N.Z.* **119 E3** 44 28 S 168 4 E
Awarua Pt., *N.Z.* **119 E3** 44 15 S 168 5 E
Awasa, L., *Ethiopia* **95 F4** 7 0N 38 30 E
Awash, *Ethiopia* **90 F3** 9 1N 40 10 E
Awash →, *Ethiopia* **95 E5** 11 45N 41 5 E
Awaso, *Ghana* **100 D4** 6 15N 2 22W
Awatere →, *N.Z.* **119 B9** 41 37 S 174 10 E
Awbārī, *Libya* **96 C2** 26 46N 12 57 E
Awbārī □, *Libya* **96 C2** 26 35N 12 46 E
Awe, L., *U.K.* **18 E3** 56 17N 5 16W
Aweil, *Sudan* **95 F2** 8 42N 27 20 E
Awgu, *Nigeria* **101 D6** 6 4N 7 24 E
Awjilah, *Libya* **96 C4** 29 8N 21 7 E
Aworro, *Papua N. G.* **120 D2** 7 43 S 143 11 E
Ax-les-Thermes, *France* **24 F5** 42 44N 1 50 E
Axel, *Neths.* **21 F3** 51 16N 3 55 E
Axel Heiberg I., *Canada* **124 A10** 80 0N 90 0W
Axim, *Ghana* **100 E4** 4 51N 2 15W
Axinim, *Brazil* **153 D6** 4 2 S 59 22W
Axintele, *Romania* **46 E7** 44 37N 26 47 E
Axioma, *Brazil* **157 B5** 6 45 S 64 31W
Axiós →, *Greece* **44 D4** 40 57N 22 35 E
Axminster, *U.K.* **17 G4** 50 46N 3 0W
Axvall, *Sweden* **15 F7** 58 23N 13 34 E
Aÿ, *France* **23 C11** 49 3N 4 1 E
Ay →, *Russia* **54 C6** 56 8N 57 40 E
Ayaantang, *Eq. Guin.* **102 B2** 1 58N 10 24 E
Ayabaca, *Peru* **156 A2** 4 40 S 79 53W
Ayabe, *Japan* **63 B7** 35 20N 135 20 E
Ayacucho, *Argentina* **158 D4** 37 5 S 58 20W
Ayacucho, *Peru* **156 C3** 13 0 S 74 0W
Ayaguz, *Kazakstan* **56 E9** 48 10N 80 10 E
Ayakkuduk, *Uzbekistan* **55 C2** 41 12N 65 12 E
Ayakudi, *India* **83 J3** 10 28N 77 56 E
Ayala, *Phil.* **71 H3** 6 57N 121 57 E
Ayamonte, *Spain* **37 H3** 37 12N 7 24W
Ayan, *Russia* **57 D14** 56 30N 138 16 E
Ayancık, *Turkey* **88 B6** 41 57N 34 35 E
Ayapel, *Colombia* **152 B2** 8 19N 75 9W
Ayas, *Turkey* **88 B5** 40 2N 32 21 E
Ayaviri, *Peru* **156 C3** 14 50 S 70 35W
Āybak, *Afghan.* **79 A3** 36 15N 68 5 E
Aybastı, *Turkey* **88 B7** 40 41N 37 23 E
Aydim, W. →, *Oman* **87 C6** 18 8N 53 8 E
Aydın, *Turkey* **88 D2** 37 51N 27 51 E
Aydyrlinskiy, *Russia* **54 E7** 52 3N 59 50 E
Aye, *Belgium* **21 H6** 50 14N 5 18 E
Ayenngré, *Togo* **101 D5** 8 40N 1 1 E
Ayer's Cliff, *Canada* **137 A12** 45 10N 72 3W
Ayers Rock, *Australia* **113 E5** 25 23 S 131 5 E
Ayiá, *Greece* **44 E4** 39 43N 22 45 E
Ayia Aikateríni, Ákra, *Greece* **32 A3** 39 50N 19 50 E
Ayía Ánna, *Greece* **45 F5** 38 52N 23 24 E
Ayia Dhéka, *Greece* **32 D6** 35 3N 24 58 E
Ayia Gálini, *Greece* **32 D6** 35 6N 24 41 E
Ayía Marína, *Kásos, Greece* **45 J8** 35 27N 26 53 E
Ayía Marína, *Leros, Greece* **45 G8** 37 11N 26 48 E
Ayia Napa, *Cyprus* **32 E13** 34 59N 34 0 E
Ayía Paraskeví, *Greece* **44 E8** 39 14N 26 16 E
Ayia Phyla, *Cyprus* **32 E12** 34 43N 33 1 E
Ayía Rouméli, *Greece* **45 J5** 35 14N 23 58 E
Ayia Varvára, *Greece* **32 D7** 35 8N 25 1 E
Ayiássos, *Greece* **45 E8** 39 5N 26 23 E
Áyion Óros, *Greece* **44 D6** 40 25N 24 6 E
Áyios Amvrósios, *Cyprus* **32 D12** 35 20N 33 35 E
Áyios Andréas, *Greece* **45 G4** 37 21N 22 45 E
Áyios Evstrátios, *Greece* **44 E6** 39 34N 24 58 E
Áyios Ioánnis, Ákra, *Greece* **32 D7** 35 20N 25 40 E
Áyios Isidhoros, *Greece* **32 C9** 36 9N 27 51 E
Áyios Kiríkos, *Greece* **45 G8** 37 34N 26 17 E
Áyios Matthaíos, *Greece* **32 B3** 39 30N 19 47 E
Áyios Mírono, *Greece* **45 J7** 35 15N 25 1 E
Áyios Nikólaos, *Greece* **32 D7** 35 11N 25 41 E
Áyios Pétros, *Greece* **45 F2** 38 38N 20 33 E
Áyios Seryios, *Cyprus* **32 D12** 35 12N 33 53 E
Ayios Theodhoros, *Cyprus* **32 D13** 35 22N 34 1 E
Áyios Yeóryios, *Greece* **45 G5** 37 28N 23 57 E
Aykathonisi, *Greece* **45 G8** 37 28N 27 0 E
Aykino, *Russia* **48 B8** 62 15N 49 56 E
Aylesbury, *U.K.* **17 F7** 51 49N 0 49W
Aylmer, *Canada* **136 D4** 42 46N 80 59W
Aylmer, L., *Canada* **126 B8** 64 0N 110 8W
'Ayn al Ghazālah, *Libya* **96 B4** 32 10N 23 20 E
Ayn Zālah, *Iraq* **89 D10** 36 45N 42 35 E
Ayna, *Spain* **35 G2** 38 34N 2 3W
Aynāt, *Yemen* **87 C5** 16 4N 49 9 E
Ayni, *Tajikistan* **55 D4** 39 23N 68 32 E
Ayolas, *Paraguay* **158 B4** 27 10 S 56 59W
Ayom, *Sudan* **95 F2** 7 49N 28 23 E
Ayon, Ostrov, *Russia* **57 C17** 69 50N 169 0 E
Ayora, *Spain* **35 F3** 39 3N 1 3W
Ayr, *Australia* **114 B4** 19 35 S 147 25 E
Ayr, *U.K.* **18 F4** 55 28N 4 38W
Ayr →, *U.K.* **18 F4** 55 28N 4 38W
Ayrancı, *Turkey* **88 D5** 37 21N 33 41 E
Ayre, Pt. of, *U.K.* **16 C3** 54 25N 4 21W
Aysha, *Ethiopia* **95 E5** 10 50N 42 23 E
Aytos, *Bulgaria* **43 E12** 42 42N 27 16 E
Aytoska Planina, *Bulgaria* **43 E12** 42 45N 27 30 E
Ayu, Kepulauan, *Indonesia* **73 A4** 0 35N 131 5 E
Ayutla, *Guatemala* **148 D1** 14 40N 92 10W
Ayutla, *Mexico* **147 D5** 16 58N 99 17W
Ayvacık, *Turkey* **88 C2** 39 36N 26 24 E
Ayvalık, *Turkey* **88 C2** 39 20N 26 46 E
Aywaille, *Belgium* **21 H7** 50 28N 5 40 E
Az Zabdānī, *Syria* **91 B5** 33 43N 36 5 E
Aẓ Ẓāhirīyah, *West Bank* **91 D3** 31 25N 34 58 E
Aẓ Ẓahrān, *Si. Arabia* **85 E6** 26 10N 50 7 E
Az Zarqā, *Jordan* **91 C5** 32 5N 36 4 E
Az Zāwiyah, *Libya* **96 B2** 32 52N 12 56 E
Az Zaydīyah, *Yemen* **86 D3** 15 20N 43 1 E
Az Zībār, *Iraq* **89 D11** 36 52N 44 4 E
Az-Zilfī, *Si. Arabia* **84 E5** 26 12N 44 52 E
Az Zubayr, *Iraq* **84 D5** 30 26N 47 40 E
Az Zuqur, *Yemen* **86 D3** 14 0N 42 45 E
Az Zuwaytīnah, *Libya* **96 B4** 30 58N 20 7 E
Azambuja, *Portugal* **37 F2** 39 4N 8 51W
Azamgarh, *India* **81 F10** 26 5N 83 13 E
Azangaro, *Peru* **156 C3** 14 55 S 70 13W
Azaouak, Vallée de l', *Mali* **101 B5** 15 50N 3 20 E
Āzār Shahr, *Iran* **89 D11** 37 45N 45 59 E
Azarān, *Iran* **89 D12** 37 25N 47 16 E
Azärbayjan = Azerbaijan ■, *Asia* **53 K9** 40 20N 48 0 E
Āzarbāyjān-e Gharbī □, *Iran* **84 B5** 37 0N 44 30 E
Āzarbāyjān-e Sharqī □, *Iran* **84 B5** 37 20N 47 0 E
Azare, *Nigeria* **101 C7** 11 55N 10 10 E
Azay-le-Rideau, *France* **22 E7** 47 16N 0 30 E
A'zāz, *Syria* **88 D7** 36 36N 37 4 E
Azazga, *Algeria* **99 A5** 36 48N 4 22 E
Azbine = Aïr, *Niger* **97 E1** 18 30N 8 0 E
Azefal, *Mauritania* **98 D2** 21 0N 14 45W
Azeffoun, *Algeria* **99 A5** 36 51N 4 26 E
Azemmour, *Morocco* **98 B3** 33 20N 9 20W
Azerbaijan ■, *Asia* **53 K9** 40 20N 48 0 E
Azerbaijchan = Azerbaijan ■, *Asia* **53 K9** 40 20N 48 0 E
Azezo, *Ethiopia* **95 E4** 12 28N 37 15 E

Barbacoas 171

Balaton, *Hungary* **31 E10** 46 50N 17 40 E
Balatonfüred, *Hungary* **31 E10** 46 58N 17 54 E
Balatonszentgyörgy, *Hungary* **31 E10** 46 41N 17 19 E
Balayan, *Phil.* **70 E3** 13 57N 120 44 E
Balazote, *Spain* **35 G2** 38 54N 2 9W
Balbalan, *Phil.* **70 C3** 17 27N 121 12 E
Balbi, Mt., *Papua N. G.* **120 C8** 5 55 S 154 58 E
Balbina, Reprêsa de, *Brazil* **153 D6** 2 0 S 59 30W
Balboa, *Panama* **148 E4** 8 57N 79 34W
Balbriggan, *Ireland* **19 C5** 53 37N 6 11W
Balcarce, *Argentina* **158 D4** 38 0 S 58 10W
Balcarres, *Canada* **131 C8** 50 50N 103 35W
Balchik, *Bulgaria* **43 D13** 43 28N 28 11 E
Balclutha, *N.Z.* **119 G4** 46 15 S 169 45 E
Bald Hd., *Australia* **113 G2** 35 6 S 118 1 E
Bald I., *Australia* **113 F2** 34 57 S 118 27 E
Bald Knob, *U.S.A.* **139 H9** 35 19N 91 34W
Baldock L., *Canada* **131 B9** 56 33N 97 57W
Baldwin, *Fla., U.S.A.* **135 K4** 30 18N 81 59W
Baldwin, *Mich., U.S.A.* **134 D3** 43 54N 85 51W
Baldwinsville, *U.S.A.* **137 C8** 43 10N 76 20W
Baldy Peak, *U.S.A.* **143 K9** 33 54N 109 34W
Bale, *Croatia* **39 C10** 45 4N 13 46 E
Bale □, *Ethiopia* **95 F5** 6 20N 41 30 E
Baleares □, *Spain* **34 F7** 39 30N 3 0 E
Baleares, Is., *Spain* **33 B10** 39 30N 3 0 E
Balearic Is. = Baleares, Is., *Spain* **33 B10** 39 30N 3 0 E
Baleia, Pta. da, *Brazil* **155 E4** 17 40 S 39 7W
Balen, *Belgium* **21 F6** 51 10N 5 10 E
Băleni, *Romania* **46 D8** 45 48N 27 51 E
Baler, *Phil.* **70 D3** 15 46N 121 34 E
Baler Bay, *Phil.* **70 D3** 15 50N 121 35 E
Balerna, *Switz.* **29 E8** 45 52N 9 0 E
Baleshwar, *India* **82 D8** 21 35N 87 3 E
Balezino, *Russia* **52 B11** 58 2N 53 6 E
Balfate, *Honduras* **148 C2** 15 48N 86 25W
Balfe's Creek, *Australia* **114 C4** 20 12 S 145 55 E
Balfour Channel, *Solomon Is.* **121 M9** 8 43 S 157 27 E
Balharshah, *India* **82 E4** 19 50N 79 23 E
Bali, *Cameroon* **101 D6** 5 54N 10 0 E
Balí, *Greece* **32 D6** 35 25N 24 47 E
Bali, *Indonesia* **75 D4** 8 20 S 115 0 E
Bali □, *Indonesia* **75 D4** 8 20 S 115 0 E
Bali, Selat, *Indonesia* **75 D4** 8 18 S 114 25 E
Balicuatro Is., *Phil.* **70 E5** 12 39N 124 24 E
Baligród, *Poland* **31 B15** 49 20N 22 17 E
Balikeşir, *Turkey* **88 C2** 39 35N 27 58 E
Balikpapan, *Indonesia* **75 C5** 1 10 S 116 55 E
Balimbing, *Phil.* **71 J2** 5 5N 119 58 E
Balimo, *Papua N. G.* **120 E2** 8 6 S 142 57 E
Baling, *Malaysia* **77 K3** 5 41N 100 55 E
Balintang Channel, *Phil.* **70 B3** 19 49N 121 40 E
Balintang Is., *Phil.* **70 B4** 19 58N 122 9 E
Baliton, *Phil.* **71 J5** 5 44N 125 14 E
Baliza, *Brazil* **157 D7** 16 0 S 52 20W
Baljurshi, *Si. Arabia* **86 C3** 19 51N 41 33 E
Balk, *Neths.* **20 C7** 52 54N 5 35 E
Balkan Mts. = Stara Planina, *Bulgaria* **43 D8** 43 15N 23 0 E
Balkh □, *Afghan.* **79 A2** 36 50N 67 0 E
Balkhash = Balqash, *Kazakstan* **56 E8** 46 50N 74 50 E
Balkhash, Ozero = Balqash Köl, *Kazakstan* **56 E8** 46 0N 74 50 E
Ballachulish, *U.K.* **18 E3** 56 41N 5 8W
Balladonia, *Australia* **113 F3** 32 27 S 123 51 E
Ballara, *Australia* **116 B4** 32 19 S 140 45 E
Ballarat, *Australia* **115 F3** 37 33 S 143 50 E
Ballard, L., *Australia* **113 E3** 29 20 S 120 40 E
Ballater, *U.K.* **18 D5** 57 3N 3 3W
Balldale, *Australia* **117 C7** 35 50 S 146 33 E
Ballenas, Canal de, *Mexico* **146 B2** 29 10N 113 45W
Balleny Is., *Antarctica* **7 C11** 66 30 S 163 0 E
Ballesteros, *Phil.* **70 B3** 18 25N 121 31 E
Ballia, *India* **81 G11** 25 46N 84 12 E
Ballidu, *Australia* **113 F2** 30 35 S 116 45 E
Ballina, *Australia* **115 D5** 28 50 S 153 31 E
Ballina, *Mayo, Ireland* **19 B2** 54 7N 9 9W
Ballina, *Tipp., Ireland* **19 D3** 52 49N 8 26W
Ballinasloe, *Ireland* **19 C3** 53 20N 8 13W
Ballinger, *U.S.A.* **139 K5** 31 45N 99 57W
Ballinrobe, *Ireland* **19 C2** 53 38N 9 13W
Ballinskelligs B., *Ireland* **19 E1** 51 48N 10 13W
Ballon, *France* **22 D7** 48 10N 0 14 E
Ballycastle, *U.K.* **19 A5** 55 12N 6 15W
Ballymena, *U.K.* **19 B5** 54 52N 6 17W
Ballymena □, *U.K.* **19 B5** 54 53N 6 18W
Ballymoney, *U.K.* **19 A5** 55 5N 6 31W
Ballymoney □, *U.K.* **19 A5** 55 5N 6 23W
Ballyshannon, *Ireland* **19 B3** 54 30N 8 11W
Balmaceda, *Chile* **160 C2** 46 0 S 71 50W
Balmazújváros, *Hungary* **31 D14** 47 37N 21 21 E
Balmhorn, *Switz.* **28 D5** 46 26N 7 42 E
Balmoral, *Australia* **116 D4** 37 15 S 141 48 E
Balmoral, *U.K.* **18 D5** 57 3N 3 13W
Balmorhea, *U.S.A.* **139 K3** 30 59N 103 45W
Balombo, *Angola* **103 E2** 12 21 S 14 46 E
Balonne →, *Australia* **115 D4** 28 47 S 147 56 E
Balqash, *Kazakstan* **56 E8** 46 50N 74 50 E
Balqash Köl, *Kazakstan* **56 E8** 46 0N 74 50 E
Balrampur, *India* **81 F10** 27 30N 82 20 E
Balranald, *Australia* **116 C5** 34 38 S 143 33 E
Balş, *Romania* **46 E5** 44 22N 24 5 E
Balsapuerto, *Peru* **156 B2** 5 48 S 76 33W
Balsas, *Mexico* **147 D5** 18 0N 99 40W
Balsas →, *Maranhão, Brazil* **154 C3** 7 15 S 44 35W
Balsas →, *Tocantins, Brazil* **154 C2** 9 58 S 47 52W
Balsas →, *Mexico* **146 D4** 17 55N 102 10W
Bålsta, *Sweden* **14 E11** 59 35N 17 30 E
Balsthal, *Switz.* **28 B5** 47 19N 7 41 E
Balston Spa, *U.S.A.* **137 D11** 43 0N 73 52W
Balta, *Romania* **46 E3** 44 54N 22 38 E
Balta, *Ukraine* **51 H5** 48 2N 29 45 E
Balta, *U.S.A.* **138 A4** 48 10N 100 2W
Baltanás, *Spain* **36 D6** 41 56N 4 15W
Bălţi, *Moldova* **51 J4** 47 48N 28 0 E
Baltic Sea, *Europe* **13 H18** 57 0N 19 0 E
Baltîm, *Egypt* **94 H7** 31 35N 31 10 E
Baltimore, *Ireland* **19 E2** 51 29N 9 22W
Baltimore, *U.S.A.* **134 F7** 39 17N 76 37W
Baltit, *Pakistan* **81 A6** 36 15N 74 40 E
Baltiysk, *Russia* **13 J18** 54 41N 19 58 E
Baltrum, *Germany* **26 B3** 53 43N 7 24 E
Baluchistan □, *Pakistan* **79 D2** 27 30N 65 0 E
Balud, *Phil.* **70 E4** 12 2N 123 12 E
Balurghat, *India* **81 G13** 25 15N 88 44 E
Balvi, *Latvia* **13 H22** 57 8N 27 15 E
Balya, *Turkey* **88 C2** 39 44N 27 35 E
Balygychan, *Russia* **57 C16** 63 56N 154 12 E
Balzar, *Ecuador* **152 D2** 2 2 S 79 54W
Bam, *Iran* **85 D8** 29 7N 58 14 E
Bama, *China* **68 E6** 24 8N 107 12 E
Bama, *Nigeria* **101 C7** 11 33N 13 41 E
Bamako, *Mali* **100 C3** 12 34N 7 55W
Bamba, *Mali* **101 B4** 17 5N 1 24W
Bamba, *Zaïre* **103 D3** 5 45 S 18 23 E
Bambam, *Phil.* **70 D3** 15 40N 120 20 E
Bambamarca, *Peru* **156 B2** 6 36 S 78 32W
Bambang, *Phil.* **70 C3** 16 23N 121 6 E
Bambari, *C.A.R.* **102 A4** 5 40N 20 35 E
Bambaroo, *Australia* **114 B4** 18 50 S 146 10 E
Bamberg, *Germany* **27 F6** 49 54N 10 54 E
Bamberg, *U.S.A.* **135 J5** 33 18N 81 2W
Bambesi, *Ethiopia* **95 F3** 9 45N 34 40 E
Bambey, *Senegal* **100 C1** 14 42N 16 28W
Bambili, *Zaïre* **106 B2** 3 40N 26 0 E
Bambuí, *Brazil* **155 F2** 20 1 S 45 58W
Bamenda, *Cameroon* **101 D7** 5 57N 10 11 E
Bamfield, *Canada* **130 D3** 48 45N 125 10W
Bāmīān □, *Afghan.* **79 B2** 35 0N 67 0 E
Bamiancheng, *China* **67 C13** 43 15N 124 2 E
Bamingui, *C.A.R.* **102 A4** 7 34N 20 11 E
Bamkin, *Cameroon* **101 D7** 6 3N 11 27 E
Bampūr, *Iran* **85 E9** 27 15N 60 21 E
Ban Aranyaprathet, *Thailand* **76 F4** 13 41N 102 30 E
Ban Ban, *Laos* **76 C4** 19 31N 103 30 E
Ban Bang Hin, *Thailand* **77 H2** 9 32N 98 35 E
Ban Chiang Klang, *Thailand* **76 C3** 19 25N 100 55 E
Ban Chik, *Laos* **76 D4** 17 15N 102 22 E
Ban Choho, *Thailand* **76 E4** 15 2N 102 9 E
Ban Dan Lan Hoi, *Thailand* **76 D2** 17 0N 99 35 E
Ban Don = Surat Thani, *Thailand* **77 H2** 9 6N 99 20 E
Ban Don, *Vietnam* **76 F6** 12 53N 107 48 E
Ban Don, Ao, *Thailand* **77 H2** 9 20N 99 25 E
Ban Dong, *Thailand* **76 C3** 19 30N 100 59 E
Ban Hong, *Thailand* **76 C2** 18 18N 98 50 E
Ban Kaeng, *Thailand* **76 D3** 17 29N 100 7 E
Ban Keun, *Laos* **76 C4** 18 22N 102 35 E
Ban Khai, *Thailand* **76 F3** 12 46N 101 18 E
Ban Kheun, *Laos* **76 B3** 20 13N 101 7 E
Ban Khlong Kua, *Thailand* **77 J3** 6 57N 100 8 E
Ban Khuan Mao, *Thailand* **77 J2** 7 50N 99 37 E
Ban Khun Yuam, *Thailand* **76 C1** 18 49N 97 57 E
Ban Ko Yai Chim, *Thailand* **77 G2** 11 17N 99 26 E
Ban Kok, *Thailand* **76 D4** 16 40N 103 40 E
Ban Laem, *Thailand* **76 F2** 13 13N 99 59 E
Ban Lao Ngam, *Laos* **76 E6** 15 28N 106 10 E
Ban Le Kathe, *Thailand* **76 E2** 15 49N 98 53 E
Ban Mae Chedi, *Thailand* **76 C2** 19 11N 99 31 E
Ban Mae Laeng, *Thailand* **76 B2** 20 1N 99 17 E
Ban Mae Sariang, *Thailand* **76 C1** 18 10N 97 56 E
Ban Mê Thuôt = Buon Me Thuot, *Vietnam* **76 F7** 12 40N 108 3 E
Ban Mi, *Thailand* **76 E3** 15 3N 100 32 E
Ban Muong Mo, *Laos* **76 C4** 19 4N 103 58 E
Ban Na Mo, *Laos* **76 D5** 17 7N 105 40 E
Ban Na San, *Thailand* **77 H2** 8 53N 99 52 E
Ban Na Tong, *Laos* **76 B3** 20 56N 101 47 E
Ban Nam Bac, *Laos* **76 B4** 20 38N 102 20 E
Ban Nam Ma, *Laos* **76 A3** 22 2N 101 37 E
Ban Ngang, *Laos* **76 E6** 15 59N 106 11 E
Ban Nong Bok, *Laos* **76 D5** 17 5N 104 48 E
Ban Nong Boua, *Laos* **76 E6** 15 40N 106 33 E
Ban Nong Pling, *Thailand* **76 E3** 15 40N 100 10 E
Ban Pak Chan, *Thailand* **77 G2** 10 32N 98 51 E
Ban Phai, *Thailand* **76 D4** 16 4N 102 44 E
Ban Pong, *Thailand* **76 F2** 13 50N 99 55 E
Ban Ron Phibun, *Thailand* **77 H2** 8 9N 99 51 E
Ban Sanam Chai, *Thailand* **77 J3** 7 33N 100 25 E
Ban Sangkha, *Thailand* **76 E4** 14 37N 103 52 E
Ban Tak, *Thailand* **76 D2** 17 2N 99 4 E
Ban Tako, *Thailand* **76 E4** 14 5N 102 40 E
Ban Tha Dua, *Thailand* **76 D2** 17 59N 98 39 E
Ban Tha Li, *Thailand* **76 D3** 17 37N 101 25 E
Ban Tha Nun, *Thailand* **77 H2** 8 12N 98 18 E
Ban Thahine, *Laos* **76 E5** 14 12N 105 33 E
Ban Xien Kok, *Laos* **76 B3** 20 54N 100 39 E
Ban Yen Nhan, *Vietnam* **76 B6** 20 57N 106 2 E
Baña, Punta de la, *Spain* **34 E5** 40 33N 0 40 E
Banā, W. →, *Yemen* **86 D4** 13 3N 45 24 E
Banaba, *Kiribati* **122 H8** 0 45 S 169 50 E
Bañalbufar, *Spain* **33 B9** 39 42N 2 31 E
Banalia, *Zaïre* **106 B2** 1 32N 25 5 E
Banam, *Cambodia* **77 G5** 11 20N 105 17 E
Banamba, *Mali* **100 C3** 13 29N 7 22W
Banana, *Australia* **114 C5** 24 28 S 150 8 E
Bananal, I. do, *Brazil* **155 D1** 11 30 S 50 30W
Banaras = Varanasi, *India* **81 G10** 25 22N 83 0 E
Banas →, *Gujarat, India* **80 H4** 23 45N 71 25 E
Banas →, *Mad. P., India* **81 G9** 24 15N 81 30 E
Bânâs, Ras, *Egypt* **94 C4** 23 57N 35 50 E
Banaz, *Turkey* **88 C3** 38 44N 29 46 E
Banbān, *Si. Arabia* **84 E5** 25 1N 46 35 E
Banbridge, *U.K.* **19 B5** 54 22N 6 16W
Banbridge □, *U.K.* **19 B5** 54 21N 6 16W
Banbury, *U.K.* **17 E6** 52 4N 1 20W
Banchory, *U.K.* **18 D6** 57 3N 2 29W
Bancroft, *Canada* **128 C4** 45 3N 77 51W
Band, *Romania* **46 C5** 46 30N 24 25 E
Band Bonī, *Iran* **85 E8** 25 30N 59 33 E
Band-e Torkestān, *Afghan.* **79 B2** 35 30N 64 0 E
Band Qīr, *Iran* **85 D6** 31 39N 48 53 E
Banda, *Cameroon* **102 B2** 3 58N 14 32 E
Banda, *India* **81 G9** 25 30N 80 26 E
Banda, Kepulauan, *Indonesia* **73 B3** 4 37 S 129 50 E
Banda Aceh, *Indonesia* **74 A1** 5 35N 95 20 E
Banda Banda, Mt., *Australia* **117 A10** 31 10 S 152 28 E
Banda Elat, *Indonesia* **73 C4** 5 40 S 133 5 E
Banda Is. = Banda, Kepulauan, *Indonesia* **73 B3** 4 37 S 129 50 E
Banda Sea, *Indonesia* **72 C3** 6 0 S 130 0 E
Bandai-San, *Japan* **60 F10** 37 36N 140 4 E
Bandama →, *Ivory C.* **100 D3** 6 32N 5 30W
Bandān, *Iran* **85 D9** 31 23N 60 44 E
Bandanaira, *Indonesia* **73 B3** 4 32 S 129 54 E
Bandanwara, *India* **80 F6** 26 9N 74 38 E
Bandar = Machilipatnam, *India* **83 F5** 16 12N 81 8 E
Bandār 'Abbās, *Iran* **85 E8** 27 15N 56 15 E
Bandar-e Anzalī, *Iran* **89 D13** 37 30N 49 30 E
Bandar-e Bushehr = Būshehr, *Iran* **85 D6** 28 55N 50 55 E
Bandar-e Chārak, *Iran* **85 E7** 26 45N 54 20 E
Bandar-e Deylam, *Iran* **85 D6** 30 5N 50 10 E
Bandar-e Khomeynı, *Iran* **85 D6** 30 30N 49 5 E
Bandar-e Lengeh, *Iran* **85 E7** 26 35N 54 58 E
Bandar-e Maqām, *Iran* **85 E7** 26 56N 53 29 E
Bandar-e Ma'shur, *Iran* **85 D6** 30 35N 49 10 E
Bandar-e Nakhīlū, *Iran* **85 E7** 26 58N 53 30 E
Bandar-e Rīg, *Iran* **85 D6** 29 29N 50 38 E
Bandar-e Torkeman, *Iran* **85 B7** 37 0N 54 10 E
Bandar Maharani = Muar, *Malaysia* **77 L4** 2 3N 102 34 E
Bandar Penggaram = Batu Pahat, *Malaysia* **77 M4** 1 50N 102 56 E
Bandar Seri Begawan, *Brunei* **75 B4** 4 52N 115 0 E
Bandawe, *Malawi* **107 E3** 11 58 S 34 5 E
Bande, *Belgium* **21 H6** 50 10N 5 25 E
Bande, *Spain* **36 C3** 42 3N 7 58W
Bandeira, Pico da, *Brazil* **155 F3** 20 26 S 41 47W
Bandeirante, *Brazil* **155 D1** 13 41 S 50 48W
Bandera, *Argentina* **158 B3** 28 55 S 62 20W
Bandera, *U.S.A.* **139 L5** 29 44N 99 5W
Banderas, B. de, *Mexico* **146 C3** 20 40N 105 30W
Bandia →, *India* **82 E5** 19 2N 80 28 E
Bandiagara, *Mali* **100 C4** 14 12N 3 29W
Bandırma, *Turkey* **88 B3** 40 20N 28 0 E
Bandon, *Ireland* **19 E3** 51 44N 8 44W
Bandon →, *Ireland* **19 E3** 51 43N 8 37W
Bandoua, *C.A.R.* **102 B4** 4 39N 21 42 E
Bandula, *Mozam.* **107 F3** 19 0 S 33 7 E
Bandundu, *Zaïre* **102 C3** 3 15 S 17 22 E
Bandung, *Indonesia* **75 D3** 6 54 S 107 36 E
Bandya, *Australia* **113 E3** 27 40 S 122 5 E
Băneasa, *Romania* **46 D8** 45 56N 27 55 E
Bāneh, *Iran* **89 E11** 35 59N 45 53 E
Bañeres, *Spain* **35 G4** 38 44N 0 38W
Banes, *Cuba* **149 B4** 21 0N 75 42W
Banff, *Canada* **130 C5** 51 10N 115 34W
Banff, *U.K.* **18 D6** 57 40N 2 33W
Banff Nat. Park, *Canada* **130 C5** 51 30N 116 15W
Banfora, *Burkina Faso* **100 C4** 10 40N 4 40W
Bang Fai →, *Laos* **76 D5** 16 57N 104 45 E
Bang Hieng →, *Laos* **76 D5** 16 10N 105 10 E
Bang Krathum, *Thailand* **76 D3** 16 34N 100 18 E
Bang Lamung, *Thailand* **76 F3** 13 3N 100 56 E
Bang Mun Nak, *Thailand* **76 D3** 16 2N 100 23 E
Bang Pa In, *Thailand* **76 E3** 14 14N 100 35 E
Bang Rakam, *Thailand* **76 D3** 16 45N 100 7 E
Bang Saphan, *Thailand* **77 G2** 11 14N 99 28 E
Bangala Dam, *Zimbabwe* **107 G3** 21 7 S 31 25 E
Bangalore, *India* **83 H3** 12 59N 77 40 E
Bangante, *Cameroon* **101 D7** 5 8N 10 32 E
Bangaon, *India* **81 H13** 23 0N 88 47 E
Bangassou, *C.A.R.* **102 B4** 4 55N 23 7 E
Bangeta, Mt., *Papua N. G.* **120 D4** 6 21 S 147 3 E
Banggai, Kepulauan, *Indonesia* **72 B2** 1 40 S 123 30 E
Banggai Arch., *Indonesia* **72 B2** 2 0 S 123 15 E
Banggi, P., *Malaysia* **75 A5** 7 17N 117 12 E
Banghāzī, *Libya* **96 B4** 32 11N 20 3 E
Banghāzī □, *Libya* **96 B4** 32 7N 20 4 E
Bangil, *Indonesia* **75 D4** 7 36 S 112 50 E
Bangjang, *Sudan* **95 E3** 11 23N 32 41 E
Bangka, P., *Sulawesi, Indonesia* **72 A3** 1 50N 125 5 E
Bangka, P., *Sumatera, Indonesia* **74 C3** 2 0 S 105 50 E
Bangka, Selat, *Indonesia* **74 C3** 2 30 S 105 30 E
Bangkalan, *Indonesia* **75 D4** 7 2 S 112 46 E
Bangkinang, *Indonesia* **74 B2** 0 18N 101 5 E
Bangko, *Indonesia* **74 C2** 2 5 S 102 9 E
Bangkok, *Thailand* **76 F3** 13 45N 100 35 E
Bangladesh ■, *Asia* **78 C3** 24 0N 90 0 E
Bangolo, *Ivory C.* **100 D3** 7 1N 7 29W
Bangong Co, *India* **81 B8** 35 50N 79 20 E
Bangor, *Down, U.K.* **19 B6** 54 40N 5 40W
Bangor, *Gwynedd, U.K.* **16 D3** 53 14N 4 8W
Bangor, *Maine, U.S.A.* **129 D6** 44 48N 68 46W
Bangor, *Mich., U.S.A.* **141 B10** 42 18N 86 7W
Bangor, *Pa., U.S.A.* **137 F9** 40 52N 75 13W
Bangu, *Zaïre* **102 C3** 0 3 S 19 12 E
Bangued, *Phil.* **70 C3** 17 40N 120 37 E
Bangui, *C.A.R.* **102 B3** 4 23N 18 35 E
Bangui, *Phil.* **70 B3** 18 32N 120 46 E
Banguru, *Zaïre* **106 B2** 0 30N 27 10 E
Bangweulu, L., *Zambia* **107 E3** 11 0 S 30 0 E
Bangweulu Swamp, *Zambia* **107 E3** 11 20 S 30 15 E
Bani, *Dom. Rep.* **149 C5** 18 16N 70 22W
Bani, *Phil.* **70 C2** 16 11N 119 52 E
Bani →, *Mali* **100 C4** 14 30N 4 12W
Bani, Djebel, *Morocco* **98 C3** 29 16N 8 0W
Bani Bangou, *Niger* **101 B5** 15 3N 2 42 E
Banī Sa'd, *Iraq* **89 F11** 33 34N 44 32 E
Banī Sār, *Si. Arabia* **86 B3** 20 6N 41 27 E
Banī Walīd, *Libya* **96 B2** 31 36N 13 53 E
Bania, *Ivory C.* **100 D4** 9 4N 3 6W
Baniara, *Papua N. G.* **120 E5** 9 44 S 149 54 E
Banihal Pass, *India* **81 C6** 33 30N 75 12 E
Banīnah, *Libya* **96 B4** 32 0N 20 12 E
Bāniyās, *Syria* **88 E6** 35 10N 36 0 E
Banja Luka, *Bos.-H.* **42 C2** 44 49N 17 11 E
Banjar, *Indonesia* **75 D3** 7 24 S 108 30 E
Banjarmasin, *Indonesia* **75 C4** 3 20 S 114 35 E
Banjarnegara, *Indonesia* **75 D3** 7 24 S 109 42 E
Banjul, *Gambia* **100 C1** 13 28N 16 40W
Banka Banka, *Australia* **114 B1** 18 50 S 134 0 E
Banket, *Zimbabwe* **107 F3** 17 27 S 30 19 E
Bankilaré, *Niger* **101 C5** 14 35N 0 44 E
Bankipore, *India* **81 G11** 25 35N 85 10 E
Banks, Is., *Vanuatu* **121 C5** 13 50 S 167 30 E
Banks I., *B.C., Canada* **130 C3** 53 20N 130 0W
Banks I., *N.W.T., Canada* **126 A7** 73 15N 121 30W
Banks I., *Papua N. G.* **120 F2** 10 10 S 142 15 E
Banks Pen., *N.Z.* **119 D8** 43 45 S 173 15 E
Banks Str., *Australia* **114 G4** 40 40 S 148 10 E
Bankura, *India* **81 H12** 23 11N 87 18 E
Bankya, *Bulgaria* **42 E8** 42 43N 23 8 E
Bann →, *Arm., U.K.* **19 B5** 54 30N 6 31W
Bann →, *L'derry., U.K.* **19 A5** 55 8N 6 41W
Banna, *Phil.* **70 C3** 17 59N 120 39 E
Bannalec, *France* **22 E3** 47 57N 3 42W
Bannang Sata, *Thailand* **77 J3** 6 16N 101 16 E
Bannerton, *Australia* **116 C5** 34 42 S 142 47 E
Banning, *U.S.A.* **145 M10** 33 56N 116 53W
Banningville = Bandundu, *Zaïre* **102 C3** 3 15 S 17 22 E
Bannockburn, *Canada* **136 B7** 44 39N 77 33W
Bannockburn, *U.K.* **18 E5** 56 5N 3 55W
Bannockburn, *Zimbabwe* **107 G2** 20 17 S 29 48 E
Bannu, *Pakistan* **79 B3** 33 0N 70 18 E
Bañolas, *Spain* **34 C7** 42 16N 2 44 E
Banon, *France* **25 D9** 44 2N 5 38 E
Baños de la Encina, *Spain* **37 G7** 38 10N 3 46W
Baños de Molgas, *Spain* **36 C3** 42 15N 7 40W
Bánovce, *Slovak Rep.* **31 C11** 48 44N 18 16 E
Bansilan □, *Phil.* **71 H3** 6 40N 121 40 E
Banská Bystrica, *Slovak Rep.* **31 C12** 48 46N 19 14 E
Banská Štiavnica, *Slovak Rep.* **31 C11** 48 25N 18 55 E
Bansko, *Bulgaria* **43 F8** 41 52N 23 28 E
Banswara, *India* **80 H6** 23 32N 74 24 E
Bantayan, *Phil.* **71 F4** 11 10N 123 43 E
Bantayan I., *Phil.* **71 F4** 11 13N 123 44 E
Banten, *Indonesia* **74 D3** 6 5 S 106 8 E
Banton I., *Phil.* **70 E4** 12 56N 122 4 E
Bantry, *Ireland* **19 E2** 51 41N 9 27W
Bantry B., *Ireland* **19 E2** 51 37N 9 44W
Bantul, *Indonesia* **75 D4** 7 55 S 110 19 E
Bantva, *India* **80 J4** 21 29N 70 12 E
Bantval, *India* **83 H2** 12 55N 75 0 E
Banya, *Bulgaria* **43 E9** 42 33N 24 50 E
Banyak, Kepulauan, *Indonesia* **74 B1** 2 10N 97 10 E
Banyo, *Cameroon* **101 D7** 6 52N 11 45 E
Banyuls-sur-Mer, *France* **24 F7** 42 28N 3 8 E
Banyumas, *Indonesia* **75 D3** 7 32 S 109 18 E
Banyuwangi, *Indonesia* **75 D4** 8 13 S 114 21 E
Banzare Coast, *Antarctica* **7 C9** 68 0 S 125 0 E
Banzyville = Mobayi, *Zaïre* **102 B4** 4 15N 21 8 E
Bao Ha, *Vietnam* **76 A5** 22 11N 104 21 E
Bao Lac, *Vietnam* **76 A5** 22 57N 105 40 E
Bao Loc, *Vietnam* **77 G6** 11 32N 107 48 E
Bao'an = Shenzhen, *China* **69 F10** 22 27N 114 10 E
Baocheng, *China* **66 H4** 33 12N 106 56 E
Baode, *China* **66 E6** 39 1N 111 5 E
Baodi, *China* **67 E9** 39 38N 117 20 E
Baoding, *China* **66 E8** 38 50N 115 28 E
Baoji, *China* **66 G4** 34 20N 107 5 E
Baojing, *China* **68 C7** 28 45N 109 41 E
Baokang, *China* **69 B8** 31 54N 111 12 E
Baoro, *C.A.R.* **102 A3** 5 40N 15 58 E
Baoshan, *Shanghai, China* **69 B13** 31 27N 121 26 E
Baoshan, *Yunnan, China* **68 E2** 25 10N 99 5 E
Baotou, *China* **66 D6** 40 32N 110 2 E
Baoying, *China* **67 H10** 33 17N 119 20 E
Bap, *India* **80 F5** 27 23N 72 18 E
Bapatla, *India* **83 G5** 15 55N 80 30 E
Bapaume, *France* **23 B9** 50 7N 2 50 E
Bāqerābād, *Iran* **85 C6** 33 2N 51 58 E
Ba'qūbah, *Iraq* **89 F11** 33 45N 44 50 E
Baquedano, *Chile* **158 A2** 23 20 S 69 52W
Bar, *Montenegro, Yug.* **42 E4** 42 8N 19 8 E
Bar, *Ukraine* **51 H4** 49 4N 27 40 E
Bar Bigha, *India* **81 G11** 25 21N 85 47 E
Bar Harbor, *U.S.A.* **129 D6** 44 23N 68 13W
Bar-le-Duc, *France* **23 D12** 48 47N 5 10 E
Bar-sur-Aube, *France* **23 D11** 48 14N 4 40 E
Bar-sur-Seine, *France* **23 D11** 48 7N 4 20 E
Barabai, *Indonesia* **75 C5** 2 32 S 115 34 E
Barabinsk, *Russia* **56 D8** 55 20N 78 20 E
Baraboo, *U.S.A.* **138 D10** 43 28N 89 45W
Baracaldo, *Spain* **34 B2** 43 18N 2 59W
Baracoa, *Cuba* **149 B5** 20 20N 74 30W
Baradero, *Argentina* **158 C4** 33 52 S 59 29W
Baradine, *Australia* **117 A8** 30 56 S 149 4 E
Baraga, *U.S.A.* **138 B10** 46 47N 88 30W
Barahona, *Dom. Rep.* **149 C5** 18 13N 71 7W
Barahona, *Spain* **34 D2** 41 17N 2 39W
Baraka →, *Sudan* **94 D4** 18 13N 37 35 E
Barakot, *India* **81 J11** 21 33N 84 59 E
Barakpur, *India* **81 H13** 22 44N 88 30 E
Barakula, *Australia* **115 D5** 26 30 S 150 33 E
Baralaba, *Australia* **114 C4** 24 13 S 149 50 E
Baralzon L., *Canada* **131 B9** 60 0N 98 3W
Baram →, *Malaysia* **75 B4** 4 35N 113 58 E
Baramati, *India* **82 E2** 18 11N 74 33 E
Baramba, *India* **82 D7** 20 25N 85 23 E
Barameiya, *Sudan* **94 D4** 18 32N 36 38 E
Baramula, *India* **81 B6** 34 15N 74 20 E
Baran, *India* **80 G7** 25 9N 76 40 E
Baranavichy, *Belarus* **51 F4** 53 10N 26 0 E
Baranoa, *Colombia* **152 A3** 10 48N 74 55W
Baranof I., *U.S.A.* **130 B1** 57 0N 135 0W
Baranów Sandomierski, *Poland* **47 E8** 50 29N 21 30 E
Baranya □, *Hungary* **31 F11** 46 0N 18 15 E
Barão de Cocais, *Brazil* **155 E3** 19 56 S 43 28W
Barão de Grajaú, *Brazil* **154 C3** 6 45 S 43 1W
Barão de Melgaço, *Mato Grosso, Brazil* **157 D6** 16 14 S 55 52W
Barão de Melgaço, *Rondônia, Brazil* **157 C5** 11 50 S 60 45W
Baraolt, *Romania* **46 C6** 46 5N 25 34 E
Barapasi, *Indonesia* **73 B5** 2 15 S 137 5 E
Barapina, *Papua N. G.* **120 D8** 6 21 S 155 25 E
Barasat, *India* **81 H13** 22 46N 88 31 E
Barat Daya, Kepulauan, *Indonesia* **72 C3** 7 30 S 128 0 E
Barataria B., *U.S.A.* **139 L10** 29 20N 89 55W
Baraut, *India* **80 E7** 29 13N 77 7 E
Baraya, *Colombia* **152 C2** 3 10N 75 4W
Barbacan, *Phil.* **71 F2** 10 20N 119 21 E
Barbacena, *Brazil* **155 F3** 21 15 S 43 56W
Barbacoas, *Colombia* **152 C2** 1 45N 78 0W

174 Ben Lomond

Ben Lomond, Tas., Australia 114 G4 41 38 S 147 42 E
Ben Lomond, U.K. 18 E4 56 11N 4 38W
Ben Luc, Vietnam 77 G6 10 39N 106 29 E
Ben Macdhui, U.K. 18 D5 57 4N 3 40W
Ben Mhor, U.K. 18 D1 57 15N 7 18W
Ben More, Arg. & Bute, U.K. 18 E2 56 26N 6 1W
Ben More, Stirl., U.K. 18 E4 56 23N 4 32W
Ben More Assynt, U.K. 18 C4 58 8N 4 52W
Ben Nevis, U.K. 18 E4 56 48N 5 1W
Ben Ohau Ra., N.Z. 119 E5 44 1 S 170 4 E
Ben Quang, Vietnam 76 D6 17 3N 106 55 E
Ben Slimane, Morocco 98 B3 33 38N 7 7W
Ben Tre, Vietnam 77 G6 10 3N 106 36 E
Ben Vorlich, U.K. 18 E4 56 21N 4 14W
Ben Wyvis, U.K. 18 D4 57 40N 4 35W
Bena, Nigeria 101 C6 11 20N 5 50 E
Bena Dibele, Zaïre 103 C4 4 4 S 22 50 E
Bena-Leka, Zaïre 103 D4 5 8 S 22 10 E
Bena-Tshadi, Zaïre 103 C4 4 40 S 22 49 E
Benāb, Iran 89 D12 37 20N 46 4 E
Benadir, Somali Rep. 108 D2 1 30N 44 30 E
Benagalbón, Spain 37 J6 36 45N 4 15W
Benagerie, Australia 116 A4 31 25 S 140 22 E
Benahmed, Morocco 98 B3 33 4N 7 9W
Benalla, Australia 117 D7 36 30 S 146 0 E
Benambra, Mt., Australia 117 D7 36 31 S 147 34 E
Benamejí, Spain 37 H6 37 16N 4 33W
Benares = Varanasi, India 81 G10 25 22N 83 0 E
Bénat, C., France 25 E10 43 5N 6 22 E
Benavente, Portugal 37 G2 38 59N 8 49W
Benavente, Spain 36 C5 42 2N 5 43W
Benavides, Spain 36 C5 42 30N 5 54W
Benavides, U.S.A. 139 M5 27 36N 98 25W
Benbecula, U.K. 18 D1 57 26N 7 21W
Benbonyathe, Australia 116 A3 30 25 S 139 11 E
Bencubbin, Australia 113 F2 30 48 S 117 52 E
Bend, U.S.A. 142 D3 44 4N 121 19W
Bendela, Zaïre 102 C3 3 18 S 17 36 E
Bender Beila, Somali Rep. 108 C4 9 30N 50 48 E
Bender Merchagno, Somali Rep. 108 B4 11 41N 50 34 E
Bendering, Australia 113 F2 32 23 S 118 18 E
Bendery = Tighina, Moldova 51 J5 46 50N 29 30 E
Bendigo, Australia 116 D6 36 40 S 144 15 E
Bendorf, Germany 26 E3 50 25N 7 35 E
Benē Beraq, Israel 91 C3 32 6N 34 51 E
Beneden Knijpe, Neths. 20 C7 52 58N 5 59 E
Beneditinos, Brazil 154 C3 5 27 S 42 22W
Benedito Leite, Brazil 154 C3 7 13 S 44 34W
Bénéna, Mali 100 C4 13 9N 4 17W
Benenitra, Madag. 105 C8 23 27 S 45 5 E
Benešŏv, Czech. 30 B7 49 46N 14 41 E
Bénestroff, France 23 D13 48 54N 6 45 E
Benet, France 24 B3 46 22N 0 35W
Benevento, Italy 41 A7 41 8N 14 45 E
Benfeld, France 23 D14 48 22N 7 34 E
Benga, Mozam. 107 F3 16 11 S 33 40 E
Bengal, Bay of, Ind. Oc. 58 H12 15 0N 90 0 E
Bengbu, China 67 H9 32 58N 117 20 E
Benghazi = Banghāzī, Libya 96 B4 32 11N 20 3 E
Bengkalis, Indonesia 74 B2 1 30N 102 10 E
Bengkulu, Indonesia 74 C2 3 50 S 102 12 E
Bengkulu □, Indonesia 74 C2 3 48 S 102 16 E
Bengough, Canada 131 D7 49 25N 105 10W
Benguela, Angola 103 E2 12 37 S 13 25 E
Benguela □, Angola 103 E2 12 0 S 13 30 E
Benguerir, Morocco 98 B3 32 16N 7 56W
Benguérua, I., Mozam. 105 C6 21 58 S 35 28 E
Benguet □, Phil. 70 C3 16 30N 120 40 E
Benha, Egypt 94 H7 30 26N 31 8 E
Beni, Zaïre 106 B2 0 30N 29 27 E
Beni □, Bolivia 157 C4 14 0 S 65 0W
Beni →, Bolivia 157 C4 10 23 S 65 24W
Beni Abbès, Algeria 99 B4 30 5N 2 5W
Beni-Haoua, Algeria 99 A5 36 30N 1 30 E
Beni Mazâr, Egypt 94 J7 28 32N 30 44 E
Beni Mellal, Morocco 98 B3 32 21N 6 21W
Beni Ounif, Algeria 99 B4 32 0N 1 10W
Beni Saf, Algeria 99 A4 35 17N 1 15W
Beni Suef, Egypt 94 J7 29 5N 31 6 E
Beniah L., Canada 130 A6 63 23N 112 17W
Benicarló, Spain 34 E5 40 23N 0 23 E
Benicia, U.S.A. 144 G4 38 3N 122 9W
Benidorm, Spain 35 G4 38 33N 0 9W
Benidorm, Islote de, Spain 35 G4 38 31N 0 9W
Benin ■, Africa 101 D5 10 0N 2 0 E
Benin, Bight of, W. Afr. 101 D5 5 0N 3 0 E
Benin City, Nigeria 101 D6 6 20N 5 31 E
Benisa, Spain 35 G5 38 43N 0 3 E
Benitses, Greece 32 A3 39 32N 19 55 E
Benjamin Aceval, Paraguay 158 A4 24 58 S 57 34W
Benjamin Constant, Brazil 152 D3 4 40 S 70 15W
Benjamin Hill, Mexico 146 A2 30 10N 111 10W
Benkelman, U.S.A. 138 E4 40 3N 101 32W
Benkovac, Croatia 39 D12 44 2N 15 37 E
Benlidi, Australia 114 C3 24 35 S 144 50 E
Benmore Pk., N.Z. 119 E5 44 25 S 170 8 E
Bennebroek, Neths. 20 D5 52 19N 4 36 E
Bennekom, Neths. 20 D7 52 0N 5 41 E
Bennett, Canada 130 B2 59 56N 134 53W
Bennett, L., Australia 112 D5 22 50 S 131 2 E
Bennett, Ostrov, Russia 57 B15 76 21N 148 56 E
Bennettsville, U.S.A. 135 H6 34 37N 79 41W
Bennington, U.S.A. 137 D11 43 0N 71 55W
Bénodet, France 22 E2 47 53N 4 7W
Benoni, S. Africa 105 D4 26 11 S 28 18 E
Benoud, Algeria 99 B5 32 20N 0 16 E
Benoy, Chad 97 G3 8 59N 16 19 E
Benque Viejo, Belize 147 D7 17 5N 89 8W
Bensheim, Germany 27 F4 49 40N 8 38 E
Benson, U.S.A. 143 L8 31 58N 110 18W
Bent, Iran 85 E8 26 20N 59 31 E
Benteng, Indonesia 72 C2 6 10 S 120 30 E
Bentinck I., Australia 114 B2 17 3 S 139 35 E
Bentiu, Sudan 95 F2 9 10N 29 55 E
Bento Gonçalves, Brazil 159 B5 29 10 S 51 31W
Benton, Ark., U.S.A. 139 H8 34 34N 92 35W
Benton, Calif., U.S.A. 144 H8 37 48N 118 32W
Benton, Ill., U.S.A. 140 G8 38 0N 88 55W
Benton Harbor, U.S.A. 141 B10 42 6N 86 27W
Bentu Liben, Ethiopia 95 F4 8 32N 38 21 E
Bentung, Malaysia 77 L3 3 31N 101 55 E
Benue □, Nigeria 101 D6 7 20N 8 45 E
Benue →, Nigeria 101 D6 7 48N 6 46 E
Benxi, China 67 D12 41 20N 123 48 E
Benzdorp, Surinam 153 C7 3 44N 54 5W
Beo, Indonesia 72 A3 4 25N 126 50 E
Beograd, Serbia, Yug. 42 C5 44 50N 20 37 E
Beowawe, U.S.A. 142 F5 40 35N 116 29W
Bepan Jiang →, China 68 E6 24 55N 106 5 E
Beppu, Japan 62 D3 33 15N 131 30 E
Beppu-Wan, Japan 62 D3 33 18N 131 34 E
Beqaa Valley = Al Biqā □, Lebanon 91 A5 34 10N 36 10 E
Bera, Bangla. 78 C2 24 5N 89 37 E
Berati, Albania 44 D1 40 43N 19 59 E
Berau →, Indonesia 75 B5 2 10N 117 42 E
Berau, Teluk, Indonesia 73 B4 2 30 S 132 30 E
Berber, Sudan 94 D3 18 0N 34 0 E
Berbera, Somali Rep. 108 B3 10 30N 45 2 E
Berbérati, C.A.R. 102 B3 4 15N 15 40 E
Berberia, C. del, Spain 33 C7 38 39N 1 24 E
Berbice →, Guyana 153 B6 6 20N 57 32W
Berceto, Italy 38 D7 44 31N 9 51 E
Berchtesgaden, Germany 27 H8 47 38N 13 0 E
Berck-Plage, France 23 B8 50 25N 1 36 E
Berdale, Somali Rep. 108 C3 7 4N 47 51 E
Berdichev = Berdychiv, Ukraine 51 H5 49 57N 28 30 E
Berdsk, Russia 56 D9 54 47N 83 2 E
Berdyansk, Ukraine 51 J9 46 45N 36 50 E
Berdyaush, Russia 54 D7 55 9N 59 9 E
Berdychiv, Ukraine 51 H5 49 57N 28 30 E
Berea, U.S.A. 134 G3 37 34N 84 17W
Berebere, Indonesia 72 A3 2 25N 128 45 E
Bereda, Somali Rep. 108 B4 11 45N 51 0 E
Berehove, Ukraine 51 H2 48 15N 22 35 E
Bereina, Papua N. G. 120 E4 8 39 S 146 30 E
Berekum, Ghana 100 D4 7 29N 2 34W
Berenice, Egypt 94 C4 24 2N 35 25 E
Berens →, Canada 131 C9 52 25N 97 2W
Berens I., Canada 131 C9 52 18N 97 18W
Berens River, Canada 131 C9 52 25N 97 0W
Berestechko, Ukraine 51 G3 50 22N 25 5 E
Bereşti, Romania 46 C8 46 6N 27 50 E
Beretău →, Romania 46 B2 47 10N 21 50 E
Berettyo →, Hungary 31 E14 46 59N 21 7 E
Berettyóújfalu, Hungary 31 D14 47 13N 21 33 E
Berevo, Mahajanga, Madag. 105 B7 17 14 S 44 17 E
Berevo, Toliara, Madag. 105 B7 19 44 S 44 58 E
Bereza, Belarus 51 F3 52 31N 24 51 E
Berezhany, Ukraine 51 H3 49 26N 24 58 E
Berezina = Byarezina →, Belarus 51 F6 52 33N 30 14 E
Berezivka, Ukraine 51 J6 47 14N 30 55 E
Berezna, Ukraine 51 G6 51 35N 31 46 E
Berezniki, Russia 54 B6 59 24N 56 46 E
Berezovo, Russia 48 B11 64 0N 65 0 E
Berga, Spain 34 C6 42 6N 1 48 E
Bergama, Turkey 88 C2 39 8N 27 15 E
Bergambacht, Neths. 20 E5 51 56N 4 48 E
Bérgamo, Italy 38 C6 45 41N 9 43 E
Bergantiños, Spain 36 B2 43 20N 8 40W
Bergara, Spain 34 B2 43 9N 2 28W
Bergedorf, Germany 26 B6 53 28N 10 6 E
Bergeijk, Neths. 21 F6 51 19N 5 21 E
Bergen, Germany 26 A9 54 25N 13 25 E
Bergen, Neths. 20 C5 52 40N 4 43 E
Bergen, Norway 13 F11 60 20N 5 20 E
Bergen, U.S.A. 136 C7 43 5N 77 57W
Bergen-op-Zoom, Neths. 21 F4 51 28N 4 18 E
Bergerac, France 24 D4 44 51N 0 30 E
Bergheim, Germany 26 E2 50 57N 6 38 E
Berghem, Neths. 20 E7 51 46N 5 33 E
Bergisch Gladbach, Germany 26 E3 50 59N 7 8 E
Bergschenhoek, Neths. 20 E5 51 59N 4 30 E
Bergsjö, Sweden 14 C11 61 59N 17 3 E
Bergues, France 23 B9 50 58N 2 24 E
Bergum, Neths. 20 B7 53 13N 5 59 E
Bergville, S. Africa 105 D4 28 52 S 29 18 E
Berhala, Selat, Indonesia 74 C2 1 0 S 104 15 E
Berhampore = Baharampur, India 81 G13 24 2N 88 27 E
Berhampur, India 82 E7 19 15N 84 54 E
Berheci →, Romania 46 C8 46 7N 27 19 E
Bering Sea, Pac. Oc. 126 C1 58 0N 171 0 E
Bering Strait, U.S.A. 126 B3 65 30N 169 0W
Beringen, Belgium 21 F6 51 3N 5 14 E
Beringen, Switz. 29 A7 47 38N 8 34 E
Beringovskiy, Russia 57 C18 63 3N 179 19 E
Berisso, Argentina 158 C4 34 56 S 57 50W
Berja, Spain 35 J2 36 50N 2 56W
Berkane, Morocco 99 B4 34 52N 2 20W
Berkel →, Neths. 20 D8 52 8N 6 12 E
Berkeley, U.K. 17 F5 51 41N 2 27W
Berkeley, U.S.A. 144 H4 37 52N 122 16W
Berkeley Springs, U.S.A. 134 F6 39 38N 78 14W
Berkhout, Neths. 20 C5 52 38N 4 59 E
Berkner I., Antarctica 7 D18 79 30 S 50 0W
Berkovitsa, Bulgaria 43 D8 43 16N 23 8 E
Berkshire □, U.K. 17 F6 51 25N 1 17W
Berlaar, Belgium 21 F5 51 7N 4 39 E
Berland →, Canada 130 C5 54 0N 116 50W
Berlanga, Spain 37 G5 38 17N 5 50W
Berlare, Belgium 21 F4 51 2N 4 2 E
Berlenga, I., Portugal 37 F1 39 25N 9 30W
Berlin, Germany 26 C9 52 30N 13 25 E
Berlin, Md., U.S.A. 134 F8 38 20N 75 13W
Berlin, N.H., U.S.A. 137 B13 44 28N 71 11W
Berlin, Wis., U.S.A. 134 D1 43 58N 88 57W
Bermeja, Sierra, Spain 37 J5 36 30N 5 11W
Bermejo →, Formosa, Argentina 158 B4 26 51 S 58 23W
Bermejo →, San Juan, Argentina 158 C2 32 30 S 67 30W
Bermeo, Spain 34 B2 43 25N 2 47W
Bermillo de Sayago, Spain 36 D4 41 22N 6 8W
Bermuda ■, Atl. Oc. 8 E2 32 45N 65 0W
Bern, Switz. 28 C4 46 57N 7 28 E
Bern □, Switz. 28 C5 46 45N 7 40 E
Bernado, U.S.A. 143 J10 34 30N 106 53W
Bernalda, Italy 41 B9 40 24N 16 41 E
Bernalillo, U.S.A. 143 J10 35 18N 106 33W
Bernam →, Malaysia 74 B2 3 45N 101 5 E
Bernardo de Irigoyen, Argentina 159 B5 26 15 S 53 40W
Bernardo O'Higgins □, Chile 158 C1 34 15 S 70 45W
Bernasconi, Argentina 158 D3 37 55 S 63 44W
Bernau, Bayern, Germany 27 H8 47 47N 12 22 E
Bernau, Brandenburg, Germany 26 C9 52 40N 13 35 E
Bernay, France 22 C7 49 5N 0 35 E
Bernburg, Germany 26 D7 51 47N 11 44 E
Berndorf, Austria 30 D9 47 59N 16 1 E
Berne = Bern, Switz. 28 C4 46 57N 7 28 E
Berne = Bern □, Switz. 28 C5 46 45N 7 40 E
Berne, U.S.A. 141 D12 40 39N 84 57W
Berner Alpen, Switz. 28 D5 46 27N 7 35 E
Bernese Oberland = Oberland, Switz. 28 C5 46 35N 7 38 E
Bernier I., Australia 113 D1 24 50 S 113 12 E
Bernina, Piz, Switz. 29 D9 46 20N 9 54 E
Bernissart, Belgium 21 H3 50 28N 3 39 E
Bernkastel-Kues, Germany 27 F3 49 55N 7 3 E
Beroroha, Madag. 105 C8 21 40 S 45 10 E
Béroubouay, Benin 101 C5 10 34N 2 46 E
Beroun, Czech. 30 B7 49 57N 14 5 E
Berounka →, Czech. 30 B7 50 0N 14 22 E
Berovo, Macedonia 42 F7 41 38N 22 51 E
Berrahal, Algeria 99 A6 36 54N 7 33 E
Berre, Étang de, France 25 E9 43 27N 5 5 E
Berrechid, Morocco 98 B3 33 18N 7 36W
Berri, Australia 116 C4 34 14 S 140 35 E
Berriane, Algeria 99 B5 32 50N 3 46 E
Berrien Springs, U.S.A. 141 C10 41 57N 86 20W
Berrigan, Australia 117 C6 35 38 S 145 49 E
Berriwillock, Australia 116 C5 35 36 S 142 59 E
Berrouaghia, Algeria 99 A5 36 10N 2 53 E
Berry, Australia 117 C9 34 46 S 150 43 E
Berry, France 23 F8 46 50N 2 0 E
Berry, U.S.A. 141 F12 38 31N 84 23W
Berry Is., Bahamas 148 A4 25 40N 77 50W
Berryessa L., U.S.A. 144 G4 38 31N 122 6W
Berryville, U.S.A. 139 G8 36 22N 93 34W
Bersenbrück, Germany 26 C3 52 34N 7 56 E
Bershad, Ukraine 51 H5 48 22N 29 31 E
Berthold, U.S.A. 138 A4 48 19N 101 44W
Berthoud, U.S.A. 138 E2 40 19N 105 5W
Bertincourt, France 23 B9 50 5N 2 58 E
Bertoua, Cameroon 102 B2 4 30N 13 45 E
Bertrand, U.S.A. 138 E5 40 32N 99 38W
Bertrange, Lux. 21 J8 49 37N 6 3 E
Bertrix, Belgium 21 J6 49 51N 5 15 E
Beruri, Brazil 153 D5 3 54 S 61 22W
Berwick, U.S.A. 137 E8 41 3N 76 14W
Berwick-upon-Tweed, U.K. 16 B5 55 46N 2 0W
Berwyn Mts., U.K. 16 E4 52 54N 3 26W
Beryslav, Ukraine 51 J7 46 50N 33 30 E
Berzasca, Romania 42 C6 44 39N 21 58 E
Berzence, Hungary 31 E10 46 12N 17 11 E
Besal, Pakistan 81 B5 35 4N 73 56 E
Besalampy, Madag. 105 B7 16 43 S 44 29 E
Besançon, France 23 E13 47 15N 6 2 E
Besar, Indonesia 75 C5 2 40 S 116 0 E
Besar, Gunong, Malaysia 74 A2 5 10N 101 18 E
Beshenkovichi, Belarus 50 E5 55 2N 29 29 E
Beška, Serbia, Yug. 42 B5 45 8N 20 6 E
Beskids = Beskydy, Europe 31 B11 49 35N 18 40 E
Beskydy, Europe 31 B11 49 35N 18 40 E
Beslan, Russia 53 J7 43 15N 44 28 E
Besna Kobila, Serbia, Yug. 42 E7 42 31N 22 10 E
Besnard L., Canada 131 B7 55 25N 106 0W
Besni, Turkey 88 D7 37 41N 37 52 E
Besor, N. →, Egypt 91 D3 31 28N 34 22 E
Beşparmak Daği, Turkey 45 G9 37 32N 27 30 E
Bessa Monteiro, Angola 103 D2 7 7 S 13 44 E
Bessarabiya, Moldova 51 J5 47 0N 28 10 E
Bessarabka = Basarabeasca, Moldova 51 J5 46 21N 28 58 E
Bessèges, France 25 D8 44 18N 4 8 E
Bessemer, Ala., U.S.A. 135 J2 33 24N 86 58W
Bessemer, Mich., U.S.A. 138 B9 46 29N 90 3W
Bessin, France 22 C5 49 18N 1 0W
Bessines-sur-Gartempe, France 24 B5 46 6N 1 22 E
Best, Neths. 21 E6 51 31N 5 23 E
Bet She'an, Israel 91 C4 32 30N 35 30 E
Bet Shemesh, Israel 91 D3 31 44N 35 0 E
Bet Tadjine, Djebel, Algeria 98 C4 29 0N 3 30W
Betafo, Madag. 105 B8 19 50 S 46 51 E
Betancuria, Canary Is. 33 F5 28 25N 14 3W
Betanzos, Bolivia 157 D4 19 34 S 65 27W
Betanzos, Spain 36 B2 43 15N 8 12W
Bétaré Oya, Cameroon 102 A2 5 40N 14 5 E
Bétera, Spain 34 F4 39 35N 0 28W
Bethal, S. Africa 105 D4 26 27 S 29 28 E
Bethanien, Namibia 104 D2 26 31 S 17 8 E
Bethany, Ill., U.S.A. 141 E8 39 39N 88 45W
Bethany, Mo., U.S.A. 140 D2 40 16N 94 2W
Bethel, Alaska, U.S.A. 126 B3 60 48N 161 45W
Bethel, Ohio, U.S.A. 141 F12 38 58N 84 5W
Bethel, Vt., U.S.A. 137 C12 43 50N 72 38W
Bethel Park, U.S.A. 136 F4 40 20N 80 1W
Bethlehem = Bayt Lahm, West Bank 91 D4 31 43N 35 12 E
Bethlehem, S. Africa 105 D4 28 14 S 28 18 E
Bethlehem, U.S.A. 137 F9 40 37N 75 23W
Bethulie, S. Africa 104 E4 30 30 S 25 59 E
Béthune, France 23 B9 50 30N 2 38 E
Béthune →, France 22 C8 49 53N 1 9 E
Bethungra, Australia 117 C7 34 45 S 147 51 E
Betijoque, Venezuela 152 B3 9 23N 70 44W
Betim, Brazil 155 E3 19 58 S 44 7W
Betioky, Madag. 105 C7 23 48 S 44 20 E
Beton-Bazoches, France 23 D10 48 42N 3 15 E
Betong, Thailand 77 K3 5 45N 101 5 E
Betoota, Australia 114 D3 25 45 S 140 42 E
Betroka, Madag. 105 C8 23 16 S 46 0 E
Betsiamites, Canada 129 C6 48 56N 68 40W
Betsiamites →, Canada 129 C6 48 56N 68 38W
Betsiboka →, Madag. 105 B8 16 3 S 46 36 E
Bettembourg, Lux. 21 J8 49 31N 6 6 E
Bettendorf, U.S.A. 140 C6 41 32N 90 30W
Bettiah, India 81 F11 26 48N 84 33 E
Béttola, Italy 38 D6 44 47N 9 36 E
Betul, India 82 D3 21 58N 77 59 E
Betung, Malaysia 75 B4 1 24N 111 31 E
Betzdorf, Germany 26 E3 50 46N 7 52 E
Beuca, Romania 46 E5 44 14N 24 56 E
Beuil, France 25 D10 44 6N 6 59 E
Beulah, U.S.A. 138 B4 47 16N 101 47W
Beuvron →, France 22 E8 47 29N 1 15 E
Beveren, Belgium 21 F4 51 12N 4 16 E
Beverley, Australia 113 F2 32 9 S 116 56 E
Beverley, U.K. 16 D7 53 51N 0 26W
Beverlo, Belgium 21 F6 51 7N 5 13 E
Beverly, Mass., U.S.A. 137 D14 42 33N 70 53W
Beverly, Wash., U.S.A. 142 C4 46 50N 119 56W
Beverly Hills, U.S.A. 145 L8 34 4N 118 25W
Beverwijk, Neths. 20 D5 52 28N 4 38 E
Bex, Switz. 28 D4 46 15N 7 0 E
Bey Dağları, Turkey 88 D4 36 38N 30 29 E
Beya, Russia 57 D10 52 40N 92 30 E
Beyānlū, Iran 84 C5 36 0N 47 51 E
Beyin, Ghana 100 D4 5 1N 2 41W
Beykoz, Turkey 43 F14 41 8N 29 7 E
Beyla, Guinea 100 D3 8 30N 8 38W
Beynat, France 24 C5 45 8N 1 44 E
Beyneu, Kazakstan 49 E10 45 18N 55 9 E
Beypazarı, Turkey 88 B4 40 10N 31 56 E
Beypore →, India 83 J2 11 10N 75 47 E
Beyşehir, Turkey 88 D4 37 41N 31 43 E
Beyşehir Gölü, Turkey 88 D4 37 41N 31 33 E
Beytüşşebap, Turkey 89 D10 37 35N 43 10 E
Bezdan, Serbia, Yug. 42 B3 45 50N 18 57 E
Bezhetsk, Russia 52 B3 57 47N 36 39 E
Bezhitsa, Russia 48 D5 53 19N 34 17 E
Béziers, France 24 E7 43 20N 3 12 E
Bezwada = Vijayawada, India 83 F5 16 31N 80 39 E
Bhadarwah, India 81 C6 32 58N 75 46 E
Bhadra →, India 83 H2 14 0N 75 20 E
Bhadrakh, India 82 D8 21 10N 86 30 E
Bhadravati, India 83 H2 13 49N 75 40 E
Bhagalpur, India 81 G12 25 10N 87 0 E
Bhainsa, India 82 E3 19 10N 77 58 E
Bhairab →, Bangla. 78 D2 22 51N 89 34 E
Bhairab Bazar, Bangla. 78 C3 24 4N 90 58 E
Bhakkar, Pakistan 79 C3 31 40N 71 5 E
Bhakra Dam, India 80 D7 31 30N 76 45 E
Bhamo, Burma 78 C6 24 15N 97 15 E
Bhamragarh, India 82 E5 19 30N 80 40 E
Bhandara, India 82 D4 21 5N 79 42 E
Bhanrer Ra., India 80 H8 23 40N 79 45 E
Bharat = India ■, Asia 59 G11 20 0N 78 0 E
Bharatpur, India 80 F7 27 15N 77 30 E
Bharuch, India 82 D1 21 47N 73 0 E
Bhatghar L., India 82 E1 18 10N 73 48 E
Bhatiapara Ghat, Bangla. 78 D2 23 13N 89 42 E
Bhatinda, India 80 D6 30 15N 74 57 E
Bhatkal, India 83 H2 13 58N 74 35 E
Bhatpara, India 81 H13 22 50N 88 25 E
Bhattiprolu, India 83 F5 16 7N 80 45 E
Bhaun, Pakistan 80 C5 32 55N 72 40 E
Bhaunagar = Bhavnagar, India 80 J5 21 45N 72 10 E
Bhavani, India 83 J3 11 27N 77 43 E
Bhavani →, India 83 J4 11 0N 78 15 E
Bhavnagar, India 80 J5 21 45N 72 10 E
Bhawanipatna, India 82 E5 19 55N 80 10 E
Bhera, Pakistan 80 C5 32 29N 72 57 E
Bhilsa = Vidisha, India 80 H7 23 28N 77 53 E
Bhilwara, India 80 G6 25 25N 74 38 E
Bhima →, India 82 F3 16 25N 77 17 E
Bhimavaram, India 83 F5 16 30N 81 30 E
Bhimbar, Pakistan 81 C6 32 59N 74 3 E
Bhind, India 81 F8 26 30N 78 46 E
Bhiwandi, India 82 E1 19 20N 73 0 E
Bhiwani, India 80 E7 28 50N 76 9 E
Bhola, Bangla. 78 D3 22 45N 90 35 E
Bhongir, India 82 F4 17 30N 78 56 E
Bhopal, India 80 H7 23 20N 77 30 E
Bhor, India 82 E1 18 12N 73 53 E
Bhubaneshwar, India 82 D7 20 15N 85 50 E
Bhuj, India 80 H3 23 15N 69 49 E
Bhumiphol Dam = Phumiphon, Khuan, Thailand 76 D2 17 15N 98 58 E
Bhusaval, India 82 D2 21 3N 75 46 E
Bhutan ■, Asia 78 B3 27 25N 90 30 E
Biá →, Brazil 152 D4 3 28 S 67 23W
Biafra, B. of = Bonny, Bight of, Africa 101 E6 3 30N 9 20 E
Biak, Indonesia 73 B5 1 10 S 136 6 E
Biała, Poland 47 E4 50 24N 17 40 E
Biała →, Białystok, Poland 47 B10 53 11N 23 4 E
Biała →, Tarnów, Poland 31 A13 50 3N 20 55 E
Biała Piska, Poland 47 B9 53 37N 22 5 E
Biała Podlaska, Poland 47 C10 52 4N 23 6 E
Biała Podlaska □, Poland 47 D10 52 0N 23 0 E
Biała Rawska, Poland 47 D7 51 48N 20 29 E
Białobrzegi, Poland 47 C8 52 27N 21 3 E
Białogard, Poland 47 A2 54 2N 15 58 E
Białowieża, Poland 47 C10 52 41N 23 49 E
Biały Bór, Poland 47 B3 53 53N 16 51 E
Białystok, Poland 47 B10 53 10N 23 10 E
Białystok □, Poland 47 B10 53 9N 23 10 E
Biancavilla, Italy 41 E7 37 38N 14 52 E
Bīārjmand, Iran 85 B7 36 6N 55 53 E
Biaro, Indonesia 72 A3 2 5N 125 26 E
Biarritz, France 24 E2 43 29N 1 33W
Biasca, Switz. 29 D7 46 22N 8 58 E
Biba, Egypt 94 J7 28 55N 31 0 E
Bibai, Japan 60 C10 43 19N 141 52 E
Bibala, Angola 103 E2 14 44 S 13 24 E
Bibane, Bahiret el, Tunisia 96 B2 33 16N 11 13 E
Bibassé, Gabon 102 B2 1 27N 11 37 E
Bibbiena, Italy 39 E8 43 42N 11 49 E
Bibby I., Canada 131 A10 61 55N 93 0W
Biberach, Germany 27 G5 48 5N 9 47 E
Biberist, Switz. 28 B5 47 11N 7 34 E
Bibey →, Spain 36 C3 42 24N 7 13W
Bibiani, Ghana 100 D4 6 30N 2 8W
Bibile, Sri Lanka 83 L5 7 10N 81 25 E
Biboohra, Australia 114 B4 16 56 S 145 25 E
Bibungwa, Zaïre 106 C2 2 40 S 28 15 E
Bic, Canada 129 C6 48 20N 68 41W
Bicaj, Albania 44 C2 41 58N 20 25 E
Bicaz, Romania 46 C7 46 53N 26 5 E
Biccari, Italy 41 A8 41 23N 15 12 E
Bichena, Ethiopia 95 E4 10 28N 38 10 E
Bichvinta, Georgia 53 J5 43 9N 40 21 E
Bickerton I., Australia 114 A2 13 45 S 136 10 E
Bicknell, Ind., U.S.A. 141 F9 38 47N 87 19W
Bicknell, Utah, U.S.A. 143 G8 38 20N 111 33W
Bida, Nigeria 101 D6 9 3N 5 58 E

Blacks Harbour 175

Bida, *Zaïre* **102 B3** 4 55N 19 56 E
Bidar, *India* **82 F3** 17 55N 77 35 E
Biddeford, *U.S.A.* **129 D5** 43 30N 70 28W
Biddwara, *Ethiopia* **95 F4** 5 11N 38 34 E
Bideford, *U.K.* **17 F3** 51 1N 4 13W
Bidon 5 = Poste Maurice Cortier, *Algeria* **99 D5** 22 14N 1 2 E
Bidor, *Malaysia* **77 K3** 4 6N 101 15 E
Bidura, *Australia* **116 C5** 34 10 S 143 21 E
Bié □, *Angola* **103 E3** 12 30 S 17 0 E
Bié, Planalto de, *Angola* **103 E3** 12 0 S 16 0 E
Bieber, *U.S.A.* **142 F3** 41 7N 121 8W
Biebrza →, *Poland* **47 B9** 53 13N 22 25 E
Biecz, *Poland* **31 B14** 49 44N 21 15 E
Biel, *Switz.* **28 B4** 47 8N 7 14 E
Bielawa, *Poland* **47 E3** 50 43N 16 37 E
Bielé Karpaty, *Europe* **31 B10** 49 5N 18 0 E
Bielefeld, *Germany* **26 C4** 52 1N 8 33 E
Bielersee, *Switz.* **28 B4** 47 6N 7 5 E
Biella, *Italy* **38 C5** 45 34N 8 3 E
Bielsk Podlaski, *Poland* **47 C10** 52 47N 23 12 E
Bielsko-Biała, *Poland* **31 B12** 49 50N 19 2 E
Bielsko-Biała □, *Poland* **31 B12** 49 45N 19 15 E
Bien Hoa, *Vietnam* **77 G6** 10 57N 106 49 E
Bienfait, *Canada* **131 D8** 49 10N 102 50W
Bienne = Biel, *Switz.* **28 B4** 47 8N 7 14 E
Bienvenida, *Spain* **37 G4** 38 18N 6 12W
Bienvenue, *Fr. Guiana* **153 C7** 3 0N 52 30W
Bienville, L., *Canada* **128 A5** 55 5N 72 40W
Biescas, *Spain* **34 C4** 42 37N 0 20W
Biese →, *Germany* **26 C7** 52 53N 11 46 E
Biesiesfontein, *S. Africa* **104 E2** 30 57 S 17 58 E
Bietigheim, *Germany* **27 G5** 48 58N 9 8 E
Bievre, *Belgium* **21 J6** 49 57N 5 1 E
Biferno →, *Italy* **41 A8** 41 59N 15 2 E
Bifoum, *Gabon* **102 C2** 0 20 S 10 23 E
Big →, *Canada* **129 B8** 54 50N 58 55W
Big →, *U.S.A.* **140 F6** 38 28N 90 37W
Big B., *Canada* **129 A7** 55 43N 60 35W
Big B., *N.Z.* **119 E3** 44 28 S 168 4 E
Big Bear City, *U.S.A.* **145 L10** 34 16N 116 51W
Big Bear Lake, *U.S.A.* **145 L10** 34 15N 116 56W
Big Beaver, *Canada* **131 D7** 49 10N 105 10W
Big Belt Mts., *U.S.A.* **142 C8** 46 30N 111 25W
Big Bend, *Swaziland* **105 D5** 26 50 S 31 58 E
Big Bend National Park, *U.S.A.* **139 L3** 29 20N 103 5W
Big Black →, *U.S.A.* **139 J9** 32 3N 91 4W
Big Blue →, *Ind., U.S.A.* **141 E11** 39 12N 85 56W
Big Blue →, *Kans., U.S.A.* **138 F6** 39 35N 96 34W
Big Cr. →, *Canada* **130 C4** 51 42N 122 41W
Big Creek, *U.S.A.* **144 H7** 37 11N 119 14W
Big Cypress Swamp, *U.S.A.* **135 M5** 26 12N 81 10W
Big Falls, *U.S.A.* **138 A8** 48 12N 93 48W
Big Fork →, *U.S.A.* **138 A8** 48 31N 93 43W
Big Horn Mts. = Bighorn Mts., *U.S.A.* **142 D10** 44 30N 107 30W
Big Lake, *U.S.A.* **139 K4** 31 12N 101 28W
Big Moose, *U.S.A.* **137 C10** 43 49N 74 58W
Big Muddy →, *U.S.A.* **140 G8** 38 0N 89 0W
Big Muddy Cr. →, *U.S.A.* **138 A2** 48 8N 104 36W
Big Pine, *U.S.A.* **144 H8** 37 10N 118 17W
Big Piney, *U.S.A.* **142 E8** 42 32N 110 7W
Big Quill L., *Canada* **131 C8** 51 55N 104 50W
Big Rapids, *U.S.A.* **134 D3** 43 42N 85 29W
Big River, *Canada* **131 C7** 53 50N 107 0W
Big Run, *U.S.A.* **136 F6** 40 57N 78 55W
Big Sable Pt., *U.S.A.* **134 C2** 44 3N 86 1W
Big Sand L., *Canada* **131 B9** 57 45N 99 45W
Big Sandy, *U.S.A.* **142 B8** 48 11N 110 7W
Big Sandy Cr. →, *U.S.A.* **138 F3** 38 7N 102 29W
Big Sioux →, *U.S.A.* **138 D6** 42 29N 96 27W
Big Spring, *U.S.A.* **139 J4** 32 15N 101 28W
Big Springs, *U.S.A.* **138 E3** 41 4N 102 5W
Big Stone City, *U.S.A.* **138 C6** 45 18N 96 28W
Big Stone Gap, *U.S.A.* **135 G4** 36 52N 82 47W
Big Stone L., *U.S.A.* **138 C6** 45 30N 96 35W
Big Sur, *U.S.A.* **144 J5** 36 15N 121 48W
Big Timber, *U.S.A.* **142 D9** 45 50N 109 57W
Big Trout L., *Canada* **128 B1** 53 40N 90 0W
Biğa, *Turkey* **88 B2** 40 13N 27 14 E
Bigadiç, *Turkey* **88 C3** 39 22N 28 7 E
Biganos, *France* **24 D3** 44 39N 0 59W
Bigfork, *U.S.A.* **142 B6** 48 4N 114 4W
Biggar, *Canada* **131 C7** 52 4N 108 0W
Biggar, *U.K.* **18 F5** 55 38N 3 32W
Bigge I., *Australia* **112 B4** 14 35 S 125 10 E
Biggenden, *Australia* **115 D5** 25 31 S 152 4 E
Biggs, *U.S.A.* **144 F5** 39 25N 121 43W
Bighorn, *U.S.A.* **142 C10** 46 10N 107 27W
Bighorn →, *U.S.A.* **142 C10** 46 10N 107 28W
Bighorn Mts., *U.S.A.* **142 D10** 44 30N 107 30W
Bignona, *Senegal* **100 C1** 12 52N 16 14W
Bigorre, *France* **24 E4** 43 10N 0 5 E
Bigstone L., *Canada* **131 C9** 53 42N 95 44W
Biguglia, Étang de, *France* **25 F13** 42 36N 9 29 E
Bigwa, *Tanzania* **106 D4** 7 10 S 39 10 E
Bihać, *Bos.-H.* **39 D12** 44 49N 15 57 E
Bihar, *India* **81 G11** 25 5N 85 40 E
Bihar □, *India* **81 G11** 25 0N 86 0 E
Biharamulo, *Tanzania* **106 C3** 2 25 S 31 25 E
Biharamulo □, *Tanzania* **106 C3** 2 30 S 31 20 E
Biharkeresztes, *Hungary* **31 D14** 47 8N 21 44 E
Bihor □, *Romania* **46 C3** 47 0N 22 10 E
Bihor, Munţii, *Romania* **46 C3** 46 29N 22 47 E
Bijagós, Arquipélago dos, *Guinea-Biss.* **100 C1** 11 15N 16 10W
Bijaipur, *India* **80 F7** 26 2N 77 20 E
Bijapur, *Karnataka, India* **82 F2** 16 50N 75 55 E
Bijapur, *Mad. P., India* **82 E5** 18 50N 80 50 E
Bījār, *Iran* **89 E12** 35 52N 47 35 E
Bijeljina, *Bos.-H.* **42 C4** 44 46N 19 17 E
Bijelo Polje, *Montenegro, Yug.* **42 D4** 43 1N 19 45 E
Bijie, *China* **68 D5** 27 20N 105 16 E
Bijni, *India* **78 B3** 26 30N 90 40 E
Bijnor, *India* **80 E8** 29 27N 78 11 E
Bikaner, *India* **80 E5** 28 2N 73 18 E
Bikapur, *India* **81 F10** 26 30N 82 7 E
Bikeqi, *China* **66 D6** 40 43N 111 20 E
Bikfayyā, *Lebanon* **91 B4** 33 55N 35 41 E
Bikin, *Russia* **57 E14** 46 50N 134 20 E
Bikin →, *Russia* **60 A7** 46 51N 134 2 E
Bikini Atoll, *Pac. Oc.* **122 F8** 12 0N 167 30 E
Bikoro, *Zaïre* **102 C3** 0 48 S 18 15 E
Bikoué, *Cameroon* **101 E7** 3 55N 11 50 E
Bila Tserkva, *Ukraine* **51 H6** 49 45N 30 10 E
Bilara, *India* **80 F5** 26 14N 73 53 E
Bilaspara, *India* **81 B3** 26 13N 90 14 E
Bilaspur, *Mad. P., India* **81 H10** 22 2N 82 15 E
Bilaspur, *Punjab, India* **80 D7** 31 19N 76 50 E
Biläsuvar, *Azerbaijan* **89 C13** 39 27N 48 32 E
Bilauk Taungdan, *Thailand* **76 F2** 13 0N 99 0 E
Bilbao, *Spain* **34 B2** 43 16N 2 56W
Bilbeis, *Egypt* **94 H7** 30 25N 31 34 E
Bilbo = Bilbao, *Spain* **34 B2** 43 16N 2 56W
Bilbor, *Romania* **46 B6** 47 6N 25 30 E
Bíldudalur, *Iceland* **12 D2** 65 41N 23 36W
Bileća, *Bos.-H.* **42 E3** 42 53N 18 27 E
Bilecik, *Turkey* **88 B4** 40 5N 30 5 E
Biłgoraj, *Poland* **47 E9** 50 33N 22 42 E
Bilhorod-Dnistrovskyy, *Ukraine* **51 J6** 46 11N 30 23 E
Bilibino, *Russia* **57 C17** 68 3N 166 20 E
Bilibiza, *Mozam.* **107 E5** 12 30 S 40 20 E
Bilin, *Burma* **78 G6** 17 14N 97 15 E
Bilir, *Russia* **57 C14** 65 40N 131 20 E
Biliran I., *Phil.* **71 F5** 11 35N 124 28 E
Bilishti, *Albania* **44 D3** 40 37N 21 2 E
Bill, *U.S.A.* **138 D2** 43 14N 105 16W
Billabalong, *Australia* **113 E2** 27 25 S 115 49 E
Billiluna, *Australia* **112 C4** 19 37 S 127 41 E
Billingham, *U.K.* **16 C6** 54 36N 1 17W
Billings, *U.S.A.* **142 D9** 45 47N 108 30W
Billiton Is. = Belitung, *Indonesia* **75 C3** 3 10 S 107 50 E
Billom, *France* **24 C7** 45 43N 3 20 E
Bilma, *Niger* **97 E2** 18 50N 13 30 E
Bilo Gora, *Croatia* **42 B2** 45 53N 17 15 E
Biloela, *Australia* **114 C5** 24 24 S 150 31 E
Bilohirsk, *Ukraine* **51 K8** 45 3N 34 35 E
Biloku, *Guyana* **153 C6** 1 50N 58 25W
Bilopillya, *Ukraine* **51 G8** 51 14N 34 20 E
Biloxi, *U.S.A.* **139 K10** 30 24N 88 53W
Bilpa Morea Claypan, *Australia* **114 D2** 25 0 S 140 0 E
Bilthoven, *Neths.* **20 D6** 52 8N 5 12 E
Biltine, *Chad* **97 F4** 14 40N 20 50 E
Bilugyun, *Burma* **78 G6** 16 24N 97 32 E
Bilyana, *Australia* **114 B4** 18 5 S 145 50 E
Bilyarsk, *Russia* **52 C10** 54 58N 50 22 E
Bilzen, *Belgium* **21 G7** 50 52N 5 31 E
Bima, *Indonesia* **75 D5** 8 22 S 118 49 E
Bimban, *Egypt* **94 C3** 24 24N 32 54 E
Bimberi Pk., *Australia* **117 C8** 35 44 S 148 51 E
Bimbila, *Ghana* **101 D5** 8 54N 0 5 E
Bimbo, *C.A.R.* **102 B3** 4 15N 18 33 E
Bimini Is., *Bahamas* **148 A4** 25 42N 79 25W
Bin Xian, *Heilongjiang, China* **67 B14** 45 42N 127 32 E
Bin Xian, *Shaanxi, China* **66 G5** 35 2N 108 4 E
Bina-Etawah, *India* **80 G8** 24 13N 78 14 E
Bināb, *Iran* **89 D13** 36 35N 48 41 E
Binaiya, *Indonesia* **73 B3** 3 11 S 129 26 E
Binalbagan, *Phil.* **71 F4** 10 12N 122 50 E
Binalong, *Australia* **117 C8** 34 40 S 148 39 E
Bīnālūd, Kūh-e, *Iran* **85 B8** 36 30N 58 30 E
Binatang, *Malaysia* **75 B4** 2 10N 111 40 E
Binbee, *Australia* **114 C4** 20 19 S 147 56 E
Binche, *Belgium* **21 H4** 50 26N 4 10 E
Binchuan, *China* **68 E3** 25 42N 100 38 E
Binda, *Australia* **115 D4** 27 52 S 147 21 E
Binda, *Zaïre* **103 D2** 5 52 S 13 14 E
Bindle, *Australia* **115 D4** 27 40 S 148 45 E
Bindoy, *Phil.* **71 G4** 9 48N 123 5 E
Bindura, *Zimbabwe* **107 F3** 17 18 S 31 18 E
Bingara, *N.S.W., Australia* **115 D5** 29 52 S 150 36 E
Bingara, *Queens., Australia* **115 D3** 28 10 S 144 37 E
Bingen, *Germany* **27 F3** 49 57N 7 55 E
Bingerville, *Ivory C.* **100 D4** 5 18N 3 49W
Bingham, *U.S.A.* **129 C6** 45 3N 69 53W
Bingham Canyon, *U.S.A.* **142 F7** 40 32N 112 9W
Binghamton, *U.S.A.* **137 D9** 42 6N 75 55W
Bingöl, *Turkey* **89 C9** 38 53N 40 29 E
Bingöl Dağları, *Turkey* **89 C9** 39 16N 41 9 E
Binh Dinh = An Nhon, *Vietnam* **76 F7** 13 55N 109 7 E
Binh Khe, *Vietnam* **76 F7** 13 57N 108 51 E
Binh Son, *Vietnam* **76 E7** 15 20N 108 40 E
Binhai, *China* **67 G10** 34 2N 119 49 E
Binisatua, *Spain* **33 B11** 39 50N 4 11 E
Binjai, *Indonesia* **74 B1** 3 20N 98 30 E
Binnaway, *Australia* **117 A8** 31 28 S 149 24 E
Binongko, *Indonesia* **72 C2** 5 55 S 123 55 E
Binscarth, *Canada* **131 C8** 50 37N 101 17W
Bintan, *Indonesia* **74 B2** 1 0N 104 0 E
Bintuni, *Indonesia* **73 B4** 2 7 S 133 32 E
Binyang, *China* **68 F7** 23 12N 108 47 E
Binz, *Germany* **26 A9** 54 24N 13 35 E
Binza, *Zaïre* **103 C3** 4 21 S 15 14 E
Binzert = Bizerte, *Tunisia* **96 A1** 37 15N 9 50 E
Bío Bío □, *Chile* **158 D1** 37 35 S 72 0W
Biograd, *Croatia* **39 E12** 43 56N 15 29 E
Bioko, *Eq. Guin.* **101 E6** 3 30N 8 40 E
Biokovo, *Croatia* **42 D2** 43 23N 17 0 E
Biougra, *Morocco* **98 B3** 30 15N 9 14W
Bir, *India* **82 E2** 19 4N 75 46 E
Bir, Ras, *Djibouti* **95 E5** 12 0N 43 20 E
Bîr Abu Hashim, *Egypt* **94 C3** 23 42N 34 6 E
Bîr Abu M'nqar, *Egypt* **94 B2** 26 33N 27 33 E
Bîr Abu Muḥammad, *Egypt* **91 F3** 29 44N 34 14 E
Bi'r ad Dabbāghāt, *Jordan* **91 E4** 30 26N 35 32 E
Bîr Adal Deib, *Sudan* **94 C4** 22 35N 36 10 E
Bi'r al Butayyihāt, *Jordan* **91 F4** 29 47N 35 20 E
Bi'r al Mārī, *Jordan* **91 E4** 30 4N 35 33 E
Bi'r al Qattār, *Jordan* **91 F4** 29 47N 35 32 E
Bir 'Ali, *Yemen* **87 D5** 14 1N 48 20 E
Bir Aouine, *Tunisia* **96 B1** 32 25N 9 18 E
Bîr 'Asal, *Egypt* **94 B3** 25 55N 34 20 E
Bir Autrun, *Sudan* **94 D2** 18 15N 26 40 E
Bîr Beiḍa, *Egypt* **91 E3** 30 25N 34 29 E
Bi'r Dhu'fān, *Libya* **96 B2** 31 59N 14 32 E
Bîr Diqnash, *Egypt* **94 A2** 31 3N 25 23 E
Bir el Abbes, *Algeria* **98 C3** 26 7N 6 9W
Bîr el 'Abd, *Egypt* **91 D2** 31 2N 33 0 E
Bir el Ater, *Algeria* **99 B6** 34 46N 8 3 E
Bîr el Basur, *Egypt* **94 B2** 29 51N 25 49 E
Bîr el Biarât, *Egypt* **91 F3** 29 30N 34 43 E
Bîr el Duweidar, *Egypt* **91 E1** 30 56N 32 32 E
Bîr el Garârât, *Egypt* **91 D2** 31 3N 33 34 E
Bîr el Gellaz, *Egypt* **94 A2** 30 50N 26 40 E
Bîr el Heisi, *Egypt* **91 F3** 29 22N 34 36 E
Bîr el Jafir, *Egypt* **91 E1** 30 50N 32 41 E
Bîr el Mâlḥi, *Egypt* **91 E2** 30 38N 33 19 E
Bîr el Shaqqa, *Egypt* **94 A2** 30 54N 25 1 E
Bîr el Thamâda, *Egypt* **91 E2** 30 12N 33 27 E
Bîr Fuad, *Egypt* **94 A2** 30 35N 26 28 E
Bir Gara, *Chad* **97 F3** 13 11N 15 58 E
Bîr Gebeil Ḥiṣn, *Egypt* **91 E2** 30 2N 33 18 E
Bi'r Ghadīr, *Syria* **91 A6** 34 6N 37 3 E
Bîr Haimur, *Egypt* **94 C3** 22 45N 33 40 E
Bîr Ḥasana, *Egypt* **91 E2** 30 29N 33 46 E
Bi'r Īdimah, *Si. Arabia* **86 C4** 18 31N 44 12 E
Bi'r Jadīd, *Iraq* **84 C4** 34 1N 42 54 E
Bir Jdid, *Morocco* **98 B3** 33 26N 8 0W
Bîr Kanayis, *Egypt* **94 C3** 24 59N 33 15 E
Bîr Kaseiba, *Egypt* **91 E2** 31 0N 33 17 E
Bîr Kerawein, *Egypt* **94 B2** 27 10N 28 25 E
Bîr Lahfân, *Egypt* **91 D2** 31 0N 33 51 E
Bir Lahrache, *Algeria* **99 B6** 32 1N 8 12 E
Bîr Madkûr, *Egypt* **91 E1** 30 44N 32 33 E
Bîr Maql, *Egypt* **94 C3** 23 7N 33 40 E
Bîr Misaha, *Egypt* **94 C2** 22 13N 27 59 E
Bir Mogrein, *Mauritania* **98 C2** 25 10N 11 25W
Bîr Murr, *Egypt* **94 C3** 23 28N 30 10 E
Bi'r Muṭribah, *Kuwait* **84 D5** 29 54N 47 17 E
Bîr Nakheila, *Egypt* **94 C3** 24 1N 30 50 E
Bîr Qaṭia, *Egypt* **91 E1** 30 58N 32 45 E
Bîr Qatrani, *Egypt* **94 A2** 30 55N 26 10 E
Bîr Ranga, *Egypt* **94 C4** 24 25N 35 15 E
Bîr Sahara, *Egypt* **94 C2** 22 54N 28 40 E
Bîr Seiyâla, *Egypt* **94 B3** 26 10N 33 50 E
Bir Semguine, *Morocco* **98 B3** 30 1N 5 39W
Bîr Shalatein, *Egypt* **94 C4** 23 5N 35 25 E
Bîr Shebb, *Egypt* **94 C2** 22 25N 29 40 E
Bîr Shût, *Egypt* **94 C4** 23 50N 35 15 E
Bi'r Tamis, *Yemen* **87 C5** 16 45N 48 48 E
Bîr Terfawi, *Egypt* **94 C2** 22 57N 28 55 E
Bîr Umm Qubûr, *Egypt* **94 C3** 24 35N 34 2 E
Bîr Ungât, *Egypt* **94 C3** 22 8N 33 48 E
Bîr Za'farâna, *Egypt* **94 J8** 29 10N 32 40 E
Bîr Zāmūs, *Libya* **96 D3** 24 16N 15 6 E
Bîr Zeidûn, *Egypt* **94 B3** 25 45N 33 40 E
Bira, *Indonesia* **73 B4** 2 3 S 132 2 E
Bîra, *Romania* **46 B8** 47 2N 27 3 E
Biramféro, *Guinea* **100 C3** 11 40N 9 10W
Birao, *C.A.R.* **102 A4** 10 20N 22 47 E
Birawa, *Zaïre* **106 C2** 2 20 S 28 48 E
Bîrca, *Romania* **46 F4** 43 59N 23 36 E
Birch Hills, *Canada* **131 C7** 52 59N 105 25W
Birch I., *Canada* **131 C9** 52 26N 99 54W
Birch L., *N.W.T., Canada* **130 A5** 62 4N 116 33W
Birch L., *Ont., Canada* **128 B1** 51 23N 92 18W
Birch L., *U.S.A.* **128 C1** 47 45N 91 51W
Birch Mts., *Canada* **130 B6** 57 30N 113 10W
Birch River, *Canada* **131 C8** 52 24N 101 6W
Birchip, *Australia* **116 C5** 35 56 S 142 55 E
Birchiş, *Romania* **46 D3** 45 58N 22 9 E
Birchwood, *N.Z.* **119 F2** 45 55 S 167 53 E
Bird, *Canada* **131 B10** 56 30N 94 13W
Bird City, *U.S.A.* **138 F4** 39 45N 101 32W
Bird I. = Aves, I. de, *W. Indies* **149 C7** 15 45N 63 55W
Birdaard, *Neths.* **20 B7** 53 18N 5 53 E
Birdlip, *U.K.* **17 F5** 51 50N 2 5W
Birds, *U.S.A.* **141 F9** 38 50N 87 40W
Birdseye, *U.S.A.* **141 F10** 38 19N 86 42W
Birdsville, *Australia* **114 D2** 25 51 S 139 20 E
Birdum, *Australia* **112 C5** 15 39 S 133 13 E
Birecik, *Turkey* **89 D8** 37 2N 38 0 E
Birein, *Israel* **91 E3** 30 50N 34 28 E
Bireuen, *Indonesia* **74 A1** 5 14N 96 39 E
Birifo, *Gambia* **100 C2** 13 30N 14 0W
Birigui, *Brazil* **159 A5** 21 18 S 50 16W
Birini, *C.A.R.* **102 A4** 7 51N 22 24 E
Birkenfeld, *Germany* **27 F3** 49 38N 7 9 E
Birkenhead, *N.Z.* **118 C3** 36 49 S 174 46 E
Birkenhead, *U.K.* **16 D4** 53 23N 3 2W
Birket Qârûn, *Egypt* **94 J7** 29 30N 30 40 E
Birkfeld, *Austria* **30 D8** 47 21N 15 45 E
Birkhadem, *Algeria* **99 A5** 36 43N 3 3 E
Bîrlad, *Romania* **46 C8** 46 15N 27 38 E
Birlik, *Kazakstan* **55 A6** 44 5N 73 31 E
Birmingham, *U.K.* **17 E6** 52 29N 1 52W
Birmingham, *Ala., U.S.A.* **135 J2** 33 31N 86 48W
Birmingham, *Iowa, U.S.A.* **140 D5** 40 53N 91 57W
Birmitrapur, *India* **82 C7** 22 24N 84 46 E
Birni Ngaouré, *Niger* **101 C5** 13 5N 2 51 E
Birni Nkonni, *Niger* **101 C6** 13 55N 5 15 E
Birnin Gwari, *Nigeria* **101 C6** 11 0N 6 45 E
Birnin Kebbi, *Nigeria* **101 C5** 12 32N 4 12 E
Birnin Kudu, *Nigeria* **101 C6** 11 30N 9 29 E
Birobidzhan, *Russia* **57 E14** 48 50N 132 50 E
Birougou, Mts., *Gabon* **102 C2** 1 51 S 12 20 E
Birr, *Ireland* **19 C4** 53 6N 7 54W
Birrie →, *Australia* **115 D4** 29 43 S 146 37 E
Birs →, *Switz.* **28 B5** 47 24N 7 32 E
Birsilpur, *India* **80 E5** 28 11N 72 15 E
Birsk, *Russia* **54 D5** 55 25N 55 30 E
Birtin, *Romania* **46 C3** 46 59N 22 31 E
Birtle, *Canada* **131 C8** 50 30N 101 5W
Biryuchiy, *Ukraine* **51 J8** 46 10N 35 0 E
Biržai, *Lithuania* **13 H21** 56 11N 24 45 E
Bîrzava, *Romania* **46 C2** 46 7N 21 59 E
Birzebugga, *Malta* **32 D2** 35 49N 14 32 E
Bisa, *Indonesia* **72 B3** 1 15 S 127 28 E
Bisáccia, *Italy* **41 A8** 41 1N 15 22 E
Bisacquino, *Italy* **40 E6** 37 42N 13 15 E
Bisai, *Japan* **63 B8** 35 16N 136 44 E
Bisalpur, *India* **81 E8** 28 14N 79 48 E
Bisbee, *U.S.A.* **143 L9** 31 27N 109 55W
Biscarrosse et de Parentis, Étang de, *France* **24 D2** 44 21N 1 10W
Biscay, B. of, *Atl. Oc.* **8 D8** 45 0N 2 0W
Biscayne B., *U.S.A.* **135 N5** 25 40N 80 12W
Biscéglie, *Italy* **41 A9** 41 14N 16 30 E
Bischofshofen, *Austria* **30 D6** 47 26N 13 14 E
Bischofswerda, *Germany* **26 D10** 51 7N 14 10 E
Bischofszell, *Switz.* **29 B8** 47 29N 9 15 E
Bischwiller, *France* **23 D14** 48 46N 7 50 E
Biscoe Bay, *Antarctica* **7 D13** 77 0 S 152 0W
Biscoe Is., *Antarctica* **7 C17** 66 0 S 67 0W
Biscostasing, *Canada* **128 C3** 47 18N 82 9W
Biscucuy, *Venezuela* **152 B4** 9 22N 69 59W
Biševo, *Croatia* **39 F13** 42 57N 16 3 E
Bisha, *Eritrea* **95 D4** 15 30N 37 31 E
Bishah, W. →, *Si. Arabia* **86 B3** 21 24N 43 26 E
Bishan, *China* **68 C6** 29 33N 106 12 E
Bishkek, *Kyrgyzstan* **55 B7** 42 54N 74 46 E
Bishnupur, *India* **81 H12** 23 8N 87 20 E
Bisho, *S. Africa* **105 E4** 32 50 S 27 23 E
Bishop, *Calif., U.S.A.* **144 H8** 37 22N 118 24W
Bishop, *Tex., U.S.A.* **139 M6** 27 35N 97 48W
Bishop Auckland, *U.K.* **16 C6** 54 39N 1 40W
Bishop's Falls, *Canada* **129 C8** 49 2N 55 30W
Bishop's Stortford, *U.K.* **17 F8** 51 52N 0 10 E
Bisignano, *Italy* **41 C9** 39 31N 16 17 E
Bisina, L., *Uganda* **106 B3** 1 38N 33 56 E
Biskra, *Algeria* **99 B6** 34 50N 5 44 E
Biskupiec, *Poland* **47 B7** 53 53N 20 58 E
Bismarck, *Mo., U.S.A.* **140 G6** 37 46N 90 38W
Bismarck, *N. Dak., U.S.A.* **138 B4** 46 48N 100 47W
Bismarck Arch., *Papua N. G.* **120 B5** 2 30 S 150 0 E
Bismarck Ra., *Papua N. G.* **120 C3** 5 35 S 145 0 E
Bismarck Sea, *Papua N. G.* **120 C4** 4 10 S 146 50 E
Bismark, *Germany* **26 C7** 52 40N 11 33 E
Bismil, *Turkey* **89 D9** 37 51N 40 40 E
Biso, *Uganda* **106 B3** 1 44N 31 26 E
Bison, *U.S.A.* **138 C3** 45 31N 102 28W
Bīsotūn, *Iran* **89 E12** 34 23N 47 26 E
Bispgården, *Sweden* **14 A10** 63 2N 16 40 E
Bissagos = Bijagós, Arquipélago dos, *Guinea-Biss.* **100 C1** 11 15N 16 10W
Bissau, *Guinea-Biss.* **100 C1** 11 45N 15 45W
Bissett, *Canada* **131 C9** 51 2N 95 41W
Bissikrima, *Guinea* **100 C2** 10 50N 10 58W
Bistcho L., *Canada* **130 B5** 59 45N 118 50W
Bistreţu, *Romania* **46 F4** 43 54N 23 23 E
Bistrica = Ilirska-Bistrica, *Slovenia* **39 C11** 45 34N 14 14 E
Bistriţa, *Romania* **46 B5** 47 9N 24 35 E
Bistriţa →, *Romania* **46 C7** 46 30N 26 57 E
Bistriţa Năsăud □, *Romania* **46 B5** 47 15N 24 30 E
Bistriţei, Munţii, *Romania* **46 B6** 47 15N 25 40 E
Biswan, *India* **81 F9** 27 29N 81 2 E
Bisztynek, *Poland* **47 A7** 54 8N 20 53 E
Bitam, *Gabon* **102 B2** 2 5N 11 25 E
Bitburg, *Germany* **27 F2** 49 58N 6 31 E
Bitche, *France* **23 C14** 49 2N 7 25 E
Bithynia, *Turkey* **88 B4** 40 40N 31 0 E
Bitkine, *Chad* **97 F3** 11 59N 18 13 E
Bitlis, *Turkey* **89 C10** 38 20N 42 3 E
Bitola, *Macedonia* **42 F6** 41 5N 21 10 E
Bitolj = Bitola, *Macedonia* **42 F6** 41 5N 21 10 E
Bitonto, *Italy* **41 A9** 41 6N 16 41 E
Bitter Creek, *U.S.A.* **142 F9** 41 33N 108 33W
Bitter L. = Buheirat-Murrat-el-Kubra, *Egypt* **94 H8** 30 18N 32 26 E
Bitterfeld, *Germany* **26 D8** 51 37N 12 20 E
Bitterfontein, *S. Africa* **104 E2** 31 1 S 18 32 E
Bitterroot →, *U.S.A.* **142 C6** 46 52N 114 7W
Bitterroot Range, *U.S.A.* **142 D6** 46 0N 114 20W
Bitterwater, *U.S.A.* **144 J6** 36 23N 121 0W
Bitti, *Italy* **40 B2** 40 29N 9 23 E
Bittou, *Burkina Faso* **101 C4** 11 17N 0 18W
Biu, *Nigeria* **101 C7** 10 40N 12 3 E
Bivolari, *Romania* **46 B8** 47 31N 27 27 E
Bivolu, *Romania* **46 B6** 47 16N 25 58 E
Biwa-Ko, *Japan* **63 B8** 35 15N 136 10 E
Biwabik, *U.S.A.* **138 B8** 47 32N 92 21W
Bixad, *Romania* **46 B4** 47 56N 23 28 E
Biyang, *China* **66 H7** 32 38N 113 21 E
Biylikol, Ozero, *Kazakstan* **55 B5** 43 5N 70 45 E
Biysk, *Russia* **56 D9** 52 40N 85 0 E
Bizana, *S. Africa* **105 E4** 30 50 S 29 52 E
Bizen, *Japan* **62 C6** 34 43N 134 8 E
Bizerte, *Tunisia* **96 A1** 37 15N 9 50 E
Bjargtangar, *Iceland* **12 D1** 65 30N 24 30W
Bjelasica, *Montenegro, Yug.* **42 E4** 42 50N 19 40 E
Bjelašnica, *Bos.-H.* **42 D3** 43 43N 18 9 E
Bjelovar, *Croatia* **42 B1** 45 56N 16 49 E
Bjerringbro, *Denmark* **15 H3** 56 23N 9 39 E
Bjervamoen, *Norway* **14 E3** 59 17N 9 5 E
Bjørnevatn, *Norway* **12 B23** 69 40N 30 0 E
Bjørnøya, *Arctic* **6 B8** 74 30N 19 0 E
Bjuv, *Sweden* **15 H6** 56 5N 12 55 E
Blace, *Serbia, Yug.* **42 D6** 43 18N 21 17 E
Blachownia, *Poland* **47 E5** 50 49N 18 56 E
Black = Da →, *Vietnam* **76 B5** 21 15N 105 20 E
Black →, *Canada* **136 B5** 44 42N 79 19W
Black →, *Ark., U.S.A.* **139 H9** 35 38N 91 20W
Black →, *N.Y., U.S.A.* **137 C8** 43 59N 76 4W
Black →, *Wis., U.S.A.* **138 D9** 43 57N 91 22W
Black Diamond, *Canada* **130 C6** 50 45N 114 14W
Black Forest = Schwarzwald, *Germany* **27 H4** 48 30N 8 20 E
Black Hills, *U.S.A.* **138 C3** 44 0N 103 45W
Black I., *Canada* **131 C9** 51 12N 96 30W
Black L., *Canada* **131 B7** 59 12N 105 15W
Black L., *U.S.A.* **134 C3** 45 28N 84 16W
Black Mesa, *U.S.A.* **139 G3** 36 58N 102 58W
Black Mountain, *Australia* **117 A9** 30 18 S 151 39 E
Black Mt. = Mynydd Du, *U.K.* **17 F4** 51 52N 3 50W
Black Mts., *U.K.* **17 F4** 51 55N 3 7W
Black Range, *U.S.A.* **143 K10** 33 15N 107 50W
Black River, *Jamaica* **148 C4** 18 0N 77 50W
Black River Falls, *U.S.A.* **138 C9** 44 18N 90 51W
Black Rock, *Australia* **116 B3** 32 50 S 138 44 E
Black Sea, *Eurasia* **49 F6** 43 30N 35 0 E
Black Volta →, *Africa* **100 D4** 8 41N 1 33W
Black Warrior →, *U.S.A.* **135 J2** 32 32N 87 51W
Blackall, *Australia* **114 C4** 24 25 S 145 45 E
Blackball, *N.Z.* **119 C6** 42 22 S 171 26 E
Blackbull, *Australia* **114 B3** 17 55 S 141 45 E
Blackburn, *U.K.* **16 D5** 53 45N 2 29W
Blackduck, *U.S.A.* **138 B7** 47 44N 94 33W
Blackfoot, *U.S.A.* **142 E7** 43 11N 112 21W
Blackfoot →, *U.S.A.* **142 C7** 46 52N 113 53W
Blackfoot River Reservoir, *U.S.A.* **142 E8** 43 0N 111 43W
Blackie, *Canada* **130 C6** 50 36N 113 37W
Blackpool, *U.K.* **16 D4** 53 49N 3 3W
Blackriver, *U.S.A.* **136 B1** 44 46N 83 17W
Blacks Harbour, *Canada* **129 C6** 45 3N 66 49W

Bragança 177

Bondeno, *Italy* 39 D8 44 53N 11 25 E
Bondo, *Zaïre* 102 B4 3 55N 23 53 E
Bondoukou, *Ivory C.* 100 D4 8 2N 2 47W
Bondowoso, *Indonesia* 75 D4 7 55 S 113 49 E
Bone, Teluk, *Indonesia* 72 B2 4 10 S 120 50 E
Bonefro, *Italy* 41 A7 41 42N 14 55 E
Bonerate, *Indonesia* 72 C2 7 25 S 121 5 E
Bonerate, Kepulauan, *Indonesia* 72 C2 6 30 S 121 10 E
Bo'ness, *U.K.* 18 E5 56 1N 3 37W
Bonete, Cerro, *Argentina* 158 B2 27 55 S 68 40W
Bong Son = Hoai Nhon, *Vietnam* 76 E7 14 28N 109 1 E
Bongabon, *Phil.* 70 D3 15 38N 121 8 E
Bongabong, *Phil.* 70 E3 12 45N 121 29 E
Bongandanga, *Zaïre* 102 B4 1 24N 21 3 E
Bongo, *Zaïre* 102 C3 1 47 S 17 41 E
Bongor, *Chad* 97 F3 10 35N 15 20 E
Bongouanou, *Ivory C.* 100 D4 6 42N 4 15W
Bonham, *U.S.A.* 139 J6 33 35N 96 11W
Bonheiden, *Belgium* 21 F5 51 1N 4 32 E
Bonifacio, *France* 25 G13 41 24N 9 10 E
Bonifacio, Bouches de, *Medit. S.* 40 A2 41 12N 9 15 E
Bonin Is. = Ogasawara Gunto, *Pac. Oc.* 58 G18 27 0N 142 0 E
Bonke, *Ethiopia* 95 F4 6 5N 37 16 E
Bonn, *Germany* 26 E3 50 46N 7 6 E
Bonnat, *France* 24 B5 46 20N 1 54 E
Bonne Terre, *U.S.A.* 139 G9 37 55N 90 33W
Bonners Ferry, *U.S.A.* 142 B5 48 42N 116 19W
Bonnétable, *France* 22 D7 48 11N 0 25 E
Bonneuil-Matours, *France* 22 F7 46 41N 0 34 E
Bonneval, *France* 22 D8 48 11N 1 24 E
Bonneville, *France* 25 B10 46 4N 6 24 E
Bonney, L., *Australia* 116 D4 37 50 S 140 20 E
Bonnie Doon, *Australia* 117 D6 37 2 S 145 53 E
Bonnie Downs, *Australia* 114 C3 22 7 S 143 50 E
Bonnie Rock, *Australia* 113 F2 30 29 S 118 22 E
Bonny, *Nigeria* 101 E6 4 25N 7 13 E
Bonny →, *Nigeria* 101 E6 4 20N 7 10 E
Bonny, Bight of, *Africa* 101 E6 3 30N 9 20 E
Bonny-sur-Loire, *France* 23 E9 47 33N 2 50 E
Bonnyville, *Canada* 131 C6 54 20N 110 45W
Bonobono, *Phil.* 71 G1 8 40N 117 36 E
Bonoi, *Indonesia* 73 B5 1 45 S 137 41 E
Bonorva, *Italy* 40 B1 40 25N 8 46 E
Bonsall, *U.S.A.* 145 M9 33 16N 117 14W
Bontang, *Indonesia* 75 B5 0 10N 117 30 E
Bonthain, *Indonesia* 72 C1 5 34 S 119 56 E
Bonthe, *S. Leone* 100 D2 7 30N 12 33W
Bontoc, *Phil.* 70 C3 17 7N 120 58 E
Bontosunggu, *Indonesia* 72 C1 5 41 S 119 42 E
Bonyeri, *Ghana* 100 D4 5 1N 2 46W
Bonyhád, *Hungary* 31 E11 46 18N 18 32 E
Bonython Ra., *Australia* 112 D4 23 40 S 128 45 E
Bookabie, *Australia* 113 F5 31 50 S 132 41 E
Booker, *U.S.A.* 139 G4 36 27N 100 32W
Boolaboolka L., *Australia* 116 B5 32 38 S 143 10 E
Boolarra, *Australia* 117 E7 38 20 S 146 20 E
Boolcoomata, *Australia* 116 A4 31 57 S 140 33 E
Booleroo Centre, *Australia* 116 B3 32 53 S 138 21 E
Booligal, *Australia* 117 B6 33 58 S 144 53 E
Boom, *Belgium* 21 F4 51 6N 4 20 E
Boonah, *Australia* 115 D5 27 58 S 152 41 E
Boone, *Iowa, U.S.A.* 140 B3 42 4N 93 53W
Boone, *N.C., U.S.A.* 135 G5 36 13N 81 41W
Booneville, *Ark., U.S.A.* 139 H8 35 8N 93 55W
Booneville, *Miss., U.S.A.* 135 H1 34 39N 88 34W
Boonville, *Calif., U.S.A.* 144 F3 39 1N 123 22W
Boonville, *Ind., U.S.A.* 141 F9 38 3N 87 16W
Boonville, *Mo., U.S.A.* 140 F4 38 58N 92 44W
Boonville, *N.Y., U.S.A.* 137 C9 43 29N 75 20W
Booral, *Australia* 117 B9 32 30 S 151 56 E
Boorindal, *Australia* 115 E4 30 22 S 146 11 E
Booroomugga, *Australia* 117 A7 31 17 S 146 27 E
Boorowa, *Australia* 117 C8 34 28 S 148 44 E
Boothia, Gulf of, *Canada* 127 A11 71 0N 90 0W
Boothia Pen., *Canada* 126 A10 71 0N 94 0W
Bootle, *U.K.* 16 D4 53 28N 3 1W
Boué, *Gabon* 102 C2 0 5 S 11 55 E
Boppard, *Germany* 27 E3 50 13N 7 35 E
Boquerón □, *Paraguay* 157 E5 23 0 S 60 0W
Boquete, *Panama* 148 E3 8 46N 82 27W
Boquilla, Presa de la, *Mexico* 146 B3 27 40N 105 30W
Boquillas del Carmen, *Mexico* 146 B4 29 17N 102 53W
Bor, *Czech.* 30 B5 49 41N 12 45 E
Bor, *Russia* 52 B7 56 28N 43 59 E
Bor, *Serbia, Yug.* 42 C7 44 5N 22 7 E
Bôr, *Sudan* 95 F3 6 10N 31 40 E
Bor, *Turkey* 88 D6 37 54N 34 32 E
Bor Mashash, *Israel* 91 D3 31 7N 34 50 E
Boradā →, *Syria* 91 B5 33 33N 36 34 E
Borah Peak, *U.S.A.* 142 D7 44 8N 113 47W
Borama, *Somali Rep.* 108 C2 9 55N 43 7 E
Borang, *Sudan* 95 G3 4 50N 30 59 E
Borangapara, *India* 78 C3 25 14N 90 14 E
Borås, *Sweden* 15 G6 57 43N 12 56 E
Borāzjān, *Iran* 85 D6 29 22N 51 10 E
Borba, *Brazil* 153 D6 4 12 S 59 34W
Borba, *Portugal* 37 G3 38 50N 7 26W
Borbon, *Phil.* 71 F5 10 50N 124 2 E
Borborema, Planalto da, *Brazil* 154 C4 7 0 S 37 0W
Borçka, *Turkey* 89 B9 41 25N 41 41 E
Borculo, *Neths.* 20 D9 52 7N 6 31 E
Bord Khūn-e Now, *Iran* 85 D6 28 3N 51 28 E
Borda, C., *Australia* 116 C2 35 45 S 136 34 E
Bordeaux, *France* 24 D3 44 50N 0 36W
Borden, *Australia* 113 F2 34 3 S 118 12 E
Borden, *Canada* 129 C7 46 18N 63 47W
Borden I., *Canada* 6 B2 78 30N 111 30W
Borders □, *U.K.* 18 F6 55 35N 2 50W
Bordertown, *Australia* 116 D4 36 19 S 140 45 E
Borðeyri, *Iceland* 12 D3 65 12N 21 6W
Bordighera, *Italy* 38 E4 43 46N 7 39 E
Bordj bou Arreridj, *Algeria* 99 A5 36 4N 4 45 E
Bordj Bourguiba, *Tunisia* 96 B2 32 12N 10 2 E
Bordj Fly Ste. Marie, *Algeria* 98 C4 27 19N 2 32W
Bordj-in-Eker, *Algeria* 99 D6 24 9N 5 3 E
Bordj Menaiel, *Algeria* 99 A5 36 46N 3 43 E
Bordj Messouda, *Algeria* 99 B6 30 12N 9 25 E
Bordj Nili, *Algeria* 99 B5 33 28N 3 2 E
Bordj Omar Driss, *Algeria* 99 C6 28 10N 6 40 E
Bordj Sif Fatima, *Algeria* 99 B6 31 6N 8 41 E
Bordj-Tarat, *Algeria* 99 C6 25 55N 9 3 E
Bordj Zelfana, *Algeria* 99 B5 32 27N 4 15 E
Bordoba, *Kyrgyzstan* 55 D6 39 31N 73 16 E
Borea Creek, *Australia* 117 C7 35 5 S 146 35 E
Borek Wielkopolski, *Poland* 47 D4 51 54N 17 11 E
Boremore, *Australia* 117 B8 33 15 S 149 0 E
Boren Kapuas, Pegunungan, *Malaysia* 75 B4 1 25N 113 15 E
Borensberg, *Sweden* 15 F9 58 34N 15 17 E
Borgå = Porvoo, *Finland* 13 F21 60 24N 25 40 E
Borgarfjörður, *Iceland* 12 D7 65 31N 13 49W
Borgarnes, *Iceland* 12 D3 64 32N 21 55W
Børgefjellet, *Norway* 12 D15 65 20N 13 45 E
Borger, *Neths.* 20 C9 52 54N 6 44 E
Borger, *U.S.A.* 139 H4 35 39N 101 24W
Borgerhout, *Belgium* 21 F4 51 12N 4 28 E
Borghamn, *Sweden* 15 F8 58 23N 14 41 E
Borgholm, *Sweden* 13 H17 56 52N 16 39 E
Bórgia, *Italy* 41 D9 38 49N 16 30 E
Borgloon, *Belgium* 21 G6 50 48N 5 21 E
Borgo San Dalmazzo, *Italy* 38 D4 44 20N 7 30 E
Borgo San Lorenzo, *Italy* 39 E8 43 57N 11 23 E
Borgo Valsugano, *Italy* 39 B8 46 3N 11 27 E
Borgomanero, *Italy* 38 C5 45 42N 8 28 E
Borgonovo Val Tidone, *Italy* 38 C6 45 1N 9 26 E
Borgorose, *Italy* 39 F10 42 11N 13 13 E
Borgosésia, *Italy* 38 C5 45 43N 8 16 E
Borgvattnet, *Sweden* 14 A9 63 26N 15 48 E
Borikhane, *Laos* 76 C4 18 33N 103 43 E
Borisoglebsk, *Russia* 52 E6 51 27N 42 5 E
Borisov = Barysaw, *Belarus* 50 E5 54 17N 28 28 E
Borisovka, *Kazakstan* 55 B4 43 15N 68 10 E
Borisovka, *Russia* 52 E3 50 36N 36 1 E
Borja, *Peru* 152 D2 4 20 S 77 40W
Borja, *Spain* 34 D3 41 48N 1 34W
Borjas Blancas, *Spain* 34 D5 41 31N 0 52 E
Borjomi, *Georgia* 53 K6 41 48N 43 28 E
Borken, *Germany* 26 D2 51 50N 6 52 E
Borkou, *Chad* 97 E3 18 15N 18 50 E
Borkum, *Germany* 26 B2 53 34N 6 40 E
Borlänge, *Sweden* 13 F16 60 29N 15 26 E
Borley, C., *Antarctica* 7 C5 66 15 S 52 30 E
Bormida →, *Italy* 38 D5 44 23N 8 13 E
Bórmio, *Italy* 38 B7 46 28N 10 22 E
Born, *Neths.* 21 F7 51 2N 5 49 E
Borna, *Germany* 26 D8 51 7N 12 29 E
Borndiep, *Neths.* 20 B7 53 27N 5 35 E
Borne, *Neths.* 20 D9 52 18N 6 46 E
Bornem, *Belgium* 21 F4 51 6N 4 14 E
Borneo, *E. Indies* 75 B4 1 0N 115 0 E
Bornholm, *Denmark* 13 J16 55 10N 15 0 E
Borno □, *Nigeria* 101 C7 11 30N 13 0 E
Bornos, *Spain* 37 J5 36 48N 5 42W
Bornu Yassa, *Nigeria* 101 C7 12 14N 12 25 E
Borobudur, *Indonesia* 75 D4 7 36 S 110 13 E
Borodino, *Russia* 52 C2 55 31N 35 40 E
Borogontsy, *Russia* 57 C14 62 42N 131 8 E
Boromo, *Burkina Faso* 100 C4 11 45N 2 58W
Boron, *U.S.A.* 145 L9 35 0N 117 39W
Boronga Is., *Burma* 78 F4 19 58N 93 6 E
Borongan, *Phil.* 71 F5 11 37N 125 26 E
Bororen, *Australia* 114 C5 24 13 S 151 33 E
Borotangba Mts., *C.A.R.* 95 F1 6 30N 25 0 E
Borovan, *Bulgaria* 43 D8 43 27N 23 45 E
Borovichi, *Russia* 50 C7 58 25N 33 55 E
Borovsk, *Russia* 52 C3 55 12N 36 24 E
Borovsk, *Russia* 54 B6 59 43N 56 40 E
Borrego Springs, *U.S.A.* 145 M10 33 15N 116 23W
Borriol, *Spain* 34 E4 40 4N 0 4W
Borroloola, *Australia* 114 B2 16 4 S 136 17 E
Borşa, *Romania* 46 B5 47 41N 24 50 E
Borsod-Abaúj-Zemplén □, *Hungary* 31 C13 48 20N 21 0 E
Borssele, *Neths.* 21 F3 51 26N 3 45 E
Bort-les-Orgues, *France* 24 C6 45 24N 2 29 E
Borth, *U.K.* 17 E3 52 29N 4 2W
Borūjerd, *Iran* 89 F13 33 55N 48 50 E
Boryslav, *Ukraine* 51 H2 49 18N 23 28 E
Boryspil, *Ukraine* 51 G6 50 21N 30 59 E
Borzhomi = Borjomi, *Georgia* 53 K6 41 48N 43 28 E
Borzna, *Ukraine* 51 G7 51 18N 32 26 E
Borzya, *Russia* 57 D12 50 24N 116 31 E
Bosa, *Italy* 40 B1 40 18N 8 30 E
Bosaga, *Turkmenistan* 55 E2 37 33N 65 41 E
Bosanska Brod, *Bos.-H.* 42 B3 45 10N 18 0 E
Bosanska Dubica, *Bos.-H.* 39 C13 45 10N 16 50 E
Bosanska Gradiška, *Bos.-H.* 42 B2 45 10N 17 15 E
Bosanska Kostajnica, *Bos.-H.* 39 C13 45 11N 16 33 E
Bosanska Krupa, *Bos.-H.* 39 D13 44 53N 16 10 E
Bosanski Novi, *Bos.-H.* 39 C13 45 2N 16 22 E
Bosanski Šamac, *Bos.-H.* 42 B3 45 3N 18 29 E
Bosansko Grahovo, *Bos.-H.* 39 D13 44 12N 16 26 E
Bosansko Petrovac, *Bos.-H.* 39 D13 44 35N 16 21 E
Bosaso, *Somali Rep.* 108 B3 11 12N 49 18 E
Bosavi, Mt., *Papua N. G.* 120 D2 6 30 S 142 49 E
Boscastle, *U.K.* 17 G3 50 41N 4 42W
Boscobel, *U.S.A.* 140 A6 43 8N 90 42W
Boscotrecase, *Italy* 41 B7 40 46N 14 28 E
Bose, *China* 68 F6 23 53N 106 35 E
Boshan, *China* 67 F9 36 28N 117 49 E
Boshof, *S. Africa* 104 D4 28 31 S 25 13 E
Boshrūyeh, *Iran* 85 C8 33 50N 57 30 E
Bosilegrad, *Serbia, Yug.* 42 E7 42 30N 22 27 E
Boskoop, *Neths.* 20 D5 52 4N 4 40 E
Boskovice, *Czech.* 31 B9 49 29N 16 40 E
Bosna →, *Bos.-H.* 42 B3 45 4N 18 29 E
Bosna i Hercegovina = Bosnia-Herzegovina ■, *Europe* 42 D2 44 0N 17 0 E
Bosnia-Herzegovina ■, *Europe* 42 D2 44 0N 17 0 E
Bosnik, *Indonesia* 73 B5 1 5 S 136 10 E
Bōsō-Hantō, *Japan* 63 B12 35 20N 140 20 E
Bosobolo, *Zaïre* 102 B3 4 15N 19 50 E
Bosporus = Karadeniz Boğazı, *Turkey* 88 B3 41 10N 29 10 E
Bossangoa, *C.A.R.* 102 A3 6 35N 17 30 E
Bossembélé, *C.A.R.* 102 A3 5 25N 17 40 E
Bossembélé II, *C.A.R.* 102 A3 5 41N 16 38 E
Bossier City, *U.S.A.* 139 J8 32 31N 93 44W
Bosso, *Niger* 97 F2 13 43N 13 19 E
Bostānābād, *Iran* 89 D12 37 50N 46 50 E
Bosten Hu, *China* 64 B3 41 55N 87 40 E
Boston, *Phil.* 71 H6 7 52N 126 22 E
Boston, *U.K.* 16 E7 52 59N 0 2W
Boston, *U.S.A.* 137 D13 42 22N 71 4W
Boston Bar, *Canada* 130 D4 49 52N 121 30W
Bosusulu, *Zaïre* 102 B4 0 50N 20 45 E
Bosut →, *Croatia* 42 B3 45 20N 18 45 E
Boswell, *Canada* 130 D5 49 28N 116 45W
Boswell, *Ind., U.S.A.* 141 D9 40 31N 87 23W
Boswell, *Okla., U.S.A.* 139 H7 34 2N 95 52W
Boswell, *Pa., U.S.A.* 136 F5 40 10N 79 2W
Bosworth, *U.S.A.* 140 E3 39 28N 93 20W
Botad, *India* 80 H4 22 15N 71 40 E
Botan →, *Turkey* 89 D10 37 57N 42 2 E
Botany B., *Australia* 115 E5 34 0 S 151 14 E
Botene, *Laos* 76 D3 17 35N 101 12 E
Botevgrad, *Bulgaria* 43 E8 42 55N 23 47 E
Bothaville, *S. Africa* 104 D4 27 23 S 26 34 E
Bothnia, G. of, *Europe* 12 E19 63 0N 20 15 E
Bothwell, *Australia* 114 G4 42 20 S 147 1 E
Bothwell, *Canada* 136 D3 42 38N 81 52W
Boticas, *Portugal* 36 D3 41 41N 7 40W
Botletle →, *Botswana* 104 C3 20 10 S 23 15 E
Botlikh, *Russia* 53 J8 42 39N 46 11 E
Botolan, *Phil.* 70 D3 15 17N 120 1 E
Botoroaga, *Romania* 46 E6 44 8N 25 32 E
Botoşani, *Romania* 46 B7 47 42N 26 41 E
Botoşani □, *Romania* 46 B7 47 50N 26 50 E
Botro, *Ivory C.* 100 D3 7 51N 5 19W
Botswana ■, *Africa* 104 C3 22 0 S 24 0 E
Bottineau, *U.S.A.* 138 A4 48 50N 100 27W
Bottrop, *Germany* 21 E9 51 31N 6 58 E
Botucatu, *Brazil* 159 A6 22 55 S 48 30W
Botwood, *Canada* 129 C8 49 6N 55 23W
Bou Alam, *Algeria* 99 B5 33 50N 1 26 E
Bou Ali, *Algeria* 99 C4 27 11N 0 4W
Bou Djébéha, *Mali* 100 B4 18 25N 2 45W
Bou Guema, *Algeria* 99 C5 28 49N 0 19 E
Bou Ismael, *Algeria* 99 A5 36 38N 2 42 E
Bou Izakarn, *Morocco* 98 C3 29 12N 9 46W
Boû Lanouâr, *Mauritania* 98 D1 21 12N 16 34W
Bou Saâda, *Algeria* 99 A5 35 11N 4 9 E
Bou Salem, *Tunisia* 96 A1 36 45N 9 2 E
Bouaké, *Ivory C.* 100 D3 7 40N 5 2W
Bouanga, *Congo* 102 C3 2 7 S 16 8 E
Bouar, *C.A.R.* 102 A3 6 0N 15 40 E
Bouârfa, *Morocco* 99 B4 32 32N 1 58W
Bouca, *C.A.R.* 102 A3 6 45N 18 25 E
Boucau, *France* 24 E2 43 32N 1 29W
Boucaut B., *Australia* 114 A1 12 0 S 134 25 E
Bouches-du-Rhône □, *France* 25 E9 43 37N 5 2 E
Bouda, *Algeria* 99 C4 27 50N 0 27W
Boudenib, *Morocco* 98 B4 31 59N 3 31W
Boudry, *Switz.* 28 C3 46 57N 6 50 E
Boufarik, *Algeria* 99 A5 36 34N 2 58 E
Bougainville, C., *Australia* 112 B4 13 57 S 126 4 E
Bougainville I., *Solomon Is.* 121 L8 6 0 S 155 0 E
Bougainville Reef, *Australia* 114 B4 15 30 S 147 5 E
Bougainville Str., *Solomon Is.* 121 L9 6 40 S 156 10 E
Bougaroun, C., *Algeria* 99 A6 37 6N 6 30 E
Bougie = Bejaia, *Algeria* 99 A6 36 42N 5 2 E
Bougouni, *Mali* 100 C3 11 30N 7 20W
Bouillon, *Belgium* 21 J6 49 44N 5 3 E
Bouïra, *Algeria* 99 A5 36 20N 3 59 E
Boulder, *Colo., U.S.A.* 138 E2 40 1N 105 17W
Boulder, *Mont., U.S.A.* 142 C7 46 14N 112 7W
Boulder City, *U.S.A.* 145 K12 35 59N 114 50W
Boulder Creek, *U.S.A.* 144 H4 37 7N 122 7W
Boulder Dam = Hoover Dam, *U.S.A.* 145 K12 36 1N 114 44W
Boulembo, *Gabon* 102 C2 1 26 S 12 0 E
Bouli, *Mauritania* 100 B2 15 17N 12 18W
Boulia, *Australia* 114 C2 22 52 S 139 51 E
Bouligny, *France* 23 C12 49 17N 5 45 E
Boulogne →, *France* 22 E5 47 12N 1 47W
Boulogne-sur-Gesse, *France* 24 E4 43 18N 0 38 E
Boulogne-sur-Mer, *France* 23 B8 50 42N 1 36 E
Bouloire, *France* 22 E7 47 59N 0 45 E
Bouloupari, *N. Cal.* 121 U20 21 52 S 166 4 E
Boulsa, *Burkina Faso* 101 C4 12 39N 0 34W
Boultoum, *Niger* 97 F2 14 45N 10 25 E
Boumalne, *Morocco* 98 B3 31 25N 6 0W
Boun Neua, *Laos* 76 B3 21 38N 101 54 E
Boun Tai, *Laos* 76 B3 21 23N 101 58 E
Bouna, *Ivory C.* 100 D4 9 10N 3 0W
Boundary Peak, *U.S.A.* 144 H8 37 51N 118 21W
Boundiali, *Ivory C.* 100 D3 9 30N 6 20W
Bountiful, *U.S.A.* 142 F8 40 53N 111 53W
Bounty Is., *Pac. Oc.* 122 M9 48 0 S 178 30 E
Bourail, *N. Cal.* 121 U19 21 34 S 165 30 E
Bourbeuse →, *U.S.A.* 140 F6 38 24N 90 53W
Bourbon, *U.S.A.* 141 C10 41 18N 86 7W
Bourbon-Lancy, *France* 24 B7 46 37N 3 45 E
Bourbon-l'Archambault, *France* 24 B7 46 36N 3 4 E
Bourbonnais, *France* 24 B7 46 28N 3 0 E
Bourbonne-les-Bains, *France* 23 E12 47 54N 5 45 E
Bourem, *Mali* 101 B4 17 0N 0 24W
Bourg, *France* 24 C3 45 3N 0 34W
Bourg-Argental, *France* 25 C8 45 18N 4 32 E
Bourg-de-Péage, *France* 25 C9 45 2N 5 3 E
Bourg-en-Bresse, *France* 25 B9 46 13N 5 12 E
Bourg-St.-Andéol, *France* 25 D8 44 23N 4 39 E
Bourg-St.-Maurice, *France* 25 C10 45 35N 6 46 E
Bourg-St.-Pierre, *Switz.* 28 E4 45 57N 7 12 E
Bourganeuf, *France* 24 C5 45 57N 1 45 E
Bourges, *France* 23 E9 47 9N 2 25 E
Bourget, *Canada* 137 A9 45 26N 75 9W
Bourget, L. du, *France* 25 C9 45 44N 5 52 E
Bourgneuf, B. de, *France* 22 E4 47 3N 2 10W
Bourgneuf-en-Retz, *France* 22 E5 47 2N 1 58W
Bourgogne, *France* 23 F11 47 0N 4 50 E
Bourgoin-Jallieu, *France* 25 C9 45 36N 5 17 E
Bourgueil, *France* 22 E7 47 17N 0 10 E
Bourke, *Australia* 115 E4 30 8 S 145 55 E
Bournemouth, *U.K.* 17 G6 50 43N 1 52W
Bourriot-Bergonce, *France* 24 D3 44 7N 0 14W
Bouse, *U.S.A.* 145 M13 33 56N 114 0W
Boussac, *France* 24 B6 46 22N 2 13 E
Boussens, *France* 24 E4 43 12N 0 58 E
Bousso, *Chad* 97 F3 10 34N 16 52 E
Boussu, *Belgium* 21 H3 50 26N 3 48 E
Boutilimit, *Mauritania* 100 B2 17 45N 14 40W
Boutonne →, *France* 24 C3 45 54N 0 50W
Bouvet I. = Bouvetøya, *Antarctica* 9 P9 54 26 S 3 24 E
Bouvetøya, *Antarctica* 9 P9 54 26 S 3 24 E
Bouznika, *Morocco* 98 B3 33 46N 7 6W
Bouzonville, *France* 23 C13 49 17N 6 32 E
Bova Marina, *Italy* 41 E8 37 56N 15 55 E
Bovalino Marina, *Italy* 41 D9 38 10N 16 10 E
Bovec, *Slovenia* 39 B10 46 20N 13 33 E
Bovenkarspel, *Neths.* 20 C6 52 41N 5 14 E
Bovigny, *Belgium* 21 H7 50 12N 5 55 E
Bovill, *U.S.A.* 142 C5 46 51N 116 24W
Bovino, *Italy* 41 A8 41 15N 15 20 E
Bow Island, *Canada* 130 D6 49 50N 111 23W
Bowbells, *U.S.A.* 138 A3 48 48N 102 15W
Bowdle, *U.S.A.* 138 C5 45 27N 99 39W
Bowelling, *Australia* 113 F2 33 25 S 116 30 E
Bowen, *Australia* 114 C4 20 0 S 148 16 E
Bowen Mts., *Australia* 117 D7 37 0 S 147 50 E
Bowie, *Ariz., U.S.A.* 143 K9 32 19N 109 29W
Bowie, *Tex., U.S.A.* 139 J6 33 34N 97 51W
Bowkān, *Iran* 89 D12 36 31N 46 12 E
Bowland, Forest of, *U.K.* 16 D5 54 0N 2 30W
Bowling Green, *Ky., U.S.A.* 134 G2 36 59N 86 27W
Bowling Green, *Mo., U.S.A.* 140 E5 39 21N 91 12W
Bowling Green, *Ohio, U.S.A.* 141 C13 41 23N 83 39W
Bowling Green, C., *Australia* 114 B4 19 19 S 147 25 E
Bowman, *U.S.A.* 138 B3 46 11N 103 24W
Bowman I., *Antarctica* 7 C8 65 0 S 104 0 E
Bowmans, *Australia* 116 C3 34 10 S 138 17 E
Bowmanville, *Canada* 128 D4 43 55N 78 41W
Bowmore, *U.K.* 18 F2 55 45N 6 17W
Bowral, *Australia* 117 C9 34 26 S 150 27 E
Bowraville, *Australia* 115 E5 30 37 S 152 52 E
Bowron →, *Canada* 130 C4 54 3N 121 50W
Bowser L., *Canada* 130 B3 56 30N 129 30W
Bowsman, *Canada* 131 C8 52 14N 101 12W
Bowutu Mts., *Papua N. G.* 120 D4 7 45 S 147 10 E
Bowwood, *Zambia* 107 F2 17 5 S 26 20 E
Boxholm, *Sweden* 15 F9 58 12N 15 3 E
Boxmeer, *Neths.* 21 E7 51 38N 5 56 E
Boxtel, *Neths.* 21 E6 51 36N 5 20 E
Boyabat, *Turkey* 88 B6 41 28N 34 47 E
Boyabo, *Zaïre* 102 B3 3 43N 18 46 E
Boyaca = Casanare □, *Colombia* 152 B3 5 30N 72 0W
Boyce, *U.S.A.* 139 K8 31 23N 92 40W
Boyer →, *Canada* 130 B5 58 27N 115 57W
Boyer, C., *N. Cal.* 121 U22 21 37 S 168 6 E
Boyle, *Ireland* 19 C3 53 59N 8 18W
Boyne →, *Ireland* 19 C5 53 43N 6 15W
Boyne City, *U.S.A.* 134 C3 45 13N 85 1W
Boyni Qara, *Afghan.* 79 A2 36 20N 67 0 E
Boynton Beach, *U.S.A.* 135 M5 26 32N 80 4W
Boyolali, *Indonesia* 75 D4 7 32 S 110 35 E
Boyoma, Chutes, *Zaïre* 102 B5 0 35N 25 23 E
Boyup Brook, *Australia* 113 F2 33 50 S 116 23 E
Boz Dağ, *Turkey* 88 D3 37 18N 29 11 E
Boz Dağları, *Turkey* 88 C3 38 20N 28 0 E
Bozburun, *Turkey* 88 D3 36 43N 28 8 E
Bozcaada, *Turkey* 88 C2 39 49N 26 3 E
Bozdoğan, *Turkey* 88 D3 37 40N 28 17 E
Bozeman, *U.S.A.* 142 D8 45 41N 111 2W
Bozen = Bolzano, *Italy* 39 B8 46 31N 11 22 E
Bozene, *Zaïre* 102 B3 2 56N 19 12 E
Boźepole Wielkopolski, *Poland* 47 A4 54 33N 17 56 E
Boževac, *Serbia, Yug.* 42 C6 44 32N 21 24 E
Bozkır, *Turkey* 88 D5 37 11N 32 14 E
Bozouls, *France* 24 D6 44 28N 2 43 E
Bozoum, *C.A.R.* 102 A3 6 25N 16 35 E
Bozova, *Turkey* 89 D8 37 21N 38 32 E
Bozovici, *Romania* 46 E3 44 56N 22 1 E
Bozüyük, *Turkey* 88 C4 39 54N 30 3 E
Bra, *Italy* 38 D4 44 42N 7 51 E
Brabant □, *Belgium* 21 G5 50 46N 4 30 E
Brabant L., *Canada* 131 B8 55 58N 103 43W
Brabrand, *Denmark* 15 H4 56 9N 10 7 E
Brač, *Croatia* 39 E13 43 20N 16 40 E
Bracadale, L., *U.K.* 18 D2 57 20N 6 30W
Bracciano, *Italy* 39 F9 42 6N 12 10 E
Bracciano, L. di, *Italy* 39 F9 42 7N 12 14 E
Bracebridge, *Canada* 128 C4 45 2N 79 19W
Brach, *Libya* 96 C2 27 31N 14 20 E
Bracieux, *France* 23 E8 47 30N 1 30 E
Bräcke, *Sweden* 14 B9 62 45N 15 26 E
Brackettville, *U.S.A.* 139 L4 29 19N 100 25W
Bracki Kanal, *Croatia* 39 E13 43 24N 16 40 E
Brad, *Romania* 46 C3 46 10N 22 50 E
Brádano →, *Italy* 41 B9 40 23N 16 51 E
Bradenton, *U.S.A.* 135 M4 27 30N 82 34W
Bradford, *Canada* 136 B5 44 7N 79 34W
Bradford, *U.K.* 16 D6 53 47N 1 45W
Bradford, *Ill., U.S.A.* 140 C7 41 11N 89 39W
Bradford, *Ohio, U.S.A.* 141 D12 40 8N 84 27W
Bradford, *Pa., U.S.A.* 136 E6 41 58N 78 38W
Bradford, *Vt., U.S.A.* 137 C12 43 59N 72 9W
Brădiceni, *Romania* 46 D4 45 3N 23 4 E
Bradley, *Ark., U.S.A.* 139 J8 33 6N 93 39W
Bradley, *Calif., U.S.A.* 144 K6 35 52N 120 48W
Bradley, *Ill., U.S.A.* 141 C9 41 9N 87 52W
Bradley, *S. Dak., U.S.A.* 138 C6 45 5N 97 39W
Bradley Institute, *Zimbabwe* 107 F3 17 7 S 31 25 E
Bradore Bay, *Canada* 129 B8 51 27N 57 18W
Bradshaw, *Australia* 112 C5 15 21 S 130 16 E
Brady, *U.S.A.* 139 K5 31 9N 99 20W
Brædstrup, *Denmark* 15 J3 55 58N 9 37 E
Braemar, *Australia* 116 B3 33 12 S 139 35 E
Braeside, *Canada* 137 A8 45 28N 76 24W
Braga, *Portugal* 36 D2 41 35N 8 25W
Braga □, *Portugal* 36 D2 41 30N 8 30W
Bragado, *Argentina* 158 D3 35 2 S 60 27W
Bragança, *Brazil* 154 B2 1 0 S 47 2W
Bragança, *Portugal* 36 D4 41 48N 6 50W

178 Bragança

Bragança □, Portugal 36 D4 41 30N 6 45W
Bragança Paulista, Brazil 159 A6 22 55 S 46 32W
Brahmanbaria, Bangla. 78 D3 23 58N 91 15 E
Brahmani →, India 82 D8 20 39N 86 46 E
Brahmaputra →, India 78 D2 23 58N 89 50 E
Braich-y-pwll, U.K. 16 E3 52 47N 4 46W
Braidwood, Australia 117 C8 35 27 S 149 49 E
Brăila, Romania 46 D8 45 19N 27 59 E
Brăila □, Romania 46 D8 45 5N 27 30 E
Braine-l'Alleud, Belgium 21 G4 50 42N 4 23 E
Braine-le-Comte, Belgium 21 G4 50 37N 4 8 E
Brainerd, U.S.A. 138 B7 46 22N 94 12W
Braintree, U.K. 17 F8 51 53N 0 34 E
Braintree, U.S.A. 137 D14 42 13N 71 0W
Brak →, S. Africa 104 D3 29 35 S 22 55 E
Brake, Germany 26 B4 53 20N 8 28 E
Brakel, Germany 26 D5 51 42N 9 11 E
Brakel, Neths. 20 E6 51 49N 5 5 E
Brakwater, Namibia 104 C2 22 28 S 17 3 E
Brålanda, Sweden 15 F6 58 34N 12 21 E
Bralorne, Canada 130 C4 50 50N 122 50W
Bramberg, Germany 27 E6 50 6N 10 40 E
Bramming, Denmark 15 J2 55 28N 8 42 E
Brämön, Sweden 14 B11 62 14N 17 40 E
Brampton, Canada 128 D4 43 45N 79 45W
Bramsche, Germany 26 C3 52 24N 7 59 E
Bramwell, Australia 114 A3 12 8 S 142 37 E
Branco →, Brazil 153 D5 1 20 S 61 50W
Branco, C., Brazil 154 C5 7 9 S 34 47W
Brande, Denmark 15 J3 55 57N 9 8 E
Brandenburg = Neubrandenburg, Germany 26 B9 53 33N 13 15 E
Brandenburg, Germany 26 C8 52 25N 12 33 E
Brandenburg, U.S.A. 141 G10 38 0N 86 10W
Brandenburg □, Germany 26 C9 52 50N 13 0 E
Brandfort, S. Africa 104 D4 28 40 S 26 30 E
Brandon, Canada 131 D9 49 50N 99 57W
Brandon, U.S.A. 137 C11 43 48N 73 4W
Brandon B., Ireland 19 D1 52 17N 10 8W
Brandon Mt., Ireland 19 D1 52 15N 10 15W
Brandsen, Argentina 158 D4 35 10 S 58 15W
Brandval, Norway 14 D6 60 19N 12 1 E
Brandvlei, S. Africa 104 E3 30 25 S 20 30 E
Brandýs, Czech. 30 A7 50 10N 14 40 E
Branford, U.S.A. 137 E12 41 17N 72 49W
Braniewo, Poland 47 A6 54 25N 19 50 E
Bransfield Str., Antarctica 7 C18 63 0 S 59 0W
Brańsk, Poland 47 C9 52 45N 22 50 E
Branson, Colo., U.S.A. 139 G3 37 1N 103 53W
Branson, Mo., U.S.A. 139 G8 36 39N 93 13W
Brantford, Canada 128 D3 43 10N 80 15W
Brantôme, France 24 C4 45 22N 0 39 E
Branxholme, Australia 116 D4 37 52 S 141 49 E
Branxton, Australia 117 B9 32 38 S 151 21 E
Branzi, Italy 38 B6 46 0N 9 46 E
Bras d'Or, L., Canada 129 C7 45 50N 60 50W
Brasil, Planalto, Brazil 150 E6 18 0 S 46 30W
Brasiléia, Brazil 156 C4 11 0 S 68 45W
Brasília, Brazil 155 E2 15 47 S 47 55W
Brasília Legal, Brazil 153 D6 3 49 S 55 36W
Braslaw, Belarus 13 J22 55 38N 27 0 E
Braslovce, Slovenia 39 B12 46 21N 15 3 E
Braşov, Romania 46 D6 45 38N 25 35 E
Braşov □, Romania 46 D6 45 45N 25 15 E
Brass, Nigeria 101 E6 4 35N 6 14 E
Brass →, Nigeria 101 E6 4 15N 6 13 E
Brassac-les-Mines, France 24 C7 45 24N 3 20 E
Brasschaat, Belgium 21 F4 51 19N 4 27 E
Brassey, Banjaran, Malaysia 75 B5 5 0N 117 15 E
Brassey Ra., Australia 113 E3 25 8 S 122 15 E
Brasstown Bald, U.S.A. 135 H4 34 53N 83 49W
Brastad, Sweden 13 G14 58 23N 11 30 E
Bratan = Morozov, Bulgaria 43 E10 42 30N 25 10 E
Bratislava, Slovak Rep. 31 C10 48 10N 17 7 E
Bratsigovo, Bulgaria 43 E9 42 1N 24 22 E
Bratsk, Russia 57 D11 56 10N 101 30 E
Brattleboro, U.S.A. 137 D12 42 51N 72 34W
Bratunac, Bos.-H. 42 C4 44 13N 19 21 E
Braunau, Austria 30 C6 48 15N 13 3 E
Braunschweig, Germany 26 C6 52 15N 10 31 E
Braunton, U.K. 17 F3 51 7N 4 10W
Brava, Somali Rep. 108 D2 1 20N 44 8 E
Bråviken, Sweden 14 F10 58 38N 16 32 E
Bravo del Norte →, Mexico 146 B5 25 57N 97 9W
Bravo del Norte, R. → = Grande, Rio →, U.S.A. 139 N6 25 58N 97 9W
Brawley, U.S.A. 145 N11 32 59N 115 31W
Bray, Ireland 19 C5 53 13N 6 7W
Bray, Mt., Australia 114 A1 14 0 S 134 30 E
Bray, Pays de, France 23 C8 49 46N 1 26 E
Bray-sur-Seine, France 23 D10 48 25N 3 14 E
Braymer, U.S.A. 140 E3 39 35N 93 48W
Brazeau →, Canada 130 C5 52 55N 115 14W
Brazil, U.S.A. 141 E9 39 32N 87 8W
Brazil ■, S. Amer. 155 D2 12 0 S 50 0W
Brazilian Highlands = Brasil, Planalto, Brazil 150 E6 18 0 S 46 30W
Brazo Sur →, S. Amer. 158 B4 25 21 S 57 42W
Brazos →, U.S.A. 139 L7 28 53N 95 23W
Brazzaville, Congo 103 C3 4 9 S 15 12 E
Brčko, Bos.-H. 42 C3 44 54N 18 46 E
Brda →, Poland 47 B5 53 8N 18 8 E
Brea, Peru 156 A1 4 40 S 81 7W
Breadalbane, Australia 114 C2 23 50 S 139 35 E
Breadalbane, U.K. 18 E4 56 30N 4 15W
Breaden, L., Australia 113 E4 25 51 S 125 28 E
Breaksea Sd., N.Z. 119 F1 45 35 S 166 35 E
Bream B., N.Z. 118 B3 35 56 S 174 28 E
Bream Hd., N.Z. 118 B3 35 51 S 174 36 E
Bream Tail, N.Z. 118 C3 36 3 S 174 36 E
Breas, Chile 158 B1 25 29 S 70 24W
Brebes, Indonesia 75 D3 6 52 S 109 3 E
Brechin, Canada 136 B5 44 32N 79 10W
Brechin, U.K. 18 E6 56 44N 2 39W
Brecht, Belgium 21 F5 51 21N 4 38 E
Breckenridge, Colo., U.S.A. 142 G10 39 29N 106 3W
Breckenridge, Minn., U.S.A. 138 B6 46 16N 96 35W
Breckenridge, Mo., U.S.A. 140 E3 39 46N 93 48W
Breckenridge, Tex., U.S.A. 139 J5 32 45N 98 54W
Breckland, U.K. 17 E8 52 30N 0 40 E
Brecknock, Pen., Chile 160 D2 54 35 S 71 30W
Břeclav, Czech. 31 C9 48 46N 16 53 E
Brecon, U.K. 17 F4 51 57N 3 23W
Brecon Beacons, U.K. 17 F4 51 53N 3 26W
Breda, Neths. 21 E5 51 35N 4 45 E
Bredasdorp, S. Africa 104 E3 34 33 S 20 2 E
Bredbo, Australia 117 C8 35 58 S 149 10 E
Bredene, Belgium 21 F1 51 14N 2 59 E
Bredstedt, Germany 26 A4 54 37N 8 55 E
Bredy, Russia 54 E8 52 26N 60 21 E
Bree, Belgium 21 F7 51 8N 5 35 E
Breezand, Neths. 20 C5 52 53N 4 49 E
Bregalnica →, Macedonia 42 F7 41 43N 22 9 E
Bregenz, Austria 30 D2 47 30N 9 45 E
Bregovo, Bulgaria 42 C7 44 9N 22 39 E
Bréhal, France 22 D5 48 53N 1 30W
Bréhat, I. de, France 22 D4 48 51N 3 0W
Breiðafjörður, Iceland 12 D2 65 15N 23 15W
Breil-sur-Roya, France 25 E11 43 56N 7 31 E
Breisach, Germany 27 G3 48 1N 7 36 E
Brejinho de Nazaré, Brazil 154 D2 11 1 S 48 34W
Brejo, Brazil 154 B3 3 41 S 42 47W
Bremen, Germany 26 B4 53 4N 8 47 E
Bremen □, Germany 26 B4 53 4N 8 50 E
Bremer I., Australia 114 A2 12 5 S 136 45 E
Bremerhaven, Germany 26 B4 53 33N 8 36 E
Bremerton, U.S.A. 144 C4 47 34N 122 38W
Bremervörde, Germany 26 B5 53 29N 9 8 E
Bremsnes, Norway 14 A1 63 6N 7 40 E
Brenes, Spain 37 H5 37 32N 5 54W
Brenham, U.S.A. 139 K6 30 10N 96 24W
Brenner P., Austria 30 D4 47 2N 11 30 E
Breno, Italy 38 C7 45 57N 10 18 E
Brent, Canada 128 C4 46 2N 78 29W
Brent, U.K. 17 F7 51 33N 0 16W
Brenta →, Italy 39 C9 45 11N 12 18 E
Brentwood, U.K. 17 F8 51 37N 0 19 E
Brentwood, U.S.A. 137 F11 40 47N 73 15W
Bréscia, Italy 38 C7 45 33N 10 15 E
Breskens, Neths. 21 F3 51 23N 3 33 E
Breslau = Wrocław, Poland 47 D4 51 5N 17 5 E
Bresle →, France 22 B8 50 4N 1 22 E
Bresles, France 23 C9 49 25N 2 13 E
Bressanone, Italy 39 B8 46 43N 11 39 E
Bressay, U.K. 18 A7 60 9N 1 6W
Bresse, France 23 F12 46 50N 5 10 E
Bressuire, France 22 F6 46 51N 0 30W
Brest, Belarus 51 F2 52 10N 23 40 E
Brest, France 22 D2 48 24N 4 31W
Brest-Litovsk = Brest, Belarus 51 F2 52 10N 23 40 E
Bretagne, France 22 D4 48 10N 3 0W
Bretçu, Romania 46 C7 46 7N 26 18 E
Breteuil, Eure, France 22 D7 48 50N 0 53 E
Breteuil, Oise, France 23 C9 49 38N 2 18 E
Breton, Canada 130 C6 53 7N 114 28W
Breton, Pertuis, France 24 B2 46 17N 1 25W
Breton Sd., U.S.A. 139 L10 29 35N 89 15W
Brett, C., N.Z. 118 B3 35 10 S 174 20 E
Bretten, Germany 27 F4 49 2N 8 42 E
Breukelen, Neths. 20 D6 52 10N 5 0 E
Brevard, U.S.A. 135 H4 35 14N 82 44W
Breves, Brazil 154 B1 1 40 S 50 29W
Brevik, Norway 14 E3 59 4N 9 42 E
Brewarrina, Australia 115 D4 30 0 S 146 51 E
Brewer, U.S.A. 129 D6 44 48N 68 46W
Brewer, Mt., U.S.A. 144 J8 36 44N 118 28W
Brewster, N.Y., U.S.A. 137 E11 41 23N 73 37W
Brewster, Wash., U.S.A. 142 B4 48 6N 119 47W
Brewster, Kap, Greenland 6 B6 70 7N 22 0W
Brewton, U.S.A. 135 K2 31 7N 87 4W
Breyten, S. Africa 105 D4 26 16 S 30 0 E
Brezhnev = Naberezhnyye Chelny, Russia 52 C11 55 42N 52 19 E
Brežice, Slovenia 39 C12 45 54N 15 35 E
Brézina, Algeria 99 B5 33 4N 1 14 E
Březnice, Czech. 30 B6 49 32N 13 57 E
Breznik, Bulgaria 42 E7 42 44N 22 50 E
Brezno, Slovak Rep. 31 C12 48 50N 19 40 E
Brezovo, Bulgaria 43 E10 42 21N 25 5 E
Bria, C.A.R. 102 A4 6 30N 21 58 E
Briançon, France 25 D10 44 54N 6 39 E
Briare, France 23 E9 47 38N 2 45 E
Bribbaree, Australia 117 C7 34 10 S 147 51 E
Bribie I., Australia 115 D5 27 0 S 153 10 E
Bricquebec, France 22 C5 49 28N 1 38W
Bridgehampton, U.S.A. 137 F12 40 56N 72 19W
Bridgend, U.K. 17 F4 51 30N 3 34W
Bridgend □, U.K. 17 F4 51 36N 3 36W
Bridgeport, Calif., U.S.A. 144 G7 38 15N 119 14W
Bridgeport, Conn., U.S.A. 137 E11 41 11N 73 12W
Bridgeport, Nebr., U.S.A. 138 E3 41 40N 103 6W
Bridgeport, Tex., U.S.A. 139 J6 33 13N 97 45W
Bridger, U.S.A. 142 D9 45 18N 108 55W
Bridgeton, U.S.A. 134 F8 39 26N 75 14W
Bridgetown, Australia 113 F2 33 58 S 116 7 E
Bridgetown, Barbados 149 D8 13 5N 59 30W
Bridgetown, Canada 129 D6 44 55N 65 18W
Bridgewater, Australia 116 D5 36 36 S 143 59 E
Bridgewater, Canada 129 D7 44 25N 64 31W
Bridgewater, Mass., U.S.A. 137 E14 41 59N 70 58W
Bridgewater, S. Dak., U.S.A. 138 D6 43 33N 97 30W
Bridgewater, C., Australia 116 E4 38 23 S 141 23 E
Bridgman, U.S.A. 141 C10 41 57N 86 33W
Bridgnorth, U.K. 17 E5 52 32N 2 25W
Bridgton, U.S.A. 137 B14 44 3N 70 42W
Bridgwater, U.K. 17 F4 51 8N 2 59W
Bridlington, U.K. 16 C7 54 5N 0 12W
Bridport, Australia 114 G4 40 59 S 147 23 E
Bridport, U.K. 17 G5 50 44N 2 45W
Brie, Plaine de la, France 23 D10 48 35N 3 10 E
Brie-Comte-Robert, France 23 D9 48 40N 2 35 E
Briec, France 22 D2 48 6N 4 0W
Brielle, Neths. 20 E4 51 54N 4 10 E
Brienne-le-Château, France 23 D11 48 24N 4 30 E
Brienon-sur-Armançon, France 23 E10 47 59N 3 38 E
Brienz, Switz. 28 C6 46 46N 8 2 E
Brienzersee, Switz. 28 C5 46 44N 7 53 E
Brig, Switz. 28 D5 46 18N 7 59 E
Brigg, U.K. 16 D7 53 34N 0 28W
Briggsdale, U.S.A. 138 E2 40 38N 104 20W
Brigham City, U.S.A. 142 F7 41 31N 112 1W
Bright, Australia 117 D7 36 42 S 146 56 E
Brighton, Australia 116 C3 35 5 S 138 30 E
Brighton, Canada 128 D4 44 2N 77 44W
Brighton, U.K. 17 G7 50 49N 0 7W
Brighton, Colo., U.S.A. 138 F2 39 59N 104 49W
Brighton, Ill., U.S.A. 140 E6 39 2N 90 8W
Brighton, Iowa, U.S.A. 140 C5 41 10N 91 49W
Brightwater, N.Z. 119 B8 41 22 S 173 9 E
Brignogan-Plage, France 22 D2 48 40N 4 20W
Brignoles, France 25 E10 43 25N 6 5 E
Brihuega, Spain 34 E2 40 45N 2 52W
Brikama, Gambia 100 C1 13 15N 16 45W
Brilliant, Canada 130 D5 49 19N 117 38W
Brilliant, U.S.A. 136 F4 40 15N 80 39W
Brilon, Germany 26 D4 51 23N 8 25 E
Brim, Australia 116 D5 36 3 S 142 27 E
Brimfield, U.S.A. 140 D7 40 50N 89 53W
Bríndisi, Italy 41 B10 40 39N 17 55 E
Brinje, Croatia 39 D12 45 0N 15 9 E
Brinkley, U.S.A. 139 H9 34 53N 91 12W
Brinkworth, Australia 116 B3 33 42 S 138 26 E
Brinnon, U.S.A. 144 C4 47 41N 122 54W
Brion, I., Canada 129 C7 47 46N 61 26W
Brionne, France 22 C7 49 11N 0 43 E
Brionski, Croatia 39 D10 44 55N 13 45 E
Brioude, France 24 C7 45 18N 3 24 E
Briouze, France 22 D6 48 42N 0 23W
Brisbane, Australia 115 D5 27 25 S 153 2 E
Brisbane →, Australia 115 D5 27 24 S 153 9 E
Brisighella, Italy 39 D8 44 13N 11 46 E
Bristol, U.K. 17 F5 51 26N 2 35W
Bristol, Conn., U.S.A. 137 E12 41 40N 72 57W
Bristol, Pa., U.S.A. 137 F10 40 6N 74 51W
Bristol, R.I., U.S.A. 137 E13 41 40N 71 16W
Bristol, S. Dak., U.S.A. 138 C6 45 21N 97 45W
Bristol, Tenn., U.S.A. 135 G4 36 36N 82 11W
Bristol □, U.K. 17 F5 51 27N 2 36W
Bristol B., U.S.A. 126 C4 58 0N 160 0W
Bristol Channel, U.K. 17 F3 51 18N 4 30W
Bristol I., Antarctica 7 B1 58 45 S 28 0W
Bristol L., U.S.A. 143 J5 34 23N 116 50W
Bristow, U.S.A. 139 H6 35 50N 96 23W
British Columbia □, Canada 130 C3 55 0N 125 15W
British Isles, Europe 10 E5 54 0N 4 0W
Brits, S. Africa 105 D4 25 37 S 27 48 E
Britstown, S. Africa 104 E3 30 37 S 23 30 E
Britt, Canada 128 C3 45 46N 80 34W
Britt, U.S.A. 140 A3 43 6N 93 48W
Brittany = Bretagne, France 22 D4 48 10N 3 0W
Britton, U.S.A. 138 C6 45 48N 97 45W
Brive-la-Gaillarde, France 24 C5 45 10N 1 32 E
Briviesca, Spain 34 C1 42 32N 3 19W
Brixen = Bressanone, Italy 39 B8 46 43N 11 39 E
Brixton, Australia 114 C3 23 32 S 144 57 E
Brlik = Birlik, Kazakstan 55 A6 44 5N 73 31 E
Brlik, Kazakstan 55 B6 43 40N 73 49 E
Brno, Czech. 31 B9 49 10N 16 35 E
Bro, Sweden 14 E11 59 31N 17 38 E
Broach = Bharuch, India 82 D1 21 47N 73 0 E
Broad →, U.S.A. 135 J5 34 1N 81 4W
Broad Arrow, Australia 113 F3 30 23 S 121 15 E
Broad B., U.K. 18 C2 58 14N 6 18W
Broad Haven, Ireland 19 B2 54 20N 9 55W
Broad Law, U.K. 18 F5 55 30N 3 21W
Broad Sd., Australia 114 C4 22 0 S 149 45 E
Broadford, Australia 117 D6 37 14 S 145 4 E
Broadhurst Ra., Australia 112 D3 22 30 S 122 30 E
Broads, The, U.K. 16 E9 52 45N 1 30 E
Broadus, U.S.A. 138 C2 45 27N 105 25W
Broadview, Canada 131 C8 50 22N 102 35W
Broager, Denmark 15 K3 54 53N 9 40 E
Broaryd, Sweden 15 G7 57 7N 13 15 E
Brochet, Canada 131 B8 57 53N 101 40W
Brochet, L., Canada 131 B8 58 36N 101 35W
Brock, Canada 131 C7 51 26N 108 43W
Brocken, Germany 26 D6 51 47N 10 37 E
Brocklehurst, Australia 117 B8 32 9 S 148 38 E
Brockport, U.S.A. 136 C7 43 13N 77 56W
Brockton, U.S.A. 137 D13 42 5N 71 1W
Brockville, Canada 128 D4 44 35N 75 41W
Brockway, Mont., U.S.A. 138 B2 47 18N 105 45W
Brockway, Pa., U.S.A. 136 E6 41 15N 78 47W
Brocton, U.S.A. 136 D5 42 23N 79 26W
Brod, Macedonia 42 F6 41 35N 21 17 E
Brodarevo, Serbia, Yug. 42 D4 43 14N 19 44 E
Brodeur Pen., Canada 127 A11 72 30N 88 10W
Brodhead, U.S.A. 140 B7 42 37N 89 22W
Brodick, U.K. 18 F3 55 35N 5 9W
Brodnica, Poland 47 B6 53 15N 19 25 E
Brody, Ukraine 51 G3 50 5N 25 10 E
Broechem, Belgium 21 F5 51 11N 4 38 E
Broek, Neths. 20 D6 52 26N 5 0 E
Broek op Langedijk, Neths. 20 C5 52 41N 4 49 E
Brogan, U.S.A. 142 D5 44 15N 117 31W
Broglie, France 22 C7 49 2N 0 30 E
Brok, Poland 47 C8 52 43N 21 52 E
Broken Arrow, U.S.A. 139 G7 36 3N 95 48W
Broken Bow, Nebr., U.S.A. 138 E5 41 24N 99 38W
Broken Bow, Okla., U.S.A. 139 H7 34 2N 94 44W
Broken Hill = Kabwe, Zambia 107 E2 14 30 S 28 29 E
Broken Hill, Australia 116 A4 31 58 S 141 29 E
Brokind, Sweden 15 F9 58 13N 15 42 E
Brokopondo, Surinam 153 B7 5 3N 54 59W
Brokopondo □, Surinam 153 C6 4 30N 55 30W
Bromfield, U.K. 17 E5 52 24N 2 45W
Bromley, U.K. 17 F8 51 24N 0 2 E
Bronaugh, U.S.A. 140 G2 37 41N 94 28W
Brønderslev, Denmark 15 G3 57 16N 9 57 E
Brong-Ahafo □, Ghana 100 D4 7 50N 2 0W
Bronkhorstspruit, S. Africa 105 D4 25 46 S 28 45 E
Brønnøysund, Norway 12 D15 65 28N 12 14 E
Bronson, U.S.A. 141 C11 41 52N 85 12W
Bronte, Italy 41 E7 37 47N 14 50 E
Bronte, U.S.A. 139 K4 31 53N 100 18W
Bronte Park, Australia 114 G4 42 8 S 146 30 E
Brook Park, U.S.A. 136 E4 41 24N 80 51W
Brookes Point, Phil. 71 G1 8 47N 117 50 E
Brookfield, U.S.A. 140 E3 39 47N 93 4W
Brookhaven, U.S.A. 139 K9 31 35N 90 26W
Brookings, Oreg., U.S.A. 142 E1 42 3N 124 17W
Brookings, S. Dak., U.S.A. 138 C6 44 19N 96 48W
Brooklin, Canada 136 C6 43 55N 78 55W
Brooklyn, U.S.A. 140 C4 41 44N 92 27W
Brooklyn Park, U.S.A. 138 C8 45 6N 93 23W
Brookmere, Canada 130 D4 49 52N 120 53W
Brooks, Canada 130 C6 50 35N 111 55W
Brooks B., Canada 130 C3 50 15N 127 55W
Brooks L., Canada 131 A7 61 55N 106 35W
Brooks Ra., U.S.A. 126 B5 68 40N 147 0W
Brookston, U.S.A. 141 D10 40 36N 86 52W
Brooksville, Fla., U.S.A. 135 L4 28 33N 82 23W
Brooksville, Ky., U.S.A. 141 F12 38 41N 84 4W
Brookville, U.S.A. 141 E11 39 25N 85 1W
Brooloo, Australia 115 D5 26 30 S 152 43 E
Broom, L., U.K. 18 D3 57 55N 5 15W
Broome, Australia 112 C3 18 0 S 122 15 E
Broomehill, Australia 113 F2 33 51 S 117 39 E
Broons, France 22 D4 48 20N 2 16W
Brora, U.K. 18 C5 58 0N 3 52W
Brora →, U.K. 18 C5 58 0N 3 51W
Brosna →, Ireland 19 C4 53 14N 7 58W
Broşteni, Romania 46 B6 47 14N 25 43 E
Brotas de Macaúbas, Brazil 155 D3 12 0 S 42 38W
Brothers, U.S.A. 142 E3 43 49N 120 36W
Brøttum, Norway 14 C4 61 2N 10 34 E
Brou, France 22 D8 48 13N 1 11 E
Brouage, Ramparts de, France 24 C2 45 52N 1 4W
Brough, U.K. 16 C5 54 32N 2 18W
Broughams Gate, Australia 116 A4 30 51 S 140 59 E
Broughton, U.S.A. 141 G8 37 56N 88 27W
Broughton Island, Canada 127 B13 67 33N 63 0W
Broughty Ferry, U.K. 18 E6 56 29N 2 51W
Broumov, Czech. 31 A9 50 35N 16 20 E
Brouwershaven, Neths. 20 E3 51 45N 3 55 E
Brouwershavensche Gat, Neths. 20 E3 51 46N 3 50 E
Brovary, Ukraine 51 G6 50 34N 30 48 E
Brovst, Denmark 15 G3 57 6N 9 31 E
Browerville, U.S.A. 138 B7 46 5N 94 52W
Brown, Mt., Australia 116 B2 32 30 S 138 0 E
Brown, Pt., Australia 115 E1 32 32 S 133 50 E
Brown Willy, U.K. 17 G3 50 35N 4 37W
Brownfield, U.S.A. 139 J3 33 11N 102 17W
Browning, Ill., U.S.A. 140 D6 40 8N 90 22W
Browning, Mo., U.S.A. 140 D3 40 3N 93 12W
Browning, Mont., U.S.A. 142 B7 48 34N 113 1W
Browning Pass, N.Z. 119 C6 42 55 S 171 22 E
Brownlee, Canada 131 C7 50 43N 106 1W
Brownsburg, U.S.A. 141 E10 39 51N 86 24W
Brownstown, U.S.A. 141 F10 38 53N 86 3W
Brownsville, Oreg., U.S.A. 142 D2 44 24N 122 59W
Brownsville, Tenn., U.S.A. 139 H10 35 36N 89 16W
Brownsville, Tex., U.S.A. 139 N6 25 54N 97 30W
Brownsweg, Surinam 153 B6 5 5N 55 15W
Brownwood, U.S.A. 139 K5 31 43N 98 59W
Brownwood, L., U.S.A. 139 K5 31 51N 98 35W
Browse I., Australia 112 B3 14 7 S 123 33 E
Broye →, Switz. 28 C3 46 52N 6 58 E
Brozas, Spain 37 F4 39 37N 6 47W
Bruas, Malaysia 77 K3 4 30N 100 47 E
Bruay-en-Artois, France 23 B9 50 29N 2 33 E
Bruce, Mt., Australia 112 D2 22 37 S 118 8 E
Bruce B., N.Z. 119 D4 43 35 S 169 42 E
Bruce Pen., Canada 136 A3 45 0N 81 30W
Bruce Rock, Australia 113 F2 31 52 S 118 8 E
Bruche →, France 23 D14 48 34N 7 43 E
Bruchsal, Germany 27 F4 49 7N 8 35 E
Bruck an der Leitha, Austria 31 C9 48 1N 16 47 E
Bruck an der Mur, Austria 30 D8 47 24N 15 16 E
Brue →, U.K. 17 F5 51 13N 2 59W
Brugelette, Belgium 21 G3 50 35N 3 52 E
Bruges = Brugge, Belgium 21 F2 51 13N 3 13 E
Brugg, Switz. 28 B6 47 29N 8 11 E
Brugge, Belgium 21 F2 51 13N 3 13 E
Brühl, Germany 26 E2 50 49N 6 54 E
Bruinisse, Neths. 21 E4 51 40N 4 5 E
Brûlé, Canada 130 C5 53 15N 117 58W
Brûlon, France 22 E6 47 58N 0 15W
Brûly, Belgium 21 J5 49 58N 4 32 E
Brumado, Brazil 155 D3 14 14 S 41 40W
Brumado →, Brazil 155 D3 14 13 S 41 40W
Brumath, France 23 D14 48 43N 7 40 E
Brummen, Neths. 20 D8 52 5N 6 10 E
Brumunddal, Norway 14 D4 60 53N 10 56 E
Brunchilly, Australia 114 B1 18 50 S 134 30 E
Brundidge, U.S.A. 135 K3 31 43N 85 49W
Bruneau, U.S.A. 142 E6 42 53N 115 48W
Bruneau →, U.S.A. 142 E6 42 56N 115 57W
Bruneck = Brunico, Italy 39 B8 46 48N 11 56 E
Brunei = Bandar Seri Begawan, Brunei 75 B4 4 52N 115 0 E
Brunei ■, Asia 75 B4 4 50N 115 0 E
Brunette Downs, Australia 114 B2 18 40 S 135 55 E
Brunflo, Sweden 14 A8 63 5N 14 50 E
Brunico, Italy 39 B8 46 48N 11 56 E
Brünig, P., Switz. 28 C6 46 46N 8 8 E
Brunkeberg, Norway 14 E2 59 26N 8 28 E
Brunna, Sweden 14 E11 59 52N 17 25 E
Brunnen, Switz. 29 C7 46 59N 8 37 E
Brunner, L., N.Z. 119 C6 42 37 S 171 27 E
Bruno, Canada 131 C7 52 20N 105 30W
Brunsbüttel, Germany 26 B5 53 53N 9 6 E
Brunssum, Neths. 21 G7 50 57N 5 59 E
Brunswick = Braunschweig, Germany 26 C6 52 15N 10 31 E
Brunswick, Ga., U.S.A. 135 K5 31 10N 81 30W
Brunswick, Maine, U.S.A. 129 D6 43 55N 69 58W
Brunswick, Md., U.S.A. 134 F7 39 19N 77 38W
Brunswick, Mo., U.S.A. 140 E3 39 26N 93 8W
Brunswick, Ohio, U.S.A. 136 E3 41 14N 81 51W
Brunswick, Pen. de, Chile 160 D2 53 30 S 71 30W
Brunswick B., Australia 112 C3 15 15 S 124 50 E
Brunswick Junction, Australia 113 F2 33 15 S 115 50 E
Bruntál, Czech. 31 B10 50 0N 17 27 E
Bruny I., Australia 114 G4 43 20 S 147 15 E
Brus Laguna, Honduras 148 C3 15 47N 84 35W

Businga 179

Brusartsi, Bulgaria 42 D8 43 40N 23 5 E
Brush, U.S.A. 138 E3 40 15N 103 37W
Brushton, U.S.A. 137 B10 44 50N 74 31W
Brusio, Switz. 29 D10 46 14N 10 8 E
Brusque, Brazil 159 B6 27 5 S 49 0W
Brussel, Belgium 21 G4 50 51N 4 21 E
Brussels = Brussel, Belgium 21 G4 50 51N 4 21 E
Brussels, Canada 136 C3 43 44N 81 15W
Brustem, Belgium 21 G6 50 48N 5 14 E
Bruthen, Australia 117 D7 37 42 S 147 50 E
Bruxelles = Brussel, Belgium 21 G4 50 51N 4 21 E
Bruyères, France 23 D13 48 10N 6 40 E
Brwinów, Poland 47 C7 52 9N 20 40 E
Bryagovo, Bulgaria 43 F10 41 58N 25 8 E
Bryan, Ohio, U.S.A. 141 C12 41 28N 84 33W
Bryan, Tex., U.S.A. 139 K6 30 40N 96 22W
Bryan, Mt., Australia 116 B3 33 30 S 139 0 E
Bryanka, Ukraine 51 H10 48 32N 38 45 E
Bryansk, Russia 52 D2 53 13N 34 25 E
Bryansk, Russia 53 H8 44 20N 47 10 E
Bryanskoye = Bryansk, Russia 53 H8 44 20N 47 10 E
Bryant, U.S.A. 138 C6 44 35N 97 28W
Bryne, Norway 13 G11 58 44N 5 38 E
Bryson City, U.S.A. 135 H4 35 26N 83 27W
Bryukhovetskaya, Russia 53 H4 45 48N 39 0 E
Brza Palanka, Serbia, Yug. 42 C7 44 28N 22 27 E
Brzava →, Serbia, Yug. 42 B5 45 21N 20 45 E
Brzeg, Poland 47 E4 50 52N 17 30 E
Brzeg Din, Poland 47 D3 51 16N 16 41 E
Brześć Kujawski, Poland 47 C5 52 36N 18 55 E
Brzesko, Poland 31 B13 49 59N 20 34 E
Brzeszcze, Poland 31 B12 49 59N 19 10 E
Brzeziny, Poland 47 D6 51 49N 19 42 E
Brzozów, Poland 31 B15 49 41N 22 3 E
Bsharri, Lebanon 91 A5 34 15N 36 0 E
Bū Athlah, Libya 96 B3 30 9N 15 39 E
Bū Baqarah, U.A.E. 85 E8 25 35N 56 25 E
Bu Craa, W. Sahara 98 C2 26 45N 12 50W
Bū Ḩasā, U.A.E. 85 F7 23 30N 53 20 E
Bua Yai, Thailand 76 E4 15 33N 102 26 E
Buad I., Phil. 71 F5 11 40N 124 51 E
Buala, Solomon Is. 121 M10 8 10 S 159 35 E
Buapinang, Indonesia 72 B2 4 40 S 121 30 E
Buba, Guinea-Biss. 100 C2 11 40N 14 59W
Bubanda, Zaïre 102 B3 4 14N 19 38 E
Bubanza, Burundi 106 C2 3 6 S 29 23 E
Būbiyān, Kuwait 85 D6 29 45N 48 15 E
Bucak, Turkey 88 D4 37 28N 30 36 E
Bucaramanga, Colombia 152 B3 7 0N 73 0W
Bucas Grande I., Phil. 71 G5 9 40N 125 57 E
Buccaneer Arch., Australia 112 C3 16 7 S 123 20 E
Bucchiánico, Italy 39 F11 42 18N 14 11 E
Bucecea, Romania 46 B7 47 47N 26 28 E
Buchach, Ukraine 51 H3 49 5N 25 25 E
Buchan, Australia 117 D8 37 30 S 148 12 E
Buchan, U.K. 18 D6 57 32N 2 21W
Buchan Ness, U.K. 18 D7 57 29N 1 46W
Buchanan, Canada 131 C8 51 40N 102 45W
Buchanan, Liberia 100 D2 5 57N 10 2W
Buchanan, U.S.A. 141 C10 41 50N 86 22W
Buchanan, L., Queens., Australia 114 C4 21 35 S 145 52 E
Buchanan, L., W. Austral., Australia 113 E3 25 33 S 123 2 E
Buchanan, L., U.S.A. 139 K5 30 45N 98 25W
Buchanan Cr. →, Australia 114 B2 19 13 S 136 33 E
Buchans, Canada 129 C8 48 50N 56 52W
Bucharest = Bucureşti, Romania 46 E7 44 27N 26 10 E
Buchholz, Germany 26 B5 53 19N 9 52 E
Buchloe, Germany 27 G6 48 1N 10 44 E
Buchon, Pt., U.S.A. 144 K6 35 15N 120 54W
Buchs, Switz. 29 B8 47 10N 9 28 E
Bückeburg, Germany 26 C5 52 16N 9 7 E
Buckeye, U.S.A. 143 K7 33 22N 112 35W
Buckhannon, U.S.A. 134 F5 39 0N 80 8W
Buckhaven, U.K. 18 E5 56 11N 3 3W
Buckie, U.K. 18 D6 57 41N 2 58W
Buckingham, Canada 128 C4 45 37N 75 24W
Buckingham, U.K. 17 F7 51 59N 0 57W
Buckingham B., Australia 114 A2 12 10 S 135 40 E
Buckingham Canal, India 83 G5 14 0N 80 5 E
Buckinghamshire □, U.K. 17 F7 51 53N 0 55W
Buckland, U.S.A. 141 D12 40 37N 84 16W
Buckle Hd., Australia 112 B4 14 26 S 127 52 E
Buckleboo, Australia 116 B2 32 54 S 136 12 E
Buckley, Ill., U.S.A. 141 D8 40 36N 88 2W
Buckley, Wash., U.S.A. 142 C2 47 10N 122 2W
Buckley →, Australia 114 C2 20 10 S 138 49 E
Bucklin, Kans., U.S.A. 139 G5 37 33N 99 38W
Bucklin, Mo., U.S.A. 140 E4 39 47N 92 53W
Bucks L., U.S.A. 144 F5 39 54N 121 12W
Buco Zau, Angola 103 C2 4 46 S 12 33 E
Bucquoy, France 23 B9 50 9N 2 43 E
Buctouche, Canada 129 C7 46 30N 64 45W
Bucureşti, Romania 46 E7 44 27N 26 10 E
Bucyrus, U.S.A. 141 D14 40 48N 82 59W
Budafok, Hungary 31 D12 47 26N 19 2 E
Budalin, Burma 78 D5 22 20N 95 10 E
Budapest, Hungary 31 D12 47 29N 19 5 E
Budaun, India 81 E8 28 5N 79 10 E
Budd Coast, Antarctica 7 C8 68 0 S 112 0 E
Buddabadah, Australia 117 A7 31 56 S 147 14 E
Buddusò, Italy 40 B2 40 35N 9 15 E
Bude, U.K. 17 G3 50 49N 4 34W
Budel, Neths. 21 F7 51 17N 5 34 E
Budennovsk, Russia 53 H7 44 50N 44 10 E
Budeşti, Romania 46 E7 44 13N 26 30 E
Budge Budge = Baj Baj, India 81 H13 22 30N 88 5 E
Budgewoi, Australia 117 B9 33 13 S 151 34 E
Budia, Spain 34 E2 40 38N 2 46W
Budjala, Zaïre 102 B3 2 50N 19 40 E
Búdrio, Italy 39 D8 44 32N 11 32 E
Budva, Montenegro, Yug. 42 E3 42 17N 18 50 E
Budzyń, Poland 47 C3 52 54N 16 59 E
Buea, Cameroon 101 E6 4 10N 9 9 E
Buellton, U.S.A. 145 L6 34 37N 120 12W
Buena Park, U.S.A. 145 M9 33 52N 117 59W
Buena Vista, Bolivia 157 D5 17 27 S 63 40W
Buena Vista, Colo., U.S.A. 143 G10 38 51N 106 8W
Buena Vista, Va., U.S.A. 134 G6 37 44N 79 21W
Buena Vista L., U.S.A. 145 K7 35 12N 119 18W
Buenaventura, Colombia 152 C2 3 53N 77 4W
Buenaventura, Mexico 146 B3 29 50N 107 30W
Buenaventura, B. de, Colombia 152 C2 3 48N 77 17W
Buenavista, Luzon, Phil. 70 E4 13 35N 122 34 E
Buenavista, Mindanao, Phil. 71 G5 8 59N 125 24 E
Buenavista, Zamboanga del S., Phil. 71 H4 7 15N 122 16 E
Buendía, Pantano de, Spain 34 E2 40 25N 2 43W
Buenópolis, Brazil 155 E3 17 54 S 44 11W
Buenos Aires, Argentina 158 C4 34 30 S 58 20W
Buenos Aires, Colombia 152 C3 1 36N 73 18W
Buenos Aires, Costa Rica 148 E3 9 10N 83 20W
Buenos Aires □, Argentina 158 D4 36 30 S 60 0W
Buenos Aires, L., Chile 160 C2 46 35 S 72 30W
Buesaco, Colombia 152 C2 1 23N 77 9W
Buffalo, Mo., U.S.A. 139 G8 37 39N 93 6W
Buffalo, N.Y., U.S.A. 136 D6 42 53N 78 53W
Buffalo, Okla., U.S.A. 139 G5 36 50N 99 38W
Buffalo, S. Dak., U.S.A. 138 C3 45 35N 103 33W
Buffalo, Wyo., U.S.A. 142 D10 44 21N 106 42W
Buffalo →, Canada 130 A5 60 5N 115 5W
Buffalo Head Hills, Canada 130 B5 57 25N 115 55W
Buffalo L., Canada 130 C6 52 27N 112 54W
Buffalo Narrows, Canada 131 B7 55 51N 108 29W
Buffels →, S. Africa 104 D2 29 36 S 17 3 E
Buford, U.S.A. 135 H4 34 10N 84 0W
Bug → = Buh →, Ukraine 51 J6 46 59N 31 58 E
Bug →, Poland 47 C8 52 31N 21 5 E
Buga, Colombia 152 C2 4 0N 76 15W
Buganda, Uganda 106 C3 0 0 31 30 E
Buganga, Uganda 106 C3 0 3 S 32 0 E
Bugasan, Phil. 71 H5 7 27N 124 14 E
Bugasong, Phil. 71 F4 11 3N 122 4 E
Bugeat, France 24 C5 45 36N 1 55 E
Bugel, Tanjung, Indonesia 75 D4 6 26 S 111 3 E
Buggenhout, Belgium 21 F4 51 1N 4 12 E
Bugibba, Malta 32 D1 35 57N 14 25 E
Bugojno, Bos.-H. 42 C2 44 2N 17 25 E
Bugsuk, Phil. 71 G1 8 15N 117 15 E
Buguey, Phil. 70 B3 18 17N 121 50 E
Bugulma, Russia 54 D4 54 33N 52 48 E
Buguma, Nigeria 101 E6 4 42N 6 55 E
Bugun Shara, Mongolia 64 B5 49 0N 104 0 E
Buguruslan, Russia 54 E4 53 39N 52 26 E
Buh →, Ukraine 51 J6 46 59N 31 58 E
Buhăeşti, Romania 46 C8 46 47N 27 32 E
Buheirat-Murrat-el-Kubra, Egypt 94 H8 30 18N 32 26 E
Buhl, Idaho, U.S.A. 142 E6 42 36N 114 46W
Buhl, Minn., U.S.A. 138 B8 47 30N 92 46W
Buhuşi, Romania 46 C7 46 41N 26 45 E
Buick, U.S.A. 139 G9 37 38N 91 2W
Builth Wells, U.K. 17 E4 52 9N 3 25W
Buin, Papua N. G. 121 L8 6 48 S 155 42 E
Buinsk, Russia 52 C9 55 0N 48 18 E
Buíque, Brazil 154 C4 8 37 S 37 9W
Buir Nur, Mongolia 65 B6 47 50N 117 42 E
Buis-les-Baronnies, France 25 D9 44 17N 5 16 E
Buitenpost, Neths. 20 B8 53 15N 6 9 E
Buitrago, Spain 36 E7 40 58N 3 38W
Bujalance, Spain 37 H6 37 54N 4 23W
Buján, Spain 36 C2 42 59N 8 36W
Bujanovac, Serbia, Yug. 42 E6 42 28N 21 44 E
Bujaraloz, Spain 34 D4 41 29N 0 10W
Buje, Croatia 39 C10 45 24N 13 39 E
Bujumbura, Burundi 106 C2 3 16 S 29 18 E
Bük, Hungary 31 D9 47 22N 16 45 E
Buk, Poland 47 C3 52 21N 16 30 E
Buka I., Papua N. G. 120 C8 5 10 S 154 35 E
Bukachacha, Russia 57 D12 52 55N 116 50 E
Bukama, Zaïre 107 D2 9 10 S 25 50 E
Bukavu, Zaïre 106 C2 2 20 S 28 52 E
Bukene, Tanzania 106 C3 4 15 S 32 48 E
Bukhara = Bukhoro, Uzbekistan 55 D2 39 48N 64 25 E
Bukhoro, Uzbekistan 55 D2 39 48N 64 25 E
Bukidnon □, Phil. 71 G5 8 0N 125 0 E
Bukima, Tanzania 106 C3 1 50 S 33 25 E
Bukit Mertajam, Malaysia 77 K3 5 22N 100 28 E
Bukittinggi, Indonesia 74 C2 0 20 S 100 20 E
Bukkapatnam, India 83 G3 14 14N 77 46 E
Bukoba, Tanzania 106 C3 1 20 S 31 49 E
Bukoba □, Tanzania 106 C3 1 30 S 32 0 E
Bukowno, Poland 31 A12 50 17N 19 35 E
Bukuru, Nigeria 101 D6 9 42N 8 48 E
Bukuya, Uganda 106 B3 0 40N 31 52 E
Bula, Guinea-Biss. 100 C1 12 7N 15 43W
Bula, Indonesia 73 B4 3 6 S 130 30 E
Bulacan, Phil. 70 E3 13 40N 120 21 E
Bulacan □, Phil. 70 D3 15 0N 121 5 E
Bülach, Switz. 29 A7 47 31N 8 32 E
Bulahdelah, Australia 117 B10 32 23 S 152 13 E
Bulalacao, Phil. 70 E3 12 31N 121 26 E
Bulan, Phil. 70 E4 12 40N 123 52 E
Bulanash, Russia 54 C9 57 16N 62 0 E
Bulancak, Turkey 89 B8 40 56N 38 14 E
Bulandshahr, India 80 E7 28 28N 77 51 E
Bulanık, Turkey 89 C10 39 4N 42 14 E
Bulanovo, Russia 54 E5 52 27N 55 10 E
Bûlâq, Egypt 94 B3 25 10N 30 38 E
Bulawayo, Zimbabwe 107 G2 20 7 S 28 32 E
Buldan, Turkey 88 C3 38 2N 28 50 E
Buldana, India 82 D3 20 30N 76 18 E
Buldon, Phil. 71 H5 7 33N 124 25 E
Bulgar, Russia 52 C9 54 57N 49 4 E
Bulgaria ■, Europe 43 E10 42 35N 25 30 E
Bulgroo, Australia 115 D3 25 47 S 143 58 E
Bulgunnia, Australia 115 E1 30 10 S 134 53 E
Bulhale, Somali Rep. 108 C3 5 20N 46 29 E
Bulhar, Somali Rep. 108 B2 10 25N 44 30 E
Buli, Teluk, Indonesia 72 A3 1 5N 128 25 E
Buliluyan, C., Phil. 71 G1 8 20N 117 15 E
Bulki, Ethiopia 95 F4 6 11N 36 31 E
Bulkley →, Canada 130 B3 55 15N 127 40W
Bull Shoals L., U.S.A. 139 G8 36 22N 92 35W
Bullange, Belgium 21 H8 50 24N 6 15 E
Bullaque →, Spain 37 G6 38 59N 4 17W
Bullara, Australia 112 D1 22 40 S 114 3 E
Bullaring, Australia 113 F2 32 30 S 117 45 E
Bullas, Spain 35 G3 38 2N 1 40W
Bulle, Switz. 28 C4 46 37N 7 3 E
Buller →, N.Z. 119 B6 41 44 S 171 36 E
Buller, Mt., Australia 117 D7 37 10 S 146 28 E
Buller Gorge, N.Z. 119 B7 41 40 S 172 10 E
Bulli, Australia 117 C9 34 15 S 150 57 E
Bullock Creek, Australia 114 B3 17 43 S 144 31 E
Bulloo →, Australia 115 D3 28 43 S 142 30 E
Bulloo Downs, Queens., Australia 115 D3 28 31 S 142 57 E
Bulloo Downs, W. Austral., Australia 112 D2 24 0 S 119 32 E
Bulloo L., Australia 115 D3 28 43 S 142 25 E
Bulls, N.Z. 118 G4 40 10 S 175 24 E
Bully-les-Mines, France 23 B9 50 27N 2 44 E
Bulnes, Chile 158 D1 36 42 S 72 19W
Bulo Burti, Somali Rep. 108 D3 3 50N 45 33 E
Bulo Ghedudo, Somali Rep. 108 D2 2 52N 43 1 E
Bulolo, Papua N. G. 120 D4 7 10 S 146 40 E
Bulongo, Zaïre 103 C4 4 45 S 21 30 E
Bulpunga, Australia 116 B4 33 47 S 141 45 E
Bulqiza, Albania 44 C2 41 30N 20 21 E
Bulsar = Valsad, India 82 D1 20 40N 72 58 E
Bultfontein, S. Africa 104 D4 28 18 S 26 10 E
Buluan, L., Phil. 71 H5 6 40N 124 49 E
Buluangan, Phil. 71 F4 10 24N 123 20 E
Bulukumba, Indonesia 72 C2 5 33 S 120 11 E
Bulun, Russia 57 B13 70 37N 127 30 E
Bulunghur, Uzbekistan 55 D3 39 46N 67 16 E
Bulungu, Zaïre 103 D4 6 4 S 21 54 E
Bulus, Russia 57 C13 63 10N 129 10 E
Bulusan, Phil. 70 E5 12 45N 124 8 E
Bumba, Zaïre 102 B4 2 13N 22 30 E
Bumbiri I., Tanzania 106 C3 1 40 S 31 55 E
Bumhkang, Burma 78 B6 26 51N 97 40 E
Bumhpa Bum, Burma 78 B6 26 51N 97 14 E
Bumi →, Zimbabwe 107 F2 17 0 S 28 20 E
Bumtang →, Bhutan 78 B3 26 56N 90 53 E
Buna, Kenya 106 B4 2 58N 39 30 E
Buna, Papua N. G. 120 E5 8 42 S 148 27 E
Bunawan, Agusan del S., Phil. 71 G5 8 12N 125 57 E
Bunawan, Davao del S., Phil. 71 H5 7 14N 125 38 E
Bunazi, Tanzania 106 C3 1 3 S 31 23 E
Bunbah, Khalīj, Libya 96 B4 32 20N 23 15 E
Bunbury, Australia 113 F2 33 20 S 115 35 E
Buncrana, Ireland 19 A4 55 8N 7 27W
Bundaberg, Australia 115 C5 24 54 S 152 22 E
Bünde, Germany 26 C4 52 11N 8 35 E
Bundey →, Australia 114 C2 21 46 S 135 37 E
Bundi, India 80 G6 25 30N 75 35 E
Bundooma, Australia 114 C1 24 54 S 134 16 E
Bundoran, Ireland 19 B3 54 28N 8 16W
Bundukia, Sudan 95 F3 5 14N 30 55 E
Bundure, Australia 117 C7 35 10 S 146 1 E
Bung Kan, Thailand 76 C4 18 23N 103 37 E
Bungatakada, Japan 62 D3 33 35N 131 25 E
Bungendore, Australia 117 C8 35 14 S 149 30 E
Bungil Cr. →, Australia 114 D4 27 5 S 149 5 E
Bungo, Gunong, Malaysia 75 B4 1 16N 110 9 E
Bungo-Suidō, Japan 62 E4 33 0N 132 15 E
Bungoma, Kenya 106 B3 0 34N 34 34 E
Bungu, Tanzania 106 D4 7 35 S 39 0 E
Bunia, Zaïre 106 B3 1 35N 30 20 E
Bunji, Pakistan 81 B6 35 45N 74 40 E
Bunker Hill, Ill., U.S.A. 140 E7 39 3N 89 57W
Bunker Hill, Ind., U.S.A. 141 D10 40 40N 86 6W
Bunkie, U.S.A. 139 K8 30 57N 92 11W
Bunnell, U.S.A. 135 L5 29 28N 81 16W
Bunnik, Neths. 20 D6 52 4N 5 12 E
Bunnythorpe, N.Z. 118 G4 40 16 S 175 39 E
Buñol, Spain 35 F4 39 25N 0 47W
Bunsbeek, Belgium 21 G5 50 50N 4 56 E
Bunschoten, Neths. 20 D6 52 14N 5 22 E
Buntok, Indonesia 75 C4 1 40 S 114 58 E
Bununu, Nigeria 101 D6 9 51N 9 32 E
Bununu Dass, Nigeria 101 C6 10 5N 9 31 E
Bünyan, Turkey 88 C6 38 51N 35 51 E
Bunyu, Indonesia 75 B5 3 35N 117 50 E
Bunza, Nigeria 101 C5 12 8N 4 0 E
Buol, Indonesia 72 A2 1 15N 121 32 E
Buon Brieng, Vietnam 76 F7 13 9N 108 12 E
Buon Me Thuot, Vietnam 76 F7 12 40N 108 3 E
Buong Long, Cambodia 76 F6 13 44N 106 59 E
Buorkhaya, Mys, Russia 57 B14 71 50N 132 40 E
Buqayq, Si. Arabia 85 E6 26 0N 49 45 E
Buqbua, Egypt 94 A2 31 29N 25 29 E
Bur Acaba, Somali Rep. 108 D2 3 12N 44 20 E
Bûr Fuad, Egypt 94 H8 31 15N 32 20 E
Bur Ghibi, Somali Rep. 108 D3 3 56N 45 7 E
Bûr Safâga, Egypt 94 B3 26 43N 33 57 E
Bûr Sa'îd, Egypt 94 H8 31 16N 32 18 E
Bûr Sûdân, Sudan 94 D4 19 32N 37 9 E
Bûr Taufiq, Egypt 94 J8 29 54N 32 32 E
Bura, Kenya 106 C4 1 4 S 39 58 E
Buran, Somali Rep. 108 B3 10 14N 48 44 E
Burao, Somali Rep. 108 C3 9 32N 45 32 E
Burāq, Syria 91 B5 33 11N 36 29 E
Buras, U.S.A. 139 L10 29 22N 89 32W
Burauen, Phil. 71 F5 10 58N 124 53 E
Buraydah, Si. Arabia 84 E5 26 20N 44 8 E
Burbank, U.S.A. 145 L8 34 11N 118 19W
Burcher, Australia 117 B7 33 30 S 147 16 E
Burdekin →, Australia 114 B4 19 38 S 147 25 E
Burdeos Bay, Phil. 70 D4 14 44N 122 6 E
Burdett, Canada 130 D6 49 50N 111 32W
Burdur, Turkey 88 D4 37 45N 30 17 E
Burdur Gölü, Turkey 88 D4 37 44N 30 10 E
Burdwan = Barddhaman, India 81 H12 23 14N 87 39 E
Bure, Ethiopia 95 E4 10 40N 37 4 E
Bure →, U.K. 16 E9 52 38N 1 43 E
Büren, Germany 26 D4 51 33N 8 35 E
Buren, Neths. 20 E6 51 55N 5 20 E
Bureya →, Russia 57 E13 49 27N 129 30 E
Burford, Canada 136 C4 43 7N 80 27W
Burg, Germany 26 C7 52 16N 11 51 E
Burg auf Fehmarn, Germany 26 A7 54 28N 11 9 E
Burg el Arab, Egypt 94 H6 30 54N 29 32 E
Burg et Tuyur, Sudan 94 C2 20 55N 27 56 E
Burg Stargard, Germany 26 B9 53 29N 13 18 E
Burgas, Bulgaria 43 E12 42 33N 27 29 E
Burgaski Zaliv, Bulgaria 43 E12 42 30N 27 39 E
Burgdorf, Germany 26 C5 52 27N 10 1 E
Burgdorf, Switz. 28 B5 47 3N 7 37 E
Burgenland □, Austria 31 D9 47 20N 16 20 E
Burgeo, Canada 129 C8 47 37N 57 38W
Burgersdorp, S. Africa 104 E4 31 0 S 26 20 E
Burges, Mt., Australia 113 F3 30 50 S 121 5 E
Burghausen, Germany 27 G8 48 9N 12 49 E
Búrgio, Italy 40 E6 37 36N 13 17 E
Bürglen, Switz. 29 C7 46 53N 8 40 E
Burglengenfeld, Germany 27 F8 49 12N 12 2 E
Burgo de Osma, Spain 34 D1 41 35N 3 4W
Burgohondo, Spain 36 E6 40 26N 4 47W
Burgos, Ilocos N., Phil. 70 B3 18 31N 120 39 E
Burgos, Pangasinan, Phil. 70 C2 16 4N 119 52 E
Burgos, Spain 34 C1 42 21N 3 41W
Burgos □, Spain 34 C1 42 21N 3 42W
Burgstädt, Germany 26 E8 50 54N 12 49 E
Burgsvik, Sweden 13 H18 57 3N 18 19 E
Burguillos del Cerro, Spain 37 G4 38 23N 6 35W
Burgundy = Bourgogne, France 23 F11 47 0N 4 50 E
Burhaniye, Turkey 88 C2 39 30N 26 58 E
Burhanpur, India 82 D3 21 18N 76 14 E
Burhou, U.K. 22 C4 49 45N 2 15W
Buri Pen., Eritrea 95 D4 15 25N 39 55 E
Burias, Phil. 70 E4 12 55N 123 5 E
Burias Pass, Phil. 70 E4 13 0N 123 15 E
Burica, Pta., Costa Rica 148 E3 8 3N 82 51W
Burigi, L., Tanzania 106 C3 2 2 S 31 22 E
Burin, Canada 129 C8 47 1N 55 14W
Buriram, Thailand 76 E4 15 0N 103 0 E
Buriti Alegre, Brazil 155 E2 18 9 S 49 3W
Buriti Bravo, Brazil 154 C3 5 50 S 43 50W
Buriti dos Lopes, Brazil 154 B3 3 10 S 41 52W
Burj Sāfitā, Syria 88 E7 34 48N 36 7 E
Burji, Ethiopia 95 F4 5 29N 37 51 E
Burkburnett, U.S.A. 139 H5 34 6N 98 34W
Burke, U.S.A. 142 C6 47 31N 115 49W
Burke →, Australia 114 C2 23 12 S 139 33 E
Burketown, Australia 114 B2 17 45 S 139 33 E
Burkettsville, U.S.A. 141 D12 40 21N 84 39W
Burkina Faso ■, Africa 100 C4 12 0N 1 0W
Burk's Falls, Canada 128 C4 45 37N 79 24W
Burley, U.S.A. 142 E7 42 32N 113 48W
Burli, Kazakstan 54 F4 51 25N 52 40 E
Burlingame, U.S.A. 144 H4 37 35N 122 21W
Burlington, Canada 136 C5 43 18N 79 45W
Burlington, Colo., U.S.A. 138 F3 39 18N 102 16W
Burlington, Ill., U.S.A. 141 B8 42 3N 88 33W
Burlington, Iowa, U.S.A. 140 D5 40 49N 91 14W
Burlington, Kans., U.S.A. 138 F7 38 12N 95 45W
Burlington, Ky., U.S.A. 141 E12 39 2N 84 43W
Burlington, N.C., U.S.A. 135 G6 36 6N 79 26W
Burlington, N.J., U.S.A. 137 F10 40 4N 74 51W
Burlington, Vt., U.S.A. 137 B11 44 29N 73 12W
Burlington, Wash., U.S.A. 144 B4 48 28N 122 20W
Burlington, Wis., U.S.A. 134 D1 42 41N 88 17W
Burlyu-Tyube, Kazakstan 56 E8 46 30N 79 10 E
Burma ■, Asia 78 E6 21 0N 96 30 E
Burnaby I., Canada 130 C2 52 25N 131 19W
Burnamwood, Australia 117 A6 31 7 S 144 53 E
Burnet, U.S.A. 139 K5 30 45N 98 14W
Burney, U.S.A. 142 F3 40 53N 121 40W
Burngup, Australia 113 F2 33 2 S 118 42 E
Burnham, U.S.A. 136 F7 40 38N 77 34W
Burnie, Australia 114 G4 41 4 S 145 56 E
Burnley, U.K. 16 D5 53 47N 2 14W
Burnoye, Kazakstan 55 B5 42 36N 70 47 E
Burns, Oreg., U.S.A. 142 E4 43 35N 119 3W
Burns, Wyo., U.S.A. 138 E2 41 12N 104 21W
Burns Lake, Canada 130 C3 54 20N 125 45W
Burnside →, Canada 126 B9 66 51N 108 4W
Burnside, L., Australia 113 E3 25 22 S 123 0 E
Burnsville, U.S.A. 138 C8 44 47N 93 17W
Burnt River, Canada 136 B6 44 41N 78 42W
Burntwood →, Canada 131 B9 56 8N 96 34W
Burntwood L., Canada 131 B8 55 22N 100 26W
Burqān, Kuwait 84 D5 29 0N 47 57 E
Burra, Australia 116 B3 33 40 S 138 55 E
Burragorang, L., Australia 117 B9 33 52 S 150 37 E
Burramurra, Australia 114 C2 20 25 S 137 15 E
Burreli, Albania 44 C2 41 36N 20 1 E
Burren Junction, Australia 115 E4 30 7 S 148 59 E
Burrendong, L., Australia 117 B8 32 45 S 149 10 E
Burrendong Dam, Australia 115 E4 32 39 S 149 6 E
Burriana, Spain 34 F4 39 50N 0 4W
Burrinjuck Res., Australia 117 C8 35 0 S 148 36 E
Burro, Serranías del, Mexico 146 B4 29 0N 102 0W
Burruyacú, Argentina 158 B3 26 30 S 64 40W
Burry Port, U.K. 17 F3 51 41N 4 15W
Bursa, Turkey 88 B3 40 15N 29 5 E
Burseryd, Sweden 15 G7 57 12N 13 17 E
Burstall, Canada 131 C7 50 39N 109 54W
Burton, U.S.A. 141 B13 43 0N 83 40W
Burton L., Canada 128 B4 54 45N 78 20W
Burton upon Trent, U.K. 16 E6 52 48N 1 38W
Burtundy, Australia 116 B5 33 45 S 142 15 E
Buru, Indonesia 72 B3 3 30 S 126 30 E
Buruanga, Phil. 71 F3 11 51N 121 53 E
Burullus, Bahra el, Egypt 94 H7 31 25N 31 0 E
Burūm, Yemen 87 D5 14 22N 48 59 E
Burûn, Râs, Egypt 91 D2 31 14N 33 7 E
Burunday, Kazakstan 55 B8 43 20N 76 51 E
Burundi ■, Africa 106 C3 3 15 S 30 0 E
Bururi, Burundi 106 C2 3 57 S 29 37 E
Burutu, Nigeria 101 D6 5 20N 5 29 E
Burwell, U.S.A. 138 E5 41 47N 99 8W
Bury, U.K. 16 D5 53 35N 2 17W
Bury St. Edmunds, U.K. 17 E8 52 15N 0 43 E
Buryatia □, Russia 57 D11 53 0N 110 0 E
Buryn, Ukraine 51 G7 51 13N 33 50 E
Burzenin, Poland 47 D5 51 28N 18 47 E
Busalla, Italy 38 D5 44 34N 8 57 E
Busango Swamp, Zambia 107 E2 14 15 S 25 45 E
Buşayrah, Syria 89 E9 35 9N 40 26 E
Buşayyah, Iraq 84 D5 30 0N 46 10 E
Busca, Italy 38 D4 44 31N 7 29 E
Bushati, Albania 44 C1 41 58N 19 34 E
Būshehr, Iran 85 D6 28 55N 50 55 E
Būshehr □, Iran 85 D6 28 20N 51 45 E
Bushell, Canada 131 B7 59 31N 108 45W
Bushenyi, Uganda 106 C3 0 35 S 30 10 E
Bushire = Būshehr, Iran 85 D6 28 55N 50 55 E
Bushnell, Ill., U.S.A. 138 E9 40 33N 90 31W
Bushnell, Nebr., U.S.A. 138 E3 41 14N 103 54W
Busia □, Kenya 106 B3 0 25N 34 6 E
Busie, Ghana 100 C4 10 29N 2 22W
Businga, Zaïre 102 B4 3 16N 20 59 E

180 Buskerud fylke

Buskerud fylke □, *Norway* **14 D3** 60 13N 9 0 E
Busko Zdrój, *Poland* **47 E7** 50 28N 20 42 E
Buskul, *Kazakstan* **54 E8** 53 45N 61 12 E
Buslei, *Ethiopia* **108 C2** 5 28N 44 25 E
Busovača, *Bos.-H.* **42 C2** 44 6N 17 53 E
Busra ash Shām, *Syria* **91 C5** 32 30N 36 25 E
Bussang, *France* **23 E13** 47 50N 6 50 E
Busselton, *Australia* **113 F2** 33 42 S 115 15 E
Busseto, *Italy* **38 D7** 44 59N 10 2 E
Bussigny, *Switz.* **28 C3** 46 33N 6 33 E
Bussum, *Neths.* **20 D6** 52 16N 5 10 E
Bustamante, B., *Argentina* **160 C3** 45 5 S 66 18W
Busto, C., *Spain* **36 B4** 43 34N 6 28W
Busto Arsízio, *Italy* **38 C5** 45 37N 8 51 E
Busu-Djanoa, *Zaïre* **102 B4** 1 43N 21 23 E
Busuanga, *Phil.* **70 E2** 12 10N 120 0 E
Busuanga, *Phil.* **70 E2** 12 14N 119 52 E
Büsum, *Germany* **26 A4** 54 7N 8 51 E
Buta, *Zaïre* **106 B1** 2 50N 24 53 E
Butare, *Rwanda* **106 C2** 2 31 S 29 52 E
Butaritari, *Kiribati* **122 G9** 3 30N 174 0 E
Bute, *Australia* **116 B3** 33 51 S 138 2 E
Bute, *U.K.* **18 F3** 55 48N 5 2W
Bute Inlet, *Canada* **130 C4** 50 40N 124 53W
Butemba, *Uganda* **106 B3** 1 9N 31 37 E
Butembo, *Zaïre* **106 B2** 0 9N 29 18 E
Butera, *Italy* **41 E7** 37 11N 14 11 E
Bütgenbach, *Belgium* **21 H8** 50 26N 6 12 E
Butha Qi, *China* **65 B7** 48 0N 122 32 E
Buthidaung, *Burma* **78 E4** 20 52N 92 32 E
Butiaba, *Uganda* **106 B3** 1 50N 31 20 E
Butkhāk, *Afghan.* **79 B3** 34 30N 69 22 E
Butler, *Ind., U.S.A.* **141 C12** 41 26N 84 52W
Butler, *Ky., U.S.A.* **141 F12** 38 47N 84 22W
Butler, *Mo., U.S.A.* **140 F2** 38 16N 94 20W
Butler, *Pa., U.S.A.* **136 F5** 40 52N 79 54W
Butom Odrzánski, *Poland* **47 D2** 51 44N 15 48 E
Buton, *Indonesia* **72 C2** 5 0 S 122 45 E
Bütschwil, *Switz.* **29 B8** 47 23N 9 5 E
Butte, *Mont., U.S.A.* **142 C7** 46 0N 112 32W
Butte, *Nebr., U.S.A.* **138 D5** 42 58N 98 51W
Butte Creek →, *U.S.A.* **144 F5** 39 12N 121 56W
Butterworth = Gcuwa,
S. Africa **105 E4** 32 20 S 28 11 E
Butterworth, *Malaysia* **77 K3** 5 24N 100 23 E
Buttfield, Mt., *Australia* **113 D4** 24 45 S 128 9 E
Button B., *Canada* **131 B10** 58 45N 94 23W
Buttonwillow, *U.S.A.* **145 K7** 35 24N 119 28W
Butty Hd., *Australia* **113 F3** 33 54 S 121 39 E
Butuan, *Phil.* **71 G5** 8 57N 125 33 E
Butuku-Luba, *Eq. Guin.* **101 E6** 3 29N 8 33 E
Butulan, *Phil.* **71 J5** 5 38N 125 26 E
Butung = Buton,
Indonesia **72 C2** 5 0 S 122 45 E
Buturlinovka, *Russia* **52 E5** 50 50N 40 35 E
Butzbach, *Germany* **26 E4** 50 25N 8 40 E
Bützow, *Germany* **26 B7** 53 50N 11 58 E
Buug, *Phil.* **71 H4** 7 40N 123 2 E
Buxar, *India* **81 G10** 25 34N 83 58 E
Buxton, *Guyana* **153 B6** 6 48N 58 2W
Buxton, *U.K.* **16 D6** 53 16N 1 54W
Buxy, *France* **23 F11** 46 44N 4 40 E
Buy, *Russia* **52 A5** 58 28N 41 28 E
Buynaksk, *Russia* **53 J8** 42 48N 47 7 E
Büyük Kemikli Burun,
Turkey **44 D8** 40 20N 26 15 E
Büyük Menderes →,
Turkey **88 D2** 37 28N 27 11 E
Büyükçekmece, *Turkey* **88 B3** 41 2N 28 35 E
Buzançais, *France* **22 F8** 46 54N 1 25 E
Buzău, *Romania* **46 D7** 45 10N 26 50 E
Buzău □, *Romania* **46 D7** 45 20N 26 30 E
Buzău →, *Romania* **46 D8** 45 26N 27 44 E
Buzău, Pasul, *Romania* **46 D7** 45 35N 26 12 E
Buzen, *Japan* **62 D3** 33 35N 131 5 E
Buzet, *Croatia* **39 C10** 45 24N 13 58 E
Buzi →, *Mozam.* **107 F3** 19 50 S 34 43 E
Buziaş, *Romania* **46 D2** 45 38N 21 36 E
Buzuluk, *Russia* **54 E4** 52 48N 52 12 E
Buzuluk →, *Russia* **52 E6** 50 15N 42 7 E
Buzzards Bay, *U.S.A.* **137 E14** 41 45N 70 37W
Bwagaoia, *Papua N. G.* **120 F7** 10 40 S 152 52 E
Bwana Mkubwe, *Zaïre* **107 E2** 13 8 S 28 38 E
Byala, *Ruse, Bulgaria* **43 D10** 43 28N 25 44 E
Byala, *Varna, Bulgaria* **43 E12** 42 53N 27 55 E
Byala Slatina, *Bulgaria* **43 D8** 43 26N 23 55 E
Byarezina →, *Belarus* **51 F6** 52 33N 30 14 E
Bychawa, *Poland* **47 D9** 51 1N 22 36 E
Byczyna, *Poland* **47 D5** 51 7N 18 12 E
Bydgoszcz, *Poland* **47 B5** 53 10N 18 0 E
Bydgoszcz □, *Poland* **47 B4** 53 16N 17 33 E
Byelarus = Belarus ■,
Europe **50 F4** 53 30N 27 0 E
Byelorussia = Belarus ■,
Europe **50 F4** 53 30N 27 0 E
Byers, *U.S.A.* **138 F2** 39 43N 104 14W
Byesville, *U.S.A.* **136 G3** 39 58N 81 32W
Byhalia, *U.S.A.* **139 H10** 34 52N 89 41W
Bykhaw, *Belarus* **50 F6** 53 31N 30 14 E
Bykhov = Bykhaw,
Belarus **50 F6** 53 31N 30 14 E
Bykovo, *Russia* **52 F7** 49 50N 45 25 E
Bylas, *U.S.A.* **143 K8** 33 8N 110 7W
Bylderup-Bov, *Denmark* **15 K3** 54 57N 9 6 E
Bylot I., *Canada* **127 A12** 73 13N 78 34W
Byrd, C., *Antarctica* **7 C17** 69 38 S 76 7W
Byro, *Australia* **113 E2** 26 5 S 116 11 E
Byrock, *Australia* **117 A7** 30 40 S 146 27 E
Byron, *U.S.A.* **140 B7** 42 8N 89 15W
Byron Bay, *Australia* **115 D5** 28 43 S 153 37 E
Byrranga, Gory, *Russia* **57 B11** 75 0N 100 0 E
Byrranga Mts. =
Byrranga, Gory, *Russia* **57 B11** 75 0N 100 0 E
Byrum, *Denmark* **15 G5** 57 16N 11 0 E
Byske, *Sweden* **12 D19** 64 57N 21 11 E
Byske älv →, *Sweden* **12 D19** 64 57N 21 13 E
Bystrovka, *Kyrgyzstan* **55 B7** 42 47N 75 42 E
Bystrzyca →, *Lublin,*
Poland **47 D9** 51 21N 22 46 E
Bystrzyca →, *Wrocław,*
Poland **47 D3** 51 12N 16 55 E
Bystrzyca Kłodzka, *Poland* **47 E3** 50 19N 16 39 E
Bytom, *Poland* **47 E5** 50 25N 18 54 E
Bytów, *Poland* **47 A4** 54 10N 17 30 E
Byumba, *Rwanda* **106 C3** 1 35 S 30 4 E
Bzenec, *Czech.* **31 C10** 48 58N 17 18 E
Bzura →, *Poland* **47 C7** 52 25N 20 15 E

C

Ca →, *Vietnam* **76 C5** 18 45N 105 45 E
Ca Mau = Quan Long,
Vietnam **77 H5** 9 7N 105 8 E
Ca Mau, Mui = Bai Bung,
Mui, *Vietnam* **77 H5** 8 38N 104 44 E
Ca Na, *Vietnam* **77 G7** 11 20N 108 54 E
Caacupé, *Paraguay* **158 B4** 25 23 S 57 5W
Caála, *Angola* **103 E3** 12 46 S 15 30 E
Caamano Sd., *Canada* **130 C3** 52 55N 129 25W
Caapiranga, *Brazil* **153 D5** 3 18 S 61 13W
Caazapá, *Paraguay* **158 B4** 26 8 S 56 19W
Caazapá □, *Paraguay* **159 B4** 26 10 S 56 0W
Cabadbaran, *Phil.* **71 G5** 9 10N 125 38 E
Cabagan, *Phil.* **70 C3** 17 26N 121 46 E
Cabalian, *Phil.* **71 F5** 10 16N 125 10 E
Caballeria, C. de, *Spain* **33 A11** 40 5N 4 5 E
Cabana, *Peru* **156 B2** 8 25 S 78 5W
Cabanaconde, *Peru* **156 D3** 15 38 S 71 58W
Cabañaquinta, *Spain* **36 B5** 43 10N 5 38W
Cabanatuan, *Phil.* **70 D3** 15 30N 120 58 E
Cabanes, *Spain* **34 E5** 40 9N 0 2 E
Cabangon, *Phil.* **70 D3** 15 10N 120 3 E
Cabanillas, *Peru* **156 D3** 15 36 S 70 28W
Cabano, *Canada* **129 C6** 47 40N 68 56W
Čabar, *Croatia* **39 C11** 45 36N 14 39 E
Cabarroquis, *Phil.* **70 C3** 16 50N 121 30 E
Cabarruyan I., *Phil.* **70 C2** 16 18N 119 59 E
Cabazon, *U.S.A.* **145 M10** 33 55N 116 47W
Cabcaben, *Phil.* **70 D3** 14 27N 120 35 E
Cabedelo, *Brazil* **154 C5** 7 0 S 34 50W
Cabery, *U.S.A.* **141 D8** 41 0N 88 12W
Cabeza del Buey, *Spain* **37 G5** 38 44N 5 13W
Cabildo, *Chile* **158 C1** 32 30 S 71 5W
Cabimas, *Venezuela* **152 A3** 10 23N 71 25W
Cabinda, *Angola* **103 D2** 5 33 S 12 11 E
Cabinda □, *Angola* **103 D2** 5 0 S 12 30 E
Cabinet Mts., *U.S.A.* **142 C6** 48 0N 115 30W
Cabiri, *Angola* **103 D2** 8 52 S 13 39 E
Cabo Blanco, *Argentina* **160 C3** 47 15 S 65 47W
Cabo Frio, *Brazil* **155 F3** 22 51 S 42 3W
Cabo Pantoja, *Peru* **152 D2** 1 0 S 75 10W
Cabo Raso, *Argentina* **160 B3** 44 20 S 65 15W
Cabonga, Réservoir,
Canada **128 C4** 47 20N 76 40W
Cabool, *U.S.A.* **139 G8** 37 7N 92 6W
Caboolture, *Australia* **115 D5** 27 5 S 152 58 E
Cabora Bassa Dam =
Cahora Bassa Dam,
Mozam. **107 F3** 15 20 S 32 50 E
Caborca, *Mexico* **146 A2** 30 40N 112 10W
Cabot, Mt., *U.S.A.* **137 B13** 44 30N 71 25W
Cabot Str., *Canada* **129 C8** 47 15N 59 40W
Cabra, *Spain* **37 H6** 37 30N 4 28W
Cabra del Santo Cristo,
Spain **35 H1** 37 42N 3 16W
Cábras, *Italy* **40 C1** 39 56N 8 32 E
Cabrera, *Spain* **33 B9** 39 8N 2 57 E
Cabrera, Sierra, *Spain* **36 C4** 42 12N 6 40W
Cabri, *Canada* **131 C7** 50 35N 108 25W
Cabriel →, *Spain* **35 F3** 39 14N 1 3W
Cabruta, *Venezuela* **152 B4** 7 50N 66 10W
Cabucgayan, *Phil.* **71 F5** 11 29N 124 34 E
Cabugao, *Phil.* **70 C3** 17 48N 120 27 E
Cabulauan Is., *Phil.* **71 F3** 11 25N 120 8 E
Caburan = Jose Abad
Santos, *Phil.* **71 J5** 5 55N 125 39 E
Cabuyaro, *Colombia* **152 C3** 4 18N 72 49W
Čacabelos, *Spain* **36 C4** 42 36N 6 44W
Čačak, *Serbia, Yug.* **42 D5** 43 54N 20 20 E
Cacao, *Fr. Guiana* **153 C7** 4 33N 52 26W
Cáceres, *Brazil* **157 D6** 16 5 S 57 40W
Cáceres, *Colombia* **152 B2** 7 35N 75 20W
Cáceres, *Spain* **37 F4** 39 26N 6 23W
Cáceres □, *Spain* **37 F4** 39 45N 6 0W
Cache Bay, *Canada* **128 C4** 46 22N 80 0W
Cache Cr. →, *U.S.A.* **144 G5** 38 42N 121 42W
Cachepo, *Portugal* **37 H3** 37 20N 7 49W
Cachéu, *Guinea-Biss.* **100 C1** 12 14N 16 8W
Cachi, *Argentina* **158 B2** 25 5 S 66 10W
Cachimbo, *Brazil* **157 B7** 8 57 S 54 54W
Cachimbo, Serra do,
Brazil **157 B6** 9 30 S 55 30W
Cachingues, *Angola* **103 E3** 13 5 S 16 43 E
Cachoeira, *Brazil* **155 D4** 12 30 S 39 0W
Cachoeira Alta, *Brazil* **155 E1** 18 48 S 50 58W
Cachoeira de Itapemirim,
Brazil **155 F3** 20 51 S 41 7W
Cachoeira do Sul, *Brazil* **159 C5** 30 3 S 52 53W
Cachoeiro do Arari, *Brazil* **154 B2** 1 1 S 48 58W
Cachopo, *Portugal* **37 H3** 37 20N 7 49W
Cachuela Esperanza,
Bolivia **157 C4** 10 32 S 65 38W
Cacólo, *Angola* **103 E3** 10 9 S 19 21 E
Caconda, *Angola* **103 E3** 13 48 S 15 8 E
Cacongo, *Angola* **103 D2** 5 11 S 12 5 E
Caçu, *Brazil* **155 E1** 18 37 S 51 4W
Cacula, *Angola* **103 E2** 14 29 S 14 10 E
Caculé, *Brazil* **155 D3** 14 30 S 42 13W
Cacuso, *Angola* **103 D3** 9 25 S 15 45 E
Čadarache, *France* **25 E9** 43 41N 5 43 E
Čadca, *Slovak Rep.* **31 B11** 49 26N 18 45 E
Caddo, *U.S.A.* **139 H6** 34 7N 96 16W
Cadell Cr. →, *Australia* **114 C3** 22 35 S 141 51 E
Cadenazzo, *Switz.* **29 D7** 46 9N 8 57 E
Cader Idris, *U.K.* **16 E4** 52 42N 3 53W
Cadí, Sierra del, *Spain* **34 C6** 42 17N 1 42 E
Cadibarrawirracanna, L.,
Australia **115 D2** 28 52 S 135 27 E
Cadillac, *Canada* **128 C4** 48 14N 78 23W
Cadillac, *France* **24 D3** 44 38N 0 20W
Cadillac, *U.S.A.* **134 C3** 44 15N 85 24W
Cadiz, *Phil.* **71 F4** 10 57N 123 15 E
Cádiz, *Spain* **37 J4** 36 30N 6 20W
Cadiz, *U.S.A.* **136 F4** 40 22N 81 0W
Cádiz □, *Spain* **37 J5** 36 36N 5 45W
Cádiz, G. de, *Spain* **37 J4** 36 40N 7 0W
Cadney Park, *Australia* **115 D1** 27 55 S 134 3 E
Cadomin, *Canada* **130 C5** 53 2N 117 20W
Cadotte →, *Canada* **130 B5** 56 43N 117 10W
Cadours, *France* **24 E5** 43 44N 1 2 E
Cadoux, *Australia* **113 F2** 30 46 S 117 7 E
Caen, *France* **22 C6** 49 10N 0 22W
Caernarfon, *U.K.* **16 D3** 53 8N 4 16W
Caernarfon B., *U.K.* **16 D3** 53 4N 4 40W
Caernarvon = Caernarfon,
U.K. **16 D3** 53 8N 4 16W
Caerphilly, *U.K.* **17 F4** 51 35N 3 13W
Caerphilly □, *U.K.* **17 F4** 51 37N 3 12W
Caesarea, *Israel* **91 C3** 32 30N 34 53 E
Caeté, *Brazil* **155 E3** 19 55 S 43 40W
Caetité, *Brazil* **155 D3** 13 50 S 42 32W
Cafayate, *Argentina* **158 B2** 26 2 S 66 0W
Cafifi, *Colombia* **152 B3** 5 13N 71 4W
Cafu, *Angola* **103 F3** 16 30 S 15 8 E
Cagayan □, *Phil.* **70 B3** 18 0N 121 50 E
Cagayan →, *Phil.* **70 B3** 18 25N 121 42 E
Cagayan de Oro, *Phil.* **71 G5** 8 30N 124 40 E
Cagayan Is., *Phil.* **71 G3** 9 40N 121 16 E
Cagayan Sulu I., *Phil.* **71 H2** 7 1N 118 30 E
Cagli, *Italy* **39 E9** 43 33N 12 39 E
Cágliari, *Italy* **40 C2** 39 13N 9 7 E
Cágliari, G. di, *Italy* **40 C2** 39 8N 9 11 E
Cagnano Varano, *Italy* **41 A8** 41 49N 15 47 E
Cagnes-sur-Mer, *France* **25 E11** 43 40N 7 9 E
Caguán →, *Colombia* **152 D3** 0 8 S 74 18W
Caguas, *Puerto Rico* **149 C6** 18 14N 66 2W
Caha Mts., *Ireland* **19 E2** 51 45N 9 40W
Cahama, *Angola* **103 F2** 16 17 S 14 19 E
Caher, *Ireland* **19 D4** 52 22N 7 56W
Caherciveen, *Ireland* **19 E1** 51 56N 10 14W
Cahora Bassa Dam,
Mozam. **107 F3** 15 20 S 32 50 E
Cahore Pt., *Ireland* **19 D5** 52 33N 6 12W
Cahors, *France* **24 D5** 44 27N 1 27 E
Cahuapanas, *Peru* **156 B2** 5 15 S 77 0W
Cahuinari →, *Colombia* **152 D3** 1 21 S 70 44W
Cahul, *Moldova* **51 K5** 45 50N 28 15 E
Cai Bau, Dao, *Vietnam* **76 B6** 21 10N 107 27 E
Cai Nuoc, *Vietnam* **77 H5** 8 56N 105 1 E
Caia, *Mozam.* **107 F4** 17 51 S 35 24 E
Caiabis, Serra dos, *Brazil* **157 C6** 11 30 S 56 30W
Caianda, *Angola* **103 E4** 11 2 S 23 31 E
Caiapó, Serra do, *Brazil* **157 D7** 17 0 S 52 0W
Caiapônia, *Brazil* **157 D7** 16 57 S 51 49W
Caibarién, *Cuba* **148 B4** 22 30N 79 30W
Caibiran, *Phil.* **71 F5** 11 34N 124 35 E
Caicara, *Bolívar,*
Venezuela **152 B4** 7 38N 66 10W
Caicara, *Monagas,*
Venezuela **153 B5** 9 52N 63 38W
Caicó, *Brazil* **154 C4** 6 20 S 37 0W
Caicos Is., *W. Indies* **149 B5** 21 40N 71 40W
Caicos Passage, *W. Indies* **149 B5** 22 45N 72 45W
Cailloma, *Peru* **156 D3** 15 9 S 71 45W
Caine →, *Bolivia* **157 D4** 18 23 S 65 21W
Caird Coast, *Antarctica* **7 D1** 75 0 S 25 0W
Cairn Gorm, *U.K.* **18 D5** 57 7N 3 39W
Cairn Toul, *U.K.* **18 D5** 57 3N 3 44W
Cairngorm Mts., *U.K.* **18 D5** 57 6N 3 42W
Cairns, *Australia* **114 B4** 16 57 S 145 45 E
Cairo = El Qâhira, *Egypt* **94 H7** 30 1N 31 14 E
Cairo, *Ga., U.S.A.* **135 K3** 30 52N 84 13W
Cairo, *Ill., U.S.A.* **139 G10** 37 0N 89 11W
Cairo Montenotte, *Italy* **38 D5** 44 23N 8 16 E
Caithness, Ord of, *U.K.* **18 C5** 58 8N 3 36W
Caiundo, *Angola* **103 F3** 15 50 S 17 28 E
Caiza, *Bolivia* **157 E4** 20 2 S 65 40W
Cajabamba, *Peru* **156 B2** 7 38 S 78 4W
Cajamarca, *Peru* **156 B2** 7 5 S 78 28W
Cajamarca □, *Peru* **156 B2** 6 15 S 78 50W
Cajapió, *Brazil* **154 B3** 2 58 S 44 48W
Cajarc, *France* **24 D5** 44 29N 1 50 E
Cajatambo, *Peru* **156 C2** 10 30 S 77 2W
Cajàzeiras, *Brazil* **154 C4** 6 52 S 38 30W
Čajetina, *Serbia, Yug.* **42 D4** 43 47N 19 42 E
Cajidiocan, *Phil.* **70 E4** 12 22N 122 41 E
Čajniče, *Bos.-H.* **42 D4** 43 34N 19 5 E
Çakirgol, *Turkey* **89 B8** 40 33N 39 40 E
Čakovec, *Croatia* **39 B13** 46 23N 16 26 E
Çal, *Turkey* **88 C3** 38 4N 29 23 E
Cala, *Spain* **37 H4** 37 59N 6 21W
Cala →, *Spain* **37 H4** 37 38N 6 5W
Cala Cadolar, Punta de,
Spain **35 G6** 38 38N 1 35 E
Cala d'Or, *Spain* **33 B10** 39 23N 3 14 E
Cala Figuera, C., *Spain* **33 B9** 39 27N 2 31 E
Cala Forcat, *Spain* **33 A10** 40 0N 3 47 E
Cala Mayor, *Spain* **33 B9** 39 33N 2 37 E
Cala Mezquida, *Spain* **33 B11** 39 55N 4 16 E
Cala Millor, *Spain* **33 B10** 39 35N 3 22 E
Cala Ratjada, *Spain* **33 B10** 39 43N 3 27 E
Calabanga, *Phil.* **70 E4** 13 42N 123 17 E
Calabar, *Nigeria* **101 E6** 4 57N 8 20 E
Calabozo, *Venezuela* **152 B4** 9 0N 67 28W
Calábria □, *Italy* **41 C9** 39 0N 16 30 E
Calaburras, Pta. de, *Spain* **37 J6** 36 30N 4 38W
Calaceite, *Spain* **34 D5** 41 1N 0 11 E
Calacota, *Bolivia* **156 D4** 17 16 S 68 38W
Calafat, *Romania* **46 F3** 43 58N 22 59 E
Calafate, *Argentina* **160 D2** 50 19 S 72 15W
Calahorra, *Spain* **34 C3** 42 18N 1 59W
Calais, *France* **23 B8** 50 57N 1 56 E
Calais, *U.S.A.* **129 C6** 45 11N 67 17W
Calais, Pas de, *France* **23 B8** 50 30N 1 20 E
Calalaste, Cord. de,
Argentina **158 B2** 25 0 S 67 0W
Calalayan, *Phil.* **71 F2** 11 30N 119 38 E
Calama, *Brazil* **157 B5** 8 0 S 62 50W
Calama, *Chile* **158 A2** 22 30 S 68 55W
Calamar, *Bolívar,*
Colombia **152 A3** 10 15N 74 55W
Calamar, *Vaupés,*
Colombia **152 C3** 1 58N 72 32W
Calamarca, *Bolivia* **156 D4** 16 55 S 68 9W
Calamba, *Cavite, Phil.* **71 G4** 8 35N 123 39 E
Calamba, *Misamis, Phil.* **71 F4** 10 11N 123 17 E
Calamba, *Negros, Phil.* **70 D3** 14 13N 121 10 E
Calamian Group, *Phil.* **71 F2** 11 50N 119 55 E
Calamocha, *Spain* **34 E3** 40 50N 1 17W
Calán Porter, *Spain* **33 B11** 39 52N 4 8 E
Calañas, *Spain* **37 H4** 37 40N 6 53W
Calanda, *Spain* **34 E4** 40 56N 0 15W
Calandagan I., *Phil.* **71 F3** 10 39N 120 15 E
Calandula, *Angola* **103 D3** 9 6 S 15 57 E
Calang, *Indonesia* **74 B1** 4 37N 95 37 E
Calangiánus, *Italy* **40 B2** 40 56N 9 11 E
Calanscio, Sarīr, *Libya* **96 C4** 27 30N 22 30 E
Calapan, *Phil.* **70 E3** 13 25N 121 7 E
Calape, *Phil.* **71 G4** 9 54N 123 52 E
Călăraşi, *Romania* **46 E8** 44 12N 27 20 E
Călăraşi □, *Romania* **46 E8** 44 10N 27 0 E
Calasparra, *Spain* **35 G3** 38 14N 1 41W
Calatafimi, *Italy* **40 E5** 37 55N 12 52 E
Calatagan, *Phil.* **70 E3** 13 50N 120 38 E
Calatayud, *Spain* **34 D3** 41 20N 1 40W
Calato = Kálathos, *Greece* **45 H10** 36 9N 28 8 E
Calauag, *Phil.* **70 E4** 13 55N 122 15 E
Calavà, C., *Italy* **41 D7** 38 11N 14 55 E
Calavite, C., *Phil.* **70 E3** 13 26N 120 20 E
Calavite Pass, *Phil.* **70 E3** 13 36N 120 25 E
Calayan, *Phil.* **70 B3** 19 16N 121 28 E
Calayan I., *Phil.* **70 B3** 19 20N 121 27 E
Calbayog, *Phil.* **70 E5** 12 4N 124 38 E
Calbe, *Germany* **26 D7** 51 54N 11 46 E
Calca, *Peru* **156 C3** 13 22 S 72 0W
Calcasieu L., *U.S.A.* **139 L8** 29 55N 93 18W
Calci, *Italy* **38 E7** 43 44N 10 31 E
Calcutta, *India* **81 H13** 22 36N 88 24 E
Caldaro, *Italy* **39 B8** 46 25N 11 14 E
Caldas □, *Colombia* **152 B2** 5 15N 75 30W
Caldas da Rainha,
Portugal **37 F1** 39 24N 9 8W
Caldas de Reyes, *Spain* **36 C2** 42 36N 8 39W
Caldas Novas, *Brazil* **155 E2** 17 45 S 48 38W
Calder →, *U.K.* **16 D6** 53 44N 1 22W
Caldera, *Chile* **158 B1** 27 5 S 70 55W
Caldwell, *Idaho, U.S.A.* **142 E5** 43 40N 116 41W
Caldwell, *Kans., U.S.A.* **139 G6** 37 2N 97 37W
Caldwell, *Tex., U.S.A.* **139 K6** 30 32N 96 42W
Caledon, *S. Africa* **104 E2** 34 14 S 19 26 E
Caledon →, *S. Africa* **104 E4** 30 31 S 26 5 E
Caledon B., *Australia* **114 A2** 12 45 S 137 0 E
Caledonia, *Canada* **136 C5** 43 7N 79 58W
Caledonia, *Mo., U.S.A.* **140 G6** 37 45N 90 46W
Caledonia, *N.Y., U.S.A.* **136 D7** 42 58N 77 51W
Calella, *Spain* **34 D7** 41 37N 2 40 E
Calemba, *Angola* **104 B2** 16 0 S 15 44 E
Calenzana, *France* **25 F12** 42 31N 8 51 E
Caleta Olivia, *Argentina* **160 C3** 46 25 S 67 25W
Calexico, *U.S.A.* **145 N11** 32 40N 115 30W
Calf of Man, *U.K.* **16 C3** 54 3N 4 48W
Calgary, *Canada* **130 C6** 51 0N 114 10W
Calheta, *Madeira* **33 D2** 32 44N 17 11W
Calhoun, *U.S.A.* **135 H3** 34 30N 84 57W
Cali, *Colombia* **152 C2** 3 25N 76 35W
Calicut, *India* **83 J2** 11 15N 75 43 E
Caliente, *U.S.A.* **143 H6** 37 37N 114 31W
California, *Mo., U.S.A.* **140 F4** 38 38N 92 34W
California, *Pa., U.S.A.* **136 F5** 40 4N 79 54W
California □, *U.S.A.* **143 H4** 37 30N 119 30W
California, Baja, *Mexico* **146 A1** 32 10N 115 12W
California, Baja,
T.N. □ = Baja
California □, *Mexico* **146 B2** 30 0N 115 0W
California, Baja, T.S. □ =
Baja California Sur □,
Mexico **146 B2** 25 50N 111 50W
California, G. de, *Mexico* **146 B2** 27 0N 111 0W
California City, *U.S.A.* **145 K9** 35 10N 117 55W
California Hot Springs,
U.S.A. **145 K8** 35 51N 118 41W
Călimăneşti, *Romania* **46 D5** 45 14N 24 20 E
Călimani, Munţii,
Romania **46 B5** 47 12N 25 0 E
Călineşti, *Romania* **46 D5** 45 21N 24 18 E
Calingasta, *Argentina* **158 C2** 31 15 S 69 30W
Calinog, *Phil.* **71 F4** 11 7N 122 32 E
Calintaan, *Phil.* **70 E3** 12 35N 120 57 E
Calipatria, *U.S.A.* **145 M11** 33 8N 115 31W
Calistoga, *U.S.A.* **144 G4** 38 35N 122 35W
Calitri, *Italy* **41 B8** 40 54N 15 26 E
Calitzdorp, *S. Africa* **104 E3** 33 33 S 21 42 E
Callabonna, L., *Australia* **115 D3** 29 40 S 140 5 E
Callac, *France* **22 D3** 48 25N 3 27W
Callan, *Ireland* **19 D4** 52 32N 7 24W
Callander, *U.K.* **18 E4** 56 15N 4 13W
Callang, *Phil.* **70 C3** 17 2N 121 38 E
Callantsoog, *Neths.* **20 C5** 52 50N 4 42 E
Callao, *Peru* **156 C2** 12 0 S 77 0W
Callaway, *U.S.A.* **138 E5** 41 18N 99 56W
Callender, *U.S.A.* **140 B2** 42 22N 94 17W
Calles, *Mexico* **147 C5** 23 2N 98 42W
Callide, *Australia* **114 C5** 24 18 S 150 28 E
Calling Lake, *Canada* **130 B6** 55 15N 113 12W
Calliope, *Australia* **114 C5** 24 0 S 151 16 E
Callosa de Ensarriá, *Spain* **35 G4** 38 40N 0 8W
Callosa de Segura, *Spain* **35 G4** 38 7N 0 53W
Calmar, *U.S.A.* **140 A5** 43 11N 91 52W
Calola, *Angola* **103 F3** 16 25 S 17 48 E
Calolbon, *Phil.* **70 E5** 13 36N 124 6 E
Caloocan, *Phil.* **70 D3** 14 39N 120 58 E
Calore →, *Italy* **41 A7** 41 11N 14 28 E
Caloundra, *Australia* **115 D5** 26 45 S 153 10 E
Calpe, *Spain* **35 G5** 38 39N 0 3 E
Calpella, *U.S.A.* **144 F3** 39 14N 123 12W
Calpine, *U.S.A.* **144 F6** 39 40N 120 27W
Calstock, *Canada* **128 C3** 49 47N 84 9W
Caltabellotta, *Italy* **40 E6** 37 34N 13 13 E
Caltagirone, *Italy* **41 E7** 37 14N 14 31 E
Caltanissetta, *Italy* **41 E7** 37 29N 14 4 E
Calucinga, *Angola* **103 E3** 11 18 S 16 12 E
Calulo, *Angola* **103 E2** 10 1 S 14 56 E
Calumet, *U.S.A.* **134 B1** 47 14N 88 27W
Calunda, *Angola* **103 E4** 12 7 S 23 36 E
Caluquembe, *Angola* **103 E2** 13 47 S 14 44 E
Caluso, *Italy* **38 C4** 45 18N 7 53 E
Caluya I., *Phil.* **71 F3** 11 55N 121 34 E
Calvados □, *France* **22 C6** 49 5N 0 15W
Calvert, *U.S.A.* **139 K6** 30 59N 96 40W
Calvert →, *Australia* **114 B2** 16 17 S 137 44 E
Calvert Hills, *Australia* **114 B2** 17 15 S 137 20 E
Calvert I., *Canada* **130 C3** 51 30N 128 0W
Calvert Ra., *Australia* **112 D3** 24 0 S 122 30 E
Calvi, *France* **25 F12** 42 34N 8 45 E
Calvillo, *Mexico* **146 C4** 21 51N 102 43W
Calvinia, *S. Africa* **104 E2** 31 28 S 19 45 E
Calw, *Germany* **27 G4** 48 42N 8 44 E
Calwa, *U.S.A.* **144 J7** 36 42N 119 46W
Calzada Almuradiel, *Spain* **35 G1** 38 32N 3 28W
Calzada de Calatrava,
Spain **37 G7** 38 42N 3 46W
Cam →, *U.K.* **17 E8** 52 21N 0 16 E
Cam Lam, *Vietnam* **77 G7** 11 54N 109 10 E
Cam Pha, *Vietnam* **76 B6** 21 7N 107 18 E
Cam Ranh, *Vietnam* **77 G7** 11 54N 109 12 E
Cam Xuyen, *Vietnam* **76 C6** 18 15N 106 0 E
Camabatela, *Angola* **103 D3** 8 20 S 15 26 E
Camacã, *Brazil* **155 E4** 15 24 S 39 30W

184 Changhŭngni

Changhŭngni, N. Korea 67 D15 40 24N 128 19 E
Changi, Malaysia 74 B2 1 23N 103 59 E
Changjiang, China 76 C7 19 20N 108 55 E
Changjin, N. Korea 67 D14 40 23N 127 15 E
Changjin-chŏsuji, N. Korea 67 D14 40 30N 127 15 E
Changle, China 69 E12 25 59N 119 27 E
Changli, China 67 E10 39 40N 119 13 E
Changling, China 67 B12 44 20N 123 58 E
Changlun, Malaysia 77 J3 6 25N 100 26 E
Changning, Hunan, China 69 D9 26 28N 112 22 E
Changning, Yunnan, China 68 E2 24 45N 99 30 E
Changping, China 66 D9 40 14N 116 12 E
Changsha, China 69 C9 28 12N 113 0 E
Changshan, China 69 C12 28 55N 118 27 E
Changshou, China 68 C6 29 51N 107 8 E
Changshu, China 69 B13 31 38N 120 43 E
Changshun, China 68 D6 26 3N 106 25 E
Changtai, China 69 E11 24 35N 117 42 E
Changting, China 69 E11 25 50N 116 22 E
Changwu, China 66 G4 35 10N 107 45 E
Changxing, China 69 B12 31 0N 119 55 E
Changyang, China 69 B8 30 30N 111 10 E
Changyi, China 67 F10 36 40N 119 30 E
Changyŏn, N. Korea 67 E13 38 15N 125 6 E
Changyuan, China 66 G8 35 15N 114 42 E
Changzhi, China 66 F7 36 10N 113 6 E
Changzhou, China 69 B12 31 47N 119 58 E
Chanhanga, Angola 103 F2 16 0S 14 8 E
Chanlar = Xanlar, Azerbaijan 53 K8 40 37N 46 12 E
Channapatna, India 83 H3 12 40N 77 15 E
Channel Is., U.K. 17 H5 49 19N 2 24W
Channel Is., U.S.A. 145 M7 33 40N 119 15W
Channel-Port aux Basques, Canada 129 C8 47 30N 59 9W
Channing, Mich., U.S.A. 134 B1 46 9N 88 5W
Channing, Tex., U.S.A. 139 H3 35 41N 102 20W
Chantada, Spain 36 C3 42 36N 7 46W
Chanthaburi, Thailand 76 F4 12 38N 102 12 E
Chantilly, France 23 C9 49 12N 2 29 E
Chantonnay, France 22 F5 46 40N 1 3W
Chantrey Inlet, Canada 126 B10 67 48N 96 20W
Chanute, U.S.A. 139 G7 37 41N 95 27W
Chanza →, Spain 37 H3 37 32N 7 30W
Chao Hu, China 69 B11 31 30N 117 30 E
Chao Phraya →, Thailand 76 F3 13 32N 100 36 E
Chao Phraya Lowlands, Thailand 76 E3 15 30N 100 0 E
Chao Xian, China 69 B11 31 38N 117 50 E
Chao'an, China 69 F11 23 42N 116 32 E
Chaocheng, China 66 F8 36 4N 115 37 E
Chaoyang, Guangdong, China 69 F11 23 17N 116 30 E
Chaoyang, Liaoning, China 67 D11 41 35N 120 22 E
Chapada dos Guimarães, Brazil 157 D6 15 26S 55 45W
Chapala, Mozam. 107 F4 15 50S 37 35 E
Chapala, L. de, Mexico 146 C4 20 10N 103 20W
Chaparé →, Bolivia 157 D5 15 58S 64 42W
Chaparmukh, India 78 B4 26 12N 92 31 E
Chaparral, Colombia 152 C2 3 43N 75 28W
Chapayev, Kazakstan 52 E10 50 25N 51 10 E
Chapayevsk, Russia 52 D9 53 0N 49 40 E
Chapecó, Brazil 159 B5 27 14S 52 41W
Chapel Hill, U.S.A. 135 H6 35 55N 79 4W
Chapetsk →, Russia 54 B3 58 36N 50 4 E
Chapin, U.S.A. 140 E6 39 46N 90 24W
Chapleau, Canada 128 C3 47 50N 83 24W
Chaplin, Canada 131 C7 50 28N 106 40W
Chaplino, Ukraine 51 H9 48 8N 36 15 E
Chaplygin, Russia 52 D5 53 15N 40 0 E
Chapra = Chhapra, India 81 G11 25 48N 84 44 E
Châr, Mauritania 98 D2 21 32N 12 45W
Chara, Russia 57 D12 56 54N 118 20 E
Charadai, Argentina 158 B4 27 35S 59 55W
Charagua, Bolivia 157 D5 19 45S 63 10W
Charalá, Colombia 152 B3 6 17N 73 10W
Charambirá, Punta, Colombia 152 C2 4 16N 77 32W
Charaña, Bolivia 156 D4 17 30S 69 25W
Charantsavan, Armenia 53 K7 40 35N 44 41 E
Charapita, Colombia 152 D3 0 37S 74 21W
Charata, Argentina 158 B3 27 13S 61 14W
Charcas, Mexico 146 C4 23 10N 101 20W
Charcoal L., Canada 131 B8 58 49N 102 22W
Chard, U.K. 17 G5 50 52N 2 58W
Chardara, Kazakstan 55 C3 41 16N 67 59 E
Chardara, Step, Kazakstan 55 B4 42 20N 68 0 E
Chardarinskoye Vdkhr., Kazakstan 55 C4 41 10N 68 15 E
Chardon, U.S.A. 136 E3 41 35N 81 12W
Charduar, India 78 B4 26 51N 92 46 E
Chardzhou = Chärjew, Turkmenistan 55 D1 39 6N 63 34 E
Charente □, France 24 C4 45 50N 0 16 E
Charente →, France 24 C2 45 57N 1 5W
Charente-Maritime □, France 24 C3 45 45N 0 45W
Chari →, Chad 97 F2 12 58N 14 31 E
Chārīkār, Afghan. 79 B3 35 0N 69 10 E
Chariton, U.S.A. 140 C3 41 1N 93 19W
Chariton →, U.S.A. 140 E4 39 19N 92 58W
Charity, Guyana 153 B6 7 24N 58 36W
Chärjew, Turkmenistan 55 D1 39 6N 63 34 E
Charkhari, India 81 G8 25 24N 79 45 E
Charkhi Dadri, India 80 E7 28 37N 76 17 E
Charleroi, Belgium 21 H4 50 24N 4 27 E
Charleroi, U.S.A. 136 F5 40 9N 79 57W
Charles, C., U.S.A. 134 G8 37 7N 75 58W
Charles City, U.S.A. 140 A4 43 4N 92 41W
Charles L., Canada 131 B6 59 50N 110 33W
Charles Sound, N.Z. 119 F2 45 2S 167 4 E
Charles Town, U.S.A. 134 F7 39 17N 77 52W
Charleston, Ill., U.S.A. 141 E8 39 30N 88 10W
Charleston, Miss., U.S.A. 139 H9 34 1N 90 4W
Charleston, Mo., U.S.A. 139 G10 36 55N 89 21W
Charleston, S.C., U.S.A. 135 J6 32 46N 79 56W
Charleston, W. Va., U.S.A. 134 F5 38 21N 81 38W
Charleston Peak, U.S.A. 145 J11 36 16N 115 42W
Charlestown, S. Africa 105 D4 27 26S 29 53 E
Charlestown, U.S.A. 141 F11 38 27N 85 40W
Charlesville, Zaïre 103 D4 5 27S 20 59 E
Charleville = Rath Luirc, Ireland 19 D3 52 21N 8 40W
Charleville, Australia 115 D4 26 24S 146 15 E
Charleville-Mézières, France 23 C11 49 44N 4 40 E
Charlevoix, U.S.A. 134 C3 45 19N 85 16W
Charlieu, France 25 B8 46 10N 4 10 E
Charlotte, Mich., U.S.A. 141 B12 42 34N 84 50W
Charlotte, N.C., U.S.A. 135 H5 35 13N 80 51W
Charlotte Amalie, Virgin Is. 149 C7 18 21N 64 56W
Charlotte Harbor, U.S.A. 135 M4 26 50N 82 10W
Charlottesville, U.S.A. 134 F6 38 2N 78 30W
Charlottetown, Canada 129 C7 46 14N 63 8W
Charlton, Australia 116 D5 36 16S 143 24 E
Charlton, U.S.A. 138 E8 40 59N 93 20W
Charlton I., Canada 128 B4 52 0N 79 20W
Charmes, France 23 D13 48 22N 6 17 E
Charny, Canada 129 C5 46 43N 71 15W
Charolles, France 25 B8 46 27N 4 16 E
Chârost, France 23 F9 46 58N 2 7 E
Charouine, Algeria 99 C4 29 0N 0 15W
Charre, Mozam. 107 F4 17 13S 35 10 E
Charroux, France 24 B4 46 9N 0 25 E
Charsadda, Pakistan 80 B4 34 7N 71 45 E
Charters Towers, Australia 114 C4 20 5S 146 13 E
Chartres, France 22 D8 48 29N 1 30 E
Charvakskoye Vdkhr., Uzbekistan 55 C5 41 35N 70 0 E
Chascomús, Argentina 158 D4 35 30S 58 0W
Chasefu, Zambia 107 E3 11 55S 33 8 E
Chaslands Mistake, N.Z. 119 G4 46 38S 169 22 E
Chasovnya-Uchurskaya, Russia 57 D14 57 15N 132 50 E
Chasseneuil-sur-Bonnieure, France 24 C4 45 52N 0 29 E
Chāt, Iran 85 B7 37 59N 55 16 E
Chatal Balkan = Udvoy Balkan, Bulgaria 43 E11 42 50N 26 50 E
Château-Arnoux, France 25 D10 44 6N 6 0 E
Château-Chinon, France 23 E10 47 4N 3 56 E
Château d'Oex, Switz. 28 D4 46 28N 7 8 E
Château-du-Loir, France 22 E7 47 40N 0 25 E
Château-Gontier, France 22 E6 47 50N 0 48W
Château-la-Vallière, France 22 E7 47 30N 0 20 E
Château-Landon, France 23 D9 48 8N 2 40 E
Château-Porcien, France 23 C11 49 31N 4 13 E
Château-Renault, France 22 E7 47 36N 0 56 E
Château-Salins, France 23 D13 48 50N 6 30 E
Château-Thierry, France 23 C10 49 3N 3 20 E
Châteaubourg, France 22 D5 48 7N 1 25W
Châteaubriant, France 22 E5 47 43N 1 23W
Châteaudun, France 22 D8 48 3N 1 20 E
Châteaugiron, France 22 D5 48 3N 1 30W
Châteaulin, France 22 D2 48 11N 4 8W
Châteaumeillant, France 24 B6 46 35N 2 12 E
Châteauneuf-du-Faou, France 22 D3 48 11N 3 50W
Châteauneuf-en-Thymerais, France 22 D8 48 35N 1 13 E
Châteauneuf-sur-Charente, France 24 C3 45 36N 0 3W
Châteauneuf-sur-Cher, France 23 F9 46 52N 2 18 E
Châteauneuf-sur-Loire, France 23 E9 47 52N 2 13 E
Châteaurenard, Bouches-du-Rhône, France 25 E8 43 53N 4 51 E
Châteaurenard, Loiret, France 23 E9 47 56N 2 55 E
Châteauroux, France 23 F8 46 50N 1 40 E
Châtel-St.-Denis, Switz. 28 C3 46 32N 6 54 E
Châtelaillon-Plage, France 24 B2 46 5N 1 5W
Châtelaudren, France 22 D4 48 33N 2 59W
Chatelet, Belgium 21 H5 50 24N 4 32 E
Châtelguyon, France 24 C7 45 55N 3 4 E
Châtellerault, France 22 F7 46 50N 0 30 E
Châtelus-Malvaleix, France 24 B6 46 18N 2 1 E
Chatfield, U.S.A. 138 D9 43 51N 92 11W
Chatham, N.B., Canada 129 C6 47 2N 65 28W
Chatham, Ont., Canada 128 D3 42 24N 82 11W
Chatham, U.K. 17 F8 51 22N 0 32 E
Chatham, Ill., U.S.A. 140 E7 39 40N 89 42W
Chatham, La., U.S.A. 139 J8 32 18N 92 27W
Chatham, N.Y., U.S.A. 137 D11 42 21N 73 36W
Chatham, I., Chile 160 D2 50 40S 74 25W
Chatham Is., Pac. Oc. 122 M10 44 0S 176 40W
Chatham Str., U.S.A. 130 B2 57 0N 134 40W
Châtillon, Italy 38 C4 45 45N 7 37 E
Châtillon-Coligny, France 23 E9 47 50N 2 51 E
Châtillon-en-Bazois, France 23 E10 47 3N 3 39 E
Châtillon-en-Diois, France 25 D9 44 41N 5 29 E
Châtillon-sur-Indre, France 22 F8 46 59N 1 10 E
Châtillon-sur-Loire, France 23 E9 47 35N 2 44 E
Châtillon-sur-Marne, France 23 C10 49 6N 3 44 E
Châtillon-sur-Seine, France 23 E11 47 50N 4 33 E
Chatkal →, Uzbekistan 55 C5 41 38N 70 1 E
Chatkalskiy Khrebet, Kyrgyzstan 55 C5 41 30N 70 45 E
Chatmohar, Bangla. 81 G13 24 15N 89 15 E
Chatra, India 81 G11 24 12N 84 56 E
Chatrapur, India 82 E7 19 22N 85 2 E
Chats, L. des, Canada 137 A8 45 30N 76 20W
Chatsworth, Canada 136 B4 44 27N 80 54W
Chatsworth, U.S.A. 141 D8 40 45N 88 18W
Chatsworth, Zimbabwe 107 F3 19 38S 31 13 E
Chatta-Hantō, Japan 63 C8 34 45N 136 55 E
Chattahoochee →, U.S.A. 135 K3 30 54N 84 57W
Chattanooga, U.S.A. 135 H3 35 3N 85 19W
Chaturat, Thailand 76 E3 15 40N 101 51 E
Chatyrkel, Ozero, Kyrgyzstan 55 C7 40 40N 75 18 E
Chatyrtash, Kyrgyzstan 55 C8 40 55N 76 25 E
Chau Doc, Vietnam 77 G5 10 42N 105 7 E
Chaudanne, Barr. de, France 25 E10 43 51N 6 32 E
Chaudes-Aigues, France 24 D7 44 51N 3 1 E
Chauffailles, France 25 B8 46 13N 4 20 E
Chauk, Burma 78 E5 20 53N 94 49 E
Chaukan Pass, Burma 78 B6 27 8N 97 10 E
Chaulnes, France 23 C9 49 48N 2 47 E
Chaumont, France 23 D12 48 7N 5 8 E
Chaumont, U.S.A. 137 B8 44 4N 76 8W
Chaumont-en-Vexin, France 23 C8 49 16N 1 53 E
Chaumont-sur-Loire, France 22 E8 47 29N 1 11 E
Chaunay, France 24 B4 46 13N 0 9 E
Chauny, France 23 C10 49 37N 3 12 E
Chausey, Is., France 22 D5 48 52N 1 49W
Chaussin, France 23 F12 46 59N 5 22 E
Chautauqua L., U.S.A. 136 D5 42 10N 79 24W
Chauvigny, France 22 F7 46 34N 0 39 E
Chauvin, Canada 131 C6 52 45N 110 10W
Chavantina, Brazil 157 C7 14 40S 52 21W
Chaves, Brazil 154 B2 0 15S 49 55W
Chaves, Portugal 36 D3 41 45N 7 32W
Chavuma, Zambia 103 E4 13 4S 22 40 E
Chawang, Thailand 77 H2 8 25N 99 30 E
Chayan, Kazakstan 55 B4 43 5N 69 25 E
Chayek, Kyrgyzstan 55 C7 41 55N 74 30 E
Chaykovskiy, Russia 54 C5 56 47N 54 9 E
Chazelles-sur-Lyon, France 25 C8 45 39N 4 22 E
Chazuta, Peru 156 B2 6 30S 76 0W
Chazy, U.S.A. 137 B11 44 53N 73 26W
Cheb, Czech. 30 A5 50 9N 12 28 E
Chebanse, U.S.A. 141 C9 41 0N 87 54W
Chebarkul, Russia 54 D8 55 0N 60 25 E
Cheboksarskoye Vdkhr., Russia 52 B8 56 13N 46 58 E
Cheboksary, Russia 52 B8 56 8N 47 12 E
Cheboygan, U.S.A. 134 C3 45 39N 84 29W
Chebsara, Russia 50 C10 59 10N 38 59 E
Chech, Erg, Africa 98 D4 25 0N 2 15W
Chechaouen, Morocco 98 A3 35 9N 5 15W
Chechen, Ostrov, Russia 53 H8 43 59N 47 40 E
Chechenia □, Russia 53 J7 43 30N 45 29 E
Checheno-Ingush Republic = Chechenia □, Russia 53 J7 43 30N 45 29 E
Chechnya = Chechenia □, Russia 53 J7 43 30N 45 29 E
Chechon, S. Korea 67 F15 37 8N 128 12 E
Chęciny, Poland 47 E7 50 46N 20 28 E
Checleset B., Canada 130 C3 50 5N 127 35W
Checotah, U.S.A. 139 H7 35 28N 95 31W
Chedabucto B., Canada 129 C7 45 25N 61 8W
Cheduba I., Burma 78 F4 18 45N 93 40 E
Cheepie, Australia 115 D4 26 33S 145 1 E
Chef-Boutonne, France 24 B3 46 7N 0 4W
Chegdomyn, Russia 57 D14 51 7N 133 1 E
Chegga, Mauritania 98 C3 25 27N 5 40W
Chegutu, Zimbabwe 107 F3 18 10S 30 14 E
Chehalis, U.S.A. 144 D4 46 40N 122 58W
Cheiron, Mt., France 25 E10 43 49N 6 58 E
Cheju Do, S. Korea 67 H14 33 29N 126 34 E
Chekalin, Russia 52 C3 54 10N 36 10 E
Chekiang = Zhejiang □, China 69 C13 29 0N 120 0 E
Chel = Kuru, Bahr el →, Sudan 95 F2 8 10N 26 50 E
Chela, Sa. da, Angola 103 F2 16 20S 13 20 E
Chelan, U.S.A. 142 C4 47 51N 120 1W
Chelan, L., U.S.A. 142 C3 48 11N 120 30W
Cheleken, Turkmenistan 49 G9 39 34N 53 16 E
Chelforó, Argentina 160 A3 39 0S 66 33W
Chéliff, O. →, Algeria 99 A5 36 0N 0 8 E
Chelkar = Shalqar, Kazakstan 56 E6 47 48N 59 39 E
Chelkar Tengiz, Solonchak, Kazakstan 56 E7 48 5N 63 7 E
Chellala Dahrania, Algeria 99 B5 33 2N 0 1 E
Chelles, France 23 D9 48 52N 2 33 E
Chełm, Poland 47 D10 51 8N 23 30 E
Chełm □, Poland 47 D10 51 15N 23 30 E
Chełmek, Poland 31 A12 50 6N 19 16 E
Chełmno, Poland 47 B5 53 20N 18 30 E
Chelmsford, U.K. 17 F8 51 44N 0 29 E
Chełmża, Poland 47 B5 53 10N 18 39 E
Chelsea, Australia 117 E6 38 5S 145 8 E
Chelsea, Mich., U.S.A. 141 B12 42 19N 84 1W
Chelsea, Okla., U.S.A. 139 G7 36 32N 95 26W
Chelsea, Vt., U.S.A. 137 C12 43 59N 72 27W
Cheltenham, U.K. 17 F5 51 54N 2 4W
Chelva, Spain 34 F4 39 45N 1 0W
Chelyabinsk, Russia 54 D8 55 10N 61 24 E
Chelyuskin, C., Russia 58 B14 77 30N 103 0 E
Chemainus, Canada 130 D4 48 55N 123 42W
Chembar = Belinskiy, Russia 52 D6 53 0N 43 25 E
Chemillé, France 22 E6 47 14N 0 45W
Chemnitz, Germany 26 E8 50 51N 12 54 E
Chemult, U.S.A. 142 E3 43 14N 121 47W
Chen, Gora, Russia 57 C15 65 16N 141 50 E
Chen Xian, China 69 E9 25 47N 113 1 E
Chenab →, Pakistan 79 C3 30 23N 71 2 E
Chenachane, O. →, Algeria 98 C4 25 20N 3 20W
Chenango Forks, U.S.A. 137 D9 42 15N 75 51W
Chencha, Ethiopia 95 F4 6 15N 37 32 E
Chenchiang = Zhenjiang, China 69 A12 32 11N 119 26 E
Chênée, Belgium 21 G7 50 37N 5 37 E
Cheney, U.S.A. 142 C5 47 30N 117 35W
Cheng Xian, China 66 H3 33 43N 105 42 E
Chengalpattu, India 83 H4 12 42N 79 58 E
Chengbu, China 69 D8 26 18N 110 16 E
Chengcheng, China 66 G5 35 8N 109 56 E
Chengchou = Zhengzhou, China 66 G7 34 45N 113 34 E
Chengde, China 67 D9 40 59N 117 58 E
Chengdong Hu, China 69 A11 32 15N 116 20 E
Chengdu, China 68 B5 30 38N 104 2 E
Chengele, India 78 A6 28 47N 96 16 E
Chenggong, China 68 E4 24 52N 102 56 E
Chenggu, China 66 H4 33 10N 107 21 E
Chengjiang, China 68 E4 24 39N 103 0 E
Chengkou, China 68 B7 31 54N 108 31 E
Ch'engtu = Chengdu, China 68 B5 30 38N 104 2 E
Chengwu, China 66 G8 34 58N 115 50 E
Chengxi Hu, China 69 A11 32 15N 116 10 E
Chengyang, China 67 F11 36 18N 120 21 E
Chenjiagang, China 67 G10 34 23N 119 47 E
Chenkán, Mexico 147 D6 19 8N 90 58W
Chenoa, U.S.A. 141 D8 40 45N 88 43W
Chenxi, China 69 C8 28 2N 110 12 E
Cheo Reo, Vietnam 76 F7 13 25N 108 28 E
Cheom Ksan, Cambodia 76 E5 14 13N 104 56 E
Chepelare, Bulgaria 43 F9 41 44N 24 40 E
Chepén, Peru 156 B2 7 15S 79 23W
Chépénéhé, Vanuatu 121 K5 20 47S 167 9 E
Chepes, Argentina 158 C2 31 20S 66 35W
Chepo, Panama 148 E4 9 10N 79 6W
Cheptsa →= Chapetsk →, Russia 54 B3 58 36N 50 4 E
Cheptulil, Mt., Kenya 106 B4 1 25N 35 35 E
Chequamegon B., U.S.A. 138 B9 46 40N 90 30W
Cher □, France 23 E9 47 10N 2 30 E
Cher →, France 22 E7 47 21N 0 29 E
Cheran, India 78 C3 25 45N 90 44 E
Cherasco, Italy 38 D4 44 39N 7 51 E
Cheratte, Belgium 21 G7 50 40N 5 41 E
Cheraw, U.S.A. 135 H6 34 42N 79 53W
Cherbourg, France 22 C5 49 39N 1 40W
Cherchell, Algeria 99 A5 36 35N 2 12 E
Cherdakly, Russia 52 C9 54 25N 48 50 E
Cherdyn, Russia 54 A6 60 24N 56 29 E
Cheremkhovo, Russia 57 D11 53 8N 103 1 E
Cherepanovo, Russia 56 D9 54 15N 83 30 E
Cherepovets, Russia 50 C9 59 5N 37 55 E
Chergui, Chott ech, Algeria 99 B5 34 21N 0 25 E
Cherikov = Cherykaw, Belarus 50 F6 53 32N 31 20 E
Cherkasy, Ukraine 51 H7 49 27N 32 4 E
Cherkessk, Russia 53 H6 44 15N 42 5 E
Cherlak, Russia 56 D8 54 15N 74 55 E
Chermoz, Russia 54 B6 58 46N 56 10 E
Chernak, Kazakstan 55 B4 43 24N 68 2 E
Chernaya, Russia 57 B9 70 30N 89 10 E
Chernaya Kholunitsa, Russia 54 B3 58 57N 51 39 E
Cherni, Bulgaria 43 E8 42 35N 23 18 E
Chernigov = Chernihiv, Ukraine 51 G6 51 28N 31 20 E
Chernihiv, Ukraine 51 G6 51 28N 31 20 E
Chernikovsk, Russia 48 D10 54 48N 56 8 E
Chernivtsi, Ukraine 51 H3 48 15N 25 52 E
Chernobyl = Chornobyl, Ukraine 51 G6 51 20N 30 15 E
Chernogorsk, Russia 57 D10 53 49N 91 18 E
Chernomorskoye = Chornomorske, Ukraine 51 K7 45 31N 32 40 E
Chernovtsy = Chernivtsi, Ukraine 51 H3 48 15N 25 52 E
Chernushka, Russia 54 C6 56 29N 56 3 E
Chernyakhovsk, Russia 13 J19 54 36N 21 48 E
Chernyanka, Russia 52 E3 50 56N 37 49 E
Chernyshovskiy, Russia 57 C12 63 0N 112 30 E
Chernyy Otrog, Russia 54 F6 51 53N 56 0 E
Chernyye Zemli, Russia 53 H8 46 10N 46 0 E
Cherokee, Iowa, U.S.A. 138 D7 42 45N 95 33W
Cherokee, Okla., U.S.A. 139 G5 36 45N 98 21W
Cherokees, Lake O' The, U.S.A. 139 G7 36 28N 95 2W
Cherquenco, Chile 160 A2 38 35S 72 0W
Cherry Creek, U.S.A. 142 G6 39 54N 114 53W
Cherry Valley, U.S.A. 145 M10 33 59N 116 57W
Cherryvale, U.S.A. 139 G7 37 16N 95 33W
Cherskiy, Russia 57 C17 68 45N 161 18 E
Cherskogo Khrebet, Russia 57 C15 65 0N 143 0 E
Chertkovo, Russia 52 F5 49 25N 40 19 E
Cherven, Belarus 50 F5 53 45N 28 28 E
Cherven-Bryag, Bulgaria 43 D9 43 17N 24 7 E
Chervonohrad, Ukraine 51 G3 50 25N 24 10 E
Cherwell →, U.K. 17 F6 51 44N 1 14W
Cherykaw, Belarus 50 F6 53 32N 31 20 E
Chesapeake, U.S.A. 134 G7 36 50N 76 17W
Chesapeake B., U.S.A. 134 F7 38 0N 76 10W
Cheshire □, U.K. 16 D5 53 14N 2 30W
Cheshskaya Guba, Russia 48 A8 67 20N 47 0 E
Cheslatta L., Canada 130 C3 53 49N 125 20W
Chesley, Canada 136 B3 44 17N 81 5W
Cheste, Spain 35 F4 39 30N 0 41W
Chester, U.K. 16 D5 53 12N 2 53W
Chester, Calif., U.S.A. 142 F3 40 19N 121 14W
Chester, Ill., U.S.A. 139 G10 37 55N 89 49W
Chester, Mont., U.S.A. 142 B8 48 31N 110 58W
Chester, Pa., U.S.A. 134 F8 39 51N 75 22W
Chester, S.C., U.S.A. 135 H5 34 43N 81 12W
Chesterfield, U.K. 16 D6 53 15N 1 25W
Chesterfield, Is., N. Cal. 122 J7 19 52S 158 15 E
Chesterfield Inlet, Canada 126 B10 63 30N 90 45W
Chesterton Ra., Australia 115 D4 25 30S 147 27 E
Chesterville, Canada 137 A9 45 6N 75 14W
Chesuncook L., U.S.A. 129 C6 46 0N 69 21W
Chéticamp, Canada 129 C7 46 37N 60 59W
Chetumal, B. de, Mexico 147 D7 18 40N 88 10W
Chetwynd, Canada 130 B4 55 45N 121 36W
Chevanceaux, France 24 C3 45 18N 0 14W
Cheviot, U.S.A. 141 E12 39 10N 84 37W
Cheviot, The, U.K. 16 B5 55 29N 2 9W
Cheviot Hills, U.K. 16 B5 55 20N 2 30W
Cheviot Ra., Australia 114 D3 25 20S 143 45 E
Chew Bahir, Ethiopia 95 G4 4 40N 36 50 E
Chewelah, U.S.A. 142 B5 48 17N 117 43W
Cheyenne, Okla., U.S.A. 139 H5 35 37N 99 40W
Cheyenne, Wyo., U.S.A. 138 E2 41 8N 104 49W
Cheyenne →, U.S.A. 138 C4 44 41N 101 18W
Cheyenne Wells, U.S.A. 138 F3 38 49N 102 21W
Cheyne B., Australia 113 F2 34 35S 118 50 E
Chhabra, India 80 G7 24 40N 76 54 E
Chhapra, India 81 G11 25 48N 84 44 E
Chhata, India 80 F7 27 42N 77 30 E
Chhatak, Bangla. 78 C3 25 5N 91 37 E
Chhatarpur, India 81 G8 24 55N 79 35 E
Chhep, Cambodia 76 F5 13 45N 105 24 E
Chhindwara, India 81 H8 22 2N 78 59 E
Chhlong, Cambodia 77 F5 12 15N 105 58 E
Chhuk, Cambodia 77 G5 10 46N 104 28 E
Chi →, Thailand 76 E5 15 11N 104 43 E
Chiai, Taiwan 69 F13 23 29N 120 25 E
Chiali, Taiwan 69 F13 23 10N 120 11 E
Chiamussu = Jiamusi, China 65 B8 46 40N 130 26 E
Chiang Dao, Thailand 76 C2 19 22N 98 58 E
Chiang Kham, Thailand 76 C3 19 32N 100 18 E
Chiang Khan, Thailand 76 D3 17 52N 101 36 E
Chiang Khong, Thailand 76 B3 20 17N 100 24 E
Chiang Mai, Thailand 76 C2 18 47N 98 59 E
Chiang Saen, Thailand 76 B3 20 16N 100 5 E
Chiange, Angola 103 F2 15 35S 13 40 E
Chiapa →, Mexico 147 D6 16 42N 93 0W
Chiapa de Corzo, Mexico 147 D6 16 42N 93 0W
Chiapas □, Mexico 147 D6 17 0N 92 45W
Chiaramonte Gulfi, Italy 41 E7 37 2N 14 42 E
Chiaravalle, Italy 39 E10 43 36N 13 19 E

Corfu, Str of 187

Colesberg, S. Africa 104 E4 30 45 S 25 5 E
Colesburg, U.S.A. 140 B5 42 38N 91 12W
Coleville, U.S.A. 144 G7 38 34N 119 30W
Colfax, Calif., U.S.A. 144 F6 39 6N 120 57W
Colfax, Ill., U.S.A. 141 D8 40 34N 88 37W
Colfax, Ind., U.S.A. 141 D10 40 12N 86 40W
Colfax, La., U.S.A. 139 K8 31 31N 92 42W
Colfax, Wash., U.S.A. 142 C5 46 53N 117 22W
Colhué Huapi, L., Argentina 160 C3 45 30 S 69 0W
Cólico, Italy 38 B6 46 8N 9 22 E
Coligny, France 25 B9 46 23N 5 21 E
Coligny, S. Africa 105 D4 26 17 S 26 15 E
Colima, Mexico 146 D4 19 14N 103 43W
Colima □, Mexico 146 D4 19 10N 103 40W
Colima, Nevado de, Mexico 146 D4 19 35N 103 45W
Colina, Chile 158 C1 33 13 S 70 45W
Colina do Norte, Guinea-Biss. 100 C2 12 28N 15 0W
Colinas, Goiás, Brazil 155 D2 14 15 S 48 2W
Colinas, Maranhão, Brazil 154 C3 6 0 S 44 10W
Colinton, Australia 117 C8 35 50 S 149 10 E
Coll, U.K. 18 E2 56 39N 6 34W
Collaguasi, Chile 158 A2 21 5 S 68 45W
Collarada, Peña, Spain 34 C4 42 43N 0 29W
Collarenebri, Australia 115 D4 29 33 S 148 34 E
Collbran, U.S.A. 143 G10 39 14N 107 58W
Colle di Val d'Elsa, Italy 39 E8 43 25N 11 7 E
Colle Salvetti, Italy 38 E7 43 34N 10 27 E
Colle Sannita, Italy 41 A7 41 22N 14 50 E
Collécchio, Italy 38 D7 44 45N 10 13 E
Colleen Bawn, Zimbabwe 107 G2 21 0 S 29 12 E
College Park, U.S.A. 135 J3 33 40N 84 27W
College Station, U.S.A. 139 K6 30 37N 96 21W
Collette, Canada 129 C6 46 40N 65 30W
Collie, N.S.W., Australia 117 A8 31 41 S 148 18 E
Collie, W. Austral., Australia 113 F2 33 22 S 116 8 E
Collier B., Australia 112 C3 16 10 S 124 15 E
Collier Ra., Australia 112 D2 24 45 S 119 10 E
Colline Metallifere, Italy 38 E7 43 10N 11 0 E
Collingwood, Canada 128 D3 44 29N 80 13W
Collingwood, N.Z. 119 A7 40 41 S 172 40 E
Collins, Canada 128 B2 50 17N 89 27W
Collins, U.S.A. 140 G3 37 54N 93 37W
Collinsville, Australia 114 C4 20 30 S 147 56 E
Collinsville, U.S.A. 140 F7 38 40N 89 59W
Collipulli, Chile 158 D1 37 55 S 72 30W
Collo, Algeria 99 A6 36 58N 6 37 E
Collonges, France 25 B9 46 9N 5 52 E
Collooney, Ireland 19 B3 54 11N 8 29W
Colmar, France 23 D14 48 5N 7 20 E
Colmars, France 25 D10 44 11N 6 39 E
Colmenar, Spain 37 J6 36 54N 4 20W
Colmenar de Oreja, Spain 34 E1 40 6N 3 25W
Colmenar Viejo, Spain 36 E7 40 39N 3 47W
Colne, U.K. 16 D5 53 51N 2 9W
Colo →, Australia 117 B9 33 25 S 150 52 E
Cologna Véneta, Italy 39 C8 45 18N 11 23 E
Cologne = Köln, Germany 26 E2 50 56N 6 57 E
Colom, I., Spain 33 B11 39 58N 4 16 E
Coloma, U.S.A. 144 G6 38 48N 120 53W
Colomb-Béchar = Béchar, Algeria 99 B4 31 38N 2 18W
Colombey-les-Belles, France 23 D12 48 32N 5 54 E
Colombey-les-Deux-Églises, France 23 D11 48 13N 4 50 E
Colômbia, Brazil 155 F2 20 10 S 48 40W
Colombia ■, S. Amer. 152 C3 3 45N 73 0W
Colombian Basin, S. Amer. 124 H12 14 0N 76 0W
Colombier, Switz. 28 C3 46 58N 6 53 E
Colombo, Sri Lanka 83 L4 6 56N 79 58 E
Colome, U.S.A. 138 D5 43 16N 99 43W
Colón, Argentina 158 C4 32 12 S 58 10W
Colón, Cuba 148 B3 22 42N 80 54W
Colón, Panama 148 E4 9 20N 79 54W
Colón, Peru 156 A1 5 0 S 81 0W
Colona, Australia 113 F5 31 38 S 132 4 E
Colonella, Italy 39 F10 42 52N 13 50 E
Colonia, Uruguay 158 C4 34 25 S 57 50W
Colonia de San Jordi, Spain 33 B9 39 19N 2 59 E
Colonia Dora, Argentina 158 B3 28 34 S 62 59W
Colonial Heights, U.S.A. 134 G7 37 15N 77 25W
Colonne, C. delle, Italy 41 C10 39 2N 17 12 E
Colonsay, Canada 131 C7 51 59N 105 52W
Colonsay, U.K. 18 E2 56 5N 6 12W
Colorado □, U.S.A. 143 G10 39 30N 105 30W
Colorado →, Argentina 160 A4 39 50 S 62 8W
Colorado →, N. Amer. 143 L6 31 45N 114 40W
Colorado →, U.S.A. 139 L7 28 36N 95 59W
Colorado City, U.S.A. 139 J4 32 24N 100 52W
Colorado Desert, U.S.A. 132 D3 34 20N 116 0W
Colorado Plateau, U.S.A. 143 H8 37 0N 111 0W
Colorado River Aqueduct, U.S.A. 145 L12 34 17N 114 10W
Colorado Springs, U.S.A. 138 F2 38 50N 104 49W
Colorno, Italy 38 D7 44 56N 10 23 E
Colotlán, Mexico 146 C4 22 6N 103 16W
Colquechaca, Bolivia 157 D4 18 40 S 66 1W
Colton, N.Y., U.S.A. 137 B10 44 33N 74 56W
Colton, Wash., U.S.A. 142 C5 46 34N 117 8W
Columbia, Ill., U.S.A. 140 F6 38 27N 90 12W
Columbia, La., U.S.A. 139 J8 32 6N 92 5W
Columbia, Miss., U.S.A. 139 K10 31 15N 89 50W
Columbia, Mo., U.S.A. 140 F4 38 57N 92 20W
Columbia, Pa., U.S.A. 137 F8 40 2N 76 30W
Columbia, S.C., U.S.A. 135 H5 34 0N 81 2W
Columbia, Tenn., U.S.A. 135 H2 35 37N 87 2W
Columbia →, U.S.A. 142 C1 46 15N 124 5W
Columbia, C., Canada 6 A4 83 0N 70 0W
Columbia, District of □, U.S.A. 134 F7 38 55N 77 0W
Columbia, Mt., Canada 130 C5 52 8N 117 20W
Columbia Basin, U.S.A. 142 C4 46 45N 119 5W
Columbia Falls, U.S.A. 142 B6 48 23N 114 11W
Columbia Heights, U.S.A. 138 C8 45 3N 93 15W
Columbiana, U.S.A. 136 F4 40 53N 80 42W
Columbretes, Is., Spain 34 F5 39 50N 0 50 E
Columbus, Ga., U.S.A. 135 J3 32 28N 84 59W
Columbus, Ind., U.S.A. 141 E11 39 13N 85 55W
Columbus, Kans., U.S.A. 139 G7 37 10N 94 50W
Columbus, Miss., U.S.A. 135 J1 33 30N 88 25W
Columbus, Mont., U.S.A. 142 D9 45 38N 109 15W
Columbus, N. Dak., U.S.A. 138 A3 48 54N 102 47W
Columbus, N. Mex., U.S.A. 143 L10 31 50N 107 38W
Columbus, Nebr., U.S.A. 138 E6 41 26N 97 22W
Columbus, Ohio, U.S.A. 141 E13 39 58N 83 0W
Columbus, Tex., U.S.A. 139 L6 29 42N 96 33W
Columbus, Wis., U.S.A. 138 D10 43 21N 89 1W
Columbus Grove, U.S.A. 141 D12 40 55N 84 4W
Columbus Junction, U.S.A. 140 C5 41 17N 91 22W
Colunga, Spain 36 B5 43 29N 5 16W
Colusa, U.S.A. 144 F4 39 13N 122 1W
Colville, U.S.A. 142 B5 48 33N 117 54W
Colville →, U.S.A. 126 A4 70 25N 150 30W
Colville, C., N.Z. 118 C4 36 29 S 175 21 E
Colwyn Bay, U.K. 16 D4 53 18N 3 44W
Coma, Ethiopia 95 F4 8 29N 36 53 E
Comácchio, Italy 39 D9 44 42N 12 11 E
Comalcalco, Mexico 147 D6 18 16N 93 13W
Comallo, Argentina 160 B2 41 0 S 70 5W
Comana, Romania 46 E7 44 10N 26 10 E
Comanche, Okla., U.S.A. 139 H6 34 22N 97 58W
Comanche, Tex., U.S.A. 139 K5 31 54N 98 36W
Comandante Luis Piedrabuena, Argentina 160 C3 49 59 S 68 54W
Comănești, Romania 46 C7 46 25N 26 26 E
Comarapa, Bolivia 157 D5 17 54 S 64 29W
Comayagua, Honduras 148 D2 14 25N 87 37W
Combahee →, U.S.A. 135 J5 32 30N 80 31W
Combara, Australia 117 A8 31 10 S 148 22 E
Combeaufontaine, France 23 E12 47 38N 5 54 E
Comber, Canada 136 D2 42 14N 82 33W
Combermere Bay, Burma 78 F4 19 37N 93 34 E
Comblain-au-Pont, Belgium 21 H7 50 29N 5 35 E
Combles, France 23 B9 50 2N 2 50 E
Combourg, France 22 D5 48 25N 1 46W
Comboyne, Australia 117 A10 31 34 S 152 27 E
Combronde, France 24 C7 45 58N 3 5 E
Comeragh Mts., Ireland 19 D4 52 18N 7 34W
Comet, Australia 114 C4 23 36 S 148 38 E
Comilla, Bangla. 78 D3 23 28N 91 10 E
Comines, Belgium 21 G1 50 46N 3 0 E
Comino, Malta 32 C1 36 2N 14 20 E
Comino, C., Italy 40 B2 40 32N 9 49 E
Cómiso, Italy 41 F7 36 56N 14 36 E
Comitán, Mexico 147 D6 16 18N 92 9W
Commentry, France 24 B6 46 20N 2 46 E
Commerce, Ga., U.S.A. 135 H4 34 12N 83 28W
Commerce, Tex., U.S.A. 139 J7 33 15N 95 54W
Commercy, France 23 D12 48 43N 5 34 E
Commewijne □, Surinam 153 B7 5 25N 54 45W
Committee B., Canada 127 B11 68 30N 86 30W
Commonwealth B., Antarctica 7 C10 67 0 S 144 0 E
Commoron Cr. →, Australia 115 D5 28 22 S 150 8 E
Communism Pk. = Kommunizma, Pik, Tajikistan 55 D6 39 0N 72 2 E
Como, Italy 38 C6 45 47N 9 5 E
Como, L. di, Italy 38 B6 46 0N 9 11 E
Comodoro Rivadavia, Argentina 160 C3 45 50 S 67 40W
Comorin, C., India 83 K3 8 3N 77 40 E
Comoriște, Romania 46 D2 45 10N 21 35 E
Comoro Is. = Comoros ■, Ind. Oc. 92 H8 12 10 S 44 15 E
Comoros ■, Ind. Oc. 92 H8 12 10 S 44 15 E
Comox, Canada 130 D4 49 42N 124 55W
Compiègne, France 23 C9 49 24N 2 50 E
Comporta, Portugal 37 G2 38 22N 8 46W
Compostela, Mexico 146 C4 21 15N 104 53W
Compostela, Phil. 71 H6 7 40N 126 2 E
Comprida, I., Brazil 159 A6 24 50 S 47 42W
Compton, U.S.A. 145 M8 33 54N 118 13W
Compton Downs, Australia 115 E4 30 28 S 146 30 E
Comrat, Moldova 51 J5 46 18N 28 40 E
Con Cuong, Vietnam 76 C5 19 2N 104 54 E
Con Son, Vietnam 77 H6 8 41N 106 37 E
Cona Niyeu, Argentina 160 B3 41 58 S 67 0W
Conakry, Guinea 100 D2 9 29N 13 49W
Conara Junction, Australia 114 G4 41 50 S 147 26 E
Conargo, Australia 117 C6 35 16 S 145 10 E
Concarneau, France 22 E3 47 52N 3 56W
Conceição, Brazil 154 C4 7 33 S 38 31W
Conceição, Mozam. 107 F4 18 47 S 36 7 E
Conceição da Barra, Brazil 155 E4 18 35 S 39 45W
Conceição do Araguaia, Brazil 154 C2 8 0 S 49 2W
Conceição do Canindé, Brazil 154 C3 7 54 S 41 34W
Concepción, Argentina 158 B2 27 20 S 65 35W
Concepción, Bolivia 157 D5 16 15 S 62 8W
Concepción, Chile 158 D1 36 50 S 73 0W
Concepción, Mexico 147 D6 18 15N 90 5W
Concepción, Paraguay 158 A4 23 22 S 57 26W
Concepción, Peru 156 C2 11 54 S 75 19W
Concepción □, Chile 158 D1 37 0 S 72 30W
Concepción →, Mexico 146 A2 30 32N 113 2W
Concepción, Est. de, Chile 160 D2 50 30 S 74 55W
Concepción, L., Bolivia 157 D5 17 20 S 61 20W
Concepción, Punta, Mexico 146 B2 26 55N 111 59W
Concepción del Oro, Mexico 146 C4 24 40N 101 30W
Concepción del Uruguay, Argentina 158 C4 32 35 S 58 20W
Conception, Pt., U.S.A. 145 L6 34 27N 120 28W
Conception B., Namibia 104 C1 23 55 S 14 22 E
Conception I., Bahamas 149 B4 23 52N 75 9W
Concession, Zimbabwe 107 F3 17 27 S 30 56 E
Conchas Dam, U.S.A. 139 H2 35 22N 104 11W
Conche, Canada 129 B8 50 55N 55 58W
Conches-en-Ouche, France 22 D7 48 58N 0 56 E
Concho, U.S.A. 143 J9 34 28N 109 36W
Concho →, U.S.A. 139 K5 31 34N 99 43W
Conchos →, Chihuahua, Mexico 146 B4 29 32N 105 0W
Conchos →, Tamaulipas, Mexico 147 B5 25 9N 98 35W
Concord, Calif., U.S.A. 144 H4 37 59N 122 2W
Concord, Mich., U.S.A. 141 B12 42 11N 84 38W
Concord, N.C., U.S.A. 135 H5 35 25N 80 35W
Concord, N.H., U.S.A. 137 C13 43 12N 71 32W
Concordia, Argentina 158 C4 31 20 S 58 2W
Concórdia, Brazil 152 D4 4 36 S 66 36W
Concordia, Mexico 146 C3 23 18N 106 2W
Concordia, Kans., U.S.A. 138 F6 39 34N 97 40W
Concordia, Mo., U.S.A. 140 F3 38 59N 93 34W
Concots, France 24 D5 44 26N 1 40 E
Concrete, U.S.A. 142 B3 48 32N 121 45W
Condah, Australia 116 D4 37 57 S 141 44 E
Condamine, Australia 115 D5 26 56 S 150 9 E
Condat, France 24 C6 45 21N 2 46 E
Condé, Angola 103 E2 10 50 S 14 37 E
Conde, Brazil 155 D4 11 49 S 37 37W
Conde, U.S.A. 138 C5 45 9N 98 6W
Condé-sur-l'Escaut, France 23 B10 50 26N 3 34 E
Condé-sur-Noireau, France 22 D6 48 51N 0 33W
Condeúba, Brazil 155 D3 14 52 S 42 0W
Condobolin, Australia 115 E4 33 4 S 147 6 E
Condom, France 24 E4 43 57N 0 22 E
Condon, U.S.A. 142 D3 45 14N 120 11W
Condove, Italy 38 C4 45 7N 7 18 E
Conegliano, Italy 39 C9 45 53N 12 18 E
Conejera, I., Spain 33 B9 39 11N 2 58 E
Conejos, Mexico 146 B4 26 14N 103 53W
Conflans-en-Jarnisy, France 23 C12 49 10N 5 52 E
Confolens, France 24 B4 46 2N 0 40 E
Confuso →, Paraguay 158 B4 25 9 S 57 34W
Congjiang, China 68 E7 25 43N 108 52 E
Congleton, U.K. 16 D5 53 10N 2 13W
Congo = Zaïre →, Africa 103 D2 6 4 S 12 24 E
Congo, Brazil 154 C4 7 48 S 36 40W
Congo (Kinshasa) = Zaïre ■, Africa 103 C4 3 0 S 23 0 E
Congo ■, Africa 102 C3 1 0 S 16 0 E
Congo Basin, Africa 92 G6 0 10 S 24 30 E
Congonhas, Brazil 155 F3 20 30 S 43 52W
Congress, U.S.A. 143 J7 34 9N 112 51W
Conil, Spain 37 J4 36 17N 6 10W
Coniston, Canada 128 C3 46 29N 80 51W
Conjeeveram = Kanchipuram, India 83 H4 12 52N 79 45 E
Conjuboy, Australia 114 B3 18 35 S 144 35 E
Conklin, Canada 131 B6 55 38N 111 5W
Conlea, Australia 115 E3 30 7 S 144 35 E
Conn, L., Ireland 19 B2 54 3N 9 15W
Connacht □, Ireland 19 C3 53 43N 9 12W
Conneaut, U.S.A. 136 E4 41 57N 80 34W
Connecticut □, U.S.A. 137 E12 41 30N 72 45W
Connecticut →, U.S.A. 137 E12 41 16N 72 20W
Connell, U.S.A. 142 C4 46 40N 118 52W
Connellsville, U.S.A. 136 F5 40 1N 79 35W
Connemara, Ireland 19 C2 53 29N 9 45W
Connemaugh →, U.S.A. 136 F5 40 28N 79 19W
Conner, Phil. 70 C3 17 48N 121 19 E
Connerré, France 22 D7 48 3N 0 30 E
Connersville, U.S.A. 141 E11 39 39N 85 8W
Connors Ra., Australia 114 C4 21 40 S 149 10 E
Conoble, Australia 117 B6 32 55 S 144 33 E
Cononaco →, Ecuador 152 D2 1 32 S 75 35W
Cononbridge, U.K. 18 D4 57 34N 4 27W
Conquest, Canada 131 C7 51 32N 107 14W
Conrad, Iowa, U.S.A. 140 B4 42 14N 92 52W
Conrad, Mont., U.S.A. 142 B8 48 10N 111 57W
Conran, C., Australia 117 D8 37 49 S 148 44 E
Conroe, U.S.A. 139 K7 30 19N 95 27W
Conselheiro Lafaiete, Brazil 155 F3 20 40 S 43 48W
Conselheiro Pena, Brazil 155 E3 19 10 S 41 30W
Consort, Canada 131 C6 52 1N 110 46W
Constance = Konstanz, Germany 27 H5 47 40N 9 10 E
Constance, L. = Bodensee, Europe 29 A8 47 35N 9 25 E
Constanța, Romania 46 E9 44 14N 28 38 E
Constanța □, Romania 46 E9 44 15N 28 15 E
Constantina, Spain 37 H5 37 51N 5 40W
Constantine, Algeria 99 A6 36 25N 6 42 E
Constantine, U.S.A. 141 C11 41 50N 85 40W
Constitución, Chile 158 D1 35 20 S 72 30W
Constitución, Uruguay 158 C4 31 0 S 57 50W
Consuegra, Spain 37 F7 39 28N 3 36W
Consul, Canada 131 D7 49 20N 109 30W
Contact, U.S.A. 142 F6 41 46N 114 45W
Contai, India 81 J12 21 54N 87 46 E
Contamana, Peru 156 B3 7 19 S 74 55W
Contarina, Italy 39 C9 45 0N 12 13 E
Contas →, Brazil 155 D4 14 17 S 39 1W
Contes, France 25 E11 43 49N 7 19 E
Conthey, Switz. 28 D4 46 14N 7 18 E
Continental, U.S.A. 141 C12 41 6N 84 16W
Contoocook, U.S.A. 137 C13 43 13N 71 45W
Contra Costa, Mozam. 105 D5 25 9 S 33 30 E
Contres, France 22 E8 47 24N 1 26 E
Contrexéville, France 23 D12 48 10N 5 53 E
Contumaza, Peru 156 B2 7 23 S 78 57W
Convención, Colombia 152 B3 8 28N 73 21W
Conversano, Italy 41 B10 40 58N 17 7 E
Converse, U.S.A. 141 D11 40 35N 85 52W
Convoy, U.S.A. 141 D12 40 55N 84 43W
Conway = Conwy, U.K. 16 D4 53 17N 3 50W
Conway = Conwy →, U.K. 16 D4 53 17N 3 50W
Conway, Ark., U.S.A. 139 H8 35 5N 92 26W
Conway, N.H., U.S.A. 137 C13 43 59N 71 7W
Conway, S.C., U.S.A. 135 J6 33 51N 79 3W
Conway, L., Australia 115 D2 28 17 S 135 35 E
Conwy, U.K. 16 D4 53 17N 3 50W
Conwy →, U.K. 16 D4 53 17N 3 50W
Coober Pedy, Australia 115 D1 29 1 S 134 43 E
Cooch Behar = Koch Bihar, India 78 B2 26 22N 89 29 E
Coodardy, Australia 113 E2 27 15 S 117 39 E
Cook, Australia 113 F5 30 37 S 130 25 E
Cook, U.S.A. 138 B8 47 49N 92 39W
Cook, B., Chile 160 E2 55 10 S 70 0W
Cook, Mt., N.Z. 119 D5 43 36 S 170 9 E
Cook Inlet, U.S.A. 126 C4 60 0N 152 0W
Cook Is., Pac. Oc. 123 J11 17 0 S 160 0W
Cook Strait, N.Z. 118 H3 41 15 S 174 29 E
Cooke Plains, Australia 116 C3 35 23 S 139 34 E
Cookeville, U.S.A. 135 G3 36 10N 85 30W
Cookhouse, S. Africa 104 E4 32 44 S 25 47 E
Cookshire, Canada 137 A13 45 25N 71 38W
Cookstown, U.K. 19 B5 54 39N 6 45W
Cookstown □, U.K. 19 B5 54 40N 6 43W
Cooksville, Canada 136 C5 43 36N 79 35W
Cooktown, Australia 114 B4 15 30 S 145 16 E
Coolabah, Australia 117 A7 31 1 S 146 43 E
Cooladdi, Australia 115 D4 26 37 S 145 23 E
Coolah, Australia 117 A8 31 48 S 149 41 E
Coolamon, Australia 117 C7 34 46 S 147 8 E
Coolangatta, Australia 115 D5 28 11 S 153 29 E
Coolgardie, Australia 113 F3 30 55 S 121 8 E
Coolibah, Australia 112 C5 15 33 S 130 56 E
Coolidge, U.S.A. 143 K8 32 59N 111 31W
Coolidge Dam, U.S.A. 143 K8 33 0N 110 20W
Cooma, Australia 117 D8 36 12 S 149 8 E
Coon Rapids, Iowa, U.S.A. 140 C2 41 53N 94 41W
Coon Rapids, Minn., U.S.A. 138 C8 45 9N 93 19W
Coonabarabran, Australia 117 A8 31 14 S 149 18 E
Coonalpyn, Australia 116 C3 35 43 S 139 52 E
Coonamble, Australia 117 A8 30 56 S 148 27 E
Coonana, Australia 113 F3 31 0 S 123 0 E
Coondapoor, India 83 H2 13 42N 74 40 E
Coongie, Australia 115 D3 27 9 S 140 8 E
Coongoola, Australia 115 D4 27 43 S 145 51 E
Cooninie, L., Australia 115 D2 26 4 S 139 59 E
Coonoor, India 83 J3 11 21N 76 45 E
Cooper, U.S.A. 139 J7 33 23N 95 42W
Cooper →, U.S.A. 135 J6 32 50N 79 56W
Cooper Cr. →, N. Terr., Australia 110 C5 12 7 S 132 41 E
Cooper Cr. →, S. Austral., Australia 115 D2 28 29 S 137 46 E
Cooperstown, N. Dak., U.S.A. 138 B5 47 27N 98 8W
Cooperstown, N.Y., U.S.A. 137 D10 42 42N 74 56W
Coopersville, U.S.A. 141 A11 43 4N 85 57W
Coorabie, Australia 113 F5 31 54 S 132 18 E
Coorabulka, Australia 114 C3 23 41 S 140 20 E
Coorow, Australia 113 E2 29 53 S 116 2 E
Cooroy, Australia 115 D5 26 22 S 152 54 E
Coos Bay, U.S.A. 142 E1 43 22N 124 13W
Cootamundra, Australia 117 C8 34 36 S 148 1 E
Cootehill, Ireland 19 B4 54 4N 7 5W
Cooyar, Australia 115 D5 26 59 S 151 51 E
Cooyeana, Australia 114 C2 24 29 S 138 45 E
Copahue Paso, Argentina 158 D1 37 49 S 71 8W
Copainalá, Mexico 147 D6 17 8N 93 11W
Copán, Honduras 148 D2 14 50N 89 9W
Copatana, Brazil 152 D4 2 48 S 67 4W
Cope, U.S.A. 138 F3 39 40N 102 51W
Cope, C., Spain 35 H3 37 26N 1 28W
Cope Cope, Australia 116 D5 36 27 S 143 5 E
Copenhagen = København, Denmark 15 J6 55 41N 12 34 E
Copertino, Italy 41 B11 40 16N 18 3 E
Copeville, Australia 116 C3 34 47 S 139 51 E
Copiapó, Chile 158 B1 27 30 S 70 20W
Copiapó →, Chile 158 B1 27 19 S 70 56W
Copley, Australia 116 A3 30 36 S 138 26 E
Copp L., Canada 130 A6 60 14N 114 40W
Copparo, Italy 39 D8 44 54N 11 49 E
Coppename →, Surinam 153 B6 5 48N 55 55W
Copper Center, U.S.A. 126 B5 61 58N 145 18W
Copper Cliff, Canada 128 C3 46 28N 81 4W
Copper Harbor, U.S.A. 134 B2 47 28N 87 53W
Copper Queen, Zimbabwe 107 F2 17 29 S 29 18 E
Copperbelt □, Zambia 107 E2 13 15 S 27 30 E
Coppermine = Kuglugtuk, Canada 126 B8 67 50N 115 5W
Coppermine →, Canada 126 B8 67 49N 116 4W
Copperopolis, U.S.A. 144 H6 37 58N 120 38W
Coquet →, U.K. 16 B6 55 20N 1 32W
Coquilhatville = Mbandaka, Zaïre 102 B3 0 1N 18 18 E
Coquille, U.S.A. 142 E1 43 11N 124 11W
Coquimbo, Chile 158 B1 30 0 S 71 20W
Coquimbo □, Chile 158 C1 31 0 S 71 0W
Corabia, Romania 46 F5 43 48N 24 30 E
Coração de Jesus, Brazil 155 E3 16 43 S 44 22W
Coracora, Peru 156 D3 15 5 S 73 45W
Coradi, Is., Italy 41 B10 40 27N 17 10 E
Coral Bay, Phil. 71 G1 8 25N 117 20 E
Coral Gables, U.S.A. 135 N5 25 45N 80 16W
Coral Harbour, Canada 127 B11 64 8N 83 10W
Coral Sea, Pac. Oc. 122 J7 15 0 S 150 0 E
Coral Springs, U.S.A. 135 M5 26 16N 80 13W
Coralville, U.S.A. 140 C5 41 40N 91 35W
Coralville Res., U.S.A. 140 C5 41 50N 91 40W
Corantijn →, Surinam 153 B6 5 50N 57 8W
Coraopolis, U.S.A. 136 F4 40 31N 80 10W
Corato, Italy 41 A9 41 9N 16 25 E
Corbeil-Essonnes, France 23 D9 48 36N 2 26 E
Corbie, France 23 C9 49 54N 2 30 E
Corbières, France 24 F6 42 55N 2 35 E
Corbigny, France 23 E10 47 16N 3 40 E
Corbin, U.S.A. 134 G3 36 57N 84 6W
Corbion, Belgium 21 J6 49 48N 5 0 E
Corbones →, Spain 37 H5 37 36N 5 39W
Corby, U.K. 17 E7 52 30N 0 41W
Corby Glen, U.K. 17 E7 52 49N 0 30W
Corcaigh = Cork, Ireland 19 E3 51 54N 8 29W
Corcoles →, Spain 35 F1 39 40N 3 18W
Corcoran, U.S.A. 144 J7 36 6N 119 33W
Corcubión, Spain 36 C1 42 56N 9 12W
Cordele, U.S.A. 135 K4 31 58N 83 47W
Cordell, U.S.A. 139 H5 35 17N 98 59W
Cordenons, Italy 39 C9 45 59N 12 42 E
Cordes, France 24 D5 44 5N 1 57 E
Cordisburgo, Brazil 155 E3 19 7 S 44 21W
Córdoba, Argentina 158 C3 31 20 S 64 10W
Córdoba, Mexico 147 D5 18 50N 97 0W
Córdoba, Spain 37 H6 37 50N 4 50W
Córdoba □, Argentina 158 C3 31 22 S 64 15W
Córdoba □, Colombia 152 B2 8 20N 75 40W
Córdoba □, Spain 37 G6 38 5N 5 0W
Córdoba, Sierra de, Argentina 158 C3 31 10 S 64 25W
Cordon, Phil. 70 C3 16 42N 121 32 E
Cordova, Ala., U.S.A. 135 J2 33 46N 87 11W
Cordova, Alaska, U.S.A. 126 B5 60 33N 145 45W
Cordova, Ill., U.S.A. 140 C6 41 41N 90 19W
Corella, Spain 34 C3 42 7N 1 48W
Corella →, Australia 114 B3 19 34 S 140 47 E
Coremas, Brazil 154 C4 7 1 S 37 58W
Corentyne →, Guyana 153 B6 5 50N 57 8W
Corfield, Australia 114 C3 21 40 S 143 21 E
Corfu = Kérkira, Greece 32 A3 39 38N 19 50 E
Corfu, Str of, Greece 32 A4 39 34N 20 0 E

188 Corgo

Corgo, *Spain* **36 C3** 42 56N 7 25W
Corguinho, *Brazil* **157 D7** 19 53 S 54 52W
Cori, *Italy* **40 A5** 41 39N 12 55 E
Coria, *Spain* **36 F4** 39 58N 6 33W
Coricudgy, *Australia* **117 B9** 32 51 S 150 24 E
Corigliano Cálabro, *Italy* **41 C9** 39 36N 16 31 E
Coringa Is., *Australia* **114 B4** 16 58 S 149 58 E
Corinna, *Australia* **114 G4** 41 35 S 145 10 E
Corinth = Kórinthos, *Greece* **45 G4** 37 56N 22 55 E
Corinth, *Ky., U.S.A.* **141 F12** 38 30N 84 34W
Corinth, *Miss., U.S.A.* **135 H1** 34 56N 88 31W
Corinth, *N.Y., U.S.A.* **137 C11** 43 15N 73 49W
Corinth, G. of = Korinthiakós Kólpos, *Greece* **45 F4** 38 16N 22 30 E
Corinth Canal, *Greece* **45 G4** 37 58N 23 0 E
Corinto, *Brazil* **155 E3** 18 20 S 44 30W
Corinto, *Nic.* **148 D2** 12 30N 87 10W
Corj □, *Romania* **46 D4** 45 5N 23 25 E
Cork, *Ireland* **19 E3** 51 54N 8 29W
Cork □, *Ireland* **19 E3** 51 57N 8 40W
Cork Harbour, *Ireland* **19 E3** 51 47N 8 16W
Corlay, *France* **22 D3** 48 20N 3 5W
Corleone, *Italy* **40 E6** 37 49N 13 18 E
Corleto Perticara, *Italy* **41 B9** 40 23N 16 2 E
Çorlu, *Turkey* **88 B2** 41 11N 27 49 E
Cormack L., *Canada* **130 A4** 60 56N 121 37W
Cormóns, *Italy* **39 C10** 45 58N 13 28 E
Cormorant, *Canada* **131 C8** 54 14N 100 35W
Cormorant L., *Canada* **131 C8** 54 15N 100 50W
Corn Is. = Maiz, Is. del, *Nic.* **148 D3** 12 15N 83 4W
Cornélio Procópio, *Brazil* **159 A5** 23 7 S 50 40W
Cornell, *Ill., U.S.A.* **141 D8** 41 0N 88 44W
Cornell, *Wis., U.S.A.* **138 C9** 45 10N 91 9W
Corner Brook, *Canada* **129 C8** 48 57N 57 58W
Cornești, *Moldova* **51 J5** 47 21N 28 1 E
Corníglio, *Italy* **38 D7** 44 29N 10 5 E
Corning, *Ark., U.S.A.* **139 G9** 36 25N 90 35W
Corning, *Calif., U.S.A.* **142 G2** 39 56N 122 11W
Corning, *Iowa, U.S.A.* **140 D2** 40 59N 94 44W
Corning, *N.Y., U.S.A.* **136 D7** 42 9N 77 3W
Corno, Monte, *Italy* **39 F10** 42 28N 13 34 E
Cornwall, *Canada* **128 C5** 45 2N 74 44W
Cornwall □, *U.K.* **17 G3** 50 26N 4 40W
Corny Pt., *Australia* **116 C2** 34 55 S 137 0 E
Coro, *Venezuela* **152 A4** 11 25N 69 41W
Coroaci, *Brazil* **155 E3** 18 35 S 42 17W
Coroatá, *Brazil* **154 B3** 4 8 S 44 0W
Coroban, *Somali Rep.* **108 D2** 3 58N 42 44 E
Corocoro, *Bolivia* **156 D4** 17 15 S 68 28W
Corocoro, I., *Venezuela* **153 B5** 8 30N 60 10W
Coroico, *Bolivia* **156 D4** 16 0 S 67 50W
Coromandel, *Brazil* **155 E2** 18 28 S 47 13W
Coromandel, *N.Z.* **118 C4** 36 45 S 175 31 E
Coromandel Coast, *India* **83 H5** 12 30N 81 0 E
Coromandel Pen., *N.Z.* **118 C4** 37 0 S 175 45 E
Coromandel Ra., *N.Z.* **118 C4** 37 0 S 175 40 E
Coron, *Phil.* **70 E3** 12 1N 120 12 E
Coron Bay, *Phil.* **71 F3** 11 54N 120 8 E
Coron I., *Phil.* **71 F3** 11 55N 120 14 E
Corona, *Australia* **115 E3** 31 16 S 141 24 E
Corona, *Calif., U.S.A.* **145 M9** 33 53N 117 34W
Corona, *N. Mex., U.S.A.* **143 J11** 34 15N 105 36W
Coronado, *U.S.A.* **145 N9** 32 41N 117 11W
Coronado, B. de, *Costa Rica* **148 E3** 9 0N 83 40W
Coronados, G. de los, *Chile* **160 B2** 41 40 S 74 0W
Coronados, Is. los, *U.S.A.* **145 N9** 32 25N 117 15W
Coronation, *Canada* **130 C6** 52 5N 111 27W
Coronation Gulf, *Canada* **126 B8** 68 25N 110 0W
Coronation I., *Antarctica* **7 C18** 60 45 S 46 0W
Coronation I., *U.S.A.* **130 B2** 55 52N 134 20W
Coronation Is., *Australia* **112 B3** 14 57 S 124 55 E
Coronda, *Argentina* **158 C3** 31 58 S 60 56W
Coronel, *Chile* **158 D1** 37 0 S 73 10W
Coronel Bogado, *Paraguay* **158 B4** 27 11 S 56 18W
Coronel Dorrego, *Argentina* **158 D3** 38 40 S 61 10W
Coronel Fabriciano, *Brazil* **155 E3** 19 31 S 42 38W
Coronel Murta, *Brazil* **155 E3** 16 37 S 42 11W
Coronel Oviedo, *Paraguay* **158 B4** 25 24 S 56 30W
Coronel Ponce, *Brazil* **157 D6** 15 34 S 55 1W
Coronel Pringles, *Argentina* **158 D3** 38 0 S 61 30W
Coronel Suárez, *Argentina* **158 D3** 37 30 S 61 52W
Coronel Vidal, *Argentina* **158 D4** 37 28 S 57 45W
Corongo, *Peru* **156 B2** 8 30 S 77 53W
Coronie □, *Surinam* **153 B6** 5 55N 56 20W
Coropuna, Nevado, *Peru* **156 D3** 15 30 S 72 41W
Çorovoda, *Albania* **44 D2** 40 31N 20 14 E
Corowa, *Australia* **117 C7** 35 58 S 146 21 E
Corozal, *Belize* **147 D7** 18 23N 88 23W
Corozal, *Colombia* **152 B2** 9 19N 75 18W
Corps, *France* **25 D9** 44 50N 5 56 E
Corpus, *Argentina* **159 B4** 27 10 S 55 30W
Corpus Christi, *U.S.A.* **139 M6** 27 47N 97 24W
Corpus Christi, L., *U.S.A.* **139 L6** 28 2N 97 52W
Corque, *Bolivia* **156 D4** 18 20 S 67 41W
Corral, *Chile* **160 A2** 39 52 S 73 26W
Corral de Almaguer, *Spain* **34 F1** 39 45N 3 10W
Corralejo, *Canary Is.* **33 F6** 28 43N 13 53W
Corréggio, *Italy* **38 D7** 44 46N 10 47 E
Corrente, *Brazil* **154 D2** 10 27 S 45 10W
Corrente →, *Brazil* **155 D3** 13 8 S 43 28W
Correntes →, *Brazil* **157 D6** 17 38 S 55 8W
Correntes, C. das, *Mozam.* **105 C6** 24 6 S 35 34 E
Correntina, *Brazil* **155 D3** 13 20 S 44 39W
Corrèze □, *France* **24 C5** 45 20N 1 45 E
Corrèze →, *France* **24 C5** 45 10N 1 28 E
Corrib, L., *Ireland* **19 C2** 53 27N 9 16W
Corrientes, *Argentina* **158 B4** 27 30 S 58 45W
Corrientes □, *Argentina* **158 B4** 28 0 S 57 0W
Corrientes →, *Argentina* **158 C4** 30 42 S 59 38W
Corrientes →, *Peru* **152 D3** 3 43 S 74 35W
Corrientes, C., *Colombia* **152 B2** 5 30N 77 34W
Corrientes, C., *Cuba* **148 B3** 21 43N 84 30W
Corrientes, C., *Mexico* **146 C3** 20 25N 105 42W
Corrigan, *U.S.A.* **139 K7** 31 0N 94 52W
Corrigin, *Australia* **113 F2** 32 20 S 117 53 E
Corrowidgie, *Australia* **117 D8** 36 56 S 148 50 E
Corry, *U.S.A.* **136 E5** 41 55N 79 39W
Corryong, *Australia* **117 D7** 36 12 S 147 53 E
Corse, *France* **25 F13** 42 0N 9 0 E
Corse, C., *France* **25 E13** 43 1N 9 25 E
Corse-du-Sud □, *France* **25 G13** 41 45N 9 0 E
Corsica = Corse, *France* **25 F13** 42 0N 9 0 E
Corsicana, *U.S.A.* **139 J6** 32 6N 96 28W
Corte, *France* **25 F13** 42 19N 9 11 E
Corte do Pinto, *Portugal* **37 H3** 37 42N 7 29W
Cortegana, *Spain* **37 H4** 37 52N 6 49W
Cortes, *Phil.* **71 G6** 9 17N 126 11 E
Cortez, *U.S.A.* **143 H9** 37 21N 108 35W
Cortina d'Ampezzo, *Italy* **39 B9** 46 32N 12 8 E
Cortland, *U.S.A.* **137 D8** 42 36N 76 11W
Cortona, *Italy* **39 E8** 43 16N 11 59 E
Coruche, *Portugal* **37 G2** 38 57N 8 30W
Çoruh →, *Turkey* **53 K5** 41 38N 41 38 E
Çorum, *Turkey* **88 B6** 40 30N 34 57 E
Corumbá, *Brazil* **157 D6** 19 0 S 57 30W
Corumbá →, *Brazil* **155 E2** 18 19 S 48 55W
Corumbá de Goiás, *Brazil* **155 E2** 16 0 S 48 50W
Corumbaíba, *Brazil* **155 E2** 18 9 S 48 34W
Corund, *Romania* **46 C6** 46 30N 25 13 E
Corunna = La Coruña, *Spain* **36 B2** 43 20N 8 25W
Corunna, *U.S.A.* **141 B12** 42 59N 84 7W
Corvallis, *U.S.A.* **142 D2** 44 34N 123 16W
Corvette, L. de la, *Canada* **128 B5** 53 25N 74 3W
Corydon, *Ind., U.S.A.* **141 F10** 38 13N 86 7W
Corydon, *Iowa, U.S.A.* **140 D3** 40 46N 93 19W
Corydon, *Ky., U.S.A.* **141 G9** 37 44N 87 43W
Cosalá, *Mexico* **146 C3** 24 28N 106 40W
Cosamaloapan, *Mexico* **147 D5** 18 23N 95 50W
Cosenza, *Italy* **41 C9** 39 18N 16 15 E
Coșereni, *Romania* **46 E7** 44 38N 26 35 E
Coshocton, *U.S.A.* **136 F3** 40 16N 81 51W
Cosmo Newberry, *Australia* **113 E3** 28 0 S 122 54 E
Cosne-sur-Loire, *France* **23 E9** 47 24N 2 54 E
Coso Junction, *U.S.A.* **145 J9** 36 3N 117 57W
Coso Pk., *U.S.A.* **145 J9** 36 13N 117 44W
Cospeito, *Spain* **36 B3** 43 12N 7 34W
Cosquín, *Argentina* **158 C3** 31 15 S 64 30W
Cossato, *Italy* **38 C5** 45 34N 8 10 E
Cossé-le-Vivien, *France* **22 E6** 47 57N 0 54W
Cosson →, *France* **22 E8** 47 30N 1 15 E
Costa Blanca, *Spain* **35 G4** 38 25N 0 10W
Costa Brava, *Spain* **34 D8** 41 30N 3 0 E
Costa del Sol, *Spain* **37 J6** 36 30N 4 30W
Costa Dorada, *Spain* **34 E6** 41 12N 1 15 E
Costa Mesa, *U.S.A.* **145 M9** 33 38N 117 55W
Costa Rica ■, *Cent. Amer.* **148 D3** 10 0N 84 0W
Costa Smeralda, *Italy* **40 A2** 41 5N 9 35 E
Costigliole d'Asti, *Italy* **38 D5** 44 47N 8 11 E
Costilla, *U.S.A.* **143 H11** 36 59N 105 32W
Coștiui, *Romania* **46 B5** 47 53N 24 2 E
Cosumnes →, *U.S.A.* **144 G5** 38 16N 121 26W
Coswig, *Germany* **26 D8** 51 53N 12 27 E
Cotabato, *Phil.* **71 H5** 7 14N 124 15 E
Cotabena, *Australia* **116 A3** 31 42 S 138 11 E
Cotacajes →, *Bolivia* **156 D4** 16 0 S 67 1W
Cotagaita, *Bolivia* **158 A2** 20 45 S 65 40W
Cotahuasi, *Peru* **156 D3** 15 12 S 72 50W
Côte d'Azur, *France* **25 E11** 43 25N 7 10 E
Côte-d'Ivoire ■ = Ivory Coast ■, *Africa* **100 D3** 7 30N 5 0W
Côte d'Or, *France* **23 E11** 47 10N 4 50 E
Côte-d'Or □, *France* **23 E11** 47 30N 4 50 E
Coteau des Prairies, *U.S.A.* **138 C6** 45 20N 97 50W
Coteau du Missouri, *U.S.A.* **138 B4** 47 0N 100 0W
Coteau Landing, *Canada* **137 A10** 45 15N 74 13W
Cotegipe, *Brazil* **155 D3** 12 2 S 44 15W
Cotentin, *France* **22 C5** 49 15N 1 30W
Côtes-d'Armor □, *France* **22 D4** 48 25N 2 40W
Côtes de Meuse, *France* **23 C12** 49 15N 5 22 E
Côtes-du-Nord = Côtes-d'Armor □, *France* **22 D4** 48 25N 2 40W
Cotiella, *Spain* **34 C5** 42 31N 0 19 E
Cotillo, *Canary Is.* **33 F5** 28 41N 14 1W
Cotina →, *Bos.-H.* **42 D3** 43 36N 18 50 E
Cotoca, *Bolivia* **157 D5** 17 49 S 63 3W
Cotonou, *Benin* **101 D5** 6 20N 2 25 E
Cotopaxi, *Ecuador* **152 D2** 0 40 S 78 30W
Cotopaxi □, *Ecuador* **152 D2** 0 5 S 78 55W
Cotronei, *Italy* **41 C9** 39 9N 16 47 E
Cotswold Hills, *U.K.* **17 F5** 51 42N 2 10W
Cottage Grove, *U.S.A.* **142 E2** 43 48N 123 3W
Cottbus, *Germany* **26 D10** 51 45N 14 20 E
Cottingham, *U.K.* **16 C5** 53 47N 0 23W
Cottonwood, *U.S.A.* **143 J7** 34 45N 112 1W
Cotulla, *U.S.A.* **139 L5** 28 26N 99 14W
Coubre, Pte. de la, *France* **24 C2** 45 42N 1 15W
Couches, *France* **23 F11** 46 53N 4 30 E
Couço, *Portugal* **37 G2** 38 59N 8 17W
Coudersport, *U.S.A.* **136 E6** 41 46N 78 1W
Couedic, C. du, *Australia* **116 D2** 36 5 S 136 40 E
Couëron, *France* **22 E5** 47 13N 1 44W
Couesnon →, *France* **22 D5** 48 38N 1 32W
Couhé, *France* **24 B4** 46 17N 0 11 E
Coulanges-sur-Yonne, *France* **23 E10** 47 31N 3 33 E
Coulee City, *U.S.A.* **142 C4** 47 37N 119 17W
Coulman I., *Antarctica* **7 D11** 73 35 S 170 0 E
Coulommiers, *France* **23 D10** 48 50N 3 3 E
Coulon →, *France* **25 E9** 43 51N 5 6 E
Coulonge →, *Canada* **128 C4** 45 52N 76 46W
Coulonges-sur-l'Autize, *France* **24 B3** 46 29N 0 36W
Coulterville, *Calif., U.S.A.* **144 H6** 37 43N 120 12W
Coulterville, *Ill., U.S.A.* **140 F7** 38 11N 89 36W
Council, *Alaska, U.S.A.* **126 B3** 64 55N 163 45W
Council, *Idaho, U.S.A.* **142 D5** 44 44N 116 26W
Council Bluffs, *U.S.A.* **138 E7** 41 16N 95 52W
Council Grove, *U.S.A.* **138 F6** 38 40N 96 29W
Coupeville, *U.S.A.* **144 B4** 48 13N 122 41W
Courantyne →, *S. Amer.* **153 B6** 5 55N 57 5W
Courcelles, *Belgium* **21 H4** 50 28N 4 22 E
Courçon, *France* **24 B3** 46 15N 0 50W
Couronne, C., *France* **25 E9** 43 19N 5 3 E
Cours-la-Ville, *France* **25 B8** 46 7N 4 19 E
Coursan, *France* **24 E7** 43 14N 3 4 E
Courseulles-sur-Mer, *France* **22 C6** 49 20N 0 29W
Court-St.-Etienne, *Belgium* **21 G5** 50 38N 4 34 E
Courtenay, *Canada* **130 D3** 49 45N 125 0W
Courtland, *U.S.A.* **144 G5** 38 20N 121 34W
Courtrai = Kortrijk, *Belgium* **21 G2** 50 50N 3 17 E
Courtright, *Canada* **136 D2** 42 49N 82 28W
Courville-sur-Eure, *France* **22 D8** 48 28N 1 15 E
Coushatta, *U.S.A.* **139 J8** 32 1N 93 21W
Coutances, *France* **22 C5** 49 3N 1 28W
Couterne, *France* **22 D6** 48 30N 0 25W
Coutras, *France* **24 C3** 45 3N 0 8W
Coutts, *Canada* **130 D6** 49 0N 111 57W
Couvet, *Switz.* **28 C3** 46 57N 6 38 E
Couvin, *Belgium* **21 H4** 50 3N 4 29 E
Covarrubias, *Spain* **34 C1** 42 4N 3 31W
Covasna, *Romania* **46 D7** 45 50N 26 10 E
Covasna □, *Romania* **46 D7** 45 50N 26 0 E
Coveñas, *Colombia* **152 B2** 9 24N 75 44W
Coventry, *U.K.* **17 E6** 52 25N 1 28W
Coventry L., *Canada* **131 A7** 61 15N 106 15W
Covilhã, *Portugal* **36 E3** 40 17N 7 31W
Covington, *Ga., U.S.A.* **135 J4** 33 36N 83 51W
Covington, *Ind., U.S.A.* **141 D9** 40 9N 87 24W
Covington, *Ky., U.S.A.* **141 E12** 39 5N 84 31W
Covington, *Ohio, U.S.A.* **141 D12** 40 7N 84 21W
Covington, *Okla., U.S.A.* **139 G6** 36 18N 97 35W
Covington, *Tenn., U.S.A.* **139 H10** 35 34N 89 39W
Cowal, L., *Australia* **117 B7** 33 40 S 147 25 E
Cowan, *Canada* **131 C8** 52 5N 100 45W
Cowan, L., *Australia* **113 F3** 31 45 S 121 45 E
Cowan L., *Canada* **131 C7** 54 0N 107 15W
Cowangie, *Australia* **116 C4** 35 12 S 141 26 E
Cowansville, *Canada* **137 A12** 45 14N 72 46W
Cowarie, *Australia* **115 D2** 27 45 S 138 15 E
Cowcowing Lakes, *Australia* **113 F2** 30 55 S 117 20 E
Cowden, *U.S.A.* **141 E8** 39 15N 88 52W
Cowdenbeath, *U.K.* **18 E5** 56 7N 3 21W
Cowell, *Australia* **116 B2** 33 39 S 136 56 E
Cowes, *U.K.* **17 G6** 50 45N 1 18W
Cowl Cowl, *Australia* **117 B6** 33 36 S 145 18 E
Cowlitz →, *U.S.A.* **144 D4** 46 6N 122 55W
Cowra, *Australia* **117 B8** 33 49 S 148 42 E
Coxilha Grande, *Brazil* **159 B5** 28 18 S 51 30W
Coxim, *Brazil* **157 D7** 18 30 S 54 55W
Coxim →, *Brazil* **157 D7** 18 34 S 54 46W
Cox's Bazar, *Bangla.* **78 E3** 21 26N 91 59 E
Cox's Cove, *Canada* **129 C8** 49 7N 58 5W
Coyame, *Mexico* **146 B3** 29 28N 105 6W
Coyote Wells, *U.S.A.* **145 N11** 32 44N 115 58W
Coyuca de Benítez, *Mexico* **147 D4** 17 1N 100 8W
Coyuca de Catalan, *Mexico* **146 D4** 18 18N 100 41W
Cozad, *U.S.A.* **138 E5** 40 52N 99 59W
Cozumel, *Mexico* **147 C7** 20 31N 86 55W
Cozumel, I. de, *Mexico* **147 C7** 20 30N 86 40W
Craboon, *Australia* **117 B8** 32 3 S 149 30 E
Cracow = Kraków, *Poland* **31 A12** 50 4N 19 57 E
Cracow, *Australia* **115 D5** 25 17 S 150 17 E
Cradock, *S. Africa* **104 E4** 32 8 S 25 36 E
Craig, *Alaska, U.S.A.* **130 B2** 55 29N 133 9W
Craig, *Colo., U.S.A.* **142 F10** 40 31N 107 33W
Craigavon, *U.K.* **19 B5** 54 27N 6 23W
Craigmore, *Zimbabwe* **107 G3** 20 28 S 32 50 E
Crailsheim, *Germany* **27 F6** 49 8N 10 5 E
Craiova, *Romania* **46 E4** 44 21N 23 48 E
Cramsie, *Australia* **114 C3** 23 20 S 144 15 E
Cranberry Portage, *Canada* **131 C8** 54 35N 101 23W
Cranbrook, *Tas., Australia* **114 G4** 42 0 S 148 5 E
Cranbrook, *W. Austral., Australia* **113 F2** 34 18 S 117 33 E
Cranbrook, *Canada* **130 D5** 49 30N 115 46W
Crandon, *U.S.A.* **138 C10** 45 34N 88 54W
Crane, *Oreg., U.S.A.* **142 E4** 43 25N 118 35W
Crane, *Tex., U.S.A.* **139 K3** 31 24N 102 21W
Cranston, *U.S.A.* **137 E13** 41 47N 71 26W
Craon, *France* **22 E6** 47 50N 0 58W
Craonne, *France* **23 C10** 49 27N 3 46 E
Craponne-sur-Arzon, *France* **24 C7** 45 19N 3 51 E
Crasna, *Romania* **46 C8** 46 32N 27 51 E
Crasna →, *Romania* **46 B3** 47 44N 22 35 E
Crasnei, Munții, *Romania* **46 C4** 47 0N 23 20 E
Crater L., *U.S.A.* **142 E2** 42 56N 122 6W
Crater Mt., *Papua N. G.* **120 D3** 6 37 S 145 7 E
Crater Pt., *Papua N. G.* **120 C7** 5 25 S 152 9 E
Crateús, *Brazil* **154 C3** 5 10 S 40 39W
Crati →, *Italy* **41 C9** 39 43N 16 31 E
Crato, *Brazil* **154 C4** 7 10 S 39 25W
Crato, *Portugal* **37 F3** 39 16N 7 39W
Cravo Norte, *Colombia* **152 B3** 6 18N 70 12W
Cravo Norte →, *Colombia* **152 B3** 6 18N 70 12W
Crawford, *U.S.A.* **138 D3** 42 41N 103 25W
Crawfordsville, *U.S.A.* **141 D10** 40 2N 86 54W
Crawley, *U.K.* **17 F7** 51 7N 0 11W
Crazy Mts., *U.S.A.* **142 C8** 46 12N 110 20W
Crean L., *Canada* **131 C7** 54 5N 106 9W
Crécy-en-Brie, *France* **23 D9** 48 50N 2 53 E
Crécy-en-Ponthieu, *France* **23 B8** 50 15N 1 53 E
Crediton, *Canada* **136 C3** 43 17N 81 33W
Credo, *Australia* **113 F3** 30 28 S 120 45 E
Cree →, *Canada* **131 B7** 58 57N 105 47W
Cree →, *U.K.* **18 G4** 54 55N 4 25W
Cree L., *Canada* **131 B7** 57 30N 106 30W
Creede, *U.S.A.* **143 H10** 37 51N 106 56W
Creel, *Mexico* **146 B3** 27 45N 107 38W
Creighton, *U.S.A.* **138 D6** 42 28N 97 54W
Creil, *France* **23 C9** 49 15N 2 29 E
Crema, *Italy* **38 C6** 45 22N 9 41 E
Cremona, *Italy* **38 C7** 45 7N 10 2 E
Crepaja, *Serbia, Yug.* **42 B5** 45 1N 20 38 E
Crepori →, *Brazil* **157 B6** 5 42 S 57 8W
Crépy, *France* **23 C10** 49 35N 3 32 E
Crépy-en-Valois, *France* **23 C9** 49 14N 2 54 E
Cres, *Croatia* **39 D11** 44 58N 14 25 E
Cresbard, *U.S.A.* **138 C5** 45 10N 98 57W
Crescent, *Okla., U.S.A.* **139 H6** 35 57N 97 36W
Crescent, *Oreg., U.S.A.* **142 E3** 43 28N 121 42W
Crescent City, *U.S.A.* **142 F1** 41 45N 124 12W
Crescentino, *Italy* **38 C5** 45 11N 8 6 E
Crespino, *Italy* **39 D8** 44 59N 11 53 E
Crespo, *Argentina* **158 C3** 32 2 S 60 19W
Cressy, *Australia* **116 E5** 38 2 S 143 40 E
Crest, *France* **25 D9** 44 44N 5 2 E
Cresta, Mt., *Phil.* **70 C4** 17 17N 122 6 E
Crested Butte, *U.S.A.* **143 G10** 38 52N 106 59W
Crestline, *Calif., U.S.A.* **145 L9** 34 14N 117 18W
Crestline, *Ohio, U.S.A.* **136 F2** 40 47N 82 44W
Creston, *Canada* **130 D5** 49 10N 116 31W
Creston, *Calif., U.S.A.* **144 K6** 35 32N 120 33W
Creston, *Iowa, U.S.A.* **140 C2** 41 4N 94 22W
Creston, *Wash., U.S.A.* **142 C4** 47 46N 118 31W
Crestview, *Calif., U.S.A.* **144 H8** 37 46N 118 58W
Crestview, *Fla., U.S.A.* **135 K2** 30 46N 86 34W
Creswick, *Australia* **116 D5** 37 25 S 143 58 E
Crete = Kríti, *Greece* **32 D7** 35 15N 25 0 E
Crete, *U.S.A.* **138 E6** 40 38N 96 58W
Crete, Sea of, *Greece* **45 H6** 36 0N 25 0 E
Cretin, C., *Papua N. G.* **120 D4** 6 40 S 147 53 E
Creus, C. de, *Spain* **34 C8** 42 20N 3 19 E
Creuse □, *France* **24 B6** 46 10N 2 0 E
Creuse →, *France* **24 B4** 47 0N 0 34 E
Creuzburg, *Germany* **26 D6** 51 3N 10 14 E
Crevalcore, *Italy* **39 D8** 44 43N 11 9 E
Crèvecœur-le-Grand, *France* **23 C9** 49 37N 2 5 E
Crevillente, *Spain* **35 G4** 38 12N 0 48W
Crewe, *U.K.* **16 D5** 53 6N 2 26W
Criciúma, *Brazil* **159 B6** 28 40 S 49 23W
Cridersville, *U.S.A.* **141 D12** 40 39N 84 9W
Crieff, *U.K.* **18 E5** 56 22N 3 50W
Crikvenica, *Croatia* **39 C11** 45 11N 14 40 E
Crimea □, *Ukraine* **51 K8** 45 30N 33 10 E
Crimean Pen. = Krymskyy Pivostriv, *Ukraine* **51 K8** 45 0N 34 0 E
Crimmitschau, *Germany* **26 E8** 50 48N 12 24 E
Cristal, Mts. de, *Gabon* **102 B2** 0 30N 10 30 E
Cristalândia, *Brazil* **154 D2** 10 36 S 49 11W
Cristești, *Romania* **46 B7** 47 15N 26 33 E
Cristino Castro, *Brazil* **154 C3** 8 49 S 44 13W
Crișul Alb →, *Romania* **42 A6** 46 42N 21 17 E
Crișul Negru →, *Romania* **46 C2** 46 42N 21 16 E
Crișul Repede →, *Romania* **46 C1** 46 55N 20 59 E
Crittenden, *U.S.A.* **141 F12** 38 47N 84 36W
Crivitz, *Germany* **26 B7** 53 34N 11 39 E
Crixás, *Brazil* **155 D2** 14 27 S 49 58W
Crna Gora = Montenegro □, *Yugoslavia* **42 E4** 42 40N 19 20 E
Crna Gora, *Serbia, Yug.* **42 E6** 42 10N 21 30 E
Crna Reka →, *Macedonia* **42 F6** 41 33N 21 59 E
Crna Trava, *Serbia, Yug.* **42 E7** 42 49N 22 19 E
Crni Drim →, *Macedonia* **42 F5** 41 17N 20 40 E
Crni Timok →, *Serbia, Yug.* **42 D7** 43 53N 22 15 E
Crnoljeva Planina, *Serbia, Yug.* **42 E6** 42 20N 21 0 E
Črnomelj, *Slovenia* **39 C12** 45 33N 15 10 E
Croagh Patrick, *Ireland* **19 C2** 53 46N 9 40W
Croatia ■, *Europe* **39 C13** 45 20N 16 0 E
Crocker, *U.S.A.* **140 G4** 37 57N 92 16W
Crocker, Banjaran, *Malaysia* **75 A5** 5 40N 116 30 E
Crockett, *U.S.A.* **139 K7** 31 19N 95 27W
Crocodile = Krokodil →, *Mozam.* **105 D5** 25 14 S 32 18 E
Crocodile Is., *Australia* **114 A1** 12 3 S 134 58 E
Crocq, *France* **24 C6** 45 52N 2 21 E
Croisette, C., *France* **25 E9** 43 14N 5 22 E
Croisic, Pte. du, *France* **22 E4** 47 19N 2 31W
Croix, L. La, *Canada* **128 C1** 48 20N 92 15W
Croker, C., *Australia* **112 B5** 10 58 S 132 35 E
Croker I., *Australia* **112 B5** 11 12 S 132 32 E
Cromarty, *Canada* **131 B10** 58 3N 94 9W
Cromarty, *U.K.* **18 D4** 57 40N 4 2W
Cromer, *U.K.* **16 E9** 52 56N 1 17 E
Cromwell, *N.Z.* **119 F4** 45 3 S 169 14 E
Cronat, *France* **23 F10** 46 43N 3 40 E
Cronulla, *Australia* **117 C9** 34 3 S 151 8 E
Crooked →, *Canada* **130 C4** 54 50N 122 54W
Crooked →, *U.S.A.* **142 D3** 44 32N 121 16W
Crooked I., *Bahamas* **149 B5** 22 50N 74 10W
Crooked Island Passage, *Bahamas* **149 B5** 23 0N 74 30W
Crookston, *Minn., U.S.A.* **138 B6** 47 47N 96 37W
Crookston, *Nebr., U.S.A.* **138 D4** 42 56N 100 45W
Crooksville, *U.S.A.* **134 F4** 39 46N 82 6W
Crookwell, *Australia* **117 C8** 34 28 S 149 24 E
Crosby, *Minn., U.S.A.* **138 B8** 46 29N 93 58W
Crosby, *N. Dak., U.S.A.* **131 D8** 48 55N 103 18W
Crosby, *Pa., U.S.A.* **136 E6** 41 45N 78 23W
Crosbyton, *U.S.A.* **139 J4** 33 40N 101 14W
Cross →, *Nigeria* **101 E6** 4 42N 8 21 E
Cross City, *U.S.A.* **135 L4** 29 38N 83 7W
Cross Fell, *U.K.* **16 C5** 54 43N 2 28W
Cross L., *Canada* **131 C9** 54 45N 97 30W
Cross Plains, *U.S.A.* **139 J5** 32 8N 99 11W
Cross River □, *Nigeria* **101 D6** 6 0N 8 0 E
Cross Sound, *U.S.A.* **126 C6** 58 0N 135 0W
Cross Timbers, *U.S.A.* **140 F3** 38 1N 93 14W
Crossett, *U.S.A.* **139 J9** 33 8N 91 58W
Crossfield, *Canada* **130 C6** 51 25N 114 0W
Crosshaven, *Ireland* **19 E3** 51 47N 8 17W
Crossley, Mt., *N.Z.* **119 C7** 42 50 S 172 5 E
Crossville, *U.S.A.* **141 F8** 38 10N 88 4W
Croton-on-Hudson, *U.S.A.* **137 E11** 41 12N 73 55W
Crotone, *Italy* **41 C10** 39 5N 17 8 E
Crow →, *Canada* **130 B4** 59 41N 124 20W
Crow Agency, *U.S.A.* **142 D10** 45 36N 107 28W
Crow Hd., *Ireland* **19 E1** 51 35N 10 9W
Crowell, *U.S.A.* **139 J5** 33 59N 99 43W
Crowl Creek, *Australia* **117 B6** 32 0 S 145 30 E
Crowley, *La., U.S.A.* **139 K8** 30 13N 92 22W
Crowley, L., *U.S.A.* **144 H8** 37 35N 118 42W
Crown Point, *U.S.A.* **141 C9** 41 25N 87 22W
Crows Landing, *U.S.A.* **144 H5** 37 23N 121 6W
Crows Nest, *Australia* **115 D5** 27 16 S 152 4 E
Crowsnest Pass, *Canada* **130 D6** 49 40N 114 40W
Croydon, *Australia* **114 B3** 18 13 S 142 14 E
Croydon, *U.K.* **17 F7** 51 22N 0 5W
Crozet Is., *Ind. Oc.* **109 J4** 46 27 S 52 0 E
Crozon, *France* **22 D2** 48 15N 4 30W
Cruz, C., *Cuba* **148 C4** 19 50N 77 50W
Cruz Alta, *Brazil* **159 B5** 28 45 S 53 40W
Cruz das Almas, *Brazil* **155 D4** 12 0 S 39 6W
Cruz de Malta, *Brazil* **154 C3** 8 15 S 40 20W
Cruz del Eje, *Argentina* **158 C3** 30 45 S 64 50W
Cruzeiro, *Brazil* **155 F2** 22 33 S 45 0W
Cruzeiro do Oeste, *Brazil* **159 A5** 23 46 S 53 4W
Cruzeiro do Sul, *Brazil* **156 B3** 7 35 S 72 35W
Cry L., *Canada* **130 B3** 58 45N 129 0W

Dame Marie 189

Crystal Bay, *U.S.A.* **144 F7** 39 15N 120 0W
Crystal Brook, *Australia* **116 B3** 33 21 S 138 12 E
Crystal City, *Mo., U.S.A.* **140 F6** 38 13N 90 23W
Crystal City, *Tex., U.S.A.* **139 L5** 28 41N 99 50W
Crystal Falls, *U.S.A.* **134 B1** 46 5N 88 20W
Crystal Lake, *U.S.A.* **141 B8** 42 14N 88 19W
Crystal River, *U.S.A.* **135 L4** 28 54N 82 35W
Crystal Springs, *U.S.A.* **139 K9** 31 59N 90 21W
Csongrád, *Hungary* **31 E13** 46 43N 20 12 E
Csongrád □, *Hungary* **31 E13** 46 32N 20 15 E
Csorna, *Hungary* **31 D10** 47 38N 17 18 E
Csurgo, *Hungary* **31 E10** 46 16N 17 9 E
Cu Lao Hon, *Vietnam* **77 G7** 10 54N 108 18 E
Cua Rao, *Vietnam* **76 C5** 19 16N 104 27 E
Cuácua →, *Mozam.* **107 F4** 17 54 S 37 0 E
Cuamato, *Angola* **103 F3** 17 2 S 15 7 E
Cuamba, *Mozam.* **107 E4** 14 45 S 36 22 E
Cuando →, *Angola* **103 F4** 17 30 S 23 15 E
Cuando Cubango □, *Angola* **103 F3** 16 25 S 20 0 E
Cuangar, *Angola* **103 F3** 17 36 S 18 39 E
Cuango, *Angola* **103 D3** 6 15 S 16 42 E
Cuanza →, *Angola* **103 D2** 9 2 S 13 30 E
Cuanza Norte □, *Angola* **103 D2** 8 50 S 14 30 E
Cuanza Sul □, *Angola* **103 E2** 10 50 S 14 50 E
Cuarto →, *Argentina* **158 C3** 33 25 S 63 2W
Cuatrociénegas, *Mexico* **146 B4** 26 59N 102 5W
Cuauhtémoc, *Mexico* **146 B3** 28 25N 106 52W
Cuba, *Portugal* **37 G3** 38 10N 7 54W
Cuba, *Mo., U.S.A.* **140 F5** 38 4N 91 24W
Cuba, *N. Mex., U.S.A.* **143 J10** 36 1N 107 4W
Cuba, *N.Y., U.S.A.* **136 D6** 42 13N 78 17W
Cuba ■, *W. Indies* **148 B4** 22 0N 79 0W
Cuba City, *U.S.A.* **140 B6** 42 36N 90 26W
Cubal, *Angola* **103 E2** 12 26 S 14 3 E
Cuballing, *Australia* **113 F2** 32 50 S 117 10 E
Cubango →, *Africa* **103 F4** 18 50 S 22 25 E
Cubanja, *Angola* **103 E4** 14 49 S 21 20 E
Cubia, *Angola* **103 F4** 15 58 S 21 42 E
Çubuk, *Turkey* **88 B5** 40 14N 33 3 E
Cuchi, *Angola* **103 E3** 14 37 S 16 58 E
Cuchillo-Có, *Argentina* **160 A4** 38 20 S 64 37W
Cuchivero →, *Venezuela* **152 B4** 7 40N 65 57W
Cuchumatanes, Sierra de los, *Guatemala* **148 C1** 15 35N 91 25W
Cucuí, *Brazil* **152 C4** 1 12N 66 50W
Cucurpe, *Mexico* **146 A2** 30 20N 110 43W
Cucurrupí, *Colombia* **152 C2** 4 23N 76 56W
Cúcuta, *Colombia* **152 B3** 7 54N 72 31W
Cudahy, *U.S.A.* **141 B9** 42 58N 87 52W
Cudalbi, *Romania* **46 D8** 45 46N 27 41 E
Cuddalore, *India* **83 J4** 11 46N 79 45 E
Cuddapah, *India* **83 G4** 14 30N 78 47 E
Cuddapan, L., *Australia* **114 D3** 25 45 S 141 26 E
Cudgewa, *Australia* **117 D7** 36 10 S 147 42 E
Cudillero, *Spain* **36 B4** 43 33N 6 9W
Cue, *Australia* **113 E2** 27 25 S 117 54 E
Cuéllar, *Spain* **36 D6** 41 23N 4 21W
Cuemba, *Angola* **103 E3** 11 50 S 17 42 E
Cuenca, *Ecuador* **152 D2** 2 50 S 79 9W
Cuenca, *Spain* **34 E2** 40 5N 2 10W
Cuenca □, *Spain* **34 F2** 40 0N 2 0W
Cuenca, Serranía de, *Spain* **34 F3** 39 55N 1 50W
Cuerdo del Pozo, Pantano de la, *Spain* **34 D2** 41 51N 2 44W
Cuernavaca, *Mexico* **147 D5** 18 55N 99 15W
Cuero, *U.S.A.* **139 L6** 29 6N 97 17W
Cuers, *France* **25 E10** 43 14N 6 5 E
Cuervo, *U.S.A.* **139 H2** 35 2N 104 25W
Cuesmes, *Belgium* **21 H3** 50 26N 3 56 E
Cuevas, Cerro, *Bolivia* **157 E4** 22 0 S 65 12W
Cuevas del Almanzora, *Spain* **35 H3** 37 18N 1 58W
Cuevo, *Bolivia* **157 E5** 20 15 S 63 30W
Cugir, *Romania* **46 D4** 45 48N 23 25 E
Cuiabá, *Brazil* **157 D6** 15 30 S 56 0W
Cuiabá →, *Brazil* **157 D6** 17 5 S 56 36W
Cuilco, *Guatemala* **148 C1** 15 24N 91 58W
Cuillin Hills, *U.K.* **18 D2** 57 13N 6 15W
Cuillin Sd., *U.K.* **18 D2** 57 4N 6 20W
Cuima, *Angola* **103 E3** 13 25 S 15 45 E
Cuiseaux, *France* **25 B9** 46 30N 5 22 E
Cuité, *Brazil* **154 C4** 6 29 S 36 9W
Cuito →, *Angola* **103 F4** 18 1 S 20 48 E
Cuito Cuanavale, *Angola* **103 F3** 15 10 S 19 10 E
Cuitzeo, L. de, *Mexico* **146 D4** 19 55N 101 5W
Cuiuni →, *Brazil* **153 D5** 0 45 S 63 7W
Cuivre →, *U.S.A.* **140 F6** 38 55N 90 44W
Cuivre, West Fork →, *U.S.A.* **140 E6** 39 2N 90 58W
Cujmir, *Romania* **46 E3** 44 13N 22 57 E
Cukai, *Malaysia* **77 K4** 4 13N 103 25 E
Culaba, *Phil.* **71 F5** 11 40N 124 32 E
Culan, *France* **24 B6** 46 34N 2 20 E
Culasi, *Phil.* **71 F4** 11 26N 122 3 E
Culauan, *Phil.* **71 J5** 5 58N 125 40 E
Culbertson, *U.S.A.* **138 A2** 48 9N 104 31W
Culburra, *Australia* **116 C3** 35 50 S 139 58 E
Culcairn, *Australia* **115 F4** 35 41 S 147 3 E
Culebra, Sierra de la, *Spain* **36 D4** 41 55N 6 20W
Culemborg, *Neths.* **20 E6** 51 58N 5 14 E
Culfa, *Azerbaijan* **89 C11** 38 57N 45 38 E
Culgoa, *Australia* **116 C5** 35 44 S 143 6 E
Culgoa →, *Australia* **115 D4** 29 56 S 146 20 E
Culiacán, *Mexico* **146 C3** 24 50N 107 23W
Culiacán →, *Mexico* **146 C3** 24 30N 107 42W
Culion, *Phil.* **71 F3** 11 54N 120 1 E
Culiseu →, *Brazil* **157 C7** 12 14 S 53 17W
Cúllar de Baza, *Spain* **35 H2** 37 35N 2 34W
Cullarin Ra., *Australia* **117 C8** 34 30 S 149 30 E
Cullen, *U.K.* **18 D6** 57 42N 2 49W
Cullen Pt., *Australia* **114 A3** 11 57 S 141 54 E
Cullera, *Spain* **35 F4** 39 9N 0 17W
Cullman, *U.S.A.* **135 H2** 34 11N 86 51W
Culloden, *U.K.* **18 D4** 57 30N 4 9W
Cullom, *U.S.A.* **141 D8** 40 53N 88 16W
Culoz, *France* **25 C9** 45 47N 5 46 E
Culpataro, *Australia* **116 B6** 33 40 S 144 22 E
Culpeper, *U.S.A.* **134 F7** 38 30N 78 0W
Culuene →, *Brazil* **157 C7** 12 56 S 52 51W
Culver, *U.S.A.* **141 C10** 41 13N 86 25W
Culver, Pt., *Australia* **113 F3** 32 54 S 124 43 E
Culverden, *N.Z.* **119 C7** 42 47 S 172 49 E
Cuma, *Angola* **103 E3** 12 52 S 15 5 E
Cumali, *Turkey* **45 H9** 36 42N 27 28 E
Cumaná, *Venezuela* **153 A5** 10 30N 64 5W
Cumare, *Colombia* **152 C3** 0 49N 72 32W
Cumari, *Brazil* **155 E2** 18 16 S 48 11W
Cumberland, *Canada* **130 D3** 49 40N 125 0W
Cumberland, *Iowa, U.S.A.* **140 C2** 41 16N 94 52W
Cumberland, *Md., U.S.A.* **134 F6** 39 39N 78 46W
Cumberland, *Wis., U.S.A.* **138 C8** 45 32N 92 1W
Cumberland →, *U.S.A.* **135 G2** 36 15N 87 0W
Cumberland, C., *Vanuatu* **121 D4** 14 39 S 166 37 E
Cumberland I., *U.S.A.* **135 K5** 30 50N 81 25W
Cumberland Is., *Australia* **114 C4** 20 35 S 149 10 E
Cumberland L., *Canada* **131 C8** 54 3N 102 18W
Cumberland Pen., *Canada* **127 B13** 67 0N 64 0W
Cumberland Plateau, *U.S.A.* **135 H3** 36 0N 85 0W
Cumberland Sd., *Canada* **127 B13** 65 30N 66 0W
Cumborah, *Australia* **115 D4** 29 40 S 147 45 E
Cumbres Mayores, *Spain* **37 G4** 38 4N 6 39W
Cumbria □, *U.K.* **16 C5** 54 42N 2 52W
Cumbrian Mts., *U.K.* **16 C4** 54 30N 3 0W
Cumbum, *India* **83 G4** 15 40N 79 10 E
Cuminá →, *Brazil* **153 D6** 1 30 S 56 0W
Cuminapanema →, *Brazil* **153 D7** 1 9 S 54 54W
Cummings Mt., *U.S.A.* **145 K8** 35 2N 118 34W
Cummins, *Australia* **115 E2** 34 16 S 135 43 E
Cumnock, *Australia* **117 B8** 32 59 S 148 46 E
Cumnock, *U.K.* **18 F4** 55 28N 4 17W
Cumpas, *Mexico* **146 A3** 30 0N 109 48W
Cumplida, Pta., *Canary Is.* **33 F2** 28 50N 17 48W
Çumra, *Turkey* **88 D5** 37 34N 32 45 E
Cuncumén, *Chile* **158 C1** 31 53 S 70 38W
Cundeelee, *Australia* **113 F3** 30 43 S 123 26 E
Cunderdin, *Australia* **113 F2** 31 37 S 117 12 E
Cundinamarca □, *Colombia* **152 C3** 5 0N 74 0W
Cunene □, *Angola* **103 F3** 16 30 S 15 0 E
Cunene →, *Angola* **103 F2** 17 20 S 11 50 E
Cúneo, *Italy* **38 D4** 44 23N 7 32 E
Cunhinga, *Angola* **103 E3** 12 11 S 16 47 E
Cunillera, I., *Spain* **33 C7** 38 59N 1 13 E
Cunjamba, *Angola* **103 F4** 15 27 S 20 10 E
Cunlhat, *France* **24 C7** 45 38N 3 32 E
Cunnamulla, *Australia* **115 D4** 28 2 S 145 38 E
Cuorgnè, *Italy* **38 C4** 45 23N 7 39 E
Cupar, *Canada* **131 C8** 50 57N 104 10W
Cupar, *U.K.* **18 E5** 56 19N 3 1W
Cupica, G. de, *Colombia* **152 B2** 6 25N 77 30W
Ćuprija, *Serbia, Yug.* **42 D6** 43 57N 21 26 E
Curaçá, *Brazil* **154 C4** 8 59 S 39 54W
Curaçao, *Neth. Ant.* **149 D6** 12 10N 69 0W
Curacautín, *Chile* **160 A2** 38 26 S 71 53W
Curahuara de Carangas, *Bolivia* **156 D4** 17 52 S 68 26W
Curanilahue, *Chile* **158 D1** 37 29 S 73 28W
Curaray →, *Peru* **152 D3** 2 20 S 74 5W
Curatabaca, *Venezuela* **153 B5** 6 19N 62 51W
Cure →, *France* **23 E10** 47 40N 3 41 E
Curepto, *Chile* **158 D1** 35 8 S 72 1W
Curiapo, *Venezuela* **153 B5** 8 33N 61 5W
Curicó, *Chile* **158 C1** 34 55 S 71 20W
Curicó □, *Chile* **158 C1** 34 50 S 71 15W
Curicuriari →, *Brazil* **152 D4** 0 14 S 66 48W
Curimatá, *Brazil* **154 D3** 10 2 S 44 17W
Curiplaya, *Colombia* **152 C3** 0 16N 74 52W
Curitiba, *Brazil* **159 B6** 25 20 S 49 10W
Currabubula, *Australia* **117 A9** 31 16 S 150 44 E
Currais Novos, *Brazil* **154 C4** 6 13 S 36 30W
Curralinho, *Brazil* **154 B2** 1 45 S 49 46W
Currant, *U.S.A.* **142 G6** 38 51N 115 32W
Curranyalpa, *Australia* **117 A6** 30 53 S 144 39 E
Curraweena, *Australia* **117 A6** 30 47 S 145 54 E
Currawilla, *Australia* **114 D3** 25 10 S 141 20 E
Current →, *U.S.A.* **139 G9** 36 15N 90 55W
Currie, *Australia* **114 F3** 39 56 S 143 53 E
Currie, *U.S.A.* **142 F6** 40 16N 114 45W
Currituck Sd., *U.S.A.* **135 G8** 36 20N 75 52W
Cursole, *Somali Rep.* **108 D3** 2 14N 45 25 E
Curtea de Argeş, *Romania* **46 D5** 45 12N 24 42 E
Curtis, *Spain* **36 B2** 43 7N 8 4W
Curtis, *U.S.A.* **138 E4** 40 38N 100 31W
Curtis Group, *Australia* **114 F4** 39 30 S 146 37 E
Curtis I., *Australia* **114 C5** 23 35 S 151 10 E
Curuá →, *Pará, Brazil* **153 D7** 2 24 S 54 5W
Curuá →, *Pará, Brazil* **157 B7** 5 23 S 54 22W
Curuá, I., *Brazil* **154 A1** 0 48N 50 10W
Curuaés →, *Brazil* **157 B7** 7 30 S 54 45W
Curuápanema →, *Brazil* **153 D6** 2 25 S 55 2W
Curuçá, *Brazil* **154 B2** 0 43 S 47 50W
Curuguaty, *Paraguay* **159 A4** 24 31 S 55 42W
Çürüksu Çayi →, *Turkey* **88 E3** 37 27N 27 11 E
Curup, *Indonesia* **74 C2** 4 26 S 102 13 E
Curupira, Serra, *S. Amer.* **153 C5** 1 25N 64 30W
Cururu →, *Brazil* **157 B6** 7 12 S 58 3W
Cururupu, *Brazil* **154 B3** 1 50 S 44 50W
Curuzú Cuatiá, *Argentina* **158 B4** 29 50 S 58 5W
Curvelo, *Brazil* **155 E3** 18 45 S 44 27W
Curyo, *Australia* **116 C5** 35 50 S 142 47 E
Cushing, *U.S.A.* **139 H6** 35 59N 96 46W
Cushing, Mt., *Canada* **130 B3** 57 35N 126 57W
Cusihuiriáchic, *Mexico* **146 B3** 28 10N 106 50W
Cusna, Mte., *Italy* **38 D7** 44 17N 10 23 E
Cusset, *France* **24 B7** 46 8N 3 28 E
Custer, *U.S.A.* **138 D3** 43 46N 103 36W
Cut Bank, *U.S.A.* **142 B7** 48 38N 112 20W
Cutervo, *Peru* **156 B2** 6 25 S 78 55W
Cuthbert, *U.S.A.* **135 K3** 31 46N 84 48W
Cutler, *U.S.A.* **144 J7** 36 31N 119 17W
Cutral-Có, *Argentina* **160 A3** 38 58 S 69 15W
Cutro, *Italy* **41 C9** 39 2N 16 59 E
Cuttaburra →, *Australia* **115 D3** 29 43 S 144 22 E
Cuttack, *India* **82 D7** 20 25N 85 57 E
Cuvelai, *Angola* **103 F3** 15 44 S 15 50 E
Cuvier, C., *Australia* **113 D1** 23 14 S 113 22 E
Cuvier I., *N.Z.* **118 C4** 36 27 S 175 50 E
Cuxhaven, *Germany* **26 B4** 53 51N 8 41 E
Cuyabeno, *Ecuador* **152 D2** 0 16 S 75 53W
Cuyahoga Falls, *U.S.A.* **136 E3** 41 8N 81 29W
Cuyapo, *Phil.* **70 D3** 15 46N 120 40 E
Cuyo, *Phil.* **71 F3** 10 50N 121 5 E
Cuyo East Pass, *Phil.* **71 F3** 11 0N 120 30 E
Cuyo I., *Phil.* **71 F3** 10 51N 121 2 E
Cuyo West Pass, *Phil.* **71 F3** 11 0N 120 30 E
Cuyuni →, *Guyana* **153 B6** 6 23N 58 41W
Cuzco, *Bolivia* **156 E4** 20 0 S 66 50W
Cuzco, *Peru* **156 C3** 13 32 S 72 0W
Cuzco □, *Peru* **156 C3** 13 31 S 71 59W
Čvrsnica, *Bos.-H.* **42 D2** 43 36N 17 35 E
Cwmbran, *U.K.* **17 F4** 51 39N 3 2W
Cyangugu, *Rwanda* **106 C2** 2 29 S 28 54 E
Cybinka, *Poland* **47 C1** 52 12N 14 46 E
Cyclades = Kikládhes, *Greece* **45 G6** 37 20N 24 30 E
Cygnet, *Australia* **114 G4** 43 8 S 147 1 E
Cynthiana, *U.S.A.* **141 F12** 38 23N 84 18W
Cypress Hills, *Canada* **131 D7** 49 40N 109 30W
Cyprus ■, *Asia* **32 E12** 35 0N 33 0 E
Cyrenaica, *Libya* **96 B4** 27 0N 23 0 E
Cyrene = Shaḥḥāt, *Libya* **96 B4** 32 48N 21 54 E
Czaplinek, *Poland* **47 B3** 53 34N 16 14 E
Czar, *Canada* **131 C6** 52 27N 110 50W
Czarna →, *Piotrkow Trybunalski, Poland* **47 D6** 51 18N 19 55 E
Czarna →, *Tarnobrzeg, Poland* **47 E8** 50 3N 21 21 E
Czarna Woda, *Poland* **47 B5** 53 51N 18 6 E
Czarne, *Poland* **47 B3** 53 42N 16 58 E
Czarnków, *Poland* **47 C3** 52 55N 16 38 E
Czech Rep. ■, *Europe* **30 B7** 50 0N 15 0 E
Czechowice-Dziedzice, *Poland* **31 B11** 49 54N 18 59 E
Czeladz, *Poland* **47 E6** 50 16N 19 2 E
Czempiń, *Poland* **47 C3** 52 9N 16 33 E
Czeremcha, *Poland* **47 C10** 52 31N 23 21 E
Czersk, *Poland* **47 B4** 53 46N 17 58 E
Czerwieńsk, *Poland* **47 C2** 52 1N 15 13 E
Czerwionka, *Poland* **31 A11** 50 7N 18 37 E
Częstochowa, *Poland* **47 E6** 50 49N 19 7 E
Częstochowa □, *Poland* **47 E6** 50 45N 19 0 E
Człopa, *Poland* **47 B3** 53 6N 16 6 E
Człuchów, *Poland* **47 B4** 53 41N 17 22 E
Czyzew, *Poland* **47 C9** 52 48N 22 19 E

D

Da →, *Vietnam* **76 B5** 21 15N 105 20 E
Da Hinggan Ling, *China* **65 B7** 48 0N 121 0 E
Da Lat, *Vietnam* **77 G7** 11 56N 108 25 E
Da Nang, *Vietnam* **76 D7** 16 4N 108 13 E
Da Qaidam, *China* **64 C4** 37 50N 95 15 E
Da Yunhe →, *China* **67 G11** 34 25N 120 5 E
Da'an, *China* **67 B13** 45 30N 124 7 E
Daap, *Phil.* **71 H4** 7 4N 122 12 E
Daarlerveen, *Neths.* **20 D9** 52 26N 6 34 E
Dab'a, Râs el, *Egypt* **94 H6** 31 3N 28 31 E
Daba Shan, *China* **68 B7** 32 0N 109 0 E
Dabai, *Nigeria* **101 C6** 11 25N 5 15 E
Dabajuro, *Venezuela* **152 A3** 11 2N 70 40W
Dabakala, *Ivory C.* **100 D4** 8 15N 4 20W
Dabaro, *Somali Rep.* **108 C3** 6 21N 48 43 E
Dabeiba, *Colombia* **152 B2** 7 1N 76 16W
Dabhoi, *India* **80 H5** 22 10N 73 20 E
Dąbie, *Konin, Poland* **47 C5** 52 5N 18 50 E
Dąbie, *Szczecin, Poland* **47 B1** 53 27N 14 45 E
Dabie Shan, *China* **69 B10** 31 20N 115 20 E
Dabo, *Indonesia* **74 C2** 0 30 S 104 33 E
Dabola, *Guinea* **100 C2** 10 50N 11 5W
Dabou, *Ivory C.* **100 D4** 5 20N 4 23W
Daboya, *Ghana* **101 D4** 9 30N 1 20W
Dabrowa Górnicza, *Poland* **47 E6** 50 15N 19 10 E
Dabrowa Tarnówska, *Poland* **31 A13** 50 10N 20 59 E
Dąbrówno, *Poland* **47 B7** 53 27N 20 2 E
Dabu, *China* **69 E11** 24 22N 116 41 E
Dabung, *Malaysia* **77 K4** 5 23N 102 1 E
Dabus →, *Ethiopia* **95 E4** 10 48N 35 10 E
Dacato →, *Ethiopia* **95 F5** 7 25N 42 40 E
Dacca = Dhaka, *Bangla.* **78 D3** 23 43N 90 26 E
Dacca = Dhaka □, *Bangla.* **78 C3** 24 25N 90 25 E
Dachau, *Germany* **27 G7** 48 15N 11 26 E
Dadale, *Solomon Is.* **121 M10** 8 7 S 159 6 E
Dadanawa, *Guyana* **153 C6** 2 50N 59 30W
Daday, *Turkey* **88 B5** 41 28N 33 27 E
Dade City, *U.S.A.* **135 L4** 28 22N 82 11W
Dades, Oued →, *Morocco* **98 B3** 30 58N 6 44W
Dadiya, *Nigeria* **101 D7** 9 35N 11 24 E
Dadra and Nagar Haveli □, *India* **82 D1** 20 5N 73 0 E
Dadri = Charkhi Dadri, *India* **80 E7** 28 37N 76 17 E
Dadu, *Pakistan* **79 D2** 26 45N 67 45 E
Dadu He →, *China* **68 C4** 29 31N 103 46 E
Dăeni, *Romania* **46 E9** 44 51N 28 10 E
Daet, *Phil.* **70 D4** 14 2N 122 55 E
Dafang, *China* **68 D5** 27 9N 105 39 E
Dagana, *Senegal* **100 B1** 16 30N 15 35W
Dagash, *Sudan* **94 D3** 19 19N 33 25 E
Dagestan □, *Russia* **53 J8** 42 30N 47 0 E
Dagestanskiye Ogni, *Russia* **53 J9** 42 6N 48 12 E
Dagg Sd., *N.Z.* **119 F1** 45 23 S 166 45 E
Daggett, *U.S.A.* **145 L10** 34 52N 116 52W
Daghestan Republic = Dagestan □, *Russia* **53 J8** 42 30N 47 0 E
Daghfeli, *Sudan* **94 D3** 19 18N 32 40 E
Dağlıq Qarabağ = Nagorno-Karabakh, *Azerbaijan* **89 C12** 39 55N 46 45 E
Dagö = Hiiumaa, *Estonia* **13 G20** 58 50N 22 45 E
Dagu, *China* **67 E9** 38 59N 117 40 E
Dagua, *Papua N. G.* **120 B2** 3 27 S 143 20 E
Daguan, *China* **68 D4** 27 43N 103 56 E
Dagupan, *Phil.* **70 C3** 16 3N 120 20 E
Dahab, *Egypt* **94 B3** 28 31N 34 31 E
Dahlak Kebir, *Eritrea* **90 D3** 15 50N 40 10 E
Dahlenburg, *Germany* **26 B6** 53 11N 10 44 E
Dahlgren, *U.S.A.* **141 F8** 38 12N 88 41W
Dahlonega, *U.S.A.* **135 H4** 34 32N 83 59W
Dahme, *Germany* **26 D9** 51 52N 13 25 E
Dahod, *India* **80 H6** 22 50N 74 15 E
Dahomey = Benin ■, *Africa* **101 D5** 10 0N 2 0 E
Dahong Shan, *China* **69 B9** 31 25N 113 0 E
Dahra, *Senegal* **100 B1** 15 22N 15 30W
Dahra, Massif de, *Algeria* **99 A5** 36 7N 1 21 E
Dahy, Nafūd ad, *Si. Arabia* **86 B4** 22 0N 45 25 E
Dai Hao, *Vietnam* **76 C6** 18 1N 106 25 E
Dai-Sen, *Japan* **62 B5** 35 22N 133 32 E
Dai Shan, *China* **69 B14** 30 25N 122 10 E
Dai Xian, *China* **66 E7** 39 4N 112 58 E
Daicheng, *China* **66 E9** 38 42N 116 38 E
Daigo, *Japan* **63 A12** 36 46N 140 21 E
Daimanji-San, *Japan* **62 A5** 36 14N 133 20 E
Daimiel, *Spain* **35 F1** 39 5N 3 35W
Daingean, *Ireland* **19 C4** 53 18N 7 17W
Daingkog, *China* **68 A1** 32 30N 97 58 E
Daintree, *Australia* **114 B4** 16 20 S 145 20 E
Daiō-Misaki, *Japan* **63 C8** 34 15N 136 45 E
Dairût, *Egypt* **94 B3** 27 34N 30 43 E
Daisetsu-Zan, *Japan* **60 C11** 43 30N 142 57 E
Daitari, *India* **82 D7** 21 10N 85 46 E
Daito, *Japan* **62 B4** 35 19N 132 58 E
Dajarra, *Australia* **114 C2** 21 42 S 139 30 E
Dajin Chuan →, *China* **68 B3** 31 16N 101 59 E
Dak Dam, *Cambodia* **76 F6** 12 20N 107 21 E
Dak Nhe, *Vietnam* **76 E6** 15 28N 107 48 E
Dak Pek, *Vietnam* **76 E6** 15 4N 107 44 E
Dak Song, *Vietnam* **77 F6** 12 19N 107 35 E
Dak Sui, *Vietnam* **76 E6** 14 55N 107 43 E
Dakar, *Senegal* **100 C1** 14 34N 17 29W
Dakhla, *W. Sahara* **98 D1** 23 50N 15 53W
Dakhla, El Wâhât el-, *Egypt* **94 B2** 25 30N 28 50 E
Dakhovskaya, *Russia* **49 F7** 44 13N 40 13 E
Dakingari, *Nigeria* **101 C5** 11 37N 4 1 E
Dakor, *India* **80 H5** 22 45N 73 11 E
Dakoro, *Niger* **101 C6** 14 31N 6 46 E
Dakota City, *Iowa, U.S.A.* **140 B2** 42 43N 94 12W
Dakota City, *Nebr., U.S.A.* **138 D6** 42 25N 96 25W
Đakovica, *Serbia, Yug.* **42 E5** 42 22N 20 26 E
Đakovo, *Croatia* **42 B3** 45 19N 18 24 E
Dala, *Angola* **103 E4** 11 3 S 20 17 E
Dala, *Solomon Is.* **121 M11** 8 30 S 160 41 E
Dalaba, *Guinea* **100 C2** 10 42N 12 15W
Dalachi, *China* **66 F3** 36 48N 105 0 E
Dalaguete, *Phil.* **71 G4** 9 46N 123 32 E
Dalai Nur, *China* **66 C9** 43 20N 116 45 E
Dālakī, *Iran* **85 D6** 29 26N 51 17 E
Dalälven, *Sweden* **13 F17** 60 12N 16 43 E
Dalaman, *Turkey* **88 D3** 36 48N 28 47 E
Dalaman →, *Turkey* **88 D3** 36 41N 28 43 E
Dalandzadgad, *Mongolia* **66 C3** 43 27N 104 30 E
Dalanganem Is., *Phil.* **71 F3** 10 40N 120 17 E
Dalarna, *Sweden* **13 F16** 61 0N 14 0 E
Dalat, *Malaysia* **75 B4** 2 44N 111 56 E
Dālbandīn, *Pakistan* **79 C2** 29 0N 64 23 E
Dalbeattie, *U.K.* **18 G5** 54 56N 3 50W
Dalbosjön, *Sweden* **15 F6** 58 40N 12 45 E
Dalby, *Australia* **115 D5** 27 10 S 151 17 E
Dalby, *Sweden* **15 J7** 55 40N 13 22 E
Dale, *U.S.A.* **141 F10** 38 10N 86 59W
Dalen, *Neths.* **20 C9** 52 42N 6 46 E
Dalen, *Norway* **14 E2** 59 26N 8 0 E
Dalet, *Burma* **78 F4** 19 59N 93 51 E
Daletme, *Burma* **78 E4** 21 36N 92 46 E
Daleville, *U.S.A.* **141 D11** 40 7N 85 33W
Dalfsen, *Neths.* **20 C8** 52 31N 6 16 E
Dalga, *Egypt* **94 B3** 27 39N 30 41 E
Dalgān, *Iran* **85 E8** 27 31N 59 19 E
Dalhart, *U.S.A.* **139 G3** 36 4N 102 31W
Dalhousie, *Canada* **129 C6** 48 5N 66 26W
Dalhousie, *India* **80 C6** 32 38N 75 58 E
Dali, *Shaanxi, China* **66 G5** 34 48N 109 58 E
Dali, *Yunnan, China* **68 E3** 25 40N 100 10 E
Dalian, *China* **67 E11** 38 50N 121 40 E
Daliang Shan, *China* **68 D4** 28 0N 102 45 E
Dalias, *Spain* **35 J2** 36 49N 2 52W
Daling He →, *China* **67 D11** 40 55N 121 40 E
Dāliyat el Karmel, *Israel* **91 C4** 32 43N 35 2 E
Dalj, *Croatia* **42 B3** 45 29N 18 59 E
Dalkeith, *U.K.* **18 F5** 55 54N 3 4W
Dall I., *U.S.A.* **130 C2** 54 59N 133 25W
Dallarnil, *Australia* **115 D5** 25 19 S 152 2 E
Dallas, *Oreg., U.S.A.* **142 D2** 44 55N 123 19W
Dallas, *Tex., U.S.A.* **139 J6** 32 47N 96 49W
Dallas Center, *U.S.A.* **140 C3** 41 41N 93 58W
Dallas City, *U.S.A.* **140 D5** 40 38N 91 10W
Dallol, *Ethiopia* **95 E5** 14 14N 40 17 E
Dalmacija, *Croatia* **42 D2** 43 20N 17 0 E
Dalmatia = Dalmacija, *Croatia* **42 D2** 43 20N 17 0 E
Dalmatovo, *Russia* **54 C9** 56 16N 62 56 E
Dalmellington, *U.K.* **18 F4** 55 19N 4 23W
Dalnegorsk, *Russia* **57 E14** 44 32N 135 33 E
Dalnerechensk, *Russia* **57 E14** 45 50N 133 40 E
Daloa, *Ivory C.* **100 D3** 7 0N 6 30W
Dalou Shan, *China* **68 C6** 28 15N 107 0 E
Dalsjöfors, *Sweden* **15 G7** 57 46N 13 5 E
Dalskog, *Sweden* **15 F6** 58 44N 12 18 E
Dalsland, *Sweden* **13 G14** 58 50N 12 15 E
Daltenganj, *India* **81 G11** 24 0N 84 4 E
Dalton, *Canada* **128 C3** 48 11N 84 1W
Dalton, *Ga., U.S.A.* **135 H3** 34 46N 84 58W
Dalton, *Mass., U.S.A.* **137 D11** 42 28N 73 11W
Dalton, *Nebr., U.S.A.* **138 E3** 41 25N 102 58W
Dalton Iceberg Tongue, *Antarctica* **7 C9** 66 15 S 121 30 E
Dalupiri I., *Cagayan, Phil.* **70 B3** 19 5N 121 12 E
Dalupiri I., *N. Samar, Phil.* **70 E5** 12 25N 124 16 E
Dalvík, *Iceland* **12 D4** 65 58N 18 32W
Daly →, *Australia* **112 B5** 13 35 S 130 19 E
Daly City, *U.S.A.* **144 H4** 37 42N 122 28W
Daly L., *Canada* **131 B7** 56 32N 105 39W
Daly Waters, *Australia* **114 B1** 16 15 S 133 24 E
Dam Doi, *Vietnam* **77 H5** 8 50N 105 12 E
Dam Ha, *Vietnam* **76 B6** 21 21N 107 36 E
Daman, *India* **82 D1** 20 25N 72 57 E
Daman □, *India* **82 D1** 20 25N 72 58 E
Dāmaneh, *Iran* **85 C6** 33 1N 50 29 E
Damanhûr, *Egypt* **94 H7** 31 0N 30 30 E
Damanzhuang, *China* **66 E9** 38 5N 116 35 E
Damar, *Indonesia* **72 C3** 7 7 S 128 40 E
Damara, *C.A.R.* **102 B3** 4 58N 18 42 E
Damaraland, *Namibia* **104 C2** 21 0 S 17 0 E
Damascus = Dimashq, *Syria* **91 B5** 33 30N 36 18 E
Damaturu, *Nigeria* **101 C7** 11 45N 11 55 E
Damāvand, *Iran* **85 C7** 35 47N 52 0 E
Damāvand, Qolleh-ye, *Iran* **85 C7** 35 56N 52 10 E
Damba, *Angola* **103 D3** 6 44 S 15 20 E
Dame Marie, *Haiti* **149 C5** 18 36N 74 26W

190 Dāmghān

Dāmghān, *Iran* 85 B7 36 10N 54 17 E
Dămienesti, *Romania* 46 C8 46 44N 27 1 E
Damietta = Dumyât, *Egypt* 94 H7 31 24N 31 48 E
Daming, *China* 66 F8 36 15N 115 6 E
Damīr Qābū, *Syria* 84 B4 36 58N 41 51 E
Dammam = Ad Dammām, *Si. Arabia* 85 E6 26 20N 50 5 E
Dammarie, *France* 22 D8 48 20N 1 30 E
Dammartin-en-Goële, *France* 23 C9 49 3N 2 41 E
Dammastock, *Switz.* 29 C6 46 38N 8 24 E
Damme, *Germany* 26 C4 52 32N 8 11 E
Damodar →, *India* 81 H12 23 17N 87 35 E
Damoh, *India* 81 H8 23 50N 79 28 E
Damous, *Algeria* 99 A5 36 31N 1 42 E
Dampier, *Australia* 112 D2 20 41 S 116 42 E
Dampier, Selat, *Indonesia* 73 B4 0 40 S 131 0 E
Dampier Arch., *Australia* 112 D2 20 38 S 116 32 E
Dampier Str., *Papua N. G.* 120 C5 5 50 S 148 0 E
Damqawt, *Yemen* 87 C6 16 34N 52 50 E
Damrei, Chuor Phnum, *Cambodia* 77 G4 11 30N 103 0 E
Damville, *France* 22 D8 48 51N 1 5 E
Damvillers, *France* 23 C12 49 20N 5 21 E
Dan-Gulbi, *Nigeria* 101 C6 11 40N 6 15 E
Dana, *Indonesia* 72 D2 11 0 S 122 52 E
Dana, L., *Canada* 128 B4 50 53N 77 20W
Dana, Mt., *U.S.A.* 144 H7 37 54N 119 12W
Danakil Depression, *Ethiopia* 95 E5 12 45N 41 0 E
Danao, *Cebu, Phil.* 71 F5 10 31N 124 1 E
Danao, *Sorsogon, Phil.* 70 E4 12 44N 123 51 E
Danbury, *U.S.A.* 137 E11 41 24N 73 28W
Danby L., *U.S.A.* 143 J6 34 13N 115 5W
Dand, *Afghan.* 80 D1 31 28N 65 32 E
Dandaragan, *Australia* 113 F2 30 40 S 115 40 E
Dandeldhura, *Nepal* 81 E9 29 20N 80 35 E
Dandenong, *Australia* 117 E6 38 0 S 145 15 E
Dandong, *China* 67 D13 40 10N 124 20 E
Danfeng, *China* 66 H6 33 45N 110 25 E
Danforth, *U.S.A.* 129 C6 45 40N 67 52W
Dangan Liedao, *China* 69 F10 22 2N 114 8 E
Dangara, *Tajikistan* 55 D4 38 6N 69 22 E
Danger Is. = Pukapuka, *Cook Is.* 123 J11 10 53 S 165 49W
Danger Pt., *S. Africa* 104 E2 34 40 S 19 17 E
Dangla, *Ethiopia* 95 E4 11 18N 36 56 E
Dangora, *Nigeria* 101 C6 11 30N 8 7 E
Dangrek, Phnom, *Thailand* 76 E5 14 15N 105 0 E
Dangriga, *Belize* 147 D7 17 0N 88 13W
Dangshan, *China* 66 G9 34 27N 116 22 E
Dangtu, *China* 69 B12 31 32N 118 25 E
Dangyang, *China* 69 B8 30 52N 111 44 E
Daniel, *U.S.A.* 142 E8 42 52N 110 4W
Daniel's Harbour, *Canada* 129 B8 50 13N 57 35W
Danielskuil, *S. Africa* 104 D3 28 11 S 23 33 E
Danielson, *U.S.A.* 137 E13 41 48N 71 53W
Danilov, *Russia* 52 A5 58 16N 40 13 E
Danilovgrad, *Montenegro, Yug.* 42 E4 42 38N 19 9 E
Danilovka, *Russia* 52 E7 50 25N 44 12 E
Daning, *China* 66 F6 36 28N 110 45 E
Danissa, *Kenya* 106 B5 3 15N 40 58 E
Danja, *Nigeria* 101 C6 11 21N 7 30 E
Danje-ia-Menha, *Angola* 103 D2 9 32 S 14 39 E
Ḑank, *Oman* 87 B7 23 33N 56 16 E
Dankalwa, *Nigeria* 101 C7 11 52N 12 12 E
Dankama, *Nigeria* 101 C6 13 20N 7 44 E
Dankov, *Russia* 52 D4 53 20N 39 5 E
Danleng, *China* 68 B4 30 1N 103 31 E
Danlí, *Honduras* 148 D2 14 4N 86 35W
Dannemora, *U.S.A.* 137 B11 44 43N 73 44W
Dannenberg, *Germany* 26 B7 53 6N 11 5 E
Dannevirke, *N.Z.* 118 G5 40 12 S 176 8 E
Dannhauser, *S. Africa* 105 D5 28 0 S 30 3 E
Danot, *Ethiopia* 108 C3 7 33N 45 17 E
Dansville, *U.S.A.* 136 D7 42 34N 77 42W
Dantan, *India* 81 J12 21 57N 87 20 E
Dante, *Somali Rep.* 108 B4 10 25N 51 16 E
Danube = Dunărea →, *Europe* 51 K5 45 20N 29 40 E
Danube →, *Europe* 46 D10 45 20N 29 40 E
Danubyu, *Burma* 78 G5 17 15N 95 35 E
Danukandi, *Bangla.* 78 D3 23 32N 90 43 E
Danvers, *U.S.A.* 137 D14 42 34N 70 56W
Danville, *Ill., U.S.A.* 141 D9 40 8N 87 37W
Danville, *Ind., U.S.A.* 141 E10 39 46N 86 32W
Danville, *Ky., U.S.A.* 141 G12 37 39N 84 46W
Danville, *Va., U.S.A.* 135 G6 36 36N 79 23W
Danyang, *China* 69 B12 32 0N 119 31 E
Danzhai, *China* 68 D6 26 11N 107 48 E
Danzig = Gdańsk, *Poland* 47 A5 54 22N 18 40 E
Dao, *Antique, Phil.* 71 F3 10 30N 121 57 E
Dao, *Capiz, Phil.* 71 F4 11 24N 122 41 E
Dão →, *Portugal* 36 E2 40 20N 8 11W
Dao Xian, *China* 69 E8 25 36N 111 31 E
Daocheng, *China* 68 C3 29 0N 100 10 E
Daora, *W. Sahara* 98 C2 27 5N 12 59W
Daoud = Aïn Beïda, *Algeria* 99 A6 35 50N 7 29 E
Daoulas, *France* 22 D2 48 22N 4 17W
Dapa, *Phil.* 71 G6 9 46N 126 3 E
Dapaong, *Togo* 101 C5 10 55N 0 16 E
Dapitan, *Phil.* 71 G4 8 39N 123 25 E
Daqing Shan, *China* 66 D6 40 40N 111 0 E
Daqu Shan, *China* 69 B14 30 25N 122 20 E
Dar Banda, *Africa* 92 F6 8 0N 23 0 E
Dar el Beida = Casablanca, *Morocco* 98 B3 33 36N 7 36W
Dar es Salaam, *Tanzania* 106 D4 6 50 S 39 12 E
Dar Mazār, *Iran* 85 D8 29 14N 57 20 E
Dar'ā, *Syria* 91 C5 32 36N 36 7 E
Dar'ā □, *Syria* 91 C5 32 55N 36 10 E
Dārāb, *Iran* 85 D7 28 50N 54 30 E
Darabani, *Romania* 46 A7 48 10N 26 39 E
Daraj, *Libya* 96 B2 30 10N 10 28 E
Dārān, *Iran* 85 C6 32 59N 50 24 E
Daraut Kurgan, *Kyrgyzstan* 55 D6 39 33N 72 11 E
Daravica, *Serbia, Yug.* 42 E5 42 32N 20 8 E
Daraw, *Egypt* 94 C3 24 22N 32 51 E
Dārayyā, *Syria* 91 B5 33 28N 36 15 E
Darazo, *Nigeria* 101 C7 11 1N 10 24 E
Darband, *Pakistan* 80 B5 34 20N 72 50 E
Darband, Kūh-e, *Iran* 85 D8 31 34N 57 8 E
Darbhanga, *India* 81 F11 26 15N 85 55 E
Darburruk, *Somali Rep.* 108 C2 9 44N 44 31 E
Darby, *U.S.A.* 142 C6 46 1N 114 11W
Darda, *Croatia* 42 B3 45 40N 18 41 E
Dardanelle, *Ark., U.S.A.* 139 H8 35 13N 93 9W
Dardanelle, *Calif., U.S.A.* 144 G7 38 20N 119 50W
Dardanelles = Çanakkale Boğazı, *Turkey* 88 B2 40 17N 26 32 E
Darende, *Turkey* 88 C7 38 31N 37 30 E
Dārestān, *Iran* 85 D8 29 9N 58 42 E
Darfield, *N.Z.* 119 D7 43 29 S 172 7 E
Darfo, *Italy* 38 C7 45 53N 10 11 E
Dârfûr, *Sudan* 92 E6 13 40N 24 0 E
Dargai, *Pakistan* 79 B3 34 25N 71 55 E
Dargan Ata, *Uzbekistan* 56 E7 40 29N 62 10 E
Dargaville, *N.Z.* 118 B2 35 57 S 173 52 E
Darhan Muminggan Lianheqi, *China* 66 D6 41 40N 110 28 E
Dari, *Sudan* 95 F3 5 48N 30 26 E
Darıca, *Turkey* 88 B3 40 45N 29 23 E
Darién, G. del, *Colombia* 152 B2 9 0N 77 0W
Darién, Serranía del, *Colombia* 152 B2 8 30N 77 30W
Dariganga, *Mongolia* 66 B7 45 21N 113 45 E
Darinskoye, *Kazakstan* 52 E10 51 20N 51 44 E
Darjeeling = Darjiling, *India* 81 F13 27 3N 88 18 E
Darjiling, *India* 81 F13 27 3N 88 18 E
Dark Cove, *Canada* 129 C9 48 47N 54 13W
Darkan, *Australia* 113 F2 33 20 S 116 43 E
Darke Peak, *Australia* 116 B2 33 27 S 136 12 E
Darkhazīneh, *Iran* 85 D6 31 54N 48 39 E
Darkot Pass, *Pakistan* 81 A5 36 45N 73 26 E
Darling →, *Australia* 116 C4 34 4 S 141 54 E
Darling Downs, *Australia* 115 D5 27 30 S 150 30 E
Darling Ra., *Australia* 113 F2 32 30 S 116 0 E
Darlington, *U.K.* 16 C6 54 32N 1 33W
Darlington, *S.C., U.S.A.* 135 H6 34 18N 79 52W
Darlington, *Wis., U.S.A.* 140 B6 42 41N 90 7W
Darlington, L., *S. Africa* 104 E4 33 10 S 25 9 E
Darlot, L., *Australia* 113 E3 27 48 S 121 35 E
Darłowo, *Poland* 47 A3 54 25N 16 25 E
Dărmănești, *Romania* 46 C7 46 21N 26 33 E
Darmstadt, *Germany* 27 F4 49 51N 8 39 E
Darnah, *Libya* 96 B4 32 45N 22 45 E
Darnah □, *Libya* 96 B4 31 0N 23 40 E
Darnall, *S. Africa* 105 D5 29 23 S 31 18 E
Darnétal, *France* 22 C8 49 25N 1 10 E
Darney, *France* 23 D13 48 5N 6 2 E
Darnick, *Australia* 116 B5 32 48 S 143 38 E
Darnley, C., *Antarctica* 7 C6 68 0 S 69 0 E
Darnley B., *Canada* 126 B7 69 30N 123 30W
Daroca, *Spain* 34 D3 41 9N 1 25W
Darr, *Australia* 114 C3 23 13 S 144 7 E
Darr →, *Australia* 114 C3 23 39 S 143 50 E
Darran Mts., *N.Z.* 119 E2 44 37 S 167 59 E
Darrington, *U.S.A.* 142 B3 48 15N 121 36W
Darsana, *Bangla.* 78 D2 23 35N 88 48 E
Darsi, *India* 83 G4 15 46N 79 44 E
Darsser Ort, *Germany* 26 A8 54 28N 12 32 E
Dart →, *U.K.* 17 G4 50 24N 3 39W
Dart, C., *Antarctica* 7 D14 73 6 S 126 20W
Dartmoor, *Australia* 116 D4 37 56 S 141 19 E
Dartmoor, *U.K.* 17 G4 50 38N 3 57W
Dartmouth, *Australia* 114 C3 23 31 S 144 44 E
Dartmouth, *Canada* 129 D7 44 40N 63 30W
Dartmouth, *U.K.* 17 G4 50 21N 3 36W
Dartmouth, L., *Australia* 115 D4 26 4 S 145 18 E
Dartuch, C., *Spain* 33 B10 39 55N 3 49 E
Daru, *Papua N. G.* 120 E2 9 3 S 143 13 E
Daruvar, *Croatia* 42 B2 45 35N 17 14 E
Darvaza, *Turkmenistan* 56 E6 40 11N 58 24 E
Darvel, Teluk, *Malaysia* 75 B5 4 50N 118 20 E
Darwha, *India* 82 D3 20 15N 77 45 E
Darwin, *Australia* 112 B5 12 25 S 130 51 E
Darwin, *U.S.A.* 145 J9 36 15N 117 35W
Darwin, Mt., *Chile* 160 D3 54 47 S 69 55W
Darwin River, *Australia* 112 B5 12 50 S 130 58 E
Daryapur, *India* 82 D3 20 55N 77 20 E
Daryoi Amu = Amudarya →, *Uzbekistan* 56 E6 43 58N 59 34 E
Dās, *U.A.E.* 85 E7 25 20N 53 30 E
Dashetai, *China* 66 D5 41 0N 109 5 E
Dashhowuz, *Turkmenistan* 56 E6 41 49N 59 58 E
Dashkesan = Daşkäsän, *Azerbaijan* 53 K7 40 25N 46 0 E
Dasht, *Iran* 85 B8 37 17N 56 7 E
Dasht →, *Pakistan* 79 D1 25 10N 61 40 E
Dasht-i-Nawar, *Afghan.* 80 C3 33 52N 68 0 E
Daska, *Pakistan* 80 C6 32 20N 74 20 E
Daşkäsän, *Azerbaijan* 53 K7 40 25N 46 0 E
Dassa-Zoume, *Benin* 101 D5 7 46N 2 14 E
Datça, *Turkey* 88 D2 36 46N 27 40 E
Datia, *India* 81 G8 25 39N 78 27 E
Datian, *China* 69 E11 25 40N 117 50 E
Datong, *Anhui, China* 69 B11 30 48N 117 44 E
Datong, *Shanxi, China* 66 D7 40 6N 113 18 E
Dattapur = Dhamangaon, *India* 82 D4 20 45N 78 15 E
Datu, Tanjung, *Indonesia* 75 B3 2 5N 109 39 E
Datu Piang, *Phil.* 71 H5 7 2N 124 30 E
Datuk, Tanjong, *Malaysia* 75 B3 2 5N 109 39 E
Daugava →, *Latvia* 13 H21 57 4N 24 3 E
Daugavpils, *Latvia* 13 J22 55 53N 26 32 E
Daulatabad, *India* 82 E2 19 57N 75 15 E
Daule, *Ecuador* 152 D2 1 56 S 79 56W
Daule →, *Ecuador* 152 D2 2 10 S 79 52W
Daulpur, *India* 80 F7 26 45N 77 59 E
Daun, *Germany* 27 E2 50 11N 6 49 E
Daund, *India* 82 E2 18 26N 74 40 E
Dauphin, *Canada* 131 C8 51 9N 100 5W
Dauphin I., *U.S.A.* 135 K1 30 15N 88 11W
Dauphin L., *Canada* 131 C9 51 20N 99 45W
Dauphiné, *France* 25 C9 45 15N 5 25 E
Daura, *Borno, Nigeria* 101 C7 11 31N 11 24 E
Daura, *Kaduna, Nigeria* 101 C6 13 2N 8 21 E
Dausa, *India* 80 F7 26 52N 76 20 E
Däväçi, *Azerbaijan* 53 K9 41 15N 48 57 E
Davangere, *India* 83 G2 14 25N 75 55 E
Davao, *Phil.* 71 H5 7 0N 125 40 E
Davao □, *Phil.* 71 H5 7 0N 125 55 E
Davao, G. of, *Phil.* 71 H5 6 30N 125 48 E
Davao del Sur □, *Phil.* 71 H5 6 30N 125 25 E
Davao Oriental □, *Phil.* 71 H6 7 10N 126 30 E
Dāvar Panāh, *Iran* 85 E9 27 25N 62 15 E
Davenport, *Calif., U.S.A.* 144 H4 37 1N 122 12W
Davenport, *Iowa, U.S.A.* 140 C6 41 32N 90 35W
Davenport, *Wash., U.S.A.* 142 C4 47 39N 118 9W
Davenport Downs, *Australia* 114 C3 24 8 S 141 7 E
Davenport Ra., *Australia* 114 C1 20 28 S 134 0 E
David, *Panama* 148 E3 8 30N 82 30W
David City, *U.S.A.* 138 E6 41 15N 97 8W
David Gorodok = Davyd Haradok, *Belarus* 51 F4 52 4N 27 8 E
Davidson, *Canada* 131 C7 51 16N 105 59W
Davis, *U.S.A.* 144 G5 38 33N 121 44W
Davis Dam, *U.S.A.* 145 K12 35 11N 114 34W
Davis Inlet, *Canada* 129 A7 55 50N 60 59W
Davis Mts., *U.S.A.* 139 K2 30 50N 103 55W
Davis Sea, *Antarctica* 7 C7 66 0 S 92 0 E
Davis Str., *N. Amer.* 127 B14 65 0N 58 0W
Davlekanovo, *Russia* 54 D5 54 13N 55 3 E
Davos, *Switz.* 29 C9 46 48N 9 49 E
Davy L., *Canada* 131 B7 58 53N 108 18W
Davyd Haradok, *Belarus* 51 F4 52 4N 27 8 E
Dawa →, *Ethiopia* 95 G5 4 11N 42 6 E
Dawaki, *Bauchi, Nigeria* 101 D6 9 25N 9 33 E
Dawaki, *Kano, Nigeria* 101 C6 12 5N 8 23 E
Dawes Ra., *Australia* 114 C5 24 40 S 150 40 E
Dawna Range, *Burma* 78 G7 16 30N 98 30 E
Dawnyein, *Burma* 78 G5 15 54N 95 36 E
Dawqah, *Si. Arabia* 86 C3 19 36N 40 54 E
Dawson, *Canada* 126 B6 64 10N 139 30W
Dawson, *Ga., U.S.A.* 135 K3 31 46N 84 27W
Dawson, *N. Dak., U.S.A.* 138 B5 46 52N 99 45W
Dawson, I., *Chile* 160 D2 53 50 S 70 50W
Dawson Creek, *Canada* 130 B4 55 45N 120 15W
Dawson Inlet, *Canada* 131 A10 61 50N 93 25W
Dawson Ra., *Australia* 114 C4 24 30 S 149 48 E
Dawu, *China* 68 B3 30 55N 101 10 E
Dawwah, *Oman* 87 B7 20 33N 58 48 E
Dax, *France* 24 E2 43 44N 1 3W
Daxian, *China* 68 B6 31 15N 107 23 E
Daxin, *China* 68 F6 22 50N 107 11 E
Daxindian, *China* 67 F11 37 30N 120 50 E
Daxinggou, *China* 67 C15 43 25N 129 40 E
Daxue Shan, *Sichuan, China* 68 B3 30 30N 101 30 E
Daxue Shan, *Yunnan, China* 68 F2 23 42N 99 48 E
Dayao, *China* 68 E3 25 43N 101 20 E
Daye, *China* 69 B10 30 6N 114 58 E
Dayi, *China* 68 B4 30 41N 103 29 E
Daylesford, *Australia* 116 D6 37 21 S 144 9 E
Dayong, *China* 69 C8 29 11N 110 30 E
Dayr az Zawr, *Syria* 89 E9 35 20N 40 5 E
Daysland, *Canada* 130 C6 52 50N 112 20W
Dayton, *Iowa, U.S.A.* 140 B2 42 14N 94 6W
Dayton, *Ky., U.S.A.* 141 E12 39 47N 84 28W
Dayton, *Nev., U.S.A.* 144 F7 39 14N 119 36W
Dayton, *Ohio, U.S.A.* 134 F3 39 45N 84 12W
Dayton, *Pa., U.S.A.* 136 F5 40 53N 79 15W
Dayton, *Tenn., U.S.A.* 135 H3 35 30N 85 1W
Dayton, *Wash., U.S.A.* 142 C4 46 19N 117 59W
Daytona Beach, *U.S.A.* 135 L5 29 13N 81 1W
Dayu, *China* 69 E10 25 24N 114 22 E
Dayville, *U.S.A.* 142 D4 44 28N 119 32W
Dazhu, *China* 68 B6 30 41N 107 15 E
Dazu, *China* 68 C5 29 40N 105 42 E
De Aar, *S. Africa* 104 E3 30 39 S 24 0 E
De Bilt, *Neths.* 20 D6 52 6N 5 11 E
De Forest, *U.S.A.* 140 A7 43 15N 89 20W
De Funiak Springs, *U.S.A.* 135 K2 30 43N 86 7W
De Grey, *Australia* 112 D2 20 12 S 119 12 E
De Grey →, *Australia* 112 D2 20 12 S 119 13 E
De Kalb, *U.S.A.* 138 E10 41 56N 88 46W
De Koog, *Neths.* 20 B5 53 6N 4 46 E
De Land, *U.S.A.* 135 L5 29 2N 81 18W
De Leon, *U.S.A.* 139 J5 32 7N 98 32W
De Panne, *Belgium* 21 F1 51 6N 2 34 E
De Pere, *U.S.A.* 134 C1 44 27N 88 4W
De Queen, *U.S.A.* 139 H7 34 2N 94 21W
De Quincy, *U.S.A.* 139 K8 30 27N 93 26W
De Ridder, *U.S.A.* 139 K8 30 51N 93 17W
De Rijp, *Neths.* 20 C5 52 33N 4 51 E
De Smet, *U.S.A.* 138 C6 44 23N 97 33W
De Soto, *U.S.A.* 140 F6 38 8N 90 34W
De Tour Village, *U.S.A.* 134 C4 46 0N 83 56W
De Witt, *Ark., U.S.A.* 139 H9 34 18N 91 20W
De Witt, *Iowa, U.S.A.* 140 C6 41 49N 90 33W
De Witt, *Mich., U.S.A.* 141 B12 42 51N 84 34W
Dead Sea, *Asia* 91 D4 31 30N 35 30 E
Deadwood, *U.S.A.* 138 C3 44 23N 103 44W
Deadwood L., *Canada* 130 B3 59 10N 128 30W
Deakin, *Australia* 113 F4 30 46 S 128 58 E
Deal, *U.K.* 17 F9 51 13N 1 25 E
Deal I., *Australia* 114 F4 39 30 S 147 20 E
Dealesville, *S. Africa* 104 D4 28 41 S 25 44 E
De'an, *China* 69 C10 29 21N 115 46 E
Dean, Forest of, *U.K.* 17 F5 51 45N 2 33W
Deán Funes, *Argentina* 158 C3 30 20 S 64 20W
Dearborn, *Mich., U.S.A.* 128 D3 42 19N 83 11W
Dearborn, *Mo., U.S.A.* 140 E2 39 32N 94 46W
Dease →, *Canada* 130 B3 59 56N 128 32W
Dease L., *Canada* 130 B2 58 40N 130 5W
Dease Lake, *Canada* 130 B2 58 25N 130 6W
Death Valley, *U.S.A.* 145 J10 36 15N 116 50W
Death Valley Junction, *U.S.A.* 145 J10 36 20N 116 25W
Death Valley National Monument, *U.S.A.* 145 J10 36 45N 117 15W
Deauville, *France* 22 C7 49 23N 0 2 E
Deba Habe, *Nigeria* 101 C7 10 14N 11 20 E
Debak, *Malaysia* 75 B4 1 34N 111 25 E
Debaltsevo, *Ukraine* 51 H10 48 22N 38 26 E
Debao, *China* 68 F6 23 21N 106 46 E
Debar, *Macedonia* 42 F5 41 31N 20 30 E
Debden, *Canada* 131 C7 53 30N 106 50W
Debdou, *Morocco* 99 B4 33 59N 3 0W
Dębica, *Poland* 31 A14 50 2N 21 25 E
Dęblin, *Poland* 47 D8 51 34N 21 50 E
Debno, *Poland* 47 C1 52 44N 14 41 E
Débo, L., *Mali* 100 B4 15 14N 4 15W
Debolt, *Canada* 130 B5 55 12N 118 1W
Deborah East, L., *Australia* 113 F2 30 45 S 119 0 E
Deborah West, L., *Australia* 113 F2 30 45 S 118 50 E
Debrc, *Serbia, Yug.* 42 C4 44 38N 19 53 E
Debre Birhan, *Ethiopia* 95 F4 9 41N 39 31 E
Debre Markos, *Ethiopia* 95 E4 10 20N 37 40 E
Debre May, *Ethiopia* 95 E4 11 20N 37 25 E
Debre Sina, *Ethiopia* 95 F4 9 51N 39 50 E
Debre Tabor, *Ethiopia* 95 E4 11 50N 38 26 E
Debre Zebit, *Ethiopia* 95 E4 11 48N 38 30 E
Debrecen, *Hungary* 31 D14 47 33N 21 42 E
Dečani, *Serbia, Yug.* 42 E5 42 30N 20 10 E
Decatur, *Ala., U.S.A.* 135 H2 34 36N 86 59W
Decatur, *Ga., U.S.A.* 135 J3 33 47N 84 18W
Decatur, *Ill., U.S.A.* 140 E8 39 51N 88 57W
Decatur, *Ind., U.S.A.* 141 D12 40 50N 84 56W
Decatur, *Mich., U.S.A.* 141 B11 42 7N 85 58W
Decatur, *Tex., U.S.A.* 139 J6 33 14N 97 35W
Decazeville, *France* 24 D6 44 34N 2 15 E
Deccan, *India* 82 F4 18 0N 79 0 E
Deception, Mt., *Australia* 116 A3 30 42 S 138 16 E
Deception L., *Canada* 131 B8 56 33N 104 13W
Dechang, *China* 68 D4 27 25N 102 11 E
Děčín, *Czech.* 30 A7 50 47N 14 12 E
Decize, *France* 23 F10 46 50N 3 28 E
Deckerville, *U.S.A.* 136 C2 43 32N 82 44W
Decollatura, *Italy* 41 C9 39 3N 16 21 E
Decorah, *U.S.A.* 138 D9 43 18N 91 48W
Deda, *Romania* 46 C5 46 56N 24 50 E
Dedaye, *Burma* 78 G5 16 24N 95 53 E
Dedéagach = Alexandroúpolis, *Greece* 44 D7 40 50N 25 54 E
Dedemsvaart, *Neths.* 20 C8 52 36N 6 28 E
Dedham, *U.S.A.* 137 D13 42 15N 71 10W
Dédougou, *Burkina Faso* 100 C4 12 30N 3 25W
Dedovichi, *Russia* 50 D5 57 32N 29 56 E
Deduru Oya, *Sri Lanka* 83 L4 7 32N 79 50 E
Dedza, *Malawi* 107 E3 14 20 S 34 20 E
Dee →, *C. of Aberd., U.K.* 18 D6 57 9N 2 5W
Dee →, *Wales, U.K.* 16 D4 53 22N 3 17W
Deep B., *Canada* 130 A5 61 15N 116 35W
Deep Lead, *Australia* 116 D5 37 0 S 142 43 E
Deep River, *U.S.A.* 140 C4 41 35N 92 22W
Deep Well, *Australia* 114 C1 24 20 S 134 0 E
Deepwater, *Australia* 115 D5 29 25 S 151 51 E
Deepwater, *U.S.A.* 140 F3 38 16N 93 47W
Deer →, *Canada* 131 B10 58 23N 94 13W
Deer Lake, *Nfld., Canada* 129 C8 49 11N 57 27W
Deer Lake, *Ont., Canada* 131 C10 52 36N 94 20W
Deer Lodge, *U.S.A.* 142 C7 46 24N 112 44W
Deer Park, *Ohio, U.S.A.* 141 E12 39 13N 84 23W
Deer Park, *Wash., U.S.A.* 142 C5 47 57N 117 28W
Deer River, *U.S.A.* 138 B8 47 20N 93 48W
Deeral, *Australia* 114 B4 17 14 S 145 55 E
Deerdepoort, *S. Africa* 104 C4 24 37 S 26 27 E
Deerlijk, *Belgium* 21 G2 50 51N 3 22 E
Deferiet, *U.S.A.* 137 B9 44 2N 75 41W
Defiance, *U.S.A.* 141 C12 41 17N 84 22W
Dêgê, *China* 68 B2 31 44N 98 39 E
Degebe →, *Portugal* 37 G3 38 13N 7 29W
Degeh Bur, *Ethiopia* 108 C2 8 11N 43 31 E
Degema, *Nigeria* 101 E6 4 50N 6 48 E
Degersheim, *Switz.* 29 B8 47 23N 9 12 E
Deggendorf, *Germany* 27 G8 48 50N 12 57 E
Deh Bīd, *Iran* 85 D7 30 39N 53 11 E
Deh-e Shīr, *Iran* 85 D7 31 29N 53 45 E
Dehaj, *Iran* 85 D7 30 42N 54 53 E
Dehak, *Iran* 79 D1 27 11N 62 37 E
Dehdez, *Iran* 85 D6 31 43N 50 17 E
Dehestān, *Iran* 85 D7 28 30N 55 35 E
Dehgolān, *Iran* 89 E12 35 17N 47 25 E
Dehibat, *Tunisia* 96 B2 32 0N 10 47 E
Dehiwala, *Sri Lanka* 83 L4 6 50N 79 51 E
Dehlorān, *Iran* 89 F12 32 41N 47 16 E
Dehnow-e Kūhestān, *Iran* 85 E8 27 58N 58 32 E
Dehra Dun, *India* 80 D8 30 20N 78 4 E
Dehri, *India* 81 G11 24 50N 84 15 E
Dehua, *China* 69 E12 25 26N 118 14 E
Dehui, *China* 67 B13 44 30N 125 40 E
Deinze, *Belgium* 21 G3 50 59N 3 32 E
Dej, *Romania* 46 B4 47 10N 23 52 E
Dejiang, *China* 68 C7 28 18N 108 7 E
Dekemhare, *Eritrea* 95 D4 15 6N 39 0 E
Dekese, *Zaïre* 102 C4 3 24 S 21 24 E
Dekhkanabad, *Uzbekistan* 55 D3 38 21N 66 30 E
Dekoa, *C.A.R.* 102 A3 6 19N 19 4 E
Del Carmen, *Phil.* 71 G6 9 50N 126 0 E
Del Mar, *U.S.A.* 145 N9 32 58N 117 16W
Del Norte, *U.S.A.* 143 H10 37 41N 106 21W
Del Rio, *U.S.A.* 139 L4 29 22N 100 54W
Delai, *Sudan* 94 D4 17 21N 36 6 E
Delano, *U.S.A.* 145 K7 35 46N 119 15W
Delareyville, *S. Africa* 104 D4 26 41 S 25 26 E
Delavan, *Ill., U.S.A.* 140 D7 40 22N 89 33W
Delavan, *Wis., U.S.A.* 138 D10 42 38N 88 39W
Delaware, *U.S.A.* 141 D13 40 18N 83 4W
Delaware □, *U.S.A.* 134 F8 39 0N 75 20W
Delaware →, *U.S.A.* 134 F8 39 15N 75 20W
Delaware B., *U.S.A.* 133 C12 39 0N 75 10W
Delčevo, *Macedonia* 42 F7 41 58N 22 46 E
Delegate, *Australia* 117 D8 37 4 S 148 56 E
Delémont, *Switz.* 28 B4 47 22N 7 20 E
Delft, *Neths.* 20 D4 52 1N 4 22 E
Delft I., *Sri Lanka* 83 K4 9 30N 79 40 E
Delfzijl, *Neths.* 20 B9 53 20N 6 55 E
Delgado, C., *Mozam.* 107 E5 10 45 S 40 40 E
Delgerhet, *Mongolia* 66 B6 45 50N 110 30 E
Delgo, *Sudan* 94 C3 20 6N 30 40 E
Delhi, *Canada* 136 D4 42 51N 80 30W
Delhi, *India* 80 E7 28 38N 77 17 E
Delhi, *U.S.A.* 137 D10 42 17N 74 55W
Deli Jovan, *Serbia, Yug.* 42 C7 44 13N 22 9 E
Delia, *Canada* 130 C6 51 38N 112 23W
Delice, *Turkey* 88 C6 39 54N 34 2 E
Delice →, *Turkey* 49 G5 39 45N 34 15 E
Delicias, *Mexico* 146 B3 28 10N 105 30W
Delījān, *Iran* 85 C6 33 59N 50 40 E
Déline, *Canada* 126 B7 65 10N 123 30W
Delitzsch, *Germany* 26 D8 51 31N 12 20 E
Dell City, *U.S.A.* 143 L11 31 56N 105 12W
Dell Rapids, *U.S.A.* 138 D6 43 50N 96 43W
Delle, *France* 23 E14 47 30N 7 2 E
Dellys, *Algeria* 99 A5 36 57N 3 57 E
Delmar, *Iowa, U.S.A.* 140 C6 42 0N 90 37W
Delmar, *N.Y., U.S.A.* 137 D11 42 37N 73 47W
Delmenhorst, *Germany* 26 B4 53 3N 8 37 E
Delmiro Gouveia, *Brazil* 154 C4 9 24 S 38 6W
Delnice, *Croatia* 39 C11 45 23N 14 50 E
Delong, Ostrova, *Russia* 57 B15 76 40N 149 20 E
Deloraine, *Australia* 114 G4 41 30 S 146 40 E
Deloraine, *Canada* 131 D8 49 15N 100 29W
Delphi, *Greece* 45 F4 38 28N 22 30 E

Dzhambul, Gora 193

Douvaine, France 25 B10 46 19N 6 16 E
Douz, Tunisia 96 B1 33 25N 9 0 E
Douze →, France 24 E3 43 54N 0 30W
Dove →, U.K. 16 E6 52 51N 1 36W
Dove Creek, U.S.A. 143 H9 37 46N 108 54W
Dover, Australia 114 G4 43 18 S 147 2 E
Dover, U.K. 17 F9 51 7N 1 19 E
Dover, Del., U.S.A. 134 F8 39 10N 75 32W
Dover, Ky., U.S.A. 141 F13 38 43N 83 52W
Dover, N.H., U.S.A. 137 C14 43 12N 70 56W
Dover, N.J., U.S.A. 137 F10 40 53N 74 34W
Dover, Ohio, U.S.A. 136 F3 40 32N 81 29W
Dover, Pt., Australia 113 F4 32 32 S 125 32 E
Dover, Str. of, Europe 22 B8 51 0N 1 30 E
Dover-Foxcroft, U.S.A. 129 C6 45 11N 69 13W
Dover Plains, U.S.A. 137 E11 41 43N 73 35W
Dovey = Dyfi →, U.K. 17 E4 52 32N 4 3W
Dovrefjell, Norway 14 B3 62 15N 9 33 E
Dow Rūd, Iran 85 C6 33 28N 49 4 E
Dowa, Malawi 107 E3 13 38 S 33 58 E
Dowagiac, U.S.A. 141 C10 41 59N 86 6W
Dowgha'i, Iran 85 B8 36 54N 58 32 E
Dowlat Yār, Afghan. 79 B2 34 30N 65 45 E
Dowlatābād, Farāh, Afghan. 79 B1 32 47N 62 40 E
Dowlatābād, Fāryāb, Afghan. 79 A2 36 26N 64 55 E
Dowlatābād, Iran 85 D8 28 20N 56 40 E
Down □, U.K. 19 B6 54 23N 6 2W
Downers Grove, U.S.A. 141 C8 41 48N 88 1W
Downey, Calif., U.S.A. 145 M8 33 56N 118 7W
Downey, Idaho, U.S.A. 142 E7 42 26N 112 7W
Downham Market, U.K. 17 E8 52 37N 0 23 E
Downieville, U.S.A. 144 F6 39 34N 120 50W
Downing, U.S.A. 140 D4 40 29N 92 22W
Downpatrick, U.K. 19 B6 54 20N 5 43W
Downpatrick Hd., Ireland 19 B2 54 20N 9 21W
Dowsārī, Iran 85 D8 28 25N 57 59 E
Dowshī, Afghan. 79 B3 35 35N 68 43 E
Doyle, U.S.A. 144 E6 40 2N 120 6W
Doylestown, U.S.A. 137 F9 40 21N 75 10W
Draa, C., Morocco 98 C2 28 47N 11 0W
Draa, Oued →, Morocco 98 C2 28 40N 11 10W
Drac →, France 25 C9 45 12N 5 42 E
Drachten, Neths. 20 B8 53 7N 6 5 E
Drăgăneşti, Romania 46 E5 44 9N 24 32 E
Drăgăneşti-Viaşca, Romania 46 E6 44 5N 25 33 E
Dragaš, Serbia, Yug. 42 E5 42 5N 20 35 E
Drăgăşani, Romania 46 E5 44 39N 24 17 E
Dragichyn, Belarus 51 F3 52 15N 25 8 E
Dragina, Serbia, Yug. 42 C4 44 30N 19 25 E
Dragocvet, Serbia, Yug. 42 D6 43 58N 21 15 E
Dragoman, Prokhod, Bulgaria 42 E7 42 58N 22 53 E
Dragonera, I., Spain 33 B9 39 35N 2 19 E
Dragovishtitsa, Bulgaria 42 E7 42 22N 22 39 E
Draguignan, France 25 E10 43 32N 6 27 E
Drain, U.S.A. 142 E2 43 40N 123 19W
Drake, Australia 115 D5 28 55 S 152 25 E
Drake, U.S.A. 138 B4 47 55N 100 23W
Drake Passage, S. Ocean 7 B17 58 0 S 68 0W
Drakensberg, S. Africa 105 E4 31 0 S 28 0 E
Dráma, Greece 44 C6 41 9N 24 10 E
Dráma □, Greece 44 C6 41 20N 24 0 E
Drammen, Norway 14 E4 59 42N 10 12 E
Drangajökull, Iceland 12 C2 66 9N 22 15W
Drangedal, Norway 14 E3 59 6N 9 3 E
Dranov, Ostrov, Romania 46 E10 44 55N 29 30 E
Dras, India 81 B6 34 25N 75 48 E
Drau = Drava →, Croatia 31 F11 45 33N 18 55 E
Drava →, Croatia 31 F11 45 33N 18 55 E
Draveil, France 23 D9 48 41N 2 25 E
Dravograd, Slovenia 39 B12 46 36N 15 5 E
Drawa →, Poland 47 C2 52 52N 15 59 E
Drawno, Poland 47 B2 53 13N 15 46 E
Drawsko Pomorskie, Poland 47 B2 53 35N 15 50 E
Drayton Plains, U.S.A. 141 B13 42 42N 83 23W
Drayton Valley, Canada 130 C6 53 12N 114 58W
Dreibergen, Neths. 20 D6 52 3N 5 17 E
Dren, Serbia, Yug. 42 D5 43 8N 20 44 E
Drenthe □, Neths. 20 C9 52 52N 6 40 E
Drentsche Hoofdvaart, Neths. 20 C8 52 39N 6 4 E
Drepanum, C., Cyprus 32 E11 34 54N 32 19 E
Dresden, Canada 136 D2 42 35N 82 11W
Dresden, Germany 26 D9 51 3N 13 44 E
Dreux, France 22 D8 48 44N 1 23 E
Drexel, U.S.A. 141 E12 39 45N 84 18W
Drezdenko, Poland 47 C2 52 50N 15 49 E
Driel, Neths. 20 E7 51 57N 5 49 E
Driffield, U.K. 16 C7 54 0N 0 26W
Driftwood, U.S.A. 136 E6 41 20N 78 8W
Driggs, U.S.A. 142 E8 43 44N 111 6W
Drin i zi →, Albania 44 C2 41 37N 20 28 E
Drina →, Bos.-H. 42 C4 44 53N 19 21 E
Drincea →, Romania 46 E3 44 20N 22 55 E
Drînceni, Romania 46 C9 46 49N 28 10 E
Drini →, Albania 44 B2 42 1N 19 38 E
Drinjača →, Bos.-H. 42 C4 44 15N 19 8 E
Drissa = Vyerkhnyadzvinsk, Belarus 50 E4 55 45N 27 58 E
Drivstua, Norway 14 B3 62 26N 9 47 E
Drniš, Croatia 39 E13 43 51N 16 10 E
Drøbak, Norway 14 E4 59 39N 10 39 E
Drobin, Poland 47 C6 52 42N 19 58 E
Drochia, Moldova 51 H4 48 2N 27 48 E
Drogheda, Ireland 19 C5 53 43N 6 22W
Drogichin = Dragichyn, Belarus 51 F3 52 15N 25 8 E
Drogobych = Drohobych, Ukraine 51 H2 49 20N 23 30 E
Drohiczyn, Poland 47 C9 52 24N 22 39 E
Drohobych, Ukraine 51 H2 49 20N 23 30 E
Droichead Atha = Drogheda, Ireland 19 C5 53 43N 6 22W
Droichead Nua, Ireland 19 C5 53 11N 6 48W
Droitwich, U.K. 17 E5 52 16N 2 8W
Drôme □, France 25 D9 44 38N 5 15 E
Drôme →, France 25 D8 44 46N 4 46 E
Dromedary, C., Australia 117 D9 36 17 S 150 10 E
Dronero, Italy 38 D4 44 29N 7 22 E
Dronfield, Australia 114 C3 21 12 S 140 3 E
Dronne →, France 24 C3 45 2N 0 9W
Dronninglund, Denmark 15 G4 57 10N 10 19 E
Dronrijp, Neths. 20 B7 53 11N 5 39 E
Dropt →, France 24 D3 44 35N 0 6W
Drosendorf, Austria 30 C8 48 52N 15 37 E
Drouin, Australia 117 E6 38 10 S 145 53 E
Drouzhba, Bulgaria 43 D13 43 15N 28 0 E
Drumbo, Canada 136 C4 43 16N 80 35W
Drumheller, Canada 130 C6 51 25N 112 40W
Drummond, U.S.A. 142 C7 46 40N 113 9W
Drummond I., U.S.A. 128 C3 46 1N 83 39W
Drummond Pt., Australia 115 E2 34 9 S 135 16 E
Drummond Ra., Australia 114 C4 23 45 S 147 10 E
Drummondville, Canada 128 C5 45 55N 72 25W
Drumright, U.S.A. 139 H6 35 59N 96 36W
Drunen, Neths. 21 E6 51 41N 5 8 E
Druskininkai, Lithuania 13 J20 54 3N 23 58 E
Drut →, Belarus 51 F6 53 8N 30 5 E
Druten, Neths. 20 E7 51 53N 5 36 E
Druya, Belarus 50 E4 55 45N 27 28 E
Druzhina, Russia 57 C15 68 14N 145 18 E
Drvar, Bos.-H. 39 D13 44 21N 16 23 E
Drvenik, Croatia 39 E13 43 27N 16 3 E
Drwęca →, Poland 47 C5 53 0N 18 42 E
Dry Tortugas, U.S.A. 148 B3 24 38N 82 55W
Dryanovo, Bulgaria 43 E10 42 59N 25 28 E
Dryden, Canada 131 D10 49 47N 92 50W
Dryden, U.S.A. 139 K3 30 3N 102 7W
Drygalski I., Antarctica 7 C7 66 0 S 92 0 E
Drysdale →, Australia 112 B4 13 59 S 126 51 E
Drysdale I., Australia 114 A2 11 41 S 136 0 E
Drzewiczka →, Poland 47 D7 51 36N 20 36 E
Dschang, Cameroon 101 D7 5 32N 10 3 E
Du Bois, U.S.A. 136 E6 41 8N 78 46W
Du Quoin, U.S.A. 140 F7 38 1N 89 14W
Duanesburg, U.S.A. 137 D10 42 45N 74 11W
Duaringa, Australia 114 C4 23 42 S 149 42 E
Ḑubā, Si. Arabia 84 E2 27 10N 35 40 E
Dubai = Dubayy, U.A.E. 85 E7 25 18N 55 20 E
Dubăsari, Moldova 51 J5 47 15N 29 10 E
Dubăsari Vdkhr., Moldova 51 J5 47 30N 29 0 E
Dubawnt →, Canada 131 A8 64 33N 100 6W
Dubawnt, L., Canada 131 A8 63 4N 101 42W
Dubayy, U.A.E. 85 E7 25 18N 55 20 E
Dubbeldam, Neths. 20 E5 51 47N 4 43 E
Dubbo, Australia 117 B8 32 11 S 148 35 E
Dubele, Zaïre 106 B2 2 56N 29 35 E
Dübendorf, Switz. 29 B7 47 24N 8 37 E
Dubica, Croatia 39 C13 45 11N 16 48 E
Dublin, Ireland 19 C5 53 21N 6 15W
Dublin, Ga., U.S.A. 135 J4 32 32N 82 54W
Dublin, Tex., U.S.A. 139 J5 32 5N 98 21W
Dublin □, Ireland 19 C5 53 24N 6 20W
Dublin B., Ireland 19 C5 53 18N 6 5W
Dubna, Russia 52 B3 56 44N 37 10 E
Dubno, Ukraine 51 G3 50 25N 25 45 E
Dubois, Idaho, U.S.A. 142 D7 44 10N 112 14W
Dubois, Ind., U.S.A. 141 F10 38 27N 86 48W
Dubossary = Dubăsari, Moldova 51 J5 47 15N 29 10 E
Dubossary Vdkhr. = Dubăsari Vdkhr., Moldova 51 J5 47 30N 29 0 E
Dubovka, Russia 53 F7 49 5N 44 50 E
Dubovskoye, Russia 53 G6 47 28N 42 46 E
Dubrajpur, India 81 H12 23 48N 87 25 E
Dubréka, Guinea 100 D2 9 46N 13 31W
Dubrovitsa = Dubrovytsya, Ukraine 51 G4 51 31N 26 35 E
Dubrovnik, Croatia 42 E3 42 39N 18 6 E
Dubrovskoye, Russia 57 D12 58 55N 111 10 E
Dubrovytsya, Ukraine 51 G4 51 31N 26 35 E
Dubulu, Zaïre 102 B4 4 18N 20 16 E
Dubuque, U.S.A. 140 B6 42 30N 90 41W
Duchang, China 69 C11 29 18N 116 12 E
Duchesne, U.S.A. 142 F8 40 10N 110 24W
Duchess, Australia 114 C2 21 20 S 139 50 E
Ducie I., Pac. Oc. 123 K15 24 40 S 124 48W
Duck Cr. →, Australia 112 D2 22 37 S 116 53 E
Duck Lake, Canada 131 C7 52 50N 106 16W
Duck Mountain Prov. Park, Canada 131 C8 51 45N 101 0W
Duckwall, Mt., U.S.A. 144 H6 37 58N 120 7W
Düdelange, Lux. 21 K8 49 29N 6 5 E
Duderstadt, Germany 26 D6 51 31N 10 15 E
Dudhnai, India 78 C3 25 59N 90 47 E
Düdingen, Switz. 28 C4 46 52N 7 12 E
Dudinka, Russia 57 C9 69 30N 86 13 E
Dudley, U.K. 17 E5 52 31N 2 5W
Dudna →, India 82 E3 19 17N 76 54 E
Dudo, Somali Rep. 108 C4 9 20N 50 12 E
Dudub, Ethiopia 108 C3 6 55N 46 43 E
Duenas, Phil. 71 F4 11 4N 122 37 E
Dueñas, Spain 36 D6 41 52N 4 33W
Dueré, Brazil 155 D2 11 20 S 49 17W
Duero = Douro →, Europe 36 D2 41 8N 8 40W
Dūfah, W. →, Si. Arabia 86 C3 18 45N 41 25 E
Duffel, Belgium 21 F5 51 6N 4 30 E
Dufftown, U.K. 18 D5 57 27N 3 8W
Dufourspitz, Switz. 28 E5 45 56N 7 52 E
Dugger, U.S.A. 141 E9 39 4N 87 18W
Dugi Otok, Croatia 39 E12 44 0N 15 3 E
Dugiuma, Somali Rep. 108 D2 1 15N 42 34 E
Dugo Selo, Croatia 39 C13 45 51N 16 18 E
Duifken Pt., Australia 114 A3 12 33 S 141 38 E
Duisburg, Germany 26 D2 51 26N 6 45 E
Duitama, Colombia 152 B3 5 50N 73 2W
Duiveland, Neths. 21 E4 51 38N 4 0 E
Duiwelskloof, S. Africa 105 C5 23 42 S 30 10 E
Dukati, Albania 44 D1 40 16N 19 32 E
Dūkdamīn, Iran 85 C8 35 59N 57 43 E
Duke I., U.S.A. 130 C2 54 50N 131 20W
Dukelský Průsmyk, Slovak Rep. 31 B14 49 25N 21 42 E
Dukhān, Qatar 85 E6 25 25N 50 50 E
Dukhovshchina, Russia 50 E7 55 15N 32 27 E
Duki, Pakistan 79 C3 30 14N 68 25 E
Dukla, Poland 31 B14 49 30N 21 35 E
Duku, Bauchi, Nigeria 101 C7 10 43N 10 43 E
Duku, Sokoto, Nigeria 101 C5 11 11N 4 55 E
Dulag, Phil. 71 F5 10 57N 125 2 E
Dulce →, Argentina 158 C3 30 32 S 62 33W
Dulce, G., Costa Rica 148 E3 8 40N 83 20W
Dulf, Iraq 84 C5 35 7N 45 51 E
Dŭlgopol, Bulgaria 43 D12 43 3N 27 22 E
Duliu, China 66 E9 39 2N 116 55 E
Dullewala, Pakistan 80 D4 31 50N 71 25 E
Dülmen, Germany 26 D3 51 49N 7 17 E
Dulovo, Bulgaria 43 D12 43 48N 27 9 E
Dulq Maghār, Syria 89 D8 36 22N 38 39 E
Dululu, Australia 114 C5 23 48 S 150 15 E
Duluth, U.S.A. 138 B8 46 47N 92 6W
Dum Dum, India 81 H13 22 39N 88 33 E
Dum Hadjer, Chad 97 F3 13 18N 19 41 E
Dūmā, Lebanon 91 A4 34 12N 35 50 E
Dūmā, Syria 91 B5 33 34N 36 24 E
Dumaguete, Phil. 71 G4 9 17N 123 15 E
Dumai, Indonesia 74 B2 1 35N 101 28 E
Dumalinao, Phil. 71 H4 7 49N 123 23 E
Dumanguilas Bay, Phil. 71 H4 7 34N 123 4 E
Dumaran, Phil. 71 F2 10 33N 119 50 E
Dumas, Ark., U.S.A. 139 J9 33 53N 91 29W
Dumas, Tex., U.S.A. 139 H4 35 52N 101 58W
Dumbarton, U.K. 18 F4 55 57N 4 33W
Dumbea, N. Cal. 121 V20 22 10 S 166 27 E
Dumbleyung, Australia 113 F2 33 17 S 117 42 E
Dumbo, Angola 103 E3 14 6 S 17 24 E
Dumbrăveni, Romania 46 C5 46 14N 24 34 E
Dumfries, U.K. 18 F5 55 4N 3 37W
Dumfries & Galloway □, U.K. 18 F5 55 9N 3 58W
Dumingag, Phil. 71 G4 8 20N 123 20 E
Dumka, India 81 G12 24 12N 87 15 E
Dümmer See, Germany 26 C4 52 31N 8 20 E
Dumoine →, Canada 128 C4 46 13N 77 51W
Dumoine L., Canada 128 C4 46 55N 77 55W
Dumraon, India 81 G11 25 33N 84 8 E
Dumyât, Egypt 94 H7 31 24N 31 48 E
Dumyât, Masabb, Egypt 94 H7 31 28N 31 51 E
Dún Dealgan = Dundalk, Ireland 19 B5 54 1N 6 24W
Dun Laoghaire, Ireland 19 C5 53 17N 6 8W
Dun-le-Palestel, France 24 B5 46 18N 1 39 E
Dun-sur-Auron, France 23 F9 46 53N 2 33 E
Duna = Dunărea →, Europe 51 K5 45 20N 29 40 E
Duna →, Hungary 31 F11 45 51N 18 48 E
Dunaföldvár, Hungary 31 E11 46 50N 18 57 E
Dunaj = Dunărea →, Europe 51 K5 45 20N 29 40 E
Dunaj →, Slovak Rep. 31 D11 47 50N 18 50 E
Dunajec →, Poland 31 A13 50 15N 20 44 E
Dunajska Streda, Slovak Rep. 31 D10 48 0N 17 37 E
Dunapatai, Hungary 31 E12 46 39N 19 4 E
Dunărea →, Europe 51 K5 45 20N 29 40 E
Dunaszekcsö, Hungary 31 E11 46 6N 18 45 E
Dunaújváros, Hungary 31 E11 47 0N 18 57 E
Dunav = Dunărea →, Europe 51 K5 45 20N 29 40 E
Dunav →, Serbia, Yug. 42 C6 44 47N 20 20 E
Dunavtsi, Bulgaria 42 D7 43 57N 22 53 E
Dunay, Russia 60 C6 42 52N 132 22 E
Dunback, N.Z. 119 F5 45 23 S 170 36 E
Dunbar, Australia 114 B3 16 0 S 142 22 E
Dunbar, U.K. 18 E6 56 0N 2 31W
Dunblane, U.K. 18 E5 56 11N 3 58W
Duncan, Canada 130 D4 48 45N 123 40W
Duncan, Ariz., U.S.A. 143 K9 32 43N 109 6W
Duncan, Okla., U.S.A. 139 H6 34 30N 97 57W
Duncan, L., Canada 128 B4 53 29N 77 58W
Duncan L., Canada 130 A6 62 51N 113 58W
Duncan Town, Bahamas 148 B4 22 15N 75 45W
Duncannon, U.S.A. 136 F7 40 23N 77 2W
Dundalk, Canada 136 B4 44 10N 80 24W
Dundalk, Ireland 19 B5 54 1N 6 24W
Dundalk Bay, Ireland 19 C5 53 55N 6 15W
Dundas, Canada 128 D4 43 17N 79 59W
Dundas, L., Australia 113 F3 32 35 S 121 50 E
Dundas I., Canada 130 C2 54 30N 130 50W
Dundas Str., Australia 112 B5 11 15 S 131 35 E
Dundee, S. Africa 105 D5 28 11 S 30 15 E
Dundee, U.K. 18 E6 56 28N 2 59W
Dundee, U.S.A. 141 C13 41 57N 83 40W
Dundee City □, U.K. 18 E6 56 30N 2 58W
Dundgovĭ □, Mongolia 66 B4 45 10N 106 0 E
Dundoo, Australia 115 D3 27 40 S 144 37 E
Dundrum, U.K. 19 B6 54 16N 5 52W
Dundrum B., U.K. 19 B6 54 13N 5 47W
Dundwara, India 81 F8 27 48N 79 9 E
Dunedin, N.Z. 119 F5 45 50 S 170 33 E
Dunedin, U.S.A. 135 L4 28 1N 82 47W
Dunedin →, Canada 130 B4 59 30N 124 5W
Dunfermline, U.K. 18 E5 56 5N 3 27W
Dungannon, Canada 136 C3 43 51N 81 36W
Dungannon, U.K. 19 B5 54 31N 6 46W
Dungannon □, U.K. 19 B5 54 30N 6 55W
Dungarpur, India 80 H5 23 52N 73 45 E
Dungarvan, Ireland 19 D4 52 5N 7 37W
Dungarvan Harbour, Ireland 19 D4 52 4N 7 35W
Dungeness, U.K. 17 G8 50 54N 0 59 E
Dungo, L. do, Angola 103 F3 17 15 S 19 0 E
Dungog, Australia 117 B9 32 22 S 151 46 E
Dungu, Zaïre 106 B2 3 40N 28 32 E
Dungunâb, Sudan 94 C4 21 10N 37 9 E
Dungunâb, Khalij, Sudan 94 C4 21 5N 37 12 E
Dunhinda Falls, Sri Lanka 83 L5 7 5N 81 6 E
Dunhua, China 67 C15 43 20N 128 14 E
Dunhuang, China 64 B4 40 8N 94 36 E
Dunières, France 25 C8 45 13N 4 20 E
Dunk I., Australia 114 B4 17 59 S 146 29 E
Dunkeld, Australia 116 D5 37 40 S 142 22 E
Dunkeld, U.K. 18 E5 56 34N 3 35W
Dunkerque, France 23 A9 51 2N 2 20 E
Dunkery Beacon, U.K. 17 F4 51 9N 3 36W
Dunkirk = Dunkerque, France 23 A9 51 2N 2 20 E
Dunkirk, U.S.A. 136 D5 42 29N 79 20W
Dunkuj, Sudan 95 E3 12 50N 32 49 E
Dunkwa, Central, Ghana 100 D4 6 0N 1 47W
Dunkwa, Central, Ghana 101 D4 5 30N 1 0W
Dunlap, U.S.A. 138 E7 41 51N 95 36W
Dúnleary = Dun Laoghaire, Ireland 19 C5 53 17N 6 8W
Dunmanus B., Ireland 19 E2 51 31N 9 50W
Dunmara, Australia 114 B1 16 42 S 133 25 E
Dunmore, U.S.A. 137 E9 41 25N 75 38W
Dunmore Hd., Ireland 19 D1 52 10N 10 35W
Dunmore Town, Bahamas 148 A4 25 30N 76 39W
Dunn, U.S.A. 135 H6 35 19N 78 37W
Dunnellon, U.S.A. 135 L4 29 3N 82 28W
Dunnet Hd., U.K. 18 C5 58 40N 3 21W
Dunning, U.S.A. 138 E4 41 50N 100 6W
Dunnville, Canada 136 D5 42 54N 79 36W
Dunolly, Australia 116 D5 36 51 S 143 44 E
Dunoon, U.K. 18 F4 55 57N 4 56W
Dunqul, Egypt 94 C3 23 26N 31 37 E
Duns, U.K. 18 F6 55 47N 2 20W
Dunseith, U.S.A. 138 A4 48 50N 100 3W
Dunsmuir, U.S.A. 142 F2 41 13N 122 16W
Dunstable, U.K. 17 F7 51 53N 0 32W
Dunstan Mts., N.Z. 119 E4 44 53 S 169 35 E
Dunster, Canada 130 C5 53 8N 119 50W
Duntroon, N.Z. 119 E5 44 51 S 170 40 E
Dunvegan L., Canada 131 A7 60 8N 107 10W
Duolun, China 66 C9 42 12N 116 28 E
Duong Dong, Vietnam 77 G4 10 13N 103 58 E
Dupax, Phil. 70 C3 16 17N 121 5 E
Dupree, U.S.A. 138 C4 45 4N 101 35W
Dupuyer, U.S.A. 142 B7 48 13N 112 30W
Duqm, Oman 87 C7 19 39N 57 42 E
Duque de Caxias, Brazil 155 F3 22 45 S 43 19W
Duque de York, I., Chile 160 D1 50 37 S 75 25W
Durack →, Australia 112 C4 15 33 S 127 52 E
Durack Ra., Australia 112 C4 16 50 S 127 40 E
Durağan, Turkey 88 B6 41 25N 35 3 E
Durance →, France 25 E8 43 55N 4 45 E
Durand, Ill., U.S.A. 140 B7 42 26N 89 20W
Durand, Mich., U.S.A. 141 B13 42 55N 83 59W
Durango = Victoria de Durango, Mexico 146 C4 24 3N 104 39W
Durango, Spain 34 B2 43 13N 2 40W
Durango, U.S.A. 143 H10 37 16N 107 53W
Durango □, Mexico 146 C4 25 0N 105 0W
Duranillin, Australia 113 F2 33 30 S 116 45 E
Durant, Iowa, U.S.A. 140 C6 41 36N 90 54W
Durant, Okla., U.S.A. 139 J6 33 59N 96 25W
Duratón →, Spain 36 D6 41 37N 4 7W
Durazno, Uruguay 158 C4 33 25 S 56 31W
Durazzo = Durrësi, Albania 44 C1 41 19N 19 28 E
Durban, France 24 F6 42 59N 2 49 E
Durban, S. Africa 105 D5 29 49 S 31 1 E
Durbo, Somali Rep. 108 B4 11 37N 50 20 E
Dúrcal, Spain 37 J7 37 0N 3 34W
Đurđevac, Croatia 42 A2 46 2N 17 3 E
Düren, Germany 26 E2 50 48N 6 29 E
Durg, India 82 D5 21 15N 81 22 E
Durgapur, India 81 H12 23 30N 87 20 E
Durham, Canada 128 D3 44 10N 80 49W
Durham, U.K. 16 C6 54 47N 1 34W
Durham, Calif., U.S.A. 144 F5 39 39N 121 48W
Durham, N.C., U.S.A. 135 G6 35 59N 78 54W
Durham □, U.K. 16 C6 54 42N 1 45W
Durham Downs, Australia 115 D4 26 6 S 149 5 E
Ḑurmā, Si. Arabia 86 A4 24 37N 46 8 E
Durmitor, Montenegro, Yug. 42 D4 43 10N 19 0 E
Durness, U.K. 18 C4 58 34N 4 45W
Durrësi, Albania 44 C1 41 19N 19 28 E
Durrie, Australia 114 D3 25 40 S 140 15 E
Dursunbey, Turkey 88 C3 39 35N 28 37 E
Durtal, France 22 E6 47 40N 0 18W
Duru, Zaïre 106 B2 4 14N 28 50 E
D'Urville, Tanjung, Indonesia 73 B5 1 28 S 137 54 E
D'Urville I., N.Z. 119 A8 40 50 S 173 55 E
Duryea, U.S.A. 137 E9 41 20N 75 45W
Dusa Mareb, Somali Rep. 108 C3 5 30N 46 15 E
Dûsh, Egypt 94 C3 24 35N 30 41 E
Dushak, Turkmenistan 56 F7 37 13N 60 1 E
Dushan, China 68 E6 25 48N 107 30 E
Dushanbe, Tajikistan 55 D4 38 33N 68 48 E
Dusheti, Georgia 53 J7 42 10N 44 42 E
Dusky Sd., N.Z. 119 F1 45 47 S 166 30 E
Dussejour, C., Australia 112 B4 14 45 S 128 13 E
Düsseldorf, Germany 26 D2 51 14N 6 47 E
Dussen, Neths. 20 E5 51 44N 4 59 E
Duszniki-Zdrój, Poland 47 E3 50 24N 16 24 E
Dutch Harbor, U.S.A. 126 C3 53 53N 166 32W
Dutlwe, Botswana 104 C3 23 58 S 23 46 E
Dutsan Wai, Nigeria 101 C6 10 50N 8 10 E
Dutton, Canada 136 D3 42 39N 81 30W
Dutton →, Australia 114 C3 20 44 S 143 10 E
Duved, Sweden 14 A6 63 24N 12 55 E
Duvno, Bos.-H. 42 D2 43 42N 17 13 E
Duyun, China 68 D6 26 18N 107 29 E
Düzce, Turkey 88 B4 40 50N 31 10 E
Duzdab = Zāhedān, Iran 85 D9 29 30N 60 50 E
Dve Mogili, Bulgaria 43 D10 43 35N 25 55 E
Dvina, Severnaya →, Russia 48 B7 64 32N 40 30 E
Dvinsk = Daugavpils, Latvia 13 J22 55 53N 26 32 E
Dvinskaya Guba, Russia 48 B6 65 0N 39 0 E
Dvor, Croatia 39 C13 45 4N 16 22 E
Dvorce, Czech. 31 B10 49 50N 17 34 E
Dvur Králové, Czech. 30 A8 50 27N 15 50 E
Dwarka, India 80 H3 22 18N 69 8 E
Dwellingup, Australia 113 F2 32 43 S 116 4 E
Dwight, Canada 136 A5 45 20N 79 1W
Dwight, U.S.A. 141 C8 41 5N 88 26W
Dyatkovo, Russia 52 D2 53 40N 34 27 E
Dyatlovo = Dzyatlava, Belarus 50 F3 53 28N 25 28 E
Dyer, U.S.A. 141 G10 37 24N 86 13W
Dyer, C., Canada 127 B13 66 40N 61 0W
Dyer Plateau, Antarctica 7 D17 70 45 S 65 30W
Dyerbeldzhin, Kyrgyzstan 55 C7 41 13N 74 54 E
Dyersburg, U.S.A. 139 G10 36 3N 89 23W
Dyersville, U.S.A. 140 B5 42 29N 91 8W
Dyfi →, U.K. 17 E4 52 32N 4 3W
Dyje →, Czech. 31 C9 48 37N 16 56 E
Dyle →, Belgium 21 G5 50 58N 4 41 E
Dymer, Ukraine 51 G6 50 47N 30 18 E
Dynevor Downs, Australia 115 D3 28 10 S 144 20 E
Dynów, Poland 31 B15 49 50N 22 11 E
Dysart, Canada 131 C8 50 57N 104 2W
Dyurtyuli, Russia 54 D5 55 9N 54 40 E
Dzamin Üüd, Mongolia 66 C6 43 50N 111 58 E
Dzerzhinsk, Russia 52 B6 56 14N 43 30 E
Dzhalal-Abad = Jalal-Abad, Kyrgyzstan 55 C6 40 56N 73 0 E
Dzhalinda, Russia 57 D13 53 26N 124 0 E
Dzhambeyty, Kazakstan 54 F4 50 16N 52 35 E
Dzhambul = Zhambyl, Kazakstan 55 B5 42 54N 71 22 E
Dzhambul, Gora = Zhambyl, Gora, Kazakstan 55 A6 44 54N 73 0 E

194 Dzhankoy

Dzhankoy, *Ukraine* **51 K8** 45 40N 34 20 E
Dzhanybek, *Kazakstan* **52 F8** 49 25N 46 50 E
Dzhardzhan, *Russia* **57 C13** 68 10N 124 10 E
Dzharkurgan = Jarqŭrghon, *Uzbekistan* **55 E3** 37 31N 67 25 E
Dzharylhach, Ostriv, *Ukraine* **51 J7** 46 2N 32 55 E
Dzhetygara = Zhetiqara, *Kazakstan* **56 D7** 52 11N 61 12 E
Dzhetym, Khrebet, *Kyrgyzstan* **55 C8** 41 30N 77 0 E
Dzhezkazgan = Zhezqazghan, *Kazakstan* **56 E7** 47 44N 67 40 E
Dzhizak = Jizzakh, *Uzbekistan* **55 C3** 40 6N 67 50 E
Dzhugdzur, Khrebet, *Russia* **57 D14** 57 30N 138 0 E
Dzhuma, *Uzbekistan* **55 D3** 39 42N 66 40 E
Dzhumgoltau, Khrebet, *Kyrgyzstan* **55 B7** 42 15N 74 30 E
Dzhungarskiye Vorota, *Kazakstan* **64 B3** 45 0N 82 0 E
Dzhvari = Jvari, *Georgia* **53 J6** 42 42N 42 4 E
Działdowa, *Poland* **47 B7** 53 15N 20 15 E
Działoszyce, *Poland* **47 E7** 50 22N 20 20 E
Działoszyn, *Poland* **47 D5** 51 6N 18 50 E
Dzierzgoń, *Poland* **47 B6** 53 58N 19 20 E
Dzierzoniów, *Poland* **47 E3** 50 45N 16 39 E
Dzilam de Bravo, *Mexico* **147 C7** 21 24N 88 53W
Dzioua, *Algeria* **99 B6** 33 14N 5 14 E
Dzisna, *Belarus* **50 E5** 55 34N 28 12 E
Dzisna →, *Belarus* **50 E5** 55 34N 28 12 E
Dziwnów, *Poland* **47 A1** 54 2N 14 45 E
Dzungaria = Junggar Pendi, *China* **64 B3** 44 30N 86 0 E
Dzungarian Gates = Dzhungarskiye Vorota, *Kazakstan* **64 B3** 45 0N 82 0 E
Dzuumod, *Mongolia* **64 B5** 47 45N 106 58 E
Dzyarzhynsk, *Belarus* **50 F4** 53 40N 27 1 E
Dzyatlava, *Belarus* **50 F3** 53 28N 25 28 E

E

Eabamet, L., *Canada* **128 B2** 51 30N 87 46W
Eads, *U.S.A.* **138 F3** 38 29N 102 47W
Eagle, *U.S.A.* **142 G10** 39 39N 106 50W
Eagle →, *Canada* **129 B8** 53 36N 57 26W
Eagle Butte, *U.S.A.* **138 C4** 45 0N 101 10W
Eagle Cr. →, *U.S.A.* **141 F11** 38 36N 85 4W
Eagle Grove, *U.S.A.* **140 B3** 42 40N 93 54W
Eagle L., *Calif., U.S.A.* **142 F3** 40 39N 120 45W
Eagle L., *Maine, U.S.A.* **129 C6** 46 20N 69 22W
Eagle Lake, *U.S.A.* **139 L6** 29 35N 96 20W
Eagle Mountain, *U.S.A.* **145 M11** 33 49N 115 27W
Eagle Nest, *U.S.A.* **143 H11** 36 33N 105 16W
Eagle Pass, *U.S.A.* **139 L4** 28 43N 100 30W
Eagle Pk., *U.S.A.* **144 G7** 38 10N 119 25W
Eagle Pt., *Australia* **112 C3** 16 11 S 124 23 E
Eagle River, *U.S.A.* **138 C10** 45 55N 89 15W
Eagleville, *U.S.A.* **140 D3** 40 28N 93 59W
Ealing, *U.K.* **17 F7** 51 31N 0 20W
Earaheedy, *Australia* **113 E3** 25 34 S 121 29 E
Earl Grey, *Canada* **131 C8** 50 57N 104 43W
Earle, *U.S.A.* **139 H9** 35 16N 90 28W
Earlimart, *U.S.A.* **145 K7** 35 53N 119 16W
Earlville, *U.S.A.* **141 C8** 41 35N 88 55W
Earn →, *U.K.* **18 E5** 56 21N 3 18W
Earn, L., *U.K.* **18 E4** 56 23N 4 13W
Earnslaw, Mt., *N.Z.* **119 E3** 44 32 S 168 27 E
Earth, *U.S.A.* **139 H3** 34 14N 102 24W
Easley, *U.S.A.* **135 H4** 34 50N 82 36W
East Angus, *Canada* **129 C5** 45 30N 71 40W
East Aurora, *U.S.A.* **136 D6** 42 46N 78 37W
East Ayrshire □, *U.K.* **18 F4** 55 26N 4 11W
East B., *U.S.A.* **139 L10** 29 0N 89 15W
East Beskids = Vychodné Beskydy, *Europe* **51 H2** 49 20N 22 0 E
East Brady, *U.S.A.* **136 F5** 40 59N 79 36W
East C., *N.Z.* **118 D7** 37 42 S 178 35 E
East C., *Papua N. G.* **120 F6** 10 13 S 150 53 E
East Chicago, *U.S.A.* **141 C9** 41 38N 87 27W
East China Sea, *Asia* **65 C7** 30 5N 126 0 E
East Coast Bays, *N.Z.* **118 C3** 36 46 S 174 46 E
East Coulee, *Canada* **130 C6** 51 23N 112 27W
East Dubuque, *U.S.A.* **140 B6** 42 30N 90 39W
East Dunbartonshire □, *U.K.* **18 F4** 55 57N 4 13W
East Falkland, *Falk. Is.* **160 D5** 51 30 S 58 30W
East Grand Forks, *U.S.A.* **138 B6** 47 56N 97 1W
East Greenwich, *U.S.A.* **137 E13** 41 40N 71 27W
East Hartford, *U.S.A.* **137 E12** 41 46N 72 39W
East Helena, *U.S.A.* **142 C8** 46 35N 111 56W
East Indies, *Asia* **58 K15** 0 0 120 0 E
East Jordan, *U.S.A.* **134 C3** 45 10N 85 7W
East Lansing, *U.S.A.* **141 B12** 42 44N 84 29W
East Liverpool, *U.S.A.* **136 F4** 40 37N 80 35W
East London, *S. Africa* **105 E4** 33 0 S 27 55 E
East Lothian □, *U.K.* **18 F6** 55 58N 2 44W
East Lynne, *Australia* **117 C9** 35 35 S 150 16 E
East Main = Eastmain, *Canada* **128 B4** 52 10N 78 30W
East Moline, *U.S.A.* **140 C6** 41 32N 90 26W
East Orange, *U.S.A.* **137 F10** 40 46N 74 13W
East Pacific Ridge, *Pac. Oc.* **123 J17** 15 0 S 110 0W
East Palestine, *U.S.A.* **136 F4** 40 50N 80 33W
East Peoria, *U.S.A.* **140 D7** 40 40N 89 34W
East Pine, *Canada* **130 B4** 55 48N 120 12W
East Point, *U.S.A.* **135 J3** 33 41N 84 27W
East Providence, *U.S.A.* **137 E13** 41 49N 71 23W
East Pt., *Canada* **129 C7** 46 27N 61 58W
East Renfrewshire □, *U.K.* **18 F4** 55 46N 4 21W
East Retford = Retford, *U.K.* **16 D7** 53 19N 0 56W
East Riding □, *U.K.* **16 D7** 53 55N 0 30W
East St. Louis, *U.S.A.* **140 F6** 38 37N 90 9W
East Schelde → = Oosterschelde, *Neths.* **21 E4** 51 33N 4 0 E
East Siberian Sea, *Russia* **57 B17** 73 0N 160 0 E
East Stroudsburg, *U.S.A.* **137 E9** 41 1N 75 11W
East Sussex □, *U.K.* **17 G8** 50 56N 0 19 E
East Tawas, *U.S.A.* **134 C4** 44 17N 83 29W
East Toorale, *Australia* **115 E4** 30 27 S 145 28 E
East Troy, *U.S.A.* **141 B8** 42 47N 88 24W
East Walker →, *U.S.A.* **144 G7** 38 52N 119 10W
Eastbourne, *N.Z.* **118 H3** 41 19 S 174 55 E
Eastbourne, *U.K.* **17 G8** 50 46N 0 18 E
Eastend, *Canada* **131 D7** 49 32N 108 50W
Easter Islands = Pascua, I. de, *Pac. Oc.* **123 K17** 27 0 S 109 0W
Eastern □, *Kenya* **106 B4** 0 0 38 30 E
Eastern □, *Uganda* **106 B3** 1 50N 33 45 E
Eastern Cape □, *S. Africa* **104 E4** 32 0 S 26 0 E
Eastern Cr. →, *Australia* **114 C3** 20 40 S 141 35 E
Eastern Ghats, *India* **83 J4** 14 0N 78 50 E
Eastern Group = Lau Group, *Fiji* **121 A3** 17 0 S 178 30W
Eastern Group, *Australia* **113 F3** 33 30 S 124 30 E
Eastern Province □, *S. Leone* **100 D2** 8 15N 11 0W
Eastern Samar □, *Phil.* **71 F5** 11 40N 125 40 E
Eastern Transvaal = Mpumalanga □, *S. Africa* **105 B5** 26 0 S 30 0 E
Easterville, *Canada* **131 C9** 53 8N 99 49W
Easthampton, *U.S.A.* **137 D12** 42 16N 72 40W
Eastland, *U.S.A.* **139 J5** 32 24N 98 49W
Eastleigh, *U.K.* **17 G6** 50 58N 1 21W
Eastmain, *Canada* **128 B4** 52 10N 78 30W
Eastmain →, *Canada* **128 B4** 52 27N 78 26W
Eastman, *Canada* **137 A12** 45 18N 72 19W
Eastman, *Ga., U.S.A.* **135 J4** 32 12N 83 11W
Eastman, *Wis., U.S.A.* **140 A5** 43 10N 91 1W
Easton, *Md., U.S.A.* **134 F7** 38 47N 76 5W
Easton, *Pa., U.S.A.* **137 F9** 40 41N 75 13W
Easton, *Wash., U.S.A.* **144 C5** 47 14N 121 11W
Eastport, *U.S.A.* **129 D6** 44 56N 67 0W
Eastsound, *U.S.A.* **144 B4** 48 42N 122 55W
Eaton, *Colo., U.S.A.* **138 E2** 40 32N 104 42W
Eaton, *Ohio, U.S.A.* **141 E12** 39 45N 84 38W
Eaton Rapids, *U.S.A.* **141 B12** 42 31N 84 39W
Eatonia, *Canada* **131 C7** 51 13N 109 25W
Eatonton, *U.S.A.* **135 J4** 33 20N 83 23W
Eatontown, *U.S.A.* **137 F10** 40 19N 74 4W
Eatonville, *U.S.A.* **144 D4** 46 52N 122 16W
Eau Claire, *Fr. Guiana* **153 C7** 3 30N 53 40W
Eau Claire, *U.S.A.* **138 C9** 44 49N 91 30W
Eauze, *France* **24 E4** 43 53N 0 7 E
Ebagoola, *Australia* **114 A3** 14 15 S 143 12 E
Eban, *Nigeria* **101 D5** 9 40N 4 50 E
Ebangalakata, *Zaïre* **102 C4** 0 29 S 21 29 E
Ebbw Vale, *U.K.* **17 F4** 51 46N 3 12W
Ebebiyín, *Eq. Guin.* **102 B2** 2 9N 11 20 E
Ebeggui, *Algeria* **99 C6** 26 2N 6 0 E
Ebel, *Gabon* **102 B2** 0 7N 11 5 E
Ebeltoft, *Denmark* **13 H14** 56 12N 10 41 E
Ebensburg, *U.S.A.* **136 F6** 40 29N 78 44W
Ebensee, *Austria* **30 D6** 47 48N 13 46 E
Eber Gölü, *Turkey* **88 C4** 38 38N 31 11 E
Eberbach, *Germany* **27 F4** 49 28N 8 59 E
Eberswalde-Finow, *Germany* **26 C9** 52 50N 13 49 E
Ebetsu, *Japan* **60 C10** 43 7N 141 34 E
Ebian, *China* **68 C4** 29 11N 103 13 E
Ebikon, *Switz.* **29 B6** 47 5N 8 21 E
Ebingen, *Germany* **27 G5** 48 13N 9 1 E
Ebino, *Japan* **62 E2** 32 2N 130 48 E
Ebnat-Kappel, *Switz.* **29 B8** 47 16N 9 7 E
Eboli, *Italy* **41 B8** 40 39N 15 2 E
Ebolowa, *Cameroon* **101 E7** 2 55N 11 10 E
Ebrach, *Germany* **27 F6** 49 51N 10 29 E
Ébrié, Lagune, *Ivory C.* **100 D4** 5 12N 4 26W
Ebro →, *Spain* **34 E5** 40 43N 0 54 E
Ebro, Pantano del, *Spain* **36 B7** 43 0N 3 58W
Ebstorf, *Germany* **26 B6** 53 2N 10 24 E
Ecaussines-d' Enghien, *Belgium* **21 G4** 50 35N 4 11 E
Eceabat, *Turkey* **88 B2** 40 11N 26 21 E
Ech Cheliff, *Algeria* **99 A5** 36 10N 1 20 E
Echallens, *Switz.* **28 C3** 46 38N 6 38 E
Echeng, *China* **69 B10** 30 23N 114 50 E
Echigo-Sammyaku, *Japan* **61 F9** 36 50N 139 50 E
Echizen-Misaki, *Japan* **63 B7** 35 59N 135 57 E
Echmiadzin = Yejmiadzin, *Armenia* **53 K7** 40 12N 44 19 E
Echo Bay, *N.W.T., Canada* **126 B8** 66 5N 117 55W
Echo Bay, *Ont., Canada* **128 C3** 46 29N 84 4W
Echoing →, *Canada* **131 B10** 55 51N 92 5W
Echt, *Neths.* **21 F7** 51 7N 5 52 E
Echternach, *Lux.* **21 J8** 49 49N 6 25 E
Echuca, *Australia* **117 D6** 36 10 S 144 20 E
Ecija, *Spain* **37 H5** 37 30N 5 10W
Eckernförde, *Germany* **26 A5** 54 28N 9 50 E
Eclipse Is., *Australia* **112 B4** 13 54 S 126 19 E
Écommoy, *France* **22 E7** 47 50N 0 17 E
Ecoporanga, *Brazil* **155 E3** 18 23 S 40 50W
Écos, *France* **23 C8** 49 9N 1 35 E
Écouché, *France* **22 D6** 48 42N 0 10W
Ecuador ■, *S. Amer.* **152 D2** 2 0 S 78 0W
Écueillé, *France* **22 E8** 47 5N 1 21 E
Ed, *Sweden* **15 F5** 58 55N 11 55 E
Ed Dabbura, *Sudan* **94 D3** 17 40N 34 15 E
Ed Dâmer, *Sudan* **94 D3** 17 27N 34 0 E
Ed Debba, *Sudan* **94 D3** 18 0N 30 51 E
Ed-Déffa, *Egypt* **94 A2** 30 40N 26 30 E
Ed Deim, *Sudan* **95 E2** 10 10N 28 20 E
Ed Dueim, *Sudan* **95 E3** 14 0N 32 10 E
Edah, *Australia* **113 E2** 28 16 S 117 10 E
Edam, *Canada* **131 C7** 53 11N 108 46W
Edam, *Neths.* **20 C6** 52 31N 5 3 E
Edapally, *India* **83 J4** 11 19N 78 3 E
Eday, *U.K.* **18 B6** 59 11N 2 47W
Edd, *Eritrea* **90 E3** 14 0N 41 38 E
Eddrachillis B., *U.K.* **18 C3** 58 17N 5 14W
Eddystone, *U.K.* **17 G3** 50 11N 4 16W
Eddystone Pt., *Australia* **114 G4** 40 59 S 148 20 E
Eddyville, *U.S.A.* **140 C4** 41 9N 92 38W
Ede, *Neths.* **20 D7** 52 4N 5 40 E
Ede, *Nigeria* **101 D5** 7 45N 4 29 E
Édea, *Cameroon* **101 E7** 3 51N 10 9 E
Edegem, *Belgium* **21 F4** 51 10N 4 27 E
Edehon L., *Canada* **131 A9** 60 25N 97 15W
Edekel, Adrar, *Algeria* **99 D6** 23 56N 6 47 E
Eden, *Australia* **117 D8** 37 3 S 149 55 E
Eden, *N.C., U.S.A.* **135 G6** 36 29N 79 53W
Eden, *N.Y., U.S.A.* **136 D6** 42 39N 78 55W
Eden, *Tex., U.S.A.* **139 K5** 31 13N 99 51W
Eden, *Wyo., U.S.A.* **142 E9** 42 3N 109 26W
Eden →, *U.K.* **16 C4** 54 57N 3 1W
Eden L., *Canada* **131 B8** 56 38N 100 15W
Edenburg, *S. Africa* **104 D4** 29 43 S 25 58 E
Edendale, *N.Z.* **119 G3** 46 19 S 168 48 E
Edendale, *S. Africa* **105 D5** 29 39 S 30 18 E
Edenderry, *Ireland* **19 C4** 53 21N 7 4W
Edenton, *U.S.A.* **135 G7** 36 4N 76 39W
Edenville, *S. Africa* **105 D4** 27 37 S 27 34 E
Eder →, *Germany* **26 D5** 51 12N 9 28 E
Eder-Stausee, *Germany* **26 D4** 51 10N 8 57 E
Edgar, *U.S.A.* **138 E5** 40 22N 97 58W
Edgartown, *U.S.A.* **137 E14** 41 23N 70 31W
Edge Hill, *U.K.* **17 E6** 52 8N 1 26W
Edgecumbe, *N.Z.* **118 D5** 37 59 S 176 47 E
Edgefield, *U.S.A.* **135 J5** 33 47N 81 56W
Edgeley, *U.S.A.* **138 B5** 46 22N 98 43W
Edgemont, *U.S.A.* **138 D3** 43 18N 103 50W
Edgeøya, *Svalbard* **6 B9** 77 45N 22 30 E
Edgerton, *Ohio, U.S.A.* **141 C12** 41 27N 84 45W
Edgerton, *Wis., U.S.A.* **140 B7** 42 50N 89 4W
Edgewood, *U.S.A.* **141 F8** 38 55N 88 40W
Édhessa, *Greece* **44 D4** 40 48N 22 5 E
Edievale, *N.Z.* **119 F4** 45 49 S 169 22 E
Edina, *Liberia* **100 D2** 6 0N 10 10W
Edina, *U.S.A.* **140 D4** 40 10N 92 11W
Edinburg, *Ill., U.S.A.* **140 E7** 39 39N 89 23W
Edinburg, *Ind., U.S.A.* **141 E11** 39 21N 85 58W
Edinburg, *Tex., U.S.A.* **139 M5** 26 18N 98 10W
Edinburgh, *U.K.* **18 F5** 55 57N 3 13W
Ediniţa, *Moldova* **51 H4** 48 9N 27 18 E
Edirne, *Turkey* **88 B2** 41 40N 26 34 E
Edison, *U.S.A.* **144 B4** 48 33N 122 27W
Edithburgh, *Australia* **116 C2** 35 5 S 137 43 E
Edjeleh, *Algeria* **99 C6** 28 38N 9 50 E
Edjudina, *Australia* **113 E3** 29 48 S 122 23 E
Edmeston, *U.S.A.* **137 D9** 42 42N 75 15W
Edmond, *U.S.A.* **139 H6** 35 39N 97 29W
Edmonds, *U.S.A.* **144 C4** 47 49N 122 23W
Edmonton, *Australia* **114 B4** 17 2 S 145 46 E
Edmonton, *Canada* **130 C6** 53 30N 113 30W
Edmund L., *Canada* **131 C10** 54 45N 93 17W
Edmundston, *Canada* **129 C6** 47 23N 68 20W
Edna, *U.S.A.* **139 L6** 28 59N 96 39W
Edna Bay, *U.S.A.* **130 B2** 55 55N 133 40W
Edo □, *Nigeria* **101 D6** 6 30N 6 0 E
Edolo, *Italy* **38 B7** 46 10N 10 21 E
Edremit, *Turkey* **88 C2** 39 34N 27 0 E
Edremit Körfezi, *Turkey* **88 C2** 39 30N 26 45 E
Edsbyn, *Sweden* **14 C9** 61 23N 15 49 E
Edsele, *Sweden* **14 A10** 63 25N 16 32 E
Edson, *Canada* **130 C5** 53 35N 116 28W
Eduardo Castex, *Argentina* **158 D3** 35 50 S 64 18W
Edward →, *Australia* **116 C5** 35 5 S 143 30 E
Edward, L., *Africa* **106 C2** 0 25 S 29 40 E
Edward I., *Canada* **128 C2** 48 22N 88 37W
Edward River, *Australia* **114 A3** 14 59 S 141 26 E
Edward VII Land, *Antarctica* **7 E13** 80 0 S 150 0W
Edwards, *U.S.A.* **145 L9** 34 55N 117 51W
Edwards →, *U.S.A.* **140 C6** 41 9N 90 59W
Edwards Plateau, *U.S.A.* **139 K4** 30 45N 101 20W
Edwardsburg, *U.S.A.* **141 C10** 41 48N 86 6W
Edwardsport, *U.S.A.* **141 F9** 38 49N 87 15W
Edwardsville, *Ill., U.S.A.* **140 F7** 38 49N 89 58W
Edwardsville, *Pa., U.S.A.* **137 E9** 41 15N 75 56W
Edzo, *Canada* **130 A5** 62 49N 116 4W
Eefde, *Neths.* **20 D8** 52 10N 6 13 E
Eekloo, *Belgium* **21 F3** 51 11N 3 33 E
Eel →, *Ind., U.S.A.* **141 E10** 39 7N 86 57W
Eel →, *Ind., U.S.A.* **141 D10** 40 45N 86 22W
Eelde, *Neths.* **20 B9** 53 8N 6 34 E
Eem →, *Neths.* **20 D6** 52 16N 5 20 E
Eems →, *Neths.* **20 B9** 53 26N 6 57 E
Eems Kanaal, *Neths.* **20 B9** 53 18N 6 46 E
Eenrum, *Neths.* **20 B8** 53 22N 6 28 E
Eernegem, *Belgium* **21 F2** 51 8N 3 2 E
Eerste Valthermond, *Neths.* **20 C9** 52 53N 6 58 E
Efate, I., *Vanuatu* **121 G6** 17 40 S 168 25 E
Eferding, *Austria* **30 C7** 48 18N 14 1 E
Eferi, *Algeria* **99 D6** 24 30N 9 28 E
Effingham, *U.S.A.* **141 E8** 39 7N 88 33W
Effretikon, *Switz.* **29 B7** 47 25N 8 42 E
Eforie Sud, *Romania* **46 E9** 44 1N 28 37 E
Ega →, *Spain* **34 C3** 42 19N 1 55W
Égadi, Ísole, *Italy* **40 E5** 37 55N 12 16 E
Eganville, *Canada* **128 C4** 45 32N 77 5W
Egeland, *U.S.A.* **138 A5** 48 38N 99 6W
Egenolf L., *Canada* **131 B9** 59 3N 100 0W
Eger = Cheb, *Czech.* **30 A5** 50 9N 12 28 E
Eger, *Hungary* **31 D13** 47 53N 20 27 E
Eger →, *Hungary* **31 D13** 47 38N 20 50 E
Egersund, *Norway* **13 G12** 58 26N 6 1 E
Egg L., *Canada* **131 B7** 55 5N 105 30W
Eggenburg, *Austria* **30 C8** 48 38N 15 50 E
Eggenfelden, *Germany* **27 G8** 48 23N 12 46 E
Eggiwil, *Switz.* **28 C5** 46 52N 7 47 E
Egherta, *Somali Rep.* **108 D2** 2 4N 43 11 E
Éghezée, *Belgium* **21 G5** 50 35N 4 55 E
Eginbah, *Australia* **112 D2** 20 53 S 119 47 E
Egito, *Angola* **103 E2** 12 4 S 13 58 E
Égletons, *France* **24 C6** 45 24N 2 3 E
Eglisau, *Switz.* **29 A7** 47 35N 8 31 E
Egmond-aan-Zee, *Neths.* **20 C5** 52 37N 4 38 E
Egmont, C., *N.Z.* **118 F2** 39 16 S 173 45 E
Egmont, Mt., *N.Z.* **118 F3** 39 17 S 174 5 E
Eğridir, *Turkey* **88 D4** 37 52N 30 51 E
Eğridir Gölü, *Turkey* **88 D4** 37 53N 30 50 E
Egtved, *Denmark* **15 J3** 55 38N 9 18 E
Éguas →, *Brazil* **155 D3** 13 26 S 44 14W
Egume, *Nigeria* **101 D6** 7 30N 7 14 E
Éguzon, *France* **24 B5** 46 27N 1 33 E
Egvekinot, *Russia* **57 C19** 66 19N 179 50W
Egyek, *Hungary* **31 D13** 47 39N 20 52 E
Egypt ■, *Africa* **94 J7** 28 0N 31 0 E
Eha Amufu, *Nigeria* **101 D6** 6 30N 7 46 E
Ehime □, *Japan* **62 D4** 33 30N 132 40 E
Ehingen, *Germany* **27 G5** 48 16N 9 43 E
Ehrenberg, *U.S.A.* **145 M12** 33 36N 114 31W
Ehrwald, *Austria* **30 D3** 47 24N 10 56 E
Eibar, *Spain* **34 B2** 43 11N 2 28W
Eibergen, *Neths.* **20 D9** 52 6N 6 39 E
Eichstätt, *Germany* **27 G7** 48 54N 11 11 E
Eider →, *Germany* **26 A4** 54 19N 8 57 E
Eidsvold, *Australia* **115 D5** 25 25 S 151 12 E
Eidsvoll, *Norway* **13 F14** 60 19N 11 14 E
Eifel, *Germany* **27 E2** 50 15N 6 50 E
Eiffel Flats, *Zimbabwe* **107 F3** 18 20 S 30 0 E
Eigg, *U.K.* **18 E2** 56 54N 6 10W
Eighty Mile Beach, *Australia* **112 C3** 19 30 S 120 40 E
Eil, *Somali Rep.* **108 C3** 8 0N 49 50 E
Eil, L., *U.K.* **18 E3** 56 51N 5 16W
Eildon, *Australia* **117 D6** 37 14 S 145 55 E
Eildon, L., *Australia* **115 F4** 37 10 S 146 0 E
Eileen L., *Canada* **131 A7** 62 16N 107 37W
Eilenburg, *Germany* **26 D8** 51 27N 12 36 E
Ein el Luweiqa, *Sudan* **95 E3** 14 5N 33 50 E
Einasleigh, *Australia* **114 B3** 18 32 S 144 5 E
Einasleigh →, *Australia* **114 B3** 17 30 S 142 17 E
Einbeck, *Germany* **26 D5** 51 49N 9 53 E
Eindhoven, *Neths.* **21 F6** 51 26N 5 28 E
Einsiedeln, *Switz.* **29 B7** 47 7N 8 46 E
Eire = Ireland ■, *Europe* **19 D4** 53 50N 7 52W
Eiríksjökull, *Iceland* **12 D3** 64 46N 20 24W
Eirlandsche Gat, *Neths.* **20 B5** 53 12N 4 54 E
Eirunepé, *Brazil* **156 B4** 6 35 S 69 53W
Eisden, *Belgium* **21 G7** 50 59N 5 42 E
Eisenach, *Germany* **26 E6** 50 58N 10 19 E
Eisenberg, *Germany* **26 E7** 50 58N 11 54 E
Eisenerz, *Austria* **30 D7** 47 32N 14 54 E
Eisenhüttenstadt, *Germany* **26 C10** 52 9N 14 38 E
Eisenkappel, *Austria* **30 E7** 46 29N 14 36 E
Eisenstadt, *Austria* **31 D9** 47 51N 16 31 E
Eiserfeld, *Germany* **26 E3** 50 49N 7 59 E
Eisfeld, *Germany* **26 E6** 50 25N 10 54 E
Eisleben, *Germany* **26 D7** 51 32N 11 32 E
Eivissa = Ibiza, *Spain* **33 C7** 38 54N 1 26 E
Ejby, *Denmark* **15 J3** 55 25N 9 56 E
Eje, Sierra del, *Spain* **36 C4** 42 24N 6 54W
Ejea de los Caballeros, *Spain* **34 C3** 42 7N 1 9W
Ejutla, *Mexico* **147 D5** 16 34N 96 44W
Ekalaka, *U.S.A.* **138 C2** 45 53N 104 33W
Ekalla, *Gabon* **102 C2** 1 27 S 14 0 E
Ekanga, *Zaïre* **102 C4** 2 23 S 23 14 E
Ekawasaki, *Japan* **62 D4** 33 13N 132 46 E
Ekeren, *Belgium* **21 F4** 51 17N 4 25 E
Eket, *Nigeria* **101 E6** 4 38N 7 56 E
Eketahuna, *N.Z.* **118 G4** 40 38 S 175 43 E
Ekhínos, *Greece* **44 C7** 41 16N 25 1 E
Ekibastuz, *Kazakstan* **56 D8** 51 50N 75 10 E
Ekimchan, *Russia* **57 D14** 53 0N 133 0 E
Ekoli, *Zaïre* **102 C4** 0 23 S 24 13 E
Eksel, *Belgium* **21 F6** 51 9N 5 24 E
Eksjö, *Sweden* **13 H16** 57 40N 14 58 E
Ekwan →, *Canada* **128 B3** 53 12N 82 15W
Ekwan Pt., *Canada* **128 B3** 53 16N 82 7W
El Aaiún, *W. Sahara* **98 C2** 27 9N 13 12W
El Aargub, *Mauritania* **98 D1** 23 37N 15 52W
El Abiodh-Sidi-Cheikh, *Algeria* **99 B5** 32 53N 0 31 E
El Adde, *Somali Rep.* **108 D3** 2 35N 46 9 E
El 'Agrûd, *Egypt* **91 E3** 30 14N 34 24 E
El Aïoun, *Morocco* **99 B4** 34 33N 2 30W
El 'Aiyat, *Egypt* **94 J7** 29 36N 31 15 E
El Alamein, *Egypt* **94 H6** 30 48N 28 58 E
El Alto, *Peru* **156 A1** 4 15 S 81 14W
El 'Aqaba, W. →, *Egypt* **91 E2** 30 7N 33 54 E
El 'Arag, *Egypt* **94 B2** 28 40N 26 20 E
El Arahal, *Spain* **37 H5** 37 15N 5 33W
El Arenal, *Spain* **33 B9** 39 30N 2 45 E
El Aricha, *Algeria* **99 B4** 34 13N 1 10W
El Arīhā, *West Bank* **91 D4** 31 52N 35 27 E
El Arish, *Australia* **114 B4** 17 35 S 146 1 E
El 'Arîsh, *Egypt* **91 D2** 31 8N 33 50 E
El 'Arîsh, W. →, *Egypt* **91 D2** 31 8N 33 47 E
El Arrouch, *Algeria* **99 A6** 36 37N 6 53 E
El Asnam = Ech Cheliff, *Algeria* **99 A5** 36 10N 1 20 E
El Astillero, *Spain* **36 B7** 43 24N 3 49W
El Badâri, *Egypt* **94 B3** 27 4N 31 25 E
El Bahrein, *Egypt* **94 B2** 28 30N 26 25 E
El Ballâs, *Egypt* **94 B3** 26 2N 32 43 E
El Balyana, *Egypt* **94 B3** 26 10N 32 3 E
El Banco, *Colombia* **152 B3** 9 0N 73 58W
El Baqeir, *Sudan* **94 D3** 18 40N 33 40 E
El Barco de Ávila, *Spain* **36 E5** 40 21N 5 31W
El Barco de Valdeorras, *Spain* **36 C4** 42 23N 6 58W
El Bauga, *Sudan* **94 D3** 18 18N 33 52 E
El Baúl, *Venezuela* **152 B4** 8 57N 68 17W
El Bawiti, *Egypt* **94 J6** 28 25N 28 45 E
El Bayadh, *Algeria* **99 B5** 33 40N 1 1 E
El Bierzo, *Spain* **36 C4** 42 45N 6 30W
El Bluff, *Nic.* **148 D3** 11 59N 83 40W
El Bolsón, *Argentina* **160 B2** 41 55 S 71 30W
El Bonillo, *Spain* **35 G2** 38 57N 2 35W
El Brûk, W. →, *Egypt* **91 E2** 30 15N 33 50 E
El Buheirat □, *Sudan* **95 F2** 7 0N 30 0 E
El Bur, *Somali Rep.* **108 D3** 4 40N 46 37 E
El Caín, *Argentina* **160 B3** 41 38 S 68 19W
El Cajon, *U.S.A.* **145 N10** 32 48N 116 58W
El Callao, *Venezuela* **153 B5** 7 18N 61 50W
El Camp, *Spain* **34 D6** 41 5N 1 10 E
El Campo, *U.S.A.* **139 L6** 29 12N 96 16W
El Carmen, *Bolivia* **157 C5** 13 40 S 63 55W
El Carmen, *Venezuela* **152 C4** 1 16N 66 52W
El Castillo, *Spain* **37 H4** 37 41N 6 19W
El Centro, *U.S.A.* **145 N11** 32 48N 115 34W
El Cerro, *Bolivia* **157 D5** 17 30 S 61 40W
El Cerro, *Spain* **37 H4** 37 45N 6 57W
El Cocuy, *Colombia* **152 B3** 6 25N 72 27W
El Compadre, *Mexico* **145 N10** 32 20N 116 14W
El Corcovado, *Argentina* **160 B2** 43 25 S 71 35W
El Coronil, *Spain* **37 H5** 37 5N 5 38W
El Cuy, *Argentina* **160 A3** 39 55 S 68 25W
El Cuyo, *Mexico* **147 C7** 21 30N 87 40W
El Dab'a, *Egypt* **94 H6** 31 0N 28 27 E
El Daheir, *Egypt* **91 D3** 31 13N 34 10 E
El Dambahaddo, *Somali Rep.* **108 D3** 3 17N 46 40 E
El Deir, *Egypt* **94 B3** 25 25N 32 20 E
El Dere, *Ethiopia* **108 C2** 5 6N 43 5 E
El Dere, *Somali Rep.* **108 D3** 3 50N 47 8 E
El Dere, *Somali Rep.* **108 C3** 5 22N 46 11 E
El Descanso, *Mexico* **145 N10** 32 12N 116 58W
El Desemboque, *Mexico* **146 A2** 30 30N 112 57W
El Dilingat, *Egypt* **94 H7** 30 50N 30 31 E
El Diviso, *Colombia* **152 C2** 1 22N 78 14W
El Djem, *Tunisia* **96 A2** 35 18N 10 42 E
El Djouf, *Mauritania* **92 D3** 20 0N 9 0W
El Dorado, *Ark., U.S.A.* **139 J8** 33 12N 92 40W

English Bazar 195

El Dorado, *Kans., U.S.A.* **139 G6** 37 49N 96 52W
El Dorado, *Venezuela* **153 B5** 6 55N 61 37W
El Eglab, *Algeria* **98 C4** 26 20N 4 30W
El Escorial, *Spain* **36 E6** 40 35N 4 7W
El Eulma, *Algeria* **99 A6** 36 9N 5 42 E
El Faiyûm, *Egypt* **94 J7** 29 19N 30 50 E
El Fâsher, *Sudan* **95 E2** 13 33N 25 26 E
El Fashn, *Egypt* **94 J7** 28 50N 30 54 E
El Ferrol, *Spain* **36 B2** 43 29N 8 15W
El Fifi, *Sudan* **95 E1** 10 4N 25 0 E
El Fud, *Ethiopia* **108 C2** 7 15N 42 52 E
El Fuerte, *Mexico* **146 B3** 26 30N 108 40W
El Gal, *Somali Rep.* **108 B4** 10 58N 50 20 E
El Gebir, *Sudan* **95 E2** 13 40N 29 40 E
El Gedida, *Egypt* **94 B2** 25 40N 28 30 E
El Geneina = Al Junaynah, *Sudan* **97 F4** 13 27N 22 45 E
El Geteina, *Sudan* **95 E3** 14 50N 32 27 E
El Gezira □, *Sudan* **95 E3** 15 0N 33 0 E
El Gîza, *Egypt* **94 H7** 30 0N 31 10 E
El Goléa, *Algeria* **99 B5** 30 30N 2 50 E
El Hadeb, *W. Sahara* **98 C2** 25 51N 13 0W
El Hadjira, *Algeria* **99 B6** 32 36N 5 30 E
El Hagiz, *Sudan* **95 D4** 15 15N 35 50 E
El Hajeb, *Morocco* **98 B3** 33 43N 5 13W
El Hammam, *Egypt* **94 H6** 30 52N 29 25 E
El Hammâmi, *Mauritania* **98 D2** 23 3N 11 30W
El Hamurre, *Somali Rep.* **108 C3** 7 13N 48 54 E
El Hank, *Mauritania* **98 D3** 24 30N 7 0W
El Hasian, *W. Sahara* **98 C2** 26 20N 14 0W
El Hawata, *Sudan* **95 E3** 13 25N 34 42 E
El Heiz, *Egypt* **94 B2** 27 50N 28 40 E
El 'Idisât, *Egypt* **94 B3** 25 30N 32 35 E
El Iskandarîya, *Egypt* **94 H6** 31 13N 29 58 E
El Jadida, *Morocco* **98 B3** 33 11N 8 17W
El Jebelein, *Sudan* **95 E3** 12 40N 32 55 E
El Kab, *Sudan* **94 D3** 19 27N 32 46 E
El Kabrît, G., *Egypt* **91 F2** 29 42N 33 16 E
El Kala, *Algeria* **99 A6** 36 50N 8 30 E
El Kalâa, *Morocco* **98 B3** 32 4N 7 27W
El Kamlin, *Sudan* **95 D3** 15 3N 33 11 E
El Kantara, *Algeria* **99 A6** 35 14N 5 45 E
El Kantara, *Tunisia* **96 B2** 33 45N 10 58 E
El Karaba, *Sudan* **94 D3** 18 32N 33 41 E
El Kef, *Tunisia* **96 A1** 36 12N 8 47 E
El Khandaq, *Sudan* **94 D3** 18 30N 30 30 E
El Khârga, *Egypt* **94 B3** 25 30N 30 33 E
El Khartûm, *Sudan* **95 D3** 15 31N 32 35 E
El Khartûm □, *Sudan* **95 D3** 16 0N 33 0 E
El Khartûm Bahrî, *Sudan* **95 D3** 15 40N 32 31 E
El Khroub, *Algeria* **99 A6** 36 10N 6 55 E
El Kseur, *Algeria* **99 A5** 36 46N 4 49 E
El Ksiba, *Morocco* **98 B3** 32 45N 6 1W
El Kuntilla, *Egypt* **91 E3** 30 1N 34 45 E
El Laqâwa, *Sudan* **95 E2** 11 25N 29 1 E
El Laqeita, *Egypt* **94 B3** 25 50N 33 15 E
El Leiya, *Sudan* **95 D4** 16 15N 35 28 E
El Mafâza, *Sudan* **95 E3** 13 38N 34 30 E
El Mahalla el Kubra, *Egypt* **94 H7** 31 0N 31 0 E
El Mahârîq, *Egypt* **94 B3** 25 35N 30 35 E
El Mahmûdîya, *Egypt* **94 H7** 31 10N 30 32 E
El Maitén, *Argentina* **160 B2** 42 3 S 71 10W
El Maiz, *Algeria* **99 C4** 28 19N 0 9W
El-Maks el-Bahari, *Egypt* **94 C3** 24 30N 30 40 E
El Manshâh, *Egypt* **94 B3** 26 26N 31 50 E
El Mansour, *Algeria* **99 C4** 27 47N 0 14W
El Mansûra, *Egypt* **94 H7** 31 0N 31 19 E
El Mantico, *Venezuela* **153 B5** 7 38N 62 45W
El Manzala, *Egypt* **94 H7** 31 10N 31 50 E
El Marâgha, *Egypt* **94 B3** 26 35N 31 10 E
El Masid, *Sudan* **95 D3** 15 15N 33 0 E
El Matariya, *Egypt* **94 H8** 31 15N 32 0 E
El Medano, *Canary Is.* **33 F3** 28 3N 16 32W
El Meghaier, *Algeria* **99 B6** 33 55N 5 58 E
El Meraguen, *Algeria* **99 C4** 28 0N 0 7W
El Metemma, *Sudan* **95 D3** 16 50N 33 10 E
El Miamo, *Venezuela* **153 B5** 7 39N 61 46W
El Milagro, *Argentina* **158 C2** 30 59 S 65 59W
El Milia, *Algeria* **99 A6** 36 51N 6 13 E
El Minyâ, *Egypt* **94 J7** 28 7N 30 33 E
El Molar, *Spain* **34 E1** 40 42N 3 45W
El Monte, *U.S.A.* **145 L8** 34 4N 118 1W
El Mreyye, *Mauritania* **100 B3** 18 0N 6 0W
El Nido, *Phil.* **71 F2** 11 10N 119 25 E
El Obeid, *Sudan* **95 E3** 13 8N 30 10 E
El Odaiya, *Sudan* **95 E2** 12 8N 28 12 E
El Oro, *Mexico* **147 D4** 19 48N 100 8W
El Oro □, *Ecuador* **152 D2** 3 30 S 79 50W
El Oued, *Algeria* **99 B6** 33 20N 6 58 E
El Palmar, *Bolivia* **157 D5** 17 50 S 63 9W
El Palmar, *Venezuela* **153 B5** 7 58N 61 53W
El Palmito, Presa, *Mexico* **146 B3** 25 40N 105 30W
El Panadés, *Spain* **34 D6** 41 10N 1 30 E
El Pardo, *Spain* **36 E7** 40 31N 3 47W
El Paso, *Ill., U.S.A.* **140 D7** 40 44N 89 1W
El Paso, *Tex., U.S.A.* **143 L10** 31 45N 106 29W
El Paso Robles, *U.S.A.* **144 K6** 35 38N 120 41W
El Pedernoso, *Spain* **35 F2** 39 29N 2 45W
El Pedroso, *Spain* **37 H5** 37 51N 5 45W
El Pobo de Dueñas, *Spain* **34 E3** 40 46N 1 39W
El Portal, *U.S.A.* **144 H7** 37 41N 119 47W
El Porvenir, *Mexico* **146 A3** 31 15N 105 51W
El Prat de Llobregat, *Spain* **34 D7** 41 18N 2 3 E
El Progreso, *Honduras* **148 C2** 15 26N 87 51W
El Provencío, *Spain* **35 F2** 39 23N 2 35W
El Pueblito, *Mexico* **146 B3** 29 3N 105 4W
El Pueblo, *Canary Is.* **33 F2** 28 36N 17 47W
El Puerto de Santa María, *Spain* **37 J4** 36 36N 6 13W
El Qâhira, *Egypt* **94 H7** 30 1N 31 14 E
El Qantara, *Egypt* **91 E1** 30 51N 32 20 E
El Qasr, *Egypt* **94 B2** 25 44N 28 42 E
El Quseima, *Egypt* **91 E3** 30 40N 34 15 E
El Qusîya, *Egypt* **94 B3** 27 29N 30 44 E
El Râshda, *Egypt* **94 B2** 25 36N 28 57 E
El Reno, *U.S.A.* **139 H6** 35 32N 97 57W
El Ribero, *Spain* **36 C2** 42 30N 8 30W
El Rîdisiya, *Egypt* **94 C3** 24 56N 32 51 E
El Rio, *U.S.A.* **145 L7** 34 14N 119 10W
El Ronquillo, *Spain* **37 H4** 37 44N 6 10W
El Roque, Pta., *Canary Is.* **33 F4** 28 10N 15 25W
El Rosarito, *Mexico* **146 B2** 28 38N 114 4W
El Rubio, *Spain* **37 H5** 37 22N 5 0W
El Saff, *Egypt* **94 J7** 29 34N 31 16 E
El Saheira, W. →, *Egypt* **91 E2** 30 5N 33 25 E
El Salto, *Mexico* **146 C3** 23 47N 105 22W
El Salvador ■, *Cent. Amer.* **148 D2** 13 50N 89 0W
El Sancejo, *Spain* **37 H5** 37 4N 5 6W
El Sauce, *Nic.* **148 D2** 13 0N 86 40W
El Shallal, *Egypt* **94 C3** 24 0N 32 53 E
El Simbillawein, *Egypt* **94 H7** 30 48N 31 13 E
El Sombrero, *Venezuela* **152 B4** 9 23N 67 3W
El Suweis, *Egypt* **94 J8** 29 58N 32 31 E
El Tamarâni, W. →, *Egypt* **91 E3** 30 7N 34 43 E
El Thamad, *Egypt* **91 F3** 29 40N 34 28 E
El Tigre, *Venezuela* **153 B5** 8 44N 64 15W
El Tîh, G., *Egypt* **91 F2** 29 40N 33 50 E
El Tîna, Khalîg, *Egypt* **91 D1** 31 10N 32 40 E
El Tocuyo, *Venezuela* **152 B4** 9 47N 69 48W
El Tofo, *Chile* **158 B1** 29 22 S 71 18W
El Tránsito, *Chile* **158 B1** 28 52 S 70 17W
El Tûr, *Egypt* **94 J8** 28 14N 33 36 E
El Turbio, *Argentina* **160 D2** 51 45 S 72 5W
El Uinle, *Somali Rep.* **108 D2** 3 4N 41 42 E
El Uqsur, *Egypt* **94 B3** 25 41N 32 38 E
El Vado, *Spain* **34 D1** 41 2N 3 18W
El Vallés, *Spain* **34 D7** 41 35N 2 20 E
El Venado, *Mexico* **146 C4** 22 56N 101 10W
El Vigía, *Venezuela* **152 B3** 8 38N 71 39W
El Wabeira, *Egypt* **91 F2** 29 34N 33 6 E
El Wak, *Kenya* **106 B5** 2 49N 40 56 E
El Wak, *Somali Rep.* **108 D2** 2 44N 41 1 E
El Waqf, *Egypt* **94 B3** 25 45N 32 15 E
El Wâsta, *Egypt* **94 J7** 29 19N 31 12 E
El Weguet, *Ethiopia* **95 F5** 5 28N 42 17 E
El Wuz, *Sudan* **95 D3** 15 5N 30 7 E
Elafónisos, *Greece* **45 H4** 36 29N 22 56 E
Elaine, *Australia* **116 D6** 37 44 S 144 2 E
Elamanchili, *India* **82 F6** 17 33N 82 50 E
Elands, *Australia* **117 A10** 31 37 S 152 20 E
Élassa, *Greece* **45 J8** 35 18N 26 21 E
Elassón, *Greece* **44 E4** 39 53N 22 12 E
Elat, *Israel* **91 F3** 29 30N 34 56 E
Eláthia, *Greece* **45 F4** 38 37N 22 46 E
Elâzığ, *Turkey* **89 C8** 38 37N 39 14 E
Elba, *Italy* **38 F7** 42 46N 10 17 E
Elba, *U.S.A.* **135 K2** 31 25N 86 4W
Elbasani, *Albania* **44 C2** 41 9N 20 9 E
Elbe, *U.S.A.* **144 D4** 46 45N 122 10W
Elbe →, *Europe* **26 B4** 53 50N 9 0 E
Elbe-Seiten Kanal, *Germany* **26 C6** 52 45N 10 32 E
Elberfeld, *U.S.A.* **141 F9** 38 10N 87 27W
Elbert, Mt., *U.S.A.* **143 G10** 39 7N 106 27W
Elberta, *U.S.A.* **134 C2** 44 37N 86 14W
Elberton, *U.S.A.* **135 H4** 34 7N 82 52W
Elbeuf, *France* **22 C8** 49 17N 1 2 E
Elbing = Elbląg, *Poland* **47 A6** 54 10N 19 25 E
Elbistan, *Turkey* **88 C7** 38 13N 37 15 E
Elbląg, *Poland* **47 A6** 54 10N 19 25 E
Elbląg □, *Poland* **47 A6** 54 15N 19 30 E
Elbow, *Canada* **131 C7** 51 7N 106 35W
Elbrus, *Asia* **53 J6** 43 21N 42 30 E
Elburg, *Neths.* **20 D7** 52 26N 5 50 E
Elburn, *U.S.A.* **141 C8** 41 54N 88 28W
Elburz Mts. = Alborz, Reshteh-ye Kūhhā-ye, *Iran* **85 C7** 36 0N 52 0 E
Elche, *Spain* **35 G4** 38 15N 0 42W
Elche de la Sierra, *Spain* **35 G2** 38 27N 2 3W
Elcho I., *Australia* **114 A2** 11 55 S 135 45 E
Elda, *Spain* **35 G4** 38 29N 0 47W
Eldon, *Mo., U.S.A.* **140 F4** 38 21N 92 35W
Eldon, *Wash., U.S.A.* **144 C3** 47 33N 123 3W
Eldora, *U.S.A.* **140 B3** 42 22N 93 5W
Eldorado, *Argentina* **159 B5** 26 28 S 54 43W
Eldorado, *Canada* **131 B7** 59 35N 108 30W
Eldorado, *Mexico* **146 C3** 24 20N 107 22W
Eldorado, *Ill., U.S.A.* **141 G8** 37 49N 88 26W
Eldorado, *Tex., U.S.A.* **139 K4** 30 52N 100 36W
Eldorado Springs, *U.S.A.* **139 G8** 37 52N 94 1W
Eldoret, *Kenya* **106 B4** 0 30N 35 17 E
Eldred, *U.S.A.* **136 E6** 41 58N 78 23W
Eldridge, *U.S.A.* **140 C6** 41 39N 90 35W
Elea, C., *Cyprus* **32 D13** 35 19N 34 4 E
Electra, *U.S.A.* **139 H5** 34 2N 98 55W
Elefantes →, *Mozam.* **105 C5** 24 10 S 32 40 E
Elefantes, G., *Chile* **160 C2** 46 28 S 73 49W
Elektrogorsk, *Russia* **52 C4** 55 56N 38 50 E
Elektrostal, *Russia* **52 C4** 55 41N 38 32 E
Elele, *Nigeria* **101 D6** 5 5N 6 50 E
Elena, *Bulgaria* **43 E10** 42 55N 25 53 E
Elephant Butte Reservoir, *U.S.A.* **143 K10** 33 9N 107 11W
Elephant I., *Antarctica* **7 C18** 61 0 S 55 0W
Elephant Pass, *Sri Lanka* **83 K5** 9 35N 80 25 E
Elesbão Veloso, *Brazil* **154 C3** 6 13 S 42 8W
Eleshnitsa, *Bulgaria* **43 F8** 41 52N 23 36 E
Eleşkirt, *Turkey* **89 C10** 39 50N 42 50 E
Eleuthera, *Bahamas* **148 A4** 25 0N 76 20W
Elevsís, *Greece* **45 F5** 38 4N 23 26 E
Elevtheroúpolis, *Greece* **44 D6** 40 52N 24 20 E
Elgepiggen, *Norway* **14 B5** 62 10N 11 21 E
Elgeyo-Marakwet □, *Kenya* **106 B4** 0 45N 35 30 E
Elgg, *Switz.* **29 B7** 47 29N 8 52 E
Elgin, *N.B., Canada* **129 C6** 45 48N 65 10W
Elgin, *Ont., Canada* **137 B8** 44 36N 76 13W
Elgin, *U.K.* **18 D5** 57 39N 3 19W
Elgin, *Ill., U.S.A.* **141 B8** 42 2N 88 17W
Elgin, *N. Dak., U.S.A.* **138 B4** 46 24N 101 51W
Elgin, *Nebr., U.S.A.* **138 E5** 41 59N 98 5W
Elgin, *Nev., U.S.A.* **143 H6** 37 21N 114 32W
Elgin, *Oreg., U.S.A.* **142 D5** 45 34N 117 55W
Elgin, *Tex., U.S.A.* **139 K6** 30 21N 97 22W
Elgon, Mt., *Africa* **106 B3** 1 10N 34 30 E
Eliase, *Indonesia* **73 C4** 8 21 S 130 48 E
Elida, *U.S.A.* **139 J3** 33 57N 103 39W
Elikón, *Greece* **45 F4** 38 18N 22 45 E
Elim, *S. Africa* **104 E2** 34 35 S 19 45 E
Elin Pelin, *Bulgaria* **43 E8** 42 40N 23 36 E
Elisabethville = Lubumbashi, *Zaïre* **107 E2** 11 40 S 27 28 E
Eliseu Martins, *Brazil* **154 C3** 8 13 S 43 42W
Elista, *Russia* **53 G7** 46 16N 44 14 E
Elizabeth, *Australia* **116 C3** 34 42 S 138 41 E
Elizabeth, *Ill., U.S.A.* **140 B6** 42 19N 90 13W
Elizabeth, *N.J., U.S.A.* **137 F10** 40 40N 74 13W
Elizabeth City, *U.S.A.* **135 G7** 36 18N 76 14W
Elizabethton, *U.S.A.* **135 G4** 36 21N 82 13W
Elizabethtown, *Ky., U.S.A.* **134 G3** 37 42N 85 52W
Elizabethtown, *N.Y., U.S.A.* **137 B11** 44 13N 73 36W
Elizabethtown, *Pa., U.S.A.* **137 F8** 40 9N 76 36W
Elizondo, *Spain* **34 B3** 43 12N 1 30W
Ełk, *Poland* **47 B9** 53 50N 22 21 E
Ełk →, *Poland* **47 B9** 53 41N 22 28 E
Elk City, *U.S.A.* **139 H5** 35 25N 99 25W
Elk Creek, *U.S.A.* **144 F4** 39 36N 122 32W
Elk Grove, *U.S.A.* **144 G5** 38 25N 121 22W
Elk Island Nat. Park, *Canada* **130 C6** 53 35N 112 59W
Elk Lake, *Canada* **128 C3** 47 40N 80 25W
Elk Point, *Canada* **131 C6** 53 54N 110 55W
Elk River, *Idaho, U.S.A.* **142 C5** 46 47N 116 11W
Elk River, *Minn., U.S.A.* **138 C8** 45 18N 93 35W
Elkader, *U.S.A.* **140 B5** 42 51N 91 24W
Elkedra, *Australia* **114 C2** 21 9 S 135 33 E
Elkedra →, *Australia* **114 C2** 21 8 S 136 22 E
Elkhart, *Ind., U.S.A.* **141 C11** 41 41N 85 58W
Elkhart, *Kans., U.S.A.* **139 G4** 37 0N 101 54W
Elkhart →, *U.S.A.* **141 C11** 41 41N 85 58W
Elkhorn, *Canada* **131 D8** 49 59N 101 14W
Elkhorn, *U.S.A.* **141 B8** 42 40N 88 33W
Elkhorn →, *U.S.A.* **138 E6** 41 8N 96 19W
Elkhovo, *Bulgaria* **43 E11** 42 10N 26 40 E
Elkin, *U.S.A.* **135 G5** 36 15N 80 51W
Elkins, *U.S.A.* **134 F6** 38 55N 79 51W
Elko, *Canada* **130 D5** 49 20N 115 10W
Elko, *U.S.A.* **142 F6** 40 50N 115 46W
Ell, L., *Australia* **113 E4** 29 13 S 127 46 E
Ellecom, *Neths.* **20 D8** 52 2N 6 6 E
Ellef Ringnes I., *Canada* **6 B2** 78 30N 102 2W
Ellendale, *Australia* **112 C3** 17 56 S 124 48 E
Ellendale, *U.S.A.* **138 B5** 46 0N 98 32W
Ellensburg, *U.S.A.* **142 C3** 46 59N 120 34W
Ellenville, *U.S.A.* **137 E10** 41 43N 74 24W
Ellerston, *Australia* **117 A9** 31 49 S 151 20 E
Ellery, Mt., *Australia* **117 D8** 37 28 S 148 47 E
Ellesmere, L., *N.Z.* **119 H7** 47 47 S 172 28 E
Ellesmere I., *Canada* **124 B11** 79 30N 80 0W
Ellesmere Port, *U.K.* **16 D5** 53 17N 2 54W
Ellettsville, *U.S.A.* **141 E10** 39 14N 86 38W
Ellezelles, *Belgium* **21 G3** 50 44N 3 42 E
Ellice Is. = Tuvalu ■, *Pac. Oc.* **122 H9** 8 0 S 178 0 E
Ellinwood, *U.S.A.* **138 F5** 38 21N 98 35W
Elliot, *Australia* **114 B1** 17 33 S 133 32 E
Elliot, *S. Africa* **105 E4** 31 22 S 27 48 E
Elliot Lake, *Canada* **128 C3** 46 25N 82 35W
Elliotdale = Xhora, *S. Africa* **105 E4** 31 55 S 28 38 E
Ellis, *U.S.A.* **138 F5** 38 56N 99 34W
Elliston, *Australia* **115 E1** 33 39 S 134 53 E
Ellisville, *U.S.A.* **139 K10** 31 36N 89 12W
Ellon, *U.K.* **18 D6** 57 22N 2 4W
Ellore = Eluru, *India* **82 F5** 16 48N 81 8 E
Ells →, *Canada* **130 B6** 57 18N 111 40W
Ellsworth, *U.S.A.* **138 F5** 38 44N 98 14W
Ellsworth Land, *Antarctica* **7 D16** 76 0 S 89 0W
Ellsworth Mts., *Antarctica* **7 D16** 78 30 S 85 0W
Ellwangen, *Germany* **27 G6** 48 57N 10 8 E
Ellwood City, *U.S.A.* **136 F4** 40 52N 80 17W
Elm, *Switz.* **29 C8** 46 54N 9 10 E
Elma, *Canada* **131 D9** 49 52N 95 55W
Elma, *U.S.A.* **144 D3** 47 0N 123 25W
Elmadağ, *Turkey* **88 C5** 39 55N 33 14 E
Elmalı, *Turkey* **88 D3** 36 44N 29 56 E
Elmer, *U.S.A.* **140 E4** 39 57N 92 39W
Elmhurst, *U.S.A.* **141 C9** 41 53N 87 56W
Elmina, *Ghana* **101 D4** 5 5N 1 21W
Elmira, *Canada* **136 C4** 43 36N 80 33W
Elmira, *U.S.A.* **136 D8** 42 6N 76 48W
Elmore, *Australia* **116 D6** 36 30 S 144 37 E
Elmore, *Calif., U.S.A.* **145 M11** 33 7N 115 49W
Elmore, *Minn., U.S.A.* **141 C13** 41 29N 83 18W
Elmshorn, *Germany* **26 B5** 53 43N 9 40 E
Elmvale, *Canada* **136 B5** 44 35N 79 52W
Elmwood, *U.S.A.* **140 D6** 40 47N 89 58W
Elne, *France* **24 F6** 42 36N 2 58 E
Elnora, *U.S.A.* **141 F9** 38 53N 87 5W
Elora, *Canada* **136 C4** 43 41N 80 26W
Elorza, *Venezuela* **152 B4** 7 3N 69 31W
Elos, *Greece* **45 H4** 36 46N 22 43 E
Eloúnda, *Greece* **32 D7** 35 16N 25 42 E
Eloy, *U.S.A.* **143 K8** 32 45N 111 33W
Éloyes, *France* **23 D13** 48 6N 6 36 E
Elrose, *Canada* **131 C7** 51 12N 108 0W
Elsas, *Canada* **128 C3** 48 32N 82 55W
Elsie, *U.S.A.* **144 E3** 45 52N 123 36W
Elsinore = Helsingør, *Denmark* **15 H6** 56 2N 12 35 E
Elsinore, *Australia* **117 A6** 31 35 S 145 11 E
Elsinore, *U.S.A.* **143 G7** 38 41N 112 9W
Elspe, *Germany* **26 D4** 51 10N 8 1 E
Elspeet, *Neths.* **20 D7** 52 17N 5 48 E
Elst, *Neths.* **20 E7** 51 55N 5 51 E
Elster →, *Germany* **26 D7** 51 25N 11 57 E
Elsterwerda, *Germany* **26 D9** 51 27N 13 31 E
Elten, *Neths.* **20 E8** 51 52N 6 9 E
Eltham, *Australia* **117 D6** 37 43 S 145 12 E
Eltham, *N.Z.* **118 F3** 39 26 S 174 19 E
Elton, *Russia* **53 F8** 49 5N 46 52 E
Elton, Ozero, *Russia* **53 F8** 49 5N 46 42 E
Eluru, *India* **82 F5** 16 48N 81 8 E
Elvas, *Portugal* **37 G3** 38 50N 7 10W
Elven, *France* **22 E4** 47 44N 2 36W
Elverum, *Norway* **14 D5** 60 53N 11 34 E
Elvire →, *Australia* **112 C4** 17 51 S 128 11 E
Elvo →, *Italy* **38 C5** 45 23N 8 21 E
Elvran, *Norway* **14 A5** 63 24N 11 3 E
Elwood, *Ill., U.S.A.* **141 C8** 41 24N 88 7W
Elwood, *Ind., U.S.A.* **141 D11** 40 17N 85 50W
Elwood, *Nebr., U.S.A.* **138 E5** 40 36N 99 52W
Elx = Elche, *Spain* **35 G4** 38 15N 0 42W
Ely, *U.K.* **17 E8** 52 24N 0 16 E
Ely, *Minn., U.S.A.* **138 B9** 47 55N 91 51W
Ely, *Nev., U.S.A.* **142 G6** 39 15N 114 54W
Elyria, *U.S.A.* **136 E2** 41 22N 82 7W
Elyrus, *Greece* **45 J5** 35 15N 23 45 E
Elz →, *Germany* **27 G3** 48 18N 7 44 E
Emai, *Vanuatu* **121 G6** 17 4 S 168 24 E
Emāmrūd, *Iran* **85 B7** 36 30N 55 0 E
Emba = Embi, *Kazakstan* **56 E6** 48 50N 58 8 E
Emba → = Embi →, *Kazakstan* **49 E9** 46 55N 53 28 E
Embarcación, *Argentina* **158 A3** 23 10 S 64 0W
Embarras →, *U.S.A.* **141 F9** 38 39N 87 37W
Embarras Portage, *Canada* **131 B6** 58 27N 111 28W
Embetsu, *Japan* **60 B10** 44 44N 141 47 E
Embi, *Kazakstan* **56 E6** 48 50N 58 8 E
Embi →, *Kazakstan* **49 E9** 46 55N 53 28 E
Embira →, *Brazil* **156 B3** 7 19 S 70 15W
Embóna, *Greece* **32 C9** 36 13N 27 51 E
Embrach, *Switz.* **29 A7** 47 30N 8 36 E
Embrun, *France* **25 D10** 44 34N 6 30 E
Embu, *Kenya* **106 C4** 0 32 S 37 38 E
Embu □, *Kenya* **106 C4** 0 30 S 37 35 E
Emden, *Germany* **26 B3** 53 21N 7 12 E
Emerald, *Australia* **114 C4** 23 32 S 148 10 E
Emerson, *Canada* **131 D9** 49 0N 97 10W
Emery, *U.S.A.* **143 G8** 38 55N 111 15W
Emet, *Turkey* **88 C3** 39 20N 29 15 E
Emi Koussi, *Chad* **97 E3** 19 45N 18 55 E
Emilia-Romagna □, *Italy* **38 D7** 44 45N 11 0 E
Emilius, Mte., *Italy* **38 C4** 45 45N 7 20 E
Eminabad, *Pakistan* **80 C6** 32 2N 74 8 E
Emine, Nos, *Bulgaria* **43 E12** 42 40N 27 56 E
Eminence, *U.S.A.* **141 F11** 38 22N 85 11W
Emirdağ, *Turkey* **88 C4** 39 2N 31 8 E
Emlenton, *U.S.A.* **136 E5** 41 11N 79 43W
Emlichheim, *Germany* **26 C2** 52 37N 6 51 E
Emme →, *Switz.* **28 B5** 47 14N 7 32 E
Emmeloord, *Neths.* **20 C7** 52 44N 5 46 E
Emmen, *Neths.* **20 C9** 52 48N 6 57 E
Emmendingen, *Germany* **27 G3** 48 6N 7 51 E
Emmental, *Switz.* **28 C4** 46 55N 7 20 E
Emmer-Compascuum, *Neths.* **20 C10** 52 49N 7 2 E
Emmerich, *Germany* **26 D2** 51 50N 6 14 E
Emmet, *Australia* **114 C3** 24 45 S 144 30 E
Emmetsburg, *U.S.A.* **140 A2** 43 7N 94 41W
Emmett, *U.S.A.* **142 E5** 43 52N 116 30W
Emőd, *Hungary* **31 D13** 47 57N 20 47 E
Emona, *Bulgaria* **43 E12** 42 43N 27 53 E
Empalme, *Mexico* **146 B2** 28 1N 110 49W
Empangeni, *S. Africa* **105 D5** 28 50 S 31 52 E
Empedrado, *Argentina* **158 B4** 28 0 S 58 46W
Emperor Seamount Chain, *Pac. Oc.* **122 D9** 40 0N 170 0 E
Empoli, *Italy* **38 E7** 43 43N 10 57 E
Emporia, *Kans., U.S.A.* **138 F6** 38 25N 96 11W
Emporia, *Va., U.S.A.* **135 G7** 36 42N 77 32W
Emporium, *U.S.A.* **136 E6** 41 31N 78 14W
Empress, *Canada* **131 C6** 50 57N 110 0W
Emptinne, *Belgium* **21 H6** 50 19N 5 8 E
Empty Quarter = Rub' al Khali, *Si. Arabia* **87 C5** 18 0N 48 0 E
Ems →, *Germany* **26 B3** 53 20N 7 12 E
Emsdale, *Canada* **136 A5** 45 32N 79 19W
Emsdetten, *Germany* **26 C3** 52 10N 7 32 E
Emu, *Australia* **116 D5** 36 44 S 143 26 E
Emu, *China* **67 C15** 43 40N 128 6 E
Emu Park, *Australia* **114 C5** 23 13 S 150 50 E
'En 'Avrona, *Israel* **91 F3** 29 43N 35 0 E
En Nahud, *Sudan* **95 E2** 12 45N 28 25 E
Ena, *Japan* **63 B9** 35 25N 137 25 E
Ena-San, *Japan* **63 B9** 35 26N 137 36 E
Enafors, *Sweden* **14 A6** 63 17N 12 20 E
Enambú, *Colombia* **152 C3** 1 1N 70 17W
Enana, *Namibia* **104 B2** 17 30 S 16 23 E
Enånger, *Sweden* **14 C11** 61 30N 17 9 E
Enaratoli, *Indonesia* **73 B5** 3 55 S 136 21 E
Enard B., *U.K.* **18 C3** 58 5N 5 20W
Enare = Inarijärvi, *Finland* **12 B22** 69 0N 28 0 E
Encantadas, Serra, *Brazil* **159 C5** 30 40 S 53 0W
Encarnación, *Paraguay* **159 B4** 27 15 S 55 50W
Encarnación de Diaz, *Mexico* **146 C4** 21 30N 102 13W
Enchi, *Ghana* **100 D4** 5 53N 2 48W
Encinal, *U.S.A.* **139 L5** 28 2N 99 21W
Encinitas, *U.S.A.* **145 M9** 33 3N 117 17W
Encino, *U.S.A.* **143 J11** 34 39N 105 28W
Encontrados, *Venezuela* **152 B3** 9 3N 72 14W
Encounter B., *Australia* **116 C3** 35 45 S 138 45 E
Encruzilhada, *Brazil* **155 E3** 15 31 S 40 54W
Ende, *Indonesia* **72 C2** 8 45 S 121 40 E
Endeavour, *Canada* **131 C8** 52 10N 102 39W
Endeavour Str., *Australia* **114 A3** 10 45 S 142 0 E
Endelave, *Denmark* **15 J4** 55 46N 10 18 E
Enderbury I., *Kiribati* **122 H10** 3 8 S 171 5W
Enderby, *Canada* **130 C5** 50 35N 119 10W
Enderby I., *Australia* **112 D2** 20 35 S 116 30 E
Enderby Land, *Antarctica* **7 C5** 66 0 S 53 0 E
Enderlin, *U.S.A.* **138 B6** 46 38N 97 36W
Endicott, *N.Y., U.S.A.* **137 D8** 42 6N 76 4W
Endicott, *Wash., U.S.A.* **142 C5** 46 56N 117 41W
Endimari →, *Brazil* **156 B4** 8 46 S 66 7W
Endröd, *Hungary* **31 E13** 46 55N 20 47 E
Endyalgout I., *Australia* **112 B5** 11 40 S 132 35 E
Ene →, *Peru* **156 C3** 11 10 S 74 18W
Energetik, *Russia* **54 F7** 51 45N 58 45 E
Enewetak Atoll, *Pac. Oc.* **122 F8** 11 30N 162 15 E
Enez, *Turkey* **88 B2** 40 45N 26 5 E
Enfield, *U.K.* **17 F7** 51 38N 0 5W
Enfield, *U.S.A.* **141 F8** 38 6N 88 20W
Engadin, *Switz.* **27 J6** 46 45N 10 10 E
Engaño, C., *Dom. Rep.* **149 C6** 18 30N 68 20W
Engaño, C., *Phil.* **70 B4** 18 35N 122 23 E
Engcobo, *S. Africa* **105 E4** 31 37 S 28 0 E
Engelberg, *Switz.* **29 C6** 46 48N 8 26 E
Engels, *Russia* **52 E8** 51 28N 46 6 E
Engemann L., *Canada* **131 B7** 58 0N 106 55W
Enger, *Norway* **14 D4** 60 35N 10 20 E
Enggano, *Indonesia* **74 D2** 5 20 S 102 40 E
Enghien, *Belgium* **21 G4** 50 37N 4 2 E
Engil, *Morocco* **98 B4** 33 12N 4 32W
Engkilili, *Malaysia* **75 B4** 1 3N 111 42 E
England, *U.S.A.* **139 H9** 34 33N 91 58W
England □, *U.K.* **11 E5** 53 0N 2 0W
Englee, *Canada* **129 B8** 50 45N 56 5W
Englefield, *Australia* **116 D4** 37 21 S 141 48 E
Englehart, *Canada* **128 C4** 47 49N 79 52W
Engler L., *Canada* **131 B7** 59 8N 106 52W
Englewood, *Colo., U.S.A.* **138 F2** 39 39N 104 59W
Englewood, *Kans., U.S.A.* **139 G5** 37 2N 99 59W
Englewood, *Ohio, U.S.A.* **141 E12** 39 53N 84 18W
English, *U.S.A.* **141 F10** 38 20N 86 28W
English →, *Canada* **131 C10** 50 35N 93 30W
English →, *U.S.A.* **140 C5** 41 29N 91 32W
English Bazar = Ingraj Bazar, *India* **81 G13** 24 58N 88 10 E

Ferreñafe 197

Excideuil, *France* **24 C5** 45 20N 1 4 E
Exe →, *U.K.* **17 G4** 50 41N 3 29W
Exeter, *Canada* **136 C3** 43 21N 81 29W
Exeter, *U.K.* **17 G4** 50 43N 3 31W
Exeter, *Calif., U.S.A.* **144 J7** 36 18N 119 9W
Exeter, *N.H., U.S.A.* **137 D14** 42 59N 70 57W
Exeter, *Nebr., U.S.A.* **138 E6** 40 39N 97 27W
Exira, *U.S.A.* **140 C2** 41 35N 94 52W
Exloo, *Neths.* **20 C9** 52 53N 6 52 E
Exmes, *France* **22 D7** 48 45N 0 10 E
Exmoor, *U.K.* **17 F4** 51 12N 3 45W
Exmouth, *Australia* **112 D1** 21 54 S 114 10 E
Exmouth, *U.K.* **17 G4** 50 37N 3 25W
Exmouth G., *Australia* **112 D1** 22 15 S 114 15 E
Expedition Ra., *Australia* **114 C4** 24 30 S 149 12 E
Extremadura □, *Spain* **37 F4** 39 30N 6 5W
Exuma Sound, *Bahamas* **148 B4** 24 30N 76 20W
Eyasi, L., *Tanzania* **106 C4** 3 30 S 35 0 E
Eyeberry L., *Canada* **131 A8** 63 8N 104 43W
Eyemouth, *U.K.* **18 F6** 55 52N 2 5W
Eygurande, *France* **24 C6** 45 40N 2 26 E
Eyjafjörður, *Iceland* **12 C4** 66 15N 18 30W
Eymet, *France* **24 D4** 44 40N 0 25 E
Eymoutiers, *France* **24 C5** 45 40N 1 45 E
Eynesil, *Turkey* **89 B8** 41 4N 39 9 E
Eyre, *Australia* **113 F4** 32 15 S 126 18 E
Eyre (North), L., *Australia* **115 D2** 28 30 S 137 20 E
Eyre (South), L., *Australia* **115 D2** 29 18 S 137 25 E
Eyre, L., *Australia* **110 F6** 29 30 S 137 26 E
Eyre Cr. →, *Australia* **115 D2** 26 40 S 139 0 E
Eyre Mts., *N.Z.* **119 F3** 45 25 S 168 25 E
Eyre Pen., *Australia* **115 E2** 33 30 S 136 17 E
Eysturoy, *Færoe Is.* **12 E9** 62 13N 6 54W
Eyvānkī, *Iran* **85 C6** 35 24N 51 56 E
Ez Zeidab, *Sudan* **94 D3** 17 25N 33 55 E
Ezcaray, *Spain* **34 C2** 42 19N 3 0W
Ezine, *Turkey* **88 C2** 39 48N 26 20 E
Ezmul, *Mauritania* **98 D1** 22 15N 15 40W
Ezouza →, *Cyprus* **32 E11** 34 44N 32 27 E

F

F.Y.R.O.M. = Macedonia ■, *Europe* **42 F6** 41 53N 21 40 E
Fabens, *U.S.A.* **143 L10** 31 30N 106 10W
Fåborg, *Denmark* **15 J4** 55 6N 10 15 E
Fabriano, *Italy* **39 E9** 43 20N 12 54 E
Făcăeni, *Romania* **46 E8** 44 32N 27 53 E
Facatativá, *Colombia* **152 C3** 4 49N 74 22W
Fachi, *Niger* **97 E2** 18 6N 11 34 E
Facture, *France* **24 D3** 44 39N 0 58W
Fada, *Chad* **97 E4** 17 13N 21 34 E
Fada-n-Gourma, *Burkina Faso* **101 C5** 12 10N 0 30 E
Fadd, *Hungary* **31 E11** 46 28N 18 49 E
Faddeyevskiy, Ostrov, *Russia* **57 B15** 76 0N 144 0 E
Fadghāmī, *Syria* **89 E9** 35 53N 40 52 E
Fadlab, *Sudan* **94 D3** 17 42N 34 2 E
Faenza, *Italy* **39 D8** 44 17N 11 53 E
Færoe Is. = Føroyar, *Atl. Oc.* **12 F9** 62 0N 7 0W
Fafa, *Mali* **101 B5** 15 22N 0 48 E
Fafe, *Portugal* **36 D2** 41 27N 8 11W
Faga, *W. Samoa* **121 W23** 13 39 S 172 8W
Fagam, *Nigeria* **101 C7** 11 1N 10 1 E
Fagamalo, *W. Samoa* **121 W23** 13 25 S 172 21W
Făgăras, *Romania* **46 D5** 45 48N 24 58 E
Făgăras, Munții, *Romania* **46 D5** 45 40N 24 40 E
Fågelsjö, *Sweden* **14 C8** 61 50N 14 35 E
Fagersta, *Sweden* **13 F16** 60 1N 15 46 E
Făget, *Romania* **46 D3** 45 52N 22 10 E
Făget, Munții, *Romania* **46 B4** 47 40N 23 10 E
Fagnano, L., *Argentina* **160 D3** 54 30 S 68 0W
Fagnano Castello, *Italy* **41 C9** 39 34N 16 3 E
Fagnières, *France* **23 D11** 48 58N 4 20 E
Fahlīān, *Iran* **85 D6** 30 11N 51 28 E
Fahr, *Yemen* **87 D6** 12 26N 54 8 E
Fahraj, *Kermān, Iran* **85 D8** 29 0N 59 0 E
Fahraj, *Yazd, Iran* **85 D7** 31 46N 54 36 E
Faial, *Madeira* **33 D3** 32 47N 16 53W
Faido, *Switz.* **29 D7** 46 29N 8 48 E
Fair Hd., *U.K.* **19 A5** 55 14N 6 9W
Fair Oaks, *U.S.A.* **144 G5** 38 39N 121 16W
Fairbank, *U.S.A.* **143 L8** 31 43N 110 11W
Fairbanks, *U.S.A.* **126 B5** 64 51N 147 43W
Fairborn, *U.S.A.* **141 E12** 39 49N 84 2W
Fairbury, *Ill., U.S.A.* **141 D8** 40 45N 88 31W
Fairbury, *Nebr., U.S.A.* **138 E6** 40 8N 97 11W
Faire, *Phil.* **70 C3** 17 53N 121 34 E
Fairfax, *Ohio, U.S.A.* **141 E13** 39 5N 83 37W
Fairfax, *Okla., U.S.A.* **139 G6** 36 34N 96 42W
Fairfield, *Australia* **117 B9** 33 53 S 150 57 E
Fairfield, *Ala., U.S.A.* **135 J2** 33 29N 86 55W
Fairfield, *Calif., U.S.A.* **144 G4** 38 15N 122 3W
Fairfield, *Conn., U.S.A.* **137 E11** 41 9N 73 16W
Fairfield, *Idaho, U.S.A.* **142 E6** 43 21N 114 44W
Fairfield, *Ill., U.S.A.* **141 F8** 38 23N 88 22W
Fairfield, *Iowa, U.S.A.* **140 C5** 40 56N 91 57W
Fairfield, *Mont., U.S.A.* **142 C8** 47 37N 111 59W
Fairfield, *Ohio, U.S.A.* **141 E12** 39 21N 84 34W
Fairfield, *Tex., U.S.A.* **139 K7** 31 44N 96 10W
Fairford, *Canada* **131 C9** 51 37N 98 38W
Fairhope, *U.S.A.* **135 K2** 30 31N 87 54W
Fairlie, *N.Z.* **119 E5** 44 5 S 170 49 E
Fairmead, *U.S.A.* **144 H6** 37 5N 120 10W
Fairmont, *Minn., U.S.A.* **138 D7** 43 39N 94 28W
Fairmont, *W. Va., U.S.A.* **134 F5** 39 29N 80 9W
Fairmount, *U.S.A.* **145 L8** 34 45N 118 26W
Fairplay, *U.S.A.* **143 G11** 39 15N 106 2W
Fairport, *U.S.A.* **136 C7** 43 6N 77 27W
Fairport Harbor, *U.S.A.* **136 E3** 41 45N 81 17W
Fairview, *Australia* **114 B3** 15 31 S 144 17 E
Fairview, *Canada* **130 B5** 56 5N 118 25W
Fairview, *Mont., U.S.A.* **138 B2** 47 51N 104 3W
Fairview, *Okla., U.S.A.* **139 G5** 36 16N 98 29W
Fairview, *Utah, U.S.A.* **142 G8** 39 50N 111 0W
Fairweather, Mt., *U.S.A.* **126 C6** 58 55N 137 32W
Faisalabad, *Pakistan* **79 C4** 31 30N 73 5 E
Faith, *U.S.A.* **138 C3** 45 2N 102 2W
Faizabad, *India* **81 F10** 26 45N 82 10 E
Faizpur, *India* **82 D2** 21 14N 75 49 E
Fajardo, *Puerto Rico* **149 C6** 18 20N 65 39W
Fakam, *Yemen* **86 C3** 16 38N 43 49 E
Fakfak, *Indonesia* **73 B4** 3 0 S 132 15 E
Fakiya, *Bulgaria* **43 E12** 42 10N 27 6 E
Fakobli, *Ivory C.* **100 D3** 7 23N 7 23W
Fakse, *Denmark* **15 J6** 55 15N 12 8 E
Fakse Bugt, *Denmark* **15 J6** 55 11N 12 15 E
Fakse Ladeplads, *Denmark* **15 J6** 55 11N 12 9 E
Faku, *China* **67 C12** 42 32N 123 21 E
Falaise, *France* **22 D6** 48 54N 0 12W
Falaise, Mui, *Vietnam* **76 C5** 19 6N 105 45 E
Falakrón Óros, *Greece* **44 C5** 41 15N 23 58 E
Falam, *Burma* **78 D4** 23 0N 93 45 E
Falces, *Spain* **34 C3** 42 24N 1 48W
Fălciu, *Romania* **46 C9** 46 17N 28 7 E
Falcón □, *Venezuela* **152 A4** 11 0N 69 50W
Falcon, C., *Algeria* **99 A4** 35 50N 0 50W
Falcón, C., *Spain* **33 C7** 38 50N 1 23 E
Falcon Dam, *U.S.A.* **139 M5** 26 50N 99 20W
Falconara Marittima, *Italy* **39 E10** 43 37N 13 24 E
Falconer, *U.S.A.* **136 D5** 42 7N 79 13W
Faléa, *Mali* **100 C2** 12 16N 11 17W
Falelatai, *W. Samoa* **121 W24** 13 55 S 171 59W
Falelima, *W. Samoa* **121 W23** 13 32 S 172 41W
Falenki, *Russia* **54 B3** 58 22N 51 35 E
Faleshty = Făleşti, *Moldova* **51 J4** 47 32N 27 44 E
Făleşti, *Moldova* **51 J4** 47 32N 27 44 E
Falfurrias, *U.S.A.* **139 M5** 27 14N 98 9W
Falher, *Canada* **130 B5** 55 44N 117 15W
Falirakí, *Greece* **32 C10** 36 22N 28 12 E
Falkenberg, *Germany* **26 D9** 51 35N 13 14 E
Falkenberg, *Sweden* **15 H6** 56 54N 12 30 E
Falkensee, *Germany* **26 C9** 52 14N 13 4 E
Falkenstein, *Germany* **26 E8** 50 28N 12 20 E
Falkirk, *U.K.* **18 F5** 56 0N 3 47W
Falkirk □, *U.K.* **18 F5** 55 58N 3 49W
Falkland, East, I., *Falk. Is.* **160 D5** 51 40 S 58 30W
Falkland, West, I., *Falk. Is.* **160 D4** 51 40 S 60 0W
Falkland Is. □, *Atl. Oc.* **160 D5** 51 30 S 59 0W
Falkland Sd., *Falk. Is.* **160 D5** 52 0 S 60 0W
Falkonéra, *Greece* **45 H5** 36 50N 23 52 E
Falköping, *Sweden* **15 F7** 58 12N 13 33 E
Fall River, *U.S.A.* **137 E13** 41 43N 71 10W
Fall River Mills, *U.S.A.* **142 F3** 41 3N 121 26W
Fallbrook, *U.S.A.* **143 K5** 33 25N 117 12W
Fallbrook, *Calif., U.S.A.* **145 M9** 33 23N 117 15W
Fallon, *Mont., U.S.A.* **138 B2** 46 50N 105 8W
Fallon, *Nev., U.S.A.* **142 G4** 39 28N 118 47W
Falls City, *Nebr., U.S.A.* **138 E7** 40 3N 95 36W
Falls City, *Oreg., U.S.A.* **142 D2** 44 52N 123 26W
Falls Creek, *U.S.A.* **136 E6** 41 9N 78 48W
Falmouth, *Jamaica* **148 C4** 18 30N 77 40W
Falmouth, *U.K.* **17 G2** 50 9N 5 5W
Falmouth, *U.S.A.* **141 F12** 38 41N 84 20W
False B., *S. Africa* **104 E2** 34 15 S 18 40 E
False Divi Pt., *India* **83 G5** 15 43N 80 50 E
Falset, *Spain* **34 D5** 41 7N 0 50 E
Falso, C., *Honduras* **148 C3** 15 12N 83 21W
Falster, *Denmark* **15 K5** 54 45N 11 55 E
Falsterbo, *Sweden* **15 J6** 55 23N 12 50 E
Fălticeni, *Romania* **46 B7** 47 21N 26 20 E
Falun, *Sweden* **13 F16** 60 37N 15 37 E
Famagusta, *Cyprus* **32 D12** 35 8N 33 55 E
Famagusta Bay, *Cyprus* **32 D13** 35 15N 34 0 E
Famatina, Sierra de, *Argentina* **158 B2** 27 30 S 68 0W
Family L., *Canada* **131 C9** 51 54N 95 27W
Famoso, *U.S.A.* **145 K7** 35 37N 119 12W
Fan Xian, *China* **66 G8** 35 55N 115 38 E
Fana, *Mali* **100 C3** 13 0N 6 56W
Fanárion, *Greece* **44 E3** 39 24N 21 47 E
Fandriana, *Madag.* **105 C8** 20 14 S 47 21 E
Fang, *Thailand* **76 C2** 19 55N 99 13 E
Fang Xian, *China* **69 A8** 32 3N 110 40 E
Fangchang, *China* **69 B12** 31 5N 118 4 E
Fangcheng, *Guangxi Zhuangzu, China* **68 G7** 21 42N 108 21 E
Fangcheng, *Henan, China* **66 H7** 33 18N 112 59 E
Fangliao, *Taiwan* **69 F13** 22 22N 120 38 E
Fangshan, *China* **66 E6** 38 3N 111 25 E
Fangzi, *China* **67 F10** 36 33N 119 10 E
Fani i Madh →, *Albania* **44 C2** 41 56N 20 16 E
Fanjiatun, *China* **67 C13** 43 40N 125 15 E
Fannich, L., *U.K.* **18 D4** 57 38N 4 59W
Fannūj, *Iran* **85 E8** 26 35N 59 38 E
Fanny Bay, *Canada* **130 D4** 49 37N 124 48W
Fanø, *Denmark* **15 J2** 55 25N 8 25 E
Fano, *Italy* **39 E10** 43 50N 13 1 E
Fanshaw, *U.S.A.* **130 B2** 57 11N 133 30W
Fanshi, *China* **66 E7** 39 12N 113 20 E
Fao = Al Fāw, *Iraq* **85 D6** 30 0N 48 30 E
Faqirwali, *Pakistan* **80 E5** 29 27N 73 0 E
Fara in Sabina, *Italy* **39 F9** 42 12N 12 43 E
Farab, *Turkmenistan* **55 D1** 39 9N 63 36 E
Faradje, *Zaïre* **106 B2** 3 50N 29 45 E
Farafangana, *Madag.* **105 C8** 22 49 S 47 50 E
Farâfra, El Wâhât el-, *Egypt* **94 B2** 27 15N 28 20 E
Farāh, *Afghan.* **79 B1** 32 20N 62 7 E
Farāh □, *Afghan.* **79 B1** 32 25N 62 10 E
Farahalana, *Madag.* **105 A9** 14 26 S 50 10 E
Faraid, Gebel, *Egypt* **94 C4** 23 33N 35 19 E
Faramana, *Burkina Faso* **100 C4** 11 56N 4 45W
Faranah, *Guinea* **100 C2** 10 3N 10 45W
Farasān, Jazā'ir, *Si. Arabia* **86 C3** 16 45N 41 55 E
Farasan Is. = Farasān, Jazā'ir, *Si. Arabia* **86 C3** 16 45N 41 55 E
Faratsiho, *Madag.* **105 B8** 19 24 S 46 57 E
Farbarachi, *Somali Rep.* **108 D3** 2 30N 45 30 E
Fardes →, *Spain* **35 H1** 37 35N 3 0W
Fareham, *U.K.* **17 G6** 50 51N 1 11W
Farewell, C., *N.Z.* **119 A7** 40 29 S 172 43 E
Farewell C. = Farvel, Kap, *Greenland* **124 D15** 59 48N 43 55W
Farewell Spit, *N.Z.* **119 A8** 40 35 S 173 0 E
Farghona, *Uzbekistan* **55 C5** 40 23N 71 19 E
Farghonskaya Dolina, *Uzbekistan* **55 C5** 40 50N 71 30 E
Fargo, *U.S.A.* **138 B6** 46 53N 96 48W
Fār'iah, W. al →, *West Bank* **91 C4** 32 12N 35 27 E
Faribault, *U.S.A.* **138 C8** 44 18N 93 16W
Faridkot, *India* **80 D6** 30 44N 74 45 E
Faridpur, *Bangla.* **78 D2** 23 15N 89 55 E
Färila, *Sweden* **14 C9** 61 48N 15 50 E
Farim, *Guinea-Biss.* **100 C1** 12 27N 15 9W
Farīmān, *Iran* **85 C8** 35 40N 59 49 E
Farina, *Australia* **115 E2** 30 3 S 138 15 E
Farinha →, *Brazil* **154 C2** 6 51 S 47 30W
Fariones, Pta., *Canary Is.* **33 E6** 29 13N 13 28W
Fâriskûr, *Egypt* **94 H7** 31 20N 31 43 E
Farmakonisi, *Greece* **45 G9** 37 17N 27 8 E
Farmer City, *U.S.A.* **141 D8** 40 15N 88 39W
Farmersburg, *U.S.A.* **141 E9** 39 15N 87 23W
Farmerville, *U.S.A.* **139 J8** 32 47N 92 24W
Farmington, *Calif., U.S.A.* **144 H6** 37 55N 120 59W
Farmington, *Ill., U.S.A.* **140 D6** 40 42N 90 0W
Farmington, *Iowa, U.S.A.* **140 D5** 40 38N 91 44W
Farmington, *Mo., U.S.A.* **140 G6** 37 47N 90 25W
Farmington, *N.H., U.S.A.* **137 C13** 43 24N 71 4W
Farmington, *N. Mex., U.S.A.* **143 H9** 36 44N 108 12W
Farmington, *Utah, U.S.A.* **142 F8** 41 0N 111 12W
Farmington →, *U.S.A.* **137 E12** 41 51N 72 38W
Farmland, *U.S.A.* **141 D11** 40 15N 85 5W
Farmville, *U.S.A.* **134 G6** 37 18N 78 24W
Farnborough, *U.K.* **17 F7** 51 16N 0 45W
Farne Is., *U.K.* **16 B6** 55 38N 1 37W
Farnham, *Canada* **137 A12** 45 17N 72 59W
Faro, *Brazil* **153 D6** 2 10 S 56 39W
Faro, *Portugal* **37 H3** 37 2N 7 55W
Fårö, *Sweden* **13 H18** 57 55N 19 5 E
Faro □, *Portugal* **37 H2** 37 12N 8 10W
Farquhar, C., *Australia* **113 D1** 23 50 S 113 36 E
Farquhar Is., *Seychelles* **109 F4** 11 0 S 52 0 E
Farrars Cr. →, *Australia* **114 D3** 25 35 S 140 43 E
Farrāshband, *Iran* **85 D7** 28 57N 52 5 E
Farrell, *U.S.A.* **136 E4** 41 13N 80 30W
Farrell Flat, *Australia* **116 B3** 33 48 S 138 48 E
Farrokhī, *Iran* **85 C8** 33 50N 59 31 E
Farruch, C., *Spain* **33 B10** 39 47N 3 21 E
Farrukhabad-cum-Fatehgarh, *India* **81 F8** 27 30N 79 32 E
Fārs □, *Iran* **85 D7** 29 30N 55 0 E
Fársala, *Greece* **44 E4** 39 17N 22 23 E
Fārsī, *Afghan.* **79 B1** 33 47N 63 15 E
Farsø, *Denmark* **15 H3** 56 46N 9 19 E
Farsund, *Norway* **13 G12** 58 5N 6 55 E
Fartak, Râs, *Si. Arabia* **84 D2** 28 5N 34 34 E
Fartak, Ra's, *Yemen* **87 D6** 15 38N 52 15 E
Fartura, Serra da, *Brazil* **159 B5** 26 21 S 52 52W
Faru, *Nigeria* **101 C6** 12 48N 6 12 E
Fārūj, *Iran* **85 B8** 37 14N 58 14 E
Farum, *Denmark* **15 J6** 55 49N 12 21 E
Farvel, Kap, *Greenland* **124 D15** 59 48N 43 55W
Farwell, *U.S.A.* **139 H3** 34 23N 103 2W
Fāryāb □, *Afghan.* **79 B2** 36 0N 65 0 E
Fasā, *Iran* **85 D7** 29 0N 53 39 E
Fasano, *Italy* **41 B10** 40 50N 17 22 E
Fashoda, *Sudan* **95 F3** 9 50N 32 2 E
Fastiv, *Ukraine* **51 G5** 50 7N 29 57 E
Fastnet Rock, *Ireland* **19 E2** 51 22N 9 37W
Fastov = Fastiv, *Ukraine* **51 G5** 50 7N 29 57 E
Fatagar, Tanjung, *Indonesia* **73 B4** 2 46 S 131 57 E
Fatehgarh, *India* **81 F8** 27 25N 79 35 E
Fatehpur, *Raj., India* **80 F6** 28 0N 74 40 E
Fatehpur, *Ut. P., India* **81 G9** 25 56N 81 13 E
Fatesh, *Russia* **52 D2** 52 8N 35 57 E
Fatick, *Senegal* **100 C1** 14 19N 16 27W
Fatima, *Canada* **129 C7** 47 24N 61 53W
Fátima, *Portugal* **37 F2** 39 37N 8 39W
Fatoya, *Guinea* **100 C3** 11 37N 9 10W
Fatsa, *Turkey* **88 B7** 41 2N 37 31 E
Faucille, Col de la, *France* **25 B10** 46 22N 6 2 E
Faulkton, *U.S.A.* **138 C5** 45 2N 99 8W
Faulquemont, *France* **23 C13** 49 3N 6 36 E
Fauquembergues, *France* **23 B9** 50 36N 2 5 E
Faure I., *Australia* **113 E1** 25 52 S 113 50 E
Făurei, *Romania* **46 D8** 45 6N 27 19 E
Fauresmith, *S. Africa* **104 D4** 29 44 S 25 17 E
Fauro, *Solomon Is.* **121 L9** 6 55 S 156 7 E
Fauske, *Norway* **12 C16** 67 17N 15 25 E
Fauvillers, *Belgium* **21 J7** 49 51N 5 40 E
Favara, *Italy* **40 E6** 37 19N 13 39 E
Favaritx, C., *Spain* **33 A11** 40 0N 4 15 E
Favignana, *Italy* **40 E5** 37 56N 12 20 E
Favignana, I., *Italy* **40 E5** 37 56N 12 19 E
Favourable Lake, *Canada* **128 B1** 52 50N 93 39W
Fawn →, *Canada* **128 A2** 55 20N 87 35W
Fawnskin, *U.S.A.* **145 L10** 34 16N 116 56W
Faxaflói, *Iceland* **12 D2** 64 29N 23 0W
Faya-Largeau, *Chad* **97 E3** 17 58N 19 6 E
Fayaoué, *Vanuatu* **121 K4** 20 38 S 166 33 E
Fayd, *Si. Arabia* **84 E4** 27 1N 42 52 E
Fayence, *France* **25 E10** 43 38N 6 42 E
Fayette, *Ala., U.S.A.* **135 J2** 33 41N 87 50W
Fayette, *Iowa, U.S.A.* **140 B5** 42 51N 91 48W
Fayette, *Mo., U.S.A.* **140 E4** 39 9N 92 41W
Fayette, *Ohio, U.S.A.* **141 C12** 41 40N 84 20W
Fayetteville, *Ark., U.S.A.* **139 G7** 36 4N 94 10W
Fayetteville, *N.C., U.S.A.* **135 H6** 35 3N 78 53W
Fayetteville, *Tenn., U.S.A.* **135 H2** 35 9N 86 34W
Fayón, *Spain* **34 D5** 41 15N 0 20 E
Fazenda Libongo, *Angola* **103 D2** 8 24 S 13 24 E
Fazenda Nova, *Brazil* **155 E1** 16 11 S 50 48W
Fazilka, *India* **80 D6** 30 27N 74 2 E
Fazilpur, *Pakistan* **80 E4** 29 18N 70 29 E
Fdérik, *Mauritania* **98 D2** 22 40N 12 45W
Feale →, *Ireland* **19 D2** 52 27N 9 37W
Fear, C., *U.S.A.* **135 J7** 33 50N 77 58W
Feather →, *U.S.A.* **142 G3** 38 47N 121 36W
Feather Falls, *U.S.A.* **144 F5** 39 36N 121 16W
Featherston, *N.Z.* **118 H4** 41 6 S 175 20 E
Featherstone, *Zimbabwe* **107 F3** 18 42 S 30 55 E
Fécamp, *France* **22 C7** 49 45N 0 22 E
Fedala = Mohammedia, *Morocco* **98 B3** 33 44N 7 21W
Federación, *Argentina* **158 C4** 31 0 S 57 55W
Fedeshkūh, *Iran* **85 D7** 28 49N 53 50 E
Fedjadj, Chott el, *Tunisia* **96 B1** 33 52N 9 14 E
Fehérgyarmat, *Hungary* **31 D15** 48 0N 22 30 E
Fehmarn, *Germany* **26 A7** 54 27N 11 7 E
Fehmarn Bælt, *Europe* **13 J14** 54 35N 11 20 E
Fei Xian, *China* **67 G9** 35 18N 117 59 E
Feijó, *Brazil* **156 B3** 8 9 S 70 21W
Feilding, *N.Z.* **118 G4** 40 13 S 175 35 E
Feira de Santana, *Brazil* **155 D4** 12 15 S 38 57W
Feixiang, *China* **66 F8** 36 30N 114 45 E
Fejér □, *Hungary* **31 D11** 47 9N 18 30 E
Fejø, *Denmark* **15 K5** 54 55N 11 30 E
Feke, *Turkey* **88 D6** 37 48N 35 56 E
Fekete →, *Hungary* **31 F11** 45 47N 18 15 E
Felanitx, *Spain* **33 B10** 39 28N 3 9 E
Feldbach, *Austria* **30 E8** 46 57N 15 52 E
Feldberg, *Baden-W., Germany* **27 H3** 47 52N 8 0 E
Feldberg, *Mecklenburg-Vorpommern, Germany* **26 B9** 53 20N 13 25 E
Feldkirch, *Austria* **30 D2** 47 15N 9 37 E
Feldkirchen, *Austria* **30 E7** 46 44N 14 6 E
Felicity, *U.S.A.* **141 F12** 38 51N 84 6W
Felipe Carrillo Puerto, *Mexico* **147 D7** 19 38N 88 3W
Felixlândia, *Brazil* **155 E3** 18 47 S 44 55W
Felixstowe, *U.K.* **17 F9** 51 58N 1 23 E
Felletin, *France* **24 C6** 45 53N 2 11 E
Felton, *U.K.* **16 B6** 55 18N 1 42W
Felton, *U.S.A.* **144 H4** 37 3N 122 4W
Feltre, *Italy* **39 B8** 46 1N 11 54 E
Femø, *Denmark* **15 K5** 54 58N 11 35 E
Femunden, *Norway* **14 B5** 62 10N 11 53 E
Fen He →, *China* **66 G6** 35 36N 110 42 E
Fenelon Falls, *Canada* **136 B6** 44 32N 78 45W
Feneroa, *Ethiopia* **95 E4** 13 5N 39 3 E
Feng Xian, *Jiangsu, China* **66 G9** 34 43N 116 35 E
Feng Xian, *Shaanxi, China* **66 H4** 33 54N 106 40 E
Fengári, *Greece* **44 D7** 40 25N 25 32 E
Fengcheng, *Jiangxi, China* **69 C10** 28 12N 115 48 E
Fengcheng, *Liaoning, China* **67 D13** 40 28N 124 5 E
Fengdu, *China* **68 C6** 29 55N 107 41 E
Fengfeng, *China* **66 F8** 36 28N 114 8 E
Fenggang, *China* **68 D6** 27 57N 107 47 E
Fenghua, *China* **69 C13** 29 40N 121 25 E
Fenghuang, *China* **68 D7** 27 57N 109 29 E
Fenghuangzui, *China* **68 A7** 33 30N 109 23 E
Fengjie, *China* **68 B7** 31 5N 109 36 E
Fengkai, *China* **69 F8** 23 24N 111 30 E
Fengle, *China* **69 B9** 31 29N 112 29 E
Fengning, *China* **66 D9** 41 10N 116 33 E
Fengqing, *China* **68 E2** 24 38N 99 55 E
Fengqiu, *China* **66 G8** 35 2N 114 25 E
Fengrun, *China* **67 E10** 39 48N 118 8 E
Fengshan, *Guangxi Zhuangzu, China* **68 E7** 24 39N 109 15 E
Fengshan, *Guangxi Zhuangzu, China* **68 E6** 24 31N 107 3 E
Fengtai, *Anhui, China* **69 A11** 32 50N 116 40 E
Fengtai, *Beijing, China* **66 E9** 39 50N 116 18 E
Fengxian, *China* **69 B13** 30 55N 121 26 E
Fengxiang, *China* **66 G4** 34 29N 107 25 E
Fengxin, *China* **69 C10** 28 41N 115 18 E
Fengyang, *China* **67 H9** 32 51N 117 29 E
Fengyi, *China* **68 E3** 25 37N 100 20 E
Fengzhen, *China* **66 D7** 40 25N 113 2 E
Feni Is., *Papua N. G.* **120 C7** 4 0 S 153 40 E
Fenit, *Ireland* **19 D2** 52 17N 9 51W
Fennimore, *U.S.A.* **140 B6** 42 59N 90 39W
Fenny, *Bangla.* **78 D3** 22 55N 91 32 E
Feno, C. de, *France* **25 G12** 41 58N 8 33 E
Fenoarivo Afovoany, *Madag.* **105 B8** 18 26 S 46 34 E
Fenoarivo Atsinanana, *Madag.* **105 B8** 17 22 S 49 25 E
Fens, The, *U.K.* **16 E8** 52 38N 0 2W
Fenton, *U.S.A.* **141 B13** 42 48N 83 42W
Fenxi, *China* **66 F6** 36 40N 111 31 E
Fenyang, *China* **66 F6** 37 18N 111 48 E
Fenyi, *China* **69 D10** 27 45N 114 47 E
Feodosiya, *Ukraine* **51 K8** 45 2N 35 16 E
Fer, C. de, *Algeria* **99 A6** 37 3N 7 10 E
Ferdows, *Iran* **85 C8** 33 58N 58 2 E
Fère-Champenoise, *France* **23 D10** 48 45N 3 59 E
Fère-en-Tardenois, *France* **23 C10** 49 10N 3 30 E
Ferentino, *Italy* **40 A6** 41 42N 13 15 E
Ferfer, *Somali Rep.* **108 C3** 5 4N 45 9 E
Fergana = Farghona, *Uzbekistan* **55 C5** 40 23N 71 19 E
Ferganskaya Dolina = Farghonskaya Dolina, *Uzbekistan* **55 C5** 40 50N 71 30 E
Ferganskiy Khrebet, *Kyrgyzstan* **55 C6** 41 0N 73 50 E
Fergus, *Canada* **128 D3** 43 43N 80 24W
Fergus Falls, *U.S.A.* **138 B6** 46 17N 96 4W
Ferguson, *U.S.A.* **140 F6** 38 45N 90 18W
Fergusson I., *Papua N. G.* **120 E6** 9 30 S 150 45 E
Fériana, *Tunisia* **96 B1** 34 59N 8 33 E
Feričanci, *Croatia* **42 B3** 45 32N 18 0 E
Ferkane, *Algeria* **99 B6** 34 37N 7 26 E
Ferkéssédougou, *Ivory C.* **100 D3** 9 35N 5 6W
Ferlach, *Austria* **30 E7** 46 32N 14 18 E
Ferland, *Canada* **128 B2** 50 19N 88 27W
Ferlo, Vallée du, *Senegal* **100 B2** 15 15N 14 15W
Fermanagh □, *U.K.* **19 B4** 54 21N 7 40W
Fermo, *Italy* **39 E10** 43 10N 13 43 E
Fermoselle, *Spain* **36 D4** 41 19N 6 27W
Fermoy, *Ireland* **19 D3** 52 9N 8 16W
Fernán Nuñéz, *Spain* **37 H6** 37 40N 4 44W
Fernández, *Argentina* **158 B3** 27 55 S 63 50W
Fernandina Beach, *U.S.A.* **135 K5** 30 40N 81 27W
Fernando de Noronha, *Brazil* **154 B5** 4 0 S 33 10W
Fernando Póo = Bioko, *Eq. Guin.* **101 E6** 3 30N 8 40 E
Fernandópolis, *Brazil* **155 F1** 20 16 S 50 14W
Ferndale, *Calif., U.S.A.* **142 F1** 40 35N 124 16W
Ferndale, *Wash., U.S.A.* **144 B4** 48 51N 122 36W
Fernie, *Canada* **130 D5** 49 30N 115 5W
Fernlees, *Australia* **114 C4** 23 51 S 148 7 E
Fernley, *U.S.A.* **142 G4** 39 36N 119 15W
Feroke, *India* **83 J2** 11 9N 75 46 E
Ferozepore = Firozpur, *India* **80 D6** 30 55N 74 40 E
Férrai, *Greece* **44 D8** 40 53N 26 10 E
Ferrandina, *Italy* **41 B9** 40 29N 16 27 E
Ferrara, *Italy* **39 D8** 44 50N 11 35 E
Ferrato, C., *Italy* **40 C2** 39 18N 9 38 E
Ferreira do Alentejo, *Portugal* **37 G2** 38 4N 8 6W
Ferreñafe, *Peru* **156 B2** 6 42 S 79 50W

Furness 199

Fort Rupert = Waskaganish, Canada 128 B4 51 30N 78 40W
Fort St. James, Canada 130 C4 54 30N 124 10W
Fort St. John, Canada 130 B4 56 15N 120 50W
Fort Sandeman, Pakistan 79 C3 31 20N 69 31 E
Fort Saskatchewan, Canada 130 C6 53 40N 113 15W
Fort Scott, U.S.A. 139 G7 37 50N 94 42W
Fort Severn, Canada 128 A2 56 0N 87 40W
Fort Shevchenko, Kazakstan 53 H10 44 35N 50 23 E
Fort Simpson, Canada 130 A4 61 45N 121 15W
Fort Smith, Canada 130 B6 60 0N 111 51W
Fort Smith, U.S.A. 139 H7 35 23N 94 25W
Fort Stanton, U.S.A. 143 K11 33 30N 105 31W
Fort Stockton, U.S.A. 139 K3 30 53N 102 53W
Fort Sumner, U.S.A. 139 H2 34 28N 104 15W
Fort Thomas, U.S.A. 141 E12 39 5N 84 27W
Fort Trinquet = Bir Mogrein, Mauritania 98 C2 25 10N 11 25W
Fort Valley, U.S.A. 135 J4 32 33N 83 53W
Fort Vermilion, Canada 130 B5 58 24N 116 0W
Fort Walton Beach, U.S.A. 135 K2 30 25N 86 36W
Fort Wayne, U.S.A. 141 C11 41 4N 85 9W
Fort William, U.K. 18 E3 56 49N 5 7W
Fort Worth, U.S.A. 139 J6 32 45N 97 18W
Fort Yates, U.S.A. 138 B4 46 5N 100 38W
Fort Yukon, U.S.A. 126 B5 66 34N 145 16W
Fortaleza, Bolivia 156 C4 12 6 S 66 49W
Fortaleza, Brazil 154 B4 3 45 S 38 35W
Forteau, Canada 129 B8 51 28N 56 58W
Forth →, U.K. 18 E5 56 9N 3 50W
Forth, Firth of, U.K. 18 E6 56 5N 2 55W
Forthassa Rharbia, Algeria 99 B4 32 52N 1 18W
Fortín Coronel Eugenio Garay, Paraguay 157 E5 20 31 S 62 8W
Fortín Garrapatal, Paraguay 157 E5 21 27 S 61 30W
Fortín General Pando, Paraguay 157 D6 19 45 S 59 47W
Fortín Madrejón, Paraguay 157 E6 20 45 S 59 52W
Fortín Uno, Argentina 160 A3 38 50 S 65 18W
Fortore →, Italy 39 G12 41 55N 15 17 E
Fortrose, N.Z. 119 G3 46 38 S 168 45 E
Fortrose, U.K. 18 D4 57 35N 4 9W
Fortuna, Spain 35 G3 38 11N 1 7W
Fortuna, Calif., U.S.A. 142 F1 40 36N 124 9W
Fortuna, N. Dak., U.S.A. 138 A3 48 55N 103 47W
Fortune B., Canada 129 C8 47 30N 55 22W
Fos-sur-Mer, France 25 E8 43 26N 4 56 E
Foshan, China 69 F9 23 4N 113 5 E
Fosna, Norway 12 E14 63 50N 10 20 E
Fosnavåg, Norway 13 E11 62 22N 5 38 E
Fossacésia, Italy 39 F11 42 15N 14 29 E
Fossano, Italy 38 D4 44 33N 7 43 E
Fosses-la-Ville, Belgium 21 H5 50 24N 4 41 E
Fossil, U.S.A. 142 D3 45 0N 120 9W
Fossilbrook, Australia 114 B3 17 47 S 144 29 E
Fossombrone, Italy 39 E9 43 41N 12 48 E
Fosston, U.S.A. 138 B7 47 35N 95 45W
Foster, Canada 137 A12 45 17N 72 30W
Foster, U.S.A. 141 F12 38 48N 84 13W
Foster →, Canada 131 B7 55 47N 105 49W
Fosters Ra., Australia 114 C1 21 35 S 133 48 E
Fostoria, U.S.A. 141 C13 41 10N 83 25W
Fotuha'a, Tonga 121 P13 19 49 S 174 44W
Fougamou, Gabon 102 C2 1 16 S 10 30 E
Fougères, France 22 D5 48 21N 1 14W
Foul Pt., Sri Lanka 83 K5 8 35N 81 18 E
Foula, U.K. 18 A6 60 10N 2 5W
Foulness I., U.K. 17 F8 51 36N 0 55 E
Foulpointe, Madag. 105 B8 17 41 S 49 31 E
Foulwind, C., N.Z. 119 B6 41 45 S 171 28 E
Foum Assaka, Morocco 98 C2 29 8N 10 24W
Foum Zguid, Morocco 98 B3 30 2N 6 59W
Foumban, Cameroon 101 D7 5 45N 10 50 E
Foundiougne, Senegal 100 C1 14 5N 16 32W
Fountain, Colo., U.S.A. 138 F2 38 41N 104 42W
Fountain, Utah, U.S.A. 142 G8 39 41N 111 37W
Fountain Springs, U.S.A. 145 K8 35 54N 118 51W
Fourchambault, France 23 E10 47 2N 3 3 E
Fourchu, Canada 129 C7 45 43N 60 17W
Fouriesburg, S. Africa 104 D4 28 38 S 28 14 E
Fourmies, France 23 B11 50 1N 4 2 E
Fournás, Greece 45 E3 39 3N 21 52 E
Foúrnoi, Greece 45 G8 37 36N 26 32 E
Fours, France 23 F10 46 50N 3 42 E
Fouta Djalon, Guinea 100 C2 11 20N 12 10W
Foux, Cap-à-, Haiti 149 C5 19 43N 73 27W
Foveaux Str., N.Z. 119 G3 46 42 S 168 10 E
Fowey, U.K. 17 G3 50 20N 4 39W
Fowler, Calif., U.S.A. 144 J7 36 38N 119 41W
Fowler, Colo., U.S.A. 138 F2 38 8N 104 2W
Fowler, Ind., U.S.A. 141 D9 40 37N 87 19W
Fowler, Kans., U.S.A. 139 G4 37 23N 100 12W
Fowler, Mich., U.S.A. 141 B12 43 0N 84 45W
Fowlers B., Australia 113 F5 31 59 S 132 34 E
Fowlerton, U.S.A. 139 L5 28 28N 98 48W
Fowlerville, U.S.A. 141 B12 42 40N 84 4W
Fowman, Iran 89 D13 37 13N 49 19 E
Fox →, Canada 131 B10 56 3N 93 18W
Fox Valley, Canada 131 C7 50 30N 109 25W
Foxe Basin, Canada 127 B12 66 0N 77 0W
Foxe Chan., Canada 127 B11 65 0N 80 0W
Foxe Pen., Canada 127 B12 65 0N 76 0W
Foxhol, Neths. 20 B9 53 10N 6 43 E
Foxpark, U.S.A. 142 F10 41 5N 106 9W
Foxton, N.Z. 118 G4 40 29 S 175 18 E
Foyle, Lough, U.K. 19 A4 55 7N 7 4W
Foynes, Ireland 19 D2 52 37N 9 7W
Foz, Spain 36 B3 43 33N 7 20W
Fóz do Cunene, Angola 103 F2 17 15 S 11 48 E
Foz do Gregório, Brazil 156 B3 6 47 S 70 44W
Foz do Iguaçu, Brazil 159 B5 25 30 S 54 30W
Foz do Riosinho, Brazil 156 B3 7 11 S 71 50W
Frackville, U.S.A. 137 F8 40 47N 76 14W
Fraga, Spain 34 D5 41 32N 0 21 E
Fraire, Belgium 21 H5 50 16N 4 31 E
Frameries, Belgium 21 H3 50 24N 3 54 E
Framingham, U.S.A. 137 D13 42 17N 71 25W
Frampol, Poland 47 E9 50 41N 22 40 E
Franca, Brazil 155 F2 20 33 S 47 30W
Francavilla al Mare, Italy 39 F11 42 25N 14 17 E
Francavilla Fontana, Italy 41 B10 40 32N 17 35 E
France ■, Europe 11 F6 47 0N 3 0 E
Frances, Australia 116 D4 36 41 S 140 55 E
Frances →, Canada 130 A3 60 16N 129 10W
Frances L., Canada 130 A3 61 23N 129 30W
Francés Viejo, C., Dom. Rep. 149 C6 19 40N 69 55W
Francesville, U.S.A. 141 D10 40 59N 86 53W
Franceville, Gabon 102 C2 1 40 S 13 32 E
Franche-Comté, France 23 F12 46 50N 5 55 E
Franches Montagnes, Switz. 28 B4 47 10N 7 0 E
Francisco de Orellana, Ecuador 152 D2 0 28 S 76 58W
Francisco I. Madero, Coahuila, Mexico 146 B4 25 48N 103 18W
Francisco I. Madero, Durango, Mexico 146 C4 24 32N 104 22W
Francisco Sá, Brazil 155 E3 16 28 S 43 30W
Francistown, Botswana 105 C4 21 7 S 27 33 E
Francofonte, Italy 41 E7 37 14N 14 53 E
François, Canada 129 C8 47 35N 56 45W
François L., Canada 130 C3 54 0N 125 30W
Francorchamps, Belgium 21 H7 50 27N 5 57 E
Franeker, Neths. 20 B7 53 12N 5 33 E
Frankado, Djibouti 95 E5 12 30N 43 12 E
Frankenberg, Germany 26 D4 51 3N 8 48 E
Frankenthal, Germany 27 F4 49 32N 8 21 E
Frankenwald, Germany 27 E7 50 20N 11 30 E
Frankford, U.S.A. 140 E5 39 29N 91 19W
Frankfort, S. Africa 105 D4 27 17 S 28 30 E
Frankfort, Ind., U.S.A. 141 D10 40 17N 86 31W
Frankfort, Kans., U.S.A. 138 F6 39 42N 96 25W
Frankfort, Ky., U.S.A. 141 F12 38 12N 84 52W
Frankfort, Mich., U.S.A. 134 C2 44 38N 86 14W
Frankfort, Ohio, U.S.A. 141 E13 39 24N 83 11W
Frankfurt, Brandenburg, Germany 26 C10 52 20N 14 32 E
Frankfurt, Hessen, Germany 27 E4 50 7N 8 41 E
Fränkische Alb, Germany 27 F7 49 10N 11 23 E
Fränkische Rezal →, Germany 27 F7 49 11N 11 1 E
Fränkische Saale →, Germany 27 E5 50 3N 9 42 E
Fränkische Schweiz, Germany 27 F7 49 26N 11 16 E
Frankland →, Australia 113 G2 35 0 S 116 48 E
Franklin, Ill., U.S.A. 140 E6 39 37N 90 3W
Franklin, Ind., U.S.A. 141 E10 39 29N 86 3W
Franklin, Ky., U.S.A. 135 G2 36 43N 86 35W
Franklin, La., U.S.A. 139 L9 29 48N 91 30W
Franklin, Mass., U.S.A. 137 D13 42 5N 71 24W
Franklin, N.H., U.S.A. 137 C13 43 27N 71 39W
Franklin, Nebr., U.S.A. 138 E5 40 6N 98 57W
Franklin, Ohio, U.S.A. 141 E12 39 34N 84 18W
Franklin, Pa., U.S.A. 136 E5 41 24N 79 50W
Franklin, Tenn., U.S.A. 135 H2 35 55N 86 52W
Franklin, Va., U.S.A. 135 G7 36 41N 76 56W
Franklin, W. Va., U.S.A. 134 F6 38 39N 79 20W
Franklin B., Canada 126 B7 69 45N 126 0W
Franklin D. Roosevelt L., U.S.A. 142 B4 48 18N 118 9W
Franklin I., Antarctica 7 D11 76 10 S 168 30 E
Franklin L., U.S.A. 142 F6 40 25N 115 22W
Franklin Mts., Canada 126 B7 65 0N 125 0W
Franklin Mts., N.Z. 119 E2 44 55 S 167 45 E
Franklin Str., Canada 126 A10 72 0N 96 0W
Franklinton, U.S.A. 139 K9 30 51N 90 9W
Franklinville, U.S.A. 136 D6 42 20N 78 27W
Franklyn Mt., N.Z. 119 C7 42 4 S 172 42 E
Franks Pk., U.S.A. 142 E9 43 58N 109 18W
Frankston, Australia 117 E6 38 8 S 145 8 E
Frankton Junc., N.Z. 118 D4 37 47 S 175 16 E
Fränsta, Sweden 14 B10 62 30N 16 11 E
Frantsa Iosifa, Zemlya, Russia 56 A6 82 0N 55 0 E
Franz, Canada 128 C3 48 25N 84 30W
Franz Josef Land = Frantsa Iosifa, Zemlya, Russia 56 A6 82 0N 55 0 E
Franzburg, Germany 26 A8 54 11N 12 51 E
Frascati, Italy 40 A5 41 48N 12 41 E
Fraser →, B.C., Canada 130 D4 49 7N 123 11W
Fraser →, Nfld., Canada 129 A7 56 39N 62 10W
Fraser, Mt., Australia 113 E2 25 35 S 118 20 E
Fraser I., Australia 115 D5 25 15 S 153 10 E
Fraser Lake, Canada 130 C4 54 0N 124 50W
Fraserburg, S. Africa 104 E3 31 55 S 21 30 E
Fraserburgh, U.K. 18 D6 57 42N 2 1W
Fraserdale, Canada 128 C3 49 55N 81 37W
Frasertown, N.Z. 118 E6 38 58 S 177 28 E
Frashëri, Albania 44 D2 40 23N 20 26 E
Frasne, France 23 F13 46 50N 6 10 E
Frauenfeld, Switz. 29 A7 47 34N 8 54 E
Fray Bentos, Uruguay 158 C4 33 10 S 58 15W
Frazier Downs, Australia 112 C3 18 48 S 121 42 E
Frechilla, Spain 36 C6 42 8N 4 50W
Fredericia, Denmark 15 J3 55 34N 9 45 E
Frederick, Md., U.S.A. 134 F7 39 25N 77 25W
Frederick, Okla., U.S.A. 139 H5 34 23N 99 1W
Frederick, S. Dak., U.S.A. 138 C5 45 50N 98 31W
Frederick Sd., U.S.A. 130 B2 57 10N 134 0W
Fredericksburg, Tex., U.S.A. 139 K5 30 16N 98 52W
Fredericksburg, Va., U.S.A. 134 F7 38 18N 77 28W
Fredericktown, U.S.A. 139 G9 37 34N 90 18W
Frederico I. Madero, Presa, Mexico 146 B3 28 7N 105 40W
Fredericton, Canada 129 C6 45 57N 66 40W
Fredericton Junc., Canada 129 C6 45 41N 66 40W
Frederikshåb, Greenland 6 C5 62 0N 49 43W
Frederikshavn, Denmark 15 G4 57 28N 10 31 E
Frederikssund, Denmark 15 J6 55 50N 12 3 E
Frederiksted, Virgin Is. 149 C7 17 43N 64 53W
Fredonia, Ariz., U.S.A. 143 H7 36 57N 112 32W
Fredonia, Kans., U.S.A. 139 G7 37 32N 95 49W
Fredonia, N.Y., U.S.A. 136 D5 42 26N 79 20W
Fredrikstad, Norway 14 E4 59 13N 10 57 E
Free State □, S. Africa 104 D4 28 30 S 27 0 E
Freeburg, U.S.A. 140 F5 38 19N 91 56W
Freehold, U.S.A. 137 F10 40 16N 74 17W
Freel Peak, U.S.A. 144 G7 38 52N 119 54W
Freeland, U.S.A. 137 E9 41 1N 75 54W
Freels, C., Canada 129 C9 49 15N 53 30W
Freeman, Calif., U.S.A. 145 K9 35 35N 117 53W
Freeman, Mo., U.S.A. 140 F2 38 37N 94 30W
Freeman, S. Dak., U.S.A. 138 D6 43 21N 97 26W
Freeport, Bahamas 148 A4 26 30N 78 47W
Freeport, Canada 129 D6 44 15N 66 20W
Freeport, Ill., U.S.A. 140 B7 42 17N 89 36W
Freeport, N.Y., U.S.A. 137 F11 40 39N 73 35W
Freeport, Tex., U.S.A. 139 L7 28 57N 95 21W
Freetown, S. Leone 100 D2 8 30N 13 17W
Frégate, L., Canada 128 B5 53 15N 74 45W
Fregenal de la Sierra, Spain 37 G4 38 10N 6 39W
Fregene, Italy 40 A5 41 51N 12 12 E
Fréhel, C., France 22 D4 48 40N 2 20W
Freiberg, Germany 26 E9 50 55N 13 20 E
Freibourg = Fribourg, Switz. 28 C4 46 49N 7 9 E
Freiburg, Baden-W., Germany 27 H3 47 59N 7 51 E
Freiburg, Niedersachsen, Germany 26 B5 53 49N 9 16 E
Freiburger Alpen, Switz. 28 C4 46 37N 7 10 E
Freire, Chile 160 A2 38 54 S 72 38W
Freirina, Chile 158 B1 28 30 S 71 10W
Freising, Germany 27 G7 48 24N 11 45 E
Freistadt, Austria 30 C7 48 30N 14 30 E
Freital, Germany 26 E9 51 0N 13 39 E
Fréjus, France 25 E10 43 25N 6 44 E
Fremantle, Australia 113 F2 32 7 S 115 47 E
Fremont, Calif., U.S.A. 144 H4 37 32N 121 57W
Fremont, Ind., U.S.A. 141 C12 41 44N 84 56W
Fremont, Mich., U.S.A. 134 D3 43 28N 85 57W
Fremont, Nebr., U.S.A. 138 E6 41 26N 96 30W
Fremont, Ohio, U.S.A. 141 C13 41 21N 83 7W
Fremont →, U.S.A. 143 G8 38 24N 110 42W
Fremont L., U.S.A. 142 E9 42 57N 109 48W
French Camp, U.S.A. 144 H5 37 53N 121 16W
French Creek →, U.S.A. 136 E5 41 24N 79 50W
French Guiana ■, S. Amer. 153 C7 4 0N 53 0W
French I., Australia 117 E6 38 20 S 145 22 E
French Lick, U.S.A. 141 F10 38 33N 86 37W
French Pass, N.Z. 119 A8 40 55 S 173 55 E
French Polynesia ■, Pac. Oc. 123 J13 20 0 S 145 0W
Frenchburg, U.S.A. 141 G13 37 57N 83 38W
Frenchglen, U.S.A. 142 E4 42 50N 118 55W
Frenchman Butte, Canada 131 C7 53 35N 109 38W
Frenchman Cr. →, Mont., U.S.A. 142 B10 48 31N 107 10W
Frenchman Cr. →, Nebr., U.S.A. 138 E4 40 14N 100 50W
Frenda, Algeria 99 A5 35 2N 1 1 E
Fresco →, Brazil 157 B7 7 15 S 51 30W
Freshfield, C., Antarctica 7 C10 68 25 S 151 10 E
Fresnay-sur-Sarthe, France 22 D7 48 17N 0 1 E
Fresnillo, Mexico 146 C4 23 10N 103 0W
Fresno, U.S.A. 144 J7 36 44N 119 47W
Fresno Alhandiga, Spain 36 E5 40 42N 5 37W
Fresno Reservoir, U.S.A. 142 B9 48 36N 109 57W
Freudenstadt, Germany 27 G4 48 27N 8 24 E
Freux, Belgium 21 J6 49 59N 5 27 E
Frévent, France 23 B9 50 15N 2 17 E
Frew →, Australia 114 C2 20 0 S 135 38 E
Frewena, Australia 114 B2 19 25 S 135 25 E
Freycinet Pen., Australia 114 G4 42 10 S 148 25 E
Freyming-Merlebach, France 23 C13 49 8N 6 48 E
Freyung, Germany 27 G9 48 48N 13 31 E
Fria, Guinea 100 C2 10 27N 13 38W
Fria, C., Namibia 104 B1 18 0 S 12 0 E
Friant, U.S.A. 144 J7 36 59N 119 43W
Frías, Argentina 158 B2 28 40 S 65 5W
Fribourg, Switz. 28 C4 46 49N 7 9 E
Fribourg □, Switz. 28 C4 46 40N 7 0 E
Frick, Switz. 28 A6 47 31N 8 1 E
Friday Harbor, U.S.A. 144 B3 48 32N 123 1W
Friedberg, Bayern, Germany 27 G6 48 21N 10 59 E
Friedberg, Hessen, Germany 27 E4 50 19N 8 45 E
Friedland, Germany 26 B9 53 40N 13 33 E
Friedrichshafen, Germany 27 H5 47 39N 9 30 E
Friedrichskoog, Germany 26 A4 54 0N 8 53 E
Friedrichstadt, Germany 26 A5 54 23N 9 6 E
Friendly Is. = Tonga ■, Pac. Oc. 121 P13 19 50 S 174 30W
Friesach, Austria 30 E7 46 57N 14 24 E
Friesack, Germany 26 C8 52 44N 12 34 E
Friesche Wad, Neths. 20 B7 53 22N 5 44 E
Friesland □, Neths. 20 B7 53 5N 5 50 E
Friesoythe, Germany 26 B3 53 1N 7 51 E
Frillesås, Sweden 15 G6 57 20N 12 12 E
Frio →, U.S.A. 139 L5 28 26N 98 11W
Frio, C., Brazil 150 F6 22 50 S 41 50W
Friona, U.S.A. 139 H3 34 38N 102 43W
Frisian Is., Europe 26 B2 53 30N 6 0 E
Fristad, Sweden 15 G7 57 50N 13 0 E
Fritch, U.S.A. 139 H4 35 38N 101 36W
Fritsla, Sweden 15 G6 57 33N 12 47 E
Fritzlar, Germany 26 D5 51 7N 9 16 E
Friuli-Venézia Giulia □, Italy 39 B10 46 0N 13 0 E
Frobisher B., Canada 127 B13 62 30N 66 0W
Frobisher Bay = Iqaluit, Canada 127 B13 63 44N 68 31W
Frobisher L., Canada 131 B7 56 20N 108 15W
Frogmore, Australia 117 C8 34 15 S 148 52 E
Frohavet, Norway 12 E13 64 0N 9 30 E
Froid, U.S.A. 138 A2 48 20N 104 30W
Froid-Chapelle, Belgium 21 H4 50 9N 4 19 E
Frolovo, Russia 52 F6 49 45N 43 40 E
Fromberg, U.S.A. 142 D9 45 24N 108 54W
Frombork, Poland 47 A6 54 21N 19 41 E
Frome, U.K. 17 F5 51 14N 2 19W
Frome, L., Australia 116 A3 30 45 S 139 45 E
Frome Downs, Australia 116 A3 31 13 S 139 45 E
Frómista, Spain 36 C6 42 16N 4 25W
Front Range, U.S.A. 142 G11 40 25N 105 45W
Front Royal, U.S.A. 134 F6 38 55N 78 12W
Fronteira, Portugal 37 F3 39 3N 7 39W
Fronteiras, Brazil 154 C3 7 5 S 40 37W
Frontera, Canary Is. 33 G2 27 47N 17 59W
Frontera, Mexico 147 D6 18 30N 92 40W
Frontignan, France 24 E7 43 27N 3 45 E
Frosinone, Italy 40 A6 41 38N 13 19 E
Frosolone, Italy 41 A7 41 36N 14 27 E
Frostburg, U.S.A. 134 F6 39 39N 78 56W
Frostisen, Norway 12 B17 68 14N 17 10 E
Frouard, France 23 D13 48 47N 6 8 E
Frøya, Norway 12 E13 63 43N 8 40 E
Fruges, France 23 B9 50 30N 2 8 E
Frumoasa, Romania 46 C6 46 28N 25 48 E
Frunze = Bishkek, Kyrgyzstan 55 B7 42 54N 74 46 E
Fruška Gora, Serbia, Yug. 42 B4 45 7N 19 30 E
Frutal, Brazil 155 F2 20 0 S 49 0W
Frutigen, Switz. 28 C5 46 35N 7 38 E
Frýdek-Místek, Czech. 31 B11 49 40N 18 20 E
Frýdlant, Severočeský, Czech. 30 A8 50 56N 15 9 E
Frýdlant, Severomoravsky, Czech. 31 B11 49 35N 18 20 E
Fryvaldov = Jeseník, Czech. 31 B10 50 0N 17 8 E
Fthiótis □, Greece 45 F4 38 50N 22 25 E
Fu Jiang →, China 68 C6 30 0N 106 16 E
Fu Xian, Liaoning, China 67 E11 39 38N 121 58 E
Fu Xian, Shaanxi, China 66 F5 36 0N 109 20 E
Fu'an, China 69 D12 27 11N 119 36 E
Fubian, China 68 B4 31 17N 102 22 E
Fucécchio, Italy 38 E7 43 44N 10 48 E
Fucheng, China 66 F9 37 50N 116 10 E
Fuchou = Fuzhou, China 69 D12 26 5N 119 16 E
Fuchū, Hiroshima, Japan 62 C5 34 34N 133 14 E
Fūchū, Tōkyō, Japan 63 B11 35 40N 139 29 E
Fuchuan, China 69 E8 24 50N 111 5 E
Fuchun Jiang →, China 69 B13 30 5N 120 5 E
Fúcino, Conca del, Italy 39 F10 42 1N 13 31 E
Fuding, China 69 D13 27 20N 120 12 E
Fuencaliente, Canary Is. 33 F2 28 28N 17 50W
Fuencaliente, Spain 37 G6 38 25N 4 18W
Fuencaliente, Pta., Canary Is. 33 F2 28 27N 17 51W
Fuengirola, Spain 37 J6 36 32N 4 41W
Fuente Alamo, Albacete, Spain 35 G3 38 44N 1 24W
Fuente Álamo, Murcia, Spain 35 H3 37 42N 1 6W
Fuente de Cantos, Spain 37 G4 38 15N 6 18W
Fuente del Maestre, Spain 37 G4 38 31N 6 28W
Fuente el Fresno, Spain 37 F7 39 14N 3 46W
Fuente Ovejuna, Spain 37 G5 38 15N 5 25W
Fuentes de Andalucía, Spain 37 H5 37 28N 5 20W
Fuentes de Ebro, Spain 34 D4 41 31N 0 38W
Fuentes de León, Spain 37 G4 38 5N 6 32W
Fuentes de Oñoro, Spain 36 E4 40 33N 6 52W
Fuentesaúco, Spain 36 D5 41 15N 5 30W
Fuerte →, Mexico 146 B3 25 50N 109 25W
Fuerte Olimpo, Paraguay 158 A4 21 0 S 57 51W
Fuerteventura, Canary Is. 33 F6 28 30N 14 0W
Fufeng, China 66 G4 34 22N 108 0 E
Fuga I., Phil. 70 B3 18 52N 121 20 E
Fughmah, Yemen 87 C5 16 9N 49 26 E
Fugong, China 68 D2 27 5N 98 47 E
Fugou, China 66 G8 34 3N 114 25 E
Fugu, China 66 E6 39 2N 111 3 E
Fuhai, China 64 B3 47 2N 87 25 E
Fuḩaymī, Iraq 89 E10 34 16N 42 10 E
Fuji, Japan 63 B10 35 9N 138 39 E
Fuji-San, Japan 63 B10 35 22N 138 44 E
Fuji-yoshida, Japan 63 B10 35 30N 138 46 E
Fujian □, China 69 E12 26 0N 118 0 E
Fujieda, Japan 63 C10 34 52N 138 16 E
Fujinomiya, Japan 63 B10 35 10N 138 40 E
Fujioka, Japan 63 A11 36 15N 139 5 E
Fujisawa, Japan 63 B11 35 22N 139 29 E
Fukaya, Japan 63 A11 36 12N 139 12 E
Fukien = Fujian □, China 69 E12 26 0N 118 0 E
Fukuchiyama, Japan 63 B7 35 19N 135 9 E
Fukue-Shima, Japan 61 H4 32 40N 128 45 E
Fukui, Japan 63 A8 36 5N 136 10 E
Fukui □, Japan 63 B8 36 0N 136 12 E
Fukuma, Japan 62 D2 33 46N 130 28 E
Fukuoka, Japan 62 D2 33 39N 130 21 E
Fukuoka □, Japan 62 D2 33 30N 131 0 E
Fukuroi, Japan 63 C9 34 45N 137 55 E
Fukushima, Japan 60 F10 37 44N 140 28 E
Fukushima □, Japan 60 F10 37 30N 140 15 E
Fukuyama, Japan 62 C5 34 35N 133 20 E
Fulda, Germany 26 E5 50 32N 9 41 E
Fulda →, Germany 26 D5 51 25N 9 39 E
Fuling, China 68 C6 29 40N 107 20 E
Fullerton, Calif., U.S.A. 145 M9 33 53N 117 56W
Fullerton, Nebr., U.S.A. 138 E5 41 22N 97 58W
Fulongquan, China 67 B13 44 20N 124 42 E
Fulton, Ill., U.S.A. 140 C6 41 52N 90 11W
Fulton, Ind., U.S.A. 141 D10 40 57N 86 16W
Fulton, Mo., U.S.A. 140 F5 38 52N 91 57W
Fulton, N.Y., U.S.A. 137 C8 43 19N 76 25W
Fulton, Tenn., U.S.A. 135 G1 36 31N 88 53W
Fuluälven →, Sweden 14 C7 61 18N 13 4 E
Fulufjället, Sweden 14 C6 61 32N 12 41 E
Fumay, France 23 C11 49 58N 4 40 E
Fumel, France 24 D4 44 30N 0 58 E
Fumin, China 68 E4 25 10N 102 20 E
Funabashi, Japan 63 B12 35 45N 140 0 E
Funafuti, Pac. Oc. 111 B14 8 30 S 179 0 E
Funchal, Madeira 33 D3 32 38N 16 54W
Fundación, Colombia 152 A3 10 31N 74 11W
Fundão, Brazil 155 E3 19 55 S 40 24W
Fundão, Portugal 36 E3 40 8N 7 30W
Fundy, B. of, Canada 129 D6 45 0N 66 0W
Funing, Hebei, China 67 E10 39 53N 119 12 E
Funing, Jiangsu, China 67 H10 33 45N 119 50 E
Funing, Yunnan, China 68 F5 23 35N 105 45 E
Funiu Shan, China 66 H7 33 30N 112 20 E
Funsi, Ghana 100 C4 10 21N 1 54W
Funtua, Nigeria 101 C6 11 30N 7 18 E
Fuping, Hebei, China 66 E8 38 48N 114 12 E
Fuping, Shaanxi, China 66 G5 34 42N 109 10 E
Fuqing, China 69 E12 25 41N 119 21 E
Fuquan, China 68 D6 26 40N 107 27 E
Fur, Denmark 15 H3 56 50N 9 0 E
Furano, Japan 60 C11 43 21N 142 23 E
Furāt, Nahr al →, Asia 84 D5 31 0N 47 25 E
Fūrg, Iran 85 D7 28 18N 55 13 E
Furkapass, Switz. 29 C7 46 34N 8 35 E
Furmanov, Russia 52 B5 57 10N 41 9 E
Furmanovka, Kazakstan 55 A6 44 17N 72 57 E
Furmanovo, Kazakstan 52 F9 49 42N 49 25 E
Furnás, Spain 33 B8 39 3N 1 32 E
Furnas, Représa de, Brazil 155 F2 20 50 S 45 30W
Furneaux Group, Australia 114 G4 40 10 S 147 50 E
Furness, U.K. 16 C4 54 14N 3 8W

200 Furqlus

Furqlus, *Syria* **91 A6** 34 36N 37 8 E
Fürstenau, *Germany* **26 C3** 52 31N 7 40 E
Fürstenberg, *Germany* **26 D3** 53 10N 13 8 E
Fürstenfeld, *Austria* **30 D9** 47 3N 16 3 E
Fürstenfeldbruck, *Germany* **27 G7** 48 11N 11 15 E
Fürstenwalde, *Germany* **26 C10** 52 22N 14 3 E
Fürth, *Germany* **27 F6** 49 28N 10 59 E
Furth im Wald, *Germany* **27 F8** 49 18N 12 50 E
Furtwangen, *Germany* **27 G4** 48 2N 8 12 E
Furukawa, *Japan* **60 E10** 38 34N 140 58 E
Furusund, *Sweden* **14 E12** 59 40N 18 55 E
Fury and Hecla Str., *Canada* **127 B11** 69 56N 84 0W
Fusagasuga, *Colombia* **152 C3** 4 21N 74 22W
Fuscaldo, *Italy* **41 C9** 39 25N 16 2 E
Fushan, *Shandong, China* **67 F11** 37 30N 121 15 E
Fushan, *Shanxi, China* **66 G6** 35 58N 111 51 E
Fushë Arrëzi, *Albania* **44 B2** 42 4N 20 2 E
Fushun, *Liaoning, China* **67 D12** 41 50N 123 56 E
Fushun, *Sichuan, China* **68 C5** 29 13N 104 52 E
Fusio, *Switz.* **29 D7** 46 27N 8 40 E
Fusong, *China* **67 C14** 42 20N 127 15 E
Füssen, *Germany* **27 H6** 47 34N 10 42 E
Fusui, *China* **68 F6** 22 40N 107 56 E
Futago-Yama, *Japan* **62 D3** 33 35N 131 36 E
Futrono, *Chile* **160 B2** 40 8S 72 24W
Futuna, *Wall. & F. Is.* **122 J9** 14 25 S 178 20 E
Fuwa, *Egypt* **94 H7** 31 12N 30 33 E
Fuxin, *China* **67 C11** 42 5N 121 48 E
Fuyang, *Anhui, China* **66 H8** 33 0N 115 48 E
Fuyang, *Zhejiang, China* **69 B12** 30 5N 119 57 E
Fuyang He →, *China* **66 E9** 38 12N 117 0 E
Fuying Dao, *China* **69 D13** 26 34N 120 9 E
Fuyu, *China* **67 B13** 45 12N 124 43 E
Fuyuan, *China* **68 E5** 25 40N 104 16 E
Füzesgyarmat, *Hungary* **31 D14** 47 6N 21 14 E
Fuzhou, *China* **69 D12** 26 5N 119 16 E
Fylde, *U.K.* **16 D5** 53 50N 2 58W
Fyn, *Denmark* **15 J4** 55 20N 10 30 E
Fyne, L., *U.K.* **18 F3** 55 59N 5 23W
Fyns Amtskommune □, *Denmark* **15 J4** 55 15N 10 30 E
Fyresvatn, *Norway* **14 E2** 59 6N 8 10 E

G

Gaanda, *Nigeria* **101 C7** 10 10N 12 27 E
Gabarin, *Nigeria* **101 C7** 11 8N 10 27 E
Gabas →, *France* **24 E3** 43 46N 0 42W
Gabela, *Angola* **103 E2** 11 0S 14 24 E
Gabès, *Tunisia* **96 B2** 33 53N 10 2 E
Gabès, G. de, *Tunisia* **96 B2** 34 0N 10 30 E
Gabgaba, W. →, *Egypt* **94 C3** 22 10N 33 5 E
Gabin, *Poland* **47 C6** 52 23N 19 41 E
Gabon ■, *Africa* **102 C2** 0 10 S 10 0 E
Gaborone, *Botswana* **104 C4** 24 45 S 25 57 E
Gabriels, *U.S.A.* **137 B10** 44 26N 74 12W
Gābrīk, *Iran* **85 E8** 25 44N 58 28 E
Gabro, *Ethiopia* **108 C2** 6 18N 43 16 E
Gabrovo, *Bulgaria* **43 E10** 42 52N 25 19 E
Gacé, *France* **22 D7** 48 49N 0 20 E
Gāch Sār, *Iran* **85 B6** 36 7N 51 19 E
Gachsārān, *Iran* **85 D6** 30 15N 50 45 E
Gacko, *Bos.-H.* **42 D3** 43 10N 18 33 E
Gadag, *India* **83 G2** 15 30N 75 45 E
Gadamai, *Sudan* **95 D4** 17 11N 36 10 E
Gadap, *Pakistan* **80 G2** 25 5N 67 28 E
Gadarwara, *India* **81 H8** 22 50N 78 50 E
Gadebusch, *Germany* **26 B7** 53 42N 11 7 E
Gadein, *Sudan* **95 F2** 8 10N 28 45 E
Gadhada, *India* **80 J4** 22 0N 71 35 E
Gadmen, *Switz.* **29 C6** 46 45N 8 16 E
Gádor, Sierra de, *Spain* **35 J2** 36 57N 2 45W
Gadsden, *Ala., U.S.A.* **135 H2** 34 1N 86 1W
Gadsden, *Ariz., U.S.A.* **143 K6** 32 33N 114 47W
Gadwal, *India* **83 F3** 16 10N 77 50 E
Gadyach = Hadyach, *Ukraine* **51 G8** 50 21N 34 0 E
Gadzi, *C.A.R.* **102 B3** 4 47N 16 42 E
Găeşti, *Romania* **46 E6** 44 48N 25 19 E
Gaeta, *Italy* **40 A6** 41 12N 13 35 E
Gaeta, G. di, *Italy* **40 A6** 41 6N 13 30 E
Gaffney, *U.S.A.* **135 H5** 35 5N 81 39W
Gafsa, *Tunisia* **96 B1** 34 24N 8 43 E
Gagarin, *Russia* **52 C2** 55 38N 35 0 E
Gagetown, *Canada* **129 C6** 45 46N 66 10W
Gagino, *Russia* **52 C7** 55 15N 45 1 E
Gagliano del Capo, *Italy* **41 C11** 39 50N 18 22 E
Gagnoa, *Ivory C.* **100 D3** 6 56N 5 16W
Gagnon, *Canada* **129 B6** 51 50N 68 5W
Gagnon, L., *Canada* **131 A6** 62 3N 110 27W
Gagra, *Georgia* **53 J5** 43 20N 40 10 E
Gahini, *Rwanda* **106 C3** 1 50 S 30 30 E
Gahmar, *India* **81 G10** 25 27N 83 49 E
Gai Xian, *China* **67 D12** 40 22N 122 20 E
Gaibanda, *Bangla.* **78 C2** 25 20N 89 36 E
Gaïdhouronísi, *Greece* **32 E7** 34 53N 25 41 E
Gail, *U.S.A.* **139 J4** 32 46N 101 27W
Gail →, *Austria* **30 E6** 46 36N 13 53 E
Gaillac, *France* **24 E5** 43 54N 1 54 E
Gaillimh = Galway, *Ireland* **19 C2** 53 17N 9 3W
Gaillon, *France* **22 C8** 49 10N 1 20 E
Gaimán, *Argentina* **160 B3** 43 10 S 65 25W
Gaines, *U.S.A.* **136 E7** 41 46N 77 35W
Gainesville, *Fla., U.S.A.* **135 L4** 29 40N 82 20W
Gainesville, *Ga., U.S.A.* **135 H4** 34 18N 83 50W
Gainesville, *Mo., U.S.A.* **139 G8** 36 36N 92 26W
Gainesville, *Tex., U.S.A.* **139 J6** 33 38N 97 8W
Gainsborough, *U.K.* **16 D7** 53 24N 0 46W
Gairdner, L., *Australia* **116 A2** 31 30 S 136 0 E
Gairloch, L., *U.K.* **18 D3** 57 43N 5 45W
Gais, *Switz.* **29 B8** 47 22N 9 27 E
Gaj, *Croatia* **42 B2** 45 28N 17 3 E
Gakuch, *Pakistan* **81 A5** 36 7N 73 45 E
Gal Laghet, *Somali Rep.* **108 D3** 4 9N 47 10 E
Gal Oya Res., *Sri Lanka* **83 L5** 7 5N 81 30 E
Gal Tardo, *Somali Rep.* **108 D3** 3 37N 45 58 E
Galachipa, *Bangla.* **78 D3** 22 8N 90 26 E
Galán, Cerro, *Argentina* **158 B2** 25 55 S 66 52W
Galana →, *Kenya* **106 C5** 3 9S 40 8 E
Galangue, *Angola* **103 E3** 13 42 S 16 9 E
Galangue, Serra, *Angola* **103 E3** 14 18 S 15 52 E
Galanta, *Slovak Rep.* **31 C10** 48 11N 17 45 E
Galápagos, *Pac. Oc.* **150 D1** 0 0 91 0W
Galashiels, *U.K.* **18 F6** 55 37N 2 49W
Galatás, *Greece* **45 G5** 37 30N 23 26 E
Galatea, *N.Z.* **118 E5** 38 24 S 176 45 E
Galaţi, *Romania* **46 D9** 45 27N 28 2 E
Galaţi □, *Romania* **46 D8** 45 45N 27 30 E
Galatia, *Turkey* **88 C5** 39 30N 33 0 E
Galatina, *Italy* **41 B11** 40 10N 18 10 E
Galátone, *Italy* **41 B11** 40 9N 18 4 E
Galax, *U.S.A.* **135 G5** 36 40N 80 56W
Galaxídhion, *Greece* **45 F4** 38 22N 22 23 E
Galbraith, *Australia* **114 B3** 16 25 S 141 30 E
Galcaio, *Somali Rep.* **90 F4** 6 30N 47 30 E
Galdhøpiggen, *Norway* **14 C2** 61 38N 8 18 E
Galeana, *Mexico* **146 C4** 24 50N 100 4W
Galela, *Indonesia* **72 A3** 1 50N 127 49 E
Galena, *U.S.A.* **140 B6** 42 25N 90 26W
Galera, *Spain* **35 H2** 37 45N 2 33W
Galera, Pta., *Chile* **160 A2** 39 59 S 73 43W
Galera Point, *Trin. & Tob.* **149 D7** 10 8N 61 0W
Galesburg, *Ill., U.S.A.* **140 D6** 40 57N 90 22W
Galesburg, *Mich., U.S.A.* **141 B11** 42 17N 85 26W
Galeton, *U.S.A.* **136 E7** 41 44N 77 39W
Galgasc, *Somali Rep.* **108 D2** 0 11N 41 38 E
Galheirão →, *Brazil* **155 D2** 12 23 S 45 5W
Galheiros, *Brazil* **155 D2** 13 18 S 46 25W
Gali, *Georgia* **53 J5** 42 37N 41 46 E
Galicea Mare, *Romania* **46 E4** 44 4N 23 19 E
Galich, *Russia* **52 A6** 58 22N 42 24 E
Galiche, *Bulgaria* **43 D8** 43 34N 23 50 E
Galicia □, *Spain* **36 C3** 42 43N 7 45W
Galien, *U.S.A.* **141 C10** 41 48N 86 30W
Galilee = Hagalil, *Israel* **91 C4** 32 53N 35 18 E
Galilee, L., *Australia* **114 C4** 22 20 S 145 50 E
Galilee, Sea of = Yam Kinneret, *Israel* **91 C4** 32 45N 35 35 E
Galinoporni, *Cyprus* **32 D13** 35 31N 34 18 E
Galion, *U.S.A.* **136 F2** 40 44N 82 47W
Galite, Is. de la, *Tunisia* **99 A6** 37 30N 8 59 E
Galiuro Mts., *U.S.A.* **143 K8** 32 30N 110 20W
Gallabat, *Sudan* **95 E4** 12 58N 36 11 E
Gallarate, *Italy* **38 C5** 45 40N 8 48 E
Gallardon, *France* **23 D8** 48 32N 1 42 E
Gallatin, *Mo., U.S.A.* **140 E3** 39 55N 93 58W
Gallatin, *Tenn., U.S.A.* **135 G2** 36 24N 86 27W
Galle, *Sri Lanka* **83 L5** 6 5N 80 10 E
Gállego →, *Spain* **34 D4** 41 39N 0 51W
Gallegos →, *Argentina* **160 D3** 51 35 S 69 0W
Galley Hd., *Ireland* **19 E3** 51 32N 8 55W
Galliate, *Italy* **38 C5** 45 29N 8 42 E
Gallinas, Pta., *Colombia* **152 A3** 12 28N 71 40W
Gallipoli = Gelibolu, *Turkey* **88 B2** 40 28N 26 43 E
Gallípoli, *Italy* **41 B11** 40 3N 17 58 E
Gallipolis, *U.S.A.* **134 F4** 38 49N 82 12W
Gällivare, *Sweden* **12 C19** 67 9N 20 40 E
Gallo, C., *Italy* **40 D6** 38 13N 13 19 E
Gallocanta, L. de, *Spain* **34 E3** 40 58N 1 30W
Galloway, *U.K.* **18 G4** 55 1N 4 29W
Galloway, Mull of, *U.K.* **18 G4** 54 39N 4 52W
Gallup, *U.S.A.* **143 J9** 35 32N 108 45W
Gallur, *Spain* **34 D3** 41 52N 1 19W
Gallyaaral, *Uzbekistan* **55 C3** 40 2N 67 35 E
Galong, *Australia* **117 C8** 34 37 S 148 34 E
Galt, *Calif., U.S.A.* **144 G5** 38 15N 121 18W
Galt, *Mo., U.S.A.* **140 D3** 40 8N 93 23W
Galtström, *Sweden* **14 B11** 62 10N 17 30 E
Galtür, *Austria* **30 E3** 46 58N 10 11 E
Galty Mts., *Ireland* **19 D3** 52 22N 8 10W
Galtymore, *Ireland* **19 D3** 52 21N 8 11W
Galva, *U.S.A.* **140 C6** 41 10N 90 3W
Galvarino, *Chile* **160 A2** 38 24 S 72 47W
Galve de Sorbe, *Spain* **34 D1** 41 13N 3 10W
Galveston, *Ind., U.S.A.* **141 D10** 40 35N 86 11W
Galveston, *Tex., U.S.A.* **139 L7** 29 18N 94 48W
Galveston B., *U.S.A.* **139 L7** 29 36N 94 50W
Gálvez, *Argentina* **158 C3** 32 0S 61 14W
Gálvez, *Spain* **37 F6** 39 42N 4 16W
Galway, *Ireland* **19 C2** 53 17N 9 3W
Galway □, *Ireland* **19 C2** 53 22N 9 1W
Galway B., *Ireland* **19 C2** 53 13N 9 10W
Gam, *Indonesia* **73 B4** 0 27 S 130 36 E
Gam →, *Vietnam* **76 B5** 21 55N 105 12 E
Gamagori, *Japan* **63 C9** 34 50N 137 14 E
Gamari, L., *Ethiopia* **95 E5** 11 32N 41 40 E
Gamawa, *Nigeria* **101 C7** 12 10N 10 31 E
Gamay, *Phil.* **70 E5** 12 23N 125 18 E
Gamay Bay, *Phil.* **70 E5** 12 21N 125 21 E
Gamba, *Angola* **103 E3** 11 42 S 17 14 E
Gambaga, *Ghana* **101 C4** 10 30N 0 28W
Gambat, *Pakistan* **80 F3** 27 17N 68 26 E
Gambela, *Ethiopia* **95 F3** 8 14N 34 38 E
Gambia ■, *W. Afr.* **100 C1** 13 25N 16 0W
Gambia →, *W. Afr.* **100 C1** 13 28N 16 34W
Gambier, C., *Australia* **112 B5** 11 56 S 130 57 E
Gambier Is., *Australia* **116 C2** 35 3 S 136 30 E
Gambo, *C.A.R.* **102 B4** 4 39N 22 16 E
Gamboli, *Pakistan* **80 E3** 29 53N 68 24 E
Gamboma, *Congo* **102 C3** 1 55 S 15 52 E
Gamboula, *C.A.R.* **102 B3** 4 8N 15 9 E
Gambuta, *Indonesia* **72 A2** 0 30N 123 20 E
Gamerco, *U.S.A.* **143 J9** 35 34N 108 46W
Gamlakarleby = Kokkola, *Finland* **12 E20** 63 50N 23 8 E
Gammon →, *Canada* **131 C9** 51 24N 95 44W
Gammouda, *Tunisia* **96 A1** 35 3N 9 39 E
Gamoda-Saki, *Japan* **62 D6** 33 50N 134 45 E
Gamu-Gofa □, *Ethiopia* **95 F4** 5 40N 36 40 E
Gan, *France* **24 E3** 43 12N 0 27W
Gan Gan, *Argentina* **160 B3** 42 30 S 68 10W
Gan Goriama, Mts., *Cameroon* **101 D7** 7 44N 12 45 E
Gan Jiang →, *China* **69 C10** 29 15N 116 0 E
Ganado, *Ariz., U.S.A.* **143 J9** 35 43N 109 33W
Ganado, *Tex., U.S.A.* **139 L6** 29 2N 96 31W
Gananoque, *Canada* **128 D4** 44 20N 76 10W
Ganāveh, *Iran* **85 D6** 29 35N 50 35 E
Gäncä, *Azerbaijan* **53 K8** 40 45N 46 20 E
Gand = Gent, *Belgium* **21 F3** 51 2N 3 42 E
Ganda, *Angola* **103 E2** 13 3 S 14 35 E
Gandak →, *India* **81 G11** 25 39N 85 13 E
Gandara, *Phil.* **70 E5** 12 1N 124 49 E
Gandava, *Pakistan* **79 C2** 28 32N 67 32 E
Gander, *Canada* **129 C9** 48 58N 54 35W
Gander L., *Canada* **129 C9** 48 58N 54 35W
Ganderowe Falls, *Zimbabwe* **107 F2** 17 20 S 29 10 E
Gandesa, *Spain* **34 D5** 41 3N 0 26 E
Gandhi Sagar, *India* **80 G6** 24 40N 75 40 E
Gandi, *Nigeria* **101 C6** 12 55N 5 49 E
Gandía, *Spain* **35 G4** 38 58N 0 9W
Gandino, *Italy* **38 C6** 45 49N 9 54 E
Gando, Pta., *Canary Is.* **33 G4** 27 55N 15 22W
Gandole, *Nigeria* **101 D7** 8 28N 11 35 E
Gandu, *Brazil* **155 D4** 13 45 S 39 30W
Ganedidalem = Gani, *Indonesia* **72 B3** 0 48 S 128 14 E
Ganetti, *Sudan* **94 D3** 18 0N 31 10 E
Ganga →, *India* **81 H14** 23 20N 90 30 E
Ganga, Mouths of the, *India* **81 J13** 21 30N 90 0 E
Ganganagar, *India* **80 E5** 29 56N 73 56 E
Gangapur, *India* **80 F7** 26 32N 76 49 E
Gangara, *Niger* **97 F1** 14 35N 8 29 E
Gangaw, *Burma* **78 D5** 22 5N 94 5 E
Gangawati, *India* **83 G3** 15 30N 76 36 E
Ganges = Ganga →, *India* **81 H14** 23 20N 90 30 E
Ganges, *France* **24 E7** 43 56N 3 42 E
Gangoh, *India* **80 E7** 29 46N 77 18 E
Gangtok, *India* **78 B2** 27 20N 88 37 E
Gangu, *China* **66 G3** 34 40N 105 15 E
Gangyao, *China* **67 B14** 44 12N 126 37 E
Gani, *Indonesia* **72 B3** 0 48 S 128 14 E
Ganj, *India* **81 F8** 27 45N 78 57 E
Gannat, *France* **24 B7** 46 7N 3 11 E
Gannett Peak, *U.S.A.* **142 E9** 43 11N 109 39W
Gannvalley, *U.S.A.* **138 C5** 44 2N 98 59W
Ganongga, *Solomon Is.* **121 M9** 8 5 S 156 35 E
Ganquan, *China* **66 F5** 36 20N 109 20 E
Gänserdorf, *Austria* **31 C9** 48 20N 16 43 E
Ganshui, *China* **68 C6** 28 40N 106 40 E
Gansu □, *China* **66 G3** 36 0N 104 0 E
Ganta, *Liberia* **100 D3** 7 15N 8 59W
Gantheaume, C., *Australia* **116 D2** 36 4 S 137 32 E
Gantheaume B., *Australia* **113 E1** 27 40 S 114 10 E
Gantsevichi = Hantsavichy, *Belarus* **51 F4** 52 49N 26 30 E
Ganyem, *Indonesia* **73 B6** 2 46 S 140 12 E
Ganyu, *China* **67 G10** 34 50N 119 8 E
Ganyushkino, *Kazakstan* **53 G9** 46 35N 49 20 E
Ganzhou, *China* **69 E10** 25 51N 114 56 E
Gao, *Mali* **101 B5** 18 0N 1 0 E
Gao Xian, *China* **68 C5** 28 21N 104 32 E
Gao'an, *China* **69 C10** 28 26N 115 17 E
Gaohe, *China* **69 F9** 22 46N 112 57 E
Gaohebu, *China* **69 B11** 30 43N 116 49 E
Gaokeng, *China* **69 D9** 27 40N 113 58 E
Gaolan Dao, *China* **69 G9** 21 55N 113 10 E
Gaoligong Shan, *China* **68 E2** 24 45N 98 45 E
Gaomi, *China* **67 F10** 36 20N 119 42 E
Gaoping, *China* **66 G7** 35 45N 112 55 E
Gaotang, *China* **66 F9** 36 50N 116 15 E
Gaoua, *Burkina Faso* **100 C4** 10 20N 3 8W
Gaoual, *Guinea* **100 C2** 11 45N 13 25W
Gaoxiong = Kaohsiung, *Taiwan* **69 F13** 22 35N 120 16 E
Gaoyang, *China* **66 E8** 38 40N 115 45 E
Gaoyou, *China* **69 A12** 32 47N 119 26 E
Gaoyou Hu, *China* **67 H10** 32 45N 119 20 E
Gaoyuan, *China* **67 F9** 37 8N 117 58 E
Gaozhou, *China* **69 G8** 21 58N 110 50 E
Gap, *France* **25 D10** 44 33N 6 5 E
Gapan, *Phil.* **70 D3** 15 19N 120 57 E
Gar, *China* **64 C2** 32 10N 79 58 E
Garabogazköl Aylagy, *Turkmenistan* **49 F9** 41 0N 53 30 E
Garachico, *Canary Is.* **33 F3** 28 22N 16 46W
Garachiné, *Panama* **148 E4** 8 0N 78 12W
Garad, *Somali Rep.* **108 C3** 6 57N 49 24 E
Garafia, *Canary Is.* **33 F2** 28 48N 17 57W
Garajonay, *Canary Is.* **33 F2** 28 7N 17 14W
Garanhuns, *Brazil* **154 C4** 8 50 S 36 30W
Garawe, *Liberia* **100 E3** 4 35N 8 0W
Garba Harre, *Somali Rep.* **108 D2** 3 19N 42 13 E
Garba Tula, *Kenya* **106 B4** 0 30N 38 32 E
Garbagududu, *Ethiopia* **108 C2** 6 12N 43 50 E
Garber, *U.S.A.* **139 G6** 36 26N 97 35W
Garberville, *U.S.A.* **142 F2** 40 6N 123 48W
Garça, *Brazil* **155 F2** 22 14 S 49 37W
Garças →, *Mato Grosso, Brazil* **157 D7** 15 54 S 52 16W
Garças →, *Pernambuco, Brazil* **154 C4** 8 43 S 39 41W
Garchitorena, *Phil.* **70 E4** 13 52N 123 40 E
Garcia Hernandez, *Phil.* **71 G5** 9 37N 124 18 E
Garcias, *Brazil* **157 E7** 20 34 S 52 13W
Gard, *Somali Rep.* **108 C3** 9 30N 49 6 E
Gard □, *France* **25 D8** 44 2N 4 10 E
Gard →, *France* **25 E8** 43 51N 4 37 E
Garda, L. di, *Italy* **38 C7** 45 40N 10 41 E
Gardanne, *France* **25 E9** 43 27N 5 27 E
Garde L., *Canada* **131 A7** 62 50N 106 13W
Gardelegen, *Germany* **26 C7** 52 32N 11 24 E
Garden City, *Kans., U.S.A.* **139 G4** 37 58N 100 53W
Garden City, *Mo., U.S.A.* **140 F2** 38 34N 94 12W
Garden City, *Tex., U.S.A.* **139 K4** 31 52N 101 29W
Garden Grove, *U.S.A.* **145 M9** 33 47N 117 55W
Gardēz, *Afghan.* **79 B3** 33 37N 69 9 E
Gardhíki, *Greece* **45 F3** 38 50N 21 55 E
Gardiner, *U.S.A.* **142 D8** 45 2N 110 22W
Gardiners I., *U.S.A.* **137 E12** 41 6N 72 6W
Gardner, *Ill., U.S.A.* **141 C8** 41 12N 88 17W
Gardner, *Mass., U.S.A.* **137 D13** 42 34N 71 59W
Gardner Canal, *Canada* **130 C3** 53 27N 128 8W
Gardnerville, *U.S.A.* **144 G7** 38 56N 119 45W
Gardno, Jezioro, *Poland* **47 A4** 54 40N 17 7 E
Gare Tigre, *Fr. Guiana* **153 C7** 4 58N 53 9W
Garešnica, *Croatia* **42 B1** 45 36N 16 56 E
Garéssio, *Italy* **38 D5** 44 12N 8 2 E
Garey, *U.S.A.* **145 L6** 34 53N 120 19W
Garfield, *U.S.A.* **142 C5** 47 1N 117 9W
Gargaliánoi, *Greece* **45 G3** 37 4N 21 38 E
Gargan, Mt., *France* **24 C5** 45 37N 1 39 E
Gargano, Mte., *Italy* **41 A8** 41 43N 15 43 E
Gargouna, *Mali* **101 B5** 15 56N 0 13 E
Garhshankar, *India* **80 D7** 31 13N 76 11 E
Gari, *Russia* **54 B9** 59 26N 62 21 E
Garibaldi Prov. Park, *Canada* **130 D4** 49 50N 122 40W
Garies, *S. Africa* **104 E2** 30 32 S 17 59 E
Garigliano →, *Italy* **40 A6** 41 13N 13 45 E
Garissa, *Kenya* **106 C4** 0 25 S 39 40 E
Garissa □, *Kenya* **106 C5** 0 20 S 40 0 E
Garkida, *Nigeria* **101 C7** 10 27N 12 36 E
Garko, *Nigeria* **101 C6** 11 45N 8 53 E
Garland, *Tex., U.S.A.* **139 J6** 32 55N 96 38W
Garland, *Utah, U.S.A.* **142 F7** 41 47N 112 10W
Garlasco, *Italy* **38 C5** 45 12N 8 55 E
Garm, *Tajikistan* **55 D5** 39 0N 70 20 E
Garmāb, *Iran* **85 C8** 35 25N 56 45 E
Garmisch-Partenkirchen, *Germany* **27 H7** 47 30N 11 6 E
Garmsār, *Iran* **85 C7** 35 20N 52 25 E
Garner, *U.S.A.* **140 A3** 43 6N 93 36W
Garnett, *U.S.A.* **138 F7** 38 17N 95 14W
Garo Hills, *India* **81 G14** 25 30N 90 30 E
Garoe, *Somali Rep.* **108 C3** 8 25N 48 33 E
Garonne →, *France* **24 C3** 45 2N 0 36W
Garonne, Canal Latéral à la →, *France* **24 D4** 44 15N 0 18 E
Garoua, *Cameroon* **101 D7** 9 19N 13 21 E
Garrel, *Germany* **26 C3** 52 57N 8 1 E
Garrett, *U.S.A.* **141 C11** 41 21N 85 8W
Garrigue, *France* **24 E7** 43 40N 3 55 E
Garrison, *Ky., U.S.A.* **141 F13** 38 36N 83 10W
Garrison, *Mont., U.S.A.* **142 C7** 46 31N 112 49W
Garrison, *N. Dak., U.S.A.* **138 B4** 47 40N 101 25W
Garrison, *Tex., U.S.A.* **139 K7** 31 49N 94 30W
Garrison Res. = Sakakawea, L., *U.S.A.* **138 B3** 47 30N 101 25W
Garrovillas, *Spain* **37 F4** 39 40N 6 33W
Garrucha, *Spain* **35 H3** 37 11N 1 49W
Garry →, *U.K.* **18 E5** 56 44N 3 47W
Garry, L., *Canada* **126 B9** 65 58N 100 18W
Garsen, *Kenya* **106 C5** 2 20 S 40 5 E
Garson L., *Canada* **131 B6** 56 19N 110 2W
Gartempe →, *France* **24 B4** 46 47N 0 49 E
Gartz, *Germany* **26 B10** 53 13N 14 22 E
Garu, *Ghana* **101 C4** 10 55N 0 11W
Garub, *Namibia* **104 D2** 26 37 S 16 0 E
Garut, *Indonesia* **75 D3** 7 14 S 107 53 E
Garvão, *Portugal* **37 H2** 37 42N 8 21W
Garvie Mts., *N.Z.* **119 F3** 45 30 S 168 50 E
Garwa = Garoua, *Cameroon* **101 D7** 9 19N 13 21 E
Garwa, *India* **81 G10** 24 11N 83 47 E
Garwolin, *Poland* **47 D8** 51 55N 21 38 E
Gary, *U.S.A.* **141 C9** 41 36N 87 20W
Garz, *Germany* **26 A9** 54 19N 13 20 E
Garzê, *China* **68 B3** 31 38N 100 1 E
Garzón, *Colombia* **152 C2** 2 10N 75 40W
Gas City, *U.S.A.* **141 D11** 40 29N 85 37W
Gas-San, *Japan* **60 E10** 38 32N 140 1 E
Gasan, *Phil.* **70 E3** 13 19N 121 51 E
Gasan Kuli = Esenguly, *Turkmenistan* **56 F6** 37 37N 53 59 E
Gascogne, *France* **24 E4** 43 45N 0 20 E
Gascogne, G. de, *Europe* **34 B2** 44 0N 2 0W
Gasconade, *U.S.A.* **140 F5** 38 40N 91 34W
Gasconade →, *U.S.A.* **140 F5** 38 41N 91 33W
Gascony = Gascogne, *France* **24 E4** 43 45N 0 20 E
Gascoyne →, *Australia* **113 D1** 24 52 S 113 37 E
Gascoyne Junc. T.O., *Australia* **113 E2** 25 2 S 115 17 E
Gascueña, *Spain* **34 E2** 40 18N 2 31W
Gash, Wadi →, *Ethiopia* **95 D4** 16 48N 35 51 E
Gashaka, *Nigeria* **101 D7** 7 20N 11 29 E
Gasherbrum, *Pakistan* **81 B7** 35 40N 76 40 E
Gashua, *Nigeria* **101 C7** 12 54N 11 0 E
Gaspé, *Canada* **129 C7** 48 52N 64 30W
Gaspé, C. de, *Canada* **129 C7** 48 48N 64 7W
Gaspé, Pén. de, *Canada* **129 C6** 48 45N 65 40W
Gaspésie, Parc Prov. de la, *Canada* **129 C6** 48 55N 65 50W
Gassaway, *U.S.A.* **134 F5** 38 41N 80 47W
Gasselte, *Neths.* **20 C9** 52 58N 6 48 E
Gasselternijveen, *Neths.* **20 C9** 52 59N 6 51 E
Gàssino Torinese, *Italy* **38 C4** 45 8N 7 50 E
Gassol, *Nigeria* **101 D7** 8 34N 10 25 E
Gasteiz = Vitoria, *Spain* **34 C2** 42 50N 2 41W
Gastonia, *U.S.A.* **135 H5** 35 16N 81 11W
Gastoúni, *Greece* **45 G3** 37 51N 21 15 E
Gastoúri, *Greece* **44 E1** 39 34N 19 54 E
Gastre, *Argentina* **160 B3** 42 20 S 69 15W
Gata, C., *Cyprus* **32 E12** 34 34N 33 2 E
Gata, C. de, *Spain* **35 J2** 36 41N 2 13W
Gata, Sierra de, *Spain* **36 E4** 40 20N 6 45W
Gataga →, *Canada* **130 B3** 58 35N 126 59W
Gătaia, *Romania* **46 D2** 45 26N 21 30 E
Gatchina, *Russia* **50 C6** 59 35N 30 9 E
Gates, *U.S.A.* **136 C7** 43 9N 77 42W
Gateshead, *U.K.* **16 C6** 54 57N 1 35W
Gatesville, *U.S.A.* **139 K6** 31 26N 97 45W
Gaths, *Zimbabwe* **107 G3** 20 2 S 30 32 E
Gatico, *Chile* **158 A1** 22 29 S 70 20W
Gâtinais, *France* **23 D9** 48 5N 2 40 E
Gâtine, Hauteurs de, *France* **24 B3** 46 35N 0 45W
Gatineau →, *Canada* **128 C4** 45 27N 75 42W
Gatineau, Parc de la, *Canada* **128 C4** 45 40N 76 0W
Gattaran, *Phil.* **70 B3** 18 4N 121 38 E
Gattinara, *Italy* **38 C5** 45 37N 8 22 E
Gatukai, *Solomon Is.* **121 M10** 8 45 S 158 15 E
Gatun, L., *Panama* **148 E4** 9 7N 79 56W
Gatyana, *S. Africa* **105 E4** 32 16 S 28 31 E
Gau, *Fiji* **121 B2** 18 2 S 179 18 E
Gaua, *Vanuatu* **121 D5** 14 15 S 167 30 E
Gaucín, *Spain* **37 J5** 36 31N 5 19W
Gauer L., *Canada* **131 B9** 57 0N 97 50W
Gauhati, *India* **81 F14** 26 10N 91 45 E
Gauja →, *Latvia* **13 H21** 57 10N 24 16 E
Gaula →, *Norway* **12 E14** 63 21N 10 14 E
Gaurain-Ramecroix, *Belgium* **21 G3** 50 36N 3 30 E
Gaurdak, *Turkmenistan* **55 E3** 37 50N 66 4 E
Gausta, *Norway* **14 E2** 59 48N 8 40 E
Gauteng □, *S. Africa* **105 D4** 26 0S 28 0 E
Gāv Koshī, *Iran* **85 D8** 28 38N 57 12 E
Gavá, *Spain* **34 D6** 41 18N 2 1 E
Gāvakān, *Iran* **85 D7** 29 37N 53 10 E
Gavarnie, *France* **24 F3** 42 44N 0 1W
Gavāter, *Iran* **85 E9** 25 10N 61 31 E
Gāvbandī, *Iran* **85 E7** 27 12N 53 4 E
Gavdhopoúla, *Greece* **32 E6** 34 56N 24 0 E
Gávdhos, *Greece* **32 E6** 34 50N 24 5 E

Ginosa 201

Gavere, *Belgium* **21 G3** 50 55N 3 40 E
Gavião, *Portugal* **37 F3** 39 28N 7 56W
Gaviota, *U.S.A.* **145 L6** 34 29N 120 13W
Gävle, *Sweden* **13 F17** 60 40N 17 9 E
Gävleborgs län □, *Sweden* **14 C10** 61 30N 16 15 E
Gavorrano, *Italy* **38 F7** 42 55N 10 54 E
Gavray, *France* **22 D5** 48 55N 1 20W
Gavrilov Yam, *Russia* **52 B4** 57 18N 39 49 E
Gávrion, *Greece* **45 G6** 37 54N 24 44 E
Gawachab, *Namibia* **104 D2** 27 4 S 17 55 E
Gawai, *Burma* **78 B6** 27 56N 97 30 E
Gawilgarh Hills, *India* **82 D3** 21 15N 76 45 E
Gawler, *Australia* **116 C3** 34 30 S 138 42 E
Gaxun Nur, *China* **64 B5** 42 22N 100 30 E
Gay, *Russia* **54 F7** 51 27N 58 27 E
Gaya, *India* **81 G11** 24 47N 85 4 E
Gaya, *Niger* **101 C5** 11 52N 3 28 E
Gaya, *Nigeria* **101 C6** 11 57N 9 0 E
Gaylord, *U.S.A.* **134 C3** 45 2N 84 41W
Gayndah, *Australia* **115 D5** 25 35 S 151 32 E
Gayny, *Russia* **54 A5** 60 18N 54 19 E
Gaysin = Haysyn, *Ukraine* **51 H5** 48 57N 29 25 E
Gayvoron = Hayvoron, *Ukraine* **51 H5** 48 22N 29 52 E
Gaza, *Gaza Strip* **91 D3** 31 30N 34 28 E
Gaza □, *Mozam.* **105 C5** 23 10 S 32 45 E
Gaza Strip □, *Asia* **91 D3** 31 29N 34 25 E
Gazaoua, *Niger* **97 F1** 13 32N 7 55 E
Gāzbor, *Iran* **85 D8** 28 5N 58 51 E
Gazelle Pen., *Papua N. G.* **120 C6** 4 40 S 152 0 E
Gazi, *Zaïre* **106 B1** 1 3N 24 30 E
Gaziantep, *Turkey* **88 D7** 37 6N 37 23 E
Gazipaşa, *Turkey* **88 D5** 36 16N 32 18 E
Gazli, *Uzbekistan* **56 E7** 40 14N 63 24 E
Gbarnga, *Liberia* **100 D3** 7 19N 9 13W
Gbekebo, *Nigeria* **101 D5** 6 20N 4 56 E
Gboko, *Nigeria* **101 D6** 7 17N 9 4 E
Gbongan, *Nigeria* **101 D5** 7 28N 4 20 E
Gcuwa, *S. Africa* **105 E4** 32 20 S 28 11 E
Gdańsk, *Poland* **47 A5** 54 22N 18 40 E
Gdańsk □, *Poland* **47 A5** 54 10N 18 30 E
Gdańska, Zatoka, *Poland* **47 A6** 54 30N 19 20 E
Gdov, *Russia* **13 G22** 58 48N 27 55 E
Gdynia, *Poland* **47 A5** 54 35N 18 33 E
Gebe, *Indonesia* **73 A3** 0 5N 129 25 E
Gebeit Mine, *Sudan* **94 C4** 21 3N 36 29 E
Gebze, *Turkey* **88 B3** 40 47N 29 25 E
Gecha, *Ethiopia* **95 F4** 7 30N 35 18 E
Gedaref, *Sudan* **95 E4** 14 2N 35 28 E
Gede, Tanjung, *Indonesia* **74 D3** 6 46 S 105 12 E
Gedinne, *Belgium* **21 J5** 49 59N 4 56 E
Gediz, *Turkey* **88 C3** 39 1N 29 24 E
Gediz →, *Turkey* **88 C2** 38 35N 26 48 E
Gedo, *Ethiopia* **95 F4** 9 2N 37 25 E
Gèdre, *France* **24 F4** 42 47N 0 2 E
Gedser, *Denmark* **15 K5** 54 35N 11 55 E
Gedser Odde, *Denmark* **15 K5** 54 30N 11 58 E
Geegully Cr. →, *Australia* **112 C3** 18 32 S 123 41 E
Geel, *Belgium* **21 F5** 51 10N 4 59 E
Geelong, *Australia* **116 E6** 38 10 S 144 22 E
Geelvink Chan., *Australia* **113 E1** 28 30 S 114 0 E
Geer →, *Belgium* **21 G7** 50 51N 5 42 E
Geesthacht, *Germany* **26 B6** 53 26N 10 22 E
Geffen, *Neths.* **20 E6** 51 44N 5 28 E
Geidam, *Nigeria* **101 C7** 12 57N 11 57 E
Geikie →, *Canada* **131 B8** 57 45N 103 52W
Geili, *Sudan* **95 D3** 16 1N 32 37 E
Geilo, *Norway* **14 D2** 60 32N 8 14 E
Geinica, *Slovak Rep.* **31 C13** 48 51N 20 55 E
Geisingen, *Germany* **27 H4** 47 54N 8 38 E
Geislingen, *Germany* **27 G5** 48 37N 9 50 E
Geita, *Tanzania* **106 C3** 2 48 S 32 12 E
Geita □, *Tanzania* **106 C3** 2 50 S 32 10 E
Gejiu, *China* **68 F4** 23 20N 103 10 E
Gel →, *Sudan* **95 F2** 7 5N 29 10 E
Gel River, *Sudan* **95 F2** 7 5N 29 10 E
Gela, *Italy* **41 E7** 37 4N 14 15 E
Gela, G. di, *Italy* **41 F7** 37 0N 14 20 E
Geladi, *Ethiopia* **108 C3** 6 59N 46 30 E
Gelderland □, *Neths.* **20 D8** 52 5N 6 10 E
Geldermalsen, *Neths.* **20 E6** 51 53N 5 17 E
Geldern, *Germany* **26 D2** 51 31N 6 20 E
Geldrop, *Neths.* **21 F7** 51 25N 5 32 E
Geleen, *Neths.* **21 G7** 50 57N 5 49 E
Gelehun, *S. Leone* **100 D2** 8 20N 11 40W
Gelendost, *Turkey* **88 C4** 38 7N 31 1 E
Gelendzhik, *Russia* **53 H4** 44 33N 38 10 E
Gelib, *Somali Rep.* **108 D2** 0 29N 42 46 E
Gelibolu, *Turkey* **88 B2** 40 28N 26 43 E
Gelidonya Burnu, *Turkey* **88 D4** 36 12N 30 24 E
Gelnhausen, *Germany* **27 E5** 50 11N 9 11 E
Gelsenkirchen, *Germany* **26 D3** 51 32N 7 1 E
Gelting, *Germany* **26 A5** 54 45N 9 53 E
Gemas, *Malaysia* **77 L4** 2 37N 102 36 E
Gembloux, *Belgium* **21 G5** 50 34N 4 43 E
Gemena, *Zaïre* **102 B3** 3 13N 19 48 E
Gemerek, *Turkey* **88 C7** 39 15N 36 10 E
Gemert, *Neths.* **21 E7** 51 33N 5 41 E
Gemlik, *Turkey* **88 B3** 40 26N 29 9 E
Gemona del Friuli, *Italy* **39 B10** 46 16N 13 9 E
Gemsa, *Egypt* **94 B3** 27 39N 33 35 E
Gemünden, *Germany* **27 E5** 50 3N 9 42 E
Genale, *Ethiopia* **95 F4** 6 0N 39 30 E
Genale, *Somali Rep.* **108 D2** 1 48N 44 42 E
Genappe, *Belgium* **21 G4** 50 37N 4 30 E
Genç, *Turkey* **89 C9** 38 44N 40 34 E
Gençay, *France* **24 B4** 46 23N 0 23 E
Gendringen, *Neths.* **20 E8** 51 52N 6 21 E
Gendt, *Neths.* **20 E7** 51 53N 5 59 E
Geneina, Gebel, *Egypt* **94 J8** 29 2N 33 55 E
Genemuiden, *Neths.* **20 C8** 52 38N 6 2 E
General Acha, *Argentina* **158 D3** 37 20 S 64 38W
General Alvear, *Buenos Aires, Argentina* **158 D3** 36 0 S 60 0W
General Alvear, *Mendoza, Argentina* **158 D2** 35 0 S 67 40W
General Artigas, *Paraguay* **158 B4** 26 52 S 56 16W
General Belgrano, *Argentina* **158 D4** 36 35 S 58 47W
General Cabrera, *Argentina* **158 C3** 32 53 S 63 52W
General Carrera, L., *Chile* **160 C2** 46 35 S 72 0W
General Cepeda, *Mexico* **146 B4** 25 23N 101 27W
General Conesa, *Argentina* **160 B4** 40 6 S 64 25W
General Guido, *Argentina* **158 D4** 36 40 S 57 50W
General Juan Madariaga, *Argentina* **158 D4** 37 0 S 57 0W
General La Madrid, *Argentina* **158 D3** 37 17 S 61 20W
General Lorenzo Vintter, *Argentina* **160 B4** 40 45 S 64 26W
General Luna, *Phil.* **70 E4** 13 41N 122 10 E
General MacArthur, *Phil.* **71 F5** 11 18N 125 28 E
General Martin Miguel de Güemes, *Argentina* **158 A3** 24 50 S 65 0W
General Paz, *Argentina* **158 B4** 27 45 S 57 36W
General Pico, *Argentina* **158 D3** 35 45 S 63 50W
General Pinedo, *Argentina* **158 B3** 27 15 S 61 20W
General Pinto, *Argentina* **158 C3** 34 45 S 61 50W
General Sampaio, *Brazil* **154 B4** 4 2 S 39 29W
General Santos, *Phil.* **71 H5** 6 5N 125 14 E
General Tinio, *Phil.* **70 D3** 15 39N 121 10 E
General Toshevo, *Bulgaria* **43 D13** 43 42N 28 6 E
General Trevino, *Mexico* **147 B5** 26 14N 99 29W
General Trías, *Mexico* **146 B3** 28 21N 106 22W
General Viamonte, *Argentina* **158 D3** 35 1 S 61 3W
General Villegas, *Argentina* **158 D3** 35 5 S 63 0W
General Vintter, L., *Argentina* **160 B2** 43 55 S 71 40W
Generoso, Mte., *Switz.* **29 E8** 45 56N 9 2 E
Genesee, *Idaho, U.S.A.* **142 C5** 46 33N 116 56W
Genesee, *Pa., U.S.A.* **136 E7** 41 59N 77 54W
Genesee →, *U.S.A.* **136 C7** 43 16N 77 36W
Geneseo, *Ill., U.S.A.* **140 C6** 41 27N 90 9W
Geneseo, *Kans., U.S.A.* **138 F5** 38 31N 98 10W
Geneseo, *N.Y., U.S.A.* **136 D7** 42 48N 77 49W
Geneva = Genève, *Switz.* **28 D2** 46 12N 6 9 E
Geneva, *Ala., U.S.A.* **135 K3** 31 2N 85 52W
Geneva, *Ill., U.S.A.* **141 C8** 41 53N 88 18W
Geneva, *Ind., U.S.A.* **141 D12** 40 36N 84 58W
Geneva, *N.Y., U.S.A.* **136 D7** 42 52N 76 59W
Geneva, *Nebr., U.S.A.* **138 E6** 40 32N 97 36W
Geneva, *Ohio, U.S.A.* **136 E4** 41 48N 80 57W
Geneva, L. = Léman, L., *Europe* **28 D3** 46 26N 6 30 E
Geneva, L., *U.S.A.* **141 B8** 42 38N 88 30W
Genève, *Switz.* **28 D2** 46 12N 6 9 E
Genève □, *Switz.* **28 D2** 46 10N 6 10 E
Geng, *Afghan.* **79 C1** 31 22N 61 28 E
Gengenbach, *Germany* **27 G4** 48 24N 8 0 E
Gengma, *China* **68 F2** 23 32N 99 20 E
Genichesk = Henichesk, *Ukraine* **51 J8** 46 12N 34 50 E
Genil →, *Spain* **37 H5** 37 42N 5 19W
Génissiat, Barr. de, *France* **25 B9** 46 1N 5 48 E
Genk, *Belgium* **21 G7** 50 58N 5 32 E
Genkai-Nada, *Japan* **62 D2** 34 0N 130 0 E
Genlis, *France* **23 E12** 47 11N 5 12 E
Gennargentu, Mti. del, *Italy* **40 C2** 40 1N 9 19 E
Gennep, *Neths.* **21 E7** 51 41N 5 59 E
Gennes, *France* **22 E6** 47 20N 0 17W
Genoa = Génova, *Italy* **38 D5** 44 25N 8 57 E
Genoa, *Australia* **117 D8** 37 29 S 149 35 E
Genoa, *Ill., U.S.A.* **141 B8** 42 6N 88 42W
Genoa, *N.Y., U.S.A.* **137 D8** 42 40N 76 32W
Genoa, *Nebr., U.S.A.* **138 E6** 41 27N 97 44W
Genoa, *Nev., U.S.A.* **144 F7** 39 2N 119 50W
Genoa →, *Argentina* **160 B2** 44 55 S 70 5W
Genoa City, *U.S.A.* **141 B8** 42 30N 88 20W
Génova, *Italy* **38 D5** 44 25N 8 57 E
Génova, G. di, *Italy* **38 E6** 44 0N 9 0 E
Gent, *Belgium* **21 F3** 51 2N 3 42 E
Gentbrugge, *Belgium* **21 F3** 51 3N 3 47 E
Genthin, *Germany* **26 C8** 52 25N 12 9 E
Gentio do Ouro, *Brazil* **154 D3** 11 25 S 42 30W
Geographe B., *Australia* **113 F2** 33 30 S 115 15 E
Geographe Chan., *Australia* **113 D1** 24 30 S 113 0 E
Geokchay = Göyçay, *Azerbaijan* **53 K8** 40 42N 47 43 E
Georga, Zemlya, *Russia* **56 A5** 80 30N 49 0 E
George, *S. Africa* **104 E3** 33 58 S 22 29 E
George →, *Canada* **129 A6** 58 49N 66 10W
George, L., *N.S.W., Australia* **117 C8** 35 10 S 149 25 E
George, L., *S. Austral., Australia* **116 D4** 37 25 S 140 0 E
George, L., *W. Austral., Australia* **112 D3** 22 45 S 123 40 E
George, L., *Uganda* **106 B3** 0 5N 30 10 E
George, L., *Fla., U.S.A.* **135 L5** 29 17N 81 36W
George, L., *N.Y., U.S.A.* **137 C11** 43 37N 73 33W
George Gill Ra., *Australia* **112 D5** 24 22 S 131 45 E
George River = Kangiqsualujjuaq, *Canada* **127 C13** 58 30N 65 59W
George Sound, *N.Z.* **119 E2** 44 52 S 167 25 E
George Town, *Bahamas* **148 B4** 23 33N 75 47W
George Town, *Malaysia* **77 K3** 5 25N 100 15 E
George V Land, *Antarctica* **7 C10** 69 0 S 148 0 E
George VI Sound, *Antarctica* **7 D17** 71 0 S 68 0W
George West, *U.S.A.* **139 L5** 28 20N 98 7W
Georgetown, *Australia* **114 B3** 18 17 S 143 33 E
Georgetown, *Ont., Canada* **128 D4** 43 40N 79 56W
Georgetown, *P.E.I., Canada* **129 C7** 46 13N 62 24W
Georgetown, *Cayman Is.* **148 C3** 19 20N 81 24W
Georgetown, *Gambia* **100 C2** 13 30N 14 47W
Georgetown, *Guyana* **153 B6** 6 50N 58 12W
Georgetown, *Calif., U.S.A.* **144 G6** 38 54N 120 50W
Georgetown, *Colo., U.S.A.* **142 G11** 39 42N 105 42W
Georgetown, *Ill., U.S.A.* **141 E9** 39 59N 87 38W
Georgetown, *Ky., U.S.A.* **141 F12** 38 13N 84 33W
Georgetown, *Ohio, U.S.A.* **141 F13** 38 52N 83 54W
Georgetown, *S.C., U.S.A.* **135 J6** 33 23N 79 17W
Georgetown, *Tex., U.S.A.* **139 K6** 30 38N 97 41W
Georgi Dimitrov, *Bulgaria* **43 E8** 42 15N 23 54 E
Georgi Dimitrov, Yazovir, *Bulgaria* **43 E10** 42 37N 25 18 E
Georgia □, *U.S.A.* **135 J4** 32 50N 83 15W
Georgia ■, *Asia* **53 J6** 42 0N 43 0 E
Georgia, Str. of, *Canada* **130 D4** 49 25N 124 0W
Georgian B., *Canada* **128 C3** 45 15N 81 0W
Georgina →, *Australia* **114 C2** 23 30 S 139 47 E
Georgina Downs, *Australia* **114 C2** 21 10 S 137 40 E
Georgiu-Dezh = Liski, *Russia* **52 E4** 51 3N 39 30 E
Georgiyevka, *Kazakstan* **55 B7** 43 3N 74 43 E
Georgiyevsk, *Russia* **53 H6** 44 12N 43 28 E
Gera, *Germany* **26 E8** 50 53N 12 4 E
Geraardsbergen, *Belgium* **21 G3** 50 45N 3 53 E
Geral, Serra, *Bahia, Brazil* **155 D3** 14 0 S 41 0W
Geral, Serra, *Goiás, Brazil* **154 D2** 11 15 S 46 30W
Geral, Serra, *Sta. Catarina, Brazil* **159 B6** 26 25 S 50 0W
Geral de Goiás, Serra, *Brazil* **155 D2** 12 0 S 46 0W
Geral do Paranã Serra, *Brazil* **155 E2** 15 0 S 47 30W
Gerald, *U.S.A.* **140 F5** 38 24N 91 20W
Geraldine, *N.Z.* **119 E6** 44 5 S 171 15 E
Geraldine, *U.S.A.* **142 C8** 47 36N 110 16W
Geraldton, *Australia* **113 E1** 28 48 S 114 32 E
Geraldton, *Canada* **128 C2** 49 44N 86 59W
Geranium, *Australia* **116 C4** 35 23 S 140 11 E
Gérardmer, *France* **23 D13** 48 3N 6 50 E
Gercüş, *Turkey* **89 D9** 37 34N 41 23 E
Gerede, *Turkey* **88 B5** 40 45N 32 10 E
Gereshk, *Afghan.* **79 C2** 31 47N 64 35 E
Gérgal, *Spain* **35 H2** 37 7N 2 31W
Gerik, *Malaysia* **77 K3** 5 50N 101 15 E
Gering, *U.S.A.* **138 E3** 41 50N 103 40W
Gerlach, *U.S.A.* **142 F4** 40 39N 119 21W
Gerlachovka, *Slovak Rep.* **31 B13** 49 11N 20 7 E
Gerlogubi, *Ethiopia* **108 C3** 6 53N 45 3 E
German Planina, *Macedonia* **42 E7** 42 20N 22 0 E
Germansen Landing, *Canada* **130 B4** 55 43N 124 40W
Germantown, *U.S.A.* **141 E12** 39 38N 84 22W
Germany ■, *Europe* **26 E6** 51 0N 10 0 E
Germersheim, *Germany* **27 F4** 49 12N 8 22 E
Germī, *Iran* **89 C13** 39 1N 48 3 E
Germiston, *S. Africa* **105 D4** 26 15 S 28 10 E
Gernsheim, *Germany* **27 F4** 49 45N 8 30 E
Gero, *Japan* **63 B9** 35 48N 137 14 E
Gerolstein, *Germany* **27 E2** 50 13N 6 39 E
Gerolzhofen, *Germany* **27 F6** 49 54N 10 21 E
Gerona, *Spain* **34 D7** 41 58N 2 46 E
Gerona □, *Spain* **34 C7** 42 11N 2 30 E
Gérouville, *Belgium* **21 J6** 49 37N 5 26 E
Gerrard, *Canada* **130 C5** 50 30N 117 17W
Gerringong, *Australia* **117 C9** 34 46 S 150 47 E
Gers □, *France* **24 E4** 43 35N 0 30 E
Gers →, *France* **24 D4** 44 9N 0 39 E
Gersfeld, *Germany* **26 E5** 50 27N 9 56 E
Gersoppa Falls, *India* **83 G2** 14 12N 74 46 E
Gerze, *Turkey* **88 B6** 41 48N 35 12 E
Geseke, *Germany* **26 D4** 51 38N 8 31 E
Geser, *Indonesia* **73 B4** 3 50 S 130 54 E
Gesso →, *Italy* **38 D4** 44 24N 7 33 E
Gestro, Wabi →, *Ethiopia* **95 G5** 4 12N 42 2 E
Gesves, *Belgium* **21 H6** 50 24N 5 4 E
Getafe, *Spain* **36 E7** 40 18N 3 44W
Gethsémani, *Canada* **129 B7** 50 13N 60 40W
Gettysburg, *Pa., U.S.A.* **134 F7** 39 50N 77 14W
Gettysburg, *S. Dak., U.S.A.* **138 C5** 45 1N 99 57W
Getz Ice Shelf, *Antarctica* **7 D14** 75 0 S 130 0W
Geul →, *Neths.* **21 G7** 50 53N 5 43 E
Geureudong, Mt., *Indonesia* **74 B1** 4 13N 96 42 E
Geurie, *Australia* **117 B8** 32 22 S 148 50 E
Gevaş, *Turkey* **89 C10** 38 15N 43 6 E
Gévaudan, *France* **24 D7** 44 40N 3 40 E
Gevgelija, *Macedonia* **42 F7** 41 9N 22 30 E
Gévora →, *Spain* **37 G4** 38 53N 6 57W
Gex, *France* **25 B10** 46 21N 6 3 E
Geyikli, *Turkey* **44 E8** 39 50N 26 12 E
Geyser, *U.S.A.* **142 C8** 47 16N 110 30W
Geyserville, *U.S.A.* **144 G4** 38 42N 122 54W
Geyve, *Turkey* **88 B4** 40 30N 30 18 E
Ghâbat el Arab = Wang Kai, *Sudan* **95 F2** 9 3N 29 23 E
Ghaghara →, *India* **81 G11** 25 45N 84 40 E
Ghalat, *Oman* **87 B7** 21 6N 58 53 E
Ghalla, Wadi el →, *Sudan* **95 E2** 10 25N 27 32 E
Ghallamane, *Mauritania* **98 D3** 23 15N 10 0W
Ghana ■, *W. Afr.* **101 D4** 8 0N 1 0W
Ghansor, *India* **81 H9** 22 39N 80 1 E
Ghanzi, *Botswana* **104 C3** 21 50 S 21 34 E
Ghanzi □, *Botswana* **104 C3** 21 50 S 21 45 E
Gharb el Istiwa'iya □, *Sudan* **95 F2** 5 0N 30 0 E
Gharbîya, Es Sahrâ el, *Egypt* **94 B2** 27 40N 26 30 E
Ghard Abû Muharik, *Egypt* **94 B2** 26 50N 30 0 E
Ghardaïa, *Algeria* **99 B5** 32 20N 3 37 E
Ghârib, G., *Egypt* **94 J8** 28 6N 32 54 E
Gharm, W. →, *Oman* **87 C7** 19 57N 57 38 E
Gharyān, *Libya* **96 B2** 32 10N 13 0 E
Gharyān □, *Libya* **96 B2** 30 35N 13 0 E
Ghat, *Libya* **96 D2** 24 59N 10 11 E
Ghatal, *India* **81 H12** 22 40N 87 46 E
Ghatampur, *India* **81 F9** 26 8N 80 13 E
Ghatere, *Solomon Is.* **121 L10** 7 55 S 159 0 E
Ghatprabha →, *India* **83 F2** 16 15N 75 20 E
Ghaţţī, *Si. Arabia* **84 D3** 31 16N 37 31 E
Ghawdex = Gozo, *Malta* **32 C1** 36 3N 14 13 E
Ghayl, *Si. Arabia* **86 B4** 21 40N 46 20 E
Ghayl Bā Wazīr, *Yemen* **87 D5** 14 47N 49 22 E
Ghazal, Bahr el →, *Chad* **97 F3** 13 0N 15 47 E
Ghazâl, Bahr el →, *Sudan* **95 F3** 9 31N 30 25 E
Ghazaouet, *Algeria* **99 A4** 35 8N 1 50W
Ghaziabad, *India* **80 E7** 28 42N 77 26 E
Ghazipur, *India* **81 G10** 25 38N 83 35 E
Ghaznī, *Afghan.* **79 B3** 33 30N 68 28 E
Ghaznī □, *Afghan.* **79 B3** 32 10N 68 20 E
Ghedi, *Italy* **38 C7** 45 24N 10 16 E
Ghelari, *Romania* **46 D3** 45 38N 22 45 E
Ghèlinsor, *Somali Rep.* **108 C3** 6 28N 46 39 E
Ghent = Gent, *Belgium* **21 F3** 51 2N 3 42 E
Gheorghe Gheorghiu-Dej = Oneşti, *Romania* **46 C7** 46 17N 26 47 E
Gheorgheni, *Romania* **46 C6** 46 43N 25 41 E
Ghergani, *Romania* **46 E6** 44 37N 25 37 E
Gherla, *Romania* **46 B4** 47 2N 23 57 E
Ghilarza, *Italy* **40 B1** 40 7N 8 50 E
Ghisonaccia, *France* **25 F13** 42 1N 9 26 E
Ghisoni, *France* **25 F13** 42 7N 9 12 E
Ghizao, *Afghan.* **80 C1** 33 20N 65 44 E
Ghizar →, *Pakistan* **81 A5** 36 15N 73 43 E
Ghod →, *India* **82 E2** 18 30N 74 35 E
Ghogha, *India* **80 J5** 21 40N 72 20 E
Ghot Ogrein, *Egypt* **94 A2** 31 10N 25 20 E
Ghotaru, *India* **80 F4** 27 20N 70 1 E
Ghotki, *Pakistan* **80 E3** 28 5N 69 21 E
Ghowr □, *Afghan.* **79 B2** 34 0N 64 20 E
Ghudaf, W. al →, *Iraq* **89 F10** 32 56N 43 30 E
Ghudāmis, *Libya* **96 B1** 30 11N 9 29 E
Ghughri, *India* **81 H9** 22 39N 80 41 E
Ghugus, *India* **82 E4** 19 58N 79 12 E
Ghulam Mohammad Barrage, *Pakistan* **80 G3** 25 30N 68 20 E
Ghurayrah, *Si. Arabia* **86 C3** 18 37N 42 41 E
Ghūriān, *Afghan.* **79 B1** 34 17N 61 25 E
Gia Dinh, *Vietnam* **77 G6** 10 49N 106 42 E
Gia Lai = Pleiku, *Vietnam* **76 F7** 13 57N 108 0 E
Gia Nghia, *Vietnam* **77 G6** 11 58N 107 42 E
Gia Ngoc, *Vietnam* **76 E7** 14 50N 108 58 E
Gia Vuc, *Vietnam* **76 E7** 14 42N 108 34 E
Giamama, *Somali Rep.* **108 D2** 0 4N 42 44 E
Giannutri, *Italy* **38 F8** 42 15N 11 6 E
Giant Forest, *U.S.A.* **144 J8** 36 36N 118 43W
Giant Mts. = Krkonoše, *Czech.* **30 A8** 50 50N 15 35 E
Giants Causeway, *U.K.* **19 A5** 55 16N 6 29W
Giarabub = Al Jaghbūb, *Libya* **96 C4** 29 42N 24 38 E
Giarre, *Italy* **41 E8** 37 43N 15 11 E
Giaveno, *Italy* **38 C4** 45 2N 7 21 E
Gibara, *Cuba* **148 B4** 21 9N 76 11W
Gibb River, *Australia* **112 C4** 16 26 S 126 26 E
Gibbon, *U.S.A.* **138 E5** 40 45N 98 51W
Gibe →, *Ethiopia* **95 F4** 7 20N 37 36 E
Gibellina, *Italy* **40 E6** 37 47N 12 58 E
Gibraléon, *Spain* **37 H4** 37 23N 6 58W
Gibraltar ■, *Europe* **37 J5** 36 7N 5 22W
Gibraltar, Str. of, *Medit. S.* **37 K5** 35 55N 5 40W
Gibson City, *U.S.A.* **141 D8** 40 28N 88 22W
Gibson Desert, *Australia* **112 D4** 24 0 S 126 0 E
Gibsonburg, *U.S.A.* **141 C13** 41 23N 83 19W
Gibsons, *Canada* **130 D4** 49 24N 123 32W
Gibsonville, *U.S.A.* **144 F6** 39 46N 120 54W
Giddalur, *India* **83 G4** 15 20N 78 57 E
Giddings, *U.S.A.* **139 K6** 30 11N 96 56W
Gidole, *Ethiopia* **95 F4** 5 40N 37 25 E
Gien, *France* **23 E9** 47 40N 2 36 E
Giessen, *Germany* **26 E4** 50 34N 8 41 E
Gieten, *Neths.* **20 B9** 53 1N 6 46 E
Gīfān, *Iran* **85 B8** 37 54N 57 28 E
Gifatin, Geziret, *Egypt* **94 B3** 27 10N 33 50 E
Gifford Creek, *Australia* **112 D2** 24 3 S 116 16 E
Gifhorn, *Germany* **26 C6** 52 30N 10 33 E
Gifu, *Japan* **63 B8** 35 30N 136 45 E
Gifu □, *Japan* **63 B8** 35 40N 137 0 E
Gigant, *Russia* **53 G5** 46 28N 41 20 E
Giganta, Sa. de la, *Mexico* **146 B2** 25 30N 111 30W
Gigen, *Bulgaria* **43 D9** 43 40N 24 28 E
Gigha, *U.K.* **18 F3** 55 42N 5 44W
Giglei, *Somali Rep.* **108 C3** 5 25N 45 20 E
Giglio, *Italy* **38 F7** 42 20N 10 52 E
Gigmoto, *Phil.* **70 E5** 13 47N 124 23 E
Gignac, *France* **24 E7** 43 39N 3 32 E
Gigüela →, *Spain* **35 F1** 39 8N 3 44W
Gijón, *Spain* **36 B5** 43 32N 5 42W
Gil I., *Canada* **130 C3** 53 12N 129 15W
Gila →, *U.S.A.* **143 K6** 32 43N 114 33W
Gila Bend, *U.S.A.* **143 K7** 32 57N 112 43W
Gila Bend Mts., *U.S.A.* **143 K7** 33 10N 113 0W
Gīlān □, *Iran* **85 B6** 37 0N 50 0 E
Gilău, *Romania* **46 C4** 46 45N 23 23 E
Gilbert →, *Australia* **114 B3** 16 35 S 141 15 E
Gilbert Is., *Kiribati* **122 G9** 1 0N 172 0 E
Gilbert Plains, *Canada* **131 C8** 51 9N 100 28W
Gilbert River, *Australia* **114 B3** 18 9 S 142 52 E
Gilberton, *Australia* **114 B3** 19 16 S 143 35 E
Gilbués, *Brazil* **154 C2** 9 50 S 45 21W
Gilf el Kebîr, Hadabat el, *Egypt* **94 C2** 23 50N 25 50 E
Gilford I., *Canada* **130 C3** 50 40N 126 30W
Gilgandra, *Australia* **117 A8** 31 43 S 148 39 E
Gilgil, *Kenya* **106 C4** 0 30 S 36 20 E
Gilgit, *India* **81 B6** 35 50N 74 15 E
Gilgit →, *Pakistan* **81 B6** 35 44N 74 37 E
Gilgunnia, *Australia* **117 B7** 32 26 S 146 2 E
Giljeva Planina, *Serbia, Yug.* **42 D4** 43 9N 20 0 E
Gillam, *Canada* **131 B10** 56 20N 94 40W
Gilleleje, *Denmark* **15 H6** 56 8N 12 19 E
Gillen, L., *Australia* **113 E3** 26 11 S 124 38 E
Gilles, L., *Australia* **116 B2** 32 50 S 136 45 E
Gillespie, *U.S.A.* **140 E7** 39 8N 89 49W
Gillespies Pt., *N.Z.* **119 D4** 43 24 S 169 49 E
Gillette, *U.S.A.* **138 C2** 44 18N 105 30W
Gilliat, *Australia* **114 C3** 20 40 S 141 28 E
Gillingham, *U.K.* **17 F8** 51 23N 0 33 E
Gilly, *Belgium* **21 H4** 50 25N 4 29 E
Gilman, *U.S.A.* **141 D9** 40 46N 88 0W
Gilman City, *U.S.A.* **140 D3** 40 8N 93 53W
Gilmer, *U.S.A.* **139 J7** 32 44N 94 57W
Gilmore, *Australia* **117 C8** 35 20 S 148 12 E
Gilmore, L., *Australia* **113 F3** 32 29 S 121 37 E
Gilmour, *Canada* **128 D4** 44 48N 77 37W
Gilo →, *Ethiopia* **95 F3** 8 10N 33 15 E
Gilort →, *Romania* **46 E4** 44 38N 23 32 E
Gilroy, *U.S.A.* **144 H5** 37 1N 121 34W
Giluwe, Mt., *Papua N. G.* **120 D2** 6 8 S 143 52 E
Gilze, *Neths.* **21 E5** 51 32N 4 57 E
Gimbi, *Ethiopia* **95 F4** 9 3N 35 42 E
Gimigliano, *Italy* **41 D9** 38 58N 16 32 E
Gimli, *Canada* **131 C9** 50 40N 97 0W
Gimone →, *France* **24 E5** 44 0N 1 6 E
Gimont, *France* **24 E4** 43 38N 0 52 E
Gin →, *Sri Lanka* **83 L5** 6 5N 80 7 E
Gin Gin, *Australia* **115 D5** 25 0 S 151 58 E
Ginâh, *Egypt* **94 B3** 25 21N 30 30 E
Ginatilan, *Phil.* **71 G4** 9 34N 123 19 E
Gindie, *Australia* **114 C4** 23 44 S 148 8 E
Gingin, *Australia* **113 F2** 31 22 S 115 54 E
Gîngiova, *Romania* **46 F4** 43 54N 23 50 E
Gingoog, *Phil.* **71 G5** 8 50N 125 7 E
Ginir, *Ethiopia* **90 F3** 7 6N 40 40 E
Ginosa, *Italy* **41 B9** 40 35N 16 45 E

204 Great Victoria Desert

Great Victoria Desert, Australia 113 E4 29 30 S 126 30 E
Great Wall, China 66 E5 38 30N 109 30 E
Great Whernside, U.K. 16 C6 54 10N 1 58W
Great Yarmouth, U.K. 16 E9 52 37N 1 44 E
Greater Antilles, W. Indies 149 C5 17 40N 74 0W
Greater London □, U.K. 17 F7 51 31N 0 6W
Greater Manchester □, U.K. 16 D5 53 30N 2 15W
Grebbestad, Sweden 15 F5 58 42N 11 15 E
Grebenka = Hrebenka, Ukraine 51 G7 50 9N 32 22 E
Greco, C., Cyprus 32 E13 34 57N 34 5 E
Greco, Mte., Italy 40 A6 41 48N 14 0 E
Gredos, Sierra de, Spain 36 E5 40 20N 5 0W
Greece, U.S.A. 136 C7 43 13N 77 41W
Greece ■, Europe 44 D5 40 0N 23 0 E
Greeley, Colo., U.S.A. 138 E2 40 25N 104 42W
Greeley, Nebr., U.S.A. 138 E5 41 33N 98 32W
Green →, Ky., U.S.A. 134 G2 37 54N 87 30W
Green →, Utah, U.S.A. 143 G9 38 11N 109 53W
Green B., U.S.A. 134 C2 45 0N 87 30W
Green Bay, U.S.A. 134 C2 44 31N 88 0W
Green C., Australia 117 D9 37 13 S 150 1 E
Green City, U.S.A. 140 D4 40 16N 92 57W
Green Cove Springs, U.S.A. 135 L5 29 59N 81 42W
Green Is., Papua N. G. 120 C8 4 35 S 154 10 E
Green Island Bay, Phil. 71 F2 10 12N 119 22 E
Green River, U.S.A. 143 G8 38 59N 110 10W
Greenbank, U.S.A. 144 B4 48 6N 122 34W
Greenbush, Mich., U.S.A. 136 B1 44 35N 83 19W
Greenbush, Minn., U.S.A. 138 A6 48 42N 96 11W
Greencastle, U.S.A. 141 E10 39 38N 86 52W
Greene, Iowa, U.S.A. 140 B4 42 54N 92 48W
Greene, N.Y., U.S.A. 137 D9 42 20N 75 46W
Greenfield, Calif., U.S.A. 144 J5 36 19N 121 15W
Greenfield, Calif., U.S.A. 145 K8 35 15N 119 0W
Greenfield, Ill., U.S.A. 140 E6 39 21N 90 12W
Greenfield, Ind., U.S.A. 141 E11 39 47N 85 46W
Greenfield, Iowa, U.S.A. 140 C2 41 18N 94 28W
Greenfield, Mass., U.S.A. 137 D12 42 35N 72 36W
Greenfield, Mo., U.S.A. 139 G8 37 25N 93 51W
Greenfield, Ohio, U.S.A. 141 E13 39 21N 83 23W
Greenfield Park, Canada 137 A11 45 29N 73 29W
Greenland ■, N. Amer. 124 C15 66 0N 45 0W
Greenland Sea, Arctic 6 B7 73 0N 10 0W
Greenock, U.K. 18 F4 55 57N 4 46W
Greenore, Ireland 19 B5 54 2N 6 8W
Greenore Pt., Ireland 19 D5 52 14N 6 19W
Greenough →, Australia 113 E1 28 51 S 114 38 E
Greenport, U.S.A. 137 E12 41 6N 72 22W
Greensboro, Ga., U.S.A. 135 J4 33 35N 83 11W
Greensboro, N.C., U.S.A. 135 G6 36 4N 79 48W
Greensburg, Ind., U.S.A. 141 E11 39 20N 85 29W
Greensburg, Kans., U.S.A. 139 G5 37 36N 99 18W
Greensburg, Pa., U.S.A. 136 F5 40 18N 79 33W
Greentown, U.S.A. 141 D11 40 29N 85 58W
Greenup, U.S.A. 141 E8 39 15N 88 10W
Greenville, Liberia 100 D3 5 1N 9 6W
Greenville, Ala., U.S.A. 135 K2 31 50N 86 38W
Greenville, Calif., U.S.A. 144 E6 40 8N 120 57W
Greenville, Ill., U.S.A. 140 F7 38 53N 89 25W
Greenville, Ind., U.S.A. 141 F11 38 22N 85 59W
Greenville, Maine, U.S.A. 129 C6 45 28N 69 35W
Greenville, Mich., U.S.A. 141 A11 43 11N 85 15W
Greenville, Miss., U.S.A. 139 J9 33 24N 91 4W
Greenville, N.C., U.S.A. 135 H7 35 37N 77 23W
Greenville, Ohio, U.S.A. 141 D12 40 6N 84 38W
Greenville, Pa., U.S.A. 136 E4 41 24N 80 23W
Greenville, S.C., U.S.A. 135 H4 34 51N 82 24W
Greenville, Tenn., U.S.A. 135 G4 36 13N 82 51W
Greenville, Tex., U.S.A. 139 J6 33 8N 96 7W
Greenwater Lake Prov. Park, Canada 131 C8 52 32N 103 30W
Greenwich, U.K. 17 F8 51 29N 0 1 E
Greenwich, Conn., U.S.A. 137 E11 41 2N 73 38W
Greenwich, N.Y., U.S.A. 137 C11 43 5N 73 30W
Greenwich, Ohio, U.S.A. 136 E2 41 2N 82 31W
Greenwood, Canada 130 D5 49 10N 118 40W
Greenwood, Ind., U.S.A. 141 E10 39 37N 86 7W
Greenwood, Miss., U.S.A. 139 J9 33 31N 90 11W
Greenwood, S.C., U.S.A. 135 H4 34 12N 82 10W
Greenwood, Mt., Australia 112 B5 13 48 S 130 4 E
Gregório →, Brazil 156 B3 6 50 S 70 46W
Gregory, U.S.A. 138 D5 43 14N 99 20W
Gregory →, Australia 114 B2 17 53 S 139 17 E
Gregory, L., S. Austral., Australia 115 D2 28 55 S 139 0 E
Gregory, L., W. Austral., Australia 113 E2 25 38 S 119 58 E
Gregory Downs, Australia 114 B2 18 35 S 138 45 E
Gregory L., Australia 112 D4 20 0 S 127 40 E
Gregory Ra., Queens., Australia 114 B3 19 30 S 143 40 E
Gregory Ra., W. Austral., Australia 112 D3 21 20 S 121 12 E
Greiffenberg, Germany 26 B9 53 5N 13 57 E
Greifswald, Germany 26 A9 54 5N 13 23 E
Greifswalder Bodden, Germany 26 A9 54 12N 13 35 E
Grein, Austria 30 C7 48 14N 14 51 E
Greiner Wald, Austria 30 C7 48 30N 15 0 E
Greiz, Germany 26 E8 50 39N 12 10 E
Gremikha, Russia 48 A6 67 59N 39 47 E
Gremyachinsk, Russia 54 B6 58 34N 57 51 E
Grenå, Denmark 15 H4 56 25N 10 53 E
Grenada, U.S.A. 139 J10 33 47N 89 49W
Grenada ■, W. Indies 149 D7 12 10N 61 40W
Grenade, France 24 E5 43 47N 1 17 E
Grenadines, W. Indies 149 D7 12 40N 61 20W
Grenchen, Switz. 28 B4 47 12N 7 24 E
Grenen, Denmark 15 G4 57 44N 10 40 E
Grenfell, Australia 117 B8 33 52 S 148 8 E
Grenfell, Canada 131 C8 50 30N 102 56W
Grenoble, France 25 C9 45 12N 5 42 E
Grenora, U.S.A. 138 A3 48 37N 103 56W
Grenville, C., Australia 114 A3 12 0 S 143 13 E
Grenville Chan., Canada 130 C3 53 40N 129 46W
Gréoux-les-Bains, France 25 E9 43 45N 5 52 E
Gresham, U.S.A. 144 E4 45 30N 122 26W
Gresik, Indonesia 75 D4 7 13 S 112 38 E
Grëssoney St. Jean, Italy 38 C4 45 49N 7 47 E
Gretna Green, U.K. 18 F5 55 1N 3 3W
Grevelingen Krammer, Neths. 20 E4 51 44N 4 0 E
Greven, Germany 26 C3 52 6N 7 37 E
Grevená, Greece 44 D3 40 4N 21 25 E
Grevená □, Greece 44 D3 40 2N 21 25 E
Grevenbroich, Germany 26 D2 51 5N 6 35 E
Grevenmacher, Lux. 21 J8 49 41N 6 26 E
Grevesmühlen, Germany 26 B7 53 52N 11 12 E
Grevie, Sweden 15 H6 56 22N 12 46 E
Grey →, N.Z. 119 C6 42 27 S 171 12 E
Grey, C., Australia 114 A2 13 0 S 136 35 E
Grey Ra., Australia 115 D3 27 0 S 143 30 E
Grey Res., Canada 129 C8 48 20N 56 30W
Greybull, U.S.A. 142 D9 44 30N 108 3W
Greymouth, N.Z. 119 C6 42 29 S 171 13 E
Greytown, N.Z. 118 H4 41 5 S 175 29 E
Greytown, S. Africa 105 D5 29 1 S 30 36 E
Gribanovskiy, Russia 52 E5 51 28N 41 50 E
Gribbell I., Canada 130 C3 53 23N 129 0W
Gridley, U.S.A. 144 F5 39 22N 121 42W
Griekwastad, S. Africa 104 D3 28 49 S 23 15 E
Griffin, U.S.A. 135 J3 33 15N 84 16W
Griffith, Australia 117 C7 34 18 S 146 2 E
Grijpskerk, Neths. 20 B8 53 16N 6 18 E
Grillby, Sweden 14 E11 59 38N 17 15 E
Grimari, C.A.R. 102 A4 5 43N 20 6 E
Grimaylov = Hrymayliv, Ukraine 51 H4 49 20N 26 5 E
Grimbergen, Belgium 21 G4 50 56N 4 22 E
Grimes, U.S.A. 144 F5 39 4N 121 54W
Grimma, Germany 26 D8 51 14N 12 43 E
Grimmen, Germany 26 A9 54 7N 13 3 E
Grimsby, Canada 136 C5 43 12N 79 34W
Grimsby, U.K. 16 D7 53 34N 0 5W
Grimselpass, Switz. 29 C6 46 34N 8 23 E
Grímsey, Iceland 12 C5 66 33N 17 58W
Grimshaw, Canada 130 B5 56 10N 117 40W
Grimstad, Norway 15 F2 58 20N 8 35 E
Grindelwald, Switz. 28 C6 46 38N 8 2 E
Grindsted, Denmark 15 J2 55 46N 8 55 E
Grindu, Romania 46 E7 44 44N 26 50 E
Grinnell, U.S.A. 140 C4 41 45N 92 43W
Griñón, Spain 36 E7 40 13N 3 51W
Grintavec, Slovenia 39 B11 46 22N 14 32 E
Grip, Norway 14 A1 63 16N 7 37 E
Gris-Nez, C., France 23 B8 50 52N 1 35 E
Grisolles, France 24 E5 43 49N 1 19 E
Grisons = Graubünden □, Switz. 29 C9 46 45N 9 30 E
Grivegnée, Belgium 21 G7 50 37N 5 36 E
Grmeč Planina, Bos.-H. 39 D13 44 43N 16 16 E
Groais I., Canada 129 B8 50 55N 55 35W
Groblersdal, S. Africa 105 D4 25 15 S 29 25 E
Grobming, Austria 30 D6 47 27N 13 54 E
Grocka, Serbia, Yug. 42 C5 44 40N 20 42 E
Gródek, Poland 47 B10 53 6N 23 40 E
Grodkow, Poland 47 E4 50 43N 17 21 E
Grodno = Hrodna, Belarus 50 F2 53 42N 23 52 E
Grodzisk Mázowiecki, Poland 47 C7 52 7N 20 37 E
Grodzisk Wielkopolski, Poland 47 C3 52 15N 16 22 E
Grodzyanka = Hrodzyanka, Belarus 50 F5 53 31N 28 42 E
Groenlo, Neths. 20 D9 52 2N 6 37 E
Groesbeck, U.S.A. 139 K6 31 31N 96 31W
Groesbeek, Neths. 20 E7 51 47N 5 58 E
Groix, France 22 E3 47 38N 3 29W
Groix, I. de, France 22 E3 47 38N 3 28W
Grójec, Poland 47 D7 51 50N 20 58 E
Grolloo, Neths. 20 C9 52 56N 6 41 E
Gronau, Niedersachsen, Germany 26 C5 52 5N 9 47 E
Gronau, Nordrhein-Westfalen, Germany 26 C3 52 12N 7 2 E
Grong, Norway 12 D15 64 25N 12 8 E
Groningen, Neths. 20 B9 53 15N 6 35 E
Groningen, Surinam 153 B6 5 48N 55 28W
Groningen □, Neths. 20 B9 53 16N 6 40 E
Groninger Wad, Neths. 20 B9 53 27N 6 30 E
Gronsveld, Neths. 21 G7 50 49N 5 44 E
Groom, U.S.A. 139 H4 35 12N 101 6W
Groot →, S. Africa 104 E3 33 45 S 24 36 E
Groot Berg →, S. Africa 104 E2 32 47 S 18 8 E
Groot-Brakrivier, S. Africa 104 E3 34 2 S 22 18 E
Groot-Kei →, S. Africa 105 E4 32 41 S 28 22 E
Groot Vis →, S. Africa 104 E4 33 28 S 27 5 E
Groote Eylandt, Australia 114 A2 14 0 S 136 40 E
Grootebroek, Neths. 20 C6 52 41N 5 13 E
Grootfontein, Namibia 104 B2 19 31 S 18 6 E
Grootlaagte →, Africa 104 C3 20 55 S 21 27 E
Grootvloer, S. Africa 104 E3 30 0 S 20 40 E
Gros C., Canada 130 A6 61 59N 113 32W
Grosa, Pta., Spain 33 B8 39 6N 1 36 E
Grósio, Italy 38 B7 46 18N 10 16 E
Grosne →, France 25 B8 46 42N 4 56 E
Gross Glockner, Austria 30 D5 47 5N 12 40 E
Grossenbrode, Germany 26 A7 54 21N 11 4 E
Grossenhain, Germany 26 D9 51 17N 13 32 E
Grosseto, Italy 38 F8 42 46N 11 8 E
Grossgerungs, Austria 30 C7 48 34N 14 57 E
Groswater B., Canada 129 B8 54 20N 57 40W
Grote Gette →, Neths. 21 G6 50 51N 5 6 E
Grote Nete →, Belgium 21 F5 51 8N 4 34 E
Groton, Conn., U.S.A. 137 E12 41 21N 72 5W
Groton, S. Dak., U.S.A. 138 C5 45 27N 98 6W
Grottáglie, Italy 41 B10 40 32N 17 26 E
Grottaminarda, Italy 41 A8 41 4N 15 2 E
Grottammare, Italy 39 F10 42 59N 13 52 E
Grouard Mission, Canada 130 B5 55 33N 116 9W
Grouin, Pte. du, France 22 D5 48 43N 1 51W
Groundhog →, Canada 128 C3 48 45N 82 58W
Grouse Creek, U.S.A. 142 F7 41 42N 113 53W
Grouw, Neths. 20 B7 53 5N 5 51 E
Grove City, Ohio, U.S.A. 141 E13 39 53N 83 6W
Grove City, Pa., U.S.A. 136 E4 41 10N 80 5W
Groveland, U.S.A. 144 H6 37 50N 120 14W
Grover City, U.S.A. 145 K6 35 7N 120 37W
Grover Hill, U.S.A. 141 C12 41 1N 84 29W
Groveton, N.H., U.S.A. 137 B13 44 36N 71 31W
Groveton, Tex., U.S.A. 139 K7 31 4N 95 8W
Grožnjan, Croatia 39 C10 45 22N 13 43 E
Groznyy, Russia 53 J7 43 20N 45 45 E
Grubbenvorst, Neths. 21 F8 51 25N 6 9 E
Grubišno Polje, Croatia 42 B2 45 44N 17 12 E
Grudovo, Bulgaria 43 E12 42 21N 27 10 E
Grudusk, Poland 47 B7 53 3N 20 38 E
Grudziądz, Poland 47 B5 53 30N 18 47 E
Gruissan, France 24 E7 43 8N 3 7 E
Grumo Áppula, Italy 41 A9 41 1N 16 42 E
Grünberg, Germany 26 E4 50 35N 8 58 E
Grundy Center, U.S.A. 140 B4 42 22N 92 47W
Gruver, U.S.A. 139 G4 36 16N 101 24W
Gruyères, Switz. 28 C4 46 35N 7 4 E
Gruža, Serbia, Yug. 42 D5 43 54N 20 46 E
Gryazi, Russia 52 D4 52 30N 39 58 E
Gryazovets, Russia 50 C11 58 50N 40 10 E
Grybów, Poland 31 B13 49 36N 20 55 E
Gryfice, Poland 47 B2 53 55N 15 13 E
Gryfino, Poland 47 B1 53 16N 14 29 E
Gryfow Sl., Poland 47 D2 51 2N 15 24 E
Gstaad, Switz. 28 D4 46 28N 7 18 E
Gua Musang, Malaysia 77 K3 4 53N 101 58 E
Guacanayabo, G. de, Cuba 148 B4 20 40N 77 20W
Guacara, Venezuela 152 A4 10 14N 67 53W
Guachípas →, Argentina 158 B2 25 40 S 65 30W
Guachiría →, Colombia 152 B3 5 27N 70 36W
Guadajoz →, Spain 37 H6 37 50N 4 51W
Guadalajara, Mexico 146 C4 20 40N 103 20W
Guadalajara, Spain 34 E1 40 37N 3 12W
Guadalajara □, Spain 34 E2 40 47N 2 30W
Guadalcanal, Solomon Is. 121 M11 9 32 S 160 12 E
Guadalcanal, Spain 37 G5 38 5N 5 52W
Guadalén →, Spain 37 G7 38 5N 3 32W
Guadales, Argentina 158 C2 34 30 S 67 55W
Guadalete →, Spain 37 J4 36 35N 6 13W
Guadalhorce →, Spain 37 J6 36 41N 4 27W
Guadalimar →, Spain 35 G1 38 5N 3 28W
Guadalmena →, Spain 35 G2 38 19N 2 56W
Guadalmez →, Spain 37 G5 38 46N 5 4W
Guadalope →, Spain 34 D4 41 15N 0 3W
Guadalquivir →, Spain 37 J4 36 47N 6 22W
Guadalupe = Guadeloupe ■, W. Indies 149 C7 16 20N 61 40W
Guadalupe, Brazil 154 C3 6 44 S 43 47W
Guadalupe, Mexico 145 N10 32 4N 116 32W
Guadalupe, Spain 37 F5 39 27N 5 17W
Guadalupe, U.S.A. 145 L6 34 59N 120 33W
Guadalupe →, Mexico 145 N10 32 6N 116 51W
Guadalupe →, U.S.A. 139 L6 28 27N 96 47W
Guadalupe, Sierra de, Spain 37 F5 39 28N 5 30W
Guadalupe Bravos, Mexico 146 A3 31 20N 106 10W
Guadalupe I., Pac. Oc. 124 G8 29 0N 118 50W
Guadalupe Peak, U.S.A. 143 L11 31 50N 104 52W
Guadalupe y Calvo, Mexico 146 B3 26 6N 106 58W
Guadarrama, Sierra de, Spain 36 E6 41 0N 4 0W
Guadauta, Georgia 53 J5 43 7N 40 32 E
Guadeloupe ■, W. Indies 149 C7 16 20N 61 40W
Guadeloupe Passage, W. Indies 149 C7 16 50N 62 15W
Guadiamar →, Spain 37 J4 36 55N 6 24W
Guadiana →, Portugal 37 H3 37 14N 7 22W
Guadiana Menor →, Spain 35 H1 37 56N 3 15W
Guadiaro →, Spain 37 J5 36 17N 5 17W
Guadiato →, Spain 37 H5 37 48N 5 5W
Guadiela →, Spain 34 E2 40 22N 2 49W
Guadix, Spain 35 H1 37 18N 3 11W
Guafo, Boca del, Chile 160 B2 43 35 S 74 0W
Guafo, I., Chile 160 B2 43 35 S 74 50W
Guainía □, Colombia 152 C4 2 30N 69 0W
Guainía →, Colombia 152 C4 2 1N 67 7W
Guaíra, Brazil 159 A5 24 5 S 54 10W
Guaitecas, Is., Chile 160 B2 44 0 S 74 30W
Guajará-Mirim, Brazil 157 C4 10 50 S 65 20W
Guajira □, Colombia 152 A3 11 30N 72 30W
Guajira, Pen. de la, Colombia 152 A3 12 0N 72 0W
Gualaceo, Ecuador 152 D2 2 54 S 78 47W
Gualán, Guatemala 148 C2 15 8N 89 22W
Gualdo Tadino, Italy 39 E9 43 14N 12 47 E
Gualeguay, Argentina 158 C4 33 10 S 59 14W
Gualeguaychú, Argentina 158 C4 33 3 S 59 31W
Gualicho, Salina, Argentina 160 B3 40 25 S 65 20W
Gualjaina, Argentina 160 B2 42 45 S 70 30W
Guam ■, Pac. Oc. 121 R15 13 27N 144 45 E
Guamá, Brazil 154 B2 1 37 S 47 29W
Guamá →, Brazil 154 B2 1 29 S 48 30W
Guamblin, I., Chile 160 B1 44 50 S 75 0W
Guaminí, Argentina 158 D3 37 1 S 62 28W
Guamote, Ecuador 152 D2 1 56 S 78 43W
Guampí, Sierra de, Venezuela 153 B4 6 0N 65 35W
Guamúchil, Mexico 146 B3 25 25N 108 3W
Guan Xian, China 68 B4 31 2N 103 38 E
Guanabacoa, Cuba 148 B3 23 8N 82 18W
Guanacaste, Cordillera del, Costa Rica 148 D2 10 40N 85 4W
Guanaceví, Mexico 146 B3 25 40N 106 0W
Guanahani = San Salvador, Bahamas 149 B5 24 0N 74 40W
Guanajay, Cuba 148 B3 22 56N 82 42W
Guanajuato, Mexico 146 C4 21 0N 101 20W
Guanajuato □, Mexico 146 C4 20 40N 101 20W
Guanambi, Brazil 155 D3 14 13 S 42 47W
Guanare, Venezuela 152 B4 8 42N 69 12W
Guanare →, Venezuela 152 B4 8 13N 67 46W
Guandacol, Argentina 158 B2 29 30 S 68 40W
Guane, Cuba 148 B3 22 10N 84 7W
Guang'an, China 68 B6 30 28N 106 35 E
Guangchang, China 69 D11 26 50N 116 21 E
Guangde, China 69 B12 30 54N 119 25 E
Guangdong □, China 69 F9 23 0N 113 0 E
Guangfeng, China 69 C12 28 20N 118 15 E
Guanghan, China 68 B5 30 58N 104 17 E
Guanghua, China 69 A8 32 22N 111 38 E
Guangji, China 69 C10 29 52N 115 30 E
Guangling, China 66 E8 39 47N 114 22 E
Guangning, China 69 F9 23 40N 112 22 E
Guangrao, China 67 F10 37 5N 118 25 E
Guangshun, China 68 D6 26 8N 106 21 E
Guanguan Peninsula, Phil. 71 H6 6 50N 126 19 E
Guangwu, China 66 F3 37 48N 105 57 E
Guangxi Zhuangzu Zizhiqu □, China 68 E7 24 0N 109 0 E
Guangyuan, China 68 A5 32 26N 105 51 E
Guangze, China 69 D11 27 30N 117 12 E
Guangzhou, China 69 F9 23 5N 113 10 E
Guanhães, Brazil 155 E3 18 47 S 42 57W
Guanipa →, Venezuela 153 B5 9 56N 62 26W
Guanling, China 68 E5 25 56N 105 35 E
Guannan, China 67 G10 34 8N 119 21 E
Guanta, Venezuela 153 A5 10 14N 64 36W
Guantánamo, Cuba 149 B4 20 10N 75 14W
Guantao, China 66 F8 36 42N 115 25 E
Guanyang, China 69 E8 25 30N 111 8 E
Guanyun, China 67 G10 34 20N 119 18 E
Guapí, Colombia 152 C2 2 36N 77 54W
Guápiles, Costa Rica 148 D3 10 10N 83 46W
Guaporé →, Brazil 157 C4 11 55 S 65 4W
Guaqui, Bolivia 156 D4 16 41 S 68 54W
Guara, Sierra de, Spain 34 C4 42 19N 0 15W
Guarabira, Brazil 154 C4 6 51 S 35 29W
Guaranda, Ecuador 152 D2 1 36 S 79 0W
Guarapari, Brazil 155 F3 20 40 S 40 30W
Guarapuava, Brazil 155 G1 25 20 S 51 30W
Guaratinguetá, Brazil 159 A6 22 49 S 45 9W
Guaratuba, Brazil 159 B6 25 53 S 48 38W
Guarda, Portugal 36 E3 40 32N 7 20W
Guarda □, Portugal 36 E3 40 40N 7 20W
Guardafui, C. = Asir, Ras, Somali Rep. 108 B4 11 55N 51 10 E
Guardamar del Segura, Spain 35 G4 38 5N 0 39W
Guardavalle, Italy 41 D9 38 30N 16 30 E
Guardiagrele, Italy 39 F11 42 11N 14 13 E
Guardo, Spain 36 C6 42 47N 4 50W
Guareña, Spain 37 G4 38 51N 6 6W
Guareña →, Spain 36 D5 41 29N 5 23W
Guaria □, Paraguay 158 B4 25 45 S 56 30W
Guárico □, Venezuela 152 B4 8 40N 66 35W
Guarrojo →, Colombia 152 C3 4 6N 70 42W
Guarujá, Brazil 159 A6 24 2 S 46 25W
Guarus, Brazil 155 F3 21 44 S 41 20W
Guasave, Mexico 146 B3 25 34N 108 27W
Guascama, Pta., Colombia 152 C2 2 32N 78 24W
Guasdualito, Venezuela 152 B3 7 15N 70 44W
Guasipati, Venezuela 153 B5 7 28N 61 54W
Guasopa, Papua N. G. 120 E7 9 12 S 152 56 E
Guastalla, Italy 38 D7 44 55N 10 39 E
Guatemala, Guatemala 148 D1 14 40N 90 22W
Guatemala ■, Cent. Amer. 148 C1 15 40N 90 30W
Guatire, Venezuela 152 A4 10 28N 66 32W
Guaviare □, Colombia 152 C3 2 0N 72 30W
Guaviare →, Colombia 152 C4 4 3N 67 44W
Guaxupé, Brazil 159 A6 21 10 S 47 5W
Guayabero →, Colombia 152 C3 2 36N 72 47W
Guayama, Puerto Rico 149 C6 17 59N 66 7W
Guayaneco, Arch., Chile 160 C1 47 45 S 75 10W
Guayaquil, Ecuador 152 D2 2 15 S 79 52W
Guayaquil, G. de, Ecuador 152 D1 3 10 S 81 0W
Guayaramerín, Bolivia 157 C4 10 48 S 65 23W
Guayas →, Ecuador 152 D2 2 36 S 79 52W
Guaymas, Mexico 146 B2 27 59N 110 54W
Guazhou, China 69 A12 32 17N 119 21 E
Guba, Zaïre 107 E2 10 38 S 26 27 E
Gubakha, Russia 54 B6 58 52N 57 36 E
Gûbâl, Madîq, Egypt 94 B3 27 30N 34 0 E
Gubam, Papua N. G. 120 E1 8 39 S 141 53 E
Gubat, Phil. 70 E5 12 55N 124 7 E
Gúbbio, Italy 39 E9 43 21N 12 35 E
Gubin, Poland 47 D1 51 57N 14 43 E
Gubio, Nigeria 101 C7 12 30N 12 42 E
Gubkin, Russia 52 E3 51 17N 37 32 E
Guča, Serbia, Yug. 42 D5 43 46N 20 15 E
Gudalur, India 83 J3 11 30N 76 29 E
Gudata = Guadauta, Georgia 53 J5 43 7N 40 32 E
Gudbrandsdalen, Norway 13 F14 61 33N 10 10 E
Gudenå →, Denmark 15 H3 56 29N 10 13 E
Gudermes, Russia 53 J8 43 24N 46 5 E
Gudivada, India 83 F5 16 30N 81 3 E
Gudiyattam, India 83 H4 12 57N 78 55 E
Gudur, India 83 G4 14 12N 79 55 E
Guebwiller, France 23 E14 47 55N 7 12 E
Guecho, Spain 34 B2 43 21N 2 59W
Guékédou, Guinea 100 D2 8 40N 10 5W
Guelma, Algeria 99 A6 36 25N 7 29 E
Guelph, Canada 128 D3 43 35N 80 20W
Guemar, Algeria 99 B6 33 30N 6 49 E
Guéméné-Penfao, France 22 E5 47 38N 1 50W
Guéméné-sur-Scorff, France 22 D3 48 4N 3 13W
Guéné, Benin 101 C5 11 44N 3 16 E
Güepi, Peru 152 D2 0 9 S 75 10W
Guer, France 22 E4 47 54N 2 8W
Güer Aike, Argentina 160 D3 51 39 S 69 35W
Guera Pk., Chad 97 F3 11 55N 18 12 E
Guérande, France 22 E4 47 20N 2 26W
Guercif, Morocco 99 B4 34 14N 3 21W
Guéréda, Chad 97 F4 14 31N 22 5 E
Guéret, France 24 B5 46 11N 1 51 E
Guérigny, France 23 E10 47 6N 3 10 E
Guerneville, U.S.A. 144 G4 38 30N 123 0W
Guernica, Spain 34 B2 43 19N 2 40W
Guernsey, U.K. 17 H5 49 26N 2 35W
Guernsey, U.S.A. 138 D2 42 19N 104 45W
Guerrara, Oasis, Algeria 99 B5 32 51N 4 22 E
Guerrara, Saoura, Algeria 99 C4 28 5N 0 8W
Guerrero □, Mexico 147 D5 17 30N 100 0W
Guerzim, Algeria 99 C4 29 39N 1 40W
Gueugnon, France 25 B8 46 36N 4 4 E
Gueydan, U.S.A. 139 K8 30 2N 92 31W
Gûgher, Iran 85 D8 29 28N 56 27 E
Guglionesi, Italy 41 A7 41 55N 14 55 E
Gui Jiang →, China 69 F8 23 30N 111 15 E
Gui Xian, China 68 F7 23 8N 109 35 E
Guia, Canary Is. 33 F4 28 8N 15 38W
Guia de Isora, Canary Is. 33 F3 28 12N 16 46W
Guia Lopes da Laguna, Brazil 159 A4 21 26 S 56 7W
Guiana, S. Amer. 150 C4 5 10N 60 40W
Guichi, China 69 B11 30 39N 117 27 E
Guider, Cameroon 101 D7 9 56N 13 57 E
Guidimouni, Niger 97 F1 13 42N 9 31 E
Guiding, China 68 D6 26 34N 107 11 E
Guidong, China 69 D9 26 7N 113 57 E
Guiglo, Ivory C. 100 D3 6 45N 7 30W
Guijá, Mozam. 105 C5 24 27 S 33 0 E
Guijo de Coria, Spain 36 E4 40 6N 6 28W
Guildford, U.K. 17 F7 51 14N 0 34W
Guilford, U.S.A. 129 C6 45 10N 69 23W

Hamakita 205

Guilin, *China* 69 **E8** 25 18N 110 15 E
Guillaumes, *France* 25 **D10** 44 5N 6 52 E
Guillestre, *France* 25 **D10** 44 39N 6 40 E
Guilvinec, *France* 22 **E2** 47 48N 4 17W
Güimar, *Canary Is.* 33 **F3** 28 18N 16 24W
Guimarães, *Brazil* 154 **B3** 2 9 S 44 42W
Guimarães, *Portugal* 36 **D2** 41 28N 8 24W
Guimaras, *Phil.* 71 **F4** 10 35N 122 37 E
Guimba, *Phil.* 70 **D3** 15 40N 120 46 E
Guinda, *U.S.A.* 144 **G4** 38 50N 122 12W
Guindulman, *Phil.* 71 **G5** 9 46N 124 29 E
Guinea, *Africa* 92 **F4** 8 0N 8 0 E
Guinea ■, *W. Afr.* 100 **C2** 10 20N 11 30W
Guinea, Gulf of, *Atl. Oc.* 101 **E5** 3 0N 2 30 E
Guinea-Bissau ■, *Africa* 100 **C2** 12 0N 15 0W
Güines, *Cuba* 148 **B3** 22 50N 82 0W
Guingamp, *France* 22 **D3** 48 34N 3 10W
Guinobatan, *Phil.* 70 **E4** 13 11N 123 36 E
Guiom, *Phil.* 71 **F4** 11 59N 123 44 E
Guipavas, *France* 22 **D2** 48 26N 4 29W
Guiping, *China* 69 **F8** 23 21N 110 2 E
Guipúzcoa □, *Spain* 34 **B2** 43 12N 2 15W
Guir, O. →, *Algeria* 99 **B4** 31 29N 2 17W
Guiratinga, *Brazil* 157 **D7** 16 21 S 53 45W
Güiria, *Venezuela* 153 **A5** 10 32N 62 18W
Guiscard, *France* 23 **C10** 49 40N 3 1 E
Guise, *France* 23 **C10** 49 52N 3 35 E
Guitiriz, *Spain* 36 **B3** 43 11N 7 50W
Guiuan, *Phil.* 71 **F5** 11 5N 125 55 E
Guixi, *China* 69 **C11** 28 16N 117 15 E
Guiyang, *Guizhou, China* 68 **D6** 26 32N 106 40 E
Guiyang, *Hunan, China* 69 **E9** 25 46N 112 42 E
Guizhou □, *China* 68 **D6** 27 0N 107 0 E
Gujan-Mestras, *France* 24 **D2** 44 38N 1 4W
Gujarat □, *India* 80 **H4** 23 20N 71 0 E
Gujiang, *China* 69 **D10** 27 11N 114 47 E
Gujranwala, *Pakistan* 79 **B4** 32 10N 74 12 E
Gujrat, *Pakistan* 79 **B4** 32 40N 74 2 E
Gukovo, *Russia* 53 **F5** 48 1N 39 58 E
Gulargambone, *Australia* 117 **A8** 31 20 S 148 30 E
Gulbarga, *India* 82 **F3** 17 20N 76 50 E
Gulbene, *Latvia* 13 **H22** 57 8N 26 52 E
Gulcha, *Kyrgyzstan* 55 **C6** 40 19N 73 26 E
Guledagudda, *India* 83 **F2** 16 3N 75 48 E
Gulf, The, *Asia* 85 **E6** 27 0N 50 0 E
Gulfport, *U.S.A.* 139 **K10** 30 22N 89 6W
Gulgong, *Australia* 117 **B8** 32 20 S 149 49 E
Gulin, *China* 68 **C5** 28 1N 105 50 E
Gulistan, *Pakistan* 80 **D2** 30 30N 66 35 E
Guliston, *Uzbekistan* 55 **C4** 40 29N 68 46 E
Gull Lake, *Canada* 131 **C7** 50 10N 108 29W
Gullegem, *Belgium* 21 **G2** 50 51N 3 13 E
Güllük, *Turkey* 88 **D2** 37 14N 27 35 E
Gulma, *Nigeria* 101 **C5** 12 40N 4 23 E
Gulmarg, *India* 81 **B6** 34 3N 74 25 E
Gülnar, *Turkey* 88 **D5** 36 19N 33 24 E
Gulnare, *Australia* 116 **B3** 33 27 S 138 27 E
Gulpen, *Neths.* 21 **G7** 50 49N 5 53 E
Gülpinar, *Turkey* 44 **E8** 39 32N 26 10 E
Gülşehir, *Turkey* 88 **C6** 38 44N 34 37 E
Gulshad, *Kazakstan* 56 **E8** 46 45N 74 25 E
Gulsvik, *Norway* 14 **D3** 60 24N 9 38 E
Gulu, *Uganda* 106 **B3** 2 48N 32 17 E
Gŭlŭbovo, *Bulgaria* 43 **E10** 42 8N 25 55 E
Gulwe, *Tanzania* 106 **D4** 6 30 S 36 25 E
Gulyaypole = Hulyaypole, *Ukraine* 51 **J9** 47 45N 36 21 E
Gum Lake, *Australia* 116 **B5** 32 42 S 143 9 E
Gumaca, *Phil.* 70 **E4** 13 55N 122 6 E
Gumal →, *Pakistan* 80 **D4** 31 40N 71 50 E
Gumbaz, *Pakistan* 80 **D3** 30 2N 69 0 E
Gumel, *Nigeria* 101 **C6** 12 39N 9 22 E
Gumiel de Hizán, *Spain* 34 **D1** 41 46N 3 41W
Gumlu, *Australia* 114 **B4** 19 53 S 147 41 E
Gumma □, *Japan* 63 **A10** 36 30N 138 20 E
Gummersbach, *Germany* 26 **D3** 51 1N 7 34 E
Gummi, *Nigeria* 101 **C6** 12 4N 5 9 E
Gümüşhaciköy, *Turkey* 88 **B6** 40 50N 35 18 E
Gümüşhane, *Turkey* 89 **B8** 40 30N 39 30 E
Gumzai, *Indonesia* 73 **C4** 5 28 S 134 42 E
Guna, *Ethiopia* 95 **E4** 11 50N 37 40 E
Guna, *India* 80 **G7** 24 40N 77 19 E
Gundagai, *Australia* 117 **C8** 35 3 S 148 6 E
Gundelfingen, *Germany* 27 **G6** 48 19N 10 22 E
Gundih, *Indonesia* 75 **D4** 7 10 S 110 56 E
Gundlakamma →, *India* 83 **G5** 15 30N 80 15 E
Gunebang, *Australia* 117 **B7** 33 1 S 146 38 E
Güneydoğu Toroslar, *Turkey* 89 **C9** 38 20N 40 30 E
Gungal, *Australia* 117 **B9** 32 17 S 150 32 E
Gungu, *Zaïre* 103 **D3** 5 43 S 19 20 E
Gunisao →, *Canada* 131 **C9** 53 56N 97 53W
Gunisao L., *Canada* 131 **C9** 53 33N 96 15W
Gunnbjørn Fjeld, *Greenland* 6 **C6** 68 55N 29 47W
Gunnedah, *Australia* 117 **A9** 30 59 S 150 15 E
Gunniguldrie, *Australia* 117 **B7** 33 10 S 146 8 E
Gunningbar Cr. →, *Australia* 117 **A7** 31 14 S 147 6 E
Gunnison, *Colo., U.S.A.* 143 **G10** 38 33N 106 56W
Gunnison, *Utah, U.S.A.* 142 **G8** 39 9N 111 49W
Gunnison →, *U.S.A.* 143 **G9** 39 4N 108 35W
Gunpowder, *Australia* 114 **B2** 19 42 S 139 22 E
Guntakal, *India* 83 **G3** 15 11N 77 27 E
Guntersville, *U.S.A.* 135 **H2** 34 21N 86 18W
Guntong, *Malaysia* 77 **K3** 4 36N 101 3 E
Guntur, *India* 83 **F5** 16 23N 80 30 E
Gunungapi, *Indonesia* 72 **C3** 6 45 S 126 30 E
Gunungsitoli, *Indonesia* 74 **B1** 1 15N 97 30 E
Gunupur, *India* 82 **E6** 19 5N 83 50 E
Günz →, *Germany* 27 **G6** 48 27N 10 16 E
Gunza, *Angola* 103 **E2** 10 50 S 13 50 E
Günzburg, *Germany* 27 **G6** 48 26N 10 17 E
Gunzenhausen, *Germany* 27 **F6** 49 7N 10 44 E
Guo He →, *China* 67 **H9** 32 59N 117 10 E
Guoyang, *China* 66 **H9** 33 32N 116 12 E
Gupis, *Pakistan* 81 **A5** 36 15N 73 20 E
Gura Humorului, *Romania* 46 **B6** 47 35N 25 53 E
Gura-Teghii, *Romania* 46 **D7** 45 30N 26 25 E
Gurag, *Ethiopia* 95 **F4** 8 20N 38 20 E
Gurdaspur, *India* 80 **C6** 32 5N 75 31 E
Gurdon, *U.S.A.* 139 **J8** 33 55N 93 9W
Gurgaon, *India* 80 **E7** 28 27N 77 1 E
Gürgentepe, *Turkey* 88 **B7** 40 51N 37 50 E
Gurghiu, Munţii, *Romania* 46 **C6** 46 41N 25 15 E
Gurgueia →, *Brazil* 154 **C3** 6 50 S 43 24W
Gurha, *India* 80 **G4** 25 12N 71 39 E
Guri, Embalse de, *Venezuela* 153 **B5** 7 50N 62 52W
Gurjaani, *Georgia* 53 **K7** 41 43N 45 52 E
Gurk →, *Austria* 30 **E7** 46 35N 14 31 E
Gurkha, *Nepal* 81 **E11** 28 5N 84 40 E
Gurley, *Australia* 115 **D4** 29 45 S 149 48 E
Gurnee, *U.S.A.* 141 **B9** 42 22N 87 55W
Gürpınar, *Turkey* 89 **C10** 38 18N 43 25 E
Gurué, *Mozam.* 107 **F4** 15 25 S 36 58 E
Gurun, *Malaysia* 77 **K3** 5 49N 100 27 E
Gürün, *Turkey* 88 **C7** 38 43N 37 15 E
Gurupá, *Brazil* 153 **D7** 1 25 S 51 35W
Gurupá, I. Grande de, *Brazil* 153 **D7** 1 25 S 51 45W
Gurupi, *Brazil* 155 **D2** 11 43 S 49 4W
Gurupi →, *Brazil* 154 **B2** 1 13 S 46 6W
Gurupi, Serra do, *Brazil* 154 **C2** 5 0 S 47 50W
Guryev = Atyraū, *Kazakstan* 49 **E9** 47 5N 52 0 E
Gus-Khrustalnyy, *Russia* 52 **C5** 55 42N 40 44 E
Gusau, *Nigeria* 101 **C6** 12 12N 6 40 E
Gusev, *Russia* 13 **J20** 54 35N 22 10 E
Gushan, *China* 67 **E12** 39 50N 123 35 E
Gushgy, *Turkmenistan* 56 **F7** 35 20N 62 18 E
Gushi, *China* 69 **A10** 32 11N 115 41 E
Gushiago, *Ghana* 101 **D4** 9 55N 0 15W
Gusinje, *Montenegro, Yug.* 42 **E4** 42 35N 19 50 E
Gusinoozersk, *Russia* 57 **D11** 51 16N 106 27 E
Gúspini, *Italy* 40 **C1** 39 32N 8 37 E
Güssing, *Austria* 31 **D9** 47 3N 16 20 E
Gustanj, *Slovenia* 39 **B11** 46 36N 14 59 E
Gustine, *U.S.A.* 144 **H6** 37 16N 121 0W
Güstrow, *Germany* 26 **B8** 53 47N 12 10 E
Gusum, *Sweden* 15 **F10** 58 16N 16 30 E
Guta = Kalárovo, *Slovak Rep.* 31 **D11** 47 54N 18 0 E
Gütersloh, *Germany* 26 **D4** 51 54N 8 24 E
Gutha, *Australia* 113 **E2** 28 58 S 115 55 E
Guthalongra, *Australia* 114 **B4** 19 52 S 147 50 E
Guthrie, *U.S.A.* 139 **H6** 35 53N 97 25W
Guthrie Center, *U.S.A.* 140 **C2** 41 41N 94 30W
Gutian, *China* 69 **D12** 26 32N 118 43 E
Gutiérrez, *Bolivia* 157 **D5** 19 25 S 63 34W
Guttannen, *Switz.* 29 **C6** 46 38N 8 18 E
Guttenberg, *U.S.A.* 140 **B5** 42 47N 91 6W
Guyana ■, *S. Amer.* 153 **B6** 5 0N 59 0W
Guyane française ■ = French Guiana ■, *S. Amer.* 153 **C7** 4 0N 53 0W
Guyang, *China* 66 **D6** 41 0N 110 5 E
Guyenne, *France* 24 **D4** 44 30N 0 40 E
Guymon, *U.S.A.* 139 **G4** 36 41N 101 29W
Guyra, *Australia* 115 **E5** 30 15 S 151 40 E
Guyuan, *Hebei, China* 66 **D8** 41 37N 115 40 E
Guyuan, *Ningxia Huizu, China* 66 **F4** 36 0N 106 20 E
Guzar, *Uzbekistan* 55 **D3** 38 36N 66 15 E
Guzhang, *China* 68 **C7** 28 42N 109 58 E
Guzhen, *China* 67 **H9** 33 22N 117 18 E
Guzmán, L. de, *Mexico* 146 **A3** 31 25N 107 25W
Gvardeysk, *Russia* 13 **J19** 54 39N 21 5 E
Gvardeyskoye, *Ukraine* 51 **K8** 45 7N 34 1 E
Gwa, *Burma* 78 **G5** 17 36N 94 34 E
Gwaai, *Zimbabwe* 107 **F2** 19 15 S 27 45 E
Gwabegar, *Australia* 117 **A8** 30 31 S 149 0 E
Gwadabawa, *Nigeria* 101 **C6** 13 28N 5 15 E
Gwādar, *Pakistan* 79 **D1** 25 10N 62 18 E
Gwagwada, *Nigeria* 101 **C6** 10 15N 7 15 E
Gwalia, *Australia* 113 **E3** 28 54 S 121 20 E
Gwalior, *India* 80 **F8** 26 12N 78 10 E
Gwanda, *Zimbabwe* 107 **G2** 20 55 S 29 0 E
Gwandu, *Nigeria* 101 **C5** 12 30N 4 41 E
Gwane, *Zaïre* 106 **B2** 4 45N 25 48 E
Gwaram, *Nigeria* 101 **C7** 10 15N 10 25 E
Gwarzo, *Nigeria* 101 **C6** 12 20N 8 55 E
Gwda →, *Poland* 47 **B3** 53 3N 16 44 E
Gweebarra B., *Ireland* 19 **B3** 54 51N 8 23W
Gweedore, *Ireland* 19 **A3** 55 3N 8 13W
Gweru, *Zimbabwe* 107 **F2** 19 28 S 29 45 E
Gwi, *Nigeria* 101 **D6** 9 0N 7 10 E
Gwinn, *U.S.A.* 134 **B2** 46 19N 87 27W
Gwio Kura, *Nigeria* 101 **C7** 12 40N 11 2 E
Gwol, *Ghana* 100 **C4** 10 58N 1 59W
Gwoza, *Nigeria* 101 **C7** 11 5N 13 40 E
Gwydir →, *Australia* 115 **D4** 29 27 S 149 48 E
Gwynedd □, *U.K.* 16 **E3** 52 52N 4 10W
Gyandzha = Gäncä, *Azerbaijan* 53 **K8** 40 45N 46 20 E
Gyaring Hu, *China* 64 **C4** 34 50N 97 40 E
Gydanskiy P-ov., *Russia* 56 **C8** 70 0N 78 0 E
Gympie, *Australia* 115 **D5** 26 11 S 152 38 E
Gyobingauk, *Burma* 78 **F5** 18 13N 95 39 E
Gyoda, *Japan* 63 **A11** 36 10N 139 30 E
Gyoma, *Hungary* 31 **E13** 46 56N 20 50 E
Gyöngyös, *Hungary* 31 **D12** 47 48N 19 56 E
Györ, *Hungary* 31 **D10** 47 41N 17 40 E
Györ-Sopron □, *Hungary* 31 **D10** 47 40N 17 20 E
Gypsum Palace, *Australia* 116 **B6** 32 37 S 144 9 E
Gypsum Pt., *Canada* 130 **A6** 61 53N 114 35W
Gypsumville, *Canada* 131 **C9** 51 45N 98 40W
Gyula, *Hungary* 31 **E14** 46 38N 21 17 E
Gyumri, *Armenia* 53 **K6** 40 47N 43 50 E
Gyzylarbat, *Turkmenistan* 56 **F6** 39 4N 56 23 E
Gzhatsk = Gagarin, *Russia* 52 **C2** 55 38N 35 0 E

H

Ha 'Arava →, *Israel* 91 **E4** 30 50N 35 20 E
Ha Coi, *Vietnam* 76 **B6** 21 26N 107 46 E
Ha Dong, *Vietnam* 76 **B5** 20 58N 105 46 E
Ha Giang, *Vietnam* 76 **A5** 22 50N 104 59 E
Ha Tien, *Vietnam* 77 **G5** 10 23N 104 29 E
Ha Tinh, *Vietnam* 76 **C5** 18 20N 105 54 E
Ha Trung, *Vietnam* 76 **C5** 19 58N 105 50 E
Haacht, *Belgium* 21 **G5** 50 59N 4 37 E
Ha'afeva, *Tonga* 121 **P13** 19 57 S 174 43W
Haag, *Germany* 27 **G8** 48 9N 12 11 E
Haaksbergen, *Neths.* 20 **D9** 52 9N 6 45 E
Haaltert, *Belgium* 21 **G4** 50 55N 4 1 E
Haamstede, *Neths.* 21 **E3** 51 42N 3 45 E
Ha'ano, *Tonga* 121 **P13** 19 41 S 174 18W
Ha'apai Group, *Tonga* 121 **P13** 19 47 S 174 27W
Haapsalu, *Estonia* 13 **G20** 58 56N 23 30 E
Haarlem, *Neths.* 20 **D5** 52 23N 4 39 E
Haast, *N.Z.* 119 **D4** 43 51 S 169 1 E
Haast →, *N.Z.* 119 **D4** 43 50 S 169 2 E
Haast Bluff, *Australia* 112 **D5** 23 22 S 132 0 E
Haast Pass, *N.Z.* 119 **E4** 44 6 S 169 21 E
Haastrecht, *Neths.* 20 **E5** 52 0N 4 47 E
Hab Nadi Chauki, *Pakistan* 80 **G2** 25 0N 66 50 E
Ḥabarūt, *Yemen* 87 **C6** 17 18N 52 44 E
Habaswein, *Kenya* 106 **B4** 1 2N 39 30 E
Ḥabawnah, W. →, *Si. Arabia* 86 **C4** 17 57N 44 58 E
Habay, *Canada* 130 **B5** 58 50N 118 44W
Habay-la-Neuve, *Belgium* 21 **J7** 49 44N 5 38 E
Ḥabbān, *Yemen* 86 **D4** 14 21N 47 5 E
Ḥabbānīyah, *Iraq* 89 **F10** 33 17N 43 29 E
Ḥabbānīyah, Hawr al, *Iraq* 89 **F10** 33 17N 43 29 E
Habiganj, *Bangla.* 78 **C3** 24 24N 91 30 E
Haboro, *Japan* 60 **B10** 44 22N 141 42 E
Haccourt, *Belgium* 21 **G7** 50 44N 5 40 E
Hachenburg, *Germany* 26 **E3** 50 40N 7 49 E
Hachijō-Jima, *Japan* 63 **D11** 33 5N 139 45 E
Hachinohe, *Japan* 60 **D10** 40 30N 141 29 E
Hachiōji, *Japan* 63 **B11** 35 40N 139 20 E
Hachŏn, *N. Korea* 67 **D15** 41 29N 129 2 E
Hachy, *Belgium* 21 **J7** 49 42N 5 41 E
Hacıbektaş, *Turkey* 88 **C6** 38 56N 34 33 E
Hacılar, *Turkey* 88 **C6** 38 38N 35 26 E
Hackensack, *U.S.A.* 137 **F10** 40 53N 74 3W
Hadali, *Pakistan* 80 **C5** 32 16N 72 11 E
Hadarba, Ras, *Sudan* 94 **C4** 22 4N 36 51 E
Hadarom □, *Israel* 91 **E3** 31 0N 35 0 E
Ḥadbaram, *Oman* 87 **C6** 17 27N 55 15 E
Hadd, R'as al, *Oman* 87 **B7** 22 35N 59 50 E
Ḥaddā, *Si. Arabia* 86 **B2** 21 27N 39 34 E
Haddington, *U.K.* 18 **F6** 55 57N 2 47W
Haddon Rig, *Australia* 117 **A7** 31 27 S 147 52 E
Haded Plain, *Somali Rep.* 108 **C3** 9 46N 48 2 E
Hadejia, *Nigeria* 101 **C7** 12 30N 10 5 E
Hadejia →, *Nigeria* 101 **C7** 12 50N 10 51 E
Haden, *Australia* 115 **D5** 27 13 S 151 54 E
Hadera, *Israel* 91 **C3** 32 27N 34 55 E
Hadera, N. →, *Israel* 91 **C3** 32 28N 34 52 E
Haderslev, *Denmark* 15 **J3** 55 15N 9 30 E
Hadházteglás, *Hungary* 31 **D14** 47 40N 21 40 E
Hadhramaut = Haḍramawt, *Yemen* 87 **D5** 15 30N 49 30 E
Hadım, *Turkey* 88 **D5** 36 58N 32 26 E
Hadjeb El Aïoun, *Tunisia* 96 **A1** 35 21N 9 32 E
Hadong, *S. Korea* 67 **G14** 35 5N 127 44 E
Haḍramawt, *Yemen* 87 **D5** 15 30N 49 30 E
Haḍramawt, W. →, *Yemen* 87 **D5** 16 0N 48 53 E
Ḥadrānīyah, *Iraq* 84 **C4** 35 38N 43 14 E
Hadrian's Wall, *U.K.* 16 **C5** 55 0N 2 30W
Hadsten, *Denmark* 15 **H4** 56 19N 10 3 E
Hadsund, *Denmark* 15 **H4** 56 44N 10 8 E
Hadyach, *Ukraine* 51 **G8** 50 21N 34 0 E
Haeju, *N. Korea* 67 **E13** 38 3N 125 45 E
Haenam, *S. Korea* 67 **G14** 34 34N 126 35 E
Haerhpin = Harbin, *China* 67 **B14** 45 48N 126 40 E
Hafar al Bāṭin, *Si. Arabia* 84 **D5** 28 32N 45 52 E
Hafik, *Turkey* 88 **C7** 39 51N 37 23 E
Ḥafīrat al 'Aydā, *Si. Arabia* 84 **E3** 26 26N 39 12 E
Ḥafit, *Oman* 87 **B6** 23 59N 55 49 E
Hafizabad, *Pakistan* 80 **C5** 32 5N 73 40 E
Haflong, *India* 78 **C4** 25 10N 93 5 E
Hafnarfjörður, *Iceland* 12 **D3** 64 4N 21 57W
Hafun, Ras, *Somali Rep.* 90 **E5** 10 29N 51 30 E
Hagalil, *Israel* 91 **C4** 32 53N 35 18 E
Hagari →, *India* 83 **G3** 15 40N 77 0 E
Hagdan, *Phil.* 71 **F4** 11 20N 123 54 E
Hagen, *Germany* 26 **D3** 51 21N 7 27 E
Hagenow, *Germany* 26 **B7** 53 26N 11 12 E
Hagerman, *U.S.A.* 139 **J2** 33 7N 104 20W
Hagerstown, *Ind., U.S.A.* 141 **E11** 39 55N 85 10W
Hagerstown, *Md., U.S.A.* 134 **F7** 39 39N 77 43W
Hagetmau, *France* 24 **E3** 43 39N 0 37W
Hagfors, *Sweden* 13 **F15** 60 3N 13 45 E
Häggenås, *Sweden* 14 **A8** 63 24N 14 55 E
Hagi, *Japan* 62 **C3** 34 30N 131 22 E
Hagolan, *Syria* 91 **B4** 33 0N 35 45 E
Hagondange-Briey, *France* 23 **C13** 49 16N 6 11 E
Hagonoy, *Phil.* 70 **D3** 14 50N 120 44 E
Hags Hd., *Ireland* 19 **D2** 52 57N 9 28W
Hague, C. de la, *France* 22 **C5** 49 44N 1 56W
Hague, The = 's-Gravenhage, *Neths.* 20 **D4** 52 7N 4 17 E
Haguenau, *France* 23 **D14** 48 49N 7 47 E
Hai □, *Tanzania* 106 **C4** 3 10 S 37 10 E
Hai Duong, *Vietnam* 76 **B6** 20 56N 106 19 E
Hai'an, *Guangdong, China* 69 **G8** 20 18N 110 11 E
Hai'an, *Jiangsu, China* 69 **A13** 32 37N 120 27 E
Haicheng, *Fujian, China* 69 **E11** 24 23N 117 48 E
Haicheng, *Liaoning, China* 67 **D12** 40 50N 122 45 E
Haidar Khel, *Afghan.* 80 **C3** 33 58N 68 38 E
Haifa = Ḥefa, *Israel* 91 **C3** 32 46N 35 0 E
Haifeng, *China* 69 **F10** 22 58N 115 10 E
Haig, *Australia* 113 **F4** 30 55 S 126 10 E
Haiger, *Germany* 26 **E4** 50 43N 8 12 E
Haikang, *China* 69 **G8** 20 52N 110 8 E
Haikou, *China* 65 **D6** 20 1N 110 16 E
Ḥā'il, *Si. Arabia* 84 **E4** 27 28N 41 45 E
Hailakandi, *India* 78 **C4** 24 42N 92 34 E
Hailar, *China* 65 **B6** 49 10N 119 38 E
Hailey, *U.S.A.* 142 **E6** 43 31N 114 19W
Haileybury, *Canada* 128 **C4** 47 30N 79 38W
Hailin, *China* 67 **B15** 44 37N 129 30 E
Hailing Dao, *China* 69 **G8** 21 35N 111 47 E
Hailong, *China* 67 **C13** 42 32N 125 40 E
Hailuoto, *Finland* 12 **D21** 65 3N 24 45 E
Haimen, *Guangdong, China* 69 **F11** 23 15N 116 38 E
Haimen, *Jiangsu, China* 69 **B13** 31 52N 121 10 E
Haimen, *Zhejiang, China* 69 **C13** 28 40N 121 24 E
Hainan □, *China* 65 **E5** 19 0N 109 30 E
Hainaut □, *Belgium* 21 **H4** 50 30N 4 0 E
Hainburg, *Austria* 31 **C9** 48 9N 16 56 E
Haines, *U.S.A.* 142 **D5** 44 55N 117 56W
Haines City, *U.S.A.* 135 **L5** 28 7N 81 38W
Haines Junction, *Canada* 130 **A1** 60 45N 137 30W
Hainfeld, *Austria* 30 **C8** 48 3N 15 48 E
Haining, *China* 69 **B13** 30 28N 120 40 E
Haiphong, *Vietnam* 64 **D5** 20 47N 106 41 E
Haiti ■, *W. Indies* 149 **C5** 19 0N 72 30W
Haiya Junction, *Sudan* 94 **D4** 18 20N 36 21 E
Haiyan, *China* 69 **B13** 30 28N 120 58 E
Haiyang, *China* 67 **F11** 36 47N 121 9 E
Haiyuan, *Guangxi Zhuangzu, China* 68 **F6** 22 8N 107 35 E
Haiyuan, *Ningxia Huizu, China* 66 **F3** 36 35N 105 52 E
Haizhou, *China* 67 **G10** 34 37N 119 7 E
Haizhou Wan, *China* 67 **G10** 34 50N 119 20 E
Hajar Bangar, *Sudan* 97 **F4** 10 40N 22 45 E
Hajdú-Bihar □, *Hungary* 31 **D14** 47 30N 21 30 E
Hajdúböszörmény, *Hungary* 31 **D14** 47 40N 21 30 E
Hajdúdurog, *Hungary* 31 **D14** 47 48N 21 30 E
Hajdúnánás, *Hungary* 31 **D14** 47 50N 21 26 E
Hajdúsámson, *Hungary* 31 **D14** 47 37N 21 42 E
Hajdúszoboszló, *Hungary* 31 **D14** 47 27N 21 22 E
Hajiganj, *Bangla.* 78 **D3** 23 15N 90 50 E
Hajipur, *India* 81 **G11** 25 45N 85 13 E
Ḥajjah, *Yemen* 86 **D3** 15 42N 43 36 E
Ḥājjī Muḥsin, *Iraq* 84 **C5** 32 35N 45 29 E
Ḥājjīābād, *Eşfahan, Iran* 85 **C7** 33 41N 54 50 E
Ḥājjīābād, *Hormozgān, Iran* 85 **D7** 28 19N 55 55 E
Hajnówka, *Poland* 47 **C10** 52 47N 23 35 E
Ḥajrah, *Si. Arabia* 86 **B3** 20 14N 41 3 E
Haka, *Burma* 78 **D4** 22 39N 93 37 E
Hakansson, Mts., *Zaïre* 103 **D5** 8 40 S 25 45 E
Håkantorp, *Sweden* 15 **F6** 58 18N 12 55 E
Hakataramea, *N.Z.* 119 **E5** 44 43 S 170 30 E
Ḥakkan, *Oman* 87 **B7** 20 22N 58 47 E
Hakkâri, *Turkey* 89 **D10** 37 34N 43 44 E
Hakkâri Dağları, *Turkey* 89 **C10** 38 2N 42 58 E
Hakken-Zan, *Japan* 63 **C7** 34 10N 135 54 E
Hakodate, *Japan* 60 **D10** 41 45N 140 44 E
Hakota, *Japan* 63 **A12** 36 5N 140 30 E
Haku-San, *Japan* 63 **A8** 36 9N 136 46 E
Hakui, *Japan* 61 **F8** 36 53N 136 47 E
Hakun, *Burma* 78 **B5** 26 46N 95 42 E
Hala, *Pakistan* 79 **D3** 25 43N 68 20 E
Ḥalab, *Syria* 88 **D7** 36 10N 37 15 E
Ḥalaban, *Si. Arabia* 86 **B4** 23 29N 44 23 E
Ḥalabjah, *Iraq* 89 **E11** 35 10N 45 58 E
Halaib, *Sudan* 94 **C4** 22 12N 36 30 E
Halanzy, *Belgium* 21 **J7** 49 33N 5 44 E
Hālat 'Ammār, *Si. Arabia* 84 **D3** 29 10N 36 4 E
Halbā, *Lebanon* 91 **A5** 34 34N 36 6 E
Halberstadt, *Germany* 26 **D7** 51 54N 11 3 E
Halcombe, *N.Z.* 118 **G4** 40 8 S 175 30 E
Halcon, Mt., *Phil.* 70 **E3** 13 0N 121 30 E
Halden, *Norway* 14 **E5** 59 9N 11 23 E
Haldensleben, *Germany* 26 **C7** 52 17N 11 24 E
Haldwani, *India* 81 **E8** 29 31N 79 30 E
Hale, *U.S.A.* 140 **E3** 39 36N 93 20W
Hale →, *Australia* 114 **C2** 24 56 S 135 53 E
Haleakala Crater, *U.S.A.* 132 **H16** 20 43N 156 16W
Halen, *Belgium* 21 **G6** 50 57N 5 6 E
Haleyville, *U.S.A.* 135 **H2** 34 14N 87 37W
Half Assini, *Ghana* 100 **D4** 5 1N 2 50W
Halfmoon Bay, *N.Z.* 119 **G3** 46 50 S 168 5 E
Halfway →, *Canada* 130 **B4** 56 12N 121 32W
Haliburton, *Canada* 128 **C4** 45 3N 78 30W
Halicarnassus, *Turkey* 45 **G9** 37 3N 27 30 E
Halifax, *Australia* 114 **B4** 18 32 S 146 22 E
Halifax, *Canada* 129 **D7** 44 38N 63 35W
Halifax, *U.K.* 16 **D6** 53 43N 1 52W
Halifax B., *Australia* 114 **B4** 18 50 S 147 0 E
Halifax I., *Namibia* 104 **D2** 26 38 S 15 4 E
Halīl →, *Iran* 85 **E8** 27 40N 58 30 E
Halin, *Somali Rep.* 108 **C3** 9 6N 48 37 E
Hall, *Austria* 30 **D4** 47 17N 11 30 E
Hall Beach, *Canada* 127 **B11** 68 46N 81 12W
Hall Pt., *Australia* 112 **C3** 15 40 S 124 23 E
Halland, *Sweden* 13 **H15** 57 8N 12 47 E
Hallands län □, *Sweden* 15 **H6** 56 50N 12 50 E
Hallands Väderö, *Sweden* 15 **H6** 56 27N 12 34 E
Hallandsås, *Sweden* 15 **H7** 56 22N 13 0 E
Halle, *Belgium* 21 **G4** 50 44N 4 13 E
Halle, *Nordrhein-Westfalen, Germany* 26 **C4** 52 3N 8 22 E
Halle, *Sachsen-Anhalt, Germany* 26 **D7** 51 30N 11 56 E
Hällefors, *Sweden* 13 **G16** 59 47N 14 31 E
Hallein, *Austria* 30 **D6** 47 40N 13 5 E
Hällekis, *Sweden* 15 **F7** 58 38N 13 27 E
Hallett, *Australia* 116 **B3** 33 25 S 138 55 E
Hallettsville, *U.S.A.* 139 **L6** 29 27N 96 57W
Hällevadsholm, *Sweden* 15 **F5** 58 35N 11 33 E
Hallia →, *India* 82 **F4** 16 55N 79 20 E
Halliday, *U.S.A.* 138 **B3** 47 21N 102 20W
Halliday L., *Canada* 131 **A7** 61 21N 108 56W
Hallim, *S. Korea* 67 **H14** 33 24N 126 15 E
Hallingdalselva →, *Norway* 13 **F13** 60 40N 8 50 E
Hallock, *U.S.A.* 131 **D9** 48 47N 96 57W
Halls Creek, *Australia* 112 **C4** 18 16 S 127 38 E
Hallsberg, *Sweden* 13 **G16** 59 5N 15 7 E
Hallstahammar, *Sweden* 14 **E10** 59 38N 16 15 E
Hallstatt, *Austria* 30 **D6** 47 33N 13 38 E
Hallstead, *U.S.A.* 137 **E9** 41 58N 75 45W
Halmahera, *Indonesia* 72 **A3** 0 40N 128 0 E
Halmeu, *Romania* 46 **B4** 47 57N 23 2 E
Halmstad, *Sweden* 15 **H6** 56 41N 12 52 E
Halq el Oued, *Tunisia* 96 **A2** 36 53N 10 18 E
Hals, *Denmark* 15 **H4** 56 59N 10 18 E
Halsafjorden, *Norway* 14 **A2** 63 5N 8 10 E
Hälsingborg = Helsingborg, *Sweden* 15 **H6** 56 3N 12 42 E
Hälsingland, *Sweden* 13 **F16** 61 40N 16 5 E
Halstad, *U.S.A.* 138 **B6** 47 21N 96 50W
Haltdalen, *Norway* 14 **B5** 62 56N 11 8 E
Haltern, *Germany* 26 **D3** 51 44N 7 11 E
Halti, *Finland* 12 **B19** 69 17N 21 18 E
Halul, *Qatar* 85 **E7** 25 40N 52 40 E
Ḥalvān, *Iran* 85 **C8** 33 57N 56 15 E
Ham, *France* 23 **C10** 49 45N 3 4 E
Ham Tan, *Vietnam* 77 **G6** 10 40N 107 45 E
Ham Yen, *Vietnam* 76 **A5** 22 4N 105 3 E
Hamab, *Namibia* 104 **D2** 28 7 S 19 16 E
Hamad, *Sudan* 95 **D3** 15 20N 33 32 E
Hamada, *Japan* 62 **C4** 34 56N 132 4 E
Hamadān, *Iran* 89 **E13** 34 52N 48 32 E
Hamadān □, *Iran* 85 **C6** 35 0N 49 0 E
Hamadia, *Algeria* 99 **A5** 35 28N 1 57 E
Hamāh, *Syria* 88 **E7** 35 5N 36 40 E
Hamakita, *Japan* 63 **C9** 34 45N 137 47 E

Hayden, Colo., U.S.A. 142 F10 40 30N 107 16W
Haydon, Australia 114 B3 18 0S 141 30E
Hayes, U.S.A. 138 C4 44 23N 101 1W
Hayes →, Canada 131 B10 57 3N 92 12W
Hayjān, Yemen 86 C4 16 40N 44 5E
Haymā', Oman 87 C7 19 56N 56 19E
Haymana, Turkey 88 C5 39 26N 32 31E
Haynan, Yemen 87 D5 15 50N 48 18E
Haynesville, U.S.A. 139 J8 32 58N 93 8W
Hayrabolu, Turkey 88 B2 41 12N 27 5E
Ḩayrān, Yemen 86 C3 16 8N 43 5E
Hays, Canada 130 C6 50 6N 111 48W
Hays, U.S.A. 138 F5 38 53N 99 20W
Ḩays, Yemen 86 D3 13 56N 43 29E
Haysville, U.S.A. 141 F10 38 28N 86 55W
Haysyn, Ukraine 51 H5 48 57N 29 25E
Hayvoron, Ukraine 51 H5 48 22N 29 52E
Hayward, Calif., U.S.A. 144 H4 37 40N 122 5W
Hayward, Wis., U.S.A. 138 B9 46 1N 91 29W
Haywards Heath, U.K. 17 F7 51 0N 0 5W
Ḩayy, Oman 87 B7 20 46N 58 18E
Hazafon □, Israel 91 C4 32 40N 35 20E
Hazarām, Kūh-e, Iran 85 D8 29 30N 57 18E
Hazard, U.S.A. 134 G4 37 15N 83 12W
Hazaribag, India 81 H11 23 58N 85 26E
Hazaribag Road, India 81 G11 24 12N 85 57E
Hazebrouck, France 23 B9 50 42N 2 31E
Hazelton, Canada 130 B3 55 20N 127 42W
Hazelton, U.S.A. 138 B4 46 29N 100 17W
Hazen, N. Dak., U.S.A. 138 B4 47 18N 101 38W
Hazen, Nev., U.S.A. 142 G4 39 34N 119 3W
Hazerswoude, Neths. 20 D5 52 5N 4 36E
Hazlehurst, Ga., U.S.A. 135 K4 31 52N 82 36W
Hazlehurst, Miss., U.S.A. 139 K9 31 52N 90 24W
Hazleton, Ind., U.S.A. 141 F9 38 29N 87 33W
Hazleton, Pa., U.S.A. 137 F9 40 57N 75 59W
Hazlett, L., Australia 112 D4 21 30S 128 48E
Ḩazor, Israel 91 B4 33 2N 35 32E
He Xian, Anhui, China 69 B12 31 45N 118 20E
He Xian, Guangxi Zhuangzu, China 69 E8 24 27N 111 30E
Head of Bight, Australia 113 F5 31 30S 131 25E
Headlands, Zimbabwe 107 F3 18 15S 32 2E
Healdsburg, U.S.A. 144 G4 38 37N 122 52W
Healdton, U.S.A. 139 H6 34 14N 97 29W
Healesville, Australia 117 D6 37 35S 145 30E
Heanor, U.K. 16 D6 53 1N 1 21W
Heard I., Ind. Oc. 109 K6 53 0S 74 0E
Hearne, U.S.A. 139 K6 30 53N 96 36W
Hearne B., Canada 131 A9 60 10N 99 10W
Hearne L., Canada 130 A6 62 20N 113 10W
Hearst, Canada 128 C3 49 40N 83 41W
Heart →, U.S.A. 138 B4 46 46N 100 50W
Heart's Content, Canada 129 C9 47 54N 53 27W
Heath →, Bolivia 156 C4 12 31S 68 38W
Heath Mts., N.Z. 119 F2 45 39S 167 9E
Heath Pt., Canada 129 C7 49 8N 61 40W
Heath Steele, Canada 129 C6 47 17N 66 5W
Heathcote, Australia 117 D6 36 56S 144 45E
Heavener, U.S.A. 139 H7 34 53N 94 36W
Hebbronville, U.S.A. 139 M5 27 18N 98 41W
Hebei □, China 66 E9 39 0N 116 0E
Hebel, Australia 115 D4 28 58S 147 47E
Heber, U.S.A. 145 N11 32 44N 115 32W
Heber Springs, U.S.A. 139 H9 35 30N 92 2W
Hebert, Canada 131 C7 50 30N 107 10W
Hebgen L., U.S.A. 142 D8 44 52N 111 20W
Hebi, China 66 G8 35 57N 114 7E
Hebrides, U.K. 18 D1 57 30N 7 0W
Hebron = Al Khalīl, West Bank 91 D4 31 32N 35 6E
Hebron, Canada 127 C13 58 5N 62 30W
Hebron, N. Dak., U.S.A. 138 B3 46 54N 102 3W
Hebron, Nebr., U.S.A. 138 E6 40 10N 97 35W
Hecate Str., Canada 130 C2 53 10N 130 30W
Hechi, China 68 E7 24 40N 108 2E
Hechingen, Germany 27 G4 48 21N 8 57E
Hechtel, Belgium 21 F6 51 8N 5 22E
Hechuan, China 68 B6 30 2N 106 12E
Hecla, U.S.A. 138 C5 45 53N 98 9W
Hecla I., Canada 131 C9 51 10N 96 43W
Heddal, Norway 14 E3 59 36N 9 9E
Hédé, France 22 D5 48 18N 1 49W
Hede, Sweden 14 B7 62 23N 13 30E
Hedemora, Sweden 13 F16 60 18N 15 58E
Hedgehope, N.Z. 119 G3 46 12S 168 34E
Hedley, U.S.A. 139 H4 34 52N 100 39W
Hedmark fylke □, Norway 14 C5 61 17N 11 40E
Hedrick, U.S.A. 140 C4 41 11N 92 19W
Hedrum, Norway 14 E4 59 8N 10 4E
Heeg, Neths. 20 C7 52 58N 5 37E
Heegermeer, Neths. 20 C7 52 56N 5 32E
Heemskerk, Neths. 20 C5 52 31N 4 40E
Heemstede, Neths. 20 D5 52 22N 4 37E
Heer, Neths. 21 G7 50 50N 5 43E
Heerde, Neths. 20 D8 52 24N 6 2E
's Heerenburg, Neths. 20 E8 51 53N 6 16E
Heerenveen, Neths. 20 C7 52 57N 5 55E
Heerhugowaard, Neths. 20 C5 52 40N 4 51E
Heerlen, Neths. 21 G7 50 55N 5 58E
Heers, Belgium 21 G6 50 45N 5 18E
Heesch, Neths. 20 E7 51 44N 5 32E
Heestert, Belgium 21 G2 50 47N 3 25E
Heeze, Neths. 21 F7 51 23N 5 35E
Ḩefa, Israel 91 C3 32 46N 35 0E
Ḩefa □, Israel 91 C4 32 40N 35 0E
Hefei, China 69 B11 31 52N 117 18E
Hegang, China 65 B8 47 20N 130 19E
Hegyalja, Hungary 31 C14 48 25N 21 25E
Heichengzhen, China 66 F4 36 24N 106 3E
Heide, Germany 26 A5 54 11N 9 6E
Heidelberg, Germany 27 F4 49 24N 8 42E
Heidelberg, S. Africa 104 E3 34 6S 20 59E
Heidenheim, Germany 27 G6 48 41N 10 9E
Heigun-To, Japan 62 D4 33 47N 132 14E
Heijing, China 68 E3 25 22N 101 44E
Heilbron, S. Africa 105 D4 27 16S 27 59E
Heilbronn, Germany 27 F5 49 9N 9 13E
Heiligenblut, Austria 30 D5 47 2N 12 51E
Heiligenhafen, Germany 26 A6 54 22N 10 59E
Heiligenstadt, Germany 26 D6 51 22N 10 8E
Heilongjiang □, China 67 B14 48 0N 126 0E
Heilunkiang = Heilongjiang □, China 67 B14 48 0N 126 0E
Heimaey, Iceland 12 E3 63 26N 20 17W
Heino, Neths. 20 D8 52 26N 6 14E
Heinola, Finland 13 F22 61 13N 26 2E
Heinsch, Belgium 21 J7 49 42N 5 44E
Heinsun, Burma 78 C5 25 52N 95 35E
Heirnkut, Burma 78 C5 25 14N 94 44E
Heishan, China 67 D12 41 40N 122 5E
Heishui, Liaoning, China 67 C10 42 8N 119 30E
Heishui, Sichuan, China 68 A4 32 4N 103 2E
Heist, Belgium 21 F2 51 20N 3 15E
Heist-op-den-Berg, Belgium 21 F5 51 5N 4 44E
Hejaz = Al Ḩijāz, Si. Arabia 86 A2 26 0N 37 30E
Hejian, China 66 E9 38 25N 116 5E
Hejiang, China 68 C5 28 43N 105 46E
Hejin, China 66 G6 35 35N 110 42E
Hekelgem, Belgium 21 G4 50 55N 4 7E
Hekımhan, Turkey 88 C7 38 50N 37 55E
Hekinan, Japan 63 C9 34 52N 137 0E
Hekla, Iceland 12 E4 63 56N 19 35W
Hekou, Gansu, China 66 F2 36 10N 103 28E
Hekou, Guangdong, China 69 F9 23 13N 112 45E
Hekou, Yunnan, China 64 D5 22 30N 103 59E
Hel, Poland 47 A5 54 37N 18 47E
Helagsfjället, Sweden 14 B6 62 54N 12 25E
Helan Shan, China 66 E3 38 30N 105 55E
Helchteren, Belgium 21 F6 51 4N 5 22E
Helden, Neths. 21 F7 51 19N 6 0E
Helechosa, Spain 37 F6 39 22N 4 53W
Helena, Ark., U.S.A. 139 H9 34 32N 90 36W
Helena, Mont., U.S.A. 142 C7 46 36N 112 2W
Helendale, U.S.A. 145 L9 34 44N 117 19W
Helensburgh, Australia 117 C9 34 11S 151 1E
Helensburgh, U.K. 18 E4 56 1N 4 43W
Helensville, N.Z. 118 C3 36 41S 174 29E
Helgeland, Norway 12 C15 66 7N 13 29E
Helgeroa, Norway 14 F3 59 0N 9 45E
Helgoland, Germany 26 A3 54 10N 7 53E
Heligoland = Helgoland, Germany 26 A3 54 10N 7 53E
Heligoland B. = Deutsche Bucht, Germany 26 A4 54 15N 8 0E
Heliopolis, Egypt 94 H7 30 6N 31 17E
Hella, Iceland 12 E3 63 50N 20 24W
Hellebæk, Denmark 15 H6 56 4N 12 32E
Hellendoorn, Neths. 20 D8 52 24N 6 27E
Hellevoetsluis, Neths. 20 E4 51 50N 4 8E
Hellín, Spain 35 G3 38 31N 1 40W
Helmand □, Afghan. 79 C2 31 20N 64 0E
Helmand →, Afghan. 79 C1 31 12N 61 34E
Helme →, Germany 26 D7 51 20N 11 21E
Helmond, Neths. 21 F7 51 29N 5 41E
Helmsdale, U.K. 18 C5 58 7N 3 39W
Helmstedt, Germany 26 C7 52 16N 11 0E
Helnæs, Denmark 15 J4 55 9N 10 2E
Helong, China 67 C15 42 40N 129 0E
Helper, U.S.A. 142 G8 39 41N 110 51W
Helsingborg, Sweden 15 H6 56 3N 12 42E
Helsinge, Denmark 15 H6 56 2N 12 12E
Helsingfors = Helsinki, Finland 13 F21 60 15N 25 3E
Helsingør, Denmark 15 H6 56 2N 12 35E
Helsinki, Finland 13 F21 60 15N 25 3E
Helska, Mierzeja, Poland 47 A5 54 45N 18 40E
Helston, U.K. 17 G2 50 6N 5 17W
Helvellyn, U.K. 16 C4 54 32N 3 1W
Helvoirt, Neths. 21 E6 51 38N 5 14E
Helwân, Egypt 94 J7 29 50N 31 20E
Hemavati →, India 83 H3 12 30N 76 20E
Hemet, U.S.A. 145 M10 33 45N 116 58W
Hemingford, U.S.A. 138 D3 42 19N 103 4W
Hemphill, U.S.A. 139 K8 31 20N 93 51W
Hempstead, U.S.A. 139 K6 30 6N 96 5W
Hemse, Sweden 13 H18 57 15N 18 22E
Hemsö, Sweden 14 B12 62 43N 18 5E
Hen & Chickens Is., N.Z. 118 B3 35 58S 174 45E
Henan □, China 66 G8 34 0N 114 0E
Henares →, Spain 34 E1 40 24N 3 30W
Henashi-Misaki, Japan 60 D9 40 37N 139 51E
Hendaye, France 24 E2 43 23N 1 47W
Hendek, Turkey 88 B4 40 48N 30 44E
Henderson, Argentina 158 D3 36 18S 61 43W
Henderson, Ky., U.S.A. 141 G9 37 50N 87 35W
Henderson, N.C., U.S.A. 135 G6 36 20N 78 25W
Henderson, Nev., U.S.A. 145 J12 36 2N 114 59W
Henderson, Tenn., U.S.A. 135 H1 35 26N 88 38W
Henderson, Tex., U.S.A. 139 J7 32 9N 94 48W
Hendersonville, U.S.A. 135 H4 35 19N 82 28W
Hendījān, Iran 85 D6 30 14N 49 43E
Hendon, Australia 115 D5 28 5S 151 50E
Hendorf, Romania 46 C5 46 4N 24 55E
Heng Xian, China 68 F7 22 40N 109 17E
Hengcheng, China 66 E4 38 18N 106 28E
Hengdaohezi, China 67 B15 44 52N 129 0E
Hengelo, Gelderland, Neths. 20 D8 52 3N 6 19E
Hengelo, Overijssel, Neths. 20 D9 52 16N 6 48E
Hengfeng, China 69 C10 28 12N 115 48E
Hengshan, Hunan, China 69 D9 27 16N 112 45E
Hengshan, Shaanxi, China 66 F5 37 58N 109 5E
Hengshui, China 66 F8 37 41N 115 40E
Hengyang, Hunan, China 69 D9 26 52N 112 33E
Hengyang, Hunan, China 69 D9 26 59N 112 22E
Henichesk, Ukraine 51 J8 46 12N 34 50E
Hénin-Beaumont, France 23 B9 50 25N 2 58E
Henlopen, C., U.S.A. 134 F8 38 48N 75 6W
Hennan, Sweden 14 B9 62 3N 15 46E
Hennebont, France 22 E3 47 49N 3 19W
Hennenman, S. Africa 104 D4 27 59S 27 1E
Hennepin, U.S.A. 140 C7 41 15N 89 21W
Hennessey, U.S.A. 139 G6 36 6N 97 54W
Hennigsdorf, Germany 26 C9 52 38N 13 12E
Henrichemont, France 23 E9 47 20N 2 30E
Henrietta, U.S.A. 139 J5 33 49N 98 12W
Henrietta, Ostrov, Russia 57 B16 77 6N 156 30E
Henrietta Maria, C., Canada 128 A3 55 9N 82 20W
Henry, U.S.A. 140 C7 41 7N 89 22W
Henryetta, U.S.A. 139 H6 35 27N 95 59W
Hensall, Canada 136 C3 43 26N 81 30W
Hentiyn Nuruu, Mongolia 65 B5 48 30N 108 30E
Henty, Australia 115 F4 35 30S 147 0E
Henzada, Burma 78 G5 17 38N 95 26E
Hephaestia, Greece 44 E7 39 55N 25 14E
Heping, China 69 E10 24 29N 115 0E
Heppner, U.S.A. 142 D4 45 21N 119 33W
Hepu, China 68 G7 21 40N 109 12E
Hepworth, Canada 136 B3 44 37N 81 9W
Heqing, China 68 D3 26 37N 100 11E
Hequ, China 66 E6 39 20N 111 15E
Héraðsflói, Iceland 12 D6 65 42N 14 12W
Héraðsvötn →, Iceland 12 D4 65 45N 19 25W
Herald Cays, Australia 114 B4 16 58S 149 9E
Herāt, Afghan. 79 B1 34 20N 62 7E
Herāt □, Afghan. 79 B1 35 0N 62 0E
Hérault □, France 24 E7 43 34N 3 15E
Hérault →, France 24 E7 43 17N 3 26E
Herbault, France 22 E8 47 36N 1 8E
Herbert →, Australia 114 B4 18 31S 146 17E
Herbert Downs, Australia 114 C2 23 7S 139 9E
Herberton, Australia 114 B4 17 20S 145 25E
Herbertsville, N.Z. 118 G5 40 30S 176 33E
Herbignac, France 22 E4 47 27N 2 18W
Herborn, Germany 26 E4 50 40N 8 18E
Herby, Poland 47 E5 50 45N 18 50E
Hercegnovi, Montenegro, Yug. 42 E3 42 30N 18 33E
Herculaneum, U.S.A. 140 F6 38 16N 90 23W
Herðubreið, Iceland 12 D5 65 11N 16 21W
Hereford, U.K. 17 E5 52 4N 2 43W
Hereford, U.S.A. 139 H3 34 49N 102 24W
Hereford and Worcester □, U.K. 17 E5 52 10N 2 30W
Herefoss, Norway 15 F2 58 32N 8 23E
Herekino, N.Z. 118 B2 35 18S 173 11E
Herent, Belgium 21 G5 50 54N 4 40E
Herentals, Belgium 21 F5 51 12N 4 51E
Herenthout, Belgium 21 F5 51 8N 4 45E
Herfølge, Denmark 15 J6 55 26N 12 9E
Herford, Germany 26 C4 52 7N 8 39E
Héricourt, France 23 E13 47 32N 6 45E
Herington, U.S.A. 138 F6 38 40N 96 57W
Herisau, Switz. 29 B8 47 22N 9 17E
Hérisson, France 24 B6 46 32N 2 42E
Herk →, Belgium 21 G6 50 56N 5 12E
Herkenbosch, Neths. 21 F8 51 9N 6 4E
Herkimer, U.S.A. 137 D10 43 0N 74 59W
Herlong, U.S.A. 144 E6 40 8N 120 8W
Herm, U.K. 22 C4 49 30N 2 28W
Hermagor-Pressegger See, Austria 30 E6 46 38N 13 23E
Herman, U.S.A. 138 C6 45 49N 96 9W
Hermann, U.S.A. 138 F9 38 42N 91 27W
Hermannsburg, Germany 26 C6 52 50N 10 5E
Hermannsburg Mission, Australia 112 D5 23 57S 132 45E
Hermanus, S. Africa 104 E2 34 27S 19 12E
Herment, France 24 C6 45 45N 2 24E
Hermidale, Australia 117 A7 31 30S 146 42E
Hermiston, U.S.A. 142 D4 45 51N 119 17W
Hermitage, N.Z. 119 D5 43 44S 170 5E
Hermitage, U.S.A. 140 G3 37 56N 93 19W
Hermite, I., Chile 160 E3 55 50S 68 0W
Hermon, Mt. = Ash Shaykh, J., Lebanon 91 B4 33 25N 35 50E
Hermosillo, Mexico 146 B2 29 10N 111 0W
Hernád →, Hungary 31 D14 47 56N 21 8E
Hernandarias, Paraguay 159 B5 25 20S 54 40W
Hernandez, U.S.A. 144 J6 36 24N 120 46W
Hernando, Argentina 158 C3 32 28S 63 40W
Hernando, U.S.A. 139 H10 34 50N 90 0W
Herne, Belgium 21 G4 50 44N 4 2E
Herne, Germany 21 E10 51 32N 7 14E
Herne Bay, U.K. 17 F9 51 21N 1 8E
Herning, Denmark 15 H2 56 8N 8 58E
Heroica = Caborca, Mexico 146 A2 30 40N 112 10W
Heroica Nogales = Nogales, Mexico 146 A2 31 20N 110 56W
Heron Bay, Canada 128 C2 48 40N 86 25W
Herradura, Pta. de la, Canary Is. 33 F5 28 26N 14 8W
Herreid, U.S.A. 138 C4 45 50N 100 4W
Herrera, Spain 37 H6 37 26N 4 55W
Herrera de Alcántar, Spain 37 F3 39 39N 7 25W
Herrera de Pisuerga, Spain 36 C6 42 35N 4 20W
Herrera del Duque, Spain 37 F5 39 10N 5 3W
Herrick, Australia 114 G4 41 5S 147 55E
Herrin, U.S.A. 139 G10 37 48N 89 2W
Herrljunga, Sweden 15 F7 58 5N 13 1E
Hersbruck, Germany 27 F7 49 30N 11 26E
Herseaux, Belgium 21 G2 50 43N 3 15E
Herselt, Belgium 21 F5 51 3N 4 53E
Hersonissos, Greece 32 D7 35 18N 25 22E
Herstal, Belgium 21 G7 50 40N 5 38E
Hertford, U.K. 17 F7 51 48N 0 4W
Hertfordshire □, U.K. 17 F7 51 51N 0 5W
's-Hertogenbosch, Neths. 21 E6 51 42N 5 17E
Hertzogville, S. Africa 104 D4 28 9S 25 30E
Hervás, Spain 36 E5 40 16N 5 52W
Herve, Belgium 21 G7 50 38N 5 48E
Herwijnen, Neths. 20 E6 51 50N 5 7E
Herzberg, Brandenburg, Germany 26 D9 51 41N 13 14E
Herzberg, Niedersachsen, Germany 26 D6 51 38N 10 20E
Herzele, Belgium 21 G3 50 53N 3 53E
Herzliyya, Israel 91 C3 32 10N 34 50E
Herzogenbuchsee, Switz. 28 B5 47 11N 7 42E
Herzogenburg, Austria 30 C8 48 17N 15 41E
Ḩeşār, Fārs, Iran 85 D6 29 52N 50 16E
Ḩeşār, Markazī, Iran 85 C6 35 50N 49 12E
Hesdin, France 23 B9 50 21N 2 2E
Hesel, Germany 26 B3 53 18N 7 36E
Heshui, China 66 G5 36 0N 108 0E
Heshun, China 66 F7 37 22N 113 32E
Hesperange, Lux. 21 J8 49 35N 6 10E
Hesperia, U.S.A. 145 L9 34 25N 117 18W
Hesse = Hessen □, Germany 26 E5 50 30N 9 0E
Hessen □, Germany 26 E5 50 30N 9 0E
Hetch Hetchy Aqueduct, U.S.A. 144 H5 37 29N 122 19W
Hettinger, U.S.A. 138 C3 46 0N 102 42W
Hettstedt, Germany 26 D7 51 39N 11 31E
Heugem, Neths. 21 G7 50 49N 5 42E
Heule, Belgium 21 G2 50 51N 3 15E
Heusden, Belgium 21 F6 51 2N 5 17E
Heusden, Neths. 20 E6 51 44N 5 8E
Hève, C. de la, France 22 C7 49 30N 0 5E
Heverlee, Belgium 21 G5 50 52N 4 42E
Heves □, Hungary 31 D13 47 50N 20 0E
Hewett, C., Canada 127 A13 70 16N 67 45W
Hexham, U.K. 16 C5 54 58N 2 4W
Hexi, Yunnan, China 68 E4 24 9N 102 38E
Hexi, Zhejiang, China 69 D12 27 58N 119 38E
Hexigten Qi, China 67 C9 43 18N 117 30E
Ḩeydarābād, Iran 85 D7 30 33N 55 38E
Heyfield, Australia 117 D7 37 59S 146 47E
Heysham, U.K. 16 C5 54 3N 2 53W
Heythuysen, Neths. 21 F7 51 15N 5 55E
Heyuan, China 69 F10 23 39N 114 40E
Heywood, Australia 116 E4 38 8S 141 37E
Heze, China 66 G8 35 14N 115 20E
Hezhang, China 68 D5 27 8N 104 41E
Hi-no-Misaki, Japan 62 B4 35 26N 132 38E
Hi Vista, U.S.A. 145 L9 34 45N 117 46W
Hialeah, U.S.A. 135 N5 25 50N 80 17W
Hiawatha, Kans., U.S.A. 138 F7 39 51N 95 32W
Hiawatha, Utah, U.S.A. 142 G8 39 29N 111 1W
Hibbing, U.S.A. 138 B8 47 25N 92 56W
Hibbs B., Australia 114 G4 42 35S 145 15E
Hibernia Reef, Australia 112 B3 12 0S 123 23E
Hibiki-Nada, Japan 62 C2 34 0N 130 0E
Hickory, U.S.A. 135 H5 35 44N 81 21W
Hicks, Pt., Australia 117 D8 37 49S 149 17E
Hicks Bay, N.Z. 118 D7 37 34S 178 21E
Hicksville, N.Y., U.S.A. 137 F11 40 46N 73 32W
Hicksville, Ohio, U.S.A. 141 C12 41 18N 84 46W
Hida, Romania 46 B4 47 10N 23 19E
Hida-Gawa →, Japan 63 B9 35 26N 137 3E
Hida-Sammyaku, Japan 63 A9 36 30N 137 40E
Hida-Sanchi, Japan 63 A9 36 10N 137 0E
Hidaka, Japan 62 B6 35 30N 134 44E
Hidaka-Sammyaku, Japan 60 C11 42 35N 142 45E
Hidalgo, Mexico 147 C5 24 15N 99 26W
Hidalgo, U.S.A. 141 E8 39 9N 88 9W
Hidalgo □, Mexico 147 C5 20 30N 99 10W
Hidalgo, Presa M., Mexico 146 B3 26 30N 108 35W
Hidalgo, Pta. del, Canary Is. 33 F3 28 33N 16 19W
Hidalgo del Parral, Mexico 146 B3 26 58N 105 40W
Hiddensee, Germany 26 A9 54 32N 13 6E
Hidrolândia, Brazil 155 E2 17 0S 49 15W
Hieflau, Austria 30 D7 47 36N 14 46E
Hiendelaencina, Spain 34 D1 41 5N 3 0W
Hienghène, N. Cal. 121 T18 20 41S 164 56E
Hierro, Canary Is. 33 G1 27 44N 18 0W
Higashi-matsuyama, Japan 63 A11 36 2N 139 25E
Higashiajima-San, Japan 60 F10 37 40N 140 10E
Higashiōsaka, Japan 63 C7 34 40N 135 37E
Higasi-Suidō, Japan 62 D1 34 0N 129 30E
Higbee, U.S.A. 140 E4 39 19N 92 31W
Higgins, U.S.A. 139 G4 36 7N 100 2W
Higgins Corner, U.S.A. 144 F5 39 2N 121 5W
Higginsville, Australia 113 F3 31 42S 121 38E
Higginsville, U.S.A. 140 E3 39 4N 93 43W
High Atlas = Haut Atlas, Morocco 98 B3 32 30N 5 0W
High I., Canada 129 A7 56 40N 61 10W
High Island, U.S.A. 139 L7 29 34N 94 24W
High Level, Canada 130 B5 58 31N 117 8W
High Point, U.S.A. 135 H6 35 57N 80 0W
High Prairie, Canada 130 B5 55 30N 116 30W
High River, Canada 130 C6 50 30N 113 50W
High Springs, U.S.A. 135 L4 29 50N 82 36W
High Tatra = Tatry, Slovak Rep. 31 B12 49 20N 20 0E
High Veld, Africa 92 J6 27 0S 27 0E
High Wycombe, U.K. 17 F7 51 37N 0 45W
Highbank, N.Z. 119 D6 43 37S 171 45E
Highbury, Australia 114 B3 16 25S 143 9E
Highland, Ill., U.S.A. 140 F7 38 44N 89 41W
Highland, Ind., U.S.A. 141 C9 41 33N 87 28W
Highland, Wis., U.S.A. 140 A6 43 5N 90 22W
Highland □, U.K. 18 D4 57 17N 4 21W
Highland Park, U.S.A. 141 B9 42 11N 87 48W
Highmore, U.S.A. 138 C5 44 31N 99 27W
Highrock L., Canada 131 B7 57 5N 105 32W
Higüay, Dom. Rep. 149 C6 18 37N 68 42W
Hihya, Egypt 94 H7 30 40N 31 36E
Hiiumaa, Estonia 13 G20 58 50N 22 45E
Híjar, Spain 34 D4 41 10N 0 27W
Ḩijāz □, Si. Arabia 86 A2 24 0N 40 0E
Hijāz, Jabal al, Si. Arabia 86 C3 19 45N 41 55E
Hiji, Japan 62 D3 33 22N 131 32E
Hijken, Neths. 20 C8 52 54N 6 30E
Hijo = Tagum, Phil. 71 H5 7 33N 125 53E
Hikari, Japan 62 D3 33 58N 131 58E
Hiketa, Japan 62 C6 34 13N 134 24E
Hiko, U.S.A. 144 H11 37 32N 115 14W
Hikone, Japan 63 B8 35 15N 136 10E
Hikurangi, N.Z. 118 B3 35 36S 174 17E
Hikurangi, Mt., N.Z. 118 E5 38 21S 176 52E
Hilawng, Burma 78 E4 21 23N 93 48E
Hildburghausen, Germany 27 E6 50 25N 10 42E
Hildesheim, Germany 26 C5 52 9N 9 56E
Hill →, Australia 113 F2 30 23S 115 3E
Hill City, Idaho, U.S.A. 142 E6 43 18N 115 3W
Hill City, Kans., U.S.A. 138 F5 39 22N 99 51W
Hill City, Minn., U.S.A. 138 B8 46 59N 93 36W
Hill City, S. Dak., U.S.A. 138 D3 43 56N 103 35W
Hill End, Australia 117 E7 38 1S 146 9E
Hill Island L., Canada 131 A7 60 30N 109 50W
Hillared, Sweden 15 G7 57 37N 13 10E
Hillcrest Center, U.S.A. 145 K8 35 23N 118 57W
Hillegom, Neths. 20 D5 52 18N 4 35E
Hillerød, Denmark 15 J6 55 56N 12 19E
Hilli, Bangla. 78 C2 25 17N 89 1E
Hillingdon, U.K. 17 F7 51 32N 0 27W
Hillman, U.S.A. 134 C4 45 4N 83 54W
Hillmond, Canada 131 C7 53 26N 109 41W
Hillsboro, Ill., U.S.A. 140 E7 39 9N 89 29W
Hillsboro, Iowa, U.S.A. 140 D5 40 50N 91 42W
Hillsboro, Kans., U.S.A. 138 F6 38 21N 97 12W
Hillsboro, Mo., U.S.A. 140 F6 38 14N 90 34W
Hillsboro, N. Dak., U.S.A. 138 B6 47 26N 97 3W
Hillsboro, N.H., U.S.A. 137 C13 43 7N 71 54W
Hillsboro, N. Mex., U.S.A. 143 K10 32 55N 107 34W
Hillsboro, Ohio, U.S.A. 141 E13 39 12N 83 37W
Hillsboro, Oreg., U.S.A. 144 E4 45 31N 122 59W
Hillsboro, Tex., U.S.A. 139 J6 32 1N 97 8W
Hillsborough, Grenada 149 D7 12 28N 61 28W
Hillsdale, Mich., U.S.A. 141 C12 41 56N 84 38W
Hillsdale, N.Y., U.S.A. 137 D11 42 11N 73 30W
Hillside, Australia 112 D2 21 45S 119 23E
Hillsport, Canada 128 C2 49 27N 85 34W
Hillston, Australia 117 B6 33 30S 145 31E
Hilo, U.S.A. 132 J17 19 44N 155 5W

208 Hilton

Hilton, U.S.A. 136 C7 43 17N 77 48W
Hilvan, Turkey 89 D8 37 34N 38 58 E
Hilvarenbeek, Neths. 21 F6 51 29N 5 8 E
Hilversum, Neths. 20 D6 52 14N 5 10 E
Himachal Pradesh □, India 80 D7 31 30N 77 0 E
Himalaya, Asia 81 E11 29 0N 84 0 E
Himamaylan, Phil. 71 F4 10 6N 122 52 E
Himara, Albania 44 D1 40 8N 19 43 E
Hime-Jima, Japan 62 D3 33 43N 131 40 E
Himeji, Japan 62 C6 34 50N 134 40 E
Himi, Japan 63 A8 36 50N 136 55 E
Himmerland, Denmark 15 H3 56 45N 9 30 E
Ḩimş, Syria 91 A5 34 40N 36 45 E
Ḩims □, Syria 91 A5 34 30N 37 0 E
Hinatuan, Phil. 71 G6 8 23N 126 20 E
Hinatuan Passage, Phil. 71 G5 9 45N 125 47 E
Hinche, Haiti 149 C5 19 9N 72 1W
Hinchinbrook I., Australia 114 B4 18 20 S 146 15 E
Hinckley, U.K. 17 E6 52 33N 1 22W
Hinckley, U.S.A. 142 G7 39 20N 112 40W
Hindås, Sweden 15 G6 57 42N 12 27 E
Hindaun, India 80 F7 26 44N 77 5 E
Hindmarsh, L., Australia 116 D4 36 5 S 141 55 E
Hindol, India 82 D7 20 40N 85 10 E
Hinds, N.Z. 119 D6 43 59 S 171 36 E
Hindsholm, Denmark 15 J4 55 30N 10 40 E
Hindu Bagh, Pakistan 79 C2 30 56N 67 50 E
Hindu Kush, Asia 79 B3 36 0N 71 0 E
Hindupur, India 83 H3 13 49N 77 32 E
Hines Creek, Canada 130 B5 56 20N 118 40W
Hinganghat, India 82 D4 20 30N 78 52 E
Hingeon, Belgium 21 G5 50 32N 4 59 E
Hingham, U.S.A. 142 B8 48 33N 110 25W
Hingoli, India 82 E3 19 41N 77 15 E
Hinigaran, Phil. 71 F4 10 16N 122 50 E
Hinis, Turkey 89 C9 39 22N 41 43 E
Hinna = Imi, Ethiopia 90 F3 6 28N 42 10 E
Hinna, Nigeria 101 C7 10 25N 11 35 E
Hinnøya, Norway 12 B16 68 35N 15 50 E
Hino, Japan 63 C8 35 0N 136 15 E
Hinojosa del Duque, Spain 37 G5 38 30N 5 9W
Hinokage, Japan 62 E3 32 39N 131 24 E
Hinsdale, U.S.A. 142 B10 48 24N 107 5W
Hinterrhein →, Switz. 29 C8 46 40N 9 25 E
Hinton, Canada 130 C5 53 26N 117 34W
Hinton, U.S.A. 134 G5 37 40N 80 54W
Hinuangan, Phil. 71 F5 10 25N 125 12 E
Hinwil, Switz. 29 B7 47 18N 8 51 E
Hınzır Burnu, Turkey 88 D6 36 19N 35 46 E
Hippolytushoef, Neths. 20 C5 52 54N 4 58 E
Hirado, Japan 62 D1 33 22N 129 33 E
Hirado-Shima, Japan 62 D1 33 20N 129 30 E
Hirakarta, Japan 63 C7 34 48N 135 40 E
Hirakud, India 82 D6 21 32N 83 51 E
Hirakud Dam, India 82 D6 21 32N 83 45 E
Hirata, Japan 62 B4 35 24N 132 49 E
Hiratsuka, Japan 63 B11 35 19N 139 21 E
Hirfanlı Baraji, Turkey 88 C5 39 18N 33 31 E
Hirhafok, Algeria 99 D6 23 49N 5 45 E
Hîrlău, Romania 46 B7 47 23N 26 55 E
Hiromi, Japan 62 D4 33 13N 132 36 E
Hiroo, Japan 60 C11 42 17N 143 19 E
Hirosaki, Japan 60 D10 40 34N 140 28 E
Hiroshima, Japan 62 C4 34 24N 132 30 E
Hiroshima □, Japan 62 C4 34 50N 133 0 E
Hiroshima-Wan, Japan 62 C4 34 5N 132 20 E
Hirsholmene, Denmark 15 G4 57 30N 10 36 E
Hirson, France 23 C11 49 55N 4 4 E
Hîrşova, Romania 46 E8 44 40N 27 59 E
Hirtshals, Denmark 15 G3 57 36N 9 57 E
Hisar, India 80 E6 29 12N 75 45 E
Hisb →, Iraq 84 D5 31 45N 44 17 E
Ḩismá, Si. Arabia 84 D3 28 30N 36 0 E
Ḩisn al 'Abr, Yemen 86 C4 16 8N 47 14 E
Ḩişn al Qarn, Yemen 87 D5 15 8N 49 7 E
Hispaniola, W. Indies 149 C5 19 0N 71 0W
Hīt, Iraq 89 F10 33 38N 42 49 E
Hita, Japan 62 D2 33 20N 130 58 E
Hitachi, Japan 63 A12 36 36N 140 39 E
Hitachiota, Japan 63 A12 36 30N 140 30 E
Hitchin, U.K. 17 F7 51 58N 0 16W
Hitoyoshi, Japan 62 E2 32 13N 130 45 E
Hitra, Norway 12 E13 63 30N 8 45 E
Hitzacker, Germany 26 B7 53 9N 11 2 E
Hiu, Vanuatu 121 C4 13 10 S 166 35 E
Hiuchi-Nada, Japan 62 C5 34 5N 133 20 E
Ḩiyyon, N. →, Israel 91 E4 30 25N 35 10 E
Hjalmar L., Canada 131 A7 61 33N 109 25W
Hjälmare kanal, Sweden 14 E9 59 20N 15 59 E
Hjälmaren, Sweden 14 E9 59 18N 15 40 E
Hjartdal, Norway 14 E2 59 37N 8 41 E
Hjerkinn, Norway 14 B3 62 13N 9 33 E
Hjørring, Denmark 15 G3 57 29N 9 59 E
Hjortkvarn, Sweden 15 F9 58 54N 15 26 E
Hkakabo Razi, Burma 78 B6 28 17N 97 46 E
Hko-ut, Burma 78 E7 20 58N 98 2 E
Hkyenhpa, Burma 78 B6 27 43N 97 25 E
Hlaingbwe, Burma 78 G6 17 8N 97 50 E
Hlinsko, Czech. 30 B8 49 45N 15 54 E
Hlohovec, Slovak Rep. 31 C10 48 26N 17 49 E
Hluhluwe, S. Africa 105 D5 28 1 S 32 15 E
Hlukhiv, Ukraine 51 G7 51 40N 33 58 E
Hlwaze, Burma 78 F6 18 54N 96 37 E
Hlyboka, Ukraine 51 H3 48 5N 25 56 E
Hlybokaye, Belarus 50 E4 55 10N 27 45 E
Ho, Ghana 101 D5 6 37N 0 27 E
Ho Chi Minh City = Phanh Bho Ho Chi Minh, Vietnam 77 G6 10 58N 106 40 E
Ho Thuong, Vietnam 76 C5 19 32N 105 48 E
Hoa Binh, Vietnam 76 B5 20 50N 105 20 E
Hoa Da, Vietnam 77 G7 11 16N 108 40 E
Hoa Hiep, Vietnam 77 G5 11 34N 105 51 E
Hoai Nhon, Vietnam 76 E7 14 28N 109 1 E
Hoang Lien Son, Vietnam 76 A4 22 0N 104 0 E
Hoare B., Canada 127 B13 65 17N 62 30W
Hobart, Australia 114 G4 42 50 S 147 21 E
Hobart, Ind., U.S.A. 141 C9 41 32N 87 15W
Hobart, Okla., U.S.A. 139 H5 35 1N 99 6W
Hobbs, U.S.A. 139 J3 32 42N 103 8W
Hobbs Coast, Antarctica 7 D14 74 50 S 131 0W
Hobo, Colombia 152 C2 2 35N 75 30W
Hoboken, Belgium 21 F4 51 11N 4 21 E
Hoboken, U.S.A. 137 F10 40 45N 74 4W
Hobro, Denmark 15 H3 56 39N 9 46 E
Hobscheid, Lux. 21 J7 49 42N 5 57 E
Hoburgen, Sweden 13 H18 56 55N 18 7 E
Hochdorf, Switz. 29 B6 47 10N 8 17 E
Hochschwab, Austria 30 D8 47 35N 15 0 E
Höchstadt, Germany 27 F6 49 42N 10 47 E
Hockenheim, Germany 27 F4 49 19N 8 32 E
Hodaka-Dake, Japan 63 A9 36 17N 137 39 E
Hodgson, Canada 131 C9 51 13N 97 36W
Hódmezövásárhely, Hungary 31 E13 46 28N 20 22 E
Hodna, Chott el, Algeria 99 A5 35 26N 4 43 E
Hodna, Monts du, Algeria 99 A5 35 52N 4 42 E
Hodonín, Czech. 31 C10 48 50N 17 10 E
Hoeamdong, N. Korea 67 C16 42 30N 130 16 E
Hœdic, I. de, France 22 E4 47 20N 2 53W
Hoegaarden, Belgium 21 G5 50 47N 4 53 E
Hoek van Holland, Neths. 20 E4 52 0N 4 7 E
Hoeksche Waard, Neths. 20 E4 51 46N 4 25 E
Hoenderloo, Neths. 20 D7 52 7N 5 52 E
Hoengsŏng, S. Korea 67 F14 37 29N 127 59 E
Hoensbroek, Neths. 21 G7 50 55N 5 55 E
Hoeryong, N. Korea 67 C15 42 30N 129 45 E
Hoeselt, Belgium 21 G6 50 51N 5 29 E
Hoeven, Neths. 21 E5 51 35N 4 35 E
Hoeyang, N. Korea 67 E14 38 43N 127 36 E
Hof, Germany 27 E7 50 19N 11 55 E
Hofgeismar, Germany 26 D5 51 29N 9 23 E
Hofmeyr, S. Africa 104 E4 31 39 S 25 50 E
Höfn, Iceland 12 D6 64 15N 15 13W
Hofors, Sweden 13 F17 60 31N 16 15 E
Hofsjökull, Iceland 12 D4 64 49N 18 48W
Hōfu, Japan 62 C3 34 3N 131 34 E
Hogan Group, Australia 114 F4 39 13 S 147 1 E
Hogansville, U.S.A. 135 J3 33 10N 84 55W
Hogeland, U.S.A. 142 B9 48 51N 108 40W
Hogenakai Falls, India 83 H3 12 6N 77 50 E
Hoggar = Ahaggar, Algeria 99 D6 23 0N 6 30 E
Hōgo-Kaikyō, Japan 62 D3 33 20N 131 58 E
Högsäter, Sweden 15 F6 58 38N 12 5 E
Hogsty Reef, Bahamas 149 B5 21 41N 73 48W
Hoh →, U.S.A. 144 C2 47 45N 124 29W
Hohe Rhön, Germany 27 E5 50 24N 9 58 E
Hohe Tauern, Austria 30 D5 47 11N 12 40 E
Hohe Venn, Belgium 21 H8 50 30N 6 5 E
Hohenau, Austria 31 C9 48 36N 16 55 E
Hohenems, Austria 30 D2 47 22N 9 42 E
Hohenstein-Ernstthal, Germany 26 E8 50 48N 12 42 E
Hohenwald, U.S.A. 135 H2 35 33N 87 33W
Hohenwestedt, Germany 26 A5 54 5N 9 40 E
Hohhot, China 66 D6 40 52N 111 40 E
Hóhlakas, Greece 32 D9 35 57N 27 53 E
Hohoe, Ghana 101 D5 7 8N 0 32 E
Hoi An, Vietnam 76 E7 15 30N 108 19 E
Hoi Xuan, Vietnam 76 B5 20 25N 105 9 E
Hoisington, U.S.A. 138 F5 38 31N 98 47W
Højer, Denmark 15 K2 54 58N 8 42 E
Hōjō, Japan 62 D4 33 58N 132 46 E
Hökerum, Sweden 15 G7 57 51N 13 16 E
Hokianga Harbour, N.Z. 118 B2 35 31 S 173 22 E
Hokitika, N.Z. 119 C5 42 42 S 171 0 E
Hokkaidō □, Japan 60 C11 43 30N 143 0 E
Hokksund, Norway 14 E3 59 48N 9 54 E
Hol-Hol, Djibouti 95 E5 11 20N 42 50 E
Hola Pristan, Ukraine 51 J7 46 29N 32 32 E
Holbæk, Denmark 15 J5 55 43N 11 43 E
Holbrook, Australia 117 C7 35 42 S 147 18 E
Holbrook, U.S.A. 143 J8 34 54N 110 10W
Holden, Canada 130 C6 53 13N 112 11W
Holden, Mo., U.S.A. 140 F3 38 43N 94 1W
Holden, Utah, U.S.A. 142 G7 39 6N 112 16W
Holdenville, U.S.A. 139 H6 35 5N 96 24W
Holder, Australia 116 C3 34 21 S 140 0 E
Holderness, U.K. 16 D7 53 45N 0 5W
Holdfast, Canada 131 C7 50 58N 105 25W
Holdich, Argentina 160 C3 45 57 S 68 13W
Holdrege, U.S.A. 138 E5 40 26N 99 23W
Hole-Narsipur, India 83 H3 12 48N 76 16 E
Holešov, Czech. 31 B10 49 20N 17 35 E
Holgate, U.S.A. 141 C12 41 15N 84 8W
Holguín, Cuba 148 B4 20 50N 76 20W
Holič, Slovak Rep. 31 C10 48 49N 17 10 E
Hollabrunn, Austria 30 C9 48 34N 16 5 E
Hollams Bird I., Namibia 104 C1 24 40 S 14 30 E
Holland, U.S.A. 141 B10 42 47N 86 7W
Hollandia = Jayapura, Indonesia 73 B6 2 28 S 140 38 E
Hollandsch Diep, Neths. 21 E5 51 41N 4 30 E
Hollandsch IJssel →, Neths. 20 E5 51 55N 4 34 E
Hollfeld, Germany 27 F7 49 56N 11 18 E
Hollidaysburg, U.S.A. 136 F6 40 26N 78 24W
Hollis, U.S.A. 139 H5 34 41N 99 55W
Hollister, Calif., U.S.A. 144 J5 36 51N 121 24W
Hollister, Idaho, U.S.A. 142 E6 42 21N 114 35W
Hollum, Neths. 20 B7 53 26N 5 38 E
Holly, Colo., U.S.A. 138 F3 38 3N 102 7W
Holly, Mich., U.S.A. 141 B13 42 48N 83 38W
Holly Hill, U.S.A. 135 L5 29 16N 81 3W
Holly Springs, U.S.A. 139 H10 34 46N 89 27W
Hollywood, Calif., U.S.A. 143 J4 34 7N 118 25W
Hollywood, Fla., U.S.A. 135 N5 26 1N 80 9W
Holm, Sweden 14 B10 62 40N 16 40 E
Holman Island, Canada 126 A8 70 42N 117 41W
Hólmavík, Iceland 12 D3 65 42N 21 40W
Holmes Reefs, Australia 114 B4 16 27 S 148 0 E
Holmestrand, Norway 14 E4 59 31N 10 14 E
Holmsbu, Norway 14 E4 59 32N 10 27 E
Holmsjön, Sweden 14 B9 62 26N 15 20 E
Holmsland Klit, Denmark 15 J2 56 0N 8 5 E
Holmsund, Sweden 12 E19 63 41N 20 20 E
Holod, Romania 46 C3 46 49N 22 8 E
Holroyd →, Australia 114 A3 14 10 S 141 36 E
Holstebro, Denmark 15 H2 56 22N 8 37 E
Holsworthy, U.K. 17 G3 50 48N 4 22W
Holte, Denmark 15 J6 55 50N 12 29 E
Holten, Neths. 20 D8 52 17N 6 26 E
Holton, Canada 129 B8 54 31N 57 12W
Holton, U.S.A. 138 F7 39 28N 95 44W
Holtville, U.S.A. 145 N11 32 49N 115 23W
Holwerd, Neths. 20 B7 53 22N 5 54 E
Holy Cross, U.S.A. 126 B4 62 12N 159 46W
Holy I., Angl., U.K. 16 D3 53 17N 4 37W
Holy I., Northumb., U.K. 16 B6 55 40N 1 47W
Holyhead, U.K. 16 D3 53 18N 4 38W
Holyoke, Colo., U.S.A. 138 E3 40 35N 102 18W
Holyoke, Mass., U.S.A. 137 D12 42 12N 72 37W
Holyrood, Canada 129 C9 47 27N 53 8W
Holzkirchen, Germany 27 H7 47 52N 11 42 E
Holzminden, Germany 26 D5 51 50N 9 28 E
Homa Bay, Kenya 106 C3 0 36 S 34 30 E
Homa Bay □, Kenya 106 C3 0 50 S 34 30 E
Homalin, Burma 78 C5 24 55N 95 0 E
Homand, Iran 85 C8 32 28N 59 37 E
Homberg, Germany 26 D5 51 2N 9 25 E
Hombori, Mali 101 B4 15 20N 1 38W
Homburg, Germany 27 F3 49 28N 7 18 E
Home B., Canada 127 B13 68 40N 67 10W
Home Hill, Australia 114 B4 19 43 S 147 25 E
Home Reef, Tonga 121 P13 18 59 S 174 47W
Homedale, U.S.A. 142 E5 43 37N 116 56W
Homer, Alaska, U.S.A. 126 C4 59 39N 151 33W
Homer, Ill., U.S.A. 141 D9 40 4N 87 57W
Homer, La., U.S.A. 139 J8 32 48N 93 4W
Homer, Mich., U.S.A. 141 B12 42 9N 84 49W
Homestead, Australia 114 C4 20 20 S 145 40 E
Homestead, Fla., U.S.A. 135 N5 25 28N 80 29W
Homestead, Oreg., U.S.A. 142 D5 45 2N 116 51W
Homewood, Calif., U.S.A. 144 F6 39 4N 120 8W
Homewood, Ill., U.S.A. 141 C9 41 34N 87 40W
Hominy, U.S.A. 139 G6 36 25N 96 24W
Homnabad, India 82 F3 17 45N 77 11 E
Homoine, Mozam. 105 C6 23 55 S 35 8 E
Homoljske Planina, Serbia, Yug. 42 C6 44 10N 21 45 E
Homonhan I., Phil. 71 F5 10 44N 125 43 E
Homorod, Romania 46 C6 46 5N 25 15 E
Homs = Ḩimş, Syria 91 A5 34 40N 36 45 E
Homyel, Belarus 51 F6 52 28N 31 0 E
Hon Chong, Vietnam 77 G5 10 25N 104 30 E
Hon Me, Vietnam 76 C5 19 23N 105 56 E
Hon Quan, Vietnam 77 G6 11 40N 106 50 E
Honan = Henan □, China 66 G8 34 0N 114 0 E
Honbetsu, Japan 60 C11 43 7N 143 37 E
Honcut, U.S.A. 144 F5 39 20N 121 32W
Honda, Colombia 152 B3 5 12N 74 45W
Honda Bay, Phil. 71 G2 9 53N 118 49 E
Hondeklipbaai, S. Africa 104 E2 30 19 S 17 17 E
Hondo, Japan 62 E2 32 27N 130 12 E
Hondo, U.S.A. 139 L5 29 21N 99 9W
Hondo →, Belize 147 D7 18 25N 88 21W
Honduras ■, Cent. Amer. 148 D2 14 40N 86 30W
Honduras, G. de, Caribbean 148 C2 16 50N 87 0W
Hønefoss, Norway 13 F14 60 10N 10 18 E
Honesdale, U.S.A. 137 E9 41 34N 75 16W
Honey L., U.S.A. 144 E6 40 15N 120 19W
Honfleur, France 22 C7 49 25N 0 13 E
Hong Gai, Vietnam 76 B6 20 57N 107 5 E
Hong He →, China 66 H8 32 25N 115 35 E
Hong Kong ■, Asia 69 F10 22 11N 114 14 E
Hong'an, China 69 B10 31 20N 114 40 E
Hongchŏn, S. Korea 67 F14 37 44N 127 53 E
Hongha →, Vietnam 64 D5 22 0N 104 0 E
Honghai Wan, China 69 F10 22 40N 115 0 E
Honghu, China 69 C9 29 50N 113 30 E
Hongjiang, China 68 D7 27 7N 109 59 E
Hongliu He →, China 66 F5 38 0N 109 50 E
Hongor, Mongolia 66 B7 45 45N 112 50 E
Hongsa, Laos 76 C3 19 43N 101 20 E
Hongshui He →, China 68 F7 23 48N 109 30 E
Hongsŏng, S. Korea 67 F14 36 37N 126 38 E
Hongtong, China 66 F6 36 16N 111 40 E
Honguedo, Détroit d', Canada 129 C7 49 15N 64 0W
Hongwon, N. Korea 67 E14 40 0N 127 56 E
Hongya, China 68 C4 29 57N 103 22 E
Hongyuan, China 68 A4 32 51N 102 40 E
Hongze Hu, China 67 H10 33 15N 118 35 E
Honiara, Solomon Is. 121 M10 9 27 S 159 57 E
Honiton, U.K. 17 G4 50 47N 3 11W
Honjō, Akita, Japan 60 E10 39 23N 140 3 E
Honjō, Gumma, Japan 63 A11 36 14N 139 11 E
Honkawane, Japan 63 B10 35 5N 138 5 E
Honkorâb, Ras, Egypt 94 C4 24 35N 35 10 E
Honningsvåg, Norway 12 A21 70 59N 25 59 E
Honolulu, U.S.A. 132 H16 21 19N 157 52W
Honshū, Japan 61 G9 36 0N 138 0 E
Hontoria del Pinar, Spain 34 D1 41 50N 3 10W
Hood, Mt., U.S.A. 142 D3 45 23N 121 42W
Hood, Pt., Australia 113 F2 34 23 S 119 34 E
Hood Pt., Papua N. G. 120 F4 10 4 S 147 45 E
Hood River, U.S.A. 142 D3 45 43N 121 31W
Hoodsport, U.S.A. 144 C3 47 24N 123 9W
Hooge, Germany 26 A4 54 34N 8 33 E
Hoogerheide, Neths. 21 F4 51 26N 4 20 E
Hoogeveen, Neths. 20 C8 52 44N 6 28 E
Hoogeveensche Vaart, Neths. 20 C8 52 42N 6 12 E
Hoogezand, Neths. 20 B9 53 11N 6 45 E
Hooghly → = Hugli →, India 81 J13 21 56N 88 4 E
Hooghly-Chinsura = Chunchura, India 81 H13 22 53N 88 27 E
Hoogkerk, Neths. 20 B9 53 13N 6 30 E
Hooglede, Belgium 21 G2 50 59N 3 5 E
Hoogstraten, Belgium 21 F5 51 24N 4 46 E
Hoogvliet, Neths. 20 E4 51 52N 4 21 E
Hook Hd., Ireland 19 D5 52 7N 6 56W
Hook I., Australia 114 C4 20 4 S 149 0 E
Hook of Holland = Hoek van Holland, Neths. 20 E4 52 0N 4 7 E
Hooker, U.S.A. 139 G4 36 52N 101 13W
Hooker Creek, Australia 112 C5 18 23 S 130 38 E
Hoopeston, U.S.A. 141 D9 40 28N 87 40W
Hoopstad, S. Africa 104 D4 27 50 S 25 55 E
Hoorn, Neths. 20 C6 52 38N 5 4 E
Hoover Dam, U.S.A. 145 K12 36 1N 114 44W
Hooversville, U.S.A. 136 F6 40 9N 78 55W
Hop Bottom, U.S.A. 137 E9 41 42N 75 46W
Hopa, Turkey 89 B9 41 28N 41 30 E
Hope, Canada 130 D4 49 25N 121 25W
Hope, Ariz., U.S.A. 145 M13 33 43N 113 42W
Hope, Ark., U.S.A. 139 J8 33 40N 93 36W
Hope, Ind., U.S.A. 141 E11 39 18N 85 46W
Hope, N. Dak., U.S.A. 138 B6 47 19N 97 43W
Hope, L., Australia 115 D2 28 24 S 139 18 E
Hope, Pt., U.S.A. 126 B3 68 20N 166 50W
Hope Pass, N.Z. 119 C7 42 36 S 172 6 E
Hope Town, Bahamas 148 A4 26 35N 76 57W
Hopedale, Canada 129 A7 55 28N 60 13W
Hopefield, S. Africa 104 E2 33 3 S 18 22 E
Hopei = Hebei □, China 66 E9 39 0N 116 0 E
Hopelchén, Mexico 147 D7 19 46N 89 50W
Hopetoun, Vic., Australia 116 C5 35 42 S 142 22 E
Hopetoun, W. Austral., Australia 113 F3 33 57 S 120 7 E
Hopetown, S. Africa 104 D3 29 34 S 24 3 E
Hopin, Burma 78 C6 24 58N 96 30 E
Hopkins, Mich., U.S.A. 141 B11 42 37N 85 46W
Hopkins, Mo., U.S.A. 140 D2 40 33N 94 49W
Hopkins, L., Australia 112 D4 24 15 S 128 35 E
Hopkinsville, U.S.A. 135 G2 36 52N 87 29W
Hopland, U.S.A. 144 G3 38 58N 123 7W
Hoptrup, Denmark 15 J3 55 11N 9 28 E
Hoquiam, U.S.A. 144 D3 46 59N 123 53W
Hōrai, Japan 63 C9 34 58N 137 32 E
Horasan, Turkey 89 B10 40 3N 42 11 E
Horazdovice, Czech. 30 B6 49 19N 13 42 E
Horcajo de Santiago, Spain 34 F1 39 50N 3 1W
Horden Hills, Australia 112 D5 20 15 S 130 0 E
Hordio, Somali Rep. 108 B4 10 33N 51 6 E
Horezu, Romania 46 D5 45 6N 24 0 E
Horgen, Switz. 29 B7 47 15N 8 35 E
Horgoš, Serbia, Yug. 42 A5 46 10N 20 0 E
Horice, Czech. 30 A8 50 21N 15 39 E
Horinger, China 66 D6 40 28N 111 48 E
Horki, Belarus 50 E6 54 17N 30 59 E
Horlick Mts., Antarctica 7 E15 84 0 S 102 0W
Horlivka, Ukraine 51 H10 48 19N 38 5 E
Hormoz, Iran 85 E7 27 35N 55 0 E
Hormoz, Jaz. ye, Iran 85 E8 27 8N 56 28 E
Hormuz, Str. of, The Gulf 85 E8 26 30N 56 30 E
Horn, Austria 30 C8 48 39N 15 40 E
Horn, Iceland 12 C2 66 28N 22 28W
Horn, Neths. 21 F7 51 12N 5 57 E
Horn →, Canada 130 A5 61 30N 118 1W
Horn, Cape = Hornos, C. de, Chile 160 E3 55 50 S 67 30W
Horn, Is., Wall. & F. Is. 111 C15 14 16 S 178 6W
Horn Head, Ireland 19 A3 55 14N 8 0W
Horn I., Australia 114 A3 10 37 S 142 17 E
Horn I., U.S.A. 135 K1 30 14N 88 39W
Horn Mts., Canada 130 A5 62 15N 119 15W
Hornachuelos, Spain 37 H5 37 50N 5 14W
Hornavan, Sweden 12 C17 66 15N 17 30 E
Hornbæk, Denmark 15 H6 56 5N 12 26 E
Hornbeck, U.S.A. 139 K8 31 20N 93 24W
Hornbrook, U.S.A. 142 F2 41 55N 122 33W
Hornburg, Germany 26 C6 52 2N 10 37 E
Hornby, N.Z. 119 D7 43 33 S 172 33 E
Horncastle, U.K. 16 D7 53 13N 0 7W
Hornell, U.S.A. 136 D7 42 20N 77 40W
Hornell L., Canada 130 A5 62 20N 119 25W
Hornepayne, Canada 128 C3 49 14N 84 48W
Hornitos, U.S.A. 144 H6 37 30N 120 14W
Hornos, C. de, Chile 160 E3 55 50 S 67 30W
Hornoy, France 23 C8 49 50N 1 54 E
Hornsby, Australia 117 B9 33 42 S 151 2 E
Hornsea, U.K. 16 D7 53 55N 0 11W
Hornslandet, Sweden 14 C11 61 35N 17 37 E
Hornslet, Denmark 15 H4 56 18N 10 19 E
Hornu, Belgium 21 H3 50 26N 3 50 E
Hörnum, Germany 26 A4 54 45N 8 17 E
Horobetsu, Japan 60 C10 42 24N 141 6 E
Horodenka, Ukraine 51 H3 48 41N 25 29 E
Horodnya, Ukraine 51 G6 51 55N 31 33 E
Horodok, Khmelnytskyy, Ukraine 51 H4 49 10N 26 34 E
Horodok, Lviv, Ukraine 51 H2 49 46N 23 32 E
Horodyshche, Ukraine 51 H6 49 17N 31 27 E
Horokhiv, Ukraine 51 G3 50 30N 24 45 E
Horovice, Czech. 30 B6 49 48N 13 53 E
Horqin Youyi Qianqi, China 67 A12 46 5N 122 3 E
Horqueta, Paraguay 158 A4 23 15 S 56 55W
Horred, Sweden 15 G6 57 22N 12 28 E
Horse Creek, U.S.A. 138 E3 41 57N 105 10W
Horse Is., Canada 129 B8 50 15N 55 50W
Horsefly L., Canada 130 C4 52 25N 121 0W
Horsens, Denmark 15 J3 55 52N 9 51 E
Horsens Fjord, Denmark 15 J4 55 50N 10 0 E
Horsham, Australia 116 D5 36 44 S 142 13 E
Horsham, U.K. 17 F7 51 4N 0 20W
Horšovský Týn, Czech. 30 B5 49 31N 12 58 E
Horst, Neths. 21 F8 51 27N 6 3 E
Horten, Norway 14 E4 59 25N 10 32 E
Hortobágy →, Hungary 31 D14 47 30N 21 6 E
Horton, U.S.A. 138 F7 39 40N 95 32W
Horton →, Canada 126 B7 69 56N 126 52W
Horw, Switz. 29 B6 47 1N 8 19 E
Horwood, L., Canada 128 C3 48 5N 82 20W
Hosaina, Ethiopia 95 F4 7 30N 37 47 E
Hosdurga, India 83 H3 13 49N 76 17 E
Ḩoseynābād, Khuzestān, Iran 85 C6 32 45N 48 20 E
Ḩoseynābād, Kordestān, Iran 89 E12 35 33N 47 8 E
Hoshangabad, India 80 H7 22 45N 77 45 E
Hoshiarpur, India 80 D6 31 30N 75 58 E
Hosingen, Lux. 21 H8 50 1N 6 6 E
Hoskins, Papua N. G. 120 C6 5 29 S 150 27 E
Hosmer, U.S.A. 138 C5 45 34N 99 28W
Hososhima, Japan 62 E3 32 26N 131 40 E
Hospental, Switz. 29 C7 46 37N 8 34 E
Hospet, India 83 G3 15 15N 76 20 E
Hospitalet de Llobregat, Spain 34 D7 41 21N 2 6 E
Hoste, I., Chile 160 E3 55 0 S 69 0W
Hostens, France 24 D3 44 30N 0 40W
Hot, Thailand 76 C2 18 8N 98 29 E
Hot Creek Range, U.S.A. 142 G5 38 40N 116 20W
Hot Springs, Ark., U.S.A. 139 H8 34 31N 93 3W
Hot Springs, S. Dak., U.S.A. 138 D3 43 26N 103 29W
Hotagen, Sweden 12 E16 63 50N 14 30 E
Hotan, China 64 C2 37 25N 79 55 E
Hotazel, S. Africa 104 D3 27 17 S 22 58 E
Hotchkiss, U.S.A. 143 G10 38 48N 107 43W
Hotham, C., Australia 112 B5 12 2 S 131 18 E
Hoting, Sweden 12 D17 64 8N 16 15 E
Hotolishti, Albania 44 C2 41 10N 20 25 E
Hotte, Massif de la, Haiti 149 C5 18 30N 73 45W
Hottentotsbaai, Namibia 104 D1 26 8 S 14 59 E
Hotton, Belgium 21 H6 50 16N 5 26 E
Houailou, N. Cal. 121 U19 21 17 S 165 38 E
Houat, I. de, France 22 E4 47 24N 2 58W
Houck, U.S.A. 143 J9 35 20N 109 10W
Houdan, France 23 D8 48 48N 1 35 E
Houdeng-Goegnies, Belgium 21 H4 50 29N 4 10 E

210 Ibrāhīm

Ibrāhīm →, *Lebanon* ... **91 A4** 34 4N 35 38 E
'Ibrī, *Oman* ... **87 B7** 23 14N 56 30 E
İbriktepe, *Turkey* ... **44 C8** 41 2N 26 33 E
Ibshawâi, *Egypt* ... **94 J7** 29 21N 30 40 E
Ibu, *Indonesia* ... **72 A3** 1 35N 127 33 E
Ibuki-Sanchi, *Japan* ... **63 B8** 35 25N 136 18 E
Iburg, *Germany* ... **26 C4** 52 10N 8 3 E
Ibusuki, *Japan* ... **62 F2** 31 12N 130 40 E
Icá, *Peru* ... **156 C2** 14 0 S 75 48W
Ica □, *Peru* ... **156 C2** 14 20 S 75 30W
Iça →, *Brazil* ... **156 A4** 2 55 S 67 58W
Icabarú, *Venezuela* ... **153 C5** 4 20N 61 45W
Icabarú →, *Venezuela* .. **153 C5** 4 45N 62 15W
Içana, *Brazil* ... **152 C4** 0 21N 67 19W
Içana →, *Brazil* ... **152 C4** 0 26N 67 19W
Icatu, *Brazil* ... **154 B3** 2 46 S 44 4W
Içel = Mersin, *Turkey* ... **88 D6** 36 51N 34 36 E
Iceland ■, *Europe* ... **12 D4** 64 45N 19 0W
Icha, *Russia* ... **57 D16** 55 30N 156 0 E
Ich'ang = Yichang, *China* **69 B8** 30 40N 111 20 E
Ichchapuram, *India* ... **82 E7** 19 10N 84 40 E
Ichihara, *Japan* ... **63 B12** 35 28N 140 5 E
Ichikawa, *Japan* ... **63 B11** 35 44N 139 55 E
Ichilo →, *Bolivia* ... **157 D5** 15 57 S 64 50W
Ichinohe, *Japan* ... **60 D10** 40 13N 141 17 E
Ichinomiya, *Gifu, Japan* . **63 B8** 35 18N 136 48 E
Ichinomiya, *Kumamoto, Japan* ... **62 E3** 32 58N 131 5 E
Ichinoseki, *Japan* ... **60 E10** 38 55N 141 8 E
Ichnya, *Ukraine* ... **51 G7** 50 52N 32 24 E
Ichŏn, *S. Korea* ... **67 F14** 37 17N 127 27 E
Icht, *Morocco* ... **98 C3** 29 6N 8 54W
Ichtegem, *Belgium* ... **21 F2** 51 5N 3 1 E
Icó, *Brazil* ... **154 C4** 6 24 S 38 51W
Icod, *Canary Is.* ... **33 F3** 28 22N 16 43W
Icoraci, *Brazil* ... **154 B2** 1 18 S 48 28W
Icy Str., *U.S.A.* ... **130 B1** 58 20N 135 30W
Ida Grove, *U.S.A.* ... **138 D7** 42 21N 95 28W
Ida Valley, *Australia* ... **113 E3** 28 42 S 120 29 E
Idabel, *U.S.A.* ... **139 J7** 33 54N 94 50W
Idaga Hamus, *Ethiopia* .. **95 E4** 14 13N 39 48 E
Idah, *Nigeria* ... **101 D6** 7 5N 6 40 E
Idaho □, *U.S.A.* ... **142 D6** 45 0N 115 0W
Idaho City, *U.S.A.* ... **142 E6** 43 50N 115 50W
Idaho Falls, *U.S.A.* ... **142 E7** 43 30N 112 2W
Idaho Springs, *U.S.A.* ... **142 G11** 39 45N 105 31W
Idanha-a-Nova, *Portugal* . **36 F3** 39 50N 7 15W
Idar-Oberstein, *Germany* **27 F3** 49 43N 7 16 E
Idd el Ghanam, *Sudan* .. **97 F4** 11 30N 24 19 E
Iddan, *Somali Rep.* ... **108 C3** 6 10N 48 55 E
Idehan, *Libya* ... **96 C2** 27 10N 11 30 E
Idehan Marzūq, *Libya* ... **96 D2** 24 50N 13 51 E
Idelès, *Algeria* ... **99 D6** 23 50N 5 53 E
Idfû, *Egypt* ... **94 C3** 24 55N 32 49 E
Ídhi Óros, *Greece* ... **32 D6** 35 15N 24 45 E
Ídhra, *Greece* ... **45 G5** 37 20N 23 28 E
Idi, *Indonesia* ... **74 A1** 5 2N 97 37 E
Idiofa, *Zaïre* ... **103 C3** 4 55 S 19 42 E
Idku, Bahra el, *Egypt* ... **94 H7** 31 18N 30 18 E
Idlib, *Syria* ... **88 E7** 35 55N 36 36 E
Idria, *U.S.A.* ... **144 J6** 36 25N 120 41W
Idrija, *Slovenia* ... **39 B11** 46 0N 14 5 E
Idritsa, *Russia* ... **50 D5** 56 17N 28 53 E
Idstein, *Germany* ... **27 E4** 50 12N 8 17 E
Idutywa, *S. Africa* ... **105 E4** 32 8 S 28 18 E
Ieper, *Belgium* ... **21 G1** 50 51N 2 53 E
Ierápetra, *Greece* ... **32 E7** 35 0N 25 44 E
Ierissós, *Greece* ... **44 D5** 40 22N 23 52 E
Ierissóu Kólpos, *Greece* .. **44 D5** 40 27N 23 57 E
Ierzu, *Italy* ... **40 C2** 39 47N 9 31 E
Ieshima-Shotō, *Japan* ... **62 C6** 34 40N 134 32 E
Iesi, *Italy* ... **39 E10** 43 31N 13 14 E
Ifach, Punta, *Spain* ... **35 G5** 38 38N 0 5 E
'Ifāl, W. al →, *Si. Arabia* **84 D2** 28 7N 35 3 E
Ifanadiana, *Madag.* ... **105 C8** 21 19 S 47 39 E
Ife, *Nigeria* ... **101 D5** 7 30N 4 31 E
Iférouâne, *Niger* ... **97 E1** 19 5N 8 24 E
Iffley, *Australia* ... **114 B3** 18 53 S 141 12 E
Ifni, *Morocco* ... **98 C2** 29 29N 10 12W
Ifon, *Nigeria* ... **101 D6** 6 58N 5 40 E
Iforas, Adrar des, *Mali* .. **101 B5** 19 40N 1 40 E
Ifould, L., *Australia* ... **113 F5** 30 52 S 132 6 E
Ifrane, *Morocco* ... **98 B3** 33 33N 5 7W
Ifugao □, *Phil.* ... **70 C3** 16 40N 121 10 E
Iga, *Japan* ... **63 C8** 34 45N 136 10 E
Iganga, *Uganda* ... **106 B3** 0 37N 33 28 E
Igara Paraná →, *Colombia* ... **152 D3** 2 9 S 71 47W
Igarapava, *Brazil* ... **155 F2** 20 3 S 47 47W
Igarapé Açu, *Brazil* ... **154 B2** 1 4 S 47 33W
Igarapé-Mirim, *Brazil* ... **154 B2** 1 59 S 48 58W
Igarka, *Russia* ... **56 C9** 67 30N 86 33 E
Igatimi, *Paraguay* ... **159 A4** 24 5 S 55 40W
Igatpuri, *India* ... **82 E1** 19 40N 73 35 E
Igbetti, *Nigeria* ... **101 D5** 8 44N 4 8 E
Igbo-Ora, *Nigeria* ... **101 D5** 7 29N 3 15 E
Igboho, *Nigeria* ... **101 D5** 8 53N 3 50 E
Iğdır, *Turkey* ... **89 C11** 39 55N 44 2 E
Iggesund, *Sweden* ... **14 C11** 61 39N 17 10 E
Ighil Izane, *Algeria* ... **99 A5** 35 44N 0 31 E
Iglésias, *Italy* ... **40 C1** 39 19N 8 32 E
Igli, *Algeria* ... **99 B4** 30 25N 2 19W
Iglino, *Russia* ... **54 D6** 54 50N 56 26 E
Igloolik, *Canada* ... **127 B11** 69 20N 81 49W
Igma, Gebel el, *Egypt* ... **94 J8** 28 55N 34 0 E
Ignace, *Canada* ... **128 C1** 49 30N 91 40W
İğneada Burnu, *Turkey* .. **88 B3** 41 53N 28 2 E
Igoumenítsa, *Greece* ... **44 E2** 39 32N 20 18 E
Igra, *Russia* ... **52 B11** 57 33N 53 7 E
Iguaçu →, *Brazil* ... **159 B5** 25 36 S 54 36W
Iguaçu, Cat. del, *Brazil* .. **159 B5** 25 41 S 54 26W
Iguaçu Falls = Iguaçu, Cat. del, *Brazil* ... **159 B5** 25 41 S 54 26W
Iguala, *Mexico* ... **147 D5** 18 20N 99 40W
Igualada, *Spain* ... **34 D6** 41 37N 1 37 E
Iguape, *Brazil* ... **155 F2** 24 43 S 47 33W
Iguassu = Iguaçu →, *Brazil* ... **159 B5** 25 36 S 54 36W
Iguatu, *Brazil* ... **154 C4** 6 20 S 39 18W
Iguéla, *Gabon* ... **102 C1** 2 0 S 9 16 E
Iguig, *Phil.* ... **70 C3** 17 45N 121 44 E
Igunga □, *Tanzania* ... **106 C3** 4 20 S 33 45 E
Iheya-Shima, *Japan* ... **61 L3** 27 4N 127 58 E
Ihiala, *Nigeria* ... **101 D6** 5 51N 6 55 E
Ihosy, *Madag.* ... **105 C8** 22 24 S 46 8 E
Ihotry, L., *Madag.* ... **105 C7** 21 56 S 43 41 E
Ii, *Finland* ... **12 D21** 65 19N 25 22 E
Ii-Shima, *Japan* ... **61 L3** 26 43N 127 47 E
Iida, *Japan* ... **63 B9** 35 35N 137 50 E
Iijoki →, *Finland* ... **12 D21** 65 20N 25 20 E
Iisalmi, *Finland* ... **12 E22** 63 32N 27 10 E
Iiyama, *Japan* ... **61 F9** 36 51N 138 22 E
Iizuka, *Japan* ... **62 D2** 33 38N 130 42 E
Ijâfene, *Mauritania* ... **98 D3** 20 40N 8 0W
Ijebu-Igbo, *Nigeria* ... **101 D5** 6 56N 4 1 E
Ijebu-Ode, *Nigeria* ... **101 D5** 6 47N 3 58 E
IJmuiden, *Neths.* ... **20 D5** 52 28N 4 35 E
IJssel →, *Neths.* ... **20 C7** 52 35N 5 50 E
IJsselmeer, *Neths.* ... **20 C6** 52 45N 5 20 E
IJsselmuiden, *Neths.* ... **20 C7** 52 34N 5 57 E
IJsselstein, *Neths.* ... **20 D6** 52 1N 5 2 E
Ijuí →, *Brazil* ... **159 B4** 27 58 S 55 20W
Ijūin, *Japan* ... **62 F2** 31 37N 130 24 E
IJzendijke, *Neths.* ... **21 F3** 51 19N 3 37 E
IJzer →, *Belgium* ... **21 F1** 51 9N 2 44 E
Ik →, *Russia* ... **54 D4** 55 41N 53 29 E
Ikale, *Nigeria* ... **101 D6** 7 40N 5 37 E
Ikare, *Nigeria* ... **101 D6** 7 32N 5 40 E
Ikaría, *Greece* ... **45 G8** 37 35N 26 10 E
Ikast, *Denmark* ... **15 H3** 56 8N 9 10 E
Ikawa, *Japan* ... **63 B10** 35 13N 138 15 E
Ikeda, *Japan* ... **62 C5** 34 1N 133 48 E
Ikeja, *Nigeria* ... **101 D5** 6 36N 3 23 E
Ikela, *Zaïre* ... **102 C4** 1 6 S 23 6 E
Ikenge, *Zaïre* ... **102 C3** 0 8 S 18 8 E
Ikerre-Ekiti, *Nigeria* ... **101 D6** 7 25N 5 19 E
Ikhtiman, *Bulgaria* ... **43 E8** 42 27N 23 48 E
Iki, *Japan* ... **62 D1** 33 45N 129 42 E
Iki-Kaikyō, *Japan* ... **62 D1** 33 40N 129 45 E
Ikimba L., *Tanzania* ... **106 C3** 1 30 S 31 20 E
Ikire, *Nigeria* ... **101 D5** 7 23N 4 15 E
Ikitsuki-Shima, *Japan* ... **62 D1** 33 23N 129 26 E
İkizdere, *Turkey* ... **89 B9** 40 46N 40 32 E
Ikom, *Nigeria* ... **101 D6** 6 0N 8 42 E
Ikopa →, *Madag.* ... **105 B8** 16 45 S 46 40 E
Ikot Ekpene, *Nigeria* ... **101 D6** 5 12N 7 40 E
'Ikrimah, *Libya* ... **96 B4** 32 2N 23 41 E
Ikungu, *Tanzania* ... **106 C3** 1 33 S 33 42 E
Ikuno, *Japan* ... **62 B6** 35 10N 134 48 E
Ikurun, *Nigeria* ... **101 D5** 7 54N 4 40 E
Ila, *Nigeria* ... **101 D5** 8 0N 4 39 E
Ilagan, *Phil.* ... **70 C3** 17 7N 121 53 E
Īlām, *Iran* ... **89 F12** 33 36N 46 36 E
Ilam, *Nepal* ... **81 F12** 26 58N 87 58 E
Ilan, *Taiwan* ... **69 E13** 24 45N 121 44 E
Ilanskiy, *Russia* ... **57 D10** 56 14N 96 3 E
Ilanz, *Switz.* ... **29 C8** 46 46N 9 12 E
Ilaro, *Nigeria* ... **101 D5** 6 53N 3 3 E
Iława, *Poland* ... **47 B6** 53 36N 19 34 E
Ilayangudi, *India* ... **83 K4** 9 34N 78 37 E
Ilbilbie, *Australia* ... **114 C4** 21 45 S 149 20 E
Ile-à-la-Crosse, *Canada* .. **131 B7** 55 27N 107 53W
Ile-à-la-Crosse, Lac, *Canada* ... **131 B7** 55 40N 107 45W
Île-de-France, *France* ... **23 D9** 49 0N 2 20 E
Ilebo, *Zaïre* ... **103 C4** 4 17 S 20 55 E
Ileje □, *Tanzania* ... **107 D3** 9 30 S 33 25 E
Ilek, *Russia* ... **54 F4** 51 32N 53 21 E
Ilek →, *Russia* ... **54 F4** 51 30N 53 22 E
Ilero, *Nigeria* ... **101 D5** 8 0N 3 20 E
Ilesha, *Kwara, Nigeria* ... **101 D5** 8 57N 3 28 E
Ilesha, *Oyo, Nigeria* ... **101 D5** 7 37N 4 40 E
Ilford, *Canada* ... **131 B9** 56 4N 95 35W
Ilfracombe, *Australia* ... **114 C3** 23 30 S 144 30 E
Ilfracombe, *U.K.* ... **17 F3** 51 12N 4 8W
Ilgaz, *Turkey* ... **88 B5** 40 55N 33 37 E
Ilgaz Dağları, *Turkey* ... **88 B5** 41 10N 33 50 E
Ilgın, *Turkey* ... **88 C4** 38 16N 31 55 E
Ilha Grande, *Brazil* ... **153 D4** 0 27 S 65 2W
Ilha Grande, B. da, *Brazil* **155 F3** 23 9 S 44 30W
Ílhavo, *Portugal* ... **36 E2** 40 33N 8 43W
Ilhéus, *Brazil* ... **155 D4** 14 49 S 39 2W
Ili →, *Kazakstan* ... **55 A8** 45 53N 77 10 E
Ilia, *Romania* ... **46 D3** 45 57N 22 40 E
Ilía □, *Greece* ... **45 G3** 37 45N 21 35 E
Iliç, *Turkey* ... **89 C8** 39 27N 38 33 E
Ilich, *Kazakstan* ... **55 C4** 40 50N 68 27 E
Ilichevsk, *Azerbaijan* ... **89 C11** 39 22N 45 5 E
Iliff, *U.S.A.* ... **138 E3** 40 45N 103 4W
Iligan, *Phil.* ... **71 G5** 8 12N 124 13 E
Iligan Bay, *Phil.* ... **71 G5** 8 25N 124 5 E
Ilíki, L., *Greece* ... **45 F5** 38 24N 23 15 E
Ilin I., *Phil.* ... **70 E3** 12 14N 121 5 E
Iliodhrómia, *Greece* ... **44 E5** 39 12N 23 50 E
Ilion, *U.S.A.* ... **137 D9** 43 1N 75 2W
Ilirska-Bistrica, *Slovenia* . **39 C11** 45 34N 14 14 E
Ilkal, *India* ... **83 G3** 15 57N 76 8 E
Ilkeston, *U.K.* ... **16 E6** 52 58N 1 19W
Illampu = Ancohuma, Nevada, *Bolivia* ... **156 D4** 16 0 S 68 50W
Illana B., *Phil.* ... **71 H4** 7 35N 123 45 E
Illapel, *Chile* ... **158 C1** 32 0 S 71 10W
Ille-et-Vilaine □, *France* . **22 D5** 48 10N 1 30W
Ille-sur-Têt, *France* ... **24 F6** 42 40N 2 38 E
Iller →, *Germany* ... **27 G5** 48 23N 9 58 E
Illescas, *Spain* ... **36 E7** 40 8N 3 51W
Illetas, *Spain* ... **33 B9** 39 32N 2 35 E
Illichivsk, *Ukraine* ... **51 J6** 46 20N 30 35 E
Illiers-Combray, *France* .. **22 D8** 48 18N 1 15 E
Illimani, *Bolivia* ... **156 D4** 16 30 S 67 50W
Illinois □, *U.S.A.* ... **140 D7** 40 15N 89 30W
Illinois →, *U.S.A.* ... **140 F6** 38 58N 90 28W
Illiopolis, *U.S.A.* ... **140 E7** 39 51N 89 15W
Illium = Troy, *Turkey* ... **88 C2** 39 57N 26 12 E
Illizi, *Algeria* ... **99 C6** 26 31N 8 32 E
Illora, *Spain* ... **37 H7** 37 17N 3 53W
Ilm →, *Germany* ... **26 D7** 51 6N 11 40 E
Ilmajoki, *Finland* ... **13 E20** 62 44N 22 34 E
Ilmen, Ozero, *Russia* ... **50 C6** 58 15N 31 10 E
Ilmenau, *Germany* ... **26 E6** 50 41N 10 54 E
Ilo, *Peru* ... **156 D3** 17 40 S 71 20W
Ilobu, *Nigeria* ... **101 D5** 7 45N 4 25 E
Ilocos Norte □, *Phil.* ... **70 B3** 18 10N 120 45 E
Ilocos Sur □, *Phil.* ... **70 C3** 17 20N 120 35 E
Iloilo, *Phil.* ... **71 F4** 10 45N 122 33 E
Iloilo □, *Phil.* ... **71 F4** 11 0N 122 40 E
Ilok, *Croatia* ... **42 B4** 45 15N 19 20 E
Ilora, *Nigeria* ... **101 D5** 7 45N 3 50 E
Ilorin, *Nigeria* ... **101 D5** 8 30N 4 35 E
Ilovatka, *Russia* ... **52 E7** 50 30N 45 50 E
Ilovlya, *Russia* ... **53 F7** 49 15N 44 2 E
Ilovlya →, *Russia* ... **53 F7** 49 14N 44 0 E
Iłowa, *Poland* ... **47 D2** 51 30N 15 10 E
Ilubabor □, *Ethiopia* ... **95 F3** 7 25N 35 0 E
Ilva Mică, *Romania* ... **46 B5** 47 17N 24 40 E
Ilwaco, *U.S.A.* ... **144 D2** 46 19N 124 3W
Ilwaki, *Indonesia* ... **72 C3** 7 55 S 126 30 E
Ilyichevsk = Illichivsk, *Ukraine* ... **51 J6** 46 20N 30 35 E
Iłża, *Poland* ... **47 D8** 51 10N 21 15 E
Iłżanka →, *Poland* ... **47 D8** 51 14N 21 48 E
Imabari, *Japan* ... **62 C5** 34 4N 133 0 E
Imaichi, *Japan* ... **63 A11** 36 43N 139 46 E
Imaloto →, *Madag.* ... **105 C8** 23 27 S 45 13 E
İmamoğlu, *Turkey* ... **88 D6** 37 15N 35 38 E
Imandra, Ozero, *Russia* . **48 A5** 67 30N 33 0 E
Imari, *Japan* ... **62 D1** 33 15N 129 52 E
Imasa, *Sudan* ... **94 D4** 18 0N 36 12 E
Imathía □, *Greece* ... **44 D4** 40 30N 22 15 E
Imatra, *Finland* ... **50 B5** 61 12N 28 48 E
Imbâbah, *Egypt* ... **94 H7** 30 5N 31 12 E
Imbabura □, *Ecuador* ... **152 C2** 0 30N 78 45W
Imbaimadai, *Guyana* ... **153 B5** 5 44N 60 17W
Imbler, *U.S.A.* ... **142 D5** 45 28N 117 58W
Imdahane, *Morocco* ... **98 B3** 32 8N 7 0W
imeni 26 Bakinskikh Komissarov = Neftçala, *Azerbaijan* ... **89 C13** 39 19N 49 12 E
imeni 26 Bakinskikh Komissarov, *Turkmenistan* ... **49 G9** 39 22N 54 10 E
Imeni Panfilova, *Kazakstan* ... **55 B8** 43 23N 77 7 E
Imeni Poliny Osipenko, *Russia* ... **57 D14** 52 30N 136 29 E
Imeri, Serra, *Brazil* ... **152 C4** 0 50N 65 25W
Imerimandroso, *Madag.* .. **105 B8** 17 26 S 48 35 E
Imesan, *Mauritania* ... **98 D1** 22 54N 15 30W
Imi, *Ethiopia* ... **90 F3** 6 28N 42 10 E
Imishly = Imişli, *Azerbaijan* ... **53 L9** 39 55N 48 4 E
Imişli, *Azerbaijan* ... **53 L9** 39 55N 48 4 E
Imitek, *Morocco* ... **98 C3** 29 43N 8 10W
Imlay, *U.S.A.* ... **142 F4** 40 40N 118 9W
Imlay City, *U.S.A.* ... **136 C1** 43 2N 83 5W
Immenstadt, *Germany* ... **27 H6** 47 33N 10 13 E
Immingham, *U.K.* ... **16 D7** 53 37N 0 13W
Immokalee, *U.S.A.* ... **135 M5** 26 25N 81 25W
Imo □, *Nigeria* ... **101 D6** 5 30N 7 10 E
Imola, *Italy* ... **39 D8** 44 20N 11 42 E
Imotski, *Croatia* ... **42 D2** 43 27N 17 12 E
Imperatriz, *Amazonas, Brazil* ... **156 B4** 5 18 S 67 11W
Imperatriz, *Maranhão, Brazil* ... **154 C2** 5 30 S 47 29W
Impéria, *Italy* ... **38 E5** 43 53N 8 3 E
Imperial, *Canada* ... **131 C7** 51 21N 105 28W
Imperial, *Peru* ... **156 C2** 13 4 S 76 21W
Imperial, *Calif., U.S.A.* ... **145 N11** 32 51N 115 34W
Imperial, *Nebr., U.S.A.* ... **138 E4** 40 31N 101 39W
Imperial Beach, *U.S.A.* .. **145 N9** 32 35N 117 8W
Imperial Dam, *U.S.A.* ... **145 N12** 32 55N 114 25W
Imperial Reservoir, *U.S.A.* ... **145 N12** 32 53N 114 28W
Imperial Valley, *U.S.A.* .. **145 N11** 33 0N 115 30W
Imperieuse Reef, *Australia* **112 C2** 17 36 S 118 50 E
Impfondo, *Congo* ... **102 B3** 1 40N 18 0 E
Imphal, *India* ... **78 C4** 24 48N 93 56 E
Imphy, *France* ... **24 B7** 46 55N 3 16 E
İmranlı, *Turkey* ... **89 C8** 39 54N 38 7 E
İmroz = Gökçeada, *Turkey* ... **88 B1** 40 10N 25 50 E
Imst, *Austria* ... **30 D3** 47 15N 10 44 E
Imuruan B., *Phil.* ... **71 F2** 10 40N 119 10 E
In Belbel, *Algeria* ... **99 C5** 27 55N 1 12 E
In Delimane, *Mali* ... **101 B5** 15 52N 1 31 E
In Rhar, *Algeria* ... **99 C5** 27 10N 1 59 E
In Salah, *Algeria* ... **99 C5** 27 10N 2 32 E
In Tallak, *Mali* ... **101 B5** 16 19N 3 15 E
Ina, *Japan* ... **63 B9** 35 50N 137 55 E
Ina-Bonchi, *Japan* ... **63 B9** 35 45N 137 58 E
Inagauan, *Phil.* ... **71 G2** 9 33N 118 39 E
Inajá, *Brazil* ... **154 C4** 8 54 S 37 49W
Inangahua Junction, *N.Z.* **119 B6** 41 52 S 171 59 E
Inanwatan, *Indonesia* ... **73 B4** 2 10 S 132 14 E
Iñapari, *Peru* ... **156 C4** 11 0 S 69 40W
Inarajan, *Guam* ... **121 R15** 13 16N 144 45 E
Inari, *Finland* ... **12 B22** 68 54N 27 5 E
Inarijärvi, *Finland* ... **12 B22** 69 0N 28 0 E
Inawashiro-Ko, *Japan* ... **60 F10** 37 29N 140 6 E
Inazawa, *Japan* ... **63 B8** 35 15N 136 47 E
Inca, *Spain* ... **33 B9** 39 43N 2 54 E
Incaguasi, *Chile* ... **158 B1** 29 12 S 71 5W
İnce Burun, *Turkey* ... **88 A6** 42 7N 34 56 E
İncekum Burnu, *Turkey* .. **88 D5** 36 13N 33 57 E
Inchon, *S. Korea* ... **67 F14** 37 27N 126 40 E
Incio, *Spain* ... **36 C3** 42 39N 7 21W
Incirliova, *Turkey* ... **88 D2** 37 50N 27 41 E
Incomáti →, *Mozam.* ... **105 D5** 25 46 S 32 43 E
Inda Silase, *Ethiopia* ... **95 E4** 14 10N 38 15 E
Indalsälven →, *Sweden* .. **14 B11** 62 36N 17 30 E
Indaw, *Burma* ... **78 C6** 24 15N 96 5 E
Indbir, *Ethiopia* ... **95 F4** 8 7N 37 52 E
Independence, *Calif., U.S.A.* ... **144 J8** 36 48N 118 12W
Independence, *Iowa, U.S.A.* ... **140 B5** 42 28N 91 54W
Independence, *Kans., U.S.A.* ... **139 G7** 37 14N 95 42W
Independence, *Ky., U.S.A.* ... **141 F12** 38 57N 84 33W
Independence, *Mo., U.S.A.* ... **140 E2** 39 6N 94 25W
Independence, *Oreg., U.S.A.* ... **142 D2** 44 51N 123 11W
Independence Fjord, *Greenland* ... **6 A6** 82 10N 29 0W
Independence Mts., *U.S.A.* ... **142 F5** 41 20N 116 0W
Independência, *Brazil* ... **154 C3** 5 23 S 40 19W
Independenţa, *Romania* ... **46 D8** 45 25N 27 42 E
Index, *U.S.A.* ... **144 C5** 47 50N 121 33W
India ■, *Asia* ... **59 G11** 20 0N 78 0 E
Indian →, *U.S.A.* ... **135 M5** 27 59N 80 34W
Indian Cabins, *Canada* .. **130 B5** 59 52N 117 40W
Indian Harbour, *Canada* . **129 B8** 54 27N 57 13W
Indian Head, *Canada* ... **131 C8** 50 30N 103 41W
Indian Ocean ... **58 K11** 5 0 S 75 0 E
Indian Springs, *U.S.A.* ... **145 J11** 36 35N 115 40W
Indiana, *U.S.A.* ... **136 F5** 40 37N 79 9W
Indiana □, *U.S.A.* ... **141 D11** 40 0N 86 0W
Indianapolis, *U.S.A.* ... **141 E10** 39 46N 86 9W
Indianola, *Iowa, U.S.A.* .. **140 C3** 41 22N 93 34W
Indianola, *Miss., U.S.A.* . **139 J9** 33 27N 90 39W
Indiapora, *Brazil* ... **155 E1** 19 57 S 50 17W
Indiga, *Russia* ... **48 A8** 67 38N 49 9 E
Indigirka →, *Russia* ... **57 B15** 70 48N 148 54 E
Indija, *Serbia, Yug.* ... **42 B5** 45 6N 20 7 E
Indio, *U.S.A.* ... **145 M10** 33 43N 116 13W
Indispensable Strait, *Solomon Is.* ... **121 M11** 9 0 S 160 30 E
Indonesia ■, *Asia* ... **75 C4** 5 0 S 115 0 E
Indore, *India* ... **80 H6** 22 42N 75 53 E
Indramayu, *Indonesia* ... **75 D3** 6 20 S 108 19 E
Indravati →, *India* ... **82 E5** 19 20N 80 20 E
Indre □, *France* ... **23 F8** 46 50N 1 39 E
Indre →, *France* ... **22 E7** 47 16N 0 11 E
Indre-et-Loire □, *France* . **22 E7** 47 20N 0 40 E
Indungo, *Angola* ... **103 E3** 14 48 S 16 17 E
Indus →, *Pakistan* ... **79 D2** 24 20N 67 47 E
Indus, Mouth of the, *Pakistan* ... **79 E3** 24 0N 68 0 E
Industry, *U.S.A.* ... **140 D6** 40 20N 90 36W
İnebolu, *Turkey* ... **88 B5** 41 55N 33 40 E
İnegöl, *Turkey* ... **88 B3** 40 5N 29 31 E
Inés, Mt., *Argentina* ... **160 C3** 48 30 S 69 40W
Ineu, *Romania* ... **46 C2** 46 26N 21 51 E
Inezgane, *Morocco* ... **98 B3** 30 25N 9 29W
Infanta, *Phil.* ... **70 D3** 14 45N 121 39 E
Infantes, *Spain* ... **35 G1** 38 43N 3 1W
Infiernillo, Presa del, *Mexico* ... **146 D4** 18 9N 102 0W
Infiesto, *Spain* ... **36 B5** 43 21N 5 21W
Inganda, *Zaïre* ... **102 C4** 0 5 S 20 57 E
Ingapirca, *Ecuador* ... **152 D2** 2 38 S 78 56W
Ingelmunster, *Belgium* ... **21 G2** 50 56N 3 16 E
Ingende, *Zaïre* ... **102 C3** 0 12 S 18 57 E
Ingeniero Jacobacci, *Argentina* ... **160 B3** 41 20 S 69 36W
Ingenio, *Canary Is.* ... **33 G4** 27 55N 15 26W
Ingenio Santa Ana, *Argentina* ... **158 B2** 27 25 S 65 40W
Ingersoll, *Canada* ... **136 C4** 43 4N 80 55W
Ingham, *Australia* ... **114 B4** 18 43 S 146 10 E
Ingichka, *Uzbekistan* ... **55 D2** 39 47N 65 58 E
Ingleborough, *U.K.* ... **16 C5** 54 10N 2 22W
Inglewood, *Queens., Australia* ... **115 D5** 28 25 S 151 2 E
Inglewood, *Vic., Australia* **116 D5** 36 29 S 143 53 E
Inglewood, *N.Z.* ... **118 F3** 39 9 S 174 14 E
Inglewood, *U.S.A.* ... **145 M8** 33 58N 118 21W
Ingólfshöfði, *Iceland* ... **12 E5** 63 48N 16 39W
Ingolstadt, *Germany* ... **27 G7** 48 46N 11 26 E
Ingomar, *U.S.A.* ... **142 C10** 46 35N 107 23W
Ingonish, *Canada* ... **129 C7** 46 42N 60 18W
Ingore, *Guinea-Biss.* ... **100 C1** 12 24N 15 48W
Ingraj Bazar, *India* ... **81 G13** 24 58N 88 10 E
Ingrid Christensen Coast, *Antarctica* ... **7 C6** 69 30 S 76 0 E
Ingul → = Inhul →, *Ukraine* ... **51 J7** 46 50N 32 0 E
Ingulec = Inhulec, *Ukraine* ... **51 J7** 47 42N 33 14 E
Ingulets → = Inhulets →, *Ukraine* .. **51 J7** 46 46N 32 47 E
Inguri → = Enguri →, *Georgia* ... **53 J5** 42 27N 41 38 E
Ingushetia □, *Russia* ... **53 J7** 43 20N 44 50 E
Ingwavuma, *S. Africa* ... **105 D5** 27 9 S 31 59 E
Inhaca, I., *Mozam.* ... **105 D5** 26 1 S 32 57 E
Inhafenga, *Mozam.* ... **105 C5** 20 36 S 33 53 E
Inhambane, *Mozam.* ... **105 C6** 23 54 S 35 30 E
Inhambane □, *Mozam.* .. **105 C5** 22 30 S 34 20 E
Inhambupe, *Brazil* ... **155 D4** 11 47 S 38 21W
Inhaminga, *Mozam.* ... **107 F4** 18 26 S 35 0 E
Inharrime, *Mozam.* ... **105 C6** 24 30 S 35 0 E
Inharrime →, *Mozam.* ... **105 C6** 24 30 S 35 0 E
Inhul →, *Ukraine* ... **51 J7** 46 50N 32 0 E
Inhulec, *Ukraine* ... **51 J7** 47 42N 33 14 E
Inhulets →, *Ukraine* ... **51 J7** 46 46N 32 47 E
Inhuma, *Brazil* ... **154 C3** 6 40 S 41 42W
Inhumas, *Brazil* ... **155 E2** 16 22 S 49 30W
Iniesta, *Spain* ... **35 F3** 39 27N 1 45W
Ining = Yining, *China* ... **56 E9** 43 58N 81 10 E
Inini □, *Fr. Guiana* ... **153 C7** 4 0N 53 0W
Inírida →, *Colombia* ... **152 C4** 3 55N 67 52W
Inishbofin, *Ireland* ... **19 C1** 53 37N 10 13W
Inishmore, *Ireland* ... **19 C2** 53 8N 9 45W
Inishowen Pen., *Ireland* .. **19 A4** 55 14N 7 15W
Injune, *Australia* ... **115 D4** 25 53 S 148 32 E
Inklin, *Canada* ... **130 B2** 58 56N 133 5W
Inklin →, *Canada* ... **130 B2** 58 50N 133 10W
Inkom, *U.S.A.* ... **142 E7** 42 48N 112 15W
Inle L., *Burma* ... **78 E6** 20 30N 96 58 E
Inn →, *Austria* ... **27 G9** 48 35N 13 28 E
Innamincka, *Australia* ... **115 D3** 27 44 S 140 46 E
Inner Hebrides, *U.K.* ... **18 D2** 57 0N 6 30W
Inner Mongolia = Nei Monggol Zizhiqu □, *China* ... **66 C6** 42 0N 112 0 E
Inner Sound, *U.K.* ... **18 D3** 57 30N 5 55W
Innerkip, *Canada* ... **136 C4** 43 13N 80 42W
Innerkirchen, *Switz.* ... **28 C6** 46 43N 8 14 E
Innerste →, *Germany* ... **26 C5** 52 45N 9 40 E
Innetalling I., *Canada* ... **128 A4** 56 0N 79 0W
Innisfail, *Australia* ... **114 B4** 17 33 S 146 5 E
Innisfail, *Canada* ... **130 C6** 52 0N 113 57W
In'no-shima, *Japan* ... **62 C5** 34 19N 133 10 E
Innsbruck, *Austria* ... **30 D4** 47 16N 11 23 E
Inny →, *Ireland* ... **19 C4** 53 30N 7 50W
Ino, *Japan* ... **62 D5** 33 33N 133 26 E
Inocência, *Brazil* ... **155 E1** 19 47 S 51 48W
Inongo, *Zaïre* ... **102 C3** 1 55 S 18 30 E
Inoni, *Congo* ... **102 C3** 3 4 S 15 39 E
Inoucdjouac = Inukjuak, *Canada* ... **127 C12** 58 25N 78 15W
Inowrocław, *Poland* ... **47 C5** 52 50N 18 12 E
Inpundong, *N. Korea* ... **67 D14** 41 25N 126 34 E
Inquisivi, *Bolivia* ... **156 D4** 16 50 S 67 10W
Ins, *Switz.* ... **28 B4** 47 1N 7 7 E
Inscription, C., *Australia* **113 E1** 25 29 S 112 59 E
Insein, *Burma* ... **78 G6** 16 50N 96 5 E
Însurăţei, *Romania* ... **46 E8** 44 50N 27 40 E
Inta, *Russia* ... **48 A11** 66 5N 60 8 E
Intendente Alvear, *Argentina* ... **158 D3** 35 12 S 63 32W
Interior, *U.S.A.* ... **138 D4** 43 44N 101 59W
Interlaken, *Switz.* ... **23 F14** 46 41N 7 50 E

212 Izmayil

Izmayil, Ukraine 51 K5 45 22N 28 46 E
İzmir, Turkey 88 C2 38 25N 27 8 E
İzmit, Turkey 88 B3 40 45N 29 50 E
Iznajar, Spain 37 H6 37 15N 4 19W
Iznalloz, Spain 35 H1 37 24N 3 30W
İznik, Turkey 88 B3 40 23N 29 46 E
İznik Gölü, Turkey 88 B3 40 27N 29 30 E
Izobil'nyy, Russia 53 H5 45 25N 41 44 E
Izola, Slovenia 39 C10 45 32N 13 39 E
Izozog, Bañados de, Bolivia 157 D5 18 48 S 62 10W
Izra, Syria 91 C5 32 51N 36 15 E
Iztochni Rodopi, Bulgaria 43 F10 41 45N 25 30 E
Izu-Hantō, Japan 63 C10 34 45N 139 0 E
Izu-Shotō, Japan 61 G10 34 30N 140 0 E
Izuhara, Japan 62 C1 34 12N 129 17 E
Izumi, Japan 62 E2 32 5N 130 22 E
Izumi-sano, Japan 63 C7 34 23N 135 18 E
Izumiotsu, Japan 63 C7 34 30N 135 24 E
Izumo, Japan 62 B4 35 20N 132 46 E
Izyaslav, Ukraine 51 G4 50 5N 26 50 E
Izyum, Ukraine 51 H9 49 12N 37 19 E

J

J.F. Rodrigues, Brazil 154 B1 2 55 S 50 20W
Jaba, Ethiopia 95 F4 6 20N 35 7 E
Jabal el Awlîya, Sudan 95 D3 15 10N 32 31 E
Jabal Lubnān, Lebanon 91 B4 33 45N 35 40 E
Jabalón →, Spain 37 G6 38 53N 4 5W
Jabalpur, India 81 H8 23 9N 79 58 E
Jabbūl, Syria 84 B3 36 4N 37 30 E
Jablah, Syria 88 E6 35 20N 36 0 E
Jablanac, Croatia 39 D11 44 42N 14 56 E
Jablonec, Czech. 30 A8 50 43N 15 10 E
Jablonica, Slovak Rep. 31 C10 48 37N 17 26 E
Jabłonowo, Poland 47 B6 53 23N 19 10 E
Jaboatão, Brazil 154 C4 8 7 S 35 1W
Jabonga, Phil. 71 G5 9 20N 125 32 E
Jaboticabal, Brazil 159 A6 21 15 S 48 17W
Jabukovac, Serbia, Yug. 42 C7 44 22N 22 21 E
Jaburu, Brazil 157 B5 5 30 S 64 0W
Jaca, Spain 34 C4 42 35N 0 33W
Jacaré →, Brazil 154 D3 10 3 S 42 13W
Jacareí, Brazil 159 A6 23 20 S 46 0W
Jacarèzinho, Brazil 159 A6 23 5 S 49 58W
Jáchymov, Czech. 30 A5 50 22N 12 55 E
Jaciara, Brazil 157 D7 15 59 S 54 57W
Jacinto, Brazil 155 E3 16 10 S 40 17W
Jaciparaná, Brazil 157 B5 9 15 S 64 23W
Jackman, U.S.A. 129 C5 45 35N 70 17W
Jacksboro, U.S.A. 139 J5 33 14N 98 15W
Jackson, Australia 115 D4 26 39 S 149 39 E
Jackson, Ala., U.S.A. 135 K2 31 31N 87 53W
Jackson, Calif., U.S.A. 144 G6 38 21N 120 46W
Jackson, Ky., U.S.A. 134 G4 37 33N 83 23W
Jackson, Mich., U.S.A. 141 B12 42 15N 84 24W
Jackson, Minn., U.S.A. 138 D7 43 37N 95 1W
Jackson, Miss., U.S.A. 139 J9 32 18N 90 12W
Jackson, Mo., U.S.A. 139 G10 37 23N 89 40W
Jackson, Ohio, U.S.A. 134 F4 39 3N 82 39W
Jackson, Tenn., U.S.A. 135 H1 35 37N 88 49W
Jackson, Wyo., U.S.A. 142 E8 43 29N 110 46W
Jackson, C., N.Z. 119 A9 40 59 S 174 20 E
Jackson B., N.Z. 119 D3 43 58 S 168 42 E
Jackson Center, U.S.A. 141 D12 40 27N 84 4W
Jackson Hd., N.Z. 119 D3 43 58 S 168 37 E
Jackson L., U.S.A. 142 E8 43 52N 110 36W
Jacksons, N.Z. 119 C6 42 46 S 171 32 E
Jacksonville, Ala., U.S.A. 135 J3 33 49N 85 46W
Jacksonville, Calif., U.S.A. 144 H6 37 52N 120 24W
Jacksonville, Fla., U.S.A. 135 K5 30 20N 81 39W
Jacksonville, Ill., U.S.A. 140 E6 39 44N 90 14W
Jacksonville, N.C., U.S.A. 135 H7 34 45N 77 26W
Jacksonville, Oreg., U.S.A. 142 E2 42 19N 122 57W
Jacksonville, Tex., U.S.A. 139 K7 31 58N 95 17W
Jacksonville Beach, U.S.A. 135 K5 30 17N 81 24W
Jacmel, Haiti 149 C5 18 14N 72 32W
Jacob Lake, U.S.A. 143 H7 36 43N 112 13W
Jacobabad, Pakistan 79 C3 28 20N 68 29 E
Jacobina, Brazil 154 D3 11 11 S 40 30W
Jacques-Cartier, Mt., Canada 129 C6 48 57N 66 0W
Jacqueville, Ivory C. 100 D4 5 12N 4 25W
Jacuí →, Brazil 159 C5 30 2 S 51 15W
Jacumba, U.S.A. 145 N10 32 37N 116 11W
Jacundá →, Brazil 154 B1 1 57 S 50 26W
Jade, Germany 26 B4 53 20N 8 14 E
Jadebusen, Germany 26 B4 53 29N 8 12 E
Jadoigne, Belgium 21 G5 50 43N 4 52 E
Jadotville = Likasi, Zaïre 107 E2 10 55 S 26 48 E
Jadovnik, Serbia, Yug. 42 D4 43 20N 19 45 E
Jadów, Poland 47 C8 52 28N 21 38 E
Jadraque, Spain 34 E2 40 55N 2 55W
Jādū, Libya 96 B2 32 0N 12 0 E
Jaén, Peru 156 B2 5 25 S 78 40W
Jaén, Spain 37 H7 37 44N 3 43W
Jaén □, Spain 37 H7 37 50N 3 30W
Jafène, Africa 98 D3 20 35N 5 30W
Jaffa = Tel Aviv-Yafo, Israel 91 C3 32 4N 34 48 E
Jaffa, C., Australia 116 D3 36 58 S 139 40 E
Jaffna, Sri Lanka 83 K5 9 45N 80 2 E
Jagadhri, India 80 D7 30 10N 77 20 E
Jagadishpur, India 81 G11 25 30N 84 21 E
Jagdalpur, India 82 E5 19 3N 82 0 E
Jagersfontein, S. Africa 104 D4 29 44 S 25 27 E
Jagst →, Germany 27 F5 49 14N 9 10 E
Jagtial, India 82 E4 18 50N 79 0 E
Jaguaquara, Brazil 155 D4 13 32 S 39 58W
Jaguariaíva, Brazil 159 A6 24 10 S 49 50W
Jaguaribe, Brazil 154 C4 5 53 S 38 37W
Jaguaribe →, Brazil 154 B4 4 25 S 37 45W
Jaguaruana, Brazil 154 B4 4 50 S 37 47W
Jagüey Grande, Cuba 148 B3 22 35N 81 7W
Jagungal, Mt., Australia 117 D8 36 8 S 148 22 E
Jahangirabad, India 80 E8 28 19N 78 4 E
Jahrom, Iran 85 D7 28 30N 53 31 E
Jaicós, Brazil 154 C3 7 21 S 41 8W
Jailolo, Indonesia 72 A3 1 5N 127 30 E
Jailolo, Selat, Indonesia 73 A3 0 5N 129 5 E
Jaintiapur, Bangla. 78 C4 25 8N 92 7 E
Jaipur, India 80 F6 27 0N 75 50 E
Jäjarm, Iran 85 B8 36 58N 56 27 E
Jajce, Bos.-H. 42 C2 44 19N 17 17 E
Jajpur, India 82 D8 20 53N 86 22 E
Jakarta, Indonesia 74 D3 6 9 S 106 49 E
Jakobstad = Pietarsaari, Finland 12 E20 63 40N 22 43 E
Jakupica, Macedonia 42 F6 41 45N 21 22 E
Jal, U.S.A. 139 J3 32 7N 103 12W
Jalal-Abad, Kyrgyzstan 55 C6 40 56N 73 0 E
Jalalabad, Afghan. 79 B3 34 30N 70 29 E
Jalalabad, India 81 F8 27 41N 79 42 E
Jalalpur Jattan, Pakistan 80 C6 32 38N 74 11 E
Jalama, U.S.A. 145 L6 34 29N 120 29W
Jalapa, Guatemala 148 D2 14 39N 89 59W
Jalapa Enríquez, Mexico 147 D5 19 32N 96 55W
Jalasjärvi, Finland 13 E20 62 29N 22 47 E
Jalaun, India 81 F8 26 8N 79 25 E
Jaldak, Afghan. 79 C2 31 58N 66 43 E
Jales, Brazil 155 F1 20 10 S 50 33W
Jaleswar, Nepal 81 F11 26 38N 85 48 E
Jalgaon, Maharashtra, India 82 D3 21 2N 76 31 E
Jalgaon, Maharashtra, India 82 D2 21 0N 75 42 E
Jalhay, Belgium 21 G7 50 33N 5 58 E
Jalībah, Iraq 84 D5 30 35N 46 32 E
Jalingo, Nigeria 101 D7 8 55N 11 25 E
Jalisco □, Mexico 146 C4 20 0N 104 0W
Jalkot, Pakistan 81 B5 35 14N 73 24 E
Jallas →, Spain 36 C1 42 54N 9 8W
Jalna, India 82 E2 19 48N 75 38 E
Jalón →, Spain 34 D3 41 47N 1 4W
Jalpa, Mexico 146 C4 21 38N 102 58W
Jalpaiguri, India 78 B2 26 32N 88 46 E
Jalq, Iran 79 D1 27 35N 62 46 E
Jaluit I., Pac. Oc. 122 G8 6 0N 169 30 E
Jalūlā, Iraq 89 E11 34 16N 45 10 E
Jamaari, Nigeria 101 C6 11 44N 9 53 E
Jamaica, U.S.A. 140 C2 41 51N 94 18W
Jamaica ■, W. Indies 148 C4 18 10N 77 30W
Jamalpur, Bangla. 78 C2 24 52N 89 56 E
Jamalpur, India 81 G12 25 18N 86 28 E
Jamalpurganj, India 81 H13 23 2N 88 1 E
Jamanxim →, Brazil 157 A6 4 43 S 56 18W
Jamari, Brazil 157 B5 8 45 S 63 27W
Jamari →, Brazil 157 B5 8 27 S 63 30W
Jambe, Indonesia 73 B4 1 15 S 132 10 E
Jambes, Belgium 21 H5 50 27N 4 52 E
Jambi, Indonesia 74 C2 1 38 S 103 30 E
Jambi □, Indonesia 74 C2 1 30 S 102 30 E
Jambusar, India 80 H5 22 3N 72 51 E
James →, U.S.A. 138 D6 42 52N 97 18W
James B., Canada 127 C11 51 30N 80 0W
James Ras., Australia 112 D5 24 10 S 132 30 E
James Ross I., Antarctica 7 C18 63 58 S 57 50W
Jamesport, U.S.A. 140 E3 39 58N 93 48W
Jamestown, Australia 116 B3 33 10 S 138 32 E
Jamestown, S. Africa 104 E4 31 6 S 26 45 E
Jamestown, Ind., U.S.A. 141 E10 39 56N 86 38W
Jamestown, Ky., U.S.A. 134 G3 36 59N 85 4W
Jamestown, Mo., U.S.A. 140 F4 38 48N 92 30W
Jamestown, N. Dak., U.S.A. 138 B5 46 54N 98 42W
Jamestown, N.Y., U.S.A. 136 D5 42 6N 79 14W
Jamestown, Ohio, U.S.A. 141 E13 39 39N 83 33W
Jamestown, Pa., U.S.A. 136 E4 41 29N 80 27W
Jamestown, Tenn., U.S.A. 135 G3 36 26N 84 56W
Jamīlābād, Iran 85 C6 34 24N 48 28 E
Jamiltepec, Mexico 147 D5 16 17N 97 49W
Jamkhandi, India 82 F2 16 30N 75 15 E
Jammalamadugu, India 83 G4 14 51N 78 25 E
Jammerbugt, Denmark 15 G3 57 15N 9 20 E
Jammu, India 80 C6 32 43N 74 54 E
Jammu & Kashmir □, India 81 B7 34 25N 77 0 E
Jamnagar, India 80 H4 22 30N 70 6 E
Jamner, India 82 D2 20 45N 75 52 E
Jamoigne, Belgium 21 J6 49 41N 5 24 E
Jampur, Pakistan 79 C3 29 39N 70 40 E
Jamrud, Pakistan 79 B3 33 59N 71 24 E
Jämsä, Finland 13 F21 61 53N 25 10 E
Jamshedpur, India 81 H12 22 44N 86 12 E
Jamtara, India 81 H12 23 59N 86 49 E
Jämtland, Sweden 12 E15 63 31N 14 0 E
Jämtlands län □, Sweden 14 B7 62 40N 13 50 E
Jamuna →, Bangla. 78 D2 23 51N 89 45 E
Jamurki, Bangla. 78 C3 24 9N 90 2 E
Jan L., Canada 131 C8 54 56N 102 55W
Jan Mayen, Arctic 6 B7 71 0N 9 0W
Janakkala, Finland 13 F21 60 54N 24 36 E
Janaúba, Brazil 155 E3 15 48 S 43 19W
Janaucu, I., Brazil 154 A1 0 30N 50 10W
Jand, Pakistan 80 C5 33 30N 72 6 E
Janda, L. de la, Spain 37 J5 36 15N 5 45W
Jandaia, Brazil 155 E1 17 6 S 50 7W
Jandaq, Iran 85 C7 34 3N 54 22 E
Jandia, Canary Is. 33 F5 28 6N 14 21W
Jandia, Pta. de, Canary Is. 33 F5 28 3N 14 31W
Jandiatuba →, Brazil 152 D4 3 28 S 68 42W
Jandola, Pakistan 80 C4 32 20N 70 9 E
Jandowae, Australia 115 D5 26 45 S 151 7 E
Jandrain-Jandrenouilles, Belgium 21 G5 50 40N 4 58 E
Jándula →, Spain 37 G6 38 3N 4 6W
Jane Pk., N.Z. 119 F3 45 15 S 168 20 E
Janesville, U.S.A. 140 B7 42 41N 89 1W
Janga, Ghana 101 C4 10 5N 1 0W
Jango, Brazil 157 E6 20 27 S 55 29W
Jangoon, India 82 F4 17 44N 79 5 E
Janhtang Ga, Burma 78 B6 26 32N 96 38 E
Jānī Kheyl, Afghan. 79 B3 32 46N 68 24 E
Janikowo, Poland 47 C5 52 45N 18 7 E
Janīn, West Bank 91 C4 32 28N 35 18 E
Janinà = Ioánnina □, Greece 44 E2 39 39N 20 57 E
Janiuay, Phil. 71 F4 10 58N 122 30 E
Janja, Bos.-H. 42 C4 44 40N 19 17 E
Janjevo, Serbia, Yug. 42 E6 42 35N 21 19 E
Janjina, Croatia 42 E2 42 58N 17 25 E
Janos, Mexico 146 A3 30 45N 108 10W
Jánoshalma, Hungary 31 E12 46 18N 19 21 E
Jánosháza, Hungary 31 D10 47 8N 17 12 E
Jánossomorja, Hungary 31 D10 47 47N 17 11 E
Janów, Poland 47 E6 50 44N 19 27 E
Janów Lubelski, Poland 47 E9 50 48N 22 23 E
Janów Podlaski, Poland 47 C10 52 11N 23 11 E
Janowiec Wielkopolski, Poland 47 C4 52 45N 17 30 E
Januária, Brazil 155 E3 15 25 S 44 25W
Janub Dârfûr □, Sudan 95 E2 11 0N 25 0 E
Janub Kordofân □, Sudan 95 E3 12 0N 30 0 E
Janubio, Canary Is. 33 F6 28 56N 13 50W
Janville, France 23 D8 48 10N 1 50 E
Janzé, France 22 E5 47 55N 1 28W
Jaora, India 80 H6 23 40N 75 10 E
Japan ■, Asia 61 G8 36 0N 136 0 E
Japan, Sea of, Asia 60 E7 40 0N 135 0 E
Japan Trench, Pac. Oc. 58 F18 32 0N 142 0 E
Japen = Yapen, Indonesia 73 B5 1 50 S 136 0 E
Japurá →, Brazil 152 D4 3 8 S 65 46W
Jaque, Panama 152 B2 7 27N 78 8W
Jarābulus, Syria 89 D8 36 49N 38 1 E
Jaraguá, Brazil 155 E2 15 45 S 49 20W
Jaraguari, Brazil 157 E7 20 9 S 54 35W
Jaraicejo, Spain 37 F5 39 40N 5 49W
Jaraiz, Spain 36 E5 40 4N 5 45W
Jarama →, Spain 34 E1 40 24N 3 32W
Jaramānah, Syria 88 F7 33 29N 36 21 E
Jaramillo, Argentina 160 C3 47 10 S 67 7W
Jarandilla, Spain 36 E5 40 8N 5 39W
Jaranwala, Pakistan 79 C4 31 15N 73 26 E
Jarash, Jordan 91 C4 32 17N 35 54 E
Jarauçu →, Brazil 153 D7 1 48 S 52 22W
Jardas al 'Abīd, Libya 96 B4 32 18N 20 59 E
Jardim, Brazil 158 A4 21 28 S 56 2W
Jardín →, Spain 35 G2 38 50N 2 10W
Jardines de la Reina, Is., Cuba 148 B4 20 50N 78 50W
Jargalang, China 67 C12 43 5N 122 55 E
Jargalant = Hovd, Mongolia 64 B4 48 2N 91 37 E
Jargeau, France 23 E9 47 50N 2 1 E
Jari →, Brazil 153 D7 1 9 S 51 54W
Jarīr, W. al →, Si. Arabia 84 E4 25 38N 42 30 E
Jarmen, Germany 26 B9 53 54N 13 20 E
Jarnac, France 24 C3 45 40N 0 11W
Jarny, France 23 C12 49 9N 5 53 E
Jaro, Phil. 71 F5 11 11N 124 47 E
Jarocin, Poland 47 D4 51 59N 17 29 E
Jaroměr, Czech. 30 A8 50 22N 15 52 E
Jarosław, Poland 31 A15 50 2N 22 42 E
Järpås, Sweden 15 F6 58 23N 12 57 E
Järpen, Sweden 14 A7 63 21N 13 26 E
Jarqūrghon, Uzbekistan 55 E3 37 31N 67 25 E
Jarrahdale, Australia 113 F2 32 24 S 116 5 E
Jarres, Plaine des, Laos 76 C4 19 27N 103 10 E
Jarso, Ethiopia 95 F4 5 15N 37 30 E
Jartai, China 66 E3 39 45N 105 48 E
Jaru, Brazil 157 C5 10 26 S 62 27W
Jaru →, Brazil 157 C5 10 5 S 61 59W
Jarud Qi, China 67 B11 44 28N 120 50 E
Järvenpää, Finland 13 F21 60 29N 25 5 E
Jarvis, Canada 136 D4 42 53N 80 6W
Jarvis I., Pac. Oc. 123 H12 0 15 S 159 55W
Jarvornik, Czech. 31 A10 50 23N 17 2 E
Jarwa, India 81 F10 27 38N 82 30 E
Jaša Tomić, Serbia, Yug. 42 B5 45 26N 20 50 E
Jasaan, Phil. 71 G5 8 39N 124 45 E
Jasien, Poland 47 D2 51 46N 15 0 E
Jāsimīyah, Iraq 89 F11 33 45N 44 41 E
Jasin, Malaysia 77 L4 2 20N 102 26 E
Jāsk, Iran 85 E8 25 38N 57 45 E
Jasło, Poland 31 B14 49 45N 21 30 E
Jason, Is., Falk. Is. 160 D4 51 0 S 61 0W
Jasonville, U.S.A. 141 E9 39 10N 87 12W
Jasper, Alta., Canada 130 C5 52 55N 118 5W
Jasper, Ont., Canada 137 B9 44 52N 75 57W
Jasper, Ala., U.S.A. 135 J2 33 50N 87 17W
Jasper, Fla., U.S.A. 135 K4 30 31N 82 57W
Jasper, Ind., U.S.A. 141 F10 38 24N 86 56W
Jasper, Minn., U.S.A. 138 D6 43 51N 96 24W
Jasper, Tex., U.S.A. 139 K8 30 56N 94 1W
Jasper Nat. Park, Canada 130 C5 52 50N 118 8W
Jastrebarsko, Croatia 39 C12 45 41N 15 39 E
Jastrowie, Poland 47 B3 53 26N 16 49 E
Jastrzębie Zdrój, Poland 31 B11 49 57N 18 35 E
Jászapáti, Hungary 31 D13 47 32N 20 10 E
Jászárokszállás, Hungary 31 D13 47 39N 20 1 E
Jászberény, Hungary 31 D12 47 30N 19 55 E
Jászkiser, Hungary 31 D13 47 27N 20 20 E
Jászladány, Hungary 31 D13 47 23N 20 10 E
Jataí, Brazil 155 E1 17 58 S 51 48W
Jatapu →, Brazil 153 D6 2 13 S 58 17W
Jati, Pakistan 80 G3 24 20N 68 19 E
Jatibarang, Indonesia 75 D3 6 28 S 108 18 E
Jatinegara, Indonesia 74 D3 6 13 S 106 52 E
Játiva, Spain 35 G4 39 0N 0 32W
Jatobal, Brazil 154 B2 4 35 S 49 33W
Jáu, Angola 103 F2 15 12 S 13 31 E
Jaú, Brazil 159 A6 22 10 S 48 30W
Jaú →, Brazil 153 D5 1 54 S 61 26W
Jauaperí →, Brazil 153 D5 1 26 S 61 35W
Jauche, Belgium 21 G5 50 41N 4 57 E
Jauja, Peru 156 C2 11 45 S 75 15W
Jaunpur, India 81 G10 25 46N 82 44 E
Jauru →, Brazil 157 D6 16 22 S 57 46W
Java = Jawa, Indonesia 75 D4 7 0 S 110 0 E
Java Sea, Indonesia 75 C3 4 35 S 107 15 E
Java Trench, Ind. Oc. 74 D2 9 0 S 105 0 E
Javadi Hills, India 83 H4 12 40N 78 40 E
Jávea, Spain 35 G5 38 48N 0 10 E
Javhlant = Ulyasutay, Mongolia 64 B4 47 56N 97 28 E
Javier, I., Chile 160 C2 47 5 S 74 25W
Javla, India 82 F2 17 18N 75 9 E
Javron, France 22 D6 48 25N 0 25W
Jawa, Indonesia 75 D4 7 0 S 110 0 E
Jawf, W. al →, Yemen 86 D4 15 50N 45 30 E
Jawor, Poland 47 D3 51 4N 16 11 E
Jaworzno, Poland 31 A12 50 13N 19 11 E
Jay, U.S.A. 139 G7 36 25N 94 48W
Jaya, Puncak, Indonesia 73 B5 3 57 S 137 17 E
Jayanca, Peru 156 B2 6 24 S 79 50W
Jayanti, India 78 B2 26 45N 89 40 E
Jayapura, Indonesia 73 B6 2 28 S 140 38 E
Jayawijaya, Pegunungan, Indonesia 73 B5 5 0 S 139 0 E
Jayrūd, Syria 88 F7 33 49N 36 44 E
Jayton, U.S.A. 139 J4 33 15N 100 34W
Jazīreh-ye Shīf, Iran 85 D6 29 4N 50 54 E
Jazminal, Mexico 146 C4 24 56N 101 25W
Jazzīn, Lebanon 91 B4 33 31N 35 35 E
Jean, U.S.A. 145 K11 35 47N 115 20W
Jean Marie River, Canada 130 A4 61 32N 120 38W
Jean Rabel, Haiti 149 C5 19 50N 73 5W
Jeanerette, U.S.A. 139 L9 29 55N 91 40W
Jeanette, Ostrov, Russia 57 B16 76 43N 158 0 E
Jeannette, U.S.A. 136 F5 40 20N 79 36W
Jebba, Morocco 98 A4 35 11N 4 43W
Jebba, Nigeria 101 D5 9 9N 4 48 E
Jebel, Bahr el →, Sudan 95 F3 9 30N 30 25 E
Jebel Qerri, Sudan 95 D3 16 16N 32 50 E
Jeberos, Peru 156 B2 5 15 S 76 10W
Jedburgh, U.K. 18 F6 55 29N 2 33W
Jedda = Jiddah, Si. Arabia 86 B2 21 29N 39 10 E
Jedlicze, Poland 31 B14 49 43N 21 40 E
Jedlnia-Letnisko, Poland 47 D8 51 25N 21 19 E
Jędrzejów, Poland 47 E7 50 35N 20 15 E
Jedwabne, Poland 47 B9 53 17N 22 18 E
Jedway, Canada 130 C2 52 17N 131 14W
Jeetzel →, Germany 26 B7 53 9N 11 3 E
Jefferson, Iowa, U.S.A. 140 B2 42 1N 94 23W
Jefferson, Ohio, U.S.A. 136 E4 41 44N 80 46W
Jefferson, Tex., U.S.A. 139 J7 32 46N 94 21W
Jefferson, Wis., U.S.A. 138 D10 43 0N 88 48W
Jefferson, Mt., Nev., U.S.A. 142 G5 38 51N 117 0W
Jefferson, Mt., Oreg., U.S.A. 142 D3 44 41N 121 48W
Jefferson City, Mo., U.S.A. 140 F4 38 34N 92 10W
Jefferson City, Tenn., U.S.A. 135 G4 36 7N 83 30W
Jeffersontown, U.S.A. 141 F11 38 12N 85 35W
Jeffersonville, Ind., U.S.A. 141 F11 38 17N 85 44W
Jeffersonville, Ohio, U.S.A. 141 E13 39 39N 83 34W
Jega, Nigeria 101 C5 12 15N 4 23 E
Jēkabpils, Latvia 13 H21 56 29N 25 57 E
Jelenia Góra, Poland 47 E2 50 50N 15 45 E
Jelenia Góra □, Poland 47 D2 51 0N 15 30 E
Jelgava, Latvia 13 H20 56 41N 23 49 E
Jelica, Serbia, Yug. 42 D5 43 50N 20 17 E
Jelli, Sudan 95 F3 5 25N 31 45 E
Jellicoe, Canada 128 C2 49 40N 87 30W
Jelšava, Slovak Rep. 31 C13 48 37N 20 15 E
Jemaja, Indonesia 74 B3 3 5N 105 45 E
Jemaluang, Malaysia 77 L4 2 16N 103 52 E
Jemappes, Belgium 21 H3 50 27N 3 54 E
Jember, Indonesia 75 D4 8 11 S 113 41 E
Jemeppe, Belgium 21 G7 50 37N 5 30 E
Jemnice, Czech. 30 B8 49 1N 15 34 E
Jena, Germany 26 E7 50 54N 11 35 E
Jena, U.S.A. 139 K8 31 41N 92 8W
Jenbach, Austria 30 D4 47 24N 11 47 E
Jendouba, Tunisia 96 A1 36 29N 8 47 E
Jenkins, U.S.A. 134 G4 37 10N 82 38W
Jenner, U.S.A. 144 G3 38 27N 123 7W
Jennings, La., U.S.A. 139 K8 30 13N 92 40W
Jennings, Mo., U.S.A. 140 F6 38 43N 90 16W
Jennings →, Canada 130 B2 59 38N 132 5W
Jepara, Indonesia 75 D3 7 40 S 109 14 E
Jeparit, Australia 116 D5 36 8 S 142 1 E
Jequié, Brazil 155 D3 13 51 S 40 5W
Jequitaí →, Brazil 155 E3 17 4 S 44 50W
Jequitinhonha, Brazil 155 E3 16 30 S 41 0W
Jequitinhonha →, Brazil 155 E4 15 51 S 38 53W
Jerada, Morocco 99 B4 34 17N 2 10W
Jerantut, Malaysia 77 L4 3 56N 102 22 E
Jérémie, Haiti 149 C5 18 40N 74 10W
Jeremoabo, Brazil 154 D4 10 4 S 38 21W
Jerez, Punta, Mexico 147 C5 22 58N 97 40W
Jerez de García Salinas, Mexico 146 C4 22 39N 103 0W
Jerez de la Frontera, Spain 37 J4 36 41N 6 7W
Jerez de los Caballeros, Spain 37 G4 38 20N 6 45W
Jericho = Arīḥā, Syria 84 C3 35 49N 36 35 E
Jericho = El Arīḥā, West Bank 91 D4 31 52N 35 27 E
Jericho, Australia 114 C4 23 38 S 146 6 E
Jerichow, Germany 26 C8 52 30N 12 1 E
Jerico Springs, U.S.A. 140 G2 37 37N 94 1W
Jerilderie, Australia 117 C6 35 20 S 145 41 E
Jermyn, U.S.A. 137 E9 41 31N 75 31W
Jerome, U.S.A. 143 J8 34 45N 112 7W
Jersey, U.K. 17 H5 49 11N 2 7W
Jersey City, U.S.A. 137 F10 40 44N 74 4W
Jersey Shore, U.S.A. 136 E7 41 12N 77 15W
Jerseyville, U.S.A. 140 E6 39 7N 90 20W
Jerusalem, Israel 91 D4 31 47N 35 10 E
Jervis B., Australia 117 C9 35 8 S 150 46 E
Jesenice, Slovenia 39 B11 46 28N 14 3 E
Jeseník, Czech. 31 B10 50 0N 17 8 E
Jesenké, Slovak Rep. 31 C13 48 20N 20 10 E
Jesselton = Kota Kinabalu, Malaysia 75 A5 6 0N 116 4 E
Jessnitz, Germany 26 D8 51 40N 12 18 E
Jessore, Bangla. 78 D2 23 10N 89 10 E
Jesup, Ga., U.S.A. 135 K5 31 36N 81 53W
Jesup, Iowa, U.S.A. 140 B4 42 29N 92 4W
Jesús, Peru 156 B2 7 15 S 78 25W
Jesús Carranza, Mexico 147 D5 17 28N 95 1W
Jesús María, Argentina 158 C3 30 59 S 64 5W
Jetafe, Phil. 71 F5 10 9N 124 9 E
Jetmore, U.S.A. 139 F5 38 4N 99 54W
Jetpur, India 80 J4 21 45N 70 10 E
Jette, Belgium 21 G4 50 53N 4 20 E
Jevnaker, Norway 14 D4 60 15N 10 26 E
Jewell, U.S.A. 140 B3 42 20N 93 39W
Jewett, Ohio, U.S.A. 136 F3 40 22N 81 2W
Jewett, Tex., U.S.A. 139 K6 31 22N 96 9W
Jewett City, U.S.A. 137 E13 41 36N 72 0W
Jeyḥūnābād, Iran 85 C6 34 58N 48 59 E
Jeypore, India 82 E6 18 50N 82 38 E
Jeziorak, Jezioro, Poland 47 B6 53 40N 19 35 E
Jeziorany, Poland 47 B7 53 58N 20 46 E
Jeziorka →, Poland 47 D7 51 59N 20 57 E
Jhajjar, India 80 E7 28 37N 76 42 E
Jhal Jhao, Pakistan 79 D2 26 20N 65 35 E
Jhalakati, Bangla. 78 D3 22 39N 90 12 E
Jhalawar, India 80 G7 24 40N 76 10 E
Jhang Maghiana, Pakistan 79 C4 31 15N 72 22 E
Jhansi, India 81 G8 25 30N 78 36 E
Jharia, India 81 H12 23 45N 86 26 E
Jharsuguda, India 82 D7 21 56N 84 5 E
Jhelum, Pakistan 79 B4 33 0N 73 45 E

Kabondo 213

Jhelum →, Pakistan 80 D5 31 20N 72 10 E
Jhunjhunu, India 80 E6 28 10N 75 30 E
Ji Xian, Hebei, China 66 F8 37 35N 115 30 E
Ji Xian, Henan, China 66 G8 35 22N 114 5 E
Ji Xian, Shanxi, China 66 F6 36 7N 110 40 E
Jia Xian, Henan, China 66 H7 33 59N 113 12 E
Jia Xian, Shaanxi, China 66 E6 38 12N 110 28 E
Jiading, China 69 B13 31 22N 121 15 E
Jiahe, China 69 E9 25 38N 112 19 E
Jialing Jiang →, China 68 C6 29 30N 106 20 E
Jiamusi, China 65 B8 46 40N 130 26 E
Ji'an, Jiangxi, China 69 D10 27 6N 114 59 E
Ji'an, Jilin, China 67 D14 41 5N 126 10 E
Jianchang, China 67 D11 40 55N 120 35 E
Jianchangying, China 67 D10 40 10N 118 50 E
Jianchuan, China 68 D2 26 38N 99 55 E
Jiande, China 69 C12 29 23N 119 15 E
Jiangbei, China 68 C6 29 40N 106 34 E
Jiangcheng, China 68 F3 22 36N 101 52 E
Jiangdi, China 68 D4 26 57N 103 37 E
Jiange, China 68 A5 32 4N 105 32 E
Jiangjin, China 68 C6 29 14N 106 14 E
Jiangkou, China 68 D7 27 40N 108 49 E
Jiangle, China 69 D11 26 42N 117 23 E
Jiangling, China 69 B9 30 25N 112 12 E
Jiangmen, China 69 F9 22 32N 113 0 E
Jiangshan, China 69 C12 28 40N 118 37 E
Jiangsu □, China 67 H10 33 0N 120 0 E
Jiangxi □, China 69 D10 27 30N 116 0 E
Jiangyin, China 69 B13 31 54N 120 17 E
Jiangyong, China 69 E8 25 20N 111 22 E
Jiangyou, China 68 B5 31 44N 104 43 E
Jianhe, China 68 D7 26 37N 108 31 E
Jianli, China 69 C9 29 46N 112 56 E
Jianning, China 69 D11 26 50N 116 50 E
Jian'ou, China 69 D12 27 3N 118 17 E
Jianshi, China 68 B7 30 37N 109 38 E
Jianshui, China 68 F4 23 36N 102 43 E
Jianyang, Fujian, China 69 D12 27 20N 118 5 E
Jianyang, Sichuan, China 68 B5 30 24N 104 33 E
Jiao Xian, China 67 F11 36 18N 120 1 E
Jiaohe, Hebei, China 66 E9 38 2N 116 20 E
Jiaohe, Jilin, China 67 C14 43 40N 127 22 E
Jiaoling, China 69 E11 24 41N 116 12 E
Jiaozhou Wan, China 67 F11 36 5N 120 10 E
Jiaozuo, China 66 G7 35 16N 113 12 E
Jiashan, China 69 A11 32 46N 117 59 E
Jiawang, China 67 G9 34 28N 117 26 E
Jiaxiang, China 66 G9 35 25N 116 20 E
Jiaxing, China 69 B13 30 49N 120 45 E
Jiayi = Chiai, Taiwan 69 F13 23 29N 120 25 E
Jiayu, China 69 C9 29 55N 113 55 E
Jibão, Serra do, Brazil 155 D3 14 48 S 45 0W
Jibiya, Nigeria 101 C6 13 5N 7 12 E
Jibou, Romania 46 B4 47 15N 23 17 E
Jibuti = Djibouti ■, Africa 90 E3 12 0N 43 0 E
Jicarón, I., Panama 148 E3 7 10N 81 50W
Jičín, Czech. 30 A8 50 25N 15 28 E
Jiddah, Si. Arabia 86 B2 21 29N 39 10 E
Jieshou, China 66 H8 33 18N 115 22 E
Jiexiu, China 66 F6 37 2N 111 55 E
Jieyang, China 69 F11 23 35N 116 21 E
Jigawa □, Nigeria 101 C6 12 0N 9 45 E
Jiggalong, Australia 112 D3 23 21 S 120 47 E
Jihlava, Czech. 30 B8 49 28N 15 35 E
Jihlava →, Czech. 30 C9 48 55N 16 36 E
Jihočeský □, Czech. 30 B7 49 8N 14 35 E
Jihomoravský □, Czech. 31 B9 49 5N 16 30 E
Jijel, Algeria 99 A6 36 52N 5 50 E
Jijiga, Ethiopia 108 C2 9 20N 42 50 E
Jijona, Spain 35 G4 38 34N 0 30W
Jikamshi, Nigeria 101 C6 12 12N 7 45 E
Jilin, China 67 C14 43 44N 126 30 E
Jilin □, China 67 C13 44 0N 127 0 E
Jiloca →, Spain 34 D3 41 21N 1 39W
Jilong = Chilung, Taiwan 69 E13 25 3N 121 45 E
Jílové, Czech. 30 B7 49 52N 14 29 E
Jima, Ethiopia 95 F4 7 40N 36 47 E
Jimbolia, Romania 46 D1 45 47N 20 43 E
Jimena de la Frontera, Spain 37 J5 36 27N 5 24W
Jimenbuen, Australia 117 D8 36 42 S 148 53 E
Jiménez, Mexico 146 B4 27 10N 104 54W
Jimenez, Phil. 71 G4 8 20N 123 50 E
Jimo, China 67 F11 36 23N 120 30 E
Jin Jiang →, China 69 C10 28 24N 115 48 E
Jin Xian, Hebei, China 66 E8 38 2N 115 2 E
Jin Xian, Liaoning, China 67 E11 38 55N 121 42 E
Jinan, China 66 F9 36 38N 117 1 E
Jincheng, China 66 G7 35 29N 112 50 E
Jinchuan, China 68 B4 31 30N 102 3 E
Jind, India 80 E7 29 19N 76 22 E
Jindabyne, Australia 117 D8 36 25 S 148 35 E
Jindrichuv Hradeç, Czech. 30 B8 49 10N 15 2 E
Jing He →, China 66 G5 34 27N 109 4 E
Jing Shan, China 69 B8 31 20N 111 35 E
Jing Xian, Anhui, China 69 B12 30 38N 118 25 E
Jing Xian, Hunan, China 68 D7 26 33N 109 40 E
Jing'an, China 69 C10 28 50N 115 17 E
Jingbian, China 66 F5 37 20N 108 30 E
Jingchuan, China 66 G4 35 20N 107 20 E
Jingde, China 69 B12 30 15N 118 27 E
Jingdezhen, China 69 C11 29 20N 117 11 E
Jingdong, China 68 E3 24 23N 100 47 E
Jinggu, China 68 F3 23 35N 100 41 E
Jinghai, China 66 E9 38 55N 116 55 E
Jinghong, China 68 F3 22 0N 100 45 E
Jingjiang, China 69 A13 32 2N 120 16 E
Jingle, China 66 E6 38 20N 111 55 E
Jingmen, China 69 B9 31 0N 112 10 E
Jingning, China 66 G3 35 30N 105 43 E
Jingpo Hu, China 67 C15 43 55N 128 55 E
Jingshan, China 69 B9 31 1N 113 7 E
Jingtai, China 66 F3 37 10N 104 6 E
Jingxi, China 68 F6 23 8N 106 27 E
Jingxing, China 66 E8 38 2N 114 8 E
Jingyang, China 66 G5 34 30N 108 50 E
Jingyu, China 67 C14 42 25N 126 45 E
Jingyuan, China 66 F3 36 30N 104 40 E
Jingziguan, China 66 H6 33 15N 111 0 E
Jinhua, China 69 C12 29 8N 119 38 E
Jining, Nei Mongol Zizhiqu, China 66 D7 41 5N 113 0 E
Jining, Shandong, China 66 G9 35 22N 116 34 E
Jinja, Uganda 106 B3 0 25N 33 12 E
Jinjang, Malaysia 77 L3 3 13N 101 39 E
Jinji, China 66 F4 37 58N 106 8 E
Jinjiang, Fujian, China 69 E12 24 43N 118 33 E
Jinjiang, Yunnan, China 68 D3 26 14N 100 34 E
Jinjie, China 68 F6 23 15N 107 18 E
Jinjini, Ghana 100 D4 7 26N 3 42W
Jinkou, China 69 B10 30 20N 114 8 E
Jinmen Dao, China 69 E12 24 25N 118 25 E
Jinning, China 68 E4 24 38N 102 38 E
Jinotega, Nic. 148 D2 13 6N 85 59W
Jinotepe, Nic. 148 D2 11 50N 86 10W
Jinping, Guizhou, China 68 D7 26 41N 109 10 E
Jinping, Yunnan, China 68 F4 22 45N 103 18 E
Jinsha, China 68 D6 27 29N 106 12 E
Jinsha Jiang →, China 68 C5 28 50N 104 36 E
Jinshan, China 69 B13 30 54N 121 10 E
Jinshi, China 69 C8 29 40N 111 50 E
Jintan, China 69 B12 31 42N 119 36 E
Jintotolo Channel, Phil. 71 F4 11 48N 123 5 E
Jinxi, Jiangxi, China 69 D11 27 56N 116 45 E
Jinxi, Liaoning, China 67 D11 40 52N 120 50 E
Jinxian, China 69 C11 28 26N 116 17 E
Jinxiang, China 66 G9 35 5N 116 22 E
Jinyun, China 69 C13 28 35N 120 5 E
Jinzhai, China 69 B10 31 40N 115 53 E
Jinzhou, China 67 D11 41 5N 121 3 E
Jiparaná →, Brazil 157 B5 8 3 S 62 52W
Jipijapa, Ecuador 152 D1 1 0 S 80 40W
Jiquilpan, Mexico 146 D4 19 57N 102 42W
Jirwān, Si. Arabia 87 B5 23 27N 50 53 E
Jishan, China 66 G6 35 34N 110 58 E
Jishou, China 68 C7 28 21N 109 43 E
Jishui, China 69 D10 27 12N 115 8 E
Jisr ash Shughūr, Syria 88 E7 35 49N 36 18 E
Jitarning, Australia 113 F2 32 48 S 117 57 E
Jitra, Malaysia 77 J3 6 16N 100 25 E
Jiu →, Romania 46 F4 43 47N 23 48 E
Jiudengkou, China 66 E4 39 56N 106 40 E
Jiujiang, Guangdong, China 69 F9 22 50N 113 0 E
Jiujiang, Jiangxi, China 69 C10 29 42N 115 58 E
Jiuling Shan, China 69 C10 28 40N 114 40 E
Jiulong, China 68 C3 28 57N 101 31 E
Jiutai, China 67 B13 44 10N 125 50 E
Jiuxiangcheng, China 66 H8 33 12N 114 50 E
Jiuxincheng, China 66 E8 39 17N 115 59 E
Jiuyuhang, China 69 B12 30 18N 119 56 E
Jixi, Anhui, China 69 B12 30 5N 118 34 E
Jixi, Heilongjiang, China 67 B16 45 20N 130 50 E
Jiyang, China 67 F9 37 0N 117 12 E
Jīz', W. →, Yemen 87 C6 16 12N 52 14 E
Jīzān, Si. Arabia 86 C3 17 0N 42 20 E
Jize, China 66 F8 36 54N 114 56 E
Jizera →, Czech. 30 A7 50 10N 14 43 E
Jizō-Zaki, Japan 62 B5 35 34N 133 20 E
Jizzakh, Uzbekistan 55 C3 40 6N 67 50 E
Joaçaba, Brazil 159 B5 27 5 S 51 31W
Joaíma, Brazil 155 E3 16 39 S 41 2W
João, Brazil 154 B1 2 46 S 50 59W
João Amaro, Brazil 155 D3 12 46 S 40 22W
João Câmara, Brazil 154 C4 5 32 S 35 48W
João Pessoa, Brazil 154 C5 7 10 S 34 52W
João Pinheiro, Brazil 155 E2 17 45 S 46 10W
Joaquim Távora, Brazil 155 F2 23 30 S 49 58W
Joaquín V. González, Argentina 158 B3 25 10 S 64 0W
Jobourg, Nez de, France 22 C5 49 41N 1 57W
Jódar, Spain 35 H1 37 50N 3 21W
Jodhpur, India 80 F5 26 23N 73 8 E
Joensuu, Finland 48 B4 62 37N 29 49 E
Jœuf, France 23 C13 49 12N 6 0 E
Jofane, Mozam. 105 C5 21 15 S 34 18 E
Jõgeva, Estonia 13 G22 58 45N 26 24 E
Joggins, Canada 129 C7 45 42N 64 27W
Jogjakarta = Yogyakarta, Indonesia 75 D4 7 49 S 110 22 E
Jōhana, Japan 63 A8 36 30N 136 57 E
Johannesburg, S. Africa 105 D4 26 10 S 28 2 E
Johannesburg, U.S.A. 145 K9 35 22N 117 38W
Jōhen, Japan 62 E4 32 58N 132 32 E
John Day, U.S.A. 142 D4 44 25N 118 57W
John Day →, U.S.A. 142 D3 45 44N 120 39W
John H. Kerr Reservoir, U.S.A. 135 G6 36 36N 78 18W
John o' Groats, U.K. 18 C5 58 38N 3 4W
Johnnie, U.S.A. 145 J10 36 25N 116 5W
John's Ra., Australia 114 C1 21 55 S 133 23 E
Johnson, U.S.A. 139 G4 37 34N 101 45W
Johnson City, Ill., U.S.A. 140 G8 37 49N 88 56W
Johnson City, N.Y., U.S.A. 137 D9 42 7N 75 58W
Johnson City, Tenn., U.S.A. 135 G4 36 19N 82 21W
Johnson City, Tex., U.S.A. 139 K5 30 17N 98 25W
Johnsonburg, U.S.A. 136 E6 41 29N 78 41W
Johnsondale, U.S.A. 145 K8 35 58N 118 32W
Johnson's Crossing, Canada 130 A2 60 29N 133 18W
Johnsonville, N.Z. 118 H3 41 13 S 174 48 E
Johnston, L., Australia 113 F3 32 25 S 120 30 E
Johnston Falls = Mambilima Falls, Zambia 107 E2 10 31 S 28 45 E
Johnston I., Pac. Oc. 123 F11 17 10N 169 8W
Johnstone Str., Canada 130 C3 50 28N 126 0W
Johnstown, N.Y., U.S.A. 137 C10 43 0N 74 22W
Johnstown, Pa., U.S.A. 136 F6 40 20N 78 55W
Johor □, Malaysia 74 B2 2 5N 103 20 E
Johor Baharu, Malaysia 77 M4 1 28N 103 46 E
Jõhvi, Estonia 13 G22 59 22N 27 27 E
Joigny, France 23 E10 47 58N 3 20 E
Joinville, Brazil 159 B6 26 15 S 48 55W
Joinville, France 23 D12 48 27N 5 10 E
Joinville I., Antarctica 7 C18 65 0 S 55 30W
Jojutla, Mexico 147 D5 18 37N 99 11W
Jokkmokk, Sweden 12 C18 66 35N 19 50 E
Jökulsá á Bru →, Iceland 12 D6 65 40N 14 16W
Jökulsá á Fjöllum →, Iceland 12 C5 66 10N 16 30W
Jolfā, Āzarbājān-e Sharqī, Iran 89 C11 38 57N 45 38 E
Jolfā, Eşfahan, Iran 85 C6 32 58N 51 37 E
Joliet, U.S.A. 141 C8 41 32N 88 5W
Joliette, Canada 128 C5 46 3N 73 24W
Jolo, Phil. 71 H3 6 0N 121 0 E
Jolo Group, Phil. 71 J3 6 0N 121 9 E
Jolon, U.S.A. 144 K5 35 58N 121 9W
Jomalig, Phil. 70 D4 14 42N 122 22 E
Jombang, Indonesia 75 D4 7 33 S 112 14 E
Jomda, China 68 B2 31 28N 98 12 E
Jome, Indonesia 72 B3 1 16 S 127 30 E
Jomfruland, Norway 15 F3 58 52N 9 36 E
Jönåker, Sweden 15 F10 58 44N 16 40 E
Jonava, Lithuania 13 J21 55 8N 24 12 E
Jones, Phil. 70 C3 16 33N 121 42 E
Jones Sound, Canada 6 B3 76 0N 85 0W
Jonesboro, Ark., U.S.A. 139 H9 35 50N 90 42W
Jonesboro, Ill., U.S.A. 139 G10 37 27N 89 16W
Jonesboro, La., U.S.A. 139 J8 32 15N 92 43W
Jonesburg, U.S.A. 140 F5 38 51N 91 18W
Jonesport, U.S.A. 129 D6 44 32N 67 37W
Jonesville, Ind., U.S.A. 141 E11 39 5N 85 54W
Jonesville, Mich., U.S.A. 141 C12 41 59N 84 40W
Jonglei, Sudan 95 F3 6 25N 30 50 E
Jonglei □, Sudan 95 F3 7 30N 32 30 E
Joniškis, Lithuania 13 H20 56 13N 23 35 E
Jönköping, Sweden 13 H16 57 45N 14 10 E
Jonquière, Canada 129 C5 48 27N 71 14W
Jonsberg, Sweden 15 F10 58 30N 16 48 E
Jonsered, Sweden 15 G6 57 45N 12 10 E
Jonzac, France 24 C3 45 27N 0 28W
Joplin, U.S.A. 139 G7 37 6N 94 31W
Jordan, U.S.A. 142 C10 47 19N 106 55W
Jordan ■, Asia 91 E5 31 0N 36 0 E
Jordan →, Asia 91 D4 31 48N 35 32 E
Jordan Valley, U.S.A. 142 E5 42 59N 117 3W
Jordânia, Brazil 155 E3 15 55 S 40 11W
Jordanów, Poland 31 B12 49 41N 19 49 E
Jorge, C., Chile 160 D1 51 40 S 75 35W
Jorhat, India 78 B5 26 45N 94 12 E
Jorm, Afghan. 79 A3 36 50N 70 52 E
Jörn, Sweden 12 D19 65 4N 20 1 E
Jorong, Indonesia 75 C4 3 58 S 114 56 E
Jørpeland, Norway 13 G11 59 3N 6 1 E
Jorquera →, Chile 158 B2 28 3 S 69 58W
Jos, Nigeria 101 D6 9 53N 8 51 E
Jošanička Banja, Serbia, Yug. 42 D5 43 24N 20 47 E
Jose Abad Santos, Phil. 71 J5 5 55N 125 39 E
José Batlle y Ordóñez, Uruguay 159 C4 33 20 S 55 10W
José de San Martín, Argentina 160 B2 44 4 S 70 26W
Jose Panganiban, Phil. 70 D4 14 17N 122 41 E
Joseni, Romania 46 C6 46 42N 25 29 E
Joseph, U.S.A. 142 D5 45 21N 117 14W
Joseph, L., Nfld., Canada 129 B6 52 45N 65 18W
Joseph, L., Ont., Canada 136 A5 45 10N 79 44W
Joseph Bonaparte G., Australia 112 B4 14 35 S 128 50 E
Joseph City, U.S.A. 143 J8 34 57N 110 20W
Joshua Tree, U.S.A. 145 L10 34 8N 116 19W
Joshua Tree National Monument, U.S.A. 145 M10 33 55N 116 0W
Josselin, France 22 E4 47 57N 2 33W
Jostedalsbreen, Norway 13 F12 61 40N 6 59 E
Jotunheimen, Norway 14 C2 61 35N 8 25 E
Jourdanton, U.S.A. 139 L5 28 55N 98 33W
Joure, Neths. 20 C7 52 58N 5 48 E
Joussard, Canada 130 B5 55 22N 115 50W
Joutseno, Finland 50 B5 61 7N 28 31 E
Jovellanos, Cuba 148 B3 22 40N 81 10W
Jovellar, Phil. 70 E4 13 4N 123 36 E
Jowai, India 78 C4 25 26N 92 12 E
Jowzjān □, Afghan. 79 A2 36 10N 66 0 E
Joyeuse, France 25 D8 44 29N 4 16 E
Józefów, Poland 47 C8 52 10N 21 11 E
Ju Xian, China 67 F10 36 35N 118 20 E
Juan Aldama, Mexico 146 C4 24 20N 103 23W
Juan Bautista Alberdi, Argentina 158 C3 34 26 S 61 48W
Juan de Fuca Str., Canada 144 B2 48 15N 124 0W
Juan de Nova, Ind. Oc. 105 B7 17 3 S 43 45 E
Juan Fernández, Arch. de, Pac. Oc. 150 G2 33 50 S 80 0W
Juan José Castelli, Argentina 158 B3 25 27 S 60 57W
Juan L. Lacaze, Uruguay 158 C4 34 26 S 57 25W
Juanjuí, Peru 156 B2 7 10 S 76 45W
Juankoski, Finland 12 E23 63 3N 28 19 E
Juárez, Argentina 158 D4 37 40 S 59 43W
Juárez, Mexico 145 N11 32 20N 115 57W
Juárez, Sierra de, Mexico 146 A1 32 0N 116 0W
Juatinga, Ponta de, Brazil 155 F3 23 17 S 44 30W
Juàzeiro, Brazil 154 C3 9 30 S 40 30W
Juàzeiro do Norte, Brazil 154 C4 7 10 S 39 18W
Jubay, Phil. 71 F5 11 33N 124 18 E
Jubayl, Lebanon 91 A4 34 5N 35 39 E
Jubbah, Si. Arabia 84 D4 28 2N 40 56 E
Jubbulpore = Jabalpur, India 81 H8 23 9N 79 58 E
Jübek, Germany 26 A5 54 33N 9 22 E
Jubga, Russia 53 H4 44 19N 38 48 E
Jubilee L., Australia 113 E4 29 0 S 126 50 E
Juby, C., Morocco 98 C2 28 0N 12 59W
Júcar →, Spain 35 F4 39 5N 0 10W
Júcaro, Cuba 148 B4 21 37N 78 51W
Juchitán, Mexico 147 D5 16 27N 95 5W
Judaea = Har Yehuda, Israel 91 D3 31 35N 34 57 E
Judenburg, Austria 30 D7 47 12N 14 38 E
Judith →, U.S.A. 142 C9 47 44N 109 39W
Judith, Pt., U.S.A. 137 E13 41 22N 71 29W
Judith Gap, U.S.A. 142 C9 46 41N 109 45W
Jufari →, Brazil 153 D5 1 13 S 62 0W
Jugoslavia = Yugoslavia ■, Europe 42 D5 44 0N 20 0 E
Juigalpa, Nic. 148 D2 12 6N 85 26W
Juillac, France 24 C5 45 20N 1 19 E
Juist, Germany 26 B2 53 40N 6 59 E
Juiz de Fora, Brazil 155 F3 21 43 S 43 19W
Jujuy □, Argentina 158 A2 23 20 S 65 40W
Julesburg, U.S.A. 138 E3 40 59N 102 16W
Juli, Peru 156 D4 16 10 S 69 25W
Julia Cr. →, Australia 114 C3 20 0 S 141 11 E
Julia Creek, Australia 114 C3 20 39 S 141 44 E
Juliaca, Peru 156 D3 15 25 S 70 10W
Julian, U.S.A. 145 M10 33 4N 116 38W
Julian Alps = Julijske Alpe, Slovenia 39 B11 46 15N 14 1 E
Julianakanaal, Neths. 21 F7 51 6N 5 52 E
Julianatop, Surinam 153 C6 3 40N 56 30W
Julianehåb, Greenland 6 C5 60 43N 46 0W
Jülich, Germany 26 E2 50 55N 6 22 E
Julierpass, Switz. 29 D9 46 28N 9 32 E
Julijske Alpe, Slovenia 39 B11 46 15N 14 1 E
Julimes, Mexico 146 B3 28 25N 105 27W
Jullundur, India 80 D6 31 20N 75 40 E
Julu, China 66 F8 37 15N 115 2 E
Jumbo, Zimbabwe 107 F3 17 30 S 30 58 E
Jumbo Pk., U.S.A. 145 J12 36 12N 114 11W
Jumentos Cays, Bahamas 149 B4 23 0N 75 40W
Jumet, Belgium 21 H4 50 27N 4 25 E
Jumilla, Spain 35 G3 38 28N 1 19W
Jumla, Nepal 81 E10 29 15N 82 13 E
Jumna = Yamuna →, India 81 G9 25 30N 81 53 E
Junagadh, India 80 J4 21 30N 70 30 E
Junaynah, Si. Arabia 86 B4 22 33N 46 18 E
Junction, Tex., U.S.A. 139 K5 30 29N 99 46W
Junction, Utah, U.S.A. 143 G7 38 14N 112 13W
Junction B., Australia 114 A1 11 52 S 133 55 E
Junction City, Kans., U.S.A. 138 F6 39 2N 96 50W
Junction City, Oreg., U.S.A. 142 D2 44 13N 123 12W
Junction Pt., Australia 114 A1 11 45 S 133 50 E
Jundah, Australia 114 C3 24 46 S 143 2 E
Jundiaí, Brazil 159 A6 24 30 S 47 0W
Juneau, U.S.A. 126 C6 58 18N 134 25W
Junee, Australia 117 C7 34 53 S 147 35 E
Jungfrau, Switz. 28 C5 46 32N 7 58 E
Junggar Pendi, China 64 B3 44 30N 86 0 E
Junglinster, Lux. 21 J8 49 43N 6 15 E
Jungshahi, Pakistan 80 G2 24 52N 67 44 E
Juniata →, U.S.A. 136 F7 40 30N 77 40W
Junín, Argentina 158 C3 34 33 S 60 57W
Junín, Peru 156 C2 11 12 S 76 0W
Junín □, Peru 156 C3 11 30 S 75 0W
Junín de los Andes, Argentina 160 A2 39 45 S 71 0W
Jūniyah, Lebanon 91 B4 33 59N 35 38 E
Junnar, India 82 E1 19 12N 73 58 E
Juntura, U.S.A. 142 E4 43 45N 118 5W
Juparanã, L., Brazil 155 E3 19 16 S 40 8W
Jupiter →, Canada 129 C7 49 29N 63 37W
Juquiá, Brazil 155 F2 24 19 S 47 38W
Jur, Nahr el →, Sudan 95 F2 8 45N 29 15 E
Jura = Jura, Mts. du, Europe 23 F13 46 40N 6 5 E
Jura = Schwäbische Alb, Germany 27 G5 48 20N 9 30 E
Jura, U.K. 18 F3 56 0N 5 50W
Jura □, France 23 F12 46 47N 5 45 E
Jura, Mts. du, Europe 23 F13 46 40N 6 5 E
Jura, Sd. of, U.K. 18 F3 55 57N 5 45W
Jura Suisse, Switz. 28 B3 47 10N 7 0 E
Jurado, Colombia 152 B2 7 7N 77 46W
Jurbarkas, Lithuania 13 J20 55 6N 22 47 E
Jurilovca, Romania 46 E9 44 46N 28 52 E
Jūrmala, Latvia 13 H20 56 58N 23 34 E
Jurong, China 69 B12 31 57N 119 9 E
Juruá →, Brazil 152 D4 2 37 S 65 44W
Juruena, Brazil 157 C6 13 0 S 58 10W
Juruena →, Brazil 157 B6 7 20 S 58 3W
Juruti, Brazil 153 D6 2 9 S 56 4W
Jussey, France 23 E12 47 50N 5 55 E
Justo Daract, Argentina 158 C2 33 52 S 65 12W
Jutaí, Brazil 156 B4 5 11 S 68 54W
Jutaí →, Brazil 152 D4 2 43 S 66 57W
Jüterbog, Germany 26 D9 51 59N 13 5 E
Juticalpa, Honduras 148 D2 14 40N 86 12W
Jutland = Jylland, Denmark 15 H3 56 25N 9 30 E
Jutphaas, Neths. 20 D6 52 2N 5 6 E
Juventud, I. de la, Cuba 148 B3 21 40N 82 40W
Juvigny-sous-Andaine, France 22 D6 48 32N 0 30W
Juvisy-sur-Orge, France 23 D9 48 42N 2 22 E
Jūy Zar, Iran 89 F12 33 50N 46 18 E
Juye, China 66 G9 35 22N 116 5 E
Juzennecourt, France 23 D11 48 10N 4 58 E
Jvari, Georgia 53 J6 42 42N 42 4 E
Jylland, Denmark 15 H3 56 25N 9 30 E
Jyväskylä, Finland 13 E21 62 14N 25 50 E

K

K2, Pakistan 81 B7 35 58N 76 32 E
Kaala-Gomén, N. Cal. 121 T18 20 40 S 164 25 E
Kaap Plateau, S. Africa 104 D3 28 30 S 24 0 E
Kaapkruis, Namibia 104 C1 21 55 S 13 57 E
Kaapstad = Cape Town, S. Africa 104 E2 33 55 S 18 22 E
Kaatsheuvel, Neths. 21 E6 51 39N 5 2 E
Kabacan, Phil. 71 H5 7 8N 124 49 E
Kabaena, Indonesia 72 C2 5 15 S 122 0 E
Kabala, S. Leone 100 D2 9 38N 11 37W
Kabale, Uganda 106 C3 1 15 S 30 0 E
Kabalo, Zaïre 103 D5 6 0 S 27 0 E
Kabambare, Zaïre 106 C2 4 41 S 27 39 E
Kabango, Zaïre 107 D2 8 35 S 28 30 E
Kabanjahe, Indonesia 74 B1 3 6N 98 30 E
Kabankalan, Phil. 71 G4 9 59N 122 49 E
Kabara, Mali 100 B4 16 40N 2 50W
Kabardinka, Russia 53 H4 44 40N 37 57 E
Kabardino-Balkar Republic = Kabardino Balkaria □, Russia 53 J6 43 30N 43 30 E
Kabardino Balkaria □, Russia 53 J6 43 30N 43 30 E
Kabare, Indonesia 73 B4 0 4 S 130 58 E
Kabarega Falls, Uganda 106 B3 2 15N 31 30 E
Kabasalan, Phil. 71 H4 7 47N 122 44 E
Kabba, Nigeria 101 D6 7 50N 6 3 E
Kabe, Japan 62 C4 34 31N 132 31 E
Kabi, Niger 97 F2 13 30N 12 35 E
Kabin Buri, Thailand 76 F3 13 57N 101 43 E
Kabinakagami L., Canada 128 C3 48 54N 84 25W
Kabīr, Zab al →, Iraq 89 D10 36 1N 43 24 E
Kabkabīyah, Sudan 97 F4 13 50N 24 0 E
Kablungu, C., Papua N. G. 120 D6 6 20 S 150 1 E
Kabna, Sudan 94 D3 19 6N 32 40 E
Kabo, C.A.R. 102 A3 7 35N 18 38 E
Kabompo, Zambia 107 E1 13 36 S 24 14 E
Kabondo, Zaïre 103 D5 8 58 S 25 40 E

216 Katav Ivanovsk

Katav Ivanovsk, Russia 54 D7 54 45N 58 12 E
Katavi Swamp, Tanzania 106 D3 6 50 S 31 10 E
Kataysk, Russia 54 C9 56 20N 62 30 E
Katchiungo, Angola 103 E3 12 35 S 16 13 E
Kateríni, Greece 44 D4 40 18N 22 37 E
Katherîna, Gebel, Egypt 94 J8 28 30N 33 57 E
Katherine, Australia 112 B5 14 27 S 132 20 E
Kathiawar, India 80 H4 22 20N 71 0 E
Kathikas, Cyprus 32 E11 34 55N 32 25 E
Kati, Mali 100 C3 12 41N 8 4W
Katihar, India 81 G12 25 34N 87 36 E
Katikati, N.Z. 118 D4 37 32 S 175 57 E
Katima Mulilo, Zambia 104 B3 17 28 S 24 13 E
Katimbira, Malawi 107 E3 12 40 S 34 0 E
Katingan = Mendawai →, Indonesia 75 C4 3 30 S 113 0 E
Katiola, Ivory C. 100 D3 8 10N 5 10W
Katipunan, Phil. 71 G4 8 31N 123 17 E
Katlanovo, Macedonia 42 F6 41 52N 21 40 E
Katmandu, Nepal 81 F11 27 45N 85 20 E
Kato Akhaïa, Greece 45 F3 38 8N 21 33 E
Káto Arkhánai, Greece 32 D7 35 15N 25 10 E
Káto Khorió, Greece 32 D7 35 3N 25 47 E
Kato Pyrgos, Cyprus 32 D11 35 11N 32 41 E
Káto Stavros, Greece 44 D5 40 39N 23 43 E
Katol, India 82 D4 21 17N 78 38 E
Katompe, Zaïre 103 D5 6 2 S 26 23 E
Katonga →, Uganda 106 B3 0 34N 31 50 E
Katoomba, Australia 117 B9 33 41 S 150 19 E
Katowice, Poland 47 E6 50 17N 19 5 E
Katowice □, Poland 47 E6 50 10N 19 0 E
Katrine, L., U.K. 18 E4 56 15N 4 30W
Katrineholm, Sweden 14 E10 59 9N 16 12 E
Katsepe, Madag. 105 B8 15 45 S 46 15 E
Katsina, Nigeria 101 C6 13 0N 7 32 E
Katsina □, Nigeria 101 C6 12 30N 7 30 E
Katsina Ala →, Nigeria 101 D6 7 10N 9 20 E
Katsumoto, Japan 62 D1 33 51N 129 42 E
Katsuta, Japan 63 A12 36 25N 140 31 E
Katsuura, Japan 63 B12 35 10N 140 20 E
Katsuyama, Japan 63 A8 36 3N 136 30 E
Kattakurgan, Uzbekistan 55 D3 39 55N 66 15 E
Kattaviá, Greece 32 D9 35 57N 27 46 E
Kattegat, Denmark 15 H5 57 0N 11 20 E
Katumba, Zaïre 103 D5 7 40 S 25 17 E
Katungu, Kenya 106 C5 2 55 S 40 3 E
Katwa, India 81 H13 23 30N 88 5 E
Katwijk-aan-Zee, Neths. 20 D4 52 12N 4 24 E
Katy, Poland 47 D3 51 2N 16 45 E
Kauai, U.S.A. 132 H15 22 3N 159 30W
Kauai Channel, U.S.A. 132 H15 21 45N 158 50W
Kaub, Germany 27 E3 50 5N 7 46 E
Kaufbeuren, Germany 27 H6 47 53N 10 57 E
Kaufman, U.S.A. 139 J6 32 35N 96 19W
Kauhajoki, Finland 13 E20 62 25N 22 10 E
Kaukauna, U.S.A. 134 C1 44 17N 88 17W
Kaukauveld, Namibia 104 C3 20 0 S 20 15 E
Kaunas, Lithuania 13 J20 54 54N 23 54 E
Kaunghein, Burma 78 C5 25 41N 95 26 E
Kaupalatmada, Mt., Indonesia 72 B3 3 30 S 126 10 E
Kaura Namoda, Nigeria 101 C6 12 37N 6 33 E
Kautokeino, Norway 12 B20 69 0N 23 4 E
Kavacha, Russia 57 C17 60 16N 169 51 E
Kavadarci, Macedonia 42 F7 41 26N 22 3 E
Kavaja, Albania 44 C1 41 11N 19 33 E
Kavak, Turkey 88 B7 41 4N 36 3 E
Kavalerovo, Russia 60 B7 44 15N 135 4 E
Kavali, India 83 G5 14 55N 80 1 E
Kavála, Greece 44 D6 40 57N 24 28 E
Kavála □, Greece 44 C6 41 5N 24 30 E
Kavála Kólpos, Greece 44 D6 40 50N 24 25 E
Kavār, Iran 85 D7 29 11N 52 44 E
Kavarna, Bulgaria 43 D13 43 26N 28 22 E
Kavieng, Papua N. G. 120 B6 2 36 S 150 51 E
Kavkaz, Russia 53 H3 45 20N 36 40 E
Kavos, Greece 32 B4 39 23N 20 3 E
Kavoúsi, Greece 45 J7 35 7N 25 51 E
Kaw, Fr. Guiana 153 C7 4 30N 52 15W
Kawa, Sudan 95 E3 13 42N 32 34 E
Kawachi-Nagano, Japan 63 C7 34 28N 135 31 E
Kawagama L., Canada 136 A6 45 18N 78 45W
Kawagoe, Japan 63 B11 35 55N 139 29 E
Kawaguchi, Japan 63 B11 35 52N 139 45 E
Kawaihae, U.S.A. 132 H17 20 3N 155 50W
Kawakawa, N.Z. 118 B3 35 23 S 174 6 E
Kawambwa, Zambia 107 D2 9 48 S 29 3 E
Kawanoe, Japan 62 C5 34 1N 133 34 E
Kawarau, N.Z. 119 F3 45 3 S 168 45 E
Kawardha, India 81 J9 22 0N 81 17 E
Kawasaki, Japan 63 B11 35 35N 139 42 E
Kawau I., N.Z. 118 C3 36 25 S 174 52 E
Kaweka Ra., N.Z. 118 F5 39 17 S 176 19 E
Kawene, Canada 128 C1 48 45N 91 15W
Kawerau, N.Z. 118 E5 38 7 S 176 42 E
Kawhia Harbour, N.Z. 118 E3 38 5 S 174 51 E
Kawio, Kepulauan, Indonesia 72 A3 4 30N 125 30 E
Kawit, Phil. 71 H3 6 57N 121 58 E
Kawkabān, Yemen 86 D3 15 30N 43 54 E
Kawkareik, Burma 78 G7 16 33N 98 14 E
Kawlin, Burma 78 D5 23 47N 95 41 E
Kawthoolei = Kawthule □, Burma 78 G6 18 0N 97 30 E
Kawthule □, Burma 78 G6 18 0N 97 30 E
Kawya, Burma 78 C6 24 50N 94 58 E
Kay, Russia 54 B4 59 57N 52 59 E
Kaya, Burkina Faso 101 C4 13 4N 1 10W
Kayah □, Burma 78 F6 19 15N 97 15 E
Kayan, Burma 78 E6 16 54N 96 34 E
Kayan →, Indonesia 75 B5 2 55N 117 35 E
Kayankulam, India 83 K3 9 10N 76 33 E
Kayapa, Phil. 70 C3 16 22N 120 53 E
Kaycee, U.S.A. 142 E10 43 43N 106 38W
Kayeli, Indonesia 72 B3 3 20 S 127 10 E
Kayenta, U.S.A. 143 H8 36 44N 110 15W
Kayes, Congo 103 C2 4 25 S 11 41 E
Kayes, Mali 100 C2 14 25N 11 30W
Kayima, S. Leone 100 D2 8 54N 11 15W
Kayl, Lux. 21 K8 49 29N 6 2 E
Kayoa, Indonesia 72 A3 0 1N 127 28 E
Kayomba, Zambia 107 E1 13 11 S 24 2 E
Kayoro, Ghana 101 C4 11 0N 1 28W
Kayrakkumskoye Vdkhr., Tajikistan 55 C4 40 20N 70 0 E
Kayrunnera, Australia 115 E3 30 40 S 142 30 E
Kaysatskoye, Russia 52 F8 49 47N 46 49 E
Kayseri, Turkey 88 C6 38 45N 35 30 E
Kaysville, U.S.A. 142 F8 41 2N 111 56W
Kayuagung, Indonesia 74 C2 3 24 S 104 50 E
Kazachye, Russia 57 B14 70 52N 135 58 E
Kazakstan ■, Asia 56 E7 50 0N 70 0 E
Kazan, Russia 52 C9 55 50N 49 10 E
Kazan-Rettō, Pac. Oc. 122 E6 25 0N 141 0 E
Kazanlŭk, Bulgaria 43 E10 42 38N 25 20 E
Kazanskaya, Russia 52 F5 49 50N 41 10 E
Kazarman, Kyrgyzstan 55 C6 41 24N 73 59 E
Kazatin = Kozyatyn, Ukraine 51 H5 49 45N 28 50 E
Kazbek, Russia 53 J7 42 42N 44 30 E
Kāzerūn, Iran 85 D6 29 38N 51 40 E
Kazhim, Russia 54 A3 60 21N 51 33 E
Kazi Magomed = Qazimämmäd, Azerbaijan 53 K9 40 3N 49 0 E
Kazimierz Dolny, Poland 47 D8 51 19N 21 57 E
Kazimierza Wielka, Poland 47 E7 50 15N 20 30 E
Kazincbarcika, Hungary 31 C13 48 17N 20 36 E
Kazo, Japan 63 A11 36 7N 139 36 E
Kaztalovka, Kazakstan 52 F9 49 47N 48 43 E
Kazu, Burma 78 C6 25 27N 97 46 E
Kazumba, Zaïre 103 D4 6 25 S 22 5 E
Kazuno, Japan 60 D10 40 10N 140 45 E
Kazym →, Russia 56 C7 63 54N 65 50 E
Kcynia, Poland 47 C4 53 0N 17 30 E
Ke-hsi Mansam, Burma 78 E6 21 56N 97 50 E
Ké-Macina, Mali 100 C3 13 58N 5 22W
Kéa, Greece 45 G6 37 35N 24 22 E
Keams Canyon, U.S.A. 143 J8 35 49N 110 12W
Kearney, Mo., U.S.A. 140 E2 39 22N 94 22W
Kearney, Nebr., U.S.A. 138 E5 40 42N 99 5W
Keban, Turkey 89 C8 38 50N 38 50 E
Keban Baraji, Turkey 89 C8 38 41N 38 33 E
Kebbi □, Nigeria 101 C6 11 30N 8 30 E
Kébi, Ivory C. 100 D3 9 18N 6 37W
Kebili, Tunisia 96 B1 33 47N 9 0 E
Kebnekaise, Sweden 12 C18 67 53N 18 33 E
Kebri Dehar, Ethiopia 108 C2 6 45N 44 17 E
Kebumen, Indonesia 75 D3 7 42 S 109 40 E
Kecel, Hungary 31 E12 46 31N 19 16 E
Kechika →, Canada 130 B3 59 41N 127 12W
Kecskemét, Hungary 31 E12 46 57N 19 42 E
Kedada, Ethiopia 95 F4 5 25N 35 58 E
Kedah □, Malaysia 74 A2 5 50N 100 40 E
Kedgwick, Canada 129 C6 47 40N 67 20W
Kédhros Óros, Greece 32 D6 35 11N 24 37 E
Kedia Hill, Botswana 104 C3 21 28 S 24 37 E
Kediniai, Lithuania 13 J21 55 15N 24 2 E
Kediri, Indonesia 75 D4 7 51 S 112 1 E
Kédougou, Senegal 100 C2 12 35N 12 10W
Kedzierzyn, Poland 47 E5 50 20N 18 12 E
Keeler, U.S.A. 144 J9 36 29N 117 52W
Keeley L., Canada 131 C7 54 54N 108 8W
Keeling Is. = Cocos Is., Ind. Oc. 109 F8 12 10 S 96 55 E
Keene, Calif., U.S.A. 145 K8 35 13N 118 33W
Keene, N.H., U.S.A. 137 D12 42 56N 72 17W
Keeper Hill, Ireland 19 D3 52 45N 8 16W
Keer-Weer, C., Australia 114 A3 14 0 S 141 32 E
Keerbergen, Belgium 21 F5 51 1N 4 38 E
Keeseville, U.S.A. 137 B11 44 29N 73 30W
Keeten Mastgat, Neths. 21 E4 51 36N 4 0 E
Keetmanshoop, Namibia 104 D2 26 35 S 18 8 E
Keewatin, U.S.A. 138 B8 47 24N 93 5W
Keewatin □, Canada 131 A10 63 20N 95 0W
Keewatin →, Canada 131 B8 56 29N 100 46W
Kefa □, Ethiopia 95 F4 6 55N 36 30 E
Kefallinía, Greece 45 F2 38 20N 20 30 E
Kefamenanu, Indonesia 72 C2 9 28 S 124 29 E
Keffi, Nigeria 101 D6 8 55N 7 43 E
Keflavík, Iceland 12 D2 64 2N 22 35W
Keg River, Canada 130 B5 57 54N 117 55W
Kegalla, Sri Lanka 83 L5 7 15N 80 21 E
Kegaska, Canada 129 B7 50 9N 61 18W
Kehl, Germany 27 G3 48 34N 7 50 E
Keighley, U.K. 16 D6 53 52N 1 54W
Keila, Estonia 13 G21 59 18N 24 25 E
Keimoes, S. Africa 104 D3 28 41 S 20 59 E
Keita, Niger 101 C6 14 46N 5 56 E
Keitele, Finland 12 E22 63 10N 26 20 E
Keith, Australia 116 D4 36 6 S 140 20 E
Keith, U.K. 18 D6 57 32N 2 57W
Keith Arm, Canada 126 B7 64 20N 122 15W
Keithsburg, U.S.A. 140 C6 41 6N 90 56W
Kejser Franz Joseph Fjord = Kong Franz Joseph Fd., Greenland 6 B6 73 30N 24 30W
Kekaygyr, Kyrgyzstan 55 C7 40 42N 75 32 E
Kekri, India 80 G6 26 0N 75 10 E
Kël, Russia 57 C13 69 30N 124 10 E
Kelamet, Eritrea 95 D4 16 0N 38 30 E
Kelan, China 66 E6 38 43N 111 31 E
Kelang, Malaysia 77 L3 3 2N 101 26 E
Kelani Ganga →, Sri Lanka 83 L4 6 58N 79 50 E
Kelantan □, Malaysia 74 A2 5 10N 102 0 E
Kelantan →, Malaysia 77 J4 6 13N 102 14 E
Këlcyra, Albania 44 D2 40 22N 20 12 E
Keles →, Kazakstan 55 C4 41 1N 68 37 E
Kelheim, Germany 27 G7 48 54N 11 52 E
Kelibia, Tunisia 96 A2 36 50N 11 3 E
Kelkit, Turkey 89 B8 40 7N 39 16 E
Kelkit →, Turkey 88 B7 40 45N 36 32 E
Kellé, Congo 102 C2 0 8 S 14 38 E
Keller, U.S.A. 142 B4 48 5N 118 41W
Kellerberrin, Australia 113 F2 31 36 S 117 38 E
Kellett, C., Canada 6 B1 72 0N 126 0W
Kelleys I., U.S.A. 136 E2 41 36N 82 42W
Kellogg, U.S.A. 142 C5 47 32N 116 7W
Kells = Ceanannus Mor, Ireland 19 C5 53 44N 6 53W
Kélo, Chad 97 G3 9 10N 15 45 E
Kelokedhara, Cyprus 32 E11 34 48N 32 39 E
Kelowna, Canada 130 D5 49 50N 119 25W
Kelsey Bay, Canada 130 C3 50 25N 126 0W
Kelseyville, U.S.A. 144 G4 38 59N 122 50W
Kelso, N.Z. 119 F3 45 54 S 169 15 E
Kelso, U.K. 18 F6 55 36N 2 26W
Kelso, U.S.A. 144 D4 46 9N 122 54W
Keltemashat, Kazakstan 55 B5 42 25N 70 8 E
Keluang, Malaysia 77 L4 2 3N 103 18 E
Kelvington, Canada 131 C8 52 10N 103 30W
Kem, Russia 48 B5 65 0N 34 38 E
Kem →, Russia 48 B5 64 57N 34 41 E
Kem-Kem, Morocco 98 B4 30 40N 4 30W
Kema, Indonesia 72 A3 1 22N 125 8 E
Kemah, Turkey 89 C8 39 32N 39 5 E
Kemaliye, Turkey 89 C8 39 16N 38 29 E
Kemano, Canada 130 C3 53 35N 128 0W
Kemapyu, Burma 78 F6 18 49N 97 19 E
Kemasik, Malaysia 77 K4 4 25N 103 27 E
Kembé, C.A.R. 102 B4 4 36N 21 54 E
Kembolcha, Ethiopia 95 E4 11 2N 39 42 E
Kemer, Turkey 88 D4 36 35N 30 33 E
Kemerovo, Russia 56 D9 55 20N 86 5 E
Kemi, Finland 12 D21 65 44N 24 34 E
Kemi älv = Kemijoki →, Finland 12 D21 65 47N 24 32 E
Kemijärvi, Finland 12 C22 66 43N 27 22 E
Kemijoki →, Finland 12 D21 65 47N 24 32 E
Kemmel, Belgium 21 G1 50 47N 2 50 E
Kemmerer, U.S.A. 142 F8 41 48N 110 32W
Kemmuna = Comino, Malta 32 C1 36 2N 14 20 E
Kemp, L., U.S.A. 139 J5 33 46N 99 9W
Kemp Land, Antarctica 7 C5 69 0 S 55 0 E
Kempsey, Australia 117 A10 31 1 S 152 50 E
Kempt, L., Canada 128 C5 47 25N 74 22W
Kempten, Germany 27 H6 47 45N 10 17 E
Kempton, U.S.A. 141 D10 40 17N 86 14W
Kemptville, Canada 128 C4 45 0N 75 38W
Kenadsa, Algeria 99 B4 31 48N 2 26W
Kendal, Indonesia 75 D4 6 56 S 110 14 E
Kendal, U.K. 16 C5 54 20N 2 44W
Kendall, Australia 117 A10 31 35 S 152 44 E
Kendall →, Australia 114 A3 14 4 S 141 35 E
Kendallville, U.S.A. 141 C11 41 27N 85 16W
Kendari, Indonesia 72 B2 3 50 S 122 30 E
Kendawangan, Indonesia 75 C4 2 32 S 110 17 E
Kende, Nigeria 101 C5 11 30N 4 12 E
Kendenup, Australia 113 F2 34 30 S 117 38 E
Kendervicës, Mal e., Albania 44 D1 40 15N 19 52 E
Kendrapara, India 82 D8 20 35N 86 30 E
Kendrew, S. Africa 104 E3 32 32 S 24 30 E
Kendrick, U.S.A. 142 C5 46 37N 116 39W
Kene Thao, Laos 76 D3 17 44N 101 10 E
Kenedy, U.S.A. 139 L6 28 49N 97 51W
Kenema, S. Leone 100 D2 7 50N 11 14W
Keng Kok, Laos 76 D5 16 26N 105 12 E
Keng Tawng, Burma 78 E7 20 45N 98 18 E
Kengeni, Zaïre 102 C3 2 59 S 17 36 E
Kenge, Zaïre 103 C3 4 50 S 17 4 E
Kengeja, Tanzania 106 D4 5 26 S 39 45 E
Kenhardt, S. Africa 104 D3 29 19 S 21 12 E
Kenimekh, Uzbekistan 55 C2 40 16N 65 7 E
Kenitra, Morocco 98 B3 34 15N 6 40W
Kenli, China 67 F10 37 30N 118 20 E
Kenmare, Ireland 19 E2 51 53N 9 36W
Kenmare, U.S.A. 138 A3 48 41N 102 5W
Kenmare →, Ireland 19 E2 51 48N 9 51W
Kennebec, U.S.A. 138 D5 43 54N 99 52W
Kennedy, Zimbabwe 107 F2 18 52 S 27 10 E
Kennedy Ra., Australia 113 D2 24 45 S 115 10 E
Kenner, U.S.A. 139 L9 29 59N 90 15W
Kennet →, U.K. 17 F7 51 27N 0 57W
Kenneth Ra., Australia 112 D2 23 50 S 117 8 E
Kennett, U.S.A. 139 G9 36 14N 90 3W
Kennewick, U.S.A. 142 C4 46 12N 119 7W
Kénogami, Canada 129 C5 48 25N 71 15W
Kenogami →, Canada 128 B3 51 6N 84 28W
Kenora, Canada 131 D10 49 47N 94 29W
Kenosha, U.S.A. 141 B9 42 35N 87 49W
Kensington, Canada 129 C7 46 28N 63 34W
Kensington, U.S.A. 138 F5 39 46N 99 2W
Kensington Downs, Australia 114 C3 22 31 S 144 19 E
Kent, Ohio, U.S.A. 136 E3 41 9N 81 22W
Kent, Oreg., U.S.A. 142 D3 45 12N 120 42W
Kent, Tex., U.S.A. 139 K2 31 4N 104 13W
Kent, Wash., U.S.A. 144 C4 47 23N 122 14W
Kent □, U.K. 17 F8 51 12N 0 40 E
Kent Group, Australia 114 F4 39 30 S 147 20 E
Kent Pen., Canada 126 B9 68 30N 107 0W
Kentau, Kazakstan 55 B4 43 32N 68 36 E
Kentland, U.S.A. 141 D9 40 46N 87 27W
Kenton, U.S.A. 141 D13 40 39N 83 37W
Kentucky, Australia 117 A9 30 45 S 151 28 E
Kentucky □, U.S.A. 134 G3 37 0N 84 0W
Kentucky →, U.S.A. 141 F11 38 41N 85 11W
Kentucky L., U.S.A. 135 G2 37 1N 88 16W
Kentville, Canada 129 C7 45 6N 64 29W
Kentwood, U.S.A. 139 K9 30 56N 90 31W
Kenya ■, Africa 106 B4 1 0N 38 0 E
Kenya, Mt., Kenya 106 C4 0 10 S 37 18 E
Kenzou, Cameroon 102 B3 4 10N 15 2 E
Keo Neua, Deo, Vietnam 76 C5 18 23N 105 10 E
Keokuk, U.S.A. 140 D5 40 24N 91 24W
Keosauqua, U.S.A. 140 D5 40 44N 91 58W
Keota, U.S.A. 140 C5 41 22N 91 57W
Kep, Cambodia 77 G5 10 29N 104 19 E
Kep, Vietnam 76 B6 21 24N 106 16 E
Kepi, Indonesia 73 C5 6 32 S 139 19 E
Kepice, Poland 47 A3 54 16N 16 51 E
Kepler Mts., N.Z. 119 F2 45 25 S 167 20 E
Kępno, Poland 47 D4 51 18N 17 58 E
Kerala □, India 83 J3 11 0N 76 15 E
Kerama-Rettō, Japan 61 L3 26 5N 127 15 E
Keran, Pakistan 81 B5 34 35N 73 59 E
Kerang, Australia 116 C5 35 40 S 143 55 E
Keratéa, Greece 45 G5 37 48N 23 58 E
Keraudren, C., Australia 112 C2 19 58 S 119 45 E
Kerava, Finland 13 F21 60 25N 25 5 E
Keravat, Papua N. G. 120 C7 4 17 S 152 2 E
Kerch, Ukraine 51 K9 45 20N 36 20 E
Kerchenskiy Proliv, Black Sea 51 K9 45 10N 36 30 E
Kerchoual, Mali 101 B5 17 12N 0 20 E
Kerema, Papua N. G. 120 D3 7 58 S 145 50 E
Kerempe Burnu, Turkey 88 A5 42 2N 33 20 E
Keren, Eritrea 95 D4 15 45N 38 28 E
Kerewan, Gambia 100 C1 13 29N 16 10W
Kerguelen, Ind. Oc. 109 J5 49 15 S 69 10 E
Keri, Greece 45 G2 37 40N 20 49 E
Keri Kera, Sudan 95 E3 12 21N 32 42 E
Kericho, Kenya 106 C4 0 22 S 35 15 E
Kericho □, Kenya 106 C4 0 30 S 35 15 E
Kerikeri, N.Z. 118 B2 35 12 S 173 59 E
Kerinci, Indonesia 74 C2 1 40 S 101 15 E
Kerkdriel, Neths. 20 E6 51 47N 5 20 E
Kerkenna, Is., Tunisia 96 B2 34 48N 11 11 E
Kerki, Turkmenistan 55 E2 37 50N 65 12 E
Kerkinítis, Límni, Greece 44 C5 41 12N 23 10 E
Kérkira, Greece 32 A3 39 38N 19 50 E
Kerkrade, Neths. 21 G8 50 53N 6 4 E
Kerma, Sudan 94 D3 19 33N 30 32 E
Kermadec Is., Pac. Oc. 122 K10 30 0 S 178 15W
Kermadec Trench, Pac. Oc. 122 L10 30 30 S 176 0W
Kermān, Iran 85 D8 30 15N 57 1 E
Kerman, U.S.A. 144 J6 36 43N 120 4W
Kermān □, Iran 85 D8 30 0N 57 0 E
Kermānshāh = Bākhtarān, Iran 89 E12 34 23N 47 0 E
Kerme Körfezi, Turkey 88 D2 36 55N 27 50 E
Kermen, Bulgaria 43 E11 42 30N 26 16 E
Kermit, U.S.A. 139 K3 31 52N 103 6W
Kern →, U.S.A. 145 K7 35 16N 119 18W
Kerns, Switz. 29 C6 46 54N 8 17 E
Kernville, U.S.A. 145 K8 35 45N 118 26W
Keroh, Malaysia 77 K3 5 43N 101 1 E
Kerrobert, Canada 131 C7 51 56N 109 8W
Kerrville, U.S.A. 139 K5 30 3N 99 8W
Kerry □, Ireland 19 D2 52 7N 9 35W
Kerry Hd., Ireland 19 D2 52 25N 9 56W
Kersa, Ethiopia 95 F5 9 28N 41 48 E
Kerteminde, Denmark 15 J4 55 28N 10 39 E
Kertosono, Indonesia 75 D4 7 38 S 112 9 E
Kerulen →, Asia 65 B6 48 48N 117 0 E
Kerzaz, Algeria 99 C4 29 29N 1 37W
Kerzers, Switz. 28 C4 46 59N 7 12 E
Kesagami →, Canada 128 B4 51 40N 79 45W
Kesagami L., Canada 128 B3 50 23N 80 15W
Keşan, Turkey 88 B2 40 49N 26 38 E
Kesch, Piz, Switz. 29 C9 46 38N 9 53 E
Kesennuma, Japan 60 E10 38 54N 141 35 E
Keshit, Iran 85 D8 29 43N 58 17 E
Keşiş Dağ, Turkey 89 C8 39 47N 39 46 E
Keskin, Turkey 88 C5 39 40N 33 36 E
Kessel, Belgium 21 F5 51 8N 4 38 E
Kessel, Neths. 21 F8 51 17N 6 3 E
Kessel-Lo, Belgium 21 G5 50 53N 4 43 E
Kestell, S. Africa 105 D4 28 17 S 28 42 E
Kestenga, Russia 48 A5 65 50N 31 45 E
Kesteren, Neths. 20 E7 51 56N 5 34 E
Keswick, U.K. 16 C4 54 36N 3 8W
Keszthely, Hungary 31 E10 46 50N 17 15 E
Ket →, Russia 56 D9 58 55N 81 32 E
Keta, Ghana 101 D5 5 49N 1 0 E
Ketapang, Indonesia 75 C4 1 55 S 110 0 E
Ketchikan, U.S.A. 126 C6 55 21N 131 39W
Ketchum, U.S.A. 142 E6 43 41N 114 22W
Kete Krachi, Ghana 101 D4 7 46N 0 1W
Ketef, Khalîg Umm el, Egypt 94 C4 23 40N 35 35 E
Ketelmeer, Neths. 20 C7 52 36N 5 46 E
Keti Bandar, Pakistan 80 G2 24 8N 67 27 E
Ketri, India 80 E6 28 1N 75 50 E
Kętrzyn, Poland 47 A8 54 7N 21 22 E
Kettering, U.K. 17 E7 52 24N 0 43W
Kettering, U.S.A. 141 E12 39 41N 84 10W
Kettle →, Canada 131 B11 56 40N 89 34W
Kettle Falls, U.S.A. 142 B4 48 37N 118 3W
Kettleman City, U.S.A. 144 J7 36 1N 119 58W
Kety, Poland 31 B12 49 51N 19 16 E
Keuruu, Finland 13 E21 62 16N 24 41 E
Kevin, U.S.A. 142 B8 48 45N 111 58W
Kewanee, U.S.A. 140 C7 41 14N 89 56W
Kewanna, U.S.A. 141 C10 41 1N 86 25W
Kewaunee, U.S.A. 134 C2 44 27N 87 31W
Keweenaw B., U.S.A. 134 B1 47 0N 88 15W
Keweenaw Pen., U.S.A. 134 B2 47 30N 88 0W
Keweenaw Pt., U.S.A. 134 B2 47 25N 87 43W
Key Harbour, Canada 128 C3 45 50N 80 45W
Key West, U.S.A. 133 F10 24 33N 81 48W
Keyesport, U.S.A. 140 F7 38 45N 89 17W
Keyser, U.S.A. 134 F6 39 26N 78 59W
Keystone, U.S.A. 138 D3 43 54N 103 25W
Keytesville, U.S.A. 140 E4 39 26N 92 56W
Kez, Russia 54 C4 57 55N 53 46 E
Kezhma, Russia 57 D11 58 59N 101 9 E
Kežmarok, Slovak Rep. 31 B13 49 10N 20 28 E
Khabarovo, Russia 56 C7 69 30N 60 30 E
Khabarovsk, Russia 57 E14 48 30N 135 5 E
Khabr, Iran 85 D8 28 51N 56 22 E
Khābūr →, Syria 89 E9 35 17N 40 35 E
Khachmas = Xaçmaz, Azerbaijan 53 K9 41 31N 48 42 E
Khachrod, India 80 H6 23 25N 75 20 E
Khadari, W. el →, Sudan 95 E2 10 29N 27 15 E
Khadro, Pakistan 80 F3 26 11N 68 50 E
Khadyzhensk, Russia 53 H4 44 26N 39 32 E
Khadzhilyangar, India 81 B8 35 45N 79 20 E
Khagaria, India 81 G12 25 30N 86 32 E
Khaipur, Bahawalpur, Pakistan 80 E5 29 34N 72 17 E
Khaipur, Hyderabad, Pakistan 80 F3 27 32N 68 49 E
Khair, India 80 F7 27 57N 77 46 E
Khairabad, India 81 F9 27 33N 80 47 E
Khairagarh, India 81 J9 21 27N 81 2 E
Khairpur, Pakistan 79 D3 27 32N 68 49 E
Khāk Dow, Afghan. 79 B2 34 57N 67 16 E
Khakassia □, Russia 56 D9 53 0N 90 0 E
Khakhea, Botswana 104 C3 24 48 S 23 22 E
Khalach, Turkmenistan 55 D2 38 4N 64 52 E
Khalafābād, Iran 85 D6 30 54N 49 24 E
Khalfallah, Algeria 99 B5 34 20N 0 16 E
Khalfūt, Yemen 87 D6 15 52N 52 10 E
Khalilabad, India 81 F10 26 48N 83 5 E
Khalīlī, Iran 85 E7 27 38N 53 17 E
Khalkhāl, Iran 89 D13 37 37N 48 32 E
Khálki, Greece 44 E4 39 36N 22 30 E
Khalkidhikí □, Greece 44 D5 40 25N 23 20 E
Khalkís, Greece 45 F5 38 27N 23 42 E
Khalmer-Sede = Tazovskiy, Russia 56 C8 67 30N 78 44 E
Khalmer Yu, Russia 48 A12 67 58N 65 1 E
Khalturin, Russia 54 B2 58 40N 48 50 E
Khalūf, Oman 90 C6 20 30N 58 13 E
Kham Keut, Laos 76 C5 18 15N 104 43 E
Khamaria, India 82 C5 23 10N 80 52 E
Khamas Country, Botswana 104 C4 21 45 S 26 30 E
Khambat, G. of, India 80 J5 20 45N 72 30 E
Khambhaliya, India 80 H3 22 14N 69 41 E

Kipling 217

Khambhat, India 80 H5 22 23N 72 33 E
Khamgaon, India 82 D3 20 42N 76 37 E
Khamilonísion, Greece 45 J8 35 50N 26 15 E
Khamīr, Iran 85 E7 26 57N 55 36 E
Khamir, Yemen 86 C3 16 2N 44 0 E
Khamīs Mushayṭ, Si. Arabia 86 C3 18 18N 42 44 E
Khammam, India 82 F5 17 11N 80 6 E
Khamsa, Egypt 91 E1 30 27N 32 23 E
Khān Abū Shāmat, Syria 91 B5 33 39N 36 53 E
Khān Azād, Iraq 84 C5 33 7N 44 22 E
Khān Mujiddah, Iraq 84 C4 32 21N 43 48 E
Khān Shaykhūn, Syria 88 E7 35 26N 36 38 E
Khān Yūnis, Gaza Strip 91 D3 31 21N 34 18 E
Khānābād, Afghan. 79 A3 36 45N 69 5 E
Khanabad, Uzbekistan 55 C5 40 59N 70 38 E
Khānaqīn, Iraq 89 E11 34 23N 45 25 E
Khānbāghī, Iran 85 B7 36 10N 55 25 E
Khandrá, Greece 45 J8 35 3N 26 8 E
Khandwa, India 82 D3 21 49N 76 22 E
Khandyga, Russia 57 C14 62 42N 135 35 E
Khāneh, Iran 84 B5 36 41N 45 8 E
Khanewal, Pakistan 79 C3 30 20N 71 55 E
Khanh Duong, Vietnam 76 F7 12 44N 108 44 E
Khaniá, Greece 32 D6 35 30N 24 4 E
Khaniá □, Greece 32 D6 35 30N 24 0 E
Khaníon, Kólpos, Greece 32 D5 35 33N 23 55 E
Khanka, Ozero, Asia 57 E14 45 0N 132 24 E
Khankendy = Xankändi, Azerbaijan 89 C12 39 52N 46 49 E
Khanna, India 80 D7 30 42N 76 16 E
Khanpur, Pakistan 79 C3 28 42N 70 35 E
Khantau, Kazakstan 55 A6 44 13N 73 48 E
Khanty-Mansiysk, Russia 56 C7 61 0N 69 0 E
Khapalu, Pakistan 81 B7 35 10N 76 20 E
Khapcheranga, Russia 57 E12 49 42N 112 24 E
Kharabali, Russia 53 G8 47 25N 47 15 E
Kharagpur, India 81 H12 22 20N 87 25 E
Khárakas, Greece 32 D7 35 1N 25 7 E
Kharan Kalat, Pakistan 79 C2 28 34N 65 21 E
Kharānaq, Iran 85 C7 32 20N 54 45 E
Kharda, India 82 E2 18 40N 75 34 E
Khardung La, India 81 B7 34 20N 77 43 E
Khârga, El Wâhât el, Egypt 94 B3 25 10N 30 35 E
Khargon, India 82 D2 21 45N 75 40 E
Kharit, Wadi el →, Egypt 94 C3 24 26N 33 3 E
Khārk, Jazireh, Iran 85 D6 29 15N 50 28 E
Kharkiv, Ukraine 51 H9 49 58N 36 20 E
Kharkov = Kharkiv, Ukraine 51 H9 49 58N 36 20 E
Kharmanli, Bulgaria 43 F10 41 55N 25 55 E
Kharovsk, Russia 50 C11 59 56N 40 13 E
Kharta, Turkey 88 B3 40 55N 29 7 E
Khartoum = El Khartûm, Sudan 95 D3 15 31N 32 35 E
Khasan, Russia 60 C5 42 25N 130 40 E
Khasavyurt, Russia 53 J8 43 16N 46 40 E
Khāsh, Iran 85 D9 28 15N 61 15 E
Khashm el Girba, Sudan 95 E4 14 59N 35 58 E
Khashuri, Georgia 53 J6 42 3N 43 35 E
Khasi Hills, India 78 C3 25 30N 91 30 E
Khaskovo, Bulgaria 43 F10 41 56N 25 30 E
Khatanga, Russia 57 B11 72 0N 102 20 E
Khatanga →, Russia 57 B11 72 55N 106 0 E
Khatauli, India 80 E7 29 17N 77 43 E
Khātūnābād, Iran 85 C6 35 30N 51 40 E
Khatyrchi, Uzbekistan 55 C2 40 2N 65 58 E
Khatyrka, Russia 57 C18 62 3N 175 15 E
Khavast, Uzbekistan 55 C4 40 10N 68 49 E
Khawlaf, Ra's, Yemen 87 D6 12 40N 54 7 E
Khay', Si. Arabia 86 C3 18 45N 41 24 E
Khaybar, Harrat, Si. Arabia 84 E4 25 45N 40 0 E
Khaydarken, Kyrgyzstan 55 D5 39 57N 71 20 E
Khāzimiyah, Iraq 84 C4 34 46N 43 37 E
Khazzân Jabal el Awliyâ, Sudan 95 D3 15 24N 32 20 E
Khe Bo, Vietnam 76 C5 19 8N 104 41 E
Khe Long, Vietnam 76 B5 21 29N 104 46 E
Khed, Maharashtra, India 82 F1 17 43N 73 27 E
Khed, Maharashtra, India 82 E1 18 51N 73 56 E
Khekra, India 80 E7 28 52N 77 20 E
Khemarak Phouminville, Cambodia 77 G4 11 37N 102 59 E
Khemis Miliana, Algeria 99 A5 36 11N 2 14 E
Khemissèt, Morocco 98 B3 33 50N 6 1W
Khemmarat, Thailand 76 D5 16 10N 105 15 E
Khenāmān, Iran 85 D8 30 27N 56 29 E
Khenchela, Algeria 99 A6 35 28N 7 11 E
Khenifra, Morocco 98 B3 32 58N 5 46W
Kherrata, Algeria 99 A6 36 27N 5 13 E
Khérson, Greece 44 C4 41 5N 22 47 E
Kherson, Ukraine 51 J7 46 35N 32 35 E
Khersónisos Akrotíri, Greece 32 D6 35 30N 24 10 E
Kheta →, Russia 57 B11 71 54N 102 6 E
Khiliomódhion, Greece 45 G4 37 48N 22 51 E
Khilok, Russia 57 D12 51 30N 110 45 E
Khimki, Russia 52 C3 55 50N 37 20 E
Khíos, Greece 45 F8 38 27N 26 9 E
Khirbat Qanāfār, Lebanon 91 B4 33 39N 35 43 E
Khisar-Momina Banya, Bulgaria 43 E9 42 30N 24 44 E
Khiuma = Hiiumaa, Estonia 13 G20 58 50N 22 45 E
Khiva, Uzbekistan 56 E7 41 30N 60 18 E
Khīyāv, Iran 84 B5 38 30N 47 45 E
Khlebarovo, Bulgaria 43 D11 43 37N 26 15 E
Khlong Khlung, Thailand 76 D2 16 12N 99 43 E
Khmelnik, Ukraine 51 H4 49 33N 27 58 E
Khmelnitskiy = Khmelnytskyy, Ukraine 51 H4 49 23N 27 0 E
Khmelnytskyy, Ukraine 51 H4 49 23N 27 0 E
Khmer Rep. = Cambodia ■, Asia 76 F5 12 15N 105 0 E
Khoai, Hon, Vietnam 77 H5 8 26N 104 50 E
Khodoriv, Ukraine 51 H3 49 24N 24 19 E
Khodzent = Khudzhand, Tajikistan 55 C4 40 17N 69 37 E
Khojak P., Afghan. 79 C2 30 55N 66 30 E
Khok Kloi, Thailand 77 H2 8 17N 98 19 E
Khok Pho, Thailand 77 J3 6 43N 101 6 E
Kholm, Afghan. 79 A2 36 45N 67 40 E
Kholm, Russia 50 D6 57 10N 31 15 E
Kholmsk, Russia 57 E15 47 40N 142 5 E
Khomas Hochland, Namibia 104 C2 22 40 S 16 0 E
Khomeyn, Iran 85 C6 33 40N 50 7 E
Khon Kaen, Thailand 76 D4 16 30N 102 47 E
Khong, Laos 76 E5 14 7N 105 51 E
Khong Sedone, Laos 76 E5 15 34N 105 49 E
Khonuu, Russia 57 C15 66 30N 143 12 E
Khoper →, Russia 52 F6 49 30N 42 20 E
Khor el 'Atash, Sudan 95 E3 13 20N 34 15 E
Khóra, Greece 45 G3 37 3N 21 42 E
Khóra Sfakíon, Greece 32 D6 35 15N 24 9 E
Khorāsān □, Iran 85 C8 34 0N 58 0 E
Khorat = Nakhon Ratchasima, Thailand 76 E4 14 59N 102 12 E
Khorat, Cao Nguyen, Thailand 76 E4 15 30N 102 50 E
Khorb el Ethel, Algeria 98 C3 28 30N 6 17W
Khorixas, Namibia 104 C1 20 16 S 14 59 E
Khorol, Ukraine 51 H7 49 48N 33 15 E
Khorramābād, Khorāsān, Iran 85 C8 35 6N 57 57 E
Khorramābād, Lorestān, Iran 89 F13 33 30N 48 25 E
Khorrāmshahr, Iran 85 D6 30 29N 48 15 E
Khorugh, Tajikistan 55 E5 37 30N 71 36 E
Khosravī, Iran 85 D6 30 48N 51 28 E
Khosrowābād, Khuzestān, Iran 85 D6 30 10N 48 25 E
Khosrowābād, Kordestān, Iran 89 E12 35 31N 47 38 E
Khosūyeh, Iran 85 D7 28 32N 54 26 E
Khotyn, Ukraine 51 H4 48 31N 26 27 E
Khouribga, Morocco 98 B3 32 58N 6 57W
Khowai, Bangla. 78 C3 24 5N 91 40 E
Khoyniki, Belarus 51 G5 51 54N 29 55 E
Khrami →, Georgia 53 K7 41 25N 45 0 E
Khrenovoye, Russia 52 E5 51 4N 40 16 E
Khristianá, Greece 45 H7 36 14N 25 13 E
Khromtau, Kazakstan 54 F7 50 17N 58 27 E
Khrysokhou B., Cyprus 32 D11 35 6N 32 25 E
Khtapodhiá, Greece 45 G7 37 24N 25 34 E
Khu Khan, Thailand 76 E5 14 42N 104 12 E
Khudrah, W. →, Yemen 87 C5 18 10N 50 20 E
Khudzhand, Tajikistan 55 C4 40 17N 69 37 E
Khuff, Si. Arabia 84 E5 24 55N 44 53 E
Khūgīānī, Qandahar, Afghan. 79 C2 31 34N 66 32 E
Khūgīānī, Qandahar, Afghan. 79 C2 31 28N 65 14 E
Khulayṣ, Si. Arabia 86 B2 22 9N 39 19 E
Khulna, Bangla. 78 D2 22 45N 89 34 E
Khulna □, Bangla. 78 D2 22 25N 89 35 E
Khulo, Georgia 53 K6 41 33N 42 19 E
Khumago, Botswana 104 C3 20 26 S 24 32 E
Khumrah, Si. Arabia 86 B2 21 22N 39 13 E
Khūnsorkh, Iran 85 E8 27 9N 56 7 E
Khūr, Iran 85 C8 32 55N 58 18 E
Khurai, India 80 G8 24 3N 78 23 E
Khuraydah, Yemen 87 D5 15 33N 48 18 E
Khurayṣ, Si. Arabia 85 E6 25 6N 48 2 E
Khūrīyā Mūrīyā, Jazā 'ir, Oman 87 C6 17 30N 55 58 E
Khurja, India 80 E7 28 15N 77 58 E
Khūsf, Iran 85 C8 32 46N 58 53 E
Khushab, Pakistan 79 B4 32 20N 72 20 E
Khust, Ukraine 51 H2 48 10N 23 18 E
Khuzdar, Pakistan 79 D2 27 52N 66 30 E
Khūzestān □, Iran 85 D6 31 0N 49 0 E
Khvājeh, Iran 84 B5 38 9N 46 35 E
Khvājeh Moḥammad, Kūh-e, Afghan. 79 A3 36 22N 70 17 E
Khvalynsk, Russia 52 D9 52 30N 48 2 E
Khvānsār, Iran 85 D7 29 56N 54 8 E
Khvatovka, Russia 52 D8 52 24N 46 32 E
Khvor, Iran 85 C7 33 45N 55 0 E
Khvorgū, Iran 85 E8 27 34N 56 27 E
Khvormūj, Iran 85 D6 28 40N 51 30 E
Khvoy, Iran 89 C11 38 35N 45 0 E
Khvoynaya, Russia 52 A2 58 58N 34 28 E
Khyber Pass, Afghan. 79 B3 34 10N 71 8 E
Kia, Solomon Is. 121 L10 7 32 S 158 26 E
Kiabukwa, Zaïre 103 D4 8 40 S 24 48 E
Kiadho →, India 82 E3 19 37N 77 40 E
Kiama, Australia 117 C9 34 40 S 150 50 E
Kiamba, Phil. 71 H5 6 2N 124 46 E
Kiambi, Zaïre 106 D2 7 15 S 28 0 E
Kiambu, Kenya 106 C4 1 8 S 36 50 E
Kiangsi = Jiangxi □, China 69 D10 27 30N 116 0 E
Kiangsu = Jiangsu □, China 67 H10 33 0N 120 0 E
Kiáton, Greece 45 F4 38 2N 22 43 E
Kibæk, Denmark 15 H2 56 2N 8 51 E
Kibanga Port, Uganda 106 B3 0 10N 32 58 E
Kibangou, Congo 102 C2 3 26 S 12 22 E
Kibara, Tanzania 106 C3 2 8 S 33 30 E
Kibare, Mts., Zaïre 106 D2 8 25 S 27 10 E
Kibawe, Phil. 71 H5 7 34N 125 0 E
Kibombo, Zaïre 103 C5 3 57 S 25 53 E
Kibondo, Tanzania 106 C3 3 35 S 30 45 E
Kibondo □, Tanzania 106 C3 4 0 S 30 55 E
Kibumbu, Burundi 106 C2 3 32 S 29 45 E
Kibungu, Rwanda 106 C3 2 10 S 30 32 E
Kibuye, Burundi 106 C2 3 39 S 29 59 E
Kibuye, Rwanda 106 C2 2 3 S 29 21 E
Kibwesa, Tanzania 106 D2 6 30 S 29 58 E
Kibwezi, Kenya 106 C4 2 27 S 37 57 E
Kičevo, Macedonia 42 F5 41 34N 20 59 E
Kichiga, Russia 57 D17 59 50N 163 5 E
Kicking Horse Pass, Canada 130 C5 51 28N 116 16W
Kidal, Mali 101 B5 18 26N 1 22 E
Kidapawan, Phil. 71 H5 7 1N 125 3 E
Kidderminster, U.K. 17 E5 52 24N 2 15W
Kidete, Tanzania 106 D4 6 25 S 37 17 E
Kidira, Senegal 100 C2 14 28N 12 13W
Kidnappers, C., N.Z. 118 F6 39 38 S 177 5 E
Kidston, Australia 114 B3 18 52 S 144 8 E
Kidugallo, Tanzania 106 D4 6 49 S 38 15 E
Kidurong, Tanjong, Malaysia 75 B4 3 16N 113 3 E
Kiel, Germany 26 A6 54 19N 10 8 E
Kiel Canal = Nord-Ostsee-Kanal →, Germany 26 A5 54 12N 9 32 E
Kielce, Poland 47 E7 50 52N 20 42 E
Kielce □, Poland 47 E7 50 40N 20 40 E
Kieldrecht, Belgium 21 F4 51 17N 4 11 E
Kieler Bucht, Germany 26 A6 54 35N 10 25 E
Kien Binh, Vietnam 77 H5 9 55N 105 19 E
Kien Tan, Vietnam 77 G5 10 7N 105 17 E
Kienge, Zaïre 107 E2 10 30 S 27 30 E
Kiessé, Niger 101 C5 13 29N 4 1 E
Kieta, Papua N. G. 120 D8 6 12 S 155 36 E
Kiev = Kyyiv, Ukraine 51 G6 50 30N 30 28 E
Kiffa, Mauritania 100 B2 16 37N 11 24W
Kifisiá, Greece 45 F5 38 4N 23 49 E
Kifissós →, Greece 45 F5 38 35N 23 20 E
Kifrī, Iraq 89 E11 34 45N 45 0 E
Kigali, Rwanda 106 C3 1 59 S 30 4 E
Kigarama, Tanzania 106 C3 1 1 S 31 50 E
Kigoma □, Tanzania 106 D2 5 0 S 30 0 E
Kigoma-Ujiji, Tanzania 106 C2 4 55 S 29 36 E
Kigomasha, Ras, Tanzania 106 C4 4 58 S 38 58 E
Kihee, Australia 115 D3 27 23 S 142 37 E
Kihikihi, N.Z. 118 E4 38 2 S 175 22 E
Kihnu, Estonia 13 G21 58 9N 24 1 E
Kii-Hantō, Japan 63 D7 34 0N 135 45 E
Kii-Sanchi, Japan 63 C8 34 20N 136 0 E
Kii-Suidō, Japan 62 D6 33 40N 134 45 E
Kikaiga-Shima, Japan 61 K4 28 19N 129 59 E
Kikinda, Serbia, Yug. 42 B5 45 50N 20 30 E
Kikládhes, Greece 45 G6 37 20N 24 30 E
Kikládhes □, Greece 45 G6 37 0N 25 0 E
Kikoira, Australia 117 B7 33 39 S 146 40 E
Kikori, Papua N. G. 120 D3 7 25 S 144 15 E
Kikori →, Papua N. G. 120 D3 7 38 S 144 20 E
Kikuchi, Japan 62 E2 32 59N 130 47 E
Kikwit, Zaïre 103 D3 5 0 S 18 45 E
Kila' Drosh, Pakistan 79 B3 35 33N 71 52 E
Kilakkarai, India 83 K4 9 12N 78 47 E
Kílalki, Greece 45 H9 36 15N 27 35 E
Kilauea Crater, U.S.A. 132 J17 19 25N 155 17W
Kilchberg, Switz. 29 B7 47 18N 8 33 E
Kilcoy, Australia 115 D5 26 59 S 152 30 E
Kildare, Ireland 19 C5 53 9N 6 55W
Kildare □, Ireland 19 C5 53 10N 6 50W
Kilembe, Zaïre 103 D3 5 42 S 19 55 E
Kilgore, U.S.A. 139 J7 32 23N 94 53W
Kilifi, Kenya 106 C4 3 40 S 39 48 E
Kilifi □, Kenya 106 C4 3 30 S 39 40 E
Kilimanjaro, Tanzania 106 C4 3 7 S 37 20 E
Kilimanjaro □, Tanzania 106 C4 4 0 S 38 0 E
Kilimli, Turkey 88 B4 41 28N 31 50 E
Kilinailau Is., Papua N. G. 120 C8 4 45 S 155 20 E
Kilindini, Kenya 106 C4 4 4 S 39 40 E
Kilis, Turkey 88 D7 36 42N 37 6 E
Kiliya, Ukraine 51 K5 45 28N 29 16 E
Kilju, N. Korea 67 D15 40 57N 129 25 E
Kilkee, Ireland 19 D2 52 41N 9 39W
Kilkenny, Ireland 19 D4 52 39N 7 15W
Kilkenny □, Ireland 19 D4 52 35N 7 15W
Kilkieran B., Ireland 19 C2 53 20N 9 41W
Kilkís, Greece 44 D4 40 58N 22 57 E
Kilkís □, Greece 44 C4 41 5N 22 50 E
Killala, Ireland 19 B2 54 13N 9 12W
Killala B., Ireland 19 B2 54 16N 9 8W
Killaloe, Ireland 19 D3 52 48N 8 28W
Killaloe Sta., Canada 136 A7 45 33N 77 25W
Killam, Canada 130 C6 52 47N 111 51W
Killarney, Australia 115 D5 28 20 S 152 18 E
Killarney, Canada 128 C3 45 55N 81 30W
Killarney, Ireland 19 D2 52 4N 9 30W
Killarney, Lakes of, Ireland 19 E2 52 0N 9 30W
Killary Harbour, Ireland 19 C2 53 38N 9 52W
Killdeer, Canada 131 D7 49 6N 106 22W
Killdeer, U.S.A. 138 B3 47 26N 102 48W
Killeen, U.S.A. 139 K6 31 7N 97 44W
Killiecrankie, Pass of, U.K. 18 E5 56 44N 3 46W
Killin, U.K. 18 E4 56 28N 4 19W
Killíni, Ilía, Greece 45 G3 37 55N 21 8 E
Killíni, Korinthía, Greece 45 G4 37 54N 22 25 E
Killybegs, Ireland 19 B3 54 38N 8 26W
Kilmarnock, U.K. 18 F4 55 37N 4 29W
Kilmez, Russia 52 B10 56 58N 50 55 E
Kilmez →, Russia 52 B10 56 58N 50 28 E
Kilmore, Australia 117 D6 37 25 S 144 53 E
Kilondo, Tanzania 107 D3 9 45 S 34 20 E
Kilosa, Tanzania 106 D4 6 48 S 37 0 E
Kilosa □, Tanzania 106 D4 6 48 S 37 0 E
Kilrush, Ireland 19 D2 52 38N 9 29W
Kilwa □, Tanzania 107 D4 9 0 S 39 0 E
Kilwa Kisiwani, Tanzania 107 D4 8 58 S 39 32 E
Kilwa Kivinje, Tanzania 107 D4 8 45 S 39 25 E
Kilwa Masoko, Tanzania 107 D4 8 55 S 39 30 E
Kim, U.S.A. 139 G3 37 15N 103 21W
Kimaam, Indonesia 73 C5 7 58 S 138 53 E
Kimamba, Tanzania 106 D4 6 45 S 37 10 E
Kimba, Australia 116 B2 33 8 S 136 23 E
Kimball, Nebr., U.S.A. 138 E3 41 14N 103 40W
Kimball, S. Dak., U.S.A. 138 D5 43 45N 98 57W
Kimbe, Papua N. G. 120 C6 5 33 S 150 11 E
Kimbe B., Papua N. G. 120 C6 5 15 S 150 30 E
Kimberley, Australia 116 B4 32 50 S 141 4 E
Kimberley, Canada 130 D5 49 40N 115 59W
Kimberley, S. Africa 104 D3 28 43 S 24 46 E
Kimberley Downs, Australia 112 C3 17 24 S 124 22 E
Kimberley Plateau, Australia 110 D4 16 20 S 127 0 E
Kimberly, U.S.A. 142 E6 42 32N 114 22W
Kimchaek, N. Korea 67 D15 40 40N 129 10 E
Kimchŏn, S. Korea 67 F15 36 11N 128 4 E
Kími, Greece 45 F6 38 38N 24 6 E
Kimje, S. Korea 67 G14 35 48N 126 45 E
Kimmirut, Canada 127 B13 62 50N 69 50W
Kímolos, Greece 45 H6 36 48N 24 37 E
Kimovsk, Russia 52 C3 54 0N 38 29 E
Kimparana, Mali 100 C4 12 48N 5 0W
Kimry, Russia 52 B3 56 55N 37 15 E
Kimsquit, Canada 130 C3 52 45N 126 57W
Kimstad, Sweden 15 F9 58 35N 15 58 E
Kimvula, Zaïre 103 D3 5 44 S 15 58 E
Kinabalu, Gunong, Malaysia 75 A5 6 3N 116 14 E
Kínaros, Greece 45 H8 36 59N 26 15 E
Kinaskan L., Canada 130 B2 57 38N 130 8W
Kinbasket L., Canada 130 C5 52 0N 118 10W
Kincaid, Canada 131 D7 49 40N 107 0W
Kincaid, U.S.A. 140 E7 39 35N 89 25W
Kincardine, Canada 128 D3 44 10N 81 40W
Kinda, Kasai Or., Zaïre 103 D5 9 18 S 25 4 E
Kinda, Shaba, Zaïre 103 C4 4 47 S 21 48 E
Kinder Scout, U.K. 16 D6 53 24N 1 52W
Kindersley, Canada 131 C7 51 30N 109 10W
Kindia, Guinea 100 C2 10 0N 12 52W
Kindu, Zaïre 102 C5 2 55 S 25 50 E
Kinel, Russia 52 D10 53 15N 50 40 E
Kineshma, Russia 52 B6 57 30N 42 5 E
Kinesi, Tanzania 106 C3 1 25 S 33 50 E
King, L., Australia 113 F2 33 10 S 119 35 E
King, Mt., Australia 114 D4 25 10 S 147 30 E
King City, Calif., U.S.A. 144 J5 36 13N 121 8W
King City, Mo., U.S.A. 140 D2 40 3N 94 31W
King Cr. →, Australia 114 C2 24 35 S 139 30 E
King Edward →, Australia 112 B4 14 14 S 126 35 E
King Frederick VI Land = Kong Frederik VI.s Kyst, Greenland 6 C5 63 0N 43 0W
King George B., Falk. Is. 160 D4 51 30 S 60 30W
King George I., Antarctica 7 C18 60 0 S 60 0W
King George Is., Canada 127 C11 57 20N 80 30W
King I., Australia 114 F3 39 50 S 144 0 E
King I., Canada 130 C3 52 10N 127 40W
King Leopold Ras., Australia 112 C4 17 30 S 125 45 E
King Sd., Australia 112 C3 16 50 S 123 20 E
King William I., Canada 126 B10 69 10N 97 25W
King William's Town, S. Africa 104 E4 32 51 S 27 22 E
Kingaroy, Australia 115 D5 26 32 S 151 51 E
Kingfisher, U.S.A. 139 H6 35 52N 97 56W
Kingirbān, Iraq 84 C5 34 40N 44 54 E
Kingisepp = Kuressaare, Estonia 13 G20 58 15N 22 30 E
Kingisepp, Russia 50 C5 59 25N 28 40 E
Kingking, Phil. 71 H5 7 9N 125 54 E
Kingman, Ariz., U.S.A. 145 K12 35 12N 114 4W
Kingman, Ind., U.S.A. 141 E9 39 58N 87 18W
Kingman, Kans., U.S.A. 139 G5 37 39N 98 7W
Kingoonya, Australia 115 E2 30 55 S 135 19 E
Kings →, U.S.A. 144 J7 36 3N 119 50W
Kings Canyon National Park, U.S.A. 144 J8 36 50N 118 40W
King's Lynn, U.K. 16 E8 52 45N 0 24 E
Kings Mountain, U.S.A. 135 H5 35 15N 81 20W
King's Peak, U.S.A. 142 F8 40 46N 110 27W
Kingsbridge, U.K. 17 G4 50 17N 3 47W
Kingsburg, U.S.A. 144 J7 36 31N 119 33W
Kingsbury, U.S.A. 141 C10 41 31N 86 42W
Kingscote, Australia 116 C2 35 40 S 137 38 E
Kingscourt, Ireland 19 C5 53 55N 6 48W
Kingsley, U.S.A. 138 D7 42 35N 95 58W
Kingsport, U.S.A. 135 G4 36 33N 82 33W
Kingston, Canada 128 D4 44 14N 76 30W
Kingston, Jamaica 148 C4 18 0N 76 50W
Kingston, N.Z. 119 F3 45 20 S 168 43 E
Kingston, Mo., U.S.A. 140 E2 39 39N 94 2W
Kingston, N.Y., U.S.A. 137 E10 41 56N 73 59W
Kingston, Pa., U.S.A. 137 E9 41 16N 75 54W
Kingston, R.I., U.S.A. 137 E13 41 29N 71 30W
Kingston Pk., U.S.A. 145 K11 35 45N 115 54W
Kingston South East, Australia 116 D3 36 51 S 139 55 E
Kingston upon Hull, U.K. 16 D7 53 45N 0 21W
Kingston upon Hull □, U.K. 16 D7 53 45N 0 21W
Kingston-upon-Thames, U.K. 17 F7 51 24N 0 17W
Kingstown, Australia 117 A9 30 29 S 151 6 E
Kingstown, St. Vincent 149 D7 13 10N 61 10W
Kingstree, U.S.A. 135 J6 33 40N 79 50W
Kingsville, Canada 128 D3 42 2N 82 45W
Kingsville, U.S.A. 139 M6 27 31N 97 52W
Kingussie, U.K. 18 D4 57 6N 4 2W
Kınık, Turkey 88 C2 39 5N 27 23 E
Kinistino, Canada 131 C7 52 57N 105 2W
Kinkala, Congo 103 C2 4 18 S 14 49 E
Kinki □, Japan 63 D8 33 45N 136 0 E
Kinleith, N.Z. 118 E4 38 20 S 175 56 E
Kinmount, Canada 136 B6 44 48N 78 45W
Kinmundy, U.S.A. 141 F8 38 46N 88 51W
Kinna, Sweden 15 G6 57 32N 12 42 E
Kinnaird, Canada 130 D5 49 17N 117 39W
Kinnairds Hd., U.K. 18 D7 57 43N 2 1W
Kinnared, Sweden 15 G7 57 2N 13 7 E
Kinnarodden, Norway 10 A11 71 8N 27 40 E
Kino, Mexico 146 B2 28 45N 111 59W
Kinogitan, Phil. 71 G5 9 0N 124 48 E
Kinoje →, Canada 128 B3 52 8N 81 25W
Kinomoto, Japan 63 B8 35 30N 136 13 E
Kinoni, Uganda 106 C3 0 41 S 30 28 E
Kinrooi, Belgium 21 F7 51 9N 5 45 E
Kinross, U.K. 18 E5 56 13N 3 25W
Kinsale, Ireland 19 E3 51 42N 8 31W
Kinsale, Old Hd. of, Ireland 19 E3 51 37N 8 33W
Kinsha = Chang Jiang →, China 69 B13 31 48N 121 10 E
Kinshasa, Zaïre 103 C3 4 20 S 15 15 E
Kinsley, U.S.A. 139 G5 37 55N 99 25W
Kinston, U.S.A. 135 H7 35 16N 77 35W
Kintampo, Ghana 101 D4 8 5N 1 41W
Kintap, Indonesia 75 C5 3 51 S 115 13 E
Kintore Ra., Australia 112 D4 23 15 S 128 47 E
Kintyre, U.K. 18 F3 55 30N 5 35W
Kintyre, Mull of, U.K. 18 F3 55 17N 5 47W
Kinu, Burma 78 D5 22 46N 95 37 E
Kinu-Gawa →, Japan 63 B11 35 36N 139 57 E
Kinushseo →, Canada 128 A3 55 15N 83 45W
Kinuso, Canada 130 B5 55 20N 115 25W
Kinyangiri, Tanzania 106 C3 4 25 S 34 37 E
Kinzig →, Germany 27 G3 48 36N 7 49 E
Kinzua, U.S.A. 136 E6 41 52N 78 58W
Kinzua Dam, U.S.A. 136 E5 41 53N 79 0W
Kióni, Greece 45 F2 38 27N 20 41 E
Kiosk, Canada 128 C4 46 6N 78 53W
Kiowa, Kans., U.S.A. 139 G5 37 1N 98 29W
Kiowa, Okla., U.S.A. 139 H7 34 43N 95 54W
Kipahigan L., Canada 131 B8 55 20N 101 55W
Kipanga, Tanzania 106 D4 6 15 S 35 20 E
Kiparissía, Greece 45 G3 37 15N 21 40 E
Kiparissiakós Kólpos, Greece 45 G3 37 25N 21 25 E
Kipembawe, Tanzania 106 D3 7 38 S 33 27 E
Kipengere Ra., Tanzania 107 D3 9 12 S 34 15 E
Kipili, Tanzania 106 D3 7 28 S 30 32 E
Kipini, Kenya 106 C5 2 30 S 40 32 E
Kipling, Canada 131 C8 50 6N 102 38W

218 Kippure

Kippure, *Ireland* **19 C5** 53 11N 6 21W
Kipungot, *Phil.* **71 H5** 6 24N 124 4 E
Kipushi, *Zaïre* **107 E2** 11 48 S 27 12 E
Kira Kira, *Solomon Is.* **121 N11** 10 27 S 161 56 E
Kirandul, *India* **82 E5** 18 33N 81 10 E
Kiratpur, *India* **80 E8** 29 32N 78 12 E
Kirchberg, *Switz.* **28 B5** 47 5N 7 35 E
Kirchhain, *Germany* **26 E4** 50 47N 8 56 E
Kirchheim, *Germany* **27 G5** 48 39N 9 27 E
Kirchheim-Bolanden, *Germany* **27 F4** 49 40N 8 0 E
Kirchschlag, *Austria* **31 D9** 47 30N 16 19 E
Kirensk, *Russia* **57 D11** 57 50N 107 55 E
Kirgella Rocks, *Australia* **113 F3** 30 5 S 122 50 E
Kirghizia ■ = Kyrgyzstan ■, *Asia* **55 C7** 42 0N 75 0 E
Kirghizstan = Kyrgyzstan ■, *Asia* **55 C7** 42 0N 75 0 E
Kirgiziya Steppe, *Eurasia* **54 G4** 50 0N 55 0 E
Kiri, *Zaïre* **102 C3** 1 29 S 19 0 E
Kiri Buru, *India* **82 D7** 22 0N 85 0 E
Kiribati ■, *Pac. Oc.* **122 H10** 5 0 S 180 0 E
Kırıkhan, *Turkey* **88 D7** 36 31N 36 21 E
Kırıkkale, *Turkey* **88 C5** 39 51N 33 32 E
Kirikopuni, *N.Z.* **118 B3** 35 50 S 174 1 E
Kirillov, *Russia* **50 C10** 59 49N 38 24 E
Kirin = Jilin, *China* **67 C14** 43 44N 126 30 E
Kirin = Jilin □, *China* **67 C13** 44 0N 127 0 E
Kirindi →, *Sri Lanka* **83 L5** 6 15N 81 20 E
Kirishi, *Russia* **50 C7** 59 28N 31 59 E
Kirishima-Yama, *Japan* **62 F2** 31 58N 130 55 E
Kiritimati, *Kiribati* **123 G12** 1 58N 157 27W
Kırka, *Turkey* **88 C4** 39 16N 30 31 E
Kirkcaldy, *U.K.* **18 E5** 56 7N 3 9W
Kirkcudbright, *U.K.* **18 G4** 54 50N 4 2W
Kirkee, *India* **82 E1** 18 34N 73 56 E
Kirkenær, *Norway* **14 D6** 60 27N 12 3 E
Kirkenes, *Norway* **12 B23** 69 40N 30 5 E
Kirkintilloch, *U.K.* **18 F4** 55 56N 4 8W
Kirkjubæjarklaustur, *Iceland* **12 E4** 63 47N 18 4W
Kirkkonummi, *Finland* **13 F21** 60 8N 24 26 E
Kirkland, *Ariz., U.S.A.* **143 J7** 34 25N 112 43W
Kirkland, *Ill., U.S.A.* **141 B8** 42 6N 88 51W
Kirkland Lake, *Canada* **128 C3** 48 9N 80 2W
Kırklareli, *Turkey* **88 B2** 41 44N 27 15 E
Kirklin, *U.S.A.* **141 D10** 40 12N 86 22W
Kirkliston Ra., *N.Z.* **119 E5** 44 25 S 170 34 E
Kirksville, *U.S.A.* **140 D4** 40 12N 92 35W
Kirkūk, *Iraq* **89 E11** 35 30N 44 21 E
Kirkwall, *U.K.* **18 C6** 58 59N 2 58W
Kirkwood, *S. Africa* **104 E4** 33 22 S 25 15 E
Kirkwood, *U.S.A.* **140 F6** 38 35N 90 24W
Kirlampudi, *India* **82 F6** 17 12N 82 12 E
Kirn, *Germany* **27 F3** 49 47N 7 26 E
Kirov, *Russia* **52 C2** 54 3N 34 20 E
Kirov, *Russia* **54 B2** 58 35N 49 40 E
Kirovabad = Gäncä, *Azerbaijan* **53 K8** 40 45N 46 20 E
Kirovakan = Vanadzor, *Armenia* **53 K7** 40 48N 44 30 E
Kirovo, *Uzbekistan* **55 C5** 40 26N 70 36 E
Kirovo-Chepetsk, *Russia* **54 B3** 58 28N 50 0 E
Kirovograd = Kirovohrad, *Ukraine* **51 H7** 48 35N 32 20 E
Kirovohrad, *Ukraine* **51 H7** 48 35N 32 20 E
Kirovsk = Babadayhan, *Turkmenistan* **56 F7** 37 42N 60 23 E
Kirovsk, *Russia* **48 A5** 67 32N 33 41 E
Kirovskiy, *Kazakstan* **55 A9** 44 52N 78 12 E
Kirovskiy, *Russia* **53 H9** 45 51N 48 11 E
Kirovskiy, *Kamchatka, Russia* **57 D16** 54 27N 155 42 E
Kirovskiy, *Primorsk, Russia* **60 B6** 45 7N 133 30 E
Kirovskoye, *Kyrgyzstan* **55 B5** 42 39N 71 35 E
Kirriemuir, *U.K.* **18 E6** 56 41N 3 1W
Kirs, *Russia* **54 B4** 59 21N 52 14 E
Kirsanov, *Russia* **52 D6** 52 35N 42 40 E
Kırşehir, *Turkey* **88 C6** 39 14N 34 5 E
Kirtachi, *Niger* **101 C5** 12 52N 2 30 E
Kīrteh, *Afghan.* **79 B1** 32 15N 63 0 E
Kirthar Range, *Pakistan* **79 D2** 27 0N 67 0 E
Kiruna, *Sweden* **12 C19** 67 52N 20 15 E
Kirundu, *Zaïre* **102 C5** 0 50 S 25 35 E
Kirup, *Australia* **113 F2** 33 40 S 115 50 E
Kirya, *Russia* **52 C8** 55 8N 46 55 E
Kiryū, *Japan* **63 A11** 36 24N 139 20 E
Kisaga, *Tanzania* **106 C3** 4 30 S 34 23 E
Kisalaya, *Nic.* **148 D3** 14 40N 84 3W
Kisambo, *Zaïre* **103 D3** 6 25 S 18 14 E
Kisámou, Kólpos, *Greece* **32 D5** 35 30N 23 38 E
Kisanga, *Zaïre* **106 B2** 2 30N 26 35 E
Kisangani, *Zaïre* **106 B2** 0 35N 25 15 E
Kisantu, *Zaïre* **103 D3** 5 7 S 15 5 E
Kisar, *Indonesia* **72 C3** 8 5 S 127 10 E
Kisaran, *Indonesia* **74 B1** 3 0N 99 37 E
Kisarawe, *Tanzania* **106 D4** 6 53 S 39 0 E
Kisarawe □, *Tanzania* **106 D4** 7 3 S 39 0 E
Kisarazu, *Japan* **63 B11** 35 23N 139 55 E
Kisbér, *Hungary* **31 D11** 47 30N 18 2 E
Kiselevsk, *Russia* **56 D9** 54 5N 86 39 E
Kishanganga →, *Pakistan* **81 B5** 34 18N 73 28 E
Kishanganj, *India* **81 F13** 26 3N 88 14 E
Kishangarh, *India* **80 F4** 27 50N 70 30 E
Kishi, *Nigeria* **101 D5** 9 1N 3 52 E
Kishinev = Chişinău, *Moldova* **51 J5** 47 0N 28 50 E
Kishiwada, *Japan* **63 C7** 34 28N 135 22 E
Kishorganj, *Bangla.* **78 C3** 24 26N 90 40 E
Kishtwar, *India* **81 C6** 33 20N 75 48 E
Kishwaukee →, *U.S.A.* **140 B7** 42 12N 89 8W
Kisii, *Kenya* **106 C3** 0 40 S 34 45 E
Kisii □, *Kenya* **106 C3** 0 40 S 34 45 E
Kisiju, *Tanzania* **106 D4** 7 23 S 39 19 E
Kisir, *Turkey* **89 B10** 41 0N 43 5 E
Kisizi, *Uganda* **106 C2** 1 0 S 29 58 E
Kiska I., *U.S.A.* **126 C1** 51 59N 177 30 E
Kiskatinaw →, *Canada* **130 B4** 56 8N 120 10W
Kiskittogisu L., *Canada* **131 C9** 54 13N 98 20W
Kiskomárom = Zalakomár, *Hungary* **31 E10** 46 33N 17 10 E
Kiskörös, *Hungary* **31 E12** 46 37N 19 20 E
Kiskundorozsma, *Hungary* **31 E13** 46 16N 20 5 E
Kiskunfélegyháza, *Hungary* **31 E12** 46 42N 19 53 E
Kiskunhalas, *Hungary* **31 E12** 46 28N 19 37 E
Kiskunmajsa, *Hungary* **31 E12** 46 30N 19 48 E
Kislovodsk, *Russia* **53 J6** 43 50N 42 45 E
Kismayu = Chisimaio, *Somali Rep.* **108 E2** 0 22 S 42 32 E
Kiso-Gawa →, *Japan* **63 B8** 35 20N 136 45 E
Kiso-Sammyaku, *Japan* **63 B9** 35 45N 137 45 E
Kisofukushima, *Japan* **63 B9** 35 52N 137 43 E
Kisoro, *Uganda* **106 C2** 1 17 S 29 48 E
Kispest, *Hungary* **31 D12** 47 27N 19 9 E
Kissidougou, *Guinea* **100 D2** 9 5N 10 5W
Kissimmee, *U.S.A.* **135 L5** 28 18N 81 24W
Kissimmee →, *U.S.A.* **135 M5** 27 9N 80 52W
Kississing L., *Canada* **131 B8** 55 10N 101 20W
Kissónerga, *Cyprus* **32 E11** 34 49N 32 24 E
Kistanje, *Croatia* **39 E12** 43 58N 15 55 E
Kisújszállás, *Hungary* **31 D13** 47 12N 20 50 E
Kisuki, *Japan* **62 B4** 35 17N 132 54 E
Kisumu, *Kenya* **106 C3** 0 3 S 34 45 E
Kisvárda, *Hungary* **31 C15** 48 14N 22 4 E
Kiswani, *Tanzania* **106 C4** 4 5 S 37 57 E
Kiswere, *Tanzania* **107 D4** 9 27 S 39 30 E
Kit Carson, *U.S.A.* **138 F3** 38 46N 102 48W
Kita, *Mali* **100 C3** 13 5N 9 25W
Kita-Ura, *Japan* **63 A12** 36 0N 140 34 E
Kitab, *Uzbekistan* **55 D3** 39 7N 66 52 E
Kitaibaraki, *Japan* **61 F10** 36 50N 140 45 E
Kitakami, *Japan* **60 E10** 39 20N 141 10 E
Kitakami-Gawa →, *Japan* **60 E10** 38 25N 141 19 E
Kitakami-Sammyaku, *Japan* **60 E10** 39 30N 141 30 E
Kitakata, *Japan* **60 F9** 37 39N 139 52 E
Kitakyūshū, *Japan* **62 D2** 33 50N 130 50 E
Kitale, *Kenya* **106 B4** 1 0N 35 0 E
Kitami, *Japan* **60 C11** 43 48N 143 54 E
Kitami-Sammyaku, *Japan* **60 B11** 44 22N 142 43 E
Kitangiri, L., *Tanzania* **106 C3** 4 5 S 34 20 E
Kitano-Kaikyō, *Japan* **62 C6** 34 17N 134 58 E
Kitaotao, *Phil.* **71 H5** 7 40N 125 1 E
Kitaya, *Tanzania* **107 E5** 10 38 S 40 8 E
Kitcharao, *Phil.* **71 G5** 9 27N 125 36 E
Kitchener, *Australia* **113 F3** 30 55 S 124 8 E
Kitchener, *Canada* **128 D3** 43 27N 80 29W
Kitee, *Finland* **50 A6** 62 5N 30 8 E
Kitega = Gitega, *Burundi* **106 C2** 3 26 S 29 56 E
Kitengo, *Zaïre* **103 D4** 7 26 S 24 8 E
Kiteto □, *Tanzania* **106 C4** 5 0 S 37 0 E
Kitgum, *Uganda* **106 B3** 3 17N 32 52 E
Kíthira, *Greece* **45 H5** 36 8N 23 0 E
Kíthnos, *Greece* **45 G6** 37 26N 24 27 E
Kiti, *Cyprus* **32 E12** 34 50N 33 34 E
Kiti, C., *Cyprus* **32 E12** 34 48N 33 36 E
Kitikmeot □, *Canada* **126 A9** 70 0N 110 0W
Kitimat, *Canada* **130 C3** 54 3N 128 38W
Kitinen →, *Finland* **12 C22** 67 14N 27 27 E
Kitiyab, *Sudan* **95 D3** 17 13N 33 35 E
Kítros, *Greece* **44 D4** 40 22N 22 34 E
Kitsuki, *Japan* **62 D3** 33 25N 131 37 E
Kittakittaooloo, L., *Australia* **115 D2** 28 3 S 138 14 E
Kittanning, *U.S.A.* **136 F5** 40 49N 79 31W
Kittatinny Mts., *U.S.A.* **137 E10** 41 0N 75 0W
Kittery, *U.S.A.* **135 D10** 43 5N 70 45W
Kittilä, *Finland* **12 C21** 67 40N 24 51 E
Kitui, *Kenya* **106 C4** 1 17 S 38 0 E
Kitui □, *Kenya* **106 C4** 1 30 S 38 25 E
Kitwe, *Zambia* **107 E2** 12 54 S 28 13 E
Kitzbühel, *Austria* **30 D5** 47 27N 12 24 E
Kitzingen, *Germany* **27 F6** 49 44N 10 9 E
Kivarli, *India* **80 G5** 24 33N 72 46 E
Kivertsi, *Ukraine* **51 G3** 50 50N 25 28 E
Kividhes, *Cyprus* **32 E11** 34 46N 32 51 E
Kivotós, *Greece* **44 D3** 40 13N 21 26 E
Kivu □, *Zaïre* **106 C2** 3 10 S 27 0 E
Kivu, L., *Zaïre* **106 C2** 1 48 S 29 0 E
Kiwai I., *Papua N. G.* **120 E2** 8 35 S 143 30 E
Kiyev = Kyyiv, *Ukraine* **51 G6** 50 30N 30 28 E
Kiyevskoye Vdkhr. = Kyyivske Vdskh., *Ukraine* **51 G6** 51 0N 30 25 E
Kizel, *Russia* **54 B6** 59 3N 57 40 E
Kiziguru, *Rwanda* **106 C3** 1 46 S 30 23 E
Kızıl Irmak →, *Turkey* **88 B6** 41 44N 35 58 E
Kizil Jilga, *India* **81 B8** 35 26N 78 50 E
Kizil Yurt, *Russia* **53 J8** 43 13N 46 54 E
Kızılcahamam, *Turkey* **88 B5** 40 30N 32 30 E
Kızılhisar, *Turkey* **88 D3** 37 32N 29 17 E
Kızılırmak, *Turkey* **88 B5** 40 21N 33 59 E
Kizilskoye, *Russia* **54 E7** 52 44N 58 54 E
Kızıltepe, *Turkey* **89 D9** 37 12N 40 35 E
Kizimkazi, *Tanzania* **106 D4** 6 28 S 39 30 E
Kizlyar, *Russia* **53 J8** 43 51N 46 40 E
Kizyl-Arvat = Gyzylarbat, *Turkmenistan* **56 F6** 39 4N 56 23 E
Kjellerup, *Denmark* **15 H3** 56 17N 9 25 E
Kjölur, *Iceland* **12 D4** 64 50N 19 25W
Kladanj, *Bos.-H.* **42 C3** 44 14N 18 42 E
Kladnica, *Serbia, Yug.* **42 D5** 43 23N 20 2 E
Kladno, *Czech.* **30 A7** 50 10N 14 7 E
Kladovo, *Serbia, Yug.* **42 C7** 44 36N 22 33 E
Klaeng, *Thailand* **76 F3** 12 47N 101 39 E
Klagan, *Malaysia* **75 A5** 5 58N 117 27 E
Klagenfurt, *Austria* **30 E7** 46 38N 14 20 E
Klagshamn, *Sweden* **15 J6** 55 32N 12 53 E
Klagstorp, *Sweden* **15 J7** 55 22N 13 23 E
Klaìpėda, *Lithuania* **13 J19** 55 43N 21 10 E
Klaksvík, *Færoe Is.* **12 E9** 62 14N 6 35W
Klamath →, *U.S.A.* **142 F1** 41 33N 124 5W
Klamath Falls, *U.S.A.* **142 E3** 42 13N 121 46W
Klamath Mts., *U.S.A.* **142 F2** 41 20N 123 0W
Klangklang, *Burma* **78 D4** 22 41N 93 26 E
Klanjec, *Croatia* **39 B12** 46 3N 15 45 E
Klappan →, *Canada* **130 B3** 58 0N 129 43W
Klarälven →, *Sweden* **13 G15** 59 23N 13 32 E
Klaten, *Indonesia* **75 D4** 7 43 S 110 36 E
Klatovy, *Czech.* **30 B6** 49 23N 13 18 E
Klausen = Chiusa, *Italy* **39 B8** 46 38N 11 34 E
Klawer, *S. Africa* **104 E2** 31 44 S 18 36 E
Klawock, *U.S.A.* **130 B2** 55 33N 133 6W
Klazienaveen, *Neths.* **20 C10** 52 44N 7 0 E
Kłecko, *Poland* **47 C4** 52 38N 17 25 E
Kleczew, *Poland* **47 C5** 52 22N 18 9 E
Kleena Kleene, *Canada* **130 C4** 52 0N 124 59W
Klein, *U.S.A.* **142 C9** 46 24N 108 33W
Klein-Karas, *Namibia* **104 D2** 27 33 S 18 7 E
Kleine Gette →, *Belgium* **21 G6** 50 51N 5 6 E
Kleine Nete →, *Belgium* **21 F5** 51 12N 4 46 E
Klekovača, *Bos.-H.* **39 D13** 44 25N 16 32 E
Klenovec, *Macedonia* **42 F5** 41 32N 20 49 E
Klenovec, *Slovak Rep.* **31 C12** 48 36N 19 54 E
Klerksdorp, *S. Africa* **104 D4** 26 53 S 26 38 E
Kleszczele, *Poland* **47 C10** 52 35N 23 19 E
Kletnya, *Russia* **50 F7** 53 23N 33 12 E
Kletsk = Klyetsk, *Belarus* **51 F4** 53 5N 26 45 E
Kletskiy, *Russia* **53 F6** 49 16N 43 11 E
Kleve, *Germany* **26 D2** 51 47N 6 7 E
Klickitat, *U.S.A.* **142 D3** 45 49N 121 9W
Klickitat →, *U.S.A.* **144 E5** 45 42N 121 17W
Klidhes, *Cyprus* **32 D13** 35 42N 34 36 E
Klimovichi, *Belarus* **50 F6** 53 36N 32 0 E
Klin, *Russia* **52 B3** 56 20N 36 48 E
Klinaklini →, *Canada* **130 C3** 51 21N 125 40W
Kling, *Phil.* **71 J5** 5 58N 124 42 E
Klintsy, *Russia* **51 F7** 52 50N 32 10 E
Klipdale, *S. Africa* **104 E2** 34 19 S 19 57 E
Klipplaat, *S. Africa* **104 E3** 33 1 S 24 22 E
Klisura, *Bulgaria* **43 E9** 42 40N 24 28 E
Klitmøller, *Denmark* **15 G2** 57 3N 8 30 E
Kljajićevo, *Serbia, Yug.* **42 B4** 45 45N 19 17 E
Ključ, *Bos.-H.* **39 D13** 44 32N 16 48 E
Kłobuck, *Poland* **47 E5** 50 55N 18 55 E
Kłodawa, *Poland* **47 C5** 52 15N 18 55 E
Kłodzko, *Poland* **47 E3** 50 28N 16 38 E
Kloetinge, *Neths.* **21 F3** 51 30N 3 56 E
Klondike, *Canada* **126 B6** 64 0N 139 26W
Kloosterzande, *Neths.* **21 F4** 51 22N 4 1 E
Klosi, *Albania* **44 C2** 41 28N 20 10 E
Klosterneuburg, *Austria* **31 C9** 48 18N 16 19 E
Klosters, *Switz.* **29 C9** 46 52N 9 52 E
Kloten, *Switz.* **29 B7** 47 27N 8 35 E
Klötze, *Germany* **26 C7** 52 37N 11 10 E
Klouto, *Togo* **101 D5** 6 57N 0 44 E
Kluane L., *Canada* **126 B6** 61 15N 138 40W
Kluczbork, *Poland* **47 E5** 50 58N 18 12 E
Klundert, *Neths.* **21 E5** 51 40N 4 32 E
Klyetsk, *Belarus* **51 F4** 53 5N 26 45 E
Klyuchevskaya, Gora, *Russia* **57 D17** 55 50N 160 30 E
Knaresborough, *U.K.* **16 C6** 54 1N 1 28W
Knee L., *Man., Canada* **131 B10** 55 3N 94 45W
Knee L., *Sask., Canada* **131 B7** 55 51N 107 0W
Kneïss, Is., *Tunisia* **96 B2** 34 22N 10 18 E
Knesselare, *Belgium* **21 F2** 51 9N 3 26 E
Knezha, *Bulgaria* **43 D9** 43 30N 24 5 E
Knić, *Serbia, Yug.* **42 D5** 43 53N 20 45 E
Knight Inlet, *Canada* **130 C3** 50 45N 125 40W
Knighton, *U.K.* **17 E4** 52 21N 3 3W
Knights Ferry, *U.S.A.* **144 H6** 37 50N 120 40W
Knights Landing, *U.S.A.* **144 G5** 38 48N 121 43W
Knightstown, *U.S.A.* **141 E11** 39 48N 85 32W
Knin, *Croatia* **39 D13** 44 1N 16 17 E
Knittelfeld, *Austria* **30 D7** 47 13N 14 51 E
Knjaževac, *Serbia, Yug.* **42 D7** 43 35N 22 18 E
Knob, C., *Australia* **113 F2** 34 32 S 119 16 E
Knockmealdown Mts., *Ireland* **19 D4** 52 14N 7 56W
Knokke, *Belgium* **21 F2** 51 20N 3 17 E
Knossós, *Greece* **32 D7** 35 16N 25 10 E
Knox, *U.S.A.* **141 C10** 41 18N 86 37W
Knox, C., *Canada* **130 C2** 54 11N 133 5W
Knox City, *U.S.A.* **139 J5** 33 25N 99 49W
Knox Coast, *Antarctica* **7 C8** 66 30 S 108 0 E
Knoxville, *Iowa, U.S.A.* **140 C4** 41 19N 93 6W
Knoxville, *Tenn., U.S.A.* **135 H4** 35 58N 83 55W
Knurów, *Poland* **31 A11** 50 13N 18 38 E
Knutshø, *Norway* **14 B3** 62 18N 9 41 E
Knysna, *S. Africa* **104 E3** 34 2 S 23 2 E
Knyszyn, *Poland* **47 B9** 53 20N 22 56 E
Ko Kha, *Thailand* **76 C2** 18 11N 99 24 E
Kō-Saki, *Japan* **62 C1** 34 5N 129 13 E
Ko Tao, *Thailand* **77 G2** 10 6N 99 48 E
Koartac = Quaqtaq, *Canada* **127 B13** 60 55N 69 40W
Koba, *Aru, Indonesia* **73 C4** 6 37 S 134 37 E
Koba, *Bangka, Indonesia* **74 C3** 2 26 S 106 14 E
Kobarid, *Slovenia* **39 B10** 46 15N 13 30 E
Kobayashi, *Japan* **62 F2** 31 56N 130 59 E
Kobdo = Hovd, *Mongolia* **64 B4** 48 2N 91 37 E
Kōbe, *Japan* **63 C7** 34 45N 135 10 E
Kobelyaky, *Ukraine* **51 H8** 49 11N 34 9 E
København, *Denmark* **15 J6** 55 41N 12 34 E
Kōbi-Sho, *Japan* **61 M1** 25 56N 123 41 E
Koblenz, *Germany* **27 E3** 50 21N 7 36 E
Koblenz, *Switz.* **28 A6** 47 37N 8 14 E
Kobo, *Ethiopia* **95 E4** 12 2N 39 56 E
Kobo, *Zaïre* **103 C3** 4 54 S 17 9 E
Kobroor, Kepulauan, *Indonesia* **73 C4** 6 10 S 134 30 E
Kobryn, *Belarus* **51 F3** 52 15N 24 22 E
Kobuchizawa, *Japan* **63 B10** 35 52N 138 19 E
Kobuleti, *Georgia* **53 K5** 41 55N 41 45 E
Kobylin, *Poland* **47 D4** 51 43N 17 12 E
Kobyłka, *Poland* **47 C8** 52 21N 21 10 E
Kobylkino, *Russia* **52 C6** 54 8N 43 56 E
Kocaeli = İzmit, *Turkey* **88 B3** 40 45N 29 50 E
Kočane, *Serbia, Yug.* **42 D6** 43 12N 21 52 E
Kočani, *Macedonia* **42 F7** 41 55N 22 25 E
Koçarlı, *Turkey* **45 G9** 37 45N 27 43 E
Koceljevo, *Serbia, Yug.* **42 C4** 44 28N 19 50 E
Kočevje, *Slovenia* **39 C11** 45 39N 14 50 E
Koch Bihar, *India* **78 B2** 26 22N 89 29 E
Kochang, *S. Korea* **67 G14** 35 41N 127 55 E
Kochas, *India* **81 G10** 25 15N 83 56 E
Kocher →, *Germany* **27 F5** 49 13N 9 12 E
Kocheya, *Russia* **57 D13** 52 32N 120 42 E
Kōchi, *Japan* **62 D5** 33 30N 133 35 E
Kōchi □, *Japan* **62 D5** 33 40N 133 30 E
Kōchi-Heiya, *Japan* **62 D5** 33 28N 133 30 E
Kochiu = Gejiu, *China* **68 F4** 23 20N 103 10 E
Kochkor-Ata, *Kyrgyzstan* **55 C6** 41 1N 72 29 E
Kochkorka, *Kyrgyzstan* **55 B7** 42 13N 75 46 E
Kock, *Poland* **47 D9** 51 38N 22 27 E
Kodaira, *Japan* **63 B11** 35 44N 139 29 E
Koddiyar B., *Sri Lanka* **83 K5** 8 33N 81 15 E
Kodiak, *U.S.A.* **126 C4** 57 47N 152 24W
Kodiak I., *U.S.A.* **126 C4** 57 30N 152 45W
Kodinar, *India* **80 J4** 20 46N 70 46 E
Kodori →, *Georgia* **53 J5** 42 47N 41 10 E
Koekelare, *Belgium* **21 F1** 51 5N 2 59 E
Koersel, *Belgium* **21 F6** 51 3N 5 17 E
Koes, *Namibia* **104 D2** 26 0 S 19 15 E
Koffiefontein, *S. Africa* **104 D4** 29 30 S 25 0 E
Kofiau, *Indonesia* **73 B3** 1 11 S 129 50 E
Köflach, *Austria* **30 D8** 47 4N 15 5 E
Koforidua, *Ghana* **101 D4** 6 3N 0 17W
Kōfu, *Japan* **63 B10** 35 40N 138 30 E
Koga, *Japan* **63 A11** 36 11N 139 43 E
Kogaluk →, *Canada* **129 A7** 56 12N 61 44W
Kogan, *Australia* **115 D5** 27 2 S 150 40 E
Køge, *Denmark* **13 J15** 55 27N 12 11 E
Kogi □, *Nigeria* **101 D6** 7 45N 6 45 E
Kogin Baba, *Nigeria* **101 D7** 7 55N 11 35 E
Koh-i-Bābā, *Afghan.* **79 B2** 34 30N 67 0 E
Koh-i-Khurd, *Afghan.* **80 C1** 33 30N 65 59 E
Kohat, *Pakistan* **79 B3** 33 40N 71 29 E
Kohima, *India* **78 C5** 25 35N 94 10 E
Kohkīlūyeh va Būyer Aḩmadi □, *Iran* **85 D6** 31 30N 50 30 E
Kohler Ra., *Antarctica* **7 D15** 77 0 S 110 0W
Kohtla-Järve, *Estonia* **13 G22** 59 20N 27 20 E
Kohukohu, *N.Z.* **118 B2** 35 22 S 173 38 E
Koillismaa, *Finland* **12 D23** 65 44N 28 36 E
Koin-dong, *N. Korea* **67 D14** 40 28N 126 18 E
Kojetin, *Czech.* **31 B10** 49 21N 17 20 E
Kojima, *Japan* **62 C5** 34 30N 133 50 E
Kōjo, *Japan* **62 C5** 34 33N 133 55 E
Kojŏ, *N. Korea* **67 E14** 38 58N 127 58 E
Kojonup, *Australia* **113 F2** 33 48 S 117 10 E
Kojūr, *Iran* **85 B6** 36 23N 51 43 E
Kok Yangak, *Kyrgyzstan* **55 C6** 41 2N 73 12 E
Koka, *Sudan* **94 C3** 20 5N 30 35 E
Kokand = Qŭqon, *Uzbekistan* **55 C5** 40 30N 70 57 E
Kokanee Glacier Prov. Park, *Canada* **130 D5** 49 47N 117 10W
Kokas, *Indonesia* **73 B4** 2 42 S 132 26 E
Kokava, *Slovak Rep.* **31 C12** 48 35N 19 50 E
Kokchetav = Kökshetaū, *Kazakstan* **56 D7** 53 20N 69 25 E
Kokemäenjoki →, *Finland* **13 F19** 61 32N 21 44 E
Kokerite, *Guyana* **153 B6** 7 12N 59 35W
Kokhma, *Russia* **52 B5** 56 57N 41 8 E
Kokiri, *N.Z.* **119 C6** 42 29 S 171 25 E
Kokkola, *Finland* **12 E20** 63 50N 23 8 E
Koko, *Nigeria* **101 C5** 11 28N 4 29 E
Kokoda, *Papua N. G.* **120 E4** 8 54 S 147 47 E
Kokolopozo, *Ivory C.* **100 D3** 5 8N 6 5W
Kokomo, *U.S.A.* **141 D10** 40 29N 86 8W
Kokonau, *Indonesia* **73 B5** 4 43 S 136 26 E
Kokopo, *Papua N. G.* **120 C7** 4 22 S 152 19 E
Kokoro, *Niger* **101 C5** 14 12N 0 55 E
Koksan, *N. Korea* **67 E14** 38 46N 126 40 E
Koksengir, Gora, *Kazakstan* **55 A2** 44 21N 65 6 E
Kökshetaū, *Kazakstan* **56 D7** 53 20N 69 25 E
Koksoak →, *Canada* **127 C13** 58 30N 68 10W
Kokstad, *S. Africa* **105 E4** 30 32 S 29 29 E
Kokubu, *Japan* **62 F2** 31 44N 130 46 E
Kokuora, *Russia* **57 B15** 71 35N 144 50 E
Kola, *Indonesia* **73 C4** 5 35 S 134 30 E
Kola, *Russia* **48 A5** 68 45N 33 8 E
Kola Pen. = Kolskiy Poluostrov, *Russia* **48 A6** 67 30N 38 0 E
Kolachel, *India* **83 K3** 8 10N 77 15 E
Kolahoi, *India* **81 B6** 34 12N 75 22 E
Kolahun, *Liberia* **100 D2** 8 15N 10 4W
Kolaka, *Indonesia* **72 B2** 4 3 S 121 46 E
Kolar, *India* **83 H4** 13 12N 78 15 E
Kolar Gold Fields, *India* **83 H4** 12 58N 78 16 E
Kolari, *Finland* **12 C20** 67 20N 23 48 E
Kolašin, *Montenegro, Yug.* **42 E4** 42 50N 19 31 E
Kolby Kås, *Denmark* **15 J4** 55 48N 10 32 E
Kolchugino = Leninsk-Kuznetskiy, *Russia* **56 D9** 54 44N 86 10 E
Kolchugino, *Russia* **52 B4** 56 17N 39 22 E
Kolda, *Senegal* **100 C2** 12 55N 14 57W
Kolding, *Denmark* **15 J3** 55 30N 9 29 E
Kole, *Zaïre* **102 C4** 3 16 S 22 42 E
Koléa, *Algeria* **99 A5** 36 38N 2 46 E
Kolepom = Yos Sudarso, Pulau, *Indonesia* **73 C5** 8 0 S 138 30 E
Kolguyev, Ostrov, *Russia* **48 A8** 69 20N 48 30 E
Kolham, *Neths.* **20 B9** 53 11N 6 44 E
Kolhapur, *India* **82 F2** 16 43N 74 15 E
Kolia, *Ivory C.* **100 D3** 9 46N 6 28W
Kolín, *Czech.* **30 A8** 50 2N 15 9 E
Kolind, *Denmark* **15 H4** 56 21N 10 34 E
Kolkas Rags, *Latvia* **13 H20** 57 46N 22 37 E
Kölleda, *Germany* **26 D7** 51 11N 11 15 E
Kollegal, *India* **83 H3** 12 9N 77 9 E
Kolleru L., *India* **82 F5** 16 40N 81 10 E
Kollum, *Neths.* **20 B8** 53 17N 6 10 E
Kolmanskop, *Namibia* **104 D2** 26 45 S 15 14 E
Köln, *Germany* **26 E2** 50 56N 6 57 E
Kolno, *Poland* **47 B8** 53 25N 21 56 E
Koło, *Poland* **47 C5** 52 14N 18 40 E
Kołobrzeg, *Poland* **47 A2** 54 10N 15 35 E
Kolokani, *Mali* **100 C3** 13 35N 7 45W
Kolombangara, *Solomon Is.* **121 M9** 8 0 S 157 5 E
Kolomna, *Russia* **52 C4** 55 8N 38 45 E
Kolomyya, *Ukraine* **51 H3** 48 31N 25 2 E
Kolondiéba, *Mali* **100 C3** 11 5N 6 54W
Kolonodale, *Indonesia* **72 B2** 2 3 S 121 25 E
Kolosib, *India* **78 C4** 24 15N 92 45 E
Kolpashevo, *Russia* **56 D9** 58 20N 83 5 E
Kolpino, *Russia* **50 C6** 59 44N 30 39 E
Kolpny, *Russia* **52 D3** 52 17N 37 1 E
Kolskiy Poluostrov, *Russia* **48 A6** 67 30N 38 0 E
Kolskiy Zaliv, *Russia* **48 A5** 69 23N 34 0 E
Kolubara →, *Serbia, Yug.* **42 C5** 44 35N 20 15 E
Kolumna, *Poland* **47 D6** 51 36N 19 14 E
Koluszki, *Poland* **47 D6** 51 45N 19 46 E
Kolwezi, *Zaïre* **107 E2** 10 40 S 25 25 E
Kolyma →, *Russia* **57 C17** 69 30N 161 0 E
Kolymskoye Nagorye, *Russia* **57 C16** 63 0N 157 0 E
Kôm Ombo, *Egypt* **94 C3** 24 25N 32 52 E
Komagene, *Japan* **63 B9** 35 44N 137 58 E
Komaki, *Japan* **63 B8** 35 17N 136 55 E
Komandorskiye Is. = Komandorskiye Ostrova, *Russia* **57 D17** 55 0N 167 0 E
Komandorskiye Ostrova, *Russia* **57 D17** 55 0N 167 0 E
Komárno, *Slovak Rep.* **31 D11** 47 49N 18 5 E
Komárom, *Hungary* **31 D11** 47 43N 18 7 E
Komárom □, *Hungary* **31 D11** 47 35N 18 20 E
Komatipoort, *S. Africa* **105 D5** 25 25 S 31 55 E
Komatou Yialou, *Cyprus* **32 D13** 35 25N 34 8 E
Komatsu, *Japan* **63 A8** 36 25N 136 30 E

Kranídhion 219

Komatsujima, Japan 62 D6 34 0N 134 35 E
Kombissiri, Burkina Faso 101 C4 12 4N 1 20W
Kombo, Gabon 102 C2 0 20S 12 22 E
Kombori, Burkina Faso 100 C4 13 26N 3 56W
Kombóti, Greece 44 E3 39 6N 21 5 E
Komen, Slovenia 39 C10 45 49N 13 45 E
Komenda, Ghana 101 D4 5 4N 1 28W
Komi □, Russia 48 B10 64 0N 55 0 E
Komiža, Croatia 39 E13 43 3N 16 11 E
Komló, Hungary 31 E11 46 15N 18 16 E
Kommamur Canal, India 83 G5 16 0N 80 25 E
Kommunarsk = Alchevsk, Ukraine 51 H10 48 30N 38 45 E
Kommunizma, Pik, Tajikistan 55 D6 39 0N 72 2 E
Komodo, Indonesia 72 C1 8 37S 119 20 E
Komoé, Ivory C. 100 D4 5 12N 3 44W
Komono, Congo 102 C2 3 10S 13 20 E
Komoran, Pulau, Indonesia 73 C5 8 18S 138 45 E
Komoro, Japan 63 A10 36 19N 138 26 E
Komotini, Greece 44 C7 41 9N 25 26 E
Komovi, Montenegro, Yug. 42 E4 42 41N 19 39 E
Kompasberg, S. Africa 104 E3 31 45S 24 32 E
Kompong Bang, Cambodia 77 F5 12 24N 104 40 E
Kompong Cham, Cambodia 77 F5 12 0N 105 30 E
Kompong Chhnang, Cambodia 77 F5 12 20N 104 35 E
Kompong Chikreng, Cambodia 76 F5 13 5N 104 18 E
Kompong Kleang, Cambodia 76 F5 13 6N 104 8 E
Kompong Luong, Cambodia 77 G5 11 49N 104 48 E
Kompong Pranak, Cambodia 76 F5 13 35N 104 55 E
Kompong Som, Cambodia 77 G4 10 38N 103 30 E
Kompong Som, Chhung, Cambodia 77 G4 10 50N 103 32 E
Kompong Speu, Cambodia 77 G5 11 26N 104 32 E
Kompong Sralao, Cambodia 76 E5 14 5N 105 46 E
Kompong Thom, Cambodia 76 F5 12 35N 104 51 E
Kompong Trabeck, Cambodia 76 F5 13 6N 105 14 E
Kompong Trabeck, Cambodia 77 G5 11 9N 105 28 E
Kompong Trach, Cambodia 77 G5 11 25N 105 48 E
Kompong Tralach, Cambodia 77 G5 11 54N 104 47 E
Komrat = Comrat, Moldova 51 J5 46 18N 28 40 E
Komsberg, S. Africa 104 E3 32 40S 20 45 E
Komsomolabad, Tajikistan 55 D4 38 50N 69 55 E
Komsomolets, Kazakstan 54 E9 53 45N 62 2 E
Komsomolets, Ostrov, Russia 57 A10 80 30N 95 0 E
Komsomolsk, Russia 52 B5 57 2N 40 20 E
Komsomolsk, Russia 57 D14 50 30N 137 0 E
Komsomolsk, Turkmenistan 55 D1 39 2N 63 36 E
Komsomolskiy, Russia 52 C7 54 27N 45 33 E
Konakovo, Russia 52 B3 56 40N 36 51 E
Konarhá □, Afghan. 79 B3 35 30N 71 3 E
Konārī, Iran 85 D6 28 13N 51 36 E
Konawa, U.S.A. 139 H6 34 58N 96 45W
Konch, India 81 G8 26 0N 79 10 E
Kondagaon, India 82 E5 19 35N 81 35 E
Kondakovo, Russia 57 C16 69 36N 152 0 E
Konde, Tanzania 106 C4 4 57S 39 45 E
Kondiá, Greece 44 E7 39 49N 25 10 E
Kondinin, Australia 113 F2 32 34S 118 8 E
Kondo, Zaïre 103 D2 5 35S 13 0 E
Kondoa, Tanzania 106 C4 4 55S 35 50 E
Kondoa □, Tanzania 106 D4 5 0S 36 0 E
Kondókali, Greece 32 A3 39 38N 19 51 E
Kondopaga, Russia 50 A8 62 12N 34 17 E
Kondratyevo, Russia 57 D10 57 22N 98 15 E
Kondrovo, Russia 52 C2 54 48N 35 56 E
Konduga, Nigeria 101 C7 11 35N 13 26 E
Kondukur, India 83 G4 15 12N 79 57 E
Koné, N. Cal. 121 U18 21 4S 164 52 E
Köneürgench, Turkmenistan 56 E6 42 19N 59 10 E
Konevo, Russia 50 A10 62 8N 39 20 E
Kong, Ivory C. 100 D4 8 54N 4 36W
Kong →, Cambodia 76 F5 13 32N 105 58 E
Kong, Koh, Cambodia 77 G4 11 20N 103 0 E
Kong Christian IX.s Land, Greenland 6 C6 68 0N 36 0W
Kong Christian X.s Land, Greenland 6 B6 74 0N 29 0W
Kong Franz Joseph Fd., Greenland 6 B6 73 30N 24 30W
Kong Frederik IX.s Land, Greenland 6 C5 67 0N 52 0W
Kong Frederik VI.s Kyst, Greenland 6 C5 63 0N 43 0W
Kong Frederik VIII.s Land, Greenland 6 B6 78 30N 26 0W
Kong Oscar Fjord, Greenland 6 B6 72 20N 24 0W
Kongbo, C.A.R. 102 B4 4 44N 21 23 E
Kongeå →, Denmark 15 J3 55 23N 8 39 E
Kongju, S. Korea 67 F14 36 30N 127 0 E
Kongkemul, Indonesia 75 B4 1 52N 112 11 E
Konglu, Burma 78 B6 27 13N 97 57 E
Kongolo, Kasai Or., Zaïre 103 D4 5 26S 24 49 E
Kongolo, Shaba, Zaïre 106 D2 5 22S 27 0 E
Kongor, Sudan 95 F3 7 1N 31 27 E
Kongoussi, Burkina Faso 101 C4 13 19N 1 32W
Kongsberg, Norway 14 E3 59 39N 9 39 E
Kongsvinger, Norway 14 D6 60 12N 12 2 E
Kongwa, Tanzania 106 D4 6 11S 36 26 E
Koni, Zaïre 107 E2 10 40S 27 11 E
Koni, Mts., Zaïre 107 E2 10 36S 27 10 E
Koniecpol, Poland 47 E6 50 46N 19 40 E
Königsberg = Kaliningrad, Russia 13 J19 54 42N 20 32 E
Königslutter, Germany 26 C6 52 15N 10 49 E
Königswusterhausen, Germany 26 C9 52 19N 13 38 E
Konin, Poland 47 C5 52 12N 18 15 E
Konin □, Poland 47 C5 52 15N 18 30 E
Konispoli, Albania 44 E2 39 42N 20 10 E
Kónitsa, Greece 44 D2 40 5N 20 48 E
Köniz, Switz. 28 C4 46 56N 7 25 E
Konjic, Bos.-H. 42 D2 43 42N 17 58 E
Konjice, Slovenia 39 B12 46 20N 15 28 E
Konkiep, Namibia 104 D2 26 49S 17 15 E
Konkouré →, Guinea 100 D2 9 50N 13 42W
Könnern, Germany 26 D7 51 41N 11 47 E
Konnur, India 83 F2 16 14N 74 49 E
Kono, S. Leone 100 D2 8 30N 11 5W
Konolfingen, Switz. 28 C5 46 54N 7 38 E
Konongo, Ghana 101 D4 6 40N 1 15W
Konos, Papua N. G. 120 B6 3 10S 151 44 E
Konosha, Russia 50 B11 61 0N 40 5 E
Kōnosu, Japan 63 A11 36 3N 139 31 E
Konotop, Ukraine 51 G7 51 12N 33 7 E
Końskie, Poland 47 D7 51 15N 20 23 E
Konstantinovka = Kostyantynivka, Ukraine 51 H9 48 32N 37 39 E
Konstantinovsk, Russia 53 G5 47 33N 41 10 E
Konstantynów Łódźki, Poland 47 D6 51 45N 19 20 E
Konstanz, Germany 27 H5 47 40N 9 10 E
Kont, Iran 85 E9 26 55N 61 50 E
Kontagora, Nigeria 101 C6 10 23N 5 27 E
Kontich, Belgium 21 F4 51 8N 4 26 E
Kontum, Vietnam 76 E7 14 24N 108 0 E
Kontum, Plateau du, Vietnam 76 E7 14 30N 108 30 E
Konya, Turkey 88 D5 37 52N 32 35 E
Konya Ovasi, Turkey 88 C5 38 30N 33 5 E
Konyin, Burma 78 D5 22 58N 94 42 E
Konz, Germany 27 F2 49 42N 6 34 E
Konza, Kenya 106 C4 1 45S 37 7 E
Konzhakovskiy Kamen, Gora, Russia 54 B7 59 38N 59 8 E
Kookynie, Australia 113 E3 29 17S 121 22 E
Kooline, Australia 112 D2 22 57S 116 20 E
Kooloonong, Australia 116 C5 34 48S 143 10 E
Koolyanobbing, Australia 113 F2 30 48S 119 36 E
Koondrook, Australia 116 C6 35 33S 144 8 E
Koonibba, Australia 115 E1 31 54S 133 25 E
Koorawatha, Australia 117 C8 34 2S 148 33 E
Koorda, Australia 113 F2 30 48S 117 35 E
Kooskia, U.S.A. 142 C6 46 9N 115 59W
Kootenai →, Canada 142 B5 49 15N 117 39W
Kootenay L., Canada 130 D5 49 45N 116 50W
Kootenay Nat. Park, Canada 130 C5 51 0N 116 0W
Kootjieskolk, S. Africa 104 E3 31 15S 20 21 E
Kopa, Kazakstan 55 B7 43 31N 75 50 E
Kopanovka, Russia 53 G8 47 28N 46 50 E
Kopaonik, Serbia, Yug. 42 D6 43 10N 20 50 E
Kopargaon, India 82 E2 19 51N 74 28 E
Kópavogur, Iceland 12 D3 64 6N 21 55W
Koper, Slovenia 39 C10 45 31N 13 44 E
Kopervik, Norway 13 G11 59 17N 5 17 E
Kopeysk, Russia 54 D8 55 7N 61 37 E
Kopi, Australia 115 E2 33 24S 135 40 E
Köping, Sweden 14 E10 59 31N 16 3 E
Kopiste, Croatia 39 F13 42 48N 16 42 E
Kopliku, Albania 44 B1 42 15N 19 25 E
Köpmanholmen, Sweden 14 A12 63 10N 18 35 E
Koppal, India 83 G3 15 23N 76 5 E
Koppang, Norway 14 C5 61 34N 11 3 E
Kopperå, Norway 14 A5 63 24N 11 50 E
Koppies, S. Africa 105 D4 27 20S 27 30 E
Koppio, Australia 116 C1 34 26S 135 51 E
Koprivlen, Bulgaria 43 F8 41 36N 23 53 E
Koprivnica, Croatia 39 B13 46 12N 16 45 E
Koprivshtitsa, Bulgaria 43 E9 42 40N 24 19 E
Kopychyntsi, Ukraine 51 H3 49 7N 25 58 E
Korab, Macedonia 42 F5 41 44N 20 40 E
Korakiána, Greece 32 A3 39 42N 19 45 E
Koraput, India 82 E6 18 50N 82 40 E
Korba, India 81 H10 22 20N 82 45 E
Korbach, Germany 26 D4 51 16N 8 52 E
Korbu, G., Malaysia 77 K3 4 41N 101 18 E
Korça, Albania 44 D2 40 37N 20 50 E
Korce = Korça, Albania 44 D2 40 37N 20 50 E
Korčula, Croatia 39 F14 42 56N 16 57 E
Korčulanski Kanal, Croatia 39 E13 43 3N 16 40 E
Kord Kūy, Iran 85 B7 36 48N 54 7 E
Kord Sheykh, Iran 85 D7 28 31N 52 53 E
Kordestān □, Iran 84 C5 36 0N 47 0 E
Korea, North ■, Asia 67 E14 40 0N 127 0 E
Korea, South ■, Asia 67 F15 36 0N 128 0 E
Korea Bay, Korea 67 E13 39 0N 124 0 E
Korea Strait, Asia 67 G15 34 0N 129 30 E
Koregaon, India 82 F2 17 40N 74 10 E
Korenevo, Russia 52 E2 51 27N 34 55 E
Korenovsk, Russia 53 H4 45 30N 39 22 E
Korets, Ukraine 50 G4 50 40N 27 5 E
Korgan, Turkey 88 B7 40 44N 37 13 E
Korgus, Sudan 94 D3 19 16N 33 29 E
Korhogo, Ivory C. 100 D3 9 29N 5 28W
Koribundu, S. Leone 100 D2 7 41N 11 46W
Korim, Indonesia 73 B5 0 58S 136 10 E
Korinthía □, Greece 45 G4 37 50N 22 35 E
Korinthiakós Kólpos, Greece 45 F4 38 16N 22 30 E
Kórinthos, Greece 45 G4 37 56N 22 55 E
Korioumé, Mali 100 B4 16 35N 3 0W
Koríssa, Límni, Greece 32 B3 39 27N 19 53 E
Kōriyama, Japan 60 F10 37 24N 140 23 E
Korkino, Russia 54 D8 54 54N 61 23 E
Korkuteli, Turkey 88 D4 37 2N 30 11 E
Korla, China 64 B3 41 45N 86 4 E
Kormakiti, C., Cyprus 32 D11 35 23N 32 56 E
Körmend, Hungary 31 D9 47 5N 16 35 E
Kornat, Croatia 39 E12 43 50N 15 20 E
Korneshty = Corneşti, Moldova 51 J5 47 21N 28 1 E
Korneuburg, Austria 31 C9 48 20N 16 20 E
Kornsjø, Norway 14 F5 58 57N 11 39 E
Kornstad, Norway 14 B1 62 59N 7 27 E
Koro, Fiji 121 A2 17 19S 179 23 E
Koro, Ivory C. 100 D3 8 32N 7 30W
Koro, Mali 100 C4 14 1N 2 58W
Koro Sea, Fiji 121 A3 17 30S 179 45W
Koro Toro, Chad 97 E3 16 5N 18 30 E
Koroba, Papua N. G. 120 C2 5 44S 142 47 E
Korocha, Russia 52 E3 50 54N 37 19 E
Köroğlu Dağları, Turkey 88 B5 40 38N 33 0 E
Korogwe, Tanzania 106 D4 5 5S 38 25 E
Korogwe □, Tanzania 106 D4 5 0S 38 20 E
Koroit, Australia 116 E5 38 18S 142 24 E
Koronadal, Phil. 71 H5 6 12N 125 1 E
Korong Vale, Australia 116 D5 36 22S 143 45 E
Koróni, Greece 45 H3 36 48N 21 57 E
Korónia, Limni, Greece 44 D5 40 47N 23 37 E
Koronís, Greece 45 G7 37 12N 25 35 E
Koronowo, Poland 47 B4 53 19N 17 55 E
Körös →, Hungary 31 E13 46 43N 20 12 E
Köröstarcsa, Hungary 31 E14 46 53N 21 3 E
Korosten, Ukraine 51 G5 50 54N 28 36 E
Korostyshev, Ukraine 51 G5 50 19N 29 4 E
Korotoyak, Russia 52 E4 51 1N 39 2 E
Korraraika, Helodranon' i, Madag. 105 B7 17 45S 43 57 E
Korsakov, Russia 57 E15 46 36N 142 42 E
Korshunovo, Russia 57 D12 58 37N 110 10 E
Korsør, Denmark 13 J14 55 20N 11 9 E
Korsun Shevchenkovskiy, Ukraine 51 H6 49 26N 31 16 E
Korsze, Poland 47 A8 54 11N 21 9 E
Kortemark, Belgium 21 F2 51 2N 3 3 E
Kortessem, Belgium 21 G6 50 52N 5 23 E
Korti, Sudan 94 D3 18 6N 31 33 E
Kortrijk, Belgium 21 G2 50 50N 3 17 E
Korumburra, Australia 117 E6 38 26S 145 50 E
Korwai, India 80 G8 24 7N 78 5 E
Koryakskoye Nagorye, Russia 57 C18 61 0N 171 0 E
Koryŏng, S. Korea 67 G15 35 44N 128 15 E
Koryukovka, Ukraine 51 G7 51 46N 32 16 E
Kos, Greece 45 H9 36 50N 27 15 E
Kosa, Ethiopia 95 F4 7 50N 36 50 E
Kosa, Russia 54 B5 59 56N 55 0 E
Kosa →, Russia 54 A5 60 11N 55 10 E
Kosaya Gora, Russia 52 C3 54 10N 37 30 E
Koschagyl, Kazakstan 49 E9 46 40N 54 0 E
Kościan, Poland 47 C3 52 5N 16 40 E
Kościerzyna, Poland 47 A4 54 8N 17 59 E
Kosciusko, U.S.A. 139 J10 33 4N 89 35W
Kosciusko, Mt., Australia 117 D8 36 27S 148 16 E
Kosciusko I., U.S.A. 130 B2 56 0N 133 40W
Kösély →, Hungary 31 D14 47 25N 21 5 E
Kosgi, India 82 F3 16 58N 77 43 E
Kosha, Sudan 94 C3 20 50N 30 30 E
Koshigaya, Japan 63 B11 35 54N 139 48 E
K'oshih = Kashi, China 64 C2 39 30N 76 2 E
Koshiki-Rettō, Japan 62 F1 31 45N 129 49 E
Koshkonong L., U.S.A. 141 B8 42 52N 88 58W
Kōshoku, Japan 63 A10 36 38N 138 6 E
Koshtëbë, Kyrgyzstan 55 C7 41 5N 74 15 E
Kosi, India 80 F7 27 48N 77 29 E
Košice, Slovak Rep. 31 C14 48 42N 21 15 E
Kosjerić, Serbia, Yug. 42 D4 44 0N 19 55 E
Koskhinoú, Greece 32 C10 36 23N 28 13 E
Koslan, Russia 48 B8 63 34N 49 14 E
Kosŏng, N. Korea 67 E15 38 40N 128 22 E
Kosovo □, Serbia, Yug. 42 E5 42 30N 21 0 E
Kosovska-Mitrovica = Titova-Mitrovica, Serbia, Yug. 42 E5 42 54N 20 52 E
Kostajnica, Croatia 39 C13 45 17N 16 30 E
Kostamuksa, Russia 48 B5 62 34N 32 44 E
Kostanjevica, Slovenia 39 C12 45 51N 15 27 E
Kostelec, Czech. 31 A9 50 14N 16 35 E
Kostenets, Bulgaria 43 E8 42 15N 23 52 E
Koster, S. Africa 104 D4 25 52S 26 54 E
Kôstî, Sudan 95 E3 13 8N 32 43 E
Kostolac, Serbia, Yug. 42 C6 44 37N 21 15 E
Kostopil, Ukraine 51 G4 50 51N 26 22 E
Kostroma, Russia 52 B5 57 50N 40 58 E
Kostromskoye Vdkhr., Russia 52 B5 57 52N 40 49 E
Kostrzyn, Gorzow Wlkp., Poland 47 C1 52 35N 14 39 E
Kostrzyn, Poznań, Poland 47 C4 52 24N 17 14 E
Kostyantynivka, Ukraine 51 H9 48 32N 37 39 E
Kostyukovichi = Kastsyukovichy, Belarus 50 F7 53 20N 32 4 E
Koszalin, Poland 47 A3 54 11N 16 8 E
Koszalin □, Poland 47 B3 53 40N 16 10 E
Kőszeg, Hungary 31 D9 47 23N 16 33 E
Kot Addu, Pakistan 79 C3 30 30N 71 0 E
Kot Moman, Pakistan 80 C5 32 13N 73 0 E
Kota, India 80 G6 25 14N 75 49 E
Kota Baharu, Malaysia 77 J4 6 7N 102 14 E
Kota Belud, Malaysia 75 A5 6 21N 116 26 E
Kota Kinabalu, Malaysia 75 A5 6 0N 116 4 E
Kota Tinggi, Malaysia 77 M4 1 44N 103 53 E
Kotaagung, Indonesia 74 D2 5 38S 104 29 E
Kotabaru, Indonesia 75 C5 3 20S 116 20 E
Kotabumi, Indonesia 74 C2 4 49S 104 54 E
Kotagede, Indonesia 75 D4 7 54S 110 26 E
Kotamobagu, Indonesia 72 A2 0 57N 124 31 E
Kotaneelee →, Canada 130 A4 60 11N 123 42W
Kotawaringin, Indonesia 75 C4 2 28S 111 27 E
Kotchandpur, Bangla. 78 D2 23 24N 89 1 E
Kotcho L., Canada 130 B4 59 7N 121 12W
Kotel, Bulgaria 43 E11 42 52N 26 26 E
Kotelnich, Russia 52 A9 58 22N 48 24 E
Kotelnikovo, Russia 53 G6 47 38N 43 8 E
Kotelnyy, Ostrov, Russia 57 B14 75 10N 139 0 E
Kothagudam, India 82 F5 17 30N 80 40 E
Kothapet, India 82 E4 19 21N 79 28 E
Köthen, Germany 26 D7 51 45N 11 59 E
Kothi, India 81 G9 24 45N 80 40 E
Kotiro, Pakistan 80 F2 26 17N 67 13 E
Kotka, Finland 13 F22 60 28N 26 58 E
Kotlas, Russia 48 B8 61 17N 46 43 E
Kotlenska Planina, Bulgaria 43 E11 42 56N 26 30 E
Kotli, Pakistan 80 C5 33 30N 73 55 E
Kotmul, Pakistan 81 B6 35 32N 75 10 E
Kotohira, Japan 62 C5 34 11N 133 49 E
Kotonkoro, Nigeria 101 C6 11 3N 5 58 E
Kotor, Montenegro, Yug. 42 E3 42 25N 18 47 E
Kotor Varoš, Bos.-H. 42 C2 44 38N 17 22 E
Kotoriba, Croatia 39 B13 46 23N 16 48 E
Kotovo, Russia 52 E7 50 22N 44 45 E
Kotovsk, Russia 52 D5 52 36N 41 32 E
Kotovsk, Ukraine 51 J5 47 45N 29 35 E
Kotputli, India 80 F7 27 43N 76 12 E
Kotri, Pakistan 79 D3 25 22N 68 22 E
Kotri →, India 82 E5 19 15N 80 35 E
Kótronas, Greece 45 H4 36 38N 22 29 E
Kötschach-Mauthen, Austria 30 E6 46 41N 13 1 E
Kottayam, India 83 K3 9 35N 76 33 E
Kottur, India 83 J3 10 34N 76 56 E
Kotuy →, Russia 57 B11 71 54N 102 6 E
Kotzebue, U.S.A. 126 B3 66 53N 162 39W
Kouango, C.A.R. 102 B4 5 0N 20 10 E
Koudekerke, Neths. 21 F3 51 29N 3 33 E
Koudougou, Burkina Faso 100 C4 12 10N 2 20W
Koufonísi, Greece 32 E8 34 56N 26 8 E
Koufonísia, Greece 45 H7 36 57N 25 35 E
Kougaberge, S. Africa 104 E3 33 48S 23 50 E
Kouibli, Ivory C. 100 D3 7 15N 7 14W
Kouilou →, Congo 103 C2 4 10S 12 5 E
Kouki, C.A.R. 102 A3 7 22N 17 3 E
Koula Moutou, Gabon 102 C2 1 15S 12 25 E
Koulen, Cambodia 76 F5 13 50N 104 40 E
Koulikoro, Mali 100 C3 12 40N 7 50W
Kouloúra, Greece 32 A3 39 42N 19 54 E
Koúm-bournoú, Ákra, Greece 32 C10 36 15N 28 11 E
Koumac, N. Cal. 121 T18 20 33S 164 17 E
Koumala, Australia 114 C4 21 38S 149 15 E
Koumankou, Mali 100 C3 11 58N 6 6W
Koumbia, Burkina Faso 100 C4 11 10N 3 50W
Koumbia, Guinea 100 C2 11 48N 13 29W
Koumboum, Guinea 100 C2 10 25N 13 0W
Koumpenntoum, Senegal 100 C2 13 59N 14 34W
Koumra, Chad 97 G3 8 50N 17 35 E
Koundara, Guinea 100 C2 12 29N 13 18W
Koundé, C.A.R. 102 A2 6 7N 14 38 E
Kounradskiy, Kazakstan 56 E8 46 59N 75 0 E
Kountze, U.S.A. 139 K7 30 22N 94 19W
Koupéla, Burkina Faso 101 C4 12 11N 0 21W
Kouris →, Cyprus 32 E11 34 38N 32 54 E
Kourizo, Passe de, Chad 96 D3 22 28N 15 27 E
Kourou, Fr. Guiana 153 B7 5 9N 52 39W
Kouroussa, Guinea 100 C3 10 45N 9 45W
Koussané, Mali 100 C2 14 53N 11 14W
Kousseri, Cameroon 97 F2 12 0N 14 55 E
Koutiala, Mali 100 C3 12 25N 5 23W
Kouto, Ivory C. 100 D3 9 53N 6 25W
Kouts, U.S.A. 141 C9 41 19N 87 2W
Kouvé, Togo 101 D5 6 25N 1 25 E
Kouvola, Finland 13 F22 60 52N 26 43 E
Kovačica, Serbia, Yug. 42 B5 45 5N 20 38 E
Kovdor, Russia 48 A5 67 34N 30 24 E
Kovel, Ukraine 51 G3 51 11N 24 38 E
Kovilpatti, India 83 K3 9 10N 77 50 E
Kovin, Serbia, Yug. 42 C5 44 44N 20 59 E
Kovrov, Russia 52 B5 56 25N 41 25 E
Kovur, Andhra Pradesh, India 82 F5 17 3N 81 39 E
Kovur, Andhra Pradesh, India 83 G5 14 30N 80 1 E
Kowal, Poland 47 C6 52 32N 19 7 E
Kowalewo Pomorskie, Poland 47 B5 53 10N 18 52 E
Kowanyama, Australia 114 B3 15 29S 141 44 E
Kowghān, Afghan. 79 B1 34 12N 63 2 E
Kowkash, Canada 128 B2 50 20N 87 12W
Kowloon, H.K. 69 F10 22 20N 114 15 E
Kowŏn, N. Korea 67 E14 39 26N 127 14 E
Kōyama, Japan 62 F2 31 20N 130 56 E
Köyceğiz, Turkey 88 D3 36 57N 28 40 E
Koytash, Uzbekistan 55 C3 40 11N 67 19 E
Koyuk, U.S.A. 126 B3 64 56N 161 9W
Koyukuk →, U.S.A. 126 B4 64 55N 157 32W
Koyulhisar, Turkey 88 B7 40 20N 37 52 E
Koza, Japan 61 L3 26 19N 127 46 E
Kozan, Turkey 88 D6 37 26N 35 50 E
Kozáni, Greece 44 D3 40 19N 21 47 E
Kozáni □, Greece 44 D3 40 18N 21 45 E
Kozara, Bos.-H. 39 D14 45 0N 17 0 E
Kozarac, Bos.-H. 39 D13 44 58N 16 48 E
Kozelets, Ukraine 51 G6 50 55N 31 7 E
Kozelsk, Russia 52 C2 54 2N 35 48 E
Kozhikode = Calicut, India 83 J2 11 15N 75 43 E
Kozhva, Russia 48 A10 65 10N 57 0 E
Koziegłowy, Poland 47 E6 50 37N 19 8 E
Kozienice, Poland 47 D8 51 35N 21 34 E
Kozje, Slovenia 39 B12 46 5N 15 35 E
Kozle, Poland 47 E5 50 20N 18 8 E
Kozloduy, Bulgaria 43 D8 43 45N 23 42 E
Kozlovets, Bulgaria 43 D10 43 30N 25 20 E
Kozlovka, Russia 52 C9 55 52N 48 14 E
Kozlu, Turkey 88 B4 41 26N 31 45 E
Kozluk, Turkey 89 C9 38 11N 41 31 E
Koźmin, Poland 47 D4 51 48N 17 27 E
Kozmodemyansk, Russia 52 B8 56 20N 46 36 E
Kōzu-Shima, Japan 63 C11 34 13N 139 10 E
Kozuchów, Poland 47 D2 51 45N 15 31 E
Kozyatyn, Ukraine 51 H5 49 45N 28 50 E
Kpabia, Ghana 101 D4 9 10N 0 20W
Kpalimé, Togo 101 D5 6 57N 0 44 E
Kpandae, Ghana 101 D4 8 30N 0 2W
Kpessi, Togo 101 D5 8 4N 1 16 E
Kra, Isthmus of = Kra, Kho Khot, Thailand 77 G2 10 15N 99 30 E
Kra, Kho Khot, Thailand 77 G2 10 15N 99 30 E
Kra Buri, Thailand 77 G2 10 22N 98 46 E
Krabbendijke, Neths. 21 F4 51 26N 4 7 E
Krabi, Thailand 77 H2 8 4N 98 55 E
Kragan, Indonesia 75 D4 6 43S 111 38 E
Kragerø, Norway 14 F3 58 52N 9 25 E
Kragujevac, Serbia, Yug. 42 C5 44 2N 20 56 E
Krajenka, Poland 47 B3 53 18N 16 59 E
Krajina, Bos.-H. 39 D13 44 45N 16 35 E
Krakatau = Rakata, Pulau, Indonesia 74 D3 6 10S 105 20 E
Krakor, Cambodia 76 F5 12 32N 104 12 E
Kraków, Poland 31 A12 50 4N 19 57 E
Kraków □, Poland 31 A13 50 0N 20 0 E
Kraksaan, Indonesia 75 D4 7 43S 113 23 E
Kråkstad, Norway 14 E4 59 39N 10 55 E
Kralanh, Cambodia 76 F4 13 35N 103 25 E
Králíky, Czech. 31 A9 50 6N 16 45 E
Kraljevo, Serbia, Yug. 42 D5 43 44N 20 41 E
Kralovice, Czech. 30 B6 49 59N 13 29 E
Královský Chlmec, Slovak Rep. 31 C14 48 27N 22 0 E
Kralupy, Czech. 30 A7 50 13N 14 20 E
Kramatorsk, Ukraine 51 H9 48 50N 37 30 E
Kramfors, Sweden 14 B11 62 55N 17 48 E
Kramis, C., Algeria 99 A5 36 26N 0 45 E
Krångede, Sweden 14 A10 63 9N 16 10 E
Kraniá, Greece 44 E3 39 53N 21 18 E
Kranídhion, Greece 45 G5 37 20N 23 10 E

Labra, Peña 221

Kus Gölü, *Turkey* 88 B2 40 10N 27 55 E
Kusa, *Russia* 54 D7 55 20N 59 29 E
Kuşada Körfezı, *Turkey* 45 G9 37 56N 27 0 E
Kuşadası, *Turkey* 88 D2 37 52N 27 15 E
Kusatsu, *Gumma, Japan* 63 A10 36 37N 138 36 E
Kusatsu, *Shiga, Japan* 63 C7 34 58N 135 57 E
Kusawa L., *Canada* 130 A1 60 20N 136 13W
Kusel, *Germany* 27 F3 49 32N 7 24 E
Kushchevskaya, *Russia* 53 G4 46 33N 39 35 E
Kushikino, *Japan* 62 F2 31 44N 130 16 E
Kushima, *Japan* 62 F3 31 29N 131 14 E
Kushimoto, *Japan* 63 D7 33 28N 135 47 E
Kushiro, *Japan* 60 C12 43 0N 144 25 E
Kushiro →, *Japan* 60 C12 42 59N 144 23 E
Kūshk, *Iran* 85 D8 28 46N 56 51 E
Kushka = Gushgy, *Turkmenistan* 56 F7 35 20N 62 18 E
Kūshkī, *Īlām, Iran* 84 C5 33 31N 47 13 E
Kūshkī, *Khorāsān, Iran* 85 B8 37 2N 57 26 E
Kūshkū, *Iran* 85 E7 27 19N 53 28 E
Kushnarenkovo, *Russia* 54 D5 55 6N 55 22 E
Kushol, *India* 81 C7 33 40N 76 36 E
Kushrabat, *Uzbekistan* 55 C3 40 18N 66 32 E
Kushtia, *Bangla.* 78 D2 23 55N 89 5 E
Kushum →, *Kazakstan* 52 F10 49 20N 50 30 E
Kushva, *Russia* 54 B7 58 18N 59 45 E
Kuskokwim →, *U.S.A.* 126 B3 60 5N 162 25W
Kuskokwim B., *U.S.A.* 126 C3 59 45N 162 25W
Küsnacht, *Switz.* 29 B7 47 19N 8 35 E
Kussharo-Ko, *Japan* 60 C12 43 38N 144 21 E
Küssnacht, *Switz.* 29 B6 47 5N 8 26 E
Kustanay = Qostanay, *Kazakstan* 56 D7 53 10N 63 35 E
Kusu, *Japan* 62 D3 33 16N 131 9 E
Kut, Ko, *Thailand* 77 G4 11 40N 102 35 E
Kutacane, *Indonesia* 74 B1 3 50N 97 50 E
Kütahya, *Turkey* 88 C4 39 30N 30 2 E
Kutaisi, *Georgia* 53 J6 42 19N 42 40 E
Kutaraja = Banda Aceh, *Indonesia* 74 A1 5 35N 95 20 E
Kutch, Gulf of = Kachchh, Gulf of, *India* 80 H3 22 50N 69 15 E
Kutch, Rann of = Kachchh, Rann of, *India* 80 G4 24 0N 70 0 E
Kutina, *Croatia* 39 C13 45 29N 16 48 E
Kutiyana, *India* 80 J4 21 36N 70 2 E
Kutjevo, *Croatia* 42 B2 45 23N 17 55 E
Kutkai, *Burma* 78 D6 23 27N 97 56 E
Kutkashen, *Azerbaijan* 53 K8 40 58N 47 47 E
Kutná Hora, *Czech.* 30 B8 49 57N 15 16 E
Kutno, *Poland* 47 C6 52 15N 19 23 E
Kuttabul, *Australia* 114 C4 21 5 S 148 48 E
Kutu, *Zaïre* 102 C3 2 40 S 18 11 E
Kutum, *Sudan* 95 E1 14 10N 24 40 E
Kúty, *Slovak Rep.* 31 C10 48 40N 17 3 E
Kuujjuaq, *Canada* 127 C13 58 6N 68 15W
Kuŭp-tong, *N. Korea* 67 D14 40 45N 126 1 E
Kuurne, *Belgium* 21 G2 50 51N 3 18 E
Kuusamo, *Finland* 12 D23 65 57N 29 8 E
Kuusankoski, *Finland* 13 F22 60 55N 26 38 E
Kuvandyk, *Russia* 54 F6 51 28N 57 21 E
Kuvango, *Angola* 103 E3 14 28 S 16 20 E
Kuvasay, *Uzbekistan* 55 C5 40 18N 71 59 E
Kuvshinovo, *Russia* 52 B2 57 2N 34 11 E
Kuwait = Al Kuwayt, *Kuwait* 84 D5 29 30N 48 0 E
Kuwait ■, *Asia* 84 D5 29 30N 47 30 E
Kuwana, *Japan* 63 B8 35 5N 136 43 E
Kuybyshev = Samara, *Russia* 52 D10 53 8N 50 6 E
Kuybyshev, *Russia* 56 D8 55 27N 78 19 E
Kuybyshevo, *Ukraine* 51 J9 47 25N 36 40 E
Kuybyshevo, *Uzbekistan* 55 C5 40 20N 71 15 E
Kuybyshevskiy, *Tajikistan* 55 E4 37 52N 68 44 E
Kuybyshevskoye Vdkhr., *Russia* 52 C9 55 2N 49 30 E
Kuye He →, *China* 66 E6 38 23N 110 46 E
Kūyeh, *Iran* 84 B5 38 45N 47 57 E
Kuylyuk, *Uzbekistan* 55 C4 41 14N 69 17 E
Kūysanjaq, *Iraq* 89 D11 36 5N 44 38 E
Kuyto, Ozero, *Russia* 48 B5 65 6N 31 20 E
Kuyumba, *Russia* 57 C10 60 58N 96 59 E
Kuzey Anadolu Dağları, *Turkey* 88 B7 41 30N 35 0 E
Kuzhitturai, *India* 83 K3 8 18N 77 11 E
Kuzino, *Russia* 54 C7 57 1N 59 27 E
Kuzmin, *Serbia, Yug.* 42 B4 45 2N 19 25 E
Kuznetsk, *Russia* 52 D8 53 12N 46 40 E
Kuzomen, *Russia* 48 A6 66 22N 36 50 E
Kvænangen, *Norway* 12 A19 70 5N 21 15 E
Kvaløy, *Norway* 12 B18 69 40N 18 30 E
Kvam, *Norway* 14 C3 61 40N 9 42 E
Kvareli = Qvareli, *Georgia* 53 K7 41 57N 45 47 E
Kvarner, *Croatia* 39 D11 44 50N 14 10 E
Kvarnerič, *Croatia* 39 D11 44 43N 14 37 E
Kviteseid, *Norway* 14 E2 59 24N 8 29 E
Kwabhaca, *S. Africa* 105 E4 30 51 S 29 0 E
Kwadacha →, *Canada* 130 B3 57 28N 125 38W
Kwakhanai, *Botswana* 104 C3 21 39 S 21 16 E
Kwakoegron, *Surinam* 153 B6 5 12N 55 25W
Kwale, *Kenya* 106 C4 4 15 S 39 31 E
Kwale, *Nigeria* 101 D6 5 46N 6 26 E
Kwale □, *Kenya* 106 C4 4 15 S 39 10 E
KwaMashu, *S. Africa* 105 D5 29 45 S 30 58 E
Kwamouth, *Zaïre* 102 C3 3 9 S 16 12 E
Kwando →, *Africa* 103 F4 18 27 S 23 32 E
Kwangdaeri, *N. Korea* 67 D14 40 31N 127 32 E
Kwangju, *S. Korea* 67 G14 35 9N 126 54 E
Kwango →, *Zaïre* 102 C3 3 14 S 17 22 E
Kwangsi-Chuang = Guangxi Zhuangzu Zizhiqu □, *China* 68 E7 24 0N 109 0 E
Kwangtung = Guangdong □, *China* 69 F9 23 0N 113 0 E
Kwara □, *Nigeria* 101 D5 8 45N 4 30 E
Kwataboahegan →, *Canada* 128 B3 51 9N 80 50W
Kwatisore, *Indonesia* 73 B4 3 18 S 134 50 E
KwaZulu Natal □, *S. Africa* 105 D5 29 0 S 30 0 E
Kweichow = Guizhou □, *China* 68 D6 27 0N 107 0 E
Kwekwe, *Zimbabwe* 107 F2 18 58 S 29 48 E
Kwidzyn, *Poland* 47 B5 53 44N 18 55 E
Kwikila, *Papua N. G.* 120 E4 9 49 S 147 38 E
Kwimba □, *Tanzania* 106 C3 3 0 S 33 0 E
Kwinana New Town, *Australia* 113 F2 32 15 S 115 47 E
Kwisa →, *Poland* 47 D2 51 34N 15 24 E
Kwoka, *Indonesia* 73 B4 0 31 S 132 27 E
Kya-in-Seikkyi, *Burma* 78 G7 16 2N 98 8 E
Kyabé, *Chad* 97 G3 9 30N 19 0 E
Kyabra Cr. →, *Australia* 115 D3 25 36 S 142 55 E
Kyabram, *Australia* 115 F4 36 19 S 145 4 E
Kyaiklat, *Burma* 78 G5 16 25N 95 40 E
Kyaikmaraw, *Burma* 78 G6 16 23N 97 44 E
Kyaikthin, *Burma* 78 D5 23 32N 95 40 E
Kyaikto, *Burma* 76 D1 17 20N 97 3 E
Kyakhta, *Russia* 57 D11 50 30N 106 25 E
Kyancutta, *Australia* 115 E2 33 8 S 135 33 E
Kyangin, *Burma* 78 F5 18 20N 95 20 E
Kyaukhnyat, *Burma* 78 F6 18 15N 97 31 E
Kyaukse, *Burma* 78 E6 21 36N 96 10 E
Kyauktaw, *Burma* 78 E4 20 51N 92 59 E
Kyawkku, *Burma* 78 E6 21 48N 96 56 E
Kyburz, *U.S.A.* 144 G6 38 47N 120 18W
Kybybolite, *Australia* 116 D4 36 53 S 140 55 E
Kyeintali, *Burma* 78 G5 18 0N 94 29 E
Kyenjojo, *Uganda* 106 B3 0 40N 30 37 E
Kyidaunggan, *Burma* 78 F6 19 53N 96 12 E
Kyle Dam, *Zimbabwe* 107 G3 20 15 S 31 0 E
Kyle of Lochalsh, *U.K.* 18 D3 57 17N 5 44W
Kyll →, *Germany* 27 F2 49 48N 6 41 E
Kyllburg, *Germany* 27 E2 50 2N 6 34 E
Kymijoki →, *Finland* 13 F22 60 30N 26 55 E
Kyneton, *Australia* 116 D6 37 10 S 144 29 E
Kynuna, *Australia* 114 C3 21 37 S 141 55 E
Kyō-ga-Saki, *Japan* 63 B7 35 45N 135 15 E
Kyoga, L., *Uganda* 106 B3 1 35N 33 0 E
Kyogle, *Australia* 115 D5 28 40 S 153 0 E
Kyongju, *S. Korea* 67 G15 35 51N 129 14 E
Kyŏngsŏng, *N. Korea* 67 D15 41 35N 129 36 E
Kyōto, *Japan* 63 B7 35 0N 135 45 E
Kyōto □, *Japan* 63 B7 35 15N 135 45 E
Kyparissovouno, *Cyprus* 32 D12 35 19N 33 10 E
Kyperounda, *Cyprus* 32 E11 34 56N 32 58 E
Kyren, *Russia* 57 D11 51 45N 101 45 E
Kyrenia, *Cyprus* 32 D12 35 20N 33 20 E
Kyrgyzstan ■, *Asia* 55 C7 42 0N 75 0 E
Kyritz, *Germany* 26 C8 52 56N 12 24 E
Kyrönjoki →, *Finland* 12 E19 63 14N 21 45 E
Kyrtylakh, *Russia* 57 C13 65 30N 123 40 E
Kyshtym, *Russia* 54 D8 55 42N 60 34 E
Kystatyam, *Russia* 57 C13 67 20N 123 10 E
Kythréa, *Cyprus* 32 D12 35 15N 33 29 E
Kytlym, *Russia* 54 B7 59 30N 59 12 E
Kyu-hkok, *Burma* 78 C7 24 4N 98 4 E
Kyulyunken, *Russia* 57 C14 64 10N 137 5 E
Kyunhla, *Burma* 78 D5 23 25N 95 15 E
Kyuquot, *Canada* 130 C3 50 3N 127 25W
Kyurdamir = Kürdämir, *Azerbaijan* 53 K9 40 25N 48 3 E
Kyūshū, *Japan* 62 E3 33 0N 131 0 E
Kyūshū □, *Japan* 62 E3 33 0N 131 0 E
Kyūshū-Sanchi, *Japan* 62 E3 32 35N 131 17 E
Kyustendil, *Bulgaria* 42 E7 42 16N 22 41 E
Kyusyur, *Russia* 57 B13 70 19N 127 30 E
Kywong, *Australia* 117 C7 34 58 S 146 44 E
Kyyiv, *Ukraine* 51 G6 50 30N 30 28 E
Kyyivske Vdskh., *Ukraine* 51 G6 51 0N 30 25 E
Kyzyl, *Russia* 57 D10 51 50N 94 30 E
Kyzyl Kum, *Uzbekistan* 55 B2 42 30N 65 0 E
Kyzyl-Kyya, *Kyrgyzstan* 55 C6 40 16N 72 8 E
Kyzylsu →, *Kyrgyzstan* 55 D6 38 50N 70 0 E
Kzyl-Orda = Qyzylorda, *Kazakstan* 55 A2 44 48N 65 28 E

L

La Albuera, *Spain* 37 G4 38 45N 6 49W
La Albufera, *Spain* 35 F4 39 20N 0 27W
La Alcarria, *Spain* 34 E2 40 31N 2 45W
La Algaba, *Spain* 37 H4 37 27N 6 1W
La Almarcha, *Spain* 34 F2 39 41N 2 24W
La Almunia de Doña Godina, *Spain* 34 D3 41 29N 1 23W
La Asunción, *Venezuela* 153 A5 11 2N 63 53W
La Banda, *Argentina* 158 B3 27 45 S 64 10W
La Bañeza, *Spain* 36 C5 42 17N 5 54W
La Barca, *Mexico* 146 C4 20 20N 102 40W
La Barge, *U.S.A.* 142 E8 42 16N 110 12W
La Bassée, *France* 23 B9 50 31N 2 49 E
La Bastide-Puylaurent, *France* 24 D7 44 35N 3 55 E
La Baule, *France* 22 E4 47 17N 2 24W
La Belle, *Fla., U.S.A.* 135 M5 26 46N 81 26W
La Belle, *Mo., U.S.A.* 140 D5 40 7N 91 55W
La Biche →, *Canada* 130 B4 59 57N 123 50W
La Bisbal, *Spain* 34 D8 41 58N 3 2 E
La Blanquilla, *Venezuela* 153 A5 11 51N 64 37W
La Bomba, *Mexico* 146 A1 31 53N 115 2W
La Bresse, *France* 23 D13 48 2N 6 53 E
La Bureba, *Spain* 34 C1 42 36N 3 24W
La Cal →, *Bolivia* 157 D6 17 27 S 58 15W
La Calera, *Chile* 158 C1 32 50 S 71 10W
La Campiña, *Spain* 37 H6 37 45N 4 45W
La Canal, *Spain* 33 C7 38 51N 1 23 E
La Cañiza, *Spain* 36 C2 42 13N 8 16W
La Capelle, *France* 23 C10 49 59N 3 50 E
La Carlota, *Argentina* 158 C3 33 30 S 63 20W
La Carlota, *Phil.* 71 F4 10 25N 122 55 E
La Carolina, *Spain* 37 G7 38 17N 3 38W
La Castellana, *Phil.* 71 F4 10 20N 123 3 E
La Cavalerie, *France* 24 D7 44 1N 3 10 E
La Ceiba, *Honduras* 148 C2 15 40N 86 50W
La Chaise-Dieu, *France* 24 C7 45 18N 3 42 E
La Chaize-le-Vicomte, *France* 22 F5 46 40N 1 18W
La Chapelle d'Angillon, *France* 23 E9 47 21N 2 25 E
La Chapelle-Glain, *France* 22 E5 47 38N 1 11W
La Charité-sur-Loire, *France* 23 E10 47 10N 3 1 E
La Chartre-sur-le-Loir, *France* 22 E7 47 44N 0 34 E
La Châtaigneraie, *France* 24 B3 46 39N 0 44W
La Châtre, *France* 24 B5 46 35N 2 0 E
La Chaux de Fonds, *Switz.* 28 B3 47 7N 6 50 E
La Chorrera, *Colombia* 152 D3 0 44 S 73 1W
La Ciotat, *France* 25 E9 43 10N 5 37 E
La Clayette, *France* 25 B8 46 17N 4 19 E
La Cocha, *Argentina* 158 B2 27 50 S 65 40W
La Concepción = Ri-Aba, *Eq. Guin.* 101 E6 3 28N 8 40 E
La Concepción, *Venezuela* 152 A3 10 30N 71 50W
La Concordia, *Mexico* 147 D6 16 8N 92 38W
La Conner, *U.S.A.* 142 B2 48 23N 122 30W
La Coruña, *Spain* 36 B2 43 20N 8 25W
La Coruña □, *Spain* 36 B2 43 10N 8 30W
La Côte, *Switz.* 28 D2 46 25N 6 15 E
La Côte-St.-André, *France* 25 C9 45 24N 5 15 E
La Courtine-le-Trucq, *France* 24 C6 45 41N 2 15 E
La Crau, *France* 25 E8 43 32N 4 40 E
La Crete, *Canada* 130 B5 58 11N 116 24W
La Crosse, *Kans., U.S.A.* 138 F5 38 32N 99 18W
La Crosse, *Wis., U.S.A.* 138 D9 43 48N 91 15W
La Cruz, *Costa Rica* 148 D2 11 4N 85 39W
La Cruz, *Mexico* 146 C3 23 55N 106 54W
La Dorada, *Colombia* 152 B3 5 30N 74 40W
La Ensenada, *Chile* 160 B2 41 12 S 72 33W
La Escondida, *Mexico* 146 C5 24 6N 99 55W
La Esmeralda, *Paraguay* 158 A3 22 16 S 62 33W
La Esperanza, *Argentina* 160 B3 40 26 S 68 32W
La Esperanza, *Cuba* 148 B3 22 46N 83 44W
La Esperanza, *Honduras* 148 D2 14 15N 88 10W
La Estrada, *Spain* 36 C2 42 43N 8 27W
La Fayette, *U.S.A.* 135 H3 34 42N 85 17W
La Fé, *Cuba* 148 B3 22 2N 84 15W
La Fère, *France* 23 C10 49 39N 3 21 E
La Ferté-Bernard, *France* 22 D7 48 10N 0 40 E
La Ferté-Macé, *France* 22 D6 48 35N 0 22W
La Ferté-St.-Aubin, *France* 23 E8 47 42N 1 57 E
La Ferté-sous-Jouarre, *France* 23 D10 48 56N 3 8 E
La Ferté-Vidame, *France* 22 D7 48 37N 0 53 E
La Flèche, *France* 22 E6 47 42N 0 4W
La Foa, *N. Cal.* 121 U19 21 43 S 165 50 E
La Follette, *U.S.A.* 135 G3 36 23N 84 7W
La Fontaine, *U.S.A.* 141 D11 40 40N 85 43W
La Fregeneda, *Spain* 36 E4 40 58N 6 54W
La Fría, *Venezuela* 152 B3 8 13N 72 15W
La Fuente de San Esteban, *Spain* 36 E4 40 49N 6 15W
La Gineta, *Spain* 35 F2 39 8N 2 1W
La Gloria, *Colombia* 152 B3 8 37N 73 48W
La Gran Sabana, *Venezuela* 153 B5 5 30N 61 30W
La Grand-Combe, *France* 25 D8 44 13N 4 2 E
La Grande, *U.S.A.* 142 D4 45 20N 118 5W
La Grande-Motte, *France* 25 E8 43 23N 4 5 E
La Grange, *Calif., U.S.A.* 144 H6 37 42N 120 27W
La Grange, *Ga., U.S.A.* 135 J3 33 2N 85 2W
La Grange, *Ky., U.S.A.* 134 F3 38 25N 85 23W
La Grange, *Mo., U.S.A.* 140 D5 40 3N 91 35W
La Grange, *Tex., U.S.A.* 139 L6 29 54N 96 52W
La Grita, *Venezuela* 152 B3 8 8N 71 59W
La Guaira, *Venezuela* 152 A4 10 36N 66 56W
La Guardia, *Spain* 36 D2 41 56N 8 52W
La Gudiña, *Spain* 36 C3 42 4N 7 8W
La Güera, *Mauritania* 98 D1 20 51N 17 0W
La Guerche-de-Bretagne, *France* 22 E5 47 57N 1 16W
La Guerche-sur-l'Aubois, *France* 23 F9 46 58N 2 56 E
La Habana, *Cuba* 148 B3 23 8N 82 22W
La Harpe, *U.S.A.* 140 D6 40 35N 90 58W
La Haye-du-Puits, *France* 22 C5 49 17N 1 33W
La Horqueta, *Venezuela* 153 B5 7 55N 60 20W
La Horra, *Spain* 36 D7 41 44N 3 53W
La Independencia, *Mexico* 147 D6 16 31N 91 47W
La Isabela, *Dom. Rep.* 149 C5 19 58N 71 2W
La Jara, *U.S.A.* 143 H11 37 16N 105 58W
La Joya, *Peru* 156 D3 16 43 S 71 52W
La Junquera, *Spain* 34 C7 42 25N 2 53 E
La Junta, *U.S.A.* 139 F3 37 59N 103 33W
La Laguna, *Canary Is.* 33 F3 28 28N 16 18W
La Libertad, *Guatemala* 148 C1 16 47N 90 7W
La Libertad, *Mexico* 146 B2 29 55N 112 41W
La Libertad □, *Peru* 156 B2 8 0 S 78 30W
La Ligua, *Chile* 158 C1 32 30 S 71 16W
La Línea de la Concepción, *Spain* 37 J5 36 15N 5 23W
La Loche, *Canada* 131 B7 56 29N 109 26W
La Londe-les-Maures, *France* 25 E10 43 8N 6 14 E
La Lora, *Spain* 36 C7 42 45N 4 0W
La Loupe, *France* 22 D8 48 29N 1 1 E
La Louvière, *Belgium* 21 H4 50 27N 4 10 E
La Machine, *France* 23 F10 46 54N 3 27 E
La Maddalena, *Italy* 40 A2 41 13N 9 24 E
La Malbaie, *Canada* 129 C5 47 40N 70 10W
La Mancha, *Spain* 35 F2 39 10N 2 54W
La Mariña, *Spain* 36 B3 43 30N 7 40W
La Mesa, *Calif., U.S.A.* 145 N9 32 46N 117 3W
La Mesa, *N. Mex., U.S.A.* 143 K10 32 7N 106 42W
La Misión, *Mexico* 146 A1 32 5N 116 50W
La Moille, *U.S.A.* 140 C7 41 32N 89 17W
La Moine →, *U.S.A.* 140 E6 39 59N 90 31W
La Monte, *U.S.A.* 140 F3 38 46N 93 26W
La Mothe-Achard, *France* 22 F5 46 37N 1 40W
La Motte, *France* 25 D10 44 20N 6 3 E
La Motte-Chalançon, *France* 25 D9 44 30N 5 21 E
La Moure, *U.S.A.* 138 B5 46 21N 98 18W
La Muela, *Spain* 34 D3 41 36N 1 7W
La Mure, *France* 25 D9 44 55N 5 48 E
La Negra, *Chile* 158 A1 23 46 S 70 18W
La Neuveville, *Switz.* 28 B4 47 4N 7 6 E
La Oliva, *Canary Is.* 33 F6 28 36N 13 57W
La Oraya, *Peru* 156 C2 11 32 S 75 54W
La Orotava, *Canary Is.* 33 F3 28 22N 16 31W
La Pacaudière, *France* 24 B7 46 11N 3 52 E
La Palma, *Canary Is.* 33 F2 28 40N 17 50W
La Palma, *Panama* 148 E4 8 15N 78 0W
La Palma del Condado, *Spain* 37 H4 37 21N 6 38W
La Paloma, *Chile* 158 C1 30 35 S 71 0W
La Pampa □, *Argentina* 158 D2 36 50 S 66 0W
La Paragua, *Venezuela* 153 B5 6 50N 63 20W
La Paz, *Entre Ríos, Argentina* 158 C4 30 50 S 59 45W
La Paz, *San Luis, Argentina* 158 C2 33 30 S 67 20W
La Paz, *Bolivia* 156 D4 16 20 S 68 10W
La Paz, *Honduras* 148 D2 14 20N 87 47W
La Paz, *Mexico* 146 C2 24 10N 110 20W
La Paz, *Phil.* 70 D3 15 26N 120 45 E
La Paz □, *Bolivia* 156 D4 15 30 S 68 0W
La Paz Centro, *Nic.* 148 D2 12 20N 86 41W
La Pedrera, *Colombia* 152 D4 1 18 S 69 43W
La Perouse Str., *Asia* 60 B11 45 40N 142 0 E
La Pesca, *Mexico* 147 C5 23 46N 97 47W
La Piedad, *Mexico* 146 C4 20 20N 102 1W
La Pine, *U.S.A.* 142 E3 43 40N 121 30W
La Plant, *U.S.A.* 138 C4 45 9N 100 39W
La Plata, *Argentina* 158 D4 35 0 S 57 55W
La Plata, *Colombia* 152 C2 2 23N 75 53W
La Plata, *U.S.A.* 140 D4 40 2N 92 29W
La Plata, L., *Argentina* 160 B2 44 55 S 71 50W
La Pobla de Lillet, *Spain* 34 C6 42 16N 1 59 E
La Pola de Gordón, *Spain* 36 C5 42 51N 5 41W
La Porte, *U.S.A.* 141 C10 41 36N 86 43W
La Porte City, *U.S.A.* 140 B4 42 19N 92 12W
La Puebla, *Spain* 34 F8 39 46N 3 1 E
La Puebla de Cazalla, *Spain* 37 H5 37 10N 5 20W
La Puebla de los Infantes, *Spain* 37 H5 37 47N 5 24W
La Puebla de Montalbán, *Spain* 36 F6 39 52N 4 22W
La Puerta, *Spain* 35 G2 38 22N 2 45W
La Punt, *Switz.* 29 C9 46 35N 9 56 E
La Purísima, *Mexico* 146 B2 26 10N 112 4W
La Push, *U.S.A.* 144 C2 47 55N 124 38W
La Quiaca, *Argentina* 158 A2 22 5 S 65 35W
La Rambla, *Spain* 37 H6 37 37N 4 45W
La Reine, *Canada* 128 C4 48 50N 79 30W
La Réole, *France* 24 D3 44 35N 0 1W
La Restinga, *Canary Is.* 33 G2 27 38N 17 59W
La Rioja, *Argentina* 158 B2 29 20 S 67 0W
La Rioja □, *Argentina* 158 B2 29 30 S 67 0W
La Rioja □, *Spain* 34 C2 42 20N 2 20W
La Robla, *Spain* 36 C5 42 50N 5 41W
La Roche, *Switz.* 28 C4 46 42N 7 7 E
La Roche-Bernard, *France* 22 E4 47 31N 2 19W
La Roche-Canillac, *France* 24 C5 45 12N 1 57 E
La Roche-en-Ardenne, *Belgium* 21 H7 50 11N 5 35 E
La Roche-sur-Yon, *France* 22 F5 46 40N 1 25W
La Rochefoucauld, *France* 24 C4 45 44N 0 24 E
La Rochelle, *France* 24 B2 46 10N 1 9W
La Roda, *Albacete, Spain* 35 F2 39 13N 2 15W
La Roda, *Sevilla, Spain* 37 H6 37 12N 4 46W
La Romana, *Dom. Rep.* 149 C6 18 27N 68 57W
La Ronge, *Canada* 131 B7 55 5N 105 20W
La Rue, *U.S.A.* 141 D13 40 35N 83 23W
La Rumorosa, *Mexico* 145 N10 32 33N 116 4W
La Sabina, *Spain* 33 C7 38 44N 1 25 E
La Sagra, *Spain* 35 H2 37 57N 2 35W
La Salle, *U.S.A.* 140 C7 41 20N 89 6W
La Sanabria, *Spain* 36 C4 42 0N 6 30W
La Santa, *Canary Is.* 33 E6 29 5N 13 40W
La Sarraz, *Switz.* 28 C3 46 38N 6 32 E
La Sarre, *Canada* 128 C4 48 45N 79 15W
La Scie, *Canada* 129 C8 49 57N 55 36W
La Selva, *Spain* 34 D7 42 0N 2 45 E
La Selva Beach, *U.S.A.* 144 J5 36 56N 121 51W
La Serena, *Chile* 158 B1 29 55 S 71 10W
La Serena, *Spain* 37 G5 38 45N 5 40W
La Seyne-sur-Mer, *France* 25 E9 43 7N 5 52 E
La Sila, *Italy* 41 C9 39 15N 16 35 E
La Solana, *Spain* 35 G1 38 59N 3 14W
La Souterraine, *France* 24 B5 46 15N 1 30 E
La Spézia, *Italy* 38 D6 44 7N 9 50 E
La Suze-sur-Sarthe, *France* 22 E7 47 53N 0 2 E
La Tagua, *Colombia* 152 C3 0 3N 74 40W
La Teste, *France* 24 D2 44 37N 1 8W
La Tortuga, *Venezuela* 149 D6 11 0N 65 22W
La Tour-du-Pin, *France* 25 C9 45 33N 5 27 E
La Tranche-sur-Mer, *France* 22 F5 46 20N 1 27W
La Tremblade, *France* 24 C2 45 46N 1 8W
La Trinidad, *Phil.* 70 C3 16 28N 120 35 E
La Tuque, *Canada* 128 C5 47 30N 72 50W
La Unión, *Chile* 160 B2 40 10 S 73 0W
La Unión, *Colombia* 152 C2 1 35N 77 5W
La Unión, *El Salv.* 148 D2 13 20N 87 50W
La Unión, *Mexico* 146 D4 17 58N 101 49W
La Unión, *Peru* 156 B2 9 43 S 76 45W
La Unión, *Spain* 35 H4 37 38N 0 53W
La Union □, *Phil.* 70 C3 16 30N 120 25 E
La Urbana, *Venezuela* 152 B4 7 8N 66 56W
La Vecilla, *Spain* 36 C5 42 51N 5 27W
La Vega, *Dom. Rep.* 149 C5 19 20N 70 30W
La Vega, *Peru* 156 C2 10 41 S 77 44W
La Vela, *Venezuela* 152 A4 11 27N 69 34W
La Veleta, *Spain* 37 H7 37 1N 3 22W
La Venta, *Mexico* 147 D6 18 8N 94 3W
La Ventura, *Mexico* 146 C4 24 38N 100 54W
La Venturosa, *Colombia* 152 B4 6 8N 68 48W
La Victoria, *Venezuela* 152 A4 10 14N 67 20W
La Voulte-sur-Rhône, *France* 25 D8 44 48N 4 46 E
La Zarza, *Spain* 37 H4 37 42N 6 51W
Laa, *Austria* 31 C9 48 43N 16 23 E
Laaber →, *Germany* 27 G8 48 55N 12 30 E
Laage, *Germany* 26 B8 53 55N 12 21 E
Laba →, *Russia* 53 H4 45 11N 39 42 E
Laban, *Burma* 78 C6 25 52N 96 40 E
Labason, *Phil.* 71 G4 8 4N 122 31 E
Labastide-Murat, *France* 24 D5 44 39N 1 33 E
Labastide-Rouairoux, *France* 24 E6 43 28N 2 39 E
Labbézenga, *Mali* 101 B5 15 2N 0 48 E
Labdah = Leptis Magna, *Libya* 96 B2 32 40N 14 12 E
Labe = Elbe →, *Europe* 26 B4 53 50N 9 0 E
Labé, *Guinea* 100 C2 11 24N 12 16W
Laberec →, *Slovak Rep.* 31 C14 48 37N 21 58 E
Laberge, L., *Canada* 130 A1 61 11N 135 12W
Labian, Tanjong, *Malaysia* 75 A5 5 9N 119 13 E
Labig Pt., *Phil.* 70 B4 18 25N 122 25 E
Labin, *Croatia* 39 C11 45 5N 14 8 E
Labinsk, *Russia* 53 H5 44 40N 40 48 E
Labis, *Malaysia* 77 L4 2 22N 103 2 E
Labiszyn, *Poland* 47 C4 52 57N 17 54 E
Labo, *Phil.* 70 D4 14 9N 122 51 E
Laboe, *Germany* 26 A6 54 24N 10 13 E
Laboka, *Gabon* 102 B2 0 19N 11 32 E
Labouheyre, *France* 24 D3 44 13N 0 55W
Laboulaye, *Argentina* 158 C3 34 10 S 63 30W
Labra, Peña, *Spain* 36 B6 43 3N 4 26W

Leland Lakes 223

Laois □, *Ireland* **19 D4** 52 57N 7 36W
Laon, *France* **23 C10** 49 33N 3 35 E
Laona, *U.S.A.* **134 C1** 45 34N 88 40W
Laos ■, *Asia* **76 D5** 17 45N 105 0 E
Lapa, *Brazil* **159 B6** 25 46 S 49 44W
Lapalisse, *France* **24 B7** 46 15N 3 38 E
Lapeer, *U.S.A.* **141 A13** 43 3N 83 19W
Lapithos, *Cyprus* **32 D12** 35 21N 33 11 E
Lapland = Lappland, *Europe* **12 B21** 68 7N 24 0 E
Lapog, *Phil.* **70 C3** 17 45N 120 27 E
Laporte, *U.S.A.* **137 E8** 41 25N 76 30W
Lapovo, *Serbia, Yug.* **42 C6** 44 10N 21 2 E
Lappeenranta, *Finland* **13 F23** 61 3N 28 12 E
Lappland, *Europe* **12 B21** 68 7N 24 0 E
Laprida, *Argentina* **158 D3** 37 34 S 60 45W
Lapseki, *Turkey* **88 B2** 40 20N 26 41 E
Laptev Sea, *Russia* **57 B13** 76 0N 125 0 E
Lapua, *Finland* **12 E20** 62 58N 23 0 E
Lapuş, Munţii, *Romania* **46 B4** 47 20N 23 50 E
Lăpuşul →, *Romania* **46 B4** 47 25N 23 40 E
Łapy, *Poland* **47 C9** 52 59N 22 52 E
L'Áquila, *Italy* **39 F10** 42 22N 13 22 E
Lār, *Āzarbājān-e Sharqī, Iran* **84 B5** 38 30N 47 52 E
Lār, *Fārs, Iran* **85 E7** 27 40N 54 14 E
Lara, *Australia* **116 E6** 38 2 S 144 26 E
Lara, *Phil.* **71 G1** 8 48N 117 52 E
Lara □, *Venezuela* **152 A4** 10 10N 69 50W
Larabanga, *Ghana* **100 D4** 9 16N 1 56W
Laracha, *Spain* **36 B2** 43 15N 8 35W
Larache, *Morocco* **98 A3** 35 10N 6 5W
Laragne-Montéglin, *France* **25 D9** 44 18N 5 49 E
Laramie, *U.S.A.* **138 E2** 41 19N 105 35W
Laramie Mts., *U.S.A.* **138 E2** 42 0N 105 30W
Laranjeiras, *Brazil* **154 D4** 10 48 S 37 10W
Laranjeiras do Sul, *Brazil* **159 B5** 25 23 S 52 23W
Larantuka, *Indonesia* **72 C2** 8 21 S 122 55 E
Larap, *Phil.* **70 D4** 14 18N 122 39 E
Larat, *Indonesia* **73 C4** 7 0 S 132 0 E
L'Arbresle, *France* **25 C8** 45 50N 4 36 E
Larde, *Mozam.* **107 F4** 16 28 S 39 43 E
Larder Lake, *Canada* **128 C4** 48 5N 79 40W
Lardhos, Ákra, *Greece* **32 C10** 36 4N 28 10 E
Lardhos, Órmos, *Greece* **32 C10** 36 4N 28 2 E
Laredo, *Spain* **34 B1** 43 26N 3 28W
Laredo, *U.S.A.* **139 M5** 27 30N 99 30W
Laredo Sd., *Canada* **130 C3** 52 30N 128 53W
Laren, *Neths.* **20 D6** 52 16N 5 14 E
Larena, *Phil.* **71 G4** 9 15N 123 35 E
Largentière, *France* **25 D8** 44 34N 4 18 E
L'Argentière-la-Bessée, *France* **25 D10** 44 47N 6 33 E
Largo, *U.S.A.* **135 M4** 27 55N 82 47W
Largs, *U.K.* **18 F4** 55 47N 4 52W
Lari, *Italy* **38 E7** 43 34N 10 35 E
Lariang, *Indonesia* **72 B1** 1 26 S 119 17 E
Larimore, *U.S.A.* **138 B6** 47 54N 97 38W
Lārīn, *Iran* **85 C7** 35 55N 52 19 E
Larino, *Italy* **41 A7** 41 48N 14 54 E
Lárisa, *Greece* **44 E4** 39 36N 22 27 E
Lárisa □, *Greece* **44 E4** 39 39N 22 24 E
Larkana, *Pakistan* **79 D3** 27 32N 68 18 E
Larnaca, *Cyprus* **32 E12** 34 55N 33 38 E
Larnaca Bay, *Cyprus* **32 E12** 34 53N 33 45 E
Larne, *U.K.* **19 B6** 54 51N 5 51W
Larned, *U.S.A.* **138 F5** 38 11N 99 6W
Larochette, *Belgium* **21 J8** 49 47N 6 13 E
Laroquebrou, *France* **24 D6** 44 58N 2 12 E
Larrimah, *Australia* **112 C5** 15 35 S 133 12 E
Larsen Ice Shelf, *Antarctica* **7 C17** 67 0 S 62 0W
Larvik, *Norway* **14 E4** 59 4N 10 0 E
Laryak, *Russia* **56 C8** 61 15N 80 0 E
Larzac, Causse du, *France* **24 E7** 43 50N 3 17 E
Las Alpujarras, *Spain* **35 J1** 36 55N 3 20W
Las Animas, *U.S.A.* **138 F3** 38 4N 103 13W
Las Anod, *Somali Rep.* **108 C3** 8 26N 47 19 E
Las Blancos, *Spain* **35 H4** 37 38N 0 49W
Las Brenãs, *Argentina* **158 B3** 27 5 S 61 7W
Las Cabezas de San Juan, *Spain* **37 J5** 37 0N 5 58W
Las Chimeneas, *Mexico* **145 N10** 32 8N 116 5W
Las Coloradas, *Argentina* **160 A2** 39 34 S 70 36W
Las Cruces, *U.S.A.* **143 K10** 32 19N 106 47W
Las Flores, *Argentina* **158 D4** 36 10 S 59 7W
Las Heras, *Argentina* **158 C2** 32 51 S 68 49W
Las Horquetas, *Argentina* **160 C2** 48 14 S 71 11W
Las Khoreh, *Somali Rep.* **108 B3** 11 10N 48 20 E
Las Lajas, *Argentina* **160 A2** 38 30 S 70 25W
Las Lomas, *Peru* **156 A1** 4 40 S 80 10W
Las Lomitas, *Argentina* **158 A3** 24 43 S 60 35W
Las Marismas, *Spain* **37 H4** 37 5N 6 20W
Las Mercedes, *Venezuela* **152 B4** 9 7N 66 24W
Las Navas de la Concepción, *Spain* **37 H5** 37 56N 5 30W
Las Navas de Tolosa, *Spain* **37 G7** 38 18N 3 38W
Las Navas del Marqués, *Spain* **36 E6** 40 36N 4 20W
Las Palmas, *Argentina* **158 B4** 27 8 S 58 45W
Las Palmas, *Canary Is.* **33 F4** 28 7N 15 26W
Las Palmas →, *Mexico* **145 N10** 32 26N 116 54W
Las Piedras, *Uruguay* **159 C4** 34 44 S 56 14W
Las Pipinas, *Argentina* **158 D4** 35 30 S 57 19W
Las Plumas, *Argentina* **160 B3** 43 40 S 67 15W
Las Rosas, *Argentina* **158 C3** 32 30 S 61 35W
Las Tablas, *Panama* **148 E3** 7 49N 80 14W
Las Termas, *Argentina* **158 B3** 27 29 S 64 52W
Las Truchas, *Mexico* **146 D4** 17 57N 102 13W
Las Varillas, *Argentina* **158 C3** 31 50 S 62 50W
Las Vegas, *N. Mex., U.S.A.* **143 J11** 35 36N 105 13W
Las Vegas, *Nev., U.S.A.* **145 J11** 36 10N 115 9W
Lascano, *Uruguay* **159 C5** 33 35 S 54 12W
Lashburn, *Canada* **131 C7** 53 10N 109 40W
Lashio, *Burma* **78 D6** 22 56N 97 45 E
Lashkar, *India* **80 F8** 26 10N 78 10 E
Lashkar Gāh, *Afghan.* **79 C2** 31 35N 64 21 E
Łasin, *Poland* **47 B6** 53 30N 19 2 E
Lasíthi, *Greece* **32 D7** 35 11N 25 31 E
Lasíthi □, *Greece* **32 D7** 35 5N 25 50 E
Lask, *Poland* **47 D6** 51 34N 19 8 E
Łaskarzew, *Poland* **47 D8** 51 48N 21 36 E
Laško, *Slovenia* **39 B12** 46 10N 15 16 E
Lassance, *Brazil* **155 E3** 17 54 S 44 34W
Lassay, *France* **22 D6** 48 27N 0 30W
Lassen Pk., *U.S.A.* **142 F3** 40 29N 121 31W
Last Mountain L., *Canada* **131 C7** 51 5N 105 14W
Lastchance Cr. →, *U.S.A.* **144 E5** 40 2N 121 15W
Lastoursville, *Gabon* **102 C2** 0 55 S 12 38 E
Lastovo, *Croatia* **39 F13** 42 46N 16 55 E
Lastovski Kanal, *Croatia* **39 F13** 42 50N 17 0 E
Lat Yao, *Thailand* **76 E2** 15 45N 99 48 E
Latacunga, *Ecuador* **152 D2** 0 50 S 78 35W
Latakia = Al Lādhiqīyah, *Syria* **88 E6** 35 30N 35 45 E
Latchford, *Canada* **128 C4** 47 20N 79 50W
Late, *Tonga* **121 P13** 18 48 S 174 39W
Laterza, *Italy* **41 B9** 40 37N 16 48 E
Latham, *Australia* **113 E2** 29 44 S 116 20 E
Lathen, *Germany* **26 C3** 52 52N 7 19 E
Lathrop, *U.S.A.* **140 E2** 39 33N 94 20W
Lathrop Wells, *U.S.A.* **145 J10** 36 39N 116 24W
Latiano, *Italy* **41 B10** 40 33N 17 43 E
Latina, *Italy* **40 A5** 41 28N 12 52 E
Latisana, *Italy* **39 C10** 45 47N 13 0 E
Latium = Lazio □, *Italy* **39 F9** 42 10N 12 30 E
Laton, *U.S.A.* **144 J7** 36 26N 119 41W
Latorica →, *Slovak Rep.* **31 C14** 48 28N 21 50 E
Latouche Treville, C., *Australia* **112 C3** 18 27 S 121 49 E
Latrobe, *Australia* **114 G4** 41 14 S 146 30 E
Latrobe, *U.S.A.* **136 F5** 40 19N 79 23W
Latrónico, *Italy* **41 B9** 40 5N 16 1 E
Latur, *India* **82 E3** 18 25N 76 40 E
Latvia ■, *Europe* **13 H20** 56 50N 24 0 E
Lau Group, *Fiji* **121 A3** 17 0 S 178 30W
Lauca →, *Bolivia* **156 D4** 19 9 S 68 10W
Lauchhammer, *Germany* **26 D9** 51 29N 13 47 E
Lauenburg, *Germany* **26 B6** 53 22N 10 32 E
Läufelfingen, *Switz.* **28 B5** 47 24N 7 52 E
Laufen, *Switz.* **28 B5** 47 25N 7 30 E
Lauffen, *Germany* **27 F5** 49 4N 9 9 E
Laujar, *Spain* **35 J2** 37 0N 2 54W
Laukaa, *Finland* **13 E21** 62 24N 25 56 E
Launceston, *Australia* **114 G4** 41 24 S 147 8 E
Launceston, *U.K.* **17 G3** 50 38N 4 22W
Laune →, *Ireland* **19 D2** 52 7N 9 47W
Laupheim, *Germany* **27 G5** 48 14N 9 52 E
Laur, *Phil.* **70 D3** 15 35N 121 11 E
Laura, *Queens., Australia* **114 B3** 15 32 S 144 32 E
Laura, *S. Austral., Australia* **116 B3** 33 10 S 138 18 E
Laureana di Borrello, *Italy* **41 D9** 38 30N 16 5 E
Laurel, *Ind., U.S.A.* **141 E11** 39 31N 85 11W
Laurel, *Miss., U.S.A.* **139 K10** 31 41N 89 8W
Laurel, *Mont., U.S.A.* **142 D9** 45 40N 108 46W
Laurencekirk, *U.K.* **18 E6** 56 50N 2 28W
Laurens, *U.S.A.* **135 H4** 34 30N 82 1W
Laurentian Plateau, *Canada* **129 B6** 52 0N 70 0W
Laurentides, Parc Prov. des, *Canada* **129 C5** 47 45N 71 15W
Lauria, *Italy* **41 B8** 40 3N 15 50 E
Laurie L., *Canada* **131 B8** 56 35N 101 57W
Laurinburg, *U.S.A.* **135 H6** 34 47N 79 28W
Laurium, *U.S.A.* **134 B1** 47 14N 88 27W
Lausanne, *Switz.* **28 C3** 46 32N 6 38 E
Laut, *Indonesia* **75 B3** 4 45N 108 0 E
Laut, Pulau, *Indonesia* **75 C5** 3 40 S 116 10 E
Laut Kecil, Kepulauan, *Indonesia* **75 C5** 4 45 S 115 40 E
Lautaro, *Chile* **160 A2** 38 31 S 72 27W
Lauterbach, *Germany* **26 E5** 50 37N 9 24 E
Lauterbrunnen, *Switz.* **28 C5** 46 36N 7 55 E
Lauterecken, *Germany* **27 F3** 49 38N 7 35 E
Lautoka, *Fiji* **121 A1** 17 37 S 177 27 E
Lauwe, *Belgium* **21 G2** 50 47N 3 12 E
Lauwers, *Neths.* **20 A8** 53 32N 6 23 E
Lauwers Zee, *Neths.* **20 B8** 53 21N 6 13 E
Lauzon, *Canada* **129 C5** 46 48N 71 10W
Lava Hot Springs, *U.S.A.* **142 E7** 42 37N 112 1W
Lavadores, *Spain* **36 C2** 42 14N 8 41W
Lavagna, *Italy* **38 D6** 44 18N 9 20 E
Laval, *France* **22 D6** 48 4N 0 48W
Lavalle, *Argentina* **158 B2** 28 15 S 65 15W
Lávara, *Greece* **44 C8** 41 19N 26 22 E
Lavardac, *France* **24 D4** 44 12N 0 20 E
Lavaur, *France* **24 E5** 43 40N 1 49 E
Lavaux, *Switz.* **28 D3** 46 30N 6 45 E
Lavelanet, *France* **24 F5** 42 57N 1 51 E
Lavello, *Italy* **41 A8** 41 3N 15 48 E
Laverne, *U.S.A.* **139 G5** 36 43N 99 54W
Lavers Hill, *Australia* **116 E5** 38 40 S 143 25 E
Laverton, *Australia* **113 E3** 28 44 S 122 29 E
Lávkos, *Greece* **45 E5** 39 9N 23 14 E
Lavos, *Portugal* **36 E2** 40 6N 8 49W
Lavras, *Brazil* **155 F3** 21 20 S 45 0W
Lavre, *Portugal* **37 G2** 38 46N 8 22W
Lavrentiya, *Russia* **57 C19** 65 35N 171 0W
Lávrion, *Greece* **45 G6** 37 40N 24 4 E
Lávris, *Greece* **32 D6** 35 25N 24 40 E
Lavumisa, *Swaziland* **105 D5** 27 20 S 31 55 E
Lawa, *Phil.* **71 H5** 6 12N 125 41 E
Lawa-an, *Phil.* **71 F5** 11 51N 125 5 E
Lawas, *Malaysia* **75 B5** 4 55N 115 25 E
Lawdar, *Yemen* **86 D4** 13 53N 45 52 E
Lawele, *Indonesia* **72 C2** 5 16 S 123 3 E
Lawksawk, *Burma* **78 E6** 21 15N 96 52 E
Lawn Hill, *Australia* **114 B2** 18 36 S 138 33 E
Lawqah, *Si. Arabia* **84 D4** 29 49N 42 45 E
Lawra, *Ghana* **100 C4** 10 39N 2 51W
Lawrence, *N.Z.* **119 F4** 45 55 S 169 41 E
Lawrence, *Ind., U.S.A.* **141 E10** 39 50N 86 2W
Lawrence, *Kans., U.S.A.* **138 F7** 38 58N 95 14W
Lawrence, *Mass., U.S.A.* **137 D13** 42 43N 71 10W
Lawrenceburg, *Ind., U.S.A.* **141 E12** 39 6N 84 52W
Lawrenceburg, *Ky., U.S.A.* **141 F12** 38 2N 84 54W
Lawrenceburg, *Tenn., U.S.A.* **135 H2** 35 14N 87 20W
Lawrenceville, *Ga., U.S.A.* **135 J4** 33 57N 83 59W
Lawrenceville, *Ill., U.S.A.* **141 F9** 38 44N 87 41W
Laws, *U.S.A.* **144 H8** 37 24N 118 20W
Lawson, *U.S.A.* **140 E2** 39 26N 94 12W
Lawton, *Mich., U.S.A.* **141 B11** 42 10N 85 50W
Lawton, *Okla., U.S.A.* **139 H5** 34 37N 98 25W
Lawu, *Indonesia* **75 D4** 7 40 S 111 13 E
Laxford, L., *U.K.* **18 C3** 58 24N 5 6W
Lay →, *France* **24 B2** 46 18N 1 17W
Layht, Ra's, *Yemen* **87 D6** 12 38N 53 25 E
Laylá, *Si. Arabia* **86 B4** 22 10N 46 40 E
Laylān, *Iraq* **84 C5** 35 18N 44 31 E
Layon →, *France* **22 E6** 47 20N 0 45W
Laysan I., *Pac. Oc.* **123 E11** 25 30N 167 0W
Laytonville, *U.S.A.* **142 G2** 39 41N 123 29W
Laza, *Burma* **78 B6** 26 30N 97 38 E
Lazarevac, *Serbia, Yug.* **42 C5** 44 23N 20 17 E
Lazarevskoye, *Russia* **53 J4** 43 55N 39 21 E
Lazi, *Phil.* **71 G4** 9 8N 123 38 E
Lazio □, *Italy* **39 F9** 42 10N 12 30 E
Lazo, *Russia* **60 C6** 43 25N 133 55 E
Łazy, *Poland* **47 E6** 50 27N 19 24 E
Le Barcarès, *France* **24 F7** 42 47N 3 2 E
Le Beausset, *France* **25 E9** 43 12N 5 48 E
Le Blanc, *France* **24 B5** 46 37N 1 3 E
Le Bleymard, *France* **24 D7** 44 30N 3 42 E
Le Bourgneuf-la-Fôret, *France* **22 D6** 48 10N 0 59W
Le Bouscat, *France* **24 D3** 44 53N 0 37W
Le Brassus, *Switz.* **28 C2** 46 35N 6 13 E
Le Bugue, *France* **24 D4** 44 55N 0 56 E
Le Canourgue, *France* **24 D7** 44 26N 3 13 E
Le Cateau, *France* **23 B10** 50 7N 3 32 E
Le Chambon-Feugerolles, *France* **25 C8** 45 24N 4 19 E
Le Château-d'Oléron, *France* **24 C2** 45 54N 1 12W
Le Châtelard, *Switz.* **28 D3** 46 4N 6 57 E
Le Châtelet, *France* **24 B6** 46 38N 2 16 E
Le Châtelet-en-Brie, *France* **23 D9** 48 31N 2 48 E
Le Chesne, *France* **23 C11** 49 30N 4 45 E
Le Cheylard, *France* **25 D8** 44 55N 4 25 E
Le Claire, *U.S.A.* **140 C6** 41 36N 90 21W
Le Conquet, *France* **22 D2** 48 21N 4 46W
Le Creusot, *France* **23 F11** 46 48N 4 24 E
Le Croisic, *France* **22 E4** 47 18N 2 30W
Le Donjon, *France* **24 B7** 46 22N 3 48 E
Le Dorat, *France* **24 B5** 46 14N 1 5 E
Le François, *Martinique* **149 D7** 14 38N 60 57W
Le Grand-Lucé, *France* **22 E7** 47 52N 0 28 E
Le Grand-Pressigny, *France* **22 F7** 46 55N 0 48 E
Le Havre, *France* **22 C7** 49 30N 0 5 E
Le Lavandou, *France* **25 E10** 43 8N 6 22 E
Le Lion-d'Angers, *France* **22 E6** 47 37N 0 43W
Le Locle, *Switz.* **28 B3** 47 3N 6 44 E
Le Louroux-Béconnais, *France* **22 E6** 47 30N 0 55W
Le Luc, *France* **25 E10** 43 23N 6 21 E
Le Madonie, *Italy* **40 E6** 37 50N 13 50 E
Le Maire, Estr. de, *Argentina* **160 D4** 54 50 S 65 0W
Le Mans, *France* **22 E7** 48 0N 0 10 E
Le Mars, *U.S.A.* **138 D6** 42 47N 96 10W
Le Mêle-sur-Sarthe, *France* **22 D7** 48 31N 0 22 E
Le Merlerault, *France* **22 D7** 48 41N 0 16 E
Le Monastier-sur-Gazeille, *France* **24 D7** 44 57N 3 59 E
Le Monêtier-les-Bains, *France* **25 D10** 44 58N 6 30 E
Le Mont d'Or, *France* **23 F13** 46 45N 6 18 E
Le Mont-Dore, *France* **24 C6** 45 35N 2 49 E
Le Mont-St.-Michel, *France* **22 D5** 48 40N 1 30W
Le Moule, *Guadeloupe* **149 C7** 16 20N 61 22W
Le Muy, *France* **25 E10** 43 28N 6 34 E
Le Palais, *France* **22 E3** 47 20N 3 10W
Le Perthus, *France* **24 F6** 42 30N 2 53 E
Le Pont, *Switz.* **28 C2** 46 41N 6 20 E
Le Pouldu, *France* **22 E3** 47 41N 3 36W
Le Puy-en-Velay, *France* **24 C7** 45 3N 3 52 E
Le Quesnoy, *France* **23 B10** 50 15N 3 38 E
Le Roy, *Ill., U.S.A.* **141 D8** 40 21N 88 46W
Le Roy, *Kans., U.S.A.* **139 F7** 38 5N 95 38W
Le Sentier, *Switz.* **28 C2** 46 37N 6 15 E
Le Sueur, *U.S.A.* **138 C8** 44 28N 93 55W
Le Teil, *France* **25 D8** 44 33N 4 40 E
Le Teilleul, *France* **22 D6** 48 32N 0 53W
Le Theil, *France* **22 D7** 48 16N 0 42 E
Le Thillot, *France* **23 E13** 47 53N 6 46 E
Le Thuy, *Vietnam* **76 D6** 17 14N 106 49 E
Le Touquet-Paris-Plage, *France* **23 B8** 50 30N 1 36 E
Le Tréport, *France* **22 B8** 50 3N 1 20 E
Le Val-d'Ajol, *France* **23 E13** 47 55N 6 30 E
Le Verdon-sur-Mer, *France* **24 C2** 45 33N 1 4W
Le Vigan, *France* **24 E7** 43 59N 3 36 E
Lea →, *U.K.* **17 F7** 51 31N 0 1 E
Leach, *Cambodia* **77 F4** 12 21N 103 46 E
Lead, *U.S.A.* **138 C3** 44 21N 103 46W
Leader, *Canada* **131 C7** 50 50N 109 30W
Leadhills, *U.K.* **18 F5** 55 25N 3 45W
Leadville, *U.S.A.* **143 G10** 39 15N 106 18W
Leaf →, *U.S.A.* **139 K10** 30 59N 88 44W
Leakey, *U.S.A.* **139 L5** 29 44N 99 46W
Lealui, *Zambia* **103 F4** 15 10 S 23 2 E
Leamington, *Canada* **128 D3** 42 3N 82 36W
Leamington, *N.Z.* **118 D4** 37 55 S 175 30 E
Leamington, *U.S.A.* **142 G7** 39 32N 112 17W
Leamington Spa = Royal Leamington Spa, *U.K.* **17 E6** 52 18N 1 31W
Le'an, *China* **69 D10** 27 22N 115 48 E
Leandro Norte Alem, *Argentina* **159 B4** 27 34 S 55 15W
Learmonth, *Australia* **112 D1** 22 13 S 114 10 E
Leask, *Canada* **131 C7** 53 5N 106 45W
Leavenworth, *Ind., U.S.A.* **141 F10** 38 12N 86 21W
Leavenworth, *Kans., U.S.A.* **138 F7** 39 19N 94 55W
Leavenworth, *Wash., U.S.A.* **142 C3** 47 36N 120 40W
Leawood, *U.S.A.* **140 F2** 38 57N 94 37W
Łeba, *Poland* **47 A4** 54 45N 17 32 E
Łeba →, *Poland* **47 A4** 54 46N 17 33 E
Lebak, *Phil.* **71 H5** 6 32N 124 5 E
Lebam, *U.S.A.* **144 D3** 46 34N 123 33W
Lebane, *Serbia, Yug.* **42 E6** 42 56N 21 44 E
Lebango, *Congo* **102 B2** 0 39N 14 21 E
Lebanon, *Ill., U.S.A.* **140 F7** 38 38N 89 49W
Lebanon, *Ind., U.S.A.* **141 D10** 40 3N 86 28W
Lebanon, *Kans., U.S.A.* **138 F5** 39 49N 98 33W
Lebanon, *Ky., U.S.A.* **134 G3** 37 34N 85 15W
Lebanon, *Mo., U.S.A.* **139 G8** 37 41N 92 40W
Lebanon, *Ohio, U.S.A.* **141 E12** 39 26N 84 13W
Lebanon, *Oreg., U.S.A.* **142 D2** 44 32N 122 55W
Lebanon, *Pa., U.S.A.* **137 F8** 40 20N 76 28W
Lebanon, *Tenn., U.S.A.* **135 G2** 36 12N 86 18W
Lebanon ■, *Asia* **91 B4** 34 0N 36 0 E
Lebanon Junction, *U.S.A.* **141 G11** 37 50N 85 44W
Lebbeke, *Belgium* **21 G4** 50 58N 4 8 E
Lebec, *U.S.A.* **145 L8** 34 50N 118 52W
Lebedyan, *Russia* **52 D4** 53 0N 39 10 E
Lebedyn, *Ukraine* **51 G8** 50 35N 34 30 E
Lebomboberge, *S. Africa* **105 C5** 24 30 S 32 0 E
Lębork, *Poland* **47 A4** 54 33N 17 46 E
Lebrija, *Spain* **37 J4** 36 53N 6 5W
Łebsko, Jezioro, *Poland* **47 A4** 54 40N 17 25 E
Lebu, *Chile* **158 D1** 37 40 S 73 47W
Lecce, *Italy* **41 B11** 40 23N 18 11 E
Lecco, *Italy* **38 C6** 45 51N 9 23 E
Lecco, L. di, *Italy* **38 C6** 45 55N 9 19 E
Lécera, *Spain* **34 D4** 41 13N 0 43W
Lech, *Austria* **30 D3** 47 13N 10 9 E
Lech →, *Germany* **27 G6** 48 43N 10 56 E
Lechang, *China* **69 E9** 25 10N 113 20 E
Lechtaler Alpen, *Austria* **30 D3** 47 15N 10 30 E
Lectoure, *France* **24 E4** 43 56N 0 38 E
Łeczna, *Poland* **47 D9** 51 18N 22 53 E
Łęczyca, *Poland* **47 C6** 52 5N 19 15 E
Ledang, Gunong, *Malaysia* **74 B2** 2 22N 102 37 E
Ledbury, *U.K.* **17 E5** 52 2N 2 25W
Lede, *Belgium* **21 G3** 50 58N 3 59 E
Ledeberg, *Belgium* **21 F3** 51 2N 3 45 E
Ledeč, *Czech.* **30 B8** 49 41N 15 18 E
Ledesma, *Spain* **36 D5** 41 6N 5 59W
Ledong, *China* **76 C7** 18 41N 109 5 E
Leduc, *Canada* **130 C6** 53 15N 113 30W
Ledyczek, *Poland* **47 B3** 53 33N 16 59 E
Lee, *U.S.A.* **137 D11** 42 19N 73 15W
Lee →, *Ireland* **19 E3** 51 53N 8 56W
Lee Vining, *U.S.A.* **144 H7** 37 58N 119 7W
Leech L., *U.S.A.* **138 B7** 47 10N 94 24W
Leedey, *U.S.A.* **139 H5** 35 52N 99 21W
Leeds, *U.K.* **16 D6** 53 48N 1 33W
Leeds, *U.S.A.* **135 J2** 33 33N 86 33W
Leek, *Neths.* **20 B8** 53 10N 6 24 E
Leek, *U.K.* **16 D5** 53 7N 2 1W
Leende, *Neths.* **21 F7** 51 21N 5 33 E
Leer, *Germany* **26 B3** 53 13N 7 26 E
Leerdam, *Neths.* **20 E6** 51 54N 5 6 E
Leersum, *Neths.* **20 E6** 52 0N 5 26 E
Lee's Summit, *U.S.A.* **140 F2** 38 55N 94 23W
Leesburg, *Fla., U.S.A.* **135 L5** 28 49N 81 53W
Leesburg, *Ohio, U.S.A.* **141 E13** 39 21N 83 33W
Leeston, *N.Z.* **119 D7** 43 45 S 172 19 E
Leesville, *U.S.A.* **139 K8** 31 9N 93 16W
Leeton, *Australia* **117 C7** 34 33 S 146 23 E
Leetonia, *U.S.A.* **136 F4** 40 53N 80 45W
Leeu Gamka, *S. Africa* **104 E3** 32 47 S 21 59 E
Leeuwarden, *Neths.* **20 B7** 53 15N 5 48 E
Leeuwin, C., *Australia* **113 F2** 34 20 S 115 9 E
Leeward Is., *Atl. Oc.* **149 C7** 16 30N 63 30W
Léfini, *Congo* **102 C3** 2 55 S 15 39 E
Lefka, *Cyprus* **32 D11** 35 6N 32 51 E
Lefkoniko, *Cyprus* **32 D12** 35 18N 33 44 E
Lefors, *U.S.A.* **139 H4** 35 26N 100 48W
Lefroy, L., *Australia* **113 F3** 31 21 S 121 40 E
Łeg →, *Poland* **47 E8** 50 42N 21 50 E
Legal, *Canada* **130 C6** 53 55N 113 35W
Leganés, *Spain* **36 E7** 40 19N 3 45W
Legazpi, *Phil.* **70 E4** 13 10N 123 45 E
Legendre I., *Australia* **112 D2** 20 22 S 116 55 E
Leghorn = Livorno, *Italy* **38 E7** 43 33N 10 19 E
Legionowo, *Poland* **47 C7** 52 25N 20 50 E
Léglise, *Belgium* **21 J7** 49 48N 5 32 E
Legnago, *Italy* **39 C8** 45 11N 11 18 E
Legnano, *Italy* **38 C5** 45 36N 8 54 E
Legnica, *Poland* **47 D3** 51 12N 16 10 E
Legnica □, *Poland* **47 D3** 51 30N 16 0 E
Legrad, *Croatia* **39 B13** 46 17N 16 51 E
Legume, *Australia* **115 D5** 28 20 S 152 19 E
Leh, *India* **81 B7** 34 9N 77 35 E
Lehi, *U.S.A.* **142 F8** 40 24N 111 51W
Lehighton, *U.S.A.* **137 F9** 40 50N 75 43W
Lehliu, *Romania* **46 E7** 44 29N 26 20 E
Lehrte, *Germany* **26 C5** 52 22N 9 58 E
Lehututu, *Botswana* **104 C3** 23 54 S 21 55 E
Lei Shui →, *China* **69 D9** 26 55N 112 35 E
Leiah, *Pakistan* **79 C3** 30 58N 70 58 E
Leibnitz, *Austria* **30 E8** 46 47N 15 34 E
Leibo, *China* **68 C4** 28 11N 103 34 E
Leicester, *U.K.* **17 E6** 52 38N 1 8W
Leicestershire □, *U.K.* **17 E6** 52 41N 1 17W
Leichhardt →, *Australia* **114 B2** 17 35 S 139 48 E
Leichhardt Ra., *Australia* **114 C4** 20 46 S 147 40 E
Leiden, *Neths.* **20 D5** 52 9N 4 30 E
Leiderdorp, *Neths.* **20 D5** 52 9N 4 32 E
Leidschendam, *Neths.* **20 D4** 52 5N 4 24 E
Leie →, *Belgium* **23 A10** 51 2N 3 45 E
Leigh →, *Australia* **116 E6** 38 18 S 144 30 E
Leignon, *Belgium* **21 H6** 50 16N 5 7 E
Leiktho, *Burma* **78 F6** 19 13N 96 35 E
Leine →, *Germany* **26 C5** 52 43N 9 36 E
Leinster, *Australia* **113 E3** 27 51 S 120 36 E
Leinster □, *Ireland* **19 C4** 53 3N 7 8W
Leinster, Mt., *Ireland* **19 D5** 52 37N 6 46W
Leipzig, *Germany* **26 D8** 51 18N 12 22 E
Leiria, *Portugal* **37 F2** 39 46N 8 53W
Leiria □, *Portugal* **37 F2** 39 46N 8 53W
Leirvik, *Norway* **13 G11** 59 47N 5 28 E
Leisler, Mt., *Australia* **112 D4** 23 23 S 129 20 E
Leith, *U.K.* **18 F5** 55 59N 3 11W
Leith Hill, *U.K.* **17 F7** 51 11N 0 22W
Leitha →, *Europe* **31 D10** 47 41N 17 40 E
Leitrim, *Ireland* **19 B3** 54 0N 8 5W
Leitrim □, *Ireland* **19 B3** 54 8N 8 0W
Leiyang, *China* **69 D9** 26 27N 112 45 E
Leiza, *Spain* **34 B3** 43 5N 1 55W
Leizhou Bandao, *China* **65 D6** 21 0N 110 0 E
Leizhou Wan, *China* **69 G8** 20 50N 110 20 E
Lek →, *Neths.* **20 E5** 51 54N 4 35 E
Leka, *Norway* **12 D14** 65 5N 11 35 E
Lekáni, *Greece* **44 C6** 41 10N 24 35 E
Leke, *Belgium* **21 F1** 51 6N 2 54 E
Lekhainá, *Greece* **45 G3** 37 57N 21 16 E
Lekkerkerk, *Neths.* **20 E5** 51 54N 4 41 E
Leksula, *Indonesia* **72 B3** 3 46 S 126 31 E
Lékva Ori, *Greece* **32 D6** 35 18N 24 3 E
Leland, *U.S.A.* **139 J9** 33 24N 90 54W
Leland Lakes, *Canada* **131 A6** 60 0N 110 59W

Mackay 227

Lučenec, *Slovak Rep.* **31 C12** 48 18N 19 42 E
Lucens, *Switz.* **28 C3** 46 43N 6 51 E
Lucera, *Italy* **41 A8** 41 30N 15 20 E
Lucerne = Luzern, *Switz.* **29 B6** 47 3N 8 18 E
Lucerne, *U.S.A.* **144 F4** 39 6N 122 48W
Lucerne Valley, *U.S.A.* **145 L10** 34 27N 116 57W
Lucero, *Mexico* **146 A3** 30 49N 106 30W
Luchena →, *Spain* **35 H3** 37 44N 1 50W
Lucheng, *China* **66 F7** 36 20N 113 11 E
Lucheringo →, *Mozam.* **107 E4** 11 43 S 36 17 E
Luchiang, *Taiwan* **69 E13** 24 1N 120 22 E
Lüchow, *Germany* **26 C7** 52 58N 11 8 E
Luchuan, *China* **69 F8** 22 21N 110 12 E
Lucie →, *Surinam* **153 C6** 3 35N 57 38W
Lucira, *Angola* **103 E2** 14 0 S 12 35 E
Luckau, *Germany* **26 D9** 51 50N 13 42 E
Luckenwalde, *Germany* **26 C9** 52 5N 13 10 E
Luckey, *U.S.A.* **141 C13** 41 27N 83 29W
Lucknow, *India* **81 F9** 26 50N 81 0 E
Luçon, *France* **24 B2** 46 28N 1 10W
Lucusse, *Angola* **103 E4** 12 32 S 20 48 E
Lüda = Dalian, *China* **67 E11** 38 50N 121 40 E
Luda Kamchiya →, *Bulgaria* **43 D12** 43 3N 27 29 E
Ludbreg, *Croatia* **39 B13** 46 15N 16 38 E
Lüdenscheid, *Germany* **26 D3** 51 13N 7 37 E
Lüderitz, *Namibia* **104 D2** 26 41 S 15 8 E
Ludewe □, *Tanzania* **107 D3** 10 0 S 34 50 E
Ludhiana, *India* **80 D6** 30 57N 75 56 E
Ludian, *China* **68 D4** 27 10N 103 33 E
Luding Qiao, *China* **68 C4** 29 53N 102 12 E
Lüdinghausen, *Germany* **26 D3** 51 46N 7 27 E
Ludington, *U.S.A.* **134 D2** 43 57N 86 27W
Ludlow, *U.K.* **17 E5** 52 22N 2 42W
Ludlow, *Calif., U.S.A.* **145 L10** 34 43N 116 10W
Ludlow, *Vt., U.S.A.* **137 C12** 43 24N 72 42W
Ludus, *Romania* **46 C5** 46 29N 24 5 E
Ludvika, *Sweden* **13 F16** 60 8N 15 14 E
Ludwigsburg, *Germany* **27 G5** 48 53N 9 11 E
Ludwigshafen, *Germany* **27 F4** 49 29N 8 26 E
Ludwigslust, *Germany* **26 B7** 53 19N 11 30 E
Ludza, *Latvia* **50 D4** 56 32N 27 43 E
Lue, *Australia* **117 B8** 32 38 S 149 50 E
Luebo, *Zaïre* **103 D4** 5 21 S 21 23 E
Lueki, *Zaïre* **102 C5** 3 20 S 25 48 E
Luena, *Angola* **103 E3** 12 13 S 19 51 E
Luena, *Zaïre* **107 D2** 9 28 S 25 43 E
Luena, *Zambia* **107 E3** 10 40 S 30 25 E
Luepa, *Venezuela* **153 B5** 5 43N 61 31W
Lüeyang, *China* **66 H4** 33 22N 106 10 E
Lufeng, *Guangdong, China* **69 F10** 22 57N 115 38 E
Lufeng, *Yunnan, China* **68 E4** 25 0N 102 5 E
Lufico, *Angola* **103 D2** 6 24 S 13 23 E
Lufira →, *Zaïre* **107 D2** 9 30 S 27 0 E
Lufkin, *U.S.A.* **139 K7** 31 21N 94 44W
Lufupa, *Zaïre* **103 E4** 10 37 S 24 56 E
Luga, *Russia* **50 C5** 58 40N 29 55 E
Luga →, *Russia* **50 C5** 59 40N 28 18 E
Lugano, *Switz.* **29 D7** 46 0N 8 57 E
Lugano, L. di, *Switz.* **29 E8** 46 0N 9 0 E
Lugansk = Luhansk, *Ukraine* **51 H10** 48 38N 39 15 E
Lugard's Falls, *Kenya* **106 C4** 3 6 S 38 41 E
Lugela, *Mozam.* **107 F4** 16 25 S 36 43 E
Lugenda →, *Mozam.* **107 E4** 11 25 S 38 33 E
Lugh Ganana, *Somali Rep.* **108 D2** 3 48N 42 34 E
Lugnaquilla, *Ireland* **19 D5** 52 58N 6 28W
Lugnvik, *Sweden* **14 B11** 62 56N 17 55 E
Lugo, *Italy* **39 D8** 44 25N 11 54 E
Lugo, *Spain* **36 B3** 43 2N 7 35W
Lugo □, *Spain* **36 C3** 43 0N 7 30W
Lugoj, *Romania* **42 B6** 45 42N 21 57 E
Lugones, *Spain* **36 B5** 43 26N 5 50W
Lugovoy, *Kazakstan* **55 B6** 42 55N 72 43 E
Luhansk, *Ukraine* **51 H10** 48 38N 39 15 E
Luhe, *China* **69 A12** 32 19N 118 50 E
Luhe →, *Germany* **26 B6** 53 23N 10 13 E
Luhuo, *China* **68 B3** 31 21N 100 48 E
Luiana, *Angola* **103 F4** 17 25 S 22 59 E
Luimneach = Limerick, *Ireland* **19 D3** 52 40N 8 37W
Luino, *Italy* **38 C5** 46 0N 8 44 E
Luís Correia, *Brazil* **154 B3** 3 0 S 41 35W
Luís Gonçalves, *Brazil* **154 C1** 5 37 S 50 25W
Luitpold Coast, *Antarctica* **7 D1** 78 30 S 32 0W
Luiza, *Zaïre* **103 D4** 7 40 S 22 30 E
Luizi, *Zaïre* **106 D2** 6 0 S 27 25 E
Luján, *Argentina* **158 C4** 34 45 S 59 5W
Lujiang, *China* **69 B11** 31 20N 117 15 E
Lukala, *Zaïre* **103 D2** 5 31 S 14 32 E
Lukanga Swamp, *Zambia* **107 E2** 14 30 S 27 40 E
Lukenie →, *Zaïre* **102 C3** 3 0 S 18 50 E
Lukhisaral, *India* **81 G12** 25 11N 86 5 E
Lŭki, *Bulgaria* **43 F9** 41 50N 24 43 E
Lukk, *Libya* **96 B4** 32 1N 24 46 E
Lukolela, *Equateur, Zaïre* **102 C3** 1 10 S 17 12 E
Lukolela, *Kasai Or., Zaïre* **103 D4** 5 23 S 24 32 E
Lukosi, *Zimbabwe* **107 F2** 18 30 S 26 30 E
Lukovit, *Bulgaria* **43 D9** 43 13N 24 11 E
Łuków, *Poland* **47 D9** 51 55N 22 23 E
Lukoyanov, *Russia* **52 C7** 55 2N 44 29 E
Lule älv →, *Sweden* **12 D19** 65 35N 22 10 E
Luleå, *Sweden* **12 D20** 65 35N 22 10 E
Lüleburgaz, *Turkey* **88 B2** 41 23N 27 22 E
Luliang, *China* **68 E4** 25 0N 103 40 E
Luling, *U.S.A.* **139 L6** 29 41N 97 39W
Lulong, *China* **67 E10** 39 53N 118 51 E
Lulonga →, *Zaïre* **102 B3** 1 0N 18 10 E
Lulua →, *Zaïre* **103 C4** 4 30 S 20 30 E
Luluabourg = Kananga, *Zaïre* **103 D4** 5 55 S 22 18 E
Lumai, *Angola* **103 E4** 13 13 S 21 25 E
Lumajang, *Indonesia* **75 D4** 8 8 S 113 13 E
Lumaku, Gunong, *Malaysia* **75 B5** 4 52N 115 38 E
Lumbala Kaquengue, *Angola* **103 E4** 12 39 S 22 34 E
Lumbala N'guimbo, *Angola* **103 E4** 14 18 S 21 18 E
Lumberton, *Miss., U.S.A.* **139 K10** 31 0N 89 27W
Lumberton, *N.C., U.S.A.* **135 H6** 34 37N 79 0W
Lumberton, *N. Mex., U.S.A.* **143 H10** 36 56N 106 56W
Lumbres, *France* **23 B9** 50 40N 2 5 E
Lumbwa, *Kenya* **106 C4** 0 12 S 35 28 E
Lumding, *India* **78 C4** 25 46N 93 10 E
Lumi, *Papua N. G.* **120 B2** 3 30 S 142 2 E
Lummen, *Belgium* **21 G6** 50 59N 5 12 E
Lumsden, *N.Z.* **119 F3** 45 44 S 168 27 E
Lumut, *Malaysia* **77 K3** 4 13N 100 37 E
Lumut, Tg., *Indonesia* **74 C3** 3 50 S 105 58 E
Luna, *Luzon, Phil.* **70 B3** 18 18N 121 21 E
Luna, *Luzon, Phil.* **70 C3** 16 51N 120 23 E
Lunan, *China* **68 E4** 24 40N 103 18 E
Lunavada, *India* **80 H5** 23 8N 73 37 E
Lunca, *Romania* **46 B6** 47 22N 25 1 E
Lund, *Sweden* **15 J7** 55 44N 13 12 E
Lund, *U.S.A.* **142 G6** 38 52N 115 0W
Lunda Norte □, *Angola* **103 D3** 8 0 S 20 0 E
Lunda Sul □, *Angola* **103 D4** 10 0 S 20 0 E
Lundazi, *Zambia* **107 E3** 12 20 S 33 7 E
Lunderskov, *Denmark* **15 J3** 55 29N 9 19 E
Lundi →, *Zimbabwe* **107 G3** 21 43 S 32 34 E
Lundu, *Malaysia* **75 B3** 1 40N 109 50 E
Lundy, *U.K.* **17 F3** 51 10N 4 41W
Lune →, *U.K.* **16 C5** 54 0N 2 51W
Lüneburg, *Germany* **26 B6** 53 15N 10 24 E
Lüneburg Heath = Lüneburger Heide, *Germany* **26 C6** 53 10N 10 12 E
Lüneburger Heide, *Germany* **26 C6** 53 10N 10 12 E
Lunel, *France* **25 E8** 43 39N 4 9 E
Lünen, *Germany* **26 D3** 51 37N 7 32 E
Lunenburg, *Canada* **129 D7** 44 22N 64 18W
Lunéville, *France* **23 D13** 48 36N 6 30 E
Lunga →, *Zambia* **107 E2** 14 34 S 26 25 E
Lungern, *Switz.* **28 C6** 46 48N 8 10 E
Lungi Airport, *S. Leone* **100 D2** 8 40N 13 17W
Lunglei, *India* **78 D4** 22 55N 92 45 E
Lungngo, *Burma* **78 E4** 21 57N 93 36 E
Luni, *India* **80 F5** 26 0N 73 6 E
Luni →, *India* **80 G4** 24 41N 71 14 E
Luninets = Luninyets, *Belarus* **51 F4** 52 15N 26 50 E
Luning, *U.S.A.* **142 G4** 38 30N 118 11W
Lunino, *Russia* **52 D7** 53 38N 45 18 E
Luninyets, *Belarus* **51 F4** 52 15N 26 50 E
Lunner, *Norway* **14 D4** 60 19N 10 35 E
Lunsemfwa →, *Zambia* **107 E3** 14 54 S 30 12 E
Lunsemfwa Falls, *Zambia* **107 E2** 14 30 S 29 6 E
Lunteren, *Neths.* **20 D7** 52 5N 5 38 E
Luo He →, *China* **66 G6** 34 35N 110 20 E
Luocheng, *China* **68 E7** 24 48N 108 53 E
Luochuan, *China* **66 G5** 35 45N 109 26 E
Luoci, *China* **68 E4** 25 19N 102 18 E
Luodian, *China* **68 E6** 25 24N 106 43 E
Luoding, *China* **69 F8** 22 45N 111 40 E
Luofu, *Zaïre* **106 C2** 0 10 S 29 15 E
Luohe, *China* **66 H8** 33 32N 114 2 E
Luojiang, *China* **68 B5** 31 18N 104 33 E
Luonan, *China* **66 G6** 34 5N 110 10 E
Luoning, *China* **66 G6** 34 35N 111 40 E
Luoshan, *China* **69 A10** 32 13N 114 30 E
Luotian, *China* **69 B10** 30 46N 115 22 E
Luoyang, *China* **66 G7** 34 40N 112 26 E
Luoyuan, *China* **69 D12** 26 28N 119 30 E
Luozi, *Zaïre* **103 C2** 4 54 S 14 0 E
Luozigou, *China* **67 C16** 43 42N 130 18 E
Lupanshui, *China* **68 D5** 26 38N 104 48 E
Lupeni, *Romania* **46 D4** 45 21N 23 13 E
Lupilichi, *Mozam.* **107 E4** 11 47 S 35 13 E
Lupire, *Angola* **103 E3** 14 36 S 19 29 E
Łupków, *Poland* **31 B15** 49 15N 22 4 E
Lupoing, *China* **68 E5** 24 53N 104 21 E
Lupon, *Phil.* **71 H5** 6 54N 126 0 E
Luquan, *China* **68 E4** 25 35N 102 25 E
Luque, *Paraguay* **158 B4** 25 19 S 57 25W
Luque, *Spain* **37 H6** 37 35N 4 16W
Luray, *U.S.A.* **134 F6** 38 40N 78 28W
Lure, *France* **23 E13** 47 40N 6 30 E
Luremo, *Angola* **103 D3** 8 30 S 17 50 E
Lurgan, *U.K.* **19 B5** 54 28N 6 19W
Luri, *France* **25 F13** 42 53N 9 23 E
Luribay, *Bolivia* **156 D4** 17 6 S 67 39W
Lurin, *Peru* **156 C2** 12 17 S 76 52W
Lusaka, *Zambia* **107 F2** 15 28 S 28 16 E
Lusambo, *Zaïre* **103 C4** 4 58 S 23 28 E
Lusangaye, *Zaïre* **103 C5** 4 54 S 26 0 E
Luseland, *Canada* **131 C7** 52 5N 109 24W
Lushan, *Henan, China* **66 H7** 33 45N 112 55 E
Lushan, *Sichuan, China* **68 B4** 30 12N 102 52 E
Lushi, *China* **66 G6** 34 3N 111 3 E
Lushnja, *Albania* **44 D1** 40 55N 19 41 E
Lushoto, *Tanzania* **106 C4** 4 47 S 38 20 E
Lushoto □, *Tanzania* **106 C4** 4 45 S 38 20 E
Lushui, *China* **68 E2** 25 58N 98 44 E
Lüshun, *China* **67 E11** 38 45N 121 15 E
Lusignan, *France* **24 B4** 46 26N 0 8 E
Lusigny-sur-Barse, *France* **23 D11** 48 16N 4 15 E
Lusk, *U.S.A.* **138 D2** 42 46N 104 27W
Lussac-les-Châteaux, *France* **24 B4** 46 24N 0 43 E
Lussanvira, *Brazil* **155 F1** 20 42 S 51 7W
Luta = Dalian, *China* **67 E11** 38 50N 121 40 E
Lutembo, *Angola* **103 E4** 13 26 S 21 16 E
Luti, *Solomon Is.* **121 L9** 7 14 S 157 0 E
Luton, *U.K.* **17 F7** 51 53N 0 24W
Lutong, *Malaysia* **75 B4** 4 28N 114 0 E
Lutry, *Switz.* **28 C3** 46 31N 6 42 E
Lutselke, *Canada* **131 A6** 62 24N 110 44W
Lutsk, *Ukraine* **51 G3** 50 50N 25 15 E
Lutuai, *Angola* **103 E4** 12 41 S 20 7 E
Lützow Holmbukta, *Antarctica* **7 C4** 69 10 S 37 30 E
Lutzputs, *S. Africa* **104 D3** 28 3 S 20 40 E
Luverne, *U.S.A.* **138 D6** 43 39N 96 13W
Luvo, *Angola* **103 D2** 5 51 S 14 5 E
Luvua, *Zaïre* **103 D5** 8 48 S 25 17 E
Luvua →, *Zaïre* **106 D2** 6 50 S 27 30 E
Luwegu →, *Tanzania* **107 D4** 8 31 S 37 23 E
Luwuk, *Indonesia* **72 B2** 0 56 S 122 47 E
Luxembourg, *Lux.* **21 J8** 49 37N 6 9 E
Luxembourg □, *Belgium* **21 J7** 49 58N 5 30 E
Luxembourg ■, *Europe* **21 J8** 49 45N 6 0 E
Luxeuil-les-Bains, *France* **23 E13** 47 49N 6 24 E
Luxi, *Hunan, China* **69 C8** 28 20N 110 7 E
Luxi, *Yunnan, China* **68 E4** 24 40N 103 55 E
Luxi, *Yunnan, China* **68 E2** 24 27N 98 36 E
Luxor = El Uqsur, *Egypt* **94 B3** 25 41N 32 38 E
Luy →, *France* **24 E2** 43 39N 1 9W
Luy-de-Béarn →, *France* **24 E3** 43 39N 0 48W
Luy-de-France →, *France* **24 E3** 43 39N 0 48W
Luyi, *China* **66 H8** 33 50N 115 35 E
Luyksgestel, *Neths.* **21 F6** 51 17N 5 20 E
Luz-St.-Sauveur, *France* **24 F4** 42 53N 0 0 E
Luza, *Russia* **48 B8** 60 39N 47 10 E
Luzern, *Switz.* **29 B6** 47 3N 8 18 E
Luzern □, *Switz.* **28 B5** 47 2N 7 55 E
Luzhai, *China* **68 E7** 24 29N 109 42 E
Luzhou, *China* **68 C5** 28 52N 105 20 E
Luziânia, *Brazil* **155 E2** 16 20 S 48 0W
Luzilândia, *Brazil* **154 B3** 3 28 S 42 22W
Luzon, *Phil.* **70 C3** 16 0N 121 0 E
Luzy, *France* **23 F10** 46 47N 3 58 E
Luzzi, *Italy* **41 C9** 39 27N 16 17 E
Lviv, *Ukraine* **51 H3** 49 50N 24 0 E
Lvov = Lviv, *Ukraine* **51 H3** 49 50N 24 0 E
Lwówek, *Poland* **47 C3** 52 28N 16 10 E
Lwówek Śląski, *Poland* **47 D2** 51 7N 15 38 E
Lyakhavichy, *Belarus* **51 F4** 53 2N 26 32 E
Lyakhovskiye, Ostrova, *Russia* **57 B15** 73 40N 141 0 E
Lyaki = Läki, *Azerbaijan* **53 K8** 40 34N 47 22 E
Lyall Mt., *N.Z.* **119 F2** 45 16 S 167 32 E
Lyallpur = Faisalabad, *Pakistan* **79 C4** 31 30N 73 5 E
Lyalya →, *Russia* **54 B8** 59 9N 61 29 E
Lyaskovets, *Bulgaria* **43 D10** 43 6N 25 44 E
Lycaonia, *Turkey* **88 D5** 38 0N 33 0 E
Lychen, *Germany* **26 B9** 53 12N 13 18 E
Lychkova, *Russia* **50 D7** 57 55N 32 24 E
Lycia, *Turkey* **88 D3** 36 30N 29 30 E
Lycksele, *Sweden* **12 D18** 64 38N 18 40 E
Lycosura, *Greece* **45 G4** 37 20N 22 3 E
Lydda = Lod, *Israel* **91 D3** 31 57N 34 54 E
Lydenburg, *S. Africa* **105 D5** 25 10 S 30 29 E
Lydia, *Turkey* **88 C3** 38 48N 28 19 E
Lyell, *N.Z.* **119 B7** 41 48 S 172 4 E
Lyell I., *Canada* **130 C2** 52 40N 131 35W
Lyepyel, *Belarus* **50 E5** 54 50N 28 40 E
Lygnern, *Sweden* **15 G6** 57 30N 12 15 E
Lyman, *U.S.A.* **142 F8** 41 20N 110 18W
Lyme Regis, *U.K.* **17 G5** 50 43N 2 57W
Lymington, *U.K.* **17 G6** 50 45N 1 32W
Łyna →, *Poland* **13 J19** 54 37N 21 14 E
Lynchburg, *Ohio, U.S.A.* **141 E13** 39 15N 83 48W
Lynchburg, *Va., U.S.A.* **134 G6** 37 25N 79 9W
Lynd →, *Australia* **114 B3** 16 28 S 143 18 E
Lynd Ra., *Australia* **115 D4** 25 30 S 149 20 E
Lynden, *Canada* **136 C4** 43 14N 80 9W
Lynden, *U.S.A.* **144 B4** 48 57N 122 27W
Lyndhurst, *Queens., Australia* **114 B3** 19 12 S 144 20 E
Lyndhurst, *S. Austral., Australia* **115 E2** 30 15 S 138 18 E
Lyndon →, *Australia* **113 D1** 23 29 S 114 6 E
Lyndonville, *N.Y., U.S.A.* **136 C6** 43 20N 78 23W
Lyndonville, *Vt., U.S.A.* **137 B12** 44 31N 72 1W
Lyngdal, *Norway* **14 E3** 59 54N 9 32 E
Lyngen, *Norway* **12 B19** 69 45N 20 30 E
Lynher Reef, *Australia* **112 C3** 15 27 S 121 55 E
Lynn, *Ind., U.S.A.* **141 D12** 40 3N 84 56W
Lynn, *Mass., U.S.A.* **137 D14** 42 28N 70 57W
Lynn Canal, *U.S.A.* **130 B1** 58 50N 135 15W
Lynn Lake, *Canada* **131 B8** 56 51N 101 3W
Lynnwood, *U.S.A.* **144 C4** 47 49N 122 19W
Lynton, *U.K.* **17 F4** 51 13N 3 50W
Lyntupy, *Belarus* **13 J22** 55 4N 26 23 E
Lynx L., *Canada* **131 A7** 62 25N 106 15W
Lyø, *Denmark* **15 J4** 55 3N 10 9 E
Lyon, *France* **25 C8** 45 46N 4 50 E
Lyonnais, *France* **25 C8** 45 45N 4 15 E
Lyons = Lyon, *France* **25 C8** 45 46N 4 50 E
Lyons, *Colo., U.S.A.* **138 E2** 40 14N 105 16W
Lyons, *Ga., U.S.A.* **135 J4** 32 12N 82 19W
Lyons, *Kans., U.S.A.* **138 F5** 38 21N 98 12W
Lyons, *N.Y., U.S.A.* **136 C8** 43 5N 77 0W
Lyozna, *Belarus* **50 E6** 55 0N 30 50 E
Lyrestad, *Sweden* **15 F8** 58 48N 14 4 E
Lys = Leie →, *Belgium* **23 A10** 51 2N 3 45 E
Lysá, *Czech.* **30 A7** 50 11N 14 51 E
Lysekil, *Sweden* **15 F5** 58 17N 11 26 E
Lyskovo, *Russia* **52 B7** 56 0N 45 3 E
Lyss, *Switz.* **28 B4** 47 4N 7 19 E
Lysva, *Russia* **54 B6** 58 7N 57 49 E
Lysychansk, *Ukraine* **51 H10** 48 55N 38 30 E
Lytle, *U.S.A.* **139 L5** 29 14N 98 48W
Lyttelton, *N.Z.* **119 D7** 43 35 S 172 44 E
Lytton, *Canada* **130 C4** 50 13N 121 31W
Lyuban, *Russia* **50 C6** 59 16N 31 18 E
Lyubertsy, *Russia* **52 C3** 55 39N 37 50 E
Lyubim, *Russia* **52 A5** 58 20N 40 39 E
Lyubimets, *Bulgaria* **43 F11** 41 50N 26 5 E
Lyuboml, *Ukraine* **51 G3** 51 11N 24 4 E
Lyubotyn, *Ukraine* **51 H8** 50 0N 36 0 E
Lyubytino, *Russia* **50 C7** 58 50N 33 16 E
Lyudinovo, *Russia* **52 D2** 53 52N 34 28 E

M

Ma →, *Vietnam* **76 C5** 19 47N 105 56 E
Ma'adaba, *Jordan* **91 E4** 30 43N 35 47 E
Maamba, *Zambia* **104 B4** 17 17 S 26 28 E
Ma'ān, *Jordan* **91 E4** 30 12N 35 44 E
Ma'ān □, *Jordan* **91 F5** 30 0N 36 0 E
Maanselkä, *Finland* **12 C23** 63 52N 28 32 E
Ma'anshan, *China* **69 B12** 31 44N 118 29 E
Maarheeze, *Neths.* **21 F7** 51 19N 5 36 E
Maarianhamina, *Finland* **13 F18** 60 5N 19 55 E
Maarn, *Neths.* **20 D6** 52 3N 5 22 E
Ma'arrat an Nu'mān, *Syria* **88 E7** 35 43N 36 43 E
Maarssen, *Neths.* **20 D6** 52 9N 5 2 E
Maartensdijk, *Neths.* **20 D6** 52 9N 5 10 E
Maas →, *Neths.* **20 E5** 51 45N 4 32 E
Maasbracht, *Belgium* **21 F7** 51 9N 5 54 E
Maasbree, *Neths.* **21 F8** 51 22N 6 3 E
Maasdam, *Neths.* **20 E5** 51 48N 4 34 E
Maasdijk, *Neths.* **20 E4** 51 58N 4 13 E
Maaseik, *Belgium* **21 F7** 51 6N 5 45 E
Maasland, *Neths.* **20 E4** 51 57N 4 16 E
Maasniel, *Neths.* **21 F8** 51 12N 6 1 E
Maassluis, *Neths.* **20 E4** 51 56N 4 16 E
Maastricht, *Neths.* **21 G7** 50 50N 5 40 E
Maave, *Mozam.* **105 C5** 21 4 S 34 47 E
Ma'bar, *Yemen* **86 D4** 14 48N 44 17 E
Mabaruma, *Guyana* **153 B6** 8 10N 59 50W
Mabein, *Burma* **78 D6** 23 29N 96 37 E
Mabel L., *Canada* **130 C5** 50 35N 118 43W
Mabenge, *Zaïre* **106 B1** 4 15N 24 12 E
Mabian, *China* **68 C4** 28 47N 103 37 E
Mablethorpe, *U.K.* **16 D8** 53 20N 0 15 E
Maboma, *Zaïre* **106 B2** 2 30N 28 10 E
Maboukou, *Congo* **102 C2** 3 39 S 12 31 E
Mabrouk, *Mali* **101 B4** 19 29N 1 15W
Mabton, *U.S.A.* **142 C3** 46 13N 120 0W
Mabungo, *Somali Rep.* **108 D2** 0 49N 42 35 E
Mac Bac, *Vietnam* **77 H6** 9 46N 106 7 E
Macachín, *Argentina* **158 D3** 37 10 S 63 43W
Macaé, *Brazil* **155 F3** 22 20 S 41 43W
Macaíba, *Brazil* **154 C4** 5 51 S 35 21W
Macajuba, *Brazil* **155 D3** 12 9 S 40 22W
Macalelon, *Phil.* **70 E4** 13 45N 122 8 E
McAlester, *U.S.A.* **139 H7** 34 56N 95 46W
McAllen, *U.S.A.* **139 M5** 26 12N 98 14W
Macamic, *Canada* **128 C4** 48 45N 79 0W
Macao = Macau ■, *China* **69 F9** 22 16N 113 35 E
Macão, *Portugal* **37 F3** 39 35N 7 59W
Macapá, *Brazil* **153 C7** 0 5N 51 4W
Macará, *Ecuador* **152 D2** 4 23 S 79 57W
Macarani, *Brazil* **155 E3** 15 33 S 40 24W
Macarena, Serranía de la, *Colombia* **152 C3** 2 45N 73 55W
Macarthur, *Australia* **116 E5** 38 5 S 142 0 E
McArthur →, *Australia* **114 B2** 15 54 S 136 40 E
McArthur, Port, *Australia* **114 B2** 16 4 S 136 23 E
McArthur River, *Australia* **114 B2** 16 27 S 136 7 E
Macas, *Ecuador* **152 D2** 2 19 S 78 7W
Macate, *Peru* **156 B2** 8 48 S 78 7W
Macau, *Brazil* **154 C4** 5 15 S 36 40W
Macau ■, *China* **69 F9** 22 16N 113 35 E
Macaúbas, *Brazil* **155 D3** 13 2 S 42 42W
Macaya →, *Colombia* **152 C3** 0 59N 72 20W
McBride, *Canada* **130 C4** 53 20N 120 19W
McCall, *U.S.A.* **142 D5** 44 55N 116 6W
McCamey, *U.S.A.* **139 K3** 31 8N 102 14W
McCammon, *U.S.A.* **142 E7** 42 39N 112 12W
McCauley I., *Canada* **130 C2** 53 40N 130 15W
McCleary, *U.S.A.* **144 C3** 47 3N 123 16W
Macclesfield, *U.K.* **16 D5** 53 15N 2 8W
McClintock, *Canada* **131 B10** 57 50N 94 10W
M'Clintock Chan., *Canada* **126 A9** 72 0N 102 0W
McClintock Ra., *Australia* **112 C4** 18 44 S 127 38 E
McCloud, *U.S.A.* **142 F2** 41 15N 122 8W
McCluer I., *Australia* **112 B5** 11 5 S 133 0 E
McClure, *U.S.A.* **136 F7** 40 42N 77 19W
McClure, L., *U.S.A.* **144 H6** 37 35N 120 16W
M'Clure Str., *Canada* **124 B8** 75 0N 119 0W
McClusky, *U.S.A.* **138 B4** 47 29N 100 27W
McComb, *U.S.A.* **139 K9** 31 15N 90 27W
McConaughy, L., *U.S.A.* **138 E4** 41 14N 101 40W
McCook, *U.S.A.* **138 E4** 40 12N 100 38W
McCullough Mt., *U.S.A.* **145 K11** 35 35N 115 13W
McCusker →, *Canada* **131 B7** 55 32N 108 39W
McDame, *Canada* **130 B3** 59 44N 128 59W
McDermitt, *U.S.A.* **142 F5** 41 59N 117 43W
Macdonald, L., *Australia* **112 D4** 23 30 S 129 0 E
Macdonald, Mt., *Vanuatu* **121 G6** 17 36 S 168 23 E
McDonald Is., *Ind. Oc.* **109 K6** 53 0 S 73 0 E
Macdonnell Ranges, *Australia* **112 D5** 23 40 S 133 0 E
McDouall Peak, *Australia* **115 D1** 29 51 S 134 55 E
Macdougall L., *Canada* **126 B10** 66 0N 98 27W
McDougalls Well, *Australia* **116 A4** 31 8 S 141 15 E
MacDowell L., *Canada* **128 B1** 52 15N 92 45W
Macduff, *U.K.* **18 D6** 57 40N 2 31W
Maceda, *Spain* **36 C3** 42 16N 7 39W
Macedonia = Makedhonía □, *Greece* **44 D3** 40 39N 22 0 E
Macedonia ■, *Europe* **42 F6** 41 53N 21 40 E
Maceió, *Brazil* **154 C4** 9 40 S 35 41W
Maceira, *Portugal* **37 F2** 39 41N 8 55W
Macenta, *Guinea* **100 D3** 8 35N 9 32W
Macerata, *Italy* **39 E10** 43 18N 13 27 E
McFarland, *U.S.A.* **145 K7** 35 41N 119 14W
McFarlane →, *Canada* **131 B7** 59 12N 107 58W
Macfarlane, L., *Australia* **116 B2** 32 0 S 136 40 E
McGehee, *U.S.A.* **139 J9** 33 38N 91 24W
McGill, *U.S.A.* **142 G6** 39 23N 114 47W
Macgillycuddy's Reeks, *Ireland* **19 D2** 51 58N 9 45W
MacGregor, *Canada* **131 D9** 49 57N 98 48W
McGregor, *U.S.A.* **140 A5** 43 1N 91 11W
McGregor →, *Canada* **130 B4** 55 10N 122 0W
McGregor Ra., *Australia* **115 D3** 27 0 S 142 45 E
Mach Kowr, *Iran* **85 E9** 25 48N 61 28 E
Machacalis, *Brazil* **155 E3** 17 5 S 40 45W
Machado = Jiparaná →, *Brazil* **157 B5** 8 3 S 62 52W
Machagai, *Argentina* **158 B3** 26 56 S 60 2W
Machakos, *Kenya* **106 C4** 1 30 S 37 15 E
Machakos □, *Kenya* **106 C4** 1 30 S 37 15 E
Machala, *Ecuador* **152 D2** 3 20 S 79 57W
Machanga, *Mozam.* **105 C6** 20 59 S 35 0 E
Machattie, L., *Australia* **114 C2** 24 50 S 139 48 E
Machava, *Mozam.* **105 D5** 25 54 S 32 28 E
Machece, *Mozam.* **107 F4** 19 15 S 35 32 E
Machecoul, *France* **22 F5** 47 0N 1 49W
Machelen, *Belgium* **21 G4** 50 55N 4 26 E
Macheng, *China* **69 B10** 31 12N 115 2 E
McHenry, *U.S.A.* **141 B8** 42 21N 88 16W
Machevna, *Russia* **57 C18** 61 20N 172 20 E
Machezo, *Spain* **37 F6** 39 21N 4 20W
Machias, *U.S.A.* **129 D6** 44 43N 67 28W
Machichaco, C., *Spain* **34 B2** 43 28N 2 47W
Machichi →, *Canada* **131 B10** 57 3N 92 6W
Machico, *Madeira* **33 D3** 32 43N 16 44W
Machida, *Japan* **63 B11** 35 28N 139 23 E
Machilipatnam, *India* **83 F5** 16 12N 81 8 E
Machiques, *Venezuela* **152 A3** 10 4N 72 34W
Machupicchu, *Peru* **156 C3** 13 8 S 72 30W
Machynlleth, *U.K.* **17 E4** 52 35N 3 50W
Maciejowice, *Poland* **47 D8** 51 36N 21 26 E
McIlwraith Ra., *Australia* **114 A3** 13 50 S 143 20 E
Măcin, *Romania* **46 D9** 45 16N 28 8 E
Macina, *Mali* **100 C4** 14 50N 5 0W
McIntosh, *U.S.A.* **138 C4** 45 55N 101 21W
McIntosh L., *Canada* **131 B8** 55 45N 105 0W
Macintosh Ra., *Australia* **113 E4** 27 39 S 125 32 E
Macintyre →, *Australia* **115 D5** 28 37 S 150 47 E
Macizo Galaico, *Spain* **36 C3** 42 30N 7 30W
Mackay, *Australia* **114 C4** 21 8 S 149 11 E

Manning 229

Maktar, Tunisia 96 A1 35 48N 9 12 E
Mākū, Iran 89 C11 39 15N 44 31 E
Makum, India 78 B5 27 30N 95 23 E
Makumbi, Zaïre 103 D4 5 50 S 20 43 E
Makunda, Botswana 104 C3 22 30 S 20 7 E
Makurazaki, Japan 62 F2 31 15N 130 20 E
Makurdi, Nigeria 101 D6 7 43N 8 35 E
Makūyeh, Iran 85 D7 28 7N 53 9 E
Makwassie, S. Africa 104 D4 27 17 S 26 0 E
Mal, India 78 B2 26 51N 88 45 E
Mal B., Ireland 19 D2 52 50N 9 30W
Mal i Gjalicës së Lumës, Albania 44 B2 42 2N 20 25 E
Mal i Gribës, Albania 44 D1 40 17N 19 45 E
Mal i Nemërçkës, Albania 44 D2 40 15N 20 15 E
Mala, Peru 156 C2 12 40 S 76 38W
Mala, Pta., Panama 148 E3 7 28N 80 2W
Mala Belozërka, Ukraine 51 J8 47 12N 34 56 E
Mala Kapela, Croatia 39 D12 44 45N 15 30 E
Mala Vyska, Ukraine 51 H6 48 39N 31 36 E
Malabang, Phil. 71 H5 7 36N 124 3 E
Malabar Coast, India 83 J2 11 0N 75 0 E
Malabo = Rey Malabo, Eq. Guin. 101 E6 3 45N 8 50 E
Malabon, Phil. 70 D3 14 21N 121 0 E
Malabrigo Pt., Phil. 70 E3 13 36N 121 15 E
Malabungan, Phil. 71 G1 9 3N 117 38 E
Malacca, Str. of, Indonesia 77 L3 3 0N 101 0 E
Malacky, Slovak Rep. 31 C10 48 27N 17 0 E
Malad City, U.S.A. 142 E7 42 12N 112 15W
Maladzyechna, Belarus 50 E4 54 20N 26 50 E
Málaga, Colombia 152 B3 6 42N 72 44W
Málaga, Spain 37 J6 36 43N 4 23W
Malaga, U.S.A. 139 J2 32 14N 104 4W
Málaga □, Spain 37 J6 36 38N 4 58W
Malagarasi, Tanzania 106 D3 5 5 S 30 50 E
Malagarasi →, Tanzania 106 D2 5 12 S 29 47 E
Malagón, Spain 37 F7 39 11N 3 52W
Malagón →, Spain 37 H3 37 35N 7 29W
Malaimbandy, Madag. 105 C8 20 20 S 45 36 E
Malaita, Pac. Oc. 121 M11 9 0 S 161 0 E
Malakâl, Sudan 95 F3 9 33N 31 40 E
Malakand, Pakistan 79 B3 34 40N 71 55 E
Malakoff, U.S.A. 139 J7 32 10N 96 1W
Malakula, Vanuatu 121 F5 16 15 S 167 30 E
Malalag, Phil. 71 H5 6 36N 125 24 E
Malam, Chad 97 F4 11 27N 20 59 E
Malamyzh, Russia 57 E14 49 50N 136 50 E
Malang, Indonesia 75 D4 7 59 S 112 45 E
Malangas, Phil. 71 H4 7 37N 123 1 E
Malange □, Angola 103 D3 9 30 S 16 0 E
Malangen, Norway 12 B18 69 24N 18 37 E
Malanje, Angola 103 D3 9 36 S 16 17 E
Mälaren, Sweden 14 E11 59 30N 17 10 E
Malargüe, Argentina 158 D2 35 32 S 69 30W
Malartic, Canada 128 C4 48 9N 78 9W
Malaryta, Belarus 51 G3 51 50N 24 3 E
Malatya, Turkey 89 C8 38 25N 38 20 E
Malawali, Malaysia 75 A5 7 3N 117 18 E
Malawi ■, Africa 107 E3 11 55 S 34 0 E
Malawi, L., Africa 107 E3 12 30 S 34 30 E
Malay, Phil. 71 F3 11 54N 121 55 E
Malay Pen., Asia 77 J3 7 25N 100 0 E
Malaya Belozërka = Mala Belozërka, Ukraine 51 J8 47 12N 34 56 E
Malaya Vishera, Russia 50 C7 58 55N 32 25 E
Malaya Viska = Mala Vyska, Ukraine 51 H6 48 39N 31 36 E
Malaybalay, Phil. 71 G5 8 5N 125 7 E
Malāyer, Iran 89 E13 34 19N 48 51 E
Malaysia ■, Asia 74 B4 5 0N 110 0 E
Malazgirt, Turkey 89 C10 39 10N 42 33 E
Malbon, Australia 114 C3 21 5 S 140 17 E
Malbooma, Australia 115 E1 30 41 S 134 11 E
Malbork, Poland 47 A6 54 3N 19 1 E
Malca Dube, Ethiopia 108 C2 6 47N 42 4 E
Malcésine, Italy 38 C7 45 46N 10 48 E
Malchin, Germany 26 B8 53 44N 12 44 E
Malchow, Germany 26 B8 53 28N 12 25 E
Malcolm, Australia 113 E3 28 51 S 121 25 E
Malcolm, Pt., Australia 113 F3 33 48 S 123 45 E
Malczyce, Poland 47 D3 51 14N 16 29 E
Maldegem, Belgium 21 F2 51 14N 3 26 E
Malden, Mass., U.S.A. 137 D13 42 26N 71 4W
Malden, Mo., U.S.A. 139 G10 36 34N 89 57W
Malden I., Kiribati 123 H12 4 3 S 155 1W
Maldives ■, Ind. Oc. 58 J11 5 0N 73 0 E
Maldon, Australia 116 D6 37 0 S 144 6 E
Maldonado, Uruguay 159 C5 34 59 S 55 0W
Maldonado, Punta, Mexico 147 D5 16 19N 98 35W
Malè, Italy 38 B7 46 21N 10 55 E
Malé Karpaty, Slovak Rep. 31 C10 48 30N 17 20 E
Maléa, Ákra, Greece 45 H5 36 28N 23 7 E
Malebo, Pool, Africa 103 C3 4 17 S 15 20 E
Malegaon, India 82 D2 20 30N 74 38 E
Malei, Mozam. 107 F4 17 12 S 36 58 E
Malek Kandī, Iran 89 D12 37 9N 46 6 E
Malela, Bas Zaïre, Zaïre 103 D2 5 59 S 12 37 E
Malela, Kivu, Zaïre 103 C5 4 22 S 26 8 E
Malema, Mozam. 107 E4 14 57 S 37 20 E
Máleme, Greece 32 D5 35 31N 23 49 E
Malerkotla, India 80 D6 30 32N 75 58 E
Máles, Greece 32 D7 35 6N 25 35 E
Malesherbes, France 23 D9 48 15N 2 24 E
Maleshevska Planina, Europe 42 F8 41 38N 23 7 E
Malestroit, France 22 E4 47 49N 2 25W
Malfa, Italy 41 D7 38 35N 14 50 E
Malgobek, Russia 53 J7 43 30N 44 34 E
Malgomaj, Sweden 12 D17 64 40N 16 30 E
Malgrat, Spain 34 D7 41 39N 2 46 E
Malha, Sudan 95 D2 15 8N 25 10 E
Malheur →, U.S.A. 142 D5 44 4N 116 59W
Malheur L., U.S.A. 142 E4 43 20N 118 48W
Mali, Guinea 100 C2 12 10N 12 20W
Mali ■, Africa 100 B4 17 0N 3 0W
Mali Hka →, Burma 78 C6 25 42N 97 30 E
Mali Kanal, Serbia, Yug. 42 B4 45 36N 19 24 E
Malibu, U.S.A. 145 L8 34 2N 118 41W
Maligaya, Phil. 70 E3 12 59N 121 30 E
Malik, Indonesia 72 B2 0 39 S 123 16 E
Malili, Indonesia 72 B2 2 42 S 121 6 E
Malimba, Mts., Zaïre 106 D2 7 30 S 29 30 E
Malin Hd., Ireland 19 A4 55 23N 7 23W
Malindang, Mt., Phil. 71 G4 8 13N 123 38 E
Malindi, Kenya 106 C5 3 12 S 40 5 E
Malines = Mechelen, Belgium 21 F4 51 2N 4 29 E
Malino, Indonesia 72 A2 1 0N 121 0 E
Malinyi, Tanzania 107 D4 8 56 S 36 0 E
Malipo, China 68 F5 23 7N 104 42 E
Maliqi, Albania 44 D2 40 45N 20 48 E
Malita, Phil. 71 H5 6 19N 125 39 E
Maljenik, Serbia, Yug. 42 D6 43 59N 21 55 E
Malkapur, Maharashtra, India 82 F3 16 57N 76 17 E
Malkapur, Maharashtra, India 82 D1 20 53N 73 58 E
Malkara, Turkey 88 B2 40 53N 26 53 E
Małkinia Górna, Poland 47 C9 52 42N 22 5 E
Malko Tŭrnovo, Bulgaria 43 F12 41 59N 27 31 E
Mallacoota, Australia 117 D8 37 40 S 149 40 E
Mallacoota Inlet, Australia 117 D8 37 34 S 149 40 E
Mallaig, U.K. 18 E3 57 0N 5 50W
Mallala, Australia 116 C3 34 26 S 138 30 E
Mallard, U.S.A. 140 B2 42 56N 94 41W
Mallawan, India 81 F9 27 4N 80 12 E
Mallawi, Egypt 94 B3 27 44N 30 44 E
Malleco □, Chile 160 A2 38 10 S 72 20W
Mallemort, France 25 E9 43 43N 5 11 E
Málles Venosta, Italy 38 B7 46 41N 10 32 E
Mállia, Greece 32 D7 35 17N 25 27 E
Mallicolo = Malakula, Vanuatu 121 F5 16 15 S 167 30 E
Mallig, Phil. 70 C3 17 8N 121 42 E
Mallión, Kólpos, Greece 32 D7 35 19N 25 27 E
Mallorca, Spain 33 B10 39 30N 3 0 E
Mallorytown, Canada 137 B9 44 29N 75 53W
Mallow, Ireland 19 D3 52 8N 8 39W
Malmberget, Sweden 12 C19 67 11N 20 40 E
Malmédy, Belgium 21 H8 50 25N 6 2 E
Malmesbury, S. Africa 104 E2 33 28 S 18 41 E
Malmö, Sweden 15 J6 55 36N 12 59 E
Malmöhus län □, Sweden 15 J7 55 45N 13 30 E
Malmslätt, Sweden 15 F9 58 27N 15 33 E
Malmyzh, Russia 52 B10 56 31N 50 41 E
Malnaş, Romania 46 C6 46 2N 25 49 E
Malo, Vanuatu 121 E5 15 40 S 167 11 E
Malo Konare, Bulgaria 43 E9 42 12N 24 24 E
Maloarkhangelsk, Russia 52 D3 52 28N 36 30 E
Maloca, Brazil 153 C6 0 43N 55 57W
Maloja, Switz. 29 D9 46 25N 9 35 E
Maloja, P., Switz. 29 D9 46 23N 9 42 E
Malolos, Phil. 70 D3 14 50N 120 49 E
Malombe L., Malawi 107 E4 14 40 S 35 15 E
Malomir, Bulgaria 43 E11 42 16N 26 30 E
Malone, U.S.A. 137 B10 44 51N 74 18W
Malong, China 68 E4 25 24N 103 34 E
Malonga, Zaïre 103 E4 10 24 S 23 10 E
Malorad, Bulgaria 43 D8 43 28N 23 41 E
Måløy, Norway 13 F11 61 57N 5 6 E
Maloyaroslovets, Russia 52 C3 55 2N 36 20 E
Malozemelskaya Tundra, Russia 48 A9 67 0N 50 0 E
Malpartida, Spain 37 F4 39 26N 6 30W
Malpaso, Canary Is. 33 G1 27 43N 18 3W
Malpica, Spain 36 B2 43 19N 8 50W
Malprabha →, India 83 F3 16 20N 76 5 E
Mals = Málles Venosta, Italy 38 B7 46 41N 10 32 E
Malta, Brazil 154 C4 6 54 S 37 31W
Malta, Idaho, U.S.A. 142 E7 42 18N 113 22W
Malta, Mont., U.S.A. 142 B10 48 21N 107 52W
Malta ■, Europe 32 D1 35 50N 14 30 E
Malta Channel, Medit. S. 40 F6 36 40N 14 0 E
Maltahöhe, Namibia 104 C2 24 55 S 17 0 E
Malters, Switz. 28 B6 47 3N 8 11 E
Malton, Canada 136 C5 43 42N 79 38W
Malton, U.K. 16 C7 54 8N 0 49W
Malu'a, Solomon Is. 121 M11 8 0 S 160 0 E
Maluku, Indonesia 72 B3 1 0 S 127 0 E
Maluku □, Indonesia 72 B3 3 0 S 128 0 E
Maluku Sea = Molucca Sea, Indonesia 72 A3 2 0 S 124 0 E
Malumfashi, Nigeria 101 C6 11 48N 7 39 E
Malungun, Phil. 71 H5 6 16N 125 14 E
Maluso, Phil. 71 H3 6 33N 121 53 E
Malvalli, India 83 H3 12 28N 77 8 E
Malvan, India 83 F1 16 2N 73 30 E
Malvern, U.S.A. 139 H8 34 22N 92 49W
Malvern Hills, U.K. 17 E5 52 0N 2 19W
Malvik, Norway 14 A4 63 25N 10 40 E
Malvinas, Is. = Falkland Is. □, Atl. Oc. 160 D5 51 30 S 59 0W
Malya, Tanzania 106 C3 3 5 S 33 38 E
Malybay, Kazakstan 55 B9 43 30N 78 25 E
Malyn, Ukraine 51 G5 50 46N 29 3 E
Malyy Lyakhovskiy, Ostrov, Russia 57 B15 74 7N 140 36 E
Malyy Nimnyr, Russia 57 D13 57 50N 125 10 E
Mama, Russia 57 D12 58 18N 112 54 E
Mamadysh, Russia 52 C10 55 44N 51 23 E
Mamaia, Romania 46 E9 44 18N 28 37 E
Mamaku, N.Z. 118 E5 38 5 S 176 8 E
Mamanguape, Brazil 154 C4 6 50 S 35 4W
Mamasa, Indonesia 72 B1 2 55 S 119 20 E
Mambajao, Phil. 71 G5 9 15N 124 43 E
Mambasa, Zaïre 106 B2 1 22N 29 3 E
Mamberamo →, Indonesia 73 B5 2 0 S 137 50 E
Mambilima Falls, Zambia 107 E2 10 31 S 28 45 E
Mambirima, Zaïre 107 E2 11 25 S 27 33 E
Mambo, Tanzania 106 C4 4 52 S 38 22 E
Mambrui, Kenya 106 C5 3 5 S 40 5 E
Mamburao, Phil. 70 E3 13 13N 120 39 E
Mameigwess L., Canada 128 B2 52 35N 87 50W
Mamer, Lux. 21 J8 49 38N 6 2 E
Mamers, France 22 D7 48 21N 0 22 E
Mamfe, Cameroon 101 D6 5 50N 9 15 E
Māmī, Ra's, Yemen 87 D6 12 32N 54 30 E
Mamiña, Chile 156 E4 20 5 S 69 14W
Mámmola, Italy 41 D9 38 22N 16 14 E
Mammoth, U.S.A. 143 K8 32 43N 110 39W
Mamoré →, Bolivia 157 C4 10 23 S 65 53W
Mamou, Guinea 100 C2 10 15N 12 0W
Mamparang Mts., Phil. 70 C3 16 21N 121 28 E
Mampatá, Guinea-Biss. 100 C2 11 54N 14 53W
Mampong, Ghana 101 D4 7 6N 1 26W
Mamry, Jezioro, Poland 47 A8 54 5N 21 50 E
Mamuil Malal, Paso, S. Amer. 160 A2 39 35 S 71 28W
Mamuju, Indonesia 72 B1 2 41 S 118 50 E
Ma'mūl, Oman 87 C6 18 8N 55 16 E
Man, Ivory C. 100 D3 7 30N 7 40W
Man →, India 82 F2 17 31N 75 32 E
Man, I. of, U.K. 16 C3 54 15N 4 30W
Man Na, Burma 78 D6 23 27N 97 19 E
Man Tun, Burma 78 D7 23 52N 98 38 E
Mana, Fr. Guiana 153 B7 5 45N 53 55W
Mana →, Fr. Guiana 153 B7 5 45N 53 55W
Måna →, Norway 14 E2 59 55N 8 48 E
Manaar, G. of = Mannar, G. of, Asia 83 K4 8 30N 79 0 E
Manabí □, Ecuador 152 D1 0 40 S 80 5W
Manacacías →, Colombia 152 C3 4 23N 72 4W
Manacapuru, Brazil 153 D5 3 16 S 60 37W
Manacapuru →, Brazil 153 D5 3 18 S 60 37W
Manacor, Spain 33 B10 39 34N 3 13 E
Manado, Indonesia 72 A2 1 29N 124 51 E
Manage, Belgium 21 G4 50 31N 4 15 E
Managua, Nic. 148 D2 12 6N 86 20W
Managua, L., Nic. 148 D2 12 20N 86 30W
Manaia, N.Z. 118 F3 39 33 S 174 8 E
Manakara, Madag. 105 C8 22 8 S 48 1 E
Manakau Mt., N.Z. 119 C8 42 15 S 173 42 E
Manākhah, Yemen 86 D3 15 5N 43 44 E
Manakino, N.Z. 118 E4 38 22 S 175 47 E
Manam I., Papua N. G. 120 C3 4 5 S 145 0 E
Manama = Al Manāmah, Bahrain 85 E6 26 10N 50 30 E
Manambao →, Madag. 105 B7 17 35 S 44 0 E
Manambato, Madag. 105 A8 13 43 S 49 7 E
Manambolo →, Madag. 105 B7 19 18 S 44 22 E
Manambolosy, Madag. 105 B8 16 2 S 49 40 E
Mananara, Madag. 105 B8 16 10 S 49 46 E
Mananara →, Madag. 105 C8 23 21 S 47 42 E
Mananjary, Madag. 105 C8 21 13 S 48 20 E
Manantenina, Madag. 105 C8 24 17 S 47 19 E
Manaos = Manaus, Brazil 153 D6 3 0 S 60 0W
Manapala, Phil. 71 F4 10 58N 123 5 E
Manapire →, Venezuela 152 B4 7 42N 66 7W
Manapouri, N.Z. 119 F2 45 34 S 167 39 E
Manapouri, L., N.Z. 119 F2 45 32 S 167 32 E
Manar →, India 82 E3 18 50N 77 20 E
Manār, Jabal, Yemen 86 D4 14 2N 44 17 E
Manas, China 64 B3 44 17N 85 56 E
Manas, Somali Rep. 108 D2 2 57N 43 28 E
Manas, Gora, Kyrgyzstan 55 B5 42 22N 71 2 E
Manaslu, Nepal 81 E11 28 33N 84 33 E
Manasquan, U.S.A. 137 F10 40 8N 74 3W
Manassa, U.S.A. 143 H11 37 11N 105 56W
Manatuto, Indonesia 72 C3 8 30 S 126 1 E
Manaung, Burma 78 F4 18 45N 93 40 E
Manaus, Brazil 153 D6 3 0 S 60 0W
Manavgat, Turkey 88 D4 36 47N 31 26 E
Manawan L., Canada 131 B8 55 24N 103 14W
Manawatu →, N.Z. 118 G4 40 28 S 175 12 E
Manay, Phil. 71 H6 7 17N 126 33 E
Manbij, Syria 88 D7 36 31N 37 57 E
Mancelona, U.S.A. 134 C3 44 54N 85 4W
Mancha Real, Spain 37 H7 37 48N 3 39W
Manche □, France 22 C5 49 10N 1 20W
Manchester, U.K. 16 D5 53 29N 2 12W
Manchester, Calif., U.S.A. 144 G3 38 58N 123 41W
Manchester, Conn., U.S.A. 137 E12 41 47N 72 31W
Manchester, Ga., U.S.A. 135 J3 32 51N 84 37W
Manchester, Iowa, U.S.A. 140 B5 42 29N 91 27W
Manchester, Ky., U.S.A. 134 G4 37 9N 83 46W
Manchester, Mich., U.S.A. 141 B12 42 9N 84 2W
Manchester, N.H., U.S.A. 137 D13 42 59N 71 28W
Manchester, N.Y., U.S.A. 136 D7 42 56N 77 16W
Manchester, Vt., U.S.A. 137 C11 43 10N 73 5W
Manchester L., Canada 131 A7 61 28N 107 29W
Manchuria = Dongbei, China 67 D13 42 0N 125 0 E
Manchurian Plain, China 58 E16 47 0N 124 0 E
Manciano, Italy 39 F8 42 35N 11 31 E
Mancifa, Ethiopia 95 F5 6 53N 41 50 E
Mancora, Pta., Peru 156 A1 4 9 S 81 1W
Mand →, Iran 85 D7 28 20N 52 30 E
Manda, Chunya, Tanzania 106 D3 6 51 S 32 29 E
Manda, Ludewe, Tanzania 107 E3 10 30 S 34 40 E
Mandabé, Madag. 105 C7 21 0 S 44 55 E
Mandaguari, Brazil 159 A5 23 32 S 51 42W
Mandah, Mongolia 66 B5 44 27N 108 2 E
Mandal, Norway 13 G12 58 2N 7 25 E
Mandalay, Burma 78 D6 22 0N 96 4 E
Mandale = Mandalay, Burma 78 D6 22 0N 96 4 E
Mandalgovi, Mongolia 66 B4 45 45N 106 10 E
Mandalī, Iraq 89 F11 33 43N 45 28 E
Mandalya Körfezi, Turkey 45 G9 37 15N 27 20 E
Mandan, U.S.A. 138 B4 46 50N 100 54W
Mandaon, Phil. 70 E4 12 13N 123 17 E
Mandapeta, India 82 F5 16 47N 81 56 E
Mandar, Teluk, Indonesia 72 B1 3 35 S 119 15 E
Mandas, Italy 40 C2 39 40N 9 8 E
Mandaue, Phil. 71 F4 10 20N 123 56 E
Mandayar, Phil. 71 H6 7 34N 126 14 E
Mandelieu-la-Napoule, France 25 E10 43 34N 6 57 E
Mandera, Kenya 106 B5 3 55N 41 53 E
Mandera □, Kenya 106 B5 3 30N 41 0 E
Manderfeld, Belgium 21 H8 50 20N 6 20 E
Mandi, India 80 D7 31 39N 76 58 E
Mandimba, Mozam. 107 E4 14 20 S 35 40 E
Mandioli, Indonesia 72 B3 0 40 S 127 20 E
Mandioré, L., S. Amer. 157 D6 18 8 S 57 33W
Mandji I. = Lopez I., Gabon 102 C1 0 50 S 8 47 E
Mandla, India 81 H9 22 39N 80 30 E
Mandø, Denmark 15 J2 55 18N 8 33 E
Mandoto, Madag. 105 B8 19 34 S 46 17 E
Mandoúdhion, Greece 45 F5 38 48N 23 29 E
Mandra, Pakistan 80 C5 33 23N 73 12 E
Mandráki, Greece 45 H9 36 36N 27 11 E
Mandrare →, Madag. 105 D8 25 10 S 46 30 E
Mandritsara, Madag. 105 B8 15 50 S 48 49 E
Mandsaur, India 80 G6 24 3N 75 8 E
Mandurah, Australia 113 F2 32 36 S 115 48 E
Mandúria, Italy 41 B10 40 24N 17 38 E
Mandvi, India 80 H3 22 51N 69 22 E
Mandya, India 83 H3 12 30N 77 0 E
Mandzai, Pakistan 80 D2 30 55N 67 6 E
Mané, Burkina Faso 101 C4 12 59N 1 21W
Maneh, Iran 85 B8 37 39N 57 7 E
Manengouba, Mts., Cameroon 101 D6 5 0N 9 50 E
Maner →, India 82 E4 18 30N 79 40 E
Maneroo, Australia 114 C3 23 22 S 143 53 E
Maneroo Cr. →, Australia 114 C3 23 21 S 143 53 E
Manfalût, Egypt 94 B3 27 20N 30 52 E
Manfred, Australia 116 B5 33 19 S 143 45 E
Manfredónia, Italy 41 A8 41 38N 15 55 E
Manfredónia, G. di, Italy 41 A9 41 35N 16 5 E
Manga, Brazil 155 D3 14 46 S 43 56W
Manga, Burkina Faso 101 C4 11 40N 1 4W
Manga, Niger 97 F2 15 0N 14 0 E
Mangabeiras, Chapada das, Brazil 154 D2 10 0 S 46 30W
Mangal, Phil. 71 H3 6 25N 121 58 E
Mangalagiri, India 83 F5 16 26N 80 36 E
Mangaldai, India 78 B4 26 26N 92 2 E
Mangalia, Romania 46 F9 43 50N 28 35 E
Mangalore, Australia 117 D6 36 56 S 145 10 E
Mangalore, India 83 H2 12 55N 74 47 E
Manganeses, Spain 36 D5 41 45N 5 43W
Mangaon, India 82 E1 18 15N 73 20 E
Mangaweka, N.Z. 118 F4 39 48 S 175 47 E
Mangaweka, Mt., N.Z. 118 F5 39 49 S 176 5 E
Mange, Zaïre 102 B4 0 54N 20 30 E
Manggar, Indonesia 75 C3 2 50 S 108 10 E
Manggawitu, Indonesia 73 B4 4 8 S 133 32 E
Mangin Range, Burma 78 C5 24 15N 95 45 E
Mangkalihat, Tanjung, Indonesia 75 B5 1 2N 118 59 E
Mangla Dam, Pakistan 81 C5 33 9N 73 44 E
Manglares, C., Colombia 152 C2 1 36N 79 2W
Manglaur, India 80 E7 29 44N 77 49 E
Mangnai, China 64 C4 37 52N 91 43 E
Mango, Togo 101 C5 10 20N 0 30 E
Mangoche, Malawi 107 E4 14 25 S 35 16 E
Mangoky →, Madag. 105 C7 21 29 S 43 41 E
Mangole, Indonesia 72 B3 1 50 S 125 55 E
Mangombe, Zaïre 106 C2 1 20 S 26 48 E
Mangonui, N.Z. 118 B2 35 1 S 173 32 E
Mangualde, Portugal 36 E3 40 38N 7 48W
Mangueigne, Chad 97 F4 10 30N 21 15 E
Mangueira, L. da, Brazil 159 C5 33 0 S 52 50W
Manguéni, Hamada, Niger 96 D2 22 35N 12 40 E
Mangum, U.S.A. 139 H5 34 53N 99 30W
Mangyshlak Poluostrov, Kazakstan 56 E6 44 30N 52 30 E
Manhattan, U.S.A. 138 F6 39 11N 96 35W
Manhatten, U.S.A. 141 C9 41 26N 87 59W
Manhiça, Mozam. 105 D5 25 23 S 32 49 E
Manhuaçu, Brazil 155 F3 20 15 S 42 2W
Manhumirim, Brazil 155 F3 20 22 S 41 57W
Maní, Colombia 152 C3 4 49N 72 17W
Mania →, Madag. 105 B8 19 42 S 45 22 E
Maniago, Italy 39 B9 46 10N 12 43 E
Manica, Mozam. 105 B5 18 58 S 32 59 E
Manica e Sofala □, Mozam. 105 B5 19 10 S 33 45 E
Manicaland □, Zimbabwe 107 F3 19 0 S 32 30 E
Manicoré, Brazil 157 B5 5 48 S 61 16W
Manicoré →, Brazil 157 B5 5 51 S 61 19W
Manicouagan →, Canada 129 C6 49 30N 68 30W
Manīfah, Si. Arabia 85 E6 27 44N 49 0 E
Manifold, Australia 114 C5 22 41 S 150 40 E
Manifold, C., Australia 114 C5 22 41 S 150 50 E
Maniganggo, China 68 B2 31 56N 99 10 E
Manigotagan, Canada 131 C9 51 6N 96 18W
Manihiki, Cook Is. 123 J11 10 24 S 161 1W
Manika, Plateau de la, Zaïre 107 E2 10 0 S 25 5 E
Manikganj, Bangla. 78 D3 23 52N 90 0 E
Manila, Phil. 70 D3 14 40N 121 3 E
Manila, U.S.A. 142 F9 40 59N 109 43W
Manila B., Phil. 70 D3 14 40N 120 35 E
Manilla, Australia 117 A9 30 45 S 150 43 E
Manimpé, Mali 100 C3 14 11N 5 28W
Maningrida, Australia 114 A1 12 3 S 134 13 E
Manipur □, India 78 C4 25 0N 94 0 E
Manipur →, Burma 78 D5 23 45N 94 20 E
Manisa, Turkey 88 C2 38 38N 27 30 E
Manistee, U.S.A. 134 C2 44 15N 86 19W
Manistee →, U.S.A. 134 C2 44 15N 86 21W
Manistique, U.S.A. 134 C2 45 57N 86 15W
Manito, U.S.A. 140 D7 40 26N 89 47W
Manito L., Canada 131 C7 52 43N 109 43W
Manitoba □, Canada 131 B9 55 30N 97 0W
Manitoba, L., Canada 131 C9 51 0N 98 45W
Manitou, Canada 131 D9 49 15N 98 32W
Manitou Beach, U.S.A. 141 C12 41 58N 84 19W
Manitou I., U.S.A. 128 C2 47 25N 87 37W
Manitou Is., U.S.A. 134 C2 45 8N 86 0W
Manitou L., Canada 129 B6 50 55N 65 17W
Manitou Springs, U.S.A. 138 F2 38 52N 104 55W
Manitoulin I., Canada 128 C3 45 40N 82 30W
Manitowaning, Canada 128 C3 45 46N 81 49W
Manitowoc, U.S.A. 134 C2 44 5N 87 40W
Manitsauá-Missu →, Brazil 157 C7 10 58 S 53 20W
Manizales, Colombia 152 B2 5 5N 75 32W
Manja, Madag. 105 C7 21 26 S 44 20 E
Manjacaze, Mozam. 105 C5 24 45 S 34 0 E
Manjakandriana, Madag. 105 B8 18 55 S 47 47 E
Manjeri, India 83 J3 11 7N 76 11 E
Manjhand, Pakistan 79 D3 25 50N 68 10 E
Manjil, Iran 85 B6 36 46N 49 30 E
Manjimup, Australia 113 F2 34 15 S 116 6 E
Manjra →, India 82 E3 18 49N 77 52 E
Mankato, Kans., U.S.A. 138 F5 39 47N 98 13W
Mankato, Minn., U.S.A. 138 C8 44 10N 94 0W
Mankayan, Phil. 70 C3 16 52N 120 47 E
Mankayane, Swaziland 105 D5 26 40 S 31 4 E
Mankono, Ivory C. 100 D3 8 1N 6 10W
Mankota, Canada 131 D7 49 25N 107 5W
Manlay, Mongolia 66 B4 44 9N 107 0 E
Manlleu, Spain 34 C7 42 2N 2 17 E
Manly, Australia 117 B9 33 48 S 151 17 E
Manmad, India 82 D2 20 18N 74 28 E
Mann Ras., Australia 113 E5 26 6 S 130 5 E
Manna, Indonesia 74 C2 4 25 S 102 55 E
Mannahill, Australia 116 B3 32 25 S 140 0 E
Mannar, Sri Lanka 83 K4 9 1N 79 54 E
Mannar, G. of, Asia 83 K4 8 30N 79 0 E
Mannar I., Sri Lanka 83 K4 9 5N 79 45 E
Mannargudi, India 83 J4 10 45N 79 51 E
Mannduque □, Phil. 70 E4 13 18N 122 0 E
Männedorf, Switz. 29 B7 47 15N 8 43 E
Mannheim, Germany 27 F4 49 29N 8 29 E
Manning, Canada 130 B5 56 53N 117 39W

230 Manning

Manning, Oreg., U.S.A. 144 E3 45 45N 123 13W
Manning, S.C., U.S.A. 135 J5 33 42N 80 13W
Manning Prov. Park, Canada 130 D4 49 5N 120 45W
Manning Str., Solomon Is. 121 L10 7 30 S 158 0 E
Mannington, U.S.A. 134 F5 39 32N 80 21W
Mannu →, Italy 40 C2 39 16N 9 0 E
Mannu, C., Italy 40 B1 40 3N 8 21 E
Mannum, Australia 116 C3 34 50 S 139 20 E
Mano, S. Leone 100 D2 8 3N 12 2W
Manoa, Bolivia 157 B4 9 40 S 65 27W
Manokwari, Indonesia 73 B4 0 54 S 134 0 E
Manolás, Greece 45 F3 38 4N 21 21 E
Manolo Fortich, Phil. 71 G5 8 28N 124 50 E
Manombo, Madag. 105 C7 22 57 S 43 28 E
Manono, Zaïre 106 D2 7 15 S 27 25 E
Manosque, France 25 E9 43 49N 5 47 E
Manouane, L., Canada 129 B5 50 45N 70 45W
Manouro, Pt., Vanuatu 121 G6 17 41 S 168 36 E
Manpojin, N. Korea 67 D14 41 6N 126 24 E
Manresa, Spain 34 D6 41 48N 1 50 E
Mansa, Gujarat, India 80 H5 23 27N 72 45 E
Mansa, Punjab, India 80 E6 30 0N 75 27 E
Mansa, Zambia 107 E2 11 13 S 28 55 E
Mansalay, Phil. 70 E3 12 31N 121 26 E
Mansehra, Pakistan 80 B5 34 20N 73 15 E
Mansel I., Canada 127 B11 62 0N 80 0W
Mansfield, Australia 117 D7 37 4 S 146 6 E
Mansfield, U.K. 16 D6 53 9N 1 11W
Mansfield, La., U.S.A. 139 J8 32 2N 93 43W
Mansfield, Mass., U.S.A. 137 D13 42 2N 71 13W
Mansfield, Ohio, U.S.A. 136 F2 40 45N 82 31W
Mansfield, Pa., U.S.A. 136 E7 41 48N 77 5W
Mansfield, Wash., U.S.A. 142 C4 47 49N 119 38W
Mansi, Burma 78 C5 24 48N 95 52 E
Mansidão, Brazil 154 D3 10 43 S 44 2W
Mansilla de las Mulas, Spain 36 C5 42 30N 5 25W
Mansle, France 24 C4 45 52N 0 12 E
Manso →, Brazil 155 D2 13 50 S 47 0W
Mansoa, Guinea-Biss. 100 C1 12 0N 15 20W
Manson, U.S.A. 140 B2 42 32N 94 32W
Manson Creek, Canada 130 B4 55 37N 124 32W
Mansoura, Algeria 99 A5 36 1N 4 31 E
Manta, Ecuador 152 D1 1 0 S 80 40W
Manta, B. de, Ecuador 152 D1 0 54 S 80 44W
Mantalingajan, Mt., Phil. 71 G1 8 55N 117 45 E
Mantare, Tanzania 106 C3 2 42 S 33 13 E
Manteca, U.S.A. 144 H5 37 48N 121 13W
Mantecal, Venezuela 152 B4 7 34N 69 17W
Mantena, Brazil 155 E3 18 47 S 40 59W
Manteno, U.S.A. 141 C9 41 15N 87 50W
Manteo, U.S.A. 135 H8 35 55N 75 40W
Mantes-la-Jolie, France 23 D8 48 58N 1 41 E
Manthani, India 82 E4 18 40N 79 35 E
Manthelan, France 22 E7 47 9N 0 47 E
Manti, U.S.A. 142 G8 39 16N 111 38W
Mantiqueira, Serra da, Brazil 155 F3 22 0 S 44 0W
Manton, U.S.A. 134 C3 44 25N 85 24W
Mantorp, Sweden 15 F9 58 21N 15 20 E
Mántova, Italy 38 C7 45 9N 10 48 E
Mänttä, Finland 13 E21 62 0N 24 40 E
Mantua = Mántova, Italy 38 C7 45 9N 10 48 E
Mantung, Australia 116 C4 34 35 S 140 3 E
Manturovo, Russia 52 A7 58 23N 44 45 E
Manu, Peru 156 C3 12 10 S 70 51W
Manu →, Peru 156 C3 12 16 S 70 55W
Manua Is., Amer. Samoa 121 X25 14 13 S 169 35W
Manuae, Cook Is. 123 J12 19 30 S 159 0W
Manuel Alves →, Brazil 155 D2 11 19 S 48 28W
Manuel Alves Grande →, Brazil 154 C2 7 27 S 47 35W
Manuel Urbano, Brazil 156 B4 8 53 S 69 18W
Manui, Indonesia 72 B2 3 35 S 123 5 E
Manukau Harbour, N.Z. 118 D3 37 3 S 174 45 E
Manunui, N.Z. 118 E4 38 54 S 175 21 E
Manurewa, N.Z. 118 D3 37 1 S 174 54 E
Manuripi →, Bolivia 156 C4 11 6 S 67 36W
Manus I., Papua N. G. 120 B4 2 0 S 147 0 E
Manvi, India 83 G3 15 57N 76 59 E
Manville, U.S.A. 138 D2 42 47N 104 37W
Manwath, India 82 E3 19 19N 76 32 E
Many, U.S.A. 139 K8 31 34N 93 29W
Manyara, L., Tanzania 106 C4 3 40 S 35 50 E
Manych →, Russia 53 G5 47 13N 40 40 E
Manych-Gudilo, Ozero, Russia 53 G6 46 24N 42 38 E
Manyonga →, Tanzania 106 C3 4 10 S 34 15 E
Manyoni, Tanzania 106 D3 5 45 S 34 55 E
Manyoni □, Tanzania 106 D3 6 30 S 34 30 E
Manzai, Pakistan 79 B3 32 12N 70 15 E
Manzala, Bahra el, Egypt 94 H7 31 10N 31 56 E
Manzanares, Spain 35 F1 39 2N 3 22W
Manzaneda, Cabeza de, Spain 36 C3 42 12N 7 15W
Manzanillo, Cuba 148 B4 20 20N 77 31W
Manzanillo, Mexico 146 D4 19 0N 104 20W
Manzanillo, Pta., Panama 148 E4 9 30N 79 40W
Manzano Mts., U.S.A. 143 J10 34 40N 106 20W
Manzarīyeh, Iran 85 C6 34 53N 50 50 E
Manzhouli, China 65 B6 49 35N 117 25 E
Manzini, Swaziland 105 D5 26 30 S 31 25 E
Mao, Chad 97 F3 14 4N 15 19 E
Maoke, Pegunungan, Indonesia 73 B5 3 40 S 137 30 E
Maolin, China 67 C12 43 58N 123 30 E
Maoming, China 69 G8 21 50N 110 54 E
Maowen, China 68 B4 31 41N 103 49 E
Maoxing, China 67 B13 45 28N 124 40 E
Mapam Yumco, China 64 C3 30 45N 81 28 E
Mapastepec, Mexico 147 D6 15 26N 92 54W
Mapia, Kepulauan, Indonesia 73 A4 0 50N 134 20 E
Mapimí, Mexico 146 B4 25 50N 103 50W
Mapimí, Bolsón de, Mexico 146 B4 27 30N 104 15W
Maping, China 69 B9 31 34N 113 32 E
Mapinga, Tanzania 106 D4 6 40 S 39 12 E
Mapinhane, Mozam. 105 C6 22 20 S 35 0 E
Mapire, Venezuela 153 B5 7 45N 64 42W
Maple →, U.S.A. 141 B12 42 59N 84 57W
Maple Creek, Canada 131 D7 49 55N 109 29W
Maple Valley, U.S.A. 144 C4 47 25N 122 3W
Mapleton, U.S.A. 142 D2 44 2N 123 52W
Mapourika, L., N.Z. 119 D5 43 16 S 170 12 E
Maprik, Papua N. G. 120 B2 3 44 S 143 3 E
Mapuca, India 83 G1 15 36N 73 46 E
Mapuera →, Brazil 153 D6 1 5 S 57 2W
Maputing Baybay, Phil. 70 E4 12 45N 123 20 E
Maputo, Mozam. 105 D5 25 58 S 32 32 E
Maputo, B. de, Mozam. 105 D5 25 50 S 32 45 E
Maqiaohe, China 67 B16 44 40N 130 30 E
Maqnā, Si. Arabia 84 D2 28 25N 34 50 E
Maqran, W. →, Si. Arabia 86 B4 20 55N 47 12 E
Maqteïr, Mauritania 98 D2 21 50N 11 40W
Maqueda Channel, Phil. 70 E5 13 42N 124 1 E
Maquela do Zombo, Angola 103 D3 6 0 S 15 15 E
Maquinchao, Argentina 160 B3 41 15 S 68 50W
Maquoketa, U.S.A. 140 B6 42 4N 90 40W
Mar, Serra do, Brazil 159 B6 25 30 S 49 0W
Mar Chiquita, L., Argentina 158 C3 30 40 S 62 50W
Mar del Plata, Argentina 158 D4 38 0 S 57 30W
Mar Menor, Spain 35 H4 37 40N 0 45W
Mara, Guyana 153 B6 6 0N 57 36W
Mara, India 78 A5 28 11N 94 14 E
Mara, Tanzania 106 C3 1 30 S 34 32 E
Mara □, Tanzania 106 C3 1 45 S 34 20 E
Maraā, Brazil 152 D4 1 52 S 65 25W
Marabá, Brazil 154 C2 5 20 S 49 5W
Maracá, I. de, Brazil 153 C7 2 10N 50 30W
Maracaibo, Venezuela 152 A3 10 40N 71 37W
Maracaibo, L. de, Venezuela 152 B3 9 40N 71 30W
Maracaju, Brazil 159 A4 21 38 S 55 9W
Maracajú, Serra de, Brazil 157 E6 23 57 S 55 1W
Maracanã, Brazil 154 B2 0 46 S 47 27W
Maracás, Brazil 155 D3 13 26 S 40 18W
Maracay, Venezuela 152 A4 10 15N 67 28W
Marādah, Libya 96 C3 29 15N 19 15 E
Maradi, Niger 101 C6 13 29N 7 20 E
Maradun, Nigeria 101 C6 12 35N 6 18 E
Marāgheh, Iran 89 D12 37 30N 46 12 E
Maragogipe, Brazil 155 D4 12 46 S 38 55W
Maragondon, Phil. 70 D3 14 16N 120 44 E
Marāh, Si. Arabia 84 E5 25 0N 45 35 E
Marajó, B. de, Brazil 154 B2 1 0 S 48 30W
Marajó, I. de, Brazil 154 B2 1 0 S 49 30W
Marākand, Iran 84 B5 38 51N 45 16 E
Maralal, Kenya 106 B4 1 0N 36 38 E
Maralinga, Australia 113 F5 30 13 S 131 32 E
Marama, Australia 116 C4 35 10 S 140 10 E
Maramasike, Solomon Is. 121 M11 9 30 S 161 25 E
Marampa, S. Leone 100 D2 8 45N 12 28W
Maramureş □, Romania 46 B4 47 45N 24 0 E
Maran, Malaysia 77 L4 3 35N 102 45 E
Marana, U.S.A. 143 K8 32 27N 111 13W
Maranboy, Australia 112 B5 14 40 S 132 39 E
Maranchón, Spain 34 D2 41 6N 2 15W
Marand, Iran 89 C11 38 30N 45 45 E
Marang, Malaysia 77 K4 5 12N 103 13 E
Maranguape, Brazil 154 B4 3 55 S 38 50W
Maranhão = São Luís, Brazil 154 B3 2 39 S 44 15W
Maranhão □, Brazil 154 B2 5 0 S 46 0W
Marano, L. di, Italy 39 C10 45 44N 13 10 E
Maranoa →, Australia 115 D4 27 50 S 148 37 E
Marañón →, Peru 156 A3 4 30 S 73 35W
Marão, Mozam. 105 C5 24 18 S 34 2 E
Marapi →, Brazil 153 C6 0 37N 55 58W
Marari, Brazil 156 B4 5 43 S 67 47W
Maraş = Kahramanmaraş, Turkey 88 D7 37 37N 36 53 E
Mărăşeşti, Romania 46 D8 45 52N 27 14 E
Maratea, Italy 41 C8 39 59N 15 43 E
Marateca, Portugal 37 G2 38 34N 8 40W
Marathasa □, Cyprus 32 E11 34 59N 32 51 E
Marathókambos, Greece 45 G8 37 43N 26 42 E
Marathon, Australia 114 C3 20 51 S 143 32 E
Marathon, Canada 128 C2 48 44N 86 23W
Marathón, Greece 45 F5 38 11N 23 58 E
Marathon, Iowa, U.S.A. 140 B2 42 52N 94 59W
Marathon, N.Y., U.S.A. 137 D8 42 27N 76 2W
Marathon, Tex., U.S.A. 139 K3 30 12N 103 15W
Marathóvouno, Cyprus 32 D12 35 13N 33 37 E
Maratua, Indonesia 75 B5 2 10N 118 35 E
Maraú, Brazil 155 D4 14 6 S 39 0W
Maravatío, Mexico 146 D4 19 51N 100 25W
Marawi City, Phil. 71 G5 8 0N 124 21 E
Marāwih, U.A.E. 85 E7 24 18N 53 18 E
Marbella, Spain 37 J6 36 30N 4 57W
Marble Bar, Australia 112 D2 21 9 S 119 44 E
Marble Falls, U.S.A. 139 K5 30 35N 98 16W
Marblehead, U.S.A. 137 D14 42 30N 70 51W
Marburg, Germany 26 E4 50 47N 8 46 E
Marby, Sweden 14 A8 63 7N 14 18 E
Marcal →, Hungary 31 D10 47 41N 17 32 E
Marcali, Hungary 31 E10 46 35N 17 25 E
Marcapata, Peru 156 C3 13 31 S 70 52W
Marcaria, Italy 38 C7 45 7N 10 32 E
Marceline, U.S.A. 140 E4 39 43N 92 57W
March, U.K. 17 E8 52 33N 0 5 E
Marchal, Zaïre 103 D2 5 16 S 14 58 E
Marchand = Rommani, Morocco 98 B3 33 31N 6 40W
Marche, France 24 B5 46 5N 1 20 E
Marche □, Italy 39 E10 43 30N 13 15 E
Marche-en-Famenne, Belgium 21 H6 50 14N 5 19 E
Marchena, Spain 37 H5 37 18N 5 23W
Marches = Marche □, Italy 39 E10 43 30N 13 15 E
Marciana Marina, Italy 38 F7 42 48N 10 12 E
Marcianise, Italy 41 A7 41 2N 14 17 E
Marcigny, France 25 B8 46 17N 4 2 E
Marcillat-en-Combraille, France 24 B6 46 12N 2 38 E
Marcinelle, Belgium 21 H4 50 24N 4 26 E
Marck, France 23 B8 50 57N 1 57 E
Marckolsheim, France 23 D14 48 10N 7 30 E
Marcona, Peru 156 D2 15 10 S 75 0W
Marcos Juárez, Argentina 158 C3 32 42 S 62 5W
Marcus I. = Minami-Tori-Shima, Pac. Oc. 122 E7 24 0N 153 45 E
Marcus Necker Ridge, Pac. Oc. 122 F9 20 0N 175 0 E
Marcy, Mt., U.S.A. 137 B11 44 7N 73 56W
Mardan, Pakistan 79 B4 34 20N 72 0 E
Mardie, Australia 112 D2 21 12 S 115 59 E
Mardin, Turkey 89 D9 37 20N 40 43 E
Maré, I., N. Cal. 121 U22 21 30 S 168 0 E
Marechal Deodoro, Brazil 154 C4 9 43 S 35 54W
Maree, L., U.K. 18 D3 57 40N 5 26W
Mareeba, Australia 114 B4 16 59 S 145 28 E
Marek = Stanke Dimitrov, Bulgaria 42 E8 42 17N 23 9 E
Marek, Indonesia 72 B2 4 41 S 120 24 E
Maremma, Italy 38 F8 42 30N 11 30 E
Maréna, Mali 100 C3 14 0N 7 20W
Marenberg, Slovenia 39 B12 46 38N 15 13 E
Marengo, U.S.A. 140 C4 41 48N 92 4W
Marennes, France 24 C2 45 49N 1 7W
Marenyi, Kenya 106 C4 4 22 S 39 8 E
Marerano, Madag. 105 C7 21 23 S 44 52 E
Maréttimo, Italy 40 E5 37 58N 12 4 E
Mareuil-sur-Lay, France 24 B2 46 32N 1 14W
Marfa, U.S.A. 139 K2 30 19N 104 1W
Marfa Pt., Malta 32 D1 35 59N 14 19 E
Marganets = Marhanets, Ukraine 51 J8 47 40N 34 40 E
Margaret →, Australia 112 C4 18 9 S 125 41 E
Margaret Bay, Canada 130 C3 51 20N 127 35W
Margaret L., Canada 130 B5 58 56N 115 25W
Margaret River, Australia 112 C4 18 38 S 126 52 E
Margarita, I. de, Venezuela 153 A5 11 0N 64 0W
Margarítion, Greece 44 E2 39 22N 20 26 E
Margaritovo, Russia 60 C7 43 25N 134 45 E
Margate, S. Africa 105 E5 30 50 S 30 20 E
Margate, U.K. 17 F9 51 23N 1 23 E
Margelan = Marghilon, Uzbekistan 55 C5 40 27N 71 42 E
Margeride, Mts. de la, France 24 D7 44 43N 3 38 E
Margherita, India 78 B5 27 16N 95 40 E
Margherita di Savola, Italy 41 A9 41 22N 16 9 E
Marghilon, Uzbekistan 55 C5 40 27N 71 42 E
Marghita, Romania 46 B3 47 22N 22 22 E
Margonin, Poland 47 C4 52 58N 17 5 E
Margosatubig, Phil. 71 H4 7 34N 123 10 E
Marguerite, Canada 130 C4 52 30N 122 25W
Marhanets, Ukraine 51 J8 47 40N 34 40 E
Marhoum, Algeria 99 B4 34 27N 0 11W
Mari El □, Russia 52 B8 56 30N 48 0 E
Mari Republic □ = Mari El □, Russia 52 B8 56 30N 48 0 E
María Elena, Chile 158 A2 22 18 S 69 40W
María Grande, Argentina 158 C4 31 45 S 59 55W
Maria I., N. Terr., Australia 114 A2 14 52 S 135 45 E
Maria I., Tas., Australia 114 G4 42 35 S 148 0 E
Maria van Diemen, C., N.Z. 118 A1 34 29 S 172 40 E
Mariager, Denmark 15 H4 56 40N 10 0 E
Mariager Fjord, Denmark 15 H4 56 42N 10 19 E
Mariakani, Kenya 106 C4 3 50 S 39 27 E
Marian L., Canada 130 A5 63 0N 116 15W
Mariana Trench, Pac. Oc. 58 H18 13 0N 145 0 E
Marianao, Cuba 148 B3 23 8N 82 24W
Mariani, India 78 B5 26 39N 94 19 E
Marianna, Ark., U.S.A. 139 H9 34 46N 90 46W
Marianna, Fla., U.S.A. 135 K3 30 46N 85 14W
Mariánské Lázně, Czech. 30 B5 49 48N 12 41 E
Marias →, U.S.A. 142 C8 47 56N 110 30W
Mariato, Punta, Panama 148 E3 7 12N 80 52W
Mariazell, Austria 30 D8 47 47N 15 19 E
Ma'rib, Yemen 86 D4 15 25N 45 21 E
Maribo, Denmark 15 K5 54 48N 11 30 E
Maribor, Slovenia 39 B12 46 36N 15 40 E
Maricaban I., Phil. 70 E3 13 39N 120 53 E
Maricalom, Phil. 71 G4 9 42N 122 25 E
Marico →, Africa 104 C4 23 35 S 26 57 E
Maricopa, Ariz., U.S.A. 143 K7 33 4N 112 3W
Maricopa, Calif., U.S.A. 145 K7 35 4N 119 24W
Maricourt, Canada 127 C12 56 34N 70 49W
Marīdī, Sudan 95 G2 4 55N 29 25 E
Marīdī, Wadi →, Sudan 95 F2 6 15N 29 21 E
Marié →, Brazil 152 D4 0 27 S 66 26W
Marie Byrd Land, Antarctica 7 D14 79 30 S 125 0W
Marie-Galante, Guadeloupe 149 C7 15 56N 61 16W
Mariecourt = Kangiqsujuaq, Canada 127 B12 61 30N 72 0W
Mariefred, Sweden 14 E11 59 15N 17 12 E
Marienbad = Mariánské Lázně, Czech. 30 B5 49 48N 12 41 E
Marienberg, Germany 26 E9 50 39N 13 9 E
Marienberg, Neths. 20 D9 52 2N 6 35 E
Marienbourg, Belgium 21 H5 50 6N 4 31 E
Mariental, Namibia 104 C2 24 36 S 18 0 E
Marienville, U.S.A. 136 E5 41 28N 79 8W
Mariestad, Sweden 15 F7 58 43N 13 50 E
Marietta, Ga., U.S.A. 135 J3 33 57N 84 33W
Marietta, Ohio, U.S.A. 134 F5 39 25N 81 27W
Marieville, Canada 137 A11 45 26N 73 10W
Marignane, France 25 E9 43 25N 5 13 E
Marihatag, Phil. 71 G6 8 48N 126 18 E
Mariinsk, Russia 56 D9 56 10N 87 20 E
Mariinskiy Posad, Russia 52 B8 56 10N 47 45 E
Marijampolė, Lithuania 13 J20 54 33N 23 19 E
Marília, Brazil 159 A5 22 13 S 50 0W
Marillana, Australia 112 D2 22 37 S 119 16 E
Marimba, Angola 103 D3 8 28 S 17 8 E
Marín, Spain 36 C2 42 23N 8 42W
Marina, U.S.A. 144 J5 36 41N 121 48W
Marina di Cirò, Italy 41 C10 39 22N 17 8 E
Marina Plains, Australia 114 A3 14 37 S 143 57 E
Marinduque, Phil. 70 E3 13 25N 122 0 E
Marine City, U.S.A. 134 D4 42 43N 82 30W
Marineo, Italy 40 E6 37 57N 13 25 E
Marinette, U.S.A. 134 C2 45 6N 87 38W
Maringá, Brazil 159 A5 23 26 S 52 2W
Marinha Grande, Portugal 37 F2 39 45N 8 56W
Marion, Ala., U.S.A. 135 J2 32 38N 87 19W
Marion, Ill., U.S.A. 139 G10 37 44N 88 56W
Marion, Ind., U.S.A. 141 D11 40 32N 85 40W
Marion, Iowa, U.S.A. 140 B5 42 2N 91 36W
Marion, Kans., U.S.A. 138 F6 38 21N 97 1W
Marion, Mich., U.S.A. 134 C3 44 6N 85 9W
Marion, N.C., U.S.A. 135 H4 35 41N 82 1W
Marion, Ohio, U.S.A. 141 D13 40 35N 83 8W
Marion, S.C., U.S.A. 135 H6 34 11N 79 24W
Marion, Va., U.S.A. 135 G5 36 50N 81 31W
Marion, L., U.S.A. 135 J5 33 28N 80 10W
Marion Bay, Australia 116 C2 35 12 S 136 59 E
Marion I., Ind. Oc. 109 J2 47 0 S 38 0 E
Maripa, Venezuela 153 B4 7 26N 65 9W
Maripasoula, Fr. Guiana 153 C7 3 40N 54 4W
Maripipi I., Phil. 71 F5 11 47N 124 19 E
Mariposa, U.S.A. 144 H7 37 29N 119 58W
Mariscal Estigarribia, Paraguay 158 A3 22 3 S 60 40W
Maritime Alps = Maritimes, Alpes, Europe 25 D11 44 10N 7 10 E
Maritimes, Alpes, Europe 25 D11 44 10N 7 10 E
Maritsa = Évros →, Bulgaria 88 B2 41 40N 26 34 E
Maritsa, Bulgaria 43 E10 42 1N 25 50 E
Maritsa, Greece 32 C10 36 22N 28 10 E
Mariupol, Ukraine 51 J9 47 5N 37 31 E
Marīvān, Iran 89 E12 35 30N 46 25 E
Markah, W. →, Yemen 86 D4 14 59N 46 36 E
Markam, China 68 C2 29 42N 98 38 E
Markapur, India 83 G4 15 44N 79 19 E
Markazī □, Iran 85 C6 35 0N 49 30 E
Markdale, Canada 136 B4 44 19N 80 39W
Marke, Belgium 21 G2 50 48N 3 14 E
Marked Tree, U.S.A. 139 H9 35 32N 90 25W
Markelsdorfer Huk, Germany 26 A6 54 33N 11 0 E
Marken, Neths. 20 D6 52 26N 5 12 E
Markermeer, Neths. 20 C6 52 33N 5 15 E
Market Drayton, U.K. 16 E5 52 54N 2 29W
Market Harborough, U.K. 17 E7 52 29N 0 55W
Markham, Canada 136 C5 43 52N 79 16W
Markham →, Papua N. G. 120 D4 6 41 S 147 2 E
Markham, Mt., Antarctica 7 E11 83 0 S 164 0 E
Markham L., Canada 131 A8 62 30N 102 35W
Marki, Poland 47 C8 52 20N 21 2 E
Markleeville, U.S.A. 144 G7 38 42N 119 47W
Markoupoulon, Greece 45 G5 37 53N 23 57 E
Markovac, Serbia, Yug. 42 C6 44 14N 21 7 E
Markovo, Russia 57 C17 64 40N 169 40 E
Markoye, Burkina Faso 101 C5 14 39N 0 2 E
Marks, Russia 52 E8 51 45N 46 50 E
Marksville, U.S.A. 139 K8 31 8N 92 4W
Markt Schwaben, Germany 27 G7 48 11N 11 52 E
Marktredwitz, Germany 27 E8 50 1N 12 6 E
Marla, Australia 115 D1 27 19 S 133 33 E
Marlboro, U.S.A. 137 D13 42 19N 71 33W
Marlborough, Australia 114 C4 22 46 S 149 52 E
Marlborough Downs, U.K. 17 F6 51 27N 1 53W
Marle, France 23 C10 49 43N 3 47 E
Marlin, U.S.A. 139 K6 31 18N 96 54W
Marlow, Germany 26 A8 54 9N 12 33 E
Marlow, U.S.A. 139 H6 34 39N 97 58W
Marly-le-Grand, Switz. 28 C4 46 47N 7 10 E
Marmagao, India 83 G1 15 25N 73 56 E
Marmande, France 24 D4 44 30N 0 10 E
Marmara, Turkey 88 B2 40 35N 27 38 E
Marmara, Sea of = Marmara Denizi, Turkey 88 B3 40 45N 28 15 E
Marmara Denizi, Turkey 88 B3 40 45N 28 15 E
Marmaris, Turkey 88 D3 36 50N 28 14 E
Marmarth, U.S.A. 138 B3 46 18N 103 54W
Marmelos →, Brazil 157 B5 6 6 S 61 46W
Marmion, Mt., Australia 113 E2 29 16 S 119 50 E
Marmion L., Canada 128 C1 48 55N 91 20W
Marmolada, Mte., Italy 39 B8 46 26N 11 51 E
Marmolejo, Spain 37 G6 38 3N 4 13W
Marmora, Canada 128 D4 44 28N 77 41W
Marnay, France 23 E12 47 16N 5 48 E
Marne, Germany 26 B5 53 56N 9 0 E
Marne □, France 23 D11 48 50N 4 10 E
Marne →, France 23 D9 48 48N 2 24 E
Marneuli, Georgia 53 K7 41 30N 44 48 E
Maro, Chad 97 G3 8 30N 19 0 E
Maroa, Venezuela 152 C4 2 43N 67 33W
Maroala, Madag. 105 B8 15 23 S 47 59 E
Maroantsetra, Madag. 105 B8 15 26 S 49 44 E
Maromandia, Madag. 105 A8 14 13 S 48 5 E
Marondera, Zimbabwe 107 F3 18 5 S 31 42 E
Maroni →, Fr. Guiana 153 B7 5 30N 54 0W
Marónia, Greece 44 D7 40 53N 25 24 E
Maronne →, France 24 C5 45 5N 1 56 E
Maroochydore, Australia 115 D5 26 29 S 153 5 E
Maroona, Australia 116 D5 37 27 S 142 54 E
Maros, Indonesia 72 C1 5 0 S 119 34 E
Maros →, Hungary 31 E13 46 15N 20 13 E
Marosakoa, Madag. 105 B8 15 26 S 46 38 E
Marostica, Italy 39 C8 45 44N 11 40 E
Maroua, Cameroon 101 C7 10 40N 14 20 E
Marovoay, Madag. 105 B8 16 6 S 46 39 E
Marowijne □, Surinam 153 C7 4 0N 55 0W
Marowijne →, Surinam 153 B7 5 45N 53 58W
Marquard, S. Africa 104 D4 28 40 S 27 28 E
Marqueira, Portugal 37 G1 38 41N 9 9W
Marquesas Is. = Marquises, Is., Pac. Oc. 123 H14 9 30 S 140 0W
Marquette, U.S.A. 134 B2 46 33N 87 24W
Marquise, France 23 B8 50 50N 1 40 E
Marquises, Is., Pac. Oc. 123 H14 9 30 S 140 0W
Marra, Gebel, Sudan 95 F2 7 20N 27 35 E
Marracuene, Mozam. 105 D5 25 45 S 32 35 E
Marradi, Italy 39 D8 44 4N 11 37 E
Marrakech, Morocco 98 B3 31 9N 8 0W
Marrawah, Australia 114 G3 40 55 S 144 42 E
Marrecas, Serra das, Brazil 154 C3 9 0 S 41 0W
Marree, Australia 115 D2 29 39 S 138 1 E
Marrilla, Australia 112 D1 22 31 S 114 25 E
Marrimane, Mozam. 105 C5 22 58 S 33 34 E
Marromeu, Mozam. 105 B6 18 15 S 36 25 E
Marroquí, Punta, Spain 37 K5 36 0N 5 37W
Marrowie Cr. →, Australia 117 B6 33 23 S 145 40 E
Marrubane, Mozam. 107 F4 18 0 S 37 0 E
Marrum, Neths. 20 B7 53 19N 5 48 E
Marrupa, Mozam. 107 E4 13 8 S 37 30 E
Marsa el Brega, Libya 96 B3 30 24N 19 37 E
Marsá Matrûh, Egypt 94 A2 31 19N 27 9 E
Marsá Susah, Libya 96 B4 32 52N 21 59 E
Marsabit, Kenya 106 B4 2 18N 38 0 E
Marsabit □, Kenya 106 B4 2 45N 37 45 E
Marsala, Italy 40 E5 37 48N 12 26 E
Marsalforn, Malta 32 C1 36 4N 14 15 E
Marsberg, Germany 26 D4 51 28N 8 52 E
Marsciano, Italy 39 F9 42 54N 12 20 E
Marsden, Australia 117 B7 33 47 S 147 32 E
Marsdiep, Neths. 20 C5 52 58N 4 46 E
Marseillan, France 24 E7 43 23N 3 31 E

Mazara del Vallo 231

Marseille, France 25 E9 43 18N 5 23 E
Marseilles = Marseille, France 25 E9 43 18N 5 23 E
Marseilles, U.S.A. 141 C8 41 20N 88 43W
Marsh I., U.S.A. 139 L9 29 34N 91 53W
Marsh L., U.S.A. 138 C6 45 5N 96 0W
Marshall, Liberia 100 D2 6 8N 10 22W
Marshall, Ark., U.S.A. 139 H8 35 55N 92 38W
Marshall, Ill., U.S.A. 141 E9 39 23N 87 42W
Marshall, Mich., U.S.A. 141 B12 42 16N 84 58W
Marshall, Minn., U.S.A. 138 C7 44 25N 95 45W
Marshall, Mo., U.S.A. 140 E3 39 7N 93 12W
Marshall, Tex., U.S.A. 139 J7 32 33N 94 23W
Marshall →, Australia 114 C2 22 59 S 136 59 E
Marshall Is. ■, Pac. Oc. 122 G9 9 0N 171 0 E
Marshalltown, U.S.A. 140 B4 42 3N 92 55W
Marshfield, Mo., U.S.A. 139 G8 37 15N 92 54W
Marshfield, Wis., U.S.A. 138 C9 44 40N 90 10W
Marshūn, Iran 85 B6 36 19N 49 23 E
Mársico Nuovo, Italy 41 B8 40 25N 15 44 E
Märsta, Sweden 14 E11 59 37N 17 52 E
Marstal, Denmark 15 K4 54 51N 10 30 E
Marstrand, Sweden 15 G5 57 53N 11 35 E
Mart, U.S.A. 139 K6 31 33N 96 50W
Marta →, Italy 39 F8 42 14N 11 42 E
Martaban, Burma 78 G6 16 30N 97 35 E
Martaban, G. of, Burma 78 G6 16 5N 96 30 E
Martano, Italy 41 B11 40 12N 18 18 E
Martapura, Kalimantan, Indonesia 75 C4 3 22 S 114 47 E
Martapura, Sumatera, Indonesia 74 C2 4 19 S 104 22 E
Marte, Nigeria 101 C7 12 23N 13 46 E
Martel, France 24 D5 44 57N 1 37 E
Martelange, Belgium 21 J7 49 49N 5 43 E
Martensdale, U.S.A. 140 C3 41 23N 93 45W
Martés, Sierra, Spain 35 F4 39 20N 1 0W
Martha's Vineyard, U.S.A. 137 E14 41 25N 70 38W
Martigné-Ferchaud, France 22 E5 47 50N 1 20W
Martigny, Switz. 28 D4 46 6N 7 3 E
Martigues, France 25 E9 43 24N 5 4 E
Martil, Morocco 98 A3 35 36N 5 15W
Martin, Slovak Rep. 31 B11 49 6N 18 48 E
Martin, S. Dak., U.S.A. 138 D4 43 11N 101 44W
Martin, Tenn., U.S.A. 139 G10 36 21N 88 51W
Martín →, Spain 34 D4 41 18N 0 19W
Martin L., U.S.A. 135 J3 32 41N 85 55W
Martina, Switz. 29 C10 46 53N 10 28 E
Martina Franca, Italy 41 B10 40 42N 17 20 E
Martinborough, N.Z. 118 H4 41 14 S 175 29 E
Martinez, U.S.A. 144 G4 38 1N 122 8W
Martinho Campos, Brazil 155 E2 19 20 S 45 13W
Martinique ■, W. Indies 149 D7 14 40N 61 0W
Martinique Passage, W. Indies 149 C7 15 15N 61 0W
Martínon, Greece 45 F5 38 35N 23 15 E
Martinópolis, Brazil 159 A5 22 11 S 51 12W
Martins Ferry, U.S.A. 136 F4 40 6N 80 44W
Martinsberg, Austria 30 C8 48 22N 15 9 E
Martinsburg, Pa., U.S.A. 136 F6 40 19N 78 20W
Martinsburg, W. Va., U.S.A. 134 F7 39 27N 77 58W
Martinsville, Ill., U.S.A. 141 E9 39 20N 87 53W
Martinsville, Ind., U.S.A. 141 E10 39 26N 86 25W
Martinsville, Va., U.S.A. 135 G6 36 41N 79 52W
Marton, N.Z. 118 G4 40 4 S 175 23 E
Martorell, Spain 34 D6 41 28N 1 56 E
Martos, Spain 37 H7 37 44N 3 58W
Martūbah, Libya 96 B4 32 35N 22 46 E
Martuk, Kazakstan 54 F6 50 46N 56 31 E
Martuni, Armenia 53 K7 40 8N 45 20 E
Maru, Nigeria 101 C6 12 22N 6 22 E
Marudi, Malaysia 75 B4 4 11N 114 19 E
Ma'ruf, Afghan. 79 C2 31 30N 67 6 E
Marugame, Japan 62 C5 34 15N 133 40 E
Marúggio, Italy 41 B10 40 19N 17 34 E
Marui, Papua N. G. 120 C2 4 4 S 143 2 E
Maruia →, N.Z. 119 B7 41 47 S 172 13 E
Maruim, Brazil 154 D4 10 45 S 37 5W
Marulan, Australia 117 C9 34 43 S 150 3 E
Marum, Neths. 20 B8 53 9N 6 16 E
Marum, Mt., Vanuatu 121 F6 16 15 S 168 7 E
Marunga, Angola 103 F4 17 28 S 20 2 E
Marungu, Mts., Zaïre 106 D2 7 30 S 30 0 E
Maruoka, Japan 63 A8 36 9N 136 16 E
Marvast, Iran 85 D7 30 30N 54 15 E
Marvejols, France 24 D7 44 33N 3 19 E
Marwar, India 80 G5 25 43N 73 45 E
Mary, Turkmenistan 56 F7 37 40N 61 50 E
Mary Frances L., Canada 131 A7 63 19N 106 13W
Mary Kathleen, Australia 114 C2 20 44 S 139 48 E
Maryborough = Port Laoise, Ireland 19 C4 53 2N 7 18W
Maryborough, Queens., Australia 115 D5 25 31 S 152 37 E
Maryborough, Vic., Australia 116 D5 37 0 S 143 44 E
Maryfield, Canada 131 D8 49 50N 101 35W
Maryland □, U.S.A. 134 F7 39 0N 76 30W
Maryland Junction, Zimbabwe 107 F3 17 45 S 30 31 E
Maryport, U.K. 16 C4 54 44N 3 28W
Mary's Harbour, Canada 129 B8 52 18N 55 51W
Marystown, Canada 129 C8 47 10N 55 10W
Marysvale, U.S.A. 143 G7 38 27N 112 14W
Marysville, Canada 130 D5 49 35N 116 0W
Marysville, Calif., U.S.A. 144 F5 39 9N 121 35W
Marysville, Kans., U.S.A. 138 F6 39 51N 96 39W
Marysville, Mich., U.S.A. 136 D2 42 54N 82 29W
Marysville, Ohio, U.S.A. 141 D13 40 14N 83 22W
Marysville, Wash., U.S.A. 144 B4 48 3N 122 11W
Maryvale, Australia 115 D5 28 4 S 152 12 E
Maryville, Mo., U.S.A. 140 D2 40 21N 94 52W
Maryville, Tenn., U.S.A. 135 H4 35 46N 83 58W
Marzo, Punta, Colombia 152 B2 6 50N 77 42W
Marzūq, Libya 96 C2 25 53N 13 57 E
Masahunga, Tanzania 106 C3 2 6 S 33 18 E
Masai, Malaysia 77 M4 1 29N 103 55 E
Masai Steppe, Tanzania 106 C4 4 30 S 36 30 E
Masaka, Uganda 106 C3 0 21 S 31 45 E
Masalembo, Kepulauan, Indonesia 75 D4 5 35 S 114 30 E
Masalima, Kepulauan, Indonesia 75 D5 5 4 S 117 5 E
Masallı, Azerbaijan 89 C13 39 3N 48 40 E
Masamba, Indonesia 72 B2 2 30 S 120 15 E
Masan, S. Korea 67 G15 35 11N 128 32 E
Masanasa, Spain 35 F4 39 25N 0 25W
Masasi, Tanzania 107 E4 10 45 S 38 52 E
Masasi □, Tanzania 107 E4 10 45 S 38 50 E
Masaya, Nic. 148 D2 12 0N 86 7W
Masba, Nigeria 101 C7 10 35N 13 1 E
Masbate, Phil. 70 E4 12 21N 123 36 E
Masbate Pass, Phil. 70 E4 12 30N 123 35 E
Mascara, Algeria 99 A5 35 26N 0 6 E
Mascarene Is., Ind. Oc. 109 G4 22 0 S 55 0 E
Mascota, Mexico 146 C4 20 30N 104 50W
Mascoutah, U.S.A. 140 F7 38 29N 89 48W
Masela, Indonesia 73 C3 8 9 S 129 51 E
Maseru, Lesotho 104 D4 29 18 S 27 30 E
Mashaba, Zimbabwe 107 G3 20 2 S 30 29 E
Mashābih, Si. Arabia 84 E3 25 35N 36 30 E
Mashan, China 68 F7 23 40N 108 11 E
Masherbrum, Pakistan 81 B7 35 38N 76 18 E
Mashhad, Iran 85 B8 36 20N 59 35 E
Mashi, Nigeria 101 C6 13 0N 7 54 E
Mashiki, Japan 62 E2 32 51N 130 53 E
Mashīz, Iran 85 D8 29 56N 56 37 E
Mashkel, Hamun-i-, Pakistan 79 C1 28 30N 63 0 E
Mashki Chāh, Pakistan 79 C1 29 5N 62 30 E
Mashonaland Central □, Zimbabwe 105 B5 17 30 S 31 0 E
Mashonaland East □, Zimbabwe 105 B5 18 0 S 32 0 E
Mashonaland West □, Zimbabwe 105 B4 17 30 S 29 30 E
Mashtaga = Maştağa, Azerbaijan 53 K10 40 35N 49 57 E
Masi Manimba, Zaïre 103 C3 4 40 S 17 54 E
Masindi, Uganda 106 B3 1 40N 31 43 E
Masindi Port, Uganda 106 B3 1 43N 32 2 E
Masinloc, Phil. 70 D2 15 32N 119 57 E
Maşīrah, Khalīj, Oman 87 B7 20 10N 58 10 E
Maşīrah, Tur'at, Oman 87 B7 20 30N 58 40 E
Masisea, Peru 156 B3 8 35 S 74 22W
Masisi, Zaïre 106 C2 1 23 S 28 49 E
Masjed Soleyman, Iran 85 D6 31 55N 49 18 E
Mask, L., Ireland 19 C2 53 36N 9 22W
Maskelyne Is., Vanuatu 121 F5 16 32 S 167 49 E
Maski, India 83 G3 15 56N 76 46 E
Maslen Nos, Bulgaria 43 E12 42 18N 27 48 E
Maslinica, Croatia 39 E13 43 24N 16 13 E
Maşna'ah, Yemen 87 D5 14 27N 48 17 E
Masnou, Spain 34 D7 41 28N 2 20 E
Masoala, Tanjon' i, Madag. 105 B9 15 59 S 50 13 E
Masoarivo, Madag. 105 B7 19 3 S 44 19 E
Masohi, Indonesia 73 B3 3 20 S 128 55 E
Masomeloka, Madag. 105 C8 20 17 S 48 37 E
Mason, Mich., U.S.A. 141 B12 42 35N 84 27W
Mason, Nev., U.S.A. 144 G7 38 56N 119 8W
Mason, Ohio, U.S.A. 141 E12 39 22N 84 19W
Mason, Tex., U.S.A. 139 K5 30 45N 99 14W
Mason B., N.Z. 119 G2 46 55 S 167 45 E
Mason City, Ill., U.S.A. 140 D7 40 12N 89 42W
Mason City, Iowa, U.S.A. 140 A3 43 9N 93 12W
Maspalomas, Canary Is. 33 G4 27 46N 15 35W
Maspalomas, Pta., Canary Is. 33 G4 27 43N 15 36W
Masqat, Oman 87 B7 23 37N 58 36 E
Massa, Congo 102 C3 3 45 S 15 29 E
Massa, Italy 38 D7 44 1N 10 9 E
Massa, O. →, Morocco 98 B3 30 2N 9 40W
Massa Maríttima, Italy 38 E7 43 3N 10 52 E
Massachusetts □, U.S.A. 137 D12 42 30N 72 0W
Massachusetts B., U.S.A. 137 D14 42 20N 70 50W
Massafra, Italy 41 B10 40 35N 17 7 E
Massaguet, Chad 97 F3 12 28N 15 26 E
Massakory, Chad 97 F3 13 0N 15 49 E
Massanella, Spain 33 B9 39 48N 2 51 E
Massangena, Mozam. 105 C5 21 34 S 33 0 E
Massapê, Brazil 154 B3 3 31 S 40 19W
Massarosa, Italy 38 E7 43 52N 10 20 E
Massat, France 24 F5 42 53N 1 21 E
Massawa = Mitsiwa, Eritrea 95 D4 15 35N 39 25 E
Massena, U.S.A. 137 B10 44 56N 74 54W
Massénya, Chad 97 F3 11 21N 16 9 E
Masset, Canada 130 C2 54 2N 132 10W
Massiac, France 24 C7 45 15N 3 11 E
Massif Central, France 24 D7 44 55N 3 0 E
Massillon, U.S.A. 136 F3 40 48N 81 32W
Massinga, Mozam. 105 C6 23 15 S 35 22 E
Masson, Canada 137 A9 45 32N 75 25W
Masson I., Antarctica 7 C7 66 10 S 93 20 E
Mastābah, Si. Arabia 86 B2 20 49N 39 26 E
Maştağa, Azerbaijan 53 K10 40 35N 49 57 E
Mastanli = Momchilgrad, Bulgaria 43 F10 41 33N 25 23 E
Masterton, N.Z. 118 G4 40 56 S 175 39 E
Mástikho, Ákra, Greece 45 F8 38 10N 26 2 E
Mastuj, Pakistan 81 A5 36 20N 72 36 E
Mastung, Pakistan 79 C2 29 50N 66 56 E
Mastūrah, Si. Arabia 86 B2 23 7N 38 52 E
Masty, Belarus 50 F3 53 27N 24 38 E
Masuda, Japan 62 C3 34 40N 131 51 E
Masuika, Zaïre 103 D4 7 37 S 22 32 E
Masvingo, Zimbabwe 107 G3 20 8 S 30 49 E
Masvingo □, Zimbabwe 107 G3 21 0 S 31 30 E
Maswa □, Tanzania 106 C3 3 30 S 34 0 E
Maşyāf, Syria 88 E7 35 4N 36 20 E
Mata de São João, Brazil 155 D4 12 31 S 38 17W
Mata Utu, Wall. & F. Is. 111 C15 13 17 S 176 8W
Matabeleland North □, Zimbabwe 107 F2 19 0 S 28 0 E
Matabeleland South □, Zimbabwe 107 G2 21 0 S 29 0 E
Mataboor, Indonesia 73 B5 1 41 S 138 3 E
Matachel →, Spain 37 G4 38 50N 6 17W
Matachewan, Canada 128 C3 47 56N 80 39W
Matacuni →, Venezuela 153 C4 3 2N 65 16W
Matadi, Zaïre 103 D2 5 52 S 13 31 E
Matagalpa, Nic. 148 D2 13 0N 85 58W
Matagami, Canada 128 C4 49 45N 77 34W
Matagami, L., Canada 128 C4 49 50N 77 40W
Matagorda, U.S.A. 139 L7 28 42N 95 58W
Matagorda B., U.S.A. 139 L6 28 40N 96 0W
Matagorda I., U.S.A. 139 L6 28 15N 96 30W
Mataguinao, Phil. 70 E5 12 5N 124 55 E
Matak, P., Indonesia 77 L6 3 18N 106 16 E
Matakana, Australia 117 B6 32 59 S 145 54 E
Matakana, N.Z. 118 C3 36 21 S 174 43 E
Matakana I., N.Z. 118 C3 36 21 S 174 43 E
Matala, Angola 103 E3 14 46 S 15 4 E
Mátala, Greece 32 E6 34 59N 24 45 E
Matalaque, Peru 156 D3 16 26 S 70 49W
Matale, Sri Lanka 83 L5 7 30N 80 37 E
Matam, Phil. 71 G4 8 25N 123 19 E
Matam, Senegal 100 B2 15 34N 13 17W
Matamata, N.Z. 118 D4 37 48 S 175 47 E
Matameye, Niger 97 F1 13 26N 8 28 E
Matamoros, Campeche, Mexico 147 D6 18 50N 90 50W
Matamoros, Coahuila, Mexico 146 B4 25 33N 103 15W
Matamoros, Puebla, Mexico 147 D5 18 2N 98 17W
Matamoros, Tamaulipas, Mexico 147 B5 25 50N 97 30W
Ma'ţan as Sarra, Libya 97 D4 21 45N 22 0 E
Matana, Danau, Indonesia 72 B2 2 28 S 121 20 E
Matandu →, Tanzania 107 D3 8 45 S 34 19 E
Matane, Canada 129 C6 48 50N 67 33W
Matang, China 68 F5 23 30N 104 7 E
Matankari, Niger 101 C5 13 46N 4 1 E
Matanzas, Cuba 148 B3 23 0N 81 40W
Matapan, C. = Taínaron, Ákra, Greece 45 H4 36 22N 22 27 E
Matapédia, Canada 129 C6 48 0N 66 59W
Matara, Sri Lanka 83 M5 5 58N 80 30 E
Mataram, Indonesia 75 D5 8 41 S 116 10 E
Matarani, Peru 156 D3 17 0 S 72 10W
Mataranka, Australia 112 B5 14 55 S 133 4 E
Matarma, Râs, Egypt 91 E1 30 27N 32 44 E
Mataró, Spain 34 D7 41 32N 2 29 E
Matarraña →, Spain 34 D5 41 14N 0 22 E
Mataruška Banja, Serbia, Yug. 42 D5 43 40N 20 45 E
Mataso, Vanuatu 121 G6 17 14 S 168 26 E
Matata, N.Z. 118 D5 37 54 S 176 48 E
Matatiele, S. Africa 105 E4 30 20 S 28 49 E
Mataura, N.Z. 119 G3 46 11 S 168 51 E
Mataura →, N.Z. 119 G3 46 34 S 168 44 E
Mategua, Bolivia 157 C5 13 1 S 62 48W
Matehuala, Mexico 146 C4 23 40N 100 40W
Mateira, Brazil 155 E1 18 54 S 50 30W
Mateke Hills, Zimbabwe 107 G3 21 48 S 31 0 E
Matélica, Italy 39 E10 43 15N 13 0 E
Matera, Italy 41 B9 40 40N 16 36 E
Mátészalka, Hungary 31 D15 47 58N 22 20 E
Matetsi, Zimbabwe 107 F2 18 12 S 26 0 E
Mateur, Tunisia 96 A1 37 0N 9 40 E
Matfors, Sweden 14 B11 62 21N 17 2 E
Matha, France 24 C3 45 52N 0 20W
Matheson Island, Canada 131 C9 51 45N 96 56W
Mathis, U.S.A. 139 L6 28 6N 97 50W
Mathoura, Australia 117 C6 35 50 S 144 55 E
Mathura, India 80 F7 27 30N 77 40 E
Mati, Phil. 71 H6 6 55N 126 15 E
Mati →, Albania 44 C1 41 40N 19 35 E
Matías Romero, Mexico 147 D5 16 53N 95 2W
Matibane, Mozam. 107 E5 14 49 S 40 45 E
Matican, Phil. 71 H3 6 39N 121 53 E
Matima, Botswana 104 C3 20 15 S 24 26 E
Matiri Ra., N.Z. 119 B7 41 38 S 172 20 E
Matlock, U.K. 16 D6 53 9N 1 33W
Matmata, Tunisia 96 B1 33 37N 9 59 E
Matna, Sudan 95 E4 13 49N 35 10 E
Matnog, Phil. 70 E5 12 35N 124 5 E
Mato →, Venezuela 153 B4 7 9N 65 7W
Mato, Serrania de, Venezuela 152 B4 6 25N 65 25W
Mato Grosso □, Brazil 157 C6 14 0 S 55 0W
Mato Grosso, Planalto do, Brazil 157 C7 15 0 S 55 0W
Mato Grosso, Plateau of, Brazil 150 E5 15 0 S 54 0W
Mato Grosso do Sul □, Brazil 157 D7 18 0 S 55 0W
Matochkin Shar, Russia 56 B6 73 10N 56 40 E
Matong, Papua N. G. 120 C6 5 36 S 151 50 E
Matopo Hills, Zimbabwe 107 G2 20 36 S 28 20 E
Matopos, Zimbabwe 107 G2 20 20 S 28 29 E
Matosinhos, Portugal 36 D2 41 11N 8 42W
Matour, France 25 B8 46 19N 4 29 E
Matrah, Oman 87 B7 23 37N 58 30 E
Matsena, Nigeria 101 C7 13 5N 10 5 E
Matsesta, Russia 53 J4 43 34N 39 51 E
Matsu Tao, Taiwan 69 E13 26 9N 119 56 E
Matsubara, Japan 63 C7 34 33N 135 34 E
Matsudo, Japan 63 B11 35 47N 139 54 E
Matsue, Japan 62 B5 35 25N 133 10 E
Matsumae, Japan 60 D10 41 26N 140 7 E
Matsumoto, Japan 63 A9 36 15N 138 0 E
Matsusaka, Japan 63 C8 34 34N 136 32 E
Matsutō, Japan 63 A8 36 31N 136 34 E
Matsuura, Japan 62 D1 33 20N 129 49 E
Matsuyama, Japan 62 D4 33 45N 132 45 E
Matsuzaki, Japan 63 C10 34 43N 138 50 E
Mattagami →, Canada 128 B3 50 43N 81 29W
Mattancheri, India 83 K3 9 50N 76 15 E
Mattawa, Canada 128 C4 46 20N 78 45W
Mattawamkeag, U.S.A. 129 C6 45 32N 68 21W
Matterhorn, Switz. 28 E5 45 58N 7 39 E
Mattersburg, Austria 31 D9 47 44N 16 24 E
Matteson, U.S.A. 141 C9 41 30N 87 42W
Matthew Town, Bahamas 149 B5 20 57N 73 40W
Matthews, U.S.A. 141 D11 40 23N 85 30W
Matthew's Ridge, Guyana 153 B5 7 37N 60 10W
Mattice, Canada 128 C3 49 40N 83 20W
Mattituck, U.S.A. 137 F12 40 59N 72 32W
Mattmar, Sweden 14 A7 63 18N 13 45 E
Matuba, Mozam. 105 C5 24 28 S 32 49 E
Matucana, Peru 156 C2 11 55 S 76 25W
Matuku, Fiji 121 B2 19 10 S 179 44 E
Matun, Afghan. 80 C3 33 22N 69 58 E
Maturín, Venezuela 153 B5 9 45N 63 11W
Matutum, Mt., Phil. 71 H5 6 22N 125 5 E
Matveyev Kurgan, Russia 53 G4 47 35N 38 57 E
Mau, India 81 G10 25 56N 83 33 E
Mau Escarpment, Kenya 106 C4 0 40 S 36 0 E
Mau Ranipur, India 81 G8 25 16N 79 8 E
Mauban, Phil. 70 D3 14 12N 121 44 E
Maubeuge, France 23 B10 50 17N 3 57 E
Maubourguet, France 24 E4 43 29N 0 1 E
Maud, Pt., Australia 112 D1 23 6 S 113 45 E
Maude, Australia 116 C6 34 29 S 144 18 E
Maués, Brazil 153 D6 3 20 S 57 45W
Maui, U.S.A. 132 H16 20 48N 156 20W
Maulamyaing = Moulmein, Burma 78 G6 16 30N 97 40 E
Maule □, Chile 158 D1 36 5 S 72 30W
Mauléon-Licharre, France 24 E3 43 14N 0 54W
Maullín, Chile 160 B2 41 38 S 73 37W
Maulvibazar, Bangla. 78 C3 24 29N 91 42 E
Maumee, U.S.A. 141 C13 41 34N 83 39W
Maumee →, U.S.A. 141 C13 41 42N 83 28W
Maumere, Indonesia 72 C2 8 38 S 122 13 E
Maun, Botswana 104 B3 20 0 S 23 26 E
Mauna Kea, U.S.A. 132 J17 19 50N 155 28W
Mauna Loa, U.S.A. 132 J17 19 30N 155 35W
Maungaturoto, N.Z. 118 C3 36 6 S 174 23 E
Maungdow, Burma 78 E4 20 50N 92 21 E
Maupin, U.S.A. 142 D3 45 11N 121 5W
Maure-de-Bretagne, France 22 E5 47 53N 1 58W
Maurepas, L., U.S.A. 139 K9 30 15N 90 30W
Maures, France 25 E10 43 15N 6 15 E
Mauriac, France 24 C6 45 13N 2 19 E
Maurice, L., Australia 113 E5 29 30 S 131 0 E
Mauriceville, N.Z. 118 G4 40 45 S 175 42 E
Maurienne, France 25 C10 45 13N 6 30 E
Mauritania ■, Africa 98 D3 20 50N 10 0W
Mauritius ■, Ind. Oc. 92 J9 20 0 S 57 0 E
Mauron, France 22 D4 48 9N 2 18W
Maurs, France 24 D6 44 43N 2 12 E
Mauston, U.S.A. 138 D9 43 48N 90 5W
Mauterndorf, Austria 30 D6 47 9N 13 40 E
Mauvezin, France 24 E4 43 44N 0 53 E
Mauzé-sur-le-Mignon, France 24 B3 46 12N 0 41W
Mavaca →, Venezuela 153 C4 2 31N 65 11W
Mavelikara, India 83 K3 9 14N 76 32 E
Mavinga, Angola 103 F4 15 50 S 20 21 E
Mavli, India 80 G5 24 45N 73 55 E
Mavrova, Albania 44 D1 40 26N 19 32 E
Mavuradonha Mts., Zimbabwe 107 F3 16 30 S 31 30 E
Mawa, Zaïre 106 B2 2 45N 26 40 E
Mawana, India 80 E7 29 6N 77 58 E
Mawand, Pakistan 80 E3 29 33N 68 38 E
Mawk Mai, Burma 78 E6 20 14N 97 37 E
Mawlaik, Burma 78 D5 23 40N 94 26 E
Mawlawkho, Burma 78 G6 17 50N 97 38 E
Mawquq, Si. Arabia 84 E4 27 25N 41 8 E
Mawshij, Yemen 86 D3 13 43N 43 17 E
Mawson Coast, Antarctica 7 C6 68 30 S 63 0 E
Max, U.S.A. 138 B4 47 49N 101 18W
Maxcanú, Mexico 147 C6 20 40N 92 0W
Maxesibeni, S. Africa 105 E4 30 49 S 29 23 E
Maxhamish L., Canada 130 B4 59 50N 123 17W
Maxixe, Mozam. 105 C6 23 54 S 35 17 E
Maxville, Canada 137 A10 45 17N 74 51W
Maxwell, N.Z. 118 F3 39 51 S 174 49 E
Maxwell, U.S.A. 144 F4 39 17N 122 11W
Maxwelton, Australia 114 C3 20 43 S 142 41 E
May Downs, Australia 114 C4 22 38 S 148 55 E
May Pen, Jamaica 148 C4 17 58N 77 15W
May River, Papua N. G. 120 C1 4 19 S 141 58 E
Maya, Indonesia 75 C3 1 10 S 109 35 E
Maya, Spain 34 B3 43 12N 1 29W
Maya →, Russia 57 D14 60 28N 134 28 E
Maya Mts., Belize 147 D7 16 30N 89 0W
Mayaguana, Bahamas 149 B5 22 30N 72 44W
Mayagüez, Puerto Rico 149 C6 18 12N 67 9W
Mayahi, Niger 101 C6 13 58N 7 40 E
Mayals, Spain 34 D5 41 22N 0 30 E
Mayama, Congo 102 C2 3 51 S 14 54 E
Mayāmey, Iran 85 B7 36 24N 55 42 E
Mayang, China 68 D7 27 53N 109 49 E
Mayarí, Cuba 149 B4 20 40N 75 41W
Mayavaram = Mayuram, India 83 J4 11 3N 79 42 E
Maybell, U.S.A. 142 F9 40 31N 108 5W
Maychew, Ethiopia 95 E4 12 50N 39 31 E
Maydān, Iraq 89 E11 34 55N 45 37 E
Maydena, Australia 114 G4 42 45 S 146 30 E
Maydī, Yemen 86 C3 16 19N 42 48 E
Maydos, Turkey 44 D8 40 13N 26 20 E
Mayen, Germany 27 E3 50 19N 7 13 E
Mayenne, France 22 D6 48 20N 0 38W
Mayenne □, France 22 D6 48 10N 0 40W
Mayenne →, France 22 E6 47 30N 0 32W
Mayer, U.S.A. 143 J7 34 24N 112 14W
Mayerthorpe, Canada 130 C5 53 57N 115 8W
Mayfield, U.S.A. 135 G1 36 44N 88 38W
Mayhill, U.S.A. 143 K11 32 53N 105 29W
Maykop, Russia 53 H5 44 35N 40 10 E
Mayli-Say, Kyrgyzstan 55 C6 41 17N 72 24 E
Maymyo, Burma 76 A1 22 2N 96 28 E
Maynard, U.S.A. 144 C4 47 59N 122 55W
Maynard Hills, Australia 113 E2 28 28 S 119 49 E
Mayne →, Australia 114 C3 23 40 S 141 55 E
Maynooth, Ireland 19 C5 53 23N 6 34W
Mayo, Canada 126 B6 63 38N 135 57W
Mayo □, Ireland 19 C2 53 53N 9 3W
Mayo →, Argentina 160 C3 45 45 S 69 45W
Mayo →, Peru 156 B2 6 38 S 76 15W
Mayo Bay, Phil. 71 H6 6 56N 126 22 E
Mayo L., Canada 126 B6 63 45N 135 0W
Mayoko, Zaïre 102 C2 2 18 S 12 49 E
Mayon Volcano, Phil. 70 E4 13 15N 123 41 E
Mayor I., N.Z. 118 D5 37 16 S 176 17 E
Mayorga, Spain 36 C5 42 10N 5 16W
Mayotte, I., Mayotte 93 H8 12 50 S 45 10 E
Mayoyao, Phil. 70 C3 16 59N 121 14 E
Mayraira Pt., Phil. 70 B3 18 39N 120 51 E
Mayskiy, Russia 53 J7 43 47N 44 2 E
Mayson L., Canada 131 B7 57 55N 107 10W
Maysville, Ky., U.S.A. 141 F13 38 39N 83 46W
Maysville, Mo., U.S.A. 140 E2 39 53N 94 22W
Mayu, Indonesia 72 A3 1 30N 126 30 E
Mayumba, Gabon 102 C2 3 25 S 10 39 E
Mayuram, India 83 J4 11 3N 79 42 E
Mayville, N. Dak., U.S.A. 138 B6 47 30N 97 20W
Mayville, N.Y., U.S.A. 136 D5 42 15N 79 30W
Mayya, Russia 57 C14 61 44N 130 18 E
Mazabuka, Zambia 107 F2 15 52 S 27 44 E
Mazagán = El Jadida, Morocco 98 B3 33 11N 8 17W
Mazagão, Brazil 153 D7 0 7 S 51 16W
Mazamet, France 24 E6 43 30N 2 20 E
Mazán, Peru 152 D3 3 30 S 73 0W
Māzandarān □, Iran 85 B7 36 30N 52 0 E
Mazapil, Mexico 146 C4 24 38N 101 34W
Mazar, O. →, Algeria 99 B5 31 50N 1 36 E
Mazar-e Sharīf, Afghan. 79 A2 36 41N 67 0 E
Mazara del Vallo, Italy 40 E5 37 39N 12 35 E

232 Mazarredo

Mazarredo, *Argentina* **160 C3** 47 10 S 66 50W
Mazarrón, *Spain* **35 H3** 37 38N 1 19W
Mazarrón, G. de, *Spain* **35 H3** 37 27N 1 19W
Mazaruni →, *Guyana* **153 B6** 6 25N 58 35W
Mazatán, *Mexico* **146 B2** 29 0N 110 8W
Mazatenango, *Guatemala* **148 D1** 14 35N 91 30W
Mazatlán, *Mexico* **146 C3** 23 13N 106 25W
Mažeikiai, *Lithuania* **13 H20** 56 20N 22 20 E
Māzhān, *Iran* **85 C8** 32 30N 59 0 E
Mazīnān, *Iran* **85 B8** 36 19N 56 56 E
Mazoe, *Mozam.* **107 F3** 16 42 S 33 7 E
Mazoe →, *Mozam.* **107 F3** 16 20 S 33 30 E
Mazomanie, *U.S.A.* **140 A7** 43 11N 89 48W
Mazon, *U.S.A.* **141 C8** 41 14N 88 25W
Mazowe, *Zimbabwe* **107 F3** 17 28 S 30 58 E
Mazrûb, *Sudan* **95 E2** 14 0N 29 20 E
Mazu Dao, *China* **69 D12** 26 10N 119 55 E
Mazurian Lakes = Mazurski, Pojezierze, *Poland* **47 B7** 53 50N 21 0 E
Mazurski, Pojezierze, *Poland* **47 B7** 53 50N 21 0 E
Mazyr, *Belarus* **51 F5** 51 59N 29 15 E
Mazzarino, *Italy* **41 E7** 37 18N 14 13 E
Mba, *Fiji* **121 A1** 17 33 S 177 41 E
Mbaba, *Senegal* **100 C1** 14 59N 16 44W
Mbabane, *Swaziland* **105 D5** 26 18 S 31 6 E
Mbagne, *Mauritania* **100 B2** 16 6N 14 47W
M'bahiakro, *Ivory C.* **100 D4** 7 33N 4 19W
Mbaïki, *C.A.R.* **102 B3** 3 53N 18 1 E
Mbakana, Mt. de, *Cameroon* **102 A3** 7 57N 15 6 E
Mbala, *Zambia* **107 D3** 8 46 S 31 24 E
Mbale, *Uganda* **106 B3** 1 8N 34 12 E
Mbalmayo, *Cameroon* **101 E7** 3 33N 11 33 E
Mbamba Bay, *Tanzania* **107 E3** 11 13 S 34 49 E
Mbandaka, *Zaïre* **102 B3** 0 1N 18 18 E
Mbanga, *Cameroon* **101 E6** 4 30N 9 33 E
Mbanza Congo, *Angola* **103 D2** 6 18 S 14 16 E
Mbanza Ngungu, *Zaïre* **103 D2** 5 12 S 14 53 E
Mbarara, *Uganda* **106 C3** 0 35 S 30 40 E
Mbashe →, *S. Africa* **105 E4** 32 15 S 28 54 E
Mbatto, *Ivory C.* **100 D4** 6 28N 4 22W
Mbengga, *Fiji* **121 B2** 18 23 S 178 8 E
Mbenkuru →, *Tanzania* **107 D4** 9 25 S 39 50 E
Mberengwa, *Zimbabwe* **107 G2** 20 29 S 29 57 E
Mberengwa, Mt., *Zimbabwe* **107 G2** 20 37 S 29 55 E
Mberubu, *Nigeria* **101 D6** 6 10N 7 38 E
Mbesuma, *Zambia* **107 D3** 10 0 S 32 2 E
Mbeya, *Tanzania* **107 D3** 8 54 S 33 29 E
Mbeya □, *Tanzania* **106 D3** 8 15 S 33 30 E
Mbigou, *Gabon* **102 C2** 1 53 S 11 56 E
Mbinga, *Tanzania* **107 E4** 10 50 S 35 0 E
Mbinga □, *Tanzania* **107 E3** 10 50 S 35 0 E
Mbini □, *Eq. Guin.* **102 B2** 1 30N 10 0 E
Mboki, *C.A.R.* **95 F2** 5 19N 25 58 E
Mboli, *Zaïre* **102 B4** 4 8N 23 9 E
Mboro, *Senegal* **100 B1** 15 9N 16 54W
Mboune, *Senegal* **100 C2** 14 42N 13 34W
Mbouoma, *Congo* **102 C3** 0 52 S 15 4 E
Mbour, *Senegal* **100 C1** 14 22N 16 54W
Mbout, *Mauritania* **100 B2** 16 1N 12 38W
Mbozi □, *Tanzania* **107 D3** 9 0 S 32 50 E
Mbrés, *C.A.R.* **102 A3** 6 40N 19 48 E
Mbuji-Mayi, *Zaïre* **103 D4** 6 9 S 23 40 E
Mbulu, *Tanzania* **106 C4** 3 45 S 35 30 E
Mbulu □, *Tanzania* **106 C4** 3 52 S 35 33 E
Mburucuyá, *Argentina* **158 B4** 28 1 S 58 14W
Mcherrah, *Algeria* **98 C4** 27 0N 4 30W
Mchinja, *Tanzania* **107 D4** 9 44 S 39 45 E
Mchinji, *Malawi* **107 E3** 13 47 S 32 58 E
Mdennah, *Mauritania* **98 D3** 24 37N 6 0W
Mead, L., *U.S.A.* **145 J12** 36 1N 114 44W
Meade, *U.S.A.* **139 G4** 37 17N 100 20W
Meadow, *Australia* **113 E1** 26 35 S 114 40 E
Meadow Lake, *Canada* **131 C7** 54 10N 108 26W
Meadow Lake Prov. Park, *Canada* **131 C7** 54 27N 109 0W
Meadow Valley Wash →, *U.S.A.* **145 J12** 36 40N 114 34W
Meadville, *Mo., U.S.A.* **140 E3** 39 47N 93 18W
Meadville, *Pa., U.S.A.* **136 E4** 41 39N 80 9W
Meaford, *Canada* **128 D3** 44 36N 80 35W
Mealhada, *Portugal* **36 E2** 40 22N 8 27W
Mealy Mts., *Canada* **129 B8** 53 10N 58 0W
Meander River, *Canada* **130 B5** 59 2N 117 42W
Meares, C., *U.S.A.* **142 D2** 45 37N 124 0W
Mearim →, *Brazil* **154 B3** 3 4 S 44 35W
Meath □, *Ireland* **19 C5** 53 40N 6 57W
Meath Park, *Canada* **131 C7** 53 27N 105 22W
Meatian, *Australia* **116 C5** 35 34 S 143 21 E
Meaulne, *France* **24 B6** 46 36N 2 36 E
Meaux, *France* **23 D9** 48 58N 2 50 E
Mebechi-Gawa →, *Japan* **60 D10** 40 31N 141 31 E
Mecanhelas, *Mozam.* **107 F4** 15 12 S 35 54 E
Mecaya →, *Colombia* **152 C2** 0 29N 75 11W
Mecca = Makkah, *Si. Arabia* **86 B2** 21 30N 39 54 E
Mecca, *U.S.A.* **145 M10** 33 34N 116 5W
Mechanicsburg, *U.S.A.* **136 F8** 40 13N 77 1W
Mechanicsville, *U.S.A.* **140 C5** 41 54N 91 16W
Mechanicville, *U.S.A.* **137 D11** 42 54N 73 41W
Mechara, *Ethiopia* **95 F5** 8 36N 40 20 E
Mechelen, *Antwerpen, Belgium* **21 F4** 51 2N 4 29 E
Mechelen, *Limburg, Belgium* **21 G7** 50 58N 5 41 E
Mecheria, *Algeria* **99 B4** 33 35N 0 18W
Mechernich, *Germany* **26 E2** 50 35N 6 39 E
Mechetinskaya, *Russia* **53 G5** 46 45N 40 32 E
Mechra Benâbbou, *Morocco* **98 B3** 32 39N 7 48W
Mecidiye, *Turkey* **44 D8** 40 38N 26 32 E
Mecitözü, *Turkey* **88 B6** 40 32N 35 17 E
Mecklenburg-Vorpommern □, *Germany* **26 B8** 53 45N 12 15 E
Mecklenburger Bucht, *Germany* **26 A7** 54 20N 11 40 E
Meconta, *Mozam.* **107 E4** 14 59 S 39 50 E
Meda, *Australia* **112 C3** 17 22 S 123 59 E
Meda, *Portugal* **36 E3** 40 57N 7 18W
Medak, *India* **82 E4** 18 1N 78 15 E
Medan, *Indonesia* **74 B1** 3 40N 98 38 E
Médanos, *Argentina* **160 A4** 38 50 S 62 42W
Medanosa, Pta., *Argentina* **160 C3** 48 8 S 66 0W
Medaryville, *U.S.A.* **141 C10** 41 5N 86 55W
Medawachchiya, *Sri Lanka* **83 K5** 8 30N 80 30 E
Medéa, *Algeria* **99 A5** 36 12N 2 50 E
Mededa, *Bos.-H.* **42 D4** 43 44N 19 15 E
Médégué, *Gabon* **102 B2** 0 37N 10 8 E
Medeiros Neto, *Brazil* **155 E3** 17 20 S 40 14W
Medel, Pic, *Switz.* **29 C7** 46 34N 8 55 E
Medellín, *Colombia* **152 B2** 6 15N 75 35W
Medelpad, *Sweden* **13 E17** 62 33N 16 30 E
Medemblik, *Neths.* **20 C6** 52 46N 5 8 E
Médenine, *Tunisia* **96 B2** 33 21N 10 30 E
Mederdra, *Mauritania* **100 B1** 17 0N 15 38W
Medford, *Mass., U.S.A.* **137 D13** 42 25N 71 7W
Medford, *Oreg., U.S.A.* **142 E2** 42 19N 122 52W
Medford, *Wis., U.S.A.* **138 C9** 45 9N 90 20W
Medgidia, *Romania* **46 E9** 44 15N 28 19 E
Medi, *Sudan* **95 F3** 5 4N 30 42 E
Media Agua, *Argentina* **158 C2** 31 58 S 68 25W
Media Luna, *Argentina* **158 C2** 34 45 S 66 44W
Mediapolis, *U.S.A.* **140 C5** 41 0N 91 10W
Mediaş, *Romania* **46 C5** 46 9N 24 22 E
Medical Lake, *U.S.A.* **142 C5** 47 34N 117 41W
Medicina, *Italy* **39 D8** 44 28N 11 38 E
Medicine Bow, *U.S.A.* **142 F10** 41 54N 106 12W
Medicine Bow Pk., *U.S.A.* **142 F10** 41 21N 106 19W
Medicine Bow Ra., *U.S.A.* **142 F10** 41 10N 106 25W
Medicine Hat, *Canada* **131 D6** 50 0N 110 45W
Medicine Lake, *U.S.A.* **138 A2** 48 30N 104 30W
Medicine Lodge, *U.S.A.* **139 G5** 37 17N 98 35W
Medina = Al Madīnah, *Si. Arabia* **84 E3** 24 35N 39 52 E
Medina, *Brazil* **155 E3** 16 15 S 41 29W
Medina, *Colombia* **152 C3** 4 30N 73 21W
Medina, *N. Dak., U.S.A.* **138 B5** 46 54N 99 18W
Medina, *N.Y., U.S.A.* **136 C6** 43 13N 78 23W
Medina, *Ohio, U.S.A.* **136 E3** 41 8N 81 52W
Medina →, *U.S.A.* **139 L5** 29 16N 98 29W
Medina de Ríoseco, *Spain* **36 D5** 41 53N 5 3W
Medina del Campo, *Spain* **36 D6** 41 18N 4 55W
Medina L., *U.S.A.* **139 L5** 29 32N 98 56W
Medina-Sidonia, *Spain* **37 J5** 36 28N 5 57W
Medinaceli, *Spain* **34 D2** 41 12N 2 30W
Medinipur, *India* **81 H12** 22 25N 87 21 E
Mediterranean Sea, *Europe* **10 H7** 35 0N 15 0 E
Medjerda, O. →, *Tunisia* **96 A2** 37 7N 10 13 E
Medley, *Canada* **131 C6** 54 25N 110 16W
Mednogorsk, *Russia* **54 F6** 51 24N 57 37 E
Médoc, *France* **24 C3** 45 10N 0 50W
Medora, *U.S.A.* **141 F10** 38 49N 86 10W
Médouneu, *Gabon* **102 B2** 0 57N 10 47 E
Medstead, *Canada* **131 C7** 53 19N 108 5W
Medulin, *Croatia* **39 D10** 44 49N 13 55 E
Medveda, *Serbia, Yug.* **42 E6** 42 50N 21 32 E
Medvedevo, *Russia* **52 B8** 56 37N 47 47 E
Medveditsa →, *Russia* **49 F6** 49 35N 42 41 E
Medveditsa →, *Russia* **52 B3** 57 5N 37 30 E
Medvedok, *Russia* **52 B10** 57 20N 50 1 E
Medvezhi, Ostrava, *Russia* **57 B17** 71 0N 161 0 E
Medvezhyegorsk, *Russia* **48 B5** 63 0N 34 25 E
Medway →, *U.K.* **17 F8** 51 27N 0 46 E
Medzev, *Slovak Rep.* **31 C13** 48 43N 20 55 E
Medzilaborce, *Slovak Rep.* **31 B14** 49 17N 21 52 E
Meeberrie, *Australia* **113 E2** 26 57 S 115 51 E
Meekatharra, *Australia* **113 E2** 26 32 S 118 29 E
Meeker, *U.S.A.* **142 F10** 40 2N 107 55W
Meeniyan, *Australia* **117 E7** 38 35 S 146 0 E
Meer, *Belgium* **21 F5** 51 27N 4 45 E
Meerane, *Germany* **26 E8** 50 51N 12 27 E
Meerbeke, *Belgium* **21 G4** 50 50N 4 3 E
Meerhout, *Belgium* **21 F6** 51 7N 5 4 E
Meerle, *Belgium* **21 F5** 51 29N 4 48 E
Meersburg, *Germany* **27 H5** 47 41N 9 16 E
Meerssen, *Neths.* **21 G7** 50 53N 5 50 E
Meerut, *India* **80 E7** 29 1N 77 42 E
Meeteetse, *U.S.A.* **142 D9** 44 9N 108 52W
Meeuwen, *Belgium* **21 F7** 51 6N 5 31 E
Mega, *Ethiopia* **95 G4** 3 57N 38 19 E
Megálo Khorío, *Greece* **45 H9** 36 27N 27 24 E
Megálo Petalí, *Greece* **45 G6** 38 0N 24 15 E
Megalópolis, *Greece* **45 G4** 37 25N 22 7 E
Meganísi, *Greece* **45 F2** 38 39N 20 48 E
Mégara, *Greece* **45 G5** 37 58N 23 22 E
Megdhova →, *Greece* **45 E3** 39 10N 21 45 E
Megève, *France* **25 C10** 45 51N 6 37 E
Meghalaya □, *India* **78 C3** 25 50N 91 0 E
Meghezez, *Ethiopia* **95 F4** 9 18N 39 26 E
Meghna →, *Bangla.* **78 D3** 22 50N 90 50 E
Mégiscane, L., *Canada* **128 C4** 48 35N 75 55W
Megra, *Russia* **50 B9** 60 11N 37 14 E
Mehadia, *Romania* **46 E3** 44 56N 22 23 E
Mehaigne →, *Belgium* **21 G6** 50 32N 5 13 E
Mehaïguene, O. →, *Algeria* **99 B5** 32 15N 2 59 E
Mehedinţi □, *Romania* **46 E3** 44 40N 22 45 E
Meheisa, *Sudan* **94 D3** 19 38N 32 57 E
Mehndawal, *India* **81 F10** 26 58N 83 5 E
Mehr Jān, *Iran* **85 C7** 33 50N 55 6 E
Mehrābād, *Iran* **89 D12** 36 53N 47 55 E
Mehrān, *Iran* **89 F12** 33 7N 46 10 E
Mehrīz, *Iran* **85 D7** 31 35N 54 28 E
Mehun-sur-Yèvre, *France* **23 E9** 47 10N 2 13 E
Mei Jiang →, *China* **69 E11** 24 25N 116 35 E
Mei Xian, *Guangdong, China* **69 E11** 24 16N 116 6 E
Mei Xian, *Shaanxi, China* **66 G4** 34 18N 107 55 E
Meia Ponte →, *Brazil* **155 E2** 18 32 S 49 36W
Meicheng, *China* **69 C12** 29 29N 119 16 E
Meichengzhen, *China* **69 C8** 28 9N 111 40 E
Meichuan, *China* **69 B10** 30 8N 115 31 E
Meiganga, *Cameroon* **102 A2** 6 30N 14 25 E
Meijel, *Neths.* **21 F7** 51 21N 5 53 E
Meiktila, *Burma* **78 E5** 20 53N 95 54 E
Meilen, *Switz.* **29 B7** 47 16N 8 39 E
Meiningen, *Germany* **26 E6** 50 34N 10 25 E
Meio →, *Brazil* **155 D3** 13 36 S 44 7W
Meira, Sierra de, *Spain* **36 B3** 43 15N 7 15W
Meiringen, *Switz.* **28 C6** 46 43N 8 12 E
Meishan, *China* **68 B4** 30 3N 103 23 E
Meissen, *Germany* **26 D9** 51 9N 13 29 E
Meissner, *Germany* **26 D5** 51 14N 9 50 E
Meitan, *China* **68 D6** 27 45N 107 29 E
Mejillones, *Chile* **158 A1** 23 10 S 70 30W
Meka, *Australia* **113 E2** 27 25 S 116 48 E
Mékambo, *Gabon* **102 B2** 1 2N 13 50 E
Mekdela, *Ethiopia* **95 E4** 11 24N 39 10 E
Mekele, *Ethiopia* **95 E4** 13 33N 39 30 E
Mekhtar, *Pakistan* **79 C3** 30 30N 69 15 E
Meknès, *Morocco* **98 B3** 33 57N 5 33W
Meko, *Nigeria* **101 D5** 7 27N 2 52 E
Mekong →, *Asia* **77 H6** 9 30N 106 15 E
Mekongga, *Indonesia* **72 B2** 3 39 S 121 15 E
Mekvari = Kür →, *Azerbaijan* **89 C13** 39 29N 49 15 E
Melagiri Hills, *India* **83 H3** 12 20N 77 30 E
Melah, Sebkhet el, *Algeria* **99 C4** 29 20N 1 30W
Melaka, *Malaysia* **77 L4** 2 15N 102 15 E
Melaka □, *Malaysia* **74 B2** 2 15N 102 15 E
Mélambes, *Greece* **32 D6** 35 8N 24 40 E
Melanesia, *Pac. Oc.* **122 H7** 4 0 S 155 0 E
Melapalaiyam, *India* **83 K3** 8 39N 77 44 E
Melawi →, *Indonesia* **75 B4** 0 5N 111 29 E
Melbourne, *Australia* **117 D6** 37 50 S 145 0 E
Melbourne, *Fla., U.S.A.* **135 L5** 28 5N 80 37W
Melbourne, *Iowa, U.S.A.* **140 C3** 41 57N 93 6W
Melcher, *U.S.A.* **140 C3** 41 14N 93 15W
Melchor Múzquiz, *Mexico* **146 B4** 27 50N 101 30W
Melchor Ocampo, *Mexico* **146 C4** 24 52N 101 40W
Méldola, *Italy* **39 D9** 44 7N 12 5 E
Meldorf, *Germany* **26 A5** 54 5N 9 5 E
Meleden, *Somali Rep.* **108 B3** 10 25N 49 51 E
Melegnano, *Italy* **38 C6** 45 21N 9 19 E
Melenci, *Serbia, Yug.* **42 B5** 45 32N 20 20 E
Melenki, *Russia* **52 C5** 55 20N 41 37 E
Meleuz, *Russia* **54 E6** 52 58N 55 55 E
Mélèzes →, *Canada* **127 C12** 57 30N 71 0W
Melfi, *Chad* **97 F3** 11 0N 17 59 E
Melfi, *Italy* **41 B8** 41 0N 15 39 E
Melfort, *Canada* **131 C8** 52 50N 104 37W
Melfort, *Zimbabwe* **107 F3** 18 0 S 31 25 E
Melgaço, *Madeira* **36 C2** 42 7N 8 15W
Melgar de Fernamental, *Spain* **36 C6** 42 27N 4 17W
Melhus, *Norway* **14 A4** 63 17N 10 18 E
Melick, *Neths.* **21 F8** 51 10N 6 1 E
Melide, *Switz.* **29 E7** 45 57N 8 57 E
Meligalá, *Greece* **45 G3** 37 15N 21 59 E
Melilla, *N. Afr.* **99 A4** 35 21N 2 57W
Melipilla, *Chile* **158 C1** 33 42 S 71 15W
Mélissa, Ákra, *Greece* **32 D6** 35 6N 24 33 E
Mélissa Óros, *Greece* **45 G8** 37 32N 26 4 E
Melita, *Canada* **131 D8** 49 15N 101 0W
Mélito di Porto Salvo, *Italy* **41 E8** 37 55N 15 47 E
Melitopol, *Ukraine* **51 J8** 46 50N 35 22 E
Melk, *Austria* **30 C8** 48 13N 15 20 E
Mellansel, *Sweden* **12 E18** 63 25N 18 17 E
Melle, *Belgium* **21 G3** 51 0N 3 49 E
Melle, *France* **24 B3** 46 14N 0 10W
Melle, *Germany* **26 C4** 52 12N 8 20 E
Mellégue, O. →, *Tunisia* **96 A1** 36 36N 9 14 E
Mellen, *U.S.A.* **138 B9** 46 20N 90 40W
Mellerud, *Sweden* **15 F6** 58 41N 12 28 E
Mellette, *U.S.A.* **138 C5** 45 9N 98 30W
Mellid, *Spain* **36 C2** 42 55N 8 1W
Mellieha, *Malta* **32 D1** 35 57N 14 21 E
Mellit, *Sudan* **95 E2** 14 7N 25 34 E
Mellizo Sur, Cerro, *Chile* **160 C2** 48 33 S 73 10W
Mellrichstadt, *Germany* **27 E6** 50 25N 10 17 E
Melnik, *Bulgaria* **43 F8** 41 30N 23 25 E
Mělník, *Czech.* **30 A7** 50 22N 14 23 E
Melo, *Uruguay* **159 C5** 32 20 S 54 10W
Melolo, *Indonesia* **72 C2** 9 53 S 120 40 E
Melouprey, *Cambodia* **76 F5** 13 48N 105 16 E
Melrhir, Chott, *Algeria* **99 B6** 34 13N 6 30 E
Melrose, *N.S.W., Australia* **117 B7** 32 42 S 146 57 E
Melrose, *W. Austral., Australia* **113 E3** 27 50 S 121 15 E
Melrose, *U.K.* **18 F6** 55 36N 2 43W
Melrose, *Iowa, U.S.A.* **140 D3** 40 59N 93 3W
Melrose, *N. Mex., U.S.A.* **139 H3** 34 26N 103 38W
Mels, *Switz.* **29 B8** 47 3N 9 25 E
Melsele, *Belgium* **21 F4** 51 13N 4 17 E
Melstone, *U.S.A.* **142 C10** 46 36N 107 52W
Melsungen, *Germany* **26 D5** 51 7N 9 32 E
Melton Mowbray, *U.K.* **16 E7** 52 47N 0 54W
Melun, *France* **23 D9** 48 32N 2 39 E
Melur, *India* **83 J4** 10 2N 78 23 E
Melut, *Sudan* **95 E3** 10 30N 32 13 E
Melville, *Canada* **131 C8** 50 55N 102 50W
Melville, C., *Australia* **114 A3** 14 11 S 144 30 E
Melville, L., *Canada* **129 B8** 53 30N 60 0W
Melville B., *Australia* **114 A2** 12 0 S 136 45 E
Melville I., *Australia* **112 B5** 11 30 S 131 0 E
Melville I., *Canada* **124 B8** 75 30N 112 0W
Melville Pen., *Canada* **127 B11** 68 0N 84 0W
Melvin →, *Canada* **130 B5** 59 11N 117 31W
Mélykút, *Hungary* **31 E12** 46 11N 19 25 E
Memaliaj, *Albania* **44 D1** 40 25N 19 58 E
Memba, *Mozam.* **107 E5** 14 11 S 40 30 E
Memboro, *Indonesia* **72 C1** 9 30 S 119 30 E
Membrilla, *Spain* **35 G1** 38 59N 3 21W
Memel = Klaìpėda, *Lithuania* **13 J19** 55 43N 21 10 E
Memel, *S. Africa* **105 D4** 27 38 S 29 36 E
Memmingen, *Germany* **27 H6** 47 58N 10 10 E
Mempawah, *Indonesia* **75 B3** 0 30N 109 5 E
Memphis, *Mo., U.S.A.* **140 D4** 40 28N 92 10W
Memphis, *Tenn., U.S.A.* **139 H10** 35 8N 90 3W
Memphis, *Tex., U.S.A.* **139 H4** 34 44N 100 33W
Mena, *Ukraine* **51 G7** 51 31N 32 13 E
Mena, *U.S.A.* **139 H7** 34 35N 94 15W
Mena →, *Ethiopia* **95 F5** 5 40N 40 50 E
Menai Strait, *U.K.* **16 D3** 53 11N 4 13W
Ménaka, *Mali* **101 B5** 15 59N 2 18 E
Menaldum, *Neths.* **20 B7** 53 13N 5 40 E
Menamurtee, *Australia* **116 A5** 31 25 S 143 11 E
Menan = Chao Phraya →, *Thailand* **76 F3** 13 32N 100 36 E
Menarandra →, *Madag.* **105 D7** 25 17 S 44 30 E
Menard, *U.S.A.* **139 K5** 30 55N 99 47W
Menasha, *U.S.A.* **134 C1** 44 13N 88 26W
Menate, *Indonesia* **75 C4** 0 12 S 113 3 E
Mendawai →, *Indonesia* **75 C4** 3 30 S 113 0 E
Mende, *France* **24 D7** 44 31N 3 30 E
Mendebo, *Ethiopia* **95 F4** 7 0N 39 22 E
Mendez, *Mexico* **147 B5** 25 7N 98 34W
Mendez Nunez, *Phil.* **70 D3** 14 8N 120 54 E
Mendhar, *India* **81 C6** 33 35N 74 10 E
Mendi, *Ethiopia* **95 F4** 9 47N 35 4 E
Mendi, *Papua N. G.* **120 D2** 6 11 S 143 39 E
Mendip Hills, *U.K.* **17 F5** 51 17N 2 40W
Mendocino, *U.S.A.* **142 G2** 39 19N 123 48W
Mendocino, C., *U.S.A.* **142 F1** 40 26N 124 25W
Mendon, *U.S.A.* **141 B11** 42 0N 85 27W
Mendota, *Calif., U.S.A.* **144 J6** 36 45N 120 23W
Mendota, *Ill., U.S.A.* **140 C7** 41 33N 89 7W
Mendoza, *Argentina* **158 C2** 32 50 S 68 52W
Mendoza □, *Argentina* **158 C2** 33 0 S 69 0W
Mendrisio, *Switz.* **29 E7** 45 52N 8 59 E
Mene Grande, *Venezuela* **152 B3** 9 49N 70 56W
Menemen, *Turkey* **88 C2** 38 34N 27 3 E
Menen, *Belgium* **21 G2** 50 47N 3 7 E
Menéndez, L., *Argentina* **160 B2** 42 40 S 71 51W
Menfi, *Italy* **40 E5** 37 36N 12 58 E
Mengcheng, *China* **69 A11** 33 18N 116 31 E
Mengdingjie, *China* **68 F2** 23 31N 98 58 E
Mengeš, *Slovenia* **39 B11** 46 10N 14 35 E
Menggala, *Indonesia* **74 C3** 4 30 S 105 15 E
Menghai, *China* **68 G3** 21 49N 100 55 E
Mengíbar, *Spain* **37 H7** 37 58N 3 48W
Mengjin, *China* **66 G7** 34 55N 112 45 E
Mengla, *China* **68 G3** 21 20N 101 25 E
Menglian, *China* **68 F2** 22 21N 99 27 E
Mengoub, *Algeria* **98 C3** 29 49N 5 26W
Mengshan, *China* **69 E8** 24 14N 110 55 E
Mengyin, *China* **67 G9** 35 40N 117 58 E
Mengzhe, *China* **68 F3** 22 2N 100 15 E
Mengzi, *China* **68 F4** 23 20N 103 22 E
Menihek L., *Canada* **129 B6** 54 0N 67 0W
Menin = Menen, *Belgium* **21 G2** 50 47N 3 7 E
Menindee, *Australia* **116 B5** 32 20 S 142 25 E
Menindee L., *Australia* **116 B5** 32 20 S 142 25 E
Meningie, *Australia* **116 C3** 35 50 S 139 18 E
Menlo Park, *U.S.A.* **144 H4** 37 27N 122 12W
Menominee, *U.S.A.* **134 C2** 45 6N 87 37W
Menominee →, *U.S.A.* **134 C2** 45 6N 87 36W
Menomonee Falls, *U.S.A.* **141 A8** 43 11N 88 7W
Menomonie, *U.S.A.* **138 C9** 44 53N 91 55W
Menongue, *Angola* **103 E3** 14 48 S 17 52 E
Menorca, *Spain* **33 B11** 40 0N 4 0 E
Mentakab, *Malaysia* **77 L4** 3 29N 102 21 E
Mentawai, Kepulauan, *Indonesia* **74 C1** 2 0 S 99 0 E
Menton, *France* **25 E11** 43 50N 7 29 E
Mentone, *U.S.A.* **141 C10** 41 10N 86 2W
Mentor, *U.S.A.* **136 E3** 41 40N 81 21W
Menyamya, *Papua N. G.* **120 D3** 7 10 S 145 59 E
Menzel-Bourguiba, *Tunisia* **96 A1** 37 9N 9 49 E
Menzel Chaker, *Tunisia* **96 B2** 35 0N 10 26 E
Menzel-Temime, *Tunisia* **96 A2** 36 46N 11 0 E
Menzelinsk, *Russia* **54 D4** 55 47N 53 11 E
Menzies, *Australia* **113 E3** 29 40 S 121 2 E
Me'ona, *Israel* **91 B4** 33 1N 35 15 E
Meoqui, *Mexico* **146 B3** 28 17N 105 29W
Mepaco, *Mozam.* **107 F3** 15 57 S 30 48 E
Meppel, *Neths.* **20 C8** 52 42N 6 12 E
Meppen, *Germany* **26 C3** 52 42N 7 17 E
Mequinenza, *Spain* **34 D5** 41 22N 0 17 E
Mequon, *U.S.A.* **141 A9** 43 14N 87 59W
Mer, *France* **22 E8** 47 42N 1 30 E
Mer Rouge, *U.S.A.* **139 J9** 32 47N 91 48W
Mera Lava, *Vanuatu* **121 D6** 14 25 S 168 3 E
Merabéllou, Kólpos, *Greece* **32 D7** 35 10N 25 50 E
Merai, *Papua N. G.* **120 C7** 4 52 S 152 19 E
Meramangye, L., *Australia* **113 E5** 28 25 S 132 13 E
Meramec →, *U.S.A.* **140 F6** 38 24N 90 21W
Meran = Merano, *Italy* **39 B8** 46 40N 11 9 E
Merano, *Italy* **39 B8** 46 40N 11 9 E
Merate, *Italy* **38 C6** 45 42N 9 25 E
Merauke, *Indonesia* **73 C6** 8 29 S 140 24 E
Merbabu, *Indonesia* **75 D4** 7 30 S 110 40 E
Merbein, *Australia* **116 C5** 34 10 S 142 2 E
Merca, *Somali Rep.* **108 D2** 1 48N 44 50 E
Mercadal, *Spain* **33 B11** 39 59N 4 5 E
Mercato Saraceno, *Italy* **39 E9** 43 57N 12 12 E
Merced, *U.S.A.* **144 H6** 37 18N 120 29W
Merced Pk., *U.S.A.* **144 H7** 37 36N 119 24W
Mercedes, *Buenos Aires, Argentina* **158 C4** 34 40 S 59 30W
Mercedes, *Corrientes, Argentina* **158 B4** 29 10 S 58 5W
Mercedes, *San Luis, Argentina* **158 C2** 33 40 S 65 21W
Mercedes, *Camarines N., Phil.* **70 D4** 14 7N 123 1 E
Mercedes, *Leyte, Phil.* **71 F5** 10 41N 124 24 E
Mercedes, *Zamboanga del S., Phil.* **71 H4** 6 57N 122 9 E
Mercedes, *Uruguay* **158 C4** 33 12 S 58 0W
Merceditas, *Chile* **158 B1** 28 20 S 70 35W
Mercer, *N.Z.* **118 D4** 37 16 S 175 5 E
Mercer, *Mo., U.S.A.* **140 D3** 40 31N 93 32W
Mercer, *Pa., U.S.A.* **136 E4** 41 14N 80 15W
Merchtem, *Belgium* **21 G4** 50 58N 4 14 E
Mercier, *Bolivia* **156 C4** 10 42 S 68 5W
Mercury, *U.S.A.* **145 J11** 36 40N 115 58W
Mercury B., *N.Z.* **118 C4** 36 48 S 175 45 E
Mercury Is., *N.Z.* **118 C4** 36 37 S 175 52 E
Mercy C., *Canada* **127 B13** 65 0N 63 30W
Merdrignac, *France* **22 D4** 48 11N 2 27W
Mere, *Belgium* **21 G3** 50 55N 3 58 E
Meredith, C., *Falk. Is.* **160 D4** 52 15 S 60 40W
Meredith, L., *U.S.A.* **139 H4** 35 43N 101 33W
Meredosia, *U.S.A.* **140 E6** 39 50N 90 34W
Merefa, *Ukraine* **51 H9** 49 48N 36 3 E
Meregh, *Somali Rep.* **108 D3** 3 46N 47 18 E
Merei, *Romania* **46 D7** 45 7N 26 43 E
Merelbeke, *Belgium* **21 G3** 51 0N 3 45 E
Méréville, *France* **23 D9** 48 20N 2 5 E
Merga = Nukheila, *Sudan* **94 D2** 19 1N 26 21 E
Mergui Arch. = Myeik Kyunzu, *Burma* **77 G1** 11 30N 97 30 E
Meribah, *Australia* **116 C4** 34 43 S 140 51 E
Mérida, *Mexico* **147 C7** 20 58N 89 37W
Merida, *Phil.* **71 F5** 10 55N 124 32 E
Mérida, *Spain* **37 G4** 38 55N 6 25W
Mérida, *Venezuela* **152 B3** 8 24N 71 8W
Mérida □, *Venezuela* **152 B3** 8 30N 71 10W
Mérida, Cord. de, *Venezuela* **152 B3** 9 0N 71 0W
Meriden, *U.S.A.* **137 E12** 41 32N 72 48W
Meridian, *Calif., U.S.A.* **144 F5** 39 9N 121 55W
Meridian, *Idaho, U.S.A.* **142 E5** 43 37N 116 24W
Meridian, *Miss., U.S.A.* **135 J1** 32 22N 88 42W
Meridian, *Tex., U.S.A.* **139 K6** 31 56N 97 39W
Mering, *Germany* **27 G7** 48 16N 10 59 E
Meriruma, *Brazil* **153 C7** 1 15N 54 50W

Mindanao 233

Merke, Kazakstan 55 B6 42 52N 73 11 E
Merkel, U.S.A. 139 J4 32 28N 100 1W
Merksem, Belgium 21 F4 51 16N 4 25 E
Merksplas, Belgium 21 F5 51 22N 4 52 E
Mermaid Reef, Australia 112 C2 17 6 S 119 36 E
Mern, Denmark 15 J6 55 3N 12 3 E
Merowe, Sudan 94 D3 18 29N 31 46 E
Merredin, Australia 113 F2 31 28 S 118 18 E
Merrick, U.K. 18 F4 55 8N 4 28W
Merrickville, Canada 137 B9 44 55N 75 50W
Merrill, Oreg., U.S.A. 142 E3 42 1N 121 36W
Merrill, Wis., U.S.A. 138 C10 45 11N 89 41W
Merrillville, U.S.A. 141 C9 41 29N 87 20W
Merriman, U.S.A. 138 D4 42 55N 101 42W
Merritt, Canada 130 C4 50 10N 120 45W
Merriwa, Australia 117 B9 32 6 S 150 22 E
Merriwagga, Australia 117 B6 33 47 S 145 43 E
Merry I., Canada 128 A4 55 29N 77 31W
Merrygoen, Australia 117 A8 31 51 S 149 12 E
Merryville, U.S.A. 139 K8 30 45N 93 33W
Mersa Fatma, Eritrea 90 E3 14 57N 40 17 E
Mersch, Lux. 21 J8 49 44N 6 7 E
Merseburg, Germany 26 D7 51 22N 11 59 E
Mersey →, U.K. 16 D5 53 25N 3 1W
Merseyside □, U.K. 16 D5 53 31N 3 2W
Mersin, Turkey 88 D6 36 51N 34 36 E
Mersing, Malaysia 77 L4 2 25N 103 50 E
Merta, India 80 F6 26 39N 74 4 E
Mertert, Lux. 21 J8 49 43N 6 29 E
Merthyr Tydfil, U.K. 17 F4 51 45N 3 22W
Merthyr Tydfil □, U.K. 17 F4 51 46N 3 21W
Mértola, Portugal 37 H3 37 40N 7 40W
Mertzig, Lux. 21 J8 49 51N 6 1 E
Mertzon, U.S.A. 139 K4 31 16N 100 49W
Méru, France 23 C9 49 13N 2 8 E
Meru, Kenya 106 B4 0 3N 37 40 E
Meru, Tanzania 106 C4 3 15 S 36 46 E
Meru □, Kenya 106 B4 0 3N 37 46 E
Merville, France 23 B9 50 38N 2 38 E
Méry-sur-Seine, France 23 D10 48 31N 3 54 E
Merzifon, Turkey 88 B6 40 53N 35 32 E
Merzig, Germany 27 F2 49 26N 6 38 E
Merzouga, Erg Tin, Algeria 99 D7 24 0N 11 4 E
Mesa, U.S.A. 143 K8 33 25N 111 50W
Mesach Mellet, Libya 96 D2 24 30N 11 30 E
Mesagne, Italy 41 B10 40 34N 17 48 E
Mesanagrós, Greece 32 C9 36 1N 27 49 E
Mesaoría □, Cyprus 32 D12 35 12N 33 14 E
Mesarás, Kólpos, Greece 32 D6 35 6N 24 47 E
Meschede, Germany 26 D4 51 20N 8 18 E
Mescit, Turkey 89 B9 40 21N 41 11 E
Mesfinto, Ethiopia 95 E4 13 20N 37 22 E
Mesgouez, L., Canada 128 B4 51 20N 75 0W
Meshchovsk, Russia 52 C2 54 22N 35 17 E
Meshed = Mashhad, Iran 85 B8 36 20N 59 35 E
Meshoppen, U.S.A. 137 E8 41 36N 76 3W
Meshra er Req, Sudan 95 F2 8 25N 29 18 E
Mesick, U.S.A. 134 C3 44 24N 85 43W
Mesilinka →, Canada 130 B4 56 6N 124 30W
Mesilla, U.S.A. 143 K10 32 16N 106 48W
Meslay-du-Maine, France 22 E6 47 58N 0 33W
Mesocco, Switz. 29 D8 46 23N 9 12 E
Mesolóngion, Greece 45 F3 38 21N 21 28 E
Mesopotamia = Al Jazirah, Iraq 89 E10 33 30N 44 0 E
Mesoraca, Italy 41 C9 39 5N 16 48 E
Mésou Volímais, Greece 45 G2 37 53N 20 35 E
Mesquite, U.S.A. 143 H6 36 47N 114 6W
Mess Cr. →, Canada 130 B2 57 55N 131 14W
Messac, France 22 E5 47 49N 1 50W
Messad, Algeria 99 B5 34 8N 3 30 E
Messalo →, Mozam. 107 E4 12 25 S 39 15 E
Méssaména, Cameroon 101 E7 3 48N 12 49 E
Messancy, Belgium 21 J7 49 36N 5 49 E
Messeue, Greece 45 G3 37 12N 21 58 E
Messier, Canal, Chile 160 C2 48 20 S 74 33W
Messina, Italy 41 D8 38 11N 15 34 E
Messina, S. Africa 105 C5 22 20 S 30 5 E
Messina, Str. di, Italy 41 D8 38 15N 15 35 E
Messíni, Greece 45 G4 37 4N 22 1 E
Messínia □, Greece 45 G3 37 10N 22 0 E
Messiniakós Kólpos, Greece 45 H4 36 45N 22 5 E
Messkirch, Germany 27 H5 47 59N 9 7 E
Messonghi, Greece 32 B3 39 29N 19 56 E
Mesta →, Bulgaria 43 F9 40 54N 24 49 E
Mestà, Ákra, Greece 45 F7 38 16N 25 53 E
Mestanza, Spain 37 G6 38 35N 4 4W
Město Teplá, Czech. 30 B5 49 59N 12 52 E
Mestre, Italy 39 C9 45 29N 12 15 E
Mestre, Espigão, Brazil 155 D2 12 30 S 46 10W
Městys Zelezná Ruda, Czech. 30 B6 49 8N 13 15 E
Mesudiye, Turkey 88 B7 40 28N 37 46 E
Meta, U.S.A. 140 F4 38 19N 92 10W
Meta □, Colombia 152 C3 3 30N 73 0W
Meta →, S. Amer. 152 B4 6 12N 67 28W
Metairie, U.S.A. 139 L9 29 58N 90 10W
Metalici, Munţii, Romania 46 C3 46 15N 22 50 E
Metaline Falls, U.S.A. 142 B5 48 52N 117 22W
Metamora, U.S.A. 140 D7 40 47N 89 22W
Metán, Argentina 158 B3 25 30 S 65 0W
Metangula, Mozam. 107 E3 12 40 S 34 50 E
Metáuro →, Italy 39 E10 43 50N 13 3 E
Metema, Ethiopia 95 E4 12 56N 36 13 E
Metengobalame, Mozam. 107 E3 14 49 S 34 30 E
Méthana, Greece 45 G5 37 35N 23 23 E
Methóni, Greece 45 H3 36 49N 21 42 E
Methven, N.Z. 119 D6 43 38 S 171 40 E
Methy L., Canada 131 B7 56 28N 109 30W
Metil, Mozam. 107 F4 16 24 S 39 0 E
Metkovets, Bulgaria 43 D8 43 37N 23 10 E
Metković, Croatia 42 D2 43 6N 17 39 E
Metlakatla, U.S.A. 130 B2 55 8N 131 35W
Metlaoui, Tunisia 96 B1 34 24N 8 24 E
Metlika, Slovenia 39 C12 45 40N 15 20 E
Metro, Indonesia 74 D3 5 5 S 105 20 E
Metropolis, U.S.A. 139 G10 37 9N 88 44W
Métsovon, Greece 44 E3 39 48N 21 12 E
Mettet, Belgium 21 H5 50 19N 4 41 E
Mettuppalaiyam, India 83 J3 11 18N 76 59 E
Mettur, India 83 J3 11 48N 77 47 E
Metz, France 23 C13 49 8N 6 10 E
Meulaboh, Indonesia 74 B1 4 11N 96 3 E
Meulan, France 23 C8 49 3N 1 55 E
Meung-sur-Loire, France 23 E8 47 50N 1 40 E
Meureudu, Indonesia 74 A1 5 19N 96 10 E
Meurthe →, France 23 D13 48 47N 6 9 E
Meurthe-et-Moselle □, France 23 D13 48 52N 6 0 E
Meuse □, France 23 C12 49 8N 5 25 E
Meuse →, Europe 21 G7 50 45N 5 41 E
Meuselwitz, Germany 26 D8 51 2N 12 17 E
Meutapok, Mt., Malaysia 75 A5 5 40N 117 0 E
Mexborough, U.K. 16 D6 53 30N 1 15W
Mexia, U.S.A. 139 K6 31 41N 96 29W
Mexiana, I., Brazil 154 A2 0 0 49 30W
Mexicali, Mexico 146 A1 32 40N 115 30W
Mexican Plateau, Mexico 124 G9 25 0N 104 0W
México, Mexico 147 D5 19 20N 99 10W
Mexico, Maine, U.S.A. 137 B14 44 34N 70 33W
Mexico, Mo., U.S.A. 140 E5 39 10N 91 53W
México □, Mexico 146 D5 19 20N 99 10W
Mexico ■, Cent. Amer. 146 C4 25 0N 105 0W
Mexico, G. of, Cent. Amer. 147 C7 25 0N 90 0W
Meyenburg, Germany 26 B8 53 18N 12 14 E
Meymac, France 24 C6 45 32N 2 10 E
Meymaneh, Afghan. 79 B2 35 53N 64 38 E
Meyrargues, France 25 E9 43 38N 5 32 E
Meyrueis, France 24 D7 44 12N 3 27 E
Meyssac, France 24 C5 45 3N 1 40 E
Mezdra, Bulgaria 43 D8 43 12N 23 42 E
Mèze, France 24 E7 43 27N 3 36 E
Mezen, Russia 48 A7 65 50N 44 20 E
Mezen →, Russia 48 A7 65 44N 44 22 E
Mézene, France 25 D8 44 54N 4 11 E
Mezeş, Munţii, Romania 46 B4 47 5N 23 5 E
Mezha →, Russia 50 E6 55 44N 31 33 E
Mézidon, France 22 C6 49 5N 0 1W
Mézilhac, France 25 D8 44 49N 4 21 E
Mézin, France 24 D4 44 4N 0 16 E
Mezöberény, Hungary 31 E14 46 49N 21 3 E
Mezöfalva, Hungary 31 E11 46 55N 18 49 E
Mezöhegyes, Hungary 31 E13 46 19N 20 49 E
Mezökovácsháza, Hungary 31 E13 46 25N 20 57 E
Mezökövesd, Hungary 31 D13 47 49N 20 35 E
Mézos, France 24 D2 44 5N 1 10W
Mezötúr, Hungary 31 E13 46 58N 20 41 E
Mezquital, Mexico 146 C4 23 29N 104 23W
Mezzolombardo, Italy 38 B8 46 13N 11 5 E
Mgeta, Tanzania 107 D4 8 22 S 36 6 E
Mglin, Russia 51 F7 53 2N 32 50 E
Mhlaba Hills, Zimbabwe 107 F3 18 30 S 30 30 E
Mhow, India 80 H6 22 33N 75 50 E
Mi-Shima, Japan 62 C3 34 46N 131 9 E
Miahuatlán, Mexico 147 D5 16 21N 96 36W
Miajadas, Spain 37 F5 39 9N 5 54W
Miallo, Australia 114 B4 16 28 S 145 22 E
Miami, Ariz., U.S.A. 143 K8 33 24N 110 52W
Miami, Fla., U.S.A. 135 N5 25 47N 80 11W
Miami, Tex., U.S.A. 139 H4 35 42N 100 38W
Miami →, U.S.A. 134 F3 39 20N 84 40W
Miami Beach, U.S.A. 135 N5 25 49N 80 8W
Miamisburg, U.S.A. 141 E12 39 38N 84 17W
Mian Xian, China 66 H4 33 10N 106 32 E
Mianchi, China 66 G6 34 48N 111 48 E
Mīāndowāb, Iran 89 D12 37 0N 46 5 E
Miandrivazo, Madag. 105 B8 19 31 S 45 29 E
Mīāneh, Iran 89 D12 37 30N 47 40 E
Mianning, China 68 C4 28 32N 102 9 E
Mianwali, Pakistan 79 B3 32 38N 71 28 E
Mianyang, Hubei, China 69 B9 30 25N 113 25 E
Mianyang, Sichuan, China 68 B5 31 22N 104 47 E
Mianzhu, China 68 B5 31 22N 104 7 E
Miaoli, Taiwan 69 E13 24 37N 120 49 E
Miarinarivo, Madag. 105 B8 18 57 S 46 55 E
Miass, Russia 54 D8 54 59N 60 6 E
Miasteczko Kraj, Poland 47 B4 53 7N 17 1 E
Miastko, Poland 47 B3 54 0N 16 58 E
Micăsasa, Romania 46 C5 46 7N 24 7 E
Michael, Mt., Papua N. G. 120 D3 6 27 S 145 22 E
Michalovce, Slovak Rep. 31 C14 48 47N 21 58 E
Michelstadt, Germany 27 F5 49 40N 8 2 E
Michigan □, U.S.A. 134 C3 44 0N 85 0W
Michigan, L., U.S.A. 134 C2 44 0N 87 0W
Michigan Center, U.S.A. 141 B12 42 14N 84 20W
Michigan City, U.S.A. 141 C10 41 43N 86 54W
Michikamau L., Canada 129 B7 54 20N 63 10W
Michipicoten, Canada 128 C3 47 55N 84 55W
Michipicoten I., Canada 128 C2 47 40N 85 40W
Michoacan □, Mexico 146 D4 19 0N 102 0W
Michurin, Bulgaria 43 E12 42 9N 27 51 E
Michurinsk, Russia 52 D5 52 58N 40 27 E
Miclere, Australia 114 C4 22 34 S 147 32 E
Mico, Pta., Nic. 148 D3 12 0N 83 30W
Micronesia, Federated States of ■, Pac. Oc. 122 G7 9 0N 150 0 E
Mid-Indian Ridge, Ind. Oc. 109 H6 30 0 S 75 0 E
Midai, P., Indonesia 75 B3 3 0N 107 47 E
Midale, Canada 131 D8 49 25N 103 20W
Middagsfjället, Sweden 14 A6 63 27N 12 19 E
Middelbeers, Neths. 21 F6 51 28N 5 15 E
Middelburg, Neths. 21 F3 51 30N 3 36 E
Middelburg, Eastern Cape, S. Africa 104 E3 31 30 S 25 0 E
Middelburg, Mpumalanga, S. Africa 105 D4 25 49 S 29 28 E
Middelfart, Denmark 15 J3 55 30N 9 43 E
Middelharnis, Neths. 20 E4 51 46N 4 10 E
Middelkerke, Belgium 21 F1 51 11N 2 49 E
Middelrode, Neths. 21 E6 51 41N 5 26 E
Middelwit, S. Africa 104 C4 24 51 S 27 3 E
Middle →, U.S.A. 140 C3 41 26N 93 30W
Middle Alkali L., U.S.A. 142 F3 41 27N 120 5W
Middle Fork Feather →, U.S.A. 144 F5 38 33N 121 30W
Middle I., Australia 113 F3 34 6 S 123 11 E
Middle Loup →, U.S.A. 138 E5 41 17N 98 24W
Middle Raccoon →, U.S.A. 140 C3 41 35N 93 35W
Middleboro, U.S.A. 137 E14 41 54N 70 55W
Middleburg, N.Y., U.S.A. 137 D10 42 36N 74 20W
Middleburg, Pa., U.S.A. 136 F7 40 47N 77 3W
Middlebury, Ind., U.S.A. 141 C11 41 41N 85 42W
Middlebury, Vt., U.S.A. 137 B11 44 1N 73 10W
Middlemarch, N.Z. 119 F5 45 30 S 170 9 E
Middleport, U.S.A. 134 F4 39 0N 82 3W
Middlesboro, U.S.A. 135 G4 36 36N 83 43W
Middlesbrough, U.K. 16 C6 54 35N 1 13W
Middlesbrough □, U.K. 16 C6 54 28N 1 13W
Middlesex, Belize 148 C2 17 2N 88 31W
Middlesex, U.S.A. 137 F10 40 36N 74 30W
Middleton, Australia 114 C3 22 22 S 141 32 E
Middleton, Canada 129 D6 44 57N 65 4W
Middleton, U.S.A. 140 A7 43 6N 89 30W
Middletown, Calif., U.S.A. 144 G4 38 45N 122 37W
Middletown, Conn., U.S.A. 137 E12 41 34N 72 39W
Middletown, N.Y., U.S.A. 137 E10 41 27N 74 25W
Middletown, Ohio, U.S.A. 141 E12 39 31N 84 24W
Middletown, Pa., U.S.A. 137 F8 40 12N 76 44W
Middleville, U.S.A. 141 B11 42 43N 85 28W
Midelt, Morocco 98 B4 32 46N 4 44W
Midhirst, N.Z. 118 F3 39 17 S 174 18 E
Midi, Canal du →, France 24 E5 43 45N 1 21 E
Midi d'Ossau, Pic du, France 24 F3 42 50N 0 26W
Midland, Canada 128 D4 44 45N 79 50W
Midland, Calif., U.S.A. 145 M12 33 52N 114 48W
Midland, Mich., U.S.A. 134 D3 43 37N 84 14W
Midland, Pa., U.S.A. 136 F4 40 39N 80 27W
Midland, Tex., U.S.A. 139 K3 32 0N 102 3W
Midlands □, Zimbabwe 107 F2 19 40 S 29 0 E
Midleton, Ireland 19 E3 51 55N 8 10W
Midlothian, U.S.A. 139 J6 32 30N 97 0W
Midlothian □, U.K. 18 F5 55 51N 3 5W
Midongy, Tangorombohitr' i, Madag. 105 C8 23 30 S 47 0 E
Midongy Atsimo, Madag. 105 C8 23 35 S 47 1 E
Midou →, France 24 E3 43 54N 0 30W
Midouze →, France 24 E3 43 48N 0 51W
Midsayap, Phil. 71 H5 7 12N 124 32 E
Midu, China 68 E3 25 18N 100 30 E
Midway Is., Pac. Oc. 122 E10 28 13N 177 22W
Midway Wells, U.S.A. 145 N11 32 41N 115 7W
Midwest, U.S.A. 133 B9 42 0N 90 0W
Midwest, Wyo., U.S.A. 142 E10 43 25N 106 16W
Midwest City, U.S.A. 139 H6 35 27N 97 24W
Midwolda, Neths. 20 B9 53 12N 6 52 E
Midyat, Turkey 89 D9 37 25N 41 23 E
Midzŏr, Bulgaria 42 D7 43 24N 22 40 E
Mie □, Japan 63 C8 34 30N 136 10 E
Miechów, Poland 47 E7 50 21N 20 5 E
Miedwie, Jezioro, Poland 47 B1 53 17N 14 54 E
Międzybód, Poland 47 D4 51 25N 17 34 E
Międzychód, Poland 47 C2 52 35N 15 53 E
Międzylesie, Poland 47 E3 50 8N 16 40 E
Międzyrzec Podlaski, Poland 47 D9 51 58N 22 45 E
Międzyrzecz, Poland 47 C2 52 26N 15 35 E
Międzyzdroje, Poland 47 B1 53 56N 14 26 E
Miejska, Poland 47 D3 51 39N 16 58 E
Miélan, France 24 E4 43 27N 0 19 E
Mielec, Poland 47 E8 50 15N 21 25 E
Mienga, Angola 103 F3 17 12 S 19 48 E
Miercurea Ciuc, Romania 46 C6 46 21N 25 48 E
Mieres, Spain 36 B5 43 18N 5 48W
Mierlo, Neths. 21 F7 51 27N 5 37 E
Mieroszów, Poland 47 E3 50 40N 16 11 E
Mieso, Ethiopia 95 F5 9 15N 40 43 E
Mieszkowice, Poland 47 C1 52 47N 14 30 E
Mifflintown, U.S.A. 136 F7 40 34N 77 24W
Mifraz Ḥefa, Israel 91 C4 32 52N 35 0 E
Migdāl, Israel 91 C4 32 51N 35 30 E
Migennes, France 23 E10 47 58N 3 31 E
Migliarino, Italy 39 D8 44 46N 11 56 E
Miguel Alemán, Presa, Mexico 147 D5 18 15N 96 40W
Miguel Alves, Brazil 154 B3 4 11 S 42 55W
Miguel Calmon, Brazil 154 D3 11 26 S 40 36W
Mihaliççik, Turkey 88 C4 39 53N 31 30 E
Mihara, Japan 62 C5 34 24N 133 5 E
Mihara-Yama, Japan 63 C11 34 43N 139 23 E
Mijares →, Spain 34 F4 39 55N 0 1W
Mijas, Spain 37 J6 36 36N 4 40W
Mikese, Tanzania 106 D4 6 48 S 37 55 E
Mikha-Tskhakaya = Senaki, Georgia 53 J6 42 15N 42 7 E
Mikhailovka = Mykhaylivka, Ukraine 51 J8 47 12N 35 15 E
Mikhaylov, Russia 52 C4 54 14N 39 0 E
Mikhaylovgrad, Bulgaria 43 D8 43 27N 23 16 E
Mikhaylovka, Russia 52 E6 50 3N 43 5 E
Mikhaylovski, Russia 54 C7 56 27N 59 7 E
Mikhnevo, Russia 52 C3 55 4N 37 59 E
Miki, Hyōgo, Japan 62 C6 34 48N 134 59 E
Miki, Kagawa, Japan 62 C6 34 12N 134 7 E
Mikínai, Greece 45 G4 37 43N 22 46 E
Mikkeli, Finland 13 F22 61 43N 27 15 E
Mikkwa →, Canada 130 B6 58 25N 114 46W
Mikniya, Sudan 95 D3 17 0N 33 45 E
Mikołajki, Poland 47 B8 53 49N 21 37 E
Mikołów, Poland 31 A11 50 10N 18 50 E
Míkonos, Greece 45 G7 37 30N 25 25 E
Mikrí Préspa, Límni, Greece 44 D3 40 47N 21 3 E
Mikrón Dhérion, Greece 44 C8 41 19N 26 6 E
Mikstat, Poland 47 D4 51 32N 17 59 E
Mikulov, Czech. 31 C9 48 48N 16 39 E
Mikumi, Tanzania 106 D4 7 26 S 37 0 E
Mikun, Russia 48 B9 62 20N 50 0 E
Mikuni, Japan 63 A8 36 13N 136 9 E
Mikuni-Tōge, Japan 63 A10 36 50N 138 50 E
Mikura-Jima, Japan 63 D11 33 52N 139 36 E
Milaca, U.S.A. 138 C8 45 45N 93 39W
Milagro, Ecuador 152 D2 2 11 S 79 36W
Milagros, Phil. 70 E4 12 13N 123 30 E
Milan = Milano, Italy 38 C6 45 28N 9 12 E
Milan, Ill., U.S.A. 140 C6 41 27N 90 34W
Milan, Mich., U.S.A. 141 B13 42 5N 83 41W
Milan, Mo., U.S.A. 140 D3 40 12N 93 7W
Milan, Tenn., U.S.A. 135 H1 35 55N 88 46W
Milang, S. Austral., Australia 115 E2 32 2 S 139 10 E
Milang, S. Austral., Australia 116 C3 35 24 S 138 58 E
Milange, Mozam. 107 F4 16 3 S 35 45 E
Milano, Italy 38 C6 45 28N 9 12 E
Milâs, Turkey 88 D2 37 20N 27 50 E
Milàtos, Greece 32 D7 35 18N 25 34 E
Milazzo, Italy 41 D8 38 13N 15 15 E
Milbank, U.S.A. 138 C6 45 13N 96 38W
Milden, Canada 131 C7 51 29N 107 32W
Mildmay, Canada 136 B3 44 3N 81 7W
Mildura, Australia 116 C5 34 13 S 142 9 E
Mile, China 68 E4 24 28N 103 20 E
Miléai, Greece 44 E5 39 20N 23 9 E
Miles, Australia 115 D5 26 40 S 150 9 E
Miles, U.S.A. 139 K4 31 36N 100 11W
Miles City, U.S.A. 138 B2 46 25N 105 51W
Milestone, Canada 131 D8 49 59N 104 31W
Mileto, Italy 41 D9 38 36N 16 4 E
Miletto, Mte., Italy 41 A7 41 27N 14 22 E
Miletus, Turkey 88 D2 37 30N 27 18 E
Mileura, Australia 113 E2 26 22 S 117 20 E
Milevsko, Czech. 30 B7 49 27N 14 21 E
Milford, Calif., U.S.A. 144 E6 40 10N 120 22W
Milford, Conn., U.S.A. 137 E11 41 14N 73 3W
Milford, Del., U.S.A. 134 F8 38 55N 75 26W
Milford, Ill., U.S.A. 141 D9 40 38N 87 42W
Milford, Mass., U.S.A. 137 D13 42 8N 71 31W
Milford, Mich., U.S.A. 141 B13 42 35N 83 36W
Milford, Pa., U.S.A. 137 E10 41 19N 74 48W
Milford, Utah, U.S.A. 143 G7 38 24N 113 1W
Milford Haven, U.K. 17 F2 51 40N 5 7W
Milford Sd., N.Z. 119 E2 44 41 S 167 47 E
Milgun, Australia 113 D2 24 56 S 118 18 E
Milḥ, Baḥr al, Iraq 89 F10 32 40N 43 35 E
Miliana, Aïn Salah, Algeria 99 C5 27 20N 2 32 E
Miliana, Médéa, Algeria 99 A5 36 20N 2 15 E
Milicz, Poland 47 D4 51 31N 17 19 E
Miling, Australia 113 F2 30 30 S 116 17 E
Militello in Val di Catánia, Italy 41 E7 37 16N 14 48 E
Milk →, U.S.A. 142 B10 48 4N 106 19W
Milk, Wadi el →, Sudan 94 D3 17 55N 30 20 E
Milk River, Canada 130 D6 49 10N 112 5W
Mill, Neths. 21 E7 51 41N 5 48 E
Mill City, U.S.A. 142 D2 44 45N 122 29W
Mill I., Antarctica 7 C8 66 0 S 101 30 E
Mill Shoals, U.S.A. 141 F8 38 15N 88 21W
Mill Valley, U.S.A. 144 H4 37 54N 122 32W
Millau, France 24 D7 44 8N 3 4 E
Millbridge, Canada 136 B7 44 41N 77 36W
Millbrook, Canada 136 B6 44 10N 78 29W
Mille Lacs, L. des, Canada 128 C1 48 45N 90 35W
Mille Lacs L., U.S.A. 138 B8 46 15N 93 39W
Milledgeville, Ga., U.S.A. 135 J4 33 5N 83 14W
Milledgeville, Ill., U.S.A. 140 C7 41 58N 89 46W
Millen, U.S.A. 135 J5 32 48N 81 57W
Miller, U.S.A. 138 C5 44 31N 98 59W
Millerovo, Russia 53 F5 48 57N 40 28 E
Miller's Flat, N.Z. 119 F4 45 39 S 169 23 E
Millersburg, Ind., U.S.A. 141 C11 41 32N 85 42W
Millersburg, Ohio, U.S.A. 136 F3 40 33N 81 55W
Millersburg, Pa., U.S.A. 136 F8 40 32N 76 58W
Millerton, N.Z. 119 B6 41 39 S 171 54 E
Millerton, U.S.A. 137 E11 41 57N 73 31W
Millerton L., U.S.A. 144 J7 37 1N 119 41W
Millevaches, Plateau de, France 24 C6 45 45N 2 0 E
Millicent, Australia 116 D4 37 34 S 140 21 E
Millingen, Neths. 20 E8 51 52N 6 2 E
Millinocket, U.S.A. 129 C6 45 39N 68 43W
Millmerran, Australia 115 D5 27 53 S 151 16 E
Mills L., Canada 130 A5 61 30N 118 20W
Millsboro, U.S.A. 136 G4 40 0N 80 0W
Milltown Malbay, Ireland 19 D2 52 52N 9 24W
Millville, U.S.A. 134 F8 39 24N 75 2W
Millwood L., U.S.A. 139 J8 33 42N 93 58W
Milly-la-Forêt, France 23 D9 48 24N 2 28 E
Milna, Croatia 39 E13 43 20N 16 28 E
Milne →, Australia 114 C2 21 10 S 137 33 E
Milne Inlet, Canada 127 A11 72 30N 80 0W
Milnor, U.S.A. 138 B6 46 16N 97 27W
Milo, Canada 130 C6 50 34N 112 53W
Mílos, Greece 45 H6 36 44N 24 25 E
Miloševo, Serbia, Yug. 42 B5 45 42N 20 20 E
Miłosław, Poland 47 C4 52 12N 17 32 E
Milparinka P.O., Australia 115 D3 29 46 S 141 57 E
Milroy, U.S.A. 141 E11 39 30N 85 28W
Miltenberg, Germany 27 F5 49 41N 10 16 E
Milton, Canada 136 C5 43 31N 79 53W
Milton, N.Z. 119 G4 46 7 S 169 59 E
Milton, U.K. 18 D4 57 18N 4 32W
Milton, Calif., U.S.A. 144 G6 38 3N 120 51W
Milton, Fla., U.S.A. 135 K2 30 38N 87 3W
Milton, Iowa, U.S.A. 140 D4 40 41N 92 10W
Milton, Pa., U.S.A. 136 F8 41 1N 76 51W
Milton, Wis., U.S.A. 141 B8 42 47N 88 56W
Milton-Freewater, U.S.A. 142 D4 45 56N 118 23W
Milton Keynes, U.K. 17 E7 52 1N 0 44W
Miltou, Chad 97 F3 10 14N 17 26 E
Milverton, Canada 136 C4 43 34N 80 55W
Milwaukee, U.S.A. 141 A9 43 2N 87 55W
Milwaukee Deep, Atl. Oc. 8 G2 19 50N 68 0W
Milwaukie, U.S.A. 144 E4 45 27N 122 38W
Mim, Ghana 100 D4 6 57N 2 33W
Mimizan, France 24 D2 44 12N 1 13W
Mimon, Czech. 30 A7 50 38N 14 43 E
Mimongo, Gabon 102 C2 1 11 S 11 36 E
Mimoso, Brazil 155 E2 15 10 S 48 5W
Min Chiang →, China 69 E12 26 0N 119 35 E
Min Jiang →, China 68 C5 28 45N 104 40 E
Min-Kush, Kyrgyzstan 55 C7 41 40N 74 28 E
Min Xian, China 66 G3 34 25N 104 5 E
Mina, U.S.A. 143 G4 38 24N 118 7W
Mina Pirquitas, Argentina 158 A2 22 40 S 66 30W
Mīnā Su'ud, Si. Arabia 85 D6 28 45N 48 28 E
Mīnā'al Aḥmadī, Kuwait 85 D6 29 5N 48 10 E
Mīnāb, Iran 85 E8 27 10N 57 1 E
Minago →, Canada 131 C9 54 33N 98 59W
Minakami, Japan 63 A10 36 49N 138 59 E
Minaki, Canada 131 D10 49 59N 94 40W
Minakuchi, Japan 63 C8 34 58N 136 10 E
Minamata, Japan 62 E2 32 10N 130 30 E
Minami-Tori-Shima, Pac. Oc. 122 E7 24 0N 153 45 E
Minas, Uruguay 159 C4 34 20 S 55 10W
Minas, Sierra de las, Guatemala 148 C2 15 9N 89 31W
Minas Basin, Canada 129 C7 45 20N 64 12W
Minas de Rio Tinto, Spain 37 H4 37 42N 6 35W
Minas de San Quintín, Spain 37 G6 38 50N 4 23W
Minas Gerais □, Brazil 155 E2 18 50 S 46 0W
Minas Novas, Brazil 155 E3 17 15 S 42 36W
Minatitlán, Mexico 147 D6 17 59N 94 31W
Minbu, Burma 78 E5 20 10N 94 52 E
Minbya, Burma 78 E4 20 22N 93 16 E
Mincio →, Italy 38 C7 45 4N 10 59 E
Mindanao, Phil. 71 H5 8 0N 125 0 E

234 Mindanao Sea

Mindanao Sea = Bohol Sea, Phil. **71 G5** 9 0N 124 0 E
Mindanao Trench, Pac. Oc. **70 E5** 12 0N 126 6 E
Mindel →, Germany **27 G6** 48 31N 10 23 E
Mindelheim, Germany **27 G6** 48 2N 10 29 E
Minden, Canada **136 B6** 44 55N 78 43W
Minden, Germany **26 C4** 52 17N 8 55 E
Minden, La., U.S.A. **139 J8** 32 37N 93 17W
Minden, Nev., U.S.A. **144 G7** 38 57N 119 46W
Mindiptana, Indonesia **73 C6** 5 55 S 140 22 E
Mindon, Burma **78 F5** 19 21N 94 44 E
Mindoro, Phil. **70 E3** 13 0N 121 0 E
Mindoro Occidental □, Phil. **70 E3** 13 0N 120 55 E
Mindoro Oriental □, Phil. **70 E3** 13 0N 121 5 E
Mindoro Str., Phil. **70 E3** 12 30N 120 30 E
Mindouli, Congo **103 C2** 4 12 S 14 28 E
Mine, Japan **62 C3** 34 12N 131 7 E
Minehead, U.K. **17 F4** 51 12N 3 29W
Mineiros, Brazil **157 D7** 17 34 S 52 34W
Mineola, U.S.A. **139 J7** 32 40N 95 29W
Mineral King, U.S.A. **144 J8** 36 27N 118 36W
Mineral Point, U.S.A. **140 B6** 42 52N 90 11W
Mineral Wells, U.S.A. **139 J5** 32 48N 98 7W
Mineralnyye Vody, Russia **53 H6** 44 15N 43 8 E
Minersville, Pa., U.S.A. **137 F8** 40 41N 76 16W
Minersville, Utah, U.S.A. **143 G7** 38 13N 112 56W
Minerva, U.S.A. **136 F3** 40 44N 81 6W
Minervino Murge, Italy **41 A9** 41 5N 16 5 E
Minetto, U.S.A. **137 C8** 43 24N 76 28W
Mingäçevir, Azerbaijan **53 K8** 40 45N 47 0 E
Mingäçevir Su Anbarı, Azerbaijan **53 K8** 40 57N 46 50 E
Mingan, Canada **129 B7** 50 20N 64 0W
Mingary, Australia **116 B4** 32 8 S 140 45 E
Mingechaur = Mingäçevir, Azerbaijan **53 K8** 40 45N 47 0 E
Mingechaurskoye Vdkhr. = Mingäçevir Su Anbarı, Azerbaijan **53 K8** 40 57N 46 50 E
Mingela, Australia **114 B4** 19 52 S 146 38 E
Mingenew, Australia **113 E2** 29 12 S 115 21 E
Mingera Cr. →, Australia **114 C2** 20 38 S 137 45 E
Minggang, China **69 A10** 32 24N 114 3 E
Mingin, Burma **78 D5** 22 50N 94 30 E
Minglanilla, Spain **34 F3** 39 34N 1 38W
Minglun, China **68 E7** 25 10N 108 21 E
Mingorria, Spain **36 E6** 40 45N 4 40W
Mingt'iehkaitafan = Mintaka Pass, Pakistan **81 A6** 37 0N 74 58 E
Mingxi, China **69 D11** 26 18N 117 12 E
Mingyuegue, China **67 C15** 43 2N 128 50 E
Minho = Miño →, Spain **36 D2** 41 52N 8 40W
Minhou, China **69 E12** 26 0N 119 15 E
Minićevo, Serbia, Yug. **42 D7** 43 42N 22 18 E
Minidoka, U.S.A. **142 E7** 42 45N 113 29W
Minier, U.S.A. **140 D7** 40 26N 89 19W
Minigwal, L., Australia **113 E3** 29 31 S 123 14 E
Minilya, Australia **113 D1** 23 55 S 114 0 E
Minilya →, Australia **113 D1** 23 45 S 114 0 E
Mininera, Australia **116 D5** 37 37 S 142 58 E
Minipi, L., Canada **129 B7** 52 25N 60 45W
Minj, Papua N. G. **120 C3** 5 54 S 144 37 E
Mink L., Canada **130 A5** 61 54N 117 40W
Minlaton, Australia **116 C2** 34 45 S 137 35 E
Minna, Nigeria **101 D6** 9 37N 6 30 E
Minneapolis, Kans., U.S.A. **138 F6** 39 8N 97 42W
Minneapolis, Minn., U.S.A. **138 C8** 44 59N 93 16W
Minnedosa, Canada **131 C9** 50 14N 99 50W
Minnesota □, U.S.A. **138 B7** 46 0N 94 15W
Minnesund, Norway **14 D5** 60 23N 11 14 E
Minnie Creek, Australia **113 D2** 24 3 S 115 42 E
Minnipa, Australia **115 E2** 32 51 S 135 9 E
Minnitaki L., Canada **128 C1** 49 57N 92 10W
Mino, Japan **63 B8** 35 32N 136 55 E
Miño →, Spain **36 D2** 41 52N 8 40W
Mino-Kamo, Japan **63 B9** 35 23N 137 2 E
Mino-Mikawa-Kōgen, Japan **63 B9** 35 10N 137 23 E
Minoa, Greece **45 J7** 35 6N 25 45 E
Minobu, Japan **63 B10** 35 22N 138 26 E
Minobu-Sanchi, Japan **63 B10** 35 14N 138 20 E
Minonk, U.S.A. **140 D7** 40 54N 89 2W
Minooka, U.S.A. **141 C8** 41 27N 88 16W
Minorca = Menorca, Spain **33 B11** 40 0N 4 0 E
Minore, Australia **117 B8** 32 14 S 148 27 E
Minot, U.S.A. **138 A4** 48 14N 101 18W
Minqin, China **66 E2** 38 38N 103 20 E
Minqing, China **69 D12** 26 15N 118 50 E
Minsen, Germany **26 B3** 53 41N 7 58 E
Minsk, Belarus **50 F4** 53 52N 27 30 E
Mińsk Mazowiecki, Poland **47 C8** 52 10N 21 33 E
Minster, U.S.A. **141 D12** 40 24N 84 23W
Mintaka Pass, Pakistan **81 A6** 37 0N 74 58 E
Minthami, Burma **78 D5** 23 55N 94 16 E
Minto, U.S.A. **126 B5** 64 53N 149 11W
Minton, Canada **131 D8** 49 10N 104 35W
Mintoum, Gabon **102 B2** 0 27N 12 16 E
Minturn, U.S.A. **142 G10** 39 35N 106 26W
Minturno, Italy **40 A6** 41 15N 13 45 E
Minûf, Egypt **94 H7** 30 26N 30 52 E
Minusinsk, Russia **57 D10** 53 50N 91 20 E
Minutang, India **78 A6** 28 15N 96 30 E
Minvoul, Gabon **102 B2** 2 9N 12 8 E
Minwakh, Yemen **87 C5** 16 48N 48 6 E
Minya el Qamh, Egypt **94 H7** 30 31N 31 21 E
Minyar, Russia **54 D6** 55 4N 57 33 E
Minyip, Australia **116 D5** 36 29 S 142 36 E
Mionica, Serbia, Yug. **42 C5** 44 14N 20 6 E
Mir, Niger **97 F2** 14 5N 11 59 E
Mīr Kūh, Iran **85 E8** 26 22N 58 55 E
Mīr Shahdād, Iran **85 E8** 26 15N 58 29 E
Mira, Italy **39 C9** 45 26N 12 8 E
Mira, Portugal **36 E2** 40 26N 8 44W
Mira →, Colombia **152 C2** 1 36N 79 1W
Mira →, Portugal **37 H2** 37 43N 8 47W
Mira por vos Cay, Bahamas **149 B5** 22 9N 74 30W
Mīrābād, Afghan. **79 C1** 30 25N 61 50 E
Mirabella Eclano, Italy **41 A7** 41 2N 14 59 E
Miracema do Norte, Brazil **154 C2** 9 33 S 48 24W
Mirador, Brazil **154 C3** 6 22 S 44 22W
Miraflores, Colombia **152 C3** 1 25N 72 13W
Miraj, India **82 F2** 16 50N 74 45 E
Miram Shah, Pakistan **79 B3** 33 0N 70 2 E
Miramar, Argentina **158 D4** 38 15 S 57 50W
Miramar, Mozam. **105 C6** 23 50 S 35 35 E
Miramas, France **25 E8** 43 33N 4 59 E
Mirambeau, France **24 C3** 45 23N 0 35W
Miramichi B., Canada **129 C7** 47 15N 65 0W
Miramont-de-Guyenne, France **24 D4** 44 37N 0 21 E
Miranda, Brazil **157 E6** 20 10 S 56 15W
Miranda □, Venezuela **152 A4** 10 15N 66 25W
Miranda →, Brazil **157 D6** 19 25 S 57 20W
Miranda de Ebro, Spain **34 C2** 42 41N 2 57W
Miranda do Corvo, Spain **36 E2** 40 6N 8 20W
Miranda do Douro, Portugal **36 D4** 41 30N 6 16W
Mirande, France **24 E4** 43 31N 0 25 E
Mirandela, Portugal **36 D3** 41 32N 7 10W
Mirando City, U.S.A. **139 M5** 27 26N 99 0W
Mirándola, Italy **38 D8** 44 53N 11 4 E
Mirandópolis, Brazil **159 A5** 21 9 S 51 6W
Mirango, Malawi **107 E3** 13 32 S 34 58 E
Mirani, Australia **114 C4** 21 9 S 148 53 E
Mirano, Italy **39 C9** 45 30N 12 7 E
Mirassol, Brazil **159 A6** 20 46 S 49 28W
Mirbāţ, Oman **87 C6** 17 0N 54 45 E
Mirboo North, Australia **117 E7** 38 24 S 146 10 E
Mirear, Egypt **94 C4** 23 15N 35 41 E
Mirebeau, Côte-d'Or, France **23 E12** 47 25N 5 20 E
Mirebeau, Vienne, France **22 F7** 46 49N 0 10 E
Mirecourt, France **23 D13** 48 20N 6 10 E
Mirgorod = Myrhorod, Ukraine **51 H7** 49 58N 33 37 E
Miri, Malaysia **75 B4** 4 23N 113 59 E
Miriam Vale, Australia **114 C5** 24 20 S 151 33 E
Mirim, L., S. Amer. **159 C5** 32 45 S 52 50W
Mirimire, Venezuela **152 A4** 11 10N 68 43W
Miriti, Brazil **157 B6** 6 15 S 59 0W
Mirnyy, Russia **57 C12** 62 33N 113 53 E
Miroč, Serbia, Yug. **42 C7** 44 32N 22 16 E
Mirond L., Canada **131 B8** 55 6N 102 47W
Mirosławiec, Poland **47 B3** 53 20N 16 5 E
Mirpur, Pakistan **79 B4** 33 32N 73 56 E
Mirpur Bibiwari, Pakistan **80 E2** 28 33N 67 44 E
Mirpur Khas, Pakistan **79 D3** 25 30N 69 0 E
Mirpur Sakro, Pakistan **80 G2** 24 33N 67 41 E
Mirria, Niger **97 F1** 13 43N 9 7 E
Mirror, Canada **130 C6** 52 30N 113 7W
Mîrşani, Romania **46 E4** 44 1N 23 59 E
Mirsk, Poland **47 E2** 50 58N 15 23 E
Miryang, S. Korea **67 G15** 35 31N 128 44 E
Mirzaani, Georgia **53 K8** 41 24N 46 5 E
Mirzapur, India **81 G10** 25 10N 82 34 E
Mirzapur-cum-Vindhyachal = Mirzapur, India **81 G10** 25 10N 82 34 E
Misamis Occidental □, Phil. **71 G4** 8 20N 123 42 E
Misamis Oriental □, Phil. **71 G5** 8 45N 125 0 E
Misantla, Mexico **147 D5** 19 56N 96 50W
Misawa, Japan **60 D10** 40 41N 141 24 E
Miscou I., Canada **129 C7** 47 57N 64 31W
Mish'āb, Ra'as al, Si. Arabia **85 D6** 28 15N 48 43 E
Mishagua →, Peru **156 C3** 11 12 S 72 58W
Mishan, China **65 B8** 45 37N 131 48 E
Mishawaka, U.S.A. **141 C10** 41 40N 86 11W
Mishbih, Gebel, Egypt **94 C3** 22 38N 34 44 E
Mishima, Japan **63 B10** 35 10N 138 52 E
Mishmi Hills, India **78 A5** 29 0N 96 0 E
Misilmeri, Italy **40 D6** 38 2N 13 27 E
Misima I., Papua N. G. **120 F7** 10 40 S 152 45 E
Misión, Mexico **145 N10** 32 6N 116 53W
Misión Fagnano, Argentina **160 D3** 54 32 S 67 17W
Misiones □, Argentina **159 B5** 27 0 S 55 0W
Misiones □, Paraguay **158 B4** 27 0 S 56 0W
Miskah, Si. Arabia **84 E4** 24 49N 42 56 E
Miskitos, Cayos, Nic. **148 D3** 14 26N 82 50W
Miskolc, Hungary **31 C13** 48 7N 20 50 E
Misoke, Zaïre **106 C2** 0 42 S 28 2 E
Misool, Indonesia **73 B4** 1 52 S 130 10 E
Misrātah, Libya **96 B3** 32 24N 15 3 E
Misrātah □, Libya **96 C3** 33 30N 15 0 E
Missanabie, Canada **128 C3** 48 20N 84 6W
Missão Velha, Brazil **154 C4** 7 15 S 39 10W
Missinaibi →, Canada **128 B3** 50 43N 81 29W
Missinaibi L., Canada **128 C3** 48 23N 83 40W
Mission, S. Dak., U.S.A. **138 D4** 43 18N 100 39W
Mission, Tex., U.S.A. **139 M5** 26 13N 98 20W
Mission City, Canada **130 D4** 49 10N 122 15W
Mission Viejo, U.S.A. **145 M9** 33 36N 117 40W
Missisa L., Canada **128 B2** 52 20N 85 7W
Missisagi →, Canada **128 C3** 46 15N 83 9W
Mississinewa Res., U.S.A. **141 D10** 40 46N 86 3W
Mississippi □, U.S.A. **139 J10** 33 0N 90 0W
Mississippi →, U.S.A. **139 L10** 29 9N 89 15W
Mississippi L., Canada **137 A8** 45 5N 76 10W
Mississippi River Delta, U.S.A. **139 L9** 29 10N 89 15W
Mississippi Sd., U.S.A. **139 K10** 30 20N 89 0W
Missoula, U.S.A. **142 C6** 46 52N 114 1W
Missour, Morocco **98 B4** 33 3N 4 0W
Missouri □, U.S.A. **138 F8** 38 25N 92 30W
Missouri →, U.S.A. **138 F9** 38 49N 90 7W
Missouri Valley, U.S.A. **138 E7** 41 34N 95 53W
Mist, U.S.A. **144 E3** 45 59N 123 15W
Mistake B., Canada **131 A10** 62 8N 93 0W
Mistassini →, Canada **129 C5** 48 42N 72 20W
Mistassini L., Canada **128 B5** 51 0N 73 30W
Mistastin L., Canada **129 A7** 55 57N 63 20W
Mistatim, Canada **131 C8** 52 52N 103 22W
Mistelbach, Austria **31 C9** 48 34N 16 34 E
Misterbianco, Italy **41 E8** 37 31N 15 0 E
Mistretta, Italy **41 E7** 37 56N 14 22 E
Misty L., Canada **131 B8** 58 53N 101 40W
Misugi, Japan **63 C8** 34 31N 136 16 E
Misumi, Japan **62 E2** 32 37N 130 27 E
Misurata = Misrātah, Libya **96 B3** 32 24N 15 3 E
Mît Ghamr, Egypt **94 H7** 30 42N 31 12 E
Mitaka, Japan **63 B11** 35 40N 139 33 E
Mitan, Uzbekistan **55 C3** 40 5N 66 35 E
Mitatib, Sudan **95 D4** 15 59N 36 12 E
Mitchell, Australia **115 D4** 26 29 S 147 58 E
Mitchell, Canada **136 C3** 43 28N 81 12W
Mitchell, Ind., U.S.A. **141 F10** 38 44N 86 28W
Mitchell, Nebr., U.S.A. **138 E3** 41 57N 103 49W
Mitchell, Oreg., U.S.A. **142 D3** 44 34N 120 9W
Mitchell, S. Dak., U.S.A. **138 D5** 43 43N 98 2W
Mitchell →, Australia **114 B3** 15 12 S 141 35 E
Mitchell, Mt., U.S.A. **135 H4** 35 46N 82 16W
Mitchell Ras., Australia **114 A2** 12 49 S 135 36 E
Mitchelstown, Ireland **19 D3** 52 15N 8 16W
Mitha Tiwana, Pakistan **80 C5** 32 13N 72 6 E
Míthimna, Greece **44 E8** 39 20N 26 12 E
Mitiamo, Australia **116 D6** 36 12 S 144 15 E
Mitilíni, Greece **45 E8** 39 6N 26 35 E
Mitilinoí, Greece **45 G8** 37 42N 26 56 E
Mito, Japan **63 A12** 36 20N 140 30 E
Mitre, Mt., N.Z. **118 G4** 40 50 S 175 30 E
Mitrofanovka, Russia **52 F4** 49 58N 39 42 E
Mitrovica = Titova-Mitrovica, Serbia, Yug. **42 E5** 42 54N 20 52 E
Mitsinjo, Madag. **105 B8** 16 1 S 45 52 E
Mitsiwa, Eritrea **95 D4** 15 35N 39 25 E
Mitsiwa Channel, Eritrea **95 D5** 15 30N 40 0 E
Mitsukaidō, Japan **63 A11** 36 1N 139 59 E
Mittagong, Australia **117 C9** 34 28 S 150 29 E
Mittelland, Switz. **28 C4** 46 50N 7 23 E
Mittellandkanal →, Germany **26 C3** 52 20N 8 28 E
Mittenwalde, Germany **26 C9** 52 15N 13 31 E
Mitterteich, Germany **27 F8** 49 57N 12 14 E
Mittweida, Germany **26 E8** 50 59N 12 59 E
Mitú, Colombia **152 C3** 1 8N 70 3W
Mituas, Colombia **152 C4** 3 52N 68 49W
Mitumba, Tanzania **106 D3** 7 8 S 31 2 E
Mitumba, Chaîne des, Zaïre **106 D2** 7 0 S 27 30 E
Mitumba Mts. = Mitumba, Chaîne des, Zaïre **106 D2** 7 0 S 27 30 E
Mitwaba, Zaïre **107 D2** 8 2 S 27 17 E
Mityana, Uganda **106 B3** 0 23N 32 2 E
Mitzic, Gabon **102 B2** 0 45N 11 40 E
Miura, Japan **63 B11** 35 12N 139 40 E
Mixteco →, Mexico **147 D5** 18 11N 98 30W
Miyagi □, Japan **60 E10** 38 15N 140 45 E
Miyâh, W. el →, Egypt **94 B3** 25 0N 33 23 E
Miyah, W. el →, Syria **84 C3** 34 44N 39 57 E
Miyake-Jima, Japan **63 C11** 34 5N 139 30 E
Miyako, Japan **60 E10** 39 40N 141 59 E
Miyako-Jima, Japan **61 M2** 24 45N 125 20 E
Miyako-Rettō, Japan **61 M2** 24 24N 125 0 E
Miyakonojō, Japan **62 F3** 31 40N 131 5 E
Miyanojō, Japan **62 F2** 31 54N 130 27 E
Miyanoura-Dake, Japan **61 J5** 30 20N 130 31 E
Miyata, Japan **62 D2** 33 49N 130 42 E
Miyazaki, Japan **62 F3** 31 56N 131 30 E
Miyazaki □, Japan **62 E3** 32 30N 131 30 E
Miyazu, Japan **63 B7** 35 35N 135 10 E
Miyet, Bahr el = Dead Sea, Asia **91 D4** 31 30N 35 30 E
Miyi, China **68 D4** 26 47N 102 9 E
Miyoshi, Japan **62 C4** 34 48N 132 51 E
Miyun, China **66 D9** 40 28N 116 50 E
Miyun Shuiku, China **67 D9** 40 30N 117 0 E
Mizdah, Libya **96 B2** 31 30N 13 0 E
Mizen Hd., Cork, Ireland **19 E2** 51 27N 9 50W
Mizen Hd., Wick., Ireland **19 D5** 52 51N 6 4W
Mizhi, China **66 F6** 37 47N 110 12 E
Mizil, Romania **46 E7** 44 59N 26 29 E
Mizoram □, India **78 D4** 23 30N 92 40 E
Mizpe Ramon, Israel **91 E3** 30 34N 34 49 E
Mizuho, Japan **63 B7** 35 6N 135 17 E
Mizunami, Japan **63 B9** 35 22N 137 15 E
Mizusawa, Japan **60 E10** 39 8N 141 8 E
Mjöbäck, Sweden **15 G6** 57 28N 12 53 E
Mjölby, Sweden **15 F9** 58 20N 15 10 E
Mjörn, Sweden **15 G6** 57 55N 12 25 E
Mjøsa, Norway **14 D5** 60 40N 11 0 E
Mkata, Tanzania **106 D4** 5 45 S 38 20 E
Mkokotoni, Tanzania **106 D4** 5 55 S 39 15 E
Mkomazi, Tanzania **106 C4** 4 40 S 38 7 E
Mkomazi →, S. Africa **105 E5** 30 12 S 30 50 E
Mkulwe, Tanzania **107 D3** 8 37 S 32 20 E
Mkumbi, Ras, Tanzania **106 D4** 7 38 S 39 55 E
Mkushi, Zambia **107 E2** 14 25 S 29 15 E
Mkushi River, Zambia **107 E2** 13 32 S 29 45 E
Mkuze, S. Africa **105 D5** 27 10 S 32 0 E
Mladá Boleslav, Czech. **30 A7** 50 27N 14 53 E
Mladenovac, Serbia, Yug. **42 C5** 44 28N 20 44 E
Mlala Hills, Tanzania **106 D3** 6 50 S 31 40 E
Mlange, Malawi **107 F4** 16 2 S 35 33 E
Mlava →, Serbia, Yug. **42 C6** 44 45N 21 13 E
Mława, Poland **47 B7** 53 9N 20 25 E
Mlinište, Bos.-H. **39 D13** 44 15N 16 50 E
Mljet, Croatia **42 E2** 42 43N 17 30 E
Mljetski Kanal, Croatia **42 E2** 42 48N 17 35 E
Młynary, Poland **47 A6** 54 12N 19 46 E
Mmabatho, S. Africa **104 D4** 25 49 S 25 30 E
Mme, Cameroon **101 D7** 6 18N 10 14 E
Mo i Rana, Norway **12 C16** 66 20N 14 7 E
Moa, Indonesia **72 C3** 8 0 S 128 0 E
Moa →, S. Leone **100 D2** 6 59N 11 36W
Moab, U.S.A. **143 G9** 38 35N 109 33W
Moabi, Gabon **102 C2** 2 24 S 10 59 E
Moaco →, Brazil **156 B4** 7 41 S 68 18W
Moala, Fiji **121 B2** 18 36 S 179 53 E
Moalie Park, Australia **115 D3** 29 42 S 143 3 E
Moaña, Spain **36 C2** 42 18N 8 43W
Moba, Zaïre **106 D2** 7 0 S 29 48 E
Mobara, Japan **63 B12** 35 25N 140 18 E
Mobārakābād, Iran **85 D7** 28 24N 53 20 E
Mobārakīyeh, Iran **85 C6** 32 23N 51 37 E
Mobaye, C.A.R. **102 B4** 4 25N 21 5 E
Mobayi, Zaïre **102 B4** 4 15N 21 8 E
Moberly, U.S.A. **140 E4** 39 25N 92 26W
Moberly →, Canada **130 B4** 56 12N 120 55W
Mobile, U.S.A. **135 K1** 30 41N 88 3W
Mobile B., U.S.A. **135 K2** 30 30N 88 0W
Mobridge, U.S.A. **138 C4** 45 32N 100 26W
Mobutu Sese Seko, L. = Albert L., Africa **106 B3** 1 30N 31 0 E
Moc Chau, Vietnam **76 B5** 20 50N 104 38 E
Moc Hoa, Vietnam **77 G5** 10 46N 105 56 E
Mocaba, Sa. de, Angola **103 D3** 7 12 S 15 0 E
Mocabe Kasari, Zaïre **107 D2** 9 58 S 26 12 E
Mocajuba, Brazil **154 B2** 2 35 S 49 30W
Moçambique, Mozam. **107 F5** 15 3 S 40 42 E
Moçâmedes = Namibe, Angola **103 F2** 15 7 S 12 11 E
Mocapra →, Venezuela **152 B4** 7 56N 66 46W
Mocha, I., Chile **160 A2** 38 22 S 73 56W
Mochudi, Botswana **104 C4** 24 27 S 26 7 E
Mocimboa da Praia, Mozam. **107 E5** 11 25 S 40 20 E
Mociu, Romania **46 C5** 46 24N 24 3 E
Moclips, U.S.A. **144 C2** 47 14N 124 13W
Mocoa, Colombia **152 C2** 1 7N 76 35W
Mococa, Brazil **159 A6** 21 28 S 47 0W
Mocorito, Mexico **146 B3** 25 30N 107 53W
Moctezuma, Mexico **146 B3** 29 50N 109 0W
Moctezuma →, Mexico **147 C5** 21 59N 98 34W
Mocuba, Mozam. **107 F4** 16 54 S 36 57 E
Mocúzari, Presa, Mexico **146 B3** 27 10N 109 10W
Moda, Burma **78 C6** 24 22N 96 29 E
Modane, France **25 C10** 45 12N 6 40 E
Modasa, India **80 H5** 23 30N 73 21 E
Modave, Belgium **21 H6** 50 27N 5 18 E
Modder →, S. Africa **104 D3** 29 2 S 24 37 E
Modderrivier, S. Africa **104 D3** 29 2 S 24 38 E
Módena, Italy **38 D7** 44 40N 10 55 E
Modena, U.S.A. **143 H7** 37 48N 113 56W
Modesto, U.S.A. **144 H6** 37 39N 121 0W
Módica, Italy **41 F7** 36 52N 14 46 E
Modigliana, Italy **39 D8** 44 9N 11 47 E
Modjamboli, Zaïre **102 B4** 2 28N 22 6 E
Modlin, Poland **47 C7** 52 24N 20 41 E
Mödling, Austria **31 C9** 48 5N 16 17 E
Modo, Sudan **95 F3** 5 31N 30 33 E
Modra, Slovak Rep. **31 C10** 48 19N 17 20 E
Modriča, Bos.-H. **42 C3** 44 57N 18 17 E
Moe, Australia **117 E7** 38 12 S 146 19 E
Moebase, Mozam. **107 F4** 17 3 S 38 41 E
Moëlan-sur-Mer, France **22 E3** 47 49N 3 38W
Moengo, Surinam **153 B7** 5 45N 54 20W
Moergestel, Neths. **21 E6** 51 33N 5 11 E
Moers, Germany **21 F9** 51 27N 6 36 E
Moësa →, Switz. **29 D8** 46 12N 9 10 E
Moffat, U.K. **18 F5** 55 21N 3 27W
Moga, India **80 D6** 30 48N 75 8 E
Mogadishu = Muqdisho, Somali Rep. **108 D3** 2 2N 45 25 E
Mogador = Essaouira, Morocco **98 B3** 31 32N 9 42W
Mogadouro, Portugal **36 D4** 41 22N 6 47W
Mogalakwena →, S. Africa **105 C4** 22 38 S 28 40 E
Mogami →, Japan **60 E10** 38 45N 140 0 E
Mogán, Canary Is. **33 G4** 27 53N 15 43W
Mogaung, Burma **78 C6** 25 20N 97 0 E
Møgeltønder, Denmark **15 K2** 54 57N 8 48 E
Mogente, Spain **35 G4** 38 52N 0 45W
Mogho, Ethiopia **95 G5** 4 54N 40 16 E
Mogi das Cruzes, Brazil **159 A6** 23 31 S 46 11W
Mogi-Guaçu →, Brazil **159 A6** 20 53 S 48 10W
Mogi-Mirim, Brazil **159 A6** 22 29 S 47 0W
Mogielnica, Poland **47 D7** 51 42N 20 41 E
Mogilev = Mahilyow, Belarus **50 F6** 53 55N 30 18 E
Mogilev-Podolskiy = Mohyliv-Podilskyy, Ukraine **51 H4** 48 26N 27 48 E
Mogilno, Poland **47 C4** 52 39N 17 55 E
Mogincual, Mozam. **107 F5** 15 35 S 40 25 E
Mogliano Véneto, Italy **39 C9** 45 33N 12 14 E
Mogocha, Russia **57 D12** 53 40N 119 50 E
Mogoi, Indonesia **73 B4** 1 55 S 133 10 E
Mogok, Burma **78 D6** 23 0N 96 40 E
Mogriguy, Australia **117 B8** 32 3 S 148 40 E
Moguer, Spain **37 H4** 37 15N 6 52W
Mogumber, Australia **113 F2** 31 2 S 116 3 E
Mohács, Hungary **31 F11** 45 58N 18 41 E
Mohaka →, N.Z. **118 F6** 39 7 S 177 12 E
Mohales Hoek, Lesotho **104 E4** 30 7 S 27 26 E
Mohall, U.S.A. **138 A4** 48 46N 101 31W
Moḩammadābād, Iran **85 B8** 37 52N 59 5 E
Mohammadia, Algeria **99 A5** 35 33N 0 3 E
Mohammedia, Morocco **98 B3** 33 44N 7 21W
Mohave, L., U.S.A. **145 K12** 35 12N 114 34W
Mohawk →, U.S.A. **137 D11** 42 47N 73 41W
Möhne →, Germany **26 D3** 51 29N 7 57 E
Mohnyin, Burma **78 C6** 24 47N 96 22 E
Moholm, Sweden **15 F8** 58 37N 14 5 E
Mohoro, Tanzania **106 D4** 8 6 S 39 8 E
Mohyliv-Podilskyy, Ukraine **51 H4** 48 26N 27 48 E
Moia, Sudan **95 F2** 5 3N 28 2 E
Moidart, L., U.K. **18 E3** 56 47N 5 52W
Moinabad, India **82 F3** 17 44N 77 16 E
Moindou, N. Cal. **121 U19** 21 42 S 165 41 E
Moinești, Romania **46 C7** 46 28N 26 31 E
Moirans, France **25 C9** 45 20N 5 33 E
Moirans-en-Montagne, France **25 B9** 46 26N 5 43 E
Moíres, Greece **32 D6** 35 4N 24 56 E
Moisaküla, Estonia **13 G21** 58 3N 25 12 E
Moisie, Canada **129 B6** 50 12N 66 1W
Moisie →, Canada **129 B6** 50 14N 66 5W
Moissac, France **24 D5** 44 7N 1 5 E
Moïssala, Chad **97 G3** 8 21N 17 46 E
Moita, Portugal **37 G2** 38 38N 8 58W
Mojácar, Spain **35 H3** 37 6N 1 55W
Mojados, Spain **36 D6** 41 26N 4 40W
Mojave, U.S.A. **145 K8** 35 3N 118 10W
Mojave Desert, U.S.A. **145 L10** 35 0N 116 30W
Mojiang, China **68 F3** 23 37N 101 35 E
Mojo, Bolivia **158 A2** 21 48 S 65 33W
Mojo, Ethiopia **95 F4** 8 35N 39 5 E
Mojokerto, Indonesia **75 D4** 7 28 S 112 26 E
Mojos, Llanos de, Bolivia **157 D5** 15 10 S 65 0W
Moju →, Brazil **154 B2** 1 40 S 48 25W
Mokai, N.Z. **118 E4** 38 32 S 175 56 E
Mokambo, Zaïre **107 E2** 12 25 S 28 20 E
Mokameh, India **81 G11** 25 24N 85 55 E
Mokane, U.S.A. **140 F5** 38 41N 91 53W
Mokau, N.Z. **118 E3** 38 42 S 174 39 E
Mokau →, N.Z. **118 E3** 38 35 S 174 55 E
Mokelumne →, U.S.A. **144 G5** 38 13N 121 28W
Mokelumne Hill, U.S.A. **144 G6** 38 18N 120 43W
Mokhós, Greece **32 D7** 35 16N 25 27 E
Mokhotlong, Lesotho **105 D4** 29 22 S 29 2 E
Mokihinui →, N.Z. **119 B6** 41 33 S 171 58 E
Moknine, Tunisia **96 A2** 35 35N 10 58 E
Mokpalin, Burma **78 G6** 17 26N 96 53 E
Mokra Gora, Serbia, Yug. **42 E5** 42 50N 20 30 E
Mokronog, Slovenia **39 C12** 45 57N 15 9 E
Moksha →, Russia **52 C6** 54 45N 41 53 E
Mokshan, Russia **52 D7** 53 25N 44 35 E

Moose River 235

Mol, *Belgium* **21 F6** 51 11N 5 5 E
Mola, C. de la, *Spain* **34 F9** 39 40N 4 20 E
Mola di Bari, *Italy* **41 A10** 41 4N 17 5 E
Moláoi, *Greece* **45 H4** 36 49N 22 56 E
Molat, *Croatia* **39 D11** 44 15N 14 50 E
Molave, *Phil.* **71 G4** 8 5N 123 30 E
Molchanovo, *Russia* **56 D9** 57 40N 83 50 E
Mold, *U.K.* **16 D4** 53 9N 3 8W
Moldava nad Bodvou, *Slovak Rep.* **31 C14** 48 38N 21 0 E
Moldavia, *Romania* **46 C8** 46 30N 27 0 E
Moldavia ■ = Moldova ■, *Europe* **51 J5** 47 0N 28 0 E
Molde, *Norway* **12 E12** 62 45N 7 9 E
Moldotau, Khrebet, *Kyrgyzstan* **55 C7** 41 35N 75 0 E
Moldova ■, *Europe* **51 J5** 47 0N 28 0 E
Moldova Nouă, *Romania* **46 E2** 44 45N 21 41 E
Moldoveana, *Romania* **46 D5** 45 36N 24 45 E
Molepolole, *Botswana* **104 C4** 24 28 S 25 28 E
Moléson, *Switz.* **28 C4** 46 33N 7 1 E
Molesworth, *N.Z.* **119 C8** 42 5 S 173 16 E
Molfetta, *Italy* **41 A9** 41 12N 16 36 E
Molina de Aragón, *Spain* **34 E3** 40 46N 1 52W
Moline, *U.S.A.* **140 C6** 41 30N 90 31W
Molinella, *Italy* **39 D8** 44 37N 11 40 E
Molinos, *Argentina* **158 B2** 25 28 S 66 15W
Moliro, *Zaïre* **106 D3** 8 12 S 30 30 E
Molise □, *Italy* **39 G11** 41 38N 14 29 E
Moliterno, *Italy* **41 B8** 40 14N 15 52 E
Mollahat, *Bangla.* **81 H13** 22 56N 89 48 E
Mölle, *Sweden* **15 H6** 56 17N 12 31 E
Molledo, *Spain* **36 B6** 43 8N 4 6W
Mollendo, *Peru* **156 D3** 17 0 S 72 0W
Mollerin, L., *Australia* **113 F2** 30 30 S 117 35 E
Mollerusa, *Spain* **34 D5** 41 37N 0 54 E
Mollina, *Spain* **37 H6** 37 8N 4 38W
Mölln, *Germany* **26 B6** 53 39N 10 32 E
Mölltorp, *Sweden* **15 F8** 58 30N 14 26 E
Mölndal, *Sweden* **15 G6** 57 40N 12 3 E
Molo, *Burma* **78 D6** 23 22N 96 53 E
Molochansk, *Ukraine* **51 J8** 47 15N 35 35 E
Molochnoye, Ozero, *Ukraine* **51 J8** 46 30N 35 20 E
Molodechno = Maladzyechna, *Belarus* **50 E4** 54 20N 26 50 E
Molokai, *U.S.A.* **132 H16** 21 8N 157 0W
Moloma →, *Russia* **54 B2** 58 29N 48 33 E
Molong, *Australia* **117 B8** 33 5 S 148 54 E
Molopo →, *Africa* **104 D3** 27 30 S 20 13 E
Mólos, *Greece* **45 F4** 38 47N 22 37 E
Molotov = Perm, *Russia* **54 C6** 58 0N 56 10 E
Moloundou, *Cameroon* **102 B3** 2 8N 15 15 E
Molsheim, *France* **23 D14** 48 33N 7 29 E
Molson L., *Canada* **131 C9** 54 22N 96 40W
Molteno, *S. Africa* **104 E4** 31 22 S 26 22 E
Molu, *Indonesia* **73 C4** 6 45 S 131 40 E
Molucca Sea, *Indonesia* **72 A3** 2 0 S 124 0 E
Moluccas = Maluku, *Indonesia* **72 B3** 1 0 S 127 0 E
Molundo, *Phil.* **71 H5** 7 57N 124 23 E
Moma, *Mozam.* **107 F4** 16 47 S 39 4 E
Moma, *Zaïre* **102 C4** 1 35 S 23 52 E
Momba, *Australia* **116 A5** 30 58 S 143 30 E
Mombaça, *Brazil* **154 C4** 5 43 S 39 45W
Mombasa, *Kenya* **106 C4** 4 2 S 39 43 E
Mombetsu, *Japan* **60 B11** 44 21N 143 22 E
Mombil, *Burma* **78 B7** 27 46N 98 6 E
Mombuey, *Spain* **36 C4** 42 3N 6 20W
Momchilgrad, *Bulgaria* **43 F10** 41 33N 25 23 E
Momence, *U.S.A.* **141 C9** 41 10N 87 40W
Momi, *Zaïre* **106 C2** 1 42 S 27 0 E
Momignies, *Belgium* **21 H4** 50 2N 4 10 E
Mompog Pass, *Phil.* **70 E4** 13 34N 122 13 E
Mompós, *Colombia* **152 B3** 9 14N 74 26W
Møn, *Denmark* **15 K6** 54 57N 12 15 E
Mona, Canal de la, *W. Indies* **149 C6** 18 30N 67 45W
Mona, Isla, *Puerto Rico* **149 C6** 18 5N 67 54W
Mona, Pta., *Costa Rica* **148 E3** 9 37N 82 36W
Mona, Pta., *Spain* **37 J7** 36 43N 3 45W
Mona Quimbundo, *Angola* **103 D3** 9 55 S 19 58 E
Monach Is., *U.K.* **18 D1** 57 32N 7 40W
Monaco ■, *Europe* **25 E11** 43 46N 7 23 E
Monadhliath Mts., *U.K.* **18 D4** 57 10N 4 4W
Monagas □, *Venezuela* **153 B5** 9 20N 63 0W
Monaghan, *Ireland* **19 B5** 54 15N 6 57W
Monaghan □, *Ireland* **19 B5** 54 11N 6 56W
Monahans, *U.S.A.* **139 K3** 31 36N 102 54W
Monapo, *Mozam.* **107 E5** 14 56 S 40 19 E
Monarch Mt., *Canada* **130 C3** 51 55N 125 57W
Monastir = Bitola, *Macedonia* **42 F6** 41 5N 21 10 E
Monastir, *Tunisia* **96 A2** 35 50N 10 49 E
Moncada, *Phil.* **70 D3** 15 44N 120 34 E
Moncada, *Spain* **34 F4** 39 30N 0 24W
Moncalieri, *Italy* **38 D4** 45 0N 7 41 E
Moncalvo, *Italy* **38 C5** 45 3N 8 16 E
Monção, *Portugal* **36 C2** 42 4N 8 27W
Moncarapacho, *Portugal* **37 H3** 37 5N 7 46W
Moncayo, Sierra del, *Spain* **34 D3** 41 48N 1 50W
Monchegorsk, *Russia* **48 A5** 67 54N 32 58 E
Mönchengladbach, *Germany* **26 D2** 51 11N 6 27 E
Monchique, *Portugal* **37 H2** 37 19N 8 38W
Monclova, *Mexico* **146 B4** 26 50N 101 30W
Moncontour, *France* **22 D4** 48 22N 2 38W
Moncoutant, *France* **24 B3** 46 43N 0 35W
Moncton, *Canada* **129 C7** 46 7N 64 51W
Mondego →, *Portugal* **36 E2** 40 9N 8 52W
Mondego, C., *Portugal* **36 E2** 40 11N 8 54W
Mondeodo, *Indonesia* **72 B2** 3 34 S 122 9 E
Mondo, *Chad* **97 F3** 13 47N 15 32 E
Mondolfo, *Italy* **39 E10** 43 45N 13 6 E
Mondoñedo, *Spain* **36 B3** 43 25N 7 23W
Mondovì, *Italy* **38 D4** 44 23N 7 49 E
Mondovi, *U.S.A.* **138 C9** 44 34N 91 40W
Mondragon, *France* **25 D8** 44 13N 4 44 E
Mondragon, *Phil.* **70 E5** 12 31N 124 45 E
Mondragone, *Italy* **40 A6** 41 7N 13 53 E
Mondrain I., *Australia* **113 F3** 34 9 S 122 14 E
Monduli □, *Tanzania* **106 C4** 3 0 S 36 0 E
Monemvasía, *Greece* **45 H5** 36 41N 23 3 E
Monessen, *U.S.A.* **136 F5** 40 9N 79 54W
Monesterio, *Spain* **37 G4** 38 6N 6 15W
Monestier-de-Clermont, *France* **25 D9** 44 55N 5 38 E
Monett, *U.S.A.* **139 G8** 36 55N 93 55W
Monfalcone, *Italy* **39 C10** 45 49N 13 32 E
Monflanquin, *France* **24 D4** 44 32N 0 47 E
Monforte, *Portugal* **37 F3** 39 6N 7 25W
Monforte de Lemos, *Spain* **36 C3** 42 31N 7 33W
Mong Hta, *Burma* **78 F7** 19 50N 98 35 E
Mong Ket, *Burma* **78 D7** 23 8N 98 22 E
Mong Kung, *Burma* **78 E6** 21 35N 97 35 E
Mong Kyawt, *Burma* **78 F7** 19 56N 98 45 E
Mong Nai, *Burma* **78 E6** 20 32N 97 46 E
Mong Ping, *Burma* **78 E7** 21 22N 99 2 E
Mong Pu, *Burma* **78 E7** 20 55N 98 44 E
Mong Ton, *Burma* **78 E7** 20 17N 98 45 E
Mong Tung, *Burma* **78 D6** 22 2N 97 41 E
Mong Yai, *Burma* **78 D7** 22 21N 98 3 E
Monga, *Zaïre* **102 B4** 4 12N 22 49 E
Mongalla, *Sudan* **95 F3** 5 8N 31 42 E
Mongers, L., *Australia* **113 E2** 29 25 S 117 5 E
Monghyr = Munger, *India* **81 G12** 25 23N 86 30 E
Mongibello = Etna, *Italy* **41 E8** 37 50N 14 55 E
Mongla, *Bangla.* **78 D2** 22 8N 89 35 E
Mongngaw, *Burma* **78 D6** 22 47N 96 59 E
Mongo, *Chad* **97 F3** 12 14N 18 43 E
Mongó, *Eq. Guin.* **102 B2** 1 52N 10 10 E
Mongolia ■, *Asia* **57 E10** 47 0N 103 0 E
Mongomo, *Eq. Guin.* **102 B2** 1 38N 11 19 E
Mongonu, *Nigeria* **101 C7** 12 40N 13 32 E
Mongororo, *Chad* **97 F4** 12 3N 22 26 E
Mongu, *Zambia* **103 F4** 15 16 S 23 12 E
Môngua, *Angola* **103 F3** 16 43 S 15 20 E
Monistrol-d'Allier, *France* **24 D7** 44 58N 3 38 E
Monistrol-sur-Loire, *France* **25 C8** 45 17N 4 11 E
Monkayo, *Phil.* **71 H6** 7 50N 126 5 E
Monkey Bay, *Malawi* **107 E4** 14 7 S 35 1 E
Monkey River, *Belize* **147 D7** 16 22N 88 29W
Mońki, *Poland* **47 B9** 53 23N 22 48 E
Monkira, *Australia* **114 C3** 24 46 S 140 30 E
Monkoto, *Zaïre* **102 C4** 1 38 S 20 35 E
Monmouth, *U.K.* **17 F5** 51 48N 2 42W
Monmouth, *U.S.A.* **140 D6** 40 55N 90 39W
Monmouthshire □, *U.K.* **17 F5** 51 48N 2 54W
Mono, *Solomon Is.* **121 L8** 7 20 S 155 35 E
Mono L., *U.S.A.* **144 H7** 38 1N 119 1W
Monolith, *U.S.A.* **145 K8** 35 7N 118 22W
Monólithos, *Greece* **32 C9** 36 7N 27 45 E
Monon, *U.S.A.* **141 D10** 40 52N 86 53W
Monona, *Iowa, U.S.A.* **140 A5** 43 3N 91 23W
Monona, *Wis., U.S.A.* **140 A7** 43 4N 89 20W
Monongahela, *U.S.A.* **136 F5** 40 12N 79 56W
Monópoli, *Italy* **41 B10** 40 57N 17 18 E
Monor, *Hungary* **31 D12** 47 21N 19 27 E
Monóvar, *Spain* **35 G4** 38 28N 0 53W
Monowai, *N.Z.* **119 F2** 45 53 S 167 31 E
Monowai, L., *N.Z.* **119 F2** 45 53 S 167 25 E
Monqoumba, *C.A.R.* **102 B3** 3 33N 18 40 E
Monreal del Campo, *Spain* **34 E3** 40 47N 1 20W
Monreale, *Italy* **40 D6** 38 5N 13 17 E
Monroe, *Ga., U.S.A.* **135 J4** 33 47N 83 43W
Monroe, *Iowa, U.S.A.* **140 C3** 41 31N 93 6W
Monroe, *La., U.S.A.* **139 J8** 32 30N 92 7W
Monroe, *Mich., U.S.A.* **141 C13** 41 55N 83 24W
Monroe, *N.C., U.S.A.* **135 H5** 34 59N 80 33W
Monroe, *N.Y., U.S.A.* **137 E10** 41 20N 74 11W
Monroe, *Ohio, U.S.A.* **141 E12** 39 27N 84 22W
Monroe, *Utah, U.S.A.* **143 G7** 38 38N 112 7W
Monroe, *Wash., U.S.A.* **144 C5** 47 51N 121 58W
Monroe, *Wis., U.S.A.* **140 B7** 42 36N 89 38W
Monroe City, *U.S.A.* **140 E5** 39 39N 91 44W
Monroe Res., *U.S.A.* **141 E10** 39 1N 86 31W
Monroeville, *Ala., U.S.A.* **135 K2** 31 31N 87 20W
Monroeville, *Ind., U.S.A.* **141 D12** 40 59N 84 52W
Monroeville, *Pa., U.S.A.* **136 F5** 40 26N 79 45W
Monrovia, *Liberia* **100 D2** 6 18N 10 47W
Mons, *Belgium* **21 H3** 50 27N 3 58 E
Monsaraz, *Portugal* **37 G3** 38 28N 7 22W
Monse, *Indonesia* **72 B2** 4 0 S 123 10 E
Monsefú, *Peru* **156 B2** 6 52 S 79 52W
Monségur, *France* **24 D4** 44 38N 0 4 E
Monsélice, *Italy* **39 C8** 45 14N 11 45 E
Monster, *Neths.* **20 D4** 52 1N 4 10 E
Mont Cenis, Col du, *France* **25 C10** 45 15N 6 55 E
Mont-de-Marsan, *France* **24 E3** 43 54N 0 31W
Mont-Joli, *Canada* **129 C6** 48 37N 68 10W
Mont-Laurier, *Canada* **128 C4** 46 35N 75 30W
Mont-St.-Michel, Le = Le Mont-St.-Michel, *France* **22 D5** 48 40N 1 30W
Mont-sous-Vaudrey, *France* **23 F12** 46 58N 5 36 E
Mont-sur-Marchienne, *Belgium* **21 H4** 50 23N 4 24 E
Mont Tremblant Prov. Park, *Canada* **128 C5** 46 30N 74 30W
Montabaur, *Germany* **26 E3** 50 25N 7 50 E
Montagnac, *France* **24 E7** 43 29N 3 28 E
Montagnana, *Italy* **39 C8** 45 14N 11 28 E
Montagu, *S. Africa* **104 E3** 33 45 S 20 8 E
Montagu I., *Antarctica* **7 B1** 58 25 S 26 20W
Montague, *Canada* **129 C7** 46 10N 62 39W
Montague, *U.S.A.* **142 F2** 41 44N 122 32W
Montague, I., *Mexico* **146 A2** 31 40N 114 56W
Montague Ra., *Australia* **113 E2** 27 15 S 119 30 E
Montague Sd., *Australia* **112 B4** 14 28 S 125 20 E
Montaigu, *France* **22 F5** 46 59N 1 18W
Montalbán, *Spain* **34 E4** 40 50N 0 45W
Montalbano di Elicona, *Italy* **41 D8** 38 1N 15 0 E
Montalbano Iónico, *Italy* **41 B9** 40 17N 16 34 E
Montalbo, *Spain* **34 F2** 39 53N 2 42W
Montalcino, *Italy* **39 E8** 43 3N 11 29 E
Montalegre, *Portugal* **36 D3** 41 49N 7 47W
Montalto di Castro, *Italy* **39 F8** 42 21N 11 37 E
Montalto Uffugo, *Italy* **41 C9** 39 24N 16 9 E
Montalvo, *U.S.A.* **145 L7** 34 15N 119 12W
Montamarta, *Spain* **36 D5** 41 39N 5 49W
Montaña, *Peru* **156 B3** 6 0 S 73 0W
Montana, *Switz.* **28 D4** 46 19N 7 29 E
Montana □, *U.S.A.* **142 C9** 47 0N 110 0W
Montaña Clara, I., *Canary Is.* **33 E6** 29 17N 13 33W
Montánchez, *Spain* **37 F4** 39 15N 6 8W
Montañita, *Colombia* **152 C2** 1 22N 75 28W
Montargis, *France* **23 E9** 47 59N 2 43 E
Montauban, *France* **24 D5** 44 2N 1 21 E
Montauk, *U.S.A.* **137 E13** 41 3N 71 57W
Montauk Pt., *U.S.A.* **137 E13** 41 4N 71 52W
Montbard, *France* **23 E11** 47 38N 4 20 E
Montbéliard, *France* **23 E13** 47 31N 6 48 E
Montblanch, *Spain* **34 D6** 41 23N 1 4 E
Montbrison, *France* **25 C8** 45 36N 4 3 E
Montcalm, Pic de, *France* **24 F5** 42 40N 1 25 E
Montceau-les-Mines, *France* **23 F11** 46 40N 4 23 E
Montchanin, *France* **25 B8** 46 47N 4 30 E
Montclair, *U.S.A.* **137 F10** 40 49N 74 13W
Montcornet, *France* **23 C11** 49 40N 4 1 E
Montcuq, *France* **24 D5** 44 21N 1 13 E
Montdidier, *France* **23 C9** 49 38N 2 35 E
Monte Albán, *Mexico* **147 D5** 17 2N 96 45W
Monte Alegre, *Brazil* **153 D7** 2 0 S 54 0W
Monte Alegre de Goiás, *Brazil* **155 D2** 13 14 S 47 10W
Monte Alegre de Minas, *Brazil* **155 E2** 18 52 S 48 52W
Monte Azul, *Brazil* **155 E3** 15 9 S 42 53W
Monte Bello Is., *Australia* **112 D2** 20 30 S 115 45 E
Monte-Carlo, *Monaco* **25 E11** 43 46N 7 23 E
Monte Carmelo, *Brazil* **155 E2** 18 43 S 47 29W
Monte Caseros, *Argentina* **158 C4** 30 10 S 57 50W
Monte Comán, *Argentina* **158 C2** 34 40 S 67 53W
Monte Cristi, *Dom. Rep.* **149 C5** 19 52N 71 39W
Monte Dinero, *Argentina* **160 D3** 52 18 S 68 33W
Monte Lindo →, *Paraguay* **158 A4** 23 56 S 57 12W
Monte Quemado, *Argentina* **158 B3** 25 53 S 62 41W
Monte Redondo, *Portugal* **36 F2** 39 53N 8 50W
Monte Rio, *U.S.A.* **144 G4** 38 28N 123 0W
Monte San Giovanni Campano, *Italy* **40 A6** 41 38N 13 31 E
Monte San Savino, *Italy* **39 E8** 43 20N 11 43 E
Monte Sant' Ángelo, *Italy* **41 A8** 41 42N 15 59 E
Monte Santu, C. di, *Italy* **40 B2** 40 5N 9 44 E
Monte Vista, *U.S.A.* **143 H10** 37 35N 106 9W
Monteagudo, *Argentina* **159 B5** 27 14 S 54 8W
Monteagudo, *Bolivia* **157 D5** 19 49 S 63 59W
Montealegre, *Spain* **35 G3** 38 48N 1 17W
Montebello, *Canada* **128 C5** 45 40N 74 55W
Montebelluna, *Italy* **39 C9** 45 47N 12 3 E
Montebourg, *France* **22 C5** 49 30N 1 20W
Montecastrilli, *Italy* **39 F9** 42 39N 12 29 E
Montecatini Terme, *Italy* **38 E7** 43 53N 10 46 E
Montecito, *U.S.A.* **145 L7** 34 26N 119 40W
Montecristi, *Ecuador* **152 D1** 1 0 S 80 40W
Montecristo, *Italy* **38 F7** 42 20N 10 19 E
Montefalco, *Italy* **39 F9** 42 54N 12 39 E
Montefiascone, *Italy* **39 F9** 42 32N 12 2 E
Montefrío, *Spain* **37 H6** 37 20N 4 0W
Montegnée, *Belgium* **21 G7** 50 38N 5 31 E
Montego Bay, *Jamaica* **148 C4** 18 30N 78 0W
Montegranaro, *Italy* **39 E10** 43 14N 13 38 E
Monteiro, *Brazil* **154 C4** 7 48 S 37 2W
Monteith, *Australia* **116 C3** 35 11 S 139 23 E
Montejicar, *Spain* **35 H1** 37 33N 3 30W
Montejinnie, *Australia* **112 C5** 16 40 S 131 38 E
Montelíbano, *Colombia* **152 B2** 8 5N 75 29W
Montélimar, *France* **25 D8** 44 33N 4 45 E
Montella, *Italy* **41 B8** 40 51N 15 1 E
Montellano, *Spain* **37 J5** 36 59N 5 36W
Montello, *U.S.A.* **138 D10** 43 48N 89 20W
Montelupo Fiorentino, *Italy* **38 E8** 43 44N 11 1 E
Montemor-o-Novo, *Portugal* **37 G2** 38 40N 8 12W
Montemor-o-Velho, *Portugal* **36 E2** 40 11N 8 40W
Montemorelos, *Mexico* **147 B5** 25 11N 99 42W
Montendre, *France* **24 C3** 45 16N 0 26W
Montenegro, *Brazil* **159 B5** 29 39 S 51 29W
Montenegro □, *Yugoslavia* **42 E4** 42 40N 19 20 E
Montenero di Bisáccia, *Italy* **39 G11** 41 57N 14 47 E
Montepuez, *Mozam.* **107 E4** 13 8 S 38 59 E
Montepuez →, *Mozam.* **107 E5** 12 32 S 40 27 E
Montepulciano, *Italy* **39 E8** 43 5N 11 47 E
Montereale, *Italy* **39 F10** 42 31N 13 15 E
Montereau-Fault-Yonne, *France* **23 D9** 48 22N 2 57 E
Monterey, *Calif., U.S.A.* **144 J5** 36 37N 121 55W
Monterey, *Ind., U.S.A.* **141 C10** 41 11N 86 30W
Monterey B., *U.S.A.* **144 J5** 36 45N 122 0W
Montería, *Colombia* **152 B2** 8 46N 75 53W
Montero, *Bolivia* **157 D5** 17 20 S 63 15W
Monteros, *Argentina* **158 B2** 27 11 S 65 30W
Monterotondo, *Italy* **39 F9** 42 3N 12 37 E
Monterrey, *Mexico* **146 B4** 25 40N 100 30W
Montes Altos, *Brazil* **154 C2** 5 50 S 47 4W
Montes Claros, *Brazil* **155 E3** 16 30 S 43 50W
Montesano, *U.S.A.* **144 D3** 46 59N 123 36W
Montesárchio, *Italy* **41 A7** 41 4N 14 38 E
Montescaglioso, *Italy* **41 B9** 40 33N 16 40 E
Montesilvano Marina, *Italy* **39 F11** 42 29N 14 8 E
Montevarchi, *Italy* **39 E8** 43 31N 11 34 E
Montevideo, *Uruguay* **159 C4** 34 50 S 56 11W
Montevideo, *U.S.A.* **138 C7** 44 57N 95 43W
Montezuma, *Ind., U.S.A.* **141 E9** 39 48N 87 22W
Montezuma, *Iowa, U.S.A.* **140 C4** 41 35N 92 32W
Montfaucon, *France* **23 C12** 49 16N 5 8 E
Montfaucon-en-Velay, *France* **25 C8** 45 11N 4 20 E
Montfort, *France* **22 D5** 48 9N 1 58W
Montfort, *Neths.* **21 F7** 51 7N 5 58 E
Montfort-l'Amaury, *France* **23 D8** 48 47N 1 49 E
Montgenèvre, *France* **25 D10** 44 56N 6 43 E
Montgomery = Sahiwal, *Pakistan* **79 C4** 30 45N 73 8 E
Montgomery, *U.K.* **17 E4** 52 34N 3 8W
Montgomery, *Ala., U.S.A.* **135 J2** 32 23N 86 19W
Montgomery, *Ill., U.S.A.* **141 C8** 41 44N 88 21W
Montgomery, *W. Va., U.S.A.* **134 F5** 38 11N 81 19W
Montgomery City, *U.S.A.* **140 F5** 38 59N 91 30W
Montguyon, *France* **24 C3** 45 12N 0 12W
Monthey, *Switz.* **28 D3** 46 15N 6 56 E
Monticelli d'Ongina, *Italy* **38 C6** 45 5N 9 56 E
Monticello, *Ark., U.S.A.* **139 J9** 33 38N 91 47W
Monticello, *Fla., U.S.A.* **135 K4** 30 33N 83 52W
Monticello, *Ill., U.S.A.* **141 D8** 40 1N 88 34W
Monticello, *Ind., U.S.A.* **141 D10** 40 45N 86 46W
Monticello, *Iowa, U.S.A.* **140 B5** 42 15N 91 12W
Monticello, *Ky., U.S.A.* **135 G3** 36 50N 84 51W
Monticello, *Minn., U.S.A.* **138 C8** 45 18N 93 48W
Monticello, *Miss., U.S.A.* **139 K9** 31 33N 90 7W
Monticello, *Mo., U.S.A.* **140 D5** 40 7N 91 43W
Monticello, *N.Y., U.S.A.* **137 E10** 41 39N 74 42W
Monticello, *Utah, U.S.A.* **143 H9** 37 52N 109 21W
Montichiari, *Italy* **38 C7** 45 25N 10 23 E
Montier-en-Der, *France* **23 D11** 48 30N 4 45 E
Montignac, *France* **24 C5** 45 4N 1 10 E
Montignies-sur-Sambre, *Belgium* **21 H4** 50 24N 4 29 E
Montigny, *France* **23 C13** 49 7N 6 10 E
Montigny-sur-Aube, *France* **23 E11** 47 57N 4 45 E
Montijo, *Spain* **37 G4** 38 52N 6 39W
Montijo, Presa de, *Spain* **37 G4** 38 55N 6 26W
Montilla, *Spain* **37 H6** 37 36N 4 40W
Montlhéry, *France* **23 D9** 48 39N 2 15 E
Montluçon, *France* **24 B6** 46 22N 2 36 E
Montmagny, *Canada* **129 C5** 46 58N 70 34W
Montmarault, *France* **24 B6** 46 19N 2 57 E
Montmartre, *Canada* **131 C8** 50 14N 103 27W
Montmédy, *France* **23 C12** 49 30N 5 20 E
Montmélian, *France* **25 C10** 45 30N 6 4 E
Montmirail, *France* **23 D10** 48 51N 3 30 E
Montmoreau-St.-Cybard, *France* **24 C4** 45 23N 0 8 E
Montmorency, *Canada* **129 C5** 46 53N 71 11W
Montmorillon, *France* **24 B4** 46 26N 0 50 E
Montmort, *France* **23 D10** 48 55N 3 49 E
Monto, *Australia* **114 C5** 24 52 S 151 6 E
Montoir-sur-le-Loir, *France* **22 E7** 47 45N 0 52 E
Montório al Vomano, *Italy* **39 F10** 42 35N 13 38 E
Montoro, *Spain* **37 G6** 38 1N 4 27W
Montour Falls, *U.S.A.* **136 D8** 42 21N 76 51W
Montpelier, *Idaho, U.S.A.* **142 E8** 42 19N 111 18W
Montpelier, *Ind., U.S.A.* **141 D11** 40 33N 85 17W
Montpelier, *Ohio, U.S.A.* **141 C12** 41 35N 84 37W
Montpelier, *Vt., U.S.A.* **137 B12** 44 16N 72 35W
Montpellier, *France* **24 E7** 43 37N 3 52 E
Montpezat-de-Quercy, *France* **24 D5** 44 15N 1 30 E
Montpon-Ménestérol, *France* **24 D4** 45 0N 0 11 E
Montréal, *Canada* **128 C5** 45 31N 73 34W
Montréal, *France* **24 E6** 43 13N 2 8 E
Montreal L., *Canada* **131 C7** 54 20N 105 45W
Montreal Lake, *Canada* **131 C7** 54 3N 105 46W
Montredon-Labessonnié, *France* **24 E6** 43 45N 2 18 E
Montréjeau, *France* **24 E4** 43 6N 0 35 E
Montrésor, *France* **22 E8** 47 10N 1 10 E
Montreuil, *France* **23 B8** 50 27N 1 45 E
Montreuil-Bellay, *France* **22 E6** 47 8N 0 9W
Montreux, *Switz.* **28 D3** 46 26N 6 55 E
Montrevault, *France* **22 E5** 47 17N 1 2W
Montrevel-en-Bresse, *France* **25 B9** 46 21N 5 8 E
Montrichard, *France* **22 E8** 47 20N 1 10 E
Montrose, *U.K.* **18 E6** 56 44N 2 27W
Montrose, *Colo., U.S.A.* **143 G10** 38 29N 107 53W
Montrose, *Pa., U.S.A.* **137 E9** 41 50N 75 53W
Montrose, L., *U.S.A.* **140 F3** 38 18N 93 50W
Monts, Pte. des, *Canada* **129 C6** 49 20N 67 12W
Monts-sur-Guesnes, *France* **22 F7** 46 55N 0 13 E
Montsalvy, *France* **24 D6** 44 41N 2 30 E
Montsant, Sierra de, *Spain* **34 D5** 41 17N 1 0 E
Montsauche, *France* **23 E11** 47 13N 4 2 E
Montsech, Sierra del, *Spain* **34 C5** 42 0N 0 45 E
Montseny, *Spain* **34 D2** 41 55N 2 25W
Montserrat, *Spain* **34 D6** 41 36N 1 49 E
Montserrat ■, *W. Indies* **149 C7** 16 40N 62 10W
Montuenga, *Spain* **36 D6** 41 3N 4 38W
Montuiri, *Spain* **33 B9** 39 34N 2 59 E
Monveda, *Zaïre* **102 B4** 2 52N 21 30 E
Monyo, *Burma* **78 G5** 17 59N 95 30 E
Monywa, *Burma* **78 D5** 22 7N 95 11 E
Monza, *Italy* **38 C6** 45 35N 9 16 E
Monze, *Zambia* **107 F2** 16 17 S 27 29 E
Monze, C., *Pakistan* **79 D2** 24 47N 66 37 E
Monzón, *Spain* **34 D5** 41 52N 0 10 E
Mooi River, *S. Africa* **105 D4** 29 13 S 29 50 E
Mook, *Neths.* **20 E7** 51 46N 5 54 E
Mo'oka, *Japan* **63 A12** 36 26N 140 1 E
Moolawatana, *Australia* **115 D2** 29 55 S 139 45 E
Mooleulooloo, *Australia* **116 A4** 31 36 S 140 32 E
Mooliabeenee, *Australia* **113 F2** 31 20 S 116 2 E
Mooloogool, *Australia* **113 E2** 26 2 S 119 5 E
Moomin Cr. →, *Australia* **115 D4** 29 44 S 149 20 E
Moonah →, *Australia* **114 C2** 22 3 S 138 33 E
Moonbeam, *Canada* **128 C3** 49 20N 82 10W
Moonda, L., *Australia* **114 D3** 25 52 S 140 25 E
Moonie, *Australia* **115 D5** 27 46 S 150 20 E
Moonie →, *Australia* **115 D4** 29 19 S 148 43 E
Moonta, *Australia* **116 C2** 34 6 S 137 32 E
Moora, *Australia* **113 F2** 30 37 S 115 58 E
Mooraberree, *Australia* **114 D3** 25 13 S 140 54 E
Moorarie, *Australia* **113 E2** 25 56 S 117 35 E
Moorcroft, *U.S.A.* **138 C2** 44 16N 104 57W
Moore →, *Australia* **113 F2** 31 22 S 115 30 E
Moore, L., *Australia* **113 E2** 29 50 S 117 35 E
Moore Reefs, *Australia* **114 B4** 16 0 S 149 5 E
Moorefield, *U.S.A.* **134 F6** 39 5N 78 59W
Moores Res., *U.S.A.* **137 B13** 44 45N 71 50W
Mooresville, *Ind., U.S.A.* **141 E10** 39 37N 86 22W
Mooresville, *N.C., U.S.A.* **135 H5** 35 35N 80 48W
Moorfoot Hills, *U.K.* **18 F5** 55 44N 3 8W
Moorhead, *U.S.A.* **138 B6** 46 53N 96 45W
Moorland, *Australia* **117 A10** 31 46 S 152 38 E
Mooroopna, *Australia* **117 D6** 36 25 S 145 22 E
Moorpark, *U.S.A.* **145 L8** 34 17N 118 53W
Moorreesburg, *S. Africa* **104 E2** 33 6 S 18 38 E
Moorslede, *Belgium* **21 G2** 50 54N 3 4 E
Moosburg, *Germany* **27 G7** 48 27N 11 56 E
Moose →, *Canada* **128 B3** 51 20N 80 25W
Moose Factory, *Canada* **128 B3** 51 16N 80 32W
Moose I., *Canada* **131 C9** 51 42N 97 10W
Moose Jaw, *Canada* **131 C7** 50 24N 105 30W
Moose Jaw →, *Canada* **131 C7** 50 34N 105 18W
Moose Lake, *Canada* **131 C8** 53 43N 100 20W
Moose Lake, *U.S.A.* **138 B8** 46 27N 92 46W
Moose Mountain Cr. →, *Canada* **131 D8** 49 13N 102 12W
Moose Mountain Prov. Park, *Canada* **131 D8** 49 48N 102 25W
Moose River, *Canada* **128 B3** 50 48N 81 17W

236 Moosehead L.

Moosehead L., *U.S.A.* **129 C6** 45 38N 69 40W
Moosomin, *Canada* **131 C8** 50 9N 101 40W
Moosonee, *Canada* **128 B3** 51 17N 80 39W
Moosup, *U.S.A.* **137 E13** 41 43N 71 53W
Mopeia Velha, *Mozam.* **107 F4** 17 30 S 35 40 E
Mopipi, *Botswana* **104 C3** 21 6 S 24 55 E
Mopoi, *C.A.R.* **102 A5** 5 6N 26 54 E
Mopti, *Mali* **100 C4** 14 30N 4 0W
Moqatta, *Sudan* **95 E4** 14 38N 35 50 E
Moquegua, *Peru* **156 D3** 17 15 S 70 46W
Moquegua □, *Peru* **156 D3** 16 50 S 70 55W
Mór, *Hungary* **31 D11** 47 25N 18 12 E
Móra, *Portugal* **37 G2** 38 55N 8 10W
Mora, *Sweden* **13 F16** 61 2N 14 38 E
Mora, *Minn., U.S.A.* **138 C8** 45 53N 93 18W
Mora, *N. Mex., U.S.A.* **143 J11** 35 58N 105 20W
Mora de Ebro, *Spain* **34 D5** 41 6N 0 38 E
Mora de Rubielos, *Spain* **34 E4** 40 15N 0 45W
Mora la Nueva, *Spain* **34 D5** 41 7N 0 39 E
Morača →, *Montenegro, Yug.* **42 E4** 42 20N 19 9 E
Morada Nova, *Brazil* **154 C4** 5 7 S 38 23W
Morada Nova de Minas, *Brazil* **155 E2** 18 37 S 45 22W
Moradabad, *India* **81 E8** 28 50N 78 50 E
Morafenobe, *Madag.* **105 B7** 17 50 S 44 53 E
Morąg, *Poland* **47 B6** 53 55N 19 56 E
Moral de Calatrava, *Spain* **35 G1** 38 51N 3 33W
Moraleja, *Spain* **36 E4** 40 6N 6 43W
Morales, *Colombia* **152 C2** 2 45N 76 38W
Moramanga, *Madag.* **105 B8** 18 56 S 48 12 E
Moran, *Kans., U.S.A.* **139 G7** 37 55N 95 10W
Moran, *Wyo., U.S.A.* **142 E8** 43 53N 110 37W
Moranbah, *Australia* **114 C4** 22 1 S 148 6 E
Morano Cálabro, *Italy* **41 C9** 39 50N 16 8 E
Morant Cays, *Jamaica* **148 C4** 17 22N 76 0W
Morant Pt., *Jamaica* **148 C4** 17 55N 76 12W
Morar, L., *U.K.* **18 E3** 56 57N 5 40W
Moratalla, *Spain* **35 G3** 38 14N 1 49W
Moratuwa, *Sri Lanka* **83 L4** 6 45N 79 55 E
Morava →, *Slovak Rep.* **31 C9** 48 10N 16 59 E
Moravia, *U.S.A.* **140 D4** 40 53N 92 49W
Moravian Hts. = Ceskomoravská Vrchovina, *Czech.* **30 B8** 49 30N 15 40 E
Moravica →, *Serbia, Yug.* **42 D5** 43 52N 20 8 E
Moravice →, *Czech.* **31 B10** 49 50N 17 43 E
Moravița, *Romania* **42 B6** 45 17N 21 14 E
Moravská Třebová, *Czech.* **31 B9** 49 45N 16 40 E
Moravské Budějovice, *Czech.* **30 B8** 49 4N 15 49 E
Morawa, *Australia* **113 E2** 29 13 S 116 0 E
Morawhanna, *Guyana* **153 B6** 8 30N 59 40W
Moray □, *U.K.* **18 D5** 57 31N 3 18W
Moray Firth, *U.K.* **18 D5** 57 40N 3 52W
Morbach, *Germany* **27 F3** 49 48N 7 6 E
Morbegno, *Italy* **38 B6** 46 8N 9 34 E
Morbi, *India* **80 H4** 22 50N 70 42 E
Morbihan □, *France* **22 E4** 47 55N 2 50W
Morcenx, *France* **24 D3** 44 3N 0 55W
Mordelles, *France* **22 D5** 48 5N 1 52W
Morden, *Canada* **131 D9** 49 15N 98 10W
Mordovian Republic □ = Mordvinia □, *Russia* **52 C7** 54 20N 44 30 E
Mordovo, *Russia* **52 D5** 52 6N 40 50 E
Mordvinia □, *Russia* **52 C7** 54 20N 44 30 E
Mordy, *Poland* **47 C9** 52 13N 22 31 E
Møre og Romsdal fylke □, *Norway* **14 B2** 62 30N 8 0 E
Morea, *Australia* **116 D4** 36 45 S 141 18 E
Morea, *Greece* **10 H10** 37 45N 22 10 E
Moreau →, *U.S.A.* **138 C4** 45 18N 100 43W
Morecambe, *U.K.* **16 C5** 54 5N 2 52W
Morecambe B., *U.K.* **16 C5** 54 7N 3 0W
Moree, *Australia* **115 D4** 29 28 S 149 54 E
Morehead, *Papua N. G.* **120 E1** 8 41 S 141 41 E
Morehead, *U.S.A.* **141 F13** 38 11N 83 26W
Morehead City, *U.S.A.* **135 H7** 34 43N 76 43W
Morelia, *Mexico* **146 D4** 19 42N 101 7W
Morella, *Australia* **114 C3** 23 0 S 143 52 E
Morella, *Spain* **34 E4** 40 35N 0 5W
Morelos, *Mexico* **146 B3** 26 42N 107 40W
Morelos □, *Mexico* **147 D5** 18 40N 99 10W
Morena, Sierra, *Spain* **37 G7** 38 20N 4 0W
Morenci, *Ariz., U.S.A.* **143 K9** 33 5N 109 22W
Morenci, *Mich., U.S.A.* **141 C12** 41 43N 84 13W
Moreni, *Romania* **46 E6** 44 59N 25 36 E
Moreno Valley, *U.S.A.* **145 M10** 33 56N 116 58W
Morero, *Bolivia* **157 C4** 11 9 S 66 15W
Moreru →, *Brazil* **157 C6** 10 10 S 59 15W
Moresby I., *Canada* **130 C2** 52 30N 131 40W
Morestel, *France* **25 C9** 45 40N 5 28 E
Moret-sur-Loing, *France* **23 D9** 48 22N 2 58 E
Moreton, *Australia* **114 A3** 12 22 S 142 40 E
Moreton I., *Australia* **115 D5** 27 10 S 153 25 E
Moreuil, *France* **23 C9** 49 46N 2 30 E
Morey, *Spain* **33 B10** 39 44N 3 20 E
Morez, *France* **25 B10** 46 31N 6 2 E
Morgan, *Australia* **116 C3** 34 2 S 139 35 E
Morgan, *U.S.A.* **142 F8** 41 2N 111 41W
Morgan City, *U.S.A.* **139 L9** 29 42N 91 12W
Morgan Hill, *U.S.A.* **144 H5** 37 8N 121 39W
Morgan Vale, *Australia* **116 B4** 33 10 S 140 32 E
Morganfield, *U.S.A.* **134 G2** 37 41N 87 55W
Morganton, *U.S.A.* **135 H5** 35 45N 81 41W
Morgantown, *Ind., U.S.A.* **141 E10** 39 22N 86 16W
Morgantown, *W. Va., U.S.A.* **134 F6** 39 38N 79 57W
Morgat, *France* **22 D2** 48 15N 4 32W
Morgenzon, *S. Africa* **105 D4** 26 45 S 29 36 E
Morges, *Switz.* **28 C2** 46 31N 6 29 E
Morghak, *Iran* **85 D8** 29 7N 57 54 E
Morhange, *France* **23 D13** 48 55N 6 38 E
Mori, *Italy* **38 C7** 45 51N 10 59 E
Morialmée, *Belgium* **21 H5** 50 17N 4 35 E
Morice L., *Canada* **130 C3** 53 50N 127 40W
Morichal, *Colombia* **152 C3** 2 10N 70 34W
Morichal Largo →, *Venezuela* **153 B5** 9 27N 62 25W
Moriguchi, *Japan* **63 C7** 34 44N 135 34 E
Moriki, *Nigeria* **101 C6** 12 52N 6 30 E
Morinville, *Canada* **130 C6** 53 49N 113 41W
Morioka, *Japan* **60 E10** 39 45N 141 8 E
Moris, *Mexico* **146 B3** 28 8N 108 32W
Morisset, *Australia* **117 B9** 33 6 S 151 30 E
Morlaàs, *France* **24 E3** 43 21N 0 18W
Morlaix, *France* **22 D3** 48 36N 3 52W
Morlanwelz, *Belgium* **21 H4** 50 28N 4 15 E
Mormanno, *Italy* **41 C8** 39 53N 15 59 E
Mormant, *France* **23 D9** 48 37N 2 52 E
Mornington, *Vic., Australia* **117 E6** 38 15 S 145 5 E
Mornington, *W. Austral., Australia* **112 C4** 17 31 S 126 6 E
Mornington, I., *Chile* **160 C1** 49 50 S 75 30W
Mornington I., *Australia* **114 B2** 16 30 S 139 30 E
Mórnos →, *Greece* **45 F3** 38 25N 21 50 E
Moro, *Sudan* **95 E3** 10 50N 30 9 E
Moro G., *Phil.* **71 H4** 6 30N 123 0 E
Morobe, *Papua N. G.* **120 D4** 7 49 S 147 38 E
Morocco, *U.S.A.* **141 D9** 40 57N 87 27W
Morocco ■, *N. Afr.* **98 B3** 32 0N 5 50W
Morococha, *Peru* **156 C2** 11 40 S 76 5W
Morogoro, *Tanzania* **106 D4** 6 50 S 37 40 E
Morogoro □, *Tanzania* **106 D4** 8 0 S 37 0 E
Moroleón, *Mexico* **146 C4** 20 8N 101 32W
Morombe, *Madag.* **105 C7** 21 45 S 43 22 E
Moron, *Argentina* **158 C4** 34 39 S 58 37W
Morón, *Cuba* **148 B4** 22 8N 78 39W
Morón de Almazán, *Spain* **34 D2** 41 29N 2 27W
Morón de la Frontera, *Spain* **37 H5** 37 6N 5 28W
Morona →, *Peru* **152 D2** 4 40 S 77 10W
Morona-Santiago □, *Ecuador* **152 D2** 2 30 S 78 0W
Morondava, *Madag.* **105 C7** 20 17 S 44 17 E
Morondo, *Ivory C.* **100 D3** 8 57N 6 47W
Morong, *Phil.* **70 D3** 14 41N 120 16 E
Morongo Valley, *U.S.A.* **145 L10** 34 3N 116 37W
Moronou, *Ivory C.* **100 D4** 6 16N 4 59W
Morotai, *Indonesia* **72 A3** 2 10N 128 30 E
Moroto, *Uganda* **106 B3** 2 28N 34 42 E
Moroto Summit, *Kenya* **106 B3** 2 30N 34 43 E
Morozov, *Bulgaria* **43 E10** 42 30N 25 10 E
Morozovsk, *Russia* **53 F5** 48 25N 41 50 E
Morpeth, *U.K.* **16 B6** 55 10N 1 41W
Morphou, *Cyprus* **32 D11** 35 12N 32 59 E
Morphou Bay, *Cyprus* **32 D11** 35 15N 32 50 E
Morrelganj, *Bangla.* **78 D2** 22 28N 89 51 E
Morrilton, *U.S.A.* **139 H8** 35 9N 92 44W
Morrinhos, *Ceara, Brazil* **154 B3** 3 14 S 40 7W
Morrinhos, *Minas Gerais, Brazil* **155 E2** 17 45 S 49 10W
Morrinsville, *N.Z.* **118 D4** 37 40 S 175 32 E
Morris, *Canada* **131 D9** 49 25N 97 22W
Morris, *Ill., U.S.A.* **141 C8** 41 22N 88 26W
Morris, *Minn., U.S.A.* **138 C7** 45 35N 95 55W
Morris, Mt., *Australia* **113 E5** 26 9 S 131 4 E
Morrisburg, *Canada* **128 D4** 44 55N 75 7W
Morrison, *U.S.A.* **140 C7** 41 49N 89 58W
Morrisonville, *U.S.A.* **140 E7** 39 25N 89 27W
Morristown, *Ariz., U.S.A.* **143 K7** 33 51N 112 37W
Morristown, *Ind., U.S.A.* **141 E11** 39 40N 85 42W
Morristown, *N.J., U.S.A.* **137 F10** 40 48N 74 29W
Morristown, *S. Dak., U.S.A.* **138 C4** 45 56N 101 43W
Morristown, *Tenn., U.S.A.* **135 G4** 36 13N 83 18W
Morro, Pta., *Chile* **158 B1** 27 6 S 71 0W
Morro Bay, *U.S.A.* **144 K6** 35 22N 120 51W
Morro del Jable, *Canary Is.* **33 F5** 28 3N 14 23W
Morro do Chapéu, *Brazil* **155 D3** 11 33 S 41 9W
Morro Jable, Pta. de, *Canary Is.* **33 F5** 28 2N 14 20W
Morros, *Brazil* **154 B3** 2 52 S 44 3W
Morrosquillo, G. de, *Colombia* **148 E4** 9 35N 75 40W
Morrumbene, *Mozam.* **105 C6** 23 31 S 35 16 E
Mors, *Denmark* **15 H2** 56 50N 8 45 E
Morshansk, *Russia* **52 D5** 53 28N 41 50 E
Mörsil, *Sweden* **14 A7** 63 19N 13 40 E
Mortagne →, *France* **23 D13** 48 33N 6 27 E
Mortagne-au-Perche, *France* **22 D7** 48 31N 0 33 E
Mortagne-sur-Gironde, *France* **24 C3** 45 28N 0 47W
Mortagne-sur-Sèvre, *France* **22 F6** 46 59N 0 57W
Mortain, *France* **22 D6** 48 40N 0 57W
Mortara, *Italy* **38 C5** 45 15N 8 44 E
Mortcha, *Chad* **97 E4** 16 0N 21 10 E
Morteau, *France* **23 E13** 47 3N 6 35 E
Morteros, *Argentina* **158 C3** 30 50 S 62 0W
Mortes, R. das →, *Brazil* **155 D1** 11 45 S 50 44W
Mortlake, *Australia* **116 E5** 38 5 S 142 50 E
Morton, *Ill., U.S.A.* **140 D7** 40 37N 89 28W
Morton, *Tex., U.S.A.* **139 J3** 33 44N 102 46W
Morton, *Wash., U.S.A.* **144 D4** 46 34N 122 17W
Mortsel, *Belgium* **21 F4** 51 11N 4 27 E
Morundah, *Australia* **117 C7** 34 57 S 146 19 E
Moruya, *Australia* **117 C9** 35 58 S 150 3 E
Morvan, *France* **23 E11** 47 5N 4 3 E
Morven, *Australia* **115 D4** 26 22 S 147 5 E
Morven, *N.Z.* **119 E6** 44 50 S 171 6 E
Morvern, *U.K.* **18 E3** 56 38N 5 44W
Morwell, *Australia* **117 E7** 38 10 S 146 22 E
Moryn, *Poland* **47 C1** 52 51N 14 22 E
Morzhovets, Ostrov, *Russia* **48 A7** 66 44N 42 35 E
Mosalsk, *Russia* **52 C2** 54 30N 34 55 E
Mosbach, *Germany* **27 F5** 49 21N 9 9 E
Moščenice, *Croatia* **39 C11** 45 17N 14 16 E
Mosciano Sant' Ángelo, *Italy* **39 F10** 42 42N 13 52 E
Moscos Is., *Burma* **76 E1** 14 0N 97 30 E
Moscow = Moskva, *Russia* **52 C3** 55 45N 37 35 E
Moscow, *U.S.A.* **142 C5** 46 44N 117 0W
Mosel →, *Europe* **27 E3** 50 22N 7 36 E
Moselle = Mosel →, *Europe* **27 E3** 50 22N 7 36 E
Moselle □, *France* **23 D13** 48 59N 6 33 E
Moses Lake, *U.S.A.* **142 C4** 47 8N 119 17W
Mosgiel, *N.Z.* **119 F5** 45 53 S 170 21 E
Moshi, *Tanzania* **106 C4** 3 22 S 37 18 E
Moshi □, *Tanzania* **106 C4** 3 22 S 37 18 E
Moshupa, *Botswana* **104 C4** 24 46 S 25 29 E
Mośina, *Poland* **47 C3** 52 15N 16 50 E
Mosjøen, *Norway* **12 D15** 65 51N 13 12 E
Moskenesøya, *Norway* **12 C15** 67 58N 13 0 E
Moskenstraumen, *Norway* **12 C15** 67 47N 12 45 E
Moskva, *Russia* **52 C3** 55 45N 37 35 E
Moskva →, *Russia* **52 C4** 55 5N 38 51 E
Moslavačka Gora, *Croatia* **39 C13** 45 40N 16 37 E
Moso, *Vanuatu* **121 G6** 17 30 S 168 15 E
Mosomane, *Botswana* **104 C4** 24 2 S 26 19 E
Moson-magyaróvar, *Hungary* **31 D10** 47 52N 17 18 E
Mošorin, *Serbia, Yug.* **42 B5** 45 19N 20 4 E
Mospino, *Ukraine* **51 J9** 47 52N 38 0 E
Mosquera, *Colombia* **152 C2** 2 35N 78 24W
Mosquero, *U.S.A.* **139 H3** 35 47N 103 58W
Mosqueruela, *Spain* **34 E4** 40 21N 0 27W
Mosquitia, *Honduras* **148 C3** 15 20N 84 10W
Mosquitos, G. de los, *Panama* **148 E3** 9 15N 81 10W
Moss, *Norway* **14 E4** 59 27N 10 40 E
Moss Vale, *Australia* **117 C9** 34 32 S 150 25 E
Mossaka, *Congo* **102 C3** 1 15 S 16 45 E
Mossâmedes, *Brazil* **155 E1** 16 7 S 50 11W
Mossbank, *Canada* **131 D7** 49 56N 105 56W
Mossburn, *N.Z.* **119 F3** 45 41 S 168 15 E
Mosselbaai, *S. Africa* **104 E3** 34 11 S 22 8 E
Mossendjo, *Congo* **102 C2** 2 55 S 12 42 E
Mosses, Col des, *Switz.* **28 D4** 46 25N 7 7 E
Mossgiel, *Australia* **116 B6** 33 15 S 144 5 E
Mossman, *Australia* **114 B4** 16 21 S 145 15 E
Mossoró, *Brazil* **154 C4** 5 10 S 37 15W
Mossuril, *Mozam.* **107 E5** 14 58 S 40 42 E
Mossy →, *Canada* **131 C8** 54 5N 102 58W
Most, *Czech.* **30 A6** 50 31N 13 38 E
Mosta, *Malta* **32 D1** 35 54N 14 24 E
Moşţafáābād, *Iran* **85 C7** 33 39N 54 53 E
Mostaganem, *Algeria* **99 A5** 35 54N 0 5 E
Mostar, *Bos.-H.* **42 D2** 43 22N 17 50 E
Mostardas, *Brazil* **159 C5** 31 2 S 50 51W
Mostefa, Rass, *Tunisia* **96 A2** 36 55N 11 3 E
Mostiska = Mostyska, *Ukraine* **51 H2** 49 48N 23 4 E
Móstoles, *Spain* **36 E7** 40 19N 3 53W
Mosty = Masty, *Belarus* **50 F3** 53 27N 24 38 E
Mostyska, *Ukraine* **51 H2** 49 48N 23 4 E
Mosul = Al Mawşil, *Iraq* **89 D10** 36 15N 43 5 E
Mosulpo, *S. Korea* **67 H14** 33 20N 126 17 E
Mota, *Vanuatu* **121 C5** 13 49 S 167 42 E
Mota del Cuervo, *Spain* **34 F2** 39 30N 2 52W
Mota del Marqués, *Spain* **36 D5** 41 38N 5 11W
Mota Lava, *Vanuatu* **121 C5** 13 40 S 167 40 E
Motagua →, *Guatemala* **148 C2** 15 44N 88 14W
Motala, *Sweden* **15 F9** 58 32N 15 1 E
Motegi, *Japan* **63 A12** 36 32N 140 11 E
Motherwell, *U.K.* **18 F5** 55 47N 3 58W
Motihari, *India* **81 F11** 26 30N 84 55 E
Motilla del Palancar, *Spain* **34 F3** 39 34N 1 55W
Motiti I., *N.Z.* **118 D5** 37 38 S 176 25 E
Motnik, *Slovenia* **39 B11** 46 14N 14 54 E
Motocurunya, *Venezuela* **153 C5** 4 24N 64 5W
Motovun, *Croatia* **39 C10** 45 20N 13 50 E
Motozintla de Mendoza, *Mexico* **147 D6** 15 21N 92 14W
Motril, *Spain* **35 J1** 36 31N 3 37W
Motru →, *Romania* **46 E4** 44 32N 23 31 E
Mott, *U.S.A.* **138 B3** 46 23N 102 20W
Móttola, *Italy* **41 B10** 40 38N 17 2 E
Motu, *N.Z.* **118 E6** 38 18 S 177 40 E
Motu →, *N.Z.* **118 D6** 37 51 S 177 35 E
Motueka, *N.Z.* **119 B8** 41 7 S 173 1 E
Motueka →, *N.Z.* **119 B8** 41 5 S 173 1 E
Motul, *Mexico* **147 C7** 21 0N 89 20W
Motupena Pt., *Papua N. G.* **120 D8** 6 30 S 155 10 E
Mouanda, *Gabon* **102 C2** 1 28 S 13 7 E
Mouchalagane →, *Canada* **129 B6** 50 56N 68 41W
Moúdhros, *Greece* **44 E7** 39 50N 25 18 E
Mouding, *China* **68 E3** 25 20N 101 28 E
Moudjeria, *Mauritania* **100 B2** 17 50N 12 28W
Moudon, *Switz.* **28 C3** 46 40N 6 49 E
Mougoundou, *Congo* **102 C2** 2 40 S 12 41 E
Mouila, *Gabon* **102 C2** 1 50 S 11 0 E
Mouka, *C.A.R.* **102 A4** 7 16N 21 52 E
Moulamein, *Australia* **116 C6** 35 3 S 144 1 E
Moulianá, *Greece* **32 D7** 35 10N 25 59 E
Moulins, *France* **24 B7** 46 35N 3 19 E
Moulmein, *Burma* **78 G6** 16 30N 97 40 E
Moulmeingyun, *Burma* **78 G5** 16 23N 95 16 E
Moulouya, O. →, *Morocco* **99 A4** 35 5N 2 25W
Moulton, *Iowa, U.S.A.* **140 D4** 40 41N 92 41W
Moulton, *Tex., U.S.A.* **139 L6** 29 35N 97 9W
Moultrie, *U.S.A.* **135 K4** 31 11N 83 47W
Moultrie, L., *U.S.A.* **135 J5** 33 20N 80 5W
Mound City, *Mo., U.S.A.* **138 E7** 40 7N 95 14W
Mound City, *S. Dak., U.S.A.* **138 C4** 45 44N 100 4W
Moúnda, Ákra, *Greece* **45 F2** 38 5N 20 45 E
Moundou, *Chad* **97 G3** 8 40N 16 10 E
Moundsville, *U.S.A.* **136 G4** 39 55N 80 44W
Mounembé, *Congo* **102 C2** 3 20 S 12 32 E
Moung, *Cambodia* **76 F4** 12 46N 103 27 E
Moungoudi, *Congo* **102 C2** 2 45 S 11 46 E
Mount Airy, *U.S.A.* **135 G5** 36 31N 80 37W
Mount Albert, *Canada* **136 B5** 44 8N 79 19W
Mount Amherst, *Australia* **112 C4** 18 24 S 126 58 E
Mount Angel, *U.S.A.* **142 D2** 45 4N 122 48W
Mount Augustus, *Australia* **112 D2** 24 20 S 116 56 E
Mount Ayr, *U.S.A.* **140 D2** 40 43N 94 14W
Mount Barker, *S. Austral., Australia* **116 C3** 35 5 S 138 52 E
Mount Barker, *W. Austral., Australia* **113 F2** 34 38 S 117 40 E
Mount Beauty, *Australia* **117 D7** 36 47 S 147 10 E
Mount Carmel, *U.S.A.* **141 F9** 38 25N 87 46W
Mount Carroll, *U.S.A.* **140 B7** 42 6N 89 59W
Mount Clemens, *U.S.A.* **128 D3** 42 35N 82 53W
Mount Coolon, *Australia* **114 C4** 21 25 S 147 25 E
Mount Darwin, *Zimbabwe* **107 F3** 16 47 S 31 38 E
Mount Desert I., *U.S.A.* **129 D6** 44 21N 68 20W
Mount Dora, *U.S.A.* **135 L5** 28 48N 81 38W
Mount Douglas, *Australia* **114 C4** 21 35 S 146 50 E
Mount Eba, *Australia* **115 E2** 30 11 S 135 40 E
Mount Eden, *U.S.A.* **141 F11** 38 3N 85 9W
Mount Edgecumbe, *U.S.A.* **130 B1** 57 3N 135 21W
Mount Elizabeth, *Australia* **112 C4** 16 0 S 125 50 E
Mount Fletcher, *S. Africa* **105 E4** 30 40 S 28 30 E
Mount Forest, *Canada* **128 D3** 43 59N 80 43W
Mount Gambier, *Australia* **116 D4** 37 50 S 140 46 E
Mount Garnet, *Australia* **114 B4** 17 37 S 145 6 E
Mount Hagen, *Papua N. G.* **120 C3** 5 52 S 144 16 E
Mount Hope, *N.S.W., Australia* **117 B6** 32 51 S 145 51 E
Mount Hope, *S. Austral., Australia* **115 E2** 34 7 S 135 23 E
Mount Hope, *U.S.A.* **134 G5** 37 54N 81 10W
Mount Horeb, *U.S.A.* **140 A7** 43 1N 89 44W
Mount Howitt, *Australia* **115 D3** 26 31 S 142 16 E
Mount Isa, *Australia* **114 C2** 20 42 S 139 26 E
Mount Keith, *Australia* **113 E3** 27 15 S 120 30 E
Mount Laguna, *U.S.A.* **145 N10** 32 52N 116 25W
Mount Larcom, *Australia* **114 C5** 23 48 S 150 59 E
Mount Lofty Ra., *Australia* **116 C3** 34 35 S 139 5 E
Mount McKinley National Park, *U.S.A.* **126 B5** 63 30N 150 0W
Mount Magnet, *Australia* **113 E2** 28 2 S 117 47 E
Mount Manara, *Australia* **116 B5** 32 29 S 143 58 E
Mount Margaret, *Australia* **115 D3** 26 54 S 143 21 E
Mount Maunganui, *N.Z.* **118 D5** 37 40 S 176 14 E
Mount Molloy, *Australia* **114 B4** 16 42 S 145 20 E
Mount Monger, *Australia* **113 F3** 31 0 S 122 0 E
Mount Morgan, *Australia* **114 C5** 23 40 S 150 25 E
Mount Morris, *U.S.A.* **136 D7** 42 44N 77 52W
Mount Mulligan, *Australia* **114 B3** 16 45 S 144 47 E
Mount Narryer, *Australia* **113 E2** 26 30 S 115 55 E
Mount Olive, *U.S.A.* **140 E7** 39 4N 89 44W
Mount Olivet, *U.S.A.* **141 F12** 38 32N 84 2W
Mount Olympus = Uludağ, *Turkey* **88 B3** 40 4N 29 13 E
Mount Orab, *U.S.A.* **141 E13** 39 2N 83 55W
Mount Oxide Mine, *Australia* **114 B2** 19 30 S 139 29 E
Mount Pearl, *Canada* **129 C9** 47 31N 52 47W
Mount Perry, *Australia* **115 D5** 25 13 S 151 42 E
Mount Phillips, *Australia* **112 D2** 24 25 S 116 15 E
Mount Pleasant, *Iowa, U.S.A.* **140 D5** 40 58N 91 33W
Mount Pleasant, *Mich., U.S.A.* **134 D3** 43 36N 84 46W
Mount Pleasant, *Pa., U.S.A.* **136 F5** 40 9N 79 33W
Mount Pleasant, *S.C., U.S.A.* **135 J6** 32 47N 79 52W
Mount Pleasant, *Tenn., U.S.A.* **135 H2** 35 32N 87 12W
Mount Pleasant, *Tex., U.S.A.* **139 J7** 33 9N 94 58W
Mount Pleasant, *Utah, U.S.A.* **142 G8** 39 33N 111 27W
Mount Pocono, *U.S.A.* **137 E9** 41 7N 75 22W
Mount Pulaski, *U.S.A.* **140 D7** 40 1N 89 17W
Mount Rainier National Park, *U.S.A.* **144 D5** 46 55N 121 50W
Mount Revelstoke Nat. Park, *Canada* **130 C5** 51 5N 118 30W
Mount Robson Prov. Park, *Canada* **130 C5** 53 0N 119 0W
Mount Roskill, *N.Z.* **118 C3** 36 55 S 174 45 E
Mount Sandiman, *Australia* **113 D2** 24 25 S 115 30 E
Mount Shasta, *U.S.A.* **142 F2** 41 19N 122 19W
Mount Signal, *U.S.A.* **145 N11** 32 39N 115 37W
Mount Somers, *N.Z.* **119 D6** 43 45 S 171 27 E
Mount Sterling, *Ill., U.S.A.* **140 E6** 39 59N 90 45W
Mount Sterling, *Ky., U.S.A.* **141 F13** 38 4N 83 56W
Mount Sterling, *Ohio, U.S.A.* **141 E13** 39 43N 83 16W
Mount Surprise, *Australia* **114 B3** 18 10 S 144 17 E
Mount Union, *U.S.A.* **136 F7** 40 23N 77 53W
Mount Vernon, *Australia* **112 D2** 24 9 S 118 2 E
Mount Vernon, *Ind., U.S.A.* **138 F10** 38 17N 88 57W
Mount Vernon, *Ind., U.S.A.* **141 F8** 37 56N 87 54W
Mount Vernon, *Iowa, U.S.A.* **140 C5** 41 55N 91 23W
Mount Vernon, *N.Y., U.S.A.* **137 F11** 40 55N 73 50W
Mount Vernon, *Ohio, U.S.A.* **136 F2** 40 23N 82 29W
Mount Vernon, *Wash., U.S.A.* **144 B4** 48 25N 122 20W
Mount Victor, *Australia* **116 B3** 32 11 S 139 44 E
Mount Washington, *U.S.A.* **141 F11** 38 3N 85 33W
Mount Wellington, *N.Z.* **118 C3** 36 55 S 174 52 E
Mount Zion, *U.S.A.* **141 E8** 39 46N 88 53W
Mountain □, *Phil.* **70 C3** 17 20N 121 10 E
Mountain Center, *U.S.A.* **145 M10** 33 42N 116 44W
Mountain City, *Nev., U.S.A.* **142 F6** 41 50N 115 58W
Mountain City, *Tenn., U.S.A.* **135 G5** 36 29N 81 48W
Mountain Grove, *U.S.A.* **139 G8** 37 8N 92 16W
Mountain Home, *Ark., U.S.A.* **139 G8** 36 20N 92 23W
Mountain Home, *Idaho, U.S.A.* **142 E6** 43 8N 115 41W
Mountain Iron, *U.S.A.* **138 B8** 47 32N 92 37W
Mountain Park, *Canada* **130 C5** 52 50N 117 15W
Mountain Pass, *U.S.A.* **145 K11** 35 29N 115 35W
Mountain View, *Ark., U.S.A.* **139 H8** 35 52N 92 7W
Mountain View, *Calif., U.S.A.* **144 H4** 37 23N 122 5W
Mountainair, *U.S.A.* **143 J10** 34 31N 106 15W
Mountmellick, *Ireland* **19 C4** 53 7N 7 20W
Moura, *Australia* **114 C4** 24 35 S 149 58 E
Moura, *Brazil* **153 D5** 1 32 S 61 38W
Moura, *Portugal* **37 G3** 38 7N 7 30W
Mourão, *Portugal* **37 G3** 38 22N 7 22W
Mourdi, Dépression du, *Chad* **97 E4** 18 10N 23 0 E
Mourdiah, *Mali* **100 C3** 14 35N 7 25W
Mourenx-Ville-Nouvelle, *France* **24 E3** 43 22N 0 38W
Mouri, *Ghana* **101 D4** 5 6N 1 14W
Mourilyan, *Australia* **114 B4** 17 35 S 146 3 E
Mourmelon-le-Grand, *France* **23 C11** 49 8N 4 22 E
Mourne →, *U.K.* **19 B4** 54 52N 7 26W
Mourne Mts., *U.K.* **19 B5** 54 10N 6 0W
Mournies, *Greece* **32 D6** 35 29N 24 1 E
Mouscron, *Belgium* **21 G2** 50 45N 3 12 E
Moussoro, *Chad* **97 F3** 13 41N 16 35 E
Mouthe, *France* **23 F13** 46 44N 6 12 E

Mustahil 237

Moutier, *Switz.* 28 B4 47 16N 7 21 E
Moûtiers, *France* 25 C10 45 29N 6 32 E
Moutohara, *N.Z.* 118 E6 38 27 S 177 32 E
Moutong, *Indonesia* 72 A2 0 28N 121 13 E
Mouy, *France* 23 C9 49 18N 2 20 E
Mouzáki, *Greece* 44 E3 39 25N 21 37 E
Movas, *Mexico* 146 B3 28 10N 109 25W
Moville, *Ireland* 19 A4 55 11N 7 3W
Moweaqua, *U.S.A.* 140 E7 39 38N 89 1W
Moxhe, *Belgium* 21 G6 50 38N 5 5 E
Moxico □, *Angola* 103 E4 12 0 S 20 30 E
Moxotó →, *Brazil* 154 C4 9 19 S 38 14W
Moy →, *Ireland* 19 B3 54 8N 9 8W
Moyale, *Kenya* 90 G2 3 30N 39 0 E
Moyamba, *S. Leone* 100 D2 8 4N 12 30W
Moyen Atlas, *Morocco* 98 B3 33 0N 5 0W
Moyle □, *U.K.* 19 A5 55 10N 6 15W
Moyo, *Indonesia* 72 C1 8 10 S 117 40 E
Moyobamba, *Peru* 156 B2 6 0 S 77 0W
Moyyero →, *Russia* 57 C11 68 44N 103 42 E
Moyynty, *Kazakstan* 56 E8 47 10N 73 18 E
Mozambique = Moçambique, *Mozam.* 107 F5 15 3 S 40 42 E
Mozambique ■, *Africa* 107 F4 19 0 S 35 0 E
Mozambique Chan., *Africa* 105 B7 17 30 S 42 30 E
Mozdok, *Russia* 53 J7 43 45N 44 48 E
Mozdūrān, *Iran* 85 B9 36 9N 60 35 E
Mozhaysk, *Russia* 52 C3 55 30N 36 2 E
Mozhga, *Russia* 52 B11 56 26N 52 15 E
Mozhnābād, *Iran* 85 C9 34 7N 60 6 E
Mozirje, *Slovenia* 39 B11 46 22N 14 58 E
Mozyr = Mazyr, *Belarus* 51 F5 51 59N 29 15 E
Mpanda, *Tanzania* 106 D3 6 23 S 31 1 E
Mpanda □, *Tanzania* 106 D3 6 23 S 31 40 E
Mpésoba, *Mali* 100 C3 12 31N 5 39W
Mpika, *Zambia* 107 E3 11 51 S 31 25 E
Mpulungu, *Zambia* 107 D3 8 51 S 31 5 E
Mpumalanga, *S. Africa* 105 D5 29 50 S 30 33 E
Mpumalanga □, *S. Africa* 105 B5 26 0 S 30 0 E
Mpwapwa, *Tanzania* 106 D4 6 23 S 36 30 E
Mpwapwa □, *Tanzania* 106 D4 6 30 S 36 20 E
Mqinvartsveri = Kazbek, *Russia* 53 J7 42 42N 44 30 E
Mrągowo, *Poland* 47 B8 53 52N 21 18 E
Mramor, *Serbia, Yug.* 42 D6 43 20N 21 45 E
Mrimina, *Morocco* 98 C3 29 50N 7 9W
Mrkonjić Grad, *Bos.-H.* 42 C2 44 26N 17 4 E
Mrkopalj, *Croatia* 39 C11 45 21N 14 52 E
Mrocza, *Poland* 47 B4 53 16N 17 35 E
Msab, Oued en →, *Algeria* 99 B6 32 15N 5 0 E
Msaken, *Tunisia* 96 A2 35 49N 10 33 E
Msambansovu, *Zimbabwe* 107 F3 15 50 S 30 3 E
M'sila, *Algeria* 99 A5 35 46N 4 30 E
Msoro, *Zambia* 107 E3 13 35 S 31 50 E
Msta →, *Russia* 50 C6 58 25N 31 20 E
Mstislavl = Mstsislaw, *Belarus* 50 E6 54 0N 31 50 E
Mstsislaw, *Belarus* 50 E6 54 0N 31 50 E
Mszana Dolna, *Poland* 31 B13 49 41N 20 5 E
Mszczonów, *Poland* 47 D7 51 58N 20 33 E
Mtama, *Tanzania* 107 E4 10 17 S 39 21 E
Mtilikwe →, *Zimbabwe* 107 G3 21 9 S 31 30 E
Mtsensk, *Russia* 52 D3 53 17N 36 36 E
Mtskheta, *Georgia* 53 K7 41 52N 44 45 E
Mtubatuba, *S. Africa* 105 D5 28 30 S 32 8 E
Mtwara-Mikindani, *Tanzania* 107 E5 10 20 S 40 20 E
Mu →, *Burma* 78 E5 21 56N 95 38 E
Mu Gia, Deo, *Vietnam* 76 D5 17 40N 105 47 E
Mu Us Shamo, *China* 66 E5 39 0N 109 0 E
Muacandalo, *Angola* 103 E3 10 2 S 19 40 E
Muaná, *Brazil* 154 B2 1 25 S 49 15W
Muanda, *Zaïre* 103 D2 6 0 S 12 20 E
Muang Chiang Rai, *Thailand* 76 C2 19 52N 99 50 E
Muang Lamphun, *Thailand* 76 C2 18 40N 99 2 E
Muang Pak Beng, *Laos* 76 C3 19 54N 101 8 E
Muar, *Malaysia* 77 L4 2 3N 102 34 E
Muarabungo, *Indonesia* 74 C2 1 28 S 102 52 E
Muaraenim, *Indonesia* 74 C2 3 40 S 103 50 E
Muarajuloi, *Indonesia* 75 C4 0 12 S 114 3 E
Muarakaman, *Indonesia* 75 C5 0 2 S 116 45 E
Muaratebo, *Indonesia* 74 C2 1 30 S 102 26 E
Muaratembesi, *Indonesia* 74 C2 1 42 S 103 8 E
Muaratewe, *Indonesia* 75 C4 0 58 S 114 52 E
Mubarakpur, *India* 81 F10 26 6N 83 18 E
Mubarraz = Al Mubarraz, *Si. Arabia* 85 E6 25 30N 49 40 E
Mubende, *Uganda* 106 B3 0 33N 31 22 E
Mubi, *Nigeria* 101 C7 10 18N 13 16 E
Mubur, P., *Indonesia* 77 L6 3 20N 106 12 E
Mucajaí →, *Brazil* 153 C5 2 25N 60 52W
Mucajaí, Serra do, *Brazil* 153 C5 2 23N 61 10W
Mucari, *Angola* 103 D3 9 30 S 16 54 E
Muchachos, Roque de los, *Canary Is.* 33 F2 28 44N 17 52W
Mücheln, *Germany* 26 D7 51 17N 11 47 E
Muchinga Mts., *Zambia* 107 E3 11 30 S 31 30 E
Muchkapskiy, *Russia* 52 E6 51 52N 42 28 E
Muck, *U.K.* 18 E2 56 50N 6 15W
Muckadilla, *Australia* 115 D4 26 35 S 148 23 E
Muco →, *Colombia* 152 C3 4 15N 70 21W
Mucoma, *Angola* 103 F2 15 18 S 13 39 E
Muconda, *Angola* 103 E4 10 31 S 21 15 E
Mucuim →, *Brazil* 157 B5 6 33 S 64 18W
Mucur, *Turkey* 88 C6 39 3N 34 22 E
Mucura, *Brazil* 153 D5 2 31 S 62 43W
Mucuri, *Brazil* 155 E4 18 0 S 39 36W
Mucurici, *Brazil* 155 E3 18 6 S 40 31W
Mucusso, *Angola* 103 F4 18 1 S 21 25 E
Muda, *Canary Is.* 33 F6 28 34N 13 57W
Mudan Jiang →, *China* 67 A15 46 20N 129 30 E
Mudanjiang, *China* 67 B15 44 38N 129 30 E
Mudanya, *Turkey* 88 B3 40 25N 28 50 E
Muddy Cr. →, *U.S.A.* 143 H8 38 24N 110 42W
Mudgee, *Australia* 117 B8 32 32 S 149 31 E
Mudjatik →, *Canada* 131 B7 56 1N 107 36W
Mudon, *Burma* 78 G6 16 15N 97 44 E
Mudugh, *Somali Rep.* 108 C3 7 0N 47 30 E
Mudurnu, *Turkey* 88 B4 40 27N 31 12 E
Muecate, *Mozam.* 107 E4 14 55 S 39 40 E
Muêda, *Mozam.* 107 E4 11 36 S 39 28 E
Mueller Ra., *Australia* 112 C4 18 18 S 126 46 E
Muende, *Mozam.* 107 E3 14 28 S 33 0 E
Muerto, Mar, *Mexico* 147 D6 16 10N 94 10W
Muertos, Punta de los, *Spain* 35 J3 36 57N 1 54W
Mufindi □, *Tanzania* 107 D4 8 30 S 35 20 E
Mufu Shan, *China* 69 C10 29 20N 114 30 E
Mufulira, *Zambia* 107 E2 12 32 S 28 15 E
Mufumbiro Range, *Africa* 106 C2 1 25 S 29 30 E
Mugardos, *Spain* 36 B2 43 27N 8 15W
Muge, *Portugal* 37 F2 39 3N 8 40W
Muge →, *Portugal* 37 F2 39 8N 8 44W
Múggia, *Italy* 39 C10 45 36N 13 46 E
Mughayrā', *Si. Arabia* 84 D3 29 17N 37 41 E
Mugi, *Japan* 62 D6 33 40N 134 25 E
Mugia, *Spain* 36 B1 43 3N 9 10W
Mugila, Mts., *Zaïre* 106 D2 7 0 S 28 50 E
Muğla, *Turkey* 88 D3 37 15N 28 22 E
Mŭglizh, *Bulgaria* 43 E10 42 37N 25 32 E
Mugu, *Nepal* 81 E10 29 45N 82 30 E
Muhammad, Râs, *Egypt* 94 B3 27 44N 34 16 E
Muhammad Qol, *Sudan* 94 C4 20 53N 37 9 E
Muhammadabad, *India* 81 F10 26 4N 83 25 E
Muḩayriqah, *Si. Arabia* 86 B4 23 59N 45 4 E
Muhesi →, *Tanzania* 106 D4 7 0 S 35 20 E
Muheza □, *Tanzania* 106 C4 5 0 S 39 0 E
Mühldorf, *Germany* 27 G8 48 14N 12 32 E
Mühlhausen, *Germany* 26 D6 51 12N 10 27 E
Mühlig Hofmann fjell, *Antarctica* 7 D3 72 30 S 5 0 E
Muhos, *Finland* 12 D22 64 47N 25 59 E
Muhu, *Estonia* 13 G20 58 36N 23 11 E
Muhutwe, *Tanzania* 106 C3 1 35 S 31 45 E
Muiden, *Neths.* 20 D6 52 20N 5 4 E
Muikamachi, *Japan* 61 F9 37 15N 138 50 E
Muine Bheag, *Ireland* 19 D5 52 42N 6 58W
Muiños, *Spain* 36 D3 41 58N 7 59W
Muir, L., *Australia* 113 F2 34 30 S 116 40 E
Mukacheve, *Ukraine* 51 H2 48 27N 22 45 E
Mukachevo = Mukacheve, *Ukraine* 51 H2 48 27N 22 45 E
Mukah, *Malaysia* 75 B4 2 55N 112 5 E
Mukawwa, Geziret, *Egypt* 94 C4 23 55N 35 53 E
Mukdahan, *Thailand* 76 D5 16 32N 104 43 E
Mukden = Shenyang, *China* 67 D12 41 48N 123 27 E
Mukhtolovo, *Russia* 52 C6 55 29N 43 15 E
Mukhtuya = Lensk, *Russia* 57 C12 60 48N 114 55 E
Mukinbudin, *Australia* 113 F2 30 55 S 118 5 E
Mukishi, *Zaïre* 103 D4 8 30 S 24 44 E
Mukomuko, *Indonesia* 74 C2 2 30 S 101 10 E
Mukomwenze, *Zaïre* 106 D2 6 49 S 27 15 E
Mukry, *Turkmenistan* 55 E2 37 54N 65 12 E
Muktsar, *India* 80 D6 30 30N 74 30 E
Mukur, *Afghan.* 80 C2 32 50N 67 42 E
Mukutawa →, *Canada* 131 C9 53 10N 97 24W
Mukwela, *Zambia* 107 F2 17 0 S 26 40 E
Mukwonago, *U.S.A.* 141 B8 42 52N 88 20W
Mula, *Spain* 35 G3 38 3N 1 33W
Mula →, *India* 82 E2 18 34N 74 21 E
Mulanay, *Phil.* 70 E4 13 31N 122 24 E
Mulange, *Zaïre* 106 C2 3 40 S 27 10 E
Mulberry Grove, *U.S.A.* 140 F7 38 56N 89 16W
Mulchén, *Chile* 158 D1 37 45 S 72 20W
Mulde →, *Germany* 26 D8 51 53N 12 15 E
Muldraugh, *U.S.A.* 141 G11 37 56N 85 59W
Mule Creek, *U.S.A.* 138 D2 43 19N 104 8W
Muleba, *Tanzania* 106 C3 1 50 S 31 37 E
Muleba □, *Tanzania* 106 C3 2 0 S 31 30 E
Mulegns, *Switz.* 29 C9 46 32N 9 38 E
Muleshoe, *U.S.A.* 139 H3 34 13N 102 43W
Mulga Valley, *Australia* 116 A4 31 8 S 141 3 E
Mulgathing, *Australia* 115 E1 30 15 S 134 8 E
Mulgrave, *Canada* 129 C7 45 38N 61 31W
Mulgrave I., *Papua N. G.* 120 F2 10 5 S 142 10 E
Mulhacén, *Spain* 35 H1 37 4N 3 20W
Mülheim, *Germany* 26 D3 51 25N 6 54 E
Mulhouse, *France* 23 E14 47 40N 7 20 E
Muli, *China* 68 D3 27 52N 101 8 E
Mulifanua, *W. Samoa* 121 W24 13 50 S 171 59W
Muling, *China* 67 B16 44 35N 130 10 E
Mull, *U.K.* 18 E3 56 25N 5 56W
Mullaittvu, *Sri Lanka* 83 K5 9 15N 80 49 E
Mullen, *U.S.A.* 138 D4 42 3N 101 1W
Mullengudgery, *Australia* 117 A7 31 43 S 147 23 E
Mullens, *U.S.A.* 134 G5 37 35N 81 23W
Muller, Pegunungan, *Indonesia* 75 B4 0 30N 113 30 E
Mullet Pen., *Ireland* 19 B1 54 13N 10 2W
Mullewa, *Australia* 113 E2 28 29 S 115 30 E
Müllheim, *Germany* 27 H3 47 47N 7 36 E
Mulligan →, *Australia* 114 C2 25 0 S 139 0 E
Mullin, *U.S.A.* 139 K5 31 33N 98 40W
Mullingar, *Ireland* 19 C4 53 31N 7 21W
Mullins, *U.S.A.* 135 H6 34 12N 79 15W
Mullumbimby, *Australia* 115 D5 28 30 S 153 30 E
Mulobezi, *Zambia* 107 F2 16 45 S 25 7 E
Mulshi L., *India* 82 E1 18 30N 73 48 E
Multai, *India* 82 D4 21 50N 78 21 E
Multan, *Pakistan* 79 C3 30 15N 71 36 E
Multrå, *Sweden* 14 A11 63 10N 17 24 E
Mulu, Gunong, *Malaysia* 75 B4 4 3N 114 56 E
Mulumbe, Mts., *Zaïre* 107 D2 8 40 S 27 30 E
Mulungushi Dam, *Zambia* 107 E2 14 48 S 28 48 E
Mulvane, *U.S.A.* 139 G6 37 29N 97 15W
Mulwad, *Sudan* 94 D3 18 45N 30 39 E
Mulwala, *Australia* 117 C7 35 59 S 146 0 E
Mumbaī = Bombay, *India* 82 E1 18 55N 72 50 E
Mumbondo, *Angola* 103 E2 10 9 S 14 15 E
Mumbwa, *Zambia* 107 E2 15 0 S 27 0 E
Mumeng, *Papua N. G.* 120 D4 7 1 S 146 37 E
Mumra, *Russia* 53 H8 45 45N 47 41 E
Mun →, *Thailand* 76 E5 15 19N 105 30 E
Muna, *Indonesia* 72 B2 5 0 S 122 30 E
Munamagi, *Estonia* 13 H22 57 43N 27 4 E
Münchberg, *Germany* 27 E7 50 11N 11 47 E
Müncheberg, *Germany* 26 C10 52 30N 14 9 E
München, *Germany* 27 G7 48 8N 11 34 E
Munchen-Gladbach = Mönchengladbach, *Germany* 26 D2 51 11N 6 27 E
Muncho Lake, *Canada* 130 B3 59 0N 125 50W
Munchŏn, *N. Korea* 67 E14 39 14N 127 19 E
Münchwilen, *Switz.* 29 B7 47 28N 8 59 E
Muncie, *U.S.A.* 141 D11 40 12N 85 23W
Muncoonie, L., *Australia* 114 D2 25 12 S 138 40 E
Munda, *Solomon Is.* 121 M9 8 20 S 157 16 E
Mundakayam, *India* 83 K3 9 30N 76 50 E
Mundala, *Indonesia* 73 B6 4 30 S 141 0 E
Mundare, *Canada* 130 C6 53 35N 112 20W
Munday, *U.S.A.* 139 J5 33 27N 99 38W
Münden, *Germany* 26 D5 51 25N 9 38 E
Mundiwindi, *Australia* 112 D3 23 47 S 120 9 E
Mundo →, *Spain* 35 G2 38 30N 2 15W
Mundo Novo, *Brazil* 155 D3 11 50 S 40 29W
Mundra, *India* 80 H3 22 54N 69 48 E
Mundrabilla, *Australia* 113 F4 31 52 S 127 51 E
Munducurus, *Brazil* 153 D6 4 47 S 58 16W
Munenga, *Angola* 103 E2 10 2 S 14 41 E
Munera, *Spain* 35 F2 39 2N 2 29W
Muneru →, *India* 83 F5 16 45N 80 3 E
Mungallala, *Australia* 115 D4 26 28 S 147 34 E
Mungallala Cr. →, *Australia* 115 D4 28 53 S 147 5 E
Mungana, *Australia* 114 B3 17 8 S 144 27 E
Mungaoli, *India* 80 G8 24 24N 78 7 E
Mungari, *Mozam.* 107 F3 17 12 S 33 30 E
Mungbere, *Zaïre* 106 B2 2 36N 28 28 E
Munger, *India* 81 G12 25 23N 86 30 E
Mungindi, *Australia* 115 D4 28 58 S 149 1 E
Munhango, *Angola* 103 E3 12 10 S 18 38 E
Munich = München, *Germany* 27 G7 48 8N 11 34 E
Munising, *U.S.A.* 134 B2 46 25N 86 40W
Munka-Ljungby, *Sweden* 15 H6 56 16N 12 58 E
Munkedal, *Sweden* 15 F5 58 28N 11 40 E
Munku-Sardyk, *Russia* 57 D11 51 45N 100 20 E
Münnerstadt, *Germany* 27 E6 50 14N 10 12 E
Munoz, *Phil.* 70 D3 15 43N 120 54 E
Muñoz Gamero, Pen., *Chile* 160 D2 52 30 S 73 5W
Munro, *Australia* 117 D7 37 56 S 147 11 E
Munroe L., *Canada* 131 B9 59 13N 98 35W
Munsan, *S. Korea* 67 F14 37 51N 126 48 E
Munshiganj, *Bangla.* 78 D3 23 33N 90 32 E
Münsingen, *Switz.* 28 C5 46 52N 7 32 E
Munster, *France* 23 D14 48 2N 7 8 E
Munster, *Niedersachsen, Germany* 26 C6 52 58N 10 5 E
Münster, *Nordrhein-Westfalen, Germany* 26 D3 51 58N 7 37 E
Münster, *Switz.* 29 D6 46 29N 8 17 E
Munster □, *Ireland* 19 D3 52 18N 8 44W
Muntadgin, *Australia* 113 F2 31 45 S 118 33 E
Muntele Mare, *Romania* 46 C4 46 30N 23 12 E
Muntok, *Indonesia* 74 C3 2 5 S 105 10 E
Munyama, *Zambia* 107 F2 16 5 S 28 31 E
Munzur Dağları, *Turkey* 89 C8 39 30N 39 10 E
Muong Beng, *Laos* 76 B3 20 23N 101 46 E
Muong Boum, *Vietnam* 76 A4 22 24N 102 49 E
Muong Et, *Laos* 76 B5 20 49N 104 1 E
Muong Hai, *Laos* 76 B3 21 3N 101 49 E
Muong Hiem, *Laos* 76 B4 20 5N 103 22 E
Muong Houn, *Laos* 76 B3 20 8N 101 23 E
Muong Hung, *Vietnam* 76 B4 20 56N 103 53 E
Muong Kau, *Laos* 76 E5 15 6N 105 47 E
Muong Khao, *Laos* 76 C4 19 38N 103 32 E
Muong Khoua, *Laos* 76 B4 21 5N 102 31 E
Muong Liep, *Laos* 76 C3 18 29N 101 40 E
Muong May, *Laos* 76 E6 14 49N 106 56 E
Muong Ngeun, *Laos* 76 B3 20 36N 101 3 E
Muong Ngoi, *Laos* 76 B4 20 43N 102 41 E
Muong Nhie, *Vietnam* 76 A4 22 12N 102 28 E
Muong Nong, *Laos* 76 D6 16 22N 106 30 E
Muong Ou Tay, *Laos* 76 A3 22 7N 101 48 E
Muong Oua, *Laos* 76 C3 18 18N 101 20 E
Muong Peun, *Laos* 76 B4 20 13N 103 52 E
Muong Phalane, *Laos* 76 D5 16 39N 105 34 E
Muong Phieng, *Laos* 76 C3 19 6N 101 32 E
Muong Phine, *Laos* 76 D6 16 32N 106 2 E
Muong Sai, *Laos* 76 B3 20 42N 101 59 E
Muong Saiapoun, *Laos* 76 C3 18 24N 101 31 E
Muong Sen, *Vietnam* 76 C5 19 24N 104 8 E
Muong Sing, *Laos* 76 B3 21 11N 101 9 E
Muong Son, *Laos* 76 B4 20 27N 103 19 E
Muong Soui, *Laos* 76 C4 19 33N 102 52 E
Muong Va, *Laos* 76 B4 21 53N 102 19 E
Muong Xia, *Vietnam* 76 B5 20 19N 104 50 E
Muonio, *Finland* 12 C20 67 57N 23 40 E
Muonionjoki →, *Finland* 12 C20 67 11N 23 34 E
Muotathal, *Switz.* 29 C7 46 58N 8 46 E
Mupa, *Angola* 103 F3 16 5 S 15 50 E
Muping, *China* 67 F11 37 22N 121 36 E
Muqaddam, Wadi →, *Sudan* 94 D3 18 4N 31 30 E
Muqdisho, *Somali Rep.* 108 D3 2 2N 45 25 E
Muqshin, W. →, *Oman* 87 C6 19 44N 55 14 E
Muquequete, *Angola* 103 E2 14 50 S 14 16 E
Mur →, *Austria* 30 E9 46 18N 16 52 E
Mur-de-Bretagne, *France* 22 D4 48 12N 3 0W
Mura →, *Slovenia* 39 B13 46 30N 16 33 E
Muradiye, *Turkey* 89 C10 39 0N 43 44 E
Murakami, *Japan* 60 E9 38 14N 139 29 E
Murallón, Cuerro, *Chile* 160 C2 49 48 S 73 30W
Muralto, *Switz.* 29 D7 46 11N 8 49 E
Muranda, *Rwanda* 106 C2 1 52 S 29 20 E
Murang'a, *Kenya* 106 C4 0 45 S 37 9 E
Murashi, *Russia* 54 B2 59 30N 49 0 E
Murat, *France* 24 C6 45 7N 2 53 E
Murat →, *Turkey* 89 C9 38 46N 40 0 E
Muratlı, *Turkey* 88 B2 41 10N 27 29 E
Murau, *Austria* 30 D7 47 6N 14 10 E
Muravera, *Italy* 40 C2 39 25N 9 34 E
Murayama, *Japan* 60 E10 38 30N 140 25 E
Murban, *U.A.E.* 85 F7 23 50N 53 45 E
Murça, *Portugal* 36 D3 41 24N 7 28W
Murchison, *N.Z.* 119 B7 41 49 S 172 21 E
Murchison →, *Australia* 113 E1 27 45 S 114 0 E
Murchison, Mt., *Antarctica* 7 D11 73 0 S 168 0 E
Murchison Falls = Kabarega Falls, *Uganda* 106 B3 2 15N 31 30 E
Murchison House, *Australia* 113 E1 27 39 S 114 14 E
Murchison Mt., *N.Z.* 119 D6 43 0 S 171 22 E
Murchison Mts., *N.Z.* 119 F2 45 13 S 167 23 E
Murchison Ra., *Australia* 114 C1 20 0 S 134 10 E
Murchison Rapids, *Malawi* 107 F3 15 55 S 34 35 E
Murcia, *Spain* 35 G3 38 5N 1 10W
Murcia □, *Spain* 35 H3 37 50N 1 30W
Murdo, *U.S.A.* 138 D4 43 53N 100 43W
Murdoch Pt., *Australia* 114 A3 14 37 S 144 55 E
Mureş □, *Romania* 46 C5 46 45N 24 40 E
Mureş →, *Romania* 46 C1 46 15N 20 13 E
Mureşul = Mureş →, *Romania* 46 C1 46 15N 20 13 E
Muret, *France* 24 E5 43 30N 1 20 E
Murfatlar, *Romania* 46 E9 44 10N 28 26 E
Murfreesboro, *U.S.A.* 135 H2 35 51N 86 24W
Murg, *Switz.* 29 B8 47 6N 9 13 E
Murg →, *Germany* 27 G4 48 55N 8 10 E
Murgab = Murghob, *Tajikistan* 55 D7 38 10N 74 2 E
Murgeni, *Romania* 46 C9 46 12N 28 1 E
Murgenthal, *Switz.* 28 B5 47 16N 7 50 E
Murghob, *Tajikistan* 55 D7 38 10N 74 2 E
Murgon, *Australia* 115 D5 26 15 S 151 54 E
Murgoo, *Australia* 113 E2 27 24 S 116 28 E
Muri, *Switz.* 29 B6 47 17N 8 21 E
Muria, *Indonesia* 75 D4 6 36 S 110 53 E
Muriaé, *Brazil* 155 F3 21 8 S 42 23W
Murias de Paredes, *Spain* 36 C4 42 52N 6 11W
Murici, *Brazil* 154 C4 9 19 S 35 56W
Muriége, *Angola* 103 D4 9 58 S 21 11 E
Muriel Mine, *Zimbabwe* 107 F3 17 14 S 30 40 E
Murila, *Angola* 103 E4 10 44 S 20 20 E
Müritz-see, *Germany* 26 B8 53 25N 12 42 E
Murka, *Kenya* 106 C4 3 27 S 38 0 E
Murmansk, *Russia* 48 A5 68 57N 33 10 E
Murmerwoude, *Neths.* 20 B8 53 18N 6 0 E
Murnau, *Germany* 27 H7 47 40N 11 12 E
Muro, *France* 25 F12 42 34N 8 54 E
Muro, *Spain* 33 B10 39 44N 3 3 E
Muro, C. de, *France* 25 G12 41 44N 8 37 E
Muro Lucano, *Italy* 41 B8 40 45N 15 29 E
Murom, *Russia* 52 C6 55 35N 42 3 E
Muroran, *Japan* 60 C10 42 25N 141 0 E
Muros, *Spain* 36 C1 42 45N 9 5W
Muros y de Noya, Ría de, *Spain* 36 C2 42 45N 9 0W
Muroto, *Japan* 62 D6 33 18N 134 9 E
Muroto-Misaki, *Japan* 62 D6 33 15N 134 10 E
Murowana Goślina, *Poland* 47 C4 52 35N 17 0 E
Murphy, *U.S.A.* 142 E5 43 13N 116 33W
Murphys, *U.S.A.* 144 G6 38 8N 120 28W
Murphysboro, *U.S.A.* 139 G10 37 46N 89 20W
Murrat, *Sudan* 94 D2 18 51N 29 33 E
Murray, *Iowa, U.S.A.* 140 C3 41 3N 93 57W
Murray, *Ky., U.S.A.* 135 G1 36 37N 88 19W
Murray, *Utah, U.S.A.* 142 F8 40 40N 111 53W
Murray →, *Australia* 116 C3 35 20 S 139 22 E
Murray →, *Canada* 130 B4 56 11N 120 45W
Murray, L., *Papua N. G.* 120 D1 7 0 S 141 35 E
Murray, L., *U.S.A.* 135 H5 34 3N 81 13W
Murray Bridge, *Australia* 116 C3 35 6 S 139 14 E
Murray Downs, *Australia* 114 C1 21 4 S 134 40 E
Murray Harbour, *Canada* 129 C7 46 0N 62 28W
Murraysburg, *S. Africa* 104 E3 31 58 S 23 47 E
Murrayville, *U.S.A.* 140 E6 39 35N 90 15W
Murree, *Pakistan* 80 C5 33 56N 73 28 E
Murrieta, *U.S.A.* 145 M9 33 33N 117 13W
Murrin Murrin, *Australia* 113 E3 28 58 S 121 33 E
Murrumbidgee →, *Australia* 116 C5 34 43 S 143 12 E
Murrumburrah, *Australia* 117 C8 34 32 S 148 22 E
Murrurundi, *Australia* 117 A9 31 42 S 150 51 E
Murshid, *Sudan* 94 C3 21 40N 31 10 E
Murshidabad, *India* 81 G13 24 11N 88 19 E
Murska Sobota, *Slovenia* 39 B13 46 39N 16 12 E
Murtazapur, *India* 82 D3 20 40N 77 25 E
Murten, *Switz.* 28 C4 46 56N 7 4 E
Murtensee, *Switz.* 28 C4 46 56N 7 7 E
Murtle L., *Canada* 130 C5 52 8N 119 38W
Murtoa, *Australia* 116 D5 36 35 S 142 28 E
Murtosa, *Portugal* 36 E2 40 44N 8 40W
Muru →, *Brazil* 156 B3 8 9 S 70 45W
Murungu, *Tanzania* 106 C3 4 12 S 31 10 E
Murupara, *N.Z.* 118 E5 38 28 S 176 42 E
Murwara, *India* 81 H9 23 46N 80 28 E
Murwillumbah, *Australia* 115 D5 28 18 S 153 27 E
Mürz →, *Austria* 30 D8 47 30N 15 25 E
Mürzzuschlag, *Austria* 30 D8 47 36N 15 41 E
Muş, *Turkey* 89 C9 38 45N 41 30 E
Musa, *Zaïre* 102 B3 2 40N 19 18 E
Musa →, *Papua N. G.* 120 E5 9 3 S 148 55 E
Mûsa, G., *Egypt* 94 J8 28 33N 33 59 E
Musa Khel, *Pakistan* 79 C3 30 59N 69 52 E
Mūsá Qal'eh, *Afghan.* 79 B2 32 20N 64 50 E
Musala, *Bulgaria* 43 E8 42 13N 23 37 E
Musala, *Indonesia* 74 B1 1 41N 98 28 E
Musan, *N. Korea* 67 C15 42 12N 129 12 E
Musangu, *Zaïre* 103 E4 10 28 S 23 55 E
Musasa, *Tanzania* 106 C3 3 25 S 31 30 E
Musashino, *Japan* 63 B11 35 42N 139 34 E
Musay'īd, *Qatar* 85 E6 25 0N 51 33 E
Musaymīr, *Yemen* 86 D4 13 27N 44 37 E
Muscat = Masqat, *Oman* 87 B7 23 37N 58 36 E
Muscat & Oman = Oman ■, *Asia* 87 B7 23 0N 58 0 E
Muscatine, *U.S.A.* 140 C5 41 25N 91 3W
Muscoda, *U.S.A.* 140 A6 43 11N 90 27W
Musel, *Spain* 36 B5 43 34N 5 42W
Musgrave, *Australia* 114 A3 14 47 S 143 30 E
Musgrave Ras., *Australia* 113 E5 26 0 S 132 0 E
Mushie, *Zaïre* 102 C3 2 56 S 16 55 E
Mushin, *Nigeria* 101 D5 6 32N 3 21 E
Musi →, *India* 82 F4 16 41N 79 40 E
Musi →, *Indonesia* 74 C2 2 20 S 104 56 E
Muskeg →, *Canada* 130 A4 60 20N 123 20W
Muskegon, *U.S.A.* 141 A10 43 14N 86 16W
Muskegon →, *U.S.A.* 134 D2 43 14N 86 21W
Muskegon Heights, *U.S.A.* 141 A10 43 12N 86 16W
Muskogee, *U.S.A.* 139 H7 35 45N 95 22W
Muskwa →, *Canada* 130 B4 58 47N 122 48W
Muslīmiyah, *Syria* 84 B3 36 19N 37 12 E
Musmar, *Sudan* 94 D4 18 13N 35 40 E
Musofu, *Zambia* 107 E2 13 30 S 29 0 E
Musoma, *Tanzania* 106 C3 1 30 S 33 48 E
Musoma □, *Tanzania* 106 C3 1 50 S 34 30 E
Musquaro, L., *Canada* 129 B7 50 38N 61 5W
Musquodoboit Harbour, *Canada* 129 D7 44 50N 63 9W
Mussau I., *Papua N. G.* 120 A5 1 30 S 149 40 E
Musselburgh, *U.K.* 18 F5 55 57N 3 2W
Musselkanaal, *Neths.* 20 C10 52 57N 7 0 E
Musselshell →, *U.S.A.* 142 C10 47 21N 107 57W
Mussende, *Angola* 103 E3 10 32 S 16 5 E
Mussidan, *France* 24 C4 45 2N 0 22 E
Mussolo, *Angola* 103 D3 9 59 S 17 19 E
Mussomeli, *Italy* 40 E6 37 35N 13 45 E
Musson, *Belgium* 21 J7 49 33N 5 42 E
Mussoorie, *India* 80 D8 30 27N 78 6 E
Mussuco, *Angola* 103 F3 17 2 S 19 3 E
Mustafakemalpaşa, *Turkey* 88 B3 40 2N 28 24 E
Mustahil, *Ethiopia* 108 C2 5 16N 44 45 E

238 Mustang

Mustang, Nepal 81 E10 29 10N 83 55 E
Musters, L., Argentina 160 C3 45 20 S 69 25W
Musudan, N. Korea 67 D15 40 50N 129 43 E
Muswellbrook, Australia 117 B9 32 16 S 150 56 E
Muszyna, Poland 31 B13 49 22N 20 55 E
Mût, Egypt 94 B2 25 28N 28 58 E
Mut, Turkey 88 D5 36 40N 33 28 E
Mutanda, Mozam. 105 C5 21 0 S 33 34 E
Mutanda, Zambia 107 E2 12 24 S 26 13 E
Mutare, Zimbabwe 107 F3 18 58 S 32 38 E
Mu'tariḍah, Al 'Urūq al, Si. Arabia 87 B6 21 15N 54 0 E
Muting, Indonesia 73 C6 7 23 S 140 20 E
Mutooroo, Australia 116 B4 32 26 S 140 55 E
Mutoray, Russia 57 C11 60 56N 101 0 E
Mutoto, Zaïre 103 D4 5 42 S 22 42 E
Mutshatsha, Zaïre 103 E4 10 35 S 24 20 E
Mutsu, Japan 60 D10 41 5N 140 55 E
Mutsu-Wan, Japan 60 D10 41 5N 140 55 E
Muttaburra, Australia 114 C3 22 38 S 144 29 E
Muttama, Australia 117 C8 34 46 S 148 8 E
Mutuáli, Mozam. 107 E4 14 55 S 37 0 E
Mutunópolis, Brazil 155 D2 13 40 S 49 15W
Muvatupusha, India 83 K3 9 53N 76 35 E
Muweilih, Egypt 91 E3 30 42N 34 19 E
Muxima, Angola 103 D2 9 33 S 13 58 E
Muy Muy, Nic. 148 D2 12 39N 85 36W
Muyinga, Burundi 106 C3 3 14 S 30 33 E
Muynak, Uzbekistan 56 E6 43 44N 59 10 E
Muyunkum, Peski, Kazakstan 55 A5 44 12N 71 0 E
Muzaffarabad, Pakistan 81 B5 34 25N 73 30 E
Muzaffargarh, Pakistan 79 C3 30 5N 71 14 E
Muzaffarnagar, India 80 E7 29 26N 77 40 E
Muzaffarpur, India 81 F11 26 7N 85 23 E
Muzeze, Angola 103 F3 15 3 S 17 43 E
Muzhi, Russia 56 C7 65 25N 64 40 E
Muzillac, France 22 E4 47 35N 2 30W
Muzkol, Khrebet, Tajikistan 55 D6 38 22N 73 20 E
Muzon, C., U.S.A. 130 C2 54 40N 132 42W
Mvadhi-Ousyé, Gabon 102 B2 1 13N 13 12 E
Mvam, Gabon 102 C1 0 13 S 9 39 E
Mvôlô, Sudan 95 F2 6 2N 29 53 E
Mvuma, Zimbabwe 107 F3 19 16 S 30 30 E
Mvurwi, Zimbabwe 107 F3 17 0 S 30 57 E
Mwadui, Tanzania 106 C3 3 26 S 33 32 E
Mwambo, Tanzania 107 E5 10 30 S 40 22 E
Mwandi, Zambia 107 F1 17 30 S 24 51 E
Mwanza, Tanzania 106 C3 2 30 S 32 58 E
Mwanza, Zaïre 103 D5 7 55 S 26 43 E
Mwanza, Zambia 107 F1 16 58 S 24 28 E
Mwanza □, Tanzania 106 C3 2 0 S 33 0 E
Mwaya, Tanzania 107 D3 9 32 S 33 55 E
Mweelrea, Ireland 19 C2 53 39N 9 49W
Mweka, Zaïre 103 C4 4 50 S 21 34 E
Mwendjila, Zaïre 103 D3 7 12 S 18 51 E
Mwene, Zaïre 103 D4 6 35 S 22 27 E
Mwenezi, Zimbabwe 107 G3 21 15 S 30 48 E
Mwenezi →, Mozam. 107 G3 22 40 S 31 50 E
Mwenga, Zaïre 106 C2 3 1 S 28 28 E
Mweru, L., Zambia 107 D2 9 0 S 28 40 E
Mweza Range, Zimbabwe 107 G3 21 0 S 30 0 E
Mwilambwe, Zaïre 103 D5 8 7 S 25 5 E
Mwimbi, Tanzania 107 D3 8 38 S 31 39 E
Mwinilunga, Zambia 107 E1 11 43 S 24 25 E
My Tho, Vietnam 77 G6 10 29N 106 23 E
Mya, O. →, Algeria 99 B5 30 46N 4 54 E
Myajlar, India 80 F4 26 15N 70 20 E
Myanaung, Burma 78 F5 18 18N 95 22 E
Myanmar = Burma ■, Asia 78 E6 21 0N 96 30 E
Myaungmya, Burma 78 G5 16 30N 94 40 E
Myeik Kyunzu, Burma 77 G1 11 30N 97 30 E
Myerstown, U.S.A. 137 F8 40 22N 76 19W
Myingyan, Burma 78 E5 21 30N 95 20 E
Myitkyina, Burma 78 C6 25 24N 97 26 E
Myittha →, Burma 78 D5 23 12N 94 17 E
Myjava, Slovak Rep. 31 C10 48 41N 17 37 E
Mykhaylivka, Ukraine 51 J8 47 12N 35 15 E
Mykines, Færoe Is. 12 E9 62 7N 7 35W
Mykolayiv, Ukraine 51 J7 46 58N 32 0 E
Mymensingh, Bangla. 78 C3 24 45N 90 24 E
Myndus, Turkey 45 G9 37 3N 27 14 E
Mynydd Du, U.K. 17 F4 51 52N 3 50W
Mynzhilgi, Gora, Kazakstan 55 B4 43 48N 68 51 E
Mýrdalsjökull, Iceland 12 E4 63 40N 19 6W
Myrhorod, Ukraine 51 H7 49 58N 33 37 E
Myroodah, Australia 112 C3 18 7 S 124 16 E
Myrtle Beach, U.S.A. 135 J6 33 42N 78 53W
Myrtle Creek, U.S.A. 142 E2 43 1N 123 17W
Myrtle Point, U.S.A. 142 E1 43 4N 124 8W
Myrtleford, Australia 117 D7 36 34 S 146 44 E
Myrtou, Cyprus 32 D12 35 18N 33 4 E
Mysen, Norway 14 E5 59 33N 11 20 E
Mysia, Turkey 88 C2 39 50N 27 0 E
Myslenice, Poland 31 B12 49 51N 19 57 E
Myślibórz, Poland 47 C1 52 55N 14 50 E
Mysłowice, Poland 31 A12 50 15N 19 12 E
Mysore = Karnataka □, India 83 H3 13 15N 77 0 E
Mysore, India 83 H3 12 17N 76 41 E
Mystic, Conn., U.S.A. 137 E13 41 21N 71 58W
Mystic, Iowa, U.S.A. 140 D4 40 47N 92 57W
Myszków, Poland 47 E6 50 45N 19 22 E
Myszyniec, Poland 47 B8 53 23N 21 21 E
Mythen, Switz. 29 B7 47 2N 8 42 E
Mytishchi, Russia 52 C3 55 50N 37 50 E
Myton, U.S.A. 142 F8 40 12N 110 4W
Mývatn, Iceland 12 D5 65 36N 17 0W
Mže →, Czech. 30 B6 49 46N 13 24 E
Mzimba, Malawi 107 E3 11 55 S 33 39 E
Mzimkulu →, S. Africa 105 E5 30 44 S 30 28 E
Mzimvubu →, S. Africa 105 E4 31 38 S 29 33 E
Mzuzu, Malawi 107 E3 11 30 S 33 55 E

N

N' Dioum, Senegal 100 B2 16 31N 14 39W
Na Hearadh = Harris, U.K. 18 D2 57 50N 6 55W
Na-lang, Burma 78 D6 22 42N 97 33 E
Na Noi, Thailand 76 C3 18 19N 100 43 E
Na Phao, Laos 76 D5 17 35N 105 44 E
Na Sam, Vietnam 76 A6 22 3N 106 37 E
Na San, Vietnam 76 B5 21 12N 104 2 E
Naab →, Germany 27 F8 49 1N 12 2 E
Naaldwijk, Neths. 20 E4 51 59N 4 13 E
Na'am, Sudan 95 F2 9 42N 28 27 E
Naantali, Finland 13 F19 60 29N 22 2 E
Naarden, Neths. 20 D6 52 18N 5 9 E
Naas, Ireland 19 C5 53 12N 6 40W
Nababiep, S. Africa 104 D2 29 36 S 17 46 E
Nabadwip = Navadwip, India 81 H13 23 34N 88 20 E
Nabari, Japan 63 C8 34 37N 136 5 E
Nabawa, Australia 113 E1 28 30 S 114 48 E
Nabberu, L., Australia 113 E3 25 50 S 120 30 E
Nabburg, Germany 27 F8 49 27N 12 11 E
Naberezhnyye Chelny, Russia 52 C11 55 42N 52 19 E
Nabeul, Tunisia 96 A2 36 30N 10 44 E
Nabha, India 80 D7 30 26N 76 14 E
Nabīd, Iran 85 D8 29 40N 57 38 E
Nabire, Indonesia 73 B5 3 15 S 135 26 E
Nabisar, Pakistan 80 G3 25 8N 69 40 E
Nabisipi →, Canada 129 B7 50 14N 62 13W
Nabiswera, Uganda 106 B3 1 27N 32 15 E
Nablus = Nābulus, West Bank 91 C4 32 14N 35 15 E
Naboomspruit, S. Africa 105 C4 24 32 S 28 40 E
Nabua, Phil. 70 E4 13 24N 123 22 E
Nābulus, West Bank 91 C4 32 14N 35 15 E
Nabunturan, Phil. 71 H5 7 35N 125 58 E
Nacala, Mozam. 107 E5 14 31 S 40 34 E
Nacala-Velha, Mozam. 107 E5 14 32 S 40 34 E
Nacaome, Honduras 148 D2 13 31N 87 30W
Nacaroa, Mozam. 107 E4 14 22 S 39 56 E
Naches, U.S.A. 142 C3 46 44N 120 42W
Naches →, U.S.A. 144 D6 46 38N 120 31W
Nachikatsuura, Japan 63 D7 33 33N 135 58 E
Nachingwea, Tanzania 107 E4 10 23 S 38 49 E
Nachingwea □, Tanzania 107 E4 10 30 S 38 30 E
Nachna, India 80 F4 27 34N 71 41 E
Náchod, Czech. 31 A9 50 25N 16 8 E
Nacimiento Reservoir, U.S.A. 144 K6 35 46N 120 53W
Nacka, Sweden 14 E12 59 17N 18 12 E
Nackara, Australia 116 B3 32 48 S 139 12 E
Naco, Mexico 146 A3 31 20N 109 56W
Naco, U.S.A. 143 L9 31 20N 109 57W
Nacogdoches, U.S.A. 139 K7 31 36N 94 39W
Nácori Chico, Mexico 146 B3 29 39N 109 1W
Nacozari, Mexico 146 A3 30 24N 109 39W
Nadi, Sudan 94 D3 18 40N 33 41 E
Nadiad, India 80 H5 22 41N 72 56 E
Nădlac, Romania 46 C1 46 10N 20 50 E
Nador, Morocco 99 A4 35 14N 2 58W
Nadur, Malta 32 C1 36 2N 14 17 E
Nadūshan, Iran 85 C7 32 2N 53 35 E
Nadvirna, Ukraine 51 H3 48 37N 24 30 E
Nadvoitsy, Russia 48 B5 63 52N 34 14 E
Nadvornaya = Nadvirna, Ukraine 51 H3 48 37N 24 30 E
Nadym, Russia 56 C8 65 35N 72 42 E
Nadym →, Russia 56 C8 66 12N 72 0 E
Nærbø, Norway 13 G11 58 40N 5 39 E
Næstved, Denmark 15 J5 55 13N 11 44 E
Nafada, Nigeria 101 C7 11 8N 11 20 E
Näfels, Switz. 29 B8 47 6N 9 4 E
Naftshahr, Iran 89 E11 34 0N 45 30 E
Nafud Desert = An Nafūd, Si. Arabia 84 D4 28 15N 41 0 E
Nafūsah, Jabal, Libya 96 B2 32 12N 12 30 E
Nag Hammâdi, Egypt 94 B3 26 2N 32 18 E
Naga, Cebu, Phil. 71 F4 10 13N 123 45 E
Naga, Luzon, Phil. 70 E4 13 38N 123 15 E
Naga, Zamboanga del S., Phil. 71 H4 7 46N 122 45 E
Naga, Kreb en, Africa 98 D3 24 12N 6 0W
Naga-Shima, Kagoshima, Japan 62 E2 32 10N 130 9 E
Naga-Shima, Yamaguchi, Japan 62 D4 33 49N 132 5 E
Nagagami →, Canada 128 C3 49 40N 84 40W
Nagahama, Ehime, Japan 62 D4 33 36N 132 29 E
Nagahama, Shiga, Japan 63 B8 35 23N 136 16 E
Nagai, Japan 60 E10 38 6N 140 2 E
Nagaland □, India 78 B5 26 0N 94 30 E
Nagambie, Australia 117 D6 36 47 S 145 10 E
Nagano, Japan 63 A10 36 40N 138 10 E
Nagano □, Japan 63 A10 36 15N 138 0 E
Nagaoka, Japan 61 F9 37 27N 138 51 E
Nagappattinam, India 83 J4 10 46N 79 51 E
Nagar Parkar, Pakistan 80 G4 24 28N 70 46 E
Nagara →, Japan 63 B8 35 40N 136 43 E
Nagari Hills, India 83 H4 13 3N 79 45 E
Nagarjuna Sagar, India 83 F4 16 35N 79 17 E
Nagasaki, Japan 62 E1 32 47N 129 50 E
Nagasaki □, Japan 62 E1 32 50N 129 40 E
Nagato, Japan 62 C3 34 19N 131 5 E
Nagaur, India 80 F5 27 15N 73 45 E
Nagbhir, India 82 D4 20 34N 79 55 E
Nagercoil, India 83 K3 8 12N 77 26 E
Nagina, India 81 E8 29 30N 78 30 E
Nagīneh, Iran 85 C8 34 20N 57 15 E
Nagir, Pakistan 81 A6 36 12N 74 42 E
Nagold, Germany 27 G4 48 32N 8 43 E
Nagold →, Germany 27 G4 48 52N 8 42 E
Nagoorin, Australia 114 C5 24 17 S 151 15 E
Nagorno-Karabakh, Azerbaijan 89 C12 39 55N 46 45 E
Nagornyy, Russia 57 D13 55 58N 124 57 E
Nagorsk, Russia 54 B3 59 18N 50 48 E
Nagoya, Japan 63 B8 35 10N 136 50 E
Nagpur, India 82 D4 21 8N 79 10 E
Nagua, Dom. Rep. 149 C6 19 23N 69 50W
Nagyatád, Hungary 31 E10 46 14N 17 22 E
Nagyecsed, Hungary 31 D15 47 53N 22 24 E
Nagykanizsa, Hungary 31 E10 46 28N 17 0 E
Nagykörös, Hungary 31 D12 47 5N 19 48 E
Nagyléta, Hungary 31 D14 47 23N 21 55 E
Naha, Japan 61 L3 26 13N 127 42 E
Nahanni Butte, Canada 130 A4 61 2N 123 31W
Nahanni Nat. Park, Canada 130 A3 61 15N 125 0W
Nahariyya, Israel 88 F6 33 1N 35 5 E
Nahāvand, Iran 89 E13 34 10N 48 22 E
Nahe →, Germany 27 F3 49 58N 7 54 E
Nahīya, W. →, Egypt 94 J7 28 55N 31 0 E
Nahlin, Canada 130 B2 58 55N 131 38W
Nahuel Huapi, L., Argentina 160 B2 41 0 S 71 32W
Naicá, Mexico 146 B3 27 53N 105 31W
Naicam, Canada 131 C8 52 30N 104 30W
Nā'ifah, Si. Arabia 90 D5 19 59N 50 46 E
Naila, Germany 27 E7 50 19N 11 42 E
Nain, Canada 129 A7 56 34N 61 40W
Nā'īn, Iran 85 C7 32 54N 53 0 E
Naini Tal, India 81 E8 29 30N 79 30 E
Naintré, France 22 F7 46 46N 0 29 E
Naipu, Romania 46 E6 44 12N 25 47 E
Nairn, U.K. 18 D5 57 35N 3 53W
Nairobi, Kenya 106 C4 1 17 S 36 48 E
Naissaar, Estonia 13 G21 59 34N 24 29 E
Naivasha, Kenya 106 C4 0 40 S 36 30 E
Naivasha, L., Kenya 106 C4 0 48 S 36 20 E
Najac, France 24 D5 44 14N 1 58 E
Najafābād, Iran 85 C6 32 40N 51 15 E
Nájera, Spain 34 C2 42 26N 2 48W
Najerilla →, Spain 34 C2 42 32N 2 48W
Najibabad, India 80 E8 29 40N 78 20 E
Najin, N. Korea 67 C16 42 12N 130 15 E
Najmah, Si. Arabia 85 E6 26 42N 50 6 E
Naju, S. Korea 67 G14 35 3N 126 43 E
Naka →, Japan 63 A12 36 20N 140 36 E
Nakadōri-Shima, Japan 61 H4 32 57N 129 4 E
Nakalagba, Zaïre 106 B2 2 50N 27 58 E
Nakama, Japan 62 D2 33 56N 130 43 E
Nakaminato, Japan 63 A12 36 21N 140 36 E
Nakamura, Japan 62 E4 32 59N 132 56 E
Nakanai Mts., Papua N. G. 120 C6 5 40 S 151 0 E
Nakano, Japan 63 A10 36 45N 138 22 E
Nakano-Shima, Japan 61 K4 29 51N 129 52 E
Nakanojō, Japan 63 A10 36 35N 138 51 E
Nakashibetsu, Japan 60 C12 43 33N 144 59 E
Nakatsu, Japan 62 D3 33 34N 131 15 E
Nakatsugawa, Japan 63 B9 35 29N 137 30 E
Nakfa, Eritrea 95 D4 16 40N 38 32 E
Nakhichevan = Naxçıvan, Azerbaijan 89 C11 39 12N 45 15 E
Nakhichevan Republic □ = Naxçıvan □, Azerbaijan 89 C11 39 25N 45 26 E
Nakhl, Egypt 91 F2 29 55N 33 43 E
Nakhl-e Taqī, Iran 85 E7 27 28N 52 36 E
Nakhodka, Russia 57 E14 42 53N 132 54 E
Nakhon Nayok, Thailand 76 E3 14 12N 101 13 E
Nakhon Pathom, Thailand 76 F3 13 49N 100 3 E
Nakhon Phanom, Thailand 76 D5 17 23N 104 43 E
Nakhon Ratchasima, Thailand 76 E4 14 59N 102 12 E
Nakhon Sawan, Thailand 76 E3 15 35N 100 10 E
Nakhon Si Thammarat, Thailand 77 H3 8 29N 100 0 E
Nakhon Thai, Thailand 76 D3 17 5N 100 44 E
Nakina, B.C., Canada 130 B2 59 12N 132 52W
Nakina, Ont., Canada 128 B2 50 10N 86 40W
Nakło nad Noteią, Poland 47 B4 53 9N 17 38 E
Nakodar, India 80 D6 31 8N 75 31 E
Nakskov, Denmark 15 K5 54 50N 11 8 E
Näkten, Sweden 14 B8 62 48N 14 38 E
Naktong →, S. Korea 67 G15 35 7N 128 57 E
Nakuru, Kenya 106 C4 0 15 S 36 4 E
Nakuru □, Kenya 106 C4 0 15 S 35 5 E
Nakuru, L., Kenya 106 C4 0 23 S 36 5 E
Nakusp, Canada 130 C5 50 20N 117 45W
Nal →, Pakistan 79 D2 25 20N 65 30 E
Nalchik, Russia 53 J6 43 30N 43 33 E
Nälden, Sweden 14 A8 63 21N 14 14 E
Nälsjön, Sweden 14 A8 63 25N 14 15 E
Nalerigu, Ghana 101 C4 10 35N 0 25W
Nalgonda, India 82 F4 17 6N 79 15 E
Nalhati, India 81 G12 24 17N 87 52 E
Nalinnes, Belgium 21 H4 50 19N 4 27 E
Nallamalai Hills, India 83 G4 15 30N 78 50 E
Nallıhan, Turkey 88 B4 40 11N 31 20 E
Nalón →, Spain 36 B4 43 32N 6 4W
Nālūt, Libya 96 B2 31 54N 11 0 E
Nam Can, Vietnam 77 H5 8 46N 104 59 E
Nam Co, China 64 C4 30 30N 90 45 E
Nam Dinh, Vietnam 76 B6 20 25N 106 5 E
Nam Du, Hon, Vietnam 77 H5 9 41N 104 21 E
Nam Ngum Dam, Laos 76 C4 18 35N 102 34 E
Nam-Phan, Vietnam 77 G6 10 30N 106 0 E
Nam Phong, Thailand 76 D4 16 42N 102 52 E
Nam Tha, Laos 76 B3 20 58N 101 30 E
Nam Tok, Thailand 76 E2 14 21N 99 4 E
Namachire, Angola 103 E4 11 26 S 22 43 E
Namacunde, Angola 103 F3 17 18 S 15 50 E
Namacurra, Mozam. 105 B6 17 30 S 36 50 E
Namak, Daryācheh-ye, Iran 85 C7 34 30N 52 0 E
Namak, Kavir-e, Iran 85 C8 34 30N 57 30 E
Namakkal, India 83 J4 11 13N 78 13 E
Namaland, Namibia 104 C2 24 30 S 17 0 E
Namangan, Uzbekistan 55 C5 41 0N 71 40 E
Namapa, Mozam. 107 E4 13 43 S 39 50 E
Namaqualand, S. Africa 104 D2 30 0 S 17 25 E
Namasagali, Uganda 106 B3 1 2N 33 0 E
Namatanai, Papua N. G. 120 B7 3 40 S 152 29 E
Namber, Indonesia 73 B4 1 2 S 134 49 E
Nambour, Australia 115 D5 26 32 S 152 58 E
Nambouwalu, Fiji 121 A2 17 0 S 178 45 E
Nambucca Heads, Australia 117 A10 30 37 S 153 0 E
Namcha Barwa, China 64 D4 29 40N 95 10 E
Namche Bazar, Nepal 81 F12 27 51N 86 47 E
Namchonjŏm, N. Korea 67 E14 38 15N 126 26 E
Namêche, Belgium 21 H6 50 28N 5 0 E
Namecunda, Mozam. 107 E4 14 54 S 37 37 E
Nameh, Indonesia 75 B5 2 34N 116 21 E
Nameponda, Mozam. 107 F4 15 50 S 39 50 E
Namerikawa, Japan 63 A9 36 46N 137 20 E
Náměšť nad Oslavou, Czech. 31 B9 49 12N 16 10 E
Námestovo, Slovak Rep. 31 B12 49 24N 19 25 E
Nametil, Mozam. 107 F4 15 40 S 39 21 E
Namew L., Canada 131 C8 54 14N 101 56W
Namhsan, Burma 78 D6 22 48N 97 2 E
Namib Desert = Namibwoestyn, Namibia 104 C2 22 30 S 15 0 E
Namibe, Angola 103 F2 15 7 S 12 11 E
Namibe □, Angola 103 F2 16 35 S 12 30 E
Namibia ■, Africa 104 C2 22 0 S 18 9 E
Namibwoestyn, Namibia 104 C2 22 30 S 15 0 E
Namīn, Iran 89 C13 38 25N 48 30 E
Namkhan, Burma 78 D6 23 50N 97 41 E
Namlea, Indonesia 72 B3 3 18 S 127 5 E
Namoi →, Australia 117 A8 30 12 S 149 30 E
Namous, O. en →, Algeria 99 B4 31 0N 0 15W
Nampa, U.S.A. 142 E5 43 34N 116 34W
Nampō-Shotō, Japan 61 J10 32 0N 140 0 E
Nampula, Mozam. 107 F4 15 6 S 39 15 E
Namrole, Indonesia 72 B3 3 46 S 126 46 E
Namsen →, Norway 12 D14 64 28N 11 37 E
Namsos, Norway 12 D14 64 29N 11 30 E
Namtsy, Russia 57 C13 62 43N 129 37 E
Namtu, Burma 78 D6 23 5N 97 28 E
Namtumbo, Tanzania 107 E4 10 30 S 36 4 E
Namu, Canada 130 C3 51 52N 127 50W
Namuac, Phil. 70 B3 18 37N 121 10 E
Namur, Belgium 21 H5 50 27N 4 52 E
Namur □, Belgium 21 H6 50 17N 5 0 E
Namutoni, Namibia 104 B2 18 49 S 16 55 E
Namwala, Zambia 107 F2 15 44 S 26 30 E
Namwŏn, S. Korea 67 G14 35 23N 127 23 E
Namysłów, Poland 47 D4 51 6N 17 42 E
Nan, Thailand 76 C3 18 48N 100 46 E
Nan →, Thailand 76 E3 15 42N 100 9 E
Nan Xian, China 69 C9 29 20N 112 22 E
Nana, Romania 46 E7 44 17N 26 34 E
Nanaimo, Canada 130 D4 49 10N 124 0W
Nanam, N. Korea 67 D15 41 44N 129 40 E
Nanan, China 69 E12 24 59N 118 21 E
Nanango, Australia 115 D5 26 40 S 152 0 E
Nan'ao, China 69 F11 23 28N 117 5 E
Nanao, Japan 61 F8 37 0N 137 0 E
Nanbu, China 68 B6 31 18N 106 3 E
Nanchang, China 69 C10 28 42N 115 55 E
Nancheng, China 69 D11 27 33N 116 35 E
Nanching = Nanjing, China 69 A12 32 2N 118 47 E
Nanchong, China 68 B6 30 43N 106 2 E
Nanchuan, China 68 C6 29 9N 107 6 E
Nancy, France 23 D13 48 42N 6 12 E
Nanda Devi, India 81 D8 30 23N 79 59 E
Nandan, China 68 E6 24 58N 107 29 E
Nandan, Japan 62 C6 34 10N 134 42 E
Nanded, India 82 E3 19 10N 77 20 E
Nandewar Ra., Australia 115 E5 30 15 S 150 35 E
Nandi □, Kenya 106 B4 0 15N 35 0 E
Nandikotkur, India 83 G4 15 52N 78 18 E
Nandura, India 82 D3 20 52N 76 25 E
Nandurbar, India 82 D2 21 20N 74 15 E
Nandyal, India 83 G4 15 30N 78 30 E
Nanfeng, Guangdong, China 69 F8 23 45N 111 47 E
Nanfeng, Jiangxi, China 69 D11 27 12N 116 28 E
Nanga, Australia 113 E1 26 7 S 113 45 E
Nanga-Eboko, Cameroon 101 E7 4 41N 12 22 E
Nanga Parbat, Pakistan 81 B6 35 10N 74 35 E
Nangade, Mozam. 107 E4 11 5 S 39 36 E
Nangapinoh, Indonesia 75 C4 0 20 S 111 44 E
Nangarhár □, Afghan. 79 B3 34 20N 70 0 E
Nangatayap, Indonesia 75 C4 1 32 S 110 34 E
Nangeya Mts., Uganda 106 B3 3 30N 33 30 E
Nangis, France 23 D10 48 33N 3 1 E
Nangong, China 66 F8 37 23N 115 22 E
Nangwarry, Australia 116 D4 37 33 S 140 48 E
Nanhua, China 68 E3 25 13N 101 21 E
Nanhuang, China 67 F11 36 58N 121 48 E
Nanhui, China 69 B13 31 5N 121 44 E
Nanjangud, India 83 H3 12 6N 76 43 E
Nanjeko, Zambia 107 F1 15 31 S 23 30 E
Nanji Shan, China 69 D13 27 27N 121 4 E
Nanjian, China 68 E3 25 2N 100 25 E
Nanjiang, China 68 A6 32 28N 106 51 E
Nanjing, Fujian, China 69 E11 24 25N 117 20 E
Nanjing, Jiangsu, China 69 A12 32 2N 118 47 E
Nanjirinji, Tanzania 107 D4 9 41 S 39 5 E
Nankana Sahib, Pakistan 80 D5 31 27N 73 38 E
Nankang, China 69 E10 25 40N 114 45 E
Nanking = Nanjing, China 69 A12 32 2N 118 47 E
Nankoku, Japan 62 D5 33 39N 133 44 E
Nanling, China 69 B12 30 55N 118 20 E
Nanning, China 68 F7 22 48N 108 20 E
Nannup, Australia 113 F2 33 59 S 115 48 E
Nanpan Jiang →, China 68 E6 25 10N 106 5 E
Nanpara, India 81 F9 27 52N 81 33 E
Nanpi, China 66 E9 38 2N 116 45 E
Nanping, Fujian, China 69 D12 26 38N 118 10 E
Nanping, Henan, China 69 C9 29 55N 112 3 E
Nanri Dao, China 69 E12 25 15N 119 25 E
Nanripe, Mozam. 107 E4 13 52 S 38 52 E
Nansei-Shotō = Ryūkyū-rettō, Japan 61 M2 26 0N 126 0 E
Nansen Sd., Canada 6 A3 81 0N 91 0W
Nansio, Tanzania 106 C3 2 3 S 33 4 E
Nant, France 24 D7 44 1N 3 18 E
Nantes, France 22 E5 47 12N 1 33W
Nanteuil-le-Haudouin, France 23 C9 49 9N 2 48 E
Nantiat, France 24 B5 46 1N 1 11 E
Nanticoke, U.S.A. 137 E8 41 12N 76 0W
Nanton, Canada 130 C6 50 21N 113 46W
Nantong, China 69 A13 32 1N 120 52 E
Nantua, France 25 B9 46 10N 5 35 E
Nantucket I., U.S.A. 124 E12 41 16N 70 5W
Nanuku Passage, Fiji 121 A3 16 45 S 179 15W
Nanuque, Brazil 155 E3 17 50 S 40 21W
Nanutarra, Australia 112 D2 22 32 S 115 30 E
Nanxiong, China 69 E10 25 6N 114 15 E
Nanyang, China 66 H7 33 11N 112 30 E
Nanyi Hu, China 69 B12 31 5N 119 0 E
Nan'yō, Japan 62 C3 34 3N 131 49 E
Nanyuan, China 66 E9 39 44N 116 22 E
Nanyuki, Kenya 106 B4 0 2N 37 4 E
Nanzhang, China 69 B8 31 45N 111 50 E
Nao, C. de la, Spain 35 G5 38 44N 0 14 E
Naococane L., Canada 129 B5 52 50N 70 45W
Naoetsu, Japan 61 F9 37 12N 138 10 E
Naogaon, Bangla. 78 C2 24 52N 88 52 E
Náousa, Greece 44 D4 40 42N 22 9 E
Naozhou Dao, China 69 G8 20 55N 110 20 E
Napa, U.S.A. 144 G4 38 18N 122 17W
Napa →, U.S.A. 144 G4 38 10N 122 19W
Napanee, Canada 128 D4 44 15N 77 0W
Napanoch, U.S.A. 137 E10 41 44N 74 22W
Nape, Laos 76 C5 18 18N 105 6 E
Nape Pass = Keo Neua, Deo, Vietnam 76 C5 18 23N 105 10 E
Naperville, U.S.A. 141 C8 41 46N 88 9W

Neumarkt-Sankt Veit 239

Napf, *Switz.* 28 B5 47 1N 7 56 E
Napier, *N.Z.* 118 F5 39 30 S 176 56 E
Napier Broome B., *Australia* 112 B4 14 2 S 126 37 E
Napier Downs, *Australia* 112 C3 17 11 S 124 36 E
Napier Pen., *Australia* 114 A2 12 4 S 135 43 E
Naples = Nápoli, *Italy* 41 B7 40 50N 14 15 E
Naples, *U.S.A.* 135 M5 26 8N 81 48W
Napo, *China* 68 F5 23 22N 105 50 E
Napo □, *Ecuador* 152 D2 0 30 S 77 0W
Napo →, *Peru* 152 D3 3 20 S 72 40W
Napoleon, *N. Dak., U.S.A.* 138 B5 46 30N 99 46W
Napoleon, *Ohio, U.S.A.* 141 C12 41 23N 84 8W
Nápoli, *Italy* 41 B7 40 50N 14 15 E
Nápoli, G. di, *Italy* 41 B7 40 43N 14 10 E
Napopo, *Zaïre* 106 B2 4 15N 28 0 E
Nappa Merrie, *Australia* 115 D3 27 36 S 141 7 E
Nappanee, *U.S.A.* 141 C11 41 27N 86 0W
Naqâda, *Egypt* 94 B3 25 53N 32 42 E
Naqadeh, *Iran* 89 D11 36 57N 45 23 E
Naqqāsh, *Iran* 85 C6 35 40N 49 6 E
Nara, *Japan* 63 C7 34 40N 135 49 E
Nara, *Mali* 100 B3 15 10N 7 20W
Nara □, *Japan* 63 C7 34 30N 136 0 E
Nara Canal, *Pakistan* 80 G3 24 30N 69 20 E
Nara Visa, *U.S.A.* 139 H3 35 37N 103 6W
Naracoorte, *Australia* 116 D4 36 58 S 140 45 E
Naradhan, *Australia* 117 B7 33 34 S 146 17 E
Narasapur, *India* 83 F5 16 26N 81 40 E
Narasaropet, *India* 83 F5 16 14N 80 4 E
Narathiwat, *Thailand* 77 J3 6 30N 101 48 E
Narayanganj, *Bangla.* 78 D3 23 40N 90 33 E
Narayanpet, *India* 82 F3 16 45N 77 30 E
Narbonne, *France* 24 E7 43 11N 3 0 E
Narcea →, *Spain* 36 B4 43 33N 6 44W
Nardīn, *Iran* 85 B7 37 3N 55 59 E
Nardò, *Italy* 41 B11 40 11N 18 2 E
Narembeen, *Australia* 113 F2 32 7 S 118 24 E
Nares Str., *Arctic* 124 A13 80 0N 70 0W
Naretha, *Australia* 113 F3 31 0 S 124 45 E
Narew, *Poland* 47 C10 52 55N 23 31 E
Narew →, *Poland* 47 C7 52 26N 20 41 E
Nari →, *Pakistan* 80 E2 28 0N 67 40 E
Narindra, Helodranon' i, *Madag.* 105 A8 14 55 S 47 30 E
Narino □, *Colombia* 152 C2 1 30N 78 0W
Narita, *Japan* 63 B12 35 47N 140 19 E
Narmada →, *India* 80 J5 21 38N 72 36 E
Narman, *Turkey* 89 B9 40 26N 41 57 E
Narmland, *Sweden* 13 F15 60 0N 13 30 E
Narnaul, *India* 80 E7 28 5N 76 11 E
Narni, *Italy* 39 F9 42 30N 12 30 E
Naro, *Ghana* 100 C4 10 22N 2 27W
Naro, *Italy* 40 E6 37 18N 13 47 E
Naro Fominsk, *Russia* 52 C3 55 23N 36 43 E
Narodnaya, *Russia* 48 A10 65 5N 59 58 E
Narok, *Kenya* 106 C4 1 55 S 35 52 E
Narok □, *Kenya* 106 C4 1 20 S 36 30 E
Narón, *Spain* 36 B2 43 32N 8 9W
Narooma, *Australia* 117 D9 36 14 S 150 4 E
Narowal, *Pakistan* 79 B4 32 6N 74 52 E
Narrabri, *Australia* 115 E4 30 19 S 149 46 E
Narran →, *Australia* 115 D4 28 37 S 148 12 E
Narrandera, *Australia* 117 C7 34 42 S 146 31 E
Narraway →, *Canada* 130 B5 55 44N 119 55W
Narrogin, *Australia* 113 F2 32 58 S 117 14 E
Narromine, *Australia* 117 B8 32 12 S 148 12 E
Narsampet, *India* 82 F4 17 57N 79 58 E
Narsimhapur, *India* 81 H8 22 54N 79 14 E
Nartkala, *Russia* 53 J6 43 33N 43 51 E
Naruto, *Kantō, Japan* 62 C6 34 11N 134 37 E
Narutō, *Shikoku, Japan* 63 B12 35 36N 140 25 E
Naruto-Kaikyō, *Japan* 62 C6 34 14N 134 39 E
Narva, *Estonia* 50 C5 59 23N 28 12 E
Narva →, *Russia* 13 G22 59 27N 28 2 E
Narvacan, *Phil.* 70 C3 17 25N 120 28 E
Narvik, *Norway* 12 B17 68 28N 17 26 E
Narvskoye Vdkhr., *Russia* 50 C5 59 18N 28 14 E
Narwana, *India* 80 E7 29 39N 76 6 E
Naryan-Mar, *Russia* 48 A9 67 42N 53 12 E
Naryilco, *Australia* 115 D3 28 37 S 141 53 E
Narym, *Russia* 56 D9 59 0N 81 30 E
Narymskoye, *Kazakstan* 56 E9 49 10N 84 15 E
Naryn, *Kyrgyzstan* 55 C7 41 26N 75 58 E
Naryn →, *Uzbekistan* 55 C5 40 52N 71 36 E
Nasa, *Norway* 12 C16 66 29N 15 23 E
Nasarawa, *Nigeria* 101 D6 8 32N 7 41 E
Năsăud, *Romania* 46 B5 47 19N 24 29 E
Nasawa, *Vanuatu* 121 E6 15 0 S 168 0 E
Naseby, *N.Z.* 119 F5 45 1 S 170 10 E
Naselle, *U.S.A.* 144 D3 46 22N 123 49W
Naser, Buheirat en, *Egypt* 94 C3 23 0N 32 30 E
Nashua, *Iowa, U.S.A.* 140 B4 42 57N 92 32W
Nashua, *Mont., U.S.A.* 142 B10 48 8N 106 22W
Nashua, *N.H., U.S.A.* 137 D13 42 45N 71 28W
Nashville, *Ark., U.S.A.* 139 J8 33 57N 93 51W
Nashville, *Ga., U.S.A.* 135 K4 31 12N 83 15W
Nashville, *Ill., U.S.A.* 140 F7 38 21N 89 23W
Nashville, *Ind., U.S.A.* 141 E10 39 12N 86 15W
Nashville, *Mich., U.S.A.* 141 B11 42 36N 85 5W
Nashville, *Tenn., U.S.A.* 135 G2 36 10N 86 47W
Našice, *Croatia* 42 B3 45 32N 18 4 E
Nasielsk, *Poland* 47 C7 52 35N 20 50 E
Nasik, *India* 82 E1 19 58N 73 50 E
Nasipit, *Phil.* 71 G5 8 57N 125 19 E
Nasirabad, *India* 80 F6 26 15N 74 45 E
Naskaupi →, *Canada* 129 B7 53 47N 60 51W
Naso, *Italy* 41 D7 38 7N 14 47 E
Naso Pt., *Phil.* 71 F3 10 25N 121 57 E
Naṣrīān-e Pā'īn, *Iran* 84 C5 32 52N 46 52 E
Nass →, *Canada* 130 B3 55 0N 129 40W
Nassau, *Bahamas* 148 A4 25 5N 77 20W
Nassau, *U.S.A.* 137 D11 42 31N 73 37W
Nassau, B., *Chile* 160 E3 55 20 S 68 0W
Nasser, L. = Naser, Buheirat en, *Egypt* 94 C3 23 0N 32 30 E
Nasser City = Kôm Ombo, *Egypt* 94 C3 24 25N 32 52 E
Nassian, *Ivory C.* 100 D4 8 28N 3 28W
Nässjö, *Sweden* 13 H16 57 39N 14 42 E
Nasugbu, *Phil.* 70 D3 14 5N 120 38 E
Näsviken, *Sweden* 14 C10 61 46N 16 52 E
Nata, *Botswana* 104 C4 20 12 S 26 12 E
Natagaima, *Colombia* 152 C2 3 37N 75 6W
Natal, *Brazil* 154 C4 5 47 S 35 13W
Natal, *Canada* 130 D6 49 43N 114 51W
Natal, *Indonesia* 74 B1 0 35N 99 7 E
Natalinci, *Serbia, Yug.* 42 C5 44 15N 20 49 E
Naṭanz, *Iran* 85 C6 33 30N 51 55 E
Natashquan, *Canada* 129 B7 50 14N 61 46W
Natashquan →, *Canada* 129 B7 50 7N 61 50W
Natchez, *U.S.A.* 139 K9 31 34N 91 24W
Natchitoches, *U.S.A.* 139 K8 31 46N 93 5W
Naters, *Switz.* 28 D5 46 19N 7 58 E
Natewa B., *Fiji* 121 A2 16 35 S 179 40 E
Nathalia, *Australia* 117 D6 36 1 S 145 13 E
Nathdwara, *India* 80 G5 24 55N 73 50 E
Nati, Pta., *Spain* 33 A10 40 3N 3 50 E
Natimuk, *Australia* 116 D4 36 42 S 142 0 E
Nation →, *Canada* 130 B4 55 30N 123 32W
National City, *U.S.A.* 145 N9 32 41N 117 6W
Natitingou, *Benin* 101 C5 10 20N 1 26 E
Natividad, I., *Mexico* 146 B1 27 50N 115 10W
Natogyi, *Burma* 78 E5 21 25N 95 39 E
Natoma, *U.S.A.* 138 F5 39 11N 99 2W
Natonin, *Phil.* 70 C3 17 6N 121 18 E
Natron, L., *Tanzania* 106 C4 2 20 S 36 0 E
Natrona Heights, *U.S.A.* 136 F5 40 37N 79 44W
Natrûn, W. el →, *Egypt* 94 H7 30 25N 30 13 E
Natuna Besar, Kepulauan, *Indonesia* 77 L7 4 0N 108 15 E
Natuna Is. = Natuna Besar, Kepulauan, *Indonesia* 77 L7 4 0N 108 15 E
Natuna Selatan, Kepulauan, *Indonesia* 75 B3 2 45N 109 0 E
Natural Bridge, *U.S.A.* 137 B9 44 5N 75 30W
Naturaliste, C., *Australia* 114 G4 40 50 S 148 15 E
Natya, *Australia* 116 C5 34 57 S 143 13 E
Nau, *Tajikistan* 55 C4 40 9N 69 22 E
Nau Qala, *Afghan.* 80 B3 34 5N 68 5 E
Naubinway, *U.S.A.* 128 C2 46 6N 85 27W
Naucelle, *France* 24 D6 44 13N 2 20 E
Nauders, *Austria* 30 E3 46 54N 10 30 E
Nauen, *Germany* 26 C8 52 36N 12 52 E
Naugatuck, *U.S.A.* 137 E11 41 30N 73 3W
Naujan, *Phil.* 70 E3 13 20N 121 18 E
Naumburg, *Germany* 26 D7 51 9N 11 47 E
Nā'ūr at Tunayb, *Jordan* 91 D4 31 48N 35 57 E
Nauru ■, *Pac. Oc.* 122 H8 1 0 S 166 0 E
Naushahra = Nowshera, *Pakistan* 79 B3 34 0N 72 0 E
Nausori, *Fiji* 121 B2 18 2 S 178 32 E
Nauta, *Peru* 152 D3 4 31 S 73 35W
Nautla, *Mexico* 147 C5 20 20N 96 50W
Nauvoo, *U.S.A.* 140 D5 40 33N 91 23W
Nava, *Mexico* 146 B4 28 25N 100 46W
Nava del Rey, *Spain* 36 D5 41 22N 5 6W
Navacerrada, Puerto de, *Spain* 36 E7 40 47N 4 0W
Navadwip, *India* 81 H13 23 34N 88 20 E
Navahermosa, *Spain* 37 F6 39 41N 4 28W
Navahrudak, *Belarus* 50 F3 53 40N 25 50 E
Navajo Reservoir, *U.S.A.* 143 H10 36 48N 107 36W
Naval, *Phil.* 71 F5 11 34N 124 23 E
Navalcarnero, *Spain* 36 E6 40 17N 4 5W
Navalmoral de la Mata, *Spain* 36 F5 39 52N 5 33W
Navalvillar de Pela, *Spain* 37 F5 39 9N 5 24W
Navan = An Uaimh, *Ireland* 19 C5 53 39N 6 41W
Navapolatsk, *Belarus* 50 E5 55 32N 28 37 E
Navarino, I., *Chile* 160 E3 55 0 S 67 40W
Navarra □, *Spain* 34 C3 42 40N 1 40W
Navarre, *U.S.A.* 136 F3 40 43N 81 31W
Navarrenx, *France* 24 E3 43 20N 0 45W
Navarro →, *U.S.A.* 144 F3 39 11N 123 45W
Navasota, *U.S.A.* 139 K6 30 23N 96 5W
Navassa, *W. Indies* 149 C4 18 30N 75 0W
Nave, *Italy* 38 C7 45 35N 10 17 E
Naver →, *U.K.* 18 C4 58 32N 4 14W
Navia, *Spain* 36 B4 43 35N 6 42W
Navia →, *Spain* 36 B4 43 15N 6 50W
Navia de Suarna, *Spain* 36 C4 42 58N 6 59W
Navidad, *Chile* 158 C1 33 57 S 71 50W
Navlya, *Russia* 52 D2 52 53N 34 30 E
Navoi = Nawoiy, *Uzbekistan* 55 C2 40 9N 65 22 E
Navojoa, *Mexico* 146 B3 27 0N 109 30W
Navolato, *Mexico* 146 C3 24 47N 107 42W
Návpaktos, *Greece* 45 F3 38 23N 21 50 E
Návplion, *Greece* 45 G4 37 33N 22 50 E
Navrongo, *Ghana* 101 C4 10 51N 1 3W
Navsari, *India* 82 D1 20 57N 72 59 E
Nawa Kot, *Pakistan* 80 E4 28 21N 71 24 E
Nawabganj, *Bangla.* 78 C2 24 35N 88 14 E
Nawabganj, *Ut. P., India* 81 F9 26 56N 81 14 E
Nawabganj, *Ut. P., India* 81 E8 28 32N 79 40 E
Nawabshah, *Pakistan* 79 D3 26 15N 68 25 E
Nawada, *India* 81 G11 24 50N 85 33 E
Nāwah, *Afghan.* 79 B2 32 19N 67 53 E
Nawakot, *Nepal* 81 F11 27 55N 85 10 E
Nawalgarh, *India* 80 F6 27 50N 75 15 E
Nawanshahr, *India* 81 C6 32 33N 74 48 E
Nawapara, *India* 82 D6 20 46N 82 33 E
Nawāṣīf, Harrat, *Si. Arabia* 86 B3 21 20N 42 10 E
Nawi, *Sudan* 94 D3 18 32N 30 50 E
Nawng Hpa, *Burma* 78 D7 22 30N 98 30 E
Nawoiy, *Uzbekistan* 55 C2 40 9N 65 22 E
Nawş, Ra's, *Oman* 87 C6 17 15N 55 16 E
Naxçıvan, *Azerbaijan* 89 C11 39 12N 45 15 E
Naxçıvan □, *Azerbaijan* 89 C11 39 25N 45 26 E
Náxos, *Greece* 45 G7 37 8N 25 25 E
Nay, *France* 24 E3 43 10N 0 18W
Nāy Band, *Iran* 85 E7 27 20N 52 40 E
Naya →, *Colombia* 152 C2 3 13N 77 22W
Nayakhan, *Russia* 57 C16 61 56N 159 0 E
Nayarit □, *Mexico* 146 C4 22 0N 105 0W
Nayé, *Senegal* 100 C2 14 28N 12 12W
Nayong, *China* 68 D5 26 50N 105 20 E
Nayoro, *Japan* 60 B11 44 21N 142 28 E
Nayyāl, W. →, *Si. Arabia* 84 D3 28 35N 39 4 E
Nazaré, *Bahia, Brazil* 155 D4 13 2 S 39 0W
Nazaré, *Pará, Brazil* 157 B7 6 25 S 52 29W
Nazaré, *Tocantins, Brazil* 154 C2 6 23 S 47 40W
Nazaré, *Portugal* 37 F1 39 36N 9 4W
Nazareth = Nazerat, *Israel* 91 C4 32 42N 35 17 E
Nazas, *Mexico* 146 B4 25 10N 104 6W
Nazas →, *Mexico* 146 B4 25 35N 103 25W
Naze, The, *U.K.* 17 F9 51 53N 1 18 E
Nazerat, *Israel* 91 C4 32 42N 35 17 E
Nāzīk, *Iran* 89 C11 39 1N 45 4 E
Nazilli, *Turkey* 88 D3 37 55N 28 15 E
Nazir Hat, *Bangla.* 78 D3 22 35N 91 49 E
Nazko, *Canada* 130 C4 53 1N 123 37W
Nazko →, *Canada* 130 C4 53 7N 123 34W
Nazret, *Ethiopia* 95 F4 8 32N 39 22 E
Nazwá, *Oman* 87 B7 22 56N 57 32 E
Nchanga, *Zambia* 107 E2 12 30 S 27 49 E
Ncheu, *Malawi* 107 E3 14 50 S 34 47 E
Ndala, *Tanzania* 106 C3 4 45 S 33 15 E
Ndalatando, *Angola* 103 D2 9 12 S 14 48 E
Ndali, *Benin* 101 D5 9 50N 2 46 E
Ndareda, *Tanzania* 106 C4 4 12 S 35 30 E
Ndélé, *C.A.R.* 102 A4 8 25N 20 36 E
Ndendé, *Gabon* 102 C2 2 22 S 11 23 E
Ndjamena, *Chad* 97 F2 12 10N 14 59 E
Ndjolé, *Gabon* 102 C2 0 10 S 10 45 E
Ndola, *Zambia* 107 E2 13 0 S 28 34 E
Ndoto Mts., *Kenya* 106 B4 2 0N 37 0 E
Ndoua, C., *N. Cal.* 121 V20 22 24 S 166 56 E
Nduguti, *Tanzania* 106 C3 4 18 S 34 41 E
Nduindui, *Vanuatu* 121 E5 15 24 S 167 46 E
Nea →, *Norway* 14 A5 63 15N 11 0 E
Néa Epídhavros, *Greece* 45 G5 37 40N 23 7 E
Néa Flippiás, *Greece* 44 E2 39 12N 20 53 E
Néa Kallikrátia, *Greece* 44 D5 40 21N 23 1 E
Néa Víssi, *Greece* 44 C8 41 34N 26 33 E
Neagari, *Japan* 63 A8 36 26N 136 25 E
Neagh, Lough, *U.K.* 19 B5 54 37N 6 25W
Neah Bay, *U.S.A.* 144 B2 48 22N 124 37W
Neale, L., *Australia* 112 D5 24 15 S 130 0 E
Neamț □, *Romania* 46 C7 47 0N 26 20 E
Neápolis, *Kozan, Greece* 44 D3 40 20N 21 24 E
Neápolis, *Kríti, Greece* 32 D7 35 15N 25 37 E
Neápolis, *Lakonia, Greece* 45 H5 36 27N 23 8 E
Near Is., *U.S.A.* 126 C1 53 0N 172 0 E
Neath, *U.K.* 17 F4 51 39N 3 48W
Neath Port Talbot □, *U.K.* 17 F4 51 42N 3 45W
Nebbou, *Burkina Faso* 101 C4 11 9N 1 51W
Nebine Cr. →, *Australia* 115 D4 29 27 S 146 56 E
Nebitdag, *Turkmenistan* 49 G9 39 30N 54 22 E
Nebolchy, *Russia* 50 C7 59 8N 33 18 E
Nebraska □, *U.S.A.* 138 E5 41 30N 99 30W
Nebraska City, *U.S.A.* 138 E7 40 41N 95 52W
Nébrodi, Monti, *Italy* 41 E7 37 54N 14 35 E
Necedah, *U.S.A.* 138 C9 44 2N 90 4W
Nechako →, *Canada* 130 C4 53 30N 122 44W
Neches →, *U.S.A.* 139 L8 29 58N 93 51W
Neckar →, *Germany* 27 F4 49 27N 8 29 E
Necochea, *Argentina* 158 D4 38 30 S 58 50W
Nectar Brook, *Australia* 116 B2 32 43 S 137 57 E
Nedelišće, *Croatia* 39 B13 46 23N 16 22 E
Neder Rijn →, *Neths.* 20 E8 51 57N 6 2 E
Nederbrakel, *Belgium* 21 G3 50 48N 3 46 E
Nederweert, *Neths.* 21 F7 51 17N 5 45 E
Nédha →, *Greece* 45 G3 37 25N 21 45 E
Nedroma, *Algeria* 99 A4 35 1N 1 45W
Nee Soon, *Singapore* 74 B2 1 24N 103 49 E
Neede, *Neths.* 20 D9 52 8N 6 37 E
Needles, *U.S.A.* 145 L12 34 51N 114 37W
Needles, The, *U.K.* 17 G6 50 39N 1 35W
Needles Pt., *N.Z.* 118 C4 36 3 S 175 25 E
Ñeembucú □, *Paraguay* 158 B4 27 0 S 58 0W
Neemuch = Nimach, *India* 80 G6 24 30N 74 56 E
Neenah, *U.S.A.* 134 C1 44 11N 88 28W
Neepawa, *Canada* 131 C9 50 15N 99 30W
Neer, *Neths.* 21 F7 51 16N 5 59 E
Neerpelt, *Belgium* 21 F6 51 13N 5 26 E
Nefta, *Tunisia* 96 B1 33 53N 7 50 E
Neftah Sidi Boubekeur, *Algeria* 99 A5 35 1N 0 4 E
Neftçala, *Azerbaijan* 89 C13 39 19N 49 12 E
Neftegorsk, *Russia* 53 H4 44 25N 39 45 E
Neftekamsk, *Russia* 54 C5 56 6N 54 17 E
Neftekumsk, *Russia* 53 H7 44 46N 44 50 E
Neftenbach, *Switz.* 29 A7 47 32N 8 41 E
Neftyannyye Kamni, *Azerbaijan* 49 F9 40 20N 50 55 E
Negapatam = Nagappattinam, *India* 83 J4 10 46N 79 51 E
Negaunee, *U.S.A.* 134 B2 46 30N 87 36W
Negele, *Ethiopia* 90 F2 5 20N 39 36 E
Negeri Sembilan □, *Malaysia* 74 B2 2 45N 102 10 E
Negev Desert = Hanegev, *Israel* 91 E3 30 50N 35 0 E
Negoiul, Vf., *Romania* 46 D5 45 38N 24 35 E
Negombo, *Sri Lanka* 83 L4 7 12N 79 50 E
Negotin, *Serbia, Yug.* 42 C7 44 16N 22 37 E
Negotino, *Macedonia* 42 F7 41 29N 22 9 E
Negra, Peña, *Spain* 36 C4 42 11N 6 30W
Negra, Pta., *Mauritania* 98 D1 22 54N 16 18W
Negra, Pta., *Peru* 156 B1 6 6 S 81 10W
Negra Pt., *Phil.* 70 B3 18 40N 120 50 E
Negrais C., *Burma* 78 G5 16 0N 94 12 E
Negreira, *Spain* 36 C2 42 54N 8 45W
Negrești, *Romania* 46 C8 46 50N 27 30 E
Négrine, *Algeria* 99 B6 34 30N 7 30 E
Negro →, *Argentina* 160 B4 41 2 S 62 47W
Negro →, *Bolivia* 157 C5 14 11 S 63 7W
Negro →, *Brazil* 153 D6 3 0 S 60 0W
Negro →, *Uruguay* 159 C4 33 24 S 58 22W
Negros, *Phil.* 71 G4 9 30N 122 40 E
Negru Vodă, *Romania* 46 F9 43 47N 28 21 E
Nehalem →, *U.S.A.* 144 E3 45 40N 123 56W
Nehāvand, *Iran* 85 C6 35 56N 49 31 E
Nehbandān, *Iran* 85 D9 31 35N 60 5 E
Neheim, *Germany* 26 D3 51 27N 7 58 E
Nehoiașu, *Romania* 46 D7 45 24N 26 20 E
Nei Monggol Zizhiqu □, *China* 66 C6 42 0N 112 0 E
Neiafu, *Tonga* 121 P14 18 39 S 173 59W
Neidpath, *Canada* 131 C7 50 12N 107 20W
Neihart, *U.S.A.* 142 C8 47 0N 110 44W
Neijiang, *China* 68 C5 29 35N 104 55 E
Neilrex, *Australia* 117 A8 31 44 S 149 20 E
Neilton, *U.S.A.* 142 C2 47 25N 123 53W
Neiqiu, *China* 66 F8 37 15N 114 30 E
Neira de Jusá, *Spain* 36 C3 42 53N 7 14W
Neiva, *Colombia* 152 C2 2 56N 75 18W
Neixiang, *China* 66 H6 33 10N 111 52 E
Nejanilini L., *Canada* 131 B9 59 33N 97 48W
Nejo, *Ethiopia* 95 F4 9 30N 35 28 E
Nekā, *Iran* 85 B7 36 39N 53 19 E
Nekemte, *Ethiopia* 95 F4 9 4N 36 30 E
Nêkheb, *Egypt* 94 B3 25 10N 32 48 E
Neksø, *Denmark* 13 J16 55 4N 15 8 E
Nelas, *Portugal* 36 E3 40 32N 7 52W
Nelia, *Australia* 114 C3 20 39 S 142 12 E
Nelidovo, *Russia* 50 D7 56 13N 32 49 E
Neligh, *U.S.A.* 138 D5 42 8N 98 2W
Nelkan, *Russia* 57 D14 57 40N 136 4 E
Nellikuppam, *India* 83 J4 11 46N 79 43 E
Nellore, *India* 83 G4 14 27N 79 59 E
Nelma, *Russia* 57 E14 47 39N 139 0 E
Nelson, *Canada* 130 D5 49 30N 117 20W
Nelson, *N.Z.* 119 B8 41 18 S 173 16 E
Nelson, *U.K.* 16 D5 53 50N 2 13W
Nelson, *U.S.A.* 143 J7 35 31N 113 19W
Nelson →, *Canada* 131 C9 54 33N 98 2W
Nelson, C., *Australia* 116 E4 38 26 S 141 32 E
Nelson, C., *Papua N. G.* 120 E5 9 0 S 149 20 E
Nelson, Estrecho, *Chile* 160 D2 51 30 S 75 0W
Nelson Forks, *Canada* 130 B4 59 30N 124 0W
Nelson House, *Canada* 131 B9 55 47N 98 51W
Nelson L., *Canada* 131 B8 55 48N 100 7W
Nelspoort, *S. Africa* 104 E3 32 7 S 23 0 E
Nelspruit, *S. Africa* 105 D5 25 29 S 30 59 E
Néma, *Mauritania* 100 B3 16 40N 7 15W
Neman, *Russia* 13 J20 55 2N 22 2 E
Neman →, *Lithuania* 13 J19 55 25N 21 10 E
Neméa, *Greece* 45 G4 37 49N 22 40 E
Nemeiben L., *Canada* 131 B7 55 20N 105 20W
Nemira, *Romania* 46 C7 46 17N 26 19 E
Nemours, *France* 23 D9 48 16N 2 40 E
Nemunas = Neman →, *Lithuania* 13 J19 55 25N 21 10 E
Nemuro, *Japan* 60 C12 43 20N 145 35 E
Nemuro-Kaikyō, *Japan* 60 C12 43 30N 145 30 E
Nemuy, *Russia* 57 D14 55 40N 136 9 E
Nen Jiang →, *China* 67 B13 45 28N 124 30 E
Nenagh, *Ireland* 19 D3 52 52N 8 11W
Nenana, *U.S.A.* 126 B5 64 34N 149 5W
Nenasi, *Malaysia* 77 L4 3 9N 103 23 E
Nendiarene, Pte., *N. Cal.* 121 T18 20 14 S 164 19 E
Nene →, *U.K.* 16 E8 52 49N 0 11 E
Nenjiang, *China* 65 B7 49 10N 125 10 E
Neno, *Malawi* 107 F3 15 25 S 34 40 E
Neodesha, *U.S.A.* 139 G7 37 25N 95 41W
Neoga, *U.S.A.* 141 E8 39 19N 88 27W
Néon Petrítsi, *Greece* 44 C5 41 16N 23 15 E
Neópolis, *Brazil* 154 D4 10 18 S 36 35W
Neosho, *U.S.A.* 139 G7 36 52N 94 22W
Neosho →, *U.S.A.* 139 H7 36 48N 95 18W
Nepal ■, *Asia* 81 F11 28 0N 84 30 E
Nepalganj, *Nepal* 81 E9 28 5N 81 40 E
Nephi, *U.S.A.* 142 G8 39 43N 111 50W
Nephin, *Ireland* 19 B2 54 1N 9 22W
Nepomuk, *Czech.* 30 B6 49 29N 13 35 E
Neptune, *U.S.A.* 137 F10 40 13N 74 2W
Néra →, *Romania* 42 C6 44 48N 21 25 E
Nérac, *France* 24 D4 44 8N 0 21 E
Nerastro, Sarīr, *Libya* 96 D4 24 20N 20 37 E
Nerchinsk, *Russia* 57 D12 52 0N 116 39 E
Nerchinskiy Zavod, *Russia* 57 D12 51 20N 119 40 E
Nereju, *Romania* 46 D7 45 43N 26 43 E
Nerekhta, *Russia* 52 B5 57 26N 40 38 E
Néret L., *Canada* 129 B5 54 45N 70 44W
Neretva →, *Croatia* 42 D2 43 1N 17 27 E
Neretvanski Kanal, *Croatia* 42 D2 43 7N 17 10 E
Neringa, *Lithuania* 13 J19 55 30N 21 5 E
Nerja, *Spain* 37 J7 36 43N 3 55W
Nerl →, *Russia* 52 B5 56 11N 40 34 E
Nerokoúrou, *Greece* 32 D6 35 29N 24 3 E
Nerpio, *Spain* 35 G2 38 11N 2 16W
Nerva, *Spain* 37 H4 37 42N 6 30W
Nes, *Neths.* 20 B7 53 26N 5 47 E
Nesbyen, *Norway* 14 D3 60 34N 9 6 E
Nesebŭr, *Bulgaria* 43 E12 42 41N 27 46 E
Nesland, *Norway* 14 E1 59 31N 7 59 E
Neslandsvatn, *Norway* 14 F3 58 57N 9 10 E
Nesle, *France* 23 C9 49 45N 2 53 E
Nesodden, *Norway* 14 E4 59 48N 10 40 E
Nesque →, *France* 25 E8 43 59N 4 59 E
Ness, L., *U.K.* 18 D4 57 15N 4 32W
Nesslau, *Switz.* 29 B8 47 14N 9 13 E
Nesterov, *Ukraine* 51 G2 50 4N 23 58 E
Nestórion, *Greece* 44 D3 40 24N 21 5 E
Néstos →, *Greece* 44 C6 41 20N 24 35 E
Nesvizh = Nyasvizh, *Belarus* 51 F4 53 14N 26 38 E
Netanya, *Israel* 91 C3 32 20N 34 51 E
Nète →, *Belgium* 21 F4 51 7N 4 14 E
Netherdale, *Australia* 114 C4 21 10 S 148 33 E
Netherlands ■, *Europe* 20 E6 52 0N 5 30 E
Netherlands Antilles ■, *W. Indies* 152 A4 12 15N 69 0W
Netley Gap, *Australia* 116 B3 32 43 S 139 59 E
Neto →, *Italy* 41 C10 39 12N 17 9 E
Netrakona, *Bangla.* 78 C3 24 53N 90 47 E
Nettancourt, *France* 23 D11 48 51N 4 57 E
Nettilling L., *Canada* 127 B12 66 30N 71 0W
Nettuno, *Italy* 40 A5 41 27N 12 39 E
Netzahualcoyotl, Presa, *Mexico* 147 D6 17 10N 93 30W
Neu-Isenburg, *Germany* 27 E4 50 3N 8 42 E
Neu-Ulm, *Germany* 27 G6 48 22N 10 0 E
Neubrandenburg, *Germany* 26 B9 53 33N 13 15 E
Neubukow, *Germany* 26 A7 54 2N 11 39 E
Neuburg, *Germany* 27 G7 48 44N 11 11 E
Neuchâtel, *Switz.* 28 C3 47 0N 6 55 E
Neuchâtel □, *Switz.* 28 C3 47 0N 6 55 E
Neuchâtel, Lac de, *Switz.* 28 C3 46 53N 6 50 E
Neudau, *Austria* 30 D9 47 11N 16 6 E
Neuenegg, *Switz.* 28 C4 46 54N 7 18 E
Neuenhaus, *Germany* 26 C2 52 30N 6 58 E
Neuf-Brisach, *France* 23 D14 48 1N 7 30 E
Neufahrn, *Germany* 27 G8 48 41N 12 11 E
Neufchâteau, *Belgium* 21 J6 49 50N 5 25 E
Neufchâteau, *France* 23 D12 48 21N 5 40 E
Neufchâtel-en-Bray, *France* 22 C8 49 44N 1 26 E
Neufchâtel-sur-Aisne, *France* 23 C11 49 26N 4 1 E
Neuhaus, *Germany* 26 B6 53 17N 10 56 E
Neuhausen, *Switz.* 29 A7 47 41N 8 37 E
Neuillé-Pont-Pierre, *France* 22 E7 47 33N 0 33 E
Neuilly-St.-Front, *France* 23 C10 49 10N 3 15 E
Neukalen, *Germany* 26 B8 53 49N 12 46 E
Neumarkt, *Germany* 27 F7 49 26N 11 27 E
Neumarkt-Sankt Veit, *Germany* 27 G8 48 22N 12 30 E

240 Neumünster

Neumünster, Germany 26 A5 54 4N 9 58 E
Neung-sur-Beuvron, France 23 E8 47 30N 1 50 E
Neunkirchen, Austria 30 D9 47 43N 16 4 E
Neunkirchen, Germany 27 F3 49 20N 7 9 E
Neuquén, Argentina 160 A3 38 55 S 68 0W
Neuquén □, Argentina 158 D2 38 0 S 69 50W
Neuquén →, Argentina 160 A3 38 59 S 68 0W
Neuruppin, Germany 26 C8 52 55N 12 48 E
Neuse →, U.S.A. 135 H7 35 6N 76 29W
Neusiedl, Austria 31 D9 47 57N 16 50 E
Neusiedler See, Austria 31 D9 47 50N 16 47 E
Neuss, Germany 21 F9 51 11N 6 42 E
Neussargues-Moissac, France 24 C7 45 9N 3 0 E
Neustadt, Baden-W., Germany 27 H4 47 54N 8 12 E
Neustadt, Bayern, Germany 27 F8 49 44N 12 10 E
Neustadt, Bayern, Germany 27 G7 48 48N 11 46 E
Neustadt, Bayern, Germany 27 F6 49 34N 10 37 E
Neustadt, Bayern, Germany 27 E7 50 19N 11 7 E
Neustadt, Brandenburg, Germany 26 C8 52 50N 12 27 E
Neustadt, Hessen, Germany 26 E5 50 51N 9 9 E
Neustadt, Niedersachsen, Germany 26 C5 52 30N 9 30 E
Neustadt, Rhld-Pfz., Germany 27 F4 49 21N 8 10 E
Neustadt, Schleswig-Holstein, Germany 26 A6 54 6N 10 49 E
Neustadt, Thüringen, Germany 26 E7 50 45N 11 43 E
Neustrelitz, Germany 26 B9 53 21N 13 4 E
Neuvic, France 24 C6 45 23N 2 16 E
Neuville, Belgium 21 H5 50 11N 4 32 E
Neuville-aux-Bois, France 23 D9 48 4N 2 3 E
Neuville-de-Poitou, France 24 B4 46 41N 0 15 E
Neuville-sur-Saône, France 25 C8 45 52N 4 51 E
Neuvy-le-Roi, France 22 E7 47 36N 0 36 E
Neuvy-St.-Sépulchre, France 24 B5 46 35N 1 48 E
Neuvy-sur-Barangeon, France 23 E9 47 20N 2 15 E
Neuwerk, Germany 26 B4 53 55N 8 30 E
Neuwied, Germany 26 E3 50 26N 7 29 E
Neva →, Russia 50 C6 59 50N 30 30 E
Nevada, Iowa, U.S.A. 140 B3 42 1N 93 27W
Nevada, Mo., U.S.A. 139 G7 37 51N 94 22W
Nevada □, U.S.A. 142 G5 39 0N 117 0W
Nevada, Sierra, Spain 35 H1 37 3N 3 15W
Nevada, Sierra, U.S.A. 142 G3 39 0N 120 30W
Nevada City, U.S.A. 144 F6 39 16N 121 1W
Nevado, Cerro, Argentina 158 D2 35 30 S 68 32W
Nevanka, Russia 57 D10 56 31N 98 55 E
Nevasa, India 82 E2 19 34N 75 0 E
Nevel, Russia 50 D5 56 0N 29 55 E
Nevele, Belgium 21 F3 51 3N 3 33 E
Nevers, France 23 F10 47 0N 3 9 E
Nevertire, Australia 117 A7 31 50 S 147 44 E
Nevesinje, Bos.-H. 42 D3 43 14N 18 6 E
Neville, Canada 131 D7 49 58N 107 39W
Nevinnomyssk, Russia 53 H6 44 40N 42 0 E
Nevis, W. Indies 149 C7 17 0N 62 30W
Nevrokop = Gotse Delchev, Bulgaria 43 F8 41 43N 23 46 E
Nevşehir, Turkey 88 C6 38 33N 34 40 E
Nevyansk, Russia 54 C8 57 30N 60 13 E
New →, Guyana 153 C6 3 20N 57 37W
New Albany, Ind., U.S.A. 141 F11 38 18N 85 49W
New Albany, Miss., U.S.A. 139 H10 34 29N 89 0W
New Albany, Pa., U.S.A. 137 E8 41 36N 76 27W
New Amsterdam, Guyana 153 B6 6 15N 57 36W
New Angledool, Australia 115 D4 29 5 S 147 55 E
New Athens, U.S.A. 140 F7 38 19N 89 53W
New Bedford, U.S.A. 137 E14 41 38N 70 56W
New Berlin, Ill., U.S.A. 140 E7 39 44N 89 55W
New Berlin, Wis., U.S.A. 141 B8 42 59N 88 6W
New Bern, U.S.A. 135 H7 35 7N 77 3W
New Bethlehem, U.S.A. 136 E5 41 0N 79 20W
New Bloomfield, U.S.A. 136 F7 40 25N 77 11W
New Boston, U.S.A. 139 J7 33 28N 94 25W
New Braunfels, U.S.A. 139 L5 29 42N 98 8W
New Brighton, N.Z. 119 D7 43 29 S 172 43 E
New Brighton, U.S.A. 136 F4 40 42N 80 19W
New Britain, Papua N. G. 120 C6 5 50 S 150 20 E
New Britain, U.S.A. 137 E12 41 40N 72 47W
New Brunswick, U.S.A. 137 F10 40 30N 74 27W
New Brunswick □, Canada 129 C6 46 50N 66 30W
New Buffalo, U.S.A. 141 C10 41 47N 86 45W
New Bussa, Nigeria 101 D5 9 53N 4 31 E
New Caledonia ■, Pac. Oc. 121 U19 21 0 S 165 0 E
New Canton, U.S.A. 140 E5 39 37N 91 8W
New Carlisle, Ind., U.S.A. 141 C10 41 45N 86 32W
New Carlisle, Ohio, U.S.A. 141 E12 39 56N 84 2W
New Castle, Ind., U.S.A. 141 E11 39 55N 85 22W
New Castle, Ky., U.S.A. 141 F11 38 26N 85 10W
New Castle, Pa., U.S.A. 136 E4 41 0N 80 21W
New City, U.S.A. 137 E11 41 9N 73 59W
New Cumberland, U.S.A. 136 F4 40 30N 80 36W
New Cuyama, U.S.A. 145 L7 34 57N 119 38W
New Delhi, India 80 E7 28 37N 77 13 E
New Denver, Canada 130 D5 50 0N 117 25W
New Don Pedro Reservoir, U.S.A. 144 H6 37 43N 120 24W
New England, U.S.A. 138 B3 46 32N 102 52W
New England Ra., Australia 115 E5 30 20 S 151 45 E
New Forest, U.K. 17 G6 50 53N 1 34W
New Franklin, U.S.A. 140 E4 39 1N 92 44W
New Georgia Is., Solomon Is. 121 M9 8 15 S 157 30 E
New Glarus, U.S.A. 140 B7 42 49N 89 38W
New Glasgow, Canada 129 C7 45 35N 62 36W
New Guinea, Oceania 58 K17 4 0 S 136 0 E
New Hamburg, Canada 136 C4 43 23N 80 42W
New Hampshire □, U.S.A. 137 C13 44 0N 71 30W
New Hampton, U.S.A. 140 A4 43 3N 92 19W
New Hanover, Papua N. G. 120 B6 2 30 S 150 10 E
New Hanover, S. Africa 105 D5 29 22 S 30 31 E
New Harmony, U.S.A. 141 F9 38 8N 87 56W
New Haven, Conn., U.S.A. 137 E12 41 18N 72 55W
New Haven, Ill., U.S.A. 141 G8 37 55N 88 8W
New Haven, Ind., U.S.A. 141 C11 41 4N 85 1W
New Haven, Mich., U.S.A. 136 D2 42 44N 82 48W
New Haven, Mo., U.S.A. 140 F5 38 37N 91 13W
New Hazelton, Canada 130 B3 55 20N 127 30W
New Hebrides = Vanuatu ■, Pac. Oc. 121 E6 15 0 S 168 0 E
New Iberia, U.S.A. 139 K9 30 1N 91 49W
New Ireland, Papua N. G. 120 B6 3 20 S 151 50 E
New Jersey □, U.S.A. 137 F10 40 0N 74 30W
New Kensington, U.S.A. 136 F5 40 34N 79 46W
New Lexington, U.S.A. 134 F4 39 43N 82 13W
New Liskeard, Canada 128 C4 47 31N 79 41W
New London, Conn., U.S.A. 137 E12 41 22N 72 6W
New London, Iowa, U.S.A. 140 D5 40 55N 91 24W
New London, Minn., U.S.A. 138 C7 45 18N 94 56W
New London, Mo., U.S.A. 140 E5 39 35N 91 24W
New London, Ohio, U.S.A. 136 E2 41 5N 82 24W
New London, Wis., U.S.A. 138 C10 44 23N 88 45W
New Madison, U.S.A. 141 E12 39 58N 84 43W
New Madrid, U.S.A. 139 G10 36 36N 89 32W
New Meadows, U.S.A. 142 D5 44 58N 116 18W
New Melones L., U.S.A. 144 H6 37 57N 120 31W
New Mexico □, U.S.A. 143 J10 34 30N 106 0W
New Miami, U.S.A. 141 E12 39 26N 84 32W
New Milford, Conn., U.S.A. 137 E11 41 35N 73 25W
New Milford, Pa., U.S.A. 137 E9 41 52N 75 44W
New Norcia, Australia 113 F2 30 57 S 116 13 E
New Norfolk, Australia 114 G4 42 46 S 147 2 E
New Orleans, U.S.A. 139 K9 29 58N 90 4W
New Palestine, U.S.A. 141 E11 39 45N 85 52W
New Paris, U.S.A. 141 E12 39 51N 84 48W
New Pekin, U.S.A. 141 F10 38 31N 86 2W
New Philadelphia, U.S.A. 136 F3 40 30N 81 27W
New Plymouth, N.Z. 118 F3 39 4 S 174 5 E
New Plymouth, U.S.A. 142 E5 43 58N 116 49W
New Providence, Bahamas 148 A4 25 25N 78 35W
New Radnor, U.K. 17 E4 52 15N 3 9W
New Richmond, Ohio, U.S.A. 141 F12 38 57N 84 17W
New Richmond, Wis., U.S.A. 138 C8 45 7N 92 32W
New Roads, U.S.A. 139 K9 30 42N 91 26W
New Rochelle, U.S.A. 137 F11 40 55N 73 47W
New Rockford, U.S.A. 138 B5 47 41N 99 8W
New Ross, Ireland 19 D5 52 23N 6 57W
New Salem, U.S.A. 138 B4 46 51N 101 25W
New Scone, U.K. 18 E5 56 25N 3 24W
New Sharon, U.S.A. 140 C4 41 28N 92 39W
New Siberian Is. = Novaya Sibir, Ostrov, Russia 57 B16 75 10N 150 0 E
New Siberian Is. = Novosibirskiye Ostrova, Russia 57 B15 75 0N 142 0 E
New Smyrna Beach, U.S.A. 135 L5 29 1N 80 56W
New South Wales □, Australia 115 E4 33 0 S 146 0 E
New Springs, Australia 113 E3 25 49 S 120 1 E
New Town, U.S.A. 138 A3 47 59N 102 30W
New Ulm, U.S.A. 138 C7 44 19N 94 28W
New Vienna, U.S.A. 141 E13 39 19N 83 42W
New Virginia, U.S.A. 140 C3 41 11N 93 44W
New Washington, Phil. 71 F4 11 39N 122 26 E
New Waterford, Canada 129 C7 46 13N 60 4W
New Westminster, Canada 130 D4 49 13N 122 55W
New York □, U.S.A. 137 D9 43 0N 75 0W
New York City, U.S.A. 137 F11 40 45N 74 0W
New Zealand ■, Oceania 118 G5 40 0 S 176 0 E
Newala, Tanzania 107 E4 10 58 S 39 18 E
Newala □, Tanzania 107 E4 10 46 S 39 20 E
Newark, Del., U.S.A. 134 F8 39 41N 75 46W
Newark, N.J., U.S.A. 137 F10 40 44N 74 10W
Newark, N.Y., U.S.A. 136 C7 43 3N 77 6W
Newark, Ohio, U.S.A. 136 F2 40 3N 82 24W
Newark-on-Trent, U.K. 16 D7 53 5N 0 48W
Newaygo, U.S.A. 134 D3 43 25N 85 48W
Newberg, Mo., U.S.A. 140 G5 37 55N 91 54W
Newberg, Oreg., U.S.A. 142 D2 45 18N 122 58W
Newberry, Mich., U.S.A. 134 B3 46 21N 85 30W
Newberry, S.C., U.S.A. 135 H5 34 17N 81 37W
Newberry Springs, U.S.A. 145 L10 34 50N 116 41W
Newbridge = Droichead Nua, Ireland 19 C5 53 11N 6 48W
Newbrook, Canada 130 C6 54 24N 112 57W
Newburgh, Ind., U.S.A. 141 G9 37 57N 87 24W
Newburgh, N.Y., U.S.A. 137 E10 41 30N 74 1W
Newbury, U.K. 17 F6 51 24N 1 20W
Newbury, U.S.A. 137 B12 43 19N 72 3W
Newburyport, U.S.A. 137 D14 42 49N 70 53W
Newcastle, Australia 117 B9 33 0 S 151 46 E
Newcastle, Canada 129 C6 47 1N 65 38W
Newcastle, S. Africa 105 D4 27 45 S 29 58 E
Newcastle, U.K. 19 B6 54 13N 5 54W
Newcastle, Calif., U.S.A. 144 G5 38 53N 121 8W
Newcastle, Wyo., U.S.A. 138 D2 43 50N 104 11W
Newcastle Emlyn, U.K. 17 E3 52 2N 4 28W
Newcastle Ra., Australia 112 C5 15 45 S 130 15 E
Newcastle-under-Lyme, U.K. 16 D5 53 1N 2 14W
Newcastle-upon-Tyne, U.K. 16 C6 54 58N 1 36W
Newcastle Waters, Australia 114 B1 17 30 S 133 28 E
Newdegate, Australia 113 F2 33 6 S 119 0 E
Newell, U.S.A. 138 C3 44 43N 103 25W
Newfoundland □, Canada 129 B8 53 0N 58 0W
Newfoundland I., N. Amer. 124 E14 49 0N 55 0W
Newhalem, U.S.A. 130 D4 48 40N 121 15W
Newhall, U.S.A. 145 L8 34 23N 118 32W
Newham, U.K. 17 F8 51 31N 0 3 E
Newhaven, U.K. 17 G8 50 47N 0 3 E
Newkirk, U.S.A. 139 G6 36 53N 97 3W
Newman, Australia 112 D2 23 18 S 119 45 E
Newman, Calif., U.S.A. 144 H5 37 19N 121 1W
Newman, Ill., U.S.A. 141 E9 39 48N 87 59W
Newmarket, Canada 136 B5 44 3N 79 28W
Newmarket, Ireland 19 D3 52 13N 9 0W
Newmarket, U.K. 17 E8 52 15N 0 25 E
Newmarket, U.S.A. 137 C14 43 5N 70 56W
Newnan, U.S.A. 135 J3 33 23N 84 48W
Newport, I. of W., U.K. 17 G6 50 42N 1 17W
Newport, Newp., U.K. 17 F5 51 35N 3 0W
Newport, Ark., U.S.A. 139 H9 35 37N 91 16W
Newport, Ind., U.S.A. 141 E9 39 53N 87 25W
Newport, Ky., U.S.A. 141 E12 39 5N 84 30W
Newport, N.H., U.S.A. 137 C12 43 22N 72 10W
Newport, Oreg., U.S.A. 142 D1 44 39N 124 3W
Newport, Pa., U.S.A. 136 F7 40 29N 77 8W
Newport, R.I., U.S.A. 137 E13 41 29N 71 19W
Newport, Tenn., U.S.A. 135 H4 35 58N 83 11W
Newport, Vt., U.S.A. 137 B12 44 56N 72 13W
Newport, Wash., U.S.A. 142 B5 48 11N 117 3W
Newport □, U.K. 17 F4 51 33N 3 1W
Newport Beach, U.S.A. 145 M9 33 37N 117 56W
Newport News, U.S.A. 134 G7 36 59N 76 25W
Newquay, U.K. 17 G2 50 25N 5 6W
Newry, U.K. 19 B5 54 11N 6 21W
Newry & Mourne □, U.K. 19 B5 54 10N 6 15W
Newton, Ill., U.S.A. 141 F8 38 59N 88 10W
Newton, Iowa, U.S.A. 140 C3 41 42N 93 3W
Newton, Mass., U.S.A. 137 D13 42 21N 71 12W
Newton, Miss., U.S.A. 139 J10 32 19N 89 10W
Newton, N.C., U.S.A. 135 H5 35 40N 81 13W
Newton, N.J., U.S.A. 137 E10 41 3N 74 45W
Newton, Tex., U.S.A. 139 K8 30 51N 93 46W
Newton Abbot, U.K. 17 G4 50 32N 3 37W
Newton Boyd, Australia 115 D5 29 45 S 152 16 E
Newton Stewart, U.K. 18 G4 54 57N 4 30W
Newtonmore, U.K. 18 D4 57 4N 4 8W
Newtown, U.K. 17 E4 52 31N 3 19W
Newtown, U.S.A. 140 D3 40 22N 93 20W
Newtownabbey □, U.K. 19 B6 54 45N 6 0W
Newtownards, U.K. 19 B6 54 36N 5 42W
Newville, U.S.A. 136 F7 40 10N 77 24W
Nexon, France 24 C5 45 41N 1 11 E
Neya, Russia 52 A6 58 21N 43 49 E
Neyrīz, Iran 85 D7 29 15N 54 19 E
Neyshābūr, Iran 85 B8 36 10N 58 50 E
Neyyattinkara, India 83 K3 8 26N 77 5 E
Nezhin = Nizhyn, Ukraine 51 G6 51 5N 31 55 E
Nezperce, U.S.A. 142 C5 46 14N 116 14W
Ngabang, Indonesia 75 B3 0 23N 109 55 E
Ngabordamlu, Tanjung, Indonesia 73 C4 6 56 S 134 11 E
N'Gage, Angola 103 D3 7 46 S 15 15 E
Ngaiphaipi, Burma 78 D4 22 14N 93 15 E
Ngambé, Cameroon 101 D7 5 48N 11 29 E
Ngami Depression, Botswana 104 C3 20 30 S 22 46 E
Ngamo, Zimbabwe 107 F2 19 3 S 27 32 E
Nganjuk, Indonesia 75 D4 7 32 S 111 55 E
Ngao, Thailand 76 C2 18 46N 99 59 E
Ngaoundéré, Cameroon 102 A2 7 15N 13 35 E
Ngapara, N.Z. 119 E5 44 57 S 170 46 E
Ngara, Tanzania 106 C3 2 29 S 30 40 E
Ngara □, Tanzania 106 C3 2 29 S 30 40 E
Ngaruawahia, N.Z. 118 D4 37 42 S 175 11 E
Ngaruroro →, N.Z. 118 F5 39 34 S 176 55 E
Ngatapa, N.Z. 118 E6 38 32 S 177 45 E
Ngathainggyaung, Burma 78 G5 17 24N 95 5 E
Ngauruhoe, Mt., N.Z. 118 F4 39 13 S 175 45 E
Ngawi, Indonesia 75 D4 7 24 S 111 26 E
Nggela, Solomon Is. 121 M11 9 5 S 160 15 E
Nghia Lo, Vietnam 76 B5 21 33N 104 28 E
Ngidinga, Zaïre 103 D3 5 37 S 15 17 E
Ngo, Congo 102 C3 2 29 S 15 45 E
N'Gola, Angola 103 E2 14 10 S 14 30 E
Ngoma, Malawi 107 E3 13 8 S 33 45 E
Ngomahura, Zimbabwe 107 G3 20 26 S 30 43 E
Ngomba, Tanzania 107 D3 8 20 S 32 53 E
Ngongotaha, N.Z. 118 E5 38 5 S 176 12 E
Ngop, Sudan 95 F3 6 17N 30 9 E
Ngoring Hu, China 64 C4 34 55N 97 5 E
Ngorkou, Mali 100 B4 15 40N 3 41W
Ngorongoro, Tanzania 106 C4 3 11 S 35 32 E
Ngouri, Chad 97 F3 13 38N 15 22 E
Ngourti, Niger 97 E2 15 19N 13 12 E
Ngozi, Burundi 106 C2 2 54 S 29 50 E
Ngudu, Tanzania 106 C3 2 58 S 33 25 E
Nguigmi, Niger 97 F2 14 20N 13 20 E
Ngukurr, Australia 114 A1 14 44 S 134 44 E
Ngunga, Tanzania 106 C3 3 37 S 33 37 E
Nguru, Nigeria 101 C7 12 56N 10 29 E
Nguru Mts., Tanzania 106 D4 6 0 S 37 30 E
Nguyen Binh, Vietnam 76 A5 22 39N 105 56 E
Nha Trang, Vietnam 77 F7 12 16N 109 10 E
Nhacoongo, Mozam. 105 C6 24 18 S 35 14 E
Nhamaabué, Mozam. 107 F4 17 25 S 35 5 E
Nhambiquara, Brazil 157 C6 12 50 S 59 49W
Nhamundá, Brazil 153 D6 2 14 S 56 43W
Nhamundá →, Brazil 153 D6 2 12 S 56 41W
Nhangutazi, L., Mozam. 105 C5 24 0 S 34 30 E
Nhecolândia, Brazil 157 D6 19 17 S 56 58W
Nhill, Australia 116 D4 36 18 S 141 40 E
Nho Quan, Vietnam 76 B5 20 18N 105 45 E
Nhulunbuy, Australia 114 A2 12 10 S 137 20 E
Nhundo, Angola 103 E4 14 25 S 21 23 E
Nia-nia, Zaïre 106 B2 1 30N 27 40 E
Niafounké, Mali 100 B4 16 0N 4 5W
Niagara, U.S.A. 134 C1 45 45N 88 0W
Niagara Falls, Canada 128 D4 43 7N 79 5W
Niagara Falls, U.S.A. 136 C6 43 5N 79 4W
Niagara-on-the-Lake, Canada 136 C5 43 15N 79 4W
Niah, Malaysia 75 B4 3 58N 113 46 E
Niamey, Niger 101 C5 13 27N 2 6 E
Nianforando, Guinea 100 D2 9 37N 10 36W
Nianfors, Sweden 14 C10 61 36N 16 46 E
Niangara, Zaïre 106 B2 3 42N 27 50 E
Niangua →, U.S.A. 140 G4 38 0N 92 48W
Nias, Indonesia 74 B1 1 0N 97 30 E
Niassa □, Mozam. 107 E4 13 30 S 36 0 E
Nibāk, Si. Arabia 87 A5 24 25N 50 50 E
Nibbiano, Italy 38 D6 44 54N 9 19 E
Nibe, Denmark 15 H3 56 59N 9 38 E
Nicaragua ■, Cent. Amer. 148 D2 11 40N 85 30W
Nicaragua, L. de, Nic. 148 D2 12 0N 85 30W
Nicastro, Italy 41 D9 38 59N 16 19 E
Nice, France 25 E11 43 42N 7 14 E
Niceville, U.S.A. 135 K2 30 31N 86 30W
Nichinan, Japan 62 F3 31 38N 131 23 E
Nicholás, Canal, W. Indies 148 B3 23 30N 80 5W
Nicholasville, U.S.A. 141 G12 37 53N 84 34W
Nichols, U.S.A. 137 D8 42 1N 76 22W
Nicholson, Australia 112 C4 18 2 S 128 54 E
Nicholson, U.S.A. 137 E9 41 37N 75 47W
Nicholson →, Australia 114 B2 17 31 S 139 36 E
Nicholson Ra., Australia 113 E2 27 15 S 116 45 E
Nickerie □, Surinam 153 C6 4 0N 57 0W
Nickerie →, Surinam 153 B6 5 58N 57 0W
Nicobar Is., Ind. Oc. 58 J13 9 0N 93 0 E
Nicoclí, Colombia 152 B2 8 26N 76 48W
Nicola, Canada 130 C4 50 12N 120 40W
Nicolet, Canada 128 C5 46 17N 72 35W
Nicolls Town, Bahamas 148 A4 25 8N 78 0W
Nicopolis, Greece 45 E2 39 2N 20 37 E
Nicosia, Cyprus 32 D12 35 10N 33 25 E
Nicosia, Italy 41 E7 37 45N 14 24 E
Nicótera, Italy 41 D8 38 33N 15 56 E
Nicoya, Costa Rica 148 D2 10 9N 85 27W
Nicoya, G. de, Costa Rica 148 E3 10 0N 85 0W
Nicoya, Pen. de, Costa Rica 148 E2 9 45N 85 40W
Nidau, Switz. 28 B4 47 7N 7 15 E
Nidd →, U.K. 16 C6 53 59N 1 23W
Nidda, Germany 26 E5 50 23N 9 1 E
Nidda →, Germany 27 E4 50 17N 8 48 E
Nidwalden □, Switz. 29 C6 46 50N 8 25 E
Nidzica, Poland 47 B7 53 25N 20 28 E
Niebüll, Germany 26 A4 54 46N 8 48 E
Nied →, Germany 23 C13 49 23N 6 40 E
Niederaula, Germany 26 E5 50 47N 9 36 E
Niederbipp, Switz. 28 B5 47 16N 7 42 E
Niederbronn-les-Bains, France 23 D14 48 57N 7 39 E
Niedere Tauern, Austria 30 D7 47 20N 14 0 E
Niederösterreich □, Austria 30 C8 48 25N 15 40 E
Niedersachsen □, Germany 26 C5 53 8N 9 0 E
Niefang, Eq. Guin. 102 B2 1 50N 10 14 E
Niekerkshoop, S. Africa 104 D3 29 19 S 22 51 E
Niel, Belgium 21 F4 51 7N 4 20 E
Niellé, Ivory C. 100 C3 10 5N 5 38W
Niem, C.A.R. 102 A3 6 12N 15 14 E
Niemba, Zaïre 106 D2 5 58 S 28 24 E
Niemcza, Poland 47 E3 50 42N 16 47 E
Niemen = Neman →, Lithuania 13 J19 55 25N 21 10 E
Niemodlin, Poland 47 E4 50 38N 17 38 E
Niemur, Australia 116 C6 35 17 S 144 9 E
Nienburg, Germany 26 C5 52 39N 9 13 E
Niepołomice, Poland 31 A13 50 3N 20 13 E
Niers →, Germany 26 D2 51 43N 5 57 E
Niesen, Switz. 28 C5 46 38N 7 39 E
Niesky, Germany 26 D10 51 17N 14 49 E
Nieszawa, Poland 47 C5 52 52N 18 50 E
Nieu Bethesda, S. Africa 104 E3 31 51 S 24 34 E
Nieuw-Amsterdam, Neths. 20 C9 52 43N 6 52 E
Nieuw Amsterdam, Surinam 153 B6 5 53N 55 5W
Nieuw Beijerland, Neths. 20 E4 51 49N 4 20 E
Nieuw-Dordrecht, Neths. 20 C9 52 45N 6 59 E
Nieuw Loosdrecht, Neths. 20 D6 52 12N 5 8 E
Nieuw Nickerie, Surinam 153 B6 6 0N 56 59W
Nieuw-Schoonebeek, Neths. 20 C10 52 39N 7 0 E
Nieuw-Vennep, Neths. 20 D5 52 16N 4 38 E
Nieuw-Vossemeer, Neths. 21 E4 51 34N 4 12 E
Nieuwe-Niedorp, Neths. 20 C5 52 44N 4 54 E
Nieuwe-Pekela, Neths. 20 B9 53 5N 6 58 E
Nieuwe-Schans, Neths. 20 B10 53 11N 7 12 E
Nieuwendijk, Neths. 20 E5 51 46N 4 55 E
Nieuwerkerken, Belgium 21 G6 50 52N 5 12 E
Nieuwkoop, Neths. 20 D5 52 9N 4 48 E
Nieuwleusen, Neths. 20 C8 52 34N 6 17 E
Nieuwnamen, Neths. 21 F4 51 18N 4 9 E
Nieuwolda, Neths. 20 B9 53 15N 6 58 E
Nieuwoudtville, S. Africa 104 E2 31 23 S 19 7 E
Nieuwpoort, Belgium 21 F1 51 8N 2 45 E
Nieuwveen, Neths. 20 D5 52 12N 4 46 E
Nieves, Spain 36 C2 42 7N 8 26W
Nieves, Pico de las, Canary Is. 33 G4 27 57N 15 35W
Nièvre □, France 23 E10 47 10N 3 40 E
Nigata, Japan 62 C4 34 13N 132 39 E
Niğde, Turkey 88 D6 37 58N 34 40 E
Nigel, S. Africa 105 D4 26 27 S 28 25 E
Niger □, Nigeria 101 C6 10 0N 5 30 E
Niger ■, W. Afr. 97 E2 17 30N 10 0 E
Niger →, W. Afr. 101 D6 5 33N 6 33 E
Nigeria ■, W. Afr. 101 D6 8 30N 8 0 E
Nightcaps, N.Z. 119 F3 45 57 S 168 2 E
Nigrita, Greece 44 D5 40 56N 23 29 E
Nihtaur, India 81 E8 29 20N 78 23 E
Nii-Jima, Japan 63 C11 34 20N 139 15 E
Niigata, Japan 60 F9 37 58N 139 0 E
Niigata □, Japan 61 F9 37 15N 138 45 E
Niihama, Japan 62 D5 33 55N 133 16 E
Niihau, U.S.A. 132 H14 21 54N 160 9W
Niimi, Japan 62 C5 34 59N 133 28 E
Niitsu, Japan 60 F9 37 48N 139 7 E
Nījar, Spain 35 J2 36 53N 2 15W
Nijil, Jordan 91 E4 30 32N 35 33 E
Nijkerk, Neths. 20 D7 52 13N 5 30 E
Nijlen, Belgium 21 F5 51 10N 4 40 E
Nijmegen, Neths. 20 E7 51 50N 5 52 E
Nijverdal, Neths. 20 D8 52 22N 6 28 E
Nīk Pey, Iran 89 D13 36 50N 48 10 E
Nike, Nigeria 101 D6 6 26N 7 29 E
Nikiniki, Indonesia 72 C2 9 49 S 124 30 E
Nikítas, Greece 44 D5 40 13N 23 34 E
Nikki, Benin 101 D5 9 58N 3 12 E
Nikkō, Japan 63 A11 36 45N 139 35 E
Nikolayev = Mykolayiv, Ukraine 51 J7 46 58N 32 0 E
Nikolayevsk, Russia 52 E7 50 0N 45 35 E
Nikolayevsk-na-Amur, Russia 57 D15 53 8N 140 44 E
Nikolsk, Russia 52 D8 53 49N 46 4 E
Nikolskoye, Russia 57 D17 55 12N 166 0 E
Nikopol, Bulgaria 43 D9 43 43N 24 54 E
Nikopol, Ukraine 51 J8 47 35N 34 25 E
Niksar, Turkey 88 B7 40 31N 37 2 E

North West Frontier 241

Nīkshahr, *Iran* **85 E9** 26 15N 60 10 E
Nikšić, *Montenegro, Yug.* **42 E3** 42 50N 18 57 E
Nîl, Nahr en →, *Africa* **94 H7** 30 10N 31 6 E
Nîl el Abyad →, *Sudan* **95 D3** 15 38N 32 31 E
Nîl el Azraq →, *Sudan* **95 D3** 15 38N 32 31 E
Niland, *U.S.A.* **145 M11** 33 14N 115 31W
Nile = Nîl, Nahr en →, *Africa* **94 H7** 30 10N 31 6 E
Nile Delta, *Egypt* **94 H7** 31 40N 31 0 E
Niles, *U.S.A.* **136 E4** 41 11N 80 46W
Nilgiri Hills, *India* **83 J3** 11 30N 76 30 E
Nilo Peçanha, *Brazil* **155 D4** 13 37 S 39 6W
Nilpena, *Australia* **116 A3** 30 58 S 138 20 E
Nimach, *India* **80 G6** 24 30N 74 56 E
Nimbahera, *India* **80 G6** 24 37N 74 45 E
Nîmes, *France* **25 E8** 43 50N 4 23 E
Nimfaíon, Ákra = Pínnes, Ákra, *Greece* **44 D6** 40 5N 24 20 E
Nimmitabel, *Australia* **117 D8** 36 29 S 149 15 E
Nimule, *Sudan* **95 G3** 3 32N 32 3 E
Nin, *Croatia* **39 D12** 44 16N 15 12 E
Nīnawá, *Iraq* **89 D10** 36 25N 43 10 E
Ninda, *Angola* **103 E4** 14 47 S 21 24 E
Nindigully, *Australia* **115 D4** 28 21 S 148 50 E
Ninemile, *U.S.A.* **130 B2** 56 0N 130 7W
Ninety Mile Beach, *N.Z.* **118 A1** 34 48 S 173 0 E
Ninety Mile Beach, The, *Australia* **117 E7** 38 15 S 147 24 E
Nineveh = Nīnawá, *Iraq* **89 D10** 36 25N 43 10 E
Ning Xian, *China* **66 G4** 35 30N 107 58 E
Ningaloo, *Australia* **112 D1** 22 41 S 113 41 E
Ning'an, *China* **67 B15** 44 22N 129 20 E
Ningbo, *China* **69 C13** 29 51N 121 28 E
Ningcheng, *China* **67 D10** 41 32N 119 53 E
Ningde, *China* **69 D12** 26 38N 119 23 E
Ningdu, *China* **69 D10** 26 25N 115 59 E
Ninggang, *China* **69 D9** 26 42N 113 55 E
Ningguo, *China* **69 B12** 30 35N 119 0 E
Ninghai, *China* **69 C13** 29 15N 121 27 E
Ninghua, *China* **69 D11** 26 14N 116 45 E
Ningjin, *China* **66 F8** 37 35N 114 57 E
Ningjing Shan, *China* **68 B2** 30 0N 98 20 E
Ninglang, *China* **68 D3** 27 20N 100 55 E
Ningling, *China* **66 G8** 34 25N 115 22 E
Ningming, *China* **68 F6** 22 8N 107 4 E
Ningnan, *China* **68 D4** 27 5N 102 36 E
Ningpo = Ningbo, *China* **69 C13** 29 51N 121 28 E
Ningqiang, *China* **66 H4** 32 47N 106 15 E
Ningshan, *China* **66 H5** 33 21N 108 21 E
Ningsia Hui A.R. = Ningxia Huizu Zizhiqu □, *China* **66 E3** 38 0N 106 0 E
Ningwu, *China* **66 E7** 39 0N 112 18 E
Ningxia Huizu Zizhiqu □, *China* **66 E3** 38 0N 106 0 E
Ningxiang, *China* **69 C9** 28 15N 112 30 E
Ningyang, *China* **66 G9** 35 47N 116 45 E
Ningyuan, *China* **69 E8** 25 37N 111 57 E
Ninh Binh, *Vietnam* **76 B5** 20 15N 105 55 E
Ninh Giang, *Vietnam* **76 B6** 20 44N 106 24 E
Ninh Hoa, *Vietnam* **76 F7** 12 30N 109 7 E
Ninh Ma, *Vietnam* **76 F7** 12 48N 109 21 E
Ninove, *Belgium* **21 G4** 50 51N 4 2 E
Nioaque, *Brazil* **159 A4** 21 5 S 55 50W
Niobrara, *U.S.A.* **138 D6** 42 45N 98 2W
Niobrara →, *U.S.A.* **138 D6** 42 46N 98 3W
Nioki, *Zaïre* **102 C3** 2 47 S 17 40 E
Niono, *Mali* **100 C3** 14 15N 6 0W
Nioro du Rip, *Senegal* **100 C1** 13 40N 15 50W
Nioro du Sahel, *Mali* **100 B3** 15 15N 9 30W
Niort, *France* **24 B3** 46 19N 0 29W
Nipa, *Papua N. G.* **120 D2** 6 9 S 143 29 E
Nipani, *India* **83 F2** 16 20N 74 25 E
Nipawin, *Canada* **131 C8** 53 20N 104 0W
Nipawin Prov. Park, *Canada* **131 C8** 54 0N 104 37W
Nipigon, *Canada* **128 C2** 49 0N 88 17W
Nipigon, L., *Canada* **128 C2** 49 50N 88 30W
Nipin →, *Canada* **131 B7** 55 46N 108 35W
Nipishish L., *Canada* **129 B7** 54 12N 60 45W
Nipissing L., *Canada* **128 C4** 46 20N 80 0W
Nipomo, *U.S.A.* **145 K6** 35 3N 120 29W
Nipton, *U.S.A.* **145 K11** 35 28N 115 16W
Niquelândia, *Brazil* **155 D2** 14 33 S 48 23W
Nīr, *Iran* **89 C12** 38 2N 47 59 E
Nira →, *India* **82 F2** 17 58N 75 8 E
Nirasaki, *Japan* **63 B10** 35 42N 138 27 E
Nirmal, *India* **82 E4** 19 3N 78 20 E
Nirmali, *India* **81 F12** 26 20N 86 35 E
Niš, *Serbia, Yug.* **42 D6** 43 19N 21 58 E
Nisa, *Portugal* **37 F3** 39 30N 7 41W
Nisāb, *Si. Arabia* **84 D5** 29 11N 44 43 E
Nişāb, *Yemen* **86 D4** 14 25N 46 29 E
Nišava →, *Serbia, Yug.* **42 D6** 43 20N 21 46 E
Niscemi, *Italy* **41 E7** 37 9N 14 23 E
Nishi-Sonogi-Hantō, *Japan* **62 E1** 32 55N 129 45 E
Nishinomiya, *Japan* **63 C7** 34 45N 135 20 E
Nishin'omote, *Japan* **61 J5** 30 43N 130 59 E
Nishio, *Japan* **63 C9** 34 52N 137 3 E
Nishiwaki, *Japan* **62 C6** 34 59N 134 58 E
Nísíros, *Greece* **45 H9** 36 35N 27 12 E
Niskibi →, *Canada* **128 A2** 56 29N 88 9W
Nisko, *Poland* **47 E9** 50 35N 22 7 E
Nispen, *Neths.* **21 F4** 51 29N 4 28 E
Nisporeni, *Moldova* **46 B9** 47 4N 28 10 E
Nisqually →, *U.S.A.* **144 C4** 47 6N 122 42W
Nissáki, *Greece* **32 A3** 39 43N 19 52 E
Nissan →, *Sweden* **15 H6** 56 40N 12 51 E
Nissedal, *Norway* **14 E2** 59 10N 8 30 E
Nisser, *Norway* **14 E2** 59 7N 8 28 E
Nissum Bredning, *Denmark* **13 H13** 56 40N 8 20 E
Nissum Fjord, *Denmark* **15 H2** 56 20N 8 11 E
Nistelrode, *Neths.* **21 E7** 51 42N 5 34 E
Nistru = Dnister →, *Europe* **51 J6** 46 18N 30 17 E
Nisutlin →, *Canada* **130 A2** 60 14N 132 34W
Nitchequon, *Canada* **129 B5** 53 10N 70 58W
Niterói, *Brazil* **155 F3** 22 52 S 43 0W
Nith →, *U.K.* **18 F5** 55 14N 3 33W
Nitra, *Slovak Rep.* **31 C11** 48 19N 18 4 E
Nitra →, *Slovak Rep.* **31 D11** 47 46N 18 10 E
Nittedal, *Norway* **14 D4** 60 1N 10 57 E
Nittenau, *Germany* **27 F8** 49 12N 12 16 E
Niuafo'ou, *Tonga* **111 D15** 15 30 S 175 58W
Niue, *Cook Is.* **123 J11** 19 2 S 169 54W
Niulan Jiang →, *China* **68 D4** 27 30N 103 5 E
Niut, *Indonesia* **75 B4** 0 55N 110 6 E
Niutou Shan, *China* **69 C13** 29 5N 121 59 E
Niuzhuang, *China* **67 D12** 40 58N 122 28 E
Nivala, *Finland* **12 E21** 63 56N 24 57 E
Nivelles, *Belgium* **21 G4** 50 35N 4 20 E
Nivernais, *France* **23 E10** 47 15N 3 30 E
Nixon, *U.S.A.* **139 L6** 29 16N 97 46W
Nizam Sagar, *India* **82 E3** 18 10N 77 58 E
Nizamabad, *India* **82 E4** 18 45N 78 7 E
Nizamghat, *India* **78 A5** 28 20N 95 45 E
Nizhne Kolymsk, *Russia* **57 C17** 68 34N 160 55 E
Nizhne-Vartovsk, *Russia* **56 C8** 60 56N 76 38 E
Nizhneangarsk, *Russia* **57 D11** 55 47N 109 30 E
Nizhnegorskiy = Nyzhnohirskyy, *Ukraine* **51 K8** 45 27N 34 38 E
Nizhnekamsk, *Russia* **52 C10** 55 38N 51 49 E
Nizhnekamskoye Vdkhr., *Russia* **54 D4** 55 56N 52 56 E
Nizhneudinsk, *Russia* **57 D10** 54 54N 99 3 E
Nizhneyansk, *Russia* **57 B14** 71 26N 136 4 E
Nizhniy Chir, *Russia* **53 F6** 48 22N 43 5 E
Nizhniy Lomov, *Russia* **52 D6** 53 34N 43 38 E
Nizhniy Novgorod, *Russia* **52 B7** 56 20N 44 0 E
Nizhniy Tagil, *Russia* **54 C7** 57 55N 59 57 E
Nizhniye Sergi, *Russia* **54 C7** 56 40N 59 18 E
Nizhnyaya Salda, *Russia* **54 B8** 58 8N 60 42 E
Nizhyn, *Ukraine* **51 G6** 51 5N 31 55 E
Nizip, *Turkey* **88 D7** 37 5N 37 50 E
Nízké Tatry, *Slovak Rep.* **31 C12** 48 55N 19 30 E
Nizza Monferrato, *Italy* **38 D5** 44 46N 8 21 E
Njakwa, *Malawi* **107 E3** 11 1 S 33 56 E
Njanji, *Zambia* **107 E3** 14 25 S 31 46 E
Njinjo, *Tanzania* **107 D4** 8 48 S 38 54 E
Njombe, *Tanzania* **107 D3** 9 20 S 34 50 E
Njombe □, *Tanzania* **107 D3** 9 20 S 34 49 E
Njombe →, *Tanzania* **106 D4** 6 56 S 35 6 E
Nkambe, *Cameroon* **101 D7** 6 35N 10 40 E
Nkana, *Zambia* **107 E2** 12 50 S 28 8 E
Nkawkaw, *Ghana* **101 D4** 6 36N 0 49W
Nkayi, *Zimbabwe* **107 F2** 19 41 S 29 20 E
Nkhota Kota, *Malawi* **107 E3** 12 56 S 34 15 E
Nkolabona, *Gabon* **102 B2** 1 14N 11 43 E
Nkone, *Zaïre* **102 C4** 1 2 S 22 20 E
Nkongsamba, *Cameroon* **101 E6** 4 55N 9 55 E
Nkunga, *Zaïre* **103 C3** 4 41 S 18 34 E
Nkurenkuru, *Namibia* **104 B2** 17 42 S 18 32 E
Nkwanta, *Ghana* **100 D4** 6 10N 2 10W
Noakhali = Maijdi, *Bangla.* **78 D3** 22 48N 91 10 E
Noatak, *U.S.A.* **126 B3** 67 34N 162 58W
Nobel, *Canada* **136 A4** 45 25N 80 6W
Nobeoka, *Japan* **62 E3** 32 36N 131 41 E
Nōbi-Heiya, *Japan* **63 B8** 35 15N 136 45 E
Noble, *U.S.A.* **141 F8** 38 42N 88 14W
Noblejas, *Spain* **34 F1** 39 58N 3 26W
Noblesville, *U.S.A.* **141 D11** 40 3N 86 1W
Noce →, *Italy* **38 B8** 46 9N 11 4 E
Nocera Inferiore, *Italy* **41 B7** 40 44N 14 38 E
Nocera Terinese, *Italy* **41 C9** 39 2N 16 9 E
Nocera Umbra, *Italy* **39 E9** 43 5N 12 47 E
Noci, *Italy* **41 B10** 40 48N 17 7 E
Nockatunga, *Australia* **115 D3** 27 42 S 142 42 E
Nocona, *U.S.A.* **139 J6** 33 47N 97 44W
Nocrich, *Romania* **46 D5** 45 55N 24 26 E
Noda, *Japan* **63 B11** 35 56N 139 52 E
Noel, *U.S.A.* **139 G7** 36 33N 94 29W
Nogal Valley, *Somali Rep.* **108 C3** 8 35N 48 35 E
Nogales, *Mexico* **146 A2** 31 20N 110 56W
Nogales, *U.S.A.* **143 L8** 31 20N 110 56W
Nogat →, *Poland* **47 A6** 54 17N 19 17 E
Nōgata, *Japan* **62 D2** 33 48N 130 44 E
Nogent-en-Bassigny, *France* **23 D12** 48 1N 5 20 E
Nogent-le-Rotrou, *France* **22 D7** 48 20N 0 50 E
Nogent-sur-Seine, *France* **23 D10** 48 30N 3 30 E
Noggerup, *Australia* **113 F2** 33 32 S 116 5 E
Noginsk, *Moskva, Russia* **52 C4** 55 50N 38 25 E
Noginsk, *Sib., Russia* **57 C10** 64 30N 90 50 E
Nogoa →, *Australia* **114 C4** 23 40 S 147 55 E
Nogoyá, *Argentina* **158 C4** 32 24 S 59 48W
Nógrád □, *Hungary* **31 D12** 48 0N 19 30 E
Nogueira de Ramuin, *Spain* **36 C3** 42 21N 7 43W
Noguera Pallaresa →, *Spain* **34 D5** 41 55N 0 55 E
Noguera Ribagorzana →, *Spain* **34 D5** 41 40N 0 43 E
Nohar, *India* **80 E6** 29 11N 74 49 E
Noing, *Phil.* **71 J5** 5 40N 125 28 E
Noire, Montagne, *France* **24 E6** 43 28N 2 18 E
Noire, Mt., *France* **22 D3** 48 11N 3 40W
Noirétable, *France* **24 C7** 45 48N 3 46 E
Noirmoutier, I. de, *France* **22 F4** 46 58N 2 10W
Noirmoutier-en-l'Ile, *France* **22 F4** 47 0N 2 14W
Nojane, *Botswana* **104 C3** 23 15 S 20 14 E
Nojima-Zaki, *Japan* **63 C11** 34 54N 139 53 E
Nok Kundi, *Pakistan* **79 C1** 28 50N 62 45 E
Nokaneng, *Botswana* **104 B3** 19 40 S 22 17 E
Nokhtuysk, *Russia* **57 C12** 60 0N 117 45 E
Nokia, *Finland* **13 F20** 61 30N 23 30 E
Nokomis, *Canada* **131 C8** 51 35N 105 0W
Nokomis, *U.S.A.* **140 E7** 39 18N 89 18W
Nokomis L., *Canada* **131 B8** 57 0N 103 0W
Nokou, *Chad* **97 F2** 14 35N 14 47 E
Nol, *Sweden* **15 G6** 57 56N 12 5 E
Nola, *C.A.R.* **102 B3** 3 35N 16 4 E
Nola, *Italy* **41 B7** 40 55N 14 33 E
Nolay, *France* **23 F11** 46 58N 4 35 E
Noli, C. di, *Italy* **38 D5** 44 12N 8 25 E
Nolinsk, *Russia* **52 B9** 57 28N 49 57 E
Noma Omuramba →, *Namibia* **104 B3** 18 52 S 20 53 E
Noma-Saki, *Japan* **62 F2** 31 25N 130 7 E
Nomad, *Papua N. G.* **120 D2** 6 19 S 142 13 E
Noman L., *Canada* **131 A7** 62 15N 108 55W
Nombre de Dios, *Panama* **148 E4** 9 34N 79 28W
Nome, *U.S.A.* **126 B3** 64 30N 165 25W
Nomo-Zaki, *Japan* **62 E1** 32 35N 129 44 E
Nomuka, *Tonga* **121 Q13** 20 17 S 174 48W
Nomuka Group, *Tonga* **121 Q13** 20 20 S 174 48W
Nonacho L., *Canada* **131 A7** 61 42N 109 40W
Nonancourt, *France* **22 D8** 48 47N 1 11 E
Nonant-le-Pin, *France* **22 D7** 48 42N 0 12 E
Nonda, *Australia* **114 C3** 20 40 S 142 28 E
Nong Chang, *Thailand* **76 E2** 15 23N 99 51 E
Nong Het, *Laos* **76 C4** 19 29N 103 59 E
Nong Khai, *Thailand* **76 D4** 17 50N 102 46 E
Nong'an, *China* **67 B13** 44 25N 125 5 E
Nongoma, *S. Africa* **105 D5** 27 58 S 31 35 E
Nonoava, *Mexico* **146 B3** 27 28N 106 44W
Nonoc I., *Phil.* **71 G5** 9 51N 125 37 E
Nonthaburi, *Thailand* **76 F3** 13 51N 100 34 E
Nontron, *France* **24 C4** 45 31N 0 40 E
Nonza, *France* **25 F13** 42 47N 9 21 E
Noonamah, *Australia* **112 B5** 12 40 S 131 4 E
Noonan, *U.S.A.* **138 A3** 48 54N 103 1W
Noondoo, *Australia* **115 D4** 28 35 S 148 30 E
Noonkanbah, *Australia* **112 C3** 18 30 S 124 50 E
Noord-Bergum, *Neths.* **20 B8** 53 14N 6 1 E
Noord Brabant □, *Neths.* **21 E6** 51 40N 5 0 E
Noord Holland □, *Neths.* **20 D5** 52 30N 4 45 E
Noordbeveland, *Neths.* **21 E3** 51 35N 3 50 E
Noordeloos, *Neths.* **20 E5** 51 55N 4 56 E
Noordhollandsch Kanaal, *Neths.* **20 C5** 52 55N 4 48 E
Noordhorn, *Neths.* **20 B8** 53 16N 6 24 E
Noordoostpolder, *Neths.* **20 C7** 52 45N 5 45 E
Noordwijk aan Zee, *Neths.* **20 D4** 52 14N 4 26 E
Noordwijk-Binnen, *Neths.* **20 D4** 52 14N 4 27 E
Noordwijkerhout, *Neths.* **20 D5** 52 16N 4 30 E
Noordzee Kanaal, *Neths.* **20 D5** 52 28N 4 35 E
Noorwolde, *Neths.* **20 C8** 52 54N 6 8 E
Nootka, *Canada* **130 D3** 49 38N 126 38W
Nootka I., *Canada* **130 D3** 49 32N 126 42W
Nóqui, *Angola* **103 D2** 5 55 S 13 30 E
Nora, *Eritrea* **95 D5** 16 6N 40 4 E
Nora Springs, *U.S.A.* **140 A4** 43 9N 93 1W
Noranda, *Canada* **128 C4** 48 20N 79 0W
Norborne, *U.S.A.* **140 E3** 39 18N 93 40W
Nórcia, *Italy* **39 F10** 42 48N 13 5 E
Norco, *U.S.A.* **145 M9** 33 56N 117 33W
Nord □, *France* **23 B10** 50 15N 3 30 E
Nord-Ostsee-Kanal →, *Germany* **26 A5** 54 12N 9 32 E
Nordagutu, *Norway* **14 E3** 59 25N 9 20 E
Nordaustlandet, *Svalbard* **6 B9** 79 14N 23 0 E
Nordborg, *Denmark* **15 J3** 55 5N 9 50 E
Nordby, *Århus, Denmark* **15 J4** 55 58N 10 32 E
Nordby, *Ribe, Denmark* **15 J2** 55 27N 8 24 E
Norddeich, *Germany* **26 B3** 53 36N 7 9 E
Nordegg, *Canada* **130 C5** 52 29N 116 5W
Norden, *Germany* **26 B3** 53 35N 7 12 E
Nordenham, *Germany* **26 B4** 53 30N 8 30 E
Norderhov, *Norway* **14 D4** 60 7N 10 17 E
Norderney, *Germany* **26 B3** 53 42N 7 9 E
Nordfjord, *Norway* **13 F11** 61 55N 5 30 E
Nordfriesische Inseln, *Germany* **26 A4** 54 40N 8 20 E
Nordhausen, *Germany* **26 D6** 51 30N 10 47 E
Nordhorn, *Germany* **26 C3** 52 26N 7 4 E
Norðoyar, *Færoe Is.* **12 E9** 62 17N 6 35W
Nordjyllands Amtskommune □, *Denmark* **15 H4** 57 0N 10 0 E
Nordkapp, *Norway* **12 A21** 71 10N 25 50 E
Nordkapp, *Svalbard* **6 A9** 80 31N 20 0 E
Nordkinn = Kinnarodden, *Norway* **10 A11** 71 8N 27 40 E
Nordkinn-halvøya, *Norway* **12 A22** 70 55N 27 40 E
Nördlingen, *Germany* **27 G6** 48 48N 10 30 E
Nordrhein-Westfalen □, *Germany* **26 D3** 51 45N 7 30 E
Nordstrand, *Germany* **26 A4** 54 30N 8 52 E
Nordvik, *Russia* **57 B12** 74 2N 111 32 E
Nore, *Norway* **14 D3** 60 10N 9 0 E
Norefjell, *Norway* **14 D3** 60 16N 9 29 E
Norembega, *Canada* **128 C3** 48 59N 80 43W
Noresund, *Norway* **14 D3** 60 11N 9 37 E
Norfolk, *Nebr., U.S.A.* **138 D6** 42 2N 97 25W
Norfolk, *Va., U.S.A.* **134 G7** 36 51N 76 17W
Norfolk □, *U.K.* **16 E9** 52 39N 0 54 E
Norfolk Broads, *U.K.* **16 E9** 52 30N 1 15 E
Norfolk I., *Pac. Oc.* **122 K8** 28 58 S 168 3 E
Norfork Res., *U.S.A.* **139 G8** 36 13N 92 15W
Norg, *Neths.* **20 B8** 53 4N 6 28 E
Norilsk, *Russia* **57 C9** 69 20N 88 6 E
Norley, *Australia* **115 D3** 27 45 S 143 48 E
Norma, Mt., *Australia* **114 C3** 20 55 S 140 42 E
Normal, *U.S.A.* **140 D8** 40 31N 88 59W
Norman, *U.S.A.* **139 H6** 35 13N 97 26W
Norman →, *Australia* **114 B3** 19 18 S 141 51 E
Norman Wells, *Canada* **126 B7** 65 17N 126 51W
Normanby, *N.Z.* **118 F3** 39 32 S 174 18 E
Normanby →, *Australia* **114 A3** 14 23 S 144 10 E
Normanby I., *Papua N. G.* **120 F6** 10 5 S 151 5 E
Normandie, *France* **22 D7** 48 45N 0 10 E
Normandie, Collines de, *France* **22 D6** 48 45N 0 45W
Normandin, *Canada* **128 C5** 48 49N 72 31W
Normandy = Normandie, *France* **22 D7** 48 45N 0 10 E
Normanhurst, Mt., *Australia* **113 E3** 25 4 S 122 30 E
Normanton, *Australia* **114 B3** 17 40 S 141 10 E
Normanville, *Australia* **116 C3** 35 27 S 138 18 E
Norquay, *Canada* **131 C8** 51 53N 102 5W
Norquinco, *Argentina* **160 B2** 41 51 S 70 55W
Norrbotten □, *Sweden* **12 C19** 66 30N 22 30 E
Nørre Åby, *Denmark* **15 J3** 55 27N 9 52 E
Nørre Nebel, *Denmark* **15 J2** 55 47N 8 17 E
Norre Vorupør, *Denmark* **15 H2** 56 58N 8 22 E
Nørresundby, *Denmark* **15 G3** 57 5N 9 52 E
Norris, *U.S.A.* **142 D8** 45 34N 111 41W
Norris City, *U.S.A.* **141 G8** 37 59N 88 20W
Norristown, *U.S.A.* **137 F9** 40 7N 75 21W
Norrköping, *Sweden* **15 F10** 58 37N 16 11 E
Norrland, *Sweden* **13 E16** 62 15N 15 45 E
Norrtälje, *Sweden* **14 E12** 59 46N 18 42 E
Norseman, *Australia* **113 F3** 32 8 S 121 43 E
Norsewood, *N.Z.* **118 G5** 40 3 S 176 13 E
Norsholm, *Sweden* **15 F9** 58 31N 15 59 E
Norsk, *Russia* **57 D14** 52 30N 130 5 E
Norsup, *Vanuatu* **121 F5** 16 3 S 167 24 E
Norte, Pta., *Argentina* **160 B4** 42 5 S 63 46W
Norte, Pta. del, *Canary Is.* **33 G2** 27 51N 17 57W
Norte de Santander □, *Colombia* **152 B3** 8 0N 73 0W
Nortelândia, *Brazil* **157 C6** 14 25 S 56 48W
North Adams, *U.S.A.* **137 D11** 42 42N 73 7W
North Atlantic Ocean, *Atl. Oc.* **8 F4** 30 0N 50 0W
North Ayrshire □, *U.K.* **18 F4** 55 45N 4 44W
North Baltimore, *U.S.A.* **141 C13** 41 11N 83 41W
North Battleford, *Canada* **131 C7** 52 50N 108 17W
North Bay, *Canada* **128 C4** 46 20N 79 30W
North Belcher Is., *Canada* **128 A4** 56 50N 79 50W
North Bend, *Canada* **130 D4** 49 50N 121 27W
North Bend, *Oreg., U.S.A.* **142 E1** 43 24N 124 14W
North Bend, *Pa., U.S.A.* **136 E7** 41 20N 77 42W
North Bend, *Wash., U.S.A.* **144 C5** 47 30N 121 47W
North Berwick, *U.K.* **18 E6** 56 4N 2 42W
North Berwick, *U.S.A.* **137 C14** 43 18N 70 44W
North C., *Canada* **129 C7** 47 2N 60 20W
North C., *N.Z.* **118 A2** 34 23 S 173 4 E
North C., *Papua N. G.* **120 B6** 2 32 S 150 50 E
North Canadian →, *U.S.A.* **139 H7** 35 16N 95 31W
North Cape = Nordkapp, *Norway* **12 A21** 71 10N 25 50 E
North Cape = Nordkapp, *Svalbard* **6 A9** 80 31N 20 0 E
North Caribou L., *Canada* **128 B1** 52 50N 90 40W
North Carolina □, *U.S.A.* **135 H5** 35 30N 80 0W
North Channel, *Canada* **128 C3** 46 0N 83 0W
North Channel, *U.K.* **18 G3** 55 13N 5 52W
North Charleston, *U.S.A.* **135 J6** 32 53N 79 58W
North Chicago, *U.S.A.* **141 B9** 42 19N 87 51W
North College Hill, *U.S.A.* **141 E12** 39 13N 84 33W
North Cotabato □, *Phil.* **71 H5** 7 10N 125 0 E
North Dakota □, *U.S.A.* **138 B5** 47 30N 100 15W
North Dandalup, *Australia* **113 F2** 32 30 S 115 57 E
North Down □, *U.K.* **19 B6** 54 40N 5 45W
North Downs, *U.K.* **17 F8** 51 19N 0 21 E
North East, *U.S.A.* **136 D5** 42 13N 79 50W
North East Frontier Agency = Arunachal Pradesh □, *India* **78 A5** 28 0N 95 0 E
North East Lincolnshire □, *U.K.* **16 D7** 53 34N 0 2W
North East Providence Chan., *W. Indies* **148 A4** 26 0N 76 0W
North Eastern □, *Kenya* **106 B5** 1 30N 40 0 E
North English, *U.S.A.* **140 C4** 41 31N 92 5W
North Esk →, *U.K.* **18 E6** 56 46N 2 24W
North European Plain, *Europe* **10 E10** 55 0N 25 0 E
North Fabius →, *U.S.A.* **140 E5** 39 54N 91 30W
North Foreland, *U.K.* **17 F9** 51 22N 1 28 E
North Fork, *U.S.A.* **144 H7** 37 14N 119 21W
North Fork, Salt →, *U.S.A.* **140 E5** 39 26N 91 53W
North Fork American →, *U.S.A.* **144 G5** 38 57N 120 59W
North Fork Feather →, *U.S.A.* **144 F5** 38 33N 121 30W
North Frisian Is. = Nordfriesische Inseln, *Germany* **26 A4** 54 40N 8 20 E
North Henik L., *Canada* **131 A9** 61 45N 97 40W
North Highlands, *U.S.A.* **144 G5** 38 40N 121 23W
North Horr, *Kenya* **106 B4** 3 20N 37 8 E
North I., *Kenya* **106 B4** 4 5N 36 5 E
North I., *N.Z.* **118 E4** 38 0 S 175 0 E
North Judson, *U.S.A.* **141 C10** 41 13N 86 46W
North Kingsville, *U.S.A.* **136 E4** 41 54N 80 42W
North Knife →, *Canada* **131 B10** 58 53N 94 45W
North Koel →, *India* **81 G10** 24 45N 83 50 E
North Korea ■, *Asia* **67 E14** 40 0N 127 0 E
North Lakhimpur, *India* **78 B5** 27 14N 94 7 E
North Lanarkshire □, *U.K.* **18 F5** 55 52N 3 56W
North Las Vegas, *U.S.A.* **145 J11** 36 12N 115 7W
North Liberty, *U.S.A.* **141 C10** 41 32N 86 26W
North Lincolnshire □, *U.K.* **16 D7** 53 36N 0 30W
North Little Rock, *U.S.A.* **139 H8** 34 45N 92 16W
North Loup →, *U.S.A.* **138 E5** 41 17N 98 24W
North Magnetic Pole, *Canada* **6 B2** 77 58N 102 8W
North Manchester, *U.S.A.* **141 D11** 41 0N 85 46W
North Minch, *U.K.* **18 C3** 58 5N 5 55W
North Nahanni →, *Canada* **130 A4** 62 15N 123 20W
North Olmsted, *U.S.A.* **136 E3** 41 25N 81 56W
North Ossetia □, *Russia* **53 J7** 43 30N 44 30 E
North Pagai, I. = Pagai Utara, *Indonesia* **74 C2** 2 35 S 100 0 E
North Palisade, *U.S.A.* **144 H8** 37 6N 118 31W
North Platte, *U.S.A.* **138 E4** 41 8N 100 46W
North Platte →, *U.S.A.* **138 E4** 41 7N 100 42W
North Pole, *Arctic* **6 A** 90 0N 0 0 E
North Portal, *Canada* **131 D8** 49 0N 102 33W
North Powder, *U.S.A.* **142 D5** 45 2N 117 55W
North Pt., *Canada* **129 C7** 47 5N 64 0W
North Pt., *Vanuatu* **121 D6** 14 56 S 168 6 E
North Rhine Westphalia □ = Nordrhein-Westfalen □, *Germany* **26 D3** 51 45N 7 30 E
North Ronaldsay, *U.K.* **18 B6** 59 22N 2 26W
North Saskatchewan →, *Canada* **131 C7** 53 15N 105 5W
North Sea, *Europe* **10 D6** 56 0N 4 0 E
North Somerset □, *U.K.* **17 F5** 51 24N 2 45W
North Sporades = Voríai Sporádhes, *Greece* **45 E5** 39 15N 23 30 E
North Sydney, *Canada* **129 C7** 46 12N 60 15W
North Taranaki Bight, *N.Z.* **118 E3** 38 50 S 174 15 E
North Thompson →, *Canada* **130 C4** 50 40N 120 20W
North Tonawanda, *U.S.A.* **136 C6** 43 2N 78 53W
North Troy, *U.S.A.* **137 B12** 45 0N 72 24W
North Truchas Pk., *U.S.A.* **143 J11** 36 0N 105 30W
North Twin I., *Canada* **128 B3** 53 20N 80 0W
North Tyne →, *U.K.* **16 C5** 55 0N 2 8W
North Uist, *U.K.* **18 D1** 57 40N 7 15W
North Vancouver, *Canada* **130 D4** 49 25N 123 3W
North Vernon, *U.S.A.* **141 E11** 39 0N 85 38W
North Wabasca L., *Canada* **130 B6** 56 0N 113 55W
North Walsham, *U.K.* **16 E9** 52 50N 1 22 E
North Webster, *U.S.A.* **141 C11** 41 25N 85 48W
North-West □, *S. Africa* **104 D4** 27 0 S 25 0 E
North West C., *Australia* **112 D1** 21 45 S 114 9 E
North West Christmas I. Ridge, *Pac. Oc.* **123 G11** 6 30N 165 0W
North West Frontier □, *Pakistan* **79 B3** 34 0N 72 0 E

242 North West Highlands

North West Highlands, U.K. 18 D3 57 33N 4 58W
North West Providence Channel, W. Indies 148 A4 26 0N 78 0W
North West River, Canada 129 B7 53 30N 60 10W
North West Territories □, Canada 126 B9 67 0N 110 0W
North Western □, Zambia 107 E2 13 30 S 25 30 E
North York Moors, U.K. 16 C7 54 23N 0 53W
North Yorkshire □, U.K. 16 C6 54 15N 1 25W
Northallerton, U.K. 16 C6 54 20N 1 26W
Northam, S. Africa 104 C4 24 56 S 27 18 E
Northampton, Australia 113 E1 28 27 S 114 33 E
Northampton, U.K. 17 E7 52 15N 0 53W
Northampton, Mass., U.S.A. 137 D12 42 19N 72 38W
Northampton, Pa., U.S.A. 137 F9 40 41N 75 30W
Northampton Downs, Australia 114 C4 24 35 S 145 48 E
Northamptonshire □, U.K. 17 E7 52 16N 0 55W
Northbridge, U.S.A. 137 D13 42 9N 71 39W
Northcliffe, Australia 113 F2 34 39 S 116 7 E
Northeim, Germany 26 D6 51 42N 10 0 E
Northern □, Malawi 107 E3 11 0 S 34 0 E
Northern □, Uganda 106 B3 3 5N 32 30 E
Northern □, Zambia 107 E3 10 30 S 31 0 E
Northern Cape □, S. Africa 104 D3 30 0 S 20 0 E
Northern Circars, India 82 F6 17 30N 82 30 E
Northern Indian L., Canada 131 B9 57 20N 97 20W
Northern Ireland □, U.K. 19 B5 54 45N 7 0W
Northern Light, L., Canada 128 C1 48 15N 90 39W
Northern Marianas ■, Pac. Oc. 122 F6 17 0N 145 0 E
Northern Province □, S. Leone 100 D2 9 15N 11 30W
Northern Samar □, Phil. 70 E5 12 30N 124 40 E
Northern Territory □, Australia 112 D5 20 0 S 133 0 E
Northern Transvaal □, S. Africa 105 C4 24 0 S 29 0 E
Northfield, U.S.A. 138 C8 44 27N 93 9W
Northland □, N.Z. 118 B2 35 30 S 173 30 E
Northome, U.S.A. 138 B7 47 52N 94 17W
Northport, Ala., U.S.A. 135 J2 33 14N 87 35W
Northport, Mich., U.S.A. 134 C3 45 8N 85 37W
Northport, Wash., U.S.A. 142 B5 48 55N 117 48W
Northumberland □, U.K. 16 B5 55 12N 2 0W
Northumberland, C., Australia 116 E4 38 5 S 140 40 E
Northumberland Is., Australia 114 C4 21 30 S 149 50 E
Northumberland Str., Canada 129 C7 46 20N 64 0W
Northwich, U.K. 16 D5 53 15N 2 31W
Northwood, Iowa, U.S.A. 138 D8 43 27N 93 13W
Northwood, N. Dak., U.S.A. 138 B6 47 44N 97 34W
Norton, U.S.A. 138 F5 39 50N 99 53W
Norton, Zimbabwe 107 F3 17 52 S 30 40 E
Norton Sd., U.S.A. 126 B3 63 50N 164 0W
Norton Shores, U.S.A. 141 A10 43 8N 86 15W
Nortorf, Germany 26 A5 54 10N 9 50 E
Norwalk, Calif., U.S.A. 145 M8 33 54N 118 5W
Norwalk, Conn., U.S.A. 137 E11 41 7N 73 22W
Norwalk, Ohio, U.S.A. 136 E2 41 15N 82 37W
Norway, U.S.A. 134 C2 45 47N 87 55W
Norway ■, Europe 12 E14 63 0N 11 0 E
Norway House, Canada 131 C9 53 59N 97 50W
Norwegian Sea, Atl. Oc. 8 B9 66 0N 1 0 E
Norwich, Canada 136 D4 42 59N 80 36W
Norwich, U.K. 16 E9 52 38N 1 18 E
Norwich, Conn., U.S.A. 137 E12 41 31N 72 5W
Norwich, N.Y., U.S.A. 137 D9 42 32N 75 32W
Norwood, Canada 136 B7 44 23N 77 59W
Norwood, U.S.A. 141 E12 39 10N 84 27W
Noshiro, Japan 60 D10 40 12N 140 0 E
Nosivka, Ukraine 51 G6 50 50N 31 37 E
Nosok, Russia 56 B9 70 10N 82 20 E
Nosovka = Nosivka, Ukraine 51 G6 50 50N 31 37 E
Noss Hd., U.K. 18 C5 58 28N 3 3W
Nossa Senhora da Glória, Brazil 154 D4 10 14 S 37 25W
Nossa Senhora das Dores, Brazil 154 D4 10 29 S 37 13W
Nossa Senhora do Livramento, Brazil 157 D6 15 48 S 56 22W
Nossebro, Sweden 15 F6 58 12N 12 43 E
Nossob →, S. Africa 104 D3 26 55 S 20 45 E
Nosy Boraha, Madag. 105 B8 16 50 S 49 55 E
Nosy Varika, Madag. 105 C8 20 35 S 48 32 E
Noteć →, Poland 47 C2 52 44N 15 26 E
Notigi Dam, Canada 131 B9 56 40N 99 10W
Notikewin →, Canada 130 B5 57 2N 117 38W
Notios Evvoïkos Kólpos, Greece 45 F5 38 20N 24 0 E
Noto, Italy 41 F8 36 53N 15 4 E
Noto, G. di, Italy 41 F8 36 50N 15 12 E
Notodden, Norway 14 E3 59 35N 9 17 E
Notre-Dame, Canada 129 C7 46 18N 64 46W
Notre Dame B., Canada 129 C8 49 45N 55 30W
Notre Dame de Koartac = Quaqtaq, Canada 127 B13 60 55N 69 40W
Notre Dame d'Ivugivic = Ivujivik, Canada 127 B12 62 24N 77 55W
Notsé, Togo 101 D5 7 0N 1 17 E
Nottaway →, Canada 128 B4 51 22N 78 55W
Nøtterøy, Norway 14 E4 59 14N 10 24 E
Nottingham, U.K. 16 E6 52 58N 1 10W
Nottinghamshire □, U.K. 16 D7 53 10N 1 3W
Nottoway →, U.S.A. 134 G7 36 33N 76 55W
Notwane →, Botswana 104 C4 23 35 S 26 58 E
Nouâdhibou, Mauritania 98 D1 20 54N 17 0W
Nouâdhibou, Ras, Mauritania 98 D1 20 50N 17 0W
Nouakchott, Mauritania 100 B1 18 9N 15 58W
Nouméa, N. Cal. 122 K8 22 17 S 166 30 E
Noupoort, S. Africa 104 E3 31 10 S 24 57 E
Nouveau Comptoir = Wemindji, Canada 128 B4 53 0N 78 49W
Nouvelle-Calédonie = New Caledonia ■, Pac. Oc. 121 U19 21 0 S 165 0 E
Nouzonville, France 23 C11 49 48N 4 44 E
Nová Baňa, Slovak Rep. 31 C11 48 28N 18 39 E
Nová Bystřice, Czech. 30 B8 49 2N 15 8 E
Nova Casa Nova, Brazil 154 C3 9 25 S 41 5W
Nova Cruz, Brazil 154 C4 6 28 S 35 25W
Nova Era, Brazil 155 E3 19 45 S 43 3W
Nova Esperança, Brazil 159 A5 23 8 S 52 24W
Nova Friburgo, Brazil 155 F3 22 16 S 42 30W
Nova Gaia = Cambundi-Catembo, Angola 103 E3 10 10 S 17 35 E
Nova Gradiška, Croatia 42 B2 45 17N 17 28 E
Nova Granada, Brazil 155 F2 20 30 S 49 20W
Nova Iguaçu, Brazil 155 F3 22 45 S 43 28W
Nova Iorque, Brazil 154 C3 7 0 S 44 5W
Nova Kakhovka, Ukraine 51 J7 46 42N 33 27 E
Nova Lamego, Guinea-Biss. 100 C2 12 19N 14 11W
Nova Lima, Brazil 159 A7 19 59 S 43 51W
Nova Lisboa = Huambo, Angola 103 E3 12 42 S 15 54 E
Nova Lusitânia, Mozam. 107 F3 19 50 S 34 34 E
Nova Mambone, Mozam. 105 C6 21 0 S 35 3 E
Nova Odesa, Ukraine 51 J6 47 19N 31 47 E
Nova Paka, Czech. 30 A8 50 29N 15 30 E
Nova Ponte, Brazil 155 E2 19 8 S 47 41W
Nova Scotia □, Canada 129 C7 45 10N 63 0W
Nova Sofala, Mozam. 105 C5 20 7 S 34 42 E
Nova Varoš, Serbia, Yug. 42 D4 43 29N 19 48 E
Nova Venécia, Brazil 155 E3 18 45 S 40 24W
Nova Vida, Brazil 157 C5 10 11 S 62 47W
Nova Zagora, Bulgaria 43 E10 42 32N 25 59 E
Novaci, Macedonia 42 F6 41 5N 21 29 E
Novaci, Romania 46 D4 45 10N 23 42 E
Novaleksandrovskaya = Novoaleksandrovsk, Russia 53 H5 45 29N 41 17 E
Novannenskiy = Novoannenskiy, Russia 52 E6 50 32N 42 39 E
Novara, Italy 38 C5 45 28N 8 38 E
Novato, U.S.A. 144 G4 38 6N 122 35W
Novaya Kakhovka = Nova Kakhovka, Ukraine 51 J7 46 42N 33 27 E
Novaya Kazanka, Kazakstan 53 F9 48 56N 49 36 E
Novaya Ladoga, Russia 50 B7 60 7N 32 16 E
Novaya Lyalya, Russia 54 B8 59 4N 60 45 E
Novaya Sibir, Ostrov, Russia 57 B16 75 10N 150 0 E
Novaya Zemlya, Russia 56 B6 75 0N 56 0 E
Nové Město, Slovak Rep. 31 C10 48 45N 17 50 E
Nové Zámky, Slovak Rep. 31 C11 48 2N 18 8 E
Novelda, Spain 35 G4 38 24N 0 45W
Novellara, Italy 38 D7 44 51N 10 44 E
Novelty, U.S.A. 140 D4 40 1N 92 12W
Noventa Vicentina, Italy 39 C8 45 17N 11 32 E
Novgorod, Russia 50 C6 58 30N 31 25 E
Novgorod-Severskiy = Novhorod-Siverskyy, Ukraine 51 G7 52 2N 33 10 E
Novhorod-Siverskyy, Ukraine 51 G7 52 2N 33 10 E
Novi Bečej, Serbia, Yug. 42 B5 45 36N 20 10 E
Novi Grad, Croatia 39 C10 45 19N 13 33 E
Novi Kneževa, Serbia, Yug. 42 A5 46 4N 20 8 E
Novi Krichim, Bulgaria 43 E9 42 8N 24 31 E
Novi Lígure, Italy 38 D5 44 46N 8 47 E
Novi Pazar, Bulgaria 43 D12 43 25N 27 15 E
Novi Pazar, Serbia, Yug. 42 D5 43 12N 20 28 E
Novi Sad, Serbia, Yug. 42 B4 45 18N 19 52 E
Novi Vinodolski, Croatia 39 C11 45 10N 14 48 E
Novigrad, Croatia 39 D12 44 10N 15 32 E
Noville, Belgium 21 H7 50 4N 5 46 E
Novinger, U.S.A. 140 D4 40 14N 92 43W
Novo Acôrdo, Brazil 154 D2 10 10 S 46 48W
Novo Aripuanã, Brazil 153 E5 5 8 S 60 22W
Nôvo Cruzeiro, Brazil 155 E3 17 29 S 41 53W
Nôvo Hamburgo, Brazil 159 B5 29 37 S 51 7W
Novo Horizonte, Brazil 155 F2 21 25 S 49 10W
Novo Mesto, Slovenia 39 C12 45 47N 15 12 E
Novo Remanso, Brazil 154 C3 9 41 S 42 4W
Novo-Sergiyevskiy, Russia 54 E4 52 5N 53 38 E
Novoaleksandrovsk, Russia 53 H5 45 29N 41 17 E
Novoalekseyevka, Kazakstan 54 F5 50 8N 55 39 E
Novoannenskiy, Russia 52 E6 50 32N 42 39 E
Novoataysk, Russia 56 D9 53 30N 84 0 E
Novoazovsk, Ukraine 51 J10 47 15N 38 4 E
Novocheboksarsk, Russia 52 B8 56 5N 47 27 E
Novocherkassk, Russia 53 G5 47 27N 40 15 E
Novodevichye, Russia 52 D9 53 37N 48 50 E
Novogrudok = Navahrudak, Belarus 50 F3 53 40N 25 50 E
Novohrad-Volynskyy, Ukraine 51 G4 50 34N 27 35 E
Novokachalinsk, Russia 60 B6 45 5N 132 0 E
Novokazalinsk = Zhangaqazaly, Kazakstan 56 E7 45 48N 62 6 E
Novokhopersk, Russia 52 E5 51 5N 41 39 E
Novokuybyshevsk, Russia 52 D9 53 7N 49 58 E
Novokuznetsk, Russia 56 D9 53 45N 87 10 E
Novomirgorod, Ukraine 51 H6 48 45N 31 33 E
Novomoskovsk, Russia 52 C4 54 5N 38 15 E
Novomoskovsk, Ukraine 51 H8 48 33N 35 17 E
Novoorsk, Russia 54 F7 51 21N 59 2 E
Novopolotsk = Navapolatsk, Belarus 50 E5 55 32N 28 37 E
Novorossiysk, Russia 53 H3 44 43N 37 46 E
Novorossiyskoye, Kazakstan 54 F7 50 13N 58 0 E
Novorybnoye, Russia 57 B11 72 50N 105 50 E
Novorzhev, Russia 50 D5 57 3N 29 25 E
Novoselytsya, Ukraine 51 H4 48 14N 26 15 E
Novoshakhtinsk, Russia 53 G4 47 46N 39 58 E
Novosibirsk, Russia 56 D9 55 0N 83 5 E
Novosibirskiye Ostrova, Russia 57 B15 75 0N 142 0 E
Novosil, Russia 52 D3 52 59N 37 2 E
Novosineglazovskiy, Russia 54 D8 55 2N 61 21 E
Novosokolniki, Russia 50 D6 56 20N 30 2 E
Novotitarovskaya, Russia 53 H4 45 17N 39 2 E
Novotroitsk, Russia 54 F7 51 10N 58 15 E
Novotroitskoye, Kazakstan 55 B6 43 42N 73 46 E
Novoukrayinka, Ukraine 51 H6 48 25N 31 30 E
Novouljanovsk, Russia 52 C9 54 8N 48 24 E
Novouzensk, Russia 52 E9 50 32N 48 17 E
Novovolynsk, Ukraine 51 G3 50 45N 24 4 E
Novovoronezhskiy, Russia 52 E4 51 19N 39 13 E
Novovyatsk, Russia 54 B2 58 24N 49 45 E
Novozybkov, Russia 51 F6 52 30N 32 0 E
Novska, Croatia 42 B2 45 19N 17 0 E
Novy Bug = Novyy Buh, Ukraine 51 J7 47 34N 32 29 E
Nový Bydzov, Czech. 30 A8 50 14N 15 29 E
Novy Dwór Mazowiecki, Poland 47 C7 52 26N 20 44 E
Nový Jičín, Czech. 31 B11 49 30N 18 2 E
Novyy Afon, Georgia 53 J5 43 7N 40 50 E
Novyy Buh, Ukraine 51 J7 47 34N 32 29 E
Novyy Oskol, Russia 52 E3 50 44N 37 55 E
Novyy Port, Russia 56 C8 67 40N 72 30 E
Now Shahr, Iran 85 B6 36 40N 51 30 E
Nowa Deba, Poland 47 E8 50 26N 21 41 E
Nowa Huta, Poland 31 A13 50 5N 20 30 E
Nowa Nowa, Australia 117 D8 37 44 S 148 3 E
Nowa Ruda, Poland 47 E3 50 35N 16 30 E
Nowa Skalmierzyce, Poland 47 D5 51 43N 18 0 E
Nowa Sól, Poland 47 D2 51 48N 15 44 E
Nowbarān, Iran 85 C6 35 8N 49 42 E
Nowe, Poland 47 B5 53 41N 18 44 E
Nowe Miasteczko, Poland 47 D2 51 42N 15 42 E
Nowe Miasto, Poland 47 D7 51 38N 20 34 E
Nowe Miasto Lubawskie, Poland 47 B6 53 27N 19 33 E
Nowe Warpno, Poland 47 B1 53 42N 14 18 E
Nowendoc, Australia 117 A9 31 32 S 151 44 E
Nowghāb, Iran 85 C8 33 53N 59 4 E
Nowgong, India 78 B4 26 20N 92 50 E
Nowingi, Australia 116 C5 34 33 S 142 15 E
Nowogard, Poland 47 B2 53 41N 15 10 E
Nowogród, Poland 47 B8 53 14N 21 53 E
Nowra, Australia 117 C9 34 53 S 150 35 E
Nowshera, Pakistan 79 B3 34 0N 72 0 E
Nowy Dwór, Białystok, Poland 47 B10 53 40N 23 30 E
Nowy Dwór, Gdańsk, Poland 47 A6 54 13N 19 7 E
Nowy Korczyn, Poland 47 E7 50 19N 20 48 E
Nowy Sącz, Poland 31 B13 49 40N 20 41 E
Nowy Sącz □, Poland 31 B13 49 30N 20 30 E
Nowy Staw, Poland 47 A6 54 13N 19 2 E
Nowy Tomyśl, Poland 47 C3 52 19N 16 10 E
Noxen, U.S.A. 137 E8 41 25N 76 4W
Noxon, U.S.A. 142 C6 48 0N 115 43W
Noya, Spain 36 C2 42 48N 8 53W
Noyant, France 22 E7 47 30N 0 6 E
Noyers, France 23 E10 47 40N 4 0 E
Noyes I., U.S.A. 130 B2 55 30N 133 40W
Noyon, France 23 C9 49 34N 2 59 E
Noyon, Mongolia 66 C2 43 2N 102 4 E
Nozay, France 22 E5 47 34N 1 38W
Nsa, O. en →, Algeria 99 B6 32 28N 5 24 E
Nsa, Plateau de, Congo 102 C3 2 26 S 15 20 E
Nsah, Congo 102 C3 2 22 S 15 19 E
Nsanje, Malawi 107 F4 16 55 S 35 12 E
Nsawam, Ghana 101 D4 5 50N 0 24W
Nsomba, Zambia 107 E2 10 45 S 29 51 E
Nsopzup, Burma 78 C6 25 51N 97 30 E
Nsukka, Nigeria 101 D6 6 51N 7 29 E
Ntoum, Gabon 102 B1 0 22N 9 47 E
Nu Jiang →, China 68 C1 29 58N 97 25 E
Nu Shan, China 68 D2 26 0N 99 20 E
Nuba Mts. = Nubah, Jibalan, Sudan 95 E3 12 0N 31 0 E
Nubah, Jibalan, Sudan 95 E3 12 0N 31 0 E
Nubia, Africa 92 D7 21 0N 32 0 E
Nubian Desert = Nûbîya, Es Sahrâ En, Sudan 94 C3 21 30N 33 30 E
Nûbîya, Es Sahrâ En, Sudan 94 C3 21 30N 33 30 E
Nuble □, Chile 158 D1 37 0 S 72 0W
Nuboai, Indonesia 73 B5 2 10 S 136 30 E
Nubra →, India 81 B7 34 35N 77 35 E
Nueces →, U.S.A. 139 M6 27 51N 97 30W
Nueltin L., Canada 131 A9 60 30N 99 30W
Nuenen, Neths. 21 F7 51 29N 5 33 E
Nueva, I., Chile 160 E3 55 13 S 66 30W
Nueva Antioquia, Colombia 152 B4 6 5N 69 26W
Nueva Asunción □, Paraguay 158 A3 21 0 S 61 0W
Nueva Ecija □, Phil. 70 D3 15 35N 121 0 E
Nueva Esparta □, Venezuela 153 A5 11 0N 64 0W
Nueva Gerona, Cuba 148 B3 21 53N 82 49W
Nueva Imperial, Chile 160 A2 38 45 S 72 58W
Nueva Palmira, Uruguay 158 C4 33 52 S 58 20W
Nueva Rosita, Mexico 146 B4 28 0N 101 11W
Nueva San Salvador, El Salv. 148 D2 13 40N 89 18W
Nueva Vizcaya □, Phil. 70 C3 16 20N 121 20 E
Nuéve de Julio, Argentina 158 D3 35 30 S 61 0W
Nuevitas, Cuba 148 B4 21 30N 77 20W
Nuevo, G., Argentina 160 B4 43 0 S 64 30W
Nuevo Guerrero, Mexico 147 B5 26 34N 99 15W
Nuevo Laredo, Mexico 147 B5 27 30N 99 30W
Nuevo León □, Mexico 146 C4 25 0N 100 0W
Nuevo Mundo, Cerro, Bolivia 156 E4 21 55 S 66 53W
Nuevo Rocafuerte, Ecuador 152 D2 0 55 S 75 27W
Nugget Pt., N.Z. 119 G4 46 27 S 169 50 E
Nugrus, Gebel, Egypt 94 C3 24 47N 34 35 E
Nuhaka, N.Z. 118 F6 39 3 S 177 45 E
Nuits-St.-Georges, France 23 E11 47 10N 4 56 E
Nukey Bluff, Australia 115 E2 32 26 S 135 29 E
Nukheila, Sudan 94 D2 19 1N 26 21 E
Nukhuyb, Iraq 89 F10 32 4N 42 3 E
Nuku'alofa, Tonga 121 Q14 21 10 S 174 0W
Nukus, Uzbekistan 56 E6 42 27N 59 41 E
Nuland, Neths. 20 E6 51 44N 5 26 E
Nulato, U.S.A. 126 B4 64 43N 158 6W
Nules, Spain 34 F4 39 51N 0 9W
Nullagine →, Australia 112 D3 21 20 S 120 20 E
Nullarbor, Australia 113 F5 31 28 S 130 55 E
Nullarbor Plain, Australia 113 F4 31 10 S 129 0 E
Numalla, L., Australia 115 D3 28 43 S 144 20 E
Numan, Nigeria 101 D7 9 29N 12 3 E
Numansdorp, Neths. 20 E4 51 43N 4 26 E
Numata, Japan 63 A11 36 45N 139 4 E
Numatinna →, Sudan 95 F2 7 38N 27 20 E
Numazu, Japan 63 B10 35 7N 138 51 E
Numbulwar, Australia 114 A2 14 15 S 135 45 E
Numfoor, Indonesia 73 B4 1 0 S 134 50 E
Numurkah, Australia 117 D6 36 5 S 145 26 E
Nunaksaluk I., Canada 129 A7 55 49N 60 20W
Nuneaton, U.K. 17 E6 52 32N 1 27W
Nungo, Mozam. 107 E4 13 23 S 37 43 E
Nungwe, Tanzania 106 C3 2 48 S 32 2 E
Nunivak I., U.S.A. 126 B3 60 10N 166 30W
Nunkun, India 81 C7 33 57N 76 2 E
Nunspeet, Neths. 20 D7 52 21N 5 45 E
Núoro, Italy 40 B2 40 20N 9 20 E
Nuqayy, Jabal, Libya 96 D3 23 11N 19 30 E
Nuqūb, Yemen 86 D4 14 59N 45 48 E
Nuquí, Colombia 152 B2 5 42N 77 17W
Nūrābād, Iran 85 E8 27 47N 57 12 E
Nurata, Uzbekistan 55 C2 40 33N 65 41 E
Nuratau, Khrebet, Uzbekistan 55 C3 40 40N 66 30 E
Nure →, Italy 38 C6 45 3N 9 49 E
Nuremberg = Nürnberg, Germany 27 F7 49 27N 11 3 E
Nūrestān, Afghan. 79 B3 35 30N 70 45 E
Nuri, Mexico 146 B3 28 2N 109 22W
Nurina, Australia 113 F4 30 56 S 126 33 E
Nuriootpa, Australia 116 C3 34 27 S 139 0 E
Nurlat, Russia 52 C10 54 29N 50 45 E
Nurmes, Finland 12 E23 63 33N 29 10 E
Nürnberg, Germany 27 F7 49 27N 11 3 E
Nurran, L. = Terewah, L., Australia 115 D4 29 52 S 147 35 E
Nurrari Lakes, Australia 113 E5 29 1 S 130 5 E
Nurri, Italy 40 C2 39 43N 9 14 E
Nurzec →, Poland 47 C9 52 37N 22 25 E
Nusa Barung, Indonesia 75 D4 8 10 S 113 30 E
Nusa Kambangan, Indonesia 75 D3 7 40 S 108 10 E
Nusa Tenggara Barat □, Indonesia 75 D5 8 50 S 117 30 E
Nusa Tenggara Timur □, Indonesia 72 C2 9 30 S 122 0 E
Nusaybin, Turkey 89 D9 37 3N 41 10 E
Nushki, Pakistan 79 C2 29 35N 66 0 E
Nutak, Canada 127 C13 57 28N 61 59W
Nuth, Neths. 21 G7 50 55N 5 53 E
Nutwood Downs, Australia 114 B1 15 49 S 134 10 E
Nuuk = Godthåb, Greenland 127 B14 64 10N 51 35W
Nuwakot, Nepal 81 E10 28 10N 83 55 E
Nuwara Eliya, Sri Lanka 83 L5 6 58N 80 48 E
Nuweiba', Egypt 94 B3 28 59N 34 39 E
Nuweveldberge, S. Africa 104 E3 32 10 S 21 45 E
Nuyts, C., Australia 113 F5 32 2 S 132 21 E
Nuyts Arch., Australia 115 E1 32 35 S 133 20 E
Nuzvid, India 82 F5 16 47N 80 53 E
Nxau-Nxau, Botswana 104 B3 18 57 S 21 4 E
Nyaake, Liberia 100 E3 4 52N 7 37W
Nyack, U.S.A. 137 E11 41 5N 73 55W
Nyadal, Sweden 14 B11 62 48N 17 59 E
Nyah West, Australia 116 C5 35 16 S 143 21 E
Nyahanga, Tanzania 106 C3 2 20 S 33 37 E
Nyahua, Tanzania 106 D3 5 25 S 33 23 E
Nyahururu, Kenya 106 B4 0 2N 36 27 E
Nyainqentanglha Shan, China 64 D3 30 0N 90 0 E
Nyakanazi, Tanzania 106 C3 3 2 S 31 10 E
Nyakrom, Ghana 101 D4 5 40N 0 50W
Nyâlâ, Sudan 95 E1 12 2N 24 58 E
Nyamandhlovu, Zimbabwe 107 F2 19 55 S 28 16 E
Nyambiti, Tanzania 106 C3 2 48 S 33 27 E
Nyamwaga, Tanzania 106 C3 1 27 S 34 33 E
Nyandekwa, Tanzania 106 C3 3 57 S 32 32 E
Nyanding →, Sudan 95 F3 8 40N 32 41 E
Nyandoma, Russia 50 B11 61 40N 40 12 E
Nyanga →, Gabon 102 C2 2 58 S 10 15 E
Nyangana, Namibia 104 B3 18 0 S 20 40 E
Nyanguge, Tanzania 106 C3 2 30 S 33 12 E
Nyankpala, Ghana 101 D4 9 21N 0 58W
Nyanza, Burundi 106 C2 4 21 S 29 36 E
Nyanza, Rwanda 106 C2 2 20 S 29 42 E
Nyanza □, Kenya 106 C3 0 10 S 34 15 E
Nyarling →, Canada 130 A6 60 41N 113 23W
Nyasa, L. = Malawi, L., Africa 107 E3 12 30 S 34 30 E
Nyasvizh, Belarus 51 F4 53 14N 26 38 E
Nyaunglebin, Burma 78 G6 17 52N 96 42 E
Nyazepetrovsk, Russia 54 C7 56 3N 59 36 E
Nyazura, Zimbabwe 107 F3 18 40 S 32 16 E
Nyazwidzi →, Zimbabwe 107 F3 20 0 S 31 17 E
Nyborg, Denmark 15 J4 55 18N 10 47 E
Nybro, Sweden 13 H16 56 44N 15 55 E
Nyda, Russia 56 C8 66 40N 72 58 E
Nyeri, Kenya 106 C4 0 23 S 36 56 E
Nyerol, Sudan 95 F3 8 41N 32 1 E
Nyhem, Sweden 14 B9 62 54N 15 37 E
Nyiel, Sudan 95 F3 6 9N 31 13 E
Nyinahin, Ghana 100 D4 6 43N 2 3W
Nyírbátor, Hungary 31 D15 47 49N 22 9 E
Nyíregyháza, Hungary 31 D14 47 58N 21 47 E
Nykøbing, Storstrøm, Denmark 15 K5 54 56N 11 52 E
Nykøbing, Vestsjælland, Denmark 15 J5 55 55N 11 40 E
Nykøbing, Viborg, Denmark 15 H2 56 48N 8 51 E
Nyköping, Sweden 15 F11 58 45N 17 0 E
Nykvarn, Sweden 14 E11 59 11N 17 25 E
Nyland, Sweden 14 A11 63 1N 17 45 E
Nylstroom, S. Africa 105 C4 24 42 S 28 22 E
Nymagee, Australia 117 B7 32 7 S 146 20 E
Nymburk, Czech. 30 A8 50 10N 15 1 E
Nynäshamn, Sweden 14 F11 58 54N 17 57 E
Nyngan, Australia 115 E4 31 30 S 147 8 E
Nyoman = Neman →, Lithuania 13 J19 55 25N 21 10 E
Nyon, Switz. 28 D2 46 23N 6 14 E
Nyong →, Cameroon 101 E6 3 17N 9 54 E
Nyons, France 25 D9 44 22N 5 10 E
Nyora, Australia 117 E6 38 20 S 145 41 E
Nyord, Denmark 15 J6 55 4N 12 13 E
Nyou, Burkina Faso 101 C4 12 42N 2 1W
Nysa, Poland 47 E4 50 30N 17 22 E
Nysa →, Europe 26 C10 52 4N 14 46 E
Nyssa, U.S.A. 142 E5 43 53N 117 0W
Nysted, Denmark 15 K5 54 40N 11 44 E
Nytva, Russia 54 C5 57 56N 55 20 E

Oliver 243

Nyūgawa, Japan 62 D5 33 56N 133 5 E
Nyunzu, Zaïre 106 D2 5 57 S 27 58 E
Nyurbe, Russia 57 C12 63 17N 118 28 E
Nyzhnohirskyy, Ukraine 51 K8 45 27N 34 38 E
Nzega, Tanzania 106 C3 4 10 S 33 12 E
Nzega □, Tanzania 106 C3 4 10 S 33 10 E
N'Zérékoré, Guinea 100 D3 7 49N 8 48W
Nzeto, Angola 103 D2 7 10 S 12 52 E
Nzilo, Chutes de, Zaïre 103 E5 10 18 S 25 27 E
Nzubuka, Tanzania 106 C3 4 45 S 32 50 E

O

Ō-Shima, Fukuoka, Japan 62 D2 33 54N 130 25 E
Ō-Shima, Nagasaki, Japan 62 C1 34 29N 129 33 E
Ō-Shima, Shizuoka, Japan 63 C11 34 44N 139 24 E
Oacoma, U.S.A. 138 D5 43 48N 99 24W
Oahe, L., U.S.A. 138 C4 44 27N 100 24W
Oahe Dam, U.S.A. 138 C4 44 27N 100 24W
Oahu, U.S.A. 132 H16 21 28N 157 58W
Oak Creek, Colo., U.S.A. 142 F10 40 16N 106 57W
Oak Creek, Wis., U.S.A. 141 B9 42 52N 87 55W
Oak Harbor, U.S.A. 144 B4 48 18N 122 39W
Oak Hill, U.S.A. 134 G5 37 59N 81 9W
Oak Lawn, U.S.A. 141 C9 41 43N 87 44W
Oak Park, U.S.A. 141 C9 41 53N 87 47W
Oak Ridge, U.S.A. 135 G3 36 1N 84 16W
Oak View, U.S.A. 145 L7 34 24N 119 18W
Oakan-Dake, Japan 60 C12 43 27N 144 10 E
Oakbank, Australia 116 B4 33 4 S 140 33 E
Oakdale, Calif., U.S.A. 144 H6 37 46N 120 51W
Oakdale, La., U.S.A. 139 K8 30 49N 92 40W
Oakengates, U.K. 16 E5 52 41N 2 26W
Oakes, U.S.A. 138 B5 46 8N 98 6W
Oakesdale, U.S.A. 142 C5 47 8N 117 15W
Oakey, Australia 115 D5 27 25 S 151 43 E
Oakford, U.S.A. 140 D7 40 6N 89 58W
Oakham, U.K. 16 E7 52 40N 0 43W
Oakhurst, U.S.A. 144 H7 37 19N 119 40W
Oakland, Calif., U.S.A. 144 H4 37 49N 122 16W
Oakland, Ill., U.S.A. 141 E8 39 39N 88 2W
Oakland, Oreg., U.S.A. 142 E2 43 25N 123 18W
Oakland City, U.S.A. 141 F9 38 20N 87 21W
Oaklands, Australia 117 C7 35 34 S 146 10 E
Oakley, Idaho, U.S.A. 142 E7 42 15N 113 53W
Oakley, Kans., U.S.A. 138 F4 39 8N 100 51W
Oakley Creek, Australia 117 A8 31 37 S 149 46 E
Oakover →, Australia 112 D3 21 0 S 120 40 E
Oakridge, U.S.A. 142 E2 43 45N 122 28W
Oaktown, U.S.A. 141 F9 38 52N 87 27W
Oakville, U.S.A. 144 D3 46 51N 123 14W
Oakwood, U.S.A. 141 C12 41 6N 84 23W
Oamaru, N.Z. 119 F5 45 5 S 170 59 E
Oamishirasato, Japan 63 B12 35 31N 140 18 E
Oarai, Japan 63 A12 36 21N 140 34 E
Oasis, Calif., U.S.A. 145 M10 33 28N 116 6W
Oasis, Nev., U.S.A. 144 H9 37 29N 117 55W
Oates Land, Antarctica 7 C11 69 0 S 160 0 E
Oatman, U.S.A. 145 K12 35 1N 114 19W
Oaxaca, Mexico 147 D5 17 2N 96 40W
Oaxaca □, Mexico 147 D5 17 0N 97 0W
Ob →, Russia 56 C7 66 45N 69 30 E
Oba, Canada 128 C3 49 4N 84 7W
Obala, Cameroon 101 E7 4 9N 11 32 E
Obama, Fukui, Japan 63 B7 35 30N 135 45 E
Obama, Nagasaki, Japan 62 E2 32 43N 130 13 E
Oban, U.K. 18 E3 56 25N 5 29W
Obbia, Somali Rep. 108 C3 5 25N 48 30 E
Obdam, Neths. 20 C5 52 41N 4 55 E
Obed, Canada 130 C5 53 30N 117 10W
Ober-Aagau, Switz. 28 B5 47 10N 7 45 E
Obera, Argentina 159 B4 27 21 S 55 2W
Oberalppass, Switz. 29 C7 46 39N 8 35 E
Oberalpstock, Switz. 29 C7 46 45N 8 47 E
Oberammergau, Germany 27 H7 47 36N 11 4 E
Oberdrauburg, Austria 30 E5 46 44N 12 58 E
Oberengadin, Switz. 29 C9 46 35N 9 55 E
Oberentfelden, Switz. 28 B6 47 21N 8 2 E
Oberhausen, Germany 26 D2 51 28N 6 51 E
Oberkirch, Germany 27 G4 48 31N 8 4 E
Oberland, Switz. 28 C5 46 35N 7 38 E
Oberlin, Kans., U.S.A. 138 F4 39 49N 100 32W
Oberlin, La., U.S.A. 139 K8 30 37N 92 46W
Oberlin, Ohio, U.S.A. 136 E2 41 18N 82 13W
Obernai, France 23 D14 48 28N 7 30 E
Oberndorf, Germany 27 G4 48 17N 8 34 E
Oberon, Australia 117 B8 33 45 S 149 52 E
Oberösterreich □, Austria 30 C6 48 10N 14 0 E
Oberpfälzer Wald, Germany 27 F8 49 30N 12 30 E
Obersiggenthal, Switz. 29 B6 47 29N 8 18 E
Oberstdorf, Germany 27 H6 47 24N 10 15 E
Oberting, Gabon 102 C1 0 22 S 9 46 E
Oberwil, Switz. 28 A5 47 32N 7 33 E
Obi, Kepulauan, Indonesia 72 B3 1 23 S 127 45 E
Obi Is. = Obi, Kepulauan, Indonesia 72 B3 1 23 S 127 45 E
Obiaruku, Nigeria 101 D6 5 51N 6 9 E
Óbidos, Brazil 153 D6 1 50 S 55 30W
Óbidos, Portugal 37 F1 39 19N 9 10W
Obihiro, Japan 60 C11 42 56N 143 12 E
Obilatu, Indonesia 72 B3 1 25 S 127 20 E
Obilnoye, Russia 53 G7 47 32N 44 30 E
Obing, Germany 27 H8 48 0N 12 24 E
Obisfelde, Germany 26 C6 52 27N 10 57 E
Objat, France 24 C5 45 16N 1 24 E
Oblong, U.S.A. 141 E9 39 0N 87 55W
Obluchye, Russia 57 E14 49 1N 131 4 E
Obninsk, Russia 52 C3 55 8N 36 37 E
Obo, C.A.R. 102 A5 5 20N 26 32 E
Obo, Ethiopia 95 G4 3 46N 38 52 E
Oboa, Mt., Uganda 106 B3 1 45N 34 45 E
Obock, Djibouti 95 E5 12 0N 43 20 E
Oborniki, Poland 47 C3 52 39N 16 50 E
Oborniki Śląskie, Poland 47 D3 51 17N 16 53 E
Obouya, Congo 102 C3 0 56 S 15 43 E
Oboyan, Russia 52 E3 51 15N 36 21 E
Obozerskaya = Obozerskiy, Russia 56 C5 63 34N 40 21 E
Obozerskiy, Russia 56 C5 63 34N 40 21 E
Obrenovac, Serbia, Yug. 42 C5 44 40N 20 11 E
Obrovac, Croatia 39 D12 44 11N 15 41 E
Obruk, Turkey 88 C5 38 7N 33 12 E
Observatory Inlet, Canada 130 B3 55 10N 129 54W
Obshchi Syrt, Russia 54 E4 52 0N 53 0 E
Obskaya Guba, Russia 56 C8 69 0N 73 0 E
Obuasi, Ghana 101 D4 6 17N 1 40W
Obubra, Nigeria 101 D6 6 8N 8 20 E
Obwalden □, Switz. 28 C6 46 55N 8 15 E
Obzor, Bulgaria 43 E12 42 50N 27 52 E
Ocala, U.S.A. 135 L4 29 11N 82 8W
Ocamo →, Venezuela 153 C4 2 48N 65 14W
Ocampo, Mexico 146 B3 28 9N 108 24W
Ocaña, Colombia 152 B3 8 15N 73 20W
Ocaña, Spain 34 F1 39 55N 3 30W
Oconomowoc, U.S.A. 138 D10 43 7N 88 30W
Ocate, U.S.A. 139 G2 36 11N 105 3W
Occidental, Cordillera, Colombia 152 C3 5 0N 76 0W
Occidental, Cordillera, Peru 156 C3 14 0 S 74 0W
Ocean City, N.J., U.S.A. 134 F8 39 17N 74 35W
Ocean City, Wash., U.S.A. 144 C2 47 4N 124 10W
Ocean I. = Banaba, Kiribati 122 H8 0 45 S 169 50 E
Ocean Park, U.S.A. 144 D2 46 30N 124 3W
Oceano, U.S.A. 145 K6 35 6N 120 37W
Oceanport, U.S.A. 137 F10 40 19N 74 3W
Oceanside, U.S.A. 145 M9 33 12N 117 23W
Ochagavia, Spain 34 C3 42 55N 1 5W
Ochakiv, Ukraine 51 J6 46 37N 31 33 E
Ochamchira, Georgia 53 J5 42 46N 41 32 E
Ochamps, Belgium 21 J6 49 56N 5 16 E
Ocher, Russia 54 C5 57 53N 54 42 E
Ochiai, Japan 62 B5 35 1N 133 45 E
Ochil Hills, U.K. 18 E5 56 14N 3 40W
Ochre River, Canada 131 C9 51 4N 99 47W
Ochsenfurt, Germany 27 F6 49 40N 10 4 E
Ochsenhausen, Germany 27 G5 48 4N 9 57 E
Ocilla, U.S.A. 135 K4 31 36N 83 15W
Ocmulgee →, U.S.A. 135 K4 31 58N 82 33W
Ocna Mureş, Romania 46 C4 46 23N 23 55 E
Ocna Sibiului, Romania 46 D5 45 52N 24 2 E
Ocnele Mari, Romania 46 D5 45 8N 24 18 E
Ocniţa, Moldova 51 H4 48 25N 27 30 E
Ocoña, Peru 156 D3 16 26 S 73 8W
Ocoña →, Peru 156 D3 16 28 S 73 8W
Oconee →, U.S.A. 135 K4 31 58N 82 33W
Oconomowoc, U.S.A. 141 A8 43 7N 88 30W
Oconto, U.S.A. 134 C2 44 53N 87 52W
Oconto Falls, U.S.A. 134 C1 44 52N 88 9W
Ocosingo, Mexico 147 D6 17 10N 92 15W
Ocotal, Nic. 148 D2 13 41N 86 31W
Ocotlán, Mexico 146 C4 20 21N 102 42W
Ocquier, Belgium 21 H6 50 24N 5 24 E
Ócreza →, Portugal 37 F3 39 32N 7 50W
Ócsa, Hungary 31 D12 47 17N 19 15 E
Octave, U.S.A. 143 J7 34 10N 112 43W
Octeville, France 22 C5 49 38N 1 40W
Ocumare del Tuy, Venezuela 152 A4 10 7N 66 46W
Ocuri, Bolivia 157 D4 18 45 S 65 50W
Oda, Ghana 101 D4 5 50N 0 51W
Oda, Ehime, Japan 62 D4 33 36N 132 53 E
Ōda, Shimane, Japan 62 B4 35 11N 132 30 E
Oda, J., Sudan 94 C4 20 21N 36 39 E
Ódáðahraun, Iceland 12 D5 65 5N 17 0W
Ödåkra, Sweden 15 H6 56 7N 12 45 E
Odate, Japan 60 D10 40 16N 140 34 E
Odawara, Japan 63 B11 35 20N 139 6 E
Odda, Norway 13 F12 60 3N 6 35 E
Odder, Denmark 15 J4 55 58N 10 10 E
Oddur, Somali Rep. 108 D2 4 11N 43 52 E
Ödeborg, Sweden 15 F5 58 32N 11 58 E
Odei →, Canada 131 B9 56 6N 96 54W
Odell, U.S.A. 141 D8 41 0N 88 31W
Odemira, Portugal 37 H2 37 35N 8 40W
Ödemiş, Turkey 88 C3 38 15N 28 0 E
Odendaalsrus, S. Africa 104 D4 27 48 S 26 45 E
Odense, Denmark 15 J4 55 22N 10 23 E
Odenwald, Germany 27 F5 49 35N 9 0 E
Oder →, Germany 26 B10 53 33N 14 38 E
Oderzo, Italy 39 C9 45 47N 12 29 E
Odesa, Ukraine 51 J6 46 30N 30 45 E
Odessa = Odesa, Ukraine 51 J6 46 30N 30 45 E
Odessa, Canada 137 B8 44 17N 76 43W
Odessa, Mo., U.S.A. 140 F3 39 0N 93 57W
Odessa, Tex., U.S.A. 139 K3 31 52N 102 23W
Odessa, Wash., U.S.A. 142 C4 47 20N 118 41W
Odiakwe, Botswana 104 C4 20 12 S 25 17 E
Odiel →, Spain 37 H4 37 10N 6 55W
Odienné, Ivory C. 100 D3 9 30N 7 34W
Odintsovo, Russia 52 C3 55 39N 37 15 E
Odiongan, Phil. 70 E3 12 24N 121 59 E
Odobeşti, Romania 46 D8 45 43N 27 4 E
Odolanów, Poland 47 D4 51 34N 17 40 E
O'Donnell, Phil. 70 D3 15 21N 120 27 E
O'Donnell, U.S.A. 139 J4 32 58N 101 50W
Odoorn, Neths. 20 C9 52 51N 6 51 E
Odorheiu Secuiesc, Romania 46 C6 46 21N 25 21 E
Odoyevo, Russia 52 D3 53 56N 36 42 E
Odra = Oder →, Germany 26 B10 53 33N 14 38 E
Odra →, Poland 47 B1 53 33N 14 38 E
Odra →, Spain 36 C6 42 14N 4 17W
Odweina, Somali Rep. 108 C3 9 25N 45 4 E
Odžaci, Serbia, Yug. 42 B4 45 30N 19 17 E
Odžak, Bos.-H. 42 B3 45 3N 18 18 E
Odzi, Zimbabwe 105 B5 19 0 S 32 20 E
Oedelem, Belgium 21 F2 51 10N 3 21 E
Oegstgeest, Neths. 20 D4 52 11N 4 29 E
Oeiras, Brazil 154 C3 7 0 S 42 8W
Oeiras, Portugal 37 G1 38 41N 9 18W
Oelrichs, U.S.A. 138 D3 43 11N 103 14W
Oelsnitz, Germany 26 E8 50 24N 12 11 E
Oelwein, U.S.A. 138 D9 42 41N 91 55W
Oenpelli, Australia 112 B5 12 20 S 133 4 E
Of, Turkey 89 B9 40 59N 40 23 E
O'Fallon, U.S.A. 140 F6 38 49N 90 42W
Ofanto →, Italy 41 A9 41 22N 16 13 E
Offa, Nigeria 101 D5 8 13N 4 42 E
Offaly □, Ireland 19 C4 53 15N 7 30W
Offenbach, Germany 27 E4 50 6N 8 44 E
Offenburg, Germany 27 G3 48 28N 7 56 E
Offerdal, Sweden 14 A8 63 28N 14 0 E
Offida, Italy 39 F10 42 56N 13 41 E
Offranville, France 22 C8 49 52N 1 1 E
Ofidhousa, Greece 45 H8 36 33N 26 8 E
Ofotfjorden, Norway 12 B17 68 27N 17 0 E
Ofu, Amer. Samoa 121 X25 14 11 S 169 41W
Ōfunato, Japan 60 E10 39 4N 141 43 E
Oga, Japan 60 E9 39 55N 139 50 E
Oga-Hantō, Japan 60 E9 39 58N 139 47 E
Ogaden, Ethiopia 108 C3 7 30N 45 30 E
Ogahalla, Canada 128 B2 50 6N 85 51W
Ōgaki, Japan 63 B8 35 21N 136 37 E
Ogallala, U.S.A. 138 E4 41 8N 101 43W
Ogan →, Indonesia 74 C2 3 1 S 104 44 E
Ogasawara Gunto, Pac. Oc. 58 G18 27 0N 142 0 E
Ogbomosho, Nigeria 101 D5 8 1N 4 11 E
Ogden, Iowa, U.S.A. 140 B2 42 2N 94 2W
Ogden, Utah, U.S.A. 142 F7 41 13N 111 58W
Ogdensburg, U.S.A. 137 B9 44 42N 75 30W
Ogeechee →, U.S.A. 135 K5 31 50N 81 3W
Ogilby, U.S.A. 145 N12 32 49N 114 50W
Oglesby, U.S.A. 140 C7 41 18N 89 4W
Oglio →, Italy 38 C7 45 2N 10 39 E
Ogmore, Australia 114 C4 22 37 S 149 35 E
Ognon →, France 23 E12 47 16N 5 28 E
Ogoamas, Indonesia 72 A2 0 50N 120 5 E
Ogoja, Nigeria 101 D6 6 38N 8 39 E
Ogoki →, Canada 128 B2 51 38N 85 57W
Ogoki L., Canada 128 B2 50 50N 87 10W
Ogoki Res., Canada 128 B2 50 45N 88 15W
Ogooué →, Gabon 102 C1 1 0 S 9 0 E
Ogori, Japan 62 C3 34 6N 131 24 E
Ogosta →, Bulgaria 43 D8 43 48N 23 55 E
Ogowe = Ogooué →, Gabon 102 C1 1 0 S 9 0 E
Ogr = Sharafa, Sudan 95 E2 11 59N 27 7 E
Ograźden, Macedonia 42 F7 41 30N 22 50 E
Ogre, Latvia 13 H21 56 49N 24 36 E
Ogrein, Sudan 94 D3 17 55N 34 50 E
Ogulin, Croatia 39 C12 45 16N 15 16 E
Ogun □, Nigeria 101 D5 7 0N 3 0 E
Oguni, Japan 62 D3 33 11N 131 8 E
Oguta, Nigeria 101 D6 5 44N 6 44 E
Ogwashi-Uku, Nigeria 101 D6 6 15N 6 30 E
Ogwe, Nigeria 101 E6 5 0N 7 14 E
Ohai, N.Z. 119 F3 45 55 S 168 0 E
Ohakune, N.Z. 118 F4 39 24 S 175 24 E
Ohanet, Algeria 99 C6 28 44N 8 46 E
Ōhara, Japan 63 B12 35 15N 140 23 E
Ohata, Japan 60 D10 41 24N 141 10 E
Ohau, L., N.Z. 119 E4 44 15 S 169 53 E
Ohaupo, N.Z. 118 D4 37 56 S 175 20 E
Ohey, Belgium 21 H6 50 26N 5 8 E
Ohio □, U.S.A. 134 E3 40 15N 82 45W
Ohio →, U.S.A. 134 G1 36 59N 89 8W
Ohio City, U.S.A. 141 D12 40 46N 84 37W
Ohiwa Harbour, N.Z. 118 D6 37 59 S 177 10 E
Ohre →, Czech. 30 A7 50 30N 14 10 E
Ohre →, Germany 26 C7 52 18N 11 46 E
Ohrid, Macedonia 42 F5 41 8N 20 52 E
Ohridsko Jezero, Macedonia 42 F5 41 8N 20 52 E
Ohrigstad, S. Africa 105 C5 24 39 S 30 36 E
Öhringen, Germany 27 F5 49 12N 9 31 E
Ohura, N.Z. 118 E3 38 51 S 174 59 E
Oiapoque →, Brazil 153 C7 4 8N 51 40W
Oikou, China 67 E9 38 35N 117 42 E
Oil City, U.S.A. 136 E5 41 26N 79 42W
Oildale, U.S.A. 145 K7 35 25N 119 1W
Oinousa, Greece 45 F8 38 33N 26 14 E
Oirschot, Neths. 21 E6 51 30N 5 18 E
Oise □, France 23 C9 49 28N 2 30 E
Oise →, France 23 D9 49 0N 2 4 E
Oisterwijk, Neths. 21 E6 51 35N 5 12 E
Ōita, Japan 62 D3 33 14N 131 36 E
Ōita □, Japan 62 D3 33 15N 131 30 E
Oiticica, Brazil 154 C3 5 3 S 41 5W
Ojai, U.S.A. 145 L7 34 27N 119 15W
Ojinaga, Mexico 146 B4 29 34N 104 25W
Ojiya, Japan 61 F9 37 18N 138 48 E
Ojos del Salado, Cerro, Argentina 158 B2 27 0 S 68 40W
Oka →, Russia 52 B7 56 20N 43 59 E
Okaba, Indonesia 73 C5 8 6 S 139 42 E
Okahandja, Namibia 104 C2 22 0 S 16 59 E
Okahukura, N.Z. 118 E4 38 48 S 175 14 E
Okaihau, N.Z. 118 B2 35 19 S 173 47 E
Okanagan L., Canada 130 C5 50 0N 119 30W
Okandja, Gabon 102 C2 0 35 S 13 45 E
Okanogan, U.S.A. 142 B4 48 22N 119 35W
Okanogan →, U.S.A. 142 B4 48 6N 119 44W
Okány, Hungary 31 E14 46 52N 21 21 E
Okapa, Papua N. G. 120 D3 6 38 S 145 39 E
Okaputa, Namibia 104 C2 20 5 S 17 0 E
Okara, Pakistan 79 C4 30 50N 73 31 E
Okarito, N.Z. 119 D5 43 15 S 170 9 E
Okato, N.Z. 118 F2 39 12 S 173 53 E
Okaukuejo, Namibia 104 B2 19 10 S 16 0 E
Okavango Swamps, Botswana 104 B3 18 45 S 22 45 E
Okawa, Japan 62 D2 33 9N 130 21 E
Okawville, U.S.A. 140 F7 38 26N 89 33W
Okaya, Japan 63 A10 36 5N 138 10 E
Okayama, Japan 62 C5 34 40N 133 54 E
Okayama □, Japan 62 C5 35 0N 133 50 E
Okazaki, Japan 63 C9 34 57N 137 10 E
Oke-Iho, Nigeria 101 D5 8 1N 3 18 E
Okeechobee, U.S.A. 135 M5 27 15N 80 50W
Okeechobee, L., U.S.A. 135 M5 27 0N 80 50W
Okefenokee Swamp, U.S.A. 135 K4 30 40N 82 20W
Okehampton, U.K. 17 G3 50 44N 4 0W
Okene, Nigeria 101 D6 7 32N 6 11 E
Oker →, Germany 26 C6 52 32N 10 22 E
Okha, Russia 57 D15 53 40N 143 0 E
Ókhi Óros, Greece 45 F6 38 5N 24 25 E
Okhotsk, Russia 57 D15 59 20N 143 10 E
Okhotsk, Sea of, Asia 57 D15 55 0N 145 0 E
Okhotskiy Perevoz, Russia 57 C14 61 52N 135 35 E
Okhtyrka, Ukraine 51 G8 50 25N 35 0 E
Oki-no-Shima, Japan 62 E4 32 44N 132 33 E
Oki-Shotō, Japan 62 A5 36 5N 133 15 E
Okiep, S. Africa 104 D2 29 39 S 17 53 E
Okigwi, Nigeria 101 D6 5 52N 7 20 E
Okija, Nigeria 101 D6 5 54N 6 55 E
Okinawa □, Japan 61 L3 26 40N 128 0 E
Okinawa-Guntō, Japan 61 L3 26 40N 128 0 E
Okinawa-Jima, Japan 61 L4 26 32N 128 0 E
Okino-erabu-Shima, Japan 61 L4 27 21N 128 33 E
Okitipupa, Nigeria 101 D5 6 31N 4 50 E
Oklahoma □, U.S.A. 139 H6 35 20N 97 30W
Oklahoma City, U.S.A. 139 H6 35 30N 97 30W
Okmulgee, U.S.A. 139 H7 35 37N 95 58W
Oknitsa = Ocniţa, Moldova 51 H4 48 25N 27 30 E
Okolo, Uganda 106 B3 2 37N 31 8 E
Okolona, Ky., U.S.A. 141 F11 38 8N 85 41W
Okolona, Miss., U.S.A. 139 H10 34 0N 88 45W
Okonek, Poland 47 B3 53 32N 16 51 E
Okrika, Nigeria 101 E6 4 40N 7 10 E
Oksovskiy, Russia 48 B6 62 33N 39 57 E
Oktabrsk = Oktyabrsk, Kazakstan 54 G6 49 28N 57 25 E
Oktyabr, Kazakstan 55 B8 43 41N 77 12 E
Oktyabrsk, Kazakstan 54 G6 49 28N 57 25 E
Oktyabrsk, Russia 52 D9 53 11N 48 40 E
Oktyabrskiy = Aktsyabrski, Belarus 51 F5 52 38N 28 53 E
Oktyabrskiy, Russia 53 G5 47 30N 40 4 E
Oktyabrskiy, Russia 54 C6 56 31N 57 12 E
Oktyabrskiy, Russia 54 D4 54 28N 53 28 E
Oktyabrskoy Revolyutsii, Os., Russia 57 B10 79 30N 97 0 E
Oktyabrskoye = Zhovtneve, Ukraine 51 J7 46 54N 32 3 E
Oktyabrskoye, Russia 54 D9 54 26N 62 44 E
Oktyabrskoye, Russia 56 C7 62 28N 66 3 E
Ōkuchi, Japan 62 E2 32 4N 130 37 E
Okulovka, Russia 50 C7 58 25N 33 19 E
Okuru, N.Z. 119 D3 43 55 S 168 55 E
Okushiri-Tō, Japan 60 C9 42 15N 139 30 E
Okuta, Nigeria 101 D5 9 14N 3 12 E
Okwa →, Botswana 104 C3 22 30 S 23 0 E
Ola, U.S.A. 139 H8 35 2N 93 13W
Ólafsfjörður, Iceland 12 C4 66 4N 18 39W
Ólafsvík, Iceland 12 D2 64 53N 23 43W
Olancha, U.S.A. 145 J8 36 17N 118 1W
Olancha Pk., U.S.A. 145 J8 36 15N 118 7W
Olanchito, Honduras 148 C2 15 30N 86 30W
Öland, Sweden 13 H17 56 45N 16 38 E
Olargues, France 24 E6 43 34N 2 53 E
Olary, Australia 116 B4 32 18 S 140 19 E
Olascoaga, Argentina 158 D3 35 15 S 60 39W
Olathe, U.S.A. 138 F7 38 53N 94 49W
Olavarría, Argentina 158 D3 36 55 S 60 20W
Oława, Poland 47 E4 50 57N 17 20 E
Ólbia, Italy 40 B2 40 55N 9 31 E
Ólbia, G. di, Italy 40 B2 40 55N 9 39 E
Old Bahama Chan. = Bahama, Canal Viejo de, W. Indies 148 B4 22 10N 77 30W
Old Baldy Pk. = San Antonio, Mt., U.S.A. 145 L9 34 17N 117 38W
Old Cork, Australia 114 C3 22 57 S 141 52 E
Old Crow, Canada 126 B6 67 30N 139 55W
Old Dale, U.S.A. 145 L11 34 8N 115 47W
Old Dongola, Sudan 94 D3 18 11N 30 44 E
Old Fletton, U.K. 17 E7 52 33N 0 14W
Old Forge, N.Y., U.S.A. 137 C10 43 43N 74 58W
Old Forge, Pa., U.S.A. 137 E9 41 22N 75 45W
Old Fort →, Canada 131 B6 58 36N 110 24W
Old Shinyanga, Tanzania 106 C3 3 33 S 33 27 E
Old Speck Mt., U.S.A. 137 B14 44 34N 70 57W
Old Town, U.S.A. 129 D6 44 56N 68 39W
Old Wives L., Canada 131 C7 50 5N 106 0W
Oldbury, U.K. 17 F5 51 38N 2 33W
Oldcastle, Ireland 19 C4 53 46N 7 10W
Oldeani, Tanzania 106 C4 3 22 S 35 35 E
Oldenburg, Niedersachsen, Germany 26 B4 53 9N 8 13 E
Oldenburg, Schleswig-Holstein, Germany 26 A6 54 17N 10 52 E
Oldenzaal, Neths. 20 D9 52 19N 6 53 E
Oldham, U.K. 16 D5 53 33N 2 7W
Oldman →, Canada 130 D6 49 57N 111 42W
Olds, Canada 130 C6 51 50N 114 10W
Olean, U.S.A. 136 D6 42 5N 78 26W
Olecko, Poland 47 A9 54 2N 22 31 E
Oléggio, Italy 38 C5 45 36N 8 38 E
Oleiros, Portugal 36 F3 39 56N 7 56W
Olekma →, Russia 57 C13 60 22N 120 42 E
Olekminsk, Russia 57 C13 60 25N 120 30 E
Oleksandriya, Ukraine 51 H7 48 42N 33 3 E
Oleksandriya, Ukraine 51 G4 50 37N 26 19 E
Oleksandrovka, Ukraine 51 H7 48 55N 32 20 E
Olema, U.S.A. 144 G4 38 3N 122 47W
Olen, Belgium 21 F5 51 9N 4 52 E
Olenegorsk, Russia 48 A5 68 9N 33 18 E
Olenek, Russia 57 C12 68 28N 112 18 E
Olenek →, Russia 57 B13 73 0N 120 10 E
Olenino, Russia 52 B1 56 15N 33 30 E
Oléron, I. d', France 24 C2 45 55N 1 15W
Oleśnica, Poland 47 D4 51 13N 17 22 E
Olesno, Poland 47 E5 50 51N 18 26 E
Olevsk, Ukraine 51 G4 51 12N 27 39 E
Olga, Russia 57 E14 43 50N 135 14 E
Olga, L., Canada 128 C4 49 47N 77 15W
Olga, Mt., Australia 113 E5 25 20 S 130 50 E
Ølgod, Denmark 15 J2 55 49N 8 36 E
Olhão, Portugal 37 H3 37 3N 7 48W
Olib, Croatia 39 D11 44 23N 14 44 E
Oliena, Italy 40 B2 40 16N 9 24 E
Oliete, Spain 34 D4 41 1N 0 41W
Olifants →, Africa 105 C5 23 57 S 31 58 E
Olifantshoek, S. Africa 104 D3 27 57 S 22 42 E
Ólimbos, Greece 45 J9 35 44N 27 11 E
Ólimbos, Óros, Greece 44 D4 40 6N 22 23 E
Olímpia, Brazil 159 A6 20 44 S 48 54W
Olin, U.S.A. 140 B5 42 0N 91 9W
Olinda, Brazil 154 C5 8 1 S 34 51W
Olindiná, Brazil 154 D4 11 22 S 38 21W
Olite, Spain 34 C3 42 29N 1 40W
Oliva, Argentina 158 C3 32 0 S 63 38W
Oliva, Spain 35 G4 38 58N 0 9W
Oliva, Punta del, Spain 36 B5 43 37N 5 28W
Oliva de la Frontera, Spain 37 G4 38 17N 6 54W
Olivares, Spain 34 F2 39 46N 2 20W
Olive Hill, U.S.A. 141 F13 38 18N 83 13W
Olivehurst, U.S.A. 144 F5 39 6N 121 34W
Oliveira, Brazil 155 F3 20 39 S 44 50W
Oliveira de Azemeis, Portugal 36 E2 40 49N 8 29W
Oliveira dos Brejinhos, Brazil 155 D3 12 19 S 42 54W
Olivenza, Spain 37 G3 38 41N 7 9W
Oliver, Canada 130 D5 49 13N 119 37W

244 Oliver L.

Oliver L., *Canada* 131 B8 56 56N 103 22W
Olivine Ra., *N.Z.* 119 E3 44 15 S 168 30 E
Olivone, *Switz.* 29 C7 46 32N 8 57 E
Olkhovka, *Russia* 52 F7 49 48N 44 32 E
Olkusz, *Poland* 47 E6 50 18N 19 33 E
Ollagüe, *Chile* 158 A2 21 15 S 68 10W
Olloy, *Belgium* 21 H5 50 5N 4 36 E
Olmaliq, *Uzbekistan* 55 C4 40 50N 69 35 E
Olmedo, *Spain* 36 D6 41 20N 4 43W
Olmos, *Peru* 156 B2 5 59 S 79 46W
Olney, *Ill., U.S.A.* 141 F8 38 44N 88 5W
Olney, *Tex., U.S.A.* 139 J5 33 22N 98 45W
Oloma, *Cameroon* 101 E7 3 29N 11 19 E
Olomane →, *Canada* 129 B7 50 14N 60 37W
Olombo, *Congo* 102 C3 1 18 S 15 53 E
Olomouc, *Czech.* 31 B10 49 38N 17 12 E
Olonets, *Russia* 50 B7 61 0N 32 54 E
Olongapo, *Phil.* 70 D3 14 50N 120 18 E
Oloron, Gave d' →, *France* 24 E2 43 33N 1 5W
Oloron-Ste.-Marie, *France* 24 E3 43 11N 0 38W
Olot, *Spain* 34 C7 42 11N 2 30 E
Olovo, *Bos.-H.* 42 C3 44 8N 18 35 E
Olovyannaya, *Russia* 57 D12 50 58N 115 35 E
Oloy →, *Russia* 57 C16 66 29N 159 29 E
Olpe, *Germany* 26 D3 51 2N 7 51 E
Olshanka, *Ukraine* 51 H6 48 16N 30 58 E
Olshany, *Ukraine* 51 G8 50 3N 35 53 E
Olst, *Neths.* 20 D8 52 20N 6 7 E
Olsztyn, *Poland* 47 B7 53 48N 20 29 E
Olsztyn □, *Poland* 47 B7 54 0N 21 0 E
Olsztynek, *Poland* 47 B7 53 34N 20 19 E
Olt □, *Romania* 46 E5 44 20N 24 30 E
Olt →, *Romania* 46 F5 43 43N 24 51 E
Olten, *Switz.* 28 B5 47 21N 7 53 E
Olteniţa, *Romania* 46 E7 44 7N 26 42 E
Olton, *U.S.A.* 139 H3 34 11N 102 8W
Oltu, *Turkey* 89 B9 40 35N 41 58 E
Olur, *Turkey* 89 B10 40 49N 42 8 E
Olutanga, *Phil.* 71 H4 7 26N 122 54 E
Olutanga I., *Phil.* 71 H4 7 22N 122 52 E
Olvega, *Spain* 34 D3 41 47N 2 0W
Olvera, *Spain* 37 J5 36 55N 5 18W
Olymbos, *Cyprus* 32 D12 35 21N 33 45 E
Olympia, *Greece* 45 G3 37 39N 21 39 E
Olympia, *U.S.A.* 144 D4 47 3N 122 53W
Olympic Mts., *U.S.A.* 144 C3 47 55N 123 45W
Olympic Nat. Park, *U.S.A.* 144 C3 47 48N 123 30W
Olympus, *Cyprus* 32 E11 34 56N 32 52 E
Olympus, Mt. = Ólimbos, Óros, *Greece* 44 D4 40 6N 22 23 E
Olympus, Mt., *U.S.A.* 144 C3 47 48N 123 43W
Olyphant, *U.S.A.* 137 E9 41 27N 75 36W
Om →, *Russia* 56 D8 54 59N 73 22 E
Om Hajer, *Eritrea* 95 E4 14 20N 36 41 E
Om Koi, *Thailand* 76 D2 17 48N 98 22 E
Ōma, *Japan* 60 D10 41 45N 141 5 E
Ōmachi, *Japan* 63 A9 36 30N 137 50 E
Omae-Zaki, *Japan* 63 C10 34 36N 138 14 E
Ōmagari, *Japan* 60 E10 39 27N 140 29 E
Omagh, *U.K.* 19 B4 54 36N 7 19W
Omagh □, *U.K.* 19 B4 54 35N 7 15W
Omaha, *U.S.A.* 138 E7 41 17N 95 58W
Omak, *U.S.A.* 142 B4 48 25N 119 31W
Omalos, *Greece* 32 D5 35 19N 23 55 E
Oman ■, *Asia* 87 B7 23 0N 58 0 E
Oman, G. of, *Asia* 85 E8 24 30N 58 30 E
Omapere, *N.Z.* 118 B2 35 37 S 173 25 E
Omar Combon, *Somali Rep.* 108 D3 3 10N 45 47 E
Omaruru, *Namibia* 104 C2 21 26 S 16 0 E
Omaruru →, *Namibia* 104 C1 22 7 S 14 15 E
Omate, *Peru* 156 D3 16 45 S 71 0W
Ombai, Selat, *Indonesia* 72 C2 8 30 S 124 50 E
Omboué, *Gabon* 102 C1 1 35 S 9 15 E
Ombrone →, *Italy* 38 F8 42 42N 11 5 E
Omchi, *Chad* 97 D3 21 22N 17 53 E
Omdurmân, *Sudan* 95 D3 15 40N 32 28 E
Ōme, *Japan* 63 B11 35 47N 139 15 E
Omegna, *Italy* 38 C5 45 53N 8 24 E
Omeonga, *Zaïre* 102 C4 3 40 S 24 22 E
Ometepe, I. de, *Nic.* 148 D2 11 32N 85 35W
Ometepec, *Mexico* 147 D5 16 39N 98 23W
Ōmi-Shima, *Ehime, Japan* 62 C5 34 15N 133 0 E
Ōmi-Shima, *Yamaguchi, Japan* 62 C3 34 25N 131 9 E
Omihachiman, *Japan* 63 B8 35 7N 136 3 E
Ominato, *Japan* 60 D10 41 17N 141 10 E
Omineca →, *Canada* 130 B4 56 3N 124 16W
Omiš, *Croatia* 39 E13 43 28N 16 40 E
Omišalj, *Croatia* 39 C11 45 13N 14 32 E
Omitara, *Namibia* 104 C2 22 16 S 18 2 E
Ōmiya, *Japan* 63 B11 35 54N 139 38 E
Omme Å →, *Denmark* 15 J2 55 56N 8 32 E
Ommen, *Neths.* 20 C8 52 31N 6 26 E
Ömnögovĭ □, *Mongolia* 66 C3 43 15N 104 0 E
Omo →, *Ethiopia* 95 F4 6 25N 36 10 E
Omodhos, *Cyprus* 32 E11 34 51N 32 48 E
Omolon →, *Russia* 57 C16 68 42N 158 36 E
Omono-Gawa →, *Japan* 60 E10 39 46N 140 3 E
Omsk, *Russia* 56 D8 55 0N 73 12 E
Omsukchan, *Russia* 57 C16 62 32N 155 48 E
Ōmu, *Japan* 60 B11 44 34N 142 58 E
Omul, Vf., *Romania* 46 D6 45 27N 25 29 E
Omulew →, *Poland* 47 B8 53 5N 21 33 E
Ōmura, *Japan* 62 E1 32 56N 129 57 E
Ōmura-Wan, *Japan* 62 E1 32 57N 129 52 E
Omurtag, *Bulgaria* 43 D11 43 8N 26 26 E
Ōmuta, *Japan* 62 D2 33 5N 130 26 E
Omutninsk, *Russia* 54 B4 58 45N 52 4 E
On, *Belgium* 21 H6 50 11N 5 18 E
On-Take, *Japan* 62 F2 31 35N 130 39 E
Oña, *Spain* 34 C1 42 43N 3 25W
Onaga, *U.S.A.* 138 F6 39 29N 96 10W
Onalaska, *U.S.A.* 138 D9 43 53N 91 14W
Onamia, *U.S.A.* 138 B8 46 4N 93 40W
Onancock, *U.S.A.* 134 G8 37 43N 75 45W
Onang, *Indonesia* 72 B1 3 2 S 118 49 E
Onaping L., *Canada* 128 C3 47 3N 81 30W
Onarga, *U.S.A.* 141 D8 40 43N 88 1W
Onarhā, *Afghan.* 79 B3 35 30N 71 0 E
Oñate, *Spain* 34 B2 43 3N 2 25W
Onavas, *Mexico* 146 B3 28 28N 109 30W
Onawa, *U.S.A.* 138 D6 42 2N 96 6W
Onaway, *U.S.A.* 134 C3 45 21N 84 14W
Oncesti, *Romania* 46 F6 43 56N 25 52 E
Oncócua, *Angola* 103 F2 16 30 S 13 25 E
Onda, *Spain* 34 F4 39 55N 0 17W
Ondaejin, *N. Korea* 67 D15 41 34N 129 40 E
Ondangua, *Namibia* 104 B2 17 57 S 16 4 E
Ondárroa, *Spain* 34 B2 43 19N 2 25W
Ondas →, *Brazil* 155 D3 12 8 S 44 55W
Ondava →, *Slovak Rep.* 31 C14 48 27N 21 48 E
Onderdijk, *Neths.* 20 C6 52 45N 5 8 E
Ondjiva, *Angola* 103 F3 16 48 S 15 50 E
Ondo, *Japan* 62 C4 34 11N 132 32 E
Ondo, *Nigeria* 101 D5 7 4N 4 47 E
Ondo □, *Nigeria* 101 D6 7 0N 5 0 E
Öndörshil, *Mongolia* 66 B5 45 13N 108 5 E
Öndverðarnes, *Iceland* 12 D1 64 52N 24 0W
Onega, *Russia* 48 B6 64 0N 38 10 E
Onega →, *Russia* 48 B6 63 58N 38 2 E
Onega, G. of = Onezhskaya Guba, *Russia* 48 B6 64 24N 36 38 E
Onega, L. = Onezhskoye Ozero, *Russia* 50 B8 61 44N 35 22 E
Onehunga, *N.Z.* 118 C3 36 55 S 174 48 E
Oneida, *Ill., U.S.A.* 140 C6 41 4N 90 13W
Oneida, *N.Y., U.S.A.* 137 C9 43 6N 75 39W
Oneida L., *U.S.A.* 137 C9 43 12N 75 54W
O'Neill, *U.S.A.* 138 D5 42 27N 98 39W
Onekotan, Ostrov, *Russia* 57 E16 49 25N 154 45 E
Onema, *Zaïre* 103 C4 4 35 S 24 30 E
Oneonta, *Ala., U.S.A.* 135 J2 33 57N 86 28W
Oneonta, *N.Y., U.S.A.* 137 D9 42 27N 75 4W
Onerahi, *N.Z.* 118 B3 35 45 S 174 22 E
Oneşti, *Romania* 46 C7 46 17N 26 47 E
Onezhskaya Guba, *Russia* 48 B6 64 24N 36 38 E
Onezhskoye Ozero, *Russia* 50 B8 61 44N 35 22 E
Ongarue, *N.Z.* 118 E4 38 42 S 175 19 E
Ongea Levu, *Fiji* 121 B3 19 8 S 178 24W
Ongerup, *Australia* 113 F2 33 58 S 118 28 E
Ongjin, *N. Korea* 67 F13 37 56N 125 21 E
Ongkharak, *Thailand* 76 E3 14 8N 101 1 E
Ongniud Qi, *China* 67 C10 43 0N 118 38 E
Ongoka, *Zaïre* 106 C2 1 20 S 26 0 E
Ongole, *India* 83 G5 15 33N 80 2 E
Ongon, *Mongolia* 66 B7 45 41N 113 5 E
Onguren, *Russia* 57 D11 53 38N 107 36 E
Onhaye, *Belgium* 21 H5 50 15N 4 50 E
Oni, *Georgia* 53 J6 42 33N 43 26 E
Onida, *U.S.A.* 138 C4 44 42N 100 4W
Onilahy →, *Madag.* 105 C7 23 34 S 43 45 E
Onitsha, *Nigeria* 101 D6 6 6N 6 42 E
Onmaka, *Burma* 78 D6 22 17N 96 41 E
Ono, *Fiji* 121 B2 18 55 S 178 29 E
Ono, *Fukui, Japan* 63 B8 35 59N 136 29 E
Ono, *Hyōgo, Japan* 62 C6 34 51N 134 56 E
Onoda, *Japan* 62 C3 34 2N 131 25 E
Onoke, L., *N.Z.* 118 H4 41 22 S 175 8 E
Onomichi, *Japan* 62 C5 34 25N 133 12 E
Onpyŏng-ni, *S. Korea* 67 H14 33 25N 126 55 E
Ons, Is. d', *Spain* 36 C2 42 23N 8 55W
Onsala, *Sweden* 15 G6 57 26N 12 0 E
Onslow, *Australia* 112 D2 21 40 S 115 12 E
Onslow B., *U.S.A.* 135 H7 34 20N 77 15W
Onstwedde, *Neths.* 20 B10 53 2N 7 4 E
Ontake-San, *Japan* 63 B9 35 53N 137 29 E
Ontaneda, *Spain* 36 B7 43 12N 3 57W
Ontario, *Calif., U.S.A.* 145 L9 34 4N 117 39W
Ontario, *Oreg., U.S.A.* 142 D5 44 2N 116 58W
Ontario □, *Canada* 128 B2 48 0N 83 0W
Ontario, L., *U.S.A.* 128 D4 43 20N 78 0W
Onteniente, *Spain* 35 G4 38 50N 0 35W
Ontonagon, *U.S.A.* 138 B10 46 52N 89 19W
Ontur, *Spain* 35 G3 38 38N 1 29W
Onyx, *U.S.A.* 145 K8 35 41N 118 14W
Oodnadatta, *Australia* 115 D2 27 33 S 135 30 E
Ooldea, *Australia* 113 F5 30 27 S 131 50 E
Ooltgensplaat, *Neths.* 21 E4 51 41N 4 21 E
Oombulgurri, *Australia* 112 C4 15 15 S 127 45 E
Oona River, *Canada* 130 C2 53 57N 130 16W
Oordegem, *Belgium* 21 G3 50 58N 3 54 E
Oorindi, *Australia* 114 C3 20 40 S 141 1 E
Oost-Vlaanderen □, *Belgium* 21 F3 51 5N 3 50 E
Oost-Vlieland, *Neths.* 20 B6 53 18N 5 4 E
Oostakker, *Belgium* 21 F3 51 6N 3 46 E
Oostburg, *Neths.* 21 F3 51 19N 3 30 E
Oostduinkerke, *Belgium* 21 F1 51 7N 2 41 E
Oostelijk-Flevoland, *Neths.* 20 C7 52 31N 5 38 E
Oostende, *Belgium* 21 F1 51 15N 2 54 E
Oosterbeek, *Neths.* 20 E7 51 59N 5 51 E
Oosterdijk, *Neths.* 20 C6 52 44N 5 14 E
Oosterend, *Friesland, Neths.* 20 B6 53 24N 5 23 E
Oosterend, *Noord-Holland, Neths.* 20 B5 53 5N 4 52 E
Oosterhout, *Neths.* 21 E5 51 39N 4 47 E
Oosterschelde, *Neths.* 21 E4 51 33N 4 0 E
Oosterwolde, *Neths.* 20 B8 53 0N 6 17 E
Oosterzele, *Belgium* 21 G3 50 57N 3 48 E
Oostkamp, *Belgium* 21 F2 51 9N 3 14 E
Oostmalle, *Belgium* 21 F5 51 18N 4 44 E
Oostrozebekke, *Belgium* 21 G2 50 55N 3 21 E
Oostvleteven, *Belgium* 21 G1 50 56N 2 45 E
Oostvoorne, *Neths.* 20 E4 51 55N 4 5 E
Oostzaan, *Neths.* 20 D5 52 26N 4 52 E
Ootacamund, *India* 83 J3 11 30N 76 44 E
Ootha, *Australia* 117 B7 33 6 S 147 29 E
Ootmarsum, *Neths.* 20 D9 52 24N 6 54 E
Ootsa L., *Canada* 130 C3 53 50N 126 2W
Opaka, *Bulgaria* 43 D11 43 28N 26 10 E
Opala, *Russia* 57 D16 51 58N 156 30 E
Opala, *Zaïre* 102 C4 0 40 S 24 20 E
Opalenica, *Poland* 47 C3 52 18N 16 24 E
Opan, *Bulgaria* 43 E10 42 13N 25 41 E
Opanake, *Sri Lanka* 83 L5 6 35N 80 40 E
Opapa, *N.Z.* 118 F5 39 47 S 176 42 E
Opasatika, *Canada* 128 C3 49 30N 82 50W
Opasquia, *Canada* 131 C10 53 16N 93 34W
Opatija, *Croatia* 39 C11 45 21N 14 17 E
Opatów, *Poland* 47 E8 50 50N 21 27 E
Opava, *Czech.* 31 B10 49 57N 17 58 E
Opeinde, *Neths.* 20 B8 53 8N 6 4 E
Opelousas, *U.S.A.* 139 K8 30 32N 92 5W
Opémisca, L., *Canada* 128 C5 49 56N 74 52W
Open Bay Is., *N.Z.* 119 D3 43 51 S 168 51 E
Opglabbeek, *Belgium* 21 F7 51 3N 5 35 E
Opheim, *U.S.A.* 142 B10 48 51N 106 24W
Ophthalmia Ra., *Australia* 112 D2 23 15 S 119 30 E
Opi, *Nigeria* 101 D6 6 36N 7 28 E
Opinaca →, *Canada* 128 B4 52 15N 78 2W
Opinaca L., *Canada* 128 B4 52 39N 76 20W
Opiskotish, L., *Canada* 129 B6 53 10N 67 50W
Oploo, *Neths.* 21 E7 51 37N 5 52 E
Opmeer, *Neths.* 20 C5 52 42N 4 57 E
Opobo, *Nigeria* 101 E6 4 35N 7 34 E
Opochka, *Russia* 50 D5 56 42N 28 45 E
Opoczno, *Poland* 47 D7 51 22N 20 18 E
Opol, *Phil.* 71 G5 8 31N 124 34 E
Opole, *Poland* 47 E4 50 42N 17 58 E
Opole □, *Poland* 47 E4 50 40N 17 56 E
Opon = Capu-Lapu, *Phil.* 71 F4 10 20N 123 55 E
Oporto = Porto, *Portugal* 36 D2 41 8N 8 40W
Opotiki, *N.Z.* 118 E6 38 1 S 177 19 E
Opp, *U.S.A.* 135 K2 31 17N 86 16W
Oppdal, *Norway* 13 E13 62 35N 9 41 E
Oppenheim, *Germany* 27 F4 49 51N 8 21 E
Opperdoes, *Neths.* 20 C6 52 45N 5 4 E
Óppido Mamertina, *Italy* 41 D8 38 16N 15 59 E
Oppland fylke □, *Norway* 14 C3 61 15N 9 40 E
Oppstad, *Norway* 14 D5 60 17N 11 40 E
Oprtalj, *Croatia* 39 C10 45 23N 13 50 E
Opua, *N.Z.* 118 B3 35 19 S 174 9 E
Opunake, *N.Z.* 118 F2 39 26 S 173 52 E
Opuzen, *Croatia* 42 D2 43 1N 17 34 E
Oquawka, *U.S.A.* 140 D6 40 56N 90 57W
Ora, *Cyprus* 32 E12 34 51N 33 12 E
Ora, *Italy* 39 B8 46 20N 11 18 E
Ora Banda, *Australia* 113 F3 30 20 S 121 0 E
Oracle, *U.S.A.* 143 K8 32 37N 110 46W
Oradea, *Romania* 46 B2 47 2N 21 58 E
Öræfajökull, *Iceland* 12 D5 64 2N 16 39W
Orahovac, *Serbia, Yug.* 42 E5 42 24N 20 40 E
Orahovica, *Croatia* 42 B2 45 35N 17 52 E
Orai, *India* 81 G8 25 58N 79 30 E
Oraison, *France* 25 E9 43 55N 5 55 E
Oral = Zhayyq →, *Kazakstan* 49 E9 47 0N 51 48 E
Oral, *Kazakstan* 52 E10 51 20N 51 20 E
Oran, *Algeria* 99 A4 35 45N 0 39W
Oran, *Argentina* 158 A3 23 10 S 64 20W
Orange = Oranje →, *S. Africa* 104 D2 28 41 S 16 28 E
Orange, *Australia* 117 B8 33 15 S 149 7 E
Orange, *France* 25 D8 44 8N 4 47 E
Orange, *Calif., U.S.A.* 145 M9 33 47N 117 51W
Orange, *Mass., U.S.A.* 137 D12 42 35N 72 19W
Orange, *Tex., U.S.A.* 139 K8 30 6N 93 44W
Orange, *Va., U.S.A.* 134 F6 38 15N 78 7W
Orange, C., *Brazil* 153 C7 4 20N 51 30W
Orange Cove, *U.S.A.* 144 J7 36 38N 119 19W
Orange Free State □ = Free State □, *S. Africa* 104 D4 28 30 S 27 0 E
Orange Grove, *U.S.A.* 139 M6 27 58N 97 56W
Orange Walk, *Belize* 147 D7 18 6N 88 33W
Orangeburg, *U.S.A.* 135 J5 33 30N 80 52W
Orangeville, *Canada* 128 D3 43 55N 80 5W
Orangeville, *U.S.A.* 140 B7 42 28N 89 39W
Orani, *Phil.* 70 D3 14 49N 120 32 E
Oranienburg, *Germany* 26 C9 52 45N 13 14 E
Oranje →, *S. Africa* 104 D2 28 41 S 16 28 E
Oranje Vrystaat □ = Free State □, *S. Africa* 104 D4 28 30 S 27 0 E
Oranjemund, *Namibia* 104 D2 28 38 S 16 29 E
Oranjerivier, *S. Africa* 104 D3 29 40 S 24 12 E
Oras, *Phil.* 70 E5 12 9N 125 28 E
Orašje, *Bos.-H.* 42 B3 45 1N 18 42 E
Orăştie, *Romania* 46 D4 45 50N 23 10 E
Oraşul Stalin = Braşov, *Romania* 46 D6 45 38N 25 35 E
Orava →, *Slovak Rep.* 31 B12 49 24N 19 20 E
Oravita, *Romania* 42 B6 45 2N 21 43 E
Orawia, *N.Z.* 119 G2 46 1 S 167 50 E
Orb →, *France* 24 E7 43 15N 3 18 E
Orba →, *Italy* 38 D5 44 53N 8 37 E
Ørbæk, *Denmark* 15 J4 55 17N 10 39 E
Orbe, *Switz.* 28 C3 46 43N 6 32 E
Orbec, *France* 22 C7 49 1N 0 23 E
Orbetello, *Italy* 39 F8 42 27N 11 13 E
Órbigo →, *Spain* 36 C5 42 5N 5 42W
Orbost, *Australia* 117 D8 37 40 S 148 29 E
Orce, *Spain* 35 H2 37 44N 2 28W
Orce →, *Spain* 35 H2 37 44N 2 28W
Orchies, *France* 23 B10 50 28N 3 14 E
Orchila, I., *Venezuela* 152 A4 11 48N 66 10W
Orco →, *Italy* 38 C4 45 10N 7 52 E
Orcopampa, *Peru* 156 D3 15 20 S 72 23W
Orcutt, *U.S.A.* 145 L6 34 52N 120 27W
Ord →, *Australia* 112 C4 15 33 S 128 15 E
Ord, Mt., *Australia* 112 C4 17 20 S 125 34 E
Ordenes, *Spain* 36 B2 43 5N 8 29W
Orderville, *U.S.A.* 143 H7 37 17N 112 38W
Ording = St-Peter-Ording, *Germany* 26 A4 54 20N 8 36 E
Ordos = Mu Us Shamo, *China* 66 E5 39 0N 109 0 E
Ordu, *Turkey* 88 B7 40 55N 37 53 E
Ordubad, *Azerbaijan* 89 C12 38 54N 46 1 E
Orduña, *Álava, Spain* 34 C7 42 58N 2 58 E
Orduña, *Granada, Spain* 35 H1 37 20N 3 30W
Ordway, *U.S.A.* 138 F3 38 13N 103 46W
Ordzhonikidze = Vladikavkaz, *Russia* 53 J7 43 0N 44 35 E
Ordzhonikidze, *Kazakstan* 54 E8 52 27N 61 39 E
Ordzhonikidze, *Ukraine* 51 J8 47 39N 34 3 E
Ordzhonikidze, *Uzbekistan* 55 C4 41 21N 69 22 E
Ordzhonikidzeabad, *Tajikistan* 55 D4 38 34N 69 1 E
Ore, *Zaïre* 106 B2 3 17N 29 30 E
Ore Mts. = Erzgebirge, *Germany* 26 E9 50 27N 12 55 E
Orealla, *Guyana* 153 B6 5 15N 57 23W
Orebić, *Croatia* 42 D2 43 0N 17 11 E
Örebro, *Sweden* 13 G16 59 20N 15 18 E
Oregon, *Ill., U.S.A.* 140 B7 42 1N 89 20W
Oregon, *Ohio, U.S.A.* 141 C13 41 38N 83 25W
Oregon, *Wis., U.S.A.* 140 B7 42 56N 89 23W
Oregon □, *U.S.A.* 142 E3 44 0N 121 0W
Oregon City, *U.S.A.* 144 E4 45 21N 122 36W
Orekhov = Orikhiv, *Ukraine* 51 J8 47 30N 35 48 E
Orekhovo-Zuyevo, *Russia* 52 C4 55 50N 38 55 E
Orel, *Russia* 52 D3 52 57N 36 3 E
Orel →, *Ukraine* 51 H8 48 30N 34 39 E
Orellana, Canal de, *Spain* 37 F5 39 2N 6 0W
Orellana, Pantano de, *Spain* 37 F5 39 5N 5 10W
Orellana la Vieja, *Spain* 37 F5 39 1N 5 32W
Orem, *U.S.A.* 142 F8 40 19N 111 42W
Ören, *Turkey* 88 D2 37 3N 27 57 E
Orenburg, *Russia* 54 F5 51 45N 55 6 E
Orense, *Spain* 36 C3 42 19N 7 55W
Orense □, *Spain* 36 C3 42 15N 7 51W
Orepuki, *N.Z.* 119 G2 46 19 S 167 46 E
Orestiás, *Greece* 44 C8 41 30N 26 33 E
Øresund, *Europe* 15 J6 55 45N 12 45 E
Oreti →, *N.Z.* 119 G3 46 28 S 168 14 E
Orford Ness, *U.K.* 17 E9 52 5N 1 35 E
Organà, *Spain* 34 C6 42 13N 1 20 E
Organos, Pta. de los, *Canary Is.* 33 F2 28 12N 17 17W
Orgaz, *Spain* 37 F7 39 39N 3 53W
Orgeyev = Orhei, *Moldova* 51 J5 47 24N 28 50 E
Orgon, *France* 25 E9 43 47N 5 3 E
Orgūn, *Afghan.* 79 B3 32 55N 69 12 E
Orhaneli, *Turkey* 88 C3 39 54N 28 59 E
Orhangazi, *Turkey* 88 B3 40 29N 29 18 E
Orhei, *Moldova* 51 J5 47 24N 28 50 E
Orhon Gol →, *Mongolia* 64 A5 50 21N 106 0 E
Ória, *Italy* 41 B10 40 30N 17 38 E
Orient, *Australia* 115 D3 28 7 S 142 50 E
Orient, *U.S.A.* 140 C2 41 12N 94 25W
Oriental, Cordillera, *Bolivia* 157 D4 17 0 S 66 0W
Oriental, Cordillera, *Colombia* 152 B3 6 0N 73 0W
Oriente, *Argentina* 158 D3 38 44 S 60 37W
Origny-Ste.-Benoîte, *France* 23 C10 49 50N 3 30 E
Orihuela, *Spain* 35 G4 38 7N 0 55W
Orihuela del Tremedal, *Spain* 34 E3 40 33N 1 39W
Orikhiv, *Ukraine* 51 J8 47 30N 35 48 E
Oriku, *Albania* 44 D1 40 20N 19 30 E
Orinduik, *Guyana* 153 C5 4 40N 60 3W
Orinoco →, *Venezuela* 153 B5 9 15N 61 30W
Orion, *U.S.A.* 140 C6 41 21N 90 23W
Orissa □, *India* 82 D6 20 0N 84 0 E
Orissaare, *Estonia* 13 G20 58 34N 23 5 E
Oristano, *Italy* 40 C1 39 54N 8 36 E
Oristano, G. di, *Italy* 40 C1 39 50N 8 29 E
Orituco →, *Venezuela* 152 B4 8 45N 67 27W
Orizaba, *Mexico* 147 D5 18 51N 97 6W
Orizare, *Bulgaria* 43 E12 42 44N 27 39 E
Orizona, *Brazil* 155 E2 17 3 S 48 18W
Orjen, *Bos.-H.* 42 E3 42 35N 18 34 E
Orjiva, *Spain* 35 J1 36 53N 3 24W
Orkanger, *Norway* 14 A3 63 18N 9 52 E
Örkelljunga, *Sweden* 15 H7 56 17N 13 17 E
Örkény, *Hungary* 31 D12 47 9N 19 26 E
Orkla →, *Norway* 14 A3 63 18N 9 51 E
Orkney, *S. Africa* 104 D4 26 58 S 26 40 E
Orkney □, *U.K.* 18 C6 59 2N 3 13W
Orkney Is., *U.K.* 18 C6 59 0N 3 0W
Orla, *Poland* 47 C10 52 42N 23 20 E
Orland, *Calif., U.S.A.* 144 F4 39 45N 122 12W
Orland, *Ind., U.S.A.* 141 C11 41 47N 85 12W
Orlando, *U.S.A.* 135 L5 28 33N 81 23W
Orlando, C. d', *Italy* 41 D7 38 10N 14 43 E
Orléanais, *France* 23 E9 48 0N 2 0 E
Orléans, *France* 23 E8 47 54N 1 52 E
Orleans, *U.S.A.* 137 B12 44 49N 72 12W
Orléans, I. d', *Canada* 129 C5 46 54N 70 58W
Orlice →, *Czech.* 30 A9 50 5N 16 10 E
Orlické Hory, *Czech.* 31 A9 50 15N 16 30 E
Orlov, *Slovak Rep.* 31 B13 49 17N 20 51 E
Orlov Gay, *Russia* 52 E9 50 56N 48 19 E
Orlovat, *Serbia, Yug.* 42 B5 45 14N 20 33 E
Ormara, *Pakistan* 79 D2 25 16N 64 33 E
Ormea, *Italy* 38 D4 44 9N 7 54 E
Ormília, *Greece* 44 D5 40 16N 23 39 E
Ormoc, *Phil.* 71 F5 11 0N 124 37 E
Ormond, *N.Z.* 118 E6 38 33 S 177 56 E
Ormond Beach, *U.S.A.* 135 L5 29 17N 81 3W
Ormondville, *N.Z.* 118 G5 40 5 S 176 19 E
Ormož, *Slovenia* 39 B13 46 25N 16 10 E
Ormstown, *Canada* 137 A11 45 8N 74 0W
Ornans, *France* 23 E13 47 7N 6 10 E
Orne □, *France* 22 D7 48 40N 0 5 E
Orne →, *France* 22 C6 49 18N 0 15W
Orneta, *Poland* 47 A7 54 8N 20 9 E
Ørnhøj, *Denmark* 15 H2 56 13N 8 34 E
Ornö, *Sweden* 14 E12 59 4N 18 24 E
Örnsköldsvik, *Sweden* 14 A12 63 17N 18 40 E
Oro, *N. Korea* 67 D14 40 1N 127 27 E
Oro →, *Mexico* 146 B3 25 35N 105 2W
Oro Grande, *U.S.A.* 145 L9 34 36N 117 20W
Orobie, Alpi, *Italy* 38 B6 46 7N 10 0 E
Orocué, *Colombia* 152 C3 4 48N 71 20W
Orodo, *Nigeria* 101 D6 5 34N 7 4 E
Orogrande, *U.S.A.* 143 K10 32 24N 106 5W
Orol, *Spain* 36 B3 43 34N 7 39W
Orol Dengizi = Aral Sea, *Asia* 56 E7 44 30N 60 0 E
Oromocto, *Canada* 129 C6 45 54N 66 29W
Oron, *Nigeria* 101 E6 4 48N 8 14 E
Oron, *Switz.* 28 C3 46 34N 6 50 E
Orono, *Canada* 136 C6 43 59N 78 37W
Oropesa, *Spain* 36 F5 39 57N 5 10W
Oroqen Zizhiqi, *China* 65 A7 50 34N 123 43 E
Oroquieta, *Phil.* 71 G4 8 32N 123 44 E
Orós, *Brazil* 154 C4 6 15 S 38 55W
Orosei, G. di, *Italy* 40 B2 40 15N 9 44 E
Orosháza, *Hungary* 31 E13 46 32N 20 42 E
Orote Pen., *Guam* 121 R15 13 26N 144 38 E
Orotukan, *Russia* 57 C16 62 16N 151 42 E
Oroville, *Calif., U.S.A.* 144 F5 39 31N 121 33W
Oroville, *Wash., U.S.A.* 142 B4 48 56N 119 26W
Oroville, L., *U.S.A.* 144 F5 39 33N 121 29W
Orrick, *U.S.A.* 140 E2 39 13N 94 7W
Orroroo, *Australia* 116 B3 32 43 S 138 38 E
Orrville, *U.S.A.* 136 F3 40 50N 81 46W
Orsara di Púglia, *Italy* 41 A8 41 17N 15 16 E
Orsha, *Belarus* 50 E6 54 30N 30 25 E
Orsières, *Switz.* 28 D4 46 2N 7 9 E
Orsk, *Russia* 54 F7 51 12N 58 34 E
Ørslev, *Denmark* 15 J5 55 3N 11 56 E
Orsogna, *Italy* 39 F11 42 13N 14 17 E
Orşova, *Romania* 46 E3 44 41N 22 25 E
Ørsted, *Denmark* 15 H4 56 30N 10 20 E
Orta, L. d', *Italy* 38 C5 45 49N 8 24 E
Orta Nova, *Italy* 41 A8 41 19N 15 42 E
Ortaca, *Turkey* 88 D3 36 49N 28 45 E

Pegnitz 247

Paradhísi, *Greece* **32 C10** 36 18N 28 7 E
Paradip, *India* **82 D8** 20 15N 86 35 E
Paradise, *Calif., U.S.A.* **144 F5** 39 46N 121 37W
Paradise, *Mont., U.S.A.* **142 C6** 47 23N 114 48W
Paradise, *Nev., U.S.A.* **145 J11** 36 9N 115 10W
Paradise →, *Canada* **129 B8** 53 27N 57 19W
Paradise Valley, *U.S.A.* **142 F5** 41 30N 117 32W
Parado, *Indonesia* **75 D5** 8 42 S 118 30 E
Paradyz, *Poland* **47 D7** 51 19N 20 2 E
Paragould, *U.S.A.* **139 G9** 36 3N 90 29W
Paraguá →, *Bolivia* **157 C5** 13 34 S 61 53W
Paragua →, *Venezuela* **153 B5** 6 55N 62 55W
Paraguaçu →, *Brazil* **155 D4** 12 45 S 38 54W
Paraguaçu Paulista, *Brazil* **159 A5** 22 22 S 50 35W
Paraguaipoa, *Venezuela* **152 A3** 11 21N 71 57W
Paraguaná, Pen. de, *Venezuela* **152 A3** 12 0N 70 0W
Paraguarí, *Paraguay* **158 B4** 25 36 S 57 0W
Paraguarí □, *Paraguay* **158 B4** 26 0 S 57 10W
Paraguay ■, *S. Amer.* **158 A4** 23 0 S 57 0W
Paraguay →, *Paraguay* **158 B4** 27 18 S 58 38W
Paraíba = João Pessoa, *Brazil* **154 C5** 7 10 S 34 52W
Paraíba □, *Brazil* **154 C4** 7 0 S 36 0W
Paraíba do Sul →, *Brazil* **155 F3** 21 37 S 41 3W
Parainen, *Finland* **13 F20** 60 18N 22 18 E
Paraiso, *Mexico* **147 D6** 18 24N 93 14W
Parak, *Iran* **85 E7** 27 38N 52 25 E
Parakhino Paddubye, *Russia* **50 C7** 58 26N 33 10 E
Parakou, *Benin* **101 D5** 9 25N 2 40 E
Parakylia, *Australia* **116 A2** 30 24 S 136 25 E
Paralimni, *Cyprus* **32 D12** 35 2N 33 58 E
Parálion-Astrous, *Greece* **45 G4** 37 25N 22 45 E
Paramakkudi, *India* **83 K4** 9 31N 78 39 E
Paramaribo, *Surinam* **153 B6** 5 50N 55 10W
Parambu, *Brazil* **154 C3** 6 13 S 40 43W
Paramillo, Nudo del, *Colombia* **152 B2** 7 4N 75 55W
Paramirim, *Brazil* **155 D3** 13 26 S 42 15W
Paramirim →, *Brazil* **155 D3** 11 34 S 43 18W
Paramithiá, *Greece* **44 E2** 39 30N 20 35 E
Paramushir, Ostrov, *Russia* **57 D16** 50 24N 156 0 E
Paran →, *Israel* **91 E4** 30 20N 35 10 E
Paraná, *Argentina* **158 C3** 31 45 S 60 30W
Paranã, *Brazil* **155 D2** 12 30 S 47 48W
Paraná □, *Brazil* **159 A5** 24 30 S 51 0W
Paraná →, *Argentina* **158 C4** 33 43 S 59 15W
Paranaguá, *Brazil* **159 B6** 25 30 S 48 30W
Paranaíba →, *Brazil* **155 F1** 20 6 S 51 4W
Paranapanema →, *Brazil* **159 A5** 22 40 S 53 9W
Paranapiacaba, Serra do, *Brazil* **159 A6** 24 31 S 48 35W
Paranavaí, *Brazil* **159 A5** 23 4 S 52 56W
Parang, *Jolo, Phil.* **71 J3** 5 55N 120 54 E
Parang, *Mindanao, Phil.* **71 H5** 7 23N 124 16 E
Parangaba, *Brazil* **154 B4** 3 45 S 38 33W
Parangippettai, *India* **83 J4** 11 30N 79 38 E
Paraparauma, *N.Z.* **118 G4** 40 57 S 175 3 E
Parapóla, *Greece* **45 H5** 36 55N 23 27 E
Paraspóri, Ákra, *Greece* **45 J9** 35 55N 27 15 E
Paratinga, *Brazil* **155 D3** 12 40 S 43 10W
Paratoo, *Australia* **116 B3** 32 42 S 139 20 E
Parattah, *Australia* **114 G4** 42 22 S 147 23 E
Paraúna, *Brazil* **155 E1** 16 55 S 50 26W
Paray-le-Monial, *France* **25 B8** 46 27N 4 7 E
Parbati →, *India* **80 G7** 25 50N 76 30 E
Parbatipur, *Bangla.* **78 C2** 25 39N 88 55 E
Parbhani, *India* **82 E3** 19 8N 76 52 E
Parchim, *Germany* **26 B7** 53 26N 11 52 E
Parczew, *Poland* **47 D9** 51 40N 22 52 E
Pardes Hanna, *Israel* **91 C3** 32 28N 34 57 E
Pardilla, *Spain* **36 D7** 41 33N 3 43W
Pardo →, *Bahia, Brazil* **155 E4** 15 40 S 39 0W
Pardo →, *Mato Grosso, Brazil* **159 A5** 21 46 S 52 9W
Pardo →, *Minas Gerais, Brazil* **155 E3** 15 48 S 44 48W
Pardo →, *São Paulo, Brazil* **155 F2** 20 10 S 48 38W
Pardubice, *Czech.* **30 A8** 50 3N 15 45 E
Pare, *Indonesia* **75 D4** 7 43 S 112 12 E
Pare □, *Tanzania* **106 C4** 4 10 S 38 0 E
Pare Mts., *Tanzania* **106 C4** 4 0 S 37 45 E
Parecis, Serra dos, *Brazil* **157 C6** 13 0 S 60 0W
Paredes de Nava, *Spain* **36 C6** 42 9N 4 42W
Pareh, *Iran* **84 B5** 38 52N 45 42 E
Parelhas, *Brazil* **154 C4** 6 41 S 36 39W
Paren, *Russia* **57 C17** 62 30N 163 15 E
Parengarenga Harbour, *N.Z.* **118 A1** 34 31 S 173 0 E
Parent, *Canada* **128 C5** 47 55N 74 35W
Parent, L., *Canada* **128 C4** 48 31N 77 1W
Parentis-en-Born, *France* **24 D2** 44 21N 1 4W
Parepare, *Indonesia* **72 B1** 4 0 S 119 40 E
Parfino, *Russia* **50 D6** 57 59N 31 34 E
Pargo, Pta. do, *Madeira* **33 D2** 32 49N 17 17W
Parguba, *Russia* **48 B5** 62 20N 34 27 E
Paria, G. de, *Venezuela* **153 A5** 10 20N 62 0W
Paria, Pen. de, *Venezuela* **153 A5** 10 50N 62 30W
Pariaguán, *Venezuela* **153 B5** 8 51N 64 34W
Pariaman, *Indonesia* **74 C2** 0 47 S 100 11 E
Paricatuba, *Brazil* **153 D5** 4 26 S 61 53W
Paricutín, Cerro, *Mexico* **146 D4** 19 28N 102 15W
Parigi, *Java, Indonesia* **75 D3** 7 42 S 108 29 E
Parigi, *Sulawesi, Indonesia* **72 B2** 0 50 S 120 5 E
Parika, *Guyana* **153 B6** 6 50N 58 20W
Parikkala, *Finland* **50 B5** 61 33N 29 31 E
Parima, Serra, *Brazil* **153 C5** 2 30N 64 0W
Parinari, *Peru* **156 A3** 4 35 S 74 25W
Pariñas, Pta., *S. Amer.* **150 D2** 4 30 S 82 0W
Parincea, *Romania* **46 C8** 46 27N 27 9 E
Parîngul Mare, *Romania* **46 D4** 45 20N 23 37 E
Parintins, *Brazil* **153 D6** 2 40 S 56 50W
Paris, *Canada* **128 D3** 43 12N 80 25W
Paris, *France* **23 D9** 48 50N 2 20 E
Paris, *Idaho, U.S.A.* **142 E8** 42 14N 111 24W
Paris, *Ill., U.S.A.* **141 E9** 39 36N 87 42W
Paris, *Ky., U.S.A.* **141 F12** 38 13N 84 15W
Paris, *Mo., U.S.A.* **140 E5** 39 29N 92 0W
Paris, *Tenn., U.S.A.* **135 G1** 36 18N 88 19W
Paris, *Tex., U.S.A.* **139 J7** 33 40N 95 33W
Paris, Ville de □, *France* **23 D9** 48 50N 2 20 E
Parish, *U.S.A.* **137 C8** 43 25N 76 8W
Pariti, *Indonesia* **72 D2** 10 15 S 123 45 E
Park, *U.S.A.* **144 B4** 48 45N 122 18W
Park City, *U.S.A.* **142 F8** 40 39N 111 30W
Park Falls, *U.S.A.* **138 C9** 45 56N 90 27W
Park Forest, *U.S.A.* **141 C9** 41 29N 87 40W
Park Range, *U.S.A.* **142 G10** 40 0N 106 30W
Park Rapids, *U.S.A.* **138 B7** 46 55N 95 4W
Park Ridge, *U.S.A.* **141 B9** 42 2N 87 51W
Park River, *U.S.A.* **138 A6** 48 24N 97 45W
Park Rynie, *S. Africa* **105 E5** 30 25 S 30 45 E
Parkā Bandar, *Iran* **85 E8** 25 55N 59 35 E
Parkano, *Finland* **13 E20** 62 1N 23 0 E
Parkent, *Uzbekistan* **55 C4** 41 18N 69 40 E
Parker, *Ariz., U.S.A.* **145 L12** 34 9N 114 17W
Parker, *S. Dak., U.S.A.* **138 D6** 43 24N 97 8W
Parker Dam, *U.S.A.* **145 L12** 34 18N 114 8W
Parkersburg, *Iowa, U.S.A.* **140 B4** 42 35N 92 47W
Parkersburg, *W. Va., U.S.A.* **134 F5** 39 16N 81 34W
Parkerview, *Canada* **131 C8** 51 21N 103 18W
Parkes, *Australia* **117 B8** 33 9 S 148 11 E
Parkfield, *U.S.A.* **144 K6** 35 54N 120 26W
Parkhar, *Tajikistan* **55 E4** 37 30N 69 34 E
Parkland, *U.S.A.* **144 C4** 47 9N 122 26W
Parkside, *Canada* **131 C7** 53 10N 106 33W
Parkston, *U.S.A.* **138 D5** 43 24N 97 59W
Parksville, *Canada* **130 D4** 49 20N 124 21W
Parlakimidi, *India* **82 E7** 18 45N 84 5 E
Parli, *India* **82 E3** 18 50N 76 35 E
Parma, *Italy* **38 D7** 44 48N 10 20 E
Parma, *Idaho, U.S.A.* **142 E5** 43 47N 116 57W
Parma, *Ohio, U.S.A.* **136 E3** 41 23N 81 43W
Parma →, *Italy* **38 D7** 44 56N 10 26 E
Parnaguá, *Brazil* **154 D3** 10 10 S 44 38W
Parnaíba, *Piauí, Brazil* **154 B3** 2 54 S 41 47W
Parnaíba, *São Paulo, Brazil* **157 D7** 19 34 S 51 14W
Parnaíba →, *Brazil* **154 B3** 3 0 S 41 50W
Parnamirim, *Brazil* **154 C4** 8 5 S 39 34W
Parnarama, *Brazil* **154 C3** 5 31 S 43 6W
Parnassós, *Greece* **45 F4** 38 35N 22 30 E
Parnassus, *N.Z.* **119 C8** 42 42 S 173 23 E
Párnis, *Greece* **45 F5** 38 14N 23 45 E
Párnon Óros, *Greece* **45 G4** 37 15N 22 45 E
Parnu, *Estonia* **13 G21** 58 28N 24 33 E
Parola, *India* **82 D2** 20 47N 75 7 E
Paroo →, *Australia* **115 E3** 31 28 S 143 32 E
Páros, *Greece* **45 G7** 37 5N 25 12 E
Parowan, *U.S.A.* **143 H7** 37 51N 112 50W
Parpaillon, *France* **25 D10** 44 30N 6 40 E
Parral, *Chile* **158 D1** 36 10 S 71 52W
Parramatta, *Australia* **117 B9** 33 48 S 151 1 E
Parras, *Mexico* **146 B4** 25 30N 102 20W
Parrett →, *U.K.* **17 F5** 51 12N 3 1W
Parris I., *U.S.A.* **135 J5** 32 20N 80 41W
Parrsboro, *Canada* **129 C7** 45 30N 64 25W
Parry Is., *Canada* **124 B8** 77 0N 110 0W
Parry Sound, *Canada* **128 C3** 45 20N 80 0W
Parsberg, *Germany* **27 F7** 49 10N 11 43 E
Parseta →, *Poland* **47 A2** 54 11N 15 34 E
Parshall, *U.S.A.* **138 B3** 47 57N 102 8W
Parsnip →, *Canada* **130 B4** 55 10N 123 2W
Parsons, *U.S.A.* **139 G7** 37 20N 95 16W
Parsons Ra., *Australia* **114 A2** 13 30 S 135 15 E
Partabpur, *India* **82 E5** 20 0N 80 42 E
Partanna, *Italy* **40 E5** 37 43N 12 53 E
Parthenay, *France* **22 F6** 46 38N 0 16W
Partinico, *Italy* **40 D6** 38 3N 13 7 E
Partur, *India* **82 E3** 19 40N 76 14 E
Paru →, *Brazil* **153 D7** 1 33 S 52 38W
Parú →, *Venezuela* **152 C4** 4 20N 66 27W
Paru de Oeste →, *Brazil* **153 C6** 1 30N 56 0W
Parubcan, *Phil.* **70 E4** 13 43N 123 45 E
Parucito →, *Venezuela* **152 B4** 5 18N 65 59W
Parur, *India* **83 J3** 10 13N 76 14 E
Paruro, *Peru* **156 C3** 13 45 S 71 50W
Parvān □, *Afghan.* **79 B3** 35 0N 69 0 E
Parvatipuram, *India* **82 E6** 18 50N 83 25 E
Parys, *S. Africa* **104 D4** 26 52 S 27 29 E
Pas-de-Calais □, *France* **23 B9** 50 30N 2 10 E
Pasadena, *Calif., U.S.A.* **145 L8** 34 9N 118 9W
Pasadena, *Tex., U.S.A.* **139 L7** 29 43N 95 13W
Pasaje, *Ecuador* **152 D2** 3 23 S 79 50W
Pasaje →, *Argentina* **158 B3** 25 39 S 63 56W
Pasay, *Phil.* **70 D3** 14 33N 121 0 E
Pascagoula, *U.S.A.* **139 K10** 30 21N 88 33W
Pascagoula →, *U.S.A.* **139 K10** 30 23N 88 37W
Paşcani, *Romania* **46 B7** 47 14N 26 45 E
Pasco, *U.S.A.* **142 C4** 46 14N 119 6W
Pasco □, *Peru* **156 C2** 10 40 S 75 0W
Pasco, Cerro de, *Peru* **156 C2** 10 45 S 76 10W
Pascua, I. de, *Pac. Oc.* **123 K17** 27 0 S 109 0W
Pasewalk, *Germany* **26 B10** 53 30N 13 58 E
Pasfield L., *Canada* **131 B7** 58 24N 105 20W
Pasha →, *Russia* **50 B7** 60 29N 32 55 E
Pashiwari, *Pakistan* **81 B6** 34 40N 75 10 E
Pashiya, *Russia* **54 B7** 58 33N 58 26 E
Pashmakli = Smolyan, *Bulgaria* **43 F9** 41 36N 24 38 E
Pasighat, *India* **78 A5** 28 4N 95 21 E
Pasinler, *Turkey* **89 C9** 39 59N 41 41 E
Pasir Mas, *Malaysia* **74 A2** 6 2N 102 8 E
Pasirian, *Indonesia* **75 D4** 8 13 S 113 8 E
Paskūh, *Iran* **85 E9** 27 34N 61 39 E
Pasłeka →, *Poland* **47 A6** 54 26N 19 46 E
Pasley, C., *Australia* **113 F3** 33 52 S 123 35 E
Pašman, *Croatia* **39 E12** 43 58N 15 20 E
Pasmore →, *Australia* **116 A3** 31 5 S 139 49 E
Pasni, *Pakistan* **79 D1** 25 15N 63 27 E
Paso Cantinela, *Mexico* **145 N11** 32 33N 115 47W
Paso de Indios, *Argentina* **160 B3** 43 55 S 69 0W
Paso de los Libres, *Argentina* **158 B4** 29 44 S 57 10W
Paso de los Toros, *Uruguay* **158 C4** 32 45 S 56 30W
Paso Flores, *Argentina* **160 B2** 40 35 S 70 38W
Paso Robles, *U.S.A.* **143 J3** 35 38N 120 41W
Pasorapa, *Bolivia* **157 D5** 18 16 S 64 37W
Paspébiac, *Canada* **129 C6** 48 3N 65 17W
Pasrur, *Pakistan* **80 C6** 32 16N 74 43 E
Passage West, *Ireland* **19 E3** 51 52N 8 21W
Passaic, *U.S.A.* **137 F10** 40 51N 74 7W
Passau, *Germany* **27 G9** 48 34N 13 28 E
Passendale, *Belgium* **21 G2** 50 54N 3 2 E
Passero, C., *Italy* **41 F8** 36 41N 15 10 E
Passi, *Phil.* **71 F4** 11 6N 122 38 E
Passo Fundo, *Brazil* **159 B5** 28 10 S 52 20W
Passos, *Brazil* **155 F2** 20 45 S 46 37W
Passow, *Germany* **26 B10** 53 8N 14 6 E
Passwang, *Switz.* **28 B5** 47 22N 7 41 E
Passy, *France* **25 C10** 45 55N 6 41 E
Pastavy, *Belarus* **13 J22** 55 4N 26 50 E
Pastaza □, *Ecuador* **152 D2** 2 0 S 77 0W
Pastaza →, *Peru* **152 D2** 4 50 S 76 52W
Pastęk, *Poland* **47 A6** 54 3N 19 41 E
Pasto, *Colombia* **152 C2** 1 13N 77 17W
Pastos Bons, *Brazil* **154 C3** 6 36 S 44 5W
Pastrana, *Spain* **34 E2** 40 27N 2 53W
Pasuquin, *Phil.* **70 B3** 18 20N 120 37 E
Pasuruan, *Indonesia* **75 D4** 7 40 S 112 44 E
Pasym, *Poland* **47 B7** 53 48N 20 49 E
Pásztó, *Hungary* **31 D12** 47 52N 19 43 E
Patagonia, *Argentina* **160 C2** 45 0 S 69 0W
Patagonia, *U.S.A.* **143 L8** 31 33N 110 45W
Patambar, *Iran* **85 D9** 29 45N 60 17 E
Patan, *Gujarat, India* **82 F1** 17 22N 73 57 E
Patan, *Maharashtra, India* **80 H5** 23 54N 72 14 E
Patani, *Indonesia* **72 A3** 0 20N 128 50 E
Pataudi, *India* **80 E7** 28 18N 76 48 E
Patay, *France* **23 D8** 48 2N 1 40 E
Patchewollock, *Australia* **116 C5** 35 22 S 142 12 E
Patchogue, *U.S.A.* **137 F11** 40 46N 73 1W
Patea, *N.Z.* **118 F3** 39 45 S 174 30 E
Pategi, *Nigeria* **101 D6** 8 50N 5 45 E
Patensie, *S. Africa* **104 E3** 33 46 S 24 49 E
Paternò, *Italy* **41 E7** 37 34N 14 54 E
Pateros, *U.S.A.* **142 B4** 48 3N 119 54W
Paterson, *Australia* **117 B9** 32 35 S 151 36 E
Paterson, *U.S.A.* **137 F10** 40 55N 74 11W
Paterson Inlet, *N.Z.* **119 G3** 46 56 S 168 12 E
Paterson Ra., *Australia* **112 D3** 21 45 S 122 10 E
Paterswolde, *Neths.* **20 B9** 53 9N 6 34 E
Pathankot, *India* **80 C6** 32 18N 75 45 E
Patharghata, *Bangla.* **78 D2** 22 2N 89 58 E
Pathfinder Reservoir, *U.S.A.* **142 E10** 42 28N 106 51W
Pathiu, *Thailand* **77 G2** 10 42N 99 19 E
Pathum Thani, *Thailand* **76 E3** 14 1N 100 32 E
Pati, *Indonesia* **75 D4** 6 45 S 111 1 E
Pati Pt., *Guam* **121 R15** 13 40N 144 50 E
Patía, *Colombia* **152 C2** 2 4N 77 4W
Patía →, *Colombia* **152 C2** 2 13N 78 40W
Patiala, *India* **80 D7** 30 23N 76 26 E
Patine Kouka, *Senegal* **100 C2** 12 45N 13 45W
Pativilca, *Peru* **156 C2** 10 42 S 77 48W
Patkai Bum, *India* **78 B5** 27 0N 95 30 E
Pátmos, *Greece* **45 G8** 37 21N 26 36 E
Patna, *India* **81 G11** 25 35N 85 12 E
Patnongon, *Phil.* **71 F3** 10 55N 122 0 E
Patnos, *Turkey* **89 C10** 39 13N 42 51 E
Patonga, *Uganda* **106 B3** 2 45N 33 15 E
Patos, *Brazil* **154 C4** 6 55 S 37 16W
Patos, L. dos, *Brazil* **159 C5** 31 20 S 51 0W
Patos de Minas, *Brazil* **155 E2** 18 35 S 46 32W
Patosi, *Albania* **44 D1** 40 42N 19 38 E
Patquía, *Argentina* **158 C2** 30 2 S 66 55W
Pátrai, *Greece* **45 F3** 38 14N 21 47 E
Pátraikós Kólpos, *Greece* **45 F3** 38 17N 21 30 E
Patras = Pátrai, *Greece* **45 F3** 38 14N 21 47 E
Patricio Lynch, I., *Chile* **160 C1** 48 35 S 75 30W
Patrocínio, *Brazil* **155 E2** 18 57 S 47 0W
Patta, *Kenya* **106 C5** 2 10 S 41 0 E
Pattada, *Italy* **40 B2** 40 35N 9 6 E
Pattanapuram, *India* **83 K3** 9 6N 76 50 E
Pattani, *Thailand* **77 J3** 6 48N 101 15 E
Patten, *U.S.A.* **129 C6** 46 0N 68 38W
Patterson, *Calif., U.S.A.* **144 H5** 37 28N 121 8W
Patterson, *La., U.S.A.* **139 L9** 29 42N 91 18W
Patterson, Mt., *U.S.A.* **144 G7** 38 29N 119 20W
Patteson, Passage, *Vanuatu* **121 E6** 15 26 S 168 12 E
Patti, *India* **80 D6** 31 17N 74 54 E
Patti, *Italy* **41 D7** 38 8N 14 58 E
Pattoki, *Pakistan* **80 D5** 31 5N 73 52 E
Patton, *U.S.A.* **136 F6** 40 38N 78 39W
Pattonsburg, *U.S.A.* **140 D2** 40 3N 94 8W
Pattukkattai, *India* **83 J4** 10 25N 79 20 E
Patu, *Brazil* **154 C4** 6 6 S 37 38W
Patuakhali, *Bangla.* **78 D3** 22 20N 90 25 E
Patuca →, *Honduras* **148 C3** 15 50N 84 18W
Patuca, Punta, *Honduras* **148 C3** 15 49N 84 14W
Pâturages, *Belgium* **21 H3** 50 25N 3 52 E
Pátzcuaro, *Mexico* **146 D4** 19 30N 101 40W
Pau, *France* **24 E3** 43 19N 0 25W
Pau, Gave de →, *France* **24 E2** 43 33N 1 12W
Pau d' Arco, *Brazil* **154 C2** 7 30 S 49 22W
Pau dos Ferros, *Brazil* **154 C4** 6 7 S 38 10W
Paucartambo, *Peru* **156 C3** 13 19 S 71 35W
Pauillac, *France* **24 C3** 45 11N 0 46W
Pauini, *Brazil* **156 B4** 7 40 S 66 58W
Pauini →, *Brazil* **153 D5** 1 42 S 62 50W
Pauk, *Burma* **78 E5** 21 27N 94 30 E
Paul I., *Canada* **129 A7** 56 30N 61 20W
Paul Isnard, *Fr. Guiana* **153 C7** 4 47N 54 1W
Paulding, *U.S.A.* **141 C12** 41 8N 84 35W
Paulhan, *France* **24 E7** 43 33N 3 28 E
Paulis = Isiro, *Zaïre* **106 B2** 2 53N 27 40 E
Paulista, *Brazil* **154 C5** 7 57 S 34 53W
Paulistana, *Brazil* **154 C3** 8 9 S 41 9W
Paullina, *U.S.A.* **138 D7** 42 59N 95 41W
Paulo Afonso, *Brazil* **154 C4** 9 21 S 38 15W
Paulo de Faria, *Brazil* **155 F2** 20 2 S 49 24W
Paulpietersburg, *S. Africa* **105 D5** 27 23 S 30 50 E
Pauls Valley, *U.S.A.* **139 H6** 34 44N 97 13W
Pauma Valley, *U.S.A.* **145 M10** 33 16N 116 58W
Paungde, *Burma* **78 F5** 18 29N 95 30 E
Pauni, *India* **82 D4** 20 48N 79 40 E
Pausa, *Peru* **156 D3** 15 16 S 73 22W
Pauto →, *Colombia* **152 B3** 5 9N 70 55W
Pāveh, *Iran* **89 E12** 35 3N 46 22 E
Pavelets, *Russia* **52 D4** 53 49N 39 14 E
Pavia, *Italy* **38 C6** 45 7N 9 8 E
Pāvilosta, *Latvia* **13 H19** 56 53N 21 14 E
Pavlikeni, *Bulgaria* **43 D10** 43 14N 25 20 E
Pavlodar, *Kazakstan* **56 D8** 52 33N 77 0 E
Pavlograd = Pavlohrad, *Ukraine* **51 H8** 48 30N 35 52 E
Pavlohrad, *Ukraine* **51 H8** 48 30N 35 52 E
Pavlovo, *Oka, Russia* **52 C6** 55 58N 43 5 E
Pavlovo, *Sakha, Russia* **57 C12** 63 5N 115 25 E
Pavlovsk, *Russia* **52 E5** 50 26N 40 5 E
Pavlovskaya, *Russia* **53 G4** 46 17N 39 47 E
Pavlovskiy-Posad, *Russia* **52 C4** 55 47N 38 42 E
Pavullo nel Frignano, *Italy* **38 D7** 44 20N 10 50 E
Pavuvu, *Solomon Is.* **121 M10** 9 4 S 159 8 E
Paw Paw, *U.S.A.* **141 B11** 42 13N 85 53W
Pawahku, *Burma* **78 B7** 26 11N 98 40 E
Pawan →, *Indonesia* **75 C4** 1 55 S 110 0 E
Pawhuska, *U.S.A.* **139 G6** 36 40N 96 20W
Pawling, *U.S.A.* **137 E11** 41 34N 73 36W
Pawnee, *Ill., U.S.A.* **140 E7** 39 36N 89 35W
Pawnee, *Okla., U.S.A.* **139 G6** 36 20N 96 48W
Pawnee City, *U.S.A.* **138 E6** 40 7N 96 9W
Pawpaw, *U.S.A.* **140 C8** 41 41N 88 59W
Pawtucket, *U.S.A.* **137 E13** 41 53N 71 23W
Paximádhia, *Greece* **32 D6** 35 0N 24 35 E
Paxoí, *Greece* **44 E2** 39 14N 20 12 E
Paxton, *Ill., U.S.A.* **141 D8** 40 27N 88 6W
Paxton, *Nebr., U.S.A.* **138 E4** 41 7N 101 21W
Payakumbuh, *Indonesia* **74 C2** 0 20 S 100 35 E
Payerne, *Switz.* **28 C3** 46 49N 6 56 E
Payette, *U.S.A.* **142 D5** 44 5N 116 56W
Paymogo, *Spain* **37 H3** 37 44N 7 21W
Payne, *U.S.A.* **141 C12** 41 5N 84 44W
Payne Bay = Kangirsuk, *Canada* **127 B13** 60 0N 70 0W
Paynes Find, *Australia* **113 E2** 29 15 S 117 42 E
Paynesville, *Liberia* **100 D2** 6 20N 10 45W
Paynesville, *U.S.A.* **138 C7** 45 23N 94 43W
Paysandú, *Uruguay* **158 C4** 32 19 S 58 8W
Payson, *Ariz., U.S.A.* **143 J8** 34 14N 111 20W
Payson, *Utah, U.S.A.* **142 F8** 40 3N 111 44W
Paz →, *Guatemala* **148 D1** 13 44N 90 10W
Paz, B. la, *Mexico* **146 C2** 24 15N 110 25W
Pāzanān, *Iran* **85 D6** 30 35N 49 59 E
Pazar, *Turkey* **89 B9** 41 10N 40 50 E
Pazarcık, *Turkey* **88 D7** 37 30N 37 17 E
Pazardzhik, *Bulgaria* **43 E9** 42 12N 24 20 E
Pazaryolu, *Turkey* **89 B9** 40 21N 40 47 E
Pazin, *Croatia* **39 C10** 45 14N 13 56 E
Pazña, *Bolivia* **156 D4** 18 36 S 66 55W
Pčinja →, *Macedonia* **42 F6** 41 50N 21 45 E
Pe Ell, *U.S.A.* **144 D3** 46 34N 123 18W
Peabody, *U.S.A.* **137 D14** 42 31N 70 56W
Peace →, *Canada* **130 B6** 59 0N 111 25W
Peace Point, *Canada* **130 B6** 59 7N 112 27W
Peace River, *Canada* **130 B5** 56 15N 117 18W
Peach Springs, *U.S.A.* **143 J7** 35 32N 113 25W
Peak, The = Kinder Scout, *U.K.* **16 D6** 53 24N 1 52W
Peak Downs, *Australia* **114 C4** 22 55 S 148 5 E
Peak Downs Mine, *Australia* **114 C4** 22 17 S 148 11 E
Peak Hill, *N.S.W., Australia* **117 B8** 32 47 S 148 11 E
Peak Hill, *W. Austral., Australia* **113 E2** 25 35 S 118 43 E
Peak Ra., *Australia* **114 C4** 22 50 S 148 20 E
Peake, *Australia* **116 C3** 35 25 S 139 55 E
Peake Cr. →, *Australia* **115 D2** 28 2 S 136 7 E
Peale, Mt., *U.S.A.* **143 G9** 38 26N 109 14W
Pearblossom, *U.S.A.* **145 L9** 34 30N 117 55W
Pearl, *U.S.A.* **140 E6** 39 28N 90 38W
Pearl →, *U.S.A.* **139 K10** 30 11N 89 32W
Pearl Banks, *Sri Lanka* **83 K4** 8 45N 79 45 E
Pearl City, *Hawaii, U.S.A.* **132 H16** 21 24N 157 59W
Pearl City, *Ill., U.S.A.* **140 B7** 42 16N 89 50W
Pearsall, *U.S.A.* **139 L5** 28 54N 99 6W
Pearse I., *Canada* **130 C2** 54 52N 130 14W
Peary Land, *Greenland* **6 A6** 82 40N 33 0W
Pease →, *U.S.A.* **139 H5** 34 12N 99 2W
Pebane, *Mozam.* **107 F4** 17 10 S 38 8 E
Pebas, *Peru* **152 D3** 3 10 S 71 46W
Pebble, I., *Falk. Is.* **160 D5** 51 20 S 59 40W
Pebble Beach, *U.S.A.* **144 J5** 36 34N 121 57W
Peć, *Serbia, Yug.* **42 E5** 42 40N 20 17 E
Peçanha, *Brazil* **155 E3** 18 33 S 42 34W
Pecatonica, *U.S.A.* **140 B7** 42 19N 89 22W
Pecatonica →, *U.S.A.* **140 B7** 42 26N 89 12W
Péccioli, *Italy* **38 E7** 43 33N 10 43 E
Pechea, *Romania* **46 D8** 45 36N 27 49 E
Pechenga, *Russia* **48 A5** 69 29N 31 4 E
Pechenizhyn, *Ukraine* **51 H3** 48 30N 24 48 E
Pechiguera, Pta., *Canary Is.* **33 F6** 28 51N 13 53W
Pechnezhskoye Vdkhr., *Ukraine* **51 G9** 50 5N 36 54 E
Pechora →, *Russia* **48 A9** 68 13N 54 15 E
Pechorskaya Guba, *Russia* **48 A9** 68 40N 54 0 E
Pecica, *Romania* **46 C2** 46 10N 21 3 E
Pečka, *Serbia, Yug.* **42 C4** 44 18N 19 33 E
Pécora, C., *Italy* **40 C1** 39 27N 8 23 E
Pečory, *Russia* **13 H22** 57 48N 27 40 E
Pecos, *U.S.A.* **139 K3** 31 26N 103 30W
Pecos →, *U.S.A.* **139 L3** 29 42N 101 22W
Pécs, *Hungary* **31 E11** 46 5N 18 15 E
Peddapalli, *India* **82 E4** 18 40N 79 24 E
Peddapuram, *India* **82 F6** 17 6N 82 8 E
Pedder, L., *Australia* **114 G4** 42 55 S 146 10 E
Peddie, *S. Africa* **105 E4** 33 14 S 27 7 E
Pédernales, *Dom. Rep.* **149 C5** 18 2N 71 44W
Pedieos →, *Cyprus* **32 D12** 35 10N 33 54 E
Pedirka, *Australia* **115 D2** 26 40 S 135 14 E
Pedra Azul, *Brazil* **155 E3** 16 2 S 41 17W
Pedra Grande, Recifes de, *Brazil* **155 E4** 17 45 S 38 58W
Pedras Negras, *Brazil* **157 C5** 12 51 S 62 54W
Pedreiras, *Brazil* **154 B3** 4 32 S 44 40W
Pedro Afonso, *Brazil* **154 C2** 9 0 S 48 10W
Pedro Cays, *Jamaica* **148 C4** 17 5N 77 48W
Pedro Chico, *Colombia* **152 C3** 1 4N 70 25W
Pedro de Valdivia, *Chile* **158 A2** 22 55 S 69 38W
Pedro Juan Caballero, *Paraguay* **159 A4** 22 30 S 55 40W
Pedro Muñoz, *Spain* **35 F2** 39 25N 2 56W
Pedrógão Grande, *Portugal* **36 F2** 39 55N 8 9W
Peebinga, *Australia* **116 C4** 34 52 S 140 57 E
Peebles, *U.K.* **18 F5** 55 40N 3 11W
Peebles, *U.S.A.* **141 F13** 38 57N 83 24W
Peekskill, *U.S.A.* **137 E11** 41 17N 73 55W
Peel, *U.K.* **16 C3** 54 13N 4 40W
Peel →, *Australia* **117 A9** 30 50 S 150 29 E
Peel →, *Canada* **126 B6** 67 0N 135 0W
Peelwood, *Australia* **117 C8** 34 7 S 149 27 E
Peene →, *Germany* **26 A9** 54 9N 13 46 E
Peera Peera Poolanna L., *Australia* **115 D2** 26 30 S 138 0 E
Peers, *Canada* **130 C5** 53 40N 116 0W
Pegasus Bay, *N.Z.* **119 D8** 43 20 S 173 10 E
Peggau, *Austria* **30 D8** 47 12N 15 21 E
Pegnitz, *Germany* **27 F7** 49 44N 11 31 E
Pegnitz →, *Germany* **27 F6** 49 30N 10 59 E

250 Platte

Platte →, Nebr., U.S.A. 124 E10 41 4N 95 53W
Platte City, U.S.A. 140 E2 39 22N 94 47W
Platteville, Colo., U.S.A. 138 E2 40 13N 104 49W
Platteville, Wis., U.S.A. 140 B6 42 44N 90 29W
Plattling, Germany 27 G8 48 46N 12 53 E
Plattsburg, U.S.A. 140 E2 39 34N 94 27W
Plattsburgh, U.S.A. 137 B11 44 42N 73 28W
Plattsmouth, U.S.A. 138 E7 41 1N 95 53W
Plau, Germany 26 B8 53 27N 12 15 E
Plauen, Germany 26 E8 50 30N 12 8 E
Plav, Montenegro, Yug. 42 E4 42 38N 19 57 E
Plavinas, Latvia 13 H21 56 35N 25 46 E
Plavnica, Montenegro, Yug. 42 E4 42 20N 19 13 E
Plavsk, Russia 52 D3 53 40N 37 18 E
Playa Blanca, Canary Is. 33 F6 28 55N 13 37W
Playa Blanca Sur, Canary Is. 33 F6 28 51N 13 50W
Playa de las Americas, Canary Is. 33 F3 28 5N 16 43W
Playa de Mogán, Canary Is. 33 G4 27 48N 15 47W
Playa del Inglés, Canary Is. 33 G4 27 45N 15 33W
Playa Esmerelda, Canary Is. 33 F5 28 8N 14 16W
Playgreen L., Canada 131 C9 54 0N 98 15W
Pleasant Bay, Canada 129 C7 46 51N 60 48W
Pleasant Hill, Calif., U.S.A. 144 H4 37 57N 122 4W
Pleasant Hill, Ill., U.S.A. 140 E6 39 27N 90 52W
Pleasant Hill, Mo., U.S.A. 140 F2 38 47N 94 16W
Pleasant Hills, Australia 117 C7 35 28 S 146 50 E
Pleasant Pt., N.Z. 119 E6 44 16 S 171 9 E
Pleasanton, U.S.A. 139 L5 28 58N 98 29W
Pleasantville, Iowa, U.S.A. 140 C3 41 23N 93 18W
Pleasantville, N.J., U.S.A. 134 F8 39 24N 74 32W
Pleasure Ridge Park, U.S.A. 141 F11 38 9N 85 50W
Pléaux, France 24 C6 45 8N 2 13 E
Pleiku, Vietnam 76 F7 13 57N 108 0 E
Plélan-le-Grand, France 22 D4 48 0N 2 7W
Plémet-la-Pierre, France 22 D4 48 11N 2 36W
Pléneuf-Val-André, France 22 D4 48 35N 2 32W
Pleniţa, Romania 46 E4 44 14N 23 10 E
Plenty →, Australia 114 C2 23 25 S 136 31 E
Plenty, B. of, N.Z. 118 D6 37 45 S 177 0 E
Plentywood, U.S.A. 138 A2 48 47N 104 34W
Plesetsk, Russia 48 B7 62 43N 40 20 E
Plessisville, Canada 129 C5 46 14N 71 47W
Plestin-les-Grèves, France 22 D3 48 40N 3 39W
Pleszew, Poland 47 D4 51 53N 17 47 E
Pleternica, Croatia 42 B2 45 17N 17 48 E
Pletipi L., Canada 129 B5 51 44N 70 6W
Pleven, Bulgaria 43 D9 43 26N 24 37 E
Plevlja, Montenegro, Yug. 42 D4 43 21N 19 21 E
Ploče = Kardeljovo, Croatia 42 D2 43 4N 17 26 E
Plock, Poland 47 C6 52 32N 19 40 E
Plock □, Poland 47 C6 52 30N 19 45 E
Plöcken Passo, Italy 39 B9 46 37N 12 57 E
Ploegsteert, Belgium 21 G1 50 44N 2 53 E
Ploemeur, France 22 E3 47 44N 3 26W
Ploërmel, France 22 E4 47 55N 2 26W
Ploieşti, Romania 46 E7 44 57N 26 5 E
Plomárion, Greece 45 F8 38 58N 26 24 E
Plombières-les-Bains, France 23 E13 47 58N 6 27 E
Plomin, Croatia 39 C11 45 8N 14 10 E
Plön, Germany 26 A6 54 9N 10 24 E
Plöner See, Germany 26 A6 54 10N 10 22 E
Plonge, Lac la, Canada 131 B7 55 8N 107 20W
Płońsk, Poland 47 C7 52 37N 20 21 E
Płoty, Poland 47 B2 53 48N 15 18 E
Plouaret, France 22 D3 48 37N 3 28W
Plouay, France 22 E3 47 55N 3 21W
Ploučnice →, Czech. 30 A7 50 46N 14 13 E
Ploudalmézeau, France 22 D2 48 34N 4 41W
Plougasnou, France 22 D3 48 42N 3 49W
Plouha, France 22 D4 48 41N 2 57W
Plouhinec, France 22 E2 48 0N 4 29W
Plovdiv, Bulgaria 43 E9 42 8N 24 44 E
Plum, U.S.A. 136 F5 40 29N 79 47W
Plum I., U.S.A. 137 E12 41 11N 72 12W
Plumas, U.S.A. 144 F7 39 45N 119 4W
Plummer, U.S.A. 142 C5 47 20N 116 53W
Plumtree, Zimbabwe 107 G2 20 27 S 27 55 E
Plunge, Lithuania 13 J19 55 53N 21 59 E
Pluvigner, France 22 E3 47 46N 3 1W
Plymouth, U.K. 17 G3 50 22N 4 10W
Plymouth, Calif., U.S.A. 144 G6 38 29N 120 51W
Plymouth, Ill., U.S.A. 140 D6 40 18N 90 58W
Plymouth, Ind., U.S.A. 141 C10 41 21N 86 19W
Plymouth, Mass., U.S.A. 137 E14 41 57N 70 40W
Plymouth, N.C., U.S.A. 135 H7 35 52N 76 43W
Plymouth, N.H., U.S.A. 137 C13 43 46N 71 41W
Plymouth, Pa., U.S.A. 137 E9 41 14N 75 57W
Plymouth, Wis., U.S.A. 134 D2 43 45N 87 59W
Plynlimon = Pumlumon Fawr, U.K. 17 E4 52 28N 3 46W
Plyusa, Russia 50 C5 58 28N 29 27 E
Plyusa →, Russia 50 C5 59 4N 28 6 E
Plyussa = Plyusa, Russia 50 C5 58 28N 29 27 E
Plyussa → = Plyusa →, Russia 50 C5 59 4N 28 6 E
Plzeň, Czech. 30 B6 49 45N 13 22 E
Pniewy, Poland 47 C3 52 31N 16 16 E
Pô, Burkina Faso 101 C4 11 14N 1 5W
Po →, Italy 39 D9 44 57N 12 4 E
Po, Foci del, Italy 39 D9 44 55N 12 30 E
Po Hai = Bo Hai, China 67 E10 39 0N 119 0 E
Po Hai, China 58 F15 38 30N 119 0 E
Pobé, Benin 101 D5 7 0N 2 56 E
Pobeda, Russia 57 C15 65 12N 146 12 E
Pobedino, Russia 57 E15 49 51N 142 49 E
Pobedy Pik, Kyrgyzstan 56 E8 40 45N 79 58 E
Pobiedziska, Poland 47 C4 52 29N 17 11 E
Pobla de Segur, Spain 34 C5 42 15N 0 58 E
Pobladura de Valle, Spain 36 C5 42 6N 5 44W
Pocahontas, Ark., U.S.A. 139 G9 36 16N 90 58W
Pocahontas, Ill., U.S.A. 140 F7 38 50N 89 33W
Pocahontas, Iowa, U.S.A. 140 B2 42 44N 94 40W
Pocatello, U.S.A. 142 E7 42 52N 112 27W
Počátky, Czech. 30 B8 49 15N 15 14 E
Pochep, Russia 51 F7 52 58N 33 29 E
Pochinki, Russia 52 C7 54 41N 44 59 E
Pochinok, Russia 50 E7 54 28N 32 29 E
Pöchlarn, Austria 30 C8 48 12N 15 12 E
Pochutla, Mexico 147 D5 15 50N 96 31W
Poci, Venezuela 153 B5 5 57N 61 29W
Pocinhos, Brazil 154 C4 7 4 S 36 3W
Pocito Casas, Mexico 146 B2 28 32N 111 6W
Poções, Brazil 155 D3 14 31 S 40 21W
Pocomoke City, U.S.A. 134 F8 38 5N 75 34W
Poconé, Brazil 157 D6 16 15 S 56 37W
Poços de Caldas, Brazil 159 A6 21 50 S 46 33W
Poddebice, Poland 47 D5 51 54N 18 58 E
Poděbrady, Czech. 30 A8 50 9N 15 8 E
Podensac, France 24 D3 44 40N 0 22W
Podgorač, Croatia 42 B3 45 27N 18 13 E
Podgorica, Montenegro, Yug. 42 E4 42 30N 19 19 E
Podilska Vysochyna, Ukraine 51 H4 49 0N 28 0 E
Podkamennaya Tunguska →, Russia 57 C10 61 50N 90 13 E
Podlapac, Croatia 39 D12 44 37N 15 47 E
Podmokly, Czech. 30 A7 50 48N 14 10 E
Podoleni, Romania 46 C7 46 46N 26 39 E
Podolínec, Slovak Rep. 31 B13 49 16N 20 31 E
Podolsk, Russia 52 C3 55 25N 37 30 E
Podor, Senegal 100 B1 16 40N 15 2W
Podporozhy, Russia 50 B8 60 55N 34 2 E
Podravska Slatina, Croatia 42 B2 45 42N 17 45 E
Podu Turcului, Romania 46 C8 46 11N 27 25 E
Podujevo, Serbia, Yug. 42 E6 42 54N 21 10 E
Poel, Germany 26 B7 54 0N 11 25 E
Pofadder, S. Africa 104 D2 29 10 S 19 22 E
Pogamasing, Canada 128 C3 46 55N 81 50W
Poggiardo, Italy 41 B11 40 3N 18 23 E
Poggibonsi, Italy 39 E8 43 28N 11 9 E
Pogoanele, Romania 46 E8 44 55N 27 0 E
Pogorzela, Poland 47 D4 51 50N 17 12 E
Pogoso, Zaïre 103 D3 6 46 S 17 12 E
Pogradeci, Albania 44 D2 40 57N 20 37 E
Pogranitšnyi, Russia 60 B5 44 25N 131 24 E
Poh, Indonesia 72 B2 0 46 S 122 51 E
Pohang, S. Korea 67 F15 36 1N 129 23 E
Pohjanmaa, Finland 12 E20 62 58N 22 50 E
Pohnpei, Pac. Oc. 122 G7 6 55N 158 10 E
Pohorelá, Slovak Rep. 31 C13 48 50N 20 2 E
Pohořelice, Czech. 31 C9 48 59N 16 31 E
Pohorje, Slovenia 39 B12 46 30N 15 20 E
Poiana Mare, Romania 46 F4 43 57N 23 5 E
Poiana Ruscăi, Munţii, Romania 46 D3 45 45N 22 25 E
Poindimié, N. Cal. 121 T19 20 56 S 165 20 E
Poinsett, C., Antarctica 7 C8 65 42 S 113 18 E
Point Edward, Canada 128 D3 43 0N 82 30W
Point Pass, Australia 116 C3 34 5 S 139 5 E
Point Pedro, Sri Lanka 83 K5 9 50N 80 15 E
Point Pleasant, N.J., U.S.A. 137 F10 40 5N 74 4W
Point Pleasant, W. Va., U.S.A. 134 F4 38 51N 82 8W
Pointe-à-la Hache, U.S.A. 139 L10 29 35N 89 55W
Pointe-à-Pitre, Guadeloupe 149 C7 16 10N 61 30W
Pointe Noire, Congo 103 C2 4 48 S 11 53 E
Poirino, Italy 38 D4 44 56N 7 48 E
Poisonbush Ra., Australia 112 D3 22 30 S 121 30 E
Poissy, France 23 D9 48 55N 2 2 E
Poitiers, France 22 F7 46 35N 0 20 E
Poitou, France 24 B3 46 40N 0 10W
Poitou, Seuil du, France 24 B4 46 20N 0 10 E
Poix de Picardie, France 23 C8 49 47N 1 58 E
Poix-Terron, France 23 C11 49 38N 4 38 E
Pojoaque Valley, U.S.A. 143 J11 35 54N 106 1W
Pokataroo, Australia 115 D4 29 30 S 148 36 E
Pokhvistnevo, Russia 52 D11 53 36N 52 0 E
Poko, Sudan 95 F3 5 41N 31 55 E
Poko, Zaïre 106 B2 3 7N 26 52 E
Pokrov, Russia 52 C4 55 55N 39 7 E
Pokrovka, Kyrgyzstan 55 B9 42 20N 78 0 E
Pokrovsk = Engels, Russia 52 E8 51 28N 46 6 E
Pokrovsk, Russia 57 C13 61 29N 129 0 E
Pokrovsk-Uralskiy, Russia 54 A7 60 10N 59 49 E
Pokrovskoye, Russia 53 G4 47 25N 38 54 E
Pol, Spain 36 B3 43 9N 7 20W
Pola = Pula, Croatia 39 D10 44 54N 13 57 E
Pola, Russia 50 D7 57 55N 32 0 E
Pola de Allande, Spain 36 B4 43 16N 6 37W
Pola de Lena, Spain 36 B5 43 10N 5 49W
Pola de Siero, Spain 36 B5 43 24N 5 39W
Pola de Somiedo, Spain 36 B4 43 5N 6 15W
Polacca, U.S.A. 143 J8 35 50N 110 23W
Polan, Iran 85 E9 25 30N 61 10 E
Poland ■, Europe 47 D7 52 0N 20 0 E
Polanów, Poland 47 A3 54 7N 16 41 E
Polatlı, Turkey 88 C5 39 36N 32 9 E
Polatsk, Belarus 50 E5 55 30N 28 50 E
Polcura, Chile 158 D1 37 17 S 71 43W
Połczyn Zdrój, Poland 47 B3 53 47N 16 5 E
Polden Hills, U.K. 17 F5 51 7N 2 50W
Polessk, Russia 13 J19 54 50N 21 8 E
Polesye = Pripet Marshes, Europe 51 F5 52 10N 28 10 E
Polevskoy, Russia 54 C8 56 26N 60 11 E
Polgar, Hungary 31 D14 47 54N 21 6 E
Pŏlgyo-ri, S. Korea 67 G14 34 51N 127 21 E
Poli, Cameroon 102 A2 8 34N 13 15 E
Políaigos, Greece 45 H6 36 45N 24 38 E
Policastro, G. di, Italy 41 C8 40 0N 15 35 E
Police, Poland 47 B1 53 33N 14 33 E
Polička, Czech. 31 B9 49 43N 16 15 E
Polignano a Mare, Italy 41 A10 41 0N 17 13 E
Poligny, France 23 F12 46 50N 5 42 E
Políkhnitas, Greece 45 E8 39 4N 26 10 E
Polillo, Phil. 70 D3 14 43N 121 56 E
Polillo Is., Phil. 70 D4 14 56N 122 0 E
Polillo Strait, Phil. 70 D3 14 44N 121 51 E
Polis, Cyprus 32 D11 35 2N 32 26 E
Polístena, Italy 41 D9 38 24N 16 4 E
Políyiros, Greece 44 D5 40 23N 23 25 E
Polk, U.S.A. 136 E5 41 22N 79 56W
Polkowice, Poland 47 D3 51 29N 16 3 E
Polla, Italy 41 B8 40 31N 15 29 E
Pollachi, India 83 J3 10 35N 77 0 E
Pollensa, Spain 33 B10 39 54N 3 1 E
Pollensa, B. de, Spain 33 B10 39 53N 3 8 E
Póllica, Italy 41 B8 40 11N 15 3 E
Pollino, Mte., Italy 41 C9 39 55N 16 11 E
Pollock, U.S.A. 138 C4 45 55N 100 17W
Polna, Russia 50 C5 58 31N 28 5 E
Polnovat, Russia 56 C7 63 50N 65 54 E
Polo, Ill., U.S.A. 140 C7 41 59N 89 35W
Polo, Mo., U.S.A. 140 E2 39 33N 94 3W
Pology, Ukraine 51 J9 47 29N 36 15 E
Polonne, Ukraine 51 G4 50 6N 27 30 E
Polonnoye = Polonne, Ukraine 51 G4 50 6N 27 30 E
Polski Trŭmbesh, Bulgaria 43 D10 43 20N 25 38 E
Polsko Kosovo, Bulgaria 43 D10 43 23N 25 38 E
Polson, U.S.A. 142 C6 47 41N 114 9W
Poltava, Ukraine 51 H8 49 35N 34 35 E
Põltsamaa, Estonia 13 G21 58 41N 25 58 E
Polunochnoye, Russia 48 B11 60 52N 60 25 E
Polur, India 83 H4 12 32N 79 11 E
Põlva, Estonia 13 G22 58 3N 27 3 E
Polyanovgrad, Bulgaria 43 E11 42 39N 26 59 E
Polyarny, Russia 48 A5 69 8N 33 20 E
Polynesia, Pac. Oc. 123 H11 10 0 S 162 0W
Polynésie française = French Polynesia ■, Pac. Oc. 123 J13 20 0 S 145 0W
Pomarance, Italy 38 E7 43 18N 10 52 E
Pomárico, Italy 41 B9 40 31N 16 33 E
Pomaro, Mexico 146 D4 18 20N 103 18W
Pombal, Brazil 154 C4 6 45 S 37 50W
Pombal, Portugal 36 F2 39 55N 8 40W
Pómbia, Greece 32 D6 35 0N 24 51 E
Pomeroy, Ohio, U.S.A. 134 F4 39 2N 82 2W
Pomeroy, Wash., U.S.A. 142 C5 46 28N 117 36W
Pomichna, Ukraine 51 H6 48 13N 31 36 E
Pomio, Papua N. G. 120 C6 5 32 S 151 33 E
Pomme de Terre L., U.S.A. 140 G3 37 54N 93 19W
Pomona, U.S.A. 145 L9 34 4N 117 45W
Pomorie, Bulgaria 43 E12 42 32N 27 41 E
Pomos, Cyprus 32 D11 35 9N 32 33 E
Pomos, C., Cyprus 32 D11 35 10N 32 33 E
Pompano Beach, U.S.A. 135 M5 26 14N 80 8W
Pompei, Italy 41 B7 40 45N 14 30 E
Pompey, France 23 D13 48 46N 6 6 E
Pompeys Pillar, U.S.A. 142 D10 45 59N 107 57W
Ponape = Pohnpei, Pac. Oc. 122 G7 6 55N 158 10 E
Ponask, L., Canada 128 B1 54 0N 92 41W
Ponass L., Canada 131 C8 52 16N 103 58W
Ponca, U.S.A. 138 D6 42 34N 96 43W
Ponca City, U.S.A. 139 G6 36 42N 97 5W
Ponce, Puerto Rico 149 C6 18 1N 66 37W
Ponchatoula, U.S.A. 139 K9 30 26N 90 26W
Poncheville, L., Canada 128 B4 50 10N 76 55W
Poncin, France 25 B9 46 6N 5 25 E
Pond, U.S.A. 145 K7 35 43N 119 20W
Pond Inlet, Canada 127 A12 72 40N 77 0W
Pondicherry, India 83 J4 11 59N 79 50 E
Pondooma, Australia 116 B2 33 29 S 136 59 E
Pondrôme, Belgium 21 H6 50 6N 5 0 E
Ponds, I. of, Canada 129 B8 53 27N 55 52W
Ponérihouen, N. Cal. 121 U19 21 5 S 165 24 E
Ponferrada, Spain 36 C4 42 32N 6 35W
Pongo, Wadi →, Sudan 95 F2 8 42N 27 40 E
Poniatowa, Poland 47 D9 51 11N 22 3 E
Poniec, Poland 47 D3 51 48N 16 50 E
Ponikva, Slovenia 39 B12 46 16N 15 26 E
Ponnaiyar →, India 83 J4 11 50N 79 45 E
Ponnani, India 83 J2 10 45N 75 59 E
Ponneri, India 83 H5 13 20N 80 15 E
Ponnuru, India 83 F5 16 5N 80 34 E
Ponoka, Canada 130 C6 52 42N 113 40W
Ponomarevka, Russia 54 E5 53 19N 54 8 E
Ponorogo, Indonesia 75 D4 7 52 S 111 27 E
Ponot, Phil. 71 G4 8 25N 123 0 E
Ponoy, Russia 48 A7 67 0N 41 13 E
Ponoy →, Russia 48 A7 66 59N 41 17 E
Pons, France 24 C3 45 35N 0 34W
Pons, Spain 34 D6 41 55N 1 12 E
Ponsul →, Portugal 37 F3 39 40N 7 31W
Pont-à-Celles, Belgium 21 G4 50 30N 4 22 E
Pont-à-Mousson, France 23 D13 48 54N 6 1 E
Pont-Audemer, France 22 C7 49 21N 0 30 E
Pont-Aven, France 22 E3 47 51N 3 47W
Pont Canavese, Italy 38 C4 45 25N 7 36 E
Pont-de-Roide, France 23 E13 47 23N 6 45 E
Pont-de-Salars, France 24 D6 44 18N 2 44 E
Pont-de-Vaux, France 23 F11 46 26N 4 56 E
Pont-de-Veyle, France 25 B8 46 17N 4 53 E
Pont-l'Abbé, France 22 E2 47 52N 4 15W
Pont-l'Évêque, France 22 C7 49 18N 0 11 E
Pont-St.-Esprit, France 25 D8 44 16N 4 40 E
Pont-Saint-Martin, Italy 38 C4 45 36N 7 48 E
Pont-sur-Yonne, France 23 D10 48 18N 3 10 E
Ponta de Pedras, Brazil 154 B2 1 23 S 48 52W
Ponta do Sol, Madeira 33 D2 32 42N 17 7W
Ponta Grossa, Brazil 159 B5 25 7 S 50 10W
Ponta Pora, Brazil 159 A4 22 20 S 55 35W
Pontacq, France 24 E3 43 11N 0 8W
Pontailler-sur-Saône, France 23 E12 47 13N 5 25 E
Pontal →, Brazil 154 C3 9 8 S 40 12W
Pontalina, Brazil 155 E2 17 31 S 49 27W
Pontarlier, France 23 F13 46 54N 6 20 E
Pontassieve, Italy 39 E8 43 46N 11 26 E
Pontaubault, France 22 D5 48 40N 1 20W
Pontaumur, France 24 C6 45 52N 2 40 E
Pontcharra, France 25 C10 45 26N 6 1 E
Pontchartrain L., U.S.A. 139 K9 30 5N 90 5W
Pontchâteau, France 22 E4 47 25N 2 5W
Ponte Alta, Serra do, Brazil 155 E2 19 42 S 47 40W
Ponte Alta do Norte, Brazil 154 D2 10 45 S 47 34W
Ponte Branca, Brazil 157 D7 16 27 S 52 40W
Ponte da Barca, Portugal 36 D2 41 48N 8 25W
Ponte de Sor, Portugal 37 F3 39 17N 7 57W
Ponte dell'Ólio, Italy 38 D6 44 52N 9 39 E
Ponte di Legno, Italy 38 B7 46 16N 10 31 E
Ponte do Lima, Portugal 36 D2 41 46N 8 35W
Ponte do Pungué, Mozam. 107 F3 19 30 S 34 33 E
Ponte-Leccia, France 25 F13 42 28N 9 13 E
Ponte nelle Alpi, Italy 39 B9 46 11N 12 16 E
Ponte Nova, Brazil 155 F3 20 25 S 42 54W
Ponte San Pietro, Italy 38 C6 45 42N 9 35 E
Pontebba, Italy 39 B10 46 30N 13 18 E
Pontecorvo, Italy 40 A6 41 27N 13 40 E
Pontedera, Italy 38 E7 43 40N 10 38 E
Pontefract, U.K. 16 D6 53 42N 1 18W
Ponteix, Canada 131 D7 49 46N 107 29W
Pontelandolfo, Italy 41 A7 41 17N 14 41 E
Pontevedra, Negros, Phil. 71 F4 10 22N 122 52 E
Pontevedra, Panay, Phil. 71 F4 11 29N 122 50 E
Pontevedra, Spain 36 C2 42 26N 8 40W
Pontevedra □, Spain 36 C2 42 25N 8 39W
Pontevedra, R. de →, Spain 36 C2 42 22N 8 45W
Pontevico, Italy 38 C7 45 16N 10 5 E
Pontiac, Ill., U.S.A. 138 E10 40 53N 88 38W
Pontiac, Mich., U.S.A. 141 B13 42 38N 83 18W
Pontian Kecil, Malaysia 77 M4 1 29N 103 23 E
Pontianak, Indonesia 75 C3 0 3 S 109 15 E
Pontine Is. = Ponziane, Ísole, Italy 40 B5 40 55N 12 57 E
Pontine Mts. = Kuzey Anadolu Dağları, Turkey 88 B7 41 30N 35 0 E
Pontínia, Italy 40 A6 41 25N 12 55 E
Pontivy, France 22 D4 48 5N 2 58W
Pontoise, France 23 C9 49 3N 2 5 E
Ponton →, Canada 130 B5 58 27N 116 11W
Pontorson, France 22 D5 48 34N 1 30W
Pontrémoli, Italy 38 D6 44 22N 9 53 E
Pontresina, Switz. 29 D9 46 29N 9 48 E
Pontrieux, France 22 D3 48 42N 3 10W
Pontypool, Canada 136 B6 44 6N 78 38W
Pontypool, U.K. 17 F4 51 42N 3 2W
Pontypridd, U.K. 17 F4 51 36N 3 20W
Ponza, Italy 40 B5 40 54N 12 58 E
Ponziane, Ísole, Italy 40 B5 40 55N 12 57 E
Poochera, Australia 115 E1 32 43 S 134 51 E
Poole, U.K. 17 G6 50 43N 1 59W
Pooley I., Canada 130 C3 52 45N 128 15W
Poona = Pune, India 82 E1 18 29N 73 57 E
Poona Bayabao, Phil. 71 H5 7 56N 124 17 E
Poonamallee, India 83 H5 13 3N 80 10 E
Pooncarie, Australia 116 B5 33 22 S 142 31 E
Poonindie, Australia 116 C1 34 34 S 135 54 E
Poopelloe L., Australia 116 A6 31 40 S 144 0 E
Poopó, Bolivia 156 D4 18 23 S 66 59W
Poopó, L. de, Bolivia 156 D4 18 30 S 67 35W
Poor Knights Is., N.Z. 118 B3 35 29 S 174 43 E
Popanyinning, Australia 113 F2 32 40 S 117 2 E
Popayán, Colombia 152 C2 2 27N 76 36W
Poperinge, Belgium 21 G1 50 51N 2 42 E
Popigay, Russia 57 B12 72 1N 110 39 E
Popilta, L., Australia 116 B4 33 10 S 141 42 E
Popina, Bulgaria 43 C11 44 7N 26 57 E
Popio L., Australia 116 B4 33 10 S 141 52 E
Poplar, U.S.A. 138 A2 48 7N 105 12W
Poplar →, Man., Canada 131 C9 53 0N 97 19W
Poplar →, N.W.T., Canada 130 A4 61 22N 121 52W
Poplar Bluff, U.S.A. 139 G9 36 46N 90 24W
Poplarville, U.S.A. 139 K10 30 51N 89 32W
Popocatépetl, Volcán, Mexico 147 D5 19 2N 98 38W
Popokabaka, Zaïre 103 D3 5 41 S 16 40 E
Pópoli, Italy 39 F10 42 10N 13 50 E
Popondetta, Papua N. G. 120 E5 8 48 S 148 17 E
Popovača, Croatia 39 C13 45 30N 16 41 E
Popovo, Bulgaria 43 D11 43 21N 26 18 E
Poppel, Belgium 21 F6 51 27N 5 2 E
Poprád, Slovak Rep. 31 B13 49 3N 20 18 E
Poprád →, Slovak Rep. 31 B13 49 38N 20 42 E
Poradaha, Bangla. 78 D2 23 51N 89 1 E
Porali →, Pakistan 79 D2 25 35N 66 26 E
Porangaba, Brazil 156 B3 8 48 S 70 36W
Porangahau, N.Z. 118 G5 40 17 S 176 37 E
Porangatu, Brazil 155 D2 13 26 S 49 10W
Porbandar, India 80 J3 21 44N 69 43 E
Porce →, Colombia 152 B3 7 28N 74 53W
Porcher I., Canada 130 C2 53 50N 130 30W
Porco, Bolivia 157 D4 19 50 S 65 59W
Porcos →, Brazil 155 D2 12 42 S 45 7W
Porcuna, Spain 37 H6 37 52N 4 11W
Porcupine →, Canada 131 B8 59 11N 104 46W
Porcupine →, U.S.A. 126 B5 66 34N 145 19W
Pordenone, Italy 39 C9 45 57N 12 39 E
Pordim, Bulgaria 43 D9 43 23N 24 51 E
Poreč, Croatia 39 C10 45 14N 13 36 E
Porecatu, Brazil 155 F1 22 43 S 51 24W
Poretskoye, Russia 52 C8 55 9N 46 21 E
Pori, Finland 13 F19 61 29N 21 48 E
Porí, Greece 45 J5 35 58N 23 13 E
Porkhov, Russia 50 D5 57 45N 29 38 E
Porlamar, Venezuela 153 A5 10 57N 63 51W
Porlezza, Italy 38 B6 46 2N 9 7 E
Porma →, Spain 36 C5 42 49N 5 28W
Pornic, France 22 E4 47 7N 2 5W
Poronaysk, Russia 57 E15 49 13N 143 0 E
Póros, Greece 45 G5 37 30N 23 30 E
Poroshiri-Dake, Japan 60 C11 42 41N 142 52 E
Poroszló, Hungary 31 D13 47 39N 20 40 E
Poroto Mts., Tanzania 107 D3 9 0 S 33 30 E
Porpoise B., Antarctica 7 C9 66 0 S 127 0 E
Porquerolles, I. de, France 25 F10 43 0N 6 13 E
Porrentruy, Switz. 28 B4 47 25N 7 6 E
Porreras, Spain 33 B10 39 31N 3 2 E
Porretta, Passo di, Italy 38 D7 44 2N 10 56 E
Porsangen, Norway 12 A21 70 40N 25 40 E
Porsgrunn, Norway 14 E3 59 10N 9 40 E
Port Adelaide, Australia 116 C3 34 46 S 138 30 E
Port Alberni, Canada 130 D4 49 14N 124 50W
Port Albert, Australia 117 E7 38 42 S 146 42 E
Port Alfred, Canada 129 C5 48 18N 70 53W
Port Alfred, S. Africa 104 E4 33 36 S 26 55 E
Port Alice, Canada 130 C3 50 20N 127 25W
Port Allegany, U.S.A. 136 E6 41 48N 78 17W
Port Allen, U.S.A. 139 K9 30 27N 91 12W
Port Alma, Australia 114 C5 23 38 S 150 53 E
Port Angeles, U.S.A. 144 B3 48 7N 123 27W
Port Antonio, Jamaica 148 C4 18 10N 76 30W
Port Aransas, U.S.A. 139 M6 27 50N 97 4W
Port Arthur = Lüshun, China 67 E11 38 45N 121 15 E
Port Arthur, Australia 114 G4 43 7 S 147 50 E
Port Arthur, U.S.A. 139 L8 29 54N 93 56W
Port au Port B., Canada 129 C8 48 40N 58 50W
Port-au-Prince, Haiti 149 C5 18 40N 72 20W
Port Augusta, Australia 116 B2 32 30 S 137 50 E
Port Augusta West, Australia 116 B2 32 29 S 137 29 E
Port Austin, U.S.A. 128 D3 44 3N 83 1W
Port Bell, Uganda 106 B3 0 18N 32 35 E
Port Bergé Vaovao, Madag. 105 B8 15 33 S 47 40 E
Port Blandford, Canada 129 C9 48 20N 54 10W

Pretoria 251

Port Bou, *Spain* **34 C8** 42 25N 3 9 E
Port Bouët, *Ivory C.* **100 D4** 5 16N 3 57W
Port Bradshaw, *Australia* **114 A2** 12 30 S 137 20 E
Port Broughton, *Australia* **116 B2** 33 37 S 137 56 E
Port Burwell, *Canada* **128 D3** 42 40N 80 48W
Port Campbell, *Australia* **116 E5** 38 37 S 143 1 E
Port Canning, *India* **81 H13** 22 23N 88 40 E
Port-Cartier, *Canada* **129 B6** 50 2N 66 50W
Port Chalmers, *N.Z.* **119 F5** 45 49 S 170 30 E
Port Charles, *N.Z.* **118 C4** 36 33 S 175 30 E
Port Chester, *U.S.A.* **137 F11** 41 0N 73 40W
Port Clements, *Canada* **130 C2** 53 40N 132 10W
Port Clinton, *U.S.A.* **141 C14** 41 31N 82 56W
Port Colborne, *Canada* **128 D4** 42 50N 79 10W
Port Coquitlam, *Canada* **130 D4** 49 15N 122 45W
Port Credit, *Canada* **136 C5** 43 33N 79 35W
Port Curtis, *Australia* **114 C5** 23 57 S 151 20 E
Port Dalhousie, *Canada* **136 C5** 43 13N 79 16W
Port Darwin, *Australia* **112 B5** 12 24 S 130 45 E
Port Darwin, *Falk. Is.* **160 D5** 51 50 S 59 0W
Port Davey, *Australia* **114 G4** 43 16 S 145 55 E
Port-de-Bouc, *France* **25 E8** 43 24N 4 59 E
Port-de-Paix, *Haiti* **149 C5** 19 50N 72 50W
Port Dickson, *Malaysia* **77 L3** 2 30N 101 49 E
Port Douglas, *Australia* **114 B4** 16 30 S 145 30 E
Port Dover, *Canada* **136 D4** 42 47N 80 12W
Port Edward, *Canada* **130 C2** 54 12N 130 10W
Port Elgin, *Canada* **128 D3** 44 25N 81 25W
Port Elizabeth, *S. Africa* **104 E4** 33 58 S 25 40 E
Port Ellen, *U.K.* **18 F2** 55 38N 6 11W
Port-en-Bessin, *France* **22 C6** 49 21N 0 45W
Port Erin, *U.K.* **16 C3** 54 5N 4 45W
Port Essington, *Australia* **112 B5** 11 15 S 132 10 E
Port Etienne = Nouâdhibou, *Mauritania* **98 D1** 20 54N 17 0W
Port Fairy, *Australia* **116 E5** 38 22 S 142 12 E
Port Fitzroy, *N.Z.* **118 C4** 36 8 S 175 20 E
Port Fouâd = Bûr Fuad, *Egypt* **94 H8** 31 15N 32 20 E
Port Gamble, *U.S.A.* **144 C4** 47 51N 122 35W
Port-Gentil, *Gabon* **102 C1** 0 40 S 8 50 E
Port Gibson, *U.S.A.* **139 K9** 31 58N 90 59W
Port Glasgow, *U.K.* **18 F4** 55 56N 4 41W
Port Harcourt, *Nigeria* **101 E6** 4 40N 7 10 E
Port Hardy, *Canada* **130 C3** 50 41N 127 30W
Port Harrison = Inukjuak, *Canada* **127 C12** 58 25N 78 15W
Port Hawkesbury, *Canada* **129 C7** 45 36N 61 22W
Port Hedland, *Australia* **112 D2** 20 25 S 118 35 E
Port Henry, *U.S.A.* **137 B11** 44 3N 73 28W
Port Hood, *Canada* **129 C7** 46 0N 61 32W
Port Hope, *Canada* **128 D4** 43 56N 78 20W
Port Hueneme, *U.S.A.* **145 L7** 34 7N 119 12W
Port Huron, *U.S.A.* **134 D4** 42 58N 82 26W
Port Iliç, *Azerbaijan* **89 C13** 38 53N 48 47 E
Port Isabel, *U.S.A.* **139 M6** 26 5N 97 12W
Port Jefferson, *U.S.A.* **137 F11** 40 57N 73 3W
Port Jervis, *U.S.A.* **137 E10** 41 22N 74 41W
Port-Joinville, *France* **22 F4** 46 45N 2 23W
Port Katon, *Russia* **53 G4** 46 52N 38 46 E
Port Kelang = Pelabuhan Kelang, *Malaysia* **77 L3** 3 0N 101 23 E
Port Kembla, *Australia* **117 C9** 34 52 S 150 49 E
Port Kenny, *Australia* **115 E1** 33 10 S 134 41 E
Port-la-Nouvelle, *France* **24 E7** 43 1N 3 3 E
Port Lairge = Waterford, *Ireland* **19 D4** 52 15N 7 8W
Port Laoise, *Ireland* **19 C4** 53 2N 7 18W
Port Lavaca, *U.S.A.* **139 L6** 28 37N 96 38W
Port-Leucate, *France* **24 F7** 42 53N 3 3 E
Port Lincoln, *Australia* **116 C1** 34 42 S 135 52 E
Port Loko, *S. Leone* **100 D2** 8 48N 12 46W
Port Louis, *France* **22 E3** 47 42N 3 22W
Port Louis, *Mauritius* **109 G4** 20 10 S 57 30 E
Port Lyautey = Kenitra, *Morocco* **98 B3** 34 15N 6 40W
Port MacDonnell, *Australia* **116 E4** 38 5 S 140 48 E
Port Macquarie, *Australia* **117 A10** 31 25 S 152 25 E
Port Maria, *Jamaica* **148 C4** 18 25N 76 55W
Port Mellon, *Canada* **130 D4** 49 32N 123 31W
Port-Menier, *Canada* **129 C7** 49 51N 64 15W
Port Morant, *Jamaica* **148 C4** 17 54N 76 19W
Port Moresby, *Papua N. G.* **120 E4** 9 24 S 147 8 E
Port Mourant, *Guyana* **153 B6** 6 15N 57 20W
Port Mouton, *Canada* **129 D7** 43 58N 64 50W
Port Musgrave, *Australia* **114 A3** 11 55 S 141 50 E
Port-Navalo, *France* **22 E4** 47 34N 2 54W
Port Nelson, *Canada* **131 B10** 57 3N 92 36W
Port Nicholson, *N.Z.* **118 H3** 41 20 S 174 52 E
Port Nolloth, *S. Africa* **104 D2** 29 17 S 16 52 E
Port Nouveau-Québec = Kangiqsualujjuaq, *Canada* **127 C13** 58 30N 65 59W
Port O'Connor, *U.S.A.* **139 L6** 28 26N 96 24W
Port of Spain, *Trin. & Tob.* **149 D7** 10 40N 61 31W
Port Orchard, *U.S.A.* **144 C4** 47 32N 122 38W
Port Orford, *U.S.A.* **142 E1** 42 45N 124 30W
Port Pegasus, *N.Z.* **119 H2** 47 12 S 167 41 E
Port Perry, *Canada* **128 D4** 44 6N 78 56W
Port Phillip B., *Australia* **115 F3** 38 10 S 144 50 E
Port Pirie, *Australia* **116 B3** 33 10 S 138 1 E
Port Pólnocny, *Poland* **47 A5** 54 25N 18 42 E
Port Radium = Echo Bay, *Canada* **126 B8** 66 5N 117 55W
Port Renfrew, *Canada* **130 D4** 48 30N 124 20W
Port Roper, *Australia* **114 A2** 14 45 S 135 25 E
Port Rowan, *Canada* **128 D3** 42 40N 80 30W
Port Safaga = Bûr Safâga, *Egypt* **94 B3** 26 43N 33 57 E
Port Said = Bûr Sa'îd, *Egypt* **94 H8** 31 16N 32 18 E
Port St. Joe, *U.S.A.* **135 L3** 29 49N 85 18W
Port St. Johns, *S. Africa* **105 E4** 31 38 S 29 33 E
Port-St.-Louis-du-Rhône, *France* **25 E8** 43 23N 4 49 E
Port San Vicente, *Phil.* **70 B4** 18 30N 122 8 E
Port Sanilac, *U.S.A.* **128 D3** 43 26N 82 33W
Port Saunders, *Canada* **129 B8** 50 40N 57 18W
Port Severn, *Canada* **136 B5** 44 48N 79 43W
Port Shepstone, *S. Africa* **105 E5** 30 44 S 30 28 E
Port Simpson, *Canada* **130 C2** 54 30N 130 20W
Port Stanley = Stanley, *Falk. Is.* **160 D5** 51 40 S 59 51W
Port Stanley, *Canada* **128 D3** 42 40N 81 10W
Port Sudan = Bûr Sûdân, *Sudan* **94 D4** 19 32N 37 9 E
Port-sur-Saône, *France* **23 E13** 47 42N 6 2 E
Port Talbot, *U.K.* **17 F4** 51 35N 3 47W
Port Taufîq = Bûr Taufiq, *Egypt* **94 J8** 29 54N 32 32 E
Port Townsend, *U.S.A.* **144 B4** 48 7N 122 45W
Port-Vendres, *France* **24 F7** 42 32N 3 8 E
Port Victoria, *Australia* **116 C2** 34 30 S 137 29 E
Port Vila, *Pac. Oc.* **111 D12** 17 45 S 168 18 E
Port Vladimir, *Russia* **48 A5** 69 25N 33 6 E
Port Wakefield, *Australia* **116 C3** 34 12 S 138 10 E
Port Washington, *U.S.A.* **134 D2** 43 23N 87 53W
Port Weld, *Malaysia* **77 K3** 4 50N 100 38 E
Portachuelo, *Bolivia* **157 D5** 17 10 S 63 20W
Portadown, *U.K.* **19 B5** 54 25N 6 27W
Portage, *Mich., U.S.A.* **141 B11** 42 12N 85 35W
Portage, *Wis., U.S.A.* **138 D10** 43 33N 89 28W
Portage →, *U.S.A.* **141 C14** 41 31N 83 5W
Portage La Prairie, *Canada* **131 D9** 49 58N 98 18W
Portageville, *U.S.A.* **139 G10** 36 26N 89 42W
Portalegre, *Portugal* **37 F3** 39 19N 7 25W
Portalegre □, *Portugal* **37 F3** 39 20N 7 40W
Portales, *U.S.A.* **139 H3** 34 11N 103 20W
Portarlington, *Ireland* **19 C4** 53 9N 7 14W
Porteirinha, *Brazil* **155 E3** 15 44 S 43 2W
Portel, *Brazil* **154 B1** 1 57 S 50 49W
Portel, *Portugal* **37 G3** 38 19N 7 41W
Porter, *U.S.A.* **141 C9** 41 36N 87 4W
Porter L., *N.W.T., Canada* **131 A7** 61 41N 108 5W
Porter L., *Sask., Canada* **131 B7** 56 20N 107 20W
Porterville, *S. Africa* **104 E2** 33 0 S 19 0 E
Porterville, *U.S.A.* **144 J8** 36 4N 119 1W
Porthcawl, *U.K.* **17 F4** 51 29N 3 42W
Porthill, *U.S.A.* **142 B5** 48 59N 116 30W
Portile de Fier, *Europe* **46 E3** 44 42N 22 30 E
Portimão, *Portugal* **37 H2** 37 8N 8 32W
Portland, *N.S.W., Australia* **117 B8** 33 20 S 150 0 E
Portland, *Vic., Australia* **116 E4** 38 20 S 141 35 E
Portland, *Canada* **137 B8** 44 42N 76 12W
Portland, *Conn., U.S.A.* **137 E12** 41 34N 72 38W
Portland, *Ind., U.S.A.* **141 D12** 40 26N 84 59W
Portland, *Maine, U.S.A.* **129 D5** 43 39N 70 16W
Portland, *Mich., U.S.A.* **141 B12** 42 52N 84 54W
Portland, *Oreg., U.S.A.* **144 E4** 45 32N 122 37W
Portland, I. of, *U.K.* **17 G5** 50 33N 2 26W
Portland B., *Australia* **116 E4** 38 15 S 141 45 E
Portland Bill, *U.K.* **17 G5** 50 31N 2 28W
Portland I., *N.Z.* **118 F6** 39 20 S 177 51 E
Portland Prom., *Canada* **127 C12** 58 40N 78 33W
Portlands Roads, *Australia* **114 A3** 12 36 S 143 25 E
Portneuf, *Canada* **129 C5** 46 43N 71 55W
Pôrto, *Brazil* **154 B3** 3 54 S 42 42W
Porto, *France* **25 F12** 42 16N 8 42 E
Porto, *Portugal* **36 D2** 41 8N 8 40W
Porto □, *Portugal* **36 D2** 41 8N 8 20W
Porto, G. de, *France* **25 F12** 42 17N 8 34 E
Pôrto Acre, *Brazil* **156 B4** 9 34 S 67 31W
Pôrto Alegre, *Pará, Brazil* **153 D7** 4 22 S 52 44W
Pôrto Alegre, *Rio Grande do S., Brazil* **159 C5** 30 5 S 51 10W
Porto Amboim = Gunza, *Angola* **103 E2** 10 50 S 13 50 E
Porto Argentera, *Italy* **38 D4** 44 15N 7 27 E
Porto Azzurro, *Italy* **38 F7** 42 46N 10 24 E
Porto Botte, *Italy* **40 C1** 39 3N 8 33 E
Pôrto Cajueiro, *Brazil* **157 C6** 11 3 S 55 53W
Porto Civitanova, *Italy* **39 E10** 43 19N 13 44 E
Porto Cristo, *Spain* **33 B10** 39 33N 3 20 E
Pôrto da Fôlha, *Brazil* **154 C4** 9 55 S 37 17W
Pôrto de Móz, *Brazil* **153 D7** 1 41 S 52 13W
Pôrto de Pedras, *Brazil* **154 C4** 9 10 S 35 17W
Pôrto des Meinacos, *Brazil* **157 C7** 12 33 S 53 7W
Porto Empédocle, *Italy* **40 E6** 37 17N 13 32 E
Pôrto Esperança, *Brazil* **157 D6** 19 37 S 57 29W
Pôrto Esperidão, *Brazil* **157 D6** 15 51 S 58 28W
Pôrto Franco, *Brazil* **154 C2** 6 20 S 47 24W
Porto Garibaldi, *Italy* **39 D9** 44 41N 12 14 E
Pôrto Grande, *Brazil* **153 C7** 0 42N 51 24W
Pôrto Jofre, *Brazil* **157 D6** 17 20 S 56 48W
Pórto Lágo, *Greece* **44 D7** 40 58N 25 6 E
Porto Mendes, *Brazil* **159 A5** 24 30 S 54 15W
Porto Moniz, *Madeira* **33 D2** 32 52N 17 11W
Pôrto Murtinho, *Brazil* **157 E6** 21 45 S 57 55W
Pôrto Nacional, *Brazil* **154 D2** 10 40 S 48 30W
Porto Novo, *Benin* **101 D5** 6 23N 2 42 E
Porto Petro, *Spain* **33 B10** 39 22N 3 13 E
Porto Recanati, *Italy* **39 E10** 43 26N 13 40 E
Porto San Giórgio, *Italy* **39 E10** 43 11N 13 48 E
Pôrto Santana, *Brazil* **153 D7** 0 3 S 51 11W
Porto Santo Stéfano, *Italy* **38 F8** 42 26N 11 7 E
Pôrto São José, *Brazil* **159 A5** 22 43 S 53 10W
Pôrto Seguro, *Brazil* **155 E4** 16 26 S 39 5W
Porto Tolle, *Italy* **39 D9** 44 56N 12 22 E
Porto Tórres, *Italy* **40 B1** 40 50N 8 24 E
Pôrto União, *Brazil* **159 B5** 26 10 S 51 10W
Pôrto Válter, *Brazil* **156 B3** 8 15 S 72 40W
Porto-Vecchio, *France* **25 G13** 41 35N 9 16 E
Pôrto Velho, *Brazil* **157 B5** 8 46 S 63 54W
Portobelo, *Panama* **148 E4** 9 35N 79 42W
Portoferráio, *Italy* **38 F7** 42 48N 10 20 E
Portogruaro, *Italy* **39 C9** 45 47N 12 50 E
Portola, *U.S.A.* **144 F6** 39 49N 120 28W
Portomaggiore, *Italy* **39 D8** 44 42N 11 48 E
Portoscuso, *Italy* **40 C1** 39 12N 8 24 E
Portovénere, *Italy* **38 D6** 44 3N 9 51 E
Portoviéjo, *Ecuador* **152 D1** 1 7 S 80 28W
Portpatrick, *U.K.* **18 G3** 54 51N 5 7W
Portree, *U.K.* **18 D2** 57 25N 6 12W
Portrush, *U.K.* **19 A5** 55 12N 6 40W
Portsall, *France* **22 D2** 48 37N 4 45W
Portsmouth, *Domin.* **149 C7** 15 34N 61 27W
Portsmouth, *U.K.* **17 G6** 50 48N 1 6W
Portsmouth, *N.H., U.S.A.* **137 C14** 43 5N 70 45W
Portsmouth, *Ohio, U.S.A.* **134 F4** 38 44N 82 57W
Portsmouth, *R.I., U.S.A.* **137 E13** 41 36N 71 15W
Portsmouth, *Va., U.S.A.* **134 G7** 36 50N 76 18W
Portsoy, *U.K.* **18 D6** 57 41N 2 41W
Porttipahtan tekojärvi, *Finland* **12 B22** 68 5N 26 40 E
Portugal ■, *Europe* **36 F3** 40 0N 8 0W
Portugalete, *Spain* **34 B1** 43 19N 3 4W
Portuguesa □, *Venezuela* **152 B4** 9 10N 69 15W
Portumna, *Ireland* **19 C3** 53 6N 8 14W
Portville, *U.S.A.* **136 D6** 42 3N 78 20W
Porvenir, *Bolivia* **156 C4** 11 10 S 68 50W
Porvenir, *Chile* **160 D2** 53 10 S 70 16W
Porvoo, *Finland* **13 F21** 60 24N 25 40 E
Porzuna, *Spain* **37 F6** 39 9N 4 9W
Posada →, *Italy* **40 B2** 40 39N 9 45 E
Posadas, *Argentina* **159 B4** 27 30 S 55 50W
Posadas, *Spain* **37 H5** 37 47N 5 11W
Poschiavo, *Switz.* **29 D10** 46 19N 10 4 E
Posets, *Spain* **34 C5** 42 39N 0 25 E
Poseyville, *U.S.A.* **141 F9** 38 10N 87 47W
Poshan = Boshan, *China* **67 F9** 36 28N 117 49 E
Posht-e-Badam, *Iran* **85 C7** 33 2N 55 23 E
Posídhion, Ákra, *Greece* **44 E5** 39 57N 23 30 E
Posidium, *Greece* **45 J9** 35 30N 27 10 E
Poso, *Indonesia* **72 B2** 1 20 S 120 55 E
Poso, Danau, *Indonesia* **72 B2** 1 52 S 120 35 E
Posoegroenoe, *Surinam* **153 C6** 4 23N 55 43W
Posong, *S. Korea* **67 G14** 34 46N 127 5 E
Posse, *Brazil* **155 D2** 14 4 S 46 18W
Possel, *C.A.R.* **102 A3** 5 5N 19 10 E
Possession I., *Antarctica* **7 D11** 72 4 S 172 0 E
Pössneck, *Germany* **26 E7** 50 42N 11 35 E
Post, *U.S.A.* **139 J4** 33 12N 101 23W
Post Falls, *U.S.A.* **142 C5** 47 43N 116 57W
Postavy = Pastavy, *Belarus* **13 J22** 55 4N 26 50 E
Poste Maurice Cortier, *Algeria* **99 D5** 22 14N 1 2 E
Postmasburg, *S. Africa* **104 D3** 28 18 S 23 5 E
Postojna, *Slovenia* **39 C11** 45 46N 14 12 E
Poston, *U.S.A.* **145 M12** 34 0N 114 24W
Postville, *U.S.A.* **140 A5** 43 5N 91 34W
Potamós, *Andikíthira, Greece* **45 H4** 35 52N 23 15 E
Potamós, *Kíthira, Greece* **45 H4** 36 15N 22 58 E
Potchefstroom, *S. Africa* **104 D4** 26 41 S 27 7 E
Potcoava, *Romania* **46 E5** 44 30N 24 39 E
Poté, *Brazil* **155 E3** 17 49 S 41 49W
Poteau, *U.S.A.* **139 H7** 35 3N 94 37W
Poteet, *U.S.A.* **139 L5** 29 2N 98 35W
Potelu, Lacul, *Romania* **46 F5** 43 44N 24 20 E
Potenza, *Italy* **41 B8** 40 38N 15 48 E
Potenza →, *Italy* **39 E10** 43 25N 13 40 E
Potenza Picena, *Italy* **39 E10** 43 22N 13 37 E
Poteriteri, L., *N.Z.* **119 G2** 46 5 S 167 10 E
Potes, *Spain* **36 B6** 43 15N 4 42W
Potgietersrus, *S. Africa* **105 C4** 24 10 S 28 55 E
Poti, *Georgia* **53 J5** 42 10N 41 38 E
Potiraguá, *Brazil* **155 E4** 15 36 S 39 53W
Potiskum, *Nigeria* **101 C7** 11 39N 11 2 E
Potlogi, *Romania* **46 E6** 44 34N 25 34 E
Potomac →, *U.S.A.* **134 F7** 38 0N 76 23W
Potosí, *Bolivia* **157 D4** 19 38 S 65 50W
Potosi, *U.S.A.* **140 G6** 37 56N 90 47W
Potosí □, *Bolivia* **156 E4** 20 31 S 67 0W
Potosi Mt., *U.S.A.* **145 K11** 35 57N 115 29W
Pototan, *Phil.* **71 F4** 10 54N 122 38 E
Potrerillos, *Chile* **158 B2** 26 30 S 69 30W
Potsdam, *Germany* **26 C9** 52 25N 13 4 E
Potsdam, *U.S.A.* **137 B10** 44 40N 74 59W
Pottenstein, *Germany* **27 F7** 49 46N 11 24 E
Potter, *U.S.A.* **138 E3** 41 13N 103 19W
Pottery Hill = Abû Ballas, *Egypt* **94 C2** 24 26N 27 36 E
Pottstown, *U.S.A.* **137 F9** 40 15N 75 39W
Pottsville, *U.S.A.* **137 F8** 40 41N 76 12W
P'otzu, *Taiwan* **69 F13** 23 30N 120 25 E
Pouancé, *France* **22 E5** 47 44N 1 10W
Pouce Coupé, *Canada* **130 B4** 55 40N 120 10W
Pouembout, *N. Cal.* **121 U18** 21 8 S 164 53 E
Poughkeepsie, *U.S.A.* **137 E11** 41 42N 73 56W
Pouilly-sur-Loire, *France* **23 E9** 47 17N 2 57 E
Poulaphouca Res., *Ireland* **19 C5** 53 8N 6 30W
Poulsbo, *U.S.A.* **144 C4** 47 44N 122 39W
Poum, *N. Cal.* **121 T18** 20 14 S 164 2 E
Poumadji, *C.A.R.* **102 A4** 5 56N 22 10 E
Pounga-Nganda, *Gabon* **102 C2** 2 58 S 10 51 E
Pourri, Mt., *France* **25 C10** 45 32N 6 52 E
Pouso Alegre, *Mato Grosso, Brazil* **157 C6** 11 46 S 57 16W
Pouso Alegre, *Minas Gerais, Brazil* **159 A6** 22 14 S 45 57W
Pouzauges, *France* **22 F6** 46 47N 0 50W
Povenets, *Russia* **48 B5** 62 50N 34 50 E
Poverty B., *N.Z.* **118 E7** 38 43 S 178 2 E
Povlen, *Serbia, Yug.* **42 C4** 44 9N 19 44 E
Póvoa de Lanhosa, *Portugal* **36 D2** 41 33N 8 15W
Póvoa de Varzim, *Portugal* **36 D2** 41 25N 8 46W
Povorino, *Russia* **52 E6** 51 12N 42 5 E
Powassan, *Canada* **128 C4** 46 5N 79 25W
Poway, *U.S.A.* **145 N9** 32 58N 117 2W
Powder →, *U.S.A.* **138 B2** 46 45N 105 26W
Powder River, *U.S.A.* **142 E10** 43 2N 106 59W
Powell, *U.S.A.* **142 D9** 44 45N 108 46W
Powell L., *U.S.A.* **143 H8** 36 57N 111 29W
Powell River, *Canada* **130 D4** 49 50N 124 35W
Powers, *Mich., U.S.A.* **134 C2** 45 41N 87 32W
Powers, *Oreg., U.S.A.* **142 E1** 42 53N 124 4W
Powers Lake, *U.S.A.* **138 A3** 48 34N 102 39W
Powys □, *U.K.* **17 E4** 52 20N 3 20W
Poxoreu, *Brazil* **157 D7** 15 50 S 54 23W
Poya, *N. Cal.* **121 U19** 21 19 S 165 7 E
Poyang Hu, *China* **69 C11** 29 5N 116 20 E
Poyarkovo, *Russia* **57 E13** 49 36N 128 41 E
Poysdorf, *Austria* **31 C9** 48 40N 16 37 E
Poza de la Sal, *Spain* **34 C1** 42 35N 3 31W
Poza Rica, *Mexico* **147 C5** 20 33N 97 27W
Pozanti, *Turkey* **88 D6** 37 25N 34 50 E
Požarevac, *Serbia, Yug.* **42 C6** 44 35N 21 18 E
Požega, *Serbia, Yug.* **42 D5** 43 53N 20 2 E
Pozhva, *Russia* **54 B6** 59 5N 56 5 E
Poznań, *Poland* **47 C3** 52 25N 16 55 E
Poznań □, *Poland* **47 C4** 52 30N 17 0 E
Pozo, *U.S.A.* **145 K6** 35 20N 120 24W
Pozo Alcón, *Spain* **35 H2** 37 42N 2 56W
Pozo Almonte, *Chile* **156 E4** 20 10 S 69 50W
Pozo Colorado, *Paraguay* **158 A4** 23 30 S 58 45W
Pozo del Dátil, *Mexico* **146 B2** 30 0N 112 15W
Pozoblanco, *Spain* **37 G6** 38 23N 4 51W
Pozorrubio, *Phil.* **70 C3** 16 7N 120 33 E
Pozuzo, *Peru* **156 C2** 10 5 S 75 35W
Pozzallo, *Italy* **41 F7** 36 43N 14 51 E
Pozzuoli, *Italy* **41 B7** 40 49N 14 7 E
Pra →, *Ghana* **101 D4** 5 1N 1 37W
Prabuty, *Poland* **47 B6** 53 47N 19 15 E
Prača, *Bos.-H.* **42 D3** 43 47N 18 43 E
Prachatice, *Czech.* **30 B7** 49 1N 14 0 E
Prachin Buri, *Thailand* **76 E3** 14 0N 101 25 E
Prachuap Khiri Khan, *Thailand* **77 G2** 11 49N 99 48 E
Pradelles, *France* **24 D7** 44 46N 3 52 E
Pradera, *Colombia* **152 C2** 3 25N 76 15W
Prades, *France* **24 F6** 42 38N 2 23 E
Prado, *Brazil* **155 E4** 17 20 S 39 13W
Prado del Rey, *Spain* **37 J5** 36 48N 5 33W
Præstø, *Denmark* **15 J6** 55 8N 12 2 E
Pragersko, *Slovenia* **39 B12** 46 27N 15 42 E
Prague = Praha, *Czech.* **30 A7** 50 5N 14 22 E
Praha, *Czech.* **30 A7** 50 5N 14 22 E
Prahecq, *France* **24 B3** 46 19N 0 26W
Prahita →, *India* **82 E4** 19 0N 79 55 E
Prahova □, *Romania* **46 D6** 45 10N 26 0 E
Prahova →, *Romania* **46 E6** 44 50N 25 50 E
Prahovo, *Serbia, Yug.* **42 C7** 44 18N 22 39 E
Praia, *C. Verde Is.* **8 G6** 14 55N 23 30W
Praia, *C. Verde Is.* **93 E1** 17 0N 25 0W
Praid, *Romania* **46 C6** 46 32N 25 10 E
Prainha, *Amazonas, Brazil* **157 B5** 7 10 S 60 30W
Prainha, *Pará, Brazil* **153 D7** 1 45 S 53 30W
Prairie, *Australia* **114 C3** 20 50 S 144 35 E
Prairie →, *U.S.A.* **139 H5** 34 30N 99 23W
Prairie City, *U.S.A.* **142 D4** 44 28N 118 43W
Prairie du Chien, *U.S.A.* **140 A5** 43 3N 91 9W
Prairie du Rocher, *U.S.A.* **140 F6** 38 5N 90 6W
Prairies, *Canada* **126 C9** 52 0N 108 0W
Pramánda, *Greece* **44 E3** 39 32N 21 8 E
Pran Buri, *Thailand* **76 F2** 12 23N 99 55 E
Prang, *Ghana* **101 D4** 8 1N 0 56W
Prasonísi, Ákra, *Greece* **32 D9** 35 42N 27 46 E
Praszka, *Poland* **47 D5** 51 5N 18 31 E
Prata, *Brazil* **155 E2** 19 25 S 48 54W
Pratapgarh, *India* **80 G6** 24 2N 74 40 E
Prática di Mare, *Italy* **40 A5** 41 40N 12 26 E
Prätigau, *Switz.* **29 C9** 46 56N 9 44 E
Prato, *Italy* **38 E8** 43 53N 11 6 E
Prátola Peligna, *Italy* **39 F10** 42 6N 13 52 E
Pratovécchio, *Italy* **39 E8** 43 44N 11 43 E
Prats-de-Mollo-la-Preste, *France* **24 F6** 42 25N 2 27 E
Pratt, *U.S.A.* **139 G5** 37 39N 98 44W
Pratteln, *Switz.* **28 A5** 47 31N 7 41 E
Prattville, *U.S.A.* **135 J2** 32 28N 86 29W
Pravara →, *India* **82 E2** 19 35N 74 45 E
Pravdinsk, *Russia* **52 B6** 56 29N 43 28 E
Pravia, *Spain* **36 B4** 43 30N 6 12W
Praya, *Indonesia* **75 D5** 8 39 S 116 17 E
Pré-en-Pail, *France* **22 D6** 48 28N 0 12W
Pré-Saint-Didier, *Italy* **38 C4** 45 46N 6 59 E
Precordillera, *Argentina* **158 C2** 30 0 S 69 1W
Predáppio, *Italy* **39 D8** 44 6N 11 59 E
Predazzo, *Italy* **39 B8** 46 19N 11 36 E
Predejane, *Serbia, Yug.* **42 E7** 42 51N 22 9 E
Preeceville, *Canada* **131 C8** 51 57N 102 40W
Préfailles, *France* **22 E4** 47 9N 2 11W
Pregonero, *Venezuela* **152 B3** 8 1N 71 46W
Pregrada, *Croatia* **39 B12** 46 11N 15 45 E
Preiļi, *Latvia* **13 H22** 56 18N 26 43 E
Preko, *Croatia* **39 D12** 44 7N 15 14 E
Prelate, *Canada* **131 C7** 50 51N 109 24W
Prelog, *Croatia* **39 B13** 46 18N 16 32 E
Premier, *Canada* **130 B3** 56 4N 129 56W
Premont, *U.S.A.* **139 M5** 27 22N 98 7W
Premuda, *Croatia* **39 D11** 44 20N 14 36 E
Prenj, *Bos.-H.* **42 D2** 43 33N 17 53 E
Prenjasi, *Albania* **44 C2** 41 6N 20 32 E
Prentice, *U.S.A.* **138 C9** 45 33N 90 17W
Prenzlau, *Germany* **26 B9** 53 19N 13 50 E
Preobrazheniye, *Russia* **60 C6** 42 54N 133 54 E
Přerov, *Czech.* **31 B10** 49 28N 17 27 E
Presanella, *Italy* **38 B7** 46 13N 10 40 E
Prescott, *Canada* **128 D4** 44 45N 75 30W
Prescott, *Ariz., U.S.A.* **143 J7** 34 33N 112 28W
Prescott, *Ark., U.S.A.* **139 J8** 33 48N 93 23W
Preservation Inlet, *N.Z.* **119 G1** 46 8 S 166 35 E
Preševo, *Serbia, Yug.* **42 E6** 42 19N 21 39 E
Presho, *U.S.A.* **138 D4** 43 54N 100 3W
Presicce, *Italy* **41 C11** 39 54N 18 16 E
Presidencia de la Plaza, *Argentina* **158 B4** 27 0 S 59 50W
Presidencia Roque Saenz Peña, *Argentina* **158 B3** 26 45 S 60 30W
Presidente Epitácio, *Brazil* **155 F1** 21 56 S 52 6W
Presidente Hayes □, *Paraguay* **158 A4** 24 0 S 59 0W
Presidente Hermes, *Brazil* **157 C5** 11 17 S 61 55W
Presidente Prudente, *Brazil* **159 A5** 22 5 S 51 25W
Presidente Roxas, *Phil.* **71 F4** 11 26N 122 56 E
Presidio, *Mexico* **146 B4** 29 29N 104 23W
Presidio, *U.S.A.* **139 L2** 29 34N 104 22W
Preslav, *Bulgaria* **43 D11** 43 10N 26 52 E
Preslavska Planina, *Bulgaria* **43 D11** 43 10N 26 45 E
Prešov, *Slovak Rep.* **31 C14** 49 0N 21 15 E
Prespa, *Bulgaria* **43 F9** 41 44N 24 55 E
Prespa, L. = Prespansko Jezero, *Macedonia* **44 D3** 40 55N 21 0 E
Prespansko Jezero, *Macedonia* **44 D3** 40 55N 21 0 E
Presque Isle, *U.S.A.* **129 C6** 46 41N 68 1W
Presseger See, *Austria* **30 E6** 46 37N 13 26 E
Prestbury, *U.K.* **17 F5** 51 54N 2 2W
Prestea, *Ghana* **100 D4** 5 22N 2 7W
Presteigne, *U.K.* **17 E5** 52 17N 3 0W
Přeštice, *Czech.* **30 B6** 49 34N 13 20 E
Presto, *Bolivia* **157 D5** 18 55 S 64 56W
Preston, *Canada* **136 C4** 43 23N 80 21W
Preston, *U.K.* **16 D5** 53 46N 2 42W
Preston, *Idaho, U.S.A.* **142 E8** 42 6N 111 53W
Preston, *Iowa, U.S.A.* **140 B6** 42 3N 90 24W
Preston, *Minn., U.S.A.* **138 D8** 43 40N 92 5W
Preston, *Nev., U.S.A.* **142 G6** 38 55N 115 4W
Preston, C., *Australia* **112 D2** 20 51 S 116 12 E
Prestonpans, *U.K.* **18 F6** 55 58N 2 58W
Prestwick, *U.K.* **18 F4** 55 29N 4 37W
Prêto →, *Amazonas, Brazil* **153 D5** 0 8 S 64 6W
Prêto →, *Bahia, Brazil* **154 D3** 11 21 S 43 52W
Prêto do Igapó-Açu →, *Brazil* **153 D6** 4 26 S 59 48W
Pretoria, *S. Africa* **105 D4** 25 44 S 28 12 E

252 Preuilly-sur-Claise

Preuilly-sur-Claise, France 22 F7 46 51N 0 56 E
Préveza, Greece 45 F2 38 57N 20 47 E
Préveza □, Greece 44 E2 39 20N 20 40 E
Priazovskoye, Ukraine 51 J8 46 44N 35 40 E
Pribilof Is., Bering S. 6 D17 56 0N 170 0W
Priboj, Serbia, Yug. 42 D4 43 35N 19 32 E
Příbram, Czech. 30 B7 49 41N 14 2 E
Price, U.S.A. 142 G8 39 36N 110 49W
Price I., Canada 130 C3 52 23N 128 41W
Prichard, U.S.A. 135 K1 30 44N 88 5W
Priego, Spain 34 E2 40 26N 2 21W
Priego de Córdoba, Spain 37 H6 37 27N 4 12W
Priekule, Latvia 13 H19 56 26N 21 35 E
Prien, Germany 27 H8 47 51N 12 20 E
Prienai, Lithuania 13 J20 54 40N 23 55 E
Prieska, S. Africa 104 D3 29 40 S 22 42 E
Priest →, U.S.A. 142 B5 48 12N 116 54W
Priest L., U.S.A. 142 B5 48 35N 116 52W
Priest Valley, U.S.A. 144 J6 36 10N 120 39W
Priestly, Canada 130 C3 54 8N 125 20W
Prieto Diaz, Phil. 70 E5 13 2N 124 12 E
Prievidza, Slovak Rep. 31 C11 48 46N 18 36 E
Prijedor, Bos.-H. 39 D13 44 58N 16 41 E
Prijepolje, Serbia, Yug. 42 D4 43 27N 19 40 E
Prikaspiyskaya Nizmennost = Caspian Depression, Eurasia 53 G9 47 0N 48 0 E
Prikubanskaya Nizmennost, Russia 53 H4 45 39N 38 33 E
Prilep, Macedonia 42 F6 41 21N 21 37 E
Priluki = Pryluky, Ukraine 51 G7 50 30N 32 24 E
Prime Seal I., Australia 114 G4 40 3 S 147 43 E
Primeira Cruz, Brazil 154 B3 2 30 S 43 26W
Primorsk, Russia 50 B5 60 22N 28 37 E
Primorsko, Bulgaria 43 E12 42 15N 27 44 E
Primorsko-Akhtarsk, Russia 53 G4 46 2N 38 10 E
Primorskoye, Ukraine 51 J9 46 48N 36 20 E
Primrose L., Canada 131 C7 54 55N 109 45W
Prince Albert, Canada 131 C7 53 15N 105 50W
Prince Albert, S. Africa 104 E3 33 12 S 22 2 E
Prince Albert Mts., Antarctica 7 D11 76 0 S 161 30 E
Prince Albert Nat. Park, Canada 131 C7 54 0N 106 25W
Prince Albert Pen., Canada 126 A8 72 30N 116 0W
Prince Albert Sd., Canada 126 A8 70 25N 115 0W
Prince Alfred, C., Canada 6 B1 74 20N 124 40W
Prince Charles I., Canada 127 B12 67 47N 76 12W
Prince Charles Mts., Antarctica 7 D6 72 0 S 67 0 E
Prince Edward I. □, Canada 129 C7 46 20N 63 20W
Prince Edward Is., Ind. Oc. 109 J2 46 35 S 38 0 E
Prince George, Canada 130 C4 53 55N 122 50W
Prince of Wales, C., U.S.A. 124 C3 65 36N 168 5W
Prince of Wales I., Australia 114 A3 10 40 S 142 10 E
Prince of Wales I., Canada 126 A10 73 0N 99 0W
Prince of Wales I., U.S.A. 130 B2 55 47N 132 50W
Prince Patrick I., Canada 6 B2 77 0N 120 0W
Prince Regent Inlet, Canada 6 B3 73 0N 90 0W
Prince Rupert, Canada 130 C2 54 20N 130 20W
Princenhage, Neths. 21 F5 51 9N 4 45 E
Princesa Isabel, Brazil 154 C4 7 44 S 38 0W
Princess Charlotte B., Australia 114 A3 14 25 S 144 0 E
Princess May Ras., Australia 112 C4 15 30 S 125 30 E
Princess Royal I., Canada 130 C3 53 0N 128 40W
Princeton, Canada 130 D4 49 27N 120 30W
Princeton, Calif., U.S.A. 144 F4 39 24N 122 1W
Princeton, Ill., U.S.A. 140 C7 41 23N 89 28W
Princeton, Ind., U.S.A. 141 F9 38 21N 87 34W
Princeton, Ky., U.S.A. 134 G2 37 7N 87 53W
Princeton, Mo., U.S.A. 140 D3 40 24N 93 35W
Princeton, N.J., U.S.A. 137 F10 40 21N 74 39W
Princeton, W. Va., U.S.A. 134 G5 37 22N 81 6W
Princeville, U.S.A. 140 D7 40 56N 89 46W
Principe, I. de, Atl. Oc. 102 B1 1 37N 7 27 E
Principe Chan., Canada 130 C2 53 28N 130 0W
Principe da Beira, Brazil 157 C5 12 20 S 64 30W
Prineville, U.S.A. 142 D3 44 18N 120 51W
Prins Harald Kyst, Antarctica 7 D4 70 0 S 35 1 E
Prinsesse Astrid Kyst, Antarctica 7 D3 70 45 S 12 30 E
Prinsesse Ragnhild Kyst, Antarctica 7 D4 70 15 S 27 30 E
Prinzapolca, Nic. 148 D3 13 20N 83 35W
Prior, C., Spain 36 B2 43 34N 8 17W
Priozersk, Russia 50 B6 61 2N 30 7 E
Pripet → = Prypyat →, Europe 51 G6 51 20N 30 15 E
Pripet Marshes, Europe 51 F5 52 10N 28 10 E
Pripyat Marshes = Pripet Marshes, Europe 51 F5 52 10N 28 10 E
Pripyats = Prypyat →, Europe 51 G6 51 20N 30 15 E
Prislop, Pasul, Romania 46 B6 47 37N 25 15 E
Pristen, Russia 52 E3 51 15N 36 44 E
Priština, Serbia, Yug. 42 E6 42 40N 21 13 E
Pritzwalk, Germany 26 B8 53 9N 12 10 E
Privas, France 25 D8 44 45N 4 37 E
Priverno, Italy 40 A6 41 28N 13 11 E
Privolzhsk, Russia 52 B5 57 23N 41 16 E
Privolzhskaya Vozvyshennost, Russia 52 E7 51 0N 46 0 E
Privolzhskiy, Russia 52 E8 51 25N 46 3 E
Privolzhye, Russia 52 D9 52 52N 48 33 E
Priyutnoye, Russia 53 G6 46 12N 43 40 E
Priyutovo, Russia 54 E4 53 55N 53 59 E
Prizren, Serbia, Yug. 42 E5 42 13N 20 45 E
Prizzi, Italy 40 E6 37 43N 13 26 E
Prnjavor, Bos.-H. 42 C2 44 52N 17 43 E
Probolinggo, Indonesia 75 D4 7 46 S 113 13 E
Prochowice, Poland 47 D3 51 17N 16 20 E
Procida, Italy 41 B7 40 46N 14 2 E
Proddatur, India 83 G4 14 45N 78 30 E
Prodhromos, Cyprus 32 E11 34 57N 32 50 E
Proença-a-Nova, Portugal 37 F3 39 45N 7 54W
Prof. Van Blommestein Meer, Surinam 153 C6 4 45N 55 5W
Profítis Ilías, Greece 32 C9 36 17N 27 56 E
Profondeville, Belgium 21 H5 50 23N 4 52 E
Progreso, Mexico 147 C7 21 20N 89 40W
Prokhladnyy, Russia 53 J7 43 50N 44 2 E
Prokletije, Albania 44 B1 42 30N 19 45 E
Prokopyevsk, Russia 56 D9 54 0N 86 45 E
Prokuplje, Serbia, Yug. 42 D6 43 16N 21 36 E
Proletarsk, Russia 53 G5 46 42N 41 50 E
Proletarskaya = Proletarsk, Russia 53 G5 46 42N 41 50 E
Prome = Pyè, Burma 78 F5 18 49N 95 13 E
Prophet →, Canada 130 B4 58 48N 122 40W
Prophetstown, U.S.A. 140 C7 41 40N 89 56W
Propriá, Brazil 154 D4 10 13 S 36 51W
Propriano, France 25 G12 41 41N 8 52 E
Proserpine, Australia 114 C4 20 21 S 148 36 E
Prosna, Poland 47 D5 51 1N 18 30 E
Prosperidad, Phil. 71 G5 8 34N 125 52 E
Prosser, U.S.A. 142 C4 46 12N 119 46W
Prostějov, Czech. 31 B10 49 30N 17 9 E
Prostki, Poland 47 B9 53 42N 22 25 E
Proston, Australia 115 D5 26 8 S 151 32 E
Proszowice, Poland 31 A13 50 13N 20 16 E
Protection, U.S.A. 139 G5 37 12N 99 29W
Próti, Greece 45 G3 37 5N 21 32 E
Provadiya, Bulgaria 43 D12 43 12N 27 30 E
Proven, Belgium 21 G1 50 54N 2 40 E
Provence, France 25 E9 43 40N 5 46 E
Providence, Ky., U.S.A. 134 G2 37 24N 87 46W
Providence, R.I., U.S.A. 137 E13 41 49N 71 24W
Providence Bay, Canada 128 C3 45 41N 82 15W
Providence C., N.Z. 119 F1 45 59 S 166 29 E
Providence Mts., U.S.A. 143 J6 35 10N 115 15W
Providencia, Ecuador 152 D2 0 28 S 76 28W
Providencia, I. de, Colombia 148 D3 13 25N 81 26W
Provideniya, Russia 57 C19 64 23N 173 18W
Provins, France 23 D10 48 33N 3 15 E
Provo, U.S.A. 142 F8 40 14N 111 39W
Provost, Canada 131 C6 52 25N 110 20W
Prozor, Bos.-H. 42 D2 43 50N 17 34 E
Prudentópolis, Brazil 155 G1 25 12 S 50 57W
Prud'homme, Canada 131 C7 52 20N 105 54W
Prudnik, Poland 47 E4 50 20N 17 38 E
Prüm, Germany 27 E2 50 12N 6 25 E
Pruszcz Gdański, Poland 47 A5 54 17N 18 40 E
Pruszków, Poland 47 C7 52 9N 20 49 E
Prut →, Romania 46 D9 45 28N 28 10 E
Pruzhany, Belarus 51 F3 52 33N 24 28 E
Prvič, Croatia 39 D11 44 55N 14 47 E
Prydz B., Antarctica 7 C6 69 0 S 74 0 E
Pryluky, Ukraine 51 G7 50 30N 32 24 E
Pryor, U.S.A. 139 G7 36 19N 95 19W
Prypyat →, Europe 51 G6 51 20N 30 15 E
Przasnysz, Poland 47 B7 53 2N 20 45 E
Przedbórz, Poland 47 D6 51 6N 19 53 E
Przedecz, Poland 47 C5 52 20N 18 53 E
Przemyśl, Poland 31 B15 49 50N 22 45 E
Przeworsk, Poland 31 A15 50 6N 22 32 E
Przewóz, Poland 47 D1 51 28N 14 57 E
Przhevalsk, Kyrgyzstan 55 B9 42 30N 78 20 E
Przysuchla, Poland 47 D7 51 22N 20 38 E
Psakhná, Greece 45 F5 38 34N 23 35 E
Psará, Greece 45 F7 38 37N 25 38 E
Psathoúra, Greece 44 E6 39 30N 24 12 E
Psel →, Ukraine 51 H7 49 10N 33 37 E
Pserimos, Greece 45 H9 36 56N 27 12 E
Psíra, Greece 32 D7 35 12N 25 52 E
Pskem →, Uzbekistan 55 C5 41 38N 70 1 E
Pskemskiy Khrebet, Uzbekistan 55 C5 42 0N 70 45 E
Pskent, Uzbekistan 55 C4 40 54N 69 20 E
Pskov, Russia 50 D5 57 50N 28 25 E
Pskovskoye, Ozero, Russia 13 H22 58 0N 27 58 E
Psunj, Croatia 42 B2 45 25N 17 19 E
Pszczyna, Poland 31 B11 49 59N 18 58 E
Pteleón, Greece 45 E4 39 3N 22 57 E
Ptich = Ptsich →, Belarus 51 F5 52 9N 28 52 E
Ptolemaís, Greece 44 D3 40 30N 21 43 E
Ptsich →, Belarus 51 F5 52 9N 28 52 E
Ptuj, Slovenia 39 B12 46 28N 15 50 E
Ptujska Gora, Slovenia 39 B12 46 23N 15 47 E
Pu Xian, China 66 F6 36 24N 111 6 E
Pua, Thailand 76 C3 19 11N 100 55 E
Puán, Argentina 158 D3 37 30 S 62 45W
Pu'an, China 68 E5 25 46N 104 57 E
Puan, S. Korea 67 G14 35 44N 126 44 E
Pu'apu'a, W. Samoa 121 W23 13 34 S 172 9W
Pubei, China 68 F7 22 16N 109 31 E
Pucacuro →, Peru 152 D3 3 20 S 74 58W
Pucallpa, Peru 156 B3 8 25 S 74 30W
Pucará, Bolivia 157 D5 18 43 S 64 11W
Pucará, Peru 156 D3 15 5 S 70 24W
Pucarani, Bolivia 156 D4 16 23 S 68 30W
Pucheng, China 69 D12 27 59N 118 31 E
Pucheni, Romania 46 D6 45 12N 25 17 E
Pucio Pt., Phil. 71 F3 11 46N 121 51 E
Pučišće, Croatia 39 E13 43 22N 16 43 E
Puck, Poland 47 A5 54 45N 18 23 E
Pucka, Zatoka, Poland 47 A5 54 30N 18 40 E
Pudasjärvi, Finland 12 D22 65 23N 26 53 E
Puding, China 68 D5 26 18N 105 44 E
Pudozh, Russia 50 B9 61 48N 36 32 E
Pudtol, Phil. 70 B3 18 13N 121 22 E
Pudukkottai, India 83 J4 10 28N 78 47 E
Puebla, Mexico 147 D5 19 3N 98 12W
Puebla □, Mexico 147 D5 18 30N 98 0W
Puebla de Alcocer, Spain 37 G5 38 59N 5 14W
Puebla de Don Fadrique, Spain 35 H2 37 58N 2 25W
Puebla de Don Rodrigo, Spain 37 F6 39 5N 4 37W
Puebla de Guzmán, Spain 37 H3 37 37N 7 15W
Puebla de Sanabria, Spain 36 C4 42 4N 6 38W
Puebla de Trives, Spain 36 C3 42 20N 7 10W
Puebla del Caramiñal, Spain 36 C2 42 37N 8 56W
Pueblo, U.S.A. 138 F2 38 16N 104 37W
Pueblo Hundido, Chile 158 B1 26 20 S 70 5W
Pueblo Nuevo, Venezuela 152 B3 8 26N 71 26W
Puelches, Argentina 158 D2 38 5 S 65 51W
Puelén, Argentina 158 D2 37 32 S 67 38W
Puente Alto, Chile 158 C1 33 32 S 70 35W
Puente del Arzobispo, Spain 36 F5 39 48N 5 10W
Puente-Genil, Spain 37 H6 37 22N 4 47W
Puente la Reina, Spain 34 C3 42 40N 1 49W
Puenteareas, Spain 36 C2 42 10N 8 28W
Puentedeume, Spain 36 B2 43 24N 8 10W
Puentes de Garcia Rodriguez, Spain 36 B3 43 27N 7 50W
Pu'er, China 68 F3 23 0N 101 15 E
Puerco →, U.S.A. 143 J10 34 22N 107 50W
Puerta Galera, Phil. 70 E3 13 30N 120 57 E
Puerto, Canary Is. 33 F2 28 5N 17 20W
Puerto Acosta, Bolivia 156 D4 15 32 S 69 15W
Puerto Aisén, Chile 160 C2 45 27 S 73 0W
Puerto Ángel, Mexico 147 D5 15 40N 96 29W
Puerto Arista, Mexico 147 D6 15 56N 93 48W
Puerto Armuelles, Panama 148 E3 8 20N 82 51W
Puerto Ayacucho, Venezuela 152 B4 5 40N 67 35W
Puerto Barrios, Guatemala 148 C2 15 40N 88 32W
Puerto Bermejo, Argentina 158 B4 26 55 S 58 34W
Puerto Bermúdez, Peru 156 C3 10 20 S 74 58W
Puerto Bolívar, Ecuador 152 D2 3 19 S 79 55W
Puerto Cabello, Venezuela 152 A4 10 28N 68 1W
Puerto Cabezas, Nic. 148 D3 14 0N 83 30W
Puerto Cabo Gracias á Dios, Nic. 148 D3 15 0N 83 10W
Puerto Capaz = Jebba, Morocco 98 A4 35 11N 4 43W
Puerto Carreño, Colombia 152 B4 6 12N 67 22W
Puerto Castilla, Honduras 148 C2 16 0N 86 0W
Puerto Chicama, Peru 156 B2 7 45 S 79 20W
Puerto Coig, Argentina 160 D3 50 54 S 69 15W
Puerto Cortes, Costa Rica 148 E3 8 55N 84 0W
Puerto Cortés, Honduras 148 C2 15 51N 88 0W
Puerto Cumarebo, Venezuela 152 A4 11 29N 69 30W
Puerto de Alcudia, Spain 33 B10 39 50N 3 7 E
Puerto de Andraitx, Spain 33 B9 39 32N 2 23 E
Puerto de Cabrera, Spain 33 B9 39 8N 2 56 E
Puerto de Gran Tarajal, Canary Is. 33 F5 28 13N 14 1W
Puerto de la Cruz, Canary Is. 33 F3 28 24N 16 32W
Puerto de Pozo Negro, Canary Is. 33 F6 28 19N 13 55W
Puerto de Sóller, Spain 33 B9 39 48N 2 42 E
Puerto del Carmen, Canary Is. 33 F6 28 55N 13 38W
Puerto del Rosario, Canary Is. 33 F6 28 30N 13 52W
Puerto Deseado, Argentina 160 C3 47 55 S 66 0W
Puerto Guaraní, Paraguay 157 E6 21 18 S 57 55W
Puerto Heath, Bolivia 156 C4 12 34 S 68 39W
Puerto Huitoto, Colombia 152 C3 0 18N 74 3W
Puerto Inca, Peru 156 B3 9 22 S 74 54W
Puerto Juárez, Mexico 147 C7 21 11N 86 49W
Puerto La Cruz, Venezuela 153 A5 10 13N 64 38W
Puerto Leguízamo, Colombia 152 D3 0 12 S 74 46W
Puerto Limón, Colombia 152 C3 3 23N 73 30W
Puerto Lobos, Argentina 160 B3 42 0 S 65 3W
Puerto López, Colombia 152 C3 4 5N 72 58W
Puerto Lumbreras, Spain 35 H3 37 34N 1 48W
Puerto Madryn, Argentina 160 B3 42 48 S 65 4W
Puerto Maldonado, Peru 156 C4 12 30 S 69 10W
Puerto Manotí, Cuba 148 B4 21 22N 76 50W
Puerto Mazarrón, Spain 35 H3 37 34N 1 15W
Puerto Mercedes, Colombia 152 C3 1 11N 72 53W
Puerto Miraña, Colombia 152 D3 1 20 S 70 19W
Puerto Montt, Chile 160 B2 41 28 S 73 0W
Puerto Morelos, Mexico 147 C7 20 49N 86 52W
Puerto Nariño, Colombia 152 C4 4 56N 67 48W
Puerto Natales, Chile 160 D2 51 45 S 72 15W
Puerto Nuevo, Colombia 152 B4 5 53N 69 56W
Puerto Nutrias, Venezuela 152 B4 8 5N 69 18W
Puerto Ordaz, Venezuela 153 B5 8 16N 62 44W
Puerto Padre, Cuba 148 B4 21 13N 76 35W
Puerto Páez, Venezuela 152 B4 6 13N 67 28W
Puerto Peñasco, Mexico 146 A2 31 20N 113 33W
Puerto Pinasco, Paraguay 158 A4 22 36 S 57 50W
Puerto Pirámides, Argentina 160 B4 42 35 S 64 20W
Puerto Plata, Dom. Rep. 149 C5 19 48N 70 45W
Puerto Pollensa, Spain 33 B10 39 54N 3 4 E
Puerto Portillo, Peru 156 B3 9 45 S 72 42W
Puerto Princesa, Phil. 71 G2 9 46N 118 45 E
Puerto Quellón, Chile 160 B2 43 7 S 73 37W
Puerto Quepos, Costa Rica 148 E3 9 29N 84 6W
Puerto Real, Spain 37 J4 36 33N 6 12W
Puerto Rico, Bolivia 156 C4 11 5 S 67 38W
Puerto Rico, Canary Is. 33 G4 27 47N 15 42W
Puerto Rico ■, W. Indies 149 C6 18 15N 66 45W
Puerto Rico Trench, Atl. Oc. 149 C6 19 50N 66 0W
Puerto Saavedra, Chile 160 A2 38 47 S 73 24W
Puerto Sastre, Paraguay 158 A4 22 2 S 57 55W
Puerto Siles, Bolivia 157 C4 12 48 S 65 5W
Puerto Suárez, Bolivia 157 D6 18 58 S 57 52W
Puerto Tejada, Colombia 152 C2 3 14N 76 24W
Puerto Umbría, Colombia 152 C2 0 52N 76 33W
Puerto Vallarta, Mexico 146 C3 20 36N 105 15W
Puerto Varas, Chile 160 B2 41 19 S 72 59W
Puerto Villazón, Bolivia 157 C5 13 32 S 61 57W
Puerto Wilches, Colombia 152 B3 7 21N 73 54W
Puertollano, Spain 37 G6 38 43N 4 7W
Puertomarin, Spain 36 C3 42 48N 7 36W
Puesto Cunambo, Peru 152 D2 2 10 S 76 0W
Pueyrredón, L., Argentina 160 C2 47 20 S 72 0W
Pugachev, Russia 52 D9 52 0N 48 49 E
Puge, China 68 D4 27 20N 102 31 E
Puge, Tanzania 106 C3 4 45 S 33 11 E
Puget Sound, U.S.A. 142 C2 47 50N 122 30W
Puget-Théniers, France 25 E10 43 58N 6 53 E
Púglia □, Italy 41 B9 41 15N 16 15 E
Pugo, Phil. 70 C3 16 8N 121 15 E
Pugŏdong, N. Korea 67 C16 42 5N 130 0 E
Pugu, Tanzania 106 D4 6 55 S 39 4 E
Pūgūnzī, Iran 85 E8 25 49N 59 10 E
Puha, N.Z. 118 E6 38 30 S 177 50 E
Pui, Romania 46 D4 45 30N 23 4 E
Puica, Peru 156 C3 15 0 S 72 33W
Puieşti, Romania 46 C8 46 25N 27 33 E
Puig Mayor, Spain 33 B9 39 48N 2 47 E
Puigcerdá, Spain 34 C6 42 24N 1 50 E
Puigmal, Spain 34 C7 42 23N 2 7 E
Puigpuñent, Spain 33 B9 39 38N 2 32 E
Puisaye, Collines de la, France 23 E10 47 37N 3 20 E
Puiseaux, France 23 D9 48 11N 2 30 E
Pujilí, Ecuador 152 D2 0 57 S 78 41W
Pujon-chosuji, N. Korea 67 D14 40 35N 127 35 E
Puka, Albania 44 B1 42 2N 19 53 E
Pukaki L., N.Z. 119 E5 44 4 S 170 1 E
Pukapuka, Cook Is. 123 J11 10 53 S 165 49W
Pukatawagan, Canada 131 B8 55 45N 101 20W
Pukchin, N. Korea 67 D13 40 12N 125 45 E
Pukchŏng, N. Korea 67 D15 40 14N 128 10 E
Pukearuhe, N.Z. 118 E3 38 55 S 174 31 E
Pukekohe, N.Z. 118 D3 37 12 S 174 55 E
Puketeraki Ra., N.Z. 119 C7 42 58 S 172 13 E
Puketoi Ra., N.Z. 118 G5 40 30 S 176 5 E
Pukeuri, N.Z. 119 F6 45 4 S 171 2 E
Pukou, China 69 A12 32 7N 118 38 E
Pula, Croatia 39 D10 44 54N 13 57 E
Pula, Italy 40 D2 39 0N 9 0 E
Pulacayo, Bolivia 156 E4 20 25 S 66 41W
Pulaski, N.Y., U.S.A. 137 C8 43 34N 76 8W
Pulaski, Tenn., U.S.A. 135 H2 35 12N 87 2W
Pulaski, Va., U.S.A. 134 G5 37 3N 80 47W
Puławy, Poland 47 D8 51 23N 21 59 E
Pulga, U.S.A. 144 F5 39 48N 121 29W
Pulgaon, India 82 D4 20 44N 78 21 E
Pulicat, L., India 83 H5 13 40N 80 15 E
Puliyangudi, India 83 K3 9 11N 77 24 E
Pullabooka, Australia 117 B7 33 44 S 147 46 E
Pullman, U.S.A. 142 C5 46 44N 117 10W
Pulog, Phil. 70 C3 16 40N 120 50 E
Púlpito do Sul, Angola 103 F2 15 46 S 12 0 E
Pultusk, Poland 47 C8 52 43N 21 6 E
Pülümür, Turkey 89 C8 39 30N 39 51 E
Pulupandan, Phil. 71 F4 10 31N 122 48 E
Pumlumon Fawr, U.K. 17 E4 52 28N 3 46W
Puna, Bolivia 157 D4 19 45 S 65 28W
Puná, I., Ecuador 152 D1 2 55 S 80 5W
Punakha, Bhutan 78 B2 27 42N 89 52 E
Punalur, India 83 K3 9 0N 76 56 E
Punasar, India 80 F5 27 6N 73 6 E
Punata, Bolivia 157 D4 17 32 S 65 50W
Punch, India 81 C6 33 48N 74 4 E
Pune, India 82 E1 18 29N 73 57 E
Pungsan, N. Korea 67 D15 40 50N 128 9 E
Pungue, Ponte de, Mozam. 107 F3 19 0 S 34 0 E
Puning, China 69 F11 23 20N 116 12 E
Punjab □, India 80 D6 31 0N 76 0 E
Punjab □, Pakistan 79 C4 32 0N 74 30 E
Puno, Peru 156 D3 15 55 S 70 3W
Punta Alta, Argentina 160 A4 38 53 S 62 4W
Punta Arenas, Chile 160 D2 53 10 S 71 0W
Punta Cardón, Venezuela 152 A3 11 38N 70 14W
Punta Coles, Peru 156 D3 17 43 S 71 23W
Punta de Bombón, Peru 156 D3 17 10 S 71 48W
Punta de Díaz, Chile 158 B1 28 0 S 70 45W
Punta Delgado, Argentina 160 B4 42 43 S 63 38W
Punta Gorda, Belize 147 D7 16 10N 88 45W
Punta Gorda, U.S.A. 135 M5 26 56N 82 3W
Punta Prieta, Mexico 146 B2 28 58N 114 17W
Punta Prima, Spain 33 B11 39 48N 4 16 E
Puntabie, Australia 115 E1 32 12 S 134 13 E
Puntarenas, Costa Rica 148 E3 10 0N 84 50W
Punto Fijo, Venezuela 152 A3 11 50N 70 13W
Punxsatawney, U.S.A. 136 F5 40 57N 78 59W
Puqi, China 69 C9 29 40N 113 50 E
Puquio, Peru 156 C3 14 45 S 74 10W
Pur →, Russia 56 C8 67 31N 77 55 E
Purace, Vol., Colombia 152 C2 2 21N 76 23W
Puračić, Bos.-H. 42 C3 44 33N 18 28 E
Puralia = Puruliya, India 81 H12 23 17N 86 24 E
Purari →, Papua N. G. 120 D3 7 49 S 145 0 E
Purbeck, Isle of, U.K. 17 G5 50 39N 1 59W
Purcell, U.S.A. 139 H6 35 1N 97 22W
Purchena Tetica, Spain 35 H2 37 21N 2 21W
Puri, India 82 E7 19 50N 85 58 E
Purificación, Colombia 152 C3 3 51N 74 55W
Purmerend, Neths. 20 C5 52 32N 4 58 E
Purna →, India 82 E3 19 6N 77 2 E
Purnia, India 81 G12 25 45N 87 31 E
Purukcahu, Indonesia 75 C4 0 35 S 114 35 E
Puruliya, India 81 H12 23 17N 86 24 E
Purus →, Brazil 153 D5 3 42 S 61 28W
Puruvesi, Finland 50 B5 61 50N 29 30 E
Pŭrvomay, Bulgaria 43 E10 42 8N 25 17 E
Purwakarta, Indonesia 75 D3 6 35 S 107 29 E
Purwodadi, Jawa, Indonesia 75 D4 7 7 S 110 55 E
Purwodadi, Jawa, Indonesia 75 D3 7 51 S 110 0 E
Purwokerto, Indonesia 75 D3 7 25 S 109 14 E
Purworejo, Indonesia 75 D4 7 43 S 110 2 E
Puryŏng, N. Korea 67 C15 42 5N 129 43 E
Pus →, India 82 E3 19 55N 77 55 E
Pusad, India 82 E3 19 56N 77 36 E
Pusan, S. Korea 67 G15 35 5N 129 0 E
Pushchino, Russia 57 D16 54 10N 158 0 E
Pushkin, Russia 50 C6 59 45N 30 25 E
Pushkino, Russia 52 E8 51 16N 47 0 E
Pushkino, Russia 52 B3 56 2N 37 49 E
Püspökladány, Hungary 31 D14 47 19N 21 6 E
Pustoshka, Russia 50 D5 56 20N 29 30 E
Puszczykowo, Poland 47 C3 52 18N 16 49 E
Putahow L., Canada 131 B8 59 54N 100 40W
Putao, Burma 78 B6 27 28N 97 30 E
Putaruru, N.Z. 118 E4 38 2 S 175 50 E
Putbus, Germany 26 A9 54 22N 13 28 E
Puţeni, Romania 46 D8 45 49N 27 42 E
Putian, China 69 E12 25 23N 119 0 E
Putignano, Italy 41 B10 40 51N 17 7 E
Putina, Peru 156 C4 14 55 S 69 55W
Puting, Tanjung, Indonesia 75 C4 3 31 S 111 46 E
Putlitz, Germany 26 B8 53 15N 12 2 E
Putna, Romania 46 B6 47 50N 25 33 E
Putna →, Romania 46 D8 45 42N 27 26 E
Putnam, U.S.A. 137 E13 41 55N 71 55W
Putnok, Hungary 31 C13 48 18N 20 26 E
Putorana, Gory, Russia 57 C10 69 0N 95 0 E
Putorino, N.Z. 118 F5 39 4 S 176 58 E
Putre, Chile 156 D4 18 12 S 69 35W
Puttalam Lagoon, Sri Lanka 83 K4 8 15N 79 45 E
Putte, Neths. 21 F4 51 22N 4 24 E
Putten, Neths. 20 D7 52 16N 5 36 E
Puttgarden, Germany 26 A7 54 30N 11 10 E
Puttur, India 83 H2 12 46N 75 12 E
Putty, Australia 117 B9 32 57 S 150 42 E
Putumayo →, S. Amer. 152 D4 3 7 S 67 58W
Putuo, China 69 C14 29 56N 122 20 E

Race, C. 253

Putussibau, *Indonesia* **75 B4** 0 50N 112 56 E
Pututahi, *N.Z.* **118 E6** 38 39 S 177 53 E
Puurs, *Belgium* **21 F4** 51 5N 4 17 E
Puy-de-Dôme, *France* **24 C6** 45 46N 2 57 E
Puy-de-Dôme □, *France* **24 C7** 45 40N 3 5 E
Puy-Guillaume, *France* **24 C7** 45 57N 3 29 E
Puy-l'Évêque, *France* **24 D5** 44 31N 1 9 E
Puyallup, *U.S.A.* **144 C4** 47 12N 122 18W
Puyang, *China* **66 G8** 35 40N 115 1 E
Puyehue, *Chile* **160 B2** 40 40 S 72 37W
Puylaurens, *France* **24 E6** 43 35N 2 0 E
Puyo, *Ecuador* **152 D2** 1 28 S 77 59W
Puysegur Pt., *N.Z.* **119 G1** 46 9 S 166 37 E
Pūzeh Rīg, *Iran* **85 E8** 27 20N 58 40 E
Pwani □, *Tanzania* **106 D4** 7 0 S 39 0 E
Pweto, *Zaïre* **107 D2** 8 25 S 28 51 E
Pwinbyu, *Burma* **78 E5** 20 23N 94 40 E
Pwllheli, *U.K.* **16 E3** 52 53N 4 25W
Pya-ozero, *Russia* **48 A5** 66 5N 30 58 E
Pyana →, *Russia* **52 C8** 55 43N 46 1 E
Pyandzh, *Tajikistan* **55 E4** 37 14N 69 6 E
Pyandzh →, *Afghan.* **79 A2** 37 15N 67 15 E
Pyandzh →, *Tajikistan* **55 E4** 37 6N 68 20 E
Pyapon, *Burma* **78 G5** 16 20N 95 40 E
Pyasina →, *Russia* **57 B9** 73 30N 87 0 E
Pyatigorsk, *Russia* **53 H6** 44 2N 43 6 E
Pyatykhatky, *Ukraine* **51 H7** 48 28N 33 38 E
Pyaye, *Burma* **78 F5** 19 12N 95 10 E
Pydna, *Greece* **44 D4** 40 20N 22 34 E
Pyè, *Burma* **78 F5** 18 49N 95 13 E
Pyetrikaw, *Belarus* **51 F5** 52 11N 28 29 E
Pyhäjoki, *Finland* **12 D21** 64 28N 24 14 E
Pyinbauk, *Burma* **78 F5** 19 10N 95 12 E
Pyinmana, *Burma* **78 F6** 19 45N 96 12 E
Pyla, C., *Cyprus* **32 E12** 34 56N 33 51 E
Pyŏktong, *N. Korea* **67 D13** 40 50N 125 50 E
Pyŏnggang, *N. Korea* **67 E14** 38 24N 127 17 E
Pyŏngtaek, *S. Korea* **67 F14** 37 1N 127 4 E
P'yŏngyang, *N. Korea* **67 E13** 39 0N 125 30 E
Pyote, *U.S.A.* **139 K3** 31 32N 103 8W
Pyramid L., *U.S.A.* **142 G4** 40 1N 119 35W
Pyramid Pk., *U.S.A.* **145 J10** 36 25N 116 37W
Pyramids, *Egypt* **94 J7** 29 58N 31 9 E
Pyrénées, *Europe* **24 F4** 42 45N 0 18 E
Pyrénées-Atlantiques □, *France* **24 E3** 43 10N 0 50W
Pyrénées-Orientales □, *France* **24 F6** 42 35N 2 26 E
Pyryatyn, *Ukraine* **51 G7** 50 15N 32 25 E
Pyrzyce, *Poland* **47 B1** 53 10N 14 55 E
Pytalovo, *Russia* **50 D4** 57 5N 27 55 E
Pyttegga, *Norway* **14 B1** 62 13N 7 42 E
Pyu, *Burma* **78 F6** 18 30N 96 28 E
Pyzdry, *Poland* **47 C4** 52 11N 17 42 E

Q

Qaanaaq = Thule, *Greenland* **6 B4** 77 40N 69 0W
Qabirri →, *Azerbaijan* **53 K8** 41 3N 46 17 E
Qabr Hūd, *Yemen* **87 C5** 16 9N 49 34 E
Qachasnek, *S. Africa* **105 E4** 30 6 S 28 42 E
Qādib, *Yemen* **87 D6** 12 37N 53 57 E
Qa'el Jafr, *Jordan* **91 E5** 30 20N 36 25 E
Qa'emābād, *Iran* **85 D9** 31 44N 60 2 E
Qā'emshahr, *Iran* **85 B7** 36 30N 52 53 E
Qagan Nur, *China* **66 C8** 43 30N 114 55 E
Qahar Youyi Zhongqi, *China* **66 D7** 41 12N 112 40 E
Qahremānshahr = Bākhtarān, *Iran* **89 E12** 34 23N 47 0 E
Qaidam Pendi, *China* **64 C4** 37 0N 95 0 E
Qajarīyeh, *Iran* **85 D6** 31 1N 48 22 E
Qala, Ras il, *Malta* **32 C1** 36 1N 14 20 E
Qala-i-Jadid, *Afghan.* **80 D2** 31 1N 66 25 E
Qala Yangi, *Afghan.* **80 B2** 34 20N 66 30 E
Qalācheh, *Afghan.* **79 B2** 35 30N 67 43 E
Qalansīyah, *Yemen* **87 D6** 12 41N 53 29 E
Qalāt, *Afghan.* **79 B2** 32 15N 66 58 E
Qal'at al Akhḑar, *Si. Arabia* **84 E3** 28 0N 37 10 E
Qal'at Bīshah, *Si. Arabia* **86 C3** 20 0N 42 36 E
Qal'at Dīzah, *Iraq* **89 D11** 36 11N 45 7 E
Qal'at Sukkar, *Iraq* **89 G12** 31 51N 46 5 E
Qal'eh Darreh, *Iran* **84 B5** 38 47N 47 2 E
Qal'eh-ye Best, *Afghan.* **79 C2** 31 30N 64 21 E
Qal'eh-ye Now, *Afghan.* **79 B1** 35 0N 63 5 E
Qal'eh-ye Panjeh, *Afghan.* **79 A4** 37 0N 72 35 E
Qal'eh-ye Sarkari, *Afghan.* **79 B2** 35 54N 67 17 E
Qal'eh-ye Valī, *Afghan.* **79 B1** 35 46N 63 45 E
Qalyûb, *Egypt* **94 H7** 30 12N 31 11 E
Qamar, Ghubbat al, *Yemen* **87 C6** 16 20N 52 30 E
Qamar, Jabal al, *Oman* **87 C6** 16 48N 53 15 E
Qamdo, *China* **68 B1** 31 15N 97 6 E
Qamruddin Karez, *Pakistan* **79 C3** 31 45N 68 20 E
Qandahār, *Afghan.* **79 C2** 31 32N 65 30 E
Qandahār □, *Afghan.* **79 C2** 31 0N 65 0 E
Qapān, *Iran* **85 B7** 37 40N 55 47 E
Qapshaghay, *Kazakstan* **55 B8** 43 51N 77 14 E
Qapshaghay Bögeni, *Kazakstan* **55 B8** 43 45N 77 50 E
Qaqortoq = Julianehåb, *Greenland* **6 C5** 60 43N 46 0W
Qâra, *Egypt* **94 B2** 29 38N 26 30 E
Qarā', Jabal al, *Oman* **87 C6** 17 15N 54 15 E
Qara Qash →, *India* **81 B8** 35 0N 78 30 E
Qarabutaq, *Kazakstan* **54 G8** 49 59N 60 14 E
Qaraçala, *Azerbaijan* **53 L9** 39 45N 48 53 E
Qaraghandy, *Kazakstan* **56 E8** 49 50N 73 10 E
Qārah, *Si. Arabia* **84 D4** 29 55N 40 3 E
Qarataū, *Kazakstan* **55 B5** 43 10N 70 28 E
Qarāvol, *Afghan.* **79 A3** 37 14N 68 46 E
Qardud, *Sudan* **95 E2** 10 20N 29 56 E
Qareh →, *Iran* **89 C12** 39 25N 47 22 E
Qareh Tekān, *Iran* **85 B6** 36 38N 49 29 E
Qarqan He →, *China* **64 C3** 39 30N 88 30 E
Qarqaraly, *Kazakstan* **56 E8** 49 26N 75 30 E
Qarrasa, *Sudan* **95 E3** 14 38N 32 5 E
Qarshi, *Uzbekistan* **55 D2** 38 53N 65 48 E
Qartabā, *Lebanon* **91 A4** 34 4N 35 50 E
Qaryat al Gharab, *Iraq* **84 D5** 31 27N 44 48 E
Qaryat al 'Ulyā, *Si. Arabia* **84 E5** 27 33N 47 42 E
Qaskeleng, *Kazakstan* **55 B8** 43 20N 76 35 E
Qasr 'Amra, *Jordan* **84 D3** 31 48N 36 35 E
Qaşr Bū Hadi, *Libya* **96 B3** 31 1N 16 45 E
Qaşr-e Qand, *Iran* **85 E9** 26 15N 60 45 E
Qasr Farâfra, *Egypt* **94 B2** 27 0N 28 1 E
Qat Lesh, *Afghan.* **79 B2** 34 40N 66 18 E
Qa'ṭabah, *Yemen* **86 D4** 13 51N 44 42 E
Qatanā, *Syria* **91 B5** 33 26N 36 4 E
Qaţānan, Ra's, *Yemen* **87 D6** 12 21N 53 33 E
Qatar ■, *Asia* **85 E6** 25 30N 51 15 E
Qatlīsh, *Iran* **85 B8** 37 50N 57 19 E
Qattâra, *Egypt* **94 A2** 30 12N 27 3 E
Qattâra, Munkhafed el, *Egypt* **94 B2** 29 30N 27 30 E
Qattâra Depression = Qattâra, Munkhafed el, *Egypt* **94 B2** 29 30N 27 30 E
Qawām al Ḩamzah, *Iraq* **84 D5** 31 43N 44 58 E
Qāyen, *Iran* **85 C8** 33 40N 59 10 E
Qazaqstan = Kazakstan ■, *Asia* **56 E7** 50 0N 70 0 E
Qazimämmäd, *Azerbaijan* **53 K9** 40 3N 49 0 E
Qazvin, *Iran* **85 B6** 36 15N 50 0 E
Qena, *Egypt* **94 B3** 26 10N 32 43 E
Qena, W. →, *Egypt* **94 B3** 26 12N 32 44 E
Qeqertarsuaq = Disko, *Greenland* **124 C14** 69 45N 53 30W
Qeqertarsuaq = Godhavn, *Greenland* **6 C5** 69 15N 53 38W
Qeshlāq, *Iran* **89 E12** 34 55N 46 28 E
Qeshm, *Iran* **85 E8** 26 55N 56 10 E
Qezi'ot, *Israel* **91 E3** 30 52N 34 26 E
Qi Xian, *China* **66 G8** 34 40N 114 48 E
Qian Gorlos, *China* **67 B13** 45 5N 124 42 E
Qian Xian, *China* **66 G5** 34 31N 108 15 E
Qiancheng, *China* **68 D7** 27 12N 109 50 E
Qianjiang, *Guangxi Zhuangzu, China* **68 F7** 23 38N 108 58 E
Qianjiang, *Hubei, China* **69 B9** 30 24N 112 55 E
Qianjiang, *Sichuan, China* **68 C7** 29 33N 108 47 E
Qianshan, *China* **69 B11** 30 37N 116 35 E
Qianwei, *China* **68 C4** 29 13N 103 56 E
Qianxi, *China* **68 D6** 27 3N 106 3 E
Qianyang, *Hunan, China* **69 D8** 27 18N 110 10 E
Qianyang, *Shaanxi, China* **66 G4** 34 40N 107 8 E
Qianyang, *Zhejiang, China* **69 B12** 30 11N 119 25 E
Qiaojia, *China* **68 D4** 26 56N 102 58 E
Qibā', *Si. Arabia* **84 E5** 27 24N 44 20 E
Qichun, *China* **69 B10** 30 18N 115 25 E
Qidong, *Hunan, China* **69 D9** 26 49N 112 7 E
Qidong, *Jiangsu, China* **69 B13** 31 48N 121 38 E
Qijiang, *China* **68 C6** 28 57N 106 35 E
Qila Saifullāh, *Pakistan* **79 C3** 30 45N 68 17 E
Qilian Shan, *China* **64 C4** 38 30N 96 0 E
Qimen, *China* **69 C11** 29 50N 117 42 E
Qin He →, *China* **66 G7** 35 1N 113 22 E
Qin Jiang →, *China* **69 D10** 26 15N 115 55 E
Qin Ling = Qinling Shandi, *China* **66 H5** 33 50N 108 10 E
Qināb, W. →, *Yemen* **87 C5** 17 55N 49 59 E
Qin'an, *China* **66 G3** 34 48N 105 40 E
Qing Xian, *China* **66 E9** 38 35N 116 45 E
Qingcheng, *China* **67 F9** 37 15N 117 40 E
Qingdao, *China* **67 F11** 36 5N 120 20 E
Qingfeng, *China* **66 G8** 35 52N 115 8 E
Qinghai □, *China* **64 C4** 36 0N 98 0 E
Qinghai Hu, *China* **64 C5** 36 40N 100 10 E
Qinghecheng, *China* **67 D13** 41 15N 124 30 E
Qinghemen, *China* **67 D11** 41 48N 121 25 E
Qingjian, *China* **66 F6** 37 8N 110 8 E
Qingjiang, *Jiangsu, China* **67 H10** 33 30N 119 2 E
Qingjiang, *Jiangxi, China* **69 C10** 28 4N 115 29 E
Qingliu, *China* **69 D11** 26 11N 116 48 E
Qinglong, *China* **68 E5** 25 49N 105 12 E
Qingping, *China* **68 D6** 26 39N 107 47 E
Qingpu, *China* **69 B13** 31 10N 121 6 E
Qingshui, *China* **66 G4** 34 48N 106 8 E
Qingshuihe, *China* **66 E6** 39 55N 111 35 E
Qingtian, *China* **69 C13** 28 12N 120 15 E
Qingtongxia Shuiku, *China* **66 F3** 37 50N 105 58 E
Qingxi, *China* **68 D7** 27 8N 108 43 E
Qingxu, *China* **66 F7** 37 34N 112 22 E
Qingyang, *Anhui, China* **69 B11** 30 38N 117 50 E
Qingyang, *Gansu, China* **66 F4** 36 2N 107 55 E
Qingyi Jiang →, *China* **68 C4** 29 32N 103 44 E
Qingyuan, *Guangdong, China* **69 F9** 23 40N 112 59 E
Qingyuan, *Liaoning, China* **67 C13** 42 10N 124 55 E
Qingyuan, *Zhejiang, China* **69 D12** 27 36N 119 3 E
Qingyun, *China* **67 F9** 37 45N 117 20 E
Qingzhen, *China* **68 D6** 26 31N 106 25 E
Qinhuangdao, *China* **67 E10** 39 56N 119 30 E
Qinling Shandi, *China* **66 H5** 33 50N 108 10 E
Qinshui, *China* **66 G7** 35 40N 112 8 E
Qinyang, *China* **66 G7** 35 7N 112 57 E
Qinyuan, *China* **66 F7** 36 29N 112 20 E
Qinzhou, *China* **68 G7** 21 58N 108 38 E
Qionghai, *China* **76 C8** 19 15N 110 26 E
Qionglai, *China* **68 B4** 30 25N 103 31 E
Qionglai Shan, *China* **68 B4** 31 0N 102 30 E
Qiongshan, *China* **76 C8** 19 51N 110 26 E
Qiongzhou Haixia, *China* **76 B8** 20 10N 110 15 E
Qiqihar, *China* **57 E13** 47 26N 124 0 E
Qirâiya, W. →, *Egypt* **91 E3** 30 27N 34 0 E
Qiryat Ata, *Israel* **91 C4** 32 47N 35 6 E
Qiryat Gat, *Israel* **91 D3** 31 32N 34 46 E
Qiryat Mal'akhi, *Israel* **91 D3** 31 44N 34 44 E
Qiryat Shemona, *Israel* **91 B4** 33 13N 35 35 E
Qiryat Yam, *Israel* **91 C4** 32 51N 35 4 E
Qishan, *China* **66 G4** 34 25N 107 38 E
Qishn, *Yemen* **87 D5** 15 26N 51 40 E
Qitai, *China* **64 B3** 44 2N 89 35 E
Qitbīt, W. →, *Oman* **87 C6** 19 15N 54 23 E
Qiubei, *China* **68 E5** 24 2N 104 12 E
Qixia, *China* **67 F11** 37 17N 120 52 E
Qiyang, *China* **69 D8** 26 35N 111 50 E
Qızılağac Körfäzi, *Azerbaijan* **89 C13** 39 9N 49 0 E
Qojūr, *Iran* **84 B5** 36 12N 47 55 E
Qom, *Iran* **85 C6** 34 40N 51 0 E
Qomsheh, *Iran* **85 D6** 32 0N 51 55 E
Qondūz, *Afghan.* **79 A3** 36 50N 68 50 E
Qondūz □, *Afghan.* **79 A3** 36 50N 68 50 E
Qorveh, *Iran* **89 E12** 35 10N 47 48 E
Qostanay, *Kazakstan* **56 D7** 53 10N 63 35 E
Qoṭūr, *Iran* **89 C11** 38 28N 44 25 E
Qu Jiang →, *China* **68 B6** 30 1N 106 24 E
Qu Xian, *Sichuan, China* **68 B6** 30 48N 106 58 E
Qu Xian, *Zhejiang, China* **69 C12** 28 57N 118 54 E
Quairading, *Australia* **113 F2** 32 0 S 117 21 E
Quakenbrück, *Germany* **26 C3** 52 41N 7 57 E
Quakertown, *U.S.A.* **137 F9** 40 26N 75 21W
Qualeup, *Australia* **113 F2** 33 48 S 116 48 E
Quambatook, *Australia* **116 C5** 35 49 S 143 34 E
Quambone, *Australia* **117 A7** 30 57 S 147 53 E
Quamby, *Australia* **114 C3** 20 22 S 140 17 E
Quan Long, *Vietnam* **77 H5** 9 7N 105 8 E
Quanah, *U.S.A.* **139 H5** 34 18N 99 44W
Quandialla, *Australia* **117 C7** 34 1 S 147 47 E
Quang Ngai, *Vietnam* **76 E7** 15 13N 108 58 E
Quang Yen, *Vietnam* **76 B6** 20 56N 106 52 E
Quannan, *China* **69 E10** 24 45N 114 33 E
Quantock Hills, *U.K.* **17 F4** 51 8N 3 10W
Quanzhou, *Fujian, China* **69 E12** 24 55N 118 34 E
Quanzhou, *Guangxi Zhuangzu, China* **69 E8** 25 57N 111 5 E
Quaqtaq, *Canada* **127 B13** 60 55N 69 40W
Quaraí, *Brazil* **158 C4** 30 15 S 56 20W
Quarré-les-Tombes, *France* **23 E10** 47 21N 4 0 E
Quartu Sant'Elena, *Italy* **40 C2** 39 15N 9 10 E
Quartzsite, *U.S.A.* **145 M12** 33 40N 114 13W
Quatsino, *Canada* **130 C3** 50 30N 127 40W
Quatsino Sd., *Canada* **130 C3** 50 25N 127 58W
Quba, *Azerbaijan* **53 K9** 41 21N 48 32 E
Qūchān, *Iran* **85 B8** 37 10N 58 27 E
Queanbeyan, *Australia* **117 C8** 35 17 S 149 14 E
Québec, *Canada* **129 C5** 46 52N 71 13W
Québec □, *Canada* **129 B6** 48 0N 74 0W
Quedlinburg, *Germany* **26 D7** 51 47N 11 8 E
Queen Alexandra Ra., *Antarctica* **7 E11** 85 0 S 170 0 E
Queen Charlotte, *Canada* **130 C2** 53 15N 132 2W
Queen Charlotte Bay, *Falk. Is.* **160 D4** 51 50 S 60 40W
Queen Charlotte Is., *Canada* **130 C2** 53 20N 132 10W
Queen Charlotte Sd., *N.Z.* **119 B9** 41 10 S 174 15 E
Queen Charlotte Str., *Canada* **130 C3** 51 0N 128 0W
Queen City, *U.S.A.* **140 D4** 40 25N 92 34W
Queen Elizabeth Is., *Canada* **124 B10** 76 0N 95 0W
Queen Elizabeth Nat. Park, *Uganda* **106 C3** 0 0 30 0 E
Queen Mary Land, *Antarctica* **7 D7** 70 0 S 95 0 E
Queen Maud G., *Canada* **126 B9** 68 15N 102 30W
Queen Maud Land, *Antarctica* **7 D3** 72 30 S 12 0 E
Queen Maud Mts., *Antarctica* **7 E13** 86 0 S 160 0W
Queens Chan., *Australia* **112 C4** 15 0 S 129 30 E
Queenscliff, *Australia* **115 F3** 38 16 S 144 39 E
Queensland □, *Australia* **114 C3** 22 0 S 142 0 E
Queenstown, *Australia* **114 G4** 42 4 S 145 35 E
Queenstown, *N.Z.* **119 F3** 45 1 S 168 40 E
Queenstown, *S. Africa* **104 E4** 31 52 S 26 52 E
Queets, *U.S.A.* **144 C2** 47 32N 124 20W
Queguay Grande →, *Uruguay* **158 C4** 32 9 S 58 9W
Queimadas, *Brazil* **154 D4** 11 0 S 39 38W
Queiros, C., *Vanuatu* **121 D5** 14 55 S 167 1 E
Quela, *Angola* **103 D3** 9 10 S 16 56 E
Quelimane, *Mozam.* **107 F4** 17 53 S 36 58 E
Quelpart = Cheju Do, *S. Korea* **67 H14** 33 29N 126 34 E
Quemado, *N. Mex., U.S.A.* **143 J9** 34 20N 108 30W
Quemado, *Tex., U.S.A.* **139 L4** 28 58N 100 35W
Quemoy = Chinmen, *Taiwan* **69 E13** 24 26N 118 19 E
Quemú-Quemú, *Argentina* **158 D3** 36 3 S 63 36W
Quequén, *Argentina* **158 D4** 38 30 S 58 30W
Querco, *Peru* **156 C3** 13 50 S 74 52W
Querétaro, *Mexico* **146 C4** 20 36N 100 23W
Querétaro □, *Mexico* **146 C5** 20 30N 100 0W
Querfurt, *Germany* **26 D7** 51 23N 11 35 E
Quesada, *Spain* **35 H1** 37 51N 3 4W
Queshan, *China* **66 H8** 32 55N 114 2 E
Quesnel, *Canada* **130 C4** 53 0N 122 30W
Quesnel →, *Canada* **130 C4** 52 58N 122 29W
Quesnel L., *Canada* **130 C4** 52 30N 121 20W
Questa, *U.S.A.* **143 H11** 36 42N 105 36W
Questembert, *France* **22 E4** 47 40N 2 28W
Quetena, *Bolivia* **156 E4** 22 10 S 67 25W
Quetico Prov. Park, *Canada* **128 C1** 48 30N 91 45W
Quetrequile, *Argentina* **160 B3** 41 33 S 69 22W
Quetta, *Pakistan* **79 C2** 30 15N 66 55 E
Quevedo, *Ecuador* **152 D2** 1 2 S 79 29W
Quezaltenango, *Guatemala* **148 D1** 14 50N 91 30W
Quezon □, *Phil.* **70 D3** 14 40N 121 30 E
Quezon City, *Phil.* **70 D3** 14 38N 121 0 E
Qufār, *Si. Arabia* **84 E4** 27 26N 41 37 E
Qui Nhon, *Vietnam* **76 F7** 13 40N 109 13 E
Quibala, *Angola* **103 E2** 10 46 S 14 59 E
Quibaxe, *Angola* **103 D2** 8 24 S 14 27 E
Quibdo, *Colombia* **152 B2** 5 42N 76 40W
Quiberon, *France* **22 E3** 47 29N 3 9W
Quíbor, *Venezuela* **152 B4** 9 56N 69 37W
Quick, *Canada* **130 C3** 54 36N 126 54W
Quickborn, *Germany* **26 B5** 53 42N 9 52 E
Quiet L., *Canada* **130 A2** 61 5N 133 5W
Quiévrain, *Belgium* **21 H3** 50 24N 3 41 E
Quiindy, *Paraguay* **158 B4** 25 58 S 57 14W
Quila, *Mexico* **146 C3** 24 23N 107 13W
Quilán, C., *Chile* **160 B2** 43 15 S 74 30W
Quilcene, *U.S.A.* **144 C4** 47 49N 122 53W
Quilengues, *Angola* **103 E2** 14 12 S 14 12 E
Quilimarí, *Chile* **158 C1** 32 5 S 71 30W
Quilino, *Argentina* **158 C3** 30 14 S 64 29W
Quillabamba, *Peru* **156 C3** 12 50 S 72 50W
Quillacollo, *Bolivia* **156 D4** 17 26 S 66 17W
Quillagua, *Chile* **158 A2** 21 40 S 69 40W
Quillaicillo, *Chile* **158 C1** 31 17 S 71 40W
Quillan, *France* **24 F6** 42 53N 2 10 E
Quillebeuf-sur-Seine, *France* **22 C7** 49 28N 0 30 E
Quillota, *Chile* **158 C1** 32 54 S 71 16W
Quilmes, *Argentina* **158 C4** 34 43 S 58 15W
Quilon, *India* **83 K3** 8 50N 76 38 E
Quilpie, *Australia* **115 D3** 26 35 S 144 11 E
Quilpué, *Chile* **158 C1** 33 5 S 71 33W
Quilua, *Mozam.* **107 F4** 16 17 S 39 54 E
Quimbele, *Angola* **103 D3** 6 17 S 16 41 E
Quimbonge, *Angola* **103 D3** 8 36 S 18 30 E
Quime, *Bolivia* **156 D4** 17 2 S 67 15W
Quimilí, *Argentina* **158 B3** 27 40 S 62 30W
Quimper, *France* **22 D2** 48 0N 4 9W
Quimperlé, *France* **22 E3** 47 53N 3 33W
Quinault →, *U.S.A.* **144 C2** 47 21N 124 18W
Quincemil, *Peru* **156 C3** 13 15 S 70 40W
Quincy, *Calif., U.S.A.* **144 F6** 39 56N 120 57W
Quincy, *Fla., U.S.A.* **135 K3** 30 35N 84 34W
Quincy, *Ill., U.S.A.* **138 F9** 39 56N 91 23W
Quincy, *Mass., U.S.A.* **137 D14** 42 15N 71 0W
Quincy, *Wash., U.S.A.* **142 C4** 47 22N 119 56W
Quines, *Argentina* **158 C2** 32 13 S 65 48W
Quinga, *Mozam.* **107 F5** 15 49 S 40 15 E
Quingey, *France* **23 E12** 47 7N 5 52 E
Quiniluban Group, *Phil.* **71 F3** 11 27N 120 48 E
Quintana de la Serena, *Spain* **37 G5** 38 45N 5 40W
Quintana Roo □, *Mexico* **147 D7** 19 0N 88 0W
Quintanar de la Orden, *Spain* **34 F1** 39 36N 3 5W
Quintanar de la Sierra, *Spain* **34 D2** 41 57N 2 55W
Quintanar del Rey, *Spain* **35 F3** 39 21N 1 56W
Quintero, *Chile* **158 C1** 32 45 S 71 30W
Quintin, *France* **22 D4** 48 26N 2 56W
Quinto, *Spain* **34 D4** 41 25N 0 32W
Quinyambie, *Australia* **115 E3** 30 15 S 141 0 E
Quípar →, *Spain* **35 G3** 38 15N 1 40W
Quipungo, *Angola* **103 E2** 14 37 S 14 40 E
Quirihue, *Chile* **158 D1** 36 15 S 72 35W
Quirimbo, *Angola* **103 E2** 10 36 S 14 12 E
Quirindi, *Australia* **117 A9** 31 28 S 150 40 E
Quirino □, *Phil.* **70 C3** 16 15N 121 40 E
Quiroga, *Spain* **36 C3** 42 28N 7 18W
Quiruvilca, *Peru* **156 B2** 8 1 S 78 19W
Quissac, *France* **25 E8** 43 55N 4 0 E
Quissanga, *Mozam.* **107 E5** 12 24 S 40 28 E
Quitapa, *Angola* **103 E3** 10 20 S 18 19 E
Quitilipi, *Argentina* **158 B3** 26 50 S 60 13W
Quitman, *Ga., U.S.A.* **135 K4** 30 47N 83 34W
Quitman, *Miss., U.S.A.* **135 J1** 32 2N 88 44W
Quitman, *Tex., U.S.A.* **139 J7** 32 48N 95 27W
Quito, *Ecuador* **152 D2** 0 15 S 78 35W
Quixadá, *Brazil* **154 B4** 4 55 S 39 0W
Quixaxe, *Mozam.* **107 F5** 15 17 S 40 4 E
Quixeramobim, *Brazil* **154 C4** 5 12 S 39 17W
Quixinge, *Angola* **103 D2** 9 52 S 14 23 E
Quizenga, *Angola* **103 D3** 9 21 S 15 28 E
Qujing, *China* **68 E4** 25 32N 103 41 E
Qul'ân, Jazâ'ir, *Egypt* **94 C4** 24 22N 35 31 E
Qumbu, *S. Africa* **105 E4** 31 10 S 28 48 E
Quneitra, *Syria* **91 B4** 33 7N 35 48 E
Qunfudh, *Yemen* **87 C5** 16 39N 49 33 E
Qŭnghirot, *Uzbekistan* **56 E6** 43 6N 58 54 E
Quoin I., *Australia* **112 B4** 14 54 S 129 32 E
Quoin Pt., *S. Africa* **104 E2** 34 46 S 19 37 E
Quondong, *Australia* **116 B4** 33 6 S 140 18 E
Quorn, *Australia* **116 B3** 32 25 S 138 5 E
Qŭqon, *Uzbekistan* **55 C5** 40 30N 70 57 E
Qurein, *Sudan* **95 E3** 13 30N 34 50 E
Qŭrghonteppa, *Tajikistan* **55 E4** 37 50N 68 47 E
Qurnat as Sawdā', *Lebanon* **91 A5** 34 18N 36 6 E
Qûs, *Egypt* **94 B3** 25 55N 32 50 E
Qusar, *Azerbaijan* **53 K9** 41 25N 48 26 E
Qusaybah, *Iraq* **89 E9** 34 24N 40 59 E
Quşay'ir, *Yemen* **87 D5** 14 55N 50 20 E
Quseir, *Egypt* **94 B3** 26 7N 34 16 E
Qūshchī, *Iran* **89 D11** 37 59N 45 3 E
Quthing, *Lesotho* **105 E4** 30 25 S 27 36 E
Qūṭīābād, *Iran* **89 E13** 35 47N 48 30 E
Quwo, *China* **66 G6** 35 38N 111 25 E
Quyang, *China* **66 E8** 38 35N 114 40 E
Quynh Nhai, *Vietnam* **76 B4** 21 49N 103 33 E
Quzi, *China* **66 F4** 36 20N 107 20 E
Qvareli, *Georgia* **53 K7** 41 57N 45 47 E
Qytet Stalin = Kuçova, *Albania* **44 D1** 40 47N 19 57 E
Qyzylorda, *Kazakstan* **55 A2** 44 48N 65 28 E

R

Ra, Ko, *Thailand* **77 H2** 9 13N 98 16 E
Råå, *Sweden* **15 J6** 56 0N 12 45 E
Raab, *Austria* **30 C6** 48 21N 13 39 E
Raahe, *Finland* **12 D21** 64 40N 24 28 E
Raalte, *Neths.* **20 D8** 52 23N 6 16 E
Raamsdonksveer, *Neths.* **21 E5** 51 43N 4 52 E
Raasay, *U.K.* **18 D2** 57 25N 6 4W
Raasay, Sd. of, *U.K.* **18 D2** 57 30N 6 8W
Rab, *Croatia* **39 D11** 44 45N 14 45 E
Raba, *Indonesia* **72 C1** 8 36 S 118 55 E
Rába →, *Hungary* **31 D10** 47 38N 17 38 E
Raba →, *Poland* **31 A13** 50 8N 20 30 E
Rabaçal →, *Portugal* **36 D3** 41 30N 7 12W
Rabah, *Nigeria* **101 C6** 13 5N 5 30 E
Rabai, *Kenya* **106 C4** 3 50 S 39 31 E
Rabaraba, *Papua N. G.* **120 E5** 9 58 S 149 49 E
Rabastens, *France* **24 E5** 43 50N 1 43 E
Rabastens-de-Bigorre, *France* **24 E4** 43 23N 0 9 E
Rabat, *Malta* **32 D1** 35 53N 14 25 E
Rabat, *Morocco* **98 B3** 34 2N 6 48W
Rabaul, *Papua N. G.* **120 C7** 4 24 S 152 18 E
Rabbit →, *Canada* **130 B3** 59 41N 127 12W
Rabbit Lake, *Canada* **131 C7** 53 8N 107 46W
Rabbitskin →, *Canada* **130 A4** 61 47N 120 42W
Rābigh, *Si. Arabia* **86 B2** 22 50N 39 5 E
Rabka, *Poland* **31 B12** 49 37N 19 59 E
Rābor, *Iran* **85 D8** 29 17N 56 55 E
Rača, *Serbia, Yug.* **42 C5** 44 14N 21 0 E
Răcale, *Italy* **41 C11** 39 57N 18 6 E
Racalmuto, *Italy* **40 E6** 37 24N 13 44 E
Răcăşdia, *Romania* **42 C6** 44 59N 21 36 E
Racconigi, *Italy* **38 D4** 44 46N 7 46 E
Raccoon →, *U.S.A.* **140 C3** 41 35N 93 37W
Raccoon Cr. →, *U.S.A.* **141 E9** 39 47N 87 23W
Race, C., *Canada* **129 C9** 46 40N 53 5W

Rio Negro 255

Redcliffe, Mt., Australia **113 E3** 28 30 S 121 30 E
Reddersburg, S. Africa **104 D4** 29 41 S 26 10 E
Redding, U.S.A. **142 F2** 40 35N 122 24W
Redditch, U.K. **17 E6** 52 18N 1 55W
Redenção, Brazil **154 B4** 4 13 S 38 43W
Redfield, U.S.A. **138 C5** 44 53N 98 31W
Redkey, U.S.A. **141 D11** 40 21N 85 9W
Redkino, Russia **52 B3** 56 39N 36 16 E
Redknife →, Canada **130 A5** 61 14N 119 22W
Redlands, U.S.A. **145 M9** 34 4N 117 11W
Redmond, Australia **113 F2** 34 55 S 117 40 E
Redmond, Oreg., U.S.A. **142 D3** 44 17N 121 11W
Redmond, Wash., U.S.A. **144 C4** 47 41N 122 7W
Redon, France **22 E4** 47 40N 2 6W
Redonda, Antigua **149 C7** 16 58N 62 19W
Redondela, Spain **36 C2** 42 15N 8 38W
Redondo, Portugal **37 G3** 38 39N 7 37W
Redondo Beach, U.S.A. **145 M8** 33 50N 118 23W
Redrock Pt., Canada **130 A5** 62 11N 115 2W
Redruth, U.K. **17 G2** 50 14N 5 14W
Redvers, Canada **131 D8** 49 35N 101 40W
Redwater, Canada **130 C6** 53 55N 113 6W
Redwood, U.S.A. **137 B9** 44 18N 75 48W
Redwood City, U.S.A. **144 H4** 37 30N 122 15W
Redwood Falls, U.S.A. **138 C7** 44 32N 95 7W
Ree, L., Ireland **19 C4** 53 35N 8 0W
Reed, L., Canada **131 C8** 54 38N 100 30W
Reed City, U.S.A. **134 D3** 43 53N 85 31W
Reeder, U.S.A. **138 B3** 46 7N 102 57W
Reedley, U.S.A. **144 J7** 36 36N 119 27W
Reedsburg, U.S.A. **138 D9** 43 32N 90 0W
Reedsport, U.S.A. **142 E1** 43 42N 124 6W
Reedy Creek, Australia **116 D4** 36 58 S 140 2 E
Reefton, Australia **117 C7** 34 15 S 147 27 E
Reefton, N.Z. **119 C6** 42 6 S 171 51 E
Refahiye, Turkey **89 C8** 39 54N 38 47 E
Refugio, U.S.A. **139 L6** 28 18N 97 17W
Rega →, Poland **47 A2** 54 10N 15 18 E
Regalbuto, Italy **41 E7** 37 39N 14 38 E
Regen, Germany **27 G9** 48 58N 13 8 E
Regen →, Germany **27 F8** 49 1N 12 6 E
Regeneração, Brazil **154 C3** 6 15 S 42 41W
Regensburg, Germany **27 F8** 49 1N 12 6 E
Regensdorf, Switz. **29 B6** 47 26N 8 28 E
Réggio di Calábria, Italy **41 D8** 38 6N 15 39 E
Réggio nell'Emília, Italy **38 D7** 44 43N 10 36 E
Regina, Canada **131 C8** 50 27N 104 35W
Régina, Fr. Guiana **153 C7** 4 19N 52 8W
Registro, Brazil **159 A6** 24 29 S 47 49W
Reguengos de Monsaraz, Portugal **37 G3** 38 25N 7 32W
Rehar →, India **81 H10** 23 55N 82 40 E
Rehoboth, Namibia **104 C2** 23 15 S 17 4 E
Rehovot, Israel **91 D3** 31 54N 34 48 E
Rei-Bouba, Cameroon **102 A2** 8 40N 14 15 E
Reichenbach, Germany **26 E8** 50 37N 12 17 E
Reichenbach, Switz. **28 C5** 46 38N 7 42 E
Reid, Australia **113 F4** 30 49 S 128 26 E
Reid River, Australia **114 B4** 19 40 S 146 48 E
Reiden, Switz. **28 B5** 47 14N 7 59 E
Reidsville, U.S.A. **135 G6** 36 21N 79 40W
Reigate, U.K. **17 F7** 51 14N 0 12W
Reillo, Spain **34 F3** 39 54N 1 53W
Reims, France **23 C11** 49 15N 4 1 E
Reina Adelaida, Arch., Chile **160 D2** 52 20 S 74 0W
Reinach, Aargau, Switz. **28 B6** 47 14N 8 11 E
Reinach, Basel, Switz. **28 B5** 47 29N 7 35 E
Reinbeck, U.S.A. **140 B4** 42 19N 92 36W
Reindeer →, Canada **131 B8** 55 36N 103 11W
Reindeer I., Canada **131 C9** 52 30N 98 0W
Reindeer L., Canada **131 B8** 57 15N 102 15W
Reinga, C., N.Z. **118 A1** 34 25 S 172 43 E
Reinosa, Spain **36 B6** 43 2N 4 15W
Reinosa, Paso, Spain **36 C6** 42 56N 4 10W
Reitdiep, Neths. **20 B8** 53 20N 6 20 E
Reitz, S. Africa **105 D4** 27 48 S 28 29 E
Reivilo, S. Africa **104 D3** 27 36 S 24 8 E
Rejmyre, Sweden **15 F9** 58 50N 15 55 E
Rejowiec Fabryczny, Poland **47 D10** 51 5N 23 17 E
Reka →, Slovenia **39 C11** 45 40N 14 0 E
Rekinniki, Russia **57 C17** 60 51N 163 40 E
Rekovac, Serbia, Yug. **42 D6** 43 51N 21 3 E
Reliance, Canada **131 A7** 63 0N 109 20W
Remad, Oued →, Algeria **99 B4** 33 28N 1 20W
Rémalard, France **22 D7** 48 26N 0 47 E
Remarkable, Mt., Australia **116 B3** 32 48 S 138 10 E
Rembang, Indonesia **75 D4** 6 42 S 111 21 E
Rembau, Malaysia **74 B2** 2 35N 102 6 E
Remchi, Algeria **99 A4** 35 2N 1 26W
Remedios, Colombia **152 B3** 7 2N 74 41W
Remedios, Panama **148 E3** 8 15N 81 50W
Remeshk, Iran **85 E8** 26 55N 58 50 E
Remetea, Romania **46 C6** 46 45N 25 29 E
Remich, Lux. **21 J8** 49 32N 6 22 E
Remington, U.S.A. **141 D9** 40 46N 87 9W
Rémire, Fr. Guiana **153 C7** 4 53N 52 17W
Remiremont, France **23 D13** 48 2N 6 36 E
Remo, Ethiopia **95 F5** 6 48N 41 20 E
Remontnoye, Russia **53 G6** 46 34N 43 37 E
Remoulins, France **25 E8** 43 55N 4 35 E
Remscheid, Germany **26 D3** 51 11N 7 12 E
Ren Xian, China **66 F8** 37 8N 114 40 E
Renascença, Brazil **152 D4** 3 50 S 66 21W
Rend Lake, U.S.A. **140 F8** 38 2N 88 58W
Rende, Italy **41 C9** 39 20N 16 11 E
Rendeux, Belgium **21 H7** 50 14N 5 30 E
Rendína, Greece **45 E3** 39 4N 21 58 E
Rendova, Solomon Is. **121 M9** 8 33 S 157 17 E
Rendsburg, Germany **26 A5** 54 17N 9 39 E
Rene, Russia **57 C19** 66 2N 179 25W
Renfrew, Canada **128 C4** 45 30N 76 40W
Renfrew, U.K. **18 F4** 55 52N 4 24W
Renfrewshire □, U.K. **18 F4** 55 49N 4 38W
Rengat, Indonesia **74 C2** 0 30 S 102 45 E
Rengo, Chile **158 C1** 34 24 S 70 50W
Renhua, China **69 E9** 25 5N 113 40 E
Renhuai, China **68 D6** 27 48N 106 24 E
Reni, Ukraine **51 K5** 45 28N 28 15 E
Renigunta, India **83 H4** 13 38N 79 30 E
Renk, Sudan **95 E3** 11 50N 32 50 E
Renkum, Neths. **20 E7** 51 58N 5 43 E
Renmark, Australia **116 C4** 34 11 S 140 43 E
Rennell, Solomon Is. **121 N11** 11 40 S 160 10 E
Rennell Sd., Canada **130 C2** 53 23N 132 35W
Renner Springs T.O., Australia **114 B1** 18 20 S 133 47 E
Rennes, France **22 D5** 48 7N 1 41W
Rennes, Bassin de, France **22 E5** 48 0N 1 30W
Reno, U.S.A. **144 F7** 39 31N 119 48W
Reno →, Italy **39 D9** 44 38N 12 16 E
Renovo, U.S.A. **136 E7** 41 20N 77 45W
Renqiu, China **66 E9** 38 43N 116 5 E
Rensselaer, Ind., U.S.A. **141 D9** 40 57N 87 9W
Rensselaer, N.Y., U.S.A. **137 D11** 42 38N 73 45W
Rentería, Spain **34 B3** 43 19N 1 54W
Renton, U.S.A. **144 C4** 47 29N 122 12W
Renwick, N.Z. **119 B8** 41 30 S 173 51 E
Réo, Burkina Faso **100 C4** 12 28N 2 35W
Reotipur, India **81 G10** 25 33N 83 45 E
Repalle, India **83 F5** 16 2N 80 45 E
Répcelak, Hungary **31 D10** 47 24N 17 1 E
Republic, Mich., U.S.A. **134 B2** 46 25N 87 59W
Republic, Wash., U.S.A. **142 B4** 48 39N 118 44W
Republican →, U.S.A. **138 F6** 39 4N 96 48W
Republican City, U.S.A. **138 E5** 40 6N 99 13W
Republiek, Surinam **153 B6** 5 30N 55 13W
Repulse Bay, Canada **127 B11** 66 30N 86 30W
Requena, Peru **156 B3** 5 5 S 73 52W
Requena, Spain **35 F3** 39 30N 1 4W
Resadiye = Datça, Turkey **88 D2** 36 46N 27 40 E
Reşadiye, Turkey **88 B7** 40 23N 37 20 E
Resele, Sweden **14 A11** 63 20N 17 5 E
Resen, Macedonia **42 F6** 41 5N 21 0 E
Reserve, Canada **131 C8** 52 28N 102 39W
Reserve, U.S.A. **143 K9** 33 43N 108 45W
Resht = Rasht, Iran **89 D13** 37 20N 49 40 E
Resistencia, Argentina **158 B4** 27 30 S 59 0W
Reşiţa, Romania **42 B6** 45 18N 21 53 E
Resko, Poland **47 B2** 53 47N 15 25 E
Resolution I., Canada **127 B13** 61 30N 65 0W
Resolution I., N.Z. **119 F1** 45 40 S 166 40 E
Resplandes, Brazil **154 C2** 6 17 S 45 13W
Resplendor, Brazil **155 E3** 19 20 S 41 15W
Ressano Garcia, Mozam. **105 D5** 25 25 S 32 0 E
Reston, Canada **131 D8** 49 33N 101 6W
Reszel, Poland **47 A8** 54 4N 21 10 E
Retalhuleu, Guatemala **148 D1** 14 33N 91 46W
Reteag, Romania **46 B5** 47 10N 24 0 E
Retenue, L. de, Zaïre **107 E2** 11 0 S 27 0 E
Retford, U.K. **16 D7** 53 19N 0 56W
Rethel, France **23 C11** 49 30N 4 20 E
Rethem, Germany **26 C5** 52 47N 9 22 E
Réthímnon, Greece **32 D6** 35 18N 24 30 E
Réthímnon □, Greece **32 D6** 35 23N 24 28 E
Retiche, Alpi, Switz. **29 D10** 46 30N 10 0 E
Retie, Belgium **21 F6** 51 16N 5 5 E
Retiers, France **22 E5** 47 55N 1 23W
Retortillo, Spain **36 E4** 40 48N 6 21W
Rétság, Hungary **31 D12** 47 58N 19 10 E
Reuland, Belgium **21 H8** 50 12N 6 8 E
Réunion ■, Ind. Oc. **92 J9** 21 0 S 56 0 E
Reus, Spain **34 D6** 41 10N 1 5 E
Reusel, Neths. **21 F6** 51 21N 5 9 E
Reuss →, Switz. **29 B6** 47 16N 8 24 E
Reutlingen, Germany **27 G5** 48 29N 9 12 E
Reutte, Austria **30 D3** 47 29N 10 42 E
Reuver, Neths. **21 F8** 51 17N 6 5 E
Reval = Tallinn, Estonia **13 G21** 59 22N 24 48 E
Revda, Russia **54 C7** 56 48N 59 57 E
Revel, France **24 E6** 43 28N 2 0 E
Revelganj, India **81 G11** 25 50N 84 40 E
Revelstoke, Canada **130 C5** 51 0N 118 10W
Reventazón, Peru **156 B1** 6 10 S 80 58W
Revigny-sur-Ornain, France **23 D11** 48 49N 4 59 E
Revilla Gigedo, Is., Pac. Oc. **124 H8** 18 40N 112 0W
Revillagigedo I., U.S.A. **130 B2** 55 50N 131 20W
Revin, France **23 C11** 49 55N 4 39 E
Revolyutsii, Pik, Tajikistan **55 D6** 38 31N 72 21 E
Revuè →, Mozam. **107 F3** 19 50 S 34 0 E
Rewa, India **81 G9** 24 33N 81 25 E
Rewa →, Guyana **153 C6** 3 19N 58 42W
Rewari, India **80 E7** 28 15N 76 40 E
Rexburg, U.S.A. **142 E8** 43 49N 111 47W
Rey, Iran **85 C6** 35 35N 51 25 E
Rey, Rio del →, Nigeria **101 E6** 4 30N 8 48 E
Rey Malabo, Eq. Guin. **101 E6** 3 45N 8 50 E
Reyðarfjörður, Iceland **12 D6** 65 2N 14 13W
Reyes, Bolivia **156 C4** 14 19 S 67 23W
Reyes, Pt., U.S.A. **144 H3** 38 0N 123 0W
Reyhanlı, Turkey **88 D7** 36 16N 36 35 E
Reykjahlið, Iceland **12 D5** 65 40N 16 55W
Reykjanes, Iceland **12 E2** 63 48N 22 40W
Reykjavík, Iceland **12 D3** 64 10N 21 57W
Reynolds, Canada **131 D9** 49 40N 95 55W
Reynolds, U.S.A. **140 C6** 41 20N 90 40W
Reynolds Ra., Australia **112 D5** 22 30 S 133 0 E
Reynoldsville, U.S.A. **136 E6** 41 5N 78 58W
Reynosa, Mexico **147 B5** 26 5N 98 18W
Rēzekne, Latvia **13 H22** 56 30N 27 17 E
Rezh, Russia **54 C8** 57 23N 61 24 E
Rezovo, Bulgaria **43 E13** 42 0N 28 0 E
Rezvān, Iran **85 E8** 27 34N 56 6 E
Rgotina, Serbia, Yug. **42 C7** 44 1N 22 17 E
Rhamnus, Greece **45 F6** 38 12N 24 3 E
Rharis, O. →, Algeria **99 C6** 26 0N 5 4 E
Rhayader, U.K. **17 E4** 52 18N 3 29W
Rheden, Neths. **20 D8** 52 3N 6 3 E
Rhein, Canada **131 C8** 51 25N 102 15W
Rhein →, Europe **20 E8** 51 52N 6 2 E
Rhein-Main-Donau-Kanal, Germany **27 F7** 49 1N 11 27 E
Rheinbach, Germany **26 E2** 50 38N 6 57 E
Rheine, Germany **26 C3** 52 17N 7 26 E
Rheineck, Switz. **29 B9** 47 28N 9 31 E
Rheinfelden, Switz. **28 A5** 47 32N 7 47 E
Rheinland-Pfalz □, Germany **27 E2** 50 0N 7 0 E
Rheinsberg, Germany **26 B8** 53 6N 12 54 E
Rheinwaldhorn, Switz. **29 D8** 46 30N 9 3 E
Rhenen, Neths. **20 E7** 51 58N 5 33 E
Rheriss, Oued →, Morocco **98 B4** 30 50N 4 34W
Rheydt, Germany **26 D2** 51 10N 6 26 E
Rhin = Rhein →, Europe **20 E8** 51 52N 6 2 E
Rhinau, France **23 D14** 48 19N 7 43 E
Rhine = Rhein →, Europe **20 E8** 51 52N 6 2 E
Rhineland-Palatinate □ = Rheinland-Pfalz □, Germany **27 E2** 50 0N 7 0 E
Rhinelander, U.S.A. **138 C10** 45 38N 89 25W
Rhino Camp, Uganda **106 B3** 3 0N 31 22 E
Rhir, Cap, Morocco **98 B3** 30 38N 9 54W
Rhisnes, Belgium **21 G5** 50 31N 4 48 E
Rho, Italy **38 C6** 45 32N 9 2 E
Rhode Island □, U.S.A. **137 E13** 41 40N 71 30W
Rhodes = Ródhos, Greece **32 C10** 36 15N 28 10 E
Rhodesia = Zimbabwe ■, Africa **107 F2** 19 0 S 30 0 E
Rhodope Mts. = Rhodopi Planina, Bulgaria **43 F9** 41 40N 24 20 E
Rhodopi Planina, Bulgaria **43 F9** 41 40N 24 20 E
Rhön = Hohe Rhön, Germany **27 E5** 50 24N 9 58 E
Rhondda, U.K. **17 F4** 51 39N 3 31W
Rhondda Cynon Taff □, U.K. **17 F4** 51 42N 3 27W
Rhône □, France **25 C8** 45 54N 4 35 E
Rhône →, France **25 E8** 43 28N 4 42 E
Rhum, U.K. **18 E2** 57 0N 6 20W
Rhyl, U.K. **16 D4** 53 20N 3 29W
Rhymney, U.K. **17 F4** 51 46N 3 17W
Ri-Aba, Eq. Guin. **101 E6** 3 28N 8 40 E
Riachão, Brazil **154 C2** 7 20 S 46 37W
Riacho de Santana, Brazil **155 D3** 13 37 S 42 57W
Rialma, Brazil **155 E2** 15 18 S 49 34W
Riang, India **78 B4** 27 31N 92 56 E
Riaño, Spain **36 C5** 42 59N 5 0W
Rians, France **25 E9** 43 37N 5 44 E
Riansares →, Spain **34 F1** 39 32N 3 18W
Riasi, India **81 C6** 33 10N 74 50 E
Riau □, Indonesia **74 B2** 0 0 102 35 E
Riau, Kepulauan, Indonesia **74 B2** 0 30N 104 20 E
Riau Arch. = Riau, Kepulauan, Indonesia **74 B2** 0 30N 104 20 E
Riaza, Spain **34 D1** 41 18N 3 30W
Riaza →, Spain **34 D1** 41 42N 3 55W
Riba de Saelices, Spain **34 E2** 40 55N 2 17W
Ribadavia, Spain **36 C2** 42 17N 8 8W
Ribadeo, Spain **36 B3** 43 35N 7 5W
Ribadesella, Spain **36 B5** 43 30N 5 7W
Ribamar, Brazil **154 B3** 2 33 S 44 3W
Ribas, Spain **34 C7** 42 19N 2 15 E
Ribas do Rio Pardo, Brazil **157 E7** 20 27 S 53 46W
Ribāţ, Yemen **86 D4** 14 18N 44 15 E
Ribble →, U.K. **16 C5** 53 52N 2 25W
Ribe, Denmark **15 J2** 55 19N 8 44 E
Ribeauvillé, France **23 D14** 48 10N 7 20 E
Ribécourt, France **23 C9** 49 30N 2 55 E
Ribeira, Spain **36 C2** 42 36N 8 58W
Ribeira Brava, Madeira **33 D2** 32 41N 17 4W
Ribeira do Pombal, Brazil **154 D4** 10 50 S 38 32W
Ribeirão Prêto, Brazil **159 A6** 21 10 S 47 50W
Ribeiro Gonçalves, Brazil **154 C2** 7 32 S 45 14W
Ribemont, France **23 C10** 49 47N 3 27 E
Ribera, Italy **40 E6** 37 30N 13 16 E
Ribérac, France **24 C4** 45 15N 0 20 E
Riberalta, Bolivia **157 C4** 11 0 S 66 0W
Ribnica, Slovenia **39 C11** 45 45N 14 45 E
Rîbniţa, Moldova **51 J5** 47 45N 29 0 E
Ribnitz-Damgarten, Germany **26 A8** 54 15N 12 27 E
Ričany, Czech. **30 B7** 50 0N 14 40 E
Riccarton, N.Z. **119 D7** 43 32 S 172 37 E
Riccia, Italy **41 A7** 41 30N 14 50 E
Riccione, Italy **39 D9** 43 59N 12 39 E
Rice, U.S.A. **145 L12** 34 5N 114 51W
Rice L., Canada **136 B6** 44 12N 78 10W
Rice Lake, U.S.A. **138 C9** 45 30N 91 44W
Rich, Morocco **98 B4** 32 16N 4 30W
Rich Hill, U.S.A. **139 F7** 38 6N 94 22W
Richards Bay, S. Africa **105 D5** 28 48 S 32 6 E
Richards L., Canada **131 B7** 59 10N 107 10W
Richardson →, Canada **131 B6** 58 25N 111 14W
Richardson Mts., N.Z. **119 E3** 44 49 S 168 34 E
Richardson Springs, U.S.A. **144 F5** 39 51N 121 46W
Richardton, U.S.A. **138 B3** 46 53N 102 19W
Riche, C., Australia **113 F2** 34 36 S 118 47 E
Richelieu, France **22 E7** 47 0N 0 20 E
Richey, U.S.A. **138 B2** 47 39N 105 4W
Richfield, Idaho, U.S.A. **142 E6** 43 3N 114 9W
Richfield, Utah, U.S.A. **143 G8** 38 46N 112 5W
Richford, U.S.A. **137 B12** 45 0N 72 40W
Richibucto, Canada **129 C7** 46 42N 64 54W
Richland, Ga., U.S.A. **135 J3** 32 5N 84 40W
Richland, Iowa, U.S.A. **140 C4** 41 13N 92 0W
Richland, Mo., U.S.A. **140 G4** 37 51N 92 26W
Richland, Oreg., U.S.A. **142 D5** 44 46N 117 10W
Richland, Wash., U.S.A. **142 C4** 46 17N 119 18W
Richland Center, U.S.A. **138 D9** 43 21N 90 23W
Richlands, U.S.A. **134 G5** 37 6N 81 48W
Richmond, N.S.W., Australia **117 B9** 33 35 S 150 42 E
Richmond, Queens., Australia **114 C3** 20 43 S 143 8 E
Richmond, N.Z. **119 B8** 41 20 S 173 12 E
Richmond, U.K. **16 C6** 54 25N 1 43W
Richmond, Calif., U.S.A. **144 H4** 37 56N 122 21W
Richmond, Ind., U.S.A. **141 E12** 39 50N 84 53W
Richmond, Ky., U.S.A. **141 G12** 37 45N 84 18W
Richmond, Mich., U.S.A. **136 D2** 42 49N 82 45W
Richmond, Mo., U.S.A. **138 F8** 39 17N 93 58W
Richmond, Tex., U.S.A. **139 L7** 29 35N 95 46W
Richmond, Utah, U.S.A. **142 F8** 41 56N 111 48W
Richmond, Va., U.S.A. **134 G7** 37 33N 77 27W
Richmond, Mt., N.Z. **119 B8** 41 32 S 173 22 E
Richmond Ra., Australia **115 D5** 29 0 S 152 45 E
Richmond Ra., N.Z. **119 B8** 41 32 S 173 22 E
Richmond-upon-Thames, U.K. **17 F7** 51 27N 0 17W
Richterswil, Switz. **29 B7** 47 13N 8 43 E
Richton, U.S.A. **135 K1** 31 16N 88 56W
Richwood, Ohio, U.S.A. **141 D13** 40 26N 83 18W
Richwood, W. Va., U.S.A. **134 F5** 38 14N 80 32W
Ricla, Spain **34 D3** 41 31N 1 24W
Ricupe, Angola **103 E4** 14 37 S 21 25 E
Ridā', Yemen **86 D4** 14 25N 44 50 E
Ridder = Leninogorsk, Kazakstan **56 D9** 50 20N 83 30 E
Ridderkerk, Neths. **20 E5** 51 52N 4 35 E
Riddes, Switz. **28 D4** 46 11N 7 14 E
Ridge Farm, U.S.A. **141 E9** 39 54N 87 39W
Ridgecrest, U.S.A. **145 K9** 35 38N 117 40W
Ridgedale, Canada **131 C8** 53 0N 104 10W
Ridgefield, U.S.A. **144 E4** 45 49N 122 45W
Ridgeland, U.S.A. **135 J5** 32 29N 80 59W
Ridgelands, Australia **114 C5** 23 16 S 150 17 E
Ridgetown, Canada **128 D3** 42 26N 81 52W
Ridgeville, U.S.A. **141 D11** 40 18N 85 2W
Ridgewood, U.S.A. **137 F10** 40 59N 74 7W
Ridgway, Ill., U.S.A. **141 G8** 37 48N 88 16W
Ridgway, Pa., U.S.A. **136 E6** 41 25N 78 44W
Riding Mountain Nat. Park, Canada **131 C8** 50 50N 100 0W
Ridley, Mt., Australia **113 F3** 33 12 S 122 7 E
Ried, Austria **30 C6** 48 14N 13 30 E
Riedlingen, Germany **27 G5** 48 9N 9 28 E
Riel, Neths. **21 E6** 51 31N 5 1 E
Rienza →, Italy **39 B8** 46 49N 11 47 E
Riesa, Germany **26 D9** 51 17N 13 17 E
Riesco, I., Chile **160 D2** 52 55 S 72 40W
Riesi, Italy **41 E7** 37 17N 14 5 E
Riet →, S. Africa **104 D3** 29 0 S 23 54 E
Rieti, Italy **39 F9** 42 24N 12 51 E
Rieupeyroux, France **24 D6** 44 19N 2 12 E
Riez, France **25 E10** 43 49N 6 6 E
Riffe L., U.S.A. **144 D4** 46 32N 122 26W
Rifle, U.S.A. **142 G10** 39 32N 107 47W
Rift Valley □, Kenya **106 B4** 0 20N 36 0 E
Rig Rig, Chad **97 F2** 14 13N 14 25 E
Rīga, Latvia **13 H21** 56 53N 24 8 E
Riga, G. of, Latvia **13 H20** 57 40N 23 45 E
Rīgān, Iran **85 D8** 28 37N 58 58 E
Rīgas Jūras Līcis = Riga, G. of, Latvia **13 H20** 57 40N 23 45 E
Rigaud, Canada **137 A10** 45 29N 74 18W
Rigby, U.S.A. **142 E8** 43 40N 111 55W
Rīgestān □, Afghan. **79 C2** 30 15N 65 0 E
Riggins, U.S.A. **142 D5** 45 25N 116 19W
Rignac, France **24 D6** 44 25N 2 16 E
Rigolet, Canada **129 B8** 54 10N 58 23W
Riihimäki, Finland **13 F21** 60 45N 24 48 E
Riiser-Larsen-halvøya, Antarctica **7 C4** 68 0 S 35 0 E
Rijau, Nigeria **101 C6** 11 8N 5 17 E
Rijeka, Croatia **39 C11** 45 20N 14 21 E
Rijeka Crnojevica, Montenegro, Yug. **42 E4** 42 24N 19 1 E
Rijen, Neths. **21 E5** 51 35N 4 55 E
Rijkevorsel, Belgium **21 F5** 51 21N 4 46 E
Rijn →, Neths. **20 D4** 52 12N 4 21 E
Rijnsberg, Neths. **20 D4** 52 11N 4 27 E
Rijsbergen, Neths. **21 E5** 51 31N 4 41 E
Rijssen, Neths. **20 D9** 52 19N 6 31 E
Rijswijk, Neths. **20 D4** 52 4N 4 22 E
Rikā', W. ar →, Si. Arabia **86 B4** 22 25N 44 50 E
Rike, Ethiopia **95 E4** 10 50N 39 53 E
Rikuzentakada, Japan **60 E10** 39 0N 141 40 E
Rila, Bulgaria **43 E8** 42 7N 23 7 E
Rila Planina, Bulgaria **42 E8** 42 10N 23 0 E
Riley, U.S.A. **142 E4** 43 32N 119 28W
Rima →, Nigeria **101 C6** 13 4N 5 10 E
Rimah, Wadi ar →, Si. Arabia **84 E4** 26 5N 41 30 E
Rimavská Sobota, Slovak Rep. **31 C13** 48 22N 20 2 E
Rimbey, Canada **130 C6** 52 35N 114 15W
Rimbo, Sweden **14 E12** 59 44N 18 21 E
Rimi, Nigeria **101 C6** 12 58N 7 43 E
Rímini, Italy **39 D9** 44 3N 12 33 E
Rîmna →, Romania **46 D8** 45 36N 27 3 E
Rîmnicu Sărat, Romania **46 D8** 45 26N 27 3 E
Rîmnicu Vîlcea, Romania **46 D5** 45 9N 24 21 E
Rimouski, Canada **129 C6** 48 27N 68 30W
Rimrock, U.S.A. **144 D5** 46 38N 121 10W
Rinca, Indonesia **72 C1** 8 45 S 119 35 E
Rincón de Romos, Mexico **146 C4** 22 14N 102 18W
Rinconada, Argentina **158 A2** 22 26 S 66 10W
Ringarum, Sweden **15 F10** 58 21N 16 26 E
Ringe, Denmark **15 J4** 55 13N 10 28 E
Ringgold Is., Fiji **121 A3** 16 15 S 179 25W
Ringim, Nigeria **101 C6** 12 13N 9 10 E
Ringkøbing, Denmark **15 H2** 56 5N 8 15 E
Ringling, U.S.A. **142 C8** 46 16N 110 49W
Ringsaker, Norway **14 D4** 60 54N 10 45 E
Ringsted, Denmark **15 J5** 55 25N 11 46 E
Ringvassøy, Norway **12 B18** 69 56N 19 15 E
Rinía, Greece **45 G7** 37 23N 25 13 E
Rinjani, Indonesia **75 D5** 8 24 S 116 28 E
Rinteln, Germany **26 C5** 52 10N 9 3 E
Río, Punta del, Spain **35 J2** 36 49N 2 24W
Rio Branco, Brazil **156 B4** 9 58 S 67 49W
Río Branco, Uruguay **159 C5** 32 40 S 53 40W
Rio Brilhante, Brazil **159 A5** 21 48 S 54 33W
Río Bueno, Chile **160 B2** 40 19 S 72 58W
Río Chico, Venezuela **152 A4** 10 19N 65 59W
Rio Claro, Brazil **159 A6** 22 19 S 47 35W
Rio Claro, Trin. & Tob. **149 D7** 10 20N 61 25W
Río Colorado, Argentina **160 A4** 39 0 S 64 0W
Río Cuarto, Argentina **158 C3** 33 10 S 64 25W
Rio das Pedras, Mozam. **105 C6** 23 8 S 35 28 E
Rio de Contas, Brazil **155 D3** 13 36 S 41 48W
Rio de Janeiro, Brazil **155 F3** 23 0 S 43 12W
Rio de Janeiro □, Brazil **155 F3** 22 50 S 43 0W
Rio do Prado, Brazil **155 E3** 16 35 S 40 34W
Rio do Sul, Brazil **159 B6** 27 13 S 49 37W
Río Gallegos, Argentina **160 D3** 51 35 S 69 15W
Río Grande, Argentina **160 D3** 53 50 S 67 45W
Río Grande, Bolivia **156 E4** 20 51 S 67 17W
Rio Grande, Brazil **159 C5** 32 0 S 52 20W
Río Grande, Mexico **146 C4** 23 50N 103 2W
Río Grande, Nic. **148 D3** 12 54N 83 33W
Rio Grande →, U.S.A. **139 N6** 25 57N 97 9W
Rio Grande City, U.S.A. **139 M5** 26 23N 98 49W
Río Grande del Norte →, N. Amer. **133 E7** 26 0N 97 0W
Rio Grande do Norte □, Brazil **154 C4** 5 40 S 36 0W
Rio Grande do Sul □, Brazil **159 C5** 30 0 S 53 0W
Río Hato, Panama **148 E3** 8 22N 80 10W
Río Lagartos, Mexico **147 C7** 21 36N 88 10W
Rio Largo, Brazil **154 C4** 9 28 S 35 50W
Rio Maior, Portugal **37 F2** 39 19N 8 57W
Rio Marina, Italy **38 F7** 42 49N 10 25 E
Río Mayo, Argentina **160 C2** 45 40 S 70 15W
Río Mulatos, Bolivia **156 D4** 19 40 S 66 50W
Río Muni = Mbini □, Eq. Guin. **102 B2** 1 30N 10 0 E
Rio Negro, Brazil **159 B6** 26 0 S 49 55W

Sabugal 257

Roseville, *Calif., U.S.A.* . **144 G5** 38 45N 121 17W
Roseville, *Ill., U.S.A.* ... **140 D6** 40 44N 90 40W
Roseville, *Mich., U.S.A.* . **141 B14** 42 30N 82 56W
Rosewood, *N.S.W., Australia* .... **117 C7** 35 38 S 147 52 E
Rosewood, *N. Terr., Australia* .... **112 C4** 16 28 S 128 58 E
Rosewood, *Queens., Australia* .... **115 D5** 27 38 S 152 36 E
Roshkhvär, *Iran* .... **85 C8** 34 58N 59 37 E
Rosières-en-Santerre, *France* .... **23 C9** 49 49N 2 42 E
Rosignano Maríttimo, *Italy* **38 E7** 43 24N 10 28 E
Rosignol, *Guyana* **153 B6** 6 15N 57 30W
Roşiori de Vede, *Romania* **46 E6** 44 9N 25 0 E
Rositsa, *Bulgaria* .... **43 D12** 43 57N 27 57 E
Rositsa →, *Bulgaria* .... **43 D10** 43 10N 25 30 E
Roskilde, *Denmark* ..... **15 J6** 55 38N 12 3 E
Roskilde Amtskommune □, *Denmark* .... **15 J6** 55 35N 12 5 E
Roskilde Fjord, *Denmark* **15 J6** 55 50N 12 2 E
Roslavl, *Russia* .... **50 F7** 53 57N 32 55 E
Roslyn, *Australia* .... **117 C8** 34 29 S 149 37 E
Rosmaninhal, *Portugal* .. **37 F3** 39 44N 7 5W
Rosmead, *S. Africa* ..... **104 E4** 31 29 S 25 8 E
Røsnæs, *Denmark* ...... **15 J4** 55 44N 10 55 E
Rosolini, *Italy* .... **41 F7** 36 49N 14 57 E
Rosporden, *France* **22 E3** 47 57N 3 50W
Ross, *Australia* .... **114 G4** 42 2 S 147 30 E
Ross, *N.Z.* .... **119 C5** 42 53 S 170 49 E
Ross I., *Antarctica* ...... **7 D11** 77 30 S 168 0 E
Ross Ice Shelf, *Antarctica* **7 E12** 80 0 S 180 0 E
Ross L., *U.S.A.* **142 B3** 48 44N 121 4W
Ross-on-Wye, *U.K.* **17 F5** 51 54N 2 34W
Ross Sea, *Antarctica* .... **7 D11** 74 0 S 178 0 E
Rossa, *Switz.* .... **29 D8** 46 23N 9 8 E
Rossan Pt., *Ireland* **19 B3** 54 42N 8 47W
Rossano Cálabro, *Italy* .. **41 C9** 39 36N 16 39 E
Rossburn, *Canada* **131 C8** 50 40N 100 49W
Rosseau, *Canada* **136 A5** 45 16N 79 39W
Rossel, C., *Vanuatu* .... **121 K4** 20 23 S 166 36 E
Rossford, *U.S.A.* **141 C13** 41 36N 83 34W
Rossignol, L., *Canada* .. **128 B5** 52 43N 73 40W
Rossignol Res., *Canada* . **129 D6** 44 12N 65 10W
Rossland, *Canada* **130 D5** 49 6N 117 50W
Rosslare, *Ireland* **19 D5** 52 17N 6 24W
Rosslau, *Germany* ...... **26 D8** 51 52N 12 15 E
Rosso, *Mauritania* **100 B1** 16 40N 15 45W
Rosso, C., *France* ...... **25 F12** 42 13N 8 32 E
Rossosh, *Russia* .... **52 E4** 50 15N 39 28 E
Rossport, *Canada* **128 C2** 48 50N 87 30W
Rossum, *Neths.* .... **20 E6** 51 48N 5 20 E
Røssvatnet, *Norway* ..... **12 D16** 65 45N 14 5 E
Rossville, *Australia* ..... **114 B4** 15 48 S 145 15 E
Rossville, *U.S.A.* **141 D10** 40 25N 86 36W
Røst, *Norway* .... **12 C15** 67 32N 12 0 E
Rostāq, *Afghan.* .... **79 A3** 37 7N 69 49 E
Rosthern, *Canada* **131 C7** 52 40N 106 20W
Rostock, *Germany* ...... **26 A8** 54 5N 12 8 E
Rostov, *Don, Russia* .... **53 G4** 47 15N 39 45 E
Rostov, *Yarosl., Russia* .. **52 B4** 57 14N 39 25 E
Rostrenen, *France* **22 D3** 48 14N 3 21W
Roswell, *Ga., U.S.A.* ... **135 H3** 34 2N 84 22W
Roswell, *N. Mex., U.S.A.* **139 J2** 33 24N 104 32W
Rosyth, *U.K.* **18 E5** 56 2N 3 25W
Rota, *Spain* **37 J4** 36 37N 6 20W
Rotälven →, *Sweden* ... **14 C8** 61 15N 14 3 E
Rotan, *U.S.A.* **139 J4** 32 51N 100 28W
Rotem, *Belgium* .... **21 F7** 51 3N 5 45 E
Rotenburg, *Germany* .... **26 B5** 53 6N 9 25 E
Roth, *Germany* .... **27 F7** 49 15N 11 5 E
Rothaargebirge, *Germany* **26 E4** 51 2N 8 13 E
Rothenburg, *Switz.* ..... **29 B6** 47 6N 8 16 E
Rothenburg ob der Tauber, *Germany* ..... **27 F6** 49 23N 10 11 E
Rother →, *U.K.* .... **17 G8** 50 59N 0 45 E
Rotherham, *U.K.* **16 D6** 53 26N 1 20W
Rothes, *U.K.* **18 D5** 57 32N 3 13W
Rothesay, *Canada* **129 C6** 45 23N 66 0W
Rothesay, *U.K.* **18 F3** 55 50N 5 3W
Rothrist, *Switz.* .... **28 B5** 47 18N 7 54 E
Roti, *Indonesia* .... **72 D2** 10 50 S 123 0 E
Roto, *Australia* .... **117 B6** 33 0 S 145 30 E
Roto Aira L., *N.Z.* ..... **118 F4** 39 3 S 175 45 E
Rotoehu L., *N.Z.* .... **118 E5** 38 1 S 176 32 E
Rotoiti, L., *N.Z.* .... **118 E5** 38 2 S 176 26 E
Rotoiti L., *N.Z.* .... **119 B7** 41 51 S 172 49 E
Rotoma L., *N.Z.* .... **118 E5** 38 2 S 176 35 E
Rotondella, *Italy* .... **41 B9** 40 10N 16 31 E
Rotoroa, L., *N.Z.* .... **119 B7** 41 55 S 172 39 E
Rotorua, *N.Z.* .... **118 E5** 38 9 S 176 16 E
Rotorua, L., *N.Z.* .... **118 E5** 38 5 S 176 18 E
Rotselaar, *Belgium* ...... **21 G5** 50 57N 4 42 E
Rott →, *Germany* ...... **27 G9** 48 27N 13 25 E
Rotten →, *Switz.* .... **28 D5** 46 18N 7 36 E
Rottenburg, *Germany* .... **27 G4** 48 28N 8 55 E
Rottenmann, *Austria* .... **30 D7** 47 31N 14 22 E
Rotterdam, *Neths.* ...... **20 E5** 51 55N 4 30 E
Rottnest I., *Australia* ... **113 F2** 32 0 S 115 27 E
Rottumeroog, *Neths.* ..... **20 A9** 53 33N 6 34 E
Rottweil, *Germany* ...... **27 G4** 48 9N 8 37 E
Rotuma, *Fiji* .... **122 J9** 12 25 S 177 5 E
Roubaix, *France* .... **23 B10** 50 40N 3 10 E
Roudnice, *Czech.* .... **30 A7** 50 25N 14 15 E
Rouen, *France* .... **22 C8** 49 27N 1 4 E
Rouergue, *France* .... **24 D5** 44 15N 2 30 E
Rough Ridge, *N.Z.* ...... **119 F4** 45 10 S 169 55 E
Rouillac, *France* **24 C3** 45 47N 0 4W
Rouleau, *Canada* **131 C8** 50 10N 104 56W
Round Mountain, *U.S.A.* **142 G5** 38 43N 117 4W
Round Mt., *Australia* .... **115 E5** 30 26 S 152 16 E
Roundup, *U.S.A.* **142 C9** 46 27N 108 33W
Roura, *Fr. Guiana* **153 C7** 4 44N 52 20W
Rousay, *U.K.* **18 B5** 59 10N 3 2W
Rouses Point, *U.S.A.* **137 B11** 44 59N 73 22W
Roussillon, *Isère, France* . **25 C8** 45 24N 4 49 E
Roussillon, *Pyrénées-Or., France* .... **24 F6** 42 30N 2 35 E
Roussin, C., *N. Cal.* .... **121 U21** 21 20 S 167 59 E
Rouveen, *Neths.* .... **20 C8** 52 37N 6 11 E
Rouxville, *S. Africa* ..... **104 E4** 30 25 S 26 50 E
Rouyn, *Canada* **128 C4** 48 20N 79 0W
Rovaniemi, *Finland* ..... **12 C21** 66 29N 25 41 E
Rovato, *Italy* .... **38 C7** 45 34N 10 0 E
Rovenki, *Ukraine* .... **51 H10** 48 5N 39 21 E
Rovereto, *Italy* .... **38 C8** 45 53N 11 3 E
Rovigo, *Italy* .... **39 C8** 45 4N 11 47 E
Rovinari, *Romania* ...... **46 E4** 44 56N 23 10 E
Rovinj, *Croatia* .... **39 C10** 45 5N 13 40 E
Rovira, *Colombia* **152 C2** 4 15N 75 20W
Rovno = Rivne, *Ukraine* **51 G4** 50 40N 26 10 E
Rovnoye, *Russia* .... **52 E8** 50 52N 46 3 E
Rovuma →, *Tanzania* .. **107 E5** 10 29 S 40 28 E
Row'ān, *Iran* .... **85 C6** 35 8N 48 51 E
Rowena, *Australia* ...... **115 D4** 29 48 S 148 55 E
Rowes, *Australia* .... **117 D8** 37 0 S 149 6 E
Rowley Shoals, *Australia* **112 C2** 17 30 S 119 0 E
Roxa, *Guinea-Biss.* **100 C1** 11 15N 15 45W
Roxas = Barbacan, *Phil.* **71 F2** 10 20N 119 21 E
Roxas, *Capiz, Phil.* ..... **71 F4** 11 36N 122 49 E
Roxas, *Isabela, Phil.* .... **70 C3** 17 8N 121 36 E
Roxas, *Mindoro, Phil.* ... **70 E3** 12 35N 121 31 E
Roxboro, *U.S.A.* **135 G6** 36 24N 78 59W
Roxborough Downs, *Australia* .... **114 C2** 22 30 S 138 45 E
Roxburgh, *N.Z.* .... **119 F4** 45 33 S 169 19 E
Roxen, *Sweden* .... **15 F9** 58 30N 15 40 E
Roy, *Mont., U.S.A.* **142 C9** 47 20N 108 58W
Roy, *N. Mex., U.S.A.* ... **139 H2** 35 57N 104 12W
Roy Hill, *Australia* ..... **112 D2** 22 37 S 119 58 E
Roya, Peña, *Spain* **34 E4** 40 25N 0 40W
Royal Center, *U.S.A.* ... **141 D10** 40 52N 86 30W
Royal Leamington Spa, *U.K.* **17 E6** 52 18N 1 31W
Royal Tunbridge Wells, *U.K.* .... **17 F8** 51 7N 0 16 E
Royalla, *Australia* ...... **117 C8** 35 30 S 149 9 E
Royan, *France* **24 C2** 45 37N 1 2W
Roye, *France* .... **23 C9** 49 42N 2 48 E
Røyken, *Norway* .... **14 E4** 59 45N 10 23 E
Rožaj, *Montenegro, Yug.* **42 E5** 42 50N 20 15 E
Rózan, *Poland* .... **47 C8** 52 52N 21 25 E
Rozay-en-Brie, *France* ... **23 D9** 48 41N 2 58 E
Rozdilna, *Ukraine* ...... **51 J6** 46 50N 30 2 E
Rozhyshche, *Ukraine* .... **51 G3** 50 54N 25 15 E
Rožňava, *Slovak Rep.* ... **31 C13** 48 37N 20 35 E
Rozogi, *Poland* .... **47 B8** 53 48N 21 9 E
Rozoy-sur-Serre, *France* . **23 C11** 49 40N 4 8 E
Rozwadów, *Poland* ...... **47 E9** 50 37N 22 2 E
Rrësheni, *Albania* ...... **44 C1** 41 47N 19 49 E
Rrogozhino, *Albania* .... **44 C1** 41 2N 19 50 E
Rtanj, *Serbia, Yug.* ..... **42 D6** 43 45N 21 50 E
Rtishchevo, *Russia* ..... **52 D6** 52 18N 43 46 E
Rúa, *Spain* **36 C3** 42 24N 7 6W
Ruacaná, *Angola* .... **103 F2** 17 20 S 14 12 E
Ruahine Ra., *N.Z.* ...... **118 F5** 39 55 S 176 2 E
Ruamahanga →, *N.Z.* .. **118 H4** 41 24 S 175 8 E
Ruapehu, *N.Z.* .... **118 F4** 39 17 S 175 35 E
Ruapuke I., *N.Z.* .... **119 G3** 46 46 S 168 31 E
Ruâq, W. →, *Egypt* .... **91 F2** 30 0N 33 49 E
Ruatoria, *N.Z.* .... **118 D7** 37 55 S 178 20 E
Ruawai, *N.Z.* .... **118 C2** 36 8 S 173 59 E
Rub' al Khali, *Si. Arabia* **87 C5** 18 0N 48 0 E
Rubeho Mts., *Tanzania* .. **106 D4** 6 50 S 36 25 E
Rubezhnoye = Rubizhne, *Ukraine* .... **51 H10** 49 6N 38 25 E
Rubh a' Mhail, *U.K.* **18 F2** 55 56N 6 8W
Rubha Hunish, *U.K.* **18 D2** 57 42N 6 20W
Rubha Robhanais = Lewis, Butt of, *U.K.* .. **18 C2** 58 31N 6 16W
Rubiataba, *Brazil* ...... **155 E2** 15 8 S 49 48W
Rubicon →, *U.S.A.* **144 G5** 38 53N 121 4W
Rubicone →, *Italy* ...... **39 D9** 44 8N 12 28 E
Rubinéia, *Brazil* .... **155 F1** 20 13 S 51 2W
Rubino, *Ivory C.* **100 D4** 6 4N 4 18W
Rubio, *Venezuela* **152 B3** 7 43N 72 22W
Rubizhne, *Ukraine* ...... **51 H10** 49 6N 38 25 E
Rubtsovsk, *Russia* ...... **56 D9** 51 30N 81 10 E
Ruby L., *U.S.A.* **142 F6** 40 10N 115 28W
Ruby Mts., *U.S.A.* **142 F6** 40 30N 115 20W
Rucheng, *China* .... **69 E9** 25 33N 113 38 E
Ruciane-Nida, *Poland* .... **47 B8** 53 40N 21 32 E
Rud, *Norway* .... **14 D4** 60 1N 10 1 E
Rūd Sar, *Iran* .... **85 B6** 37 8N 50 18 E
Ruda Śląska, *Poland* ..... **47 E5** 50 16N 18 50 E
Rudall, *Australia* .... **116 B2** 33 43 S 136 17 E
Rudall →, *Australia* .... **112 D3** 22 34 S 122 13 E
Rūdbār, *Afghan.* .... **79 C1** 30 9N 62 36 E
Ruden, *Germany* .... **26 A9** 54 13N 13 47 E
Rüdersdorf, *Germany* .... **26 C9** 52 27N 13 47 E
Rudewa, *Tanzania* ...... **107 E3** 10 7 S 34 40 E
Rudkøbing, *Denmark* .... **15 K4** 54 56N 10 41 E
Rudna, *Poland* .... **47 D3** 51 30N 16 17 E
Rudnichnyy, *Russia* ..... **48 C9** 59 38N 52 26 E
Rudnik, *Bulgaria* .... **43 E12** 42 36N 27 30 E
Rudnik, *Poland* .... **47 E9** 50 26N 22 15 E
Rudnik, *Serbia, Yug.* .... **42 C5** 44 7N 20 35 E
Rudnogorsk, *Russia* ..... **57 D11** 57 15N 103 42 E
Rudnya, *Russia* .... **50 E6** 54 55N 31 7 E
Rudnyy, *Kazakstan* ...... **54 E9** 52 57N 63 7 E
Rudo, *Bos.-H.* .... **42 D4** 43 41N 19 23 E
Rudolf, Ostrov, *Russia* ... **56 A6** 81 45N 58 30 E
Rudolstadt, *Germany* .... **26 E7** 50 44N 11 19 E
Rudong, *China* .... **69 A13** 32 20N 121 12 E
Rudozem, *Bulgaria* ...... **43 F9** 41 29N 24 51 E
Rudyard, *U.S.A.* **134 B3** 46 14N 84 36W
Rue, *France* .... **23 B8** 50 15N 1 40 E
Ruelle, *France* .... **24 C4** 45 41N 0 14 E
Rufa'a, *Sudan* .... **95 E3** 14 44N 33 22 E
Ruffec, *France* .... **24 B4** 46 2N 0 12 E
Rufiji □, *Tanzania* ..... **106 D4** 8 0 S 38 30 E
Rufiji →, *Tanzania* ..... **106 D4** 7 50 S 39 15 E
Rufino, *Argentina* ...... **158 C3** 34 20 S 62 50W
Rufisque, *Senegal* **100 C1** 14 40N 17 15W
Rufunsa, *Zambia* .... **107 F2** 15 4 S 29 34 E
Rugao, *China* .... **69 A13** 32 23N 120 31 E
Rugby, *U.K.* **17 E6** 52 23N 1 16W
Rugby, *U.S.A.* **138 A5** 48 22N 100 0W
Rügen, *Germany* .... **26 A9** 54 22N 13 24 E
Rugles, *France* .... **22 D7** 48 50N 0 40 E
Ruhea, *Bangla.* .... **78 B2** 26 10N 88 25 E
Ruhengeri, *Rwanda* ..... **106 C2** 1 30 S 29 36 E
Ruhla, *Germany* .... **26 E6** 50 54N 10 23 E
Ruhland, *Germany* ...... **26 D9** 51 27N 13 52 E
Ruhnu saar, *Estonia* .... **13 H20** 57 48N 23 15 E
Ruhr →, *Germany* ...... **26 D2** 51 27N 6 43 E
Ruhuhu →, *Tanzania* ... **107 E3** 10 31 S 34 34 E
Rui Barbosa, *Brazil* ..... **155 D3** 12 18 S 40 27W
Rui'an, *China* .... **69 D13** 27 47N 120 40 E
Ruichang, *China* .... **69 C10** 29 40N 115 39 E
Ruidosa, *U.S.A.* **139 L2** 29 59N 104 41W
Ruidoso, *U.S.A.* **143 K11** 33 20N 105 41W
Ruili, *China* .... **68 E1** 24 1N 97 43 E
Ruinen, *Neths.* .... **20 C8** 52 46N 6 21 E
Ruinerwold, *Neths.* ..... **20 C8** 52 44N 6 15 E
Ruiten A Kanaal →, *Neths.* .... **20 C10** 52 54N 7 8 E
Ruivo, Pico, *Madeira* **33 D3** 32 45N 16 56W
Ruj, *Bulgaria* .... **42 E7** 42 52N 22 42 E
Rujen, *Macedonia* ...... **42 E7** 42 9N 22 30 E
Rujm Tal'at al Jamā'ah, *Jordan* .... **91 E4** 30 24N 35 30 E
Ruk, *Pakistan* .... **80 F3** 27 50N 68 42 E
Rukwa □, *Tanzania* ..... **106 D3** 7 0 S 31 30 E
Rukwa L., *Tanzania* .... **106 D3** 8 0 S 32 20 E
Rulhieres, C., *Australia* .. **112 B4** 13 56 S 127 22 E
Rulles, *Belgium* .... **21 J7** 49 43N 5 32 E
Rum = Rhum, *U.K.* **18 E2** 57 0N 6 20W
Rum Cay, *Bahamas* **149 B5** 23 40N 74 58W
Rum Jungle, *Australia* ... **112 B5** 13 0 S 130 59 E
Ruma, *Serbia, Yug.* ..... **42 B4** 45 0N 19 50 E
Rumāḥ, *Yemen* .... **86 D3** 13 34N 43 52 E
Rumāḥ, *Si. Arabia* ...... **84 E5** 25 29N 47 10 E
Rumania = Romania ■, *Europe* .... **46 C5** 46 0N 25 0 E
Rumaylah, *Iraq* .... **84 D5** 30 47N 47 37 E
Rumaylah, 'Urūq ar, *Si. Arabia* .... **86 B4** 21 0N 47 30 E
Rumbalara, *Australia* .... **114 D1** 25 20 S 134 29 E
Rumbêk, *Sudan* .... **95 F2** 6 54N 29 37 E
Rumbeke, *Belgium* ...... **21 G2** 50 56N 3 10 E
Rumburk, *Czech.* .... **30 A7** 50 57N 14 32 E
Rumelange, *Lux.* .... **21 K8** 49 27N 6 2 E
Rumford, *U.S.A.* **137 B14** 44 33N 70 33W
Rumia, *Poland* .... **47 A5** 54 37N 18 25 E
Rumilly, *France* .... **25 C9** 45 53N 5 56 E
Rumoi, *Japan* .... **60 C10** 43 56N 141 39 E
Rumonge, *Burundi* ...... **106 C2** 3 59 S 29 26 E
Rumsey, *Canada* **130 C6** 51 51N 112 48W
Rumula, *Australia* ...... **114 B4** 16 35 S 145 20 E
Rumuruti, *Kenya* .... **106 B4** 0 17N 36 32 E
Runan, *China* .... **66 H8** 33 0N 114 30 E
Runanga, *N.Z.* .... **119 C6** 42 25 S 171 15 E
Runaway, C., *N.Z.* ..... **118 D6** 37 32 S 177 59 E
Runcorn, *U.K.* **16 D5** 53 21N 2 44W
Rungwa, *Tanzania* ...... **106 D3** 6 55 S 33 32 E
Rungwa →, *Tanzania* ... **106 D3** 7 36 S 31 50 E
Rungwe, *Tanzania* ...... **107 D3** 9 11 S 33 32 E
Rungwe □, *Tanzania* .... **107 D3** 9 25 S 33 32 E
Runka, *Nigeria* .... **101 C6** 12 28N 7 20 E
Runton Ra., *Australia* ... **112 D3** 23 31 S 123 6 E
Ruokolahti, *Finland* ..... **50 B5** 61 17N 28 50 E
Ruoqiang, *China* .... **64 C3** 38 55N 88 10 E
Rupa, *India* .... **78 B4** 27 15N 92 21 E
Rupar, *India* .... **80 D7** 31 2N 76 38 E
Rupat, *Indonesia* .... **74 B2** 1 45N 101 40 E
Rupea, *Romania* .... **46 C6** 46 2N 25 13 E
Rupert →, *Canada* **128 B4** 51 29N 78 45W
Rupert House = Waskaganish, *Canada* . **128 B4** 51 30N 78 40W
Rupsa, *Bangla.* .... **78 E2** 21 44N 89 30 E
Rupununi →, *Guyana* .. **153 C6** 4 3N 58 35W
Rur →, *Germany* .... **26 E2** 51 11N 5 59 E
Rurrenabaque, *Bolivia* ... **156 C4** 14 30 S 67 32W
Rus →, *Spain* **35 F2** 39 30N 2 30W
Rusambo, *Zimbabwe* .... **107 F3** 16 30 S 32 4 E
Rusape, *Zimbabwe* ...... **107 F3** 18 35 S 32 8 E
Ruschuk = Ruse, *Bulgaria* **43 D10** 43 48N 25 59 E
Ruse, *Bulgaria* .... **43 D10** 43 48N 25 59 E
Ruşețu, *Romania* .... **46 E8** 44 57N 27 14 E
Rushan, *China* .... **67 F11** 36 56N 121 30 E
Rushden, *U.K.* **17 E7** 52 18N 0 35W
Rushford, *U.S.A.* **138 D9** 43 49N 91 46W
Rushville, *Ill., U.S.A.* ... **140 D6** 40 7N 90 34W
Rushville, *Ind., U.S.A.* .. **141 E11** 39 37N 85 27W
Rushville, *Nebr., U.S.A.* . **138 D3** 42 43N 102 28W
Rushworth, *Australia* .... **117 D6** 36 32 S 145 1 E
Russas, *Brazil* .... **154 B4** 4 55 S 37 50W
Russell, *Canada* **131 C8** 50 50N 101 20W
Russell, *N.Z.* .... **118 B3** 35 16 S 174 10 E
Russell, *U.S.A.* **138 F5** 38 54N 98 52W
Russell Is., *Solomon Is.* . **121 M10** 9 4 S 159 12 E
Russell L., *Man., Canada* **131 B8** 56 15N 101 30W
Russell L., *N.W.T., Canada* **130 A5** 63 5N 115 44W
Russellkonda, *India* ..... **82 E7** 19 57N 84 42 E
Russellville, *Ala., U.S.A.* **135 H2** 34 30N 87 44W
Russellville, *Ark., U.S.A.* **139 H8** 35 17N 93 8W
Russellville, *Ky., U.S.A.* . **135 G2** 36 51N 86 53W
Russi, *Italy* .... **39 D9** 44 22N 12 2 E
Russia ■, *Eurasia* ...... **57 C11** 62 0N 105 0 E
Russian →, *U.S.A.* **144 G3** 38 27N 123 8W
Russiaville, *U.S.A.* **141 D10** 40 25N 86 16W
Russkaya Polyana, *Kazakstan* .... **56 D8** 53 47N 73 53 E
Russkoye Ustie, *Russia* .. **6 B15** 71 0N 149 0 E
Rust, *Austria* .... **31 D9** 47 49N 16 42 E
Rustam, *Pakistan* .... **80 B5** 34 25N 72 13 E
Rustam Shahr, *Pakistan* . **80 F2** 26 58N 66 6 E
Rustavi, *Georgia* .... **53 K7** 41 30N 45 0 E
Rustenburg, *S. Africa* ... **104 D4** 25 41 S 27 14 E
Ruston, *U.S.A.* **139 J8** 32 32N 92 38W
Ruswil, *Switz.* .... **28 B6** 47 5N 8 8 E
Rutana, *Burundi* .... **106 C2** 3 55 S 30 0 E
Rute, *Spain* **37 H6** 37 19N 4 23W
Ruteng, *Indonesia* ...... **72 C2** 8 35 S 120 30 E
Ruth, *Mich., U.S.A.* **136 C2** 43 42N 82 45W
Ruth, *Nev., U.S.A.* **142 G6** 39 17N 114 59W
Rutherford, *U.S.A.* **144 G4** 38 26N 122 24W
Rutherglen, *Australia* ... **117 D7** 36 5 S 146 29 E
Rutherglen, *U.K.* **18 F4** 55 49N 4 13W
Rüti, *Switz.* .... **29 B7** 47 16N 8 51 E
Rutigliano, *Italy* .... **41 A10** 41 1N 17 0 E
Rutland Plains, *Australia* **114 B3** 15 38 S 141 43 E
Rutledge →, *Canada* **131 A6** 61 4N 112 0W
Rutledge L., *Canada* **131 A6** 61 33N 110 47W
Rutqa, W. →, *Syria* .... **89 E9** 34 30N 41 3 E
Rutshuru, *Zaïre* .... **106 C2** 1 13 S 29 25 E
Ruurlo, *Neths.* .... **20 D8** 52 5N 6 24 E
Ruvo di Púglia, *Italy* .... **41 A9** 41 7N 16 29 E
Ruvu, *Tanzania* .... **106 D4** 6 49 S 38 43 E
Ruvu →, *Tanzania* ..... **106 D4** 6 23 S 38 52 E
Ruvuma □, *Tanzania* ... **107 E4** 10 20 S 36 0 E
Ruwais, *U.A.E.* .... **85 E7** 24 5N 52 50 E
Ruwenzori, *Africa* ...... **106 B2** 0 30N 29 55 E
Ruyigi, *Burundi* .... **106 C3** 3 29 S 30 15 E
Ruyuan, *China* .... **69 E9** 24 46N 113 16 E
Ruzayevka, *Russia* ...... **52 C7** 54 4N 45 0 E
Růžhevo Konare, *Bulgaria* **43 E9** 42 23N 24 46 E
Ružomberok, *Slovak Rep.* **31 B12** 49 3N 19 17 E
Rwanda ■, *Africa* ...... **106 C3** 2 0 S 30 0 E
Ry, *Denmark* .... **15 H3** 56 5N 9 45 E
Ryakhovo, *Bulgaria* ..... **43 D11** 43 58N 26 18 E
Ryan, L., *U.K.* **18 G3** 55 0N 5 2W
Ryazan, *Russia* .... **52 C4** 54 40N 39 40 E
Ryazhsk, *Russia* .... **52 D5** 53 45N 40 3 E
Rybache = Rybachye, *Kazakstan* .... **56 E9** 46 40N 81 20 E
Rybachiy Poluostrov, *Russia* .... **48 A5** 69 43N 32 0 E
Rybachye = Ysyk-Köl, *Kyrgyzstan* .... **55 B8** 42 26N 76 12 E
Rybachye, *Kazakstan* .... **56 E9** 46 40N 81 20 E
Rybinsk, *Russia* .... **52 A4** 58 5N 38 50 E
Rybinskoye Vdkhr., *Russia* .... **50 C10** 58 30N 38 25 E
Rybnik, *Poland* .... **31 A11** 50 6N 18 32 E
Rybnitsa = Rîbnița, *Moldova* .... **51 J5** 47 45N 29 0 E
Rybnoye, *Russia* .... **52 C4** 54 45N 39 30 E
Rychwał, *Poland* .... **47 C5** 52 4N 18 10 E
Ryde, *U.K.* **17 G6** 50 43N 1 9W
Ryderwood, *U.S.A.* **144 D3** 46 23N 123 3W
Rydöbruk, *Sweden* ...... **15 H7** 56 58N 13 7 E
Rydułtowy, *Poland* ...... **31 A11** 50 4N 18 23 E
Rydzyna, *Poland* .... **47 D3** 51 47N 16 39 E
Rye, *U.K.* .... **17 G8** 50 57N 0 45 E
Rye →, *U.K.* **16 C7** 54 11N 0 44W
Rye Patch Reservoir, *U.S.A.* **142 F4** 40 28N 118 19W
Ryegate, *U.S.A.* **142 C9** 46 18N 109 15W
Ryki, *Poland* .... **47 D8** 51 38N 21 56 E
Rylsk, *Russia* .... **52 E2** 51 36N 34 43 E
Rylstone, *Australia* ..... **117 B8** 32 46 S 149 58 E
Rymanów, *Poland* .... **31 B14** 49 35N 21 51 E
Ryn, *Poland* .... **47 B8** 53 57N 21 34 E
Ryn Peski, *Kazakstan* ... **53 G9** 47 30N 49 0 E
Ryōhaku-Sanchi, *Japan* .. **63 A8** 36 9N 136 49 E
Ryōthu, *Japan* .... **60 E9** 38 5N 138 26 E
Rypin, *Poland* .... **47 B6** 53 3N 19 25 E
Ryūgasaki, *Japan* .... **63 B12** 35 54N 140 11 E
Ryūkyū Is. = Ryūkyū-rettō, *Japan* .... **61 M2** 26 0N 126 0 E
Ryūkyū-rettō, *Japan* .... **61 M2** 26 0N 126 0 E
Rzepin, *Poland* .... **47 C1** 52 20N 14 49 E
Rzeszów, *Poland* .... **31 A14** 50 5N 21 58 E
Rzeszów □, *Poland* ..... **31 B15** 50 0N 22 0 E
Rzhev, *Russia* .... **52 B2** 56 20N 34 20 E

S

Sa, *Thailand* .... **76 C3** 18 34N 100 45 E
Sa Dec, *Vietnam* .... **77 G5** 10 20N 105 46 E
Sa-koi, *Burma* .... **78 F6** 19 54N 97 3 E
Sa'ādatābād, *Fārs, Iran* .. **85 D7** 30 10N 53 5 E
Sa'ādatābād, *Kermān, Iran* **85 D7** 28 3N 55 53 E
Saale →, *Germany* ..... **26 D7** 51 56N 11 54 E
Saaler Bodden, *Germany* **26 A8** 54 20N 12 27 E
Saalfeld, *Germany* ...... **26 E7** 50 38N 11 21 E
Saalfelden, *Austria* ..... **30 D5** 47 25N 12 51 E
Saane →, *Switz.* .... **28 B4** 47 8N 7 10 E
Saar →, *Europe* .... **23 C13** 49 41N 6 32 E
Saarbrücken, *Germany* .. **27 F2** 49 14N 6 59 E
Saarburg, *Germany* ..... **27 F2** 49 36N 6 32 E
Saaremaa, *Estonia* ..... **13 G20** 58 30N 22 30 E
Saarijärvi, *Finland* ..... **13 E21** 62 43N 25 16 E
Saariselkä, *Finland* ..... **12 B23** 68 16N 28 15 E
Saarland □, *Germany* ... **23 C13** 49 20N 7 0 E
Saarlouis, *Germany* ..... **27 F2** 49 18N 6 45 E
Saas Fee, *Switz.* .... **28 D5** 46 7N 7 56 E
Sab 'Ābar, *Syria* .... **88 F7** 33 46N 37 41 E
Saba, *W. Indies* **149 C7** 17 42N 63 26W
Šabac, *Serbia, Yug.* ..... **42 C4** 44 48N 19 42 E
Sabadell, *Spain* .... **34 D7** 41 28N 2 7 E
Sabae, *Japan* .... **63 B8** 35 57N 136 11 E
Sabah □, *Malaysia* ..... **75 A5** 6 0N 117 0 E
Sabak Bernam, *Malaysia* . **77 L3** 3 46N 100 58 E
Sabalān, Kūhhā-ye, *Iran* . **89 C12** 38 15N 47 45 E
Sábana de la Mar, *Dom. Rep.* **149 C6** 19 7N 69 24W
Sábanalarga, *Colombia* .. **152 A3** 10 38N 74 55W
Sabang, *Indonesia* ...... **74 A1** 5 50N 95 15 E
Sabangan, *Phil.* .... **70 C3** 17 0N 120 55 E
Sabará, *Brazil* .... **155 E3** 19 55 S 43 46W
Sabari →, *India* .... **82 F5** 17 35N 81 16 E
Sab'atayn, Ramlat as, *Yemen* .... **86 D4** 15 30N 46 10 E
Sabattis, *U.S.A.* **137 B10** 44 6N 74 40W
Sabáudia, *Italy* .... **40 A6** 41 18N 13 2 E
Sabaya, *Bolivia* .... **156 D4** 19 1 S 68 23W
Sabāyā, Jaz., *Si. Arabia* . **86 C3** 18 35N 41 3 E
Saberania, *Indonesia* .... **73 B5** 2 5 S 138 18 E
Sabhah, *Libya* .... **96 C2** 27 9N 14 29 E
Sabhah □, *Libya* .... **96 C2** 26 0N 14 0 E
Sabie, *S. Africa* .... **105 D5** 25 10 S 30 48 E
Sabina, *U.S.A.* **141 E13** 39 29N 83 38W
Sabinal, *Mexico* **146 A3** 30 58N 107 25W
Sabinal, *U.S.A.* **139 L5** 29 19N 99 28W
Sabinal, Punta del, *Spain* **35 J2** 36 43N 2 44W
Sabinas, *Mexico* **146 B4** 27 50N 101 10W
Sabinas →, *Mexico* **146 B4** 27 37N 100 42W
Sabinas Hidalgo, *Mexico* . **146 B4** 26 33N 100 10W
Sabine →, *U.S.A.* **139 L8** 29 59N 93 47W
Sabine L., *U.S.A.* **139 L8** 29 53N 93 51W
Sabine Pass, *U.S.A.* **139 L8** 29 44N 93 54W
Sabinópolis, *Brazil* ..... **155 E3** 18 40 S 43 6W
Sabinov, *Slovak Rep.* .... **31 B14** 49 6N 21 5 E
Sabirabad, *Azerbaijan* ... **53 K9** 40 5N 48 30 E
Sabkhat Tāwurghā', *Libya* **96 B3** 31 48N 15 30 E
Sabkhet el Bardawil, *Egypt* .... **91 D2** 31 10N 33 15 E
Sablayan, *Phil.* .... **70 E3** 12 50N 120 50 E
Sable, C., *Canada* **129 D6** 43 29N 65 38W
Sable, C., *U.S.A.* **133 E10** 25 9N 81 8W
Sable I., *Canada* **129 D8** 44 0N 60 0W
Sablé-sur-Sarthe, *France* . **22 E6** 47 50N 0 20W
Saboeiro, *Brazil* .... **154 C4** 6 32 S 39 54W
Sabor →, *Portugal* **36 D3** 41 10N 7 7W
Sabou, *Burkina Faso* **100 C4** 12 1N 2 15W
Sabrātah, *Libya* .... **96 B2** 32 47N 12 29 E
Sabria, *Tunisia* .... **96 B1** 33 22N 8 45 E
Sabrina Coast, *Antarctica* **7 C9** 68 0 S 120 0 E
Sabtang I., *Phil.* .... **70 A3** 20 19N 121 52 E
Sabugal, *Portugal* **36 E3** 40 20N 7 5W

Samui, Ko 259

St. Neots, U.K. **17 E7** 52 14N 0 15W
St.-Nicolas-de-Port, France **23 D13** 48 38N 6 18 E
St. Niklass = Sint Niklaas, Belgium **21 F4** 51 10N 4 9 E
St. Niklaus, Switz. **28 D5** 46 10N 7 49 E
St.-Omer, France **23 B9** 50 45N 2 15 E
St-Pacome, Canada **129 C6** 47 24N 69 58W
St.-Palais-sur-Mer, France **24 C2** 45 38N 1 5W
St-Pamphile, Canada **129 C6** 46 58N 69 48W
St.-Pardoux-la-Rivière, France **24 C4** 45 29N 0 45 E
St. Paris, U.S.A. **141 D13** 40 8N 83 58W
St. Pascal, Canada **129 C6** 47 32N 69 48W
St. Paul, Canada **130 C6** 54 0N 111 17W
St. Paul, Ind., U.S.A. **141 E11** 39 26N 85 38W
St. Paul, Minn., U.S.A. **138 C8** 44 57N 93 6W
St. Paul, Nebr., U.S.A. **138 E5** 41 13N 98 27W
St. Paul, I., Ind. Oc. **109 H6** 38 55 S 77 34 E
St.-Paul-de-Fenouillet, France **24 F6** 42 48N 2 30 E
St. Paul I., Canada **129 C7** 47 12N 60 9W
St.-Paul-lès-Dax, France **24 E2** 43 44N 1 3W
St.-Péray, France **25 D8** 44 57N 4 50 E
St.-Père-en-Retz, France **22 E4** 47 11N 2 2W
St. Peter, U.S.A. **138 C8** 44 20N 93 57W
St-Peter-Ording, Germany **26 A4** 54 20N 8 36 E
St. Peter Port, U.K. **17 H5** 49 26N 2 33W
St. Peters, N.S., Canada **129 C7** 45 40N 60 53W
St. Peters, P.E.I., Canada **129 C7** 46 25N 62 35W
St. Petersburg = Sankt-Peterburg, Russia **50 C6** 59 55N 30 20 E
St. Petersburg, U.S.A. **135 M4** 27 46N 82 39W
St.-Philbert-de-Grand-Lieu, France **22 E5** 47 2N 1 39W
St.-Pierre, St- P. & M. **129 C8** 46 46N 56 12W
St. Pierre, Seychelles **109 E3** 9 20 S 46 0 E
St-Pierre, L., Canada **128 C5** 46 12N 72 52W
St.-Pierre-d'Oléron, France **24 C2** 45 57N 1 19W
St.-Pierre-Église, France **22 C5** 49 40N 1 24W
St.-Pierre-en-Port, France **22 C7** 49 48N 0 30 E
St.-Pierre et Miquelon □, St- P. & M. **129 C8** 46 55N 56 10W
St.-Pierre-le-Moûtier, France **23 F10** 46 47N 3 7 E
St.-Pierre-sur-Dives, France **22 C6** 49 2N 0 1W
St.-Pieters Leew, Belgium **21 G4** 50 47N 4 16 E
St.-Pol-de-Léon, France **22 D2** 48 41N 4 0W
St.-Pol-sur-Mer, France **23 A9** 51 1N 2 20 E
St.-Pol-sur-Ternoise, France **23 B9** 50 23N 2 20 E
St.-Pons, France **24 E6** 43 30N 2 45 E
St.-Pourçain-sur-Sioule, France **24 B7** 46 18N 3 18 E
St.-Quay-Portrieux, France **22 D4** 48 39N 2 51W
St.-Quentin, France **23 C10** 49 50N 3 16 E
St.-Rambert-d'Albon, France **25 C8** 45 17N 4 49 E
St.-Raphaël, France **25 E10** 43 25N 6 46 E
St. Regis, U.S.A. **142 C6** 47 18N 115 6W
St.-Rémy-de-Provence, France **25 E8** 43 48N 4 50 E
St.-Renan, France **22 D2** 48 26N 4 37W
St.-Saëns, France **22 C8** 49 41N 1 16 E
St.-Sauveur-en-Puisaye, France **23 E10** 47 37N 3 12 E
St.-Sauveur-le-Vicomte, France **22 C5** 49 23N 1 32W
St.-Savin, France **24 B4** 46 34N 0 53 E
St.-Savinien, France **24 C3** 45 53N 0 42W
St. Sebastien, Tanjon' i, Madag. **105 A8** 12 26 S 48 44 E
St.-Seine-l'Abbaye, France **23 E11** 47 26N 4 47 E
St.-Sernin-sur-Rance, France **24 E6** 43 54N 2 35 E
St.-Servan-sur-Mer, France **22 D4** 48 38N 2 2W
St.-Sever, France **24 E3** 43 45N 0 35W
St.-Sever-Calvados, France **22 D5** 48 50N 1 3W
St-Siméon, Canada **129 C6** 47 51N 69 54W
St. Stephen, Canada **129 C6** 45 16N 67 17W
St.-Sulpice, France **24 E5** 43 46N 1 41 E
St.-Sulpice-Laurière, France **24 B5** 46 3N 1 29 E
St.-Syprien, France **24 F7** 42 37N 3 2 E
St.-Thégonnec, France **22 D3** 48 31N 3 57W
St. Thomas, Canada **128 D3** 42 45N 81 10W
St. Thomas I., Virgin Is. **149 C7** 18 20N 64 55W
St-Tite, Canada **128 C5** 46 45N 72 34W
St.-Tropez, France **25 E10** 43 17N 6 38 E
St. Troud = Sint Truiden, Belgium **21 G6** 50 48N 5 10 E
St.-Vaast-la-Hougue, France **22 C5** 49 35N 1 17W
St.-Valéry-en-Caux, France **22 C7** 49 52N 0 43 E
St.-Valéry-sur-Somme, France **23 B8** 50 11N 1 38 E
St.-Vallier, France **25 C8** 45 11N 4 50 E
St.-Vallier-de-Thiey, France **25 E10** 43 42N 6 51 E
St.-Varent, France **22 F6** 46 53N 0 13W
St. Vincent = São Vicente, C. Verde Is. **8 G6** 18 0N 26 1W
St. Vincent, W. Indies **149 D7** 13 10N 61 10W
St. Vincent, G., Australia **116 C3** 35 0 S 138 0 E
St. Vincent & the Grenadines ■, W. Indies **149 D7** 13 0N 61 10W
St.-Vincent-de-Tyrosse, France **24 E2** 43 39N 1 19W
St. Vincent Passage, W. Indies **149 D7** 13 30N 61 0W
St-Vith, Belgium **21 H8** 50 17N 6 9 E
St.-Yrieix-la-Perche, France **24 C5** 45 31N 1 12 E
Ste.-Adresse, France **22 C7** 49 31N 0 5 E
Ste-Agathe-des-Monts, Canada **128 C5** 46 3N 74 17W
Ste-Anne de Beaupré, Canada **129 C5** 47 2N 70 58W
Ste-Anne-des-Monts, Canada **129 C6** 49 8N 66 30W
Ste-Croix, Switz. **28 C3** 46 49N 6 34 E
Ste.-Enimie, France **24 D7** 44 22N 3 26 E
Ste.-Foy-la-Grande, France **24 D4** 44 50N 0 13 E
Ste. Genevieve, U.S.A. **140 G6** 37 59N 90 2W
Ste.-Hermine, France **24 B2** 46 32N 1 4W
Ste.-Livrade-sur-Lot, France **24 D4** 44 24N 0 36 E
Ste-Marguerite →, Canada **129 B6** 50 9N 66 36W
Ste.-Marie, Martinique **149 D7** 14 48N 61 1W
Ste.-Marie-aux-Mines, France **23 D14** 48 15N 7 12 E
Ste-Marie de la Madeleine, Canada **129 C5** 46 26N 71 0W
Ste.-Maure-de-Touraine, France **22 E7** 47 7N 0 37 E
Ste.-Maxime, France **25 E10** 43 19N 6 39 E
Ste.-Menehould, France **23 C11** 49 5N 4 54 E
Ste.-Mère-Église, France **22 C5** 49 24N 1 19W
Ste.-Rose, Guadeloupe **149 C7** 16 20N 61 45W
Ste. Rose du Lac, Canada **131 C9** 51 4N 99 30W
Saintes, France **24 C3** 45 45N 0 37W
Saintes, I. des, Guadeloupe **149 C7** 15 50N 61 35W
Stes.-Maries-de-la-Mer, France **25 E8** 43 26N 4 26 E
Saintonge, France **24 C3** 45 40N 0 50W
Saipan, Pac. Oc. **122 F6** 15 12N 145 45 E
Sairecábur, Cerro, Bolivia **158 A2** 22 43 S 67 54W
Saitama □, Japan **63 A11** 36 25N 139 30 E
Saito, Japan **62 E3** 32 3N 131 24 E
Sajama, Bolivia **156 D4** 18 7 S 69 0W
Sajan, Serbia, Yug. **42 B5** 45 50N 20 20 E
Sajó, Hungary **31 C13** 48 12N 20 44 E
Sajum, India **81 C8** 33 20N 79 0 E
Sak →, S. Africa **104 E3** 30 52 S 20 25 E
Sakai, Japan **63 C7** 34 30N 135 30 E
Sakaide, Japan **62 C5** 34 15N 133 50 E
Sakaiminato, Japan **62 B5** 35 38N 133 11 E
Sakākah, Si. Arabia **84 D4** 30 0N 40 8 E
Sakakawea, L., U.S.A. **138 B3** 47 30N 101 25W
Sakami, L., Canada **128 B4** 53 15N 77 0W
Sâkâne, 'Erg i-n, Mali **98 D4** 20 30N 1 30W
Sakania, Zaïre **107 E2** 12 43 S 28 30 E
Sakarya = Adapazarı, Turkey **88 B4** 40 48N 30 25 E
Sakarya →, Turkey **88 B4** 41 7N 30 39 E
Sakashima-Guntō, Japan **61 M2** 24 46N 124 0 E
Sakata, Japan **60 E9** 38 55N 139 50 E
Sakchu, N. Korea **67 D13** 40 23N 125 2 E
Sakeny →, Madag. **105 C8** 20 0 S 45 25 E
Sakété, Benin **101 D5** 6 40N 2 45 E
Sakha □, Russia **57 C13** 62 0N 130 0 E
Sakhalin, Russia **57 D15** 51 0N 143 0 E
Sakhalinskiy Zaliv, Russia **57 D15** 54 0N 141 0 E
Sakhi Gopal, India **82 E7** 19 58N 85 50 E
Şaki, Azerbaijan **53 K8** 41 10N 47 5 E
Šakiai, Lithuania **13 J20** 54 59N 23 0 E
Sakmara →, Russia **54 F5** 51 46N 55 1 E
Sakon Nakhon, Thailand **76 D5** 17 10N 104 9 E
Sakrand, Pakistan **80 F3** 26 10N 68 15 E
Sakri, India **82 D2** 21 2N 74 20 E
Sakrivier, S. Africa **104 E3** 30 54 S 20 28 E
Sakskøbing, Denmark **15 K5** 54 49N 11 39 E
Saku, Japan **63 A10** 36 17N 138 31 E
Sakuma, Japan **63 B9** 35 3N 137 49 E
Sakura, Japan **63 B12** 35 43N 140 14 E
Sakurai, Japan **63 C7** 34 30N 135 51 E
Saky, Ukraine **51 K7** 45 9N 33 34 E
Sal →, Russia **53 G5** 47 31N 40 45 E
Šal'a, Slovak Rep. **31 C10** 48 10N 17 50 E
Sala, Sweden **13 G17** 59 58N 16 35 E
Sala Consilina, Italy **41 B8** 40 23N 15 36 E
Sala-y-Gómez, Pac. Oc. **123 K17** 26 28 S 105 28W
Salaberry-de-Valleyfield, Canada **128 C5** 45 15N 74 8W
Saladas, Argentina **158 B4** 28 15 S 58 40W
Saladillo, Argentina **158 D4** 35 40 S 59 55W
Salado →, Buenos Aires, Argentina **158 D4** 35 44 S 57 22W
Salado →, La Pampa, Argentina **160 A3** 37 30 S 67 0W
Salado →, Río Negro, Argentina **160 B3** 41 34 S 65 3W
Salado →, Santa Fe, Argentina **158 C3** 31 40 S 60 41W
Salado →, Mexico **146 B5** 26 52N 99 19W
Salaga, Ghana **101 D4** 8 31N 0 31W
Şalāḥ, Syria **91 C5** 32 40N 36 45 E
Sălaj □, Romania **46 B4** 47 15N 23 0 E
Sálakhos, Greece **32 C9** 36 17N 27 57 E
Salala, Liberia **100 D2** 6 42N 10 7W
Salala, Sudan **94 C4** 21 17N 36 16 E
Salālah, Oman **87 C6** 16 56N 53 59 E
Salamanca, Chile **158 C1** 31 46 S 70 59W
Salamanca, Spain **36 E5** 40 58N 5 39W
Salamanca, U.S.A. **136 D6** 42 10N 78 43W
Salamanca □, Spain **36 E5** 40 57N 5 40W
Salāmatābād, Iran **84 C5** 35 39N 47 50 E
Salamina, Colombia **152 B2** 5 25N 75 29W
Salamis, Cyprus **32 D12** 35 11N 33 54 E
Salamís, Greece **45 G5** 37 56N 23 30 E
Salamonie L., U.S.A. **141 D11** 40 46N 85 37W
Salar de Atacama, Chile **158 A2** 23 30 S 68 25W
Salar de Uyuni, Bolivia **156 E4** 20 30 S 67 45W
Sălard, Romania **46 B3** 47 12N 22 3 E
Salas, Spain **36 B4** 43 25N 6 15W
Salas de los Infantes, Spain **34 C1** 42 2N 3 17W
Salatiga, Indonesia **75 D4** 7 19 S 110 30 E
Salavat, Russia **54 E5** 53 21N 55 55 E
Salaverry, Peru **156 B2** 8 15 S 79 0W
Salawati, Indonesia **73 B4** 1 7 S 130 52 E
Salay, Phil. **71 G5** 8 52N 124 47 E
Salayar, Indonesia **72 C2** 6 7 S 120 30 E
Salazar →, Spain **34 C3** 42 40N 1 20W
Salbris, France **23 E9** 47 25N 2 3 E
Salcia, Romania **46 F5** 43 56N 24 55 E
Salcombe, U.K. **17 G4** 50 14N 3 47W
Saldaña, Spain **36 C6** 42 32N 4 48W
Saldanha, S. Africa **104 E2** 33 0 S 17 58 E
Saldanha B., S. Africa **104 E2** 33 6 S 18 0 E
Saldus, Latvia **13 H20** 56 38N 22 30 E
Sale, Australia **117 E7** 38 6 S 147 6 E
Salé, Morocco **98 B3** 34 3N 6 48W
Sale, U.K. **16 D5** 53 26N 2 19W
Salekhard, Russia **48 A12** 66 30N 66 35 E
Salem, India **83 J4** 11 40N 78 11 E
Salem, Ill., U.S.A. **140 F8** 38 38N 88 57W
Salem, Ind., U.S.A. **141 F10** 38 36N 86 6W
Salem, Mass., U.S.A. **137 D14** 42 31N 70 53W
Salem, Mo., U.S.A. **139 G9** 37 39N 91 32W
Salem, N.J., U.S.A. **134 F8** 39 34N 75 28W
Salem, Ohio, U.S.A. **136 F4** 40 54N 80 52W
Salem, Oreg., U.S.A. **142 D2** 44 56N 123 2W
Salem, S. Dak., U.S.A. **138 D6** 43 44N 97 23W
Salem, Va., U.S.A. **134 G5** 37 18N 80 3W
Salemi, Italy **40 E5** 37 49N 12 48 E
Salernes, France **25 E10** 43 34N 6 15 E
Salerno, Italy **41 B7** 40 41N 14 47 E
Salerno, G. di, Italy **41 B7** 40 32N 14 42 E
Salford, U.K. **16 D5** 53 30N 2 18W
Salgir →, Ukraine **51 K8** 45 38N 35 1 E
Salgótarján, Hungary **31 C12** 48 5N 19 47 E
Salgueiro, Brazil **154 C4** 8 4 S 39 6W
Salida, U.S.A. **132 C5** 38 32N 106 0W
Salies-de-Béarn, France **24 E3** 43 28N 0 56W
Şalif, Yemen **86 D3** 15 18N 42 41 E
Salihli, Turkey **88 C3** 38 28N 28 8 E
Salihorsk, Belarus **51 F4** 52 51N 27 27 E
Salin, Burma **78 E5** 20 35N 94 40 E
Salina, Italy **41 D7** 38 34N 14 50 E
Salina, U.S.A. **138 F6** 38 50N 97 37W
Salina Cruz, Mexico **147 D5** 16 10N 95 10W
Salinas, Brazil **155 E3** 16 10 S 42 10W
Salinas, Chile **158 A2** 23 31 S 69 29W
Salinas, Ecuador **152 D1** 2 10 S 80 58W
Salinas, U.S.A. **144 J5** 36 40N 121 39W
Salinas →, Guatemala **147 D6** 16 28N 90 31W
Salinas →, U.S.A. **144 J5** 36 45N 121 48W
Salinas, B. de, Nic. **148 D2** 11 4N 85 45W
Salinas, C. de, Spain **33 B10** 39 16N 3 4 E
Salinas, Pampa de las, Argentina **158 C2** 31 58 S 66 42W
Salinas Ambargasta, Argentina **158 B3** 29 0 S 65 0W
Salinas de Hidalgo, Mexico **146 C4** 22 30N 101 40W
Salinas Grandes, Argentina **158 B2** 30 0 S 65 0W
Saline →, Ark., U.S.A. **139 J8** 33 10N 92 8W
Saline →, Kans., U.S.A. **138 F6** 38 52N 97 30W
Salines, Spain **33 B10** 39 21N 3 3 E
Salinópolis, Brazil **154 B2** 0 40 S 47 20W
Salins-les-Bains, France **23 F12** 46 58N 5 52 E
Salir, Portugal **37 H2** 37 14N 8 2W
Salisbury = Harare, Zimbabwe **107 F3** 17 43 S 31 2 E
Salisbury, Australia **116 C3** 34 46 S 138 40 E
Salisbury, U.K. **17 F6** 51 4N 1 47W
Salisbury, Md., U.S.A. **134 F8** 38 22N 75 36W
Salisbury, Mo., U.S.A. **140 E4** 39 25N 92 48W
Salisbury, N.C., U.S.A. **135 H5** 35 40N 80 29W
Salisbury Plain, U.K. **17 F6** 51 14N 1 55W
Săliște, Romania **46 D4** 45 45N 23 56 E
Salitre →, Brazil **154 C3** 9 29 S 40 39W
Salka, Nigeria **101 C5** 10 20N 4 58 E
Şalkhad, Syria **91 C5** 32 29N 36 43 E
Salla, Finland **12 C23** 66 50N 28 49 E
Sallent, Spain **34 D6** 41 49N 1 54 E
Salles-Curan, France **24 D6** 44 11N 2 48 E
Salling, Denmark **15 H2** 56 40N 8 55 E
Sallisaw, U.S.A. **139 H7** 35 28N 94 47W
Sallom Junction, Sudan **94 D4** 19 17N 37 6 E
Salluit, Canada **127 B12** 62 14N 75 38W
Salmās, Iran **89 C11** 38 11N 44 47 E
Salmerón, Spain **34 E2** 40 33N 2 29W
Salmo, Canada **130 D5** 49 10N 117 20W
Salmon, U.S.A. **142 D7** 45 11N 113 54W
Salmon →, Canada **130 C4** 54 3N 122 40W
Salmon →, U.S.A. **142 D5** 45 51N 116 47W
Salmon Arm, Canada **130 C5** 50 40N 119 15W
Salmon Falls, U.S.A. **142 E6** 42 48N 114 59W
Salmon Gums, Australia **113 F3** 32 59 S 121 38 E
Salmon Res., Canada **129 C8** 48 5N 56 0W
Salmon River Mts., U.S.A. **142 D6** 45 0N 114 30W
Salo, Finland **13 F20** 60 22N 23 10 E
Salò, Italy **38 C7** 45 36N 10 31 E
Salobreña, Spain **37 J7** 36 44N 3 35W
Salome, U.S.A. **145 M13** 33 47N 113 37W
Salon-de-Provence, France **25 E9** 43 39N 5 6 E
Salonica = Thessaloníki, Greece **44 D4** 40 38N 22 58 E
Salonta, Romania **46 C2** 46 49N 21 42 E
Salor →, Spain **37 F3** 39 39N 7 3W
Salou, C., Spain **34 D6** 41 3N 1 10 E
Salpausselkä, Finland **13 F22** 61 0N 27 0 E
Salsacate, Argentina **158 C2** 31 20 S 65 5W
Salses, France **24 F6** 42 50N 2 55 E
Salsette I., India **82 E1** 19 5N 72 50 E
Salsk, Russia **53 G5** 46 28N 41 30 E
Salso →, Italy **40 E6** 37 6N 13 57 E
Salsomaggiore Terme, Italy **38 D6** 44 49N 9 59 E
Salt →, Canada **130 B6** 60 0N 112 25W
Salt →, Ariz., U.S.A. **143 K7** 33 23N 112 19W
Salt →, Mo., U.S.A. **140 E5** 39 28N 91 4W
Salt Creek, Australia **116 D3** 36 8 S 139 38 E
Salt Fork Arkansas →, U.S.A. **139 G6** 36 36N 97 3W
Salt Lake City, U.S.A. **142 F8** 40 45N 111 53W
Salt Range, Pakistan **80 C5** 32 30N 72 25 E
Salta, Argentina **158 A2** 24 57 S 65 25W
Salta □, Argentina **158 A2** 24 48 S 65 30W
Saltcoats, U.K. **18 F4** 55 38N 4 47W
Saltee Is., Ireland **19 D5** 52 7N 6 37W
Saltfjellet, Norway **12 C16** 66 40N 15 15 E
Saltfjorden, Norway **12 C16** 67 15N 14 10 E
Saltholm, Denmark **15 J6** 55 38N 12 43 E
Saltillo, Mexico **146 B4** 25 25N 101 0W
Salto, Argentina **158 C3** 34 20 S 60 15W
Salto, Uruguay **158 C4** 31 27 S 57 50W
Salto da Divisa, Brazil **155 E4** 16 0 S 39 57W
Salton City, U.S.A. **145 M11** 33 29N 115 51W
Salton Sea, U.S.A. **145 M11** 33 15N 115 45W
Saltpond, Ghana **101 D4** 5 15N 1 3W
Saltsjöbaden, Sweden **14 E12** 59 15N 18 20 E
Saltville, U.S.A. **134 G5** 36 53N 81 46W
Saluda →, U.S.A. **135 H5** 34 1N 81 4W
Salûm, Egypt **94 A2** 31 31N 25 7 E
Salûm, Khâlig el, Egypt **94 A2** 31 35N 25 24 E
Salur, India **82 E6** 18 27N 83 18 E
Salut, Is. du, Fr. Guiana **153 B7** 5 15N 52 35W
Saluzzo, Italy **38 D4** 44 39N 7 29 E
Salvacion, Phil. **71 G2** 9 56N 118 47 E
Salvación, B., Chile **160 D1** 50 50 S 75 10W
Salvador, Brazil **155 D4** 13 0 S 38 30W
Salvador, Canada **131 C7** 52 10N 109 32W
Salvador, L., U.S.A. **139 L9** 29 43N 90 15W
Salvaterra, Brazil **154 B2** 0 46 S 48 31W
Salvaterra de Magos, Portugal **37 F2** 39 1N 8 47W
Salvisa, U.S.A. **141 G12** 37 54N 84 51W
Sálvora, I., Spain **36 C2** 42 30N 8 58W
Salween →, Burma **78 G6** 16 31N 97 37 E
Salyan, Azerbaijan **89 C13** 39 33N 48 59 E
Salyersville, U.S.A. **134 G4** 37 45N 83 4W
Salza →, Austria **30 D7** 47 40N 14 43 E
Salzach →, Austria **30 C5** 48 12N 12 56 E
Salzburg, Austria **30 D6** 47 48N 13 2 E
Salzburg □, Austria **30 D6** 47 15N 13 0 E
Salzgitter, Germany **26 C6** 52 9N 10 19 E
Salzwedel, Germany **26 C7** 52 52N 11 10 E
Sam, Gabon **102 B2** 0 58N 11 16 E
Sam Neua, Laos **76 B5** 20 29N 104 5 E
Sam Ngao, Thailand **76 D2** 17 18N 99 0 E
Sam Rayburn Reservoir, U.S.A. **139 K7** 31 4N 94 5W
Sam Son, Vietnam **76 C5** 19 44N 105 54 E
Sam Teu, Laos **76 C5** 19 59N 104 38 E
Sama, Russia **56 C7** 60 12N 60 22 E
Sama de Langreo, Spain **36 B5** 43 18N 5 40W
Samacimbo, Angola **103 E3** 13 33 S 16 59 E
Samagaltay, Russia **57 D10** 50 36N 95 3 E
Samā'il, Oman **87 B7** 23 40N 57 50 E
Samaipata, Bolivia **157 D5** 18 9 S 63 52W
Samal, Phil. **71 H5** 7 5N 125 42 E
Samal I., Phil. **71 H5** 7 3N 125 44 E
Samales Group, Phil. **71 J3** 6 0N 122 0 E
Samalkot, India **82 F6** 17 3N 82 13 E
Samâlût, Egypt **94 J7** 28 20N 30 42 E
Samana, India **80 D7** 30 10N 76 13 E
Samana Cay, Bahamas **149 B5** 23 3N 73 45W
Samandağı, Turkey **88 D6** 36 5N 35 59 E
Samanga, Tanzania **107 D4** 8 20 S 39 13 E
Samangān □, Afghan. **79 A3** 36 15N 68 3 E
Samangwa, Zaïre **103 C4** 4 23 S 24 10 E
Samani, Japan **60 C11** 42 7N 142 56 E
Samar, Phil. **71 E5** 12 0N 125 0 E
Samar □, Phil. **71 F5** 11 50N 125 0 E
Samar Sea, Phil. **70 E5** 12 0N 124 15 E
Samara, Russia **52 D10** 53 8N 50 6 E
Samara →, Russia **52 D10** 53 10N 50 4 E
Samara →, Ukraine **51 H8** 48 28N 35 7 E
Samarai, Papua N. G. **120 F6** 10 39 S 150 41 E
Samaria = Shōmrōn, West Bank **91 C4** 32 15N 35 13 E
Samariá, Greece **32 D5** 35 17N 23 58 E
Samarinda, Indonesia **75 C5** 0 30 S 117 9 E
Samarkand = Samarqand, Uzbekistan **55 D3** 39 40N 66 55 E
Samarqand, Uzbekistan **55 D3** 39 40N 66 55 E
Sāmarrā, Iraq **89 E10** 34 12N 43 52 E
Samastipur, India **81 G11** 25 50N 85 50 E
Samatan, France **24 E4** 43 29N 0 55 E
Samaúma, Brazil **157 B5** 7 50 S 60 2W
Şamaxi, Azerbaijan **53 K9** 40 38N 48 37 E
Samba, India **81 C6** 32 32N 75 10 E
Samba, Zaïre **103 C5** 4 38 S 26 22 E
Samba Caju, Angola **103 D3** 8 46 S 15 24 E
Sambaíba, Brazil **154 C2** 7 8 S 45 21W
Sambalpur, India **82 D7** 21 28N 84 4 E
Sambar, Tanjung, Indonesia **75 C4** 2 59 S 110 19 E
Sambas, Indonesia **75 B3** 1 20N 109 20 E
Sambava, Madag. **105 A9** 14 16 S 50 10 E
Sambawizi, Zimbabwe **107 F2** 18 24 S 26 13 E
Sambhal, India **81 E8** 28 35N 78 37 E
Sambhar, India **80 F6** 26 52N 75 6 E
Sambiase, Italy **41 D9** 38 58N 16 17 E
Sambir, Ukraine **51 H2** 49 30N 23 10 E
Sambonifacio, Italy **38 C8** 45 24N 11 16 E
Sambor, Cambodia **76 F6** 12 46N 106 0 E
Sambre →, Europe **21 H5** 50 27N 4 52 E
Sambuca di Sicília, Italy **40 E6** 37 39N 13 7 E
Samburu □, Kenya **106 B4** 1 10N 37 0 E
Samchŏk, S. Korea **67 F15** 37 30N 129 10 E
Samchonpo, S. Korea **67 G15** 35 0N 128 6 E
Same, Tanzania **106 C4** 4 2 S 37 38 E
Samedan, Switz. **29 C9** 46 32N 9 52 E
Samer, France **23 B8** 50 38N 1 44 E
Samfya, Zambia **107 E2** 11 22 S 29 31 E
Samḩan, Jabal, Oman **87 C6** 17 12N 54 55 E
Sámi, Greece **45 F2** 38 15N 20 39 E
Şämkir, Azerbaijan **53 K8** 40 50N 46 0 E
Samnah, Si. Arabia **84 E3** 25 10N 37 15 E
Samnaun, Switz. **29 C10** 46 57N 10 22 E
Samnū, Libya **96 C2** 27 15N 14 55 E
Samo Alto, Chile **158 C1** 30 22 S 71 0W
Samoan Is., Pac. Oc. **121 X24** 14 0 S 171 0W
Samobor, Croatia **39 C12** 45 47N 15 44 E
Samoëns, France **25 B10** 46 5N 6 45 E
Samokov, Bulgaria **43 E8** 42 18N 23 35 E
Samoorombón, B., Argentina **158 D4** 36 5 S 57 20W
Samorogouan, Burkina Faso **100 C4** 11 21N 4 57W
Sámos, Greece **45 G8** 37 45N 26 50 E
Samoš, Serbia, Yug. **42 B5** 45 13N 20 49 E
Samos, Spain **36 C3** 42 44N 7 20W
Samosir, Indonesia **74 B1** 2 55N 98 50 E
Samothráki, Évros, Greece **44 D7** 40 28N 25 28 E
Samothráki, Ionioi Nísoi, Greece **44 E1** 39 48N 19 31 E
Samothráki, Kérkira, Greece **32 A3** 39 48N 19 31 E
Samoylovka, Russia **52 E6** 51 12N 43 43 E
Sampa, Ghana **100 D4** 8 0N 2 36W
Sampacho, Argentina **158 C3** 33 20 S 64 50W
Sampang, Indonesia **75 D4** 7 11 S 113 13 E
Samper de Calanda, Spain **34 D4** 41 11N 0 28W
Sampit, Indonesia **75 C4** 2 34 S 113 0 E
Sampit →, Indonesia **75 C4** 2 44 S 112 54 E
Sampit, Teluk, Indonesia **75 C4** 3 5 S 113 3 E
Samrée, Belgium **21 H7** 50 13N 5 39 E
Samrong, Cambodia **76 E4** 14 15N 103 30 E
Samrong, Thailand **76 E3** 15 10N 100 40 E
Samsø, Denmark **15 J4** 55 50N 10 35 E
Samsø Bælt, Denmark **15 J4** 55 45N 10 45 E
Samsonovo, Turkmenistan **55 E2** 37 53N 65 15 E
Samsun, Turkey **88 B7** 41 15N 36 22 E
Samsun Dağı, Turkey **45 G9** 37 45N 27 10 E
Samtredia, Georgia **53 J6** 42 7N 42 24 E
Samui, Ko, Thailand **77 H3** 9 30N 100 0 E

260 Samur

Samur →, *Russia* **53 K9** 41 53N 48 32 E
Samurskiy Khrebet, *Russia* **53 K8** 41 55N 47 11 E
Samusole, *Zaïre* **103 E4** 10 2 S 24 0 E
Samut Prakan, *Thailand* **76 F3** 13 32N 100 40 E
Samut Sakhon, *Thailand* **76 F3** 13 31N 100 13 E
Samut Songkhram →, *Thailand* **76 F3** 13 24N 100 1 E
Samwari, *Pakistan* **80 E2** 28 30N 66 46 E
San, *Mali* **100 C4** 13 15N 4 57W
San →, *Cambodia* **76 F5** 13 32N 105 57 E
San →, *Poland* **31 A14** 50 45N 21 51 E
San Adrián, C. de, *Spain* **36 B2** 43 21N 8 50W
San Agustín, *Colombia* **152 C2** 1 53N 76 16W
San Agustin, C., *Phil.* **71 H6** 6 20N 126 13 E
San Agustín de Valle Fértil, *Argentina* **158 C2** 30 35 S 67 30W
San Ambrosio, *Pac. Oc.* **150 F3** 26 28 S 79 53W
San Andreas, *U.S.A.* **144 G6** 38 12N 120 41W
San Andres, *Phil.* **70 E4** 13 19N 122 41 E
San Andrés, I. de, *Caribbean* **148 D3** 12 42N 81 46W
San Andres Mts., *U.S.A.* **143 K10** 33 0N 106 30W
San Andrés Tuxtla, *Mexico* **147 D5** 18 30N 95 20W
San Angelo, *U.S.A.* **139 K4** 31 28N 100 26W
San Anselmo, *U.S.A.* **144 H4** 37 59N 122 34W
San Antonio, *Belize* **147 D7** 16 15N 89 2W
San Antonio, *Chile* **158 C1** 33 40 S 71 40W
San Antonio, *Phil.* **70 D3** 14 57N 120 5 E
San Antonio, *Spain* **33 C7** 38 59N 1 19 E
San Antonio, *N. Mex., U.S.A.* **143 K10** 33 55N 106 52W
San Antonio, *Tex., U.S.A.* **139 L5** 29 25N 98 30W
San Antonio, *Venezuela* **152 C4** 3 30N 66 44W
San Antonio →, *U.S.A.* **139 L6** 28 30N 96 54W
San Antonio, C., *Argentina* **158 D4** 36 15 S 56 40W
San Antonio, C., *Cuba* **148 B3** 21 50N 84 57W
San Antonio, C. de, *Spain* **35 G5** 38 48N 0 12 E
San Antonio, Mt., *U.S.A.* **145 L9** 34 17N 117 38W
San Antonio Bay, *Phil.* **71 G1** 8 38N 117 35 E
San Antonio de los Baños, *Cuba* **148 B3** 22 54N 82 31W
San Antonio de los Cobres, *Argentina* **158 A2** 24 10 S 66 17W
San Antonio Oeste, *Argentina* **160 B4** 40 40 S 65 0W
San Arcángelo, *Italy* **41 B9** 40 14N 16 14 E
San Ardo, *U.S.A.* **144 J6** 36 1N 120 54W
San Augustín, *Canary Is.* **33 G4** 27 47N 15 32W
San Augustine, *U.S.A.* **139 K7** 31 30N 94 7W
San Bartolomé, *Canary Is.* **33 F6** 28 59N 13 37W
San Bartolomé de Tirajana, *Canary Is.* **33 G4** 27 54N 15 34W
San Bartolomeo in Galdo, *Italy* **41 A8** 41 24N 15 1 E
San Benedetto del Tronto, *Italy* **39 F10** 42 57N 13 53 E
San Benedetto Po, *Italy* **38 C7** 45 2N 10 55 E
San Benedicto, I., *Mexico* **146 D2** 19 18N 110 49W
San Benito, *U.S.A.* **139 M6** 26 8N 97 38W
San Benito →, *U.S.A.* **144 J5** 36 53N 121 34W
San Benito Mt., *U.S.A.* **144 J6** 36 22N 120 37W
San Bernardino, *U.S.A.* **145 L9** 34 7N 117 19W
San Bernardino, Paso del, *Switz.* **29 D8** 46 28N 9 11 E
San Bernardino Mts., *U.S.A.* **145 L10** 34 10N 116 45W
San Bernardino Str., *Phil.* **70 E5** 13 0N 125 0 E
San Bernardo, *Chile* **158 C1** 33 40 S 70 50W
San Bernardo, I. de, *Colombia* **152 B2** 9 45N 75 50W
San Blas, *Mexico* **146 B3** 26 4N 108 46W
San Blas, Arch. de, *Panama* **148 E4** 9 50N 78 31W
San Blas, C., *U.S.A.* **135 L3** 29 40N 85 21W
San Borja, *Bolivia* **156 C4** 14 50 S 66 52W
San Buenaventura, *Bolivia* **156 C4** 14 28 S 67 35W
San Buenaventura, *Mexico* **146 B4** 27 5N 101 32W
San Carlos = Butuku-Luba, *Eq. Guin.* **101 E6** 3 29N 8 33 E
San Carlos, *Argentina* **158 C2** 33 50 S 69 0W
San Carlos, *Bolivia* **157 D5** 17 24 S 63 45W
San Carlos, *Chile* **158 D1** 36 10 S 72 0W
San Carlos, *Mexico* **146 B4** 29 0N 100 54W
San Carlos, *Nic.* **148 D3** 11 12N 84 50W
San Carlos, *Negros, Phil.* **71 F4** 10 29N 123 25 E
San Carlos, *Pangasinan, Phil.* **70 D3** 15 55N 120 20 E
San Carlos, *Spain* **33 B8** 39 3N 1 34 E
San Carlos, *Uruguay* **159 C5** 34 46 S 54 58W
San Carlos, *U.S.A.* **143 K8** 33 21N 110 27W
San Carlos, *Amazonas, Venezuela* **152 C4** 1 55N 67 4W
San Carlos, *Cojedes, Venezuela* **152 B4** 9 40N 68 36W
San Carlos de Bariloche, *Argentina* **160 B2** 41 10 S 71 25W
San Carlos de la Rápita, *Spain* **34 E5** 40 37N 0 35 E
San Carlos del Zulia, *Venezuela* **152 B3** 9 1N 71 55W
San Carlos L., *U.S.A.* **143 K8** 33 11N 110 32W
San Cataldo, *Italy* **40 E6** 37 29N 13 59 E
San Celoni, *Spain* **34 D7** 41 42N 2 30 E
San Clemente, *Chile* **158 D1** 35 30 S 71 29W
San Clemente, *Spain* **35 F2** 39 24N 2 25W
San Clemente, *U.S.A.* **145 M9** 33 26N 117 37W
San Clemente I., *U.S.A.* **145 N8** 32 53N 118 29W
San Costanzo, *Italy* **39 E10** 43 46N 13 4 E
San Cristóbal, *Argentina* **158 C3** 30 20 S 61 10W
San Cristóbal, *Colombia* **152 D3** 2 18 S 73 2W
San Cristóbal, *Dom. Rep.* **149 C5** 18 25N 70 6W
San Cristóbal, *Mexico* **147 D6** 16 50N 92 33W
San Cristóbal, *Solomon Is.* **121 N11** 10 30 S 161 0 E
San Cristóbal, *Spain* **33 B11** 39 57N 4 3 E
San Cristóbal, *Venezuela* **152 B3** 7 46N 72 14W
San Damiano d'Asti, *Italy* **38 D5** 44 50N 8 4 E
San Daniele del Friuli, *Italy* **39 B10** 46 9N 13 0 E
San Demétrio Corone, *Italy* **41 C9** 39 34N 16 22 E
San Diego, *Calif., U.S.A.* **145 N9** 32 43N 117 9W
San Diego, *Tex., U.S.A.* **139 M5** 27 46N 98 14W
San Diego, C., *Argentina* **160 D3** 54 40 S 65 10W
San Diego de la Unión, *Mexico* **146 C4** 21 28N 100 52W
San Dimitri, Ras, *Malta* **32 C1** 36 4N 14 11 E
San Dionosio, *Phil.* **71 F4** 11 16N 123 6 E
San Doná di Piave, *Italy* **39 C9** 45 38N 12 34 E
San Elpídio a Mare, *Italy* **39 E10** 43 16N 13 41 E
San Emilio, *Phil.* **70 C3** 17 14N 120 37 E
San Estanislao, *Paraguay* **158 A4** 24 39 S 56 26W
San Esteban de Gormaz, *Spain* **34 D1** 41 34N 3 13W
San Fabian, *Phil.* **70 C3** 16 5N 120 25 E
San Felice sul Panaro, *Italy* **38 D8** 44 50N 11 8 E
San Felipe, *Chile* **158 C1** 32 43 S 70 42W
San Felipe, *Colombia* **152 C4** 1 55N 67 6W
San Felipe, *Mexico* **146 A2** 31 0N 114 52W
San Felipe, *Phil.* **70 D3** 15 4N 120 4 E
San Felipe, *Venezuela* **152 A4** 10 20N 68 44W
San Felipe →, *U.S.A.* **145 M11** 33 12N 115 49W
San Felíu de Guíxols, *Spain* **34 D8** 41 45N 3 1 E
San Felíu de Llobregat, *Spain* **34 D7** 41 23N 2 2 E
San Félix, *Pac. Oc.* **150 F2** 26 23 S 80 0W
San Fernando, *Chile* **158 C1** 34 30 S 71 0W
San Fernando, *Mexico* **146 B1** 29 55N 115 10W
San Fernando, *Cebu, Phil.* **71 F4** 10 10N 123 42 E
San Fernando, *La Union, Phil.* **70 C3** 16 40N 120 23 E
San Fernando, *Pampanga, Phil.* **70 D3** 15 5N 120 37 E
San Fernando, *Tablas, Phil.* **70 E4** 12 18N 122 36 E
San Fernando, *Baleares, Spain* **33 C7** 38 42N 1 28 E
San Fernando, *Cádiz, Spain* **37 J4** 36 28N 6 17W
San Fernando, *Trin. & Tob.* **149 D7** 10 20N 61 30W
San Fernando, *U.S.A.* **145 L8** 34 17N 118 26W
San Fernando →, *Mexico* **146 C5** 24 55N 98 10W
San Fernando de Apure, *Venezuela* **152 B4** 7 54N 67 15W
San Fernando de Atabapo, *Venezuela* **152 C4** 4 3N 67 42W
San Fernando di Púglia, *Italy* **41 A9** 41 18N 16 5 E
San Francisco, *Argentina* **158 C3** 31 30 S 62 5W
San Francisco, *Bolivia* **157 D4** 15 16 S 65 31W
San Francisco, *Cebu, Phil.* **71 F5** 10 39N 124 23 E
San Francisco, *Leyte, Phil.* **71 F5** 10 4N 125 9 E
San Francisco, *Mindanao, Phil.* **71 G5** 8 30N 125 56 E
San Francisco, *U.S.A.* **144 H4** 37 47N 122 25W
San Francisco →, *U.S.A.* **143 K9** 32 59N 109 22W
San Francisco, Paso de, *S. Amer.* **158 B2** 27 0 S 68 0W
San Francisco de Macorîs, *Dom. Rep.* **149 C5** 19 19N 70 15W
San Francisco del Monte de Oro, *Argentina* **158 C2** 32 36 S 66 8W
San Francisco del Oro, *Mexico* **146 B3** 26 52N 105 50W
San Francisco Javier, *Spain* **33 C7** 38 42N 1 26 E
San Francisco Solano, Pta., *Colombia* **152 B2** 6 18N 77 29W
San Fratello, *Italy* **41 D7** 38 1N 14 36 E
San Gabriel, *Ecuador* **152 C2** 0 36N 77 49W
San Gavino Monreale, *Italy* **40 C1** 39 33N 8 47 E
San Gil, *Colombia* **152 B3** 6 33N 73 8W
San Gimignano, *Italy* **38 E8** 43 28N 11 2 E
San Giórgio di Nogaro, *Italy* **39 C10** 45 50N 13 13 E
San Giórgio Iónico, *Italy* **41 B10** 40 27N 17 23 E
San Giovanni Bianco, *Italy* **38 C6** 45 52N 9 39 E
San Giovanni in Fiore, *Italy* **41 C9** 39 15N 16 42 E
San Giovanni in Persiceto, *Italy* **39 D8** 44 38N 11 11 E
San Giovanni Rotondo, *Italy* **41 A8** 41 42N 15 44 E
San Giovanni Valdarno, *Italy* **39 E8** 43 34N 11 32 E
San Giuliano Terme, *Italy* **38 E7** 43 46N 10 26 E
San Gorgonio Mt., *U.S.A.* **145 L10** 34 7N 116 51W
San Gottardo, P. del, *Switz.* **29 C7** 46 33N 8 33 E
San Gregorio, *Uruguay* **159 C4** 32 37 S 55 40W
San Gregorio, *U.S.A.* **144 H4** 37 20N 122 23W
San Guiseppe Iato, *Italy* **40 E6** 37 57N 13 11 E
San Ignacio, *Belize* **147 D7** 17 10N 89 0W
San Ignacio, *Bolivia* **157 D5** 16 20 S 60 55W
San Ignacio, *Mexico* **146 B2** 27 27N 113 0W
San Ignacio, *Paraguay* **158 B4** 26 52 S 57 3W
San Ignacio, L., *Mexico* **146 B2** 26 50N 113 11W
San Ildefonso, *Phil.* **70 D3** 15 5N 120 56 E
San Ildefonso, C., *Phil.* **70 C4** 16 0N 122 1 E
San Isidro, *Argentina* **158 C4** 34 29 S 58 31W
San Jacinto, *Colombia* **152 B2** 9 50N 75 8W
San Jacinto, *Phil.* **70 E4** 12 34N 123 44 E
San Jacinto, *U.S.A.* **145 M10** 33 47N 116 57W
San Jaime, *Spain* **33 B11** 39 54N 4 4 E
San Javier, *Misiones, Argentina* **159 B4** 27 55 S 55 5W
San Javier, *Santa Fe, Argentina* **158 C4** 30 40 S 59 55W
San Javier, *Beni, Bolivia* **157 C5** 14 34 S 64 42W
San Javier, *Santa Cruz, Bolivia* **157 D5** 16 18 S 62 30W
San Javier, *Chile* **158 D1** 35 40 S 71 45W
San Javier, *Spain* **35 H4** 37 49N 0 50W
San Jerónimo, Sa. de, *Colombia* **152 B2** 8 0N 75 50W
San Jeronimo Taviche, *Mexico* **147 D5** 16 38N 96 32W
San Joaquín, *Bolivia* **157 C5** 13 4 S 64 49W
San Joaquin, *Phil.* **71 F4** 10 35N 122 8 E
San Joaquin, *U.S.A.* **144 J6** 36 36N 120 11W
San Joaquín, *Venezuela* **152 A4** 10 16N 67 47W
San Joaquín →, *Bolivia* **157 C5** 13 8 S 63 41W
San Joaquin →, *U.S.A.* **144 G5** 38 4N 121 51W
San Joaquin Valley, *U.S.A.* **144 J6** 37 20N 121 0W
San Jordi, *Spain* **33 B9** 39 33N 2 46 E
San Jorge, *Argentina* **158 C3** 31 54 S 61 50W
San Jorge, *Spain* **33 C7** 38 54N 1 24 E
San Jorge, B. de, *Mexico* **146 A2** 31 20N 113 20W
San Jorge, G., *Argentina* **160 C3** 46 0 S 66 0W
San Jorge, G. de, *Spain* **34 E4** 40 53N 1 2 E
San Jorge, G. of, *Argentina* **150 H4** 46 0 S 66 0W
San José, *Bolivia* **157 D5** 17 53 S 60 50W
San José, *Costa Rica* **148 E3** 9 55N 84 2W
San José, *Guatemala* **148 D1** 14 0N 90 50W
San José, *Mexico* **146 C2** 25 0N 110 50W
San Jose, *Phil.* **70 D3** 15 45N 120 55 E
San José, *Spain* **33 C7** 38 55N 1 18 E
San Jose, *Calif., U.S.A.* **144 H5** 37 20N 121 53W
San Jose, *Ill., U.S.A.* **140 D7** 40 18N 89 36W
San Jose →, *U.S.A.* **143 J10** 34 25N 106 45W
San Jose de Buenovista, *Phil.* **70 E3** 12 27N 121 4 E
San José de Feliciano, *Argentina* **158 C4** 30 26 S 58 46W
San José de Jáchal, *Argentina* **158 C2** 30 15 S 68 46W
San José de Mayo, *Uruguay* **158 C4** 34 27 S 56 40W
San José de Ocune, *Colombia* **152 C3** 4 15N 70 20W
San José de Uchapiamonas, *Bolivia* **156 C4** 14 13 S 68 5W
San José del Cabo, *Mexico* **146 C3** 23 0N 109 40W
San José del Guaviare, *Colombia* **152 C3** 2 35N 72 38W
San José do Anauá, *Brazil* **153 C5** 0 58N 61 22W
San Juan, *Argentina* **158 C2** 31 30 S 68 30W
San Juan, *Colombia* **152 B2** 8 46N 76 32W
San Juan, *Mexico* **146 C4** 21 20N 102 50W
San Juan, *Ica, Peru* **156 D2** 15 22 S 75 7W
San Juan, *Puno, Peru* **156 C4** 14 2 S 69 19W
San Juan, *Luzon, Phil.* **70 C3** 16 40N 120 20 E
San Juan, *Mindanao, Phil.* **71 G6** 8 25N 126 20 E
San Juan, *Puerto Rico* **149 C6** 18 28N 66 7W
San Juan □, *Argentina* **158 C2** 31 9 S 69 0W
San Juan →, *Argentina* **158 C2** 32 20 S 67 25W
San Juan →, *Bolivia* **157 E4** 21 2 S 65 19W
San Juan →, *Colombia* **152 C2** 4 3N 77 27W
San Juan →, *Nic.* **148 D3** 10 56N 83 42W
San Juan →, *U.S.A.* **143 H8** 37 16N 110 26W
San Juan →, *Venezuela* **153 A5** 10 14N 62 38W
San Juan, C., *Eq. Guin.* **102 B1** 1 5N 9 20 E
San Juan Bautista, *Paraguay* **158 B4** 26 37 S 57 6W
San Juan Bautista, *Spain* **33 B8** 39 5N 1 31 E
San Juan Bautista, *U.S.A.* **144 J5** 36 51N 121 32W
San Juan Bautista Valle Nacional, *Mexico* **147 D5** 17 47N 96 19W
San Juan Capistrano, *U.S.A.* **145 M9** 33 30N 117 40W
San Juan Cr. →, *U.S.A.* **144 J5** 35 40N 120 22W
San Juan de Guadalupe, *Mexico* **146 C4** 24 38N 102 44W
San Juan de los Morros, *Venezuela* **152 B4** 9 55N 67 21W
San Juan del César, *Colombia* **152 A3** 10 46N 73 1W
San Juan del Norte, *Nic.* **148 D3** 10 58N 83 40W
San Juan del Norte, B. de, *Nic.* **148 D3** 11 0N 83 40W
San Juan del Puerto, *Spain* **37 H4** 37 20N 6 50W
San Juan del Río, *Mexico* **147 C5** 20 25N 100 0W
San Juan del Sur, *Nic.* **148 D2** 11 20N 85 51W
San Juan I., *U.S.A.* **144 B3** 48 32N 123 5W
San Juan Mts., *U.S.A.* **143 H10** 37 30N 107 0W
San Julián, *Argentina* **160 C3** 49 15 S 67 45W
San Julian, *Phil.* **71 F5** 11 45N 125 27 E
San Just, Sierra de, *Spain* **34 E4** 40 45N 0 49W
San Justo, *Argentina* **158 C3** 30 47 S 60 30W
San Kamphaeng, *Thailand* **76 C2** 18 45N 99 8 E
San Lázaro, C., *Mexico* **146 C2** 24 50N 112 18W
San Lázaro, Sa., *Mexico* **146 C3** 23 25N 110 0W
San Leandro, *U.S.A.* **144 H4** 37 44N 122 9W
San Leonardo, *Spain* **34 D1** 41 51N 3 5W
San Lorenzo, *Argentina* **158 C3** 32 45 S 60 45W
San Lorenzo, *Beni, Bolivia* **157 D4** 15 22 S 65 48W
San Lorenzo, *Tarija, Bolivia* **157 E5** 21 26 S 64 47W
San Lorenzo, *Ecuador* **152 C2** 1 15N 78 50W
San Lorenzo, *Paraguay* **158 B4** 25 20 S 57 32W
San Lorenzo, *Spain* **33 B10** 39 37N 3 17 E
San Lorenzo, *Venezuela* **152 B3** 9 47N 71 4W
San Lorenzo →, *Mexico* **146 C3** 24 15N 107 24W
San Lorenzo, I., *Mexico* **146 B2** 28 35N 112 50W
San Lorenzo, I., *Peru* **156 C2** 12 7 S 77 15W
San Lorenzo, Mt., *Argentina* **160 C2** 47 40 S 72 20W
San Lorenzo de la Parrilla, *Spain* **34 F2** 39 51N 2 22W
San Lorenzo de Morunys, *Spain* **34 C6** 42 8N 1 35 E
San Lucas, *Bolivia* **157 E4** 20 5 S 65 7W
San Lucas, *Baja Calif. S., Mexico* **146 C3** 22 53N 109 54W
San Lucas, *Baja Calif. S., Mexico* **146 B2** 27 10N 112 14W
San Lucas, *U.S.A.* **144 J5** 36 8N 121 1W
San Lucas, C., *Mexico* **146 C3** 22 50N 110 0W
San Lúcido, *Italy* **41 C9** 39 18N 16 3 E
San Luis, *Argentina* **158 C2** 33 20 S 66 20W
San Luis, *Cuba* **148 B3** 22 17N 83 46W
San Luis, *Guatemala* **148 C2** 16 14N 89 27W
San Luis, *U.S.A.* **143 H11** 37 12N 105 25W
San Luis □, *Argentina* **158 C2** 34 0 S 66 0W
San Luis, I., *Mexico* **146 B2** 29 58N 114 26W
San Luis, L. de, *Bolivia* **157 C5** 13 45 S 64 0W
San Luis, Sierra de, *Argentina* **158 C2** 32 30 S 66 10W
San Luis de la Paz, *Mexico* **146 C4** 21 19N 100 32W
San Luis Obispo, *U.S.A.* **145 K6** 35 17N 120 40W
San Luis Potosí, *Mexico* **146 C4** 22 9N 100 59W
San Luis Potosí □, *Mexico* **146 C4** 22 10N 101 0W
San Luis Reservoir, *U.S.A.* **144 H5** 37 4N 121 5W
San Luis Río Colorado, *Mexico* **146 A2** 32 29N 114 58W
San Manuel, *Phil.* **70 C3** 16 4N 120 40 E
San Marco Argentano, *Italy* **41 C9** 39 33N 16 7 E
San Marco dei Cavoti, *Italy* **41 A7** 41 18N 14 53 E
San Marco in Lámis, *Italy* **41 A8** 41 43N 15 38 E
San Marcos, *Colombia* **152 B2** 8 39N 75 8W
San Marcos, *Guatemala* **148 D1** 14 59N 91 52W
San Marcos, *Mexico* **146 B2** 27 13N 112 6W
San Marcos, *U.S.A.* **139 L6** 29 53N 97 56W
San Marino ■, *Europe* **39 E9** 43 56N 12 25 E
San Martín, *Argentina* **158 C2** 33 5 S 68 28W
San Martín, *Colombia* **152 C3** 3 42N 73 42W
San Martín →, *Bolivia* **157 C5** 13 8 S 63 43W
San Martín, L., *Argentina* **160 C2** 48 50 S 72 50W
San Martín de los Andes, *Argentina* **160 B2** 40 10 S 71 20W
San Martín de Valdeiglesias, *Spain* **36 E6** 40 21N 4 24W
San Martino de Calvi, *Italy* **38 C6** 45 57N 9 41 E
San Mateo, *Agusan del N., Phil.* **71 G5** 8 48N 125 33 E
San Mateo, *Isabela, Phil.* **70 C3** 16 54N 121 33 E
San Mateo, *Baleares, Spain* **33 B7** 39 3N 1 23 E
San Mateo, *Valencia, Spain* **34 E5** 40 28N 0 10 E
San Mateo, *U.S.A.* **144 H4** 37 34N 122 19W
San Matías, *Bolivia* **157 D6** 16 25 S 58 20W
San Matías, G., *Argentina* **160 B4** 41 30 S 64 0W
San Miguel = Linapacan, *Phil.* **71 F2** 11 30N 119 52 E
San Miguel, *El Salv.* **148 D2** 13 30N 88 12W
San Miguel, *Panama* **148 E4** 8 27N 78 55W
San Miguel, *Lanao del N., Phil.* **71 G5** 9 3N 125 59 E
San Miguel, *Lanao del S., Phil.* **71 G5** 8 13N 124 14 E
San Miguel, *Spain* **33 B7** 39 3N 1 26 E
San Miguel, *U.S.A.* **144 K6** 35 45N 120 42W
San Miguel, *Venezuela* **152 B4** 9 40N 65 11W
San Miguel →, *Bolivia* **157 C5** 13 52 S 63 56W
San Miguel →, *S. Amer.* **152 C2** 0 25N 76 30W
San Miguel de Huachi, *Bolivia* **156 D4** 15 40 S 67 15W
San Miguel de Salinas, *Spain* **35 H4** 37 59N 0 47W
San Miguel de Tucumán, *Argentina* **158 B2** 26 50 S 65 20W
San Miguel del Monte, *Argentina* **158 D4** 35 23 S 58 50W
San Miguel I., *U.S.A.* **145 L6** 34 2N 120 23W
San Miguel Is., *Phil.* **71 H2** 7 45N 118 28 E
San Miniato, *Italy* **38 E7** 43 41N 10 51 E
San Narciso, *Quezon, Phil.* **70 E4** 13 34N 122 34 E
San Narciso, *Zambales, Phil.* **70 D3** 15 2N 120 3 E
San Nicolás, *Canary Is.* **33 G4** 27 58N 15 47W
San Nicolas, *Phil.* **70 B3** 18 10N 120 36 E
San Nicolás de los Arroyas, *Argentina* **158 C3** 33 25 S 60 10W
San Nicolas I., *U.S.A.* **145 M7** 33 15N 119 30W
San Onofre, *Colombia* **152 B2** 9 44N 75 32W
San Onofre, *U.S.A.* **145 M9** 33 22N 117 34W
San Pablo, *Bolivia* **158 A2** 21 43 S 66 38W
San Pablo, *Isabela, Phil.* **70 C3** 17 27N 121 48 E
San Pablo, *Laguna, Phil.* **70 D3** 14 11N 121 31 E
San Páolo di Civitate, *Italy* **41 A8** 41 44N 15 15 E
San Pascual, *Phil.* **70 E4** 13 8N 122 59 E
San Pedro, *Buenos Aires, Argentina* **159 B5** 26 30 S 54 10W
San Pedro, *Jujuy, Argentina* **158 A3** 24 12 S 64 55W
San Pedro, *Colombia* **152 C3** 4 56N 71 53W
San-Pédro, *Ivory C.* **100 E3** 4 50N 6 33W
San Pedro, *Mexico* **146 C2** 23 55N 110 17W
San Pedro, *Peru* **156 C3** 14 49 S 74 5W
San Pedro □, *Paraguay* **158 A4** 24 0 S 57 0W
San Pedro →, *Chihuahua, Mexico* **146 B3** 28 20N 106 10W
San Pedro →, *Michoacan, Mexico* **146 D4** 19 23N 103 51W
San Pedro →, *Nayarit, Mexico* **146 C3** 21 45N 105 30W
San Pedro →, *U.S.A.* **143 K8** 32 59N 110 47W
San Pedro, Pta., *Chile* **158 B1** 25 30 S 70 38W
San Pedro, Sierra de, *Spain* **37 F4** 39 18N 6 40W
San Pedro Channel, *U.S.A.* **145 M8** 33 30N 118 25W
San Pedro de Arimena, *Colombia* **152 C3** 4 37N 71 42W
San Pedro de Atacama, *Chile* **158 A2** 22 55 S 68 15W
San Pedro de Jujuy, *Argentina* **158 A3** 24 12 S 64 55W
San Pedro de las Colonias, *Mexico* **146 B4** 25 50N 102 59W
San Pedro de Lloc, *Peru* **156 B2** 7 15 S 79 28W
San Pedro de Macorís, *Dom. Rep.* **149 C6** 18 30N 69 18W
San Pedro del Norte, *Nic.* **148 D3** 13 4N 84 33W
San Pedro del Paraná, *Paraguay* **158 B4** 26 43 S 56 13W
San Pedro del Pinatar, *Spain* **35 H4** 37 50N 0 50W
San Pedro Mártir, Sierra, *Mexico* **146 A1** 31 0N 115 30W
San Pedro Mixtepec, *Mexico* **147 D5** 16 2N 97 7W
San Pedro Ocampo = Melchor Ocampo, *Mexico* **146 C4** 24 52N 101 40W
San Pedro Sula, *Honduras* **148 C2** 15 30N 88 0W
San Pieto, *Italy* **40 C1** 39 8N 8 17 E
San Pietro Vernótico, *Italy* **41 B11** 40 29N 18 0 E
San Quintín, *Mexico* **146 A1** 30 29N 115 57W
San Rafael, *Argentina* **158 C2** 34 40 S 68 21W
San Rafael, *Calif., U.S.A.* **144 H4** 37 58N 122 32W
San Rafael, *N. Mex., U.S.A.* **143 J10** 35 7N 107 53W
San Rafael, *Venezuela* **152 A3** 10 58N 71 46W
San Rafael Mt., *U.S.A.* **145 L7** 34 41N 119 52W
San Rafael Mts., *U.S.A.* **145 L7** 34 40N 119 50W
San Ramón, *Bolivia* **157 C5** 13 17 S 64 43W
San Ramón, *Peru* **156 C2** 11 8 S 75 20W
San Ramón de la Nueva Orán, *Argentina* **158 A3** 23 10 S 64 20W
San Remo, *Italy* **38 E4** 43 49N 7 46 E
San Román, C., *Venezuela* **152 A3** 12 12N 70 0W
San Roque, *Argentina* **158 B4** 28 25 S 58 45W
San Roque, *Phil.* **70 E5** 12 37N 124 52 E
San Roque, *Spain* **37 J5** 36 17N 5 21W

Santiago 261

San Rosendo, *Chile* 158 **D1** 37 16 S 72 43W
San Saba, *U.S.A.* 139 **K5** 31 12N 98 43W
San Salvador, *Bahamas* 149 **B5** 24 0N 74 40W
San Salvador, *El Salv.* 148 **D2** 13 40N 89 10W
San Salvador, *Spain* 33 **B10** 39 27N 3 11 E
San Salvador de Jujuy, *Argentina* 158 **A3** 24 10 S 64 48W
San Salvador I., *Bahamas* 149 **B5** 24 0N 74 32W
San Sebastián, *Argentina* 160 **D3** 53 10 S 68 30W
San Sebastián, *Spain* 34 **B3** 43 17N 1 58W
San Sebastián, *Venezuela* 152 **B4** 9 57N 67 11W
San Sebastian de la Gomera, *Canary Is.* 33 **F2** 28 5N 17 7W
San Serra, *Spain* 33 **B10** 39 43N 3 13 E
San Serverino Marche, *Italy* 39 **E10** 43 13N 13 10 E
San Simeon, *U.S.A.* 144 **K5** 35 39N 121 11W
San Simon, *U.S.A.* 143 **K9** 32 16N 109 14W
San Stéfano di Cadore, *Italy* 39 **B9** 46 34N 12 33 E
San Telmo, *Mexico* 146 **A1** 30 58N 116 6W
San Telmo, *Spain* 33 **B9** 39 35N 2 21 E
San Teodoro, *Phil.* 70 **E3** 13 26N 121 1 E
San Tiburcio, *Mexico* 146 **C4** 24 8N 101 32W
San Valentin, Mte., *Chile* 160 **C2** 46 30 S 73 30W
San Vicente de Alcántara, *Spain* 37 **F3** 39 22N 7 8W
San Vicente de la Barquera, *Spain* 36 **B6** 43 23N 4 29W
San Vicente del Caguán, *Colombia* 152 **C3** 2 7N 74 46W
San Vincenzo, *Italy* 38 **E7** 43 6N 10 32 E
San Vito, *Italy* 40 **C2** 39 26N 9 32 E
San Vito, C., *Italy* 40 **D5** 38 11N 12 41 E
San Vito al Tagliamento, *Italy* 39 **C9** 45 54N 12 52 E
San Vito Chietino, *Italy* 39 **F11** 42 18N 14 27 E
San Vito dei Normanni, *Italy* 41 **B10** 40 39N 17 42 E
San Yanaro, *Colombia* 152 **C4** 2 47N 69 42W
San Ygnacio, *U.S.A.* 139 **M5** 27 3N 99 26W
Saña, *Peru* 156 **B2** 6 54 S 79 36W
Sana', *Yemen* 86 **D4** 15 27N 44 12 E
Sana —►, *Bos.-H.* 39 **C13** 45 3N 16 23 E
Sanaba, *Burkina Faso* 100 **C4** 12 25N 3 47W
Şanāfīr, *Si. Arabia* 94 **B3** 27 56N 34 42 E
Sanaga —►, *Cameroon* 101 **E6** 3 35N 9 38 E
Sanaloa, Presa, *Mexico* 146 **C3** 24 50N 107 20W
Sanām, *Si. Arabia* 86 **B4** 23 40N 44 45 E
Sanana, *Indonesia* 72 **B3** 2 4 S 125 58 E
Sanand, *India* 80 **H5** 22 59N 72 25 E
Sanandaj, *Iran* 89 **E12** 35 18N 47 1 E
Sanandita, *Bolivia* 158 **A3** 21 40 S 63 45W
Sanary-sur-Mer, *France* 25 **E9** 43 7N 5 49 E
Sanāw, *Yemen* 87 **C5** 17 50N 51 5 E
Sanawad, *India* 80 **H7** 22 11N 76 5 E
Sanbe-San, *Japan* 62 **B4** 35 6N 132 38 E
Sancellas, *Spain* 33 **B9** 39 39N 2 54 E
Sancergues, *France* 23 **E9** 47 10N 2 54 E
Sancerre, *France* 23 **E9** 47 20N 2 50 E
Sancerrois, Collines du, *France* 23 **E9** 47 20N 2 40 E
Sancha He —►, *China* 68 **D6** 26 48N 106 7 E
Sanchahe, *China* 67 **B14** 44 50N 126 2 E
Sánchez, *Dom. Rep.* 149 **C6** 19 15N 69 36W
Sanchor, *India* 80 **G4** 24 45N 71 55 E
Sanco Pt., *Phil.* 71 **G6** 8 15N 126 27 E
Sancoins, *France* 23 **F9** 46 47N 2 55 E
Sancti-Spíritus, *Cuba* 148 **B4** 21 52N 79 33W
Sancy, Puy de, *France* 24 **C6** 45 32N 2 50 E
Sand —►, *S. Africa* 105 **C5** 22 25 S 30 5 E
Sand Cr. —►, *U.S.A.* 141 **E11** 39 3N 85 51W
Sand Springs, *U.S.A.* 139 **G6** 36 9N 96 7W
Sanda, *Japan* 63 **C7** 34 53N 135 14 E
Sandakan, *Malaysia* 75 **A5** 5 53N 118 4 E
Sandalwood, *Australia* 116 **C4** 34 55 S 140 9 E
Sandan = Sambor, *Cambodia* 76 **F6** 12 46N 106 0 E
Sandanski, *Bulgaria* 43 **F8** 41 35N 23 16 E
Sandaré, *Mali* 100 **C2** 14 40N 10 15W
Sanday, *U.K.* 18 **B6** 59 16N 2 31W
Sandefjord, *Norway* 14 **E4** 59 10N 10 15 E
Sanders, *Ariz., U.S.A.* 143 **J9** 35 13N 109 20W
Sanders, *Ky., U.S.A.* 141 **F12** 38 40N 84 56W
Sanderson, *U.S.A.* 139 **K3** 30 9N 102 24W
Sanderston, *Australia* 116 **C3** 34 46 S 139 15 E
Sandfly L., *Canada* 131 **B7** 55 43N 106 6W
Sandgate, *Australia* 115 **D5** 27 18 S 153 3 E
Sandía, *Peru* 156 **C4** 14 10 S 69 30W
Sandıklı, *Turkey* 88 **C4** 38 30N 30 20 E
Sandnes, *Norway* 13 **G11** 58 50N 5 45 E
Sandness, *U.K.* 18 **A7** 60 18N 1 40W
Sandnessjøen, *Norway* 12 **C15** 66 2N 12 38 E
Sandoa, *Zaïre* 103 **D4** 9 41 S 23 0 E
Sandomierz, *Poland* 47 **E8** 50 40N 21 43 E
Sandona, *Colombia* 152 **C2** 1 17N 77 28W
Sandongo, *Angola* 103 **F4** 15 30 S 21 28 E
Sandoval, *U.S.A.* 140 **F7** 38 37N 89 7W
Sandover —►, *Australia* 114 **C2** 21 43 S 136 32 E
Sandoy, *Færoe Is.* 12 **F9** 61 52N 6 46W
Sandpoint, *U.S.A.* 142 **B5** 48 17N 116 33W
Sandringham, *U.K.* 16 **E8** 52 51N 0 31 E
Sandslån, *Sweden* 14 **A11** 63 2N 17 49 E
Sandspit, *Canada* 130 **C2** 53 14N 131 49W
Sandstone, *Australia* 113 **E2** 27 59 S 119 16 E
Sandu, *China* 68 **E6** 26 0N 107 52 E
Sandusky, *Mich., U.S.A.* 128 **D3** 43 25N 82 50W
Sandusky, *Ohio, U.S.A.* 136 **E2** 41 27N 82 42W
Sandusky —►, *U.S.A.* 141 **C14** 41 27N 83 0W
Sandvig, *Sweden* 15 **J8** 55 18N 14 47 E
Sandviken, *Sweden* 13 **F17** 60 38N 16 46 E
Sandwich, *U.S.A.* 141 **C8** 41 39N 88 37W
Sandwich, C., *Australia* 114 **B4** 18 14 S 146 18 E
Sandwich B., *Canada* 129 **B8** 53 40N 57 15W
Sandwich B., *Namibia* 104 **C1** 23 25 S 14 20 E
Sandy, *Nev., U.S.A.* 145 **K11** 35 49N 115 36W
Sandy, *Oreg., U.S.A.* 144 **E4** 45 24N 122 16W
Sandy, *Utah, U.S.A.* 142 **F8** 40 35N 111 50W
Sandy Bight, *Australia* 113 **F3** 33 50 S 123 20 E
Sandy C., *Queens., Australia* 114 **C5** 24 42 S 153 15 E
Sandy C., *Tas., Australia* 114 **G3** 41 25 S 144 45 E
Sandy Cay, *Bahamas* 149 **B4** 23 13N 75 18W
Sandy Cr. —►, *U.S.A.* 142 **F9** 41 51N 109 47W
Sandy L., *Canada* 128 **B1** 53 2N 93 0W
Sandy Lake, *Canada* 128 **B1** 53 0N 93 15W
Sandy Narrows, *Canada* 131 **B8** 55 5N 103 4W
Sanford, *Fla., U.S.A.* 135 **L5** 28 48N 81 16W
Sanford, *Maine, U.S.A.* 137 **C14** 43 27N 70 47W
Sanford, *N.C., U.S.A.* 135 **H6** 35 29N 79 10W
Sanford —►, *Australia* 113 **E2** 27 22 S 115 53 E
Sanford, Mt., *U.S.A.* 126 **B5** 62 13N 144 8W
Sang-i-Masha, *Afghan.* 80 **C2** 33 8N 67 27 E
Sanga, *Mozam.* 107 **E4** 12 22 S 35 21 E
Sanga —►, *Congo* 102 **C3** 1 5 S 17 0 E
Sanga-Tolon, *Russia* 57 **C15** 61 50N 149 40 E
Sangamner, *India* 82 **E2** 19 37N 74 15 E
Sangamon —►, *U.S.A.* 140 **D6** 40 7N 90 20W
Sangar, *Afghan.* 80 **C1** 32 56N 65 30 E
Sangar, *Russia* 57 **C13** 64 2N 127 31 E
Sangar Sarai, *Afghan.* 80 **B4** 34 27N 70 35 E
Sangasangadalam, *Indonesia* 75 **C5** 0 36 S 117 13 E
Sangatte, *France* 23 **B8** 50 56N 1 44 E
Sangay, *Ecuador* 152 **D2** 2 0 S 78 20W
Sange, *Zaïre* 106 **D2** 6 58 S 28 21 E
Sangeang, *Indonesia* 72 **C1** 8 12 S 119 6 E
Sanger, *U.S.A.* 144 **J7** 36 42N 119 33W
Sangerhausen, *Germany* 26 **D7** 51 28N 11 18 E
Sanggan He —►, *China* 66 **E9** 38 12N 117 15 E
Sanggau, *Indonesia* 75 **B4** 0 5N 110 30 E
Sangihe, Kepulauan, *Indonesia* 72 **A3** 3 0N 126 0 E
Sangihe, P., *Indonesia* 72 **A3** 3 45N 125 30 E
Sangju, *S. Korea* 67 **F15** 36 25N 128 10 E
Sangkapura, *Indonesia* 75 **D4** 5 52 S 112 40 E
Sangkhla, *Thailand* 76 **E2** 14 57N 98 28 E
Sangli, *India* 82 **F2** 16 55N 74 33 E
Sangmélina, *Cameroon* 101 **E7** 2 57N 12 1 E
Sangonera —►, *Spain* 35 **H3** 37 59N 1 4W
Sangpang Bum, *Burma* 78 **B5** 26 30N 95 50 E
Sangre de Cristo Mts., *U.S.A.* 139 **G2** 37 0N 105 0W
Sangro —►, *Italy* 39 **F11** 42 14N 14 32 E
Sangudo, *Canada* 130 **C6** 53 50N 114 54W
Sangue —►, *Brazil* 157 **C6** 11 1 S 58 39W
Sangüesa, *Spain* 34 **C3** 42 37N 1 17W
Sanguinaires, Is., *France* 25 **G12** 41 51N 8 36 E
Sangzhi, *China* 69 **C8** 29 25N 110 12 E
Sanhala, *Ivory C.* 100 **C3** 10 3N 6 51W
Sanje, *Uganda* 106 **C3** 0 49 S 31 30 E
Sanjiang, *China* 68 **E7** 25 48N 109 37 E
Sanjo, *Japan* 60 **F9** 37 37N 138 57 E
Sankarankovil, *India* 83 **K3** 9 10N 77 35 E
Sankeshwar, *India* 83 **F2** 16 23N 74 32 E
Sankosh —►, *India* 78 **B2** 26 24N 89 47 E
Sankt Andrä, *Austria* 30 **E7** 46 46N 14 50 E
Sankt Antönien, *Switz.* 29 **C9** 46 58N 9 48 E
Sankt Blasien, *Germany* 27 **H4** 47 47N 8 7 E
Sankt Gallen, *Switz.* 29 **B8** 47 26N 9 22 E
Sankt Gallen □, *Switz.* 29 **B8** 47 25N 9 22 E
Sankt Goar, *Germany* 27 **E3** 50 12N 7 43 E
Sankt Ingbert, *Germany* 27 **F3** 49 16N 7 6 E
Sankt Johann, *Salzburg, Austria* 30 **D6** 47 22N 13 12 E
Sankt Johann, *Tirol, Austria* 30 **D5** 47 30N 12 25 E
Sankt Margrethen, *Switz.* 29 **B9** 47 28N 9 37 E
Sankt Moritz, *Switz.* 29 **D9** 46 30N 9 50 E
Sankt-Peterburg, *Russia* 50 **C6** 59 55N 30 20 E
Sankt Pölten, *Austria* 30 **C8** 48 12N 15 38 E
Sankt Valentin, *Austria* 30 **C7** 48 11N 14 33 E
Sankt Veit, *Austria* 30 **E7** 46 54N 14 22 E
Sankt Wendel, *Germany* 27 **F3** 49 27N 7 9 E
Sankt Wolfgang, *Austria* 30 **D6** 47 43N 13 27 E
Sankuru —►, *Zaïre* 103 **C4** 4 17 S 20 25 E
Sanliurfa, *Turkey* 89 **D8** 37 12N 38 50 E
Sanlúcar de Barrameda, *Spain* 37 **J4** 36 46N 6 21W
Sanlúcar la Mayor, *Spain* 37 **H4** 37 26N 6 18W
Sanluri, *Italy* 40 **C1** 39 34N 8 54 E
Sanmenxia, *China* 66 **G6** 34 47N 111 12 E
Sanming, *China* 69 **D11** 26 15N 117 40 E
Sannan, *Japan* 63 **B7** 35 2N 135 1 E
Sannaspos, *S. Africa* 104 **D4** 29 6 S 26 34 E
Sannicandro Gargánico, *Italy* 41 **A8** 41 50N 15 34 E
Sannidal, *Norway* 14 **F3** 58 55N 9 15 E
Sannieshof, *S. Africa* 104 **D4** 26 30 S 25 47 E
Sannīn, J., *Lebanon* 91 **B4** 33 57N 35 52 E
Sano, *Japan* 63 **A11** 36 19N 139 35 E
Sanok, *Poland* 31 **B15** 49 35N 22 10 E
Sanquhar, *U.K.* 18 **F5** 55 22N 3 54W
Sansanding Dam, *Mali* 100 **C3** 13 48N 6 0W
Sansepolcro, *Italy* 39 **E9** 43 34N 12 8 E
Sansha, *China* 69 **D13** 26 58N 120 12 E
Sanshui, *China* 69 **F9** 23 10N 112 56 E
Sanski Most, *Bos.-H.* 39 **D13** 44 46N 16 40 E
Sansui, *China* 68 **D7** 26 58N 108 39 E
Santa, *Peru* 156 **B2** 8 59 S 78 40W
Sant' Ágata de Goti, *Italy* 41 **A7** 41 6N 14 30 E
Sant' Ágata di Militello, *Italy* 41 **D7** 38 2N 14 8 E
Santa Ana, *Beni, Bolivia* 157 **C4** 13 50 S 65 40W
Santa Ana, *Santa Cruz, Bolivia* 157 **D6** 18 43 S 58 44W
Santa Ana, *Santa Cruz, Bolivia* 157 **D5** 16 37 S 60 43W
Santa Ana, *Ecuador* 152 **D1** 1 16 S 80 20W
Santa Ana, *El Salv.* 148 **D2** 14 0N 89 31W
Santa Ana, *Mexico* 146 **A2** 30 31N 111 8W
Santa Ana, *Phil.* 70 **B4** 18 28N 122 20 E
Santa Ana, *U.S.A.* 145 **M9** 33 46N 117 52W
Santa Ana —►, *Venezuela* 152 **B3** 9 30N 71 57W
Sant' Ángelo Lodigiano, *Italy* 38 **C6** 45 14N 9 25 E
Sant' Antíoco, *Italy* 40 **C1** 39 2N 8 30 E
Sant' Arcángelo di Romagna, *Italy* 39 **D9** 44 4N 12 26 E
Santa Bárbara, *Colombia* 152 **B2** 5 53N 75 35W
Santa Barbara, *Honduras* 148 **D2** 14 53N 88 14W
Santa Bárbara, *Mexico* 146 **B3** 26 48N 105 50W
Santa Barbara, *Phil.* 71 **F4** 10 50N 122 32 E
Santa Bárbara, *Spain* 34 **E5** 40 42N 0 29 E
Santa Barbara, *U.S.A.* 145 **L7** 34 25N 119 42W
Santa Bárbara, *Venezuela* 152 **B3** 7 47N 71 10W
Santa Bárbara, Mt., *Spain* 35 **H2** 37 23N 2 50W
Santa Barbara Channel, *U.S.A.* 145 **L7** 34 15N 120 0W
Santa Barbara I., *U.S.A.* 145 **M7** 33 29N 119 2W
Santa Catalina, *Colombia* 152 **A2** 10 36N 75 17W
Santa Catalina, *Mexico* 146 **B2** 25 40N 110 50W
Santa Catalina, Gulf of, *U.S.A.* 145 **N9** 33 10N 117 50W
Santa Catalina I., *U.S.A.* 145 **M8** 33 23N 118 25W
Santa Catarina □, *Brazil* 159 **B6** 27 25 S 48 30W
Santa Catarina, I. de, *Brazil* 159 **B6** 27 30 S 48 40W
Santa Caterina Villarmosa, *Italy* 41 **E7** 37 35N 14 2 E
Santa Cecília, *Brazil* 159 **B5** 26 56 S 50 18W
Santa Clara, *Cuba* 148 **B4** 22 20N 80 0W
Santa Clara, *Calif., U.S.A.* 144 **H5** 37 21N 121 57W
Santa Clara, *Utah, U.S.A.* 143 **H7** 37 8N 113 39W
Santa Clara de Olimar, *Uruguay* 159 **C5** 32 50 S 54 54W
Santa Clotilde, *Peru* 152 **D3** 2 33 S 73 45W
Santa Coloma de Farners, *Spain* 34 **D7** 41 50N 2 39 E
Santa Coloma de Gramanet, *Spain* 34 **D7** 41 27N 2 13 E
Santa Comba, *Spain* 36 **B2** 43 2N 8 49W
Santa Croce Camerina, *Italy* 41 **F7** 36 50N 14 31 E
Santa Croce di Magliano, *Italy* 41 **A7** 41 42N 14 59 E
Santa Cruz, *Argentina* 160 **D3** 50 0 S 68 32W
Santa Cruz, *Bolivia* 157 **D5** 17 43 S 63 10W
Santa Cruz, *Brazil* 154 **C4** 6 13 S 36 1W
Santa Cruz, *Chile* 158 **C1** 34 38 S 71 27W
Santa Cruz, *Costa Rica* 148 **D2** 10 15N 85 35W
Santa Cruz, *Madeira* 33 **D3** 32 42N 16 46W
Santa Cruz, *Peru* 156 **B2** 5 40 S 75 56W
Santa Cruz, *Davao del S., Phil.* 71 **H5** 6 50N 125 25 E
Santa Cruz, *Laguna, Phil.* 70 **D3** 14 20N 121 24 E
Santa Cruz, *Marinduque, Phil.* 70 **E4** 13 28N 122 2 E
Santa Cruz, *U.S.A.* 144 **J4** 36 58N 122 1W
Santa Cruz, *Venezuela* 153 **B5** 8 3N 64 27W
Santa Cruz □, *Argentina* 160 **C3** 49 0 S 70 0W
Santa Cruz □, *Bolivia* 157 **D5** 17 43 S 63 10W
Santa Cruz —►, *Argentina* 160 **D3** 50 10 S 68 20W
Santa Cruz Cabrália, *Brazil* 155 **E4** 16 17 S 39 2W
Santa Cruz de la Palma, *Canary Is.* 33 **F2** 28 41N 17 46W
Santa Cruz de Mudela, *Spain* 35 **G1** 38 39N 3 28W
Santa Cruz de Tenerife, *Canary Is.* 33 **F3** 28 28N 16 15W
Santa Cruz del Norte, *Cuba* 148 **B3** 23 9N 81 55W
Santa Cruz del Retamar, *Spain* 36 **E6** 40 8N 4 14W
Santa Cruz del Sur, *Cuba* 148 **B4** 20 44N 78 0W
Santa Cruz do Rio Pardo, *Brazil* 159 **A6** 22 54 S 49 37W
Santa Cruz do Sul, *Brazil* 159 **B5** 29 42 S 52 25W
Santa Cruz I., *Solomon Is.* 122 **J8** 10 30 S 166 0 E
Santa Cruz I., *U.S.A.* 145 **M7** 34 1N 119 43W
Santa Domingo, Cay, *Bahamas* 148 **B4** 21 25N 75 15W
Santa Elena, *Argentina* 158 **C4** 30 58 S 59 47W
Santa Elena, *Ecuador* 152 **D1** 2 16 S 80 52W
Santa Elena, C., *Costa Rica* 148 **D2** 10 54N 85 56W
Sant' Eufémia, G. di, *Italy* 41 **D9** 38 51N 16 4 E
Santa Eugenia, Pta., *Mexico* 146 **B1** 27 50N 115 5W
Santa Eulalia, *Spain* 33 **C8** 38 59N 1 32 E
Santa Fe, *Argentina* 158 **C3** 31 35 S 60 41W
Santa Fe, *Nueva Viscaya, Phil.* 70 **C3** 16 10N 120 57 E
Santa Fe, *Tablas, Phil.* 70 **E4** 12 10N 122 0 E
Santa Fe, *Spain* 37 **H7** 37 11N 3 43W
Santa Fe, *U.S.A.* 143 **J11** 35 41N 105 57W
Santa Fé □, *Argentina* 158 **C3** 31 50 S 60 55W
Santa Filomena, *Brazil* 154 **C2** 9 6 S 45 50W
Santa Galdana, *Spain* 33 **B10** 39 56N 3 58 E
Santa Gertrudis, *Spain* 33 **B7** 39 0N 1 26 E
Santa Helena, *Brazil* 154 **B2** 2 14 S 45 18W
Santa Helena de Goiás, *Brazil* 155 **E1** 17 53 S 50 35W
Santa Inês, *Brazil* 155 **D4** 13 17 S 39 48W
Santa Inés, *Baleares, Spain* 33 **B7** 39 3N 1 21 E
Santa Inés, *Extremadura, Spain* 37 **G5** 38 32N 5 37W
Santa Inés, I., *Chile* 160 **D2** 54 0 S 73 0W
Santa Isabel = Rey Malabo, *Eq. Guin.* 101 **E6** 3 45N 8 50 E
Santa Isabel, *Argentina* 158 **D2** 36 10 S 66 54W
Santa Isabel, *Brazil* 155 **D1** 11 45 S 51 30W
Santa Isabel, *Solomon Is.* 121 **M10** 8 0 S 159 0 E
Santa Isabel, Pico, *Eq. Guin.* 101 **E6** 3 36N 8 49 E
Santa Isabel do Araguaia, *Brazil* 154 **C2** 6 7 S 48 19W
Santa Isabel do Morro, *Brazil* 155 **D1** 11 34 S 50 40W
Santa Lucía, *Corrientes, Argentina* 158 **B4** 28 58 S 59 5W
Santa Lucía, *San Juan, Argentina* 158 **C2** 31 30 S 68 30W
Santa Lucia, *Phil.* 70 **C3** 17 7N 120 27 E
Santa Lucía, *Spain* 35 **H4** 37 35N 0 58W
Santa Lucía, *Uruguay* 158 **C4** 34 27 S 56 24W
Santa Lucia Range, *U.S.A.* 144 **K5** 36 0N 121 20W
Santa Magdalena, I., *Mexico* 146 **C2** 24 40N 112 15W
Santa Margarita, *Argentina* 158 **D3** 38 28 S 61 35W
Santa Margarita, *Mexico* 146 **C2** 24 30N 111 50W
Santa Margarita, *Spain* 33 **B10** 39 42N 3 6 E
Santa Margarita, *U.S.A.* 144 **K6** 35 23N 120 37W
Santa Margarita —►, *U.S.A.* 145 **M9** 33 13N 117 23W
Santa Margherita, *Italy* 38 **D6** 44 20N 9 11 E
Santa María, *Argentina* 158 **B2** 26 40 S 66 0W
Santa Maria, *Brazil* 159 **B5** 29 40 S 53 48W
Santa Maria, *Ilocos S., Phil.* 70 **C3** 17 22N 120 29 E
Santa Maria, *Isabela, Phil.* 70 **C3** 17 28N 121 45 E
Santa Maria, *Spain* 33 **B9** 39 38N 2 47 E
Santa Maria, *Switz.* 29 **C10** 46 36N 10 25 E
Santa Maria, *U.S.A.* 145 **L6** 34 57N 120 26W
Santa María —►, *Mexico* 146 **A3** 31 0N 107 14W
Santa María, B. de, *Mexico* 146 **B3** 25 10N 108 40W
Santa Maria, C. de, *Portugal* 37 **J3** 36 58N 7 53W
Santa Maria Cápua Vétere, *Italy* 41 **A7** 41 5N 14 15 E
Santa Maria da Vitória, *Brazil* 155 **D3** 13 24 S 44 12W
Santa María de Ipire, *Venezuela* 153 **B4** 8 49N 65 19W
Santa Maria di Leuca, C., *Italy* 41 **C11** 39 47N 18 22 E
Santa Maria do Suaçuí, *Brazil* 155 **E3** 18 12 S 42 25W
Santa Maria dos Marmelos, *Brazil* 157 **B5** 6 7 S 61 51W
Santa María la Real de Nieva, *Spain* 36 **D6** 41 4N 4 24W
Santa Marta, *Colombia* 152 **A3** 11 15N 74 13W
Santa Marta, *Spain* 37 **G4** 38 37N 6 39W
Santa Marta, Ría de, *Spain* 36 **B3** 43 44N 7 45W
Santa Marta, Sierra Nevada de, *Colombia* 152 **A3** 10 55N 73 50W
Santa Marta Grande, C., *Brazil* 159 **B6** 28 43 S 48 50W
Santa Maura = Levkás, *Greece* 45 **F2** 38 40N 20 43 E
Santa Monica, *U.S.A.* 145 **M8** 34 1N 118 29W
Santa Olalla, *Huelva, Spain* 37 **H4** 37 54N 6 14W
Santa Olalla, *Toledo, Spain* 36 **E6** 40 2N 4 25W
Sant' Onofrio, *Italy* 41 **D9** 38 42N 16 10 E
Santa Pola, *Spain* 35 **G4** 38 13N 0 35W
Santa Ponsa, *Spain* 33 **B9** 39 30N 2 28 E
Santa Quitéria, *Brazil* 154 **B3** 4 20 S 40 10W
Santa Rita, *U.S.A.* 143 **K10** 32 48N 108 4W
Santa Rita, *Guarico, Venezuela* 152 **B4** 8 8N 66 16W
Santa Rita, *Zulia, Venezuela* 152 **A3** 10 32N 71 32W
Santa Rita do Araquaia, *Brazil* 157 **D7** 17 20 S 53 12W
Santa Rosa, *La Pampa, Argentina* 158 **D3** 36 40 S 64 17W
Santa Rosa, *San Luis, Argentina* 158 **C2** 32 21 S 65 10W
Santa Rosa, *Bolivia* 156 **C4** 10 36 S 67 20W
Santa Rosa, *Brazil* 159 **B5** 27 52 S 54 29W
Santa Rosa, *Colombia* 152 **C4** 3 32N 69 48W
Santa Rosa, *Ecuador* 152 **D2** 3 27 S 79 58W
Santa Rosa, *Peru* 156 **C3** 14 30 S 70 50W
Santa Rosa, *Phil.* 70 **D3** 15 25N 120 57 E
Santa Rosa, *Calif., U.S.A.* 144 **G4** 38 26N 122 43W
Santa Rosa, *N. Mex., U.S.A.* 139 **H2** 34 57N 104 41W
Santa Rosa, *Venezuela* 152 **C4** 1 29N 66 55W
Santa Rosa de Cabal, *Colombia* 152 **C2** 4 52N 75 38W
Santa Rosa de Copán, *Honduras* 148 **D2** 14 47N 88 46W
Santa Rosa de Osos, *Colombia* 152 **B2** 6 39N 75 28W
Santa Rosa de Río Primero, *Argentina* 158 **C3** 31 8 S 63 20W
Santa Rosa de Viterbo, *Colombia* 152 **B3** 5 53N 72 59W
Santa Rosa del Palmar, *Bolivia* 157 **D5** 16 54 S 62 24W
Santa Rosa I., *Calif., U.S.A.* 145 **M6** 33 58N 120 6W
Santa Rosa I., *Fla., U.S.A.* 135 **K2** 30 20N 86 50W
Santa Rosa Range, *U.S.A.* 142 **F5** 41 45N 117 40W
Santa Rosalía, *Mexico* 146 **B2** 27 20N 112 20W
Santa Sofia, *Italy* 39 **E8** 43 57N 11 54 E
Santa Sylvina, *Argentina* 158 **B3** 27 50 S 61 10W
Santa Tecla = Nueva San Salvador, *El Salv.* 148 **D2** 13 40N 89 18W
Santa Teresa, *Argentina* 158 **C3** 33 25 S 60 47W
Santa Teresa, *Brazil* 155 **E3** 19 55 S 40 36W
Santa Teresa, *Mexico* 147 **B5** 25 17N 97 51W
Santa Teresa, *Venezuela* 153 **C5** 4 43N 61 4W
Santa Teresa di Riva, *Italy* 41 **E8** 37 57N 15 22 E
Santa Teresa Gallura, *Italy* 40 **A2** 41 14N 9 11 E
Santa Vitória, *Brazil* 155 **E1** 18 50 S 50 8W
Santa Vitória do Palmar, *Brazil* 159 **C5** 33 32 S 53 25W
Santa Ynez —►, *U.S.A.* 145 **L6** 35 41N 120 36W
Santa Ynez Mts., *U.S.A.* 145 **L6** 34 30N 120 0W
Santa Ysabel, *U.S.A.* 145 **M10** 33 7N 116 40W
Santadi, *Italy* 40 **C1** 39 5N 8 43 E
Santahar, *Bangla.* 78 **C2** 24 48N 88 59 E
Santai, *China* 68 **B5** 31 5N 104 58 E
Santaluz, *Brazil* 154 **D4** 11 15 S 39 22W
Santana, *Brazil* 155 **D3** 13 2 S 44 5W
Santana, *Madeira* 33 **D3** 32 48N 16 52W
Santana, Coxilha de, *Brazil* 159 **C4** 30 50 S 55 35W
Santana do Ipanema, *Brazil* 154 **C4** 9 22 S 37 14W
Santana do Livramento, *Brazil* 159 **C4** 30 55 S 55 30W
Santanayi, *Spain* 33 **B10** 39 20N 3 5 E
Santander, *Colombia* 152 **C2** 3 1N 76 28W
Santander, *Phil.* 71 **G4** 9 25N 123 20 E
Santander, *Spain* 36 **B7** 43 27N 3 51W
Santander Jiménez, *Mexico* 147 **C5** 24 11N 98 29W
Santaquin, *U.S.A.* 142 **G8** 39 59N 111 47W
Santarém, *Brazil* 153 **D7** 2 25 S 54 42W
Santarém, *Portugal* 37 **F2** 39 12N 8 42W
Santarém □, *Portugal* 37 **F2** 39 10N 8 40W
Santaren Channel, *W. Indies* 148 **B4** 24 0N 79 30W
Santee, *U.S.A.* 145 **N10** 32 50N 116 58W
Santéramo in Colle, *Italy* 41 **B9** 40 48N 16 45 E
Santerno —►, *Italy* 39 **D8** 44 34N 11 58 E
Santhià, *Italy* 38 **C5** 45 22N 8 10 E
Santiago, *Bolivia* 157 **D6** 18 19 S 59 34W
Santiago, *Brazil* 159 **B5** 29 11 S 54 52W
Santiago, *C. Verde Is.* 8 **G6** 15 10N 23 30W
Santiago, *Chile* 158 **C1** 33 24 S 70 40W
Santiago, *Panama* 148 **E3** 8 0N 81 0W
Santiago, *Peru* 156 **C2** 14 11 S 75 43W
Santiago, *Ilocos S., Phil.* 70 **C3** 17 18N 120 27 E
Santiago, *Isabela, Phil.* 70 **C3** 16 41N 121 33 E
Santiago □, *Chile* 158 **C1** 33 30 S 70 50W
Santiago —►, *Mexico* 124 **G9** 25 11N 105 26W
Santiago —►, *Peru* 152 **D2** 4 27 S 77 38W

Senftenberg 263

Sayan, Zapadnyy, Russia 57 D10 52 30N 94 0 E
Saydā, Lebanon 91 B4 33 35N 35 25 E
Sayghān, Afghan. 79 B2 35 10N 67 55 E
Sayhan-Ovoo, Mongolia 66 B2 45 27N 103 54 E
Sayhandulaan, Mongolia 66 B5 44 40N 109 1 E
Sayḥut, Yemen 87 D5 15 12N 51 10 E
Saykhin, Kazakstan 53 F8 48 50N 46 47 E
Saylorville L., U.S.A. 140 C3 41 48N 93 46W
Saynshand, Mongolia 66 B6 44 55N 110 11 E
Sayō, Japan 62 C6 34 59N 134 22 E
Sayre, Okla., U.S.A. 139 H5 35 18N 99 38W
Sayre, Pa., U.S.A. 137 E8 41 59N 76 32W
Sayula, Mexico 146 D4 19 50N 103 40W
Saywūn, Yemen 87 D5 15 56N 48 47 E
Sazanit, Albania 44 D1 40 30N 19 20 E
Sázava →, Czech. 30 B7 49 53N 14 24 E
Sazin, Pakistan 81 B5 35 35N 73 30 E
Sazlika →, Bulgaria 43 F10 41 59N 25 50 E
Sbeïtla, Tunisia 96 A1 35 12N 9 7 E
Scaër, France 22 D3 48 2N 3 42W
Scafell Pike, U.K. 16 C4 54 27N 3 14W
Scalea, Italy 41 C8 39 49N 15 47 E
Scalpay, U.K. 18 D2 57 52N 6 40W
Scandia, Canada 130 C6 50 20N 112 0W
Scandiano, Italy 38 D7 44 36N 10 43 E
Scandinavia, Europe 10 C8 64 0N 12 0 E
Scansano, Italy 39 F8 42 41N 11 20 E
Scapa Flow, U.K. 18 C5 58 53N 3 3W
Scappoose, U.S.A. 144 E4 45 45N 122 53W
Scarborough, Trin. & Tob. 149 D7 11 11N 60 42W
Scarborough, U.K. 16 C7 54 17N 0 24W
Scargill, N.Z. 119 C7 42 56 S 172 58 E
Scarsdale, Australia 116 D5 37 41 S 143 39 E
Scebeli, Wabi →, Somali Rep. 95 G5 2 0N 44 0 E
Šćedro, Croatia 39 E13 43 6N 16 43 E
Scenic, U.S.A. 138 D3 43 47N 102 33W
Schaalsee, Germany 26 B6 53 36N 10 55 E
Schaan, Liech. 29 B9 47 10N 9 31 E
Schaesberg, Neths. 21 G8 50 54N 6 0 E
Schaffen, Belgium 21 G6 51 0N 5 5 E
Schaffhausen, Switz. 29 A7 47 42N 8 39 E
Schaffhausen □, Switz. 29 A7 47 42N 8 36 E
Schagen, Neths. 20 C5 52 49N 4 48 E
Schaijk, Neths. 20 E7 51 44N 5 38 E
Schalkhaar, Neths. 20 D8 52 17N 6 12 E
Schalkwijk, Neths. 20 E6 52 0N 5 11 E
Schangnau, Switz. 28 C5 46 50N 7 47 E
Schänis, Switz. 29 B8 47 10N 9 3 E
Schärding, Austria 30 C6 48 27N 13 27 E
Scharhörn, Germany 26 B4 53 57N 8 24 E
Scharnitz, Austria 30 D4 47 23N 11 15 E
Schaumburg, U.S.A. 141 B8 42 2N 88 5W
Scheessel, Germany 26 B5 53 10N 9 29 E
Schefferville, Canada 129 B6 54 48N 66 50W
Scheibbs, Austria 30 C8 48 1N 15 9 E
Schelde →, Belgium 21 F4 51 15N 4 16 E
Schell City, U.S.A. 140 F2 38 1N 94 7W
Schell Creek Ra., U.S.A. 142 G6 39 15N 114 30W
Schenectady, U.S.A. 137 D11 42 49N 73 57W
Scherfede, Germany 26 D5 51 32N 9 2 E
Scherpenheuvel, Belgium 21 G5 50 58N 4 58 E
Scherpenisse, Neths. 21 E4 51 33N 4 6 E
Scherpenzeel, Neths. 20 D7 52 5N 5 30 E
Schesaplana, Switz. 29 B9 47 5N 9 43 E
Schesslitz, Germany 27 F7 49 58N 11 1 E
Scheveningen, Neths. 20 D4 52 6N 4 16 E
Schiedam, Neths. 20 E4 51 55N 4 25 E
Schiermonnikoog, Neths. 20 B8 53 30N 6 15 E
Schiers, Switz. 29 C9 46 58N 9 41 E
Schifferstadt, Germany 27 F4 49 23N 8 22 E
Schifflange, Lux. 21 K8 49 30N 6 1 E
Schijndel, Neths. 21 E6 51 37N 5 27 E
Schiltigheim, France 23 D14 48 35N 7 45 E
Schio, Italy 39 C8 45 43N 11 21 E
Schipbeek, Neths. 20 D8 52 14N 6 10 E
Schipluiden, Neths. 20 E4 51 59N 4 19 E
Schirmeck, France 23 D14 48 29N 7 12 E
Schladming, Austria 30 D6 47 23N 13 41 E
Schlanders = Silandro, Italy 38 B7 46 38N 10 46 E
Schlei →, Germany 26 A5 54 40N 10 0 E
Schleiden, Germany 26 E2 50 31N 6 28 E
Schleiz, Germany 26 E7 50 35N 11 49 E
Schleswig, Germany 26 A5 54 31N 9 34 E
Schleswig-Holstein □, Germany 26 A5 54 30N 9 30 E
Schlieren, Switz. 29 B6 47 26N 8 27 E
Schlüchtern, Germany 27 E5 50 20N 9 32 E
Schmalkalden, Germany 26 E6 50 44N 10 26 E
Schmölln, Brandenburg, Germany 26 B10 53 17N 14 5 E
Schmölln, Thüringen, Germany 26 E8 50 54N 12 19 E
Schneeberg, Austria 30 D8 47 47N 15 48 E
Schneeberg, Germany 26 E8 50 35N 12 38 E
Schneider, U.S.A. 141 C9 41 13N 87 28W
Schoenberg, Belgium 21 H8 50 17N 6 16 E
Schofield, U.S.A. 138 C10 44 54N 89 36W
Scholls, U.S.A. 144 E4 45 24N 122 56W
Schönberg, Mecklenburg-Vorpommern, Germany 26 B6 53 52N 10 56 E
Schönberg, Schleswig-Holstein, Germany 26 A6 54 23N 10 21 E
Schönebeck, Germany 26 C7 52 2N 11 44 E
Schönenwerd, Switz. 28 B5 47 23N 8 0 E
Schongau, Germany 27 H6 47 47N 10 53 E
Schöningen, Germany 26 C6 52 8N 10 56 E
Schoolcraft, U.S.A. 141 B11 42 7N 85 38W
Schoondijke, Neths. 21 F3 51 21N 3 33 E
Schoonebeek, Neths. 20 C9 52 39N 6 52 E
Schoonhoven, Neths. 20 E5 51 57N 4 51 E
Schoorl, Neths. 20 C5 52 42N 4 42 E
Schortens, Germany 26 B3 53 31N 7 56 E
Schoten, Belgium 21 F5 51 16N 4 30 E
Schouten I., Australia 114 G4 42 20 S 148 20 E
Schouten Is. = Supiori, Indonesia 73 B5 1 0 S 136 0 E
Schouwen, Neths. 21 E3 51 43N 3 45 E
Schramberg, Germany 27 G4 48 13N 8 22 E
Schrankogl, Austria 30 D4 47 3N 11 7 E
Schreckhorn, Switz. 28 C6 46 36N 8 7 E
Schreiber, Canada 128 C2 48 45N 87 20W
Schrobenhausen, Germany 27 G7 48 34N 11 16 E
Schruns, Austria 30 D2 47 5N 9 56 E
Schuler, Canada 131 C6 50 20N 110 6W
Schuls, Switz. 29 C10 46 48N 10 18 E
Schumacher, Canada 128 C3 48 30N 81 16W
Schüpfen, Switz. 28 B4 47 2N 7 24 E
Schüpfheim, Switz. 28 C6 46 57N 8 2 E
Schurz, U.S.A. 142 G4 38 57N 118 49W
Schuyler, U.S.A. 138 E6 41 27N 97 4W
Schuylkill Haven, U.S.A. 137 F8 40 37N 76 11W
Schwabach, Germany 27 F7 49 19N 11 2 E
Schwäbisch Gmünd, Germany 27 G5 48 48N 9 47 E
Schwäbisch Hall, Germany 27 F5 49 6N 9 44 E
Schwäbische Alb, Germany 27 G5 48 20N 9 30 E
Schwabmünchen, Germany 27 G6 48 10N 10 46 E
Schwanden, Switz. 29 C8 46 58N 9 5 E
Schwandorf, Germany 27 F8 49 20N 12 7 E
Schwaner, Pegunungan, Indonesia 75 C4 1 0 S 112 30 E
Schwarmstedt, Germany 26 C5 52 31N 9 38 E
Schwarzach →, Austria 30 E5 46 56N 12 35 E
Schwärze, Germany 26 C9 52 50N 13 49 E
Schwarze Elster →, Germany 26 D8 51 48N 12 50 E
Schwarzenberg, Germany 26 E8 50 32N 12 47 E
Schwarzenburg, Switz. 28 C4 46 49N 7 20 E
Schwarzwald, Germany 27 H4 48 30N 8 20 E
Schwaz, Austria 30 D4 47 20N 11 44 E
Schwedt, Germany 26 B10 53 3N 14 16 E
Schweinfurt, Germany 27 E6 50 3N 10 14 E
Schweizer Mittelland, Switz. 28 C4 47 0N 7 15 E
Schweizer-Reneke, S. Africa 104 D4 27 11 S 25 18 E
Schwenningen = Villingen-Schwenningen, Germany 27 G4 48 3N 8 26 E
Schwerin, Germany 26 B7 53 36N 11 22 E
Schweriner See, Germany 26 B7 53 43N 11 28 E
Schwetzingen, Germany 27 F4 49 23N 8 35 E
Schwyz, Switz. 29 B7 47 2N 8 39 E
Schwyz □, Switz. 29 B7 47 2N 8 39 E
Sciacca, Italy 40 E6 37 31N 13 3 E
Sciao, Somali Rep. 108 D3 3 26N 45 21 E
Scicli, Italy 41 F7 36 47N 14 42 E
Scilla, Italy 41 D8 38 15N 15 43 E
Scilly, Isles of, U.K. 17 H1 49 56N 6 22W
Ścinawa, Poland 47 D3 51 25N 16 26 E
Scione, Greece 44 E5 39 57N 23 36 E
Scioto →, U.S.A. 134 F4 38 44N 83 1W
Scobey, U.S.A. 138 A2 48 47N 105 25W
Scone, Australia 117 B9 32 5 S 150 52 E
Scórdia, Italy 41 E7 37 18N 14 51 E
Scoresbysund, Greenland 6 B6 70 20N 23 0W
Scorno, Punta dello, Italy 40 A1 41 7N 8 19 E
Scotia, Calif., U.S.A. 142 F1 40 29N 124 6W
Scotia, N.Y., U.S.A. 137 D11 42 50N 73 58W
Scotia Sea, Antarctica 7 B18 56 5 S 56 0W
Scotland, U.S.A. 138 D6 43 9N 97 43W
Scotland □, U.K. 18 E5 57 0N 4 0W
Scotland Neck, U.S.A. 135 G7 36 8N 77 25W
Scott, C., Australia 112 B4 13 30 S 129 49 E
Scott City, U.S.A. 138 F4 38 29N 100 54W
Scott Glacier, Antarctica 7 C8 66 15 S 100 5 E
Scott I., Antarctica 7 C11 67 0 S 179 0 E
Scott Inlet, Canada 127 A12 71 0N 71 0W
Scott Is., Canada 130 C3 50 48N 128 40W
Scott L., Canada 131 B7 59 55N 106 18W
Scott Reef, Australia 112 B3 14 0 S 121 50 E
Scottburgh, S. Africa 105 E5 30 15 S 30 47 E
Scottdale, U.S.A. 136 F5 40 6N 79 35W
Scottsbluff, U.S.A. 138 E3 41 52N 103 40W
Scottsboro, U.S.A. 135 H2 34 40N 86 2W
Scottsburg, U.S.A. 141 F11 38 41N 85 47W
Scottsdale, Australia 114 G4 41 9 S 147 31 E
Scottsdale, U.S.A. 143 K7 33 29N 111 56W
Scottsville, Ky., U.S.A. 135 G2 36 45N 86 11W
Scottsville, N.Y., U.S.A. 136 C7 43 2N 77 47W
Scottville, U.S.A. 134 D2 43 58N 86 17W
Scranton, Iowa, U.S.A. 140 B2 42 1N 94 33W
Scranton, Pa., U.S.A. 137 E9 41 25N 75 40W
Scugog, L., Canada 136 B6 44 10N 78 55W
Scunthorpe, U.K. 16 D7 53 36N 0 39W
Scuol, Switz. 29 C10 46 48N 10 17 E
Scusciuban, Somali Rep. 108 B4 10 18N 50 12 E
Scutari = Üsküdar, Turkey 49 F4 41 0N 29 5 E
Seabra, Brazil 155 D3 12 25 S 41 46W
Seabrook, L., Australia 113 F2 30 55 S 119 40 E
Seaford, U.S.A. 134 F8 38 39N 75 37W
Seaforth, Canada 128 D3 43 35N 81 25W
Seagraves, U.S.A. 139 J3 32 57N 102 34W
Seal →, Canada 131 B10 59 4N 94 48W
Seal Cove, Canada 129 C8 49 57N 56 22W
Seal L., Canada 129 B7 54 20N 61 30W
Sealy, U.S.A. 139 L6 29 47N 96 9W
Seaman, U.S.A. 141 F13 38 57N 83 34W
Searchlight, U.S.A. 145 K12 35 28N 114 55W
Searcy, U.S.A. 139 H9 35 15N 91 44W
Searles L., U.S.A. 145 K9 35 44N 117 21W
Seaside, Calif., U.S.A. 144 J5 36 37N 121 50W
Seaside, Oreg., U.S.A. 144 E3 46 0N 123 56W
Seaspray, Australia 117 E7 38 25 S 147 15 E
Seattle, U.S.A. 144 C4 47 36N 122 20W
Seaview Ra., Australia 114 B4 18 40 S 145 45 E
Seaward Kaikouras, Mts., N.Z. 119 C8 42 10 S 173 44 E
Sebangka, Indonesia 74 B2 0 7N 104 36 E
Sebastián Vizcaíno, B., Mexico 146 B2 28 0N 114 30W
Sebastopol = Sevastopol, Ukraine 51 K7 44 35N 33 30 E
Sebastopol, U.S.A. 144 G4 38 24N 122 49W
Sebderat, Eritrea 95 D4 15 26N 36 42 E
Sebdou, Algeria 99 B4 34 38N 1 19W
Seben, Turkey 88 B4 40 24N 31 34 E
Sebeş, Romania 46 D4 45 58N 23 34 E
Sebeşului, Munţii, Romania 46 D4 45 36N 23 40 E
Sebewaing, U.S.A. 134 D4 43 44N 83 27W
Sebezh, Russia 50 D5 56 14N 28 22 E
Sebha = Sabhah, Libya 96 C2 27 9N 14 29 E
Sébi, Mali 100 B4 15 50N 4 12W
Şebinkarahisar, Turkey 89 B8 40 22N 38 28 E
Sebiş, Romania 46 C3 46 23N 22 13 E
Sebkhet Te-n-Dghâmcha, Mauritania 100 B1 18 30N 15 55W
Sebkra Azzel Mati, Algeria 99 C5 26 10N 0 43 E
Sebkra Mekerghene, Algeria 99 C5 26 21N 1 30 E
Seblat, Indonesia 74 C2 3 14 S 101 38 E
Sebnitz, Germany 26 E10 50 58N 14 15 E
Sebou, Oued →, Morocco 98 B3 34 16N 6 40W
Sebring, Fla., U.S.A. 135 M5 27 30N 81 27W
Sebring, Ohio, U.S.A. 136 F3 40 55N 81 2W
Sebringville, Canada 136 C3 43 24N 81 4W
Sebta = Ceuta, N. Afr. 98 A3 35 52N 5 18W
Sebuku, Indonesia 75 C5 3 30 S 116 25 E
Sebuku, Teluk, Malaysia 75 B5 4 0N 118 10 E
Sečanj, Serbia, Yug. 42 B5 45 25N 20 47 E
Secchia →, Italy 38 C8 45 4N 11 0 E
Sechelt, Canada 130 D4 49 25N 123 42W
Sechura, Peru 156 B1 5 39 S 80 50W
Sechura, Desierto de, Peru 156 B1 6 0 S 80 30W
Seclin, France 23 B10 50 33N 3 2 E
Secondigny, France 22 F6 46 37N 0 26W
Sečovce, Slovak Rep. 31 C14 48 42N 21 40 E
Secretary I., N.Z. 119 F1 45 15 S 166 56 E
Secunderabad, India 82 F4 17 28N 78 30 E
Sécure →, Bolivia 157 D5 15 10 S 64 52W
Sedalia, U.S.A. 140 F3 38 42N 93 14W
Sedan, Australia 116 C3 34 34 S 139 19 E
Sedan, France 23 C11 49 43N 4 57 E
Sedan, U.S.A. 139 G6 37 8N 96 11W
Sedano, Spain 34 C1 42 43N 3 49W
Seddon, N.Z. 119 B9 41 40 S 174 7 E
Seddonville, N.Z. 119 B7 41 33 S 172 1 E
Sedeh, Fārs, Iran 85 D7 30 45N 52 11 E
Sedeh, Khorāsān, Iran 85 C8 33 20N 59 14 E
Sederot, Israel 91 D3 31 32N 34 37 E
Sedgewick, Canada 130 C6 52 48N 111 41W
Sedhiou, Senegal 100 C1 12 44N 15 30W
Sedičany, Czech. 30 B7 49 40N 14 25 E
Sedico, Italy 39 B9 46 8N 12 6 E
Sedienie, Bulgaria 43 E9 42 16N 24 33 E
Sedley, Canada 131 C8 50 10N 104 0W
Sedova, Pik, Russia 56 B6 73 29N 54 58 E
Sedrata, Algeria 99 A6 36 7N 7 31 E
Sedro Woolley, U.S.A. 144 B4 48 30N 122 14W
Sedrun, Switz. 29 C7 46 36N 8 47 E
Sedziszów Małapolski, Poland 31 A14 50 5N 21 45 E
Seebad Ahlbeck, Germany 26 B10 53 56N 14 10 E
Seefeld, Austria 30 D4 47 19N 11 13 E
Seehausen, Germany 26 C7 52 54N 11 45 E
Seeheim, Namibia 104 D2 26 50 S 17 45 E
Seekoei →, S. Africa 104 E4 30 18 S 25 1 E
Seelow, Germany 26 C10 52 32N 14 23 E
Sées, France 22 D7 48 38N 0 10 E
Seesen, Germany 26 D6 51 54N 10 10 E
Sefadu, S. Leone 100 D2 8 35N 10 58W
Seferihisar, Turkey 88 C2 38 10N 26 50 E
Séfeto, Mali 100 C3 14 8N 9 49W
Sefrou, Morocco 98 B4 33 52N 4 52W
Sefton, N.Z. 119 D7 43 15 S 172 41 E
Sefuri-San, Japan 62 D2 33 28N 130 18 E
Sefwi Bekwai, Ghana 100 D4 6 10N 2 25W
Seg-ozero, Russia 48 B5 63 20N 33 46 E
Segag, Ethiopia 108 C2 7 39N 42 50 E
Segamat, Malaysia 77 L4 2 30N 102 50 E
Segarcea, Romania 46 E4 44 6N 23 43 E
Segbwema, S. Leone 100 D2 8 0N 11 0W
Seget, Indonesia 73 B4 1 24 S 130 58 E
Segezha, Russia 48 B5 63 44N 34 19 E
Seggueur, O. →, Algeria 99 B5 32 14N 1 48 E
Segonzac, France 24 C3 45 36N 0 14W
Segorbe, Spain 34 F4 39 50N 0 30W
Ségou, Mali 100 C3 13 30N 6 16W
Segovia = Coco →, Cent. Amer. 148 D3 15 0N 83 8W
Segovia, Colombia 152 B3 7 7N 74 42W
Segovia, Spain 36 E6 40 57N 4 10W
Segovia □, Spain 36 E6 40 55N 4 10W
Segré, France 22 E6 47 40N 0 52W
Segre →, Spain 34 D5 41 40N 0 43 E
Séguéla, Ivory C. 100 D3 7 55N 6 40W
Seguin, U.S.A. 139 L6 29 34N 97 58W
Segundo →, Argentina 158 C3 30 53 S 62 44W
Segura →, Spain 35 G4 38 3N 0 44W
Segura, Sierra de, Spain 35 G2 38 5N 2 45W
Seh Qal'eh, Iran 85 C8 33 40N 58 24 E
Sehitwa, Botswana 104 C3 20 30 S 22 30 E
Sehore, India 80 H7 23 10N 77 5 E
Sehwan, Pakistan 79 D2 26 28N 67 53 E
Şeica Mare, Romania 46 C5 46 1N 24 7 E
Seikpyu, Burma 78 E5 20 54N 94 48 E
Seiland, Norway 12 A20 70 25N 23 15 E
Seiling, U.S.A. 139 G5 36 9N 98 56W
Seille →, Moselle, France 23 C13 49 7N 6 11 E
Seille →, Saône-et-Loire, France 25 B8 46 31N 4 57 E
Seilles, Belgium 21 G6 50 30N 5 6 E
Sein, I. de, France 22 D2 48 2N 4 52W
Seinäjoki, Finland 13 E20 62 40N 22 51 E
Seine →, France 22 C7 49 26N 0 26 E
Seine, B. de la, France 22 C6 49 40N 0 40W
Seine-et-Marne □, France 23 D9 48 45N 3 0 E
Seine-Maritime □, France 22 C7 49 40N 1 0 E
Seine-St.-Denis □, France 23 D9 48 58N 2 24 E
Seini, Romania 46 B4 47 44N 23 21 E
Seistan, Iran 85 D9 30 50N 61 0 E
Sejerø, Denmark 15 J5 55 54N 11 9 E
Sejerø Bugt, Denmark 15 J5 55 53N 11 15 E
Sejny, Poland 47 A10 54 6N 23 21 E
Seka, Ethiopia 95 F4 8 10N 36 52 E
Sekayu, Indonesia 74 C2 2 51 S 103 51 E
Seke, Tanzania 106 C3 3 20 S 33 31 E
Seke-Banza, Zaïre 103 D2 5 20 S 13 16 E
Sekenke, Tanzania 106 C3 4 18 S 34 11 E
Seki, Japan 63 B8 35 29N 136 55 E
Sekigahara, Japan 63 B8 35 22N 136 28 E
Sekondi-Takoradi, Ghana 100 E4 4 58N 1 45W
Seksna, Russia 50 C10 59 13N 38 30 E
Sekuma, Botswana 104 C3 24 36 S 23 50 E
Selah, U.S.A. 142 C3 46 39N 120 32W
Selama, Malaysia 77 K3 5 12N 100 42 E
Selangor □, Malaysia 74 B2 3 10N 101 30 E
Selárgius, Italy 40 C2 39 16N 9 10 E
Selaru, Indonesia 73 C4 8 9 S 131 0 E
Selb, Germany 27 E8 50 10N 12 7 E
Selby, U.K. 16 D6 53 47N 1 5W
Selby, U.S.A. 138 C4 45 31N 100 2W
Selca, Croatia 39 E13 43 20N 16 50 E
Selçuk, Turkey 88 D2 37 56N 27 22 E
Selden, U.S.A. 138 F4 39 33N 100 34W
Sele →, Italy 41 B7 40 29N 14 56 E
Selemdzha →, Russia 57 D13 51 42N 128 53 E
Selenga = Selenge Mörön →, Asia 64 A5 52 16N 106 16 E
Selenge, Zaïre 102 C3 1 58 S 18 11 E
Selenge Mörön →, Asia 64 A5 52 16N 106 16 E
Selenica, Albania 44 D1 40 33N 19 39 E
Selenter See, Germany 26 A6 54 18N 10 26 E
Sélestat, France 23 D14 48 16N 7 26 E
Seletan, Tg., Indonesia 75 C4 4 10 S 114 40 E
Selevac, Serbia, Yug. 42 C5 44 28N 20 52 E
Selfridge, U.S.A. 138 B4 46 2N 100 56W
Sélibabi, Mauritania 100 B2 15 10N 12 15W
Seliger, Ozero, Russia 52 B1 57 15N 33 0 E
Seligman, U.S.A. 143 J7 35 20N 112 53W
Şelim, Turkey 89 B10 40 30N 42 46 E
Selîma, El Wâhât el, Sudan 94 C2 21 22N 29 19 E
Selinda Spillway, Botswana 104 B3 18 35 S 23 10 E
Selinoús, Greece 45 G3 37 35N 21 37 E
Selizharovo, Russia 52 B1 56 51N 33 27 E
Seljord, Norway 14 E2 59 30N 8 40 E
Selkirk, Canada 131 C9 50 10N 96 55W
Selkirk, U.K. 18 F6 55 33N 2 50W
Selkirk I., Canada 131 C9 53 20N 99 6W
Selkirk Mts., Canada 130 C5 51 15N 117 40W
Selles-sur-Cher, France 23 E8 47 16N 1 33 E
Selliá, Greece 32 D6 35 12N 24 23 E
Sellières, France 23 F12 46 50N 5 32 E
Sells, U.S.A. 143 L8 31 55N 111 53W
Sellye, Hungary 31 F10 45 52N 17 51 E
Selma, Ala., U.S.A. 135 J2 32 25N 87 1W
Selma, Calif., U.S.A. 144 J7 36 34N 119 37W
Selma, N.C., U.S.A. 135 H6 35 32N 78 17W
Selmer, U.S.A. 135 H1 35 10N 88 36W
Selo, Greece 44 C7 41 10N 25 53 E
Selong, Indonesia 75 D5 8 39 S 116 32 E
Selongey, France 23 E12 47 36N 5 11 E
Selowandoma Falls, Zimbabwe 107 G3 21 15 S 31 50 E
Selpele, Indonesia 73 B4 0 1 S 130 5 E
Selsey Bill, U.K. 17 G7 50 44N 0 47W
Seltso, Russia 52 D2 53 22N 34 4 E
Seltz, France 23 D15 48 54N 8 4 E
Selu, Indonesia 73 C4 7 32 S 130 55 E
Sélune →, France 22 D5 48 38N 1 22W
Selva, Argentina 158 B3 29 50 S 62 0W
Selva, Italy 39 B8 46 33N 11 46 E
Selva, Spain 34 D6 41 13N 1 8 E
Selvas, Brazil 156 B4 6 30 S 67 0W
Selwyn, Australia 114 C3 21 32 S 140 30 E
Selwyn L., Canada 131 A8 60 0N 104 30W
Selwyn Passage, Vanuatu 121 F6 16 3 S 168 12 E
Selwyn Ra., Australia 114 C3 21 10 S 140 0 E
Selyatyn, Ukraine 46 B6 47 50N 25 12 E
Semani →, Albania 44 D1 40 47N 19 30 E
Semara, W. Sahara 98 C2 26 48N 11 41W
Semarang, Indonesia 75 D4 7 0 S 110 26 E
Sematan, Malaysia 75 B3 1 48N 109 46 E
Semau, Indonesia 72 D2 10 13 S 123 22 E
Sembabule, Uganda 106 C3 0 4 S 31 25 E
Sembé, Congo 102 B2 1 39N 14 36 E
Şemdinli, Turkey 89 D11 37 18N 44 35 E
Sémé, Senegal 100 B2 15 4N 13 41W
Semeih, Sudan 95 E3 12 43N 30 53 E
Semenov, Russia 52 B7 56 43N 44 30 E
Semenovka, Ukraine 51 H7 49 37N 33 10 E
Semenovka, Ukraine 51 F7 52 8N 32 36 E
Semeru, Indonesia 75 D4 8 4 S 112 55 E
Semey, Kazakstan 56 D9 50 30N 80 10 E
Semikarakorskiy, Russia 53 G5 47 30N 40 48 E
Semiluki, Russia 52 E4 51 41N 39 2 E
Seminoe Reservoir, U.S.A. 142 E10 42 9N 106 55W
Seminole, Okla., U.S.A. 139 H6 35 14N 96 41W
Seminole, Tex., U.S.A. 139 J3 32 43N 102 39W
Semiozernoye, Kazakstan 56 D7 52 22N 64 8 E
Semipalatinsk = Semey, Kazakstan 56 D9 50 30N 80 10 E
Semirara I., Phil. 70 E3 12 4N 121 23 E
Semirara Is., Phil. 71 F3 12 0N 121 20 E
Semisopochnoi I., U.S.A. 126 C2 51 55N 179 36 E
Semitau, Indonesia 75 B4 0 29N 111 57 E
Semiyarka, Kazakstan 56 D8 50 55N 78 23 E
Semiyarskoye = Semiyarka, Kazakstan 56 D8 50 55N 78 23 E
Semmering P., Austria 30 D8 47 41N 15 45 E
Semnān, Iran 85 C7 35 40N 53 23 E
Semnān □, Iran 85 C7 36 0N 54 0 E
Semois →, Europe 21 J5 49 53N 4 44 E
Sempang Mengayou, Tanjong, Malaysia 75 A5 7 0N 116 40 E
Semporna, Malaysia 75 B5 4 30N 118 33 E
Semuda, Indonesia 75 C4 2 51 S 112 58 E
Semur-en-Auxois, France 23 E11 47 30N 4 20 E
Sena, Bolivia 156 C4 11 32 S 67 11W
Senā, Iran 85 D6 28 27N 51 36 E
Sena, Mozam. 107 F3 17 25 S 35 0 E
Sena →, Bolivia 156 C4 11 31 S 67 11W
Sena Madureira, Brazil 156 B4 9 5 S 68 45W
Senador Pompeu, Brazil 154 C4 5 40 S 39 20W
Senaja, Malaysia 75 A5 6 45N 117 3 E
Senaki, Georgia 53 J6 42 15N 42 7 E
Senanga, Zambia 104 B3 16 2 S 23 14 E
Senatobia, U.S.A. 139 H10 34 37N 89 58W
Sendafa, Ethiopia 95 F4 9 11N 39 3 E
Sendai, Kagoshima, Japan 62 F2 31 50N 130 20 E
Sendai, Miyagi, Japan 60 E10 38 15N 140 53 E
Sendai-Wan, Japan 60 E10 38 15N 141 0 E
Sendamangalam, India 83 J4 11 17N 78 17 E
Sendenhorst, Germany 26 D3 51 50N 7 49 E
Sendurjana, India 82 D4 21 32N 78 17 E
Senec, Slovak Rep. 31 C10 48 12N 17 23 E
Seneca, Oreg., U.S.A. 142 D4 44 8N 118 58W
Seneca, S.C., U.S.A. 135 H4 34 41N 82 57W
Seneca Falls, U.S.A. 137 D8 42 55N 76 48W
Seneca L., U.S.A. 136 D8 42 40N 76 54W
Seneffe, Belgium 21 G4 50 32N 4 16 E
Senegal ■, W. Afr. 100 C2 14 30N 14 30W
Senegal →, W. Afr. 100 B1 15 48N 16 32W
Senegambia, Africa 92 E2 12 45N 12 0W
Senekal, S. Africa 105 D4 28 20 S 27 36 E
Senftenberg, Germany 26 D10 51 32N 14 0 E

266 Siler City

Siler City, *U.S.A.* **135 H6** 35 44N 79 28W
Sileru →, *India* **82 F5** 17 49N 81 24 E
Silet, *Algeria* **99 D5** 22 44N 4 37 E
Silgarhi Doti, *Nepal* **81 E9** 29 15N 81 0 E
Silghat, *India* **78 B4** 26 35N 93 0 E
Silifke, *Turkey* **88 D5** 36 22N 33 58 E
Siliguri = Shiliguri, *India* **78 B2** 26 45N 88 25 E
Siling Co, *China* **64 C3** 31 50N 89 20 E
Silíqua, *Italy* **40 C1** 39 18N 8 48 E
Silistra, *Bulgaria* **43 C12** 44 6N 27 19 E
Silivri, *Turkey* **88 B3** 41 4N 28 14 E
Siljan, *Sweden* **13 F16** 60 55N 14 45 E
Silkeborg, *Denmark* **15 H3** 56 10N 9 32 E
Sillajhuay, Cordillera, *Chile* **156 D4** 19 46 S 68 40W
Sillamäe, *Estonia* **13 G22** 59 24N 27 45 E
Sillé-le-Guillaume, *France* **22 D6** 48 10N 0 8W
Sillustani, *Peru* **156 D3** 15 50 S 70 7W
Siloam Springs, *U.S.A.* **139 G7** 36 11N 94 32W
Silopi, *Turkey* **89 D10** 37 15N 42 27 E
Silsbee, *U.S.A.* **139 K7** 30 21N 94 11W
Šilute, *Lithuania* **13 J19** 55 21N 21 33 E
Silva Porto = Kuito, *Angola* **103 E3** 12 22 S 16 55 E
Silvan, *Turkey* **89 C9** 38 7N 41 2 E
Silvaplana, *Switz.* **29 D9** 46 28N 9 48 E
Silver City, *N. Mex., U.S.A.* **143 K9** 32 46N 108 17W
Silver City, *Nev., U.S.A.* **142 G4** 39 15N 119 48W
Silver Cr. →, *U.S.A.* **142 E4** 43 16N 119 13W
Silver Creek, *U.S.A.* **136 D5** 42 33N 79 10W
Silver Grove, *U.S.A.* **141 E12** 39 2N 84 24W
Silver L., *Calif., U.S.A.* **144 G6** 38 39N 120 6W
Silver L., *Calif., U.S.A.* **145 K10** 35 21N 116 7W
Silver Lake, *Ind., U.S.A.* **141 C11** 41 4N 85 53W
Silver Lake, *Oreg., U.S.A.* **142 E3** 43 8N 121 3W
Silver Lake, *Wis., U.S.A.* **141 B8** 42 33N 88 13W
Silver Streams, *S. Africa* **104 D3** 28 20 S 23 33 E
Silverton, *Australia* **116 A4** 31 52 S 141 10 E
Silverton, *Colo., U.S.A.* **143 H10** 37 49N 107 40W
Silverton, *Tex., U.S.A.* **139 H4** 34 28N 101 19W
Silves, *Portugal* **37 H2** 37 11N 8 26W
Silvi Marina, *Italy* **39 F11** 42 34N 14 5 E
Silvia, *Colombia* **152 C2** 2 37N 76 21W
Silvies →, *U.S.A.* **142 E4** 43 34N 119 2W
Silvolde, *Neths.* **20 E8** 51 55N 6 23 E
Silvretta-Gruppe, *Switz.* **29 C10** 46 50N 10 6 E
Silwa Bahari, *Egypt* **94 C3** 24 45N 32 55 E
Silz, *Austria* **30 D3** 47 16N 10 56 E
Sim, C., *Morocco* **98 B3** 31 26N 9 51W
Simanggang, *Malaysia* **75 B4** 1 15N 111 32 E
Simao, *China* **68 F3** 22 47N 101 5 E
Simão Dias, *Brazil* **154 D4** 10 44 S 37 49W
Simara I., *Phil.* **70 E4** 12 48N 122 3 E
Simard, L., *Canada* **128 C4** 47 40N 78 40W
Şimareh →, *Iran* **89 F12** 33 9N 47 41 E
Simărtin, *Romania* **46 C6** 46 19N 25 58 E
Simav, *Turkey* **88 C3** 39 4N 28 58 E
Simba, *Tanzania* **106 C4** 2 10 S 37 36 E
Simbach, *Germany* **27 G9** 48 16N 13 2 E
Simbirsk, *Russia* **52 C9** 54 20N 48 25 E
Simbo, *Tanzania* **106 C2** 4 51 S 29 41 E
Simcoe, *Canada* **128 D3** 42 50N 80 20W
Simcoe, L., *Canada* **128 D4** 44 25N 79 20W
Simenga, *Russia* **57 C11** 62 42N 108 25 E
Simeto →, *Italy* **41 E8** 37 24N 15 6 E
Simeulue, *Indonesia* **74 B1** 2 45N 95 45 E
Simferopol, *Ukraine* **51 K8** 44 55N 34 3 E
Sími, *Greece* **45 H9** 36 35N 27 50 E
Simi Valley, *U.S.A.* **145 L8** 34 16N 118 47W
Simikot, *Nepal* **81 E9** 30 0N 81 50 E
Simití, *Colombia* **152 B3** 7 58N 73 57W
Simitli, *Bulgaria* **42 F8** 41 52N 23 7 E
Simla, *India* **80 D7** 31 2N 77 9 E
Şimleu-Silvaniei, *Romania* **46 B3** 47 17N 22 50 E
Simme →, *Switz.* **28 C4** 46 38N 7 25 E
Simmern, *Germany* **27 F3** 49 58N 7 30 E
Simmie, *Canada* **131 D7** 49 56N 108 6W
Simmler, *U.S.A.* **145 K7** 35 21N 119 59W
Simões, *Brazil* **154 C3** 7 36 S 40 49W
Simojoki →, *Finland* **12 D21** 65 35N 25 1 E
Simojovel, *Mexico* **147 D6** 17 12N 92 38W
Simonette →, *Canada* **130 B5** 55 9N 118 15W
Simonstown, *S. Africa* **104 E2** 34 14 S 18 26 E
Simontornya, *Hungary* **31 E11** 46 45N 18 33 E
Simpangkiri →, *Indonesia* **74 B1** 2 50N 97 40 E
Simplício Mendes, *Brazil* **154 C3** 7 51 S 41 54W
Simplon, *Switz.* **28 D6** 46 12N 8 4 E
Simplon P., *Switz.* **28 D6** 46 15N 8 3 E
Simplon Tunnel, *Switz.* **28 D6** 46 15N 8 7 E
Simpson Desert, *Australia* **114 D2** 25 0 S 137 0 E
Simpungdong, *N. Korea* **67 D15** 40 56N 129 29 E
Simrishamn, *Sweden* **13 J16** 55 33N 14 22 E
Simunjan, *Malaysia* **75 B4** 1 25N 110 45 E
Simushir, Ostrov, *Russia* **57 E16** 46 50N 152 30 E
Sina →, *India* **82 F2** 17 30N 75 55 E
Sinabang, *Indonesia* **74 B1** 2 30N 96 24 E
Sinadogo, *Somali Rep.* **108 C3** 5 50N 47 0 E
Sinai = Es Sînâ', *Egypt* **94 J8** 29 0N 34 0 E
Sinai, Mt. = Mûsa, G., *Egypt* **94 J8** 28 33N 33 59 E
Sinai Peninsula, *Egypt* **91 F2** 29 30N 34 0 E
Sinaia, *Romania* **46 D6** 45 21N 25 38 E
Sinait, *Phil.* **70 C3** 17 52N 120 27 E
Sinako, Mt., *Phil.* **71 H5** 7 30N 125 17 E
Sinaloa □, *Mexico* **146 C3** 25 0N 107 30W
Sinaloa de Levya, *Mexico* **146 B3** 25 50N 108 20W
Sinalunga, *Italy* **39 E8** 43 12N 11 44 E
Sinan, *China* **68 D7** 27 56N 108 13 E
Sînandrei, *Romania* **46 D2** 45 52N 21 13 E
Sinarádhes, *Greece* **32 A3** 39 34N 19 51 E
Sīnāwan, *Libya* **96 B2** 31 0N 10 37 E
Sinbaungwe, *Burma* **78 F5** 19 43N 95 10 E
Sinbo, *Burma* **78 C6** 24 46N 97 3 E
Sincan, *Turkey* **88 B5** 39 58N 32 36 E
Sincé, *Colombia* **152 B2** 9 15N 75 9W
Sincelejo, *Colombia* **152 B2** 9 18N 75 24W
Sinchang, *N. Korea* **67 D15** 40 7N 128 28 E
Sinchang-ni, *N. Korea* **67 E14** 39 24N 126 8 E
Sinclair, *U.S.A.* **142 F10** 41 47N 107 7W
Sinclair Mills, *Canada* **130 C4** 54 5N 121 40W
Sincorá, Serra do, *Brazil* **155 D3** 13 30 S 41 0W
Sind, *Pakistan* **80 G3** 26 0N 68 30 E
Sind □, *Pakistan* **79 D3** 26 0N 69 0 E
Sind →, *India* **81 B6** 34 18N 74 45 E
Sind Sagar Doab, *Pakistan* **80 D4** 32 0N 71 30 E
Sindal, *Denmark* **15 G4** 57 28N 10 10 E
Sindangan, *Phil.* **71 G4** 8 10N 123 5 E
Sindangan Bay, *Phil.* **71 G4** 8 11N 122 50 E
Sindangbarang, *Indonesia* **75 D3** 7 27 S 107 1 E
Sinde, *Zambia* **107 F2** 17 28 S 25 51 E
Sinegorskiy, *Russia* **53 G5** 47 55N 40 52 E
Sinelnikovo = Synelnykove, *Ukraine* **51 H8** 48 25N 35 30 E
Sines, *Portugal* **37 H2** 37 56N 8 51W
Sines, C. de, *Portugal* **37 H2** 37 58N 8 53W
Sineu, *Spain* **33 B10** 39 38N 3 1 E
Sinewit, Mt., *Papua N. G.* **120 C7** 4 44 S 152 2 E
Sinfra, *Ivory C.* **100 D3** 6 35N 5 56W
Sing Buri, *Thailand* **76 E3** 14 53N 100 25 E
Singa, *Sudan* **95 E3** 13 10N 33 57 E
Singanallur, *India* **83 J3** 11 2N 77 1 E
Singapore ■, *Asia* **77 M4** 1 17N 103 51 E
Singapore, Straits of, *Asia* **77 M5** 1 15N 104 0 E
Singaraja, *Indonesia* **75 D5** 8 6 S 115 10 E
Singen, *Germany* **27 H4** 47 45N 8 50 E
Singida, *Tanzania* **106 C3** 4 49 S 34 48 E
Singida □, *Tanzania* **106 D3** 6 0 S 34 30 E
Singitikós Kólpos, *Greece* **44 D5** 40 6N 24 0 E
Singkaling Hkamti, *Burma* **78 C5** 26 0N 95 39 E
Singkawang, *Indonesia* **75 B3** 1 0N 108 57 E
Singleton, *Australia* **117 B9** 32 33 S 151 0 E
Singleton, Mt., *N. Terr., Australia* **112 D5** 22 0 S 130 46 E
Singleton, Mt., *W. Austral., Australia* **113 E2** 29 27 S 117 15 E
Singoli, *India* **80 G6** 25 0N 75 22 E
Singora = Songkhla, *Thailand* **77 J3** 7 13N 100 37 E
Singosan, *N. Korea* **67 E14** 38 52N 127 25 E
Sinhung, *N. Korea* **67 D14** 40 11N 127 34 E
Sînî □, *Egypt* **91 F2** 30 0N 34 0 E
Siniátsikon, Óros, *Greece* **44 D3** 40 25N 21 35 E
Siniloan, *Phil.* **70 D3** 14 25N 121 27 E
Siniscóla, *Italy* **40 B2** 40 34N 9 41 E
Sinj, *Croatia* **39 E13** 43 42N 16 39 E
Sinjai, *Indonesia* **72 C2** 5 7 S 120 20 E
Sinjajevina, *Montenegro, Yug.* **42 E4** 42 57N 19 22 E
Sinjār, *Iraq* **89 D9** 36 19N 41 52 E
Sinkat, *Sudan* **94 D4** 18 55N 36 49 E
Sinkiang Uighur = Xinjiang Uygur Zizhiqu □, *China* **64 B3** 42 0N 86 0 E
Sinmak, *N. Korea* **67 E14** 38 25N 126 14 E
Sinnai, *Italy* **40 C2** 39 18N 9 13 E
Sinnar, *India* **82 E2** 19 48N 74 0 E
Sinni →, *Italy* **41 B9** 40 9N 16 41 E
Sînnicolau Maré, *Romania* **42 A5** 46 5N 20 39 E
Sinnuris, *Egypt* **94 J7** 29 26N 30 31 E
Sinoe, L., *Romania* **46 E9** 44 35N 28 50 E
Sinop, *Turkey* **88 A6** 42 1N 35 11 E
Sinpo, *N. Korea* **67 E15** 40 0N 128 13 E
Sins, *Switz.* **29 B6** 47 12N 8 24 E
Sinsk, *Russia* **57 C13** 61 8N 126 48 E
Sint-Amandsberg, *Belgium* **21 F3** 51 4N 3 45 E
Sint Annaland, *Neths.* **21 E4** 51 36N 4 6 E
Sint Annaparoch, *Neths.* **20 B7** 53 16N 5 40 E
Sint-Denijs, *Belgium* **21 G2** 50 45N 3 23 E
Sint Eustatius, I., *Neth. Ant.* **149 C7** 17 30N 62 59W
Sint-Genesius-Rode, *Belgium* **21 G4** 50 45N 4 22 E
Sint-Gillis-Waas, *Belgium* **21 F4** 51 13N 4 6 E
Sint-Huibrechts-Lille, *Belgium* **21 F6** 51 13N 5 29 E
Sint-Katelinje-Waver, *Belgium* **21 F5** 51 5N 4 32 E
Sint-Kruis, *Belgium* **21 F2** 51 13N 3 15 E
Sint-Laureins, *Belgium* **21 F3** 51 14N 3 32 E
Sint Maarten, I., *W. Indies* **149 C7** 18 4N 63 4W
Sint-Michiels, *Belgium* **21 F2** 51 11N 3 15 E
Sint Nicolaasga, *Neths.* **20 C7** 52 55N 5 45 E
Sint Niklaas, *Belgium* **21 F4** 51 10N 4 9 E
Sint Oedenrode, *Neths.* **21 E6** 51 35N 5 29 E
Sint Pancras, *Neths.* **20 C5** 52 40N 4 48 E
Sint Philipsland, *Neths.* **21 E4** 51 37N 4 10 E
Sint Truiden, *Belgium* **21 G6** 50 48N 5 10 E
Sint Willebrord, *Neths.* **21 E5** 51 33N 4 33 E
Sîntana, *Romania* **46 C2** 46 20N 21 30 E
Sintang, *Indonesia* **75 B4** 0 5N 111 35 E
Sintjohannesga, *Neths.* **20 C7** 52 55N 5 52 E
Sinton, *U.S.A.* **139 L6** 28 2N 97 31W
Sintra, *Portugal* **37 G1** 38 47N 9 25W
Sinugif, *Somali Rep.* **108 C3** 8 33N 48 59 E
Sinŭiju, *N. Korea* **67 D13** 40 5N 124 24 E
Sinyukha →, *Ukraine* **51 H6** 48 3N 30 51 E
Siocon, *Phil.* **71 H4** 7 40N 122 10 E
Siófok, *Hungary* **31 E11** 46 54N 18 3 E
Sioma, *Zambia* **104 B3** 16 25 S 23 28 E
Sion, *Switz.* **28 D4** 46 14N 7 20 E
Sioux City, *U.S.A.* **138 D6** 42 30N 96 24W
Sioux Falls, *U.S.A.* **138 D6** 43 33N 96 44W
Sioux Lookout, *Canada* **128 B1** 50 10N 91 50W
Sipalay, *Phil.* **71 G4** 9 45N 122 24 E
Šipan, *Croatia* **42 E2** 42 45N 17 52 E
Sipang, Tanjong, *Malaysia* **75 B4** 1 48N 110 20 E
Siping, *China* **67 C13** 43 8N 124 21 E
Sipiwesk L., *Canada* **131 B9** 55 5N 97 35W
Sipocot, *Phil.* **70 E4** 13 46N 122 58 E
Sipura, *Indonesia* **74 C1** 2 18 S 99 40 E
Siquia →, *Nic.* **148 D3** 12 10N 84 20W
Siquijor, *Phil.* **71 G4** 9 12N 123 35 E
Siquijor □, *Phil.* **71 G4** 9 11N 123 35 E
Siquirres, *Costa Rica* **148 D3** 10 6N 83 30W
Siquisique, *Venezuela* **152 A4** 10 34N 69 42W
Sir Edward Pellew Group, *Australia* **114 B2** 15 40 S 137 10 E
Sir Graham Moore Is., *Australia* **112 B4** 13 53 S 126 34 E
Sira, *India* **83 H3** 13 41N 76 49 E
Sira →, *Norway* **13 G12** 58 23N 6 34 E
Siracusa, *Italy* **41 E8** 37 4N 15 17 E
Sirajganj, *Bangla.* **81 G13** 24 25N 89 47 E
Sirakoro, *Mali* **100 C3** 12 41N 9 14W
Şiran, *Turkey* **89 B8** 40 11N 39 7 E
Sirasso, *Ivory C.* **100 D3** 9 16N 6 6W
Siraway, *Phil.* **71 H4** 7 34N 122 8 E
Sīrdān, *Iran* **89 D13** 36 39N 49 12 E
Sirdaryo = Syrdarya →, *Kazakstan* **56 E7** 46 3N 61 0 E
Sirdaryo, *Uzbekistan* **55 C4** 40 50N 68 40 E
Sirer, *Spain* **33 C7** 38 56N 1 22 E
Siret, *Romania* **46 B7** 47 55N 26 5 E
Siret →, *Romania* **46 D9** 45 24N 28 1 E
Şiria, *Romania* **46 C2** 46 16N 21 38 E
Sirik, Tanjong, *Malaysia* **75 B4** 2 47N 111 15 E
Sirino, Mte., *Italy* **41 B8** 40 7N 15 50 E
Sirkali = Sirkazhi, *India* **83 J4** 11 15N 79 41 E
Sirkazhi, *India* **83 J4** 11 15N 79 41 E
Sírna, *Greece* **45 H8** 36 22N 26 42 E
Sirnach, *Switz.* **29 B7** 47 28N 8 59 E
Şirnak, *Turkey* **89 D10** 37 32N 42 28 E
Sirohi, *India* **80 G5** 24 52N 72 53 E
Široki Brijeg, *Bos.-H.* **42 D2** 43 21N 17 36 E
Sironj, *India* **80 G7** 24 5N 77 39 E
Síros, *Greece* **45 G6** 37 28N 24 57 E
Sirrayn, *Si. Arabia* **86 C3** 19 38N 40 36 E
Sirretta Pk., *U.S.A.* **145 K8** 35 56N 118 19W
Sirsa, *India* **80 E6** 29 33N 75 4 E
Sirsi, *India* **83 G2** 14 40N 74 49 E
Siruela, *Spain* **37 G5** 38 58N 5 3W
Sisak, *Croatia* **39 C13** 45 30N 16 21 E
Sisaket, *Thailand* **76 E5** 15 8N 104 23 E
Sisante, *Spain* **35 F2** 39 25N 2 12W
Sisargas, Is., *Spain* **36 B2** 43 21N 8 50W
Sishen, *S. Africa* **104 D3** 27 47 S 22 59 E
Sishui, *Henan, China* **66 G7** 34 48N 113 15 E
Sishui, *Shandong, China* **67 G9** 35 42N 117 18 E
Sisipuk L., *Canada* **131 B8** 55 45N 101 50W
Sisophon, *Cambodia* **76 F4** 13 38N 102 59 E
Sissach, *Switz.* **28 B5** 47 27N 7 48 E
Sisseton, *U.S.A.* **138 C6** 45 40N 97 3W
Sissonne, *France* **23 C10** 49 34N 3 51 E
Sīstān va Balūchestān □, *Iran* **85 E9** 27 0N 62 0 E
Sisteron, *France* **25 D9** 44 12N 5 57 E
Sisters, *U.S.A.* **142 D3** 44 18N 121 33W
Sitamarhi, *India* **81 F11** 26 37N 85 30 E
Sitapur, *India* **81 F9** 27 38N 80 45 E
Siteki, *Swaziland* **105 D5** 26 32 S 31 58 E
Sitges, *Spain* **34 D6** 41 17N 1 47 E
Sithoniá, *Greece* **44 D5** 40 0N 23 45 E
Sitía, *Greece* **32 D8** 35 13N 26 6 E
Sítio da Abadia, *Brazil* **155 D2** 14 48 S 46 16W
Sitka, *U.S.A.* **126 C6** 57 3N 135 20W
Sitoti, *Botswana* **104 C3** 23 15 S 23 40 E
Sitra, *Egypt* **94 B2** 28 40N 26 53 E
Sittang Myit →, *Burma* **78 G6** 17 20N 96 45 E
Sittard, *Neths.* **21 G7** 51 0N 5 52 E
Sittaung, *Burma* **78 C5** 24 10N 94 35 E
Sittensen, *Germany* **26 B5** 53 17N 9 32 E
Sittona, *Eritrea* **95 E4** 14 25N 37 23 E
Sittwe, *Burma* **78 E4** 20 18N 92 45 E
Siuna, *Nic.* **148 D3** 13 37N 84 45W
Siuri, *India* **81 H12** 23 50N 87 34 E
Sivaganga, *India* **83 K4** 9 50N 78 28 E
Sivagiri, *India* **83 K3** 9 16N 77 26 E
Sivakasi, *India* **83 K3** 9 24N 77 47 E
Sivana, *India* **80 E8** 28 37N 78 6 E
Sīvand, *Iran* **85 D7** 30 5N 52 55 E
Sivas, *Turkey* **88 C7** 39 43N 36 58 E
Siverek, *Turkey* **89 D8** 37 50N 39 19 E
Sivomaskinskiy, *Russia* **48 A11** 66 40N 62 35 E
Sivrihisar, *Turkey* **88 C4** 39 30N 31 35 E
Sivry, *Belgium* **21 H4** 50 10N 4 12 E
Sîwa, *Egypt* **94 B2** 29 11N 25 31 E
Sîwa, El Wâhât es, *Egypt* **94 B2** 29 10N 25 30 E
Siwa Oasis, *Egypt* **92 D6** 29 10N 25 30 E
Siwalik Range, *Nepal* **81 F10** 28 0N 83 0 E
Siwan, *India* **81 F11** 26 13N 84 21 E
Siyâl, Jazâ'ir, *Egypt* **94 C4** 22 49N 36 12 E
Siyäzän, *Azerbaijan* **53 K9** 41 3N 49 10 E
Sizewell, *U.K.* **17 E9** 52 12N 1 37 E
Siziwang Qi, *China* **66 D6** 41 25N 111 40 E
Sjælland, *Denmark* **15 J5** 55 30N 11 30 E
Sjællands Odde, *Denmark* **15 J5** 55 58N 11 24 E
Själevad, *Sweden* **14 A12** 63 18N 18 36 E
Sjarinska Banja, *Yugoslavia* **42 E6** 42 45N 21 38 E
Sjenica, *Serbia, Yug.* **42 D4** 43 16N 20 0 E
Sjoa, *Norway* **14 C3** 61 41N 9 33 E
Sjöbo, *Sweden* **15 J7** 55 37N 13 45 E
Sjösa, *Sweden* **15 F11** 58 47N 17 4 E
Sjumen = Šumen, *Bulgaria* **43 D11** 43 18N 26 55 E
Skadarsko Jezero, *Montenegro, Yug.* **42 E4** 42 10N 19 20 E
Skadovsk, *Ukraine* **51 J7** 46 17N 32 52 E
Skaftafell, *Iceland* **12 D5** 64 1N 17 0W
Skagafjörður, *Iceland* **12 D4** 65 54N 19 35W
Skagastølstindane, *Norway* **13 F12** 61 28N 7 52 E
Skagaströnd, *Iceland* **12 D3** 65 50N 20 19W
Skagen, *Denmark* **15 G4** 57 43N 10 35 E
Skagerrak, *Denmark* **15 G3** 57 30N 9 0 E
Skagit →, *U.S.A.* **144 B4** 48 23N 122 22W
Skagway, *U.S.A.* **130 B1** 59 28N 135 19W
Skala-Podilska, *Ukraine* **51 H4** 48 50N 26 15 E
Skala Podolskaya = Skala-Podilska, *Ukraine* **51 H4** 48 50N 26 15 E
Skalat, *Ukraine* **51 H3** 49 23N 25 55 E
Skalbmierz, *Poland* **47 E7** 50 20N 20 25 E
Skalica, *Slovak Rep.* **31 C10** 48 50N 17 15 E
Skalni Dol = Kamenyak, *Bulgaria* **43 D11** 43 24N 26 57 E
Skals, *Denmark* **15 H3** 56 34N 9 24 E
Skanderborg, *Denmark* **15 H3** 56 2N 9 55 E
Skåne, *Sweden* **13 J15** 55 59N 13 30 E
Skanör, *Sweden* **15 J6** 55 24N 12 50 E
Skantzoúra, *Greece* **45 E6** 39 5N 24 6 E
Skara, *Sweden* **13 G15** 58 25N 13 30 E
Skardu, *Pakistan* **81 B6** 35 20N 75 44 E
Skarrild, *Denmark* **15 J2** 55 58N 8 53 E
Skarszewy, *Poland* **47 A5** 54 4N 18 25 E
Skaryszew, *Poland* **47 D8** 51 19N 21 15 E
Skarzysko-Kamienna, *Poland* **47 D7** 51 7N 20 52 E
Skebokvarn, *Sweden* **14 E10** 59 7N 16 45 E
Skeena →, *Canada* **130 C2** 54 9N 130 5W
Skeena Mts., *Canada* **130 B3** 56 40N 128 30W
Skegness, *U.K.* **16 D8** 53 9N 0 20 E
Skeldon, *Guyana* **153 B6** 5 55N 57 20W
Skellefte älv →, *Sweden* **12 D19** 64 45N 21 10 E
Skellefteå, *Sweden* **12 D19** 64 45N 20 50 E
Skelleftehamn, *Sweden* **12 D19** 64 40N 21 9 E
Skender Vakuf, *Bos.-H.* **42 C2** 44 29N 17 22 E
Skene, *Sweden* **15 G6** 57 30N 12 37 E
Skerries, The, *U.K.* **16 D3** 53 25N 4 36W
Skhíza, *Greece* **45 H3** 36 41N 21 40 E
Skhoinoúsa, *Greece* **45 H7** 36 53N 25 31 E
Ski, *Norway* **14 E4** 59 43N 10 52 E
Skíathos, *Greece* **45 E5** 39 12N 23 30 E
Skibbereen, *Ireland* **19 E2** 51 33N 9 16W
Skiddaw, *U.K.* **16 C4** 54 39N 3 9W
Skien, *Norway* **14 E3** 59 12N 9 35 E
Skierniewice, *Poland* **47 D7** 51 58N 20 10 E
Skierniewice □, *Poland* **47 D7** 52 0N 20 10 E
Skikda, *Algeria* **99 A6** 36 50N 6 58 E
Skillet →, *U.S.A.* **141 F8** 38 5N 88 5W
Skilloura, *Cyprus* **32 D12** 35 14N 33 10 E
Skinári, Ákra, *Greece* **45 G2** 37 56N 20 40 E
Skipton, *Australia* **116 D5** 37 39 S 143 40 E
Skipton, *U.K.* **16 D5** 53 58N 2 3W
Skirmish Pt., *Australia* **114 A1** 11 59 S 134 17 E
Skiropoúla, *Greece* **45 F6** 38 50N 24 21 E
Skíros, *Greece* **45 F6** 38 55N 24 34 E
Skivarp, *Sweden* **15 J7** 55 26N 13 34 E
Skive, *Denmark* **15 H3** 56 33N 9 2 E
Skjálfandafljót →, *Iceland* **12 D5** 65 59N 17 25W
Skjálfandi, *Iceland* **12 C5** 66 5N 17 30W
Skjeberg, *Norway* **14 E5** 59 12N 11 12 E
Skjern, *Denmark* **15 J2** 55 57N 8 30 E
Skoczów, *Poland* **31 B11** 49 49N 18 45 E
Škofja Loka, *Slovenia* **39 B11** 46 9N 14 19 E
Skoghall, *Sweden* **13 G15** 59 20N 13 30 E
Skoki, *Poland* **47 C4** 52 40N 17 11 E
Skokie, *U.S.A.* **141 B9** 42 3N 87 45W
Skole, *Ukraine* **51 H2** 49 3N 23 30 E
Skópelos, *Greece* **45 E5** 39 9N 23 47 E
Skopí, *Greece* **32 D8** 35 11N 26 2 E
Skopin, *Russia* **52 D4** 53 55N 39 32 E
Skopje, *Macedonia* **42 E6** 42 1N 21 32 E
Skórcz, *Poland* **47 B5** 53 47N 18 30 E
Skövde, *Sweden* **13 G15** 58 24N 13 50 E
Skovorodino, *Russia* **57 D13** 54 0N 124 0 E
Skowhegan, *U.S.A.* **129 D6** 44 46N 69 43W
Skownan, *Canada* **131 C9** 51 58N 99 35W
Skradin, *Croatia* **39 E12** 43 52N 15 53 E
Skreanäs, *Sweden* **15 H6** 56 52N 12 35 E
Skrwa →, *Poland* **47 C6** 52 35N 19 32 E
Skull, *Ireland* **19 E2** 51 32N 9 34W
Skultorp, *Sweden* **15 F7** 58 24N 13 51 E
Skunk →, *U.S.A.* **140 D5** 40 42N 91 7W
Skuodas, *Lithuania* **13 H19** 56 16N 21 33 E
Skurup, *Sweden* **15 J7** 55 28N 13 30 E
Skutskär, *Sweden* **14 D11** 60 37N 17 25 E
Skvyra, *Ukraine* **51 H5** 49 44N 29 40 E
Skwierzyna, *Poland* **47 C2** 52 33N 15 30 E
Skye, *U.K.* **18 D2** 57 15N 6 10W
Skykomish, *U.S.A.* **142 C3** 47 42N 121 22W
Skyros = Skíros, *Greece* **45 F6** 38 55N 24 34 E
Slættaratindur, *Færoe Is.* **12 E9** 62 18N 7 1W
Slagelse, *Denmark* **15 J5** 55 23N 11 19 E
Slagharen, *Neths.* **20 C9** 52 37N 6 34 E
Slamannon, *Australia* **116 B5** 32 1 S 143 41 E
Slamet, *Indonesia* **75 D3** 7 16 S 109 8 E
Slaney →, *Ireland* **19 D5** 52 26N 6 33W
Slangerup, *Denmark* **15 J6** 55 50N 12 11 E
Slănic, *Romania* **46 D6** 45 14N 25 58 E
Slankamen, *Serbia, Yug.* **42 B5** 45 8N 20 15 E
Slano, *Croatia* **42 E2** 42 48N 17 53 E
Slantsy, *Russia* **50 C5** 59 7N 28 5 E
Slany, *Czech.* **30 A7** 50 13N 14 6 E
Slate Is., *Canada* **128 C2** 48 40N 87 0W
Slater, *U.S.A.* **140 E3** 39 13N 93 4W
Slatina, *Romania* **46 E5** 44 28N 24 22 E
Slaton, *U.S.A.* **139 J4** 33 26N 101 39W
Slave →, *Canada* **130 A6** 61 18N 113 39W
Slave Coast, *W. Afr.* **101 D5** 6 0N 2 30 E
Slave Lake, *Canada* **130 B6** 55 17N 114 43W
Slave Pt., *Canada* **130 A5** 61 11N 115 56W
Slavgorod, *Russia* **56 D8** 53 1N 78 37 E
Slavinja, *Serbia, Yug.* **42 D7** 43 9N 22 50 E
Slavkov, *Czech.* **31 B9** 49 10N 16 52 E
Slavonska Požega, *Croatia* **42 B2** 45 20N 17 40 E
Slavonski Brod, *Croatia* **42 B3** 45 11N 18 0 E
Slavuta, *Ukraine* **51 G4** 50 15N 27 2 E
Slavyanka, *Russia* **60 C5** 42 53N 131 21 E
Slavyansk = Slovyansk, *Ukraine* **51 H9** 48 55N 37 36 E
Slavyansk-na-Kubani, *Russia* **53 H4** 45 15N 38 11 E
Sława, *Poland* **47 D3** 51 52N 16 2 E
Slawharad, *Belarus* **50 F6** 53 27N 31 0 E
Sławno, *Poland* **47 A3** 54 20N 16 41 E
Sławoborze, *Poland* **47 B2** 53 55N 15 42 E
Sleaford, *U.K.* **16 E7** 53 0N 0 24W
Sleaford B., *Australia* **115 E2** 34 55 S 135 45 E
Sleat, Sd. of, *U.K.* **18 D3** 57 5N 5 47W
Sleeper Is., *Canada* **127 C11** 58 30N 81 0W
Sleepy Eye, *U.S.A.* **138 C7** 44 18N 94 43W
Sleidinge, *Belgium* **21 F3** 51 8N 3 41 E
Sleman, *Indonesia* **75 D4** 7 40 S 110 20 E
Slemon L., *Canada* **130 A5** 63 13N 116 4W
Ślesin, *Poland* **47 C5** 52 22N 18 14 E
Slidell, *U.S.A.* **139 K10** 30 17N 89 47W
Sliedrecht, *Neths.* **20 E5** 51 50N 4 45 E
Sliema, *Malta* **32 D2** 35 54N 14 30 E
Slieve Aughty, *Ireland* **19 C3** 53 4N 8 30W
Slieve Bloom, *Ireland* **19 C4** 53 4N 7 40W
Slieve Donard, *U.K.* **19 B6** 54 11N 5 55W
Slieve Gullion, *U.K.* **19 B5** 54 7N 6 26W
Slieve Mish, *Ireland* **19 D2** 52 12N 9 50W
Slievenamon, *Ireland* **19 D4** 52 25N 7 34W
Sligeach = Sligo, *Ireland* **19 B3** 54 16N 8 28W
Sligo, *Ireland* **19 B3** 54 16N 8 28W
Sligo □, *Ireland* **19 B3** 54 8N 8 42W
Sligo B., *Ireland* **19 B3** 54 18N 8 40W
Slijpe, *Belgium* **21 F1** 51 9N 2 51 E
Slikkerveer, *Neths.* **20 E5** 51 53N 4 36 E
Slite, *Sweden* **13 H18** 57 42N 18 48 E
Sliven, *Bulgaria* **43 E11** 42 42N 26 19 E
Slivnitsa, *Bulgaria* **42 E8** 42 50N 23 0 E
Sljeme, *Croatia* **39 C12** 45 57N 15 58 E
Sloan, *U.S.A.* **145 K11** 35 57N 115 13W
Sloansville, *U.S.A.* **137 D10** 42 45N 74 22W
Slobodskoy, *Russia* **54 B3** 58 40N 50 6 E
Slobozia, *Argeş, Romania* **46 E6** 44 30N 25 14 E
Slobozia, *Ialomiţa, Romania* **46 E8** 44 34N 27 23 E
Slocan, *Canada* **130 D5** 49 48N 117 28W
Slochteren, *Neths.* **20 B9** 53 12N 6 48 E
Slöinge, *Sweden* **15 H6** 56 51N 12 42 E
Słomniki, *Poland* **47 E7** 50 16N 20 4 E
Slonim, *Belarus* **51 F3** 53 4N 25 19 E
Slotermeer, *Neths.* **20 C7** 52 55N 5 38 E
Slough, *U.K.* **17 F7** 51 30N 0 36W
Sloughhouse, *U.S.A.* **144 G5** 38 26N 121 12W

Sujangarh 269

Stassfurt, Germany 26 D7 51 51N 11 35 E
Staszów, Poland 47 E8 50 33N 21 10 E
State Center, U.S.A. 140 B3 42 1N 93 10W
State College, U.S.A. 136 F7 40 48N 77 52W
Stateline, U.S.A. 144 G7 38 57N 119 56W
Staten, I. = Estados, I. de Los, Argentina 160 D4 54 40 S 64 30W
Staten, I., Argentina 150 J4 54 40 S 64 0W
Staten I., U.S.A. 137 F10 40 35N 74 9W
Statesboro, U.S.A. 135 J5 32 27N 81 47W
Statesville, U.S.A. 135 H5 35 47N 80 53W
Stauffer, U.S.A. 145 L7 34 45N 119 3W
Staunton, Ill., U.S.A. 140 E7 39 1N 89 47W
Staunton, Va., U.S.A. 134 F6 38 9N 79 4W
Stavanger, Norway 13 G11 58 57N 5 40 E
Staveley, N.Z. 119 D6 43 40 S 171 32 E
Stavelot, Belgium 21 H7 50 23N 5 55 E
Stavenhagen, Germany 26 B8 53 42N 12 54 E
Stavenisse, Neths. 21 E4 51 35N 4 1 E
Staveren, Neths. 20 C6 52 53N 5 22 E
Stavern, Norway 14 F4 59 0N 10 1 E
Stavre, Sweden 14 B9 62 51N 15 19 E
Stavropol, Russia 53 H6 45 5N 42 0 E
Stavros, Cyprus 32 D11 35 1N 32 38 E
Stavrós, Greece 32 D6 35 12N 24 45 E
Stavros, Ákra, Greece 32 D6 35 26N 24 58 E
Stavroúpolis, Greece 44 C6 41 12N 24 45 E
Stawell, Australia 116 D5 37 5 S 142 47 E
Stawell →, Australia 114 C3 20 20 S 142 55 E
Stawiski, Poland 47 B9 53 22N 22 9 E
Stawiszyn, Poland 47 D5 51 56N 18 4 E
Stayner, Canada 136 B4 44 25N 80 5W
Steamboat Springs, U.S.A. 142 F10 40 29N 106 50W
Stębark, Poland 47 B7 53 30N 20 10 E
Stebleva, Albania 44 C2 41 18N 20 33 E
Steckborn, Switz. 29 A7 47 44N 8 59 E
Steele, U.S.A. 138 B5 46 51N 99 55W
Steelton, U.S.A. 136 F8 40 14N 76 50W
Steelville, U.S.A. 139 G9 37 58N 91 22W
Steen River, Canada 130 B5 59 40N 117 12W
Steenbergen, Neths. 21 E4 51 35N 4 19 E
Steenkool = Bintuni, Indonesia 73 B4 2 7 S 133 32 E
Steenvoorde, France 23 B9 50 48N 2 33 E
Steenwijk, Neths. 20 C8 52 47N 6 7 E
Steep Pt., Australia 113 E1 26 8 S 113 8 E
Steep Rock, Canada 131 C9 51 30N 98 48W
Ştefăneşti, Romania 46 B8 47 44N 27 15 E
Stefanie L. = Chew Bahir, Ethiopia 95 G4 4 40N 36 50 E
Stefansson Bay, Antarctica 7 C5 67 20 S 59 8 E
Steffisburg, Switz. 28 C5 46 47N 7 38 E
Stege, Denmark 15 K6 55 0N 12 18 E
Steiermark □, Austria 30 D8 47 26N 15 0 E
Steigerwald, Germany 27 F6 49 44N 10 26 E
Steilacoom, U.S.A. 144 C4 47 10N 122 36W
Stein, Neths. 21 G7 50 58N 5 45 E
Steinbach, Canada 131 D9 49 32N 96 40W
Steinfort, Lux. 21 J7 49 39N 5 55 E
Steinfurt, Germany 26 C3 52 9N 7 20 E
Steinheim, Germany 26 D5 51 51N 9 5 E
Steinhuder Meer, Germany 26 C5 52 29N 9 21 E
Steinkjer, Norway 12 D14 64 1N 11 31 E
Steinkopf, S. Africa 104 D2 29 18 S 17 43 E
Stekene, Belgium 21 F4 51 12N 4 2 E
Stellarton, Canada 129 C7 45 32N 62 30W
Stellenbosch, S. Africa 104 E2 33 58 S 18 50 E
Stellendam, Neths. 20 E4 51 49N 4 1 E
Stelvio, Paso dello, Italy 38 B7 46 32N 10 27 E
Stemshaug, Norway 14 A2 63 19N 8 44 E
Stendal, Germany 26 C7 52 36N 11 53 E
Stene, Belgium 21 F1 51 12N 2 56 E
Stenstorp, Sweden 15 F7 58 17N 13 45 E
Steornabhaigh = Stornoway, U.K. 18 C2 58 13N 6 23W
Stepanakert = Xankändi, Azerbaijan 89 C12 39 52N 46 49 E
Stepanavan, Armenia 53 K7 41 1N 44 23 E
Stephen, U.S.A. 138 A6 48 27N 96 53W
Stephens, C., N.Z. 119 A8 40 42 S 173 58 E
Stephens Creek, Australia 116 A4 31 50 S 141 30 E
Stephens I., Canada 130 C2 54 10N 130 45W
Stephens I., N.Z. 119 A9 40 40 S 174 1 E
Stephenville, Canada 129 C8 48 31N 58 35W
Stephenville, U.S.A. 139 J5 32 13N 98 12W
Stepnica, Poland 47 B1 53 38N 14 36 E
Stepnoi = Elista, Russia 53 G7 46 16N 44 14 E
Stepnoye, Russia 54 D8 54 4N 60 26 E
Stepnyak, Kazakstan 56 D8 52 50N 70 50 E
Steppe, Asia 58 D9 50 0N 50 0 E
Stereá Ellas □, Greece 45 F4 38 50N 22 0 E
Sterkstroom, S. Africa 104 E4 31 32 S 26 32 E
Sterling, Colo., U.S.A. 138 E3 40 37N 103 13W
Sterling, Ill., U.S.A. 140 C7 41 48N 89 42W
Sterling, Kans., U.S.A. 138 F5 38 13N 98 12W
Sterling City, U.S.A. 139 K4 31 51N 101 0W
Sterling Heights, U.S.A. 141 B13 42 35N 83 0W
Sterling Run, U.S.A. 136 E6 41 25N 78 12W
Sterlitamak, Russia 54 E6 53 40N 56 0 E
Šternberg, Germany 26 B7 53 42N 11 50 E
Šternberk, Czech. 31 B10 49 45N 17 15 E
Stérnes, Greece 32 D6 35 30N 24 9 E
Sterzing = Vipiteno, Italy 39 B8 46 54N 11 26 E
Stettin = Szczecin, Poland 47 B1 53 27N 14 27 E
Stettiner Haff, Germany 26 B10 53 47N 14 15 E
Stettler, Canada 130 C6 52 19N 112 40W
Steubenville, U.S.A. 136 F4 40 22N 80 37W
Stevens Point, U.S.A. 138 C10 44 31N 89 34W
Stevenson, U.S.A. 144 E5 45 42N 121 53W
Stevenson L., Canada 131 C9 53 55N 96 0W
Stevns Klint, Denmark 15 J6 55 17N 12 28 E
Steward, U.S.A. 140 C7 41 51N 89 1W
Stewardson, U.S.A. 141 E8 39 16N 88 38W
Stewart, B.C., Canada 130 B3 55 56N 129 57W
Stewart, N.W.T., Canada 126 B6 63 19N 139 26W
Stewart, U.S.A. 144 F7 39 5N 119 46W
Stewart, C., Australia 114 A1 11 57 S 134 56 E
Stewart, I., Chile 160 D2 54 50 S 71 15W
Stewart I., N.Z. 119 G2 46 58 S 167 54 E
Stewarts Point, U.S.A. 144 G3 38 39N 123 24W
Stewartsville, U.S.A. 140 E2 39 45N 94 30W
Stewiacke, Canada 129 C7 45 9N 63 22W
Steynsburg, S. Africa 104 E4 31 15 S 25 49 E
Steyr, Austria 30 C7 48 3N 14 25 E
Steyr →, Austria 30 C7 48 17N 14 15 E
Steytlerville, S. Africa 104 E3 33 17 S 24 19 E
Stia, Italy 39 E8 43 48N 11 42 E
Stiens, Neths. 20 B7 53 16N 5 46 E
Stigler, U.S.A. 139 H7 35 15N 95 8W
Stigliano, Italy 41 B9 40 24N 16 14 E
Stigsnæs, Denmark 15 J5 55 13N 11 18 E
Stigtomta, Sweden 15 F10 58 47N 16 48 E
Stikine →, Canada 130 B2 56 40N 132 30W
Stilfontein, S. Africa 104 D4 26 51 S 26 50 E
Stilís, Greece 45 F4 38 55N 22 47 E
Stillwater, N.Z. 119 C6 42 27 S 171 20 E
Stillwater, Minn., U.S.A. 138 C8 45 3N 92 49W
Stillwater, N.Y., U.S.A. 137 D11 42 55N 73 41W
Stillwater, Okla., U.S.A. 139 G6 36 7N 97 4W
Stillwater Range, U.S.A. 142 G4 39 50N 118 5W
Stilwell, U.S.A. 139 H7 35 49N 94 38W
Štimfalías, L., Greece 45 G4 37 51N 22 27 E
Štip, Macedonia 42 F7 41 42N 22 10 E
Stíra, Greece 45 F6 38 9N 24 14 E
Stirling, Australia 114 B3 17 12 S 141 35 E
Stirling, Canada 130 D6 49 30N 112 30W
Stirling, N.Z. 119 G4 46 14 S 169 49 E
Stirling, U.K. 18 E5 56 8N 3 57W
Stirling □, U.K. 18 E4 56 12N 4 18W
Stirling Ra., Australia 113 F2 34 23 S 118 0 E
Stittsville, Canada 137 A9 45 15N 75 55W
Stjernøya, Norway 12 A20 70 20N 22 40 E
Stjørdalshalsen, Norway 12 E14 63 29N 10 51 E
Stockach, Germany 27 H5 47 50N 9 1 E
Stockbridge, U.S.A. 141 B12 42 27N 84 11W
Stockerau, Austria 31 C9 48 24N 16 12 E
Stockett, U.S.A. 142 C8 47 21N 111 10W
Stockholm, Sweden 14 E12 59 20N 18 3 E
Stockholms län □, Sweden 14 E12 59 30N 18 20 E
Stockhorn, Switz. 28 C5 46 42N 7 33 E
Stockport, U.K. 16 D5 53 25N 2 9W
Stockton, Australia 117 B9 32 50 S 151 47 E
Stockton, Calif., U.S.A. 144 H5 37 58N 121 17W
Stockton, Ill., U.S.A. 140 B6 42 21N 90 1W
Stockton, Kans., U.S.A. 138 F5 39 26N 99 16W
Stockton, Mo., U.S.A. 139 G8 37 42N 93 48W
Stockton-on-Tees, U.K. 16 C6 54 35N 1 19W
Stockton-on-Tees □, U.K. 16 C6 54 35N 1 19W
Stockvik, Sweden 14 B11 62 17N 17 23 E
Stoczek Łukowski, Poland 47 D8 51 58N 21 58 E
Stöde, Sweden 14 B10 62 28N 16 35 E
Stogovo, Macedonia 42 F5 41 31N 20 38 E
Stoke, N.Z. 119 B8 41 19 S 173 14 E
Stoke on Trent, U.K. 16 D5 53 1N 2 11W
Stokes Bay, Canada 128 C3 45 0N 81 28W
Stokes Pt., Australia 114 G3 40 10 S 143 56 E
Stokes Ra., Australia 112 C5 15 50 S 130 50 E
Stokksnes, Iceland 12 D6 64 14N 14 58W
Stokmarknes, Norway 12 B16 68 34N 14 54 E
Stolac, Bos.-H. 42 D2 43 8N 17 59 E
Stolberg, Germany 26 E2 50 47N 6 13 E
Stolbovaya, Russia 57 C16 64 50N 153 50 E
Stolbovoy, Ostrov, Russia 57 D17 74 44N 135 14 E
Stolbtsy = Stowbtsy, Belarus 50 F4 53 30N 26 43 E
Stolin, Belarus 51 G4 51 53N 26 50 E
Stolnici, Romania 46 E5 44 31N 24 48 E
Stolwijk, Neths. 20 E5 51 59N 4 47 E
Stomíon, Greece 32 D5 35 21N 23 32 E
Ston, Croatia 42 E2 42 51N 17 43 E
Stonehaven, U.K. 18 E6 56 59N 2 12W
Stonehenge, Australia 114 C3 24 22 S 143 17 E
Stonewall, Canada 131 C9 50 10N 97 19W
Stonington, U.S.A. 140 E7 39 44N 89 12W
Stony L., Man., Canada 131 B9 58 51N 98 40W
Stony L., Ont., Canada 136 B6 44 30N 78 5W
Stony Rapids, Canada 131 B7 59 16N 105 50W
Stony Tunguska = Podkamennaya Tunguska →, Russia 57 C10 61 50N 90 13 E
Stonyford, U.S.A. 144 F4 39 23N 122 33W
Stopnica, Poland 47 E7 50 27N 20 57 E
Stora Lulevatten, Sweden 12 C18 67 10N 19 30 E
Storavan, Sweden 12 D18 65 45N 18 10 E
Stord, Norway 13 G11 59 52N 5 23 E
Store Bælt, Denmark 15 J5 55 20N 11 0 E
Store Creek, Australia 117 B8 32 54 S 149 6 E
Store Heddinge, Denmark 15 J6 55 18N 12 23 E
Støren, Norway 14 A4 63 3N 10 18 E
Storm B., Australia 114 G4 43 10 S 147 30 E
Storm Lake, U.S.A. 138 D7 42 39N 95 13W
Stormberge, S. Africa 104 E4 31 16 S 26 17 E
Stormsrivier, S. Africa 104 E3 33 59 S 23 52 E
Stornoway, U.K. 18 C2 58 13N 6 23W
Storozhinets = Storozhynets, Ukraine 51 H3 48 14N 25 45 E
Storozhynets, Ukraine 51 H3 48 14N 25 45 E
Storsjö, Sweden 14 B7 62 49N 13 5 E
Storsjøen, Hedmark, Norway 14 D5 60 20N 11 40 E
Storsjøen, Hedmark, Norway 14 C5 61 30N 11 14 E
Storsjön, Sweden 14 B7 63 9N 14 30 E
Storstrøms Amtskommune □, Denmark 15 K5 54 50N 11 45 E
Storuman, Sweden 12 D17 65 5N 17 10 E
Storuman, sjö, Sweden 12 D17 65 13N 16 50 E
Story City, U.S.A. 140 B3 42 11N 93 36W
Stoughton, Canada 131 D8 49 40N 103 0W
Stoughton, U.S.A. 140 B8 42 55N 89 13W
Stour →, Dorset, U.K. 17 G5 50 43N 1 47W
Stour →, Here. & Worcs., U.K. 17 E5 52 21N 2 17W
Stour →, Kent, U.K. 17 F9 51 18N 1 22 E
Stour →, Suffolk, U.K. 17 F9 51 57N 1 4 E
Stourbridge, U.K. 17 E5 52 28N 2 8W
Stout, L., Canada 131 C10 52 0N 94 40W
Stove Pipe Wells Village, U.S.A. 145 J9 36 35N 117 11W
Stowbtsy, Belarus 50 F4 53 30N 26 43 E
Stowmarket, U.K. 17 E9 52 12N 1 0 E
Strabane, U.K. 19 B4 54 50N 7 27W
Strabane □, U.K. 19 B4 54 45N 7 25W
Stracin, Macedonia 42 E7 42 13N 22 2 E
Stradella, Italy 38 C6 45 5N 9 18 E
Strahan, Australia 114 G4 42 9 S 145 20 E
Strakonice, Czech. 30 B6 49 15N 13 53 E
Straldzha, Bulgaria 43 E11 42 35N 26 40 E
Stralsund, Germany 26 A9 54 18N 13 4 E
Strand, S. Africa 104 E2 34 9 S 18 48 E
Stranda, Møre og Romsdal, Norway 13 E12 62 19N 6 58 E
Stranda, Nord-Trøndelag, Norway 12 E14 63 33N 10 14 E
Strangford L., U.K. 19 B6 54 30N 5 37W
Strängnäs, Sweden 14 E11 59 23N 17 2 E
Strangsville, U.S.A. 136 E3 41 19N 81 50W
Stranraer, U.K. 18 G3 54 54N 5 1W
Strasbourg, Canada 131 C8 51 4N 104 55W
Strasbourg, France 23 D14 48 35N 7 42 E
Strasburg, Germany 26 B9 53 30N 13 43 E
Strasburg, U.S.A. 138 B4 46 8N 100 10W
Strassen, Lux. 21 J8 49 37N 6 4 E
Stratford, N.S.W., Australia 117 B9 32 7 S 151 55 E
Stratford, Vic., Australia 117 D7 37 59 S 147 7 E
Stratford, Canada 128 D3 43 23N 81 0W
Stratford, N.Z. 118 F3 39 20 S 174 19 E
Stratford, Calif., U.S.A. 144 J7 36 11N 119 49W
Stratford, Conn., U.S.A. 137 E11 41 12N 73 8W
Stratford, Tex., U.S.A. 139 G3 36 20N 102 4W
Stratford-upon-Avon, U.K. 17 E6 52 12N 1 42W
Strath Spey, U.K. 18 D5 57 9N 3 49W
Strathalbyn, Australia 116 C3 35 13 S 138 53 E
Strathcona Prov. Park, Canada 130 D3 49 38N 125 40W
Strathmore, Australia 114 B3 17 50 S 142 35 E
Strathmore, Canada 130 C6 51 5N 113 18W
Strathmore, U.K. 18 E5 56 37N 3 7W
Strathmore, U.S.A. 144 J7 36 9N 119 4W
Strathnaver, Canada 130 C4 53 20N 122 33W
Strathpeffer, U.K. 18 D4 57 35N 4 32W
Strathroy, Canada 128 D3 42 58N 81 38W
Strathy Pt., U.K. 18 C4 58 36N 4 1W
Stratton, U.S.A. 138 F3 39 19N 102 36W
Straubing, Germany 27 G8 48 52N 12 34 E
Straumnes, Iceland 12 C2 66 26N 23 8W
Strausberg, Germany 26 C9 52 35N 13 54 E
Strawberry Point, U.S.A. 140 B5 42 41N 91 32W
Strawberry Reservoir, U.S.A. 142 F8 40 8N 111 9W
Strawn, U.S.A. 139 J5 32 33N 98 30W
Strážnice, Czech. 31 C10 48 54N 17 19 E
Streaky B., Australia 115 E1 32 48 S 134 13 E
Streaky Bay, Australia 115 E1 32 51 S 134 18 E
Streator, U.S.A. 138 E10 41 8N 88 50W
Středočeský □, Czech. 30 B7 49 55N 14 30 E
Středoslovenský □, Slovak Rep. 31 C12 48 30N 19 15 E
Streé, Belgium 21 H4 50 17N 4 18 E
Streeter, U.S.A. 138 B5 46 39N 99 21W
Streetsville, Canada 136 C5 43 35N 79 42W
Strehaia, Romania 46 E4 44 37N 23 10 E
Strelcha, Bulgaria 43 E9 42 25N 24 19 E
Strelka, Russia 57 D10 58 5N 93 3 E
Streng →, Cambodia 76 F4 13 12N 103 37 E
Strésa, Italy 38 C5 45 52N 8 28 E
Streymoy, Færoe Is. 12 E9 62 8N 7 5W
Strezhevoy, Russia 56 C8 60 42N 77 34 E
Střibro, Czech. 30 B6 49 44N 13 2 E
Strickland →, Papua N. G. 120 D1 7 35 S 141 36 E
Strijen, Neths. 20 E5 51 45N 4 33 E
Strimón →, Greece 44 D5 40 46N 23 51 E
Strimonikós Kólpos, Greece 44 D5 40 33N 24 0 E
Stroeder, Argentina 160 B4 40 12 S 62 37W
Strofádhes, Greece 45 G3 37 15N 21 0 E
Strömbacka, Sweden 14 C10 61 58N 16 44 E
Strómboli, Italy 41 D8 38 47N 15 13 E
Stromeferry, U.K. 18 D3 57 21N 5 33W
Stromness, U.K. 18 C5 58 58N 3 17W
Stromsburg, U.S.A. 138 E6 41 7N 97 36W
Strömstad, Sweden 13 G14 58 56N 11 10 E
Strömsund, Sweden 12 E16 63 51N 15 33 E
Stronghurst, U.S.A. 140 D6 40 45N 90 55W
Stróngoli, Italy 41 C10 39 16N 17 3 E
Stronsay, U.K. 18 B6 59 7N 2 35W
Stropkov, Slovak Rep. 31 B14 49 13N 21 39 E
Stroud, U.K. 17 F5 51 45N 2 13W
Stroud Road, Australia 117 B9 32 18 S 151 57 E
Stroudsburg, U.S.A. 137 F9 40 59N 75 12W
Stroumbi, Cyprus 32 E11 34 53N 32 29 E
Struer, Denmark 15 H2 56 30N 8 35 E
Struga, Macedonia 42 F5 41 13N 20 44 E
Strugi Krasnyye, Russia 50 C5 58 21N 29 1 E
Strumica, Macedonia 42 F7 41 28N 22 41 E
Strumica →, Europe 42 F8 41 20N 23 22 E
Struthers, Canada 128 C2 48 41N 85 51W
Struthers, U.S.A. 136 E4 41 4N 80 39W
Stryama, Bulgaria 43 E9 42 16N 24 54 E
Stryker, U.S.A. 142 B6 48 41N 114 46W
Stryków, Poland 47 D6 51 55N 19 33 E
Stryy, Ukraine 51 H2 49 16N 23 48 E
Strzegom, Poland 47 E3 50 58N 16 20 E
Strzelce Krajeńskie, Poland 47 C2 52 52N 15 33 E
Strzelce Opolskie, Poland 47 E5 50 31N 18 18 E
Strzelecki Cr. →, Australia 115 D2 29 37 S 139 59 E
Strzelin, Poland 47 E4 50 46N 17 2 E
Strzelno, Poland 47 C5 52 35N 18 9 E
Strzybnica, Poland 47 E5 50 28N 18 48 E
Strzyżów, Poland 31 B14 49 52N 21 47 E
Stuart, Fla., U.S.A. 135 M5 27 12N 80 15W
Stuart, Iowa, U.S.A. 140 C2 41 30N 94 19W
Stuart, Nebr., U.S.A. 138 D5 42 36N 99 8W
Stuart →, Canada 130 C4 54 0N 123 35W
Stuart Bluff Ra., Australia 112 D5 22 50 S 131 52 E
Stuart L., Canada 130 C4 54 30N 124 30W
Stuart Mts., N.Z. 119 F2 45 2 S 167 39 E
Stuart Ra., Australia 115 D1 29 10 S 134 56 E
Stubbekøbing, Denmark 15 K6 54 53N 12 9 E
Stuben, Austria 30 D3 47 10N 10 8 E
Studen Kladenets, Yazovir, Bulgaria 43 F10 41 37N 25 30 E
Studholme, N.Z. 119 E6 44 42 S 171 9 E
Stugun, Sweden 14 A9 63 10N 15 40 E
Stull, L., Canada 128 B1 54 24N 92 34W
Stung Treng, Cambodia 76 F5 13 31N 105 58 E
Stupart →, Canada 131 B10 56 0N 93 25W
Stupino, Russia 52 C4 54 57N 38 2 E
Sturgeon B., Canada 131 C9 52 0N 97 50W
Sturgeon Bay, U.S.A. 134 C2 44 50N 87 23W
Sturgeon Falls, Canada 128 C4 46 25N 79 57W
Sturgeon L., Alta., Canada 130 B5 55 6N 117 32W
Sturgeon L., Ont., Canada 128 B1 50 0N 90 45W
Sturgeon L., Ont., Canada 136 B6 44 28N 78 43W
Sturgis, Mich., U.S.A. 141 C11 41 48N 85 25W
Sturgis, S. Dak., U.S.A. 138 C3 44 25N 103 31W
Štúrovo, Slovak Rep. 31 D11 47 48N 18 41 E
Sturt Cr. →, Australia 112 C4 19 8 S 127 50 E
Sturt Creek, Australia 112 C4 19 12 S 128 8 E
Sturts Meadows, Australia 116 A4 31 18 S 141 42 E
Stutterheim, S. Africa 104 E4 32 33 S 27 28 E
Stuttgart, Germany 27 G5 48 48N 9 11 E
Stuttgart, U.S.A. 139 H9 34 30N 91 33W
Stuyvesant, U.S.A. 137 D11 42 23N 73 45W
Stykkishólmur, Iceland 12 D2 65 2N 22 40W
Styria = Steiermark □, Austria 30 D8 47 26N 15 0 E
Su-no-Saki, Japan 63 C11 34 58N 139 45 E
Su Xian, China 66 H9 33 41N 116 59 E
Suai, Indonesia 72 C3 9 21 S 125 17 E
Suakin, Sudan 94 D4 19 8N 37 20 E
Sual, Phil. 70 C3 16 4N 120 5 E
Suan, N. Korea 67 E14 38 42N 126 22 E
Suapure →, Venezuela 152 B4 6 48N 67 1W
Suaqui, Mexico 146 B3 29 12N 109 41W
Suatá →, Venezuela 153 B4 7 52N 65 22W
Subang, Indonesia 75 D3 6 34 S 107 45 E
Subansiri →, India 78 B4 26 48N 93 50 E
Subayhah, Si. Arabia 84 D3 30 2N 38 50 E
Subi, Indonesia 75 B3 2 58N 108 50 E
Subiaco, Italy 39 G10 41 56N 13 5 E
Subotica, Serbia, Yug. 42 A4 46 6N 19 39 E
Success, Canada 131 C7 50 28N 108 6W
Suceava, Romania 46 B7 47 38N 26 16 E
Suceava □, Romania 46 B6 47 37N 25 40 E
Suceava →, Romania 46 B7 47 38N 26 16 E
Sucha-Beskidzka, Poland 31 B12 49 44N 19 35 E
Suchan, Poland 47 B2 53 18N 15 18 E
Suchan, Russia 60 C6 43 8N 133 9 E
Suchedniów, Poland 47 D7 51 3N 20 49 E
Suchitoto, El Salv. 148 D2 13 56N 89 0W
Suchou = Suzhou, China 69 B13 31 19N 120 38 E
Süchow = Xuzhou, China 67 G9 34 18N 117 10 E
Suchowola, Poland 47 B10 53 33N 23 3 E
Sucio →, Colombia 152 B2 7 27N 77 7W
Suck →, Ireland 19 C3 53 17N 8 3W
Suckling, Mt., Papua N. G. 120 E5 9 49 S 148 53 E
Sucre, Bolivia 157 D4 19 0 S 65 15W
Sucre, Colombia 152 B3 8 49N 74 44W
Sucre □, Colombia 152 B2 8 50N 75 40W
Sucre □, Venezuela 153 A5 10 25N 63 30W
Sucuaro, Colombia 152 C4 4 34N 68 50W
Sućuraj, Croatia 39 E14 43 10N 17 8 E
Sucuriju, Brazil 154 A2 1 39N 49 57W
Sucuriú →, Brazil 157 E7 20 47 S 51 38W
Sud, Pte., Canada 129 C7 49 3N 62 14W
Sud-Ouest, Pte. du, Canada 129 C7 49 23N 63 36W
Suda →, Russia 50 C9 59 0N 37 40 E
Sudak, Ukraine 51 K8 44 51N 34 57 E
Sudan, U.S.A. 139 H3 34 4N 102 32W
Sudan ■, Africa 95 E3 15 0N 30 0 E
Sudbury, Canada 128 C3 46 30N 81 0W
Sudbury, U.K. 17 E8 52 2N 0 45 E
Sûdd, Sudan 95 F2 8 20N 30 0 E
Suddie, Guyana 153 B6 7 8N 58 29W
Süderbrarup, Germany 26 A5 54 38N 9 45 E
Süderlügum, Germany 26 A4 54 52N 8 54 E
Süderoogsand, Germany 26 A4 54 27N 8 28 E
Sudeten Mts. = Sudety, Europe 31 A9 50 20N 16 45 E
Sudety, Europe 31 A9 50 20N 16 45 E
Suðuroy, Færoe Is. 12 F9 61 32N 6 50W
Sudi, Tanzania 107 E4 10 11 S 39 57 E
Sudirman, Pegunungan, Indonesia 73 B5 4 30 S 137 0 E
Sudiţi, Romania 46 E8 44 35N 27 38 E
Sudogda, Russia 52 C5 55 55N 40 50 E
Sudr, Egypt 94 J8 29 40N 32 42 E
Sudzha, Russia 52 E2 51 14N 35 17 E
Sueca, Spain 35 F4 39 12N 0 21W
Suedala, Sweden 15 J7 55 30N 13 15 E
Suez = El Suweis, Egypt 94 J8 29 58N 32 31 E
Suez, G. of = Suweis, Khalîg el, Egypt 94 J8 28 40N 33 0 E
Suez Canal = Suweis, Qanâ es, Egypt 94 H8 31 0N 32 20 E
Suffield, Canada 131 C6 50 12N 111 10W
Suffolk, U.S.A. 134 G7 36 44N 76 35W
Suffolk □, U.K. 17 E9 52 16N 1 0 E
Sufi-Kurgan, Kyrgyzstan 55 C6 40 2N 73 30 E
Suga no-Sen, Japan 62 B6 35 25N 134 25 E
Sugag, Romania 46 D4 45 47N 23 37 E
Sugar →, Ill., U.S.A. 140 B7 42 26N 89 12W
Sugar →, Ind., U.S.A. 141 E9 39 50N 87 23W
Sugar City, U.S.A. 138 F3 38 14N 103 40W
Sugar Cr. →, U.S.A. 140 D7 40 9N 89 38W
Sugbai Passage, Phil. 71 J3 5 22N 120 33 E
Suğla Gölü, Turkey 88 D5 37 20N 32 0 E
Sugluk = Salluit, Canada 127 B12 62 14N 75 38W
Sugny, Belgium 21 J5 49 49N 4 54 E
Suhaia, L., Romania 46 F6 43 45N 25 15 E
Suhār, Oman 85 E8 24 20N 56 40 E
Sühbaatar □, Mongolia 66 B8 45 30N 114 0 E
Suhl, Germany 26 E6 50 36N 10 42 E
Suhr, Switz. 28 B6 47 22N 8 5 E
Şuhut, Turkey 88 C4 38 31N 30 32 E
Sui Xian, Henan, China 66 G8 34 25N 115 2 E
Sui Xian, Henan, China 69 B9 31 42N 113 24 E
Suiá Missu →, Brazil 157 C7 11 13 S 53 15W
Suichang, China 69 C12 28 29N 119 15 E
Suichuan, China 69 D10 26 20N 114 32 E
Suide, China 66 F6 37 30N 110 12 E
Suifenhe, China 67 B16 44 25N 131 10 E
Suihua, China 65 B7 46 32N 126 55 E
Suijiang, China 68 C4 28 40N 103 59 E
Suining, Hunan, China 69 D8 26 35N 110 10 E
Suining, Jiangsu, China 67 H9 33 56N 117 58 E
Suining, Sichuan, China 68 B5 30 26N 105 35 E
Suiping, China 66 H7 33 10N 113 59 E
Suippes, France 23 C11 49 8N 4 30 E
Suir →, Ireland 19 D4 52 16N 7 9W
Suita, Japan 63 C7 34 45N 135 32 E
Suixi, China 69 G8 21 19N 110 18 E
Suiyang, Guizhou, China 68 D6 27 58N 107 18 E
Suiyang, Heilongjiang, China 67 B16 44 30N 130 56 E
Suizhong, China 67 D11 40 21N 120 20 E
Sujangarh, India 80 F6 27 42N 74 31 E

270 Sujica

Sujica, Bos.-H. 42 D2 43 52N 17 11 E
Sukabumi, Indonesia 74 D3 6 56 S 106 50 E
Sukadana, Kalimantan, Indonesia 75 C4 1 10 S 110 0 E
Sukadana, Sumatera, Indonesia 74 D3 5 5 S 105 33 E
Sukagawa, Japan 61 F10 37 17N 140 23 E
Sukaraja, Indonesia 75 C4 2 28 S 110 25 E
Sukarnapura = Jayapura, Indonesia 73 B6 2 28 S 140 38 E
Sukchŏn, N. Korea 67 E13 39 22N 125 35 E
Sukhindol, Bulgaria 43 D10 43 11N 25 10 E
Sukhinichi, Russia 52 C2 54 8N 35 10 E
Sukhona →, Russia 48 C6 61 15N 46 39 E
Sukhothai, Thailand 76 D2 17 1N 99 49 E
Sukhoy Log, Russia 54 C9 56 55N 62 1 E
Sukhumi = Sokhumi, Georgia 53 J5 43 0N 41 0 E
Sukkur, Pakistan 79 D3 27 42N 68 54 E
Sukkur Barrage, Pakistan 80 F3 27 40N 68 50 E
Sukma, India 82 E5 18 24N 81 45 E
Sukovo, Serbia, Yug. 42 D7 43 4N 22 37 E
Sukumo, Japan 62 E4 32 56N 132 44 E
Sukunka →, Canada 130 B4 55 45N 121 15W
Sul, Canal do, Brazil 154 B2 0 10 S 48 30W
Sula →, Ukraine 51 H7 49 40N 32 41 E
Sula, Kepulauan, Indonesia 72 B3 1 45 S 125 0 E
Sulaco →, Honduras 148 C2 15 2N 87 44W
Sulaiman Range, Pakistan 80 D3 30 30N 69 50 E
Sulak →, Russia 53 J8 43 20N 47 34 E
Sūlār, Iran 85 D6 31 53N 51 54 E
Sulawesi □, Indonesia 72 B2 2 0 S 120 0 E
Sulawesi Sea = Celebes Sea, Indonesia 72 A2 3 0N 123 0 E
Sulechów, Poland 47 C2 52 5N 15 40 E
Sulęcin, Poland 47 C2 52 26N 15 10 E
Sulejów, Poland 47 D6 51 26N 19 53 E
Sulejówek, Poland 47 C8 52 13N 21 17 E
Sulgen, Switz. 29 A8 47 33N 9 7 E
Sulima, S. Leone 100 D2 6 58N 11 32W
Sulina, Romania 46 D10 45 10N 29 40 E
Sulina, Braţul →, Romania 46 D10 45 10N 29 20 E
Sulingen, Germany 26 C4 52 41N 8 48 E
Suliţa, Romania 46 B7 47 39N 26 59 E
Sulitjelma, Norway 12 C17 67 9N 16 3 E
Sułkowice, Poland 31 B12 49 50N 19 49 E
Sullana, Peru 156 A1 4 52 S 80 39W
Sullivan, Ill., U.S.A. 138 F10 39 36N 88 37W
Sullivan, Ind., U.S.A. 141 E9 39 6N 87 24W
Sullivan, Mo., U.S.A. 140 F5 38 13N 91 10W
Sullivan Bay, Canada 130 C3 50 55N 126 50W
Sully, U.S.A. 140 C4 41 34N 92 50W
Sully-sur-Loire, France 23 E9 47 45N 2 20 E
Sulmierzyce, Poland 47 D4 51 37N 17 32 E
Sulmona, Italy 39 F10 42 3N 13 55 E
Sulphur, La., U.S.A. 139 K8 30 14N 93 23W
Sulphur, Okla., U.S.A. 139 H6 34 31N 96 58W
Sulphur Pt., Canada 130 A6 60 56N 114 48W
Sulphur Springs, U.S.A. 139 J7 33 8N 95 36W
Sulphur Springs Draw →, U.S.A. 139 J4 32 12N 101 36W
Sulsul, Ethiopia 108 C2 5 5N 44 50 E
Sultan, Canada 128 C3 47 36N 82 47W
Sultan, U.S.A. 144 C5 47 52N 121 49W
Sultan Dağları, Turkey 88 C4 38 20N 31 20 E
Sultan Kudarat □, Phil. 71 H5 6 30N 124 10 E
Sultan sa Barongis, Phil. 71 H5 6 45N 124 35 E
Sultanpur, India 81 F10 26 18N 82 4 E
Sultsa, Russia 48 B8 63 27N 46 2 E
Sulu □, Phil. 71 J3 5 30N 120 30 E
Sulu Arch., Phil. 71 J3 6 0N 121 0 E
Sulu Sea, E. Indies 71 G3 8 0N 120 0 E
Sülüklü, Turkey 88 C5 38 53N 32 20 E
Sülüktü, Kyrgyzstan 55 D4 39 56N 69 34 E
Sululta, Ethiopia 95 F4 9 10N 38 43 E
Suluova, Turkey 88 B6 40 46N 35 32 E
Suluq, Libya 96 B4 31 44N 20 14 E
Sulyukta = Sülüktü, Kyrgyzstan 55 D4 39 56N 69 34 E
Sulzbach, Germany 27 F3 49 18N 7 3 E
Sulzbach-Rosenberg, Germany 27 F7 49 30N 11 44 E
Sulzberger Ice Shelf, Antarctica 7 D10 78 0 S 150 0 E
Sumalata, Indonesia 72 A2 1 0N 122 31 E
Sumampa, Argentina 158 B3 29 25 S 63 29W
Sumatera □, Indonesia 74 B2 0 40N 100 20 E
Sumatra = Sumatera □, Indonesia 74 B2 0 40N 100 20 E
Sumatra, U.S.A. 142 C10 46 37N 107 33W
Sumba, Indonesia 72 C1 9 45 S 119 35 E
Sumba, Selat, Indonesia 72 C1 9 0 S 118 40 E
Sumbawa, Indonesia 72 C1 8 26 S 117 30 E
Sumbawa Besar, Indonesia 72 C1 8 30 S 117 26 E
Sumbawanga □, Tanzania 106 D3 8 0 S 31 30 E
Sumbe, Angola 103 E2 11 10 S 13 48 E
Sumburgh Hd., U.K. 18 B7 59 52N 1 17W
Sumdo, India 81 B8 35 6N 78 41 E
Sumé, Brazil 154 C4 7 39 S 36 55W
Sumedang, Indonesia 75 D3 6 52 S 107 55 E
Sümeg, Hungary 31 E10 46 59N 17 20 E
Šumen, Bulgaria 43 D11 43 18N 26 55 E
Sumenep, Indonesia 75 D4 7 1 S 113 52 E
Sumgait = Sumqayıt, Azerbaijan 53 K9 40 34N 49 38 E
Sumisu-Jima, Japan 63 F12 31 27N 140 3 E
Sumiswald, Switz. 28 B5 47 2N 7 44 E
Summer L., U.S.A. 142 E3 42 50N 120 45W
Summerland, Canada 130 D5 49 32N 119 41W
Summerside, Canada 129 C7 46 24N 63 47W
Summerville, Ga., U.S.A. 135 H3 34 29N 85 21W
Summerville, S.C., U.S.A. 135 J5 33 1N 80 11W
Summit Lake, Canada 130 C4 54 20N 122 40W
Summit Peak, U.S.A. 143 H10 37 21N 106 42W
Sumner, N.Z. 119 D7 43 35 S 172 48 E
Sumner, Ill., U.S.A. 141 F9 38 42N 87 53W
Sumner, Iowa, U.S.A. 140 B4 42 51N 92 6W
Sumner, Wash., U.S.A. 144 C4 47 12N 122 14W
Sumner L., N.Z. 119 C7 42 42 S 172 15 E
Sumoto, Japan 62 C6 34 21N 134 54 E
Sumpangbinangae, Indonesia 72 B1 4 24 S 119 36 E
Šumperk, Czech. 31 B9 49 59N 17 0 E
Sumprabum, Burma 78 B6 26 33N 97 36 E
Sumqayıt, Azerbaijan 53 K9 40 34N 49 38 E
Sumter, U.S.A. 135 J5 33 55N 80 21W
Sumy, Ukraine 51 G8 50 57N 34 50 E
Sun City, Ariz., U.S.A. 143 K7 33 36N 112 17W
Sun City, Calif., U.S.A. 145 M9 33 42N 117 11W
Sun Prairie, U.S.A. 140 A7 43 11N 89 13W
Sunagawa, Japan 60 C10 43 29N 141 55 E
Sunan, N. Korea 67 E13 39 15N 125 40 E
Sunart, L., U.K. 18 E3 56 42N 5 43W
Sunburst, U.S.A. 142 B8 48 53N 111 55W
Sunbury, Australia 117 D6 37 35 S 144 44 E
Sunbury, U.S.A. 137 F8 40 52N 76 48W
Sunchales, Argentina 158 C3 30 58 S 61 35W
Suncho Corral, Argentina 158 B3 27 55 S 63 27W
Sunchon, S. Korea 67 G14 34 52N 127 31 E
Suncook, U.S.A. 137 C13 43 8N 71 27W
Sunda, Selat, Indonesia 74 D3 6 20 S 105 30 E
Sunda Is., Indonesia 58 K14 5 0 S 105 0 E
Sunda Str. = Sunda, Selat, Indonesia 74 D3 6 20 S 105 30 E
Sundance, U.S.A. 138 C2 44 24N 104 23W
Sundarbans, The, Asia 78 E2 22 0N 89 0 E
Sundargarh, India 82 C7 22 4N 84 5 E
Sundays = Sondags →, S. Africa 104 E4 33 44 S 25 51 E
Sundbyberg, Sweden 14 E11 59 22N 17 58 E
Sunderland, Canada 136 B5 44 16N 79 4W
Sunderland, U.K. 16 C6 54 55N 1 23W
Sundre, Canada 130 C6 51 49N 114 38W
Sundridge, Canada 128 C4 45 45N 79 25W
Sunds, Denmark 15 H3 56 13N 9 1 E
Sundsjö, Sweden 14 B9 62 59N 15 9 E
Sundsvall, Sweden 14 B11 62 23N 17 17 E
Sung Hei, Vietnam 77 G6 10 20N 106 2 E
Sungai Kolok, Thailand 77 J3 6 2N 101 58 E
Sungai Lembing, Malaysia 77 L4 3 55N 103 3 E
Sungai Patani, Malaysia 77 K3 5 37N 100 30 E
Sungaigerong, Indonesia 74 C2 2 59 S 104 52 E
Sungailiat, Indonesia 74 C3 1 51 S 106 8 E
Sungaipenuh, Indonesia 74 C2 2 1 S 101 20 E
Sungaitiram, Indonesia 75 C5 0 45 S 117 8 E
Sungari = Songhua Jiang →, China 65 B8 47 45N 132 30 E
Sungguminasa, Indonesia 72 C1 5 17 S 119 30 E
Sunghua Chiang = Songhua Jiang →, China 65 B8 47 45N 132 30 E
Sungikai, Sudan 95 E2 12 20N 29 51 E
Sungurlu, Turkey 88 B6 40 12N 34 21 E
Sunja, Croatia 39 C13 45 21N 16 35 E
Sunkar, Gora, Kazakstan 55 A6 44 15N 73 50 E
Sunndalsøra, Norway 13 E13 62 40N 8 33 E
Sunnyside, Utah, U.S.A. 142 G8 39 34N 110 23W
Sunnyside, Wash., U.S.A. 142 C3 46 20N 120 0W
Sunnyvale, U.S.A. 144 H4 37 23N 122 2W
Sunray, U.S.A. 139 G4 36 1N 101 49W
Sunshine, Australia 117 D6 37 48 S 144 52 E
Suntar, Russia 57 C12 62 15N 117 30 E
Sunyani, Ghana 100 D4 7 21N 2 22W
Suō-Nada, Japan 62 D3 33 50N 131 30 E
Suomenselkä, Finland 12 E21 62 52N 24 0 E
Suomussalmi, Finland 12 D23 64 54N 29 10 E
Suoyarvi, Russia 50 A7 62 3N 32 20 E
Supai, U.S.A. 143 H7 36 15N 112 41W
Supamo →, Venezuela 153 B5 6 48N 61 50W
Supaul, India 81 F12 26 10N 86 40 E
Supe, Peru 156 C2 11 0 S 77 30W
Superior, Ariz., U.S.A. 143 K8 33 18N 111 6W
Superior, Mont., U.S.A. 142 C6 47 12N 114 53W
Superior, Nebr., U.S.A. 138 E5 40 1N 98 4W
Superior, Wis., U.S.A. 138 B8 46 44N 92 6W
Superior, L., U.S.A. 128 C2 47 0N 87 0W
Supetar, Croatia 39 E13 43 25N 16 32 E
Suphan Buri, Thailand 76 E3 14 14N 100 10 E
Suphan Dağı, Turkey 89 C10 38 54N 42 48 E
Supiori, Indonesia 73 B5 1 0 S 136 0 E
Supraśl, Poland 47 B10 53 13N 23 19 E
Supung Sk., China 67 D13 40 35N 124 50 E
Sūq 'Abs, Yemen 86 D3 16 0N 43 12 E
Sūq Suwayq, Si. Arabia 84 E3 24 23N 38 27 E
Suqian, China 67 H10 33 54N 118 8 E
Sūr, Lebanon 91 B4 33 19N 35 16 E
Sur, Pt., U.S.A. 144 J5 36 18N 121 54W
Sura →, Russia 52 C8 56 6N 46 0 E
Surab, Pakistan 79 C2 28 25N 66 15 E
Surabaja = Surabaya, Indonesia 75 D4 7 17 S 112 45 E
Surabaya, Indonesia 75 D4 7 17 S 112 45 E
Suraia, Romania 46 D8 45 40N 27 25 E
Surakarta, Indonesia 75 D4 7 35 S 110 48 E
Surakhany, Azerbaijan 53 K10 40 25N 50 1 E
Surandai, India 83 K3 8 58N 77 26 E
Šurany, Slovak Rep. 31 C11 48 6N 18 10 E
Surat, Australia 115 D4 27 10 S 149 6 E
Surat, India 82 D1 21 12N 72 55 E
Surat Thani, Thailand 77 H2 9 6N 99 20 E
Suratgarh, India 80 E5 29 18N 73 55 E
Suraz, Poland 47 C9 52 57N 22 57 E
Surazh, Belarus 50 E6 55 25N 30 44 E
Surazh, Russia 51 F7 53 5N 32 27 E
Surduc, Romania 46 B4 47 15N 23 25 E
Surduc Pasul, Romania 46 D4 45 21N 23 23 E
Surdulica, Serbia, Yug. 42 E7 42 41N 22 11 E
Sûre = Sauer →, Germany 21 J9 49 44N 6 31 E
Surendranagar, India 80 H4 22 45N 71 40 E
Surf, U.S.A. 145 L6 34 41N 120 36W
Surgères, France 24 B3 46 7N 0 47W
Surgut, Russia 56 C8 61 14N 73 20 E
Surhuisterveen, Neths. 20 B8 53 11N 6 10 E
Surianu, Romania 46 D4 45 33N 23 31 E
Suriapet, India 82 F4 17 10N 79 40 E
Surigao, Phil. 71 G5 9 47N 125 29 E
Surigao del Norte □, Phil. 71 G5 10 0N 125 40 E
Surigao del Sur □, Phil. 71 G6 8 45N 126 0 E
Surigao Strait, Phil. 71 F5 10 15N 125 23 E
Surin, Thailand 76 E4 14 50N 103 34 E
Surin Nua, Ko, Thailand 77 H1 9 30N 97 55 E
Surinam ■, S. Amer. 153 C6 4 0N 56 0W
Suriname □, Surinam 153 B6 5 30N 55 0W
Suriname ■ = Surinam ■, S. Amer. 153 C6 4 0N 56 0W
Suriname →, Surinam 153 B6 5 50N 55 15W
Surkhandarya →, Uzbekistan 55 E3 37 12N 67 20 E
Sürmaq, Iran 85 D7 31 3N 52 48 E
Sürmene, Turkey 89 B9 41 0N 40 1 E
Surovikino, Russia 53 F6 48 32N 42 55 E
Surprise L., Canada 130 B2 59 40N 133 15W
Surrey □, U.K. 17 F7 51 15N 0 31W
Sursee, Switz. 28 B6 47 11N 8 6 E
Sursk, Russia 52 D7 53 3N 45 40 E
Surskoye, Russia 52 C8 54 30N 46 44 E
Surt, Libya 96 B3 31 11N 16 39 E
Surt, Al Hammadah al, Libya 96 B3 30 0N 17 50 E
Surt, Khalīj, Libya 96 B3 31 40N 18 30 E
Surtsey, Iceland 12 E3 63 20N 20 30W
Surubim, Brazil 154 C4 7 50 S 35 45W
Sürüç, Turkey 89 D8 36 58N 38 25 E
Surud Ad, Somali Rep. 108 B3 10 42N 47 9 E
Suruga-Wan, Japan 63 C10 34 45N 138 30 E
Surumu →, Brazil 153 C5 3 22N 60 19W
Susa, Italy 38 C4 45 8N 7 3 E
Suså →, Denmark 15 J5 55 12N 11 42 E
Sušac, Croatia 39 F13 42 46N 16 30 E
Susak, Croatia 39 D11 44 30N 14 18 E
Susaki, Japan 62 D5 33 22N 133 17 E
Susamyr, Kyrgyzstan 55 B6 42 12N 73 58 E
Susamyrtau, Khrebet, Kyrgyzstan 55 B6 42 8N 73 15 E
Süsangerd, Iran 89 G13 31 35N 48 6 E
Susanino, Russia 57 D15 52 50N 140 14 E
Susanville, U.S.A. 142 F3 40 25N 120 39W
Susch, Switz. 29 C10 46 46N 10 5 E
Suşehri, Turkey 89 B8 40 10N 38 6 E
Sušice, Czech. 30 B6 49 17N 13 30 E
Susong, China 69 B11 30 10N 116 5 E
Susquehanna →, U.S.A. 137 G8 39 33N 76 5W
Susquehanna Depot, U.S.A. 137 E9 41 57N 75 36W
Susques, Argentina 158 A2 23 35 S 66 25W
Sussex, Canada 129 C6 45 45N 65 37W
Sussex, U.S.A. 137 E10 41 13N 74 37W
Sussex, E. □, U.K. 17 G8 51 0N 0 20 E
Sussex, W. □, U.K. 17 G7 51 0N 0 30W
Susteren, Neths. 21 F7 51 4N 5 51 E
Sustut →, Canada 130 B3 56 20N 127 30W
Susubona, Solomon Is. 121 M10 8 19 S 159 27 E
Susuman, Russia 57 C15 62 47N 148 10 E
Susunu, Indonesia 73 B4 3 20 S 133 25 E
Susurluk, Turkey 88 C3 39 54N 28 8 E
Susuz, Turkey 89 B10 40 46N 43 8 E
Susz, Poland 47 B6 53 44N 19 20 E
Sütçüler, Turkey 88 D4 37 29N 30 57 E
Şuţeşti, Romania 46 D8 45 13N 27 27 E
Sutherland, Australia 117 C9 34 2 S 151 4 E
Sutherland, S. Africa 104 E3 32 24 S 20 40 E
Sutherland, U.S.A. 138 E4 41 10N 101 8W
Sutherland Falls, N.Z. 119 E2 44 48 S 167 46 E
Sutherlin, U.S.A. 142 E2 43 23N 123 19W
Sutivan, Croatia 39 E13 43 23N 16 30 E
Sutlej →, Pakistan 79 C3 29 23N 71 3 E
Sutter, U.S.A. 144 F5 39 10N 121 45W
Sutter Creek, U.S.A. 144 G6 38 24N 120 48W
Sutton, Canada 137 A12 45 6N 72 37W
Sutton, N.Z. 119 F5 45 34 S 170 8 E
Sutton, U.S.A. 138 E6 40 36N 97 52W
Sutton →, Canada 128 A3 55 15N 83 45W
Sutton in Ashfield, U.K. 16 D6 53 8N 1 16W
Suttor →, Australia 114 C4 21 36 S 147 2 E
Suttsu, Japan 60 C10 42 48N 140 14 E
Su'u, Solomon Is. 121 M11 9 11 S 160 56 E
Suva, Fiji 121 B2 18 6 S 178 30 E
Suva Gora, Macedonia 42 F6 41 45N 21 3 E
Suva Planina, Serbia, Yug. 42 D7 43 10N 22 5 E
Suva Reka, Serbia, Yug. 42 E5 42 21N 20 50 E
Suvo Rudīste, Serbia, Yug. 42 D5 43 17N 20 49 E
Suvorov, Russia 52 C3 54 7N 36 30 E
Suvorov Is. = Suwarrow Is., Cook Is. 123 J11 15 0 S 163 0W
Suvorovo, Bulgaria 43 D12 43 20N 27 35 E
Suwa, Japan 63 A10 36 2N 138 8 E
Suwa-Ko, Japan 63 A10 36 3N 138 5 E
Suwałki, Poland 47 A9 54 8N 22 59 E
Suwałki □, Poland 47 B9 54 0N 22 30 E
Suwannaphum, Thailand 76 E4 15 33N 103 47 E
Suwannee →, U.S.A. 135 L4 29 17N 83 10W
Suwanose-Jima, Japan 61 K4 29 38N 129 43 E
Suwarrow Is., Cook Is. 123 J11 15 0 S 163 0W
Suwayq aş Şuqban, Iraq 84 D5 31 32N 46 7 E
Suweis, Khalîg el, Egypt 94 J8 28 40N 33 0 E
Suweis, Qanâ es, Egypt 94 H8 31 0N 32 20 E
Suwŏn, S. Korea 67 F14 37 17N 127 1 E
Suyo, Phil. 70 C3 16 59N 120 31 E
Suzak, Kazakstan 55 A4 44 9N 68 27 E
Suzaka, Japan 63 A10 36 39N 138 19 E
Suzdal, Russia 52 B5 56 29N 40 26 E
Suzhou, China 69 B13 31 19N 120 38 E
Suzu, Japan 61 F8 37 25N 137 17 E
Suzu-Misaki, Japan 61 F8 37 31N 137 21 E
Suzuka, Japan 63 C8 34 55N 136 36 E
Suzuka-Sam, Japan 63 B8 35 5N 136 30 E
Suzzara, Italy 38 C7 45 0N 10 45 E
Svalbard, Arctic 6 B8 78 0N 17 0 E
Svalöv, Sweden 15 J7 55 57N 13 8 E
Svappavaara, Sweden 12 C19 67 40N 21 3 E
Svarstad, Norway 14 E3 59 27N 9 56 E
Svartisen, Norway 12 C15 66 40N 13 50 E
Svartvik, Sweden 14 B11 62 19N 17 24 E
Svatove, Ukraine 51 H10 49 22N 38 15 E
Svatovo = Svatove, Ukraine 51 H10 49 22N 38 15 E
Svay Chek, Cambodia 76 F4 13 48N 102 58 E
Svay Rieng, Cambodia 77 G5 11 5N 105 48 E
Svealand □, Sweden 13 G16 59 55N 15 0 E
Sveg, Sweden 13 E16 62 2N 14 21 E
Svendborg, Denmark 15 J4 55 4N 10 35 E
Svene, Norway 14 E3 59 45N 9 31 E
Svenljunga, Sweden 15 G7 57 29N 13 5 E
Svenstrup, Denmark 15 H3 56 58N 9 50 E
Sverdlovsk = Yekaterinburg, Russia 54 C8 56 50N 60 30 E
Sverdlovsk, Ukraine 51 H10 48 5N 39 47 E
Sverdrup Is., Canada 124 B10 79 0N 97 0W
Svetac, Croatia 39 E12 43 3N 15 43 E
Sveti Ivan Zelina, Croatia 39 C13 45 57N 16 16 E
Sveti Jurij, Slovenia 39 B12 46 14N 15 24 E
Sveti Lenart, Slovenia 39 B12 46 36N 15 48 E
Sveti Nikola, Prokhad, Europe 42 D7 43 27N 22 6 E
Sveti Nikole, Macedonia 42 F6 41 51N 21 56 E
Sveti Trojica, Slovenia 39 B12 46 37N 15 50 E
Svetlaya, Russia 60 A9 46 33N 138 18 E
Svetlogorsk = Svyetlahorsk, Belarus 51 F5 52 38N 29 46 E
Svetlograd, Russia 53 H6 45 25N 42 58 E
Svetlovodsk = Svitlovodsk, Ukraine 51 H7 49 2N 33 13 E
Svetlyy, Russia 54 F8 50 48N 60 51 E
Svetozarevo, Serbia, Yug. 42 C6 44 5N 21 15 E
Svidník, Slovak Rep. 31 B14 49 20N 21 37 E
Svilaja Planina, Croatia 39 E13 43 49N 16 31 E
Svilajnac, Serbia, Yug. 42 C6 44 15N 21 11 E
Svilengrad, Bulgaria 43 F11 41 49N 26 12 E
Svir →, Russia 50 B7 60 30N 32 48 E
Sviritsa, Russia 50 B7 60 29N 32 51 E
Svishtov, Bulgaria 43 D10 43 36N 25 23 E
Svislach, Belarus 51 F3 53 3N 24 2 E
Svitava →, Czech. 31 B9 49 30N 16 37 E
Svitavy, Czech. 31 B9 49 47N 16 28 E
Svitlovodsk, Ukraine 51 H7 49 2N 33 13 E
Svobodnyy, Russia 57 D13 51 20N 128 0 E
Svoge, Bulgaria 43 E8 42 59N 23 23 E
Svolvær, Norway 12 B16 68 15N 14 34 E
Svratka →, Czech. 31 B9 49 11N 16 38 E
Svrljig, Serbia, Yug. 42 D7 43 25N 22 6 E
Svyetlahorsk, Belarus 51 F5 52 38N 29 46 E
Swa, Burma 78 F6 19 15N 96 17 E
Swa Tende, Zaïre 103 D3 7 9 S 17 7 E
Swabian Alps = Schwäbische Alb, Germany 27 G5 48 20N 9 30 E
Swainsboro, U.S.A. 135 J4 32 36N 82 20W
Swakopmund, Namibia 104 C1 22 37 S 14 30 E
Swale →, U.K. 16 C6 54 5N 1 20W
Swalmen, Neths. 21 F8 51 13N 6 2 E
Swan Hill, Australia 116 C5 35 20 S 143 33 E
Swan Hills, Canada 130 C5 54 42N 115 24W
Swan Is., W. Indies 148 C3 17 22N 83 57W
Swan L., Canada 131 C8 52 30N 100 40W
Swan Reach, Australia 116 C3 34 35 S 139 37 E
Swan River, Canada 131 C8 52 10N 101 16W
Swanage, U.K. 17 G6 50 36N 1 58W
Swansea, Australia 117 B9 33 3 S 151 35 E
Swansea, U.K. 17 F4 51 37N 3 57W
Swansea □, U.K. 17 F3 51 38N 4 3W
Swar →, Pakistan 81 B5 34 40N 72 5 E
Swartberge, S. Africa 104 E3 33 20 S 22 0 E
Swartmodder, S. Africa 104 D3 28 1 S 20 32 E
Swartruggens, S. Africa 104 D4 25 39 S 26 42 E
Swarzędz, Poland 47 C4 52 25N 17 4 E
Swastika, Canada 128 C3 48 7N 80 6W
Swatow = Shantou, China 69 F11 23 18N 116 40 E
Swaziland ■, Africa 105 D5 26 30 S 31 30 E
Sweden ■, Europe 13 G16 57 0N 15 0 E
Swedru, Ghana 101 D4 5 32N 0 41W
Sweet Home, U.S.A. 142 D2 44 24N 122 44W
Sweet Springs, U.S.A. 140 F3 38 58N 93 25W
Sweetwater, Nev., U.S.A. 144 G7 38 27N 119 9W
Sweetwater, Tex., U.S.A. 139 J4 32 28N 100 25W
Sweetwater →, U.S.A. 142 E10 42 31N 107 2W
Swellendam, S. Africa 104 E3 34 1 S 20 26 E
Swider →, Poland 47 C8 52 6N 21 14 E
Świdnica, Poland 47 E3 50 50N 16 30 E
Świdnik, Poland 47 D9 51 13N 22 39 E
Świdwin, Poland 47 B2 53 47N 15 49 E
Świebodzice, Poland 47 E3 50 51N 16 20 E
Świebodzin, Poland 47 C2 52 15N 15 31 E
Świecie, Poland 47 B5 53 25N 18 30 E
Świętokrzyskie, Góry, Poland 47 E7 51 0N 20 30 E
Swift Current, Canada 131 C7 50 20N 107 45W
Swiftcurrent →, Canada 131 C7 50 38N 107 44W
Swilly, L., Ireland 19 A4 55 12N 7 33W
Swindle, I., Canada 130 C3 52 30N 128 35W
Swindon, U.K. 17 F6 51 34N 1 46W
Swinemünde = Świnoujście, Poland 47 B1 53 54N 14 16 E
Świnoujście, Poland 47 B1 53 54N 14 16 E
Switzerland ■, Europe 28 D6 46 30N 8 0 E
Swords, Ireland 19 C5 53 28N 6 13W
Syasstroy, Russia 50 B7 60 9N 32 33 E
Sychevka, Russia 52 C2 55 59N 34 16 E
Syców, Poland 47 D4 51 19N 17 40 E
Sydney, Australia 117 B9 33 53 S 151 10 E
Sydney, Canada 129 C7 46 7N 60 7W
Sydney Mines, Canada 129 C7 46 18N 60 15W
Sydprøven, Greenland 6 C5 60 30N 45 35W
Sydra, G. of = Surt, Khalīj, Libya 96 B3 31 40N 18 30 E
Syeverodonetsk, Ukraine 51 H10 48 58N 38 35 E
Syke, Germany 26 C4 52 55N 8 50 E
Syktyvkar, Russia 48 B9 61 45N 50 40 E
Sylacauga, U.S.A. 135 J2 33 10N 86 15W
Sylarna, Sweden 12 E15 63 2N 12 13 E
Sylhet, Bangla. 78 C3 24 54N 91 52 E
Sylt, Germany 26 A4 54 54N 8 22 E
Sylva →, Russia 54 B6 58 0N 56 54 E
Sylvan Lake, Canada 130 C6 52 20N 114 3W
Sylvania, Ga., U.S.A. 135 J5 32 45N 81 38W
Sylvania, Ohio, U.S.A. 141 C13 41 43N 83 42W
Sylvester, U.S.A. 135 K4 31 32N 83 50W
Sym, Russia 56 C9 60 20N 88 18 E
Symón, Mexico 146 C4 24 42N 102 35W
Synelnykove, Ukraine 51 H8 48 25N 35 30 E
Synnott Ra., Australia 112 C4 16 30 S 125 20 E
Syracuse, Ind., U.S.A. 141 C11 41 26N 85 45W
Syracuse, Kans., U.S.A. 139 F4 37 59N 101 45W
Syracuse, N.Y., U.S.A. 137 C8 43 3N 76 9W
Syrdarya = Sirdaryo, Uzbekistan 55 C4 40 50N 68 40 E
Syrdarya →, Kazakstan 56 E7 46 3N 61 0 E
Syria ■, Asia 89 E8 35 0N 38 0 E
Syriam, Burma 78 G6 16 44N 96 19 E
Syrian Desert = Ash Shām, Bādiyat, Asia 58 F7 32 0N 40 0 E
Sysert, Russia 54 C8 56 29N 60 49 E
Syul'dzhyukyor, Russia 57 C12 63 14N 113 32 E
Syutkya, Bulgaria 43 F9 41 50N 24 16 E
Syzran, Russia 52 D9 53 12N 48 30 E
Szabolcs-Szatmár □, Hungary 31 C14 48 2N 21 45 E
Szamocin, Poland 47 B4 53 2N 17 7 E
Szamos →, Hungary 31 C15 48 7N 22 20 E
Szaraz →, Hungary 31 E13 46 28N 20 44 E
Szarvas, Hungary 31 E13 46 50N 20 38 E
Szazhalombatta, Hungary 31 D11 47 20N 18 58 E
Szczawnica, Poland 31 B13 49 26N 20 30 E
Szczebrzeszyn, Poland 47 E9 50 42N 22 59 E
Szczecin, Poland 47 B1 53 27N 14 27 E
Szczecin □, Poland 47 B1 53 25N 14 32 E
Szczecinek, Poland 47 B3 53 43N 16 41 E

Tanay 271

Szczekocimy, Poland 47 E6 50 38N 19 48 E
Szczucin, Poland 47 E8 50 18N 21 4 E
Szczuczyn, Poland 47 B9 53 36N 22 19 E
Szczytno, Poland 47 B8 53 33N 21 0 E
Szechwan = Sichuan □, China 68 B5 31 0N 104 0 E
Szécsény, Hungary 31 C12 48 7N 19 30 E
Szeged, Hungary 31 E13 46 16N 20 10 E
Szeghalom, Hungary 31 D14 47 1N 21 10 E
Székesfehérvár, Hungary 31 D11 47 15N 18 25 E
Szekszárd, Hungary 31 E11 46 22N 18 42 E
Szendrö, Hungary 31 C13 48 24N 20 41 E
Szentendre, Hungary 31 D12 47 39N 19 4 E
Szentes, Hungary 31 E13 46 39N 20 21 E
Szentgotthárd, Hungary 31 E9 46 58N 16 19 E
Szentlörinc, Hungary 31 E11 46 3N 18 1 E
Szerencs, Hungary 31 C14 48 10N 21 12 E
Szigetvár, Hungary 31 E10 46 3N 17 46 E
Szikszó, Hungary 31 C13 48 12N 20 56 E
Szkwa →, Poland 47 B8 53 11N 21 43 E
Szlichtyngowa, Poland 47 D3 51 42N 16 15 E
Szob, Hungary 31 D11 47 48N 18 53 E
Szolnok, Hungary 31 D13 47 10N 20 15 E
Szolnok □, Hungary 31 D13 47 15N 20 30 E
Szombathely, Hungary 31 D9 47 14N 16 38 E
Szprotawa, Poland 47 D2 51 33N 15 35 E
Sztum, Poland 47 B6 53 55N 19 1 E
Sztutowo, Poland 47 A6 54 20N 19 15 E
Szubin, Poland 47 B4 53 1N 17 45 E
Szydłowiec, Poland 47 D7 51 15N 20 51 E
Szypliszki, Poland 47 A10 54 17N 23 2 E

T

't Harde, Neths. 20 D7 52 24N 5 54 E
't Zandt, Neths. 20 B9 53 22N 6 46 E
Ta Khli Khok, Thailand 76 E3 15 18N 100 20 E
Ta Lai, Vietnam 77 G6 11 24N 107 23 E
Tabacal, Argentina 158 A3 23 15 S 64 15W
Tabaco, Phil. 70 E4 13 22N 123 44 E
Tabagné, Ivory C. 100 D4 7 59N 3 4W
Ţābah, Si. Arabia 84 E4 26 55N 42 38 E
Tabajara, Brazil 157 B5 8 56 S 62 8W
Tabalos, Peru 156 B2 6 26 S 76 37W
Tabango, Phil. 71 F5 11 19N 124 22 E
Tabar Is., Papua N. G. 120 B7 2 50 S 152 0 E
Tabarca, I. de, Spain 35 G4 38 17N 0 30W
Tabarka, Tunisia 96 A1 36 56N 8 46 E
Ţabas, Khorāsān, Iran 85 C9 32 48N 60 12 E
Ţabas, Khorāsān, Iran 85 C8 33 35N 56 55 E
Tabasará, Serranía de, Panama 148 E3 8 35N 81 40W
Tabasco □, Mexico 147 D6 17 45N 93 30W
Tabatinga, Serra da, Brazil 154 D3 10 30 S 44 0W
Tabayin, Burma 78 D5 22 42N 95 20 E
Tabāzīn, Iran 85 D8 31 12N 57 54 E
Tabelbala, Kahal de, Algeria 99 C4 28 47N 2 0W
Taber, Canada 130 D6 49 47N 112 8W
Tabernas, Spain 35 H2 37 4N 2 26W
Tabernes de Valldigna, Spain 35 F4 39 5N 0 13W
Tabi, Angola 103 D2 8 10 S 13 18 E
Tabira, Brazil 154 C4 7 35 S 37 33W
Tablas, Phil. 70 E4 12 25N 122 2 E
Tablas Strait, Phil. 70 E3 12 40N 121 48 E
Table B. = Tafelbaai, S. Africa 104 E2 33 35 S 18 25 E
Table B., Canada 129 B8 53 40N 56 25W
Table Grove, U.S.A. 140 D6 40 20N 90 27W
Table Mt., S. Africa 104 E2 34 0 S 18 22 E
Tableland, Australia 112 C4 17 16 S 126 51 E
Tabletop, Mt., Australia 114 C4 23 24 S 147 11 E
Tabogon, Phil. 71 F5 10 57N 124 2 E
Tábor, Czech. 30 B7 49 25N 14 39 E
Tabora, Tanzania 106 D3 5 2 S 32 50 E
Tabora □, Tanzania 106 D3 5 0 S 33 0 E
Tabou, Ivory C. 100 E3 4 30N 7 20W
Tabrīz, Iran 89 C12 38 7N 46 20 E
Tabuaeran, Pac. Oc. 123 G12 3 51N 159 22W
Tabuelan, Phil. 71 F4 10 49N 123 52 E
Tabuenca, Spain 34 D3 41 42N 1 33W
Tabuk, Phil. 70 C3 17 24N 121 25 E
Tabūk, Si. Arabia 84 D3 28 23N 36 36 E
Tabwemasana, Mt., Vanuatu 121 E4 15 20 S 166 44 E
Tacámbaro de Codallos, Mexico 146 D4 19 14N 101 28W
Tacheng, China 64 B3 46 40N 82 58 E
Tachia, Taiwan 69 E13 24 25N 120 28 E
Tachibana-Wan, Japan 62 E2 32 45N 130 7 E
Tachikawa, Japan 63 B11 35 42N 139 25 E
Tach'ing Shan = Daqing Shan, China 66 D6 40 40N 111 0 E
Táchira □, Venezuela 152 B3 8 7N 72 15W
Tachov, Czech. 30 B5 49 47N 12 39 E
Tácina →, Italy 41 D9 38 57N 16 55 E
Tacloban, Phil. 71 F5 11 15N 124 58 E
Tacna, Peru 156 D3 18 0 S 70 20W
Tacna □, Peru 156 D3 17 40 S 70 20W
Tacoma, U.S.A. 144 C4 47 14N 122 26W
Tacuarembó, Uruguay 159 C4 31 45 S 56 0W
Tacutu →, Brazil 153 C5 3 1N 60 29W
Tademaït, Plateau du, Algeria 99 C5 28 30N 2 30 E
Tadent, O. →, Algeria 99 D6 22 25N 6 40 E
Tadjerdjeri, O. →, Algeria 99 C6 26 0N 8 0 E
Tadjerouna, Algeria 99 B5 33 31N 2 3 E
Tadjettaret, O. →, Algeria 99 D6 21 20N 7 22 E
Tadjmout, Oasis, Algeria 99 B5 33 52N 2 30 E
Tadjmout, Saoura, Algeria 99 C5 25 37N 3 48 E
Tadjoura, Djibouti 90 E3 11 50N 42 55 E
Tadjoura, Golfe de, Djibouti 95 E5 11 50N 43 0 E
Tadmor, N.Z. 119 B7 41 27 S 172 45 E
Tadotsu, Japan 62 C5 34 16N 133 45 E
Tadoule, L., Canada 131 B9 58 36N 98 20W
Tadoussac, Canada 129 C6 48 11N 69 42W
Tadzhikistan = Tajikistan ■, Asia 55 D5 38 30N 70 0 E
Taechŏn-ni, S. Korea 67 F14 36 21N 126 36 E
Taegu, S. Korea 67 G15 35 50N 128 37 E
Taegwan, N. Korea 67 D13 40 13N 125 12 E
Taejŏn, S. Korea 67 F14 36 20N 127 28 E
Tafalla, Spain 34 C3 42 30N 1 41W
Tafar, Sudan 95 F2 6 52N 28 15 E
Tafassasset, O. →, Algeria 99 D6 22 0N 9 57 E
Tafelbaai, S. Africa 104 E2 33 35 S 18 25 E
Tafelney, C., Morocco 98 B3 31 3N 9 51W
Tafermaar, Indonesia 73 C4 6 47 S 134 10 E
Taffermit, Morocco 98 C3 29 37N 9 15W
Tafí Viejo, Argentina 158 B2 26 43 S 65 17W
Tafīhān, Iran 85 D7 29 25N 52 39 E
Tafiré, Ivory C. 100 D3 9 4N 5 4W
Tafnidilt, Morocco 98 C2 28 47N 10 58W
Tafraoute, Morocco 98 C3 29 50N 8 58W
Taft, Iran 85 D7 31 45N 54 14 E
Taft, Phil. 71 F5 11 57N 125 30 E
Taft, Calif., U.S.A. 145 K7 35 8N 119 28W
Taft, Tex., U.S.A. 139 M6 27 59N 97 24W
Taga, W. Samoa 121 W23 13 46 S 172 28W
Taga Dzong, Bhutan 78 B2 27 5N 89 55 E
Tagana-an, Phil. 71 G5 9 42N 125 35 E
Taganrog, Russia 53 G4 47 12N 38 50 E
Taganrogskiy Zaliv, Russia 53 G4 47 0N 38 30 E
Tagânt, Mauritania 100 B2 18 20N 11 0W
Tagap Ga, Burma 78 B6 26 56N 96 13 E
Tagapula I., Phil. 70 E5 12 4N 124 12 E
Tagatay, Phil. 70 D3 14 6N 120 56 E
Tagauayan I., Phil. 71 F3 10 58N 121 13 E
Tagbilaran, Phil. 71 G4 9 39N 123 51 E
Tage, Papua N. G. 120 D2 6 19 S 143 20 E
Tággia, Italy 38 E4 43 52N 7 51 E
Taghzout, Morocco 98 B4 33 30N 4 49W
Tagish, Canada 130 A2 60 19N 134 16W
Tagish L., Canada 130 A2 60 10N 134 20W
Tagkawayan, Phil. 70 E4 13 58N 122 32 E
Tagliacozzo, Italy 39 F10 42 4N 13 14 E
Tagliamento →, Italy 39 C10 45 38N 13 6 E
Táglio di Po, Italy 39 D9 45 0N 12 12 E
Tagna, Colombia 152 D3 2 24 S 70 37W
Tago, Phil. 71 G6 9 2N 126 13 E
Tago, Mt., Phil. 71 G5 8 23N 125 5 E
Tagomago, I. de, Spain 33 B8 39 2N 1 39 E
Taguatinga, Brazil 155 D3 12 16 S 42 26W
Tagudin, Phil. 70 C3 16 56N 120 27 E
Tagula, Papua N. G. 120 F7 11 22 S 153 15 E
Tagula I., Papua N. G. 120 F7 11 30 S 153 30 E
Tagum, Phil. 71 H5 7 33N 125 53 E
Tagus = Tejo →, Europe 37 G1 38 40N 9 24W
Tahakopa, N.Z. 119 G4 46 30 S 169 23 E
Tahala, Morocco 98 B4 34 0N 4 28W
Tahan, Gunong, Malaysia 77 K4 4 34N 102 17 E
Tahānah-ye sūr Gol, Afghan. 79 C2 31 43N 67 53 E
Tahara, Japan 63 C9 34 40N 137 16 E
Tahat, Algeria 99 D6 23 18N 5 33 E
Tāherī, Iran 85 E7 27 43N 52 20 E
Tahiti, Pac. Oc. 123 J13 17 37 S 149 27W
Tahoe, L., U.S.A. 144 G6 39 6N 120 2W
Tahoe City, U.S.A. 144 F6 39 10N 120 9W
Taholah, U.S.A. 144 C2 47 21N 124 17W
Tahora, N.Z. 118 F3 39 2 S 174 49 E
Tahoua, Niger 101 C6 14 57N 5 16 E
Tahta, Egypt 94 B3 26 44N 31 32 E
Tahtalı Dağları, Turkey 88 C7 38 20N 36 0 E
Tahuamanu →, Bolivia 156 C4 11 6 S 67 36W
Tahulandang, Indonesia 72 A3 2 27N 125 23 E
Tahuna, Indonesia 72 A3 3 38N 125 30 E
Taï, Ivory C. 100 D3 5 55N 7 30W
Tai Shan, China 67 F9 36 25N 117 20 E
Tai Xian, China 69 A13 32 30N 120 7 E
Tai'an, China 67 F9 36 12N 117 8 E
Taibei = T'aipei, Taiwan 69 E13 25 2N 121 30 E
Taibique, Canary Is. 33 G2 27 42N 17 58W
Taibus Qi, China 66 D8 41 54N 115 22 E
T'aichung, Taiwan 69 E13 24 9N 120 37 E
Taieri →, N.Z. 119 G5 46 3 S 170 12 E
Taiga Madema, Libya 96 D3 23 46N 15 25 E
Taigu, China 66 F7 37 28N 112 30 E
Taihang Shan, China 66 G7 36 0N 113 30 E
Taihape, N.Z. 118 F4 39 41 S 175 48 E
Taihe, Anhui, China 66 H8 33 20N 115 42 E
Taihe, Jiangxi, China 69 D10 26 47N 114 52 E
Taihu, China 69 B11 30 22N 116 20 E
Taijiang, China 68 D7 26 39N 108 21 E
Taikang, China 66 G8 34 5N 114 50 E
Taikkyi, Burma 78 G6 17 20N 96 0 E
Tailem Bend, Australia 116 C3 35 12 S 139 29 E
Tailfingen, Germany 27 G5 48 15N 9 1 E
Taimyr Peninsula = Taymyr, Poluostrov, Russia 57 B11 75 0N 100 0 E
Tain, U.K. 18 D4 57 49N 4 4W
T'ainan, Taiwan 69 F13 23 0N 120 10 E
Taínaron, Ákra, Greece 45 H4 36 22N 22 27 E
Tainggyo, Burma 78 G5 17 49N 94 29 E
Taining, China 69 D11 26 54N 117 9 E
Taintignies, Belgium 21 G2 50 33N 3 22 E
Taiobeiras, Brazil 155 E3 15 49 S 42 14W
T'aipei, Taiwan 69 E13 25 2N 121 30 E
Taiping, China 69 B12 30 15N 118 6 E
Taiping, Malaysia 77 K3 4 51N 100 44 E
Taipingzhen, China 66 H6 33 35N 111 42 E
Taipu, Brazil 154 C4 5 37 S 35 36W
Tairbeart = Tarbert, U.K. 18 D2 57 54N 6 49W
Taisha, Japan 62 B4 35 24N 132 40 E
Taishan, China 69 F9 22 14N 112 41 E
Taishun, China 69 D12 27 30N 119 42 E
Taita □, Kenya 106 C4 4 0 S 38 30 E
Taita Hills, Kenya 106 C4 3 25 S 38 15 E
Taitao, C., Chile 160 C1 45 53 S 75 5W
Taitao, Pen. de, Chile 160 C2 46 30 S 75 0W
T'aitung, Taiwan 69 F13 22 43N 121 4 E
Taivalkoski, Finland 12 D23 65 33N 28 12 E
Taiwan ■, Asia 69 F13 23 30N 121 0 E
Taixing, China 69 A13 32 11N 120 0 E
Taïyetos Óros, Greece 45 H4 37 0N 22 23 E
Taiyiba, Israel 91 C4 32 36N 35 27 E
Taiyuan, China 66 F7 37 52N 112 33 E
Taizhong = T'aichung, Taiwan 69 E13 24 9N 120 37 E
Taizhou, China 69 A12 32 28N 119 55 E
Taizhou Liedao, China 69 C13 28 30N 121 55 E
Ta'izz, Yemen 86 D4 13 35N 44 2 E
Tājābād, Iran 85 D7 30 2N 54 24 E
Tajapuru, Furo do, Brazil 154 B1 1 50 S 50 25W
Tajarḥī, Libya 96 D2 24 21N 14 28 E
Tajikistan ■, Asia 55 D5 38 30N 70 0 E
Tajima, Japan 61 F9 37 12N 139 46 E
Tajimi, Japan 63 B9 35 19N 137 8 E
Tajo = Tejo →, Europe 37 G1 38 40N 9 24W
Tajrīsh, Iran 85 C6 35 48N 51 25 E
Tājūrā, Libya 96 B2 32 51N 13 21 E
Tak, Thailand 76 D2 16 52N 99 8 E
Takāb, Iran 89 D12 36 24N 47 7 E
Takachiho, Japan 62 E3 32 42N 131 18 E
Takada, Japan 61 F9 37 7N 138 15 E
Takahagi, Japan 61 F10 36 43N 140 45 E
Takahashi, Japan 62 C5 34 51N 133 39 E
Takaka, N.Z. 119 A7 40 51 S 172 50 E
Takamatsu, Japan 62 C6 34 20N 134 5 E
Takanabe, Japan 62 E3 32 8N 131 30 E
Takaoka, Japan 63 A8 36 47N 137 0 E
Takapau, N.Z. 118 G5 40 2 S 176 21 E
Takapuna, N.Z. 118 C3 36 47 S 174 47 E
Takasago, Japan 62 C6 34 45N 134 48 E
Takasaki, Japan 63 A10 36 20N 139 0 E
Takase, Japan 62 C5 34 7N 133 48 E
Takatsuki, Japan 63 C7 34 51N 135 37 E
Takaungu, Kenya 106 C4 3 38 S 39 52 E
Takawa, Japan 62 D2 33 38N 130 51 E
Takayama, Japan 63 A9 36 18N 137 11 E
Takayama-Bonchi, Japan 63 B9 36 0N 137 18 E
Take-Shima, Japan 61 J5 30 49N 130 26 E
Takefu, Japan 63 B8 35 50N 136 10 E
Takehara, Japan 62 C4 34 21N 132 55 E
Takengon, Indonesia 74 B1 4 45N 96 50 E
Takeo, Cambodia 77 G5 10 59N 104 47 E
Takeo, Japan 62 D2 33 12N 130 1 E
Tåkern, Sweden 15 F8 58 22N 14 45 E
Tākestān, Iran 85 C6 36 0N 49 40 E
Taketa, Japan 62 E3 32 58N 131 24 E
Takh, India 81 C7 33 6N 77 32 E
Takhār □, Afghan. 79 A3 36 40N 70 0 E
Takhman, Cambodia 77 G5 11 29N 104 57 E
Taki, Papua N. G. 120 D8 6 29 S 155 52 E
Takikawa, Japan 60 C10 43 33N 141 54 E
Takla L., Canada 130 B3 55 15N 125 45W
Takla Landing, Canada 130 B3 55 30N 125 50W
Takla Makan = Taklamakan Shamo, China 64 C3 38 0N 83 0 E
Taklamakan Shamo, China 64 C3 38 0N 83 0 E
Taku, Japan 62 D2 33 18N 130 3 E
Taku →, Canada 130 B2 58 30N 133 50W
Takum, Nigeria 101 D6 7 18N 9 36 E
Takuma, Japan 62 C5 34 13N 133 40 E
Takundi, Zaïre 103 C3 4 45 S 16 34 E
Takuran, Phil. 71 H4 7 51N 123 34 E
Takutu →, Guyana 153 C5 3 1N 60 29W
Tal Halāl, Iran 85 D7 28 54N 55 1 E
Tala, Uruguay 159 C4 34 21 S 55 46W
Talachyn, Belarus 50 E5 54 25N 29 42 E
Talacogan, Phil. 71 G5 8 32N 125 39 E
Talagante, Chile 158 C1 33 40 S 70 50W
Talaïnt, Morocco 98 C3 29 41N 9 40W
Talak, Niger 101 B6 18 0N 5 0 E
Talakag, Phil. 71 G5 8 16N 124 37 E
Talamanca, Cordillera de, Cent. Amer. 148 E3 9 20N 83 20W
Talara, Peru 156 A1 4 38 S 81 18W
Talas, Kyrgyzstan 55 B6 42 30N 72 13 E
Talas, Turkey 88 C6 38 41N 35 33 E
Talas →, Kazakstan 55 B5 44 0N 70 20 E
Talasea, Papua N. G. 120 C6 5 20 S 150 2 E
Talasskiy Alatau, Khrebet, Kyrgyzstan 55 B6 42 15N 72 0 E
Talâta, Egypt 91 E1 30 36N 32 20 E
Talata Mafara, Nigeria 101 C6 12 38N 6 4 E
Talaud, Kepulauan, Indonesia 72 A3 4 30N 127 10 E
Talaud Is. = Talaud, Kepulauan, Indonesia 72 A3 4 30N 127 10 E
Talavera de la Reina, Spain 36 F6 39 55N 4 46W
Talawana, Australia 112 D3 22 51 S 121 9 E
Talawgyi, Burma 78 C6 25 4N 97 19 E
Talayan, Phil. 71 H5 6 52N 124 24 E
Talbert, Sillon de, France 22 D3 48 53N 3 5W
Talbot, C., Australia 112 B4 13 48 S 126 43 E
Talbragar →, Australia 117 B8 32 12 S 148 37 E
Talca, Chile 158 D1 35 28 S 71 40W
Talca □, Chile 158 D1 35 20 S 71 46W
Talcahuano, Chile 158 D1 36 40 S 73 10W
Talcher, India 82 D7 21 0N 85 18 E
Talcho, Niger 101 C5 14 44N 3 28 E
Taldy Kurgan = Taldyqorghan, Kazakstan 56 E8 45 10N 78 45 E
Taldyqorghan, Kazakstan 56 E8 45 10N 78 45 E
Tālesh, Iran 89 D13 37 58N 48 58 E
Ţalesh, Kūhhā-ye, Iran 89 D13 37 42N 48 55 E
Talgar, Kazakstan 55 B8 43 19N 77 15 E
Talgar, Pik, Kazakstan 55 B8 43 5N 77 20 E
Talguharai, Sudan 94 D4 18 19N 35 56 E
Tali Post, Sudan 95 F3 5 55N 30 44 E
Talibon, Phil. 71 F5 10 9N 124 20 E
Talibong, Ko, Thailand 77 J2 7 15N 99 23 E
Talihina, U.S.A. 139 H7 34 45N 95 3W
Talikota, India 83 F3 16 29N 76 17 E
Talimardzhan, Turkmenistan 55 D2 38 23N 65 37 E
Talisay, Phil. 71 F4 10 44N 122 58 E
Talisayan, Phil. 71 G5 9 0N 124 55 E
Talitsa, Russia 54 C9 57 0N 63 43 E
Taliwang, Indonesia 72 C1 8 50 S 116 55 E
Tall 'Afar, Iraq 89 D10 36 22N 42 27 E
Tall 'Asūr, West Bank 91 D4 31 59N 35 17 E
Tall Kalakh, Syria 91 A5 34 41N 36 15 E
Talla, Egypt 94 J7 28 5N 30 43 E
Talladega, U.S.A. 135 J2 33 26N 86 6W
Tallahassee, U.S.A. 135 K3 30 27N 84 17W
Tallangatta, Australia 117 D7 36 15 S 147 19 E
Tallarook, Australia 117 D6 37 5 S 145 6 E
Tallawang, Australia 117 B8 32 12 S 149 28 E
Tallering Pk., Australia 113 E2 28 6 S 115 37 E
Tallinn, Estonia 13 G21 59 22N 24 48 E
Tallulah, U.S.A. 139 J9 32 25N 91 11W
Tălmaciu, Romania 46 D5 45 38N 24 19 E
Talmest, Morocco 98 B3 31 48N 9 21W
Talmont, France 24 B2 46 27N 1 37W
Talne, Ukraine 51 H6 48 50N 30 44 E
Talnoye = Talne, Ukraine 51 H6 48 50N 30 44 E
Taloda, India 82 D2 21 34N 74 11 E
Talodi, Sudan 95 E3 10 35N 30 22 E
Talomo, Phil. 71 H5 7 3N 125 32 E
Talovaya, Russia 52 E5 51 6N 40 45 E
Taloyoak, Canada 126 B10 69 32N 93 32W
Talpa de Allende, Mexico 146 C4 20 23N 104 51W
Tālqān, Afghan. 79 A3 36 44N 69 33 E
Talsi, Latvia 13 H20 57 10N 22 30 E
Talsinnt, Morocco 99 B4 32 33N 3 27W
Taltal, Chile 158 B1 25 23 S 70 33W
Taltson →, Canada 130 A6 61 24N 112 46W
Talwood, Australia 115 D4 28 29 S 149 29 E
Talyawalka Cr. →, Australia 116 B5 32 28 S 142 22 E
Tam Chau, Vietnam 77 G5 10 48N 105 12 E
Tam Ky, Vietnam 76 E7 15 34N 108 29 E
Tam Quan, Vietnam 76 E7 14 35N 109 3 E
Tama, U.S.A. 140 C4 41 58N 92 35W
Tamala, Australia 113 E1 26 42 S 113 47 E
Tamalameque, Colombia 152 B3 8 52N 73 49W
Tamale, Ghana 101 D4 9 22N 0 50W
Taman, Russia 53 H3 45 14N 36 41 E
Tamana, Japan 62 E2 32 58N 130 32 E
Tamanar, Morocco 98 B3 31 1N 9 46W
Tamano, Japan 62 C5 34 29N 133 59 E
Tamanrasset, Algeria 99 D6 22 50N 5 30 E
Tamanrasset, O. →, Algeria 99 D5 22 0N 2 0 E
Tamanthi, Burma 78 C5 25 19N 95 17 E
Tamaqua, U.S.A. 137 F9 40 48N 75 58W
Tamar →, U.K. 17 G3 50 27N 4 15W
Támara, Colombia 152 B3 5 50N 72 10W
Tamarang, Australia 117 A9 31 27 S 150 5 E
Tamarinda, Spain 33 B10 39 55N 3 49 E
Tamarite de Litera, Spain 34 D5 41 52N 0 25 E
Tamaroa, U.S.A. 140 F7 38 8N 89 14W
Tamashima, Japan 62 C5 34 32N 133 40 E
Tamási, Hungary 31 E11 46 40N 18 18 E
Tamaské, Niger 101 C6 14 49N 5 43 E
Tamaulipas □, Mexico 147 C5 24 0N 99 0W
Tamaulipas, Sierra de, Mexico 147 C5 23 30N 98 20W
Tamazula, Mexico 146 C3 24 55N 106 58W
Tamazunchale, Mexico 147 C5 21 16N 98 47W
Tamba-Dabatou, Guinea 100 C2 11 50N 10 40W
Tambacounda, Senegal 100 C2 13 45N 13 40W
Tambelan, Kepulauan, Indonesia 74 B3 1 0N 107 30 E
Tambellup, Australia 113 F2 34 4 S 117 37 E
Tambo, Australia 114 C4 24 54 S 146 14 E
Tambo, Peru 156 C3 12 57 S 74 1W
Tambo →, Peru 156 C3 10 42 S 73 47W
Tambo de Mora, Peru 156 C2 13 30 S 76 8W
Tambobamba, Peru 156 C3 13 54 S 72 8W
Tambohorano, Madag. 105 B7 17 30 S 43 58 E
Tambopata →, Peru 156 C4 13 21 S 69 36W
Tambora, Indonesia 72 C1 8 12 S 118 5 E
Tamboritha, Mt., Australia 117 D7 37 31 S 146 40 E
Tambov, Russia 52 D5 52 45N 41 28 E
Tambre →, Spain 36 C2 42 49N 8 53W
Tambuku, Indonesia 75 D4 7 8 S 113 40 E
Tambun Sigumbal, Phil. 71 H3 6 5N 121 47 E
Tamburâ, Sudan 95 F2 5 40N 27 25 E
Tambuyukan, Gunong, Malaysia 75 A5 6 13N 116 39 E
Tâmchekket, Mauritania 100 B2 17 25N 10 40W
Tamdybulak, Uzbekistan 55 C2 41 46N 64 36 E
Tame, Colombia 152 B3 6 28N 71 44W
Tamega →, Portugal 36 D2 41 5N 8 21W
Tamelelt, Morocco 98 B3 31 50N 7 32W
Tamenglong, India 78 C4 25 0N 93 35 E
Tamerlanovka, Kazakstan 55 B4 42 36N 69 17 E
Tamerza, Tunisia 96 B1 34 23N 7 58 E
Tamiahua, L. de, Mexico 147 C5 21 30N 97 30W
Tamil Nadu □, India 83 J3 11 0N 77 0 E
Tamines, Belgium 21 H5 50 26N 4 36 E
Tamis →, Serbia, Yug. 46 E1 44 51N 20 39 E
Tamluk, India 81 H12 22 18N 87 58 E
Tammerfors = Tampere, Finland 13 F20 61 30N 23 50 E
Tammisaari, Finland 13 F20 60 0N 23 26 E
Tamo Abu, Pegunungan, Malaysia 75 B5 3 10N 115 5 E
Tampa, U.S.A. 135 M4 27 57N 82 27W
Tampa B., U.S.A. 135 M4 27 50N 82 30W
Tampere, Finland 13 F20 61 30N 23 50 E
Tampico, Mexico 147 C5 22 20N 97 50W
Tampico, U.S.A. 140 C7 41 38N 89 47W
Tampin, Malaysia 77 L4 2 28N 102 13 E
Tamrah, Si. Arabia 86 B4 20 24N 45 25 E
Tamri, Morocco 98 B3 30 49N 9 50W
Tamrida = Qādib, Yemen 87 D6 12 37N 53 57 E
Tamsweg, Austria 30 D6 47 7N 13 49 E
Tamuja →, Spain 37 F4 39 38N 6 29W
Tamworth, Australia 117 A9 31 7 S 150 58 E
Tamworth, U.K. 17 E6 52 39N 1 41W
Tamyang, S. Korea 67 G14 35 19N 126 59 E
Tan An, Vietnam 77 G6 10 32N 106 25 E
Tan-tan, Morocco 98 C2 28 29N 11 1W
Tana →, Kenya 106 C5 2 32 S 40 31 E
Tana →, Norway 12 A23 70 30N 28 14 E
Tana, L., Ethiopia 95 E4 13 5N 37 30 E
Tana River, Kenya 106 C4 2 0 S 39 30 E
Tanabe, Japan 63 D7 33 44N 135 22 E
Tanabi, Brazil 155 F2 20 37 S 49 37W
Tanafjorden, Norway 12 A23 70 45N 28 25 E
Tanaga, Pta., Canary Is. 33 G1 27 42N 18 10W
Tanagro →, Italy 41 B8 40 38N 15 14 E
Tanah Merah, Malaysia 74 A2 5 48N 102 9 E
Tanahbala, Indonesia 74 C1 0 30 S 98 30 E
Tanahgrogot, Indonesia 75 C5 1 55 S 116 15 E
Tanahjampea, Indonesia 72 C2 7 10 S 120 35 E
Tanahmasa, Indonesia 74 C1 0 12 S 98 39 E
Tanahmerah, Indonesia 73 C6 6 5 S 140 16 E
Tanakura, Japan 61 F10 37 10N 140 20 E
Tanami, Australia 112 C4 19 59 S 129 43 E
Tanami Desert, Australia 112 C5 18 50 S 132 0 E
Tanana, U.S.A. 126 B4 65 10N 152 4W
Tanana →, U.S.A. 126 B4 65 10N 151 58W
Tananarive = Antananarivo, Madag. 105 B8 18 55 S 47 31 E
Tanannt, Morocco 98 B3 31 54N 6 56W
Tánaro →, Italy 38 C5 44 55N 8 40 E
Tanauan, Batangas, Phil. 70 D3 14 5N 121 10 E
Tanauan, Leyte, Phil. 71 F5 11 7N 125 1 E
Tanaunella, Italy 40 B2 40 42N 9 45 E
Tanay, Phil. 70 D3 14 30N 121 17 E

Tiveden, *Sweden* **15 F8** 58 50N 14 30 E
Tiverton, *U.K.* **17 G4** 50 54N 3 29W
Tívoli, *Italy* **39 G9** 41 58N 12 45 E
Tiwī, *Oman* **87 B7** 22 45N 59 12 E
Tiyo, *Eritrea* **95 E5** 14 41N 40 15 E
Tizga, *Morocco* **98 B3** 32 1N 5 9W
Ti'zi N'Isli, *Morocco* **98 B3** 32 28N 5 47W
Tizi-Ouzou, *Algeria* **99 A5** 36 42N 4 3 E
Tizimín, *Mexico* **147 C7** 21 0N 88 1W
Tiznados →, *Venezuela* **152 B4** 8 16N 67 47W
Tiznit, *Morocco* **98 C3** 29 48N 9 45W
Tjeggelvas, *Sweden* **12 C17** 66 37N 17 45 E
Tjeukemeer, *Neths.* **20 C7** 52 53N 5 48 E
Tjirebon = Cirebon, *Indonesia* **75 D3** 6 45 S 108 32 E
Tjøme, *Norway* **14 E4** 59 8N 10 26 E
Tjonger Kanaal, *Neths.* **20 C7** 52 52N 5 52 E
Tjörn, *Sweden* **15 G5** 58 0N 11 35 E
Tkibuli = Tqibuli, *Georgia* **53 J6** 42 26N 43 0 E
Tkvarcheli = Tqvarcheli, *Georgia* **53 J5** 42 47N 41 42 E
Tlacotalpan, *Mexico* **147 D5** 18 37N 95 40W
Tlahualilo, *Mexico* **146 B4** 26 20N 103 30W
Tlaquepaque, *Mexico* **146 C4** 20 39N 103 19W
Tlaxcala, *Mexico* **147 D5** 19 20N 98 14W
Tlaxcala □, *Mexico* **147 D5** 19 30N 98 20W
Tlaxiaco, *Mexico* **147 D5** 17 18N 97 40W
Tlell, *Canada* **130 C2** 53 34N 131 56W
Tlemcen, *Algeria* **99 B4** 34 52N 1 21W
Tleta Sidi Bouguedra, *Morocco* **98 B3** 32 16N 9 59W
Tłuszcz, *Poland* **47 C8** 52 25N 21 25 E
Tlyarata, *Russia* **53 J8** 42 9N 46 26 E
Tmassah, *Libya* **96 C3** 26 19N 15 51 E
Tnine d'Anglou, *Morocco* **98 C3** 29 50N 9 50W
To Bong, *Vietnam* **76 F7** 12 45N 109 16 E
To-Shima, *Japan* **63 C11** 34 31N 139 17 E
Toad →, *Canada* **130 B4** 59 25N 124 57W
Toamasina, *Madag.* **105 B8** 18 10 S 49 25 E
Toamasina □, *Madag.* **105 B8** 18 0 S 49 0 E
Toay, *Argentina* **158 D3** 36 43 S 64 38W
Toba, *Japan* **63 C8** 34 30N 136 51 E
Toba Kakar, *Pakistan* **79 C3** 31 30N 69 0 E
Toba Tek Singh, *Pakistan* **80 D5** 30 55N 72 25 E
Tobago, *W. Indies* **149 D7** 11 10N 60 30W
Tobarra, *Spain* **35 G3** 38 37N 1 44W
Tobelo, *Indonesia* **72 A3** 1 45N 127 56 E
Tobermorey, *Australia* **114 C2** 22 12 S 138 0 E
Tobermory, *Canada* **128 C3** 45 12N 81 40W
Tobermory, *U.K.* **18 E2** 56 38N 6 5W
Tobin, *U.S.A.* **144 F5** 39 55N 121 19W
Tobin, L., *Australia* **112 D4** 21 45 S 125 49 E
Tobin L., *Canada* **131 C8** 53 35N 103 30W
Toblach = Dobbiaco, *Italy* **39 B9** 46 44N 12 14 E
Toboali, *Indonesia* **74 C3** 3 0 S 106 25 E
Tobol, *Kazakstan* **54 E9** 52 40N 62 39 E
Tobol →, *Russia* **56 D7** 58 10N 68 12 E
Toboli, *Indonesia* **72 B2** 0 38 S 120 5 E
Tobolsk, *Russia* **56 D7** 58 15N 68 10 E
Toboso, *Phil.* **71 F4** 10 43N 123 31 E
Tobruk = Tubruq, *Libya* **96 B4** 32 7N 23 55 E
Tobyhanna, *U.S.A.* **137 E9** 41 11N 75 25W
Tobyl = Tobol →, *Russia* **56 D7** 58 10N 68 12 E
Tocache Nuevo, *Peru* **156 B2** 8 9 S 76 26W
Tocantínia, *Brazil* **154 C2** 9 33 S 48 22W
Tocantinópolis, *Brazil* **154 C2** 6 20 S 47 25W
Tocantins □, *Brazil* **154 D2** 10 0 S 48 0W
Tocantins →, *Brazil* **154 B2** 1 45 S 49 10W
Toccoa, *U.S.A.* **135 H4** 34 35N 83 19W
Toce →, *Italy* **38 C5** 45 56N 8 29 E
Tochigi, *Japan* **63 A11** 36 25N 139 45 E
Tochigi □, *Japan* **63 A11** 36 45N 139 45 E
Tocina, *Spain* **37 H5** 37 37N 5 44W
Tocopilla, *Chile* **158 A1** 22 5 S 70 10W
Tocumwal, *Australia* **117 C6** 35 51 S 145 31 E
Tocuyo →, *Venezuela* **152 A4** 11 3N 68 23W
Tocuyo de la Costa, *Venezuela* **152 A4** 11 2N 68 23W
Todd →, *Australia* **114 C2** 24 52 S 135 48 E
Todeli, *Indonesia* **72 B2** 1 38 S 124 34 E
Todenyang, *Kenya* **106 B4** 4 35N 35 56 E
Todi, *Italy* **39 F9** 42 47N 12 24 E
Tödi, *Switz.* **29 C7** 46 48N 8 55 E
Todos os Santos, B. de, *Brazil* **155 D4** 12 48 S 38 38W
Todos Santos, *Mexico* **146 C2** 23 27N 110 13W
Todtnau, *Germany* **27 H3** 47 49N 7 56 E
Toecé, *Burkina Faso* **101 C4** 11 50N 1 16W
Toetoes B., *N.Z.* **119 G3** 46 42 S 168 41 E
Tofield, *Canada* **130 C6** 53 25N 112 40W
Tofino, *Canada* **130 D3** 49 11N 125 55W
Töfsingdalens nationalpark, *Sweden* **14 B6** 62 15N 12 44 E
Toftlund, *Denmark* **15 J3** 55 11N 9 2 E
Tofua, *Tonga* **121 P13** 19 45 S 175 5W
Toga, *Vanuatu* **121 C4** 13 26 S 166 42 E
Tōgane, *Japan* **63 B12** 35 33N 140 22 E
Togba, *Mauritania* **100 B2** 17 26N 10 12W
Togbo, *C.A.R.* **102 A3** 6 0N 17 27 E
Toggenburg, *Switz.* **29 B8** 47 16N 9 9 E
Togian, Kepulauan, *Indonesia* **72 B2** 0 20 S 121 50 E
Togliatti, *Russia* **52 D9** 53 32N 49 24 E
Togo ■, *W. Afr.* **101 D5** 8 30N 1 35 E
Togtoh, *China* **66 D6** 40 15N 111 10 E
Toguzak →, *Kazakstan* **54 D9** 54 3N 62 44 E
Tohma →, *Turkey* **88 C7** 38 29N 38 23 E
Tōhoku □, *Japan* **60 E10** 39 50N 141 45 E
Toi, *Japan* **63 C10** 34 54N 138 47 E
Toinya, *Sudan* **95 F2** 6 17N 29 46 E
Tojikiston = Tajikistan ■, *Asia* **55 D5** 38 30N 70 0 E
Tojo, *Indonesia* **72 B2** 1 20 S 121 15 E
Tōjō, *Japan* **62 C5** 34 53N 133 16 E
Tok →, *Russia* **54 E4** 52 46N 52 22 E
Toka, *Guyana* **153 C6** 3 58N 59 17W
Tokaanu, *N.Z.* **118 E4** 38 58 S 175 46 E
Tokachi-Dake, *Japan* **60 C11** 43 17N 142 5 E
Tokachi-Gawa →, *Japan* **60 C11** 42 44N 143 42 E
Tokai, *Japan* **63 B8** 35 2N 136 55 E
Tokaj, *Hungary* **31 C14** 48 8N 21 27 E
Tokala, *Indonesia* **72 B2** 1 30 S 121 40 E
Tōkamachi, *Japan* **61 F9** 37 8N 138 43 E
Tokanui, *N.Z.* **119 G3** 46 34 S 168 56 E
Tokar, *Sudan* **94 D4** 18 27N 37 56 E
Tokara-Rettō, *Japan* **61 K4** 29 37N 129 43 E
Tokarahi, *N.Z.* **119 E5** 44 56 S 170 39 E
Tokashiki-Shima, *Japan* **61 L3** 26 11N 127 21 E
Tokat, *Turkey* **88 B7** 40 22N 36 35 E
Tŏkchŏn, *N. Korea* **67 E14** 39 45N 126 18 E
Tokeland, *U.S.A.* **144 D3** 46 42N 123 59W
Tokelau Is., *Pac. Oc.* **122 H10** 9 0 S 171 45W
Toki, *Japan* **63 B9** 35 18N 137 8 E
Tokmak, *Kyrgyzstan* **55 B7** 42 49N 75 15 E
Tokmak, *Ukraine* **51 J8** 47 16N 35 42 E
Toko Ra., *Australia* **114 C2** 23 5 S 138 20 E
Tokomaru Bay, *N.Z.* **118 E7** 38 8 S 178 22 E
Tokoname, *Japan* **63 C8** 34 53N 136 51 E
Tokoro-Gawa →, *Japan* **60 B12** 44 7N 144 5 E
Tokoroa, *N.Z.* **118 E4** 38 13 S 175 50 E
Tokorozawa, *Japan* **63 B11** 35 47N 139 28 E
Toktogul, *Kyrgyzstan* **55 C6** 41 50N 72 50 E
Toku, *Tonga* **121 P13** 18 10 S 174 11W
Tokuji, *Japan* **62 C3** 34 11N 131 42 E
Tokuno-Shima, *Japan* **61 L4** 27 56N 128 55 E
Tokushima, *Japan* **62 C6** 34 4N 134 34 E
Tokushima □, *Japan* **62 D6** 33 55N 134 0 E
Tokuyama, *Japan* **62 C3** 34 3N 131 50 E
Tōkyō, *Japan* **63 B11** 35 45N 139 45 E
Tōkyō □, *Japan* **63 B11** 35 40N 139 30 E
Tōkyō-Wan, *Japan* **63 B11** 35 25N 139 47 E
Tokzār, *Afghan.* **79 B2** 35 52N 66 26 E
Tolaga Bay, *N.Z.* **118 E7** 38 21 S 178 20 E
Tolbukhin = Dobrich, *Bulgaria* **43 D12** 43 37N 27 49 E
Toledo, *Phil.* **71 F4** 10 23N 123 38 E
Toledo, *Spain* **36 F6** 39 50N 4 2W
Toledo, *Ill., U.S.A.* **141 E8** 39 16N 88 15W
Toledo, *Iowa, U.S.A.* **140 B4** 42 0N 92 35W
Toledo, *Ohio, U.S.A.* **141 C13** 41 39N 83 33W
Toledo, *Oreg., U.S.A.* **142 D2** 44 37N 123 56W
Toledo, *Wash., U.S.A.* **142 C2** 46 26N 122 51W
Toledo, Montes de, *Spain* **37 F6** 39 33N 4 20W
Tolentino, *Italy* **39 E10** 43 12N 13 17 E
Tolga, *Algeria* **99 B6** 34 40N 5 22 E
Tolga, *Norway* **14 B5** 62 26N 11 1 E
Toliara, *Madag.* **105 C7** 23 21 S 43 40 E
Toliara □, *Madag.* **105 C8** 21 0 S 45 0 E
Tolima, *Colombia* **152 C2** 4 40N 75 19W
Tolima □, *Colombia* **152 C2** 3 45N 75 15W
Tolitoli, *Indonesia* **72 A2** 1 5N 120 50 E
Tolkamer, *Neths.* **20 E8** 51 52N 6 6 E
Tolkmicko, *Poland* **47 A6** 54 19N 19 31 E
Tollhouse, *U.S.A.* **144 H7** 37 1N 119 24W
Tolmachevo, *Russia* **50 C5** 58 56N 29 51 E
Tolmezzo, *Italy* **39 B10** 46 24N 13 1 E
Tolmin, *Slovenia* **39 B10** 46 11N 13 45 E
Tolna, *Hungary* **31 E11** 46 25N 18 48 E
Tolna □, *Hungary* **31 E11** 46 30N 18 30 E
Tolo, *Zaïre* **102 C3** 2 55 S 18 34 E
Tolo, Teluk, *Indonesia* **72 B2** 2 20 S 122 10 E
Tolochin = Talachyn, *Belarus* **50 E5** 54 25N 29 42 E
Tolong Bay, *Phil.* **71 G4** 9 20N 122 49 E
Tolono, *U.S.A.* **141 E8** 39 59N 88 16W
Tolosa, *Spain* **34 B2** 43 8N 2 5W
Tolox, *Spain* **37 J6** 36 41N 4 54W
Toltén, *Chile* **160 A2** 39 13 S 74 14W
Toluca, *Mexico* **147 D5** 19 20N 99 40W
Tolybay, *Kazakstan* **54 F9** 50 31N 62 19 E
Tom Burke, *S. Africa* **105 C4** 23 5 S 28 0 E
Tom Price, *Australia* **112 D2** 22 40 S 117 48 E
Tomah, *U.S.A.* **138 D9** 43 59N 90 30W
Tomahawk, *U.S.A.* **138 C10** 45 28N 89 44W
Tomakomai, *Japan* **60 C10** 42 38N 141 36 E
Tomales, *U.S.A.* **144 G4** 38 15N 122 53W
Tomales B., *U.S.A.* **144 G3** 38 15N 123 58W
Tomanlivi, *Fiji* **121 A2** 17 37 S 178 1 E
Tomar, *Portugal* **37 F2** 39 36N 8 25W
Tómaros Óros, *Greece* **44 E2** 39 29N 20 48 E
Tomarza, *Turkey* **88 C6** 38 27N 35 48 E
Tomás Barrón, *Bolivia* **156 D4** 17 35 S 67 31W
Tomaszów Mazowiecki, *Poland* **47 D6** 51 30N 19 57 E
Tomatlán, *Mexico* **146 D3** 19 56N 105 15W
Tombador, Serra do, *Brazil* **157 C6** 12 0 S 58 0W
Tombé, *Sudan* **95 F3** 5 53N 31 40 E
Tombigbee →, *U.S.A.* **135 K2** 31 8N 87 57W
Tombôco, *Angola* **103 D2** 6 48 S 13 18 E
Tombouctou, *Mali* **100 B4** 16 50N 3 0W
Tombstone, *U.S.A.* **143 L8** 31 43N 110 4W
Tombua, *Angola* **103 F2** 15 55 S 11 55 E
Tomé, *Chile* **158 D1** 36 36 S 72 57W
Tomé-Açu, *Brazil* **154 B2** 2 25 S 48 9W
Tomelilla, *Sweden* **15 J7** 55 33N 13 58 E
Tomelloso, *Spain* **35 F1** 39 10N 3 2W
Tomingley, *Australia* **117 B8** 32 26 S 148 16 E
Tomini, *Indonesia* **72 A2** 0 30N 120 30 E
Tomini, Teluk, *Indonesia* **72 B2** 0 10 S 122 0 E
Tominian, *Mali* **100 C4** 13 17N 4 35W
Tomiño, *Spain* **36 D2** 41 59N 8 46W
Tomkinson Ras., *Australia* **113 E4** 26 11 S 129 5 E
Tommot, *Russia* **57 D13** 59 4N 126 20 E
Tomnavoulin, *U.K.* **18 D5** 57 19N 3 19W
Tomnop Ta Suos, *Cambodia* **77 G5** 11 20N 104 15 E
Tomo, *Colombia* **152 C4** 2 38N 67 32W
Tomo, *Japan* **62 C5** 34 23N 133 23 E
Tomo →, *Colombia* **152 B4** 5 20N 67 48W
Tomobe, *Japan* **63 A12** 36 20N 140 20 E
Tomorit, *Albania* **44 D2** 40 42N 20 11 E
Toms Place, *U.S.A.* **144 H8** 37 34N 118 41W
Toms River, *U.S.A.* **137 G10** 39 58N 74 12W
Tomsk, *Russia* **56 D9** 56 30N 85 5 E
Tonalá, *Mexico* **147 D6** 16 8N 93 41W
Tonale, Passo del, *Italy* **38 B7** 46 15N 10 35 E
Tonalea, *U.S.A.* **143 H8** 36 19N 110 56W
Tonami, *Japan* **63 A8** 36 40N 136 58 E
Tonantins, *Brazil* **152 D4** 2 45 S 67 45W
Tonasket, *U.S.A.* **142 B4** 48 42N 119 26W
Tonate, *Fr. Guiana* **153 C7** 5 0N 52 28W
Tonawanda, *U.S.A.* **136 D6** 43 1N 78 53W
Tonbridge, *U.K.* **17 F8** 51 11N 0 17 E
Tondano, *Indonesia* **72 A2** 1 35N 124 54 E
Tondela, *Portugal* **36 E2** 40 31N 8 5W
Tønder, *Denmark* **15 K2** 54 58N 8 50 E
Tondi, *India* **83 K4** 9 45N 79 4 E
Tondi Kiwindi, *Niger* **101 C5** 14 28N 2 2 E
Tondibi, *Mali* **101 B4** 16 39N 0 14W
Tonekābon, *Iran* **85 B6** 36 45N 51 12 E
Tong Xian, *China* **66 E9** 39 55N 116 35 E
Tonga ■, *Pac. Oc.* **121 P13** 19 50 S 174 30W
Tonga Trench, *Pac. Oc.* **122 J10** 18 0 S 173 0W
Tongaat, *S. Africa* **105 D5** 29 33 S 31 9 E
Tongala, *Australia* **117 D6** 36 14 S 144 56 E
Tong'an, *China* **69 E12** 24 37N 118 8 E
Tongareva, *Cook Is.* **123 H12** 9 0 S 158 0W
Tongatapu, *Tonga* **121 Q14** 21 10 S 174 0W
Tongatapu Group, *Tonga* **121 Q13** 21 0 S 175 0W
Tongbai, *China* **69 A9** 32 20N 113 23 E
Tongcheng, *Anhui, China* **69 B11** 31 4N 116 56 E
Tongcheng, *Hubei, China* **69 C9** 29 15N 113 50 E
Tongchŏn-ni, *N. Korea* **67 E14** 39 50N 127 25 E
Tongchuan, *China* **66 G5** 35 6N 109 3 E
Tongdao, *China* **68 D7** 26 10N 109 42 E
Tongeren, *Belgium* **21 G6** 50 47N 5 28 E
Tonggu, *China* **69 C10** 28 31N 114 20 E
Tongguan, *China* **66 G6** 34 40N 110 25 E
Tonghai, *China* **68 E4** 24 10N 102 53 E
Tonghua, *China* **67 D13** 41 42N 125 58 E
Tongjiang, *China* **68 B6** 31 58N 107 11 E
Tongjosŏn Man, *N. Korea* **67 E14** 39 30N 128 0 E
Tongking, G. of = Tonkin, G. of, *Asia* **64 E5** 20 0N 108 0 E
Tongliang, *China* **68 C6** 29 50N 106 3 E
Tongliao, *China* **67 C12** 43 38N 122 18 E
Tongling, *China* **69 B11** 30 55N 117 48 E
Tonglu, *China* **69 C12** 29 45N 119 37 E
Tongnae, *S. Korea* **67 G15** 35 12N 129 5 E
Tongnan, *China* **68 B5** 30 9N 105 50 E
Tongoa, *Vanuatu* **121 F6** 16 54 S 168 34 E
Tongobory, *Madag.* **105 C7** 23 32 S 44 20 E
Tongoy, *Chile* **158 C1** 30 16 S 71 31W
Tongren, *China* **68 D7** 27 43N 109 11 E
Tongres = Tongeren, *Belgium* **21 G6** 50 47N 5 28 E
Tongsa Dzong, *Bhutan* **78 B3** 27 31N 90 31 E
Tongue, *U.K.* **18 C4** 58 29N 4 25W
Tongue →, *U.S.A.* **138 B2** 46 25N 105 52W
Tongwei, *China* **66 G3** 35 0N 105 5 E
Tongxin, *China* **66 F3** 36 59N 105 58 E
Tongyang, *N. Korea* **67 E14** 39 9N 126 53 E
Tongyu, *China* **67 B12** 44 45N 123 4 E
Tongzi, *China* **68 C6** 28 9N 106 49 E
Tonica, *U.S.A.* **140 C7** 41 13N 89 4W
Tonj, *Sudan* **95 F2** 7 20N 28 44 E
Tonk, *India* **80 F6** 26 6N 75 54 E
Tonkawa, *U.S.A.* **139 G6** 36 41N 97 18W
Tonkin = Bac Phan, *Vietnam* **76 B5** 22 0N 105 0 E
Tonkin, G. of, *Asia* **64 E5** 20 0N 108 0 E
Tonlé Sap, *Cambodia* **76 F4** 13 0N 104 0 E
Tonnay-Charente, *France* **24 C3** 45 56N 0 55W
Tonneins, *France* **24 D4** 44 23N 0 19 E
Tonnerre, *France* **23 E10** 47 51N 3 59 E
Tönning, *Germany* **26 A4** 54 19N 8 56 E
Tono, *Japan* **60 E10** 39 19N 141 32 E
Tonopah, *U.S.A.* **143 G5** 38 4N 117 14W
Tonoshō, *Japan* **62 C6** 34 29N 134 11 E
Tonosí, *Panama* **148 E3** 7 20N 80 20W
Tønsberg, *Norway* **14 E4** 59 19N 10 25 E
Tonumea, *Tonga* **121 Q13** 20 30 S 174 30W
Tonya, *Turkey* **89 B8** 40 53N 39 16 E
Tonzang, *Burma* **78 D4** 23 36N 93 42 E
Tonzi, *Burma* **78 C5** 24 39N 94 57 E
Tooele, *U.S.A.* **142 F7** 40 32N 112 18W
Toolondo, *Australia* **116 D4** 36 58 S 141 58 E
Toompine, *Australia* **115 D3** 27 15 S 144 19 E
Toongi, *Australia* **117 B8** 32 28 S 148 30 E
Toonpan, *Australia* **114 B4** 19 28 S 146 48 E
Toora, *Australia* **117 E7** 38 39 S 146 23 E
Toora-Khem, *Russia* **57 D10** 52 28N 96 17 E
Toowoomba, *Australia* **115 D5** 27 32 S 151 56 E
Top-ozero, *Russia* **48 A5** 65 35N 32 0 E
Topalu, *Romania* **46 E9** 44 31N 28 3 E
Topaz, *U.S.A.* **144 G7** 38 41N 119 30W
Topeka, *U.S.A.* **138 F7** 39 3N 95 40W
Topki, *Russia* **56 D9** 55 20N 85 35 E
Topl'a →, *Slovak Rep.* **31 C14** 48 45N 21 45 E
Topley, *Canada* **130 C3** 54 49N 126 18W
Toplica →, *Serbia, Yug.* **42 D6** 43 15N 21 49 E
Toplița, *Romania* **46 C6** 46 55N 25 20 E
Topocalma, Pta., *Chile* **158 C1** 34 10 S 72 2W
Topock, *U.S.A.* **145 L12** 34 46N 114 29W
Topola, *Serbia, Yug.* **42 C5** 44 17N 20 41 E
Topolčane, *Macedonia* **42 F6** 41 14N 21 56 E
Topol'čany, *Slovak Rep.* **31 C11** 48 35N 18 12 E
Topolnitsa →, *Bulgaria* **43 E9** 42 11N 24 18 E
Topolobampo, *Mexico* **146 B3** 25 40N 109 4W
Topolovgrad, *Bulgaria* **43 E11** 42 5N 26 20 E
Topolvătu Mare, *Romania* **42 B6** 45 46N 21 41 E
Toppenish, *U.S.A.* **142 C3** 46 23N 120 19W
Topusko, *Croatia* **39 C12** 45 18N 15 59 E
Toquepala, *Peru* **156 D3** 17 24 S 70 25W
Torá, *Spain* **34 D6** 41 49N 1 25 E
Tora Kit, *Sudan* **95 E3** 11 2N 32 36 E
Toraka Vestale, *Madag.* **105 B7** 16 20 S 43 58 E
Torata, *Peru* **156 D3** 17 23 S 70 1W
Torbalı, *Turkey* **88 C2** 38 10N 27 21 E
Torbay, *Canada* **129 C9** 47 40N 52 42W
Torbay, *U.K.* **17 G4** 50 26N 3 31W
Tørdal, *Norway* **14 E2** 59 10N 8 45 E
Tordesillas, *Spain* **36 D6** 41 30N 5 0W
Tordoya, *Spain* **36 B2** 43 6N 8 36W
Töreboda, *Sweden* **15 F8** 58 41N 14 7 E
Torfaen □, *U.K.* **17 F4** 51 43N 3 3W
Torgau, *Germany* **26 D8** 51 34N 13 0 E
Torgelow, *Germany* **26 B9** 53 37N 13 59 E
Torhout, *Belgium* **21 F2** 51 5N 3 7 E
Tori, *Ethiopia* **95 F3** 7 53N 33 35 E
Tori-Shima, *Japan* **61 J10** 30 29N 140 19 E
Torigni-sur-Vire, *France* **22 C6** 49 3N 0 58W
Torija, *Spain* **34 E1** 40 44N 3 2W
Torin, *Mexico* **146 B2** 27 33N 110 15W
Toriñana, C., *Spain* **36 B1** 43 3N 9 17W
Torino, *Italy* **38 C4** 45 3N 7 40 E
Torit, *Sudan* **95 G3** 4 27N 32 31 E
Torkamān, *Iran* **89 D12** 37 35N 47 23 E
Torkovichi, *Russia* **50 C6** 58 51N 30 21 E
Tormac, *Romania* **42 B6** 45 30N 21 30 E
Tormes →, *Spain* **36 D4** 41 18N 6 29W
Tornado Mt., *Canada* **130 D6** 49 55N 114 40W
Tornala, *Slovak Rep.* **31 C13** 48 25N 20 20 E
Torne älv →, *Sweden* **12 D21** 65 50N 24 12 E
Torneå = Tornio, *Finland* **12 D21** 65 50N 24 12 E
Torneträsk, *Sweden* **12 B18** 68 24N 19 15 E
Tornio, *Finland* **12 D21** 65 50N 24 12 E
Tornionjoki →, *Finland* **12 D21** 65 50N 24 12 E
Tornquist, *Argentina* **158 D3** 38 8 S 62 15W
Toro, *Baleares, Spain* **33 B11** 39 59N 4 8 E
Toro, *Zamora, Spain* **36 D5** 41 35N 5 24W
Torö, *Sweden* **15 F11** 58 48N 17 50 E
Toro, Cerro del, *Chile* **158 B2** 29 10 S 69 50W
Toro Pk., *U.S.A.* **145 M10** 33 34N 116 24W
Törökszentmiklós, *Hungary* **31 D13** 47 11N 20 27 E
Toroníios Kólpos, *Greece* **44 D5** 40 5N 23 30 E
Toronto, *Australia* **117 B9** 33 0 S 151 30 E
Toronto, *Canada* **128 D4** 43 39N 79 20W
Toronto, *U.S.A.* **136 F4** 40 28N 80 36W
Toropets, *Russia* **50 D6** 56 30N 31 40 E
Tororo, *Uganda* **106 B3** 0 45N 34 12 E
Toros Dağları, *Turkey* **88 D5** 37 0N 32 30 E
Torotoro, *Bolivia* **157 D4** 18 7 S 65 46W
Torpshammar, *Sweden* **14 B10** 62 29N 16 20 E
Torquay, *Australia* **116 E6** 38 20 S 144 19 E
Torquay, *Canada* **131 D8** 49 9N 103 30W
Torquay, *U.K.* **17 G4** 50 27N 3 32W
Torquemada, *Spain* **36 C6** 42 2N 4 19W
Torralba de Calatrava, *Spain* **37 F7** 39 1N 3 44W
Torrance, *U.S.A.* **145 M8** 33 50N 118 19W
Torrão, *Portugal* **37 G2** 38 16N 8 11W
Torre Annunziata, *Italy* **41 B7** 40 45N 14 27 E
Tôrre de Moncorvo, *Portugal* **36 D3** 41 12N 7 8W
Torre del Greco, *Italy* **41 B7** 40 47N 14 22 E
Torre del Mar, *Spain* **37 J6** 36 44N 4 6W
Torre-Pacheco, *Spain* **35 H4** 37 44N 0 57W
Torre Péllice, *Italy* **38 D4** 44 49N 7 13 E
Torreblanca, *Spain* **34 E5** 40 14N 0 12 E
Torrecampo, *Spain* **37 G6** 38 29N 4 41W
Torrecilla en Cameros, *Spain* **34 C2** 42 15N 2 38W
Torredembarra, *Spain* **34 D6** 41 9N 1 24 E
Torredonjimeno, *Spain* **37 H7** 37 46N 3 57W
Torrejoncillo, *Spain* **36 F4** 39 54N 6 28W
Torrelaguna, *Spain* **34 E1** 40 50N 3 38W
Torrelavega, *Spain* **36 B6** 43 20N 4 5W
Torremaggiore, *Italy* **41 A8** 41 41N 15 17 E
Torremolinos, *Spain* **37 J6** 36 38N 4 30W
Torrens, L., *Australia* **116 A2** 31 0 S 137 50 E
Torrens Cr. →, *Australia* **114 C4** 22 23 S 145 9 E
Torrens Creek, *Australia* **114 C4** 20 48 S 145 3 E
Torrente, *Spain* **35 F4** 39 27N 0 28W
Torrenueva, *Spain* **35 G1** 38 38N 3 22W
Torreón, *Mexico* **146 B4** 25 33N 103 26W
Torreperogil, *Spain* **35 G1** 38 2N 3 17W
Torres, *Mexico* **146 B2** 28 46N 110 47W
Torres, Is., *Vanuatu* **121 C4** 13 15 S 166 37 E
Torres Novas, *Portugal* **37 F2** 39 27N 8 33W
Torres Strait, *Australia* **120 E2** 9 50 S 142 20 E
Torres Vedras, *Portugal* **37 F1** 39 5N 9 15W
Torrevieja, *Spain* **35 H4** 37 59N 0 42W
Torrey, *U.S.A.* **143 G8** 38 18N 111 25W
Torridge →, *U.K.* **17 G3** 51 0N 4 13W
Torridon, L., *U.K.* **18 D3** 57 35N 5 50W
Torrijos, *Phil.* **70 E4** 13 19N 122 5 E
Torrijos, *Spain* **36 F6** 39 59N 4 18W
Torrington, *Conn., U.S.A.* **137 E11** 41 48N 73 7W
Torrington, *Wyo., U.S.A.* **138 D2** 42 4N 104 11W
Torroella de Montgrí, *Spain* **34 C8** 42 2N 3 8 E
Torrox, *Spain* **37 J7** 36 46N 3 57W
Tórshavn, *Færoe Is.* **12 E9** 62 5N 6 56W
Torsö, *Sweden* **15 F7** 58 48N 13 45 E
Tortola, *Virgin Is.* **149 C7** 18 19N 64 45W
Tórtoles de Esgueva, *Spain* **36 D6** 41 49N 4 2W
Tortona, *Italy* **38 D5** 44 54N 8 52 E
Tortoreto, *Italy* **39 F10** 42 48N 13 55 E
Tortorici, *Italy* **41 D7** 38 2N 14 49 E
Tortosa, *Spain* **34 E5** 40 49N 0 31 E
Tortosa, C. de, *Spain* **34 E5** 40 41N 0 52 E
Tortosendo, *Portugal* **36 E3** 40 15N 7 31W
Tortue, I. de la, *Haiti* **149 B5** 20 5N 72 57W
Tortum, *Turkey* **89 B9** 40 19N 41 35 E
Ţorūd, *Iran* **85 C7** 35 25N 55 5 E
Torugart, Pereval = Turugart, Pereval, *Kyrgyzstan* **55 C7** 40 32N 75 24 E
Torul, *Turkey* **89 B8** 40 34N 39 18 E
Toruń, *Poland* **47 B5** 53 2N 18 39 E
Toruń □, *Poland* **47 B6** 53 20N 19 0 E
Torup, *Sweden* **15 H7** 56 57N 13 5 E
Tory I., *Ireland* **19 A3** 55 16N 8 14W
Torysa →, *Slovak Rep.* **31 C14** 48 39N 21 21 E
Torzhok, *Russia* **52 B2** 57 5N 34 55 E
Tosa, *Japan* **62 D5** 33 24N 133 23 E
Tosa-Shimizu, *Japan* **62 E4** 32 52N 132 58 E
Tosa-Wan, *Japan* **62 D5** 33 15N 133 30 E
Tosa-yamada, *Japan* **62 D5** 33 36N 133 38 E
Toscana □, *Italy* **38 E8** 43 25N 11 0 E
Toscano, Arcipelago, *Italy* **38 F7** 42 30N 10 30 E
Toshkent, *Uzbekistan* **55 C4** 41 20N 69 10 E
Tosno, *Russia* **50 C6** 59 38N 30 46 E
Tossa, *Spain* **34 D7** 41 43N 2 56 E
Tostado, *Argentina* **158 B3** 29 15 S 61 50W
Tostedt, *Germany* **26 B5** 53 17N 9 42 E
Tostón, Pta. de, *Canary Is.* **33 F5** 28 42N 14 2W
Tosu, *Japan* **62 D2** 33 22N 130 31 E
Tosya, *Turkey* **88 B6** 41 1N 34 2 E
Toszek, *Poland* **47 E5** 50 27N 18 32 E
Totana, *Spain* **35 H3** 37 45N 1 30W
Toten, *Norway* **14 D4** 60 40N 10 40 E
Toteng, *Botswana* **104 C3** 20 22 S 22 58 E
Tôtes, *France* **22 C8** 49 41N 1 3 E
Tótkomlós, *Hungary* **31 E13** 46 24N 20 45 E
Totma, *Russia* **48 C7** 60 0N 42 40 E
Totnes, *U.K.* **17 G4** 50 26N 3 42W
Totness, *Surinam* **153 B6** 5 53N 56 19W
Totonicapán, *Guatemala* **148 D1** 14 58N 91 12W
Totora, *Bolivia* **157 D4** 17 42 S 65 9W
Totoya, I., *Fiji* **121 B3** 18 57 S 179 50W
Totskoye, *Russia* **54 E4** 52 32N 52 45 E
Totten Glacier, *Antarctica* **7 C8** 66 45 S 116 10 E
Tottenham, *Australia* **117 B7** 32 14 S 147 21 E
Tottenham, *Canada* **136 B5** 44 1N 79 49W
Tottori, *Japan* **62 B6** 35 30N 134 15 E
Tottori □, *Japan* **62 B6** 35 30N 134 12 E
Touat, *Algeria* **99 C5** 27 27N 0 30 E
Touba, *Ivory C.* **100 D3** 8 22N 7 40W
Toubkal, Djebel, *Morocco* **98 B3** 31 0N 8 0W
Toucy, *France* **23 E10** 47 44N 3 15 E
Tougan, *Burkina Faso* **100 C4** 13 11N 2 58W
Touggourt, *Algeria* **99 B6** 33 6N 6 4 E
Tougué, *Guinea* **100 C2** 11 25N 11 50W
Touho, *N. Cal.* **121 T19** 20 47 S 165 14 E
Toukmatine, *Algeria* **99 D6** 24 49N 7 11 E
Toul, *France* **23 D12** 48 40N 5 53 E

Uzhgorod = Uzhhorod, *Ukraine* **51 H2** 48 36N 22 18 E
Uzhhorod, *Ukraine* **51 H2** 48 36N 22 18 E
Uzlovaya, *Russia* **52 D4** 54 0N 38 5 E
Uzun-Agach, *Kazakstan* **55 B8** 43 35N 76 20 E
Uzunköprü, *Turkey* **88 B2** 41 16N 26 43 E
Uzwil, *Switz.* **29 B8** 47 26N 9 9 E

V

Vaal →, *S. Africa* **104 D3** 29 4 S 23 38 E
Vaal Dam, *S. Africa* **105 D4** 27 0 S 28 14 E
Vaals, *Neths.* **21 G8** 50 46N 6 1 E
Vaalwater, *S. Africa* **105 C4** 24 15 S 28 8 E
Vaasa, *Finland* **12 E19** 63 6N 21 38 E
Vaassen, *Neths.* **20 D7** 52 17N 5 58 E
Vabre, *France* **24 E6** 43 42N 2 24 E
Vác, *Hungary* **31 D12** 47 49N 19 10 E
Vacaria, *Brazil* **159 B5** 28 31 S 50 52W
Vacaville, *U.S.A.* **144 G5** 38 21N 121 59W
Vaccarès, Étang de, *France* **25 E8** 43 32N 4 34 E
Vach → = Vakh →, *Russia* **56 C8** 60 45N 76 45 E
Vache, Î.-à-, *Haiti* **149 C5** 18 2N 73 35W
Vadnagar, *India* **80 H5** 23 47N 72 40 E
Vado Lígure, *Italy* **38 D5** 44 17N 8 26 E
Vadodara, *India* **80 H5** 22 20N 73 10 E
Vadsø, *Norway* **12 A23** 70 3N 29 50 E
Vadstena, *Sweden* **15 F8** 58 28N 14 54 E
Vaduz, *Liech.* **29 B9** 47 8N 9 31 E
Værøy, *Norway* **12 C15** 67 40N 12 40 E
Vágar, *Færoe Is.* **12 E9** 62 5N 7 15W
Vagney, *France* **23 E13** 48 1N 6 43 E
Vagnhärad, *Sweden* **14 F11** 58 57N 17 33 E
Vagos, *Portugal* **36 E2** 40 33N 8 42W
Vågsfjorden, *Norway* **12 B17** 68 50N 16 50 E
Váh →, *Slovak Rep.* **31 D11** 47 43N 18 7 E
Vahsel B., *Antarctica* **7 D1** 75 0 S 35 0W
Váï, *Greece* **32 D8** 35 15N 26 18 E
Vaigach, *Russia* **56 B6** 70 10N 59 0 E
Vaigai →, *India* **83 K4** 9 15N 79 10 E
Vaiges, *France* **22 D6** 48 2N 0 30W
Vaihingen, *Germany* **27 G4** 48 54N 8 57 E
Vaijapur, *India* **82 E2** 19 58N 74 45 E
Vaikam, *India* **83 K3** 9 45N 76 25 E
Vailly-sur-Aisne, *France* **23 C10** 49 24N 3 31 E
Vaippar →, *India* **83 K4** 9 0N 78 25 E
Vaison-la-Romaine, *France* **25 D9** 44 14N 5 4 E
Vajpur, *India* **82 D1** 21 24N 73 17 E
Vakarel, *Bulgaria* **43 E8** 42 35N 23 40 E
Vakfikebir, *Turkey* **89 B8** 41 2N 39 17 E
Vakh →, *Russia* **56 C8** 60 45N 76 45 E
Vakhsh →, *Tajikistan* **55 E4** 37 6N 68 18 E
Vakhtan, *Russia* **52 B8** 57 53N 46 47 E
Vál, *Hungary* **31 D11** 47 22N 18 40 E
Val-de-Marne □, *France* **23 D9** 48 45N 2 28 E
Val-d'Oise □, *France* **23 C9** 49 5N 2 10 E
Val d'Or, *Canada* **128 C4** 48 7N 77 47W
Val Marie, *Canada* **131 D7** 49 15N 107 45W
Valaam, *Russia* **50 B6** 61 22N 30 57 E
Valadares, *Portugal* **36 D2** 41 5N 8 38W
Valahia, *Romania* **46 E5** 44 35N 25 0 E
Valais □, *Switz.* **28 D5** 46 12N 7 45 E
Valais, Alpes du, *Switz.* **28 D5** 46 5N 7 35 E
Valandovo, *Macedonia* **42 F7** 41 19N 22 34 E
Valašské Meziříčí, *Czech.* **31 B10** 49 29N 17 59 E
Valáxa, *Greece* **45 F6** 38 50N 24 29 E
Vâlcani, *Romania* **42 A5** 46 0N 20 26 E
Valcheta, *Argentina* **160 B3** 40 40 S 66 8W
Valdagno, *Italy* **39 C8** 45 39N 11 18 E
Valdahon, *France* **23 E13** 47 8N 6 21 E
Valday, *Russia* **52 B1** 57 58N 33 9 E
Valdayskaya Vozvyshennost, *Russia* **52 B1** 57 0N 33 30 E
Valdeazogues →, *Spain* **37 G6** 38 45N 4 55W
Valdemarsvik, *Sweden* **15 F10** 58 14N 16 40 E
Valdepeñas, *Ciudad Real, Spain* **37 G7** 38 43N 3 25W
Valdepeñas, *Jaén, Spain* **37 H7** 37 33N 3 47W
Valderaduey →, *Spain* **36 D5** 41 31N 5 42W
Valderrobres, *Spain* **34 E5** 40 53N 0 9 E
Valdés, Pen., *Argentina* **160 B4** 42 30 S 63 45W
Valdez, *Ecuador* **152 C2** 1 15N 79 0W
Valdez, *U.S.A.* **126 B5** 61 7N 146 16W
Valdivia, *Chile* **160 A2** 39 50 S 73 14W
Valdivia, *Colombia* **152 B2** 7 11N 75 27W
Valdivia □, *Chile* **160 B2** 40 0 S 73 0W
Valdobbiádene, *Italy* **39 C9** 45 17N 12 0 E
Valdosta, *U.S.A.* **135 K4** 30 50N 83 17W
Valdoviño, *Spain* **36 B2** 43 36N 8 8W
Valdres, *Norway* **14 D3** 61 5N 9 5 E
Vale, *Georgia* **53 K6** 41 30N 42 58 E
Vale, *U.S.A.* **142 E5** 43 59N 117 15W
Vale of Glamorgan □, *U.K.* **17 F4** 51 28N 3 25W
Valea lui Mihai, *Romania* **46 B3** 47 32N 22 11 E
Valença, *Brazil* **155 D4** 13 20 S 39 5W
Valença, *Portugal* **36 C2** 42 1N 8 34W
Valença do Piauí, *Brazil* **154 C3** 6 20 S 41 45W
Valençay, *France* **23 E8** 47 9N 1 34 E
Valence, *Drôme, France* **25 D8** 44 57N 4 54 E
Valence, *Tarn-et-Garonne, France* **24 D4** 44 6N 0 53 E
Valencia, *Phil.* **71 H5** 7 57N 125 3 E
Valencia, *Spain* **35 F4** 39 27N 0 23W
Valencia, *Venezuela* **152 A4** 10 11N 68 0W
Valencia □, *Spain* **35 F4** 39 20N 0 40W
Valencia, G. de, *Spain* **35 F5** 39 30N 0 20 E
Valencia de Alcántara, *Spain* **37 F3** 39 25N 7 14W
Valencia de Don Juan, *Spain* **36 C5** 42 17N 5 31W
Valencia del Ventoso, *Spain* **37 G4** 38 15N 6 29W
Valencia Harbour, *Ireland* **19 E1** 51 56N 10 19W
Valencia I., *Ireland* **19 E1** 51 54N 10 22W
Valenciennes, *France* **23 B10** 50 20N 3 34 E
Văleni, *Romania* **46 E5** 44 15N 24 45 E
Valensole, *France* **25 E9** 43 50N 5 59 E
Valentim, Sa. do, *Brazil* **154 C3** 6 0 S 43 30W
Valentin, *Russia* **60 C7** 43 8N 134 17 E
Valentine, *Nebr., U.S.A.* **138 D4** 42 52N 100 33W
Valentine, *Tex., U.S.A.* **139 K2** 30 35N 104 30W
Valenza, *Italy* **38 C5** 45 1N 8 38 E
Valera, *Venezuela* **152 B3** 9 19N 70 37W
Valga, *Estonia* **13 H22** 57 47N 26 2 E
Valguarnera Caropepe, *Italy* **41 E7** 37 30N 14 23 E
Valier, *U.S.A.* **142 B7** 48 18N 112 16W
Valinco, G. de, *France* **25 G12** 41 40N 8 52 E
Valjevo, *Serbia, Yug.* **42 C4** 44 18N 19 53 E
Valka, *Latvia* **13 H21** 57 42N 25 57 E
Valkeakoski, *Finland* **13 F20** 61 16N 24 2 E
Valkenburg, *Neths.* **21 G7** 50 52N 5 50 E
Valkenswaard, *Neths.* **21 F6** 51 21N 5 29 E
Vall de Uxó, *Spain* **34 F4** 39 49N 0 15W
Valla, *Sweden* **14 E10** 59 2N 16 20 E
Valladolid, *Mexico* **147 C7** 20 40N 88 11W
Valladolid, *Spain* **36 D6** 41 38N 4 43W
Valladolid □, *Spain* **36 D6** 41 38N 4 43W
Vallata, *Italy* **41 A8** 41 2N 15 15 E
Valldemosa, *Spain* **33 B9** 39 43N 2 37 E
Valle d'Aosta □, *Italy* **38 C4** 45 45N 7 15 E
Valle de Arán, *Spain* **34 C5** 42 50N 0 55 E
Valle de Cabuérniga, *Spain* **36 B6** 43 14N 4 18W
Valle de la Pascua, *Venezuela* **152 B4** 9 13N 66 0W
Valle de las Palmas, *Mexico* **145 N10** 32 20N 116 43W
Valle de Santiago, *Mexico* **146 C4** 20 25N 101 15W
Valle de Suchil, *Mexico* **146 C4** 23 38N 103 55W
Valle de Zaragoza, *Mexico* **146 B3** 27 28N 105 49W
Valle del Cauca □, *Colombia* **152 C2** 3 45N 76 30W
Valle Fértil, Sierra del, *Argentina* **158 C2** 30 20 S 68 0W
Valle Hermoso, *Mexico* **147 B5** 25 35N 97 40W
Vallecas, *Spain* **36 E7** 40 23N 3 41W
Valledupar, *Colombia* **152 A3** 10 29N 73 15W
Vallehermoso, *Canary Is.* **33 F2** 28 10N 17 15W
Vallejo, *U.S.A.* **144 G4** 38 7N 122 14W
Vallenar, *Chile* **158 B1** 28 30 S 70 50W
Valleraugue, *France* **24 D7** 44 6N 3 39 E
Vallet, *France* **22 E5** 47 10N 1 15W
Valletta, *Malta* **32 D2** 35 54N 14 31 E
Valley Center, *U.S.A.* **145 M9** 33 13N 117 2W
Valley City, *U.S.A.* **138 B6** 46 55N 98 0W
Valley Falls, *U.S.A.* **142 E3** 42 29N 120 17W
Valley Park, *U.S.A.* **140 F6** 38 33N 90 29W
Valley Springs, *U.S.A.* **144 G6** 38 12N 120 50W
Valley Station, *U.S.A.* **141 F11** 38 6N 85 52W
Valley Wells, *U.S.A.* **145 K11** 35 27N 115 46W
Valleyview, *Canada* **130 B5** 55 5N 117 17W
Valli di Comácchio, *Italy* **39 D9** 44 40N 12 15 E
Vallimanca, Arroyo, *Argentina* **158 D4** 35 40 S 59 10W
Vallo della Lucánia, *Italy* **41 B8** 40 14N 15 16 E
Vallon-Pont-d'Arc, *France* **25 D8** 44 24N 4 24 E
Vallorbe, *Switz.* **28 C2** 46 42N 6 20 E
Valls, *Spain* **34 D6** 41 18N 1 15 E
Vallsta, *Sweden* **14 C10** 61 31N 16 22 E
Valmaseda, *Spain* **34 B1** 43 11N 3 12W
Valmeyer, *U.S.A.* **140 F6** 38 18N 90 19W
Valmiera, *Latvia* **13 H21** 57 37N 25 29 E
Valmont, *France* **22 C7** 49 45N 0 30 E
Valmontone, *Italy* **40 A5** 41 46N 12 57 E
Valmy, *France* **23 C11** 49 5N 4 45 E
Valnera, Mte., *Spain* **34 B1** 43 9N 3 40W
Valognes, *France* **22 C5** 49 30N 1 28W
Valona = Vlóra, *Albania* **44 D1** 40 32N 19 28 E
Valongo, *Portugal* **36 D2** 41 8N 8 30W
Valozhyn, *Belarus* **50 E4** 54 3N 26 30 E
Valpaços, *Portugal* **36 D3** 41 36N 7 17W
Valparaíso, *Chile* **158 C1** 33 2 S 71 40W
Valparaíso, *Mexico* **146 C4** 22 50N 103 32W
Valparaiso, *U.S.A.* **141 C9** 41 28N 87 4W
Valparaíso □, *Chile* **158 C1** 33 2 S 71 40W
Valpovo, *Croatia* **42 B3** 45 39N 18 25 E
Valréas, *France* **25 D8** 44 24N 5 0 E
Vals, *Switz.* **29 C8** 46 39N 9 11 E
Vals →, *S. Africa* **104 D4** 27 23 S 26 30 E
Vals, Tanjung, *Indonesia* **73 C5** 8 26 S 137 25 E
Vals-les-Bains, *France* **25 D8** 44 42N 4 24 E
Valsad, *India* **82 D1** 20 40N 72 58 E
Valskog, *Sweden* **14 E9** 59 27N 15 57 E
Válta, *Greece* **44 D5** 40 3N 23 25 E
Valtellina, *Italy* **38 B6** 46 11N 9 55 E
Valuyki, *Russia* **52 E4** 50 10N 38 5 E
Valverde, *Canary Is.* **33 G2** 27 48N 17 55W
Valverde del Camino, *Spain* **37 H4** 37 35N 6 47W
Valverde del Fresno, *Spain* **36 E4** 40 15N 6 51W
Vama, *Romania* **46 B6** 47 34N 25 42 E
Vammala, *Finland* **13 F20** 61 20N 22 54 E
Vámos, *Greece* **32 D6** 35 24N 24 13 E
Vamsadhara →, *India* **82 E7** 18 21N 84 8 E
Van, *Turkey* **89 C10** 38 30N 43 20 E
Van, L. = Van Gölü, *Turkey* **89 C10** 38 30N 43 0 E
Van Alstyne, *U.S.A.* **139 J6** 33 25N 96 35W
Van Bruyssel, *Canada* **129 C5** 47 56N 72 9W
Van Buren, *Canada* **129 C6** 47 10N 67 55W
Van Buren, *Ark., U.S.A.* **139 H7** 35 26N 94 21W
Van Buren, *Maine, U.S.A.* **135 B11** 47 10N 67 58W
Van Buren, *Mo., U.S.A.* **139 G9** 37 0N 91 1W
Van Canh, *Vietnam* **76 F7** 13 37N 109 0 E
Van Diemen, C., *N. Terr., Australia* **112 B5** 11 9 S 130 24 E
Van Diemen, C., *Queens., Australia* **114 B2** 16 30 S 139 46 E
Van Diemen G., *Australia* **112 B5** 11 45 S 132 0 E
Van Gölü, *Turkey* **89 C10** 38 30N 43 0 E
Van Horn, *U.S.A.* **139 K2** 31 3N 104 50W
Van Horne, *U.S.A.* **140 B4** 42 1N 92 4W
Van Ninh, *Vietnam* **76 F7** 12 42N 109 14 E
Van Rees, Pegunungan, *Indonesia* **73 B5** 2 35 S 138 15 E
Van Tassell, *U.S.A.* **138 D2** 42 40N 104 5W
Van Tivu, *India* **83 K4** 8 51N 78 15 E
Van Wert, *U.S.A.* **141 D12** 40 52N 84 35W
Van Yen, *Vietnam* **76 B5** 21 4N 104 42 E
Vanadzor, *Armenia* **53 K7** 40 48N 44 30 E
Vanavara, *Russia* **57 C11** 60 22N 102 16 E
Vanceburg, *U.S.A.* **141 F13** 38 36N 83 19W
Vancouver, *Canada* **130 D4** 49 15N 123 10W
Vancouver, *U.S.A.* **144 E4** 45 38N 122 40W
Vancouver, C., *Australia* **113 G2** 35 2 S 118 11 E
Vancouver I., *Canada* **130 D3** 49 50N 126 0W
Vandalia, *Ill., U.S.A.* **140 F7** 38 58N 89 6W
Vandalia, *Mo., U.S.A.* **140 E5** 39 19N 91 29W
Vandalia, *Ohio, U.S.A.* **141 E12** 39 54N 84 12W
Vandavasi, *India* **83 H4** 12 30N 79 30 E
Vandeloos B., *Sri Lanka* **83 K5** 8 0N 81 45 E
Vandenburg, *U.S.A.* **145 L6** 34 35N 120 33W
Vanderbijlpark, *S. Africa* **105 D4** 26 42 S 27 54 E
Vandergrift, *U.S.A.* **136 F5** 40 36N 79 34W
Vanderhoof, *Canada* **130 C4** 54 0N 124 0W
Vanderkloof Dam, *S. Africa* **104 E3** 30 4 S 24 40 E
Vanderlin I., *Australia* **114 B2** 15 44 S 137 2 E
Vandyke, *Australia* **114 C4** 24 10 S 147 51 E
Vänern, *Sweden* **15 F7** 58 47N 13 30 E
Vänersborg, *Sweden* **15 F6** 58 26N 12 19 E
Vang Vieng, *Laos* **76 C4** 18 58N 102 32 E
Vanga, *Kenya* **106 C4** 4 35 S 39 12 E
Vangaindrano, *Madag.* **105 C8** 23 21 S 47 36 E
Vanguard, *Canada* **131 D7** 49 55N 107 20W
Vangunu, *Solomon Is.* **121 M10** 8 40 S 158 5 E
Vanier, *Canada* **128 C4** 45 27N 75 40W
Vanimo, *Papua N. G.* **120 B1** 2 42 S 141 21 E
Vanivilasa Sagara, *India* **83 H3** 13 45N 76 30 E
Vaniyambadi, *India* **83 H4** 12 46N 78 44 E
Vankleek Hill, *Canada* **128 C5** 45 32N 74 40W
Vanna, *Norway* **12 A18** 70 6N 19 50 E
Vännäs, *Sweden* **12 E18** 63 58N 19 48 E
Vannes, *France* **22 E4** 47 40N 2 47W
Vanoise, Massif de la, *France* **25 C10** 45 25N 6 40 E
Vanrhynsdorp, *S. Africa* **104 E2** 31 36 S 18 44 E
Vanrook, *Australia* **114 B3** 16 57 S 141 57 E
Vansbro, *Sweden* **13 F16** 60 32N 14 15 E
Vansittart B., *Australia* **112 B4** 14 3 S 126 17 E
Vantaa, *Finland* **13 F21** 60 18N 24 58 E
Vanthli, *India* **80 J4** 21 28N 70 25 E
Vanua Levu, *Fiji* **121 A2** 16 33 S 179 15 E
Vanuatu ■, *Pac. Oc.* **121 E6** 15 0 S 168 0 E
Vanwyksvlei, *S. Africa* **104 E3** 30 18 S 21 49 E
Vanzylsrus, *S. Africa* **104 D3** 26 52 S 22 4 E
Vapnyarka, *Ukraine* **51 H5** 48 32N 28 45 E
Var □, *France* **25 E10** 43 27N 6 18 E
Var →, *France* **25 E11** 43 39N 7 12 E
Vara, *Sweden* **15 F6** 58 16N 12 55 E
Varada →, *India* **83 G2** 15 0N 75 40 E
Varades, *France* **22 E5** 47 25N 1 1W
Varáita →, *Italy* **38 D4** 44 9N 7 53 E
Varallo, *Italy* **38 C5** 45 49N 8 15 E
Varanasi, *India* **81 G10** 25 22N 83 0 E
Varanger-halvøya, *Norway* **12 A23** 70 25N 29 30 E
Varangerfjorden, *Norway* **12 A23** 70 3N 29 25 E
Varaždin, *Croatia* **39 B13** 46 20N 16 20 E
Varazze, *Italy* **38 D5** 44 22N 8 34 E
Varberg, *Sweden* **15 G6** 57 6N 12 20 E
Vardar = Axiós →, *Greece* **44 D4** 40 57N 22 35 E
Varde, *Denmark* **15 J2** 55 38N 8 29 E
Varde Å →, *Denmark* **15 J2** 55 35N 8 19 E
Vardø, *Norway* **12 A24** 70 23N 31 5 E
Varel, *Germany* **26 B4** 53 23N 8 8 E
Varella, Mui, *Vietnam* **76 F7** 12 54N 109 26 E
Varėna, *Lithuania* **13 J21** 54 12N 24 30 E
Varennes-sur-Allier, *France* **24 B7** 46 19N 3 24 E
Vareš, *Bos.-H.* **42 C3** 44 12N 18 23 E
Varese, *Italy* **38 C5** 45 48N 8 50 E
Varese Lígure, *Italy* **38 D6** 44 49N 9 45 E
Vårgårda, *Sweden* **15 F6** 58 2N 12 49 E
Vargem Bonita, *Brazil* **155 F2** 20 20 S 46 22W
Vargem Grande, *Brazil* **154 B3** 3 33 S 43 56W
Varginha, *Brazil* **159 A6** 21 33 S 45 25W
Vargön, *Sweden* **15 F6** 58 22N 12 20 E
Variadero, *U.S.A.* **139 H2** 35 43N 104 17W
Varillas, *Chile* **158 A1** 24 0 S 70 10W
Väring, *Sweden* **15 F8** 58 30N 14 0 E
Varkaus, *Finland* **13 E22** 62 19N 27 50 E
Varna, *Bulgaria* **43 D12** 43 13N 27 56 E
Varna, *Russia* **54 E8** 53 24N 60 58 E
Varna, *U.S.A.* **140 C7** 41 2N 89 14W
Varna →, *India* **82 F2** 16 48N 74 32 E
Värnamo, *Sweden* **13 H16** 57 10N 14 3 E
Varnsdorf, *Czech.* **30 A7** 50 55N 14 35 E
Värö, *Sweden* **15 G6** 57 16N 12 11 E
Vars, *Canada* **137 A9** 45 21N 75 21W
Varsseveld, *Neths.* **20 E8** 51 56N 6 29 E
Varto, *Turkey* **89 C9** 39 10N 41 27 E
Varvarin, *Serbia, Yug.* **42 D6** 43 43N 21 20 E
Varzaneh, *Iran* **85 C7** 32 25N 52 40 E
Várzea Alegre, *Brazil* **154 C4** 6 47 S 39 17W
Várzea da Palma, *Brazil* **155 E3** 17 36 S 44 44W
Várzea Grande, *Brazil* **157 D6** 15 39 S 56 8W
Varzi, *Italy* **38 D6** 44 49N 9 12 E
Varzo, *Italy* **38 B5** 46 12N 8 15 E
Varzy, *France* **23 E10** 47 22N 3 20 E
Vas □, *Hungary* **31 D9** 47 10N 16 55 E
Vasa Barris →, *Brazil* **154 D4** 11 10 S 37 10W
Vásárosnamény, *Hungary* **31 C15** 48 9N 22 19 E
Vascâo →, *Portugal* **37 H3** 37 31N 7 31W
Vaşcău, *Romania* **46 C3** 46 28N 22 30 E
Vascongadas = País Vasco □, *Spain* **34 C2** 42 50N 2 45W
Vāshīr, *Afghan.* **79 B1** 32 16N 63 51 E
Vasht = Khāsh, *Iran* **85 D9** 28 15N 61 15 E
Vasilevichi, *Belarus* **51 F5** 52 15N 29 50 E
Vasilikón, *Greece* **45 F5** 38 25N 23 40 E
Vasilkov = Vasylkiv, *Ukraine* **51 G6** 50 7N 30 15 E
Vaslui, *Romania* **46 C8** 46 38N 27 42 E
Vaslui □, *Romania* **46 C8** 46 30N 27 45 E
Vassar, *Canada* **131 D9** 49 10N 95 55W
Vassar, *U.S.A.* **134 D4** 43 22N 83 35W
Västerås, *Sweden* **14 E10** 59 37N 16 38 E
Västerbotten, *Sweden* **12 D18** 64 36N 20 4 E
Västerdalälven →, *Sweden* **13 F16** 60 30N 14 7 E
Västernorrlands län □, *Sweden* **14 A11** 63 30N 17 30 E
Västervik, *Sweden* **13 H17** 57 43N 16 33 E
Västmanland, *Sweden* **13 G16** 59 45N 16 20 E
Vasto, *Italy* **39 F11** 42 8N 14 40 E
Vasvár, *Hungary* **31 D9** 47 3N 16 47 E
Vasylkiv, *Ukraine* **51 G6** 50 7N 30 15 E
Vatan, *France* **23 E8** 47 4N 1 50 E
Vaté = Efate, I., *Vanuatu* **121 G6** 17 40 S 168 25 E
Vathí, *Itháki, Greece* **45 F2** 38 18N 20 40 E
Vathí, *Sámos, Greece* **45 G9** 37 46N 27 1 E
Váthia, *Greece* **45 H4** 36 29N 22 29 E
Vatican City ■, *Europe* **39 G9** 41 54N 12 27 E
Vaticano, C., *Italy* **41 D8** 38 37N 15 50 E
Vatili, *Cyprus* **32 D12** 35 6N 33 40 E
Vatin, *Serbia, Yug.* **42 B6** 45 12N 21 20 E
Vatnajökull, *Iceland* **12 D5** 64 30N 16 48W
Vatnås, *Norway* **14 E3** 59 58N 9 37 E
Vatólakkos, *Greece* **32 D5** 35 27N 23 53 E
Vatoloha, *Madag.* **105 B8** 17 52 S 47 48 E
Vatomandry, *Madag.* **105 B8** 19 20 S 48 59 E
Vatra-Dornei, *Romania* **46 B6** 47 22N 25 22 E
Vättern, *Sweden* **15 F8** 58 25N 14 30 E
Vättis, *Switz.* **29 C8** 46 55N 9 27 E
Vatulele, *Fiji* **121 B1** 18 33 S 177 37 E
Vaucluse □, *France* **25 E9** 43 50N 5 20 E
Vaucouleurs, *France* **23 D12** 48 37N 5 40 E
Vaud □, *Switz.* **28 C2** 46 35N 6 30 E
Vaughn, *Mont., U.S.A.* **142 C8** 47 33N 111 33W
Vaughn, *N. Mex., U.S.A.* **143 J11** 34 36N 105 13W
Vaulruz, *Switz.* **28 C3** 46 38N 6 58 E
Vaupés = Uaupés →, *Brazil* **152 C4** 0 2N 67 16W
Vaupes □, *Colombia* **152 C3** 1 0N 71 0W
Vauvert, *France* **25 E8** 43 42N 4 17 E
Vauxhall, *Canada* **130 C6** 50 5N 112 9W
Vava'u, *Tonga* **121 P14** 18 36 S 174 0W
Vavoua, *Ivory C.* **100 D3** 7 23N 6 29W
Vawkavysk, *Belarus* **51 F3** 53 9N 24 30 E
Vaxholm, *Sweden* **14 E12** 59 25N 18 20 E
Växjö, *Sweden* **13 H16** 56 52N 14 50 E
Vaygach, Ostrov, *Russia* **56 C6** 70 0N 60 0 E
Váyia, Ákra, *Greece* **32 C10** 36 15N 28 11 E
Vazovgrad, *Bulgaria* **43 E9** 42 39N 24 45 E
Veadeiros, *Brazil* **155 D2** 14 7 S 47 31W
Vechta, *Germany* **26 C4** 52 44N 8 17 E
Vechte →, *Neths.* **20 C8** 52 34N 6 6 E
Vecsés, *Hungary* **31 D12** 47 26N 19 19 E
Vedaranniyam, *India* **83 J4** 10 25N 79 50 E
Veddige, *Sweden* **15 G6** 57 17N 12 20 E
Vedea →, *Romania* **46 F6** 43 53N 25 59 E
Vedia, *Argentina* **158 C3** 34 30 S 61 31W
Vedra, I. del, *Spain* **33 C7** 38 52N 1 12 E
Vedrin, *Belgium* **21 G5** 50 30N 4 52 E
Veendam, *Neths.* **20 B9** 53 5N 6 52 E
Veenendaal, *Neths.* **20 D7** 52 2N 5 34 E
Veerle, *Belgium* **21 F5** 51 4N 4 59 E
Vefsna →, *Norway* **12 D15** 65 48N 13 10 E
Vega, *Norway* **12 D14** 65 40N 11 55 E
Vega, *U.S.A.* **139 H3** 35 15N 102 26W
Vegadeo, *Spain* **36 B3** 43 27N 7 4W
Veghel, *Neths.* **21 E7** 51 37N 5 32 E
Vegorritis, Límni, *Greece* **44 D3** 40 45N 21 45 E
Vegreville, *Canada* **130 C6** 53 30N 112 5W
Vegusdal, *Norway* **15 F2** 58 32N 8 10 E
Veii, *Italy* **39 F9** 42 0N 12 24 E
Veitch, *Australia* **116 C4** 34 39 S 140 31 E
Vejen, *Denmark* **15 J3** 55 30N 9 9 E
Vejer de la Frontera, *Spain* **37 J5** 36 15N 5 59W
Vejle, *Denmark* **15 J3** 55 43N 9 30 E
Vejle Fjord, *Denmark* **15 J3** 55 40N 9 50 E
Vela Luka, *Croatia* **39 F13** 42 59N 16 44 E
Velanai I., *Sri Lanka* **83 K4** 9 45N 79 45 E
Velas, C., *Costa Rica* **148 D2** 10 21N 85 52W
Velasco, Sierra de, *Argentina* **158 B2** 29 20 S 67 10W
Velay, Mts. du, *France* **24 D7** 45 0N 3 40 E
Velddrif, *S. Africa* **104 E2** 32 42 S 18 11 E
Veldegem, *Belgium* **21 F2** 51 7N 3 10 E
Velden, *Neths.* **21 F8** 51 25N 6 10 E
Veldhoven, *Neths.* **21 F6** 51 24N 5 25 E
Velebit Planina, *Croatia* **39 D12** 44 50N 15 20 E
Velebitski Kanal, *Croatia* **39 D11** 44 45N 14 55 E
Veleka →, *Bulgaria* **43 E12** 42 4N 27 58 E
Velenje, *Slovenia* **39 B12** 46 23N 15 8 E
Velestínon, *Greece* **44 E4** 39 23N 22 43 E
Velež, *Bos.-H.* **42 D3** 43 19N 18 2 E
Vélez, *Colombia* **152 B3** 6 1N 73 41W
Vélez Blanco, *Spain* **35 H2** 37 41N 2 5W
Vélez Málaga, *Spain* **37 J6** 36 48N 4 5W
Vélez Rubio, *Spain* **35 H2** 37 41N 2 5W
Velhas →, *Brazil* **155 E3** 17 13 S 44 49W
Velik Jastrebac, *Serbia, Yug.* **42 D6** 43 25N 21 30 E
Velika, *Croatia* **42 B2** 45 27N 17 40 E
Velika Gorica, *Croatia* **39 C13** 45 44N 16 5 E
Velika Gradište, *Serbia, Yug.* **42 C6** 44 46N 21 29 E
Velika Kapela, *Croatia* **39 C12** 45 10N 15 5 E
Velika Kladuša, *Bos.-H.* **39 C12** 45 11N 15 48 E
Velika Morava →, *Serbia, Yug.* **42 C6** 44 43N 21 3 E
Velika Plana, *Serbia, Yug.* **42 C6** 44 20N 21 1 E
Velikaya →, *Russia* **50 D5** 57 48N 28 10 E
Velikaya Kema, *Russia* **60 B8** 45 30N 137 12 E
Velikaya Lepetikha, *Ukraine* **51 J7** 47 2N 33 58 E
Veliké Kapušany, *Slovak Rep.* **31 C15** 48 34N 22 5 E
Velike Lašče, *Slovenia* **39 C11** 45 49N 14 45 E
Veliki Backu Kanal, *Serbia, Yug.* **42 B4** 45 45N 19 15 E
Veliki Popović, *Serbia, Yug.* **42 C6** 44 8N 21 18 E
Veliki Ustyug, *Russia* **48 B8** 60 47N 46 20 E
Velikiye Luki, *Russia* **50 D6** 56 25N 30 32 E
Veliko Tŭrnovo, *Bulgaria* **43 D10** 43 5N 25 41 E
Velikonda Range, *India* **83 G4** 14 45N 79 10 E
Velingrad, *Bulgaria* **43 E8** 42 4N 23 58 E
Velino, Mte., *Italy* **39 F10** 42 9N 13 23 E
Velizh, *Russia* **50 E6** 55 36N 31 11 E
Velké Karlovice, *Czech.* **31 B11** 49 20N 18 17 E
Velke Meziřici, *Czech.* **30 B9** 49 21N 16 1 E
Vel'ký Žitný ostrov, *Slovak Rep.* **31 C10** 48 5N 17 20 E
Vella G., *Solomon Is.* **121 M9** 8 0 S 156 50 E
Vella Lavella, *Solomon Is.* **121 L9** 7 45 S 156 40 E
Vellar →, *India* **83 J4** 11 30N 79 36 E
Velletri, *Italy* **40 A5** 41 41N 12 47 E
Vellinge, *Sweden* **15 J7** 55 29N 13 0 E
Vellore, *India* **83 H4** 12 57N 79 10 E
Velp, *Neths.* **20 D7** 52 0N 5 59 E
Velsen-Noord, *Neths.* **20 D5** 52 27N 4 40 E
Velsk, *Russia* **50 B11** 61 10N 42 5 E
Velten, *Germany* **26 C9** 52 42N 13 10 E
Veluwe Meer, *Neths.* **20 D7** 52 24N 5 44 E
Velva, *U.S.A.* **138 A4** 48 4N 100 56W
Velvendós, *Greece* **44 D4** 40 15N 22 6 E
Vembanad L., *India* **83 K3** 9 36N 76 15 E
Veme, *Norway* **14 D4** 60 14N 10 7 E
Ven, *Sweden* **15 J6** 55 55N 12 45 E

282 Vrena

Vrena, *Sweden* **15 F10** 58 54N 16 41 E
Vrgorac, *Croatia* **42 D2** 43 12N 17 20 E
Vrhnika, *Slovenia* **39 C11** 45 58N 14 15 E
Vriddhachalam, *India* **83 J4** 11 30N 79 20 E
Vrīdi, *Ivory C.* **100 D4** 5 15N 4 3W
Vries, *Neths.* **20 B9** 53 5N 6 35 E
Vriezenveen, *Neths.* **20 D9** 52 25N 6 38 E
Vrindavan, *India* **80 F7** 27 37N 77 40 E
Vrises, *Greece* **32 D6** 35 23N 24 13 E
Vrnograč, *Bos.-H.* **39 C12** 45 10N 15 57 E
Vrondádhes, *Greece* **45 F8** 38 25N 26 7 E
Vroomshoop, *Neths.* **20 D9** 52 27N 6 34 E
Vrpolje, *Croatia* **42 B3** 45 13N 18 24 E
Vršac, *Serbia, Yug.* **42 B6** 45 8N 21 18 E
Vrsacki Kanal, *Serbia, Yug.* **42 B5** 45 15N 21 0 E
Vryburg, *S. Africa* **104 D3** 26 55 S 24 45 E
Vryheid, *S. Africa* **105 D5** 27 45 S 30 47 E
Vsetín, *Czech.* **31 B11** 49 20N 18 0 E
Vu Liet, *Vietnam* **76 C5** 18 43N 105 23 E
Vucha →, *Bulgaria* **43 E9** 42 10N 24 26 E
Vučitrn, *Serbia, Yug.* **42 E5** 42 49N 20 59 E
Vught, *Neths.* **21 E6** 51 38N 5 20 E
Vukovar, *Croatia* **42 B3** 45 21N 18 59 E
Vulcan, *Canada* **130 C6** 50 25N 113 15W
Vulcan, *Romania* **46 D4** 45 23N 23 17 E
Vulcan, *U.S.A.* **134 C2** 45 47N 87 53W
Vulcaneşti, *Moldova* **51 K5** 45 35N 28 30 E
Vulcano, *Italy* **41 D7** 38 24N 14 58 E
Vŭlchedruma, *Bulgaria* **43 D8** 43 42N 23 27 E
Vulci, *Italy* **39 F8** 42 23N 11 37 E
Vulkaneshty = Vulcaneşti, *Moldova* **51 K5** 45 35N 28 30 E
Vunduzi →, *Mozam.* **107 F3** 18 56 S 34 1 E
Vung Tau, *Vietnam* **77 G6** 10 21N 107 4 E
Vunisea, *Fiji* **121 B2** 19 3 S 178 10 E
Vŭrbitsa, *Bulgaria* **43 E11** 42 59N 26 40 E
Vurshets, *Bulgaria* **43 D8** 43 15N 23 23 E
Vutcani, *Romania* **46 C8** 46 26N 27 59 E
Vuyyuru, *India* **83 F5** 16 28N 80 50 E
Vyara, *India* **82 D1** 21 8N 73 28 E
Vyartsilya, *Russia* **48 A6** 62 8N 30 45 E
Vyatka = Kirov, *Russia* **54 B2** 58 35N 49 40 E
Vyatka →, *Russia* **52 C10** 55 37N 51 28 E
Vyatskiye Polyany, *Russia* **52 B10** 56 14N 51 5 E
Vyazemskiy, *Russia* **57 E14** 47 32N 134 45 E
Vyazma, *Russia* **52 C2** 55 10N 34 15 E
Vyazniki, *Russia* **52 B6** 56 10N 42 10 E
Vyborg, *Russia* **50 B5** 60 43N 28 47 E
Vychegda →, *Russia* **48 B8** 61 18N 46 36 E
Vychodné Beskydy, *Europe* **51 H2** 49 20N 22 0 E
Východočeský □, *Czech.* **30 A8** 50 20N 15 45 E
Východoslovenský □, *Slovak Rep.* **31 C14** 48 50N 21 0 E
Vyerkhnyadzvinsk, *Belarus* **50 E4** 55 45N 27 58 E
Vyg-ozero, *Russia* **48 B5** 63 47N 34 29 E
Vyksa, *Russia* **52 C6** 55 19N 42 11 E
Vylkove, *Ukraine* **51 K5** 45 28N 29 32 E
Vynohradiv, *Ukraine* **51 H2** 48 9N 23 2 E
Vypin, *India* **83 J3** 10 10N 76 15 E
Vyrnwy, L., *U.K.* **16 E4** 52 48N 3 31W
Vyshniy Volochek, *Russia* **52 B2** 57 30N 34 30 E
Vyshzha = imeni 26 Bakinskikh Komissarov, *Turkmenistan* **49 G9** 39 22N 54 10 E
Vyškov, *Czech.* **31 B10** 49 17N 17 0 E
Vysoké Mýto, *Czech.* **31 B9** 49 58N 16 10 E
Vysokovsk, *Russia* **52 B3** 56 22N 36 30 E
Vyšší Brod, *Czech.* **30 C7** 48 37N 14 19 E
Vytegra, *Russia* **50 B9** 61 0N 36 27 E

W

W.A.C. Bennett Dam, *Canada* **130 B4** 56 2N 122 6W
Wa, *Ghana* **100 C4** 10 7N 2 25W
Waal →, *Neths.* **20 E6** 51 37N 5 0 E
Waalwijk, *Neths.* **21 E6** 51 42N 5 4 E
Waarschoot, *Belgium* **21 F3** 51 10N 3 36 E
Waasmunster, *Belgium* **21 F4** 51 6N 4 5 E
Wabag, *Papua N. G.* **120 C2** 5 32 S 143 40 E
Wabakimi L., *Canada* **128 B2** 50 38N 89 45W
Wabana, *Canada* **129 C9** 47 40N 53 0W
Wabao, C., *N. Cal.* **121 U21** 21 35 S 167 53 E
Wabasca, *Canada* **130 B6** 55 57N 113 56W
Wabash, *U.S.A.* **141 D11** 40 48N 85 49W
Wabash →, *U.S.A.* **134 G1** 37 48N 88 2W
Wabawng, *Burma* **78 B6** 26 20N 97 25 E
Wabeno, *U.S.A.* **134 C1** 45 26N 88 39W
Wabi →, *Ethiopia* **95 F5** 7 45N 40 50 E
Wabigoon L., *Canada* **131 D10** 49 44N 92 44W
Wabowden, *Canada* **131 C9** 54 55N 98 38W
Wąbrzeźno, *Poland* **47 B5** 53 16N 18 57 E
Wabu Hu, *China* **69 A11** 32 20N 116 50 E
Wabuk Pt., *Canada* **128 A2** 55 20N 85 5W
Wabush, *Canada* **129 B6** 52 55N 66 52W
Wabuska, *U.S.A.* **142 G4** 39 9N 119 11W
Wachtebeke, *Belgium* **21 F3** 51 11N 3 52 E
Wächtersbach, *Germany* **27 E5** 50 14N 9 17 E
Waco, *U.S.A.* **139 K6** 31 33N 97 9W
Waconichi, L., *Canada* **128 B5** 50 8N 74 0W
Wad Ban Naqa, *Sudan* **95 D3** 16 32N 33 9 E
Wad Banda, *Sudan* **95 E2** 13 10N 27 56 E
Wad el Haddad, *Sudan* **95 E3** 13 50N 33 30 E
Wad en Nau, *Sudan* **95 E3** 14 10N 33 34 E
Wad Hamid, *Sudan* **95 D3** 16 30N 32 45 E
Wâd Medanî, *Sudan* **95 E3** 14 28N 33 30 E
Wad Thana, *Pakistan* **79 D2** 27 22N 66 23 E
Wadai, *Africa* **92 E5** 12 0N 19 0 E
Wadayama, *Japan* **62 B6** 35 19N 134 52 E
Waddān, *Libya* **96 C3** 29 9N 16 10 E
Waddeneilanden, *Neths.* **20 B6** 53 25N 5 10 E
Waddenzee, *Neths.* **20 B6** 53 6N 5 10 E
Wadderin Hill, *Australia* **113 F2** 32 0 S 118 25 E
Waddington, *U.S.A.* **137 B9** 44 52N 75 12W
Waddington, Mt., *Canada* **130 C3** 51 23N 125 15W
Waddinxveen, *Neths.* **20 D5** 52 2N 4 40 E
Waddy Pt., *Australia* **115 C5** 24 58 S 153 21 E
Wadena, *Canada* **131 C8** 51 57N 103 47W
Wadena, *U.S.A.* **138 B7** 46 26N 95 8W
Wädenswil, *Switz.* **29 B7** 47 14N 8 40 E
Wadesboro, *U.S.A.* **135 H5** 34 58N 80 5W
Wadhams, *Canada* **130 C3** 51 30N 127 30W
Wādī as Sīr, *Jordan* **91 D4** 31 56N 35 49 E
Wādī ash Shāṭi', *Libya* **96 C2** 27 30N 15 0 E
Wādī Banī Walīd, *Libya* **96 B2** 31 49N 14 0 E
Wadi Gemâl, *Egypt* **94 C4** 24 35N 35 10 E
Wadi Halfa, *Sudan* **94 C3** 21 53N 31 19 E
Wadian, *China* **69 A9** 32 42N 112 29 E
Wadim, *Oman* **87 B7** 22 40N 57 21 E
Wadlew, *Poland* **47 D6** 51 31N 19 23 E
Wadowice, *Poland* **31 B12** 49 52N 19 30 E
Wadsworth, *U.S.A.* **142 G4** 39 38N 119 17W
Waegwan, *S. Korea* **67 G15** 35 59N 128 23 E
Wafrah, *Si. Arabia* **84 D5** 28 33N 47 56 E
Wagenberg, *Neths.* **21 E5** 51 40N 4 46 E
Wageningen, *Neths.* **20 E7** 51 58N 5 40 E
Wageningen, *Surinam* **153 B6** 5 50N 56 50W
Wager B., *Canada* **127 B11** 65 26N 88 40W
Wager Bay, *Canada* **127 B10** 65 56N 90 49W
Wagga Wagga, *Australia* **117 C7** 35 7 S 147 24 E
Waghete, *Indonesia* **73 B5** 4 10 S 135 50 E
Wagin, *Australia* **113 F2** 33 17 S 117 25 E
Wagon Mound, *U.S.A.* **139 G2** 36 1N 104 42W
Wagoner, *U.S.A.* **139 G7** 35 58N 95 22W
Wagrowiec, *Poland* **47 C4** 52 48N 17 11 E
Wah, *Pakistan* **79 B4** 33 45N 72 40 E
Wahai, *Indonesia* **73 B3** 2 48 S 129 35 E
Waharoa, *N.Z.* **118 D4** 37 46 S 175 45 E
Wahiawa, *U.S.A.* **132 H15** 21 30N 158 2W
Wâḥid, *Egypt* **91 E1** 30 48N 32 21 E
Wahnai, *Afghan.* **80 C1** 32 40N 65 50 E
Wahoo, *U.S.A.* **138 E6** 41 13N 96 37W
Wahpeton, *U.S.A.* **138 B6** 46 16N 96 36W
Wahratta, *Australia* **116 A4** 31 58 S 141 50 E
Wai, *India* **82 F1** 17 56N 73 57 E
Wai, Koh, *Cambodia* **77 H4** 9 55N 102 55 E
Waiai →, *N.Z.* **119 G2** 46 12 S 167 38 E
Waiapu →, *N.Z.* **118 D7** 37 47 S 178 29 E
Waiau, *N.Z.* **119 C8** 42 39 S 173 5 E
Waiau →, *N.Z.* **119 C8** 42 47 S 173 22 E
Waiawe Ganga →, *Sri Lanka* **83 L5** 6 15N 81 0 E
Waibeem, *Indonesia* **73 B4** 0 30 S 132 59 E
Waiblingen, *Germany* **27 G5** 48 49N 9 18 E
Waidhofen, *Niederösterreich, Austria* **30 C8** 48 49N 15 17 E
Waidhofen, *Niederösterreich, Austria* **30 D7** 47 57N 14 46 E
Waigeo, *Indonesia* **73 B4** 0 20 S 130 40 E
Waihao →, *N.Z.* **119 E6** 44 52 S 171 11 E
Waihao Downs, *N.Z.* **119 E5** 44 48 S 170 55 E
Waiheke I., *N.Z.* **118 C4** 36 48 S 175 6 E
Waihi, *N.Z.* **118 D4** 37 23 S 175 52 E
Waihola, *N.Z.* **119 G5** 46 1 S 170 8 E
Waihola L., *N.Z.* **119 F5** 45 59 S 170 8 E
Waihou →, *N.Z.* **118 D4** 37 15 S 175 40 E
Waika, *Zaïre* **102 C5** 2 22 S 25 42 E
Waikabubak, *Indonesia* **72 C1** 9 45 S 119 25 E
Waikaia, *N.Z.* **119 F3** 45 44 S 168 51 E
Waikaka, *N.Z.* **119 F4** 45 55 S 169 1 E
Waikare, L., *N.Z.* **118 D4** 37 26 S 175 13 E
Waikareiti, L., *N.Z.* **118 E6** 38 43 S 177 10 E
Waikaremoana, *N.Z.* **118 E6** 38 42 S 177 12 E
Waikaremoana L., *N.Z.* **118 E6** 38 49 S 177 9 E
Waikari, *N.Z.* **119 C7** 42 58 S 172 41 E
Waikato →, *N.Z.* **118 D3** 37 23 S 174 43 E
Waikerie, *Australia* **116 C3** 34 9 S 140 0 E
Waikiekie, *N.Z.* **118 B3** 35 57 S 174 16 E
Waikokopu, *N.Z.* **118 F6** 39 3 S 177 52 E
Waikouaiti, *N.Z.* **119 F5** 45 36 S 170 41 E
Waikouaiti Downs, *N.Z.* **119 F5** 45 30 S 170 30 E
Waimakariri →, *N.Z.* **119 D7** 43 24 S 172 42 E
Waimangaroa, *N.Z.* **119 B6** 41 43 S 171 46 E
Waimarie, *N.Z.* **119 B6** 41 35 S 171 58 E
Waimate, *N.Z.* **119 E6** 44 45 S 171 3 E
Waimea Plain, *N.Z.* **119 F3** 45 55 S 168 35 E
Waimes, *Belgium* **21 H8** 50 25N 6 7 E
Wainganga →, *India* **82 E4** 18 50N 79 55 E
Waingapu, *Indonesia* **72 C2** 9 35 S 120 11 E
Waingmaw, *Burma* **78 C6** 25 21N 97 26 E
Waini →, *Guyana* **153 B6** 8 20N 59 50W
Wainuiomata, *N.Z.* **118 H3** 41 17 S 174 56 E
Wainwright, *Canada* **131 C6** 52 50N 110 50W
Wainwright, *U.S.A.* **126 A3** 70 38N 160 2W
Waiotapu, *N.Z.* **118 E5** 38 21 S 176 25 E
Waiouru, *N.Z.* **118 F4** 39 28 S 175 41 E
Waipa →, *N.Z.* **118 E4** 38 16 S 175 21 E
Waipahi, *N.Z.* **119 G4** 46 6 S 169 15 E
Waipapa Pt., *N.Z.* **119 G3** 46 40 S 168 51 E
Waipara, *N.Z.* **119 D7** 43 3 S 172 46 E
Waipawa, *N.Z.* **118 F5** 39 56 S 176 38 E
Waipiro, *N.Z.* **118 E7** 38 2 S 178 22 E
Waipu, *N.Z.* **118 B3** 35 59 S 174 29 E
Waipukurau, *N.Z.* **118 G5** 40 1 S 176 33 E
Wairakei, *N.Z.* **118 E5** 38 37 S 176 6 E
Wairarapa, L., *N.Z.* **118 H4** 41 14 S 175 15 E
Wairau →, *N.Z.* **119 B9** 41 32 S 174 7 E
Wairio, *N.Z.* **119 F3** 45 59 S 168 3 E
Wairoa, *N.Z.* **118 F6** 39 3 S 177 25 E
Wairoa →, *Hawke's Bay, N.Z.* **118 F6** 39 4 S 177 25 E
Wairoa →, *Northland, N.Z.* **118 C2** 36 5 S 173 59 E
Waitaha, *N.Z.* **119 D5** 43 0 S 170 45 E
Waitaki →, *N.Z.* **119 E6** 44 56 S 171 7 E
Waitaki Plains, *N.Z.* **119 E5** 44 22 S 170 0 E
Waitara, *N.Z.* **118 E3** 38 59 S 174 15 E
Waitara →, *N.Z.* **118 E3** 38 59 S 174 14 E
Waitchie, *Australia* **116 C5** 35 22 S 143 8 E
Waitoa, *N.Z.* **118 D4** 37 37 S 175 35 E
Waitotara, *N.Z.* **118 F3** 39 49 S 174 44 E
Waitotara →, *N.Z.* **118 F3** 39 51 S 174 41 E
Waitsburg, *U.S.A.* **142 C5** 46 16N 118 9W
Waiuku, *N.Z.* **118 D3** 37 15 S 174 45 E
Waiyevo, *Fiji* **121 A3** 16 48 S 179 59W
Wajima, *Japan* **61 F8** 37 30N 137 0 E
Wajir, *Kenya* **106 B5** 1 42N 40 5 E
Wajir □, *Kenya* **106 B5** 1 42N 40 20 E
Waka, *Zaïre* **102 B4** 1 1N 20 13 E
Wakarusa, *U.S.A.* **141 C10** 41 32N 86 1W
Wakasa, *Japan* **62 B6** 35 20N 134 24 E
Wakasa-Wan, *Japan* **63 B7** 35 40N 135 30 E
Wakatipu, L., *N.Z.* **119 F3** 45 5 S 168 33 E
Wakaw, *Canada* **131 C7** 52 39N 105 44W
Wakayama, *Japan* **63 C7** 34 15N 135 15 E
Wakayama-ken □, *Japan* **63 D7** 33 50N 135 30 E
Wake, *Japan* **62 C6** 34 48N 134 8 E
Wake Forest, *U.S.A.* **135 H6** 35 59N 78 30W
Wake I., *Pac. Oc.* **122 F8** 19 18N 166 36 E
Wakefield, *N.Z.* **119 B8** 41 24 S 173 5 E
Wakefield, *U.K.* **16 D6** 53 41N 1 29W
Wakefield, *Mass., U.S.A.* **137 D13** 42 30N 71 4W
Wakefield, *Mich., U.S.A.* **138 B10** 46 29N 89 56W
Wakeham Bay = Maricourt, *Canada* **127 C12** 56 34N 70 49W
Wakema, *Burma* **78 G5** 16 30N 95 11 E
Wakkanai, *Japan* **60 B10** 45 28N 141 35 E
Wakkerstroom, *S. Africa* **105 D5** 27 24 S 30 10 E
Wakool, *Australia* **116 C6** 35 28 S 144 23 E
Wakool →, *Australia* **116 C5** 35 5 S 143 33 E
Wakre, *Indonesia* **73 B4** 0 19 S 131 5 E
Waku, *Papua N. G.* **120 D5** 6 5 S 149 9 E
Wakuach L., *Canada* **129 A6** 55 34N 67 32W
Walamba, *Zambia* **107 E2** 13 30 S 28 42 E
Wałbrzych, *Poland* **47 E3** 50 45N 16 18 E
Walbury Hill, *U.K.* **17 F6** 51 21N 1 28W
Walcha, *Australia* **117 A9** 30 55 S 151 31 E
Walcha Road, *Australia* **117 A9** 30 55 S 151 24 E
Walcheren, *Neths.* **21 E3** 51 30N 3 35 E
Walcott, *U.S.A.* **142 F10** 41 46N 106 51W
Wałcz, *Poland* **47 B3** 53 17N 16 27 E
Wald, *Switz.* **29 B7** 47 17N 8 56 E
Waldbröl, *Germany* **26 E3** 50 52N 7 37 E
Waldburg Ra., *Australia* **112 D2** 24 40 S 117 35 E
Waldeck, *Germany* **26 D5** 51 12N 9 4 E
Walden, *Colo., U.S.A.* **142 F10** 40 44N 106 17W
Walden, *N.Y., U.S.A.* **137 E10** 41 34N 74 11W
Waldenburg, *Switz.* **28 B5** 47 23N 7 45 E
Waldport, *U.S.A.* **142 D1** 44 26N 124 4W
Waldron, *U.S.A.* **139 H7** 34 54N 94 5W
Waldshut, *Germany* **27 H4** 47 37N 8 13 E
Walembele, *Ghana* **100 C4** 10 30N 1 58W
Walensee, *Switz.* **29 B8** 47 7N 9 13 E
Walenstadt, *Switz.* **29 B8** 47 8N 9 19 E
Wales □, *U.K.* **17 E4** 52 19N 4 43W
Walewale, *Ghana* **101 C4** 10 21N 0 50W
Walgett, *Australia* **115 E4** 30 0 S 148 5 E
Walgreen Coast, *Antarctica* **7 D15** 75 15 S 105 0W
Walhalla, *Australia* **117 D7** 37 56 S 146 29 E
Walhalla, *U.S.A.* **131 D9** 48 55N 97 55W
Walker, *Minn., U.S.A.* **138 B7** 47 6N 94 35W
Walker, *Mo., U.S.A.* **140 G2** 37 54N 94 14W
Walker L., *Man., Canada* **131 C9** 54 42N 95 57W
Walker L., *Qué., Canada* **129 B6** 50 20N 67 11W
Walker L., *U.S.A.* **142 G4** 38 42N 118 43W
Walkerston, *Australia* **114 C4** 21 11 S 149 8 E
Walkerton, *Canada* **136 B3** 44 10N 81 10W
Walkerton, *U.S.A.* **141 C10** 41 28N 86 29W
Wall, *U.S.A.* **138 C3** 44 0N 102 8W
Walla Walla, *Australia* **117 C7** 35 45 S 146 54 E
Walla Walla, *U.S.A.* **142 C4** 46 4N 118 20W
Wallabadah, *Australia* **114 B3** 17 57 S 142 15 E
Wallace, *Idaho, U.S.A.* **142 C6** 47 28N 115 56W
Wallace, *N.C., U.S.A.* **135 H7** 34 44N 77 59W
Wallace, *Nebr., U.S.A.* **138 E4** 40 50N 101 10W
Wallaceburg, *Canada* **128 D3** 42 34N 82 23W
Wallacetown, *N.Z.* **119 G3** 46 21 S 168 19 E
Wallachia = Valahia, *Romania* **46 E5** 44 35N 25 0 E
Wallal, *Australia* **115 D4** 26 32 S 146 7 E
Wallal Downs, *Australia* **112 C3** 19 47 S 120 40 E
Wallambin, L., *Australia* **113 F2** 30 57 S 117 35 E
Wallaroo, *Australia* **116 B2** 33 56 S 137 39 E
Wallasey, *U.K.* **16 D4** 53 25N 3 2W
Walldürn, *Germany* **27 F5** 49 34N 9 22 E
Wallerawang, *Australia* **117 B9** 33 25 S 150 4 E
Wallhallow, *Australia* **114 B2** 17 50 S 135 50 E
Wallingford, *U.S.A.* **137 E12** 41 27N 72 50W
Wallis & Futuna, Is., *Pac. Oc.* **122 J10** 13 18 S 176 10W
Wallisellen, *Switz.* **29 B7** 47 25N 8 36 E
Wallowa, *U.S.A.* **142 D5** 45 34N 117 32W
Wallowa Mts., *U.S.A.* **142 D5** 45 20N 117 30W
Wallsend, *Australia* **117 B9** 32 55 S 151 40 E
Wallsend, *U.K.* **16 C6** 54 59N 1 31W
Wallula, *U.S.A.* **142 C4** 46 5N 118 54W
Wallumbilla, *Australia* **115 D4** 26 33 S 149 9 E
Walmsley, L., *Canada* **131 A7** 63 25N 108 36W
Walney, I. of, *U.K.* **16 C4** 54 6N 3 15W
Walnut, *U.S.A.* **140 C7** 41 33N 89 36W
Walnut Creek, *U.S.A.* **144 H4** 37 54N 122 4W
Walnut Ridge, *U.S.A.* **139 G9** 36 4N 90 57W
Walpeup, *Australia* **116 C5** 35 7 S 142 2 E
Walsall, *U.K.* **17 E6** 52 35N 1 58W
Walsenburg, *U.S.A.* **139 G2** 37 38N 104 47W
Walsh, *U.S.A.* **139 G3** 37 23N 102 17W
Walsh →, *Australia* **114 B3** 16 31 S 143 42 E
Walsh P.O., *Australia* **114 B3** 16 40 S 144 0 E
Walshoutem, *Belgium* **21 G6** 50 43N 5 4 E
Walsrode, *Germany* **26 C5** 52 51N 9 35 E
Waltair, *India* **82 F6** 17 44N 83 23 E
Walterboro, *U.S.A.* **135 J5** 32 55N 80 40W
Walters, *U.S.A.* **139 H5** 34 22N 98 19W
Waltershausen, *Germany* **26 E6** 50 54N 10 33 E
Waltham, *U.S.A.* **137 D13** 42 23N 71 14W
Waltham Station, *Canada* **128 C4** 45 57N 76 57W
Waltman, *U.S.A.* **142 E10** 43 4N 107 12W
Walton, *Ky., U.S.A.* **141 F12** 38 52N 84 37W
Walton, *N.Y., U.S.A.* **137 D9** 42 10N 75 8W
Waltonville, *U.S.A.* **140 F7** 38 13N 89 2W
Walu, *Burma* **78 B7** 26 28N 98 2 E
Walvisbaai, *Namibia* **104 C1** 23 0 S 14 28 E
Walwa, *Australia* **117 C7** 35 59 S 147 44 E
Wamba, *Kenya* **106 B4** 0 58N 37 19 E
Wamba, *Zaïre* **106 B2** 2 10N 27 57 E
Wamego, *U.S.A.* **138 F6** 39 12N 96 18W
Wamena, *Indonesia* **73 B5** 4 4 S 138 57 E
Wamulan, *Indonesia* **72 B3** 3 27 S 126 7 E
Wan Hat, *Burma* **78 E6** 20 14N 97 53 E
Wan Kinghao, *Burma* **78 E7** 21 34N 98 17 E
Wan Lai-kam, *Burma* **78 E7** 21 21N 98 22 E
Wan Tup, *Burma* **78 E7** 21 13N 98 42 E
Wan Xian, *China* **66 E8** 38 47N 115 7 E
Wana, *Pakistan* **79 B3** 32 20N 69 32 E
Wanaaring, *Australia* **115 D3** 29 38 S 144 9 E
Wanaka, *N.Z.* **119 E4** 44 42 S 169 9 E
Wanaka L., *N.Z.* **119 E4** 44 33 S 169 7 E
Wan'an, *China* **69 D10** 26 26N 114 49 E
Wanapiri, *Indonesia* **73 B5** 4 30 S 135 59 E
Wanapitei L., *Canada* **128 C3** 46 45N 80 40W
Wanbi, *Australia* **116 C4** 34 46 S 140 17 E
Wandaik, *Guyana* **153 C6** 4 27N 59 35W
Wandandian, *Australia* **117 C9** 35 6 S 150 30 E
Wandarrie, *Australia* **113 E2** 27 50 S 117 52 E
Wandel Sea = McKinley Sea, *Arctic* **6 A7** 82 0N 0 0 E
Wanderer, *Zimbabwe* **107 F3** 19 36 S 30 1 E
Wandoan, *Australia* **115 D4** 26 5 S 149 55 E
Wandre, *Belgium* **21 G7** 50 40N 5 39 E
Wanfercée-Baulet, *Belgium* **21 H5** 50 28N 4 35 E
Wanfu, *China* **67 D12** 40 8N 122 38 E
Wang →, *Thailand* **76 D2** 17 8N 99 2 E
Wang Kai, *Sudan* **95 F2** 9 3N 29 23 E
Wang Noi, *Thailand* **76 E3** 14 13N 100 44 E
Wang Saphung, *Thailand* **76 D3** 17 18N 101 46 E
Wang Thong, *Thailand* **76 D3** 16 50N 100 26 E
Wanga, *Zaïre* **106 B2** 2 58N 29 12 E
Wangal, *Indonesia* **73 C4** 6 8 S 134 9 E
Wanganella, *Australia* **117 C6** 35 6 S 144 49 E
Wanganui, *N.Z.* **118 F4** 39 56 S 175 3 E
Wanganui →, *W. Coast, N.Z.* **119 D5** 43 3 S 170 26 E
Wanganui →, *Wanganui-Manawatu, N.Z.* **118 F4** 39 55 S 175 4 E
Wangaratta, *Australia* **117 D7** 36 21 S 146 19 E
Wangary, *Australia* **115 E2** 34 35 S 135 29 E
Wangcang, *China* **68 A6** 32 18N 106 20 E
Wangdu, *China* **66 E8** 38 40N 115 7 E
Wangdu Phodrang, *Bhutan* **78 B2** 27 28N 89 54 E
Wangerooge, *Germany* **26 B3** 53 47N 7 54 E
Wangi, *Kenya* **106 C5** 1 58 S 40 58 E
Wangiwangi, *Indonesia* **72 C2** 5 22 S 123 37 E
Wangjiang, *China* **69 B11** 30 10N 116 42 E
Wangmo, *China* **68 E6** 25 11N 106 5 E
Wangqing, *China* **67 C15** 43 12N 129 42 E
Wankaner, *India* **80 H4** 22 35N 71 0 E
Wanless, *Canada* **131 C8** 54 11N 101 21W
Wannian, *China* **69 C11** 28 42N 117 4 E
Wanon Niwat, *Thailand* **76 D4** 17 38N 103 46 E
Wanquan, *China* **66 D8** 40 50N 114 40 E
Wanrong, *China* **66 G6** 35 25N 110 50 E
Wanshan, *China* **68 D7** 27 30N 109 12 E
Wanshengchang, *China* **68 C6** 28 57N 106 53 E
Wanssum, *Neths.* **21 E8** 51 32N 6 5 E
Wanstead, *N.Z.* **118 G5** 40 8 S 176 30 E
Wanxian, *China* **68 B7** 30 42N 108 20 E
Wanyin, *Burma* **78 E6** 20 23N 97 15 E
Wanyuan, *China* **68 A7** 32 4N 108 3 E
Wanzai, *China* **69 C10** 28 7N 114 30 E
Wanze, *Belgium* **21 G6** 50 32N 5 13 E
Wapakoneta, *U.S.A.* **141 D12** 40 34N 84 12W
Wapato, *U.S.A.* **142 C3** 46 27N 120 25W
Wapawekka L., *Canada* **131 C8** 54 55N 104 40W
Wapello, *U.S.A.* **140 C5** 41 11N 91 11W
Wapikopa L., *Canada* **128 B2** 52 56N 87 53W
Wappingers Falls, *U.S.A.* **137 E11** 41 36N 73 55W
Wapsipinicon →, *U.S.A.* **140 C6** 41 44N 90 19W
Warabi, *Japan* **63 B11** 35 49N 139 41 E
Warangal, *India* **82 F4** 17 58N 79 35 E
Waratah, *Australia* **114 G4** 41 30 S 145 30 E
Waratah B., *Australia* **115 F4** 38 54 S 146 5 E
Warburg, *Germany* **26 D5** 51 28N 9 11 E
Warburton, *Vic., Australia* **117 D6** 37 47 S 145 42 E
Warburton, *W. Austral., Australia* **113 E4** 26 8 S 126 35 E
Warburton Ra., *Australia* **113 E4** 25 55 S 126 28 E
Ward, *N.Z.* **119 B9** 41 49 S 174 11 E
Ward →, *Australia* **115 D4** 26 28 S 146 6 E
Ward Cove, *U.S.A.* **130 B2** 55 25N 132 43W
Ward Hunt, C., *Papua N. G.* **120 E5** 8 2 S 148 10 E
Ward Hunt Str., *Papua N. G.* **120 E6** 9 30 S 150 0 E
Ward Mt., *U.S.A.* **144 H8** 37 12N 118 54W
Warden, *S. Africa* **105 D4** 27 50 S 29 0 E
Wardha, *India* **82 D4** 20 45N 78 39 E
Wardlow, *Canada* **130 C6** 50 56N 111 31W
Wards River, *Australia* **117 B9** 32 11 S 151 56 E
Ware, *Canada* **130 B3** 57 26N 125 41W
Ware, *U.S.A.* **137 D12** 42 16N 72 14W
Waregem, *Belgium* **21 G2** 50 53N 3 27 E
Wareham, *U.S.A.* **137 E14** 41 46N 70 43W
Waremme, *Belgium* **21 G6** 50 43N 5 15 E
Waren, *Germany* **26 B8** 53 31N 12 40 E
Warendorf, *Germany* **26 D3** 51 57N 7 59 E
Warialda, *Australia* **115 D5** 29 29 S 150 33 E
Wariap, *Indonesia* **73 B4** 1 30 S 134 5 E
Warin Chamrap, *Thailand* **76 E5** 15 12N 104 53 E
Warka, *Poland* **47 D8** 51 47N 21 12 E
Warkopi, *Indonesia* **73 B4** 1 12 S 134 9 E
Warkworth, *N.Z.* **118 C3** 36 24 S 174 41 E
Warley, *U.K.* **17 E6** 52 30N 1 59W
Warm Springs, *U.S.A.* **143 G5** 38 10N 116 20W
Warman, *Canada* **131 C7** 52 19N 106 30W
Warmbad, *Namibia* **104 D2** 28 25 S 18 42 E
Warmbad, *S. Africa* **105 C4** 24 51 S 28 19 E
Warmenhuizen, *Neths.* **20 C5** 52 43N 4 44 E
Warmeriville, *France* **23 C11** 49 20N 4 13 E
Warmond, *Neths.* **20 D5** 52 12N 4 30 E
Warnambool Downs, *Australia* **114 C3** 22 48 S 142 52 E
Warnemünde, *Germany* **26 A8** 54 10N 12 4 E
Warner, *Canada* **130 D6** 49 17N 112 12W
Warner Mts., *U.S.A.* **142 F3** 41 40N 120 15W
Warner Robins, *U.S.A.* **135 J4** 32 37N 83 36W
Warnes, *Bolivia* **157 D5** 17 30 S 63 10W
Warneton, *Belgium* **21 G1** 50 45N 2 57 E
Warnow →, *Germany* **26 A8** 54 6N 12 9 E
Warnsveld, *Neths.* **20 D8** 52 8N 6 14 E
Waroona, *Australia* **113 F2** 32 50 S 115 58 E
Warora, *India* **82 D4** 20 14N 79 1 E
Warracknabeal, *Australia* **116 D5** 36 9 S 142 26 E
Warragul, *Australia* **117 E6** 38 10 S 145 58 E
Warrawagine, *Australia* **112 D3** 20 51 S 120 42 E
Warrego →, *Australia* **115 E4** 30 24 S 145 21 E
Warrego Ra., *Australia* **114 C4** 24 58 S 146 0 E
Warren, *Australia* **117 A7** 31 42 S 147 51 E
Warren, *Ark., U.S.A.* **139 J8** 33 37N 92 4W
Warren, *Ill., U.S.A.* **140 B7** 42 29N 90 0W
Warren, *Mich., U.S.A.* **141 B13** 42 30N 83 0W
Warren, *Minn., U.S.A.* **138 A6** 48 12N 96 46W
Warren, *Ohio, U.S.A.* **136 E4** 41 14N 80 49W
Warren, *Pa., U.S.A.* **136 E5** 41 51N 79 9W
Warrenpoint, *U.K.* **19 B5** 54 6N 6 15W
Warrensburg, *Ill., U.S.A.* **140 E7** 39 56N 89 4W
Warrensburg, *Mo., U.S.A.* **138 F8** 38 46N 93 44W
Warrenton, *S. Africa* **104 D3** 28 9 S 24 47 E
Warrenton, *Mo., U.S.A.* **140 F5** 38 49N 91 9W
Warrenton, *Oreg., U.S.A.* **144 D3** 46 10N 123 56W
Warrenville, *Australia* **115 D4** 25 48 S 147 22 E
Warri, *Nigeria* **101 D6** 5 30N 5 41 E
Warrina, *Australia* **115 D2** 28 12 S 135 50 E
Warrington, *N.Z.* **119 F5** 45 43 S 170 35 E
Warrington, *U.K.* **16 D5** 53 24N 2 35W

West Wyalong 283

Warrington, *U.S.A.* **135 K2** 30 23N 87 17W
Warrnambool, *Australia* **116 E5** 38 25 S 142 30 E
Warroad, *U.S.A.* **138 A7** 48 54N 95 19W
Warsa, *Indonesia* **73 B5** 0 47 S 135 55 E
Warsaw = Warszawa, *Poland* **47 C8** 52 13N 21 0 E
Warsaw, *Ill., U.S.A.* **140 D5** 40 22N 91 26W
Warsaw, *Ind., U.S.A.* **141 C11** 41 14N 85 51W
Warsaw, *Ky., U.S.A.* **141 F12** 38 47N 84 54W
Warsaw, *Mo., U.S.A.* **140 F3** 38 15N 93 23W
Warsaw, *N.Y., U.S.A.* **136 D6** 42 45N 78 8W
Warsaw, *Ohio, U.S.A.* **140 F2** 40 20N 82 0W
Warstein, *Germany* **26 D4** 51 26N 8 22 E
Warszawa, *Poland* **47 C8** 52 13N 21 0 E
Warszawa □, *Poland* **47 C7** 52 30N 21 0 E
Warta, *Poland* **47 D5** 51 43N 18 38 E
Warta →, *Poland* **47 C1** 52 35N 14 39 E
Warthe = Warta →, *Poland* **47 C1** 52 35N 14 39 E
Waru, *Indonesia* **73 B4** 3 30 S 130 36 E
Warud, *India* **82 D4** 21 30N 78 16 E
Warwick, *Australia* **115 D5** 28 10 S 152 1 E
Warwick, *U.K.* **17 E6** 52 18N 1 35W
Warwick, *U.S.A.* **137 E13** 41 42N 71 28W
Warwickshire □, *U.K.* **17 E6** 52 14N 1 38W
Wasaga Beach, *Canada* **136 B4** 44 31N 80 1W
Wasatch Ra., *U.S.A.* **142 F8** 40 30N 111 15W
Wasbank, *S. Africa* **105 D5** 28 15 S 30 9 E
Wasco, *Calif., U.S.A.* **145 K7** 35 36N 119 20W
Wasco, *Oreg., U.S.A.* **142 D3** 45 36N 120 42W
Waseca, *U.S.A.* **138 C8** 44 5N 93 30W
Wasekamio L., *Canada* **131 B7** 56 45N 108 45W
Wash, The, *U.K.* **16 E8** 52 58N 0 20 E
Washago, *Canada* **136 B5** 44 45N 79 20W
Washburn, *Ill., U.S.A.* **140 D7** 40 55N 89 17W
Washburn, *N. Dak., U.S.A.* **138 B4** 47 17N 101 2W
Washburn, *Wis., U.S.A.* **138 B9** 46 40N 90 54W
Washim, *India* **82 D3** 20 3N 77 0 E
Washington, *D.C., U.S.A.* **134 F7** 38 54N 77 2W
Washington, *Ga., U.S.A.* **135 J4** 33 44N 82 44W
Washington, *Ind., U.S.A.* **141 F9** 38 40N 87 10W
Washington, *Iowa, U.S.A.* **140 C5** 41 18N 91 42W
Washington, *Mo., U.S.A.* **140 F5** 38 33N 91 1W
Washington, *N.C., U.S.A.* **135 H7** 35 33N 77 3W
Washington, *N.J., U.S.A.* **137 F10** 40 46N 74 59W
Washington, *Pa., U.S.A.* **136 F4** 40 10N 80 15W
Washington, *Utah, U.S.A.* **143 H7** 37 8N 113 31W
Washington □, *U.S.A.* **142 C3** 47 30N 120 30W
Washington, Mt., *U.S.A.* **137 B13** 44 16N 71 18W
Washington Court House, *U.S.A.* **141 E13** 39 32N 83 26W
Washington I., *U.S.A.* **134 C2** 45 23N 86 54W
Washougal, *U.S.A.* **144 E4** 45 35N 122 21W
Washuk, *Pakistan* **79 D2** 27 42N 64 45 E
Wasian, *Indonesia* **73 B4** 1 47 S 133 19 E
Wasilków, *Poland* **47 B10** 53 12N 23 13 E
Wasior, *Indonesia* **73 B4** 2 43 S 134 30 E
Waskaganish, *Canada* **128 B4** 51 30N 78 40W
Waskaiowaka, L., *Canada* **131 B9** 56 33N 96 23W
Waskesiu Lake, *Canada* **131 C7** 53 55N 106 5W
Wasmes, *Belgium* **21 H3** 50 25N 3 50 E
Waspik, *Neths.* **21 E5** 51 41N 4 57 E
Wassen, *Switz.* **29 C7** 46 42N 8 36 E
Wassenaar, *Neths.* **20 D4** 52 8N 4 24 E
Wasserburg, *Germany* **27 G8** 48 3N 12 14 E
Wasserkuppe, *Germany* **26 E5** 50 29N 9 55 E
Wassy, *France* **23 D11** 48 30N 4 58 E
Waswanipi, *Canada* **128 C4** 49 40N 76 29W
Waswanipi, L., *Canada* **128 C4** 49 35N 76 40W
Watangpone, *Indonesia* **72 B2** 4 29 S 120 25 E
Watansoppeng, *Indonesia* **72 B1** 4 10 S 119 56 E
Water Park Pt., *Australia* **114 C5** 22 56 S 150 47 E
Water Valley, *U.S.A.* **139 H10** 34 10N 89 38W
Waterberge, *S. Africa* **105 C4** 24 10 S 28 0 E
Waterbury, *Conn., U.S.A.* **137 E11** 41 33N 73 3W
Waterbury, *Vt., U.S.A.* **137 B12** 44 20N 72 46W
Waterbury L., *Canada* **131 B8** 58 10N 104 22W
Waterdown, *Canada* **136 C5** 43 20N 79 53W
Waterford, *Canada* **136 D4** 42 56N 80 17W
Waterford, *Ireland* **19 D4** 52 15N 7 8W
Waterford, *Calif., U.S.A.* **144 H6** 37 38N 120 46W
Waterford, *Wis., U.S.A.* **141 B8** 42 46N 88 13W
Waterford □, *Ireland* **19 D4** 52 10N 7 40W
Waterford Harbour, *Ireland* **19 D5** 52 8N 6 58W
Waterhen L., *Man., Canada* **131 C9** 52 10N 99 40W
Waterhen L., *Sask., Canada* **131 C7** 54 28N 108 25W
Wateringen, *Neths.* **20 D4** 52 2N 4 16 E
Waterloo, *Belgium* **21 G4** 50 43N 4 25 E
Waterloo, *Ont., Canada* **128 D3** 43 30N 80 32W
Waterloo, *Qué., Canada* **137 A12** 45 22N 72 32W
Waterloo, *S. Leone* **100 D2** 8 26N 13 8W
Waterloo, *Ill., U.S.A.* **140 F6** 38 20N 90 9W
Waterloo, *Ind., U.S.A.* **141 C11** 41 26N 85 1W
Waterloo, *Iowa, U.S.A.* **140 B4** 42 30N 92 21W
Waterloo, *N.Y., U.S.A.* **136 D8** 42 54N 76 52W
Waterloo, *Wis., U.S.A.* **140 A8** 43 11N 88 59W
Waterman, *U.S.A.* **141 C8** 41 46N 88 47W
Watermeal-Boitsford, *Belgium* **21 G4** 50 48N 4 25 E
Watersmeet, *U.S.A.* **138 B10** 46 16N 89 11W
Waterton-Glacier International Peace Park, *U.S.A.* **142 B7** 48 45N 115 0W
Watertown, *Conn., U.S.A.* **137 E11** 41 36N 73 7W
Watertown, *N.Y., U.S.A.* **137 C9** 43 59N 75 55W
Watertown, *S. Dak., U.S.A.* **138 C6** 44 54N 97 7W
Watertown, *Wis., U.S.A.* **138 D10** 43 12N 88 43W
Waterval-Boven, *S. Africa* **105 D5** 25 40 S 30 18 E
Waterville, *Canada* **137 A13** 45 16N 71 54W
Waterville, *Maine, U.S.A.* **129 D6** 44 33N 69 38W
Waterville, *N.Y., U.S.A.* **137 D9** 42 56N 75 23W
Waterville, *Pa., U.S.A.* **136 E7** 41 19N 77 21W
Waterville, *Wash., U.S.A.* **142 C3** 47 39N 120 4W
Watervliet, *Belgium* **21 F3** 51 17N 3 38 E
Watervliet, *Mich., U.S.A.* **141 B10** 42 11N 86 18W
Watervliet, *N.Y., U.S.A.* **137 D11** 42 44N 73 42W
Wates, *Indonesia* **75 D4** 7 51 S 110 10 E
Watford, *Canada* **136 D3** 42 57N 81 53W
Watford, *U.K.* **17 F7** 51 40N 0 24W
Watford City, *U.S.A.* **138 B3** 47 48N 103 17W
Wathaman →, *Canada* **131 B8** 57 16N 102 59W
Watheroo, *Australia* **113 F2** 30 15 S 116 0 E
Wating, *China* **66 G4** 35 40N 106 38 E
Watkins Glen, *U.S.A.* **136 D8** 42 23N 76 52W
Watling I. = San Salvador, *Bahamas* **149 B5** 24 0N 74 40W
Watonga, *U.S.A.* **139 H5** 35 51N 98 25W
Watou, *Belgium* **21 G1** 50 51N 2 38 E
Watrous, *Canada* **131 C7** 51 40N 105 25W
Watrous, *U.S.A.* **139 H2** 35 48N 104 59W
Watsa, *Zaïre* **106 B2** 3 4N 29 30 E
Watseka, *U.S.A.* **141 D9** 40 47N 87 44W
Watson, *Australia* **113 F5** 30 29 S 131 31 E
Watson, *Canada* **131 C8** 52 10N 104 30W
Watson Lake, *Canada* **130 A3** 60 6N 128 49W
Watsonville, *U.S.A.* **144 J5** 36 55N 121 45W
Wattenwil, *Switz.* **28 C5** 46 46N 7 30 E
Wattiwarriganna Cr. →, *Australia* **115 D2** 28 57 S 136 10 E
Wattwil, *Switz.* **29 B8** 47 18N 9 6 E
Watuata = Batuata, *Indonesia* **72 C2** 6 12 S 122 42 E
Watubela, Kepulauan, *Indonesia* **73 B4** 4 28 S 131 35 E
Watubela Is. = Watubela, Kepulauan, *Indonesia* **73 B4** 4 28 S 131 35 E
Wau, *Papua N. G.* **120 D4** 7 21 S 146 47 E
Wau, *Sudan* **93 F6** 7 45N 28 1 E
Waubach, *Neths.* **21 G8** 50 55N 6 3 E
Waubamik, *Canada* **136 A4** 45 27N 80 1W
Waubay, *U.S.A.* **138 C6** 45 20N 97 18W
Waubra, *Australia* **116 D5** 37 21 S 143 39 E
Wauchope, *Australia* **117 A10** 31 28 S 152 45 E
Wauchula, *U.S.A.* **135 M5** 27 33N 81 49W
Waugh, *Canada* **131 D9** 49 40N 95 11W
Waukarlycarly, L., *Australia* **112 D3** 21 18 S 121 56 E
Waukegan, *U.S.A.* **141 B9** 42 22N 87 50W
Waukesha, *U.S.A.* **141 B8** 43 1N 88 14W
Waukon, *U.S.A.* **138 D9** 43 16N 91 29W
Wauneta, *U.S.A.* **138 E4** 40 25N 101 23W
Waupaca, *U.S.A.* **138 C10** 44 21N 89 5W
Waupun, *U.S.A.* **138 D10** 43 38N 88 44W
Waurika, *U.S.A.* **139 H6** 34 10N 98 0W
Wausau, *U.S.A.* **138 C10** 44 58N 89 38W
Wauseon, *U.S.A.* **141 C12** 41 33N 84 8W
Wautoma, *U.S.A.* **138 C10** 44 4N 89 18W
Wauwatosa, *U.S.A.* **141 A9** 43 3N 88 0W
Wave Hill, *Australia* **112 C5** 17 32 S 131 0 E
Waveland, *U.S.A.* **141 E9** 39 53N 87 3W
Waveney →, *U.K.* **17 E9** 52 35N 1 39 E
Waverley, *N.Z.* **118 F3** 39 46 S 174 37 E
Waverly, *Ill., U.S.A.* **140 E7** 39 36N 89 57W
Waverly, *Iowa, U.S.A.* **140 B4** 42 44N 92 29W
Waverly, *Mo., U.S.A.* **140 E3** 39 13N 93 31W
Waverly, *N.Y., U.S.A.* **137 D8** 42 1N 76 32W
Wavre, *Belgium* **21 G5** 50 43N 4 38 E
Wavreille, *Belgium* **21 H6** 50 7N 5 15 E
Wâw, *Sudan* **95 F2** 7 45N 28 1 E
Wāw al Kabīr, *Libya* **96 C3** 25 20N 16 43 E
Wāw an Nāmūs, *Libya* **96 D3** 24 55N 17 46 E
Wawa, *Canada* **128 C3** 47 59N 84 47W
Wawa, *Nigeria* **101 D5** 9 54N 4 27 E
Wawa, *Sudan* **94 C3** 20 30N 30 22 E
Wawanesa, *Canada* **131 D9** 49 36N 99 40W
Wawasee, L., *U.S.A.* **141 C11** 41 24N 85 42W
Wawoi →, *Papua N. G.* **120 D2** 7 48 S 143 16 E
Wawona, *U.S.A.* **144 H7** 37 32N 119 39W
Waxahachie, *U.S.A.* **139 J6** 32 24N 96 51W
Way, L., *Australia* **113 E3** 26 45 S 120 16 E
Wayabula Rau, *Indonesia* **72 A3** 2 29N 128 17 E
Wayatinah, *Australia* **114 G4** 42 19 S 146 27 E
Waycross, *U.S.A.* **135 K4** 31 13N 82 21W
Wayi, *Sudan* **95 F3** 5 8N 30 10 E
Wayland, *U.S.A.* **141 B11** 42 40N 85 39W
Wayne, *Nebr., U.S.A.* **138 D6** 42 14N 97 1W
Wayne, *W. Va., U.S.A.* **134 F4** 38 13N 82 27W
Wayne City, *U.S.A.* **141 F8** 38 21N 88 35W
Waynesboro, *Ga., U.S.A.* **135 J4** 33 6N 82 1W
Waynesboro, *Miss., U.S.A.* **135 K1** 31 40N 88 39W
Waynesboro, *Pa., U.S.A.* **134 F7** 39 45N 77 35W
Waynesboro, *Va., U.S.A.* **134 F6** 38 4N 78 53W
Waynesburg, *U.S.A.* **134 F5** 39 54N 80 11W
Waynesville, *Mo., U.S.A.* **140 G4** 37 50N 92 12W
Waynesville, *N.C., U.S.A.* **135 H4** 35 28N 82 58W
Waynesville, *Ohio, U.S.A.* **141 E12** 39 32N 84 5W
Waynoka, *U.S.A.* **139 G5** 36 35N 98 53W
Wazay, *Afghan.* **79 B3** 33 22N 69 26 E
Wāzin, *Libya* **96 B2** 31 58N 10 40 E
Wazirabad, *Pakistan* **80 C6** 32 30N 74 8 E
Wda →, *Poland* **47 B5** 53 25N 18 29 E
We, *Indonesia* **74 A1** 5 51N 95 18 E
Weald, The, *U.K.* **17 F8** 51 4N 0 20 E
Wear →, *U.K.* **16 C6** 54 55N 1 23W
Weatherford, *Okla., U.S.A.* **139 H5** 35 32N 98 43W
Weatherford, *Tex., U.S.A.* **139 J6** 32 46N 97 48W
Weaubleau, *U.S.A.* **140 G3** 37 54N 93 32W
Weaverville, *U.S.A.* **142 F2** 40 44N 122 56W
Webb City, *U.S.A.* **139 G7** 37 9N 94 28W
Weber, *N.Z.* **118 G5** 40 24 S 176 20 E
Webo = Nyaake, *Liberia* **100 E3** 4 52N 7 37W
Webster, *Mass., U.S.A.* **137 D13** 42 3N 71 53W
Webster, *N.Y., U.S.A.* **136 C7** 43 13N 77 26W
Webster, *S. Dak., U.S.A.* **138 C6** 45 20N 97 31W
Webster, *Wis., U.S.A.* **138 C8** 45 53N 92 22W
Webster City, *U.S.A.* **140 B3** 42 28N 93 49W
Webster Green, *U.S.A.* **138 F9** 38 38N 90 20W
Webster Springs, *U.S.A.* **134 F5** 38 29N 80 25W
Weda, *Indonesia* **72 A3** 0 21N 127 50 E
Weda, Teluk, *Indonesia* **72 A3** 0 30N 127 50 E
Weddell I., *Falk. Is.* **160 D4** 51 50 S 61 0W
Weddell Sea, *Antarctica* **7 D1** 72 30 S 40 0W
Wedderburn, *Australia* **116 D5** 36 26 S 143 33 E
Wedel, *Germany* **26 B5** 53 34N 9 42 E
Wedgeport, *Canada* **129 D6** 43 44N 65 59W
Wedza, *Zimbabwe* **107 F3** 18 40 S 31 33 E
Wee Elwah, *Australia* **117 B6** 33 2 S 145 14 E
Wee Waa, *Australia* **115 E4** 30 11 S 149 26 E
Weed, *U.S.A.* **142 F2** 41 25N 122 23W
Weed Heights, *U.S.A.* **144 G7** 38 59N 119 13W
Weedsport, *U.S.A.* **137 C8** 43 3N 76 35W
Weedville, *U.S.A.* **136 E6** 41 17N 78 30W
Weemelah, *Australia* **115 D4** 29 2 S 149 15 E
Weenen, *S. Africa* **105 D5** 28 48 S 30 7 E
Weener, *Germany* **26 B3** 53 9N 7 20 E
Weert, *Neths.* **21 F7** 51 15N 5 43 E
Weesp, *Neths.* **20 D6** 52 18N 5 2 E
Weggis, *Switz.* **29 B6** 47 2N 8 26 E
Wegierska-Gorka, *Poland* **31 B12** 49 36N 19 7 E
Wegliniec, *Poland* **47 D2** 51 18N 15 10 E
Węgorzewo, *Poland* **47 A8** 54 13N 21 43 E
Węgrów, *Poland* **47 C9** 52 24N 22 0 E
Wehl, *Neths.* **20 E8** 51 58N 6 13 E
Wei He →, *Hebei, China* **66 F8** 36 10N 115 45 E
Wei He →, *Shaanxi, China* **66 G6** 34 38N 110 15 E
Weichang, *China* **67 D9** 41 58N 117 49 E
Weichuan, *China* **66 G7** 34 20N 113 59 E
Weida, *Germany* **26 E8** 50 46N 12 2 E
Weiden, *Germany* **27 F8** 49 41N 12 10 E
Weifang, *China* **67 F10** 36 44N 119 7 E
Weihai, *China* **67 F12** 37 30N 122 6 E
Weilburg, *Germany* **26 E4** 50 28N 8 17 E
Weilheim, *Germany* **27 H7** 47 50N 11 9 E
Weimar, *Germany* **26 E7** 50 58N 11 19 E
Weinan, *China* **66 G5** 34 31N 109 29 E
Weinfelden, *Switz.* **29 A8** 47 34N 9 6 E
Weingarten, *Germany* **27 H5** 47 47N 9 39 E
Weinheim, *Germany* **27 F4** 49 32N 8 39 E
Weining, *China* **68 D5** 26 50N 104 17 E
Weipa, *Australia* **114 A3** 12 40 S 141 50 E
Weir →, *Australia* **115 D4** 28 20 S 149 50 E
Weir →, *Canada* **131 B10** 56 54N 93 21W
Weir River, *Canada* **131 B10** 56 49N 94 6W
Weirton, *U.S.A.* **136 F4** 40 24N 80 35W
Weisen, *Switz.* **29 C9** 46 42N 9 43 E
Weiser, *U.S.A.* **142 D5** 44 10N 117 0W
Weishan, *Shandong, China* **67 G9** 34 47N 117 5 E
Weishan, *Yunnan, China* **68 E3** 25 12N 100 20 E
Weissenburg, *Germany* **27 F6** 49 2N 10 58 E
Weissenfels, *Germany* **26 D8** 51 11N 12 0 E
Weisshorn, *Switz.* **28 D5** 46 7N 7 43 E
Weissmies, *Switz.* **28 D6** 46 8N 8 1 E
Weisstannen, *Switz.* **29 C8** 46 59N 9 22 E
Weisswasser, *Germany* **26 D10** 51 30N 14 36 E
Weiswampach, *Belgium* **21 H8** 50 8N 6 5 E
Wéitra, *Austria* **30 C7** 48 41N 14 54 E
Weixi, *China* **68 D2** 27 10N 99 10 E
Weixin, *China* **68 D5** 27 48N 105 3 E
Weiyuan, *China* **66 G3** 35 7N 104 10 E
Weiz, *Austria* **30 D8** 47 13N 15 39 E
Weizhou Dao, *China* **68 G7** 21 0N 109 5 E
Wejherowo, *Poland* **47 A5** 54 35N 18 12 E
Wekusko L., *Canada* **131 C9** 54 40N 99 50W
Welbourn Hill, *Australia* **115 D1** 27 21 S 134 6 E
Welch, *U.S.A.* **134 G5** 37 26N 81 35W
Weldya, *Ethiopia* **95 E4** 11 50N 39 34 E
Welega □, *Ethiopia* **95 F3** 9 25N 34 20 E
Welkenraedt, *Belgium* **21 G7** 50 39N 5 58 E
Welkite, *Ethiopia* **95 F4** 8 15N 37 42 E
Welkom, *S. Africa* **104 D4** 28 0 S 26 46 E
Welland, *Canada* **128 D4** 43 0N 79 15W
Welland →, *U.K.* **16 E7** 52 51N 0 5W
Wellen, *Belgium* **21 G6** 50 50N 5 21 E
Wellesley Is., *Australia* **114 B2** 16 42 S 139 30 E
Wellin, *Belgium* **21 H6** 50 5N 5 6 E
Wellingborough, *U.K.* **17 E7** 52 19N 0 41W
Wellington, *Australia* **117 B8** 32 35 S 148 59 E
Wellington, *Canada* **128 D4** 43 57N 77 20W
Wellington, *N.Z.* **118 H3** 41 19 S 174 46 E
Wellington, *S. Africa* **104 E2** 33 38 S 19 1 E
Wellington, *Shrops., U.K.* **16 E5** 52 42N 2 30W
Wellington, *Somst., U.K.* **17 G4** 50 58N 3 13W
Wellington, *Colo., U.S.A.* **138 E2** 40 42N 105 0W
Wellington, *Kans., U.S.A.* **139 G6** 37 16N 97 24W
Wellington, *Mo., U.S.A.* **140 E3** 39 8N 93 59W
Wellington, *Nev., U.S.A.* **144 G7** 38 45N 119 23W
Wellington, *Ohio, U.S.A.* **136 E2** 41 10N 82 13W
Wellington, *Tex., U.S.A.* **139 H4** 34 51N 100 13W
Wellington □, *N.Z.* **118 G4** 41 0 S 175 30 E
Wellington, I., *Chile* **160 C2** 49 30 S 75 0W
Wellington, L., *Australia* **117 E7** 38 6 S 147 20 E
Wells, *U.K.* **17 F5** 51 13N 2 39W
Wells, *Maine, U.S.A.* **137 C14** 43 20N 70 35W
Wells, *Minn., U.S.A.* **138 D8** 43 45N 93 43W
Wells, *Nev., U.S.A.* **142 F6** 41 7N 114 58W
Wells, L., *Australia* **113 E3** 26 44 S 123 15 E
Wells Gray Prov. Park, *Canada* **130 C4** 52 30N 120 15W
Wells-next-the-Sea, *U.K.* **16 E8** 52 57N 0 51 E
Wells River, *U.S.A.* **137 B12** 44 9N 72 4W
Wellsboro, *U.S.A.* **136 E7** 41 45N 77 18W
Wellsburg, *U.S.A.* **136 F4** 40 16N 80 37W
Wellsford, *N.Z.* **118 C3** 36 16 S 174 32 E
Wellsville, *Mo., U.S.A.* **140 E5** 39 4N 91 34W
Wellsville, *N.Y., U.S.A.* **136 D7** 42 7N 77 57W
Wellsville, *Ohio, U.S.A.* **136 F4** 40 36N 80 39W
Wellsville, *Utah, U.S.A.* **142 F8** 41 38N 111 56W
Wellton, *U.S.A.* **143 K6** 32 40N 114 8W
Welmel, Wabi →, *Ethiopia* **95 F5** 5 38N 40 47 E
Wełna →, *Poland* **47 C4** 52 46N 17 32 E
Welo, *Somali Rep.* **108 C3** 9 25N 48 55 E
Welo □, *Ethiopia* **95 E4** 11 50N 39 48 E
Wels, *Austria* **30 C7** 48 9N 14 1 E
Welshpool, *U.K.* **17 E4** 52 39N 3 8W
Wem, *U.K.* **16 E5** 52 52N 2 44W
Wembere →, *Tanzania* **106 C3** 4 10 S 34 15 E
Wemindji, *Canada* **128 B4** 53 0N 78 49W
Wemmel, *Belgium* **21 G4** 50 55N 4 18 E
Wen Xian, *Gansu, China* **66 H3** 32 43N 104 36 E
Wen Xian, *Henan, China* **66 G7** 34 55N 113 5 E
Wenatchee, *U.S.A.* **142 C3** 47 25N 120 19W
Wenchang, *China* **76 C8** 19 38N 110 42 E
Wencheng, *China* **69 D13** 27 46N 120 4 E
Wenchi, *Ghana* **100 D4** 7 46N 2 8W
Wenchow = Wenzhou, *China* **69 C13** 28 0N 120 38 E
Wenchuan, *China* **68 B4** 31 22N 103 35 E
Wendell, *U.S.A.* **142 E6** 42 47N 114 42W
Wenden, *U.S.A.* **145 M13** 33 49N 113 33W
Wendeng, *China* **67 F12** 37 15N 122 5 E
Wendesi, *Indonesia* **73 B4** 2 30 S 134 17 E
Wendo, *Ethiopia* **95 F4** 6 40N 38 27 E
Wendover, *U.S.A.* **142 F6** 40 44N 114 2W
Wenduine, *Belgium* **21 F2** 51 18N 3 5 E
Weng'an, *China* **68 D6** 27 5N 107 25 E
Wengcheng, *China* **69 E9** 24 22N 113 50 E
Wengen, *Switz.* **28 C5** 46 37N 7 55 E
Wengyuan, *China* **69 E10** 24 20N 114 9 E
Wenjiang, *China* **68 B4** 30 44N 103 55 E
Wenling, *China* **69 C13** 28 21N 121 20 E
Wenlock →, *Australia* **114 A3** 12 2 S 141 55 E
Wenona, *U.S.A.* **140 C7** 41 3N 89 3W
Wenshan, *China* **68 F5** 23 20N 104 18 E
Wenshang, *China* **66 G9** 35 45N 116 30 E
Wenshui, *Guizhou, China* **68 C6** 28 27N 106 28 E
Wenshui, *Shanxi, China* **66 F7** 37 26N 112 1 E
Wensu, *China* **64 B3** 41 15N 80 10 E
Wentworth, *Australia* **116 C4** 34 2 S 141 54 E
Wentzville, *U.S.A.* **140 F6** 38 49N 90 51W
Wenut, *Indonesia* **73 B4** 3 11 S 133 19 E
Wenxi, *China* **66 G6** 35 20N 111 10 E
Wenzhou, *China* **69 C13** 28 0N 120 38 E
Weott, *U.S.A.* **142 F2** 40 20N 123 55W
Wepener, *S. Africa* **104 D4** 29 42 S 27 3 E
Werbomont, *Belgium* **21 H7** 50 23N 5 41 E
Werda, *Botswana* **104 D3** 25 24 S 23 15 E
Werdau, *Germany* **26 E8** 50 45N 12 22 E
Werder, *Ethiopia* **108 C3** 6 58N 45 1 E
Werder, *Germany* **26 C8** 52 23N 12 55 E
Werdohl, *Germany* **26 D3** 51 15N 7 46 E
Wereilu, *Ethiopia* **95 E4** 10 40N 39 28 E
Weri, *Indonesia* **73 B4** 3 10 S 132 38 E
Werkendam, *Neths.* **20 E5** 51 50N 4 53 E
Werne, *Germany* **26 D3** 51 39N 7 38 E
Werneck, *Germany* **27 F6** 49 58N 10 5 E
Wernigerode, *Germany* **26 D6** 51 50N 10 47 E
Werra →, *Germany* **26 D5** 51 24N 9 39 E
Werribee, *Australia* **116 D6** 37 54 S 144 40 E
Werrimull, *Australia* **116 C4** 34 25 S 141 38 E
Werris Creek, *Australia* **117 A9** 31 18 S 150 38 E
Wersar, *Indonesia* **73 B4** 1 30 S 131 55 E
Wertach →, *Germany* **27 G6** 48 22N 10 54 E
Wertheim, *Germany* **27 F5** 49 45N 9 32 E
Wertingen, *Germany* **27 G6** 48 33N 10 41 E
Wervershoof, *Neths.* **20 C6** 52 44N 5 10 E
Wervik, *Belgium* **21 G2** 50 47N 3 3 E
Wesel, *Germany* **26 D2** 51 39N 6 37 E
Weser →, *Germany* **26 B4** 53 36N 8 28 E
Wesiri, *Indonesia* **72 C3** 7 30 S 126 30 E
Wesley Vale, *U.S.A.* **143 J10** 35 3N 106 2W
Wesleyville, *Canada* **129 C9** 49 8N 53 36W
Wesleyville, *U.S.A.* **136 D4** 42 9N 80 0W
Wessel, C., *Australia* **114 A2** 10 59 S 136 46 E
Wessel Is., *Australia* **114 A2** 11 10 S 136 45 E
Wesselburen, *Germany* **26 A4** 54 13N 8 54 E
Wessem, *Neths.* **21 F7** 51 11N 5 49 E
Wessington, *U.S.A.* **138 C5** 44 27N 98 42W
Wessington Springs, *U.S.A.* **138 C5** 44 5N 98 34W
West, *U.S.A.* **139 K6** 31 48N 97 6W
West Allis, *U.S.A.* **141 A10** 43 1N 88 0W
West B., *U.S.A.* **139 L10** 29 3N 89 22W
West Baines →, *Australia* **112 C4** 15 38 S 129 59 E
West Bank □, *Asia* **91 C4** 32 6N 35 13 E
West Bend, *U.S.A.* **134 D1** 43 25N 88 11W
West Bengal □, *India* **81 H12** 23 0N 88 0 E
West Beskids = Západné Beskydy, *Europe* **31 B12** 49 30N 19 0 E
West Branch, *U.S.A.* **134 C3** 44 17N 84 14W
West Bromwich, *U.K.* **17 E5** 52 32N 1 59W
West Cape Howe, *Australia* **113 G2** 35 8 S 117 36 E
West Carrollton, *U.S.A.* **141 E12** 39 40N 84 17W
West Chazy, *U.S.A.* **137 B11** 44 49N 73 28W
West Chester, *U.S.A.* **134 F8** 39 58N 75 36W
West Chicago, *U.S.A.* **141 C8** 41 53N 88 12W
West Columbia, *U.S.A.* **139 L7** 29 9N 95 39W
West Covina, *U.S.A.* **145 L9** 34 4N 117 54W
West Des Moines, *U.S.A.* **140 C3** 41 35N 93 43W
West Dunbartonshire □, *U.K.* **18 F4** 55 59N 4 30W
West End, *Bahamas* **148 A4** 26 41N 78 58W
West Falkland, *Falk. Is.* **160 D4** 51 40 S 60 0W
West Fjord = Vestfjorden, *Norway* **12 C15** 67 55N 14 0 E
West Frankfort, *U.S.A.* **140 G8** 37 54N 88 55W
West Hartford, *U.S.A.* **137 E12** 41 45N 72 44W
West Haven, *U.S.A.* **137 E12** 41 17N 72 57W
West Helena, *U.S.A.* **139 H9** 34 33N 90 38W
West Ice Shelf, *Antarctica* **7 C7** 67 0 S 85 0 E
West Indies, *Cent. Amer.* **149 C7** 15 0N 65 0W
West Lafayette, *U.S.A.* **141 D10** 40 27N 86 55W
West Liberty, *Iowa, U.S.A.* **140 C5** 41 34N 91 16W
West Liberty, *Ky., U.S.A.* **141 G13** 37 55N 83 16W
West Liberty, *Ohio, U.S.A.* **141 D13** 40 15N 83 45W
West Lorne, *Canada* **136 D3** 42 36N 81 36W
West Lothian □, *U.K.* **18 F5** 55 54N 3 36W
West Lunga →, *Zambia* **107 E1** 13 6 S 24 39 E
West Manchester, *U.S.A.* **141 E12** 39 55N 84 38W
West Memphis, *U.S.A.* **139 H9** 35 9N 90 11W
West Midlands □, *U.K.* **17 E6** 52 26N 2 0W
West Mifflin, *U.S.A.* **136 F5** 40 22N 79 52W
West Milton, *U.S.A.* **141 E12** 39 58N 84 20W
West Monroe, *U.S.A.* **139 J8** 32 31N 92 9W
West Newton, *U.S.A.* **136 F5** 40 14N 79 46W
West Nicholson, *Zimbabwe* **107 G2** 21 2 S 29 20 E
West Palm Beach, *U.S.A.* **135 M5** 26 43N 80 3W
West Plains, *U.S.A.* **139 G9** 36 44N 91 51W
West Point, *Ga., U.S.A.* **135 J3** 32 53N 85 11W
West Point, *Ill., U.S.A.* **140 D5** 40 15N 91 11W
West Point, *Iowa, U.S.A.* **140 D5** 40 43N 91 27W
West Point, *Ky., U.S.A.* **141 G11** 37 59N 85 57W
West Point, *Miss., U.S.A.* **135 J1** 33 36N 88 39W
West Point, *Nebr., U.S.A.* **138 E6** 41 51N 96 43W
West Point, *Va., U.S.A.* **134 G7** 37 32N 76 48W
West Pokot □, *Kenya* **106 B4** 1 30N 35 15 E
West Pt. = Ouest, Pte., *Canada* **129 C7** 49 52N 64 40W
West Pt., *Australia* **116 C1** 35 1 S 135 56 E
West Road →, *Canada* **130 C4** 53 18N 122 53W
West Rutland, *U.S.A.* **137 C11** 43 38N 73 5W
West Salem, *U.S.A.* **141 F8** 38 31N 88 1W
West Schelde = Westerschelde →, *Neths.* **21 F2** 51 25N 3 25 E
West Seneca, *U.S.A.* **136 D6** 42 51N 78 48W
West Siberian Plain, *Russia* **58 C11** 62 0N 75 0 E
West Sussex □, *U.K.* **17 G7** 50 55N 0 30W
West Terre Haute, *U.S.A.* **141 E9** 39 28N 87 27W
West-Terschelling, *Neths.* **20 B6** 53 22N 5 13 E
West Union, *Iowa, U.S.A.* **140 B5** 42 57N 91 49W
West Union, *Ohio, U.S.A.* **141 F13** 38 48N 83 33W
West Unity, *U.S.A.* **141 C12** 41 35N 84 26W
West Valley City, *U.S.A.* **142 F8** 40 42N 111 57W
West Virginia □, *U.S.A.* **134 F5** 38 45N 80 30W
West-Vlaanderen □, *Belgium* **21 G2** 51 0N 3 0 E
West Walker →, *U.S.A.* **144 G7** 38 54N 119 9W
West Wyalong, *Australia* **117 B7** 33 56 S 147 10 E

284 West Yellowstone

West Yellowstone, U.S.A. 142 D8 44 40N 111 6W
West Yorkshire □, U.K. 16 D6 53 45N 1 40W
Westall Pt., Australia 115 E1 32 55 S 134 4 E
Westbrook, Maine, U.S.A. 135 D10 43 41N 70 22W
Westbrook, Tex., U.S.A. 139 J4 32 21N 101 1W
Westbury, Australia 114 G4 41 30 S 146 51 E
Westby, U.S.A. 138 A2 48 52N 104 3W
Westend, U.S.A. 145 K9 35 42N 117 24W
Westerbork, Neths. 20 C9 52 51N 6 37 E
Westerland, Germany 13 J13 54 54N 8 17 E
Western □, Kenya 106 B3 0 30N 34 30 E
Western □, Uganda 106 B3 1 45N 31 30 E
Western □, Zambia 107 F1 15 15 S 24 30 E
Western Australia □, Australia 113 E2 25 0 S 118 0 E
Western Cape □, S. Africa 104 E3 34 0 S 20 0 E
Western Dvina = Daugava →, Latvia 13 H21 57 4N 24 3 E
Western Ghats, India 83 H2 14 0N 75 0 E
Western Isles □, U.K. 18 D1 57 30N 7 10W
Western River, Australia 116 C2 35 42 S 136 56 E
Western Sahara ■, Africa 98 D2 25 0N 13 0W
Western Samoa ■, Pac. Oc. 121 X24 14 0 S 172 0W
Westernport, U.S.A. 134 F6 39 29N 79 3W
Westerschelde →, Neths. 21 F2 51 25N 3 25 E
Westerstede, Germany 26 B3 53 15N 7 55 E
Westervoort, Neths. 20 E7 51 58N 5 59 E
Westerwald, Germany 26 E4 50 38N 7 56 E
Westfield, Ill., U.S.A. 141 E8 39 27N 88 0W
Westfield, Ind., U.S.A. 141 D10 40 2N 86 8W
Westfield, Mass., U.S.A. 137 D12 42 7N 72 45W
Westfield, N.Y., U.S.A. 136 D5 42 20N 79 35W
Westfield, Pa., U.S.A. 136 E7 41 55N 77 32W
Westgat, Neths. 21 E3 51 39N 3 44 E
Westhope, U.S.A. 138 A4 48 55N 101 1W
Westkapelle, Belgium 21 F2 51 19N 3 19 E
Westkapelle, Neths. 21 E2 51 31N 3 28 E
Westland, U.S.A. 141 B13 42 15N 83 20W
Westland Bight, N.Z. 119 C5 42 55 S 170 5 E
Westlock, Canada 130 C6 54 9N 113 55W
Westmalle, Belgium 21 F5 51 18N 4 42 E
Westmeath □, Ireland 19 C4 53 33N 7 34W
Westminster, U.S.A. 134 F7 39 34N 76 59W
Westmorland, U.S.A. 143 K6 33 2N 115 37W
Weston, Malaysia 75 A5 5 10N 115 35 E
Weston, Ohio, U.S.A. 141 C13 41 21N 83 47W
Weston, Oreg., U.S.A. 142 D4 45 49N 118 26W
Weston, W. Va., U.S.A. 134 F5 39 2N 80 28W
Weston I., Canada 128 B4 52 33N 79 36W
Weston-super-Mare, U.K. 17 F5 51 21N 2 58W
Westphalia, U.S.A. 140 F5 38 26N 92 0W
Westport, Canada 137 B8 44 40N 76 25W
Westport, Ireland 19 C2 53 48N 9 31W
Westport, N.Z. 119 B6 41 46 S 171 37 E
Westport, Ind., U.S.A. 141 E11 39 11N 85 34W
Westport, Oreg., U.S.A. 144 D3 46 8N 123 23W
Westport, Wash., U.S.A. 142 C1 46 53N 124 6W
Westray, Canada 131 C8 53 36N 101 24W
Westray, U.K. 18 B6 59 18N 3 0W
Westree, Canada 128 C3 47 26N 81 34W
Westville, Calif., U.S.A. 144 F6 39 8N 120 42W
Westville, Ill., U.S.A. 141 D9 40 2N 87 38W
Westville, Ind., U.S.A. 141 C10 41 35N 86 55W
Westville, Okla., U.S.A. 139 G7 35 58N 94 40W
Westwood, U.S.A. 142 F3 40 18N 121 0W
Wetar, Indonesia 72 C3 7 30 S 126 30 E
Wetaskiwin, Canada 130 C6 52 55N 113 24W
Wethersfield, U.S.A. 137 E12 41 42N 72 40W
Wetlet, Burma 78 D5 22 20N 95 53 E
Wetteren, Belgium 21 G3 51 0N 3 52 E
Wettingen, Switz. 29 B6 47 28N 8 20 E
Wetzikon, Switz. 29 B7 47 19N 8 48 E
Wetzlar, Germany 26 E4 50 32N 8 31 E
Wevelgem, Belgium 21 G2 50 49N 3 12 E
Wewak, Papua N. G. 120 B2 3 38 S 143 41 E
Wewoka, U.S.A. 139 H6 35 9N 96 30W
Wexford, Ireland 19 D5 52 20N 6 28W
Wexford □, Ireland 19 D5 52 20N 6 25W
Wexford Harbour, Ireland 19 D5 52 20N 6 25W
Weyburn, Canada 131 D8 49 40N 103 50W
Weyburn L., Canada 130 A5 63 0N 117 59W
Weyer, Austria 30 D7 47 51N 14 40 E
Weyib →, Ethiopia 95 F5 7 15N 40 15 E
Weymouth, Canada 129 D6 44 30N 66 1W
Weymouth, U.K. 17 G5 50 37N 2 28W
Weymouth, U.S.A. 137 D14 42 13N 70 58W
Weymouth, C., Australia 114 A3 12 37 S 143 27 E
Wezemaal, Belgium 21 G5 50 57N 4 45 E
Wezep, Neths. 20 D7 52 28N 6 0 E
Wha Ti, Canada 126 B8 63 8N 117 16W
Whakamaru, N.Z. 118 E4 38 23 S 175 50 E
Whakatane, N.Z. 118 D6 37 57 S 177 1 E
Whakatane →, N.Z. 118 D6 37 57 S 177 1 E
Whale →, Canada 129 A6 58 15N 67 40W
Whale Cove, Canada 131 A10 62 11N 92 36W
Whales, B. of, Antarctica 7 D12 78 0 S 165 0W
Whalsay, U.K. 18 A7 60 22N 0 59W
Whangaehu →, N.Z. 118 G4 40 3 S 175 6 E
Whangamata, N.Z. 118 D4 37 12 S 175 53 E
Whangamomona, N.Z. 118 F3 39 8 S 174 44 E
Whangarei, N.Z. 118 B3 35 43 S 174 21 E
Whangarei Harb., N.Z. 118 B3 35 45 S 174 28 E
Whangaroa Harb., N.Z. 118 B2 35 4 S 173 46 E
Whangaruru Harb., N.Z. 118 B3 35 24 S 174 23 E
Wharanui, N.Z. 119 B9 41 55 S 174 6 E
Wharfe →, U.K. 16 D6 53 51N 1 9W
Wharfedale, U.K. 16 C5 54 6N 2 1W
Wharton, N.J., U.S.A. 137 F10 40 54N 74 35W
Wharton, Pa., U.S.A. 136 E6 41 31N 78 1W
Wharton, Tex., U.S.A. 139 L6 29 19N 96 6W
Whataroa, N.Z. 119 D5 43 18 S 170 24 E
Whataroa →, N.Z. 119 D5 43 7 S 170 16 E
Wheatfield, U.S.A. 141 C9 41 13N 87 4W
Wheatland, Calif., U.S.A. 144 F5 39 1N 121 25W
Wheatland, Ind., U.S.A. 141 F9 38 40N 87 19W
Wheatland, Wyo., U.S.A. 138 D2 42 3N 104 58W
Wheatley, Canada 136 D2 42 6N 82 27W
Wheaton, Ill., U.S.A. 141 C8 41 52N 88 6W
Wheaton, Minn., U.S.A. 138 C6 45 48N 96 30W
Wheelbarrow Pk., U.S.A. 144 H10 37 26N 116 5W
Wheeler, Oreg., U.S.A. 142 D2 45 41N 123 53W
Wheeler, Tex., U.S.A. 139 H4 35 27N 100 16W
Wheeler →, Canada 131 B7 57 25N 105 30W
Wheeler Pk., N. Mex., U.S.A. 143 H11 36 34N 105 25W
Wheeler Pk., Nev., U.S.A. 143 G6 38 57N 114 15W
Wheeler Ridge, U.S.A. 145 L8 35 0N 118 57W
Wheeling, U.S.A. 136 F4 40 4N 80 43W
Whernside, U.K. 16 C5 54 14N 2 24W
Whidbey I., U.S.A. 130 D4 48 12N 122 17W
Whiskey Gap, Canada 130 D6 49 0N 113 3W
Whiskey Jack L., Canada 131 B8 58 23N 101 55W
Whistleduck Cr. →, Australia 114 C2 20 15 S 135 18 E
Whitby, Canada 136 C6 43 52N 78 56W
Whitby, U.K. 16 C7 54 29N 0 37W
Whitcombe Pass, N.Z. 119 D5 43 13 S 170 55 E
White →, Ark., U.S.A. 139 J9 33 57N 91 5W
White →, Ind., U.S.A. 141 F9 38 25N 87 45W
White →, S. Dak., U.S.A. 138 D5 43 42N 99 27W
White →, Utah, U.S.A. 142 F9 40 4N 109 41W
White →, Wash., U.S.A. 144 C4 47 12N 122 15W
White, East Fork →, U.S.A. 141 F9 38 33N 87 14W
White, L., Australia 112 D4 21 9 S 128 56 E
White B., Canada 129 B8 50 0N 56 35W
White Bear Res., Canada 129 C8 48 10N 57 5W
White Bird, U.S.A. 142 D5 45 46N 116 18W
White Butte, U.S.A. 138 B3 46 23N 103 18W
White City, U.S.A. 138 F6 38 48N 96 44W
White Cliffs, Australia 116 A5 30 50 S 143 10 E
White Deer, U.S.A. 139 H4 35 26N 101 10W
White Hall, U.S.A. 140 E6 39 26N 90 24W
White Haven, U.S.A. 137 E9 41 4N 75 47W
White Horse, Vale of, U.K. 17 F6 51 37N 1 30W
White I., N.Z. 118 D6 37 30 S 177 13 E
White L., Canada 137 A8 45 18N 76 31W
White L., U.S.A. 139 L8 29 44N 92 30W
White Mts., Calif., U.S.A. 144 H8 37 30N 118 15W
White Mts., N.H., U.S.A. 137 B13 44 15N 71 15W
White Nile = Nîl el Abyad →, Sudan 95 D3 15 38N 32 31 E
White Nile Dam = Khazzân Jabal el Awliyâ, Sudan 95 D3 15 24N 32 20 E
White Otter L., Canada 128 C1 49 5N 91 55W
White Pass, Canada 130 B1 59 40N 135 3W
White Pass, U.S.A. 144 D5 46 38N 121 24W
White Pigeon, U.S.A. 141 C11 41 48N 85 39W
White Plains, U.S.A. 137 E11 41 2N 73 46W
White River, Canada 128 C2 48 35N 85 20W
White River, S. Africa 105 D5 25 20 S 31 0 E
White River, U.S.A. 138 D4 43 34N 100 45W
White Russia = Belarus ■, Europe 50 F4 53 30N 27 0 E
White Sea = Beloye More, Russia 48 A6 66 30N 38 0 E
White Sulphur Springs, Mont., U.S.A. 142 C8 46 33N 110 54W
White Sulphur Springs, W. Va., U.S.A. 134 G5 37 48N 80 18W
White Swan, U.S.A. 144 D6 46 23N 120 44W
White Volta →, Ghana 101 D4 9 10N 1 15W
Whitecliffs, N.Z. 119 D6 43 26 S 171 55 E
Whitecourt, Canada 130 C5 54 10N 115 45W
Whiteface, U.S.A. 139 J3 33 36N 102 37W
Whitefield, U.S.A. 137 B13 44 23N 71 37W
Whitefish, U.S.A. 142 B6 48 25N 114 20W
Whitefish Bay, U.S.A. 141 A9 43 23N 87 54W
Whitefish L., Canada 131 A7 62 41N 106 48W
Whitefish Point, U.S.A. 134 B3 46 45N 84 59W
Whitegull, L., Canada 129 A7 55 27N 64 17W
Whitehall, Mich., U.S.A. 134 D2 43 24N 86 21W
Whitehall, Mont., U.S.A. 142 D7 45 52N 112 6W
Whitehall, N.Y., U.S.A. 137 C11 43 33N 73 24W
Whitehall, Wis., U.S.A. 138 C9 44 22N 91 19W
Whitehaven, U.K. 16 C4 54 33N 3 35W
Whitehorse, Canada 130 A1 60 43N 135 3W
Whiteman, U.S.A. 140 F3 38 45N 93 40W
Whiteman Ra., Papua N. G. 120 C5 5 55 S 150 0 E
Whitemark, Australia 114 G4 40 7 S 148 3 E
Whitemouth, Canada 131 D9 49 57N 95 58W
Whiteplains, Liberia 100 D2 6 28N 10 40W
Whitesboro, N.Y., U.S.A. 137 C9 43 7N 75 18W
Whitesboro, Tex., U.S.A. 139 J6 33 39N 96 54W
Whiteshell Prov. Park, Canada 131 C9 50 0N 95 40W
Whiteside, U.S.A. 140 E5 39 12N 91 2W
Whiteside, Canal, Chile 160 D2 53 55 S 70 15W
Whitetail, U.S.A. 138 A2 48 54N 105 10W
Whiteville, U.S.A. 135 H6 34 20N 78 42W
Whitewater, U.S.A. 141 B8 42 50N 88 44W
Whitewater Baldy, U.S.A. 143 K9 33 20N 108 39W
Whitewater L., Canada 128 B2 50 50N 89 10W
Whitewood, Australia 114 C3 21 28 S 143 30 E
Whitewood, Canada 131 C8 50 20N 102 20W
Whitfield, Australia 117 D7 36 42 S 146 24 E
Whithorn, U.K. 18 G4 54 44N 4 26W
Whitianga, N.Z. 118 C4 36 47 S 175 41 E
Whiting, U.S.A. 141 C9 41 41N 87 29W
Whitman, U.S.A. 137 D14 42 5N 70 56W
Whitmire, U.S.A. 135 H5 34 30N 81 37W
Whitney, Canada 128 C4 45 31N 78 14W
Whitney, Mt., U.S.A. 144 J8 36 35N 118 18W
Whitney Point, U.S.A. 137 D9 42 20N 75 58W
Whitstable, U.K. 17 F9 51 21N 1 3 E
Whitsunday I., Australia 114 C4 20 15 S 149 4 E
Whittemore, U.S.A. 140 A2 43 4N 94 26W
Whittier, U.S.A. 145 M8 33 58N 118 3W
Whittlesea, Australia 117 D6 37 27 S 145 9 E
Whitwell, U.S.A. 135 H3 35 12N 85 31W
Wholdaia L., Canada 131 A8 60 43N 104 20W
Whyalla, Australia 116 B2 33 2 S 137 30 E
Whyjonta, Australia 115 D3 29 41 S 142 28 E
Wiarton, Canada 128 D3 44 40N 81 10W
Wiawso, Ghana 100 D4 6 10N 2 25W
Wiazów, Poland 47 E4 50 50N 17 10 E
Wibaux, U.S.A. 138 B2 46 59N 104 11W
Wichabai, Guyana 153 C6 2 57N 59 35W
Wichian Buri, Thailand 76 E3 15 39N 101 7 E
Wichita, U.S.A. 139 G6 37 42N 97 20W
Wichita Falls, U.S.A. 139 J5 33 54N 98 30W
Wick, U.K. 18 C5 58 26N 3 5W
Wickenburg, U.S.A. 143 K7 33 58N 112 44W
Wickepin, Australia 113 F2 32 50 S 117 30 E
Wickham, C., Australia 114 F3 39 35 S 143 57 E
Wickliffe, U.S.A. 136 E3 41 36N 81 28W
Wicklow, Ireland 19 D5 52 59N 6 3W
Wicklow □, Ireland 19 D5 52 57N 6 25W
Wicklow Hd., Ireland 19 D5 52 58N 6 0W
Widawa, Poland 47 D5 51 27N 18 51 E
Widawka, Poland 47 D6 51 7N 19 36 E
Widgiemooltha, Australia 113 F3 31 30 S 121 34 E
Widnes, U.K. 16 D5 53 23N 2 45W
Więcbork, Poland 47 B4 53 21N 17 30 E
Wiedenbrück, Germany 26 D4 51 52N 8 15 E
Wiehl, Germany 26 E3 50 56N 7 34 E
Wiek, Germany 26 A9 54 37N 13 17 E
Wielbark, Poland 47 B7 53 24N 20 55 E
Wieleń, Poland 47 C3 52 53N 16 9 E
Wieliczka, Poland 31 B13 50 0N 20 5 E
Wieluń, Poland 47 D5 51 15N 18 34 E
Wien, Austria 31 C9 48 12N 16 22 E
Wiener Neustadt, Austria 31 D9 47 49N 16 16 E
Wieprz →, Koszalin, Poland 47 A3 54 26N 16 35 E
Wieprz →, Lublin, Poland 47 D8 51 34N 21 49 E
Wierden, Neths. 20 D9 52 22N 6 35 E
Wiers, Belgium 21 H3 50 30N 3 32 E
Wieruszów, Poland 47 D5 51 19N 18 9 E
Wiesbaden, Germany 27 E4 50 4N 8 14 E
Wiesental, Germany 27 F4 49 13N 8 31 E
Wigan, U.K. 16 D5 53 33N 2 38W
Wiggins, Colo., U.S.A. 138 E2 40 14N 104 4W
Wiggins, Miss., U.S.A. 139 K10 30 51N 89 8W
Wight, I. of □, U.K. 17 G6 50 40N 1 20W
Wigry, Jezioro, Poland 47 A10 54 2N 23 8 E
Wigtown, U.K. 18 G4 54 53N 4 27W
Wigtown B., U.K. 18 G4 54 46N 4 15W
Wijchen, Neths. 20 E7 51 48N 5 44 E
Wijhe, Neths. 20 D8 52 23N 6 8 E
Wijk bij Duurstede, Neths. 20 E6 51 59N 5 21 E
Wil, Switz. 29 B8 47 28N 9 3 E
Wilamowice, Poland 31 B12 49 55N 19 9 E
Wilangee, Australia 116 A4 31 28 S 141 20 E
Wilber, U.S.A. 138 E6 40 29N 96 58W
Wilberforce, Canada 136 A6 45 2N 78 13W
Wilberforce, C., Australia 114 A2 11 54 S 136 35 E
Wilburton, U.S.A. 139 H7 34 55N 95 19W
Wilcannia, Australia 116 A5 31 30 S 143 26 E
Wilcox, U.S.A. 136 E6 41 35N 78 41W
Wildbad, Germany 27 G4 48 44N 8 33 E
Wildcat →, U.S.A. 141 D10 40 28N 86 52W
Wildervank, Neths. 20 B9 53 5N 6 52 E
Wildeshausen, Germany 26 C4 52 54N 8 27 E
Wildhorn, Switz. 28 D4 46 22N 7 21 E
Wildon, Austria 30 E8 46 52N 15 31 E
Wildrose, Calif., U.S.A. 145 J9 36 14N 117 11W
Wildrose, N. Dak., U.S.A. 138 A3 48 38N 103 11W
Wildspitze, Austria 30 E3 46 53N 10 53 E
Wildstrubel, Switz. 28 D5 46 24N 7 32 E
Wildwood, U.S.A. 134 F8 38 59N 74 50W
Wilga →, Poland 47 D8 51 52N 21 18 E
Wilgaroon, Australia 117 A6 30 52 S 145 42 E
Wilge →, S. Africa 105 D4 27 3 S 28 20 E
Wilhelm, Mt., Papua N. G. 120 C3 5 50 S 145 1 E
Wilhelm II Coast, Antarctica 7 C7 68 0 S 90 0 E
Wilhelm-Pieck-Stadt-Guben, Germany 26 D10 51 57N 14 42 E
Wilhelmina, Geb., Surinam 153 C6 3 50N 56 30W
Wilhelmina Kanaal, Neths. 21 E6 51 36N 5 6 E
Wilhelmsburg, Austria 30 C8 48 6N 15 36 E
Wilhelmshaven, Germany 26 B4 53 31N 8 7 E
Wilhelmstal, Namibia 104 C2 21 58 S 16 21 E
Wilkes-Barre, U.S.A. 137 E9 41 15N 75 53W
Wilkesboro, U.S.A. 135 G5 36 9N 81 10W
Wilkie, Canada 131 C7 52 27N 108 42W
Wilkinsburg, U.S.A. 136 F5 40 26N 79 53W
Wilkinson Lakes, Australia 113 E5 29 40 S 132 39 E
Willamina, U.S.A. 142 D2 45 5N 123 29W
Willamulka, Australia 116 B2 33 55 S 137 52 E
Willandra Billabong Creek →, Australia 116 B6 33 22 S 145 52 E
Willapa B., U.S.A. 142 C2 46 40N 124 0W
Willapa Hills, U.S.A. 144 D3 46 35N 123 25W
Willard, N. Mex., U.S.A. 143 J10 34 36N 106 2W
Willard, Utah, U.S.A. 142 F7 41 25N 112 2W
Willaura, Australia 116 D5 37 31 S 142 45 E
Willbriggie, Australia 117 C7 34 28 S 146 2 E
Willcox, U.S.A. 143 K9 32 15N 109 50W
Willebroek, Belgium 21 F4 51 4N 4 22 E
Willemstad, Neth. Ant. 149 D6 12 5N 69 0W
Willeroo, Australia 112 C5 15 14 S 131 37 E
William →, Canada 131 B7 59 8N 109 19W
William, Mt., Australia 116 D5 37 17 S 142 35 E
William Creek, Australia 115 D2 28 58 S 136 22 E
Williambury, Australia 113 D2 23 45 S 115 12 E
Williams, Australia 113 F2 33 2 S 116 52 E
Williams, Ariz., U.S.A. 143 J7 35 15N 112 11W
Williams, Calif., U.S.A. 144 F4 39 9N 122 9W
Williams Lake, Canada 130 C4 52 10N 122 10W
Williamsburg, Ky., U.S.A. 135 G3 36 44N 84 10W
Williamsburg, Pa., U.S.A. 136 F6 40 28N 78 12W
Williamsburg, Va., U.S.A. 134 G7 37 17N 76 44W
Williamsfield, U.S.A. 140 D6 40 55N 90 1W
Williamson, N.Y., U.S.A. 136 C7 43 14N 77 11W
Williamson, W. Va., U.S.A. 134 G4 37 41N 82 17W
Williamsport, Ind., U.S.A. 141 D9 40 17N 87 17W
Williamsport, Pa., U.S.A. 136 E7 41 15N 77 0W
Williamston, Mich., U.S.A. 141 B12 42 41N 84 17W
Williamston, N.C., U.S.A. 135 H7 35 51N 77 4W
Williamstown, Australia 117 D6 37 51 S 144 52 E
Williamstown, Ky., U.S.A. 141 F12 38 38N 84 34W
Williamstown, Mass., U.S.A. 137 D11 42 41N 73 12W
Williamstown, N.Y., U.S.A. 137 C9 43 26N 75 53W
Williamsville, Ill., U.S.A. 140 E7 39 57N 89 33W
Williamsville, Mo., U.S.A. 139 G9 36 58N 90 33W
Willimantic, U.S.A. 137 E12 41 43N 72 13W
Willis Group, Australia 114 B5 16 18 S 150 0 E
Willisau, Switz. 28 B6 47 7N 8 0 E
Willisburg, U.S.A. 141 G11 37 49N 85 8W
Williston, S. Africa 104 E3 31 20 S 20 53 E
Williston, Fla., U.S.A. 135 L4 29 23N 82 27W
Williston, N. Dak., U.S.A. 138 A3 48 9N 103 37W
Williston L., Canada 130 B4 56 0N 124 0W
Willits, U.S.A. 142 G2 39 25N 123 21W
Willmar, U.S.A. 138 C7 45 7N 95 3W
Willoughby, U.S.A. 136 E3 41 39N 81 24W
Willow Bunch, Canada 131 D7 49 20N 105 35W
Willow L., Canada 130 A5 62 10N 119 8W
Willow Lake, U.S.A. 138 C6 44 38N 97 38W
Willow Springs, U.S.A. 139 G8 37 0N 91 58W
Willow Tree, Australia 117 A9 31 40 S 150 45 E
Willow Wall, The, China 67 C12 42 10N 122 0 E
Willowlake →, Canada 130 A4 62 42N 123 8W
Willowmore, S. Africa 104 E3 33 15 S 23 30 E
Willows, Australia 114 C4 23 39 S 147 25 E
Willows, U.S.A. 144 F4 39 31N 122 12W
Willowvale = Gatyana, S. Africa 105 E4 32 16 S 28 31 E
Wills, L., Australia 112 D4 21 25 S 128 51 E
Wills Cr. →, Australia 114 C3 22 43 S 140 2 E
Wills Point, U.S.A. 139 J7 32 43N 96 1W
Willunga, Australia 116 C3 35 15 S 138 30 E
Wilmette, U.S.A. 134 D2 42 5N 87 42W
Wilmington, Australia 116 B3 32 39 S 138 7 E
Wilmington, Del., U.S.A. 134 F8 39 45N 75 33W
Wilmington, Ill., U.S.A. 141 C8 41 18N 88 9W
Wilmington, N.C., U.S.A. 135 H7 34 14N 77 55W
Wilmington, Ohio, U.S.A. 141 E13 39 27N 83 50W
Wilpena Cr. →, Australia 116 A3 31 25 S 139 29 E
Wilrijk, Belgium 21 F4 51 9N 4 22 E
Wilsall, U.S.A. 142 D8 45 59N 110 38W
Wilson, U.S.A. 135 H7 35 44N 77 55W
Wilson →, Queens., Australia 115 D3 27 38 S 141 24 E
Wilson →, W. Austral., Australia 112 C4 16 48 S 128 16 E
Wilson Bluff, Australia 113 F4 31 41 S 129 0 E
Wilson Str., Solomon Is. 121 M9 8 0 S 156 39 E
Wilsons Promontory, Australia 117 E7 38 55 S 146 25 E
Wilster, Germany 26 B5 53 55N 9 23 E
Wilton, U.K. 17 F6 51 5N 1 51W
Wilton, U.S.A. 138 B4 47 10N 100 47W
Wilton →, Australia 114 A1 14 45 S 134 33 E
Wiltshire □, U.K. 17 F6 51 18N 1 53W
Wiltz, Lux. 21 J7 49 57N 5 55 E
Wiluna, Australia 113 E3 26 36 S 120 14 E
Wimereux, France 23 B8 50 45N 1 37 E
Wimmera →, Australia 116 D4 36 8 S 141 56 E
Winam G., Kenya 106 C3 0 20 S 34 15 E
Winamac, U.S.A. 141 C10 41 3N 86 36W
Winburg, S. Africa 104 D4 28 30 S 27 2 E
Winchelsea, Australia 116 E6 38 10 S 144 1 E
Winchendon, U.S.A. 137 D12 42 41N 72 3W
Winchester, N.Z. 119 E6 44 11 S 171 17 E
Winchester, U.K. 17 F6 51 4N 1 18W
Winchester, Conn., U.S.A. 137 E11 41 53N 73 9W
Winchester, Idaho, U.S.A. 142 C5 46 14N 116 38W
Winchester, Ill., U.S.A. 140 E6 39 38N 90 27W
Winchester, Ind., U.S.A. 141 D12 40 10N 84 59W
Winchester, Ky., U.S.A. 141 G12 38 0N 84 11W
Winchester, N.H., U.S.A. 137 D12 42 46N 72 23W
Winchester, Nev., U.S.A. 145 J11 36 6N 115 10W
Winchester, Ohio, U.S.A. 141 F13 38 57N 83 40W
Winchester, Tenn., U.S.A. 135 H2 35 11N 86 7W
Winchester, Va., U.S.A. 134 F6 39 11N 78 10W
Wind →, U.S.A. 142 E9 43 12N 108 12W
Wind Point, U.S.A. 141 B9 42 47N 87 46W
Wind River Range, U.S.A. 142 E9 43 0N 109 30W
Windau = Ventspils, Latvia 13 H19 57 25N 21 32 E
Windber, U.S.A. 136 F6 40 14N 78 50W
Windermere, L., U.K. 16 C5 54 22N 2 56W
Windfall, Canada 130 C5 54 12N 116 13W
Windfall, U.S.A. 141 D11 40 22N 85 57W
Windflower L., Canada 130 A5 62 52N 118 30W
Windhoek, Namibia 104 C2 22 35 S 17 4 E
Windischgarsten, Austria 30 D7 47 42N 14 21 E
Windom, U.S.A. 138 D7 43 52N 95 7W
Windorah, Australia 114 D3 25 24 S 142 36 E
Window Rock, U.S.A. 143 J9 35 41N 109 3W
Windrush →, U.K. 17 F6 51 43N 1 24W
Windsor, Australia 117 B9 33 37 S 150 50 E
Windsor, N.S., Canada 129 D7 44 59N 64 5W
Windsor, Nfld., Canada 129 C8 48 57N 55 40W
Windsor, Ont., Canada 128 D3 42 18N 83 0W
Windsor, N.Z. 119 E5 44 59 S 170 49 E
Windsor, U.K. 17 F7 51 29N 0 36W
Windsor, Colo., U.S.A. 138 E2 40 29N 104 54W
Windsor, Conn., U.S.A. 137 E12 41 50N 72 39W
Windsor, Ill., U.S.A. 141 E8 39 26N 88 36W
Windsor, Mo., U.S.A. 140 F3 38 32N 93 31W
Windsor, N.Y., U.S.A. 137 D9 42 5N 75 37W
Windsor, Vt., U.S.A. 137 C12 43 29N 72 24W
Windsorton, S. Africa 104 D3 28 16 S 24 44 E
Windward Is., W. Indies 149 D7 13 0N 61 0W
Windward Passage = Vientos, Paso de los, Caribbean 149 C5 20 0N 74 0W
Windy L., Canada 131 A8 60 20N 100 2W
Winefred L., Canada 131 B6 55 30N 110 30W
Winejok, Sudan 95 F2 9 1N 27 30 E
Winfield, Iowa, U.S.A. 140 C5 41 7N 91 26W
Winfield, Kans., U.S.A. 139 G6 37 15N 96 59W
Winfield, Mo., U.S.A. 140 E6 39 0N 90 44W
Wingate Mts., Australia 112 B5 14 25 S 130 40 E
Wingen, Australia 117 A9 31 54 S 150 54 E
Wingene, Belgium 21 F2 51 3N 3 17 E
Wingham, Australia 117 A10 31 48 S 152 22 E
Wingham, Canada 128 D3 43 55N 81 20W
Winifred, U.S.A. 142 C9 47 34N 109 23W
Winisk, Canada 128 A2 55 20N 85 15W
Winisk →, Canada 128 A2 55 17N 85 5W
Winisk L., Canada 128 B2 52 55N 87 22W
Wink, U.S.A. 139 K3 31 45N 103 9W
Winkler, Canada 131 D9 49 10N 97 56W
Winklern, Austria 30 E5 46 52N 12 52 E
Winlock, U.S.A. 144 D4 46 30N 122 56W
Winneba, Ghana 101 D4 5 25N 0 36W
Winnebago, Ill., U.S.A. 140 B7 42 16N 89 15W
Winnebago, Minn., U.S.A. 138 D7 43 46N 94 10W
Winnebago, L., U.S.A. 134 D1 44 0N 88 26W
Winnecke Cr. →, Australia 112 C5 18 35 S 131 34 E
Winnemucca, U.S.A. 142 F5 40 58N 117 44W
Winnemucca L., U.S.A. 142 F4 40 7N 119 21W
Winner, U.S.A. 138 D5 43 22N 99 52W
Winnett, U.S.A. 142 C9 47 0N 108 21W
Winnfield, U.S.A. 139 K8 31 56N 92 38W
Winnibigoshish, L., U.S.A. 138 B7 47 27N 94 13W
Winning, Australia 112 D1 23 9 S 114 30 E
Winnipeg, Canada 131 D9 49 54N 97 9W

286 Xinjin

Xinjin, *Liaoning, China* **67 E11** 39 25N 121 58 E
Xinjin, *Sichuan, China* **68 B4** 30 24N 103 47 E
Xinkai He →, *China* **67 C12** 43 32N 123 35 E
Xinle, *China* **66 E8** 38 25N 114 40 E
Xinlitun, *China* **67 D12** 42 0N 122 8 E
Xinlong, *China* **68 B3** 30 57N 100 12 E
Xinmin, *China* **67 D12** 41 59N 122 50 E
Xinning, *China* **69 D8** 26 28N 110 50 E
Xinping, *China* **68 E3** 24 5N 101 59 E
Xinshao, *China* **69 D8** 27 21N 111 26 E
Xintai, *China* **67 G9** 35 55N 117 45 E
Xintian, *China* **69 E9** 25 55N 112 13 E
Xinxiang, *China* **66 G7** 35 18N 113 50 E
Xinxing, *China* **69 F9** 22 35N 112 15 E
Xinyang, *China* **69 A10** 32 6N 114 3 E
Xinye, *China* **69 A9** 32 30N 112 21 E
Xinyi, *China* **69 F8** 22 25N 111 0 E
Xinyu, *China* **69 D10** 27 49N 114 58 E
Xinzhan, *China* **67 C14** 43 50N 127 18 E
Xinzheng, *China* **66 G7** 34 20N 113 45 E
Xinzhou, *China* **69 B10** 30 50N 114 48 E
Xiong Xian, *China* **66 E9** 38 59N 116 8 E
Xiongyuecheng, *China* **67 D12** 40 12N 122 5 E
Xiping, *Henan, China* **66 H8** 33 22N 114 5 E
Xiping, *Henan, China* **66 H6** 33 25N 111 8 E
Xiping, *Zhejiang, China* **69 C12** 28 16N 119 29 E
Xique-Xique, *Brazil* **154 D3** 10 50 S 42 40W
Xiruá →, *Brazil* **156 B4** 6 3 S 67 50W
Xishui, *China* **69 B10** 30 30N 115 15 E
Xituozhen, *China* **68 B7** 30 22N 108 11 E
Xiuning, *China* **69 C12** 29 45N 118 10 E
Xiuren, *China* **69 E8** 24 27N 110 12 E
Xiushan, *China* **68 C7** 28 25N 108 57 E
Xiushui, *China* **69 C10** 29 2N 114 33 E
Xiuwen, *China* **68 D6** 26 49N 106 32 E
Xiuyan, *China* **67 D12** 40 18N 123 11 E
Xixia, *China* **66 H6** 33 25N 111 29 E
Xixiang, *China* **66 H4** 33 0N 107 44 E
Xiyang, *China* **66 F7** 37 38N 113 38 E
Xizang □, *China* **64 C3** 32 0N 88 0 E
Xlendi, *Malta* **32 C1** 36 1N 14 12 E
Xu Jiang →, *China* **69 D11** 28 0N 116 25 E
Xuan Loc, *Vietnam* **77 G6** 10 56N 107 14 E
Xuancheng, *China* **69 B12** 30 56N 118 43 E
Xuan'en, *China* **68 C7** 30 0N 109 30 E
Xuanhan, *China* **68 B6** 31 18N 107 38 E
Xuanhua, *China* **66 D8** 40 40N 115 2 E
Xuchang, *China* **66 G7** 34 2N 113 48 E
Xudat, *Azerbaijan* **53 K9** 41 38N 48 41 E
Xuefeng Shan, *China* **69 D8** 27 5N 110 35 E
Xuejiaping, *China* **69 B8** 31 39N 110 16 E
Xun Jiang →, *China* **69 F8** 23 35N 111 30 E
Xun Xian, *China* **66 G8** 35 42N 114 33 E
Xundian, *China* **68 E4** 25 36N 103 15 E
Xunwu, *China* **69 E10** 24 54N 115 37 E
Xunyang, *China* **66 H5** 32 48N 109 22 E
Xunyi, *China* **66 G5** 35 8N 108 20 E
Xupu, *China* **69 D8** 27 53N 110 32 E
Xushui, *China* **66 E8** 39 2N 115 40 E
Xuwen, *China* **69 G8** 20 20N 110 10 E
Xuyen Moc, *Vietnam* **77 G6** 10 34N 107 25 E
Xuyong, *China* **68 C5** 28 10N 105 22 E
Xuzhou, *China* **67 G9** 34 18N 117 10 E
Xylophagou, *Cyprus* **32 E12** 34 54N 33 51 E

Y

Ya Xian, *China* **76 C7** 18 14N 109 29 E
Yaamba, *Australia* **114 C5** 23 8 S 150 22 E
Ya'an, *China* **68 C4** 29 58N 103 5 E
Yaapeet, *Australia* **116 C5** 35 45 S 142 3 E
Yabassi, *Cameroon* **101 E6** 4 30N 9 57 E
Yabba North, *Australia* **117 D6** 36 13 S 145 42 E
Yabelo, *Ethiopia* **95 G4** 4 50N 38 8 E
Yablanitsa, *Bulgaria* **43 D9** 43 2N 24 5 E
Yablonovy Ra. = Yablonovyy Khrebet, *Russia* **57 D12** 53 0N 114 0 E
Yablonovyy Khrebet, *Russia* **57 D12** 53 0N 114 0 E
Yabrai Shan, *China* **66 E2** 39 40N 103 0 E
Yabrūd, *Syria* **91 B5** 33 58N 36 39 E
Yacheng, *China* **65 E5** 18 22N 109 6 E
Yacuiba, *Bolivia* **158 A3** 22 0 S 63 43W
Yacuma →, *Bolivia* **157 C4** 13 38 S 65 23W
Yadgir, *India* **82 F3** 16 45N 77 5 E
Yadkin →, *U.S.A.* **135 H5** 35 29N 80 9W
Yadrin, *Russia* **52 C8** 55 57N 46 12 E
Yagaba, *Ghana* **101 C4** 10 14N 1 20W
Yagodnoye, *Russia* **57 C15** 62 33N 149 40 E
Yagoua, *Cameroon* **102 A3** 10 20N 15 13 E
Yaguas →, *Peru* **152 D3** 2 45 S 70 10W
Yaha, *Thailand* **77 J3** 6 29N 101 8 E
Yahila, *Zaïre* **102 B4** 0 13N 24 28 E
Yahk, *Canada* **130 D5** 49 6N 116 10W
Yahotyn, *Ukraine* **51 G6** 50 17N 31 46 E
Yahuma, *Zaïre* **102 B4** 1 0N 23 10 E
Yahyalı, *Turkey* **88 C6** 38 5N 35 2 E
Yaita, *Japan* **61 F9** 36 48N 139 56 E
Yaiza, *Canary Is.* **33 F6** 28 57N 13 46W
Yaizu, *Japan* **63 C10** 34 52N 138 20 E
Yajiang, *China* **68 B3** 30 2N 100 57 E
Yajua, *Nigeria* **101 C7** 11 27N 12 49 E
Yakage, *Japan* **62 C5** 34 37N 133 35 E
Yakamba, *Zaïre* **102 B3** 2 42N 19 38 E
Yakima, *U.S.A.* **142 C3** 46 36N 120 31W
Yakima →, *U.S.A.* **142 C3** 47 0N 120 30W
Yako, *Burkina Faso* **100 C4** 12 59N 2 15W
Yakoma, *Zaïre* **102 B4** 4 5N 22 27 E
Yakoruda, *Bulgaria* **43 E8** 42 1N 23 39 E
Yakovlevka, *Russia* **60 B6** 44 26N 133 28 E
Yakshur Bodya, *Russia* **54 C4** 57 11N 53 7 E
Yaku-Shima, *Japan* **61 J5** 30 20N 130 30 E
Yakutat, *U.S.A.* **126 C6** 59 33N 139 44W
Yakutia = Sakha □, *Russia* **57 C13** 62 0N 130 0 E
Yakutsk, *Russia* **57 C13** 62 5N 129 50 E
Yala, *Thailand* **77 J3** 6 33N 101 18 E
Yalbalgo, *Australia* **113 E1** 25 10 S 114 45 E
Yalboroo, *Australia* **114 C4** 20 50 S 148 40 E
Yale, *U.S.A.* **136 C2** 43 8N 82 48W
Yalgoo, *Australia* **113 E2** 28 16 S 116 39 E
Yali, *Zaïre* **102 B4** 0 4N 21 3 E
Yaligimba, *Zaïre* **102 B4** 2 13N 22 56 E
Yalinga, *C.A.R.* **102 A4** 6 33N 23 10 E
Yalkubul, Punta, *Mexico* **147 C7** 21 32N 88 37W
Yalleroi, *Australia* **114 C4** 24 3 S 145 42 E
Yalobusha →, *U.S.A.* **139 J9** 33 33N 90 10W
Yaloke, *C.A.R.* **102 A3** 5 19N 17 5 E
Yalong Jiang →, *China* **68 D3** 26 40N 101 55 E
Yalova, *Turkey* **88 B3** 40 41N 29 15 E
Yalpuh, Ozero, *Ukraine* **46 D9** 45 30N 28 41 E
Yalta, *Ukraine* **51 K8** 44 30N 34 10 E
Yalu Jiang →, *China* **67 E13** 40 0N 124 22 E
Yalutorovsk, *Russia* **56 D7** 56 41N 66 12 E
Yalvaç, *Turkey* **88 C4** 38 17N 31 10 E
Yam Ha Melah = Dead Sea, *Asia* **91 D4** 31 30N 35 30 E
Yam Kinneret, *Israel* **91 C4** 32 45N 35 35 E
Yamada, *Japan* **62 D2** 33 33N 130 49 E
Yamaga, *Japan* **62 D2** 33 1N 130 41 E
Yamagata, *Japan* **60 E10** 38 15N 140 15 E
Yamagata □, *Japan* **60 E10** 38 30N 140 0 E
Yamagawa, *Japan* **62 F2** 31 12N 130 39 E
Yamaguchi, *Japan* **62 C3** 34 10N 131 32 E
Yamaguchi □, *Japan* **62 C3** 34 20N 131 40 E
Yamal, Poluostrov, *Russia* **56 B8** 71 0N 70 0 E
Yamal Pen. = Yamal, Poluostrov, *Russia* **56 B8** 71 0N 70 0 E
Yamanaka, *Japan* **63 A8** 36 15N 136 22 E
Yamanashi □, *Japan* **63 B10** 35 40N 138 40 E
Yamantau, Gora, *Russia* **54 D7** 54 15N 58 6 E
Yamato, *Japan* **63 B11** 35 27N 139 25 E
Yamatotakada, *Japan* **63 C7** 34 31N 135 45 E
Yamazaki, *Japan* **62 B6** 35 0N 134 32 E
Yamba, *N.S.W., Australia* **115 D5** 29 26 S 153 23 E
Yamba, *S. Austral., Australia* **116 C4** 34 10 S 140 52 E
Yambah, *Australia* **114 C1** 23 10 S 133 50 E
Yambarran Ra., *Australia* **112 C5** 15 10 S 130 25 E
Yambata, *Zaïre* **102 B4** 2 26N 21 58 E
Yâmbiô, *Sudan* **95 G2** 4 35N 28 16 E
Yambol, *Bulgaria* **43 E11** 42 30N 26 36 E
Yamdena, *Indonesia* **73 C4** 7 45 S 131 20 E
Yame, *Japan* **62 D2** 33 13N 130 35 E
Yamethin, *Burma* **78 E6** 20 29N 96 18 E
Yamil, *Nigeria* **101 C6** 12 53N 8 4 E
Yamma-Yamma, L., *Australia* **115 D3** 26 16 S 141 20 E
Yamoussoukro, *Ivory C.* **100 D3** 6 49N 5 17W
Yampa →, *U.S.A.* **142 F9** 40 32N 108 59W
Yampi Sd., *Australia* **112 C3** 16 8 S 123 38 E
Yampil, *Moldova* **51 H5** 48 15N 28 15 E
Yampol = Yampil, *Moldova* **51 H5** 48 15N 28 15 E
Yamrat, *Nigeria* **101 C6** 10 11N 9 55 E
Yamrukchal, *Bulgaria* **43 E9** 42 44N 24 52 E
Yamuna →, *India* **81 G9** 25 30N 81 53 E
Yamzho Yumco, *China* **64 D4** 28 48N 90 35 E
Yan, *Nigeria* **101 C7** 10 5N 12 11 E
Yan →, *Sri Lanka* **83 K5** 9 0N 81 10 E
Yana →, *Russia* **57 B14** 71 30N 136 0 E
Yanac, *Australia* **116 D4** 36 8 S 141 25 E
Yanagawa, *Japan* **62 D2** 33 10N 130 24 E
Yanahara, *Japan* **62 C6** 34 58N 134 2 E
Yanai, *Japan* **62 D4** 33 58N 132 7 E
Yanam, *India* **82 F6** 16 47N 82 15 E
Yan'an, *China* **66 F5** 36 35N 109 26 E
Yanaul, *Russia* **54 C5** 56 25N 55 0 E
Yanbian, *China* **68 D3** 26 47N 101 31 E
Yanbu 'al Baḩr, *Si. Arabia* **84 F3** 24 0N 38 5 E
Yancannia, *Australia* **115 E3** 30 12 S 142 35 E
Yanchang, *China* **66 F6** 36 43N 110 1 E
Yancheng, *Henan, China* **66 H7** 33 35N 114 0 E
Yancheng, *Jiangsu, China* **67 H11** 33 23N 120 8 E
Yanchi, *China* **66 F4** 37 48N 107 20 E
Yanchuan, *China* **66 F6** 36 51N 110 10 E
Yanco, *Australia* **117 C7** 34 38 S 146 27 E
Yanco Cr. →, *Australia* **117 C6** 35 14 S 145 35 E
Yandal, *Australia* **113 E3** 27 35 S 121 10 E
Yandanooka, *Australia* **113 E2** 29 18 S 115 29 E
Yandaran, *Australia* **114 C5** 24 43 S 152 6 E
Yandé, I., *N. Cal.* **121 T17** 20 3 S 163 49 E
Yandina, *Solomon Is.* **121 M10** 9 7 S 159 13 E
Yandja, *Zaïre* **102 C3** 1 41 S 17 43 E
Yandongi, *Zaïre* **102 B4** 2 51N 22 16 E
Yandoon, *Burma* **78 G5** 17 0N 95 40 E
Yanfeng, *China* **68 E3** 25 52N 101 8 E
Yanfolila, *Mali* **100 C3** 11 11N 8 9W
Yang Xian, *China* **66 H4** 33 15N 107 30 E
Yangambi, *Zaïre* **106 B1** 0 47N 24 20 E
Yangbi, *China* **68 E2** 25 41N 99 58 E
Yangcheng, *China* **66 G7** 35 28N 112 22 E
Yangch'ü = Taiyuan, *China* **66 F7** 37 52N 112 33 E
Yangchun, *China* **69 F8** 22 11N 111 48 E
Yanggao, *China* **66 D7** 40 21N 113 55 E
Yanggu, *China* **66 F8** 36 8N 115 43 E
Yangibazar, *Kyrgyzstan* **55 C5** 41 40N 70 53 E
Yangikishlak, *Uzbekistan* **55 C3** 40 25N 67 10 E
Yangiyul, *Uzbekistan* **55 C4** 41 0N 69 3 E
Yangjiang, *China* **69 G8** 21 50N 111 59 E
Yangliuqing, *China* **67 E9** 39 2N 117 5 E
Yangon = Rangoon, *Burma* **78 G6** 16 45N 96 20 E
Yangping, *China* **69 B8** 31 12N 111 25 E
Yangpingguan, *China* **66 H4** 32 58N 106 5 E
Yangquan, *China* **66 F7** 37 58N 113 31 E
Yangshan, *China* **69 E9** 24 30N 112 40 E
Yangshuo, *China* **69 E8** 24 48N 110 29 E
Yangtze Kiang = Chang Jiang →, *China* **69 B13** 31 48N 121 10 E
Yangxin, *China* **69 C10** 29 50N 115 12 E
Yangyang, *S. Korea* **67 E15** 38 4N 128 38 E
Yangyuan, *China* **66 D8** 40 1N 114 10 E
Yangzhou, *China* **69 A12** 32 21N 119 26 E
Yanhe, *China* **68 C7** 28 31N 108 29 E
Yanji, *China* **67 C15** 42 59N 129 30 E
Yanjin, *China* **68 C5** 28 5N 104 18 E
Yanjing, *China* **68 C2** 29 7N 98 33 E
Yankton, *U.S.A.* **138 D6** 42 53N 97 23W
Yanna, *Australia* **115 D4** 26 58 S 146 0 E
Yanonge, *Zaïre* **102 B4** 0 35N 24 38 E
Yanqi, *China* **64 B3** 42 5N 86 35 E
Yanqing, *China* **66 D8** 40 30N 115 58 E
Yanshan, *Hebei, China* **67 E9** 38 4N 117 22 E
Yanshan, *Jiangxi, China* **69 C11** 28 15N 117 41 E
Yanshan, *Yunnan, China* **68 F5** 23 35N 104 20 E
Yanshou, *China* **67 B15** 45 28N 128 22 E
Yantabulla, *Australia* **115 D4** 29 21 S 145 0 E
Yantai, *China* **67 F11** 37 34N 121 22 E
Yanting, *China* **68 B5** 31 11N 105 24 E
Yantra →, *Bulgaria* **43 D10** 43 40N 25 37 E
Yanwa, *China* **68 D2** 27 35N 98 55 E
Yanykurgan, *Kazakstan* **55 B3** 43 50N 68 48 E
Yanyuan, *China* **68 D3** 27 25N 101 30 E
Yanzhou, *China* **66 G9** 35 35N 116 49 E
Yao, *Chad* **97 F3** 12 56N 17 33 E
Yao, *Japan* **63 C7** 34 32N 135 36 E
Yao Xian, *China* **66 G5** 34 55N 108 59 E
Yao Yai, Ko, *Thailand* **77 J2** 8 0N 98 35 E
Yao'an, *China* **68 E3** 25 31N 101 18 E
Yaodu, *China* **68 A5** 32 45N 105 22 E
Yaoundé, *Cameroon* **101 E7** 3 50N 11 35 E
Yaowan, *China* **67 G10** 34 15N 118 3 E
Yap I., *Pac. Oc.* **122 G5** 9 30N 138 10 E
Yapen, *Indonesia* **73 B5** 1 50 S 136 0 E
Yapen, Selat, *Indonesia* **73 B5** 1 20 S 136 10 E
Yappar →, *Australia* **114 B3** 18 22 S 141 16 E
Yaqui →, *Mexico* **146 B2** 27 37N 110 39W
Yar, *Russia* **54 B4** 58 14N 52 5 E
Yar-Sale, *Russia* **56 C8** 66 50N 70 50 E
Yaracuy □, *Venezuela* **152 A4** 10 20N 68 45W
Yaracuy →, *Venezuela* **152 A4** 10 33N 68 15W
Yaraka, *Australia* **114 C3** 24 53 S 144 3 E
Yaransk, *Russia* **52 B8** 57 22N 47 49 E
Yardea P.O., *Australia* **115 E2** 32 23 S 135 32 E
Yare →, *U.K.* **17 E9** 52 35N 1 38 E
Yaremcha, *Ukraine* **51 H3** 48 27N 24 33 E
Yarensk, *Russia* **48 B8** 62 11N 49 15 E
Yarí →, *Colombia* **152 D3** 0 20 S 72 20W
Yaritagua, *Venezuela* **152 A4** 10 5N 69 8W
Yarkand = Shache, *China* **64 C2** 38 20N 77 10 E
Yarker, *Canada* **137 B8** 44 23N 76 46W
Yarkhun →, *Pakistan* **81 A5** 36 17N 72 30 E
Yarmouth, *Canada* **129 D6** 43 50N 66 7W
Yarmūk →, *Syria* **91 C4** 32 42N 35 40 E
Yaroslavl, *Russia* **52 B4** 57 35N 39 55 E
Yarqa, W. →, *Egypt* **91 F2** 30 0N 33 49 E
Yarra Yarra Lakes, *Australia* **113 E2** 29 40 S 115 45 E
Yarraden, *Australia* **114 A3** 14 17 S 143 15 E
Yarraloola, *Australia* **112 D2** 21 33 S 115 52 E
Yarram, *Australia* **117 E7** 38 29 S 146 39 E
Yarraman, *Australia* **115 D5** 26 50 S 152 0 E
Yarranvale, *Australia* **115 D4** 26 50 S 145 20 E
Yarras, *Australia* **117 A10** 31 25 S 152 20 E
Yarrawonga, *Australia* **117 D6** 36 0 S 146 0 E
Yarrowmere, *Australia* **114 C4** 21 27 S 145 53 E
Yarto, *Australia* **116 C5** 35 28 S 142 16 E
Yartsevo, *Russia* **50 E7** 55 6N 32 43 E
Yartsevo, *Russia* **57 C10** 60 20N 90 0 E
Yarumal, *Colombia* **152 B2** 6 58N 75 24W
Yasawa, *Fiji* **121 A1** 16 47 S 177 31 E
Yasawa Group, *Fiji* **121 A1** 17 0 S 177 23 E
Yaselda, *Belarus* **51 F4** 52 7N 26 28 E
Yashbum, *Yemen* **86 D4** 14 19N 46 56 E
Yashi, *Nigeria* **101 C6** 12 23N 7 54 E
Yashiro-Jima, *Japan* **62 D4** 33 55N 132 15 E
Yashkul, *Russia* **53 G7** 46 11N 45 21 E
Yasin, *Pakistan* **81 A5** 36 24N 73 23 E
Yasinovataya, *Ukraine* **51 H9** 48 7N 37 57 E
Yasinski, L., *Canada* **128 B4** 53 16N 77 35W
Yasinya, *Ukraine* **51 H3** 48 16N 24 21 E
Yasnyy, *Russia* **54 F7** 51 1N 59 58 E
Yasothon, *Thailand* **76 E5** 15 50N 104 10 E
Yass, *Australia* **117 C8** 34 49 S 148 54 E
Yasugi, *Japan* **62 B5** 35 26N 133 15 E
Yata →, *Bolivia* **157 C4** 10 29 S 65 26W
Yatağan, *Turkey* **88 D3** 37 20N 28 10 E
Yates Center, *U.S.A.* **139 G7** 37 53N 95 44W
Yates Pt., *N.Z.* **119 E2** 44 29 S 167 49 E
Yathkyed L., *Canada* **131 A9** 62 40N 98 0W
Yathong, *Australia* **117 B6** 32 37 S 145 33 E
Yatsuo, *Japan* **63 A9** 36 34N 137 8 E
Yatsushiro, *Japan* **62 E2** 32 30N 130 40 E
Yatsushiro-Kai, *Japan* **62 E2** 32 30N 130 25 E
Yatta Plateau, *Kenya* **106 C4** 2 0 S 38 0 E
Yauca, *Peru* **156 D3** 15 39 S 74 35W
Yauya, *Peru* **156 B2** 8 59 S 77 17W
Yauyos, *Peru* **156 C2** 12 19 S 75 50W
Yaval, *India* **82 D2** 21 10N 75 42 E
Yavan, *Tajikistan* **55 D4** 38 19N 69 2 E
Yavari →, *Peru* **156 A3** 4 21 S 70 2W
Yavatmal, *India* **82 D4** 20 20N 78 15 E
Yavne, *Israel* **91 D3** 31 52N 34 45 E
Yavoriv, *Ukraine* **51 H2** 49 55N 23 20 E
Yavorov = Yavoriv, *Ukraine* **51 H2** 49 55N 23 20 E
Yavuzeli, *Turkey* **88 D7** 37 18N 37 24 E
Yawatahama, *Japan* **62 D4** 33 27N 132 24 E
Yawri B., *S. Leone* **100 D2** 8 22N 13 0W
Yaxi, *China* **68 D6** 27 33N 106 41 E
Yayama-Rettō, *Japan* **61 M1** 24 30N 123 40 E
Yazagyo, *Burma* **78 D5** 23 30N 94 6 E
Yazd, *Iran* **85 D7** 31 55N 54 27 E
Yazd □, *Iran* **85 D7** 32 0N 55 0 E
Yazdān, *Iran* **79 B1** 33 30N 60 50 E
Yazoo →, *U.S.A.* **139 J9** 32 22N 90 54W
Yazoo City, *U.S.A.* **139 J9** 32 51N 90 25W
Ybbs, *Austria* **30 C8** 48 12N 15 4 E
Yding Skovhøj, *Denmark* **13 J13** 55 59N 9 46 E
Ydrim, *Yemen* **86 D4** 14 20N 44 22 E
Ye Xian, *Henan, China* **66 H7** 33 35N 113 25 E
Ye Xian, *Shandong, China* **67 F10** 37 8N 119 57 E
Yea, *Australia* **117 D6** 37 14 S 145 26 E
Yealering, *Australia* **113 F2** 32 36 S 117 36 E
Yearinan, *Australia* **117 A8** 31 10 S 149 11 E
Yebbi-Souma, *Chad* **97 D3** 21 7N 17 54 E
Yechŏn, *S. Korea* **67 F15** 36 39N 128 27 E
Yecla, *Spain* **35 G3** 38 35N 1 5W
Yécora, *Mexico* **146 B3** 28 20N 108 58W
Yedashe, *Burma* **78 F6** 19 10N 96 20 E
Yedintsy = Edinița, *Moldova* **51 H4** 48 9N 27 18 E
Yeeda, *Australia* **112 C3** 17 31 S 123 38 E
Yeelanna, *Australia* **115 E2** 34 9 S 135 45 E
Yefremov, *Russia* **52 D4** 53 8N 38 3 E
Yeghegnadzor, *Armenia* **89 C11** 39 44N 45 19 E
Yegorlyk →, *Russia* **53 G5** 46 35N 41 57 E
Yegorlykskaya, *Russia* **53 G5** 46 35N 40 35 E
Yegoryevsk, *Russia* **52 C4** 55 27N 38 55 E
Yegros, *Paraguay* **158 B4** 26 20 S 56 25W
Yehuda, Midbar, *Israel* **91 D4** 31 35N 35 15 E
Yei, *Sudan* **95 G3** 4 9N 30 40 E
Yei, Nahr →, *Sudan* **95 F3** 6 15N 30 13 E
Yejmiadzin, *Armenia* **53 K7** 40 12N 44 19 E
Yekaterinburg, *Russia* **54 C8** 56 50N 60 30 E
Yekaterinodar = Krasnodar, *Russia* **53 H4** 45 5N 39 0 E
Yekumbe, *Zaïre* **102 C4** 1 2 S 23 27 E
Yelabuga, *Russia* **52 C11** 55 45N 52 4 E
Yelan, *Russia* **52 E6** 50 55N 43 43 E
Yelandur, *India* **83 H3** 12 6N 77 0 E
Yelanskoye, *Russia* **57 C13** 61 25N 128 0 E
Yelarbon, *Australia* **115 D5** 28 33 S 150 38 E
Yelatma, *Russia* **52 C5** 55 0N 41 45 E
Yelcho, L., *Chile* **160 B2** 43 18 S 72 18W
Yelets, *Russia* **52 D4** 52 40N 38 30 E
Yélimané, *Mali* **100 B2** 15 9N 10 34W
Yelizavetgrad = Kirovohrad, *Ukraine* **51 H7** 48 35N 32 20 E
Yelizavetinka, *Russia* **54 F7** 51 46N 59 45 E
Yell, *U.K.* **18 A7** 60 35N 1 5W
Yell Sd., *U.K.* **18 A7** 60 33N 1 15W
Yellamanchilli = Elamanchili, *India* **82 F6** 17 33N 82 50 E
Yellow Sea, *China* **67 G12** 35 0N 123 0 E
Yellowhead Pass, *Canada* **130 C5** 52 53N 118 25W
Yellowknife, *Canada* **130 A6** 62 27N 114 29W
Yellowknife →, *Canada* **130 A6** 62 31N 114 19W
Yellowstone →, *U.S.A.* **138 B3** 47 59N 103 59W
Yellowstone L., *U.S.A.* **142 D8** 44 27N 110 22W
Yellowstone National Park, *U.S.A.* **142 D8** 44 40N 110 30W
Yellowtail Res., *U.S.A.* **142 D9** 45 6N 108 8W
Yelnya, *Russia* **50 E7** 54 35N 33 15 E
Yelsk, *Belarus* **51 G5** 51 50N 29 10 E
Yelvertoft, *Australia* **114 C2** 20 13 S 138 45 E
Yelwa, *Nigeria* **101 C5** 10 49N 4 41 E
Yemanzhelinsk, *Russia* **54 D8** 54 58N 61 18 E
Yembongo, *Zaïre* **102 B3** 3 12N 19 2 E
Yemen ■, *Asia* **86 D4** 15 0N 44 0 E
Yen Bai, *Vietnam* **76 B5** 21 42N 104 52 E
Yenakiyeve, *Ukraine* **51 H10** 48 15N 38 15 E
Yenakiyevo = Yenakiyeve, *Ukraine* **51 H10** 48 15N 38 15 E
Yenangyaung, *Burma* **78 E5** 20 30N 95 0 E
Yenanma, *Burma* **78 F5** 19 46N 94 49 E
Yenbo = Yanbu 'al Baḩr, *Si. Arabia* **84 F3** 24 0N 38 5 E
Yenda, *Australia* **117 C7** 34 13 S 146 14 E
Yendéré, *Ivory C.* **100 C4** 10 12N 4 59W
Yendi, *Ghana* **101 D4** 9 29N 0 1W
Yengo, *Congo* **102 B3** 0 22N 15 29 E
Yenice, *Ankara, Turkey* **88 C5** 39 14N 32 42 E
Yenice, *Çanakkale, Turkey* **88 C2** 39 55N 27 17 E
Yenice →, *Turkey* **88 D6** 37 37N 35 33 E
Yenisaía, *Greece* **44 C6** 41 1N 24 57 E
Yenişehir, *Turkey* **88 B3** 40 16N 29 38 E
Yenisey →, *Russia* **56 B9** 71 50N 82 40 E
Yeniseysk, *Russia* **57 D10** 58 27N 92 13 E
Yeniseyskiy Zaliv, *Russia* **56 B9** 72 20N 81 0 E
Yennádhi, *Greece* **32 C9** 36 2N 27 56 E
Yenne, *France* **25 C9** 45 43N 5 44 E
Yenotayevka, *Russia* **53 G8** 47 15N 47 0 E
Yenyuka, *Russia* **57 D13** 57 57N 121 15 E
Yeo, L., *Australia* **113 E3** 28 0 S 124 30 E
Yeola, *India* **82 D2** 20 2N 74 30 E
Yeoryioúpolis, *Greece* **32 D6** 35 20N 24 15 E
Yeoval, *Australia* **117 B8** 32 47 S 148 40 E
Yeovil, *U.K.* **17 G5** 50 57N 2 38W
Yepes, *Spain* **34 F1** 39 55N 3 39W
Yeppoon, *Australia* **114 C5** 23 5 S 150 47 E
Yeráki, *Greece* **45 H4** 37 0N 22 42 E
Yerbent, *Turkmenistan* **56 F6** 39 30N 58 50 E
Yerbogachen, *Russia* **57 C11** 61 16N 108 0 E
Yerevan, *Armenia* **53 K7** 40 10N 44 31 E
Yerilla, *Australia* **113 E3** 29 24 S 121 47 E
Yerköy, *Turkey* **88 C6** 39 38N 34 28 E
Yerla →, *India* **82 F2** 16 50N 74 30 E
Yermak, *Kazakstan* **56 D8** 52 2N 76 55 E
Yermakovo, *Russia* **57 D13** 52 25N 126 20 E
Yermo, *U.S.A.* **145 L10** 34 54N 116 50W
Yerofey Pavlovich, *Russia* **57 D13** 54 0N 122 0 E
Yerólakkos, *Cyprus* **32 D12** 35 11N 33 15 E
Yeropol, *Russia* **57 C17** 65 15N 168 40 E
Yeropótamos →, *Greece* **32 D6** 35 3N 24 50 E
Yeroskipos, *Cyprus* **32 E11** 34 46N 32 28 E
Yerseke, *Neths.* **21 F4** 51 29N 4 3 E
Yershov, *Russia* **52 E9** 51 23N 48 27 E
Yerunaja, Cerro, *Peru* **156 C2** 10 16 S 76 55W
Yerushalayim = Jerusalem, *Israel* **91 D4** 31 47N 35 10 E
Yerville, *France* **22 C7** 49 40N 0 53 E
Yes Tor, *U.K.* **17 G4** 50 41N 4 0W
Yesagyo, *Burma* **78 E5** 21 38N 95 14 E
Yesan, *S. Korea* **67 F14** 36 41N 126 51 E
Yeşilhisar, *Turkey* **88 C6** 38 20N 35 5 E
Yeşilırmak →, *Turkey* **88 B7** 41 22N 36 37 E
Yeşilkent, *Turkey* **88 D7** 36 57N 36 12 E
Yesnogorsk, *Russia* **52 C3** 54 32N 37 38 E
Yeso, *U.S.A.* **139 H2** 34 26N 104 37W
Yessentuki, *Russia* **53 H6** 44 5N 42 53 E
Yessey, *Russia* **57 C11** 68 29N 102 10 E
Yeste, *Spain* **35 G2** 38 22N 2 19W
Yeu, I. d', *France* **22 F4** 46 42N 2 20W
Yevlakh = Yevlax, *Azerbaijan* **53 K8** 40 39N 47 7 E
Yevlax, *Azerbaijan* **53 K8** 40 39N 47 7 E
Yevpatoriya, *Ukraine* **51 K7** 45 15N 33 20 E
Yeya →, *Russia* **53 G4** 46 40N 38 40 E
Yeysk, *Russia* **53 G4** 46 40N 38 12 E
Yezd = Yazd, *Iran* **85 D7** 31 55N 54 27 E
Yezerishche, *Belarus* **50 E5** 55 50N 29 59 E
Yhati, *Paraguay* **158 B4** 25 45 S 56 35W
Yhú, *Paraguay* **159 B4** 25 0 S 56 0W
Yi →, *Uruguay* **158 C4** 33 7 S 57 8W
Yi 'Allaq, G., *Egypt* **91 E2** 30 22N 33 32 E
Yi He →, *China* **67 G10** 34 10N 118 8 E
Yi Xian, *Anhui, China* **69 C11** 29 55N 117 57 E
Yi Xian, *Hebei, China* **66 E8** 39 20N 115 30 E
Yi Xian, *Liaoning, China* **67 D11** 41 30N 121 22 E
Yialí, *Greece* **45 H9** 36 41N 27 11 E
Yialiás →, *Cyprus* **32 D12** 35 9N 33 44 E
Yi'allaq, G., *Egypt* **94 H8** 30 21N 33 31 E
Yialousa, *Cyprus* **32 D13** 35 32N 34 10 E
Yiáltra, *Greece* **45 F4** 38 51N 22 59 E
Yianisádhes, *Greece* **32 D8** 35 20N 26 10 E
Yiannitsa, *Greece* **44 D4** 40 46N 22 24 E
Yibin, *China* **68 C5** 28 45N 104 32 E
Yichang, *China* **69 B8** 30 40N 111 20 E
Yicheng, *Henan, China* **69 B9** 31 41N 112 12 E
Yicheng, *Shanxi, China* **66 G6** 35 42N 111 40 E
Yichuan, *China* **66 F6** 36 2N 110 10 E
Yichun, *Heilongjiang, China* **65 B7** 47 44N 128 52 E
Yichun, *Jiangxi, China* **69 D10** 27 48N 114 22 E

Zaragoza 287

Yidhá, Greece 44 D4 40 35N 22 53 E
Yidu, Hubei, China 69 B8 30 25N 111 27 E
Yidu, Shandong, China 67 F10 36 43N 118 28 E
Yidun, China 68 B2 30 22N 99 21 E
Yihuang, China 69 D11 27 30N 116 12 E
Yijun, China 66 G5 35 28N 109 8 E
Yıldızeli, Turkey 88 C7 39 51N 36 36 E
Yilehuli Shan, China 65 A7 51 20N 124 20 E
Yiliang, Yunnan, China 68 D5 27 38N 104 2 E
Yiliang, Yunnan, China 68 E4 24 56N 103 11 E
Yilong, China 68 B6 31 34N 106 23 E
Yimen, China 68 E4 24 40N 102 10 E
Yimianpo, China 67 B15 45 7N 128 2 E
Yinchuan, China 66 E4 38 30N 106 15 E
Yindarlgooda, L., Australia 113 F3 30 40 S 121 52 E
Ying He →, China 66 H9 32 30N 116 30 E
Ying Xian, China 66 E7 39 32N 113 10 E
Yingcheng, China 69 B9 30 56N 113 35 E
Yingde, China 69 E9 24 10N 113 25 E
Yingjiang, China 68 E1 24 41N 97 55 E
Yingjing, China 68 C4 29 41N 102 52 E
Yingkou, China 67 D12 40 37N 122 18 E
Yingshan, Henan, China 69 B9 31 35N 113 50 E
Yingshan, Hubei, China 69 B10 30 41N 115 32 E
Yingshan, Sichuan, China 68 B6 31 4N 106 35 E
Yingshang, China 69 A11 32 38N 116 12 E
Yining, China 56 E9 43 58N 81 10 E
Yinjiang, China 68 C7 28 1N 108 21 E
Yinnietharra, Australia 112 D2 24 39 S 116 12 E
Yiofiros →, Greece 32 D7 35 20N 25 6 E
Yioúra, Notios Aiyaíon, Greece 45 G6 37 32N 24 40 E
Yioúra, Thessalía, Greece 44 E6 39 23N 24 10 E
Yipinglang, China 68 E3 25 10N 101 52 E
Yirga Alem, Ethiopia 95 F4 6 48N 38 22 E
Yishan, China 68 E7 24 28N 108 38 E
Yishui, China 67 G10 35 47N 118 30 E
Yíthion, Greece 45 H4 36 46N 22 34 E
Yitiaoshan, China 66 F3 37 5N 104 2 E
Yitong, China 67 C13 43 13N 125 20 E
Yiwu, China 69 C13 29 20N 120 3 E
Yixing, China 69 B12 31 21N 119 48 E
Yiyang, Henan, China 66 G7 34 27N 112 10 E
Yiyang, Hunan, China 69 C9 28 35N 112 18 E
Yiyang, Jiangxi, China 69 C11 28 22N 117 20 E
Yizhang, China 69 E9 25 27N 112 57 E
Yizheng, China 69 A12 32 18N 119 10 E
Yli-Kitka, Finland 12 C23 66 8N 28 30 E
Ylitornio, Finland 12 C20 66 19N 23 39 E
Ylivieska, Finland 12 D21 64 4N 24 28 E
Yngaren, Sweden 15 F10 58 50N 16 35 E
Ynykchanskiy, Russia 57 C14 60 15N 137 35 E
Yoakum, U.S.A. 139 L6 29 17N 97 9W
Yobe □, Nigeria 101 C7 12 0N 11 30 E
Yobuko, Japan 62 D1 33 32N 129 54 E
Yog Pt., Phil. 70 D5 14 6N 124 12 E
Yogan, Togo 101 D5 6 23N 1 30 E
Yogyakarta, Indonesia 75 D4 7 49 S 110 22 E
Yogyakarta □, Indonesia 75 D4 7 48 S 110 22 E
Yoho Nat. Park, Canada 130 C5 51 25N 116 30W
Yojoa, L. de, Honduras 148 D2 14 53N 88 0W
Yŏju, S. Korea 67 F14 37 20N 127 35 E
Yokadouma, Cameroon 102 B2 3 26N 14 55 E
Yōkaichiba, Japan 63 B12 35 42N 140 33 E
Yokkaichi, Japan 63 C8 34 55N 136 38 E
Yoko, Cameroon 101 D7 5 32N 12 20 E
Yokohama, Japan 63 B11 35 27N 139 28 E
Yokosuka, Japan 63 B11 35 20N 139 40 E
Yokote, Japan 60 E10 39 20N 140 30 E
Yola, Nigeria 101 D7 9 10N 12 29 E
Yolaina, Cordillera de, Nic. 148 D3 11 30N 84 0W
Yolombo, Zaïre 102 C4 1 36 S 23 12 E
Yombi, Gabon 102 C2 1 26 S 10 37 E
Yonago, Japan 62 B5 35 25N 133 19 E
Yonaguni-Jima, Japan 61 M1 24 27N 123 0 E
Yŏnan, N. Korea 67 F14 37 55N 126 11 E
Yonezawa, Japan 60 F10 37 57N 140 4 E
Yong Peng, Malaysia 77 L4 2 0N 103 3 E
Yong Sata, Thailand 77 J2 7 8N 99 41 E
Yongampo, N. Korea 67 E13 39 56N 124 23 E
Yong'an, China 69 E11 25 59N 117 25 E
Yongcheng, China 66 H9 33 55N 116 20 E
Yŏngchŏn, S. Korea 67 G15 35 58N 128 56 E
Yongchuan, China 68 C5 29 17N 105 55 E
Yongchun, China 69 E12 25 16N 118 20 E
Yongdeng, China 66 F2 36 38N 103 25 E
Yongding, China 69 E11 24 43N 116 45 E
Yŏngdŏk, S. Korea 67 F15 36 24N 129 22 E
Yŏngdŭngpo, S. Korea 67 F14 37 31N 126 54 E
Yongfeng, China 69 D10 27 20N 115 22 E
Yongfu, China 68 E7 24 59N 109 59 E
Yonghe, China 66 F6 36 46N 110 38 E
Yŏnghŭng, N. Korea 67 E14 39 31N 127 18 E
Yongji, China 66 G6 34 52N 110 28 E
Yŏngju, S. Korea 67 F15 36 50N 128 40 E
Yongkang, Yunnan, China 68 E2 24 9N 99 20 E
Yongkang, Zhejiang, China 69 C13 28 55N 120 2 E
Yongnian, China 66 F8 36 47N 114 29 E
Yongning, Guangxi Zhuangzu, China 68 F7 22 44N 108 28 E
Yongning, Ningxia Huizu, China 66 E4 38 15N 106 14 E
Yongping, China 68 E2 25 27N 99 38 E
Yongqing, China 66 E9 39 25N 116 28 E
Yongren, China 68 D3 26 4N 101 40 E
Yongshan, China 68 C4 28 11N 103 35 E
Yongsheng, China 68 D3 26 38N 100 46 E
Yongshun, China 68 C7 29 2N 109 51 E
Yongtai, China 69 E12 25 49N 118 58 E
Yŏngwŏl, S. Korea 67 F15 37 11N 128 28 E
Yongxin, China 69 D10 26 58N 114 15 E
Yongxing, China 69 D9 26 9N 113 8 E
Yongxiu, China 69 C10 29 2N 115 42 E
Yonibana, S. Leone 100 D2 8 30N 12 19W
Yonkers, U.S.A. 137 F11 40 56N 73 54W
Yonne □, France 23 E10 47 50N 3 40 E
Yonne →, France 23 D9 48 23N 2 58 E
York, Australia 113 F2 31 52 S 116 47 E
York, U.K. 16 D6 53 58N 1 6W
York, Ala., U.S.A. 135 J1 32 29N 88 18W
York, Nebr., U.S.A. 138 E6 40 52N 97 36W
York, Pa., U.S.A. 134 F7 39 58N 76 44W
York □, U.K. 16 D6 53 58N 1 6W
York, C., Australia 114 A3 10 42 S 142 31 E
York, Kap, Greenland 6 B4 75 55N 66 25W
York Sd., Australia 112 B4 15 0 S 125 5 E
Yorke Pen., Australia 116 C2 34 50 S 137 40 E
Yorkshire Wolds, U.K. 16 D7 54 8N 0 31W
Yorkton, Canada 131 C8 51 11N 102 28W
Yorktown, U.S.A. 139 L6 28 59N 97 30W
Yorkville, Calif., U.S.A. 144 G3 38 52N 123 13W
Yorkville, Ill., U.S.A. 141 C8 41 38N 88 27W
Yornup, Australia 113 F2 34 2 S 116 10 E
Yoro, Honduras 148 C2 15 9N 87 7W
Yoron-Jima, Japan 61 L4 27 2N 128 26 E
Yos Sudarso, Pulau, Indonesia 73 C5 8 0 S 138 30 E
Yosemite National Park, U.S.A. 144 H7 37 45N 119 40W
Yosemite Village, U.S.A. 144 H7 37 45N 119 35W
Yoshii, Japan 62 D1 33 16N 129 46 E
Yoshimatsu, Japan 62 E2 32 0N 130 47 E
Yoshkar Ola, Russia 52 B8 56 38N 47 55 E
Yŏsu, S. Korea 67 G14 34 47N 127 45 E
Yotala, Bolivia 157 D4 19 10 S 65 17W
Yotvata, Israel 91 F4 29 55N 35 2 E
You Xian, China 69 D9 27 1N 113 17 E
Youbou, Canada 130 D4 48 53N 124 13W
Youghal, Ireland 19 E4 51 56N 7 52W
Youghal B., Ireland 19 E4 51 55N 7 49W
Youkounkoun, Guinea 100 C2 12 35N 13 11W
Young, Australia 117 C8 34 19 S 148 18 E
Young, Canada 131 C7 51 47N 105 45W
Young, Uruguay 158 C4 32 44 S 57 36W
Young Ra., N.Z. 119 E4 44 10 S 169 30 E
Younghusband, L., Australia 116 A2 30 50 S 136 5 E
Younghusband Pen., Australia 116 D3 36 0 S 139 25 E
Youngstown, Canada 131 C6 51 35N 111 10W
Youngstown, N.Y., U.S.A. 136 C5 43 15N 79 3W
Youngstown, Ohio, U.S.A. 136 E4 41 6N 80 39W
Youngsville, U.S.A. 136 E5 41 51N 79 19W
Youssoufia, Morocco 98 B3 32 16N 8 31W
Youxi, China 69 D12 26 10N 118 13 E
Youyang, China 68 C7 28 47N 108 42 E
Youyu, China 66 D7 40 10N 112 20 E
Yoweragabbie, Australia 113 E2 28 14 S 117 39 E
Yowrie, Australia 117 D8 36 17 S 149 46 E
Yozgat, Turkey 88 C6 39 51N 34 47 E
Ypané →, Paraguay 158 A4 23 29 S 57 19W
Yport, France 22 C7 49 45N 0 15 E
Ypres = Ieper, Belgium 21 G1 50 51N 2 53 E
Ypsilanti, U.S.A. 141 B13 42 14N 83 37W
Yreka, U.S.A. 142 F2 41 44N 122 38W
Ysabel Chan., Papua N. G. 120 B5 2 0 S 150 0 E
Ysleta, U.S.A. 143 L10 31 45N 106 24W
Yssingeaux, France 25 C8 45 9N 4 8 E
Ystad, Sweden 15 J7 55 26N 13 50 E
Ysyk-Köl, Kyrgyzstan 55 B8 42 26N 76 12 E
Ysyk-Köl, Ozero, Kyrgyzstan 55 B8 42 25N 77 15 E
Ythan →, U.K. 18 D7 57 19N 1 59W
Ytterhogdal, Sweden 14 B8 62 12N 14 56 E
Ytyk Kyuyel, Russia 57 C14 62 30N 133 45 E
Yu Jiang →, China 65 D6 23 22N 110 3 E
Yu Xian, Hebei, China 66 E8 39 50N 114 35 E
Yu Xian, Henan, China 66 G7 34 10N 113 28 E
Yu Xian, Shanxi, China 66 E7 38 5N 113 20 E
Yuan Jiang →, Hunan, China 69 C8 28 55N 111 50 E
Yuan Jiang →, Yunnan, China 68 F4 22 20N 103 59 E
Yuan'an, China 69 B8 31 3N 111 34 E
Yuanjiang, Hunan, China 69 C9 28 47N 112 21 E
Yuanjiang, Yunnan, China 68 F4 23 32N 102 0 E
Yüanli, Taiwan 69 E13 24 27N 120 39 E
Yüanlin, Taiwan 69 F13 23 45N 120 30 E
Yuanlin, Taiwan 69 F13 23 58N 120 30 E
Yuanling, China 69 C8 28 29N 110 22 E
Yuanmou, China 68 E3 25 42N 101 53 E
Yuanqu, China 66 G6 35 18N 111 40 E
Yuanyang, Henan, China 66 G7 35 3N 113 58 E
Yuanyang, Yunnan, China 68 F4 23 10N 102 43 E
Yuat →, Papua N. G. 120 C2 4 10 S 143 52 E
Yuba →, U.S.A. 144 F5 39 8N 121 36W
Yuba City, U.S.A. 144 F5 39 8N 121 37W
Yūbari, Japan 60 C10 43 4N 141 59 E
Yūbetsu, Japan 60 B11 44 13N 143 50 E
Yucatán □, Mexico 147 C7 21 30N 86 30W
Yucatán, Canal de, Caribbean 148 B2 22 0N 86 30W
Yucatán, Península de, Mexico 124 H11 19 30N 89 0W
Yucatán Basin, Cent. Amer. 124 H11 19 0N 86 0W
Yucatan Str. = Yucatán, Canal de, Caribbean 148 B2 22 0N 86 30W
Yucca, U.S.A. 145 L12 34 52N 114 9W
Yucca Valley, U.S.A. 145 L10 34 8N 116 27W
Yucheng, China 66 F9 36 55N 116 32 E
Yuci, China 66 F7 37 42N 112 46 E
Yudino, Russia 56 D7 55 10N 67 55 E
Yudu, China 69 E10 25 59N 115 30 E
Yuendumu, Australia 112 D5 22 16 S 131 49 E
Yueqing, China 69 C13 28 9N 120 59 E
Yueqing Wan, China 69 C13 28 5N 121 20 E
Yuexi, Anhui, China 69 B11 30 50N 116 20 E
Yuexi, Sichuan, China 68 C4 28 37N 102 26 E
Yueyang, China 69 C9 29 21N 113 5 E
Yufu-Dake, Japan 62 D3 33 17N 131 33 E
Yugan, China 69 C11 28 43N 116 37 E
Yugoslavia ■, Europe 42 D5 44 0N 20 0 E
Yuhuan, China 69 C13 28 9N 121 12 E
Yujiang, China 69 C11 28 10N 116 43 E
Yukhnov, Russia 52 C2 54 44N 35 15 E
Yūki, Japan 63 A11 36 18N 139 53 E
Yukon →, U.S.A. 126 B3 62 32N 163 54W
Yukon Territory □, Canada 126 B6 63 0N 135 0W
Yüksekova, Turkey 89 D11 37 34N 44 16 E
Yukti, Russia 57 C11 63 26N 105 42 E
Yukuhashi, Japan 62 D2 33 44N 130 59 E
Yule →, Australia 112 D2 20 41 S 118 17 E
Yuli, Nigeria 101 D7 9 44N 10 12 E
Yulin, Guangxi Zhuangzu, China 69 F8 22 40N 110 8 E
Yulin, Shaanxi, China 66 E5 38 20N 109 30 E
Yuma, Ariz., U.S.A. 145 N12 32 43N 114 37W
Yuma, Colo., U.S.A. 138 E3 40 8N 102 43W
Yuma, B. de, Dom. Rep. 149 C6 18 20N 68 35W
Yumali, Australia 116 C3 35 32 S 139 45 E
Yumbe, Uganda 106 B3 3 28N 31 15 E
Yumbi, Zaïre 106 C2 1 12 S 26 15 E
Yumbo, Colombia 152 C2 3 35N 76 28W
Yumen, China 64 C4 39 50N 97 30 E
Yumurtalık, Turkey 88 D6 36 45N 35 43 E
Yun Ho →, China 67 E9 39 10N 117 10 E
Yun Xian, Hubei, China 69 A8 32 50N 110 46 E
Yun Xian, Yunnan, China 68 E3 24 27N 100 8 E
Yunak, Turkey 88 C4 38 49N 31 43 E
Yunan, China 69 F8 23 12N 111 30 E
Yuncheng, Henan, China 66 G8 35 36N 115 57 E
Yuncheng, Shanxi, China 66 G6 35 2N 111 0 E
Yundamindra, Australia 113 E3 29 15 S 122 6 E
Yunfu, China 69 F9 22 50N 112 5 E
Yungas, Bolivia 157 D4 17 0 S 66 0W
Yungay, Chile 158 D1 37 10 S 72 5W
Yungay, Peru 156 B2 9 2 S 77 45W
Yunhe, China 69 C12 28 8N 119 33 E
Yunlin, Taiwan 69 F13 23 42N 120 30 E
Yunling, China 68 D2 27 0N 99 20 E
Yunlong, China 68 E2 25 57N 99 13 E
Yunmeng, China 69 B9 31 2N 113 43 E
Yunnan □, China 68 E4 25 0N 102 0 E
Yunomae, Japan 62 E2 32 12N 130 59 E
Yunotso, Japan 62 B4 35 5N 132 21 E
Yunquera de Henares, Spain 34 E1 40 47N 3 11W
Yunta, Australia 116 B3 32 34 S 139 36 E
Yunxi, China 66 H6 33 0N 110 22 E
Yunxiao, China 69 F11 23 59N 117 18 E
Yunyang, China 68 B7 30 58N 108 54 E
Yuping, China 68 D7 27 13N 108 56 E
Yupukarri, Guyana 153 C6 3 45N 59 20W
Yupyongdong, N. Korea 67 D15 41 49N 128 53 E
Yuqing, China 68 D6 27 13N 107 53 E
Yur, Russia 57 D14 59 52N 137 41 E
Yurgao, Russia 56 D9 55 42N 84 51 E
Yuribei, Russia 56 B8 71 8N 76 58 E
Yurimaguas, Peru 156 B2 5 55 S 76 7W
Yurla, Russia 54 B5 59 22N 54 21 E
Yurya, Russia 54 B2 59 1N 49 13 E
Yuryev-Polskiy, Russia 52 B4 56 30N 39 40 E
Yuryevets, Russia 52 B6 57 25N 43 2 E
Yuryung Kaya, Russia 57 B12 72 48N 113 23 E
Yuryuzan, Russia 54 D7 54 57N 58 28 E
Yuscarán, Honduras 148 D2 13 58N 86 45W
Yushanzhen, China 68 C7 29 28N 108 22 E
Yushe, China 66 F7 37 4N 112 58 E
Yushu, Jilin, China 67 B14 44 43N 126 38 E
Yushu, Qinghai, China 64 C4 33 5N 96 55 E
Yusufeli, Turkey 89 B9 40 50N 41 33 E
Yutai, China 66 G9 35 0N 116 45 E
Yutian, China 67 E9 39 53N 117 45 E
Yuxarı Qarabağ = Nagorno-Karabakh, Azerbaijan 89 C12 39 55N 46 45 E
Yuxi, China 68 E4 24 30N 102 35 E
Yuyao, China 69 B13 30 3N 121 10 E
Yuzawa, Japan 60 E10 39 10N 140 30 E
Yuzha, Russia 52 B6 56 34N 42 1 E
Yuzhno-Sakhalinsk, Russia 57 E15 46 58N 142 45 E
Yuzhno-Surkhanskoye Vdkhr., Uzbekistan 55 E3 37 53N 67 42 E
Yuzhnouralsk, Russia 54 D8 54 26N 61 15 E
Yvelines □, France 23 D8 48 40N 1 45 E
Yverdon, Switz. 28 C3 46 47N 6 39 E
Yvetot, France 22 C7 49 37N 0 44 E
Yvonand, Switz. 28 C3 46 48N 6 44 E

Z

Zaalayskiy Khrebet, Asia 55 D6 39 20N 73 0 E
Zaamslag, Neths. 21 F3 51 19N 3 55 E
Zaan →, Neths. 20 D5 52 25N 4 52 E
Zaandam, Neths. 20 D5 52 26N 4 49 E
Zab, Monts du, Algeria 99 B6 34 55N 5 0 E
Žabalj, Serbia, Yug. 42 B5 45 21N 20 5 E
Žabari, Serbia, Yug. 42 C6 44 22N 21 15 E
Zabarjad, Egypt 94 C4 23 40N 36 12 E
Zabaykalsk, Russia 57 E12 49 40N 117 25 E
Zabid, Yemen 86 D3 14 0N 43 10 E
Zabīd, W. →, Yemen 86 D3 14 7N 43 6 E
Ząbkowice Śląskie, Poland 47 E3 50 35N 16 50 E
Žabljak, Montenegro, Yug. 42 D4 43 18N 19 7 E
Zabłudów, Poland 47 B10 53 0N 23 19 E
Żabno, Poland 31 A13 50 9N 20 53 E
Zābol, Iran 85 D9 31 0N 61 32 E
Zābol □, Afghan. 79 B2 32 0N 67 0 E
Zābolī, Iran 85 E9 27 10N 61 35 E
Zabré, Burkina Faso 101 C4 11 12N 0 36W
Zabrze, Poland 47 E5 50 18N 18 50 E
Zacapa, Guatemala 148 D2 14 59N 89 31W
Zacapu, Mexico 146 D4 19 50N 101 43W
Zacatecas, Mexico 146 C4 22 49N 102 34W
Zacatecas □, Mexico 146 C4 23 30N 103 0W
Zacatecoluca, El Salv. 148 D2 13 29N 88 51W
Zacoalco, Mexico 146 C4 20 14N 103 33W
Zacualtipán, Mexico 147 C5 20 39N 98 36W
Zadar, Croatia 39 D12 44 8N 15 14 E
Zadawa, Nigeria 101 C7 11 33N 10 19 E
Zadetkyi Kyun, Burma 77 H2 10 0N 98 25 E
Zadonsk, Russia 52 D4 52 25N 38 56 E
Zafarqand, Iran 85 C7 33 11N 52 29 E
Zafora, Greece 45 H8 36 5N 26 24 E
Zafra, Spain 37 G4 38 26N 6 30W
Żagań, Poland 47 D2 51 39N 15 22 E
Zagazig, Egypt 94 H7 30 40N 31 30 E
Zāgheh, Iran 85 C6 33 30N 48 42 E
Zaghouan, Tunisia 96 A2 36 23N 10 10 E
Zaglivérion, Greece 44 D5 40 36N 23 15 E
Zaglou, Algeria 99 C4 27 17N 0 3W
Zagnanado, Benin 101 D5 7 18N 2 28 E
Zagorá, Greece 44 E5 39 27N 23 6 E
Zagora, Morocco 98 B3 30 22N 5 51W
Zagórów, Poland 47 C4 52 10N 17 54 E
Zagorsk = Sergiyev Posad, Russia 52 B4 56 20N 38 10 E
Zagórz, Poland 31 B15 49 30N 22 14 E
Zagreb, Croatia 39 C12 45 50N 16 0 E
Zāgros, Kūhhā-ye, Iran 85 C6 33 45N 48 5 E
Zagros Mts. = Zāgros, Kūhhā-ye, Iran 85 C6 33 45N 48 5 E
Žagubica, Serbia, Yug. 42 C6 44 15N 21 47 E
Zaguinaso, Ivory C. 100 C3 10 1N 6 14W
Zagyva →, Hungary 31 D13 47 5N 20 4 E
Zāhedān, Fārs, Iran 85 D7 28 46N 53 52 E
Zāhedān, Sīstān va Balūchestān, Iran 85 D9 29 30N 60 50 E
Zahirabad, India 82 F3 17 43N 77 37 E
Zahlah, Lebanon 91 B4 33 52N 35 50 E
Zahna, Germany 26 D8 51 55N 12 49 E
Zahrez Chergui, Algeria 99 A5 35 11N 3 31 E
Zahrez Rharbi, Algeria 99 B5 34 50N 2 55 E
Zailiyskiy Alatau, Khrebet, Kazakstan 55 B8 43 5N 77 0 E
Zainsk, Russia 52 C11 55 18N 52 4 E
Zaire □, Angola 103 D2 7 0 S 14 0 E
Zaïre ■, Africa 103 C4 3 0 S 23 0 E
Zaïre →, Africa 103 D2 6 4 S 12 24 E
Zaječar, Serbia, Yug. 42 D7 43 53N 22 18 E
Zakamensk, Russia 57 D11 50 23N 103 17 E
Zakani, Zaïre 102 B4 2 33N 23 16 E
Zakataly = Zaqatala, Azerbaijan 53 K8 41 38N 46 35 E
Zakavkazye, Asia 49 F7 42 0N 44 0 E
Zakhodnaya Dzvina = Daugava →, Latvia 13 H21 57 4N 24 3 E
Zākhū, Iraq 89 D10 37 10N 42 50 E
Zákinthos, Greece 45 G2 37 47N 20 57 E
Zaklików, Poland 47 E9 50 46N 22 7 E
Zakopane, Poland 31 B12 49 18N 19 57 E
Zakroczym, Poland 47 C7 52 26N 20 38 E
Zákros, Greece 32 D8 35 6N 26 10 E
Zala, Angola 103 D2 7 52 S 13 42 E
Zala □, Hungary 31 E9 46 42N 16 50 E
Zala →, Hungary 31 E10 46 43N 17 16 E
Zalaegerszeg, Hungary 31 E9 46 53N 16 47 E
Zalakomár, Hungary 31 E10 46 33N 17 10 E
Zalalövö, Hungary 31 E9 46 51N 16 35 E
Zalamea de la Serena, Spain 37 G5 38 40N 5 38W
Zalamea la Real, Spain 37 H4 37 41N 6 38W
Zalău, Romania 46 B4 47 12N 23 3 E
Zalazna, Russia 54 B4 58 39N 52 31 E
Žalec, Slovenia 39 B12 46 16N 15 10 E
Zaleshchiki = Zalishchyky, Ukraine 51 H3 48 45N 25 45 E
Zalew Wiślany, Poland 47 A6 54 20N 19 50 E
Zalewo, Poland 47 B6 53 50N 19 41 E
Zalīm, Si. Arabia 86 B3 22 43N 42 10 E
Zalingei, Sudan 97 F4 12 51N 23 29 E
Zalishchyky, Ukraine 51 H3 48 45N 25 45 E
Zaltan, Jabal, Libya 96 C3 28 46N 19 45 E
Zaltbommel, Neths. 20 E6 51 48N 5 15 E
Zambales □, Phil. 70 D3 15 20N 120 10 E
Zambales Mts., Phil. 70 D3 15 45N 120 5 E
Zambeke, Zaïre 106 B2 2 8N 25 17 E
Zambeze →, Africa 107 F4 18 35 S 36 20 E
Zambezi = Zambeze →, Africa 107 F4 18 35 S 36 20 E
Zambezi, Zambia 103 E4 13 30 S 23 15 E
Zambezia □, Mozam. 107 F4 16 15 S 37 30 E
Zambia ■, Africa 107 E2 15 0 S 28 0 E
Zamboanga, Phil. 71 H4 6 59N 122 3 E
Zamboanga del Norte □, Phil. 71 G4 8 0N 123 0 E
Zamboanga del Sur □, Phil. 71 H4 7 40N 123 0 E
Zamboanguita, Phil. 71 G4 9 6N 123 12 E
Zambrano, Colombia 152 B3 9 45N 74 49W
Zambrów, Poland 47 C9 52 59N 22 14 E
Zametchino, Russia 52 D6 53 30N 42 30 E
Zamora, Ecuador 152 D2 4 4 S 78 58W
Zamora, Mexico 146 C4 20 0N 102 21W
Zamora, Spain 36 D5 41 30N 5 45W
Zamora □, Spain 36 D5 41 30N 5 46W
Zamora-Chinchipe □, Ecuador 152 D2 4 15 S 78 50W
Zamość, Poland 47 E10 50 43N 23 15 E
Zamość □, Poland 47 E10 50 40N 23 10 E
Zamuro, Sierra del, Venezuela 153 C5 4 0N 62 30W
Zamzam, W. →, Libya 96 B2 30 58N 14 48 E
Zan, Ghana 101 D4 9 26N 0 17W
Zanaga, Congo 102 C2 2 48 S 13 48 E
Záncara →, Spain 35 F1 39 18N 3 18W
Zandijk, Neths. 20 D5 52 28N 4 49 E
Zandvoort, Neths. 20 D5 52 22N 4 32 E
Zanesville, U.S.A. 136 G2 39 56N 82 1W
Zangābād, Iran 84 B5 38 26N 46 44 E
Zangue →, Mozam. 107 F4 17 50 S 35 21 E
Zanjān, Iran 89 D13 36 40N 48 35 E
Zanjān □, Iran 85 B6 37 20N 49 30 E
Zannone, Italy 40 B6 40 58N 13 3 E
Zante = Zákinthos, Greece 45 G2 37 47N 20 57 E
Zanthus, Australia 113 F3 31 2 S 123 34 E
Zanzibar, Tanzania 106 D4 6 12 S 39 12 E
Zanzūr, Libya 96 B2 32 55N 13 1 E
Zaouiet El-Kala = Bordj Omar Driss, Algeria 99 C6 28 10N 6 40 E
Zaouiet Reggane, Algeria 99 C5 26 32N 0 3 E
Zaoyang, China 69 A9 32 10N 112 45 E
Zaozhuang, China 67 G9 34 50N 117 35 E
Zap Suyu = Kabīr, Zab al →, Iraq 89 D10 36 1N 43 24 E
Zapadna Morava →, Serbia, Yug. 42 D6 43 38N 21 30 E
Zapadnaya Dvina, Russia 50 D7 56 15N 32 3 E
Zapadnaya Dvina → = Daugava →, Latvia 13 H21 57 4N 24 3 E
Západné Beskydy, Europe 31 B12 49 30N 19 0 E
Zapadni Rodopi, Bulgaria 43 F8 41 50N 24 0 E
Západočeský □, Czech. 30 B6 49 35N 13 0 E
Západoslovenský □, Slovak Rep. 31 C10 48 30N 17 30 E
Zapala, Argentina 160 A2 39 0 S 70 5W
Zapaleri, Cerro, Bolivia 158 A2 22 49 S 67 11W
Zapata, U.S.A. 139 M5 26 55N 99 16W
Zapatón →, Spain 37 G4 39 0N 6 49W
Zapiga, Chile 156 D4 19 40 S 69 55W
Zapolyarnyy, Russia 48 A5 69 26N 30 51 E
Zaporizhzhya, Ukraine 51 J8 47 50N 35 10 E
Zaporozhye = Zaporizhzhya, Ukraine 51 J8 47 50N 35 10 E
Zapponeta, Italy 41 A8 41 27N 15 57 E
Zaqatala, Azerbaijan 53 K8 41 38N 46 35 E
Zara, Turkey 88 C7 39 58N 37 43 E
Zaragoza, Colombia 152 B3 7 30N 74 52W

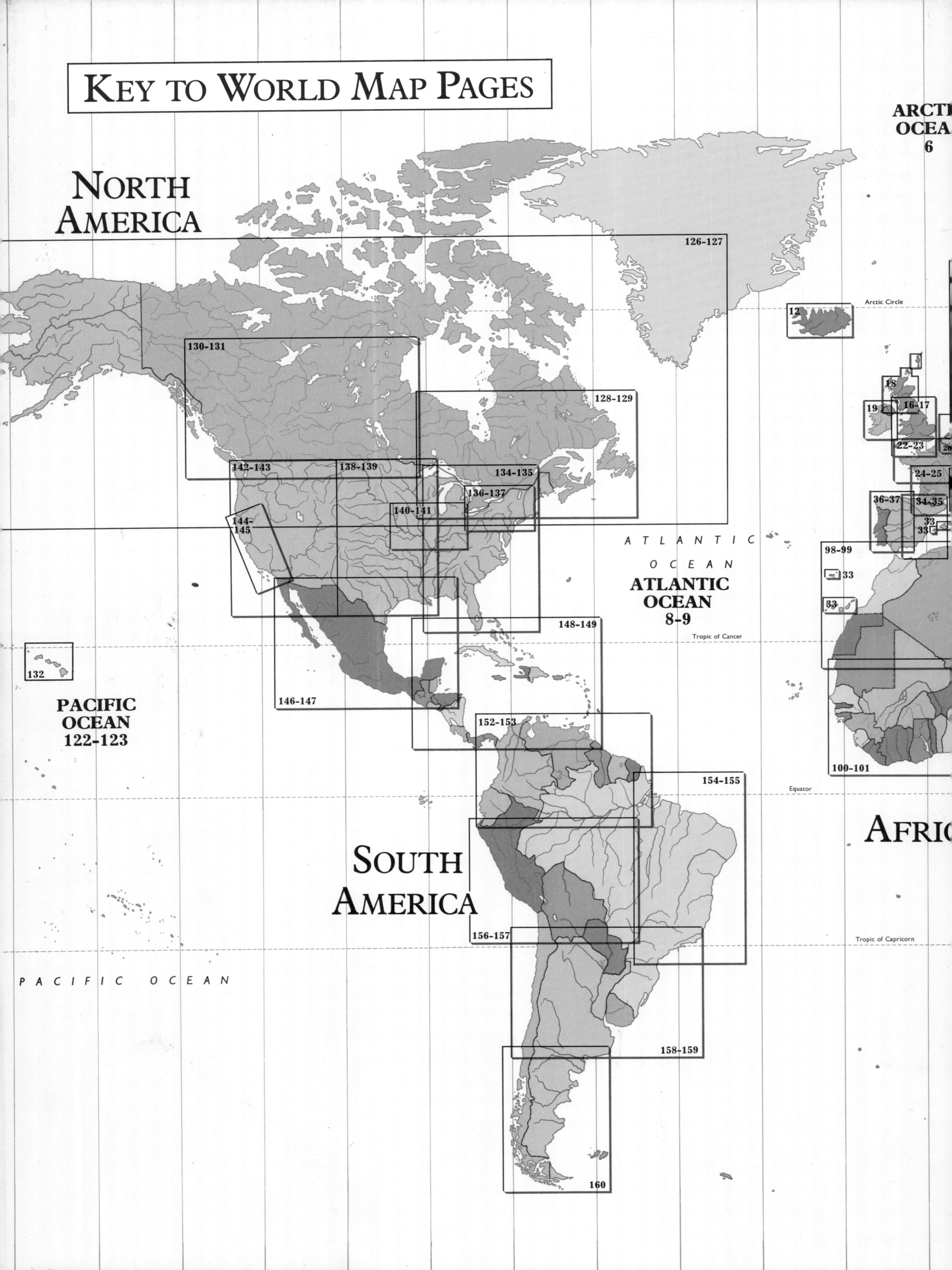

KEY TO WORLD MAP PAGES

NORTH AMERICA

ARCTIC OCEAN 6

Arctic Circle

126-127

12

130-131

128-129

142-143   138-139   134-135

136-137

140-141

144-145

18

19   16-17

22-23   20

24-25

ATLANTIC OCEAN   36-37   34-35

33   33

ATLANTIC OCEAN 8-9   98-99

33   33

Tropic of Cancer

148-149

132

PACIFIC OCEAN 122-123

146-147

152-153

100-101

154-155   Equator

SOUTH AMERICA

AFRICA

Tropic of Capricorn

156-157

PACIFIC OCEAN

158-159

160